1996

VOLUME I

HERITAGE OF
AMERICAN LITERATURE
BEGINNINGS TO THE CIVIL WAR

VOLUME I

HERITAGE OF
AMERICAN LITERATURE
BEGINNINGS TO THE CIVIL WAR

James E. Miller, Jr.
The University of Chicago

With the assistance of
Kathleen Farley

HBJ

HARCOURT BRACE JOVANOVICH, PUBLISHERS
San Diego New York Chicago Austin Washington, D.C.
London Sydney Tokyo Toronto

HERITAGE OF AMERICAN LITERATURE, VOLUME I

Cover: (left to right) **Ralph Waldo Emerson,** HBJ Picture Library, courtesy of the Library of Congress, Washington, D.C.; **Herman Melville,** HBJ Picture Library; courtesy of Brown Brothers, Sterling, Pa.; **Margaret Fuller,** The Bettmann Archive, New York, N.Y.; **Louisa May Alcott,** Culver Pictures, Inc., New York, N.Y.; **Frederick Douglass,** The Bettmann Archive, New York, N.Y.

Back cover: James E. Miller, Jr., courtesy of the author. Photo by Kathleen Farley.

ISBN: 0-15-535697-6

Library of Congress Catalog Card Number: 90-82129

Printed in the United States of America

Copyrights and Acknowledgments and Illustration Credits appear on pages 2029–31, which constitute a continuation of the copyright page.

PREFACE

Heritage of American Literature presents a survey of the travel narratives, exploration and discovery accounts, religious and political tracts, formal and informal essays, humor and wit, fiction, poetry, and drama inspired by America from Columbus's "discovery" in 1492 up to the 1990s. It stretches from Captain John Smith, William Bradford, Ann Bradstreet, and Phillis Wheatley to T. S. Eliot, William Faulkner, Ralph Ellison, and Flannery O'Connor. In the opening pages may be found Dekanawidah's *Iroquois Constitution* alongside Columbus's Letter on Discovery, and in the closing pages may be found poems, fiction, and drama by Gary Soto, Maxine Hong Kingston, and Sam Shepard. In these 500 years, the country has not ceased to elicit the awe and wonder expressed by Columbus on first setting eyes on its virgin lands. And in this long stretch of time, the American imagination has not yet provided final answers to such nagging questions as that posed by St. John de Crèvecoeur in the eighteenth century: "What is an American?"

Whereas Crèvecoeur introduced the notion of the new country as a "melting pot," the contemporary imagination is more likely to compare America to a varicolored patchwork quilt. In a world beset by so many upheavals and disruptions, Americans are more likely now to set off in search of their roots than to leave them lost in the soil of the past. Whatever the truth of these metaphors—melting pot, patchwork quilt, roots—there can be no gainsaying that American writers and their works are made up of a multiplicity and variety that constitute their unique character and richness. Americans may be justly proud of their literature, and moreover will come to know themselves and discover their identity through encountering and experiencing that literature extensively and deeply. This anthology was designed to provide such an encounter, such an experience. Its special features include the following:

1. *Interrelated Clusters of Literary Works.* Instead of arranging selections haphazardly in accord with the authors' birth years, *Heritage of American Literature* groups them in clusters where, read together, they explicate, complement, or give resonance to each other. For example, in Volume I will be found a cluster entitled "Personal Accounts of High Adventure," which brings Mary Rowlandson's exciting account of her Indian captivity together with Sarah Kemble Knight's later hazardous trip alone from Boston to New York. Also in Volume I, "Emerging Feminist Perspectives" presents a group of important, innovative, and often skeptical or ironic women writers, ranging from Margaret Fuller and Elizabeth Cady Stanton to Rebecca Harding Davis and Louisa May Alcott. Volume I concludes with the cluster "Slavery and the Civil War," bringing together the protests and slave narratives of such gifted writers as David Walker, Frederick Douglass, and Harriet A. Jacobs, and concluding with Abraham Lincoln and Walt Whitman. Similar groupings found in Volume II include "Emerging Feminist Fiction" (from Constance Fenimore Woolson to Charlotte Perkins Gilman), "Personal Voice and View: Diaries, Autobiographies, Essays" (from Sarah Winnemucca Hopkins to William James), and "Autobiographies: Modes of Remembering" (from Gertrude Stein to Richard Wright).

2. *Balance in Selections between the Traditional and the New. Heritage of American Literature* includes, as the names listed above suggest, many writers from

the past who are new to the canon, especially women and minority writers (Native Americans, blacks, Chicanos, Asian-Americans, and others). They are represented generously in both Volumes I and II, but not at the sacrifice of writers who have long had a place in the canon, such as the familiar nineteenth-century traditional poets William Cullen Bryant, Henry Wadsworth Longfellow, John Greenleaf Whittier, Oliver Wendell Holmes, James Russell Lowell, and even the less familiar Jones Very and Frederick Goddard Tuckerman. *Heritage* is organized in such a way as to make possible a variety of approaches by the reader. For example, such central nineteenth-century writers as Edgar Allan Poe, Nathaniel Hawthorne, Herman Melville, Ralph Waldo Emerson, Walt Whitman, and Emily Dickinson are represented fully enough to satisfy those who wish to concentrate on the major writers in their approach. For the modernist period, although numerous poets, novelists, and essayists are represented, copious space is reserved for such leading figures in poetry as Ezra Pound, T. S. Eliot, Robert Frost, Wallace Stevens, William Carlos Williams, Marianne Moore, Hart Crane, and Langston Hughes, and in fiction for Willa Cather, Sherwood Anderson, Katherine Anne Porter, Jean Toomer, F. Scott Fitzgerald, William Faulkner, Ernest Hemingway, John Steinbeck, and Eudora Welty.

3. *Integrity of Individual Selections. Heritage of American Literature* has opted for novellas and one-act plays over space-gulping novels and full-length plays in the conviction that, in a literary survey, variety is of the essence. Thus Stephen Crane's *Maggie: A Girl of the Streets*, Willa Cather's, "Neighbour Rosicky," William Faulkner's "Spotted Horses," Saul Bellow's "A Silver Dish," Carson McCullers's *Ballad of the Sad Café*, and John Updike's "Pigeon Feathers" are all included. By presenting only one-act dramas, *Heritage* offers more dramatists than any other anthology of American literature, including Susan Glaspell, Eugene O'Neill, Thornton Wilder, Tennessee Williams, Arthur Miller, Edward Albee, and Sam Shepard. *Heritage* includes no excerpts of novels for the sake of sampling, but rather chooses whole works in the belief that only a work in its totality can offer a genuine experience on which to base a critical or value judgment. Wherever possible, *Heritage* adopts the same approach to poems, and thus includes the whole not only of T. S. Eliot's *The Waste Land*, but also of Ezra Pound's *Hugh Selwyn Mauberley*, William Carlos Williams's *Desert Music*, Allen Tate's " Ode to the Confederate Dead," Robert Lowell's "For the Union Dead," and Charles Wright's *Tattoos*.

4. *Supportive Editorial Apparatus.* All of the introductions, biographies, headnotes, and footnotes in *Heritage* are aimed at assisting students in the reading and understanding of literary texts. Enough history, social and political background, and literary currents and movements are covered in the six section introductions to clarify questions that naturally arise out of the selections. For example, it is important to understand something of the nature of Calvinism as carried to America by the Puritans in order to comprehend Cotton Mather, Jonathan Edwards, and even Benjamin Franklin. A similar understanding of the nature of naturalism as it was discussed in Stephen Crane's day is useful to the reading of *Maggie: A Girl of the Streets*. The introductions are thus meant to support and enhance the reader's experience of the literature. The biographies serve the same purpose: the personal lives of the authors are dealt with fully and frankly, but focus is generally on the aesthetic or artistic ideas and principles espoused by the writers. Often these theories or notions help in the understanding of a work far more than details of the writer's daily life. When a work seems to assume or demand some background before beginning the reading, *Heritage* provides a comprehensive headnote—as, for example, in

the case of Benjamin Franklin's *Autobiography*, T. S. Eliot's *The Waste Land*, and Hart Crane's *The Bridge*. Commentary by authors on specific stories, poems or essays—sometimes on whole works, sometimes on particular lines, stanzas, characters, or events—may be found in headnotes or footnotes. Footnotes themselves, defining, explaining, or clarifying, have been supplied in quantity to be sure that they are there when they are wanted. In short, the editorial apparatus is included to be used when it is needed by a reader determined to experience the literary selections to the full.

Note on Titles, Texts, Dates, and Headnotes: Titles of selections are originals as bestowed by the authors except for those in brackets, which have been supplied by the editor. Texts of some selections from the seventeenth and eighteenth centuries, identified in each instance, have been modernized in spelling, punctuation, and syntax, either by the editors of editions reprinted here or by the editor of this anthology. Omissions from texts are indicated by ellipses. The dates of first publication are listed after the selections to the right; if more than one date is found in this position, the first indicates the year of magazine publication and the second date indicates the first appearance in book form; the dates of composition, if they are known, are placed after the selections to the left; exceptions to this pattern of dating are indicated with the texts. Headnotes are flagged by the appearance of a dingbat (🕭).

Heritage of American Literature has, in a sense, been forty years in the making. I had my first experience with the survey of American literature while a student at the University of Oklahoma (1939–42). When I left the University of Chicago with my graduate degrees and started my academic career at the University of Michigan in 1949, I began to teach both halves of the survey of American literature, and when I went to the University of Nebraska in 1953, I continued to teach the survey. Moreover, I taught the survey abroad, in Italy, Japan, and France. When, coming full circle, I returned to the University of Chicago in 1962, I again taught the survey, and this very year I have taught American literature from the Civil War (Whitman) to the present (Pynchon).

Many years ago, I began a plan for compiling an anthology of American literature, but the idea was set aside for other more pressing projects. I decided to return to the notion of making an anthology some five years ago because I suddenly had a yearning to see the field in its totality or wholeness, and in depth, as I had once glimpsed it years ago as a graduate student. The making of this anthology has been a kind of return to intellectual roots and a labor of academic love. In creating it, I began to remember my graduate courses in American literature at the University of Chicago with Professors Walter Blair, Napier Wilt, and Robert Streeter. Something of their eclecticism, pragmatism, common sense, and humor have helped shape the project.

But *Heritage of American Literature* has the stamp of my particular perspective on it throughout. By sheer force of will, I turned myself into a generalist, absorbing what I could from the scholarship and criticism of others, but always coming back in the end to my own feelings, sensibility, and field of vision. I began with the conviction that an anthology created from beginning to end out of a single, continuous, and coherent point of view—that is, my own—would have its own value. I have finished the anthology with that conviction intact.

To express gratitude to all of those who have in some way contributed to the making of this anthology would require me to write my autobiography. This I cannot do. But I can name those who have been most immediately helpful. They belong (or belonged) to the editorial and production staff of

This I cannot do. But I can name those who have been most immediately helpful. They belong (or belonged) to the editorial and production staff of Harcourt Brace Jovanovich—Paul Nockleby, Bill McLane, Karen Allanson, Robert Watrous, Eleanor Garner, Don Fujimoto, Diane Southworth, Michael Kleist, Pat Gonzalez, Diana Reynolds, Candy Young, and Diane Pella. My thanks go also to those reviewers who provided valuable critiques of this anthology—Thomas Buell, Portland State University; Philip Furia, University of Minnesota; Frank Hodgins, University of Illinois, Urbana; Virginia M. Kouidis, Auburn University; Jerome Loving, Texas A & M University; Mitchel E. Summerlin, John C. Calhoun State Community College; and Patricia Lee Yongue, University of Houston. My collaborator and constant assistant, Kathleen Farley, has helped at every turn and crisis in the project, and has offered emotional support as well as technical assistance throughout. She has thus earned her place on the title page. In an enterprise as complicated and vast as this one, it would be absurd to claim for myself all the anthology's merits; but it would be equally absurd to imply that the blemishes belong to anyone else but myself.

JAMES E. MILLER, JR.
1990

CONTENTS

PART II: FOUNDATIONS: THE NEW NATION (1765–1830)

PART III: FRUITION: THE COMING OF AGE (1830–1865)

VOLUME I

HERITAGE OF
AMERICAN LITERATURE
BEGINNINGS TO THE CIVIL WAR

PART I

BEGINNINGS:
THE COLONIES (1608–1765)

PROLOGUE

After sailing westward for thirty-three days, Christopher Columbus and his men gazed out in awe at land on October 11, 1492. From the time he described to his sponsors, King Ferdinand and Queen Isabel of Spain, the abundant fruits hanging on the trees, the fertile lands lying idle, the rivers and streams bearing fish and gold, the rich honey and exotic spices readily available, the great mines producing quantities of copper and gold—from the time these dazzling descriptions of the newly discovered continent spread across Europe, the collective imagination became fixed on a dream of an earthly paradise where human aspirations would be fulfilled, whether for gold or God, for material wealth or spiritual freedom, for isolation and solitude or community and utopia. Often the conflicting elements of desire were so intertwined as to become inseparable, rendering the American dream from its birth indefinable.

Columbus believed until his death that he had discovered the westward route to India. He could not have imagined that the two continents opened by him to European exploration contained ancient civilizations, some of them like the Mayan in southern Mexico and Guatemala already lost in history; others, like the Aztecs in Mexico and the Incas in Peru ruling vast areas of endless prairies and soaring mountains; and still others, like the Iroquois in northern New York living under an oral constitution, governing the League of the Five Nations, that prized peace and the democratic ideal of equality.

Columbus's discovery, leading to successive waves of European migration, was to disrupt forever whatever tranquility of social order, whatever structures of civilized intercourse then existent on the two American continents. Spanish explorers like Hernando Cortés (1485–1547), Francisco Pizarro (1470?–1541), and Francisco Vásquez de Coronado (1510–1554) paved the way for Spanish settlements in Mexico, South America, and the southwestern areas of the United States beginning in the sixteenth century. And at about the same time French adventurers and missionaries like Jacques Cartier (1491–1557), Samuel de Champlain (1567?–1635), and Robert de La Salle (1643–1687) opened up Canada and the vast Mississippi Valley, running through the center of the United States from Lake Michigan to the Gulf of Mexico, to French settlement.

THE BRITISH SETTLEMENT

In this context, the British appear to be late starters in the international scramble for the lands of the New World. Moreover, one of the first British attempts at colonization was a disaster. An expedition sent out by Sir Walter

Raleigh established a settlement on Roanoke Island (now part of North Carolina) in 1587, but in 1591 a supply ship from England found no trace of the colony. In 1608, however, the British succeeded in establishing their first permanent colony at Jamestown, Virginia, in an expedition commissioned by King James I. The resourceful John Smith, then twenty-six years old, accompanied that expedition and quickly became a forceful leader in the colony. It needed firm leadership, inasmuch as it was made up in the main of "poor gentlemen, tradesmen, serving-men, libertines, and such like ten times more fit to spoil a commonwealth than . . . to begin one." Such was John Smith's opinion, recorded in one of the several works he wrote of his experience in Virginia.

It was John Smith's *Description of New England* (1616) that helped lure the Pilgrims to the New World, using for the voyage his *Map of Virginia with a Description of the Country* (1612) to find a place to locate. But the colonists of Plymouth Plantation, arriving in New England in 1620, and those of Massachusetts Bay, settling there ten years later, differed radically from those of Jamestown, foreshadowing differences between the American North and the American South that endure in other forms to this day. If the southern colonists were motivated mainly by a desire for adventure and hopes for private gain and personal pleasure, those to the north considered themselves religious Pilgrims voyaging to the promised land.

As citizens of the sixteenth century they were all in some sense products of the Renaissance and the Reformation. The Renaissance witnessed the transition from the Medieval to the modern world, renewed interest in the classical period and Greek scholarship, and the dissemination of learning as never before through the invention of movable type by Johann Gutenberg (in the mid-1400s). With its awakened curiosity in this world as against the Medieval period's emphasis on the *next,* the Renaissance had led to the discovery of America and the extensive explorations of it that followed. Through the miraculous process of printing, the books that flowed from the explorers and travellers to their home countries were bringing news of an existent world never before imagined and satisfying curiosities only recently inflamed. Even adventurers and libertines were shaped by the lively spirit of the Renaissance; as certainly were the Pilgrims and Puritans, especially in their devotion to learning, their love of Latin, Greek, and Hebrew, and their enthusiasm for books on all subjects, including the sciences.

All of the colonists, too, were products of the Reformation, that movement of reform which swept through the Holy Roman Catholic Church, destroying its unity and creating its adversaries in the form of protesting *Protestant* sects that proliferated in the process of splintering off from one another—a process continuing even into the present. The leading figures of the Reformation were Martin Luther (1483–1546), famed for nailing to the church door in Wittenberg, Germany, in 1517, his ninety-five theses attacking the Catholic practices of selling indulgences; and John Calvin (1509–1564), banished from Paris for his heretical—that is, Reformation—views, and celebrated by Protestants for his publication of *Institutes of the Christian Religion* (1536), countering Catholic dogma with a Reformation theology. Henry VIII, King of England (r. 1509–47), came into conflict with the Pope because of his desire to divorce a wife who could not give him a male heir. The conflict led to the creation in England of a national church separate from the Catholic Church.

By dint of being born in England, one became a member of the official

Church of England. Just as the Catholic Church was intolerant of heretical beliefs, so was the Church of England. Protestants who believed that the Church of England had retained too many of the Catholic images, forms, and rituals worked to purify it, to return it to the simple Word of God, and thus became known as Puritans. The official Church of England harassed and persecuted the Puritans, and those among them radical enough to propose breaking away and separating from the Church became known as Separatists.

THE AMERICAN PURITANS

Separatists was the name applied to the Puritans who set off from England to Holland in 1608, and from thence to Plymouth in New England in 1620, self-styled Pilgrims in search of religious freedom outside of the jurisdiction of English ecclesiastical authority. The beliefs they brought with them derived ultimately from John Calvin's *Institutes of the Christian Religion*. They shared these beliefs with other Puritans, including those who came to Massachusetts Bay in 1630, leading a major migration from England as persecutions were intensified. But these later immigrants were Non-Separatist Independents who hoped to achieve freedom without the radical break with the established church that the Separatists had made.

In spite of their close doctrinal relationships, the Plymouth Puritans and the Massachusetts Bay Puritans differed fundamentally in their forms of church governance. The Plymouth Puritans were *Congregationalists:* authority was vested not in an ecclesiastical hierarchy or small group of church elders, but in the congregation itself in a way that can only be described as fundamentally democratic in form. The Massachusetts Bay Puritans, as Non-Separatists and thus linked to an ecclesiastical hierarchy, were led by a group who were considered presbyters (or elders): the form of governance was *Presbyterian*. In short, in Plymouth religious authority came from the church members themselves, while in Massachusetts Bay it was imposed from above. As the populations interspersed and colonies merged, New England churches tended to adopt a modified Congregationalism (called the New England Way) in which local churches maintained their independence with decisions made by the congregations, but with neighboring churches participating in the ordination and installation of ministers.

The doctrines ("five points") of Calvinism adopted by the Puritans and established at the Synod of Dort in 1619 in Holland are straightforward, simple, and interlinked. The basic tenet is belief in the *total depravity* of humankind, stemming from Adam and Eve's disobedience to God in the Garden of Eden by eating the forbidden fruit, thus bestowing on all descendants an inescapable innate evil and corruption. But through the intercession of Jesus Christ, God provided a *limited atonement* for a select number—not all—of his creatures, in an *unconditional election*. Those so fortunate to be of these elect are subject to *irresistible grace* and scheduled for salvation, a happy fate unaffected one way or another by acts of those saved. The *perseverance of the saints* (that is, the elect) determines their final salvation, regardless of their weaknesses or "falls." And those not of the elect are scheduled for damnation, a terrible fate equally unaffected by the acts of those damned. A truly omnipotent God, through predestination, controls all events and thus determines those destined for heaven and those destined for hell.

Belief in these doctrines was accompanied by a belief in *covenant theology*. In the beginning God made a contract, or covenant, with his creatures Adam and Eve, which promised salvation through obedience and good works. When they were lured into eating the forbidden fruit by Satan, they broke the covenant and were banished from the Garden of Eden. But God out of his infinite goodness made another contract, this time with Abraham—the covenant of grace. This covenant was offered through God's sacrifice of his Son, Jesus Christ, who took on the sins of the world in his death. According to this second covenant, humankind may achieve salvation not through good works but only through God's grace, granted to those of the elect. In Puritan theology, *conversion* was not a change from a state of damnation (impossible because of predestination), but, rather, a spiritual awakening to membership among the elect, predetermined from the beginning.

The Puritans who came to America were zealous in their belief in the Bible as the Word of God, and in the tenets of Calvinism as firmly supported by that Word. Moreover, they felt that theirs was a special destiny in world history, that they were assigned by God to play out a special role in a cosmic drama. Just as the Old Testament had prefigured the New Testament by its *typology*—setting forth types that are repeated, actions that are paralleled, prophecies and promises that are fulfilled—so both Old and New Testaments prefigured the Puritan's voyaging to the New World: Moses and Christ prefigured such Puritan leaders as William Bradford and John Winthrop; the children of Israel's exodus from bondage in Egypt was paralleled by the flight of the Puritans from persecution in England; the Israelites' wandering journey in search of the promised land was paralleled by the Pilgrims' wandering journey to Holland and then to the New World wilderness in search of religious freedom; and the Israelites' discovery of their promised land in Canaan (Palestine) prefigured the Puritans' settlement in New England—constituting for them the New Canaan. When John Winthrop, the leader of the Puritans sailing to New England on the *Arbella* in 1630, delivered to his assembled flock his sermon "A Model of Christian Charity," he cast himself in the role of Moses and his flock in the role of the children of Israel, and he exhorted them that they must make their settlement in New England an exemplary community for all mankind: "For we must consider that we shall be as a city upon a hill."

It is not without significance that at the moment of the founding of America, the founders were filled with a keen sense of their destiny and the transcendent importance of their actions and their legacy. Although many of the terms of description would change, that sense of destiny, that ideal of being or becoming that "city upon a hill" as a model for all the world, has endured deep into the twentieth century, lodged as it is deep in the American psyche.

HERETICS, INDIANS, WITCHES

Just as the Church of England considered the Puritans heretical, so the Puritans considered those who challenged their fixed dogmas heretical. Roger Williams was among the first to question the very basis of the Puritan theocracy in which religion and government were united in the state, tolerating no dissenting belief, and the minister became the ruler through application of the Bible as law. Williams argued for separation of church and state and called for toleration of all beliefs, even atheism. He was banished from the Massachusetts Bay Colony in 1635 and established his own settlement at Providence, Rhode Island, in 1636. Antinomianism reared its threatening head in the form of the courageous Anne Hutchinson. Antinomianism held that under the covenant of grace, moral law was irrelevant because faith alone would lead to salvation. Anne Hutchinson spread such a belief, maintaining that God revealed Himself to her by an indwelling Holy Spirit—thus challenging ministerial authority which held the sole source of the knowledge of God to be the Holy Bible, the Word of God. She was banished and went to Rhode Island in 1638. Many people found an appealing common sense in Arminianism. Named after the Dutch theologian, Jacobus Arminius (1560–1609), Arminianism maintained that "good works" could play a part in the achievement of salvation—thus challenging the Calvinist doctrine of predestination. Arminianism was much easier for some people—particularly those haunted by possible damnation—to understand and believe than the abstract doctrines of predestination and the covenant of grace.

The Indians were described in the early accounts of settlement in the New World as both friends and foes. Jamestown leader John Smith was held captive for a time by Chief Powhatan, and the colonists in turn held captive the Chief's daughter Pocahontas. After the resolution of differences and reconciliation, Pocahontas led her tribe in helping the colonists through their time of great want and suffering. Similarly in Plymouth, the Indians helped the Puritans in their hard times. But as the colonists grew in numbers, encroaching on the ancestral homes and lands of the Indians in both the North and the South, conflict became inevitable. A few colonists, like Roger Williams in New England, questioned the right of the king of England to grant charters to lands the crown did not own. Williams was easy to deal with by banishment. But the Indians were not so easily dismissed.

The Puritans saw the "savages" as playing a hostile role in the cosmic religious drama unfolding: the New World wilderness had been taken over by Satan as his empire, and its natives had made a diabolical covenant with him to war against God's chosen people and to defeat the plans for the building of a city of God, or New Canaan, in the middle of the devil's domain. Like the Israelites of old, those come to the New World were to have their loyalty and faith tested by Satan himself. This view of the Indians, rendering them something less than human, made conflict likely and bloodletting probable, especially if the Indians committed acts that aroused the anger of the settlers.

The first major incident was the war with the Pequots in 1637, precipitated by the increasing and seemingly endless dispossession of the Indians of their lands. The colonists' superior weapons and strategy prevailed. In the climactic battle at Mystic, Connecticut, the Pequots' wigwams were set on fire, and those who were not burned to death were killed by musket fire when they tried to escape. The historian of the colonists, Captain John Mason, wrote of the slaughter in the battle he helped to plan: "Thus did the Lord judge among the heathen, filling the place with dead bodies."

King Philip's War of 1675–76 brought the defeat (or retreat) of the Indians and left the land open to unobstructed colonist settlement. King Philip was the English name given to an Indian chieftan of the Wampanoags, who brought together a number of tribes with the specific aim of obliterating the white settlements. They had particular grievances, but underlying them was the increasing white encroachment on Indian lands. Again the settlers' superior arms won the day. Over three thousand Indians were killed, and King Philip taken, drawn and quartered, and his head placed on a pole for public display. Organized Indian attacks diminished. Mary Rowlandson, taken by the Indians in 1676, wrote in her *Narrative of the Captivity* (1682) of the pagan victory celebration she witnessed on her first night as prisoner (she was "captive" for over eleven weeks): the Indians were "a company of hell-hounds, roaring, singing, ranting, and insulting, as if they would have torn our very hearts out; yet the Lord by His almighty power preserved a number of us from death." The battle lines of colonists and Indians were precisely the battle lines of God and Satan. All was enacted according to God's predesigned plan, including the final defeat of the Indians.

In 1692, an outbreak of witchcraft in Salem spread fear throughout the colony. Charges were brought against the offenders. The governor appointed a special tribunal (Nathaniel Hawthorne's ancestor served as a member), and guilt was found in nineteen cases. Those found guilty were hanged. In *Wonders of the Invisible World* (1693), Cotton Mather simply expressed the assumptions and beliefs of the colonies when he attributed the witchcraft to Satan and his "possessed" confederates: "Now, by these confessions [of the "witches" at Salem] 'tis agreed that the Devil has made a dreadful knot of witches in the country . . . that these witches have driven a trade of commissioning their confederate spirits to do all sorts of mischief to the neighbors. . . .: yea, that at prodigious witch-meetings, the wretches have proceeded so far as to concert and consult the methods of rooting out the Christian religion from this country, and setting up instead of it perhaps a more gross diabolism than ever the world saw before."

With heretics in active opposition, with Satan-inspired Indians in open rebellion, with the devil sending out his witches to confuse, delude, and persecute the colonists, it is no wonder that the Puritans saw themselves as protagonists in a cosmic drama. They were God's soldiers in a life and death struggle against Satan's legions, with their New World City of God hanging in the balance.

GROWTH, DECLINE, THE GREAT AWAKENING

The story of New World settlement during its first century is the story of its rapid growth into a culturally varied and religiously diverse population through immigration, the gradual dilution and decline of the Puritan theocracy, and sporadic attempts to revive the faith resulting in such phenomena as the Great Awakening.

The British migration to the New World that began with the settlement of Jamestown in Virginia in 1607, Plymouth in New England in 1620, and Massachusetts Bay in 1630, increased markedly in the following two decades. A major reason was the intensifying royal persecution of the Puritans in England. But with Charles I's loss of power that brought his death and the establishment of the Commonwealth in 1649, migration slowed because the British government became sympathetic to the Puritans. With the fall of the Commonwealth and the Restoration of Charles II in 1660—and the reassumption of power of the Church of England—circumstances were again reversed, and removal from England to the New World increased again.

But by this time, the motivations for migration to the New World had become mixed. Indeed, by the time of the second generation of Puritans, the cohesiveness and unity of the original theocracy had slackened. In *Of Plymouth*

Plantation, William Bradford lamented that by the early 1630s prosperity had brought dispersal of the population and growing interest in owning cattle and land. He concluded: "I fear [this] will be the ruin of New England, at least of the churches of God there, and will provoke the Lord's displeasure against them." This doubt about the future of the Puritans' shining city on a hill became a recurring theme of the aging first-generation Puritans.

Not only were the successive generations of the original Puritan settlers dispersing, successive immigrants, representing a variety of nationalities, religious beliefs, and attitudes, were also diluting the original English and Puritan concentration. The Dutch began settling in the 1620s along the Hudson River in New York, and the Swedes and Finns in the 1630s in the Delaware Valley. Catholics fleeing persecution found a refuge in Lord Baltimore's Maryland in the mid-1630s. The Quakers were favored by William Penn in the 1680s with a haven in Pennsylvania, a colony dedicated to religious freedom. Germans, French, and Jews from Germany and Portugal soon joined the growing migration to the New World. Colonists numbered more than 250,000 in 1700; by 1750 they numbered around one and a half million diverse inhabitants.

As the population increased, there were advances in technology and growth of institutions that supported learning—and encouraged diversity of opinion. The first American printing press was established at Cambridge, Massachusetts, in 1639; the first book *(The Bay Psalm Book)* appeared in 1640. The first newspaper appeared in Boston in 1690, but lasted for only four days. Another began publication in Boston in 1704—and survived. In 1636, the Puritans established Harvard College to prepare young men for the ministry. In 1693, Virginia established William and Mary College. Yale College followed in 1701, the College of New Jersey (later, Princeton) in 1746, and King's College (later, Columbia) in 1754. Gradually the religious purposes imposed on the colleges at their founding became diffuse, and the curriculum adapted to changing interests, times, and populations.

By the time the impressively learned Puritans Cotton Mather (1663–1728) and Jonathan Edwards (1703–1758) appeared on the scene, Puritanism had passed the pinnacle of its power. The Puritans themselves were the first to note and record the decline of religious fervor and the increase in sin and wickedness among them. Michael Wigglesworth, for example, wrote "God's Controversy with New England" in response to a terrible drought that laid waste the crops throughout the colony in 1662. A subtitle of the poem succinctly captured the latter-day Puritans' view of their melancholy fate: "New-England planted, prospered, declining, threatened, punished." God speaks sternly to his chosen people, the Puritans:

> . . . how is it that I find
> Instead of holiness carnality,
> Instead of heavenly frames an earthly mind,
> For burning zeal luke-warm indifferency,
> For flaming love, key-cold dead-heartedness,
> For temperance (in meat, and drink, and clothes) excess?

God's accusations of "deceit, contention, and strife,/False-dealing, covetousness, hypocrisy" continue for many stanzas. Wigglesworth's poem is but one of many contemporary writings revealing the later Puritans' deepening sense of betrayal of the founders' dream: the creation of the New Canaan in fulfillment of God's plan. They did not realize that the Puritanism of the past was doomed by the tide of non-Puritan immigration, the new learning in an age of enlightenment, the quickening colonial interest in trade and commerce, and other historical currents they did not understand and could not control.

The general slackening of religious commitment, along with the decline of Puritanism, no doubt contributed to the intense efforts at religious revival that resulted in the Great Awakening in the late 1730s and into the 1740s. Religious fervor swept through the colonies, the flames fanned by such itinerant ministers as the famed British Methodist George Whitefield (1714–1770), who could address outdoor crowds numbering in the thousands (Benjamin Franklin calculated in his *Autobiography* that Whitefield's voice would carry effectively to an audience of 30,000). In fact, the Great Awakening was foreshadowed by a revival that took place in the early 1730s in Northampton, Massachusetts, centered in Jonathan Edwards's church. There the numbers and nature of the "conversions" were such as to inspire Edwards to examine and describe them in one of his most widely read works, *A Faithful Narrative of the Surprising Works of God* (1737). There was some concern that the intense emotionalism inspired in the converted might be the duplicitous work of the devil, intended to deceive and mock the ministers. Edwards described one of his flock, his Uncle Hawley, who committed suicide in his depression after becoming convinced that he was a member not of the elect but of the damned.

The Great Awakening may well seem in retrospect to be the dying gasp of the Puritans' bold and mighty effort to build a New Jerusalem in the New World wilderness. Religious feeling did not disappear in the colonies, but took different forms. The Quakers believed that each individual was morally informed by God through an "inner light." Deists found their revelation not in an infallible Bible but in nature itself. Older religious groups—Catholics, Jews—brought their ancient faiths with them to the New World. Practical interests such as commerce, taxes, and politics came to the forefront of concern. Gradually the ideal of separation of church and state evolved, perhaps inevitable in such a pluralistic society. The idea of a United States was slowly gathering strength, consciously and unconsciously, for the ordeal of birth.

COLONIAL LITERATURE

Colonial literature with its focus on religious experience, questions, and controversy, may seem quite removed from modern American concerns and preoccupations. But in fact it has much to tell us about ourselves. In it are to be found the roots of the American character, intellect, and imagination. Indeed, many of the ideas and issues that gripped the Puritan mind, when translated from a religious to a secular vocabulary and context, remain alive today—as, for example, predestination survives in discussions of social, economic, or psychological determinism.

Few other countries of the world are as accessible through their literature as America. America was established shortly after the invention of the printing press and was settled by a literate and learned people involved in an enterprise they believed to have world and cosmic implications. They were eager to leave accounts of their momentous activities to a posterity that, they believed, would see them as Old Testament figures present at the "beginning." It would be a radical mistake to set aside colonial literature because it exists mainly in "non-imaginative" genres, because it has no fiction or drama, and because the poetry itself tends always to be religious. Colonial literature is, in fact, a very rich embodiment of the colonial and Puritan imagination. No novel's action could compete in interest with the life lived by the Puritan, lured by Satan and enticed by vice, unsure of membership in the elect, horrified at the prospects of damnation, a sinner held in the hands of an angry God. This vision of the human plight is imaginatively embodied in every form of Puritan literature.

ACCOUNTS OF THE FOUNDING

Many early works of the colonial imagination come together (and interrelate in their nature) as accounts of the founding of the colonies. Works like John Smith's *A Description of New England* (1616) and *The General History of Virginia* (1624) combine elements of the sociological study, the promotional tract, and the historical record, describing for Europeans an exotic and abundant land that could provide the necessities of life with a minimum of toil. Such works lured the Puritans to the New World, where they discovered difficulties they had not expected and suffered deprivations they had not imagined. William Bradford was obsessed with getting an account of the Pilgrims' experience down on paper because he believed that the events constituted a beginning of a momentous religious action that would have its conclusion in the distant future. The epic nature of his *Of Plymouth Plantation* (written 1630–50) is no doubt different in reality from what Bradford intended, but in such passages as those describing the Mayflower Compact, the "Starving Time," and the first Thanksgiving, he provided the American imagination with its most enduring founding myths.

Like Bradford, John Winthrop, first governor of the Massachusetts Bay Colony, felt compelled to set down a record of events that would shake the world. He kept a journal, but it was for the public record, and when it was published it was entitled *The History of New England* (written 1630–49). It is a day-by-day account and provides fascinating glimpses, from the Puritan perspective, of dissenters Anne Hutchinson and Roger Williams, along with much else. It is, however, Edward Johnson who most directly adopted and most fully adapted the epic form in his *The Wonder-Working Providence of Sion's Saviour in New England* (1654), casting Jesus Christ in the role of epic hero gripped in battle with Satan, the fate of Sion (another designation for New Canaan, or New England) hanging in the balance. Johnson did not hesitate to affirm and reaffirm the cosmic significance of the events taking place in the early seventeenth century in the New England wilderness.

DISCOURSE AND DEBATE ON BELIEFS

Most Puritan intellectual energy was poured into religious discourse, especially sermons and religious arguments, forms for which the modern age has limited enthusiasm. Some of the best examples of straightforward discourse on points of doctrine are Thomas Shepard's little essay "The Covenant of Grace" and Increase Mather's brief discussion of predestination, "What Sinners Can Do Towards Their Own Conversion." Shepard's piece is full of sweet reason; man deserves "to be driven up and down the world as a vagabond," yet "Almighty God . . . must take Himself to us, and us to Himself, more sure and near than even before" by His covenant of grace. Increase

Mather's brief discussion argues the paradoxical proposition that sinners who are predestined to be damned must place the blame only on themselves. Without conceding that God is the least bit less than "absolute sovereign," Mather affirms that sinners may do much towards their own conversion by leaving off their sinning ways and taking on the ways of faith: "Sinners should consider of death, that the thing is certain, and the time uncertain, and that they run an infinite hazzard if they neglect making sure of an interest in Christ one day longer." By the time readers finish this sermon-like essay, they may well be convinced that predestination and free will are distinguishable only by the most subtle of metaphysical niceties of thought.

By far the largest body of literature to survive the colonial period is a vast number of sermons. Examples of writing in the sermon form that might be compared with Increase Mather's piece are (from the earlier period) John Winthrop's "A Model of Christian Charity" (1630) and (from a later time) Jonathan Edwards's "A Divine and Supernatural Light" (1734) and "Sinners in the Hands of an Angry God" (1741). In the New England churches, pulpits were elevated and the sermons delivered from a lofty height. It was not uncommon for the sermon to last for two hours, causing wit Nathaniel Ward to remark: "We have a strong weakness in New England that when we speak we know not how to conclude. We make many ends before we make an end." If it seems remarkable that the congregations not only came to church but listened attentively to the sermons, it must be recalled that there were no public entertainments for Puritans to attend—and few private ones for that matter. The occasion of the sermon was often the high point of the week for the community, absorbing the whole intellectual, emotional, and psychological being of both minister and listener.

Some of the most engaging religious writing is polemical. The Puritans argued with each other on points of doctrine with a passion verging on violence. They used sarcasm, wit, invective—and intelligence. One of the most fascinating debates that went on was over the question of tolerance of dissenting religious beliefs when Roger Williams took the side of tolerance and the Puritan establishment (particularly John Cotton and Nathaniel Ward), the side of the existent intolerance. Roger Williams manages to get in his very title the intensity he felt on the issue—*The Bloody Tenet of Persecution for Cause of Conscience* (1644)—and in the first of twelve propositions he sets forth in his Preface, he infuses his style with his indignation: "First, That the blood of so many hundred thousand souls of protestants and papists, spilled in the wars of present and former ages, for their respective consciences, is not required nor accepted by Jesus Christ the Prince of Peace." Nathaniel Ward, in *The Simple Cobbler of Aggawam* (1647), is sly, witty, and oblique in his reply. He suggests that anyone tolerant of the "adversaries of God's truth" is somehow on the side of Satan, who "loves to fish in roiled waters": "If the devil might have his free option, I believe he would ask nothing else but liberty to enfranchise all false religions and to embondage the truth." This exchange is serious debate, but at the same time it is entertaining intellectual fencing.

Another religious debate that drew attention was over Congregationalism. In 1705 an anonymous pamphlet (later traced to Cotton Mather) appeared whose veiled intent was to call into question the radically democratic form of government of the New England churches. It suggests the need to diminish control by the congregations, to decrease the independence of the churches one from another, and to increase the power of the clergy. John Wise was moved to attack these proposals in a basically democratic text, *A Vindication of the Government of New-England Churches* (1717), which rings with such sentences as: "The end of all good government is to cultivate humanity, and promote the happiness of all, and the good of every man in all his rights, his life, liberty, estate, honor, etc. without injury or abuse done to any."

In any discussion of the Puritan contribution to American character and institutions, the documents of Puritan debates must loom large. Both Roger Williams and John Wise were Puritans, to some extent dissenting from those established in power. In clarifying and sharpening their ideas in argument, their legacy is a vital one: Williams in his dedication to religious tolerance and the radical notion of the separation of church and state; Wise in his dedication to democracy and the radical notion that the purposes of government include the cultivation of "humanity," the promotion of "the happiness of all," the preservation of the rights of "every man" to "life, liberty, estate, honor." Williams and Wise make us realize how profound and complex the Puritan heritage is.

DIARIES: PURITAN GENTLEMAN, PLANTATION ARISTOCRAT

Some of the most interesting colonial writing turns up in the diaries, which were written not for publication but for a variety of private and personal reasons. The Puritans, of course, were concerned for the daily state of their souls and were constantly on watch for small signs in daily life that revealed the veiled destinies of the individuals or the hidden purposes of God. But diaries have been kept throughout history by individuals who define and explore and complete their identities through daily stints of writing about the self and personal experience. Diaries and journals have many elements in common. But a cursory examination of the notable diaries of Michael Wigglesworth, Cotton Mather, and Jonathan Edwards and the important journals of John Winthrop, Mary Rowlandson, and Sarah Kemble Knight suggests that the diary is centripetal, tending inward to the private-most self, while the journal is centrifugal, tending outward to exterior experience and public event. The difference is implicit in a remark set down by Jonathan Edwards in his diary that he was bent on "narrowly searching out all the subtle subterfuges" of his "thought."

Two remarkable diaries survive from the colonial period, one from the Massachusetts Bay Colony written by Samuel Sewall and the other from the colony of Virginia by William Byrd. Both diaries narrate much of the outer experience of these prominent leaders but both also reveal much of their inner, intimate feelings and desires, meditations, and motives. Neither was intended (at least on the conscious level) for publication: Sewall's diary did not appear until the latter part of the nineteenth century and Byrd's not until the middle of the twentieth. Read side by side, these diaries suggest much about the major character differences between the North and the South, the religious focus of the one as against the religious unconcern of the other, the sexual restraint as against sexual capriciousness, moral anguish as against moral incuriosity. But Sewall and Byrd share, among other traits, a keen awareness of the price of things, a love of books and learning, a concern for social and political order. Differences between the American North and South originated in the beginning with the differences in motivation between the New England Puritans and the Virginia adventurers and gentlemen. The differences were perpetuated by the patterns of settlement: New England developed as a series of small towns made up of people of more or less equal means sharing (or disputing) religious views; Virginia developed as a collection of large plantations separated by great distances with a slave- or worker-based economy supporting a wealthy, cultured elite.

POETRY

The one traditional imaginative genre the colonists produced in quantity was poetry. Indeed, the first book published on the first printing press established in America (1639) was *The Bay Psalm Book* (1640). Richard Mather was one of the translators and John Cotton wrote the Preface, giving the book the imprimatur of the Founding Fathers. Cotton said in his Preface: "If . . . the verses are not always so smooth and elegant as some may desire or expect, let them consider that God's Altar needs not our polishings . . . for we have respected rather a plain translation, than to smooth our verses with the sweetness of any paraphrase, and so have attended conscience rather than elegance, fidelity rather than poetry . . . so we may sing in Sion the Lord's songs of praise according to his own will." It is easy to ridicule such inverted lines as "The Lord to me a shepherd is," but refinement of expression was secondary to singability inspired by religious fervor. Some of the finest Puritan wit is found in poetic tributes to the dead in epitaphs and threnodies, genres much admired during the period. Two lines from a threnody for a man named Stone suggest how the poet could be carried away by multiplying puns: "Whetstone, that edgified the obtusest mind;/Loadstone, that drew the iron heart unkind." Ever practical, New Englanders discovered in *The New England Primer* (*c.* 1683) a way to teach the ABCs and points of Puritan dogma simultaneously—in rhymes that could be chanted by children: "In Adam's fall/We sinned all."

With poetry so prominent at the beginning of life in education, in religious experience throughout life, and at the end in memorial rituals, it is no wonder that the colonies could produce some impressive poets that command attention. From New England these include Anne Bradstreet, Michael Wigglesworth, and Edward Taylor. In the South (Maryland)—and a radically different poet from the Puritan poets of the North—is Ebenezer Cooke, gentleman adventurer and tobacco agent. These are the poets who emerge from the mass. In 1726, Cotton Mather in *Manuductio ad Ministerium* felt it necessary to warn his readers against "a boundless and sickly appetite for the reading of poems, which now the rickety nation swarms withal."

At the beginning of American literature stands Anne Bradstreet. She was, as Adrienne Rich has said, "the first non-didactic American poet, the first to give an embodiment to American nature, the first in whom personal intention appears to precede Puritan dogma as an impulse in verse. . . . The web of her sensibility stretches almost invisibly within the framework of Puritan literary convention; its texture is essentially both Puritan and feminine." Had we come to know Anne Bradstreet's poetry only through the poems published (without her permission or knowledge) in *The Tenth Muse, Lately Sprung Up in America* (1650), we would pay her little attention today. Even she, in "The Author to Her Book," conceiving her volume as a child, wittily discusses the difficulties of revision:

> Yet being mine own, at length affection would
> Thy blemishes amend, if so I could;
> I washed thy face, but more defects I saw,
> And rubbing off a spot still made a flaw.

It is, however, in her later poetry that she achieved distinction. She gave up imitating her literary models and wrote poems about seizure of a fever, a child's death, an absent husband, the burning of the family house, a walk in the woods, thoughts of death before giving birth to a child. These poems have the power still today to arrest attention and enter into the reader's imaginative concerns and awareness.

In his *Day of Doom* (1662), Michael Wigglesworth wrote the most popular book of poetry in the Puritan period and one of the most popular (if we calculate the percentage of readers in the entire population) in the history of America. Moses Coit Tyler noted that the poem "attributes to the Divine Being a character the most execrable and loathsome to be met with, perhaps, in any literature, Christian or pagan." But the New England Puritans knew this Divine Being well from the sermons they heard in their churches—the kind of sermon that Jonathan Edwards's "Sinners in the Hands of an Angry God" has come to symbolize. There is surely something in human psychology that fixes attention with grim fascination on scenes of intense suffering in hell: visitors to the Vatican's Sistine Chapel in Rome gaze in awe at Michelangelo's ceiling portraying God's creation of Adam, but they stand transfixed in rapt horror at Michelangelo's wall of the Last Judgment, in which stripped sinners pursued by demons are tumbling into the fiery pits of hell. One can imagine a Puritan family gathered around the table at night, reading by a flickering candle—

> With iron bonds they bind their hands
>   and cursed feet together,
> And cast them all, both great and small,
>   into that lake forever.
> Where day and night, without respite,
>   they wail, and cry, and howl
> For tort'ring pain, which they sustain
>   in body and in soul.

The ballad measure has been ridiculed, but for oral recitation, and with the right reader, it can be very effective in underscoring the concrete and vivid depictions of punishment and suffering.

In contrast with Anne Bradstreet and Michael Wigglesworth, Edward Taylor was virtually unknown as a poet in his lifetime. His poems in manuscript were not discovered and published until the twentieth century. Now his reputation has soared beyond those of the other poets of the period, not because he hit upon an original subject matter (his subjects are always some aspect of orthodox Puritanism), but because of the startling—often dazzling—word, image, or metaphor he summons to his purpose: "God's tender bowels run/ Out streams of grace" ("Meditation Eight," First Series); "Words are befouled, thought's filthy fumes that smoke/From smutty huts, like will-a-wisps that rise/From quagmires, run o'er bogs where frogs do croak" ("Meditation 43," Second Series); "Lord put these nipples then my mouth into/And suckle me therewith I humbly pray" ("Meditation 150," Second Series); "Upon what base was fixed the lathe, where-in/He turned this globe, and riggaled it so trim ("Preface," *God's Determinations*); "Make me, O Lord, Thy spinning wheel complete./Thy holy word my distaff make for me" ("Huswifery"); "When in this knot [the true love-knot of marriage] I planted was, my stock/Soon knotted and a manly flower outbrake" ("Upon Wedlock and Death of Children").

Such astonishing diction, imagery, metaphor, and conceit have caused critics to cite Taylor as a metaphysical poet, in the tradition of his English counterparts such as George Herbert and John Donne. But one critic, Norman S. Grabo, asserts with considerable justification: "None of the metaphysicals relies so heavily on allegory as Taylor does; and, as a result, his poetry is rooted as firmly in the Middle Ages as it is in his own century. But beyond his era, his method with images anticipates Emily Dickinson, Gerard Manley Hopkins, and a number of recent writers. . . . His strange ability to remind readers of others—from Clement of Alexandria to Walt Whitman—frees Taylor from the narrow designation 'metaphysical' and associates him with major writers in the entire stream of Christian, English, and American literature."

To turn from Bradstreet, Wigglesworth, and Taylor to Ebenezer Cooke is to turn from tense Puritan soul-searching to relaxed cavalier scalawaggery, from the sober, sin-hating North to the sunny, fun-loving South, from serious concentration on the next life to satiric portrayal of this life. *The Sot-Weed Factor: Or, a Voyage to Maryland* (1708) is the inverse of a promotional tract for America. The sot-weed factor (tobacco agent) who is the speaker of the poem begins by lamenting his departure from England for Maryland:

> Condemned by fate to wayward curse,
> Of friends unkind, and empty purse,
> Plagues worse than filled Pandora's box,
> I took my leave of Albion's rocks. . . .

And he concludes by placing a "dreadful curse" on this New World travesty of a civilized country:

> May wrath divine then lay those regions waste
> Where no man's faithful, nor a woman chaste.

In between the opening anguish at removal from England and the closing curse bestowed on America, Cooke provides a picaresque account of crude frontier life in Maryland, with emphasis on discomforts, stupidities, drunkenness, and injustice. At one point in his travels he is taken in by a settler and finally, wearily, goes to bed. Suddenly a cat begins a fight with a pig, dogs begin to bark, then a fox (reynard) pursues ducks and geese into the room—

> Raging, I jumped upon the floor,
> And like a drunken sailor swore;
> With sword I fiercely laid about,
> And soon dispersed the feathered rout,
> The poultry out of window flew,
> And reynard cautiously withdrew.
> The dogs who this encounter heard,
> Fiercely themselves to aid me reared,
> And to the place of combat run,
> Exactly as the field was won,
> Fretting and hot as roasted capon,
> And greasy as a flitch of bacon.

The scene is a comedy, verging on the slapstick; the descriptions are deft, the metaphors apt; and the rhyming couplet and rollicking meter match the satiric voice and tone. But though the poem is marvelously comic, it clearly provides authentic glimpses of New World frontier life. As Edward H. Cohen has written of Ebenezer Cooke: "Coarse though his writing may sometimes be, it is charged with a wholesome native flavor. It uses the idiom of a lost people and keeps alive their forgotten way of life."

JOURNALS: PERSONAL ACCOUNTS OF HIGH ADVENTURE

During the colonial period, journals of actual adventure filled the role played by fiction in a later day. Real events were strange and exciting enough to compete with any invention by a literary imagination. These narratives were read avidly both at home and abroad for the information about life in the New World wilderness they contained and for the sheer pleasure of vicarious experience they inspired. Two of the best examples of this anomalous literary genre are Mary Rowlandson's *Narrative of the Captivity* and Sarah Kembel Knight's *Journal*.

Mary Rowlandson's account of her captivity among the Indians for over eleven weeks in 1676 was one of the subgenre of literature widely read during the colonial period. The "captivity narratives" were popular for a variety of reasons: they were filled with action, violence, conflict, suspense; since they were written by survivors, they were all in some way confirmation of the remarkable providence of God (God's "promises displayed" was a part of Rowlandson's title); they manifested archetypal patterns of good against evil, fulfilling readers' assumptions that the hostile Indians were under control of the devil and the settlers creatures of God. Mary Rowlandson's account was no doubt especially fascinating because she was a vulnerable member of the "weaker sex" with babes in arms when captured. Her story was full of pathos, particularly as she related the occasion of her child's death. And readers surely read her narrative with dreadful anticipation of how the virile Indians might victimize her. Early in the narrative, she refers to the "master" who took her over as his possession, but she does not reveal until near the end of her narrative the answer to the question on every reader's mind: "O the wonderful power of God that I have seen, and the experience that I have had. I have been in the midst of those roaring lions, and savage bears, that feared neither God, nor man, nor the devil, by night and day, alone and in company, sleeping all sorts together, and yet not one of them ever offered me the least abuse of unchastity to me, in word or action. Though some are ready to say I speak it for my own credit; but I speak it in the presence of God, and to His glory." This is not the only point of the account at which a subtext emerges actually countering the recurring surface exclamations about the cruelty and savagery of the Indians.

Sarah Kemble Knight's *Journal*, kept on her trip from Boston to New York in 1704–05, belongs to that literary subgenre, the travel narrative. It was not published until 1825, at a time when the hazardous journey of the rapidly receding and distant past already seemed strange. Today, when the same distance Madam Knight travelled may be covered by jet liner in thirty minutes, her journey seems even more exotic. If something has been gained by the rapid transportation, something has also been lost—as Madam Knight reveals in the colorful details of her account of the food and beds of the inns she visited and of the quirks and oddities of characters she encountered. Not a small part of the interest of her narrative resides in the fact that she was a woman travelling alone, thus finding it necessary to hire male companions to accompany her over the most dangerous parts of the countryside. She emerges from her own narrative an independent and forceful woman, capable of making her way and holding her own without the constant attendance of a man— an early example of those "pioneer women" whose part in the settling and development of America has been largely overlooked.

PHILOSOPHERS AND DIVINES:
COTTON MATHER AND JONATHAN EDWARDS

By the time of the appearance of the most brilliant Puritan theologians who were most adept in explicating and defending points of Calvinistic dogma, the Puritan dominance of the New England colonies was on the wane. Perhaps it was because Puritanism was gradually being displaced from the center of colonial life that Cotton Mather and Jonathan Edwards were all the more zealous in defending and propping up the old faith of the early Puritans. Theirs was a lost cause, but by dedicating themselves so wholeheartedly to it, they established themselves as important thinkers and philosophers standing at the beginnings of American literature. They may be attacked, as they have been, but they cannot be dislodged from the niches they occupy: their awesome achievements are too firmly fixed, their commanding presences too deeply embedded in the American psyche and spirit.

A few of Cotton Mather's 450 works continue to have appeal. His massive *Magnalia Christi Americana* (1702), purported *Ecclesiastical History of New England* from 1620 to 1698, is in reality an American epic perpetuating the myths of the Founders, accepting them in their self-appointed roles as Moses-figures leading a chosen people into the wilderness in search of the promised land, New Canaan. His *Wonders of the Invisible World* (1693) continues to fascinate not because it is persuasive in its affirmation of the existence of witches and its defense of the 1692 witch trials in Salem, but because of the eerie light it throws on the underside of American politics and behavior, the perverse propensity to launch "witch hunts" whenever confronted with adversaries of entrenched truths and established dogmas. *Bonifacius: An Essay Upon the Good* (1710) strikes later readers as a peculiarly American book in its attempt to create systematic procedures for "doing good" and in its pragmatism in reducing abstract virtue to concrete experience by focusing on behavior in the relationship of the self to the self, to spouse, to children, and to neighbors. In its admonishments about the self and practicality about relations with others, it links Mather with such later American writers as Benjamin Franklin and Henry David Thoreau.

But it is perhaps in his personal presence that Mather will continue to engage our imagination. As one critic, Babette M. Levy, has concluded: "He [Mather] would put first his efforts to preserve New England's Congregational churches, to keep alive the memory of the spirit and dedication of the first settlers. . . . Later generations, with different values, might look with gentle eyes upon his advocacy of kindness to children, to the mentally ill, to the slave. . . [and upon] his careful plan for communal happiness with every man, according to his ability and place in life, doing good to all." Mather's estate was meager when he died because he had been so generous in life. But his library, the largest in the colonies, testified to his intellectual—and moral—dedication.

Jonathan Edwards is popularly remembered, and often condemned, for his one notorious sermon, "Sinners in the Hands of an Angry God" (1741). But as one critic, James Carse, has pointed out, "His sermons were meant to terrify. They were for his time what Picasso's 'Guernica' is for ours." It is, moreover, useful to balance Edwards's lurid evocation of the tortures of hell with his subtler, softer delineations of the fulfillments of heaven: in notable sermons like "A Divine and Supernatural Light" (1734), terror is displaced by a quiet spiritual rapture and the imagery is as enthralling as his imagery of hell is repellant. It is unlikely that Edwards's account of his own awakening to religious feeling, his "Personal Narrative" (published after his death), will be displaced from its prominent position among spiritual autobiographies. And his *Faithful Narrative of the Surprising Works of God* (1737) will surely continue to fascinate readers who are interested in detailed accounts of religious ecstasy and conversion, whether as spiritual or psychological phenomena. Edwards's *The Nature of True Virtue* (written in 1755, published in 1765), like Mather's or Franklin's attempts to define the good, will always find an audience. Less certain of endurance, perhaps, are the late, long works whose very titles indicate their purposes of defending doctrines fading from the forefront of religious debate in Edwards's own time: *A Careful and Strict Enquiry into the Modern Prevailing Notions of that Freedom of the Will which is supposed to be Essential to Moral Agency, Virtue and Vice, Reward and Punishment, Praise and Blame* (1754); and *The Great Christian Doctrine of Original Sin Defended* (1758). Whatever the defects of these works, they do not suffer from the weaknesses of previous Puritan treatises in relying fundamentally on Biblical quotation for "proof"; they are carefully crafted arguments of a keen mind ready to engage the enlightened reader with "proofs" of reason.

Edwards's work is more likely than Mather's to engage the modern imagination on its own terms (rather than as curiosities in myth-making). But even so, he is vulnerable to criticism. One critic, Peter Gay, writes: "Far from being the first modern American. . . he was the last medieval American—at least among the intellectuals." Other contemporary critics have been less harsh. David Levin writes of the lively experience of reading Edwards: "We feel the passionate strength of a pious mind, driving the intellect forward to the Lord's work." And John E. Smith says of Edwards's conception of "religious affections": "Edwards's calm word in the midst of 'much noise about religion' is that religion must not be lifeless and it must be something more than doctrine or good conduct." Robert Lowell, one of the preeminent sensibilities of modern poetry, has written:

> White wig and black coat
> all cut from one cloth,
> and designed
> like your mind!
>
> I love you faded,
> old, exiled and afraid
> to leave your last flock, a dozen
> Houssatonic Indian children;
>
> afraid to leave
> all your writing, writing, writing,
> denying the Freedom of the Will.

Edwards's powerful presence, it seems, is not easily dislodged from the American imagination.

ADDITIONAL READING

Moses Coit Tyler, *A History of American Literature, 1607–1765*, 1878.
Frederick Jackson Turner, *The Frontier in American History*, 1920.

Vernon L. Parrington, *Main Currents in American Thought*, Vol. 1, 1927.

Samuel Eliot Morison, *Builders of the Bay Colony*, 1930, 1963.

Perry Miller, *The New England Mind: The Seventeenth Century*, 1939.

John Bakeless, *The Eyes of Discovery: America as Seen by the First Explorers*, 1950.

Henry Nash Smith, *The Virgin Land: The American West as Symbol and Myth*, 1950.

Kenneth B. Murdock, "The Colonial and Revolutionary Period," *The Literature of the American People*, ed. Arthur Hobson Quinn, 1951.

Perry Miller, *The New England Mind: From Colony to Province*, 1953.

Perry Miller, *Errand into the Wilderness*, 1956.

Samuel Eliot Morison, *The Intellectual Life of Colonial New England*, 1956.

Daniel J. Boorstin, *The Americans: The Colonial Experience*, 1958.

Howard Mumford Jones, *O Strange New World: American Culture, The Formative Years*, 1964.

Daniel B. Shea, *Spiritual Autobiography in Early America*, 1968.

Samuel Eliot Morison, *The European Discovery of America: The Northern Voyages*, A.D. *500–1600*, 1971.

Everett Emerson, ed., *Major Writers of Early American Literature*, 1972.

Sacvan Bercovitch, ed., *Typology and Early American Literature*, 1972.

Larzer Ziff, *Puritanism in America: New Culture in a New World*, 1973.

Richard Slotkin, *Regeneration Through Violence: The Mythology of the American Frontier, 1600–1860*, 1973.

Samuel Eliot Morison, *The European Discovery of America: The Southern Voyages*, 1974.

Sacvan Bercovitch, *The American Puritan Imagination: Essays in Revaluation*, 1974.

Sacvan Bercovitch, *The Puritan Origins of the American Self*, 1975.

Everett H. Emerson, *Puritanism in America, 1620–1750*, 1977.

John Seelye, *Prophetic Waters: The River in Early American Life and Literature*, 1977.

Sacvan Bercovitch, *The American Jeremiad*, 1978.

Wayne Franklin, *Discoverers, Explorers, Settlers: The Diligent Writers in Early America*, 1979.

Alden T. Vaughan and Edward W. Clark, eds., *Puritans Among the Indians: Accounts of Captivity and Redemption, 1676–1724*, 1981.

Patricia Caldwell, *The Puritan Conversion Narrative: The Beginnings of American Expression*, 1983.

Philip F. Gura, *A Glimpse of Sion's Glory: Puritan Radicalism in New England, 1620–1660*, 1983.

Earl N. Harbert and Robert A. Rees, eds., *Fifteen American Authors Before 1900: Bibliographical Essays on Research and Criticism*, 1984; includes Edward Taylor and Jonathan Edwards.

Alan Heimert and Andrew Delbanco, eds., *The Puritans in America: A Narrative Anthology*, 1985.

Douglas Robinson, *American Apocalypses: The Image of the End of the World in American Literature*, 1985.

Albert J. Von Frank, *The Sacred Game: Provincialism and Frontier Consciousness in American Literature, 1630–1860*, 1986.

Emory Elliott, gen. ed., *Columbia Literary History of the United States*, 1988.

PROLOGUE: ON THE EVE OF AMERICA'S DISCOVERY

JOHN BAKELESS   CHRISTOPHER COLUMBUS
DEKANAWIDAH

It was on the night of October 11, 1492, that Christopher Columbus and the men of his three small ships, the *Pinta*, the *Niña*, and the *Santa María*, saw land after a long voyage across the unknown Atlantic. What was this newly discovered land like at this transcendent moment in American history? Were the inhabitants savage or civilized? What were the impressions of those explorers who first set eyes on the New World? Gathered together in this Prologue are three selections: a panoramic view of what was happening on the mysterious continent, imaginatively recreated in 1950 by a modern American historian, John Bakeless; an excerpt of the Constitution of the League of the Five Iroquois Nations, formulated some time around 1450 by the Iroquois Chief Dekanawidah; and the first impressions of the New World and its inhabitants written shortly after the "discovery" by Christopher Columbus in a letter of 1493.

from The Eyes of Discovery

[ON THE EVE OF AMERICA'S DISCOVERY]

It is interesting to think of the vast continent as it lay for a few hours before dawn in the darkness of that moonlit October night and of its unconcerned red inhabitants, still ignorant of that momentous instant. In Mexico, only a few hundred miles west of San Salvador, where Columbus landed, the Aztec civilization was at its height of grace, cruelty, and power, though already showing faint signs of corruption at its heart. The Lord Montezuma, or his predecessor, slept quietly, not guessing that a Cortez would follow a Columbus.

In the southwestern United States, where dawn was at that moment not yet ready to break, the peaceful Indians of the Pueblos would wake to the life they had been living for at least a thousand years, worshipping the rain-gods with ceremonial dances, harvesting their crops, managing their irrigation, fearing nothing. Were not their painted deserts a protection? Undisturbed in their majesty, giant redwoods that had been growing when Rome was still an empire, looked through the fogs toward the Pacific waves breaking on the California coast. Northward, on the Columbia, Chinook and Klamath had relaxed from the ardors of the salmon fishing. From the Rockies to the forests of Pennsylvania black, gigantic buffalo herds were beginning to stir in the morning and think of grass and forage. Wolf, cougar, lynx, weasel, wildcat, fox were nearly ready to den up for their daytime rest. Between the Mississippi and the Pacific, the giant grizzlies prowled, lords of plain and mountain, certain of their power, contemptuous of the frail, red creatures who, with bows and arrows, occasionally disturbed them briefly. And over it all, through the autumn night, swept the miraculous millions of the migrant birds.

Just west of the Mississippi, in their leather tepees, dwelt the Sioux, a rather weak tribe who had as yet never dreamed of the horses, the mounted buffalo-hunting, the cavalry war that would make them the rich and powerful terrors of the plains. Through Canada, about the Great Lakes, into New England and down the coast, ranged various Algonkian tribes, hunters, trappers, canoemen. In upper New York State the great Iroquois statesmen, Dekanáwida and Hayowentha had only recently established the League of the Iroquois, the Five Nations, who were just beginning to develop their power, when on that fateful October morning *Pinta* fired the signal gun that marked the coming of the master race and the red man's loss of a continent that he had held since the last glacier.

There were not really very many of these red men. Some parts of the huge continent were wholly empty. Even where powerful tribes controlled the forests or the plains, the land seemed empty to invaders who came from settled Europe.

To all appearance, the life of the whole great continent, that fateful October morning in 1492 was wholly unchanged. Save on one insignificant island, there was no stir that day and no excitement. Yet the arrival of these three small ships, bobbing in the warm blue waves off San Salvador, meant that all this life of plains, mountains, lakes, and forests was now an insubstantial pageant soon to fade.

John Bakeless, *1950*

DEKANAWIDAH
(1450?)

The first American literature was the literature of the native Americans—or Indians, as Columbus called them, believing they were natives of India. The literature survived through a strong oral tradition: sacred and secular texts were passed down by word of mouth through succeeding generations. The Iroquois Constitution was formulated at the time of the creation of the League of the Five Nations: some historians say 1390 A.D., others 1450, and still others have set the date as late as 1570. Since the Iroquois themselves have asserted that the time was before the appearance of the white man, scholars have tended to settle on 1450. The five tribes of the Iroquois League were the Mohawk, Oneida, Onondaga, Cayuga, and Seneca. Later (in 1712) the Tuscarora joined the League.

The leaders in bringing the Iroquois League into being were Dekanawidah and Hiawatha (Henry Wadsworth Longfellow used the latter's name but not his deeds in his poem "Hiawatha," 1855); but the words of the "Law of the Great Peace"—the Iroquois Constitution—are attributed to Dekanawidah. Many scholars, including Benjamin Franklin, have pointed to the possible influence of the Iroquois Constitution on the Constitution of the United States, to come some 300 years later, in 1787. Both documents appear dedicated to the democratic ideal.

The Iroquois Constitution is not only a political document, but, because of its brilliant use of metaphor and imagery, also a work of literature. The following poetic version is "adapted" by the poet William Brandon from various prose versions and perhaps captures the spirit of the original oral version as it was spoken or chanted and passed down through many generations before being put into print.

ADDITIONAL READING

Paul A. W. Wallace, *The White Roots of Peace*, 1946, 1968; Roy Harvey Pearce, *The Savages of America: A Study of the Indian and the Idea of Civilization*, 1953, 1965; Paula Gunn Allen, ed., *Studies in American Indian Literature*, 1983; John Bierhorst, ed., *The Sacred Path: Spells, Prayers & Power Songs of the American Indians*, 1983.

TEXT

The Magic World: American Indian Songs and Poems, selected and edited with an introduction by William Brandon, 1971. (Part I was adapted from William N. Fenton, ed., *Parker on the Iroquois*, 1968; Part II was adapted from Paul A. W. Wallace, *The White Roots of Peace*, 1946.) Variant spellings of the Indian names have been retained in Brandon's text.

from The Iroquois Constitution

[THE TREE OF THE GREAT PEACE]

I. THE TREE (*c.* 1450)

I am Dekanawideh and with the chiefs of the Five Nations
I plant the Tree of the Great Peace. . . .

Roots have spread out from the Tree of the Great Peace. . . .
the Great White Roots of Peace. . . .

Any man of any nation   5
may trace the roots to their source and be welcome
to shelter
beneath the Great Peace. . . .

I
Dekanawideh   10
and the chiefs of our Five Nations of the Great Peace
we now uproot the tallest pine

    into the cavity thereby made
    we cast all weapons of war

    Into the depths of the earth   15
    into the deep underneath. . . .

    we cast all weapons of war

We bury them from sight forever. . . .
and we plant again the tree. . . .

Thus shall the Great Peace be established. . . .   20

II. DEGANAWIDAH'S LAST MESSAGE (*c.* 1450)

We bind ourselves together
(said Deganawidah)
by taking hold of each other's hands. . . .

Our strength shall be in union
our way the way of reason   5
righteousness and peace. . . .

Hearken, O chiefs, that peace may continue unto future days. . . .

Have courage. . . .

Think not so much of present advantage
as the future welfare of the people. . . .   10

When you administer the Law
your skins must be seven thumbs thick
so the envious darts of your enemies may
not penetrate. . . .

Be of strong mind   15
O chiefs
carry no anger. . . .

Think not forever of yourselves nor of your own generation. . . .

Think of those yet unborn whose faces are coming
from beneath the ground. . . .   20

CHRISTOPHER COLUMBUS
(1451–1506)

Christopher Columbus was awed by his first view of America—by the "trees of a thousand shapes" and "little birds of a thousand kinds"; by the lands "so beautiful and fat for planting and sowing"; by the inhabitants who "go naked as their mothers bore them," who were honest, of "a very keen intelligence," and in their unbelievable generosity displayed "as much love as if they were giving their hearts." Columbus described his impressions on his return voyage on board the *Niña,* in a letter dated February 15, 1493, and sent from Lisbon on March 14, 1493. Sometimes called "Columbus's Letter to Santangel" or to "Raphael Sanchez" (officials of the Aragon Kingdom), it is, in fact, Columbus's report to Ferdinand and Isabella. As biographer Samuel Eliot Morison (*Christopher Columbus, Mariner,* 1942, 1955) observes, the letter "is not only the first of all *Americana;* it is a vital document for the Admiral himself, relating what he wished important people to think about his discovery, appealing alike to their piety and their cupidity, and concealing matters that he did not care to be broadcast, such as the near mutiny of his men, the loss of his flagship, and the disloyalty of Martin Alonso Pinzon [Captain of the *Pinta* who tried to be the first on returning to Spain to relay the news of the discovery to the King and Queen]."

Select details of Columbus's life have become enshrined in the legends of the origins and founding of America—the discovery of a new world by him and his men on the fragile craft the *Niña, Pinta,* and *Santa María* when in search of India, the continual struggle to finance this and other voyages, Columbus's imprisonment and poverty when he had fallen out of favor, and his dying unaware of what he had really discovered (not some cluster of islands near China, but a new continent bounded by oceans). Columbus's letter has fired the imagination of later Americans who have tried to conjure up what he saw—a virgin country yet untouched by the discoverers and settlers. Such poets as Walt Whitman (in "Passage to India," 1871, and "Prayer of Columbus," 1874) and Hart Crane (in *The Bridge,* 1930) have enlisted Columbus as a mythic or archetypal figure in their epic visions. In Columbus's discovery, in his description of the new land in this letter, are to be found the embryonic elements of the American dream.

ADDITIONAL READING

Journals and Other Documents on the Life and Voyages of Christopher Columbus, ed. Samuel Eliot Morison, 1963.

Washington Irving, *A History of the Life and Voyages of Christopher Columbus,* 1828; Samuel Eliot Morison, *Admiral of the Ocean Sea: A Life of Christopher Columbus,* 2 vols., 1942; Björn Landström, *Columbus: The Story of Don Cristóbal Colon,* 1966, tr. 1967; Ernle Dusgate Bradford, *Christopher Columbus,* 1973.

TEXT

"Columbus's Letter on His First Voyage," translated by Samuel Eliot Morison in his *Christopher Columbus, Mariner,* 1955. Morison's translation is based on the first Spanish edition (1493), correcting errors made in various Latin translations; Morison also used a surviving abstract of the Journal in which Columbus recorded his initial impressions of the New World. All the numbered footnotes are Morison's, with editor's explanations in brackets; asterisks indicate editor's notes, included in brackets.

[1493 LETTER ON DISCOVERY: LOFTY LANDS MOST BEAUTIFUL, OF A THOUSAND SHAPES]

SIR, since I know that you will take pleasure at the great victory with which Our Lord has crowned my voyage, I write this to you, from which you will learn how in twenty[1] days I reached the Indies with the fleet which the most illustrious King and Queen, our lords, gave to me. And there I found very many islands filled with people without number, and of them all I have taken possession for their Highnesses, by proclamation and with the royal standard displayed, and nobody objected. To the first island which I found I gave the name *Sant Salvador*, in remembrance of His Heavenly Majesty, who marvelously hath given all this; the Indians call it *Guanahani*. To the second I gave the name *Isla de Santa Maria de Concepción;* to the third, *Ferrandina;* to the fourth, *La Isla Bella;*[2] to the fifth, *La Isla Juana;* and so to each one I gave a new name.

When I reached Juana, I followed its coast to the westward, and I found it to be so long that I thought it must be the mainland, the province of Catayo.[3] And since there were neither towns nor cities on the coast, but only small villages, with the people of which I could not have speech because they all fled forthwith, I went forward on the same course, thinking that I should not fail to find great cities and towns. And, at the end of many leagues, seeing that there was no change and that the coast was bearing me to the north, which was contrary to my desire since winter was already beginning and I proposed to go thence to the south, and as moreover the wind was favorable, I determined not to wait for a change of weather and backtracked to a notable harbor;[4] and thence I sent two men upcountry to learn if there were a king or great cities. They traveled for three days and found an infinite number of small villages and people without number, but nothing of importance; hence they returned.

I understood sufficiently from other Indians, whom I had already taken, that continually[5] this land was an island, and so I followed its coast eastwards 107 leagues up to where it ended. And from that cape I saw toward the east another island, distant 18 leagues from the former, to which I at once gave the name *La Spañola*.* And I went there and followed its northern part, as I had in the case of Juana, to the eastward for 178 great leagues in a straight line. As Juana, so all the others are very fertile[6] to an excessive degree, and this one especially. In it there are many harbors on the coast of the sea, incomparable to others which I know in Christendom, and numerous rivers, good and large, which is marvelous. Its lands are lofty and in it there are very many sierras and very high mountains, to which the island *Centrefrei*[7] is not comparable. All are most beautiful, of a thousand shapes, and all accessible and filled with trees of a thousand kinds and tall, and they seem to touch the sky; and I am told that they never lose their foliage, which I can believe, for I saw them as green and beautiful as they are in Spain in May, and some of them were flowering, some with fruit, and some in another condition, according to their quality. And there were singing the nightingale and other little birds of a thousand kinds in the month of November, there where I went. There are palm trees of six or eight kinds, which are a wonder to behold on account of their beautiful variety, and so are the other trees and fruits and herbs; therein are marvelous pine groves, and extensive champaign* country; and there is honey, and there are many kinds of birds and a great variety of fruits. Upcoun-

---

[1]*Veinte*. Probably a misprint for *treinte*, or xxxiii. The actual time, . . . was thirty-three days. All other numerals in the original text are Roman.
[2]Misprint for *Isabela*, the name he gave to Crooked Island. Conception was Rum Cay; Ferrandina, Long Island; and Juana, Cuba.
[3]Meaning, a province of China.
[4]Puerto Gibara.

[5]*Continuamente*. Not clear whether he meant that the Indians told him continually that Cuba was an island, or what.
*[Later abbreviated to *Española* and corrupted to Hispaniola, present-day Haiti and the Dominican Republic—Ed.]
[6]*Fortissimas*. Probably a printer's error for *fertilissimas*.
[7]An obvious misprint for Tenerife [largest of the Canary Islands—Ed.].
*[Level and open—Ed.]

try there are many mines of metals, and the population is innumerable. *La Spañola* is marvelous, the sierras and the mountains and the plains and the champaigns and the lands are so beautiful and fat for planting and sowing, and for livestock of every sort, and for building towns and cities. The harbors of the sea here are such as you could not believe in without seeing them, and so the rivers, many and great, and good streams, the most of which bear gold. And the trees and fruits and plants have great differences from those of La Juana; in this there are many spices and great mines of gold and of other metals.

The people of this island and of all the other islands which I have found and seen, or have not seen, all go naked, men and women, as their mothers bore them, except that some women cover one place only with the leaf of a plant or with a net of cotton which they make for that. They have no iron or steel or weapons, nor are they capable of using them, although they are well-built people of handsome stature, because they are wonderfully timorous. They have no other arms than arms of canes, [cut] when they are in seed time, to the ends of which they fix a sharp little stick; and they dare not make use of these, for oftentimes it has happened that I have sent ashore two or three men to some town to have speech, and people without number have come out to them, and as soon as they saw them coming, they fled; even a father would not stay for his son; and this not because wrong has been done to anyone; on the contrary, at every point where I have been and have been able to have speech, I have given them of all that I had, such as cloth and many other things, without receiving anything for it; but they are like that, timid beyond cure. It is true that after they have been reassured and have lost this fear, they are so artless and so free with all they possess, that no one would believe it without having seen it. Of anything they have, if you ask them for it, they never say no; rather they invite the person to share it, and show as much love as if they were giving their hearts; and whether the thing be of value or of small price, at once they are content with whatever little thing of whatever kind may be given to them. I forbade that they should be given things so worthless as pieces of broken crockery and broken glass, and ends of straps, although when they were able to get them, they thought they had the best jewel in the world; thus it was ascertained that a sailor for a strap received gold to the weight of two and a half *castellanos*,[8] and others much more for other things which were worth much less; yea, for new *blancas*,[9] for them they would give all that they had, although it might be two or three castellanos' weight of gold or an *arrova*[10] or two of spun cotton; they even took pieces of the broken hoops of the wine casks and, like animals, gave what they had, so that it seemed to me to be wrong and I forbade it, and I gave them a thousand good, pleasing things which I had brought, in order that they might be fond of us, and furthermore might be made Christians and be inclined to the love and service of their Highnesses and of the whole Castilian nation, and try to help us and to give us of the things which they have in abundance and which are necessary to us. And they know neither sect nor idolatry, with the exception that all believe that the source of all power and goodness is in the sky, and they believe very firmly that I, with these ships and people, came from the sky, and in this belief they everywhere received me, after they had overcome their fear. And this does not result from their being ignorant, for they are of a very keen intelligence and men who navigate all those seas, so that it is marvelous the good account they give of everything, but because they have never seen people clothed or ships like ours.

---

[8]$7.50, or a guinea and a half in gold.
[9]A copper coin worth half a maravedi, about a third of a cent.
[10]A weight equivalent to 25 lbs., or 11½ kilos.

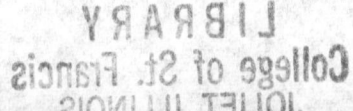

And as soon as I arrived in the Indies, in the first island which I found, I took by force some of them in order that they might learn [Castilian] and give me information of what they had in those parts; it so worked out that they soon understood us, and we them, either by speech or signs, and they have been very serviceable. I still have them with me, and they are still of the opinion that I come from the sky, in spite of all the intercourse which they have had with me, and they were the first to announce this wherever I went, and the others went running from house to house and to the neighboring towns with loud cries of, "Come! Come! See the people from the sky!" Then all came, men and women, as soon as they had confidence in us, so that not one, big or little, remained behind, and all brought something to eat and drink, which they gave with marvelous love. In all the islands they have very many *canoas* like rowing *fustes,* some bigger and some smaller, and some are bigger than a *fusta*[11] of eighteen benches. They are not so broad, because they are made of a single log, but a *fusta* could not keep up with them by rowing, since they make incredible speed, and in these [canoes] they navigate all those islands, which are innumerable, and carry their merchandise. Some of these canoes I have seen with 70 and 80 men in them, each one with his oar.

In all these islands, I saw no great diversity in the appearance of the people or in their manners and language, but they all understand one another, which is a very singular thing, on account of which I hope that their Highnesses will determine upon their conversion to our holy faith, towards which they are much inclined.

I have already said how I went 107 leagues in a straight line from west to east along the coast of the island Juana, and as a result of that voyage I can say that this island is larger than England and Scotland together; for, beyond these 107 leagues, there remain to the westward two provinces where I have not been, one of which they call *Auau,*[12] and there the people are born with tails. Those provinces cannot have a length of less than 50 or 60 leagues, as I could understand from those Indians whom I retain and who know all the islands. The other, *Española,* in circuit is greater than all Spain, from *Colunya* by the coast to *Fuenterauia* in Vizcaya, since I went along one side 188 great leagues in a straight line from west to east.[13] It is a desirable land and, once seen, is never to be relinquished; and in it, although of all I have taken possession for their Highnesses and all are more richly supplied than I know or could tell, I hold them all for their Highnesses, which they may dispose of as absolutely as of the realms of Castile. In this *Española,* in the most convenient place and in the best district for the gold mines and for every trade both with this continent and with that over there belonging to the *Gran Can*[Grand Khan], where there will be great trade and profit, I have taken possession of a large town to which I gave the name *La Villa de Nauidad,**
and in it I have built a fort and defenses, which already, at this moment, will be all complete, and I have left in it enough people for such a purpose, with arms and artillery and provisions for more than a year, and a *fusta,*[14] and a master of the sea in all arts[15] to build others; and great friendship with the king of that land, to such an extent that he took pride in calling me and treating me as brother; and

---

[11]A long, light boat propelled chiefly by oars, common in the Mediterranean.

[12]Thus in the Spanish folio, *Avan* in the Spanish quarto, *Anan* in the Latin translation. What Columbus probably meant was Avan, the native name of a Cuban region which gave its name to Havana. Tailed men was one of the most popular yarns of Sir John Mandeville [14th-century compiler of a book of travels filled with fictitious marvels]. Columbus and his men frequently inquired about such creatures and were "yessed" by the Indians, who probably thought they were talking about monkeys.

[13]I.e., from Collioure, a port in the Gulf of Lyons that then

belonged to Aragon, around the entire Spanish Peninsula to Fuenterrabia, the frontier town on the Bay of Biscay. Like his other estimates of land distances, this was greatly exaggerated.

*["Christmas Town," which, as Morison observes, was "the first attempt by Europeans since that of the Northmen to establish themselves in the New World."—Ed.]

[14]See note 11 above.

[15]This man must have been either Antonio de Cuéllar, carpenter of *Santa María,* or Alonso de Morales, who was *Niña's* "chips."

even if he were to change his mind and offer insult to these people, neither he nor his know the use of arms and they go naked, as I have already said, and are the most timid people in the world, so that merely the people whom I have left there could destroy all that land; and the island is without danger for their persons, if they know how to behave themselves.[16]

In all these islands, it appears, all the men are content with one woman, but to their *Maioral,* or king, they give up to twenty. It appears to me that the women work more than the men. I have been unable to learn whether they hold private property, but it appeared true to me that all took a share in anything that one had, especially in victuals.

In these islands I have so far found no human monstrosities, as many expected;[17] on the contrary, among all these people good looks are esteemed;[18] nor are they Negroes, as in Guinea, but with flowing hair, and they are not born where there is excessive force in the solar rays; it is true that the sun there has great strength, although it is distant from the Equator 26 degrees.[19] In these islands, where there are high mountains, the cold this winter was strong, but they endure it through habit and with the help of food which they eat with many and excessively hot spices. Thus I have neither found monsters nor had report of any, except in an island[20] which is the second at the entrance to the Indies, which is inhabited by a people who are regarded in all the islands as very ferocious and who eat human flesh; they have many canoes with which they range all the islands of India and pillage and take as much as they can; they are no more malformed than the others, except that they have the custom of wearing their hair long like women, and they use bows and arrows of the same stems of cane with a little piece of wood at the tip for want of iron, which they have not. They are ferocious toward these other people, who are exceeding great cowards, but I make no more account of them than of the rest. These are those who have intercourse with the women of *Matremonio,*[21] which is the first island met on the way from Spain to the Indies, in which there is not one man. These women use no feminine exercises, but bows and arrows of cane, like the abovesaid; and they arm and cover themselves with plates of copper, of which they have plenty. In another island, which they assure me is larger than *Española,* the people have no hair.[22] In this there is countless gold, and from it and from the other islands I bring with me Indios[23] as evidence.

In conclusion, to speak only of that which has been accomplished on this voyage, which was so hurried, their Highnesses can see that I shall give them as much gold as they want if their Highnesses will render me a little help; besides spice and cotton, as much as their Highnesses shall command; and gum mastic, as much as they shall order shipped, and which, up to now, has been found only in Greece, in the island of Chios, and the Seignory[24] sells it for what it pleases; and aloe wood, as much as they shall order shipped, and slaves, as many as they shall order, who will be idolaters.[25] And I believe that I have found rhubarb and cinnamon, and I shall find a thousand other things of value, which the people whom I have left

---

[16]A pretty big if! . . . they didn't; some killed each other and the rest were finished off by Caonabó [a local chief—Ed.].

[17]See above, note 12.

[18]*Mas antes es toda gente de muy lindo acatamiento.* The meaning is somewhat obscure; the Latin translator of the Letter thought that Columbus meant that the people were reverential.

[19]*Viente e seis,* a radical revision downward of the Admiral's two inaccurate calculations that the north coast of Cuba was in lat. 42° N and that of Hispaniola 34° N. Actually 21° and 20° are correct.

[20]At this point the Latin edition of the Letter introduces the name of this island, Charis. That, or Caire, was the Carib name for Dominica. Note that the Admiral's captive Indians had given him the position of this island and told him about the Caribs.

[21]Thus in both Spanish editions, *Mateunin* in the Latin edition, *Matinino* in Columbus's Journal. This was the island afterwards colonized by the French and named Martinique.

[22]What island the Admiral's informants meant by that of the bald natives can only be guessed.

[23]The first appearance in print of this name that Columbus gave to the natives of America.

[24]The government of Genoa. Columbus as a young man had made a voyage or two to Chios.

[25]I.e., the slave trade is legitimate if Christians are not the victims.

there will have discovered, for I have not delayed anywhere, provided the wind allowed me to sail, except in the town of Navidad, where I stayed [to have it] secured and well seated. And the truth is I should have done much more if the ships had served me as the occasion required.[26]

This is sufficient. And the eternal God, Our Lord, Who gives to all those who walk in His way victory over things which appear impossible, and this was notably one.[27] For although men have talked or have written of these lands, all was conjecture, without getting a look at it, but amounted only to this, that those who heard for the most part listened and judged it more a fable than that there was anything in it, however small.[28]

So, since our Redeemer has given this victory to our most illustrious King and Queen, and to their famous realms, in so great a matter, for this all Christendom ought to feel joyful and make great celebrations and give solemn thanks to the Holy Trinity with many solemn prayers for the great exaltation which it will have, in the turning of so many peoples to our holy faith, and afterwards for material benefits, since not only Spain but all Christians will hence have refreshment and profit. This is exactly what has been done,[29] though in brief.

Done in the caravel, off the Canary Islands,[30] on the fifteenth of February, year 1493.

At your service.

THE ADMIRAL

ADDITIONAL NOTE,[31] WHICH CAME
WITHIN THE LETTER

After having written this, and being in the Sea of Castile, there rose up on me so great a wind south and southwest,[32] that I was obliged to ease the ships.[33] But I ran here today into this port of Lisbon, which was the greatest wonder in the world, and whence I decided to write to their Highnesses. In all the Indies I have always found weather as in May; I went thither in 33 days and would have returned in 28 but for these tempests which detained me 23 days, beating about in this sea. Here all the seafarers say that never has there been so bad a winter or so many losses of ships.

Done on the fourteenth[34] day of March.

This letter *Colom* sent to the Keeper of the Privy Purse[35] about the islands discovered in the Indies. Contained in another for their Highnesses.

[26]An oblique reference to *Pinta's* leaving him. It will be observed that Columbus says nothing about losing his flagship.

[27]There is no verb to this sentence in either Spanish edition; the Latin ones have interpolated several pious ejaculations.

[28]He probably had in mind the *Book of Ser Marco Polo,* which most of the learned in Europe regarded as fabulous.

[29]*Segun el fecho,* a legal term meaning literally, "executed."

[30]So in both Spanish editions; doubtless a misprint, as *Niña* was already off Santa Maria of the Azores on the fifteenth, and Columbus knew perfectly well that he had been in Santa Maria before he sent the letter off.

[31]*Anima* (modern *nema*), a paper wrapped around a letter after its conclusion, and to which the seal was affixed.

[32]*Sueste,* a misprint for *sudoeste,* as may be seen from the Journal.

[33]Plural in both Spanish editions.

[34]*Quatorze.* A misprint for *quatro.*

[35]This official was Luis de Santangel, Columbus's friend. [Morison explains that Columbus was called Colom in Portugal, Colón in Spain, Christophe Colomb in France, and Cristoforo Colomb (his christened name) in Italy—Ed.]

FOUNDING: VOYAGES, ADVENTURES, VISIONS

JOHN SMITH   JOHN WINTHROP
WILLIAM BRADFORD   EDWARD JOHNSON
THOMAS MORTON

Whatever their differences—and they were fundamental—John Smith, William Bradford, Thomas Morton, John Winthrop, and Edward Johnson all were filled with a sense of participation in *beginnings*—the beginnings of a new social order founded in the New World wilderness, the beginnings of a new civilization with untold possibilities for economic, religious, political, and social reform and experimentation. They sought freedom and found in the process that one individual's freedom could prove another's constraint. And they were all driven by a sense of the transcendent importance of their actions to write personal and civic accounts—they called them histories—for a posterity that would inherit the fruits of these momentous beginnings. Looking back through more than three centuries of time, we can read of their voyages over unknown seas, their adventures in unknown lands, their visions of themselves and their destinies with the shock (in some sense) of *self*-recognition.

CAPTAIN JOHN SMITH
(1580–1631)

John Smith has survived in popular history as the English explorer saved by the beautiful Indian princess Pocahontas just as her father Chief Powhatan was signaling his warriors to beat Smith's brains out with clubs. This account, embedded deeply in the American imagination (see, for example, Hart Crane's treatment of Pocahontas in *The Bridge*) may or may not be true in all its details, its only source being John Smith himself. But whether literally true or not, the story is true in spirit to the adventurous, even swashbuckling life lived by this extraordinary man.

Smith was only twenty-six years old in 1608 when he sailed in one of the three ships commissioned by King James I to establish the first permanent English colony in Virginia (the one established at Roanoke, Virginia, by Sir Walter Raleigh in 1584 had disappeared). But by this young age he had already lived a full life of adventure. Born the son of a farmer in Willoughby (at Alford, Lincolnshire), when about sixteen he set out on his own (his father died in 1596) and spent the next ten years travelling, exploring, and fighting. He turned up in a number of countries, serving with English troops in the Netherlands, touring France and Scotland, and fighting in Hungary against the Turks. Wounded and captured, he was sent to be the slave of a young lady in Constantinople, who, out of compassion for him, sent him for safety (just as her mother was about to sell him) to her brother in "Tartaria." The brother's cruel treatment inspired Smith to escape and make his way back to Hungary. He set off on travels through Germany, Spain, and Morocco and became engaged in a sea battle off Africa. By the time he returned to England, he was a seasoned soldier and survivor. Although earlier historians cast considerable doubt on the authenticity of these events as Smith narrated them in one of his last books, *The True Travels* (1629), more recent research has tended to find Smith's account generally valid.

Smith's knock-about, adventurous life prepared him for the trials that lay ahead for the small band of men sailing forth in December 1606, to establish an English colony in Virginia. The name *Virginia*, derived from the virgin queen, Elizabeth I, then applied to all the American coast stretching north of Florida, including what is now called New England. The area was in effect a wilderness, full of unfamiliar plants and unknown animals, as well as a race of unpredictable people called Indians, most often labelled "savages." The three ships venturing boldly forth on this difficult enterprise held 105 individuals, few of them accustomed to hard work. As Smith noted in his *General History of Virginia,* besides one carpenter, two blacksmiths, two sailors, and a scattering of "laborers," "all the rest were poor gentlemen, tradesmen, serving-men, libertines, and such like ten times more fit to spoil a commonwealth than either to begin one, or but help to maintain one." The ships arrived in March 1607, in Chesapeake Bay, and the colonists immediately began to squabble over who had rightful seats on the governing Council and who was to assume leadership. The "gentlemen" neglected to plant or to build, but wasted time in search of quick wealth (especially gold) or engaged in aimless explorations. The number of settlers was reduced from 105 to 38 by January 1608.

Although at first excluded from his rightful seat on the Council, Smith set about the duties of "supply officer." Largely through his explorations and his negotiations with the Indians, and particularly through his friendship with Chief Powhatan and his daughter Pocahontas (developed after Smith's captivity by the Indians), he provided the settlers with the few supplies available. Others who ventured out into the wilderness usually came back empty-handed, or never came back at all.

Because of his resourcefulness, Smith emerged as the natural leader of the colony and was named President in 1609. Although bickering never stopped, Smith led the colonists in building shelters and bolstering defenses and in developing food supplies through farming and fishing, as well as trading with the Indians. In addition, he found time for extensive exploration of Chesapeake Bay and the Potomac River as far as the present city of Washington, D.C. He also found time to write "under a rotten tent in the wilderness, perhaps by the flickering blaze of a pine knot" what has been called by Moses Coit Tyler the "earliest book in American literature": *A True Relation of such occurrences and accidents of note as hath happened in Virginia since the first planting of that colony. . .* (1608).

Because of severe burns suffered in a powder explosion, Smith returned to England in 1609. Although he left the colony in relatively stable condition with sufficient supplies, it immediately began to decline in discipline and the winter of 1609–10 was known as "the starving time." Smith did not come back to America until 1614, and, after explorations in some areas of northern Virginia (to which he gave the name New England), he returned to England the same year. Although he set out again in 1615, he was captured by pirates, escaped to France, and returned to England, where he spent the remainder of his years writing and publishing books about his travels. The principal works are *A Description of New England* (1616), based on his travels there in 1614, and *The General History of Virginia, New England, and the Summer Isles* (1624), his longest work incorporating many of his earlier accounts.

Smith's style has the vigor, force, and energy that have enabled his books to endure as literature. His work has, moreover, firsthand descriptions of the New World and its inhabitants that (in spite of occasional exaggerations) constitute unique and valuable records for American history. But above all, Captain John Smith continues to fascinate readers because he seems to be the prototypical frontiersman—resourceful, shrewd, adaptable, tough—the kind of character out of which homespun myths are made.

ADDITIONAL READING

The Complete Works of Captain John Smith (1580–1631), 3 vols., ed. Philip L. Barbour, 1986.

Bradford Smith, *Captain John Smith: His Life and Legend*, 1953; Jay B. Hubbell, "The Smith-Pocahontas Story in Literature," *Virginia Magazine of History and Biography*, 1957; John Lankford, "Introduction," *Captain John Smith's America: Selections from His Writings*, ed. Lankford, 1967; Philip L. Barbour, *The Three Worlds of Captain John Smith*, 1971; Alden T. Vaughan, *American Genesis: Captain John Smith and the Founding of Virginia*, 1975; John Seelye, "Captain Courageous: Captain John Smith, Father of Us All," *Prophetic Waters: The River in Early American Life and Literature*, 1977.

TEXT

Travels and Works of Captain John Smith, President of Virginia and Admiral of New England, 1580–1631, ed. Edward Arber, 1884; rpt. in 2 vols. with an introduction by A. G. Bradley, 1910, 1966. Typography, punctuation, spelling, and usage have been changed to conform with contemporary English and modern printing practices.

from A Description of New England

[Recruiting Colonists]

Smith's explorations of the New England coast during his 1614 voyage led to the writing of *A Description of New England* (1616), which was designed to lure Smith's countrymen to the New World where they could seek—and find—their fortunes. The details of his description suggested a paradise of abundance. What, he asked, "can be more pleasant" for any man "than planting and building a foundation for his posterity, got from the rude earth, by God's blessing and his own industry, without prejudice to any?" Smith's books and maps were later read and used by the Pilgrims, though they rejected his offer to lead them on their 1620 voyage to the New World, choosing Miles Standish instead. Smith's imagination in *A Description of New England* vividly embodies the excitement and wonder that the New World inspired in the Old.

❧

[New England's Geography and Resources Described]

[1614] New England is that part of America in the Ocean Sea opposite to *Nova Albyon* [California] in the South Sea, discovered by the most memorable Sir Francis Drake in his voyage about the world. In regard whereto this is styled New England, being in the same latitude. New France, off it, is Northward; Southwards is Virginia, and all the adjoining continent, with New Granada, New Spain, New Andalusia, and the West Indies.

Now because I have been so oft asked such strange questions, of the goodness and greatness of those spacious tracts of land, how they can be thus long unknown or not possessed by the Spaniard, and many such like demands, I entreat your pardons if I chance to be too plain or tedious in relating my knowledge for plain men's satisfaction. . . .

Lest others may be deceived as I was or through dangerous ignorance hazard themselves as I did, I have drawn a map from point to point, isle to isle, and harbor to harbor, with the soundings, sands, rocks, and landmarks as I passed close aboard the shore in a little boat, although there [may] be many things to be observed which the haste of other affairs did cause me [to] omit. For being sent more to get present commodities than knowledge by discoveries for any future good, I had not power to search as I would; yet it will serve to direct any [that] should go that way, to safe harbors and the savage's habitations. What merchandise and commodities for their labor they may find, this following discourse shall plainly demonstrate.

Thus you may see, of this 2,000 miles more than half is yet unknown to any purpose; no, not so much as the borders of the sea are yet certainly discovered. As for the goodness and true substances of the land, we are for [the] most part yet altogether ignorant of them, unless it be those parts about the Bay of Chesapeake and Sagadahoc;[1] but only here and there we touched or have seen a little the edges of those large dominions which do stretch themselves into the main, God doth know how many thousand miles, whereof we can yet no more judge than a stranger that sails between England and France can describe the harbors and dangers, by landing here or there in some river or bay, tell thereby the goodness and substances of Spain, Italy, Germany, Bohemia, Hungary, and the rest. By this you

---

[1]Kennebec River, Maine.

may perceive how much they err that think every one who has been at Virginia understands or knows what Virginia is or that the Spaniards know one half quarter of those territories they possess, no, not so much as the true circumference of *Terra Incognita*,[2] whose large dominions may equal the greatness and goodness of America, for anything yet known. . . .

But it is not a work for everyone, to manage such an affair as makes a discovery and plants a colony. It requires all the best parts of art, judgment, courage, honesty, constancy, diligence, and industry to do but near well. Some are more proper for one thing than another, and therein are to be employed, and nothing breeds more confusion than misplacing and misemploying men in their undertakings. Columbus, Cortes, Pizarro, Soto, Magellan,[3] and the rest served more than an apprenticeship to learn how to begin their most memorable attempts in the West Indies, which to the wonder of all ages successfully they effected, when many hundreds of others far above them in the world's opinion, being instructed but by relation, came to shame and confusion in actions of small moment, who doubtless in other matters were both wise, discreet, generous, and courageous. I say not this to detract anything from their incomparable merits but to answer those questionless questions that keep us back from imitating the worthiness of their brave spirits that advanced themselves from poor soldiers to great captains, their posterity to great lords, their king to be one of the greatest potentates on earth, and the fruits of their labors, his greatest glory, power, and renown.

That part we call New England is betwixt the degrees of 41 and 45, but that part this discourse speaks of, stretches but from Penobscot[4] to Cape Cod, some seventy-five leagues[5] by a right line distant each from other, within which bounds I have seen at least forty several habitations upon the seacoast and sounded about twenty-five excellent good harbors, in many whereof there is anchorage for 500 sail of ships of any burden, in some of them for 5,000. And [I have seen] more than 200 isles overgrown with good timber of divers sorts of wood, which do make so many harbors as requires a longer time than I had, to be well discovered.

. . . . .

From Penobscot to Sagadahoc this coast is all mountainous and isles of huge rocks but overgrown with all sorts of excellent good woods for building houses, boats, barks, or ships, with an incredible abundance of most sorts of fish, much fowl, and sundry sorts of good fruits for man's use.

Betwixt Sagadahoc and Sawocatuck[6] there are but two or three sandy bays, but betwixt that and Cape Cod very many; especially the coast of Massachusetts is so indifferently mixed with high clayey or sandy cliffs in one place and then tracts of large long ledges of divers sorts, and quarries of stones in other places, so strangely divided with tinctured veins of divers colors, as freestone for building, slate for tiling, smooth stone to make furnaces and forges for glass or iron, and iron ore sufficient, conveniently, to melt in them. . . .

And surely by reason of those sandy cliffs and cliffs of rocks, both which we saw so planted with gardens and corn fields, and so well inhabited with a goodly, strong, and well proportioned people, besides the greatness of the timber growing on them, the greatness of the fish, and the moderate temper of the air (for of twenty-five, not any was sick but two that were many years diseased before they went, notwithstanding our bad lodging and accidental diet), who can but approve

---

[2]"Unknown land" (Latin).
[3]Christopher Columbus (1451–1506), Italian navigator who led the Spanish exploration of the New World; Hernando Cortés (1485–1547), Spanish conqueror of the Aztecs in Mexico; Francisco Pizarro (1470?–1541), Spanish explorer and conqueror of Peru; Hernando de Soto (1500?–1542), Spanish explorer who discovered the Missis-

sippi River in 1541; Ferdinand Magellan (1480?–1521), Portuguese navigator who led the Spanish expedition that first circumnavigated the world.
[4]Maine river and bay.
[5]About 225 miles.
[6]Old Orchard Bay, Maine.

this a most excellent place, both for health and fertility? And of all the four parts of the world that I have yet seen not inhabited, could I have but means to transport a colony, I would rather live here than anywhere, and if it did not maintain itself, were we but once indifferently well fitted, let us starve.

The main staple, from hence to be extracted for the present to produce the rest, is fish, which however it may seem a mean and a base commodity, yet who will but truly take the pains and consider the sequel, I think will allow it well worth the labor. . . . But who doth not know that the poor Hollanders, chiefly by fishing at a great charge and labor in all weathers in the open sea, are made a people so hardy and industrious, and by the vending [of] this poor commodity to the Easterlings[7] for [items] as mean, which is wood, flax, pitch, tar, rosin, cordage, and such like (which they exchange again to the French, Spaniards, Portuguese, and English, &c, for what they want), are made so mighty, strong, and rich as no state but Venice, of twice their magnitude, is so well furnished with so many fair cities, goodly towns, strong fortresses, and that abundance of shipping and all sorts of merchandise, as well of gold, silver, pearls, diamonds, precious stones, silks, velvets, and cloth of gold as [of] fish, pitch, wood, or such gross commodities? . . .

Why should we more doubt than Holland, Portugal, Spaniards, French, or other, but to do much better than they, where there is victual to feed us; wood of all sorts to build boats, ships, or barks; the fish at our doors; pitch, tar, masts, yards, and most of other necessaries only for [the] making? And here are no hard landlords to rack us with high rents or extorted fines to consume us, no tedious pleas in law to consume us with their many years' disputations for justice, no multitudes to occasion such impediments to good orders, as in popular states. So freely hath God and his Majesty bestowed those blessings on them that will attempt to obtain them, as here every man may be master and owner of his own labor and land, or the greatest part, in a small time. If he have nothing but his hands, he may set up this trade and by industry quickly grow rich, spending but half that time well which in England we abuse in idleness, worse or as ill.

· · · · · ·

And whereas it is said the Hollanders serve the Easterlings themselves and other parts that want with herring, ling, and wet cod, the Easterlings [serve] a great part of Europe with sturgeon and caviar; Capeblank, Spain, Portugal, and the Levant[8] [serve] with mullet and puttargo;[9] Newfoundland [serves] all Europe with a thin Poor John.[10] Yet all is so overlaid with fishers as the fishing decayeth and many are constrained to return with a small freight. [With] Norway and Poland [producing] pitch, tar, masts, and yards; Sweden and Russia, iron and ropes; France and Spain, canvas, wine, steel, iron, and oil; Italy and Greece, silks and fruits, I dare boldly say (because I have seen naturally growing or breeding in those parts [New England] the same materials that all those are made of), they may as well be had there [New England] or the most part of them, within the distance of 70 leagues, for some few ages, as from all those parts, using but the same means to have them as they do and with all those advantages.

First the ground is so fertile that questionless it is capable of producing any grain, fruits, or seeds you will sow or plant, growing in the regions aforenamed, but it may be, not every kind to that perfection of delicacy, or some tender plants may miscarry because the summer is not so hot, and the winter is more cold in those parts we have yet tried near the seaside, than we find in the same height in Europe or Asia. Yet I made a garden upon the top of a rocky isle in 43½°, four

---

[7]People of the Baltic coast and East Germany.
[8]Countries bordering the eastern Mediterranean Sea.

[9]Food preserve of various fish eggs.
[10]Dried fish.

leagues from the main in May, that grew so well as it served us for salads in June and July.

All sorts of cattle may here be bred and fed in the isles or peninsulas, securely for nothing. In the interim, till they increase, if need be (observing the seasons) I dare undertake to have corn enough from the savages for 300 men, for a few trifles. And if they [the savages] should be untoward (as it is most certain they are), thirty or forty good men will be sufficient to bring them all in subjection. . . .

Now young boys and girls, savages or any other, be they never such idlers, may turn, carry, and return fish without either shame or any great pain; he is very idle that is past twelve years of age and cannot do so much, and she is very old that cannot spin a thread to make engines to catch them.

· · · · ·

The waters are most pure, proceeding from the entrails of rocky mountains.

The herbs and fruits are of many sorts and kinds: as alkermes,[11] currants, or a fruit like currants, mulberries, vines, raspberries, gooseberries, plums, walnuts, chestnuts, small nuts, &c, pumpkins, gourds, strawberries, beans, peas, and maize, a kind or two of flax wherewith they make nets, lines, and ropes both small and great, very strong for their quantities.

Oak is the chief wood; of which there is great difference in regard of the soil where it grows: fir, pine, walnut, chestnut, birch, ash, elm, cypress, cedar, mulberry, plum tree, hazel, sassafras, and many other sorts.

Eagles, gripes, divers sorts of hawks, cranes, geese, brants, cormorants, ducks, sheldrakes, teal, mews, gulls, turkeys, divedappers, and many other sorts, whose names I know not.

Whales, grampus, porpoises, turbot, sturgeon, cod, hake, haddock, cole, cusk or small ling, shark, mackerel, herring, mullet, bass, pinacks, cunners, perch, eels, crabs, lobsters, mussels, whelks, oysters, and divers others, &c.

Moose, a beast bigger than a stag, deer red and fallow, beavers, wolves, foxes both black and other, raccoons, wildcats, bears, otters, martens, fitches, muskrats, and divers sorts of vermin whose names I know not.

[NEW ENGLAND'S ABUNDANCE AWAITING EUROPEAN COLONISTS]

All these and divers other good things do here, for want of use, still increase and decrease with little diminution, whereby they grow to that abundance [that] you shall scarce find any bay, shallow shore, or cove of sand where you may not take many clams, or lobsters, or both at your pleasure, and in many places load your boat if you please, nor isles where you find not fruits, birds, crabs, and mussels, or all of them for [the] taking, at a low water. And in the harbors we frequented, a little boy might take of cunners and pinacks and such delicate fish, at the ship's stern, more than six or ten can eat in a day; but with a casting net [we took] thousands when we pleased, and scarce any place but cod, cusk, halibut, mackerel, skate, or such like, a man may take with a hook or line what he will. And in divers sandy bays, a man may draw with a net great store of mullets, basses, and divers other sorts of such excellent fish, as many as his net can draw on shore. [There is] no river where there is not plenty of sturgeon, or salmon, or both, all which are to be had in abundance observing but their seasons. But if a man will go at Christmas to gather cherries in Kent, he may be deceived though there be plenty in summer; so here, these plenties have each their seasons as I have expressed.

We for the most part had little but bread and vinegar, and though the most part of July, when the fishing decayed, they worked all day, lay abroad in the isles

---

[11]Crimson insect once taken to be a berry.

all night, and lived on what they found, yet were [they] not sick. But I would wish none [to] put himself long to such plunges, except necessity constrain it. Yet worthy is that person to starve that here cannot live, if he have sense, strength, and health; for there is no such penury of these blessings in any place but that a hundred men may, in one hour or two, make their provisions for a day, and he that has experience to manage well these affairs, with forty or thirty honest industrious men, might well undertake (if they dwell in these parts) to subject the savages, and feed daily two or three hundred men with as good corn, fish, and flesh as the earth has of those kinds and yet make that labor but their pleasure, provided that they have engines that be proper for their purposes.

Who can desire more content, that has small means or but only his merit to advance his fortune, than to tread and plant that ground he has purchased by the hazard of his life? If he have but the taste of virtue and magnanimity, what to such a mind can be more pleasant than planting and building a foundation for his posterity, got from the rude earth by God's blessing and his own industry, without prejudice to any? If he have any grain of faith or zeal in religion, what can he do less hurtful to any or more agreeable to God than to seek to convert those poor savages to know Christ and humanity, whose labors with discretion will triple requite thy charge and pains? What so truly suits with honor and honesty as the discovering things unknown, erecting towns, peopling countries, informing the ignorant, reforming things unjust, teaching virtue, and gain to our native mother-country a kingdom to attend her, find employment for those that are idle because they know not what to do? [This is] so far from wronging any as to cause posterity to remember thee, and remembering thee, ever honor that remembrance with praise.

[1616] Consider: What were the beginnings and endings of the monarchies of the Chaldeans, the Syrians, the Grecians, and Romans, but this one rule: what was it they would not do for the good of the commonwealth or their Mother-city? For example, Rome: What made her such a monarchess, but only the adventures of her youth, not in riots at home, but in dangers abroad, and the justice and judgment out of their experience when they grew aged? What was their ruin and hurt but this: the excess of idleness, the fondness of parents, the want of experience in magistrates, the admiration of their undeserved honors, the contempt of true merit, their unjust jealousies, their politic incredulities, their hypocritical seeming goodness, and their deeds of secret lewdness? Finally . . . all that their predecessors got in many years, they lost in a few days. Those by their pain and virtues became lords of the world; they by their ease and vices became slaves to their servants. This is the difference between the use of arms in the field and on the monuments of stone, the golden age and the leaden age, prosperity and misery, justice and corruption, substance and shadows, words and deeds, experience and imagination, making commonwealths and marring commonwealths, the fruits of virtue and the conclusions of vice.

Then who would live at home idly (or think in himself any worth to live) only to eat, drink, and sleep, and so die? Or by consuming that carelessly [which] his friends got worthily? Or by using that miserably, that [which] maintained virtue honestly? Or for being descended nobly, pine with the vain vaunt of great kindred in penury? Or (to maintain a silly show of bravery) toil out thy heart, soul, and time basely, by shifts, tricks, cards, and dice? Or by relating news of other's actions, shark here or there for a dinner or supper; deceive thy friends, by fair promises and dissimulation, in borrowing where thou never intendest to pay; offend the laws; surfeit with excess; burden thy country; abuse thy self; despair in want and then cozen thy kindred, yea even thine own brother, and wish thy parents' death (I will not say damnation) to have their estates? Though thou seest what honors and rewards the world yet has for them [who] will seek them and worthily deserve them.

I would be sorry to offend or that any should mistake my meaning, for I wish good to all, hurt to none. But rich men for the most part are grown to that dotage, through their pride in their wealth, as though there were no accident could end it, or their life. . . .

Let this move you to embrace employment for those whose educations, spirits, and judgments want but your purses, not only to prevent such accustomed dangers, but also to gain more thereby than you have.

And you fathers, that are either so foolishly fond, or so miserably covetous, or so willfully ignorant, or so negligently careless, as that you will rather maintain your children in idle wantonness till they grow your masters or become so basely unkind as they wish nothing but your deaths, so that both sorts grow dissolute; and although you would wish them anywhere to escape the gallows and ease your cares, though they spend you here one, two, or three hundred pounds a year, you would grudge to give half so much in adventure with them to obtain an estate which in a small time, but with a little assistance of your providence, might be better than your own. But if an angel should tell you [that] any place yet unknown can afford such fortunes, you would not believe him, no more than Columbus was believed [that] there was any such land as is now the well known abounding America, much less such large regions as are yet unknown as well in America as in Africa, and Asia, and *terra incognita*, where were courses for gentlemen (and them that would be so reputed) more suiting their qualities than begging from their Prince's generous disposition, the labors of his subjects, and the very marrow of his maintenance.

I have not been so ill bred but I have tasted of plenty and pleasure as well as want and misery, nor does necessity yet or occasion of discontent force me to these endeavors, nor am I ignorant [of] what small thanks I shall have for my pains or that many would have the world imagine them to be of great judgment that can but blemish these my designs by their witty objections and detractions. Yet (I hope) my reasons with my deeds will so prevail with some that I shall not want employment in these affairs, to make the most blind see his own senselessness and incredulity, hoping that gain will make them effect that which religion, charity, and the common good cannot. It were but a poor device in me to deceive myself, much more the king, state, my friends, and country with these inducements which, seeing his Majesty has given permission, I wish all sorts of worthy, honest, industrious spirits would understand, and if they desire any further satisfaction, I will do my best to give it, not to persuade them to go only, but go with them; not leave them there, but live with them there.

I will not say, but by ill providing and undue managing, such courses may be taken [that] may make us miserable enough. But if I may have the execution of what I have projected, [then] if they want to eat, let them eat or never digest me. If I perform what I say, I desire but that reward out of the gains [which] may suit my pains, quality, and condition. And if I abuse you with my tongue, take my head for satisfaction. If any dislike at the year's end, defraying their charge, by my consent they should freely return. I fear not want of company sufficient, were it but known what I know of those countries; and by the proof of that wealth I hope yearly to return, if God please to bless me from such accidents as are beyond my power in reason to prevent. For I am not so simple to think that ever any other motive than wealth will ever erect there a commonwealth or draw company from their ease and humors at home to stay in New England to effect my purposes.

And lest any should think the toil might be insupportable, though these things may be had by labor and diligence, I assure myself there are [those] who delight extremely in vain pleasure, that take much more pains in England to enjoy it than I should do here [New England] to gain wealth sufficient, and yet I think they should not have half such sweet content, for our pleasure here is still gains; in

England [it is] charges and loss. Here nature and liberty afford us that freely which in England we want, or it costs us dearly. What pleasure can be more than (being tired with any occasion ashore, in planting vines, fruits, or herbs, in contriving their own grounds, to the pleasure of their own minds, their fields, gardens, orchards, buildings, ships, and other works, &c) to recreate themselves before their own doors, in their own boats upon the sea, where man, woman, and child, with a small hook and line, by angling may take divers sorts of excellent fish at their pleasures? And is it not pretty sport to pull up two pence, six pence, and twelve pence as fast as you can haul and veer a line? He is a very bad fisher [that] cannot kill in one day, with his hook and line, one, two, or three hundred cods, which dressed and dried, if they be sold there for ten shillings the hundred, though in England they will give more than twenty, may not both the servant, the master, and merchant be well content with this gain? If a man work but three days in seven he may get more than he can spend, unless he will be excessive. Now that carpenter, mason, gardener, tailor, smith, sailor, forgers, or what other, may they not make this a pretty recreation, though they fish but an hour in a day, to take more than they eat in a week? Or if they will not eat it, because there is so much better choice, yet sell it or change it with the fishermen or merchants for anything they want. And what sport does yield a more pleasing content and less hurt or charge than angling with a hook and crossing the sweet air from isle to isle, over the silent streams of a calm sea, wherein the most curious may find pleasure, profit, and content?

Thus, though all men be not fishers, yet all men, whatsoever, may in other matters do as well. For necessity does in these cases so rule a commonwealth, and each in their several functions, as their labors in their qualities, may be as profitable because there is a necessary mutual use of all.

For gentlemen, what exercise should more delight them than ranging daily those unknown parts, using fowling and fishing, for hunting and hawking? And yet you shall see the wild hawks give you some pleasure, in seeing them stoop (six or seven after one another) an hour or two together at the schools of fish in the fair harbors, as those ashore at a fowl, and never trouble nor torment yourselves with watching, mewing,[12] feeding, and attending them, nor kill horse and man with running and crying, "See you not a hawk?" For hunting also, the woods, lakes, and rivers afford not only chase sufficient for any that delight in that kind of toil or pleasure but such beasts to hunt that besides the delicacy of their bodies for food their skins are so rich as may well recompense thy daily labor with a captain's pay.

For laborers, if those [in England] that sow hemp, rape,[13] turnips, parsnips, carrots, cabbage, and such like, give twenty, thirty, forty, fifty shillings yearly for an acre of ground, and meat, drink, and wages to use it and yet grow rich, when better or at least as good ground may be had [in New England] and cost nothing but labor, it seems strange to me any such should there grow poor.

My purpose is not to persuade children from their parents, men from their wives, nor servants from their masters, only such as with free consent may be spared. But that each parish or village, in city or country, that will but apparel their fatherless children of thirteen or fourteen years of age, or young married people that have small wealth to live on, here by their labor [they] may live exceeding well, provided always that first there be a sufficient power to command them, houses to receive them, means to defend them, and meet[14] provisions for them; for any place may be overlain and it is most necessary to have a fortress (ere

---

[12]Supplying cages.
[13]Plant cultivated for the oil extracted from the seed.
[14]Proper.

this grow to practice) and sufficient masters (as carpenters, masons, fishers, fowlers, gardeners, husbandmen, sawyers, smiths, spinners, tailors, weavers, and such like) to take ten, twelve, or twenty, or as there is occasion, for apprentices. The masters by this may quickly grow rich; these [apprentices] may learn their trades themselves to do the like, to a general and an incredible benefit for king and country, master and servant. . . .

And who is he [that] hath judgment, courage, and any industry or quality with understanding will leave his country, his hopes at home, his certain estate, his friends, pleasures, liberty, and the preferment sweet England doth afford to all degrees were it not to advance his fortunes by enjoying his deserts, whose prosperity once appearing will encourage others? But it must be cherished as a child, till it be able to go and understand itself and not [be] corrected nor oppressed above its strength ere it know wherefore.

A child can neither perform the office nor deeds of a man of strength, nor endure that affliction he is able; nor can an apprentice at the first perform the part of a master. And if twenty years be required to make a child a man, seven years limited [to] an apprentice for his trade, if scarce an age be sufficient to make a wise man a statesman, and commonly a man dies ere he hath learned to be discreet, if perfection be so hard to be obtained as of necessity there must be practice as well as theory, let no man much condemn this paradoxical opinion to say that half seven years is scarce sufficient for a good capacity to learn in these affairs how to carry himself. And whoever shall try in these remote places the erecting of a colony shall find at the end of seven years occasion enough to use all his discretion. And in the interim all the content, rewards, gains, and hopes will be necessarily required to be given to the beginning till it be able to creep, to stand, and go, yet time enough to keep it from running; for there is no fear it will grow too fast or ever to anything except liberty, profit, honor, and prosperity there found more bind the planters of those affairs in devotion to effect it than bondage, violence, tyranny, ingratitude and such double dealing as binds freemen to become slaves and honest men [to] turn knaves, which hath ever been the ruin of the most popular commonweals and is very unlikely ever well to begin in a new. . . .

[NEW WORLD COLONIZATION: RELIGIOUS MOTIVE AND VISION]

Religion, above all things, should move us (especially the clergy), if we were religious, to show our faith by our works in converting those poor savages to the knowledge of God, seeing what pains the Spaniards take to bring them to their adulterated faith. Honor might move the gentry, the valiant, and industrious, and the hope and assurance of wealth [might move] all, if we were that [which] we would seem and be accounted. Or be we so far inferior to other nations, or our spirits so far dejected from our ancient predecessors, or our minds so [set] upon spoil, piracy, and such villany as to serve the Portuguese, Spaniard, Dutch, French, or Turk (as to the cost of Europe, too many do) rather than our God, our king, our country, and ourselves, excusing our idleness and our base complaints by want of employment, when here is such choice of all sorts, and for all degrees, in the planting and discovering these North parts of America? . . .

But, to conclude, Adam and Eve did first begin this innocent work, to plant the earth to remain to posterity, but not without labor, trouble, and industry. Noah and his family began again the second plantation; and their seed as it still increased has still planted new countries, and one country, another. And so the world to that estate [which] it is. But not without much hazard, travail, discontents, and many disasters. Had those worthy fathers and their memorable offspring not been more diligent for us now in these ages than we are to plant that yet unplanted for the after livers, had the seed of Abraham, our Savior Christ, and his apostles, exposed themselves to no more dangers to teach the gospel and the will of God than we, even we ourselves had at this present been as savage and as miserable as the most barbarous savage yet uncivilized.

The Hebrews, and Lacedoemonians, the Goths, the Grecians, the Romans, and the rest, what was it they would not undertake to enlarge their territories, enrich their subjects, resist their enemies? Those that were the founders of those great monarchies and their virtues were no silvered idle golden pharisees, but industrious iron-steeled publicans. They regarded more [to supply] provisions and necessaries for their people than jewels, riches, ease, or delight for themselves. Riches were their servants, not their masters. They ruled (as Fathers, not as tyrants) their people as children, not as slaves. There was no disaster could discourage them, and let none think they encountered not with all manner of encumbrances. And what have ever been the works of the greatest princes of the earth but planting of countries and civilizing barbarous and inhumane nations to civility and humanity, whose eternal actions fill our histories? Lastly, the Portuguese and Spaniards, whose everlasting actions before our eyes will testify with them [about] our idleness and ingratitude to all posterities and the neglect of our duties in our piety and religion [that] we owe our God, our king, and country, and want of charity to those poor savages, whose country we challenge, use, and possess, except we be but made to use and mar what our forefathers made or but only tell what they did or esteem ourselves too good to take the like pains. Was it virtue in them to provide that [which] does maintain us and baseness for us to do the like for others? Surely no.

Then seeing we are not born for ourselves but each to help [the] other, and our abilities are much alike at the hour of our birth and the minute of our death; seeing our good deeds or our bad, by faith in Christ's merits, is all we have to carry our souls to heaven or hell; seeing honor is our lives' ambition, and our ambition after death, to have an honorable memory of our life; and seeing by no means [that] we would be abated of the dignities and glories of our predecessors, let us imitate their virtues to be worthily their successors.

1616

from The General History
of Virginia, New England, and The Summer Isles

[THE POCAHONTAS STORY]

In 1607 (September) when the Jamestown Colony was on the point of starvation, with many men ill, Smith was sent into the wilderness to trade with the Indians. He was taken into captivity by Chief Powhatan's warriors and was about to be put to death when he was dramatically rescued by Powhatan's daughter, Pocahontas. Powhatan then adopted Smith, declaring that he would ever esteem him as a son. Smith left this story of Pocahontas's intervention out of his previous account of his captivity (in *A True Relation*, 1608), casting doubt in some minds as to its authenticity. About the reality of Pocahontas there can be no doubt. Later, in 1613, when relations with the Indians were strained, Pocahontas was taken prisoner and offered in ransom to Chief Powhatan in return for the colony's men, weapons, and tools that he held. Negotiations dragged on for months. Mean-time, a lonely Jamestown widower, John Rolfe, gave Pocahontas religious instructions; she converted to

Christianity and took the Christian name Rebecca. Rolfe fell in love with her and married her, with the consent of the Governor of the colony and her father in April 1614. From that point on, the relations between the settlers and the Indians were cordial. Pocahontas learned English quickly and, when she accompanied her husband to England in 1616, Smith wrote a letter to the consort of James I, Queen Anne, introducing her. She was received at court as a princess, and was a sensation.

There is a sad postscript to this triumphant visit to England. She started to return to America in 1617 but became ill and suddenly died. John Smith wrote, ". . . it pleased God at Gravesend to take this young lady to his mercy, where she made not more sorrow for her unexpected death than joy to the beholders to hear and see her make so religious and godly an end."

ॐ

[Pocahontas's Sacrifice to Save Smith]

[1607] Six or seven weeks [rather about the three weeks 16 December 1607– 8 January 1608] those barbarians kept him [Captain John Smith]* prisoner; many strange triumphs and conjurations they made of him, yet he so demeaned himself amongst them as he not only diverted them from surprising the fort but procured his own liberty and got himself and his company such estimation amongst them, that those savages admired him more than their own Quiyouckosucks.[1]

The manner how they used and delivered him is as follows: The savages having drawn from George Cassen whither Captain Smith was gone, prosecuting that opportunity they followed him with 300 bowmen, conducted by the King of Pamunkey, who in divisions searching the turnings of the river found Robinson and Emry by the fireside; those they shot full of arrows and slew. Then finding the Captain, as is said, who used the savage that was his guide as his shield (three of them being slain and divers others so galled) all the rest would not come near him. Thinking thus to have returned to his boat, regarding them, as he marched, more than his way, [he] slipped up to the middle in an oozy creek and his savage with him, yet dared they not come to him till being near dead with cold he threw away his arms. Then according to their composition[2] they drew him forth and led him to the fire where his men were slain. Diligently they chafed his benumbed limbs.

He demanding for their captain, they showed him Opechancanough,[3] King of Pamunkey, to whom he gave a round ivory double compass dial. Much they marveled at the playing of the fly[4] and needle, which they could see so plainly and yet not touch it because of the glass that covered them. But when he demonstrated by that globe-like jewel the roundness of the earth and skies, the sphere of the sun, moon, and stars, and how the sun did chase the night round about the world continually, the greatness of the land and sea, the diversity of nations, variety of complexions, and how we were to them antipodes, and many other such like matters, they all stood as amazed with admiration.

Notwithstanding, within an hour after, they tied him to a tree, and as many as could stand about him prepared to shoot him, but the King holding up the compass in his hand, they all laid down their bows and arrows and in a triumphant manner led him to Orapaks,[5] where he was after their manner kindly feasted and well used.

---

*Smith refers to himself throughout in the third person; in writing *The General History of Virginia*, he adapted works by others about the establishment of the colony and often left references to himself as he found them.
[1]"Petty gods and their affinities," according to Smith's glossary of Indian words.

[2]Order.
[3]Head of the Pamunkey tribe and half brother of the Great Powhatan, Overlord of All Tidewater Virginia.
[4]Circular disc carrying magnetic needles of the compass, marked with direction points.
[5]Indian village.

Their order in conducting him was thus: Drawing themselves all in file, the King in the midst had all their pieces and swords borne before him. Captain Smith was led after him by three great savages holding him fast by each arm, and on each side six went in file with their arrows nocked. But arriving at the town (which was but only thirty or forty hunting houses made of mats, which they remove as they please, as we our tents), all the women and children staring to behold him, the soldiers first all in file performed the form of a bissom[6] so well as could be, and on each flank, officers as sergeants to see them keep their orders. A good time they continued this exercise and then cast themselves in a ring, dancing in such several postures and singing and yelling out such hellish notes and screeches; being strangely painted, every one his quiver of arrows and at his back a club, on his arm a fox or an otter's skin or some such matter for his vambrace;[7] their heads and shoulders painted red with oil and pocones[8] mingled together, which scarlet-like color made an exceeding handsome show; [each with] his bow in his hand and the skin of a bird with her wings abroad, dried, tied on his head, a piece of copper, a white shell, a long feather with a small rattle growing at the tails of their snakes tied to it, or some such like toy. All this while, Smith and the King stood in the midst, guarded as before is said, and after three dances they all departed. Smith they conducted to a long house where thirty or forty tall fellows did guard him, and ere long more bread and venison was brought him than would have served twenty men. I think his stomach at that time was not very good; what he left they put in baskets and tied over his head. About midnight they set the meat again before him; all this time not one of them would eat a bit with him, till the next morning they brought him as much more, and then did they eat all the old and reserved the new as they had done the other, which made him think they would fat him to eat him. Yet in this desperate estate, to defend him from the cold, one Maocassater brought him his gown in requital of some beads and toys Smith had given him at his first arrival in Virginia.

Two days after, a man would have slain him (but that the guard prevented it) for the death of his son, to whom they conducted him to recover the poor man then breathing his last. Smith told them that at Jamestown he had a water [that] would do it, if they would let him fetch it, but they would not permit that, but [they] made all the preparations they could to assault Jamestown, craving his advice, and for recompense he should have life, liberty, land, and women. In part of a table book[9] he wrote his mind to them at the fort, what was intended, how they should follow that direction to affright the messengers, and without fail send him such things as he wrote for, and an inventory with them. The difficulty and danger he told the savages of, the mines, great guns, and other engines, exceedingly affrighted them, yet according to his request they went to Jamestown in as bitter weather as could be of frost and snow, and within three days returned with an answer.

But when they came to Jamestown, seeing men sally out as he had told them they would, they fled, yet in the night they came again to the same place where he had told them they should receive an answer and such things as he had promised them, which they found accordingly and with which they returned with no small expedition,[10] to the wonder of them all that heard it, that he could either divine or the paper could speak.

Then they led him to the Youghtanunds, the Mattapanients, the Payankatanks, the Nantaughtacunds, and Onawmanients[11] upon the rivers of Rappahannock and Potomac, over all those rivers and back again by divers other several nations

---

[6]Marching and countermarching in a snake-like way, from Italian *biscione*, "a large snake."
[7]Armor to protect the forearm.
[8]Bloodroot.

[9]Writing tablet.
[10]Promptness.
[11]Indian tribes ruled by Powhatan.

to the King's habitation at Pamunkey, where they entertained him with most strange and fearful conjurations.

> As if near led to hell,
> Amongst the devils to dwell.[12]

Not long after, early in a morning, a great fire was made in a long house and a mat spread on the one side as on the other; on the one they caused him to sit, and all the guard went out of the house, and presently came skipping in a great grim fellow all painted over with coal mingled with oil, and many snakes' and weasels' skins stuffed with moss, and all their tails tied together so as they met on the crown of his head in a tassel, and round about the tassel was as a coronet of feathers, the skins hanging round about his head, back, and shoulders and in a manner covered his face, with a hellish voice, and a rattle in his hand. With most strange gestures and passions he began his invocation and environed the fire with a circle of meal; which done, three more such like devils came rushing in with the like antic tricks, painted half black, half red, but all their eyes were painted white and some red strokes like mustaches along their cheeks; round about him those fiends danced a pretty while, and then came in three more as ugly as the rest, with red eyes and white strokes over their black faces; at last they all sat down right against him, three of them on the one hand of the chief priest and three on the other. Then all with their rattles began a song; which ended, the chief priest laid down five wheat corns; then, straining his arms and hands with such violence that he sweat and his veins swelled, he began a short oration; at the conclusion they all gave a short groan and then laid down three grains more. After that [they] began their song again and then another oration, ever laying down so many corns as before till they had twice encircled the fire; that done, they took a bunch of little sticks prepared for that purpose, continuing still their devotion, and at the end of every song and oration they laid down a stick betwixt the divisions of corn. Till night, neither he nor they did either eat or drink, and then they feasted merrily with the best provisions they could make. Three days they used this ceremony; the meaning whereof, they told him, was to know if he intended them well or no. The circle of meal signified their country, the circles of corn the bounds of the sea, and the sticks his country. They imagined the world to be flat and round, like a trencher, and they in the midst.[13]

After this they brought him a bag of gunpowder, which they carefully preserved till the next spring, to plant as they did their corn, because they would be acquainted with the nature of that seed.

Opitchapam,[14] the King's brother, invited him to his house, where, with as many platters of bread, fowl, and wild beasts as did environ him, he bid him welcome, but not any of them would eat a bit with him but put up all the remainder in baskets.

At his return to Opechancanough's, all the King's women and their children flocked about him for their parts,[15] as a due by custom, to be merry with such fragments.

> But his waking mind in hideous dreams did
>   oft see wondrous shapes
> Of bodies strange, and huge in growth, and
>   of stupendous makes.[16]

---

[12]Smith quotes the Roman philosopher Seneca (4 B.C.–A.D. 65) from Bishop Martin Fotherby's translation in *Atheomastix: clearing foure truthes against Atheists* (1622).
[13]Plate.
[14]Half brother of Powhatan, first in line to inherit his kingdom.

[15]I.e., share of the food.
[16]From the Roman poet Lucretius (c. 98–55 B.C.), translated by Fotherby.

At last they brought him to Werowocómoco[17] [January 5, 1608], where was Powhatan, their Emperor. Here more than two hundred of those grim courtiers stood wondering at him, as [if] he had been a monster, till Powhatan and his train had put themselves in their greatest braveries.[18] Before a fire, upon a seat like a bedstead, he sat covered with a great robe made of raccoon skins and all the tails hanging by. On either hand did sit a young wench of sixteen or eighteen years and along on each side [of] the house, two rows of men and behind them as many women, with all their heads and shoulders painted red, many of their heads bedecked with the white down of birds, but every one with something, and a great chain of white beads about their necks.

At his entrance before the King, all the people gave a great shout. The Queen of Appomattoc[19] was appointed to bring him water to wash his hands, and another brought him a bunch of feathers, instead of a towel, to dry them; having feasted him after their best barbarous manner they could, a long consultation was held, but the conclusion was, two great stones were brought before Powhatan; then as many as could laid hands on him, dragged him to them, and thereon laid his head, and being ready with their clubs, to beat out his brains. Pocahontas, the King's dearest daughter, when no entreaty could prevail, got his head in her arms and laid her own upon his to save him from death, whereat the Emperor was contented he should live to make him hatchets, and her bells, beads, and copper, for they thought him as well [capable] of all occupations as themselves. For the King himself will make his own robes, shoes, bows, arrows, pots; plant, hunt, or do anything so well as the rest.

> They say he bore a pleasant show,
> But sure his heart was sad.
> For who can pleasant be, and rest,
> That lives in fear and dread:
> And having life suspected, doth
> It still suspected lead.[20]

Two days after, Powhatan, having disguised himself in the most fearfulest manner he could, caused Captain Smith to be brought forth to a great house in the woods and there upon a mat by the fire to be left alone. Not long after, from behind a mat that divided the house, was made the most dolefulest noise he ever heard; then Powhatan, more like a devil than a man, with some two hundred more as black as himself, came unto him and told him now they were friends, and presently he should go to Jamestown to send him two great guns and a grindstone for which he would give him the country of Capahowasic[21] and forever esteem him as his son Nantaquaus.

So to Jamestown with twelve guides Powhatan sent him. That night they quartered in the woods, he still expecting (as he had done all this long time of his imprisonment) every hour to be put to one death or other, for all their feasting. But almighty God (by His divine providence) had mollified the hearts of those stern barbarians with compassion. The next morning betimes they came to the fort, where Smith having used the savages with what kindness he could, he showed Rawhunt, Powhatan's trusty servant, two demiculverins[22] and a millstone to carry [to] Powhatan; they found them somewhat too heavy, but when they did see him discharge them, being loaded with stones, among the boughs of a great tree

---

[17]Royal Court of Powhatan on the York River some 14 miles, or 6 or 7 hours (according to Smith), from Jamestown.
[18]Garments.
[19]One of 30 tribes subject to Powhatan.

[20]From the Greek dramatist Euripides (*c.* 480–405 B.C.), translated by Fotherby.
[21]Neighboring tribal territory.
[22]Heavy cannon.

loaded with icicles, the ice and branches came so tumbling down that the poor savages ran away half dead with fear. But at last we regained some conference with them and gave them such toys and sent to Powhatan, his women, and children such presents as gave them in general full content.

[POCAHONTAS'S PRESENTATION AT COURT]

[1616] During this time, the Lady Rebecca, alias Pocahontas, daughter to Powhatan, by the diligent care of Master John Rolfe, her husband, and his friends, was taught to speak such English as might well be understood, [was] well instructed in Christianity, and was become very formal and civil after our English manner. She had also by him a child which she loved most dearly, and the Treasurer and Company took order both for the maintenance of her and it; besides there were diverse persons of great rank and quality had been very kind to her. And before she arrived at London, Captain Smith, to deserve her former courtesies, made her qualities known to the Queen's most excellent Majesty and her Court, and wrote a little book to this effect to the Queen. An abstract whereof followeth:

To the most high and virtuous
Princess, Queen Anne of
Great Britain.

Most admired Queen,

The love I bear my God, my King and country, hath so oft emboldened me in the worst of extreme dangers that new honesty doth constrain me [to] presume thus far beyond myself to present your Majesty this short discourse. If ingratitude be a deadly poison to all honest virtues, I must be guilty of that crime if I should omit any means to be thankful.

So it is, that some ten years ago [i.e., Jan. 1608], being in Virginia and taken prisoner by the power of Powhatan their chief King, I received from this great Savage exceeding great courtesy, especially from his son Nantaquaus, the most manliest, comeliest, boldest spirit I ever saw in a savage, and his sister Pocahontas, the King's most dear and well-beloved daughter, being but a child of twelve or thirteen years of age, whose compassionate, pitiful heart, of my desperate estate, gave me much cause to respect her; I being the first Christian this proud King and his grim attendants ever saw, and thus enthralled in their barbarous power, I cannot say I felt the least occasion of want that was in the power of those my mortal foes to prevent, notwithstanding all their threats.

After some six weeks [or rather about three weeks] fatting amongst those savage courtiers, at the minute of my execution, she hazarded the beating out of her own brains to save mine; and not only that, but so prevailed with her father, that I was safely conducted to Jamestown, where I found about eight and thirty miserable poor and sick creatures to keep possession of all those large territories of Virginia. Such was the weakness of this poor commonwealth, as had the savages not fed us, we directly had starved. And this relief, most gracious Queen, was commonly brought us by this Lady Pocahontas.

Notwithstanding all these passages,[1] when inconstant Fortune turned our peace to war, this tender Virgin would still not spare to dare to visit us, and by her our jars[2] have been oft appeased and our wants still supplied. Were it the policy of her father thus to employ her, or the ordinance of God thus to make her his instrument, or her extraordinary affection to our nation, I know not. But of this I am sure: when her father with the utmost of his policy and power sought to sur-

---

[1]Incidents.
[2]Disagreements, most likely with the Indians.

prise me [at Werowocomoco, about January 15, 1609], having but eighteen with me, the dark night could not affright her from coming through the irksome woods, and with watered eyes [she] gave me intelligence, with her best advice to escape his fury, which had he known, he had surely slain her.

Jamestown with her wild train[3] she as freely frequented as her father's habitation. And during the time of two or three years [1608–1609], she next under God was still the instrument to preserve this colony from death, famine, and utter confusion, which if in those times [it] had once been dissolved, Virginia might have line [lain] as it was at our first arrival to this day.

Since then, this business [the colonists' relations with the Indians] having been turned and varied by many accidents from that [which] I left it at [on October 4, 1609], it is most certain [that] after a long and troublesome war after my departure betwixt her father and our Colony, all [of] which time she was not heard of, [that] about two years after [April 1613] she herself was taken prisoner. Being so detained near two years longer, the colony by that means was relieved, [and] peace concluded.

And at last rejecting her barbarous condition, [she] was married [April 1, 1614] to an English gentleman, with whom at this present she is in England, the first Christian ever of that nation, the first Virginian [who] ever spake English, or had a child in marriage by an Englishman: a matter surely, if my meaning be truly considered and well understood, worthy a Prince's understanding.

Thus, most gracious Lady, I have related to your Majesty what at your best leisure our approved histories will account [to] you at large, and done in the time of your Majesty's life; and however this might be presented [to] you from a more worthy pen, it cannot from a more honest heart. As yet, I never begged anything of the state, or any [one]; and it is my want of ability and her exceeding desert, your birth, means, and authority, her birth, virtue, want, and simplicity, doth make me thus bold, humbly to beseech your Majesty to take this knowledge of her, though it be from one so unworthy to be the reporter as myself, her husband's estate not being able to make her fit to attend your Majesty.

The most and least I can do is to tell you this, because none so oft hath tried it as myself, and [she] rather being of so great a spirit, however her stature. If she should not be well received, seeing this Kingdom may rightly have a Kingdom by her means, her present love to us and Christianity might turn to such scorn and fury as to divert all this good to the worst of evil. Where[as] finding so great a Queen should do her some honor more than she can imagine, for being so kind to your servants and subjects, would so ravish her with content, as endear her dearest blood to effect that [which] your Majesty and all the King's honest subjects most earnestly desire.

And so I humbly kiss your gracious hands. . . .

1624

---

[3]According to the *History of Travel into Virginia Britannia* by William Strachey, a contemporary of Smith's, "Pocahontas . . . sometimes resorting to our Fort, . . . [would] get the boys forth with her into the market place and make them wheel [do cartwheels]."

WILLIAM BRADFORD
(1590–1657)

Many of the most popular of American "myths of origin" are rooted in one work, William Bradford's *Of Plymouth Plantation,* written from 1630 to 1650, but not published until 1856. In it are found the first American social contract, "The Mayflower Compact"; the beginnings of that peculiarly American holiday, Thanksgiving; and the image of starch-stiff Pilgrim Fathers passing sober judgment on maypole merrymakers. Every American child learns the legends of the hardships of the Atlantic crossing of the *Mayflower* and the providential landing at Plymouth Rock—and learns too that a vital element of American character derives from the Puritan spirit and zeal that inspired the voyage and created a new society in the New World wilderness.

Called the "father of American history" by Moses Coit Tyler in the nineteenth century, Bradford seems to us now more the father of American legend and myth. In either role, he looms large in our literature and his book assumes something of the nature of a sacred (or "founding") text. This is an astonishing achievement for one who was orphaned by the time he was seven, who suffered prolonged illnesses in his youth, and who did not attend university.

The central and consuming interest of Bradford's life came into focus very early, when at the age of twelve he began attending meetings of Separatists, the outlawed religious groups who were not only Puritans but believed that the only way to attain their religious ends was to *separate* from the Church of England. In 1606, at sixteen, Bradford joined the Scrooby group of Separatists and fled with it to Holland in 1608 to escape persecution. The band of believers settled first in Amsterdam, but within a year removed to Leyden because of differences with another Separatist group.

After some ten years, the Pilgrims decided to make the radical move to the American wilderness. The reasons were many and complicated, but prominent among them was the awareness that their children (and next generation of believers) were too often being seduced by "the great licentiousness of youth" in Holland and were being "drawn away by evil examples into extravagant and dangerous courses." America was chosen because it was "devoid of all civil inhabitants, where there are only savage and brutish men, which range up and down, little otherwise than the wild beasts of the same."

Bradford sailed with the other Pilgrims from Plymouth, England, on September 1620; some two months later on November 11, the ship landed at Cape Cod, New England, instead of Virginia—as called for by an agreement with the Virginia Company of London, which had financed the trip in the expectation of profits through shipment of furs and other New World treasures. Because of the hardship of the long ocean voyage on the small, crowded ship, the Pilgrims decided to remain in New England, arriving at New Plymouth on December 16. Before disembarking, however, they drew up and signed the Mayflower Compact, in which they did "Covenant and Combine" themselves "together into a Civil Body Politic" for their "better ordering and preservation."

Their "preservation" was indeed at stake. There were "discontents and murmerings" and even "mutinous speeches" among the Pilgrims facing the hardships of a winter without housing and food. Of the 102 passengers on the *Mayflower,* four died before arriving at Plymouth (among them Bradford's wife, who jumped or fell overboard) and forty-six others through the hard winter, known as "the starving time."

The first governor of the colony, John Carver, died within a year, and Bradford was elected to take his place. He served as governor of Plymouth for the rest of his life, with the exception of a few scattered years when, as he says, "by importunity" he got off. The office was a demanding one, requiring Bradford to act not only in an administrative but also a legislative and judicial role. All questions of government, law, and justice were settled by reference to the sole authoritative document, the Bible.

Bradford guided the colony through times of want and danger to relative prosperity and harmony, the turn in fortunes symbolized by the first Thanksgiving of 1621. Through friendship with the Indians, the Pilgrims learned how to grow and store corn and how and where to catch fish. Thus began a relationship with the unpredictable "savages" that was the cause of both gratitude and uneasiness in the colony.

With a keen sense of the importance of the events in which he was a leading participant, Bradford began writing his history in 1630. He believed with the group's founders John Robinson and William Brewster that the Pilgrims were "knit together as a body in a most strict and sacred bond and covenant of the Lord," and that the Lord would "graciously prosper" their endeavors. The first part of his history is filled with a vision of ultimate success in overcoming the wiles of Satan and establishing an ideal Christian community—a veritable New Jerusalem—in the wilderness. But as time wore on, and the less zealous, more prosperous new generation replaced the old, Bradford seemed overtaken by a growing gloom. He wrote: ". . . (alas) that subtle serpent hath slyly wound in himself under fair pretences of necessity and the like, to untwist these sacred bonds and tied, and as it were insensible by degrees to dissolve, or in a great measure to weaken, the same." The church to which he had devoted his life was left, he felt, "like an ancient mother grown old and forsaken of her children."

Bradford was the first in a long line of American self-educated (or self-made) men. His history, he said at the beginning, he would "endeavor to manifest in a plain style," and with this "plain style" he is able to absorb the reader's interest in events, actions, and characters. Deprived of a formal education, he still set about the learning of Greek, Latin, and Hebrew in later life. "Though I am grown aged, yet I have had a longing desire, to see with my own eyes, something of that most ancient language, and holy tongue, in which the Law and oracles of God were written; and in which God, and angels, spoke to the holy patriarchs of old time; and what names were given to things, from the creation." Bradford held to his purpose from youth to death, and his faith in God and the Word did not waver. He died leaving a small estate, a modest house, an orchard, and a few household belongings—including a library of some 400 volumes.

ADDITIONAL READING

Samuel Eliot Morison, *Builders of the Bay Colony,* 1930, 1958; Bradford Smith, *Bradford of Plymouth,* 1951; Norman S. Grabo, "William Bradford: *Of Plymouth Plantation," Landmarks of American Literature,* ed. Hennig Cohen, 1969; Alan B. Howard, "Art and History in Bradford's *Of Plymouth Plantation," William and Mary Quarterly,* 1971; David Levin, "William Bradford: The Value of Puritan Historiography," *Major Writers of Early American Literature,* ed.

Everett Emerson, 1972; Robert Daly, "William Bradford's Vision of History," *American Literature*, 1973; Jasper Rosenmeier, " 'With My Owne Eyes': William Bradford's *Of Plymouth Plantation*," *The American Puritan Imagination: Essays in Revaluation*, ed. Sacvan Bercovitch, 1974; Perry D. Westbrook, *William Bradford*, 1978; Floyd Ogburn, Jr., *Style as Structure and Meaning: William Bradford's "Of Plymouth Plantation*," 1981.

TEXT

The manuscript of *Of Plymouth Plantation* was handed down by succeeding generations of Bradfords. It was used in manuscript form by other early historians of New England, including Cotton Mather, and was finally deposited in 1758 in the library of Old South Church of Boston. The manuscript disappeared during the War of Independence (1776–83) and was not discovered until 1855—in the Palace Library of the Bishop of London. It was published for the first time in 1856 and the manuscript itself was returned to Boston in 1897. The text used here is *Of Plymouth Plantation, 1620–1647*, ed. Samuel Eliot Morison, 1952. Footnotes from this edition are indicated by the editor's name followed by the note enclosed in quotation marks. Typography, punctuation, spelling, and usage have been changed to conform with contemporary English and modern printing practices.

from Of Plymouth Plantation

And first of the occasion and inducements thereunto; the which, that I may truly unfold, I must begin at the very root and rise of the same. The which I shall endeavour to manifest in a plain style, with singular regard unto the simple truth in all things; at least as near as my slender judgment can attain the same.

from CHAPTER I

[THE SEPARATIST INTERPRETATION OF THE REFORMATION IN ENGLAND, 1550–1607]

It is well known unto the godly and judicious, how ever since the first breaking out of the light of the gospel in our honourable nation of England, (which was the first of nations whom the Lord adorned therewith after the gross darkness of popery which had covered and overspread the Christian world), what wars and oppositions ever since, Satan hath raised, maintained and continued against the Saints,[1] from time to time, in one sort or other. Sometimes by bloody death and cruel torments; other whiles imprisonments, banishments and other hard usages; as being loath his kingdom should go down, the truth prevail and the churches of God revert to their ancient purity and recover their primitive order, liberty and beauty.

But when he could not prevail by these means against the main truths of the gospel, but that they began to take rooting in many places, being watered with the blood of the martyrs and blessed from Heaven with a gracious increase; he then began to take him to his ancient stratagems, used of old against the first Christians. That when by the bloody and barbarous persecutions of the heathen emperors he could not stop and subvert the course of the gospel, but that it speedily overspread, with a wonderful celerity, the then best known parts of the world; he then began to sow errours, heresies and wonderful dissensions amongst the professors[2] themselves, working upon their pride and ambition, with other corrupt passions incident to all mortal men, yea to the saints themselves in some measure,

---

[1] A Christian, or a church member, not one canonized by the Roman Catholic Church.
[2] One professing Christianity.

by which woeful effects followed. As not only bitter contentions and heartburnings, schisms, with other horrible confusions; but Satan took occasion and advantage thereby to foist in a number of vile ceremonies, with many unprofitable canons and decrees, which have since been as snares to many poor and peaceable souls even to this day.

So as in the ancient times, the persecutions by the heathen and their emperors was not greater than of the Christians one against other:—the Arians and other their complices against the orthodox and true Christians. As witnesseth Socrates in his second book.[3] His words are these:

> The violence truly (saith he) was no less than that of old practiced towards the Christians when they were compelled and drawn to sacrifice to idols; for many endured sundry kinds of torment, often rackings and dismembering of their joints, confiscating of their goods; some bereaved of their native soil, others departed this life under the hands of the tormentor, and some died in banishment and never saw their country again, etc.

The like method Satan hath seemed to hold in these later times, since the truth began to spring and spread after the great defection made by Antichrist, that man of sin.[4]

* * * * *

[SIMPLICITY VS. CEREMONY]

The one side laboured to have the right worship of God and discipline of Christ established in the church, according to the simplicity of the gospel, without the mixture of men's inventions; and to have and to be ruled by the laws of God's Word, dispensed in those offices, and by those officers of Pastors, Teachers and Elders, etc. according to the Scriptures. The other party, though under many colours and pretences, endeavoured to have the episcopal dignity (after the popish manner) with their large power and jurisdiction still retained; with all those courts, canons and ceremonies, together with all such livings, revenues and subordinate officers, with other such means as formerly upheld their antichristian greatness and enabled them with lordly and tyrannous power to persecute the poor servants of God. This contention was so great, as neither the honour of God, the common persecution, nor the mediation of Mr. Calvin[5] and other worthies of the Lord in those places, could prevail with those thus episcopally minded; but they proceeded by all means to disturb the peace of this poor persecuted church, even so far as to charge (very unjustly and ungodlily yet prelatelike) some of their chief opposers with rebellion and high treason against the Emperor, and other such crimes.

And this contention died not with Queen Mary, nor was left beyond the seas. But at her death these people returning into England under gracious Queen Elizabeth, many of them being preferred to bishoprics and other promotions according to their aims and desires, that inveterate hatred against the holy discipline of Christ in His church[6] hath continued to this day. Insomuch that for fear it should prevail, all plots and devices have been used to keep it out, incensing the Queen and State against it as dangerous for the commonwealth; and that it was most

[3]Socrates Scholasticus, Greek historian of the fifth century A.D., author of an Ecclesiastical History. Bradford quotes from a London edition of 1577.

[4]2 Thessalonians 2:3: "Let no man deceive you by any means: for that day shall not come, except there come a falling away first, and that man of sin be revealed, the son of perdition."

[5]John Calvin (1509–1564), French theologian who came to

believe the doctrines of the Reformation; banished from Paris, he settled in Geneva, Switzerland. He wrote *Institutes of the Christian Religion* (1536) embodying a Reformation theology that strongly influenced the Puritans.

[6]Morison: "Bradford means the Congregational discipline. His account of church history during Elizabeth's reign is of course a partisan one, unfair to the acts and the motives of everyone not in the left wing of Protestantism."

needful that the fundamental points of religion should be preached in those ignorant and superstitious times. And to win the weak and ignorant they might retain
divers harmless ceremonies; and though it were to be wished that divers things
were reformed, yet this was not a season for it. And many the like, to stop the
mouths of the more godly, to bring them on to yield to one ceremony after another, and one corruption after another; by these wiles beguiling some and corrupting others till at length they began to persecute all the zealous professors in
the land (though they knew little what this discipline meant) both by word and
deed, if they would not submit to their ceremonies and become slaves to them and
their popish trash, which have no ground in the Word of God, but are relics of
that man of sin. And the more the light of the gospel grew, the more they urged
their subscriptions to these corruptions. So as (notwithstanding all their former
pretences and fair colours) they whose eyes God had not justly blinded might easily see whereto these things tended. And to cast contempt the more upon the sincere servants of God, they opprobriously and most injuriously gave unto and imposed upon them that name of Puritans, which is said the Novatians out of pride
did assume and take unto themselves.[7] And lamentable it is to see the effects
which have followed. Religion hath been disgraced, the godly grieved, afflicted,
persecuted, and many exiled; sundry have lost their lives in prisons and other
ways. On the other hand, sin hath been countenanced; ignorance, profaneness
and atheism increased, and the papists encouraged to hope again for a day.

· · · · · ·

[DECISION TO LEAVE]

But after these things they could not long continue in any peaceable condition,
but were hunted and persecuted on every side, so as their former afflictions were
but as flea-bitings in comparison of these which now came upon them. For some
were taken and clapped up in prison, others had their houses beset and watched
night and day, and hardly escaped their hands; and the most were fain to flee and
leave their houses and habitations, and the means of their livelihood.

Yet these and many other sharper things which afterward befell them, were no
other than they looked for, and therefore were the better prepared to bear them
by the assistance of God's grace and Spirit.

Yet seeing themselves thus molested, and that there was no hope of their continuance there, by a joint consent they resolved to go into the Low Countries,
where they heard was freedom of religion for all men; as also how sundry from
London and other parts of the land had been exiled and persecuted for the same
cause, and were gone thither, and lived at Amsterdam and in other places of the
land. So after they had continued together about a year, and kept their meetings
every Sabbath in one place or other, exercising the worship of God amongst themselves, notwithstanding all the diligence and malice of their adversaries, they seeing they could no longer continue in that condition, they resolved to get over into
Holland as they could. Which was in the year 1607 and 1608; of which more at
large in the next chapter.

from CHAPTER II

[DEPARTURE INTO HOLLAND, 1608]

Being thus constrained to leave their native soil and country, their lands and
livings, and all their friends and familiar acquaintance, it was much; and thought

---

[7]Morison: "The Novatians were an obscure sect of the 3rd
century. The term *Puritan,* like *Quaker,* was originally one
of reproach, not accepted until nearly the close of the 17th
century by the people to whom it was applied. The Puritans called themselves 'God's people.' "

marvelous by many. But to go into a country they knew not but by hearsay, where they must learn a new language and get their livings they knew not how, it being a dear place and subject to the miseries of war, it was by many thought an adventure almost desperate; a case intolerable and a misery worse than death. Especially seeing they were not acquainted with trades nor traffic (by which that country doth subsist) but had only been used to a plain country life and the innocent trade of husbandry. But these things did not dismay them, though they did sometimes trouble them; for their desires were set on the ways of God and to enjoy His ordinances; but they rested on His providence, and knew Whom they had believed. Yet this was not all, for though they could not stay, yet were they not suffered to go; but the ports and havens were shut against them, so as they were fain to seek secret means of conveyance, and to bribe and fee the mariners, and give extraordinary rates for their passages.[1] And yet were they often times betrayed, many of them; and both they and their goods intercepted and surprised, and thereby put to great trouble and charge, of which I will give an instance or two and omit the rest.

There was a large company of them purposed to get passage at Boston in Lincolnshire, and for that end had hired a ship wholly to themselves and made agreement with the master to be ready at a certain day, and take them and their goods in at a convenient place, where they accordingly would all attend in readiness. So after long waiting and large expenses, though he kept not day with them, yet he came at length and took them in, in the night. But when he had them and their goods aboard, he betrayed them, having beforehand complotted with the searchers and other officers so to do; who took them, and put them into open boats, and there rifled and ransacked them, searching to their shirts for money, yea even the women further than became modesty; and then carried them back into the town and made them a spectacle and wonder to the multitude which came flocking on all sides to behold them. Being thus first, by these catchpoll[2] officers rifled and stripped of their money, books and much other goods, they were presented to the magistrates, and messengers sent to inform the Lords of the Council of them; and so they were committed to ward. Indeed the magistrates used them courteously and showed them what favour they could; but could not deliver them till order came from the Council table. But the issue was that after a month's imprisonment the greatest part were dismissed and sent to the places from whence they came; but seven of the principal were still kept in prison and bound over to the assizes.[3]

. . . . . .

But that I be not tedious in these things, I will omit the rest, though I might relate many other notable passages and troubles which they endured and underwent in these their wanderings and travels both at land and sea; but I haste to other things. Yet I may not omit the fruit that came hereby, for by these so public troubles in so many eminent places their cause became famous and occasioned many to look into the same, and their godly carriage and Christian behaviour was such as left a deep impression in the minds of many. And though some few shrunk at these first conflicts and sharp beginnings (as it was no marvel) yet many more came on with fresh courage and greatly animated others. And in the end, notwithstanding all these storms of opposition, they all gat over at length, some at one time and some at another, and some in one place and some in another, and met together again according to their desires, with no small rejoicing.[4]

[1] Morison: "In England, as in other European nations at the time, a license was required to go abroad, and such licenses were commonly refused to Roman Catholics and dissenters. This first attempt of the Scrooby congregation to flee was in the fall of 1607."

[2] One who arrests debtors.
[3] Court.
[4] Bradford was among the 125 members of the Scrooby congregation who went to Amsterdam.

from CHAPTER III

[SETTLING IN HOLLAND, 1608]

Being now come into the Low Countries, they saw many goodly and fortified cities, strongly walled and guarded with troops of armed men. Also, they heard a strange and uncouth language, and beheld the different manners and customs of the people, with their strange fashions and attires; all so far differing from that of their plain country villages (wherein they were bred and had so long lived) as it seemed they were come into a new world. But these were not the things they much looked on, or long took up their thoughts, for they had other work in hand and another kind of war to wage and maintain. For although they saw fair and beautiful cities, flowing with abundance of all sorts of wealth and riches, yet it was not long before they saw the grim and grisly face of poverty coming upon them like an armed man,[1] with whom they must buckle and encounter, and from whom they could not fly. But they were armed with faith and patience against him and all his encounters; and though they were sometimes foiled, yet by God's assistance they prevailed and got the victory.

Now when Mr. Robinson, Mr. Brewster[2] and other principal members were come over (for they were of the last and stayed to help the weakest over before them) such things were thought on as were necessary for their settling and best ordering of the church affairs.

And when they had lived at Amsterdam about a year, Mr. Robinson their pastor and some others of best discerning, seeing how Mr. John Smith and his company was already fallen into contention with the church that was there before them,[3] and no means they could use would do any good to cure the same, and also that the flames of contention were like to break out in that ancient church itself (as afterwards lamentably came to pass); which things they prudently foreseeing thought it was best to remove before they were any way engaged with the same, though they well knew it would be much to the prejudice of their outward estates, both at present and in likelihood in the future; as indeed it proved to be.

[REMOVAL TO LEYDEN]

For these and some other reasons they removed to Leyden,[4] a fair and beautiful city and of a sweet situation, but made more famous by the university wherewith it is adorned, in which of late had been so many learned men.[5] But wanting that traffic by sea which Amsterdam enjoys, it was not so beneficial for their outward means of living and estate. But being now here pitch[ed], they fell to such trades and employments as they best could, valuing peace and their spiritual comfort above any other riches whatsoever. And at length they came to raise a competent and comfortable living, but with hard and continual labour.[6]

---

[1]Proverbs 24:34: "So shall thy poverty come as one that travelleth; and thy want as an armed man."

[2]John Robinson (1576?–1625), Cambridge graduate and member of the Scrooby congregation in Nottinghamshire, England, was ordained pastor (1609) in Leyden and helped organize the emigration to America (1620), which he planned to follow, but he died in Leyden. William Brewster (1576–1644), with Richard Clyfton in 1606 at Scrooby, organized the Separatist congregation, which Bradford joined as a young man; a leader of the Pilgrims in Leyden, he was also influential in the church and colony of Plymouth.

[3]John Smith (1570?–1612), Cambridge graduate and clergyman, led his Separatist group in 1608 from Gainsborough to Amsterdam, where he later became a Mennonite Baptist, writing some of the initial principles of the General Baptists.

[4]The Burgomasters of Leyden, 25 miles southwest, gave permission to the Pilgrims to settle in February 1609; by May nearly one hundred were there.

[5]Established in 1575, the University of Leyden was then among the most preeminent Protestant universities.

[6]Morison, citing Henry Martyn Dexter's *England and Holland of the Pilgrims*, notes that the 131 English (86 of them Pilgrims) engaged in 57 occupations, most involving cloth making. Bradford was described as a fustian (cotton and flax) maker, while Brewster and Winslow printed Puritan tracts (unlicensed in England) on their printing press.

CHAPTER IV

[DECISION TO LEAVE HOLLAND]

After they had lived in this city about some eleven or twelve years (which is the more observable being the whole time of that famous truce between that state and the Spaniards)[1] and sundry of them were taken away by death and many others began to be well stricken in years (the grave mistress of Experience having taught them many things), those prudent governors with sundry of the sagest members began both deeply to apprehend their present dangers and wisely to foresee the future and think of timely remedy. In the agitation of their thoughts, and much discourse of things hereabout, at length they began to incline to this conclusion: of removal to some other place. Not out of any newfangledness or other such like giddy humor by which men are oftentimes transported to their great hurt and danger, but for sundry weighty and solid reasons, some of the chief of which I will here briefly touch.

And first, they saw and found by experience the hardness of the place and country to be such as few in comparison would come to them, and fewer that would bide it out and continue with them. For many that came to them, and many more that desired to be with them, could not endure that great labour and hard fare, with other inconveniences which they underwent and were contented with. But though they loved their persons, approved their cause and honoured their sufferings, yet they left them as it were weeping, as Orpah did her mother-in-law Naomi,[2] or as those Romans did Cato in Utica[3] who desired to be excused and borne with, though they could not all be Catos. For many, though they desired to enjoy the ordinances of God in their purity and the liberty of the gospel with them, yet (alas) they admitted of bondage with danger of conscience, rather than to endure these hardships. Yea, some preferred and chose the prisons in England rather than this liberty in Holland with these afflictions.[4] But it was thought that if a better and easier place of living could be had, it would draw many and take away these discouragements. Yea, their pastor would often say that many of those who both wrote and preached now against them, if they were in a place where they might have liberty and live comfortably, they would then practice as they did.

Secondly. They saw that though the people generally bore all these difficulties very cheerfully and with a resolute courage, being in the best and strength of their years; yet old age began to steal on many of them; and their great and continual labours, with other crosses and sorrows, hastened it before the time. So as it was not only probably thought, but apparently seen, that within a few years more they would be in danger to scatter, by necessities pressing them, or sink under their burdens, or both. And therefore according to the divine proverb, that a wise man seeth the plague when it cometh, and hideth himself, Proverbs xxii.3, so they like skillful and beaten soldiers were fearful either to be entrapped or surrounded by their enemies so as they should neither be able to fight nor fly. And therefore thought it better to dislodge betimes to some place of better advantage and less danger, if any such could be found.

Thirdly. As necessity was a taskmaster over them so they were forced to be such, not only to their servants but in a sort to their dearest children, the which as

---

[1] The Netherlands had signed a twelve-years' truce with Spain in 1609, due to end in 1621. The Pilgrims feared a Spanish victory, bringing persecution by the Inquisition.
[2] Ruth 1:14: "And they lifted up their voice, and wept again: and Orpah kissed her mother-in-law; but Ruth clave unto her."
[3] Cato of Utica (95–46 B.C.), a Roman statesman, stoic philosopher, and enemy of Julius Caesar, who killed himself upon Caesar's victory over Pompey.

[4] Morison: "It may seem strange that it should seem easier to emigrate to the American wilderness than to a Dutch city; but the Netherlands were overpopulated in relation to the economic system of that day, and the standard of living in the handicrafts, the only occupations open to English immigrants, was low."

it did not a little wound the tender hearts of many a loving father and mother, so it produced likewise sundry sad and sorrowful effects. For many of their children that were of best dispositions and gracious inclinations, having learned[5] to bear the yoke in their youth and willing to bear part of their parents' burden, were oftentimes so oppressed with their heavy labours that though their minds were free and willing, yet their bodies bowed under the weight of the same, and became decrepit in their early youth, the vigour of nature being consumed in the very bud as it were. But that which was more lamentable, and of all sorrows most heavy to be borne, was that many of their children, by these occasions and the great licentiousness of youth in that country,[6] and the manifold temptations of the place, were drawn away by evil examples into extravagant and dangerous courses, getting the reins off their necks and departing from their parents. Some became soldiers, others took upon them far voyages by sea, and others some worse courses tending to dissoluteness and the danger of their souls, to the great grief of their parents and dishonour of God. So that they saw their posterity would be in danger to degenerate and be corrupted.[7]

Lastly (and which was not least), a great hope and inward zeal they had of laying some good foundation, or at least to make some way thereunto, for the propagating and advancing the gospel of the kingdom of Christ in those remote parts of the world; yea, though they should be but even as stepping-stones unto others for the performing of so great a work.

These and some other like reasons moved them to undertake this resolution of their removal; the which they afterward prosecuted with so great difficulties, as by the sequel will appear.

The place they had thoughts on was some of those vast and unpeopled countries of America, which are fruitful and fit for habitation, being devoid of all civil inhabitants, where there are only savage and brutish men which range up and down, little otherwise than the wild beasts of the same. This proposition being made public and coming to the scanning of all, it raised many variable opinions amongst men and caused many fears and doubts amongst themselves. Some, from their reasons and hopes conceived, laboured to stir up and encourage the rest to undertake and prosecute the same; others again, out of their fears, objected against it and sought to divert from it; alleging many things, and those neither unreasonable nor unprobable; as that it was a great design and subject to many unconceivable perils and dangers; as, besides the casualties of the sea (which none can be freed from), the length of the voyage was such as the weak bodies of women and other persons worn out with age and travail (as many of them were) could never be able to endure. And yet if they should, the miseries of the land which they should be exposed unto, would be too hard to be borne and likely, some or all of them together, to consume and utterly to ruinate them. For there they should be liable to famine and nakedness and the want, in a manner, of all things. The change of air, diet and drinking of water[8] would infect their bodies with sore sicknesses and grievous diseases. And also those which should escape or overcome these difficulties should yet be in continual danger of the savage people, who are cruel, barbarous and most treacherous, being most furious in their rage

---

[5]Lamentations 3:27: "It is good for a man that he bear the yoke in his youth."

[6]Morison: "The Dutch, curiously enough, did not 'remember the Sabbath Day to keep it holy' in the strict sense that other Calvinists did. Sunday after church was a day of feasting and merrymaking, especially for children. This was one of the conditions that the English community found most obnoxious."

[7]Morison: "Both Nathaniel Morton in *New Englands Memoriall* p. 3, and Edward Winslow in *Hypocrisie Unmasked* p. 89 stressed the fear of the Pilgrims lest their children lose their language and nationality. And their fear of the Dutch 'melting pot' was well taken; for the offspring of those English Puritans who did not emigrate to New England or return to England became completely amalgamated with the local population by 1660."

[8]Morison: "It was a general opinion of the time, which Bradford on sundry occasions shows that he shared, that water was an unwholesome beverage, as indeed it was when drawn from a contaminated well in a city or farmyard. The common table beverages of poor families in England and Holland were beer and cider."

and merciless where they overcome; not being content only to kill and take away life, but delight to torment men in the most bloody manner that may be; flaying some alive with the shells of fishes, cutting off the members and joints of others by piecemeal and broiling on the coals, eat the collops[9] of their flesh in their sight whilst they live, with other cruelties horrible to be related.[10]

And surely it could not be thought but the very hearing of these things could not but move the very bowels of men to grate within them and make the weak to quake and tremble. It was further objected that it would require greater sums of money to furnish such a voyage and to fit them with necessaries, than their consumed estates would amount to; and yet they must as well look to be seconded with supplies as presently to be transported. Also many precedents of ill success and lamentable miseries befallen others in the like designs were easy to be found, and not forgotten to be alleged; besides their own experience, in their former troubles and hardships in their removal into Holland, and how hard a thing it was for them to live in that strange place, though it was a neighbour country and a civil and rich commonwealth.

It was answered, that all great and honourable actions are accompanied with great difficulties and must be both enterprised and overcome with answerable courages. It was granted the dangers were great, but not desperate. The difficulties were many, but not invincible. For though there were many of them likely, yet they were not certain. It might be sundry of the things feared might never befall; others by provident care and the use of good means might in a great measure be prevented; and all of them, through the help of God, by fortitude and patience, might either be borne or overcome. True it was that such attempts were not to be made and undertaken without good ground and reason, not rashly or lightly as many have done for curiosity or hope of gain, etc. But their condition was not ordinary, their ends were good and honourable, their calling lawful and urgent; and therefore they might expect the blessing of God in their proceeding. Yea, though they should lose their lives in this action, yet might they have comfort in the same and their endeavours would be honourable. They lived here but as men in exile and in a poor condition, and as great miseries might possibly befall them in this place; for the twelve years of truce were now out and there was nothing but beating of drums and preparing for war, the events whereof are always uncertain. The Spaniard might prove as cruel as the savages of America, and the famine and pestilence as sore here as there, and their liberty less to look out for remedy.

After many other particular things answered and alleged on both sides, it was fully concluded by the major part to put this design in execution and to prosecute it by the best means they could.

from CHAPTER V

[DECISION TO GO TO VIRGINIA]

And first after their humble prayers unto God for His direction and assistance, and a general conference held hereabout, they consulted what particular place to pitch upon and prepare for. Some (and none of the meanest) had thoughts and were earnest for Guiana, or some of those fertile places in those hot climates. Others were for some parts of Virginia, where the English had already made entrance and beginning. Those for Guiana alleged that the country was rich, fruitful, and blessed with a perpetual spring and a flourishing greenness, where vigorous nature brought forth all things in abundance and plenty without any great labour or

---

[9]Rolls.
[10]Morison: "As the Netherlands was then the principal center for the publication of illustrated narratives of voyages, the Pilgrims had a wide choice of literature from which to acquire a healthy respect for the Indians and an aversion to taking up a new abode within reach of the Spaniards."

art of man.[1] So as it must needs make the inhabitants rich, seeing less provisions of clothing and other things would serve, than in more colder and less fruitful countries must be had. As also that the Spaniards (having much more than they could possess) had not yet planted there nor anywhere very near the same. But to this it was answered that out of question the country was both fruitful and pleasant, and might yield riches and maintenance to the possessors more easily than the other; yet, other things considered, it would not be so fit for them. And first, that such hot countries are subject to grievous diseases and many noisome impediments which other more temperate places are freer from, and would not so well agree with our English bodies. Again, if they should there live and do well, the jealous Spaniard would never suffer them long, but would displant or overthrow them as he did the French in Florida, who were seated further from his richest countries; and the sooner because they should have none to protect them, and their own strength would be too small to resist so potent an enemy and so near a neighbour.

On the other hand, for Virginia it was objected that if they lived among the English which were there planted, or so near them as to be under their government, they should be in as great danger to be troubled and persecuted for the cause of religion as if they lived in England; and it might be worse. And if they lived too far off, they should neither have succour nor defense from them.

But at length the conclusion was to live as a distinct body by themselves under the general Government of Virginia; and by their friends to sue to His Majesty that he would be pleased to grant them freedom of religion. And that this might be obtained they were put in good hope by some great persons of good rank and quality that were made their friends. Whereupon two were chosen and sent into England (at the charge of the rest) to solicit this matter, who found the Virginia Company very desirous to have them go thither and willing to grant them a patent, with as ample privileges as they had or could grant to any; and to give them the best furtherance they could.[2] And some of the chief of that Company doubted not to obtain their suit of the King for liberty in religion, and to have it confirmed under the King's broad seal, according to their desires. But it proved a harder piece of work than they took it for; for though many means were used to bring it about, yet it could not be effected. For there were divers of good worth laboured with the King to obtain it, amongst whom was one of his chief secretaries, Sir Robert Naunton.[3] And some others wrought with the Archbishop to give way thereunto, but it proved all in vain. Yet thus far they prevailed, in sounding His Majesty's mind, that he would connive[4] at them and not molest them, provided they carried themselves peaceably. But to allow or tolerate them by his public authority, under his seal, they found it would not be. And this was all the chief of the Virginia Company or any other of their best friends could do in the case. Yet they persuaded them to go on, for they presumed they should not be troubled. And with this answer the messengers returned and signified what diligence had been used and to what issue things were come.

But this made a damp in the business and caused some distraction, for many were afraid that if they should unsettle themselves and put off their estates and go upon these hopes, it might prove dangerous and prove but a sandy foundation. Yea it was thought they might better have presumed hereupon without making

---

[1]Guiana was known to them as the area in South America between the Orinoco River in Venezuela and the Amazon River in Peru and Brazil.

[2]From about 1617, the Virginia Company of London granted land tracts of up to 80,000 acres, including the rights of self-government, jurisdiction, fishing, and trade with Indians, in return for populating and cultivating their land, extending to Long Island and encompassing Manhattan.

[3]A Puritan sympathizer.

[4]Pretend ignorance of any injustice.

any suit at all than, having made it, to be thus rejected. But some of the chiefest thought otherwise and that they might well proceed hereupon, and that the King's Majesty was willing enough to suffer them without molestation, though for other reasons he would not confirm it by any public act. And furthermore, if there was no security in this promise intimated, there would be no great certainty in a further confirmation of the same; for if afterwards there should be a purpose or desire to wrong them, though they had a seal as broad as the house floor it would not serve the turn; for there would be means enow found to recall or reverse it. Seeing therefore the course was probable, they must rest herein on God's providence as they had done in other things.

Upon this resolution, other messengers were dispatched, to end with the Virginia Company as well as they could. And to procure a patent with as good and ample conditions as they might by any good means obtain. As also to treat and conclude with such merchants and other friends as had manifested their forwardness to provoke to and adventure in this voyage. For which end they had instructions given them upon what conditions they should proceed with them, or else to conclude nothing without further advice.

from CHAPTER VII
[DEPARTURE FROM LEYDEN]

At length, after much travel and these debates, all things were got ready and provided. A small ship[1] was bought and fitted in Holland, which was intended as to serve to help to transport them, so to stay in the country and attend upon fishing and such other affairs as might be for the good and benefit of the colony when they came there. Another was hired at London, of burthen about 9 score,[2] and all other things got in readiness. So being ready to depart, they had a day of solemn humiliation, their pastor taking his text from Ezra viii.21: "And there at the river, by Ahava, I proclaimed a fast, that we might humble ourselves before our God, and seek of him a right way for us, and for our children, and for all our substance."[3] Upon which he spent a good part of the day very profitably and suitable to their present occasion; the rest of the time was spent in pouring out prayers to the Lord with great fervency, mixed with abundance of tears. And the time being come that they must depart, they were accompanied with most of their brethren out of the city, unto a town sundry miles off called Delftshaven, where the ship lay ready to receive them. So they left that goodly and pleasant city which had been their resting place near twelve years; but they knew they were pilgrims,[4] and looked not much on those things, but lift up their eyes to the heavens, their dearest country, and quieted their spirits.

When they came to the place they found the ship and all things ready, and such of their friends as could not come with them followed after them, and sundry also came from Amsterdam to see them shipped and to take their leave of them. That night was spent with little sleep by the most, but with friendly entertainment and Christian discourse and other real expressions of true Christian

---

[1]Bradford notes that the ship, the *Speedwell*, was "of some 60 ton."

[2]Morison: "The *Mayflower*, 190 tons."

[3]Ezra here speaks to the Jews, assembled near the settlement of Ahava, on the Tigris River, readying themselves for their move from Babylonian captivity back to Jerusalem. Bradford quotes from the Geneva Bible published in 1560 in Geneva by English Calvinist exiles. The Puritans favored its scholarly translations and marginal commentary over the Authorized King James Version of 1611.

[4]In a note Bradford cites Hebrews 11:13–16, which says, "These all died in faith, not having received the promises, but having seen them afar off, and were persuaded of them, and embraced them, and confessed that they were strangers and pilgrims on the earth. For they that say such things declare plainly that they seek a country. And truly, if they had been mindful of that country from whence they came out, they might have had opportunity to have returned. But now they desire a better country, that is, an heavenly: wherefore God is not ashamed to be called their God: for he hath prepared for them a city." Morison: "It was owing to this passage, first printed in 1669, that the *Mayflower's* company came eventually to be called the Pilgrim Fathers."

love. The next day (the wind being fair) they went aboard and their friends with them, where truly doleful was the sight of that sad and mournful parting, to see what sighs and sobs and prayers did sound amongst them, what tears did gush from every eye, and pithy speeches pierced each heart; that sundry of the Dutch strangers that stood on the quay as spectators could not refrain from tears. Yet comfortable and sweet it was to see such lively and true expressions of dear and unfeigned love. But the tide, which stays for no man, calling them away that were thus loath to depart, their reverend pastor falling down on his knees (and they all with him) with watery cheeks commended them with most fervent prayers to the Lord and His blessing. And then with mutual embraces and many tears they took their leaves one of another, which proved to be the last leave to many of them.

CHAPTER IX

[VOYAGE TO THE NEW WORLD]

September 6 [1620]. These troubles being blown over,[1] and now all being compact together in one ship, they put to sea again with a prosperous wind, which continued divers days together, which was some encouragement unto them; yet, according to the usual manner, many were afflicted with seasickness. And I may not omit here a special work of God's providence. There was a proud and very profane young man, one of the seamen, of a lusty,[2] able body, which made him the more haughty; he would alway be contemning the poor people in their sickness and cursing them daily with grievous execrations; and did not let[3] to tell them that he hoped to help to cast half of them overboard before they came to their journey's end, and to make merry with what they had; and if he were by any gently reproved, he would curse and swear most bitterly. But it pleased God before they came half seas over, to smite this young man with a grievous disease, of which he died in a desperate manner, and so was himself the first that was thrown overboard. Thus his curses light on his own head, and it was an astonishment to all his fellows for they noted it to be the just hand of God upon him.

After they had enjoyed fair winds and weather for a season, they were encountered many times with cross winds and met with many fierce storms with which the ship was shroudly[4] shaken, and her upper works made very leaky; and one of the main beams in the midships was bowed and cracked, which put them in some fear that the ship could not be able to perform the voyage. So some of the chief of the company, perceiving the mariners to fear the sufficiency of the ship as appeared by their mutterings, they entered into serious consultation with the master and other officers of the ship, to consider in time of the danger, and rather to return than to cast themselves into a desperate and inevitable peril. And truly there was great distraction and difference of opinion amongst the mariners themselves; fain would they do what could be done for their wages' sake (being now near half the seas over) and on the other hand they were loath to hazard their lives too desperately. But in examining of all opinions, the master and others affirmed they knew the ship to be strong and firm under water; and for the buckling of the main beam, there was a great iron screw the passengers brought out of Holland, which would raise the beam into his place; the which being done, the carpenter and master affirmed that with a post put under it, set firm in the lower

---

[1] In July 1620, the Pilgrims set sail from Leyden in the *Speedwell* for Southhampton, England, where some joined other emigrants on a hired ship, the *Mayflower*. The two ships embarked for Virginia in August 1620, but returned to Plymouth, England, when the *Speedwell* proved unseaworthy. They set out again on the heavier ship, the *Mayflower*, in September 1620. Bradford's date, the 6th, is that of the Old Style (Julian) calender, ten days earlier than that of the New Style (Gregorian). Both dates will be given in the footnotes.
[2] Merry, joyous; no sexual connotation.
[3] Hesitate.
[4] Wickedly, from the original form of shrewdly.

deck and otherways bound, he would make it sufficient. And as for the decks and upper works, they would caulk them as well as they could, and though with the working of the ship they would not long keep staunch, yet there would otherwise be no great danger, if they did not overpress her with sails. So they committed themselves to the will of God and resolved to proceed.

In sundry of these storms the winds were so fierce and the seas so high, as they could not bear a knot of sail, but were forced to hull[5] for divers days together. And in one of them, as they thus lay at hull in a mighty storm, a lusty young man called John Howland, coming upon some occasion above the gratings was, with a seele[6] of the ship, thrown into sea; but it pleased God that he caught hold of the topsail halyards which hung overboard and ran out at length. Yet he held his hold (though he was sundry fathoms under water) till he was hauled up by the same rope to the brim of the water, and then with a boat hook and other means got into the ship again and his life saved. And though he was something ill with it, yet he lived many years after and became a profitable member both in church and commonwealth. In all this voyage there died but one of the passengers, which was William Butten, a youth, servant to Samuel Fuller, when they drew near the coast.

But to omit other things (that I may be brief) after long beating at sea they fell with that land which is called Cape Cod;[7] the which being made and certainly known to be it, they were not a little joyful. After some deliberation had amongst themselves and with the master of the ship, they tacked about and resolved to stand for the southward (the wind and weather being fair) to find some place about Hudson's River for their habitation.[8] But after they had sailed that course about half the day, they fell amongst dangerous shoals and roaring breakers, and they were so far entangled therewith as they conceived themselves in great danger; and the wind shrinking upon them withal, they resolved to bear up again for the Cape and thought themselves happy to get out of those dangers before night overtook them, as by God's good providence they did. And the next day[9] they got into the Cape Harbor[10] where they rid in safety.

A word or two by the way of this cape. It was thus first named by Captain Gosnold and his company,[11] Anno 1602, and after by Captain Smith was called Cape James; but it retains the former name amongst seamen. Also, that point which first showed those dangerous shoals unto them they called Point Care, and Tucker's Terrour; but the French and Dutch to this day call it Malabar by reason of those perilous shoals and the losses they have suffered there.

Being thus arrived in a good harbor, and brought safe to land, they fell upon their knees and blessed the God of Heaven[12] who had brought them over the vast and furious ocean, and delivered them from all the perils and miseries thereof, again to set their feet on the firm and stable earth, their proper element. And no marvel if they were thus joyful, seeing wise Seneca was so affected with sailing a few miles on the coast of his own Italy, as he affirmed, that he had rather remain twenty years on his way by land than pass by sea to any place in a short time, so tedious and dreadful was the same unto him.[13]

But here I cannot but stay and make a pause, and stand half amazed at this poor people's present condition; and so I think will the reader, too, when he well

---

[5]Drift with the wind under a very short sail.
[6]Roll.
[7]Morison: "At daybreak 9/19 November 1620, they sighted the Highlands of Cape Cod."
[8]The Pilgrims thus were heading for the area within the boundaries authorized by the patent received from the Virginia Company, although they failed to reach it.
[9]November 11/21, 1620, 65 days out of Plymouth.

[10]Now Provincetown Harbor.
[11]Cod, so called, as Bradford notes, "Because they took much of that fish there."
[12]Daniel 2:19: "Then was the secret revealed unto Daniel in a night vision. Then Daniel blessed the God of heaven."
[13]Bradford cites Epistle 53, an allusion to a sentence in Seneca (4 B.C.–A.D. 65), Roman rhetorician.

considers the same. Being thus passed the vast ocean, and a sea of troubles before in their preparation (as may be remembered by that which went before), they had now no friends to welcome them nor inns to entertain or refresh their weather-beaten bodies; no houses or much less towns to repair to, to seek for succour. It is recorded in Scripture[14] as a mercy to the Apostle and his shipwrecked company, that the barbarians showed them no small kindness in refreshing them, but these savage barbarians, when they met with them (as after will appear) were readier to fill their sides full of arrows than otherwise. And for the season it was winter, and they that know the winters of that country know them to be sharp and violent, and subject to cruel and fierce storms, dangerous to travel to known places, much more to search an unknown coast. Besides, what could they see but a hideous and desolate wilderness, full of wild beasts and wild men—and what multitudes there might be of them they knew not. Neither could they, as it were, go up to the top of Pisgah[15] to view from this wilderness a more goodly country to feed their hopes; for which way soever they turned their eyes (save upward to the heavens) they could have little solace or content in respect of any outward objects. For summer being done, all things stand upon them with a weather-beaten face, and the whole country, full of woods and thickets, represented a wild and savage hue. If they looked behind them, there was the mighty ocean which they had passed and was now as a main bar and gulf to separate them from all the civil parts of the world. If it be said they had a ship to succour them, it is true; but what heard they daily from the master and company? But that with speed they should look out a place (with their shallop[16]) where they would be, at some near distance; for the season was such as he would not stir from thence till a safe harbor was discovered by them, where they would be, and he might go without danger; and that victuals consumed apace but he must and would keep sufficient for themselves and their return. Yea, it was muttered by some that if they got not a place in time, they would turn them and their goods ashore and leave them. Let it also be considered what weak hopes of supply and succour they left behind them, that might bear up their minds in this sad condition and trials they were under; and they could not but be very small. It is true, indeed, the affections and love of their brethren at Leyden[17] was cordial and entire towards them, but they had little power to help them or themselves; and how the case stood between them and the merchants at their coming away hath already been declared.

What could now sustain them but the Spirit of God and His grace? May not and ought not the children of these fathers rightly say: "Our fathers were Englishmen which came over this great ocean, and were ready to perish in this wilderness; but they cried unto the Lord, and He heard their voice and looked on their adversity,"[18] etc. "Let them therefore praise the Lord, because He is good: and His mercies endure forever." "Yea, let them which have been redeemed of the Lord, shew how He hath delivered them from the hand of the oppressor. When they wandered in the desert wilderness out of the way, and found no city to dwell in, both hungry and thirsty, their soul was overwhelmed in them. Let them confess before the Lord His lovingkindness and His wonderful works before the sons of men."[19]

[14]Bradford cites Acts 28; Morison cites verse 2: "And the barbarous people showed us no little kindness: for they kindled a fire, and received us every one, because of the present rain, and because of the cold."
[15]Deuteronomy 34:1–4; from Mount Pisgah, the Lord showed Moses the Promised Land.
[16]Small open boat.
[17]The town in Holland from whence they had sailed, leaving most of their fellow Separatists.
[18]Bradford cites Deuteronomy 26:5, 7, a reference to the deliverance of the Israelites from Egyptian bondage.

[19]Bradford cites Psalm 107:1–5, 8: "O give thanks unto the Lord, for he is good: for his mercy endureth forever. Let the redeemed of the Lord say so, whom he hath redeemed from the hand of the enemy; and gathered them out of the lands, from the east, and from the west, from the north, and from the south. They wandered in the wilderness in a solitary way; they found no city to dwell in. Hungry and thirsty, their soul fainted in them. Oh that men would praise the Lord for his goodness, and for his wonderful works to the children of men!"

CHAPTER X

[Searching for a Place, Encountering Indians, Settling in Plymouth]

Being thus arrived at Cape Cod the 11th[1] of November [1620], and necessity calling them to look out a place for habitation (as well as the master's and mariners' importunity); they having brought a large shallop with them out of England, stowed in quarters in the ship, they now got her out and set their carpenters to work to trim her up; but being much bruised and shattered in the ship with foul weather, they saw she would be long in mending. Whereupon a few of them tendered themselves to go by land and discover those nearest places, whilst the shallop was in mending; and the rather because as they went into that harbor there seemed to be an opening some two or three leagues off, which the master judged to be a river. It was conceived there might be some danger in the attempt, yet seeing them resolute, they were permitted to go, being sixteen of them well armed under the conduct of Captain Standish,[2] having such instructions given them as was thought meet.

They set forth the 15th[3] of November; and when they had marched about the space of a mile by the seaside, they espied five or six persons with a dog coming towards them, who were savages; but they fled from them and ran up into the woods, and the English followed them, partly to see if they could speak with them, and partly to discover if there might not be more of them lying in ambush. But the Indians seeing themselves thus followed, they again forsook the woods and ran away on the sands as hard as they could, so as they could not come near them but followed them by the track of their feet sundry miles and saw that they had come the same way. So, night coming on, they made their rendezvous and set out their sentinels, and rested in quiet that night; and the next morning followed their track till they had headed a great creek and so left the sands, and turned another way into the woods. But they still followed them by guess, hoping to find their dwellings; but they soon lost both them and themselves, falling into such thickets as were ready to tear their clothes and armor in pieces; but were most distressed for want of drink. But at length they found water and refreshed themselves, being the first New England water they drunk of, and was now in great thirst as pleasant unto them as wine or beer had been in foretimes.

Afterwards they directed their course to come to the other shore, for they knew it was a neck of land they were to cross over, and so at length got to the seaside and marched to this supposed river, and by the way found a pond of clear, fresh water, and shortly after a good quantity of clear ground where the Indians had formerly set corn, and some of their graves. And proceeding further they saw new stubble where corn had been set the same year; also they found where lately a house had been, where some planks and a great kettle was remaining, and heaps of sand newly paddled with their hands. Which, they digging up, found in them divers fair Indian baskets filled with corn, and some in ears, fair and good, of divers colours, which seemed to them a very goodly sight (having never seen any such before). This was near the place of that supposed river they came to seek, unto which they went and found it to open itself into two arms with a high cliff of sand in the entrance but more like to be creeks of salt water than any fresh, for aught they saw; and that there was good harborage for their shallop, leaving it

---

[1]November 21.

[2]Myles Standish (1584?–1656), military leader and defender of the Pilgrims, became a leader in the colony and, with John Alden, founded Duxbury (1631). Longfellow's *The Courtship of Miles Standish* (1858) has no apparent historical basis.

[3]November 25. Further details of these expeditions are found in the extracts from Bradford and Winslow's Journals, published in London in 1622 as *A Relation or Journall of the beginning and proceedings of the English Plantation setled at Plimouth in New England, by certain English Adventurers both Merchants and others*, commonly known as *Mourt's Relation*.

further to be discovered by their shallop, when she was ready. So, their time limited them being expired, they returned to the ship lest they should be in fear of their safety; and took with them part of the corn and buried up the rest. And so, like the men from Eshcol, carried with them of the fruits of the land and showed their brethren;[4] of which, and their return, they were marvelously glad and their hearts encouraged.

After this, the shallop being got ready, they set out again for the better discovery of this place, and the master of the ship desired to go himself. So there went some thirty men but found it to be no harbor for ships but only for boats. There was also found two of their houses covered with mats, and sundry of their implements in them, but the people were run away and could not be seen. Also there was found more of their corn and of their beans of various colours; the corn and beans they brought away, purposing to give them full satisfaction when they should meet with any of them as, about some six months afterward they did, to their good content.

And here is to be noted a special providence of God, and a great mercy to this poor people, that here they got seed to plant them corn the next year, or else they might have starved, for they had none nor any likelihood to get any till the season had been past, as the sequel did manifest. Neither is it likely they had had this, if the first voyage had not been made, for the ground was now all covered with snow and hard frozen; but the Lord is never wanting unto His in their greatest needs; let His holy name have all the praise.

The month of November being spent in these affairs, and much foul weather falling in, the 6th of December they sent out their shallop again with ten of their principal men[5] and some seamen, upon further discovery, intending to circulate that deep bay of Cape Cod. The weather was very cold and it froze so hard as the spray of the sea lighting on their coats, they were as if they had been glazed. Yet that night betimes they got down into the bottom of the bay, and as they drew near the shore they saw some ten or twelve Indians very busy about something. They landed about a league or two from them, and had much ado to put ashore anywhere—it lay so full of flats. Being landed, it grew late and they made themselves a barricado with logs and boughs as well as they could in the time, and set out their sentinel and betook them to rest, and saw the smoke of the fire the savages made that night. When morning was come they divided their company, some to coast along the shore in the boat, and the rest marched through the woods to see the land, if any fit place might be for their dwelling. They came also to the place where they saw the Indians the night before, and found they had been cutting up a great fish like a grampus, being some two inches thick of fat like a hog, some pieces whereof they had left by the way. And the shallop found two more of these fishes dead on the sands, a thing usual after storms in that place, by reason of the great flats of sand that lie off.

So they ranged up and down all that day, but found no people, nor any place they liked. When the sun grew low, they hasted out of the woods to meet with their shallop, to whom they made signs to come to them into a creek hard by, the

---

[4]Numbers 13:23–26: "And they came unto the brook of Eschol, and cut down from thence a branch with one cluster of grapes, and they bare it between two upon a staff; and they brought of the pomegranates, and of the figs. . . . And they went and came to Moses, and to Aaron, and to all the congregation of the children of Israel, . . . and brought back word unto them, . . . and showed them the fruit of the land."
[5]December 16. Morison: "The names of the ten (from *Mourt's Relation*) are Standish, Carver and his servant Howland, Bradford, Winslow, John and Edward Tilley, Richard Warren, Stephen Hopkins and his servant Doten; also the

pilots, John Clarke and Robert Coppin, and the master gunner and three sailors, whose names are unknown. *Mourt's Relation* states that after the return of the second exploring expedition there was much debate on board the *Mayflower* whether they should settle at Pamet River, at Agawam (the later Ipswich), which looked good on Captain John Smith's map, at Cape Ann, or at Plymouth. On the strength of the recommendations of Coppin, who had been to Plymouth on a previous voyage and offered to pilot them thither, they decided to investigate that place before deciding."

which they did at high water; of which they were very glad, for they had not seen each other all that day since the morning. So they made them a barricado as usually they did every night, with logs, stakes and thick pine boughs, the height of a man, leaving it open to leeward, partly to shelter them from the cold and wind (making their fire in the middle and lying round about it) and partly to defend them from any sudden assaults of the savages, if they should surround them; so being very weary, they betook them to rest. But about midnight they heard a hideous and great cry, and their sentinel called "Arm! arm!" So they bestirred them and stood to their arms and shot off a couple of muskets, and then the noise ceased. They concluded it was a company of wolves or such like wild beasts, for one of the seamen told them he had often heard such a noise in Newfoundland.

So they rested till about five of the clock in the morning; for the tide, and their purpose to go from thence, made them be stirring betimes. So after prayer they prepared for breakfast, and it being day dawning it was thought best to be carrying things down to the boat. But some said it was not best to carry the arms down, others said they would be the readier, for they had lapped them up in their coats from the dew; but some three or four would not carry theirs till they went themselves. Yet as it fell out, the water being not high enough, they laid them down on the bank side and came up to breakfast.

But presently, all on the sudden, they heard a great and strange cry, which they knew to be the same voices they heard in the night, though they varied their notes; and one of their company being abroad came running in and cried, "Men, Indians! Indians!" And withal, their arrows came flying amongst them. Their men ran with all speed to recover their arms, as by the good providence of God they did. In the meantime, of those that were there ready, two muskets were discharged at them, and two more stood ready in the entrance of their rendezvous but were commanded not to shoot till they could take full aim at them. And the other two charged again with all speed, for there were only four had arms there, and defended the barricado, which was first assaulted. The cry of the Indians was dreadful, especially when they saw their men run out of the rendezvous toward the shallop to recover their arms, the Indians wheeling about upon them. But some running out with coats of mail on, and cutlasses in their hands, they soon got their arms and let fly amongst them and quickly stopped their violence. Yet there was a lusty man, and no less valiant, stood behind a tree within half a musket shot, and let his arrows fly at them; he was seen [to] shoot three arrows, which were all avoided. He stood three shots of a musket, till one taking full aim at him and made the bark or splinters of the tree fly about his ears, after which he gave an extraordinary shriek and away they went, all of them. They[6] left some to keep the shallop and followed them about a quarter of a mile and shouted once or twice, and shot off two or three pieces, and so returned. This they did that they might conceive that they were not afraid of them or any way discouraged.

Thus it pleased God to vanquish their enemies and give them deliverance; and by His special providence so to dispose that not any one of them were either hurt or hit, though their arrows came close by them and on every side [of] them; and sundry of their coats, which hung up in the barricado, were shot through and through. Afterwards they gave God solemn thanks and praise for their deliverance, and gathered up a bundle of their arrows and sent them into England afterward by the master of the ship, and called that place the First Encounter.

From hence they departed and coasted all along but discerned no place likely for harbor; and therefore hasted to a place that their pilot (one Mr. Coppin who had been in the country before) did assure them was a good harbor, which he had

---

[6]I.e., the English.

been in, and they might fetch it before night; of which they were glad for it began to be foul weather.

After some hours' sailing it began to snow and rain, and about the middle of the afternoon the wind increased and the sea became very rough, and they broke their rudder, and it was as much as two men could do to steer her with a couple of oars. But their pilot bade them be of good cheer for he saw the harbor; but the storm increasing, and night drawing on, they bore what sail they could to get in, while they could see. But herewith they broke their mast in three pieces and their sail fell overboard in a very grown sea, so as they had like to have been cast away. Yet by God's mercy they recovered themselves, and having the flood[7] with them, struck into the harbor. But when it came to, the pilot was deceived in the place, and said the Lord be merciful unto them for his eyes never saw that place before; and he and the master's mate would have run her ashore in a cove full of breakers before the wind. But a lusty seaman which steered bade those which rowed, if they were men, about with her or else they were all cast away; the which they did with speed. So he bid them be of good cheer and row lustily, for there was a fair sound before them, and he doubted not but they should find one place or other where they might ride in safety. And though it was very dark and rained sore, yet in the end they got under the lee of a small island and remained there all that night in safety. But they knew not this to be an island till morning, but were divided in their minds; some would keep the boat for fear they might be amongst the Indians, others were so wet and cold they could not endure but got ashore, and with much ado got fire (all things being so wet); and the rest were glad to come to them, for after midnight the wind shifted to the northwest and it froze hard.

But though this had been a day and night of much trouble and danger unto them, yet God gave them a morning of comfort and refreshing (as usually He doth to His children) for the next day was a fair, sunshining day, and they found themselves to be on an island secure from the Indians, where they might dry their stuff, fix their pieces and rest themselves; and gave God thanks for His mercies in their manifold deliverances. And this being the last day of the week, they prepared there to keep the Sabbath.

On Monday they sounded the harbor and found it fit for shipping, and marched into the land and found divers cornfields and little running brooks, a place (as they supposed) fit for situation.[8] At least it was the best they could find, and the season and their present necessity made them glad to accept of it. So they returned to their ship again with this news to the rest of their people, which did much comfort their hearts.

On the 15th of December they weighed anchor to go to the place they had discovered, and came within two leagues of it, but were fain to bear up again; but the 16th day, the wind came fair, and they arrived safe in this harbor. And afterwards took better view of the place, and resolved where to pitch their dwelling; and the 25th day began to erect the first house for common use to receive them and their goods.[9]

---

[7] I.e., the flood tide.

[8] Morison: "Here is the only contemporary authority for the 'Landing of the Pilgrims on Plymouth Rock' on Monday, 11/21 Dec. 1620. It is clear that the landing took place from the shallop, not the *Mayflower*, which was then moored in Provincetown Harbor; that no women were involved in it, and no Indians or anyone else were on the receiving end. Nor is it clear that they landed on the large boulder since called Plymouth Rock. That boulder was identified in 1741 by Elder John Faunce, aged 95, as the 'place where the forefathers landed,' and although he probably only meant to say that they used it as a landing place, for it would have been very convenient for that purpose at half tide, every-one seems to have assumed that they 'first' landed there. The exploring party may have landed anywhere between Captain's Hill and the Rock."

[9] Morison: "*Mourt's Relation* p. 23 says that after the *Mayflower's* arrival in Plymouth Bay on 16/26 Dec. the men explored the bay again and debated whether to settle at Plymouth, the mouth of Jones River (the present Kingston) or on Clark's Island. They decided on the first because much of the land was already cleared and a fort on the hill—now Burial Hill—could command the surrounding country; and because 'a very sweet brook'—the Town Brook—'runs under the hillside.' "

from CHAPTER XI: THE REMAINDER OF ANNO 1620
[THE MAYFLOWER COMPACT]

I shall a little return back, and begin with a combination[1] made by them before they came ashore; being the first foundation of their government in this place. Occasioned partly by the discontented and mutinous speeches that some of the strangers[2] amongst them had let fall from them in the ship: That when they came ashore they would use their own liberty, for none had power to command them, the patent they had being for Virginia and not for New England, which belonged to another government, with which the Virginia Company had nothing to do. And partly that such an act by them done, this their condition considered, might be as firm as any patent, and in some respects more sure.

The form was as followeth:[3]

IN THE NAME OF GOD, AMEN.
We whose names are underwritten, the loyal subjects of our dread Sovereign Lord King James, by the Grace of God of Great Britain, France, and Ireland King, Defender of the Faith, etc.

Having undertaken, for the Glory of God and advancement of the Christian Faith and Honour of our King and Country, a Voyage to plant the First Colony in the Northern Parts of Virginia,[4] do by these presents solemnly and mutually in the presence of God and one of another, Covenant and Combine ourselves together into a Civil Body Politic, for our better ordering and preservation and furtherance of the ends aforesaid; and by virtue hereof to enact, constitute and frame such just and equal Laws, Ordinances, Acts, Constitutions and Offices, from time to time, as shall be thought most meet and convenient for the general good of the Colony, unto which we promise all due submission and obedience. In witness whereof we have hereunder subscribed our names at Cape Cod, the 11th of November, in the year of the reign of our Sovereign Lord King James, of England, France and Ireland the eighteenth, and of Scotland the fifty-fourth. Anno Domini 1620.

After this they chose, or rather confirmed, Mr. John Carver[5] (a man godly and well approved amongst them) their Governor for that year. And after they had provided a place for their goods, or common store (which were long in unlading for want of boats, foulness of the winter weather and sickness of divers) and begun some small cottages for their habitation; as time would admit, they met and consulted of laws and orders, both for their civil and military government as the necessity of their condition did require, still adding thereunto as urgent occasion in several times, and as cases did require.

In these hard and difficult beginnings they found some discontents and murmurings arise amongst some, and mutinous speeches and carriages in other; but they were soon quelled and overcome by the wisdom, patience, and just and equal carriage of things, by the Governor and better part, which clave[6] faithfully together in the main.

---

[1]Agreement. Morison notes in *An American Primer,* ed., Daniel J. Boorstin, 1966, that not until 1793 was the word "compact" applied to the *Mayflower* agreement, after the social compact theory of government in the works of Locke (1690) and Rousseau (1762) had become widely read.
[2]Those outside the church who had sailed on the *Mayflower* to find new lives in the New World.
[3]Samuel Eliot Morison, in *An American Primer,* says that the Mayflower Compact "is justly regarded as a key document in American history. It proves the determination of the small group of English emigrants to live under a rule of law, based on the consent of the people, and to set up their own civil government."

[4]That is, New England—the northern part of Virginia which John Smith explored and christened New England, popularizing the new name in his book, *A Description of New England* (1616). Both names were used for a time, but gradually after 1620, New England came into general usage.
[5]John Carver (1575?–1621). Carver had been appointed governor in England. The vote confirmed him as the Pilgrims' choice.
[6]Past of "cleave" (cleaved, adhered).

[The Starving Time]

But that which was most sad and lamentable was, that in two or three months' time half of their company died, especially in January and February, being the depth of winter, and wanting houses and other comforts; being infected with the scurvy and other diseases which this long voyage and their inaccommodate condition had brought upon them. So as there died some times two or three of a day in the foresaid time, that of 100 and odd persons, scarce fifty remained.[7] And of these, in the time of most distress, there was but six or seven sound persons who to their great commendations, be it spoken, spared no pains night nor day, but with abundance of toil and hazard of their own health, fetched them wood, made them fires, dressed them meat, made their beds, washed their loathsome clothes, clothed and unclothed them. In a word, did all the homely and necessary offices for them which dainty and queasy stomachs cannot endure to hear named; and all this willingly and cheerfully, without any grudging in the least, showing herein their true love unto their friends and brethren; a rare example and worthy to be remembered. Two of these seven were Mr. William Brewster, their reverend Elder, and Myles Standish, their Captain and military commander, unto whom myself and many others were much beholden in our low and sick condition. And yet the Lord so upheld these persons as in this general calamity they were not at all infected either with sickness or lameness. And what I have said of these I may say of many others who died in this general visitation, and others yet living; that whilst they had health, yea, or any strength continuing, they were not wanting to any that had need of them. And I doubt not but their recompense is with the Lord.

But I may not here pass by another remarkable passage not to be forgotten. As this calamity fell among the passengers that were to be left here to plant, and were hasted ashore and made to drink water that the seamen might have the more beer, and one[8] in his sickness desiring but a small can of beer, it was answered that if he were their own father he should have none. The disease began to fall amongst them[9] also, so as almost half of their company died before they went away, and many of their officers and lustiest men, as the boatswain, gunner, three quartermasters, the cook and others. At which the Master was something strucken and sent to the sick ashore and told the Governor he should send for beer for them that had need of it, though he drunk water homeward bound.

But now amongst his company there was far another kind of carriage in this misery than amongst the passengers. For they that before had been boon companions in drinking and jollity in the time of their health and welfare, began now to desert one another in this calamity, saying they would not hazard their lives for them, they should be infected by coming to help them in their cabins; and so, after they came to lie by it, would do little or nothing for them but, "if they died, let them die." But such of the passengers as were yet aboard showed them what mercy they could, which made some of their hearts relent, as the boatswain (and some others) who was a proud young man and would often curse and scoff at the passengers. But when he grew weak, they had compassion on him and helped him; then he confessed he did not deserve it at their hands, he had abused them in word and deed. "Oh!" (saith he) "you, I now see, show your love like Christians indeed one to another, but we let one another lie and die like dogs." Another lay cursing his wife, saying if it had not been for her he had never come this unlucky voyage, and anon cursing his fellows, saying he had done this and that for some of

---

[7]Morison: "Of the 102 *Mayflower* passengers who reached Cape Cod, 4 died before she made Plymouth; and by the summer of 1621 the total deaths numbered 50. Only 12 of the original 26 heads of families and 4 of the original 12 unattached men or boys were left; and of the women who reached Plymouth, all but a few died. Doubtless many of the deaths took place on board the *Mayflower* at anchor, since there was not enough shelter ashore for all; and Plymouth Harbor is so shallow that she was moored about 1½ nautical miles from the Rock."

[8]Bradford indicates in a note that he was the "one."

[9]I.e., the members of the crew.

them; he had spent so much and so much amongst them, and they were now weary of him and did not help him, having need. Another gave his companion all he had, if he died, to help him in his weakness; he went and got a little spice and made him a mess of meat once or twice. And because he died not so soon as he expected, he went amongst his fellows and swore the rogue would cozen[10] him, he would see him choked before he made him any more meat; and yet the poor fellow died before morning.

[INDIAN RELATIONS]

All this while the Indians came skulking about them, and would sometimes show themselves aloof off, but when any approached near them, they would run away; and once they stole away their tools where they had been at work and were gone to dinner. But about the 16th of March, a certain Indian came boldly amongst them and spoke to them in broken English, which they could well understand but marveled at it. At length they understood by discourse with him, that he was not of these parts, but belonged to the eastern parts where some English ships came to fish, with whom he was acquainted and could name sundry of them by their names, amongst whom he had got his language. He became profitable to them in acquainting them with many things concerning the state of the country in the east parts where he lived, which was afterwards profitable unto them; as also of the people here, of their names, number and strength, of their situation and distance from this place, and who was chief amongst them. His name was Samoset.[11] He told them also of another Indian whose name was Squanto, a native of this place, who had been in England and could speak better English than himself.

Being, after some time of entertainment and gifts dismissed, a while after he came again, and five more with him, and they brought again all the tools that were stolen away before, and made way for the coming of their great Sachem, called Massasoit. Who, about four or five days after, came with the chief of his friends and other attendance, with the aforesaid Squanto. With whom, after friendly entertainment and some gifts given him, they made a peace with him (which hath now continued this 24 years)[12] in these terms:

1. That neither he nor any of his should injure or do hurt to any of their people.

2. That if any of his did hurt to any of theirs, he should send the offender, that they might punish him.

3. That if anything were taken away from any of theirs, he should cause it to be restored; and they should do the like to his.

4. If any did unjustly war against him, they would aid him; if any did war against them, he should aid them.

5. He should send to his neighbours confederates to certify them of this, that they might not wrong them, but might be likewise comprised in the conditions of peace.

6. That when their men came to them, they should leave their bows and arrows behind them.

After these things he returned to his place called Sowams,[13] some 40 miles from this place, but Squanto continued with them and was their interpreter and was a special instrument sent of God for their good beyond their expectation. He directed them how to set their corn, where to take fish, and to procure other commodities, and was also their pilot to bring them to unknown places for their profit,

---

[10]Cheat.

[11]Morison: "Samoset was an Algonkian sagamore of Pemaquid Point, Maine, a region much frequented by English fisherman. . . ."

[12]This first American treaty with the Indians, concluded with Massasoit (1580?–1661), chief of the Wampanoag, was in force until Massasoit's son, Metacomet (called King Philip by the English) began his attacks to force the English settlers to abandon their colonies—King Philip's War (1675–76).

[13]Barrington, Rhode Island.

and never left them till he died. He was a native of this place, and scarce any left alive besides himself. He was carried away with divers others by one Hunt, a master of a ship,[14] who thought to sell them for slaves in Spain. But he got away for England and was entertained by a merchant in London, and employed to Newfoundland and other parts, and lastly brought hither into these parts by one Mr. Dermer, a gentleman employed by Sir Ferdinando Gorges and others for discovery and other designs in these parts.

·   ·   ·   ·   ·

But to return. The spring now approaching, it pleased God the mortality began to cease amongst them, and the sick and lame recovered apace, which put as [it] were new life into them, though they had borne their sad affliction with much patience and contentedness as I think any people could do. But it was the Lord which upheld them, and had beforehand prepared them; many having long borne the yoke, yea from their youth.[15] Many other smaller matters I omit, sundry of them having been already published in a journal made by one of the company,[16] and some other passages of journeys and relations already published, to which I refer those that are willing to know them more particularly.

And being now come to the 25th of March, I shall begin the year 1621.

from CHAPTER XII: ANNO 1621

[INDIAN DIPLOMACY]

Having in some sort ordered their business at home, it was thought meet to send some abroad to see their new friend Massasoit, and to bestow upon him some gratuity to bind him the faster unto them; as also that hereby they might view the country and see in what manner he lived, what strength he had about him, and how the ways were to his place, if at any time they should have occasion. So the second of July they sent Mr. Edward Winslow and Mr. Hopkins,[1] with the foresaid Squanto for their guide; who gave him a suit of clothes and a horseman's coat, with some other small things, which were kindly accepted; but they found but short commons[2] and came both weary and hungry home. For the Indians used then to have nothing so much corn as they have since the English have stored them with their hoes, and seen their industry in breaking up new grounds therewith.

They found his place to be forty miles from hence, the soil good and the people not many, being dead and abundantly wasted in the late great mortality, which fell in all these parts about three years before the coming of the English, wherein thousands of them died. They not being able to bury one another, their skulls and bones were found in many places lying still above the ground where their houses and dwellings had been, a very sad spectacle to behold. But they brought word that the Narragansetts[3] lived but on the other side of that great bay, and were a strong people and many in number, living compact together, and had not been at all touched with this wasting plague.

About the latter end of this month, one John Billington lost himself in the woods, and wandered up and down some five days, living on berries and what he could find. At length he light on an Indian plantation twenty miles south of this

---

[14]Morison: "Squanto or Tisquantum appears to have been the sole survivor of the Patuxet tribe. Kidnapped there by Capt. Thomas Hunt in 1614, he had the curious career that Bradford says; he jumped Capt. Dermer's ship in 1618 and made his way to the site of Plymouth, where he found himself to be the sole survivor of his tribe, wiped out in the pestilence of 1617."
[15]Lamentations 3:26: "It is good that a man should both hope and quietly wait for the salvation of the Lord."

[16]*Mourt's Relation;* see Ch. X, note 3 above.
[1]Morison: "Stephen Hopkins, of London, is probably the same man of that name who was wrecked in Bermuda in 1609, proceeded to Virginia next year, but did not stay long. . . ."
[2]Provisions, supplies.
[3]Algonquian-speaking Indians of great might living in what is now Rhode Island.

place, called Manomet; they conveyed him further off, to Nauset among those people that had before set upon the English when they were coasting whilst the ship lay at the Cape, as is before noted. But the Governor caused him to be inquired for among the Indians, and at length Massasoit sent word where he was, and the Governor sent a shallop for him and had him delivered. Those people also came and made their peace; and they gave full satisfaction to those whose corn they had found and taken when they were at Cape Cod.

Thus their peace and acquaintance was pretty well established with the natives about them. And there was another Indian called Hobomok come to live amongst them, a proper lusty man, and a man of account for his valour and parts amongst the Indians, and continued very faithful and constant to the English till he died. He and Squanto being gone upon business among the Indians, at their return (whether it was out of envy to them or malice to the English) there was a sachem called Corbitant, allied to Massasoit but never any good friend to the English to this day, met with them at an Indian town called Namasket, fourteen miles to the west of this place, and began to quarrel with them and offered to stab Hobomok.[4] But being a lusty man, he cleared himself of him and came running away all sweating, and told the Governor what had befallen him. And he feared they had killed Squanto, for they threatened them both; and for no other cause but because they were friends to the English and serviceable unto them. Upon this the Governor taking counsel, it was conceived not fit to be borne; for if they should suffer their friends and messengers thus to be wronged, they should have none would cleave to them, or give them any intelligence, or do them service afterwards, but next they would fall upon themselves. Whereupon it was resolved to send the Captain and fourteen men well armed, and to go and fall upon them in the night. And if they found that Squanto was killed, to cut off Corbitant's head, but not to hurt any but those that had a hand in it.

Hobomok was asked if he would go and be their guide and bring them there before day. He said he would, and bring them to the house where the man lay, and show them which was he. So they set forth the 14th of August, and beset the house round. The Captain, giving charge to let none pass out, entered the house to search for him. But he was gone away that day, so they missed him, but understood that Squanto was alive, and that he had only threatened to kill him and made an offer to stab him but did not. So they withheld and did no more hurt, and the people came trembling and brought them the best provisions they had, after they were acquainted by Hobomok what was only intended. There was three sore wounded which broke out of the house and assayed to pass through the guard. These they brought home with them, and they had their wounds dressed and cured, and sent home. After this they had many gratulations from divers sachems, and much firmer peace; yea, those of the Isles of Capawack sent to make friendship; and this Corbitant himself used the mediation of Massasoit to make his peace, but was shy to come near them a long while after.

After this, the 18th of September they sent out their shallop to the Massachusetts, with ten men and Squanto for their guide and interpreter, to discover and view that Bay and trade with the natives. The which they performed, and found kind entertainment. The people were much afraid of the Tarentines, a people to the eastward which used to come in harvest time and take away their corn, and many times kill their persons.[5] They returned in safety and brought home a good quantity of beaver, and made report of the place, wishing they had been there

[4]Morison: "Hobomok was a Wampanoag; Corbitant, sachem of the Pocasset but subject to Massasoit, lived on what is now Gardner's Neck, Swansea; Namasket was in the present township of Middleborough."
[5]Morison: "*Tarentine* was the name then used for the Al- maki Indians, who occupied the shores of Maine from Casco Bay eastward and part of New Brunswick. They were the Vikings of New England, preferring to take corn from their neighbors than to grow it."

seated. But it seems the Lord, who assigns to all men the bounds of their habitations,[6] had appointed it for another use. And thus they found the Lord to be with them in all their ways, and to bless their outgoings and incomings, for which let His holy name have the praise forever, to all posterity.

[FIRST THANKSGIVING]

They began now to gather in the small harvest they had, and to fit up their houses and dwellings against winter, being all well recovered in health and strength and had all things in good plenty. For as some were thus employed in affairs abroad, others were exercised in fishing, about cod and bass and other fish, of which they took good store, of which every family had their portion. All the summer there was no want; and now began to come in store of fowl, as winter approached, of which this place did abound when they came first (but afterward decreased by degrees). And besides waterfowl there was great store of wild turkeys, of which they took many, besides venison, etc. Besides they had about a peck a meal a week to a person, or now since harvest, Indian corn to that proportion. Which made many afterwards write so largely of their plenty here to their friends in England, which were not feigned but true reports.[7]

from CHAPTER XIV: ANNO DOM: 1623

[END OF THE "COMMON COURSE AND CONDITION"]

All this while no supply was heard of, neither knew they when they might expect any. So they began to think how they might raise as much corn as they could, and obtain a better crop than they had done, that they might not still thus languish in misery.[1] At length, after much debate of things, the Governor (with the advice of the chiefest amongst them) gave way that they should set corn every man for his own particular, and in that regard trust to themselves; in all other things to go on in the general way as before.[2] And so assigned to every family a parcel of land, according to the proportion of their number, for that end, only for present use (but made no division for inheritance) and ranged all boys and youth under some family. This had very good success, for it made all hands very industrious, so as much more corn was planted than otherwise would have been by any means the Governor or any other could use, and saved him a great deal of trouble, and gave far better content. The women now went willingly into the field, and took their little ones with them to set corn; which before would allege weakness and inability; whom to have compelled would have been thought great tyranny and oppression.

---

[6]Deuteronomy 32:8: "When the Most High divided to the nations their inheritance, when he separated the sons of Adam, he set the bounds of the people according to the number of the children of Israel." Morison: "The fur trade, economic salvation of the Colony, began in the summer of 1621 through Squanto acting as buyer. On this 'voyage to the Massachusetts' he was impatient to 'rifle the salvage women' of their beaver coats, but the Pilgrims wisely insisted on fair trade. The women 'sold their coats from their backs, and tied boughs about them, but with great shamefacedness (for indeed they are more modest than some of our English women are).' *Mourt's Relation*, p. 60."
[7]Morison: "Edward Winslow's letter of 11 Dec. 1621 to a friend in England describing this 'First Thanksgiving' is printed in *Mourt's Relation* pp. 60–5: 'Our harvest being gotten in, our Governor sent four men on fowling, that so we might after a more special manner rejoice together, after we had gathered the fruit of our labours. They four in one day killed as much fowl as, with a little help beside, served the Company almost a week. At which time, amongst other recreations, we exercised our arms, many of

the Indians coming amongst us, and amongst the rest their greatest king, Massasoit with some 90 men, whom for three days we entertained and feasted. And they went out and killed five deer which they brought to the plantation and bestowed on our Governor and upon the Captain and others.' The actual date of this festival is nowhere related. See William De Loss Love *Fast and Thanksgiving Days of New England* (1895)."
[1]Unfamiliarity with "the manner of Indian corn," mismanagement, the lack of further supplies from England, the scarcity of trading commodities and markets, theft from the Indians and among themselves—all contributed to the "misery" of the Pilgrims by the year 1623.
[2]Until this time, in accord with the wishes of the original investors in the Pilgrim's enterprise (and with Christian principles), the Pilgrims had operated communally—from each according to his ability, to each according to his needs. Property, land, houses, and cattle were owned communally. The communal system apparently failed. Private ownership, as this passage indicates, increased crop production and "had very good success."

The experience that was had in this common course and condition, tried sundry years and that amongst godly and sober men, may well evince the vanity of that conceit of Plato's and other ancients applauded by some of later times; that the taking away of property and bringing in community into a commonwealth would make them happy and flourishing; as if they were wiser than God.[3] For this community (so far as it was) was found to breed much confusion and discontent and retard much employment that would have been to their benefit and comfort. For the young men, that were most able and fit for labour and service, did repine that they should spend their time and strength to work for other men's wives and children without any recompense. The strong, or man of parts, had no more in division of victuals and clothes than he that was weak and not able to do a quarter the other could; this was thought injustice. The aged and graver men to be ranked and equalized in labours and victuals, clothes, etc., with the meaner and younger sort, thought it some indignity and disrespect unto them. And for men's wives to be commanded to do service for other men, as dressing their meat, washing their clothes, etc., they deemed it a kind of slavery, neither could many husbands well brook it. Upon the point all being to have alike, and all to do alike, they thought themselves in the like condition, and one as good as another; and so, if it did not cut off those relations that God hath set amongst men, yet it did at least much diminish and take off the mutual respects that should be preserved amongst them. And would have been worse if they had been men of another condition. Let none object this is men's corruption, and nothing to the course itself. I answer, seeing all men have this corruption in them, God in His wisdom saw another course fitter for them.

from CHAPTER XIX: ANNO DOM: 1628

[THOMAS MORTON OF MERRYMOUNT]

About some three or four years before this time, there came over one Captain Wollaston (a man of pretty[1] parts) and with him three or four more of some eminency, who brought with them a great many servants, with provisions and other implements for to begin a plantation. And pitched themselves in a place within the Massachusetts which they called after their Captain's name, Mount Wollaston. Amongst whom was one Mr. Morton,[2] who it should seem had some small adventure of his own or other men's amongst them, but had little respect amongst them, and was slighted by the meanest servants. Having continued there some time, and not finding things to answer their expectations nor profit to arise as they looked for, Captain Wollaston takes a great part of the servants and transports them to Virginia, where he puts them off at good rates, selling their time to other men; and writes back to one Mr. Rasdall (one of his chief partners and accounted their merchant) to bring another part of them to Virginia likewise, intending to put them off there as he had done the rest. And he, with the consent of the said Rasdall, appointed one Fitcher to be his Lieutenant and govern the remains of the Plantation till he or Rasdall returned to take further order thereabout. But this Morton abovesaid, having more craft than honesty (who had been a kind of pettifogger of Furnival's Inn[3]) in the others' absence watches an opportunity (commons being but hard amongst them) and got some strong drink and other junkets and made them a feast; and after they were merry, he began to tell them he

[3]Morison: "Presumably Bradford had read the gibes at Plato's *Republic* in Jean Bodin *de Republica* (1586), a copy of which is mentioned in the inventory of his estate. 'But he [Plato] understood not that by making all things thus common, a Commonweal must needs perish: for nothing can be public, where nothing is private. . . . Albeit that such a Commonweal should also be against the law of God and nature . . . which expressly forbids us to . . . desire anything that another man's is.' *The Six Bookes of a Commonweale . . . Done into English by Richard Knolles,* Book I p. 11 (London, 1606)."
[1]Crafty, ingenious.
[2]See Thomas Morton's account in this volume for his side of the controversy.
[3]Minor, unscrupulous lawyer at one of the Inns of Court in London, center for legal study and practice.

would give them good counsel. "You see," saith he, "that many of your fellows are carried to Virginia, and if you stay till this Rasdall return, you will also be carried away and sold for slaves with the rest. Therefore I would advise you to thrust out this Lieutenant Fitcher, and I, having a part in the Plantation, will receive you as my partners and consociates; so may you be free from service, and we will converse, plant, trade, and live together as equals and support and protect one another," or to like effect. This counsel was easily received, so they took opportunity and thrust Lieutenant Fitcher out o' doors, and would suffer him to come no more amongst them, but forced him to seek bread to eat and other relief from his neighbours till he could get passage for England.

After this they fell to great licentiousness and led a dissolute life, pouring out themselves into all profaneness. And Morton became Lord of Misrule,[4] and maintained (as it were) a School of Atheism. And after they had got some goods into their hands, and got much by trading with the Indians, they spent it as vainly in quaffing and drinking, both wine and strong waters in great excess (and, as some reported) £10 worth in a morning. They also set up a maypole, drinking and dancing about it many days together, inviting the Indian women for their consorts, dancing and frisking together like so many fairies, or furies, rather; and worse practices. As if they had anew revived and celebrated the feasts of the Roman goddess Flora, or the beastly practices of the mad Bacchanalians.[5] Morton likewise, to show his poetry composed sundry rhymes and verses, some tending to lasciviousness, and others to the detraction and scandal of some persons, which he affixed to this idle or idol maypole. They changed also the name of their place, and instead of calling it Mount Wollaston they call it Merry-mount, as if this jollity would have lasted ever. But this continued not long, for after Morton was sent for England (as follows to be declared) shortly after came over that worthy gentleman Mr. John Endecott,[6] who brought over a patent under the broad seal for the government of the Massachusetts. Who, visiting those parts, caused that maypole to be cut down and rebuked them for their profaneness and admonished them to look there should be better walking. So they or others now changed the name of their place again and called it Mount Dagon.[7]

Now to maintain this riotous prodigality and profuse excess, Morton, thinking himself lawless, and hearing what gain the French and fishermen made by trading of pieces,[8] powder and shot to the Indians, he as the head of this consortship began the practice of the same in these parts. And first he taught them how to use them, to charge and discharge, and what proportion of powder to give the piece, according to the size or bigness of the same; and what shot to use for fowl and what for deer. And having thus instructed them, he employed some of them to hunt and fowl for him, so as they became far more active in that employment than any of the English, by reason of their swiftness of foot and nimbleness of body, being also quick-sighted and by continual exercise well knowing the haunts of all sorts of game. So as when they saw the execution that a piece would do, and the benefit that might come by the same, they became mad (as it were) after them and would not stick to give any price they could attain to for them; accounting their bows and arrows but baubles in comparison of them.

And here I may take occasion to bewail the mischief that this wicked man began in these parts, and which since, base covetousness prevailing in men that should know better, has now at length got the upper hand and made this thing

---

[4]A title in England for a comic master of ceremonies at masques and revels.
[5]Revellers in the pagan orgies celebrating Bacchus, god of wine.
[6]John Endecott (c. 1589–1665) served as governor of Massachusetts Bay Colony beginning on his arrival in 1628 until the coming of the Winthrop party in 1630. Later he

served terms as deputy governor and as governor. He figures in Nathaniel Hawthorne's story, "Endicott and the Red Cross."
[7]The Philistine god. His temple was destroyed by Samson. Judges 16:23–31.
[8]Guns.

common, notwithstanding any laws to the contrary. So as the Indians are full of pieces all over, both fowling pieces, muskets, pistols, etc. They have also their moulds to make shot of all sorts, as musket bullets, pistol bullets, swan and goose shot, and of smaller sorts. Yea some have seen them have their screw-plates to make screw-pins[9] themselves when they want them, with sundry other implements, wherewith they are ordinarily better fitted and furnished than the English themselves. Yea, it is well known that they will have powder and shot when the English want it nor cannot get it; and that in a time of war or danger, as experience hath manifested, that when lead hath been scarce and men for their own defense would gladly have given a groat[10] a pound, which is dear enough, yet hath it been bought up and sent to other places and sold to such as trade it with the Indians at 12*d* the pound. And it is like they give 3*s* or 4*s* the pound, for they will have it at any rate. And these things have been done in the same times when some of their neighbours and friends are daily killed by the Indians, or are in danger thereof and live but at the Indians' mercy. Yea some, as they have acquainted them with all other things, have told them how gunpowder is made, and all the materials in it, and that they are to be had in their own land; and I am confident, could they attain to make saltpeter, they would teach them to make powder.

O, the horribleness of this villainy! How many both Dutch and English have been lately slain by those Indians thus furnished, and no remedy provided; nay, the evil more increased, and the blood of their brethren sold for gain (as is to be feared) and in what danger all these colonies are in is too well known. O that princes and parliaments would take some timely order to prevent this mischief and at length to suppress it by some exemplary punishment upon some of these gain-thirsty murderers, for they deserve no better title, before their colonies in these parts be overthrown by these barbarous savages thus armed with their own weapons, by these evil instruments and traitors to their neighbours and country! But I have forgot myself and have been too long in this digression; but now to return.

This Morton having thus taught them the use of pieces, he sold them all he could spare, and he and his consorts determined to send for many out of England and had by some of the ships sent for above a score. The which being known, and his neighbours meeting the Indians in the woods armed with guns in this sort, it was a terror unto them who lived stragglingly and were of no strength in any place. And other places (though more remote) saw this mischief would quickly spread over all, if not prevented. Besides, they saw they should keep no servants, for Morton would entertain any, how vile soever, and all the scum of the country or any discontents would flock to him from all places, if this nest was not broken. And they should stand in more fear of their lives and goods in short time from this wicked and debased crew than from the savages themselves.

So sundry of the chief of the straggling plantations, meeting together, agreed by mutual consent to solicit those of Plymouth (who were then of more strength than them all) to join with them to prevent the further growth of this mischief, and suppress Morton and his consorts before they grew to further head and strength. Those that joined in this action, and after contributed to the charge of sending him for England, were from Piscataqua, Naumkeag, Winnisimmet, Wessagusset, Nantasket and other places where any English were seated. Those of Plymouth being thus sought to by their messengers and letters, and weighing both their reasons and the common danger, were willing to afford them their help though themselves had least cause of fear or hurt. So, to be short, they first re-

---

[9]"Screw-plates" are tools to make the threads in screws ("screw-pins").
[10]British coin worth fourpence.

solved jointly to write to him, and in a friendly and neighbourly way to admonish him to forbear those courses, and sent a messenger with their letters to bring his answer.

But he was so high as he scorned all advice, and asked who had to do with him, he had and would trade pieces with the Indians, in despite of all, with many other scurrilous terms full of disdain. They sent to him a second time and bade him be better advised and more temperate in his terms, for the country could not bear the injury he did. It was against their common safety and against the King's proclamation. He answered in high terms as before; and that the King's proclamation was no law, demanding what penalty was upon it. It was answered, more than he could bear—His Majesty's displeasure. But insolently he persisted and said the King was dead and his displeasure with him, and many the like things. And threatened withal that if any came to molest him, let them look to themselves for he would prepare for them.

Upon which they saw there was no way but to take him by force; and having so far proceeded, now to give over would make him far more haughty and insolent. So they mutually resolved to proceed, and obtained of the Governor of Plymouth to send Captain Standish and some other aid with him, to take Morton by force. The which accordingly was done. But they found him to stand stiffly in his defense, having made fast his doors, armed his consorts, set divers dishes of powder and bullets ready on the table; and if they had not been over-armed with drink, more hurt might have been done. They summoned him to yield, but he kept his house and they could get nothing but scoffs and scorns from him. But at length, fearing they would do some violence to the house, he and some of his crew came out, but not to yield but to shoot; but they were so steeled with drink as their pieces were too heavy for them. Himself with a carbine, overcharged and almost half filled with powder and shot, as was after found, had thought to have shot Captain Standish;[11] but he stepped to him and put by his piece and took him. Neither was there any hurt done to any of either side, save that one was so drunk that he ran his own nose upon the point of a sword that one held before him, as he entered the house; but he lost but a little of his hot blood.

Morton they brought away to Plymouth, where he was kept till a ship went from the Isle of Shoals[12] for England, with which he was sent to the Council of New England, and letters written to give them information of his course and carriage. And also one was sent at their common charge to inform their Honours more particularly and to prosecute against him. But he fooled of the messenger, after he was gone from hence, and though he went for England yet nothing was done to him, not so much as rebuked, for aught was heard, but returned the next year. Some of the worst of the company were dispersed and some of the more modest kept the house till he should be heard from. But I have been too long about so unworthy a person, and bad a cause.

from CHAPTER XXIII: ANNO DOM: 1632

[Prosperity Brings Dispersal of Population]

The people of the Plantation began to grow in their outward estates, by reason of the flowing of many people into the country, especially into the Bay of the Massachusetts. By which means corn and cattle rose to a great price, by which many were much enriched and commodities grew plentiful. And yet in other regards this benefit turned to their hurt, and this accession of strength to their weakness. For now as their stocks increased and the increase vendible,[1] there was no longer any holding them together, but now they must of necessity go to their great lots.

---

[11]Captain Miles Standish, leader of the expedition against Morton and his group. Morton refers to him as "Captain Shrimp."

[12]Islands off Maine where Morton was held until he could be sent back to England.

[1]Salable.

They could not otherwise keep their cattle, and having oxen grown they must have land for plowing and tillage. And no man now thought he could live except he had cattle and a great deal of ground to keep them, all striving to increase their stocks. By which means they were scattered all over the Bay quickly and the town in which they lived compactly till now was left very thin and in a short time almost desolate.

And if this had been all, it had been less, though too much; but the church must also be divided, and those that had lived so long together in Christian and comfortable fellowship must now part and suffer many divisions. First, those that lived on their lots on the other side of the Bay, called Duxbury, they could not long bring their wives and children to the public worship and church meetings here, but with such burthen as, growing to some competent number, they sued to be dismissed and become a body of themselves. And so they were dismissed about this time, though very unwillingly.[2] But to touch this sad matter, and handle things together that fell out afterward; to prevent any further scattering from this place and weakening of the same, it was thought best to give out some good farms to special persons that would promise to live at Plymouth, and likely to be helpful to the church or commonwealth, and so tie the lands to Plymouth as farms for the same; and there they might keep their cattle and tillage by some servants and re-tain their dwellings here. And so some special lands were granted at a place gen-eral called Green's Harbor,[3] where no allotments had been in the former division, a place very well meadowed and fit to keep and rear cattle good store. But alas, this remedy proved worse than the disease; for within a few years those that had thus got footing there rent themselves away, partly by force and partly wearing the rest with importunity and pleas of necessity, so as they must either suffer them to go or live in continual opposition and contention. And other still, as they con-ceived themselves straitened[4] or to want accommodation, broke away under one pretence or other, thinking their own conceived necessity and the example of oth-ers a warrant sufficient for them. And this I fear will be the ruin of New England, at least of the churches of God there, and will provoke the Lord's displeasure against them.

from CHAPTER XXIV: ANNO DOM: 1633

[MR. ROGER WILLIAMS]

Mr. Roger Williams,[1] a man godly and zealous, having many precious parts but very unsettled in judgment, came over first to the Massachusetts;[2] but upon some discontent left that place and came hither, where he was friendly entertained ac-cording to their poor ability, and exercised his gifts amongst them and after some time was admitted a member of the church. And his teaching well approved, for the benefit whereof I still bless God and am thankful to him even for his sharpest admonitions and reproofs so far as they agreed with truth. He this year began to fall into some strange opinions, and from opinion to practice, which caused some controversy between the church and him. And in the end some discontent on his part, by occasion whereof he left them something abruptly. Yet afterwards sued for his dismission to the church of Salem, which was granted, with some caution to them concerning him and what care they ought to have of him. But he soon fell into more things there, both to their and the government's trouble and distur-

---

[2]Morison: "John Alden, Myles Standish, Jonathan Brewster and Thomas Prence were the first prominent settlers of Duxbury. Bradford's efforts to stop what would now be called 'progress' are amusing and pathetic. The great Puri-tan emigration to the Bay created such a market for corn and cattle that the compact settlement at Plymouth no longer sufficed for the increased production."
[3]Morison: "The present Marshfield."

[4]Financially hard-up.
[1]Morison: "The famous founder of Rhode Island. He ar-rived at Boston with his family in the *Lyon* in Feb. 1631. He had already preached at Salem and got into trouble with the Bay authorities before coming to Plymouth." See Roger Williams's works included in this volume.
[2]Massachusetts Bay Colony.

bance. I shall not need to name particulars; they are too well known now to all, though for a time the church here went under some hard censure by his occasion from some that afterwards smarted themselves. But he is to be pitied and prayed for; and so I shall leave the matter and desire the Lord to show him his errors and reduce him into the way of truth and give him a settled judgment and constancy in the same, for I hope he belongs to the Lord, and that He will show him mercy.

from CHAPTER XXVI: ANNO DOM: 1635

[THE GREAT HURRICANE]

This year, the 14th or 15th of August (being Saturday) was such a mighty storm of wind and rain as none living in these parts, either English or Indians, ever saw. Being like, for the time it continued, to those hurricanes and typhoons that writers make mention of in the Indies. It began in the morning a little before day, and grew not by degrees but came with violence in the beginning, to the great amazement of many. It blew down sundry houses and uncovered others. Divers vessels were lost at sea and many more in extreme danger. It caused the sea to swell to the southward of this place above 20 foot right up and down, and made many of the Indians to climb into trees for their safety. It took off the boarded roof of a house which belonged to this Plantation at Manomet, and floated it to another place, the posts still standing in the ground. And if it had continued long without the shifting of the wind, it is like it would have drowned some part of the country. It blew down many hundred thousands of trees, turning up the stronger by the roots and breaking the higher pine trees off in the middle. And the tall young oaks and walnut trees of good bigness were wound like a withe, very strange and fearful to behold. It began in the southeast and parted toward the south and east, and veered sundry ways, but the greatest force of it here was from the former quarters. It continued not (in the extremity) above five or six hours but the violence began to abate. The signs and marks of it will remain this hundred years in these parts where it was sorest. The moon suffered a great eclipse the second night after it.

from CHAPTER XXVIII: ANNO DOM: 1637

[THE PEQUOT WAR][1]

In the fore part of this year, the Pequots fell openly upon the English at Connecticut, in the lower parts of the river, and slew sundry of them as they were at work in the fields, both men and women, to the great terrour of the rest, and went away in great pride and triumph, with many high threats. They also assaulted a fort at the river's mouth, though strong and well defended; and though they did not there prevail, yet it struck them with much fear and astonishment to see their bold attempts in the face of danger. Which made them in all places to stand upon their guard and to prepare for resistance, and earnestly to solicit their friends and confederates in the Bay of Massachusetts to send them speedy aid, for they looked for more forcible assaults. Mr. Vane,[2] being then Governor, writ from their General Court to them here to join with them in this war. To which they were cordially willing. . . .

In the meantime, the Pequots, especially in the winter before, sought to make

---

[1]The Pequot War was the first large-scale clash between Indians and Colonists. The Pequots, an Algonquian-speaking tribe in Connecticut, numbering about 3,000 and under the leadership of their chief Sassacus, were warlike and threatening. But among their grievances, as Bradford makes clear, was the English encroachment on Indian lands. The superior weaponry of the English meant doom for the Pequots, who were virtually exterminated in battles which have been described as massacres. (The name "Pequot" survives in the name of Herman Melville's whaling vessel, the *Pequod,* in *Moby-Dick,* 1851.)

[2]Henry Vane (1613–1662), the governor of Massachusetts Bay Colony.

peace with the Narragansetts, and used very pernicious arguments to move them thereunto: as that the English were strangers and began to overspread their country, and would deprive them thereof in time, if they were suffered to grow and increase. And if the Narragansetts did assist the English to subdue them, they did but make way for their own overthrow, for if they were rooted out, the English would soon take occasion to subjugate them. And if they would hearken to them they should not need to fear the strength of the English, for they would not come to open battle with them but fire their houses, kill their cattle, and lie in ambush for them as they went abroad upon their occasions; and all this they might easily do without any or little danger to themselves. The which course being held, they well saw the English could not long subsist but they would either be starved with hunger or be forced to forsake the country. With many the like things; insomuch that the Narragansetts were once wavering and were half minded to have made peace with them, and joined against the English. But again, when they considered how much wrong they had received from the Pequots, and what an opportunity they now had by the help of the English to right themselves; revenge was so sweet unto them as it prevailed above all the rest, so as they resolved to join with the English against them, and did.

The Court here agreed forthwith to send fifty men at their own charge; and with as much speed as possibly they could, got them armed and had made them ready under sufficient leaders, and provided a bark to carry them provisions and tend upon them for all occasions. But when they were ready to march, with a supply from the Bay, they had word to stay; for the enemy was as good as vanquished and there would be no need.

I shall not take upon me exactly to describe their proceedings in these things, because I expect it will be fully done by themselves who best know the carriage and circumstances of things. I shall therefore but touch them in general. From Connecticut, who were most sensible of the hurt sustained and the present danger, they set out a party of men, and another party met them from the Bay, at Narragansetts', who were to join with them. The Narragansetts were earnest to be gone before the English were well rested and refreshed, especially some of them which came last. It should seem their desire was to come upon the enemy suddenly and undiscovered. There was a bark of this place, newly put in there, which was come from Connecticut, who did encourage them to lay hold of the Indians' forwardness, and to show as great forwardness as they, for it would encourage them, and expedition might prove to their great advantage. So they went on, and so ordered their march as the Indians brought them to a fort of the enemy's (in which most of their chief men were) before day.[3] They approached the same with great silence and surrounded it both with English and Indians, that they might not break out; and so assaulted them with great courage, shooting amongst them, and entered the fort with all speed. And those that first entered found sharp resistance from the enemy who both shot at and grappled with them; others ran into their houses and brought out fire and set them on fire, which soon took in their mat; and standing close together, with the wind all was quickly on a flame, and thereby more were burnt to death than was otherwise slain; It burnt their bowstrings and made them unserviceable; those that scaped the fire were slain with the sword, some hewed to pieces, others run through with their rapiers, so as they were quickly dispatched and very few escaped. It was conceived they thus destroyed about 400 at this time. It was a fearful sight to see them thus frying in the fire and the streams of blood quenching the same, and horrible was the stink and

---

[3]Morison: "Mystic Fort, on the west bank of the Mystic River near its mouth."

scent thereof; but the victory seemed a sweet sacrifice,[4] and they gave the praise thereof to God, who had wrought so wonderfully for them, thus to enclose their enemies in their hands and give them so speedy a victory over so proud and insulting an enemy.

from CHAPTER XXIX: ANNO DOM: 1638

[GREAT AND FEARFUL EARTHQUAKE]

This year, about the first or second of June, was a great and fearful earthquake. It was in this place heard before it was felt. It came with a rumbling noise or low murmur, like unto remote thunder. It came from the northward and passed southward; as the noise approached nearer, the earth began to shake and came at length with that violence as caused platters, dishes and suchlike things as stood upon shelves, to clatter and fall down. Yea, persons were afraid of the houses themselves. It so fell out that at the same time divers of the chief of this town were met together at one house, conferring with some of their friends that were upon their removal from the place, as if the Lord would hereby show the signs of His displeasure, in their shaking a-pieces and removals one from another. However, it was very terrible for the time, and as the men were set talking in the house, some women and others were without the doors, and the earth shook with that violence as they could not stand without catching hold of the posts and pales that stood next them. But the violence lasted not long. And about half an hour, or less came another noise and shaking, but neither so loud nor strong as the former, but quickly passed over and so it ceased. It was not only on the seacoast, but the Indians felt it within land, and some ships that were upon the coast were shaken by it. So powerful is the mighty hand of the Lord, as to make both the earth and sea to shake, and the mountains to tremble before Him, when He pleases. And who can stay His hand?[1]

It was observed that the summers for divers years together after this earthquake were not so hot and seasonable for the ripening of corn and other fruits as formerly, but more cold and moist, and subject to early and untimely frosts by which, many times, much Indian corn came not to maturity. But whether this was any cause I leave it to naturalists to judge.

from CHAPTER XXXII: ANNO DOM: 1642

[WICKEDNESS BREAKS FORTH]

Marvelous it may be to see and consider how some kind of wickedness did grow and break forth here, in a land where the same was so much witnessed against and so narrowly looked unto, and severely punished when it was known, as in no place more, or so much, that I have known or heard of; insomuch that they have been somewhat censured even by moderate and good men for their severity in punishments. And yet all this could not suppress the breaking out of sundry notorious sins (as this year, besides other, gives us too many sad precedents and instances), especially drunkenness and uncleanness. Not only incontinency between persons unmarried, for which many both men and women have been punished sharply enough, but some married persons also. But that which is worse, even sodomy and buggery (things fearful to name) have broke forth in this land oftener than once.

I say it may justly be marveled at and cause us to fear and tremble at the con-

---

[4]Leviticus 2:1–2: " . . . the priest shall burn the memorial . . . upon the altar, to be an offering made by fire, of a sweet savour unto the Lord."
[1]Haggai 2:6: "For thus saith the LORD of hosts: Yet once it is a little while, and I will shake the heavens, and the earth, and the sea, and the dry land." Daniel 4:35: "And all the inhabitants of the earth are reputed as nothing: and he doeth according to his will in the army of heaven, and among the inhabitants of the earth: and none can stay his hand, or say unto him, What doest thou?"

sideration of our corrupt natures, which are so hardly bridled, subdued and mortified; nay, cannot by any other means but the powerful work and grace of God's Spirit. But (besides this) one reason may be that the Devil may carry a greater spite against the churches of Christ and the gospel here, by how much the more they endeavour to preserve holiness and purity amongst them and strictly punisheth the contrary when it ariseth either in church or commonwealth; that he might cast a blemish and stain upon them in the eyes of [the] world, who use to be rash in judgment. I would rather think thus, than that Satan hath more power in these heathen lands, as some have thought, than in more Christian nations, especially over God's servants in them.

2. Another reason may be, that it may be in this case as it is with waters when their streams are stopped or dammed up. When they get passage they flow with more violence and make more noise and disturbance than when they are suffered to run quietly in their own channels; so wickedness being here more stopped by strict laws, and the same more nearly looked unto so as it cannot run in a common road of liberty as it would and is inclined, it searches everywhere and at last breaks out where it gets vent.

3. A third reason may be, here (as I am verily persuaded) is not more evils in this kind, nor nothing near so many by proportion as in other places; but they are here more discovered and seen and made public by due search, inquisition and due punishment; for the churches look narrowly to their members, and the magistrates over all, more strictly than in other places. Besides, here the people are but few in comparison of other places which are full and populous and lie hid, as it were, in a wood or thicket and many horrible evils by that means are never seen nor known; whereas here they are, as it were, brought into the light and set in the plain field, or rather on a hill, made conspicuous to the view of all.

. . . . .

[A HORRIBLE CASE OF BESTIALITY]

And after the time of the writing of these things befell a very sad accident of the like foul nature in this government, this very year, which I shall now relate. There was a youth whose name was Thomas Granger. He was servant to an honest man of Duxbury, being about 16 or 17 years of age. (His father and mother lived at the same time at Scituate.) He was this year detected of buggery, and indicted for the same, with a mare, a cow, two goats, five sheep, two calves and a turkey. Horrible it is to mention, but the truth of the history requires it. He was first discovered by one that accidentally saw his lewd practice towards the mare. (I forbear particulars.) Being upon it examined and committed, in the end he not only confessed the fact with that beast at that time, but sundry times before and at several times with all the rest of the forenamed in his indictment. And this his free confession was not only in private to the magistrates (though at first he strived to deny it) but to sundry, both ministers and others; and afterwards, upon his indictment, to the whole Court and jury; and confirmed it at his execution. And whereas some of the sheep could not so well be known by his description of them, others with them were brought before him and he declared which were they and which were not. And accordingly he was cast by the jury and condemned, and after executed about the 8th of September, 1642. A very sad spectacle it was. For first the mare and then the cow and the rest of the lesser cattle were killed before his face, according to the law, Leviticus xx.15;[1] and then he himself was executed.

---

[1]"If a man lie with a beast, he shall surely be put to death: and ye shall slay the beast."

The cattle were all cast into a great and large pit that was digged of purpose for them, and no use made of any part of them.

Upon the examination of this person and also of a former that had made some sodomitical attempts upon another, it being demanded of them how they came first to the knowledge and practice of such wickedness, the one confessed he had long used it in old England; and this youth last spoken of said he was taught it by another that had heard of such things from some in England when he was there, and they kept cattle together. By which it appears how one wicked person may infect many, and what care all ought to have what servants they bring into their families.

But it may be demanded how came it to pass that so many wicked persons and profane people should so quickly come over into this land and mix themselves amongst them? Seeing it was religious men that began the work and they came for religion's sake? I confess this may be marveled at, at least in time to come, when the reasons thereof should not be known; and the more because here was so many hardships and wants met withal. I shall therefore endeavour to give some answer hereunto.

1. And first, according to that in the gospel, it is ever to be remembered that where the Lord begins to sow good seed, there the envious man will endeavour to sow tares.[2]

2. Men being to come over into a wilderness, in which much labour and service was to be done about building and planting, etc., such as wanted help in that respect, when they could not have such as they would, were glad to take such as they could; and so, many untoward servants, sundry of them proved, that were thus brought over, both men and womenkind who, when their times were expired, became families of themselves, which gave increase hereunto.

3. Another and a main reason hereof was that men, finding so many godly disposed persons willing to come into these parts, some began to make a trade of it, to transport passengers and their goods, and hired ships for that end. And then, to make up their freight and advance their profit, cared not who the persons were, so they had money to pay them. And by this means the country became pestered with many unworthy persons who, being come over, crept into one place or other.

4. Again, the Lord's blessing usually following His people as well in outward as spiritual things (though afflictions be mixed withal) do make many to adhere to the People of God, as many followed Christ for the loaves' sake (John vi.26)[3] and a "mixed multitude" came into the wilderness with the People of God out of Egypt of old (Exodus xii.38).[4] So also there were sent by their friends, some under hope that they would be made better; others that they might be eased of such burthens, and they kept from shame at home, that would necessarily follow their dissolute courses. And thus, by one means or other, in 20 years' time it is a question whether the greater part be not grown the worser?

from CHAPTER XXXIV: ANNO DOM: 1644

[PROPOSAL TO REMOVE TO NAUSET]

Many having left this place (as is before noted) by reason of the straitness[1] and barrenness of the same and their finding of better accommodations elsewhere more suitable to their ends and minds; and sundry others still upon every occasion desiring their dismissions,[2] the church began seriously to think whether it

---

[2]Tares are weeds found in grainfields.
[3]"Jesus answered them and said, Verily, Verily, I say unto you, Ye seek me, not because ye saw the miracles, but because ye did eat of the loaves, and were filled."

[4]"And a mixed multitude went up also with them; and flocks, and herds, even very much cattle."
[1]Scarcity of resources.
[2]Release or discharge.

were not better jointly to remove to some other place than to be thus weakened and as it were insensibly dissolved.[3] Many meetings and much consultation was held hereabout, and divers were men's minds and opinions. Some were still for staying together in this place, alleging men might here live if they would be content with their condition, and that it was not for want or necessity so much that they removed as for the enriching of themselves. Others were resolute upon removal and so signified that here they could not stay; but if the church did not remove, they must. Insomuch as many were swayed rather than there should be a dissolution, to condescend to a removal if a fit place could be found that might more conveniently and comfortably receive the whole, with such accession of others as might come to them for their better strength and subsistence; and some such-like cautions and limitations.

So as, with the aforesaid provisos, the greater part consented to a removal to a place called Nauset, which had been superficially viewed and the good will of the purchasers to whom it belonged obtained, with some addition thereto from the Court. But now they began to see their errour, that they had given away already the best and most commodious places to others, and now wanted themselves. For this place was about 50 miles from hence, and at an outside of the country remote from all society; also that it would prove so strait as it would not be competent to receive the whole body, much less be capable of any addition or increase; so as, at least in a short time, they should be worse there than they are now here. The which with sundry other like considerations and inconveniences made them change their resolutions. But such as were before resolved upon removal took advantage of this agreement and went on, notwithstanding; neither could the rest hinder them, they having made some beginning.[4]

And thus was this poor church left, like an ancient mother grown old and forsaken of her children, though not in their affections yet in regard of their bodily presence and personal helpfulness; her ancient members being most of them worn away by death, and these of later time being like children translated into other families, and she like a widow left only to trust in God.[5] Thus, she that had made many rich became herself poor.[6]

from CHAPTER XXXVI: ANNO DOM: 1646

[WINSLOW'S FINAL DEPARTURE]

This year Mr. Edward Winslow[1] went into England, upon this occasion: some discontented persons under the government of the Massachusetts sought to trouble their peace and disturb, if not innovate,[2] their government by laying many scandals upon them, and intended to prosecute against them in England by petitioning and complaining to the Parliament. Also, Samuel Gorton and his company made complaints against them.[3] So as they made choice of Mr. Winslow to be

---

[3]Morison: "Bradford and likeminded Pilgrims welcomed the establishment of new towns and churches in the Colony by newcomers, as at Scituate and Taunton, but they wanted the original Plymouth church, including members of the second generation, to stick together. There was, however, a very narrow strip of arable land on Plymouth Bay; the back country was too rugged and rocky for profitable agriculture; and after the founding of Boston, ships from England found it more convenient to put in there. Boston gave them more business than Plymouth, which lay dead to windward of Cape Cod in the prevailing breezes, and where goods had to be lightered ashore instead of being landed on a wharf."

[4]Morison: "Nausset was in the first of the Old Comers' [as the Pilgrim Fathers were called in their own day] or Purchasers' reserved tracts of 1640. After looking it over twice, a committee of the Plymouth church reported that there was not enough room for all. . . ."

[5]1 Timothy 5: 5: "Now she that is a widow indeed, and desolate, trusteth in God, and continueth in supplications and prayers night and day."

[6]2 Corinthians 6:10: "As sorrowful, yet always rejoicing; as poor, yet making many rich; as having nothing, and yet possessing all things."

[1]Edward Winslow (1595–1655) had sailed to the New World on the *Mayflower*, and had later served as Governor of Plymouth Colony several times. His mission to England in 1646 was to defend the colony against charges brought by some of the discontented colonists. His mission was successful.

[2]Change.

[3]Morison: "Samuel Gorton, one of the most persistent and amusing of all troublemakers in early New England, eventually the founder of a sect, was expelled from four colonies before founding his own at Warwick, Rhode Island. . . ."

their agent to make their defense, and gave him commission and instructions for that end. In which he so carried himself as did well answer their ends and cleared them from any blame or dishonour, to the shame of their adversaries. But by reason of the great alterations in the State, he was detained longer than was expected, and afterwards fell into other employments there; so as he hath now been absent this four years, which hath been much to the weakening of this government, without whose consent he took these employments upon him.[4]

1630–50   *1856*

THOMAS MORTON
(*c.* 1579–1647)

Thomas Morton walked into history in 1627 when he and his comrades put up an eighty-foot maypole, topped with goat's horns, at their frontier trading post at Merry Mount and began dancing around it with Indian maids—drinking homebrewed beer, composing erotic poems to attach to the maypole, and boisterously celebrating Eros and Priapus. The only problem was the location of these revels—at Mount Wollaston, on Quincy Bay, just a few miles north of Plymouth Colony, sober and Puritan. Morton and his fellows had arrived at Mount Wollaston (later to be dubbed Merry Mount) some three years before, eager to engage in the fur trade with the Indians, a business that put them in competition with the Puritans. Friction had been building, as William Bradford revealed in *Of Plymouth Plantation*, where several pages were given over to the debauchery and licentious behavior at Merry Mount, led by Morton, the "Lord of Misrule." Bradford wrote with a mixture of astonishment and outrage: "They also set up a maypole, drinking and dancing about it many days together, inviting the Indian women for their consorts, dancing and frisking together like so many fairies, or furies, rather; and worse practices."

These "mad Bacchanalians" infuriated the Puritans and inspired them to intervene. They sent Captain Miles Standish to arrest Morton, held a trial at Plymouth Plantation, and shipped him back to England in 1628. There the charges were dismissed. In 1629 Morton returned to New England and this time clashed first with John Endecott and the new Puritan settlement at Salem. (Endecott had already destroyed the notorious Morton Maypole.) Next, Morton enraged the new Puritan settlement at Charlestown (established in 1630, led by John Winthrop). Morton was arrested, put in the stocks, and deprived of all his goods. For good measure the Puritans burned down his house. They then returned Morton to England for additional punishment. There he was once again released.

These events turned out to have more symbolic than literal significance and inspired Hawthorne some 200 years later to write a short story based on them: "The Maypole of Merry Mount." Hawthorne was no doubt attracted to the incidents because of their stark contrast between reason and instinct, the rational and irrational, spiritual sobriety and phallic celebration.

---

[4]Winslow decided not to return to New England but to remain in England, where the Puritans were in power and placed him in their service. This symbolic event (a Pilgrim's return to a Puritan-ruled England to remain) seems an appropriate close to Bradford's history.

Morton gave his side of the affair in his book *New English Canaan or New Canaan* in 1637. This work's three parts are devoted to a firsthand description of the Indians, an account of New England as a place for settlement—and a personal view of the clash with the Plymouth settlers in which Morton satirizes and ridicules the Puritans (Captain Miles Standish becomes Captain Shrimp).

But Morton had more in mind than satire. At the time he wrote, Charles I, anti-Puritan and pro-Catholic, was on the throne. Morton, an Anglican, hoped to make serious trouble for the Puritans. He was clearly involved in a court judgment recalling the Massachusetts Bay charter in 1637, and his book was calculated to show the Puritans as anti-royal and anti-Anglican. But events bringing the Puritans to power in England were moving too quickly for Morton. Massachusetts Bay did not lose its charter and Morton's meddling in its affairs came to nothing.

Morton seems to have disappeared from history as abruptly as he entered it. Little is known about his later life, but it is known that in 1643 he once more returned to New England, and was once more arrested and imprisoned in Boston. He was released, as John Winthrop explained: ". . . we thought not fit to inflict corporal punishment upon him, being old and crazy, but thought better to fine him and give him his liberty." Morton left Boston in 1645 for Maine, where he died in 1647.

ADDITIONAL READING

Donald F. Connors, *Thomas Morton*, 1969; John Seelye, "Womb of Nature: Thomas Morton and the Call of the Wild," *Prophetic Waters: The River in Early American Life and Literature*, 1977; Wayne Franklin, *Discoverers, Explorers, Settlers: The Diligent Writers of Early America*, 1979.

TEXT

The New English Canaan of Thomas Morton, ed. C. F. Adams, Jr., 1883. Typography, punctuation, spelling, and usage have been changed to conform with contemporary English and modern printing practices.

from The New English Canaan

[FRISKING AROUND THE MAYPOLE OF MERRY MOUNT]

BOOK III

CHAPTER XIV

OF THE REVELS OF NEW CANAAN[1]

The inhabitants of Passonagessit[2] (having translated the name of their habitation from that ancient savage name to Ma-re[3] Mount, and being resolved to have the new name confirmed for a memorial to after ages) did devise amongst themselves to have it performed in a solemn manner, with revels and merriment after

---

[1]Canaan was the Promised Land of the Israelites. Thus it was common to refer to the Puritan colonies as New Canaan, the Puritans' Promised Land.
[2]Indian name for area below Boston, where Morton established his trading post.

[3]The settlement's name was Mount Wollaston, but was often called Merry Mount, here corrupted to Ma-re Mount by Morton, suggesting the *sea* (from Latin), a *female horse*, the *goblin* that produces nightmares, as well as *merry*.

the old English custom; [they] prepared to set up a Maypole upon the festival day of Philip and Jacob,[4] and therefore brewed a barrel of excellent beer and provided a case of bottles to be spent, with other good cheer, for all comers of that day. And because they would have it in a complete form, they had prepared a song fitting to the time and present occasion. And upon May Day they brought the Maypole to the place appointed, with drums, guns, pistols, and other fitting instruments for that purpose, and there erected it with the help of savages that came thither of purpose to see the manner of our revels. A goodly pine tree of eighty feet long was reared up, with a pair of buck's horns[5] nailed on somewhat near unto the top of it, where it stood as a fair sea mark for directions how to find out the way to mine host[6] of Ma-re Mount.

And because it should more fully appear to what end it was placed there, they had a poem in readiness made, which was fixed to the Maypole to show the new name confirmed upon that plantation, which, although it were made according to the occurrence of the time, it being enigmatically composed, puzzled the Separatists[7] most pitifully to expound[8] it, which (for the better information of the reader) I have here inserted.

THE POEM[9]

Rise Oedipus, and, if thou canst, unfold
What means Charybdis underneath the mold,
When Scylla solitary on the ground
(Sitting in form of Niobe) was found,
Till Amphitrite's darling did acquaint
Grim Neptune with the tenor of her plaint,
And caused him send forth Triton with the sound
Of trumpet loud, at which the seas were found
So full of protean forms that the bold shore
Presented Scylla a new paramour
So strong as Samson and so patient
As Job himself, directed thus, by fate,
To comfort Scylla so unfortunate.
I do profess, by Cupid's beauteous mother,
Here's Scogan's choice for Scylla, and none other;
Though Scylla's sick with grief, because no sign
Can there be found of virtue masculine.
Asclepius come; I know right well
His labor's lost when you may ring her knell.
The fatal sisters' doom none can withstand,
Nor Cytherea's power, who points to land
With proclamation that the first of May
At Ma-re Mount shall be kept holiday.

---

[4]May 1, May Day; in medieval England, the Maypole rites were introduced into the spring festivals originating in ancient cultures.
[5]Horns of a goat.
[6]Throughout, Morton refers to himself in the third person as "mine host."
[7]Puritans of Plymouth Colony who, because they believed reform unlikely in the English church, wished to separate from the Church of England.
[8]Explicate.
[9]The allusions (and nonsense) in the poem were designed to puzzle and confuse the Puritans, expecting to find a scandalous set of verses. *Oedipus*, in Greek legend, answered the riddle of the sphinx, and unwittingly killed his father and married his mother. *Charybdis* was a sea monster that resembled a whirlpool; *Scylla* was a nymph changed into a sea monster—they guarded the two sides of a strait through which Odysseus had to pass on his way home from the Trojan war. *Niobe's* children were killed to punish her for her pride; she wept and continued to weep after being turned to stone. *Amphitrite* was the wife of the sea god Poseidon, whose Roman name was *Neptune;* their son was *Triton*. Proteus was the name of a sea deity from which comes the word *protean* (assuming many shapes). In the Bible, *Samson* was famed for his strength in battles against the Philistines, and *Job* for his patience in suffering the inexplicable hardships imposed by God. *Cupid's mother* was Aphrodite (whose Roman name was Venus), goddess of love. *Scogan's choice:* when an Englishman, John Scogan, was condemned to be hanged, he was given his choice of trees for use as the gallows; he liked none of them and escaped hanging. *Asclepius* was the Greek god of medicine. The *fatal sisters* were the three fates who determined the destinies of the living. *Cytherea* was another name for Aphrodite (or Venus), goddess of love.

The setting up of this Maypole was a lamentable spectacle to the precise Separatists that lived at New Plymouth. They termed it an idol; yea, they called it the Calf of Horeb[10] and stood at defiance with the place, naming it Mount Dagon,[11] threatening to make it a woeful mount and not a merry mount.

The riddle, for want of Oedipus, they could not expound, only they made some explication of part of it and said it was meant by Samson Job, the carpenter of the ship that brought over a woman to her husband that had been there long before and thrived so well that he sent for her and her children to come to him where shortly after he died, having no reason but because of the sound of those two words, when as (the truth is) the man they applied it to was altogether unknown to the author.

There was likewise a merry song made which (to make their revels more fashionable) was sung with a chorus, every man bearing his part, which they performed in a dance, hand in hand about the Maypole, while one of the company sang and filled out the good liquor, like Ganymede and Jupiter.[12]

THE SONG

Chorus.
Drink and be merry, merry, merry boys;
Let all your delight be in the Hymen's[13] joys;
Io[14] to Hymen, now the day is come,
About the merry Maypole take a room.
　Make green garlands, bring bottles out
　And fill sweet nectar freely about.
　Uncover thy head and fear no harm,
　For here's good liquor to keep it warm.
Then drink and be merry, &c.
Io to Hymen, &c.
　Nectar is a thing assigned
　By the Deity's own mind
　To cure the heart oppressed with grief,
　And of good liquors is the chief.
Then drink, &c.
Io to Hymen, &c.
　Give to the melancholy man
　A cup or two of't now and then;
　This physic will soon revive his blood,
　And make him be of a merrier mood.
Then drink, &c.
Io to Hymen, &c.
　Give to the nymph that's free from scorn
　No Irish stuff nor Scotch[15] over worn.
　Lasses in beaver coats come away,
　Ye shall be welcome to us night and day.
To drink and be merry &c.
Io to Hymen, &c.

This harmless mirth made by young men (that lived in hope to have wives brought over to them, that would save them a labor to make a voyage to fetch any

[10]The golden calf made at Mount Horeb and worshipped by the Israelites as a god until Moses intervened and destroyed the idol (Deuteronomy 9:13–21).
[11]National god of the Philistines.
[12]*Ganymede* was cupbearer to Zeus (with Roman name of *Jupiter*).
[13]Greek god of marriage.
[14]*Io* in Latin: Hail. But also, Io was beloved by Zeus, arousing the jealousy of his wife Hera, who changed her into a heifer.
[15]Irish or Scotch material or cloth.

over) was much distasted of the precise Separatists that keep much ado about the tithe of mint and cummin,[16] troubling their brains more than reason would require about things that are indifferent, and from that time sought occasion against my honest host of Ma-re Mount, to overthrow his undertakings and to destroy his plantation quite and clean. But because they presumed, with their imaginary gifts (which they haue out of Phaon's box[17]), they could expound hidden mysteries, to convince them of blindness as well in this as in other matters of more consequence, I will illustrate the poem according to the true intent of the authors of these revels, so much distasted by those moles.

Oedipus is generally received for the absolute reader of riddles, who is invoked; Scylla and Charybdis are two dangerous places for seamen to encounter, near unto Venice, and have been by poets formerly resembled to man and wife. The like license the author challenged for a pair of his nomination, the one lamenting for the loss of the other as Niobe for her children. Amphitrite is an arm of the sea, by which the news was carried up and down of a rich widow, now to be taken up or laid down. By Triton is the fame spread that caused the suitors to muster (as it had been to Penelope[18] of Greece); and, the coast lying circular, all our passage to and fro is made more convenient by sea than land. Many aimed at this mark, but he that played Proteus best and could comply with her humor must be the man that would carry her; and he had need have Samson's strength to deal with a Delilah,[19] and as much patience as Job that should come there, for a thing that I did observe in the lifetime of the former.

But marriage and hanging (they say) come by destiny, and Scogan's choice is better [than] none at all. He that played Proteus (with the help of Priapus[20]) put their noses out of joint, as the proverb is.

And this the whole company of the revelers at Ma-re Mount knew to be the true sense and exposition of the riddle that was fixed to the Maypole which the Separatists were at defiance with. Some of them affirmed that the first institution thereof was in memory of a whore, not knowing that it was a trophy erected at first in honor of Maia,[21] the Lady of Learning which they despise, vilifying the two universities with uncivil terms, accounting what is there obtained by study is but unnecessary learning, not considering that learning does enable men's minds to converse with elements of a higher nature than is to be found within the habitation of the mole.

[PURITAN ARREST OF MORTON BY "OUTRAGIOUS RIOT"]

CHAPTER XV

OF A GREAT MONSTER SUPPOSED TO BE AT MA-RE MOUNT; AND
THE PREPARATION MADE TO DESTROY IT

The Separatists, envying the prosperity and hope of the plantation at Ma-re Mount (which they perceived began to come forward and to be in a good way for gain in the beaver trade), conspired together against mine host especially (who

---

[16]Matthew 23:23: "Woe unto you, scribes and Pharisees, hypocrites! for ye pay tithe of mint and anise and cummin, and have omitted the weightier matters of the law, judgement, mercy, and faith. . . ."

[17]Box given to the aged boatman Phaon by Aphrodite for ferrying her from Lesbos to Chios; the magic elixir of the box restored his youth and beauty.

[18]Wife of Odysseus who, when he was away fighting the Trojan War, was surrounded by suitors whom she had to fend off.

[19]Judges 16:2–22; Samson loved Delilah, but she betrayed him to the Philistines.

[20]Greek deity, sponsor of fertility, often associated with the phallus.

[21]William Bradford in *Of Plymouth Plantation* describes the men frisking around the maypole at Merry Mount "as if they had anew revived and celebrated the feasts of the Roman goddess Flora, or the beastly practices of the Bacchanalians [celebrants in orgiastic rites of the god of wine, Bacchus]." To the Puritans, such feasts and practices were whorish. Morton traces the tradition of the Maypole rites to Maia, Roman goddess of spring and fertility, celebrated in the month of May, which bears her name.

was the owner of that plantation) and made up a party against him and mustered up what aid they could, accounting of him as of a great monster.

Many threatening speeches were given out both against his person and his habitation, which they divulged should be consumed with fire. And taking advantage of the time when his company (which seemed little to regard their threats) were gone up unto the inlands to trade with the savages for beaver, they set upon my honest host at a place called Wessaguscus, where, by accident, they found him. The inhabitants there were in good hope of the subversion of the plantation at Ma-re Mount (which they principally aimed at) and the rather because mine host was a man that endeavored to advance the dignity of the Church of England, which they (on the contrary part) would labor to vilify with uncivil terms, inveighing against the sacred Book of Common Prayer and mine host that used it in a laudable manner amongst his family as a practice of piety.

There he would be a means to bring sacks to their mill (such is the thirst after beaver) and helped the conspirators to surprise mine host (who was there all alone), and they charged him (because they would [like to] seem to have some reasonable cause against him, to set a gloss upon their malice) with criminal things, which indeed had been done by such a person, but was of their conspiracy. Mine host demanded of the conspirators who it was that was author of that information that seemed to be their ground for what they now intended. And because they answered they would not tell him, he as peremptorily replied that he would not say whether he had or he had not done as they had been informed.

The answer made no matter (as it seemed), whether it had been negatively or affirmatively made, for they had resolved what he would suffer, because, (as they boasted), they were now become the greater number: they had shaken off their shackles of servitude and were become masters and masterless people.

It appears they were like bears' whelps in former time when mine host's plantation was of as much strength as theirs, but now (theirs being stronger) they (like over grown bears) seemed monstrous. In brief, mine host must endure to be their prisoner until they could contrive it so that they might send him for England (as they said), there to suffer according to the merit of the fact which they intended to father upon him, supposing (belike) it would prove a heinous crime.

Much rejoicing was made that they had gotten their capital enemy (as they concluded him) whom they purposed to hamper in such sort that he should not be able to uphold his plantation at Ma-re Mount.

The conspirators sported themselves at my honest host, that meant them no hurt, and were so jocund that they feasted their bodies and fell to tippling as if they had obtained a great prize, like the Trojans when they had the custody of Epeios'[22] pinetree horse.

Mine host feigned grief and could not be persuaded either to eat or drink, because he knew emptiness would be a means to make him as watchful as the geese kept in the Roman Capital;[23] whereon, the contrary part, the conspirators would be so drowsy that he might have an opportunity to give them a slip instead of a tester.[24] Six persons of the conspiracy were set to watch him at Wessaguscus. But he kept waking, and in the dead of the night (one lying on the bed for further surety), up gets mine host and got to the second door that he was to pass, which, notwithstanding the lock, he got open and shut it after him with such violence that it affrighted some of the conspirators.

The word which was given with an alarm was, "O he's gone, he's gone, what

[22]Architect of the famed wooden horse used in the Trojan War to conceal the Greek soldiers entering the city of Troy.
[23]The geese served as guards at the Capitoline Hill. In 390 B.C. the hissing geese alerted the Romans to the approaching Gauls.
[24]A counterfeit coin instead of a sixpence.

shall we do, he's gone!" The rest (half asleep) start up in amaze and like rams, ran their heads one at another full butt in the dark.

Their grand leader, Captain Shrimp,[25] took on most furiously and tore his clothes for anger, to see the empty nest and their bird gone.

The rest were eager to have torn their hair from their heads, but it was so short that it would give them no hold.[26] Now Captain Shrimp thought in the loss of this prize (which he accounted his masterpiece) all his honor would be lost forever.

In the meantime mine host was got home to Ma-re Mount through the woods, eight miles round about the head of the river Monatoquit that parted the two plantations, finding his way by the help of the lightning (for it thundered as he went terribly), and there he prepared powder, three pounds dried, for his present employment, and four good guns for him and the two assistants left at his house, with bullets of several sizes, three hundred or thereabouts, to be used if the conspirators should pursue him thither; and these two persons promised their aids in the quarrel and confirmed that promise with health in good *rosa solis.*[27]

Now Captain Shrimp, the first captain in the land (as he supposed), must do some new act to repair this loss and to vindicate his reputation, who had sustained blemish by this oversight, begins now to study how to repair or survive his honor; in this manner, calling of council, they conclude.

He takes eight persons more to him, and (like the nine worthies[28] of New Canaan) they embark with preparation against Ma-re Mount where this monster of a man, as their phrase was, had his den; the whole number, had the rest not been from home, being but seven, would have given Captain Shrimp (a *quondam*[29] drummer) such a welcome as would have made him wish for a drum as big as Diogenes' tub,[30] that he might have crept into it out of sight.

Now the nine worthies are approached, and mine host prepared, having intelligence by a savage that hastened in love from Wessaguscus to give him notice of their intent.

One of mine host's men proved a craven; the other had proved his wits to purchase a little valor, before mine host had observed his posture.

The nine worthies coming before the den of this supposed monster (this seven-headed hydra,[31] as they termed him) and began, like Don Quixote against the windmill,[32] to beat a parley and to offer quarter if mine host would yield, for they resolved to send him to England and bade him lay by his arms.

But he (who was the son of a soldier), having taken up arms in his just defense, replied that he would not lay by those arms because they were so needful at sea, if he should be sent over. Yet, to save the effusion of so much worthy blood as would have issued out of the veins of these nine worthies of New Canaan if mine host should have played upon them out at his portholes (for they came within danger like a flock of wild geese, as if they had been tailed one to another, as colts to be sold at a fair), mine host was content to yield upon quarter and did capitulate with them in what manner it should be for more certainty, because he knew what Captain Shrimp was.

He expressed that no violence should be offered to his person, none to his goods, nor any of his household but that he should have his arms and what else was requisite for the voyage: which their herald returns, it was agreed upon and should be performed.

But mine host no sooner had set open the door and issued out, but instantly

---

[25]Captain Miles Standish was short, plump, and ruddy.
[26]The Puritans cut their hair very short.
[27]A liqueur.
[28]Morton is ironic. The Nine Worthies of history were held up as ideals: three from the Bible (Joshua, David, and Judas Maccabaeus); three from the classics (Hector, Alexander, and Julius Caesar); and three from romance (Arthur, Charlemagne, and Godfrey of Bouillon).

[29]Sometime, former.
[30]Diogenes (*c.* 412–323 B.C.), Greek philosopher who was supposed to have lived in a tub.
[31]The multiheaded Hydra in Greek mythology was killed by Hercules.
[32]In a famous episode of *Don Quixote* by Cervantes (1547–1616), the hero mistakes a windmill for a giant warrior and attacks it in battle.

Captain Shrimp and the rest of the worthies stepped to him, laid hold of his arms, and had him down; and so eagerly was every man bent against him (not regarding any agreement made with such a carnal man), that they fell upon him as if they would have eaten him; some of them were so violent that they would have a slice with scabbard, and all for haste, until an old soldier (of the Queen's, as the proverb is) that was there by accident, clapped his gun under the weapons and sharply rebuked these worthies for their unworthy practices. So the matter was taken into more deliberate consideration.

Captain Shrimp and the rest of the nine worthies made themselves (by this outrageous riot) masters of mine host of Ma-re Mount and disposed of what he had at his plantation.

This, they knew (in the eye of the savages), would add to their glory and diminish the reputation of mine honest host, whom they practiced to be rid of upon any terms, as willingly as if he had been the very hydra of the time.

CHAPTER XVI

HOW THE NINE WORTHIES PUT MINE HOST OF MA-RE MOUNT INTO THE ENCHANTED CASTLE AT PLYMOUTH AND TERRIFIED HIM WITH THE MONSTER BRIAREUS[33]

The nine worthies of New Canaan having now the law in their own hands (there being no general governor in the land, nor none of the separation that regarded the duty they owe their sovereign, whose natural born subjects they were, though translated out of Holland from whence they had learned to work all to their own ends, and make a great show of religion but no humanity), for they were now to sit in council on the cause.

And much it stood mine honest host upon to be very circumspect, and to take Eacus[34] to task; for that his voice was more allowed of than both the other; and had not mine host confounded all the arguments that Eacus could make in their defense, and confuted him that swayed the rest, they would have made him unable to drink in such manner of merriment any more. So that following this private counsel, given him by one that knew who ruled the roost, the hurricane ceased that else would split his pinnace.[35]

A conclusion was made and sentence given that mine host should be sent to England a prisoner. But when he was brought to the ships for that purpose, no man durst be so foolhardy as to undertake [to] carry him. So these worthies set mine host upon an island, without gun, powder, or shot, or dog, or so much as a knife to get anything to feed upon, or any other clothes to shelter him with at winter than a thin suit which he had on at that time. Home he could not get to Ma-re Mount. Upon this island he stayed a month at least, and was relieved by savages that took notice that mine host was a sachem[36] of Passonagessit, and would bring bottles of strong liquor to him and unite themselves into a league of brotherhood with mine host, so full of humanity are these infidels before those Christians.

From this place for England sailed mine host in a Plymouth ship (that came into the land to fish upon the coast) that landed him safe in England at Plymouth; and he stayed in England until the ordinary time for shipping to set forth for these parts, and then returned, no man being able to tax him of anything.

But the worthies (in the meantime) hoped they had been rid of him.

1635?   *1637*

---

[33]In Greek mythology, one of the giants that fought with the gods.
[34]In Greek mythology, one of the judges in the underworld. Elsewhere Morton names his judges: Samuel Fuller, Miles Standish, William Bradford.

[35]A light sailing ship.
[36]Chief.

JOHN WINTHROP
(1588–1649)

In April 1630, a large band of some 2,000 men, women, and children set out from England for the New World with charter in hand designating them the Massachusetts Bay Company; the charter meant that they were not dependent on "backers" seeking profits. They were largely well-to-do people, solid and influential citizens of Old England bent on establishing a Biblical Commonwealth—a New Canaan—in New England. They were Puritans in that they wanted to "purify" the established church of its Papist-like rituals and service; but they were not Separatists, like the Pilgrims of Plymouth Plantation, who believed the only course was to "separate" from the wicked established church.

Their leader was John Winthrop, who sailed on the lead ship, the *Arbella*. The voyage lasted about two months. Somewhere on the Atlantic, Winthrop gathered his followers together to listen to a sermon entitled "A Model of Christian Charity." In this sermon, Winthrop stressed the vital role of Christian love (charity) in creating the ideal human (and social) bond, and he stressed the importance of the principles of Christian love in the enterprise at hand—the "special commission," given by God in a covenant with the voyagers, for establishing the exemplary Christian community, or "a city upon a hill."

Although Winthrop had at one time thought of becoming a minister, he had in fact gone into legal practice. Born in Groton, England, to a prosperous family that had purchased its estate from Henry VIII, he attended Cambridge University, where he first encountered Puritanism and became a convert. When Charles I (known for his Roman Catholic sympathies) succeeded to the British throne in 1625, the lot of Puritans became ambiguous at best, and the great migration to America intensified.

Winthrop began to keep a daily journal on the voyage to America and he continued it until his death in 1649. It is clear from the nature of the entries that Winthrop wrote for the historical record, and when the *Journal* was first published in its entirety in 1825–26, it was entitled *The History of New England*.

Winthrop was memorialized by Cotton Mather in his masterwork of history *Magnalia Christi Americana* (1702) as the ideal earthly ruler and as the counterpart of Moses leading the Israelites to the Promised Land (New Canaan or Jerusalem), and of Nehemiah serving as Governor of the Israelites in Jerusalem. Winthrop was committed to the creation in the New World of a Christian society in which church and state were one, in which the Bible itself was the sole source of the law, and in which dissenting views were not tolerated. But at the same time he stands revealed in his *Journal* as a man of deep feelings, wide human sympathies, and of severe self-judgment. He proved himself a devoted, just, and worthy leader.

ADDITIONAL READING

The History of New England (Winthrop's *Journal*), 2 vols., ed. James Savage, 1825–26, revised, 1853; *The Winthrop Papers*, 5 vols., ed. Allyn B. Forbes, 1929–47.

Robert C. Winthrop, *Life and Letters of John Winthrop*, 1864–67; Samuel Eliot Morison, *Builders of the Bay Colony*, 1930; Edmund S. Morgan, *The Puritan Dilemma: The Story of John*

Winthrop, 1958; D. B. Rutman, *Winthrop's Boston,* 1965; Sacvan Bercovitch, *The Puritan Origins of the American Self,* 1975.

TEXTS

Winthrop's Journal: "History of New England," 1630–1649, ed. James Kendall Hosmer, 2 vols., 1908; "A Model of Christian Charity," *Old South Leaflets,* Old South Association, Old South Meetinghouse, No. 207, ed. Samuel Eliot Morison, 1916. Typography, punctuation, spelling, and usage have been changed to conform with contemporary English and modern printing practices.

from A MODEL OF CHRISTIAN CHARITY

Written and delivered by John Winthrop on the *Arbella* as it was sailing to New England in 1630, "A Model for Christian Charity" was lost for over two hundred years. A copy was found in the early nineteenth century among Winthrop's papers. Samuel Eliot Morison based his edition on this manuscript. The sermon presents practical advice about Christian responsibility for one's fellow beings together with a Christian vision of establishing "a city upon a hill." Part I sets forth principles that should govern Christians in their relationships with one another in community; Part II applies the principles to the "present design," that is, the creating of a new community—a city of God—in the New World wilderness.

I

[CHRISTIAN LOVE, THE BOND OF PERFECTION]

A MODEL HEREOF

God Almighty in His most holy and wise providence, hath so disposed of the condition of mankind, as in all times some must be rich, some poor, some high and eminent in power and dignity; others mean and in subjection.

THE REASON HEREOF

First, to hold conformity with the rest of His works, being delighted to show forth the glory of His wisdom in the variety and difference of the creatures; and the glory of His power, in ordering all these differences for the preservation and good of the whole; and the glory of His greatness, that as it is the glory of princes to have many officers, so this great King will have many stewards, counting Himself more honored in dispensing His gifts to man by man than if He did it by His own immediate hands.

Secondly, that He might have the more occasion to manifest the work of His Spirit: first upon the wicked in moderating and restraining them, so that the rich and mighty should not eat up the poor, nor the poor and despised rise up against their superiors and shake off their yoke; secondly in the regenerate, in exercising His graces, in them, as in the great ones, their love, mercy, gentleness, temperance, etc.; in the poor and inferior sort, their faith patience, obedience etc.

Thirdly, that every man might have need of other, and from hence they might be all knit more nearly together in the bonds of brotherly affection. From hence it appears plainly that no man is made more honorable than another or more wealthy, etc., out of any particular and singular respect to himself, but for the glory of his creator and the common good of the creature, man. Therefore God still reserves the property of these gifts to Himself as [in] Ezekiel 16.17. He there calls wealth His gold and His silver. [In] Proverbs 3.9, he claims their service as His due, honor the Lord with thy riches etc. All men being thus (by divine providence) ranked into two sorts, rich and poor; under the first are comprehended all such as are able to live comfortably by their own means duly improved; and all others are poor according to the former distribution.

There are two rules whereby we are to walk one towards another: justice and mercy. These are always distinguished in their act and in their object, yet may they both concur in the same subject in each respect; as sometimes there may be an occasion of showing mercy to a rich man in some sudden danger of distress, and also doing of mere justice to a poor man in regard of some particular contract, etc.

There is likewise a double law by which we are regulated in our conversation one towards another in both the former respects: the law of nature and the law of grace, or the moral law or the law of the Gospel, to omit the rule of justice as not properly belonging to this purpose otherwise than it may fall into consideration in some particular cases. By the first of these laws man as he was enabled so withal [is] commanded to love his neighbor as himself.[1] Upon this ground stands all the precepts of the moral law, which concerns our dealings with men. To apply this to the works of mercy, this law requires two things: first, that every man afford his help to another in every want or distress; secondly, that he performed this out of the same affection which makes him careful of his own goods, according to that of our Savior. Matthew: "Whatsoever ye would that men should do to you."[2] This was practiced by Abraham and Lot in entertaining the Angels and the old man of Gibeah.[3]

The law of grace or the Gospel hath some difference from the former, as in these respects: First, the law of nature was given to man in the estate of innocency; this of the Gospel in the estate of regeneracy.[4] Secondly, the former propounds one man to another, as the same flesh and image of God; this as a brother in Christ also, and in the communion of the same spirit and so teacheth us to put a difference between Christians and others. *Do good to all, especially to the household of faith.*[5] Upon this ground the Israelites were to put a difference between the brethren of such as were strangers though not of Canaanites.[6] Third, the law of nature could give no rules for dealing with enemies, for all are to be considered as friends in the state of innocency, but the Gospel commands love to an enemy. Proof. If thine Enemy hunger, feed him:[7] Love your Enemies, do good to them that hate you. Matthew: 5.44.

This law of the Gospel propounds likewise a difference of seasons and occasions. There is a time when a Christian must sell all and give to the poor, as they did in the Apostles' times.[8] There is a time also when a Christian (though they give not all yet) must give beyond their ability, as they of Macedonia, Corinthians: 2, 6.[9] Likewise community of perils calls for extraordinary liberality, and so doth

---

[1]Matthew 19:19.
[2]Matthew 7:12.
[3]In Genesis 18, Abraham welcomed and entertained three angels; in Genesis 19:1–14, the nephew of Abraham, Lot, saved two angels from a mob and thus escaped the destruction of Sodom. In Judges 19:15–21, the old man of Gibeah took in a traveller pursued by his enemies.
[4]The "estate of innocency" was the condition of man before the fall, brought about by Adam and Eve's sin of disobedience in eating the forbidden fruit. Christ's sacrifice through His taking on man's sins in His crucifixion redeemed all who believed in Him, restoring them to an "estate of regeneracy."
[5]Galatians 6:10.

[6]Inhabitants of ancient Palestine, Canaan, the Promised Land to which Moses led the Israelites.
[7]Proverbs 25:21.
[8]Luke 18:22: ". . . Yet lackest thou [a certain ruler who had kept the commandments] one thing: sell all that thou hast, and distribute unto the poor, and thou shalt have treasure in heaven: and come, follow me."
[9]Actually 2 Corinthians 8:2–3: ". . . in a great trial of affliction the abundance of their [the churches' of Macedonia] joy and their deep poverty abounded unto the riches of their liberality. For to their power, I bear record, yea, and beyond their power they were willing of themselves."

community in some special service for the Church. Lastly, when there is no other means whereby our Christian brother may be relieved in his distress, we must help him beyond our ability, rather than tempt God in putting him upon help by miraculous or extraordinary means.

· · · · ·

Having already set forth the practice of mercy according to the rule of God's law, it will be useful to lay open the grounds of it also, being the other part of the commandment, and that is the affection from which this exercise of mercy must arise. The apostle[10] tells us that this love is the fullfilling of the law, not that it is enough to love our brother and so no further; but in regard of the excellency of his parts giving any motion to the other as the soul to the body and the power it hath to set all the facilities on work in the outward exercise of this duty. As when we bid one make the clock strike, he doth not lay hand on the hammer, which is the immediate instrument of the sound, but sets on work the first mover or main wheel, knowing that will certainly produce the sound which he intends. So the way to draw men to works of mercy, is not by force of argument from the goodness or necessity of the work; for though this course may enforce a rational mind to some present act of mercy, as is frequent in experience, yet it cannot work such a habit in a soul, as shall make it prompt upon all occasions to produce the same effect, but by framing these affections of love in the heart which will as natively bring forth the other, as any cause doth produce effect.

The definition which the Scripture gives us of love is this: "Love is the bond of perfection."[11] First, it is a bond or ligament. Secondly it makes the work perfect. There is no body but consists of parts and that which knits these parts together gives the body its perfection, because it makes each part so contiguous to others as thereby they do mutually participate with each other, both in strength and infirmity, in pleasure and pain. To instance in the most perfect of all bodies: Christ and His church make one body. The several parts of this body, considered apart before they were united, were as disproportionate and as much disordering as so many contrary qualities or elements, but when Christ comes and by His spirit and love knits all these parts to Himself and each to other, it is become the most perfect and best proportioned body in the world. Ephesians 4.16: "Christ, by whom all the body being knit together by every joint for the furniture thereof, according to the effectual power which is in the measure of every perfection of parts," "a glorious body without spot or wrinkle," the ligaments hereof being Christ, or His love, for Christ is love (1 John 4.8). So this definition is right: "Love is the bond of perfection."

· · · · ·

If any shall object that it is not possible that love should be bred or upheld without hope of requital, it is granted; but that is not our cause; for this love is always under reward. It never gives, but it always receives with advantage; first, in regard that among the members of the same body, love and affection are reciprocal in a most equal and sweet kind of commerce. Secondly, in regard of the pleasure and content that the exercise of love carries with it, as we may see in the natural body. The mouth is at all the pains to receive and mince the food which serves for the nourishment of all the other parts of the body, yet it hath no cause to complain; for first the other parts send back by several passages a due proportion of the same nourishment, in a better form for the strengthening and comforting the mouth. Secondly, the labor of the mouth is accompanied with such

---

[10]St. Paul to the Romans 9:31.
[11]Colossians 3:14.

pleasure and content as fare exceeds the pains it takes. So is it in all the labor of love among Christians. The party loving, reaps love again, as was showed before, which the soul covets more than all the wealth in the world. Third: Nothing yields more pleasure and content to the soul than when it finds that which it may love fervently, for to love and live beloved is the soul's paradise, both here and in heaven. In the state of wedlock there be many comforts to bear out the troubles of that condition; but let such as have tried the most, say if there be any sweetness in that condition comparable to the exercise of mutual love.

From former considerations arise these conclusions.

1. First, This love among Christians is a real thing, not Imaginary.

Secondly: This love is as absolutely necessary to the being of the body of Christ, as the sinews and other ligaments of a natural body are to the being of that body.

Third: This love is a divine, spiritual nature free, active, strong, courageous, permanent; undervaluing all things beneath its proper object; and of all the graces, this makes us nearer to resemble the virtues of our heavenly father.

Fourth: It rests in the love and welfare of its beloved. For the full and certain knowledge of these truths concerning the nature, use, and excellency of this grace, that which the Holy Ghost hath left recorded, I Corinthians 13,[12] may give full satisfaction, which is needful for every true member of this lovely body of the Lord Jesus, to work upon their hearts by prayer, meditation, continual exercise at least of the special [influence] of this grace, 'til Christ be formed in them and they in him, all in each other, knit together by this bond of love.

II

[APPLICATION: "WE SHALL BE AS A CITY ON A HILL"]

It rests now to make some application of this discourse by the present design, which gave the occasion of writing of it. Herein are four things to be propounded: first the persons, secondly the work, third the end, fourth the means.

1. For the persons. We are a company professing ourselves fellow members of Christ, in which respect only though we were absent from each other many miles, and had our employments as far distant, yet we ought to account ourselves knit together by this bond of love, and live in the exercise of it, if we would have comfort of our being in Christ. This was notorious in the practice of the Christians in former times; as is testified of the Waldenses, from the mouth of one of the adversaries *Æneas Sylvius*:[13] "mutuo [ament] penè antequam norunt," they use to love any of their own religion even before they were acquainted with them.

Secondly, for the work we have in hand. It is by a mutual consent, through a special overvaluing providence and a more than an ordinary approbation of the Churches of Christ, to seek out a place of cohabitation and consortship under a due form of government both civil and ecclesiastical. In such cases as this, the care of the public must oversway all private respects, by which, not only conscience, but mere civil policy, doth bind us. For it is a true rule that particular estates cannot subsist in the ruin of the public.

---

[12]1 Corinthians 13:1–13: "Though I speak with the tongues of men and of angels, and have not charity [love], I am become as sounding brass, or a tinkling cymbal. . . . Charity suffereth long, and is kind; charity envieth not; charity vaunteth not itself, is not puffed up, Doth not behave itself unseemly, seeketh not her own, is not easily provoked, thinketh no evil; Rejoiceth not in inequity, but rejoiceth in the truth; Beareth all things, believeth all things, hopeth all things, endureth all things. . . . And now abideth faith, hope, and charity, these three; but the greatest of these is charity."

[13]Peter Waldo, a twelfth-century French merchant who gave away his property and turned to religious studies, was excommunicated for his reforming and protestant views. He and his disciples became known as Waldenses; the sect became increasingly Calvinistic by the 16th century. Pope Pius II (1405–1464), who took the name Aeneas Sylvius, wrote against them in his history; the Latin *ament* [Morison's reconstruction] should be replaced by *solent amare*.

Third. The end is to improve our lives to do more service to the Lord; the comfort and increase of the body of Christ whereof we are members; that ourselves and posterity may be the better preserved from the common corruptions of this evil world, to serve the Lord and work out our salvation under the power and purity of His holy ordinances.

Fourth, for the means whereby this must be effected. They are twofold, a conformity with the work and end we aim at. These we see are extraordinary, therefore we must not content ourselves with usual ordinary means. Whatsoever we did or ought to have done when we lived in England, the same must we do, and more also, where we go. That which the most in their churches maintain as a truth in profession only, we must bring into familiar and constant practice, as in this duty of love. We must love brotherly without dissimulation;[14] we must love one another with a pure heart fervently.[15] We must bear one another's burthens.[16] We must not look only on our own things, but also on the things of our brethren, neither must we think that the Lord will bear with such failings at our hands as he doth from those among whom we have lived; and that for three reasons.

1. In regard of the more near bond of marriage between Him and us, wherein He hath taken us to be His after a most strict and peculiar manner, which will make Him the more jealous of our love and obedience. So He tells the people of Israel, you only have I known of all the families of the earth, therefore will I punish you for your transgressions.[17] Secondly, because the Lord will be sanctified in them that come near Him. We know that there were many that corrupted the service of the Lord, some setting up altars before His own, others offering both strange fire and strange sacrifices also; yet there came no fire from heaven or other sudden judgment upon them, as did upon Nadab and Abihu,[18] who yet we may think did not sin presumptuously. Third. When God gives a special commission He looks to have it strictly observed in every article. When He gave Saul a commission to destroy Amaleck, He indented with him upon certain articles, and because he failed in one of the least, and that upon a fair pretense, it lost him the kingdom which should have been his reward if he had observed his commission.[19]

Thus stands the cause between God and us. We are entered into covenant with Him for this work. We have taken out a commission, the Lord hath given us leave to draw our own articles. We have professed to enterprise these actions, upon these and those ends, we have hereupon besought Him of favour and blessing. Now if the Lord shall please to hear us, and bring us in peace to the place we desire, then hath He ratified this covenant and sealed our commission, [and] will expect a strict performance of the articles contained in it; but if we shall neglect the observation of these articles which are the ends we have propounded, and, dissembling with our God, shall fall to embrace this present world and prosecute our carnal intentions, seeking great things for ourselves and our posterity, the Lord will surely break out in wrath against us; be revenged of such a perjured people and make us know the price of the breach of such a covenant.

Now the only way to avoid this shipwreck, and to provide for our posterity, is to follow the counsel of Micah,[20] to do justly, to love mercy, to walk humbly with

---

[14]Romans 12:9–10.
[15]1 Peter 1:22.
[16]Galatians 6:2.
[17]Amos 3:2.
[18]Leviticus 10:1–2: Nadab and Abihu, sons of Aaron, violated God's command by offering incense and a "strange fire before the Lord"; "And there went out fire from the Lord, and devoured them, and they died before the Lord." God therefore holds His chosen people to a stricter standard than "others offering both strange fire and strange sacrifices."

[19]1 Samuel 15:1–35: Saul was ordered by the Lord to destroy the Amalekites and "all that they have, . . . man and woman, infant and suckling, ox and sheep, camel and ass," but he spared their King Agag and the best of the livestock for sacrifice. His disobedience resulted in his rejection as King over Israel.
[20]Micah 6:8: "He hath shewed thee, O man, what is good; and what doth the Lord require of thee, but to do justly, and to love mercy, and to walk humbly with thy God?"

our God. For this end, we must be knit together in this work as one man. We must entertain each other in brotherly affection, we must be willing to abridge ourselves of our superfluities, for the supply of other's necessities. We must uphold a familiar commerce together in all meekness, gentleness, patience and liberality. We must delight in each other, make other's conditions our own, rejoice together, mourn together, labor and suffer together, always having before our eyes our commission and community in the work, our community as members of the same body. So shall we keep the unity of the spirit in the bond of peace.[21] The Lord will be our God, and delight to dwell among us as His own people, and will command a blessing upon us in all our ways, so that we shall see much more of His wisdom, power, goodness and truth, than formerly we have been acquainted with. We shall find that the God of Israel is among us, when ten of us shall be able to resist a thousand of our enemies; when He shall make us a praise and glory that men shall say of succeeding plantations, "the lord make it like that of NEW ENGLAND." For we must consider that we shall be as a city upon a hill.[22] The eyes of all people are upon us, so that if we shall deal falsely with our God in this work we have undertaken, and so cause Him to withdraw His present help from us, we shall be made a story and a by-word through the world. We shall open the mouths of enemies to speak evil of the ways of God, and all professors for God's sake. We shall shame the faces of many of God's worthy servants, and cause their prayers to be turned into curses upon us 'til we be consumed out of the good land whither we are agoing.

And to shut up this discourse with that exhortation of Moses, that faithful servant of the Lord, in his last farewell to Israel, Deuteronomy 30.[23] Beloved, there is now set before us life and good, death and evil, in that we are commanded this day to love the Lord our God, and to love one another, to walk in His ways and to keep His commandments and His ordinance and His laws, and the articles of our covenant with Him, that we may live and be multiplied, and that the Lord our God may bless us in the land whither we go to possess it. But if our hearts shall turn away, so that we will not obey, but shall be seduced, and worship other Gods, our pleasures and profits, and serve them; it is propounded unto us this day, we shall surely perish out of the good land whither we pass over this vast sea to possess it.

> Therefore let us choose life,
> that we and our seed
> may live by obeying His
> voice and cleaving to Him,
> for He is our life and
> our prosperity.[24]

1630   *1838*

---

[21]Ephesians 4:3: "Endeavouring to keep the unity of the Spirit in the bond of peace."

[22]Matthew 5:14: "Ye are the light of the world. A city that is set on an hill cannot be hid."

[23]Deuteronomy 30:1–20, Moses' farewell speech to the Israelites, is paraphrased by Winthrop in his conclusion. Like the Israelites, the Puritans saw themselves as on the way to the promised land. Moses had led the Israelites up to the river Jordan. It was left to his successor, Joshua, to cross the Jordan and conquer Canaan, the promised land. To the Puritans, the New World was to be a New Canaan.

[24]Deuteronomy 30:19–20: "Therefore choose life, that both thou and thy seed may live. That thou mayest love the Lord thy God, and that thou mayest obey his voice, and that thou mayest cleave unto him: for he is thy life, and the length of thy days. . . ."

from Winthrop's Journal: "History of New England"

[ROGER WILLIAMS]

[July 8, 1635] At the general court, Mr. Williams[1] of Salem was summoned, and did appear. It was laid to his charge, that, being under question before the magistracy and churches for divers dangerous opinions, viz. 1, that the magistrate ought not to punish the breach of the first table,[2] otherwise than in such cases as did disturb the civil peace; 2, that he ought not to tender an oath to an unregenerate man; 3, that a man ought not to pray with such, though wife, child, etc.; 4, that a man ought not to give thanks after the sacrament nor after meat, etc.; and that the other churches were about to write to the church of Salem to admonish him of these errors; notwithstanding the church had since called him to [the] office of a teacher. Much debate was about these things. The said opinions were adjudged by all, magistrates and ministers, (who were desired to be present,) to be erroneous, and very dangerous, and the calling of him to office, at that time, was judged a great contempt of authority. So, in fine, time was given to him and the church of Salem to consider of these things till the next general court, and then either to give satisfaction to the court, or else to expect the sentence; it being professedly declared by the ministers, (at the request of the court to give their advice,) that he who should obstinately maintain such opinions, (whereby a church might run into heresy, apostacy, or tyranny, and yet the civil magistrate could not intermeddle,) were to be removed, and that the other churches ought to request the magistrates so to do.

[January 11, 1636] The governor[3] and assistants met at Boston to consider about Mr. Williams, for that they were credibly informed, that, notwithstanding the injunction laid upon him (upon the liberty granted him to stay till the spring) not to go about to draw others to his opinions, he did use to entertain company in his house, and to preach to them, even of such points as he had been censured for; and it was agreed to send him into England by a ship then ready to depart. The reason was, because he had drawn above twenty persons to his opinion, and they were intended to erect a plantation about the Naragansett Bay,[4] from whence the infection would easily spread into these churches, (the people being, many of them, much taken with the apprehension of his godliness). Whereupon a warrant was sent to him to come presently to Boston, to be shipped, etc. He returned answer, (and divers of Salem came with it) that he could not come without hazard of his life, etc. Whereupon a pinnace was sent with commission to Capt. Underhill, etc., to apprehend him, and carry him aboard the ship, (which then rode at Natascutt;) but, when they came at his house, they found he had been gone three days before; but whither they could not learn.

He had so far prevailed at Salem, as many there (especially of devout women) did embrace his opinions, and separated from the churches, for this cause, that some of their members, going into England, did hear the ministers there, and when they came home the churches here held communion with them.

---

[1]Roger Williams. See biography and works included in this volume.
[2]The first five of the Ten Commandments (Decalogue), which are religious injunctions, are known as the first table; the last five, moral in nature, are the second table.

[3]The governor then was John Haynes (1594–1654); Winthrop, one of the assistants, was reelected governor in 1637.
[4]Williams moved his ministry to Providence Plantation, Rhode Island.

[ANNE HUTCHINSON]

[October 21, 1636] One Mrs. Hutchinson,[1] a member of the church of Boston, a woman of a ready wit and bold spirit, brought over with her two dangerous errors: 1. That the person of the Holy Ghost dwells in a justified[2] person. 2. That no sanctification[3] can help to evidence to us our justification.— From these two grew many branches; as, 1. Our union with the Holy Ghost, so as a Christian remains dead to every spiritual action, and hath no gifts nor graces, other than such as are in hypocrites, nor any other sanctification but the Holy Ghost himself.

There joined with her in these opinions a brother of hers, one Mr. Wheelwright,[4] a silenced minister sometimes in England.

[November 1, 1637] The court also sent for Mrs. Hutchinson, and charged her with divers matters, as her keeping two public lectures every week in her house, whereto sixty or eighty persons did usually resort, and for reproaching most of the ministers (viz., all except Mr. Cotton[5]) for not preaching a covenant of free grace,[6] and that they had not the seal of the spirit, nor were able ministers of the New Testament; which were clearly proved against her, though she sought to shift it off. And, after many speeches to and fro, at last she was so full as she could not contain, but vented her revelations; amongst which this was one, that she had it revealed to her, that she should come into New England, and should here be persecuted, and that God would ruin us and our posterity, and the whole state, for the same. So the court proceeded and banished her; but, because it was winter, they committed her to a private house, where she was well provided, and her own friends and the elders permitted to go to her, but none else.

[March 1, 1638] While Mrs. Hutchinson continued at Roxbury,[7] divers of the elders and others resorted to her, and finding her to persist in maintaining those gross errors beforementioned, and many others, to the number of thirty or thereabout, some of them wrote to the church at Boston, offering to make proof of the same before the church, etc., . . . ; whereupon she was called, (the magistrates being desired to give her license to come,) and the lecture was appointed to begin at ten. (The general court being then at Newtown, the governor and the treasurer, being members of Boston, were permitted to come down, but the rest of the court continued at Newtown.) When she appeared, the errors were read to her. The first was, that the souls of men are mortal by generation,[8] but, after, made immortal by Christ's purchase. This she maintained a long time; but at length she was so clearly convinced by reason and scripture, and the whole church agreeing that sufficient had been delivered for her conviction, that she yielded she had been in an error. Then they proceeded to three other errors: 1. That there was no resurrection of these bodies, and that these bodies were not united to Christ, but every person united hath a new body, etc. These were also clearly confuted, but yet she held her own; so as the church (all but two of her sons) agreed she should be admonished,[9] and because her sons would not agree to it, they were admonished also.

Mr. Cotton pronounced the sentence of admonition with great solemnity, and with much zeal and detestation of her errors and pride of spirit. The assembly

---

[1] Anne Hutchinson came with her family from England to America in 1634, drawn in part by her admiration for John Cotton. She soon gathered about her in weekly meetings a group of women to discuss the Sunday sermons. She was outspoken and persuasive, and soon she was charged with antinomianism, a belief that for the elect whose faith had provided them grace, the moral law did not apply. The Puritan leaders found Anne Hutchinson's ideas dangerous for themselves, in that her emphasis on the indwelling Holy Ghost seemed to diminish their and Scripture's authority; and for others, in that her emphasis on the inapplicability of the moral law seemed to encourage licentiousness.

[2] Of the elect.
[3] Outward holiness does not constitute evidence that one is of the elect.
[4] Rev. John Wheelwright (c. 1592–1679), brother-in-law of Anne Hutchinson.
[5] John Cotton (1584–1652), prominent minister of Boston.
[6] Grace granted freely by God, not earned by good works.
[7] Roxbury, Massachusetts, where Anne Hutchinson was then held.
[8] The process of procreation.
[9] A kind of reprimand, but a lesser punishment than banishment.

continued till eight at night, and all did acknowledge the special presence of God's spirit therein; and she was appointed to appear again the next lecture day.

[March 22, 1638] Mrs. Hutchinson appeared again; (she had been licensed by the court, in regard she had given hope of her repentance, to be at Mr. Cotton's house, that both he and Mr. Davenport[10] might have the more opportunity to deal with her;) and the articles being again read to her, and her answer required, she delivered it in writing, wherein she made a retractation of near all, but with such explanations and circumstances as gave no satisfaction to the church; so as she was required to speak further to them. Then she declared, that it was just with God to leave her to herself, as he had done, for her slighting his ordinances, both magistracy and ministry; and confessed that what she had spoken against the magistrates at the court (by way of revelation) was rash and ungrounded; and desired the church to pray for her. This gave the church good hope of her repentance; but when she was examined about some particulars, as that she had denied inherent righteousness, etc., she affirmed that it was never her judgment; and though it was proved by many testimonies, that she had been of that judgment, and so had persisted, and maintained it by argument against divers,[11] yet she impudently persisted in her affirmation, to the astonishment of all the assembly. So that, after much time and many arguments had been spent to bring her to see her sin, but all in vain, the church, with one consent, cast her out. Some moved to have her admonished[12] once more; but, it being for manifest evil in matter of conversation, it was agreed otherwise; and for that reason also the sentence was denounced by the pastor, matter of manners belonging properly to his place.

After she was excommunicated,[13] her spirits, which seemed before to be somewhat dejected, revived again, and she gloried in her sufferings, saying, that it was the greatest happiness, next to Christ, that ever befell her. Indeed, it was a happy day to the churches of Christ here, and to many poor souls, who had been seduced by her, who, by what they heard and saw that day, were (through the grace of God) brought off quite from her errors, and settled again in the truth.

At this time the good providence of God so disposed, divers of the congregation (being the chief men of the party, her husband being one) were gone to Naragansett to seek out a new place for plantation, and taking liking of one in Plymouth patent, they went thither to have it granted them; but the magistrates there, knowing their spirit, gave them a denial, but consented they might buy of the Indians an island in the Naragansett Bay.[14]

After two or three days, the governor sent a warrant to Mrs. Hutchinson to depart this jurisdiction before the last of this month, according to the order of court, and for that end set her at liberty from her former constraint, so as she was not to go forth of her own house till her departure; and upon the 28th she went by water to her farm at the Mount, where she was to take water, with Mr. Wheelwright's wife and family, to go to Pascataquack; but she changed her mind, and went by land to Providence, and so to the island in the Naragansett Bay, which her husband and the rest of that sect had purchased of the Indians, and prepared with all speed to remove unto. For the court had ordered, that, except they were gone with their families by such a time, they should be summoned to the general court, etc.

[September, 1638] Mrs. Hutchinson, being removed to the Isle of Aquidneck, in the Naragansett Bay, after her time was fulfilled, that she expected deliverance of a child, was delivered of a monstrous birth, which, being diversely related in

---

[10]John Davenport (1597–1670), Puritan minister.
[11]Several persons.
[12]A lesser punishment, thus enabling her to remain in the colony.

[13]Banished from the church and colony.
[14]Roger Williams settled in Providence; Anne Hutchinson's removal to Naragansett Bay placed them in separate places but together in Rhode Island.

the country, (and, in the open assembly at Boston, upon a lecture day, declared by Mr. Cotton to be twenty-seven several lumps of man's seed, without any alteration or mixture of anything from the woman, and thereupon gathered that it might signify her error in denying inherent righteousness, but that all was Christ in us, and nothing of ours in our faith, love, etc.) hereupon the governor wrote to Mr. Clarke, a physician and a preacher to those of the island, to know the certainty thereof. . . .[15]

[September 7, 1643] The Indians near the Dutch, having killed 15 men, as is before related, proceeded on and began to set upon the English who dwelt under the Dutch. They came to Mrs. Hutchinson's in way of friendly neighborhood,[16] as they had been accustomed, and taking their opportunity, killed her and Mr. Collins, her son-in-law, (who had been kept prisoner in Boston, as is before related,)[17] and all her family, and such of Mr. Throckmorton's and Mr. Cornhill's families as were at home; in all sixteen, and put their cattle into their houses and there burnt them. By a good providence of God, there was a boat came in there at the same instant, to which some women and children fled, and so were saved, but two of the boatmen going up to the houses were shot and killed.

These people had cast off ordinances and churches, and now at last their own people, and for larger accommodation had subjected themselves to the Dutch[18] and dwelt scatteringly near a mile asunder: and some that escaped, who had removed only for want (as they said) of hay for their cattle which increased much, now coming back again to Aquidneck, they wanted cattle for their grass.[19]

[PRICES AND PROFITS]

[November 9, 1639] At a general court held at Boston, great complaint was made of the oppression used in the country in sale of foreign commodities; and Mr. Robert Keayne,[1] who kept a shop in Boston, was notoriously above others observed and complained of; and, being convented,[2] he was charged with many particulars; in some, for taking above six-pence in the shilling profit; in some above eight-pence; and, in some small things, above two for one; and being hereof convicted (as appears by the records), he was fined £200, which came thus to pass: the deputies considered, apart, of his fine, and set it at £200; the magistrates agreed but to £100. So, the court being divided, at length it was agreed, that his fine should be £200, but he should pay but £100, and the other should be respited[3] to the further consideration of the next general court. By this means the magistrates and deputies were brought to an accord, which otherwise had not been likely, and so much trouble might have grown, and the offender escaped censure. For the cry of the country was so great against oppression, and some of the elders and magistrates had declared such detestation of the corrupt practice of this man (which was the more observable, because he was wealthy and sold dearer than most other tradesmen, and for that he was of ill report for the like covetous practice in England, that incensed the deputies very much against him). And sure the course was very evil, especial circumstances considered: 1. He being an ancient profes-

[15]Lines omitted from this entry in the Hosmer edition have been restored from the *Journal* as edited by James Savage (Boston, 1825–26; revised, 1853).
[16]Anne Hutchinson was then living in what is now Pelham Neck, near New Rochelle, New York.
[17]Anne Hutchinson's son Francis and her son-in-law Mr. Collins were both imprisoned briefly in Boston in 1641 for their heretical opinions.
[18]I.e., in New York.

[19]I.e., some of the people had returned from New York to the island of Aquidneck, where they had formerly lived, and thus escaped the massacre.
[1]Robert Keayne had lived a long time in the colony as a respected merchant. He was well connected: his daughter had married a son of Thomas Dudley (father of Anne Bradstreet and future governor of the colony).
[2]Summoned.
[3]Postponed.

sor[4] of the gospel: 2. A man of eminent parts: 3. Wealthy, and having but one child: 4. Having come over for conscience' sake, and for the advancement of the gospel here: 5. Having been formerly dealt with and admonished, both by private friends and also by some of the magistrates and elders, and having promised reformation; being a member of a church and commonwealth now in their infancy, and under the curious observation of all churches and civil states in the world. These added much aggravation to his sin in the judgment of all men of understanding. Yet most of the magistrates (though they discerned of the offence clothed with all these circumstances) would have been more moderate in their censure: 1. Because there was no law in force to limit or direct men in point of profit in their trade. 2. Because it is the common practice, in all countries, for men to make use of advantages for raising the prices of their commodities. 3. Because (though he were chiefly aimed at, yet) he was not alone in this fault. 4. Because all men through the country, in sale of cattle, corn, labor, etc., were guilty of the like excess in prices. 5. Because a certain rule could not be found out for an equal rate between buyer and seller, though much labor had been bestowed in it, and divers laws had been made, which, upon experience, were repealed, as being neither safe nor equal. Lastly, and especially, because the law of God appoints no other punishment but double restitution; and, in some cases, as where the offender freely confesseth, and brings his offering, only half added to the principal. After the court had censured him, the church of Boston called him also in question, where (as before he had done in the court) he did, with tears, acknowledge and bewail his covetous and corrupt heart, yet making some excuse for many of the particulars, which were charged upon him, as partly by pretence of ignorance of the true price of some wares, and chiefly by being misled by some false principles, as 1. That, if a man lost in one commodity, he might help himself in the price of another. 2. That if, through want of skill or other occasion, his commodity cost him more than the price of the market in England, he might then sell it for more than the price of the market in New England, etc. These things gave occasion to Mr. Cotton, in his public exercise the next lecture day, to lay open the error of such false principles, and to give some rules of direction in the case.

Some false principles were these:—

1. That a man might sell as dear as he can, and buy as cheap as he can.

2. If a man lose by casualty of sea, etc., in some of his commodities, he may raise the price of the rest.

3. That he may sell as he bought, though he paid too dear, etc., and though the commodity be fallen, etc.

4. That, as a man may take the advantage of his own skill or ability, so he may of another's ignorance or necessity.

5. Where one gives time for payment, he is to take like recompense of one as of another.

The rules for trading were these:—

1. A man may not sell above the current price, i.e., such a price as is usual in the time and place, and as another (who knows the worth of the commodity) would give for it, if he had occasion to use it; as that is called current money, which every man will take, etc.

2. When a man loseth in his commodity for want of skill, etc., he must look at it as his own fault or cross, and therefore must not lay it upon another.

3. Where a man loseth by casualty of sea, or, etc., it is a loss cast upon himself by providence, and he may not ease himself of it by casting it upon another; for so

---

[4]One who professed or believed in.

a man should seem to provide against all providences, etc., that he should never lose; but where there is a scarcity of the commodity, there men may raise their price; for now it is a hand of God upon the commodity, and not the person.

4. A man may not ask any more for his commodity than his selling price, as Ephron to Abraham,[5] the land is worth thus much.

The cause being debated by the church, some were earnest to have him excommunicated; but the most thought an admonition would be sufficient. Mr. Cotton opened the causes, which required excommunication, out of that in 1 Cor. 5: 11.[6] The point now in question was, whether these actions did declare him to be such a covetous person, etc. Upon which he showed, that it is neither the habit of covetousness, (which is in every man in some degree,) nor simply the act, that declares a man to be such, but when it appears, that a man sins against his conscience, or the very light of nature, and when it appears in a man's whole conversation. But Mr. Keayne did not appear to be such, but rather upon an error in his judgment, being led by false principles; and, beside, he is otherwise liberal, as in his hospitality, and in church communion, etc. So, in the end, the church consented to an admonition.

· · · · · ·

[A Woman's "Place," A Woman's Plight]

[April 13, 1645] Mr. Hopkins,[1] the governor of Hartford upon Connecticut, came to Boston, and brought his wife with him, (a godly young woman, and of special parts,) who was fallen into a sad infirmity, the loss of her understanding and reason, which had been growing upon her divers years, by occasion of her giving herself wholly to reading and writing, and had written many books. Her husband, being very loving and tender of her, was loath to grieve her; but he saw his error, when it was too late. For if she had attended her household affairs, and such things as belong to women, and not gone out of her way and calling to meddle in such things as are proper for men, whose minds are stronger, etc., she had kept her wits, and might have improved them usefully and honorably in the place God had set her. He brought her to Boston, and left her with her brother, one Mr. Yale, a merchant, to try what means might be had here for her. But no help could be had.[2]

· · · · · ·

[March, 1647] There fell out at this time a very sad occasion. A merchant of Plymouth in England, (whose father had been mayor there,) called [blank] Martin, being fallen into decay, came to Casco Bay, and after some time, having occasion to return into England, he left behind him two daughters, (very proper maidens and of modest behavior,) but took not that course for their safe bestowing in his absence, as the care and wisdom of a father should have done, so as the eldest of them, called Mary, twenty-two years of age, being in [the] house with one Mr. Mitton, a married man of Casco, within one quarter of a year, he was taken with her, and soliciting her chastity, obtained his desire, and having divers times committed sin with her, in the space of three months, she then removed to Boston, and put herself in service to Mrs. Bourne; and finding herself to be with child, and not

---

[5]Genesis 23:11–16: Ephron offered Abraham a burial cave for Abraham's wife Sarah; Abraham insisted on paying the established price.

[6]1 Corinthians 5:11: "But now I have written unto you not to keep company, if any man that is called a brother be a fornicator, or covetous, or an idolater, or a railer, or a drunkard, or an extortioner: with such an one no not to eat."

[1]Edward Hopkins (1600–1657) on September 5, 1631, married Anne Yale (d. 1698), sister of David Yale of Boston and Thomas Yale of New Haven, aunt of Elihu Yale, founder of Yale University.

[2]Biographical dictionaries report her death after 50 years of insanity.

able to bear the shame of it, she concealed it, and though divers did suspect it, and some told her mistress their fears, yet her behavior was so modest, and so faithful she was in her service, as her mistress would not give ear to any such report, but blamed such as told her of it. But, her time being come, she was delivered of a woman child in a back room by herself upon the 13 (December) in the night, and the child was born alive, but she kneeled upon the head of it, till she thought it had been dead, and having laid it by, the child, being strong, recovered, and cried again. Then she took it again, and used violence to it till it was quite dead. Then she put it into her chest, and having cleansed the room, she went to bed, and arose again the next day about noon, and went about her business, and so continued till the nineteenth day, that her master and mistress went on shipboard to go for England. They being gone, and she removed to another house, a midwife in the town, having formerly suspected her, and now coming to her again, found she had been delivered of a child, which, upon examination, she confessed, but said it was still-born, and so she put it into the fire. But, search being made, it was found in her chest, and when she was brought before the jury, they caused her to touch the face of it, whereupon the blood came fresh into it.[3] Whereupon she confessed the whole truth, and a surgeon, being called to search the body of the child, found a fracture in the skull. Before she was condemned, she confessed, that she had prostituted her body to another also, one Sears. She behaved herself very penitently while she was in prison, and at her death, complaining much of the hardness of her heart. She confessed, that the first and second time she committed fornication, she prayed for pardon, and promised to commit it no more; and the third time she prayed God, that if she did fall into it again, he would make her an example, and therein she justified God, as she did in the rest. Yet all the comfort God would afford her, was only trust (as she said) in his mercy through Christ. After she was turned off and had hung a space, she spake, and asked what they did mean to do. Then some stepped up, and turned the knot of the rope backward, and then she soon died.

[CREATURES, PORTENTS, LESSONS]

[July 5, 1632] At Watertown there was (in the view of divers witnesses) a great combat between a mouse and a snake; and, after a long fight, the mouse prevailed and killed the snake. The pastor of Boston, Mr. Wilson, a very sincere, holy man, hearing of it, gave this interpretation: That the snake was the devil; the mouse was a poor contemptible people, which God had brought hither, which should overcome Satan here, and dispossess him of his kingdom.

[December 15, 1640] About this time there fell out a thing worthy of observation. Mr. Winthrop the younger, one of the magistrates, having many books in a chamber where there was corn of divers sorts, had among them one wherein the Greek testament, the psalms and the common prayer[1] were bound together. He found the common prayer eaten with mice, every leaf of it, and not any of the two other touched, nor any other of his books, though there were above a thousand.

[March 5, 1643] Corn was very scarce all over the country, so as by the end of the 2d month, many families in most towns had none to eat, but were forced to live of clams, muscles, cataos, dry fish, etc.,. . . . The immediate causes of this scarcity were the cold and wet summer, especially in the time of the first harvest; also, the pigeons came in such flocks, (above 10,000 in one flock,) that beat down, and eat up a very great quantity of all sorts of English grain; much corn spent in

---

[3]A superstition of the time held that if a secret murder took place, the corpse would bleed if touched by the murderer.

[1]The Book of Common Prayer, services and prayers for worship in the Church of England.

setting out the ships, ketches, etc.; lastly, there were such abundance of mice in the barns, that devoured much there. The mice also did much spoil in orchards, eating off the bark at the bottom of the fruit trees in the time of the snow, so as never had been known the like spoil in any former winter. So many enemies doth the Lord arm against our daily bread, that we might know we are to eat it in the sweat of our brows.[2]

[December 15, 1645] At Ipswich there was a calf brought forth with one head, and three mouths, three noses, and six eyes. What these prodigies portended the Lord only knows, which in his due time he will manifest.

[August 15, 1648] The synod[3] met at Cambridge by adjournment from the (4) [June] last. Mr. Allen of Dedham preached out of Acts 15, a very godly, learned, and particular handling of near all the doctrines and applications concerning that subject with a clear discovery and refutation of such errors, objections, and scruples as had been raised about it by some young heads in the country.

It fell out, about the midst of his sermon, there came a snake into the seat, where many of the elders sate behind the preacher. It came in at the door where people stood thick upon the stairs. Divers of the elders shifted from it, but Mr. Thomson, one of the elders of Braintree, (a man of much faith,) trode upon the head of it, and so held it with his foot and staff with a small pair of grains,[4] until it was killed. This being so remarkable, and nothing falling out but by divine providence, it is out of doubt, the Lord discovered[5] somewhat of His mind in it. The serpent is the devil; the synod, the representative of the churches of Christ in New England. The devil had formerly and lately attempted their disturbance and dissolution; but their faith in the seed of the woman overcame him and crushed his head.[6]

[August 15, 1648] This month, when our first harvest was near had in, the pigeons came again all over the country, but did no harm, (harvest being just in), but proved a great blessing, it being incredible what multitudes of them were killed daily. It was ordinary for one man to kill eight or ten dozen in half a day, yea five or six dozen at one shoot, and some seven or eight. Thus the Lord showed us that he could make the same creature, which formerly had been a great chastisement, now to become a great blessing.

[NATURAL AND CIVIL LIBERTY[1]]

[July 3, 1645] I suppose something may be expected from me, upon this charge that is befallen me, which moves me to speak now to you; yet I intend not to intermeddle in the proceedings of the court, or with any of the persons concerned therein. Only I bless God, that I see an issue of this troublesome business. I also acknowledge the justice of the court, and, for mine own part, I am well satisfied, I was publicly charged, and I am publicly and legally acquitted, which is all I did expect or desire. And though this be sufficient for my justification before men, yet not so before the God, who hath seen so much amiss in my dispensations (and even in this affair) as calls me to be humble. For to be publicly and criminally charged in this court, is matter of humiliation, (and I desire to make a right use of it,) notwithstanding I be thus acquitted. If her father had spit in her face, (saith

---

[2] Genesis 3:19: "In the sweat of thy face shalt thou eat bread."
[3] Assembly of church officials. This synod of 1648 established the Congregational polity of New England, known as the Cambridge Platform.
[4] Barbed prongs of a fish spear.
[5] Revealed.
    3:15: "And I will put enmity between thee [the serpent] and the woman, and between thy seed and her seed; it shall bruise thy head, and thou shalt bruise his heel."
[1] Winthrop was forced to stand an "impeachment" trial in 1645 because of complicated charges that he had exceeded the power of his office. After he was "legally and publicly acquit of all that was laid to his charge," Winthrop made this speech to the court.

the Lord concerning Miriam,) should she not have been ashamed seven days?[2] Shame had lain upon her, whatever the occasion had been. I am unwilling to stay you from your urgent affairs, yet give me leave (upon this special occasion) to speak a little more to this assembly. It may be of some good use, to inform and rectify the judgments of some of the people, and may prevent such distempers as have arisen amongst us. The great questions that have troubled the country, are about the authority of the magistrates and the liberty of the people. It is yourselves who have called us to this office, and being called by you, we have our authority from God, in way of an ordinance, such as hath the image of God eminently stamped upon it, the contempt and violation whereof hath been vindicated with examples of divine vengeance. I entreat you to consider, that when you choose magistrates, you take them from among yourselves, men subject to like passions as you are. Therefore when you see infirmities in us, you should reflect upon your own, and that would make you bear the more with us, and not be severe censurers of the failings of your magistrates, when you have continual experience of the like infirmities in yourselves and others. We account him a good servant, who breaks not his covenant. The covenant between you and us is the oath you have taken of us, which is to this purpose, that we shall govern you and judge your causes by the rules of God's laws and our own, according to our best skill. When you agree with a workman to build you a ship or house, etc., he undertakes as well for his skill as for his faithfulness, for it is his profession, and you pay him for both. But when you call one to be a magistrate, he doth not profess nor undertake to have sufficient skill for that office, nor can you furnish him with gifts, etc., therefore you must run the hazard of his skill and ability. But if he fail in faithfulness, which by his oath he is bound unto, that he must answer for. If it fall out that the case be clear to common apprehension, and the rule clear also, if he transgress here, the error is not in the skill, but in the evil of the will: it must be required of him. But if the case be doubtful, or the rule doubtful, to men of such understanding and parts as your magistrates are, if your magistrates should err here, yourselves must bear it.

For the other point concerning liberty, I observe a great mistake in the country about that. There is a twofold liberty, natural (I mean as our nature is now corrupt) and civil or federal. The first is common to man with beasts and other creatures. By this, man, as he stands in relation to man simply, hath liberty to do what he lists; it is a liberty to evil as well as to good. This liberty is incompatible and inconsistent with authority, and cannot endure the least restraint of the most just authority. The exercise and maintaining of this liberty makes men grow more evil, and in time to be worse than brute beasts: *omnes sumus licentia deteriores.*[3] This is that great enemy of truth and peace, that wild beast, which all the ordinances of God are bent against, to restrain and subdue it. The other kind of liberty I call civil or federal, it may also be termed moral, in reference to the covenant between God and man, in the moral law, and the politic covenants and constitutions, amongst men themselves. This liberty is the proper end and object of authority, and cannot subsist without it; and it is a liberty to that only which is good, just, and honest. This liberty you are to stand for, with the hazard (not only of your goods, but) of your lives, if need be. Whatsoever crosseth this, is not authority, but a distemper thereof. This liberty is maintained and exercised in a way of subjection to authority; it is of the same kind of liberty wherewith Christ hath made us

---

[2]Numbers 12:14: "And the Lord said unto Moses, If her father had but spit in her face, should she not be ashamed seven days? . . ."
[3]"All are weakened by excess liberty" (Latin).

free. The woman's own choice makes such a man her husband; yet being so chosen, he is her lord, and she is to be subject to him, yet in a way of liberty, not of bondage; and a true wife accounts her subjection her honor and freedom, and would not think her condition safe and free, but in her subjection to her husband's authority. Such is the liberty of the church under the authority of Christ, her king and husband; his yoke is so easy and sweet to her as a bride's ornaments; and if through frowardness or wantonness, etc., she shake it off, at any time, she is at no rest in her spirit, until she take it up again; and whether her lord smiles upon her, and embraceth her in his arms, or whether he frowns, or rebukes, or smites her, she apprehends the sweetness of his love in all, and is refreshed, supported, and instructed by every such dispensation of his authority over her. On the other side, ye know who they are that complain of this yoke and say, let us break their bands, etc., we will not have this man to rule over us. Even so, brethren, it will be between you and your magistrates. If you stand for your natural corrupt liberties, and will do what is good in your own eyes, you will not endure the least weight of authority, but will murmur, and oppose, and be always striving to shake off that yoke; but if you will be satisfied to enjoy such civil and lawful liberties, such as Christ allows you, then will you quietly and cheerfully submit unto that authority which is set over you, in all the administrations of it, for your good. Wherein, if we fail at any time, we hope we shall be willing (by God's assistance) to hearken to good advice from any of you, or in any other way of God; so shall your liberties be preserved, in upholding the honor and power of authority amongst you.

1630–49   *1825–26*

EDWARD JOHNSON
(1598–1672)

If there is an epic among the early histories of New England, Edward Johnson's *Wonder-Working Providence of Sion's Saviour in New England* (1654) must claim the title. Johnson's work, though a chronicle of New England from the founding of Salem in 1628 to the period of John Endecott's governorship in 1651, is much more a creation of the imagination. The chief character (as the title suggests) is Christ Himself, Commander-in-Chief in the war against the forces of evil—a war begun in England against "irreligious, lascivious, and Popish" persons, but played out in the New World, the colonists themselves serving as soldiers in the Lord's army doing battle against Satan. Thus Johnson conceived and wrote his history as a cosmic epic, elevating the actions of the colonists from provincial to world importance, the fate of humankind hanging in the balance. Later Americans were to appropriate, consciously or unconsciously, elements of this grandiose vision of their origins and destiny.

Johnson himself (unlettered, a ship carpenter, and farmer) seems an unlikely person to have produced such a book. An industrious citizen (and Puritan) of Herne Hill, Kent, he came to New England in 1630 to develop trade with the Indians. Shortly thereafter, he returned to England to bring his wife and seven children to America. Returning and settling in Charlestown in 1636, he founded the town of Woburn in 1640. He became a leading citizen, serving in several posts including militia captain and deputy to the General

Court. He began writing his history in 1650 and published it anonymously in England in 1654.

In the excerpts presented here, Johnson exhibits his imaginative gifts. In "The Farewell to England," he invents characters—friends—who are bidding each other good-bye before one of them departs on the voyage to the New World. Johnson draws on his own passage to describe the very real dangers of the "long and restless voyage." Christ and Satan are living presences in the entire work, locked in combat that will determine the world's destiny.

The literary historian Moses Coit Tyler has vividly characterized Johnson's book: "It is crude enough in thought and style, avowedly partisan, and pitched upon a key of wild religious rhapsody. Yet with all its limitations, it is the sincere testimony of an eye-witness and an honest man . . . a most authentic and a priceless memorial of American character and life in the heroic epoch of our earliest men." This is another way of saying that *The Wonder-Working Providence* is one of those "epic" works that created out of the historical materials of migration and settlement an enduring American myth.

ADDITIONAL READING

Moses Coit Tyler, *A History of American Literature, 1607–1765*, 1878; Sacvan Bercovitch, *The Puritan Origins of the American Self*, 1975; Cecelia Tichi, *New World, New Earth: Environmental Reform in American Literature from the Puritans through Whitman*, 1979.

TEXT

Wonder-Working Providence of Sion's Saviour in New England, ed. J. Franklin Jameson, 1910. Typography, punctuation, spelling, and usage have been changed to conform with contemporary English and modern printing practices.

from Wonder-Working Providence of Sion's Saviour in New England

BOOK I

CHAPTER I

[THE SAD CONDITION OF OLD ENGLAND]

When England began to decline in religion, like lukewarm Laodicea,[1] and instead of purging out Popery, a farther compliance was sought, not only in vain idolatrous ceremonies but also in profaning the Sabbath and, by proclamation throughout their parish churches, exasperating lewd and profane persons to celebrate a Sabbath, like the heathen, to Venus, Bacchus and Ceres,[2] insomuch that the multitude of irreligious lascivious, and Popish affected persons spread the whole land like grasshoppers—in this very time, Christ, the glorious king of His churches, raises an army out of our English nation, for freeing His people from

---

[1] Ancient city in Asia Minor whose church was chastised in Revelation 3:14–16 for being "neither cold nor hot," but "lukewarm."
[2] Goddess of Love, god of wine, goddess of agriculture in Roman mythology. Puritans objected to the English law permitting Sunday amusements. In his 1617 *Declaration of* *Sports*, James I allowed dancing, archery, May games, morris dances, Whitsun ales, the setting up of Maypoles, and other "harmless recreations," and Charles I, his successor, in 1633, insisted upon the clergy reading this *Booke of Sports* from the pulpit, punishing all who disobeyed.

their long servitude under usurping prelacy. And because every corner of England was filled with the fury of malignant adversaries, Christ creates a new England to muster up the first of His forces in, whose low condition, little number, and remoteness of place made these adversaries triumph, despising this day of small things. But in this height of their pride, the Lord Christ brought sudden and unexpected destruction upon them. Thus have you a touch of the time when this work began.

Christ Jesus, intending to manifest His kingly office toward His churches more fully than ever yet the sons of men saw, even to the uniting of Jew and Gentile churches in one faith, begins with our English nation (whose former reformation being very imperfect), doth now resolve to cast down their false foundation of prelacy, even in the height of their domineering dignity. And therefore in the year 1628, He stirs up His servants as the heralds of a king to make this proclamation for volunteers, as followeth:

"Oh yes! oh yes! oh yes! All you, the people of Christ that are here oppressed, imprisoned, and scurrilously derided, gather yourselves together, your wives, and little ones and answer to your several names as you shall be shipped for His service in the western world and more especially for planting the united colonies of New England, where you are to attend the service of the king of kings, upon the divulging of this proclamation by his heralds at arms."

Many (although otherwise willing for this service) began to object as followeth:

"Can it possibly be the mind of Christ (who formerly enabled so many soldiers of His to keep their station unto the death here) that now so many brave soldiers, disciplined by Christ Himself, the captain of our salvation, should turn their backs to the disheartening of their fellow soldiers and loss of further opportunity in gaining a great number of subjects to Christ's kingdom?"

Notwithstanding this objection, it was further proclaimed as followeth: "What creature wilt not know that Christ thy king crusheth with a rod of iron the pomp and pride of man; and must He, like man, cast and contrive to take His enemies at advantage? No, of purpose He causeth such instruments to retreat as He hath made strong for Himself, that so, His adversaries glorying in the pride of their power, insulting over the little remnant remaining, Christ causeth them to be cast down suddenly forever. And we find in stories reported, earth's princes have passed their armies at need over seas and deep torrents. Could Caesar so suddenly fetch over fresh forces from Europe to Asia, Pompey to foil?[3] How much more shall Christ, who createth all power, call over this nine hundred league ocean at His pleasure such instruments as He thinks meet to make use of in this place, from whence you are now to depart? But further, that you may not delay the voyage intended, for your full satisfaction know this is the place where the Lord will create a new heaven and a new earth in, new churches and a new commonwealth together. . . .

CHAPTER II

[THE CALL OF CHRIST'S PEOPLE TO NEW ENGLAND]

Attend to your commission, all you that are or shall hereafter be shipped for this service. Ye are with all possible speed to embark yourselves; and as for all such worthies who are hunted after as David was by Saul and his courtiers,[1] you may change your habit and ship you with what secrecy you can, carrying all things

---

[3]Gaius Julius Caesar (100–44 B.C.), Roman statesman, general, and dictator (49–44 B.C.); Gnaeus Pompeius Magnus (106–48 B.C.), Roman statesman and general, member of the First Triumverate, defeated by Caesar in 48 B.C. at Pharsalus in Greece.

[1]Saul (eleventh century B.C.), first king of Israel, succeeded by David (1010?–970? B.C.), second king of Judah and Israel. Saul unsuccessfully sought to kill David, having become jealous of David's military victories and popularity. (1 Samuel 18–20).

most needful for the voyage and service you are to be employed in after your landing. But as soon as you shall be exposed to danger of tempestuous seas, you shall forthwith show whose servants you are by calling on the name of your God, sometimes by extraordinary seeking His pleasing face in times of deep distress and publishing your Master's will and pleasure to all that voyage with you, and that is His mind to have purity in religion preferred above all dignity in the world. Your Christ hath commanded the seas they shall not swallow you, nor pirates imprison your persons or possess your goods. At your landing, see you observe the rule of His word, for neither larger nor stricter commission can He give by any; and therefore at first filling the land whither you are sent, with diligence search out the mind of God both in planting and continuing church and civil government. But be sure they be distinct, yet agreeing and helping the one to the other. Let the matter and form of your churches be such as were in the primitive times (before Antichrist's[2] kingdom prevailed), plainly pointed out by Christ and His apostles in most of their epistles to be neither national nor provincial, but gathered together in covenant of such a number as might ordinarily meet together in one place, and built of such living stones as outwardly appear saints by calling. You are also to ordain elders in every church: make you use of such as Christ hath endowed with the best gifts for that end; their call to office shall be mediate from you, but their authority and commission shall be immediate from Christ revealed in His word—which, if you shall slight, despise, or condemn, He will soon frustrate your call by taking the most able among you to honor with an everlasting crown, whom you neglected to honor on earth double as their due, or He will carry them remote from you to more infant churches. You are not to put them upon anxious cares for their daily bread, for assuredly (although it may now seem strange) you shall be fed in this wilderness whither you are to go with the flower of wheat, and wine shall be plentiful among you (but be sure you abuse it not). These doctrines, delivered from the word of God, embrace. And let not Satan delude you by persuading their learned skill is unnecessary. Soon then will the word of God be slighted as translated by such, and you shall be left bewildered with strange revelations of every fantastic brain, which to prevent here are to be shipped among you many both Godly, judicious, and learned. . . ."

CHAPTER XII

[THE FAREWELL TO ENGLAND]

And now behold the several regiments of these soldiers of Christ, as they are shipped for His service in the western world, part thereof being come to the town and port of Southampton in England, where they were to be shipped, that they might prosecute this design to the full. One ship called the *Eagle*,[1] they wholly purchase, and many more they hire, filling them with the seed of man and beast to sow this yet untilled wilderness withall, making sale of such land as they possess to the great admiration of their friends and acquaintances, who thus expostulate with them: "What, will not the large income of your yearly revenue content you, which in all reason cannot choose but be more advantageous both to you and yours than all that rocky wilderness whither you are going to run the hazard of your life? Have you not here your tables filled with great variety of food, your coffers filled with coin, your houses beautifully built and filled with all rich furniture? Or otherwise, have you not such a gainful trade as none the like in the town

---

[2]The great antagonist expected by the early church in the last days before the Second Coming of Christ. 1 John 2:18: "Little children, it is the last time: and as ye have heard that antichrist shall come, even now are there many antichrists; whereby we know that it is the last time."

[1]John Winthrop's "admiral" or flag-ship, 350 tons, on which Johnson most likely was a passenger. Its name was later changed to *Arbella*, as Johnson recounts in Chapter XIV.

where you live? Are you not enriched daily? Are not your children very well provided for as they come to years? Nay, may you not here as pithily practice the two chief duties of a Christian (if Christ give strength), namely mortification and sanctification, as in any place of the world? What helps can you have there that you must not carry from hence?"

With bold resolvedness, these stout soldiers of Christ reply: "As Death, the King of terror, with all his dreadful attendance, inhumane and barbarous tortures, doubled and trebled by all the infernal furies, has appeared but light and momentany[2] to the soldiers of Christ Jesus, so also the pleasure, profits, and honors of this world, set forth in their most glorious splendor and magnitude by the alluring lady of delight, proffering pleasant embraces, cannot entice with her siren songs such soldiers of Christ, whose arms are elevated by Him many millions above that brave warrier Ulysses."[3]

Now seeing all [that] can be said will but barely set forth the immovable resolutions that Christ continued in these men, pass on and attend with tears, if thou hast any, the following discourse, while these men, women, and children are taking their last farewell of their native country, kindred, friends, and acquaintances while the ships attend them. Many make choice of some solitary place to echo out their bowel[4]-breaking affections in bidding their friends farewell. "Dear friends," says one, "as near as my own soul doth thy love lodge in my breast, with thought of the heart-burning ravishments that thy heavenly speeches have wrought; my melting soul is poured out at present with these words." Both of them had their farther speech strangled from the depth of their inward dolor with breast-breaking sobs, till leaning their heads each on other's shoulders, they let fall the salt-dropping dews of vehement affection, striving to exceed one another, much like the departure of David and Jonathan.[5]

Having a little eased their hearts with the still streams of tears, they recovered speech again. "Ah! My much honored friend, hath Christ given thee so great a charge as to be leader of his people into that far, remote, and vast wilderness? Ay, oh, and alas, thou must die there and never shall I see thy face in the flesh again. Wert thou called to so great a task as to pass the precious ocean and hazard thy person in battle against thousands of malignant enemies there, there were hopes of thy return with triumph; but now, after two, three, or four months spent with daily expectation of swallowing waves and cruel pirates, you are to be landed among barbarous Indians, famous for nothing but cruelty, where you are like to spend your days in a famishing condition for a long space." Scarce had he uttered this, but presently he locks his friend fast in his arms; holding each other thus for some space of time, they weep again.

But as Paul to his beloved flock, the other replies: "What do you weeping and breaking my heart?[6] I am now pressed for the service of our Lord Christ to rebuild the most glorious edifice of Mount Sion in a wilderness, and as John Baptist,

---

[2]Momentary.
[3]Latin name for Odysseus, King of Ithaca and leader of the Greeks during the Trojan War, hero of Homer's epic *Odyssey*.
[4]The interior of a body, or seat of the sympathetic emotions, thus "Heart-breaking."
[5]Jonathan (eleventh century B.C.), eldest son of King Saul of Israel and friend of David (1010?–970? B.C.), second king of Judah and Israel. The account of their friendship, in 1 and 2 Samuel, came to be considered one of the most touching in all Hebrew literature. Saul, jealous of David, sought to kill him and his son because Jonathan remained David's friend. Jonathan helped David escape and the two friends parted: ". . . David arose out of a place toward the south, and fell on his face to the ground, and bowed himself three times: and they kissed one another, and wept one with another, until David exceeded. And Jonathan said to David, Go in peace, forasmuch as we have sworn both of us in the name of the LORD, saying, the LORD be between me and thee, and between my seed and thy seed for ever . . ." (1 Samuel 20:41–2).
[6]Acts 21:13. Johnson quotes sometimes from the Authorized Version (1611) or, as is the case here, from the English Geneva Bible, the work of English exiles first published in 1560. The scholarly translations and marginal commentary, designed for the laity, made it the most popular of Bibles. Calvinistic in emphasis, it was the favored Bible of the Puritans in the Virginia and Plymouth settlements.

I must cry, 'Prepare ye the way of the Lord, make his paths straight,'[7] for behold He is coming again, He is coming to destroy Antichrist and give the whore double to drink the very dregs of His wrath.[8] Then my dear friend, unfold thy hands, for thou and I have much work to do, ay, and all Christian soldiers the world throughout."

Then hand in hand they lead each other to the sandy banks of the brinish ocean, when, clenching their hands fast, they unloose not till enforced to wipe their watery eyes, whose constant streams forced a watery path upon their cheeks, which to hide from the eyes of others, they shun society for a time; but being called by occasion, whose bold backpart none can lay hold on, they thrust in among the throng now ready to take ship, where they beheld the like affections with their own among divers relations. Husbands and wives with mutual consent are now purposed to part for a time 900 leagues asunder, since some providence at present will not suffer them to go together; they resolve their tender affections shall not hinder this work of Christ. The new-married and betrothed men, exempt by the law of God from war, now will not claim their privilege, but being constrained by the love of Christ, lock up their natural affections for a time, till the Lord shall be pleased to give them a meeting in this western world, sweetly mixing it with spiritual love in the meantime. Many fathers now take their young Samuels[9] and give them to this service of Christ all their lives. Brethren, sisters, uncles, nephews, nieces, together with all kindred of blood that binds the bowels of affection in a true lover's knot, can now take their last farewell, each of other, although natural affection will still claim her right and manifest herself to be in the body by looking out at the windows in a mournful manner.

Among this company, thus disposed, doth many reverend and godly pastors of Christ present themselves, some in a seaman's habit,[10] and, their scattered sheep coming as a poor convoy, loftily take their leave of them as followeth: "What doleful days are these, when the best choice our orthodox ministers can make is to take up a perpetual banishment from their native soil, together with their wives and children; we their poor sheep they may not feed, but by stoledred[11] should they abide here. Lord Christ, here they are at thy command, they go; this is the door thou hast opened upon our earnest request, and we hope it shall never be shut. For England's sake, they are going from England to pray without ceasing for England. O England! Thou shalt find New England prayers prevailing with their God for thee, but now, woe, alas, what great hardship must these our endeared pastors endure for a long season."

With these words they lift[ed] up their voices and wept, adding many drops of salt liquor to the ebbing ocean. Then shaking hands, they bid adieu with much cordial affection to all their brethren and sisters in Christ, yet now the scorn and derision of those times, and for this their great enterprise counted as so many cracked brains. But Christ will make all the earth know the wisdom he hath endued them with, shall overtop all the human policy in the world, as the sequel we hope will show. Thus much shall suffice in general to speak of their people's farewell they took from time to time of their country and friends.

---

[7]Luke 3:4.

[8]Revelation 18:6, Geneva Bible: "Reward her [the whore of Babylon] even as she hath rewarded you, and give her double according to her works: & in the cup that she hath filled to you, fill her the double." The marginal commentary identifies the whore of Babylon as "the Antichrist, that is, the Pope with ye whole bodie of his filthie creatures, as is expounded" *The Geneva Bible: A Facsimile of the 1560 Edition* (1969), p. 120.

[9]Samuel (eleventh century B.C.), Hebrew judge, priest, prophet, and kingmaker. His mother Hannah, long barren, prayed to the Lord for a son, promising to "give him unto the Lord all the days of his life." When he was weaned, she gave him to the priest Eli to be brought up at the temple of Shiloh. God then called the young Samuel to be His prophet (1 Samuel 1–3).

[10]The nonconforming ministers were disguised as seamen in order to escape.

[11]Stealth.

CHAPTER XIV

[GOD'S PROVIDENCE IN TRANSPORTING HIS PEOPLE SAFELY]

And now [that] you have had a short survey of the charges of their New England voyages,[1] see their progress. Being safe aboard, weighing anchor and hoisting sail, they betook them to the protection of the Lord on the wide ocean. No sooner were they dispersed by reason of the wideness of the sea, but the *Arabella* (for so they called the *Eagle,* which the company purchased in honor of the Lady Arabella, wife to that godly Esquire, Izack Johnson)[2] espied four ships, as they supposed, in pursuit of them, their suspicion being the more augmented by reason of a report (when they lay in harbor) of four Dunkirk men-of-war,[3] who were said to lie waiting for their coming forth. At this fight, they make preparation, according to their present condition, comforting one another in the sweet mercies of Christ. The weaker sex betook them to the ship's hold, but the men on decks wait in a readiness for the enemy's approach, at whose courage, many of the seamen wonder, not knowing under whose command these their passengers were, even He who makes all His soldiers bold as lions.

Yet was He not minded to make trial of His people's valiancy in fight at this time, for the ships coming up with them proved to be their own countrymen and friends, at which they greatly rejoiced, seeing the good hand of their God was upon them. And [they] are further strengthened in faith to rely on Christ for the future time against all leaks, storms, rocks, sands, and all other wants a long sea voyage procures, sustaining them with all meekness and patience, yet sensible of the Lord's frowns, humbling their souls before Him, and also rejoicing in His deliverances in taking the cup of salvation, and paying the tribute of thankfulness to the most High, whose provident hand was diversely directed toward them purposely to point out the great hardships they must undergo in this their Christian warfare. And withall to tell them, although their difficulties were many and mournful, yet their victories should be much more glorious and joyful, eminently eyed of the whole world.

But now keeping their course so near as the winds will suffer them, the billows begin to grow lofty and raging and suddenly bringing them into the vale of death, covering them with the formidable floods, and dashing their bodies from side to side, hurling their unfixed goods from place to place. At these unwonted works many of these people, amazed, find such opposition in nature that her principles grow feeble and cannot digest her food, loathing all manner of meat, so that the vital parts are hindered from cooperating with the soul in spiritual duties, insomuch that both men, women, and children are in a helpless condition for present. And now is the time if ever of recounting this service they have and are about to undertake for Christ.

But He, who is very sensible of His people's infirmities, rebukes the winds and seas for their sakes, and then the reverend and godly among them begin to exhort them in the name of the Lord, and from the Lord, being fitted with such words as much encourages the work they are going about. Many of their horses and other cattle are cast overboard by the way, to the great disheartening of some, but Christ knew well how far His people's hearts would be taken off the main work with these things. And therefore, although He be very tender in providing outward

---

[1] In the previous chapter Johnson writes that the passage of people cost 95,000 pounds; the swine, goats, sheep, neat [cattle] and horse cost twelve thousand to transport, besides the price they could cost; enough food until they could harvest, 45,000 pounds; nails, glass, iron work for building, 18,000; arms, powder, bullet, match, and artillery, 22,000, the sum being 192,000 pounds.
[2] Isaac Johnson, one of the richest emigrants, and his wife

Arbella or Lady Arabella sailed to New England in 1630; both died soon after landing.
[3] Dunkirk or Dunkerque, on the northern coast of France, was a Spanish possession. From its port warships (men-of-war) and pirates attacked English commerce in the Channel in times of peace or war; England was at war with Spain until November 1630.

necessaries for His, yet rather than this great work (He intends) should be hindered, their tables shall be spread but thinly in this wilderness for a time.

After the Lord had exercised them thus several ways, He sent diseases to visit their ships, that the desert land they were now drawing near unto might not be deserted by them at first entrance, which sure it would have been by many, had not the Lord prevented by a troublesome passage.

At forty day's end or thereabout, they cast to sound the sea's depth and find them sixty fathom, by which they deem the banks of Newfoundland are near, where they, being provided with cod line and hook, haul up some store of fish to their no small refreshing. And within some space of time after, they approach the coast of New England, where they are again provided with mackerel and that which was their greater rejoicing; they discover land, at sight thereof they blessed the Lord. . . .

1650–51?   *1654*

BELIEVING: RELIGIOUS DISCOURSE
AND DEBATE

ROGER WILLIAMS   INCREASE MATHER
NATHANIEL WARD   JOHN WISE
THOMAS SHEPARD

The Puritan period may be characterized as an age of believing, but it would be wrong to assume that the believers were all alike in their beliefs. First the Puritans dissented from the Church of England, came to America, and then began to disagree with each other. Much of their intellectual energy was spent in religious discussion and debate. Roger Williams, Nathaniel Ward, Thomas Shepard, Increase Mather, and John Wise are all remembered now for books written on religious issues, but their works touch as well on still unresolved philosophical or political issues. Nathaniel Ward is slashingly witty in his astonishing damnation of religious tolerance; Thomas Shepard is appealingly gentle in his patient explanation of the often puzzling "Covenant of Grace"; and Increase Mather is self-assuredly unpliant in proclaiming determinism and free choice compatible for the errant sinner. Although we sometimes think of the Puritans as committed to the inseparability of church and state and to the rigid rule of religious authority, we find Roger Williams arguing eloquently for liberty of conscience and separation of church and state. And we discover John Wise arguing passionately for the superiority of democracy over authoritarian forms of government, for church as well as state. Thus the Puritanism that remains as residue in American thought and institutions may be found as much in its clashes and contradictions as in its often simplified or "purified" form.

ROGER WILLIAMS
(*c.* 1603–1683)

The Separatists and Puritans, themselves the victims of persecution for their beliefs, have a reputation for intolerance when confronting doctrines in conflict with their own. Roger Williams is the best example of a Separatist victimized by his fellow Puritans for his heretical views. In response, he provided America with some of the most passionate defenses for the separation of church and state; and he argued eloquently for tolerance and against persecution for religious differences.

A Londoner educated for the law at Cambridge University, Williams turned to the ministry and to Puritanism. He came to New England in 1631 and became a minister at Salem, where he was soon in conflict with the church hierarchy of Massachusetts. He decried the treatment of Indians as inferior "savages" and argued that the royal charter had granted lands to the colonists that belonged rightfully to the Indians. Such views led to his banishment, and he set out on his journey of exile in a "bitter winter season, not knowing what bread or bed did mean." In his suffering, he was befriended by the Indians. Finally he made his way in 1636 to Rhode Island, where he founded Providence.

Many of the colonists at Salem followed Williams to Providence, where the principles Williams espoused were put into practice. Church and state were separated, and the government was democratic, based on equality and deriving authority from the governed. Such liberal practices frightened other colonies, especially as Providence welcomed dissenters and free-thinkers from all over New England. In response to this hostility, Williams decided to go to England to obtain a charter, thus providing a legal basis for his settlement.

On the way to England, he began to write his first book, *A Key into the Language of America*. Although designed to be a dictionary and phrase book for the Indian languages Williams had learned, it turned out to be in addition (when published in 1643) an eccentric book of philosophic commentary, with moral observations expressed at every turn. In describing Indian ways of eating and entertaining, Williams wrote: "It is a strange truth that a man shall generally find more free entertainment and refreshing amongst these barbarians, than amongst thousands that call themselves Christians."

Williams arrived in London at a time of turmoil and civil war. While there, a six-year-old letter by John Cotton, written in justification of the persecution and banishment of Williams, was published. Williams answered Cotton's charges in a pamphlet entitled *Mr. Cotton's Letter Lately Printed, Examined, and Answered* (1644), in which he wrote: "Persecutors of men's bodies seldom or never do these men's souls good." Williams almost immediately entered another controversy, arguing passionately for separation of church and state in *Queries of Highest Consideration* (1644), a pamphlet addressed to the British parliament, which was then debating the nature of the state religion to be established. Williams wrote: ". . . we ask, whether in the constitution of a national church it can possibly be framed without a racking and tormenting of the souls as well as the bodies of persons. . . ."

Fired up by the ideas about "soul-liberty" he had clarified for himself and others in these works, Williams went on in 1644 to write his most celebrated work, *The Bloody Tenet of Persecution for Cause of Conscience*. In it he argued for

total freedom for "the most paganish, Jewish, Turkish or anti-Christian consciences and worships" for "all men in all nations and countries."

When Williams returned to Rhode Island in 1644, he became embroiled in
a struggle for control of Providence. He finally overcame his rivals, but he
spent the remainder of his life engaged in successive controversies. John Cotton attacked his *Bloody Tenet of Persecution* with *The Bloody Tenet Washed and
Made White in the Blood of the Lamb* (1647). Williams answered with *The Bloody
Tenet yet More Bloody, by Mr. Cotton's Endeavor to Wash it White in the Blood of the
Lamb* (1652).

Williams was a stubborn and often rash man. He could appear dogmatic
and arrogant in argument, unyielding and rigid in debate. At the same time
he could be warm and generous. His was a prickly personality, in the American tradition of radical dissent. His obsessive ideas about spiritual and intellectual freedom became embedded in America's founding documents and are
now an integral part of the American ideal. The fact that Williams was a Puritan holding such radical beliefs must undermine stereotypical notions of
what Puritanism was and how it contributed to the shape of the American
character.

ADDITIONAL READING

The Complete Writings of Roger Williams, 7 vols., a reprint of the 6 volume 1866–74 edition
cited below together with a seventh volume edited by Perry Miller, 1963.

Moses Coit Tyler, *A History of American Literature, 1607–1765*, 1878; Vernon L. Par-
rington, "Roger Williams, Seeker," *Main Currents in American Thought*, 1927–30; Perry
Miller, *Roger Williams: His Contribution to the American Tradition*, 1953; Ola E. Winslow, *Master
Roger Williams: A Biography*, 1957; Edmund Morgan, *Roger Williams, The Church and the State*,
1967; Henry Chupack, *Roger Williams*, 1969; John Garett, *Roger Williams: Witness Beyond
Christendom, 1603–1683*, 1970; Wallace Coyle, ed., *Roger Williams*, 1977; W. Clark Gilpin,
The Millenarian Piety of Roger Williams, 1979.

TEXTS

The Writings of Roger Williams, 6 vols., eds. J. H. Trumbull, Samuel L. Caldwell, John Russell Bartlett, 1866–74; rpt. 1963. Typography, punctuation, spelling, and usage have been
changed to conform with contemporary English and modern printing practices.

from A Key into the Language of America[1]

Of Eating and Entertainment

It is a strange truth that a man shall generally find more free entertainment
and refreshing amongst these barbarians, than amongst thousands that call themselves Christians.

---

[1]Although a dictionary of the Narragansett Indian language, Williams's little book is much more poetic and philosophic than most dictionaries, as his full title proclaims: "A
Key into the Language of America: Or, An help to the
Language of the Natives in that part of America, called
New-England. Together, with brief Observations of the
Customs, Manners and Worships, etc. of the aforesaid Natives, in Peace and War, in Life and Death. On all which
are added Spiritual Observations, General and Particular
by the Author, of chief and special use (upon all occasions)
to all the English Inhabiting those parts; yet pleasant and
profitable to the view of all men."

More particular:

> Coarse bread and water's most their fare,
> O England's diet fine;
> Thy cup run's o'er with plenteous store
> Of wholesome beer and wine.
>
> Sometimes God gives them fish or flesh,   5
> Yet they're content without;
> And what comes in, they part to friends
> And strangers round about.
>
> God's providence is rich to His,
> Let none distrustful be;   10
> In wilderness, in great distress,
> These ravens have fed me.

Of the Family Business

The sociableness of the nature of man appears in the wildest of them, who love society, families, cohabitation, and consocation of houses and towns together.

More particular:

> How busy are the sons of men?
> How full their heads and hands?
> What noise and tumults in our own,
> And eke[2] in pagan lands?
>
> Yet I have found less noise, more peace   5
> In wild America,
> Where women quickly build the house,
> And quickly move away.[3]
>
> English and Indians busy are,
> In parts of their abode: 10
> Yet both stand idle, till God's call
> Set them to work for God.

Of Their Persons and Parts of Body

Natures knows no difference between Europe[ans] and Americans in blood, birth, bodies, etc., God having of one blood made all mankind, Acts 17, and all by nature being children of wrath, Ephesians 2.

More particular:

> Boast not proud English, of thy birth and blood,
> Thy brother Indian is by birth as good.
> Of one blood God made him, and thee and all,
> As wise, as fair, as strong, as personal.

---

[2]Also.
[3]The migratory Indians changed living areas frequently, working quickly in putting up their "houses" and as swiftly carting them away. The women had primary responsibility for the living quarters.

By nature wrath's his portion, thine no more,   5
　　Till grace his soul and thine in Christ restore.
Make sure thy second birth, else thou shalt see,
　　Heaven ope to Indians wild, but shut to thee.

Of the Time of the Day

　　The sun and the moon, in the observation of all the sons of men, even the wildest, are the great directors of the day and night; as it pleased God to appoint in the first creation.

More particular:

The Indians find the sun so sweet,
　　He is a God they say;
Giving them light, and heat, and fruit,
　　And guidance all the day.

They have no help of clock or watch!   5
　　And sun they overprize.
Having those artificial helps, the sun
　　We unthankfully despise.
God is a sun and shield, a thousand times more bright;
　　Indians, or English, though they see.   10
　　　　Yet how few prize His light?

Of the Heavenly Bodies

　　The wildest sons of men hear the preaching of the heavens, the sun, moon, and stars, yet not seeking after God the Maker are justly condemned, though they never have nor despise other preaching, as the civilized world hath done.

More particular:

When sun doth rise the stars do set,
　　Yet there's no need of light,
God shines a sun most glorious,
　　When creatures all are night.

The very Indian boys can give,   5
　　To many stars their name,
And know their course and therein do
　　Excel the English tame.

English and Indians none enquire,
　　Whose hand these candles hold;   10
Who gives these stars their names Himself
　　More bright ten thousand fold.

Of Their Nakedness and Clothing

How deep are the purposes and counsels of God? What should be the reason of this mighty difference of one man's children that all the sons of men on this side[4] the way (in Europe, Asia, and Africa) should have such plenteous clothing for body, for soul! and the rest of Adam's sons and daughters on the other side, or America (some think as big as the other three) should neither have nor desire clothing for their naked souls, or bodies.

More particular:

O what a tyrant's custom long,
  How do men make a tush,[5]
At what's in use, though ne'er so foul,
  Without once shame or blush?

Many thousand proper men and women,   5
  I have seen met in one place:
Almost all naked, yet not one,
  Thought want of clothes disgrace.

Israel was naked, wearing clothes!
  The best clad Englishman,   10
Not clothed with Christ, more naked is
  Than naked Indian.

Of Their Government and Justice

The wildest of the sons of men have ever found a necessity (for preservation of themselves, their families and properties) to cast themselves into some mold or form of government.

More particular:

Adulteries, murders, robberies, thefts,
  Wild Indians punish these!
And hold the scales of justice so,
  That no man farthing[6] leese.[7]

When Indians hear the horrid filths,   5
  Of Irish, English men,
The horrid oaths and murders late,
  Thus say these Indians then,

"We wear no clothes, have many gods,
  And yet our sins are less: 10
You are barbarians, pagans wild,
  Your land's the wilderness."

---

[4]Since Williams published his book in London, "this side" refers to Europe.
[5]To make a tush: to scorn, to pooh-pooh.
[6]English coin worth one-fourth of a penny.
[7]Loses.

Of Their Marriage

God hath planted in the hearts of the wildest of the sons of men an high and honorable esteem of the marriage bed, insomuch that they universally submit unto it, and hold the violation of that bed abominable, and accordingly reap the fruit thereof in the abundant increase of posterity.

More particular:

When Indians hear that some there are,
    (That men the Papists call)
Forbidding marriage bed and yet,
    To thousand whoredomes fall:

They ask if such do go in clothes,   5
    And whether God they know?
And when they hear they're richly clad,
    Know God, yet practice so:

"No, sure, they're beasts, not men," say they,
    "Men's shame and foul disgrace,   10
Or men have mixed with beasts and so,
    Brought forth that monstrous race."

1643

from The Bloody Tenet of Persecution for Cause of Conscience

PREFACE

[Twelve Arguments for Religious Tolerance]

First, that the blood of so many hundred thousand souls of Protestants and Papists, spilt in the wars of present and former ages, for their respective consciences, is not required nor accepted by Jesus Christ the Prince of Peace.

Secondly, pregnant scriptures and arguments are throughout the work proposed against the doctrine of persecution for cause of conscience.

Thirdly, satisfactory answers are given to scriptures, and objections produced by Mr. Calvin, Beza, Mr. Cotton,[1] and the ministers of the New English churches and others former and later, tending to prove the doctrine of persecution for cause of conscience.

Fourthly, the doctrine of persecution for cause of conscience is proved guilty of all the blood of the souls crying for vengeance under the altar.[2]

Fifthly, all civil states with their officers of justice in their respective constitutions and administrations are proved essentially civil, and therefore not judges, governors, or defenders of the spiritual or Christian state and worship.

Sixthly, it is the will and command of God that (since the coming of his Son the

---

[1]John Calvin (1509–1564) and Theodore Beza (or Bèze) (1519–1605) were French Protestant theologians. Calvin went to Geneva when banished from Paris; Bèze converted to Protestantism in Geneva, and, when Calvin died, succeeded him as leader of the Reformation movement centered in Geneva. John Cotton (1584–1652), by his attacks on Williams, inspired Williams to write *The Bloody Tenet* (see Introduction).
[2]Revelation 6:9: "I saw under the altar the souls of them that were slain for the word of God, and for the testimony which they held."

Lord Jesus) a permission of the most paganish, Jewish, Turkish, or anti-Christian consciences and worships be granted to all men in all nations and countries, and that they are only to be fought against with that sword which is only (in soul matters) able to conquer, to wit, the sword of God's spirit, the word of God.

Seventhly, the state of the land of Israel, the kings and people thereof in peace and war, is proved figurative and ceremonial, and no pattern nor precedent for any kingdom or civil state in the world to follow.

Eighthly, God requireth not an uniformity of religion to be enacted and enforced in any civil state, which enforced uniformity (sooner or later) is the greatest occasion of civil war, ravishing of conscience, persecution of Christ Jesus in his servants, and of the hypocrisy and destruction of millions of souls.

Ninthly, in holding an enforced uniformity of religion in a civil state, we must necessarily disclaim our desires and hopes of the Jews' conversion to Christ.

Tenthly, an enforced uniformity of religion throughout a nation or civil state, confounds[3] the civil and religious, denies the principles of Christianity and civility and that Jesus Christ is come in the flesh.

Eleventhly, the permission[4] of other consciences and worships than a state professeth, only can (according to God) procure a firm and lasting peace (good assurance being taken according to the wisdom of the civil state for uniformity of civil obedience from all sorts).

Twelfthly, lastly, true civility and Christianity may both flourish in a state or kingdom, notwithstanding the permission of divers and contrary consciences, either of Jew or gentile.

CHAPTER II

[AGAINST PERSECUTION FOR RELIGIOUS BELIEF]

[Peace]: Dear truth, I have two sad complaints:

First, the most sober of thy witnesses, that dare to plead thy cause, how are they charged to be mine enemies, contentious, turbulent, seditious?

Secondly, thine enemies, though they speak and rail against thee, though they outragiously pursue, imprison, banish, kill thy faithful witnesses, yet how is all vermillioned o'er[1] for justice 'gainst the heretics? Yea, if they kindle coals, and blow the flames of devouring wars, that leave neither spiritual nor civil state, but burns up branch and root, yet how do all pretend an holy war? He that kills, and he that's killed, they both cry out. It is for God, and for their conscience.

'Tis true, nor one nor other seldom dare to plead the mighty Prince Christ Jesus for their author, yet both (both Protestant and Papist) pretend they have spoken with Moses and the prophets, who all, say they (before Christ came), allowed such holy persecutions, holy wars against the enemies of holy church.

Truth. Dear Peace (to ease thy first complaint) 'tis true, thy dearest sons, most like their mother, peace-keeping, peace-making sons of God, have borne and still must bear the blurs[2] of troublers of Israel, and turners of the world upside down. And 'tis true again, what Solomon once spoke: "The beginning of strife is as when one letteth out water; therefore," saith he, "leave off contention before it be meddled with."[3] This caveat should keep the banks and sluices firm and strong, [so] that strife, like a breach of waters, break not in upon the sons of men.

Yet strife must be distinguished: it is necessary or unnecessary, godly or ungodly, Christian or unChristian, etc.

It is unnecessary, unlawful, dishonorable, ungodly, unChristian, in most cases

---

[3]Fails to discern differences between.
[4]Toleration.
[1]Painted a bright red; made rosy or pretty.

[2]Smears, stains.
[3]Proverbs 17:14.

in the world, for there is a possibility of keeping sweet peace in most cases, and if it be possible, it is the express command of God that peace be kept, Rom. 13.[4]

Again, it is necessary, honorable, godly, etc. with civil and earthly weapons to defend the innocent, and to rescue the oppressed from the violent paws and jaws of oppressing persecuting Nimrods, Psal. 73. Job 29.[5]

It is as necessary, yea more honorable, godly, and Christian, to fight the fight of faith, with religious and spiritual artillery, and to contend earnestly for the faith of Jesus, once delivered to the saints against all opposers, and the gates of earth and hell, men or devils, yea against Paul himself, or an angel from heaven, if he bring any other faith or doctrine, Jude vers. 4. Gal. 1. 8.[6]

Peace. With the clashing of such arms[7] am I never wakened. Speak once again (dear Truth) to my second complaint of bloody persecution, and devouring wars, marching under the colors of upright justice, and holy zeal, etc.

Truth. Mine ears have long been filled with a threefold doleful outcry.

First, of one hundred forty four thousand virgins[8] (Rev. 14.) forced and ravished by emperors, kings, and governors to their beds of worship and religion, set up (like Absaloms[9]) on high in their several states and countries.

Secondly, the cry of those precious souls under the altar (Rev. 6) the souls of such as have been persecuted and slain for the testimony and witness of Jesus, whose blood hath been spilt like water upon the earth, and that because they have held fast the truth and witness of Jesus, against the worship of the states and times, compelling to an uniformity of state religion.

These cries of murdered virgins who can sit still and hear? Who can but run with zeal inflamed to prevent the deflowering of chaste souls, and spilling of the blood of the innocent? Humanity stirs up and prompts the sons of men to draw material swords for a virgin's chastity and life, against a ravishing murderer? And piety and Christianity must needs awaken the sons of God to draw the spiritual sword (the Word of God) to preserve the chastity and life of spiritual virgins, who abhor the spiritual defilements of false worship, Rev. 14.

Thirdly, the cry of the whole earth, made drunk with the blood of its inhabitants, slaughtering each other in their blinded zeal, for conscience, for religion, against the Catholics, against the Lutherans, etc.

What fearful cries within these twenty years of hundred thousands men, women, children, fathers, mothers, husbands, wives, brethren, sisters, old and young, high and low, plundered, ravished, slaughtered, murdered, famished? And hence these cries, that men fling away the spiritual sword and spiritual artillery (in spiritual and religious causes) and rather trust for the suppressing of each other's God, conscience, and religion (as they suppose) to an arm of flesh, and sword of steel?

Truth. Sweet Peace, what hast thou there?

Peace. Arguments against persecution for cause of conscience.

Truth. And what there?

---

[4]Romans 13:1,10: "Let every soul be subject unto the higher powers. For there is no power but of God: the powers that be are ordained of God. . . . Love worketh no ill to his neighbor: therefore love is the fulfilling of the law."
[5]Tyrants. Nimrod, son of Cush, great-grandson of Noah, "a mighty hunter before the Lord" (Genesis 10:9), considered the first empire builder in history, was seen by the Puritans as "a cruel oppressor" (Geneva Bible). Psalm 73:27: "For, lo, they that are far from Thee shall perish: Thou hast destroyed all them that go a whoring from Thee." Job 29:12, 17: " . . . I delivered the poor that cried, and the fatherless, and him that had none to help him. . . . And I brake the jaws of the wicked, and plucked the spoil out of his teeth."

[6]Jude 1:4: "For there are certain men crept in unawares, who were before of old ordained to this condemnation, ungodly men, turning the grace of our God into lasciviousness, and denying the only Lord God, and our Lord Jesus Christ." Galatians 1:8: "But though we [Paul], or an angel from heaven, preach any other gospel unto you than that which we have preached unto you, let him be accursed."
[7]That is, "spiritual artillery" rather than real guns; the weaponry of the Bible and faith, not rifles or clubs.
[8]Souls of the redeemed.
[9]Old Testament: Absalom was the son of David who plotted to overthrow his father and become king, but was himself killed in battle. Thus, a usurper or one who attempts to take control by force.

Peace. An answer to such arguments, contrarily maintaining such persecution for cause of conscience.

Truth. These arguments against such persecution, and the answer pleading for it, written (as love hopes) from godly intentions, hearts, and hands, yet in a marvelous different style and manner. The arguments against persecution in milk, the answer for it (as I may say) in blood.

The author of these arguments (against persecution) (as I have been informed) being committed by some then in power, close prisoner to Newgate,[10] for the witness of some truths of Jesus,[11] and having not the use of pen and ink, wrote these arguments in milk, on sheets of paper, brought to him by the woman his keeper from a friend in London, as the stopples[12] of his milk bottle.

On such paper written with milk nothing will appear, but the way of reading it by fire being known to this friend who received the papers, he transcribed and kept together the papers, although the author himself could not correct, nor view what himself had written.

It was in milk, tending to soul nourishment, even for babes and sucklings in Christ.

It was in milk, spiritually white, pure and innocent, like those white horses of the word of truth and meekness, and the white linen or armor of righteousness, in the army of Jesus, Rev. 6. & 19.[13]

It was in milk, soft, meek, peaceable and gentle, tending both to the peace of souls, and the peace of states and kingdoms.

Peace. The answer (though I hope out of milky pure intentions) is returned in blood;[14] bloody and slaughterous conclusions; bloody to the souls of all men, forced to the religion and worship which every civil state or commonweal agrees on, and compels all subjects to in a dissembled uniformity.

Bloody to the bodies, first of the holy witnesses of Christ Jesus, who testify against such invented worships.

Secondly, of the nations and peoples slaughtering each other for their several respective religions and consciences.

1643–44   *1644*

Letter to the Town of Providence[1]
[Defining Liberty of Conscience]

[Providence, January 1655] That ever I should speak or write a tittle, that tends to such an infinite liberty of conscience, is a mistake, and which I have ever disclaimed and abhorred. To prevent such mistakes, I shall at present only propose this case: There goes many a ship to sea, with many hundred souls in one ship, whose weal and woe in common, and is a true picture of a commonwealth, or a human combination or society. It hath fallen out sometimes, that both Papists

[10]Notorious London prison.
[11]Williams seems here to suggest that his own excommunication and banishment for his espousing "truths of Jesus" constituted a kind of imprisonment, and his writings against "persecution for cause of conscience" were produced under the handicaps, as it were, of one imprisoned.
[12]Stoppers.
[13]Revelation 6:2: "And I saw, and behold a white horse: and he that sat on him had a bow; and a crown was given unto him: and he went forth conquering, and to conquer." Revelation 19:11: "And I saw heaven opened, and behold a

white horse; and he that sat upon him was called faithful and true, and in righteousness he doth judge and make war."
[14]Williams's principal opponent, John Cotton, defended punishment and persecution of "heretics"—those who dissented from the established doctrines and dogma.
[1]Some residents of Providence asserted that those who broke civil laws for cause of conscience should not be punished. Williams saw this position as incompatible with his own and wrote this letter to set forth clearly his views on liberty of conscience and the limits of freedom.

and Protestants, Jews and Turks, may be embarked in one ship; upon which suppposal I affirm, that all the liberty of conscience, that ever I pleaded for, turns upon these two hinges—that none of the Papists, Protestants, Jews, or Turks be forced to come to the ship's prayers or worship, nor compelled from their own particular prayers or worship, if they practice any. I further add, that I never denied, that notwithstanding this liberty, the commander of this ship ought to command the ship's course, yea, and also command that justice, peace, and sobriety be kept and practiced, both among the seamen and all the passengers. If any of the seamen refuse to perform their services, or passengers to pay their freight; if any refuse to help, in person or purse, towards the common charges or defence; if any refuse to obey the common laws and orders of the ship, concerning their common peace or preservation; if any shall mutiny and rise up against their commanders and officers; if any should preach or write that there ought to be no commanders or officers, because all are equal in Christ, therefore no masters nor officers, no laws nor orders, nor corrections nor punishments; —I say, I never denied, but in such cases, whatever is pretended, the commander or commanders may judge, resist, compel, and punish such transgressors, according to their deserts and merits. This if seriously and honestly minded, may, if it so please the Father of lights, let in some light to such as willingly shut not their eyes.

I remain studious of your common peace and liberty.

Roger Williams

NATHANIEL WARD
(*c.* 1578–1652)

It is rare to find wit in Puritan writings, but the author of *The Simple Cobbler of Aggawam* is something of a humorist. He is quoted as saying once: "I have two comforts to live upon: the one is, in the perfections of Christ: the other is in the imperfections of all Christians." He often indulged in a weakness for writing verses, as in:

The world is full of care, much like unto a bubble,
Women and care, and care and women, and women and care and trouble.

Ward was born in Haverhill, Essex, into a minister's family. He studied law, but decided to enter the ministry and was appointed to the living at Stondon Massey, Essex. He was excommunicated in 1633 by Bishop William Laud for his Puritan views, and found his way to a frontier village of Massachusetts that shortly changed its Indian name of Aggawam to Ipswich. There he became minister, but because of ill health, retired in 1636. In 1641 he helped draw up the first written laws of Massachusetts, "The Body of Liberties"; it was based on common law, and succeeded in establishing a government of laws, not of men.

But Ward's most enduring work, written in 1645–46, is *The Simple Cobbler of Aggawam* (1647). He published it under the pseudonym of Theodore de La Guard; Theodore is Greek for Nathaniel, Guard is French for Ward. As the cobbler, Ward argued against religious "toleration" with greater wit (if less passion) than Roger Williams had argued against religious intolerance in *The Bloody Tenet of Persecution for Cause of Conscience* (1644). Ward was no cobbler, of course, but his title page introduced the language play and punning he used throughout his book: "The Simple Cobbler of Aggawam in America/ Willing to help mend his native country, lamentably tattered, both in the upper-leather and sole, with all the honest stitches he can take./And as willing never to be paid for his work, by old English wonted pay./It is his trade to patch all year long, gratis. Therefore I pray gentlemen keep your purses."

In his love of oddities and quirks of language, Ward sometimes stretched his prose beyond bearable limits, as for example: "If the whole conclave of hell can so compromise exadverse and diametrical contradictions as to compolitize such a multimontrous maufrey of heteroclites and quicquidlibets quietly, I trust I may say with all humble reverence, they can do more than the senate of heaven." Moses Coit Tyler quotes this passage and remarks: ". . . he will be a bold man who can affirm at sight in what language this sentence is written, or what it means."

Ward returned to England in 1647, and became involved in the religious and political struggles of the time, preaching a controversial sermon defending the king before the then anti-royal House of Commons. He spent his remaining years as a minister only a few miles from his former place at Stondon Massey.

ADDITIONAL READING

Moses Coit Tyler, *A History of American Literature, 1607–1765,* 1878; Vernon L. Parrington, "Nathaniel Ward, Elizabethan Puritan," *Main Currents in American Thought,* 1927–30; Samuel Eliot Morison, "Nathaniel Ward, Lawmaker and Wit," *Builders of the Bay Colony,* 1930.

TEXT

The Simple Cobbler of Aggawam in America, ed. P. M. Zall, 1969. Footnotes from this edition are indicated by the editor's name followed by the note enclosed in quotation marks. Typography, punctuation, spelling, and usage have been changed to conform with contemporary English and modern printing practices.

from The Simple Cobbler of Aggawam

[Satan Fishing in Roiled Waters]

Either I am in an apoplexy, or that man is in a lethargy who doth not now sensibly feel God shaking the heavens over his head and the earth underneath his feet; the heavens so, as the sun begins to turn into darkness, the moon into blood, the stars to fall down to the ground; so that little light of comfort or counsel is left to the sons of men; the earth so, as the foundations are failing, the righteous scarce know where to find rest, the inhabitants stagger like drunken men. It is in a manner dissolved both in religions and relations; and no marvel, for they have defiled it by transgressing the laws, changing the ordinances, and breaking the everlasting covenant. The truths of God are the pillars of the world whereon states and churches may stand quiet if they will; if they will not, He can easily shake them off into delusions and distractions enough.

Satan is now in his passions, he feels his passions approaching, he loves to fish in roiled[1] waters. Though that dragon cannot sting the vitals of the elect mortally, yet that Beelzebub[2] can fly-blow[3] their intellectuals miserably. The finer religion grows, the finer he spins his cobwebs; he will hold pace with Christ so long as his wits will serve him. He sees himself beaten out of gross idolatries, heresies, ceremonies, where the light breaks forth with power. He will, therefore, bestir him to prevaricate evangelical truths and ordinances, that if they will needs be walking yet they shall *laborare varicibus*[4] and not keep their path, he will put them out of time and place, assassinating for his engineers, men of Paracelsian[5] parts, well complexioned for honesty; for such are fittest to mountebank[6] his chemistry into sick churches and weak judgments.

Nor shall he need to stretch his strength overmuch in this work. Too many men, having not laid their foundations sure nor ballasted their spirits deep with humility and fear, are pressed enough of themselves to evaporate their own apprehensions. Those that are acquainted with story[7] know it has ever been so in new editions of churches: such as are least able are most busy to pudder[8] in the rubbish and to raise dust in the eyes of more steady repairers. Civil commotions make room for uncivil practices; religious mutations, for irreligious opinions; change of air discovers corrupt bodies; reformation of religion, unsound minds. He that has any well-faced fancy in his crown and does not vent it now, fears the pride of his own heart will dub him dunce forever. Such a one will trouble the whole Israel of God with his most untimely births, though he makes the bones of his vanity stick up, to the view and grief of all that are godly wise. The devil desires no better sport than to see light heads handle their heels and fetch their careers in a time when the roof of liberty stands open.

[No Toleration for Adversaries of God's Truth]

The next perplexed question with pious and ponderous men will be: What should be done for the healing of these comfortless exulcerations?[1] I am the unablest adviser of a thousand, the unworthiest of ten thousand; yet I hope I may presume to assert what follows without just offense.

First, such as have given or taken any unfriendly reports of us New English should do well to recollect themselves. We have been reputed a colluvies[2] of wild opinionists, swarmed into a remote wilderness to find elbow room for our fanatic doctrines and practices. I trust our diligence past and constant sedulity[3] against such persons and courses will plead better things for us. I dare take upon me to be the herald of New England so far as to proclaim to the world, in the name of our colony, that all Familists, Antinomians, Anabaptists,[4] and other enthusiasts shall have free liberty to keep away from us; and such as will come to be gone as fast as they can, the sooner the better.

Secondly, I dare aver that God does nowhere in His word tolerate Christian states to give toleration to such adversaries of His truth, if they have power in their hands to suppress them.

Here is lately brought us an extract of a Magna Carta,[5] so called, compiled be-

---

[1] Turbulent, agitated.
[2] Devil, from Hebrew "Lord of flies."
[3] Corrupt, contaminate.
[4] Zall: "Waste time with trifles."
[5] Like Paracelsus. Philippus Aureolus Paracelsus (c. 1493–1541) was an ingenious alchemist and physician who wrote medical and occult works.
[6] Promote through trickery or charlatanry.
[7] History.
[8] To go poking about.
[1] Ulcerations, sores.

[2] Rabble.
[3] Zealousness.
[4] *Familists* belonged to the Family of Love and believed that the chief element of religion was love; *Antinomians* believed the covenant of grace made the moral law inapplicable; *Anabaptists* proposed baptism and church membership for adult believers only.
[5] The great charter of liberties granted to the English by King John on June 15, 1215; the term is often used, as is the case here, to denote any agreement of fundamental rights.

tween the sub-planters of a West Indian island,[6] whereof the first article of con-stipulation firmly provides free stableroom and litter for all kind of consciences, be they never so dirty or jadish,[7] making it actionable—yea, treasonable—to dis-turb any man in his religion or to discommend it, whatever it be. We are very sorry to see such professed profaneness in English professors,[8] as industriously to lay their religious foundations on the ruin of true religion, which strictly binds ev-ery conscience to contend earnestly for the truth; to preserve unity of spirit, faith, and ordinances; to be all like minded, of one accord, every man to take his brother into his Christian care, to stand fast with one spirit, with one mind, striv-ing together for the faith of the Gospel; and by no means to permit heresies or erroneous opinions. But God, abhorring such loathsome beverages, hath in His righteous judgment blasted that enterprise, which might otherwise have pros-pered well, for aught I know; I presume their case is generally known ere this.

If the devil might have his free option, I believe he would ask nothing else but liberty to enfranchise all false religions and to embondage the truth; nor should he need. It is much to be feared that lax tolerations upon state pretenses and planting necessities will be the next subtle stratagem he will spread to distate[9] the truth of God and supplant the peace of the churches. Tolerations in things toler-able, exquisitely drawn out by the lines of the scripture and pencil of the spirit, are the sacred favors of truth, the due latitudes of love, the fair compartments of Christian fraternity; but irregular dispensations, dealt forth by the facilities of men, are the frontiers of error, the redoubts of schism, the perilous irritaments of carnal and spiritual enmity.

My heart has naturally detested four things: the standing of the Apocrypha[10] in the Bible; foreigners dwelling in my country to crowd out native subjects into the corners of the earth; alchemized[11] coins; tolerations of divers religions, or of one religion in segregant[12] shapes. He that willingly assents to the last, if he exam-ines his heart by daylight, his conscience will tell him he is either an atheist or a heretic or a hypocrite, or at best a captive to some lust. Poly-piety is the greatest impiety in the world. True religion is *ignis probationis* which doth *congregare homo-genea & segregare heterogenea.*[13]

Not to tolerate things merely indifferent to weak consciences argues a con-science too strong; pressed uniformity in these causes much disunity. To tolerate more than indifferents is not to deal indifferently with God; he that does it takes His scepter out of His hand and bids Him stand by. Who hath to do to institute religion but God? The power of all religion and ordinances lies in their purity, their purity in their simplicity; then are mixtures pernicious. I lived in a city[14] where a Papist preached in one church, a Lutheran in another, a Calvinist in a third; a Lutheran one part of the day, a Calvinist the other, in the same pulpit. The religion of that place was but motley and meager, their affections leopard-like.

If the whole creature should conspire to do the Creator a mischief or offer Him an insolency, it would be in nothing more than in erecting untruths against His truth, or by sophisticating His truths with human medleys. The removing of some one iota in scripture may draw out all the life and traverse all the truth of the whole Bible; but to authorize an untruth by a toleration of state is to build a

---

[6]Zall: "Probably Bermuda."
[7]Having the characteristics of a horse.
[8]Professors of the faith, believers.
[9]Deprive a thing of its position or state.
[10]Early Christian writings proposed as additions to the Bi-ble, accepted by Roman Catholics in part, but rejected by Protestants as uncanonical.

[11]Transformed by alchemy, an early chemical philosophy whose aim was to change base metals into gold.
[12]Separate.
[13]Zall: "True religion combines likenesses and separates differences in the same way as the fire used by goldsmiths to separate impurities from gold."
[14]Zall: "Probably Elbing, Prussia."

sconce[15] against the walls of heaven, to batter God out of His chair. To tell a practical lie is a great sin, but yet transient; but to set up a theoretical untruth is to warrant every lie that lies from its root to the top of every branch it hath, which are not a few.

I would willingly hope that no member of the Parliament has skillfully ingratiated himself into the hearts of the House that he might watch a time to midwife out some ungracious toleration for his own turn; and for the sake of that, some other, I would also hope that a word of general caution should not be particularly misapplied. I am the freer to suggest it because I know not one man of that mind. My aim is general, and I desire may be so accepted. Yet, good gentlemen, look well about you and remember how Tiberius played the fox with the senate of Rome and how Fabius Maximus cropped his ears for his cunning.[16]

That state is wise that will improve all pains and patience rather to compose than tolerate differences in religion. There is no divine truth but hath much celestial fire in it from the spirit of truth, nor no irreligious untruth without its proportion of antifire from the spirit of error to contradict it: the zeal of the one, the virulency of the other, must necessarily kindle combustions. Fiery diseases seated in the spirit embroil the whole frame of the body; others more external and cool are less dangerous. They which divide in religion, divide in God; they who divide in Him, divide beyond *genus generalissimum*[17] where there is no reconciliation without atonement: that is, without uniting in Him who is one, and in His truth which is also one.

Wise are those men who will be persuaded rather to live within the pale[18] of truth where they may be quiet than in the purlieus[19] where they are sure to be hunted ever and anon, do authority what it can. Every singular opinion hath a singular opinion of itself, and he that holds it a singular opinion of himself, and a simple opinion of all contrasentients.[20] He that confutes them must confute all three at once, or else he does nothing—which will not be done without more stir than the peace of the state or church can endure.

And prudent are those Christians that will rather give what may be given than hazard all by yielding nothing. To sell all peace of country to buy some peace of conscience unseasonably is more avarice than thrift, imprudence than patience: they deal not equally that set any truth of God at such a rate; but they deal wisely that will stay till the market is fallen.

My prognostics deceive me not a little if, once within three seven years, peace prove not such a pennyworth at most marts in Christendom that he that would not lay down his money, his lust, his opinion, his will—I had almost said the best flower of his crown—for it while he might have had it will tell his own heart he played the very ill husband.

[The Great Evil of Toleration of False Religion]

Concerning tolerations I may further assert:

That persecution of true religion and toleration of false are the *Jannes* and *Jambres*[1] to the kingdom of Christ, whereof the last is far the worst. Augustine's[2] tongue had not owed his mouth one pennyrent though it had never spake word more in it but this: *Nullum malum pejus libertate errandi.*[3]

---

[15]Fort.

[16]Zall: "Cicero, Livy, Plutarch, and many others tell how M. Livius (rather than Tiberius) assured the Senate that while it may be true he lost the town of which he was governor, still he deserved some credit for helping Fabius recover it. Fabius agreed: 'If you had not lost it, I never could have recaptured it.'"

[17]Zall: "The most general class."

[18]Area enclosed by a boundary.

[19]Outskirts.

[20]Those holding opposite opinions.

[1]Zall: "'As Jannes and Jambres, so do these also resist the truth: Men of corrupt minds, reprobate concerning faith,' (2 Timothy, 3:8)."

[2]St. Augustine (354–430), church father and author of *The City of God.*

[3]Zall: "No freedom is worse than the freedom of erring."

Frederick, Duke of Saxon,[4] spake not one foot beyond the mark when he said he had rather the earth should swallow him up quick than he should give a toleration to any opinion against any truth of God.

He that is willing to tolerate any religion or discrepant way of religion besides his own, unless it be in matters merely indifferent, either doubts of his own or is not sincere in it.

He that is willing to tolerate any unsound opinion, that his own may also be tolerated, though never so sound, will for a need hang God's Bible at the devil's girdle.

Every toleration of false religions or opinions hath as many errors and sins in it as all the false religions and opinions it tolerates; and one sound, one more.

That state that will give liberty of conscience in matters of religion must give liberty of conscience and conversation in their moral laws, or else the fiddle will be out of tune and some of the strings crack.

He that will rather make an irreligious quarrel with other religions than try the truth of his own valuable arguments and peaceable sufferings, either his religion or himself is irreligious.

Experience will teach churches and Christians that it is far better to live in a state united, though somewhat corrupt, than in a state whereof some part is incorrupt and all the rest divided.

I am not altogether ignorant of the eight rules given by orthodox divines about giving tolerations,[5] yet with their favor I dare affirm:

That there is no rule given by God for any state to give an affirmative toleration to any false religion or opinion whatsoever; they must connive in some cases, but may not concede in any.

That the state of England (so far as my intelligence serves) might in time have prevented with ease, and may yet without any great difficulty deny both toleration, and irregular connivances *salva Republica.*[6]

That if the state of England shall either willingly tolerate or weakly connive at such courses, the church of that kingdom will sooner become the devil's dancing-school than God's temple, the civil state a bear-garden than an exchange, the whole realm a *pays bas*[7] than an England. And what pity it is that the country which hath been the staple of truth to all Christendom should now become the aviary[8] of errors to the whole world, let every fearing heart judge.

I take liberty of conscience to be nothing but a freedom from sin and error. *Conscientia in tantum libera, in quantum ab errore liberata.*[9] And liberty of error nothing but a prison for conscience. Then small will be the kindness of a state to build such prisons for their subjects.

The scripture saith, there is nothing makes free but truth,[10] and truth saith, there is no truth but one. If the states of the world would make it their summoperous[11] care to preserve this one truth in its purity and authority it would ease you of all other political cares. I am sure Satan makes it his grand if not only task to adulterate truth; falsehood is his sole scepter whereby he first ruffled, and ever since ruined, the world.

If truth be but one, me thinks all the opinionists in England should not be all in that one truth; some of them I doubt are out. He that can extract an unity out of such a disparity, or contract such a disparity into an unity, had need be a better artist than ever was Drebbel.[12]

---

[4]Zall: "Elector of Saxony who ordered Luther imprisoned in 1521."

[5]Zall: "A convocation of Bishops, April 13-May 29, 1640, produced seventeen canons, including one on toleration."

[6]Zall: "Saving the state."

[7]*Pays bas:* the Low Countries. Zall: "The pun is on *the Low Countries* and *a low country,* in the sense of base, low down."

[8]A place for keeping birds confined.

[9]Zall: "Conscience is free insofar as it is free from error."

[10]Zall: "John 8:32; 1 Corinthians 8:4."

[11]Zall: "Utmost."

[12]Zall: "Cornelis Drebbel (1572–1634), Dutch inventor."

If two centers (as we may suppose) be in one circle, and lines drawn from both to all the points of the compass, they will certainly cross one another, and probably cut through the centers themselves.

[SPEAKING A LITTLE TO WOMEN'S FASHIONS AND A WORD TO MEN'S LONG HAIR]

Should I not keep promise in speaking a little to women's fashions, they would take it unkindly. I was loath to pester better matter with such stuff; I rather thought it meet to let them stand by themselves, like the *Quae Genus* [1] in the grammar, being deficients, or redundants, not to be brought under any rule. I shall therefore make bold for this once to borrow a little of their loose-tongued liberty, and misspend a word or two upon their long-waisted but short-skirted patience. A little use of my stirrup will do no harm.

> *Ridentem dicere verum, quid prohibet?* [2]
> Gray gravity itself can well beteam
> That language be adapted to the theme.
> He that to parrots speaks, must parrotize;
> He that instructs a fool, may act th' unwise.

It is known more than enough that I am neither niggard nor cynic to the due bravery of the true gentry; if any man mislikes a bullimong drassock [3] more than I, let him take her for his labor; I honor the woman that can honor herself with her attire; a good text always deserves a fair margin; I am not much offended if I see a trim far trimmer than she that wears it; in a word, whatever Christianity or civility will allow, I can afford with London measure. But when I hear a nugiperous [4] gentledame inquire what dress the Queen is in this week, what the nudiustertian [5] fashion of the court, with edge to be in it in all haste, whatever it be; I look at her as the very gizzard of a trifle, the product of a quarter of a cipher, the epitome of nothing, fitter to be kicked, if she were of a kickable substance, than either honored or humored.

To speak moderately, I truly confess it is beyond the ken of my understanding to conceive how those women should have any true grace or valuable virtue that have so little wit as to disfigure themselves with such exotic garbs as not only dismantles their native lovely lustre but transclouts them into gant bar-geese, [6] illshapen, shotten [7] shellfish, Egyptian hieroglyphics, or at the best into French flirts of the pastry, which a proper Englishwoman should scorn with her heels; it is no marvel they wear drails [8] on the hinder part of their heads, having nothing as it seems in the fore part but a few squirrels' brains to help them frisk from one illfavored fashion to another.

> These whim-crowned shes, these fashion-fancying wits,
> Are empty thin-brained shells and fiddling kits.

The very troublers and impoverishers of mankind! I can hardly forbear to commend to the world a saying of a lady living sometime with the Queen of Bohemia. I know not where she found it, but it is pity it should be lost:

> The world is full of care, much like unto a bubble,
> Women and care, and care and women, and women and care and trouble.

---

[1] Zall: "What gender?—a formula in elementary grammar lessons."
[2] Zall: "After Horace *Satires* I. i. 24–25: '*Ridentem dicere verum qui vetat*': 'What's to keep me from telling the truth with a laugh?'"
[3] Zall: "Drab, untidy woman."

[4] Zall: "Gossipy."
[5] Zall: "The very newest."
[6] Gaping barnacle geese.
[7] Newly spawned or used figuratively in Ward's time to mean worthless.
[8] Zall: "Long, trailing headdresses."

The verses are even enough for such odd pegmas.[9] I can make myself sick at any time with comparing the dazzling splendor wherewith our gentlewomen were embellished in some former habits, with the gut-foundered goosedom wherewith they are now surcingled[10] and debauched. We have about five or six of them in our colony; if I see any of them accidentally, I cannot cleanse my fancy of them for a month after. I have been a solitary widower almost twelve years, purposed lately to make a step over to my native country for a yoke-fellow; but when I consider how women there have tripe-wifed[11] themselves with their cladments, I have no heart to the voyage, lest their nauseous shapes and the sea should work too sorely upon my stomach. I speak sadly; methinks it should break the hearts of Englishmen to see so many goodly Englishwomen imprisoned in French cages, peering out of their hood-holes for some men of mercy to help them with a little wit; and nobody relieves them.

It is a more common than convenient saying that nine tailors make a man; it were well if nineteen could make a woman to her mind; if tailors were men indeed, well furnished but with mere moral principles, they would disdain to be led about like apes by such mimic marmosets.[12] It is a most unworthy thing for men that have bones in them to spend their lives in making fiddle-cases for futilous[13] women's fancies, which are the very pettitoes[14] of infirmity, the giblets of perquisquilian[15] toys. I am so charitable to think that most of that mystery would work the cheerfuller while they live if they might be well discharged of the tiring slavery of mis-tiring women; it is no little labor to be continually putting up Englishwomen into outlandish casks, who, if they be not shifted anew once in a few months, grow too sour for their husbands. What this trade will answer for themselves when God shall take measure of tailors' consciences is beyond my skill to imagine. There was a time when

> The joining of the red rose with the white
> Did set our state into a damask plight.

But now our roses are turned to fleur-de-lis,[16] our carnations to tulips, our gilliflowers to daisies, our city-dames to an indenominable quaemalry of overturcased things.[17] He that makes coats for the moon had need to take measure every noon; and he that makes for women, as often, to keep them from lunacy.

I have often heard divers ladies vent loud feminine complaints of the wearisome varieties and chargeable changes of fashions. I marvel themselves prefer not a bill of redress. I would Essex[18] ladies would lead the chore, for the honor of their county and persons; or rather the thrice honorable ladies of the court, whom it best beseems; who may well presume of a *le roy le veult* from our sober King, a *les seigneurs ont assentus*[19] from our prudent Peers, and the like *assentus* from our considerate, I dare not say wife-worn Commons, who I believe had much rather pass one such bill than pay so many tailors' bills as they are forced to do.

Most dear and unparalleled ladies, be pleased to attempt it; as you have the precellency[20] of the women of the world for beauty and feature, so assume the

---

[9]A pegma is a framework or stage for theatricals bearing an inscription—and thus the inscription itself.

[10]A surcingle is a girth (band) for a horse or other animal; thus, encircled.

[11]Tripe: entrails of animal or fish; tripe-wife: female tripe dresser, used contemptuously of the woman.

[12]Small monkeys.

[13]Zall: "Futile."

[14]Feet of a pig, as an article of food; used figuratively to express contempt.

[15]The giblets of perquisquilian toys: the odds and ends of worthless toys.

[16]The red rose was the emblem of the English House of Lancaster, the white of the English House of York; their

dynastic struggle (1455–85) is known as the Wars of the Roses. The fleur-de-lis (iris) is the emblem of the kings of France.

[17]Zall: "Whatever-it-is of overdecorated (over-turquoised) things."

[18]Ward's marginal note: "All the counties and shires of England have had wars in them since the Conquest, but Essex, which is only free, and should be thankful."

[19]Zall: "The king so wills it; The lords have assented. The first phrase was used by kings in signing bills passed by Parliament; the second also echoes a Parliamentary formula, beginning, 'Les prelates, seigneurs, et commons en a present parliament assembles.' "

[20]Preeminency.

honor to give and not take law from any, in matter of attire; if ye can transact so fair a motion among yourselves unanimously, I dare say they that most renite[21] will least repent. What greater honor can your honors desire than to build a promontory president to all foreign ladies, to deserve so eminently at the hands of all the English gentry present and to come; and to confute the opinion of all the wise men in the world, who never thought it possible for women to do so good a work?

If any man think I have spoken rather merrily than seriously, he is much mistaken; I have written what I write with all the indignation I can, and no more than I ought. I confess I veered my tongue to this kind of language *de industria*[22] though unwillingly, supposing those I speak to are uncapable of grave and rational arguments.

I desire all ladies and gentlewomen to understand that all this while I intend not such as through necessary modesty to avoid morose singularity, follow fashions slowly, a flight shot or two off, showing by their moderation that they rather draw countermont with their hearts,[23] than put on by their examples.

I point my pen only against the light-heeled beagles that lead the chase so fast, that they run all civility out of breath, against these ape-headed pullets which invent antique fool-fangles[24] merely for fashion and novelty's sake.

In a word, if I begin once to declaim against fashions, let men and women look well about them; there is somewhat in the business. I confess to the world, I never had grace enough to be strict in that kind; and of late years, I have found syrup of pride very wholesome in a due dose, which makes me keep such store of that drug by me that if anybody comes to me for a questionful or two about fashions, they never complain of me for giving them hard measure or under-weight.

But I address myself to those who can both hear and mend all if they please. I seriously fear, if the pious parliament do not find a time to state fashions, as ancient parliaments have done in part, God will hardly find a time to state religion or peace. They are the surquedryes[25] of pride, the wantonness of idleness, provoking sins, the certain prodromies[26] of assured judgment, Zeph. 1: 7,8.[27]

It is beyond all account how many gentlemen's and citizen's estates are deplumed by their feather-headed wives, what useful supplies the pannage[28] of England would afford other countries, what rich returns to itself, if it were not sliced out into male and female fripperies. And what a multitude of misemployed hands might be better improved in some more manly manufactures for the public weal. It is not easily credible what may be said of the preterpluralities[29] of tailors in London. I have heard an honest man say that not long since there were numbered between Temple-bar and Charing-Cross eight thousand of that trade. Let it be conjectured by that proportion how many there are in and about London, and in all England; they will appear to be very numerous. If the Parliament would please to mend women, which their husbands dare not do, there need not so many men to make and mend as there are. I hope the present doleful estate of the realm will persuade more strongly to some considerate course herein than I now can.

Knew I how to bring it in, I would speak a word to long hair, whereof I will say no more but this: if God proves not such a barber to it as He threatens, unless it be amended, Isaiah 7:20,[30] before the peace of the state and church be well settled, then let my prophecy be scorned, as a sound mind scorns the riot of that sin,

---

[21]Zall: "Resist pressure."
[22]Zall: "Diligently."
[23]Zall: "make a long uphill pull with their hearts rather than dash impetuously ahead."
[24]Silly finery.
[25]Zall: "arrogant pieces."
[26]Symptoms.
[27]Zall: "The day of the Lord is at hand . . . . In the day of the Lordes sacrifice I will visit the princes and the kinges children, and al such as weare strange clothing."
[28]Pasturage (acorns, beech-mast, etc.) for swine.
[29]Multitudes.
[30]Zall: "At the same time shall the Lord shave the haire of the head . . . with the razor that He shall hire beyond the waters: namely, with the king of the Assyrians."

and more it needs not. If those who are termed Rattle-heads and Impuritans would take up a resolution to begin in moderation of hair to the just reproach of those that are called Puritans and Round-heads,[31] I would honor their manliness as much as the other's godliness, so long as I knew what man or honor meant. If neither can find a barber's shop, let them turn in, to Psal. 68:21, Jer. 7:29, I Cor. 11: 14.[32] If it be thought no wisdom in men to distinguish themselves in the field by the scissors, let it be thought no injustice in God not to distinguish them by the sword. I had rather God should know me by my sobriety than mine enemy not know me by my vanity. He is ill kept, that is kept by his own sin. A short promise is a far safer guard than a long lock. It is an ill distinction which God is loath to look at, and His angels cannot know His saints by. Though it be not the mark of the beast, yet it may be the mark of a beast prepared to slaughter. I am sure men used not to wear such manes; I am also sure soldiers used to wear other marklets or notadoes[33] in time of battle.

1645–46   *1647*

THOMAS SHEPARD
(1605–1649)

Like so many of the great ministers of the first generation of New England Puritans, Thomas Shepard, son of a grocer in Towcester, prepared for the ministry in England at Cambridge University and obtained a "lectureship" in Essex. And there his Puritan nonconformity brought him to the attention of the fiercely anti-Puritan Bishop William Laud. Shepard has left an account of his excommunication in 1630. Laud pronounced: "I charge you that you neither preach, read, marry, bury, or exercise any ministerial function in any part of my diocese; for if you do, and I hear of it, I'll be upon your back, and follow you wherever you go in any part of this kingdom, and so everlastingly disenable you."

It is understandable why such "silenced ministers" as Shepard fled to America. Shepard arrived in New England in 1635 and became minister at Cambridge. There he helped to found Harvard College in 1636. His reputation as a preacher was great. He could describe the doctrine of the "depravity of man" with vividness: "Every natural man and woman is born full of sin, as full as a toad is of poison, as full as ever his skin can hold; mind, will, eyes, mouth, every limb of his body, and every piece of his soul, is full of sin; their hearts are bundles of sin." At the same time, Shepard had a reputation for preaching the gospel of compassion and love. Here is his description of Christ's love from his popular book, *The Sincere Convert* (1641): "As 'tis with woman when the fulness of the husband's love is seen, it knits the heart invincibly to him, and makes her do anything for him; so here. And as we say of trees, if the tree begins to wither and die, the only way is . . . water the root. Love is the next root of all grace."

---

[31]A derisive term applied to the Puritans (whose hair was close-cropped) by the Royalists during the struggle between the parliamentary party and the supporters of the king during the English Civil War (1642–49).
[32]Psalm 68:21: "But God shall wound the head of his enemies, and the hairy scalp of such an one as goeth on still in his trespasses." Jeremiah 7:29: "Cut off thine hair, O Jerusalem, and cast it away, and take up a lamentation on high places. . . . 1 Corinthians 11:14: "Doth not even nature itself teach you, that, if a man have long hair, it is a shame unto him?"
[33]Zall: "badges or insignia."

Shepard was one of the leaders in expelling the Antinomians, including Anne Hutchinson, from the Massachusetts Bay Colony. The Antinomians believed that under the doctrine of the Covenant of Grace, no moral law could apply, because the Christian was saved by faith alone through the mercy of God's grace. The Puritan brand of Protestantism put much emphasis on "covenant theology," in which it was said that there were two covenants (or contracts) made by God with His people. The first of these was the "Covenant of Works," in which God held Adam to a particular behavior under a moral law. Adam broke the law, and was expelled from Eden. God made a new contract, beginning with Abraham, that was a "Covenant of Grace"; recognizing that fallen man, naturally depraved, could not fulfill the law, the new covenant requires only that he believe—or have faith in Christ as his mediator and salvation.

The doctrine of the "Covenant of Grace" is a complex one susceptible to various interpretations—including the Antinomian, which assumes that since salvation is not a consequence of behavior, one who is saved (or is among the elect) may behave as he or she pleases. It is no wonder that the Puritans repeatedly attempted to clarify the doctrine for a sometimes confused flock. Shepard's essay, "The Covenant of Grace," appeared as a Preface to *The Gospel-Covenant: or the Covenant of Grace Opened,* a book of sermons by a fellow Puritan minister, Peter Bulkeley, published in 1651. In his brief explanation of the doctrine, Shepard's gentle temper shines through his lucid and quiet prose.

ADDITIONAL READING

Moses Coit Tyler, *A History of American Literature, 1607–1765,* 1878; Samuel Eliot Morison, "Master Thomas Shepard," *Builders of the Bay Colony,* 1930; Patricia Caldwell, *The Puritan Conversion Narrative: The Beginnings of American Expression,* 1983.

TEXT

"To the Reader [Covenant of Grace]," Preface to *The Gospel-Covenant: or the Covenant of Grace Opened* by Peter Bulkeley, 1651. Typography, punctuation, spelling, and usage have been changed to conform with contemporary English and modern printing practices.

[The Covenant of Grace]

The blessed God hath evermore delighted to reveal and communicate Himself by way of Covenant. He might have done good to man before his fall, as also since his fall, without binding Himself in the bond of Covenant; Noah, Abraham, and David, Jews, Gentiles, might have had the blessings intended, without any promise or Covenant. But the Lord's heart is so full of love (especially to His own) that it cannot be contained so long within the bounds of secrecy—*viz.* from God's eternal purpose to the actual accomplishment of good things intended—but it must aforehand overflow and break out into the many streams of a blessed Covenant. The Lord can never get near enough to His people, and thinks He can never get them near enough unto Himself, and therefore unites and binds and fastens them close to Himself, and Himself unto them, by the bonds of a Covenant. And therefore when we break our Covenant, and that will not hold us, He takes a faster bond and makes a sure and everlasting Covenant, according to Grace, not according to Works; and that shall hold His people firm unto Himself, and hold Himself close and fast unto them, that He may never depart from us.

Oh! the depth of God's grace herein; that when sinful man deserves never to have the least good word from Him, that He should open His whole heart and purpose to him in a Covenant; that when he deserves nothing else but separation from God, and to be driven up and down the world as a vagabond, or as dried leaves fallen from our God, that yet the Almighty God cannot be content with it, but must make Himself to us, and us to Himself, more sure and near than ever before! And is not this Covenant then (Christian reader) worth thy looking into and searching after? Surely never was there a time wherein the Lord calls His people to more serious searching into the nature of the Covenant than in these days.

For are there not some who cut off the entail[1] to children of those in Covenant, and so lessen and shorten the riches of grace in the Lord's free Covenant, and that in the time of more grace under the gospel than He was wont to dispense under the law? Are there not others who preach a new, or rather another gospel or Covenant—*viz*, that actual remission of sins and reconciliation with God (purchased indeed in redemption by Christ's death) is without, nay before faith; the condition (though wrought of God) of the Covenant of Grace, expressly opposed to the Law or Covenant of Works, Rom. 3:27, and ever required as the means (and therefore antecedent) to the attainment of those ends in the constant ministry of the apostles of Christ, Act. 2:38 & 10:43? Is it not time for the people of God now to pry into the secret of God's Covenant (which He reveals to them that fear Him, Psal. 25. 14) when, by clipping of it and distinguishing about it, the beautiful countenance of it begins to be changed and transformed by those angels of "new light" which once it had, when it began to be published in the simplicity of it by the Apostles of Christ (II Cor. 11.3)? Nay, is not the time come wherein the Lord of hosts seems to have a quarrel against all the world, and especially His churches and people, whom He goes on to waste by the sharpest sword that (almost) was ever drawn out? And is it not the duty of all that have the least spark of holy fear and trembling to ask and search diligently what should be the reason of this sore anger and hot displeasure, before they and theirs be consumed in the burning flames of it?

Search the scriptures, and there we shall find the cause, and see God Himself laying His finger upon that which is the sore and the wound of such times: for so it is said, Isa. 24. 1–5, "Behold, the Lord maketh the earth empty and waste, and turns it upside down, and scattereth abroad the inhabitants thereof; and it shall be as with the people, so with the priest; and the land shall be utterly spoiled." Why? "For the earth is defiled under the inhabitants thereof." Why so? "Because they have transgressed the laws, changed the ordinance, and broken the everlasting Covenant." And therefore when the Lord shall have wasted His church, and hath made it as Adnah and Zeboim,[2] when heathen nations shall ask, "Wherefore hath the Lord done all this against this land? What meaneth the heat of His great anger?", the answer is made by the Lord Himself expressly, Deut. 29. 25 : *viz.* "Because they have forsaken the Covenant of the Lord God of their fathers." And no wonder, for they that reject the Covenant of Grace, they break the league of peace between God and themselves. And hence, if acts of hostility in desolating kingdoms, churches, families and persons break out from a long-suffering God, they may easily see the cause, and that the cause and quarrel of God herein is just.

As all good things are conveyed to God's people not barely by common provi-

---

[1]Inheritance.
[2]Deuteronomy 29:23: "And that the whole land thereof is brimstone, and salt, and burning, that it is not sown, nor beareth, nor any grass groweth therein, like the overthrow of Sodom, and Gomorrah, Admah, and Zeboim, which the Lord overthrew in His anger, and in His wrath."

dence but by special Covenant, Isa. 16. 8, 9, so all the evils they meet with in this world (if in them the face of God's anger appears), upon narrow search, will be found to arise from breach of Covenant, more or less. So that if it be the great cause of all the public calamities of the church and people of God, and those calamities are already begun, and God's hand is stretched out still—was there then ever a more seasonable time and hour to study the Covenant, and so see the sin repent of it, and at last to lay hold of God's rich grace and bowels in it, lest the Lord go on and fulfill the word of His servants, and expose most pleasant lands to the doleful lamentation of a very little remnant, reserved as a few coals in the ashes, when all else is consumed?

As particular persons, when they break their Covenant, the Lord therefore breaks out against them: so, when whole churches forsake their Covenant, the Lord therefore doth sorely visit them. Sins of ignorance the Lord Jesus pities, Heb. 5. 2, and many times winks at, but sins against light He cannot endure, II Pet. 2. 21. Sins against light are great, but sins against the purpose and Covenant, nay God's Covenant, are by many degrees worse, for the soul of man rusheth most violently and strongly against God when it breaks through all the light of the mind and purposes of the will that stand in his way to keep him from sin. And is not this done by breach of Covenant? And therefore no wonder if the Lord makes His people's chain heavy by sore affliction, until they come to consider and behold this sin, and learn more fear (after they are bound to their good behavior) of breaking Covenant with God again. It is true, the Covenant effectually made can never be really broke, yet externally it may. But suppose God's churches were in greatest peace, and had a blessed rest from all their labors round about them: yet what is the child's position, but his legacy left him, written with the finger of God his father, in the New Covenant, and the blood of Jesus Christ his redeemer, in His last will and testament? What is a Christian's comfort, and where doth it chiefly lie, but in this: that the Lord hath made with him an everlasting Covenant, in all things established and sure? Which were the last breathing of the sweet singer of Israel, and the last bubblings up of the joy of his heart, II Sam. 23.5.

God the Father's eternal purposes are sealed secrets, not immediately seen, and the full and blessed accomplishments of those purposes are not yet experimentally felt. The Covenant is the midst between both God's purposes and performances, by which and in which we come to see the one before the world began, and by a blessed faith (which makes things absent, present) to enjoy the other, which shall be our glory when this world shall be burned up and all things in it shall have an end. For in God's Covenant we see with open face God's secret purpose for time past—God's purposes toward His people being, as it were, nothing else but promises concealed, and God's promises in the Covenant being nothing else but His purposes revealed. As also, in the same Covenant and promises we see performances for future, as if they were accomplishments at present. Where then is a Christian's comfort but in that Covenant, wherein two eternities (as it were) meet together, and whereby he may see accomplishments (made sure to him) of eternal glory, arising from blessed purposes of eternal grace? In a word, wherein he fastens upon God, and hath Him from everlasting to everlasting, comprehended at hand near and obvious in His words of a gracious Covenant?

The Church of God is therefore bound to bless God much for this food in season, and for the holy judicious and learned labors of this aged, experienced and precious servant of Christ Jesus, who hath taken much pains to discover—and that not in words and allegories but in the demonstration and evidence of the Spirit—the great mystery of godliness wrapped up in the Covenant, and hath now fully opened sundry knotty questions concerning the same, which happily have not been brought so fully to light until now. Which cannot but be of singular and seasonable use, to prevent apostasies from the simplicity of the Covenant and

Gospel of Christ. The sermons were preached in the remote ends of the earth and, as it were, set under a bushel, a church more remote from the numerous society of others of the saints; if now, therefore, the light be set upon a hill, 'tis where it should stand, and where Christ surely would have it put. The good Lord enlighten the minds of all those who seek for the truth by this and such like helps; and the Lord enlighten the whole world with His glory, even with the glory of His Covenant, grace and love, that His people hereby may be sealed up daily unto all fulness of assurance and peace, in these evil times.

1651

INCREASE MATHER
(1639–1723)

Increase Mather was the preeminent New England divine of his day, the era of the second-generation American Puritans. He was the author of some 130 books and he contributed essays to some 65 books edited by others. He conversed fluently in Latin and he was able to read and write Hebrew and Greek. He worked a sixteen hour day, most of the time spent in his study praying, reading, and writing. He composed his sermons early in the week, memorized them at the end, and delivered them on Sunday in the famed Mather voice without a manuscript. For good reason his biographer called him "the foremost American Puritan."

Mather was educated first at Harvard and then at Trinity College, Dublin. In 1664 he became minister of the North Church, Boston; and in 1685 he was appointed president of Harvard College. In these positions (and with his intellectual preeminence) he became the most influential figure in the Puritan colony. He was appointed in 1688 to go to England to renegotiate the colonial charter, and he returned in 1692 with a new charter naming a governor and magistrates of his choice. His role in the "witchcraft delusion" of the 1690s is ambiguous. His *Essay for the Recording of Illustrious Providences* (1684) supported the superstitions of those involved in the trials. But in *Cases of Conscience Concerning Evil Spirits* (1693), Mather disavowed the "spectral evidence" admitted by the court.

Mather's father, Richard, was a prominent minister of the "old comers," the first-generation Puritans, and he married the daughter of another, John Cotton. Increase's son and heir, Cotton Mather, gained the enduring intellectual, religious, and literary fame that eluded the father. Increase Mather's works have never been published as an "edition," and are now generally unavailable. But their plain, vigorous, and lively style makes them in some ways more readable than the voluminous works of his son.

In *Awakening Truths Tending to Conversion* (1710), Increase Mather meets head-on the knotty problem of the doctrine of the elect—or predestination: If God determines *all*, does not that total power absolve the sinner of responsibility for his sin and thus place the responsibility on God Himself? Mather's argument is subtle, and he marshals key quotations from scripture for proof. If he is not entirely convincing to a modern reader, it must be remembered that he is dealing with a contradiction in philosophy—determinism versus free will—that has never been adequately or wholly resolved.

ADDITIONAL READING

Moses Coit Tyler, *A History of American Literature, 1607–1765,* 1878; Kenneth B. Murdock, *Increase Mather, the Foremost American Puritan,* 1925; Vernon L. Parrington, "The Mather Dynasty," *Main Currents in American Thought,* 1927–30; Perry Miller, *The New England Mind: From Colony to Province,* 1953; Robert Middlekauff, *The Mathers: Three Generations of Puritan Intellectuals, 1596–1728,* 1971; Mason Lowance, *Increase Mather,* 1974; Michael Hall, *The Last American Puritan: The Life of Increase Mather,* 1987.

TEXT

Awakening Truths Tending to Conversion, 1710. Typography, punctuation, spelling, and usage have been changed to conform with contemporary English and modern printing practices.

from Awakening Truths Tending to Conversion

[WHAT SINNERS CAN DO TOWARDS THEIR OWN CONVERSION][1]

If prayerless, graceless sinners continue and perish in their unconverted estate, they ought not to lay the blame upon God, but upon themselves. There are some sinners so unreasonable and so wicked. Ask them why they don't reform their lives, "Why don't you turn over a new leaf and amend your ways and your doings"; they will answer, "God does not give me Grace. I can't convert myself, and God does not convert me." Thus do they insinuate as if God were in fault, and the blame of their unconversion to be imputed unto him. But as Elihu speaks, "Suffer me a little, and I will shew you what I have yet to say on God's behalf."[2]

I. I say, God is not bound to give sinners grace. He is an absolute sovereign and may give grace or deny grace to whom He pleases. Shall the thing formed say to him that formed it, "Why hast thou made me thus?" Has not the potter power over the clay, to make one vessel honor and another to dishonor?[3] The glorious God has a greater power over his creatures than the potter has over the clay. Wherefore, "He has mercy on whom He will have mercy, and whom He will He hardens," Romans 9:18. If He gives grace to any man in the world, it is from His sovereign good pleasure. Why were such poor fishermen as Peter, and James, and John and others as mean as they, made the subjects of saving grace, when many incomparably beyond them in learning and wisdom have been left to perish in their unbelief? Even so, because so it has seemed good in the sight of Him, who is the Lord of heaven and earth, Matthew 11:25–26. Grace is a wonderful gift of God. Sinners are enemies to Him and rebels against Him. Is He bound to bestow such a gift on His enemies when it may be too they will not so much as humbly pray unto Him for it? Indeed He sometimes has done so. Sinners that never prayed to Him, that never had one thought in their hearts of returning to Him, He has miraculously presented them with sovereign grace. So it was with the converted gentiles. Of them the Lord says, "I am sought of them that asked not for me; I am found of them that sought me not: I said, Behold me, behold me, unto a nation that was not called by my name," Isaiah 65:1. Nay, sometimes when sinners have been in the height of their resistance and rebellion, to show the exceeding

---

[1]This selection comes from Part II ("That Sinners Who Cannot Convert Themselves Ought to Pray for Converting Grace") of *Awakening Truths Tending to Conversion.* When Perry Miller and Thomas H. Johnson published an excerpt of this selection in *The Puritans* (1938), they entitled it "Predestination and Human Exertion."
[2] Job 36:2.
[3]Romans 9:21.

riches of His grace, God has then converted them. Thus it was with Saul, afterwards Paul, when he was breathing out "slaughter against the disciples of the Lord,"[4] then did God give him faith in Christ, without his praying for it. Thus also those converts in the second chapter of The Acts. Not many days before their conversion they had been murdering the Son of God. And just before the sermon began they were mocking of the preacher, and yet converted by that sermon. Such instances there have been known in the world, of men that have come to hear a sermon only to deride it, and yet have been savingly wrought upon by it. A credible author reports that two profane men drinking together, knowing that Mr. Hooker[5] was to preach, one of them said to the other, "Let us go hear how Hooker will bawl," yet was he converted by that very sermon which he went to hear with a scornful spirit. And after that had such a love for Mr. Hooker as to remove three thousand miles so that he might live under his ministry. Such examples are wonderful evidence of sovereign grace.

II. Although it is true, (as has been showed) that sinners cannot convert themselves, their "cannot" is a willful "cannot." Matthew 22:3, "They will not come." It is not said they "could not" (though they could not of themselves come to Christ) but that they "would not" come. If it were in the power of a sinner to convert himself, he would not do it. For he hates conversion. "It is abomination to fools to depart from evil," Proverbs 13:19. Psalms 50:17, "Thou hatest instruction." If they hate to be converted they will not choose it. Proverbs 1:29, "They hated knowledge, and did not choose the fear of the Lord." Their hearts are in love and in league with their lusts; yea they hate to be turned from them. They love darkness rather than light, they hate the light, neither come they to the light, John 3:19–20. Sinners are haters of God; they say and think that they love Him, but the Lord knows that they hate Him, and therefore they will not repent of their sins and believe on Christ. Christ said to the Jews, "You will not come to me that you might have life," John 5:40. No, they would die first. And why would they not come? The reason of their aversion is mentioned in verse 42, "I know you, that you have not the love of God in you." Their carnal unregenerate minds were full of enmity against God, and therefore they would not come to Jesus Christ the Son of God. They cannot convert themselves, and they are not willing that God should convert them. If sinners were willing to have grace and holiness, why do they not repair to Him for it, who alone can give it to them? A hungry man is willing to have bread, therefore he will seek after it, where ever it is to be had. When the Egyptians were hunger bitten, they went to Pharaoh, crying for bread; he bid them go to Joseph, and they did so. Thus if sinners were willing to be converted, they would cry to God to turn them; whereas there are many sinners that did never put up one earnest prayer to God in their lives, that He would bestow converting grace on them.

III. Sinners can do more towards their own conversion than they do or will do. They should give diligence to make sure of their being effectually called. They should strive to enter in at the strait gate. Conversion is the strait gate that leads unto salvation. They should labor not for the meat that perisheth, but for that which endureth to everlasting life; but they do not give diligence, they do not strive, they do not labor to obtain grace and salvation. Therefore they perish, and perish justly. Proverbs 21:25, "The desire of the slothful killeth him, for his hands refuse to labor." Men say that they desire grace, and yet their hands refuse to labor, they will be at no pains to obtain it. And this slothfulness kills them. It proves the death of their souls. "The soul of the sluggard desireth, and hath nothing, but

---

[4]Acts 9.
[5]Thomas Hooker (1586–1647), eminent and successful Puritan preacher.

the soul of the diligent shall be made fat," Proverbs 13:4. There are several things which sinners have power to do in order to their own conversion, and which they ought to do, but they will not.

(1) They have power to avoid those things which are a hindrance of conversion. *E.g.*, they can if they will forbear the outward acts of sin. By giving way to sin their hearts are hardened, and their conversion becomes the more difficult. Hebrews 3:12, "Take heed lest any of you be hardened through the deceitfulness of sin." But sinners give way to many sins which they could abstain from, if they would. A sabbath-breaker can forbear his profaning of the sabbath. An ungodly swearer can forbear his profane oaths, if he will. A liar can forbear telling such lies. Sinners can avoid the temptations which will endanger their falling into sin. He that knows that if he goes to such a place, or into such a company, he will probably be drawn into sin, ought to avoid the temptation. Proverbs 4:15, "Avoid it, turn from it, and pass away." The sinner can do so if he will, but he will not keep out of the way of temptation. A drunkard will not avoid the temptation to his sin. Proverbs 23:31, "Look not on the wine when it giveth his color." He can choose whether he will look on the wine or no; he has power to refrain, but will not. Thus men, by habituating themselves to sin, do what in them is to hinder their own conversion. Jeremiah 13:23, "Can the Ethiopian change his skin, or the leopard his spots? Then may you also do good that are accustomed to do evil." Again, evil companions hinder conversion. Alas! Alas! Alas! These have been the eternal ruin of many a young man that was in a hopeful way for conversion. He has fallen in with vain companions; they have given him bad counsel; so have convictions been stifled and the motions of God's holy spirit quenched in his soul. The word of the Lord says, "Forsake the foolish and live," Proverbs 9:6. The sinner has power to forsake them, but he will not though he dies for it.

(2) Sinners have power to wait on God in the use of means, which has a tendency to promote conversion. They can, if they will, not only forsake evil companions but associate themselves with those that are good. Then are they in the way of conversion. Proverbs 13:20, "He that walketh with wise men shall be wise: but a companion of fools shall be destroyed." That learned and holy man Dr. Goodwin,[6] in the account which he gives of his conversion, declares that when he was a young scholar in the University of Cambridge there were in that college, which he belonged unto, a "number of holy youths" (that's his expression); his associating himself with them was a happy means of furthering the work of conversion in his soul. This unconverted sinners have the power to do. Their feet are as able to carry them to a godly meeting as to an ungodly one. Reading the scripture has sometimes been the means of conversion. I could tell you of several learned Jews that were converted from their Judaism by reading the 53rd chapter of Isaiah.[7] The famous Fr. Junius[8] was converted from his atheism by reading the first chapter of John's gospel.[9] He that can read is able to read the scripture and books which promote godliness in the power of it, but a sinful creature chooses rather to misspend his time in reading vain romances, or it may be worse books. A diligent attendance to the word of God is the way to obtain converting grace. Romans 10:17, "Faith cometh by hearing, and hearing by the word of God." Sinners many times do not mind what they hear. Nay, it may be they will set themselves to sleep when God is speaking to them by His minister! And shall they then complain that

---

[6]Thomas Goodwin (1600–1680), British minister.

[7]Isaiah 53:3–5: The story of the Suffering Servant of God in this passage has often been interpreted as a foretelling of the story of Christ and his taking on the sins of the world for all humankind.

[8]Franz Junius (1545–1602), Huguenot (French Protestant) divine.

[9]John 1:1,14,17: "In the beginning was the Word, and the Word was with God, and the Word was God. . . . And the Word was made flesh, and dwelt among us, . . . full of grace and truth. . . .For the law was given by Moses, but grace and truth came by Jesus Christ."

they cannot convert themselves and that God will not convert them? Once more, serious thinking and consideration on spiritual and eternal things is oftentimes blessed unto conversion. This is what God has given men power to do, if they will use that power. They ought seriously to think what they have done, and what they are, and what their end is likely to be. If they would do so, it may be repentance would be the effect of it. I Kings 8:47, "If they shall bethink themselves, and repent, and make supplication." David says, "I thought on my ways, and turned my feet unto thy testimonies," Psalms 119:59. If men would be persuaded to think seriously, it may be they would turn. How long shall thy vain thoughts lodge within thee? A sinner will suffer vain thoughts to lodge within him, but serious and holy thoughts he will give no lodging unto, he will not suffer them to abide in his heart. Serious consideration is a duty incumbent on sinners. Haggai 1:5, "Thus saith the Lord of hosts, Consider your ways." Would the unconverted sinner consider sadly what his sinful ways have been, what numberless sins he has been guilty of, and what a fountain of sin his heart is, and whither he is going, it may be conversion would follow upon such serious consideration. Ezekial 18:28, "Because he considereth and turneth away from all his transgressions." Yes, if he is set upon considering, there is great hope that he will turn, and that he shall live, and not die. If he will be persuaded to go alone, to think and consider sadly with himself: What is my present condition? Am I in Christ, or am I not in Christ? If I should die this night, what would become of my soul? In what world must it be to all eternity? It may be such considerations would issue in conversion. Sinners should consider of death, that the thing is certain, and the time uncertain, and that they run an infinite hazard if they neglect making sure of an interest in Christ one day longer. Deuteronomy 32:29, "O that they were wise, that they would consider their latter end!" And they should consider of the eternity which follows immediately upon death. If they would do that, surely it would affect their souls. A late writer (which I have formerly mentioned) speaks of a pious man, that one in company with him, observing a more than ordinary fixedness and concern in his countenance, asked him what his thoughts were upon; he then thereupon uttered that word "For-ever," and so continued saying nothing but repeating that word, "For-ever! For-ever! For-ever!" a quarter of an hour together. His thoughts and soul were swallowed up with the consideration of eternity. And truly if an unconverted sinner could be persuaded to go alone and think seriously of eternity, if it were but for one quarter of an hour, it may be it would have an everlasting impression on his heart. This, sinners can do if they will. And if they will not do as much as this comes to, towards their own conversion and salvation, how inexcusable will they be? Their blood will be upon their own heads. Let them no more say, "God must do all, we can do nothing," and so encourage themselves to live in a careless neglect of God and of their own souls and salvation. Most certainly, although we cannot say that if men improve their natural abilities, as they ought to do, that grace will infallibly follow; yet there will not one sinner in all the reprobate world stand forth at the Day of Judgment and say, "Lord, Thou knowest I did all that possibly I could do for the obtaining grace, and for all that, Thou didst withhold it from me."

1710

JOHN WISE
(1652–1725)

"Every man must be conceived to be perfectly in his own power and dis-posal, and not to be controlled by the authority of any other. And thus every man must be acknowledged equal to every man, since all subjection and all command are equally banished on both sides; and considering all men thus at liberty, every man has a prerogative to judge for himself, *viz.* What shall be most for his behoof, happiness and well-being." "The end of all good govern-ment is to cultivate humanity, and promote the happiness of all, and the good of every man in all his rights, his life, liberty, estate, honor, etc. without injury or abuse done to any."

These words published in 1717 have a ring of familiarity to readers who know the Declaration of Independence of 1776: "We hold these truths to be self-evident, that all men are created equal, that they are endowed by their Creator with certain unalienable rights, that among these are Life, Liberty and the pursuit of Happiness."

The opening words are taken from a book entitled *A Vindication of the Gov-ernment of New England Churches* by John Wise. For good reason he has been called by Moses Coit Tyler "the first great American democrat."

Wise's father came to Roxbury in New England an indentured servant—"the most menial of stations in that aristocratic old Boston world," as Vernon Parrington observed. He served out his indenture and was able to send his son to Harvard College. Graduated in 1673, John Wise became minister of a church in Ipswich, Essex County, in 1680, where he served until his death in 1725. He was imprisoned briefly in 1687 for defying the governor of Massa-chusetts Bay, Sir Edmund Andros, by advising his countrymen against pay-ment of taxes arbitrarily imposed and without approval of a legislature.

Wise wrote his most impassioned prose in response to proposals, made anonymously (but clearly linked to Cotton Mather), that some kind of hierar-chical church government should be considered for the radically independent "congregational" form then prevailing in the colonies. Congregational doc-trine required only that an individual church be founded on a covenant of all its members and that each church be autonomous. *The Cambridge Platform* of 1648 institutionalized this doctrine and provided for only occasional joint meetings of the churches to seek counsel from each other. Thus congrega-tional churches rejected any kind of clerical hierarchy (bishoprics, for exam-ple) or governing body (such as a synod or presbytery). Congregationalism was uniquely American and, as Wise realized, basically democratic.

Wise's first work, *The Church's Quarrel Espoused* (1710), was a satirical attack on the proposal to establish a church government: "Though it be a calf now, yet in time it may grow—being of a thrifty nature—to become a sturdy ox that will know no 'whoa,' and, it may be, past the churches' skill to subdue it."

Wise's invective and ridicule were effective, but he found he had more to say on the subject in reasoned and powerfully persuasive discourse in his re-markable book *A Vindication of the Government of New England Churches* (1717). Wise's philosophy had matured and his commitment to democracy deepened. His maverick presence among the Puritan ministers, alongside those of the "establishment" such as the Mathers, indicates how complex and contradic-tory is the Puritan heritage in American thought and spirit.

ADDITIONAL READING

Moses Coit Tyler, *A History of American Literature, 1607–1765*, 1878; Vernon L. Parrington, "Village Democrat," *Main Currents in American Thought*, 1927–30; George Allan Cook, *John Wise: Early American Democrat*, 1952; Perry Miller, *The New England Mind: From Colony to Province*, 1953.

TEXT

A Vindication of the Government of New England Churches: A Facsimile Reprint [of the 1717 Edition], ed. Perry Miller, 1958. Typography, punctuation, spelling, and usage have been changed to conform with contemporary English and modern printing practices.

from A Vindication of the Government of New England Churches

PART 2: "DEMONSTRATION DEFENSE OF OUR PLATFORM, WHICH IS FOUNDED IN THE LIGHT OF NATURE"

CHAPTER I
["MAN'S NATURAL STATE OF BEING AND ORIGINAL FREEDOM"]

The divine establishment in providence of the forenamed churches[1] in their order is apparently the royal assent of the supreme monarch of the churches to the grave decisions of reason in favor of man's natural state of being and original freedom. For if we should make a new survey of the constitution[2] before named under the brightest light of nature, there is no greater example of natural wisdom in any settlement on earth, for the present and future security of human beings in all that is most valuable and grand, than in this: that it seems to me as though wise and provident nature, by the dictates of right reason, excited by the moving suggestions of humanity, and awed with the just demands of natural liberty, equity, equality and principles of self-preservation, originally drew up the scheme, and then obtained the royal approbation. And certainly it is agreeable that we attribute it to God, whether we receive it next from reason or revelation, for that each is equally an emanation of His wisdom, Prov. 20:27: "The spirit of man is the candle of the Lord, searching all the inward parts of the belly." There be many larger volumes in this dark recess called the belly to be read by that candle God has lit up. And I am very well assured the forenamed constitution is a transcript out of some of their pages, John 1:4, 9: "And the life was the light of men, which lighteth every man which cometh into the world." This admirable effect of Christ's creating power in hanging out so many lights to guide man through a dark world is as applicable to the light of reason as to that of revelation, for that the light of reason as a law and rule of right is an effect of Christ's goodness, care and creating power, as well as of revelation—though revelation is nature's law in a fairer

---

[1] Churches of New England.
[2] "The Cambridge Platform" was drawn up in Cambridge, Mass., in 1648, embodying the basic democratic principles of New England Congregationalism. It was published in 1649 as *A Platform of Church Discipline*.

and brighter edition. . . . But in the further and more distinct management of this plea, I shall:

1. Lay before the reader several principles of natural knowledge;
2. Apply or improve them in ecclesiastical affairs;
3. Infer from the premises a demonstration that these churches, if not properly formed, yet are fairly established in their present order by the law of nature.

from CHAPTER II

I shall disclose several principles of natural knowledge, plainly discovering the law of nature, or the true sentiments of natural reason, with respect to man's being and government. And in this essay I shall peculiarly confine the discourse to two heads, *viz.*

I. Of the natural (in distinction to the civil), and then,

II. Of the civil being of man. And I shall principally take Baron Puffendorff[3] for my chief guide and spokesman.

[OF THE NATURAL BEING OF MAN]

I shall consider man in a state of natural being, as a freeborn subject under the crown of heaven and owing homage to none but God Himself.

It is certain, civil government in general is a very admirable result of providence and an incomparable benefit to mankind, yet must needs be acknowledged to be the effect of human free compacts and not of divine institution. It is the produce of man's reason, of human and rational combinations, and not from any direct orders of infinite wisdom in any positive law where is drawn up this or that scheme of civil government. Government, says Lord Warrington,[4] is necessary, in that no society of men can subsist without it; and that particular form of government is necessary which best suits the temper and inclination of a people. Nothing can be God's ordinance but what He has particularly declared to be such; there is no particular form of civil government described in God's word, neither does nature prompt it. The government of the Jews was changed five times. Government is not formed by nature, as other births or productions; if it were, it would be the same in all countries, because nature keeps the same method, in the same thing, in all climates. If a commonwealth be changed into a monarchy, is it nature that forms and brings forth the monarch? Or if a royal family be wholly extinct (as in Noah's case, being not heir apparent from descent from Adam), is it nature that must go to work (with the king bees, who themselves alone preserve the royal race in that empire) to breed a monarch before the people can have a king or a government set over them? And thus we must leave kings to resolve which is their best title to their crowns, whether natural right or the constitution of government settled by human compacts, under the direction and conduct of reason.

But to proceed under the head of a state of natural being, I shall more distinctly explain the state of human nature in its original capacity, as man is placed on earth by his maker and clothed with many investitures and immunities which properly belong to man separately considered. As:

1. The prime immunity in man's state is that he is most properly the subject of the law of nature. He is the favorite animal on earth, in that this part of God's

---

[3]Baron Samuel von Pufendorf (1632–1694), German jurist and teacher whose works influenced the thought of the French political theorist Jean Jacques Rousseau (1712–1778). Pufendorf maintained that the law of nations derives from natural rights. His major works are *Elementa jurisprudentiae universalis*, "Elements of universal

jurisprudence," 1661; and *De jure naturae et gentium*, "On the law of nature and of nations," 1672.

[4]Henry Booth, Earl of Warrington (1652–1694), was well known for his outspoken defense of religious and political freedom against royal encroachment. His *Works* were published in 1694.

image—*viz.* reason—is congenate[5] with his nature, wherein, by a law immutable, instamped upon his frame, God has provided a rule for men in all their actions, obliging each one to the performance of that which is right, not only as to justice but likewise as to all other moral virtues, the which is nothing but the dictate of right reason founded in the soul of man. . . .

That which is to be drawn from man's reason, flowing from the true current of that faculty when unperverted may be said to be the law of nature; on which account, the Holy Scriptures declare it written on men's hearts. For being endowed with a soul, you may know from yourself how and what you ought to act, Rom. 2. 14: "These having not a law, are a law to themselves." So that the meaning is, when we acknowledge the law of nature to be the dictate of right reason, we must mean that the understanding of man is endowed with such a power as to be able, from the contemplation of human condition, to discover a necessity of living agreeably with this law: and likewise to find out some principle by which the precepts of it may be clearly and solidly demonstrated. The way to discover the law of nature in our own state is by a narrow watch and accurate contemplation of our natural condition and propensions. Others say this is the way to find out the law of nature: if a man any ways doubts whether what he is going to do to another man be agreeable to the law of nature, then let him suppose himself to be in that other man's room. And by this rule effectually executed, a man must be a very dull scholar to nature not to make proficiency in the knowledge of her laws.

But more particularly, in pursuing our condition for the discovery of the law of nature, this is very obvious to view, *viz.*

A principle of self-love and self-preservation is very predominant in every man's being;

A sociable disposition;

An affection or love to mankind in general.

And to give such sentiments the force of a law, we must suppose a God who takes care of all mankind, and has thus obliged each one, as a subject of higher principles of being than mere instincts. For that all law, properly considered, supposes a capable subject and a superior power; and the law of God which is binding is published by the dictates of right reason as other ways. "Therefore," says Plutarch, "to follow God and obey reason is the same thing." But moreover, that God has established the law of nature as the general rule of government is further illustrable from the many sanctions in providence, and from the peace and guilt of conscience in them that either obey or violate the law of nature. But moreover, the foundation of the law of nature with relation to government may be thus discovered: man is a creature extremely desirous of his own preservation; of himself he is plainly exposed to many wants, unable to secure his own safety and maintenance without the assistance of his fellows; and he is also able of returning kindness by the furtherance of mutual good. But yet man is often found to be malicious, insolent and easily provoked, and as powerful in effecting mischief as he is ready in designing it.

Now, that such a creature may be preserved, it is necessary that he be sociable—that is, that he be capable and disposed to unite himself to those of his own species, and to regulate himself towards them, that they may have no fair reason to do him harm, but rather incline to promote his interests and secure his rights and concerns. This then is a fundamental law of nature, that every man, as far as in him lies, do maintain a sociableness with others, agreeable with the main end and disposition of human nature in general. For this is very apparent, that reason

---

[5]Variant of congenite, congenital or inborn.

and society render man the most potent of all creatures. And finally, from the principles of sociableness it follows as a fundamental law of nature that man is not so wedded to his own interest but that he can make the common good the mark of his aim. And hence he becomes capacitated to enter into a civil state by the law of nature; for without this property in nature—*viz.* sociableness, which is for cementing of parts—every government would soon moulder and dissolve.

2. The second great immunity of man is an original liberty instamped upon his rational nature. He that intrudes upon this liberty violates the law of nature. In this discourse I shall waive the consideration of man's moral turpitude, but shall view him physically as a creature which God has made and furnished essentially with many ennobling immunities which render him the most august animal in the world; and still, whatever has happened since his creation, he remains at the upper end of nature, and as such is a creature of a very noble character. For as to his dominion, the whole frame of the lower part of the universe is devoted to his use and at his command; and his liberty under the conduct of right reason is equal with his trust.

Which liberty may be briefly considered, internally as to his mind, and externally as to his person:

The internal native liberty of man's nature in general implies a faculty of doing or omitting things according to the direction of his judgment. But in a more special meaning, this liberty does not consist in a loose and ungovernable freedom or in an unbounded license of acting. Such license is disagreeing with the condition and dignity of man, and would make man of a lower and meaner constitution than brute creatures, who in all their liberties are kept under a better and more rational government by their instincts. Therefore as Plutarch says, "Those persons only who live in obedience to reason are worthy to be accounted free; they alone live as they will who have learned what they ought to will." So that the true natural liberty of man, such as really and truly agrees to him, must be understood as he is guided and restrained by the ties of reason and laws of nature; all the rest is brutal, if not worse.

Man's external, personal, natural liberty, antecedent to all human parts or alliances, must also be considered. And so every man must be conceived to be perfectly in his own power and disposal, and not to be controlled by the authority of any other. And thus every man must be acknowledged equal to every man, since all subjection and all command are equally banished on both sides; and considering all men thus at liberty, every man has a prerogative to judge for himself, *viz.* what shall be most for his behoof, happiness and well-being.

3. The third capital immunity belonging to man's nature is an equality amongst men, which is not to be denied by the law of nature till man has resigned himself with all his rights for the sake of a civil state. And then his personal liberty and equality is to be cherished, and preserved to the highest degree, as will consist with all just distinctions amongst men of honor, and shall be agreeable with the public good. For man has a high valuation of himself, and the passion seems to lay its first foundation, not in pride, but really in the high and admirable frame and constitution of human nature. The word "Man," says my author, is thought to carry somewhat of dignity in its sound; and we commonly make use of this as the most proper and prevailing argument against a rude insulter, *viz.* "I am not a beast or a dog, but am a man as well as yourself." Since then human nature agrees equally with all persons, and since no one can live a sociable life with another that does not own or respect him as a man, it follows as a command of the law of nature, that every man esteem and treat another as one who is naturally his equal, or who is a man as well as he. There be many popular or plausible reasons that greatly illustrate this equality, *viz.* that we all derive our being from one stock, the

same common father of [the] human race. On this consideration Boethius[6] checks
the pride of the insulting nobility: . . .

> Fondly our first descent we boast;
>   If whence at first our breath we drew,
>   The common springs of life we view,
> The airy notion soon is lost.
>
> The Almighty made us equal all;
>   But he that slavishly complies
>   To do the drudgery of vice,
> Denies his high original.

And also, that our bodies are composed of matter, frail, brittle, and liable to be
destroyed by [a] thousand accidents. We all owe our existence to the same method
of propagation. The noblest mortal, in his entrance onto the stage of life, is not
distinguished by any pomp or of passage from the lowest of mankind; and our life
hastens to the same general mark: death observes no ceremony, but knocks as
loud at the barriers of the Court as at the door of the cottage.

. . . . . .

[OF THE CIVIL BEING OF MAN]

And thus we come to consider man in a civil state of being; wherein we shall
observe the great difference between a natural and political state; for in the latter
state many great disproportions appear, or at least many obvious distinctions are
soon made amongst men.

Which doctrine is to be laid open under a few heads:

1. Every man considered in a natural state must be allowed to be free and at
his own dispose; yet to suit man's inclinations to society, and in a peculiar manner
to gratify the necessity he is in of public rule and order, he is impelled to enter
into a civil community, and divests himself of his natural freedom and puts himself under government: which amongst other things comprehends the power of
life and death over him, together with authority to enjoin him some things to
which he has an utter aversion, and to prohibit him other things for which he may
have as strong an inclination, so that he may be often, under this authority,
obliged to sacrifice his private for the public good. So that, though man is inclined
to society, yet he is driven to a combination by great necessity. For that the true
and leading cause of forming governments, and yielding up natural liberty and
throwing man's equality into a common pile to be new cast by the rules of fellowship, was really and truly to guard themselves against the injuries men were liable
to interchangeably. For none so good to man as man, and yet none a greater enemy, so that,

2. The first human subject and original of civil power is the people. For as they
have a power, every man over himself in a natural state, so upon a combination
they can and do bequeath this power unto others, and settle it according as their
united discretion shall determine. For that this is very plain, that when the subject
of sovereign power is quite extinct, that power returns to the people again. And
when they are free, they may set up what species of government they please; or, if
they rather incline to it, they may subside into a state of natural being, if it be
plainly for the best. In the Eastern country of the Mogul, we have some resem-

---

[6]Boethius (c. 480–524), Roman philosopher whose greatest
work is *De Consolatione Philosophia* (*The Consolation of Philosophy*).

blance of the case: for upon the death of an absolute monarch, they live so many days without a civil head; but in that interregnum, those who survive the vacancy are glad to get into a civil state again, and usually they are in a very bloody condition when they return under the covert of a new monarch. This project is to endear the people to a tyranny, from the experience they have so lately had of an anarchy.

3. The formal reason of government is the will of a community, yielded up and surrendered to some other subject, either of one particular person or more, conveyed in the following manner:

Let us conceive in our mind a multitude of men, all naturally free and equal, going about voluntarily to erect themselves into a new commonwealth. Now, their condition being such, to bring themselves into a politic body they must needs enter into divers covenants.

They must interchangeably, each man, covenant to join in one lasting society, that they may be capable to concert the measures of their safety by a public vote.

A vote or decree must then nextly pass to set up some particular species of government over them. And if they are joined in their first compact upon absolute terms to stand to the decision of the first vote concerning the species of government, then all are bound by the majority to acquiesce in that particular form thereby settled, though their own private opinion incline them to some other model.

After a decree has specified the particular form of government, then there will be need of a new covenant, whereby those on whom sovereignty is conferred engage to take care of the common peace and welfare, and the subjects on the other hand to yield them faithful obedience. In which covenant is included that submission and union of wills by which a state may be conceived to be but one person. So that the most proper definition of a civil state is this: a civil state is a compound moral person whose will (united by those covenants before passed) is the will of all, to the end it may use and apply the strength and riches of private persons towards maintaining the common peace, security and well-being of all. Which may be conceived as though the whole state was now become but one man, in which the aforesaid covenants may be supposed, under God's providence, to be the divine fiat pronounced by God, "Let us make man."

And by way of resemblance, the aforesaid being may be thus anatomized:

The sovereign power is the soul infused, giving life and motion to the whole body.

Subordinate officers are the joints by which the body moves.

Wealth and riches are the strength.

Equity and laws are the reason.

Councilors the memory.

Salus Populi,[7] or the happiness of the people, is the end of its being, or main business to be attended and done.

Concord amongst the members and all estates is the health.

Sedition is sickness, and civil war death.

4. The parts of sovereignty may be considered; so:

As it prescribes the rule of action, it is rightly termed legislative power.

As it determines the controversies of subjects by the standard of those rules, so is it justly termed judiciary power.

As it arms the subjects against foreigners or forbids hostility, so it's called the power of peace and war.

As it takes in ministers for the discharge of business, so it is called the right of

---

[7]Health of the people.

appointing magistrates. So that all great officers and public servants must needs owe their original to the creating power of sovereignty. So that those whose right it is to create may dissolve the being of those who are created, unless they cast them into an immortal frame. And yet must needs be dissoluble if they justly forfeit their being to their creators.

5. The chief end of civil communities is that men thus conjoined may be secured against the injuries they are liable to from their own kind. For if every man could secure himself singly, it would be great folly for him to renounce his natural liberty, in which every man is his own king and protector.

[THREE FORMS OF GOVERNMENT: DEMOCRACY, ARISTOCRACY, MONARCHY]

The sovereign authority, besides that it inheres in every state as in a common and general subject, so farther, according as it resides in some one person, or in a council (consisting of some select persons or of all the members of a community) as in a proper and particular subject, so it produceth different forms of commonwealths, *viz.* such as are either simple and regular, or mixed.

The forms of a regular state are three only, which forms arise from the proper and particular subject in which the supreme power resides. As:

1. A democracy: which is when the sovereign power is lodged in a council consisting of all the members, and where every member has the privilege of a vote.

This form of government appears in the greatest part of the world to have been the most ancient. For that reason seems to show it to be most probable that when men (being originally in a condition of natural freedom and equality) had thoughts of joining in a civil body, [they] would without question be inclined to administer their common affairs by their common judgment, and so must necessarily, to gratify that inclination, establish a democracy. Neither can it be rationally imagined that fathers of families, being yet free and independent, should in a moment, or little time, take off their long delight in governing their own affairs and devolve all upon some single sovereign commander. For that it seems to have been thought more equitable that what belonged to all should be managed by all, when all had entered by compact into one community. . . .

A democracy is then erected when a number of free persons do assemble together, in order to enter into a covenant for uniting themselves in a body. And such a preparative assembly hath some appearance already of a democracy: it is a democracy in embryo properly in this respect, that every man hath the privilege freely to deliver his opinion concerning the common affairs. Yet he who dissents from the vote of the majority is not in the least obliged by what they determine, till by a second covenant a popular form be actually established. For not before then can we call it a democratical government, *viz.* till the right of determining all matters relating to the public safety is actually placed in a general assembly of the whole people, or by their own compact and mutual agreement, determine themselves the proper subject for the exercise of sovereign power.

And to complete this state, and render it capable to exert its power to answer the end of a civil state, these conditions are necessary:

That a certain time and place be assigned for assembling.

That when the assembly be orderly met, as to time and place, that then the vote of the majority must pass for the vote of the whole body.

That magistrates be appointed to exercise the authority of the whole, for the better dispatch of business of every day's occurrence; who also may with more mature diligence search into more important affairs, and if in case any thing happens of greater consequence may report it to the assembly, and be peculiarly serviceable in putting all public decrees into execution—because a large body of people is almost useless in respect of the last service, and of many others as to the more particular application and exercise of power. Therefore it is most agreeable with the law of nature that they institute their officers to act in their name and stead.

2. The second species of regular government is an aristocracy. And this is said then to be constituted when the people or assembly, united by a first covenant and having thereby cast themselves into the first rudiments of a state, do then, by common decree, devolve the sovereign power on a council, consisting of some select members. And these, having accepted of the designation, are then properly invested with sovereign command. And then an aristocracy is formed.

3. The third species of a regular government is a monarchy, which is settled when the sovereign power is conferred on some one worthy person. It differs from the former, because a monarch who is but one person in natural, as well as in moral account, and so is furnished with an immediate power of exercising sovereign command in all instances of government; but the forenamed must needs have particular time and place assigned; but the power and authority is equal in each.

• • • • •

[DEMOCRACY: "THE NOBLE GOVERNMENT"][8]

. . . But to abbreviate: it seems most agreeable with the light of nature that if there be any of the regular government settled in the church of God, it must needs be a democracy.

This is a form of government which the light of nature does highly value, and often directs to as most agreeable to the just and natural prerogatives of human beings. This was of great account in the early times of the world. And not only so, but upon the experience of several thousand years, after the world had been tumbled and tossed from one species of government to another, at a great expense of blood and treasure, many of the wise nations of the world have sheltered themselves under it again:—or at least have blendished and balanced their governments with it.

It is certainly a great truth, that man's original liberty, after it is resigned (yet under due restrictions), ought to be cherished in all wise governments; or otherwise a man, in making himself a subject, he alters himself from a free-man into a slave, which to do is repugnant to the law of nature. Also the natural equality of men amongst men must be duly favored, in that government was never established by God or nature to give one man a prerogative to insult over another. Therefore in a civil, as well as in a natural, state of being, a just equality is to be indulged, so far as that every man is bound to honor every man, which is agreeable both with nature and religion, I Pet. 2: 17: "Honor all men."

The end of all good government is to cultivate humanity and promote the happiness of all, and the good of every man in all his rights, his life, liberty, estate, honor, etc., without injury or abuse done to any. Then certainly it cannot easily be thought that a company of men, that shall enter into a voluntary compact, to hold all power in their own hands, thereby to use and improve their united force, wisdom, riches and strength for the common and particular good of every member, as is the nature of a democracy—I say, it cannot be that this sort of constitution will so readily furnish those in government with an appetite or disposition to prey upon each other, or embezzle the common stock, as some particular persons may be apt to do when set off and entrusted with the same power. And moreover, this appears very natural, that when the aforesaid government or power, settled in all, when they have elected certain capable persons to minister in their affairs, and the

---

[8]In a later passage not excerpted here, Wise says: "A democracy was the noble government which beat out all the bad weather of ten bloody persecutions under the management of antiquity."

said ministers remain accountable to the assembly, these officers must needs be under the influence of many wise cautions from their own thoughts (as well as under confinement by their commission) in their whole administration. And from thence it must needs follow that they will be more apt and inclined to steer right for the main point, *viz.* the peculiar good and benefit of the whole and every particular member fairly and sincerely. And why may not these stand for very rational pleas in church order?

For certainly if Christ has settled any form of power in His church, He has done it for His church's safety and for the benefit of every member. Then He must needs be presumed to have made choice of that government as should least expose His people to hazard, either from the fraud or arbitrary measures of particular men. And it is as plain as daylight, there is no species of government like a democracy to attain this end. . . .

1717

LIVING: PURITAN GENTLEMAN, PLANTATION ARISTOCRAT

SAMUEL SEWALL   WILLIAM BYRD

The differences between the North and the South began with the differences between the settlers of New England (dissident Separatists and non-Separatist Puritans) and the settlers of Virginia (Anglican gentlemen and adventurers). These differences may be observed in the remarkable contrast between Massachusett's Samuel Sewall and Virginia's William Byrd. Both left voluminous diaries in which they revealed themselves, their country, and their times; each has been called an American Pepys. Both were men of great wealth with a keen eye to its conservation and increase; and both served their colonies in high governmental positions. But they differ fundamentally in their views of religion, women, slaves, and Indians, as well as in their sense of themselves, their lives, their destinies. Both represent cultures that contributed to the making and shaping of modern America.

SAMUEL SEWALL
(1652–1730)

On February 6, 1718, some four months after his wife's death, Samuel Sewall wrote in his diary: "This morning wandering in my mind whether to live
a single or a married life, I had a sweet and very affectionate meditation concerning the Lord Jesus. Nothing was objected against his person, parentage,
relations, estate, house, home! Why did I not resolutely, presently close with
Him! And I cried mightily to God that He would help me so to do!" The religious focus of the passage is expected in the personal writings of Puritans;
but what is a reader to make of Sewall's finding no objections to Lord Jesus's
"person, parentage, relations, estate, house, home." The diction suggests (unconsciously perhaps) that a rigorous credit check has found Jesus a good commercial risk.

The passage reveals the tendency of second-generation Puritans to be less
intense about religious dedication and more concerned with business and
commerce. Among other things, Sewall was a banker and would have been
accustomed to credit checks. Throughout his diary he constantly set down the
cost of items he purchased (especially when they were gifts) and the amount
of charitable contributions he made. His was the generation of pragmatic Puritans who found no contradiction in a life dedicated to God and commerce,
to salvation and prosperity.

Born in England of parents with some roots and considerable property in
New England, Sewall was brought to Boston when he was nine. Witnessing in
alarm the change from Puritan to royal rule in England with the Restoration
in 1660, the family decided on a permanent move to the New World. Sewall
graduated from Harvard in 1671 (where he roomed with the poet Edward
Taylor), became a tutor there, and after three years was awarded an M.A. for
a thesis written on original sin. His marriage in 1676 to Hannah Hull, daughter of the wealthiest man in the colony, brought a large dowry that enabled
Sewall to launch his career as a merchant-banker, dealing in (among other
things) tobacco, oil, and wood. Under Sewall's shrewd management, land
speculation, money lending, and various commercial enterprises, his estate
grew enormously to mark him as a leading citizen of Massachusetts.

He held various public offices, including manager of the colony's printing
press and deputy to the General Court; he served twice as a member of the
Governing Council in 1684–86 and 1691–1725. In England during 1688–
89, he helped Increase Mather in his negotiations with William III for renewal of the Royal Charter for Massachusetts Bay Colony.

In 1692 he was appointed by Royal Governor Sir William Phips to be one
of the commissioners (John Hathorne, Nathaniel Hawthorne's ancestor, was
another) to try the accused witches in Salem. Nineteen individuals (and two
dogs) were sentenced to death and hanged. Sewall says little about the trial in
his diary, but he does record there, on January 14, 1697, his recantation. It
was read aloud that day, set aside as a day of penance for the wrongs committed in Salem, in the Old South Church while Sewall stood listening to the
words of his own confession, expressing his desire "to take the blame and
shame of the [guilt contracted]" and "asking pardon of men, and especially
desiring prayers that God . . . would pardon that sin. . . ." He was the only
person bearing responsibility in the Salem trials and executions to make a
public confession.

Sewall wrote in his diary in 1716, "I essayed June 22 to prevent Indians and Negroes being rated with horses and hogs, but could not prevail." Such entries show Sewall's human sympathies in advance of those of his compatriots. Indeed, one of the few items he published during his lifetime, *The Selling of Joseph* (1700), was a tract against slavery, the first printed in New England. The argument was simple and powerful: "It is most certain that all men, as they are the sons of Adam, are coheirs; and have equal rights unto liberty. . . ."

In 1673 Sewall began keeping his diary and he continued (with a lapse from 1677 to 1685) through 1729, the year before his death. He did not write for publication and the diary did not come to light until the middle of the nineteenth century, when it was published in three volumes (1878–82). Appearance of the *Diary* immediately established Sewall as an important literary figure of the colonial period. One reviewer called him a "Puritan Pepys," providing for the Massachusetts Bay Colony the same kind of intimate revelation of daily life that Samuel Pepys (1633–1703) had given England in his famous diary.

Sewall's accounts of his courtships after his wife's death (especially of the widow Madam Winthrop) have been so frequently reprinted without reference to Sewall's situation that he has seemed to some primarily a comic figure. It must be remembered that he had been happily married for forty-one years, that on his wife's sudden death he was a grief-stricken man, and that instead of withdrawing he set about to renew his life with continuing close relationships. His second wife, the Widow Tilley, died within less than one year of the marriage. By the time he came to court Madam Winthrop, he was a desolate, even desperate man in his loneliness. If there is something of the comic in his behavior, there is also much of human pathos. As he sets down his feelings in his *Diary*, he reveals himself as a clumsy but well-meaning 68-year-old man reaching out uncertainly for human companionship and love.

ADDITIONAL READING

The Diary of Samuel Sewall, ed. Harvey Wish, 1967.

N. H. Chamberlain, *Samuel Sewall*, 1897, rpt. 1967; Vernon L. Parrington, "Samuel Sewall, Yankee," *Main Currents in American Thought*, 1927–30; Perry Miller, *The New England Mind: From Colony to Province*, 1953; Ola E. Winslow, *Samuel Sewall of Boston*, 1964; T. B. Strandness, *Samuel Sewall, A Puritan Portrait*, 1967.

TEXT

The Diary of Samuel Sewall, 1674–1729, ed. M. Halsey Thomas, 1973. Footnotes from this edition are indicated by the editor's name followed by the notes enclosed in quotation marks. Typography, punctuation, spelling, and usage have been changed to conform with contemporary English and modern printing practices.

from The Diary of Samuel Sewall

[BIRTH AND DEATH OF A SON, 1685]

Monday, December 7, 1685. About one in the night my wife is brought to bed of a son, of which Mother Hull brings me the first news: Mrs. Weeden, midwife.[1]

Sabbath-day, December 13, 1685. Mr. Willard[2] baptizeth my son lately born, whom I named Henry:[3] David Stoddard, the son of Mr. Simeon Stoddard, was baptized next, and then several other grown children. Nurse Hill came in before the psalm was sung, and yet the child was fine and quiet: Mr. Willard preached from John 15: 8: "Herein is my Father glorified, that ye bear much fruit, so shall ye be my disciples": which is the first sermon my little son hath been present at.

December 17. One Trescot, an ancient woman of Dorchester, riding over the Neck, tide being high, her horse drowned and she hardly saved: questioned whether she may live or no. This night little Hull[4] hath a convulsion fit, as he lay with me in bed. Henry very restless.

Saturday, December 19. Mr. Willard prays with my little Henry, being very ill.

Sabbath-day, December 20. Send notes to Mr. Willard and Mr. Moodey[5] to pray for my child Henry.

Monday, about four in the morn the faint and moaning noise of my child forces me up to pray for it.

[December] 21. Monday even Mr. Moodey calls. I get him to go up and pray with my extreme sick son.

Tuesday Morn, December 22. Child makes no noise save by a kind of snoring as it breathed, and as it were slept.

Read the 16th of the first Chron.[6] in the family. Having read to my wife and nurse out of John: the fourteenth Chapter[7] fell now in course, which I read and went to prayer: By that time had done, could hear little breathing, and so about sun-rise, or little after, he fell asleep, I hope in Jesus, and that a mansion was ready for him in the Father's house. Died in Nurse Hill's lap. Nurse Hill washes and lays him out: because our private meeting[8] hath a day of prayer tomorrow, Thursday, Mr. Willard's lecture,[9] and the child dying after sunrise (weather cloudy), have determined to bury on Thursday after lecture. The Lord sanctify his dispensation, and prepare me and mine for the coming of our Lord, in whatsoever way it be. Mr. Tho. Oakes our physician for this child. Read the 16th Chap. of the First Chronicles in the Family.

Tuesday night read the 15th John in the chamber, out of which Mr. Willard took his text the day Henry was baptized: in the family, the 3[d] of Matthew,[10] both requiring fruit.

Wednesday, December 23. Go to the private fast at Brother Williams's.[11] Capt. Scottow begins and is enlarged and fervent in praying for the Church and Christ's witnesses: Made me conclude. Sung part 137. Ps.[12] But if I Jerusalem, &c. Just

---

[1]Judith (Quincy) Hull (d. 1695), mother-in-law of Sewall; Mrs. Elizabeth Weeden.

[2]Samuel Willard (1640–1707), minister of the Old South Church, Boston.

[3]Henry was the sixth child of Sewell and his wife Hannah who had a total of fourteen children; the first child, John, had died in 1678 at the age of 15 months.

[4]Hull, the fifth child, was born in July 1684.

[5]Joshua Moody (1684–1693), minister of the First Church, Boston.

[6]I Chronicles 16: David gives thanks to the Lord before the Ark of the Covenant, the cask containing the tablets of the Ten Commandments.

[7]John 14:1–2: "Let not your heart be troubled: ye believe in God, believe also in me. In my Father's house are many mansions: if it were not so, I would have told you. I go to prepare a place for you."

[8]Hull, Sewall, and their neighbors met for private prayer-meetings beginning in 1676.

[9]Each Thursday, the minister would lecture on the Bible.

[10]John 15:8:"Herein is my Father glorified, that ye bear much fruit"; Matthew 3:8: "Bring forth therefore fruits meet for repentance."

[11]Captain Nathaniel Williams (1642–1714), deacon and member of Sewall's private prayer-meeting group; Capt. Joshua Scottow, a member also.

[12]Psalm 137:1, 4, 5, 9: "By the rivers of Babylon, there we sat down, yea, we wept, when we remembered Zion. . . . How shall we sing the Lord's song in a strange land? If I forget thee, O Jerusalem, let my right hand forget her cunning. . . . Happy shall he be, that taketh and dasheth thy [Babylon's] little ones against the stones."

before I went, Brother Longfellow[13] came in, which was some exercise to me, he being so ill conditioned and so outwardly shabby. The Lord humble me. As I remember, he came so before; either upon the funeral of my father or Johnny.

Thursday, December 24, 1685. We follow little Henry to his grave: Governor and magistrates of the county here, 8 in all, beside my self, eight ministers, and several persons of note. Mr. Phillips of Rowley here. I led Sam., then Cous. Savage led mother, and Cousin Dummer led Cous. Quinsey's wife,[14] he not well. Midwife Weeden and Nurse Hill carried the corpse by turns, and so by men in its chesnut coffin 'twas set into a grave (the tomb full of water) between 4 and 5. At lecture the 21. Psalm was Sung from 8th to the end.[15] The Lord humble me kindly in respect of all my enmity against Him, and let his breaking my image in my Son be a means of it. Considerable snow this night. At night little Hull had a sore convulsion fit.[16]

[WITCHCRAFT TRIALS: INVOLVEMENT, 1692, AND RECANTATION, 1697]

April 11, 1692. Went to Salem, where, in the meeting-house, the persons accused of witchcraft were examined; was a very great assembly; 'twas awful to see how the afflicted persons were agitated. Mr. Noyes pray'd at the beginning, and Mr. Higginson concluded.[1]

August 19, 1692. This day[2] George Burrough, John Willard, John Procter, Martha Carrier and George Jacobs were executed at Salem, a very great number of spectators being present. Mr. Cotton Mather was there, Mr. Sims, Hale, Noyes, Chiever, &c. All of them said they were innocent, Carrier and all. Mr. Mather says they all died by a righteous sentence. Mr. Burrough by his speech, prayer, protestation of his innocence, did much move unthinking persons, which occasions their speaking hardly concerning his being executed.

August 25. Fast at the old *[First]* Church, respecting the witchcraft, drought, &c.

Monday, September 19, 1692. About noon, at Salem, Giles Corey was press'd to death for standing mute; much pains was used with him two days, one after another, by the Court and Capt. Gardner of Nantucket who had been of his acquaintance: but all in vain.[3]

September 20. Now I hear from Salem that about 18 years ago, he [Giles Corey] was suspected to have stampd and press'd a man to death, but was cleared. 'Twas

---

[13]Sewall's brother-in-law, William Longfellow, Ensign (d. 1690), married to Anne.

[14]Samuel Phillips, clergyman; Capt. Ephraim Savage; Capt. Jeremiah Drummer (1645–1718), silversmith; Ann (Shepard) Quincy, wife of Daniel Quincy (1650/51–1690).

[15]Psalm 21:8, 10: "Thine hand shall find out all thine enemies: thy right hand shall find out those that hate thee. . . . Their fruit shalt thou destroy from the earth, and their seed from among the children of men."

[16]He died six months later, June 1686.

[1]Sewall's first mention of the Salem witchcraft episode. In the margin of this entry he wrote: "Vae, vae, vae [Woe, woe, woe] Witchcraft." Thomas: "In the dismal and interminable winter of 1691–92, a group of bored teenage girls, and younger—the daughters, relatives, and neighbors of the Rev. Samuel Parris of Salem Village (now Danvers)—idled often in the kitchen of the parsonage to listen to the tales of Tituba, the half-Carib, half-Negro slave, and to learn voodoo tricks and spells from her. Before many of these forbidden gatherings had taken place they had worked themselves up into mass hysteria, and would put on an act of screaming, writhing, and swooning whenever there was an audience. The parents, the clergy, the doctors, had only one explanation: the girls were possessed.

Next the girls accused various crones of bewitching them and torturing them by spectral means. A special court was convened in Salem to deal with this outbreak. Feeling their power as the venerable judges attended in all seriousness to their rantings, the girls went on to accuse scores of persons, some on the basis of family and church feuds which they heard about at home, and before the summer was over nineteen of the convicted had died on the gallows."

[2]Sewall, at a later time, wrote in the margin: "Doleful! Witchcraft."

[3]Thomas: "In an open field near the Salem jail, Giles Corey, about 80 years of age, was put to death by officers of the law, who placed heavy stones on his supine body, adding them until his life was extinguished. This was in strict accord with English law, but the case stands alone in American annals. . . . Corey felt that he had no chance of acquittal of the charges of witchcraft standing against him; he also bethought his not inconsiderable land holdings which might be forfeited if he were convicted as a felon. He therefore executed a deed in Ipswich jail conveying his property to his sons-in-law, William Cleves and John Moulton, who had stood by him in his troubles. When called to court to answer the indictment of the grand jury, he stood resolutely silent."

not remembered till Anne Putnam was told of it by said Corey's spectre the sabbath-day night before execution.[4]

September 21. A petition is sent to town in behalf of Dorcas Hoar, who now confesses: accordingly an order is sent to the sheriff to forbear her execution, notwithstanding her being in the warrant to die tomorrow. This is the first condemned person who has confess'd.[5]

Thursday, September 22, 1692. William Stoughton, Esqr., John Hathorne, Esqr., Mr. Cotton Mather, and Capt. John Higginson, with my Brother St., were at our house, speaking about publishing some Trials of the Witches.[6]

[January 14, 1697]. Copy of the bill I put up on the fast day;[7] giving it to Mr. Willard as he pass'd by, and standing up at the reading of it, and bowing when finished; in the afternoon.

"Samuel Sewall, sensible of the reiterated strokes of God upon himself and family;[8] and being sensible, that as to the guilt contracted, upon the opening of the late Commission of Oyer and Terminer[9] at Salem (to which the order for this day relates) he is, upon many accounts, more concerned than any that he knows of, desires to take the blame and shame of it, asking pardon of men, and especially desiring prayers that God, who has an unlimited authority, would pardon that sin and all other his sins; personal and relative: And according to his infinite benignity, and sovereignty, not visit the sin of him, or of any other, upon himself or any of his, nor upon the land: But that He would powerfully defend him against all temptations to sin, for the future; and vouchsafe him the efficacious, saving conduct of his word and spirit."

[DEATH OF WIFE HANNAH AFTER FORTY-ONE YEARS OF Marriage, 1717]

[October 15, 1717]. My wife got some relapse by a new cold and grew very bad; sent for Mr. Oakes, and he sat up with me all night.

[October] 16. The distemper increases; yet my wife speaks to me to go to bed.

[October] 17. Thursday, I asked my wife whether twere best for me to go to lecture: she said, I can't tell; so I staid at home. Put up a note. It being my son's[1] lecture, and I absent, 'twas taken much notice of. Major Gen Winthrop[2] and his lady visit us. I thank her that she would visit my poor wife.

Friday, [October] 18. My wife grows worse and exceedingly restless. Pray'd God to look upon her. Ask'd not after my going to bed. Had the advice of Mr. Williams and Dr. Cutler.[3]

---

[4]Thomas: "Cotton Mather printed Thomas Putnam's letter to Sewall in his *Wonders of the Invisible World.* Ann Putnam, 12, was one of the aptest pupils of Tituba in the Parris kitchen, and with her mother, one of the chief accusers of the witches. Putnam wrote: 'The last night my daughter Ann was grievously tormented by witches, threatning that she should be pressed to death, before Giles Cory. But thro' the goodness of a gracious God, she had at last a little respite. Whereupon there appeared unto her (she said) a man in a winding sheet; who told her that Giles Cory had murdered him, by pressing him to death with his feet; but that the devil there appeared unto him, and covenanted with him, and promised him, he should not be hanged. The apparition said, God hardened his heart that he should not hearken to the advice of the court, and so die an easy death; because as it said, "It must be done to him as he has done to me." The apparition also said, that Giles Cory was carry'd to the Court for this, and that the jury had found the murder, and that her father knew the man, and the thing was done before she was born. . . .'"

[5]Thomas: "By reason of a strange inversion of jurisprudence which prevailed in the witchcraft court, confession insured immunity from trial or imprisonment or execution. Some fifty-five of the accused confessed their complicity with the Evil One and were allowed to go free. Dorcas

Hoar had been tried and sentenced, and her hanging was imminent before she confessed; she would have gone to the gallows except for the petition gotten up for her by influential friends, including John Hale, minister of Beverly."

[6]Cotton Mather's *The Wonders of the Invisible World.* Thomas: "Following Mather's breviates of the trials there is a statement over the names of William Stoughton and Samuel Sewall, dated at Boston, October 11, 1692, that 'Upon perusal thereof, we find the matters of fact and evidence truly reported.'"

[7]January 14, 1697, was set aside by Massachusetts as a day of atonement and fasting for the execution of the witches. Sewall was the only individual of prominence who made public confession of error.

[8]One-month-old Jane died in 1693, two-year-old Sarah died in 1696, and a son was stillborn in 1696.

[9]The Court instituted by the Governor in May 1692 "to enquire, hear and determine all manner of crimes and offenses. . . ."; it was disbanded in October 1692.

[1]Joseph Sewall (1688–1769), minister of the Old South Church (1713–58).

[2]Maj. Gen. Wait Still Winthrop (1642–1717), Chief Justice.

[3]Nathaniel Williams, Master of Boston Latin School also practiced medicine; Dr. John Cutler.

7th day, [October] 19. Call'd Dr. C. Mather to pray, which he did excellently in the dining room, having suggested good thoughts to my wife before he went down. After, Mr. Wadsworth[4] pray'd in the chamber when 'twas suppos'd my wife took little notice. About a quarter of an hour past four, my dear wife expired in the afternoon, whereby the chamber was fill'd with a flood of tears. God is teaching me a new lesson; to live a widower's life. Lord help me to learn; and be a sun and shield to me, now so much of my comfort and defense are taken away.[5]

[October] 20. I go to the public worship forenoon and afternoon. My son has much ado to read the note I put up, being overwhelm'd with tears.

[October] 21. Monday, my dear wife is embowelled and put in a cere-cloth,[6] the weather being more than ordinarily hot.

Midweek, [October] 23. My dear wife is inter'd. Bearers, Lt. Gov; Dummer, Maj. Gen. Winthrop; Col. Elisha Hutchinson, Col. Townsend; Andrew Belcher Esqr. and Simeon Stoddard Esqr. I intended Col. Taylor for a bearer, but he was from home. Had very comfortable weather. Bro. Gerrish pray'd with us when return'd from the tomb: I went into it. Gov. had a scarf and ring, and the bearers, Gov. Dudley, Brother Sewall, Hirst, Gerrish. Was very destitute for want of the help of son Hirst, and cousin Jane Green. This was the first day of the Gen. Court. Gave the deputies books. Allen's *Alarm*.[7] They sent Mr. Isa. Tay and Capt. Wadsworth to me to thank me.

[COURTSHIP OF MADAM WINTHROP, 1720]

Winthrop was not alone in wondering, as he noted in his diary in February 1718, "whether to live a single or a married life." That same month he records that Governor Dudley had "laid out," or selected Madam Winthrop as a suitable wife for him, and in March President Leverett and his wife "had laid out Madam Brown" for him. Even Cotton Mather, as Thomas notes, put pressure on Sewall to remarry, giving him a copy of the sermon he had preached to the widows (who made up a fifth of his congregation), entitled, in part, *A Brief Essay to do Good unto the Widow*. Sewall entered in his diary for March 17, 1718, these words from Mather's letter accompanying his sermon: "But your honor will allow me now at length to offer you my opinion that all the regards are not yet paid which you owe unto the *Widow*, and which are expected from you." Thus in addition to loneliness, Christian duty impelled Sewall to look for another wife.

He began to court Mrs. Dorothy Denison, a widow, in 1718. She was a reluctant object of his affection, and the courtship broke off by the end of the year. In 1719, Sewall turned his attentions to another widow, Abigail Tilley. In October, they were married, but she became gravely ill on the wedding night, spitting blood. A few months later, in May 1720, the second Mrs. Sewall died. Later in 1720, Sewall began his courtship of Madam Katherine Winthrop, widow of Major-General Wait Still Winthrop, who died in 1717. She was fifty-six years old when Sewall began courting her. Madam Winthrop's first husband, John Eyre, had died in 1700. On visiting her, Sewall often encountered children and grandchildren from her first marriage. There were three surviving children from that marriage: Katherine, who first mar-

---

[4]Benjamin Wadsworth, pastor of First Church.
[5]Thomas: "Hannah Hull Sewall was fifty-nine and had been married to our diarist for forty-one years. There is not a word of complaint, annoyance, disaccord, or disaffection in these pages."
[6]A waxed winding-sheet.

[7]Thomas: "Joseph Alleine's book, *An Alarm to Unconverted Sinners* (London, 1672), was a best-seller of the time." Sewall was following custom in giving presents to the guests and coffin bearers. His son-in-law, Grove Hirst was dying; he was the husband of Bettey Sewall, who had died the year before.

ried David Jeffries, and after his death married Dr. Oliver Noyes; Bethiah, who married John Walley; and John (thus John Eyre).

September 5 [1720]. Going to son Sewall's I there meet with Madam Winthrop, told her I was glad to meet her there, had not seen her a great while; gave her Mr. Homes's *Sermon.*[1]

[September 30]. Mr. Colman's lecture: Daughter Sewall acquaints Madam Winthrop that if she pleas'd to be within at 3. p.m. I would wait on her. She answer'd she would be at home.

[October] 1. Saturday, I dine at Mr. Stoddard's: from thence I went to Madam Winthrop's just at 3. Spake to her, saying, my loving wife died so soon and suddenly, 'twas hardly convenient for me to think of marrying again; however I came to this resolution, that I would not make my court to any person without first consulting with her. Had a pleasant discourse about 7 single persons sitting in the fore-seat[2] [September] 29th, viz. Mad[m] Rebekah Dudley, Catharine Winthrop, Bridget Usher, Deliverance Legg, Rebekah Loyd, Lydia Colman, Elizabeth Bellingham. She propounded one and another for me; but none would do, said Mrs. Loyd was about her age.

October 3. Waited on Madam Winthrop again; 'twas a little while before she came in. Her daughter Noyes being there alone with me, I said, I hoped my waiting on her mother would not be disagreeable to her. She answer'd she should not be against that that might be for her comfort. I saluted her, and told her I perceiv'd I must shortly wish her a good time; (her mother had told me, she was with child, and within a month or two of her time). By and by in came Mr. Ayers,[3] Chaplain of the Castle, and hang'd up his hat, which I was a little startled at, it seeming as if he was to lodge there. At last Madam Winthrop came in. After a considerable time, I went up to her and said, if it might not be inconvenient I desired to speak with her. She assented, and spake of going into another room; but Mr. Ayers and Mrs. Noyes presently rose up, and went out, leaving us there alone. Then I usher'd in discourse from the names in the fore-seat; at last I pray'd that Katharine *[Mrs. Winthrop]* might be the person assign'd for me. She instantly took it up in way of denial, as if she had catch'd at an opportunity to do it, saying she could not do it before she was asked. Said that was her mind unless she should change it, which she believed she should not; could not leave her children. I express'd my sorrow that she should do it so speedily, pray'd her consideration, and ask'd her when I should wait on her again. She setting no time, I mention'd that day sennight.[4] Gave her Mr. Willard's *Fountain*[5] open'd with the little print and verses; saying, I hop'd if we did well read that book, we should meet together hereafter, if we did not now. She took the book, and put it in her pocket. Took leave.

[October] 6. A little after 6. p.m. I went to Madam Winthrop's. She was not within. I gave Sarah Chickering the maid 2s, Juno, who brought in wood, 1s. Afterward the nurse came in, I gave her 18d, having no other small bill. After awhile Dr. Noyes came in with his mother; and quickly after his wife came in. They sat talking, I think, till eight a-clock. I said I fear'd I might be some interruption to their business. Dr. Noyes reply'd pleasantly: He fear'd they might be an interrup-

[1]Thomas: "*A Discourse concerning the Publick reading of the Holy Scriptures, by the Lords people in their Religious Assemblies: delivered at Tisbury August 12, 1719* by William Homes, M.A. (Edin.), minister of Chilmark, Martha's Vineyard (Boston, 1720)."
[2]A pew reserved for widows at the front of the church.

[3]Obadiah Ayers was chaplain of Castle William, fortress on Castle Island in Boston Harbor.
[4]Seven nights, a week later.
[5]Samuel Willard's *The Fountain Opened, or the Great Gospel Privilege of Having Christ Exhibited to Sinful Men* (1700).

tion to me, and went away. Madam seem'd to harp upon the same string. Must take care of her children; could not leave that house and neighbourhood where she had dwelt so long. I told her she might do her children as much or more good by bestowing what she laid out in house-keeping, upon them. Said her son would be of age the 7th of August. I said it might be inconvenient for her to dwell with her daughter-in-law, who must be mistress of the house. I gave her a piece of Mr. Belcher's cake and ginger-bread[6] wrapped up in a clean sheet of paper; told her of her father's kindness to me when treasurer, and I constable. My daughter Judith was gone from me and I was more lonesome—might help to forward one another in our journey to Canaan.[7]—Mr. Eyre came within the door; I saluted him, ask'd how Mr. Clark did, and he went away. I took leave about 9 o'clock. I told [her] I came now to refresh her memory as to Monday-night; said she had not forgot it. In discourse with her, I ask'd leave to speak with her sister; I meant to gain Madam Mico's[8] favour to persuade her sister. She seem'd surpris'd and displeas'd, and said she was in the same condition!

[October] 11. I writ a few lines to Madam Winthrop to this purpose: "Madam, these wait on you with Mr. Mayhew's Sermon, and account of the state of the Indians on Martha's Vinyard. I thank you for your unmerited favours of yesterday; and hope to have the happiness of waiting on you to-morrow before eight a-clock after noon. I pray GOD to keep you, and give you a joyfull entrance upon the two hundred and twenty ninth year of Christopher Columbus his discovery; and take leave, who am, Madam, your humble Serv[t].

S. S.

Sent this by Deacon Green, who deliver'd it to Sarah Chickering, her mistress not being at home.

[October] 12. . . . . Mrs. Anne Cotton came to door (twas before 8.) said Madam Winthrop was within, directed me into the little room, where she was full of work behind a stand; Mrs. Cotton came in and stood. Madam Winthrop pointed to her to set me a chair. Madam Winthrop's countenance was much changed from what 'twas on Monday, look'd dark and lowering. At last, the work, (black stuff or silk) was taken away, I got my chair in place, had some converse, but very cold and indifferent to what 'twas before. Ask'd her to acquit me of rudeness if I drew off her glove. Enquiring the reason, I told her 'twas great odds between handling a dead goat, and a living lady. Got it off. I told her I had one petition to ask of her, that was, that she would take off the negative she laid on me the third of October; She readily answer'd she could not, and enlarg'd upon it; She told me of it so soon as she could; could not leave her house, children, neighbours, business. I told her she might do some good to help and support me. Mentioning Mrs. Gookin, Nath, the widow Weld was spoken of; said I had visited Mrs. Denison. I told her, "Yes!" Afterward I said, If after a first and second vagary she would accept of me returning, her victorious kindness and good will would be very obliging. She thank'd me for my book, (Mr. Mayhew's *Sermon*), but said not a word of the letter. When she insisted on the negative, I pray'd there might be no more thunder and lightening, I should not sleep all night. I gave her Dr. Preston, *The Church's Marriage and the Church's Carriage*,[9] which cost me 6s at the sale. The door standing open, Mr. Ayers came in, hung up his hat, and sat down. After awhile, Madam Winthrop moving, he went out. John Eyre look'd in, I said, "How do ye," or, "your servant Mr. Eyre"; but heard no word from him. Sarah fill'd a glass of wine; she drank to me,

---

[6]Given to Sewall the day before by Jonathan Belcher (1682–1757), a wealthy merchant.
[7]The Promised Land of the Israelites; the Puritans considered New England as the New Canaan.
[8]Madam Winthrop's sister Mary, wife of John Mico, had been a widow since 1718.
[9]Thomas: "The *Golden Scepter held forth to the humble*. With

the *Church's Dignity by her Marriage. And The Church's Dutie in her Carriage*. In three Treatises . . . By the late learned and reverend Divine, John Preston (London, 1638). This was a volume of 461 pages which Sewall probably bought at the Auction Sale of Choice Books newly imported from Great Britain, sold at the Sign of the Magpy, 4 July 1720."

I to her. She sent Juno home with me with a good lantern, I gave her 6d and bid her thank her Mistress. In some of our discourse, I told her I had rather go to the stone-house adjoining to her, than to come to her against her mind. Told her the reason why I came every other night was lest I should drink too deep draughts of pleasure. She had talk'd of canary,[10] her kisses were to me better than the best canary. Explain'd the expression concerning Columbus.

[October] 17. Monday, . . . In the evening I visited Madam Winthrop, who treated me courteously, but not in clean linen as sometimes. She said, she did not know whether I would come again, or no. I ask'd her how she could so impute inconstancy to me. (I had not visited her since Wednesday night being unable to get over the indisposition received by the treatment received that night, and *I must in it* seem'd to sound like a made piece of formality.) Gave her this day's *Gazette.* . . .

[October] 18. Visited Madam Mico, who came to me in a splendid dress. I said, "It may be you have heard of my visiting Madam Winthrop," her sister. She answered, Her sister had told her of it. I ask'd her good will in the affair. She answer'd, If her sister were for it, she should not hinder it. I gave her Mr. Homes's *Sermon.* She gave me a glass of canary, entertain'd me with good discourse, and a respectful remembrance of my first wife. I took leave.

[October] 19. Midweek, visited Madam Winthrop; Sarah told me she was at Mr. Walley's, would not come home till late. I gave her Hannah's 3 oranges with her duty, not knowing whether I should find her or no. Was ready to go home: but said if I knew she was there, I would go thither. Sarah seem'd to speak with pretty good courage, She would be there. I went and found her there, with Mr. Walley and his wife in the little room below. At 7 a-clock I mentioned going home; at 8. I put on my coat, and quickly waited on her home. She found occasion to speak loud to the servant, as if she had a mind to be known. Was courteous to me; but took occasion to speak pretty earnestly about my keeping a coach: I said 'twould cost £100. per annum: she said 'twould cost but £40. Spake much against John Winthrop, his false-heartedness. . . . Came away somewhat late.

[October] 20. . . . Madam Winthrop not being at lecture, I went thither first; found her very serene with her daughter Noyes, Mrs. Dering, and the widow Shipreev sitting at a little table, she in her arm'd chair. She drank to me, and I to Mrs. Noyes. After awhile pray'd the favour to speak with her. She took one of the candles, and went into the best room, clos'd the shutters, sat down upon the couch. She told me Madam Usher had been there, and said the coach must be set on wheels, and not by rusting. She spake something of my needing a wig. Ask'd me what her sister said to me. I told her: She said, If her sister were for it, she would not hinder it. But I told her, she did not say she would be glad to have me for her brother. Said, I shall keep you in the cold, and ask her if she would be within tomorrow night, for we had had but a running feast. She said she could not tell whether she should, or no. I took leave. As were drinking at the Governour's, he said: In England the ladies minded little more than that they might have money, and coaches to ride in. I said, And New-England brooks[11] its name. At which Mr. Dudley smiled. Gov[r] said they were not quite so bad here.

[October] 21. Friday, My son, the minister, came to me p.m. by appointment and we pray one for another in the old chamber; more especially respecting my courtship. About 6. a-clock I go to Madam Winthrop's; Sarah told me her mistress was gone out, but did not tell me whither she went. She presently order'd me a fire; so I went in, having Dr. Sibb's *Bowels*[12] with me to read. I read the two first Sermons,

---

[10]Canary wine from the Canary Islands, off Spain.
[11]Bears.
[12]Thomas: "Richard Sibbes, D.D., master of St. Catherine's Hall, Cambridge, had published *Bowels Opened: Or, A Dis-* *covery Of The Neare and Deare Love, Union and Communion betwixt Christ, and the Church* in London in 1641; a third edition appeared in 1648."

still no body came in: at last about 9. a-clock Mr. John Eyre came in; I took the opportunity to say to him as I had done to Mrs. Noyes before, that I hoped my visiting his mother would not be disagreeable to him; he answered me with much respect. When 'twas after 9. a-clock he of himself said he would go and call her, she was but at one of his brothers. A while after I heard Madam Winthrop's voice, enquiring something about John. After a good while and clapping the garden door twice or thrice, she came in. I mention'd something of the lateness; she banter'd me, and said I was later. She receiv'd me courteously. I ask'd when our proceedings should be made public: She said they were like to be no more public than they were already. Offer'd me no wine that I remember. I rose up at 11 a-clock to come away, saying I would put on my coat, She offer'd not to help me. I pray'd her that Juno might light me home, she open'd the shutter, and said twas pretty light abroad; Juno was weary and gone to bed. So I came home by star-light as well as I could. At my first coming in, I gave Sarah five shillings. I wrote Mr. Eyre his name in his book with the date October 21. 1720. It cost me 8s. Jehovah jireh![13] Madam told me she had visited M. Mico, Wendell, and Wm Clark of the South *[Church]*.

October 24. I went in the hackny coach through the Common, stopped at Madam Winthrop's (had told her I would take my departure from thence). Sarah came to the door with Katie in her arms: but I did not think to take notice of the child. Call'd her mistress. I told her, being encourag'd by David Jeffries loving eyes, and sweet words, I was come to enquire whether she could find in her heart to leave that house and neighbourhood, and go and dwell with me at the south end; I think she said softly, Not yet. I told her It did not lie in my hands to keep a coach. If I should, I should be in danger to be brought to keep company with her neighbour Brooker, (he was a little before sent to prison for debt). Told her I had an antipathy against those who would pretend to give themselves; but nothing of their estate. I would a proportion of my estate with my self. And I suppos'd she would do so. As to a Periwig, my best and greatest friend, I could not possibly have a greater, began to find me with hair before I was born, and had continued to do so ever since; and I could not find in my heart to go to another. She commended the book I gave her, Dr. Preston, the *Church's Marriage;* quoted him saying 'twas inconvenient keeping out of a fashion commonly used. I said the time and tide did circumscribe my visit. She gave me a dram of black-cherry brandy, and gave me a lump of the sugar that was in it. She wish'd me a good journey. I pray'd God to keep her, and came away. Had a very pleasant journey to Salem.

[October] 31. . . . At night I visited Madam Winthrop about 6. p.m. They told me she was gone to Madam Mico's. I went thither and found she was gone; so return'd to her house, read the Epistles to the Galatians, Ephesians in Mr. Eyre's Latin Bible. After the clock struck 8, I began to read the 103. Psalm. Mr. Wendell[14] came in from his warehouse. Ask'd me if I were alone? Spake very kindly to me, offer'd me to call Madam Winthrop. I told him, She would be angry, had been at M. Mico's; he help'd me on with my coat and I came home: left the *Gazette* in the Bible, which told Sarah of, bid her present my service to M. Winthrop, and tell her I had been to wait on her if she had been at home.

November 1. I was so taken up that I could not go if I would.

November 2. Midweek, went again, and found Mrs. Alden there, who quickly went out. Gave her[15] about ½ pound of sugar almonds, cost 3s per £. Carried them on Monday. She seem'd pleas'd with them, ask'd what they cost. Spake of giving her a hundred pounds per annum if I died before her. Ask'd her what sum

---

[13]God will provide!
[14]Jacob Wendell, husband of Madam Winthrop's grand-
niece, and ancestor of Oliver Wendell Holmes.
[15]That is, Madam Winthrop.

she would give me, if she should die first? Said I would give her time to consider of it. She said she heard as if I had given all to my children by deeds of gift. I told her 'twas a mistake, Point-Judith was mine &c. That in England, I own'd, my father's desire was that it should go to my eldest son; 'twas 20£ per annum; she thought 'twas forty. I think when I seem'd to excuse pressing this, she seem'd to think 'twas best to speak of it; a long winter was coming on. Gave me a glass or two of Canary.

November 4. Friday, Went again about 7. a-clock; found there Mr. John Walley and his wife: sat discoursing pleasantly. I shew'd them Isaac Moses's *[an Indian]* writing. Madam W. serv'd comfits[16] to us. After a while a table was spread, and supper was set. I urg'd Mr. Walley to crave a blessing; but he put it upon me. About 9, they went away. I ask'd Madam what fashioned neck-lace I should present her with; she said, "None at all." I ask'd her whereabout we left off last time; mention'd what I had offer'd to give her; ask'd her what she would give me. She said she could not change her condition. She had said so from the beginning; could not be so far from her children, the lecture. Quoted the Apostle Paul affirming that a single life was better than a married.[17] I answer'd, that was for the present distress. Said she had not pleasure in things of that nature as formerly: I said, you are the fitter to make me a wife. If she held in that mind, I must go home and bewail my rashness in making more haste than good speed. However, considering the supper, I desired her to be within next Monday night, if we liv'd so long. Assented. She charg'd me with saying, that she must put away Juno, if she came to me: I utterly deny'd it; it never came in my heart; yet she insisted upon it; saying it came in upon discourse about the Indian woman that obtained her freedom this court. About 10, I said I would not disturb the good orders of her house, and came away. She not seeming pleas'd with my coming away. Spake to her about David Jeffries, had not seen him.

Monday, November 7. My son pray'd in the old chamber. Our time had been taken up by son and daughter Cooper's visit; so that I only read the 130th and 143. Psalm. 'Twas on the account of my courtship. I went to Mad. Winthrop; found her rocking her little Katie in the cradle. I excus'd my coming so late (near eight). She set me an arm'd chair and cushion; and so the cradle was between her arm'd chair and mine. Gave her the remnant of my almonds; she did not eat of them as before, but laid them away; I said I came to enquire whether she had alter'd her mind since Friday, or remained of the same mind still. She said, "Thereabouts." I told her I loved her, and was so fond as to think that she loved me: she said [she] had a great respect for me. I told her, I had made her an offer, without asking any advice; she had so many to advise with, that twas a hindrance. The fire was come to one short brand besides the block, which brand was set up in end; at last it fell to pieces, and no recruit[18] was made. She gave me a glass of wine. I think I repeated again that I would go home and bewail my rashness in making more haste than good speed. I would endeavour to contain myself, and not go on to solicit her to do that which she could not consent to. Took leave of her. As came down the steps she bid me have a care. Treated me courteously. Told her she had enter'd the 4th year of her widowhood. I had given her the News-Letter before: I did not bid her draw off her glove as sometime I had done. Her dress was not so clean as sometime it had been. Jehovah jireh![19]

Midweek, [November] 9. Dine at Bro[r] Stoddard's: were so kind as to enquire of me if they should invite M[m] Winthrop; I answer'd, "No." Thank'd my sister Stod-

---

[16]Sweetmeats containing fruits and nuts preserved in sugar.
[17]I Corinthians 7:8: "I say therefore to the unmarried and widows. It is good for them if they abide even as I."
[18]Replacement.

[19]Thomas: "*Jehovah jireh!* The Lord will provide! With this exclamation Sewall gave up his courtship. Madam Winthrop appears casually a few times more in the diary; Sewall visited her with his son, the parson, during her last illness, and he was a bearer at her funeral 5 August 1725."

dard for her courtesy. . . . She sent her servant home with me with a lantern. Madam Winthrop's shutters were open as I pass'd by.

November 11. Went not to Madam Winthrop's. This is the 2nd withdraw.

1673–1729   *1878–82*

from The Selling of Joseph[1]

[*Fourth-day, June 19, 1700.* . . . . Having been long and much dissatisfied with the trade of fetching Negroes from Guinea; at last I had a strong inclination to write something about it; but it wore off. At last reading Bayne, *Ephes.*[2] about servants, who mentions blackamoors, I began to be uneasy that I had so long neglected doing any thing. When I was thus thinking, in came Brother Belknap to shew me a petition he intended to present to the General Court for the freeing a Negro and his wife, who were unjustly held in bondage. And there is a motion by a Boston Committee to get a law that all importers of Negroes shall pay 40s *per* head, to discourage the bringing of them. And Mr. C. Mather resolves to publish a sheet to exhort masters to labour their conversion. Which makes me hope that I was call'd of God to write this apology for them; Let His blessing accompany the same.]

[AGAINST SLAVERY]

Foreasmuch as liberty is in real value next unto life: none ought to part with it themselves, or deprive others of it, but upon most mature considerations.

The numerousness of slaves at this day in the province, and the uneasiness of them under their slavery, hath put many upon thinking whether the foundation of it be firmly and well laid, so as to sustain the vast weight that is built upon it. It is most certain that all men, as they are the sons of Adam, are coheirs, and have equal right unto liberty, and all other outward comforts of life.

"God hath given the earth [with all its commodities] unto the sons of Adam," Psalm 115:16; "And hath made of one blood all nations of men for to dwell on all the face of the earth, and hath determined the times before appointed, and the bounds of their habitation, that they should seek the Lord. Forasmuch then as we are the offspring of God," etc., Acts 17: 26, 27, 29.

Now although the title given by the last Adam doth infinitely better men's estates respecting God and themselves, and grants them a most beneficial and inviolable lease under the broad seal of heaven, who were before only tenants at will: yet through the indulgence of God to our first parents after the Fall, the outward estate of all and every of their children remains the same, as to one another.

So that originally, and naturally, there is no such thing as slavery. Joseph was rightfully no more a slave to his brethren, than they were to him; and they had no more authority to sell him than they had to slay him. And if they had nothing to do to sell him, the Ishmaelites bargaining with them, and paying down twenty pieces of silver, could not make a title. Neither could Potiphar have any better interest in him than the Ishmaelites had. Gen. 37:20, 27, 28. For he that shall in this

---

[1] The story of Joseph is found in Genesis, Chapters 37–50. Joseph's brothers, resentful of the father's love for him, cast him into a pit. There he was found by travelling merchants and sold into bondage. Joseph pleased his master, Potiphar, but was accused falsely of trying to seduce Potiphar's wife. Imprisoned, he became a renowned interpreter of dreams. Eventually he prospered and forgave his brothers and comforted his father in his old age. The entry of June 19, 1700, from Samuel Sewall's *Diary* gives some background to his writing his antislavery pamphlet, *The Selling of Joseph.*

[2] Paul Baynes, *A Commentary Upon the First Chapter of the Epistle of Saint Paul to the Ephesians,* (1618).

case plead alteration of property, seems to have forfeited a great part of his own claim to humanity. There is no proportion between twenty pieces of silver and liberty. The commodity itself is the claimer. If Arabian gold be imported in any quantities, most are afraid to meddle with it, though they might have it at easy rates, lest if it should have been wrongfully taken from the owners, it should kindle a fire to the consumption of their whole estate. 'Tis pity there should be more caution used in buying a horse, or a little lifeless dust, than there is in purchasing men and women: whenas they are the offspring of God, and their liberty is,

> . . . *auro pretiosior omni.*[3]

And seeing God hath said, "He that stealeth a man and selleth him, or if he be found in his hand, he shall surely be put to death." Exod. 21:16. This law being of everlasting equity, wherein man-stealing is ranked among the most atrocious of capital crimes, what louder cry can there be made of that celebrated warning,

> *Caveat emptor!*[4]

And all things considered, it would conduce more to the welfare of the province, to have white servants for a term of years, than to have slaves for life. Few can endure to hear of a negro's being made free; and indeed they can seldom use their freedom well; yet their continual aspiring after their forbidden liberty renders them unwilling servants. And there is such a disparity in their conditions, color and hair, that they can never embody with us and grow up into orderly families, to the peopling of the land: but still remain in our body politic as a kind of extravasate[5] blood. As many negro men as there are among us, so many empty places there are in our train bands, and the places taken up of men that might make husbands for our daughters. And the sons and daughters of New England would become more like Jacob and Rachel,[6] if this slavery were thrust quite out of doors. Moreover, it is too well known what temptations masters are under, to connive at the fornication of their slaves; lest they should be obliged to find them wives or pay their fines. It seems to be practically pleaded that they might be lawless; 'tis thought much of, that the law should have satisfaction for their thefts and other immoralities; by which means, holiness to the Lord is more rarely engraven upon this sort of servitude. It is likewise most lamentable to think how, in taking negroes out of Africa and selling of them here, that which God has joined together men do boldly rend asunder; men from their country, husbands from their wives, parents from their children. How horrible is the uncleanness, immorality, if not murder, that the ships are guilty of that bring great crowds of these miserable men and women. Methinks, when we are bemoaning the barbarous usage of our friends and kinsfolk in Africa,[7] it might not be unseasonable to inquire whether we are not culpable in forcing the Africans to become slaves among ourselves. And it may be a question whether all the benefit received by negro slaves will balance the account of cash laid out upon them; and for the redemption of our own enslaved friends out of Africa. Besides all the persons and estates that have perished there.

1700   *1700*

---

[3]"More precious than all the gold in the world" (Latin).
[4]"Let the purchaser beware" (Latin).
[5]Extravasate: blood seeping out of normal vessels into nearby tissues.

[6]Jacob, successor to Isaac, married his cousin Rachel, whom he deeply loved. For a long time she was barren, but eventually bore him two sons, Joseph and Benjamin.
[7]Europeans held in slavery in Africa.

WILLIAM BYRD
(1674–1744)

William Byrd once wrote of himself: "Love broke out upon him before his beard, and he could distinguish sexes long before he could the difference between good and evil." This self-description captures the spirit of Byrd's character, especially as it is revealed in his *Secret Diary*, which he kept in a personal shorthand and which remained unknown until the twentieth century, when portions were found, deciphered, and published. It is not unusual for Byrd to reveal in his diary the most intimate details of personal behavior—October 6, 1709: "I went to the capitol where I sent for the wench to clean my room and when I came I kissed her and felt her, for which God forgive me."

Byrd's weakness for ladies was perhaps an expected part of the role he played as Virginia aristocrat, gentleman, and wit. His father built a large fortune in Virginia, and the son was sent to England when he was seven to be educated by private tutors and to study law. He returned in 1696, when he was twenty-two, with a knowledge of the classics and an ability to read Latin, Greek, and Hebrew, languages he continued to read daily. He served a term in the Virginia House of Burgesses, but returned to England in 1697 on business for his father and in service for the Virginia Assembly.

Byrd's father died in December 1704, and the son (and heir) came home in 1705 to look after the large estate, including more than 26,000 acres of land. Byrd was appointed the "receiver-general of the colony's revenues," and in 1709 took a seat on the Council of State, the highest ruling body in Virginia. In addition to these governmental duties, Byrd looked after his extensive properties. Through purchase, marriage, and other means, he continued to add land to his holdings throughout his life (at the end he owned 179,440 acres).

His Georgian manor house, "Westover," built on a grand scale, and filled with the most expensive silver, cut glass, furniture, and art imported from England, was a suitable residence for an aristocrat-gentleman at home in both the New World and Old. He spent much time in England, where he represented the colony on a variety of matters, and where he counted among his friends such prominent figures as dramatists William Wycherly, William Congreve, and Nicholas Rowe. He treasured throughout his life his membership in the Royal Society (for the Improving of Natural Knowledge), to which he was elected when he was only twenty-two.

It was not until the nineteenth century that Byrd's significant writings began to be published. His *History of the Dividing Line* was written out of an experience in 1728, when, serving on the commission appointed to determine the boundaries separating Virginia and North Carolina, he travelled with the surveyors through the swampy frontier and kept a daily account of events, including details of the sometimes scandalous behavior of the party. Using this journal (but omitting the scandal), Byrd wrote a lively narrative of the expedition, which was found among his manuscripts and published in 1841. Byrd proved himself a keen observer of his companions and of the frontier inhabitants, drifters, and Indians that they encountered. His narrative of the journey is written in a graceful style enlivened by his wit and shrewd understanding of human nature. (In 1929, the journal which Byrd kept on the trip was published as *The Secret History of the Line*. It is shorter, but much more candid in its descriptions of the men on the surveying team and their sexual exploits.)

Also published in 1841 were two other accounts Byrd left among his manuscripts. *A Progress to the Mines* grew out of his trip made in 1732 to inspect Colonel Alexander Spotswood's iron mines in western Virginia, near Fredericksburg and Germanna. *Journey to the Land of Eden* is the journal Byrd kept when he made a trip in 1733 to visit the 26,000-acre tract of land he had bought in North Carolina.

Byrd's literary reputation was enhanced with the publication in 1941 of *The Secret Diary of William Byrd of Westover, 1709–1712. Another Secret Diary* (including entries for 1739–41) was published in 1942. And *The London Diary* (1717–21) was added in 1958. The *Diaries* give insight into the daily life of the period, and they reveal the human dimension of Byrd—his frailty and vanity as well as his sagacity and generosity—as do none other of his writings. They provide informal glimpses behind the scenes of formal history much like those provided by the *Diary* of Samuel Pepys (1633–1703) for seventeenth-century England.

In spite of his busy life devoted to his great estate, to his governmental obligations, and to his role as social leader, Byrd regularly applied himself to intellectual development. His library required its own librarian, and contained volumes of philosophy, poetry, drama, as well as the latest scientific works. Over 500 volumes were in foreign languages. At his death, his library held some 4,000 volumes, vying with Cotton Mather's as the greatest in the colonies.

ADDITIONAL READING

R. C. Beatty, *William Byrd of Westover*, 1932; Louis B. Wright, *The First Gentleman of Virginia*, 1940; John Seelye, *Prophetic Waters: The River in Early American Life and Literature*, 1977; Marion Tinling, ed., *The Correspondence of Three William Byrds of Westover*, 2 vols., 1977; Wayne Franklin, *Discoverers, Explorers, Settlers: The Diligent Writers of Early America*, 1979.

TEXTS

The Secret Diary of William Byrd of Westover, 1709–1712, ed. Louis B. Wright and Marion Tinling, 1941; *Another Secret Diary of William Byrd of Westover, 1739–1741, with Letters & Literary Exercises, 1696–1726*, ed. Maude H. Woodfin, trans. and collated by Marion Tinling, 1942; *The History of the Dividing Line*, in *The Prose Works of William Byrd of Westover*, ed. Louis B. Wright, 1966. Footnotes from these editions are indicated by the editors' names followed by the notes enclosed in quotation marks. Typography, punctuation, spelling, and usage have been changed to conform with contemporary English and modern printing practices.

from The Secret Diary of William Byrd of Westover, 1709–1712

[Routines, Repetitions, and Occasional Roguery]

[1709]

[February] 22. I rose at 7 o'clock and read a chapter in Hebrew and 200 verses in Homer's *Odyssey*. I said my prayers, and ate milk for breakfast. I threatened

Anaka[1] with a whipping if she did not confess the intrigue between Daniel[2] and Nurse, but she prevented by a confession. I chided Nurse severely about it, but she denied, with an impudent face, protesting that Daniel only lay on the bed for the sake of the child. I ate nothing but beef for dinner.[3] The Doctor went to Mr. Dick Cocke who was very dangerously sick. I said my prayers. I had good health, good thoughts, and good humor, thanks be to God Almighty.

[March] 31. I rose at 6 o'clock and read a chapter in Hebrew and 200 verses in Homer's *Odyssey*. I said my prayers and ate milk for breakfast. I danced my dance.[4] Mr. Haynes came to see me and I appointed him to receive the President's tobacco. We made an end of sowing the oats. I ate nothing but boiled beef for dinner. My wife was out of humor for nothing. However I endeavored to please her again, having consideration for a woman's weakness. I played at billiards with the ladies. I read Italian. In the evening we walked about the plantation. My wife was out of order so we went to bed soon. I had good health, good thoughts, and good humor, thanks be to God Almighty. I said my prayers. This month was remarkable for abundance of rain and wind without frost.

[April] 7. I rose before 6 o'clock and read two chapters in Hebrew and 250 verses in Homer's *Odyssey* and made an end of it. I said my prayers devoutly. I ate milk for breakfast. I danced my dance. The men began to work this day to dig for brick. I settled my accounts and read Italian. I reproached my wife with ordering the old beef to be kept and the fresh beef used first, contrary to good management, on which she was pleased to be very angry and this put me out of humor. I ate nothing but boiled beef for dinner. I went away presently after dinner to look after my people. When I returned I read more Italian and then my wife came and begged my pardon and we were friends again. I read in Dr. Lister[5] again very late. I said my prayers. I had good health, good thoughts, and bad humor, unlike a philosopher.

[October] 6. I rose at 6 o'clock and said my prayers and ate milk for breakfast. Then I proceeded to Williamsburg,[6] where I found all well. I went to the capitol where I sent for the wench to clean my room and when I came I kissed her and felt her, for which God forgive me. Then I went to see the President,[7] whom I found indisposed in his ears. I dined with him on beef on beef [sic]. Then we went to his house and played at piquet[8] where Mr. Clayton[9] came to us. We had much to do to get a bottle of French wine. About 10 o'clock I went to my lodgings. I had good health but wicked thoughts, God forgive me.

[November] 2. I rose at 6 o'clock and read a chapter in Hebrew and some Greek in Lucian.[10] I said my prayers and ate milk for breakfast, and settled some accounts, and then went to court where we made an end of the business. We went to dinner about 4 o'clock and I ate boiled beef again. In the evening I went to Dr. [Barret's] where my wife came this afternoon. Here I found Mrs. Chiswell, my sister Custis,[11] and other ladies. We sat and talked till about 11 o'clock and then retired to our chambers. I played at [r-m][12] with Mrs. Chiswell and kissed her on the bed till she was angry and my wife also was uneasy about it, and cried as soon as the company was gone. I neglected to say my prayers, which I should not have done, because I ought to beg pardon for the lust I had for another man's wife. However I had good health, good thoughts, and good humor, thanks be to God Almighty.

---

[1] A black servant.
[2] Daniel Wilkinson, secretary to Byrd.
[3] Byrd had decided to eat only one dish at a meal.
[4] Did physical exercises.
[5] Martin Lister (c. 1638–1712), author of *A Journey to Paris in the Year 1698.*
[6] Capitol of the Virginia Colony.

[7] Of the State Council.
[8] A card game for two persons.
[9] John Clayton, Attorney-General of Virginia.
[10] Greek satirist of second century A.D.
[11] Wife of the clerk of the general court, Charles Chiswell. Frances Parke Custis, Byrd's wife's sister.
[12] Indecipherable shorthand entry.

[December] 25. I rose at 7 o'clock and ate milk for breakfast. I neglected to say my prayers because of my company. I ate milk for breakfast. About 11 o'clock the rest of the company ate some broiled turkey for their breakfast. Then we went to church, notwithstanding it rained a little, where Mr. Anderson preached a good sermon for the occasion. I received the Sacrament with great devoutness. After church the same company went to dine with me and I ate roast beef for dinner. In the afternoon Dick Randolph and Mr. Jackson went away and Mr. Jackson rode sidelong like a woman. Then we took a walk about the plantation, but a great fog soon drove us into the house again. In the evening we were merry with nonsense and so were my servants. I said my prayers shortly and had good health, good thoughts, and good humor, thanks be to God Almighty.

[1710]

[February] 26. I rose at 8 o'clock and read nothing because of my company. I neglected to say my prayers, for which God forgive me. I ate milk for breakfast. Then we took a walk about the plantation till it was time to go to dinner. I ate fish for dinner. In the afternoon we saw a good battle between a stallion and Robin[13] about the mare, but at last the stallion had the advantage and covered the mare three times. The Captain's bitch killed another lamb for which she was beat very much. We took another walk about the plantation. My maid Anaka was very well again, thank God, and so was Moll at the quarters. My wife was out of humor with us for going to see so filthy a sight as the horse to cover the mare. In the evening we drank a bottle of wine and were very merry till 9 o'clock. I neglected to say my prayers but had good health, good thoughts, and good humor, thanks be to God Almighty.

[March] 31. I rose at 7 o'clock and read some Greek in bed. I said my prayers and ate milk for breakfast. Then about 8 o'clock we got a-horseback and rode to Mr. Harrison's[14] and found him very ill but sensible. Here I met Mr. Bland,[15] who brought me several letters from England and among the rest two from Colonel Blakiston[16] who had endeavored to procure the government of Virginia for me at the price of £1,000 of my Lady Orkney[17] and that my Lord [agreed] but the Duke of Marlborough declared that no one but soldiers should have the government of a plantation, so I was disappointed. God's will be done. From hence I came home where I found all well, thank God. I ate fish for dinner. In the afternoon I went again with my wife to Mr. Harrison's who continued very bad so that I resolved to stay with him all night, which I did with Mr. Anderson and Nat Burwell.[18] He was in the same bad condition till he vomited and then he was more easy. In the morning early I returned home and went to bed. It is remarkable that Mrs. Burwell dreamed this night that she saw a person that with money scales weighed time and declared that there was no more than 18 pennies worth of time to come, which seems to be a dream with some significance either concerning the world or a sick person. In my letters from England I learned that the Bishop of Worcester was of opinion that in the year 1715 the city of Rome would be burnt to the ground, that before the year 1745 the popish religion would be routed out of the world, that before the year 1790 the Jews and Gentiles would be converted to the Christianity and then would begin the millenium.

---

[13]Servant in charge of stables.
[14]Benjamin Harrison, Byrd's neighbor.
[15]Richard Bland, Byrd's neighbor.
[16]Agent for Virginia in England.
[17]Wright and Tinling: "Lord George Hamilton, Earl of Orkney, was appointed in 1704 governor of Virginia for life, but never came to the colony. He died in 1737. During

that period various lieutenant governors ruled. On July 23, 1710, Alexander Spotswood received the appointment sought by Byrd."
[18]Reverend Charles Anderson, minister of Westover Parish; Nathaniel Burwell of Carter's Creek, whose wife was Elizabeth Carter.

[BIRTH AND DEATH OF A SON]

[1709]

[September] 6. About one o'clock this morning my wife was happily delivered of a son,[1] thanks be to God Almighty. I was awake in a blink and rose and my cousin Harrison[2] met me on the stairs and told me it was a boy. We drank some French wine and went to bed again and rose at 7 o'clock. I read a chapter in Hebrew and then drank chocolate with the women for breakfast. I returned God humble thanks for so great a blessing and recommended my young son to His divine protection. . . .

[September] 28. I rose at 6 o'clock and read nothing because of the company. I said my prayers shortly and ate milk for breakfast. It rained much in the night and also this morning, for which reason my company went to cards again. About 11 o'clock Mr. Anderson came and soon after Mr. Harrison, his wife, and daughter. About 12 o'clock our son was christened and his name was Parke. God grant him grace to be a good man. The two captains[3] of the men-of-war were godfathers. When this was over we played at cards again till dinner. I ate blue wing for dinner. In the afternoon we went to cards again and played till 10 o'clock. In the meanwhile Mr. Harrison and his wife and Mr. Anderson went away. My cold continued with some violence. I had good health, good thoughts, and good humor, thanks be to God Almighty. Mrs. Betty Harrison was godmother.

[1710]

[May] 27. I rose at 5 o'clock and read two chapters in Hebrew and some Greek in Anacreon.[4] I said my prayers and ate milk for breakfast. I danced my dance. Evie took a purge which worked but a little and my son had a little fever. Mr. [*i.e.* Mrs.?] Hamlin came to see them. I went about 11 o'clock to Colonel Randolph's to visit him because he was sick, and I found him better than he had been. We had bacon and green peas for dinner. I let the Colonel know anything I had was at his service and took my leave about 5 o'clock and got home about 7 where I found the boy in his fever but Evie was better, thank God Almighty. Mr. C-s was at our house to borrow a horse to go to Major Burwell's. He stayed till 9 o'clock. I neglected to say my prayers but had good health, good thoughts, and good humor, thanks be to God Almighty.

[May] 28. I rose at 6 o'clock and read two chapters in Hebrew and some Greek in the Christian part of Anacreon.[5] I said my prayers and ate bread and butter for breakfast. The boy was still ill of his fever. Joe Wilkinson came from above where all was well, thank God. We went to church and heard a sermon and received the Sacrament. I heard at church that Colonel Ludwell had lost 3 or 4 negroes more. I invited nobody home this day. I ate beans and bacon for dinner. In the afternoon I discoursed with Joe Wilkinson about my affairs and learned that all went well. In the evening Mr. G-r-l came with a heavy heart and cried on my reproaching him for staying so long in Carolina and not leaving his brother in his stead as he promised me, and offered to make me any reparation. He told me of the breaking of the dam, which was like my fortune. It put me very much out of humor. In the evening I took a walk. I said my prayers and had good health, indifferent humor, and good thoughts, thanks be to God Almighty.

[May] 29. I rose at 5 o'clock and read a chapter in Hebrew and some Greek in

---

[1]The Byrd's second child; their firstborn, Evelyn, called Evie in the diary, was born June 16, 1707.
[2]Mrs. Elizabeth Burwell Harrison, neighbor and distant relation to his wife, Lucy.
[3]Captain John Roberts, commander of the *Southsea Castle*, and Captain Cook, commander of the *Garland*, house guests whom Byrd had asked to be godfathers the night before.

[4]Anacreon (*c.* 572–488 B.C.), Greek lyric poet.
[5]Wright and Tinling: "St. Gregory of Nanzianus and other church fathers wrote so-called 'pious anacreontics.' Byrd may refer to some of these imitations of Anacreon, whose own verses are the very antithesis of Christian."

Anacreon. I said my prayers and ate milk and strawberries for breakfast. I danced my dance. I agreed with Joe Wilkinson to be my overseer four years. I ordered Mr. G-r-l to repair the break in the dam as soon as possible. Then they both went away. The boy continued very ill of the fever. I read some Italian. I ate roast mutton for dinner. In the afternoon we cut [sage].[6] My belly ached exceedingly and continued so till the evening and gave me many stools. I took a long walk about the plantation. I neglected to say my prayers but had good health, good thoughts, and good humor, thanks be to God Almighty. My boy appeared to be a little better this evening, blessed be God for it.

[May] 30. I rose at 6 o'clock and read two chapters in Hebrew and some Greek in Anacreon. I said my prayers and ate bread and butter for breakfast. I danced my dance. The boy was better, thank God, and I began to give him the bark. About 10 o'clock Captain Browne[7] came to pay for the quitrents[8] of Surry, which he had bought. Captain Posford's boat brought three pipes of wine from Williamsburg which came in good order. I ate some chicken for dinner. In the afternoon Tom Howlett[9] came. I sent Captain Posford some green peas. In the evening we thought the child better. I took a walk about the plantation. Mr. C-s returned from Major Burwell's with the horse which I lent him. I said my prayers and had good health, good thoughts, and good humor, thank God Almighty.

[May] 31. I rose at 5 o'clock and read a chapter in Hebrew and some Greek in Anacreon. I said my prayers and ate milk for breakfast. The child had a fever still. I danced my dance. I read some Italian and wrote a letter. I ate hashed mutton for dinner. In the afternoon I played at billiards with my wife and was exceedingly griped[10] in my belly. I ate as many cherries as I could get for it, but they did no good. I read more Italian, and in the evening took a walk to my cousin Harrison's, whom I found very melancholy. She told me she was much alone and little company came near her. When I returned I found the child a little better. I said my prayers and had good health, good thoughts, and good humor, thanks be to God Almighty. The weather of this month was generally cold, notwithstanding for about a week of it, it was very hot. The wind was often east and northeast and northwest, which did much injury to the fruit trees and made the weather unseasonable and the people sickly.

[June] 1. I rose at 6 o'clock and because I was not easy in my belly I took some [purge l-p of scurvy grass]. They worked but little. I read a chapter in Hebrew and some Greek in Anacreon. I said my prayers and drank some broth for breakfast. The child was a little better. Colonel Hill and Mr. Anderson called to see us on their way over the river. I wrote a letter to England. My purge worked but a little. I ate some boiled chicken for dinner. In the afternoon we played at billiards and then cut some [sage]. Then I set my closet in order. In the evening I took a walk and met the new negroes which Mr. Bland had bought for me to the number of 26 for £23 apiece. This evening the sloop likewise came from above where all was well. I said my prayers and had good health, good thoughts, and good humor, thanks be to God Almighty.

[June] 2. I rose at 6 o'clock and read a chapter in Hebrew and some Greek in Pindar.[11] I said my prayers and ate bread and butter for breakfast. I sent away the sloop to Appomattox. The child was worse and his nurse was very ill. I gave her a vomit which worked very well. Colonel Eppes called here. I ate cold mutton for dinner. In the afternoon I read some English. About 5 o'clock Robin Hix and Robin Mumford[12] came to discourse about the skin trade. We gave them some

---

[6]Probably for medicinal use.
[7]Wright and Tinling: "Probably Captain William Browne of Surry County, who speculated in land."
[8]Rents paid in lieu of service.
[9]Wright and Tinling: "Son of Mrs. Mary Byrd."

[10]Felt a sharp pain in the belly.
[11]Pindar (c. 522–443 B.C.), Greek lyric poet.
[12]Robert Hix, an Indian trader; Robert Mumford, a justice of the peace.

mutton and sallet for supper. In the evening I did not walk because of my company. Robin Hix asked me to pay £70 for two negroes which he intended to buy of John [Evans] which I agreed to in hope of gaining the trade. I neglected to say my prayers but was griped in my belly and had indifferent bad humor.

[June] 3. I rose at 6 o'clock and as soon as I came out news was brought that the child was very ill. We went out and found him just ready to die and he died about 8 o'clock in the morning. God gives and God takes away; blessed be the name of God.[13] Mrs. Harrison and Mr. Anderson and his wife and some other company came to see us in our affliction. My wife was much afflicted but submitted to His judgment better, notwithstanding I was very sensible of my loss, but God's will be done. Mr. Anderson and his wife with Mrs. B-k-r dined here. I ate roast mutton. In the afternoon I was griped in my belly very much but it grew better towards the night. In the afternoon it rained and was fair again in the evening. My poor wife and I walked in the garden. In the evening I neglected to say prayers, had indifferent health, good thoughts, and good humor, thanks be to God Almighty.

[June] 4. I rose at 6 o'clock and read nothing because I took physic which did not work. I said my prayers and ate water gruel. I had no more than two stools but was a little griped. I was so indisposed that I could not settle to anything. My wife had several fits of tears for our dear son but kept within the bounds of submission. I ate hashed mutton for dinner. In the afternoon we walked a little abroad but it was so hot we soon returned. My dinner griped me again but not so much as it did. My man Tom returned from Williamsburg and brought me letters from Green Springs and Queen's Creek. Jimmy brought a coffin from Falling Creek made of walnut tree. In the evening we took a walk. I said my prayers and had good thoughts, good humor, and indifferent good health, thank God Almighty.

[June] 5. I rose at 6 o'clock and read a chapter in Hebrew and some Greek in Pindar. I said my prayers and ate water gruel for breakfast. Mrs. Ann B-k-r came to assist my wife. I gave John W-l-r-c a note to Colonel Digges for a negro. My gripes continued still, and made me uneasy. About 12 o'clock my brother Custis came without my sister who could not come because she was big with child. He could tell no news. I ate roast veal for breakfast [*sic*]. In the afternoon I was worse of my gripes. My wife continued very melancholy, notwithstanding I comforted her as well as I could. I took a glyster[14] in the evening which worked a little. Then we walked in the garden. I said my prayers and had good thoughts, good humor, but indifferent health, thank God Almighty.

[June] 6. I rose at 6 o'clock and read two chapters in Hebrew and no Greek because we prepared to receive company for the funeral. I said my prayers and ate cake and water gruel for breakfast. About 10 o'clock Colonel Hill, Mr. Anderson and his wife came. Half an hour after my sister Duke[15] came without my brother who could not leave his business, and about 11 came my cousin Harrison with her son and daughter, Mr. C-s and Mr. Doyley. We gave them burnt claret and cake. About 2 o'clock we went with the corpse to the churchyard and as soon as the service was begun it rained very hard so that we were forced to leave the parson and go into the church porch but Mr. Anderson stayed till the service was finished. About 3 o'clock we went to dinner and I ate boiled beef for dinner. The company stayed till the evening and then went away. Mr. Custis and I took a walk about the plantation. Two of the new negroes were taken sick and I gave each of them a vomit which worked well. I said my prayers and had good health, good thoughts, and better health [*sic*], thank God Almighty.

---

[13]Job 1:21: ". . . the Lord gave, and the Lord hath taken away; blessed be the name of the Lord."
[14]A medicine injected into the rectum to cleanse the bowels.

[15]Wife of James Duke, possibly distant relations of Mrs. Byrd's.

[INDIAN TROUBLES]

The Tuscarora Indians, an Iroquois tribe of Carolina, incensed because of confiscation of their lands and kidnapping of their children as slaves, began a war with the southern settlers in 1711. The Indians had taken as their prisoners John Lawson, the surveyor general of Carolina, and a Baron de Graffenried, who happened to be with Lawson at the time. Byrd, a colonel in the Virginia militia, set out with Virginia Governor Alexander Spotswood on an expedition in October 1711, with around 1,600 troops as a show of strength to frighten the Tuscaroras into releasing their prisoners and joining the settlers against the Indians carrying on the war. These diary entries describe the meeting with the Indians at Nottoway town. The parley resulted in a treaty with the Tuscaroras in less than two months, but conflicts continued until 1713, ending with the defeat of the Indians; the remaining Tuscaroras became the sixth nation of the League of the Iroquois.

❧

[1711]

[October] 17. I rose about 7 o'clock and found the Governor up. I drank some strong water. I said a short prayer and about 8 o'clock we sat to a family breakfast and I ate some roast mutton. About 9 we took leave of Colonel Harrison and got on our horses with Captain Hal Harrison's troop to wait on us. Captain John Allen's troop met us on the road and about 3 o'clock we met Colonel Ludwell[1] and soon after got to Nottoway town where we met abundance of the militia. We had just time before night to settle our quarters and to look about us. Several of us lay in the King's cabin with the Governor, where we lay on new mats and our cabin was covered with other mats. I found my baggage well received but one of the horses was sick. No less than eight of my Henrico captains[2] came over to meet the Governor, which compliment he took very kindly. Both they and all the volunteers supped with the Governor under his marquee and I ate venison pasty. The Governor appointed a guard for the fort of about 100 men. Several of the Tributary Indians[3] came here to meet the Governor. The Doctor[4] lay with me but our lodging seemed very hard at first and we were incommoded with the smoke at first. I said a short prayer and had good health, good thoughts, and good humor, thank God Almighty. We talked almost all night. We lay in our morning gowns and breeches.

[October] 18. About break of day we were waked with the reveille and rose about 6 o'clock and then took a walk about the town to see some Indian girls, with which we played the wag. I ate some gingerbread and drank tea with the Governor for breakfast. Then we got on our horses to take a review of the militia and assigned to each county its post and gave the militia of the Isle of Wight[5] the head because we were in their county. While we were in the field the Governor modelled the horse and put commanders at the head of them. There were about 700 horse besides volunteers and about 900 foot, and there were about 30 volunteers among whom were three parsons. About noon the Governor sent about 30 horses to meet the Tuscarora Indians at the Saponie town. After the Governor had reviewed the horse on both wings he dismissed them about 4 o'clock and sent all except those appointed for the guard that they might provide themselves with lodgings in the neighborhood. About 5 we went to dinner with the Governor and I ate some venison. All the volunteers dined with the Governor. At night we

---

[1]These individuals are Byrd's fellow officers in the militia.
[2]Captains from Henrico County, Virginia, under Byrd's jurisdiction.
[3]Friendly to the colonists.

[4]Dr. William Cocke, accompanying Gov. Spotswood on the expedition.
[5]A county of Virginia.

drank a bottle till about 10 o'clock, and then went to bed. I said a short prayer and had good health, good thoughts, and good humor, thank God Almighty.

[October] 19. I rose about 6 o'clock and found it cold. We drank chocolate with the Governor and about 9 o'clock got on our horses and waited on the Governor to see him put the foot in order. [He] divided the companies and made them about 50 men each, and made captains over them, though when he came to Surry[6] he found it difficult to get captains because everybody refused the Governor and made him so angry that he swore at several which was a thing he seldom did. The Doctor went away about 10 o'clock privately with pretence of some business but it was to go to Mrs. Russell.[7] We ate gingerbread all day long and saw the Governor exercise the foot. I drew up the volunteers into a company or troop and commanded them under the name of the Governor's Guard and we placed ourselves on the right. About 3 o'clock the Tuscarora Indians came with their guard and Mr. Poythress[8] with them. He told the Governor that the Baron was alive and would be released but that Mr. Lawson was killed because he had been so foolish as to threaten the Indian that had taken him. About 6 o'clock we went to dinner and I ate some roast mutton. At night some of my troop went with me into the town to see the girls and kissed them without proceeding any further, and we had like to have been kept out by the captain of the guard. However at last they let us in and we went to bed about 2 o'clock in the morning. I neglected to say my prayers but had good health, good thoughts, and good humor, thank God Almighty.

[October] 20. I rose about 6 o'clock and drank tea with the Governor, who made use of this opportunity to make the Indians send some of their great men to the College,[9] and the Nansemonds sent two, the Nottoways two, and the Meherrins[10] two. He also demanded one from every town belonging to the Tuscaroras. About 9 the Governor mounted and we waited on him to see him exercise the horse and when all the militia was drawn up he caused the Indians to walk from one end to the other and they seemed very much afraid lest they should be killed. The Governor did nothing but wheel the foot,[11] and Colonel Ludwell and I assisted him as well as we could. About noon the Governor ordered lists to be taken of the troops and companies that the people might make their claim to be paid, because they had been on the service five days. When this was done he gave liberty to the people to go home, except a troop and company for the guard that night. Then we went and saw the Indian boys shoot and the Indian girls run for a prize. We had likewise a war dance by the men and a love dance by the women, which sports lasted till it grew dark. Then we went to supper and I ate chicken with a good stomach. We sat with the Governor till he went to bed about 11 o'clock and then we went to Major Harrison's to supper again but the Governor ordered the sentry to keep us out and in revenge about 2 o'clock in the morning we danced a [g-n-t-r][12] dance just at his bed's head. However we called for the captain of the guard and gave him a word and then we all got in except Colonel Ludwell and we kept him out about quarter of an hour. Jenny, an Indian girl, had got drunk and made us good sport. I neglected to say my prayers and had good health, good thoughts, and good humor, thank God Almighty.

[October] 21. I rose about 6 o'clock and we began to pack up our baggage in order to return. We drank chocolate with the Governor and about 10 o'clock we took leave of the Nottoway town and the Indian boys went away with us that were designed for the College. The Governor made three proposals to the Tuscaroras:

---

[6]Surrey County, Virginia.
[7]Mrs. Katherine Russell, introduced into society by Gov. Spotswood as his niece; but there were scandalous rumors about the two.
[8]Mr. Peter Poythress, an Indian trader and interpreter.

[9]William and Mary College, Williamsburg, Virginia.
[10]Various towns of the Indian tribes.
[11]March the foot soldiers in demonstration.
[12]Illegible entry.

that they would join with the English to cut off those Indians that had killed the people of Carolina, that they should have 40 shillings for every head they brought in of those guilty Indians and be paid the price of a slave for all they brought in alive, and that they should send one of the chief men's sons out of every town to the College. I waited on the Governor about ten miles and then took leave of him and he went to Mr. Cargill's[13] and I with Colonel Hill, Mr. Platt, and John Hardiman went to Colonel Harrison's[14] where we got about 3 o'clock in the afternoon. About 4 we dined and I ate some boiled beef. My man's horse was lame for which he was let blood. At night I asked a negro girl to kiss me, and when I went to bed I was very cold because I pulled off my clothes after lying in them so long. I neglected to say my prayers but had good health, good thoughts, and good humor, thank God Almighty.

[DOMESTIC AFFAIRS]

[1710]

[July] 30. I rose at 5 o'clock and wrote a letter to Major Burwell about his boat which Captain Broadwater's people had brought round and sent Tom with it. I read two chapters in Hebrew and some Greek in Thucydides.[1] I said my prayers and ate boiled milk for breakfast. I danced my dance. I read a sermon in Dr. Tillotson[2] and then took a little [nap]. I ate fish for dinner. In the afternoon my wife and I had a little quarrel which I reconciled with a flourish. Then she read a sermon in Dr. Tillotson to me. It is to be observed that the flourish was performed on the billiard table. I read a little Latin. In the evening we took a walk about the plantation. I neglected to say my prayers but had good health, good thoughts, and good humor, thanks be to God. This month there were many people sick of fever and pain in their heads; perhaps this might be caused by the cold weather which we had this month, which was indeed the coldest that ever was known in July in this country. Several of my people have been sick, but none died, thank God.

[1711]

[January] 31. I rose at 5 o'clock and read two chapters in Hebrew and some Greek in Lucian.[3] I said my prayers and ate boiled milk for breakfast. My wife quarreled with me about not sending for Mrs. Dunn[4] when it rained to [lend her John]. She threatened to kill herself but had more discretion. I danced my dance and then read some English about [love]. It rained again all the morning. I ate some roast shoat[5] for dinner. In the afternoon Nurse was taken sick of a [purging]. I took a walk to see the boatwright at work. My wife came into good humor again and we resolved to live for the future in love and peace. At night I ate some battered eggs with her and drank some cider. I said my prayers and had good health, good thoughts, and good humor, thank God Almighty. The wind was still northeast as it was when the moon was at full and since that a good deal of rain has fallen. The boy whose thigh was swollen grew worse.

[February] 5. I rose about 8 o'clock and found my cold still worse. I said my prayers and ate milk and potatoes for breakfast. My wife and I quarreled about her pulling her brows.[6] She threatened she would not go to Williamsburg[7] if she might not pull them; I refused, however, and got the better of her, and maintained my authority. About 10 o'clock we went over the river and got to Colonel Duke's about 11. There I ate some toast and canary.[8] Then we proceeded to

---

[13]Reverend John Cargill, minister of Southwark Parish, Surry.
[14]Col. Nathaniel Harrison, long time friend of Byrd's.
[1]Thucydides (*c.* 471–400 B.C.), Greek historian.
[2]John Tillotson (1630–1694), Archbishop of Canterbury and author of volumes of sermons; one of Byrd's favorite authors.
[3]Lucian (*c.* 120), Greek satirist.

[4]Wife of Parson Dunn; John, a servant.
[5]Young pig.
[6]Plucking her eyebrows.
[7]The Governor, at Williamsburg, was giving the annual ball in honor of the Queen's birthday, the great social event of the year.
[8]Wine from the Canary Islands.

Queen's Creek, where we found all well, thank God. We ate roast goose for supper. The women prepared to go to the Governor's the next day and my brother and I talked of old stories. My cold grew exceedingly bad so that I thought I should be sick. My sister gave me some sage tea and leaves of [s-m-n-k][9] which made me mad all night so that I could not sleep but was much disordered by it. I neglected to say my prayers in form but had good thoughts, good humor, and indifferent health, thank God Almighty.

[December] 30. I rose about 7 o'clock and read a chapter in Hebrew and three chapters in the Greek Testament. I said my prayers very devoutly and ate boiled milk for breakfast. The weather was very clear and warm so that my wife walked out with Mrs. Dunn and forgot dinner, for which I had a little quarrel with her and another afterwards because I was not willing to let her have a book out of the library. About 12 o'clock came Mr. Bland from Williamsburg but brought no news. He stayed to dinner and I ate some roast beef. In the afternoon we sat and talked till about 4 o'clock and then I caused my people to set him over the river and then I walked with the women about the plantation till they were very weary. At night we ate some eggs and drank some Virginia beer and talked very gravely without reading anything. However I said my prayers and spoke with all my people. I had good health, good thoughts, and good humor, thank God Almighty. I danced my dance in the morning.

[December] 31. I rose about 7 o'clock and read a chapter in Hebrew and six leaves in Lucian. I said my prayers and ate boiled milk for breakfast. The weather continued warm and clear. I settled my accounts and wrote several things till dinner. I danced my dance. I ate some turkey and chine[10] for dinner. In the afternoon I weighed some money and then read some Latin in Terence[11] and then Mr. Mumford came and told me my man Tony had been very sick but he was recovered again, thank God. He told me Robin Bolling had been like to die and that he denied that he was the first to mention the imposition on skins which he certainly did. Then he and I took a walk about the plantation. When I returned I was out of humor to find the negroes all at work in our chambers. At night I ate some broiled turkey with Mr. Mumford and we talked and were merry all the evening. I said my prayers and had good health, good thoughts, and good humor, thank God Almighty. My wife and I had a terrible quarrel about whipping Eugene[12] while Mr. Mumford was there but she had a mind to show her authority before company but I would not suffer it, which she took very ill; however for peace sake I made the first advance towards a reconciliation which I obtained with some difficulty and after abundance of crying. However it spoiled the mirth of the evening, but I was not conscious that I was to blame in that quarrel.

[1712]

[March] 2. I rose about 7 o'clock and read a chapter in Hebrew but no Greek because Mr. G-r-l was here and I wished to talk with him. I ate boiled milk for breakfast and danced my dance. I reprimanded him for drawing so many notes on me. However I told him if he would let me know his debts I would pay them provided he would let a mulatto of mine that is his apprentice come to work at Falling Creek the last two years of his service, which he agreed. I had a terrible quarrel with my wife concerning Jenny[13] that I took away from her when she was beating her with the tongs. She lifted up her hands to strike me but forbore to do it. She gave me abundance of bad words and endeavored to strangle herself, but I believe in jest only. However after acting a mad woman a long time she was passive again. I ate some roast beef for dinner. In the afternoon Mr. G-r-l went away and I took a walk about the plantation. At night we drank some cider by way of

---

[9]Herb for medicinal use.
[10]A cut of meat containing part of the backbone.
[11]Terence (*c.* 190–159 B.C.), Roman playwright.

[12]House servant, probably black; the editors note that servants could have been black or white.
[13]House servant.

reconciliation and I read nothing. I said my prayers and had good health, good thoughts, and good humor, thank God Almighty. I sent Tom to Williamsburg with some fish to the Governor and my sister Custis. My daughter was indisposed with a small fever.

[May] 22. I rose about 6 o'clock and read two chapters in Hebrew and some Greek in Lucian. I said my prayers and ate boiled milk for breakfast. I danced my dance. It rained a little this morning. My wife caused Prue[14] to be whipped violently notwithstanding I desired not, which provoked me to have Anaka whipped likewise who had deserved it much more, on which my wife flew into such a passion that she hoped she would be revenged of me. I was moved very much at this but only thanked her for the present lest I should say things foolish in my passion. I wrote more accounts to go to England. My wife was sorry for what she had said and came to ask my pardon and I forgave her in my heart but seemed to resent, that she might be the more sorry for her folly. She ate no dinner nor appeared the whole day. I ate some bacon for dinner. In the afternoon I wrote two more accounts till the evening and then took a walk in the garden. I said my prayers and was reconciled to my wife and gave her a flourish in token of it. I had good health, good thoughts, but was a little out of humor, for which God forgive me.

1941

Inamorato L'Oiseaux[1]

["The Enamored Bird"]

Never did the sun shine upon a swain who had more combustible matter in his constitution than the unfortunate Inamorato. Love broke out upon him before his beard, and he could distinguish sexes long before he could the difference betwixt good and evil. 'Tis well he had not a twin sister as Osiris[2] had, for without doubt like him he would have had an *amourette*[3] with her in his mother's belly. Love was born to him so long before reason that it has ever since slighted its rebukes, as much as old fops do the good sense of a young man.

However, this frailty has never been without some check, for Diana[4] threw such a weight of grace into the opposite scale that the balance has commonly been held very even. And if the love-scale has happened to be carried down sometimes, the counterpoise has not failed to mount it up again very suddenly. The struggle between the Senate and the plebeians in the Roman Commonwealth, or betwixt the king and the Parliament in England,[5] was never half so violent as the civil war between this hero's principles and his inclinations. Sometimes grace would be uppermost and sometimes love; neither would yield and neither could conquer. Like Caesar and Pompey,[6] one could not bear an equal nor t'other a superior.

---

[14]House servant.

[1]Woodfin: "In this character [sketch] of himself, 'The Enamored Bird,' . . . Byrd analyzed himself, for the most part with fidelity to the facts of his life as revealed in his diary, and with considerable insight into his own frailty and strength. . . . In writing a character [sketch] of himself, he was following a custom of the time. . . . The use of the plural instead of the singular in the French for *bird* was apparently a slip in his copying into this notebook, while the use of *inamorato* suggests the Italian influence in drama and music so prevalent in England at this time."

[2]Ancient Egyptian god of the underworld, associated with the vivifying powers of the sun and fertility of nature because of his annual death and resurrection, whose feminine counterpart is his sister and wife, Isis.

[3]Affair.

[4]Roman virgin goddess (twin sister of Apollo, god of the sun) of the moon, hunting, and chastity. Graceful in form, she was swift to punish her nymphs for any violation of their vows of perpetual chastity.

[5]In ancient Rome, the members of the senate and the plebians (common people) were always in conflict, as were the Crown and Parliament in seventeenth-century England.

[6]Julius Caesar (100–44 B.C.) and Pompey the Great (Gnaeus Pompeius Magnus, 106–48 B.C.), Roman generals and statesmen, were proud of themselves and envious of each other; their rivalry ended in Pompey's defeat and Caesar's dictatorship.

It must be confessed, indeed, his principles have been sometimes happily supported by the misadventures of his love, by which means its own cannon have been turned against itself. This foible has been an unhappy clog to all his fortunes and hindered him from reaching that eminence in the world, which his friends and his abilities might possibly have advanced him to. Nature gave him all the talents in the world for business except industry, which of all others is the most necessary. This is the spring and life and spirit of all preferment and makes a man bustle through all difficulty and foil all opposition. Laziness mires a man in the degree in which he was born and clogs the wheels of the finest qualifications. Fortune may make a lazy fellow great, but he will never make himself so. Diligence gives wings to ambition by which it soars up to the highest pitch of advancement. These wings Inamorato wanted, as he did constancy, which is another ingredient to raise a great fortune. To what purpose is it for a man to be always upon the wing, if he only fly backward and forward. He must go right out or else he will never go far. He should fix one certain end in his own thoughts, and towards that all his designs, and all his motions should unalterably tend.

But poor Inamorato had too much mercury[7] to fix to one thing. His brain was too hot to jog on eternally in the same dull road. He lived more by the lively movement of his passions than by the cold and unromantic dictates of reason. This made him wavering in his resolutions and inconstant after he had taken them. He would follow a scent with great eagerness for a little while, but then a fresh scent would cross it and carry him as violently another way. One while, the ease with which the judges loll in their coaches and doze upon the bench tempted him to study the law, but he was soon taken off by the rapine and mercenariness of that profession. Then the gaity of St. James's[8] made him fancy to be a courtier, but the falseness and treachery, the envy and corruption in fashion there quickly made him abandon that pursuit. When this fit was over he was charmed with the glory of serving in the army and thought it a shame for a proper fellow to live at home in ease when the liberties of Europe were in danger; but before he had provided his equipage, he was discouraged by the confinement, dependence, and barbarity of that service.

In some frolics no state appeared so happy to him as matrimony; the convenience, the tenderness, the society of that condition made him resolve upon his own ruin and set up for a wife. He fancied it too sullen, too splenetic to continue single, and too liable to the inconveniences that attend accidental and promiscuous gallantry. In this humor he'd work himself violently in love with some nymph of good sense, whose understanding forsooth might keep under all the impertinent starts of a woman's temper. And when he was in love, no man ever made so disengaging a figure. Instead of that life and gaity, that freedom and pushing confidence which hits the ladies, he would look as dismal as if he appeared before his judge and not his mistress. Venus[9] and all the graces would leave him in the lurch in the critical time when they should have assisted him most. When he ought to have had the most fire, he had the most phlegm, and he was all form and constraint when he should have the most freedom and spirit. He would look like a fool and talk like a philosopher, when both his eyes and his tongue should have sparkled with wit and waggery. He would sigh as ruefully as if he sat over a dead friend and not a live mistress.

No wonder this awkward conduct was without success, for what woman would venture upon a solemn swain that looked more like her confessor than her gallant and put her more in mind of a sullen husband than a sprightly lover? The miscar-

---

[7]Changeableness, volatility.
[8]The royal palace in London, scene of glittering social court functions.
[9]Roman goddess of love.

riage of an honorable amour never disturbed him so much, but that he would sleep and look much better in his despair than he did in the hottest of his expectation. He was not in half the jeopardy of hanging himself when he lost a mistress than he was while he was in danger of getting her. While there was hope, he would be assiduous to a fault, not considering that a little neglect in love (like saltpeter in gunpowder) serves to give force to the passion.

Whenever his bashfulness gave him leave to declare his mind, something would rise in his throat and intercept the untimely question. A woman is with more ease delivered of a huge boy than he was of the painful secret. His eyeballs would role with as much ghastliness as if he had been strangled. 'Twas melancholy to see how his heart panted, his spirits fluttered, his hands trembled, his knees knocked against one another, and the whole machine was in a deplorable confusion. You may guess how engaging a declaration must be that was attended with so many sorrowful symptoms. It moved the nymph's pity at least, if it could not move her inclination. If she could not be kind to a man to whom she had created so much disturbance, yet she could not forebear being civil.

Thus whenever Inamorato lost a mistress, he got a friend by way of equivalent, and so providence made a good bargain for him when he would have made a woeful one for himself. His person was agreeable enough though he had a certain cast of pride in his look, which clouded some of the grace of it. Hardly anybody liked him that did not know him, and nobody hated him that did. He had almost as many friends as he had acquaintance, and nobody ever fell out with him for any other reason but because they thought he neglected them.

His conversation was easy, sensible, and inoffensive, never bordering either upon profaneness or indecency. He was always tender of the modesty of those that were present and of the reputation of those that were absent. He was incapable of saying a shocking thing or of acting an unjust one. He was the never failing friend of the unfortunate, and good nature was the constantest of all his virtues. He paid his court more to obscure merit than to corrupt greatness. He never could flatter anybody, no not himself, which were two invincible bars to all preferment. He was much readier to tell people of their faults than their fine qualities, because they were already too sensible of these, whereas they were too ignorant of the first. His soul is so tuned to those things that are right that he is too ready to be moved at those that are wrong. This makes him passionate and sorely sensible of injuries, but he punishes himself more by the resentment than he does the party by revenge. If the sun go down upon his wrath, 'twill be sure to rise upon his reconciliation. An injury never festers nor rankles upon his mind, but wastes itself in the first sally of indignation.

He is frugal in all expenses upon himself that he may be generous to the distressed. He takes more pleasure to supply the wants of others than his own wantonness. His religion is more in substance than in form, and he is more forward to practice virtue than profess it. He is sincere to an indiscretion himself and therefore abhores dissimulation in other people. He can sooner be reconciled to a professed enemy than to a pretended friend. Of all cheats in the world, he has least charity for the holy cheat that makes religion bawd[10] for his interest and serves the devil in the livery of Godliness.

His memory is nothing so punctual as in performing of promises. He thinks himself as firmly bound by his word as by his hand and seal and would be as much ashamed to be put in mind of one as to be sued for the other. He knows the world perfectly well and thinks himself a citizen of it without the [. . .][11] distinctions of

[10]A prostitute.
[11]Indecipherable

kindred sect or country. He has learning without ostentation. By reading he's acquainted with ages past and with the present by voyaging and conversation.

He knew how to keep company with rakes without being infected with their vices and had the secret of giving virtue so good a grace that wit itself could not make it ridiculous. He could return from one of the convents in Drury Lane[12] with as much innocence as any of the saints from a meeting. He loved to undress wickedness of all its paint and disguise that he might loathe its deformity. His discretion never gave him an opportunity to try his courage, for he would never provoke a [. . .][13] sober man, nor be provoked by a man in drink. He never interloped with another's wife or mistress, but dealt altogether where the trade was open and free for all adventurers.

If he reflected upon anyone 'twas by irony, which a wise man would take for a banter and a fool for a compliment. His tongue was so far from embroiling the rest of his person that upon some occasions it has happily protected it. He abhores all excesses of strong drink because it wholly removes those guards that can defend a man from doing and suffering harm. He's a great friend to temperance because 'tis the security of all the other virtues. It disarms flesh and blood of those tempests with which it puts out all the lights of reason.

By talking little he is quit of a world of folly and repentance. His silence proceeds not from want of matter, but from plenty of discretion. He is so great a friend to exactness that he sometimes allows too little to the frailty of mankind. He wishes everybody so perfect that he overlooks the impossibility of reaching it in this world. He would have men angels before their time, and would bring down that perfection upon earth which is the peculiar privilege of heaven. This makes him a little too severe upon faults, which it would not be unjust to forgive. However he would not have transgressors punished to procure them pain, but reformation. It proceeds from his hatred of the fault and not of the offender.

He loves retirement, that while he is acquainted with the world, he may not be a stranger to himself. Too much company distracts his thoughts and hinders him from digesting his observations into good sense. It makes a man superficial, penetrating no deeper than the surface of things. One notice crowds out another, having no time to sink into the mind. A constant hurry of visits and conversation gives a man a habit of inadvertency, which betrays him into faults without measure and without end. For this reason he commonly reserved the morning to himself and bestowed the rest upon his business and his friends.

He often frequented the company of women, not so much to improve his mind as to polish his behavior. There is something in female conversation that softens the roughness, tames the wildness, and refines the indecency too common amongst the men. He laid it down as a maxim that without the ladies, a scholar is a pedant, a philosopher a cynic, all morality is morose, and all behavior either too formal or too licentious.

He has an excellent talent at keeping a secret, which neither love nor resentment, vanity nor lightness can ever draw from him. All the ingenious tortures of the Inquisition[14] can't force him to betray either his faith or his friend. He always thought ingratitude the most monstrous of all the vices because it makes a man unfit for society, which subsists by mutual returns of kindness.

His good nature is so universal as to extend to all brute creatures. He cannot see them ill used without the tenderest sentiments of compassion. They are helpless and must submit to all sorts of tyranny, while men have some way or other of

---

[12]Gatherings in Drury Lane, theater district of London, offering many temptations (including vice).
[13]Indecipherable.
[14]During the thirteenth century, the Roman Catholic Church established a tribunal of inquiry to find out and punish nonbelievers and heretics. The Inquisition became synonymous with bloody persecution.

righting themselves. They have no refuge, no friend, no laws to protect them from injury, but are liable to suffer by the neglect, the wantonness, and cruelty of men. This hard fate he bemoans with a very sensible concern, and the rather because they have often more merit than their oppressors.

1723   *1942*

from The History of the Dividing Line Betwixt Virginia and North Carolina, Run in the Year of Our Lord 1728[1]

[LIFE ON THE NORTH CAROLINA FRONTIER]

[1728]

[March] 10. The Sabbath happened very opportunely, to give some ease to our jaded people, who rested religiously from every work but that of cooking the kettle. We observed very few cornfields in our walks and those very small, which seemed the stranger to us because we could see no other tokens of husbandry or improvement. But upon further inquiry we were given to understand people only made corn for themselves and not for their stocks, which know very well how to get their own living. Both cattle and hogs ramble into the neighboring marshes and swamps, where they maintain themselves the whole winter long and are not fetched home till the spring. Thus these indolent wretches during one half of the year lose the advantage of the milk of their cattle, as well as their dung, and many of the poor creatures perish in the mire, into the bargain, by this ill management. Some who pique themselves more upon industry than their neighbors will now and then, in compliment to their cattle, cut down a tree whose limbs are loaded with the moss afore-mentioned. The trouble would be too great to climb the tree in order to gather this provender, but the shortest way (which in this country is always counted the best) is to fell it, just like the lazy Indians, who do the same by such trees as bear fruit and so make one harvest for all. By this bad husbandry milk is so scarce in the winter season that were a big-bellied woman[2] to long for it she would tax her longing. And, in truth, I believe this is often the case, and at the same time a very good reason why so many people in this province are marked with a custard complexion.

The only business here is raising of hogs, which is managed with the least trouble and affords the diet they are most fond of. The truth of it is, the inhabitants of North Carolina devour so much swine's flesh that it fills them full of gross humors. For want, too, of a constant supply of salt, they are commonly obliged to eat it fresh, and that begets the highest taint of scurvy. Thus, whenever a severe cold happens to constitutions thus vitiated, 'tis apt to improve into the yaws,[3] called there very justly the country distemper. This has all the symptoms of the pox, with this aggravation, that no preparation of mercury will touch it. First it seizes the throat, next the palate, and lastly shows its spite to the poor nose, of which 'tis apt in a small time treacherously to undermine the foundation. This calamity is so common and familiar here that it ceases to be a scandal, and in the disputes that happen about beauty the noses have in some companies much ado to carry it. Nay, 'tis said that once, after three good pork years, a motion had like to have

---

[1]In 1728, Byrd headed a Virginia Commission which joined a commission from North Carolina to establish the border between the two states. The survey was launched March 6, 1728, moving westward from the Atlantic shore.

[2]Woman who is pregnant.
[3]An infectious disease with ulcerating lesions.

been made in the House of Burgesses[4] that a man with a nose should be incapable of holding any place of profit in the province; which extraordinary motion could never have been intended without some hopes of a majority.

Thus, considering the foul and pernicious effects of eating swine's flesh in a hot country, it was wisely forbid and made an abomination to the Jews, who lived much in the same latitude with Carolina.

[March] 11. We ordered the surveyors early to their business, who were blessed with pretty dry grounds for three miles together. But they paid dear for it in the next two, consisting of one continued frightful pocosin,[5] which no creatures but those of the amphibious kind ever had ventured into before. This filthy quagmire did in earnest put the men's courage to a trial, and though I can't say it made them lose their patience, yet they lost their humor for joking. They kept their gravity like so many Spaniards, so that a man might then have taken his opportunity to plunge up to the chin without danger of being laughed at. However, this unusual composure of countenance could not fairly be called complaining.

Their day's work ended at the mouth of Northern's Creek, which empties itself into Northwest River; though we chose to quarter a little higher up the river near Mossy Point. This we did for the convenience of an old house to shelter our persons and baggage from the rain, which threatened us hard. We judged the thing right, for there fell an heavy shower in the night that drove the most hardy of us into the house. Though indeed our case was not much mended by retreating thither, because, that tenement having not long before been used as a pork store, the moisture of the air dissolved the salt that lay scattered on the floor and made it as wet withindoors as without. However, the swamps and marshes we were lately accustomed to had made such beavers and otters of us that nobody caught the least cold.

We had encamped so early that we found time in the evening to walk near half a mile into the woods. There we came upon a family of mulattoes that called themselves free, though by the shyness of the master of the house, who took care to keep least in sight, their freedom seemed a little doubtful. It is certain many slaves shelter themselves in this obscure part of the world, nor will any of their righteous neighbors discover them. On the contrary, they find their account in settling such fugitives on some out-of-the-way corner of their land to raise stocks for a mean and inconsiderable share, well knowing their condition makes it necessary for them to submit to any terms. Nor were these worthy borderers content to shelter runaway slaves, but debtors and criminals have often met with the like indulgence. But if the government of North Carolina have encouraged this unneighborly policy in order to increase their people, it is no more than what ancient Rome did before them, which was made a city of refuge for all debtors and fugitives and from that wretched beginning grew up in time to be mistress of great part of the world. And, considering how fortune delights in bringing great things out of small, who knows but Carolina may, one time or other, come to be the seat of some other great empire?

[March] 12. Everything had been so soaked with the rain that we were obliged to lie by a good part of the morning and dry them. However, that time was not lost, because it gave the surveyors an opportunity of platting[6] off their work and taking the course of the river. It likewise helped to recruit the spirits of the men, who had been a little harassed with yesterday's march. Notwithstanding all this, we crossed the river before noon and advanced our line three miles. It was not possi-

---

[4]Virginia's legislative body.
[5]A tract of low, swampy land, or marsh.
[6]To plat is to map or make a plan of.

ble to make more of it by reason good part of the way was either marsh or pocosin. The line cut two or three plantations, leaving part of them in Virginia and part of them in Carolina. This was a case that happened frequently, to the great inconvenience of the owners, who were therefore obliged to take out two patents and pay for a new survey in each government.

In the evening we took up our quarters in Mr. Ballance's pasture, a little above the bridge built over Northwest River. There we discharged the two piraguas,[7] which in truth had been very serviceable in transporting us over the many waters in that dirty and difficult part of our business. Our landlord had a tolerable good house and clean furniture, and yet we could not be tempted to lodge in it. We chose rather to lie in the open field, for fear of growing too tender. A clear sky, spangled with stars, was our canopy, which, being the last thing we saw before we fell asleep, gave us magnificent dreams. The truth of it is, we took so much pleasure in that natural kind of lodging that I think at the foot of the account mankind are great losers by the luxury of feather beds and warm apartments.

The curiosity of beholding so new and withal so sweet a method of encamping brought one of the Senators of North Carolina to make us a midnight visit. But he was so very clamorous in his commendations of it that the sentinel, not seeing his quality either through his habit or behavior, had like to have treated him roughly. After excusing the unseasonableness of his visit and letting us know he was a parliament man, he swore he was so taken with our lodging that he would set fire to his house as soon as he got home and teach his wife and children to lie like us in the open field.

[THE GREAT DISMAL SWAMP]

[March] 13. Early this morning our chaplain repaired to us with the men we had left at Mr. Wilson's. We had sent for them the evening before to relieve those who had the labor oar from Currituck Inlet. But to our great surprise, they petitioned not to be relieved, hoping to gain immortal reputation by being the first of mankind that ventured through the Great Dismal. But the rest being equally ambitious of the same honor, it was but fair to decide their pretensions by lot. After fortune had declared herself, those which she had excluded offered money to the happy persons to go in their stead. But Hercules would have as soon sold the glory of cleansing the Augean stables,[1] which was pretty near the same sort of work. No sooner was the controversy at an end but we sent those unfortunate fellows back to their quarters whom chance had condemned to remain upon firm land and sleep in a whole skin. In the meanwhile, the surveyors carried the line three miles, which was no contemptible day's work, considering how cruelly they were entangled with briers and gallbushes. The leaf of this last shrub bespeaks it to be of the alaternus family.

Our work ended within a quarter of a mile of the Dismal above-mentioned, where the ground began to be already full of sunken holes and slashes, which had, here and there, some few reeds growing in them. 'Tis hardly credible how little the bordering inhabitants were acquainted with this mighty swamp, notwithstanding they had lived their whole lives within smell of it. Yet, as great strangers as they were to it, they pretended to be very exact in their account of its dimensions and were positive it could not be above seven or eight miles wide, but knew no more of the matter than stargazers know of the distance of the fixed stars. At the same time, they were simple enough to amuse our men with idle stories of the

---

[7]Canoes.

[1]Hercules was assigned twelve almost impossible labors, one of which was the cleaning of the Augean stables. It held 3,000 cattle and had not been cleaned for thirty years.

lions, panthers, and alligators they were likely to encounter in that dreadful place. In short, we saw plainly there was no intelligence of this *Terra Incognita*[2] to be got but from our own experience. For that reason it was resolved to make the requisite dispositions to enter it next morning. We allotted every one of the surveyors for this painful enterprise, with twelve men to attend them. Fewer than that could not be employed in clearing the way, carrying the chain, marking the trees, and bearing the necessary bedding and provisions. Nor would the commissioners themselves have spared their persons on this occasion but for fear of adding to the poor men's burden, while they were certain they could add nothing to their resolution.

We quartered with our friend and fellow traveler, William Wilkins, who had been our faithful pilot to Currituck and lived about a mile from the place where the line ended. Everything looked so very clean and the furniture so neat that we were tempted to lodge withindoors. But the novelty of being shut up so close quite spoiled our rest, nor did we breathe so free by abundance as when we lay in the open air.

[March] 14. Before nine of the clock this morning the provisions, bedding, and other necessaries were made up into packs for the men to carry on their shoulders into the Dismal. They were victualed for eight days at full allowance, nobody doubting but that would be abundantly sufficient to carry them through that inhospitable place; nor indeed was it possible for the poor fellows to stagger under more. As it was, their loads weighed from sixty to seventy pounds, in just proportion to the strength of those who were to bear them. 'Twould have been unconscionable to have saddled them with burdens heavier than that, when they were to lug them through a filthy bog which was hardly practicable with no burden at all. Besides this luggage at their backs, they were obliged to measure the distance, mark the trees, and clear the way for the surveyors every step they went. It was really a pleasure to see with how much cheerfulness they undertook and with how much spirit they went through all this drudgery. For their greater safety, the commissioners took care to furnish them with Peruvian bark, rhubarb, and ipecacuanha,[3] in case they might happen, in that wet journey, to be taken with fevers or fluxes.

Although there was no need of example to inflame persons already so cheerful, yet to enter the people with the better grace, the author and two more of the commissioners accompanied them half a mile into the Dismal.[4] The skirts of it were thinly planted with dwarf reeds and gallbushes, but when we got into the Dismal itself we found the reeds grew there much taller and closer and, to mend the matter, were so interlaced with bamboo briers that there was no scuffling through them without the help of pioneers. At the same time we found the ground moist and trembling under our feet like a quagmire, insomuch that it was an easy matter to run a ten-foot pole up to the head in it without exerting any uncommon strength to do it. Two of the men whose burdens were the least cumbersome had orders to march before with their tomahawks and clear the way in order to make an opening for the surveyors. By their assistance we made a shift to push the line half a mile in three hours and then reached a small piece of firm land about a hundred yards wide, standing up above the rest like an island. Here the people were glad to lay down their loads and take a little refreshment, while the happy man whose lot it was to carry the jug of rum began already, like Aesop's bread carriers, to find it grow a good deal lighter.[5]

After reposing about an hour, the commissioners recommended vigor and con-

---

[2]"Unknown land" (Latin).
[3]Remedies of the time. Peruvian bark was Cinchona, used for malaria and other fevers; rhubarb was a cathartic used for constipation; ipecacuanha was an emetic to induce vomiting.

[4]Byrd and the commissioners travelled on horses and did not ordinarily follow the surveyors through the swamp.
[5]They were drinking the rum (as those in an Aesop fable must have eaten the bread).

stancy to their fellow travelers, by whom they were answered with three cheerful huzzas, in token of obedience. This ceremony was no sooner over but they took up their burdens and attended the motion of the surveyors, who, though they worked with all their might, could reach but one mile farther, the same obstacles still attending them which they had met with in the morning. However small this distance may seem to such as are used to travel at their ease, yet our poor men, who were obliged to work with an unwieldy load at their backs, had reason to think it a long way; especially in a bog where they had no firm footing but every step made a deep impression which was instantly filled with water. At the same time they were laboring with their hands to cut down the reeds, which were ten feet high, their legs were hampered with briers. Besides, the weather happened to be warm, and the tallness of the reeds kept off every friendly breeze from coming to refresh them. And indeed it was a little provoking to hear the wind whistling among the branches of the white cedars, which grew here and there amongst the reeds, and at the same time not to have the comfort to feel the least breath of it.

In the meantime the three commissioners returned out of the Dismal the same way they went in and, having joined their brethren, proceeded that night as far as Mr. Wilson's. This worthy person lives within sight of the Dismal, in the skirts whereof his stocks range and maintain themselves all the winter, and yet he knew as little of it as he did of *Terra Australis Incognita.*[6] He told us a Canterbury tale[7] of a North Briton whose curiosity spurred him a long way into this great desert, as he called it, near twenty years ago, but he, having no compass nor seeing the sun for several days together, wandered about till he was almost famished; but at last he bethought himself of a secret his countrymen make use of to pilot themselves in a dark day. He took a fat louse out of his collar and exposed it to the open day on a piece of white paper, which he brought along with him for his journal. The poor insect, having no eyelids, turned himself about till he found the darkest part of the heavens and so made the best of his way toward the North. By this direction he steered himself safe out and gave such a frightful account of the monsters he saw and the distresses he underwent that no mortal since has been hardy enough to go upon the like dangerous discovery.

[March] 15. The surveyors pursued their work with all diligence but still found the soil of the Dismal so spongy that the water oozed up into every footstep they took. To their sorrow, too, they found the reeds and briers more firmly interwoven than they did the day before. But the greatest grievance was from large cypresses which the wind had blown down and heaped upon one another. On the limbs of most of them grew sharp snags, pointing every way like so many pikes, that required much pains and caution to avoid. These trees, being evergreens and shooting their large tops very high, are easily overset by every gust of wind, because there is no firm earth to steady their roots. Thus many of them were laid prostrate, to the great encumbrance of the way. Such variety of difficulties made the business go on heavily, insomuch that from morning till night the line could advance no farther than one mile and thirty-one poles.

Never was rum, that cordial of life, found more necessary than it was in this dirty place. It did not only recruit the people's spirits, now almost jaded with fatigue, but served to correct the badness of the water and at the same time to resist the malignity of the air. Whenever the men wanted to drink, which was very often, they had nothing more to do but make a hole and the water bubbled up in a moment. But it was far from being either clear or well tasted and had, besides, a physical effect from the tincture it received from the roots of the shrubs and trees that grew in the neighborhood. . . .

[6]Australia was so marked on maps of the time.
[7]A good story to while away the time. Refers to *The Canterbury Tales* of Geoffrey Chaucer (c. 1340–1400), in which the pilgrims shorten their journey to the shrine at Canterbury by telling tales.

[Customs of the Country in North Carolina]

[March] 25. The air was chilled this morning with a smart northwest wind, which favored the Dismalites in their dirty march. They returned by the path they had made in coming out and with great industry arrived in the evening at the spot where the line had been discontinued. After so long and laborious a journey, they were glad to repose themselves on their couches of cypress bark, where their sleep was as sweet as it would have been on a bed of Finland down.

In the meantime, we who stayed behind had nothing to do but to make the best observations we could upon that part of the country. The soil of our landlord's plantation, though none of the best, seemed more fertile than any thereabouts, where the ground is near as sandy as the deserts of Africa and consequently barren. The road leading from thence to Edenton, being in distance about twenty-seven miles, lies upon a ridge called Sandy Ridge, which is so wretchedly poor that it will not bring potatoes. The pines in this part of the country are of a different species from those that grow in Virginia: their bearded leaves are much longer and their cones much larger. Each cell contains a seed of the size and figure of a black-eyed pea, which, shedding in November, is very good mast[1] for hogs and fattens them in a short time. The smallest of these pines are full of cones which are eight or nine inches long, and each affords commonly sixty or seventy seeds. This kind of mast has the advantage of all other by being more constant and less liable to be nipped by the frost or eaten by the caterpillars.

The trees also abound more with turpentine and consequently yield more tar than either the yellow or the white pine and for the same reason make more durable timber for building. The inhabitants hereabouts pick up knots of lightwood in abundance, which they burn into tar and then carry it to Norfolk or Nansemond[2] for a market. The tar made in this method is the less valuable because it is said to burn the cordage,[3] though it is full as good for all other uses as that made in Sweden and Muscovy.

Surely there is no place in the world where the inhabitants live with less labor than in North Carolina. It approaches nearer to the description of Lubberland[4] than any other, by the great felicity of the climate, the easiness of raising provisions, and the slothfulness of the people. Indian corn is of so great increase that a little pains will subsist a very large family with bread, and then they may have meat without any pains at all, by the help of the low grounds and the great variety of mast that grows on the high land. The men, for their parts, just like the Indians, impose all the work upon the poor women. They make their wives rise out of their beds early in the morning, at the same time that they lie and snore till the sun has risen one-third of his course and dispersed all the unwholesome damps. Then, after stretching and yawning for half an hour, they light their pipes, and, under the protection of a cloud of smoke, venture out into the open air; though if it happen to be never so little cold they quickly return shivering into the chimney corner. When the weather is mild, they stand leaning with both their arms upon the cornfield fence and gravely consider whether they had best go and take a small heat at the hoe but generally find reasons to put it off till another time. Thus they loiter away their lives, like Solomon's sluggard,[5] with their arms across, and at the winding up of the year scarcely have bread to eat. To speak the truth, 'tis a thorough aversion to labor that makes people file off to North Carolina, where plenty and a warm sun confirm them in their disposition to laziness for their whole lives.

[March] 26. Since we were like to be confined to this place till the people re-

---

[1]Acorns or nuts serving as food for hogs.
[2]Norfolk, Virginia, or Nansemond County, Virginia.
[3]Twisted roots or wood generally.

[4]Lubberland is a name for a fabulous utopia, a land of abundance and ease.
[5]Proverbs 6:9: "How long wilt thou sleep, O sluggard?"

turned out of the Dismal, 'twas agreed that our chaplain might safely take a turn to Edenton to preach the Gospel to the infidels there and christen their children. He was accompanied thither by Mr. Little, one of the Carolina commissioners, who, to show his regard for the church, offered to treat him on the road with a fricassee of rum. They fried half a dozen rashers of very fat bacon in a pint of rum, both which being dished up together served the company at once both for meat and drink.

Most of the rum they get in this country comes from New England and is so bad and unwholesome that it is not improperly called "kill-devil." It is distilled there from foreign molasses, which, if skillfully managed, yields near gallon for gallon. Their molasses comes from the same country and has the name of "long sugar" in Carolina, I suppose from the ropiness of it, and serves all the purposes of sugar, both in their eating and drinking. When they entertain their friends bountifully, they fail not to set before them a capacious bowl of bombo,[6] so called from the admiral of that name. This is a compound of rum and water in equal parts, made palatable with the said long sugar. As good humor begins to flow and the bowl to ebb they take care to replenish it with sheer rum, of which there always is a reserve under the table.

But such generous doings happen only when that balsam of life is plenty; for they have often such melancholy times that neither landgraves nor caciques[7] can procure one drop for their wives when they lie in or are troubled with the colic or vapors. Very few in this country have the industry to plant orchards, which, in a dearth of rum, might supply them with much better liquor. The truth is, there is one inconvenience that easily discourages lazy people from making this improvement: very often, in autumn, when the apples begin to ripen, they are visited with numerous flights of parakeets, that bite all the fruit to pieces in a moment for the sake of the kernels. The havoc they make is sometimes so great that whole orchards are laid waste, in spite of all the noises that can be made or mawkins[8] that can be dressed up to fright 'em away. These ravenous birds visit North Carolina only during the warm season and so soon as the cold begins to come on retire back toward the sun. They rarely venture so far north as Virginia, except in a very hot summer, when they visit the most southern parts of it. They are very beautiful but, like some other pretty creatures, are apt to be loud and mischievous.

[VISIT WITH THE INDIANS]

[April] 7. The next day being Sunday, we ordered notice to be sent to all the neighborhood that there would be a sermon at this place and an opportunity of christening their children. But the likelihood of rain got the better of their devotion and, what perhaps might still be a stronger motive, of their curiosity. In the morning we dispatched a runner to the Nottoway town to let the Indians know we intended them a visit that evening, and our honest landlord was so kind as to be our pilot thither, being about four miles from his house. Accordingly, in the afternoon we marched in good order to the town, where the female scouts, stationed on an eminence for that purpose, had no sooner spied us but they gave notice of our approach to their fellow citizens by continual whoops and cries, which could not possibly have been more dismal at the sight of their most implacable enemies. This signal assembled all their great men, who received us in a body and conducted us into the fort.

This fort was a square piece of ground, enclosed with substantial puncheons or

---

[6]"Bombo" from Admiral John Benbow (1653–1702).
[7]Men of high rank. Landgraves were judicial officers in the medieval period; cacique is an Indian chieftan.
[8]Variant of "malkin," a scarecrow.

strong palisades about ten feet high and leaning a little outwards to make a sca-
lade[1] more difficult. Each side of the square might be about a hundred yards
long, with loopholes at proper distances through which they may fire upon the
enemy. Within this enclosure we found bark cabins sufficient to lodge all their
people in case they should be obliged to retire thither. These cabins are no other
but close arbors made of saplings, arched at the top and covered so well with bark
as to be proof against all weather. The fire is made in the middle, according to the
Hibernian[2] fashion, the smoke whereof finds no other vent but at the door and so
keeps the whole family warm, at the expense both of their eyes and complexion.
The Indians have no standing furniture in their cabins but hurdles to repose their
persons upon which they cover with mats or deerskins. We were conducted to the
best apartments in the fort, which just before had been made ready for our reception and adorned with new mats that were very sweet and clean.

The young men had painted themselves in a hideous manner, not so much for
ornament as terror. In that frightful equipage they entertained us with sundry
war dances, wherein they endeavored to look as formidable as possible. The instrument they danced to was an Indian drum, that is, a large gourd with a skin
braced taut over the mouth of it. The dancers all sang to this music, keeping exact
time with their feet while their head and arms were screwed into a thousand menacing postures.

Upon this occasion the ladies had arrayed themselves in all their finery. They
were wrapped in their red and blue matchcoats, thrown so negligently about them
that their mahogany skins appeared in several parts, like the Lacedaemonian[3]
damsels of old. Their hair was braided with white and blue peak and hung gracefully in a large roll upon their shoulders.

This peak consists of small cylinders cut out of a conch shell, drilled through
and strung like beads. It serves them both for money and jewels, the blue being of
much greater value than the white for the same reason that Ethiopian mistresses
in France are dearer than French, because they are more scarce. The women wear
necklaces and bracelets of these precious materials when they have a mind to appear lovely. Though their complexions be a little sad-colored, yet their shapes are
very straight and well proportioned. Their faces are seldom handsome, yet they
have an air of innocence and bashfulness that with a little less dirt would not fail
to make them desirable. Such charms might have had their full effect upon men
who had been so long deprived of female conversation but that the whole winter's
soil was so crusted on the skins of those dark angels that it required a very strong
appetite to approach them. The bear's oil with which they anoint their persons all
over makes their skins soft and at the same time protects them from every species
of vermin that used to be troublesome to other uncleanly people.

We were unluckily so many that they could not well make us the compliment of
bedfellows according to the Indian rules of hospitality, though a grave matron
whispered one of the commissioners very civilly in the ear that if her daughter
had been but one year older she should have been at his devotion. It is by no
means a loss of reputation among the Indians for damsels that are single to have
intrigues with the men; on the contrary, they account it an argument of superior
merit to be liked by a great number of gallants. However, like the ladies that
game,[4] they are a little mercenary in their amours and seldom bestow their favors
out of stark love and kindness. But after these women have once appropriated

---

[1] A scaling of the walls.
[2] Irish.
[3] Lacedaemon or Sparta, city-state of ancient Greece, whose
inhabitants excelled in military skills and austere living.
[4] Engage in prostitution.

their charms by marriage, they are from thenceforth faithful to their vows and will hardly ever be tempted by an agreeable gallant or be provoked by a brutal or even by a fumbling husband to go astray.

The little work that is done among the Indians is done by the poor women, while the men are quite idle or at most employed only in the gentlemanly diversions of hunting and fishing. In this, as well as in their wars, they now use nothing but firearms, which they purchase of the English for skins. Bows and arrows are grown into disuse, except only amongst their boys. Nor is it ill policy, but on the contrary very prudent, thus to furnish the Indians with firearms, because it makes them depend entirely upon the English, not only for their trade but even for their subsistence. Besides, they were really able to do more mischief while they made use of arrows, of which they would let silently fly several in a minute with wonderful dexterity, whereas now they hardly ever discharge their firelocks more than once, which they insidiously do from behind a tree and then retire as nimbly as the Dutch horse used to do now and then formerly in Flanders.

We put the Indians to no expense but only of a little corn for our horses, for which in gratitude we cheered their hearts with what rum we had left, which they love better than they do their wives and children. Though these Indians dwell among the English and see in what plenty a little industry enables them to live, yet they choose to continue in their stupid idleness and to suffer all the inconveniences of dirt, cold, and want rather than disturb their heads with care or defile their hands with labor.

The whole number of people belonging to the Nottoway town, if you include women and children, amount to about two hundred. These are the only Indians of any consequence now remaining within the limits of Virginia. The rest are either removed or dwindled to a very inconsiderable number, either by destroying one another or else by the smallpox and other diseases. Though nothing has been so fatal to them as their ungovernable passion for rum, with which, I am sorry to say it, they have been but too liberally supplied by the English that live near them.

And here I must lament the bad success Mr. Boyle's charity has hitherto had toward converting any of these poor heathens to Christianity.[5] Many children of our neighboring Indians have been brought up in the College of William and Mary. They have been taught to read and write and been carefully instructed in the principles of the Christian religion till they came to be men. Yet after they returned home, instead of civilizing and converting the rest, they have immediately relapsed into infidelity and barbarism themselves. . . .

I am sorry I can't give a better account of the state of the poor Indians with respect to Christianity, although a great deal of pains has been and still continues to be taken with them. For my part, I must be of opinion, as I hinted before, that there is but one way of converting these poor infidels and reclaiming them from barbarity, and that is charitably to intermarry with them, according to the modern policy of the Most Christian King in Canada and Louisiana.[6] Had the English done this at the first settlement of the colony, the infidelity of the Indians had been worn out at this day with their dark complexions, and the country had swarmed with people more than it does with insects. It was certainly an unreasonable nicety that prevented their entering into so good-natured an alliance. All nations of men have the same natural dignity, and we all know that very bright talents may be lodged under a very dark skin. The principal difference between one

---

[5]Wright: "Robert Boyle, the English philosopher-scientist, left money in his will to be used for the propagation of Christianity among the heathen. James Blair used his influence with the trustees of Boyle's estate to have the College of William and Mary made the chief beneficiary of the money. Brafferton Hall, where Indians were to be schooled, was built in 1723 from this bequest."

[6]King of France.

people and another proceeds only from the different opportunities of improvement. The Indians by no means want understanding and are in their figure tall and well proportioned. Even their copper-colored complexion would admit of blanching, if not in the first, at the farthest in the second, generation. I may safely venture to say, the Indian women would have made altogether as honest wives for the first planters as the damsels they used to purchase from aboard the ships. 'Tis strange, therefore, that any good Christian should have refused a wholesome, straight bedfellow, when he might have had so fair a portion with her as the merit of saving her soul.

1728   *1841*

POETS AND RHYMERS: PIOUS PURITANS
AND SOUTHERN SATIRIST

The Bay Psalm Book	Anne Bradstreet
New England's Memorial	Michael Wigglesworth
The New England Primer	Edward Taylor
	Ebenezer Cooke

Although the New England colonists produced no fiction or drama (the Puritans of England on assuming power in the 1640s closed the theaters), they found poetry useful for their purposes. It was placed in the service of piety in *The Bay Psalm Book*, in the service of education in *The New England Primer*, and in the service of the dead in memorials and epitaphs. The Puritan colonies produced three important poets: Anne Bradstreet, the first poet and one of considerable consequence, complexity, and power, especially in her poems of personal reference; Michael Wigglesworth, the most popular as well as most hair-raising in his accounts of doomed sinners; and Edward Taylor, the most talented in dressing familiar religious beliefs in startling, often dazzling, images and metaphors.

The southern colonists were less concerned with religion and the moral usefulness of literary genres than they were with amusement, wit, and candor in the treatment of human foibles. The poet laureate of Maryland, Ebenezer Cooke, wrote a rollicking, sometimes bawdy, picaresque tale which here balances the sober seriousness of the Puritans.

POPULAR PURITAN POETRY

The Puritans were too preoccupied with the establishment of the ideal Christian society in the New World wilderness to have time for such "unreal" literary forms as drama and fiction. But for poetry they had a genuine fondness, perhaps because they could place it in the service of their and the community's struggle in this life to gain entry into the next. Thus poetry figured importantly in early life in education for the young, in mid-life in singing psalms at church services, and at the end of life in observances and rituals for the dead.

The first book published in America—in 1640—was in effect a book of poetry, designed to be sung at church services: *The Whole Book of Psalms Faithfully Translated into English Meter.* The book was commonly called *The Bay Psalm Book.* Psalm singing by the congregation came in with the Reformation, and the Massachusetts Bay Colony early decided to create its own version of the psalms, rendering them as close as possible to the original Hebrew in which they were written, and at the same time adapting them to be sung. The task was undertaken by several of the most distinguished divines of the Bay colony, including Increase Mather and John Eliot. The inversions of syntactic structures that jar the modern ear ("The Lord to me a shepherd is") serve to fit the words to the meters and rhythms of the tunes used in the Puritan services.

Much New England poetry was preserved by Nathaniel Morton (1613–1686) in his history of New England, *New England's Memorial* (1669). In writing his history, Morton quoted verbatim long passages from his Uncle William Bradford's *History of Plymouth Plantation.* When the Bradford manuscript came to light in 1855, Morton's book faded in importance. But as a ready source for many examples of early New England poetry, especially memorials, threnodies, and epitaphs written for eminent Puritan citizens when they died, Morton's work is invaluable. By browsing in his book we discover the truth of what Moses Coit Tyler remarked: "It is an extraordinary fact about these grave and substantial men of New England . . . that they all had a lurking propensity to write what they sincerely believed to be poetry. . . ." It was the extraordinary occasion of death that inspired and emboldened these closet poets to publish, unashamedly, their verses to the world.

If poetry could assist in salvation, and help in the experience of death, it could also serve education, largely, perhaps, because of its usefulness as a memory aid. In studying the alphabet, the Puritan child chanted "In Adam's fall/We sinned all," learning thus not only the letter A but also an important point of religious doctrine. *The New England Primer*, containing this and other similar verses aimed at simultaneous education and indoctrination, appeared around 1683, and in all some 5,000,000 copies bearing identical mnemonic devices and dogmas were circulated. Such a book so widely read was a powerful force in shaping a cohesive culture with a common moral and religious outlook.

ADDITIONAL READING

Moses Coit Tyler, "New England: The Verse Writers," *A History of American Literature, 1607–1765,* 1878; Samuel Marion Tucker, "The Beginnings of Verse, 1610–1808," *The Cambridge History of American Literature*, Vol. 1, 1917; Zoltán Haraszti, *The Enigma of the Bay Psalm Book*, 1956.

TEXTS

The Bay Psalm Book: A Facsimile Reprint of the First Edition of 1640, ed. Zoltán Haraszti, 1956; Nathaniel Morton, *New England's Memorial: or, A Brief Relation of the Providence of God manifested to the Planters of New England in America: with Special Reference to the First Colony Thereof, Called New Plymouth*, 1669, rpt. 1855; *The New England Primer*, ed. Paul Leicester Ford, 1727, 1897, rpt. 1962. Typography, punctuation, spelling, and usage have been changed to conform with contemporary English and modern printing practices.

from The Bay Psalm Book (1640)

Psalm 8

O Lord our God in all the earth
  how's Thy name wondrous great,
Who hast Thy glorious majesty
  above the heavens set.
Out of the mouths of sucking babes   5
  Thy strength Thou didst ordain,
That Thou mightst still the enemy,
  and them that Thee disdain.
When I Thy finger's work, Thy Heavens,
  the moon and stars consider,   10
Which Thou hast set: What's wretched man
  that Thou dost him remember?
Or what's the Son of Man, that thus
  Him visited Thou hast?
For next to angels, Thou hast him   15
  a little lower placed,
And hast with glory crowned him,
  and comely majesty:
And on Thy works hast given him
  lordly authority.   20
All hast Thou put under his feet;
  all sheep and oxen, yea,
And beasts of field, fowls of the air,
  and fishes of the sea,
And all that pass through paths of seas.   25
  O Jehovah our Lord,
How wondrously-magnificent
  is Thy name through the world?

Psalm 23

The Lord to me a shepherd is,
  want therefore shall not I.
He in the folds of tender grass,
  doth cause me down to lie.

To waters calm me gently leads,
  restore my soul doth He;
He doth in paths of righteousness
  for His name's sake lead me.
Yea though in valley of death's shade
  I walk, none ill I'll fear,
Because Thou art with me; Thy rod
  and staff my comfort are.
For me a table Thou hast spread,
  in presence of my foes.
Thou dost anoint my head with oil;
  my cup it overflows.
Goodness and mercy surely shall
  all my days follow me;
And in the Lord's house I shall dwell
  so long as days shall be.

5

10

15

20

from Nathaniel Morton, *New England's Memorial*

[Thomas Dudley Foresees His Death][1]

[1653] Mr. Thomas Dudley, who was a principal founder and pillar of the colony of Massachusetts, in New England, and sundry times governor and deputy-governor of that jurisdiction, died at his house in Roxbury, July 31, in the seventy-seventh year of his age. . . . The verses following were found in his pocket after his death, which may further illustrate his character, and give a taste of his poetical fancy. . . .

Dim eyes, deaf ears, cold stomach show
My dissolution is in view;
Eleven times seven near lived have I,
And now God calls, I willing die:
My shuttle's[2] shot, my race is run,
My sun is set, my deed is done;
My span is measured, tale is told,
My flower is faded and grown old,
My dream is vanished, shadow's fled,
My soul with Christ, my body dead;
Farewell dear wife, children and friends,
Hate heresy, make blessed ends;
Bear poverty, live with good men,
So shall we meet with joy again.

5

10

Let men of God in courts and churches watch
O'er such as do a toleration hatch;
Lest that ill egg bring forth a cockatrice,[3]
To poison all with heresy and vice.
If men be left, and otherwise combine,
My epitaph's, I died no libertine.[4]

15

20

---

[1]Thomas Dudley was the father of the poet Anne Bradstreet.
[2]Shuttle: a dart, missile, or arrow,
[3]A fabled snake hatched from a cock's egg that can kill with a look.

[4]A free thinker on religious doctrines as well as one who lives unrestrained by moral law.

from Threnodia[1] upon Our Church's Second Dark Eclipse, Happening July 20, 1663, by Death's Interposition between Us and That Great Light and Divine Plant, Mr. Samuel Stone, Late of Hartford, in New England

[A STONY THRENODY FOR SAMUEL STONE]

May nature, grace and art be found in one
So high, as to be found in few or none.
In him these three with full fraught hand contested,
With which by each he should be most invested.
The largest of the three, it was so great   5
On him, the stone was held a light complete,
A stone more than the Ebenezer[2] famed;
Stone splendent[3] diamond, right orient named;
A cordial stone, that often cheered hearts
With pleasant wit, with Gospel rich imparts;   10
Whetstone, that edgified[4] the obtusest mind;
Loadstone,[5] that drew the iron heart unkind;
A ponderous stone, that would the bottom sound
Of scripture depths, and bring out arcans[6] found;
A stone for kingly David's[7] use so fit,   15
As would not fail Goliath's front to hit;
A stone, an antidote, that brake the course
Of gangrene error, by convincing force;[8]
A stone acute, fit to divide and square;
A squared stone became Christ's building rare[9]. . . .   20
                                        E. B.[10]

An Epitaph upon the Deplored Death of That Supereminent Minister of the Gospel, Mr. Jonathan Mitchell [1668]

["FOUND FULL RIPE AND PLUCKED FOR HEAVEN"]

Here lies the darling of his time,
Mitchell expired in his prime;
Who four years short of forty-seven,
Was found full ripe and plucked for heaven.
Was full of prudent zeal and love,   5
Faith, patience, wisdom from above;
New England's stay,[1] next age's story;[2]
The church's gem; the college glory.[3]

---

[1]Variant of threnody, a poem lamenting the death of an individual.
[2]The name of the stone set up by Samuel in celebration of the victory over the Philistines (1 Samuel 7:12).
[3]Brilliant. "Orient," the east, where the sun rises; thus, shining.
[4]Sharpened.
[5]Strongly magnetic mineral, variety of magnetite.
[6]Secrets, hidden meanings.
[7]When he was a shepherd boy, David killed the giant Philistine (10½ feet tall) by a stone flung from his slingshot (1 Samuel 17).
[8]A common form of punishment for those believed to be in error was to stone them, pelting them with stones.
[9]Matthew 16:18: "And I say also unto thee, That thou art Peter, and upon this rock I will build my church."
[10]Supposed to be Edward Bulkley.
[1]Steadying support.
[2]History.
[3]Mitchell was pastor of the church at Cambridge as well as a fellow of Harvard College.

Angels may speak him; ah, not I,
(Whose worth's above hyperbole)
But for our loss, were't in my power,   10
I'd weep an everlasting shower.

J. E.[4]

from The New England Primer (*c.* 1683)

[The Alphabet]

In Adam's fall
We sinned all.

Thy life to mend,
This Book[1] attend.

The Cat doth play,
And after slay.

A Dog will bite
A thief at night.

An Eagle's flight
Is out of sight.

The idle Fool
Is whipped at school.

As runs the Glass,[2]
Man's life doth pass.

My Book and Heart
Shall never part.

Job[3] feels the rod,
Yet blesses God.

Our King the good
No man of blood.[4]

The Lion bold
the Lamb doth hold.

The Moon gives light
In time of night.

Nightingales sing.
In time of spring.

The royal Oak, it was the tree
That saved his royal majesty.[5]

Peter denies
His Lord, and cries.[6]

Queen Esther comes in royal state
To save the Jews from dismal fate.[7]

Rachel doth mourn
For her first-born.[8]

Samuel anoints
Whom God appoints.[9]

Time cuts down all,
Both great and small.

Uriah's beauteous wife
Made David seek his life.[10]

Whales in the sea,
God's voice obey.

Xerxes the great did die[11]
And so must you and I.

Youth forward slips,
Death soonest nips.

Zaccheus he
Did climb the tree
His Lord to see.[12]

---

[4]Probably the Reverend John Sherman, minister of Watertown.
[1]The Bible.
[2]Hourglass, containing sand flowing from one half to the other.
[3]Tried with a series of misfortunes, the righteous Job accepts God's will (Job 1:21).
[4]Bloodshed or hot temper.
[5]Charles II, after his defeat by Cromwell at Worcester in 1649, was hidden in the Royal Oak at Boscobel in order to effect his escape and flight to France.
[6]Matthew 26:75: "And Peter remembered the word of Jesus, which said unto him, Before the cock crow, thou shalt deny me thrice. And he went out, and wept bitterly."
[7]Esther was an orphaned Jewish girl raised in Persia. Because of her beauty she was chosen to be the consort of the Persian King Ahasuerus. When the king's prime minister, finding the Jews unsubmissive, planned to annihilate them, Esther risked her life by interceding for her people (Esther 8:1–8).

[8]Rachel was looked upon as the mother of the tribes of Israel. Jeremiah 31:15: "Thus saith the Lord; A voice was heard in Ramah, lamentation and bitter weeping; Rachel weeping for her children refused to be comforted for her children, because they *were* not."
[9]Following the Lord's will, Samuel first anointed Saul to succeed him as king; but then he became displeased with Saul's actions and, again following the choice of the Lord, anointed David king in place of Saul (1 Samuel 15, 16).
[10]A loyal soldier in David's army, Uriah was the husband of Bathsheba, beloved by David. David plotted Uriah's death in order to possess Bathsheba (2 Samuel 11, 12).
[11]Xerxes the Great (*c.* 519–465 B.C.), King of Persia (r. 486–465 B.C.), was victorious in war with the Greeks, especially in bridging the Hellespont and in the battle at Thermopylae (480 B.C.), but later defeated.
[12]Zaccheus was a tax collector in Jericho hated by his compatriots. He was short in stature and when Jesus came to Jericho, Zaccheus had to climb a tree to see him. Jesus ate with Zaccheus and brought about his reform (Luke 19).

ANNE BRADSTREET
(1612–1672)

In 1650 a book of poems entitled *The Tenth Muse Lately Sprung Up in America* was published in London. It was remarkable for two reasons: first, it was written in the New World, and indeed was the first book of poems published by an American; second, it was written by a woman, Anne Bradstreet, during a time when few women were given educations and fewer still found the time or the courage to write poetry (or any other form of literature). Anne Bradstreet had nothing to say about the publication of her book. Her brother-in-law, the Reverend John Woodbridge, had taken the manuscript to England with him and had there arranged for anonymous publication. In the book's poem on Queen Elizabeth she gave a strong "nay" to the "masculines" who dismissed women as "void of reason." That Anne Bradstreet felt the sting of criticism for her impertinence in becoming a poet is shown in the lines of one of her poems:

> I am obnoxious to each carping tongue,
> Who says my hand a needle better fits,
> A poet's pen, all scorn, I should thus wrong. . . .

She goes on to say that the "despite" (contempt) the carping tongues "cast on female wits" is such that, even if her poetry were to "prove well," "they'll say it's stol'n, or else, it was by chance." The carping tongues had, in Anne Bradstreet, met their match.

This pioneer literary figure was born in England, probably Northampton, the daughter of Thomas Dudley, who was steward for the Earl of Lincoln (a Puritan). Growing up as a privileged child in the Earl's castle of Sempringham, Anne would, no doubt, have had access to the Earl's fine library. Her familiarity with a near contemporary, Shakespeare, and with other writers indicates that she had read early and widely. In 1628, when she was sixteen, she married Simon Bradstreet, then twenty-five and (like her father) in the service of the Earl.

The Dudleys were Puritans, as was Bradstreet, and in 1630 they all sailed with John Winthrop on the *Arbella* to Massachusetts Bay. From a life of relative ease in a household of culture and social sophistication, Anne Bradstreet found herself in an undeveloped civilization with few of the graces that had surrounded her in England. Both Anne's father and her husband became prominent leaders in the new colony. Thomas Dudley succeeded John Winthrop as governor in 1649; Simon Bradstreet became governor in 1678. The Bradstreets moved several times in the New World, settling for a time in Newton (Cambridge), then Agawam (Ipswich), and finally in Merrimac (Andover). Anne bore her husband eight children. In the middle of her many household tasks she found time to write.

In "The Author to Her Book," Anne Bradstreet noted that her work had been "snatched" from her side by friends "less wise than true," who had "exposed" it to "public view." She addressed her book as a mother would address a child—"Thou ill-formed offspring of my feeble brain." And extending the conceit, she referred to her labors of revision:

> I washed thy face, but more defects I saw,
> And rubbing off a spot still made a flaw.

As a matter of fact, Anne Bradstreet did revise her poems and added to them, preparing a manuscript for a new volume. It was published in 1678, six years after her death. Critics have noted her improvement of the previously published poems and the superiority of many of the new poems, among them the long sequence on nature entitled "Contemplations." As Anne Bradstreet the poet matured, she moved out from under the influence of her first models, Sir Walter Raleigh and Seigneur Guillaume de Salluste Du Bartas, and in some ways anticipated the British Romantics and the American Transcendentalists. Especially appealing to the modern reader are the verses on domestic themes and the love poems.

As a Puritan it was natural that Anne Bradstreet would make religion and spiritual experience a subject of her poems. What is surprising is that she clearly struggled with belief. In a letter written to her children and left on her death with a manuscript of poems, many of which were not included in her published volumes, she confessed: "I have often been perplexed that I have not found that constant joy in my pilgrimage and refreshing which I supposed most of the servants of God have. . . . Many times hath Satan troubled me concerning the verity of the scriptures, many times by atheism how I could know whether there was a God: I never saw any miracles to confirm me, and those I read of how did I know but they were feigned. That there is a God my reason would soon tell me by the wondrous works that I see, the vast frame of the heaven and the earth, the order of all things night and day, summer and winter, spring and autumn, the daily providing for this great household upon the earth. . . ."

These words reveal a doubting Puritan embued with something of the spirit of a Deist, finding God's revelation not in scriptures but in nature. Anne Bradstreet's religious poetry had—considered in its entirety—a greater complexity than her contemporary readers ever suspected. Something of this complexity has been captured in a twentieth-century poet's long poem about this seventeenth-century poet—John Berryman's *Homage to Mistress Bradstreet* (1956).

ADDITIONAL READING

The Works of Anne Bradstreet in Prose and Verse, ed. John Harvard Ellis, 1867, 1932, 1962; *The Complete Works of Anne Bradstreet,* ed. Joseph R. McElrath, Jr., and Allan P. Robb, 1981.

Josephine K. Piercy, *Anne Bradstreet,* 1965; Adrienne Rich, "Anne Bradstreet and Her Poetry," *The Works of Anne Bradstreet,* ed. Jeannine Hensley, 1967; Elizabeth W. White, *Anne Bradstreet: The Tenth Muse,* 1971; Robert D. Richardson, Jr., "The Puritan Poetry of Anne Bradstreet," *The American Puritan Imagination,* ed., Sacvan Bercovitch, 1974; Ann Stanford, *Anne Bradstreet: The Worldly Puritan,* 1974; Pattie Cowell and Ann Stanford, eds., *Critical Essays on Anne Bradstreet,* 1983; Wendy Martin, *An American Triptych: Anne Bradstreet, Emily Dickinson, Adrienne Rich,* 1984.

TEXT

The Works of Anne Bradstreet, ed. Jeannine Hensley, 1967. Typography, punctuation, spelling, and usage have been changed to conform with contemporary English and modern printing practices.

The Prologue[1]

1

To sing of wars, of captains, and of kings,
Of cities founded, commonwealths begun,
For my mean pen are too superior things:
Or how they all, or each their dates have run
Let poets and historians set these forth,   5
My obscure lines shall not so dim their worth.

2

But when my wond'ring eyes and envious heart
Great Bartas'[2] sugared lines do but read o'er,
Fool I do grudge the Muses[3] did not part
'Twixt him and me that overfluent store;   10
A Bartas can do what a Bartas will
But simple I according to my skill.

3

From schoolboy's tongue no rhet'ric we expect,
Nor yet a sweet consort from broken strings,
Nor perfect beauty where's a main defect: 15
My foolish, broken, blemished Muse so sings,
And this to mend, alas, no art is able,
'Cause nature made it so irreparable.

4

Nor can I, like that fluent sweet tongued Greek,[4]
Who lisped at first, in future times speak plain.   20
By art he gladly found what he did seek,
A full requital of his striving pain.
Art can do much, but this maxim's most sure:
A weak or wounded brain admits no cure.

5

I am obnoxious to each carping tongue   25
Who says my hand a needle better fits,
A poet's pen all scorn I should thus wrong,
For such despite[5] they cast on female wits:
If what I do prove well, it won't advance,
They'll say it's stol'n, or else it was by chance.   30

6

But sure the antique Greeks were far more mild
Else of our sex, why feigned[6] they those nine
And poesy made Calliope's[7] own child;
So 'mongst the rest they placed the arts divine:

---

[1]"The Prologue" stood at the beginning of *The Tenth Muse* (1650).
[2]Guillaume du Bartas (1544–1590), French author of *The Divine Weeks and Works*, which was translated into English in 1605–07 by Joshua Sylvester.
[3]The nine Muses of Greek mythology presided over poetry, music, and the other arts.

[4]The Athenian orator Demosthenes (*c.* 385–322 B.C.), who, according to legend, walked by the sea-shore with pebbles in his mouth, practicing his speech to rid himself of his impediment.
[5]Contempt.
[6]Conceived, shaped.
[7]Calliope was the Muse of epic poetry.

But this weak knot they will full soon untie,   35
The Greeks did nought, but play the fools and lie.

7

Let Greeks be Greeks, and women what they are
Men have precedency and still excel,
It is but vain unjustly to wage war;
Men can do best, and women know it well.   40
Preeminence in all and each is yours;
Yet grant some small acknowledgement of ours.

8

And oh ye high flown quills[8] that soar the skies,
And ever with your prey still catch your praise,
If e'er you deign these lowly lines your eyes,   45

Give thyme or parsley wreath, I ask no bays;[9]
This mean and unrefined ore of mine
Will make your glist'ring gold but more to shine.

1650

In Honor of That
High and Mighty Princess
Queen Elizabeth[1] of Happy Memory

THE PROEM[2]

Although, great Queen, thou now in silence lie
Yet thy loud herald[3] Fame doth to the sky
Thy wondrous worth proclaim in every clime,
And so hath vowed while there is world or time.
So great's thy glory and thine excellence,   5
The sound thereof rapts[4] every human sense,
That men account it no impiety,
To say thou wert a fleshly deity.
Thousands bring offerings (though out of date)
Thy world of honors to accumulate;   10
'Mongst hundred hecatombs[5] of roaring verse,
Mine bleating stands before thy royal hearse.[6]
Thou never didst nor canst thou now disdain
T' accept the tribute of a loyal brain.
Thy clemency did erst[7] esteem as much   15
The acclamations of the poor as rich,
Which makes me deem my rudeness is no wrong,
Though I resound thy praises 'mongst the throng.

---

[8]Quill pens, made from feathers.
[9]A crown or wreath made of laurel leaves bestowed on victors or honored individuals, especially writers.
[1]Elizabeth Tudor (1533–1603), Queen of England (r. 1558–1603).
[2]Preface, introductory song.

[3]Royal messenger.
[4]Absorbs, engrosses; from "rap" (to enchant, enrapture).
[5]Public offerings to the gods in ancient Greece of 100 oxen.
[6]Structure over tomb or coffin on which to place epitaphs.
[7]Formerly.

THE POEM

No Phoenix[8] pen, nor Spenser's poetry,
No Speed's nor Camden's learned history,   20
Eliza's works wars, praise, can e'er compact;[9]
The world's the theatre where she did act.
No memories nor volumes can contain
The 'leven Olympiads[10] of her happy reign.
Who was so good, so just, so learn'd, so wise,   25
From all the kings on earth she won the prize.
Nor say I more than duly is her due,
Millions will testify that this is true.
She hath wiped off th' aspersion of her sex,
That women wisdom lack to play the rex.[11]   30
Spain's monarch, says not so, nor yet his host;[12]
She taught them better manners, to their cost.
The Salic law,[13] in force now had not been,
If France had ever hoped for such a queen.
But can you, doctors,[14] now this point dispute,   35
She's argument enough to make you mute.
Since first the Sun did run his ne'er run race,
And earth had, once a year, a new old face,
Since time was time, and man unmanly man,
Come show me such a Phoenix if you can.   40
Was ever people better ruled than hers?
Was ever land more happy freed from stirs?[15]
Did ever wealth in England more abound?
Her victories in foreign coasts resound;
Ships more invincible than Spain's, her foe,   45
She wracked, she sacked,[16] she sunk his Armado;
Her stately troops advanced to Lisbon's wall,
Don Anthony in's right there to install.[17]
She frankly helped Frank's brave distressed king;[18]
The states united now her fame do sing.   50
She their protectrix[19] was; they well do know
Unto our dread virago,[20] what they owe.
Her nobles sacrificed their noble blood,
Nor men nor coin she spared to do them good.
The rude untamed Irish, she did quell,   55
Before her picture the proud Tyrone[21] fell.
Had ever prince such counsellors as she?
Herself Minerva[22] caused them so to be.

---

[8]In Egyptian mythology, the Phoenix is the bird consumed by fire who rises renewed from its ashes; Edmund Spenser (1552–1599), English poet, whose great epic poem, *The Faerie Queen*, celebrates Queen Elizabeth; John Speed (1542–1629), English historian and mapmaker; William Camden (1551–1623), English historian.
[9]Condense.
[10]An Olympiad is the four-year interval between the Olympic games by which the ancient Greeks calculated dates; thus, 44 years of Elizabeth's reign.
[11]"King" (Latin).
[12]Army of King Philip II (1527–1598) of Spain, Portugal, and the Netherlands, whose Spanish Armada (fleet of warships), considered invincible, was defeated in 1588 while attempting to invade England.
[13]Originally the law code of ancient Salic Franks denying women the inheritance of "Salic land," employed by France to deny women the crown.

[14]Learned persons.
[15]Disturbances.
[16]"Wracked," destroyed; "sacked," plundered.
[17]England and France attempted to restore Don Antonio to the Portuguese crown he had claimed in Lisbon in 1581, but lost to Philip II of Spain.
[18]Elizabeth aided Henry IV, successor to Henry III in 1589, in the struggle for the French throne against the rival backed by Spain, the Pope, and members of the Holy League in France, a party favoring establishment of catholicism as the national religion and elective monarchies.
[19]Female protector.
[20]Courageous, strong woman.
[21]Hugh O'Neill, Earl of Tyrone, enlisted the aid of Spain in the Irish rebellion against England (Tyrone War, 1594–1603), but was defeated.
[22]Roman name for Pallas Athena, Greek virgin-goddess of wisdom, war, and protectress of cities.

Such captains and such soldiers never seen,
As were the subjects of our Pallas queen.   60
Her seamen through all straits the world did round;
Terra incognita[23] might know the sound.
Her Drake came laden home with Spanish gold;[24]
Her Essex took Cadiz, their Herculean hold.[25]
But time would fail me, so my tongue would too,   65
To tell of half she did, or she could do.
Semiramis[26] to her is but obscure,
More infamy than fame she did procure.
She built her glory but on Babel's walls,[27]
World's wonder for a while, but yet it falls.   70
Fierce Tomris[28] (Cyrus' headsman) Scythians' queen,
Had put her harness off, had she but seen
Our Amazon in th' Camp of Tilbury,[29]
Judging all valor and all majesty
Within that princess to have residence,   75
And prostrate yielded to her excellence.
Dido,[30] first foundress of proud Carthage walls
(Who living consummates her funerals),
A great Eliza, but compared with ours,
How vanisheth her glory, wealth, and powers.   80
Profuse, proud Cleopatra,[31] whose wrong name,
Instead of glory, proved her country's shame,
Of her what worth in stories to be seen,
But that she was a rich Egyptian queen.
Zenobya,[32] potent empress of the East,   85
And of all these without compare the best,
Whom none but great Aurelius could quell;
Yet for our Queen is no fit parallel.
She was a Phoenix queen, so shall she be,
Her ashes not revived, more Phoenix she.   90
Her personal perfections, who would tell
Must dip his pen in th' Heleconian well,[33]
Which I may not, my pride doth but aspire
To read what others write and so admire.
Now say, have women worth? or have they none?   95
Or had they some, but with our Queen is't gone?
Nay masculines, you have thus taxed[34] us long,
But she, though dead, will vindicate our wrong.
Let such as say our sex is void of reason,
Know 'tis a slander now but once was treason.   100

---

[23]"Unknown land" (Latin).
[24]Sir Francis Drake (1540–1596), English commander at the defeat of the Spanish Armada (1588).
[25]Robert Devereux, Earl of Essex (1566–1601), in 1596 helped command the successful expedition against Cadiz, an important Spanish port. "Herculean," from Hercules, in Greek and Roman mythology, the greatest of heroes, possessing superhuman strength and power.
[26]Legendary Assyrian Queen of beauty and wisdom, said to have built cities, including Babylon with its hanging gardens, and conquered many countries.
[27]Ancient Babylonia, where men erected a tower to "reach unto heaven"; in anger God destroyed it and confounded men's language. Genesis 11:1–9: "Therefore is the name of it called Babel."
[28]Queen of ancient Scythia, reputed to have killed Cyrus (600?–529 B.C.), founder of the Persian empire.
[29]In Greek mythology, Amazons were a race of female warriors. Before the defeat of the Spanish Armada at sea, and

in anticipation of invasion by the Spanish troops, Elizabeth delivered a speech to the troops at Tilbury.
[30]Legendary founder of Carthage, ancient city in North Africa, who built a pyre and leapt into the flames to escape marriage with the king of Libya. Virgil, in his epic *The Aeneid*, describes her immolation as caused by her abandonment by her lover Aeneas.
[31]Queen of Egypt (69–30 B.C.), and mistress of Julius Caesar and Mark Antony, Roman statesmen and soldiers, whose wrong name means "glory to the father."
[32]Queen of Palmyra (c. 266), ancient Syrian city, challenged the Roman Empire by invading Asia Minor and Egypt; she was defeated and captured by Roman Emperor Aurelian (Aurelianus, c. 215–275) in 272, and Palmyra was destroyed.
[33]In Greek mythology, Mount Helicon is the home of the muses, and the spring of water there, struck by the foot of the winged horse Pegasus, is the inspiration of poets.
[34]Accused.

But happy England which had such a queen;
Yea happy, happy, had those days still been.
But happiness lies in a higher sphere,
Then wonder not Eliza moves not here.
Full fraught with honor, riches and with days   105
She set, she set, like Titan[35] in his rays.
No more shall rise or set so glorious sun
Until the heaven's great revolution;[36]
If then new things their old forms shall retain,
Eliza shall rule Albion[37] once again.   110

HER EPITAPH

Here sleeps the queen, this is the royal bed
Of th' damask rose,[38] sprung from the white and red,
Whose sweet perfume fills the all-filling air.
This rose is withered, once so lovely fair.
On neither tree did grow such rose before,   115
The greater was our gain, our loss the more.

ANOTHER

Here lies the pride of queens, pattern of kings,
So blaze[39] it, Fame, here's feathers for thy wings.
Here lies the envied, yet unparalleled prince,
Whose living virtues speak (though dead long since).   120
If many worlds, as that fantastic framed,[40]
In every one be her great glory famed.

1643   1650

Contemplations

1

Some time now past in the autumnal tide,
When Phoebus[1] wanted but one hour to bed,
The trees all richly clad, yet void of pride,
Where gilded o'er by his rich golden head.
Their leaves and fruits seemed painted, but was true,   5
Of green, of red, of yellow, mixed hue;
Rapt were my senses at this delectable view.

2

I wist[2] not what to wish, yet sure thought I,
If so much excellence abide below,

---

[35]In Greek and Roman mythology, Titan, associated with the sun, was one of the family of primordial gods overthrown by the Olympian gods in the War of the Titans.
[36]The Second Coming of Christ, the Last Judgment. Revelation 19:11: "And I saw heaven opened, and behold a white horse; and he that sat upon him was called Faithful and True, and in righteousness he doth judge. . . ."
[37]Britain.
[38]Fragrant red or pink rose, a reference to the Tudor dynasty that reigned in England from Henry VII (1485) through Elizabeth I (1603). Henry VII's victory ended the

Wars of the Roses (1455–85), the dynastic wars between the Houses of York (white rose) and Lancaster (red rose).
[39]Proclaim (as with a trumpet).
[40]I.e., as that dreamer, seer, or visionary one imagined; probably refers to the theory of Nicolaus Copernicus (1473–1543), Polish astronomer, in which the earth is only one of other planets ("many worlds") revolving around the sun, a heliocentric theory of the universe challenging Ptolemy's earth-centered theory.
[1]In Greek mythology Phoebus Apollo is the god of the sun.
[2]Knew.

How excellent is He that dwells on high,   10
Whose power and beauty by his works we know?
Sure He is goodness, wisdom, glory, light,
That hath this under world so richly dight;[3]
More heaven than earth was here, no winter and no night.

3

Then on a stately oak I cast mine eye,   15
Whose ruffling top the clouds seemed to aspire;
How long since thou wast in thine infancy?
Thy strength, and stature, more thy years admire,
Hath hundred winters past since thou wast born?
Or thousand since thou brakest thy shell of horn?[4]   20
If so, all these as nought, eternity doth scorn.

4

Then higher on the glistering Sun I gazed,
Whose beams was shaded by the leafy tree;
The more I looked, the more I grew amazed,
And softly said, "What glory's like to thee?"   25
Soul of this world, this universe's eye,
No wonder some made thee a deity;
Had I not better known, alas, the same had I.

5

Thou as a bridegroom from thy chamber rushes,
And as a strong man, joys to run a race;[5]   30
The morn doth usher thee with smiles and blushes;
The Earth reflects her glances in thy face.
Birds, insects, animals with vegative,[6]
Thy heat from death and dullness doth revive,
And in the darksome womb of fruitful nature dive.   35

6

Thy swift annual and diurnal course,
Thy daily straight and yearly oblique path,
Thy pleasing fervor and thy scorching force,
All mortals here the feeling knowledge hath.
Thy presence makes it day, thy absence night,   40
Quaternal seasons caused by thy might:
Hail creature, full of sweetness, beauty, and delight.

7

Art thou so full of glory that no eye
Hath strength thy shining rays once to behold?
And is thy splendid throne erect so high,   45
As to approach it, can no earthly mould?
How full of glory then must thy Creator be,
Who gave this bright light luster unto thee?
Admired, adored for ever, be that Majesty.

---

[3]Adorned.
[4]Shell of the acorn.
[5]Psalm 19:5: The sun "is as a bridegroom coming out of his
chamber, and rejoiceth as a strong man to run a race."
[6]Vegetable.

8

Silent alone, where none or saw, or heard,   50
In pathless paths I lead my wand'ring feet,
My humble eyes to lofty skies I reared
To sing some song, my mazed[7] Muse thought meet.[8]
My great Creator I would magnify,
That nature had thus decked liberally;   55
But Ah, and Ah, again, my imbecility!

9

I heard the merry grasshopper then sing.
The black-clad cricket bear a second part;
They kept one tune and played on the same string,
Seeming to glory in their little art.   60
Shall creatures abject thus their voices raise
And in their kind resound their Maker's praise,
Whilst I, as mute, can warble forth no higher lays?

10

When present times look back to ages past,
And men in being fancy those are dead,   65
It makes things gone perpetually to last,
And calls back months and years that long since fled.
It makes a man more aged in conceit[9]
Than was Methuselah, or's grandsire great,[10]
While of their persons and their acts his mind doth treat.   70

11

Sometimes in Eden fair he seems to be,
Sees glorious Adam there made lord of all,
Fancies the apple, dangle on the tree,
That turned his sovereign to a naked thrall.[11]
Who like a miscreant's driven from that place,   75
To get his bread with pain and sweat of face,
A penalty imposed on his backsliding race.

12

Here sits our grandame in retired place,
And in her lap her bloody Cain new-born;[12]
The weeping imp oft looks her in the face,   80
Bewails his unknown hap[13] and fate forlorn;
His mother sighs to think of Paradise,
And how she lost her bliss to be more wise,
Believing him that was, and is, father of lies.

13

Here Cain and Abel come to sacrifice,   85
Fruits of the earth and fatlings each do bring,
On Abel's gift the fire descends from skies,

---

[7]Amazed.
[8]Appropriate.
[9]Conception, imagination.
[10]Methuselah's 969 years made him the longest-living man in the Bible; his grandfather lived 962 years (Genesis 5:18–27).

[11]Adam ate the apple, became ashamed of his nakedness, and lost his sovereignty in the Garden of Eden, being cast out to work like a thrall (or slave) for his food (Genesis 3).
[12]Eve holding Cain, who later will murder his brother Abel (Genesis 4:1–8).
[13]Fortune.

But no such sign on false Cain's offering;[14]
With sullen hateful looks he goes his ways,
Hath thousand thoughts to end his brother's days,   90
Upon whose blood his future good he hopes to raise.

14

There Abel keeps his sheep, no ill he thinks;
His brother comes, then acts his fratricide;
The virgin Earth of blood her first draught drinks,
But since that time she often hath been cloyed.   95
The wretch with ghastly face and dreadful mind
Thinks each he sees will serve him in his kind,
Though none on earth but kindred near then could he find.

15

Who fancies not his looks now at the bar,[15]
His face like death, his heart with horror fraught,   100
Nor malefactor ever felt like war,
When deep despair with wish of life hath fought,
Branded with guilt and crushed with treble woes,
A vagabond to Land of Nod he goes.[16]
A city builds, that walls might him secure from foes.   105

16

Who thinks not oft upon the father's ages,
Their long descent, how nephews' sons they saw,
The starry observations of those sages,
And how their precepts to their sons were law,
How Adam sighed to see his progeny,   110
Clothed all in his black sinful livery,
Who neither guilt nor yet the punishment could fly.

17

Our life compare we with their length of days
Who to the tenth of theirs doth now arrive?
And though thus short, we shorten many ways,   115
Living so little while we are alive;
In eating, drinking, sleeping, vain delight
So unawares comes on perpetual night,
And puts all pleasures vain unto eternal flight.

18

When I behold the heavens as in their prime,   120
And then the earth (though old) still clad in green,
The stones and trees, insensible of time,
Nor age nor wrinkle on their front are seen;
If winter come and greenness then do fade,
A spring returns, and they more youthful made;   125
But man grows old, lies down, remains where once he's laid.

---

[14]Cain brought an offering of "fruit of the ground" to the Lord, while Abel brought "the firstlings of his flock and of the fat thereof"; "And the Lord had respect unto Abel and to his offering" but "unto Cain and to his offering he had not respect" (Genesis 4:3–5).

[15]Place of justice.
[16]Genesis 4:16: "And Cain went out from the presence of the Lord, and dwelt in the land of Nod, on the east of Eden."

19

By birth more noble than those creatures all,
Yet seems by nature and by custom cursed,
No sooner born, but grief and care makes fall
That state obliterate he had at first;   130
Nor youth, nor strength, nor wisdom spring again,
Nor habitations long their names retain,
But in oblivion to the final day remain.

20

Shall I then praise the heavens, the trees, the earth
Because their beauty and their strength last longer?   135
Shall I wish there, or never to had birth,
Because they're bigger, and their bodies stronger?
Nay, they shall darken, perish, fade and die,
And when unmade, so ever shall they lie,
But man was made for endless immortality.   140

21

Under the cooling shadow of a stately elm
Close sat I by a goodly river's side,
Where gliding streams the rocks did overwhelm,
A lonely place, with pleasures dignified.
I once that loved the shady woods so well,   145
Now thought the rivers did the trees excel,
And if the sun would ever shine, there would I dwell.

22

While on the stealing stream I fixt mine eye,
Which to the longed-for ocean held its course,
I marked, nor crooks, nor rubs[17] that there did lie   150
Could hinder ought, but still augment its force.
"O happy flood," quoth I, "that holds thy race
Till thou arrive at thy beloved place,
Nor is it rocks or shoals that can obstruct thy pace,

23

Nor is't enough, that thou alone mayst slide,   155
But hundred brooks in thy clear waves do meet,
So hand in hand along with thee they glide
To Thetis' house,[18] where all embrace and greet.
Thou emblem true of what I count the best,
O could I lead my rivulets to rest,   160
So may we press to that vast mansion, ever blest."

24

Ye fish, which in this liquid region 'bide,
That for each season have your habitation,
Now salt, now fresh where you think best to glide
To unknown coasts to give a visitation,   165

---

[17]Neither turns nor obstacles.
[18]In Greek mythology, a Nereid or water-goddess who lived in the depths of the sea.

In lakes and ponds you leave your numerous fry;
So nature taught, and yet you know not why,
You wat'ry folk that know not your felicity.

25

Look how the wantons frisk to taste the air,
Then to the colder bottom straight they dive;
Eftsoon[19] to Neptune's[20] glassy hall repair   170
To see what trade they great ones there do drive,
Who forage o'er the spacious sea-green field,
And take the trembling prey before it yield,
Whose armor is their scales, their spreading fins their shield.   175

26

While musing thus with contemplation fed,
And thousand fancies buzzing in my brain,
The sweet-tongued Philomel[21] perched o'er my head
And chanted forth a most melodious strain
Which rapt me so with wonder and delight,   180
I judged my hearing better than my sight,
And wished me wings with her a while to take my flight.

27

"O merry Bird," said I, "that fears no snares,
That neither toils nor hoards up in thy barn,
Feels no sad thoughts nor cruciating[22] cares   185
To gain more good or shun what might thee harm.
Thy clothes ne'er wear, thy meat is everywhere,
Thy bed a bough, thy drink the water clear,
Reminds not what is past, nor what's to come dost fear."

28

"The dawning morn with songs thou dost prevent,[23]   190
Sets hundred notes unto thy feathered crew,
So each one tunes his pretty instrument,
And warbling out the old, begin anew,
And thus they pass their youth in summer season,
Then follow thee into a better region,   195
Where winter's never felt by that sweet airy legion."

29

Man at the best a creature frail and vain,
In knowledge ignorant, in strength but weak,
Subject to sorrows, losses, sickness, pain,
Each storm his state, his mind, his body break,   200
From some of these he never finds cessation,
But day or night, within, without, vexation,
Troubles from foes, from friends, from dearest, near'st
    relation.

---

[19]From time to time.
[20]Roman god of the sea.
[21]A nightingale. In Greek mythology, Philomela was
turned into a nightingale after Tereus (her brother-in-law)
raped her and cut out her tongue.

[22]Excruciating, painful.
[23]Anticipate, come before.

30

And yet this sinful creature, frail and vain,
This lump of wretchedness, of sin and sorrow,   205
This weatherbeaten vessel wracked with pain,
Joys not in hope of an eternal morrow;
Nor all his losses, crosses, and vexation,
In weight, in frequency and long duration
Can make him deeply groan for that divine translation.[24]   210

31

The mariner that on smooth waves doth glide
Sings merrily and steers his bark with ease,
As if he had command of wind and tide,
And now become great master of the seas:
But suddenly a storm spoils all the sport,   215
And makes him long for a more quiet port,
Which 'gainst all adverse winds may serve for fort.

32

So he that saileth in this world of pleasure,
Feeding on sweets, that never bit of th' sour,
That's full of friends, of honor, and of treasure,   220
Fond[25] fool, he takes this earth ev'n for heav'n's bower.
But sad affliction comes and makes him see
Here's neither honor, wealth, nor safety;
Only above is found all with security.

33

O Time the fatal wrack of mortal things,   225
That draws oblivion's curtains over kings;
Their sumptuous monuments, men know them not,
Their names without a record are forgot,
Their parts, their ports, their pomp's all laid in th' dust
Nor wit nor gold, nor buildings scape[26] time's rust;   230
But he whose name is graved in the white stone[27]
Shall last and shine when all of these are gone.

1664–65?   *1678*

The Flesh and the Spirit

In secret place where once I stood
Close by the banks of Lacrim[1] flood,
I heard two sisters reason on
Things that are past and things to come;
One flesh was called, who had her eye   5
On worldly wealth and vanity;

---

[24]Change from life to eternity through death.
[25]Foolishly naive.
[26]Escape.
[27]Revelation 2:17: "He that hath an ear, let him hear what the Spirit saith unto the churches: To him that overcometh will I give to eat of the hidden manna, and will give him a white stone, and in the stone a new name written, which no man knoweth saving he that receiveth it."
[1]River of tears. Lacrim from the Latin *lacrima*, "tear" (cf. lachrymose, tearful).

The other Spirit, who did rear
Her thoughts unto a higher sphere:
Sister, quoth Flesh, what liv'st thou on,
Nothing but meditation?   10
Doth contemplation feed thee so
Regardlessly to let earth go?
Can speculation satisfy
Notion[2] without reality?
Dost dream of things beyond the moon,   15
And dost thou hope to dwell there soon?
Hast treasures there laid up in store
That all in th' world thou count'st but poor?
Art fancy sick, or turned a sot[3]
To catch at shadows which are not?   20
Come, come, I'll show unto thy sense,
Industry hath its recompense.
What canst desire, but thou may'st see
True substance in variety?
Dost honor like? Acquire the same,   25
As some to their immortal fame,
And trophies[4] to thy name erect
Which wearing time shall ne'er deject.[5]
For riches doth thou long full sore?
Behold enough of precious store.   30
Earth hath more silver, pearls, and gold,
Than eyes can see or hands can hold.
Affect's[6] thou pleasure? Take thy fill,
Earth hath enough of what you will.
Then let not go, what thou may'st find   35
For things unknown, only in mind.

Spirit: Be still thou unregenerate part,
Disturb no more my settled heart,
For I have vowed (and so will do)
Thee as a foe still to pursue.   40
And combat with thee will and must,
Until I see thee laid in th' dust.
Sisters we are, yea, twins we be,
Yet deadly feud 'twixt thee and me;
For from one father are we not,   45
Thou by old Adam wast begot,
But my arise is from above,[7]
Whence my dear Father I do love.
Thou speak'st me fair, but hat'st me sore,
Thy flatt'ring shows I'll trust no more.   50
How oft thy slave, hast thou me made,
When I believed what thou hast said,
And never had more cause of woe
Than when I did what thou bad'st do.
I'll stop mine ears at these thy charms,   55
And count them for my deadly harms.

---

[2]Idea or thought.
[3]Sick on fancy, imagining; sot: blockhead, dolt.
[4]Memorials or monuments of victory.
[5]Cast down.

[6]Seekest.
[7]The flesh descends from Adam, but spirit comes from heaven.

Thy sinful pleasures I do hate,
Thy riches are to me no bait,
Thine honors do, nor will I love;
For my ambition lies above.   60
My greatest honor it shall be
When I am victor over thee,
And triumph shall with laurel head,[8]
When thou my captive shalt be led,
How I do live, thou need'st not scoff,   65
For I have meat thou know'st not of;[9]
The hidden manna[10] I do eat,
The word of life it is my meat.
My thoughts do yield me more content
Than can thy hours in pleasure spent.   70
Nor are they shadows which I catch,
Nor fancies vain at which I snatch,
But reach at things that are so high,
Beyond thy dull capacity;
Eternal substance I do see,   75
With which enriched I would be.
Mine eye doth pierce the heavens and see
What is invisible to thee.
My garments are not silk nor gold,
Nor such like trash which earth doth hold,   80
But royal robes I shall have on,
More glorious than the glist'ring sun;
My crown not diamonds, pearls, and gold,
But such as angels' heads enfold.
The city[11] where I hope to dwell,   85
There's none on earth can parallel;
The stately walls both high and strong,
Are made of precious jasper stone;
The gates of pearl, both rich and clear,
And angels are for porters there;   90
The streets thereof transparent gold,
Such as no eye did e'er behold;
A crystal river there doth run,
Which doth proceed from the Lamb's throne.
Of life, there are the waters sure,   95
Which shall remain forever pure,[12]
Nor sun, nor moon, they have no need,
For glory doth from God proceed.
No candle there, nor yet torchlight,
For there shall be no darksome night.   100
From sickness and infirmity
For evermore they shall be free;
Nor withering age shall e'er come there,
But beauty shall be bright and clear;

---

[8]In classical times, a wreath or crown of laurel leaves was placed on the victor's head.
[9]John 4:32: "But he [Christ] said unto them [the disciples], I have meat to eat that ye know not of."
[10]Manna is the bread sent by God to the Israelites wandering in the wilderness (Exodus 16:14–15); in Revelation 2:17, the Spirit promises spiritual food, "the hidden manna," to "him that overcometh."

[11]The holy city or "new Jerusalem" depicted in Revelation 21 and 22 is described in the remaining lines of the poem.
[12]Revelation 22:1: "And he shewed me a pure river of water of life, clear as crystal, proceeding out of the throne of God and of the Lamb."

This city pure is not for thee,   105
For things unclean there shall not be.[13]
If I of heaven may have my fill,
Take thou the world and all that will.

1660–70   *1678*

The Vanity
of All Worldly Things

As he said vanity,[1] so vain say I,
Oh! vanity, O vain all under sky;
Where is the man can say, "Lo, I have found
On brittle earth a consolation sound"?
What is't in honor to be set on high?   5
No, they like beasts and sons of men shall die,
And whilst they live, how oft doth turn their fate;
He's now a captive that was king of late.
What is't in wealth great treasures to obtain?
No, that's but labor, anxious care, and pain.   10
He heaps up riches, and he heaps up sorrow,
It's his today, but who's his heir tomorrow?
What then? Content in pleasures canst thou find?
More vain than all, that's but to grasp the wind.
The sensual senses for a time they please,   15
Meanwhile the conscience rage, who shall appease?
What is't in beauty? No that's but a snare,
They're foul enough today, that once were fair.
What is't in flow'ring youth, or manly age?
The first is prone to vice, the last to rage.   20
Where is it then, in wisdom, learning, arts?
Sure if on earth, it must be in those parts;
Yet these the wisest man of men did find
But vanity, vexation of mind.
And he that knows the most doth still bemoan   25
He knows not all that here is to be known.
What is it then? to do as stoics[2] tell,
Nor laugh, nor weep, let things go ill or well?
Such stoics are but stocks,[3] such teaching vain,
While man is man, he shall have ease or pain.   30
If not in honor, beauty, age, nor treasure,
Nor yet in learning, wisdom, youth, nor pleasure,
Where shall I climb, sound, seek, search, or find
That *summum bonum*[4] which may stay my mind?
There is a path no vulture's eye hath seen,   35
Where lion fierce, nor lion's whelps have been,
Which leads unto that living crystal fount,
Who drinks thereof, the world doth nought account.
The depth and sea have said "'tis not in me."

---

[13]Revelation 21:27: "And there shall in no wise enter into it
any thing that defileth. . . ."
[1]Ecclesiastes 1:2: "Vanity of vanities, saith the preacher,
vanity of vanities; all is vanity."

[2]Those who are indifferent to emotion, pleasure or pain,
accepting all.
[3]Stupid or slow-witted persons.
[4]"Highest good" (Latin).

With pearl and gold it shall not valued be.   40
For sapphire, onyx, topaz who would change;
It's hid from eyes of men, they count it strange.
Death and destruction the fame hath heard,
But where and what it is, from heaven's declared;
It brings to honor which shall ne'er decay,   45
It stores with wealth which time can't wear away.
It yieldeth pleasures far beyond conceit,
And truly beautifies without deceit.
Nor strength, nor wisdom, nor fresh youth shall fade,
Nor death shall see, but are immortal made.   50
This pearl of price, this tree of life, this spring,
Who is possessed of shall reign a king.
Nor change of state nor cares shall ever see,
But wear his crown unto eternity.
This satiates the soul, this stays[5] the mind,   55
And all the rest, but vanity we find.

1647–48?   *1650*

The Author to Her Book[1]

Thou ill-formed offspring of my feeble brain,
Who after birth didst by my side remain,
Till snatched from thence by friends, less wise than true,
Who thee abroad, exposed to public view,
Made thee in rags, halting to th' press to trudge,   5
Where errors were not lessened (all may judge).
At thy return my blushing was not small,
My rambling brat (in print) should mother call,
I cast thee by as one unfit for light,
Thy visage was so irksome in my sight;   10
Yet being mine own, at length affection would
Thy blemishes amend, if so I could:
I washed thy face, but more defects I saw,
And rubbing off a spot still made a flaw.
I stretched thy joints to make thee even feet,[2]   15
Yet still thou run'st more hobbling than is meet;
In better dress to trim thee was my mind,
But nought save homespun cloth i' th' house I find.
In this array 'mongst vulgars[3] may'st thou roam.
In critic's hands beware thou dost not come,   20
And take thy way where yet thou art not known;
If for thy father asked, say thou hadst none;
And for thy mother, she alas is poor,
Which caused her thus to send thee out of door.

1650–70?   *1678*

---

[5]Steadies, supports.
[1]The poem is addressed to *The Tenth Muse* (1650) published in London without Anne Bradstreet's knowledge. It appeared in her corrected second edition of 1678, published in Boston.

[2]Drew out the lines to make the metrical feet scan properly.
[3]Common people.

Before the Birth
of One of Her Children

All things within this fading world hath end,
Adversity doth still our joys attend;
No ties so strong, no friends so dear and sweet,
But with death's parting blow is sure to meet.
The sentence past is most irrevocable,   5
A common thing, yet oh, inevitable.
How soon, my Dear, death may my steps attend,
How soon't may be thy lot to lose thy friend,
We both are ignorant, yet love bids me
These farewell lines to recommend to thee,   10
That when that knot's untied that made us one,
I may seem thine, who in effect am none.
And if I see not half my days that's due,
What nature would, God grant to yours and you;
The many faults that well you know I have   15
Let be interred in my oblivious grave;
If any worth or virtue were in me,
Let that live freshly in thy memory
And when thou feel'st no grief, as I no harms,
Yet love thy dead, who long lay in thine arms.   20
And when thy loss shall be repaid with gains
Look to my little babes, my dear remains.
And if thou love thyself, or loved'st me,
These O protect from step-dame's injury.
And if chance to thine eyes shall bring this verse,   25
With some sad sighs honor my absent hearse;
And kiss this paper for thy love's dear sake,
Who with salt tears this last farewell did take.

1640–52?   1678

To My Dear
and Loving Husband

If ever two were one, then surely we.
If ever man were loved by wife, then thee;
If ever wife was happy in a man,
Compare with me, ye women, if you can.
I prize thy love more than whole mines of gold   5
Or all the riches that the East doth hold.
My love is such that rivers cannot quench,
Nor ought[1] but love from thee, give recompense.
Thy love is such I can no way repay,
The heavens reward thee manifold, I pray.   10
Then while we live, in love let's so persevere[2]
That when we live no more, we may live ever.

1641–43   1678

_____
[1] Anything.
[2] In the seventeenth century, pronounced to rhyme with "ever."

A Letter to Her Husband,
Absent upon Public Employment

My head, my heart, mine eyes, my life, nay, more,
My joy, my magazine[1] of earthly store,
If two be one, as surely thou and I,
How stayest thou there, whilst I at Ipswich[2] lie?
So many steps, head from the heart to sever,   5
If but a neck, soon should we be together.
I, like the Earth this season, mourn in black,
My Sun is gone so far in's zodiac,[3]
Whom whilst I 'joyed, nor storms, nor frost I felt,
His warmth such frigid colds did cause to melt.   10
My chilled limbs now numbed lie forlorn;
Return, return, sweet Sol,[4] from Capricorn;[5]
In this dead time, alas, what can I more
Than view those fruits[6] which through thy heat I bore?
Which sweet contentment yield me for a space,   15
True living pictures of their father's face.
O strange effect! now thou art southward gone,
I weary grow the tedious day so long;
But when thou northward to me shalt return,
I wish my Sun may never set, but burn   20
Within the Cancer[7] of my glowing breast,
The welcome house of him my dearest guest.
Where ever, ever stay, and go not thence,
Till nature's sad decree shall call thee hence;
Flesh of thy flesh, bone of thy bone,[8]   25
I here, thou there, yet both but one.

1641–43?   *1678*

Another

As loving hind[1] that (hartless)[2] wants her deer,
Scuds[3] through the woods and fern with hark'ning ear,
Perplext, in every bush and nook doth pry,
Her dearest deer, might answer ear or eye;
So doth my anxious soul, which now doth miss   5
A dearer dear (far dearer heart) than this.
Still wait with doubts, and hopes, and failing eye,
His voice to hear or person to descry.
Or as the pensive dove doth all alone

---

[1]Place of storage.
[2]Ipswich, Massachusetts, where the Bradstreets lived for a time.
[3]An imaginary path in the heavens related to the paths of the sun and moon, and encompassing the paths of the principal planets. It is divided into twelve equal parts, each of which incorporates a part of the year (about thirty days each), a constellation, and a sign—all important in astrology.
[4]Sol: sun,
[5]Capricorn the Goat, tenth sign of the Zodiac, December 22 to January 19: thus, winter.

[6]Their children.
[7]Cancer the Crab, fourth sign of the Zodiac, June 22 to July 22: thus, summer.
[8]Genesis 2:23: "And Adam said, This is now bone of my bones, and flesh of my flesh; she shall be called Woman, because she was taken out of Man."
[1]Female deer.
[2]Hart is a male deer (as well as a pun for heart).
[3]Runs swiftly.

(On withered bough) most uncouthly bemoan   10
The absence of her love and loving mate,
Whose loss hath made her so unfortunate,
Ev'n thus do I, with many a deep sad groan,
Bewail my turtle[4] true, who now is gone,
His presence and his safe return still woos,   15
With thousand doleful sighs and mournful coos.
Or as the loving mullet, that true fish,
Her fellow lost, nor joy nor life do wish,
But launches on that shore, there for to die,
Where she her captive husband doth espy.   20
Mine being gone, I lead a joyless life,
I have a loving peer,[5] yet seem no wife;
But worst of all, to him can't steer my course,
I here, he there, alas, both kept by force.
Return my dear, my joy, my only love,   25
Unto thy hind, thy mullet, and thy dove,
Who neither joys in pasture, house, nor streams,
The substance gone, O me, these are but dreams.
Together at one tree, oh let us browse,
And like two turtles roost within one house,   30
And like the mullets in one river glide,
Let's still remain but one, till death divide.
         Thy loving love and dearest dear,
         At home, abroad, and everywhere.

1641–43?   *1678*

In Reference to
Her Children, 23 June, 1659

I had eight birds hatched in one nest,
Four cocks there were, and hens the rest.
I nursed them up with pain and care,
Nor cost, nor labor did I spare,
Till at the last they felt their wing,   5
Mounted the trees, and learned to sing;
Chief of the brood then took his flight[1]
To regions far and left me quite.
My mournful chirps I after send,
Till he return, or I do end: 10
Leave not thy nest, thy dam and sire,[2]
Fly back and sing amidst this choir.
My second bird[3] did take her flight,
And with her mate flew out of sight;
Southward they both their course did bend,   15
And seasons twain they there did spend,
Till after blown by southern gales,

---

[4]Turtledove.
[5]In the first edition the word is "phere," a variant of "fere": mate, companion, spouse.
[1]Her oldest child Samuel was in England from 1657 to 1661.

[2]"Dam and Sire": mother and father.
[3]Dorothy married and lived first in Connecticut (to the south of Andover, where the Bradstreets then lived), and then in New Hampshire (to the north).

They norward steered with filled sails.
A prettier bird was no where seen,
Along the beach among the treen.[4]   20
I have a third of color white,
On whom I placed no small delight;
Coupled with mate loving and true,
Hath also bid her dam adieu;[5]
And where Aurora[6] first appears,   25
She now hath perched to spend her years.
One[7] to the academy flew
To chat among that learned crew;
Ambition moves still in his breast
That he might chant above the rest,   30
Striving for more than to do well,
That nightingales he might excel.
My fifth, whose down is yet scarce gone,[8]
Is 'mongst the shrubs and bushes flown,
And as his wings increase in strength,   35
On higher boughs he'll perch at length.
My other three still with me nest,[9]
Until they're grown, then as the rest,
Or here or there they'll take their flight,
As is ordained, so shall they light.   40
If birds could weep, then would my tears
Let others know what are my fears
Lest this my brood some harm should catch,
And be surprised for want of watch,
Whilst pecking corn and void of care,   45
They fall un'wares in fowler's snare,
Or whilst on trees they sit and sing,
Some untoward boy at them do fling,
Or whilst allured with bell and glass,
The net be spread, and caught, alas.   50
Or lest by lime-twigs[10] they be foiled,
Or by some greedy hawks be spoiled.
O would my young, ye saw my breast,
And knew what thoughts there sadly rest,
Great was my pain when I you bred,   55
Great was my care when I you fed,
Long did I keep you soft and warm,
And with my wings kept off all harm,
My cares are more and fears than ever,
My throbs such now as 'fore were never.   60
Alas, my birds, you wisdom want,
Of perils you are ignorant;
Oft times in grass, on trees, in flight,
Sore accidents on you may light.
O to your safety have an eye,   65
So happy may you live and die.
Meanwhile my days in tunes I'll spend,
Till my weak lays with me shall end.
In shady woods I'll sit and sing,

---

[4]Trees (older form of the plural of tree).
[5]Sarah married and moved to Ipswich, east of Andover.
[6]Roman goddess of dawn.
[7]Simon, then going to Harvard.

[8]Probably Dudley, her seventh child. The numbering of the children is apparently out of order.
[9]Hannah, Mercy, and John.
[10]Sticky bird-lime was used on trees to trap birds.

And things that past to mind I'll bring.   70
Once young and pleasant, as are you,
But former toys (no joys) adieu.
My age I will not once lament,
But sing, my time so near is spent.
And from the top bough take my flight   75
Into a country beyond sight,
Where old ones instantly grow young,
And there with seraphims[11] set song;
No seasons cold, nor storms they see;
But spring lasts to eternity.   80
When each of you shall in your nest
Among your young ones take your rest,
In chirping language, oft them tell,
You had a dam that loved you well,
That did what could be done for young,   85
And nursed you up till you were strong,
And 'fore she once would let you fly,
She showed you joy and misery;
Taught what was good, and what was ill,
What would save life, and what would kill.   90
Thus gone, amongst you I may live,
And dead, yet speak, and counsel give:
Farewell, my birds, farewell adieu,
I happy am, if well with you.

1659   *1678*

In Memory of My Dear Grandchild
Elizabeth Bradstreet, Who Deceased August, 1665,
Being a Year and Half Old

Farewell dear babe, my heart's too much content,
Farewell sweet babe, the pleasure of mine eye,
Farewell fair flower that for a space was lent,
Then ta'en away unto eternity.
Blest babe, why should I once bewail thy fate,   5
Or sigh thy days so soon were terminate,
Sith[1] thou art settled in an everlasting state.

2

By nature trees do rot when they are grown,
And plums and apples thoroughly ripe do fall,
And corn and grass are in their season mown,   10
And time brings down what is both strong and tall.
But plants new set to be eradicate,
And buds new blown to have so short a date,
Is by His hand alone that guides nature and fate.

1665   *1678*

---

[11]Celestial beings in the highest order of angels.
[1]Since.

Here Follows Some Verses upon the Burning of Our House July 10th, 1666

COPIED OUT OF A LOOSE PAPER

In silent night when rest I took
For sorrow near I did not look
I wakened was with thund'ring noise
And piteous shrieks of dreadful voice.
That fearful sound of "Fire!" and "Fire!"   5
Let no man know is my desire.
I, starting up, the light did spy,
And to my God my heart did cry
To strengthen me in my distress
And not to leave me succorless.   10
Then, coming out, beheld a space[1]
The flame consume my dwelling place.
And when I could no longer look,
I blest His name that gave and took,[2]
That laid my goods now in the dust.   15
Yea, so it was, and so 'twas just.
It was His own, it was not mine,
Far be it that I should repine;
He might of all justly bereft
But yet sufficient for us left.   20
When by the ruins oft I past
My sorrowing eyes aside did cast,
And here and there the places spy
Where oft I sat and long did lie:
Here stood that trunk, and there that chest,   25
There lay that store I counted best.
My pleasant things in ashes lie,
And them behold no more shall I.
Under thy roof no guest shall sit,
Nor at thy table eat a bit.   30
No pleasant tale shall e'er be told,
Nor things recounted done of old.
No candle e'er shall shine in thee,
Nor bridegroom's voice e'er heard shall be.
In silence ever shall thou lie,   35
Adieu, Adieu, all's vanity.[3]
Then straight I 'gin my heart to chide,
And did thy wealth on earth abide?
Didst fix thy hope on mold'ring dust?
The arm of flesh didst make thy trust?   40
Raise up thy thoughts above the sky
That dunghill mists away may fly.
Thou hast an house on high erect,
Framed by that mighty Architect,
With glory richly furnished,   45

---

[1] A little while.
[2] Job 1:21: "Naked came I out of my mother's womb, and naked shall I return thither: the Lord gave, and Lord hath taken away; blessed be the name of the Lord."

[3] Ecclesiastes 1:2: "Vanity of vanities, saith the preacher, vanity of vanities; all is vanity."

Stands permanent though this be fled.
It's purchased and paid for too
By Him who hath enough to do.
A price so vast as is unknown
Yet by His gift is made thine own;   50
There's wealth enough, I need no more,
Farewell, my pelf,[4] farewell my store.
The world no longer let me love,
My hope and treasure lies above.

1666   *1867*

As Weary Pilgrim

As weary pilgrim, now at rest,
  Hugs with delight his silent nest,
His wasted limbs now lie full soft
  That mirey[1] steps have trodden oft,
Blesses himself to think upon   5
  His dangers past, and travails done.
The burning sun no more shall heat,
  Nor stormy rains on him shall beat.
The briars and thorns no more shall scratch,
  Nor hungry wolves at him shall catch.   10
He erring paths no more shall tread,
  Nor wild fruits eat instead of bread.
For waters cold he doth not long
  For thirst no more shall parch his tongue.
No rugged stones his feet shall gall,   15
  Nor stumps nor rocks cause him to fall.
All cares and fears he bids farewell
  And means in safety now to dwell.
A pilgrim I, on earth perplexed
  With sins, with cares and sorrows vext,   20
By age and pains brought to decay,
  And my clay house[2] mold'ring away.
Oh, how I long to be at rest
  And soar on high among the blest.
This body shall in silence sleep,   25
  Mine eyes no more shall ever weep,
No fainting fits shall me assail,
  Nor grinding pains my body frail,
With cares and fears ne'er cumb'red be
  Nor losses know, nor sorrows see.   30
What though my flesh shall there consume,
  It is the bed Christ did perfume,
And when a few years shall be gone,
  This mortal shall be clothed upon.
A corrupt carcass down it lays,   35
  A glorious body it shall rise.

---

[4]Treasure, especially dishonestly gained.
[1]Boggy, mire-like.
[2]The body.

In weakness and dishonor sown,
   In power 'tis raised by Christ alone.
Then soul and body shall unite
   And of their Maker have the sight.   40
Such lasting joys shall there behold
   As ear ne'er heard nor tongue e'er told.
Lord make me ready for that day,
   Then come, dear Bridegroom,[3] come away.

1669   *1867*

from Meditations Divine and Moral

2

Many can speak well, but few can do well. We are better scholars in the theory than the practic[1] part, but he is a true Christian that is a proficient in both.

6

The finest bread hath the least bran, the purest honey the least wax, and the sincerest Christian the least self-love.

8

Downy beds make drowsy persons, but hard lodging keeps the eyes open; a prosperous state makes a secure Christian, but adversity makes him consider.

9

Sweet words are like honey: a little may refresh, but too much gluts the stomach.

10

Diverse children have their different natures: some are like flesh[2] which nothing but salt will keep from putrefaction, some again like tender fruits that are best preserved with sugar. Those parents are wise that can fit their nurture according to their nature.

12

Authority without wisdom is like a heavy axe without an edge: fitter to bruise than polish.

14

If we had no winter, the spring would not be so pleasant; if we did not sometimes taste of adversity, prosperity would not be so welcome.

16

That house which is not often swept makes the cleanly inhabitant soon loath it, and that heart which is not continually purifying itself is no fit temple for the spirit of God to dwell in.

---

[3]Christ, bridegroom of the soul.
[1]Practice.
[2]Meat.

19

Corn,[3] till it have past through the mill and been ground to powder, is not fit for bread. God so deals with his servants: he grinds them with grief and pain till they turn to dust, and then are they fit manchet[4] for his mansion.

26

A sore finger may disquiet the whole body, but an ulcer within destroys it; so an enemy without may disturb a commonwealth, but dissentions within overthrow it.

.34

Dim eyes are the concomitants of old age, and shortsightedness in those that are eyes of a republic fortells a declining state.

38

Some children are hardly weaned; although the teat be rubbed with wormwood[5] or mustard, they will either wipe it off, or else suck down sweet and bitter together. So is it with some Christians: let God embitter all the sweets of this life, that so they might feed upon more substantial food, yet they are so childishly sottish[6] that they are still hugging and sucking these empty breasts that God is forced to hedge up their way with thorns or lay affliction on their loins that so they might shake hands with the world, before it bid them farewell.

39

A prudent mother will not cloth her little child with a long and cumbersome garment; she easily forsees what events it is like to produce, at the best, but falls and bruises or perhaps somewhat worse. Much more will the allwise God proportion His dispensations according to the stature and strength of the person He bestows them on. Large endowments of honor, wealth, or a healthful body would quite overthrow some weak Christian; therefore God cuts their garments short to keep them in such a trim that they might run the ways of His commandment.

49

The treasures of this world may well be compared to husks, for they have no kernal in them, and they that feed upon them may soon stuff their throats, but cannot fill their bellies. They may be choked by them, but cannot be satisfied with them.

58

Sin and shame ever go together. He that would be freed from the last must be sure to shun the company of the first.

c. 1664   *1867*

---

[3]Grain.
[4]Finest white bread.

[5]Bitter plant extract.
[6]Drunken.

MICHAEL WIGGLESWORTH
(1631–1705)

In 1653, at the age of twenty-two, Michael Wigglesworth entered in his *Diary* a list of ten of his chief faults. Number eight was "want of sense and sorrow for my father's death, O Lord forgive!" He had received word of his father's death the month before, and to his horror (as his *Diary* reveals) he had found himself feeling "secretly glad." Shortly after noting such an inexplicable feeling, Wigglesworth wrote in his *Diary:* ". . . in my sleep I dream'd of the approach of the great and dreadful day of judgment." No doubt seeing himself not among the sheep bound for heaven but among the goats destined for hell, Wigglesworth was powerfully moved "to follow God with tears and cries" until he received from God His "gracious good will." How often Wigglesworth dreamed the terrible dream of the last judgment is not known, but some nine years later, he was moved to set down in his poem *The Day of Doom* one of the most vivid narratives of the depravity of sinners and the horrors of hell ever imagined.

Wigglesworth's Puritan parents brought their seven-year-old son with them to America from Yorkshire in 1638. At that time Charles I, through his zealous Archbishop of Canterbury, William Laud, was throwing in prison those who would not forswear their heretical Puritan beliefs. In a brief autobiographical sketch, the mature Michael Wigglesworth recalled the calamities the family suffered on settling in America, the principal of which was his father's developing a lameness which "grew upon him more and more to his dying day." Michael was taken out of school to get employment, losing, as he recorded, "all that I had gained in the Latin tongue." It was not until he was fourteen that he was allowed to reenter school for the learning (he wrote with a touch of bitterness) "whereto I had been designed from my infancy."

His progress in his studies was such that, at some cost to the family finances, the sixteen-year-old Michael Wigglesworth entered Harvard in 1647, and, on graduation in 1651, was invited to tutor there. He was a conscientious and popular teacher, counting among his pupils the twelve-year-old Increase Mather. He prepared himself for the ministry, and in 1654, upon obtaining an M.A., was invited to become minister at Malden, with a population of fourteen or so families.

Wigglesworth seems to have suffered ill health for most of his life. In fact, his epitaph (presumably written by Cotton Mather) spends four of its eight lines referring to Wigglesworth's frailty (as well as his practice of medicine in the latter part of his career):

> His *body* once so *thin*, was next to *none,*
> From hence he's to *unbodied spirits* flown.
> Once his rare skill did all *diseases* heal;
> And he does nothing now *uneasy* feel.

Because his bad health prevented him for long stretches from fulfilling his duties as minister, he was able to spend much time in writing. The wife he married in 1654 died in 1659. Twenty years later, in 1679, he married his twenty-eight-year-old housemaid—over the objections of the community and Increase Mather. But the marriage was so successful as to satisfy friends and win over the community, and it produced six children. On his second wife's death in 1690, Wigglesworth married a widow, who survived him.

Wigglesworth published *The Day of Doom* in 1662, and the 1,800 copies printed sold within the year. Its simple ballad measure, its long catalogue of depravities and stunning description of the agonies of sinners, its lurid depiction of hell—all assured its immediate and continuing success. Jonathan Mitchell, his tutor and pastor, wrote introductory verses for the poem (published in the 1701 edition):

> A verse may find him who a sermon flies,
> Saith Herbert well. Great truths to dress in meter.
> Becomes a preacher, who men's souls doth prize,
> That truth in sugar roll'd may taste the sweeter.

The Day of Doom, found in every Puritan household alongside the Bible, was second only to the *Bay Psalm Book* in sales during the seventeenth century. It was not eclipsed as an all-time American best-seller until the eighteenth century, when Benjamin Franklin's *The Way to Wealth* appeared in 1758.

Wigglesworth continued to write, but never repeated that initial success. In 1669 he published a work that was less bleak than *The Day of Doom* in the hope it offered for salvation: *Meat Out of the Eater; or, Meditations concerning the necessity, end, and usefulness of afflictions unto God's children, all tending to prepare them for and comfort them under the Cross.* His "God's Controversy with New England," though written in 1662 "at a time of the great drought," was not published until 1873. It is noteworthy for its depiction of pre-Puritan America as

> A waste and howling wilderness,
> Where none inhabited,
> But hellish fiends, and brutish men,
> That devils worshiped.

The Puritans brought to this darkness the "glorious gospel-shine." In the latter part of his life, Wigglesworth recovered his health sufficiently to perform his ministerial duties with regularity.

Wigglesworth's *Diary,* covering the period February 1653 to May 1657, was published in 1951. It offers remarkable glimpses into a Puritan's agonized struggle with his own depravity: "I find myself such unresistable torments of carnal lusts or provocation unto the ejection of seed that I find myself unable to read any thing to inform me about my distemper because of the prevailing or rising of my lusts." Such revelations are common in the *Diary.* Today a psychoanalyst would probably connect these strong sexual impulses with Wigglesworth's secret gladness at his father's death and discover the elements of a classic Oedipus complex. But Wigglesworth, like other Puritans, believed himself locked in struggle with the devil, doomed (if he lost) to be banished to the everlasting fires of hell on the day of judgment.

ADDITIONAL READING

The Diary of Michael Wigglesworth, ed. Edmund Morgan, 1951, 1965.

Kenneth Murdock, "Introduction," *The Day of Doom,* 1929, 1966; Richard Crowder, *No Featherbed to Heaven: A Biography of Michael Wigglesworth, 1631–1705,* 1962; Harold S. Jantz, *The First Century of New England Verse,* 1962; Richard M. Gummere, "Michael Wigglesworth: From Kill-Joy to Comforter," *Seven Wise Men of Colonial America,* 1967; Douglas Robinson, *American Apocalypse,* 1985.

TEXT

The Day of Doom; or a Poetical Description of the Great and Last Judgment, from London editions of 1666 and 1673 as edited by Harrison T. Meserole in *Seventeenth-Century American Poetry*, 1968. Typography, punctuation, spelling, and usage have been changed to conform with contemporary English and modern printing practices.

from The Day of Doom

[THE MAJESTY AND TERROR OF CHRIST'S APPEARING]

1

The Security of the World before Christ's coming to Judgment.
Luk. 12: 19

Still was the night, serene and bright,
    when all men sleeping lay;
Calm was the season, and carnal reason
    thought so 'twould last for ay.[1]
Soul, take thine ease, let sorrow cease,
    much good thou hast in store: 5
This was their song, their cups among,
    the evening before.

2

Wallowing in all kind of sin,
    vile wretches lay secure:[2]   10

Mat. 25: 5

The best of men had scarcely then
    their lamps kept in good ure.[3]
Virgins unwise, who through disguise
    amongst the best were numbered,
Had clos'd their eyes; yea, and the wise   15
    through sloth and frailty slumbered.

3

Mat. 24: 37, 38

Like as of old, when men grow bold
    Gods threatnings to contemn,[4]
Who stopt their ear, and would not hear,
    when mercy warned them: 20
But took their course, without remorse,
    til God began to power[5]
Destruction the world upon
    in a tempestuous shower.

4

They put away the evil day,   25
    and drowned their care and fears,
Till drowned were they, and swept away
    by vengeance unawares:

1 Thes. 5: 3

So at the last, whilst men sleep fast
    in their security,   30
Surprised they are in such a snare
    as cometh suddenly.

---

[1]Ever.
[2]Falsely self-assured.
[3]Condition.

[4]Mock.
[5]Pour (pronounced to rhyme with shower).

5

The Suddenness,   For at midnight brake forth a light,
Majesty, and   which turned the night to day,
Terror of Christ's   And speedily an hideous cry   35
appearing.   did all the world dismay.
Mat. 25: 6   Sinners awake, their hearts do ache,
2 Pet. 3: 10   trembling their loins surpriseth;
                           Amazed with fear, by what they hear,
                              each one of them ariseth.   40

6

                           They rush from beds with giddy heads,
                              and to their windows run,
                           Viewing this light, which shines more bright
Mat. 24: 29, 30   than doth the noon-day sun.
                           Straightway appears (they see't with tears)   45
                              the Son of God most dread;
                           Who with His train comes on amain[6]
                              To judge both quick[7] and dead.

7

                           Before His face the heav'ns gave place,
2 Pet. 3: 10   and skies are rent asunder,   50
                           With mighty voice, and hideous noise,
                              more terrible than thunder.
                           His brightness damps heav'ns glorious lamps
                              and makes them hide their heads,
                           As if afraid and quite dismayed,   55
                              they quit their wonted steads.[8]

· · · · · ·

[RESURRECTION OF THE DEAD]

17

1 Thes. 4: 16   Before His throne a trump is blown,
Resurrection of   Proclaiming the Day of Doom: 130
the Dead.   Forthwith He cries, *"Ye dead arise,*
John 5: 28, 29   *and unto judgment come."*
                           No sooner said, but 'tis obeyed;
                              Sepulchers opened are:
                           Dead bodies all rise at his call,   135
                              and's mighty power declare.

18

                           Both sea and land, at His command,
                              their dead at once surrender:
                           The fire and air constrained are
                              also their dead to tender.   140
                           The mighty word of this great Lord
                              links body and soul together

---

[6]With strength and speed.
[7]Living.
[8]They left customary places.

Both of the just, and the unjust,
    to part no more for ever.

. . . . . .

21

2 Cor. 5: 10 The
Sheep Separated
from the Goats.
Mat. 25: 32

Thus every one before the throne
    of Christ the Judge is brought,
Both righteous and impious
    that good or ill had wrought.
A separation, and differing station   165
    by Christ appointed is
(To sinners sad) 'twixt good and bad,
    'twixt heirs of woe and bliss.

22

Who are Christ's
Sheep.
Mat. 5: 10, 11

At Christ's right hand the sheep do stand,
    His holy martyrs, who   170
For His dear name suffering shame,
    calamity and woe,
Like champions stood, and with their blood
    their testimony sealed;
Whose innocence without offence,   175
    to Christ their Judge appealed.

. . . . . .

27

The Goats
described or the
several sorts of
Reprobates on the
left hand.
Mat. 24: 51

At Christ's left hand the goats do stand,
    all whining hypocrites,   210
Who for self-ends did seem Christ's friends,
    but fostered guileful sprites;[1]
Who sheep resembled, but they dissembled
    (their hearts were not sincere);
Who once did throng Christ's lambs among,   215
    but now must not come near.

28

Luk. 11: 24, 26
Heb. 6: 4, 5, 6
Heb. 10: 29

Apostates and run-aways,
    such as have Christ forsaken,
Of whom the devil, with seven more evil,[2]
    hath fresh possession taken: 220
Sinners in grain, reserved to pain
    and torments most severe:
Because 'gainst light they sinned with spite,
    are also placed there.

29

Luk. 12: 47
Prov. 1: 24, 26
Joh. 3: 19

There also stand a num'rous band,   225
    that no profession made
Of godliness, nor to redress
    their ways at all essayed:[3]

---

[1]Deceitful ghosts, apparitions.
[2]Luke 11:24–26: Christ describes the backsliding individual who, after being cleansed, finds seven other spirits
"more evil" than himself and who becomes worse than he
was at first.
[3]Tried, attempted.

Who better knew, but (sinful crew)
    Gospel and law despised;
Who all Christ's knocks withstood like blocks
    and would not be advised.

30

Moreover, there with them appear
    a number, numberless

Gal. 3: 10
1 Cor. 6: 9
Rev. 21: 8

Of great and small, vile wretches all,
    that did God's law transgress:
Idolaters, false worshippers,
    Prophaners of God's name.
Who not at all thereon did call,
    or took in vain the same.

31

Blasphemers lewd, and swearers shrewd,
    Scoffers at purity,

Exod. 20: 7
and 8

That hated God, contemned His rod,
    and loved security;
Sabbath-polluters, saints' persecutors,
    Presumptuous men and proud,

2 Thes. 1: 6, 8, 9

Who never loved those that reproved;
    all stand amongst this crowd.

32

Heb. 13: 4
1 Cor. 6: 10

Adulterers and whoremongers
    were there, with all unchaste:
There covetous, and ravenous,
    that riches got too fast:
Who used vile ways themselves to raise
    t' estates and worldly wealth,
Oppression by, or knavery,
    by force, or fraud, or stealth.

33

Moreover, there together were
    Children flagitious,[4]

Zach. 5: 3, 4
Gal. 5: 19, 20,
21

And parents who did them undo
    by nurture vicious.
False-witness-bearers, and self-forswearers,
    Murd'rers, and men of blood,
Witches, enchanters, and ale-house-haunters,
    beyond account there stood.

• • • • •

[THE WICKED BROUGHT TO THE BAR]

51

The wicked
brought to the
Bar.
Rom. 2: 3, 6, 11

The wicked are brought to the bar,[1]
    like guilty malefactors,
That oftentimes of bloody crimes
    and treasons have been actors.

---

[4]Grossly wicked.
[1]Place of judgment.

Of wicked men, none are so mean[2]
    as there to be neglected:
Nor none so high in dignity,
    as there to be respected.

52

Rev. 6: 15, 16
Isa. 30: 33

The glorious Judge will privilege
    nor emperor, nor king:
But every one that hath mis-done
    doth into judgment bring.
And every one that hath mis-done,
    the Judge impartially
Condemneth to eternal woe,
    and endless misery.

53

Thus one and all, thus great and small,
    the rich as well as poor,
And those of place as the most base,
    do stand the Judge before.
They are arraigned, and there detained,
    before Christ's judgment-seat
With trembling fear, their doom to hear,
    and feel His anger's heat.

. . . . .

57

Secret sins and
works of darkness
brought to light.
Psal. 139: 2, 4,
12
Rom. 2: 16

It's vain, moreover, for men to cover
    the least iniquity:
The Judge hath seen, and privy been
    to all their villany.
He unto light, and open sight
    the works of darkness brings:
He doth unfold both new and old,
    both known and hidden things.

58

Eccles. 12: 14

All filthy facts, and secret acts,
    however closly done,
And long concealed, are there revealed
    before the mid-day Sun.
Deeds of the night shunning the light,
    which darkest corners sought,
To fearful blame, and endless shame,
    are there most justly brought.

. . . . .

66

Thus He doth find of all mankind,
Rom. 3: 10, 12   that stand at His left hand,

---

[2]Low.

No mother's son, but hath mis-done,
   and broken God's command.
All have transgressed, even the best,
   and merited God's wrath   525
Unto their own perdition,
   and everlasting scath.[3]

67

Rom. 6: 23

Earth's dwellers all, both great and small,
   have wrought iniquity,   530
And suffer must, for it is just,
   Eternal misery.
Amongst the many there come not any,
   before the Judge's face,
That able are themselves to clear,   535
   of all this cursed race.

. . . . .

[REPROBATE INFANTS PLEAD FOR THEMSELVES]

166

*Reprobate Infants
plead for
themselves.
Rev. 20: 12, 15
compared with
Rom. 5: 12, 14
and 9: 11, 13*

Then to the bar,[1] all they drew near
   who died in Infancy,
And never had or good or bad
   effected pers'nally,
But from the womb unto the tomb   1325
   were straightway carried,
(Or at the last e're they transgressed)
   who thus began to plead:

167

Ezek. 18: 2

"If for our own transgression,
   or disobedience,   1330
We here did stand at thy left-hand
   just were the recompence:
But Adam's guilt our souls hath split,
   his fault is charged on us;
And that alone hath overthrown,   1335
   and utterly undone us.

168

Not we, but he, ate of the tree
   whose fruit was interdicted:[2]
Yet on us all of his sad Fall,
   the punishment's inflicted.   1340
How could we sin that had not been,
   or how is his sin our,
Without consent, which to prevent,
   we never had a power?

---

[3] Punishment, harm.
[1] Place of judgment.
[2] Forbidden.

169

O great Creator, why was our nature
    depraved and forlorn?   1345
Why so defiled, and made so vild[3]
    whilst we were yet unborn?
If it be just, and needs we must
    transgressors reckoned be,   1350
Psal. 51: 5   Thy mercy, Lord, to us afford,
    which sinners hath set free.

170

Behold we see Adam set free,
    and saved from his trespass,
Whose sinful Fall hath split us all,   1355
    and brought us to this pass.
Canst Thou deny us once to try,
    or grace to us to tender,[4]
When he finds grace before thy face,
    that was the chief offender?"   1360

171

Their Argument   Then answered the Judge most dread,
taken off.   "God doth such doom forbid,
Ezek. 18: 20   That men should die eternally
Rom. 5: 12, 19   for what they never did.
But what you call old Adam's Fall,   1365
    and only his trespass,
You call amiss to call it his,
    both his and yours it was.

172

He was designed of all mankind
    to be a public head,   1370
A common root, whence all should shoot,
    and stood in all their stead.
1Cor. 15: 48, 49   He stood and fell, did ill or well,
    not for himself alone,
But for you all, who now his Fall,   1375
    and trespass would disown.

173

If he had stood, then all his brood
    had been established
In God's true love, never to move,
    nor once awry to tread: 1380
Then all his race, my Father's grace,
    should have enjoyed forever,
And wicked sprites[5] by subtle sleights
    could them have harmed never.

---

[3]Vile.
[4]Offer.
[5]Spirits.

174

Would you have grieved to have received   1385
   through Adam so much good,
As had been your for evermore,
   if he at first had stood?
Would you have said, we ne'er obeyed,
   nor did Thy laws regard;   1390
It ill befits with benefits,
   us, Lord, so to reward?

175

Since then to share in his welfare,
   you could have been content,
You may with reason share in his treason,   1395
   and in the punishment.

Rom. 5: 12   Hence you were born in state forlorn,
Psa. 51: 5   with natures so depraved:
Gen. 5: 3   Death was your due, because that you
   had thus your selves behaved.   1400

    . . . . .

180

Psa. 58: 3   You sinners are, and such a share
Ro. 6: 23   as sinners may expect,
Gal. 3: 10   Such you shall have; for I do save   1435
Rom. 8: 29, 30   none but Mine own Elect.
and 11: 7   Yet to compare your sin with their,
Rev. 21: 27   who lived a longer time,
Luk. 12: 48   I do confess yours is much less,
   though every sin's a crime.   1440

181

Mat. 11: 22   A crime it is, therefore in bliss
The wicked all   you may not hope to dwell;
convinced and   But unto you I shall allow
put to silence.   the easiest room in hell."
Ro. 3: 19   The glorious King thus answering,   1445
Mat. 22: 12   they cease, and plead no longer:
Their consciences must needs confess
   His reasons are the stronger.

182

Behold the   Thus all men's pleas the Judge with ease
formidable estate   doth answer and confute,   1450
of all the ungodly,   Until that all, both great and small,
as they stand   are silenced and mute.
hopeless and   Vain hopes are cropped, all mouths are stopped,
helpless before an   sinners have nought to say,
impartial Judge,   But that 'tis just, and equal most   1455
expecting their   they should be damned for aye.
final sentence.
Rev. 6: 16, 17

    . . . . .

[THE SENTENCE OF CONDEMNATION]

201

*The Judge
pronounceth the
Sentence of
condemnation.
Mat. 25: 41*

"Ye sinful wights,[1] and cursed sprites,
    that work iniquity,
Depart together from Me for ever
    to endless misery;
Your portion take in yonder lake,   1605
    where fire and brimstone flameth:
Suffer the smart, which your desert
    as its due wages claimeth."

202

The terror of it.

Oh piercing words more sharp than swords!
    what, to depart from Thee,   1610
Whose face before for evermore
    the best of pleasures be!
What? to depart (unto our smart)
    from Thee eternally:
To be for aye banished away,   1615
    with devils' company!

203

What? to be sent to punishment,
    and flames of burning fire,
To be surrounded, and eke[2] confounded
    with God's revengeful ire.   1620
What? to abide, not for a tide
    these torments, but for ever:
To be released, or to be eased,
    not after years, but never.

204

Oh, fearful doom! now there's no room   1625
    for hope or help at all:
Sentence is passed which aye shall last,
    Christ will not it recall.
There might you hear them rent and tear
    the air with their out-cries: 1630
The hideous noise of their sad voice
    ascendeth to the skies.

205

Luk. 13: 28

They wring their hands, their caitiff-hands[3]
    and gnash their teeth for terror;
They cry, they roar for anguish sore,   1635
    and gnaw their tongues for horror.
But get away without delay,
    Christ pities not your cry:
Depart to hell, there may you yell,

Prov. 1: 26
    and roar eternally.   1640

• • • • •

---

[1]Persons.
[2]Also.
[3]Evil-hands.

207

As chaff that's dry, and dust doth fly
    before the northern wind: 1650
Right so are they chased away,
    and can no refuge find.
They hasten to the pit of woe,
Matt. 13: 41, 42   guarded by angels stout;
Who to fulfil Christ's holy will,   1655
    attend this wicked rout.[4]

208

HELL.
Mat. 25: 30 Whom having brought, as they are taught,
Mark 9: 43   unto the brink of hell,
Isa. 30: 33 (That dismal place far from Christ's face,
Rev. 21: 8   where death and darkness dwell: 1660
Where God's fierce ire kindleth the fire,
    and vengeance feeds the flame
With piles of wood, and brimstone flood,
    that none can quench the same),

209

Wicked Men and With iron bands they bind their hands,   1665
Devils cast into it   and cursed feet together,
for ever. And cast them all, both great and small,
Mat. 22: 13 and   into that lake for ever.
25: 46 Where day and night, without respite,[5]
    they wail, and cry, and howl   1670
For tort'ring pain, which they sustain
    in body and in soul.

210

Rev. 14: 10, 11 For day and night, in their despite,[6]
    their torment's smoke ascendeth.
Their pain and grief have no relief,   1675
    their anguish never endeth.
There must they lie, and never die,
    though dying every day:
There must they dying ever lie,
    and not consume away.   1680

211

Die fain[7] they would, if die they could,
    but death will not be had:
God's direful wrath their bodies hath
    forever immortal made.
They live to lie in misery,   1685
    and bear eternal woe;
And live they must whilst God is just,
    that He may plague them so.

---

[4]Milling throng.   [6]Malice.
[5]Relief.   [7]Gladly.

212

The unsufferable   But who can tell the plagues of hell,
torments of the   and torments exquisite?   1690
damned.   Who can relate their dismal state,
Luk. 16: 24   and terrors infinite?
Jude 7   Who fare the best, and feel the least,
                               yet feel that punishment
                           Whereby to nought they should be brought,   1695
                               if God did not prevent.

213

                           The least degree of misery
                               there felt's incomparable,
                           The lightest pain they there sustain
Isa. 33: 14   more than intolerable.   1700
Mark 9: 43, 44   But God's great power from hour to hour
                               upholds them in the fire,
                           That they shall not consume a jot,
                               nor by it's force expire.

· · · · · ·

216

Luk. 16: 23, 25   The pain of loss their souls doth toss,
Luk. 13: 28   and wond'rously distress,
                           To think what they have cast away
                               by willful wickedness.
                           "We might have been redeemed from sin,"   1725
                               think they, "and lived above,
                           Being possessed of heav'nly rest,
                               and joying in God's love.

217

Luk. 13: 34   But woe, woe, woe our Souls unto!
                               we would not happy be;   1730
                           And therefore bear God's vengeance here
                               to all eternity.
                           Experience and woeful sense
                               must be our painful teachers
                           Who n'ould[8] believe, nor credit give,   1735
                               unto our faithful preachers."

218

Mark 9: 44   Thus shall they lie, and wail, and cry,
Rom. 2: 15   tormented, and tormenting
                           Their galled hearts with poisoned darts
                               but now too late repenting.   1740
                           There let them dwell i' th' flames of hell
                               there leave we them to burn,
                           And back again unto the men
                               whom Christ acquits, return.

---

[8]Would not.

[THE SAINTS REJOICE]

219

The Saints rejoice
to see Judgment
executed upon the
wicked World.
Ps. 58: 10
Rev. 19: 1, 2, 3

The saints behold with courage bold,
   and thankful wonderment,
To see all those that were their foes
   thus sent to punishment:
Then do they sing unto their King
   a song of endless praise:
They praise His name, and do proclaim
   that just are all His ways.

1745

1750

220

They ascend with
Christ into
Heaven
triumphing.
Mat. 25: 46
1 Joh. 3: 2
1 Cor. 13: 12

Thus with great joy and melody
   to heav'n they all ascend,
Him there to praise with sweetest lays,[1]
   and hymns that never end,
Where with long rest they shall be blest,
   and nought shall them annoy:
Where they shall see as seen they be,
   and whom they love enjoy.

1755

1760

221

Their Eternal
happiness and
incomparable
Glory there.

O glorious place! where face to face
   Jehovah may be seen,
By such as were sinners whilere[2]
   and no dark veil between.
Where the sun shine, and light divine,
   of God's bright countenance,
Doth rest upon them every one,
   with sweetest influence.

1765

222

O blessed state of the renate![3]
   O wondrous happiness,
To which they're brought, beyond what thought
   can reach, or words express!
Rev. 21: 4
Grief's water-course, and sorrows source,
   are turned to joyful streams,
Their old distress and heaviness
   are vanished like dreams.

1770

1775

223

For God above in arms of love
   doth dearly them embrace,
Psal. 16: 11
And fills their sprites with such delights,
   and pleasures in His grace;
As shall not fail, nor yet grow stale
   through frequency of use:
Nor do they fear God's favor there,
   to forfeit by abuse.

1780

---

[1]Songs.
[2]Before, a while ago.
[3]Regenerate, reborn.

224

Heb. 12: 23	For there the saints are perfect saints,	1785
	and holy ones indeed,	
	From all the sin that dwelt within	
	their mortal bodies freed:	
	Made kings and priests to God through Christ's	
Rev. 1: 6 and	dear love's transcendency,	1790
22: 5	There to remain, and there to reign	
	with Him eternally.	

1661   *1662*

EDWARD TAYLOR
(*c.* 1642–1729)

Edward Taylor remembered his "conversion"—or religious "awakening"—as occurring when he was a small boy, listening one morning to a sister giving an "account of the creation of the world by God alone and of man especially and of the excellent state of man by creation as that he was created in the image of God and was holy and righteous and how Eve was made of Adam's rib"; of "how both were placed in . . . the Garden of Eden, a most curious place and had liberty to eat of all the trees therein *except* the tree of knowledge of good and evil"; of how "the serpent did betray them and did draw them to eat of that fruit . . . and God was angry and cast them out of the Garden of Eden . . . and so man was made a sinner and God was angry with all men for sin."

Taylor claimed that his experience in listening to this account affected him "in such a strong way" that he was "not able to express it." But "ever since," he confessed, "I have had a notion of sin and its naughtiness remain and the wrath of God on account of the same." This awakening to an intense sense of sin and of God's wrath was to be the shaping event of Taylor's life, propelling him toward a career in the ministry—and inspiring him to devote his private life to the writing of the greatest poetry written during the colonial period in America. His poems remained unpublished during his lifetime and did not see print until the twentieth century.

Taylor was probably born in Sketchley, Leicestershire, England, and he may have attended Cambridge University for a time. After the Restoration of Charles II, Taylor lost his teaching position for refusing to submit to the 1662 Act of Uniformity to the Anglican church. In 1668, at the age of twenty-six, he came to America with a letter of introduction to Increase Mather. Accepted with advanced standing, Taylor then entered Harvard, where he roomed with Samuel Sewall and came to know other leading Puritans. In 1671 he accepted an invitation to become minister at Westfield, Massachusetts, a frontier town lying about a hundred miles west of Boston. Taylor's first journey there in November was difficult, as he noted in his diary: "the snow being above Mid-Leg deep, the way unbeaten . . . and over rocks and mountains." It was in this distant town that Taylor spent his career. In his first marriage there were eight children, five of them dying in infancy. His first wife died in 1689 and Taylor remarried in 1692, a union that brought forth six children.

Although Taylor became engaged in some of the religious debates of the day, he seems to have lived a life largely undisturbed by the many energetic rivalries and violent controversies of the time. Even the attack on the colonies planned and executed in 1675–76 by the Indian chief Philip, son of Massasoit, with the intent of driving the English out of New England, left Westfield untouched—though it was quite vulnerable in its isolation on the frontier. Taylor was free most of his ministerial career to devote his private life to poetry. He shared the religious passion and intensity of the first-generation New England Puritans, but his destiny placed him in a later generation of declining religious passions and decreasing dogmatic intensities. He poured his powerful imaginative energies into his poems, conceiving himself as a "crumb of dust" designed to "hand a pen" to "gild o'er/Eternal glory with a glorious glore." The process of writing a poem was a private service of devotion; the poem achieved its end in the process, not in publication.

Taylor apparently wrote poetry all his life, experimenting with a number of different forms and genres. Many of the stylistic traits of his short lyrics (such as "Huswifery" or "Upon a Spider Catching a Fly") remind readers of the elaborate conceits and extended metaphors of the English metaphysical poets, especially John Donne and George Herbert. His *God's Determinations Touching His Elect* is cast in the form of a dialogue or debate on points of religious doctrine, with speeches by Christ, Satan, the Elect, Mercy, and Justice. There is general agreement, however, that Taylor's best poetry appears in two sequences, entitled *Preparatory Meditations before my Approach to the Lord's Supper. Chiefly upon the Doctrine preached upon the Day of administration.* The First Series contains 49 poems, the Second Series 165. Beginning in 1682, Taylor wrote the *Preparatory Meditations* at monthly intervals, continuing until 1725. They are "preparatory" in that, as Louis Martz has observed, they prepare "the preacher to receive and administer the sacrament and to deliver his sermon."

Taylor's syntax might be described as gnarled or craggy, the words used often strange and puzzling, the metaphors at once homely and exotic. Thus Taylor links with such later American poets as Emily Dickinson and Walt Whitman and their homemade language experiments. He asks in "The Preface" to *God's Determinations:* "Upon what base was fixed the lathe, wherein/ He [God] turned this globe, and riggaled it so trim?" And he also asks, "Who in this bowling alley bowled the sun?" In many of Taylor's poems, there comes a critical moment in which the poet cries out in anguish at the inadequacy of mere words to embody the profound feelings and deep realities that he is wrestling with. For example, Meditation 43, Second Series states:

> Words mental are syllabicated thought;
>   Words oral but thought whiffled in the wind.
> Words writ are inky, goose quill—slabbered drafts,
>   Although the fairest blossoms of the mind.
> Then can such glasses clear enough descry
> My love to Thee, or Thy rich deity?

It is perhaps no wonder, with this view of language and its frailties, that Taylor found the poem's value in its making, of significance only to its maker who knows and can supply the depths—or heights—it never reached.

With the exception of two stanzas of a short lyric published by Cotton Mather in 1689, Taylor's poems lay in the Yale University Library, where they had been deposited in the late eighteenth century by the then-president of

Yale, Ezra Stiles, grandson of Edward Taylor. It was not until the 1930s that Thomas H. Johnson tracked them down and published a selection. Gradually additional poems were published, and, finally, in 1960 *The Poems of Edward Taylor* appeared. It became clear only in the twentieth century that Edward Taylor was the finest American poet of the seventeenth century.

ADDITIONAL READING

Edward Taylor's Christographia, ed. Norman S. Grabo, 1962; *The Diary of Edward Taylor,* ed. Francis Murphy, 1964; *Edward Taylor's Treatise Concerning the Lord's Supper,* ed. Norman S. Grabo, 1966; *The Unpublished Writings of Edward Taylor,* 3 vols., ed. Thomas M. and Virginia L. Davis, 1981.

Norman Grabo, *Edward Taylor,* 1961; Donald Stanford, *Edward Taylor,* 1965; Karl Keller, "The Example of Edward Taylor," *The American Puritan Imagination,* ed. Sacvan Bercovitch, 1974; William J. Scheick, *The Will and the Word: Conversion in the Poetry of Edward Taylor,* 1974; Karl Keller, *The Example of Edward Taylor,* 1975; Karen Rowe, *Saint and Singer: Edward Taylor's Typology and the Poetics of Meditation,* 1986.

TEXT

All poems are from *The Poetical Works of Edward Taylor,* ed. Thomas H. Johnson, 1939, 1943, 1966, except for the following: "Upon a Wasp Chilled with Cold," and "Upon the Sweeping Flood," *The New England Quarterly* 16, 1943; "Meditation 43" (Second Series), *The Yale University Library Gazette* 29, 1954; "Meditation 23" (First Series) and "Meditation 26" (Second Series), *American Literature* 29, 1957; "Meditation 150" (Second Series) and "A Fig for Thee Oh! Death" from *The Poems of Edward Taylor,* ed. Donald E. Stanford, 1960. Some minor textual differences between the Johnson and Stanford editions have been indicated in the footnotes. Typography, punctuation, spelling, and usage have been changed to conform with contemporary English and modern printing practices.

Prologue[1]

Lord, can a crumb of earth[2] the earth outweigh,
    Outmatch all mountains, nay the crystal sky?
Embosom in't designs that shall display
    And trace into the boundless Deity?
Yea, hand[3] a pen whose moisture doth gild o'er   5
    Eternal glory with a glorious glore.[4]

If it its pen had of an angel's quill,
    And sharpened on a precious stone ground tight,
And dipped in liquid gold, and moved by skill
    In crystal leaves[5] should golden letters write,   10
It would but blot and blur, yea, jag and jar,
    Unless Thou mak'st the pen and scrivener.

I am this crumb of dust which is designed
    To make my pen unto Thy praise alone,
And my dull fancy I would gladly grind   15
    Unto an edge on Zion's precious stone,[6]

---

[1] The "Prologue" was probably written as an introduction to the *Preparatory Meditations.*
[2] This reads "crumb of dust" in Stanford.
[3] Handle, manipulate.
[4] Variant of "glory."
[5] The leaves of a book.
[6] One of the diamond-hard jewels of the new Jerusalem described in Isaiah 28:16; 1 Peter 2:6; and Revelation 21.

And write in liquid gold upon Thy name
My letters till Thy glory forth doth flame.

Let not th'attempts break down my dust I pray,
  Nor laugh Thou them to scorn, but pardon give.   20
Inspire this crumb of dust till it display
  Thy glory through't: and then Thy dust shall live.
  Its failings then Thou'lt overlook I trust,
  They being slips slipped from Thy crumb of dust.

Thy crumb of dust breathes two words from its breast,   25
  That Thou wilt guide its pen to write aright
To prove Thou art, and that Thou art the best,
  And show Thy properties to shine most bright.
  And then Thy works will shine as flowers on stems
  Or as in jewelry shops, do gems.   30

c. 1682   *1937*

from Preparatory Meditations
Before My Approach to the Lord's Supper

Meditation 1 (First Series)

What love is this of Thine, that cannot be
  In Thine infinity, O Lord, confined,
Unless it in Thy very Person see
  Infinity and finity conjoined?
  What! hath Thy Godhead, as not satisfied,   5
  Married our manhood, making it its bride?

Oh, matchless love! filling heaven to the brim!
  O'er running it: all running o'er beside
This world! Nay, overflowing hell, wherein
  For Thine elect, there rose a mighty tide!   10
  That there our veins might through Thy Person bleed,
  To quench those flames, that else would on us feed.

Oh! that Thy love might overflow my heart!
  To fire the same with love: for love I would.
But oh! my straitened[1] breast! my lifeless spark!   15
  My fireless flame! What chilly love, and cold?
  In measure small! In manner chilly! See.
  Lord blow the coal: Thy love enflame in me.

1682   *1937*

---

[1]Confined, restrained.

Meditation 6 (First Series)

Canticles 2: 1: I am . . . the lily of the valleys.

Am I Thy gold? Or purse, Lord, for Thy wealth;
  Whether in mine or mint refined for Thee?
I'm counted so, but count me o'er Thyself,
  Lest gold washed face, and brass in heart I be.
  I fear my touchstone[1] touches when I try   5
  Me, and my counted gold too overly.

Am I new minted by Thy stamp indeed?
  Mine eyes are dim; I cannot clearly see.
Be Thou my spectacles that I may read
  Thine image and inscription stamped on me.   10
  If Thy bright image do upon me stand,
  I am a golden angel[2] in Thy hand.

Lord, make my soul Thy plate: Thine image bright
  Within the circle of the same enfoil.
And on its brims in golden letters write   15
  Thy superscription in an holy style.
  Then I shall be Thy money, Thou my hoard:
  Let me Thy angel be, be Thou my Lord.

1939

Meditation 8 (First Series)

John 6:51: I am the living bread.

I kenning[1] through astronomy divine
  The world's bright battlement, wherein I spy
A golden path my pencil cannot line,
  From that bright throne unto my threshold lie.
  And while my puzzled thoughts about it pour,   5
  I find the bread of life in't at my door.

When that this bird of paradise[2] put in
  This wicker cage (my corpse) to tweedle praise
Had pecked the fruit forbade, and so did fling
  Away its food, and lost its golden days,   10
  It fell into celestial famine sore,
  And never could attain a morsel more.

Alas! Alas! Poor bird, what wilt thou do?
  This creature's field no food for souls e're gave.
And if thou knock at angels' doors, they show   15
  An empty barrel: they no soul bread have.

---

[1] A black stone formerly used to test the purity of gold or silver; the metal left a telltale color when rubbed against the stone.

[2] A British gold coin of the period.
[1] Catching sight of.
[2] The soul.

Alas! Poor bird, the world's white loaf is done,
And cannot yield thee here the smallest crumb.

In this sad state, God's tender bowels[3] run
    Out streams of grace. And He to end all strife   20
The purest wheat in heaven, His dear-dear Son,
    Grinds and kneads up into this bread of life,
Which bread of life from heaven down came and stands
Dished on thy table up by angels' hands.

Did God mold up this bread in heaven, and bake,   25
    Which from His table came, and to thine goeth?
Doth He bespeak thee thus: "This soul bread take;
    Come, eat thy fill of this, thy God's white loaf.
It's food too fine for angels; yet come, take
And eat thy fill! It's heaven's sugar cake"?   30

What grace is this knead in this loaf? This thing
    Souls are but petty things it to admire.
Ye angels, help: This fill would to the brim
    Heaven's whelmed-down[4] crystal meal bowl, yea and higher.
This bread of life dropped in my mouth doth cry: 35
"Eat, eat me, soul, and thou shalt never die."

1684   1937

Meditation 23 (First Series)

Canticles[1] 4:8: My Spouse.

Would God I in that golden city[2] were,
    With jaspers walled, all garnished, and made swash[3]
With precious stones, whose gates are pearls most clear
    And street pure gold, like to transparent glass,
    That my dull soul might be inflamed to see   5
    How saints and angels ravished are in glee.

Were I but there, and could but tell my story,
    'Twould rub those walls of precious stones more bright,
And glaze those gates of pearl with brighter glory,
    And pave the golden street with greater light.
    'Twould in fresh raptures saints and angels fling,   10
    But I poor snake crawl here, scarce[4] mudwalled in.

May my rough voice and my blunt tongue but spell[5]
    My tale (for tune they can't) perhaps there may
Some angel catch an end of't up, and tell   15

---

[3]The seat of affections, feelings, love.
[4]Turned upside down.
[1]"The Song of Solomon" (called "Canticles") consists mainly of love poetry, generally interpreted as an allegorical treatment of the love between Christ and individual Christians. Christ thus is seen commonly as the bridegroom of the Christian's soul.

[2]The holy city, the New Jerusalem, of Revelation 21.
[3]Glittering.
[4]Restricted (by being walled in).
[5]Tell.

In heaven, when he doth return that way,
  He'll make Thy palace, Lord, all over ring
With it in songs Thy saint and angels sing.

I know not how to speak't, it is so good:
  Shall mortal and immortal marry? nay,   20
Man marry God? God be a match for mud?
  The Kind of Glory wed a worm? mere clay?
  This is the case. The wonder too in bliss.
  Thy Maker is thy Husband. Hear'st thou this?

My Maker, He my Husband? Oh! strange joy!   25
  If kings wed worms and monarchs mites wed should,
Glory spouse shame, a prince a snake or fly,
  An angel court an ant, all wonder would.
  Let such wed worms, snakes, serpents, devils, flies.
  Less wonder than the wedding in our eyes.   30

I am to Christ more base than to a king,
  A mite, fly, worm, ant, serpent, devil is,
Or can be, being tumbled all in sin.
  And shall I be His spouse? How good is this?
  It is too good to be declared to thee,   35
  But not too good to be believed by me.

Yet to this wonder, this is found in me,
  I am not only base but backward clay,
When Christ doth woo; and till His Spirit be
  His Spokesman to compel me, I deny.   40
  I am so base and froward[6] to Him, He
  Appears as wonder's wonder, wedding me.

Seeing, dear Lord, it's thus, Thy Spirit take
  And send Thy Spokesman to my soul, I pray.
Thy saving grace my wedding garment make;   45
  Thy Spouse's Frame into my soul convey;
  I then shall be Thy bride espoused by Thee
  And Thou my Bridesgroom dear espoused shalt be.

1687   1957

Meditation 38 (First Series)

1 John 2: 1: And if any man sin, we have an
advocate with the Father.[1]

Oh! What a thing is man? Lord, who am I?
  That Thou shouldst give him law (Oh! golden line)
To regulate his thoughts, words, life thereby.
  And judge him wilt thereby too in Thy time.

---

[6]Disobedient.
[1]1 John 2:1: "My little children, these things write I unto you, that ye sin not. And if any man sin, we have an advocate with the Father, Jesus Christ the righteous."

A court of justice Thou in heaven hold'st,   5
To try his case while he's here housed on mold.[2]

How do Thy angels lay before Thine eye
My deeds both white and black I daily do?
How doth Thy court Thou panelest[3] there them try?
   But flesh complains. What right for this? Let's know!   10
   For right or wrong, I can't appear unto't.
   And shall a sentence pass on such a suit?

Soft; blemish not this golden bench, or place.
   Here is no bribe, nor colorings to hide,
Nor pettifogger[4] to befog the case;   15
   But justice hath her glory here well tried.
   Her spotless law all spotted cases tends,
   Without respect or disrespect them ends.

God's judge Himself, and Christ attorney is;
   The Holy Ghost registerer is found.   20
Angels the sergeants are, all creatures kiss
   The book, and do as evidence[5] abound.
   All cases pass according to pure law,
   And in the sentence is no fret[6] nor flaw.

What sayest, my soul? Here all thy deeds are tried.   25
   Is Christ thy advocate to plead thy cause?
Art thou His client? Such shall never slide.[7]
   He never lost His case: He pleads such laws
   As carry do the same, nor doth refuse
   The vilest sinner's case that doth Him choose.   30

This is His honor, not dishonor: nay,
   No *habeas-corpus*[8] 'gainst His clients came;
For all their fines His purse doth make down pay.
   He non-suits Satan's suit or casts[9] the same.
   He'll plead thy case, and not accept a fee.   35
   He'll plead *sub forma pauperis*[10] for thee.

My case is bad. Lord, be my advocate.
   My sin is red: I'm under God's arrest.
Thou hast the hit[11] of pleading; plead my state.
   Although it's bad, Thy plea will make it best.   40
   If Thou wilt plead my case before the King,
   I'll wagon loads of love and glory bring.

1690   *1937*

---

[2]This world.
[3]Empanel, as in selecting a jury.
[4]Unscrupulous lawyer.
[5]Witnesses.
[6]Vexation.
[7]Backslide, or slide into hell.

[8]Legal Latin: "You shall have the body"; writ to bring an individual before a court.
[9]That is, Christ obtains dismissal of the suit, or defeats it.
[10]Legal Latin: "In the form of a pauper"; a plea to set aside court costs.
[11]Striking expression, telling phrase; "hint" in Stanford.

Meditation 26 (Second Series)

Hebrews 9:13–14: How much more shall the blood
of Christ, etc.[1]

Unclean, unclean: My Lord undone, all vile
    Yea, all defiled: What shall Thy servant do?
Unfit for Thee, not fit for holy soil,
    Nor for communion of saints below.
      A bag of botches, lump of loathsomeness: 5
      Defiled by touch, by issue: Leprous flesh.

Thou wilt have all that enter do Thy fold
    Pure, clean, and bright, whiter than whitest snow,
Better refined than most refined gold:
    I am not so, but foul. What shall I do?   10
      Shall Thy church doors be shut, and shut out me?
      Shall not church fellowship my portion be?

How can it be? Thy churches do require
    Pure holiness. I am all filth, alas!
Shall I defile them, tumbled thus in mire?   15
    Or they me cleanse before I current pass?
      If thus they do, where is the nitre[2] bright
      And soap they offer me to wash me white?

The brisk red heifer's ashes, when calcined,[3]
    Mixed all in running water, is too weak   20
To wash away my filth; the doves assigned,
    Burnt, and sin offerings ne'er do the feat,
      But as they emblemize the fountain spring,
      Thy blood, my Lord, set ope to wash off sin.

Oh! richest grace! Are Thy rich veins then tapped   25
    To ope this holy fountain (boundless sea)
For sinners here to laver[4] off (all sapped
    With sin) their sins and sinfulness away?
      In this bright crystal crimson fountain flows
      What washeth whiter than the swan or rose.   30

Oh! wash me, Lord, in this choice fountain white
    That I may enter and not sully here
Thy church, whose floor is paved with graces bright,
    And hold church fellowship with saints most clear.
      My voice all sweet with their melodious lays[5]   35
      Shall make sweet music blossomed with Thy praise.

1698   *1960*

---

[1]Hebrews 9:13–14: "For if the blood of bulls and of goats, and the ashes of an heifer sprinkling the unclean, sanctifieth to the purifying of the flesh: How much more shall the blood of Christ, who through the eternal Spirit offered Himself without spot to God, purge your conscience from dead works to serve the living God?"

[2]A whitening agent, potassium nitrate.
[3]Turned to ashes by burning.
[4]Wash.
[5]Songs.

Meditation 43 (Second Series)

Romans 9:5: God Blessed Forever.[1]

When, Lord, I seek to show Thy praises, then
  Thy shining majesty doth stund[2] my mind,
Encramps my tongue and tongue ties fast my pen,
  That all my doings do not what's designed.
  My speech's organs are so trancified[3]   5
  My words stand startled, can't Thy praises stride.[4]

Nay speech's bloomery[5] can't, from the ore
  Of reason's mine, melt words for to define
Thy Deity, nor t'deck the reeches[6] that soar
  From love's rich vales, sweeter than honey rhymes.   10
  Words, though the finest twine of reason, are
  Too course a web for Deity to wear.

Words mental are syllabicated thoughts;[7]
  Words oral are thoughts whiffled[8] in the wind.
Words writ are inky, goose quill-slabbered[9] drafts,   15
  Although the fairest blossoms of the mind.
  Then can such glasses clear enough descry
  My love to Thee, or Thy rich Deity?

Words are befouled, thought's filthy fumes that smoke
  From smutty huts, like will-a-wisps[10] that rise   20
From quagmires, run o'er bogs where frogs do croak,
  Lead all astray led by them by the eyes.
  My muddy words so dark Thy Deity,
  And cloud Thy sun-shine and its shining sky.

Yet spare me, Lord, to use this hurden[11] ware.   25
  I have no finer stuff to use, and I
Will use it now my creed but to declare
  And most[12] Thy glorious self to beautify.
  Thou art all-God: All Godhead then is Thine,
  Although the manhood there unto doth join.   30

Thou art all Godhead bright, although there be
  Something beside the Godhead in Thee bright.
Thou art all Infinite although in Thee
  There is a nature pure, not infinite.
  Thou art Almighty, though Thy human tent   35
  Of human frailty upon earth did sent.

He needs must be the Deity most high,
  To Whom all properties essential to

---

[1]Romans 9:5: "Whose are the fathers, and of whom as concerning the flesh Christ came, who is over all. God blessed forever, Amen."
[2]Stun or stupefy (form of "stoun").
[3]Set in a trance.
[4]Bestride.
[5]The first forge in an iron works, where the metal is made into blooms (ingots).

[6]Reeks, odors.
[7]Thoughts rendered in syllables.
[8]Puffed about.
[9]Pen-slobbered.
[10]*Ignis fatuus*, a light seen at night over marshes, not a real fire; thus, false or deceptive.
[11]Coarse fabric.
[12]"Most" is conjectured by the editor, B. D. Simison.

The Godhead do belong essentially
    And not to others, nor from Godhead go.   40
    And Thou art thus, my Lord, to Godhead joined.
    We find Thee thus in Holy Writ defined.

Thou art eternal; infinite Thou art;
    Omnipotent, omniscient, e'rywhere,
All holy, just, good, gracious, true in heart,   45
    Immortal, though with mortal nature here.
    Religious worship hence belongs to Thee
    From men and angels: all, of each degree.

Be Thou my God, and make me Thine elect
    To kiss Thy feet, and worship give to Thee;   50
Accept of me, and make me Thee accept,
    So I'st[13] be safe, and Thou shalt served be.
    I'll bring Thee praise, busked up[14] in songs perfumed,
    When Thou with grace my soul hast sweetly tuned.

1701   *1954*

Meditation 150 (Second Series)

Canticles[1] 7: 3: Thy two breasts are like two young
roes that are twins.

My blessed Lord, how doth Thy beauteous spouse
    In stately stature rise in comeliness?
With her two breasts like two little roes[2] that browse
    Among the lilies in their shining dress
    Like stately milk pails ever full and flow   5
    With spiritual milk to make her babes to grow.

Celestial nectar wealthier far than wine
    Wrought in the spirit's brew house and up tund[3]
Within these vessels which are trussed up fine,
    Likened to two pretty neat twin roes that run'd[4]   10
    Most pleasantly by their dam's sides like cades[5]
    And suckle with their milk Christ's spiritual babes.

Lord, put these nipples then my mouth into
    And suckle me therewith I humbly pray;
Then with this milk Thy spiritual babe I'st grow,   15
    And these two milk pails shall themselves display
    Like to these pretty twins in pairs round neat
    And shall sing forth Thy praise over this meat.[6]

1719   *1960*

---

[13]I shall.
[14]Dressed up, adorned.
[1]"The Song of Solomon" (called "Canticles") consists of explicit love poetry usually interpreted as expressing the love between Christ as bridegroom and His bride, the individual or the church.

[2]Small deer.
[3]Casked, put in a barrel or tun.
[4]Variant of ran.
[5]Pets.
[6]The wafer of the Lord's Supper, symbolizing Christ's flesh.

from God's Determinations Touching His Elect[1]

The Preface

[ALL THINGS BEHELD IN NOTHING]

Infinity, when all things it beheld
In nothing, and of nothing all did build,
Upon what base was fixed the lathe, wherein
He turned this globe, and riggaled[2] it so trim?
Who blew the bellows of His furnace vast?   5
Or held the mold wherein the world was cast?
Who laid its corner stone? Or whose command?
Where stand the pillars upon which it stands?
Who laced and filleted[3] the earth so fine,
With rivers like green ribbons smaragdine?[4]   10
Who made the seas its selvage,[5] and it locks
Like a quilt ball[6] within a silver box?
Who spread its canopy? Or curtains spun?
Who in this bowling alley bowled the sun?
Who made it always when it rises set   15
To go at once both down, and up to get?
Who th'curtain rods made for this tapestry?
Who hung the twinkling lanterns in the sky?
Who? Who did this? Or who is He? Why, know
It's only might Almighty this did do.   20
His hand hath made this noble work which stands
His glorious handiwork not made by hands.
Who spake all things from nothing, and with ease
Can speak all things to nothing, if He please.
Whose little finger at His pleasure can   25
Out mete[7] ten thousand worlds with half a span;
Whose might Almighty can by half a looks
Root up the rocks and rock the hills by th'roots.
Can take this mighty world up in His hand,
And shake it like a squitchen[8] or a wand.   30
Whose single frown will make the heavens shake
Like as an aspen leaf the wind makes quake.
Oh! What a might is this! Whose single frown
Doth shake the world as it would shake it down?
Which all from nothing fet,[9] from nothing, all: 35
Hath all on nothing set, lets nothing fall.
Gave all to nothing man indeed, whereby
Through nothing man all might Him glorify.
In nothing is[10] embossed the brightest gem
More precious than all preciousness in them.   40
But nothing man did throw down all by sin,

---

[1]Composed perhaps around 1685, *God's Determinations* is a long poem consisting of thirty-five parts, many of them dramatic speeches often responding one to another. The full title of the poem tells something of its argument: *God's Determinations Touching His Elect: And the Elect's Combat in Their Conversion, and Coming Up to God in Christ Together with the Comfortable Effects Thereof.*
[2]Grooved.
[3]Girded with ornamental bands.

[4]Emerald green.
[5]Edge, border.
[6]Multicolored like a quilt, the ball like a ball of yarn kept in a box.
[7]Measure out.
[8]A branch or switch.
[9]Fetched.
[10]"Then" in Stanford.

And darkened that lightsome gem in him.
　　That now his brightest diamond is grown
　　Darker by far than any coalpit stone.

c. 1685   *1939*

The Frowardness of the
Elect in the Work of Conversion

Those upon whom Almighty doth intend
His all eternal glory to expend,
Lulled in the lap of sinful nature snug,
Like pearls in puddles covered o'er with mud;
Whom, if you search, perhaps some few you'll find,   5
That to notorious sins were ne'er inclined.
Some shunning some, some most, some great, some small.
Some this, that, or the other, some none at all.
But all, or almost all, you'st[1] easily find,
To all, or almost all defects inclined.   10
To revel with the rabble rout who say,
"Let's hiss this piety out of our day."
And those whose frame is made of finer twine
Stand further off from grace than wash[2] from wine.
Those who suck grace from th'breast are nigh as rare   15
As black swans that in milk white rivers are.
Grace therefore calls them all, and sweetly woos.
Some won, come in; the rest as yet refuse,
And run away. Mercy pursues apace,
Then some cast down their arms, cry quarter,[3] grace.   20
Some chased out of breath drop down with fear,
Perceiving the pursuer drawing near.
The rest pursued, divide into two ranks
And this way one, and that the other pranks.[4]

Then in comes Justice with her forces by her,   25
And doth pursue as hot as sparkling fire.
The right wing then begins to fly away.
But in the straits strong barricadoes[5] lay.
They're therefore forced to face about, and have
Their spirits quelled, and therefore quarter crave.   30
These captived thus, Justice pursues the game
With all her troops to take the other train;
Which being chased in a peninsula
And followed close, they find no other way
To make escape, but t'rally round about;   35
Which if it fail them that they get not out,
They're forced into the infernal gulf alive
Or hacked in pieces are or took captive.

---

[1]You shall.   [4]Prances, capers in an arrogant manner.
[2]Swill.   [5]Barriers.
[3]Mercy, clemency.

But spying Mercy stand with Justice, they
Cast down their weapons, and for quarter pray.   40
Their lives are therefore spared, yet they are ta'en
As th'other band, and prisoners must remain.
And so they must now Justice's captives be
On Mercy's quarrel.[6] Mercy sets not free.
    Their former captain[7] is their deadly foe.   45
    And now, poor souls, they know not what to do.

c. 1685   *1939*

Satan's Rage at
Them in Their Conversion

    Grace by the aid of Justice wins the day.
And Satan's captives captives leads away,
Who finding of their former captain's cheats,
To be rebellion, him a rebel great,
Against his rightful Sovereign, by Whom   5
He shortly shall to execution come,
They sue for pardon do at Mercy's door,
Bewailing of that war they waged before.

    Then Satan in a red-hot fiery rage
Comes bellowing, roaring ready to engage,   10
To rend, to tear to pieces small all those
Whom in the former quarrel did lose.
But's boiling poisoned madness, being by
A shield divine repelled, he thus lets fly:
"You rebels all, I will you grip and fist.   15
I'll make my jaws a mill to grind such grists.
Look not for Mercy; Mercy well doth see
You'll be more false to her than unto me.
You're the first van[1] that fell; you're traitors, foes,
And unto such grace will no trust repose.   20
You second rank are cowards; if Christ come
With you to fight His field, you'll from Him run.
You third are feeble-hearted; if Christ's crown
Must stand or fall by you, you'll fling it down.
You last did last the longest; but being ta'en,   25
Are prisoners made, and jailbirds must remain.
It had been better on the turf to die
Than in such deadly slavery to lie.
Nay, at the best you all are captive foes.
Will wisdom have no better aid than those?   30
Trust to a forced faith? To hearts well known
To be (like yours) to all black treason prone?
For when I shall let fly at you, you'll fall;
And so fall foul upon your General.

---

[6]Ground or occasion of complaint.
[7]That is, Satan.
[1]The foremost detachment or group.

He'll hang you up alive then, by and by.   35
And I'll you wrack[2] too for your treachery.
He will become your foe; you then shall be
Flanked of by Him before, behind by me.
You'st[3] stand between us two our spears to dunce.[4]
Can you offend and fence both ways at once?   40
You'll then have sharper service than the whale,
Between the swordfish and the thresher's tail.
You'll then be mauled worse than the hand that's right
Between the heads of wheelhorned rams that fight.
   What will you do when you shall squeezed be   45
   Between such monstrous giant's jaws as we?"

c. 1685   *1939*

The Soul's Groan
to Christ for Succor

Good Lord, behold this dreadful enemy
   Who makes me tremble with his fierce assaults;
I dare not trust, yet fear to give the lie,
   For in my soul, my soul finds many faults.
   And though I justify myself to's face,   5
   I do condemn myself before Thy grace.

He strives to mount my sins, and them advance
   Above Thy merits, pardons, or good will,
Thy grace to lessen, and Thy wrath t'enhance,
   As if Thou couldst not pay the sinner's bill.   10
   He chiefly injures Thy rich grace, I find,
   Though I confess my heart to sin inclined.

Those graces which Thy grace enwrought in me,
   He makes as nothing but a pack of sins.
He maketh grace no grace, but cruelty;   15
   Is grace's honeycomb a comb of stings?
   This makes me ready leave Thy grace and run,
   Which if I do, I find I am undone.

I know he is Thy cur, therefore I be
   Perplexed lest I from Thy pasture stray.   20
He bays and barks so veh'mently at me.
   Come, rate[1] this cur, Lord, break his teeth, I pray.
   Remember me, I humbly pray Thee first.
   Then halter up this cur that is so curst.

c. 1685   *1939*

---

[2]Punish, avenge.   [4]Puzzle.
[3]You shall.   [1]Berate, rebuke.

Christ's Reply

Peace, peace, my honey, do not cry,
My little darling, wipe thine eye,
   Oh cheer, cheer up, come see.
Is anything too dear, my dove,
Is anything too good, my love,   5
   To get or give for thee?

If in the several[1] thou art,
This yelper fierce will at thee bark:
   That thou art mine this shows.
As Spot barks back the sheep again   10
Before they to the pound are ta'en,
   So he and hence 'way goes.

But if this cur that bays so sore
Is broken toothed and muzzled sure,
   Fear not, my pretty heart.   15
His barking is to make thee cling
Close underneath thy Savior's wing.
   Why did my sweeten[2] start?

And if he run an inch too far,
I'll check his chain and rate[3] the cur.   20
   My chick, keep close to me.
The poles shall sooner kiss and greet,
And parallels shall sooner meet,
   Than thou shalt harmed be.

He seeks to aggravate thy sin   25
And screw them to the highest pin,
   To make thy faith to quail.
Yet mountain sins like mites should show,
And then these mites for naught should go,
   Could he but once prevail.   30

I smote thy sins upon the head.
They deadened are, though not quite dead,
   And shall not rise again.
I'll but away the guilt thereof,
And purge its filthiness clear off: 35
   My blood doth out[4] the stain.

And though thy judgment was remiss,
Thy headstrong will too willful is.
   I will renew the same.
And though thou do too frequently   40
Offend as heretofore, hereby
   I'll not severely blame.

And though thy senses do inveigle
Thy noble soul to tend the beagle,

---

[1]Divided in the self, not one with Christ.   [3]Berate, rebuke.
[2]Beloved.   [4]Remove.

That t'hunt her games forth go,   45
I'll lure her back to me, and change
Those fond affections[5] that do range
   As yelping beagles do.

Although thy sins increase their race,
And though when thou hast sought for grace,   50
   Thou fallst more than before,
If thou by true repentence rise,
And faith makes me thy sacrifice,
   I'll pardon all, though more.

Though Satan strive to block thy way   55
By all his stratagems he may,
   Come, come, though through the fire.
For hell, that gulf of fire for sins,
Is not so hot as t'burn thy shins.
   Then credit not the liar.   60

Those cursed vermin sins that crawl
All o'er thy soul, but great and small,
   Are only Satan's own;
Which he in his malignity
Unto thy soul's true sanctity   65
   In at the doors hath thrown.

And though they be rebellion high,
Ath'ism or apostasy;
   Though blasphemy it be;
Unto what quality or size,   70
Excepting one, so e'er it rise,
   Repent, I'll pardon thee.

Although thy soul was once a stall
Rich hung with Satan's nicknacks all,
   If thou repent thy sin,   75
A tabernacle in't I'll place,
Filled with God's spirit and His grace.
   Oh comfortable thing!

I dare the world there to show
A God like me, to anger slow,   80
   Whose wrath is full of grace;
Doth hate all sins both great and small,
Yet when repented, pardons all,
   Frowns with a smiling face.

As for thy outward postures each,   85
Thy gestures, actions, and thy speech,
   I eye and eying spare,
If thou repent. My grace is more
Ten thousand times still trebled o'er
   Than thou canst want or wear.   90

---

[5]Foolish emotions or feelings.

As for the wicked charge he makes
That he of every dish first takes
   Of all thy holy things:
It's false, deny the same, and say,
That which he had he stole away   95
   Out of thy offerings.

Though to thy grief, poor heart, thou find
In prayer too oft a wandering mind,
   In sermons spirits dull;
Though faith in fiery furnace flags,   100
And zeal in chilly seasons lags,
   Temptations powerful:

These faults are his, and none of thine,
So far as thou dost them decline.
   Come then receive my grace.   105
And when he buffets thee therefore
If thou my aid and grace implore
   I'll show a pleasant face.

But still look for temptations deep,
Whilst that thy noble spark doth keep   110
   Within a mudwalled cote.[6]
These white frosts and the showers that fall
Are but to whiten thee withall,
   Not rob the web they smote.

If in the fire where gold is tried   115
Thy soul is put and purified,
   Wilt thou lament thy loss?
If silver-like this fire refine
Thy soul and make it brighter shine,
   Wilt thou bewail the dross?   120

Oh! fight my field: no colors fear;
I'll be thy front, I'll be thy rear,
   Fail not: my battles fight.
Defy the tempter, and his mock.
Anchor thy heart on me thy rock.   125
   I do in thee delight.

c. 1685   *1939*

The Joy of Church
Fellowship Rightly Attended[1]

In heaven soaring up, I dropped an ear
   On earth; and oh! sweet melody:
And listening, found it was the saints who were
   Encoached for heaven that sang for joy.

---

[6]A small shelter.
[1]This is the concluding poem of *God's Determinations*.

For in Christ's coach[2] they sweetly sing,   5
   As they to glory ride therein.

Oh! joyous hearts! Enfired with holy flame!
   Is speech thus tasseled with praise?
Will not your inward fire of joy contain,
   That it in open flames doth blaze?   10
   For in Christ's coach saints sweetly sing,
   As they to glory ride therein.

And if a string do slip by chance, they soon
   Do screw it up again;[3] whereby
They set it in a more melodious tune   15
   And a diviner harmony.
   For in Christ's coach they sweetly sing,
   As they to glory ride therein.

In all their acts, public and private, nay
   And secret too, they praise impart.   20
But in their acts divine and worship, they
   With hymns do offer up their heart.
   Thus in Christ's coach they sweetly sing,
   As they to glory ride therein.

Some few not in;[4] and some whose time and place   25
   Block up this coach's way,[5] do go
As travelers afoot, and so do trace
   The road that gives them right thereto;
   While in this coach these sweetly sing,
   As they to glory ride therein.   30

c. 1685   *1937*

An Address to the
Soul Occasioned by a Rain[1]

Ye flippering[2] soul,
   Why dost between the nippers dwell?
Not stay, nor go. Not yea, nor yet control.
   Doth this do well?
     Rise journey'ng when the skies fall weeping showers.   5
     Not o'er nor under th'clouds and cloudy powers.

Not yea, nor no:
   On tiptoes thus? Why sit on thorns?
Resolve the matter. Stay thyself or go.
   Be n't both ways born.   10

---

[2]Christ's coach holds all the Christians who are of the elect; it may be taken as the church of the title.
[3]When one of the strings of a stringed instrument loosens, the musician tightens it.
[4]Those who never became Christians, but who are of the elect nevertheless.

[5]Those whose time or place made impossible their becoming Christians but who still are of the elect.
[1]Johnson's reconstruction of the title. "[When] Let by Rain" in Stanford, "Let" meaning "hindered."
[2]Swinging, vacillating.

Wager thyself against thy surpliced see,[3]
And win thy coat, or let thy coat win thee.

Is this th'effect
  To leaven[4] thus my spirits all?
To make my heart a crabtree cask direct?   15
  A verjuiced[5] hall?
    As bottle ale, whose spirits prisoned must
    When jogged, the bung[6] with violence doth burst?

Shall I be made
  A sparkling wildfire shop,   20
Where my dull spirits at the fireball trade
  Do frisk and hop?
    And while the hammer doth the anvil pay,
    The fireball matter sparkles e'ry way.

One sorry fret,[7]   25
  An anvil spark, rose higher,
And in thy temple falling, almost set
  The house on fire.
    Such fireballs dropping in the temple flame
    Burns up the building: Lord, forbid the same.   30

1939

Upon a Spider
Catching a Fly

Thou sorrow, venom elf.
  Is this thy play,
To spin a web out of thyself
  To catch a fly?
    For why?   5

I saw a pettish[1] wasp
  Fall foul therein,
Whom yet thy whorl pins[2] did not hasp[3]
  Lest he should fling
    His sting.   10

But as afraid, remote
  Didst stand hereat,
And with thy little fingers stroke
  And gently tap
    His back.   15

Thus gently him didst treat
  Lest he should pet,[4]

---

[3]"Surplice, see" in Stanford. "Surplice": a loose-fitting coat-like garment worn by those taking part in church services; "see": jurisdiction of a bishop.
[4]To spread through, causing change (fermenting).
[5]Made sour.
[6]Stopper.

[7]Worry, irritation.
[1]Petulant.
[2]Spinning pins on a spinning wheel to catch the thread.
[3]Fasten; "clasp" in Stanford.
[4]Become impulsively angry.

And in a froppish,[5] aspish[6] heat
  Should greatly fret
    Thy net.   20

Whereas the silly fly,
  Caught by its leg
Thou by the throat took'st hastily
  And 'hind the head
    Bite dead.   25

This goes to pot,[7] that not
  Nature doth call.
Strive not above what strength hath got,
  Lest in the brawl
    Thou fall.   30

This fray seems thus to us:
  Hell's spider gets
His entrails spun to whipcords[8] thus,
  And wove to nets
    And sets,   35

To tangle Adam's race
  In's stratagems
To their destructions, spoiled, made base
  By venom things,
    Damned sins.   40

But mighty, gracious Lord,
  Communicate
Thy grace to break the cord; afford
  Us glory's gate
    And state.   45

We'll nightingale sing like
  When perched on high
In glory's cage, Thy glory, bright,   50
  Yea[9] thankfully,
    For joy.

c. 1685   *1939*

Upon a Wasp
Chilled with Cold

The bear[1] that breathes the northern blast
Did numb, torpedo-like,[2] a wasp
Whose stiffened limbs encramped, lay bathing
In Sol's warm breath and shine as saving,

---

[5]Fretful, peevish.
[6]"Waspish" in Stanford.
[7]To pieces, to ruin.
[8]A strong twisted cord used for whiplashes.
[9]"And" in Stanford.

[1]Both Ursa Major (Great Bear) and Ursa Minor (Little Bear) are northern constellations, and thus seen as sources of cold northern winds.
[2]The torpedo fish, or electric ray fish, immobilizes its victims by a severe sting.

Which with her hands she chafes and slams[3]   5
Rubbing her legs, shanks, thighs, and hands.
Her pretty toes, and fingers' ends
Nipped with this breath, she out extends
Unto the sun, in great desire
To warm her digits at that fire;   10
Doth hold her temples in this state
Where pulse doth beat, and head doth ache;
Doth turn, and stretch her body small,
Doth comb her velvet capital.[4]
As if her little brain pan were   15
A volume of choice precepts clear;
As if her satin jacket hot
Contained apothecary's shop
Of nature's receipts,[5] that prevails
To remedy all her sad ails;   20
As if her velvet helmet high
Did turret[6] rationality;
She fans her wing up to the wind
As if her petticoat were lined
With reason's fleece, and hoists sail   25
And humming flies in thankful gale
Unto her dun curled[7] palace hall,
Her warm thanks offering for all.

    Lord, clear my misted sight that I
May hence view Thy divinity,   30
Some sparks whereof Thou up dost hasp[8]
Within this little downy wasp,
In whose small corporation[9] we
A school and a schoolmaster see,
Where we may learn, and easily find   35
A nimble spirit bravely mind
Her work in e'ry limb, and lace
It up neat with a vital grace,
Acting each part though ne'er so small
Here of this fustian[10] animal,   40
Till I enravished climb into
The Godhead on this ladder[11] do,
Where all my pipes inspired upraise
An heavenly music furred[12] with praise.

c. 1685   *1943*

Huswifery

Make me, O Lord, Thy spinning wheel complete.
    Thy holy word my distaff[1] make for me.
Make mine affections Thy swift flyers[2] neat,

---

[3]"Stands" in Stanford.
[4]Head.
[5]Remedies, recipes for medicines.
[6]Roof over, cover.
[7]Dark curved or rounded.
[8]Lock or close in.
[9]Body, being.

[10]Thick, twilled cloth.
[11]On the meaning of the Lord enclosed in the wasp's actions.
[12]Trimmed, ornamented.
[1]Holds the raw flax or wool.
[2]Twists the raw material into threads.

And make my soul Thy holy spool[3] to be.
My conversation make to be Thy reel,[4]   5
And reel the yarn thereon spun of Thy wheel.

Make me Thy loom[5] then, knit therein this twine;
And make Thy Holy Spirit, Lord, wind quills:[6]
Then weave the web Thyself. The yarn is fine.
Thine ordinances make my fulling mills.[7]   10
Then dye the same in heavenly colors choice,
All pinked[8] with varnished[9] flowers of paradise.

Then clothe therewith mine understanding, will,
Affections, judgment, conscience, memory,
My words and actions, that their shine may fill   15
My ways with glory and Thee glorify.
Then mine apparel shall display before Ye
That I am clothed in holy robes for glory.

1937

Upon Wedlock and Death of Children[1]

A curious knot God made in Paradise,
And drew it out enameled neatly fresh.
It was the true-love knot, more sweet than spice,
And set with all the flowers of grace's dress.
Its wedding's knot, that ne'er can be untied.   5
No Alexander's sword can it divide.[2]

The slips here planted, gay and glorious grow,
Unless an hellish breath do singe their plumes.
Here primrose, cowslips, roses, lilies blow,
With violets and pinks that void[3] perfumes,   10
Whose beauteous leaves are laced with honey dew,
And chanting birds chirp out sweet music true.

When in this knot I planted was, my stock[4]
Soon knotted, and a manly flower outbrake.
And after it my branch again did knot,   15
Brought out another flower, its sweet-breathed mate.
One knot gave tother and tother's place;
Thence chuckling smiles fought in each other's face.

But oh! a glorious hand from glory came,
Guarded with angels, soon did crop this flower,   20

---

[3]Onto which the twisted threads are first wound.
[4]Holds the finished threads.
[5]Machine for weaving thread into cloth.
[6]Hollow reeds onto which the yarn is wound.
[7]Mills where cloth is beaten and cleansed with fuller's earth or soap.
[8]Decorated.
[9]Shining.

[1]Taylor's first four children are referred to in the poem: Samuel, born August 27, 1675; Elizabeth, born December 27, 1676, died December 25, 1677; James, born October 12, 1678; Abigail, born August 6, 1681, died August 22, 1682.
[2]Alexander the Great cut the Gordian Knot with his sword.
[3]Send out.
[4]Trunk, as of a plant.

Which almost tore the root up of the same,
  At that unlooked for, dolesome, darksome hour.
In prayer to Christ perfumed it did ascend,
  And angels bright did it to heaven 'tend.

But pausing on't, this sweet perfumed my thought: 25
  Christ would in glory have a flower, choice, prime,
And having choice, chose this my branch forth brought.
  Lord, take! I thank Thee, Thou tak'st ought[5] of mine;
  It is my pledge[6] in glory; part of me
  Is now in it, Lord, glorified with Thee.   30

But praying o'er my branch, my branch did sprout,
  And bore another manly flower, and gay,
And after that, another sweet broke out,
  The which the former hand soon got away.
  But oh! the torture, vomit, screechings, groans;   35
  And six weeks' fever would pierce hearts like stones.

Grief o'er doth flow: and nature fault would find
  Were not Thy will my spell, charm, joy, and gem;
That as I said, I say, take, Lord, they're Thine.
  I piecemeal pass to glory bright in them.   40
  I joy; may I sweet flowers for glory breed,
  Whether Thou get'st them green, or lets them seed.

c. 1682   *1937*

The Ebb and Flow

When first Thou on me, Lord, wrought'st Thy sweet print,[1]
  My heart was made Thy tinder box.[2]
  My 'ffections were Thy tinder in't,
    Where fell Thy sparks by drops.
Those holy sparks of heavenly fire that came   5
Did ever catch and often out would flame.

But now my heart is made Thy censer[3] trim,
  Full of Thy golden altar's fire,
  To offer up sweet incense in
    Unto Thyself entire,
I find my tinder scarce Thy sparks can feel   10
That drop out from Thy holy flint and steel.

Hence doubts out bud for fear Thy fire in me
  'S a mocking *ignis fatuus*,[4]
  Or lest Thine altar's fire out be,
    It's hid in ashes thus.   15
Yet when the bellows of Thy Spirit blow
Away mine ashes, then Thy fire doth glow.

1937

---

[5]Nothing.
[6]Contract, security payment.
[1]Image.
[2]Box holding kindling for the fire.

[3]Incense burner.
[4]"Foolish fire" (Latin); a phosphorescent light seen at night over a marshy land, not a real fire.

Upon the Sweeping Flood

O! that I'd had a tear to've quenched that flame
   Which did dissolve the heavens above
   Into those liquid drops that came
      To drown our carnal love.
Our cheeks were dry and eyes refused to weep.   5
Tears bursting out ran down the sky's dark cheek.

Were th'heavens sick? Must we their doctors be
   And physic them with pills, our sin?
   To make them purge and vomit, see,
      And excrements out fling?   10
We've grieved them by such physic[1] that they shed
Their excrements upon our lofty heads.

1683   *1943*

A Fig for Thee Oh! Death

Thou king of terrors with thy ghastly eyes,
With butter teeth,[1] bare bones, grim looks likewise,
And grizzly hide, and clawing talons, fell,[2]
Op'ning to sinners vile, trap door of hell,
That on in sin impenitently trip,   5
The downfall art of the infernal pit.
Thou struckst thy teeth deep in my Lord's blest side,
Who dashed it out, and all its venom 'stroyed
That now thy pounderall[3] shall only dash
My flesh and bones to bits, and cask[4] shall clash.   10
Thou'rt not so frightful now to me, thy knocks
Do crack my shell. Its heavenly kernel's box
Abides most safe. Thy blows do break its shell,
Thy teeth its nut. Cracks are that on it fell.
Thence out its kernel fair and nut, by worms   15
Once vitiated out, new formed forth turns
And on the wings of some bright angel flies
Out to bright glory of God's blissful joys.
Hence thou to me with all thy ghastly face
Art not so dreadful unto me through grace.   20
I am resolved to fight thee, and ne'er yield,
Blood up to th'ears, and in the battlefield
Chasing thee hence. But not for this my flesh,
My body, my vile harlot, it's thy mess,[5]
Laboring to drown me into sin, disguise   25
By eating and by drinking such evil joys,
Though grace preserved me that I ne'er have
Surprised been nor tumbled in such grave.
Hence for my strumpet[6] I'll ne'er draw my sword
Nor thee restrain at all by iron curb   30

---

[1]Give medicine, as a laxative pill.
[1]Large, projecting buckteeth.
[2]Fierce, terrible.
[3]Pestle.

[4]Husk, the outer being or body.
[5]Concoction, contrivance.
[6]Prostitute (the body).

Nor for her safety will I 'gainst thee strive
But let thy frozen grips take her captive
And her imprison in thy dungeon cave
And grind to powder in thy mill the grave,
Which powder in thy van[7] thou'st safely keep   35
Till she hath slept out quite her fatal sleep.
When the last cock shall crow the last day[8] in
And the archangel's trumpet's sound shall ring,
Then the 'Eye Omniscient seek shall all there round
Each dust death's mill had very finely ground,   40
Which in death's smoky furnace well refined
And each to'ts fellow hath exactly joined,
Is raised up anew and made all bright
And crystallized; all top full of delight,
And entertains its soul again in bliss   45
And holy angels waiting all on this,
The soul and body now, as two true lovers
E'ry night how do they hug and kiss each other.
And going hand in hand thus through the skies
Up to eternal glory glorious rise.   50
Is this the worst thy terrors then canst, why
Then should this grimace at me terrify?
Why cam'st thou then so slowly? Mend thy pace.
Thy slowness me detains from Christ's bright face.
Although thy terrors rise to th'highest degree,   55
I still am where I was, a fig for thee.

1960

EBENEZER COOKE
(*c.* 1670– *c.* 1735)

Ebenezer Cooke's *The Sot-Weed Factor,* published in London in 1708, comes out of a tradition radically different from that of Puritan poetry with its sober focus on religious belief and doctrinal questions. Satiric, witty, often bawdy, Cooke's poem tells a picaresque tale of riotous conduct, drunken revelry, and scandalous behavior in Maryland's tobacco-growing colony that both amuses and fascinates readers. A "sot-weed factor" was a tobacco agent who accompanied goods from England to barter for the colony's "sot-weed" or tobacco. At the end of Cooke's poem, the much put-upon "hero" escapes Maryland on a ship bound for his native England, his last words a "dreadful curse" on the uncouth land and savage society:

> May wrath divine then lay those regions waste
> Where no man's faithful, nor a woman chaste.

Very little is known with certainty about Ebenezer Cooke. Apparently his grandfather acquired land in the Maryland colony in the mid-seventeenth century but continued to live in England. Ebenezer Cooke was probably born

---

[7]Grave.
[8]Last Judgment or Day of Doom.

between 1665 and 1670. There is evidence that Cooke made trips to America in the 1690s and early 1700s; his description of life among the tobacco planters of Maryland in *The Sot-Weed Factor* could, therefore, be based on observation. We know almost nothing of Cooke's education, but there are some indications that he prepared for the law. If so, his characterization of Maryland lawyers in *The Sot-Weed Factor* is written from personal insight. He describes them as "wrangling"—

> With nonsense, stuff, and false quotations,
> With brazen lies and allegations.

Ebenezer Cooke came into his inheritance at his father's death in 1711, and by the 1720s Cooke was residing in Maryland. Various contemporary references to him show that he was known as Maryland's poet laureate. He published something of a sequel to his first poem, *Sotweed Redivivus,* in 1730. This poem, more serious and less witty (or scandalous) than *The Sot-Weed Factor,* addresses the economic and other problems of the tobacco planter in the New World.

The so-called third edition of *The Sot-Weed Factor* appeared in 1731, but no copy of a second edition (if it was published) seems to have survived. In the 1731 edition, Cooke somewhat softened the satire of the original poem, dropping (for example) the final "dreadful curse" on Maryland in favor of a "wish":

> If any youngster cross the ocean,
> To sell his wares—may he with caution
> Before he pays, receive each hogshead,
> Lest he be cheated by some dogshead,
> Both of his goods and his tobacco;
> And then like me, he shall not lack woe.
>   And may that land where hospitality
> Is every planter's darling quality,
> Be by each trader kindly used,
> And may no trader be abused;
> Then each of them shall deal with pleasure,
> And each increase the other's treasure.

This cautious, slightly visionary ending seems more appropriate than the original curse for a writer who has become the poet laureate of Maryland. But unfortunately it seems to go against the grain of the victimized hero and tends to dissipate the satiric force of the poem.

The title, *The Sot-Weed Factor,* was appropriated by John Barth for his novel published in 1960 (revised 1966). In this novel Barth invents a biography for Ebenezer Cooke, endows him with a twin sister, and relates a picaresque tale very much in the eighteenth-century tradition and style.

ADDITIONAL READING

"The Maryland Muse by Ebenezer Cooke: A Facsimile with an Introduction," ed. Lawrence C. Wroth, *American Antiquarian Society Proceedings,* 44, 1934.

John Barth, *The Sot-Weed Factor,* 1960, 1966 (a modern fictional treatment); Robert D. Arner, "Ebenezer Cooke's *The Sot-Weed Factor:* The Structure of Satire," *Southern Literary Journal,* 4, 1971; J. A. Leo Lemay, *Men of Letters in Colonial Maryland,* 1972; Edward H. Cohen, *Ebenezer Cooke: The Sot-Weed Canon,* 1975.

TEXT

The Sot-Weed Factor, ed. Bernard C. Steiner, *Early Maryland Poetry, Maryland Historical Society Fund Publication*, No. 36, 1900. "This reprint carefully follows the John Carter Brown copy [of the 1708 edition at Brown University]." A few lines of the text are incomplete and the gaps have been indicated by ellipses. Footnotes written by Ebenezer Cooke are indicated by his name followed by the note enclosed in quotation marks. Typography, punctuation, spelling, and usage have been changed to conform with contemporary English and modern printing practices.

The Sot-Weed Factor:[1]
Or, a Voyage to Maryland, &c.

Condemned by fate, to wayward curse,
Of friends unkind, and empty purse,
Plagues worse than filled Pandora's box,[2]
I took my leave of Albion's[3] rocks,
With heavy heart, concerned that I   5
Was forced my native soil to fly,
And the old world must bid good-bye.

But Heaven ordained it should be so,
And to repine is vain, we know:
Freighted with fools, from Plymouth sound,[4]   10
To Maryland our ship was bound,
Where we arrived, in dreadful pain,
Shocked by the terrors of the main;
For full three months our wavering boat
Did through the surly ocean float,   15
And furious storms and threatening blasts,
Both split our sails, and sprung our masts:
Wearied, yet pleased we did escape
Such ills, we anchored at the Cape;[5]
But weighing soon, we plowed the Bay,   20
To cove[6] it in Piscataway.[7]
Intending there to open store,
I put myself and goods on shore,
Where soon repaired a numerous crew,
In shirts and drawers of Scotch-cloth blue[8]   25
With neither stocking, hat, nor shoe.
These sot-weed planters crowd the shore,
In hue as tawny as a Moor;
Figures, so strange, no God designed
To be a part of humankind: 30
But wanton nature, void of rest,
Molded the brittle clay in jest.

---

[1] The tobacco agent. "Factor," Latin for "agent"; in this case, one representing English merchants exchanging British goods for American tobacco. "Sot": one who drinks excessively; as the weed that inebriated, tobacco was known as the sot-weed.
[2] When Pandora of Greek myth opened her box, all the evils of the world escaped and plagued humankind. She was sent by Zeus as a punishment for Prometheus' theft of fire.

[3] England.
[4] City on English Channel.
[5] Cooke: "By the Cape is meant the Capes of Virginia, the first land on the coast of Virginia and Maryland."
[6] Cooke: "To cove is to lie at anchor safe in harbor."
[7] Cooke: "The Bay of Piscataway, the usual place where our ships come to an anchor in Maryland."
[8] Cooke: "The planters generally wear blue linen."

At last a fancy very odd
Took me, this was The Land of Nod,
Planted at first when vagrant Cain   35
His brother had unjustly slain;[9]
Then, conscious of the crime he'd done,
From vengeance dire, he hither run,
And in a hut supinely dwelt,
The first in furs and sot-weed dealt.   40
And ever since his time, the place
Has harbored a detested race,
Who, when they could not thrive at home,
For refuge to these worlds did roam,
In hopes by flight they might prevent   45
The devil, and his fell intent,
Obtain from triple tree[10] reprieve,
And Heaven and Hell alike deceive.

But e're their manners I display,
I think it fit I open lay   50
My entertainment by the way,
That strangers well may be aware on
What homely diet they must fare on;
To touch that shore, where no good sense is found,
But conversation's lost, and manners drowned.   55
I crossed unto the other side
A river[11] whose impetuous tide,
Those savage borders do divide,
In such a shining odd invention,
I scarce can give its due dimension.   60
The Indians call this watery waggon
Canoe,[12] a vessel none can brag on,
Cut from a poplar tree, or pine,
And fashioned like a trough for swine:
In this most noble fishing-boat,   65
I boldly put myself afloat;
Standing erect, with legs stretched wide,
We paddled to the other side;
Where being landed safe by hap,
As Sol fell into Thetis' Lap.[13]   70
A ravenous gang, bent on the stroll,
Of wolves[14] for prey, began to howl;
This put me in a panic fright,
Lest I should be devoured quite:
But as I there a musing stood   75
And quite benighted in the wood,
A female voice pierced through my ears,
Crying, "You rogue drive home the steers."
I listened to the attractive sound,
And straight a herd of cattle found   80
Drove by a youth, and homewards bound.

---

[9]After Cain killed his brother Abel, he fled to the Land of Nod (Genesis 4:16).
[10]The gallows.
[11]The Piscatay River.
[12]Cooke: "A canoe is an Indian boat cut out of the body of a poplar tree."

[13]The sun set in the sea. In Greek mythology, Thetis is an ocean nymph; Sol is Roman god of the sun.
[14]Cooke: "Wolves are very numerous in Maryland."

Cheered with the sight, I straight thought fit
To ask where I a bed might get.
The surly peasant bid me stay,
And asked from whom[15] I'd run away.   85
Surprised at such a saucy word,
I instantly lugged out my sword,
Swearing I was no fugitive,
But from Great Britain did arrive,
In hopes I better here might thrive.   90
To which he mildly made reply,
"I beg your pardon, Sir, that I
Should talk to you unmannerly;
But if you please to go with me,
To yonder house you'll welcome be."   95

Encountering soon the smoky seat,
The planter old did thus me greet:
"Whether you're come from jail or college,
You're welcome to my certain knowledge;
And if you'll please all night to stay,   100
My son shall put you in the way."
Which offer I most kindly took,
And for a seat did round me look,
When presently among the rest
He placed his unknown English guest,   105
Who found them drinking, for a whet,[16]
A cask of cider on the fret:[17]
'Til supper came upon the table,
On which I fed whilst I was able.
So after hearty entertainment,   110
Of drink and victuals, without payment,
For planters' tables, you must know,
Are free for all that come and go,
Whilst pone,[18] with milk and mush[19] well stored,
In wooden dishes graced the board,   115
With hominy[20] and cider-pap,[21]
(Which scarce an English dog would lap)
Well stuffed with fat from bacon fried,
And with molasses dulcified.
Then out our landlord pulls a pouch,   120
As greasy as the leather couch
On which he sat, and straight begun
To load with weed his Indian gun,[22]
In length scarce longer than one's finger,
Or that for which the ladies linger.   125
His pipe smoked out with awful grace,
With aspect grave and solemn pace,
The reverend Sire walks to a Chest,
Of all his furniture the best,
Closely confined within a room,   130

---

[15]Cooke: "'Tis supposed by the planters that all unknown persons are run away from some master."
[16]Something that whets the appetite.
[17]In ferment.
[18]Cooke: "Pone is bread made of Indian corn."
[19]Cooke: "Mush is a sort of hasty-pudding made with water and Indian flour."

[20]Cooke: "Hominy is a dish that is made of boiled Indian wheat [corn], eaten with molasses or bacon fat."
[21]Cooke: "Cider-pap is a sort of food made of cider and small hominy, like our oatmeal."
[22]A pipe for smoking tobacco.

Which seldom felt the weight of broom.
From thence he lugs a keg of rum,
And nodding to me, thus begun:
"I find," says he, "you don't much care
For this our Indian country fare; 135
But let me tell you, friend of mine,
You may be glad of it in time,
Though now your stomach is so fine;
And if within this land you stay,
You'll find it true what I do say." 140
This said, the rundlet[23] up he threw,
And bending backwards strongly drew;
I plucked as stoutly, for my part,
Although it made me sick at heart,
And got so soon into my head, 145
I scarce could find my way to bed;
Where I was instantly conveyed
By one that passed for chambermaid,
Though by her loose and sluttish dress,
She rather seemed a Bedlam Bess.[24] 150
Curious to know from whence she came,
I pressed her to declare her name.
She blushing seemed to hide her eyes,
And thus in civil terms replies:
"In better times, e're to this land 155
I was unhappily trepanned,[25]
Perchance as well I did appear,
As any lord or lady here,
Not then a slave for twice two year.[26]
My clothes were fashionably new, 160
Nor were my shifts of linen blue;
But things are changed: now at the hoe
I daily work, and barefoot go,
In weeding corn or feeding swine,
I spend my melancholy time. 165
Kidnapped and fooled, I hither fled,
To shun a hated nuptial bed;[27]
And, to my cost already find
Worse plagues than those I left behind."
Whatever the wanderer did profess, 170
Good faith I could not choose but guess
The cause which brought her to this place[28]
Was supping e'er the priest said grace.

Quick as my thoughts, the slave was fled,
Her candle left to show my bed, 175
Which made of feathers soft and good,
Close in the chimney corner stood.[29]
I threw me down, expecting rest,
To be in golden slumbers blest;

---

[23]Small barrel.
[24]Servant in an insane asylum (Bedlam was the most notorious madhouse in London).
[25]Ensnared, kidnapped.
[26]Cooke: "'Tis the custom for servants to be obliged for four years to very servile work, after which time they have their freedom."

[27]Cooke: "These are the general excuses made by English women, which are sold, or sell themselves to Maryland."
[28]That is, her child.
[29]Cooke: "Beds stand in the chimney-corner in this country."

But soon a noise disturbed my quiet,   180
And plagued me with nocturnal riot:
A puss, which in the ashes lay,
With grunting pig, began a fray,
And prudent dog, that feuds might cease,
Most sharply barked, to keep the peace.   185
This quarrel scarcely was decided
By stick, that ready lay provided,
But reynard,[30] arch and cunning loon,
Broke into my apartment soon,
In hot pursuit of ducks and geese,   190
With full intent the same to seize;
Their cackling 'plaints with strange surprise
Chased sleep's thick vapors from my eyes;
Raging, I jumped upon the floor,
And like a drunken sailor swore;   195
With sword I fiercely laid about,
And soon dispersed the feathered rout,
The poultry out of window flew,
And reynard cautiously withdrew.
The dogs who this encounter heard,   200
Fiercely themselves to aid me reared,
And to the place of combat run,
Exactly as the field was won,
Fretting and hot as roasted capon,
And greasy as a flitch of bacon.[31]   205
I to the orchard did repair,
To breathe the cool and open air;
Expecting there the rising day,
Extended on a bank I lay.
But fortune here, that saucy whore,   210
Disturbed me worse and plagued me more
Than she had done the night before.
Hoarse croaking frogs[32] did 'round me ring,
Such peals the dead to life would bring,
A noise might move their wooden king.[33]   215
I stuffed my ears with cotton white
For fear of being deaf outright,
And cursed the melancholy night.
But soon my vows I did recant,
And hearing as a blessing grant,   220
When a confounded rattlesnake
With hissing made my heart to ache.
Not knowing how to fly the foe,
Or whither in the dark to go,
By strange good luck I took a tree,   225
Prepared by fate to set me free,
Where, riding on a limb astride,
Night and the branches did me hide,
And I the Devil and snake defied.
Not yet from plagues exempted quite,   230

---

[30]A fox.
[31]A side of bacon.
[32]Cooke: "Frogs are called Virginia bells, and make (both in that country and Maryland) during the night a very hoarse, ungrateful noise."

[33]A pagan idol. The frogs are like the idol-worshippers of Isaiah 45:20: "They have no knowledge that set up the wood of their graven image, and pray unto a god that cannot save."

The cursed mosquitoes did me bite;
'Til rising morn, and blushing day
Drove both my fears and ills away,
And from night's terrors set me free,
Discharged from hospitable tree.   235
I did to planter's booth[34] repair,
And there at breakfast nobly fare,[35]
On rasher broiled, of infant bear;
I thought the cub delicious meat,
Which ne'er did ought but chestnuts eat,   240
Nor was young Orson's flesh the worse,
Because he sucked a pagan nurse.[36]
Our breakfast done, my landlord stout,
Handed a glass of rum about.

   Pleased with the treatment I did find,   245
I took my leave of host so kind,
Who, to oblige me, did provide
His eldest son to be my guide,
And lent me horses of his own,
A skittish colt and aged roan,   250
The four-legged prop of his wife Joan.
Steering our course in trot or pace,
We sailed directly for a place,
In Maryland of high renown,
Known by the name of Battle Town.[37]   255
To view the crowds did there resort,
Which justice made, and law their sport,
In that sagacious country court.
Scarce had we entered on the way,
Which through the woods and marshes lay,   260
But Indian strange did soon appear
In hot pursuit of wounded deer;
No mortal creature can express
His wild fantastic air and dress;
His painted skin in colors dyed,   265
His sable hair in satchel tied,
Showed savages not free from pride.
His tawny thighs and bosom bare
Disdained a useless coat to wear,
Scorned summer's heat and winter's air;   270
His manly shoulders, such as please
Widows and wives, were bathed in grease,
Of cub and bear, whose supple oil,
Prepared his limbs 'gainst heat and toil.
Thus naked Pict[38] in battle fought,   275
Or undisguised his mistress sought;
And knowing well his ware was good,
Refused to screen it with a hood.
His visage dun, and chin that ne'er
Did razor feel, nor scissors bear,   280

---

[34]Room, quarters.
[35]Fared, ate.
[36]Orson is a bear, after Italian *orso*. In *Valentine and Orson*, an old French romance, twin sons are separated, one raised at court, the other raised as a wild child, suckled by a bear.

[37]Battle Town, on Battle Creek, was the county seat of Calvert County, and was about eight miles south of Prince Frederick.
[38]Prehistoric inhabitants of Great Britain.

Or know the ornament of hair,
Looked sternly grim; surprised with fear,
I spurred my horse as he drew near.
But roan, who better knew than I,
The little cause I had to fly,   285
Seemed by his solemn step and pace,
Resolved I should the specter face,
Nor faster moved, though spurred and licked,
Than Balaam's ass by prophet kicked.[39]
"Kekicnatop,"[40] the heathen cried;   290
"How is it Tom," my friend replied.
Judging from thence the brute was civil,
I boldly faced the courteous devil,
And lugging out a dram of rum,
I gave his tawny worship some;   295
Who in his language as I guess,
(My guide informing me no less,)
Implored the devil[41] me to bless.
I thanked him for his good intent,
And forward on my journey went;   300
Discoursing as along I rode,
Whether this race was framed of God,
Or whether some malignant power,
Contrived them in an evil hour,
And from his own infernal look   305
Their dusky form and image took.
From hence we fell to argument
Whence peopled was this continent.
My friend supposed Tartarians[42] wild,
Or Chinese from their home exiled,   310
Wandering through mountains hid with snow,
And rills that in the valleys flow,
Far to the south of Mexico,
Broke through the bars which nature cast,
And wide unbeaten regions past;   315
'Til near those streams the human deluge rolled,
Which sparkling shined with glittering sands of gold;
And fetched Pizarro[43] from the Iberian shore[44]
To rob the natives of their fatal store.
I smiled to hear my young logician,   320
Thus reason like a politician;
Who ne'er by father's pains and earning
Had got, at Mother Cambridge,[45] learning;
Where lubber[46] youth just free from birch,[47]

---

[39]Numbers 22: the prophet Balaam was on his way to deliver a curse on the Israelites; but his ass stopped in a narrow passage and even though kicked would not go on. Jehovah opened Balaam's eyes and he saw the angel that his ass had seen.
[40]Cooke: "*Kekicnatop* is an Indian expression and signifies no more than this, How do you do?"
[41]Cooke: "These Indians worship the devil, and pray to him as we do to God almighty. 'Tis supposed that America was peopled from Scythia or Tartaria, which borders on China, by reason the Tartarians and Americans very much agree in their manners, arms and government. Other persons are of opinion that the Chinese first peopled the West Indies, imagining China and the southern part of America to be contiguous. Others believe that the Phoenicians, who

were very skillful mariners, first planted a colony in the isles of America, and supplied the persons left to inhabit there with women and all other necessaries, till either the death or shipwreck of the first discoverers, or some other misfortune occasioned the loss of the discovery, which had been purchased by the peril of the first adventurers."
[42]Inhabitants of Central Asia.
[43]Cooke: "Pizarro [1470?–1541] was the person that conquered Peru, a man of a most bloody disposition, base, treacherous, covetous and revengeful."
[44]Cooke: "Spanish shore."
[45]Cambridge University, Cambridge, England.
[46]Big and clumsy.
[47]Just old enough to be beyond birch-rod punishment.

Most stoutly drink to prop the church;[48]   325
Nor with gray groat[49] had taken pains
To purge his head, and cleanse his reins;
And in obedience to the college,
Had pleased himself with carnal knowledge.[50]
And though I liked the youngster's wit,   330
I judged the truth he had not hit;
And could not choose but smile to think,
What they could do for meat and drink,
Who o'er so many deserts ran,
With brats and wives in caravan;   335
Unless perchance they'd got the trick,
To eat no more than porker sick;
Or could with well-contented maws,[51]
Quarter like bears upon their paws.[52]
Thinking his reasons to confute,   340
I gravely thus commenced dispute;
And urged that though a Chinese host
Might penetrate this Indian coast,
Yet this was certainly most true,
They never could the isles subdue;   345
For knowing not to steer a boat,
They could not on the ocean float,
Or plant their sunburnt colonies,
In regions parted by the seas.
I thence inferred Phoenicians[53] old   350
Discovered first, with vessels bold,
These western shores, and planted here,
Returning once or twice a year,
With naval stores, and lasses kind,
To comfort those were left behind;   355
'Til by the winds and tempests tore,
From their intended golden shore,
They suffered shipwreck, or were drowned,
And lost the world so newly found.
But after long and learned contention,   360
We could not finish our dissention;
And when that both had talked their fill,
We had the selfsame notion still.
Thus Parson, grave, well read, and sage,
Does in dispute with priest engage;   365
The one protests they are not wise,
Who judge by sense and trust their eyes,[54]
And vows he'd burn for it at stake,
That Man may God his maker make;
The other smiles at his religion,   370

---

[48]Study at university usually led to a career in the church.
[49]Cooke: "There is a very bad custom in some colleges of giving the students a *groat and purgandas rhenes* [cleaning and purging agents; groats made from ground oats], which is usually employed to the use of the donor."
[50]Secular knowledge, rather than knowledge concerned with preparation for the ministry, as evidenced by this discussion of the Tartarian (Tartans) or Chinese migration to "this continent," America.
[51]Stomachs.

[52]Cooke: "Bears are said to live by sucking of their paws, according to the notion of some learned authors."
[53]Cooke: "The Phoenicians were the best and boldest sailors of antiquity, and indeed the only persons, in former ages, who durst venture themselves on the main sea."
[54]Cooke: "The priests argue that our senses in the point of transubstantiation ought not to be believed, for though the consecrated bread has all the accidents of bread, yet they affirm, 'tis the body of Christ, and not bread but flesh and bones."

And vows he's but a learned widgeon;[55]
And when they've emptied all their store,
From books and fathers,[56] are not more
Convinced, or wiser than before.

Scarce had we finished serious story,   375
But I espied the town before me,
And roaring planters on the ground,
Drinking of healths, in circle round.
Dismounting steed with friendly guide,
Our horses to a tree we tied,   380
And forward passed amongst the rout,
To choose convenient quarters out.
But being none were to be found,
We sat like others on the ground,
Carousing punch in open air   385
'Til crier did the court declare.
The planting rabble being met,
Their drunken worships likewise sat,
Crier proclaims the noise should cease,
And straight the lawyers broke the peace,   390
Wrangling for plaintiff and defendant,
I thought they ne'er would make an end on't,
With nonsense, stuff and false quotations,
With brazen lies, and allegations;
And in the splitting of the cause,   395
They used such motions with their paws,
As showed their zeal was strongly bent
In blows to end the argument.
A reverend judge, who to the shame,
Of all the bench, could write his name,[57]   400
At pettifogger[58] took offense,
And wondered at his impudence.
My neighbor Dash with scorn replies,
And in the face of justice flies;
The bench in fury straight divide,   405
And scribbles take, or judge's side;
The jury, lawyers, and their clients,
Contending, fight like earth-born giants.
But sheriff wily lay perdue,[59]
Hoping indictments would ensue;   410
And when . . .
A hat or wig fell in the way,
He seized 'em for the queen as stray.
The court adjourned in usual manner,
In battle, blood and fractious clamor.   415
I thought it proper to provide
A lodging for myself and guide,
So to our inn we marched away,
Which at a little distance lay;
Where all things were in such confusion,   420
I thought the world at its conclusion.

---

[55]Fresh-water ducks found in Europe and Africa.   [58]Unscrupulous lawyer.
[56]Church fathers.   [59]Out of sight.
[57]Cooke: "In the county court of Maryland, very few of the
justices of the peace can write or read."

A herd of planters on the ground,
O'erwhelmed with punch, dead drunk we found;
Others were fighting and contending,
Some burned their clothes to save the mending;   425
A few whose heads, by frequent use,
Could better bear the potent juice,
Gravely debated state affairs,
Whilst I most nimbly tripped up stairs,
Leaving my friend discoursing oddly,   430
And mixing things profane and godly.
Just then beginning to be drunk,
As from the company I slunk:
To every room and nook I crept,
In hopes I might have somewhere slept;   435
But all the bedding was possessed
By one or other drunken guest.
But after looking long about,
I found an ancient corn loft out;
Glad that I might in quiet sleep,   440
And there my bones unfractured keep.
I laid me down secure from fray,
And soundly snored 'til break of day;
When waking fresh, I sat upright
And found my shoes were vanished quite;   445
Hat, wig, and stockings, all were fled,
From this extended Indian bed.
Vexed at the loss of goods and chattel,
I swore I'd give the rascal battle,
Who had abused me in this sort,   450
And merchant-stranger made his sport.
I furiously descended ladder,
No hare in March was ever madder.[60]
In vain I searched for my apparel,
And did with host and servants quarrel;   455
For one whose mind did much aspire
To mischief, threw them in the fire.[61]
Equipped with neither hat nor shoe,
I did my coming hither rue,
And doubtful thought what I should do.   460
Then looking 'round I saw my friend
Lie naked on a table's end,
A sight so dismal to behold,
One would have thought him dead and cold,
When ringing of his bloody nose,   465
By fighting got we may suppose,
I found him not so fast asleep,
Might give his friends a cause to weep.
"Rise Oronooko,[62] rise," said I,
"And from this hell and bedlam fly."   470
My guide starts up, and in amaze,

---

[60]Hares were thought to go mad in March, the mating season.
[61]Cooke: "'Tis the custom of the planters to throw their own, or any other person's hat, wig, shoes, or stockings in the fire."
[62]Cooke: "Planters are usually called by the name of Oro-nooko, from their planting Oronooko Tobacco." *Oronooko, or the History of the Royal Slave* (c. 1688), an early antislave-trade novel by English novelist Aphra Behn (1640–1689), celebrates the virtues of the "noble savage" or primitive people. Extremely popular, it was adapted for the stage in 1695 by British dramatist Thomas Southerne (1659–1746).

With bloodshot eyes did round him gaze;
At length with many sigh and groan,
He went in search of aged roan;
But roan, though seldom used to falter,   475
Had fairly this time slipped his halter,
And not content all night to stay,
Tied up from fodder, run away.
After my guide to catch him ran,
And so I lost both horse and man;   480
Which disappointment though so great,
Did only jest and mirth create:
'Til one more civil than the rest,
In conversation far the best,
Observing that for want of roan,   485
I should be left to walk alone,
Most readily did me entreat,
To take a bottle at his seat,[63]
A favor at that time so great,
I blessed my kind propitious fate.   490
And finding soon a fresh supply
Of clothes, from storehouse kept hard by,
I mounted straight on such a steed,
Did rather curb than whipping need;
And straining at the usual rate,   495
With spur of punch which lies in pate,[64]
E'er long we lighted at the gate;
Where in an ancient cedar house,
Dwelt my new friend, a cockerouse,[65]
Whose fabric, though 'twas built of wood,   500
Had many springs and winters stood:
When sturdy oaks and lofty pines,
Were leveled with musk-melon-vines,
And plants eradicated were,
By hurricanes into the air.   505
There with good punch and apple juice,
We spent our time without abuse,
'Til Midnight in her sable vest,
Persuaded gods and men to rest;
And with a pleasing kind surprise,   510
Indulged soft slumber to my eyes.

Fierce Aethon, courser[66] of the sun,
Had half his race exactly run,
And breathed on me a furious ray,
Darting hot beams the following day,   515
When snug in blanket white, I lay.
But heat and chinches[67] raised the sinner,
Most opportunely to his dinner;
Wild fowl and fish delicious meats,
As good as Neptune's doxy[68] eats,   520

---

[63]His country residence.
[64]Spurred on by the punch he had drunk, still in his head.
[65]Cooke: "Cockerouse is a man of quality." Variant of *Cock-arouse*, title of honor among the Indians of Virginia and thus among the colonists.
[66]Cooke: "Aethon is one of the poetical horses of the sun."

Courser: swift horse. In Greek mythology, four horses pull the sun across the sky.
[67]Cooke: "Chinches are a sort of vermin like our bugs in England." Bedbugs.
[68]Mistress. Neptune is the Roman god of the sea.

Began our hospitable treat;
Fat venison followed in the rear,
And turkeys wild,[69] luxurious cheer.
But what the feast did most commend,
Was hearty welcome from my friend.   525
Thus having made a noble feast,
I eat as well as pampered priest;
Madeira strong in flowing bowls,
Filled with extreme delight our souls;
'Til wearied with a purple flood,   530
Of gen'rous wine (the giants' blood,
As poets feign) away I made
For some refreshing verdant shade;
Where musing on my rambles strange,
And fortune, which so oft did change,   535
In midst of various contemplations,
Of fancies odd and meditations,
I slumber'd long
'Til hazy night and noxious dews,
Did sleep's unwholesome fetters loose,   540
With vapors chilled and misty air,
To fireside I did repair;
Near which a jolly female crew,
Were deep engaged at Lanterloo,[70]
In Nighttrails[71] white, with dirty mien,   545
Such sights are scarce in England seen.
I thought them first some witches bent
On black designs, in dire convent;
'Til one who with affected air,
Had nicely learned to curse and swear,   550
Cried "dealing's lost, 'tis but a flam,"[72]
And vowed by G— she'd keep her Pam.[73]
When dealing through the board had run,
They asked me kindly to make one;
Not staying often to be bid,   555
I sat me down as others did;
We scarce had played a round about,
But that these Indian frows[74] fell out:
"D—m you," says one, "though now so brave,
I knew you late a four year's slave;   560
What if for planter's wife you go,
Nature designed you for the hoe."
"Rot you," replies the other straight,
"The captain kissed you for his freight;
And if the truth was known aright,   565
And how you walked the streets by night,
You'd blush, if one could blush for shame,
Who from Bridewell and Newgate[75] came."
From words they fairly fell to blows,
And being loath to interpose,   570
Or meddle in the wars of punk,[76]

---

[69]Cooke: "Wild turkeys are very good meat and prodigiously large in Maryland."
[70]A card game, sometimes called "loo."
[71]Night dresses or gowns.
[72]Deception, cheating.

[73]The knave of trumps, usually clubs in the game of loo, and the highest card in the pack.
[74]Wives, scolding women.
[75]Prisons in London.
[76]Prostitutes.

Away to bed in haste I slunk.
Waking next day with aching head,
And thirst that made me quit the bed,
I rigged myself and soon got up,   575
To cool my liver with a cup
Of Succahanah[77] fresh and clear,
Not half so good as English beer,
Which ready stood in kitchen pail,
And was, in fact, but Adam's ale.   580
For planters' cellars, you must know,
Seldom with good October[78] flow
But perry,[79] quince, and apple juice,
Spout from the tap, like any sluice,
Until the cask's grown low and stale,   585
They're forced again to gourd and pail.[80]
The soothing draught scarce down my throat,
Enough to set a ship afloat,
With cockerouse as I was sitting
I felt a fever intermitting,   590
A fiery pulse beat in my veins,
From cold I felt resembling pains;
This cursed seasoning I remember,
Lasted from March 'til cold December;
Nor could it then its quarter shift,   595
Until by carduus[81] turned adrift;
And had my doct'ress wanted skill,
Or kitchen physic[82] at her will
My father's son had lost his lands,
And never seen the Goodwin Sands:[83]   600
But thanks to fortune, and a nurse,
Whose care depended on my purse,
I saw myself in good condition,
Without the help of a physician.
At length the shivering ill relieved   605
Which long my head and heart had grieved.

  I then began to think with care,
How I might sell my British ware;
That with my freight I might comply,
Did on my Charter Party[84] lie: 610
To this intent, with guide before,
I tripped it to the eastern shore;
While riding near a sandy bay,
I met a Quaker, *yea* and *nay;*
A pious conscientious rogue,   615
As e'er wore bonnet or a brogue,
Who neither swore nor kept his word,
But cheated in the fear of God;
And when his debts he would not pay,
By light within he ran away.   620

---

[77]Cooke: "Succahanah is water." Refers to Susquehanna River.
[78]Beer brewed in October was considered excellent.
[79]Pear juice (makes an alcoholic drink).
[80]Cooke: "A gourd grows upon an Indian vine, resembling a bottle, when ripe it is hollow; this the planters make use of to drink water out of."

[81]Thistle prized as a remedy for diseases.
[82]Kitchen remedies.
[83]Never gone home to England; Goodwin Sands are shoals near the British coast.
[84]The contract between him and his merchant backers concerning the cargo he brought with him from England to barter for tobacco.

With this sly zealot, soon I struck
A bargain for my English truck,
Agreeing for ten thousand weight
Of Sot-weed good and fit for freight:
Broad Oronooko,[85] bright and sound,   625
The growth and product of his ground;
In cask that should contain complete
Five hundred of tobacco neat.
The contract thus betwixt us made,
Not well acquainted with the trade,   630
My goods I trusted to the cheat,
Whose crop was then aboard the fleet;
And going to receive my own,
I found the bird was newly flown.
Cursing this execrable slave,   635
This damned pretended godly knave,
On due revenge and justice bent,
I instantly to council went;
Unto an ambodexter quack,[86]
Who learnedly had got the knack   640
Of giving clysters,[87] making pills,
Of filling bonds, and forging wills;
And with a stock of impudence,
Supplied his want of wit and sense,
With looks demure, amazing people,   645
No wiser than a daw[88] on steeple;
My anger flushing in my face,
I stated the preceding case,
And of my money was so lavish
That he'd have poisoned half the parish   650
And hanged his father on a tree,
For such another tempting fee.
Smiling, said he, "The cause is clear,
I'll manage him, you need not fear;
The case is judged, good Sir, but look   655
In Galen, no—in my Lord Cook,[89]
I vow to God, I was mistook:
I'll take out a provincial writ,[90]
And trounce him for his knavish wit;
Upon my life we'll win the cause,   660
With all the ease I cure the yaws."[91]
Resolv'd to plague the holy brother,
I set one rogue to catch another.
To try the cause then fully bent,
Up to Annapolis[92] I went,   665
A city situate on a plain,
Where scarce a house will keep out rain;
The buildings framed with cypress rare,

---

[85]The tobacco plant.
[86]Cooke: "This fellow was an apothecary, and turned an attorney at law." Ambodexter: ambidextrous, "deceitful" as used here.
[87]Enemas.
[88]Crow or jackdaw.
[89]Galen, a second-century Greek physician; "Lord Cook," probably Sir Edward Coke (1552–1634), lord chief justice of England and author of *Institutes of the Laws of England*.
[90]Restraining order for the colonies (provinces).
[91]Cooke: "The yaws is the pox." Disease that causes a rash and splotches to break out on the skin.
[92]Cooke: "The chief of Maryland, containing about twenty-four houses."

Resembles much our Southwark Fair;[93]
But stranger here will scarcely meet,   670
With market place, exchange, or street;
And if the truth I may report,
'Tis not so large as Tottenham Court.[94]
St. Mary's[95] once was in repute,
Now here the Judges try the suit,   675
And lawyers twice a year dispute.
As oft the bench most gravely meet,
Some to get drunk, and some to eat
A swinging share of country treat.
But as for justice right or wrong,   680
Not one amongst the numerous throng
Knows what they mean, or has the heart,
To give his verdict on a stranger's part.
Now court being called by beat of drum,
The judges left their punch and rum;   685
When pettifogger doctor draws
His paper forth and opens cause;
And lest I should the better get,
Bribed quack suppressed his knavish wit.
So maid upon the downy field   690
Pretends a force and fights to yield.
The biased court without delay
Adjudged my debt in country pay,
In pipe staves, corn, or flesh of boar,[96]
Rare cargo for the English shore.   695
Raging with grief, full speed I ran
To join the fleet at Kicketan.[97]
Embarked and waiting for a wind,
I left this dreadful curse behind.

  May cannibals transported o'er the sea   700
Prey on these slaves as they have done on me;
May never merchant's trading sails explore
This cruel, this inhospitable shore;
But left abandoned by the world to starve,
May they sustain the fate they well deserve.   705
May they turn savage, or as Indians wild,
From trade, converse, and happiness exiled;
Recreant to heaven, may they adore the sun,
And into pagan superstitions run;
For vengeance ripe . . .   710
May wrath divine then lay those regions waste
Where no man's faithful,[98] nor a woman chaste.

                                                                1708

---

[93]Part of London.
[94]Near London.
[95]A town in Maryland.
[96]Cooke: "There is a law in this country, the plaintiff may pay his debt in country pay, which consists in the produce of his plantation."

[97]Cooke: "The homeward bound fleet meets here." Indian name for Hampton or Cape of Virginia.
[98]Cooke: "The author does not intend by this any of the English gentlemen resident there."

PERSONAL ACCOUNTS OF HIGH ADVENTURE: INDIAN CAPTIVITY AND HAZARDOUS JOURNEY

MARY ROWLANDSON   SARAH KEMBLE KNIGHT

Mary Rowlandson's narrative of her captivity by the Indians in Massachusetts in 1676 and Sarah Kemble Knight's narrative of her hazardous journey from Boston to New Haven and New York in 1704–05 are both remarkable pieces of writing sharply realized by observant women with an eye for telling detail and a gift for the vivid phrase or image. The writers could hardly be more different, with Mary Rowlandson's piety and concentration on the transcendent in sharp contrast with Madam Knight's wit and her interest in the common and everyday. Read together, they tell something of the changes that were taking place in New England as it moved from the seventeenth century into the eighteenth.

MARY ROWLANDSON
(*c.* 1635–*c.* 1678)

Early in the morning before sunup, the Indians surrounded the garrison in secrecy, ready for attack, careful to assure *surprise*—the most effective tactic of frontier warfare. Then they moved swiftly into the settlement, burning the houses, shooting and clubbing and slashing the startled people, braining, butchering, and disemboweling women and children as well as men. This episode could be the opening of many a western novel or movie. In fact, it actually happened on the morning of February 10, 1676, in the town of Lancaster, Massachesetts, west of Boston. Mary Rowlandson heard shots, looked out the window of her house and saw nearby houses burning. Soon the Indians were upon her and her family with "the bullets flying thick," one piercing her side and the hand and "bowels" of the child she held. She witnessed first her brother-in-law fall dead and then her oldest sister. Other horrors were to follow during her captivity by the Indians for eleven weeks and five days.

This event is but one episode in the most important Indian war in the New England colonies, King Philip's War (1675–76). The causes of the war were complex, but certainly contributing to the hostility of the Indians was the steady and continuing loss of their lands to the white colonists. Philip, a Wampanoag with the Indian name of Metacomet, had become sachem of his tribe in 1662. In 1675 a Christian Indian, spying for the colonists, was killed by the Wampanoags. In retaliation the colonists executed three Wampanoags accused of the murder.

Thus began King Philip's War, which brought together the Wampanoags with the Nipmucks and the Narragansetts. The Indians avoided direct battles but were skilled in making raids on the frontier settlements. They burned over a thousand houses and killed some six hundred colonists. Around three thousand Indians were killed. The colonists' superior weaponry prevailed and the Indians were defeated in 1676. King Philip was killed, and his body was drawn and quartered; his head was displayed on a pole in Plymouth. The colonists were then able to take over the lands without major opposition.

Mary Rowlandson was the daughter of a wealthy settler, John White, of Lancaster. In 1656 she married a congregational minister, Joseph Rowlandson. What little more we know about Mary Rowlandson we learn from her account of her captivity. Until she was taken by the Indians, she enjoyed smoking several pipefuls of tobacco a day, and she was thankful to give up the habit (a weakness, in her view) during her imprisonment. Her most prized possession during her captivity was a Bible given her by an Indian (who had taken it in a raid on a settlement). Passages applicable to her situation comforted her in her severest trials; her piety and the strength it gave her are remarkable.

After her captivity, Mary Rowlandson set about writing her account, published in 1682 under a title that emphasized its revelation and authentication of God's dependability and righteousness: *The Sovereignty and Goodness of God, Together with the Faithfulness of His Promises Displayed; Being a Narrative of the Captivity and Restoration of Mrs. Mary Rowlandson.* The ingenuity of the author in finding the providence of God revealed in the most appalling examples of human cruelty and suffering is characteristically Puritan. She sees the New England Puritan tormented and tortured by the Indians as a modern

Job, whom she quotes in her opening pages; "And I only am escaped alone to tell the News."

Her book was immensely popular both in England and America, less for its Biblical allusions than for its skill in building suspense, in portraying character, and in depicting events of terror and violence, hardship and suffering, all in vigorous, vivid prose. Her narrative together with other accounts of Indian captivity became models for later American fiction, drama, and motion pictures. James Fenimore Cooper skillfully took over the major elements of the captivity narratives for his novels, especially *The Leather-Stocking Tales.*

ADDITIONAL READING

Roy Harvey Pearce, *The Savages of America: A Study of the Indian and the Idea of Civilization,* 1953, 1965; Roy Harvey Pearce, "The Significance of the Captivity Narrative," *American Literature,* XIX, 1947; Richard VanDerBeets, ed. *Held Captive by the Indians,* 1973; Richard VanDerBeets, *The Indian Captivity Narrative: An American Genre, 1984;* Annette Kolodny, *The Land Before Her,* 1984.

TEXT

"Narrative of the Captivity of Mrs. Mary Rowlandson," *Original Narratives of Early American History, Narratives of Indian Wars, 1675–1699,* vol. XIV, ed., Charles H. Lincoln, 1913. Footnotes from this edition are indicated by the editor's name followed by the note enclosed in quotation marks. Typography, punctuation, spelling, and usage have been changed to conform with contemporary English and modern printing practices.

from A Narrative of the Captivity and Restoration of Mrs. Mary Rowlandson

[BEGINNING OF THE CAPTIVITY]

On the tenth of February 1675,[1] came the Indians with great numbers upon Lancaster: their first coming was about sunrising; hearing the noise of some guns, we looked out; several houses were burning, and the smoke ascending to heaven. There were five persons taken in one house; the father, and the mother and a sucking child, they knocked on the head; the other two they took and carried away alive. There were two others, who being out of their garrison[2] upon some occasion were set upon; one was knocked on the head, the other escaped. Another there was who running along was shot and wounded, and fell down; he begged of them his life, promising them money (as they told me) but they would not hearken to him but knocked him in head, and stripped him naked, and split open his bowels. Another, seeing many of the Indians about his barn, ventured and went out, but was quickly shot down. There were three others belonging to the same garrison who were killed; the Indians' getting up upon the roof of the barn, had advantage to shoot down upon them over their fortification. Thus these murderous wretches went on, burning, and destroying before them.

At length they came and beset our own house, and quickly it was the dolefulest day that ever mine eyes saw. The house stood upon the edge of a hill; some of the Indians got behind the hill, others into the barn, and others behind anything that

---

[1]Actually February 10, 1676, Gregorian calendar.
[2]Special buildings in the town used for defense.

could shelter them; from all which places they shot against the house, so that the bullets seemed to fly like hail; and quickly they wounded one man among us, then another, and then a third. About two hours (according to my observation, in that amazing time) they had been about the house before they prevailed to fire it (which they did with flax and hemp, which they brought out of the barn, and there being no defense about the house, only two flankers[3] at two opposite corners and one of them not finished); they fired it once and one ventured out and quenched it, but they quickly fired it again, and that took. Now is the dreadful hour come, that I have often heard of (in time of war, as it was the case of others), but now mine eyes see it. Some in our house were fighting for their lives, others wallowing in their blood, the house on fire over our heads, and the bloody heathen ready to knock us on the head, if we stirred out. Now might we hear mothers and children crying out for themselves, and one another, "Lord, what shall we do?" Then I took my children (and one of my sisters', hers) to go forth and leave the house: but as soon as we came to the door and appeared, the Indians shot so thick that the bullets rattled against the house, as if one had taken an handful of stones and threw them, so that we were fain to give back. We had six stout dogs belonging to our garrison, but none of them would stir, though another time, if any Indian had come to the door, they were ready to fly upon him and tear him down. The Lord hereby would make us the more to acknowledge His hand, and to see that our help is always in Him. But out we must go, the fire increasing, and coming along behind us, roaring, and the Indians gaping before us with their guns, spears, and hatchets to devour us. No sooner were we out of the house, but my brother-in-law (being before wounded, in defending the house, in or near the throat) fell down dead, whereat the Indians scornfully shouted, and hallowed, and were presently upon him, stripping off his clothes, the bullets flying thick, one went through my side, and the same (as would seem) through the bowels and hand of my dear child in my arms. One of my elder sister's children, named William, had then his leg broken, which the Indians perceiving, they knocked him on [the] head. Thus were we butchered by those merciless heathen, standing amazed, with the blood running down to our heels. My eldest sister being yet in the house, and seeing those woeful sights, the infidels haling mothers one way, and children another, and some wallowing in their blood; and her elder son telling her that her son William was dead, and myself was wounded, she said, "And Lord, let me die with them," which was no sooner said, but she was struck with a bullet, and fell down dead over the threshold. I hope she is reaping the fruit of her good labors, being faithful to the service of God in her place. In her younger years she lay under much trouble upon spiritual accounts, till it pleased God to make that precious scripture take hold of her heart, 2 Cor. 12:9, "And he said unto me, my Grace is sufficient for thee." More than twenty years after, I have heard her tell how sweet and comfortable that place was to her. But to return: the Indians laid hold of us, pulling me one way, and the children another, and said, "Come go along with us"; I told them they would kill me; they answered, if I were willing to go along with them, they would not hurt me.

Oh the doleful sight that now was to behold at this house! "Come, behold the works of the Lord, what desolations he has made in the Earth."[4] Of thirty-seven persons who were in this one house, none escaped either present death, or a bitter captivity, save only one, who might say as he, Job 1:15, "And I only am escaped alone to tell the News." There were twelve killed, some shot, some stabbed with their spears, some knocked down with their hatchets. When we are in prosperity,

---

[3]Fortified projections for defense.
[4]Psalm 46:8.

Oh the little that we think of such dreadful sights, and to see our dear friends and relations lie bleeding out their heart-blood upon the ground. There was one who was chopped into the head with a hatchet, and stripped naked, and yet was crawling up and down. It is a solemn sight to see so many Christians lying in their blood, some here, and some there, like a company of sheep torn by wolves, all of them stripped naked by a company of hell-hounds, roaring, singing, ranting, and insulting, as if they would have torn our very hearts out; yet the Lord by His almighty power preserved a number of us from death, for there were twenty-four of us taken alive and carried captive.

I had often before this said that if the Indians should come, I should choose rather to be killed by them than taken alive, but when it came to the trial my mind changed; their glittering weapons so daunted my spirit, that I chose rather to go along with those (as I may say) ravenous beasts, than that moment to end my days; and that I may the better declare what happened to me during that grievous captivity, I shall particularly speak of the several removes[5] we had up and down the wilderness.

The First Remove

Now away we must go with those barbarous creatures, with our bodies wounded and bleeding, and our hearts no less than our bodies. About a mile we went that night, up upon a hill within sight of the town, where they intended to lodge. There was hard by a vacant house (deserted by the English before, for fear of the Indians). I asked them whether I might not lodge in the house that night, to which they answered, "What, will you love English men still?" This was the dolefulest night that ever my eyes saw. Oh the roaring, and singing and dancing, and yelling of those black creatures in the night, which made the place a lively resemblance of hell. And as miserable was the waste that was there made of horses, cattle, sheep, swine, calves, lambs, roasting pigs, and fowl (which they had plundered in the town), some roasting, some lying and burning, and some boiling to feed our merciless enemies; who were joyful enough, though we were disconsolate. To add to the dolefulness of the former day, and the dismalness of the present night, my thoughts ran upon my losses and sad bereaved condition. All was gone, my husband gone (at least separated from me, he being in the bay;[1] and to add to my grief, the Indians told me they would kill him as he came homeward), my children gone, my relations and friends gone, our house and home and all our comforts, within door and without—all was gone (except my life), and I knew not but the next moment that might go too. There remained nothing to me but one poor wounded babe, and it seemed at present worse than death that it was in such a pitiful condition, bespeaking compassion, and I had no refreshing for it, nor suitable things to revive it. Little do many think what is the savageness and brutishness of this barbarous enemy. Ay, even those that seem to profess more than others among them, when the English have fallen into their hands.

Those seven that were killed at Lancaster the summer before upon a Sabbath day, and the one that was afterward killed upon a week day, were slain and mangled in a barbarous manner, by one-eyed John, and Marlborough's Praying Indians,[2] which Capt. Mosely brought to Boston, as the Indians told me.

---

[5]Moves; the narrative is divided into the periods from the moves into and the departures from particular sites or campgrounds.
[1]He was in Boston, in Massachusetts Bay Colony.
[2]There was a settlement of Christianized Indians at Marlborough, Massachusetts. Some colonists were skeptical that these "Praying Indians" were innocent of assaults on the English settlements. On August 30, 1675, Captain Samuel Mosely brought fifteen of these Indians in captivity to Boston, charging them with attacking Lancaster shortly before. One-eyed John was also called Monoco and Apequinash.

THE SECOND REMOVE[1]

But now, the next morning, I must turn my back upon the town, and travel with them into the vast and desolate wilderness, I knew not wither. It is not my tongue, or pen, can express the sorrows of my heart, and bitterness of my spirit that I had at this departure; but God was with me in a wonderful manner, carrying me along, and bearing up my spirit, that it did not quite fail. One of the Indians carried my poor wounded babe upon a horse; it went moaning all along, "I shall die, I shall die." I went on foot after it, with sorrow that cannot be expressed. At length I took it off the horse, and carried it in my arms till my strength failed, and I fell down with it. Then they set me upon a horse with my wounded child in my lap, and there being no furniture upon the horse's back, as we were going down a steep hill, we both fell over the horse's head, at which they, like inhumane creatures, laughed, and rejoiced to see it, though I thought we should there have ended our days, as overcome with so many difficulties. But the Lord renewed my strength still, and carried me along, that I might see more of his power; yea, so much that I could never have thought of, had I not experienced it.

After this it quickly began to snow, and when night came on, they stopped, and now down I must sit in the snow, by a little fire, and a few boughs behind me, with my sick child in my lap; and calling much for water, being now (through the wound) fallen into a violent fever. My own wound also growing so stiff that I could scarce sit down or rise up; yet so it must be, that I must sit all this cold winter night upon the cold snowy ground, with my sick child in my arms, looking that every hour would be the last of its life; and having no Christian friend near me, either to comfort or help me. Oh, I may see the wonderful power of God, that my Spirit did not utterly sink under my affliction: still the Lord upheld me with His gracious and merciful spirit, and we were both alive to see the light of the next morning.

THE THIRD REMOVE[1]

The morning being come, they prepared to go on their way. One of the Indians got up upon a horse, and they set me up behind him, with my poor sick babe in my lap. A very wearisome and tedious day I had of it; what with my own wound, and my child's being so exceeding sick, and in a lamentable condition with her wound. It may be easily judged what a poor feeble condition we were in, there being not the least crumb of refreshing that came within either of our mouths from Wednesday night to Saturday night, except only a little cold water. This day in the afternoon, about an hour by sun, we came to the place where they intended, *viz.* an Indian town, called Wenimesset, northward of Quabaug. When we were come, Oh the number of pagans (now merciless enemies) that there came about me, that I may say as David, Psalm 27:13, "I had fainted, unless I had believed, etc." The next day was the sabbath. I then remembered how careless I had been of God's holy time, how many sabbaths I had lost and misspent, and how evilly I had walked in God's sight; which lay so close unto my spirit, that it was easy for me to see how righteous it was with God to cut off the thread of my life and cast me out of His presence for ever. Yet the Lord still showed mercy to me, and upheld me; and as He wounded me with one hand, so he healed me with the other. This day there came to me one Robert Pepper (a man belonging to Rox-

---

[1]Lincoln: "The second remove was to Princeton, Mass., near Mount Wachusett."

[1]Lincoln: "The third remove, February 12–27, ended at an Indian village, Menameset (Wenimesset), on the Ware River, in what is now New Braintree. Quabaug was Brookfield."

bury) who was taken in Captain Beers his fight,[2] and had been now a considerable time with the Indians; and up with them almost as far as Albany, to see king Philip, as he told me, and was now very lately come into these parts. Hearing, I say, that I was in this Indian town, he obtained leave to come and see me. He told me he himself was wounded in the leg at Captain Beers his fight; and was not able some time to go, but as they carried him, and as he took oaken leaves and laid to his wound, and through the blessing of God he was able to travel again. Then I took oaken leaves and laid to my side, and with the blessing of God it cured me also; yet before the cure was wrought, I may say, as it is in Psalm 38:5–6 "My wounds stink and are corrupt, I am troubled, I am bowed down greatly, I go mourning all the day long." I sat much alone with a poor wounded child in my lap, which moaned night and day, having nothing to revive the body, or cheer the spirits of her, but instead of that, sometimes one Indian would come and tell me one hour that "your master will knock your child in the head," and then a second, and then a third, "your master will quickly knock your child in the head."

This was the comfort I had from them, miserable comforters are ye all, as he[3] said. Thus nine days I sat upon my knees, with my babe in my lap, till my flesh was raw again; my child being even ready to depart this sorrowful world, they bade me carry it out to another wigwam (I suppose because they would not be troubled with such spectacles) whither I went with a very heavy heart, and down I sat with the picture of death in my lap. About two hours in the night, my sweet babe like a lamb departed this life on Feb. 18, 1675.[4] It being about six years, and five months old. It was nine days from the first wounding, in this miserable condition, without any refreshing of one nature or other, except a little cold water. I cannot but take notice how, at another time, I could not bear to be in the room where any dead person was, but now the case is changed; I must and could lie down by my dead babe, side by side all the night after. I have thought since of the wonderful goodness of God to me in preserving me in the use of my reason and senses in that distressed time, that I did not use wicked and violent means to end my own miserable life. In the morning, when they understood that my child was dead, they sent for me home to my master's wigwam (by my master in this writing, must be understood Quanopin,[5] who was a Sagamore, and married King Philip's wife's sister; not that he first took me, but I was sold to him by another Narraganset Indian, who took me when first I came out of the garrison). I went to take up my dead child in my arms to carry it with me, but they bid me let it alone; there was no resisting, but go I must and leave it. When I had been at my master's wigwam, I took the first opportunity I could get to go look after my dead child. When I came I asked them what they had done with it; then they told me it was upon the hill. Then they went and showed me where it was, where I saw the ground was newly digged, and there they told me they had buried it. There I left that child in the wilderness, and must commit it, and myself also in this wilderness-condition, to Him who is above all.

God having taken away this dear child, I went to see my daughter Mary, who was at this same Indian town, at a wigwam not very far off, though we had little liberty or opportunity to see one another. She was about ten years old, and taken from the door at first by a Praying Ind. and afterward sold for a gun. When I came in sight, she would fall aweeping; at which they were provoked, and would not let me come near her, but bade me be gone; which was a heart-cutting word to

[2]Lincoln: "Captain Beers, attempting to relieve the garrison of Northfield, [Mass.], was slain with most of his men, September 4, 1675."
[3]Job 16:2: "I have heard many such things: miserable comforters are ye all."
[4]1676, Gregorian Calendar.
[5]Quanopin, an Algonquin subordinate chief (Sagamore), had three squaws, one of whom was Weetamo; Mary Rowlandson was her servant.

me. I had one child dead, another in the wilderness, I knew not where, the third they would not let me come near to: "Me (as he said) have ye bereaved of my Children, Joseph is not, and Simeon is not, and ye will take Benjamin also, all these things are against me."[6] I could not sit still in this condition, but kept walking from one place to another. And as I was going along, my heart was even overwhelmed with the thoughts of my condition, and that I should have children, and a nation which I knew not, ruled over them. Whereupon I earnestly entreated the Lord, that He would consider my low estate, and show me a token for good, and if it were His blessed will, some sign and hope of some relief.

And indeed quickly the Lord answered, in some measure, my poor prayers; for as I was going up and down mourning and lamenting my condition, my son came to me, and asked me how I did. I had not seen him before, since the destruction of the town, and I knew not where he was, till I was informed by himself, that he was amongst a smaller parcel of Indians, whose place was about six miles off. With tears in his eyes, he asked me whether his sister Sarah was dead; and told me he had seen his sister Mary; and prayed me, that I would not be troubled in reference to himself. The occasion of his coming to see me at this time, was this: there was, as I said, about six miles from us, a small plantation of Indians, where it seems he had been during his captivity; and at this time, there were some forces of the Ind. gathered out of our company, and some also from them (among whom was my son's master) to go to assault and burn Medfield.[7] In this time of the absence of his master, his dame brought him to see me. I took this to be some gracious answer to my earnest and unfeigned desire.

The next day, *viz.* to this, the Indians returned from Medfield, all the company, for those that belonged to the other small company, came through the town that now we were at. But before they came to us, Oh! the outrageous roaring and whooping that there was. They began their din about a mile before they came to us. By their noise and whooping they signified how many they had destroyed (which was at that time twenty-three). Those that were with us at home were gathered together as soon as they heard the whooping, and every time that the other went over their number, these at home gave a shout, that the very earth rung again. And thus they continued till those that had been upon the expedition were come up to the Sagamore's wigwam; and then, Oh, the hideous insulting and triumphing that there was over some Englishmen's scalps that they had taken (as their manner is) and brought with them.

I cannot but take notice of the wonderful mercy of God to me in those afflictions, in sending me a Bible. One of the Indians that came from Medfield fight, had brought some plunder, came to me, and asked me, if I would have a Bible; he had got one in his basket. I was glad of it, and asked him, whether he thought the Indians would let me read? He answered, yes. So I took the Bible, and in that melancholy time, it came into my mind to read first the 28th Chap. of Deuteronomy,[8] which I did, and when I had read it, my dark heart wrought on this manner: that there was no mercy for me, that the blessings were gone, and the curses come in their room, and that I had lost my opportunity. But the Lord helped me still to go on reading till I came to Chap. 30, the seven first verses,[9] where I found, there was mercy promised again, if we would return to Him by repentance; and though we were scattered from one end of the earth to the other, yet

---

[6]Lincoln: "The lament of Jacob in Genesis 42:36."
[7]Lincoln: "The Medfield [Mass.] fight . . . occurred on February 21; fifty houses were burned."
[8]In Deuteronomy 28:1, Moses speaks to the Israelites: "If thou shalt hearken diligently unto the voice of the Lord thy God, to observe and to do all His commandments which I command thee this day . . . the Lord thy God will set thee on high above all nations of the earth." The chapter is largely devoted to the commandments and the blessings that will flow from obedience, the afflictions from disobedience.
[9]Deuteronomy 30:1–7: Promise is made that obedience to the Lord will bring an end to captivity, a return "into the land which thy fathers possessed," and "curses upon thine enemies, and on them that hate thee, which persecuted thee."

the Lord would gather us together, and turn all those curses upon our enemies. I do not desire to live to forget this Scripture, and what comfort it was to me.

Now the Ind. began to talk of removing from this place, some one way, and some another. There were now besides myself nine English captives in this place (all of them children, except one woman). I got an opportunity to go and take my leave of them. They being to go one way, and I another, I asked them whether they were earnest with God for deliverance. They told me they did as they were able, and it was some comfort to me, that the Lord stirred up children to look to Him. The woman, *viz.* goodwife[10] Joslin, told me she should never see me again, and that she could find in her heart to run away. I wished her not to run away by any means, for we were near thirty miles from any English town, and she very big with child, and had but one week to reckon, and another child in her arms, two years old, and bad rivers there were to go over, and we were feeble, with our poor and coarse entertainment. I had my Bible with me; I pulled it out, and asked her whether she would read. We opened the Bible and lighted on Psalm 27, in which Psalm we especially took notice of that, *ver. ult.,* "Wait on the Lord, Be of good courage, and he shall strengthen thine Heart, wait I say on the Lord."[11]

♠

The Fourth through the Twentieth and last "Removes" continue the account of the hunger, abuse, fear, cold, and anguish that Mary Rowlandson suffered in her captivity. At times her "master" (the Indian responsible for overseeing her) treated her well; at other times one of his three squaws hit or threatened her. Her skill with the needle often earned her some ground nuts or bear or horse meat in return for making a shirt for a papoose. Sometimes she was confronted with irrational threats, at other times inexplicable kindnesses from the Indians. Always she found succor and hope in reading the Bible she had been given. At last the negotiations for her release began with representatives from the governor. She was asked to specify what ransom her husband might pay. With some hesitation she suggested twenty pounds. And so it was agreed. But she remained in danger until actually gaining her freedom after almost twelve weeks of captivity. After relating her "Twentieth Remove," Rowlandson paused in her narrative to comment on some "remarkable passages of Providence" she had observed while being held hostage. Especially astonishing to her was the "strange providence of God . . . in turning things about when the Indian was at the highest, and the English at the lowest" during the continuing conflict known as King Philip's War.

♠

[A FEW REMARKABLE PASSAGES OF PROVIDENCE]

But before I go any further, I would take leave to mention a few remarkable passages of providence, which I took special notice of in my afflicted time.

1. Of the fair opportunity lost in the long march, a little after the fort-fight, when our English army was so numerous, and in pursuit of the enemy, and so near as to take several and destroy them, and the enemy in such distress for food that our men might track them by their rooting in the earth for ground-nuts, whilst they were flying for their lives. I say, that then our army should want provision, and be forced to leave their pursuit and return homeward; and the very

---

[10]Equivalent of *Mrs.,* mistress of the house.
[11]Psalm 27:14. *Ver. ult.:* "last verse" (Latin).

next week the enemy came upon our town, like bears bereft of their whelps, or so many ravenous wolves, rending us and our lambs to death. But what shall I say? God seemed to leave his people to themselves, and order all things for his own holy ends. "Shall there be evil in the City and the Lord hath not done it?"[1] "They are not grieved for the affliction of Joseph, therefore shall they go captive, with the first that go captive."[2] It is the Lord's doing, and it should be marvelous in our eyes.

2. I cannot but remember how the Indians derided the slowness and dullness of the English army in its setting out. For after the desolations at Lancaster and Medfield, as I went along with them, they asked me when I thought the English army would come after them? I told them I could not tell. "It may be they will come in May," said they. Thus did they scoff at us, as if the English would be a quarter of a year getting ready.

3. Which also I have hinted before, when the English army with new supplies were sent forth to pursue after the enemy, and they understanding it, fled before them till they came to Baquaug river, where they forthwith went over safely; that that river should be impassable to the English. I can but admire to see the wonderful providence of God in preserving the heathen for further affliction to our poor country. They could go in great numbers over, but the English must stop. God had an over-ruling hand in all those things.

4. It was thought, if their corn were cut down, they would starve and die with hunger, and all their corn that could be found, was destroyed, and they driven from that little they had in store, into the woods in the midst of winter; and yet how to admiration did the Lord preserve them for his holy ends, and the destruction of many still amongst the English! strangely did the Lord provide for them, that I did not see (all the time I was among them) one man, woman, or child, die with hunger.

Though many times they would eat that, that a hog or a dog would hardly touch; yet by that God strengthened them to be a scourge to his people.

The chief and commonest food was ground-nuts. They eat also nuts and acorns, artichokes, lilly roots, ground-beans, and several other weeds and roots, that I know not.

They would pick up old bones, and cut them to pieces at the joints, and if they were full of worms and maggots, they would scald them over the fire to make the vermine come out, and then boil them, and drink up the liquor, and then beat the great ends of them in a mortar, and so eat them. They would eat horse's guts, and ears, and all sorts of wild birds which they could catch; also bear, venison, beaver, tortoise, frogs, squirrels, dogs, skunks, rattlesnakes; yea, the very bark of trees; besides all sorts of creatures, and provision which they plundered from the English. I can but stand in admiration to see the wonderful power of God in providing for such a vast number of our enemies in the wilderness, where there was nothing to be seen, but from hand to mouth. Many times in a morning, the generality of them would eat up all they had, and yet, have some further supply against they wanted. It is said Psalm 81:13–14, "Oh, that my People had hearkened to me, and Israel had walked in my ways, I should soon have subdued their Enemies, and turned my hand against their Adversaries." But now our perverse and evil carriages in the sight of the Lord, have so offended Him, that instead of turning His hand against them, the Lord feeds and nourishes them up to be a scourge to the whole land.

5. Another thing that I would observe is the strange providence of God, in turning things about when the Indian was at the highest, and the English at the

---

[1] Amos 3:6.
[2] Amos 6:6–7.

lowest. I was with the enemy eleven weeks and five days, and not one week passed without the fury of the enemy, and some desolation by fire and sword upon one place or other. They mourned (with their black faces) for their own losses, yet triumphed and rejoiced in their inhumane, and many times devilish cruelty to the English. They would boast much of their victories; saying, that in two hours time they had destroyed such a captain and his company, at such a place; and such a captain and his company in such a place; and such a captain and his company in such a place; and boast how many towns they had destroyed, and then scoff, and say they had done them a good turn to send them to Heaven so soon. Again, they would say this summer that they would knock all the rogues in the head, or drive them into the sea, or make them fly the country; thinking surely, Agag-like, "The bitterness of Death is past."[3] Now the heathen begins to think all is their own, and the poor Christian's hopes to fail (as to man) and now their eyes are more to God, and their hearts sigh heaven-ward; and to say in good earnest, "Help Lord, or we perish." When the Lord had brought his people to this, that they saw no help in anything but Himself; then He takes the quarrel into His own hand; and though they had made a pit, in their own imaginations, as deep as hell for the Christians that summer, yet the Lord hurled themselves into it. And the Lord had not so many ways before to preserve them, but now He hath as many to destroy them.

[HOMECOMING AND REUNION]

But to return again to my going home, where we may see a remarkable change of providence. At first they were all against it, except my husband would come for me, but after they assented to it, and seemed much to rejoice in it; some asked me to send them some bread, others some tobacco, others shaking me by the hand, offering me a hood and scarf to ride in; not one moving hand or tongue against it. Thus hath the Lord answered my poor desire, and the many earnest requests of others put up unto God for me. In my travels an Indian came to me and told me, if I were willing, he and his squaw would run away, and go home along with me. I told him no: I was not willing to run away, but desired to wait God's time, that I might go home quietly, and without fear. And now God hath granted me my desire. O the wonderful power of God that I have seen, and the experience that I have had. I have been in the midst of those roaring lions, and savage bears, that feared neither God, nor man, nor the devil, by night and day, alone and in company, sleeping all sorts together, and yet not one of them ever offered me the least abuse of unchastity to me, in word or action. Though some are ready to say I speak it for my own credit; but I speak it in the presence of God, and to His Glory. God's power is as great now, and as sufficient to save, as when He preserved Daniel in the lion's den; or the three children in the fiery furnace.[1] I may well say as his Psalm 107:12, "Oh give thanks unto the Lord for he is good, for his mercy endureth for ever." Let the redeemed of the Lord say so, whom he hath redeemed from the hand of the enemy, especially that I should come away in the midst of so many hundreds of enemies quietly and peaceably, and not a dog moving his tongue.

So I took my leave of them, and in coming along my heart melted into tears, more than all the while I was with them, and I was almost swallowed up with the thoughts that ever I should go home again. About the sun going down, Mr. Hoar, and myself, and the two Indians came to Lancaster, and a solemn sight it was to

---

[3]1 Samuel 15:32: When Agag, ruler of the Alalekites, was captured by Saul, his life was spared and he who thought he was going to die learned he was to live. However, Samuel called for him and told him he was to die. Agag said, "Surely the bitterness of death is past."

[1]Shadrach, Meshach, and Abednego refused to worship the golden image and were cast into the fiery furnace, but they emerged unhurt (Daniel 3:12–30).

me. There had I lived many comfortable years amongst my relations and neighbors, and now not one Christian to be seen, or one house left standing. We went on to a farmhouse that was yet standing, where we lay all night, and a comfortable lodging we had, though nothing but straw to lie on. The Lord preserved us in safety that night, and raised us up again in the morning, and carried us along, that before noon, we came to Concord. Now was I full of joy, and yet not without sorrow: joy to see such a lovely sight, so many Christians together, and some of them my neighbors. There I met with my brother, and my brother-in-law, who asked me, if I knew where his wife was? Poor heart! he had helped to bury her, and knew it not. She being shot down by the house was partly burnt, so that those who were at Boston at the desolation of the town, and came back afterward, and buried the dead, did not know her. Yet I was not without sorrow, to think how many were looking and longing, and my own children amongst the rest, to enjoy that deliverance that I had now received, and I did not know whether ever I should see them again. Being recruited[2] with food and raiment we went to Boston that day, where I met with my dear husband, but the thoughts of our dear children, one being dead, and the other we could not tell where, abated our comfort each to other. I was not before so much hemmed in with the merciless and cruel heathen, but now as much with pitiful, tender-hearted and compassionate Christians. In that poor, and distressed, and beggarly condition I was received in, I was kindly entertained in several houses. So much love I received from several (some of whom I knew, and others I knew not) that I am not capable to declare it. . . .

["WHEN OTHERS ARE SLEEPING MINE EYES ARE WEEPING"]

I can remember the time when I used to sleep quietly without workings in my thoughts, whole nights together, but now it is other ways with me. When all are fast about me, and no eye open, but His who ever waketh, my thoughts are upon things past, upon the awful dispensation of the Lord towards us, upon His wonderful power and might, in carrying of us through so many difficulties, in returning us in safety, and suffering none to hurt us. I remember, in the night season, how the other day I was in the midst of thousands of enemies, and nothing but death before me. It is then hard work to persuade myself, that ever I should be satisfied with bread again. But now we are fed with the finest of the wheat, and, as I may say, with honey out of the rock.[1] Instead of the husk, we have the fatted calf.[2] The thoughts of these things in the particulars of them, and of the love and goodness of God towards us, make it true of me, what David said of himself, Psalm 6:6, "I watered my Couch with my tears." Oh! the wonderful power of God that mine eyes have seen, affording matter enough for my thoughts to run in, that when others are sleeping mine eyes are weeping.

I have seen the extreme vanity of this world: One hour I have been in health, and wealth, wanting nothing. But the next hour in sickness and wounds, and death, having nothing but sorrow and affliction.

Before I knew what affliction meant, I was ready sometimes to wish for it. When I lived in prosperity, having the comforts of the world about me, my relations by me, my heart cheerful, and taking little care for anything, and yet seeing many, whom I preferred before myself, under many trials and afflictions, in sickness, weakness, poverty, losses, crosses, and cares of the world, I should be sometimes jealous lest I should have my portion in this life, and that scripture would come to my mind, Hebrews 12:6, "For whom the Lord loveth he chasteneth, and

---

[2]Supplied.
[1]Psalm 81:16: "He should have fed them also with the finest of the wheat; and with honey out of the rock should I have satisfied thee."

[2]Luke 15:23: "And bring thither the fatted calf, and kill it: and let us eat, and be merry."

scourgeth every Son whom he receiveth." But now I see the Lord had His time to scourge and chasten me. The portion of some is to have their afflictions by drops, now one drop and then another; but the dregs of the cup, the wine of astonishment, like a sweeping rain that leaveth no food, did the Lord prepare to be my portion. Affliction I wanted, and affliction I had, full measure (I thought), pressed down and running over. Yet I see, when God calls a person to anything, and through never so many difficulties, yet He is fully able to carry them through and make them see, and say they have been gainers thereby. And I hope I can say in some measure, as David did, "It is good for me that I have been afflicted."[3] The Lord hath showed me the vanity of these outward things. That they are the vanity of vanities, and vexation of spirit, that they are but a shadow, a blast, a bubble, and things of no continuance. That we must rely on God Himself, and our whole dependence must be upon Him. If trouble from smaller matters begin to arise in me, I have something at hand to check myself with, and say, why am I troubled? It was but the other day that if I had had the world, I would have given it for my freedom, or to have been a servant to a Christian. I have learned to look beyond present and smaller troubles, and to be quieted under them. As Moses said, Exodus 14:13, "Stand still and see the salvation of the Lord."

Finis.

1682

SARAH KEMBLE KNIGHT
(1666–1727)

In 1704 when Madam Knight set out on horseback for New Haven, Connecticut (followed by a trip to New York), she was the object of considerable astonishment. Arriving at her first lodging place, she was met by a young lady who exclaimed excitedly: "Law for me—what in the world brings you here this time a night?—I never see a woman on the road so dreadful late, in all the days of my versal [whole] life. Who are you?"

Madam Knight's absence from Boston was to last for some six months, with about two weeks on the road. Ladies then did not travel alone; she solved the problem by joining existing mail routes (posts), or by hiring male travelling companions along the way to guide her through unfamiliar—and possibly dangerous—lands. There were woods to traverse, creeks to ford, mountainous terrain to cross; and there were dangers and discomforts at every turn. Food was generally terrible: unable to eat one malodorous dish, she went to bed hungry, recording in her journal that she paid sixpence for her dinner, "which was only a smell."

Sarah Kemble Knight was thirty-eight years old when she undertook the hazardous trip recorded so meticulously and wittily in her *Journal*. Little is known of her life before her 1704 journey. Tradition has it that her father, Thomas Kemble, "was put in the stocks for 'lewd and unseemly conduct' in kissing his wife on the Sabbath, when he met her at his door after an absence of three years." When Sarah was born in 1666, her merchant father had settled in Boston; her mother's father had settled in Charlestown in 1636. Be-

---

[3]Psalm 119:71.

fore her father died in 1689, Sarah Kemble married Captain Richard Knight, a shipmaster and widower much older than she. Nothing is known of Knight after 1706, but of Sarah Kemble Knight it is known that she signed official documents that indicate her employment as a court recorder. For a time she ran a "writing-school" said to have been attended by Benjamin Franklin and Richard Mather. Her title of "Madam" was apparently bestowed on her because of her paid legal activities and her management of business affairs.

One such business affair, the settlement of a relative's estate on behalf of her cousin's widow, Mrs. Caleb Trowbridge, occasioned her celebrated journey. Although her daily stints of travelling must have been exhausting, she found time to set down in her journal descriptions of characters she encountered, accounts of dangerous or funny incidents she experienced, and anecdotes she heard. Madam Knight had a sharp eye for significant detail, and, like a traveller in a foreign land, she constantly compared the customs and mores, the business and trade practices, the food and clothes, houses and buildings with what she knew in Boston.

It is likely that Madam Knight kept her journal in shorthand, but the original manuscript has been lost. A manuscript, "neatly copied into a small book," was published in 1825, some hundred years after Madam Knight's death. The publisher obtained it from a descendant of the person who had administered the estate of Madam Knight's only daughter. We may be grateful for its survival. Few accounts of the time even attempted to set down observations of daily life such as Madam Knight recorded in her *Journal.* Her book is a valuable record, but it is also a fascinating narrative of adventurous travel.

ADDITIONAL READING

Sidney Gunn, "Sarah Kemble Knight," *Dictionary of American Biography,* 1928–36; George P. Winship, "Introductory Note," *The Journal of Madam Knight,* 1935.

TEXT

The Journal of Madam Knight, ed. George P. Winship, 1920, 1935. Typography, punctuation, spelling, and usage have been changed to conform with contemporary English and modern printing practices.

from The Journal of Madam Knight

[BEGINNING THE JOURNEY]

Monday, October the Second, 1704

About three o'clock afternoon, I began my journey from Boston to New Haven, being about two hundred miles. My kinsman, Capt. Robert Luist, waited on me as far as Dedham, where I was to meet the western post.

I visited the Rev. Mr. Belcher, the minister of the town, and tarried there till evening in hopes the post would come along. But he not coming, I resolved to go to Billingses where he used to lodge, being 12 miles further. But being ignorant of the way, Madam Belcher, seeing no persuasions of her good spouse's or hers could prevail with me to lodge there that night, very kindly went with me to the tavern, where I hoped to get my guide, and desired the hostess to inquire of her guests whether any of them would go with me. But they, being tied by the lips to a pewter engine,[1] scarcely allowed themselves time to say what clownish. . . .

[Here half a page of the ms. is gone.]

. . . Pieces of eight, I told her no, I would not be accessary to such extortion.

"Then John shan't go," says she. "No, indeed shan't he"; and held forth at that rate a long time, that I began to fear I was got among the quaking tribe,[2] believing not a limber-tongued sister among them could outdo madam hostess.

Upon this, to my no small surprise, son John arose and gravely demanded what I would give him to go with me? "Give you," says I, "are you John?" "Yes," says he, for want of a better; and behold! this John looked as old as my host, and perhaps had been a man in the last century. "Well, Mr. John," says I, "make your demands." "Why, half a piece of eight and a dram,"[3] says John. I agreed, and gave him a dram (now) in hand to bind the bargain.

My hostess catechized[4] John for going so cheap, saying his poor wife would break her heart. . . .

[Here another half page of the Ms. is gone.]

. . . His shade on his horse resembled a globe on a gate post. His habit, horse, and furniture, its looks and going incomparably answered the rest.

Thus jogging on with an easy pace, my guide telling me it was dangerous to ride hard in the night (which his horse had the sense to avoid), he entertained me with the adventures he had passed by late riding, and eminent dangers he had escaped, so that, remembering the heroes in *Parismus* and *The Knight of the Oracle*,[5] I didn't know but I had met with a prince disguised.

When we had rid about an hour, we came into a thick swamp, which by reason of a great fog, very much startled me, it being now very dark. But nothing dismayed John: he had encountered a thousand and a thousand such swamps, having a universal knowledge in the woods; and readily answered all my inquiries, which were not a few.

In about an hour, or something more, after we left the swamp, we came to Billinges, where I was to lodge. My guide dismounted and very complacently helped me down and showed the door, signing to me with his hand to go in; which I gladly did—But had not gone many steps into the room, ere I was interrogated by a young lady I understood afterwards was the eldest daughter of the family, with these, or words to this purpose (*viz.*), "Law for me—what in the world brings you here at this time a night?—I never see a woman on the road so dreadful late, in all the days of my versal[6] life. Who are you? Where are you going? I'm scared out of my wits"—with much now of the same kind. I stood aghast, preparing to reply, when in comes my guide—to him madam turned, roaring out: "Lawful heart, John, is it you?—howdy do! Where in the world are you going with this woman? Who is she?" John made no answer but sat down in the corner, fumbled out his black junk,[7] and saluted that instead of Debb; she then turned again to me and fell anew into her silly questions, without asking me to sit down.

I told her she treated me very rudely, and I did not think it my duty to answer her unmannerly questions. But to get rid of them, I told her I came there to have the post's[8] company with me tomorrow on my journey, etc. Miss stared awhile, drew a chair, bid me sit, and then ran upstairs and put on two or three rings (or else I had not seen them before) and returning, set herself just before me, show-

---

[1]I.e., using pewter mugs for drinking.
[2]Quakers.
[3]A piece of eight was a Spanish silver dollar, worth eight reals; a dram was a small (shot-glass size) glass of whiskey or brandy.
[4]Questioned, scolded.
[5]The two romances are by Emanuel Ford (fl. 1607); *Parismus, the Renowned Prince of Bohemia* (1598) and *The Famous*

History of Montelion, Knight of the Oracle, Son to the True Mirror of Princes, the Most Renowned Persicles, King of Assyria (1633?).
[6]Variant of universal (entire).
[7]Tobacco twist resembling jute, or oakum (hemp fibers used in boats for calking).
[8]Messenger for the postal service.

ing the way to reding,[9] that I might see her ornaments, perhaps to gain more respect. But her grandma's new rung sow, had it appeared, would [have] affected me as much. I paid honest John with money and dram according to contract, and dismissed him, and prayed Miss to show me where I must lodge. She conducted me to a parlor in a little back leanto, which was almost filled with the bedstead, which was so high that I was forced to climb on a chair to get up to the wretched bed that lay on it; on which having stretched my tired limbs, and laid my head on a sad-colored pillow, I began to think on the transactions of the past day.

Tuesday, October the Third

About 8 in the morning, I with the post proceeded forward without observing anything remarkable; and about two, afternoon, arrived at the post's second stage, where the western post met him and exchanged letters. Here, having called for something to eat, the woman brought in a twisted thing like a cable, but something whiter; and laying it on the board, tugged for life to bring it into a capacity to spread; which having with great pains accomplished, she served in a dish of pork and cabbage, I suppose the remains of dinner. The sauce was of a deep purple, which I thought was boiled in her dye kettle; the bread was Indian and everything on the table service agreeable to these. I, being hungry, got a little down; but my stomach was soon cloyed, and what cabbage I swallowed served me for a cud the whole day after.

Having here discharged the ordinary[10] for self and guide (as I understood was the custom), about three, afternoon, went on with my third guide, who rode very hard; and having crossed Providence ferry, we came to a river which they generally ride through. But I dared not venture; so the post got a lad and canoe to carry me to t'other side, and he rid through and led my horse. The canoe was very small and shallow, so that when we were in, she seemed ready to take in water, which greatly terrified me, and caused me to be very circumspect, sitting with my hands fast on each side, my eyes steady, not daring so much as to lodge my tongue a hair's breadth more on one side of my mouth than t'other nor so much as think on Lot's wife,[11] for a wry thought would have overset our wherry;[12] but was soon put out of this pain, by feeling the canoe on shore, which I as soon almost saluted with my feet; and rewarding my sculler, again mounted and made the best of our way forwards. The road here was very even and the day pleasant, it being now near sunset. But the post told me we had near 14 miles to ride to the next stage (where we were to lodge). I asked him of the rest of the road, foreseeing we must travel in the night. He told me there was a bad river we were to ride through, which was so very fierce a horse could sometimes hardly stem it: but it was but narrow, and we should soon be over. I cannot express the concern of mind this relation set me in: no thoughts but those of the dangerous river could entertain my imagination, and they were as formidable as various, still tormenting me with blackest ideas of my approaching fate—sometimes seeing myself drowning, otherwhiles drowned, and at the best, like a holy sister just come out of a spiritual bath in dripping garments.

Now was the glorious luminary, with his swift coursers arrived at his stage,[13] leaving poor me with the rest of this part of the lower world in darkness, with which we were soon surrounded. The only glimmering we now had was from the spangled skies, whose imperfect reflections rendered every object formidable. Each lifeless trunk, with its shattered limbs, appeared an armed enemy; and every little stump like a ravenous devourer. Nor could I so much as discern my guide, when at any distance, which added to the terror.

---

[9]Making a display of oneself (colloquial).
[10]Paid for the meal (*ordinary* was a set meal for all).
[11]In fleeing the destruction of Sodom, Lot's wife looked back and was turned into a pillar of salt (Genesis 19:26).

[12]Small boat (canoe).
[13]Night had fallen. In Greek mythology, Apollo (sun god) drives across the sky in his chariot drawn by his horses, or coursers.

Thus, absolutely lost in thought, and dying with the very thoughts of drowning, I came up with the post, who I did not see 'til even with his horse: he told me he stopped for me; and we rode on very deliberately a few paces, when we entered a thicket of trees and shrubs, and I perceived by the horse's going, we were on the descent of a hill, which, as we came nearer the bottom, 'twas totally dark with the trees that surrounded it. But I knew by the going of the horse we had entered the water, which my guide told me was the hazardous river he had told me of; and he, riding up close to my side, bid me not fear—we should be over immediately. I now rallied all the courage I was mistress of, knowing that I must either venture my fate of drowning, or be left like the children in the wood.[14] So, as the post bid me, I gave reins to my nag; and sitting as steady as just before in the canoe, in a few minutes got safe to the other side, which he told me was the Narragansett country.

Here we found great difficulty in traveling, the way being very narrow, and on each side the trees and bushes gave us very unpleasant welcomes with their branches and boughs, which we could not avoid, it being so exceeding dark. My guide, as before so now, put on harder than I, with my weary bones, could follow; so left me and the way behind him. Now returned my distressed apprehensions of the place where I was: the dolesome woods, my company next to none, going I knew not whither, and encompassed with terrifying darkness; the least of which was enough to startle a more masculine courage. Added to which the reflections, as in the afternoon of the day that my call[15] was very questionable, which, til then I had not so prudently as I ought considered. Now, coming to the foot of a hill, I found great difficulty in ascending; but being got to the top, was there amply recompensed with the friendly appearance of the kind conductress of the night, just then advancing above the horizontal line. The raptures which the sight of that fair planet produced in me, caused me, for the moment, to forget my present weariness and past toils; and inspired me for most of the remaining way with very diverting thoughts, some of which, with other occurrences of the day, I reserved to note down when I should come to my stage. My thoughts on the sight of the moon were to this purpose:

> Fair Cynthia,[16] all the homage that I may
> Unto a creature, unto thee I pay;
> In lonesome woods to meet so kind a guide,
> To me's more worth than all the world beside.
> Some joy I felt just now, when safe got o'er
> Yon surly river to this rugged shore,
> Deeming rough welcomes from these clownish trees
> Better than lodgings with Nereides.[17]
> Yet swelling fears surprise; all dark appears—
> Nothing but light can dissipate those fears.
> My fainting vitals can't lend strength to say,
> But softly whisper, O I wish 'twere day.
> The murmur hardly warmed the ambient air,
> E're thy bright aspect rescues from despair:
> Makes the old hag[18] her sable mantle loose,
> And a bright joy does through my soul diffuse.
> The boisterous trees now lend a passage free,
> And pleasant prospects thou giv'st light to see.

---

[14]Like the "babes in the wood" in the ballad: they are to be killed, but instead are abandoned overnight in the woods, where they die.
[15]Purpose for the trip.
[16]The moon; surname of Artemis or Diana, goddess of the moon in Greek and Roman mythology, who was born on Mount Cynthus.
[17]Sea nymphs, the fifty daughters of Nereus, old man of the sea in Greek mythology.
[18]Night.

From hence we kept on, with more ease than before: the way being smooth and even, the night warm and serene, and the tall and thick trees at a distance, especially when the moon glared light through the branches, filled my imagination with the pleasant delusion of a sumptuous city, filled with famous buildings and churches, with their spiring steeples, balconies, galleries and I know not what: grandeurs which I had heard of, and which the stories of foreign countries had given me the idea of.

> Here stood a lofty church—there is a steeple,
> And there the grand parade—O see the people!
> That famous castle there, were I but nigh,
> To see the mote and bridge and walls so high—
> They're very fine! says my deluded eye.

Being thus agreeably entertained without a thought of anything but thoughts themselves, I on a sudden was roused from these pleasing imaginations by the post's sounding his horn, which assured me he was arrived at the stage where we were to lodge; and that music was then most musical and agreeable to me.

Being come to Mr. Havens', I was very civilly received, and courteously entertained, in a clean comfortable house; and the good woman was very active in helping off my riding clothes, and then asked what I would eat. I told her I had some chocolate, if she would prepare it; which with the help of some milk, and a little clean brass kettle, she soon effected to my satisfaction. I then betook me to my apartment, which was a little room parted from the kitchen by a single board partition; where, after I had noted the occurrences of the past day, I went to bed, which, though pretty hard, yet neat and handsome. But I could get no sleep, because of the clamor of some of the town topers in next room, who were entered into a strong debate concerning the signification of the name of their country (*viz.*), *Narragansett*. One said it was named so by the Indians, because there grew a brier there, of a prodigious height and bigness, the like hardly ever known, called by the Indians narragansett; and quotes an Indian of so barbarous a name for his author, that I could not write it. His antagonist replied no—it was from a spring it had its name, which he well knew where it was, which was extreme cold in summer, and as hot as could be imagined in the winter, which was much resorted to by the natives, and by them called Narragansett (hot and cold), and that was the original of their place's name—with a thousand impertinances not worth notice, which he uttered with such a roaring voice and thundering blows with the fist of wickedness on the table, that it pierced my very head. I heartily fretted, and wished 'um tonguetied; but with as little success as a friend of mine once, who was (as she said) kept a whole night awake, on a journey, by a country left. and a sergeant, ensign[19] and a deacon, contriving how to bring a triangle into a square. They kept calling for t'other gill,[20] which while they were swallowing, was some intermission; but presently, like oil to fire, increased the flame. I set my candle on a chest by the bedside, and setting up, fell to my old way of composing my resentments, in the following manner:

> I ask thy aid, O potent rum!
> To charm these wrangling topers dumb.
> Thou hast their giddy brains possessed—
> The man confounded with the beast—
> And I, poor I, can get no rest.
> Intoxicate them with thy fumes:
> O still their tongues' til morning comes!

---

[19]Military ranks: left., lieutenant; ensign, lowest ranking commissioned officer.

[20]Originally, the name of the vessel that measured wine; a gill is a measure of liquid equal to a quarter pint.

And I know not but my wishes took effect; for the dispute soon ended with t'other dram; and so good night!

[LIFE IN CONNECTICUT]

Friday, October the Sixth

I got up very early, in order to hire somebody to go with me to New Haven, being in great perplexity at the thoughts of proceeding alone; which my most hospitable entertainer observing himself went, and soon returned with a young gentleman of the town, who he could confide in to go with me; and about eight this morning, with Mr. Joshua Wheeler my new guide, taking leave of this worthy gentleman, we advanced on towards Seabrook. The roads all along this way are very bad, encumbered with rocks and mountainous passages, which were very disagreeable to my tired carcass; but we went on with a moderate pace which made the journey more pleasant. But after about eight miles riding, in going over a bridge under which the river ran very swift, my horse stumbled, and very narrowly escaped falling over into the water; which extremely frightened me. But through God's goodness I met with no harm, and mounting again, in about half a mile's riding, came to an ordinary,[1] were well entertained by a woman of about seventy and vantage,[2] but of as sound intellectuals as one of seventeen. She entertained Mr. Wheeler with some passages of a wedding awhile ago at a place hard by, the bride's-groom being about her age or something above, saying his children was dreadfully against their father's marrying, which she condemned them extremely for.

From hence we went pretty briskly forward, and arrived at Saybrook ferry about two of the clock afternoon; and crossing it, we called at an inn to bait[3] (foreseeing we should not have such another opportunity 'til we come to Killingsworth). Landlady came in, with her hair about her ears, and hands at full pay[4] scratching. She told us she had some mutton which she would broil, which I was glad to hear; but I suppose forgot to wash her scratches; in a little time she brought it in; but it being pickled, and my guide said it smelled strong of head sause,[5] we left it, and paid sixpence a piece for our dinners, which was only smell.

So we put forward with all speed, and about seven at night came to Killingsworth, and were tolerably well with travelers' fare, and lodged there that night.

Saturday, October the Seventh

We set out early in the morning, and being something unacquainted with the way, having asked it of some we met, they told us we must ride a mile or two and turn down a lane on the right hand; and by their direction we rode on but not yet coming to the turning, we met a young fellow and asked him how far it was to the lane which turned down towards Guilford. He said we must ride a little further, and turn down by the corner of Uncle Sam's lot. My guide vented his spleen at the lubber;[6] and we soon came into the road, and keeping still on, without anything further remarkable, about two a clock afternoon we arrived at New Haven, where I was received with all possible respects and civility. Here I discharged Mr. Wheeler with a reward to his satisfaction, and took some time to rest after so long and toilsome a journey; and informed myself of the manners and customs of the place, and at the same time employed myself in the affair I went there upon.

They are governed by the same laws as we in Boston (or little differing) thr'out this whole Colony of Connecticut, and much the same way of church government, and many of them good, sociable people, and I hope religious too; but a little too

---

[1] Hotel or inn, serving meals.
[2] More.
[3] Take refreshments and let the horses rest.
[4] At full speed.

[5] Variant of *head souse*, or head cheese, loaf of jellied, seasoned meat.
[6] Slow, clumsy person.

much independent in their principles; and, as I have been told, were formerly in their zeal very rigid in their administration towards such as their laws made offenders, even to a harmless kiss or innocent merriment among young people; whipping being a frequent and counted an easy punishment, about which other crimes, the judges were absolute in their sentences.

• • • • •

Their diversions in this part of the country are on lecture days and training days[7] mostly; on the former there is riding from town to town.

And on training days the youth divert themselves by shooting at the target, as they call it (but it very much resembles a pillory) where he that hits nearest the white has some yards of red ribbon presented him which, being tied to his hatband, the two ends streaming down his back, he is led away in triumph, with great applause, as the winners of the Olympic games. They generally marry very young; the males oftener as I am told under twenty than above; they generally make public weddings, and have a way something singular (as they say) in some of them, *viz.* Just before joining hands the bridegroom quits the place, who is soon followed by the bridesmen, and as it were, dragged back to duty—being the reverse to the former practice among us, to steal Miss Pride.[8]

• • • • •

There are everywhere, in the towns as I passed, a number of Indians, the natives of the country, and are the most savage of all the savages of that kind that I had ever seen: little or no care taken (as I heard upon inquiry) to make them otherwise. They have in some places lands of their own, and governed by laws of their own making;—they marry many wives and at pleasure put them away, and on the least dislike or fickle humor, on either side, saying "Stand away" to one another is a sufficient divorce. And indeed those uncomely "Stand aways" are too much in vogue among the English in this (indulgent colony) as their records plentifully prove, and that on very trivial matters, of which some have been told me, but are not proper to be related by a female pen, tho some of that foolish sex have had too large a share in the story.

If the natives commit any crime on their own precincts among themselves, the English takes no cognizance of. But if on the English ground, they are punishable by our laws. They mourn for their dead by blacking their faces, and cutting their hair, after an awkward and frightful manner; but can't bear you should mention the names of their dead relations to them. They trade most for rum, for which they'd hazard their very lives; and the English fit them generally as well, by seasoning it plentifully with water.

They give the title of merchant to every trader, who rate their goods according to the time and specie they pay in: *viz.* Pay, money, pay as money, and trusting. *Pay* is grain, pork, beef, etc., at the prices set by the General Court that year; *money* is pieces of eight, riyals,[9] or Boston or Bay shillings (as they call them) or good hard money, as sometimes silver coin is termed by them; also wampum, *viz.* Indian beads which serves for change. *Pay as money* is provisions, as aforesaid, one third cheaper than as the Assembly or General Court sets it; and *Trust* as they and the merchant agree for time.

Now, when the buyer comes to ask for a commodity, sometimes before the merchant answers that he has it, he says, "is your pay ready?" Perhaps the chap replies, "Yes"; "What do you pay in?" says the merchant. The buyer having answered, then the price is set; as suppose he wants a sixpenny knife, in pay it is

---

[7]On lecture days the minister would explicate the bible; training days, mandatory military training exercises.

[8]I.e., the bride.

[9]Spanish reals, or coins.

12d—in pay as money eight pence, and hard money its own price, *viz.* 6d. It seems a very intricate way of trade and what *Lex Mercatoria*[10] had not thought of.

Being at a merchant's house, in comes a tall country fellow, with his alfogeos[11] full of tobacco; for they seldom lose their cud, but keep chewing and spitting as long as their eyes are open,—he advanced to the middle of the room, made an awkward nod, and spitting a large deal of aromatic tincture, he gave a scrape with his shovel-like shoe, leaving a small shovelful of dirt on the floor, made a full stop, hugging his own pretty body with his hands under his arms, stood staring 'round him, like a cat let out of a basket. At last, like the creature Balaam rode on,[12] he opened his mouth and said: "have you any ribbon for hatbands to sell, I pray?" The questions and answers about the pay being past, the ribbon is bro't and opened. Bumpkin simpers, cries "it's confounded gay I vow"; and beckoning to the door, in comes Joan Tawdry, dropping about 50 curtsies, and stands by him; he shows her the ribbon. "Law you," says she, "it's right gent, do you, take it, 'tis dreadful pretty." Then she enquires, "have you any hood silk, I pray?" which being brought and bought, "Have you any thread to sew it with," says she, which being accommodated with, they departed. They generally stand after they come in a great while speechless, and sometimes don't say a word till they are asked what they want, which I impute to the awe they stand in of the merchants, who they are constantly almost indebted to; and must take what they bring without liberty to choose for themselves; but they serve them as well, making the merchants stay long enough for their pay.

We may observe here the great necessity and benefit both of education and conversation; for these people have as large a portion of mother wit, and sometimes larger, than those who have been brought up in cities; but for want of improvements, render themselves almost ridiculous, as above. I should be glad if they would leave such follies, and am sure all that love clean houses (at least) would be glad on't too.

They are generally very plain in their dress, throughout all the Colony, as I saw, and follow one another in their modes; that you may know where they belong, especially the women, meet them where you will.

Their chief red letter day[13] is St. Election, which is annually observed according to charter, to choose their government: a blessing they can never be thankful enough for, as they will find, if ever it be their hard fortune to lose it.[14] The present governor in Connecticut is the Honorable John Winthrop, Esq.: a gentleman of an ancient and honorable family, whose father was governor here sometime before, and his grandfather had been governor of Massachusetts. This gentleman is a very courteous and affable person, much given to hospitality, and has by his good services gained the affection of the people as much as any who had been before him in that post.

[THE CITY OF NEW YORK]

December the Sixth

Being by this time well recruited[1] and rested after my journey, my business lying unfinished by some concerns at New York depending thereupon, my kinsman, Mr. Thomas Trowbridge of New Haven, must needs take a journey there before it could be accomplished, I resolved to go there in company with him, and a man of the town which I engaged to wait on me there. Accordingly, Dec. 6th we set out from New Haven. . . .

---

[10]Merchant law.
[11]Cheeks: cf. Spanish *alforjas*, saddle bags.
[12]The ass, which God caused to speak to Balaam, deterring him from delivering a curse on the Israelites (Numbers 22:28ff).

[13]Holiday.
[14]Reference to Massachusetts being governed at the time by appointees of the British Crown.
[1]Renewed, resupplied.

The city of New York is a pleasant, well-compacted place, situated on a commodious river which is a fine harbor for shipping. The buildings brick generally, very stately and high, though not altogether like ours in Boston. The bricks in some of the houses are of divers colors and laid in checkers, being glazed look very agreeable. The insides of them are neat to admiration, the wooden work, for only the walls are plastered, and the sumers and gist[2] are plained and kept very white scowered as so is all the partitions if made of boards. The fireplaces have no jambs (as ours have) but the backs run flush with the walls, and the hearth is of tiles and is as far out into the room at the ends as before the fire, which is generally five foot in the lower rooms, and the piece over where the mantle tree should be is made as ours with joiners' work,[3] and as I suppose is fastened to iron rods inside. The house where the vendue[4] was had chimney corners like ours, and they and the hearths were laid with the finest tile that I ever see, and the staircases laid all with white tile which is ever clean, and so are the walls of the kitchen which had a brick floor. They were making great preparations to receive their governor, Lord Cornbury from the Jerseys,[5] and for that end raised the militia to guard him on shore to the fort.

They are generally of the Church of England and have a New England gentleman for their minister, and a very fine church set out with all customary requisites. There are also a Dutch and divers conventicles as they call them, *viz.* Baptist, Quakers, &c. They are not strict in keeping the sabbath as in Boston and other places where I had been, but seem to deal with great exactness as far as I see or deal with. They are sociable to one another and courteous and civil to strangers and fare well in their houses. The English go very fashionable in their dress. But the Dutch, especially the middling sort, differ from our women, in their habit go loose, wear French muchets which are like a cap and a headband in one, leaving their ears bare, which are set out with jewels of a large size and many in number. And their fingers hooped with rings, some with large stones in them of many colors as were their pendants in their ears, which you should see very old women wear as well as young.

They have vendues very frequently and make their earnings very well by them, for they treat with good liquor liberally, and the customers drink as liberally and generally pay for't as well, by paying for that which they bid up briskly for, after the sack[6] has gone plentifully about, though sometimes good penny worths are got there. Their diversions in the winter is riding sleighs about three or four miles out of town, where they have houses of entertainment at a place called the Bowery, and some go to friends' houses who handsomely treat them. Mr. Burroughs carried his spouse and daughter and myself out to one Madame Dowes, a gentlewoman that lived at a farm house, who gave us a handsome entertainment of five or six dishes and choice beer and metheglin,[7] cider, &c. all which she said was the produce of her farm. I believe we met 50 or 60 sleighs that day—they fly with great swiftness and some are so furious that they'll turn out of the path for none except a loaden cart. Nor do they spare for any diversion the place affords, and sociable to a degree, their tables being as free to their neighbors as to themselves.

Having here transacted the affair I went upon and some other that fell in the way, after about a fortnight's stay there I left New York with no little regret.

. . . . .

---

[2]Beams and joists.
[3]Craft of high-level carpenter, or joiner, who does the finishing or painstaking interior woodwork of houses and buildings.
[4]Public auction.

[5]Royal Governor of New York and New Jersey, Edward Hyde (1661–1723).
[6]Dry white wine, often imported at this time from Spain and the Canary Islands.
[7]Alcoholic liquor made from fermented honey.

[OBSERVATIONS ON TOWNS BETWEEN NEW YORK AND NEW HAVEN]

Saturday, December Twenty-third

. . . Having rid thro a difficult river we come to Fairfield where we baited and were much refreshed as well with the good things which gratified our appetites as the time took to rest our wearied limbs, which latter I employed in enquiring concerning the town and manners of the people, &c. This is a considerable town, and filled as they say with wealthy people—have a spacious meeting house and good buildings. But the inhabitants are litigious, nor do they well agree with their minister, who (they say) is a very worthy gentleman.

They have abundance of sheep, whose very dung brings them great gain, with part of which they pay their parson's salary. And they grudge that, preferring their dung before their minister. They let out their sheep at so much they agree upon for a night; the highest bidder always carries them. And they will sufficiently dung a large quantity of land before morning, but were once bit by a sharper who had them a night and sheared them all before morning. . . .

Being got to Milford, it being late in the night, I could go no further; my fellow traveler going forward, I was invited to lodge at Mrs. _____ , a very kind and civil gentlewoman, by whom I was handsomely and kindly entertained till the next night. The people here go very plain in their apparel (more plain than I had observed in the towns I had passed) and seem to be very grave and serious. They told me there was a singing Quaker lived there, or at least had a strong inclination to be so, his spouse not at all affected that way. Some of the singing crew come there one day to visit him, who being then abroad, they sat down (to the woman's no small vexation) humming and singing and groaning after their conjuring way—says the woman, "Are you singing Quakers?" "Yea," says they—"Then take my squalling brat of a child here and sing to it," says she, "for I have almost split my throat with singing to him and can't get the rogue to sleep." They took this as a great indignation, and mediately departed. Shaking the dust from their heels, left the good woman and her child among the number of the wicked.

This is a seaport place and accommodated with a good harbor, but I had not opportunity to make particular observations because it was Sabbath day—This evening,

December 24,

I set out with the gentlewoman's son who she very civilly offered to go with me when she see no persuasions would cause me to stay which she pressingly desired, and, crossing a ferry having but nine miles to New Haven in a short time arrived there and was kindly received and well accommodated amongst my friends and relations. . . .

[RETURN TO BOSTON]

January the Sixth [1705]

Being now well recruited and fit for business I discoursed[1] the persons I was concerned with, that we might finish in order to my return to Boston. They delayed as they had hitherto done hoping to tire my patience. But I was resolute to stay and see an end of the matter let it be never so much to my disadvantage—So January 9th they come again and promise the Wednesday following to go through with the distribution of the estate which they delayed till Thursday and then came

---

[1]Told.

with new amusements.[2] But at length by the mediation of that holy good gentleman, the Rev. Mr. James Pierpont, the minister of New Haven, and with the advice and assistance of other our good friends we come to an accommodation and distribution, which having finished though not 'til February, the man that waited on me to York taking the charge of me I set out for Boston. We went from New Haven upon the ice (the ferry being not passable thereby) and the Rev. Mr. Pierpont with Madam Prout, cousin Trowbridge and divers others were taking leave, we went onward without anything remarkable till we come to New London and lodged again at Mr. Saltonstalls—and here I dismissed my guide, and my generous entertainer provided me Mr. Samuel Rogers of that place to go home with me—I stayed a day here longer than I intended by the commands of the honorable Governor Winthrop to stay and take a supper with him whose wonderful civility I may not omit. The next morning I crossed the ferry to Groton, having had the honor of the company of Madam Livingston (who is the governor's daughter) and Mary Christophers and divers others to the boat—and that night lodged at Stonington and had roast beef and pumpkin sauce for supper. The next night at Haven's and had roast fowl, and the next day we come to a river which by reason of the freshets coming down was swelled so high we feared it impassable and the rapid stream was very terrifying—However we must over and that in a small canoe. Mr. Rogers assuring me of his good conduct,[3] I after a stay of near an hour on the shore for consultation, went into the canoe, and Mr. Rogers paddled about 100 yards up the creek by the shore side, turned into the swift stream and dexterously steering her in a moment we come to the other side as swiftly passing as an arrow shot out of the bow by a strong arm. I stayed on the shore till he returned to fetch our horses, which he caused to swim over, himself bringing the furniture in the canoe. But it is past my skill to express the exceeding fright all their transactions formed in me. We were now in the colony of the Massachusetts and taking lodgings at the first inn we come to, had a pretty difficult passage the next day which was the second of March by reason of the sloughy[4] ways then thawed by the sun. Here I met Capt. John Richards of Boston who was going home, so being very glad of his company we rode something harder than hitherto, and missing my way in going up a very steep hill, my horse dropped down under me as dead; this new surprise no little hurt me, meeting it just at the entrance into Dedham from whence we intended to reach home that night. But was now obliged to get another horse there and leave my own, resolving for Boston that night if possible. But in going over the causeway at Dedham the Bridge being overflowed by the high waters coming down, I very narrowly escaped falling over into the river horse and all which 'twas almost a miracle I did not—now it grew late in the afternoon and the people having very much discouraged us about the sloughy way which they said we should find very difficult and hazardous, it so wrought on me being tired and dispirited and disappointed of my desires of going home, that I agreed to lodge there that night which we did at the house of one Draper, and the next day being March 3d we got safe home to Boston, where I found my aged and tender mother and my dear and only child in good health with open arms ready to receive me, and my kind relations and friends flocking in to welcome me and hear the story of my transactions and travels, I having this day been five months from home and now I cannot fully express my joy and satisfaction. But desire sincerely to adore my great Benefactor for thus graciously carrying forth and returning in safety his unworthy handmaid.

1704–05   *1825*

---

[2]Trivial matters causing delays.
[3]Safe handling (of the boat).
[4]Miry, boggy, muddy.

EMINENT PHILOSOPHERS AND DIVINES

(1663–1728)

Cotton Mather   Jonathan Edwards

Cotton Mather and Jonathan Edwards share the honor of being the most eminent American intellectuals and philosophers of their time. But they also share the tragedy of being not ahead of but behind their time, taking on the task of defending dogmas and doctrines central to the minds of the Puritan founding fathers but fading fast in the consciousness of succeeding generations. They may be thought of as the last of the pure Puritans. Mather found his authority in Biblical quotation; Edwards found his in reason and logic. For all that they share in belief, they differ radically in method and style of argument.

COTTON MATHER
(1663–1728)

Cotton Mather entered Harvard in 1674 when he was eleven, the youngest student ever admitted. Entrance requirements included a working knowledge of Latin and Greek. Clearly Cotton Mather was learned and brilliant, but he had one serious flaw: he stuttered. Such a flaw was a calamity for one setting out for the ministry. It was, moreover, the kind of defect that draws cruel and mirthful attention of one's fellow students. Increase Mather was concerned about his son "lest the hesitancy in his speech should make him uncapable of improvement in the work of the ministry, whereunto I had designed him." The father called his wife and the son into his study in October 1674, and with "many tears bewailed our sinfulness, and begged of God mercy in this particular."

As the maturing Cotton Mather struggled to overcome his "impediment," it was natural, given his religious environment, that he would attribute its cause to "his early wickedness and filthiness" that had "provoked" God. With a strong sense of guilt, he prayed: "Lord, I deserve, not only a stammering slowness, but also a total dumbness in my speech." Mather was gradually able to overcome his stutter sufficiently to become a successful preacher, but it appears likely that the causes of the one defect shaped other elements of his personality that remained permanent: his frequent expressions of humility belied by arrogant behavior, an erudition clearly impressive but often flaunted, a prose style sometimes embedded with so many obscure allusions and foreign quotations as to suggest a wall erected between writer and reader.

It is no wonder that Cotton Mather stammered. He lived his entire life under the shadow of his dominating forebears. His two grandfathers, Richard Mather and John Cotton, had been founders and leaders of the Massachusetts Bay Colony—both Moses-like figures bound to intimidate any child, however much a prodigy. Cotton Mather's father Increase spent sixteen hours a day in his study, writing and memorizing his sermons; he too partook of the eminence of that founding generation. Moreover, when the son began his career, he was ordained in the Old North Church, Boston, where his father was minister, and thus from 1685 until his father's death in 1723 he labored under the stern eyes and commanding presence of his father.

Mather no doubt felt the weight of a great responsibility to continue what his ancestry had begun in the founding of the New Canaan, the promised land of the New World. He had inherited their beliefs and their zeal. But he was not living in their time. The signs of change appeared at every turn. Religious consciousness and concerns were being replaced by a new passion for commerce, trade, and mercantile interests, and there was increasing unwillingness to tolerate church control of the state and the people in nonreligious and private affairs.

Mather labored mightily to shore up a weakening theocracy and bore witness to his own failure. He wrote ceaselessly, perhaps in part because of the lingering humiliation of his early stutter, but most certainly in an attempt to bolster the crumbling foundations of Puritan belief and dominance. The result was over 450 works. Most are tinged with a melancholy awareness that Mather's generation had markedly declined in morality, religious faith, and missionary zeal, thus betraying the dazzling vision of the New Jerusalem that had beckoned the founding fathers to the New World.

Mather's personal life was also beset by tragedy. His first wife died in 1702 after sixteen years of marriage. He remarried in 1703 and this second wife died in 1713 after ten years of marriage. He married a third time in 1715, and became aware in 1718 that this wife suffered periods of insanity. He had in all fifteen children; nine did not survive infancy. Only two survived him. His son Increase ("Creasy") fell in with a bad lot and his scandalous behavior became another cross for the father to bear. It is no wonder that Cotton Mather devoted much time to fasting, praying, and keeping vigils.

Magnalia Christi Americana (*The Great Works of Christ in America*, 1702) was Mather's most ambitious work. Its two large volumes of history, biography, accounts of "remarkable providences," etc., is suffused with the epic intent announced at the beginning: "I write the wonders of the Christian religion, flying from the deprivations of Europe, to the American strand. . . ." The work is a monument erected to Mather's antecedents, the founding generation.

Mather wrote *Wonders of the Inivisible World* (1693) at the request of the judges at the witchcraft trials in Salem in 1692, at which nineteen of the accused were hanged. Mather did not participate in the trials, and he warned against too heavy a reliance on spectral evidence. But his forceful writing expressing his belief in witches as possessed by Satan and placed in his hellish service did nothing to diminish the hysteria that led to the executions. The book contains some of Mather's liveliest and most fascinating passages.

Two other of Mather's books have remained in print since his death. *Bonifacius: An Essay Upon the Good*, popularly known as *Essays to Do Good*, was especially admired by Benjamin Franklin (influencing his *Dogood Papers*). And *Manuductio ad Ministerium* (*Directions for a Candidate of the Ministry*, 1726) was Mather's last important work, a kind of manual for beginning ministers, surprisingly readable, tolerant, and practical. Its passage on style has been widely reprinted.

Mather's private library was the pride of New England. When he married Elizabeth, his second wife, in 1703, he owned between 2,000 to 3,000 volumes. He continued to add books through purchase and inheritance. His son Samuel estimated the collection (no doubt including Increase Mather's library) at a total of between 7,000 and 8,000 volumes, plus a large number of manuscripts. The only library comparable in the American colonies belonged to Virginia's William Byrd and numbered about 4,000 at his death in 1744. Mather was elected to the Royal Society of London in 1713, an honor he shared with Byrd.

The *Diary of Cotton Mather*, edited in two volumes by Worthington C. Ford (1911–12; rpt. 1926, 1957), reveals a man beset by contradictions—feelings of shame, but expressions of arrogance; superstitions about inexplicable marvels, yet intense interest in the advancement of science (as in his support of the smallpox vaccination); protestations of unworthiness and humility, yet manifestations of an inordinate pride. In other words, Cotton Mather was thoroughly human, and although he failed to preserve the Puritan theocracy, he helped to create that melancholy American sense of regret at the loss of a founding dream, the disappearance of a shining possibility in the rapidly receding past.

ADDITIONAL READING

Selections from Cotton Mather, ed. Kenneth Murdock, 1926, 1960; *Magnalia Christi Americana, Books I and II*, ed. Kenneth Murdock, 1977; *Selected Letters of Cotton Mather*, ed. Kenneth Silverman, 1971.

Barrett Wendell, *Cotton Mather: The Puritan Priest*, 1891, 1926, 1963; Robert Middlekauff, *The Mathers: Three Generations of Puritan Intellectuals*, 1971; Sacvan Bercovitch, "Cotton Mather," *Major Writers of Early American Literature*, ed. Everett Emerson, 1972; Sacvan Bercovitch, *The Puritan Origins of the American Self*, 1975; David Levin, *Cotton Mather: The Young Life of the Lord's Remembrancer*, 1978; Babette M. Levy, *Cotton Mather*, 1979; Kenneth Silverman, *The Life and Times of Cotton Mather*, 1984; Mitchell Robert Breitwieser, *Cotton Mather and Benjamin Franklin: The Price of Representative Personality*, 1985.

TEXTS

Diary of Cotton Mather, ed. Worthington C. Ford, 1911–12, 1926, 1957; *The Wonders of the Invisible World*, from *The Witchcraft Delusion in New England*, 3 vols., ed. Samuel G. Drake, 1886, 1970; *Magnalia Christi Americana*, 2 vols., ed. Thomas Robbins, 1820, 1855; *Bonifacius: An Essay Upon the Good*, ed. David Levin, 1966; *Manuductio ad Ministerium*, ed. Thomas J. Holmes and Kenneth B. Murdock, 1938 (reproduced form the 1726 edition). Footnotes from these editions are indicated by the editor's name followed by the note enclosed in quotation marks. Typography, punctuation, spelling, and usage have been changed to conform with contemporary English and modern printing practices.

from Diary of Cotton Mather

The period excerpted here is February – July 1703. Cotton Mather's first wife of sixteen years, Abigail, died on December 5, 1702. The loss was devastating to Mather, then in his late thirties. Shortly after Abigails's death, Mather began to receive letters from a twenty-year-old gentlewoman, proposing marriage. Thus began a period of trial and temptation for Mather that lasted until he forced himself to break off the relationship to avoid scandal and family censure. In the meantime, he met a widow living nearby (the "lovely person," Elizabeth Hubbard, referred to at the end of this excerpt), and took her as his second wife in August 1703, regaining his equanimity and his family's approval. The *Diary* entries here reveal the astonishing emotional turmoil Mather experienced, compounded of desire, guilt, piety, and not a little sexual frustration. Although Mather never names the "young gentlewoman" of this episode in his *Diary*, biographers have identified her as Katherine Maccarty, daughter of a Boston merchant.

৯৯

[A YOUNG GENTLEWOMAN PROPOSES TO THE GRIEVING WIDOWER]

February [1703] begins with a very astonishing trial.

There is a young gentlewoman of incomparable accomplishments. No gentlewoman in the English America has had a more polite education. She is one of rare wit and sense; and of a comely aspect; and extremely winning in her conversation, and she has a mother of an extraordinary character for her piety.

This young gentlewoman first addresses me with diverse letters, and then makes me a visit at my house; wherein she gives me to understand, that she has long had a more than ordinary value for my ministry; and that since my present condition has given her more of liberty to think of me, she must confess herself charmed with my person, to such a degree, that she could not but break in upon me, with her most importunate requests, that I would make her mine; and that the highest consideration she had in it, was her eternal salvation, for if she were mine, she could not but hope the effect of it would be, that she should also be Christ's.

I endeavoured faithfully to set before her, all the discouraging circumstances attending me, that I could think of. She told me, that she had weighed all those discouragements, but was fortified and resolved with a strong faith in the mighty God, for to encounter them all. And whereas I had mention'd my way of living, in continual prayers, tears, fasts, and macerating devotions and reservations, to divert her from her proposal, she told me, that this very consideration was that which animated her; for she desired nothing so much as a share in my way of living.

I was in a great strait,[1] how to treat so polite a gentlewoman, thus applying herself unto me. I plainly told her, that I feared, whether her proposal would not meet with unsurmountable oppositions from those who had a great interest in disposing of me. However, I desired, that there might be time taken, to see what would be the wisest and fittest resolution.

In the mean time, if I could not make her my own, I should be glad of being any way instrumental, to make her the Lord's.

I turned my discourse, and my design into that channel; and with as exquisite artifice as I could use, I made my essays[2] to engage her young soul into piety.

She is not much more than twenty years old. I know she has been a very aiery[3] person. Her reputation has been under some disadvantage.

What snares may be laying for me, I know not. Much prayer with fasting and patience, must be my way to encounter them.

I think, how would my Lord Jesus Christ Himself treat a returning sinner.

I shall shortly see more into the meaning of this odd matter.

[February 12] My sore distresses and temptations, I this day carried unto the Lord; with hope of His compassions, to his tempted servant.

The chief of them lies in this: the well accomplished gentlewoman, mention'd (tho' not by name) in the close of the former year, one whom everybody does with admiration confess to be, for her charming accomplishments, an incomparable person, addressing me to make her mine, and professing a disposition unto the most holy flights of religion to lie at the bottom of her addresses. I am in the greatest straits[4] imaginable, what course to steer. Nature itself causes in me a mighty tenderness for a person so very amiable. Breeding requires me to treat her with honour and respect, and very much of deference, to all that she shall at any time ask of me. But religion, above all, obliges me, instead of a rash rejecting her conversation, to contrive rather, how I may imitate the goodness of the Lord Jesus Christ, in His dealing with such as are upon a conversion unto Him.

On the other side: I cannot but fear a fearful snare,[5] and that I may soon fall into some error in my conversation, if the point proposed unto me, be found, after all, unattainable, through the violent storm of opposition, which I cannot but foresee and suspect will be made unto it.

The dreadful confusions which I behold Heaven, even devising for me, do exceedingly break and waste my spirit. I should recover a wondrous degree of health, if I were not broken by these distresses, and grievous temptations. But

---

[1]Dilemma.
[2]Attempts.
[3]Unsubstantial, vivacious.

[4]In the greatest uncertainty.
[5]Trap.

these things cause me to spend more time than ordinary, for the most part every day, in prayers and in tears, prostrate on my study-floor before the Lord. Yea, and they cause me by night also sometimes to hold my vigils, in which I cry to God, until, and after, the middle of the night, that He would look down upon me, and help me, and save me, and not cast me off.

[February 18] *Thursday*. This day was kept as a fast, through the province. I enjoyed great assistences, in the services of the day.

As for my special soul-harassing point: I did some days ago, under my hand, vehemently beg, as for my life, that it might be desisted from, and that I might not be killed by hearing any more of it. Yet such was my flexible tenderness, as to be conquered by the importunities of several, to allow some further interviews. But I resolved, that I would make them turn chiefly upon the most glorious design in the world. I did, accordingly, and once especially, I did, with all the charms I could imagine, draw that witty gentlewoman unto tearful expressions of her consent unto all the articles in the covenant of grace, the articles of her marriage and union with the great L[ord] Redeemer. I had abundance of satisfaction in this action, whatever may be the issue of our conversation.

[February 20] *Saturday*. My grievous distresses, (occasioned especially by the late addresses made unto me, by the person formerly mentioned, and the opposition of her enemies) cause me to fall down before the Lord, with prayers and with tears continually. And because my heart is sore pained within me, to think, what I shall do, or what will be the issue of my distressing affair, I think it proper to multiply my vigils before the Lord. One of them I kept this night; and as it grew towards the morning, after I had cried unto the Lord for my relief and succour, under the temptations now harassing of me, I did again throw myself prostrate in the dust before the Lord; beseeching of Him, that if He would not hear my cries for myself, He would yet hear my cries for my flock; and hereupon I wrestled with the Lord for my great congregation, that the interests of religion might prevail mightily among them, and especially in the young people of my congregation.

It was a consolation unto me to think, that when my people were all asleep in their beds, their poor pastor should be watching, and praying and weeping for them.

The Lord, in His holy sovereignity orders it, that I am left unto great vexations from Satan, about this time; who fills me with fears, that I am a man rejected and abhored of God, and given up to the worst of delusions; and that the Lord will make no more use of me to glorify Him. I am scarce able to live under these doleful disconsolations.

And that I may be left utterly destitute of all human support, my relatives, through their extreme distaste at the talk of my respects for the person, above mentioned, and fear lest I should over-value her, do treat me with unsupportable strangeness and harshness.

"Lord, I am oppressed; undertake for me!"

[February 27] *Saturday*. I set apart this day for prayer with fasting in my study, especially to commend my distressing affair unto the Lord.

As for the ingenious child that solicits my respects unto her, I cry to the Lord, with fervency and agony and floods of tears, that she may be the Lord's; and that her union and marriage to the Lord Jesus Christ, may be the effect of the discourses I have had with her. But I also resign her, and offer her up unto the Lord; and earnestly profess unto Him, that though I set a great value upon her, yet I can deny myself every thing in the world, that the glory of His name, and my service to His name, shall oblige me to part withal. Wherefore, I continually beg of the Lord, that He will show me my duty and bring my distress to a comfortable issue.

[March 3] *Wednesday*. My dreadful distresses continue upon me.

For which cause, I set apart this day, for the duties of a secret fast before the Lord; that I may obtain direction in, and deliverance from, the distresses which do so exceedingly harass and buffet my mind, and break my soul to pieces.

As also, that I may obtain the presence of the Lord with me, in the lecture tomorrow, when I am to do a special service, for His interests.

[March 6] *Saturday*. Though I have kept one fast in my study this week already, yet I must this day keep another.

I am a most miserable man.

That young gentlewoman of so fine accomplishments, (that there is none in this land in those respects comparable to her) who has with such repeated importunity and ingenuity pressed my respects to her, that I have had much ado to steer clear of great inconveniencies, hath by the disadvantages of the company which has continually resorted unto her unhappy father's house, got but a bad name among the generality of the people; and there appears no possibility of her speedy recovery of it, be her carriage never so virtuous, and her conversion never so notorious. By an unhappy coincidence of some circumstances, there is a noise, and a mighty noise it is, made about the town, that I am engaged in a courtship to that young gentlewoman; and though I am so very innocent, (and have so much aimed at a conformity to my Lord Jesus Christ, and serviceableness to Him, in my treating of her) yet it is not easy presently to confute the rumor.

I am now under incredible disadvantages. The design of Satan, to entangle me in a match that might have proved ruinous to my family, or my ministry, is defeated, by my resolution totally to reject the addresses of the young gentlewoman to me; which I do, for the sake of the Lord Jesus Christ, whose name, I see, will suffer if I accept her; and I do it cheerfully, though she be so very charming a person.

But then, Satan has raised an horrid storm of reproach upon me, both for my earliness in courting a gentlewoman, and especially for my courting of a person whom they generally apprehend so disagreeable to my character. And there is hazard, lest my usefulness be horribly ruined, by the clamour of the rash people on this occasion, before there can be due measures taken to quiet them; and my civility to the person who has addressed me, will not let me utter what would most effectually quiet them.

I am a man greatly assaulted by Satan. Is it because I have done much against that enemy? or, are the judgments of God incessantly pursuing of me, for my miscarriages!

My Spirit is excessively broken. There is danger of my dying suddenly, with smothered griefs and fears. I know not what to do, but to pour out my soul unto the Lord, and submit unto His dreadful sovereignty and righteousness; but cry mightily unto Him, that He would yet rescue my precious opportunities to glorify the L[ord] Jesus Christ (the apple of my eye,) from the mischiefs which do threaten them.

[Breaking Off: Victory Over Flesh and Blood]

[March 15, Monday] And now, being after all due deliberation, fully satisfied, that my countenancing the proposals of coming one day to a marriage, with the gentlewoman so often mentioned in these papers, will not be consistent with my public serviceableness; but that the prejudices in the minds of the people of God against it, are insuperable, and little short of universal: I set myself to make unto the L[ord] Jesus Christ, a sacrifice of a person, who, for many charming accomplishments, has not many equals in the English America. In making of my sacrifice, I have not gone upon any inferior considerations, nor have I minded,[1] but slighted,[2] the defamatory stories, which have been uttered concerning her, as knowing how little weight there is to be laid upon popular slanders. But I have been acted[3] purely by a religious respect unto the holy name of the L[ord] Jesus Christ, and my serviceableness to His precious interests; which I had a thousand times rather die than damnify. My victory over flesh and blood in this matter, was no unhappy symptom, I hope, of regeneration in my Soul. I encouraged myself with hopes, that God would carry me well through my sacrifice, in preserving the person addressing me from any damage by her fondness for me; (but I must continue praying for her!) And that I should one day meet with some wonderful recompenses.

I struck my knife into the heart of my sacrifice by a letter to her mother.

[March 27] *Saturday.* Was ever man more tempted than the miserable Mather! Should I tell in how many forms the devil has assaulted me, and with what subtelty and energy, his assaults have been carried on, it would strike my friends with horror.

Sometimes, temptations to impurities; and sometimes to blasphemy, and atheism, and the abandonment of all religion, as a mere delusion; and sometimes, to self-destruction itself. These, even these, O miserable Mather, do follow thee, with an astonishing fury. But I fall down into the dust, on my study-floor, with tears before the Lord; and then they quickly vanish: 'tis fair weather again. "Lord! what wilt Thou do with me!"

[April 3, Saturday] I am under singular distresses. What I would on many accounts prefer, as the most eligible and honourable condition, would be to continue all the rest of my little time, in an unspotted widowhood.

But my family suffers by it, in several instances. And yet I could concoct and conquer this inconvenience, much easier than some other circumstances.

My father presses me frequently and fervently, that I would by no means take up resolutions to continue in my widowhood. My flexible temper makes it not easy for me to resist his exhortations.

But I foresee, and already suffer, a worse encumbrance. The applications, which the gentlewoman formerly mentioned in these papers, has made unto me, have occasioned very many misrepresentations of me, among a foolish people. The coarse, though just, usage that she has had from me, will also put her upon a thousand inventions. I shall be continually, every week, persecuted with some noise and nonsense carried about the town concerning me. The persecution of the lies daily invented about me, will be, I see, insupportable. All the friends I have in the world persuade me that I shall have no way to get from under these confusions, but by proceeding unto another marriage.

"Lord, help me, what shall I do? I am a miserable man."

[April 13, 14, 15] *Tuesday, Wednesday, Thursday.* The dispensations of heaven towards me, in and since the death of my lovely consort, have been very awful.

I have lately waded through dreadful temptations, and I tremble to think, what may be the next storm that will be raised upon me.

About eleven months having passed since the Lord began to take away from me the desire of my eyes, my friends begin to press my thoughts of returning to the married state. This is a point of terrible consequence. I had need use more than ordinary humiliations, and supplications, and resignations, upon an occasion so full of agony.

Though I have rarely let a week pass me without setting apart a day for prayer

---

[1] Taken into account.
[2] Discounted.
[3] Motivated.

with fasting, for now many, many months together; and I have ever now and then had my vigils, for a conversation with heaven; and every day for the most part, I have had one secret prayer more than I use to have, and lain prostrate, in the dust, with tears before the Lord, because of my distresses: Yet I thought it necessary to do something more than all of this. I resolved upon doing a thing, which I do not know to have been done, by any man living in the world. I took up a resolution, to spend no less than THREE DAYS together, in prayer with fasting in my study; and beseech the Lord thrice, knocking at the door of heaven for three days together.

[May 19, Wednesday] I preached both parts of the Lord's day at Salem, and on Monday returned home.

In my absence the young gentlewoman, to whom I have been so unkind many weeks or months ago, writes and comes to my father, and brings her good mother with her and charms the neighbours into her interests; and renews her importunities (both before and after my journey) that I would make her mine. My apprehension of damage to arise therefrom unto the holy interests of religion, fixes me still in an unalterable resolution, that I must never hearken to her proposals, whatever may be the consequence of my being so resolved. I am hereupon threatened by some with exquisite revenges and reproaches from her defeated love, and the hazards of her coming to mischief.[4] Some set the town into a new storm of obloquy upon me, and threaten me with an horrid encumbrance upon all my intentions elsewhere to return unto the married state.

Satan makes these rebukes of heaven upon me, after all my prayers, and tears, and fasts and resignations, to be an occasion of sore temptation unto me.

However, in the midst of all this temptation, my weeping soul keeps humbly professing before the Lord; that I will not give over seeking Him, though it appears as if I sought Him in vain; that I will always love Him, and serve Him, though He seems as if He would lay me by from serving Him; that though He should not rescue my opportunities of glorifying the L[ord] Jesus Christ, from the fine devices of Satan to hurt them, yet I will continue to glorify Him as much as ever I can all my days; yea, though He should leave me without hopes of arising to glory at the last. While I am thus professing before the Lord, He keeps reviving of my broken, drooping spirit, with comfortable persuasions, that He will not cast me off but that I shall see a blessed issue of all the dark dispensations that are passing over me.

[June 12] *Saturday.* The holy justice and wisdom of God, shines forth, in His awful dispensations towards me.

A lying spirit is gone forth, and the people of the town, are strangely under the influences of it.

I have the inconvenience of being a person, whom the eye and the talk of the people is very much upon. My present circumstances give them opportunities to invent and report abundance of disadvantageous falsehoods, of my being engaged in such and such courtships, wherein I am really unconcerned. But the addresses which I have had from the young gentlewoman so often mentioned in these papers, and the discourses thereby raised among the dissatisfied people, afford the greatest theme for their mischievous and malicious lying to turn upon. When all assaults upon me from that quarter have been hitherto unsuccessful at last, I am unhappily persecuted with insinuations that I had proceeded so far in countenancing that matter, I could not with honour and justice now steer clear of it, as I have done. God strangely appears for me, in this point also, by disposing the young gentlewoman, with her mother, to furnish me with their assertions: "That I

---

[4]Dangers of her reacting spitefully.

have never done any unworthy thing; but acted most honourably and righteously towards them, and as became a Christian, and a minister; and they will give all the world leave to censure them after the hardest manner in the world, if ever they should speak the contrary." Yea, they have proceeded so far beyond all bounds in my vindication, as to say: "They verily look upon Mr M⎯⎯⎯⎯r to be as great a saint of God, as any upon earth." Nevertheless, the Devil owes me a spite, and he inspires his people in this town, to whisper impertinent stories, which have a tendency to make me contemptible, and hurt my serviceableness, and strike at, yea, strike out the apple of my eye.[5] My spirit is on this occasion too much disturbed. I am encountering an hour and power of darkness. My temptations from the clamour of many people, among whom I hear the defaming of many; the desolate condition of my family, not likely to be provided for; and the desertions which my soul suffers, while I behold the dreadful frown of God upon my prayers, my fasts, my fears, my resignations, and all my endeavours to glorify Him: these things do exceedingly unhinge me, and cause me sometimes to speak unadvisedly with my lips. 'Tis well, if they do not perfectly kill me.

[July 17] *Saturday.* I set apart this day for prayer with fasting in my study, to obtain a good progress and success of the affair which I am now managing; and a deliverance from any further vexation, temptation, or encumbrance by the young gentlewoman that has vexed me with so many of her wiles, and by such exquisite methods been trying to ensnare or trouble me.

The rage of that young gentlewoman, whom out of obedience to God I have rejected, (and never more pleased God than in rejecting of her addresses to me) is transporting her[6] to threaten that she will be a thorn in my side, and contrive all possible ways to vex me, affront me, disgrace me, in my attempting a return to the married state with another gentlewoman. Instead of using other contrivances to quell the rage of a person, who is of so rare a wit but so little grace, that I may expect unknown damages from her, I carried her to the Lord Jesus Christ. I pleaded, that my Lord Jesus Christ is able to do everything; that He can restrain Satan, and all Satanic influences at His pleasure; that my temptations had already proceeded a great way; and His name would suffer, and His poor servant would sink, if he should permit them to proceed any further; and that I had out of obedience unto Him, exposed myself unto the rage, by which I was now likely to be incommoded. And I concluded still, with a triumphant faith in my Lord Jesus Christ, for my victory over the mischiefs which threatened me.

Behold, within a few days, the gentlewoman without my seeking it, sent me a letter, with a promise under her hand, that she would offer me none of those disquietments, which in her passion she had threatened. I was astonished at this work of heaven; and with the tears of a raptured soul, I offered up a sacrifice of love and praise unto the Lord.

My conversation with the lovely person,[7] to whom heaven has directed me, goes on, with pure, chaste, noble strokes, and the smiles of God upon it.

And the universal satisfaction which it has given to the people of God, through town and country, proclaims itself, to a degree which perfectly amazes me.

The extreme heat of the weather (with some other inconveniences, by the carpenters making some addition to my habitation) put me by, from keeping a fast this week, as I might else have done.

1703   *1911–12*

---

[5]Christ.
[6]I.e., her rage is inspiring or compelling.
[7]A nearby widow whom Mather has met.

from The Wonders of the Invisible World

[DECLINE OF MORALITY IN NEW ENGLAND]

Whosoever travels over this wilderness will see it richly bespangled with evangelical churches, whose pastors are holy, able, and painful overseers of their flocks, lively preachers, and virtuous livers. . . . The body of the people are hitherto so disposed that swearing, sabbath-breaking, whoring, drunkenness, and the like, do not make a gentleman, but a monster, or a goblin, in the vulgar estimation. All this notwithstanding, we must humbly confess to our God that we are miserably degenerated from the first love of our predecessors. . . .

The first planters of these colonies were a chosen generation of men, who were first so pure as to disrelish[1] many things which they thought wanted reformation elsewhere; and yet withal so peaceable that they embraced a voluntary exile in a squalid, horrid American desert, rather than to live in contentions with their brethren. Those good men imagined that they should never see the inroads of profanity or superstition. And a famous person[2] returning hence, could, in a sermon before the Parliament, profess, "I have been seven years in a country, where I never saw one man drunk, or heard one oath sworn, or beheld one beggar in the streets all the while." Such great persons as Budaeus,[3] and others, who mistook Sir Thomas More's *Utopia*[4] for a country really existent, and stirred up some divines charitably to undertake a voyage thither, might now have certainly found a truth in their mistake; New England was a true Utopia.

But alas, the children and servants of those old planters must needs afford many degenerate plants, and there is now risen up a number of people, otherwise inclined than our Joshuas[5] and the elders that out-lived them. These two things, our holy progenitors and our happy advantages, make omissions of duty and such spiritual disorders as the whole world abroad is overwhelmed with, to be as provoking in us as the most flagitious[6] wickednesses committed in other places; and the ministers of God are accordingly severe in their testimonies. But in short, those interests of the gospel, which were the errand of our fathers into these ends of the earth, have been too much neglected and postponed, and the attainments of an handsome education have been too much undervalued by multitudes that have not fallen into exorbitances of wickedness. And some, especially of our young ones, when they have got abroad from under the restraints here laid upon them, have become extravagantly and abominably vicious. Hence 'tis that the happiness of New England has been but for a time, as it was foretold, and not for a long time, as has been desired for us. A variety of calamity has long followed this plantation, and we have all the reason imaginable to ascribe it unto the rebuke of heaven upon us for our manifold apostasies.[7] We make no right use of our disasters if we do not "Remember whence we are fallen, and repent, and do the first works."[8] But yet our afflictions may come under a further consideration with us. There is a further cause of our afflictions, whose due must be given him.

---

[1]Dislike.

[2]Mr. Giles Firmin (suggested by Samuel Drake, editor of this text).

[3]Guillaume Budaeus (1468–1540), French scholar, friend of Erasmus, and Royal Librarian to Francis I.

[4]Thomas More (1478–1535) in his *Utopia* (1516) described an ideal society.

[5]Joshua was King of Judah (*c.* 638–608 B.C.). As successor to Moses, he led the Israelites to Canaan, the Promised Land (Joshua, 1–12).

[6]Heinous, infamous.

[7]Abandonment of faith.

[8]Revelation 2:5: "Remember therefore from whence thou art fallen, and repent, and do the first works."

[THE DEVIL'S PLOT TO OVERTURN THIS POOR PLANTATION]

The New Englanders are a people of God settled in those, which were once the devil's territories; and it may easily be supposed that the devil was exceedingly disturbed, when he perceived such a people here accomplishing the promise of old made unto our blessed Jesus, that He should have the utmost parts of the earth for His possession.[1] There was not a greater uproar among the Ephesians, when the Gospel was first brought among them,[2] than there was among the powers of the air (after whom those Ephesians walked) when first the silver trumpets of the Gospel here made the joyful sound. The devil thus irritated, immediately tried all sorts of methods to overturn this poor plantation: and so much of the church, as was fled into this wilderness, immediately found the serpent cast out of his mouth a flood for the carrying of it away. I believe that never were more satanical devices used for the unsettling of any people under the sun, than what have been employed for the extirpation of the vine which God has here planted,[3] casting out the heathen, and preparing a room before it, and causing it to take deep root, and fill the land, so that it sent its boughs unto the Atlantic Sea eastward, and its branches unto the Connecticut River westward, and the hills were covered with the shadow thereof. But all those attempts of hell have hitherto been abortive, many an Ebenezer[4] has been erected unto the praise of God, by his poor people here; and having obtained help from God, we continue to this day.

Wherefore the devil is now making one attempt more upon us; an attempt more difficult, more surprising, more snarled with unintelligible circumstances than any that we have hitherto encountered; an attempt so critical, that if we get well through, we shall soon enjoy halcyon days with all the vultures of hell trodden under our feet. He has wanted his incarnate legions to persecute us, as the people of God have in the other hemisphere[5] been persecuted: he has therefore drawn forth his more spiritual ones to make an attack upon us. We have been advised by some credible Christians yet alive, that a malefactor, accused of witchcraft as well as murder, and executed in this place more than forty years ago, did then give notice of an horrible plot against the country by witchcraft, and a foundation of witchcraft then laid, which if it were not seasonably discovered, would probably blow up, and pull down all the churches in the country.

And we have now with horror seen the discovery of such a witchcraft! An army of devils is horribly broke in upon the place which is the center, and after a sort, the first-born of our English settlements: and the houses of the good people there are filled with the doleful shrieks of their children and servants, tormented by invisible hands, with tortures altogether preternatural. After the mischiefs there endeavored, and since in part conquered, the terrible plague of evil angels hath made its progress into some other places, where other persons have been in like manner diabolically handled. These our poor afflicted neighbors, quickly after they become infected and infested with these demons, arrive to a capacity of discerning those which they conceive the shapes of their troublers; and notwithstanding the great and just suspicion that the demons might impose the shapes of innocent persons in their spectral exhibitions upon the sufferers (which may perhaps prove no small part of the witch-plot in the issue), yet many of the persons thus represented, being examined, several of them have been convicted of a very damnable witchcraft: yea, more than one twenty[6] have confessed, that they have

---

[1] Luke 4:5–7: When Jesus fasted in the wilderness for forty days, the devil tempted him by promising him the world.
[2] Acts 19: When St. Paul preached in Ephesus, there was an uproar of protest by the Ephesians on behalf of their "great goddess Diana."

[3] I.e., the Puritan colonies.
[4] 1 Samuel 7:12: Memorial stone set up by Samuel after defeat of the Philistines.
[5] Europe.
[6] I.e., twenty-one.

signed unto a book, which the devil showed them, and engaged in his hellish design of bewitching and ruining our land.

We know not, at least I know not, how far the delusions of Satan may be interwoven into some circumstances of the confessions; but one would think all the rules of understanding human affairs are at an end, if after so many most voluntary harmonious confessions, made by intelligent persons of all ages, in sundry towns, at several times, we must not believe the main strokes wherein those confessions all agree: especially when we have a thousand preternatural things every day before our eyes, wherein the confessors do acknowledge their concernment, and give demonstration of their being so concerned. If the devils now can strike the minds of men with any poisons of so fine a composition and operation, that scores of innocent people shall unite, in confessions of a crime, which we see actually committed, it is a thing prodigious, beyond the wonders of the former ages, and it threatens no less than a sort of a dissolution upon the world.

Now, by these confessions 'tis agreed that the Devil has made a dreadful knot[7] of witches in the country, and by the help of witches has dreadfully increased that knot: that these witches have driven a trade of commissioning their confederate spirits to do all sorts of mischiefs to the neighbors, whereupon there have ensued such mischievous consequences upon the bodies and estates of the neighborhood, as could not otherwise be accounted for: yea, that at prodigious witch-meetings, the wretches have proceeded so far as to concert and consult the methods of rooting out the Christian religion from this country, and setting up instead of it perhaps a more gross diabolism than ever the world saw before. And yet it will be a thing little short of miracle, if in so spread a business as this, the Devil should not get in some of his juggles,[8] to confound the discovery of all the rest.

[THE WITCHES' COVENANT WITH THE DEVIL]

That the devil is come down unto us with great wrath, we find, we feel, we now deplore. In many ways, for many years hath the devil been assaying to extirpate the kingdom of our Lord Jesus here. . . . The things confessed by witches, and the things endured by others, laid together, amount unto this account of our affliction. The devil, exhibiting himself ordinarily as a small black man, has decoyed a fearful knot[1] of proud, froward, ignorant, envious and malicious creatures, to lift themselves in his horrid service, by entering their names in a book by him tendered unto them. These witches, whereof above a score have now confessed and shown their deeds, and some are now tormented by the devils for confessing, have met in hellish rendezvous, wherein the confessors do say, they have had their diabolical sacraments, imitating the baptism and the supper of our Lord. In these hellish meetings, these monsters have associated themselves to do no less a thing than to destroy the kingdom of our Lord Jesus Christ in these parts of the world; and in order hereunto, first they each of them have their specters, or devils, commissioned by them, and representing of them, to be the engines[2] of their malice. By these wicked specters, they sieze poor people about the country, with various and bloody torments; and of those evidently preternatural[3] torments there are some have died. They have bewitched some, even so far as to make self-destroyers; and others are in many towns here and there languishing under their evil hands.

The people thus afflicted are miserably scratched and bitten, so that the marks are most visible to all the world, but the causes utterly invisible; and the same in-

---

[7]Group, cluster.
[8]Deceptions, tricks.
[1]Group, cluster.

[2]Agents.
[3]Supernatural.

visible furies do most visibly stick pins and hideously distort and disjoint all their members,[4] besides a thousand other sorts of plagues beyond these of any natural diseases which they give unto them. Yea, they sometimes drag the poor people out of their chambers and carry them over trees and hills, for divers miles together. A large part of the persons tortured by these diabolical specters are horribly tempted[5] by them, sometimes with fair promises, and sometimes with hard threatenings, but always with felt miseries, to sign the devil's laws in a spectral book laid before them; which two or three of these poor sufferers, being by their tiresome sufferings overcome to do, they have immediately been released from all their miseries and they appeared in specter then to torture those that were before their fellow-sufferers.

The witches which, by their covenant with the devil, are become owners of specters, are oftentimes by their own specters required and compelled to give their consent for the molestation of some, which they had no mind otherwise to fall upon; and cruel depredations are then made upon the vicinage.[6] In the prosecution of these witchcrafts, among a thousand other unaccountable things, the specters have an odd faculty of clothing the most substantial and corporeal instruments of torture with invisibility, while the wounds thereby given have been the most palpable things in the world; so that the sufferers assaulted with instruments of iron, wholly unseen to the standers-by, though, to their cost, seen by themselves, have, upon snatching, wrested the instruments out of the specter's hands, and everyone has then immediately not only beheld, but handled, an iron instrument taken by a devil from a neighbor.[7] These wicked specters have proceeded so far as to steal several quantities of money from divers people, part of which money has, before sufficient spectators, been dropped out of the air into the hands of the sufferers, while the specters have been urging them to subscribe their covenant with death.

In such extravagant ways have these wretches propounded the dragooning[8] of as many as they can, in their own combination, and the destroying of others, with lingering, spreading, deadly diseases, till our country should at last become too hot for us. Among the ghastly instances of the success which those bloody witches have had, we have seen even some of their own children so dedicated unto the devil, that in their infancy, it is found, the imps have sucked them and rendered them venemous to a prodigy.[9] We have also seen the devil's first batteries upon the town, where the first church of our Lord in this colony was gathered, producing those distractions which have almost ruined the town. We have seen likewise the plague reaching afterwards into other towns far and near, where the houses of good men have the devil's filling of them with terrible vexations!

· · · · ·

But I shall no longer detain my reader from his expected entertainment, in a brief account of the trials which have passed upon some of the malefactors lately executed at Salem, for the witchcrafts whereof they stood convicted. For my own part, I was not present at any of them; nor ever had I any personal prejudice at the persons thus brought upon the stage; much less at the surviving relations of those persons, with and for whom I would be as hearty a mourner as any man living in the world: The Lord comfort them! But having received a command[10] so to do, I can do no other than shortly relate the chief matters of fact, which oc-

---

[4]Arms, legs, etc.
[5]Lured, coerced.
[6]Vicinity.
[7]I.e., the devil-specter has stolen an iron tool from one of the neighbors and has used it in an invisible assault on his victim, but the victim snatches it and thus exhibits it to friends and neighbors.

[8]Harassing.
[9]Turned them into monstrosities.
[10]I.e., the request by the judges in the Salem witch-trials that Mather write an account explaining the sentences passed out.

curred in the trials of some that were executed, in an abridgment collected out of the court papers on this occasion put into my hands. You are to take the truth, just as it was; and the truth will hurt no good man. . . .

THE TRIAL OF MARTHA CARRIER

At The Court Of Oyer and Terminer,[1] Held By Adjournment at Salem, August 2, 1692

I. Martha Carrier was indicted for the bewitching certain persons, according to the form usual in such cases, pleading not guilty to her indictment; there were first brought in a considerable number of the bewitched persons who not only made the court sensible of an horrid witchcraft committed upon them, but also deposed that it was Martha Carrier, or her shape, that grievously tormented them, by biting, pricking, pinching and choking of them. It was further deposed that while this Carrier was on her examination before the magistrates, the poor people were so tortured that every one expected their death upon the very spot, but that upon the binding of Carrier they were eased. Moreover the look of Carrier then laid the afflicted people for dead;[2] and her touch, if her eye at the same time were off them, raised them again: which things were also now seen upon her trial. And it was testified that upon the mention of some having their necks twisted almost round, by the shape of this Carrier, she replied, "It's no matter though their necks had been twisted quite off."

II. Before the trial of this prisoner, several of her own children had frankly and fully confessed not only that they were witches themselves, but that this their mother had made them so. This confession they made with great shows of repentance, and with much demonstration of truth. They related place, time, occasion; they gave an account of journeys, meetings and mischiefs by them performed, and were very credible in what they said. Nevertheless, this evidence was not produced against the prisoner at the bar,[3] inasmuch as there was other evidence enough to proceed upon.

III. Benjamin Abbot gave his testimony that last March was a twelvemonth, this Carrier was very angry with him, upon laying out some land near her husband's: her expressions in this anger were that she would stick as close to Abbot as the bark stuck to the tree; and that he should repent of it afore seven years came to an end, so as Doctor Prescot should never cure him. These words were heard by others besides Abbot himself; who also heard her say, she would hold his nose as close to the grindstone as ever it was held since his name was Abbot. Presently after this, he was taken with a swelling in his foot, and then with a pain in his side, and exceedingly tormented. It bred into a sore, which was lanced by Doctor Prescot, and several gallons of corruption ran out of it. For six weeks it continued very bad, and then another sore bred in the groin, which was also lanced by Doctor Prescot. Another sore than bred in his groin, which was likewise cut, and put him to very great misery: he was brought unto death's door, and so remained until Carrier was taken, and carried away by the constable, from which very day he began to mend, and so grew better every day, and is well ever since.

Sarah Abbot also, his wife, testified that her husband was not only all this while afflicted in his body, but also that strange, extraordinary and unaccountable ca-

---

[1]Latin, to hear and determine; the special court appointed to try those accused of witchcraft.
[2]Her gaze bewitched her victims, placing them under her power.
[3]Court (bar of justice).

lamities befell his cattle; their death being such as they could guess at no natural reason for.

IV. Allin Toothaker testified that Richard, the son of Martha Carrier, having some difference with him, pulled him down by the hair of the head. When he rose again he was going to strike at Richard Carrier but fell down flat on his back to the ground, and had not power to stir hand or foot, until he told Carrier he yielded; and then he saw the shape of Martha Carrier go off his breast.

This Toothaker had received a wound in the wars; and he now testified that Martha Carrier told him he should never be cured. Just afore the apprehending of Carrier, he could thrust a knitting needle into his wound four inches deep; but presently after her being seized, he was thoroughly healed.

He further testified that when Carrier and he some times were at variance, she would clap her hands at him, and say he should get nothing by it; whereupon he several times lost his cattle, by strange deaths, whereof no natural causes could be given.

V. John Rogger also testified that upon the threatening words of this malicious Carrier, his cattle would be strangely bewitched; as was more particularly then described.

VI. Samuel Preston testified that about two years ago, having some difference with Martha Carrier, he lost a cow in a strange, preternatural, unusual manner; and about a month after this, the said Carrier, having again some difference with him, she told him he had lately lost a cow, and it should not be long before he lost another; which accordingly came to pass; for he had a thriving and well-kept cow, which without any known cause quickly fell down and died.

VII. Phebe Chandler testified that about a fortnight before the apprehension of Martha Carrier, on a Lord's day, while the Psalm was singing in the Church, this Carrier then took her by the shoulder and shaking her, asked her, where she lived: she made her no answer, although as Carrier, who lived next door to her father's house, could not in reason but know who she was. Quickly after this, as she was at several times crossing the fields, she heard a voice, that she took to be Martha Carrier's, and it seemed as if it was over her head. The voice told her she should within two or three days be poisoned. Accordingly, within such a little time, one half of her right hand became greatly swollen and very painful; as also part of her face: whereof she can give no account how it came. It continued very bad for some days; and several times since she has had a great pain in her breast; and been so seized on her legs that she has hardly been able to go. She added that lately, going well to the house of God, Richard, the son of Martha Carrier, looked very earnestly upon her, and immediately her hand, which had formerly been poisoned, as is abovesaid, began to pain her greatly, and she had a strange burning at her stomach; but was then struck deaf, so that she could not hear any of the prayer, or singing, till the two or three last words of the Psalm.

VIII. One Foster, who confessed her own share in the witchcraft for which the prisoner stood indicted, affirmed that she had seen the prisoner at some of their witch-meetings, and that it was this Carrier, who persuaded her to be a witch. She confessed that the Devil carried them on a pole to a witch-meeting; but the pole broke, and she hanging about Carrier's neck, they both fell down, and she then received an hurt by the fall, whereof she was not at this very time recovered.

IX. One Lacy, who likewise confessed her share in this witchcraft, now testified, that she and the prisoner were once bodily present at a witch-meeting in Salem village; and that she knew the prisoner to be a witch, and to have been at a diabolical sacrament, and that the prisoner was the undoing of her and her children by enticing them into the snare of the devil.

X. Another Lacy, who also confessed her share in this witchcraft, now testified, that the prisoner was at the witch-meeting, in Salem village, where they had bread and wine administered unto them.

XI. In the time of this prisoner's trial, one Susanna Sheldon in open court had her hands unaccountably tied together with a wheel-band[4] so fast that without cutting it, it could not be loosed: it was done by a specter; and the sufferer affirmed it was the prisoner's.

Memorandum. This rampant hag, Martha Carrier, was the person of whom the confessions of the witches, and of her own children among the rest, agreed that the devil had promised her she should be queen of hell.[5]

1692   *1693*

from Magnalia Christi Americana[1]

from A GENERAL INTRODUCTION
[THE EPIC PLAN]

I write the wonders of the Christian religion, flying from the depravations[2] of Europe to the American strand, and assisted by the holy Author of that religion, I do with all conscience of truth, required therein by Him who is the Truth itself, report the wonderful displays of His infinite power, wisdom, goodness, and faithfulness, wherewith His divine providence hath irradiated an Indian wilderness.

I relate the considerable matters that produced and attended the first settlement of colonies which have been renowned for the degree of Reformation professed and attained by evangelical churches erected in those ends of the earth, and a field being thus prepared, I proceed unto a relation of the considerable matters which have been acted thereupon.

I first introduce the actors that have in a more exemplary manner served those colonies and give remarkable occurrences in the exemplary lives of many magistrates and of more ministers who so lived as to leave unto posterity examples worthy of everlasting remembrance.

I add hereunto the notables of the only protestant university that ever shone in that hemisphere of the New World; with particular instances of Creolians[3] in our biography, provoking the whole world with virtuous objects of emulation.

I introduce then the actions of a more eminent importance that have signalized those colonies; whether the establishments, directed by their synods, with a rich variety of synodical and ecclesiastical determinations; or, the disturbances with which they have been from all sorts of temptations and enemies tempestuated,[4] and the methods by which they have still weathered out each horrible tempest.

And into the midst of these actions, I interpose an entire book, wherein there is, with all possible veracity, a collection made of memorable occurrences and amazing judgments and mercies befalling many particular persons among the people of New England.

Let my readers expect all that I have promised them in this bill of fare, and it may be that they will find themselves entertained with yet many other passages, above and beyond their expectation, deserving likewise a room in history; in all which there will be nothing but the author's too mean way of preparing so great entertainments to reproach the invitation.

---

[4]A strap that goes around a wheel, as on a spinning wheel.
[5]Martha Carrier was found guilty by the court and was hanged on August 19, 1692.
[1]*The Great Works of Christ in America,* subtitled *The Ecclesiastical History of New England from its first planting, in the year 1620, unto the year of our Lord, 1698.*

[2]Depravities, corruption.
[3]Persons who were born or settled in America but of European race. Obsolete (cf. creole).
[4]Tossed about, stricken (as in a tempest).

THE SECOND BOOK
CHAPTER I

GALEACIUS SECUNDUS.[1] THE LIFE OF WILLIAM BRADFORD, ESQ.,
GOVERNOR OF PLYMOUTH COLONY

*Omnium Somnos, illius vigilantia defendit, omnium otium
illius Labor, omnium Delicias illius Industria, omnium
vacationem illius occupatio.*[2]

I. It has been a matter of some observation that, although Yorkshire be one of
the largest shires in England, yet, for all the fires of martyrdom which were kindled in the days of Queen Mary,[3] it afforded no more fuel than one poor leaf,
namely, John Leaf, an apprentice who suffered for the doctrine of the Reformation at the same time and stake with the famous John Bradford.[4] But when the
reign of Queen Elizabeth would not admit the Reformation of worship to proceed
unto those degrees which were proposed and pursued by no small number of the
faithful in those days,[5] Yorkshire was not the least of the shires in England that
afforded suffering witnesses thereunto. The churches there gathered were
quickly molested with such a raging persecution that if the spirit of separation in
them did carry them unto a further extreme than it should have done, one blam-
able cause therefore will be found in the extremity of that persecution. Their
troubles made that cold country too hot for them, so that they were under a necessity to seek a retreat in the Low Countries; and yet the watchful malice and
fury of their adversaries rendered it almost impossible for them to find what they
sought. For them to leave their native soil, their lands, and their friends, and go
into a strange place where they must hear foreign language and live meanly and
hardly and in other employments than that of husbandry wherein they had been
educated, these must needs have been such discouragements as could have been
conquered by none save those who sought first the kingdom of God and the righteousness thereof.[6] But that which would have made these discouragements the
more unconquerable unto an ordinary faith, was the terrible zeal of their enemies
to guard all ports, and search all ships, that none of them should be carried off.

I will not relate the sad things of this kind then seen and felt by this people of
God; but only exemplify those trials with one short story. Divers of this people
having hired a Dutchman, then lying at Hull, to carry them over to Holland, he
promised faithfully to take them[7] in between Grimsby and Hull; but they coming
to the place a day or two too soon, the appearance of such a multitude alarmed
the officers of the town adjoining, who came with a great body of soldiers to seize
upon them. Now it happened that one boat full of men had been carried aboard,
while the women were yet in a bark that lay aground in a creek at low water. The
Dutchman perceiving the storm that was thus beginning ashore, swore by the sacrament that he would stay no longer for any of them; and so taking the advantage
of a fair wind then blowing, he put out to sea for Zeeland.[8] The women thus left
near Grimsby-common, bereaved of their husbands, who had been hurried from

---

[1]"The Second Galeacius" (Latin). Galeazzo Carracioli
(1517–1586), Italian religious leader who became a Protestant and was exiled from Italy; he was called a "Second
Moses."

[2]"His vigilance secures the sleep of all, his labor the leisure
of all, his industry the pleasures of all, his employment the
freedom of all" (Latin).

[3]Mary Tudor ("Bloody Mary"), daughter of Henry VIII,
who reigned from 1553 to 1558; in her attempt to restore
the Catholicism her father had banished, she executed
many Protestants, creating many martyrs.

[4]Both John Leaf and John Bradford were burned at the
stake in London on July 1, 1555.

[5]Elizabeth Tudor (r. 1558–1603), also daughter of Henry
VIII; she supported independence from Catholicism of the
Church of England established by her father, but did not
rid the Church of those Catholic elements that the Puritans
disliked.

[6]Cf. Matthew 6:33: "Seek ye first the kingdom of God, and
his righteousness."

[7]Let them board the ship.

[8]In Holland.

them, and forsaken of their neighbours, of whom none durst in this fright stay with them, were a very rueful spectacle; some crying for fear, some shaking for cold, all dragged by troops of armed and angry men from one Justice to another, till not knowing what to do with them, they even dismissed them to shift as well as they could for themselves. But by their singular afflictions, and by their Christian behaviours, the cause for which they exposed themselves did gain considerably. In the meantime, the men at sea found reason to be glad that their families were not with them, for they were surprised with an horrible tempest, which held them for fourteen days together, in seven whereof they saw not sun, moon or star, but were driven upon the coast of Norway. The mariners often despaired of life, and once with doleful shrieks gave over all, as thinking the vessel was foundered: but the vessel rose again, and when the mariners with sunk hearts often cried out, "We sink! we sink!" the passengers, without such distraction of mind, even while the water was running into their mouths and ears, would cheerfully shout, "Yet, Lord, thou canst save! Yet, Lord, thou canst save!" And the Lord accordingly brought them at last safe unto their desired haven: and not long after helped their distressed relations thither after them, where indeed they found upon almost all accounts a new world, but a world in which they found that they must live like strangers and pilgrims.

2. Among those devout people was our William Bradford, who was born Anno 1588[9] in an obscure village called Austerfield, where the people were as unacquainted with the Bible as the Jews do seem to have been with part of it in the day of Josiah,[10] a most ignorant and licentious people, and like unto their priest. Here, and in some other places, he had a comfortable inheritance left him of his honest parents, who died while he was yet a child and cast him on the education, first of his grandparents, and then of his uncles, who devoted him, like his ancestors, unto the affairs of husbandry. Soon a long sickness kept him, as he would afterwards thankfully say, from the vanities of youth and made him the fitter for what he was afterwards to undergo. When he was about a dozen years old, the reading of the Scriptures began to cause great impressions upon him; and those impressions were much assisted and improved when he came to enjoy Mr. Richard Clifton's[11] illuminating ministry, not far from his abode; he was then also further befriended by being brought into the company and fellowship of such as were then called professors, though the young man that brought him into it did after become a profane and wicked apostate. Nor could the wrath of his uncles, nor the scoff of his neighbors now turned upon him as one of the Puritans, divert him from his pious inclinations.

3. At last beholding how fearfully the evangelical and apostolical church[12] form, whereinto the churches of the primitive times were cast by the good spirit of God, had been deformed by the apostasy[13] of the succeeding times, and what little progress the Reformation had yet made in many parts of Christendom towards its recovery, he set himself by reading, by discourse, by prayer, to learn whether it was not his duty to withdraw from the communion of the parish assemblies and engage with some society of the faithful that should keep close unto the written word of God as the rule of their worship. And after many distresses of mind concerning it, he took up a very deliberate and understanding resolution of doing so, which resolution he cheerfully prosecuted, although the provoked rage of his friends tried all the ways imaginable to reclaim him from it; unto all whom his

---

[9]Bradford was born in 1590.
[10]King of Judah (*c.* 640–609 B.C.) who destroyed idolatry and repaired the Temple, thereby discovering a lost book of the Law, Deuteronomy (2 Kings 22, 23).
[11]Puritan pastor of the congregation at Scrooby joined by Bradford; died in Holland in 1616.

[12]Evangelical: the teachings of the four Gospels of the New Testament, written by the Evangelists; apostolic: the faith of the twelve Disciples (or Apostles) sent by Christ to teach the gospel. Thus, a return to the church origins in its teaching and faith.
[13]Abandonment of faith.

answer was: "Were I like to endanger my life or consume my estate by any ungodly courses, your counsels to me were very seasonable; but you know that I have been diligent and provident in my calling, and not only desirous to augment what I have, but also to enjoy it in your company, to part from which will be as great a cross as can befall me. Nevertheless, to keep a good conscience, and walk in such a way as God has prescribed in His Word, is a thing which I must prefer before you all and above life itself. Wherefore, since 'tis for a good cause that I am like to suffer the disasters which you lay before me, you have no cause to be either angry with me or sorry for me; yea, I am not only willing to part with everything that is dear to me in this world for this cause, but I am also thankful that God has given me an heart to do so, and will accept me so to suffer for Him." Some lamented him, some derided him, all dissuaded him; nevertheless the more they did it, the more fixed he was in his purpose to seek the ordinances of the gospel where they should be dispensed with most of the commanded purity; and the sudden deaths of the chief relations which thus lay at him, quickly after convinced him what a folly it had been to have quitted his profession in expectation of any satisfaction from them. So to Holland he attempted a removal.

4. Having with a great company of Christians hired a ship to transport them for Holland, the master perfidiously betrayed them into the hands of those persecutors who rifled and ransacked their goods and clapped their persons into prison at Boston,[14] where they lay for a month together. But Mr. Bradford, being a young man of about eighteen, was dismissed sooner than the rest, so that within a while he had opportunity with some others to get over to Zeeland, through perils both by land and sea not inconsiderable, where he was not long ashore ere a viper seized on his hand—that is, an officer—who carried him unto the magistrates, unto whom an envious passenger had accused him as having fled out of England. When the magistrates understood the true cause of his coming thither, they were well satisfied with him; and so he repaired joyfully unto his brethren at Amsterdam, where the difficulties to which he afterwards stooped in learning and serving of a Frenchman at the working of silks were abundantly compensated by the delight wherewith he sat under the shadow of our Lord in His purely dispensed ordinances. At the end of two years, he did, being of age to do it, convert his estate in England into money; but setting up for himself, he found some of his designs by the providence of God frowned upon, which he judged a correction bestowed by God upon him for certain decays of internal piety, whereinto he had fallen; the consumption of his estate he thought came to prevent a consumption in his virtue. But after he had resided in Holland about half a score years, he was one of those who bore a part in that hazardous and generous[15] enterprise of removing into New England, with part of the English church at Leyden, where, at their first landing his dearest consort, accidentally falling overboard, was drowned in the harbor; and the rest of his days were spent in the services and the temptations of that American wilderness.

5. Here was Mr. Bradford in the year 1621, unanimously chosen the Governor of the plantation, the difficulties whereof were such that, if he had not been a person of more than ordinary piety, wisdom, and courage, he must have sunk under them. He had with a laudable industry been laying up a treasure of experiences, and he had now occasion to use it; indeed, nothing but an experienced man could have been suitable to the necessities of the people. The potent nations of the Indians, into whose country they were come, would have cut them off, if the blessing of God upon his conduct had not quelled them; and if his prudence, justice, and moderation had not overruled them, they had been ruined by their own distem-

---

[14]In England.
[15]Courageous.

pers. One specimen of his demeanor is to this day particularly spoken of. A company of young fellows that were newly arrived were very unwilling to comply with the Governor's order for working abroad on the public account; and therefore on Christmas Day,[16] when he had called upon them, they excused themselves with a pretense that it was against their conscience to work such a day. The Governor gave them no answer, only that he could spare them till they were better informed; but by and by he found them all at play in the street, sporting themselves with various diversions; whereupon, commanding the instruments of their games to be taken from them, he effectually gave them to understand that it was against his conscience that they should play whilst others were at work, and that if they had any devotion to the day, they should show it at home in the exercises of religion and not in the streets with pastime and frolics; and this gentle reproof put a final stop to all such disorders for the future.

6. For two years together after the beginning of the Colony, whereof he was now Governor, the poor people had a great experiment of man's not living by bread alone; for when they were left all together without one morsel of bread for many months one after another, still the good providence of God relieved them and supplied them, and this for the most part out of the sea. In this low condition of affairs, there was no little exercise for the prudence and patience of the Governor, who cheerfully bore his part in all; and, that industry might not flag, he quickly set himself to settle property among the new planters, foreseeing that while the whole country laboured upon a common stock,[17] the husbandry and business of the plantation could not flourish, as Plato[18] and others long since dreamed that it would if a community were established. Certainly, if the spirit which dwelt in the old Puritans had not inspired these new planters, they had sunk under the burden of these difficulties; but our Bradford had a double portion of that spirit.

7. The plantation was quickly thrown into a storm that almost overwhelmed it by the unhappy actions of a minister[19] sent over from England by the adventurers[20] concerned for the plantation; but by the blessing of Heaven on the conduct of the Governor, they weathered out that storm. Only the adventurers, hereupon breaking to pieces, threw up all their concernments with the infant Colony; whereof they gave this as one reason, that the planters dissembled with his majesty and their friends in their petition, wherein they declared for a church discipline agreeing with the French[21] and others of the reforming churches in Europe; whereas 'twas now urged that they had admitted into their communion a person[22] who at his admission utterly renounced the churches of England (which person, by the way, was that very man who had made the complaints against them); and therefore, though they denied the name of Brownists,[23] yet they were the thing. In answer hereunto, the very words written by the Governor were these: "Whereas you tax us with dissembling about the French discipline, you do us wrong, for we both hold and practice the discipline of the French and other reformed churches (as they have published the same in the harmony of confessions) according to our

---

[16]Puritans believed that, since December 25 was not the correct birthday of Christ, Christmas day was a pagan celebration.

[17]Property belonged to the community, not the individual.

[18]Plato (427–347 B.C.), Greek philosopher who described the ideal state in *The Republic*.

[19]The Rev. John Lyford came to Plymouth in 1624 with the secret mission of reporting on the Pilgrims to their English investors. He wormed his way into the Puritans' good graces, but his hypocrisy was unmasked when his letters to the investors were intercepted and read.

[20]Backers who had put up the money for the Mayflower voyage to the New World in hopes of profit.

[21]The "French discipline" refers to the forms of ceremony and worship of the French Calvinists or Huguenots, which the English Puritans found ideal. But the New England Puritans preferred their Congregationalism, with its emphasis on independence and democracy, over the French Presbyterianism, with its government by presbyters or elders.

[22]The person was John Lyford, who had been sent by the "adventurers" (or backers) to spy on the Pilgrims.

[23]Followers of Robert Browne (c. 1550–1633), who was a leader of the Separatist movement advocating, out of despair for reform, a breaking away from the Church of England; founder of Congregationalism, with its radically democratic form of church governance.

means, in effect and substance. But whereas you would tie us up to the French discipline in every circumstance, you derogate from the liberty we have in Christ Jesus. The Apostle Paul would have none to follow him in any thing but wherein he follows Christ; much less ought any Christian or church in the world to do it. The French may err, we may err, and other churches may err, and doubtless do in many circumstances. That honor therefore belongs only to the infallible word of God and pure testament of Christ, to be propounded and followed as the only rule and pattern for direction herein to all churches and Christians. And it is too great arrogancy for any men or church to think that he or they have so sounded the word of God unto the bottom as precisely to set down the churches' discipline without error in substance or circumstance, that no other without blame may digress or differ in any thing from the same. And it is not difficult to show that the reformed churches differ in many circumstances among themselves." By which words it appears how far he was free from that rigid spirit of separation which broke to pieces the Separatists themselves in the Low Countries, unto the great scandal of the reforming churches. He was indeed a person of a well-tempered spirit, or else it had been scarce possible for him to have kept the affairs of Plymouth in so good a temper for thirty-seven years together, in every one of which he was chosen their governor except the three years wherein Mr. Winslow, and the two years wherein Mr. Prince, at the choice of the people, took a turn with him.[24]

8. The leader of a people in a wilderness had need be a Moses; and if a Moses had not led the people of Plymouth Colony, when this worthy person was their Governor, the people had never with so much unanimity and importunity still called him to lead them. Among many instances thereof, let this one piece of self-denial be told for a memorial of him, wheresoever this history shall be considered. The patent of the Colony was taken in his name, running in these terms: "To William Bradford, his heirs, associates, and assigns." But when the number of the freemen was much increased and many new townships erected, the General Court there desired of Mr. Bradford that he would make a surrender of the same into their hands, which he willingly and presently assented unto, and confirmed it according to their desire by his hand and seal, reserving no more for himself than was his proportion, with others, by agreement. But as he found the providence of heaven many ways recompensing his many acts of self-denial, so he gave this testimony to the faithfulness of the divine promises: that he had forsaken friends, houses, and lands for the sake of the gospel, and the Lord gave them him again. Here he prospered in his estate; and besides a worthy son which he had by a former wife, he had also two sons and a daughter by another whom he married in this land.

9. He was a person for study as well as action; and hence, notwithstanding the difficulties through which he passed in his youth, he attained unto a notable skill in languages; the Dutch tongue was become almost as vernacular to him as the English; the French tongue he could also manage; the Latin and the Greek he had mastered; but the Hebrew he most of all studied because, he said, he would see with his own eyes the ancient oracles of God in their native beauty. He was also well skilled in history, in antiquity, and in philosophy; and for theology he became so versed in it that he was an irrefragable[25] disputant against the errors, especially those of Anabaptism,[26] which with trouble he saw rising in his colony; wherefore he wrote some significant things for the confutation of those errors. But the crown of all was his holy, prayerful, watchful, and fruitful walk with God, wherein he was very exemplary.

---

[24]In reality, Bradford served thirty years as governor and five years as assistant.

[25]Inviolable.
[26]Opposed to infant baptism.

10. At length he fell into an indisposition of body which rendered him unhealthy for a whole winter; and as the spring advanced, his health yet more declined; yet he felt himself not what he counted sick, till one day, in the night after
which, the God of Heaven so filled his mind with ineffable consolations that he
seemed little short of Paul,[27] rapt up[28] unto the unutterable entertainments of
paradise. The next morning he told his friends that the good spirit of God had
given him a pledge of his happiness in another world and the first fruits of his
eternal glory; and on the day following, he died, May 9, 1657, in the sixty-ninth
year of his age,[29] lamented by all the colonies of New England as a common blessing and father to them all.

> *O mihi si similis contingat clausula vitae!*[30]

Plato's brief description of a governor is all that I will now leave as his character, in an

Epitaph
Νομενσ, τροφὸσ ἀγέλησ ἀυθρωπίνησ.[31]

Men are but flocks; Bradford beheld their need,
And long did them at once both rule and feed.

1693–96   *1702*

from Bonifacius: An Essay Upon the Good[1]

[DUTY TO ONESELF]

Odi sapientem qui sibi sapit.[2] The charity we are upon, why should it not begin at
home? It observes not a due decorum, if it do not so; and it will be liable to great
exceptions in its pretensions and proceedings.

This then is to be made as an early proposal.

First, let every man devise what good may be done, for the help of what is yet
amiss, in his own heart and life. It is a good note of the witty Fuller's: "He need
not complain of too little work, who hath a little world in himself to mend."[3] It
was of old complained: "No man repented him, saying, 'What have I done?' "[4] Every man upon earth may find in himself something that wants mending; and the
work of repentance is to inquire, not only, what we have done, but also, what we
have to do? Frequent self-examination is the duty and the prudence of all that
would know themselves, or would not lose themselves. The great intention of self-
examination is to find out the points wherein we are to amend our ways. A Christian that would thrive in Christianity must be no stranger to a course of meditation. Meditation, 'tis one of the masters to make a man of God. One article and
exercise in our meditation, should be, to find out, the things wherein a greater

---

[27]Paul's conversion on the Road to Damascus, in which
"suddenly there shined round about him a light from
heaven" (Acts 9:3).
[28]Enraptured.
[29]Only the sixty-seventh.
[30]"O, that life's end may be as sweet to me!" (Latin).
[31]"A shepherd-guardian of his human fold" (Greek).
[1]The full title of this most popular of all Mather's works is
*Bonifacius: An Essay Upon the Good, that is to be Devised and
Designed, by Those Who Desire to Answer the Great End of Life,
and to Do Good While They Live.* But the book has been
known in the many editions since its publication in 1710 as

Mather's *Essays to Do Good.* One of its greatest boosters was
Benjamin Franklin, who listed it along with John Bunyan's
Pilgrim's Progress among a handful of books that impressed
him deeply in his early years. He remarked of *Essays to Do
Good* in his *Autobiography* that it had given him "a turn of
thinking that had influence on some of the principal future
events" of his life.
[2]"I hate the wise man who does not know himself" (Latin).
[3]Levin: "Probably Thomas Fuller (1608–1661), English
preacher and writer noted for his epigrammatic wit."
[4]Levin: "That is, no man repents 'of his wickedness.' See
Jeremiah 8:6."

conformity to the truths upon which we have been meditating, must be endeavored. If we would be good men, we must often devise, how we may grow in knowledge, and in all goodness! It is an inquiry often to be made:

"What shall we do, that what is yet lacking in the image of God upon me, may be perfected? What shall I do, that I may live more perfectly, more watchfully, more fruitfully before the glorious Lord?"

And why should not our meditation, when we retire to that soul-enriching work of shaping the right thoughts of the righteous, expire with some resolution? Devise now, and resolve something, to strengthen your walk with God.

•   •   •   •   •

[DUTY TO CONSORT]

The useful man may now with a very good grace, extend and enlarge the sphere of his consideration. My next proposal now shall be: Let every man consider the relation, wherein the Sovereign God has placed him, and let him devise what good he may do, that may render his relatives, the better for him. One great way to prove ourselves really good, is to be relatively[1] good. By this, more than by anything in the world, it is, that we adorn the doctrine of God our Savior. It would be an excellent wisdom in a man, to make the interest he has in the good opinion and affection of anyone, an advantage to do good service for God upon them: He that has a friend will show himself indeed friendly, if he thinks, "Such an one loves me, and will hearken to me; what good shall I take advantage hence to persuade him to?"

This will take place more particularly, where the endearing ties of natural relation do give us an interest. Let us call over our several relations, and let us have devices of something that may be called heroical goodness, in our discharging of them. Why should we not, at least once or twice in a week, make this relational goodness, the subject of our inquiries, and our purposes? Particularly, let us begin with our domestic relations, and provide for those of our own house, lest we deny some glorious rules and hopes of our Christian faith, in our negligence.

First, in the conjugal relation, how agreeably may the consorts think on those words: "What knowest thou, O wife, whether thou shalt save thy husband?" Or, "How knowest thou, O man, whether thou shalt save thy wife?"

The husband will do well to think: "What shall I do, that my wife may have cause forever to bless God, for bringing her unto me?" And, "What shall I do that in my carriage[2] towards my wife, the kindness of the blessed Jesus towards His Church, may be followed and resembled?" That this question may be the more perfectly answered, Sir, sometimes ask her to help you in the answer; ask her to tell you, what she would have you to do.

But then, the Wife also will do well to think: "Wherein may I be to my husband, a wife of that character: she will do him good, and not evil, all the days of his life?"

With my married people, I will particularly leave a good note, which I find in the Memorials of Gervase Disney, Esq.[3] "Family passions cloud faith, disturb duty, darken comfort." You'll do the more good unto one another, the more this note is thought upon. When the husband and wife are always contriving to be blessings unto one another, I will say with Tertullian, "*Unde, sufficiam ad enarrandam faelicitatem ejus matrimonii!*"[4] O happy marriage!

---

[1] I.e., in all relationships with others.
[2] Conduct.
[3] Levin: "Disney was a wealthy, religious man whose book, *Some Remarkable Passages in the Holy Life and Death of Gervase Disney, Esq.* (London, 1692), was published posthumously by his brother so that readers might "see how he was wont to exercise himself, while many of his rank are for hawks and hounds, for cards and dice."
[4] Levin: "'How can I find words to express the happiness of their marriage!'" Tertullian (c. A.D. 160–230), church father, author of *Apologeticus*, a defense of Christianity written at a time of the persecution of Christians in Rome.

[DUTY TO NEIGHBORS]

All the afflicted in the neighborhood are to be thought upon. Sirs, would it be too much for you, at least once a week, to think, "What neighbor is reduced into a pinching and painful poverty? Or in any degree impoverished with heavy losses?" Think, "What neighbor is languishing with sickness; especially if sick with sore maladies, and of some continuance?" Think, "What neighbor is heartbroken with sad bereavements; bereaved of desirable relatives?" And think: "What neighbor has a soul buffeted, and buried with violent assaults of the wicked one?" But then think, "What shall be done for such neighbors?"

First, you will pity them. . . .

But this is not all. 'Tis possible, 'tis probable, you may do well to visit them; and when you visit them, comfort them. Carry them some good word, which may raise a gladness, in an heart stooping with heaviness.

And lastly. Give them all the assistances that may answer their occasions: assist them with advice to them; assist them with address to others for them. And if it be needful, bestow your alms upon them: deal thy bread to the hungry; bring to thy house the poor that are cast out; when thou seest the naked, cover him. At least, as Nazianzen's[1] charity, I pray: *Si nihil habes, da lacrymulam;*[2] if you have nothing else to bestow upon the miserable, bestow a tear or two upon their miseries. This little, is better than nothing!

Would it be amiss for you, to have always lying by you, a list of the poor in your neighborhood, or of those whose calamities may call for the assistances of the neighborhood? Such a list would often furnish you, with matter for an useful conversation, when you are talking with your friends, whom you may provoke to love and good works.

I will go on to say: Be glad of opportunities to do good in your neighborhood: yea, look out for them, lay hold on them, with a rapturous assiduity. Be sorry for all the bad circumstances of any neighbor, that bespeak your doing of good unto him. Yet, be glad, if any one tell you of them. Thank him who tells you, as having therein done you a very great civility. Let him know, that he could not by anything have more gratified you. Any civility that you can show, by lending, by watching, by—all the methods of courtesy; show it; and be glad you can show it. Show it, and give a pleasant countenance *(cum munere vultum)*[3] in the showing of it. Let your wisdom cause your face always to shine; look, not with a cloudy but a serene and shining face, upon your neighbors; and shed the rays of your courtesy upon them, with such affability, that they may see they are welcome to all you can do for them. Yea, stay not until you are told of opportunities to do good. Inquire after them; let the inquiry be solicitous, be unwearied. The incomparable pleasure, is worth an inquiry.

There was a generous pagan, who counted a day lost, if he had obliged nobody in the day. *Amici, diem perdidi!*[4] O Christian, let us try whether we can't attain to do something, for some neighbor or other, every day that comes over our head. Some do so; and with a better spirit, than ever Titus Vespasian[5] was acted withal. Thrice in the Scriptures, we find the good angels rejoicing: 'tis always, at the good of others. To rejoice in the good of others, and most of all in doing of good unto them, 'tis angelical goodness.

In moving for the devices of good neighborhood, a principal motion which I have to make, is, that you consult the spiritual interests of your neighborhood, as well as the temporal. Be concerned, lest the deceitfulness of sin undo any of the

---

[1]St. Gregory Nazianzen (*c.* 330–390), one of four Greek fathers of the Catholic Church, became Bishop of Constantinople in 379, one of the authors of the Greek hymnody.
[2]Mather follows the Latin quotation with his free translation.
[3]Mather's partial Latin version of his own English.

[4]Levin: "Friends, I have lost the day!"
[5]Roman emperor (A.D. 69–79), a generally good and constructive leader. When Vespasian spared the life of a conspiratorial republican who had insulted him, he remarked, "I will not kill a dog that barks at me."

neighbors. If there be any idle persons among them, I beseech you, cure them of their idleness; don't nourish 'em and harden 'em in that; but find employment for them. Find 'em work; set 'em to work; keep 'em to work. Then, as much of your other bounty to them, as you please.

If any children in the neighborhood, are under no education, don't allow 'em to continue so. Let care be taken, that they may be better educated; and be taught to read; and be taught their catechism; and the truths and ways of their only Savior.

Once more. If any in the neighborhood, are taking to bad courses, lovingly and faithfully admonish them. If any in the neighborhood are enemies to their own welfare, or their families; prudently dispense your admonitions unto them. If there are any prayerless families, never leave off entreating and exhorting of them, 'til you have persuaded them, to set up the worship of God. If there be any service of God, or of His people, to which any one may need to be excited, give him a tender excitation. Whatever snare you see any one in, be so kind, as to tell him of his danger to be ensnared, and save him from it. By putting of good books into the hands of your neighbors, and gaining of them a promise to read the books, who can tell, what good you may do unto them! It is possible, you may in this way, with ingenuity, and with efficacy, administer those reproofs, which you may owe unto such neighbors, as are to be reproved for their miscarriages. The books will balk nothing, that is to be said, on the subjects, that you would have the neighbors advised upon.

Finally. If there be any base houses, which threaten to debauch, and poison, and confound the neighborhood, let your charity to your neighbors, make you do all you can, for the suppression of them.

That my proposal to do good in the neighborhood, and as a neighbor may be more fully formed and followed; I will conclude it, with minding you, that a world of self-denial is to be exercised in the execution of it. You must be armed against selfishness, all selfish and squinting intentions, in your generous resolutions. . . .

The thing required by our Savior is, Do good unto such as you are never like to be the better for.[6]

1710

from Manuductio Ad Ministerium[1]

[OF STYLE]

Poetry, whereof we have now even an antediluvian piece in our hands, has from the beginning been in such request, that I must needs recommend unto you some acquaintance with it. Though some have had a soul so unmusical that they have decried all verse as being but a mere playing and fiddling upon words, all versifying as if it were more unnatural than if we should choose dancing instead of walking, and rhyme as if it were but a sort of Morris dancing[2] with bells. Yet I cannot wish you a soul that shall be wholly unpoetical. An old Horace has left us an *Art of Poetry*,[3] which you may do well to bestow a perusal on. And besides your

---

[6]Luke 6:34–35: "And if ye lend to them of whom ye hope to receive, what thank have ye? for sinners also lend to sinners, to receive as much again. But love ye your enemies, and do good, and lend, hoping for nothing again; and your reward shall be great."
[1]*Directions for a Candidate of the Ministry* (Latin). In this work, Mather surveyed the arts and sciences and proscribed suitable studies and conduct for the prospective

minister; in this excerpt he comments on literature and defends his own writing style.
[2]Variant of morrice dance, rustic dance of northern England, accompanied by a piper, with characters such as Robin Hood; originated in country festivals.
[3]Horace (65–8 B.C.), Roman poet known for his odes and for his *Ars Poetica*, setting forth rules for writing poetry.

lyric hours, I wish you may so far understand an epic poem that the beauties of an Homer and a Virgil[4] may be discerned with you. . . .

I proceed now to say, that if (under the guidance of a Vida[5]) you try your young wings now and then to see what flights you can make, at least for an epigram, it may a little sharpen your sense, and polish your style, for more important performances. For this purpose you are now even overstocked with patterns and *poemata passim.*[6] You may, like Nazianzen,[7] all your days, make a little recreation of poetry in the midst of your more painful studies. Nevertheless, I cannot but advise you, withhold thy throat from thirst. Be not so set upon poetry, as to be always poring on the passionate and measured pages. Let not what should be sauce rather than food for you, engross all your application. Beware of a boundless and sickly appetite, for the reading of the poems, which now the rickety nation swarms withal, and let not the Circean cup[8] intoxicate you. But especially preserve the chastity of your soul from the dangers you may incur, by a conversation with Muses that are no better than harlots, among which are others besides Ovid's *Epistles,*[9] which for their tendency to excite and foment impure flames, and cast coals into your bosom, deserve rather to be thrown into the fire than to be laid before the eye which a covenant should be made withal. Indeed, not merely for the impurities which they convey, but also on some other accounts, the powers of darkness have a library among us, whereof the poets have been the most numerous as well as the most venomous authors. Most of the modern plays, as well as the romances and novels and fictions, which are a sort of poems, do belong to the catalogue of this cursed library. . . .

But there is what I may rather call a parenthesis than a digression, which this may be not altogether an improper place for the introducing of.

There has been a deal of ado about a style, so much, that I must offer you my sentiments upon it. There is a way of writing wherein the author endeavors that the reader may have something to the purpose in every paragraph. There is not only a vigor sensible in every sentence, but the paragraph is embellished with profitable references, even to something beyond what is directly spoken. Formal and painful quotations are not studied, yet all that could be learnt from them is insinuated. The writer pretends not unto reading, yet he could not have writ as he does if he had not read very much in his time, and his composures are not only a cloth of gold, but also stuck with as many jewels as the gown of a Russian ambassador. This way of writing has been decried by many, and is at this day more than ever so, for the same reason, that in the old story, the grapes were decried, that they were not ripe.[10] A lazy, ignorant, conceited set of authors would persuade the whole tribe to lay aside that way of writing for the same reason that one would have persuaded his brethren to part with the encumbrance of their bushy tails. But however fashion and humor may prevail, they must not think that the club at their coffeehouse is all the world, but there will always be those who will in this case be governed by indisputable reason and who will think that the real excellency of a book will never lie in saying of little, that the less one has for his money in a book, 'tis really the more valuable for it, and that the less one is instructed in a book and the more of superfluous margin and superficial harangue and the less of substantial matter one has in it, the more 'tis to be accounted of. And if a more massy way of writing be never so much disgusted at this day, a better gust[11] will

---

[4]Homer (between twelfth and ninth century B.C.), Greek author of the epic poems, the *Iliad* and the *Odyssey;* Virgil (70–19 B.C.), Roman author of the epic, the *Aeneid.*

[5]Marco Girolamo Vida (*c.* 1480–1566), Italian poet and bishop, known for his Latin epic, *Christias.*

[6]"Poems of various kinds" (Latin).

[7]St. Gregory Nazianzen (*c.* 330–390), one of the four Greek fathers of the Catholic Church and one of the authors of the Greek hymnody.

[8]Circe was an enchantress who drugged Odysseus's men and turned them into swine (in Homer's *Odyssey*).

[9]Ovid (*c.* 43 B.C.–A.D. 17), Roman author of *Metamorphoses* and *Art of Love,* was also long considered immoral or vulgar because of his portrayal of passion, love, and lust.

[10]In one of Aesop's *Fables,* the fox sees grapes hanging high up that are temptingly ripe, but because he cannot reach them he says, "These grapes are sour."

[11]Taste.

come on, as will some other thing, *quae jam cecidere*.[12] In the meantime, nothing appears to me more impertinent and ridiculous than the modern way (I cannot say, rule; for they have none!) of criticizing. The blades that set up for critics—I know not who constituted or commissioned 'em!—they appear to me for the most part as contemptible as they are a supercilious generation. For indeed no two of them have the same style, and they are as intolerably cross-grained and severe in their censures upon one another as they are upon the rest of mankind. But while each of them, conceitedly enough, sets up for the standard of perfection, we are entirely at a loss which fire to follow. Nor can you easily find any one thing wherein they agree for their style, except perhaps a perpetual care to give us jejune[13] and empty pages, without such touches of erudition (to speak in the style of an ingenious traveler) as may make the discourses less tedious and more enriching to the mind of him that peruses them. There is much talk of a florid style obtaining among the pens that are most in vogue, but how often would it puzzle one, even with the best glasses, to find the flowers! And if they were to be chastised for it, it would be with as much of justice as Jerome was, for being a Ciceronian.[14] After all, every man will have his own style which will distinguish him as much as his gait, and if you can attain to that which I have newly described, but always writing so as to give an easy conveyance unto your ideas, I would not have you by any scourging be driven out of your gait; but if you must confess a fault in it, make a confession like that of the lad unto his father while he was beating him for his versifying.

However, since every man will have his own style, I would pray that we may learn to treat one another with mutual civilities and condescensions,[15] and handsomely indulge one another in this, as gentlemen do in other matters.

I wonder what ails people that they cannot let Cicero write in the style of Cicero and Seneca write in the (much other) style of Seneca,[16] and own that both may please in their several ways. But I will freely tell you, what has made me consider the humorists that set up for critics upon style as the most unregardable set of mortals in the world is this: Far more illustrious critics than any of those to whom I am now bidding defiance, and no less men than your Erasmuses and your Grotiuses,[17] have taxed the Greek style of the New Testament with I know not what solecisms and barbarisms (and how many learned folks have obsequiously run away with the notion) whereas 'tis an ignorant and an insolent whimsy which they have been guilty of. It may be (and particularly by an ingenious Blackwall,[18] it has been) demonstrated that the gentlemen are mistaken in every one of their pretended instances; all the unquestionable classics may be brought in to convince them of their mistakes. Those glorious oracles are as pure Greek as ever was written in the world and so correct, so noble, so sublime is their style that never anything under the cope[19] of Heaven but the Old Testament has equaled it.

1726

---

[12]"Which now to cut short" (Latin), i.e., so much for that.
[13]Barren, dull.
[14]St. Jerome (*c.* 331–420) translated the Bible into Latin (the Vulgate); Ciceronian, the style of Cicero (106–43 B.C.), that is—polished and elegant.
[15]Agreements, concessions.
[16]For Cicero see note 14; Seneca (*c.* 4 B.C.–A.D. 65), whose epigrammatic style is in marked contrast with Cicero's elegant style.

[17]Erasmus (*c.* 1467–1536) edited the Greek New Testament, with Latin translations; Grotius (Huig de Groot) (1583–1645) wrote a commentary on, and provided annotations for, the Bible.
[18]Anthony Blackwall (1674–1730) wrote *The Sacred Classics Defended* (1725).
[19]A covering, as a canopy or the sky.

JONATHAN EDWARDS
(1703–1758)

In his "Personal Narrative" (1739), Jonathan Edwards describes a moment in his youth when he walked alone, "in a solitary place" of his father's pasture, "for contemplation": "And as I was walking there, and looking up on the sky and clouds, there came into my mind so sweet a sense of the glorious *majesty* and *grace* of God, that I know not how to express." This felt presence of an "awful sweetness," this "sense of divine things," made such an imprint that Edwards remembered it always. It was well worth remembering, for it could be cited as one of those reassuring signs from God that, in Edwards's Calvinistic universe, he was not of the damned but of the elect, destined for salvation by God's *grace*. Such experiences, in short, confirmed Puritan doctrine. But ironically, to us now, they seem to be prophetic of the essential transcendental experience like that described by Emerson in *Nature*, about a century after Edwards. Emerson, solitary and wandering in the woods, suddenly felt "uplifted in infinite space": "I am nothing; I see all, the currents of the Universal Being circulate through me."

Edwards was, of course, no Transcendentalist; but he might well have been, as he has been called, a "Puritan mystic." At the same time, his range was broad enough to embrace and utilize the meticulous methods of argument and rebuttal generally used in an "age of reason." He was able to point out, in his *Freedom of the Will*, the logical absurdities of the Arminians who attacked the Calvinistic doctrine of predestination; but on the other hand he could affirm in one of his most celebrated sermons, "A Divine and Supernatural Light," that there is such a thing as "a Spiritual and Divine Light, immediately imparted to the soul by God, of a different nature from any that is obtained by natural means." Thus Edwards placed in the service of his Calvinistic faith both his rational and intuitive faculties without confronting the possibility of their contradictory nature.

Jonathan Edwards was born at East Windsor, Connecticut, a son and grandson of ministers. At the age of twelve, he wrote a scientific tract on the "flying spider" ("Of Insects") in which he displayed remarkable talents of observation and writing. He was admitted to Yale at the age of thirteen, where he completed the undergraduate program and then took two years of theology. It was at Yale that he discovered John Locke's *Essay Concerning Human Understanding* and felt the delight of a "greedy miser" in "some newly discovered treasure." In 1727 he became assistant minister to his grandfather, Reverend Solomon Stoddard, at the church in Northampton, Massachusetts. This same year he married the seventeen-year-old Sarah Pierrepont, who bore him twelve children.

On his grandfather's death two years later, Edwards became the minister. During 1734–35, his powerful preaching helped ignite the spiritual revival in Northampton that became known as the Great Awakening, a religious conflagration that swept through New England and the other colonies. Supporters of the Great Awakening believed it to be the work of God; detractors, on the other hand, were skeptical of the emotionalism and doubted the depth of its religious meaning.

Edwards spent twenty-four years as minister at Northampton, with most of his energies going into a revival of the religious dedication of the Puritan founding fathers. Such sermons as "Sinners in the Hands of an Angry God" (1741) caused despair at the prospects of eternal damnation, while others like "A Divine and Supernatural Light" (1734) inspired hope of finding within oneself the spiritual presence signaling salvation. In "A Narrative of the Surprising Conversions" (1736), Edwards recorded many cases of successful conversion; but he recorded, too, the case of the desperate "Uncle Hawley," who "laid violent hands on himself, and put an end to his life."

In the tide of the new religious fervor, Edwards felt himself on the verge of restoring the original intensity of the Puritan faith. He became more and more severe in his application of the tests of doctrine and dogma. He publicly chastized sinners, and he refused the sacrament of communion to those who had not publicly affirmed their conversion (achievement of a conviction of being of the elect, or saved). In effect, he rejected the then widely accepted practice of the "Halfway Covenant." As descendants of the original Puritans matured but had not met the strict requirements for full church membership (had not experienced "conversion"), many pastors agreed to baptize their children if the parents were not "of scandalous living" and would covenant to fulfill the duties of church membership. Gradually parents and children were allowed to participate in communion. Edwards's refusal to follow this practice enraged an already resentful congregation. The congregation rebelled, and by a large margin voted to dismiss him. He preached his farewell sermon in mid-1750.

The following year he accepted the church's call from the frontier town of Stockbridge, in western Massachusetts. There he settled into his ministry and became missionary to the Indians. But he directed his intellectual energies into the writing of a series of books defending the points of Puritan doctrine that had been challenged and diminished in the years since the founding generation. The principal of these are *Freedom of the Will* (1754), *The Great Christian Doctrine of Original Sin Defended* (1758), and *The Nature of True Virtue* (published posthumously in 1765). These works could only have been conceived and written during the twilight phase of the Puritan period, when all its doctrines had been irreversibly diluted. They differ fundamentally, however, from most previous defenses of Puritan doctrine. Before Edwards, writers "proved" points of belief by copious quotation from the Bible; Edwards used cold, calculating logic—and his was something of a steel-trap intellect. In 1757 Edwards was selected as president of the College of New Jersey (now Princeton) and he took office in early 1758. Shortly after arriving at his new post, Edwards was innoculated for smallpox. The serum was contaminated; he contracted the disease and died.

Edwards was a brilliant, even dazzling, eighteenth-century participant in seventeenth-century debates on points of religious doctrine that seem—on the surface—largely irrelevant to the twentieth-century lives of his readers. A sympathetic biographer wrote of him: "The great wrong Edwards did, which haunts us as an evil dream throughout his writings, was to assert God at the expense of humanity." But however we assess his work, it is a massive, an impressive intellectual achievement. And contemporary poet Robert Lowell apprises us of the deeper relevance of Edwards to us as Americans, and to our modern age of anxiety, in several important poems, including "Mr. Edwards and the Spider," "After the Surprising Conversions," and "Jonathan Edwards in Western Massachusetts." One critic, Richard J. Fein, has written that for Lowell, "Edwards is an authentic even if doomed voice, authentic because doomed; he makes no compromises; his vision is so intense that none can be made."

ADDITIONAL READING

Jonathan Edwards: Representative Selections, ed. Clarence H. Faust and Thomas H. Johnson, 1935, 1962; *Jonathan Edwards: Basic Writings*, ed. Ola Elizabeth Winslow, 1966.

Thomas H. Johnson, *The Printed Writings of Jonathan Edwards, 1703–1758: A Bibliography*, 1940, 1970; Perry Miller, *Jonathan Edwards*, 1949; Ola E. Winslow, *Jonathan Edwards*, 1949; A. O. Aldridge, *Jonathan Edwards*, 1964; Edward H. Davidson, *Jonathan Edwards: The Narrative of a Puritan Mind*, 1968; Roland A. Delattre, *Beauty and Sensibility in the Thought of Jonathan Edwards*, 1968; David Levin, ed., *Jonathan Edwards: A Profile*, 1969; Edward M. Griffin, *Jonathan Edwards*, 1971; Terrence Erdt, *Jonathan Edwards: Art and the Sense of the Heart*, 1980; M. X. Lesser, *Jonathan Edwards: A Reference Guide*, 1981; Paula M. Cooey, *Jonathan Edwards on Nature and Destiny: A Systematic Analysis*, 1985; R. C. De Prospo, *Theism in the Discourse of Jonathan Edwards*, 1985; Iain Hamish Murray, *Jonathan Edwards: A New Biography*, 1987; M. X. Lesser, *Jonathan Edwards*, 1988; Nathan O. Hatch and Harry S. Stout, eds., *Jonathan Edwards and the American Experience*, 1988; Allen C. Guelzo, *Edwards on the Will: A Century of American Theological Debate*, 1989.

TEXTS

The Yale University Press edition of Edwards, *The Works of Jonathan Edwards*, began under the general editorship of Perry Miller, later assumed by John E. Smith. From this edition: "Of Insects," *Scientific and Philosophical Writings*, vol. 6, ed. Wallace E. Anderson, 1980; [Narrative of Surprising Conversions], *The Great Awakening*, vol. 4, ed. C. C. Goen, 1972; selections from *Freedom of the Will*, vol. 1, ed. Paul Ramsey, 1957. "Sarah Pierrepont" and "Sinners in the Hands of an Angry God" are taken from *The Works of Jonathan Edwards*, 10 vols., ed. Sereno E. Dwight, 1829–30; "Personal Narrative," selections from "A Divine and Supernatural Light," and selections from "The Nature of True Virtue" are taken from *The Works of President Edwards*, 8 vols., ed. S. Austin, 1808; selections from *Images or Shadows of Divine Things*, ed. Perry Miller, 1948. Typography, punctuation, spelling, and usage have been changed to conform with contemporary English and modern printing practices.

Of Insects[1]

Of all insects, no one is more wonderful than the spider, especially with respect to their sagacity and admirable way of working. These spiders, for the present, shall be distinguished into those that keep in houses and those that keep in forests, upon trees, bushes, shrubs, etc.; for I take 'em to be of very different kinds and natures (there are also other sorts, some of which keep in rotten logs, hollow trees, swamps and grass).

Of these last, everyone knows the truth of their marching in the air from tree to tree, and these sometimes at five or six rods[2] distance sometimes. Nor can anyone go out amongst the trees in a dewy morning towards the latter end of August or the beginning of September, but that he shall see hundreds of webs, made conspicuous by the dew that is lodged upon them, reaching from one tree and shrub to another that stands at a considerable distance; and they may be seen well

---

[1]Written when Edwards was eleven years old, "Of Insects" is a remarkable account of the flying spider which he studied in the natural setting around him. Composed at his father's request to send to an English correspondent, the essay has rarely failed to impress readers with its perception, clarity, and meticulous analysis. Its composition is the subject of Robert Lowell's poem, "Mr. Edwards and the Spider" (1946).

[2]A rod is a measure of length equaling 16½ feet; six rods would be 99 feet.

enough by an observing eye at noonday by their glistening against the sun. And what is still more wonderful, I know I have several times seen, in a very calm and serene day at that time of year, standing behind some opaque body that shall just hide the disk of the sun and keep off his dazzling rays from my eye, multitudes of little shining webs and glistening strings of a great length, and at such a height as that one would think they were tacked to the sky by one end, were it not that they were moving and floating. And there often appears at the end of these webs a spider floating and sailing in the air with them, which I have plainly discerned in those webs that were nearer to my eye. And once [I] saw a very large spider, to my surprise, swimming in the air in this manner, and others have assured me that they often have seen spiders fly. The appearance is truly very pretty and pleasing, and it was so pleasing, as well as surprising, to me, that I resolved to endeavor to satisfy my curiosity about it, by finding out the way and manner of their doing it; being also persuaded that, if I could find out how they flew, I could easily find out how they made webs from tree to tree.

And accordingly, at a time when I was in the woods, I happened to see one of these spiders on a bush. So I went to the bush and shook it, hoping thereby to make him uneasy upon it and provoke him to leave it by flying, and took good care that he should not get off from it any other way. So I continued constantly to shake it, which made him several times let himself fall by his web a little; but he would presently creep up again, till at last he was pleased, however, to leave that bush and march along in the air to the next; but which way I did not know, nor could I conceive, but resolved to watch him more narrowly next time. So I brought [him] back to the same bush again; and to be sure that there was nothing for him to go upon the next time, I whisked about a stick I had in my hand on all sides of the bush, that I might break any web going from it, if there were any, and leave nothing else for him to go on but the clear air, and then shook the bush as before; but it was not long before he again to my surprise went to the next bush. I took him off upon my stick and, holding of him near my eye, shook the stick as I had done the bush, whereupon he let himself down a little, hanging by his web, and [I] presently perceived a web out from his tail and a good way into the air. I took hold of it with my hand and broke it off, not knowing but that I might take it out to the stick with him from the bush; but then I plainly perceived another such string to proceed out at his tail.

I now conceived I had found out the whole mystery. I repeated the trial over and over again till I was fully satisfied of his way of working, which I don't only conjecture, to be on this wise, viz.: They, when they would go from tree to tree, or would sail in the air, let themselves hang down a little way by their web; and then put out a web at their tails, which being so exceeding rare when it first comes from the spider as to be lighter than the air, so as of itself it will ascend in it (which I know by experience), the moving air takes it by the end, and by the spider's permission, pulls it out and bears it out of his tail to any length, and if the further end of it happens to catch by a tree or anything, why, there's a web for him to go over upon. And the spider immediately perceives it and feels when it touches, much after the same manner as the soul in the brain immediately perceives when any of those little nervous strings that proceed from it are in the least jarred by external things. And this very way I have seen spiders go from one thing to another, I believe fifty times at least since I first discovered it.

But if nothing is in the way of those webs to hinder their flying out at a sufficient distance, and they don't catch by anything, there will be so much of it drawn out into the air, as by its ascending force there will be enough to carry the spider with it; or, which is all one, till there is so much of this web which is rarer than the air as that the web, taken with the spider, shall take up as much or more space than the same quantity [of air]. Of which, if it be equal they together will be in perfect equilibrium or poise with the air, so as that when they are loose therein they will neither ascend or descend, but only as they are driven by the wind; but if they together be more, will ascend therein: like as a man at the bottom of the sea, if he has hold on a stick of wood, or anything that is lighter or takes up more space for the quantity of matter than the water. If it be a little piece, it may not be enough to carry him and cause him to swim therein, but if there be enough of it, it will carry him up to the surface of the water (if there be so much as that the greater rarity shall more than counterbalance the greater density of the man); and if it doth but just counterbalance, put the man anywhere in the water and there he'll keep, without ascending or descending. 'Tis just so with the spider in the air as with the man in the water, for what is lighter than the air will swim or ascend therein, as well as that which is lighter than the water swims in that. And if the spider has hold on so much of a web that the greater levity[3] of all of it shall more than counterpoise the greater gravity of the spider, so that the ascending force of the web shall be more than the descending force of the spider, the web, by its ascending, will necessarily carry the spider up unto such a height, as that the air shall be so much thinner and lighter, as that the lightness of the web with the spider shall no longer prevail.

Now perhaps here it will be asked how the spider knows when he has put out web enough, and, when he does know, how does he get himself loose from the web by which he hung to the tree. I answer: there is no occasion for the spider's knowing, for their manner is to let out their web until the ascending force of their web and the force the wind has upon it, together with the weight of the spider, shall be enough to break the web by which the spider hangs to the tree, for the stress of all these comes upon that, and nature has so provided, that just so much web as is sufficient to break, that shall be sufficient [to] carry the spider. And [this] very way I very frequently have seen spiders mount away into the air, with a vast train of glistening web before them, from a stick in my hand, and have also shewed it to others. And without doubt they do it with a great deal of their sort of pleasure.

There remain only two difficulties. The one is, how should they first begin to spin out this so fine and even a thread of their bodies? If once there is a web out it is easy to conceive how if the end of it were once out, how the air might take it and so draw it out to a greater length. But how should they at first let out of their tails the end of a fine string, whereas in all probability the web, while it is in the spider, is a certain liquor with which that great bottle tail of theirs is filled, which immediately upon its being exposed to the air turns to a dry substance and very much rarifies and extends itself. Now if it be a liquor, it is hardly conceivable how they should let out a fine string, except by expelling a small drop at the end of it; but none such can be discovered. To find out this difficulty I once got a very large spider of the sort; for in lesser ones I could not distinctly discern how they did that, nor can one discern their webs at all except they are held up against the sun or some dark place. I took this spider and held him up against an open door, which, being dark, helped me plainly to discern, and shook him. Whereupon, he let himself down by his web—as in the [first] figure, by the web *cb*—and then fixed with his tail one end of the web that he intended to let out into the air to the web by which he let himself down, at *a;* then, pulling away his tail, one end of the web was thereby drawn out, which being at first exceeding slender, the wind presently broke it at *d,* and drew it out, as in Figure the second, and it was immediately spun out to a very great length.

The other difficulty is, how when they are once carried up into the air, how

---

[3]Lightness of weight.

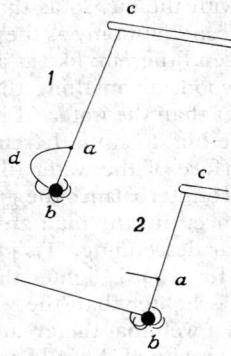

Figs. 1, 2

they get down again, or whether they are necessitated to continue, till they are beat down by some shower of rain, without any sustenance—which [is] not probable nor agreeable to nature's providence. I answer: there is a way whereby they may come down again when they please by only gathering in their webs in to them again, by which way they may come down gradually and gently. But whether that be their way or no, I can't say—but without scruple, that or a better, for we always find things done by nature as well or better than [we] can imagine beforehand.

Corol. We hence see the exuberant goodness of the Creator, who hath not only provided for all the necessities, but also for the pleasure and recreation of all sorts of creatures, and even the insects and those that are most despicable.

Another thing particularly notable and worthy of being inquired into about these webs is that they, which are so exceeding small and fine as that they cannot be discerned except held in a particular position with respect to the sun or against some dark place when held close to the eye, should appear at such a prodigious height in the air when near betwixt us and the sun, so that they must needs some often appear as big as a cable would do, if it appeared exactly *secundum rationem distantiae.*[4] To solve, we ought to consider that these webs, as they are thus posited, very vividly reflect the rays of the sun, so as to cause them to be very lightsome bodies; and then see if we can't find any parallel phenomena in other lightsome bodies. And everybody knows that a candle in the night appears exceedingly bigger at a distance than it ought to do, and we may observe in the moon towards the new, when that part of it that is not enlightened by the sun, is visible, how much the enlightened part thereof is enlarged and extended beyond the circumference of the other parts. And astronomers also know how exceedingly the fixed stars are beyond their bounds to our naked eye, so that without doubt they appear many hundreds of times bigger than they ought to do. The reason may be that the multitude and powerfulness of the rays affects a greater part of the retina than their share, that which they immediately strike upon. But we find that a light that so does when it is alone, and when no part of the retina is affected by anything else but that, so that the least impression is felt by it, won't do so—or at least not so much—in the midst of other perhaps greater light, so that other parts of the retina are filled with impressions of their own. But these webs are instances of the latter, so that this reason does not seem fully to solve this so great a magnifying, though without a doubt that helps. But the chief reason must be referred to that incurvation[5] of the rays passing by the edge of any body, which Sir Isaac Newton has proved.

---

[4]According to the calculation of the distance (Latin).
[5]Curving or bending inward. Sir Isaac Newton (1642–1727), English natural philosopher, scientist, mathemati-cian, whose *New Theory about Light and Colours* was read to the Royal Society of London in 1672.

One thing more I shall take notice of, before I dismiss this subject, concerning the end of nature in giving spiders this way of flying; which, though we have found in the corollary to be their pleasure and recreation, yet we think a greater end is at last their destruction. And what makes us think so is because that is necessarily and naturally brought to pass by it, and we shall find nothing so brought to pass by nature but what is the end of those means by which is brought to pass; and we shall further evince it by and by, by shewing the great usefulness of it. But we must show how their destruction is brought to pass by it.

I say then, that by this means almost all the spiders upon the land must necessarily be swept first and last into the sea. For we have observed already that they never fly except in fair weather; and we may now observe that it is never fair weather, neither in this country nor any other, except when the wind blows from the midland parts, and so towards the sea. So, here in New England, I have observed that they never fly except when the wind is westerly, and I never saw them fly but when they were hastening directly towards the sea. And [the] time of the flying being so long, even from the middle of August to the middle of October— though their chief time here in New England is in the time as was said before, to wit, the latter end of August and the beginning of September—and they keep flying all that while towards the sea, [they] must needs almost all of them get there before they have done. And the same indeed holds true of all other sorts of flying insects, for at that time of year the ground, trees and houses, the places of their residence in summer, being pretty chill, they leave 'em whenever the sun shines pretty warm, and mount up into the air and expand their wings to the sun. And so, flying for nothing but their ease and comfort, they suffer themselves to go that way that they find they can go with greatest ease, and so wheresoever the wind pleases. And besides, it being warmth they fly for, and it being warmer flying with the wind than against it or sideways to it—for thereby the wind has less power upon them—and as was said of spiders, they never flying but when the winds that blow from the midland parts towards the sea bring fair weather, they must necessarily, flying so long a time, all the while towards the sea, get there at last. And I very well remember, that at the same time when I have been viewing the spiders with their webs in the air, I also saw vast multitudes of flies, many of 'em at a great height, all flying the same way with the spiders and webs, directly seaward. And I have many times, at that time of year, looking westward, seen myriads of them towards sun setting, flying continually towards the sea; and this, I believe, almost everybody, if not all, of my own country will call to mind that they have also seen. And as to other sorts of flying insects, such as butterflies, millers, moths, etc., I remember that, when I was a boy, I have at the same time of year lien[6] on the ground upon my back and beheld abundance of them, all flying southeast, which I then thought were going to a warm country. So that, without any doubt, almost all manner of aerial insects, and also spiders which live upon them and are made up of them, are at the end of the year swept and wafted into the sea and buried in the ocean, and leave nothing behind them but their eggs for a new stock the next year.

Corol. 1. Hence also we may behold and admire at the wisdom of the Creator, and be convinced that is exercised about such little things, in this wonderful contrivance of annually carrying off and burying the corrupting nauseousness of our air, of which flying insects are little collections, in the bottom of the ocean where it will do no harm; and especially the strange way of bringing this about in spiders (which are collections of these collections, their food being flying insects) which want wings whereby it might be done. And what great inconveniences should we labor under if there were no such way. For spiders and flies are so exceeding mul-

---

[6]Variant of *lain*.

tiplying creatures that if they only slept or lay benumbed in [winter] and were raised again in the spring, which is commonly supposed, it would not be many years before we should be as much plagued with their vast numbers as Egypt was. And if they died for good and all in winter they, by the renewed heat of the sun, would presently again be dissipated into those nauseous vapors which they are made up of, and so would be of no use or benefit in that [in] which now they are so very serviceable.

Corol. 2. Admire also the Creator in so nicely and mathematically adjusting their multiplying nature, that notwithstanding their destruction by this means and the multitudes that are eaten by birds, that they do not decrease and so, little by little, come to nothing; and in so adjusting their destruction to their multiplication that they do neither increase, but taking one year with another, there is always just an equal number of them.

Another reason why they will not fly at any other time but when a dry wind blows, is because a moist wind moistens the web and makes it heavier than the air. And if they had the sense to stop themselves, we should have hundreds of times more spiders and flies by the seashore than anywhere else.

1715   *1890*

Sarah Pierrepont[1]

They say there is a young lady in [New Haven] who is beloved of that Great Being, who made and rules the world, and that there are certain seasons in which this Great Being, in some way or other invisible, comes to her and fills her mind with exceeding sweet delight; and that she hardly cares for any thing, except to meditate on him—that she expects after a while to be received up where he is, to be raised up out of the world and caught up into heaven; being assured that he loves her too well to let her remain at a distance from him always. There she is to dwell with him, and to be ravished with his love and delighted forever. Therefore, if you present all the world before her, with the richest of its treasures, she disregards it and cares not for it, and is unmindful of any pain or affliction. She has a strange sweetness in her mind, and singular purity in her affections; is most just and conscientious in all her conduct; and you could not persuade her to do any thing wrong or sinful, if you would give her all the world, lest she should offend this Great Being. She is of a wonderful sweetness, calmness, and universal benevolence of mind; especially after this Great God has manifested himself to her mind. She will sometimes go about from place to place, singing sweetly; and seems to be always full of joy and pleasure; and no one knows for what. She loves to be alone, walking in the fields and groves, and seems to have some one invisible always conversing with her.

1723   *1829*

---

[1]Sarah Pierrepont was only thirteen and Edwards twenty when he wrote these lines about her in a blank page of a book. Four years later, in 1727, they were united in a marriage that lasted until Edwards's death in 1758.

Personal Narrative[1]

I had a variety of concerns and exercises about my soul from my childhood; but had two more remarkable seasons of awakening, before I met with that change by which I was brought to those new dispositions, and that new sense of things, that I have since had. The first time was when I was a boy, some years before I went to college,[2] at a time of remarkable awakening in my father's congregation. I was then very much affected for many months, and concerned about the things of religion, and my soul's salvation; and was abundant in duties. I used to pray five times a day in secret, and to spend much time in religious talk with other boys, and used to meet with them to pray together. I experienced I know not what kind of delight in religion. My mind was much engaged in it, and had much self-righteous pleasure; and it was my delight to abound in religious duties. I with some of my schoolmates joined together, and built a booth in a swamp, in a very retired spot, for a place of prayer. And besides, I had particular secret places of my own in the woods, where I used to retire by myself; and was from time to time much affected. My affections[3] seemed to be lively and easily moved, and I seemed to be in my element when engaged in religious duties. And I am ready to think, many are deceived with such affections, and such a kind of delight as I then had in religion, and mistake it for grace.

But in process of time, my convictions and affections wore off; and I entirely lost all those affections and delights and left off secret prayer, at least as to any constant performance of it; and returned like a dog to his vomit, and went on in the ways of sin.[4] Indeed I was at times very uneasy, especially towards the latter part of my time at college; when it pleased God, to seize me with the pleurisy,[5] in which He brought me nigh to the grave, and shook me over the pit of hell. And yet, it was not long after my recovery, before I fell again into my old ways of sin. But God would not suffer me to go on with any quietness; I had great and violent inward struggles, till, after many conflicts with wicked inclinations, repeated resolutions, and bonds that I laid myself under by a kind of vows to God, I was brought wholly to break off all former wicked ways, and all ways of known outward sin; and to apply myself to seek salvation, and practice many religious duties; but without that kind of affection and delight which I had formerly experienced. My concern now wrought more by inward struggles and conflicts, and self-reflections. I made seeking my salvation the main business of my life. But yet, it seems to me, I sought after a miserable manner; which has made me sometimes since to question, whether ever it issued in that which was saving; being ready to doubt, whether such miserable seeking ever succeeded. I was indeed brought to seek salvation in a manner that I never was before; I felt a spirit to part with all things in the world, for an interest in Christ. My concern continued and prevailed, with many exercising thoughts and inward struggles; but yet it never seemed to be proper to express that concern by the name of terror.

From my childhood up, my mind had been full of objections against the doctrine of God's sovereignty, in choosing whom He would to eternal life, and reject-

[1]Because he mentions in "Personal Narrative" an evening in 1739, we know that Edwards wrote it some time after that year. He did not publish it during his lifetime, but his friend Samuel Hopkins found it among his papers after his death and included it in his biography, *The Life and Character of the Late Rev. Jonathan Edwards*, published in 1765. It was there entitled "An Account of His Conversion, Experiences, and Religious Exercises, Given by Himself." The elements of the Puritan conversion experience are vividly portrayed—a deep conviction of sin, an awakening to the absolute sovereignty and transfiguring presence of God, and a total surrender to Him through His grace. The experience as Edwards conveys it can only be described as ecstatic, and, in the profoundest sense, mystic.
[2]Edwards was at Yale as an undergraduate (1716–1720), a divinity school student (1720–1722), and a tutor (1724–1726).
[3]Emotions, feelings.
[4]Proverbs 26:11: "As a dog returneth to his vomit, so a fool returneth to his folly."
[5]Inflammation of the respiratory system, with painful breathing, fever, etc.

ing whom He pleased; leaving them eternally to perish, and be everlastingly tormented in hell. It used to appear like a horrible doctrine to me. But I remember the time very well, when I seemed to be convinced, and fully satisfied, as to this sovereignty of God, and His justice in thus eternally disposing of men, according to His sovereign pleasure. But never could give an account, how, or by what means, I was thus convinced, not in the least imagining at the time, nor a long time after, that there was any extraordinary influence of God's Spirit in it; but only that now I saw further, and my reason apprehended the justice and reasonableness of it. However, my mind rested in it; and it put an end to all those cavils and objections. And there has been a wonderful alteration in my mind, with respect to the doctrine of God's sovereignty, from that day to this; so that I scarce ever have found so much as the rising of an objection against it, in the most absolute sense, in God's showing mercy to whom He will show mercy, and hardening whom He will.[6] God's absolute sovereignty and justice, with respect to salvation and damnation, is what my mind seems to rest assured of, as much as of any thing that I see with my eyes; at least it is so at times. But I have often, since that first conviction, had quite another kind of sense of God's sovereignty than I had then. I have often since had not only a conviction, but a delightful conviction. The doctrine has appeared exceeding pleasant, bright, and sweet. Absolute sovereignty is what I love to ascribe to God. But my first conviction was not so.

The first instance that I remember of that sort of inward, sweet delight in God and divine things that I have lived much in since, was on reading those words, 1 Tim. 1:17, "Now unto the King eternal, immortal, invisible, the only wise God, be honor and glory forever and ever, Amen." As I read the words, there came into my soul, and was as it were diffused through it, a sense of the glory of the Divine Being; a new sense, quite different from anything I ever experienced before. Never any words of scripture seemed to me as these words did. I thought within myself, how excellent a Being that was, and how happy I should be, if I might enjoy that God, and be rapt[7] up to Him in heaven, and be as it were swallowed up in Him forever! I kept saying, and as it were singing over these words of scripture to myself; and went to pray to God that I might enjoy Him, and prayed in a manner quite different from what I used to do, with a new sort of affection. But it never came into my thought, that there was any thing spiritual, or of a saving nature in this.

From about that time, I began to have a new kind of apprehensions and ideas of Christ, and the work of redemption, and the glorious way of salvation by Him. An inward, sweet sense of these things, at times, came into my heart, and my soul was led away in pleasant views and contemplations of them. And my mind was greatly engaged to spend my time in reading and meditating on Christ, on the beauty and excellency of His person, and the lovely way of salvation by free grace in Him. I found no books so delightful to me, as those that treated of these subjects. Those words, Cant. 2:1, used to be abundantly with me, "I am the Rose of Sharon, and the Lily of the valleys." The words seemed to me, sweetly to represent the loveliness and beauty of Jesus Christ. The whole book of Canticles[8] used to be pleasant to me, and I used to be much in reading it, about that time; and found, from time to time, an inward sweetness, that would carry me away, in my contemplations. This I know not how to express otherwise, than by a calm, sweet abstraction of soul from all the concerns of this world; and sometimes a kind of vision, or fixed ideas and imaginations, of being alone in the mountains, or some solitary wilderness, far from all mankind, sweetly conversing with Christ, and rapt

---

[6]Romans 9:18: "Therefore hath He mercy on whom He will have mercy, and whom He will He hardeneth."
[7]Carried away.

[8]Song of Solomon, a poem of human love, read allegorically as the love between God and Israel or Christ and His church.

and swallowed up in God. The sense I had of divine things, would often of a sudden kindle up, as it were, a sweet burning in my heart; an ardor of soul, that I know not how to express.

Not long after I began to experience these things, I gave an account to my father of some things that had passed in my mind. I was pretty much affected by the discourse we had together; and when the discourse was ended, I walked abroad alone, in a solitary place in my father's pasture, for contemplation. And as I was walking there, and looking up on the sky and clouds, there came into my mind so sweet a sense of the glorious *majesty* and *grace* of God, that I know not how to express. I seemed to see them both in a sweet conjunction; majesty and meekness joined together; it was a sweet and gentle, and holy majesty; and also a majestic meekness; an awful sweetness; a high, and great, and holy gentleness.

After this my sense of divine things gradually increased, and became more and more lively, and had more of that inward sweetness. The appearance of every thing was altered; there seemed to be, as it were, a calm, sweet cast, or appearance of divine glory, in almost every thing. God's excellency, His wisdom, His purity and love, seemed to appear in every thing; in the sun, and moon, and stars; in the clouds and blue sky; in the grass, flowers, trees; in the water, and all nature; which used greatly to fix my mind. I often used to sit and view the moon for continuance; and in the day, spent much time in viewing the clouds and sky, to behold the sweet glory of God in these things; in the mean time, singing forth, with a low voice, my contemplations of the Creator and Redeemer. And scarce any thing, among all the works of nature, was so delightful to me as thunder and lightning; formerly, nothing had been so terrible to me. Before, I used to be uncommonly terrified with thunder, and to be struck with terror when I saw a thunder storm rising; but now, on the contrary, it rejoiced me. I felt God, so to speak, at the first appearance of a thunder storm; and used to take the opportunity, at such times, to fix myself in order to view the clouds and see the lightnings play, and hear the majestic and awful voice of God's thunder, which oftentimes was exceedingly entertaining, leading me to sweet contemplations of my great and glorious God. While thus engaged, it always seemed natural to me to sing, or chant for my meditations, or, to speak my thoughts in soliloquies with a singing voice.

I felt then great satisfaction, as to my good state; but that did not content me. I had vehement longings of soul after God and Christ, and after more holiness, wherewith my heart seemed to be full, and ready to break; which often brought to my mind the words of the Psalmist, Psalm 119:28, "My soul breaketh for the longing it hath." I often felt a mourning and lamenting in my heart, that I had not turned to God sooner, that I might have had more time to grow in grace. My mind was greatly fixed on divine things; almost perpetually in the contemplation of them. I spent most of my time in thinking of divine things, year after year; often walking alone in the woods, and solitary places, for meditation, soliloquy, and prayer, and converse with God; and it was always my manner, at such times, to sing forth my contemplations. I was almost constantly in ejaculatory prayer,[9] wherever I was. Prayer seemed to be natural to me, as the breath by which the inward burnings of my heart had vent. The delights which I now felt in the things of religion, were of an exceedingly different kind from those before mentioned, that I had when a boy; and what I then had no more notion of, than one born blind has of pleasant and beautiful colors. They were of a more inward, pure, soul-animating and refreshing nature. Those former delights never reached the heart; and did not arise from any sight of the divine excellency of the things of God; or any taste of the soul-satisfying and life-giving good there is in them.

---

[9]Abrupt, impulsive prayer.

My sense of divine things seemed gradually to increase, until I went to preach at New York,[10] which was about a year and a half after they began; and while I was there, I felt them, very sensibly, in a much higher degree than I had done before. My longings after God and holiness were much increased. Pure and humble, holy and heavenly Christianity, appeared exceedingly amiable to me. I felt a burning desire to be in every thing a complete Christian; and conformed to the blessed image of Christ, and that I might live, in all things, according to the pure sweet and blessed rules of the gospel. I had an eager thirsting after progress in these things; which put me upon pursuing and pressing after them. It was my continual strife day and night, and constant inquiry, how I should *be* more holy, and *live* more holily, and more becoming a child of God, and a disciple of Christ. I now sought an increase of grace and holiness, and a holy life, with much more earnestness, than ever I sought grace before I had it. I used to be continually examining myself, and studying and contriving for likely ways and means, how I should live holily, with far greater diligence and earnestness, than ever I pursued any thing in my life; but yet with too great a dependance on my own strength; which afterwards proved a great damage to me. My experience had not then taught me, as it has done since, my extreme feebleness and impotence, every manner of way; and the bottomless depths of secret corruption and deceit there was in my heart. However, I went on with my eager pursuit after more holiness, and conformity to Christ.

The heaven I desired was a heaven of holiness; to be with God, and to spend my eternity in divine love, and holy communion with Christ. My mind was very much taken up with contemplations on heaven, and the enjoyments there; and living there in perfect holiness, humility, and love. And it used at that time to appear a great part of the happiness of heaven, that there the saints could express their love to Christ. It appeared to me a great clog and burden, that what I felt within, I could not express as I desired. The inward ardor of my soul seemed to be hindered and pent up, and could not freely flame out as it would. I used often to think, how in heaven this principle should freely and fully vent and express itself. Heaven appeared exceedingly delightful, as a world of love; and that all happiness consisted in living in pure, humble, heavenly, divine love.

I remember the thoughts I used then to have of holiness; and said sometimes to myself, "I do certainly know that I love holiness, such as the gospel prescribes." It appeared to me, that there was nothing in it but what was ravishingly lovely; the highest beauty and amiableness—a *divine* beauty; far purer than any thing here upon earth; and that every thing else was like mire and defilement, in comparison of it.

Holiness, as I then wrote down some of my contemplations on it, appeared to me to be of a sweet, pleasant, charming, serene, calm nature; which brought an inexpressible purity, brightness, peacefulness and ravishment to the soul. In other words, that it made the soul like a field or garden of God, with all manner of pleasant flowers; all pleasant, delightful, and undisturbed; enjoying a sweet calm, and the gently vivifying beams of the sun. The soul of a true Christian, as I then wrote my meditations, appeared like such a little white flower as we see in the spring of the year; low and humble on the ground, opening its bosom to receive the pleasant beams of the sun's glory; rejoicing as it were in a calm rapture; diffusing around a sweet fragrancy; standing peacefully and lovingly, in the midst of other flowers round about; all in like manner opening their bosoms, to drink in the light of the sun. There was no part of creature holiness, that I had so great a sense of its loveliness, as humility, brokenness of heart, and poverty of spirit; and

---

[10]Edwards was in New York, assisting in a Presbyterian church, from August 1722 to April 1723.

there was nothing that I so earnestly longed for. My heart panted after this, to lie low before God, as in the dust; that I might be nothing, and that God might be ALL, that I might become as a little child.[11]

While at New York, I was sometimes much affected with reflections on my past life, considering how late it was before I began to be truly religious; and how wickedly I had lived till then; and once so as to weep abundantly, and for a considerable time together.

On January 12, 1723, I made a solemn dedication of myself to God, and wrote it down; giving up myself, and all that I had to God; to be for the future in no respect my own, to act as one that had no right to himself, in any respect. And solemnly vowed to take God for my whole portion and felicity; looking on nothing else as any part of my happiness, nor acting as if it were; and his law for the constant rule of my obedience; engaging to fight with all my might, against the world, the flesh and the devil,[12] to the end of my life. But I have reason to be infinitely humbled, when I consider how much I have failed of answering my obligation.

I had then abundance of sweet religious conversation in the family where I lived, with Mr. John Smith and his pious mother. My heart was knit in affection to those in whom were appearances of true piety; and I could bear the thoughts of no other companions, but such as were holy, and the disciples of the blessed Jesus. I had great longings for the advancement of Christ's kingdom in the world; and my secret prayer used to be, in great part, taken up in praying for it. If I heard the least hint of any thing that happened, in any part of the world, that appeared, in some respect or other, to have a favorable aspect on the interest of Christ's kingdom, my soul eagerly catched at it; and it would much animate and refresh me. I used to be eager to read public news letters, mainly for that end; to see if I could not find some news favorable to the interest of religion in the world.

I very frequently used to retire into a solitary place, on the banks of Hudson's river, at some distance from the city, for contemplation on divine things, and secret converse with God; and had many sweet hours there. Sometimes Mr. Smith and I walked there together, to converse on the things of God; and our conversation used to turn much on the advancement of Christ's kingdom in the world, and the glorious things that God would accomplish for His church in the latter days. I had then, and at other times the greatest delight in the holy scriptures, of any book whatsoever. Oftentimes in reading it, every word seemed to touch my heart. I felt a harmony between something in my heart, and those sweet and powerful words. I seemed often to see so much light exhibited by every sentence, and such a refreshing food communicated, that I could not get along in reading; often dwelling long on one sentence, to see the wonders contained in it, and yet almost every sentence seemed to be full of wonders.

I came away from New York in the month of April, 1723, and had a most bitter parting with Madam Smith and her son. My heart seemed to sink within me at leaving the family and city, where I had enjoyed so many sweet and pleasant days. I went from New York to Weathersfield,[13] by water, and as I sailed away, I kept sight of the city as long as I could. However, that night, after this sorrowful parting, I was greatly comforted in God at Westchester, where we went ashore to lodge; and had a pleasant time of it all the voyage to Saybrook.[14] It was sweet to me to think of meeting dear Christians in heaven, where we should never part more. At Saybrook we went ashore to lodge, on Saturday, and there kept the Sabbath; where I had a sweet and refreshing season, walking alone in the fields.

---

[11]Mark 10:15: "Whosoever shall not receive the kingdom of God as a little child, he shall not enter therein."
[12]*Book of Common Prayer*, "Litany": "Good Lord, deliver us. From all inordinate and sinful affections; and from all the deceits of the world, the flesh, and the devil."

[13]Wethersfield, Connecticut.
[14]Westchester in New York, Saybrook in Connecticut.

After I came home to Windsor, I remained much in a like frame of mind, as when at New York; only sometimes I felt my heart ready to sink with the thoughts of my friends at New York. My support was in contemplations on the heavenly state; as I find in my Diary of May 1, 1723. It was a comfort to think of that state, where there is fulness of joy; where reigns heavenly, calm, and delightful love, without alloy; where there are continually the dearest expressions of this love; where is the enjoyment of the persons loved, without ever parting; where those persons who appear so lovely in this world, will really be inexpressibly more lovely and full of love to us. And how sweetly will the mutual lovers join together to sing the praises of God and the Lamb![15] How will it fill us with joy to think, that this enjoyment, these sweet exercises will never cease, but will last to all eternity! I continued much in the same frame, in the general, as when at New York, till I went to New Haven as tutor to the college; particularly once at Bolton, on a journey from Boston, while walking out alone in the fields. After I went to New Haven I sunk in religion; my mind being diverted from my eager pursuits after holiness, by some affairs that greatly perplexed and distracted my thoughts.

In September, 1725, I was taken ill at New Haven, and while endeavoring to go home to Windsor, was so ill at the North Village, that I could go no further; where I lay sick for about a quarter of a year. In this sickness God was pleased to visit me again with the sweet influences of His Spirit. My mind was greatly engaged there in divine, pleasant contemplations, and longings of soul. I observed that those who watched with me, would often be looking out wishfully for the morning; which brought to my mind those words of the Psalmist, and which my soul with delight made its own language, "My soul waiteth for the Lord, more than they that watch for the morning, I say, more than they that watch for the morning,"[16] and when the light of day came in at the windows, it refreshed my soul from one morning to another. It seemed to be some image of the light of God's glory.

I remember, about that time, I used greatly to long for the conversion of some that I was concerned with; I could gladly honor them, and with delight be a servant to them, and lie at their feet, if they were but truly holy. But some time after this, I was again greatly diverted in my mind with some temporal concerns that exceedingly took up my thoughts, greatly to the wounding of my soul; and went on through various exercises, that it would be tedious to relate, which gave me much more experience of my own heart, than ever I had before.

Since I came to this town,[17] I have often had sweet complacency in God, in views of his glorious perfections and the excellency of Jesus Christ. God has appeared to me a glorious and lovely Being, chiefly on the account of His holiness. The holiness of God has always appeared to me the most lovely of all His attributes. The doctrines of God's absolute sovereignty, and free grace, in showing mercy to whom He would show mercy; and man's absolute dependance on the operations of God's Holy Spirit, have very often appeared to me as sweet and glorious doctrines. These doctrines have been much my delight. God's sovereignty has ever appeared to me, a great part of His glory. It has often been my delight to approach God, and adore him as a sovereign God, and ask sovereign mercy of Him.

I have loved the doctrines of the gospel; they have been to my soul like green pastures. The gospel has seemed to me the richest treasure; the treasure that I have most desired, and longed that it might dwell richly in me. The way of salvation by Christ has appeared, in a general way, glorious and excellent, most pleasant and most beautiful. It has often seemed to me, that it would in a great mea-

---

[15]The symbol of Christ in Revelation.
[16]Psalm 130:6.

[17]Northampton, Massachusetts. Edwards went there in 1726 to assist his grandfather, the minister of the church.

sure spoil heaven, to receive it in any other way. That text has often been affecting and delightful to me, Isaiah 32:2, "A man shall be an hiding place from the wind, and a covert from the tempest, &c."

It has often appeared to me delightful, to be united to Christ; to have Him for my Head, and to be a member of His body; also to have Christ for my teacher and prophet. I very often think with sweetness, and longings, and pantings of soul, of being a little child, taking hold of Christ, to be led by Him through the wilderness of this world. That text, Matthew 18:3, has often been sweet to me, "except ye be converted and become as little children, &c." I love to think of coming to Christ, to receive salvation of Him, poor in spirit, and quite empty of self, humbly exalting Him alone; cut off entirely from my own root, in order to grow into, and out of Christ; to have God in Christ to be all in all; and to live by faith on the Son of God, a life of humble unfeigned confidence in Him. That scripture has often been sweet to me, Psalm 115:1, "Not unto us, O Lord, not unto us, but to thy name give glory, for thy mercy and for thy truth's sake." And those words of Christ, Luke 10:21, "In that hour Jesus rejoiced in spirit, and said, I thank thee, O Father, Lord of heaven and earth, that thou hast hid these things from the wise and prudent, and hast revealed them unto babes; even so, Father, for so it seemed good in thy sight." That sovereignty of God which Christ rejoiced in, seemed to me worthy of such joy; and that rejoicing seemed to show the excellency of Christ, and of what spirit he was.

Sometimes, only mentioning a single word caused my heart to burn within me; or only seeing the name of Christ, or the name of some attribute of God. And God has appeared glorious to me, on account of the Trinity. It has made me have exalting thoughts of God, that He subsists in three persons; Father, Son, and Holy Ghost. The sweetest joys and delights I have experienced, have not been those that have arisen from a hope of my own good estate; but in a direct view of the glorious things of the gospel. When I enjoy this sweetness, it seems to carry me above the thoughts of my own estate; it seems at such times a loss that I cannot bear, to take off my eye from the glorious pleasant object I behold without me, to turn my eye in upon myself, and my own good estate.

My heart has been much on the advancement of Christ's kingdom in the world. The histories of the past advancement of Christ's kingdom have been sweet to me. When I have read histories of past ages, the pleasantest thing in all my reading has been, to read of the kingdom of Christ being promoted. And when I have expected, in my reading, to come to any such thing, I have rejoiced in the prospect, all the way as I read. And my mind has been much entertained and delighted with the scripture promises and prophecies, which relate to the future glorious advancement of Christ's kingdom upon earth.

I have sometimes had a sense of the excellent fulness of Christ, and His meetness and suitableness as a Saviour, whereby he has appeared to me, far above all, the chief of ten thousands.[18] His blood and atonement have appeared sweet, and His righteousness sweet: which was always accompanied with ardency of spirit; and inward strugglings and breathings, and groanings that cannot be uttered, to be emptied of myself, and swallowed up in Christ.

Once as I rode out into the woods for my health, in 1737, having alighted from my horse in a retired place, as my manner commonly has been, to walk for divine contemplation and prayer, I had a view that for me was extraordinary, of the glory of the Son of God, as Mediator between God and man, and his wonderful, great, full, pure and sweet grace and love, and meek and gentle condescension. This grace that appeared so calm and sweet, appeared also great above the heav-

---

[18]Song of Solomon 5:10: "My beloved is white and ruddy, the chiefest among ten thousand."

ens. The person of Christ appeared ineffably excellent with an excellency great enough to swallow up all thought and conception—which continued as near as I can judge, about an hour; which kept me the greater part of the time in a flood of tears, and weeping aloud. I felt an ardency of soul to be, what I know not otherwise how to express, emptied and annihilated; to lie in the dust, and to be full of Christ alone; to love Him with a holy and pure love, to trust in Him; to live upon Him; to serve and follow Him; and to be perfectly sanctified and made pure, with a divine and heavenly purity. I have, several other times, had views very much of the same nature, and which have had the same effects.

I have many times had a sense of the glory of the third person in the Trinity, in His office of Sanctifier; in His holy operations, communicating divine light and life to the soul. God, in the communications of His Holy Spirit, has appeared as an infinite fountain of divine glory and sweetness; being full and sufficient to fill and satisfy the soul; pouring forth itself in sweet communications; like the sun in its glory, sweetly and pleasantly diffusing light and life. And I have sometimes had an affecting sense of the excellency of the word of God, as a word of life; as the light of life; a sweet, excellent, life-giving word; accompanied with a thirsting after that word, that it might dwell richly in my heart.

Often, since I lived in this town, I have had very affecting views of my own sinfulness and vileness; very frequently to such a degree as to hold me in a kind of loud weeping, sometimes for a considerable time together; so that I have often been forced to shut myself up. I have had a vastly greater sense of my own wickedness, and the badness of my own heart, than ever I had before my conversion. It has often appeared to me, that if God should mark iniquity against me, I should appear the very worst of all mankind; of all that have been, since the beginning of the world to this time; and that I should have by far the lowest place in hell. When others, that have come to talk with me about their soul concerns, have expressed the sense they have had of their own wickedness, by saying that it seemed to them, that they were as bad as the devil himself; I thought their expression seemed exceedingly faint and feeble, to represent my wickedness.

My wickedness, as I am in myself, has long appeared to me perfectly ineffable, and swallowing up all thought and imagination; like an infinite deluge, or mountains over my head. I know not how to express better what my sins appear to me to be, than by heaping infinite upon infinite, and multiplying infinite by infinite. Very often, for these many years, these expressions are in my mind, and in my mouth, "Infinite upon infinite—Infinite upon infinite!" When I look into my heart, and take a view of my wickedness, it looks like an abyss infinitely deeper than hell. And it appears to me, that were it not for free grace, exalted and raised up to the infinite height of all the fulness and glory of the great Jehovah, and the arm of His power and grace stretched forth in all the majesty of His power, and in all the glory of His sovereignty, I should appear sunk down in my sins below hell itself, far beyond the sight of every thing, but the eye of sovereign grace, that can pierce even down to such a depth. And yet, it seems to me, that my conviction of sin is exceedingly small, and faint; it is enough to amaze me, that I have no more sense of my sin. I know certainly, that I have very little sense of my sinfulness. When I have had turns of weeping and crying for my sins, I thought I knew at the time, that my repentance was nothing to my sin.

I have greatly longed of late, for a broken heart, and to lie low before God; and, when I ask for humility, I cannot bear the thoughts of being no more humble than other Christians. It seems to me, that though their degrees of humility may be suitable for them, yet it would be a vile self-exaltation to me, not to be the lowest in humility of all mankind. Others speak of their longing to be "humbled to the dust"; that may be a proper expression for them, but I always think of myself, that I ought, and it is an expression that has long been natural for me to use in prayer, "to lie infinitely low before God." And it is affecting to think, how ignorant I was, when a young Christian, of the bottomless, infinite depths of wickedness, pride, hypocrisy and deceit, left in my heart.

I have a much greater sense of my universal, exceeding dependance on God's grace and strength, and mere good pleasure, of late, than I used formerly to have; and have experienced more of an abhorrence of my own righteousness. The very thought of any joy arising in me, on any consideration of my own amiableness, performances, or experiences, or any goodness of heart or life, is nauseous and detestable to me. And yet I am greatly afflicted with a proud and self-righteous spirit, much more sensibly than I used to be formerly. I see that serpent rising and putting forth its head continually, every where, all around me.

Though it seems to me, that, in some respects, I was a far better Christian, for two or three years after my first conversion, than I am now; and lived in a more constant delight and pleasure; yet, of late years, I have had a more full and constant sense of the absolute sovereignty of God, and a delight in that sovereignty and have had more of a sense of the glory of Christ, as a Mediator revealed in the gospel. On one Saturday night, in particular, I had such a discovery of the excellency of the gospel above all other doctrines, that I could not but say to myself, "This is my chosen light, my chosen doctrine"; and of Christ, "This is my chosen Prophet." It appeared sweet, beyond all expression, to follow Christ, and to be taught, and enlightened, and instructed by Him; to learn of Him, and live to Him. Another Saturday night (January, 1739), I had such a sense, how sweet and blessed a thing it was to walk in the way of duty; to do that which was right and meet to be done, and agreeable to the holy mind of God; that it caused me to break forth into a kind of loud weeping, which held me some time, so that I was forced to shut myself up, and fasten the doors. I could not but, as it were, cry out, "How happy are they which do that which is right in the sight of God! They are blessed indeed, they are the happy ones!" I had, at the same time, a very affecting sense, how meet and suitable it was that God should govern the world, and order all things according to his own pleasure; and I rejoiced in it, that God reigned, and that His will was done.

c. 1740   *1765*

[Narrative of Surprising Conversions]

In 1735, on learning about the religious awakening taking place in western Massachusetts, the Reverend Dr. Benjamin Colman (1673–1747), pastor of the Brattle Street Church in Boston, wrote to Jonathan Edwards in Northampton and asked for an account of what was happening. Edwards wrote this long letter in reply. Colman was so moved by Edwards's vivid descriptions of the conversions taking place that he published the letter in 1736. It created a sensation, especially in England, and Edwards was persuaded to rewrite and expand the letter, which was published in London in 1737 with the title of *A Faithful Narrative of the Surprising Works of God*. It went through numerous printings in the course of a three-year period.

The original 1735 letter, compelling in its immediacy, freshness, and brevity, is reprinted here. The text has been reprinted from *The Great Awakening* (1972), edited by C. C. Goen. His footnotes have been adapted in the notes printed here.

❧

Northampton, May 30, 1735

Dear Sir:

In answer to your desire, I here send you a particular account of the present extraordinary circumstances of this town, and the neighboring towns with respect to religion. I have observed that the town for this several years have gradually been reforming; there has appeared less and less of a party spirit, and a contentious disposition, which before had prevailed for many years between two parties in the town.[1] The young people also have been reforming more and more; they by degrees left off their frolicking, and have been observably more decent in their attendance on the public worship. The winter before last there appeared a strange flexibleness in the young people of the town, and an unusual disposition to hearken to counsel, on this occasion. It had been their manner of a long time, and for aught I know, always, to make Sabbath-day nights and lecture days to be especially times of diversion and company-keeping. I then preached a sermon on the Sabbath before the lecture, to show them the unsuitableness and inconvenience of the practice, and to persuade them to reform it; and urged it on heads of families that it should be a thing agreed among them to govern their families, and keep them in at those times. And there happened to be at my house the evening after, men that belonged to the several parts of the town, to whom I moved that they should desire the heads of families, in my name, to meet together in their several neighborhoods, that they might know each others' minds, and agree every one to restrain his family; which was done, and my motion complied with throughout the town. But the parents found little or no occasion for the exercise of government in the case; for the young people declared themselves convinced by what they had heard, and willing of themselves to comply with the counsel given them; and I suppose it was almost universally complied with thenceforward.

After this there began to be a remarkable religious concern among some farm houses at a place called Pascommuck,[2] and five or six that I hoped were savingly wrought upon there. And in April [1734] there was a very sudden and awful death of a young man in town, in the very bloom of his youth, who was violently seized with a pleurisy[3] and taken immediately out of his head, and died in two days; which much affected many young people in the town. This was followed with another death of a young married woman, who was in great distress in the beginning of her illness, but was hopefully converted before her death; so that she died full of comfort, and in a most earnest and moving manner, warning and counselling others, which I believe much contributed to the solemnizing of the spirits of the young people in the town; and there began evidently to appear more of a religious concern upon people's minds. In the fall of the year I moved to the young people that they should set up religious meetings, on evenings after lectures, which they complied with; this was followed with the death of an elderly person in the town, which was attended with very unusual circumstances, which much affected many people. About that time began the great noise that there was in this part of the country about Arminianism,[4] which seemed strangely to be overruled for the promoting of religion. People seemed to be put by it upon inquiring, with concern and engagedness of mind, what was the way of salvation, and what were the terms of our acceptance with God; and what was said publicly

---

[1] Edwards refers to what he described more fully in a letter of July 1, 1751, to the Rev. Thomas Gillespie: "In one ecclesiastical controversy in Mr. Stoddard's days, wherein the church was divided into two parties, the heat of spirit was raised to such a height, that it came to hard blows; a member of one party met the head of the opposite party, and assaulted him and beat him unmercifully."

[2] A small community three miles from Edwards's church in Northampton, where they worshipped.
[3] Inflammation of the lungs, causing fever, pain in breathing, etc.
[4] A doctrine of salvation through good works as against the Calvinistic doctrine of predestination; formulated by Jacobus Arminius (1560–1609).

on that occasion, however found fault with by many elsewhere, and ridiculed by some, was most evidently attended with a very remarkable blessing of heaven, to the souls of the people in this town, to the giving of them an universal satisfaction and engaging their minds with respect to the thing in question, the more earnestly to seek salvation in the way that had been made evident to them.

And then a concern about the great things of religion began, about the latter end of December and the beginning of January [1735], to prevail abundantly in the town, till in a very little time it became universal throughout the town, among old and young, and from the highest to the lowest. All seemed to be seized with a deep concern about their eternal salvation; all the talk in all companies, and upon occasions was upon the things of religion, and no other talk was anywhere relished; and scarcely a single person in the whole town was left unconcerned about the great things of the eternal world. Those that were wont to be the vainest, and loosest persons in town in general seemed to be seized with strong convictions. Those that were most disposed to contemn[5] vital and experimental religion, and those that had the greatest conceit of their own reason, the highest families in the town, and the oldest persons in the town, and many little children were affected remarkably; no one family that I know of, and scarcely a person, has been exempt. And the Spirit of God went on in his saving influences, to the appearance of all human reason and charity, in a truly wonderful and astonishing manner. The news of it filled the neighboring towns with talk, and there were many in them that scoffed and made a ridicule of the religion that appeared in Northampton. But it was observable that it was very frequent and common that those of other towns that came into this town, and observed how it was here, were greatly affected, and went home with wounded spirits, and were never more able to shake off the impression that it made upon them, till at length there began to appear a general concern in several of the towns in the county.

In the month of March the people in New Hadley[6] seemed to be seized with a deep concern about their salvation, all as it were at once, which has continued in a very great degree ever since. About the same time there began to appear the like concern in the west part of Suffield, which has since spread into all parts of the town. It next began to appear at Sunderland, and soon became universal, and to a very great degree. About the same time it began to appear in part of Deerfield, called Green River, and since has filled the town. It began to appear also at a part of Hatfield, and after that the whole town in the second week in April seemed to be seized at once, and there is a great and general concern there. And there gradually got in a considerable degree of the same concern into Hadley Old Society, and Mr. Hopkins' parish in [West] Springfield,[7] but it is nothing near so great as in many other places. The next place that we heard of was Northfield, where the concern is very great and general. We have heard that there is a considerable degree of it at Longmeadow, and there is something of it in Old Springfield in some parts of the society. About three weeks ago the town of Enfield were struck down as it were at once, the worst persons in the town seemed to be suddenly seized with a great degree of concern about their souls, as I have been informed. And about the same time, Mr. Bull[8] of Westfield [said] that there began to be a great alteration there, and that there had been more done in one week before that time that I spoke with him than had been done in seven years before. The people of Westfield have till now above all other places, made a scoff and derision of this concern at Northampton. There has been a great concern of a like nature at

---

[5]Scorn.

[6]A nearby community, now South Hadley. Other towns mentioned in this paragraph are in western Massachusetts, near Northampton.

[7]Samuel Hopkins (1693–1755), pastor at West Springfield,

Massachusetts, 1720–1755, was married to Edwards's oldest sister.

[8]Nehemiah Bull (1701–1740), pastor at Westfield, Massachusetts, 1726–1740.

Windsor, on the west side of the [Connecticut] River, which began about the same time that it began to be general here at Northampton; and my father[9] has told me that there is an hopeful beginning on the east side in his society. Mr. Noyes[10] writes me word that there is a considerable revival of religion at New Haven; and I have been credibly informed that there is something of it at Guilford and Lyme, as there also is at Coventry, Bolton, and a society in Lebanon called The Crank. I yesterday saw Mr. White[11] of Bolton, and also last night saw a young man that belongs to [the church at] Coventry, who gave a very remarkable account of that town, of the manner in which the rude debauched young people there were suddenly seized with a concern about their souls.

As to the nature of persons' experiences, and the influences of that spirit that there is amongst us, persons when seized with concern are brought to forsake their vices, and ill practices; the looser sort are brought to forsake and to dread their former extravagances. Persons are soon brought to have done with their old quarrels; contention and intermeddling with other men's matters seems to be dead amongst us. I believe there never was so much done at confessing of faults to each other, and making up differences, as there has lately been. Where this concern comes it immediately puts an end to differences between ministers and people: there was a considerable uneasiness at New Hadley between some of the people and their minister, but when this concern came amongst them it immediately put an end to it, and the people are now universally united to their minister. There was an exceeding alienation at Sunderland, between the minister and many of the people; but when this concern came amongst them it all vanished at once, and the people are universally united in hearty affection to their minister. There were some men at Deerfield, of turbulent spirits, that kept up an uneasiness there with Mr. Ashley;[12] but one of the chief of them has lately been influenced fully and freely to confess his fault to him, and is become his hearty friend.

People are brought off from inordinate engagedness after the world, and have been ready to run into the other extreme of too much neglecting their worldly business and to mind nothing but religion. Those that are under convictions are put upon it earnestly to inquire what they shall do to be saved, and diligently to use appointed means of grace, and apply themselves to all known duty. And those that obtain hope themselves, and the charity of others concerning their good estate, generally seem to be brought to a great sense of their own exceeding misery in a natural condition, and their utter helplessness, and insufficiency for themselves, and their exceeding wickedness and guiltiness in the sight of God; it seldom fails but that each one seems to think himself worse than anybody else, and they are brought to see that they deserve no mercy of God, that all their prayers and pains are exceeding worthless and polluted, and that God, notwithstanding all that they have done, or can do, may justly execute his eternal wrath upon them, and they seem to be brought to a lively sense of the excellency of Jesus Christ and his sufficiency and willingness to save sinners, and to be much weaned in their affections from the world, and to have their hearts filled with love to God and Christ, and a disposition to lie in the dust before him. They seem to have given [to] them a lively conviction of the truth of the Gospel, and the divine authority of the Holy Scriptures; though they can't have the exercise of this at all times alike, nor indeed of any other grace. They seem to be brought to abhor themselves for the sins of their past life, and to long to be holy, and to live holily, and to God's glory; but at the same time complain that they can do nothing, [for] they are poor

---

[9]Timothy Edwards (1669–1758), pastor at East Windsor, Connecticut, 1694–1755.
[10]Joseph Noyes (1688–1761), pastor at the First Church in New Haven, Connecticut, 1715–1761. Guilford, Lyme, Coventry, Bolton, all in Connecticut.

[11]Thomas White (1701–1763), pastor at Bolton, 1725–1763.
[12]Jonathan Ashley (1712–1780), pastor at Deerfield, Massachusetts, 1732–1780.

impotent creatures, utterly insufficient to glorify their Creator and Redeemer. They commonly seem to be much more sensible of their own wickedness after their conversion than before, so that they are often humbled by it; it seems to them that they are really become more wicked, when at the same time they are evidently full of a gracious spirit. Their remaining sin seems to be their very great burden, and many of them seem to long after heaven, that there they may be rid of sin. They generally seem to be united in dear love and affection one to another, and to have a love to all mankind. I never saw the Christian spirit in love to enemies so exemplified in all my life as I have seen it within this half year. They commonly express a great concern for others' salvation; some say that they think they are far more concerned for others' conversion, after they themselves have been converted, than ever they were for their own; several have thought (though perhaps they might be deceived in it) that they could freely die for the salvation of any soul, of the meanest of mankind, of any Indian in the woods.

This town never was so full of love, nor so full of joy, nor so full of distress as it has lately been. Some persons have had those longing desires after Jesus Christ, that have been to that degree as to take away their strength, and very much to weaken them, and make them faint. Many have been even overcome with a sense of the dying love of Christ, so that the home of the body has been ready to fail under it; there was once three pious young persons in this town talking together of the dying love of Christ, till they all fainted away; though 'tis probable the fainting of the two latter was much promoted by the fainting of the first. Many express a sense of the glory of the divine perfections, and of the excellency and fullness of Jesus Christ, and of their own littleness and unworthiness, in a manner truly wonderful and almost unparalleled; and so likewise of the excellency and wonderfulness of the way of salvation by Jesus Christ. Their esteem of the Holy Scriptures is exceedingly increased. Many of them say the Bible seems to be a new book to them, as though they never read it before. There have been some instances of persons that by only an accidental sight of the Bible, have been as much moved, it seemed to me, as a lover by the sight of his sweetheart. The preaching of the Word is greatly prized by them; they say they never heard preaching before: and so are God's Sabbaths, and ordinances, and opportunities of public worship. The Sabbath is longed for before it comes; some by only hearing the bell ring on some occasion in the week time, have been greatly moved, because it has put them in mind of its ringing to call the people together to worship God. But no part of public worship has commonly [had] such an effect on them as singing God's praises. They have a greater respect to ministers than they used to have; there is scarcely a minister preaches here but gets their esteem and affection.

The experiences of some persons lately amongst [us] have been beyond almost all that ever I heard or read of. There is a pious woman in this town that is a very modest bashful person, that was moved by what she heard of the experiences of others earnestly to seek to God to give her more clear manifestations of himself, and evidences of her own good estate, and God answered her request, and gradually gave her more and more of a sense of his glory and love, which she had with intermissions for several days, till one morning the week before last she had it to a more than ordinary degree, and it prevailed more and more till towards the middle of the day, till her nature began to sink under it, as she was alone in the house; but there came somebody into the house, and found her in an unusual, extraordinary frame. She expressed what she saw and felt to him; it came to that at last that they raised the neighbors, [for] they were afraid she would die; I went up to see her and found her perfectly sober and in the exercise of her reason, but having her nature seemingly overborne and sinking, and when she could speak expressing in a manner that can't be described the sense she had of the glory of God, and particularly of such and such perfections, and her own unworthiness, her longing to lie in the dust, sometimes her longing to go to be with Christ, and crying out of the excellency of Christ, and the wonderfulness of his dying love; and so she continued for hours together, though not always in the same degree. At some times she was able to discourse to those about her; but it seemed to me [that] if God had manifested a little more of himself to her she would immediately have sunk and her frame dissolved under it. She has since been at my house, and continues as full as she can hold, but looks on herself not as an eminent saint, but as the worst of all, and unworthy to go to speak with a minister; but yet now beyond any great doubt of her good estate.

There are two persons that belong to other towns that have had such a sense of God's exceeding greatness and majesty, that they were as it were swallowed up; they both of them told me to that purpose that if in the time of it they had had the least fear that they were not at peace with that great God, they should immediately have died. But there is a very vast variety of degrees of spiritual discoveries, that are made to those that we hope are godly, as there is also in the steps, and method of the Spirit's operation in convincing and converting sinners, and the length of time that persons are under conviction before they have comfort.

There is an alteration made in the town in a few months that strangers can scarcely conceive of; our church I believe was the largest in New England before,[13] but persons lately have thronged in, so that there are very few adult persons left out. There have been a great multitude hopefully converted; too many, I find, for me to declare abroad with credit to my judgment. The town seems to be full of the presence of God; our young people when they get together instead of frolicking as they used to do are altogether on pious subjects; 'tis so at weddings and on all occasions. The children in this and the neighboring towns have been greatly affected and influenced by the Spirit of God, and many of them hopefully changed; the youngest in this town is between nine and ten years of age. Some of them seem to be full of love to Christ and have expressed great longings after him and willingness to die, and leave father and mother and all things in the world to go to him, together with a great sense of their unworthiness and admiration at the free grace of God towards them. And there have been many old people, many above fifty and several near seventy, that seem to be wonderfully changed and hopefully newborn. The good people that have been formerly converted in the town have many of them been wonderfully enlivened and increased.

This work seems to be upon every account an extraordinary dispensation of providence. 'Tis extraordinary upon the account of [the] universality of it in affecting all sorts, high and low, rich and poor, wise and unwise, old and young, vicious and moral; 'tis very extraordinary as to the numbers that are hopefully savingly wrought upon, and particularly the number of aged persons and children and loose livers; and also on the account of the quickness of the work of the Spirit on them, for many seem to have been suddenly taken from a loose way of living, and to be so changed as to become truly holy, spiritual, heavenly persons; 'tis extraordinary as to the degrees of gracious communications, and the abundant measures in which the Spirit of God has been poured out on many persons; 'tis extraordinary as to the extent of it, God's Spirit being so remarkably poured out on so many towns at once, and its making such swift progress from place to place. The extraordinariness of the thing has been, I believe, one principal cause that people abroad have suspected it.

There have been, as I have heard, many odd and strange stories that have been carried about the country of this affair, which it is a wonder some wise men

---

[13]Northampton was the shire town of Hampshire County, which then included almost half the area of the Bay Colony. Its church had 71 members in 1669; by 1729, under Edwards's grandfather, the Reverend Samuel Stoddard, 630 had been admitted. In November 1736, Edwards claimed 620 communicant adults.

should be so ready to believe. Some indeed under great terrors of conscience have had impressions on their imaginations; and also under the power of spiritual discoveries, they have had livelily impressed ideas of Christ shedding blood for sinners, his blood running from his veins, and of Christ in his glory in heaven and such like things, but they are always taught, and have been several times taught in public not to lay the weight of their hopes on such things and many have nothing of any such imaginations. There have been several persons that have had their natures overborne under strong convictions, have trembled, and han't been able to stand, they have had such a sense of divine wrath; but there are no new doctrines embraced, but people have been abundantly established in those that we account orthodox; there is no new way of worship affected. There is no oddity of behavior prevails; people are no more superstitious about their clothes, or anything else than they used to be. Indeed, there is a great deal of talk when they are together of one another's experiences, and indeed no other is to be expected in a town where the concern of the soul is so universally the concern, and that to so great a degree. And doubtless some persons under the strength of impressions that are made on their minds and under the power of strong affections, are guilty of imprudences; their zeal may need to be regulated by more prudence, and they may need a guide to their assistance; as of old when the church of Corinth had the extraordinary gifts of the Spirit, they needed to be told by the Apostle that the spirit of the prophets were subject to the prophets, and that their gifts were to be exercised with prudence, because God was not the author of confusion but of peace [1 Cor. 14:32–33].[14] There is no unlovely oddity in people's temper prevailing with this work, but on the contrary the face of things is much changed as to the appearance of a meek, humble, amiable behavior. Indeed, the Devil has not been idle, but his hand has evidently appeared in several instances endeavoring to mimic the work of the Spirit of God and to cast a slur upon it, and no wonder. And there has hereby appeared the need of the watchful eye of skillful guides, and of wisdom from above to direct them.

There lately came up, hither a couple of ministers from Connecticut, viz. Mr. Lord[15] of [North] Preston, and Mr. Owen[16] of Groton, who had heard of the extraordinary circumstances of this and the neighboring towns, who had heard the affair well represented by some, and also had heard many reports greatly to its disadvantage, who came on purpose to see and satisfy themselves; and that they might thoroughly acquaint themselves, went about and spent [the] good part of a day in hearing the accounts of many of our new converts, and examining of them, which was greatly to their satisfaction; and they took particular notice, among other things, of the modesty with which persons gave account of themselves, and said that the one-half was not told them, and could not be told them; and that if they renounced these persons' experiences they must renounce Christianity itself. And Mr. Owen said particularly as to their impressions on their imaginations, they were quite different from what had been represented, and that they were no more than might naturally be expected in such cases.

Thus, Sir, I have given you a particular account of this affair which Satan has so much misrepresented in the country. This is a true account of the matter as far as I have opportunity to know, and I suppose I am under greater advantages to know than any person living. Having been thus long in the account, I forbear to make reflections, or to guess what God is about to do; I leave this to you, and shall only say, as I desire always to say from my heart, "To God be all the glory, whose

---

[14]"And the spirits of the prophets are subject to the prophets. For God is not the author of confusion, but of peace, as in all churches of the saints."
[15]Hezekiah Lord (1698–1761), pastor at North Preston,

Connecticut (1720–1761), was active in the revival of the 1740s, though within establishment bounds.
[16]John Owen (1699–1753), pastor at Groton, Connecticut (1726–1753), vigorously promoted the revival.

work alone it is." And let him have an interest in your prayers, who so much needs divine help at this day, and is your affectionate brother and humble servant.

Jonathan Edwards

Northampton, June 3, 1735

Since I wrote the foregoing letter, there has happened a thing of a very awful nature in the town. My Uncle Hawley,[17] the last Sabbath-day morning [June 1], laid violent hands on himself, and put an end to his life, by cutting his own throat. He had been for a considerable time greatly concerned about the condition of his soul; till, by the ordering of a sovereign providence he was suffered to fall into deep melancholy, a distemper that the family are very prone to; he was much overpowered by it; the devil took the advantage and drove him into despairing thoughts. He was kept very much awake anights, so that he had but very little sleep for two months, till he seemed not to have his faculties in his own power. He was in a great measure past a capacity of receiving advice, or being reasoned with. The coroner's inquest judged him delirious. Satan seems to be in a great rage, at this extraordinary breaking forth of the work of God. I hope it is because he knows that he has but a short time. Doubtless he had a great reach, in this violent attack of his against the whole affair. We have appointed a day of fasting in the town this week, by reason of this and other appearances of Satan's rage amongst us against poor souls.[18] I yesterday saw a woman that belongs to [the church in] Durham [Connecticut], who says there is a considerable revival of religion there.

I am yours, etc.—

J.E.

1735   *1736*

from A Divine and Supernatural Light[1]

A DIVINE AND SUPERNATURAL LIGHT, IMMEDIATELY IMPARTED TO THE SOUL BY THE SPIRIT OF GOD, SHOWN TO BE BOTH A SCRIPTURAL AND RATIONAL DOCTRINE.

> MATTHEW 16:17: And Jesus answered and said unto him, Blessed art thou, Simon Barjona: for flesh and blood hath not revealed it unto thee, but my Father which is in heaven.[2]

• • • • •

DOCTRINE

That there is such a thing as a Spiritual and Divine Light, immediately imparted to the soul by God, of a different nature from any that is obtained by natural means.

---

[17]Joseph Hawley (1682–1735), a leading merchant of Northampton, had married Rebekah Stoddard, sister of Edwards's mother.
[18]See Robert Lowell, "After the Surprising Conversions" (1946), a poem about Hawley's suicide.
[1]This sermon was delivered at Northampton in 1733 and published at the request of the congregation in 1734. It is remarkable for its revelation of affinities with the later

Transcendental thought of Ralph Waldo Emerson and others but at the same time propounding the Calvinistic doctrine of salvation only through God's grace.
[2]Christ tells the Apostle Peter (Simon, son of Jona) that his recognition of Christ as the true Son of God has come not through Peter's own faculties but through revelation by God.

In what I say on this subject, at this time, I would,

I. Show what divine light is.

II. How it is given immediately by God, and not obtained by natural means.

III. Show the truth of the doctrine.

And then conclude with a brief improvement.[3]

I. I would show what this spiritual and divine light is. And in order to it, would show,

First, In a few things what it is not. And here,

1. Those convictions that natural men may have of their sin and misery, is not this spiritual and divine light. Men in a natural condition may have convictions of the guilt that lies upon them, and of the anger of God, and their danger of divine vengeance. Some convictions are from light or sensibleness of truth. That some sinners have a greater conviction of their guilt and misery than others, is because some have more light, or more of an apprehension of truth than others. And this light and conviction may be from the Spirit of God; the Spirit convinces men of sin. But yet nature is much more concerned in it than in the communication of that spiritual and divine light that is spoken of in the doctrine; it is from the Spirit of God only as assisting natural principles, and not as infusing any new principles. Common grace differs from special, in that it influences only by assisting of nature; and not by imparting grace, or bestowing any thing above nature. The light that is obtained is wholly natural, or of no superior kind to what mere nature attains to, though more of that kind be obtained than would be obtained if men were left wholly to themselves: or, in other words, common grace only assists the faculties of the soul to do that more fully which they do by nature, as natural conscience or reason will, by mere nature, make a man sensible of guilt, and will accuse and condemn him when he has done amiss. Conscience is a principle natural to men; and the work that it doth naturally, or of itself, is to give up an apprehension of right and wrong, and to suggest to the mind the relation that there is between right and wrong, and a retribution. The Spirit of God, in those convictions which unregenerate men sometimes have, assists conscience to do this work in a further degree than it would do if they were left to themselves: He helps it against those things that tend to stupify it, and obstruct its exercise. But in the renewing and sanctifying work of the Holy Ghost, those things are wrought in the soul that are above nature, and of which there is nothing of the like kind in the soul by nature; and they are caused to exist in the soul habitually, and according to such a stated constitution or law that lays such a foundation for exercises in a continued course, as is called a principle of nature. Not only are remaining principles assisted to do their work more freely and fully, but those principles are restored that were utterly destroyed by the fall; and the mind thenceforward habitually exerts those acts that the dominion of sin had made it as wholly destitute of, as a dead body is of vital acts.

The Spirit of God acts in a very different manner in the one case, from what He doth in the other. He may indeed act upon the mind of a natural man, but He acts in the mind of a saint[4] as an indwelling vital principle. He acts upon the mind of an unregenerate person as an extrinsic, occasional agent; for in acting upon them, He doth not unite himself to them; for notwithstanding all His influences that they may be the subjects of, they are still sensual, having not the Spirit, Jude 19.[5] But He unites Himself with the mind of a saint, takes him for His temple,

---

[3]In the outline of his sermon given here, Edwards shows three main parts and a conclusion "with a brief improvement" or lesson. Part III, showing the doctrine to be "both scriptural and rational," and the conclusion are omitted here.

[4]I.e., a Christian who has experienced conversion and is thus of God's elect; often labeled a "visible saint."

[5]Jude 19: "These be they who separate themselves, sensual, having not the Spirit."

actuates and influences him as a new supernatural principle of life and action. There is this difference, that the Spirit of God, in acting in the soul of a godly man, exerts and communicates Himself there in His own proper nature. Holiness is the proper nature of the Spirit of God. The Holy Spirit operates in the minds of the godly, by uniting Himself to them, and living in them, and exerting His own nature in the exercise of their faculties. The Spirit of God may act upon a creature, and yet not in acting communicate Himself. The Spirit of God may act upon inanimate creatures; as, the Spirit "moved upon the face of the waters,"[6] in the beginning of the creation; so the Spirit of God may act upon the minds of men many ways, and communicate Himself no more than when He acts upon an inanimate creature. For instance, He may excite thoughts in them, may assist their natural reason and understanding, or may assist other natural principles, and this without any union with the soul, but may act, as it were, as upon an external object. But as He acts in His holy influences and spiritual operations, He acts in a way of peculiar communication of Himself; so that the subject is thence denominated spiritual.

2. This spiritual and divine light does not consist in any impression made upon the imagination. It is no impression upon the mind, as though one saw any thing with the bodily eyes: It is no imagination or idea of an outward light or glory, or any beauty of form or countenance, or a visible lustre or brightness of any object. The imagination may be strongly impressed with such things; but this is not spiritual light. Indeed when the mind has a lively discovery of spiritual things, and is greatly affected by the power of divine light, it may, and probably very commonly doth, much affect the imagination; so that impressions of an outward beauty or brightness may accompany those spiritual discoveries. But spiritual light is not that impression upon the imagination, but an exceeding different thing from it. Natural men may have lively impressions on their imaginations; and we cannot determine but the devil, who transforms himself into an angel of light, may cause imaginations of an outward beauty, or visible glory, and of sounds and speeches, and other such things; but these are things of a vastly inferior nature to spiritual light.

3. This spiritual light is not the suggesting of any new truths or propositions not contained in the word of God. This suggesting of new truths or doctrines to the mind, independent of any antecedent revelation of those propositions, either in word or writing, is inspiration; such as the prophets and apostles had, and such as some enthusiasts[7] pretend to. But this spiritual light that I am speaking of, is quite a different thing from inspiration: it reveals no new doctrine, it suggests no new proposition to the mind, it teaches no new thing of God, or Christ, or another world, not taught in the Bible, but only gives a due apprehension of those things that are taught in the word of God.

4. It is not every affecting view[8] that men have of the things of religion that is this spiritual and divine light. Men by mere principles of nature are capable of being affected with things that have a special relation to religion as well as other things. A person by mere nature, for instance, may be liable to be affected with the story of Jesus Christ, and the sufferings He underwent, as well as by any other tragical story: he may be the more affected with it from the interest he conceives mankind to have in it: yea, he may be affected with it without believing it; as well as a man may be affected with what he reads in a romance, or sees acted in a stage play. He may be affected with a lively and eloquent description of many pleasant things that attend the state of the blessed in heaven, as well as his imagination be entertained by a romantic description of the pleasantness of fairy land, or the like.

---

[6]Genesis 1:2: "And the spirit of God moved upon the face of the waters."

[7]Emotional but mistaken witnesses.
[8]Deeply felt impression.

And that common belief of the truth of the things of religion, that persons may have from education or otherwise, may help forward their affection. We read in Scripture of many that were greatly affected with things of a religious nature, who yet are there represented as wholly graceless, and many of them very ill[9] men. A person therefore may have affecting views of the things of religion, and yet be very destitute of spiritual light. Flesh and blood may be the author of this: one man may give another an affecting view of divine things with but common assistance; but God alone can give a spiritual discovery of them.

But I proceed to show,

Secondly, Positively what this spiritual and divine light is.

And it may be thus described: a true sense of the divine excellency of the things revealed in the word of God, and a conviction of the truth and reality of them thence arising.

This spiritual light primarily consists in the former of these, viz., a real sense and apprehension of the divine excellency of things revealed in the word of God. A spiritual and saving conviction of the truth and reality of these things, arises from such a sight of their divine excellency and glory; so that this conviction of their truth is an effect and natural consequence of this sight of their divine glory. There is therefore in this spiritual light,

1. A true sense of the divine and superlative excellency of the things of religion; a real sense of the excellency of God and Jesus Christ, and of the work of redemption, and the ways and works of God revealed in the gospel. There is a divine and superlative glory in these things; an excellency that is of a vastly higher kind, and more sublime nature than in other things; a glory greatly distinguishing them from all that is earthly and temporal. He that is spiritually enlightened truly apprehends and sees it, or has a sense of it. He does not merely rationally believe that God is glorious, but he has a sense of the gloriousness of God in his heart. There is not only a rational belief that God is holy, and that holiness is a good thing, but there is a sense of the loveliness of God's holiness. There is not only a speculatively judging that God is gracious, but a sense how amiable God is upon that account, or a sense of the beauty of this divine attribute.

There is a twofold understanding or knowledge of good that God has made the mind of man capable of. The first, that which is merely speculative and notional; as when a person only speculatively judges that any thing is, which, by the agreement of mankind, is called good or excellent, viz., that which is most to general advantage, and between which and a reward there is a suitableness, and the like. And the other is, that which consists in the sense of the heart: as when there is a sense of the beauty, amiableness, or sweetness of a thing; so that the heart is sensible of pleasure and delight in the presence of the idea of it. In the former is exercised merely the speculative faculty, or the understanding, strictly so called, or as spoken of in distinction from the will or disposition of the soul. In the latter, the will, or inclination, or heart, is mainly concerned.

Thus there is a difference between having an opinion, that God is holy and gracious, and having a sense of the loveliness and beauty of that holiness and grace. There is a difference between having a rational judgment that honey is sweet, and having a sense of its sweetness. A man may have the former, that knows not how honey tastes; but a man cannot have the latter unless he has an idea of the taste of honey in his mind. So there is a difference between believing that a person is beautiful, and having a sense of his beauty. The former may be obtained by hearsay, but the latter only by seeing the countenance. There is a wide difference between mere speculative rational judging any thing to be excel-

---

[9]Evil.

lent, and having a sense of its sweetness and beauty. The former rests only in the head, speculation only is concerned in it; but the heart is concerned in the latter. When the heart is sensible of the beauty and amiableness of a thing, it necessarily feels pleasure in the apprehension. It is implied in a person's being heartily sensible of the loveliness of a thing, that the idea of it is sweet and pleasant to his soul; which is a far different thing from having a rational opinion that it is excellent.

2. There arises from this sense of divine excellency of things contained in the word of God, a conviction of the truth and reality of them: and that either directly or indirectly.

First, Indirectly, and that two ways.

1. As the prejudices that are in the heart, against the truth of divine things, are hereby removed; so that the mind becomes susceptive of the due force of rational judgments for their truth. The mind of man is naturally full of prejudices against the truth of divine things: it is full of enmity against the doctrines of the gospel; which is a disadvantage to those arguments that prove their truth, and causes them to lose their force upon the mind. But when a person has discovered to him the divine excellency of Christian doctrines, this destroys the enmity, removes those prejudices, and sanctifies the reason, and causes it to lie open to the force of arguments for their truth.

Hence was the different effect that Christ's miracles had to convince the disciples, from what they had to convince the Scribes and Pharisees.[10] Not that they had a stronger reason, or had their reason more improved; but their reason was sanctified, and those blinding prejudices, that the Scribes and Pharisees were under, were removed by the sense they had of the excellency of Christ and his doctrine.

2. It not only removes the hindrances of reason, but positively helps reason. It makes even the speculative notions the more lively. It engages the attention of the mind, with the more fixedness and intenseness to that kind of objects; which causes it to have a clearer view of them, and enables it more clearly to see their mutual relations, and occasions it to take more notice of them. The ideas themselves that otherwise are dim and obscure, are by this means impressed with the greater strength, and have a light cast upon them; so that the mind can better judge of them. As he that beholds the objects on the face of the earth, when the light of the sun is cast upon them, is under greater advantage to discern them in their true forms and mutual relations, than he that sees them in a dim star light or twilight.

The mind having a sensibleness of the excellency of divine objects, dwells upon them with delight; and the powers of the soul are more awakened and enlivened to employ themselves in the contemplation of them, and exert themselves more fully and much more to the purpose. The beauty and sweetness of the objects draws on the faculties, and draws forth their exercises: so that reason itself is under far greater advantages for its proper and free exercises, and to attain its proper end, free of darkness and delusion. But,

Secondly. A true sense of the divine excellency of the things of God's word doth more directly and immediately convince of the truth of them; and that because the excellency of these things is so superlative. There is a beauty in them that is so divine and godlike, that is greatly and evidently distinguishing of them from things merely human, or that men are the inventors and authors of; a glory that is so high and great, that when clearly seen, commands assent to their divinity and reality. When there is an actual and lively discovery of this beauty and excel-

---

[10]Scribes were interpreters of the Jewish law and the Pharisees were a sect of ascetics who lived by the letter but not the spirit of the law. Luke 11:44: "Woe unto you, scribes and Pharisees, hypocrites!"

lency, it will not allow of any such thought as that it is an human work, or the fruit of men's invention. This evidence that they that are spiritually enlightened have of the truth of the things of religion, is a kind of intuitive and immediate evidence. They believe the doctrines of God's word to be divine, because they see divinity in them, i.e., they see a divine, and transcendent, and most evidently distinguishing glory in them; such a glory as, if clearly seen, does not leave room to doubt of their being of God, and not of men.

Such a conviction of the truth of religion as this, arising, these ways, from a sense of the divine excellency of them, is that true spiritual conviction that there is in saving faith. And this original of it, is that by which it is most essentially distinguished from that common assent, which unregenerate men are capable of.

II. I proceed now to the second thing proposed, viz., to show how this light is immediately given by God, and not obtained by natural means. And here,

1. It is not intended that the natural faculties are not made use of in it. The natural faculties are the subject of this light: and they are the subject in such a manner, that they are not merely passive, but active in it; the acts and exercises of man's understanding are concerned and made use of in it. God, in letting in this light into the soul, deals with man according to his nature, or as a rational creature; and makes use of his human faculties. But yet this light is not the less immediately from God for that; though the faculties are made use of, it is as the subject and not as the cause; and that acting of the faculties in it, is not the cause, but is either implied in the thing itself (in the light that is imparted) or is the consequence of it. As the use that we make of our eyes in beholding various objects, when the sun arises, is not the cause of the light that discovers those objects to us.

2. It is not intended that outward means have no concern in this affair. As I have observed already, it is not in this affair, as it is in inspiration, where new truths are suggested: for here is by this light only given a due apprehension of the same truths that are revealed in the word of God; and therefore it is not given without the word. The gospel is made use of in this affair: this light is "the light of the glorious gospel of Christ," 2 Cor. 4:4.[11] The gospel is as a glass, by which this light is conveyed to us, 1 Cor. 13:12:[12] "Now we see through a glass."—But,

3. When it is said that this light is given immediately by God, and not obtained by natural means, hereby is intended, that it is given by God without making use of any means that operate by their own power, or a natural force. God makes use of means; but it is not as mediate causes to produce this effect. There are not truly any second causes of it; but it is produced by God immediately. The word of God is no proper cause of this effect: It does not operate by any natural force in it. The word of God is only made use of to convey to the mind the subject matter of this saving instruction: and this indeed it doth convey to us by natural force or influence. It conveys to our minds these and those doctrines; it is the cause of the notion of them in our heads, but not of the sense of the divine excellency of them in our hearts. Indeed a person cannot have spiritual light without the word. But that does not argue, that the word properly causes that light. The mind cannot see the excellency of any doctrine, unless that doctrine be first in the mind; but the seeing of the excellency of the doctrine may be immediately from the Spirit of God; though the conveying of the doctrine or proposition itself may be by the word. So that the notions that are subject matter of this light, are conveyed to the mind by the word of God; but that due sense of the heart, wherein this light for-

---

[11]"The god of this world hath blinded the minds of them which believe not, lest the light of the glorious gospel of Christ . . . should shine unto them."

[12]1 Corinthians 13:12: "For now we see through a glass darkly; but then face to face: now I know in part: but then shall I know even as also I am known."

mally consists, is immediately by the Spirit of God. As for instance, that notion that there is a Christ, and that Christ is holy and gracious, is conveyed to the mind by the word of God: but the sense of the excellency of Christ by reason of that holiness and grace, is nevertheless immediately the work of the Holy Spirit.

. . . . .

1733   *1734*

Sinners in the Hands of an Angry God

It is ironic that the best known Puritan sermon today, "Sinners in the Hands of an Angry God," generally viewed as one of the most disquieting and threatening sermons of the colonial period, was written by one of the most composed, self-possessed preachers of the period. Edwards delivered the sermon at Enfield, Connecticut, on Sunday, July 8, 1741. According to reports, he held his sermonbook in his left hand and turned pages with his right, reading in a calm, steady voice: "Before the sermon was ended, the assembly appeared deeply impressed and bowed down, with an awful conviction of their sin and danger. There was such a breathing of distress, and weeping, that the preacher was obliged to speak to the people and desire silence, that he might be heard" (Benjamin Trumbull, *A Complete History of Connecticut*, 1797, 1818).

❧

Deuteronomy 32:35: Their foot shall slide in due time.[1]

In this verse is threatened the vengeance of God on the wicked unbelieving Israelites, who were God's visible people, and who lived under the means of grace,[2] but who, notwithstanding all God's wonderful works towards them, remained (as [in] verse 28.)[3] void of counsel, having no understanding in them. Under all the cultivations of heaven, they brought forth bitter and poisonous fruit, as in the two verses next preceding the text.[4] The expression I have chosen for my text, "Their foot shall slide in due time," seems to imply the following things, relating to the punishment and destruction to which these wicked Israelites were exposed.

1. That they were always exposed to *destruction;* as one that stands or walks in slippery places is always exposed to fall. This is implied in the manner of their destruction coming upon them, being represented by their foot sliding. The same is expressed, Psalm 73:18: "Surely thou didst set them in slippery places; thou castedst them down into destruction."

2. It implies that they were always exposed to sudden unexpected destruction. As he that walks in slippery places is every moment liable to fall, he cannot foresee

---

[1]"To me belongeth vengeance, and recompence; their foot shall slide in due time: for the day of their calamity is at hand, and the things that shall come upon them make haste."

[2]I.e., the Ten Commandments, or Decalogue. By obeying the Commandments, the Israelites could remain God's chosen people. For the Puritans, on the other hand, the "means of grace" were "the preaching of the word and the administration of the sacraments of baptism and the Lord's Supper." These means, approved by Calvinists, were formulated in the Westminster Confession of Faith (1647).

[3]Deuteronomy 32:28: "For they are a nation void of council, neither is there any understanding in them."

[4]Deuteronomy 32:32–33: "For their vine is of the vine of Sodom, and of the fields of Gomorrah: their grapes are grapes of gall, their clusters are bitter: their wine is the poison of dragons, and the cruel venom of asps."

one moment whether he shall stand or fall the next; and when he does fall, he falls at once without warning, which is also expressed in Psalm 73:18–19: "Surely thou didst set them in slippery places; thou castedst them down into destruction: How are they brought into desolation as in a moment!"

3. Another thing implied is, that they are liable to fall *of themselves,* without being thrown down by the hand of another; as he that stands or walks on slippery ground needs nothing but his own weight to throw him down.

4. That the reason why they are not fallen already, and do not fall now, is only that God's appointed time is not come. For it is said, that when that due time or appointed time comes, *their foot shall slide.* Then they shall be left to fall, as they are inclined by their own weight. God will not hold them up in these slippery places any longer, but will let them go; and then, at that very instant, they shall fall into destruction; as he that stands on such slippery declining ground, on the edge of a pit, he cannot stand alone, when he is let go he immediately falls and is lost.

The observation from the words that I would now insist upon is this. "There is nothing that keeps wicked men at any one moment out of hell, but the mere pleasure of God." By the *mere* pleasure of God, I mean His *sovereign* pleasure, His arbitrary will, restrained by no obligation, hindered by no manner of difficulty, any more than if nothing else but God's mere will had in the least degree, or in any respect whatsoever, any hand in the preservation of wicked men one moment. The truth of this observation may appear by the following considerations.

1. There is no want of *power* in God to cast wicked men into hell at any moment. Men's hands cannot be strong when God rises up. The strongest have no power to resist Him, nor can any deliver[5] out of His hands. He is not only able to cast wicked men into hell, but He can most easily do it. Sometimes an earthly prince meets with a great deal of difficulty to subdue a rebel, who has found means to fortify himself, and has made himself strong by the numbers of his followers. But it is not so with God. There is no fortress that is any defense from the power of God. Though hand join in hand, and vast multitudes of God's enemies combine and associate themselves, they are easily broken in pieces. They are as great heaps of light chaff before the whirlwind; or large quantities of dry stubble before devouring flames. We find it easy to tread on and crush a worm that we see crawling on the earth; so it is easy for us to cut or singe a slender thread that any thing hangs by: thus easy is it for God, when He pleases, to cast His enemies down to hell. What are we, that we should think to stand before Him, at Whose rebuke the earth trembles, and before Whom the rocks are thrown down?

2. They *deserve* to be cast into hell; so that divine justice never stands in the way, it makes no objection against God's using His power at any moment to destroy them. Yea, on the contrary, justice calls aloud for an infinite punishment of their sins. Divine justice says of the tree that brings forth such grapes of Sodom, "Cut it down, why cumbereth it the ground?" Luke 13:7. The sword of divine justice is every moment brandished over their heads, and it is nothing but the hand of arbitrary mercy, and God's mere will, that holds it back.

3. They are already under a sentence of *condemnation* to hell. They do not only justly deserve to be cast down thither, but the sentence of the law of God, that eternal and immutable rule of righteousness that God has fixed between Him and mankind, is gone out against them, and stands against them; so that they are bound over already to hell: John 3:18, "He that believeth not is condemned already." So that every unconverted man properly belongs to hell; that is his place;

---

[5]I.e., deliver or rescue others.

from thence he is: John 8:23, "Ye are from beneath." And thither he is bound; it is the place that justice, and God's word, and the sentence of His unchangeable law assign to him.

4. They are now the objects of that very same *anger* and wrath of God, that is expressed in the torments of hell. And the reason why they do not go down to hell at each moment, is not because God, in whose power they are, is not then very angry with them; as He is with many miserable creatures now tormented in hell, who there feel and bear the fierceness of His wrath. Yea, God is a great deal more angry with great numbers that are now on earth: yea, doubtless, with many that are now in this congregation, who it may be are at ease, than He is with many of those who are now in the flames of hell.

So that it is not because God is unmindful of their wickedness, and does not resent it, that He does not let loose His hand and cut them off. God is not altogether such an one as themselves, though they may imagine Him to be so. The wrath of God burns against them, their damnation does not slumber; the pit is prepared, the fire is made ready, the furnace is now hot, ready to receive them; the flames do now rage and glow. The glittering sword is whet,[6] and held over them, and the pit hath opened its mouth under them.

5. The *devil* stands ready to fall upon them, and seize them as his own, at what moment God shall permit him. They belong to him; he has their souls in his possession, and under his dominion. The scripture represents them as his goods, Luke 11:21.[7] The devils watch them; they are ever by them at their right hand; they stand waiting for them, like greedy hungry lions that see their prey, and expect to have it, but are for the present kept back. If God should withdraw His hand, by which they are restrained, they would in one moment fly upon their poor souls. The old serpent is gaping for them; hell opens its mouth wide to receive them; and if God should permit it, they would be hastily swallowed up and lost.

6. There are in the souls of wicked men those hellish *principles* reigning, that would presently kindle and flame out into hell fire, if it were not for God's restraints. There is laid in the very nature of carnal men, a foundation for the torments of hell. There are those corrupt principles, in reigning power in them, and in full possession of them, that are seeds of hell fire. These principles are active and powerful, exceeding violent in their nature, and if it were not for the restraining hand of God upon them, they would soon break out, they would flame out after the same manner as the same corruptions, the same enmity does in the hearts of damned souls, and would beget the same torments as they do in them. The souls of the wicked are in scripture compared to the troubled sea, Isaiah 57:20.[8] For the present, God restrains their wickedness by His mighty power, as He does the raging waves of the troubled sea, saying, "Hitherto shalt thou come, but no further;"[9] but if God should withdraw that restraining power, it would soon carry all before it. Sin is the ruin and misery of the soul; it is destructive in its nature; and if God should leave it without restraint, there would need nothing else to make the soul perfectly miserable. The corruption of the heart of man is immoderate and boundless in its fury; and while wicked men live here, it is like fire pent up by God's restraints, whereas if it were let loose, it would set on fire the course of nature; and as the heart is now a sink of sin, so if sin was not restrained, it would immediately turn the soul into a fiery oven, or a furnace of fire and brimstone.

7. It is no security to wicked men for one moment that there are no visible

---

[6]Sharpened (as with a whet-stone).
[7] "When a strong man armed keepeth his palace, his goods are in peace."

[8] "But the wicked are like the troubled sea, when it cannot rest, whose waters cast up mire and dirt."
[9]Job 38:11.

means of death at hand. It is no security to a natural man,[10] that he is now in health, and that he does not see which way he should now immediately go out of the world by any accident, and that there is no visible danger in any respect in his circumstances. The manifold and continual experience of the world in all ages, shows this is no evidence that a man is not on the very brink of eternity, and that the next step will not be into another world. The unseen, unthought-of ways and means of persons going suddenly out of the world are innumerable and inconceivable. Unconverted men walk over the pit of hell on a rotten covering, and there are innumerable places in this covering so weak that they will not bear their weight, and these places are not seen. The arrows of death fly unseen at noonday,[11] the sharpest sight cannot discern them. God has so many different unsearchable ways of taking wicked men out of the world and sending them to hell, that there is nothing to make it appear, that God had need to be at the expense of a miracle, or go out of the ordinary course of His providence, to destroy any wicked man, at any moment. All the means that there are of sinners going out of the world, are so in God's hands, and so universally and absolutely subject to His power and determination, that it does not depend at all the less on the mere will of God, whether sinners shall at any moment go to hell, than if means were never made use of or at all concerned in the case.

8. Natural men's prudence and care to preserve their own lives, or the care of others to preserve them, do not secure them a moment. To this, divine providence and universal experience do also bear testimony. There is this clear evidence that men's own wisdom is no security to them from death; that if it were otherwise we should see some difference between the wise and politic men of the world, and others, with regard to their liableness to early and unexpected death: but how is it in fact? Ecclesiastes 2:16: "How dieth the wise man? even as the fool."

9. All wicked men's pains and *contrivance* which they use to escape hell, while they continue to reject Christ, and so remain wicked men, do not secure them from hell one moment. Almost every natural man that hears of hell, flatters himself that he shall escape it; he depends upon himself for his own security; he flatters himself in what he has done, in what he is now doing, or what he intends to do. Every one lays out matters in his own mind how he shall avoid damnation, and flatters himself that he contrives well for himself, and that his schemes will not fail. They hear indeed that there are but few saved, and that the greater part of men that have died heretofore are gone to hell; but each one imagines that he lays out matters better for his own escape than others have done. He does not intend to come to that place of torment; he says within himself that he intends to take effectual care, and to order matters so for himself as not to fail.

But the foolish children of men miserably delude themselves in their own schemes, and in confidence in their own strength and wisdom; they trust to nothing but a shadow. The greater part of those who heretofore have lived under the same means of grace, and are now dead, are undoubtedly gone to hell; and it was not because they were not as wise as those who are now alive: it was not because they did not lay out matters as well for themselves to secure their own escape. If we could speak with them, and inquire of them, one by one, whether they expected, when alive, and when they used to hear about hell, ever to be the subjects of that misery, we doubtless, should hear one and another reply, "No, I never intended to come here: I had laid out matters otherwise in my mind; I thought I should contrive well for myself: I thought my scheme good. I intended to take effectual care; but it came upon me unexpected; I did not look for it at that time,

[10]Unconverted, unregenerate.
[11]Psalm 91:5: "Thou shalt not be afraid for the terror by night: nor for the arrow that flieth by day."

and in that manner; it came as a thief: Death outwitted me: God's wrath was too quick for me. Oh, my cursed foolishness! I was flattering myself, and pleasing myself with vain dreams of what I would do hereafter; and when I was saying, peace and safety, then suddenly destruction came upon me."

10. God has laid Himself under *no obligation,* by any promise to keep any natural man out of hell one moment. God certainly has made no promises either of eternal life or of any deliverance or preservation from eternal death, but what are contained in the covenant of grace,[12] the promises that are given in Christ, in whom all the promises are yea and amen. But surely they have no interest in the promises of the covenant of grace who are not the children of the covenant, who do not believe in any of the promises, and have no interest in the Mediator[13] of the covenant.

So that, whatever some have imagined and pretended about promises made to natural men's earnest seeking and knocking, it is plain and manifest that whatever pains a natural man takes in religion, whatever prayers he makes, till he believes in Christ, God is under no manner of obligation to keep him a moment from eternal destruction.

So that, thus it is that natural men are held in the hand of God, over the pit of hell; they have deserved the fiery pit, and are already sentenced to it; and God is dreadfully provoked, His anger is as great towards them as to those that are actually suffering the executions of the fierceness of His wrath in hell, and they have done nothing in the least to appease or abate that anger, neither is God in the least bound by any promise to hold them up one moment: the devil is waiting for them, hell is gaping for them, the flames gather and flash about them, and would fain lay hold on them, and swallow them up; the fire pent up in their own hearts is struggling to break out: and they have no interest in any Mediator, there are no means within reach that can be any security to them. In short, they have no refuge, nothing to take hold of; all that preserves them every moment is the mere arbitrary will, and uncovenanted, unobliged forbearance of an incensed God.

APPLICATION

The use of this awful subject may be for awakening unconverted persons in this congregation. This that you have heard is the case of every one of you that are out of Christ. That world of misery, that lake of burning brimstone, is extended abroad under you. There is the dreadful pit of the glowing flames of the wrath of God; there is hell's wide gaping mouth open; and you have nothing to stand upon, nor any thing to take hold of; there is nothing between you and hell but the air; it is only the power and mere pleasure of God that holds you up.

You probably are not sensible of this; you find you are kept out of hell, but do not see the hand of God in it; but look at other things, as the good state of your bodily constitution, your care of your own life, and the means you use for your own preservation. But indeed these things are nothing; if God should withdraw His hand, they would avail no more to keep you from falling, than the thin air to hold up a person that is suspended in it.

Your wickedness makes you as it were heavy as lead, and to tend downwards with great weight and pressure towards hell; and if God should let you go, you would immediately sink and swiftly descend and plunge into the bottomless gulf,

---

[12]The original Covenant of Works was broken by Adam and Eve in eating the forbidden fruit; the new Covenant of Grace, made with man after the Fall, requires faith in Christ as redeemer: good works are to no avail without the faith.

[13]Christ is Mediator between God and man, taking the world's sins as his own burden and thus redeeming man.

and your healthy constitution, and your own care and prudence, and best contrivance, and all your righteousness, would have no more influence to uphold you and keep you out of hell, than a spider's web would have to stop a fallen rock. Were it not for the sovereign pleasure of God, the earth would not bear you one moment; for you are a burden to it; the creation groans with you; the creature is made subject to the bondage of your corruption, not willingly; the sun does not willingly shine upon you to give you light to serve sin and Satan; the earth does not willingly yield her increase to satisfy your lusts; nor is it willingly a stage for your wickedness to be acted upon; the air does not willingly serve you for breath to maintain the flame of life in your vitals, while you spend your life in the service of God's enemies. God's creatures are good, and were made for men to serve God with, and do not willingly subserve to any other purpose, and groan when they are abused to purposes so directly contrary to their nature and end. And the world would spew you out, were it not for the sovereign hand of Him who hath subjected it in hope. There are black clouds of God's wrath now hanging directly over your heads, full of the dreadful storm, and big with thunder; and were it not for the restraining hand of God, it would immediately burst forth upon you. The sovereign pleasure of God, for the present, stays His rough wind; otherwise it would come with fury, and your destruction would come like a whirlwind, and you would be like the chaff of the summer threshing floor.

The wrath of God is like great waters that are dammed for the present; they increase more and more, and rise higher and higher, till an outlet is given; and the longer the stream is stopped, the more rapid and mighty is its course, when once it is let loose. It is true, that judgment against your evil works has not been executed hitherto; the floods of God's vengeance have been withheld; but your guilt in the meantime is constantly increasing, and you are every day treasuring up more wrath; the waters are constantly rising, and waxing more and more mighty; and there is nothing but the mere pleasure of God that holds the waters back, that are unwilling to be stopped, and press hard to go forward. If God should only withdraw His hand from the floodgate, it would immediately fly open, and the fiery floods of the fierceness and wrath of God, would rush forth with inconceivable fury, and would come upon you with omnipotent power; and if your strength were ten thousand times greater than it is, yea, ten thousand times greater than the strength of the stoutest, sturdiest devil in hell, it would be nothing to withstand or endure it.

The bow of God's wrath is bent, and the arrow made ready on the string, and justice bends the arrow at your heart, and strains the bow, and it is nothing but the mere pleasure of God, and that of an angry God, without any promise or obligation at all, that keeps the arrow one moment from being made drunk with your blood. Thus all you that never passed under a great change of heart, by the mighty power of the Spirit of God upon your souls; all you that were never born again, and made new creatures, and raised from being dead in sin, to a state of new, and before altogether unexperienced light and life, are in the hands of an angry God. However you may have reformed your life in many things, and may have had religious affections,[14] and may keep up a form of religion in your families and closets,[15] and in the house of God, it is nothing but His mere pleasure that keeps you from being this moment swallowed up in everlasting destruction. However unconvinced you may now be of the truth of what you hear, by and by you will be fully convinced of it. Those that are gone from being in the like circumstances with you, see that it was so with them; for destruction came suddenly upon most of them; when they expected nothing of it, and while they were saying,

[14]Emotions, feelings.
[15]Studies; rooms for retreat or meditation.

peace and safety: now they see, that those things on which they depended for peace and safety, were nothing but thin air and empty shadows.

The God that holds you over the pit of hell, much as one holds a spider, or some loathsome insect over the fire, abhors you, and is dreadfully provoked: His wrath towards you burns like fire; He looks upon you as worthy of nothing else but to be cast into the fire; He is of purer eyes than to bear to have you in His sight; you are ten thousand times more abominable in His eyes than the most hateful venomous serpent is in ours. You have offended Him infinitely more than ever a stubborn rebel did his prince; and yet it is nothing but His hand that holds you from falling into the fire every moment. It is to be ascribed to nothing else, that you did not go to hell the last night; that you was suffered to awake again in this world, after you closed your eyes to sleep. And there is no other reason to be given, why you have not dropped into hell since you arose in the morning, but that God's hand has held you up. There is no other reason to be given why you have not gone to hell, since you have sat here in the house of God, provoking His pure eyes by your sinful wicked manner of attending His solemn worship. Yea, there is nothing else that is to be given as a reason why you do not this very moment drop down into hell.

O sinner! Consider the fearful danger you are in: it is a great furnace of wrath, a wide and bottomless pit, full of the fire of wrath, that you are held over in the hand of that God, whose wrath is provoked and incensed as much against you, as against many of the damned in hell. You hang by a slender thread, with the flames of divine wrath flashing about it, and ready every moment to singe it, and burn it asunder; and you have no interest in any Mediator, and nothing to lay hold of to save yourself, nothing to keep off the flames of wrath, nothing of your own, nothing that you ever have done, nothing that you can do, to induce God to spare you one moment. And consider here more particularly,

1. *Whose* wrath it is: it is the wrath of the infinite God. If it were only the wrath of man, though it were of the most potent prince, it would be comparatively little to be regarded. The wrath of kings is very much dreaded, especially of absolute monarchs, who have the possessions and lives of their subjects wholly in their power, to be disposed of at their mere will. Proverbs 20:2: "The fear of a king is as the roaring of a lion: Whoso provoketh him to anger, sinneth against his own soul." The subject that very much enrages an arbitrary prince, is liable to suffer the most extreme torments that human art can invent, or human power can inflict. But the greatest earthly potentates in their greatest majesty and strength, and when clothed in their greatest terrors, are but feeble, despicable worms of the dust, in comparison of the great and almighty Creator and King of heaven and earth. It is but little that they can do, when most enraged, and when they have exerted the utmost of their fury. All the kings of the earth, before God, are as grasshoppers; they are nothing, and less than nothing: both their love and their hatred is to be despised. The wrath of the great King of kings, is as much more terrible than theirs, as His majesty is greater. Luke 12:4–5: "And I say unto you, my friends, Be not afraid of them that kill the body, and after that, have no more that they can do. But I will forewarn you whom you shall fear: fear him, which after he hath killed, hath power to cast into hell: yea, I say unto you, Fear him."

2. It is the *fierceness* of His wrath that you are exposed to. We often read of the fury of God; as in Isaiah 59:18: "According to their deeds, accordingly he will repay fury to his adversaries." So Isaiah 66:15: "For behold, the Lord will come with fire, and with his chariots like a whirlwind, to render his anger with fury, and his rebuke with flames of fire." And in many other places. So, Revelation 19:15: we read of "the wine press of the fierceness and wrath of Almighty God."[16] The

---

[16]"And he treadeth the winepress of the fierceness and wrath of Almighty God."

words are exceeding terrible. If it had only been said, "the wrath of God," the words would have implied that which is infinitely dreadful: but it is "the fierceness and wrath of God." The fury of God! the fierceness of Jehovah! Oh, how dreadful must that be! Who can utter or conceive what such expressions carry in them! But it is also "the fierceness and wrath of *Almighty* God." As though there would be a very great manifestation of His almighty power in what the fierceness of His wrath should inflict, as though omnipotence should be as it were enraged, and exerted, as men are wont to exert their strength in the fierceness of their wrath. Oh! then, what will be the consequence! What will become of the poor worms that shall suffer it! Whose hands can be strong? And whose heart can endure? To what a dreadful, inexpressible, inconceivable depth of misery must the poor creature be sunk who shall be the subject of this!

Consider this, you that are here present that yet remain in an unregenerate state. That God will execute the fierceness of His anger implies that He will inflict wrath without any pity. When God beholds the ineffable extremity of your case, and sees your torment to be so vastly disproportioned to your strength, and sees how your poor soul is crushed, and sinks down, as it were, into an infinite gloom; He will have no compassion upon you, He will not forbear the executions of His wrath, or in the least lighten His hand; there shall be no moderation or mercy, nor will God then at all stay His rough wind; He will have no regard to your welfare, nor be at all careful lest you should suffer too much in any other sense, than only that you shall *not suffer beyond what strict justice requires.* Nothing shall be withheld because it is so hard for you to bear. Ezekiel 8:18: "Therefore will I also deal in fury: mine eye shall not spare, neither will I have pity; and though they cry in mine ears with a loud voice, yet I will not hear them." Now God stands ready to pity you; this is a day of mercy; you may cry now with some encouragement of obtaining mercy. But when once the day of mercy is past, your most lamentable and dolorous cries and shrieks will be in vain; you will be wholly lost and thrown away of God as to any regard to your welfare. God will have no other use to put you to, but to suffer misery; you shall be continued in being to no other end; for you will be a vessel of wrath fitted to destruction; and there will be no other use of this vessel, but to be filled full of wrath. God will be so far from pitying you when you cry to Him, that it is said He will only "laugh and mock." Proverbs 1:25–26, &c.[17]

How awful are those words, Isaiah 63:3, which are the words of the great God: "I will tread them in mine anger, and will trample them in my fury, and their blood shall be sprinkled upon my garments, and I will stain all my raiment." It is perhaps impossible to conceive of words that carry in them greater manifestations of these three things, viz., contempt, and hatred, and fierceness of indignation. If you cry to God to pity you, He will be so far from pitying you in your doleful case, or showing you the least regard or favor, that instead of that, He will only tread you under foot. And though He will know that you cannot bear the weight of omnipotence treading upon you, yet He will not regard that, but He will crush you under His feet without mercy; He will crush out your blood, and make it fly, and it shall be sprinkled on His garments, so as to stain all His raiment. He will not only hate you, but He will have you, in the utmost contempt: no place shall be thought fit for you, but under His feet to be trodden down as the mire of the streets.

3. The *misery* you are exposed to is that which God will inflict to that end, that He might show what that wrath of Jehovah is. God hath had it on His heart to show to angels and men both how excellent His love is, and also how terrible His

---

[17]"But ye have set at nought all my counsel, and would none of my reproof: I also will laugh at your calamity; I will mock you when your fear cometh."

wrath is. Sometimes earthly kings have a mind to show how terrible their wrath is, by the extreme punishments they would execute on those that would provoke them. Nebuchadnezzar, that mighty and haughty monarch of the Chaldean empire, was willing to show his wrath when enraged with Shadrach, Meshech, and Abednego; and accordingly gave orders that the burning fiery furnace should be heated seven times hotter than it was before; doubtless, it was raised to the utmost degree of fierceness that human art could raise it.[18] But the great God is also willing to show His wrath, and magnify His awful majesty and mighty power in the extreme sufferings of His enemies. Romans 9:22: "What if God, willing to show his wrath, and to make his power known, endure with much long-suffering the vessels of wrath fitted to destruction?" And seeing this is His design, and what He has determined, even to show how terrible the restrained wrath, the fury and fierceness of Jehovah is, He will do it to effect. There will be something accomplished and brought to pass that will be dreadful with a witness. When the great and angry God hath risen up and executed His awful vengeance on the poor sinner, and the wretch is actually suffering the infinite weight and power of His indignation, then will God call upon the whole universe to behold that awful majesty and mighty power that is to be seen in it. Isaiah 33:12–14: "And the people shall be as the burnings of lime, as thorns cut up shall they be burnt in the fire. Hear ye that are far off, what I have done; ye that are near, acknowledge my might. The sinners in Zion are afraid; fearfulness hath surprised the hypocrites," &c.

Thus it will be with you that are in an unconverted state, if you continue in it; the infinite might, and majesty, and terribleness of the omnipotent God shall be magnified upon you, in the ineffable strength of your torments. You shall be tormented in the presence of the holy angels, and in the presence of the Lamb; and when you shall be in this state of suffering, the glorious inhabitants of heaven shall go forth and look on the awful spectacle, that they may see what the wrath and fierceness of the Almighty is; and when they have seen it, they will fall down and adore that great power and majesty. Isaiah 66:23–24: "And it shall come to pass, that from one new moon to another, and from one sabbath to another, shall all flesh come to worship before me, saith the Lord. And they shall go forth and look upon the carcasses of the men that have transgressed against me; for their worm shall not die, neither shall their fire be quenched, and they shall be an abhorring unto all flesh."

4. It is *everlasting* wrath. It would be dreadful to suffer this fierceness and wrath of Almighty God one moment; but you must suffer it to all eternity. There will be no end to this exquisite horrible misery. When you look forward, you shall see a long forever, a boundless duration before you, which will swallow up your thoughts, and amaze your soul; and you will absolutely despair of ever having any deliverance, any end, any mitigation, any rest at all. You will know certainly that you must wear out long ages, millions of millions of ages, in wrestling and conflicting with this almighty merciless vengeance; and then when you have so done, when so many ages have actually been spent by you in this manner, you will know that all is but a point to what remains. So that your punishment will indeed be infinite. Oh, who can express what the state of a soul in such circumstances is! All that we can possibly say about it, gives but a very feeble, faint representation of it; it is inexpressible and inconceivable: For "who knows the power of God's anger?"[19]

How dreadful is the state of those that are daily and hourly in the danger of this great wrath and infinite misery! But this is the dismal case of every soul in this congregation that has not been born again, however moral and strict, sober and

---

[18]Daniel 3:1–30.
[19]Psalm 90:11: "Who knoweth the power of thine anger? Even according to thy fear, so is thy wrath."

religious, they may otherwise be. Oh that you would consider it, whether you be young or old! There is reason to think, that there are many in this congregation now hearing this discourse, that will actually be the subjects of this very misery to all eternity. We know not who they are, or in what seats they sit, or what thoughts they now have. It may be they are now at ease, and hear all these things without much disturbance, and are now flattering themselves that they are not the persons, promising themselves that they shall escape. If they knew that there was one person, and but one, in the whole congregation, that was to be the subject of this misery, what an awful thing would it be to think of! If we knew who it was, what an awful sight would it be to see such a person! How might all the rest of the congregation lift up a lamentable and bitter cry over him! But, alas! instead of one, how many is it likely will remember this discourse in hell? And it would be a wonder, if some that are now present should not be in hell in a very short time, even before this year is out. And it would be no wonder if some persons, that now sit here, in some seats of this meeting-house, in health, quiet and secure, should be there before tomorrow morning. Those of you that finally continue in a natural condition, that shall keep out of hell longest will be there in a little time! your damnation does not slumber; it will come swiftly, and, in all probability, very suddenly upon many of you. You have reason to wonder that you are not already in hell. It is doubtless the case of some whom you have seen and known, that never deserved hell more than you, and that heretofore appeared as likely to have been now alive as you. Their case is past all hope; they are crying in extreme misery and perfect despair; but here you are in the land of the living and in the house of God, and have an opportunity to obtain salvation. What would not those poor damned hopeless souls give for one day's opportunity such as you now enjoy!

And now you have an extraordinary opportunity, a day wherein Christ has thrown the door of mercy wide open, and stands in calling and crying with a loud voice to poor sinners; a day wherein many are flocking to Him, and pressing into the kingdom of God. Many are daily coming from the east, west, north and south; many that were very lately in the same miserable condition that you are in, are now in a happy state, with their hearts filled with love to Him who has loved them, and washed them from their sins in His own blood, and rejoicing in hope of the glory of God. How awful is it to be left behind at such a day! To see so many others feasting, while you are pining and perishing! To see so many rejoicing and singing for joy of heart, while you have cause to mourn for sorrow of heart, and howl for vexation of spirit! How can you rest one moment in such a condition? Are not your souls as precious as the souls of the people at Suffield,[20] where they are flocking from day to day to Christ?

Are there not many here who have lived long in the world, and are not to this day born again? and so are aliens from the commonwealth of Israel,[21] and have done nothing ever since they have lived, but treasure up wrath against the day of wrath? Oh, sirs, your case, in an especial manner, is extremely dangerous. Your guilt and hardness of heart is extremely great. Do you not see how generally persons of your years are passed over and left, in the present remarkable and wonderful dispensation of God's mercy? You had need to consider yourselves, and awake thoroughly out of sleep. You cannot bear the fierceness and wrath of the infinite God. And you, young men, and young women, will you neglect this precious season which you now enjoy, when so many others of your age are renouncing all youthful vanities, and flocking to Christ? You especially have now an extraordinary opportunity; but if you neglect it, it will soon be with you as with those persons who spent all the precious days in youth in sin, and are now come to such

---

[20]"A town in the neighborhood" (Edwards's note).
[21]The unconverted or unregenerate who do not belong to the new chosen people, the God-designated elect of the Puritans.

a dreadful pass in blindness and hardness. And you, children, who are unconverted, do not you know that you are going down to hell, to bear the dreadful
wrath of that God, who is now angry with you every day and every night? Will you
be content to be the children of the devil, when so many other children in the
land are converted, and are become the holy and happy children of the King of
kings?

And let every one that is yet of Christ, and hanging over the pit of hell,
whether they be old men and women, or middle aged, or young people, or little
children, now hearken to the loud calls of God's word and providence. This acceptable year of the Lord, a day of such great favors to some, will doubtless be a
day of as remarkable vengeance to others. Men's hearts harden, and their guilt
increases apace at such a day as this, if they neglect their souls; and never was
there so great danger of such person being given up to hardness of heart and
blindness of mind. God seems now to be hastily gathering in His elect in all parts
of the land; and probably the greater part of adult persons that ever shall be
saved, will be brought in now in a little time, and that it will be as it was on the
great out-pouring of the Spirit upon the Jews in the apostles' days;[22] the election
will obtain, and the rest will be blinded. If this should be the case with you, you
will eternally curse this day, and will curse the day that ever you was born, to see
such a season of the pouring out of God's Spirit, and will wish that you had died
and gone to hell before you had seen it. Now undoubtedly it is, as it was in the
days of John the Baptist, the axe is in an extraordinary manner laid at the root of
the trees, that every tree which brings not forth good fruit, may be hewn down
and cast into the fire.[23]

Therefore, let everyone that is out of Christ, now awake and fly from the wrath
to come. The wrath of Almighty God is now undoubtedly hanging over a great
part of this congregation: Let every one fly out of Sodom: "Haste and escape for
your lives, look not behind you, escape to the mountain, lest you be consumed."[24]

1741   *1741*

from Freedom of the Will[1]

from SECTION 1. CONCERNING THE NATURE OF THE WILL

It may possibly be thought, that there is no great need of going about to define
or describe the "will"; this word being generally as well understood as any other
words we can use to explain it: and so perhaps it would be, had not philosophers,
metaphysicians and polemic divines brought the matter into obscurity by the
things they have said of it. But since it is so, I think it may be of some use, and will
tend to the greater clearness in the following discourse, to say a few things concerning it.

And therefore I observe, that the will (without any metaphysical refining) is
plainly, that by which the mind chooses anything. The faculty of the will is that

---

[22]In Acts 2, Peter preaches to the multitude to "repent, and
be baptized every one of you in the name of Jesus Christ";
on that "same day there were added unto them about three
thousand souls" (Acts 2:38, 41).
[23]Matthew 3:10: "And now also the axe is laid unto the
root of the trees: therefore every tree which bringeth not
forth good fruit is hewn down, and cast into the fire." The
verse is essentially the same as Luke 3:9.
[24]Genesis 19:17.

[1]The full title is explanatory: *A Careful and Strict Enquiry
into the Modern Prevailing Notions of That Freedom of the Will,
Which Is Supposed to Be Essential to Moral Agency, Virtue and
Vice, Reward and Punishment, Praise and Blame* (1754). Written at Stockbridge, the work was perhaps Edwards's most
ambitious elaboration of his theological-philosophical
stand, aimed at those who were attacking Calvinism's doctrine of predestination. It shows Edwards at his best—agile, subtle, rigorous—in intellectual dispute.

faculty or power or principle of mind by which it is capable of choosing: an act of the will is the same as an act of choosing or choice.

If any think 'tis a more perfect definition of the will, to say, that it is that by which the soul either chooses or refuses; I am content with it: though I think that 'tis enough to say, it's that by which the soul chooses: for in every act of will whatsoever, the mind chooses one thing rather than another; it chooses something rather than the contrary, or rather than the want or nonexistence of that thing. So in every act of refusal, the mind chooses the absence of the thing refused; the positive and the negative are set before the mind for its choice, and it chooses the negative; and the mind's making its choice in that case is properly the act of the will: the will's determining between the two is a voluntary determining; but that is the same thing as making a choice. So that whatever names we call the act of the will by—choosing, refusing, approving, disapproving, liking, disliking, embracing, rejecting, determining, directing, commanding, forbidding, inclining or being averse, a being pleased or displeased with—all may be reduced to this of choosing. For the soul to act voluntarily, is evermore to act electively. . . .

from Section 2. Concerning the Determination of the Will

By "determining the will," if the phrase be used with any meaning, must be intended, causing that the act of the will or choice should be thus, and not otherwise: and the will is said to be determined, when, in consequence of some action, or influence, its choice is directed to, and fixed upon a particular object. As when we speak of the determination of motion, we mean causing the motion of the body to be such a way, or in such a direction, rather than another.

To talk of the determination of the will, supposes an effect, which must have a cause. If the will be determined, there is a determiner. This must be supposed to be intended even by them that say, the will determines itself. If it be so, the will is both determiner and determined; it is a cause that acts and produces effects upon itself, and is the object of its own influence and action.

With respect to that grand inquiry, what determines the will, it would be very tedious and unnecessary at present to enumerate and examine all the various opinions, which have been advanced concerning this matter; nor is it needful that I should enter into a particular disquisition of all points debated in disputes on that question, whether the will always follows the last dictate of the understanding. It is sufficient to my present purpose to say, it is that motive, which, as it stands in the view of the mind, is the strongest, that determines the will.—But it may be necessary that I should a little explain my meaning in this.

By "motive," I mean the whole of that which moves, excites or invites the mind to volition, whether that be one thing singly, or many things conjunctly. Many particular things may concur and unite their strength to induce the mind; and when it is so, all together are as it were one complex motive. And when I speak of the "strongest motive," I have respect to the strength of the whole that operates to induce to a particular act of volition, whether that be the strength of one thing alone, or of many together.

Whatever is a motive, in this sense, must be something that is extant in the view or apprehension of the understanding, or perceiving faculty. Nothing can induce or invite the mind to will or act anything, any further than it is perceived, or is some way or other in the mind's view; for what is wholly unperceived, and perfectly out of the mind's view, can't affect the mind at all. 'Tis most evident, that nothing is in the mind, or reaches it, or takes any hold of it, any otherwise than as it is perceived or thought of.

And I think it must also be allowed by all, that everything that is properly called a motive, excitement or inducement to a perceiving willing agent, has some sort and degree of tendency, or advantage to move or excite the will, previous to the effect, or to the act of the will excited. This previous tendency of the motive is what I call the "strength" of the motive. That motive which has a less degree of previous advantage or tendency to move the will, or that appears less inviting, as it stands in the view of the mind, is what I call a "weaker motive." On the contrary, that which appears most inviting, and has, by what appears concerning it to the understanding or apprehension, the greatest degree of previous tendency to excite and induce the choice, is what I call the "strongest motive." And in this sense, I suppose the will is always determined by the strongest motive.

Things that exist in the view of the mind, have their strength, tendency or advantage to move or excite its will, from many things appertaining to the nature and circumstances of the thing viewed, the nature and circumstances of the mind that views, and the degree and manner of its view; which it would perhaps be hard to make a perfect enumeration of. But so much I think may be determined in general, without room for controversy, that whatever is perceived or apprehended by an intelligent and voluntary agent, which has the nature and influence of a motive to volition or choice, is considered or viewed *as good;* nor has it any tendency to invite or engage the election of the soul in any further degree than it appears such. For to say otherwise, would be to say, that things that appear have a tendency by the appearance they make, to engage the mind to elect them, some other way than by their appearing eligible to it; which is absurd. And therefore it must be true, in some sense, that the will always is as the greatest apparent good is. . . .

Section 5. Concerning the Notion of Liberty, and of Moral Agency

The plain and obvious meaning of the words "freedom" and "liberty," in common speech, is power, opportunity, or advantage, that anyone has, to do as he pleases. Or in other words, his being free from hindrance or impediment in the way of doing, or conducting in any respect, as he wills.[2] And the contrary to liberty, whatever name we call that by, is a person's being hindered or unable to conduct as he will, or being necessitated to do otherwise.

If this which I have mentioned be the meaning of the word "liberty," in the ordinary use of language; as I trust that none that has ever learned to talk, and is unprejudiced, will deny; then it will follow, that in propriety of speech, neither liberty, nor its contrary, can properly be ascribed to any being or thing, but that which has such a faculty, power or property, as is called "will." For that which is possessed of no such thing as will, can't have any power or opportunity of doing according to its will, nor be necessitated to act contrary to its will, nor be restrained from acting agreeably to it. And therefore to talk of liberty, or the contrary, as belonging to the very will itself, is not to speak good sense; if we judge of sense, and nonsense, by the original and proper signification of words. For the will itself is not an agent that has a will: the power of choosing, itself, has not a power of choosing. That which has the power of volition or choice is the man or the soul, and not the power of volition itself. And he that has the liberty of doing according to his will, is the agent or doer who is possessed of the will; and not the will which he is possessed of. We say with propriety, that a bird let loose has power and liberty to fly; but not that the bird's power of flying has a power and liberty of flying. To be free is the property of an agent, who is possessed of powers and faculties, as much as to be cunning, valiant, bountiful, or zealous. But these qualities are the properties of men or persons; and not the properties of properties.

---

[2]Edwards's note: "I say not only 'doing,' but 'conducting'; because a voluntary forbearing to do, sitting still, keeping silence, etc. are instances of persons' conduct, about which liberty is exercised; though they are not properly called 'doing.'"

There are two things that are contrary to this which is called liberty in common speech. One is *constraint;* the same is otherwise called force, compulsion, and coaction; which is a person's being necessitated to do a thing *contrary* to his will. The other is *restraint;* which is his being hindered, and not having power to do *according* to his will. But that which has no will, can't be the subject of these things.— I need say the less on this head, Mr. Locke having set the same thing forth, with so great clearness, in his *Essay on the Human Understanding.*[3]

But one thing more I would observe concerning what is vulgarly called liberty; namely, that power and opportunity for one to do and conduct as he will, or according to his choice, is all that is meant by it; without taking into the meaning of the word, anything of the cause or original of that choice; or at all considering how the person came to have such a volition; whether it was caused by some external motive, or internal habitual bias; whether it was determined by some internal antecedent volition, or whether it happened without a cause; whether it was necessarily connected with something foregoing, or not connected. Let the person come by his volition or choice how he will, yet, if he is able, and there is nothing in the way to hinder his pursuing and executing his will, the man is fully and perfectly free, according to the primary and common notion of freedom.

What has been said may be sufficient to shew what is meant by liberty, according to the common notions of mankind, and in the usual and primary acceptation of the word: but the word, as used by Arminians, Pelagians[4] and others, who oppose the Calvinists, has an entirely different signification. These several things belong to their notion of liberty: 1. That it consists in a self-determining power in the will, or a certain sovereignty the will has over itself, and its own acts, whereby it determines its own volitions; so as not to be dependent in its determinations, on any cause without itself, nor determined by anything prior to its own acts. 2. Indifference belongs to liberty in their notion of it, or that the mind, previous to the act of volition be, *in equilibrio.*[5] 3. Contingence is another thing that belongs and is essential to it; not in the common acceptation of the word, as that has been already explained, but as opposed to all necessity, or any fixed and certain connection with some previous ground or reason of its existence. They suppose the essence of liberty so much to consist in these things, that unless the will of man be free in this sense, he has no real freedom, how much soever he may be at liberty to act according to his will.

A moral agent is a being that is capable of those actions that have a moral quality, and which can properly be denominated good or evil in a moral sense, virtuous or vicious, commendable or faulty. To moral agency belongs a moral faculty, or sense of moral good and evil, or of such a thing as desert or worthiness of praise or blame, reward or punishment; and a capacity which an agent has of being influenced in his actions by moral inducements or motives, exhibited to the view of understanding and reason, to engage to a conduct agreeable to the moral faculty.

The sun is very excellent and beneficial in its action and influence on the earth, in warming it, and causing it to bring forth its fruits; but it is not a moral agent: its action, though good, is not virtuous or meritorious. Fire that breaks out in a city, and consumes great part of it, is very mischievous in its operation; but is not a moral agent: what it does is not faulty or sinful, or deserving of any punishment. The brute creatures are not moral agents: the actions of some of 'em are very profitable and pleasant; others are very hurtful: yet, seeing they have no moral

---

[3]John Locke (1632–1704), whose *An Essay Concerning Human Understanding* (1690) was, according to Edwards's own testimony, a major influence on him.
[4]Arminians were followers of Jacobus Arminius (1560–1609), a Dutch theologian who taught that through free will an individual could win salvation by good works; Pelagians were followers of Pelagius, a fourth-century British monk who denied the doctrine of original sin and believed in free will.
[5]"In equilibrium" (Latin).

faculty, or sense of desert, and don't act from choice guided by understanding, or with a capacity of reasoning and reflecting, but only from instinct, and are not capable of being influenced by moral inducements, their actions are not properly sinful or virtuous; nor are they properly the subjects of any such moral treatment for what they do, as moral agents are for their faults or good deeds.

Here it may be noted, that there is a circumstantial difference between the moral agency of a ruler and a subject. I call it circumstantial, because it lies only in the difference of moral inducements they are capable of being influenced by, arising from the difference of circumstances. A ruler acting in that capacity only, is not capable of being influenced by a moral law, and its sanctions of threatenings and promises, rewards and punishments, as the subject is; though both may be influenced by a knowledge of moral good and evil. And therefore the moral agency of the supreme Being, who acts only in the capacity of a ruler towards his creatures, and never as a subject, differs in that respect from the moral agency of created intelligent beings. God's actions, and particularly those which he exerts as a moral governor, have moral qualifications, are morally good in the highest degree. They are most perfectly holy and righteous; and we must conceive of him as influenced in the highest degree, by that which, above all others, is properly a moral inducement; viz. the moral good which he sees in such and such things: and therefore he is, in the most proper sense, a moral agent, the source of all moral ability and agency, the fountain and rule of all virtue and moral good; though by reason of his being supreme over all, 'tis not possible he should be under the influence of law or command, promises or threatenings, rewards or punishments, counsels or warnings. The essential qualities of a moral agent are in God, in the greatest possible perfection; such as understanding, to perceive the difference between moral good and evil; a capacity of discerning that moral worthiness and demerit, by which some things are praiseworthy, others deserving of blame and punishment; and also a capacity of choice, and choice guided by understanding, and a power of acting according to his choice or pleasure, and being capable of doing those things which are in the highest sense praiseworthy. And herein does very much consist that image of God wherein he made man (which we read of Gen. 1:26–27 and ch. 9:6),[6] by which God distinguished man from the beasts, viz. in those faculties and principles of nature, whereby he is capable of moral agency. Herein very much consists the *natural* image of God; as his *spiritual* and *moral* image, wherein man was made at first, consisted in that moral excellency, that he was endowed with.

1754

---

[6]Genesis 1:26–27: "And God said, Let us make man in our image, after our likeness: and let them have dominion over the fish of the sea, and over the fowl of the air, and over the cattle, and over all the earth, and over every creeping thing that creepeth upon the earth. So God created man in his own image, in the image of God created he him; male and female created he them." Genesis 9:6: ". . . in the image of God made he man."

from The Nature of True Virtue[1]

from CHAPTER I
[THE ESSENCE OF TRUE VIRTUE]

Whatever controversies and variety of opinions there are about the nature of virtue, yet all (excepting some skeptics, who deny any real difference between virtue and vice) mean by it, something *beautiful,* or rather some kind of *beauty,* or excellency.— It is not *all* beauty, that is called virtue; for instance, not the beauty of a building, of a flower, or of the rainbow: but some beauty belonging to Beings that have *perception* and *will.*— It is not all beauty of *mankind,* that is called virtue; for instance, not the external beauty of the countenance, or shape, gracefulness of motion, or harmony of voice: but it is a beauty that has its original seat in the mind.— But yet perhaps not *every* thing that may be called a beauty of mind, is properly called virtue. There is a beauty of understanding and speculation. There is something in the ideas and conceptions of great philosophers and statesmen, that may be called beautiful; which is a different thing from what is most commonly meant by virtue. But virtue is the beauty of those qualities and acts of the mind, that are of a *moral* nature, i.e., such as are attended with desert or worthiness of *praise,* or *blame.* Things of this sort, it is generally agreed, so far as I know, are not any thing belonging merely to speculation; but to the *disposition* and *will,* or (to use a general word, I suppose commonly well understood) the *heart.* Therefore I suppose, I shall not depart from the common opinion, when I say, that virtue is the beauty of the qualities and exercises of the heart, or those actions which proceed from them. So that when it is inquired, What is the nature of true *virtue?*—this is the same as to inquire, what that is which renders any habit, disposition, or exercise of the heart truly *beautiful.* I use the phrase *true* virtue, and speak of things *truly* beautiful, because I suppose it will generally be allowed, that there is a distinction to be made between some things which are truly virtuous, and others which only seem to be virtuous, through a partial and imperfect view of things: that some actions and dispositions appear beautiful, if considered partially and superficially, or with regard to some things belonging to them, and in some of their circumstances and tendencies, which would appear otherwise in a more extensive and comprehensive view, wherein they are seen clearly in their whole nature and the extent of their connections in the universality of things.— There is a general and a particular beauty. By a *particular* beauty, I mean that by which a thing appears beautiful when considered only with regard to its connection with, and tendency to some particular things within a limited, and, as it were, a private sphere. And a *general* beauty is that by which a thing appears beautiful when viewed most perfectly, comprehensively and universally, with regard to all its tendencies, and its connections with every thing it stands related to. The former may be without and against the latter. As, a few notes in a tune, taken only by themselves, and in their relation to one another, may be harmonious; which when considered with respect to all the notes in the tune, or the entire series of sounds they are connected with, may be very discordant and disagreeable.—(Of which more afterwards.)—*That only,* therefore, is what I mean by true virtue, which is *that,* belonging to the *heart* of an intelligent Being, that is beautiful by a *general* beauty, or

---

[1]One of Edwards's late works, *The Nature of True Virtue* was not published until 1765, after his death. It is interesting not only in rounding out Edwards's thought, locating the virtue of benevolence not in the reason but in the affec-tions, but also in connecting with such other American explorations of right conduct as Mather's *Bonifacius: An Essay Upon the Good,* Benjamin Franklin's *The Do-Good Papers,* and Emerson's essays "Love" and "Friendship."

beautiful in a comprehensive view as it is in itself, and as related to every thing that it stands in connection with. And therefore when we are inquiring concerning the nature of true virtue, viz., wherein this true and general beauty of the heart does most essentially consist—this is my answer to the inquiry:

True virtue most essentially consists in benevolence to Being in general. Or perhaps to speak more accurately, it is that consent, propensity and union of heart to Being in general, that is immediately exercised in a general good will.

The things which were before observed of the nature of true virtue, naturally lead us to such a notion of it. If it has its seat in the heart, and is the general good-ness and beauty of the disposition and exercise of that, in the most comprehensive view, considered with regard to its universal tendency, and as related to every thing that it stands in connection with; what can it consist in, but a consent and good will to Being in general?—Beauty does not consist in discord and dissent, but in consent and agreement. And if every intelligent Being is some way related to Being in general, and is a part of the universal system of existence; and so stands in connection with the whole; what can its general and true beauty be, but its union and consent with the great whole?

If any such thing can be supposed as a union of heart to some particular Being, or number of Beings, disposing it to benevolence to a private circle or system of Beings, which are but a small part of the whole; not implying a tendency to a union with the great system, and not at all inconsistent with enmity towards Being in general; this I suppose not to be of the nature of true virtue: although it may in some respects be good, and may appear beautiful in a confined and contracted view of things.—But of this more afterwards.

It is abundantly plain by the holy Scriptures, and generally allowed, not only by Christian divines, but by the more considerable deists,[2] that virtue most essentially consists in love. And I suppose, it is owned by the most considerable writers, to consist in general love of benevolence, or kind affection: though it seems to me, the meaning of some in this affair is not sufficiently explained, which perhaps oc-casions some error or confusion in discourses on this subject.

When I say, true virtue consists in love to Being in general, I shall not be likely to be understood, that no one act of the mind or exercise of love is of the nature of true virtue, but what has Being in general, or the great system of universal ex-istence, for its direct and immediate object: so that no exercise of love or kind af-fection to any one particular Being, that is but a small part of this whole, has any thing of the nature of true virtue. But, that the nature of true virtue consists in a disposition to benevolence towards Being in general. Though, from such a dispo-sition may arise exercises of love to particular Beings, as objects are presented and occasions arise. No wonder, that he who is of a generally benevolent disposition, should be more disposed than another to have his heart moved with benevolent affection to particular persons, whom he is acquainted and conversant with, and from whom arise the greatest and most frequent occasions for exciting his benev-olent temper. But my meaning is, that no affections towards particular persons or Beings are of the nature of true virtue, but such as arise from a generally benev-olent temper, or from that habit or frame of mind, wherein consists a disposition to love Being in general.

• • • • •

---

[2]Those who believed God is revealed in nature, not in the Bible. Deism flourished in America especially in the eigh-teenth century as Puritanism declined and Protestantism became more and more fragmented.

from Images or Shadows of Divine Things

Images or Shadows of Divine Things remained in manuscript until 1948, when Perry Miller edited and published it. Edwards made carefully numbered entries in a notebook over a long period of time, and tried out a series of titles: "The Images of Divine Things," "The Shadows of Divine Things," "The Book of Nature and Common Providence," "The Language and Lessons of Nature." This notebook was one of several that Edwards kept, in addition to his journal (to which he gave the provisional title "Miscellanies"). In *Images or Shadows of Divine Things,* Edwards systematically entered his inspired observations of "types" in the visible world that (in accord with the Puritan belief in "typology") represented an actual correspondence to or prefiguring of a Biblical truth or "reality." It seemed to be Edwards's purpose to demonstrate ultimately that God made the whole of the "material world" as an "imitation" or "shadow of the spiritual world." Long after the decline of Puritanism, the "typological" imagination (or habit of mind) appeared to survive in many Romantic poets, as in Ralph Waldo Emerson and his observation in *Nature* (1836): "Particular natural facts are symbols of particular spiritual facts."

[ROSES]

3. Roses grow upon briars, which is to signify that all temporal sweets are mixt with bitter. But what seems more especially to be meant by it is that pure happiness, the crown of glory, is to be come at in no other way than by bearing Christ's cross, by a life of mortification, self-denial, and labor, and bearing all things for Christ. The rose, that is chief of all flowers, is the last thing that comes out. The briary, prickly bush grows before that; the end and crown of all is the beautiful and fragrant rose.

[A GREAT AND REMARKABLE ANALOGY IN GOD'S WORKS]

8. Again it is apparent and allowed that there is a great and remarkable analogy in God's works. There is a wonderful resemblance in the effects which God produces, and consentaneity[1] in His manner of working in one thing and another throughout all nature. It is very observable in the visible world; therefore it is allowed that God does purposely make and order one thing to be in agreeableness and harmony with another. And if so, why should not we suppose that He makes the inferior in imitation of the superior, the material of the spiritual, on purpose to have a resemblance and shadow of them? We see that even in the material world, God makes one part of it strangely to agree with another, and why is it not reasonable to suppose He makes the whole as a shadow of the spiritual world?

[GRASS]

13. Thus I believe the grass and other vegetables growing and flourishing, looking green and pleasant as it were, ripening, blossoming, and bearing fruit from the influences of the heavens, the rain and wind and light and heat of the sun, to be on purpose to represent the dependence of our spiritual welfare upon

---

[1] I.e., quality of being consentaneous, thus agreeing or accordant with.

God's gracious influences and the effusions of His holy spirit. I am sure there are none of the types of the Old Testament are more lively images of spiritual things. And we find spiritual things very often compared to them in Scripture.

[THE SUN]

14. The sun's so perpetually, for so many ages, sending forth his rays in such vast profusion, without any diminution of his light and heat, is a bright image of the all-sufficiency and everlastingness of God's bounty and goodness.

[RIVERS]

15. And so likewise are rivers, which are ever flowing, that empty vast quantities of water every day and yet there is never the less to come. The spirit communicated and shed abroad, that is to say, the goodness of God, is in Scripture compared to a river, and the trees that grow and flourish by the river's side through the benefit of the water represent the saints who live upon Christ and flourish through the influences of His spirit.

[RAVENS]

61. Ravens, that with delight feed on carrion, seem to be remarkable types of devils, who with delight prey upon the souls of the dead. A dead, filthy, rotten carcass is a lively image of the soul of a wicked man, that is spiritually and exceeding filthy and abominable. Their spiritual corruption is of a far more loathsome savour than the stench of a putrefying carcass. Such souls the Devil delights in; they are his proper food. Again, dead corpses are types of the departed souls of the dead and are so used. (Isa. 66.24.[2]) Ravens don't prey on the bodies of animals till they are dead; so the Devil has not the souls of wicked men delivered into his tormenting hands and devouring jaws till they are dead. Again, the body in such circumstances being dead and in loathsome putrefaction is a lively image of a soul in the dismal state it is in under eternal death. (See Image 151.) Ravens are birds of the air that are expressly used by Christ as types of the Devil in the parable of the sower and the seed. The Devil is the prince of the power of the air, as he is called; devils are spirits of the air. The raven by its blackness represents the prince of darkness. Sin and sorrow and death are all in Scripture represented by darkness or the color black, but the Devil is the father of sin, a most foul and wicked spirit, and the prince of death and misery.

[TYPES AND ANTITYPES]

118. Images of divine things. It is with many of these images as it was with the sacrifices of old: they are often repeated, whereas the antitype is continual and never comes to pass but once. Thus sleep is an image of death that is repeated every night; so the morning is the image of the resurrection; so the spring of the year is the image of the resurrection which is repeated every year. And so of many other things that might be mentioned, they are repeated often, but the antitype is but once. The shadows are often repeated to show t[w]o things, viz.,[3] [1.] that the thing shadowed is not yet fulfilled, and 2. to signify the great importance of the antitype that we need to be so renewedly and continually put in mind of it.

---

[2]The Lord speaks: "And they shall go forth, and look upon the carcasses of the men that have transgressed against me: for their worm shall not die, neither shall their fire be quenched; and they shall be an abhorring unto all flesh."
[3]"Videlicet" (Latin): namely, that is to say.

[Blossoming and Ripening of Fruit]

171. Concerning the blossoming and ripening of fruits and other things of that nature: The first puttings forth of the tree in order to fruit make a great show and are pleasant to the eye, but the fruit then is very small and tender. Afterwards, when there is less show, the fruit is increased. So it often is at first conversion. There are flowing affections, passionate joys, that are the flower that soon falls off, etc. The fruit when young is very tender, easily hurt with frost or heat or vermin or any thing that touches it. So it is with young converts, Cant. 2.15:[4] Take us the foxes, the little foxes, that spoil the vines, for our vines have tender grapes.

Fruit on the tree or in the field is not in its fixed and ultimate state, the state where it properly answers its end, but in a state wholly subordinate and preparatory to another. So it is with the saints. The fruit while it stands in the field or hangs on the tree till fully ripe and the time of gathering comes, is in a progressive state, growing in perfection. So it is with grace in the saints. Many kinds of fruit have a great deal of bitterness and sourness while green, and much that is crude and unwholesome, which, as it ripens, becomes sweeter, the juices purer, the crude parts are removed. The burning heat of the summer sun purges away that which is crude, sour, and unwholesome, and refines the fruit and ripens it and fits it more for use, which burning heat withers and destroys those fruits that have not substance in them. So young converts have a remaining sourness and bitterness. They have a great mixture in their experiences and religious exercises, but as they ripen for heaven, they are more purified. Their experiences become purer, their tempers are more mollified and sweetened with meekness and Christian love, and this by afflictions, persecutions, and occasions of great self-denial, or in one word by the cross of Christ, whereas those trials bring hypocrites to nothing.

Green fruit hangs fast to the tree, but when it is ripe, it is loose and easily picked. Wheat, while it is green in the field, sucks and draws for nourishment from the ground, but when it is ripe, it draws no more. So a saint when ripe for heaven is weaned from the world.

[Crocodile]

177. It is observed of the CROCODILE that it cometh of an egg no bigger than a goose egg, yet grows till he is fifteen cubits long (Pliny[5] says thirty). He is also long-lived and grows as long as he lives. (See Spencer's *Similies and Sentences*, p. 68.[6]) And how terrible a creature does he become, how destructive and hard to be destroyed. So sin is comparatively easily crushed in the egg, taken in its beginning; but if let alone, what head does it get, how great and strong, terrible and destructive does it become, and hard to kill, and grows as long as it lives. So it is with sin or Satan's interest in particular persons. So it is with his interest in towns, countrys, and empires and the world of mankind. How small was Satan's interest in the old world, beginning in Cain's family, but what did it come to before the flood? How small was idolatry in its beginnings after the flood, but how did it carry the world before it afterwards, and hold it for many ages, growing stronger and greater and worse and worse? So it was with the kingdom of antichrist, and so it was with Satan's Mahometan[7] kingdom, and so it will probably be with the last apostacy before the end of time.

---

[4]I.e., The Song of Solomon.
[5]Pliny the Elder (A.D. 23–79), a Roman scholar.
[6]John Spencer, *Things New and Old, Or, A Store-House of Similies, Sentences, Allegories, Apophthegms, Adagies, Apologues,* *Divine, Morall, Politicall, etc. With their severall Applications* (1658).
[7]I.e., Islam, the religious faith of Muslims founded by Muhammad (570–632), an Arab prophet.

[SERPENTS]

181. Serpents gradually swallow many of those animals that are their prey; they are too big for them to swallow at once, but they draw them down by little and little, till they are wholly swallowed and are past recovery. This represents the way in which Satan destroys multitudes of men that have had so good an education or so much conviction and light and common grace that they are too big to be swallowed at once. It also livelily represents his way of corrupting and prevailing against Christian countrys and churches, and against even some of the saints with respect to some particular errors and corruptions that he draws them into for a season.

[A BUBBLE]

191. A bubble that is blown up, when it is come to be largest of all and full of fine colors, is near breaking, which is a lively image of earthly glory, which very commonly, when it is come to the height, is near its end and commonly goes out and vanishes away in a moment, and a proper type of the men of this world, who place their happiness in the things of this life, who, when they are most swollen with worldly prosperity and are in the midst of their honors, wealth and pleasures, and glory most in these things, do commonly die. Death dashes all their glory to pieces in a moment, Ps. 37.35, 36: I have seen the wicked in great power and spreading himself like a green bay tree, yet he passed away, and lo, he was not, yea, I sought him, but he could not be found. And many places in Job; Hos. 10.7: As for Samaria, her king is cut off as the foam upon the water.

1948

PART II

FOUNDATIONS: THE NEW NATION (1765–1830)

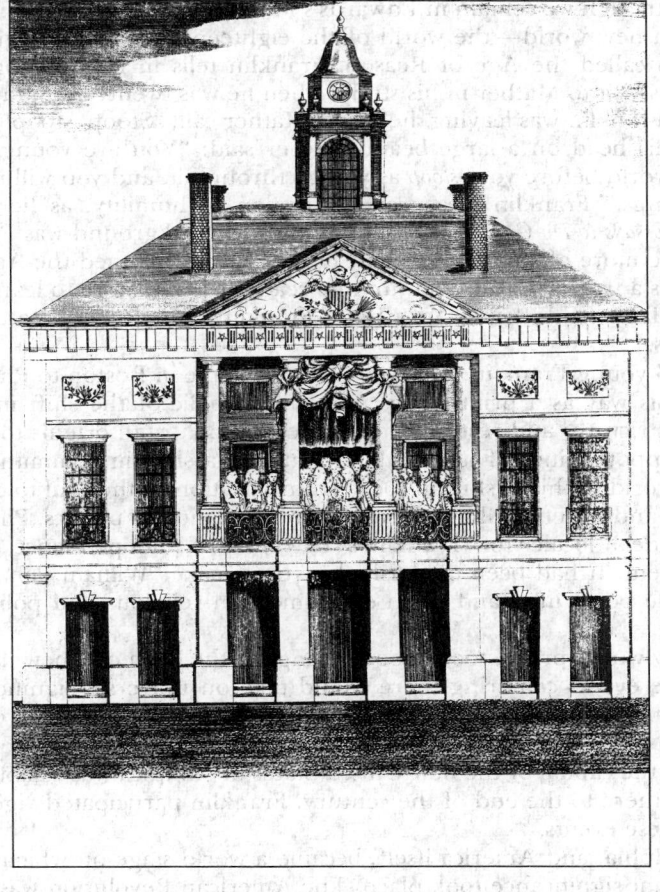

INTRODUCTION

When we move from Cotton Mather and Jonathan Edwards to Benjamin Franklin, though we remain in Edwards's Massachusetts and Mather's Boston, we enter a new world—the world of the eighteenth-century Enlightenment, sometimes called the Age of Reason. Franklin tells in his *Autobiography* the story of his visit to Mather in his study, when he was twenty and Mather sixty-three. As Franklin was leaving, he heard Mather call, "Stoop, stoop!" Franklin bumped his head on a large beam. Mather said: "You are young, and you have the world before you; *stoop* as you go through it, and you will miss many hard thumps." Franklin treasured this lesson in humility, as he treasured Mather's *Essays to Do Good*. But although his own background was Puritan, he found little more of value in Mather. Franklin's life spanned the Age of Reason, and as a true son of the century, he read the Bible more to learn from its style than from its doctrines. As a Deist, Franklin would turn to nature for his revelations.

In 1723 young Franklin ran away from his home in Boston to Philadelphia to make his way as a printer. His move is symbolic of the shift in America from the strictures and restraints of its theocratic Puritan origins to the liberties and opportunities of its republican future: a shift in commitment from the next world to this, a shift in focus from salvation of the soul to cultivation of the self and society, a shift in thought from religion to politics. Philadelphia was the ideal locale for Franklin's new life of independence and self-improvement. It had been established by the Quaker William Penn as a refuge for the persecuted and as an experiment in religious and political freedom.

The city would prove, too, a good setting for the birth of a new nation. For a time, the events centering there would take on universal significance: the Declaration of Independence was signed there in 1776; the Revolutionary War (1776–83) was directed from there; the Constitution was written there in 1787; and the capital of the new United States of America was established and remained there to the end of the century. Franklin participated vigorously in most of these events.

Philadelphia, and America itself, became a world stage on which events of transcendent significance took place. The American Revolution was the forerunner of the French Revolution (which began in 1789) and of an Age of Revolutions that would transform many societies and change many governments in the next century. The intellectual preparation for this radical change had been made by the philosophers and thinkers of the Enlightenment, some time before the change itself came about.

PROLOGUE TO AMERICAN INDEPENDENCE: THE ENLIGHTENMENT

The leaders of the American Revolution and shapers of the new nation were all themselves formed by the new zeal for knowledge ushered in by the Renaissance in the sixteenth and seventeenth centuries. Though they differed among themselves, they held a common commitment to human rights of freedom and equality and a common ideal of human fulfillment through a social compact based on mutual consent and respect. Benjamin Franklin, George Washington, John Adams, and Thomas Jefferson might differ in defining some of the abstract terms of their beliefs, but they were united in opposing tyranny and injustice.

The origins of the ideas that crystallized in the Declaration of Independence of 1776 and the American Constitution of 1787 may be found in the writings of a succession of scientists and philosophers who changed the way people saw their universe, their societies, and themselves. The seeds of this revolution in thought and perception were sewn long before by two scientists. Nicolaus Copernicus (1473–1543), a Polish astronomer, demonstrated in a work published in 1543 that the planets revolved around the sun and the earth turned on its axis. The Copernican system, the basis of modern astronomy, undermined the Ptolemaic theory that the heavenly bodies rotated about the earth, a theory that had supported the medieval Church's view of man and earth as the center of God's universe. Galileo Galilei (1564–1642), an Italian astronomer and physicist, in his investigation of the laws of motion, confirmed the Copernican theory. Both Copernicus and Galileo were condemned by the Catholic Church for their heretical views displacing the earth as the center of the universe.

In spite of the Church's opposition to scientific discoveries that upset traditional religious views of the world and universe, interest in science grew and spread in the seventeenth century. In England the Royal Society of London for Improving Natural Knowledge was established in 1660. The French Academy of Sciences was formally organized in 1666 under the sponsorship of the king of France.

England had already broken away from the Church by the time Sir Isaac Newton (1642–1727) produced his influential *Philosophiae naturalis principia mathematica (Mathematical Principles of Natural Philosophy,* 1687), which, building on Copernican theory and Galileo's laws of motion, provided a basis for a rational explanation of the universe. Newton's description of the universe as a self-regulating, clock-like machine that obeyed its own fixed laws undermined faith in a God-controlled universe as well as belief in the divine right of kings. (Benjamin Franklin describes in his *Autobiography* his unfulfilled hopes to meet Sir Isaac Newton when, as a nineteen-year-old lad in 1725, he had found himself temporarily stranded in London but eagerly in pursuit of knowledge of the world.)

The French philosopher, René Descartes (1596–1650), attempted to apply reason to metaphysics. In *Discours de la methode (Discourse on Method,* 1637) he insisted on believing nothing that could be doubted, and found that he could not doubt his own existence ("*Cogito, ergo sum*"; "I think, therefore I am"), and, moreover, that God existed as his idea and therefore, since the idea could not have come from his own experience or being, God *must* exist as the source of the idea. British philosopher John Locke (1632–1704) propounded the belief in *Essay Concerning Human Understanding* (1690) that the mind at birth was a *tabula rasa* (blank tablet) and that all ideas come from experience

and reflection. Such a notion undermined belief in original sin, predestination, and total depravity. The virtue or vice of an individual was shaped,
Locke reasoned, by environment and experience only after birth.

With traditional religious doctrine called into question, faith in social and
political institutions that claimed divine sanction began to weaken. In *Of Civil
Government: The Second Treatise* (1690), Locke set forth the notion that, in a
state of nature, all people are free and equal. He argued that a government's
only source of authority was the social contract entered into freely by individuals with those who governed. If the rulers violated the contract, the people
had the right to change the government. These radical ideas spread quickly,
and other thinkers explored their implications and ramifications.

French philosopher Jean Jacques Rousseau (1712–1778) contended in *The
Social Contract* (1762) that all governments derive their authority from a social
contract. Individuals who place themselves under control of a sovereign are
really placing themselves under control of the citizenry—in effect, themselves. The French philosopher Baron Charles de Secondant de Montesquieu
(1689–1755), in a massive comparative study of various kinds of government
entitled *L'Esprit des lois* (*The Spirit of Laws,* 1748), described the ideal form of
government as one providing for the separation of powers, with checks and
balances among the administrative, the legislative, and the judicial branches.
And the French satirist Voltaire (1694–1778), in a series of highly popular
poems, dramas, and novels (including *Candide,* 1759), spread an infectious
skepticism of all arbitrary and authoritarian institutions, social, religious, and
political.

In one of history's great symbolic moments, in 1778, at a public meeting of
the French Academy of Sciences in Paris, Voltaire (then eighty-four) and
Benjamin Franklin (seventy-two) embraced *à la française* (in the French manner) at the insistence of the assembled audience. Thus the American and
French shapers and makers of the American and French Revolutions (one
over, the other yet to begin) saluted each other to the acclaim of the crowd of
onlookers.

RELIGIOUS PLURALISM: QUAKERS, DEISTS, UNITARIANS

Although politics and government tended to displace religion as the central concern of Americans during this period, religion remained of immense
importance. Earlier in the eighteenth century, Calvinism lost its dominance.
Jonathan Edwards was the last great defender of its doctrines, and he knew
even as he wrote that they were under attack or, worse, simply ignored. Other
religious beliefs had been brought to the New World from the beginning of
its settlement, and still others developed as various religious groups split off—
or were banished from—the orthodox Puritans.

It is perhaps true, as St. John de Crèvecoeur had argued in *Letters from an
American Farmer* in 1782, that conditions on the American frontier—the thinness of population, the necessity of sharing meeting houses, the harsh demands on time and energy in obtaining food and shelter—decreased the zeal
of religious commitment and, over time, increased tolerance for other beliefs.
Certain it is that sects multiplied and, when the new government was formed
for the United States of America, no serious thought was given to endorsing a
state religion. Indeed, the Bill of Rights added to the Constitution in 1791 as
the first ten amendments guaranteed freedom of religion. A number of religious movements of the time were of significance in the realms of philosophy

and literature and had impact on social and political institutions. The most important of these were Quakerism, Deism, and Unitarianism.

Quakers received their name from their quaking or trembling when feeling the power of the Word of God. Known properly as the Society of Friends, the movement began in England under the leadership of George Fox (1624–1691), and was devoted to a simplification of religious worship, without hierarchy, formality, or institutionalization of forms. Known also as "Children of Light," the Quakers had faith that each person had an "inner light" that in effect bestowed the truth of God. There was, therefore, no need for a trained clergy or formal indoctrination. There was, instead, a lay clergy, and religious service consisted of meditative silences or comments from those "moved" to speak by the inner spirit.

When the English Quaker William Penn established the Colony of Pennsylvania in 1681, there was an influx of Quakers to America. Those who strayed into the Puritans' orbit were persecuted, but those who remained in Pennsylvania flourished. One of the important literary works of the eighteenth century was the *Journal* (1774) of Quaker John Woolman, which described in a meditative and gentle style Woolman's personal awakening to the inner light and to the immorality of slavery and war.

Deism was in many ways an intellectual counter to a Calvinistic God intimately involved in the daily affairs of each individual being, even to the extent of arbitrarily electing some to be saved and others to be damned. Deists believed in one God as Creator of the universe, but regarded Him as detached from the affairs of the world. They denied the Bible as a source of revelation and relied on reason as the principle resource for the discovery of truth; God could be perceived, not in the Bible, but in the laws governing nature. Deism was not an organized religion, but a rationalistic movement that had wide appeal during the latter eighteenth century. It inspired a variety of attitudes and views that helped to shape the events and documents of both the American and French revolutions.

In many ways, Deism was a conciliatory religious response to the scientific advances of the age. If the earth and humankind were displaced from center stage in the unfolding drama of the universe, they still played a part in the cosmic story. Newton had shown that there were immutable laws governing all of nature. As the maker of those laws, God stood revealed in them—

> All that we see, about, abroad,
> What is it all, but nature's God?

Thus wrote the Deist poet Philip Freneau in an 1815 poem. Many of the leading figures in the American Revolution were Deists, principal among them Benjamin Franklin. Always the pragmatist, Franklin kept his religious views to himself, knowing the antagonism they could provoke from a traditional believer. But he never swayed from his belief in religious pluralism and freedom of conscience. Thomas Jefferson put his Deistic views down on paper in *Notes on the State of Virginia* (1784), and they brought the charge of atheism from his enemies when he later ran for president. Thomas Paine wrote one of the most powerful defenses of Deism ever written in *The Age of Reason* (1794–95), and it provoked such violent denunciation that his last years were lived out in isolation and poverty. In America, the movement lost its momentum as a body of beliefs by the early nineteenth century, countered in part by a renewed revivalist fervor that focused on a concern for salvation and immortality. But it continued as a powerful influence in philosophic thought and in such liberal religious sects as Unitarianism.

Unitarianism, as the name implies, opposed itself to traditional Trinitarian belief in a three-fold Divinity—Father, Son, and Holy Ghost. Like Deism, it was a response to the rigidities of Calvinistic dogmas and denied doctrines of innate depravity, predestination, and eternal punishment. As a mortal human being, Christ could not have carried out the terms of the second covenant by taking on himself the sins of the world; thus Unitarianism swept aside the Calvinistic creed of atonement and salvation by faith alone. The first Unitarian Church in America was established in the Calvinistic stronghold, Boston, in 1785. And a Unitarian theologian, Henry Ware, became a professor of divinity in 1805 at the first college founded in America by the Puritans—Harvard. Unitarianism was to prove an important shaping influence on the Transcendentalism of the succeeding period.

There were, of course, other religious developments during this period. Among the sects founded was the Universalist Church of America, organized in 1790 in Philadelphia. It claimed that all human beings were the elect of God and therefore saved and that good inevitably triumphed over evil in the world. The colony of Maryland was founded as a haven for persecuted Catholics, and the first settlers had arrived as early as 1634. The first Catholic bishop in America was appointed in 1789, when there were some 30,000 Catholics in the country. Jews had come to America very early, first in the seventeenth century to Rhode Island because of its religious freedom. By 1820, there were some 3,000 Jews in America; the large immigration from Germany was to come later. Clearly the religious diversity of America was such that it would have been difficult to set any policy for the newly formed United States other than freedom of religious belief.

THE ROAD TO INDEPENDENCE

Whereas religion seemed to be the obsessive concern of Americans in the seventeenth century, politics and economics took possession of their attention in the eighteenth. No doubt events forced a shift in concern. First of all there were the problems and challenges of deciding on and winning independence. Then there was the greater challenge of holding the states together in independence and creating the brand-new governmental model of the United States of America.

The American Revolution was the first in a series of revolutions that would shake the western world at its foundations into the twentieth century. Just about the time it was resolved, the French Revolution began. And the revolutionary spirit swept through Europe repeatedly during the next century, particularly France, Germany, Italy, and Poland in 1830, and again in 1848; very few countries were left untouched by it. The major example in the early twentieth century was the Russian Revolution during the First World War. By the end of that war in 1918, few emperors, kings, or czars with autocratic power survived.

Thus the American Revolution was more an international than a national episode, with reverberations that still sound through world events. The participants seemed to be aware (as the settlers before them had been aware sailing off to the New World) that the actions in which they were engaged had a larger than local significance. Not only their fate was involved; the fate of humankind seemed to hang in the balance. No wonder they played out their roles with concerned self-consciousness, with the certitude that posterity would look back and wonder and judge.

For a long period the colonies in America seemed merely pawns in an international struggle among European-based empires. The principals were England, France, and Spain, with the first two assuming the leading roles. The wars between France and England, both marshalling Indians on their sides, lasted intermittently through the latter part of the 1600s and into the middle of the 1700s. America was often a battleground for conflicts in which the colonists were only peripherally involved. Gradually, however, they were drawn in.

In 1754, a meeting of the colonies was called in Albany, New York, to deal with problems posed by the usually friendly Iroquois who were threatening to support the French. The Albany meeting negotiated a successful treaty with the Iroquois, and then considered the Albany Plan of Union, drafted by Benjamin Franklin. This was the first proposal for a union of the colonies and would have provided a president appointed by the crown and a Council of Delegates elected by the various colonial assemblies. The plan was rejected by colonies protective of their independence and their rights to make treaties and levy taxes.

The French and Indian War (1755–63) was the last of a series of wars fought over control of the American continent. The determining battle was fought in 1759 on the Plains of Abraham, a plateau above the city of Quebec in Canada. Both the French commander Louis Montcalm and British General James Wolfe were killed in the battle, but England was the victor. In the Treaty of Paris in 1763, France ceded to Britain all of Canada and the upper Mississippi Valley.

Great Britain was now the holder of an enormous empire in the New World, but it needed money to run it. In its effort to impose taxes on the colonies, it met resistance at every turn. The colonists challenged the right of the British Parliament to levy taxes in America, asserting their sole allegiance was to the king of England. Thus the cry went up, "No taxation without representation." The Stamp Act of 1765, requiring the payment of a fee for a stamp affixed to all pamphlets, newspapers, and legal documents, was especially denounced. A congress was called—the first to be held on American initiative—to deny the right of the British Parliament to impose taxes. The issue of taxation surged to the fore again in 1773 in resentment against a tax on tea. In December, a band of patriots disguised as Indians boarded the British ships in Boston Harbor and dumped the tea overboard. The Boston Tea Party was the first of a series of events that would be elevated later from local history to national myth when Americans would recreate their origins in the national imagination. The first Continental Congress was called to Philadelphia in 1774 to issue a Declaration of Rights and Grievances aimed at England.

In 1775 open conflict broke out between England and the colonists. The British, on hearing that the colonists were collecting weapons and ammunition at Concord, Massachusetts, sent a detail to confiscate the store of munitions. Paul Revere made his famous midnight ride to alert the colonists. The British encountered American "minutemen" at Lexington, Massachusetts, but after a few shots the Americans retreated to Concord. There, in the words of Ralph Waldo Emerson's "Concord Hymn" (1837):

> By the rude bridge that arched the flood,
>   Their flag to April's breeze unfurled,
> Here once the embattled farmers stood
>   And fired the shot heard round the world.

On their retreat to Boston, the British in their red coats were easy targets for the American soldiers stealthily following them through the familiar fields and woods. Paul Revere, minutemen, Lexington, Concord, Red Coats—the colonists garnered the symbols that would galvanize the population into action.

Literature had an important role to play in the American Revolution. Even before the "shot heard round the world," the debate in the colonies had produced abundant pamphlets and broadsides arguing the issues, the patriots taking radical positions that moved toward independence, the "Tories," more cautious, searching for means of reconciliation. Such pieces as Benjamin Franklin's satire, "Rules by Which a Great Empire May Be Reduced to a Small One" (1773), were highly effective. But the work that must be given credit for decisively crystallizing feelings and precipitating action is Thomas Paine's *Common Sense,* published in January 1776, setting forth in urgent, eloquent language the colonists' rights to overthrow a tyrannical ruler and form their own government and calling for an immediate declaration of independence. It was a runaway best seller, going through innumerable printings.

In June 1776, the second Continental Congress appointed a committee of five to draft a Declaration of Independence. Benjamin Franklin, John Adams, and Thomas Jefferson served on the committee, which turned over to the thirty-three-year-old Jefferson the job of drafting the document: "We hold these truths to be self-evident, that all men are created equal, that they are endowed by their Creator with certain unalienable rights; that among these are life, liberty, and the pursuit of happiness. That to secure these rights, governments are instituted among men, deriving their just powers from the consent of the governed. . . ." These few words were the distillation of the deepest and boldest thought of Enlightenment philosophy, and would be echoed and reechoed through successive struggles for freedom throughout the world. The Declaration was approved on July 4, 1776.

THE WAR, THE CONSTITUTION, THE UNITED STATES OF AMERICA

The Revolutionary War lasted from 1776 to 1783. At first there were defeats and strategic retreats. The British occupied New York, then Philadelphia. But in 1777, the Americans defeated General John Burgoyne and his British and mercenary Hessian forces, who came down from Canada to "finish" the war. Burgoyne's defeat brought the French in on the American side. The Marquis de Lafayette persuaded the French government to send an expeditionary force of 6,000 Frenchmen to America. Next, in 1781, came the defeat of Lord Cornwallis's army at Yorktown, on the coast of Virginia. Cornwallis's surrender decided the British House of Commons to end the conflict, but the Treaty of Paris formally ending the war was not signed until 1783.

Thomas Paine placed his pen in the service of the American forces. When Washington's armies were in retreat, facing possible defeat, he wrote the first of his sixteen pamphlets entitled *The American Crisis:* "These are the times that try men's souls. . . ." Washington ordered the paper read to all his troops. It rallied them and the people, too. Poet Philip Freneau also placed his pen at the service of the Revolution, ready to celebrate a victory or lament a defeat— "On the Memorable Victory" (Capt. John Paul Jones's at sea, 1781), "To the Memory of the Brave Americans" (who died at Eutaw Springs, North Carolina, in 1781). Freneau is remembered in history as the "Poet of the American Revolution."

With the war at an end, the main source of the colonies' unity—hatred of British tyranny—disappeared. Although the colonies were held together loosely by the Articles of Confederation (devised in 1781), they started to split apart because of their diverse interests and self-concerns. States began to issue their own paper money and to institute tariffs against importation of goods. In short, there was financial and mercantile chaos. A constitutional convention was called in Philadelphia in 1787 to begin the task of writing a Constitution to provide a stronger central government. George Washington presided over the proceedings. Members included James Madison, Alexander Hamilton, and the aging Benjamin Franklin. In one of the great conciliatory speeches of his career, Franklin asked the deadlocked delegates to rise above disagreements and give unanimous consent to approval of the newly written Constitution.

But ratification by the states was by no means assured. Those who had argued with each other in writing the Constitution joined each other in persuading the various states to give their approval. In the process, Alexander Hamilton, James Madison, and John Jay came together to write some eighty-six papers entitled *The Federalist* (1787–88). They emphasized the need for a strong national government and the protections offered by the careful separation of the powers of the executive, legislative, and judiciary branches. Jefferson, who was minister to France during this period, called the *Federalist* "the best commentary on the principles of government which was ever written." The new Constitution was ratified by the ninth state, New Hampshire, in June 1788, assuring the creation of the new government. By early 1791, all thirteen of the original colonies had ratified the Constitution.

States were willing to submit to a strong central government in part because of such episodes as Shays's Rebellion, an uprising of farmers in western Massachusetts who faced foreclosure on their farms brought about largely by high taxes imposed by a distant state government. Shays and his supporters were put down, but not without armed force. The incident inspired the Connecticut Wits, a conservative "federalist" group of poets, to write a series of mock heroic satires called *The Anarchiad* (1786–87).

These clashing populist and federalist forces foreshadowed the party divisions that would appear soon after George Washington was inaugurated as the first president of the United States. Secretary of State Thomas Jefferson, considered populist and even radical by many, immediately collided with Treasury Secretary Alexander Hamilton, a strong centrist and Federalist. Jefferson was unsuccessful in advising against Hamilton's excise tax on whisky, which led eventually to the Whisky Rebellion of 1784 in western Pennsylvania. It was instigated by Scotch-Irish settlers who were making whisky out of grain that they could not transport over the mountains to market. The tax imposed by a distant government on a vital money crop struck the settlers as unfair and they forced one federal inspector to flee for his life.

The two-party system developed during Washington's two-term presidency, with the Federalists led by Hamilton allied to Washington, and the Democratic-Republicans led by Jefferson biding their time for power. The latter's support of the French Revolution outraged the Federalists. Federalists remained in power through the term of John Adams until 1800. With Jefferson's ascendancy to the presidency in 1801, the Democratic-Republicans (later called simply Democrats) held office through the administrations of James Madison (1809–17) and James Monroe (1817–25). John Quincy Adams became president (1825–29) at a time when the parties were realigning, the

Federalists turning into Whigs (eventually Republicans) and the Democratic-Republicans becoming the Democrats, the party of Andrew Jackson.

Throughout these early years of the Republic, the issues that divided the parties were economic and social, with the Federalist party supporting strong national powers and institutions, apprehensive about the judgment of the mass of people; and the Democratic or Jeffersonian party supporting states' rights and local rule, trusting the judgment of the people. With the election in 1828 of Andrew Jackson (1829–37), a folksy populist Democrat from Tennessee, the country seemed set in directions Jefferson had desired.

THE LOUISIANA PURCHASE AND WESTWARD SETTLEMENT

The first U.S. census taken in 1790, the year after Washington's election as president, counted about four million American citizens. The major cities were, in descending order of population, Philadelphia, New York, Boston, and Baltimore. The largest of these (Philadelphia) had 42,000 people, the smallest (Baltimore), 13,000. At the time of Andrew Jackson's presidency in 1830, the population had more than tripled to nearly thirteen million.

More dramatic, perhaps, was the increase in the territory of the new country. Victory over England in the Revolutionary War had awarded America the land to the east of the Mississippi River. Beyond lay the land held by Spain, whose main empire lay south in Mexico and South America. Napoleon, emerging out of the chaos of the French Revolution, had seized power in 1799 and had crowned himself emperor in 1804. Shortly after Jefferson became president, Napoleon forced Spain to cede to France the immense tract of land beyond the Mississippi. Rumors circulated that he planned a great empire there, but suddenly he decided to sell. In 1803, Jefferson "stretched the Constitution till it cracked" and bought the area for $15,000,000.

The Louisiana Purchase doubled the size of the fledgling country, adding more than a million square miles extending from the Mississippi to the Rocky Mountains and from the Gulf of Mexico to Canada. The prize of the purchase was New Orleans itself, the cosmopolitan port on the Gulf at the mouth of the Mississippi. Jefferson sent Meriwether Lewis and William Clark to explore this vast new area. They set out in 1804, following the Missouri River to its source, and returned in 1806. Their *History of the Expedition*, edited from their journals, was published in 1814.

The vast empty territories stretching to the west assured America's expansion and growth. By 1830, the United States added eleven states to the original thirteen: Vermont, 1791; Kentucky, 1792; Tennessee, 1796; Ohio, 1803; Louisiana, 1812; Indiana, 1816; Mississippi, 1817; Illinois, 1818; Alabama, 1819; Maine, 1820; and Missouri, 1821. The movement of America was westward, both physically and psychologically. That the Tennessean Andrew Jackson, himself a migrant westward from the Carolinas, could be elected president in 1828 was indicative of a radical shift in American orientation and pointed to the emergence of radically different notions of what an American political leader might be.

The presence of immense areas of unsettled land meant the continuing presence of a constantly receding frontier—that area at the border between the populated and unpopulated lands. In the old European countries, many people were consigned to perpetual poverty because of increasing populations and diminishing resources; in America, down and out people found the promise of a fresh start and a new life in the seemingly endless bounty of the westward expansion.

In *Letters from an American Farmer* (1782), St. John de Crèvecoeur contended that the American was a "new man." He was made new in part by the necessity of confronting the American wilderness. He shed his European identity and became American when he went out to hunt animals for their food and fur, or when he cleared the forests for a plot of land and planted corn and other vegetables, or when he joined together with other frontier settlers to protect themselves from Indian raids, or when he helped form a community to build a nondenominational church where all people could worship, regardless of their faith.

Crèvecoeur described the frontiersman, but it was novelist James Fenimore Cooper who raised him to the level of myth in the character of Natty Bumppo in the *Leather-Stocking Tales* (1823–41). A loner and wanderer, uneasy in civilization, living in a world half-way between the worlds of the white man and red, at ease in the woods and on the rivers and prairies, resourceful and self-reliant, tough on the outside but tender within, independent but selfless — this figure would occupy a space deep in the American imagination far into the future. It would also be fixed in the imagination of those who, wondering "What is an American?" would encounter Gary Cooper or John Wayne in one or another Hollywood "western" depicting life in America on a frontier that, though long since gone, can never be fully exorcised.

AN EMERGING AMERICAN LITERATURE

PROSE ON THE RUN: FOUR FLAWED CLASSICS

The French historian Abbé Raynal (1713–1796), believing that nature determined the vigor of plants, animals, and even human beings, exclaimed in a work published in 1770: "One must be astonished that America has not yet produced one good poet, one able mathematician, one man of genius in a single art or a simple science." Thomas Jefferson protested in *Notes on the State of Virginia* that Raynal's judgment was unfair, given America's youth and sparsity of population. But the Abbé Raynal touched a chord that would be sounded over and over in the new nation and abroad.

At the very time the Abbé Raynal was writing, works of literature of the kind he demanded were being written but not yet published. There are four books from eighteenth-century America that were to be critically acclaimed in their own time and have endured to the present as classics, flawed but extraordinary achievements. They were all written by men who were deeply engaged in other enterprises, such as establishing a new government, tilling the soil, or saving souls. America could not yet afford to support writers solely committed to writing careers. The works are Benjamin Franklin's *Autobiography* (1791–1818), John Woolman's *Journal* (1774), St. John de Crèvecoeur's *Letters from an American Farmer* (1782), and Thomas Jefferson's *Notes on the State of Virginia* (1784). All of these books were written "on the run" by men of action who had difficulty finding time to write. The books are incomplete, episodic, repetitive, contradictory, and awkwardly structured, but nobody would deny their genius. They have had enduring reputations abroad, some of them published and acclaimed in France and England before their appearance in America.

Together these four books present a picture of eighteenth-century life in America and at the same time offer insight into the nature of the "American." First and basic is Franklin's *Autobiography,* with its account of the young Franklin's life from 1706 to the 1750s, moving from Boston to Philadelphia, to England and back, and establishing the basic myth of the "rise from rags to riches" that would stereotype Americans long into the future. John Woolman's Quaker *Journal* presents an antidote to Franklin's "way to wealth" in revealing the experience of a deeply religious man who turned aside from the making of money to explore and address the moral issues of the time—slavery, displacement of the Indians, poverty. Franklin, too, had given up the making of money in midlife to devote himself to reading and science and the shaping of the new nation, but the unfinished *Autobiography* left out much of the latter half of his life.

Crèvecoeur's *Letters from an American Farmer,* in exploring the question "What Is an American?" portrays the simple, self-restoring life of the husbandman clearing the lands and then planting and harvesting crops that nourish a family and sustain a community in the wilderness of frontier America. It is, as pictured, a life with its own spiritual rewards and important for the basic values of the society. Thomas Jefferson's *Notes on the State of Virginia,* written in answer to a series of "queries" from a Frenchman, is a grab bag of facts, conjectures, and views on the country's geography, government, society, and people by a wealthy, fiercely democratic statesman who helped "invent" the United States. The book grapples with the question "What is America?" and moves with such agility from fact to essence, escaping its own confining structure, as to provide an answer both profound and complex. All four of these books taken together, with all their varied and sometimes conflicting views, can convey some sense of an answer to the puzzling, often haunting questions, "What is an American?" "What is America?" These questions have the same urgency in the twentieth century as they had in the eighteenth.

There were, of course, many other autobiographies, journals, diaries, and descriptive accounts of the time. These and other nonfiction prose forms constituted the dominant literary genres of the Revolutionary period. As the focus on religion that characterized the colonial period diminished and the concern for politics and government increased, more and more American writers were coming from the ranks of those who had trained not for the ministry but the law. *Common Sense* and the *Crisis* papers by Thomas Paine as well as *The Federalist* papers by Alexander Hamilton, James Madison, and John Jay are examples of political pamphleteering and debate that have had lasting significance. Even the new nation's governmental documents themselves—the Declaration of Independence, the Constitution, the Bill of Rights—have stimulated lively interest beyond the nation's boundaries, especially in countries undergoing the throes of their own revolutions.

The four "flawed classics" had wide audiences abroad. So did another American work published after the Revolution—John Bartram's *Travels* (1791), ostensibly a work of botany, in reality a narrative account of the author's five-year journey through the southeastern United States interlaced with a series of reflections on nature, experience, and humankind, civilized and "savage." It may serve as an example of the growing reputation of American books, inspired in part by the enormous hunger abroad for word of the New World. Bartram's *Travels* was not only read but absorbed by some of the major figures of the Romantic literary movement in Europe—including Chateaubriand in France, Coleridge and Wordsworth in England.

AN EMERGING AMERICAN POETRY: FROM CLASSIC TO ROMANTIC

For literature, the Revolutionary period was a time of transition from the forms and themes of neoclassicism to the new forms and different concerns of romanticism. The characteristic form of neoclassicism was the heroic couplet (two lines of rhymed iambic pentameter), which with its constant rhyme imposed a formal restraint on the poet; the characteristic form of romanticism was blank verse (unrhymed iambic pentameter) or some subtle variation, which allowed for a freedom with artful or submerged restraint. The dominant mode of neoclassicism was satiric, with a focus on the foibles and weaknesses of society. The dominant mode of romanticism was contemplative, with a focus on the outward and inward meaning of nature. These simplifications may serve as pointers rather than as comprehensive definitions of complex literary movements, international in scope, that embraced paradoxes and contradictions. But for those growing to maturity during the transitional period of the late eighteenth and early nineteenth centuries, the challenges were quite real. They often had to transform themselves, even start over and begin anew.

For the American poet the challenge was even greater, to comprehend the transition from a colonial country to a newly independent nation. And in a populace with little leisure to devote to the "impractical" arts, Philip Freneau caught some of the sense of despair that must have visited most writers who struggled to be poets during this time in "To an Author":

> On these bleak climes by fortune thrown,
> Where rigid reason reigns alone,
> Where lovely fancy has no sway,
> Nor magic forms about us play—
> Tell me, what has the muse to do?—

Philip Freneau found plenty to do as a poet, as his large body of collected poems shows. And he made himself over many times as a poet. He was first and foremost "Poet of the American Revolution," in which his satiric gifts proved most valuable—as in "A Political Litany" (1775). But his encounter with the tropical islands of the West Indies furnished him with the ideal materials of romantic poetry, which he embraced in his innovative long poem "The House of Night" (1779), anticipating many aspects of the romantic movement yet to emerge in Europe. He is best remembered, and perhaps rightly so, for a handful of short lyrics that show romantic melancholy and linguistic playfulness, as in "The Wild Honey Suckle," "The Indian Burying Ground," and "To a Caty-Did."

Phillis Wheatley should have found greater difficulty than Freneau in practicing as a poet. She was purchased in Boston as a domestic slave at the age of seven to attend Mrs. Wheatley. The Wheatley daughter tutored her and soon she was reading the classic English and Latin poets, and writing after their manner. And she, too, wrote enthusiastically on patriotic and Revolutionary themes, as in "To His Excellency General Washington" (1776), written when he assumed command of the Revolutionary Army. Her celebration of freedom could take an ironic and moving turn whenever she referred to her own fate, "snatched from Afric's fancied happy seat!" She asked, "And can I then but pray / Others may never feel tyrannic sway?" She was the first black American writer of note, and, as a twentieth-century critic, William H. Robinson, has said, "She proved herself a worthy black American poet-pioneer. She led the way."

Timothy Dwight (1764–1846), grandson of Jonathan Edwards, has the dubious honor of publishing the first epic poem in America, *The Conquest of Canaan* (1785). George Washington and Connecticut are made to parallel the Biblical Joshua and Canaan in 10,000 lines of heroic couplets. The poem is deeply religious, soberly patriotic, and unbelievably dull. Its failure, however, did not deter Joel Barlow from devoting much of his life to the writing of his epic poem, the second to be produced in America. Published as *The Vision of Columbus* in 1787, when Barlow was thirty-three, it reappeared in 1807 as *The Columbiad*, with its original 4,700 lines expanded to 8,350, all heroic couplets. The revision was fatal, turning a tolerable epic into an inhumanly long bore. But the impulse to write the American epic would endure, down to Walt Whitman and beyond to the present age.

Joel Barlow and Timothy Dwight were members of the Connecticut Wits, centered in Hartford, Connecticut, and made up of a number of conservative Yale graduates. Their satiric wit appeared first in the jointly written *Anarchiad* (1786–87), and gained its thrust from their rock-solid faith in Calvinism and Federalism and their opposition to the disreputable beliefs in Deism and egalitarianism. It is ironic that Joel Barlow has been consigned by literary history to this guilt by association with the Connecticut Wits, because he went on to become an admirer of the French Revolution and an associate of Thomas Jefferson and Thomas Paine—as radical as they in politics and religion. When he found time from the making of his epic, he also wrote a charming mock-epic, *The Hasty Pudding* (1796), that has found a permanent niche in the American tradition of humorous verse.

Though Freneau is sometimes called the "first American poet," William Cullen Bryant was to bear the burden of being called the "American Wordsworth." He enjoyed the title no more than Cooper enjoyed that of the "American Scott." Born a few years after the American Revolution, Bryant began in early youth to write poetry and quickly made the transition from neoclassical heroic couplet (with which he began) to romantic blank verse. He became famous with "Thanatopsis" (1817), and he endeared himself as a familiar poet with such memorable and quotable lyrics as "The Yellow Violet" (1821) and "To the Fringed Gentian" (1832). His best—and quite good—poetry is to be found in his slightly longer poems, meditations in and on nature that succeed in engaging the imagination—"Inscription for the Entrance to a Wood" (1817), "A Forest Hymn" (1825), and "The Prairies" (1833). In "The Poet" (1864), Bryant described the poet's aim as "to touch the heart or fire the blood." He clearly achieved that aim in his own time. Now it is difficult to get beyond the schoolroom image of the complacent bearded poet. To go beyond it, however, is to hear, underneath his sometimes facile affirmations, a tragic note sounded again and again in the poetry, a forlorn sense of solitude and even desolation—as in the ending of his poignant poem "The Prairies": "And I am in the wilderness alone."

AN EMERGING AMERICAN DRAMA

The Puritans found poetry compatible with their Calvinistic piety, but they believed drama and the stage were associated with Satan. The theaters, closed by the Puritans in England, were never opened in America until after the passing of Puritan dominance. It is no wonder, then, that drama was slow to develop as a literary genre. Major Robert Rogers (1731–1795), who fought in the French and Indian wars and defended Detroit against the Indian attack led by Chief Pontiac, has the distinction of writing America's first published play, *Ponteach; or, The Savages of America* (Ponteach was an early spelling for Pontiac). A blank-verse historical drama in five acts, *Ponteach* presents an account of events of the time that has been considered historically accurate, even though the character of the chief Pontiac is idealized. The honor, however, of writing the first American play actually produced in America goes to Thomas Godfrey (1736–1763). His *Prince of Parthia,* a blank-verse romantic tragedy in five acts, was produced in 1767 for one performance. The action is set on the Tigris River, near Baghdad, at the beginning of the Christian era, and tells a tale of intrigue at court between two sons of the king struggling for their father's throne and in love with the same maiden.

Even though Royall Tyler came along a bit later than these playwrights, his play *The Contrast* earns the distinction of being the first play set in America and produced in America. Tyler had never seen a play until business brought him to New York in 1787, when he went to see Richard Brinsley Sheridan's comedy *The School for Scandal.* Three weeks later, *The Contrast* was produced. Tyler was obviously influenced by the British play, but he produced a remarkably refreshing and original American comedy that has entertained audiences into the twentieth century. He introduced themes and elements of character that were recognizably American and enduring. Starting in April 1787, it ran for several performances in New York and soon had productions in other American cities.

The play was not only set in America but dealt with the events of the time. The leading character, Colonel Henry Manly, had just been through the Revolutionary War, and his patriotic fervor, sense of honor, and American frankness reflected the values of the audiences. He is in radical contrast to Billy Dimple, a decadent fortune chaser who had been turned into a fop by his education in England and his reading of Lord Chesterfield's *Letters to His Son.* The play also introduced to the stage the Yankee character of Jonathan, a shrewd country bumpkin or simpleton who always outsmarted the supersophisticated city slicker. Politically the play affirmed innocent American values and manners over the decadent values and pretentious manners of the British—reassuring Americans of the justness of their triumph in the recently concluded Revolutionary War. *The Contrast* marks the true beginning of American drama.

AN EMERGING AMERICAN FICTION

Like drama, fiction had to overcome a prejudice against it; from the Puritan period well into the eighteenth century it was thought of as untrue and immoral. Some intellectuals like Thomas Jefferson, busy with the Revolution and forming a new government, felt fiction was a falsification of life and a waste of time. But by the end of the eighteenth century American novels were being published, and in the early part of the nineteenth century American storytellers and novelists began to enjoy international reputations.

William Hill Brown (1765–1793) is generally considered the author of the first American novel, *The Power of Sympathy* (1789). Long attributed to the writer Sarah W. Morton (1759–1846), the novel, according to its Preface, was written "to expose the dangerous consequences of seduction." It is a somewhat lurid story of illicit sex, mysterious parenthood, and an incestuous marriage prevented at the last minute by exposure of the unknown blood relationship. Such sensational, sentimental, and didactic fictions were to prove popular throughout the nineteenth century and into the twentieth. One of the most popular was by Mrs. Susanna Haswell Rowson (*c.* 1762–1824), *Charlotte Temple, A Tale of Truth* (1791); it was another story of the grim consequences of seduction written "for the perusal of the young and thoughtful of the fair sex." By the 1930s it had gone through 161 editions. Less sentimental novelists who wrote in a deeper vein to explore more complex themes also achieved popularity in their time. Those of enduring significance include Hugh Henry Brackenridge, Charles Brockden Brown, Washington Irving, and James Fenimore Cooper.

Hugh Henry Brackenridge became first a lawyer and later a judge, but his one novel, *Modern Chivalry* (1792–1815), took almost a lifetime to write. His main influence is Cervantes, the primary model *Don Quixote;* however, there is a good deal of borrowing from the satire of Jonathan Swift and the narrative structures of Henry Fielding. Brackenridge's characters are Captain John Farrago (the Don Quixote figure) and his illiterate Irish servant Teague O'Regan (the Sancho Panza equivalent). The picaresque tale is set in contemporary rural America and is the first comprehensive presentation of backwoods life in American literature. The narrator is vividly present throughout this "self-conscious narrative," chatting to the reader directly about his purposes and plans. On the very first pages, he confesses that the sole purpose for his writing is to "fix the English language" by giving an "example of good English" to serve as a "model to future speakers and writers." A perceptive reader will soon discover that the purpose is also political satire, in support of the democratic ideas and ideals that may be loosely described as Jeffersonian, with a dash of Tom Paine added.

Charles Brockden Brown fell under the spell of the British writers William Godwin and his wife, Mary Wollstonecraft, liberal free thinkers of the time. It was the latter's *Vindication of the Rights of Women* (1792) that influenced Brown's first work, *Alcuin: A Dialogue.* It is a "novel of ideas" in which fictional characters explore the status, abilities, and rights of women in long conversations. Only one-half of the work appeared during Brown's lifetime (in 1798). The other half, portraying Alcuin's visit to a visionary "Paradise of Women," with its frank discussion of marriage, divorce, and sex, must have been considered too radical to print. It was published in a biography of Brown that appeared in 1815 after his death. Brown's fame rests on a series of novels written under the influence of the Gothic novels of such British writers as Mrs. Ann Radcliffe, and her *The Mysteries of Udolpho* (1794). Brown wrote four "Gothic romances" in quick order: *Wieland* (1798), *Arthur Mervyn* (1799), *Ormond* (1799), and *Edgar Huntly* (1799). Filled with horror, mystery, pathological behavior, and such pseudoscientific fads as ventriloquism, his work (particularly *Wieland*) had an international following, even among those who had influenced him.

Like Brown, Washington Irving gave up the law to devote himself to writing; but while Brown had to turn to magazine editing to make a living, Irving was able to support himself by the pen throughout his life, becoming, in effect, America's first man of letters. He gained international recognition with his satiric "Knickerbocker" *History of New York* (1809), written in an elegant, polished, witty style; and he solidified his fame with *The Sketch Book*, written in England and published first as a book there in 1820. Books of personal essays, sketches, legends and short stories followed one another until the opportunity of going to Spain arose, enabling Irving to exploit the archives there for history and biography. His *History of the Life and Voyages of Christopher Columbus* was published in 1828, and *The Conquest of Granada* in 1829. After living in the old Moorish castle, the Alhambra in Granada, he put together a series of sketches and stories that became known as his "Spanish Sketch Book"—*The Alhambra* (1832). On returning to America after a seventeen-year absence and being accused of having become a foreign writer, Irving wrote a succession of American books to underscore his American origins and allegiance. The best-known of these is *A Tour of the Prairies (1835)*, an account of his expedition through the Indian territories of the American West. He was a master of the personal essay, an accomplished satirist and comic writer, and a pioneer in the genre of the short story, leaving two masterpieces in the form, "Rip Van Winkle" and "The Legend of Sleepy Hollow."

James Fenimore Cooper came to writing fiction late, and then, according to legend, on a dare. Remarking one evening that he could write a better novel than he had just been reading to his wife, he found himself challenged. And he immediately wrote his first novel, which was a failure. But undeterred, he wrote his second, *The Spy* (1821), which was an instant success. In it he exploited his earlier experiences at sea, first on a merchant vessel, later as midshipman in the Navy. Cooper continued to write, publishing for a time a book a year. In his third novel, *The Pioneers* (1823), he hit upon the materials that would charge his imagination and fascinate readers for the rest of his career. The novel introduced Natty Bumppo, the skilled outdoorsman at home in the woods and prairies, and his closest friend and comrade, Chingachgook, a trustworthy Mohican Indian chief. Cooper created an epic of the American West from frontier and Indian legends in the *Leather-Stocking Tales,* a total of five novels that traced the life of Natty Bumppo from his vigorous manhood to his death in leathery old age. Cooper advised reading them in the chronological order of the action: *The Deerslayer* (1841), *The Last of the Mohicans* (1826), *The Pathfinder* (1840), *The Pioneers* (1823), and *The Prairie* (1827).

Although Cooper's style at times became somewhat labored and clotted, and his actions studded with exhausting chases, hairbreadth escapes, and miraculous rescues, he never failed to arouse and hold the interest of readers. The secret probably lies in the character of Natty Bumppo, the archetypal American frontiersman with whom readers could identify, envying his freedom from the restraints of civilized society and his simple life in the woods and admiring his resourcefulness, honesty, and generosity to friend and foe. Americans read Cooper at the time to find out who they were, collectively. Foreigners read him in search of the answer to that question Crèvecoeur had first posed back in 1782, "What Is an American?" Cooper seemed (and to many still seems), at least in a measure, to provide the materials for discovery.

With such writers as Cooper, Irving, and Bryant, American literature came of age. They demonstrated that "letters" could be a career in America, and that American writers could attract enthusiastic audiences abroad as well as at home. They prepared the way for a distinctively American literary culture and production.

ADDITIONAL READING

Moses Coit Tyler, *Literary History of the American Revolution, 1763–1783,* 2 vols., 1897.
Vernon L. Parrington, *Main Currents in American Thought,* Vols. I and II, 1927.
Leon Howard, *The Connecticut Wits,* 1943.
Howard Mumford Jones, *O Strange New World: American Culture, the Formative Years,* 1952.
Harry Hayden Clark, *Transitions in American Literary History,* 1953.

Russel B. Nye, *The Cultural Life of the New Nation*, 1960.
Leslie Fiedler, *Love and Death in the American Novel*, 1960, 1966.
Lewis P. Simpson, ed., *The Federalist Literary Mind*, 1962.
Perry Miller, *The Life of the Mind in America: From the Revolution to the Civil War*, 1965.
Daniel Boorstin, *The Americans: The National Experience*, 1965.
Robert Spiller, ed., *The American Literary Revolution, 1783–1837*, 1967.
Richard Slotkin, *Regeneration Through Violence: The Mythology of the American Frontier, 1600–1860*, 1973.
Annette Kolodny, *The Lay of the Land*, 1975.
Lawrence J. Friedman, *Inventors of the Promised Land*, 1975.
Kenneth Silverman, *Cultural History of the American Revolution*, 1976.
Everett Emerson, ed., *American Literature, 1764–1789: The Revolutionary Years*, 1977.
Cecelia Tichi, *New World, New Earth*, 1979.
Emory Elliott, *Revolutionary Writers: Literature and Authority in the New Republic, 1725–1810*, 1982.
Robert A. Ferguson, *Law and Letters in American Culture*, 1984.
Earl N. Harbert and Robert A. Rees, eds., *Fifteen American Authors Before 1900: Bibliographical Essays on Research and Criticism*, 1984; includes Franklin, Bryant, Irving, and Cooper.
Jane Tompkins, *Sensational Designs: The Cultural Work of American Fiction, 1790–1860*, 1985.
Lawrence Buell, *New England Literary Culture: From Revolution Through Renaissance*, 1986.
Cathy Davidson, *Revolution and the Word*, 1986.
Myra Jehlen, *American Incarnation*, 1986.
Ruth H. Bloch, *Visionary Republic: Millennial Themes in American Thought, 1756–1800*, 1986.

FROM EDWARDS TO FRANKLIN: DIVERGENCE
AND CONTINUITY

At first glance, Jonathan Edwards (born 1703) and Benjamin Franklin (born 1706) seem so radically different as to be classified irreconcilable opposites. The erudite Edwards, exiled during his late years in the crude frontier village of Stockbridge, pouring his energies into writing his subtle defenses of Puritan doctrines, seems far removed from the homespun Franklin in his seventies, exiled in a sophisticated Paris suburb, spending *his* energies in wooing French diplomats and ladies. But in many ways these two images epitomize the complex American character, with its conflicting desires to withdraw from society, or to conquer and control it; to civilize the wilderness, or to rough up the refined; to retreat inward to the self, or to venture outward to the other; to live with the soul, or to live by the flesh and the appetites. In spite of their differences, Edwards and Franklin shared many aims and convictions. Edwards's belief in man's innate depravity, including his own, had its counterpart in Franklin's assumptions about man's deviousness and egoism, even his own. Edwards's ambition, fulsomely realized, to explain to the world "The Nature of True Virtue" was matched by Franklin's ambition, realized only in foreshortened fragment in the *Autobiography,* to reveal to all the "The Art of Virtue." Edwards's zeal to show the way to "conversion" (which required application and persistence) was matched by Franklin's eagerness to show the way to wealth (which required industry and frugality). Edwards's awe at "the universal system of excellence" inspired by God's revelations in the Bible was matched by Franklin's curiosity and pleasure in the universal laws of nature inspired by his "philosophic studies." Probing beneath surface differences often reveals subterranean connections. The contradictions of American character may have their mysterious and hidden links.

BENJAMIN FRANKLIN
(1706–1790)
Philosopher Pragmatist

When Benjamin Franklin was born, January 17, 1706, Boston was a town of some 10,000 people, dominated still by a waning Puritan culture. The major concern on all sober Puritans' minds was their fate not in this world but the next. The New World was divided into scattered colonies engaging in more traffic with the mother country than in intercourse with each other. When Franklin died, April 17, 1790, in Philadelphia, this New World had become an independent nation, the United States of America, with a population of some 4,000,000 by the first census count. And the leading lights who had brought this miracle about tended to be, like Franklin, not Puritans but Deists, believing God's revelations were not in dogmas distilled from the Bible, but in laws discovered in nature. The eighteenth century was an age of rapid and radical change, and Benjamin Franklin was a true son of that century, witnessing the passing of the old, assisting at the birth of the new.

Like Whitman later, Franklin was large: he contained multitudes. His life and his achievements lend themselves to merging with the American myth, making them one and the same. His rise from rags to riches, his encouragement of industry and frugality, his cultivation of independence and selfhood, his promotion of groups and associations, his eagerness to conciliate and compromise, his willingness to serve and assist—all these traits and many more have made Franklin a legendary figure often appropriated as a patron saint by one or another movement or cause, inevitably diminishing Franklin to a caricature of his genuinely mutifaceted self.

Such a distortion of Franklin appears in the savings-bank image of him projected in much contemporary advertising: "A penny saved is a penny earned." Here Franklin appears a man obsessed with the accumulation of wealth to the point of miserliness. This view of Franklin, as the archetypal self-made American capitalist singled-mindedly bent on making more and more money, is not only ludicrous, but simply incompatible with Franklin's decision in 1748, at the age of forty-two, to "disengage" from his "private business," and with his "sufficient though moderate fortune" to spend the rest of his life in "philosophical studies." It was these studies that led to Franklin's kite experiment and publication of *Experiments and Observations on Electricity* in 1751 and his election to the British Royal Society in 1756. In his passion for "philosophical studies" Franklin is not unlike that earlier self-educated American William Bradford in his passion (at age sixty) to learn Hebrew: both Deist and Puritan wished to observe with their own eyes the laws of God.

Franklin was the youngest son in the large family of a Boston candle and soap maker. He was removed from school at the age of ten because of the expense and brought to work in his father's business. At the age of twelve he was apprenticed to his older brother James in his printing house. At the age of sixteen, Franklin submitted the first of his *Dogood Papers* to his brother's *New England Courant* (established 1721) by slipping the anonymous manuscript under the door of the printing shop one night. This and subsequent letters from "Silence Dogood" turned out to be highly popular. When his brother was briefly imprisoned for publishing an item that displeased the political authorities, Franklin took over as publisher.

Friction between the two brothers caused Franklin to set out on his own and in 1723 he made the journey to Philadelphia. With his skill as a printer he quickly obtained employment and just as quickly observed that he could run a printing shop better than any then open in Philadelphia. After a number of adventures, including a voyage to England, Franklin and a partner set themselves up as printers in Philadephia in 1728. Soon after, Franklin bought out his alcoholic partner, acquired a newspaper, *The Pennsylvania Gazette*, became printer to the Pennsylvania Assembly, and married Deborah Read, daughter of his first Philadelphia landlady. He was established, on his way to wealth, and only twenty-four years old.

He started publishing *Poor Richard's Almanac* in 1732 and created the fictional Richard Saunders as spokesman for the aphorisms that he pilfered from the world's literature: "Fish and visitors smell in three days." "Little strokes fell great oaks." "The used key is always bright." The compendium of Poor Richard's sayings, published in 1758 as *The Way to Wealth*, displaced Michael Wigglesworth's *Day of Doom* as the all-time best seller in America, making both Richard's and Franklin's names household words.

After Franklin's arrangement with his partner to retire from his business in 1748 in order to devote himself to philosophic and scientific experiment, Franklin found himself more and more called upon for public service. He was appointed to several postal positions, including deputy postmaster-general for the colonies (1753–74). He represented Pennsylvania at the Albany Congress in 1754, called to plan cooperation in the war against the French and Indians, where Franklin presented his plan for uniting the colonies. He served in England from 1757 to 1762 and again from 1764 to 1775, first representing Pennsylvania in disputes with the proprietaries (who refused to allow their large holdings in the colony to be taxed), and then representing several colonies in the dispute with England over taxation without representation. He appeared in 1766 before the British Parliament in a debate on the subject and was subjected to 174 questions; his answers were brief, simple, and pointed. But gradually he was coming to the conclusion that reconciliation was impossible.

On his return to America, he was appointed to the second Continental Congress and served on the committee to write the Declaration of Independence. Then, with war inevitable, Franklin served on the commission sent in 1776 to negotiate a treaty with France (signed in 1778), where he remained for the next nine years, becoming minister plenipotentiary of the United States to France in 1778. A widely recognized figure in France, with his rustic dress, his homespun wit and wisdom, his democratic and open manner, he was looked upon as a symbol of the Age of Reason in a country that would shortly have its own revolution.

After serving on the commission to negotiate the peace treaty with England from 1781 to 1783, Franklin returned to America in 1785 and was appointed Pennsylvania representative to the Constitutional Convention in 1787. He was now eighty-one years old. It was his speech at the close of the convention that persuaded those in attendance, no one of whom was wholly satisfied with the drafted constitution, to give it "unanimous consent" in approval.

It is difficult to convey a full sense of Franklin's accomplishments in a chronological outline of his astonishing international achievements. He invented the Franklin stove (1742), the lightning rod (1752), and bifocal spectacles (*c.* 1760). He founded or helped establish the first subscription library in America (1731), a fire company (1736), the American Philosophical Society (1743), a volunteer militia (1747), the academy that would later become the University of Pennsylvania (1749), the charitable Pennsylvania Hospital (1751), and a fire insurance company (1752).

It is no wonder that Franklin wrote only one book, and that incomplete— his *Autobiography*. It was written at four different stages in the calms between the storms of political unrest or upheaval demanding Franklin's attention and involvement. It has been called, with some justification, the first American classic. In it, Franklin tells the story of his setting about methodically learning how to write when he was an apprentice printer in his 'teens, using as a model a volume of Addison and Steele's *Spectator* he had come across. During his days as a printer, Franklin developed the habit of writing short pieces to fill his newspaper and almanac, often publishing under an assumed name; he continued the habit for the rest of his life. More than once such hoaxes as "The Speech of Polly Baker" (defending herself as she stands trial for her fifth pregnancy) were taken at face value, sometimes outraging readers. To call attention to the abuses of British colonial administration Franklin skillfully employed irony in satires like "Rules by Which a Great Empire May Be Reduced to a Small One." Such later little essays as "The Ephemera" and "The Whistle" reveal a melancholy side of Franklin's philosophy that is as moving as it is charming. His voluminous letters were written with as much care as to content and style as his literary works.

Franklin's style has been the subject of much commentary, but no one has described it better than Franklin himself in the notes he jotted down for a piece on writing: "Nothing should be expressed in two words that can be as well expressed in one . . . the whole should be as short as possible, consistent with clearness. The words should be so placed as to be agreeable to the ear in reading; summarily, it should be *smooth, clear,* and *short.*"

In its muscular grace and rugged elegance, in its terse and pungent Americanness, Franklin's style contains the elements of an American style that will run through Thoreau and Twain in the nineteenth century to Mencken and Hemingway in the twentieth. Thus if Franklin may be seen as the figure who looms largest in the creation of America, he may also be seen as casting a long shadow over the development of an American literature.

ADDITIONAL READING

Definitive edition in progress: *The Papers of Benjamin Franklin*, ed. Leonard W. Labaree, et al, 1959–. Selected writings: *Benjamin Franklin: Representative Selections*, ed. Frank L. Mott and Chester E. Jorgenson, 1936.

Phillips Russell, *Benjamin Franklin: The First Civilized American*, 1926; Carl Van Doren, *Benjamin Franklin*, 1938; Richard E. Amacher, *Benjamin Franklin*, 1962; Bruce I. Granger, *Benjamin Franklin: An American Man of Letters*, 1964; Alfred Owen Aldridge, *Benjamin Franklin, Philosopher and Man*, 1965; Roger Burlingame, *Benjamin Franklin: Envoy Extraordinary*, 1967; Claude-Anne Lopez and Eugenia W. Herbert, *The Private Franklin: The Man and His Family*, 1975; J. A. Leo Lemay, ed., *The Oldest Revolutionary*, 1976; Brian M. Barbour, *Benjamin Franklin: A Collection of Critical Essays*, 1979; Roy N. Lokken, ed., *Meet Dr. Franklin*, 1981; Willard Randall, *A Little Revenge: Benjamin Franklin and His Son*, 1984; Mitchell Robert Breitwieser, *Cotton Mather and Benjamin Franklin: The Price of Representative Personality*, 1985; Esmond Wright, *Franklin of Philadelphia*, 1986; J. A. Leo Lemay, *The Canon of Benjamin Franklin, 1722–1776*, 1986.

TEXTS

"On Literary Style" is from *The Pennsylvania Gazette*, August 2, 1733; "Old Mistresses Apologue" is from the copy in the Library of Congress; "The Ephemera," "The Whistle," and "Remarks Concerning the Savages of North America" are from the facsimile edition of *The Bagatelles from Passy* (1967) with notes by Claude-Anne Lopez; the "Speech in the Convention" is a collation of the text in Smyth and the Cornell University Library manuscript. All other selections are from *The Writings of Benjamin Franklin*, 10 vols., ed. Albert Henry Smyth (1905–07), with corrections or insertions made in some cases by comparison with the texts in *The Papers of Benjamin Franklin*, ed. Leonard W. Labaree, et al., 1959–. Typography, punctuation, spelling, and usage have been changed to conform with contemporary English and modern printing practices.

from Dogood Papers

SILENCE DOGOOD, NO. 5

[MALE AND FEMALE VICES][1]

Mulier Mulieri magis congruet. Ter.[2]

To the Author of the *New England Courant.*
Sir,

I shall here present your readers with a letter from one who informs me that I have begun at the wrong end of my business, and that I ought to begin at home, and censure the vices and follies of my own sex before I venture to meddle with yours. Nevertheless, I am resolved to dedicate this speculation to the fair tribe, and endeavor to show that Mr. Ephraim charges women with being particularly guilty of pride, idleness, &c., wrongfully, inasmuch as the men have not only as great a share in those vices as the women, but are likewise in a great measure the cause of that which the women are guilty of. I think it will be best to produce my antagonist before I encounter him.

To Mrs. Dogood.

Madam,

My design in troubling you with this letter is to desire you would begin with your own sex first: let the first volley of your resentments be directed against *female* vice; let female idleness, ignorance and folly (which are vices more peculiar to your sex than to ours) be the subject of your satires, but more especially female pride, which I think is intolerable. Here is a large field that wants cultivation, and which I believe you are able (if willing) to improve with advantage; and when you have once reformed the women, you will find it a much easier task to reform the men, because women are the prime causes of a great many male enormities. This is all at present from your friendly well-wisher,

Ephraim Censorious

---

[1]Published anonymously May 28, 1722, in *The New England Courant*, when Franklin was sixteen years old. The paper was owned by Franklin's brother James, to whom Franklin was apprenticed. Afraid that James would not print his writing, Franklin slipped the Dogood letters, fourteen in all, under the printing house door at night. Franklin had very early read Cotton Mather's *Essays to Do Good*, but his essays, like others in the *Courant*, were also influenced by the English magazine *The Spectator*. Though witty, the anything-but-silent widow Dogood's letters have a serious moral purpose, like all satire.

[2]"A woman deals much better with a woman." Terence (*c*. 190–159 B.C.), Latin dramatist, in *Phormio*, IV, v, 14.

After thanks to my correspondent for his kindness in cutting out work for me, I must assure him that I find it a very difficult matter to reprove women separate from the men; for what vice is there in which the men have not as great a share as the women? And in some have they not a far greater, as in drunkenness, swearing, &c.? And if they have, then it follows that when a vice is to be reproved, men, who are most culpable, deserve the most reprehension, and certainly, therefore, ought to have it. But we will waive this point at present, and proceed to a particular consideration of what my correspondent calls *female vice.*

As for idleness, if I should *quaere,*[3] Where are the greatest number of its votaries to be found, with us or the men? it might I believe be easily and truly answered, "With the latter." For notwithstanding the men are commonly complaining how hard they are forced to labor, only to maintain their wives in pomp and idleness, yet if you go among the women, you will learn that *they have always more work upon their hands than they are able to do,* and that "a woman's work is never done," &c. But, however, suppose we should grant for once that we are generally more idle than the men (without making any allowance for the *weakness of the sex*), I desire to know whose fault it is? Are not the men to blame for their folly in maintaining us in idleness? Who is there that can be handsomely supported in affluence, ease and pleasure by another that will choose rather to earn his bread by the sweat of his own brows? And if a man will be so fond and so foolish as to labor hard himself for a livelihood, and suffer his wife in the meantime to sit in ease and idleness, let him not blame her if she does so, for it is in a great measure his own fault.

And now for the ignorance and folly which he reproaches us with, let us see (if we are fools and ignoramuses) whose is the fault, the men's or ours. An ingenious writer, having this subject in hand, has the following words, wherein he lays the fault wholly on the men for not allowing women the advantages of education.

"I have," says he, "often thought of it as one of the most barbarous customs in the world, considering us as a civilized and Christian country, that we deny the advantages of learning to women. We reproach the sex every day with folly and impertinence, while I am confident, had they the advantages of education equal to us, they would be guilty of less than ourselves. One would wonder indeed how it should happen that women are conversible at all, since they are only beholding to natural parts[4] for all their knowledge. Their youth is spent to teach them to stitch and sew, or make baubles. They are taught to read indeed, and perhaps to write their names, or so; and that is the height of a woman's education. And I would but ask any who slight the sex for their understanding, What is a man (a gentleman, I mean) good for that is taught no more? If knowledge and understanding had been useless additions to the sex, God almighty would never have given them capacities, for he made nothing needless. What has the woman done to forfeit the privilege of being taught? Does she plague us with her pride and impertinence? Why did we not let her learn, that she might have had more wit? Shall we upbraid women with folly, when 'tis only the error of this inhuman custom that hindered them being made wiser."[5]

So much for female ignorance and folly; and now let us a little consider the pride which my correspondent thinks is *intolerable.* By this expression of his, one would think he is some dejected swain, tyrannized over by some cruel haughty nymph, who (perhaps he thinks) has no more reason to be proud than himself. *Alas-a-day!* What shall we say in this case! Why truly, if women are proud, it is cer-

---

[3] "Inquire" (Latin).
[4] I.e., their native wits.
[5] Daniel Defoe (c. 1660–1731), English novelist, in *An Essay upon Projects* (1697), with minor omissions and variations in spelling and punctuation.

tainly owing to the men still; for if they will be such *simpletons* as to humble themselves at their feet, and fill their credulous ears with extravagant praises of their wit, beauty, and other accomplishments (perhaps where there are none too), and when women are by this means persuaded that they are something more than human, what wonder is it if they carry themselves haughtily, and live extravagantly. Notwithstanding, I believe there are more instances of extravagant pride to be found among men than among women, and this fault is certainly more heinous in the former than in the latter.

Upon the whole, I conclude that it will be impossible to lash any vice of which the men are not equally guilty with the women, and consequently deserve an equal (if not greater) share in the censure. However, I exhort both to amend where both are culpable; otherwise they may expect to be severely handled by, Sir, your humble servant,

Silence Dogood

N. B. Mrs. Dogood has lately left her seat in the country and come to Boston, where she intends to tarry for the summer season, in order to complete her observations of the present reigning vices of the town.

1722   *1722*

SILENCE DOGOOD, NO. 7
[RECEIPT FOR A FUNERAL ELEGY][1]

Give me the muse, whose generous force,
Impatient of the reins,
Pursues an unattempted course,
Breaks all the critics' iron chains. Watts.[2]

To the Author of the *New England Courant.*
Sir,

It has been the complaint of many ingenious foreigners who have traveled among us, *that good poetry is not to be expected in New England.* I am apt to fancy, the reason is, not because our countrymen are altogether void of a poetical genius, nor yet because we have not those advantages of education which other countries have, but purely because we do not afford that praise and encouragement which is merited, when anything extraordinary of this kind is produced among us: upon which consideration I have determined, when I meet with a good piece of New England poetry, to give it a suitable encomium,[3] and thereby endeavor to discover[4] to the world some of its beauties, in order to encourage the author to go on, and bless the world with more and more excellent productions.

There has lately appeared among us a most excellent piece of poetry, entitled *An Elegy upon the much Lamented Death of Mrs. Mehitebel Kitel, Wife of Mr. John Kitel of Salem, etc.* It may justly be said in its praise, without flattery to the author, that it is the most *extraordinary* piece that ever was wrote in New England. The language is so soft and easy, the expression so moving and pathetic, but above all, the verse and numbers[5] so charming and natural, that it is almost beyond comparison.

---

[1]Printed in *The New England Courant,* June 25, 1722. In this recipe (receipt) for a funeral elegy, Franklin mocks the contemporary New England elegies by contrasting one written possibly by Edward Holyoke (later president of Harvard) for Mrs. Mehitable Kittle (died, September 15, 1718) with the poems of the English religious poet Isaac Watts (1674–1748). Watts experimented with a variety of poetic forms and meters in his *Horae Lyricae* or *Poems of the Lyric Kind* (1709), from which the following excerpts are taken.
[2]"The Adventurous Muse."
[3]Tribute.
[4]Disclose.
[5]Meter.

> The muse *disdains*
> *Those links and chains,*
> *Measures and rules of vulgar strains,*
> *And o'er the laws of harmony a sovereign queen she reigns.*[6]

I find no English author, ancient or modern, whose elegies may be compared with this, in respect to the elegance of style, or smoothness of rhyme; and for the affecting part, I will leave your readers to judge if ever they read any lines that would sooner make them *draw their breath* and sigh, if not shed tears, than these following.

> *Come let us mourn, for we have lost a wife, a daughter, and*
>   *a sister,*
> *Who has lately taken flight, and greatly we have missed her.*

In another place,

> *Some little time before she yielded up her breath,*
> *She said, I ne'er shall hear one sermon more on earth.*
> *She kissed her husband some little time before she expired,*
> *Then leaned her head the pillow on, just out of breath and tired.*

But the threefold appellation in the first line

> *a wife, a daughter, and a sister,*

must not pass unobserved. That line in the celebrated Watts,

> Gunston *the just, the generous, and the young,*[7]

is nothing comparable to it. The latter only mentions three qualifications of *one* person who was deceased, which therefore could raise grief and compassion but for *one*. Whereas the former *(our most excellent poet)* gives his reader a sort of an idea of the death of *three persons,* viz.

> *a wife, a daughter, and a sister,*

which is *three times* as great a loss as the death of *one,* and consequently must raise *three times* as much grief and compassion in the reader.

I should be very much straitened[8] for room, if I should attempt to discover even half the excellencies of this elegy which are obvious to me. Yet I cannot omit one observation, which is, that the author has (to his honor) invented a new species of poetry, which wants a name, and was never before known. His muse scorns to be confined to the old measures and limits, or to observe the dull rules of critics;

> *Nor Rapin gives her rules to fly, nor Purcell notes to sing.*[9]
> Watts.

Now 'tis pity that such an excellent piece should not be dignified with a particular name; and seeing it cannot justly be called either *epic, sapphic, lyric,* or *pindaric,*[10] nor any other name yet invented, I presume it may (in honor and remembrance of the dead) be called the *kitelic.* Thus much in the praise of *kitelic poetry.*

---

[6]"Watts" (Franklin's note). His quotation of "Two Happy Rivals, Devotion and the Muse" begins with the word "disdains."
[7]"To the Dear Memory of My Honored Friend, Thomas Gunston, Esq."
[8]Cramped.
[9]"The Adventurous Muse." Paul de Rapin-Thoyras (1661–

1725), French critic; Henry Purcell (1659–1695), English composer.
[10]Epic: a long narrative poem with a national or historical hero; sapphic: verse form named after Greek poet Sappho; lyric: short poem expressing personal feeling; pindaric: an ode in the complex metrical form of the Greek poet Pindar.

It is certain that those elegies which are of our own growth, (and our soil seldom produces any other sort of poetry) are by far the greatest part wretchedly dull and ridiculous. Now since it is imagined by many that our poets are honest, well-meaning fellows, who do their best, and that if they had but some instructions how to govern fancy with judgment, they would make indifferent good elegies; I shall here subjoin a receipt for that purpose, which was left me as a legacy (among other valuable rarities) by my reverend husband. It is as follows,

A RECEIPT TO MAKE A NEW ENGLAND FUNERAL ELEGY.

For the Title of your Elegy. Of these you may have enough ready made to your hands; but if you should choose to make it yourself, you must be sure not to omit the words *Aetatis Suae*,[11] which will beautify it exceedingly.

For the Subject of your Elegy. Take one of your neighbors who has lately departed this life; it is no great matter at what age the party died, but it will be best if he went away suddenly, being *killed, drowned,* or *frozen to death.*

Having chose the person, take all his virtues, excellencies, etc., and if he have not enough, you may borrow some to make up a sufficient quantity: To these add his last words, dying expressions, etc., if they are to be had; mix all these together, and be sure you *strain* them well. Then season all with a handful or two of melancholy expressions, such as *dreadful, deadly, cruel cold death, unhappy fate, weeping eyes,* etc. Have mixed all these ingredients well, put them into the empty skull of some *young Harvard* (but in case you have ne'er a one at hand, you may use your own); there let them ferment for the space of a fortnight, and by that time they will be incorporated into a body, which take out, and having prepared a sufficient quantity of double rhymes, such as, *power, flower; quiver, shiver; grieve us, leave us; tell you, excel you; expeditions, physicians; fatigue him, intrigue him;* etc. you must spread all upon paper, and if you can procure a scrap of Latin to put at the end, it will garnish it mightily; then having affixed your name at the bottom, with a *Moestus composuit,*[12] you will have an excellent elegy.

N.B. This receipt will serve when a female is the subject of your elegy, provided you borrow a greater quantity of virtues, excellencies, etc. sir, your servant,

Silence Dogood

P.S. I shall make no other answer to Hypercarpus's criticism on my last letter than this, *Mater me genuit, peperit mox filia matrem.*[13]

1722

A Witch Trial at Mount Holly[1]

Saturday last, at Mount Holly, about 8 miles from this place, near 300 people were gathered together to see an experiment or two tried on some persons accused of witchcraft. It seems the accused had been charged with making their neighbors' sheep dance in an uncommon manner, and with causing hogs to speak and sing psalms, etc., to the great terror and amazement of the king's good and peaceable subjects in this province; and the accusers, being very positive that if the

---

[11]"Of his age" (Latin).
[12]"Composed in sorrow" (Latin).
[13]"My mother bore me, and soon the daughter will bear a mother" (Latin). Hypercarpus (excessive at "carping") wrote to the newspaper objecting to Dogood's remark that

pride of apparel causes pride of heart, and arguing the reverse.
[1]Printed in *The Pennsylvania Gazette,* October 22, 1730. *The Gentleman's Magazine,* I (1731), took the item as actual fact and pirated a short account of the episode.

accused were weighed in scales against a Bible, the Bible would prove too heavy for them; or that, if they were bound and put into the river they would swim; the said accused, desirous to make innocence appear, voluntarily offered to undergo the said trials if two of the most violent of their accusers would be tried with them. Accordingly, the time and place was agreed on and advertised about the country. The accusers were one man and one woman, and the accused the same. The parties being met and the people got together, a grand consultation was held, before they proceeded to trial; in which it was agreed to use the scales first; and a committee of men were appointed to search the men, and a committee of women to search the women, to see if they had anything of weight about them, particularly pins. After the scrutiny was over a huge great Bible belonging to the Justice of the place was provided, and a lane through the populace was made from the Justice's house to the scales, which were fixed on a gallows erected for that purpose opposite to the house, that the Justice's wife and the rest of the ladies might see the trial without coming among the mob, and after the manner of moorfields a large ring was also made. Then came out of the house a grave, tall man carrying the Holy Writ before the supposed wizard[2] etc. (as solemnly as the Swordbearer of London before the Lord Mayor). The wizard was first put in the scale, and over him was read a chapter out of the Books of Moses, and then the Bible was put in the other scale (which, being kept down before, was immediately let go); but, to the great surprise of the spectators, flesh and bones came down plump, and outweighed that great good Book by abundance. After the same manner the others were served, and their lumps of mortality severally were too heavy for Moses and all the prophets and apostles. This being over, the accusers and the rest of the mob, not satisfied with this experiment, would have the trial by water. Accordingly, a most solemn procession was made to the millpond, where both accused and accusers being stripped (saving only to the women their shifts) were bound hand and foot and severally placed in the water lengthwise from the side of a barge, or flat, having for security only a rope about the middle of each, which was held by some in the flat. The accused man being thin and spare with some difficulty began to sink at last; but the rest, every one of them, swam very light upon the water. A sailor in the flat jumped out upon the back of the man accused, thinking to drive him down to the bottom; but the person bound, without any help, came up some time before the other. The woman accuser being told that she did not sink, would be ducked a second time; when she swam again as light as before. Upon which she declared that she believed the accused had bewitched her to make her so light, and that she would be ducked again a hundred times but she would duck the devil out of her. The accused man, being surprised at his own swimming, was not so confident of his innocence as before, but said, "If I am a witch, it is more than I know." The more thinking part of the spectators were of opinion that any person so bound and placed in the water (unless they were mere skin and bones) would swim, till their breath was gone, and their lungs filled with water. But it being the general belief of the populace that the women's shifts and the garters with which they were bound helped to support them, it is said they are to be tried again the next warm weather, naked.

1730

---

[2]Male witch.

On Literary Style[1]

To the Printer of the *Gazette:*

There are few men of capacity for making any considerable figure in life who have not frequent occasion to communicate their thoughts to others in *writing;* if not sometimes publicly as authors, yet continually in the management of their private affairs, both of business and friendship. And since, when ill-expressed, the most proper sentiments and justest reasoning lose much of their native force and beauty, it seems to me that there is scarce any accomplishment more necessary to a man of sense than that of *writing well* in his mother tongue. But as most other polite acquirements make a greater appearance in a man's character, this, however useful, is generally neglected or forgotten.

I believe there is no better means of learning to write well than this of attempting to entertain the public now and then in one of your papers. When the writer conceals himself, he has the advantage of hearing the censure both of friends and enemies expressed with more impartiality. And since, in some degree, it concerns the credit of the province that such things as are printed be performed tolerably well, mutual improvement seems to be the duty of all lovers of writing. I shall therefore frankly communicate the observations I have made or collected on this subject, and request those of others in return.

I have thought in general that whoever would write so as not to displease good judges should have particular regard to these three things, viz., that his performance be *smooth, clear,* and *short.* For the contrary qualities are apt to offend either the ear, the understanding, or the patience.

'Tis an observation of Dr. Swift that modern writers injure the smoothness of our tongue by omitting vowels wherever it is possible, and joining the harshest consonants together with only an apostrophe between; thus for *judged,* in itself not the smoothest of words, they say *judg'd;* for *disturbed, disturb'd,* &c.[2] It may be added to this, says another, that by changing *eth* into *s,* they have shortened one syllable in a multitude of words, and have thereby increased not only the *hissing,* too offensive before, but also the great number of monosyllables, of which, without great difficulty, a smooth sentence cannot be composed. The smoothness of a period[3] is also often hurt by parentheses, and therefore the best writers endeavor to avoid them.

To write *clearly,* not only the most expressive, but the plainest words should be chosen. In this, as well as in every other particular requisite to clearness, Dr. Tillotson[4] is an excellent example. The fondness of some writers for such words as carry with them an air of learning, renders them unintelligible to more than half their countrymen. If a man would that his writings have an effect on the generality of readers, he had better imitate that gentleman who would use no word in his works that was not well understood by his cook-maid.

A too frequent use of phrases[5] ought likewise to be avoided by him that would write clearly. They trouble the language, not only rendering it extremely difficult to foreigners, but make the meaning obscure to a great number of English readers. Phrases, like learned words, are seldom used without affectation; when, with all true judges, the simplest style is the most beautiful.

---

[1] Printed in *The Pennsylvania Gazette,* August 2, 1733, without title. The essay was one of Franklin's contributions to the Junto, the philosophic club Franklin organized for the improvement of self and society.
[2] Jonathan Swift (1667–1745) British satirist, had made such observations in the *Tatler,* no. 230 (September 1710), and *A Proposal for Correcting, Improving, and Ascertaining the English Tongue,* February 1711–12.

[3] Sentence.
[4] John Tillotson (1630–1694), Archbishop of Canterbury, wrote short sermons in simple prose that were held up as models of lucidity.
[5] An expression peculiar to a language or region or group, sometimes meaningless, trite, or high-sounding.

But supposing the most proper words and expressions chosen, the performance may yet be weak and obscure if it has not *method*. If a writer would *persuade*, he should proceed gradually from things already allowed to those from which assent is yet withheld, and make their connection manifest. If he would *inform*, he must advance regularly from things known to things unknown, distinctly without confusion, and the lower he begins the better. It is a common fault in writers to allow their readers too much knowledge. They begin with that which should be the middle, and skipping backwards and forwards, 'tis impossible for anyone but he who is perfect in the subject before to understand their work, and such an one has no occasion to read it. Perhaps a habit of using good method cannot be better acquired than by learning a little geometry or algebra.

Amplification, or the art of saying little in much, should only be allowed to speakers. If they preach, a discourse of considerable length is expected from them upon every subject they undertake, and perhaps they are not stocked with naked thoughts sufficient to furnish it out. If they plead in the courts, it is of use to speak abundance, though they reason little; for the ignorant in a jury can scarcely believe it possible that a man can talk so much and so long without being in the right. Let them have the liberty then, of repeating the same sentences in other words; let them put an adjective to every substantive, and double every substantive with a synonima;[6] for this is more agreeable than hawking, spitting, taking snuff, or any other means of concealing hesitation. Let them multiply definitions, comparisons, similitudes and examples. Permit them to make a detail of causes and effects, enumerate all the consequences, and express one-half by metaphor and circumlocution. Nay, allow the preacher too to tell us whatever a thing is negatively, before he begins to tell us what it is affirmatively; and suffer him to divide and subdivide as far as *two and fiftiethly*. All this is not intolerable while it is not written. But when a discourse is to be bound down upon paper, and subjected to the calm leisurely examination of nice[7] judgment, everything that is needless gives offense; and therefore all should be retrenched that does not directly conduce to the end designed. Had this been always done, many large and tiresome folios would have shrunk into pamphlets, and many a pamphlet into a single period. However, though a multitude of words obscure the sense, and 'tis necessary to abridge a verbose author in order to understand him; yet a writer should take especial care on the other hand that his brevity doth not hurt his perspicuity.[8]

After all, if the author does not intend his piece for general reading, he must exactly suit his style and manner to the particular taste of those he proposes for his readers. Everyone observes the different ways of writing and expression used by the different sects of religion; and can readily enough pronounce that it is improper to use some of these styles in common, or to use the common style, when we address some of these sects in particular.

To conclude, I shall venture to lay it down as a maxim, *That no piece can properly be called good, and well written, which is void of any tendency to benefit the reader, either by improving his virtue or his knowledge.* This principle every writer would do well to have in view, whenever he undertakes to write. All performances done for mere ostentation of parts are really contemptible; and withal far more subject to the severity of criticism than those more meanly written, wherein the author appears to have aimed at the good of others. For when 'tis visible to everyone that a man writes to show his wit only, all his expressions are sifted, and his sense examined, in the nicest and most ill-natured manner; and everyone is glad of an opportunity

---

[6]Synonym, a word having the same meaning.
[7]Subtle.
[8]Clarity.

to mortify him. But what a vast destruction would there be of books if they were to be saved or condemned on a trial by this rule!

Besides, pieces merely humorous are of all sorts the hardest to succeed in. If they are not natural, they are stark naught; and there can be no real humor in an affectation of humor.

Perhaps it may be said that an ill man is able to write an ill thing well; that is, having an ill design, and considering who are to be his readers, he may use the properest style and arguments to attain his point. In this sense, that is best wrote which is best adapted to the purpose of the writer.

I am apprehensive, dear readers, lest in this piece, I should be guilty of every fault I condemn and deficient in everything I recommend; so much easier it is to offer rules than to practice them. I am sure, however, of this, that I am your very sincere friend and servant.

1733

Old Mistresses Apologue

[Advice to a Young Man on the Choice of a Mistress][1]

June 25, 1745

My Dear Friend:

I know of no medicine fit to diminish the violent natural inclinations you mention; and if I did, I think I should not communicate it to you. Marriage is the proper remedy. It is the most natural state of man, and therefore the state in which you are most likely to find solid happiness. Your reasons against entering into it at present appear to me to be not well founded. The circumstantial advantages you have in view by postponing it are not only uncertain, but they are small in comparison with that of the thing itself, the being *married and settled*. It is the man and woman united that make the complete human being. Separate, she wants his force of body and strength of reason; he, her softness, sensibility and acute discernment. Together they are more likely to succeed in the world. A single man has not nearly the value he would have in that state of union. He is an incomplete animal. He resembles the odd half of a pair of scissors. If you get a prudent, healthy wife, your industry in your profession, with her good economy, will be a fortune sufficient.

But if you will not take this counsel, and persist in thinking a commerce with the sex inevitable, then I repeat my former advice that in all your amours you should *prefer old women to young ones.* You call this a paradox, and demand my reasons. They are these:

1. Because as they have more knowledge of the world and their minds are better stored with observations, their conversation is more improving and more lastingly agreeable.

2. Because when women cease to be handsome, they study to be good. To maintain their influence over men, they supply the diminution of beauty by an augmentation of utility. They learn to do a thousand services, small and great,

---

[1] This piece did not appear with Franklin's name during his lifetime. Copies (one in his hand) were left among his papers when he died. It began to be privately printed and circulated in the nineteenth century, but not included in the editions of Franklin's works. Finally, in the twentieth century, it was published in Phillips Russell's biography, *Benjamin Franklin: The First Civilized American,* in 1926; it appeared in a *Treasury of the World's Great Letters* in 1941.

and are the most tender and useful of all friends when you are sick. Thus they continue amiable. And hence there is hardly such a thing to be found as an old woman who is not a good woman.

3. Because there is no hazard of children, which irregularly produced may be attended with much inconvenience.

4. Because through more experience they are more prudent and discreet in conducting an intrigue to prevent suspicion. The commerce with them is therefore safer with regard to your reputation. And with regard to theirs, if the affair should happen to be known, considerate people might be rather inclined to excuse an old woman who would kindly take care of a young man, form his manners by her good counsels, and prevent his ruining his health and fortune among mercenary prostitutes.

5. Because in every animal that walks upright, the deficiency of the fluids that fill the muscles appears first in the highest part. The face first grows lank and wrinkled, then the neck, then the breast and arms, the lower parts continuing to the last as plump as ever; so that covering all above with a basket, and regarding only what is below the girdle, it is impossible of two women to know an old one from a young one. And as in the dark all cats are grey, the pleasure of corporal enjoyment with an old woman is at least equal, and frequently superior, every knack being by practice capable of improvement.

6. Because the sin is less. The debauching a virgin may be her ruin, and make her for life unhappy.

7. Because the compunction is less. The having made a young girl *miserable* may give you frequent bitter reflections; none of which can attend making an old woman *happy*.

8thly and lastly. They are *so grateful!!*

Thus much for my paradox. But still I advise you to marry directly; being sincerely your affectionate friend.

The Speech of Miss Polly Baker[1]

The speech of Miss Polly Baker before a Court of judicature, at Connecticut near Boston in New England; where she was prosecuted the fifth time, for having a bastard child: which influenced the Court to dispense with her punishment, and which induced one of her judges to marry her the next day.

May it please the honorable bench to indulge me in a few words: I am a poor, unhappy woman, who has no money to fee lawyers to plead for me, being hard put to it to get a tolerable living. I shall not trouble your honors with long speeches; for I have not the presumption to expect that you may, by any means, be prevailed on to deviate in your sentence from the law, in my favor. All I humbly hope is that your honors would charitably move the governor's goodness on my behalf, that my fine may be remitted. This is the fifth time, gentlemen, that I have been dragged before your court on the same account; twice I have paid heavy fines, and twice have been brought to public punishment, for want of money to pay those fines. This may have been agreeable to the laws, and I don't

[1]The first known publication of this piece was in a London newspaper, *The General Advertiser*, April 15, 1747. Taken as true, it was afterwards frequently reprinted in Britain and America. It was translated and published by the Abbé Raynal in his popular *Histoire Philosophique et Politique* (1770) and became widely known in France, even inspiring some of the revolutionary fervor for reform. Authorship was unknown until Franklin, living in Paris in the late 1770s, revealed to the surprised Abbé that he had made up the Polly Baker speech when he was a young printer and needed filler for his newspaper.

dispute it; but since laws are sometimes unreasonable in themselves, and therefore repealed; and others bear too hard on the subject in particular circumstances, and therefore there is left a power somewhere to dispense with the execution of them; I take the liberty to say that I think this law, by which I am punished, is both unreasonable in itself, and particularly severe with regard to me, who have always lived an inoffensive life in the neighborhood where I was born, and defy my enemies (if I have any) to say I ever wronged any man, woman, or child. Abstracted from the law, I cannot conceive (may it please your honors) what the nature of my offense is. I have brought five fine children into the world, at the risk of my life; I have maintained them well by my own industry, without burdening the township, and would have done it better, if it had not been for the heavy charges and fines I have paid. Can it be a crime (in the nature of things, I mean) to add to the number of the king's subjects in a new country that really wants people? I own it, I should think it a praiseworthy rather than a punishable action. I have debauched no other woman's husband, nor enticed any other youth; these things I never was charged with; nor has anyone the least cause of complaint against me, unless, perhaps, the minister, or justice, because I have had children without being married, by which they have missed a wedding fee. But can this be a fault of mine? I appeal to your honors. You are pleased to allow I don't want sense; but I must be stupefied to the last degree, not to prefer the honorable state of wedlock to the condition I have lived in. I always was and still am willing to enter into it; and doubt not my behaving well in it, having all the industry, frugality, fertility, and skill in economy appertaining to a good wife's character. I defy any person to say I ever refused an offer of that sort: on the contrary, I readily consented to the only proposal of marriage that ever was made me, which was when I was a virgin, but too easily confiding in the person's sincerity that made it, I unhappily lost my honor by trusting to his; for he got me with child, and then forsook me.

That very person, you all know, he is now become a magistrate of this country; and I had hopes he would have appeared this day on the bench, and have endeavored to moderate the Court in my favor; then I should have scorned to have mentioned it; but I must now complain of it, as unjust and unequal, that my betrayer and undoer, the first cause of all my faults and miscarriages (if they must be deemed such), should be advanced to honor and power in this government that punishes my misfortunes with stripes and infamy. I should be told, 'tis like that were there no act of Assembly in the case, the precepts of religion are violated by my transgressions. If mine is a religious offense, leave it to religious punishments. You have already excluded me from the comforts of your church communion. Is not that sufficient? You believe I have offended heaven, and must suffer eternal fire: will not that be sufficient? What need is there then of your additional fines and whipping? I own I do not think as you do, for, if I thought what you call a sin was really such, I could not presumptuously commit it. But, how can it be believed that heaven is angry at my having children, when to the little done by me toward it, God has been pleased to add his divine skill and admirable workmanship in the formation of their bodies, and crowned it by furnishing them with rational and immortal souls?

Forgive me, gentlemen, if I talk a little extravagantly on these matters; I am no divine, but if you, gentlemen, must be making laws, do not turn natural and useful actions into crimes by your prohibitions. But take into your wise consideration the great and growing number of bachelors in the country, many of whom, from the mean fear of the expenses of a family, have never sincerely and honorably courted a woman in their lives; and by their manner of living leave unproduced (which is little better than murder) hundreds of their posterity to the thousandth generation. Is not this a greater offense against the public good than mine? Compel them, then, by law, either to marriage, or to pay double the fine of fornication every year. What must poor young women do, whom custom has forbid to solicit the men, and who cannot force themselves upon husbands, when the laws take no care to provide them any, and yet severely punish them if they do their duty without them; the duty of the first and great command of nature and of nature's God, *increase and multiply;* a duty from the steady performance of which nothing has been able to deter me, but for its sake I have hazarded the loss of the public esteem, and have frequently endured public disgrace and punishment; and therefore ought, in my humble opinion, instead of a whipping, to have a statue erected to my memory.

c. 1746   *1747*

Preface to *Poor Richard Improved*, 1758

[THE WAY TO WEALTH]

Franklin began publishing *Poor Richard's Almanac* in 1733, and in 1748, he increased the literary material and renamed it *Poor Richard Improved.* In addition to the usual astronomical data, weather forecasts, etc., Franklin introduced homespun literary pieces via the fictional editor Richard Saunders, whose practical advice became very popular. In 1758, Franklin published his last issue and included a long preface by Richard who introduces Father Abraham, dispensing a lifetime's wisdom in the pithy form of Poor Richard's proverbs, gathered from all the previous issues. Of course, Poor Richard took the proverbs from Franklin, who took them from the world's literature and folklore and rendered them in his own succinct, balanced style.

The essay quickly became Franklin's best-known piece, with 145 reprintings before the end of the eighteenth century. There were twenty-eight translations into French. At some point it became popularly known as "The Way to Wealth," a title that stuck. This title and the essay's emphasis on industry, frugality, and perseverance have caused critics to assume that Franklin was shallow because of his single-minded interest in accumulation of wealth. "Procuring wealth," however, was, as Franklin tells us in the *Autobiography,* a way of "securing virtue, it being more difficult for a man in want to act always honestly, as, to use here one of those proverbs, *It is hard for an empty sack to stand upright.*"

ε&

Courteous Reader,

I have heard that nothing gives an author so great pleasure, as to find his works respectfully quoted by other learned authors. This pleasure I have seldom enjoyed; for though I have been, if I may say it without vanity, an eminent author of almanacs annually now a full quarter of a century, my brother authors in the same way, for what reason I know not, have ever been very sparing in their applauses, and no other author has taken the least notice of me, so that did not my writings produce me some solid pudding, the great deficiency of praise would have quite discouraged me.

I concluded at length, that the people were the best judges of my merit; for they buy my works; and besides, in my rambles, where I am not personally known, I have frequently heard one or other of my adages repeated, with "as

Poor Richard says" at the end on 't; this gave me some satisfaction, as it showed not only that my instructions were regarded, but discovered likewise some respect for my authority; and I own, that to encourage the practice of remembering and repeating those wise sentences, I have sometimes quoted myself with great gravity.

Judge, then, how much I must have been gratified by an incident I am going to relate to you. I stopped my horse lately where a great number of people were collected at a vendue[1] of merchant goods. The hour of sale not being come, they were conversing on the badness of the times and one of the company called to a plain clean old man, with white locks, "Pray, Father Abraham, what think you of the times? Won't these heavy taxes quite ruin the country? How shall we be ever able to pay them? What would you advise us to?" Father Abraham stood up, and replied, "If you'd have my advice, I'll give it you in short, for a *word to the wise is enough, and many words won't fill a bushel,* as Poor Richard says." They joined in desiring him to speak his mind, and gathering round him, he proceeded as follows:

"Friends," says he, "and neighbors, the taxes are indeed very heavy, and if those laid on by the government were the only ones we had to pay, we might more easily discharge them; but we have many others, and much more grievous to some of us. We are taxed twice as much by our idleness, three times as much by our pride, and four times as much by our folly; and from these taxes the commissioners cannot ease or deliver us by allowing an abatement. However, let us hearken to good advice, and something may be done for us; *God helps them that help themselves,* as Poor Richard says, in his almanac of 1733.

"It would be thought a hard government that should tax its people one-tenth part of their time, to be employed in its service. But idleness taxes many of us much more, if we reckon all that is spent in absolute sloth, or doing of nothing, with that which is spent in idle employments or amusements, that amount to nothing. Sloth, by bringing on diseases, absolutely shortens life. *Sloth, like rust, consumes faster than labor wears, while the used key is always bright,* as Poor Richard says. But *dost thou love life, then do not squander time, for that's the stuff life is made of,* as Poor Richard says. How much more than is necessary do we spend in sleep, forgetting that *The sleeping fox catches no poultry* and that *There will be sleeping enough in the grave,* as Poor Richard says. If time be of all things the most precious, *wasting time* must be, as Poor Richard says, *the greatest prodigality;* since, as he elsewhere tells us, *Lost time is never found again;* and what we call *Time enough, always proves little enough:* let us then be up and be doing, and doing to the purpose; so by diligence shall we do more with less perplexity. *Sloth makes all things difficult, but industry all easy,* as Poor Richard says; and *He that riseth late must trot all day, and shall scarce overtake his business at night;* while *Laziness travels so slowly, that poverty soon overtakes him,* as we read in Poor Richard, who adds, *Drive thy business, let not that drive thee,* and *Early to bed, and early to rise, makes a man healthy, wealthy, and wise.*

"So what signifies wishing and hoping for better times. We may make these times better, if we bestir ourselves. *Industry need not wish,* as Poor Richard says, and *He that lives upon hope will die fasting. There are no gains without pains;* then *Help hands, for I have no lands,* or if I have, they are smartly taxed. And, as Poor Richard likewise observes, *He that hath a trade hath an estate,* and *He that hath a calling, hath an office of profit and honor;* but then the trade must be worked at, and the calling well followed, or neither the estate nor the office will enable us to pay our taxes. If we are industrious, we shall never starve; for, as Poor Richard says, *At the workingman's house hunger looks in, but dares not enter.* Nor will the bailiff or the constable enter, for *Industry pays debts, while despair increaseth them,* says Poor Richard. What though you have found no treasure, nor has any rich relation left you a legacy,

[1]Sale, auction.

Diligence is the mother of goodluck, as Poor Richard says, and *God gives all things to industry.* Then *plow deep, while sluggards sleep, and you shall have corn to sell and to keep,* says Poor Dick. Work while it is called today, for you know not how much you may be hindered tomorrow, which makes Poor Richard say, *One today is worth two tomorrows,* and farther, *Have you somewhat to do tomorrow, do it today.* If you were a servant, would you not be ashamed that a good master should catch you idle? Are you then your own master, *be ashamed to catch yourself idle,* as Poor Dick says. When there is so much to be done for yourself, your family, your country, and your gracious king, be up by peep of day; *Let not the sun look down and say, Inglorious here he lies.* Handle your tools without mittens; remember that *the cat in gloves catches no mice,* as Poor Richard says. 'Tis true there is much to be done, and perhaps you are weak-handed, but stick to it steadily, and you will see great effects, for *constant dropping wears away stones,* and *by diligence and patience the mouse ate in two the cable;* and *little strokes fell great oaks,* as Poor Richard says in his almanac, the year I cannot just now remember.

"Methinks I hear some of you say, 'must a man afford himself no leisure?' I will tell thee, my friend, what Poor Richard says, *Employ thy time well if thou meanest to gain leisure;* and, *since thou art not sure of a minute, throw not away an hour.* Leisure is time for doing something useful; this leisure the diligent man will obtain, but the lazy man never; so that, as Poor Richard says *a life of leisure and a life of laziness are two things.* Do you imagine that sloth will afford you more comfort than labor? No, for as Poor Richard says, *Trouble springs from idleness, and grievous toil from needless ease. Many without labor, would live by their wits only, but they break for want of stock.* Whereas industry gives comfort, and plenty, and respect: *Fly pleasures, and they'll follow you. The diligent spinner has a large shift,*[2] and *now I have a sheep and a cow, everybody bids me good morrow;* all which is well said by Poor Richard.

"But with our industry, we must likewise be steady, settled, and careful, and oversee our own affairs with our own eyes, and not trust too much to others; for, as Poor Richard says,

> *I never saw an oft-removed tree,*
> *Nor yet an oft-removed family,*
> *That throve so well as those that settled be.*

And again, *Three removes*[3] *is as bad as a fire;* and again, *Keep thy shop, and thy shop will keep thee;* and again, *If you would have your business done, go; if not, send.* And again,

> *He that by the plough would thrive,*
> *Himself must either hold or drive.*

And again, *The eye of a master will do more work than both his hands;* and again, *Want of care does us more damage than want of knowledge;* and again, *Not to oversee workmen is to leave them your purse open.* Trusting too much to others' care is the ruin of many; for, as the almanac says, *In the affairs of this world, men are saved, not by faith, but by the want of it;* but a man's own care is profitable; for, saith Poor Dick, *Learning is to the studious,* and *Riches to the careful,* as well as *Power to the bold,* and *Heaven to the virtuous.* And farther, *If you would have a faithful servant, and one that you like, serve yourself.* And again, he adviseth to circumspection and care, even in the smallest matters, because sometimes *a little neglect may breed great mischief;* adding, *For want of a nail the shoe was lost; for want of a shoe the horse was lost; and for want of a horse the rider was lost,* being overtaken and slain by the enemy, all for want of care about a horseshoe nail.

---

[2]Wardrobe.
[3]Moves.

"So much for industry, my friends, and attention to one's own business; but to these we must add frugality, if we would make our industry more certainly successful. A man may, if he knows not how to save as he gets, *keep his nose all his life to the grindstone,* and die not worth a groat[4] at last. *A fat kitchen makes a lean will,* as Poor Richard says; and,

> *Many estates are spent in the getting,*
> *Since women for tea forsook spinning and knitting,*
> *And men for punch forsook hewing and splitting.*

If you would be wealthy, says he, in another almanac, *think of saving as well as of getting: The Indies have not made Spain rich, because her outgoes are greater than her incomes.* Away then with your expensive follies, and you will not have so much cause to complain of hard times, heavy taxes, and chargeable families; for, as Poor Dick says,

> *Women and wine, game and deceit,*
> *Make the wealth small and the wants great.*

And farther, *What maintains one vice would bring up two children.* You may think perhaps, that a little tea, or a little punch now and then, diet a little more costly, clothes a little finer, and a little entertainment now and then, can be no great matter; but remember what Poor Richard says, *Many a little makes a mickle;*[5] and farther, *Beware of little expenses; a small leak will sink a great ship;* and again, *Who dainties love shall beggars prove;* and moreover, *Fools make feasts, and wise men eat them.*

"Here you are all got together at this vendue of fineries and knicknacks. You call them goods, but if you do not take care, they will prove evils to some of you. You expect they will be sold cheap, and perhaps they may for less than they cost; but if you have no occasion for them, they must be dear to you. Remember what Poor Richard says, *Buy what thou hast no need of, and ere long thou shalt sell thy necessaries.* And again, *At a great pennyworth pause a while:* he means, that perhaps the cheapness is apparent only, and not real; or the bargain, by straightening thee[6] in thy business, may do thee more harm than good. For in another place he says, *Many have been ruined by buying good pennyworths.* Again, Poor Richard says, *'Tis foolish to lay out money in a purchase of repentance;* and yet this folly is practiced every day at vendues, for want of minding the almanac. *Wise men,* as Poor Dick says, *learn by others' harms, fools scarcely by their own;* but *Felix quem faciunt aliena pericula cautum.*[7] Many a one, for the sake of finery on the back, have gone with a hungry belly, and half-starved their families. *Silks and satins, scarlet and velvets,* as Poor Richard says, *put out the kitchen fire.*

"These are not the necessaries of life; they can scarcely be called the conveniences; and yet only because they look pretty, how many want to have them. The artificial wants of mankind thus become more numerous than the natural; and, as Poor Dick says, *For one poor person, there are an hundred indigent.* By these, and other extravagancies, the genteel are reduced to poverty, and forced to borrow of those whom they formerly despised, but who through industry and frugality have maintained their standing; in which case it appears plainly, that *a plowman on his legs is higher than a gentleman on his knees,* as Poor Richard says. Perhaps they have had a small estate left them, which they knew not the getting of; they think, ' 'Tis day, and will never be night'; that a little to be spent out of so much is not worth minding; *(a child and a fool,* as Poor Richard says, *imagine twenty shillings and twenty years can never be spent)* but, *always taking out of the meal-tub, and never putting in, soon comes*

---

[4]British coin worth four pence.
[5]Lot.
[6]Making financial difficulty for you.

[7]"Fortunate is he made careful by the mistakes of others" (Latin).

to the bottom; then as Poor Dick says, *When the well's dry, they know the worth of water.* But this they might have known before, if they had taken his advice; *If you would know the value of money, go and try to borrow some;* for, *he that goes a-borrowing goes a-sorrowing;* and indeed so does he that lends to such people, when he goes to get it in again. Poor Dick farther advises, and says,

> *Fond pride of dress is sure a very curse;*
> *E'er fancy you consult, consult your purse.*

And again, *Pride is as loud a beggar as want, and a great deal more saucy.* When you have bought one fine thing, you must buy ten more, that your appearance may be all of a piece; but Poor Dick says, *'Tis easier to suppress the first desire, than to satisfy all that follow it.* And 'tis as truly folly for the poor to ape the rich, as for the frog to swell, in order to equal the ox.

> *Great estates may venture more,*
> *But little boats should keep near shore.*

'Tis, however, a folly soon punished; for *Pride that dines on vanity sups on contempt,* as Poor Richard says. And in another place, *Pride breakfasted with plenty, dined with poverty, and supped with infamy.* And after all, of what use is this pride of appearance, for which so much is risked so much is suffered? It cannot promote health, or ease pain; it makes no increase of merit in the person, it creates envy, it hastens misfortune.

> *What is a butterfly? At best*
> *He's but a caterpillar dressed.*
> *The gaudy fop's his picture just,*

as Poor Richard says.

"But what madness must it be to run in debt for these superfluities! We are offered, by the terms of this vendue, *six months' credit;* and that perhaps has induced some of us to attend it, because we cannot spare the ready money, and hope now to be fine without it. But, ah, think what you do when you run in debt; *You give to another power over your liberty.* If you cannot pay at the time, you will be ashamed to see your creditor; you will be in fear when you speak to him; you will make poor pitiful sneaking excuses, and by degrees come to lose your veracity, and sink into base downright lying; for, as Poor Richard says, *The second vice is lying, the first is running in debt.* And again, to the same purpose, *Lying rides upon debt's back.* Whereas a free-born Englishman ought not to be ashamed or afraid to see or speak to any man living. But poverty often deprives a man of all spirit and virtue: *'Tis hard for an empty bag to stand upright,* as Poor Richard truly says.

"What would you think of that prince, or that government, who should issue an edict forbidding you to dress like a gentleman or a gentlewoman, on pain of imprisonment or servitude? Would you not say, that you are free, have a right to dress as you please, and that such an edict would be a breach of your privileges, and such a government tyrannical? And yet you are about to put yourself under that tyranny, when you run in debt for such dress! Your creditor has authority, at his pleasure to deprive you of your liberty, by confining you in gaol[8] for life, or to sell you for a servant, if you should not be able to pay him! When you have got your bargain, you may, perhaps, think little of payment; but *Creditors,* Poor Richard tells us, *have better memories than debtors;* and in another place says, *Creditors are a superstitious sect, great observers of set days and times.* The day comes round before you are aware, and the demand is made before you are prepared to satisfy it. Or,

---

[8]Jail.

if you bear your debt in mind, the term which at first seemed so long will, as it lessens, appear extremely short. Time will seem to have added wings to his heels as well as shoulders. *Those have a short Lent,* saith Poor Richard, *who owe money to be paid at Easter.* Then since, as he says, *The borrower is a slave to the lender, and the debtor to the creditor,* disdain the chain, preserve your freedom; and maintain your independency: be industrious and free; be frugal and free. At present, perhaps, you may think yourself in thriving circumstances, and that you can bear a little extravagance without injury; but,

> *For age and want, save while you may;*
> *No morning sun lasts a whole day,*

as Poor Richard says. Gain may be temporary and uncertain, but ever while you live, expense is constant and certain; and *'tis easier to build two chimneys than to keep one in fuel,* as Poor Richard says. So, *rather go to bed supperless than rise in debt.*

> *Get what you can, and what you get hold;*
> *'Tis the stone that will turn all your lead into gold,*

as Poor Richard says. And when you have got the philosopher's stone,[9] sure you will no longer complain of bad times, or the difficulty of paying taxes.

"This doctrine, my friends, is reason and wisdom; but after all, do not depend too much upon your own industry, and frugality, and prudence, though excellent things, for they may all be blasted without the blessing of heaven; and therefore, ask that blessing humbly, and be not uncharitable to those that at present seem to want it, but comfort and help them. Remember, Job suffered, and was afterwards prosperous.

"And now to conclude, *Experience keeps a dear school, but fools will learn in no other, and scarce in that;* for it is true, *we may give advice, but we cannot give conduct,* as Poor Richard says: however, remember this, *They that won't be counseled, can't be helped,* as Poor Richard says: and farther, that, *if you will not hear reason, she'll surely rap your knuckles.*"

Thus the old gentleman ended his harangue. The people heard it, and approved the doctrine, and immediately practiced the contrary, just as if it had been a common sermon; for the vendue opened, and they began to buy extravangantly, notwithstanding all his cautions and their own fear of taxes. I found the good man had thoroughly studied my almanacs, and digested all I had dropped on these topics during the course of five and twenty years. The frequent mention he made of me must have tired any one else, but my vanity was wonderfully delighted with it, though I was conscious that not a tenth part of the wisdom was my own which he ascribed to me, but rather the gleanings I had made of the sense of all ages and nations. However, I resolved to be the better for the echo of it; and though I had at first determined to buy stuff for a new coat, I went away resolved to wear my old one a little longer. Reader, if thou wilt do the same, thy profit will be as great as mine. I am, as ever, thine to serve thee,

Richard Saunders

July 7, 1757   1758

---

[9]The substance believed capable of transforming base metals into gold.

Rules by Which a Great
Empire May Be Reduced to a Small One

Presented Privately to a *late Minister,* when He Entered Upon His
Administration; and Now First Published.[1]

An ancient sage boasted that though he could not fiddle, he knew how to make
a *great city* of a *little one.*[2] The science that I, a modern simpleton, am about to
communicate is the very reverse.

I address myself to all ministers who have the management of extensive dominions, which from their very greatness are become troublesome to govern, because
the multiplicity of their affairs leaves no time for *fiddling.*

I. In the first place, gentlemen, you are to consider, that a great empire, like a
great cake, is most easily diminished at the edges. Turn your attention, therefore,
first to your remotest provinces; that, as you get rid of them, the next may follow
in order.

II. That the possibility of this separation may always exist; take special care the
provinces are never incorporated with the mother country; that they do not enjoy
the same common rights, the same privileges in commerce; and that they are governed by *severer* laws, all of *your enacting,* without allowing them any share in the
choice of the legislators. By carefully making and preserving such distinctions, you
will (to keep to my simile of the cake) act like a wise gingerbread baker, who, to
facilitate a division, cuts his dough half through in those places where, when
baked, he would have it *broken to pieces.*

III. These remote provinces have perhaps been acquired, purchased, or conquered, at the *sole expense* of the settlers, or their ancestors, without the aid of the
mother country. If this should happen to increase her *strength* by their growing
numbers ready to join in her wars, her *commerce* by their growing demand for her
manufactures, or her *naval power* by greater employment for her ships and seamen, they may probably suppose some merit in this, and that it entitles them to
some favor; you are therefore to *forget it all,* or resent it as if they had done you
injury. If they happen to be zealous whigs, friends of liberty, nurtured in revolution principles;[3] *remember all that* to their prejudice, and resolve to punish it; for
such principles, after a revolution is thoroughly established, are of *no more use,*
they are even *odious* and *abominable.*

IV. However peaceably your colonies have submitted to your government,
shown their affection to your interest, and patiently borne their grievances, you
are to *suppose* them always inclined to revolt, and treat them accordingly. Quarter
troops among them, who by their insolence may *provoke* the rising of mobs, and by
their bullets and bayonets *suppress* them.[4] By this means, like the husband who
uses his wife ill *from suspicion,* you may in time convert your *suspicions* into *realities.*

V. Remote provinces must have *governors* and *judges* to represent the Royal Person, and execute everywhere the delegated parts of his office and authority. You
ministers know, that much of the strength of government depends on the *opinion*
of the people; and much of that opinion on the choice of rulers placed immedi-

---

[1]Written in London, where Franklin served as a colonial
agent (1764–1775), and published in the London newspaper, *The Public Advertiser,* on September 11, 1773. In this
satire aimed at acquainting readers with colonial grievances, Franklin reviews the actual record of the cabinet
minister responsible for American affairs from 1768 until
1772, the Earl of Hillsborough (1718–1793). Many of
these "rules" were legislated by Parliament in the Coercive
Acts of 1774.

[2]The sage was Themistocles (*c.* 528–462 B.C.), as reported
by Greek biographer Plutarch (*c.* 46– *c.* 120) in his *Parallel
Lives.*
[3]An allusion to Whig leadership in the Glorious Revolution
of 1688, which vindicated the principles of parliamentary
government and the right of rebellion against tyranny.
[4]Governor Francis Bernard (1712–1779) requested British
troops who were quartered in Boston, leading to the Boston Massacre of 1770.

ately over them. If you send them wise and good men for governors, who study the interest of the colonists, and advance their prosperity, they will think their king wise and good, and that he wishes the welfare of his subjects. If you send them learned and upright men for judges, they will think him a lover of justice. This may attach your provinces more to his government. You are therefore to be careful whom you recommend for those offices. If you can find prodigals who have ruined their fortunes, broken gamesters or stockjobbers,[5] these may do well as *governors;* for they will probably be rapacious, and provoke the people by their extortions. Wrangling proctors[6] and pettifogging[7] lawyers, too, are not amiss; for they will be for ever disputing and quarreling with their little parliaments. If withal they should be ignorant, wrong-headed, and insolent, so much the better. Attorneys' clerks and Newgate solicitors[8] will do for *chief justices,* especially if they hold their places *during your pleasure.* And all will contribute to impress those ideas of your government that are proper for a people *you would wish to renounce it.*

VI. To confirm these impressions, and strike them deeper, whenever the injured come to the capital with complaints of maladministration, oppression, or injustice, punish such suitors with long delay, enormous expense, and a final judgment in favor of the oppressor. This will have an admirable effect every way. The trouble of future complaints will be prevented, and governors and judges will be encouraged to further acts of oppression and injustice; and thence the people may become more disaffected, *and at length desperate.*

VII. When such governors have crammed their coffers, and made themselves so odious to the people that they can no longer remain among them, with safety to their persons, recall and *reward* them with pensions. You may make them *baronets* too,[9] if that respectable order should not think fit to resent it. All will contribute to encourage new governors in the same practices, and make the supreme government *detestable.*

VIII. If, when you are engaged in war, your colonies should vie in liberal aids of men and money against the common enemy, upon your simple requisition, and give far beyond their abilities, reflect that a penny taken from them by your power is more honorable to you than a pound presented by their benevolence. Despise therefore their voluntary grants, and resolve to harass them with novel taxes.[10] They will probably complain to your parliaments that they are taxed by a body in which they have no representative, and that this is contrary to common right. They will petition for redress. Let the parliaments flout their claims, reject their petitions, refuse even to suffer the reading of them, and treat the petitioners with the utmost contempt. Nothing can have a better effect in producing the alienation proposed; for though many can forgive injuries, *none ever forgave contempt.*

IX. In laying these taxes, never regard the heavy burdens those remote people already undergo, in defending their own frontiers, supporting their own provincial governments, making new roads, building bridges, churches, and other public edifices, which in old countries have been done to your hands by your ancestors, but which occasion constant calls and demands on the purses of a new people. Forget the *restraints* you lay on their trade for *your own* benefit, and the advantage a *monopoly* of this trade gives your exacting merchants. Think nothing of the wealth those merchants and your manufacturers acquire by the colony commerce; their increased ability thereby to pay taxes at home; their accumulating, in the price of their commodities, most of those taxes, and so levying them from their consuming customers. All this, and the employment and support of thousands of

---

[5]Stockbroker, used disparagingly.
[6]Lawyers in ecclesiastical and admiralty courts.
[7]Unscrupulous.
[8]Low rank lawyers frequenting London's Newgate prison.

[9]When Governor Bernard was removed from office in Massachusetts in 1769, he was made a baronet.
[10]Such as the Stamp Act of 1765, which taxed all uses of paper.

your poor by the colonists, you are *entirely to forget.* But remember to make your arbitrary tax more grievous to your provinces, by public declarations importing that your power of taxing them has *no limits,* so that when you take from them without their consent one shilling in the pound, you have a clear right to the other nineteen. This will probably weaken every idea of *security in their property,* and convince them that under such a government *they have nothing they can call their own;* which can scarce fail of producing the *happiest consequences!*

X. Possibly, indeed, some of them might still comfort themselves, and say, "Though we have no property, we have yet *something* left that is valuable; we have constitutional *liberty,* both of person and of conscience. This king, these lords, and these Commons, who it seems are too remote from us to know us and feel for us, cannot take from us our *habeas corpus*[11] right, or our right of trial *by a jury of our neighbors.* They cannot deprive us of the exercise of our religion, alter our ecclesiastical constitutions, and compel us to be papists, if they please, or Mohammedans." To annihilate this comfort, begin by laws to perplex their commerce with infinite regulations, impossible to be remembered and observed; ordain seizures of their property for every failure; take away the trial of such property by jury, and give it to arbitrary judges of your own appointing, and of the lowest characters in the country, whose salaries and emoluments are to arise out of the duties or condemnations, and whose appointments are *during pleasure.* Then let there be a formal declaration of both Houses, that opposition to your edicts is *treason,* and that any person suspected of treason in the provinces may, according to some obsolete law, be seized and sent to the metropolis of the empire for trial; and pass an act, that those there charged with certain other offenses, shall be sent away in chains from their friends and country to be tried in the same manner for felony. Then erect a new Court of Inquisition among them, accompanied by an armed force, with instructions to transport all such suspected persons, to be ruined by the expense if they bring over evidences to prove their innocence, or be found guilty and hanged, if they can't afford it. And, lest the people should think you cannot possibly go any further, pass another solemn declaratory act,[12] that "king, lords, Commons had, hath, and of right ought to have, full power and authority to make statutes of sufficient force and validity to bind the unrepresented provinces *in all cases whatsoever.*" This will include *spiritual* with temporal, and, taken together, must operate wonderfully to your purpose, by convincing them that they are at present under a power something like that spoken of in the scriptures, which can not only *kill their bodies,* but *damn their souls* to all eternity, by compelling them, if it pleases, *to worship the Devil.*[13]

XI. To make your taxes more odious, and more likely to procure resistance, send from the capital a board of officers to superintend the collection, composed of the most *indiscreet, ill-bred,* and *insolent* you can find. Let these have large salaries out of the extorted revenue, and live in open, grating luxury upon the sweat and blood of the industrious, whom they are to worry continually with groundless and expensive prosecutions before the above-mentioned arbitrary revenue Judges, all *at the cost of the party prosecuted,* though acquitted, because *the King is to pay no costs.* Let these men, *by your order,* be exempted from all the common taxes and burdens of the province, though they and their property are protected by its laws. If any revenue officers are *suspected* of the least tenderness for the people, discard them.[14] If others are justly complained of, protect and reward them. If

---

[11]"You shall have the body," Latin for a writ to bring a party before a judge to protect against unlawful restraint.
[12]The Declaratory Act of 1766, passed when the Stamp Act was repealed, was Parliament's response to the colonist complaint against being controlled without representation. In his quotation from the act, Franklin substitutes "unrep-

resented provinces" for "colonies and people of America, subjects of the crown of Great Britain."
[13]Matthew 10: 28.
[14]John Temple (1732–1798), a customs commissioner biased toward the Americans, was dismissed in 1770.

any of the under officers behave so as to provoke the people to drub them, promote those to better offices. This will encourage others to procure for themselves such profitable drubbings, by multiplying and enlarging such provocations, and *all will work toward the end you aim at.*

XII. Another way to make your tax odious is to misapply the produce of it. If it was originally appropriated for the *defense* of the provinces, the better support of government, and the administration of justice, where it may be *necessary,* then apply none of it to that *defense,* but bestow it where it is *not necessary,* in augmented salaries or pensions to every governor who has distinguished himself by his enmity to the people, and by calumniating them to their sovereign. This will make them pay it more unwillingly, and be more apt to quarrel with those that collect it and those that imposed it, who will quarrel again with them, and all shall contribute to your *main purpose,* of making them *weary of your government.*

XIII. If the people of any province have been accustomed to support their own governors and judges to satisfaction, you are to apprehend that such governors and judges may be thereby influenced to treat the people kindly, and to do them justice. This is another reason for applying part of that revenue in larger salaries to such governors and judges, given, as their commissions are, *during your pleasure* only; forbidding them to take any salaries from their provinces; that thus the people may no longer hope any kindness from their governors, or (in Crown cases) any justice from their judges. And, as the money thus misapplied in one province is extorted from all, probably *all will resent the misapplication.*

XIV. If the parliaments of your provinces should dare to claim rights, or complain of your administration, order them to be harassed with repeated *dissolutions.*[15] If the same men are continually returned by new elections, adjourn their meetings to some country village where they cannot be accommodated, and there keep them *during pleasure;* for this, you know, is your *prerogative;* and an excellent one it is, as you may manage it to promote discontents among the people, diminish their respect, and *increase their disaffection.*

XV. Convert the brave, honest officers of your navy into pimping tidewaiters[16] and colony officers of the customs. Let those who in time of war fought gallantly in defense of the commerce of their countrymen, in peace be taught to prey upon it. Let them learn to be corrupted by great and real smugglers; but (to show their diligence) scour with armed boats every bay, harbor, river, creek, cove, or nook throughout the coast of your colonies; stop and detain every coaster, every woodboat, every fisherman, tumble their cargoes and even their ballast, inside out and upside down; and, if a pennyworth of pins is found unentered, let the whole be seized and confiscated. Thus shall the trade of your colonists suffer more from their friends in time of peace, than it did from their enemies in war. Then let these boats' crews land upon every farm in their way, rob the orchards, steal the pigs and the poultry, and insult the inhabitants. If the injured and exasperated farmers, unable to procure other justice, should attack the aggressors, drub them, and burn their boats; you are to call this *high treason* and *rebellion,* order fleets and armies into their country, and threaten to carry all the offenders three thousand miles to be hanged, drawn, and quartered.[17] *O! this will work admirably!*

XVI. If you are told of discontents in your colonies, never believe that they are general, or that you have given occasion for them; therefore do not think of applying any remedy, or of changing any offensive measure. Redress no grievance, lest they should be encouraged to demand the redress of some other grievance. Grant no request that is just and reasonable, lest they should make another that is

---

[15]Closings.
[16]Customs officers who boarded ships to prevent evasion of regulations.

[17]Such was the response to the burning of the schooner *Gaspée* on June 10, 1772.

unreasonable. Take all your informations of the state of the colonies from your governors and officers in enmity with them. Encourage and reward these *leasing-makers;*[18] secrete their lying accusations, lest they should be confuted; but act upon them as the clearest evidence, and believe nothing you hear from the friends of the people. Suppose all *their* complaints to be invented and promoted by a few factious demagogues,[19] whom if you could catch and hang, all would be quiet. Catch and hang a few of them accordingly; and the *blood of the Martyrs* shall *work miracles* in favor of your purpose.

XVII. If you see *rival nations* rejoicing at the prospect of your disunion with your provinces, and endeavoring to promote it; if they translate, publish, and applaud all the complaints of your discontented colonists,[20] at the same time privately stimulating you to severer measures, let not that *alarm* or offend you. Why should it, since you all mean *the same thing?*

XVIII. If any colony should at their own charge erect a fortress to secure their port against the fleets of a foreign enemy, get your governor to betray that fortress into your hands.[21] Never think of paying what it cost the country, for that would *look,* at least, like some regard for justice; but turn it into a citadel to awe the inhabitants and curb their commerce. If they should have lodged in such fortress the very arms they bought and used to aid you in your conquests, seize them all; 'twill provoke like *ingratitude* added to *robbery.* One admirable effect of these operations will be to discourage every other colony from erecting such defenses, and so their and your enemies may more easily invade them, to the great disgrace of your government, and of course *the furtherance of your project.*

XIX. Send armies into their country under pretense of protecting the inhabitants; but, instead of garrisoning the forts on their frontiers with those troops, to prevent incursions, demolish those forts, and order the troops into the heart of the country, that the savages may be encouraged to attack the frontiers, and that the troops may be protected by the inhabitants. This will seem to proceed from your ill will or your ignorance, and contribute further to produce and strengthen an opinion among them, *that you are no longer fit to govern them.*

XX. Lastly, invest the general of your army in the provinces with great and unconstitutional powers, and free him from the control of even your own civil governors. Let him have troops enough under his command, with all the fortresses in his possession; and who knows but (like some provincial generals in the Roman empire, and encouraged by the universal discontent you have produced) he may take it into his head to set up for himself? If he should, and you have carefully practiced these few *excellent rules* of mine, take my word for it, all the provinces will immediately join him, and you will that day (if you have not done it sooner) get rid of the trouble of governing them, and all the *plagues* attending their *commerce* and connection from thenceforth and forever.

Q.E.D.[22]

1773   *1773*

---

[18]Liars; in Scottish law, those who lie to alienate a king from his people.
[19]Divisive, unprincipled popular leaders.
[20]Since the Stamp Act, the French had published accounts of the growing Anglo-American quarrel.

[21]Castle William in Boston Harbor, delivered to the British by Governor Thomas Hutchinson (1711–1780) in September 1770.
[22]*Quod erat demonstrandum,* Latin for "which was to be demonstrated."

The Ephemera[1]

An Emblem of Human Life

Translator's Note: Madame Brillon is a very amiable lady, and one who has a distinguished talent for music; she lives at Passy where she moves in the same society as Mr. Franklin. In the summer of 1778 they had passed a day together at the Moulin-Joly,[2] *where on the same day there hovered over the river a swarm of those small flies called Ephemerae, which people call May Flies. Mr. Franklin studied them with care, and the next day sent Madame Brillon the letter of which this is the translation.*

You may remember my dear friend that when we passed that happy day together, in the delightful garden and sweet society of the *Moulin-Joly,* I stopped a little in one of our walks, and stayed some time behind the company.

We had been shown numberless skeletons of a kind of little fly, called an *Ephemera,* all whose successive generations we were told were bred and expired within the day. I happened to see a living company of them on a leaf, who appeared to be engaged in conversation.

You know I understand all the inferior animal tongues. My too great application to the study of them is the best excuse I can give for the little progress I have made in your charming language. I listened with curiosity to the discourse of these little creatures, but as they in their national vivacity spoke three or four together, I could make but little of their conversation. I found, however, by some broken expressions that I caught now and then, they were disputing warmly the merit of two foreign musicians, one a coûsin[3] and the other a musketo;[4] in which dispute they spent their time seemingly as regardless of the shortness of life as if they had been sure of living a month. Happy people, thought I! You live certainly under a wise, just and mild government, since you have no public grievances to complain of, nor any subject of contention but the perfection or imperfection of foreign music.

I turned from them to an old grey-headed one, who was single on another leaf, and talking to himself. Being amused with his soliloquy, I have put it down in writing, in hopes it will likewise amuse her I am so much indebted to, for the most pleasing of all amusements, her delicious company, and her heavenly harmony.

"It was," says he, "the opinion of learned philosophers of our race, who lived and flourished long before my time, that this vast world[5] could not itself subsist more than eighteen hours, and I think there was some foundation for that opinion, since by the apparent motion of the great luminary that gives life to all nature, and which in my time has evidently declined considerably towards the ocean[6] at the end of our earth, it must soon finish its course, and be extinguished in the waters that surround us, leaving the world in cold and darkness, necessarily producing universal death and destruction. I have lived seven of those hours, a great age, being no less than 420 minutes of time! How very few of us continue so long! I have seen generations born, flourish and expire. My present friends are the children and grandchildren of the friends of my youth, who are now alas no more! And I must soon follow them, for by the course of nature, though still in health, I cannot expect to live above seven or eight minutes longer. What now avails all my

---

[1]Written in French for Madame Brillon de Jouy, Franklin's friend and neighbor in the Paris suburb of Passy during his appointment in France as minister plenipotentiary of the United States (1776–85). This piece and other short essays like "The Whistle" are called bagatelles (or trifles) after their lightness and graceful manner. They were "published" on Franklin's own press which he installed at his residence and were circulated among friends.

[2]The "English" or informal garden of the country residence of a mutual friend, the painter Claude-Henri Watelet, on an island in the Seine.
[3]Gnat.
[4]Mosquito.
[5]"The Moulin-Joly" (Franklin's note).
[6]"The river Seine" (Franklin's note).

toil and labor in amassing honey-dew on this leaf, which I cannot live to enjoy! What the political struggles I have been in, or my philosophical studies for the benefit of our race in general! For in politics, what can law do without morals?[7] Our present race of Ephemerae will in a course of minutes become corrupt like those of other and elder bushes, and consequently as wretched. And in philosophy, how small our progress! Alas, art is long and life short![8] My friends would comfort me with the idea of a name they say I shall leave behind me, and they tell me I have lived long enough to nature and to glory.[9] But what will fame be to an *Ephemera* who no longer exists? And what will become of all history in the ten hours when the world itself, even the whole *Moulin-Joly*, shall come to its end, and be buried in universal ruin? After all my eager pursuits, no solid pleasure now remains, but the reflection of a long life spent in meaning well, the sensible conversation of a few lady *Ephemerae,* and now and then a kind smile, and a tune from the ever amiable *Brilliante.*"[10]

1778   1778?

The Whistle[1]

Passy, November 10, 1779

I received my dear friend's two letters, one for Wednesday and one for Saturday. This is again Wednesday. I do not deserve one for today, because I have not answered the former. But indolent as I am, and averse to writing, the fear of having no more of your pleasing epistles, if I do not contribute to the correspondance, obliges me to take up my pen. And as M. Brillon has kindly sent me word that he sets out tomorrow to see you, instead of spending this Wednesday evening as I have long done its namesakes, in your delightful company, I sit down to spend it in thinking of you, in writing to you, and in reading over and over again your letters.

I am charmed with your description of Paradise,[2] and with your plan of living there. And I approve much of your conclusion, that in the mean time we should draw all the good we can from this world. In my opinion, we might all draw more good from it than we do, and suffer less evil, if we would but take care *not to give too much for our whistles.* For to me it seems that most of the unhappy people we meet with are become so by neglect of that caution.

You ask what I mean? You love stories, and will excuse my telling one of myself. When I was a child of seven years old, my friends, on a holiday, filled my little pocket with halfpence. I went directly to a shop where they sold toys for children; and, being charmed with the sound of a whistle that I met by the way, in the hands of another boy, I voluntarily offered and gave all my money for it. When I

[7]*Quid leges sine moribus?* Horace (*Odes.* 3, 24, line 35. Franklin's note).
[8]Hippocrates (*Aphorisms.* 1, 1. Franklin's note).
[9]Caesar in Cicero's *Pro Marcello.* 8, 25.
[10]French for *brilliant,* suggestive of Madame Brillon's name.
[1]Franklin wrote "The Whistle" in English and in French for Madame Brillon, who had gone to visit her mother in the country. While there, she wrote to Franklin each Wednesday and Saturday, the days they would meet for tea, chess, and music at Passy.
[2]On November 1, 1779, Madame Brillon had written of the uncertainty of earthly happiness, taking comfort in her vision of paradise, where they would never part, would "live

on roasted apples only; all chess games will end in a tie, so that nobody will be sorry; the same language will be spoken by all; the English, there, will be neither unjust nor wicked; women will not be coquettish, men will be neither jealous nor too enterprising; 'King John' will be left to eat his apples in peace; perhaps he will be decent enough to offer some to his neighbors—who knows? since we shall want for nothing in paradise! . . . There shall be no gout, no nervous upsets . . . ambition, envy, conceit, jealousy, prejudices, all will vanish at the sound of a trumpet; a lasting, sweet and peaceful friendship will animate every society . . . ." Her reference to King John may point to the ravaging greed of the English King John (1167?–1216), who died, according to legend, after eating poisoned pears.

came home, whistling all over the house, much pleased with my whistle, but disturbing all the family, my brothers, sisters, and cousins, understanding the bargain I had made, told me I had given four times as much for it as it was worth, put me in mind what good things I might have bought with the rest of the money, and laughed at me so much for my folly that I cried with vexation; and the reflection gave me more chagrin than the whistle gave me pleasure.

This however was afterwards of use to me, the impression continuing on my mind; so that often when I was tempted to buy some unnecessary thing, I said to myself, *Do not give too much for the whistle;* and I saved my money.

As I grew up, came into the world, and observed the actions of men, I thought I met many *who gave too much for the whistle.*

When I saw one ambitious of court favor, sacrificing his time in attendance at levees,[3] his repose, his liberty, his virtue, and perhaps his friend to obtain it, I have said to myself, *This man gives too much for his whistle.*

When I saw another fond of popularity, constantly employing himself in political bustles, neglecting his own affairs, and ruining them by that neglect, *He pays,* says I, *too much for his whistle.*

If I knew a miser, who gave up every kind of comfortable living, all the pleasures of doing good to others, all the esteem of his fellow citizens, and the joys of benevolent friendship, for the sake of accumulating wealth, *Poor man,* says I, *you pay too much for your whistle.*

When I met with a man of pleasure, sacrificing every laudable improvement of his mind or of his fortune to mere corporeal satisfactions, and ruining his health in their pursuit, *Mistaken man,* says I, *you are providing pain for yourself instead of pleasure, you pay too much for your whistle.*

If I see one fond of appearance, of fine clothes, fine houses, fine furniture, fine equipages, all above his fortune, for which he contracts debts, and ends his career in a prison, *Alas,* says I, *he has paid too much for his whistle.*

When I saw a beautiful sweet-tempered girl married to an ill-natured brute of a husband, *What a pity,* says I, *that she should pay so much for a whistle!*

In short, I conceived that great part of the miseries of mankind were brought upon them by the false estimates they had made of the value of things, and by their *giving too much for the whistle.*

Yet I ought to have charity for these unhappy people, when I consider that with all this wisdom of which I am boasting, there are certain things in the world so tempting, for example, the apples of King John,[4] which happily are not to be bought, for if they were put to sale by auction, I might very easily be led to ruin myself in the purchase, and find that I had once more *given too much for the whistle.*

Adieu, my dearest friend, and believe me ever yours very sincerely and with unalterable affection.

1779?

---

[3]Receptions held by monarchs upon arising from bed; also, any court reception.

[4]This allusion to the apples of King John appears in other letters and seems to be a private joke between them.

Speech in the [Constitutional]
Convention at the Conclusion of Its Deliberations[1]

[A PLEA FOR DOUBT OF ONE'S INFALLIBILITY]

Mr. President,

I confess that I do not entirely approve of this Constitution at present, but, Sir, I am not sure I shall never approve it; for, having lived long, I have experienced many instances of being obliged, by better information or fuller consideration, to change opinions even on important subjects, which I once thought right, but found to be otherwise. It is therefore that the older I grow, the more apt I am to doubt my own judgment, and to pay more respect to the judgment of others. Most men, indeed, as well as most sects in religion, think themselves in possession of all truth, and that wherever others differ from them, it is so far error. Steele,[2] a Protestant, in a dedication, tells the Pope, that the only difference between our two churches in their opinions of the certainty of their doctrine, is, the Romish Church is *infallible*, and the Church of England is *never in the wrong*. But, though many private Persons think almost as highly of their own infallibility as of that of their sect, few express it so naturally as a certain French lady, who, in a little dispute with her sister, said, "I don't know how it happens, Sister, but I meet with nobody but myself that is *always* in the right." "*Je ne trouve que moi qui aie toujours raison.*"[3]

In these sentiments, Sir, I agree to this Constitution, with all its faults,—if they are such; because I think a general government necessary for us, and there is no *form* of government but what may be a blessing to the people, if well administered; and I believe, farther, that this is likely to be well administered for a course of years, and can only end in despotism, as other forms have done before it, when the people shall become so corrupted as to need despotic government, being incapable of any other. I doubt, too, whether any other convention we can obtain, may be able to make a better constitution; for, when you assemble a number of men to have the advantage of their joint wisdom, you inevitably assemble with those men all their prejudices, their passions, their errors of opinion, their local interests, and their selfish views. From such an assembly can a *perfect* production be expected? It therefore astonishes me, Sir, to find this system approaching so near to perfection as it does; and I think it will astonish our enemies, who are waiting with confidence to hear that our councils are confounded, like those of the builders of Babel, and that our states are on the point of separation, only to meet hereafter for the purpose of cutting one another's throats. Thus I consent, Sir, to this Constitution because I expect no better, and because I am not sure that it is not the best. The opinions I have had of its *errors* I sacrifice to the public good. I have never whispered a syllable of them abroad. Within these walls they were born, and here they shall die. If every one of us, in returning to our constituents, were to report the objections he has had to it, and endeavour to gain partisans in support of them, we might prevent its being generally received, and thereby lose all the salutary effects and great advantages resulting naturally in our favor among for-

---

[1] Delivered at the Constitutional Convention in Philadelphia on September 17, 1787, the day when work on drafting the constitution was completed. It was read for Franklin, 82 years old and frail, by James Wilson of the Pennsylvania delegation. Franklin had set forth a number of proposals that were rejected—a single legislature, a plural executive, unsalaried executive officers. After Franklin's speech, the Constitution was approved "by the unanimous consent of the states present."

This text from the Smyth edition has been checked against a text based on the manuscript in the Cornell University Library and missing phrases have been restored.
[2] Sir Richard Steele (1672–1729), English essayist and dramatist.
[3] The French is a translation of the preceding English.

eign nations, as well as among ourselves, from our real or apparent unanimity. Much of the strength and efficiency of any government, in procuring and securing happiness to the people, depends on *opinion,* on the general opinion of the goodness of that government, as well as of the wisdom and integrity of its governors. I hope, therefore, for our own sakes, as a part of the people, and for the sake of our posterity, that we shall act heartily and unanimously in recommending this Constitution, wherever our influence may extend, and turn our future thoughts and endeavours to the means of having it *well administered.*

On the whole, Sir, I cannot help expressing a wish, that every member of the convention who may still have objections to it, would with me on this occasion doubt a little of his own infallibility, and, to make *manifest* our *unanimity,* put his name to this instrument.

1787   *1787*

Remarks Concerning the
Savages of North America[1]

Savages we call them, because their manners differ from ours, which we think the perfection of civility; they think the same of theirs.

Perhaps, if we could examine the manners of different nations with impartiality, we should find no people so rude, as to be without any rules of politeness; nor any so polite, as not to have some remains of rudeness.

The Indian men, when young, are hunters and warriors; when old, counselors; for all their government is by counsel of the sages; there is no force, there are no prisons, no officers to compel obedience, or inflict punishment. Hence they generally study oratory, the best speaker having the most influence. The Indian women till the ground, dress the food, nurse and bring up the children, and preserve and hand down to posterity the memory of public transactions. These employments of men and women are accounted natural and honorable. Having few artificial wants, they have abundance of leisure for improvement by conversation. Our laborious manner of life, compared with theirs, they esteem slavish and base; and the learning, on which we value ourselves, they regard as frivolous and useless. An instance of this occurred at the Treaty of Lancaster, in Pennsylvania, *anno* 1744, between the government of Virginia and the Six Nations.[2] After the principal business was settled, the commissioners from Virginia acquainted the Indians by a speech, that there was at Williamsburg a college, with a fund for educating Indian youth; and that, if the chiefs of the Six Nations would send down half a dozen of their sons to that college,[3] the government would take care that they should be well provided for, and instructed in all the learning of the white people. It is one of the Indian rules of politeness not to answer a public proposition the same day that it is made; they think it would be treating it as a light matter, and that they show it respect by taking time to consider it, as of a matter important. They therefore deferred their answer till the day following; when their speaker began, by expressing their deep sense of the kindness of the Virginia government, in making them that offer; "for we know," says he, "that you highly esteem the kind of learning taught in those Colleges, and that the maintenance of our young

---

[1]Published in England as a pamphlet in 1784.
[2]A league of Iroquois tribes, Seneca, Cayuga, Oneida, Onondaga, Mohawk, and Tuscarora.
[3]College of William and Mary.

men, while with you, would be very expensive to you. We are convinced, there-fore, that you mean to do us good by your proposal, and we thank you heartily. But you, who are wise, must know that different nations have different concep-tions of things; and you will therefore not take it amiss, if our ideas of this kind of education happen not to be the same with yours. We have had some experience of it. Several of our young people were formerly brought up at the colleges of the northern provinces; they were instructed in all your sciences; but, when they came back to us, they were bad runners, ignorant of every means of living in the woods, unable to bear either cold or hunger, knew neither how to build a cabin, take a deer, or kill an enemy, spoke our language imperfectly, were therefore neither fit for hunters, warriors, nor counselors; they were totally good for nothing. We are however not the less obliged by your kind offer, though we decline accepting it; and, to show our grateful sense of it, if the gentlemen of Virginia will send us a dozen of their sons, we will take great care of their education, instruct them in all we know, and make *men* of them."

Having frequent occasions to hold public councils, they have acquired great or-der and decency in conducting them. The old men sit in the foremost ranks, the warriors in the next, and the women and children in the hindmost. The business of the women is to take exact notice of what passes, imprint it in their memories, for they have no writing, and communicate it to their children. They are the records of the council, and they preserve tradition of the stipulations in treaties a hundred years back; which, when we compare with our writings, we always find exact. He that would speak, rises. The rest observe a profound silence. When he has finished and sits down, they leave him 5 or 6 minutes to recollect, that, if he has omitted anything he intended to say, or has anything to add, he may rise again and deliver it. To interrupt another, even in common conversation, is reck-oned highly indecent. How different this is from the conduct of a polite British House of Commons, where scarce a day passes without some confusion that makes the speaker hoarse in calling *to order;* and how different from the mode of conversation in many polite companies of Europe, where, if you do not deliver your sentence with great rapidity, you are cut off in the middle of it by the impa-tient loquacity of those you converse with, and never suffered to finish it.

The politeness of these savages in conversation is indeed carried to excess, since it does not permit them to contradict or deny the truth of what is asserted in their presence. By this means they indeed avoid disputes, but then it becomes dif-ficult to know their minds, or what impression you make upon them. The mission-aries who have attempted to convert them to Christianity, all complain of this as one of the great difficulties of their mission. The Indians hear with patience the truths of the Gospel explained to them, and give their usual tokens of assent and approbation; you would think they were convinced. No such matter. It is mere civility.

A Swedish minister, having assembled the chiefs of the Susquehanah Indians, made a sermon to them, acquainting them with the principal historical facts on which our religion is founded; such as the fall of our first parents by eating an apple, the coming of Christ to repair the mischief, His miracles and suffering, &c. When he had finished, an Indian orator stood up to thank him. "What you have told us," says he, "is all very good. It is indeed bad to eat apples. It is better to make them all into cider. We are much obliged by your kindness in coming so far to tell us those things which you have heard from your mothers. In return, I will tell you some of those we have heard from ours.

"In the beginning, our fathers had only the flesh of animals to subsist on; and if their hunting was unsuccessful, they were starving. Two of our young hunters, having killed a deer, made a fire in the woods to broil some parts of it. When they were about to satisfy their hunger, they beheld a beautiful young woman descend from the clouds, and seat herself on that hill, which you see yonder among the blue mountains. They said to each other, it is a spirit that has smelled our broiling venison, and wishes to eat of it; let us offer some to her. They presented her with the tongue. She was pleased with the taste of it, and said, 'Your kindness shall be rewarded. Come to this place after thirteen moons, and you shall find something that will be of great benefit in nourishing you and your children to the latest generations.' They did so, and, to their surprise, found plants they had never seen before, but which, from that ancient time, have been constantly cultivated among us, to our great advantage. Where her right hand had touched the ground, they found maize; where her left hand had touched it, they found kidney-beans; and where her backside had sat on it, they found tobacco." The good missionary, disgusted with this idle tale, said, "What I delivered to you were sacred truths; but what you tell me is mere fable, fiction, and falsehood." The Indian, offended, replied, "My brother, it seems your friends have not done you justice in your education; they have not well instructed you in the rules of common civility. You saw that we, who understand and practice those rules, believed all your stories; why do you refuse to believe ours?"

When any of them come into our towns, our people are apt to crowd round them, gaze upon them, and incommode them, where they desire to be private; this they esteem great rudeness, and the effect of the want of instruction in the rules of civility and good manners. "We have," say they, "as much curiosity as you, and when you come into our towns, we wish for opportunities of looking at you; but for this purpose we hide ourselves behind bushes, where you are to pass, and never intrude ourselves into your company."

Their manner of entering one another's village has likewise its rules. It is reckoned uncivil in traveling strangers to enter a village abruptly, without giving notice of their approach. Therefore, as soon as they arrive within hearing, they stop and hollow,[4] remaining there till invited to enter. Two old men usually come out to them, and lead them in. There is in every village a vacant dwelling, called the strangers' house. Here they are placed, while the old men go round from hut to hut acquainting the inhabitants that strangers are arrived, who are probably hungry and weary; and every one sends them what he can spare of victuals, and skins to repose on. When the strangers are refreshed, pipes and tobacco are brought; and then, but not before, conversation begins, with inquiries who they are, whither bound, what news, &c.; and it usually ends with offers of service, if the strangers have occasion of guides, or any neccessaries for continuing their journey; and nothing is exacted for the entertainment.

The same hospitality, esteemed among them as a principal virtue, is practiced by private persons; of which Conrad Weiser, our interpreter, gave me the following instances. He had been naturalized among the Six Nations, and spoke well the Mohawk language. In going through the Indian country, to carry a message from our Governor to the Council at Onondaga, he called at the habitation of Canassatego, an old acquaintance, who embraced him, spread furs for him to sit on, placed before him some boiled beans and venison, and mixed some rum and water for his drink. When he was well refreshed, and had lit his pipe, Canassatego began to converse with him, asked how he had fared the many years since they had seen each other, whence he then came, what occasioned the journey, &c. Conrad answered all his questions; and when the discourse began to flag, the Indian, to continue it, said, "Conrad, you have lived long among the white people, and know something of their customs; I have been sometimes at Albany, and have observed that once in seven days they shut up their shops and assemble all in the great

---

[4]Yell, shout.

house; tell me what it is for? What do they do there?" "They meet there," says Conrad, "to hear and learn *good things.*" "I do not doubt," says the Indian, "that they tell you so; they have told me the same; but I doubt the truth of what they say, and I will tell you my reasons. I went lately to Albany to sell my skins and buy blankets, knives, powder, rum, &c. You know I used generally to deal with Hans Hanson; but I was a little inclined this time to try some other merchant. However, I called first upon Hans, and asked him what he would give for beaver. He said he could not give any more than four shillings a pound; 'but,' says he, 'I cannot talk on business now; this is the day when we meet together to learn *good things,* and I am going to the meeting.' So I thought to myself, 'Since we cannot do any business today, I may as well go to the meeting too,' and I went with him. There stood up a man in black, and began to talk to the people very angrily. I did not understand what he said; but, perceiving that he looked much at me and at Hanson, I imagined he was angry at seeing me there; so I went out, sat down near the house, struck fire, and lit my pipe, waiting till the meeting should break up. I thought too, that the man had mentioned something of beaver, and I suspected it might be the subject of their meeting. So, when they came out, I accosted my merchant. 'Well, Hans,' says I, 'I hope you have agreed to give more than four shillings a pound.' 'No,' says he, 'I cannot give so much; I cannot give more than three shillings and sixpence.' I then spoke to several other dealers, but they all sung the same song, three and sixpence, three and sixpence. This made it clear to me, that my suspicion was right; and, that whatever they pretended of meeting to learn *good things,* the real purpose was to consult how to cheat Indians in the price of beaver. Consider but a little, Conrad, and you must be of my opinion. If they met so often to learn *good things,* they would certainly have learned some before this time. But they are still ignorant. You know our practice. If a white man, in traveling through our country, enters one of our cabins, we all treat him as I treat you; we dry him if he is wet, we warm him if he is cold, and give him meat and drink that he may allay his thirst and hunger; and we spread soft furs for him to rest and sleep on. We demand nothing in return.[5] But, if I go into a white man's house at Albany, and ask for victuals and drink, they say, 'Where is your money?' and if I have none, they say, 'Get out, you Indian dog.' You see they have not yet learned those little *good things,* that we need no meetings to be instructed in, because our mothers taught them to us when we were children. And therefore it is impossible their meetings should be, as they say, for any such purpose, or have any such effect; they are only to contrive *the cheating of Indians in the price of beaver.*"

1784

---

[5]"It is remarkable that in all ages and countries, hospitality has been allowed as the virtue of those whom the civilized were pleased to call barbarians; the Greeks celebrated the Scythians for it. The Saracens possessed it eminently; and it is to this day the reigning virtue of the wild Arabs. St. Paul, too, in the relation of his voyage and shipwreck on the island of Melita says, 'The barbarous people showed us no little kindness; for they kindled a fire, and received us every one, because of the present rain and because of the cold' " (Acts 28:2. Franklin's note).

from Letters

TO JOSEPH HUEY[1]

[ON GOOD WORKS]

Philadelphia, June 6, 1753

Sir,

I received your kind letter of the 2nd inst,[2] and am glad to hear that you increase in strength; I hope you will continue mending till you recover your former health and firmness. Let me know whether you still use the cold bath, and what effect it has.

As to the kindness you mention, I wish it could have been of more service to you. But if it had, the only thanks I should desire is that you would always be equally ready to serve any other person that may need your assistance, and so let good offices go round, for mankind are all of a family.

For my own part, when I am employed in serving others, I do not look upon myself as conferring favors, but as paying debts. In my travels and since my settlement I have received much kindness from men, to whom I shall never have any opportunity of making the least direct return. And numberless mercies from God, who is infinitely above being benefited by our services. These kindnesses from men I can therefore only return on their fellowmen; and I can only show my gratitude for those mercies from God by a readiness to help his other children and my brethren. For I do not think that thanks and compliments, though repeated weekly, can discharge our real obligations to each other, and much less those to our Creator.

You will see in this, my notion of good works, that I am far from expecting (as you suppose) that I shall merit heaven by them. By heaven we understand a state of happiness, infinite in degree, and eternal in duration: I can do nothing to deserve such reward. He that, for giving a draught of water to a thirsty person, should expect to be paid with a good plantation would be modest in his demands compared with those who think they deserve heaven for the little good they do on earth. Even the mixed imperfect pleasures we enjoy in this world are rather from God's goodness than our merit; how much more such happiness of heaven. For my own part, I have not the vanity to think I deserve it, the folly to expect it, nor the ambition to desire it; but content myself in submitting to the will and disposal of that God who made me, who has hitherto preserved and blessed me, and in whose fatherly goodness I may well confide, that he will never make me miserable, and that even the afflictions I may at any time suffer shall tend to my benefit.

The faith you mention has doubtless its use in the world; I do not desire to see it diminished, nor would I endeavor to lessen it in any man. But I wish it were more productive of good works than I have generally seen it. I mean real good works, works of kindness, charity, mercy, and public spirit, not holiday-keeping, sermon-reading or hearing, performing church ceremonies, or making long prayers, filled with flatteries and compliments, despised even by wise men, and much less capable of pleasing the Deity. The worship of God is a duty, the hearing and reading of sermons may be useful; but if men rest in hearing and praying, as too many do, it is as if a tree should value itself on being watered and putting forth leaves, though it never produced any fruit.

---

[1]Nothing is known about the recipient except what Franklin said almost forty years later in one of the last letters he wrote, the letter of March 9, 1790, to Ezra Stiles (see following). Franklin sent a copy of this letter to Stiles as evidence of what he still believed about meriting salvation by good works rather than faith. He had written this letter in answer to Huey, "a zealous religionist, whom I had relieved in a paralytic case by electricity, and who, being afraid I should grow proud upon it, sent me his serious, though rather impertinent cautions."

[2]Instant: of the current month.

Your great Master thought much less of these outward appearances than many of his modern disciples. He preferred the doers of the Word to the mere hearers; the son that seemingly refused to obey his father and yet performed his commands, to him that professed his readiness but neglected the works;[3] the heretical but charitable samaritan to the uncharitable though orthodox priest and sanctified Levite.[4] And those who gave food to the hungry, drink to the thirsty, raiment to the naked, entertainment to the stranger, and relief to the sick, etc., though they never heard of his name, he declares shall in the last day be accepted, when those who cry "Lord, Lord," who value themselves on their faith, though great enough to perform miracles, but have neglected good works, shall be rejected.[5] He professed that he came not to call the righteous but sinners to repentance,[6] which implied his modest opinion that there were some in his time so good that they need not hear even him for improvement. But nowadays we have scarce a little parson that does not think it the duty of every man within his reach to sit under his petty ministrations, and that whoever omits them offends God. I wish to such more humility, and to you health and happiness, being

Your friend and servant,

B. Franklin

TO JOSEPH PRIESTLEY[1]

[MORE PRIDE IN KILLING THAN BEGETTING]

Passy near Paris, June 7, 1782

Dear Sir:

I received your kind letter of the seventh of April, also one of the third of May. I have always great pleasure in hearing from you, in learning that you are well, and that you continue your experiments. I should rejoice much, if I could once more recover the leisure to search with you into the works of nature; I mean the *inanimate*, not the *animate* or moral part of them; the more I discovered of the former, the more I admired them; the more I know of the latter, the more I am disgusted with them. Men I find to be a sort of beings very badly constructed, as they are generally more easily provoked than reconciled, more disposed to do mischief to each other than to make reparation, much more easily deceived than undeceived, and having more pride and even pleasure in killing than in begetting one another; for without a blush they assemble in great armies at noonday to destroy, and when they have killed as many as they can, they exaggerate the number to augment the fancied glory; but they creep into corners, or cover themselves with the darkness of night, when they mean to beget, as being ashamed of a virtuous action. A virtuous action it would be, and a vicious one the killing of them, if the species were really worth producing or preserving; but of this I begin to doubt.

I know you have no such doubts, because, in your zeal for their welfare, you are taking a great deal of pains to save their souls. Perhaps as you grow older, you may look upon this as a hopeless project, or an idle amusement, repent of having murdered in mephitic[2] air so many honest, harmless mice, and wish that to prevent mischief, you had used boys and girls instead of them. In what light we are viewed by superior beings, may be gathered from a piece of late West India[3]

---

[3]Matthew 21: 28–32.
[4]Luke 10: 29–37.
[5]Matthew 25: 35–46.
[6]Matthew 9: 13.
[1]Joseph Priestley (1733–1804), English clergyman, chemist, and friend of the American revolution, was encouraged by Franklin to complete his *History and Present State of Elec-*

tricity (1767). In 1774 he discovered "dephlogisticated air" (oxygen).
[2]Bad-smelling, poisonous.
[3]West Indies, the island chain southeast of the United States, including the Bahamas, the Greater Antilles, and the Lesser Antilles.

news, which possibly has not yet reached you. A young angel of distinction, being sent down to this world on some business for the first time, had an old courier-spirit assigned him as a guide. They arrived over the seas of Martinico,[4] in the middle of the long day of obstinate fight between the fleets of Rodney and De Grasse.[5] When, through the clouds of smoke, he saw the fire of the guns, the decks covered with mangled limbs, and bodies dead or dying; the ships sinking, burning, or blown into the air; and the quantity of pain, misery, and destruction, the crews yet alive were thus with so much eagerness dealing round to one another; he turned angrily to his guide, and said, "You blundering blockhead, you are ignorant of your business; you undertook to conduct me to the earth, and you have brought me into hell!" "No, Sir," says the guide, "I have made no mistake; this is really the earth, and these are men. Devils never treat one another in this cruel manner; they have more sense, and more of what men (vainly) call *humanity*."

But to be serious, my dear old friend, I love you as much as ever, and I love all the honest souls that meet at the London coffee house. I only wonder how it happened, that they and my other friends in England came to be such good creatures in the midst of so perverse a generation. I long to see them and you once more, and I labor for peace with more earnestness, that I may again be happy in your sweet society.

I showed your letter to the Duke de La Rochefoucault,[6] who thinks with me, the new experiments you have made are extremely curious; and he has given me thereupon a note, which I enclose, and I request you would furnish me with the answer desired.

Yesterday the Count du Nord[7] was at the Academy of Sciences, when sundry experiments were exhibited for his entertainment; among them, one by M. Lavoisier,[8] to show that the strongest fire we yet know is made in a charcoal blown upon with dephlogisticated air. In a heat so produced, he melted platina[9] presently,[10] the fire being much more powerful than that of the strongest burning mirror.[11] Adieu, and believe me ever, yours most affectionately,

B. Franklin.

TO [THOMAS PAINE?][1]

["YOU STRIKE AT THE FOUNDATION OF ALL RELIGION"]

Philadelphia, July 3, 1786[?]

Dear Sir,

I have read your manuscript with some attention. By the argument it contains against the doctrines of a particular providence, though you allow a general providence, you strike at the foundation of all religion. For without the belief of a providence, that takes cognizance of, guards, and guides, and may favor particular persons, there is no motive to worship a deity, to fear its displeasure, or to pray for its protection. I will not enter into any discussion of your principles, though you seem to desire it. At present I shall only give you my opinion, that, though

[4]Martinique, island of the Lesser Antilles.
[5]George B. Rodney (1718–1792), British admiral, in April, 1782, defeated the French fleet in the West Indies and captured the commander, François Joseph Paul de Grasse (1722–1788).
[6]Duc François de La Rochefoucauld (1613–1680), French writer known primarily for his *Maxims*.
[7]Grand Duke of Russia, later Emperor Paul I (1754–1801).
[8]Antoine Laurent Lavoisier (1743–1794), French chemist and founder of modern chemistry. After Priestley isolated "dephlogisticated air," Lavoisier explained combustion, not as the result of the release in flame of the hypothetical substance "phlogiston," but rather as the result of the combi-

nation of the burning substance with "dephlogisticated air," which Lavoisier named oxygen in 1777.
[9]Platinum.
[10]Immediately.
[11]A concave mirror used to reflect and concentrate heat, as from the sun, on a substance.
[1]Although Thomas Paine's deistical writings were not published until after this letter was written, parts of the *Age of Reason* (1793–95) existed in draft form before 1781. It is reasonable to assume, given the Franklin-Paine friendship, that Paine would have shown Franklin his work-in-progress.

your reasonings are subtle, and may prevail with some readers, you will not succeed so as to change the general sentiments of mankind on that subject, and the consequence of printing this piece will be a great deal of odium drawn upon yourself, mischief to you, and no benefit to others. He that spits against the wind, spits in his own face.

But, were you to succeed, do you imagine any good would be done by it? You yourself may find it easy to live a virtuous life, without the assistance afforded by religion; you having a clear perception of the advantages of virtue, and the disadvantages of vice, and possessing a strength of resolution sufficient to enable you to resist common temptations. But think how great a proportion of mankind consists of weak and ignorant men and women, and of inexperienced and inconsiderate youth of both sexes, who have need of the motives of religion to restrain them from vice, to support their virtue, and retain them in the practice of it till it becomes *habitual,* which is the great point for its security. And perhaps you are indebted to her originally, that is, to your religious education, for the habits of virtue upon which you now justly value yourself. You might easily display your excellent talents of reasoning upon a less hazardous subject, and thereby obtain a rank with our most distinguished authors. For among us it is not necessary, as among the Hottentots,[2] that a youth, to be received into the company of men, should prove his manhood by beating his mother.

I would advise you, therefore, not to attempt unchaining the tiger, but to burn this piece before it is seen by any other person; whereby you will save yourself a great deal of mortification from the enemies it may raise against you, and perhaps a good deal of regret and repentance. If men are so wicked as we now see them *with religion,* what would they be *if without it.* I intend this letter itself as a *proof* of my friendship, and therefore add no *professions* to it; but subscribe simply yours,

B.F.

TO EZRA STILES[1]

[MY RELIGIOUS CREDO]

Philadelphia, March 9, 1790

Reverend and Dear Sir,

I received your kind letter of January 28, and am glad you have at length received the portrait of Governor Yale from his family, and deposited it in the college library.[2] He was a great and good man, and had the merit of doing infinite service to your country by his munificence to that institution. The honor you propose doing me by placing mine in the same room with his is much too great for my deserts; but you always had a partiality for me, and to that it must be ascribed. I am however too much obliged to Yale College, the first learned society that took notice of me and adorned me with its honors,[3] to refuse a request that comes from it through so esteemed a friend. But I do not think any one of the portraits you mention, as in my possession, worthy of the place and company you propose to place it in. You have an excellent artist lately arrived. If he will undertake to make one for you, I shall cheerfully pay the expense; but he must not delay setting about it, or I may slip through his fingers, for I am now in my eighty-fifth year, and very infirm.[4]

[2]A people of South Africa.

[1]Ezra Stiles (1727–1795), grandson of the poet Edward Taylor, was a clergyman and president of Yale College. On January 28, 1790, he had written to Franklin: "I wish to know the opinion of my venerable friend concerning Jesus of Nazareth." Franklin's reply was written five weeks before he died.

[2]Elihu Yale (1649–1721), born in Boston, taken to England as a child, became an official of the East India Company and Governor of Fort Saint George, Madras, India. His gift of books, a portrait, and some goods to the college at New Haven caused the trustees to name it Yale College in 1718.

[3]Yale awarded Franklin an honorary M.A. in September 1753. Harvard had done so in July 1753, and William and Mary in April 1756.

[4]Franklin died on April 17, 1790, at age 84.

I send with this a very learned work, as it seems to me, on the ancient Samaritan coins, lately printed in Spain, and at least curious for the beauty of the impression. Please to accept it for your college library. I have subscribed for the Encyclopaedia now printing here,[5] with the intention of presenting it to the college. I shall probably depart before the work is finished, but shall leave directions for its continuance to the end. With this you will receive some of the first numbers.

You desire to know something of my religion. It is the first time I have been questioned upon it. But I cannot take your curiosity amiss, and shall endeavor in a few words to gratify it. Here is my creed. I believe in one God, Creator of the Universe. That He governs it by His providence. That He ought to be worshiped. That the most acceptable service we render to Him is doing good to His other children. That the soul of man is immortal, and will be treated with justice in another life respecting its conduct in this. These I take to be the fundamental principles of all sound religion, and I regard them as you do in whatever sect I meet with them.

As to Jesus of Nazareth, my opinion of whom you particularly desire, I think the system of morals, and his religion, as he left them to us, the best the world ever saw or is likely to see; but I apprehend it has received various corrupting changes, and I have, with most of the present dissenters[6] in England, some doubts as to his divinity; though it is a question I do not dogmatize upon, having never studied it, and think it needless to busy myself with it now, when I expect soon an opportunity of knowing the truth with less trouble. I see no harm, however, in its being believed, if that belief has the good consequence, as probably it has, of making his doctrines more respected and better observed; especially as I do not perceive, that the Supreme takes it amiss, by distinguishing the unbelievers in His government of the world with any peculiar marks of His displeasure.

I shall only add, respecting myself, that, having experienced the goodness of that Being in conducting me prosperously through a long life, I have no doubt of its continuance in the next, though without the smallest conceit of meriting such goodness. My sentiments on this head you will see in the copy of an old letter enclosed, which I wrote in answer to one from a zealous religionist, whom I had relieved in a paralytic case by electricity, and who, being afraid I should grow proud upon it, sent me his serious though rather impertinent caution.[7] I send you also the copy of another letter,[8] which will show something of my disposition relating to religion. With great and sincere esteem and affection, I am, your obliged old friend and most obedient humble servant

B. Franklin

P.S. Had not your college some present of books from the King of France? Please to let me know, if you had an expectation given you of more, and the nature of that expectation. I have a reason for the inquiry.

I confide, that you will not expose me to criticism and censure by publishing any part of his communication to you. I have ever let others enjoy their religious sentiments, without reflecting on them for those that appeared to me unsupportable and even absurd. All sects here, and we have a great variety, have experienced my good will in assisting them with subscriptions for building their new places of worship; and, as I have never opposed any of their doctrines, I hope to go out of the world in peace with them all.

[5]The third edition of the *Encyclopaedia Britannica* (1788–97) was pirated by Thomas Dobson of Philadelphia; his reprint, entitled *Encyclopaedia*, with parts rewritten to correct British bias, he called the first American edition.

[6]The Unitarians.
[7]The letter of June 6, 1753, to Joseph Huey (see previous letter).
[8]Possibly the preceding letter to Thomas Paine.

from The Autobiography

Franklin's *Autobiography* was started when he was sixty-five, written in four different stages when he could find time in a very busy career in public service, and was left unfinished at his death. Part One was written in 1771 at Twyford, a village some fifty miles from London, where Franklin was staying for two weeks at the home of a friend, taking a respite from his duties as representative of Pennsylvania and other colonies to England. He carried the story of his life to his twenty-fifth year. Part Two was written thirteen years later, when the seventy-eight-year-old Franklin was living in Passy, suburb of Paris, serving as minister plenipotentiary to France. This part dwelt on Franklin's systematic scheme to achieve moral perfection in the late 1720s and early 1730s. Parts One and Two constitute over half of the text of the *Autobiography*. Parts Three and Four, not included here, were written at age eighty-two and eighty-four, when Franklin's energies were flagging, and carry the story of his life up to 1758, when Franklin was fifty-two, breaking off just as he was about to enter the great period of his life as statesman and diplomat.

Franklin addressed his *Autobiography* to his illegitimate son, William (*c.* 1731–1813), who was at that time governor of New Jersey. Of the circumstances of his conception and birth, nothing is revealed in the *Autobiography* and almost nothing is known. Franklin's common-law marriage seems to have coincided with William's birth, and Franklin's wife, Deborah Read, took him to raise as her child. Some biographers speculate that William was really Deborah's child, born before the marriage, but announced as Franklin's natural child to protect her reputation. By the time Franklin started to write Part Two of the *Autobiography,* in 1784, he was estranged from his son because William had gone over to the British side in the Revolution. They were never reconciled, and Franklin virtually excluded William from his will.

The story of the publication of Franklin's *Autobiography* is too complicated to disentangle completely here. But a few of the details are quite interesting and useful. The story begins in 1789, one year before his death, when Franklin asked one of his grandsons to make two copies of his manuscript, one of which was sent to England (ultimately lost), the other to a friend in France, Louis Guillaume Le Veillard. Another grandson, William Temple Franklin, inherited Franklin's books, manuscripts, and papers, including a manuscript of the *Autobiography* in Franklin's handwriting. In 1791, a translation of Part One of the *Autobiography* mysteriously appeared in France (Le Veillard swore it did not come from him). In 1793, this French version was translated into English and published in England, and, later, in America. Temple Franklin brought out a supposedly reliable version in 1818; but having traded Franklin's messy original manuscript to Le Veillard for his cleaner (though less reliable) copied text, the grandson published a version with important departures from what Franklin had written. That original manuscript was in the possession of descendants of the unfortunate Le Veillard, guillotined in 1794 during the Reign of Terror in revolutionary France. John Bigelow, American minister to France in 1865–66, located and bought it, and prepared a new edition of the *Autobiography* based on it, published in 1868. It was this version that Albert Henry Smyth used for his edition of *The Writings of Benjamin Franklin* (1905–07), following the authentic text but eliminating the capricious capitalization. Parts One and Two of the *Autobiography* presented here are based on the Bigelow-Smyth text, checked against the version prepared in

1964 by Leonard W. Labaree and others for the on-going Yale edition of *The Papers of Benjamin Franklin* (1959–). Spelling, punctuation, and contractions have been minimally modernized to assure readability without distortion of the authentic text.

❧

PART ONE

I [1706–1718: ANCESTRAL ORIGINS, EARLY EDUCATION, FIRST EMPLOYMENT]

TWYFORD, *at the Bishop of St. Asaph's,* 1771.

DEAR SON, I have ever had a pleasure in obtaining any little anecdotes of my ancestors. You may remember the inquiries I made among the remains[1] of my relations when you were with me in England, and the journey I took for that purpose.[2] Now imagining it may be equally agreeable to you to know the circumstances of *my* life, many of which you are yet unacquainted with, and expecting a week's uninterrupted leisure in my present country retirement, I sit down to write them for you. To which I have besides some other inducements. Having emerged from the poverty and obscurity in which I was born and bred, to a state of affluence and some degree of reputation in the world, and having gone so far through life with a considerable share of felicity, the conducing means I made use of, which with the blessing of God so well succeeded, my posterity may like to know, as they may find some of them suitable to their own situations, and therefore fit to be imitated.

That felicity, when I reflected on it, has induced me sometimes to say that were it offered to my choice, I should have no objection to a repetition of the same life from its beginning, only asking the advantage authors have in a second edition to correct some faults of the first. So would I, if I might, besides correcting the faults, change some sinister accidents and events of it for others more favorable. But though this were denied, I should still accept the offer. However, since such a repetition is not to be expected, the next thing most like living one's life over again seems to be a *recollection* of that life, and to make that recollection as durable as possible, the putting it down in writing.

Hereby, too, I shall indulge the inclination so natural in old men, to be talking of themselves and their own past actions, and I shall indulge it without being troublesome to others, who through respect to age might think themselves obliged to give me a hearing, since this may be read or not as any one pleases. And lastly (I may as well confess it, since my denial of it will be believed by nobody), perhaps I shall a good deal gratify my own *vanity*. Indeed, I scarce ever heard or saw the introductory words, "*Without vanity I may say,*" etc., but some vain thing immediately followed. Most people dislike vanity in others, whatever share they have of it themselves; but I give it fair quarter wherever I meet with it, being persuaded that it is often productive of good to the possessor and to others that are within his sphere of action; and therefore, in many cases, it would not be quite absurd if a man were to thank God for his vanity among the other comforts of life.

And now I speak of thanking God, I desire with all humility to acknowledge that I owe the mentioned happiness of my past life to His kind providence, which lead me to the means I used and gave them success. My belief of this induces me to *hope*, though I must not *presume*, that the same goodness will still be exercised

---

[1] I.e., living relatives.
[2] Franklin and his son, on a tour of England in 1758, visited the Franklin ancestral home.

towards me in continuing that happiness, or in enabling me to bear a fatal reverse, which I may experience as others have done, the complexion of my future fortune being known to Him only and in whose power it is to bless to us even our afflictions.

The notes one of my uncles (who had the same kind of curiosity in collecting family anecdotes) once put into my hands furnished me with several particulars relating to our ancestors. From these notes I learned that the family had lived in the same village, Ecton, in Northamptonshire,[3] for three hundred years, and how much longer he knew not (perhaps from the time when the name *Franklin,* that before was the name of an order of people,[4] was assumed by them as a surname when others took surnames all over the kingdom),[5] on a freehold of about thirty acres, aided by the smith's business, which had continued in the family till his time, the eldest son being always bred to that business. A custom which he and my father both followed as to their eldest sons. When I searched the register at Ecton, I found an account of their births, marriages, and burials from the year 1555 only, there being no register kept in that parish at any time preceding. By that register I perceived that I was the youngest son of the youngest son for five generations back.

My grandfather Thomas, who was born in 1598, lived at Ecton till he grew too old to follow business longer, when he went to live with his son John, a dyer at Banbury, in Oxfordshire, with whom my father served an apprenticeship. There my grandfather died and lies buried. We saw his gravestone in 1758. His eldest son Thomas lived in the house at Ecton, and left it with the land to his only child, a daughter, who with her husband, one Fisher of Wellingborough, sold it to Mr. Isted, now lord of the manor there. My grandfather had four sons that grew up, viz. Thomas, John, Benjamin, and Josiah. I will give you what account I can of them at this distance from my papers, and if they are not lost in my absence, you will among them find many more particulars.

Thomas was bred a smith under his father, but being ingenious and encouraged in learning (as all his brothers likewise were) by an Esquire Palmer, then the principal gentleman in that parish, he qualified himself for the business of scrivener;[6] became a considerable man in the county affairs; was a chief mover of all public-spirited undertakings for the county or town of Northampton and his own village, of which many instances were told us at Ecton; and he was much taken notice of and patronized by the then Lord Halifax. He died in 1702, January 6, old style, just four years to a day before I was born.[7] The account we received of his life and character from some old people at Ecton, I remember, struck you as something extraordinary, from its similarity to what you knew of mine. "Had he died on the same day," you said, "one might have supposed a transmigration."[8]

John was bred a dyer, I believe, of woolens. Benjamin was bred a silk dyer, serving an apprenticeship at London. He was an ingenious man. I remember him well, for when I was a boy he came over to my father in Boston and lived in the house with us some years. He lived to a great age. His grandson, Samuel Franklin, now lives in Boston. He left behind him two quarto volumes, MS. of his own poetry, consisting of little occasional pieces addressed to his friends and relations, of

---

[3]Some fifty miles north of London.

[4]In feudal times, a franklin was a freeholder, a landowner free but not of noble birth holding land in the freest tenure.

[5]"Here a note," Franklin's note, but none was found with the manuscript. Temple Franklin's edition printed one, probably Franklin's, which quotes a fifteenth-century legal authority proving *Franklin* was the name of a social rank in England, and lines from Chaucer's *Canterbury Tales* describing the "country gentleman, a *Franklin.*"

[6]Copier of legal documents.

[7]In 1752, England and her colonies dropped the "old style" Julian calendar and adopted the new style Gregorian calendar, losing eleven days in the process and changing the beginning of the year from March 25 to January 1. Thus Franklin's birthday of January 6, 1705/06, old style, became January 17, 1706, with the new calendar.

[8]The soul's passing into another body after death; metempsychosis.

which the following, sent to me, is a specimen.[9] He had formed a shorthand of his own, which he taught me, but never practicing it, I have now forgot it. I was named after this uncle, there being a particular affection between him and my father. He was very pious, a great attender of sermons of the best preachers, which he took down in his shorthand, and had with him many volumes of them. He was also much of a politician, too much, perhaps, for his station. There fell lately into my hands, in London, a collection he had made of all the principal pamphlets relating to public affairs, from 1641 to 1717. Many of the volumes are wanting, as appears by the numbering, but there still remain eight volumes in folio, and twenty-four in quarto and in octavo.[10] A dealer in old books met with them and knowing me by my sometimes buying of him, he brought them to me. It seems my uncle must have left them here when he went to America, which was above fifty years since. There are many of his notes in the margins.

This obscure family of ours was early in the Reformation and continued Protestants through the reign of Queen Mary, when they were sometimes in danger of trouble on account of their zeal against popery.[11] They had got an English Bible, and to conceal and secure it, it was fastened open with tapes under and within the frame of a joint stool.[12] When my great-great-grandfather read in it to his family, he turned up the joint stool upon his knees, turning over the leaves then under the tapes. One of the children stood at the door to give notice if he saw the apparitor[13] coming, who was an officer of the spiritual court. In that case the stool was turned down again upon its feet, when the Bible remained concealed under it as before. This anecdote I had from my uncle Benjamin. The family continued all of the Church of England till about the end of Charles the Second's reign,[14] when some of the ministers that had been outed for non-conformity, holding conventicles[15] in Northamptonshire, Benjamin and Josiah adhered to them, and so continued all their lives. The rest of the family remained with the Episcopal Church.

Josiah, my father, married young, and carried his wife with three children unto New England about 1682.[16] The conventicles having been forbidden by law and frequently disturbed induced some considerable men of his acquaintance to remove to that country, and he was prevailed with to accompany them thither, where they expected to enjoy their mode of religion with freedom. By the same wife he had four children more born there, and by a second wife ten more, in all seventeen, of which I remember thirteen sitting at one time at his table, who all grew up to be men and women, and married. I was the youngest son, and the youngest child but two, and was born in Boston, New England.

My mother, the second wife, was Abiah Folger, daughter of Peter Folger, one of the first settlers of New England, of whom honorable mention is made by Cotton Mather, in his church history of that country, entitled *Magnalia Christi Americana,* as "a godly, learned Englishman," if I remember the words rightly. I have heard that he wrote sundry small occasional pieces, but only one of them was printed, which I saw now many years since. It was written in 1675, in the homespun verse of that time and people, and addressed to those then concerned in the government there. It was in favor of liberty of conscience and in behalf of the Baptists, Quakers, and other sectaries that had been under persecution, ascribing the Indian wars and other distresses that had befallen the country to that persecu-

[9]"Here insert it," Franklin's note, but no example is found with the manuscript. The Le Veillard translation contains two of Uncle Benjamin's poems, reprinted in Labaree, *Papers* I.

[10]Folio, quarto, and octavo indicate volume and page size of books. The large sheets of printer's paper were folded once to make two leaves or four pages for folios, twice to make four leaves or eight pages for quartos, and four times to make eight leaves or sixteen pages for octavos.

[11]Queen Mary, known as "Bloody Mary," tried to reinstate Roman Catholicism in England during her reign (1553–58), persecuting many Protestants in the attempt.

[12]A wooden stool whose parts are held together by pegged joints.

[13]Officer of an ecclesiastical court, charged with finding and punishing heretics.

[14]Charles II (r. 1660–85).

[15]Illegal meetings held by ministers ousted from the Church of England for not conforming to its doctrine.

[16]Really 1683.

tion, as so many judgments of God to punish so heinous an offense, and exhorting a repeal of those uncharitable laws. The whole appeared to me as written with a good deal of decent plainness and manly freedom. The six concluding lines I remember, though I have forgotten the two first of the stanza; but the purport of them was that his censures proceeded from *goodwill* and, therefore, he would be known as the author,

> because to be a libeler (says he)
>   I hate it with my heart.
> From Sherburne town[17] where now I dwell,
>   My name I do put here,
> Without offense, your real friend,
>   It is Peter Folgier.[18]

My elder brothers were all put apprentices to different trades. I was put to the grammar school at eight years of age, my father intending to devote me, as the tithe[19] of his sons, to the service of the Church. My early readiness in learning to read (which must have been very early, as I do not remember when I could not read) and the opinion of all his friends that I should certainly make a good scholar encouraged him in this purpose of his. My uncle Benjamin, too, approved of it, and proposed to give me all his shorthand volumes of sermons, I suppose as a stock to set up with, if I would learn his character.[20] I continued, however, at the grammar school not quite one year, though in that time I had risen gradually from the middle of the class of that year to be the head of it, and farther was removed into the next class above it, in order to go with that into the third at the end of the year. But my father, in the meantime, from a view of the expense of a college education, which having so large a family he could not well afford, and the mean[21] living many so educated were afterwards able to obtain—reasons that he gave to his friends in my hearing—altered his first intention, took me from the grammar school, and sent me to a school for writing and arithmetic, kept by a then famous man, Mr. George Brownell, very successful in his profession generally, and that by mild, encouraging methods. Under him I acquired fair writing pretty soon, but I failed in the arithmetic, and made no progress in it.

At ten years old I was taken home to assist my father in his business, which was that of a tallow chandler and soap boiler;[22] a business he was not bred to, but had assumed on his arrival in New England, and on finding his dying trade would not maintain his family, being in little request. Accordingly, I was employed in cutting wick for the candles, filling the dipping mold and the molds for cast candles, attending the shop, going of errands, etc.

I disliked the trade, and had a strong inclination for the sea, but my father declared against it; however, living near the water, I was much in and about it, learned early to swim well, and to manage boats; and when in a boat or canoe with other boys, I was commonly allowed to govern, especially in any case of difficulty; and upon other occasions I was generally a leader among the boys, and sometimes led them into scrapes, of which I will mention one instance, as it shows an early projecting public spirit, though not then justly conducted.

There was a salt marsh that bounded part of the mill pond, on the edge of which, at high water, we used to stand to fish for minnows. By much trampling, we had made it a mere quagmire. My proposal was to build a wharf there fit for us to stand upon, and I showed my comrades a large heap of stones, which were

---

[17]"In the Island of Nantucket" (Franklin's note).
[18]*A Looking Glass for the Times, or the Former Spirit of New England Revived in This Generation* (1676), by Peter Folger (1617–1690).

[19]Tenth.
[20]Shorthand system.
[21]Meager.
[22]Candle and soap maker.

intended for a new house near the marsh, and which would very well suit our purpose. Accordingly, in the evening, when the workmen were gone, I assembled a number of my playfellows, and working with them diligently like so many emmets,[23] sometimes two or three to a stone, we brought them all away and built our little wharf. The next morning the workmen were surprised at missing the stones, which were found in our wharf. Inquiry was made after the removers; we were discovered and complained of; several of us were corrected by our fathers; and though I pleaded the usefulness of the work, mine convinced me that nothing was useful which was not honest.

I think you may like to know something of his person and character. He had an excellent constitution of body, was of middle stature, but well set, and very strong. He was ingenious, could draw prettily, was skilled a little in music, and had a clear pleasing voice, so that when he played psalm tunes on his violin and sung withal, as he sometimes did in an evening after the business of the day was over, it was extremely agreeable to hear. He had a mechanical genius too, and on occasion was very handy in the use of other tradesmen's tools. But his great excellence lay in a sound understanding and solid judgment in prudential matters, both in private and public affairs. In the latter, indeed, he was never employed, the numerous family he had to educate and the straitness of his circumstances keeping him close to his trade; but I remember well his being frequently visited by leading people, who consulted him for his opinion in affairs of the town or of the church he belonged to and showed a good deal of respect for his judgment and advice. He was also much consulted by private persons about their affairs when any difficulty occurred, and frequently chosen an arbitrator between contending parties. At his table he liked to have, as often as he could, some sensible friend or neighbor to converse with, and always took care to start some ingenious or useful topic for discourse, which might tend to improve the minds of his children. By this means he turned our attention to what was good, just, and prudent in the conduct of life; and little or no notice was ever taken of what related to the victuals on the table, whether it was well or ill dressed, in or out of season, of good or bad flavor, preferable or inferior to this or that other thing of the kind, so that I was brought up in such a perfect inattention to those matters as to be quite indifferent what kind of food was set before me and so unobservant of it that to this day if I am asked, I can scarce tell a few hours after dinner what I dined upon. This has been a convenience to me in travelling, where my companions have been sometimes very unhappy for want of a suitable gratification of their more delicate, because better instructed, tastes and appetites.

My mother had likewise an excellent constitution. She suckled all her ten children. I never knew either my father or mother to have any sickness but that of which they died, he at eighty-nine, and she at eighty-five years of age. They lie buried together at Boston, where I some years since placed a marble stone over their grave with this inscription:

JOSIAH FRANKLIN
And
ABIAH his wife
Lie here interred.
They lived lovingly together in wedlock
Fifty-five years.
Without an estate, or any gainful employment,
By constant labor and industry,
With God's blessing,

---

[23]Ants.

> They maintained a large family
> Comfortably,
> And brought up thirteen children
> And seven grandchildren
> Reputably.
> From this instance, reader,
> Be encouraged to diligence in thy calling,
> And distrust not Providence.
> He was a pious and prudent man,
> She, a discreet and virtuous woman.
> Their youngest son,
> In filial regard to their memory,
> Places this stone.
> J. F. born 1655, died 1744, Ætat 89.
> A. F. born 1667, died 1752,——85.

By my rambling digressions I perceive myself to be grown old. I used to write more methodically. But one does not dress for private company as for a public ball. 'Tis perhaps only negligence.

To return. I continued thus employed in my father's business for two years, that is, till I was twelve years old; and my brother John, who was bred to that business, having left my father, married, and set up for himself at Rhode Island, there was all appearance that I was destined to supply his place, and be a tallow chandler. But my dislike to the trade continuing, my father was under apprehensions that if he did not find one for me more agreeable, I should break away and get to sea, as his son Josiah had done, to his great vexation. He therefore sometimes took me to walk with him, and see joiners, bricklayers, turners, braziers,[24] etc., at their work, that he might observe my inclination, and endeavor to fix it on some trade or other on land. It has ever since been a pleasure to me to see good workmen handle their tools; and it has been useful to me, having learnt so much by it as to be able to do little jobs myself in my house when a workman could not readily be got, and to construct little machines for my experiments, while the intention of making the experiment was fresh and warm in my mind. My father at last fixed upon the cutler's trade,[25] and my uncle Benjamin's son Samuel, who was bred to that business in London, being about that time established in Boston, I was sent to be with him some time on liking. But his expectations of a fee with me displeasing my father, I was taken home again.

II [1718–1723: Apprenticed as Printer, Learning to Write, Differences with Brother]

From a child I was fond of reading, and all the little money that came into my hands was ever laid out in books. Pleased with the *Pilgrim's Progress*, my first collection was of John Bunyan's works in separate little volumes.[1] I afterwards sold them to enable me to buy R. Burton's Historical Collections; they were small chapmen's books, and cheap, 40 or 50 in all.[2] My father's little library consisted chiefly of books in polemic divinity, most of which I read and have since often regretted that at a time when I had such a thirst for knowledge, more proper books had not fallen in my way, since it was now resolved I should not be a clergyman. Plutarch's

---

[24]Woodworkers, bricklayers, lathe workers, brass workers.
[25]Making, repairing, selling, and sharpening knives and cutting tools.
[1]John Bunyan (1628–1688), English Puritan preacher, author of *Pilgrim's Progress* (1678).

[2]R. Burton is the pen name of Nathaniel Crouch, who wrote simplified stories of English history sold as "penny books" by peddlers (chapmen).

Lives there was in which I read abundantly, and I still think that time spent to great advantage.[3] There was also a book of Defoe's, called an *Essay on Projects,* and another of Dr. Mather's, called *Essays to Do Good,* which perhaps gave me a turn of thinking that had an influence on some of the principal future events of my life.[4]

This bookish inclination at length determined my father to make me a printer, though he had already one son (James) of that profession. In 1717 my brother James returned from England with a press and letters to set up his business in Boston. I liked it much better than that of my father, but still had a hankering for the sea. To prevent the apprehended effect of such an inclination, my father was impatient to have me bound to my brother. I stood out some time, but at last was persuaded, and signed the indentures[5] when I was yet but twelve years old. I was to serve as an apprentice till I was twenty-one years of age, only I was to be allowed journeyman's[6] wages during the last year. In a little time I made great proficiency in the business and became a useful hand to my brother. I now had access to better books. An acquaintance with the apprentices of booksellers enabled me sometimes to borrow a small one, which I was careful to return soon and clean. Often I sat up in my room reading the greatest part of the night, when the book was borrowed in the evening and to be returned early in the morning, lest it should be missed or wanted.

And after some time an ingenious tradesman, Mr. Matthew Adams, who had a pretty collection of books, and who frequented our printing-house, took notice of me, invited me to his library, and very kindly lent me such books as I chose to read. I now took a fancy to poetry, and made some little pieces. My brother, thinking it might turn to account, encouraged me and put me on composing occasional ballads. One was called *The Lighthouse Tragedy,* and contained an account of the drowning of Captain Worthilake with his two daughters; the other was a sailor song, on the taking of *Teach* or Blackbeard, the pirate.[7] They were wretched stuff, in the Grubstreet-ballad style,[8] and when they were printed he sent me about the town to sell them. The first sold wonderfully, the event being recent, having made a great noise. This flattered my vanity. But my father discouraged me by ridiculing my performances and telling me verse-makers were generally beggars; so I escaped being a poet, most probably a very bad one. But as prose writing has been of great use to me in the course of my life, and was a principal means of my advancement, I shall tell you how, in such a situation, I acquired what little ability I have in that way.

There was another bookish lad in the town, John Collins by name, with whom I was intimately acquainted. We sometimes disputed, and very fond we were of argument, and very desirous of confuting one another, which disputatious turn, by the way, is apt to become a very bad habit, making people often extremely disagreeable in company by the contradiction that is necessary to bring it into practice; and thence, besides souring and spoiling the conversation, is productive of disgusts and perhaps enmities where you may have occasion for friendship. I had caught it by reading my father's books of dispute about religion. Persons of good sense, I have since observed, seldom fall into it, except lawyers, university men, and men of all sorts that have been bred at Edinborough.

---

[3]Plutarch (c. 46–c. 120), Greek author of *Parallel Lives,* pairing biographies of eminent Greeks and Romans.

[4]Daniel Defoe (1659–1731), English journalist and novelist, suggested social and economic reforms in *An Essay upon Projects* (1697); Cotton Mather (1663–1728), author of *Bonifacius. An Essay Upon the Good, that is to be Devised and Designed, by those Who Desire . . . to Do Good While they Live* (1710).

[5]Contract binding him to serve his brother James Franklin (1697–1735) for nine years.

[6]One who has learned his trade and is paid for each day's work.

[7]On November 3, 1718, the lighthouse keeper on Beacon Island, George Worthylake, and his wife and daughter were drowned; on November 22, 1718, Edward Teach, a famous pirate known as "Blackbeard," was killed off North Carolina.

[8]Hack work; Grub Street in London, where writers and literary hacks struggled to make a living.

A question was once, somehow or other, started between Collins and me of the propriety of educating the female sex in learning, and their abilities for study. He was of opinion that it was improper, and that they were naturally unequal to it. I took the contrary side, perhaps a little for dispute's sake. He was naturally more eloquent, had a ready plenty of words, and sometimes, as I thought, bore me down more by his fluency than by the strength of his reasons. As we parted without settling the point and were not to see one another again for some time, I sat down to put my arguments in writing, which I copied fair and sent to him. He answered and I replied. Three or four letters of a side had passed, when my father happened to find my papers and read them. Without entering into the discussion, he took occasion to talk to me about the manner of my writing, observed that though I had the advantage of my antagonist in correct spelling and pointing[9] (which I owed to the printing house), I fell far short in elegance of expression, in method, and in perspicuity, of which he convinced me by several instances. I saw the justice of his remarks, and thence grew more attentive to the *manner* in writing, and determined to endeavor at improvement.

About this time I met with an odd volume of the *Spectator*.[10] It was the third. I had never before seen any of them. I bought it, read it over and over, and was much delighted with it. I thought the writing excellent, and wished, if possible, to imitate it. With that view I took some of the papers, and, making short hints of the sentiment in each sentence, laid them by a few days, and then, without looking at the book, tried to complete the papers again by expressing each hinted sentiment at length, and as fully as it had been expressed before, in any suitable words that should come to hand.

Then I compared my *Spectator* with the original, discovered some of my faults, and corrected them. But I found I wanted a stock of words, or a readiness in recollecting and using them, which I thought I should have acquired before that time if I had gone on making verses, since the continual occasion for words of the same import, but of different length to suit the measure, or of different sound for the rhyme, would have laid me under a constant necessity of searching for variety and also have tended to fix that variety in my mind, and make me master of it. Therefore, I took some of the tales and turned them into verse; and, after a time, when I had pretty well forgotten the prose, turned them back again. I also sometimes jumbled my collections of hints into confusion, and after some weeks endeavored to reduce them into the best order, before I began to form the full sentences and complete the paper. This was to teach me method in the arrangement of thoughts. By comparing my work afterwards with the original, I discovered many faults and amended them; but I sometimes had the pleasure of fancying that in certain particulars of small import, I had been lucky enough to improve the method or the language, and this encouraged me to think I might possibly in time come to be a tolerable English writer, of which I was extremely ambitious.

My time for these exercises and for reading was at night, after work, or before work began in the morning, or on Sundays, when I contrived to be in the printing house alone, evading as much as I could the common attendance on public worship which my father used to exact of me when I was under his care, and which indeed I still thought a duty, though I could not, as it seemed to me, afford the time to practice it.

When about 16 years of age I happened to meet with a book written by one Tryon recommending a vegetable diet.[11] I determined to go into it. My brother,

---

[9]Punctuation.

[10]An English paper with essays by Joseph Addison and Richard Steele published daily from March 1711 to December 1712. Dr. Johnson characterized the style as "familiar, but not coarse, and elegant but not ostentatious."

[11]Thomas Tryon (1634–1703), English author of *The Way to Health, Long Life and Happiness, or a Discourse of Temperance* (1682, 1691).

being yet unmarried, did not keep house, but boarded himself and his apprentices in another family. My refusing to eat flesh occasioned an inconveniency, and I was frequently chid for my singularity. I made myself acquainted with Tryon's manner of preparing some of his dishes, such as boiling potatoes or rice, making hasty pudding, and a few others, and then proposed to my brother that if he would give me, weekly, half the money he paid for my board, I would board myself. He instantly agreed to it, and I presently found that I could save half what he paid me. This was an additional fund for buying books. But I had another advantage in it. My brother and the rest going from the printing house to their meals, I remained there alone, and, despatching presently my light repast (which often was no more than a biscuit or a slice of bread, a handful of raisins or a tart from the pastry cook's, and a glass of water), had the rest of the time till their return for study, in which I made the greater progress, from that greater clearness of head and quicker apprehension which usually attend temperance in eating and drinking.

And now it was that, being on some occasion made ashamed of my ignorance in figures, which I had twice failed in learning when at school, I took Cocker's book of arithmetic,[12] and went through the whole by myself with great ease. I also read Seller's and Sturmy's books of navigation,[13] and became acquainted with the little geometry they contain, but never proceeded far in that science. And I read about this time Locke on *Human Understanding,* and the *Art of Thinking,* by Messrs. du Port Royal.[14]

While I was intent on improving my language, I met with an English grammar (I think it was Greenwood's),[15] at the end of which there were two little sketches of the arts of rhetoric and logic, the latter finishing with a specimen of a dispute in the Socratic method. And soon after I procured Xenophon's *Memorable Things of Socrates,* wherein there are many instances of the same method.[16] I was charmed with it, adopted it, dropped my abrupt contradiction and positive argumentation and put on the humble inquirer and doubter. And being then, from reading Shaftesbury and Collins,[17] become a real doubter in many points of our religious doctrine, I found this method safest for myself and very embarrassing to those against whom I used it; therefore I took a delight in it, practiced it continually, and grew very artful and expert in drawing people, even of superior knowledge, into concessions, the consequences of which they did not foresee, entangling them in difficulties out of which they could not extricate themselves, and so obtaining victories that neither myself nor my cause always deserved.

I continued this method some few years, but gradually left it, retaining only the habit of expressing myself in terms of modest diffidence, never using, when I advanced anything that may possibly be disputed, the words *certainly, undoubtedly,* or any others that give the air of positiveness to an opinion; but rather say, *I conceive* or *I apprehend a thing to be so and so; it appears to me,* or *I should think it so or so, for such and such reasons;* or *I imagine it to be so;* or *it is so, if I am not mistaken.* This habit, I believe, has been of great advantage to me when I have had occasion to inculcate my opinions and persuade men into measures that I have been from time to time engaged in promoting. And, as the chief ends of conversation are to *inform* or to be *informed,* to *please* or to *persuade,* I wish well-meaning, sensible men would not lessen their power of doing good by a positive, assuming manner that seldom fails

---

[12]Edward Cocker (1631–1675), English author of many books of arithmetic.
[13]John Seller, *An Epitome of the Art of Navigation* (1681); Samuel Sturmy, *The Mariner's Magazine; or, Sturmy's Mathematical and Practical Arts* (1669).
[14]John Locke (1632–1704), English philosopher, author of *An Essay Concerning Human Understanding* (1690); Antoine Arnauld and Pierre Nicole, at the Abbey of Port Royal, Paris, *Logic: or the Art of Thinking* (1718), English translation

by John Ozell of the French *La logique ou l'art de penser* (1662).
[15]James Greenwood, *An Essay towards a Practical English Grammar* (1711).
[16]Xenophon, *The Memorable Things of Socrates,* translated by Edward Bysshe (1712).
[17]Anthony Ashley Cooper, third Earl of Shaftesbury (1671–1713), religious skeptic; Anthony Collins (1676–1729), deist.

to disgust, tends to create opposition and to defeat everyone of those purposes for which speech was given us, to wit, giving or receiving information or pleasure. For, if you would *inform,* a positive, dogmatical manner in advancing your sentiments may provoke contradiction and prevent a candid attention. If you wish information and improvement from the knowledge of others, and yet at the same time express yourself as firmly fixed in your present opinions, modest, sensible men, who do not love disputation, will probably leave you undisturbed in the possession of your error. And by such a manner, you can seldom hope to recommend yourself in *pleasing* your hearers, or to persuade those whose concurrence you desire. Pope says, judiciously,

> Men should be taught as if you taught them not,
> And things unknown proposed as things forgot,

farther recommending it to us

> To speak, though sure, with seeming diffidence.[18]

And he might have coupled with this line that which he has coupled with another, I think, less properly,

> For want of modesty is want of sense.

If you ask, why *less properly,* I must repeat the lines,

> Immodest words admit of *no* defense,
> *For* want of modesty is want of sense.[19]

Now, is not *want of sense* (where a man is so unfortunate as to want it) some apology for his *want of modesty?* and would not the lines stand more justly thus?

> Immodest words admit *but this* defense,
> That want of modesty is want of sense.

This, however, I should submit to better judgments.

My brother had, in 1720 or 1721, begun to print a newspaper. It was the second that appeared in America, and was called *The New England Courant.* The only one before it was the *Boston News Letter.*[20] I remember his being dissuaded by some of his friends from the undertaking, as not likely to succeed, one newspaper being, in their judgment, enough for America. At this time (1771) there are not less than five-and-twenty. He went on, however, with the undertaking, and after having worked in composing the types and printing off the sheets, I was employed to carry the papers through the streets to the customers.

He had some ingenious men among his friends, who amused themselves by writing little pieces for this paper, which gained it credit and made it more in demand, and these gentlemen often visited us. Hearing their conversations, and their accounts of the approbation their papers were received with, I was excited to try my hand among them. But, being still a boy, and suspecting that my brother would object to printing anything of mine in his paper if he knew it to be mine, I contrived to disguise my hand and, writing an anonymous paper, I put it in at night under the door of the printing house. It was found in the morning and communicated to his writing friends when they called in as usual. They read it,

---

[18]Alexander Pope, *An Essay on Criticism* (1711), lines 574–75, 567, with minor variations: "should" for "must" (574); "To speak" for "And speak" (567).

[19]Not by Pope, but by Wentworth Dillon, Earl of Roscommon, *Essay on Translated Verse* (1684), lines 113–14. The second line reads: "For want of decency is want of sense."

[20]*The New England Courant,* August 7, 1721, was the fifth newspaper in America. Boston's *Public Occurrences,* which published only one issue on September 25, 1690, was first; *The Boston News Letter,* April 24, 1704, was second; *The Boston Gazette,* December 21, 1719, third; and *The American Weekly Mercury,* Philadelphia, December 22, 1719, fourth.

commented on it in my hearing, and I had the exquisite pleasure of finding it met with their approbation, and that, in their different guesses at the author, none were named but men of some character among us for learning and ingenuity. I suppose now that I was rather lucky in my judges, and that perhaps they were not really so very good ones as I then esteemed them.

Encouraged, however, by this, I wrote and conveyed in the same way to the press several more papers[21] which were equally approved; and I kept my secret till my small fund of sense for such performances was pretty well exhausted, and then I discovered[22] it, when I began to be considered a little more by my brother's acquaintance, and in a manner that did not quite please him, as he thought, probably with reason, that it tended to make me too vain. And perhaps this might be one occasion of the differences that we began to have about this time. Though a brother, he considered himself as my master, and me as his apprentice, and accordingly, expected the same services from me as he would from another, while I thought he demeaned me too much in some he required of me, who from a brother expected more indulgence. Our disputes were often brought before our father, and I fancy I was either generally in the right, or else a better pleader, because the judgment was generally in my favor. But my brother was passionate, and had often beaten me, which I took extremely amiss; and, thinking my apprenticeship very tedious, I was continually wishing for some opportunity of shortening it, which at length offered in a manner unexpected.[23]

One of the pieces in our newspaper on some political point, which I have now forgotten, gave offense to the Assembly. He was taken up, censured, and imprisoned for a month by the speaker's warrant, I suppose because he would not discover his author. I too was taken up and examined before the council; but, though I did not give them any satisfaction, they contented themselves with admonishing me, and dismissed me, considering me, perhaps, as an apprentice who was bound to keep his master's secrets.

During my brother's confinement, which I resented a good deal, notwithstanding our private differences, I had the management of the paper, and I made bold to give our rulers some rubs in it, which my brother took very kindly, while others began to consider me in an unfavorable light, as a young genius that had a turn for libeling and satire. My brother's discharge was accompanied with an order of the House (a very odd one), that "James Franklin should no longer print the paper called the *New England Courant.*"

There was a consultation held in our printing house among his friends what he should do in this case. Some proposed to evade the order by changing the name of the paper; but my brother seeing inconveniences in that, it was finally concluded on as a better way to let it be printed for the future under the name of BENJAMIN FRANKLIN. And to avoid the censure of the Assembly that might fall on him, as still printing it by his apprentice, the contrivance was that my old indenture should be returned to me, with a full discharge on the back of it, to be shown on occasion; but to secure to him the benefit of my service, I was to sign new indentures for the remainder of the term, which were to be kept private. A very flimsy scheme it was; however, it was immediately executed, and the paper went on accordingly under my name for several months.[24]

At length, a fresh difference arising between my brother and me, I took upon

---

[21]The fourteen satiric letters of Silence Dogood, published in the *Courant* April 12 through October 8, 1722.
[22]Revealed.
[23]"I fancy his harsh and tyrannical treatment of me might be a means of impressing me with that aversion to arbitrary power that has stuck to me through my whole life" (Franklin's note).

[24]On June 11, 1722, James Franklin suggested that officials were slow to deal with pirates, and he was imprisoned for a month. Later, he was forbidden to publish the *Courant* without prior censorship. As a result, Benjamin Franklin was listed as the publisher until 1726, long after he had run away from Boston.

me to assert my freedom, presuming that he would not venture to produce the new indentures. It was not fair in me to take this advantage, and this I therefore reckon one of the first errata[25] of my life. But the unfairness of it weighed little with me, when under the impressions of resentment for the blows his passion too often urged him to bestow upon me, though he was otherwise not an ill-natured man. Perhaps I was too saucy and provoking.

When he found I would leave him, he took care to prevent my getting employment in any other printing house of the town, by going round and speaking to every master, who accordingly refused to give me work.

III [1723–1724: JOURNEY TO PHILADELPHIA, EMPLOYMENT BY KEIMER AS PRINTER]

I then thought of going to New York, as the nearest place where there was a printer; and I was rather inclined to leave Boston when I reflected that I had already made myself a little obnoxious to the governing party, and, from the arbitrary proceedings of the Assembly in my brother's case, it was likely I might, if I stayed, soon bring myself into scrapes; and farther, that my indiscrete disputations about religion began to make me pointed at with horror by good people as an infidel or atheist. I determined on the point, but my father now siding with my brother, I was sensible that, if I attempted to go openly, means would be used to prevent me. My friend Collins, therefore, undertook to manage a little for me. He agreed with the captain of a New York sloop for my passage, under the notion of my being a young acquaintance of his that had got a naughty girl with child, whose friends would compel me to marry her, and therefore I could not appear or come away publicly. So I sold some of my books to raise a little money, was taken on board privately, and as we had a fair wind, in three days I found myself in New York, near three hundred miles from home, a boy of but seventeen, without the least recommendation to, or knowledge of, any person in the place, and with very little money in my pocket.

My inclinations for the sea were by this time worn out, or I might now have gratified them. But, having a trade, and supposing myself a pretty good workman, I offered my service to the printer of the place, old Mr. William Bradford,[1] who had been the first printer in Pennsylvania, but removed from thence upon the quarrel of George Keith. He could give me no employment, having little to do, and help enough already. "But," says he, "My son at Philadelphia has lately lost his principal hand, Aquila Rose, by death. If you go thither, I believe he may employ you." Philadelphia was one hundred miles further. I set out, however, in a boat for Amboy,[2] leaving my chest and things to follow me round by sea.

In crossing the bay, we met with a squall that tore our rotten sails to pieces, prevented our getting into the Kill,[3] and drove us upon Long Island. In our way, a drunken Dutchman, who was a passenger too, fell overboard; when he was sinking, I reached through the water to his shock pate,[4] and drew him up, so that we got him in again. His ducking sobered him a little, and he went to sleep, taking first out of his pocket a book, which he desired I would dry for him. It proved to be my old favorite author, Bunyan's *Pilgrim's Progress*, in Dutch, finely printed on good paper, with copper cuts, a dress better than I had ever seen it wear in its own language. I have since found that it has been translated into most of the lan-

---

[25]Printer's word for errors.
[1]William Bradford (1663–1752), famed pioneer printer, was tried but not convicted in 1692 for printing the writings of the schismatic Quaker George Keith (1638–1716). In 1693, he moved to New York and became the royal printer, founding New York's first newspaper the *Gazette* in 1725. His son Andrew Bradford (1686–1742) published

the first Pennsylvania newspaper in 1719 and eventually became Franklin's competitor in Philadelphia.
[2]Perth Amboy, New Jersey.
[3]A narrow channel between Staten Island, New York, and New Jersey.
[4]Shaggy hair.

guages of Europe, and suppose it has been more generally read than any other book, except perhaps the Bible. Honest John was the first that I know of who mixed narration and dialogue, a method of writing very engaging to the reader, who in the most interesting parts finds himself, as it were, brought into the company and present at the discourse. Defoe in his *Crusoe*, his *Moll Flanders, Religious Courtship, Family Instructor*, and other pieces, has imitated it with success. And Richardson has done the same in his *Pamela*, etc.[5]

When we drew near the island, we found it was at a place where there could be no landing, there being a great surf on the stony beach. So we dropped anchor, and swung round towards the shore. Some people came down to the water edge and hallowed to us, as we did to them. But the wind was so high, and the surf so loud, that we could not hear so as to understand each other. There were canoes on the shore, and we made signs, and hallowed that they should fetch us, but they either did not understand us, or thought it impracticable. So they went away, and night coming on, we had no remedy but to wait till the wind should abate; and in the mean time the boatman and I concluded to sleep if we could; and so crowded into the scuttle, with the Dutchman, who was still wet, and the spray beating over the head of our boat, leaked through to us, so that we were soon almost as wet as he. In this manner we lay all night, with very little rest. But, the wind abating the next day, we made a shift to reach Amboy before night, having been thirty hours on the water without victuals, or any drink but a bottle of filthy rum, the water we sailed on being salt.

In the evening I found myself very feverish, and went in to bed. But, having read somewhere that cold water drank plentifully was good for a fever, I followed the prescription, sweat plentifully most of the night, my fever left me, and in the morning, crossing the ferry, I proceeded on my journey on foot, having fifty miles to Burlington,[6] where I was told I should find boats that would carry me the rest of the way to Philadelphia.

It rained very hard all the day; I was thoroughly soaked and by noon a good deal tired, so I stopped at a poor inn, where I stayed all night, beginning now to wish I had never left home. I cut so miserable a figure, too, that I found by the questions asked me I was suspected to be some runaway servant, and in danger of being taken up on that suspicion. However, I proceeded the next day and got in the evening to an inn, within eight or ten miles of Burlington, kept by one Dr. Brown.[7] He entered into conversation with me while I took some refreshment, and, finding I had read a little, became very sociable and friendly. Our acquaintance continued as long as he lived. He had been, I imagine, an itinerant doctor, for there was no town in England, or country in Europe, of which he could not give a very particular account. He had some letters,[8] and was ingenious, but much of an unbeliever, and wickedly undertook, some years after, to travesty the Bible in doggerel verse, as Cotton had done Virgil.[9] By this means he set many of the facts in a very ridiculous light, and might have hurt weak minds if his work had been published; but it never was.

At his house I lay that night, and the next morning reached Burlington, but had the mortification to find that the regular boats were gone a little before my coming, and no other expected to go before Tuesday, this being Saturday; wherefore I returned to an old woman in the town, of whom I had bought gingerbread

---

[5]Daniel Defoe's novels, *Robinson Crusoe* (1719), *Moll Flanders* (1722), and didactic works, *Religious Courtship* (1722), *The Family Instructor* (1715–18); Samuel Richardson (1689–1761), English novelist, author of *Pamela, or Virtue Rewarded* (1740). In 1744 Franklin reprinted *Pamela*, the first novel published in America.
[6]In western New Jersey on the Delaware River, eighteen miles northeast of Philadelphia.

[7]John Browne (c. 1667–1737), physician, innkeeper, and colorful freethinker.
[8]Acquaintance with literature, learning.
[9]Charles Cotton (1630–1687), English poet, wrote the burlesque poem, *Scarronides, or the First Book of Virgil Travestie* (1664).

to eat on the water, and asked her advice. She invited me to lodge at her house till a passage by water should offer; and being tired with my foot travelling, I accepted the invitation. She understanding I was a printer, would have had me stay at that town and follow my business, being ignorant of the stock necessary to begin with. She was very hospitable, gave me a dinner of ox-cheek with great good will, accepting only of a pot of ale in return. And I thought myself fixed till Tuesday should come. However, walking in the evening by the side of the river, a boat came by, which I found was going towards Philadelphia, with several people in her. They took me in, and, as there was no wind, we rowed all the way; and about midnight, not having yet seen the city, some of the company were confident we must have passed it and would row no farther; the others knew not where we were; so we put toward the shore, got into a creek, landed near an old fence, with the rails of which we made a fire, the night being cold, in October, and there we remained till daylight. Then one of the company knew the place to be Cooper's Creek, a little above Philadelphia, which we saw as soon as we got out of the creek, and arrived there about eight or nine o'clock on the Sunday morning, and landed at the Market Street wharf.[10]

I have been the more particular in this description of my journey, and shall be so of my first entry into that city, that you may in your mind compare such unlikely beginnings with the figure I have since made there. I was in my working dress, my best clothes being to come round by sea. I was dirty from my journey; my pockets were stuffed out with shirts and stockings; I knew no soul nor where to look for lodging. I was fatigued with travelling, rowing, and want of rest. I was very hungry, and my whole stock of cash consisted of a Dutch dollar and about a shilling in copper. The latter I gave the people of the boat for my passage, who at first refused it on account of my rowing; but I insisted on their taking it, a man being sometimes more generous when he has but a little money than when he has plenty, perhaps through fear of being thought to have but little.

Then I walked up the street, gazing about, till near the market house I met a boy with bread. I had made many a meal on bread, and, inquiring where he got it, I went immediately to the baker's he directed me to, in Second Street, and asked for biscuit, intending such as we had in Boston; but they, it seems, were not made in Philadelphia. Then I asked for a three-penny loaf, and was told they had none such. So not considering or knowing the difference of money, and the greater cheapness nor the names of his bread, I bade him give me three-penny worth of any sort. He gave me, accordingly, three great puffy rolls. I was surprised at the quantity, but took it, and, having no room in my pockets, walked off with a roll under each arm, and eating the other. Thus I went up Market Street as far as Fourth Street, passing by the door of Mr. Read, my future wife's father, when she, standing at the door, saw me, and thought I made, as I certainly did, a most awkward, ridiculous appearance. Then I turned and went down Chestnut Street and part of Walnut Street, eating my roll all the way, and, coming round, found myself again at Market Street wharf, near the boat I came in, to which I went for a draught of the river water; and, being filled with one of my rolls, gave the other two to a woman and her child that came down the river in the boat with us and were waiting to go farther.

Thus refreshed, I walked again up the street, which by this time had many clean-dressed people in it, who were all walking the same way. I joined them, and thereby was led into the great meetinghouse of the Quakers near the market. I sat down among them, and, after looking round awhile and hearing nothing said, being very drowsy through labor and want of rest the preceding night, I fell fast

---

[10]In October 1723, date unknown.

asleep, and continued so till the meeting broke up, when one was kind enough to rouse me. This was, therefore, the first house I was in, or slept in, in Philadelphia.

Walking down again toward the river and looking in the faces of people, I met a young Quaker man, whose countenance I liked, and, accosting him, requested he would tell me where a stranger could get lodging. We were then near the sign of the Three Mariners. "Here," says he, "is one place that entertains strangers, but it is not a reputable house; if thee wilt walk with me, I'll show thee a better." He brought me to the Crooked Billet in Water Street. Here I got a dinner; and, while I was eating it, several sly questions were asked me, as it seemed to be suspected from my youth and appearance that I might be some runaway.

After dinner, my sleepiness returned, and, being shown to a bed, I lay down without undressing, and slept till six in the evening, was called to supper, went to bed again very early, and slept soundly till the next morning. Then I made myself as tidy as I could, and went to Andrew Bradford the printer's. I found in the shop the old man his father, whom I had seen at New York, and who, travelling on horseback, had got to Philadelphia before me. He introduced me to his son, who received me civilly, gave me a breakfast, but told me he did not at present want a hand, being lately supplied with one. But there was another printer in town, lately set up, one Keimer,[11] who, perhaps, might employ me; if not, I should be welcome to lodge at his house, and he would give me a little work to do now and then till fuller business should offer.

The old gentleman said he would go with me to the new printer. And when we found him, "Neighbor," says Bradford, "I have brought to see you a young man of your business; perhaps you may want such a one." He asked me a few questions, put a composing stick[12] in my hand to see how I worked, and then said he would employ me soon, though he had just then nothing for me to do; and, taking old Bradford, whom he had never seen before, to be one of the town's people that had a good will for him, entered into a conversation on his present undertaking and prospects, while Bradford, not discovering[13] that he was the other printer's father, on Keimer's saying he expected soon to get the greatest part of the business into his own hands, drew him on by artful questions, and starting little doubts, to explain all his views, what interest he relied on, and in what manner he intended to proceed. I, who stood by and heard all, saw immediately that one of them was a crafty old sophister, and the other a mere novice. Bradford left me with Keimer, who was greatly surprised when I told him who the old man was.

Keimer's printing-house, I found, consisted of an old shattered press, and one small, worn-out font of English,[14] which he was then using himself, composing an elegy on Aquila Rose, before mentioned, an ingenious young man, of excellent character, much respected in the town, clerk of the Assembly, and a pretty poet. Keimer made verses too, but very indifferently. He could not be said to write them, for his manner was to compose them in the types directly out of his head. So there being no copy, but one pair of cases,[15] and the elegy likely to require all the letter, no one could help him. I endeavored to put his press (which he had not yet used, and of which he understood nothing) into order fit to be worked with; and, promising to come and print off his elegy as soon as he should have got it ready, I returned to Bradford's, who gave me a little job to do for the present, and there I lodged and dieted.[16] A few days after, Keimer sent for me to print off the elegy. And now he had got another pair of cases, and a pamphlet to reprint, on which he set me to work.

[11]Samuel Keimer (*c.* 1688–1742) left London for Philadelphia in 1722.
[12]Shallow tray with adjustable end in which type is set by hand.
[13]Revealing.
[14]Complete set of type in the face and size called English, two points larger than Pica.
[15]Trays of type holding small, "lower case," and capital, "upper case," letters.
[16]Boarded.

These two printers I found poorly qualified for their business. Bradford had not been bred to it, and was very illiterate; and Keimer, though something of a scholar, was a mere compositor,[17] knowing nothing of presswork. He had been one of the French Prophets,[18] and could act their enthusiastic agitations. At this time he did not profess any particular religion, but something of all on occasion; was very ignorant of the world, and had, as I afterward found, a good deal of the knave in his composition. He did not like my lodging at Bradford's while I worked with him. He had a house, indeed, but without furniture, so he could not lodge me; but he got me a lodging at Mr. Read's before mentioned, who was the owner of his house. And, my chest and clothes being come by this time, I made rather a more respectable appearance in the eyes of Miss Read than I had done when she first happened to see me eating my roll in the street.

IV [1724: The Governor's Encouragement, Trip to Boston and Back, Friendships]

I began now to have some acquaintance among the young people of the town that were lovers of reading, with whom I spent my evenings very pleasantly; and gaining money by my industry and frugality, I lived very agreeably, forgetting Boston as much as I could, and not desiring that any there should know where I resided, except my friend Collins, who was in my secret, and kept it when I wrote to him. At length, an incident happened that sent me back again much sooner than I had intended. I had a brother-in-law, Robert Holmes,[1] master of a sloop that traded between Boston and Delaware. He being at Newcastle, forty miles below Philadelphia, heard there of me, and wrote me a letter mentioning the concern of my friends in Boston at my abrupt departure, assuring me of their good will to me, and that every thing would be accommodated to my mind if I would return, to which he exhorted me very earnestly. I wrote an answer to his letter, thanked him for his advice, but stated my reasons for quitting Boston fully and in such a light as to convince him I was not so wrong as he had apprehended.

Sir William Keith,[2] governor of the province, was then at Newcastle, and Captain Holmes, happening to be in company with him when my letter came to hand, spoke to him of me, and showed him the letter. The governor read it, and seemed surprised when he was told my age. He said I appeared a young man of promising parts, and therefore should be encouraged. The printers at Philadelphia were wretched ones, and if I would set up there, he made no doubt I should succeed; for his part, he would procure me the public business and do me every other service in his power. This my brother-in-law afterwards told me in Boston, but I knew as yet nothing of it; when, one day, Keimer and I being at work together near the window, we saw the governor and another gentleman (which proved to be Colonel French,[3] of Newcastle), finely dressed, come directly across the street to our house, and heard them at the door.

Keimer ran down immediately, thinking it a visit to him. But the governor inquired for me, came up, and with a condescension and politeness I had been quite unused to, made me many compliments, desired to be acquainted with me, blamed me kindly for not having made myself known to him when I first came to the place, and would have me away with him to the tavern, where he was going with Colonel French to taste, as he said, some excellent Madeira. I was not a little surprised, and Keimer stared like a pig poisoned. I went, however, with the gov-

---

[17] Typesetter.
[18] French Protestants (Camisards) who had fled to England in 1706, inclined to self-induced trances and apocalyptic prophesies.
[1] Robert Holmes (d. before 1743) was husband of Franklin's sister Mary and captain of a ship in coastal trade.

[2] Sir William Keith (1680-1749) was governor of Pennsylvania from 1717 until 1726.
[3] John French (d. 1728) was a member of the governor's council.

ernor and Colonel French to a tavern at the corner of Third Street, and over the Madeira he proposed my setting up my business, laid before me the probabilities of success, and both he and Colonel French assured me I should have their interest and influence in procuring the public business of both governments. On my doubting whether my father would assist me in it, Sir William said he would give me a letter to him, in which he would state the advantages, and he did not doubt of prevailing with him. So it was concluded I should return to Boston in the first vessel, with the governor's letter recommending me to my father. In the mean time the intention was to be kept a secret, and I went on working with Keimer as usual, the governor sending for me now and then to dine with him, a very great honor I thought it, and conversing with me in the most affable, familiar, and friendly manner imaginable.

About the end of April, 1724, a little vessel offered for Boston. I took leave of Keimer as going to see my friends. The governor gave me an ample letter, saying many flattering things of me to my father, and strongly recommending the project of my setting up at Philadelphia as a thing that must make my fortune. We struck on a shoal in going down the bay and sprung a leak; we had a blustering time at sea and were obliged to pump almost continually, at which I took my turn. We arrived safe, however, at Boston in about a fortnight. I had been absent seven months, and my friends had heard nothing of me, for my brother Holmes was not yet returned, and had not written about me. My unexpected appearance surprised the family; all were, however, very glad to see me, and made me welcome, except my brother. I went to see him at his printing-house. I was better dressed than ever while in his service, having a genteel new suit from head to foot, a watch, and my pockets lined with near five pounds sterling in silver. He received me not very frankly, looked me all over, and turned to his work again.

The journeymen were inquisitive where I had been, what sort of a country it was, and how I liked it. I praised it much and the happy life I led in it, expressing strongly my intention of returning to it; and, one of them asking what kind of money we had there, I produced a handful of silver and spread it before them, which was a kind of raree-show[4] they had not been used to, paper being the money of Boston. Then I took an opportunity of letting them see my watch; and lastly (my brother still grum[5] and sullen), I gave them a piece of eight to drink[6] and took my leave. This visit of mine offended him extremely. For when my mother some time after spoke to him of a reconciliation, and of her wishes to see us on good terms together, and that we might live for the future as brothers, he said I had insulted him in such a manner before his people that he could never forget or forgive it. In this, however, he was mistaken.

My father received the governor's letter with some apparent surprise, but said little of it to me for some days, when Captain Holmes returning he showed it to him, asked him if he knew Keith, and what kind of man he was; adding his opinion that he must be of small discretion to think of setting a boy up in business who wanted yet three years of being at man's estate. Holmes said what he could in favor of the project, but my father was clear in the impropriety of it, and at last, gave a flat denial to it. Then he wrote a civil letter to Sir William, thanking him for the patronage he had so kindly offered me, but declining to assist me as yet in setting up, I being, in his opinion, too young to be trusted with the management of a business so important, and for which the preparation must be so expensive.

My friend and companion Collins, who was a clerk at the post office, pleased with the account I gave him of my new country, determined to go thither also.

[4]Show carried about in a box; a peepshow.
[5]Glum, morose.
[6]Spanish silver dollar to buy drinks.

And while I waited for my father's determination, he set out before me by land to Rhode Island, leaving his books, which were a pretty collection of mathematics and natural philosophy,[7] to come with mine and me to New York, where he proposed to wait for me.

My father, though he did not approve Sir William's proposition, was yet pleased that I had been able to obtain so advantageous a character from a person of such note where I had resided, and that I had been so industrious and careful as to equip myself so handsomely in so short a time; therefore, seeing no prospect of an accommodation between my brother and me, he gave his consent to my returning again to Philadelphia, advised me to behave respectfully to the people there, endeavor to obtain the general esteem, and avoid lampooning and libeling, to which he thought I had too much inclination; telling me that by steady industry and a prudent parsimony, I might save enough by the time I was one-and-twenty to set me up, and that if I came near the matter, he would help me out with the rest. This was all I could obtain, except some small gifts as tokens of his and my mother's love, when I embarked again for New York, now with their approbation and their blessing.

The sloop putting in at Newport, Rhode Island, I visited my brother John, who had been married and settled there some years. He received me very affectionately, for he always loved me. A friend of his, one Vernon, having some money due to him in Pennsylvania, about thirty-five pounds currency, desired I would receive it for him, and keep it till I had his directions what to remit it in. Accordingly, he gave me an order. This afterwards occasioned me a good deal of uneasiness.

At Newport we took in a number of passengers for New York, among which were two young women, companions, and a grave, sensible, matronlike Quaker woman with her attendants. I had shown an obliging readiness to do her some little services, which impressed her I suppose with a degree of good will towards me. Therefore, when she saw a daily growing familiarity between me and the two young women, which they appeared to encourage, she took me aside, and said, "Young man, I am concerned for thee, as thou has no friend with thee, and seems not to know much of the world, or of the snares youth is exposed to; depend upon it, those are very bad women; I can see it in all their actions, and if thee art not upon thy guard, they will draw thee into some danger; they are strangers to thee, and I advise thee, in a friendly concern for thy welfare, to have no acquaintance with them." As I seemed at first not to think so ill of them as she did, she mentioned some things she had observed and heard that had escaped my notice, but now convinced me she was right. I thanked her for her kind advice and promised to follow it. When we arrived at New York, they told me where they lived and invited me to come and see them; but I avoided it. And it was well I did; for the next day the captain missed a silver spoon and some other things that had been taken out of his cabin, and knowing that these were a couple of strumpets, he got a warrant to search their lodgings, found the stolen goods, and had the thieves punished. So, though we had escaped a sunken rock, which we scraped upon in the passage, I thought this escape of rather more importance to me.

At New York I found my friend Collins, who had arrived there some time before me. We had been intimate from children, and had read the same books together; but he had the advantage of more time for reading and studying, and a wonderful genius for mathematical learning, in which he far outstript me. While I lived in Boston, most of my hours of leisure for conversation were spent with him, and he continued a sober as well as an industrious lad, was much respected for his

---

[7]Works on nature, the physical universe.

learning by several of the clergy and other gentlemen, and seemed to promise making a good figure in life. But during my absence, he had acquired a habit of sotting with brandy; and I found by his own account, and what I heard from others, that he had been drunk every day since his arrival at New York, and behaved very oddly. He had gamed, too, and lost his money, so that I was obliged to discharge his lodgings, and defray his expenses to and at Philadelphia, which proved extremely inconvenient to me.

The then governor of New York, Burnet[8] (son of Bishop Burnet), hearing from the captain that a young man, one of his passengers, had a great many books, desired he would bring me to see him. I waited upon him accordingly and should have taken Collins with me but that he was not sober. The governor treated me with great civility, showed me his library, which was a very large one, and we had a good deal of conversation about books and authors. This was the second governor who had done me the honor to take notice of me; which, to a poor boy like me, was very pleasing.

We proceeded to Philadelphia. I received on the way Vernon's money, without which we could hardly have finished our journey. Collins wished to be employed in some counting-house; but whether they discovered his dramming[9] by his breath, or by his behavior, though he had some recommendations, he met with no success in any application, and continued lodging and boarding at the same house with me, and at my expense. Knowing I had that money of Vernon's, he was continually borrowing of me, still promising repayment as soon as he should be in business. At length he had got so much of it that I was distressed to think what I should do in case of being called on to remit it.

His drinking continued, about which we sometimes quarrelled, for, when a little intoxicated, he was very fractious. Once, in a boat on the Delaware with some other young men, he refused to row in his turn. "I will be rowed home," says he. "We will not row you," says I. "You must, or stay all night on the water," says he, "just as you please." The others said, "Let us row; what signifies it?" But my mind being soured with his other conduct, I continued to refuse. So he swore he would make me row, or throw me overboard; and coming along, stepping on the thwarts,[10] toward me, when he came up and struck at me, I clapped my hand under his crotch, and rising, pitched him headforemost into the river. I knew he was a good swimmer, and so was under little concern about him; but before he could get round to lay hold of the boat, we had with a few strokes pulled her out of his reach. And ever when he drew near the boat, we asked if he would row, striking a few strokes to slide her away from him. He was ready to die with vexation, and obstinately would not promise to row. However, seeing him at last beginning to tire, we lifted him in and brought him home dripping wet in the evening. We hardly exchang'd a civil word afterwards, and a West India captain, who had a commission to procure a tutor for the sons of a gentleman at Barbadoes,[11] happening to meet with him, agreed to carry him thither. He left me then, promising to remit me the first money he should receive in order to discharge the debt. But I never heard of him after.

The breaking into this money of Vernon's was one of the first great errata of my life. And this affair showed that my father was not much out in his judgment when he supposed me too young to manage business of importance. But Sir William, on reading his letter, said he was too prudent. There was great difference in persons, and discretion did not always accompany years, nor was youth always without it. "And since he will not set you up," says he, "I will do it myself.

---

[8]William Burnet (1688–1729), governor of New York and New Jersey (1720–28), had one of the best libraries in the colonies.
[9]Drinking.
[10]Seats across the boat.
[11]Island of the British West Indies.

Give me an inventory of the things necessary to be had from England, and I will send for them. You shall repay me when you are able; I am resolved to have a good printer here, and I am sure you must succeed." This was spoken with such an appearance of cordiality that I had not the least doubt of his meaning what he said. I had hitherto kept the proposition of my setting up, a secret in Philadelphia, and I still kept it. Had it been known that I depended on the governor, probably some friend that knew him better would have advised me not to rely on him, as I afterwards heard it as his known character to be liberal of promises which he never meant to keep. Yet, unsolicited as he was by me, how could I think his generous offers insincere? I believed him one of the best men in the world.

I presented him an inventory of a little printing-house, amounting by my computation to about one hundred pounds sterling. He liked it, but asked me if my being on the spot in England to choose the types and see that every thing was good of the kind might not be of some advantage. "Then," says he, "when there, you may make acquaintances and establish correspondences in the bookselling and stationery way." I agreed that this might be advantageous. "Then," says he, "get yourself ready to go with Annis,"[12] which was the annual ship, and the only one at that time usually passing between London and Philadelphia. But it would be some months before Annis sailed, so I continued working with Keimer, fretting about the money Collins had got from me, and in daily apprehensions of being called upon by Vernon, which, however, did not happen for some years after.

I believe I have omitted mentioning that in my first voyage from Boston, being becalmed off Block Island,[13] our people set about catching cod and hauled up a great many. Hitherto I had stuck to my resolution of not eating animal food, and on this occasion I considered, with my master Tryon, the taking every fish as a kind of unprovoked murder, since none of them had or ever could do us any injury that might justify the slaughter. All this seemed very reasonable. But I had formerly been a great lover of fish, and when this came hot out of the frying pan, it smelt admirably well. I balanced some time between principle and inclination, till I recollected that when the fish were opened, I saw smaller fish taken out of their stomachs. Then thought I, "If you eat one another, I don't see why we mayn't eat you." So I dined upon cod very heartily, and continued to eat with other people, returning only now and then occasionally to a vegetable diet. So convenient a thing it is to be a *reasonable creature,* since it enables one to find or make a reason for every thing one has a mind to do.

Keimer and I lived on a pretty good familiar footing and agreed tolerably well, for he suspected nothing of my setting up. He retained a great deal of his old enthusiasms and loved argumentation. We therefore had many disputations. I used to work him so with my Socratic method, and had trepanned[14] him so often by questions apparently so distant from any point we had in hand, and yet by degrees led to the point, and brought him into difficulties and contradictions, that at last he grew ridiculously cautious and would hardly answer me the most common question without asking first, "What do you intend to infer from that?" However, it gave him so high an opinion of my abilities in the confuting way, that he seriously proposed my being his colleague in a project he had of setting up a new sect. He was to preach the doctrines, and I was to confound all opponents. When he came to explain with me upon the doctrines, I found several conundrums[15] which I objected to, unless I might have my way a little too and introduce some of mine.

Keimer wore his beard at full length, because somewhere in the Mosaic law it is said, "Thou shalt not mar the corners of thy beard."[16] He likewise kept the Sev-

---

[12]Thomas Annis, master of the *London Hope,* on which Franklin sailed for London, November 5, 1724.
[13]Off the coast of Rhode Island.
[14]Trapped.

[15]Puzzling problems.
[16]Leviticus 19: 27: "Ye shall not round the corners of your heads, neither shalt thou mar the corners of thy beard."

enth day, Sabbath; and these two points were essentials with him. I disliked both, but agreed to admit them upon condition of his adopting the doctrine of using no animal food. "I doubt," said he, "my constitution will not bear that." I assured him it would, and that he would be the better for it. He was usually a great glutton, and I promised myself some diversion in half starving him. He agreed to try the practice, if I would keep him company. I did so, and we held it for three months. We had our victuals dressed and brought to us regularly by a woman in the neighborhood, who had from me a list of forty dishes to be prepared for us at different times, in all which there was neither fish, flesh, nor fowl, and the whim suited me the better at this time from the cheapness of it, not costing us above eighteen-pence sterling each per week. I have since kept several Lents most strictly, leaving the common diet for that, and that for the common, abruptly, without the least inconvenience, so that I think there is little in the advice of making those changes by easy gradations. I went on pleasantly, but poor Keimer suffered grievously, tired of the project, longed for the flesh pots of Egypt,[17] and ordered a roast pig. He invited me and two women friends to dine with him, but, it being brought too soon upon table, he could not resist the temptation and ate the whole before we came.

I had made some courtship during this time to Miss Read. I had a great respect and affection for her, and had some reason to believe she had the same for me; but as I was about to take a long voyage, and we were both very young, only a little above eighteen, it was thought most prudent by her mother to prevent our going too far at present, as a marriage, if it was to take place, would be more convenient after my return, when I should be, as I expected, set up in my business. Perhaps, too, she thought my expectations not so well founded as I imagined them to be.

My chief acquaintances at this time were Charles Osborne, Joseph Watson, and James Ralph, all lovers of reading. The two first were clerks to an eminent scrivener or conveyancer in the town, Charles Brogden;[18] the other was clerk to a merchant. Watson was a pious, sensible young man, of great integrity; the others rather more lax in their principles of religion, particularly Ralph, who, as well as Collins, had been unsettled by me, for which they both made me suffer. Osborne was sensible, candid, frank, sincere, and affectionate to his friends; but in literary matters, too fond of criticizing. Ralph was ingenious, genteel in his manners, and extremely eloquent; I think I never knew a prettier talker. Both of them great admirers of poetry, and began to try their hands in little pieces. Many pleasant walks we four had together on Sundays into the woods, near Schuylkill,[19] where we read to one another, and conferred on what we read.

Ralph was inclined to pursue the study of poetry, not doubting but he might become eminent in it and make his fortune by it, alleging that the best poets must, when they first began to write, make as many faults as he did. Osborne dissuaded him, assured him he had no genius for poetry, and advised him to think of nothing beyond the business he was bred to; that, in the mercantile way, though he had no stock, he might, by his diligence and punctuality, recommend himself to employment as a factor,[20] and in time acquire wherewith to trade on his own account. I approved the amusing one's self with poetry now and then, so far as to improve one's language, but no farther.

On this it was proposed that we should each of us, at our next meeting, pro-

---

[17]Pots in which meat is boiled, an allusion to Exodus 16:3: "And the children of Israel said unto them [Moses and Aaron], 'Would to God we had died by the hand of the Lord in the land of Egypt, when we sat by the flesh pots, and when we did eat bread to the full; for ye have brought us forth into this wilderness, to kill this whole assembly with hunger.' "

[18]Charles Brockden (1683–1769) held various offices including conveyancer, or drafter of deeds and leases.
[19]Schuylkill River.
[20]Business agent.

duce a piece of our own composing, in order to improve by our mutual observations, criticisms, and corrections. As language and expression were what we had in view, we excluded all considerations of invention by agreeing that the task should be a version of the eighteenth Psalm, which describes the descent of a Deity. When the time of our meeting drew nigh, Ralph called on me first, and let me know his piece was ready. I told him I had been busy, and, having little inclination, had done nothing. He then showed me his piece for my opinion, and I much approved it, as it appeared to me to have great merit. "Now," says he, "Osborne never will allow the least merit in any thing of mine, but makes 1000 criticisms out of mere envy. He is not so jealous of you, I wish, therefore, you would take this piece and produce it as yours. I will pretend not to have had time, and so produce nothing. We shall then see what he will say to it." It was agreed, and I immediately transcribed it, that it might appear in my own hand.

We met. Watson's performance was read; there were some beauties in it, but many defects. Osborne's was read. It was much better. Ralph did it justice, remarked some faults, but applauded the beauties. He himself had nothing to produce. I was backward, seemed desirous of being excused, had not had sufficient time to correct, etc., but no excuse could be admitted; produce I must. It was read and repeated; Watson and Osborne gave up the contest, and joined in applauding it. Ralph only made some criticisms and proposed some amendments, but I defended my text. Osborne was against Ralph, and told him he was no better a critic than poet, so he dropped the argument. As they two went home together, Osborne expressed himself still more strongly in favor of what he thought my production, having restrained himself before, as he said, lest I should think it flattery. "But who would have imagined," said he, "that Franklin had been capable of such a performance, such painting, such force, such fire! He has even improved the original. In his common conversation, he seems to have no choice of words; he hesitates and blunders; and yet, good God, how he writes!" When we next met, Ralph discovered the trick we had played him, and Osborne was a little laughed at.

This transaction fixed Ralph in his resolution of becoming a poet. I did all I could to dissuade him from it, but he continued scribbling verses till Pope cured him.[21] He became, however, a pretty good prose writer. More of him hereafter. But, as I may not have occasion again to mention the other two, I shall just remark here, that Watson died in my arms a few years after, much lamented, being the best of our set. Osborne went to the West Indies, where he became an eminent lawyer and made money, but died young. He and I had made a serious agreement, that the one who happened first to die should, if possible, make a friendly visit to the other, and acquaint him how he found things in that separate state. But he never fulfilled his promise.

V [1724–1726: Voyage to England, the Governor's Tricks, Employment as Printer, Life in London]

The governor, seeming to like my company, had me frequently to his house, and his setting me up was always mentioned as a fixed thing. I was to take with me letters recommendatory to a number of his friends, besides the letter of credit to furnish me with the necessary money for purchasing the press and types, paper, etc. For these letters I was appointed to call at different times, when they were to be ready, but a future time was still named. Thus he went on till the ship, whose

---

[21]James Ralph (c. 1705–1762) attacked Alexander Pope in *Sawney: an Heroic Poem Occasioned by the Dunciad* (1728). Pope, alluding to Ralph's poem *Night,* added this couplet to the second edition of his satire on ignorance, the *Dunciad:*

"Silence, ye wolves! while Ralph to Cynthia howls, / And makes night hideous—answer him, ye owls" (III, 159–60). Ralph was more successful as a political journalist and author of *The History of England* (1744–46).

departure too had been several times postponed, was on the point of sailing. Then, when I called to take my leave and receive the letters, his secretary, Dr. Bard,[1] came out to me, and said the governor was extremely busy in writing, but would be down at Newcastle[2] before the ship, and there the letters would be delivered to me.

Ralph, though married, and having one child, had determined to accompany me in this voyage. It was thought he intended to establish a correspondence and obtain goods to sell on commission; but I found afterwards, that through some discontent with his wife's relations, he purposed to leave her on their hands and never return again. Having taken leave of my friends, and interchanged some promises with Miss Read, I left Philadelphia in the ship, which anchor'd at Newcastle. The governor was there. But when I went to his lodging, the secretary came to me from him with the civillest message in the world, that he could not then see me, being engaged in business of the utmost importance, but should send the letters to me on board, wished me heartily a good voyage and a speedy return, etc. I returned on board a little puzzled, but still not doubting.

Mr. Andrew Hamilton,[3] a famous lawyer of Philadelphia, had taken passage in the same ship for himself and son, and with Mr. Denham, a Quaker merchant, and Messrs. Onion and Russel, masters of an iron work in Maryland, had engaged the great cabin; so that Ralph and I were forced to take up with a berth in the steerage, and none on board knowing us, were considered as ordinary persons. But Mr. Hamilton and his son (it was James, since governor)[4] returned from Newcastle to Philadelphia, the father being recalled by a great fee to plead for a seized ship; and, just before we sailed, Colonel French coming on board and showing me great respect, I was more taken notice of, and, with my friend Ralph, invited by the other gentlemen to come into the cabin, there being now room. Accordingly, we removed thither.

Understanding that Colonel French had brought on board the governor's despatches, I asked the captain for those letters that were to be under my care. He said all were put into the bag together and he could not then come at them; but before we landed in England I should have an opportunity of picking them out. So I was satisfied for the present, and we proceeded on our voyage. We had a sociable company in the cabin and lived uncommonly well, having the addition of all Mr. Hamilton's stores, who had laid in plentifully. In this passage Mr. Denham contracted a friendship for me that continued during his life.[5] The voyage was otherwise not a pleasant one, as we had a great deal of bad weather.

When we came into the Channel, the captain kept his word with me and gave me an opportunity of examining the bag for the governor's letters. I found none upon which my name was put as under my care. I picked out six or seven that by the handwriting I thought might be the promised letters, especially as one of them was directed to Basket, the king's printer, and another to some stationer. We arrived in London the 24th of December, 1724. I waited upon the stationer, who came first in my way, delivering the letter as from Governor Keith. "I don't know such a person," says he; but, opening the letter, "O! this is from Riddlesden.[6] I have lately found him to be a complete rascal, and I will have nothing to do with him, nor receive any letters from him." So, putting the letter into my hand, he turned on his heel and left me to serve some customer. I was surprised to find these were not the governor's letters; and, after recollecting and comparing cir-

---

[1]Dr. Patrick Baird, surgeon.
[2]Delaware.
[3]Andrew Hamilton (*c.* 1676–1741), defender of John Peter Zenger when tried for seditious libel in New York in 1735. Zenger's acquittal by jury established freedom of the press in America.
[4]James Hamilton (*c.* 1710–1783), lieutenant-governor of

Pennsylvania (1748–54, 1759–63); acting governor (May–October 1771 and July–August 1773).
[5]Thomas Denham (d. 1728), Philadelphia merchant and Franklin's benefactor.
[6]William Riddlesden (d. before 1733), felon and cheat, described by the Maryland Assembly as "a Person of a matchless Character in Infamy."

cumstances, I began to doubt his sincerity. I found my friend Denham and opened the whole affair to him. He let me into Keith's character, told me there was not the least probability that he had written any letters for me, that no one who knew him had the smallest dependence on him, and he laughed at the notion of the governor's giving me a letter of credit, having, as he said, no credit to give. On my expressing some concern about what I should do, he advised me to endeavor getting some employment in the way of my business. "Among the printers here," said he, "you will improve yourself, and when you return to America, you will set up to greater advantage."

We both of us happened to know, as well as the stationer, that Riddlesden, the attorney, was a very knave. He had half ruined Miss Read's father by persuading him to be bound for him.[7] By his letter it appeared there was a secret scheme on foot to the prejudice of Hamilton (supposed to be then coming over with us), and that Keith was concerned in it with Riddlesden. Denham, who was a friend of Hamilton's, thought he ought to be acquainted with it; so, when he arriv'd in England, which was soon after, partly from resentment and ill-will to Keith and Riddlesden, and partly from good-will to him, I waited on him, and gave him the letter. He thanked me cordially, the information being of importance to him. And from that time he became my friend, greatly to my advantage afterwards on many occasions.

But what shall we think of a governor's playing such pitiful tricks, and imposing so grossly on a poor ignorant boy! It was a habit he had acquired. He wished to please everybody; and having little to give, he gave expectations. He was otherwise an ingenious, sensible man, a pretty good writer, and a good governor for the people, though not for his constituents, the proprietaries,[8] whose instructions he sometimes disregarded. Several of our best laws were of his planning and passed during his administration.

Ralph and I were inseparable companions. We took lodgings together in Little Britain[9] at three shillings and sixpence a week, as much as we could then afford. He found some relations, but they were poor and unable to assist him. He now let me know his intentions of remaining in London, and that he never meant to return to Philadelphia. He had brought no money with him, the whole he could muster having been expended in paying his passage. I had fifteen pistoles;[10] so he borrowed occasionally of me to subsist, while he was looking out for business. He first endeavored to get into the playhouse, believing himself qualified for an actor; but Wilkes,[11] to whom he applied, advised him candidly not to think of that employment, as it was impossible he should succeed in it. Then he proposed to Roberts,[12] a publisher in Paternoster Row, to write for him a weekly paper like the *Spectator,* on certain conditions, which Roberts did not approve. Then he endeavored to get employment as a hackney writer,[13] to copy for the stationers and lawyers about the Temple,[14] but could find no vacancy.

I immediately got into work at Palmer's, then a famous printing-house in Bartholomew Close,[15] and here I continued near a year. I was pretty diligent, but spent with Ralph a good deal of my earnings in going to plays and other places of amusement. We had together consumed all my pistoles, and now just rubbed on from hand to mouth. He seemed quite to forget his wife and child, and I, by degrees, my engagements with Miss Read, to whom I never wrote more than one

---

[7]I.e., made responsible for Riddlesden's actions and debts.
[8]Owners of the colony of Pennsylvania, the William Penn family.
[9]Short London street near St. Bartholomew's Hospital and St. Paul's Cathedral.
[10]Spanish gold coin worth eighteen shillings.
[11]Robert Wilks (1665?–1732), London actor, associated with the Haymarket and Drury Lane Theatres.

[12]James Roberts (*c.* 1669–1754), eminent London printer and publisher.
[13]A hired copier of documents.
[14]Center of the London legal profession.
[15]Square off Little Britain, center of the printing business.

letter, and that was to let her know I was not likely soon to return. This was another of the great errata of my life, which I should wish to correct if I were to live it over again. In fact, by our expenses, I was constantly kept unable to pay my passage.

At Palmer's I was employed in composing for the second edition of Wollaston's *Religion of Nature*.[16] Some of his reasonings not appearing to me well founded, I wrote a little metaphysical piece in which I made remarks on them. It was entitled *A Dissertation on Liberty and Necessity, Pleasure and Pain.* I inscribed it to my friend Ralph. I printed a small number. It occasioned my being more considered by Mr. Palmer as a young man of some ingenuity, though he seriously expostulated with me upon the principles of my pamphlet, which to him appeared abominable. My printing this pamphlet was another erratum.[17]

While I lodged in Little Britain, I made an acquaintance with one Wilcox, a bookseller, whose shop was at the next door. He had an immense collection of second-hand books. Circulating libraries were not then in use; but we agreed that, on certain reasonable terms, which I have now forgotten, I might take, read, and return any of his books. This I esteemed a great advantage, and I made as much use of it as I could.

My pamphlet by some means falling into the hands of one Lyons, a surgeon, author of a book entitled *The Infallibility of Human Judgment*,[18] it occasioned an acquaintance between us. He took great notice of me, called on me often to converse on those subjects, carried me to the Horns, a pale alehouse in [blank] Lane, Cheapside, and introduced me to Dr. Mandeville, author of the *Fable of the Bees*,[19] who had a club there, of which he was the soul, being a most facetious, entertaining companion. Lyons, too, introduced me to Dr. Pemberton, at Batson's Coffee House,[20] who promised to give me an opportunity, some time or other, of seeing Sir Isaac Newton,[21] of which I was extremely desirous; but this never happened.

I had brought over a few curiosities, among which the principal was a purse made of the asbestos, which purifies by fire. Sir Hans Sloane heard of it, came to see me, and invited me to his house in Bloomsbury Square, where he showed me all his curiosities, and persuaded me to let him add that to the number, for which he paid me handsomely.[22]

In our house there lodged a young woman, a milliner, who, I think, had a shop in the Cloisters. She had been genteelly bred, was sensible and lively, and of most pleasing conversation. Ralph read plays to her in the evenings, they grew intimate, she took another lodging, and he followed her. They lived together some time, but, he being still out of business, and her income not sufficient to maintain them with her child, he took a resolution of going from London to try for a country school, which he thought himself well qualified to undertake, as he wrote an excellent hand, and was a master of arithmetic and accounts. This, however, he deemed a business below him, and confident of future better fortune, when he should be unwilling to have it known that he once was so meanly employed, he changed his name, and did me the honor to assume mine; for I soon after had a letter from him, acquainting me that he was settled in a small village (in Berkshire,

---

[16]The third edition of *The Religion of Nature Delineated* (1722), by the English Christian deist William Wollaston (1660–1772).

[17]In the pamphlet, Franklin refuted Wollaston's belief in free will and argued that virtue and vice did not exist.

[18]William Lyons, author of *The Infallibility, Dignity, and Excellence of Human Judgment* (1719).

[19]Bernard Mandeville (c. 1670–1733), Dutch physician, philosopher, and satirist, held that every virtue was really a form of selfishness in *The Fable of the Bees, or Private Vices, Public Benefits* (1714).

[20]Batson's was a favorite meeting place of physicians;

Henry Pemberton (1694–1771), author of *A View of Sir Isaac Newton's Philosophy* (1728), was helping Newton prepare the third edition of the *Principia*.

[21]Sir Isaac Newton (1642–1727), English mathematician, scientist, philosopher, who formulated the laws of gravity and motion.

[22]Sir Hans Sloane (1660–1753), physician and botanist, left his collection to the nation, which became the nucleus of the British Museum, where Franklin's purse is now. Franklin had actually written Sloane on June 2, 1725, offering to show (and sell) him his "curiosities."

I think it was, where he taught reading and writing to ten or a dozen boys, at six-pence each per week), recommending Mrs. T. to my care, and desiring me to write to him, directing for Mr. Franklin, schoolmaster, at such a place.

He continued to write frequently, sending me large specimens of an epic poem which he was then composing, and desiring my remarks and corrections. These I gave him from time to time, but endeavored rather to discourage his proceeding. One of Young's satires was then just published.[23] I copied and sent him a great part of it, which set in a strong light the folly of pursuing the muses with any hope of advancement by them. All was in vain. Sheets of the poem continued to come by every post. In the mean time, Mrs. T., having on his account lost her friends and business, was often in distresses, and used to send for me and borrow what I could spare to help her out of them. I grew fond of her company, and being at that time under no religious restraints and presuming upon my importance to her, I attempted familiarities (another erratum), which she repulsed with a proper resentment, and acquainted him with my behavior. This made a breach between us, and when he returned again to London, he let me know he thought I had can-celed all the obligations he had been under to me. So I found I was never to ex-pect his repaying me what I lent to him, or advanced for him. This, however, was not then of much consequence, as he was totally unable; and in the loss of his friendship I found myself relieved from a burthen. I now began to think of get-ting a little money beforehand, and expecting better work, I left Palmer's to work at Watts's, near Lincoln's Inn Fields, a still greater printing-house. Here I contin-ued all the rest of my stay in London.

At my first admission into this printing-house I took to working at press, imag-ining I felt a want of the bodily exercise I had been used to in America, where presswork is mixed with composing. I drank only water; the other workmen, near fifty in number, were great guzzlers of beer. On occasion, I carried up and down stairs a large form of types[24] in each hand, when others carried but one in both hands. They wondered to see, from this and several instances, that the Water-American, as they called me, was *stronger* than themselves, who drank *strong* beer. We had an alehouse boy who attended always in the house to supply the work-men. My companion at the press drank every day a pint before breakfast, a pint at breakfast with his bread and cheese, a pint between breakfast and dinner, a pint at dinner, a pint in the afternoon about six o'clock, and another when he had done his day's work. I thought it a detestable custom; but it was necessary, he supposed, to drink *strong* beer that he might be *strong* to labor. I endeavored to convince him that the bodily strength afforded by beer could only be in proportion to the grain or flour of the barley dissolved in the water of which it was made; that there was more flour in a pennyworth of bread; and therefore, if he would eat that with a pint of water, it would give him more strength than a quart of beer. He drank on, however, and had four or five shillings to pay out of his wages every Saturday night for that muddling liquor; an expense I was free from. And thus these poor devils keep themselves always under.

Watts, after some weeks, desiring to have me in the composing-room, I left the pressmen; a new *bienvenu*[25] or sum for drink, being five shillings, was demanded of me by the compositors. I thought it an imposition, as I had paid below. The master thought so too, and forbad my paying it. I stood out two or three weeks, was accordingly considered as an excommunicate, and had so many little pieces of private mischief done me, by mixing my sorts,[26] transposing my pages, breaking my matter,[27] etc., etc., if I were ever so little out of the room, and all ascribed to

---

[23]Edward Young (1683–1765), author of a series of satires entitled *Love of Fame, the Universal Passion* (1725–28).
[24]Composed type for a sheet or a page locked in an iron frame.

[25]"Welcome" (French).
[26]Letters of type.
[27]Composed type ready for printing.

the chapel ghost, which they said ever haunted those not regularly admitted, that, notwithstanding the master's protection, I found myself obliged to comply and pay the money, convinced of the folly of being on ill terms with those one is to live with continually.

I was now on a fair footing with them, and soon acquired considerable influence. I proposed some reasonable alterations in their chapel[28] laws, and carried them against all opposition. From my example, a great part of them left their muddling breakfast of beer, and bread, and cheese, finding they could with me be supplied from a neighboring house with a large porringer of hot water-gruel, sprinkled with pepper, crumbed with bread, and a bit of butter in it, for the price of a pint of beer, viz., three half-pence. This was a more comfortable as well as cheaper breakfast, and kept their heads clearer. Those who continued sotting with beer all day were often, by not paying, out of credit at the alehouse, and used to make interest with me to get beer, *their light,* as they phrased it, *being out.* I watched the pay table on Saturday night, and collected what I stood engaged for them, having to pay sometimes near thirty shillings a week on their accounts. This, and my being esteemed a pretty good riggite, that is, a jocular verbal satirist, supported my consequence in the society. My constant attendance (I never making a St. Monday)[29] recommended me to the master; and my uncommon quickness at composing occasioned my being put upon all work of dispatch, which was generally better paid. So I went on now very agreeably.

My lodging in Little Britain being too remote, I found another in Duke Street, opposite to the Romish Chapel.[30] It was two pair of stairs backwards at an Italian warehouse. A widow lady kept the house; she had a daughter, and a maid servant, and a journeyman who attended the warehouse, but lodged abroad. After sending to inquire my character at the house where I last lodged, she agreed to take me in at the same rate, three shillings and six pence per week, cheaper, as she said, from the protection she expected in having a man lodge in the house. She was a widow, an elderly woman, had been bred a Protestant, being a clergyman's daughter, but was converted to the Catholic religion by her husband, whose memory she much revered; had lived much among people of distinction, and knew a thousand anecdotes of them as far back as the times of Charles the Second. She was lame in her knees with the gout, and, therefore, seldom stirred out of her room, so sometimes wanted company; and hers was so highly amusing to me, that I was sure to spend an evening with her whenever she desired it. Our supper was only half an anchovy each, on a very little strip of bread and butter, and half a pint of ale between us. But the entertainment was in her conversation. My always keeping good hours, and giving little trouble in the family, made her unwilling to part with me; so that when I talked of a lodging I had heard of, nearer my business, for two shillings a week, which, intent as I now was on saving money, made some difference, she bid me not think of it, for she would abate me two shillings a week for the future; so I remained with her at one shilling and sixpence as long as I stayed in London.

In a garret of her house there lived a maiden lady of seventy, in the most retired manner, of whom my landlady gave me this account: that she was a Roman Catholic, had been sent abroad when young, and lodged in a nunnery with an intent of becoming a nun; but, the country not agreeing with her, she returned to England, where, there being no nunnery, she had vowed to lead the life of a nun, as near as might be done in those circumstances. Accordingly, she had given all her estate to charitable uses, reserving only twelve pounds a year to live on, and

---

[28]"A printing house is always called a chapel by the workmen" (Franklin's note).
[29]Never making Monday a holiday and staying home because of weekend dissipation.

[30]The Roman Catholic Chapel of Saints Anselm and Cecelia.

out of this sum she still gave a great deal in charity, living herself on water-gruel only, and using no fire but to boil it. She had lived many years in that garret, being permitted to remain there gratis by successive Catholic tenants of the house below, as they deemed it a blessing to have her there. A priest visited her to confess her every day. "I have asked her," says my landlady, "how she, as she lived, could possibly find so much employment for a confessor?" "Oh," said she, "it is impossible to avoid *vain thoughts.*" I was permitted once to visit her. She was cheerful and polite, and conversed pleasantly. The room was clean, but had no other furniture than a mattress, a table with a crucifix and book, a stool which she gave me to sit on, and a picture over the chimney of Saint Veronica displaying her handkerchief, with the miraculous figure of Christ's bleeding face on it, which she explained to me with great seriousness.[31] She looked pale, but was never sick; and I give it as another instance on how small an income life and health may be supported.

At Watt's printing-house I contracted an acquaintance with an ingenious young man, one Wygate; who, having wealthy relations, had been better educated than most printers, was a tolerable Latinist, spoke French, and loved reading. I taught him and a friend of his to swim at twice going into the river, and they soon became good swimmers. They introduced me to some gentlemen from the country, who went to Chelsea by water to see the College[32] and Don Saltero's curiosities.[33] In our return, at the request of the company, whose curiosity Wygate had excited, I stripped and leaped into the river, and swam from near Chelsea to Blackfriar's,[34] performing on the way many feats of activity, both upon and under water, that surprised and pleased those to whom they were novelties.

I had from a child been ever delighted with this exercise, had studied and practised all Thevenot's motions and positions,[35] added some of my own, aiming at the graceful and easy as well as the useful. All these I took this occasion of exhibiting to the company, and was much flattered by their admiration. And Wygate, who was desirous of becoming a master, grew more and more attached to me on that account, as well as from the similarity of our studies. He at length proposed to me travelling all over Europe together, supporting ourselves everywhere by working at our business. I was once inclined to it; but, mentioning it to my good friend Mr. Denham, with whom I often spent an hour when I had leisure, he dissuaded me from it, advising me to think only of returning to Pennsylvania, which he was now about to do.

I must record one trait of this good man's character. He had formerly been in business at Bristol, but failed in debt to a number of people, compounded[36] and went to America. There, by a close application to business as a merchant, he acquired a plentiful fortune in a few years. Returning to England in the ship with me, he invited his old creditors to an entertainment, at which he thanked them for the easy composition[37] they had favored him with, and, when they expected nothing but the treat, every man at the first remove[38] found under his plate an order on a banker for the full amount of the unpaid remainder with interest.

He now told me he was about to return to Philadelphia, and should carry over a great quantity of goods in order to open a store there. He proposed to take me over as his clerk, to keep his books (in which he would instruct me), copy his letters, and attend the store. He added that, as soon as I should be acquainted with mercantile business, he would promote me by sending me with a cargo of flour

---

[31]According to legend, St. Veronica handed her handkerchief to Christ on his way to Calvary; he wiped his face and gave the handkerchief back. It miraculously preserved his likeness.

[32]Probably Chelsea Hospital, designed by Christopher Wren in 1682, replacing Chelsea College.

[33]James Salter's coffee house had on exhibit Job's tears, a petrified crab, William the Conqueror's sword, etc.

[34]Some three and a half miles.

[35]Melchisédeck de Thévenot, *The Art of Swimming, Illustrated by Proper Figures* (1699).

[36]Settled his debts in part.

[37]Settlement.

[38]First removal of plates.

and bread, etc., to the West Indies, and procure me commissions from others which would be profitable; and, if I managed well, would establish me handsomely. The thing pleased me, for I was grown tired of London, remembered with pleasure the happy months I had spent in Pennsylvania, and wished again to see it; therefore I immediately agreed on the terms of fifty pounds a year, Pennsylvania money; less, indeed, than my present gettings as a compositor, but affording a better prospect.

I now took leave of printing, as I thought, for ever, and was daily employed in my new business, going about with Mr. Denham among the tradesmen to purchase various articles, and seeing them packed up, doing errands, calling upon workmen to dispatch, etc., and, when all was on board, I had a few days' leisure. On one of these days, I was, to my surprise, sent for by a great man I knew only by name, a Sir William Wyndham,[39] and I waited upon him. He had heard by some means or other of my swimming from Chelsea to Blackfriar's, and of my teaching Wygate and another young man to swim in a few hours. He had two sons about to set out on their travels; he wished to have them first taught swimming, and proposed to gratify me handsomely if I would teach them. They were not yet come to town, and my stay was uncertain, so I could not undertake it. But, from this incident, I thought it likely that if I were to remain in England and open a swimming-school, I might get a good deal of money. And it struck me so strongly that, had the overture been sooner made me, probably I should not so soon have returned to America. After many years, you and I had something of more importance to do with one of these sons of Sir William Wyndham, become Earl of Egremont, which I shall mention in its place.[40]

Thus I spent about eighteen months in London. Most part of the time I worked hard at my business, and spent but little upon myself except in seeing plays and in books. My friend Ralph had kept me poor. He owed me about twenty-seven pounds, which I was now never likely to receive; a great sum out of my small earnings. I loved him, notwithstanding, for he had many amiable qualities. I had by no means improved my fortune; but I had picked up some very ingenious acquaintance, whose conversation was of great advantage to me; and I had read considerably.

VI [1726–1727: RETURN TO PHILADELPHIA, MANAGING KEIMER'S SHOP, PRINCIPLES AND MORALS]

We sailed from Gravesend on the 23rd of July, 1726. For the incidents of the voyage, I refer you to my Journal, where you will find them all minutely related. Perhaps the most important part of that journal is the *plan* to be found in it, which I formed at sea, for regulating my future conduct in life.[1] It is the more remark-

---

[39]Sir William Wyndham (1687–1740), prominent Tory politician.

[40]Franklin never got around to doing so.

[1]The plan is lost, except for "the preamble and heads of it," which was printed by Robert Walsh in his "Life of Benjamin Franklin" (1815–17):

> Those who write of the art of poetry teach us that if we would write what may be worth the reading, we ought always, before we begin, to form a regular plan and design of our piece: otherwise, we shall be in danger of incongruity. I am apt to think it is the same as to life. I have never fixed a regular design in life; by which means it has been a confused variety of different scenes. I am now entering upon a new one: let me, therefore, make some resolutions, and form some scheme of action, that, henceforth, I may live in all respects like a rational creature.

1. It is necessary for me to be extremely frugal for some time, till I have paid what I owe.

2. To endeavor to speak truth in every instance; to give nobody expectations that are not likely to be answered, but aim at sincerity in every word and action—the most amiable excellence in a rational being.

3. To apply myself industriously to whatever business I take in hand, and not divert my mind from my business by any foolish project of growing suddenly rich; for industry and patience are the surest means of plenty.

4. I resolve to speak ill of no man whatever, not even in a matter of truth; but rather by some means excuse the faults I hear charged upon others, and upon proper occasions speak all the good I know of every body.

able, as being formed when I was so young, and yet being pretty faithfully adhered to quite through to old age.

We landed in Philadelphia on the 11th of October, where I found sundry alterations. Keith was no longer governor, being superseded by Major Gordon.[2] I met him walking the streets as a common citizen. He seemed a little ashamed at seeing me, but passed without saying any thing. I should have been as much ashamed at seeing Miss Read, had not her friends, despairing with reason of my return after the receipt of my letter, persuaded her to marry another, one Rogers, a potter, which was done in my absence. With him, however, she was never happy, and soon parted from him, refusing to cohabit with him or bear his name, it being now said that he had another wife. He was a worthless fellow, though an excellent workman, which was the temptation to her friends. He got into debt, ran away in 1727 or 1728, went to the West Indies, and died there. Keimer had got a better house, a shop well supplied with stationery, plenty of new types, a number of hands, though none good, and seemed to have a great deal of business.

Mr. Denham took a store in Water Street, where we opened our goods. I attended the business diligently, studied accounts, and grew, in a little time, expert at selling. We lodged and boarded together; he counselled me as a father, having a sincere regard for me. I respected and loved him, and we might have gone on together very happily, but, in the beginning of February, 1726/7, when I had just passed my twenty-first year, we both were taken ill. My distemper was a pleurisy, which very nearly carried me off. I suffered a good deal, gave up the point in my own mind, and was rather disappointed when I found myself recovering, regretting, in some degree, that I must now, some time or other, have all that disagreeable work to do over again. I forget what his distemper was. It held him a long time, and at length carried him off. He left me a small legacy in a nuncupative will,[3] as a token of his kindness for me, and he left me once more to the wide world; for the store was taken into the care of his executors, and my employment under him ended.

My brother-in-law, Holmes, being now at Philadelphia, advised my return to my business. And Keimer tempted me, with an offer of large wages by the year, to come and take the management of his printing-house, that he might better attend his stationer's shop. I had heard a bad character of him in London from his wife and her friends, and was not fond of having any more to do with him. I tried for farther employment as a merchant's clerk; but, not readily meeting with any, I closed again with Keimer. I found in his house these hands: Hugh Meredith,[4] a Welsh Pennsylvanian, thirty years of age, bred to country work, honest, sensible, had a great deal of solid observation, was something of a reader, but given to drink. Stephen Potts,[5] a young countryman of full age, bred to the same, of uncommon natural parts, and great wit and humor, but a little idle. These he had agreed with at extreme low wages per week, to be raised a shilling every three months, as they would deserve by improving in their business; and the expectation of these high wages, to come on hereafter, was what he had drawn them in with. Meredith was to work at press, Potts at bookbinding, which he, by agreement, was to teach them, though he knew neither one nor t'other. John——, a wild Irishman, brought up to no business, whose service, for four years, Keimer had purchased[6] from the captain of a ship; he, too, was to be made a pressman. George Webb,[7] an Oxford scholar, whose time for four years he had likewise

[2]Patrick Gordon (1664–1736), governor of Pennsylvania (1726–36).
[3]An oral will.
[4]Hugh Meredith (c. 1697–1749) became Franklin's friend and partner.

[5]Stephen Potts (d. 1758), later a bookseller and tavernkeeper.
[6]By paying for his passage in return for a contract of four years labor; an indentured worker.
[7]George Webb (born c. 1709).

bought, intending him for a compositor, of whom more presently; and David Harry,[8] a country boy, whom he had taken apprentice.

I soon perceived that the intention of engaging me at wages so much higher than he had been used to give, was to have these raw, cheap hands formed through me; and, as soon as I had instructed them, then, they being all articled to him, he should be able to do without me. I went on, however, very cheerfully, put his printing-house in order, which had been in great confusion, and brought his hands by degrees to mind their business and to do it better.

It was an odd thing to find an Oxford scholar in the situation of a bought servant. He was not more than eighteen years of age, and gave me this account of himself; that he was born in Gloucester, educated at a grammar school there, had been distinguished among the scholars for some apparent superiority in performing his part, when they exhibited plays; belonged to the Witty Club there, and had written some pieces in prose and verse, which were printed in the Gloucester newspapers. Thence he was sent to Oxford; there he continued about a year, but not well satisfied, wishing of all things to see London and become a player. At length, receiving his quarterly allowance of fifteen guineas, instead of discharging his debts he walked out of town, hid his gown in a furze bush, and footed it to London, where, having no friend to advise him, he fell into bad company, soon spent his guineas, found no means of being introduced among the players, grew necessitous, pawned his clothes, and wanted bread. Walking the street very hungry, and not knowing what to do with himself, a crimp's bill[9] was put into his hand, offering immediate entertainment and encouragement to such as would bind themselves to serve in America. He went directly, signed the indentures, was put into the ship, and came over, never writing a line to acquaint his friends what was become of him. He was lively, witty, good-natured, and a pleasant companion, but idle, thoughtless, and imprudent to the last degree.

John, the Irishman, soon ran away. With the rest I began to live very agreeably, for they all respected me, the more as they found Keimer incapable of instructing them, and that from me they learned something daily. We never worked on Saturday, that being Keimer's Sabbath, so I had two days for reading. My acquaintance with ingenious people in the town increased. Keimer himself treated me with great civility and apparent regard, and nothing now made me uneasy but my debt to Vernon, which I was yet unable to pay, being hitherto but a poor economist. He, however, kindly made no demand of it.

Our printing-house often wanted sorts,[10] and there was no letter-founder in America. I had seen types cast at James's in London,[11] but without much attention to the manner. However, I now contrived a mould, made use of the letters we had as puncheons,[12] struck the matrices[13] in lead, and thus supplied in a pretty tolerable way all deficiencies. I also engraved several things on occasion. I made the ink, I was warehouseman, and everything, in short, quite a factotum.[14]

But, however serviceable I might be, I found that my services became every day of less importance, as the other hands improved in the business. And when Keimer paid my second quarter's wages, he let me know that he felt them too heavy, and thought I should make an abatement. He grew by degrees less civil, put on more of the master, frequently found fault, was captious, and seemed ready for an outbreaking. I went on, nevertheless, with a good deal of patience, thinking that his encumbered circumstances were partly the cause. At length a

---

[8]David Harry (1708–1760).
[9]A recruitment advertisement circulated by "crimps," who lured men into military or indentured service.
[10]Letters of type. Thus, a printer "out of sorts" is angry.
[11]Type foundry owned by Thomas James, the biggest in London.

[12]Stamping or punching tools.
[13]Molds for casting type.
[14]One who does all, a jack-of-all-trades.

trifle snapped our connections; for, a great noise happening near the courthouse, I put my head out of the window to see what was the matter. Keimer, being in the street, looked up and saw me, called out to me in a loud voice and angry tone to mind my business, adding some reproachful words, that nettled me the more for their publicity, all the neighbors who were looking out on the same occasion being witnesses how I was treated. He came up immediately into the printing-house, continued the quarrel, high words passed on both sides, he gave me the quarter's warning we had stipulated, expressing a wish that he had not been obliged to so long a warning. I told him his wish was unnecessary, for I would leave him that instant; and so, taking my hat, walked out of doors, desiring Meredith, whom I saw below, to take care of some things I left, and bring them to my lodgings.

Meredith came accordingly in the evening, when we talked my affair over. He had conceived a great regard for me, and was very unwilling that I should leave the house while he remained in it. He dissuaded me from returning to my native country, which I began to think of. He reminded me that Keimer was in debt for all he possessed; that his creditors began to be uneasy; that he kept his shop miserably, sold often without profit for ready money, and often trusted without keeping accounts; that he must therefore fail, which would make a vacancy I might profit of. I objected my want of money. He then let me know that his father had a high opinion of me, and, from some discourse that had passed between them, he was sure would advance money to set us up, if I would enter into partnership with him. "My time," says he, "will be out with Keimer in the spring. By that time we may have our press and types in from London. I am sensible I am no workman. If you like it, your skill in the business shall be set against the stock I furnish, and we will share the profits equally."

The proposal was agreeable, and I consented. His father was in town and approved of it, the more as he saw I had great influence with his son, had prevailed on him to abstain long from dram-drinking, and he hoped might break him off that wretched habit entirely, when we came to be so closely connected. I gave an inventory to the father, who carried it to a merchant; the things were sent for; the secret was to be kept till they should arrive, and in the mean time I was to get work, if I could, at the other printing-house. But I found no vacancy there, and so remained idle a few days, when Keimer, on a prospect of being employed to print some paper money in New Jersey, which would require cuts and various types that I only could supply, and apprehending Bradford might engage me and get the job from him, sent me a very civil message, that old friends should not part for a few words, the effect of sudden passion, and wishing me to return. Meredith persuaded me to comply, as it would give more opportunity for his improvement under my daily instructions. So I returned, and we went on more smoothly than for some time before. The New Jersey job was obtained. I contrived a copperplate press for it, the first that had been seen in the country. I cut several ornaments and checks for the bills. We went together to Burlington,[15] where I executed the whole to satisfaction, and he received so large a sum for the work as to be enabled thereby to keep his head much longer above water.

At Burlington I made an acquaintance with many principal people of the province. Several of them had been appointed by the Assembly a committee to attend the press, and take care that no more bills were printed than the law directed. They were therefore, by turns, constantly with us, and generally he who attended, brought with him a friend or two for company. My mind having been much more improved by reading than Keimer's, I suppose it was for that reason my conversation seemed to be more valued. They had me to their houses, introduced me to

---

[15]In New Jersey.

their friends, and showed me much civility, while he, though the master, was a little neglected. In truth, he was an odd fish, ignorant of common life, fond of rudely opposing received opinions, slovenly to extreme dirtiness, enthusiastic [16] in some points of religion, and a little knavish withal.

We continued there near three months, and by that time I could reckon among my acquired friends, Judge Allen, Samuel Bustill, the secretary of the Province, Isaac Pearson, Joseph Cooper, and several of the Smiths, members of Assembly, and Isaac Decow, the surveyor-general. The latter was a shrewd, sagacious old man, who told me that he began for himself, when young, by wheeling clay for the brickmakers, learned to write after he was of age, carried the chain for surveyors, who taught him surveying, and he had now by his industry, acquired a good estate; and says he, "I foresee that you will soon work this man out of his business and make a fortune in it at Philadelphia." He had not then the least intimation of my intention to set up there or anywhere. These friends were afterwards of great use to me, as I occasionally was to some of them. They all continued their regard for me as long as they lived.

Before I enter upon my public appearance in business, it may be well to let you know the then state of my mind with regard to my principles and morals, that you may see how far those influenced the future events of my life. My parents had early given me religious impressions, and brought me through my childhood piously in the Dissenting way. But I was scarce fifteen, when, after doubting by turns of several points, as I found them disputed in the different books I read, I began to doubt of Revelation itself. Some books against Deism fell into my hands; they were said to be the substance of sermons preached at Boyle's Lectures.[17] It happened that they wrought an effect on me quite contrary to what was intended by them; for the arguments of the Deists, which were quoted to be refuted, appeared to me much stronger than the refutations. In short, I soon became a thorough Deist. My arguments perverted some others, particularly Collins and Ralph; but, each of them having afterwards wronged me greatly without the least compunction, and recollecting Keith's conduct towards me (who was another freethinker), and my own towards Vernon and Miss Read, which at times gave me great trouble, I began to suspect that this doctrine, though it might be true, was not very useful. My London pamphlet, which had for its motto these lines of Dryden:

> —Whatever is, is right.—
> Though purblind man
> Sees but a part of the chain, the nearest link,
> His eyes not carrying to the equal beam,
> That poises all above;[18]

and from the attributes of God, his infinite wisdom, goodness and power, concluded that nothing could possibly be wrong in the world, and that vice and virtue were empty distinctions, no such things existing, appeared now not so clever a performance as I once thought it; and I doubted whether some error had not insinuated itself unperceived into my argument, so as to infect all that followed, as is common in metaphysical reasonings.

I grew convinced that *truth, sincerity* and *integrity* in dealings between man and man were of the utmost importance to the felicity of life; and I formed written resolutions (which still remain in my journal book) to practice them ever while I lived. Revelation had indeed no weight with me, as such; but I entertained an

---

[16]Fanatical.

[17]Robert Boyle (1627–1691), a wealthy English chemist, established an annual lecture series to defend Christianity against attacks by skeptics.

[18]The first line is from Pope's *Essay on Man* (1733), Epistle I, line 294; the rest is from John Dryden (1631–1700), *Oedipus*, III, i, 245–48.

opinion that, though certain actions might not be bad *because* they were forbidden by it, or good *because* it commanded them, yet probably these actions might be forbidden *because* they were bad for us, or commanded *because* they were beneficial to us, in their own natures, all the circumstances of things considered. And this persuasion, with the kind hand of Providence, or some guardian angel, or accidental favorable circumstances and situations, or all together, preserved me (through this dangerous time of youth and the hazardous situations I was sometimes in among strangers, remote from the eye and advice of my father) without any *willful* gross immorality or injustice that might have been expected from my want of religion.[19] I say *willful*, because the instances I have mentioned had something of *necessity* in them, from my youth, inexperience, and the knavery of others. I had therefore a tolerable character to begin the world with, I valued it properly, and determined to preserve it.

VII [1727–1730: Setting up Partnership, the Junto, Dissolving Partnership, Paper Money]

We had not been long returned to Philadelphia before the new types arrived from London. We settled with Keimer, and left him by his consent before he heard of it. We found a house to hire near the market and took it. To lessen the rent (which was then but twenty-four pounds a year, though I have since known it to let for seventy), we took in Thomas Godfrey, a glazier,[1] and his family, who were to pay a considerable part of it to us, and we to board with them. We had scarce opened our letters and put our press in order before George House, an acquaintance of mine, brought a countryman to us, whom he had met in the street inquiring for a printer. All our cash was now expended in the variety of particulars we had been obliged to procure, and this countryman's five shillings, being our first fruits and coming so seasonably, gave me more pleasure than any crown[2] I have since earned; and from the gratitude I felt towards House has made me often more ready than perhaps I should otherwise have been to assist young beginners.

There are croakers in every country, always boding its ruin. Such a one then lived in Philadelphia, a person of note, an elderly man, with a wise look and very grave manner of speaking. His name was Samuel Mickle. This gentleman, a stranger to me, stopped one day at my door, and asked me if I was the young man who had lately opened a new printing-house. Being answered in the affirmative, he said he was sorry for me, because it was an expensive undertaking, and the expense would be lost; for Philadelphia was a sinking place, the people already half bankrupts, or near being so; all appearances to the contrary, such as new buildings and the rise of rents, being to his certain knowledge fallacious, for they were, in fact, among the things that would soon ruin us. And he gave me such a detail of misfortunes now existing, or that were soon to exist, that he left me half melancholy. Had I known him before I engaged in this business, probably I never should have done it. This man continued to live in this decaying place, and to declaim in the same strain, refusing for many years to buy a house there because all was going to destruction; and at last I had the pleasure of seeing him give five times as much for one as he might have bought it for when he first began his croaking.

I should have mentioned before, that in the autumn of the preceding year, I had formed most of my ingenious acquaintance into a club of mutual improve-

---

[19]Franklin has here crossed out: "some foolish intrigues with low women excepted, which from the expense were rather more prejudicial to me than to them."
[1]One who cuts and fits window glass. Thomas Godfrey

(1704–1749), later a member of Franklin's group, the Junto, and inventor of a quadrant for measuring altitudes in astronomy and navigation.
[2]Five-shilling coin.

ment, which we called the JUNTO.[3] We met on Friday evenings. The rules that I drew up required that every member in his turn should produce one or more queries on any point of Morals, Politics, or Natural Philosophy, to be discussed by the company, and once in three months produce and read an essay of his own writing on any subject he pleased. Our debates were to be under the direction of a president, and to be conducted in the sincere spirit of inquiry after truth, without fondness for dispute, or desire of victory; and to prevent warmth, all expressions of positiveness in opinions, or direct contradiction, were after some time made contraband, and prohibited under small pecuniary penalties.

The first members were Joseph Breintnal, a copier of deeds for the scriveners, a good-natured, friendly, middle-aged man, a great lover of poetry, reading all he could meet with, and writing some that was tolerable; very ingenious in many little Nicknackeries, and of sensible conversation. Thomas Godfrey, a self-taught mathematician, great in his way, and afterward inventor of what is now called Hadley's Quadrant. But he knew little out of his way, and was not a pleasing companion; as, like most great mathematicians I have met with, he expected universal precision in everything said, or was for ever denying or distinguishing upon trifles, to the disturbance of all conversation. He soon left us. Nicholas Scull, a surveyor, afterwards surveyor-general, who loved books, and sometimes made a few verses. William Parsons, bred a shoemaker, but, loving reading, had acquired a considerable share of mathematics, which he first studied with a view to astrology that he afterwards laughed at it. He also became surveyor-general. William Maugridge, a joiner, a most exquisite mechanic, and a solid, sensible man. Hugh Meredith, Stephen Potts, and George Webb I have characterized before. Robert Grace, a young gentleman of some fortune, generous, lively, and witty, a lover of punning and of his friends. And William Coleman, then a merchant's clerk, about my age, who had the coolest, clearest head, the best heart, and the exactest morals of almost any man I ever met with. He became afterwards a merchant of great note, and one of our provincial judges. Our friendship continued without interruption to his death, upwards of forty years. And the club continued almost as long, and was the best school of philosophy, morals, and politics that then existed in the province; for our queries, which were read the week preceding their discussion, put us on reading with attention upon the several subjects, that we might speak more to the purpose; and here, too, we acquired better habits of conversation, every thing being studied in our rules which might prevent our disgusting each other. From hence the long continuance of the club, which I shall have frequent occasion to speak further of hereafter.

But my giving this account of it here is to show something of the interest I had, every one of these exerting themselves in recommending business to us. Breintnal particularly procured us from the Quakers the printing forty sheets of their history, the rest being to be done by Keimer; and upon this we worked exceedingly hard, for the price was low.[4] It was a folio, pro patria size, in pica, with long primer notes.[5] I composed of it a sheet a day, and Meredith worked it off at press. It was often eleven at night and sometimes later before I had finished my distribution for the next day's work, for the little jobs sent in by our other friends now and then put us back. But so determined I was to continue doing a sheet a day of the folio, that one night when, having imposed my forms,[6] I thought my day's work over, one of them by accident was broken and two pages reduced to pie,[7] I immediately distributed and composed it over again before I went to bed. And

---

[3]Small group joined together by a common interest (from the Spanish *junta*).
[4]William Sewel, *The History of the Rise, Increase, and Progress of the Christian People called Quakers: Intermixed with Several Remarkable Occurrences* (1728).

[5]Folio, large pages; pica, 12-point type (1/6 inch) for the text, with the notes set in the smaller 10-point type, long primer.
[6]Locked the type in forms ready for printing.
[7]A heap.

this industry, visible to our neighbors, began to give us character and credit; particularly, I was told, that mention being made of the new printing-office at the merchants' Every-night club, the general opinion was that it must fail, there being already two printers in the place, Keimer and Bradford; but Dr. Baird (whom you and I saw many years after at his native place, St. Andrew's in Scotland) gave a contrary opinion: "For the industry of that Franklin," says he, "is superior to any thing I ever saw of the kind. I see him still at work when I go home from club, and he is at work again before his neighbors are out of bed." This struck the rest, and we soon after had offers from one of them to supply us with stationery. But as yet we did not choose to engage in shop business.

I mention this industry the more particularly and the more freely, though it seems to be talking in my own praise, that those of my posterity who shall read it may know the use of that virtue, when they see its effects in my favor throughout this relation.

George Webb, who had found a female friend that lent him wherewith to purchase his time of Keimer, now came to offer himself as a journeyman to us. We could not then employ him, but I foolishly let him know as a secret that I soon intended to begin a newspaper, and might then have work for him. My hopes of success, as I told him, were founded on this, that the then only newspaper, printed by Bradford, was a paltry thing, wretchedly managed, no way entertaining, and yet was profitable to him.[8] I therefore thought a good paper would scarcely fail of good encouragement. I requested Webb not to mention it, but he told it to Keimer, who immediately, to be beforehand with me, published proposals for printing one himself, on which Webb was to be employed. I resented this, and, to counteract them, as I could not yet begin our paper, I wrote several pieces of entertainment for Bradford's paper, under the title of the "Busy Body," which Breintnal continued some months.[9] By this means the attention of the public was fixed on that paper, and Keimer's proposals, which we burlesqued and ridiculed, were disregarded. He began his paper, however, and, after carrying it on three quarters of a year, with at most only ninety subscribers, he offered it to me for a trifle, and I, having been ready some time to go on with it, took it in hand directly; and it proved in a few years extremely profitable to me.[10]

I perceive that I am apt to speak in the singular number, though our partnership still continued. The reason may be that, in fact, the whole management of the business lay upon me. Meredith was no compositor, a poor pressman, and seldom sober. My friends lamented my connection with him, but I was to make the best of it.

Our first papers made a quite different appearance from any before in the province, a better type, and better printed; but some spirited remarks[11] of my writing, on the dispute then going on between Governor Burnet and the Massachusetts Assembly, struck the principal people, occasioned the paper and the manager of it to be much talked of, and in a few weeks brought them all to be our subscribers. Their example was followed by many, and our number went on growing continually. This was one of the first good effects of my having learned a little to scribble. Another was, that the leading men, seeing a newspaper now in the hands of one who could also handle a pen, thought it convenient to oblige and encourage me. Bradford still printed the votes, and laws, and other public busi-

---

[8]The American Weekly Mercury, begun December 22, 1719.
[9]Franklin wrote the first four pieces and parts of two others, published in February–March 1729.
[10]Keimer's paper was called The Universal Instructor in all Arts and Sciences: and Pennsylvania Gazette. When Franklin took it over on October 2, 1729, he shortened the title to The Pennsylvania Gazette and made it the most popular paper in the colonies.

[11]"Insert these remarks in a note" (Franklin's marginal note). Franklin, in the Gazette of October 9, 1792, praised the Assembly's "ardent spirit of liberty" in the dispute over the salary of William Burnet (1688–1729), governor of New York and New Jersey (1720–28) and Massachusetts (1728–29).

ness. He had printed an address of the House to the governor in a coarse, blundering manner. We reprinted it elegantly and correctly, and sent one to every member. They were sensible of the difference, it strengthened the hands of our friends in the House, and they voted us their printers for the year ensuing.

Among my friends in the House I must not forget Mr. Hamilton, before mentioned, who was then returned from England, and had a seat in it.[12] He interested himself for me strongly in that instance, as he did in many others afterward, continuing his patronage till his death.[13]

Mr. Vernon, about this time, put me in mind of the debt I owed him, but did not press me. I wrote him an ingenuous letter of acknowledgment, craved his forbearance a little longer, which he allowed me, and as soon as I was able, I paid the principal with interest and many thanks. So that *erratum* was in some degree corrected.

But now another difficulty came upon me which I had never the least reason to expect. Mr. Meredith's father, who was to have paid for our printing-house according to the expectations given me, was able to advance only one hundred pounds currency, which had been paid; and a hundred more was due to the merchant, who grew impatient, and sued us all. We gave bail, but saw that if the money could not be raised in time, the suit must soon come to a judgment and execution, and our hopeful prospects must, with us, be ruined, as the press and letters must be sold for payment, perhaps at half price.

In this distress two true friends, whose kindness I have never forgotten, nor ever shall forget while I can remember any thing, came to me separately, unknown to each other, and, without any application from me, offering each of them to advance me all the money that should be necessary to enable me to take the whole business upon myself, if that should be practicable; but they did not like my continuing the partnership with Meredith, who, as they said, was often seen drunk in the streets, and playing at low games in ale-houses, much to our discredit. These two friends were William Coleman and Robert Grace.[14] I told them I could not propose a separation while any prospect remained of the Meredith's fulfilling their part of our agreement, because I thought myself under great obligations to them for what they had done, and would do if they could. But, if they finally failed in their performance, and our partnership must be dissolved, I should then think myself at liberty to accept the assistance of my friends.

Thus the matter rested for some time, when I said to my partner, "Perhaps your father is dissatisfied at the part you have undertaken in this affair of ours and is unwilling to advance for you and me what he would for you alone. If that is the case, tell me, and I will resign the whole to you, and go about my business." "No," said he, "my father has really been disappointed and is really unable; and I am unwilling to distress him farther. I see this is a business I am not fit for. I was bred a farmer, and it was a folly in me to come to town and put myself, at thirty years of age, an apprentice to learn a new trade. Many of our Welsh people are going to settle in North Carolina, where land is cheap. I am inclined to go with them, and follow my old employment. You may find friends to assist you. If you will take the debts of the company upon you, return to my father the hundred pound he has advanced, pay my little personal debts, and give me thirty pounds and a new saddle, I will relinquish the partnership and leave the whole in your hands." I agreed to this proposal. It was drawn up in writing, signed, and sealed immediately. I gave him what he demanded, and he went soon after to Carolina, from whence he sent me next year two long letters, containing the best account

---

[12]Andrew Hamilton served as speaker of the Assembly in 1729–30 and later.
[13]"I got his son once £500" (Franklin's note).

[14]William Coleman (1704–1769) and Robert Grace (1709–1766); the latter's iron works cast Franklin's stoves, resembling fireplaces.

that had been given of that country, the climate, the soil, husbandry, etc., for in those matters he was very judicious. I printed them in the papers,[15] and they gave great satisfaction to the public.

As soon as he was gone, I recurred to my two friends; and because I would not give an unkind preference to either, I took half of what each had offered and I wanted of one, and half of the other; paid off the company debts, and went on with the business in my own name, advertising that the partnership was dissolved. I think this was in or about the year 1729.[16]

About this time there was a cry among the people for more paper money, only fifteen thousand pounds being extant in the province, and that soon to be sunk. The wealthy inhabitants opposed any addition, being against all paper currency, from an apprehension that it would depreciate, as it had done in New England, to the prejudice of all creditors. We had discussed this point in our Junto, where I was on the side of an addition, being persuaded that the first small sum struck in 1723 had done much good by increasing the trade, employment, and number of inhabitants in the province, since I now saw all the old houses inhabited, and many new ones building; whereas I remembered well, that when I first walked about the streets of Philadelphia, eating my roll, I saw most of the houses in Walnut Street between Second and Front streets with bills on their doors, "To be let"; and many likewise in Chestnut Street and other streets, which made me then think the inhabitants of the city were deserting it one after another.

Our debates possessed me so fully of the subject, that I wrote and printed an anonymous pamphlet on it, entitled "The Nature and Necessity of a Paper Currency."[17] It was well received by the common people in general; but the rich men disliked it, for it increased and strengthened the clamor for more money, and they happening to have no writers among them that were able to answer it, their opposition slackened, and the point was carried by a majority in the House. My friends there, who conceived I had been of some service, thought fit to reward me by employing me in printing the money, a very profitable job and a great help to me.[18] This was another advantage gained by my being able to write.

The utility of this currency became by time and experience so evident as never afterwards to be much disputed, so that it grew soon to fifty-five thousand pounds, and in 1739 to eighty thousand pounds, since which it arose during war to upwards of three hundred and fifty thousand pounds, trade, building, and inhabitants all the while increasing, though I now think there are limits beyond which the quantity may be hurtful.

I soon after obtained, through my friend Hamilton, the printing of the Newcastle[19] paper money, another profitable job, as I then thought it; small things appearing great to those in small circumstances. And these, to me, were really great advantages, as they were great encouragements. He procured me, also, the printing of the laws and votes of that government, which continued in my hands as long as I followed the business.

VIII [1730–1731: Expanding Business, Marriage, Subscription Library]

I now opened a little stationer's shop.[1] I had in it blanks of all sorts, the correctest that ever appeared among us, being assisted in that by my friend Breintnal. I had also paper, parchment, chapmen's books, etc. One Whitemash, a compositor I had known in London, an excellent workman, now came to me, and

---

[15]*Pennsylvania Gazette*, May 6 and 13, 1731.
[16]The exact date was July 14, 1730.
[17]*A Modest Inquiry into the Nature and Necessity of a Paper Currency* (1729).
[18]Andrew Bradford got the currency-printing contract in 1729; Franklin got the next one in 1731.

[19]New Castle (also Kent and Sussex counties, now Delaware) shared Pennsylvania's proprietary governor, but had a separate legislature. Andrew Hamilton was speaker of both legislative bodies.
[1]About July 1730.

worked with me constantly and diligently, and I took an apprentice, the son of Aquila Rose.

I began now gradually to pay off the debt I was under for the printing-house. In order to secure my credit and character as a tradesman, I took care not only to be in *reality* industrious and frugal, but to avoid all *appearances* of the contrary. I dressed plainly. I was seen at no places of idle diversion. I never went out a-fishing or shooting; a book, indeed, sometimes debauched me from my work, but that was seldom, snug, and gave no scandal; and to show that I was not above my business, I sometimes brought home the paper I purchased at the stores through the streets on a wheelbarrow. Thus being esteemed an industrious, thriving young man, and paying duly for what I bought, the merchants who imported stationery solicited my custom; others proposed supplying me with books, and I went on swimmingly. In the mean time, Keimer's credit and business declining daily, he was at last forced to sell his printing-house to satisfy his creditors. He went to Barbadoes, and there lived some years in very poor circumstances.

His apprentice, David Harry, whom I had instructed while I worked with him, set up in his place at Philadelphia, having bought his materials. I was at first apprehensive of a powerful rival in Harry, as his friends were very able, and had a good deal of interest. I therefore proposed a partnership to him, which he, fortunately for me, rejected with scorn. He was very proud, dressed like a gentleman, lived expensively, took much diversion and pleasure abroad, ran in debt, and neglected his business; upon which, all business left him; and, finding nothing to do, he followed Keimer to Barbadoes, taking the printing-house with him. There this apprentice employed his former master as a journeyman. They quarreled often. Harry went continually behindhand, and at length was forced to sell his types and return to his country work in Pennsylvania. The person that bought them employed Keimer to use them, but in a few years he died.

There remained now no competitor with me at Philadelphia but the old one, Bradford, who was rich and easy, did a little printing now and then by straggling hands, but was not very anxious about the business. However, as he kept the post-office, it was imagined he had better opportunities of obtaining news; his paper was thought a better distributer of advertisements than mine, and therefore had many more, which was a profitable thing to him and a disadvantage to me. For though I did indeed receive and send papers by the post, yet the public opinion was otherwise, for what I did send was by bribing the riders, who took them privately, Bradford being unkind enough to forbid it, which occasioned some resentment on my part; and I thought so meanly of him for it, that when I afterward came into his situation,[2] I took care never to imitate it.

I had hitherto continued to board with Godfrey, who lived in part of my house with his wife and children, and had one side of the shop for his glazier's business, though he worked little, being always absorbed in his mathematics. Mrs. Godfrey projected a match for me with a relation's daughter, took opportunities of bringing us often together, till a serious courtship on my part ensued, the girl being in herself very deserving. The old folks encouraged me by continual invitations to supper, and by leaving us together, till at length it was time to explain. Mrs. Godfrey managed our little treaty. I let her know that I expected as much money with their daughter as would pay off my remaining debt for the printing-house, which I believe was not then above a hundred pounds. She brought me word they had no such sum to spare. I said they might mortgage their house in the loan-office. The answer to this, after some days, was that they did not approve the match;

---

[2]Franklin served as postmaster at Philadelphia, beginning in 1737; he became deputy postmaster for the colonies in 1753.

that, on inquiry of Bradford, they had been informed the printing business was not a profitable one; the types would soon be worn out and more wanted; that S. Keimer and D. Harry had failed one after the other, and I should probably soon follow them; and, therefore, I was forbidden the house, and the daughter shut up.

Whether this was a real change of sentiment or only artifice, on a supposition of our being too far engaged in affection to retract, and therefore that we should steal a marriage, which would leave them at liberty to give or withhold what they pleased, I know not; but I suspected the latter, resented it, and went no more. Mrs. Godfrey brought me afterwards some more favorable accounts of their disposition, and would have drawn me on again; but I declared absolutely my resolution to have nothing more to do with that family.[3] This was resented by the Godfreys; we differed, and they removed, leaving me the whole house, and I resolved to take no more inmates.

But this affair having turned my thoughts to marriage, I looked round me and made overtures of acquaintance in other places; but soon found that, the business of a printer being generally thought a poor one, I was not to expect money with a wife, unless with such a one as I should not otherwise think agreeable. In the mean time, that hard-to-be-governed passion of youth hurried me frequently into intrigues with low women that fell in my way, which were attended with some expense and great inconvenience, besides a continual risk to my health by a distemper which of all things I dreaded, though by great good luck I escaped it.

A friendly correspondence as neighbors and old acquaintances had continued between me and Mrs. Read's family, who all had a regard for me from the time of my first lodging in their house. I was often invited there and consulted in their affairs, wherein I sometimes was of service. I pitied poor Miss Read's unfortunate situation, who was generally dejected, seldom cheerful, and avoided company. I considered my giddiness and inconstancy when in London as in a great degree the cause of her unhappiness, though the mother was good enough to think the fault more her own than mine, as she had prevented our marrying before I went thither, and persuaded the other match in my absence. Our mutual affection was revived, but there were now great objections to our union. The match was indeed looked upon as invalid, a preceding wife being said to be living in England; but this could not easily be proved, because of the distance; and, though there was a report of his death, it was not certain. Then, though it should be true, he had left many debts, which his successor might be called upon to pay. We ventured, however, over all these difficulties, and I took her to wife, September 1st, 1730.[4] None of the inconveniences happened that we had apprehended; she proved a good and faithful helpmate, assisted me much by attending the shop; we throve together, and have ever mutually endeavored to make each other happy. Thus I corrected that great *erratum* as well as I could.

About this time, our club meeting, not at a tavern, but in a little room of Mr. Grace's, set apart for that purpose, a proposition was made by me, that since our books were often referred to in our disquisitions upon the queries, it might be convenient to us to have them altogether where we met, that upon occasion they might be consulted; and by thus clubbing our books to a common library, we should, while we liked to keep them together, have each of us the advantage of using the books of all the other members, which would be nearly as beneficial as if each owned the whole. It was liked and agreed to, and we filled one end of the

---

[3]Franklin's expectation of a dowry was not unusual for the time.
[4]Technically, Deborah Read was still the wife of John Rogers as long as she had no proof he was dead or a bigamist.

The two of them could have been convicted of bigamy had Rogers turned up after their marriage. Thus, theirs was a common-law marriage, legally valid, and the children were legitimate.

room with such books as we could best spare. The number was not so great as we expected; and though they had been of great use, yet some inconveniences occurring for want of due care of them, the collection, after about a year, was separated, and each took his books home again.

And now I set on foot my first project of a public nature, that for a subscription library. I drew up the proposals, got them put into form by our great scrivener, Brockden, and, by the help of my friends in the Junto, procured fifty subscribers of forty shillings each to begin with, and ten shillings a year for fifty years, the term our company was to continue. We afterwards obtained a charter, the company being increased to one hundred. This was the mother of all the North American subscription libraries, now so numerous.[5] It is become a great thing itself, and continually increasing. These libraries have improved the general conversation of the Americans, made the common tradesmen and farmers as intelligent as most gentlemen from other countries, and perhaps have contributed in some degree to the stand so generally made throughout the colonies in defence of their privileges.

PART TWO

IX [1730–1731: Public Library, Wife as Helpmate, Religion]

Continuation of the Account of my Life, begun at Passy, near Paris, 1784.

It is some time since I received the above letters,[1] but I have been too busy till now to think of complying with the request they contain. It might, too, be much better done if I were at home among my papers, which would aid my memory, and help to ascertain dates. But my return being uncertain, and having just now a little leisure,[2] I will endeavor to recollect and write what I can; if I live to get home, it may there be corrected and improved.

Not having any copy here of what is already written, I know not whether an account is given of the means I used to establish the Philadelphia public library, which, from a small beginning, is now become so considerable, though I remember to have come down to near the time of that transaction, 1730. I will therefore begin here with an account of it, which may be struck out if found to have been already given.

At the time I established myself in Pennsylvania, there was not a good bookseller's shop in any of the colonies to the southward of Boston. In New York and Philadelphia the printers were indeed stationers; they sold only paper, etc., almanacs, ballads, and a few common school books. Those who loved reading were obliged to send for their books from England. The members of the Junto had each a few. We had left the alehouse, where we first met, and hired a room to hold our club in. I proposed that we should all of us bring our books to that room, where they would not only be ready to consult in our conferences, but become a

---

[5]The Library Company of Philadelphia (1731) was the first *subscription* library in the colonies, but other libraries, public or semipublic, had existed before.

[1]The two letters, not actually in the manuscript, are from Abel James (c. 1726–1790) and Benjamin Vaughan (1751–1835), pleading with Franklin to continue the account of his life. James, a prominent Philadelphia Quaker merchant, was a long-time friend of Franklin. Vaughan, a British merchant and diplomat, met Franklin in London before the Revolution and edited the first general collection of

Franklin's works (1779). In a memorandum prepared to introduce the letters, Franklin wrote that he was continuing his autobiography "in compliance with the advice contained in these letters, and accordingly intended for the public."

[2]Franklin's was one of the signatures on the Treaty of Peace with Great Britain, September 3, 1783, negotiated in Paris. Franklin had asked to come home, but he was requested to remain as minister. Thomas Jefferson succeeded him in May, 1785.

common benefit, each of us being at liberty to borrow such as he wished to read at home. This was accordingly done, and for some time contented us.

Finding the advantage of this little collection, I proposed to render the benefit from books more common, by commencing a public subscription library. I drew a sketch of the plan and rules that would be necessary, and got a skilful convey-ancer, Mr. Charles Brockden, to put the whole in form of articles of agreement to be subscribed, by which each subscriber engaged to pay a certain sum down for the first purchase of books and an annual contribution for increasing them. So few were the readers at that time in Philadelphia, and the majority of us so poor, that I was not able, with great industry, to find more than fifty persons, mostly young tradesmen, willing to pay down for this purpose forty shillings each, and ten shillings per annum. On this little fund we began. The books were imported. The library was opened one day in the week for lending them to the subscribers, on their promissory notes to pay double the value if not duly returned. The insti-tution soon manifested its utility, was imitated by other towns, and in other prov-inces. The libraries were augmented by donations; reading became fashionable; and our people, having no public amusements to divert their attention from study, became better acquainted with books, and in a few years were observed by strangers to be better instructed and more intelligent than people of the same rank generally are in other countries.

When we were about to sign the above-mentioned articles, which were to be binding on us, our heirs, etc., for fifty years, Mr. Brockden, the scrivener, said to us, "You are young men, but it is scarce probable that any of you will live to see the expiration of the term fixed in this instrument." A number of us, however, are yet living; but the instrument was after a few years rendered null by a charter that incorporated and gave perpetuity to the company.

The objections and reluctances I met with in soliciting the subscriptions made me soon feel the impropriety of presenting one's self as the proposer of any use-ful project, that might be supposed to raise one's reputation in the smallest degree above that of one's neighbors, when one has need of their assistance to accomplish that project. I therefore put myself as much as I could out of sight, and stated it as a scheme of a *number of friends,* who had requested me to go about and propose it to such as they thought lovers of reading. In this way my affair went on more smoothly, and I ever after practiced it on such occasions; and, from my frequent successes, can heartily recommend it. The present little sacrifice of your vanity will afterwards be amply repaid. If it remains a while uncertain to whom the merit belongs, some one more vain than yourself will be encouraged to claim it, and then even envy will be disposed to do you justice by plucking those assumed feath-ers, and restoring them to their right owner.

This library afforded me the means of improvement by constant study, for which I set apart an hour or two each day, and thus repaired in some degree the loss of the learned education my father once intended for me. Reading was the only amusement I allowed myself. I spent no time in taverns, games, or frolics of any kind. And my industry in my business continued as indefatigable as it was necessary. I was in debt for my printing-house, I had a young family coming on to be educated,[3] and I had to contend with for business two printers who were estab-lished in the place before me. My circumstances, however, grew daily easier. My original habits of frugality continuing, and my father having, among his instruc-tions to me when a boy, frequently repeated a proverb of Solomon, "Seest thou a man diligent in his calling, he shall stand before kings, he shall not stand before

---

[3]The children were Franklin's illegitimate son William (born *c.* 1731), Francis Folger (1732–1736), Sarah (born 1743).

mean men."[4] I from thence considered industry as a means of obtaining wealth and distinction, which encouraged me, though I did not think that I should ever literally stand before kings, which, however, has since happened; for I have stood before five, and even had the honor of sitting down with one, the King of Denmark, to dinner.[5]

We have an English proverb that says, "He that would thrive/Must ask his wife." It was lucky for me that I had one as much disposed to industry and frugality as myself. She assisted me cheerfully in my business, folding and stitching pamphlets, tending shop, purchasing old linen rags for the paper-makers, etc., etc. We kept no idle servants, our table was plain and simple, our furniture of the cheapest. For instance, my breakfast was a long time bread and milk (no tea), and I ate it out of a twopenny earthen porringer,[6] with a pewter spoon. But mark how luxury will enter families, and make a progress, in spite of principle. Being called one morning to breakfast, I found it in a china bowl, with a spoon of silver. They had been bought for me without my knowledge by my wife, and had cost her the enormous sum of three-and-twenty shillings, for which she had no other excuse or apology to make, but that she thought *her* husband deserved a silver spoon and china bowl as well as any of his neighbors. This was the first appearance of plate and china in our house, which afterwards, in a course of years, as our wealth increased, augmented gradually to several hundred pounds in value.

I had been religiously educated as a Presbyterian; and though some of the dogmas of that persuasion, such as the eternal decrees of God, election, reprobation, etc., appeared to me unintelligible, others doubtful, and I early absented myself from the public assemblies of the sect, Sunday being my studying day, I never was without some religious principles. I never doubted, for instance, the existence of the Deity; that he made the world, and governed it by his Providence; that the most acceptable service of God was the doing good to man; that our souls are immortal; and that all crime will be punished, and virtue rewarded, either here or hereafter. These I esteemed the essentials of every religion; and, being to be found in all the religions we had in our country, I respected them all, though with different degrees of respect, as I found them more or less mixed with other articles, which, without any tendency to inspire, promote, or confirm morality, served principally to divide us, and make us unfriendly to one another. This respect to all, with an opinion that the worst had some good effects, induced me to avoid all discourse that might tend to lessen the good opinion another might have of his own religion; and as our province increased in people, and new places of worship were continually wanted, and generally erected by voluntary contribution, my mite for such purpose, whatever might be the sect, was never refused.[7]

Though I seldom attended any public worship, I had still an opinion of its propriety, and of its utility when rightly conducted, and I regularly paid my annual subscription for the support of the only Presbyterian minister or meeting we had in Philadelphia. He used to visit me sometimes as a friend, and admonish me to attend his administrations, and I was now and then prevailed on to do so, once for five Sundays successively. Had he been in my opinion a good preacher, perhaps I might have continued, notwithstanding the occasion I had for the Sunday's leisure in my course of study. But his discourses were chiefly either polemic arguments, or explications of the peculiar doctrines of our sect, and were all to me very dry, uninteresting, and unedifying, since not a single moral principle was inculcated or

---

[4]Proverbs 22:29.
[5]Franklin was invited to dine with King Christian VI of Denmark in England in 1768. Other kings are Louis XV and Louis XVI of France, and probably George II and George III of Great Britain.

[6]Bowl for porridge.
[7]Records of the Congregation Mikveh Israel, Philadelphia, show that Franklin contributed to pay off a debt for building a synagogue.

enforced, their aim seeming to be rather to make us Presbyterians than good citizens.

At length he took for his text that verse of the fourth chapter of Philippians, "Finally, brethren, whatsoever things are true, honest, just, pure, lovely, or of good report, if there be any virtue, or any praise, think on these things."[8] And I imagined, in a sermon on such a text, we could not miss of having some morality. But he confined himself to five points only, as meant by the apostle, viz. 1. Keeping holy the Sabbath day. 2. Being diligent in reading the holy Scriptures. 3. Attending duly the public worship. 4. Partaking of the Sacrament. 5. Paying a due respect to God's ministers. These might be all good things; but, as they were not the kind of good things that I expected from that text, I despaired of ever meeting with them from any other, was disgusted, and attended his preaching no more. I had some years before composed a little Liturgy, or form of prayer, for my own private use (viz., in 1728), entitled, *Articles of Belief and Acts of Religion*. I returned to the use of this, and went no more to the public assemblies. My conduct might be blameable, but I leave it, without attempting further to excuse it; my present purpose being to relate facts, and not to make apologies for them.

X [1730s: Project for Moral Perfection, Weakness in Order, Problems with Pride]

It was about this time I conceived the bold and arduous project of arriving at moral perfection. I wished to live without committing any fault at any time; I would conquer all that either natural inclination, custom, or company might lead me into. As I knew, or thought I knew, what was right and wrong, I did not see why I might not *always* do the one and avoid the other. But I soon found I had undertaken a task of more difficulty than I had imagined. While my care was employed in guarding against one fault, I was often surprised by another. Habit took the advantage of inattention. Inclination was sometimes too strong for reason. I concluded, at length, that the mere speculative conviction that it was our interest to be completely virtuous was not sufficient to prevent our slipping; and that the contrary habits must be broken, and good ones acquired and established, before we can have any dependence on a steady, uniform rectitude of conduct. For this purpose I therefore contrived the following method.

In the various enumerations of the moral virtues I had met with in my reading, I found the catalogue more or less numerous, as different writers included more or fewer ideas under the same name. Temperance, for example, was by some confined to eating and drinking, while by others it was extended to mean the moderating every other pleasure, appetite, inclination, or passion, bodily or mental, even to our avarice and ambition. I proposed to myself, for the sake of clearness, to use rather more names, with fewer ideas annexed to each, than a few names with more ideas; and I included under thirteen names of virtues all that at that time occurred to me as necessary or desirable, and annexed to each a short precept, which fully expressed the extent I gave to its meaning.

These names of virtues, with their precepts, were:

1. TEMPERANCE.

Eat not to dullness; drink not to elevation.

2. SILENCE.

Speak not but what may benefit others or yourself; avoid trifling conversation.

---

[8]Philippians 4:8.

3. ORDER.

Let all your things have their places; let each part of your business have its time.

4. RESOLUTION.

Resolve to perform what you ought; perform without fail what you resolve.

5. FRUGALITY.

Make no expense but to do good to others or yourself; *i.e.,* waste nothing.

6. INDUSTRY.

Lose no time; be always employed in something useful; cut off all unnecessary actions.

7. SINCERITY.

Use no hurtful deceit; think innocently and justly, and, if you speak, speak accordingly.

8. JUSTICE.

Wrong none by doing injuries, or omitting the benefits that are your duty.

9. MODERATION.

Avoid extremes; forbear resenting injuries so much as you think they deserve.

10. CLEANLINESS.

Tolerate no uncleanliness in body, clothes, or habitation.

11. TRANQUILITY.

Be not disturbed at trifles, or at accidents common or unavoidable.

12. CHASTITY.

Rarely use venery but for health or offspring, never to dullness, weakness, or the injury of your own or another's peace or reputation.

13. HUMILITY.

Imitate Jesus and Socrates.

My intention being to acquire the *habitude* of all these virtues, I judged it would be well not to distract my attention by attempting the whole at once, but to fix it on one of them at a time; and, when I should be master of that, then to proceed to another, and so on, till I should have gone through the thirteen. And, as the previous acquisition of some might facilitate the acquisition of certain others, I arranged them with that view, as they stand above. *Temperance* first, as it tends to procure that coolness and clearness of head, which is so necessary where constant vigilance was to be kept up, and guard maintained against the unremitting attraction of ancient habits, and the force of perpetual temptations. This being acquired and established, *Silence* would be more easy; and my desire being to gain knowledge at the same time that I improved in virtue, and considering that in conversation it was obtained rather by the use of the ears than of the tongue, and therefore wishing to break a habit I was getting into of prattling, punning, and joking, which only made me acceptable to trifling company, I gave *Silence* the second place. This and the next, *Order,* I expected would allow me more time for attending to my project and my studies. *Resolution,* once become habitual, would keep me firm in my endeavors to obtain all the subsequent virtues; *Frugality* and *Industry*, by freeing me from my remaining debt, and producing affluence and independence, would make more easy the practice of *Sincerity* and *Justice*, etc., etc. Conceiving then, that, agreeably to the advice of Pythagoras in his *Golden Verses*,[1] daily examination would be necessary, I contrived the following method for conducting that examination.

I made a little book, in which I allotted a page for each of the virtues. I ruled each page with red ink, so as to have seven columns, one for each day of the week, marking each column with a letter for the day. I crossed these columns with thirteen red lines, marking the beginning of each line with the first letter of one of the virtues, on which line, and in its proper column, I might mark, by a little black spot, every fault I found upon examination to have been committed respecting that virtue upon that day.

Form of the pages.

TEMPERANCE.						
EAT NOT TO DULLNESS.						
DRINK NOT TO ELEVATION.						
	S.	M.	T.	W.	T.	F.	S.
T.							
S.	*	*		*		*	
O.	**	*	*		*	*	*
R.			*			*	
F.		*			*		
I.		*					
S.							
J.							
M.							
C.							
T.							
C.							
H.							

I determined to give a week's strict attention to each of the virtues successively. Thus, in the first week, my great guard was to avoid every the least offence against *Temperance*, leaving the other virtues to their ordinary chance, only marking every evening the faults of the day. Thus, if in the first week I could keep my first line, marked T, clear of spots, I supposed the habit of that virtue so much strengthened, and its opposite weakened, that I might venture extending my attention to include the next, and for the following week keep both lines clear of spots. Proceeding thus to the last, I could go through a course complete in thir-

[1]Pythagoras, Greek philosopher and mathematician of the sixth century B.C.; a marginal note indicated the insertion of verses translated: "Let sleep not close your eyes till you have thrice examined the transactions of the day: where have I strayed, what have I done, what good have I omitted?"

teen weeks, and four courses in a year. And like him who, having a garden to weed, does not attempt to eradicate all the bad herbs at once, which would exceed his reach and his strength, but works on one of the beds at a time, and, having accomplished the first, proceeds to a second, so I should have, I hoped, the encouraging pleasure of seeing on my pages the progress I made in virtue, by clearing successively my lines of their spots, till in the end, by a number of courses, I should be happy in viewing a clean book, after a thirteen weeks' daily examination.

This my little book had for its motto these lines from Addison's *Cato:*

> Here will I hold: If there is a power above us
> (And that there is, all nature cries aloud
> Through all her works), He must delight in virtue,
> And that which he delights in must be happy.[2]

Another from Cicero,

> O vitae Philosophia dux! O virtutum indagatrix expultrixque vitiorum! Unus dies, bene et ex praeceptis tuis actus, peccanti immortalitati est anteponendus.[3]

Another from the Proverbs of Solomon, speaking of wisdom or virtue:

> Length of days is in her right hand, and in her left hand riches and honor. Her ways are ways of pleasantness, and all her paths are peace.
> 3:16,17.

And conceiving God to be the fountain of wisdom, I thought it right and necessary to solicit his assistance for obtaining it; to this end I formed the following little prayer, which was prefixed to my tables of examination, for daily use.

> O powerful Goodness! bountiful Father! merciful Guide! Increase in me that wisdom which discovers my truest interests. Strengthen my resolutions to perform what that wisdom dictates. Accept my kind offices to thy other children as the only return in my power for thy continual favors to me.

I used also sometimes a little prayer which I took from Thomson's poems, viz.:

> Father of light and life, thou Good Supreme!
> O teach me what is good; teach me Thyself!
> Save me from folly, vanity, and vice,
> From every low pursuit; and fill my soul
> With knowledge, conscious peace, and virtue pure,
> Sacred, substantial, never-fading bliss![4]

The precept of *Order* requiring that *every part of my business should have its allotted time,* one page in my little book contained the following scheme of employment for the twenty-four hours of a natural day.

[2]Joseph Addison, *Cato: A Tragedy* (1713), V, i, 15–18.
[3]Marcus Tullius Cicero (106–43 B.C.) Roman philosopher and orator, in *Tusculan Disputations*, V, ii, 5 (lines omitted after *vitiorum*): "O philosophy, thou guide of life! O thou explorer of virtue and expeller of vice! . . . One day well spent and in accordance with thy lessons is to be preferred to an eternity of errors."
[4]James Thomson (1700–1748), English poet, author of *The Seasons*, "Winter" (1726), lines 218–23.

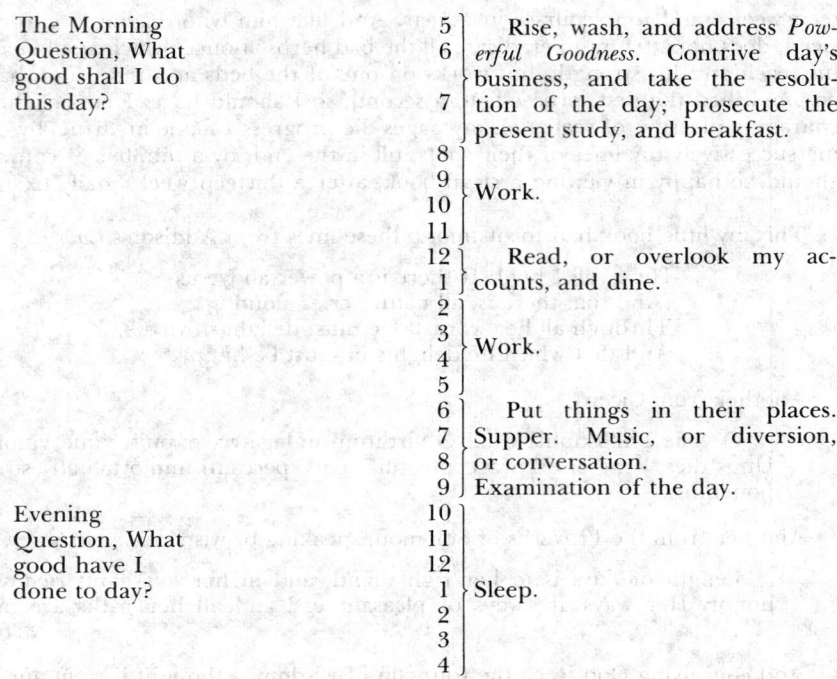

The Morning Question, What good shall I do this day?	5 6 7	Rise, wash, and address *Powerful Goodness*. Contrive day's business, and take the resolution of the day; prosecute the present study, and breakfast.
	8 9 10 11	Work.
	12 1	Read, or overlook my accounts, and dine.
	2 3 4 5	Work.
	6 7 8 9	Put things in their places. Supper. Music, or diversion, or conversation. Examination of the day.
Evening Question, What good have I done to day?	10 11 12 1 2 3 4	Sleep.

I entered upon the execution of this plan for self-examination, and continued it with occasional intermissions for some time. I was surprised to find myself so much fuller of faults than I had imagined, but I had the satisfaction of seeing them diminish. To avoid the trouble of renewing now and then my little book, which, by scraping out the marks on the paper of old faults to make room for new ones in a new course, became full of holes, I transferred my tables and precepts to the ivory leaves of a memorandum book, on which the lines were drawn with red ink that made a durable stain, and on those lines I marked my faults with a black lead pencil, which marks I could easily wipe out with a wet sponge. After a while I went through one course only in a year, and afterward only one in several years, till at length I omitted them entirely, being employed in voyages and business abroad, with a multiplicity of affairs that interfered; but I always carried my little book with me.

My scheme of ORDER gave me the most trouble; and I found that, though it might be practicable where a man's business was such as to leave him the disposition of his time, that of a journeyman printer, for instance, it was not possible to be exactly observed by a master who must mix with the world and often receive people of business at their own hours. *Order,* too, with regard to places for things, papers, etc., I found extremely difficult to acquire. I had not been early accustomed to it, and, having an exceeding good memory, I was not so sensible of the inconvenience attending want of method. This article, therefore, cost me so much painful attention, and my faults in it vexed me so much, and I made so little progress in amendment, and had such frequent relapses, that I was almost ready to give up the attempt, and content myself with a faulty character in that respect, like the man who, in buying an ax of a smith, my neighbor, desired to have the whole of its surface as bright as the edge. The smith consented to grind it bright for him if he would turn the wheel; he turned while the smith pressed the broad face of the ax hard and heavily on the stone which made the turning of it very fatiguing. The man came every now and then from the wheel to see how the work went on and at length would take his ax as it was, without farther grinding. "No," said the smith, "turn on, turn on; we shall have it bright by and by; as yet, it is only speckled." "Yes," says the man, *"but I think I like a speckled ax best."* And I believe this may have been the case with many who, having, for want of some such means as I employed, found the difficulty of obtaining good and breaking bad habits in other points of vice and virtue, have given up the struggle, and concluded that *a speckled ax was best;* for something, that pretended to be reason, was every now and then suggesting to me that such extreme nicety as I exacted of myself might be a kind of foppery in morals, which, if it were known, would make me ridiculous; that a perfect character might be attended with the inconvenience of being envied and hated; and that a benevolent man should allow a few faults in himself, to keep his friends in countenance.

In truth, I found myself incorrigible with respect to *Order;* and now I am grown old, and my memory bad, I feel very sensibly the want of it. But, on the whole, though I never arrived at the perfection I had been so ambitious of obtaining, but fell far short of it, yet I was, by the endeavor, a better and a happier man than I otherwise should have been if I had not attempted it; as those who aim at perfect writing by imitating the engraved copies, though they never reach the wished-for excellence of those copies, their hand is mended by the endeavor, and is tolerable while it continues fair and legible.

It may be well my posterity should be informed that to this little artifice, with the blessing of God, their ancestor owed the constant felicity of his life, down to his 79th year in which this is written. What reverses may attend the remainder is in the hand of Providence; but, if they arrive, the reflection on past happiness enjoyed ought to help his bearing them with more resignation. To *Temperance* he ascribes his long-continued health, and what is still left to him of a good constitution. To *Industry* and *Frugality,* the early easiness of his circumstances and acquisition of his fortune, with all that knowledge that enabled him to be a useful citizen, and obtained for him some degree of reputation among the learned. To *Sincerity* and *Justice,* the confidence of his country, and the honorable employs it conferred upon him. And to the joint influence of the whole mass of the virtues, even in the imperfect state he was able to acquire them, all that evenness of temper, and that cheerfulness in conversation, which makes his company still sought for and agreeable even to his younger acquaintance. I hope, therefore, that some of my descendants may follow the example and reap the benefit.

It will be remarked that, though my scheme was not wholly without religion, there was in it no mark of any of the distinguishing tenets of any particular sect. I had purposely avoided them; for, being fully persuaded of the utility and excellency of my method, and that it might be serviceable to people in all religions, and intending some time or other to publish it, I would not have any thing in it that should prejudice any one, of any sect, against it. I purposed writing a little comment on each virtue, in which I would have shown the advantages of possessing it, and the mischiefs attending its opposite vice; and I should have called my book THE ART OF VIRTUE, because it would have shown the means and manner of obtaining virtue, which would have distinguished it from the mere exhortation to be good, that does not instruct and indicate the means, but is like the apostle's man of verbal charity, who only, without showing to the naked and hungry how or where they might get clothes or victuals, exhorted them to be fed and clothed.— James 2:15,16.[5]

But it so happened that my intention of writing and publishing this comment was never fulfilled. I did, indeed, from time to time, put down short hints of the

---

[5]"If a brother or sister be naked, and destitute of daily food, And one of you say unto them, Depart in peace, be ye warmed and filled; notwithstanding ye give them not those things which are needful to the body; what doth it profit?"

sentiments, reasonings, etc., to be made use of in it, some of which I have still by me; but the necessary close attention to private business in the earlier part of my life, and public business since, have occasioned my postponing it; for, it being connected in my mind with *a great and extensive project* that required the whole man to execute, and which an unforeseen succession of employs prevented my attending to, it has hitherto remained unfinished.

In this piece it was my design to explain and enforce this doctrine, that vicious actions are not hurtful because they are forbidden, but forbidden because they are hurtful, the nature of man alone considered; that it was, therefore, every one's interest to be virtuous who wished to be happy even in this world; and I should, from this circumstance (there being always in the world a number of rich merchants, nobility, states, and princes, who have need of honest instruments for the management of their affairs, and such being so rare), have endeavored to convince young persons that no qualities were so likely to make a poor man's fortune as those of probity and integrity.

My list of virtues contained at first but twelve; but a Quaker friend having kindly informed me that I was generally thought proud; that my pride showed itself frequently in conversation; that I was not content with being in the right when discussing any point, but was overbearing, and rather insolent, of which he convinced me by mentioning several instances; I determined endeavoring to cure myself, if I could, of this vice or folly among the rest, and I added *Humility* to my list, giving an extensive meaning to the word.

I cannot boast of much success in acquiring the *reality* of this virtue, but I had a good deal with regard to the *appearance* of it. I made it a rule to forbear all direct contradiction to the sentiments of others, and all positive assertion of my own. I even forbid myself, agreeably to the old laws of our Junto, the use of every word or expression in the language that imported a fixed opinion, such as *certainly, undoubtedly*, etc., and I adopted, instead of them, *I conceive, I apprehend*, or *I imagine* a thing to be so or so; or it *so appears to me at present.* When another asserted something that I thought an error, I denied myself the pleasure of contradicting him abruptly, and of showing immediately some absurdity in his proposition; and in answering I began by observing that in certain cases or circumstances his opinion would be right, but in the present case there *appeared* or *seemed* to me some difference, etc. I soon found the advantage of this change in my manners; the conversations I engaged in went on more pleasantly. The modest way in which I proposed my opinions procured them a readier reception and less contradiction; I had less mortification when I was found to be in the wrong, and I more easily prevailed with others to give up their mistakes and join with me when I happened to be in the right.

And this mode, which I at first put on with some violence to natural inclination, became at length so easy, and so habitual to me, that perhaps for these fifty years past no one has ever heard a dogmatical expression escape me. And to this habit (after my character of integrity) I think it principally owing that I had early so much weight with my fellow-citizens when I proposed new institutions, or alterations in the old, and so much influence in public councils when I became a member; for I was but a bad speaker, never eloquent, subject to much hesitation in my choice of words, hardly correct in language, and yet I generally carried my points.

In reality, there is, perhaps, no one of our natural passions so hard to subdue as *Pride*. Disguise it, struggle with it, beat it down, stifle it, mortify it as much as one pleases, it is still alive, and will every now and then peep out and show itself. You will see it, perhaps, often in this history; for, even if I could conceive that I had completely overcome it, I should probably be proud of my humility.

Thus far written at Passy, 1784.

1771, 1784　　　　　　　　　　　　　　　　　　　　　　　　　　　*1868*

JOURNALS AND LETTERS

JOHN WOOLMAN   WILLIAM BARTRAM
MICHEL-GUILLAUME JEAN DE CRÈVECOEUR

Fiction is usually the place to find the creation of interesting characters and absorbing plots. But at a time when little or no fiction was written, diarists, journal keepers, and letter writers created selves or personas larger than life, and narrated adventures more absorbing than the actions found in fiction. The walking Quaker preacher John Woolman, the plain frontier farmer Michel-Guillaume Jean de Crèvecoeur, the shy poetic botanist William Bartram—all speak through their writing with still-living voices, and tell stories of their lives that continue to fascinate.

JOHN WOOLMAN
(1720–1772)

In his *Journal*, John Woolman remembers as a boy suddenly coming upon a nest of robins; when the mother robin flew about in panic, he threw a stone that killed her. Frightened by what he had done, the young Woolman then killed all the young robins, "supposing that better than to leave them to pine away and die miserably." But he found himself unable to forget his deed: "[I] could think of little else but the cruelties I had committed and was much troubled." For the thirty-six-year-old Woolman just beginning to keep his now famous *Journal*, this episode yielded a lesson—that God "hath placed a principle in the human mind which incites to exercise goodness toward every living creature."

In short, the young Woolman had experienced the flickering of the inner light—the central principle in the Quaker faith of his family. Quakers believed that all people experienced such an inner light, which came directly from God. It differed from the Calvinist's "divine and supernatural light," which spent its illumination in ratifying Calvinistic dogma or Puritan belief. The Quaker's inner light, on the other hand, illuminated the morality of human acts and brightened the path to salvation.

George Fox had founded the Society of Friends in England in the mid-1650s. Because members of the Society often shook in a kind of religious ecstasy, in "trembling before God's word," they were called "quakers," which gradually lost its satiric intent. The Quakers were persecuted by the Anglicans in England. And when they came to America they were persecuted by the Puritans, whose belief in religious freedom had limits. But William Penn was converted by George Fox to the Quaker faith, and when the crown settled debts owed to his family by making him immense land grants in the New World, Penn established the colony of Pennsylvania in 1682 as a "holy experiment" in religious and political freedom—and as a haven for the Society of Friends.

Believing every individual had access to God through the inner light, Quakers thought a trained ministry and church rituals unnecessary. Their meetings consisted of meditation in silence until members were moved to speak. They were firm believers in equality, and did not remove their hats in the presence of authorities. They refused to take oaths or to support wars. John Woolman grew up in a household in which these attitudes and beliefs were taken for granted. He was the oldest son and fourth child in a family of thirteen children, living on a farm at Rancocas, New Jersey. His education was limited to the elementary grades, but he was an avid reader, especially of the Bible.

He served as a tailor's apprentice, worked as a shop clerk and bookkeeper for a time, and then, in 1748, began his own business as a tailor and retailer in Mount Holly, New Jersey. In 1749, he felt successful enough to take a wife. His business prospered, but his interests turned more and more toward the religious life. He had been "recognized and recorded" as a minister by the Society of Friends in 1743, and he took that year the first of a number of "preaching trips" that were partly missionary in purpose.

In 1756, he confronted a personal crisis in his life in deciding what direction to take, continuing his burgeoning business or following the religious life to which he felt drawn. "My prayers," he wrote, "were put up to the Lord, who graciously heard me and gave me a heart resigned to his holy will." He gave up his shop, but continued as tailor in accord with his needs, deliberately diminished. In this same year, he began to keep his journal: "I have often felt a motion of love to leave some hints in writing of my experience of the goodness of God, and now, in the thirty-sixth year of my age, I begin this work."

This opening sentence reveals that Woolman's is no ordinary *Journal* any more than his life was an ordinary life. The *Journal*, first published in 1774, has become recognized as a classic autobiography of a soul in quiet search of the truly moral life. Its simple, plain account of the inner struggle to live a simple, plain, and devout life is moving as well as fascinating. Its frank and honest voice, its gentle manner, its straightforward and candid tone—all draw the reader into the spiritual experience recreated and explored. "The only American book I ever read twice was the *Journal* of Woolman," the English essayist Charles Lamb once remarked. "His character is one of the finest I ever met with."

Woolman's observations in his trips through the South of the corrupting influence of slavery, not only on the slaves but on the masters, led him to write *Some Considerations on the Keeping of Negroes* (Part I, 1754; Part II, 1762). It was Woolman that moved the Society of Friends, at its Philadelphia Yearly Meeting in 1758, to form a committee to prepare the way for abolishing slavery among Quakers. In 1776, the same Yearly Meeting disowned members who refused to free their slaves. One Woolman scholar, Amelia Mott Gummere, has written: "More than any other one man, Woolman aided the English-speaking nations to throw off the disgrace of slavery; and although so late as 1800, there were still 12,442 slaves held in New Jersey, of these, thanks to the labours of John Woolman, almost none were held by Friends."

Woolman's sympathies for the Indians, as well as his keen awareness of the injustices done them, are revealed throughout his *Journal*. His description of his trip into the wilderness for a visit and spiritual exchange with them at their village of Wyalusing makes for some of his journal's most serious, conscience-searching pages. His sympathies for the poor moved him to write one of the few pieces he wrote (in 1763) outside his journal—*A Plea for the Poor*, first published in 1793. It opens: "Wealth desired for its own sake obstructs the increase of virtue, and large possessions in the hands of selfish men have a bad tendency, for by their means too small a number of people are employed in things useful." In many of his concerns, he anticipates Henry David Thoreau and his notions of "economy" in *Walden* (". . . the cost of a thing is the amount of what I will call life which is required to be exchanged for it . . .").

In 1772, Woolman went to England on one of his preaching trips. He travelled throughout the country on foot and was shocked at the poverty of the workers. He was laboring among the poor at York when he died suddenly of smallpox. He had left a farewell "Epistle" to his Friends in America in 1772, to be opened in case of his death. It contained a restatement of his faith: "The necessity of an inward stillness . . . appeared clear to my mind. In true silence strength is renewed, the mind herein is weaned from all things, but as they may be enjoyed in the Divine Will, and a lowliness in outward living, opposite to worldly honor, becomes truly acceptable to us."

The Quaker poet John Greenleaf Whittier edited Woolman's *Journal* in 1871 and commented in his Introduction: "I am not unmindful of the wide difference between the appreciation of a pure and true life and the living of it, and am willing to own that in delineating a character of such moral and spiritual symmetry I have felt something like rebuke from my own words. I have been awed and solemnized by the presence of a serene and beautiful spirit redeemed of the Lord from all selfishness, and I have been made thankful for the ability to recognize and the disposition to love him. I leave the book with its readers."

ADDITIONAL READING

The Journal of John Woolman, ed. John Greenleaf Whittier, 1871 (contains important introduction); *The Journal and Essays of John Woolman*, ed. Amelia Mott Gummere, 1922 (contains biography).

Janet Whitney, *John Woolman, American Quaker*, 1942; Edwin Cady, *John Woolman*, 1965; Daniel B. Shea, *Spiritual Autobiography in Early America*, 1968; Paul Rosenblatt, *John Woolman*, 1969; Henry J. Cadbury, ed., *John Woolman in England*, 1971; Mildred B. Young, *Woolman and Blake, Prophets of Today*, 1971.

TEXT

The Journal and Major Essays of John Woolman, ed. Phillips P. Moulton, 1971.

from The Journal
[Awakening to Wickedness and the Inner Light]

1720–1742

I have often felt a motion of love to leave some hints in writing of my experience of the goodness of God, and now, in the thirty-sixth year of my age, I begin this work. I was born in Northampton, in Burlington County in West Jersey,[1] A.D. 1720, and before I was seven years old I began to be acquainted with the operations of divine love. Through the care of my parents, I was taught to read near as soon as I was capable of it, and as I went from school one Seventh Day,[2] I remember, while my companions went to play by the way, I went forward out of sight; and sitting down, I read the twenty-second chapter of the Revelations: "He showed me a river of water, clear as crystal, proceeding out of the throne of God and the Lamb, etc." And in reading it my mind was drawn to seek after that pure habitation which I then believed God had prepared for his servants. The place where I sat and the sweetness that attended my mind remains fresh in my memory.

This and the like gracious visitations had that effect upon me, that when boys used ill language it troubled me, and through the continued mercies of God I was preserved from it. The pious instructions of my parents were often fresh in my mind when I happened amongst wicked children, and was of use to me. My parents, having a large family of children, used frequently on First Days[3] after meeting to put us to read in the Holy Scriptures or some religious books, one after another, the rest sitting by without much conversation, which I have since often thought was a good practice. From what I had read and heard, I believed there

---

[1]New Jersey, originally divided into East and West Jersey; the two were united in 1702, but people continued to refer to the old designations.

[2]Saturday. Quakers used numbers to designate days and months, avoiding the use of names honoring pagan gods.
[3]Sundays.

had been in past ages people who walked in uprightness before God in a degree exceeding any that I knew, or heard of, now living; and the apprehension of there being less steadiness and firmness amongst people in this age than in past ages often troubled me while I was a child.

I had a dream about the ninth year of my age as follows: I saw the moon rise near the west and run a regular course eastward, so swift that in about a quarter of an hour she reached our meridian, when there descended from her a small cloud on a direct line to the earth, which lighted on a pleasant green about twenty yards from the door of my father's house (in which I thought I stood) and was immediately turned into a beautiful green tree. The moon appeared to run on with equal swiftness and soon set in the east, at which time the sun arose at the place where it commonly does in the summer, and shining with full radiance in a serene air, it appeared as pleasant a morning as ever I saw.

All this time I stood still in the door in an awful[4] frame of mind, and I observed that as heat increased by the rising sun, it wrought so powerfully on the little green tree that the leaves gradually withered; and before noon it appeared dry and dead. There then appeared a being, small of size, full of strength and resolution, moving swift from the north, southward, called a sun worm.[5]

Another thing remarkable in my childhood was that once, going to a neighbor's house, I saw on the way a robin sitting on her nest; and as I came near she went off, but having young ones, flew about and with many cries expressed her concern for them. I stood and threw stones at her, till one striking her, she fell down dead. At first I was pleased with the exploit, but after a few minutes was seized with horror, as having in a sportive way killed an innocent creature while she was careful for her young. I beheld her lying dead and thought those young ones for which she was so careful must now perish for want of their dam to nourish them; and after some painful considerations on the subject, I climbed up the tree, took all the young birds and killed them, supposing that better than to leave them to pine away and die miserably, and believed in this case that Scripture proverb was fulfilled, "The tender mercies of the wicked are cruel."[6] I then went on my errand, but for some hours could think of little else but the cruelties I had committed, and was much troubled.

Thus He whose tender mercies are over all His works hath placed a principle in the human mind which incites to exercise goodness toward every living creature; and this being singly attended to, people become tender-hearted and sympathizing, but being frequently and totally rejected, the mind shuts itself up in a contrary disposition.

About the twelfth year of my age, my father being abroad,[7] my mother reproved me for some misconduct, to which I made an undutiful reply; and the next First Day as I was with my father returning from meeting, he told me he understood I had behaved amiss to my mother and advised me to be more careful in future. I knew myself blameable, and in shame and confusion remained silent. Being thus awakened to a sense of my wickedness, I felt remorse in my mind, and getting home I retired and prayed to the Lord to forgive me, and do not remember that I ever after that spoke unhandsomely to either of my parents, however foolish in other things.

---

[4]Awestruck.
[5]In one version of *The Journal,* Woolman wrote here: "Though I was a child, this dream was instructive to me." Although the symbolism of the dream is obscure, it is very suggestive. A sun worm may be, in contrast with the earthworm (which feeds on the dead), the evil creature, strong and resolute like Satan, that infects the living. (Cf. Job 17:14: "I have said to corruption, Thou art my father: to the worm, Thou art my mother, and my sister.") It is possible that the tree on one level is that of Eden, the tree of life, suddenly subject to the death that Satan brought into the world by his successful temptation of Adam and Eve. Thus the dream is an oblique awakening to the active presence of evil in the universe.
[6]Proverbs 12:10.
[7]Away from home.

Having attained the age of sixteen years, I began to love wanton[8] company, and though I was preserved from profane language or scandalous conduct, still I perceived a plant in me which produced much wild grapes. Yet my merciful Father forsook me not utterly, but at times through His grace I was brought seriously to consider my ways, and the sight of my backsliding affected me with sorrow. But for want of rightly attending to the reproofs of instruction, vanity was added to vanity, and repentance to repentance; upon the whole my mind was more and more alienated from the Truth, and I hastened toward destruction. While I meditate on the gulf toward which I travelled and reflect on my youthful disobedience, for these things I weep; mine eye runneth down with water.

Advancing in age the number of my acquaintance increased, and thereby my way grew more difficult. Though I had heretofore found comfort in reading the Holy Scriptures and thinking on heavenly things, I was now estranged therefrom. I knew I was going from the flock of Christ and had no resolution to return; hence serious reflections were uneasy to me and youthful vanities and diversions my greatest pleasure. Running in this road I found many like myself, and we associated in that which is reverse to true friendship.

But in this swift race it pleased God to visit me with sickness, so that I doubted of recovering. And then did darkness, horror, and amazement with full force seize me, even when my pain and distress of body was very great. I thought it would have been better for me never to have had a being than to see the day which I now saw. I was filled with confusion, and in great affliction both of mind and body I lay and bewailed myself. I had not confidence to lift up my cries to God, whom I had thus offended, but in a deep sense of my great folly I was humbled before Him, and at length that Word which is as a fire and a hammer broke and dissolved my rebellious heart.[9] And then my cries were put up in contrition, and in the multitude of His mercies I found inward relief, and felt a close engagement that if He was pleased to restore my health, I might walk humbly before Him.

After my recovery this exercise[10] remained with me a considerable time; but by degrees giving way to youthful vanities, they gained strength, and getting with wanton young people I lost ground. The Lord had been very gracious and spoke peace to me in the time of my distress, and I now most ungratefully turned again to folly, on which account at times I felt sharp reproof but did not get low enough to cry for help. I was not so hardy as to commit things scandalous, but to exceed in vanity and promote mirth was my chief study. Still I retained a love and esteem for pious people, and their company brought an awe upon me.

My dear parents several times admonished me in the fear of the Lord, and their admonition entered into my heart and had a good effect for a season, but not getting deep enough to pray rightly, the tempter when he came found entrance. I remember once, having spent a part of the day in wantonness, as I went to bed at night there lay in a window near my bed a Bible, which I opened, and first cast my eye on the text, "We lie down in our shame, and our confusion covers us."[11] This I knew to be my case, and meeting with so unexpected a reproof, I was somewhat affected with it and went to bed under remorse of conscience, which I soon cast off again.

Thus time passed on; my heart was replenished with mirth and wantonness, while pleasing scenes of vanity were presented to my imagination till I attained the age of eighteen years, near which time I felt the judgments of God in my soul like a consuming fire, and looking over my past life the prospect was moving. I was

---

[8]Undisciplined.
[9]Jeremiah 23:29: "Is not my word like as a fire? saith the Lord; and like a hammer that breaketh the rock in pieces?"

[10]Inner turmoil of an intellectual or spiritual nature.
[11]Jeremiah 3:25.

often sad and longed to be delivered from those vanities; then again my heart was strongly inclined to them, and there was in me a sore conflict. At times I turned to folly, and then again sorrow and confusion took hold of me. In a while I resolved totally to leave off some of my vanities, but there was a secret reserve in my heart of the more refined part of them, and I was not low enough to find true peace. Thus for some months I had great trouble, there remaining in me an unsubjected will which rendered my labors fruitless, till at length through the merciful continuance of heavenly visitations I was made to bow down in spirit before the Lord.

I remember one evening I had spent some time in reading a pious author, and walking out alone I humbly prayed to the Lord for His help, that I might be delivered from all those vanities which so ensnared me. Thus being brought low, He helped me; and as I learned to bear the cross I felt refreshment to come from His presence; but not keeping in that strength which gave victory, I lost ground again, the sense of which greatly affected me; and I sought deserts and lonely places and there with tears did confess my sins to God and humbly craved help of Him. And I may say with reverence He was near to me in my troubles, and in those times of humiliation opened my ear to discipline.

I was now led to look seriously at the means by which I was drawn from the pure Truth, and learned this: that if I would live in the life which the faithful servants of God lived in, I must not go into company as heretofore in my own will, but all the cravings of sense must be governed by a divine principle. In times of sorrow and abasement these instructions were sealed upon me, and I felt the power of Christ prevail over selfish desires, so that I was preserved in a good degree of steadiness. And being young and believing at that time that a single life was best for me, I was strengthened to keep from such company as had often been a snare to me.

I kept steady to meetings,[12] spent First Days after noon chiefly in reading the Scriptures and other good books, and was early convinced in my mind that true religion consisted in an inward life, wherein the heart doth love and reverence God the Creator and learn to exercise true justice and goodness, not only toward all men but also toward the brute creatures; that as the mind was moved on an inward principle to love God as an invisible, incomprehensible being, on the same principle it was moved to love Him in all His manifestations in the visible world; that as by His breath the flame of life was kindled in all animal and sensitive creatures, to say we love God as unseen and at the same time exercise cruelty toward the least creature moving by His life, or by life derived from Him, was a contradiction in itself.

I found no narrowness respecting sects and opinions, but believed that sincere, upright-hearted people in every Society who truly loved God were accepted of Him.

As I lived under the cross and simply followed the openings[13] of Truth, my mind from day to day was more enlightened; my former acquaintance was left to judge of me as they would, for I found it safest for me to live in private and keep these things sealed up in my own breast.

While I silently ponder on that change wrought in me, I find no language equal to it nor any means to convey to another a clear idea of it. I looked upon the works of God in this visible creation and an awfulness covered me; my heart was tender and often contrite, and a universal love to my fellow creatures increased in me. This will be understood by such who have trodden in the same path. Some glances of real beauty may be seen in their faces who dwell in true meekness. There is a harmony in the sound of that voice to which divine love gives utter-

---

[12]Went to Quaker assemblies every Sunday.
[13]Intuitions (from the inner light).

ance, and some appearance of right order in their temper and conduct whose passions are fully regulated. Yet all these do not fully show forth that inward life to such who have not felt it, but this white stone and new name[14] is known rightly to such only who have it.

Now though I had been thus strengthened to bear the cross, I still found myself in great danger, having many weaknesses attending me and strong temptations to wrestle with, in the feeling whereof I frequently withdrew into private places and often with tears besought the Lord to help me, whose gracious ear was open to my cry.

All this time I lived with my parents and wrought on the plantation,[15] and having had schooling pretty well for a planter, I used to improve in winter evenings and other leisure times. And being now in the twenty-first year of my age, a man in much business shopkeeping and baking asked me if I would hire with him to tend shop and keep books. I acquainted my father with the proposal, and after some deliberation it was agreed for me to go.

At home I had lived retired, and now having a prospect of being much in the way of company, I felt frequent and fervent cries in my heart to God, the Father of Mercies, that He would preserve me from all taint and corruption, that in this more public employ I might serve Him, my gracious Redeemer, in that humility and self-denial with which I had been in a small degree exercised in a very private life.

The man who employed me furnished a shop in Mount Holly,[16] about five miles from my father's house and six from his own, and there I lived alone and tended his shop. Shortly after my settlement here I was visited by several young people, my former acquaintance, who knew not but vanities would be as agreeable to me now as ever; and at these times I cried to the Lord in secret for wisdom and strength, for I felt myself encompassed with difficulties and had fresh occasion to bewail the follies of time past in contracting a familiarity with a libertine people. And as I had now left my father's house outwardly,[17] I found my Heavenly Father to be merciful to me beyond what I can express.

By day I was much amongst people and had many trials to go through, but in evenings I was mostly alone and may with thankfulness acknowledge that in those times the spirit of supplication was often poured upon me, under which I was frequently exercised and felt my strength renewed.

In a few months after I came here, my master bought several Scotch menservants from on board a vessel and brought them to Mount Holly to sell,[18] one of which was taken sick and died. The latter part of his sickness he, being delirious, used to curse and swear most sorrowfully, and after he was buried I was left to sleep alone the next night in the same chamber where he died. I perceived in me a timorousness. I knew, however, I had not injured the man but assisted in taking care of him according to my capacity, and was not free to ask anyone on that occasion to sleep with me. Nature was feeble, but every trial was a fresh incitement to give myself up wholly to the service of God, for I found no helper like Him in times of trouble.

After a while my former acquaintance gave over expecting me as one of their company, and I began to be known to some whose conversation was helpful to me. And now, as I had experienced the love of God through Jesus Christ to redeem me from many pollutions and to be a succor to me through a sea of con-

---

[14]Revelation 2:17: "To him that overcometh will I give to eat of the hidden manna, and will give him a white stone, and in the stone a new name written, which no man knoweth saving he that receiveth it."
[15]Worked on the farm.
[16]In New Jersey.

[17]Physically (opposed to inwardly or spiritually).
[18]He bought and sold men's indentures—negotiable contracts in which the indentured man promises to work so many years in return for passage and expenses.

flicts, with which no person was fully acquainted, and as my heart was often enlarged in this heavenly principle, I felt a tender compassion for the youth who remained entangled in snares like those which had entangled me. From one month to another this love and tenderness increased, and my mind was more strongly engaged for the good of my fellow creatures.

I went to meetings in an awful frame of mind and endeavored to be inwardly acquainted with the language of the True Shepherd. And one day being under a strong exercise of spirit, I stood up and said some words in a meeting, but not keeping close to the divine opening, I said more than was required of me; and being soon sensible of my error, I was afflicted in mind some weeks without any light or comfort, even to that degree that I could take satisfaction in nothing. I remembered God and was troubled, and in the depth of my distress He had pity upon me and sent the Comforter. I then felt forgiveness for my offense, and my mind became calm and quiet, being truly thankful to my gracious Redeemer for His mercies. And after this, feeling the spring of divine love opened and a concern to speak,[19] I said a few words in a meeting, in which I found peace. This I believe was about six weeks from the first time, and as I was thus humbled and disciplined under the cross, my understanding became more strengthened to distinguish the language of the pure Spirit which inwardly moves upon the heart and taught [me] to wait in silence sometimes many weeks together, until I felt that rise which prepares the creature to stand like a trumpet through which the Lord speaks to His flock.

From an inward purifying, and steadfast abiding under it, springs a lively operative desire for the good of others. All faithful people are not called to the public ministry, but whoever are, are called to minister of that which they have tasted and handled spiritually. The outward modes of worship are various, but wherever men are true ministers of Jesus Christ it is from the operation of His spirit upon their hearts, first purifying them and thus giving them a feeling sense of the conditions of others. This truth was early fixed in my mind, and I was taught to watch the pure opening[20] and to take heed lest while I was standing to speak, my own will should get uppermost and cause me to utter words from worldly wisdom and depart from the channel of the true gospel ministry.

In the management of my outward affairs I may say with thankfulness I found Truth to be my support, and I was respected in my master's family, who came to live in Mount Holly within two year after my going there.

About the twenty-third year of my age, I had many fresh and heavenly openings in respect to the care and providence of the Almighty over His creatures in general, and over man as the most noble amongst those which are visible. And being clearly convinced in my judgment that to place my whole trust in God was best for me, I felt renewed engagements that in all things I might act on an inward principle of virtue and pursue worldly business no further than as Truth opened my way therein.

About the time called Christmas[21] I observed many people from the country and dwellers in town who, resorting to the public houses,[22] spent their time in drinking and vain sports, tending to corrupt one another, on which account I was much troubled. At one house in particular there was much disorder, and I believed it was a duty laid on me to go and speak to the master of that house. I considered I was young and that several elderly Friends in town had opportunity to see these things, and though I would gladly have been excused, yet I could not feel my mind clear.

---

[19]Moved to speak. Quaker meetings were periods of meditation broken only by comments from those who were moved by divine guidance to speak.
[20]Wait for the genuinely divine inner light.

[21]Quakers did not celebrate Christmas, believing that Christ could be reborn in the soul every day; thus all days were holy.
[22]Taverns.

The exercise was heavy, and as I was reading what the Almighty said to Ezekiel respecting his duty as a watchman,[23] the matter was set home more clearly; and then with prayer and tears I besought the Lord for His assistance, who in loving-kindness gave me a resigned heart. Then at a suitable opportunity I went to the public house, and seeing the man amongst a company, I went to him and told him I wanted to speak with him; so we went aside, and there in the fear and dread of the Almighty I expressed to him what rested on my mind, which he took kindly, and afterward showed more regard to me than before. In a few years after, he died middle-aged, and I often thought that had I neglected my duty in that case it would have given me great trouble, and I was humbly thankful to my gracious Father, who had supported me herein.

My employer, having a Negro woman, sold her and directed me to write a bill of sale, the man being waiting who bought her. The thing was sudden, and though the thoughts of writing an instrument of slavery for one of my fellow creatures felt uneasy,[24] yet I remembered I was hired by the year, that it was my master who directed me to do it, and that it was an elderly man, a member of our Society,[25] who bought her; so through weakness I gave way and wrote it, but at the executing it, I was so afflicted in my mind that I said before my master and the Friend that I believed slavekeeping to be a practice inconsistent with the Christian religion. This in some degree abated my uneasiness, yet as often as I reflected seriously upon it I thought I should have been clearer if I had desired to be excused from it as a thing against my conscience, for such it was. And some time after this a young man of our Society spake to me to write an instrument of slavery, he having lately taken a Negro into his house. I told him I was not easy to write it, for though many kept slaves in our Society, as in others, I still believed the practice was not right, and desired to be excused from writing [it]. I spoke to him in good will, and he told me that keeping slaves was not altogether agreeable to his mind, but that the slave being a gift made to his wife, he had accepted of her.

[ON SLAVERY]

1743–1748

Two things were remarkable to me in this journey.[1] First, in regard to my entertainment: When I eat, drank, and lodged free-cost with people who lived in ease on the hard labor of their slaves, I felt uneasy; and as my mind was inward to the Lord, I found, from place to place, this uneasiness return upon me at times through the whole visit. Where the masters bore a good share of the burden and lived frugal, so that their servants were well provided for and their labor moderate, I felt more easy; but where they lived in a costly way and laid heavy burdens on their slaves, my exercise[2] was often great, and I frequently had conversation with them in private concerning it. Secondly, this trade of importing them from their native country being much encouraged amongst them and the white people and their children so generally living without much labor was frequently the subject of my serious thoughts. And I saw in these southern provinces so many vices and corruptions increased by this trade and this way of life that it appeared to me as a dark gloominess hanging over the land; and though now many willingly run into it, yet in future the consequence will be grievous to posterity! I express it as it hath appeared to me, not at once nor twice, but as a matter fixed on my mind.

· · · · · ·

---

[23]Ezekial 3:17: "Son of man, I have made thee a watchman unto the house of Israel: therefore hear the word at my mouth, and give them warning from me."
[24]I.e., his conscience was troubled.
[25]Society of Friends, or Quakers.

[1]A religious journey visiting Friends and attending meetings in Pennsylvania, Virginia, North Carolina, and Maryland.
[2]Concern, inner turmoil.

1749–1756

Scrupling to do writings relative to keeping slaves having been a means of sundry small trials to me, in which I have so evidently felt my own will set aside that I think it good to mention a few of them. Tradesmen and retailers of goods, who depend on their business for a living, are naturally inclined to keep the good will of their customers; nor is it a pleasant thing for young men to be under a necessity to question the judgment or honesty of elderly men, and more especially of such who have a fair reputation. Deep-rooted customs, though wrong, are not easily altered, but it is the duty of everyone to be firm in that which they certainly know is right for them. A charitable, benevolent man, well acquainted with a Negro, may, I believe, under some certain circumstances keep him in his family as a servant on no other motives than the Negro's good; but man, as man, knows not what shall be after him, nor hath he any assurance that his children will attain to that perfection in wisdom and goodness necessary in every absolute governor. Hence it is clear to me that I ought not to be the scribe where wills are drawn in which some children are made absolute masters over others during life.

About this time an ancient man of good esteem in the neighborhood came to my house to get his will wrote. He had young Negroes, and I asking him privately how he purposed to dispose of them, he told me. I then said, "I cannot write thy will without breaking my own peace," and respectfully gave him my reasons for it. He signified that he had a choice that I should have wrote it, but as I could not consistent with my conscience, he did not desire it, and so he got it wrote by some other person. And a few years after, there being great alterations in his family, he came again to get me to write his will. His Negroes were yet young, and his son, to whom he intended to give them, was since he first spoke to me, from a libertine become a sober young man; and he supposed that I would have been free on that account to write it. We had much friendly talk on the subject and then deferred it, and a few days after, he came again and directed their freedom, and so I wrote his will.

Near the time the last-mentioned friend first spoke to me, a neighbor received a bad bruise in his body and sent for me to bleed him, which being done he desired me to write his will. I took notes, and amongst other things he told me to which of his children he gave his young Negro. I considered the pain and distress he was in and knew not how it would end, so I wrote his will, save only that part concerning his slave, and carrying it to his bedside read it to him and then told him in a friendly way that I could not write any instruments by which my fellow creatures were made slaves, without bringing trouble on my own mind. I let him know that I charged nothing for what I had done and desired to be excused from doing the other part in the way he proposed. Then we had a serious conference on the subject, and at length, he agreeing to set her free, I finished his will.

• • • • •

1757

11th day, 5th month. We crossed the rivers Potomac and Rappahannock and lodged at Port Royal.[3] And on the way, we happening in company with a colonel of the militia who appeared to be a thoughtful man, I took occasion to remark on the odds in general betwixt a people used to labor moderately for their living, training up their children in frugality and business, and those who live on the labor of slaves, the former in my view being the most happy life; with which he concurred and mentioned the trouble arising from the untoward, slothful disposition of the Negroes, adding that one of our laborers would do as much in a day as two of their slaves. I replied that free men whose minds were properly on their business found a satisfaction in improving, cultivating, and providing for their fami-

---

[3]Virginia.

lies, but Negroes, laboring to support others who claim them as their property and expecting nothing but slavery during life, had not the like inducement to be industrious.

After some further conversation I said that men having power too often misapplied it; that though we made slaves of the Negroes and the Turks made slaves of the Christians, I, however, believed that liberty was the natural right of all men equally, which he did not deny, but said the lives of the Negroes were so wretched in their own country that many of them lived better here than there. I only said, "There's great odds in regard to us on what principle we act." And so the conversation on that subject ended. And I may here add that another person some time afterward mentioned the wretchedness of the Negroes occasioned by their intestine[4] wars as an argument in favor of our fetching them away for slaves, to which I then replied: "If compassion on the Africans in regard to their domestic troubles were the real motives of our purchasing them, that spirit of tenderness being attended to would incite us to use them kindly, that as strangers brought out of affliction their lives might be happy among us; and as they are human creatures, whose souls are as precious as ours and who may receive the same help and comfort from the Holy Scriptures as we do, we could not omit suitable endeavors to instruct them therein. But while we manifest by our conduct that our views in purchasing them are to advance ourselves, and while our buying captives taken in war animates those parties to push on that war and increase desolations amongst them, to say they live unhappy in Africa is far from being an argument in our favor."

And I further said, "The present circumstances of these provinces to me appears difficult, that the slaves look like a burdensome stone to such who burden themselves with them, and that if the white people retain a resolution to prefer their outward prospects of gain to all other considerations and do not act conscientiously toward them as fellow creatures, I believe that burden will grow heavier and heavier till times change in a way disagreeable to us"—at which the person appeared very serious and owned that in considering their condition and the manner of their treatment in these provinces, he had sometimes thought it might be just in the Almighty to so order it.

[Luxury and Plain Living]

1749–1756

Until the year 1756 I continued to retail goods, besides following my trade as a tailor, about which time I grew uneasy on account of my business growing too cumbersome. I began with selling trimmings for garments and from thence proceeded to sell clothes and linens, and at length having got a considerable shop of goods, my trade increased every year and the road to large business appeared open; but I felt a stop in my mind.

Through the mercies of the Almighty I had in a good degree learned to be content with a plain way of living. I had but a small family, that on serious consideration I believed Truth did not require me to engage in much cumbrous affairs. It had been my general practice to buy and sell things really useful. Things that served chiefly to please the vain mind in people I was not easy to trade in, seldom did it, and whenever I did I found it weaken me as a Christian.

The increase of business became my burden, for though my natural inclination was toward merchandise, yet I believed Truth required me to live more free from outward cumbers, and there was now a strife in my mind between the two; and in this exercise my prayers were put up to the Lord, who graciously heard me and

---

[4]Internal.

gave me a heart resigned to His holy will. Then I lessened my outward business, and as I had opportunity told my customers of my intentions that they might consider what shop to turn to, and so in a while wholly laid down merchandise, following my trade as a tailor, myself only, having no apprentice. I also had a nursery of apple trees, in which I employed some of my time—hoeing, grafting, trimming, and inoculating.

In merchandise it is the custom where I lived to sell chiefly on credit, and poor people often get in debt, and when payment is expected, not having wherewith to pay, their creditors often sue for it at law. Having often observed occurrences of this kind, I found it good for me to advise poor people to take such goods as were most useful and not costly.

In the time of trading, I had an opportunity of seeing that too liberal a use of spirituous liquors and the custom of wearing too costly apparel lead some people into great inconveniences, and these two things appear to be often connected one with the other. For by not attending to that use of things which is consistent with universal righteousness, there is an increase of labor which extends beyond what our Heavenly Father intends for us. And by great labor, and often by much sweating in the heat, there is even amongst such who are not drunkards a craving of some liquors to revive the spirits: that partly by the wanton, luxurious drinking of some, and partly by the drinkings of others led to it through immoderate labor, very great quantities of rum are every year expended in our colonies, the greater part of which we should have no need did we steadily attend to pure wisdom.

Where men take pleasure in feeling their minds elevated with strong drink and so indulge their appetite as to disorder their understandings, neglect their duty as members in a family or civil society, and cast off all pretense to religion, their case is much to be pitied. And where such whose lives are for the most part regular, and whose examples have a strong influence on the minds of others, adhere to some customs which strongly draw toward the use of more strong liquor than pure wisdom directs to the use of, this also, as it hinders the spreading of the spirit of meekness and strengthens the hands of the more excessive drinkers, is a case to be lamented.

As the least degree of luxury hath some connection with evil, for those who profess to be disciples of Christ and are looked upon as leaders of the people, to have that mind in them which was also in Him, and so stand separate from every wrong way, is a means of help to the weaker. As I have sometimes been much spent in the heat and taken spirits to revive me, I have found by experience that in such circumstance the mind is not so calm nor so fitly disposed for divine meditation as when all such extremes are avoided, and have felt an increasing care to attend to that Holy Spirit which sets right bounds to our desires and leads those who faithfully follow it to apply all the gifts of divine providence to the purposes for which they were intended. Did such who have the care of great estates attend with singleness of heart to this Heavenly Instructor, which so opens and enlarges the mind that men love their neighbors as themselves,[1] they would have wisdom given them to manage without finding occasion to employ some people in the luxuries of life or to make it necessary for others to labor too hard. But for want of steadily regarding this principle of divine love, a selfish spirit takes place in the minds of people, which is attended with darkness and manifold confusions in the world.

In the course of my trading being somewhat troubled at the various law suits about collecting money which I saw going forward, on applying to a constable he gave me a list of his proceeding for one year as follows—to wit, served 267 war-

---

[1] Matthew 19:19: "Thou shalt love thy neighbor as thyself."

rants, 103 summonses, and 79 executions. As to writs served by the sheriff, I got no account of them.

I once had a warrant for an idle man who I believed was about to run away, which was the only time I applied to the law to recover money.

Though trading in things useful is an honest employ, yet through the great number of superfluities which are bought and sold and through the corruption of the times, they who apply to merchandise for a living have great need to be well experienced in that precept which the prophet Jeremiah laid down for his scribe: "Seekest thou great things for thyself? Seek them not."[2]

[On War]

On the 9th day, 8th month, 1757, at night, orders came to the military officers in our country, directing them to draft the militia and prepare a number of men to go off as soldiers to the relief of the English at Fort William Henry in [New] York government.[1] And in a few days there was a general review of the militia at Mount Holly, and a number of men chosen and sent off under some officers. Shortly after, there came orders to draft three times as many, to hold themselves in readiness to march when fresh orders came. And on the 17th day, 8th month, there was a meeting of the military officers at Mount Holly, who agreed on a draft, and orders were sent to the men so chosen to meet their respective captains at set times and places, those in our township to meet at Mount Holly, amongst whom were a considerable number of our Society.

My mind being affected herewith, I had fresh opportunity to see and consider the advantage of living in the real substance of religion, where practice doth harmonize with principle. Amongst the officers are men of understanding, who have some regard to sincerity where they see it; and in the execution of their office, when they have men to deal with whom they believe to be upright-hearted men, to put them to trouble on account of scruples of conscience is a painful task and likely to be avoided as much as may be easily. But where men profess to be so meek and heavenly minded and to have their trust so firmly settled in God that they cannot join in wars, and yet by their spirit and conduct in common life manifest a contrary disposition, their difficulties are great at such a time.

Officers in great anxiety endeavoring to get troops to answer the demands of their superiors, seeing men who are insincere pretend scruple of conscience in hopes of being excused from a dangerous employment, they are likely to be roughly handled. In this time of commotion some of our young men left the parts and tarried abroad till it was over. Some came and proposed to go as soldiers. Others appeared to have a real tender scruple in their minds against joining in wars and were much humbled under the apprehension of a trial so near; I had conversation with several of them to my satisfaction.

At the set time when the captain came to town some of those last-mentioned went and told in substance as follows: That they could not bear arms for conscience sake, nor could they hire any to go in their places, being resigned as to the event of it. At length the captain acquainted them all that they might return home for the present and required them to provide themselves as soldiers and to be in readiness to march when called upon. This was such a time as I had not seen before, and yet I may say with thankfulness to the Lord that I believed this trial was intended for our good, and I was favored with resignation to him. The French army, taking the fort they were besieging, destroyed it and went away. The com-

---

[2]Jeremiah 45:5.
[1]The fort was besieged by the French and their allies, the Indians, during the French and Indian War (1754–63).

pany of men first drafted, after some days march had orders to return home, and these on the second draft were no more called upon on that occasion.

The 4th day, 4th month, 1758, orders came to some officers in Mount Holly to prepare quarters a short time for about one hundred soldiers; and an officer and two other men, all inhabitants of our town, came to my house, and the officer told me that he came to speak with me to provide lodging and entertainment for two soldiers, there being six shillings a week per man allowed as pay for it. The case being new and unexpected, I made no answer suddenly but sat a time silent, my mind being inward. I was fully convinced that the proceedings in wars are inconsistent with the purity of the Christian religion, and to be hired to entertain men who were then under pay as soldiers was a difficulty with me. I expected they had legal authority for what they did, and after a short time I said to the officer, "If the men are sent here for entertainment, I believe I shall not refuse to admit them into my house, but the nature of the case is such that I expect I cannot keep them on hire." One of the men intimated that he thought I might do it consistent with my religious principles, to which I made no reply, as believing silence at that time best for me.

Though they spake of two, there came only one, who tarried at my house about two weeks and behaved himself civilly. And when the officer came to pay me I told him that I could not take pay for it, having admitted him into my house in a passive obedience to authority. I was on horseback when he spake to me, and as I turned from him he said he was obliged to me, to which I said nothing; but thinking on the expression I grew uneasy, and afterwards being near where he lived I went and told him on what grounds I refused pay for keeping the soldier.

[SCRUPLES AT COMPLICITY IN THE COMMERCE OF OPPRESSION][1]

25th day, 11th month, 1769. As an exercise with respect to a visit to Barbados hath been weighty on my mind, I may express some of the trials which have attended me. Under these trials I have at times rejoiced, in that I have felt my own self-will subjected.

I once, some years ago, retailed rum, sugar, and molasses, the fruits of the labor of slaves, but then had not much concern about them save only that the rum might be used in moderation; nor was this concern so weightily attended to as I now believe it ought to have been. But of late years being further informed respecting the oppressions too generally exercised in these islands, and thinking often on the degrees that there are in connections of interest and fellowship with the works of darkness (Eph. 5:11),[2] and feeling an increasing concern to be wholly given up to the leadings of the Holy Spirit, it hath appeared that the small gain I got by this branch of trade should be applied in promoting righteousness in the earth. And near the first motion toward a visit to Barbados, I believed the outward substance I possess should be applied in paying my passage, if I go, and providing things in a lowly way for my subsistence. But when the time drew near in which I believed it required of me to be in readiness, a difficulty arose which hath been a continued trial for some months past, under which I have with abasement of mind from day to day sought the Lord for instruction, and often had a feeling of the condition of one formerly who bewailed himself for that the Lord hid his face from him.

During these exercises my heart hath been often contrite, and I have had a tender feeling of the temptations of my fellow creatures laboring under those expen-

---

[1]Feeling called to minister to the slaves in the West Indies, Woolman prepared to sail on a trading vessel bound for Barbados, but he never made the voyage. His scruples about supporting in any degree the oppression of slaves are recorded in this journal entry that he showed to the Quaker owners of the ship.
[2]"And have no fellowship with the unfruitful works of darkness, but rather remove them."

sive customs distinguishable from "the simplicity that there is in Christ" (2 Cor. 11:3),[3] and sometimes in the renewings of gospel love have been helped to minister to others.

That which hath so closely engaged my mind in seeking to the Lord for instruction is whether, after so full information of the oppression the slaves in the West Indies lie under who raise the West India produce, as I had in reading *A Caution and Warning to Great Britain and Her Colonies,* wrote by Anthony Benezet,[4] it is right for me to take a passage in a vessel employed in the West India trade.

To trade freely with oppressors and, without laboring to dissuade from such unkind treatment, seek for gain by such traffic tends, I believe, to make them more easy respecting their conduct than they would be if the cause of universal righteousness was humbly and firmly attended to by those in general with whom they have commerce; and that complaint of the Lord by his prophet, "They have strengthened the hands of the wicked,"[5] hath very often revived in my mind, and I may here add some circumstances preceding any prospect of a visit there.

The case of David hath often been before me of late years. He longed for some water in a well beyond an army of Philistines at war with Israel, and some of his men, to please him, ventured their lives in passing through this army and brought that water. It doth not appear that the Israelites were then scarce of water, but rather that David gave way to delicacy of taste; but having thought on the danger these men were exposed to, he considered this water as their blood, and his heart smote him, [so] that he could not drink it but poured it out to the Lord.[6] And the oppression of the slaves which I have seen in several journeys southward on this continent and the report of their treatment in the West Indies hath deeply affected me, and a care to live in the spirit of peace and minister just cause of offense to none of my fellow creatures hath from time to time livingly revived on my mind, and under this exercise I for some years past declined to gratify my palate with those sugars.

I do not censure my brethren in these things, but believe the Father of Mercies, to whom all mankind by creation are equally related, hath heard the groans of these oppressed people and is preparing some to have a tender feeling of their condition. And the trading in, or frequent use of, any produce known to be raised under such lamentable oppression hath appeared to be a subject which may yet more require the serious consideration of the humble followers of Christ, the Prince of Peace. After long and mournful exercise I am now free to mention how things have opened in my mind, with desires that if it may please the Lord to further open His will to any of His children in this matter, they may faithfully follow Him in such further manifestation.

The number of those who decline the use of the West India produce on account of the hard usage of the slaves who raise it appears small, even amongst people truly pious, and the labors in Christian love on that subject of those who do, not very extensive. Was the trade from this continent to the West Indies to be quite stopped at once, I believe many there would suffer for want of bread.

Did we on this continent and the inhabitants of the West Indies generally dwell in pure righteousness, I believe a small trade between us might be right—that under these considerations, when the thoughts of wholly declining the use of trading vessels and of trying to hire a vessel to go under ballast[7] have arose in my mind, I

---

[3]"But I fear, lest by any means, as the serpent beguiled Eve through his subtlety, so your minds should be corrupted from the simplicity that is in Christ."

[4]Anthony Benezet (1713–1784), French-born Quaker and associate of Woolman, wrote influential antislavery tracts, including *A Caution and Warning to Great Britain and Her Colonies in a Short Representation of the Calamitous State of the Enslaved Negroes in the British Dominions* (1767).

[5]Ezekiel 13:22: "Because with lies ye have made the heart of the righteous sad, whom I have not made sad: and strengthened the hands of the wicked, that he should not return from his wicked way, by promising him life."

[6]2 Samuel 23:14–17.

[7]I.e., a vessel carrying only the stabilizing weight or ballast in the hold and no trading cargo.

have believed that the labors in gospel love yet bestowed in the cause of universal righteousness are not arrived to that height.

If the trade to the West Indies was no more than was consistent with pure wisdom, I believe the passage money would for good reasons be higher than it is now; and here under deep exercise of mind, I have believed that I should not take the advantage of this great trade and small passage money, but as a testimony in favor of less trading should pay more than is common for others to pay, if I go at this time.

[A VISION OF DEATH: A MYSTERY OPENED]

26th day, 8th month, 1772. Being now at George Crosfield's, in Westmoreland County in England, I feel a concern to commit to writing that which to me hath been a case uncommon. In a time of sickness with the pleurisy a little upward of two years and a half ago, I was brought so near the gates of death that I forgot my name. Being then desirous to know who I was, I saw a mass of matter of a dull gloomy color, between the south and the east, and was informed that this mass was human beings in as great misery as they could be and live, and that I was mixed in with them and henceforth might not consider myself as a distinct or separate being. In this state I remained several hours. I then heard a soft, melodious voice, more pure and harmonious than any voice I had heard with my ears before, and I believed it was the voice of an angel who spake to other angels. The words were, "*John Woolman is dead.*" I soon remembered that I once was John Woolman, and being assured that I was alive in the body, I greatly wondered what that heavenly voice could mean. I believed beyond doubting that it was the voice of an holy angel, but as yet it was a mystery to me.

I was then carried in spirit to the mines, where poor oppressed people were digging rich treasures for those called Christians, and heard them blaspheme the name of Christ, at which I was grieved, for his name to me was precious. Then I was informed that these heathens were told that those who oppressed them were the followers of Christ, and they said amongst themselves: "If Christ directed them to use us in this sort, then Christ is a cruel tyrant."

All this time the song of the angel remained a mystery, and in the morning my dear wife and some others coming to my bedside, I asked them if they knew who I was; and they, telling me I was John Woolman, thought I was only light-headed, for I told them not what the angel said, nor was I disposed to talk much to anyone, but was very desirous to get so deep that I might understand this mystery.

My tongue was often so dry that I could not speak till I had moved it about and gathered some moisture, and as I lay still for a time, at length I felt divine power prepare my mouth that I could speak, and then I said: "I am crucified with Christ, nevertheless I live; yet not I, but Christ that liveth in me, and the life I now live in the flesh is by faith in the Son of God, who loved me and gave himself for me."[1] Then the mystery was opened, and I perceived there was joy in heaven over a sinner who had repented and that that language *John Woolman is dead* meant no more than the death of my own will.

Soon after this I coughed and raised much bloody matter, which I had not during this vision, and now my natural understanding returned as before. Here I saw that people getting silver vessels to set off their tables at entertainments was often stained with worldly glory, and that in the present state of things, I should take heed how I fed myself from out of silver vessels.

Soon after my recovery I, going to our Monthly Meeting, dined at a Friend's house, where drink was brought in silver vessels and not in any other. And I,

---

[1]Galations 2:20.

wanting some drink, told him my case with weeping, and he ordered some drink for me in another vessel.

The like I went through in several Friends' houses in America and have also in England since I came here, and have cause with humble reverence to acknowledge the loving-kindness of my Heavenly Father, who hath preserved me in such a tender frame of mind that none, I believe, have ever been offended at what I have said on that occasion. John Woolman.

1756–72

                                                                                        1774

MICHEL-GUILLAUME JEAN DE CRÈVECOEUR
(1735–1813)

In 1782, while the Revolutionary War was in progress in America, a book of *Letters from an American Farmer* was published in London and became an immediate success. One of the *Letters*, entitled "What Is an American?" was eagerly taken by the British, and later by the French, as proof that human beings could, if not achieve perfection, improve themselves and their lot in something like a New World Utopia. They read the words of this American farmer: "We have no princes for whom we toil, starve, and bleed: we are the most perfect society now existing in the world. Here man is free as he ought to be; nor is this pleasing equality so transitory as many others are."

The description supported the revolutionary ideas that were in the air, especially Rousseau's notions of the superiority of the natural and primitive. What the book's readers then and later failed to notice was that, in another letter decrying the corruption of slavery in the South, this same American farmer wrote: "Would you prefer the state of men in the woods to that of men in a more improved situation? Evil preponderates in both; in the first they often eat each other for want of food, and in the other they often starve each other for want of room." Few readers have noticed, and fewer still resolved, the contradictions implicit in these two passages, primarily because the letter entitled "What Is an American?" has been so often reprinted alone that it has shaped the general impression of the book throughout its existence.

Who is this Michel-Guillaume Jean de Crèvecoeur who so powerfully posed the question of "What Is an American?" He was born French, in Caen, Normandy, in a family of the petty nobility prosperous enough to educate their son at a Jesuit school in Caen. He went to England in 1754 to visit relatives at Salisbury, and the following year sailed off to French Canada, where he enlisted in the colonial militia, serving as surveyor and cartographer. He became a lieutenant in the French army, fighting with Montcalm in the defense of Quebec in 1759 when the English forces under Wolfe attacked and routed the French. Crèvecoeur was wounded and hospitalized. Relieved from his commission, Crèvecoeur made his way south to New York, and after working as an Indian trader and surveyor, he married and settled on a farm (Pine Hill) in Orange County, northwest of New York City. Soon he began to write the *Letters* that would bring him fame.

At the outbreak of the Revolutionary War in 1775, Orange County became a battleground. Crèvecoeur was in some danger because the family he married into was Tory (British loyalists), and so was he. Hoping to return to France, he made his way to New York City in 1778, was arrested by the British and held for several months in 1779, but finally allowed to depart in 1780. Passing through London on his way to France, he took the manuscript of his book to a publisher and arranged for publication. *Letters from an American Farmer* was published there in 1782 under the pen name J. Hector St. John, "A Farmer in Pennsylvania."

In Paris, Crèvecoeur gained entrée to intellectual circles under the sponsorship of one of his father's friends, Madame d'Houdetat (whose charms had inspired the passion of Jean-Jacques Rousseau). At the end of the Revolutionary War in 1783, Benjamin Franklin used his influence to have Crèvecoeur appointed French consul for New York, New Jersey, and Connecticut.

When Crèvecoeur returned to America in 1783, he discovered that his wife was dead and Pine Hill itself destroyed during an Indian raid. He found his children still alive in Boston, where they had been taken after rescue from Orange County by a merchant who had learned of their condition. In 1785, Crèvecoeur's ill health forced him to return to France, where he found himself a celebrity, his book having been published in Paris just the year before. He prepared an expanded version for the press and then returned to America in 1787.

He enjoyed success as the French consul and influenced French-American relations. He was popular in America, accepting election to the American Philosophical Society in 1789. That same year saw the beginning of the French Revolution. Crèvecoeur returned to France in 1790, never again to return to America during the twenty-three years remaining of his life. He escaped death during the upheaval of the Reign of Terror, lived for a time in Germany, and published a book that sparked little interest (*Travels in Northern Pennsylvania and the State of New York*, 1801). He died of a heart ailment in 1813.

Crèvecoeur was, in spite of other writing, essentially a one-book author. That one book, however, has legitimate claim to be called a classic. This claim may best be understood by approaching the book as a work of fiction, in which the writer of the *Letters* is a character in process of changing his point of view, his feelings, his attitudes. The writer of the *Letters* is James, not Crèvecoeur's name. James's farm is located in Pennsylvania, where Crèvecoeur never lived. James inherited the family farm from his father—but Crèvecoeur's father never set foot in America. These are only a few of the elements that distance Crèvecoeur from James.

The epistolary genre allows for shifting moods and emotions, varied insights, and deepening of awareness. In short, the form not only allows for but demands turns and changes, conflicts and contradictions. To take one passage out of context and set it forth as Crèvecoeur's belief is much too simple. To get at Crèvecoeur's point of view, the reader must come to understand the complex fictional character he created, and the varied feelings that character experiences and the attitudes he expresses.

A recent critic, A. W. Plumstead, has summed up Crèvecoeur's achievement: "Crèvecoeur was, I believe, the first in our literature to find this dramatic voice [a lyric song of discovery of the American dream] in an imaginative work of power. Like [Henry David] Thoreau, [Mark] Twain, and [F. Scott] Fitzgerald later, he came to it honestly through his own experience, and he transmuted that experience into an art that recognized both the dream and its elusiveness. As a sketcher of life in America, he ranks with

[Thomas] Jefferson and [William] Bartram; as a symbol maker out of raw experience, however, he was unique in his time and a pathfinder for American writers to follow."

ADDITIONAL READING

Letters from an American Farmer, ed. L. Lewisohn, 1904; *Letters from an American Farmer,* ed. A. Stone, 1963; *Sketches of Eighteenth-Century America,* ed. H. L. Bourdin, R. H. Gabriel, and S. T. Williams, 1925; *Journey into Northern Pennsylvania and the State of New York,* trans. Clarissa S. Bostelmann, 1964.

Julia P. Mitchell, *St. Jean de Crèvecoeur,* 1916; D. H. Lawrence, *Studies in Classic American Literature,* 1923; Howard C. Rice, *Le Cultivateur Américain: Étude sur l'oeuvre de Saint John de Crèvecoeur,* 1932; Thomas Philbrook, *St. John de Crèvecoeur,* 1970; A. W. Plumstead, "Hector St. John de Crèvecoeur," *American Literature, 1764–1789: The Revolutionary Years,* ed. Everett Emerson, 1977; Gay Wilson Allen and Roger Asselineau, *St. John de Crèvecoeur: The Life of an American Farmer,* 1987.

TEXT

J. Hector St. John, *Letters from an American Farmer,* 1782. Typography, punctuation, spelling, and usage have been changed to conform with contemporary English.

from Letters from an American Farmer

from LETTER III: WHAT IS AN AMERICAN[1]

[AN AMERICAN DEFINED]

I wish I could be acquainted with the feelings and thoughts which must agitate the heart and present themselves to the mind of an enlightened Englishman when he first lands on this continent. He must greatly rejoice that he lived at a time to see this fair country discovered[2] and settled; he must necessarily feel a share of national pride when he views the chain of settlements which embellish these extended shores. When he says to himself, this is the work of my countrymen, who, when convulsed by factions, afflicted by a variety of miseries and wants, restless and impatient, took refuge here. They brought along with them their national genius, to which they principally owe what liberty they enjoy and what substance they possess. Here he sees the industry of his native country displayed in a new manner and traces in their works the embryos of all the arts, sciences, and ingenuity which flourish in Europe. Here he beholds fair cities, substantial villages, extensive fields, an immense country filled with decent houses, good roads, orchards, meadows, and bridges where an hundred years ago all was wild, woody, and uncultivated! What a train of pleasing ideas this fair spectacle must suggest; it is a prospect which must inspire a good citizen with the most heartfelt pleasure. The difficulty consists in the manner of viewing so extensive a scene. He is arrived on a new continent; a modern society offers itself to his contemplation, different from what he had hitherto seen. It is not composed, as in Europe, of great lords

---

[1]This most popular letter of Crèvecoeur's work addresses the question of identity that puzzled the world and haunted Americans throughout their early history. Some would say it still does.

[2]Explored.

who possess everything and of a herd of people who have nothing. Here are no aristocratical families, no courts, no kings, no bishops, no ecclesiastical dominion, no invisible power giving to a few a very visible one, no great manufactures employing thousands, no great refinements of luxury. The rich and the poor are not so far removed from each other as they are in Europe. Some few towns excepted, we are all tillers of the earth, from Nova Scotia to West Florida. We are a people of cultivators scattered over an immense territory, communicating with each other by means of good roads and navigable rivers, united by the silken bands of mild government, all respecting the laws without dreading their power, because they are equitable. We are all animated with the spirit of an industry which is unfettered and unrestrained, because each person works for himself. If he travels through our rural districts, he views not the hostile castle and the haughty mansion, contrasted with the clay-built hut and miserable cabin, where cattle and men help to keep each other warm and dwell in meanness, smoke, and indigence. A pleasing uniformity of decent competence appears throughout our habitations. The meanest of our log-houses is a dry and comfortable habitation. Lawyer or merchant are the fairest titles our towns afford; that of a farmer is the only appellation of the rural inhabitants of our country. It must take some time ere he can reconcile himself to our dictionary, which is but short in words of dignity and names of honor. There, on a Sunday, he sees a congregation of respectable farmers and their wives, all clad in neat homespun, well mounted, or riding in their own humble wagons. There is not among them an esquire, saving the unlettered magistrate. There he sees a parson as simple as his flock, a farmer who does not riot[3] on the labor of others. We have no princes for whom we toil, starve, and bleed: we are the most perfect society now existing in the world. Here man is free as he ought to be; nor is this pleasing equality so transitory as many others are. Many ages will not see the shores of our great lakes replenished with inland nations, nor the unknown bounds of North America entirely peopled. Who can tell how far it extends? Who can tell the millions of men whom it will feed and contain? For no European foot has as yet travelled half the extent of this mighty continent!

The next wish of this traveller will be to know whence came all these people. They are a mixture of English, Scotch, Irish, French, Dutch, Germans, and Swedes. From this promiscuous[4] breed, that race now called Americans have arisen. The eastern provinces[5] must indeed be excepted as being the unmixed descendants of Englishmen. I have heard many wish that they had been more intermixed also; for my part, I am no wisher and think it much better as it has happened. They exhibit a most conspicuous figure in this great and variegated picture; they too enter for a great share in the pleasing perspective displayed in these thirteen provinces. I know it is fashionable to reflect on them, but I respect them for what they have done; for the accuracy and wisdom with which they have settled their territory; for the decency of their manners; for their early love of letters; their ancient college,[6] the first in this hemisphere; for their industry, which to me who am but a farmer is the criterion of everything. There never was a people, situated as they are, who with so ungrateful a soil have done more in so short a time. Do you think that the monarchical ingredients which are more prevalent in other governments have purged them from all foul stains? Their histories assert the contrary.

In this great American asylum, the poor of Europe have by some means met together, and in consequence of various causes; to what purpose should they ask one another what countrymen they are? Alas, two thirds of them had no country.

---

[3]Live wastefully.
[4]Fruitful.

[5]New England.
[6]Harvard College, founded in 1636.

Can a wretch who wanders about, who works and starves, whose life is a continual scene of sore affliction or pinching penury, can that man call England or any other kingdom his country? A country that had no bread for him, whose fields procured him no harvest, who met with nothing but the frowns of the rich, the severity of the laws, with jails and punishments; who owned not a single foot of the extensive surface of this planet? No! Urged by a variety of motives, here they came. Everything has tended to regenerate them: new laws, a new mode of living, a new social system; here they are become men: in Europe they were as so many useless plants, wanting vegetative mould and refreshing showers; they withered, and were mowed down by want, hunger, and war; but now, by the power of transplantation, like all other plants they have taken root and flourished! Formerly they were not numbered in any civil lists of their country, except in those of the poor; here they rank as citizens. By what invisible power hath this surprising metamorphosis been performed? By that of the laws and that of their industry. The laws, the indulgent laws, protect them as they arrive, stamping on them the symbol of adoption; they receive ample rewards for their labors; these accumulated rewards procure them lands; those lands confer on them the title of freemen, and to that title every benefit is affixed which men can possibly require. This is the great operation daily performed by our laws. From whence proceed these laws? From our government. Whence that government? It is derived from the original genius and strong desire of the people ratified and confirmed by the crown. This is the great chain which links us all, this is the picture which every province exhibits, Nova Scotia excepted. There the crown has done all; either there were no people who had genius or it was not much attended to; the consequence is that the province is very thinly inhabited indeed; the power of the crown in conjunction with the mosquitoes has prevented men from settling there. Yet some parts of it flourished once, and it contained a mild, harmless set of people. But for the fault of a few leaders, the whole was banished. The greatest political error the crown ever committed in America was to cut off men from a country which wanted nothing but men![7]

What attachment can a poor European emigrant have for a country where he had nothing? The knowledge of the language, the love of a few kindred as poor as himself, were the only cords that tied him; his country is now that which gives him land, bread, protection, and consequence: *Ubi panis ibi patria*[8] is the motto of all emigrants. What, then, is the American, this new man? He is neither a European nor the descendant of a European; hence that strange mixture of blood, which you will find in no other country. I could point out to you a family whose grandfather was an Englishman, whose wife was Dutch, whose son married a French woman, and whose present four sons have now four wives of different nations. *He* is an American, who, leaving behind him all his ancient prejudices and manners, receives new ones from the new mode of life he has embraced, the new government he obeys, and the new rank he holds. He becomes an American by being received in the broad lap of our great *Alma Mater.*[9] Here individuals of all nations are melted into a new race of men, whose labors and posterity will one day cause great changes in the world. Americans are the western pilgrims who are carrying along with them that great mass of arts, sciences, vigor, and industry which began long since in the East; they will finish the great circle. The Americans were once scattered all over Europe; here they are incorporated into one of the finest systems of population which has ever appeared, and which will hereafter become

---

[7]The British took Nova Scotia in 1710 and in 1755 banished the French Acadians, many of whom ended up in the American South. Longfellow's *Evangeline* gives a poetical account of these events.

[8]"Where there is bread, there is one's fatherland" (Latin).
[9]"Nourishing Mother" (Latin).

distinct by the power of the different climates they inhabit. The American ought therefore to love this country much better than that wherein either he or his forefathers were born. Here the rewards of his industry follow with equal steps the progress of his labor; his labor is founded on the basis of nature, *self-interest;* can it want a stronger allurement? Wives and children, who before in vain demanded of him a morsel of bread, now, fat and frolicsome, gladly help their father to clear those fields whence exuberant crops are to arise to feed and to clothe them all, without any part being claimed, either by a despotic prince, a rich abbot, or a mighty lord. Here religion demands but little of him, a small voluntary salary to the minister and gratitude to God; can he refuse these? The American is a new man, who acts upon new principles; he must therefore entertain new ideas and form new opinions. From involuntary idleness, servile dependence, penury, and useless labor, he has passed to toils of a very different nature, rewarded by ample subsistence. This is an American.

[SHAPING CHARACTER DIFFERENCES, REDUCING RELIGIOUS ZEAL]

British America is divided into many provinces, forming a large association scattered along a coast 1,500 miles extent and about 200 wide. This society I would fain examine, at least such as it appears in the middle provinces; if it does not afford that variety of tinges and gradations which may be observed in Europe, we have colors peculiar to ourselves. For instance, it is natural to conceive that those who live near the sea must be very different from those who live in the woods; the intermediate space will afford a separate and distinct class.

Men are like plants; the goodness and flavor of the fruit proceeds from the peculiar soil and exposition in which they grow. We are nothing but what we derive from the air we breathe, the climate we inhabit, the government we obey, the system of religion we profess, and the nature of our employment. Here you will find but few crimes; these have acquired as yet no root among us. I wish I were able to trace all my ideas; if my ignorance prevents me from describing them properly, I hope I shall be able to delineate a few of the outlines, which is all I propose.

Those who live near the sea feed more on fish than on flesh and often encounter that boisterous element. This renders them more bold and enterprising; this leads them to neglect the confined occupations of the land. They see and converse with a variety of people; their intercourse with mankind becomes extensive. The sea inspires them with a love of traffic, a desire of transporting produce from one place to another, and leads them to a variety of resources which supply the place of labor. Those who inhabit the middle settlements, by far the most numerous, must be very different; the simple cultivation of the earth purifies them, but the indulgences of the government, the soft remonstrances of religion, the rank of independent freeholders, must necessarily inspire them with sentiments very little known in Europe among a people of the same class. What do I say? Europe has no such class of men; the early knowledge they acquire, the early bargains they make, give them a great degree of sagacity. As freemen, they will be litigious,[1] pride and obstinacy are often the cause of lawsuits; the nature of our laws and governments may be another. As citizens, it is easy to imagine that they will carefully read the newspapers, enter into every political disquisition, freely blame or censure governors and others. As farmers, they will be careful and anxious to get as much as they can, because what they get is their own. As northern men, they will love the cheerful cup. As Christians, religion curbs them not in their opinions; the general indulgence leaves every one to think for themselves in spiritual matters; the law inspects our actions; our thoughts are left to God. Industry, good

---

[1] Eager to use the laws and courts.

living, selfishness, litigiousness, country politics, the pride of freemen, religious indifference, are their characteristics. If you recede still farther from the sea, you will come into more modern settlements; they exhibit the same strong lineaments, in a ruder appearance. Religion seems to have still less influence, and their manners are less improved.

Now we arrive near the great woods, near the last inhabited districts;[2] there men seem to be placed still farther beyond the reach of government, which in some measure leaves them to themselves. How can it pervade every corner, as they were driven there by misfortunes, necessity of beginnings, desire of acquiring large tracks of land, idleness, frequent want of economy,[3] ancient debts; the re-union of such people does not afford a very pleasing spectacle. When discord, want of unity and friendship, when either drunkenness or idleness prevail in such remote districts, contention, inactivity, and wretchedness must ensue. There are not the same remedies to these evils as in a long-established community. The few magistrates they have are in general little better than the rest; they are often in a perfect state of war; that of man against man, sometimes decided by blows, sometimes by means of the law; that of man against every wild inhabitant of these venerable woods, of which they are come to dispossess them. There men appear to be no better than carnivorous animals of a superior rank, living on the flesh of wild animals when they can catch them, and when they are not able, they subsist on grain.

He who would wish to see America in its proper light and have a true idea of its feeble beginnings and barbarous rudiments must visit our extended line of frontiers, where the last settlers dwell and where he may see the first labors of settlement, the mode of clearing the earth, in all their different appearances, where men are wholly left dependent on their native tempers and on the spur of uncertain industry, which often fails when not sanctified by the efficacy of a few moral rules. There, remote from the power of example and check of shame, many families exhibit the most hideous parts of our society. They are a kind of forlorn hope, preceding by ten or twelve years the most respectable army of veterans which come after them. In that space, prosperity will polish some, vice and the law will drive off the rest, who, uniting again with others like themselves, will recede still farther, making room for more industrious people, who will finish their improvements, convert the loghouse into a convenient habitation, and rejoicing that the first heavy labors are finished, will change in a few years that hitherto barbarous country into a fine, fertile, well-regulated district. Such is our progress, such is the march of the Europeans toward the interior parts of this continent. In all societies there are off-casts; this impure part serves as our precursors or pioneers; my father himself was one of that class, but he came upon honest principles and was therefore one of the few who held fast;[4] by good conduct and temperance, he transmitted to me his fair inheritance, when not above one in fourteen of his contemporaries had the same good fortune.

Forty years ago, this smiling country was thus inhabited; it is now purged, a general decency of manners prevails throughout, and such has been the fate of our best countries.

Exclusive of those general characteristics, each province has its own, founded on the government, climate, mode of husbandry, customs, and peculiarity of circumstances. Europeans submit insensibly to these great powers and become, in the course of a few generations, not only Americans in general, but either Pennsylvanians, Virginians, or provincials under some other name. Whoever traverses the continent must easily observe those strong differences, which will grow more

---

[2] The frontier.
[3] I.e., they were extravagant in spending.

[4] Crèvecoeur is speaking in a fictional voice. His father never came to America.

evident in time. The inhabitants of Canada, Massachusetts, the middle provinces, the southern ones, will be as different as their climates; their only points of unity will be those of religion and language.

As I have endeavored to show you how Europeans become Americans, it may not be disagreeable to show you likewise how the various Christian sects introduced wear out and how religious indifference becomes prevalent. When any considerable number of a particular sect happen to dwell contiguous to each other, they immediately erect a temple and there worship the Divinity agreeably to their own peculiar ideas. Nobody disturbs them. If any new sect springs up in Europe, it may happen that many of its professors[5] will come and settle in America. As they bring their zeal with them, they are at liberty to make proselytes if they can and to build a meeting and to follow the dictates of their consciences; for neither the government nor any other power interferes. If they are peaceable subjects and are industrious, what is it to their neighbors how and in what manner they think fit to address their prayers to the Supreme Being? But if the sectaries[6] are not settled close together, if they are mixed with other denominations, their zeal will cool for want of fuel, and will be extinguished in a little time. Then, the Americans become as to religion what they are as to country, allied to all. In them the name of Englishman, Frenchman, and European is lost, and in like manner, the strict modes of Christianity as practiced in Europe are lost also. This effect will extend itself still farther hereafter, and though this may appear to you as a strange idea, yet it is a very true one. I shall be able, perhaps, hereafter to explain myself better; in the meanwhile, let the following example serve as my first justification.

Let us suppose you and I to be travelling; we observe that in this house, to the right, lives a Catholic, who prays to God as he has been taught and believes in transubstantiation;[7] he works and raises wheat, he has a large family of children, all hale and robust; his belief, his prayers, offend nobody. About one mile farther on the same road, his next neighbor may be a good, honest, plodding German Lutheran, who addresses himself to the same God, the God of all, agreeably to the modes he has been educated in, and believes in consubstantiation;[8] by so doing, he scandalizes nobody; he also works in his fields, embellishes the earth, clears swamps, etc. What has the world to do with his Lutheran principles? He persecutes nobody, and nobody persecutes him; he visits his neighbors, and his neighbors visit him. Next to him lives a seceder,[9] the most enthusiastic of all sectaries; his zeal is hot and fiery, but separated as he is from others of the same complexion, he has no congregation of his own to resort to where he might cabal and mingle religious pride with worldly obstinacy. He likewise raises good crops, his house is handsomely painted, his orchard is one of the fairest in the neighborhood. How does it concern the welfare of the country, or of the province at large, what this man's religious sentiments are, or really whether he has any at all? He is a good farmer, he is a sober, peaceable, good citizen; William Penn[10] himself would not wish for more. This is the visible character; the invisible one is only guessed at, and is nobody's business. Next, again, lives a Low Dutchman,[11] who implicitly believes the rules laid down by the synod of Dort.[12] He conceives no other idea of a clergyman than that of an hired man; if he does his work well, he will pay him the

---

[5]I.e., believers.
[6]Dissenting sects.
[7]The doctrine that the bread and wine of the communion sacrament (the Eucharist) are changed into the real body and blood of Christ.
[8]The doctrine, held by Luther, that the body and blood of Christ coexist with the Eucharistic bread and wine. In contrast, Calvin believed the Eucharistic bread and wine to be symbolic of, not changed into or coexisting with, the body and blood of Christ.

[9]Member of the Secession Church of Scotland, separated from the established church.
[10]William Penn (1644–1718), English Quaker who established the colony of Pennsylvania as an experiment in religious and political freedom.
[11]One from Holland, not Belgium.
[12]The Synod of Dort (1618) established for Protestant Reformed Churches the Calvinistic doctrine and form of church governance.

stipulated sum; if not, he will dismiss him, and do without his sermons, and let his church be shut up for years. But notwithstanding this coarse idea, you will find his house and farm to be the neatest in all the country; and you will judge by his wagon and fat horses that he thinks more of the affairs of this world than of those of the next. He is sober and laborious; therefore, he is all he ought to be as to the affairs of this life. As for those of the next, he must trust to the great Creator.

Each of these people instruct their children as well as they can, but these instructions are feeble compared to those which are given to the youth of the poorest class in Europe. Their children will therefore grow up less zealous and more indifferent in matters of religion than their parents. The foolish vanity or, rather, the fury of making proselytes is unknown here; they have no time, the seasons call for all their attention, and thus in a few years this mixed neighborhood will exhibit a strange religious medley that will be neither pure Catholicism nor pure Calvinism. A very perceptible indifference, even in the first generation, will become apparent; and it may happen that the daughter of the Catholic will marry the son of the seceder and settle by themselves at a distance from their parents. What religious education will they give their children? A very imperfect one. If there happens to be in the neighborhood any place of worship, we will suppose a Quaker's meeting; rather than not show their fine clothes, they will go to it, and some of them may perhaps attach themselves to that society. Others will remain in a perfect state of indifference; the children of these zealous parents will not be able to tell what their religious principles are, and their grandchildren still less. The neighborhood of a place of worship generally leads them to it, and the action of going thither is the strongest evidence they can give of their attachment to any sect. The Quakers are the only people who retain a fondness for their own mode of worship; for be they ever so far separated from each other, they hold a sort of communion with the society and seldom depart from its rules, at least in this country. Thus all sects are mixed, as well as all nations; thus religious indifference is imperceptibly disseminated from one end of the continent to the other, which is at present one of the strongest characteristics of the Americans. Where this will reach no one can tell; perhaps it may leave a vacuum fit to receive other systems. Persecution, religious pride, the love of contradiction, are the food of what the world commonly calls religion. These motives have ceased here; zeal in Europe is confined; here it evaporates in the great distance it has to travel; there it is a grain of powder enclosed; here it burns away in the open air and consumes without effect.

[BACK SETTLERS, FREEHOLDERS, THE AMERICANIZATION OF EUROPEANS]

But to return to our back settlers. I must tell you that there is something in the proximity of the woods which is very singular. It is with men as it is with the plants and animals that grow and live in the forests; they are entirely different from those that live in the plains. I will candidly tell you all my thoughts, but you are not to expect that I shall advance any reasons. By living in or near the woods, their actions are regulated by the wildness of the neighborhood. The deer often come to eat their grain, the wolves to destroy their sheep, the bears to kill their hogs, the foxes to catch their poultry. This surrounding hostility immediately puts the gun into their hands; they watch these animals, they kill some; and thus by defending their property, they soon become professed hunters; this is the progress;[1] once hunters, farewell to the plow. The chase renders them ferocious, gloomy, and unsocial; a hunter wants no neighbor, he rather hates them because he dreads the competition. In a little time, their success in the woods makes them

---

[1]Sequence.

neglect their tillage. They trust to the natural fecundity of the earth and therefore do little; carelessness in fencing often exposes what little they sow to destruction; they are not at home to watch; in order, therefore, to make up the deficiency, they go oftener to the woods.

That new mode of life brings along with it a new set of manners, which I cannot easily describe. These new manners being grafted on the old stock produce a strange sort of lawless profligacy, the impressions of which are indelible. The manners of the Indian natives are respectable compared with this European medley.[2] Their wives and children live in sloth and inactivity; and having no proper pursuits, you may judge what education the latter receive. Their tender minds have nothing else to contemplate but the example of their parents; like them, they grow up a mongrel breed, half civilized, half savage, except nature stamps on them some constitutional propensities. That rich, that voluptuous sentiment is gone that struck them so forcibly; the possession of their freeholds no longer conveys to their minds the same pleasure and pride. To all these reasons you must add their lonely situation, and you cannot imagine what an effect on manners the great distances they live from each other has!

Consider one of the last settlements in its first view: of what is it composed? Europeans who have not that sufficient share of knowledge they ought to have in order to prosper; people who have suddenly passed from oppression, dread of government, and fear of laws into the unlimited freedom of the woods. This sudden change must have a very great effect on most men, and on that class particularly. Eating of wild meat, whatever you may think, tends to alter their temper, though all the proof I can adduce is that I have seen it, and having no place of worship to resort to, what little society this might afford is denied them. The Sunday meetings, exclusive of religious benefits, were the only social bonds that might have inspired them with some degree of emulation in neatness. Is it, then, surprising to see men thus situated, immersed in great and heavy labors, degenerate a little? It is rather a wonder the effect is not more diffusive.[3] The Moravians and the Quakers[4] are the only instances in exception to what I have advanced. The first never settle singly, it is a colony of the society which emigrates; they carry with them their forms, worship, rules, and decency. The others never begin so hard; they are always able to buy improvements, in which there is a great advantage, for by that time the country is recovered from its first barbarity.

Thus our bad people are those who are half cultivators and half hunters; and the worst of them are those who have degenerated altogether into the hunting state. As old plowmen and new men of the woods, as Europeans and new-made Indians, they contract the vices of both; they adopt the moroseness and ferocity of a native, without his mildness or even his industry at home. If manners are not refined, at least they are rendered simple and inoffensive by tilling the earth. All our wants are supplied by it; our time is divided between labor and rest, and leaves none for the commission of great misdeeds. As hunters, it is divided between the toil of the chase, the idleness of repose, or the indulgence of inebriation. Hunting is but a licentious idle life, and if it does not always pervert good dispositions, yet, when it is united with bad luck, it leads to want: want stimulates that propensity to rapacity and injustice, too natural to needy men, which is the fatal gradation. After this explanation of the effects which follow by living in the woods, shall we yet vainly flatter ourselves with the hope of converting the Indians? We should rather begin with converting our back-settlers; and now if I dare mention the name of religion, its sweet accents would be lost in the immensity of these woods. Men thus placed are not fit either to receive or remember its mild

---

[2]Mixture.
[3]Widespread.

[4]Protestant sects, close-knit, emphasizing simplicity and personal service.

instructions; they want temples and ministers, but as soon as men cease to remain at home and begin to lead an erratic life, let them be either tawny or white, they cease to be its disciples.

Thus have I faintly and imperfectly endeavored to trace our society from the sea to our woods! Yet you must not imagine that every person who moves back acts upon the same principles or falls into the same degeneracy. Many families carry with them all their decency of conduct, purity of morals, and respect of religion, but these are scarce; the power of example is sometimes irresistible. Even among these back-settlers, their depravity is greater or less according to what nation or province they belong. Were I to adduce proofs of this, I might be accused of partiality. If there happens to be some rich intervals, some fertile bottoms, in those remote districts, the people will there prefer tilling the land to hunting and will attach themselves to it; but even on these fertile spots you may plainly perceive the inhabitants to acquire a great degree of rusticity and selfishness.

It is in consequence of this straggling situation and the astonishing power it has on manners that the back-settlers of both the Carolinas, Virginia, and many other parts have been long a set of lawless people; it has been even dangerous to travel among them. Government can do nothing in so extensive a country; better it should wink at these irregularities than that it should use means inconsistent with its usual mildness. Time will efface those stains: in proportion as the great body of population approaches them they will reform and become polished and subordinate. Whatever has been said of the four New England provinces, no such degeneracy of manners has ever tarnished their annals; their back-settlers have been kept within the bounds of decency, and government, by means of wise laws, and by the influence of religion. What a detestable idea such people must have given to the natives of the Europeans! They trade with them; the worst of people are permitted to do that which none but persons of the best characters should be employed in. They get drunk with them and often defraud the Indians. Their avarice, removed from the eyes of their superiors, knows no bounds; and aided by a little superiority of knowledge, these traders deceive them and even sometimes shed blood. Hence those shocking violations, those sudden devastations which have so often stained our frontiers, when hundreds of innocent people have been sacrificed for the crimes of a few. It was in consequence of such behavior that the Indians took the hatchet against the Virginians in 1774.[5] Thus are our first steps trodden, thus are our first trees felled, in general, by the most vicious of our people; and thus the path is opened for the arrival of a second and better class, the true American freeholders,[6] the most respectable set of people in this part of the world: respectable for their industry, their happy independence, the great share of freedom they possess, the good regulation of their families, and for extending the trade and the dominion of our mother country.

Europe contains hardly any other distinctions but lords and tenants; this fair country alone is settled by freeholders, the possessors of the soil they cultivate, members of the government they obey, and the framers of their own laws, by means of their representatives. This is a thought which you have taught me to cherish; our distance from Europe, far from diminishing, rather adds to our usefulness and consequence as men and subjects. Had our forefathers remained there, they would only have crowded it and perhaps prolonged those convulsions which had shaken it so long. Every industrious European who transports himself here may be compared to a sprout growing at the foot of a great tree; it enjoys

---

[5]White settlers along the western border of Virginia killed the family of an Indian chief. The royal governor of Virginia raised 3,000 men to crush the Shawnee Indians in what is called Lord Dunmore's War.
[6]Owners of land that may be passed on as inheritance.

and draws but a little portion of sap; wrench it from the parent roots, transplant it, and it will become a tree bearing fruit also. Colonists are therefore entitled to the consideration due to the most useful subjects; a hundred families barely existing in some parts of Scotland will here in six years cause an annual exportation of 10,000 bushels of wheat, 100 bushels being but a common quantity for an industrious family to sell if they cultivate good land. It is here, then, that the idle may be employed, the useless become useful, and the poor become rich; but by riches I do not mean gold and silver, we have but little of those metals; I mean a better sort of wealth, cleared lands, cattle, good houses, good clothes, and an increase of people to enjoy them.

There is no wonder that this country has so many charms and presents to Europeans so many temptations to remain in it. A traveller in Europe becomes a stranger as soon as he quits his own kingdom; but it is otherwise here. We know, properly speaking, no strangers; this is every person's country; the variety of our soils, situations, climates, governments, and produce hath something which must please everybody. No sooner does a European arrive, no matter of what condition, than his eyes are opened upon the fair prospect: he hears his language spoken; he retraces many of his own country manners; he perpetually hears the names of families and towns with which he is acquainted; he sees happiness and prosperity in all places disseminated; he meets with hospitality, kindness, and plenty everywhere; he beholds hardly any poor; he seldom hears of punishments and executions; and he wonders at the elegance of our towns, those miracles of industry and freedom. He cannot admire enough our rural districts, our convenient roads, good taverns, and our many accommodations; he involuntarily loves a country where everything is so lovely. When in England, he was a mere Englishman; here he stands on a larger portion of the globe, not less than its fourth part, and may see the productions of the north, in iron and naval stores; the provisions of Ireland; the grain of Egypt; the indigo, the rice of China. He does not find, as in Europe, a crowded society where every place is overstocked; he does not feel that perpetual collision of parties, that difficulty of beginning, that contention which oversets so many. There is room for everybody in America; has he any particular talent or industry? He exerts it in order to procure a livelihood, and it succeeds. Is he a merchant? The avenues of trade are infinite. Is he eminent in any respect? He will be employed and respected. Does he love a country life? Pleasant farms present themselves; he may purchase what he wants and thereby become an American farmer. Is he a laborer, sober and industrious? He need not go many miles nor receive many informations[7] before he will be hired, well fed at the table of his employer, and paid four or five times more than he can get in Europe. Does he want uncultivated lands? Thousands of acres present themselves, which he may purchase cheap. Whatever be his talents or inclinations, if they are moderate, he may satisfy them. I do not mean that every one who comes will grow rich in a little time; no, but he may procure an easy, decent maintenance by his industry. Instead of starving, he will be fed; instead of being idle, he will have employment: and these are riches enough for such men as come over here. The rich stay in Europe; it is only the middling and poor that emigrate. Would you wish to travel in independent idleness, from north to south, you will find easy access, and the most cheerful reception at every house; society without ostentation; good cheer without pride; and every decent diversion which the country affords, with little expense. It is no wonder that the European who has lived here a few years is desirous to remain; Europe with all its pomp is not to be compared to this continent for men of middle stations or laborers.

---

[7]Advertisements.

A European, when he first arrives, seems limited in his intentions, as well as in his views; but he very suddenly alters his scale; two hundred miles formerly appeared a very great distance, it is now but a trifle; he no sooner breathes our air than he forms schemes and embarks in designs he never would have thought of in his own country. There the plenitude of society confines many useful ideas and often extinguishes the most laudable schemes which here ripen into maturity. Thus Europeans become Americans.

But how is this accomplished in that crowd of low, indigent people who flock here every year from all parts of Europe? I will tell you; they no sooner arrive than they immediately feel the good effects of that plenty of provisions we possess: they fare on our best food, and are kindly entertained; their talents, character, and peculiar industry are immediately inquired into; they find countrymen everywhere disseminated, let them come from whatever part of Europe. Let me select one as an epitome of the rest; he is hired, he goes to work, and works moderately; instead of being employed by a haughty person, he finds himself with his equal, placed at the substantial table of the farmer, or else at an inferior one as good; his wages are high, his bed is not like that bed of sorrow on which he used to lie; if he behaves with propriety, and is faithful, he is caressed, and becomes as it were a member of the family. He begins to feel the effects of a sort of resurrection; hitherto he had not lived, but simply vegetated; he now feels himself a man because he is treated as such; the laws of his own country had overlooked him in his insignificancy; the laws of this cover him with their mantle. Judge what an alteration there must arise in the mind and thoughts of this man. He begins to forget his former servitude and dependence; his heart involuntarily swells and glows; this first swell inspires him with those new thoughts which constitute an American. What love can he entertain for a country where his existence was a burden to him; if he is a generous, good man, the love of this new adoptive parent will sink deep into his heart. He looks around and sees many a prosperous person who but a few years before was as poor as himself. This encourages him much; he begins to form some little scheme, the first, alas, he ever formed in his life. If he is wise, he thus spends two or three years, in which time he acquires knowledge, the use of tools, the modes of working the lands, felling trees, etc. This prepares the foundation of a good name, the most useful acquisition he can make. He is encouraged, he has gained friends; he is advised and directed; he feels bold, he purchases some land; he gives all the money he has brought over, as well as what he has earned, and trusts to the God of harvests for the discharge of the rest. His good name procures him credit. He is now possessed of the deed, conveying to him and his posterity the fee simple[8] and absolute property of two hundred acres of land, situated on such a river. What an epoch in this man's life! He is become a freeholder, from perhaps a German boor[9]—he is now an American, a Pennsylvanian, an English subject. He is naturalized, his name is enrolled with those of the other citizens of the province. Instead of being a vagrant, he has a place of residence; he is called the inhabitant of such a county, or of such a district, and for the first time in his life counts for something, for hitherto he has been a cipher. I only repeat what I have heard many say, and no wonder their hearts should glow and be agitated with a multitude of feelings, not easy to describe. From nothing to start into being; from a servant to the rank of a master; from being the slave of some despotic prince, to become a free man, invested with lands to which every municipal blessing is annexed! What a change indeed! It is in consequence of that change that he becomes an American. . . .

·　·　·　·　·

---

[8]Legal possession in perpetuity.
[9]Peasant.

After a foreigner from any part of Europe is arrived and become a citizen, let him devoutly listen to the voice of our great parent, which says to him, "Welcome to my shores, distressed European; bless the hour in which thou didst see my verdant fields, my fair navigable rivers, and my green mountains! If thou wilt work, I have bread for thee; if thou wilt be honest, sober, and industrious, I have greater rewards to confer on thee—ease and independence. I will give thee fields to feed and clothe thee, a comfortable fireside to sit by and tell thy children by what means thou hast prospered, and a decent bed to repose on. I shall endow thee beside with the immunities of a freeman. If thou wilt carefully educate thy children, teach them gratitude to God and reverence to that government, that philanthropic government, which has collected here so many men and made them happy, I will also provide for thy progeny; and to every good man this ought to be the most holy, the most powerful, the most earnest wish he can possibly form, as well as the most consolatory prospect when he dies. Go thou and work and till; thou shalt prosper, provided thou be just, grateful, and industrious."

from LETTER IX: DESCRIPTION OF CHARLESTON . . .
[THE HAPPINESS OF CHARLESTON, THE MISERY OF SLAVES]

Charleston is, in the north, what Lima[1] is in the south; both are capitals of the richest provinces of their respective hemispheres: you may therefore conjecture that both cities must exhibit the appearances necessarily resulting from riches. Peru abounding in gold, Lima is filled with inhabitants who enjoy all those gradations of pleasure, refinement, and luxury which proceed from wealth. Carolina produces commodities more valuable perhaps than gold because they are gained by greater industry; it exhibits also on our northern stage a display of riches and luxury, inferior indeed to the former, but far superior to what are to be seen in our northern towns. Its situation is admirable, being built at the confluence of two large rivers, which receive in their course a great number of inferior streams, all navigable in the spring for flat boats. Here the produce of this extensive territory concentres; here therefore is the seat of the most valuable exportation; their wharfs, their docks, their magazines,[2] are extremely convenient to facilitate this great commercial business. The inhabitants are the gayest in America; it is called the center of our beau monde[3] and is always filled with the richest planters of the province, who resort hither in quest of health and pleasure. Here is always to be seen a great number of valetudinarians[4] from the West Indies, seeking for the renovation of health, exhausted by the debilitating nature of their sun, air, and modes of living. Many of these West Indians have I seen, at thirty, loaded with the infirmities of old age; for nothing is more common in those countries of wealth than for persons to lose the abilities of enjoying the comforts of life at a time when we northern men just begin to taste the fruits of our labor and prudence. The round of pleasure and the expenses of those citizens' tables are much superior to what you would imagine: indeed, the growth of this town and province has been astonishingly rapid. It is pity that the narrowness of the neck on which it stands prevents it from increasing; and which is the reason why houses are so dear. The heat of the climate, which is sometimes very great in the interior parts of the country, is always temperate in Charleston, though sometimes when they have no sea breezes, the sun is too powerful. The climate renders excesses of all kinds very dangerous, particularly those of the table; and yet, insensible or fearless of danger, they live on and enjoy a short and a merry life. The rays of their sun seem to urge them irresistibly to dissipation and pleasure: on the contrary, the women,

---

[1] Charleston, South Carolina; Lima, Peru.
[2] Storehouses.
[3] "Fashionable society" (French).
[4] Invalids, sickly persons.

from being abstemious, reach to a longer period of life and seldom die without having had several husbands. A European at his first arrival must be greatly surprised when he sees the elegance of their houses, their sumptuous furniture, as well as the magnificence of their tables. Can he imagine himself in a country the establishment of which is so recent?

The three principal classes of inhabitants are lawyers, planters, and merchants; this is the province which has afforded to the first the richest spoils, for nothing can exceed their wealth, their power, and their influence. They have reached the *ne plus ultra*[5] of worldly felicity; no plantation is secured, no title is good, no will is valid, but what they dictate, regulate, and approve. The whole mass of provincial property is become tributary to this society, which, far above priests and bishops, disdain to be satisfied with the poor Mosaical portion of the tenth.[6] I appeal to the many inhabitants who, while contending perhaps for their right to a few hundred acres, have lost by the mazes of the law their whole patrimony. These men are more properly lawgivers than interpreters of the law and have united here, as well as in most other provinces, the skill and dexterity of the scribe with the power and ambition of the prince: who can tell where this may lead in a future day? The nature of our laws and the spirit of freedom, which often tends to make us litigious, must necessarily throw the greatest part of the property of the colonies into the hands of these gentlemen. In another century, the law will possess in the north what now the church possesses in Peru and Mexico.[7]

While all is joy, festivity, and happiness in Charleston, would you imagine that scenes of misery overspread in the country? Their ears by habit are become deaf, their hearts are hardened; they neither see, hear, nor feel for the woes of their poor slaves, from whose painful labors all their wealth proceeds. Here the horrors of slavery, the hardship of incessant toils, are unseen; and no one thinks with compassion of those showers of sweat and of tears which from the bodies of Africans daily drop and moisten the ground they till. The cracks of the whip urging these miserable beings to excessive labor are far too distant from the gay capital to be heard. The chosen race eat, drink, and live happy, while the unfortunate one grubs up the ground, raises indigo, or husks the rice, exposed to a sun full as scorching as their native one, without the support of good food, without the cordials of any cheering liquor. This great contrast has often afforded me subjects of the most afflicting meditations. On the one side, behold a people enjoying all that life affords most bewitching and pleasurable, without labor, without fatigue, hardly subjected to the trouble of wishing. With gold, dug from Peruvian mountains, they order vessels to the coasts of Guinea;[8] by virtue of that gold, wars, murders, and devastations are committed in some harmless, peaceable African neighborhood where dwelt innocent people who even knew not but that all men were black. The daughter torn from her weeping mother, the child from the wretched parents, the wife from the loving husband; whole families swept away and brought through storms and tempests to this rich metropolis! There, arranged like horses at a fair, they are branded like cattle and then driven to toil, to starve, and to languish for a few years on the different plantations of these citizens. And for whom must they work? For persons they know not, and who have no other power over them than that of violence, no other right than what this accursed metal has given them! Strange order of things! Oh, Nature, where art thou? Are not these blacks thy children as well as we? On the other side, nothing is to be seen but the most diffusive misery and wretchedness, unrelieved even in thought or wish! Day after day they drudge on without any prospect of ever reaping for

---

[5]"No more beyond, the furthest limit" (Latin).
[6]I.e., the tithe, a tenth of one's income.
[7]The Catholic Church owned extensive properties in these

two New World countries conquered and settled by the Spanish in the sixteenth and seventeenth centuries.
[8]West Africa.

themselves; they are obliged to devote their lives, their limbs, their will, and every vital exertion to swell the wealth of masters who look not upon them with half the kindness and affection with which they consider their dogs and horses. Kindness and affection are not the portion of those who till the earth, who carry burdens, who convert the logs into useful boards. This reward, simple and natural as one would conceive it, would border on humanity; and planters must have none of it!

If Negroes are permitted to become fathers, this fatal indulgence only tends to increase their misery: the poor companions of their scanty pleasures are likewise the companions of their labors; and when at some critical seasons they could wish to see them relieved, with tears in their eyes they behold them perhaps doubly oppressed, obliged to bear the burden of Nature—a fatal present—as well as that of unabated tasks. How many have I seen cursing the irresistible propensity and regretting that by having tasted of those harmless joys they had become the authors of double misery to their wives. Like their masters, they are not permitted to partake of those ineffable sensations with which Nature inspires the hearts of fathers and mothers; they must repel them all and become callous and passive. This unnatural state often occasions the most acute, the most pungent of their afflictions; they have no time, like us, tenderly to rear their helpless offspring, to nurse them on their knees, to enjoy the delight of being parents. Their paternal fondness is embittered by considering that if their children live, they must live to be slaves like themselves; no time is allowed them to exercise their pious office; the mothers must fasten them on their backs and, with this double load, follow their husbands in the fields, where they too often hear no other sound than that of the voice or whip of the taskmaster and the cries of their infants, broiling in the sun. These unfortunate creatures cry and weep like their parents, without a possibility of relief; the very instinct of the brute, so laudable, so irresistible, runs counter here to their master's interest; and to that god, all the laws of Nature must give way. Thus planters get rich; so raw, so inexperienced am I in this mode of life that were I to be possessed of a plantation, and my slaves treated as in general they are here, never could I rest in peace; my sleep would be perpetually disturbed by a retrospect of the frauds committed in Africa in order to entrap them, frauds surpassing in enormity everything which a common mind can possibly conceive. I should be thinking of the barbarous treatment they meet with on shipboard, of their anguish, of the despair necessarily inspired by their situation, when torn from their friends and relations, when delivered into the hands of a people differently colored, whom they cannot understand, carried in a strange machine over an ever agitated element, which they had never seen before, and finally delivered over to the severities of the whippers and the excessive labors of the field. Can it be possible that the force of custom should ever make me deaf to all these reflections and as insensible to the injustice of that trade and to their miseries as the rich inhabitants of this town seem to be? What, then, is man, this being who boasts so much of the excellence and dignity of his nature among that variety of unscrutable mysteries, of unsolvable problems, with which he is surrounded?

["Man, an Animal of Prey"]

. . . Is there . . . no superintending power who conducts the moral operations of the world, as well as the physical? The same sublime hand which guides the planets round the sun with so much exactness, which preserves the arrangement of the whole with such exalted wisdom and paternal care, and prevents the vast system from falling into confusion—doth it abandon mankind to all the errors, the follies, and the miseries, which their most frantic rage and their most dangerous vices and passions can produce?

The history of the earth! Doth it present anything but crimes of the most heinous nature, committed from one end of the world to the other? We observe avarice, rapine, and murder, equally prevailing in all parts. History perpetually tells us of millions of people abandoned to the caprice of the maddest princes, and of whole nations devoted to the blind fury of tyrants. Countries destroyed, nations alternately buried in ruins by other nations, some parts of the world beautifully cultivated, returned again into their pristine state, the fruits of ages of industry, the toil of thousands in a short time destroyed by few! If one corner breathes in peace for a few years, it is, in turn subjected, torn, and levelled; one would almost believe the principles of action in man, considered as the first agent of this planet, to be poisoned in their most essential parts. We certainly are not that class of beings which we vainly think ourselves to be; man, an animal of prey, seems to have rapine and the love of bloodshed implanted in his heart, nay, to hold it the most honorable occupation in society; we never speak of a hero of mathematics, a hero of knowledge or humanity, no, this illustrious appellation is reserved for the most successful butchers of the world. If nature has given us a fruitful soil to inhabit, she has refused us such inclinations and propensities as would afford us the full enjoyment of it. Extensive as the surface of this planet is, not one half of it is yet cultivated, not half replenished; she created man and placed him either in the woods or plains and provided him with passions which must forever oppose his happiness; everything is submitted to the power of the strongest; men, like the elements, are always at war; the weakest yield to the most potent; force, subtlety, and malice always triumph over unguarded honesty and simplicity. Benignity, moderation, and justice are virtues adapted only to the humble paths of life; we love to talk of virtue and to admire its beauty while in the shade of solitude and retirement, but when we step forth into active life, if it happen to be in competition with any passion or desire, do we observe it to prevail? Hence so many religious impostors have triumphed over the credulity of mankind and have rendered their frauds the creeds of succeeding generations during the course of many ages until, worn away by time, they have been replaced by new ones. Hence the most unjust war, if supported by the greatest force, always succeeds; hence the most just ones, when supported only by their justice, as often fail. Such is the ascendancy of power, the supreme arbiter of all the revolutions which we observe in this planet; so irresistible is power that it often thwarts the tendency of the most forcible causes and prevents their subsequent salutary effects, though ordained for the good of man by the Governor of the universe. Such is the perverseness of human nature; who can describe it in all its latitude?

[A Melancholy Scene]

Everywhere one part of the human species is taught the art of shedding the blood of the other, of setting fire to their dwellings, of levelling the works of their industry: half of the existence of nations regularly employed in destroying other nations. What little political felicity is to be met with here and there has cost oceans of blood to purchase, as if good was never to be the portion of unhappy man. Republics, kingdoms, monarchies, founded either on fraud or successful violence, increase by pursuing the steps of the same policy until they are destroyed in their turn, either by the influence of their own crimes or by more successful but equally criminal enemies.

If from this general review of human nature we descend to the examination of what is called civilized society, there the combination of every natural and artificial want makes us pay very dear for what little share of political felicity we enjoy. It is a strange heterogeneous assemblage of vices and virtues and of a variety of other principles, forever at war, forever jarring, forever producing some dangerous, some distressing extreme. Where do you conceive, then, that nature intended we should be happy? Would you prefer the state of men in the woods to that of men in a more improved situation? Evil preponderates in both; in the first they often eat each other for want of food, and in the other they often starve each other for want of room. For my part, I think the vices and miseries to be found in the latter exceed those of the former, in which real evil is more scarce, more supportable, and less enormous. Yet we wish to see the earth peopled, to accomplish the happiness of kingdoms, which is said to consist in numbers. Gracious God! To what end is the introduction of so many beings into a mode of existence in which they must grope amidst as many errors, commit as many crimes, and meet with as many diseases, wants, and sufferings!

The following scene will, I hope, account for these melancholy reflections and apologize for the gloomy thoughts with which I have filled this letter: my mind is, and always has been, oppressed since I became a witness to it. I was not long since invited to dine with a planter who lived three miles from —, where he then resided. In order to avoid the heat of the sun, I resolved to go on foot, sheltered in a small path leading through a pleasant wood. I was leisurely travelling along, attentively examining some peculiar plants which I had collected, when all at once I felt the air strongly agitated, though the day was perfectly calm and sultry. I immediately cast my eyes toward the cleared ground, from which I was but a small distance, in order to see whether it was not occasioned by a sudden shower, when at that instant a sound resembling a deep rough voice, uttered, as I thought, a few inarticulate monosyllables. Alarmed and surprised, I precipitately looked all round, when I perceived at about six rods distance something resembling a cage, suspended to the limbs of a tree, all the branches of which appeared covered with large birds of prey, fluttering about and anxiously endeavoring to perch on the cage. Actuated by an involuntary motion of my hands more than by any design of my mind, I fired at them; they all flew to a short distance, with a most hideous noise, when, horrid to think and painful to repeat, I perceived a Negro, suspended in the cage and left there to expire! I shudder when I recollect that the birds had already picked out his eyes; his cheek bones were bare; his arms had been attacked in several places; and his body seemed covered with a multitude of wounds. From the edges of the hollow sockets and from the lacerations with which he was disfigured, the blood slowly dropped and tinged the ground beneath. No sooner were the birds flown than swarms of insects covered the whole body of this unfortunate wretch, eager to feed on his mangled flesh and to drink his blood. I found myself suddenly arrested by the power of affright and terror; my nerves were convulsed; I trembled; I stood motionless, involuntarily contemplating the fate of this Negro in all its dismal latitude. The living spectre, though deprived of his eyes, could still distinctly hear, and in his uncouth dialect begged me to give him some water to allay his thirst. Humanity herself would have recoiled back with horror; she would have balanced whether to lessen such reliefless distress or mercifully with one blow to end this dreadful scene of agonizing torture! Had I had a ball in my gun, I certainly should have dispatched him, but finding myself unable to perform so kind an office, I sought, though trembling, to relieve him as well as I could. A shell ready fixed to a pole, which had been used by some Negroes, presented itself to me; filled it with water, and with trembling hands I guided it to the quivering lips of the wretched sufferer. Urged by the irresistible power of thirst, he endeavored to meet it, as he instinctively guessed its approach by the noise it made in passing through the bars of the cage. "Tanky you, white man; tanky you; puta some poison and give me." "How long have you been hanging there?" I asked him. "Two days, and me no die; the birds, the birds; aaah me!" Oppressed with the reflections which this shocking spectacle afforded me, I mustered strength enough to walk away and soon reached the house at which I intended to dine. There I heard that the reason for this slave's being thus punished was on account of his having killed the overseer of the plantation. They told me that the laws of self-preservation rendered such executions necessary, and supported the doctrine of slavery with the arguments generally made use of to justify the practice, with the repetition of which I shall not trouble you at present. Adieu.

from LETTER XII: DISTRESSES OF A FRONTIER MAN
[FLIGHT FROM WAR, REVERSION TO NATURE]

I wish for a change of place; the hour is come at last that I must fly from my house and abandon my farm![1] But what course shall I steer, enclosed as I am? The climate best adapted to my present situation and humor would be the polar regions, where six months' day and six months' night divide the dull year: nay, a simple aurora borealis[2] would suffice me and greatly refresh my eyes, fatigued now by so many disagreeable objects. The severity of those climates, that great gloom where melancholy dwells, would be perfectly analogous to the turn of my mind. Oh, could I remove my plantation[3] to the shores of the Oby, willingly would I dwell in the hut of a Samoyed;[4] with cheerfulness would I go and bury myself in the cavern of a Laplander.[5] Could I but carry my family along with me, I would winter at Pello, or Tobolsk,[6] in order to enjoy the peace and innocence of that country. But let me arrive under the pole, or reach the antipodes,[7] I never can leave behind me the remembrance of the dreadful scenes to which I have been witness; therefore, never can I be happy! Happy, why would I mention that sweet, that enchanting word? Once happiness was our portion; now it is gone from us, and I am afraid not to be enjoyed again by the present generation! Whichever way I look, nothing but the most frightful precipices present themselves to my view, in which hundreds of my friends and acquaintances have already perished; of all animals that live on the surface of this planet, what is man when no longer connected with society, or when he finds himself surrounded by a convulsed and a half-dissolved one? He cannot live in solitude; he must belong to some community bound by some ties, however imperfect. Men mutually support and add to the boldness and confidence of each other; the weakness of each is strengthened by the force of the whole. I had never before these calamitous times formed any such ideas; I lived on, labored and prospered, without having ever studied on what the security of my life and the foundation of my prosperity were established: I perceived them just as they left me. Never was a situation so singularly terrible as mine, in every possible respect, as a member of an extensive society, as a citizen of an inferior division of the same society, as a husband, as a father, as a man who exquisitely feels for the miseries of others as well as for his own! But alas! So much is everything now subverted among us that the very word *misery*, with which we were hardly acquainted before, no longer conveys the same ideas; or, rather, tired with feeling for the miseries of others, every one feels now for himself alone. When I consider myself as connected in all these characters, as bound by so many cords, all uniting in my heart, I am seized with a fever of the mind, I am transported beyond that degree of calmness which is necessary to delineate our thoughts. I feel as if my reason wanted to leave me, as if it would burst its poor weak tenement; again, I try to compose myself, I grow cool, and preconceiving the dreadful loss, I endeavor to retain the useful guest. . . .

---

[1]The American Revolutionary War (1775–83) is beginning, causing distress to a "frontier man" who is divided in his loyalties between England and the colonies.
[2]Northern Lights.
[3]Farm.
[4]A nomadic people living in Siberia near the Oby (or Ob) River.

[5]Nomads inhabiting Lapland in northern Scandinavia and Finland.
[6]Pello: a town in northern Finland; Tobolsk: a town in Siberia.
[7]Any two places on opposite sides of the earth.

Could not the great nation we belong to have accomplished her designs by means of her numerous armies, by means of those fleets which cover the ocean? Must those who are masters of two thirds of the trade of the world, who have in their hands the power which almighty gold can give, who possess a species of wealth that increases with their desires—must they establish their conquest with our insignificant, innocent blood!

Must I, then, bid farewell to Britain, to that renowned country? Must I renounce a name so ancient and so venerable? Alas, she herself, that once indulgent parent, forces me to take up arms against her. She herself first inspired the most unhappy citizens of our remote districts with the thoughts of shedding the blood of those whom they used to call by the name of friends and brethren. That great nation which now convulses the world, which hardly knows the extent of her Indian kingdoms, which looks toward the universal monarchy of trade, of industry, of riches, of power: why must she strew our poor frontiers with the carcasses of her friends, with the wrecks of our insignificant villages, in which there is no gold? . . .

To this great evil I must seek some sort of remedy adapted to remove or to palliate it; situated as I am, what steps should I take that will neither injure nor insult any of the parties, and at the same time save my family from that certain destruction which awaits it if I remain here much longer. Could I ensure them bread, safety, and subsistence, not the bread of idleness, but that earned by proper labor as heretofore; could this be accomplished by the sacrifice of my life, I would willingly give it up. I attest before heaven that it is only for these I would wish to live and to toil, for these whom I have brought into this miserable existence. I resemble, methinks, one of the stones of a ruined arch, still retaining that pristine form which anciently fitted the place I occupied, but the center is tumbled down; I can be nothing until I am replaced, either in the former circle or in some stronger one. I see one on a smaller scale, and at a considerable distance, but it is within my power to reach it; and since I have ceased to consider myself as a member of the ancient state now convulsed, I willingly descend into an inferior one. I will revert into a state approaching nearer to that of nature, unencumbered either with voluminous laws or contradictory codes, often galling the very necks of those whom they protect, and at the same time sufficiently remote from the brutality of unconnected savage nature. . . .

I have carefully revolved the scheme; I have considered in all its future effects and tendencies the new mode of living we must pursue, without salt, without spices, without linen, and with little other clothing; the art of hunting we must acquire, the new manners we must adopt, the new language we must speak; the dangers attending the education of my children we must endure. These changes may appear more terrific at a distance perhaps than when grown familiar by practice; what is it to us whether we eat well-made pastry or pounded àlagrichés,[8] well-roasted beef or smoked venison, cabbages or squashes? Whether we wear neat homespun or good beaver, whether we sleep on feather-beds or on bearskins? The difference is not worth attending to. The difficulty of the language, the fear of some great intoxication among the Indians, finally the apprehension lest my younger children should be caught by that singular charm, so dangerous at their tender years, are the only considerations that startle me. By what power does it come to pass that children who have been adopted when young among these people can never be prevailed on to readopt European manners? Many an anxious parent have I seen last war who at the return of the peace went to the Indian vil-

---

[8]From the French *à la grichés:* in the manner of grinding or gnashing (as teeth); *gricher* is Normandy dialect for *grincer,* meaning to grind, especially teeth.

lages where they knew their children had been carried in captivity, when to their inexpressible sorrow they found them so perfectly Indianized that many knew them no longer, and those whose more advanced ages permitted them to recollect their fathers and mothers absolutely refused to follow them and ran to their adoptive parents for protection against the effusions of love their unhappy real parents lavished on them! . . .

Let us say what we will of them, of their inferior organs, of their want of bread, etc., they are as stout and well made as the Europeans. Without temples, without priests, without kings, and without laws, they are in many instances superior to us; and the proofs of what I advance are that they live without care, sleep without inquietude, take life as it comes, bearing all its asperities with unparalleled patience, and die without any kind of apprehension for what they have done or for what they expect to meet with hereafter. What system of philosophy can give us so many necessary qualifications for happiness? They most certainly are much more closely connected with Nature than we are; they are her immediate children: the inhabitants of the woods are her undefiled offspring; those of the plains are her degenerated breed, far, very far removed from her primitive laws, from her original design. It is therefore resolved on. I will either die in the attempt or succeed; better perish all together in one fatal hour than to suffer what we daily endure.

["Behold Me under the Wigwam"]

You may therefore, by means of anticipation, behold me under the wigwam;[1] I am so well acquainted with the principal manners of these people that I entertain not the least apprehension from them. I rely more securely on their strong hospitality than on the witnessed compacts of many Europeans. As soon as possible after my arrival, I design to build myself a wigwam, after the same manner and size with the rest in order to avoid being thought singular or giving occasion for any railleries, though these people are seldom guilty of such European follies. I shall erect it hard by the lands which they propose to allot me, and will endeavor that my wife, my children, and myself may be adopted soon after our arrival. Thus becoming truly inhabitants of their village, we shall immediately occupy that rank within the pale[2] of their society, which will afford us all the amends[3] we can possibly expect for the loss we have met with by the convulsions of our own. According to their customs, we shall likewise receive names from them, by which we shall always be known. My youngest children shall learn to swim and to shoot with the bow, that they may acquire such talents as will necessarily raise them into some degree of esteem among the Indian lads of their own age; the rest of us must hunt with the hunters. I have been for several years an expert marksman; but I dread lest the imperceptible charm of Indian education may seize my younger children and give them such a propensity to that mode of life as may preclude their returning to the manners and customs of their parents. I have but one remedy to prevent this great evil, and that is to employ them in the labor of the fields as much as I can; I have even resolved to make their daily subsistence depend altogether on it. As long as we keep ourselves busy in tilling the earth, there is no fear of any of us becoming wild; it is the chase and the food it procures that have this strange effect. Excuse a simile—those hogs which range in the woods, and to whom grain is given once a week, preserve their former degree of tameness; but if, on the contrary, they are reduced to live on ground nuts and on what they can get, they soon become wild and fierce. For my part, I can plow, sow, and hunt, as occasion may require; but my wife, deprived of wool and flax, will have no room

---

[1] I.e., living as an Indian in a tepee or wigwam made of poles and animal skins.

[2] Bounds.

[3] Restitutions.

for industry;[4] what is she then to do? Like the other squaws, she must cook for us the nasaump, the ninchickè,[5] and such other preparations of corn as are customary among these people. She must learn to bake squashes and pumpkins under the ashes, to slice and smoke the meat of our own killing in order to preserve it; she must cheerfully adopt the manners and customs of her neighbors, in their dress, deportment, conduct, and internal economy, in all respects. Surely if we can have fortitude enough to quit all we have, to remove so far, and to associate with people so different from us, these necessary compliances are but subordinate parts of the scheme. The change of garments, when those they carry with them are worn out, will not be the least of my wife's and daughter's concerns, though I am in hopes that self-love will invent some sort of reparation. Perhaps you would not believe that there are in the woods looking-glasses and paint of every color; and that the inhabitants take as much pains to adorn their faces and their bodies, to fix their bracelets of silver, and plait their hair as our forefathers the Picts[6] used to do in the time of the Romans. Not that I would wish to see either my wife or daughter adopt those savage customs; we can live in great peace and harmony with them without descending to every article; the interruption of trade hath, I hope, suspended this mode of dress. My wife understands inoculation perfectly well; she inoculated all our children one after another and has successfully performed the operation on several scores of people, who, scattered here and there through our woods, were too far removed from all medical assistance. If we can persuade but one family to submit to it, and it succeeds, we shall then be as happy as our situation will admit of; it will raise her into some degree of consideration, for whoever is useful in any society will always be respected. If we are so fortunate as to carry one family through a disorder, which is the plague among these people, I trust to the force of example we shall then become truly necessary, valued, and beloved; we indeed owe every kind office to a society of men who so readily offer to admit us into their social partnership and to extend to my family the shelter of their village, the strength of their adoption, and even the dignity of their names. God grant us a prosperous beginning; we may then hope to be of more service to them than even missionaries who have been sent to preach to them a Gospel they cannot understand.

As to religion, our mode of worship will not suffer much by this removal from a cultivated country into the bosom of the woods; for it cannot be much simpler than that which we have followed here these many years, and I will with as much care as I can redouble my attention and twice a week retrace to them the great outlines of their duty to God and to man. I will read and expound to them some part of the decalogue,[7] which is the method I have pursued ever since I married. . . .

Not a word of politics shall cloud our simple conversation; tired either with the chase or the labor of the field, we shall sleep on our mats without any distressing want, having learnt to retrench every superfluous one; we shall have but two prayers to make to the Supreme Being, that He may shed His fertilizing dew on our little crops and that He will be pleased to restore peace to our unhappy country. These shall be the only subject of our nightly prayers and of our daily ejaculations; and if the labor, the industry, the frugality, the union of men, can be an agreeable offering to Him, we shall not fail to receive His paternal blessings. There I shall contemplate nature in her most wild and ample extent; I shall carefully study a species of society of which I have at present but very imperfect ideas; I will endeavor to occupy with propriety that place which will enable me to enjoy

---

[4]Such as spinning.
[5]Dishes made from corn meal, like mush or porridge. Nasaump is a variant of samp.

[6]Prehistoric people of northern England.
[7]The Ten Commandments.

the few and sufficient benefits it confers. The solitary and unconnected mode of life I have lived in my youth must fit me for this trial; I am not the first who has attempted it; Europeans did not, it is true, carry to the wilderness numerous families; they went there as mere speculators, I as a man seeking a refuge from the desolation of war. They went there to study the manner of the aborigines, I to conform to them, whatever they are; some went as visitors, as travellers; I, as a sojourner, as a fellow-hunter and laborer, go determined industriously to work up among them such a system of happiness as may be adequate to my future situation and may be a sufficient compensation for all my fatigues and for the misfortunes I have borne: I have always found it at home; I may hope likewise to find it under the humble roof of my wigwam.

c. 1770–80   *1782*

WILLIAM BARTRAM
(1739–1823)

In the Introduction to his *Travels,* published in 1791, William Bartram revealed the range and style of his observations of nature in America: "The pompous Palms of Florida, and glorious Magnolia strike us with the sense of dignity and magnificence; the expansive umbrageous Live Oak with awful veneration; the Carica papaya seems supercilious with all the harmony of beauty and gracefulness." A "sportive" plant closes one leaf on "a struggling fly," another on a worm: "Can we after viewing this object, hesitate a moment to confess, that vegetable beings are endued with some sensible faculties or attributes, familiar to those that dignify animal nature; they are organical, living, and self-moving bodies, for we see, here, in this plant, motion and volition."

At another point Bartram describes his temporary guide, a hunter, stalking two bears and killing the mother; the young cub "approached the dead body, smelled, and pawed it, and appearing in agony, fell to weeping and looking upwards, then towards us, and cried like a child." Moved by the "cries of this afflicted child, bereft of its parent," Bartram pleaded with the hunter not to kill the cub, but to no avail.

At still another point, Bartram observes an insect drama. A large spider stalks a bee sipping nectar from a flower, pounces, and the two then disappear from view: "I expected the bee had carried off his enemy, but to my surprise, they both together rebounded back again, suspended at the extremity of a long elastic thread or web, which the spider had artfully let fall, or fixed on a twig, the instant he leaped from it." The bee was devoured by the spider, who, "perhaps before night," would become "himself the delicious evening repast of a bird or lizard."

These random samples from the Introduction suggest that the secret of the popularity of Bartram's *Travels*—influencing Samuel Taylor Coleridge, William Wordsworth, Thomas Carlyle, Henry David Thoreau, Chateaubriand and others—lies not in its scientific achievement but in its literary power. An important part of that power comes through the voice we hear as we read and the personality that gradually emerges from behind the voice.

We are likely to come to know William Bartram more intimately through his *Travels* than through the assorted facts of his life that biography provides. His father, John Bartram, a Quaker, was a distinguished botanist whose famous Botanical Garden in Philadelphia was the first in North America. Benjamin Franklin offered to train William in printing or engraving, but the boy was not interested. He worked for a time with a Philadelphia merchant, then tried his hand as a trader in North Carolina.

In 1765–66 came the event that determined his life. He accompanied his father on a botanical expedition, exploring some four hundred miles of St. John's River in northern Florida. William was eager to become a farmer along the river. Some of his excellent nature sketches circulated in England and came to the attention of Dr. John Fothergill, a Quaker, physician, and renowned botanist. He offered to subsidize Bartram on his explorations if he would send back to England seeds, specimens, and drawings, and if he would keep a journal recording his observations.

Bartram spent 1773–77 travelling throughout the southeastern United States, observing plant and animal life, as well as the landscape and the natives inhabiting it. He dressed completely in leather, generally travelled alone, and carefully recorded in his journal an account of what he saw and experienced. By the Seminole Indians he was known as "Puc-Puggy," Flower-Hunter. He returned to Pennsylvania early in 1778 and began to work on the manuscripts of his journal.

In 1782 he was appointed professor of botany at the University of Pennsylvania, but for reasons of health declined the position. In 1786 he was elected to the American Philosophical Society, but never attended meetings. At last, in 1791, he published *Travels through North and South Carolina, Georgia, East and West Florida, the Cherokee Country, the Extensive Territories of the Moscogulges, or Creek Confederacy, and the Country of the Chactaws; Containing an Account of the Soil and Natural Productions of these Regions, together with Observations on the Manners of the Indians.*

This prosaic if informative title concealed the true nature of an engrossing work combining narrative skill, descriptive power, and imaginative, or poetic, depth. Translated into German, Dutch, and French, it swept through Europe attracting readers eager to learn something about this new nation, the United States. It described majestic vistas and statuesque natives in the wilderness of the New World that intensified the romantic longings of those pent up in the decadent cities of the old world.

Bartram's father died in 1777, and Bartram's older brother John inherited the Botanical Gardens, but took William in as a partner. William lived in the family home, unmarried, shy, sensitive, sometimes sickly, continuing his investigations and observations. He died suddenly in 1823, having just completed a description of a plant and stepped into the garden for a walk.

A century after Bartram published his *Travels,* the book was probably better known abroad than at home. One of the most appreciative comments on it came from the pen of Scottish essayist and historian Thomas Carlyle recommending the work to his American friend Ralph Waldo Emerson in a letter of July 8, 1851: "Do you know *Bartram's Travels*? This is of the Seventies (1770) or so; treats of *Florida* chiefly, has a wondrous kind of floundering eloquence in it; and has also grown immeasurably *old*. All American libraries ought to provide themselves with that kind of book; and keep them as a kind of *biblical* article."

ADDITIONAL READING

The Travels of William Bartram, ed. Mark Van Doren; with Introduction by John Livingston Lowes, 1928, 1940.

N. Bryllion Fagin, *William Bartram: Interpreter of the American Landscape,* 1933; Ernest Earnest, *John and William Bartram: Botanists and Explorers,* 1940; Patricia M. Medeiros, "Three Travelers: Carver, Bartram, and Woolman," *American Literature, 1764–1789: The Revolutionary Years,* ed. Everett Emerson, 1977; William J. Scheick, "Telling a Wonder: Dialectic in the Writings of John Bartram," *Pennsylvania Magazine of History and Biography,* Vol. 107, 1983.

TEXT

The Travels of William Bartram: Naturalist's Edition, ed. Francis Harper, 1958. Some punctuation and spelling have been brought into conformity with contemporary English.

from The Travels

PART I, CHAPTER V

[THE ALATAMAHA RIVER]

HAVING completed my Hortus Siccus,[1] and made up my collections of seeds and growing roots, the fruits of my late western tour, and sent them to Charleston, to be forwarded to Europe, I spent the remaining part of this season in botanical excursions to the low countries, between Carolina and East Florida, and collected seeds, roots, and specimens, making drawings of such curious subjects as could not be preserved in their native state of excellence.

During this recess from the high road of my travels, having obtained the use of a neat light cypress canoe, at Broughton Island,[2] a plantation, the property of the Hon. Henry Laurens, Esq. where I stored myself with necessaries, for the voyage, and resolved upon a trip up the Alatamaha.

I ascended this beautiful river, on whose fruitful banks the generous and true sons of liberty securely dwell, fifty miles above the white settlements.

How gently flow thy peaceful floods, O Alatamaha! How sublimely rise to view, on thy elevated shores, yon Magnolian groves, from whose tops the surrounding expanse is perfumed, by clouds of incense, blended with the exhaling balm of the Liquid-amber, and odors continually arising from circumambient aromatic groves of Illicium, Myrica, Laurus, and Bignonia.[3]

When wearied with working my canoe against the impetuous current (which becomes stronger by reason of the mighty floods of the river, with collected force, pressing through the first hilly ascents, where the shores on each side the river present to view rocky cliffs rising above the surface of the water, in nearly flat horizontal masses, washed smooth by the descending floods, and which appear to be a composition, or concrete, of sandy lime-stone) I resigned my bark to the friendly current, reserving to myself the control of the helm. My progress was rendered delightful by the sylvan elegance of the groves, cheerful meadows, and high distant forests, which in grand order presented themselves to view. The winding banks of the river, and the high projecting promontories, unfolded fresh scenes of grandeur and sublimity. The deep forests and distant hills re-echoed the cheer-

---

[1] Dried plant specimens.
[2] In Georgia at the mouth of the Alatamaha River.
[3] Bartram's generic names generally follow the classifica-

tions worked out by the great Swedish botanist Linnaeus (1707–1778). Often Bartram mixes popular and scientific names in the *Travels.*

ing social lowings of domestic herds. The air was filled with the loud and shrill whooping of the wary sharp-sighted crane. Behold, on yon decayed, defoliated Cypress tree, the solitary wood-pelican, dejectedly perched upon its utmost elevated spire; he there, like an ancient venerable sage, sets himself up as a mark of derision, for the safety of his kindred tribes. The crying-bird, another faithful guardian, screaming in the gloomy thickets, warns the feathered tribes of approaching peril; and the plumage of the swift sailing squadrons of Spanish curlews (white as the immaculate robe of innocence) gleam in the cerulean skies.

Thus secure and tranquil, and meditating on the marvellous scenes of primitive nature, as yet unmodified by the hand of man, I gently descended the peaceful stream, on whose polished surface were depicted the mutable shadows from its pensile[4] banks; whilst myriads of finny inhabitants sported in its pellucid floods.

The glorious sovereign of day, clothed in light refulgent, rolling on his gilded chariot, speeds to revisit the western realms. Grey pensive eve now admonishes us of gloomy night's hasty approach: I am roused by care to seek a place of secure repose, ere darkness comes on.

Drawing near the high shores, I ascended the steep banks, where stood a venerable oak. An ancient Indian field, verdured o'er with succulent grass, and checquered with coppices of fragrant shrubs, offers to my view the Myrica cerifera, Magnolia glauca, Laurus benzoin, Laur. Borbonia, Rhamnus frangula, Prunus Chicasaw, Prun. Lauro cerasa, and others. It was nearly encircled with an open forest of stately pines (Pinus palustris) through which appears the extensive savanna,[5] the secure range of the swift roebuck. In front of my landing, and due east, I had a fine prospect of the river and low lands on each side, which gradually widened to the sea coast, and gave me an unconfined prospect, whilst the far distant sea coast islands, like a coronet, limited the hoary horizon.

My barque being securely moored, and having reconnoitered the surrounding groves, and collected fire-wood, I spread my skins and blanket by my cheerful fire, under the protecting shade of the hospitable Live-oak, and reclined my head on my hard but healthy couch. I listened, undisturbed, to the divine hymns of the feathered songsters of the groves, whilst the softly whispering breezes faintly died away.

The sun now below the western horizon, the moon majestically rising in the east; again the tuneful birds become inspired; how melodious is the social mockbird! the groves resound the unceasing cries of the whip-poor-will; the moon about an hour above the horizon; lo! a dark eclipse[6] of her glorious brightness comes slowly on; at length, a silver thread alone encircles her temples: at this boding change, an universal silence prevails.

Nature now weary, I resigned myself to rest; the night passed over; the cool dews of the morning awake me; my fire burnt low; the blue smoke scarce rises above the moistened embers; all is gloomy: the late starry skies, now overcast by thick clouds, I am warned to rise and be going. The livid purple clouds thicken on the frowning brows of the morning; the tumultuous winds from the east now exert their power. O peaceful Alatamaha! gentle by nature! how thou art ruffled! thy wavy surface disfigures every object, presenting them obscurely to the sight, and they at length totally disappear, whilst the furious winds and sweeping rains bend the lofty groves, and prostrate the quaking grass, driving the affrighted creatures to their dens and caverns.

The tempest now relaxes, its impetus is spent, and a calm serenity gradually takes place; by noon they break away, the blue sky appears, the fulgid[7] sun-beams

---

[4]Overhanging.
[5]Treeless plain.
[6]"The air at this time being serene, and not a cloud to be

seen, I saw this annual, almost total autumnal eclipse in its highest degree of perfection" (Bartram's note).
[7]Flashing.

spread abroad their animating light, and the steady western wind resumes his peaceful reign. The waters are purified, the waves subside, and the beautiful river regains its native calmness: so it is with the varied and mutable scenes of human events on the stream of life. The higher powers and affections of the soul are so blended and connected with the inferior passions, that the most painful feelings are excited in the mind when the latter are crossed: thus in the moral system, which we have planned for our conduct, as a ladder whereby to mount to the summit of terrestrial glory and happiness, and from whence we perhaps medi- tated our flight to heaven itself, at the very moment when we vainly imagine our- selves to have attained its point, some unforeseen accident intervenes, and sur- prises us; the chain is violently shaken, we quit our hold and fall: the well contrived system at once becomes a chaos; every idea of happiness recedes; the splendor of glory darkens, and at length totally disappears; every pleasing object is defaced, all is deranged, and the flattering scene passes quite away, a gloomy cloud pervades the understanding, and when we see our progress retarded, and our best intentions frustrated, we are apt to deviate from the admonitions and convictions of virtue, to shut our eyes upon our guide and protector, doubt of his power, and despair of his assistance. But let us wait and rely on our God, who in due time will shine forth in brightness, dissipate the envious cloud, and reveal to us how finite and circumscribed is human power, when assuming to itself inde- pendent wisdom.

from PART II, CHAPTER III
[THE EPHEMERA]

Leaving Picolata,[1] I continued to ascend the river. I observed this day, during my progress up the river, incredible numbers of small flying insects, of the genus, termed by naturalists, Ephemera, continually emerging from the shallow water, near shore, some of them immediately taking their flight to the land, whilst myri- ads, crept up the grass and herbage, where remaining, for a short time, as they acquired sufficient strength, they took their flight also, following their kindred, to the main land. This resurrection from the deep, if I may so express it, commences early in the morning, and ceases after the sun is up. At evening they are seen in clouds of innumerable millions, swarming and wantoning in the still air, gradually drawing near the river, descend upon its surface, and there quickly end their day, after committing their eggs to the deep; which being for a little while tossed about, enveloped in a viscid[2] scum, are hatched, and the little larvae descend into their secure and dark habitation, in the oozy bed beneath, where they remain, gradually increasing in size, until the returning spring; they then change to a nymph, when the genial[3] heat brings them, as it were, into existence, and they again arise into the world. This fly seems to be delicious food for birds, frogs and fish. In the morning, when they arise, and in the evening, when they return, the tumult is great indeed, and the surface of the water along shore broken into bub- bles, or spirted into the air, by the contending aquatic tribes, and such is the avid- ity of the fish and frogs, that they spring into the air, after this delicious prey.

Early in the evening, after a pleasant day's voyage, I made a convenient and safe harbor, in a little lagoon, under an elevated bank, on the west shore of the river, where I shall entreat the reader's patience, whilst we behold the closing scene of the short-lived Ephemera, and communicate to each other the reflections which so singular an exhibition might rationally suggest to an inquisitive mind. Our place of observation is happily situated, under the protecting shade of majes-

---

[1]Fort Picolata, on the east side of the St. John's River in northeast Florida.
[2]Thick, sticky.
[3]Life-giving.

tic Live Oaks, glorious Magnolias and the fragrant Orange, open to the view of the great river, and still waters of the lagoon just before us.

At the cool eve's approach, the sweet enchanting melody of the feathered songsters gradually ceases, and they betake themselves to their leafy coverts for security and repose.

Solemnly and slowly move onward, to the river's shore, the rustling clouds of the Ephemera. How awful the procession! innumerable millions of winged beings, voluntarily verging on to destruction, to the brink of the grave, where they behold bands of their enemies with wide open jaws, ready to receive them. But as if insensible of their danger, gay and tranquil each meets his beloved mate, in the still air, inimitably bedecked in their new nuptial robes. What eye can trace them, in their varied wanton amorous chases, bounding and fluttering on the odoriferous air? with what peace, love and joy, do they end the last moments of their existence?

I think we may assert, without any fear of exaggeration, that there are annually of these beautiful winged beings, which rise into existence, and for a few moments take a transient view of the glory of the Creator's works, a number greater than the whole race of mankind that have ever existed since the creation; and that only, from the shores of this river. How many then must have been produced since the creation, when we consider the number of large rivers in America, in comparison with which, this river is but a brook or rivulet.

The importance of the existence of these beautiful and delicately formed little creatures, in the creation, whose frame and organization is equally wonderful, more delicate, and perhaps as complicated as that of the most perfect human being, is well worth a few moments contemplation; I mean particularly when they appear in the fly state. And if we consider the very short period, of that stage of existence, which we may reasonably suppose, to be the only space of their life that admits of pleasure and enjoyment, what a lesson doth it not afford us of the vanity of our own pursuits.

Their whole existence in this world, is but one complete year, and at least three hundred and sixty days of that time, they are in the form of an ugly grub, buried in mud, eighteen inches under water, and in this condition scarcely locomotive, as each larva or grub, has but its own narrow solitary cell, from which it never travels, or moves, but in a perpendicular progression, of a few inches, up and down, from the bottom to the surface of the mud, in order to intercept the passing atoms for its food, and get a momentary respiration of fresh air; and even here it must be perpetually on its guard, in order to escape the troops of fish and shrimps, watching to catch it, and from whom it has no escape, but by instantly retreating back into its cell. One would be apt almost to imagine them created merely for the food of fish and other animals.

from PART II, CHAPTER V
[ATTACKED BY ALLIGATORS]

. . . The little lake, which is an expansion of the river,[1] now appeared in view; on the east side are extensive marshes, and on the other high forests and Orange groves, and then a bay, lined with vast Cypress swamps, both coasts gradually approaching each other, to the opening of the river again, which is in this place about three hundred yards wide; evening now drawing on, I was anxious to reach some high bank of the river, where I intended to lodge, and agreeably to my wishes, I soon after discovered on the west shore, a little promontory, at the turn-

---

[1]Lake Dexter, the St. John's (or St. Juan's) River, in northeast Florida.

ing of the river, contracting it here to about one hundred and fifty yards in width. This promontory is a peninsula, containing about three acres of high ground, and is one entire Orange grove, with a few Live Oaks, Magnolias and Palms. Upon doubling the point, I arrived at the landing, which is a circular harbor, at the foot of the bluff, the top of which is about twelve feet high; and back of it is a large Cypress swamp, that spreads each way, the right wing forming the west coast of the little lake, and the left stretching up the river many miles, and encompassing a vast space of low grassy marshes. From this promontory, looking eastward across the river, we behold a landscape of low country, unparalleled as I think; on the left is the east coast of the little lake, which I had just passed, and from the Orange bluff at the lower end, the high forests begin, and increase in breadth from the shore of the lake, making a circular sweep to the right, and contain many hundred thousand acres of meadow, and this grand sweep of high forests encircles, as I apprehend, at least twenty miles of these green fields, interspersed with hommocks or islets of evergreen trees, where the sovereign Magnolia and lordly Palm stand conspicuous. The islets are high shelly knolls, on the sides of creeks or branches of the river, which wind about and drain off the super-abundant waters that cover these meadows, during the winter season.

The evening was temperately cool and calm. The crocodiles began to roar and appear in uncommon numbers along the shores and in the river. I fixed my camp in an open plain, near the utmost projection of the promontory, under the shelter of a large Live Oak, which stood on the highest part of the ground and but a few yards from my boat. From this open, high situation, I had a free prospect of the river, which was a matter of no trivial consideration to me, having good reason to dread the subtle attacks of the alligators,[2] who were crowding about my harbor. Having collected a good quantity of wood for the purpose of keeping up a light and smoke during the night, I began to think of preparing my supper, when, upon examining my stores, I found but a scanty provision, I thereupon determined, as the most expeditious way of supplying my necessities, to take my bob[3] and try for some trout. About one hundred yards above my harbor, began a cove or bay of the river, out of which opened a large lagoon. The mouth or entrance from the river to it was narrow, but the waters soon after spread and formed a little lake, extending into the marshes, its entrance and shores within I observed to be verged with floating lawns of the Pistia and Nymphea and other aquatic plants; these I knew were excellent haunts for trout.

The verges and islets of the lagoon were elegantly embellished with flowering plants and shrubs; the laughing coots with wings half spread were tripping over the little coves and hiding themselves in the tufts of grass; young broods of the painted summer teal, skimming the still surface of the waters, and following the watchful parent unconscious of danger, were frequently surprised by the voracious trout, and he in turn, as often by the subtle, greedy alligator. Behold him rushing forth from the flags and reeds. His enormous body swells. His plaited tail brandished high, floats upon the lake. The waters like a cataract descend from his opening jaws. Clouds of smoke issue from his dilated nostrils. The earth trembles with his thunder. When immediately from the opposite coast of the lagoon, emerges from the deep his rival champion. They suddenly dart upon each other. The boiling surface of the lake marks their rapid course, and a terrific conflict commences. They now sink to the bottom folded together in horrid wreaths. The water becomes thick and discolored. Again they rise, their jaws clap together, re-

---

[2]"I have made use of the terms alligator and crocodile indiscriminately for this animal, alligator being the country name" (Bartram's earlier note).

[3]Bartram earlier described a bob as "three large hooks . . . covered with the white hair of a deer's tail, shreds of a red garter, and some parti-colored feathers, all which form a tuft or tassel, nearly as large as one's fist, and entirely cover and conceal the hooks."

echoing through the deep surrounding forests. Again they sink, when the contest ends at the muddy bottom of the lake, and the vanquished makes a hazardous escape, hiding himself in the muddy turbulent waters and sedge on a distant shore. The proud victor exulting returns to the place of action. The shores and forests resound his dreadful roar, together with the triumphing shouts of the plaited tribes around, witnesses of the horrid combat.

My apprehensions were highly alarmed after being a spectator of so dreadful a battle; it was obvious that every delay would but tend to increase my dangers and difficulties, as the sun was near setting, and the alligators gathered around my harbor from all quarters; from these considerations I concluded to be expeditious in my trip to the lagoon, in order to take some fish. Not thinking it prudent to take my fusee[4] with me, lest I might lose it overboard in case of a battle, which I had every reason to dread before my return, I therefore furnished myself with a club for my defense, went on board, and penetrating the first line of those which surrounded my harbor, they gave way; but being pursued by several very large ones, I kept strictly on the watch, and paddled with all my might towards the entrance of the lagoon, hoping to be sheltered there from the multitude of my assailants; but ere I had half-way reached the place, I was attacked on all sides, several endeavoring to overset the canoe. My situation now became precarious to the last degree: two very large ones attacked me closely, at the same instant, rushing up with their heads and part of their bodies above the water, roaring terribly and belching floods of water over me. They struck their jaws together so close to my ears, as almost to stun me, and I expected every moment to be dragged out of the boat and instantly devoured, but I applied my weapons so effectually about me, though at random, that I was so successful as to beat them off a little; when, finding that they designed to renew the battle, I made for the shore, as the only means left me for my preservation, for, by keeping close to it, I should have my enemies on one side of me only, whereas I was before surrounded by them, and there was a probability, if pushed to the last extremity, of saving myself, by jumping out of the canoe on shore, as it is easy to outwalk them on land, although comparatively as swift as lightning in the water. I found this last expedient alone could fully answer my expectations, for as soon as I gained the shore they drew off and kept aloof. This was a happy relief, as my confidence was, in some degree, recovered by it. On recollecting myself, I discovered that I had almost reached the entrance of the lagoon, and determined to venture in, if possible to take a few fish and then return to my harbor, while day-light continued; for I could now, with caution and resolution, make my way with safety along shore, and indeed there was no other way to regain my camp, without leaving my boat and making my retreat through the marshes and reeds, which, if I could even effect, would have been in a manner throwing myself away, for then there would have been no hopes of ever recovering my bark, and returning in safety to any settlements of men. I accordingly proceeded and made good my entrance into the lagoon, though not without opposition from the alligators, who formed a line across the entrance, but did not pursue me into it, nor was I molested by any there, though there were some very large ones in a cove at the upper end. I soon caught more trout than I had present occasion for, and the air was too hot and sultry to admit of their being kept for many hours, even though salted or barbecued. I now prepared for my return to camp, which I succeeded in with but little trouble, by keeping close to the shore, yet I was opposed upon re-entering the river out of the lagoon, and pursued near to my landing (though not closely attacked) particularly by an old daring one, about twelve feet in length, who kept close after me, and when I stepped on shore

----

[4]Musket.

and turned about, in order to draw up my canoe, he rushed up near my feet and lay there for some time, looking me in the face, his head and shoulders out of water; I resolved he should pay for his temerity, and having a heavy load in my fusee, I ran to my camp, and returning with my piece, found him with his foot on the gunwale of the boat, in search of fish, on my coming up he withdrew sullenly and slowly into the water, but soon returned and placed himself in his former position, looking at me and seeming neither fearful or any way disturbed. I soon dispatched him by lodging the contents of my gun in his head, and then proceeded to cleanse and prepare my fish for supper, and accordingly took them out of the boat, laid them down on the sand close to the water, and began to scale them, when, raising my head, I saw before me, through the clear water, the head and shoulders of a very large alligator, moving slowly towards me; I instantly stepped back, when, with a sweep of his tail, he brushed off several of my fish. It was certainly most providential that I looked up at that instant, as the monster would probably, in less than a minute, have seized and dragged me into the river. This incredible boldness of the animal disturbed me greatly, supposing there could now be no reasonable safety for me during the night, but by keeping continually on the watch; I therefore, as soon as I had prepared the fish, proceeded to secure myself and effects in the best manner I could: in the first place, I hauled my bark upon the shore, almost clear out of the water, to prevent their oversetting or sinking her, after this every moveable was taken out and carried to my camp, which was but a few yards off; then ranging some dry wood in such order as was the most convenient, cleared the ground round about it, that there might be no impediment in my way, in case of an attack in the night, either from the water or the land; for I discovered by this time, that this small isthmus, from its remote situation and fruitfulness, was resorted to by bears and wolves. Having prepared myself in the best manner I could, I charged my gun and proceeded to reconnoitre my camp and the adjacent grounds; when I discovered that the peninsula and grove, at the distance of about two hundred yards from my encampment, on the land side, were invested by a Cypress swamp, covered with water, which below was joined to the shore of the little lake, and above to the marshes surrounding the lagoon, so that I was confined to an islet exceedingly circumscribed, and I found there was no other retreat for me, in case of an attack, but by either ascending one of the large Oaks, or pushing off with my boat.

It was by this time dusk, and the alligators had nearly ceased their roar, when I was again alarmed by a tumultuous noise that seemed to be in my harbor, and therefore engaged my immediate attention. Returning to my camp I found it undisturbed, and then continued on to the extreme point of the promontory, where I saw a scene, new and surprising, which at first threw my senses into such a tumult, that it was some time before I could comprehend what was the matter; however, I soon accounted for the prodigious assemblage of crocodiles at this place, which exceeded every thing of the kind I had ever heard of.

How shall I express myself so as to convey an adequate idea of it to the reader, and at the same time avoid raising suspicions of my want of veracity? Should I say, that the river (in this place) from shore to shore, and perhaps near half a mile above and below me, appeared to be one solid bank of fish, of various kinds, pushing through this narrow pass of St. Juan's into the little lake, on their return down the river, and that the alligators were in such incredible numbers, and so close together from shore to shore, that it would have been easy to have walked across on their heads, had the animals been harmless? What expressions can sufficiently declare the shocking scene that for some minutes continued, whilst this mighty army of fish were forcing the pass? During this attempt, thousands, I may say hundreds of thousands of them were caught and swallowed by the devouring alligators. I have seen an alligator take up out of the water several great fish at a time, and just squeeze them betwixt his jaws, while the tails of the great trout flapped about his eyes and lips, ere he had swallowed them. The horrid noise of their closing jaws, their plunging amidst the broken banks of fish, and rising with their prey some feet upright above the water, the floods of water and blood rushing out of their mouths, and the clouds of vapor issuing from their wide nostrils, were truly frightful. This scene continued at intervals during the night, as the fish came to the pass. After this sight, shocking and tremendous as it was, I found myself somewhat easier and more reconciled to my situation, being convinced that their extraordinary assemblage here, was owing to this annual feast of fish, and that they were so well employed in their own element, that I had little occasion to fear their paying me a visit.

It being now almost night, I returned to my camp, where I had left my fish broiling, and my kettle of rice stewing, and having with me, oil, pepper and salt, and excellent oranges hanging in abundance over my head (a valuable substitute for vinegar) I sat down and regaled myself cheerfully; having finished my repast, I re-kindled my fire for light, and whilst I was revising the notes of my past day's journey, I was suddenly roused with a noise behind me toward the main land; I sprang up on my feet, and listening, I distinctly heard some creature wading in the water of the isthmus; I seized my gun and went cautiously from my camp, directing my steps towards the noise; when I had advanced about thirty yards, I halted behind a coppice of Orange trees, and soon perceived two very large bears, which had made their way through the water, and had landed in the grove, about one hundred yards distance from me, and were advancing towards me. I waited until they were within thirty yards of me, they there began to snuff and look towards my camp, I snapped my piece, but it flashed, on which they both turned about and galloped off, plunging through the water and swamp, never halting as I suppose, until they reached fast land, as I could hear them leaping and plunging a long time; they did not presume to return again, nor was I molested by any other creature, except being occasionally awakened by the whooping of owls, screaming of bitterns, or the wood-rats running amongst the leaves. . . .

The noise of the crocodiles kept me awake the greater part of the night, but when I arose in the morning, contrary to my expectations, there was perfect peace; very few of them to be seen, and those were asleep on the shore, yet I was not able to suppress my fears and apprehensions of being attacked by them in future; and indeed yesterday's combat with them, notwithstanding I came off in a manner victorious, or at least made a safe retreat, had left sufficient impression on my mind to damp my courage, and it seemed too much for one of my strength, being alone in a very small boat to encounter such collected danger. To pursue my voyage up the river, and be obliged every evening to pass such dangerous defiles, appeared to me as perilous as running the gauntlet betwixt two rows of Indians armed with knives and fire brands; I however resolved to continue my voyage one day longer, if I possibly could with safety, and then return down the river, should I find the like difficulties to oppose. Accordingly I got every thing on board, charged my gun, and set sail cautiously along shore; as I passed by Battle lagoon,[5] I began to tremble and keep a good look out, when suddenly a huge alligator rushed out of the reeds, and with a tremendous roar, came up, and darted as swift as an arrow under my boat, emerging upright on my lee quarter, with open jaws, and belching water and smoke that fell upon me like rain in a hurricane; I laid soundly about his head with my club and beat him off, and after plunging and darting about my boat, he went off on a straight line through the water, seemingly with the rapidity of lightning, and entered the cape of the la-

[5]Mud Lake, above Lake Dexter, where he had fished the previous evening.

goon; I now employed my time to the very best advantage in paddling close along shore, but could not forbear looking now and then behind me, and presently perceived one of them coming up again; the water of the river hereabouts, was shoal and very clear, the monster came up with the usual roar and menaces, and passed close by the side of my boat, when I could distinctly see a young brood of alligators to the number of one hundred or more, following after her in a long train, they kept close together in a column without straggling off to the one side or the other, the young appeared to be of an equal size, about fifteen inches in length, almost black, with pale yellow transverse waved clouds or blotches, much like rattle snakes in colour. I now lost sight of my enemy again.

Still keeping close along shore; on turning a point or projection of the river bank, at once I beheld a great number of hillocks or small pyramids, resembling hay cocks, ranged like an encampment along the banks, they stood fifteen or twenty yards distant from the water, on a high marsh, about four feet perpendicular above the water; I knew them to be the nests of the crocodile, having had a description of them before, and now expected a furious and general attack, as I saw several large crocodiles swimming abreast of these buildings. These nests being so great a curiosity to me, I was determined at all events immediately to land and examine them. Accordingly I ran my bark on shore at one of their landing places, which was a sort of nick or little dock, from which ascended a sloping path or road up to the edge of the meadow, where their nests were, most of them were deserted, and the great thick whitish egg-shells lay broken and scattered upon the ground round about them.

The nests or hillocks are of the form of an obtuse cone, four feet high and four or five feet in diameter at their bases; they are constructed with mud, grass and herbage: at first they lay a floor of this kind of tempered mortar on the ground, upon which they deposit a layer of eggs, and upon this a stratum of mortar seven or eight inches in thickness, and then another layer of eggs, and in this manner one stratum upon another, nearly to the top: I believe they commonly lay from one to two hundred eggs in a nest: these are hatched I suppose by the heat of the sun, and perhaps the vegetable substances mixed with the earth, being acted upon by the sun, may cause a small degree of fermentation, and so increase the heat in those hillocks. The ground for several acres about these nests showed evident marks of a continual resort of alligators; the grass was every where beaten down, hardly a blade or straw was left standing; whereas, all about, at a distance, it was five or six feet high, and as thick as it could grow together. The female, as I imagine, carefully watches her own nest of eggs until they are all hatched, or perhaps while she is attending her own brood, she takes under her care and protection, as many as she can get at one time, either from her own particular nest or others: but certain it is, that the young are not left to shift for themselves, having had frequent opportunities of seeing the female alligator, leading about the shores her train of young ones, just like a hen does her brood of chickens, and she is equally assiduous and courageous in defending the young, which are under their care, and providing for their subsistence; and when she is basking upon the warm banks, with her brood around her, you may hear the young ones continually whining and barking, like young puppies. I believe but few of a brood live to the years of full growth and magnitude, as the old feed on the young as long as they can make prey of them.

The alligator when full grown is a very large and terrible creature, and of prodigious strength, activity and swiftness in the water. I have seen them twenty feet in length, and some are supposed to be twenty-two or twenty-three feet; their body is as large as that of a horse; their shape exactly resembles that of a lizard, except their tail, which is flat or cuneiform,[6] being compressed on each side, and

---

[6]Wedge-shaped.

gradually diminishing from the abdomen to the extremity, which, with the whole body is covered with horny plates or squamae, impenetrable when on the body of the live animal, even to a rifle ball, except about their head and just behind their fore-legs or arms, where it is said they are only vulnerable. The head of a full grown one is about three feet, and the mouth opens nearly the same length, the eyes are small in proportion and seem sunk deep in the head, by means of the prominency of the brows; the nostrils are large, inflated and prominent on the top, so that the head in the water, resembles, at a distance, a great chunk of wood floating about. Only the upper jaw moves, which they raise almost perpendicular, so as to form a right angle with the lower one. In the fore part of the upper jaw, on each side, just under the nostrils, are two very large, thick, strong teeth or tusks, not very sharp, but rather the shape of a cone, these are as white as the finest polished ivory, and are not covered by any skin or lips, and always in sight, which gives the creature a frightful appearance; in the lower jaw are holes opposite to these teeth, to receive them; when they clap their jaws together it causes a surprising noise, like that which is made by forcing a heavy plank with violence upon the ground, and may be heard at a great distance.

But what is yet more surprising to a stranger, is the incredible loud and terrifying roar, which they are capable of making, especially in the spring season, their breeding time; it most resembles very heavy distant thunder, not only shaking the air and waters, but causing the earth to tremble; and when hundreds and thousands are roaring at the same time, you can scarcely be persuaded, but that the whole globe is violently and dangerously agitated.

An old champion, who is perhaps absolute sovereign of a little lake or lagoon (when fifty less than himself are obliged to content themselves with swelling and roaring in little coves round about) darts forth from the reedy coverts all at once, on the surface of the waters, in a right line; at first seemingly as rapid as lightning, but gradually more slowly until he arrives at the center of the lake, when he stops; he now swells himself by drawing in wind and water through his mouth, which causes a loud sonorous rattling in the throat for near a minute, but it is immediately forced out again through his mouth and nostrils, with a loud noise, brandishing his tail in the air, and the vapor ascending from his nostrils like smoke. At other times, when swollen to an extent ready to burst, his head and tail lifted up, he spins or twirls round on the surface of the water. He acts his part like an Indian chief when rehearsing his feats of war, and then retiring, the exhibition is continued by others who dare to step forth, and strive to excel each other, to gain the attention of the favourite female.

Having gratified my curiosity at this general breeding place and nursery of crocodiles, I continued my voyage up the river without being greatly disturbed by them: in my way I observed islets or floating fields of the bright green Pistia, decorated with other amphibious plants, as Senecio Jacobea, Persicaria amphibia, Coreopsis bidens, Hydrocotile fluitans, and many others of less note. . . .

[Idyllic Scenes, Sudden Invasions]

At evening I arrived at Cedar Point,[1] my former safe and pleasant harbor, at the East cape of the Great Lake, where I had noticed some curious shrubs and plants; here I rested, and on the smooth and gentle current launch again into the little ocean of Lake George, meaning now, on my return, to coast his Western shores in search of new beauties in the bounteous kingdom of Flora.

I was however induced to deviate a little from my intended course, and touch at the enchanting little Isle of Palms. This delightful spot, planted by nature, is almost an entire grove of Palms, with a few pyramidal Magnolias, Live Oaks,

---

[1]Where the St. John's River enters Lake George in Florida.

golden Orange, and the animating Zanthoxilon; what a beautiful retreat is here! blessed unviolated spot of earth! rising from the limpid waters of the lake; its fragrant groves and blooming lawns invested and protected by encircling ranks of the Yucca gloriosa; a fascinating atmosphere surrounds this blissful garden; the balmy Lantana, ambrosial Citra, perfumed Crinum, perspiring their mingled odors, wafted through Zanthoxilon groves. I at last broke away from the enchanting spot, and stepped on board my boat, hoisted sail and soon approached the coast of the main, at the cool eve of day; then traversing a capacious semicircular cove of the lake, verged by low, extensive grassy meadows, I at length by dusk made a safe harbor, in a little lagoon, on the sea shore or strand of a bold sandy point, which descended from the surf of the lake; this was a clean sandy beach, hard and firm by the beating surf, when the wind sets from the East coast; I drew up my light vessel on the sloping shore, that she might be safe from the beating waves in case of a sudden storm of wind in the night. A few yards back the land was a little elevated, and overgrown with thickets of shrubs and low trees, consisting chiefly of Zanthoxilon, Olea Americana, Rhamus frangula, Sideroxilon, Morus, Ptelea, Halesia, Querci, Myrica cerifera and others; these groves were but low, yet sufficiently high to shelter me from the chilling dews; and being but a few yards distance from my vessel, here I fixed my encampment. A brisk wind arising from the lake, drove away the clouds of mosquitoes into the thickets. I now, with difficulty and industry, collected a sufficiency of dry wood to keep up a light during the night, and to roast some trout which I had caught when descending the river; their heads I stewed in the juice of oranges, which, with boiled rice, afforded me a wholesome and delicious supper: I hung the remainder of my broiled fish on the snags of some shrubs over my head. I at last, after reconnoitering my habitation, returned, spread abroad my skins and blanket upon the clean sands by my fire side, and betook myself to repose.

How glorious the powerful sun, minister of the Most High, in the rule and government of this earth, leaves our hemisphere, retiring from our sight beyond the western forests! I behold with gratitude his departing smiles, tinging the fleecy roseate clouds, now riding far away on the eastern horizon; behold they vanish from sight in the azure skies!

All now silent and peaceable, I suddenly fell asleep. At midnight I awake; when raising my head erect, I find myself alone in the wilderness of Florida, on the shores of Lake George. Alone indeed, but under the care of the Almighty, and protected by the invisible hand of my guardian angel.

When quite awake, I started at the heavy tread of some animal, the dry limbs of trees upon the ground crack under his feet, the close shrubby thickets part and bend under him as he rushes off.

I rekindled up my sleepy fire, lay in contact the exfoliated[2] smoking brands damp with the dew of heaven.

The bright flame ascends and illuminates the ground and groves around me.

When looking up, I found my fish carried off, though I had thought them safe on the shrubs, just over my head, but their scent, carried to a great distance by the damp nocturnal breezes, I suppose were too powerful attractions to resist.

Perhaps it may not be time lost, to rest awhile here, and reflect on the unexpected and unaccountable incident, which however pointed out to me an extraordinary deliverance, or protection of my life, from the rapacious wolf that stole my fish from over my head.

How much easier and more eligible might it have been for him to have leaped upon my breast in the dead of sleep, and torn my throat, which would have in-

---

[2]Separated.

stantly deprived me of life, and then glutted his stomach for the present with my warm blood, and dragged off my body, which would have made a feast afterwards for him and his howling associates; I say would not this have been a wiser step, than to have made protracted and circular approaches, and then after, by chance, espying the fish over my head, with the greatest caution and silence rear up, and take them off the snags one by one, then make off with them, and that so cunningly as not to awaken me until he had fairly accomplished his purpose.

The morning being clear, I set sail with a favorable breeze, coasting along the shores; when on a sudden the waters became transparent, and discovered the sandy bottom, and the several nations of fish, passing and repassing each other. Following this course I was led to the cape of the little river, descending from Six mile Springs,[3] and meandering six miles from its source, through green meadows. I entered this pellucid stream, sailing over the heads of innumerable squadrons of fish, which, although many feet deep in the water, were distinctly to be seen; I passed by charming islets of flourishing trees, as Palm, Red Bay, Ash, Maple, Nussa and others. As I approached the distant high forest on the main, the river widens, floating fields of the green Pistia surrounded me, the rapid stream winding through them. What an alluring scene was now before me! A vast basin or little lake of crystal waters, half encircled by swelling hills, clad with Orange and odoriferous Illisium groves. The towering Magnolia itself a grove, and the exalted Palm, as if conscious of their transcendent glories, tossed about their lofty heads, painting, with mutable shades, the green floating fields beneath. The social prattling coot enrobed in blue, and the squeeling water-hen, with wings half expanded, tripped after each other, over the watery mirror. . . .

["PARADISE OF FISH"]

I now directed my steps towards my encampment, in a different direction. I seated myself upon a swelling green knoll, at the head of the crystal basin. Near me, on the left, was a point or projection of an entire grove of the aromatic Illisium Floridanum; on my right and all around behind me, was a fruitful Orange grove, with Palms and Magnolias interspersed; in front, just under my feet was the enchanting and amazing crystal fountain,[1] which incessantly threw up, from dark, rocky caverns below, tons of water every minute, forming a basin, capacious enough for large shallops[2] to ride in, and a creek of four or five feet depth of water, and near twenty yards over, which meanders six miles through green meadows, pouring its limpid waters into the great Lake George, where they seem to remain pure and unmixed. About twenty yards from the upper edge of the basin, and directly opposite to the mouth or outlet to the creek, is a continual and amazing ebullition, where the waters are thrown up in such abundance and amazing force, as to jet and swell up two or three feet above the common surface: white sand and small particles of shells are thrown up with the waters, near to the top, when they diverge from the center, subside with the expanding flood, and gently sink again, forming a large rim or funnel round about the aperture or mouth of the fountain, which is a vast perforation through a bed of rocks, the ragged points of which are projected out on every side. Thus far I know to be matter of real fact, and I have related it as near as I could conceive or express myself. But there are yet remaining scenes inexpressibly admirable and pleasing.

Behold, for instance, a vast circular expanse before you, the waters of which are so extremely clear as to be absolutely diaphanous or transparent as the ether; the margin of the basin ornamented with a great variety of fruitful and floriferous

---

[3]Salt Springs, Florida.
[1]Salt Springs, Florida.
[2]Boats fitted with oars or sails for use in shallow waters.

trees, shrubs and plants, the pendant golden Orange dancing on the surface of the pellucid waters, the balmy air vibrates the melody of the merry birds, tenants of the encircling aromatic grove.

At the same instant innumerable bands of fish are seen, some clothed in the most brilliant colors; the voracious crocodile stretched along at full length, as the great trunk of a tree in size, the devouring garfish, inimical trout, and all the varieties of gilded painted bream, the barbed catfish, dreaded sting-ray, skate and flounder, spotted bass, sheeps head and ominous drum; all in their separate bands and communities, with free and unsuspicious intercourse performing their evolutions: there are no signs of enmity, no attempt to devour each other; the different bands seem peaceably and complaisantly to move a little aside, as it were to make room for others to pass by.

But behold yet something far more admirable, see whole armies descending into an abyss, into the mouth of the bubbling fountain, they disappear! are they gone forever? is it real? I raise my eyes with terror and astonishment,- - -I look down again to the fountain with anxiety, when behold them as it were emerging from the blue ether of another world, apparently at a vast distance, at their first appearance, no bigger than flies or minnows, now gradually enlarging, their brilliant colors begin to paint the fluid.

Now they come forward rapidly, and instantly emerge, with the elastic expanding column of crystalline waters, into the circular basin or funnel, see now how gently they rise, some upright, others obliquely, or seem to lay as it were on their sides, suffering themselves to be gently lifted or born up, by the expanding fluid towards the surface, sailing or floating like butterflies in the cerulean ether: then again they as gently descend, diverge and move off; when they rally, form again and rejoin their kindred tribes.

This amazing and delightful scene, though real, appears at first but as a piece of excellent painting; there seems no medium, you imagine the picture to be within a few inches of your eyes, and that you may without the least difficulty touch any one of the fish, or put your finger upon the crocodile's eye, when it really is twenty or thirty feet under water.

And although this paradise of fish, may seem to exhibit a just representation of the peaceable and happy state of nature which existed before the fall, yet in reality it is a mere representation; for the nature of the fish is the same as if they were in Lake George or the river; but here the water or element in which they live and move, is so perfectly clear and transparent, it places them all on an equality with regard to their ability to injure or escape from one another; (as all river fish of prey, or such as feed upon each other, as well as the unwieldy crocodile, take their prey by surprise; secreting themselves under covert or in ambush, until an opportunity offers, when they rush suddenly upon them:) but here is no covert, no ambush, here the trout freely passes by the very nose of the alligator and laughs in his face, and the bream by the trout.

But what is really surprising, that the consciousness of each others safety or some other latent cause, should so absolutely alter their conduct, for here is not the least attempt made to injure or disturb one another.

The sun passing below the horizon, and night approaching, I arose from my seat, and proceeding on arrived at my camp, kindled my fire, supped and reposed peaceably. And rising early, employed the fore part of the day in collecting specimens of growing roots and seeds. In the afternoon, left these Elysian[3] springs and the aromatic groves, and briskly descend the pellucid little river, re-entering the great lake. . . .

---

[3]Blissful; in Greek mythology, Elysium was the home of the blessed dead.

from PART III, CHAPTER III
[STRAWBERRY FIELDS]

. . . Soon after entering on these charming, sequestered, prolific fields, we came to a fine little river,[1] which crossing, and riding over fruitful strawberry beds and green lawns, on the sides of a circular ridge of hills in front of us, and going round the bases of this promontory, came to a fine meadow on an arm of the vale, through which meandered a brook, its humid vapors bedewing the fragrant strawberries which hung in heavy red clusters over the grassy verge; we crossed the rivulet, then rising a sloping, green, turfy ascent, alighted on the borders of a grand forest of stately trees, which we penetrated on foot a little distance to a horse-stamp, where was a large squadron of those useful creatures, belonging to my friend and companion, the trader, on the sight of whom they assembled together from all quarters; some at a distance saluted him with shrill neighings of gratitude, or came prancing up to lick the salt out of his hand; whilst the younger and more timorous came galloping onward, but coyly wheeled off, and fetching a circuit stood aloof, but as soon as their lord and master strewed the crystalline salty bait on the hard beaten ground, they all, old and young, docile and timorous, soon formed themselves in ranks and fell to licking up the delicious morsel.

It was a fine sight; more beautiful creatures I never saw; there were of them of all colors, sizes and dispositions. Every year as they become of age he sends off a troop of them down to Charleston, where they are sold to the highest bidder.

Having paid our attention to this useful part of the creation, who, if they are under our dominion, have consequently a right to our protection and favor, we returned to our trusty servants that were regaling themselves in the exuberant sweet pastures and strawberry fields in sight, and mounted again; proceeding on our return to town,[2] continued through part of this high forest skirting on the meadows; began to ascend the hills of a ridge which we were under the necessity of crossing, and having gained its summit, enjoyed a most enchanting view, a vast expanse of green meadows and strawberry fields; a meandering river gliding through, saluting in its various turnings the swelling, green, turfy knolls, embellished with parterres[3] of flowers and fruitful strawberry beds; flocks of turkeys strolling about them; herds of deer prancing in the meads or bounding over the hills; companies of young, innocent Cherokee virgins, some busily gathering the rich fragrant fruit, others having already filled their baskets, lay reclined under the shade of floriferous and fragrant native bowers of Magnolia, Azalea, Philadelphus, perfumed Calycanthus, sweet Yellow Jessamine and cerulian Glycine frutescens, disclosing their beauties to the fluttering breeze, and bathing their limbs in the cool fleeting streams; whilst other parties, more gay and libertine, were yet collecting strawberries or wantonly chasing their companions, tantalising them, staining their lips and cheeks with the rich fruit.

This sylvan scene of primitive innocence was enchanting, and perhaps too enticing for hearty young men long to continue idle spectators.

In fine, nature prevailing over reason, we wished at least to have a more active part in their delicious sports. Thus precipitately resolving, we cautiously made our approaches, yet undiscovered, almost to the joyous scene of action. Now, although we meant no other than an innocent frolic with this gay assembly of hamadryades,[4] we shall leave it to the person of feeling and sensibility to form an idea to what lengths our passions might have hurried us, thus warmed and excited, had it not been for the vigilance and care of some envious matrons who lay in ambush, and

---

[1]Burningtown Creek in southwestern North Carolina.
[2]Cowe, a Cherokee town on the Little Tennessee River in North Carolina.

[3]Patterned gardens.
[4]Wood nymphs, in classical mythology.

espying us gave the alarm, time enough for the nymphs to rally and assemble together; we however pursued and gained ground on a group of them, who had incautiously strolled to a greater distance from their guardians, and finding their retreat now like to be cut off, took shelter under cover of a little grove, but on perceiving themselves to be discovered by us, kept their station, peeping through the bushes; when observing our approaches, they confidently discovered[5] themselves and decently advanced to meet us, half unveiling their blooming faces, incarnated with the modest maiden blush, and with native innocence and cheerfulness, presented their little baskets, merrily telling us their fruit was ripe and sound.

We accepted a basket, sat down and regaled ourselves on the delicious fruit, encircled by the whole assembly of the innocently jocose sylvan nymphs; by this time the several parties under the conduct of the elder matrons, had disposed themselves in companies on the green, turfy banks.

My young companion, the trader, by concessions and suitable apologies for the bold intrusion, having compromised[6] the matter with them, engaged them to bring their collections to his house at a stipulated price, we parted friendly.

And now taking leave of these Elysian fields, we again mounted the hills, which we crossed, and traversing obliquely their flowery beds, arrived in town in the cool of the evening.

from PART IV, CHAPTER II
["LET MY SPIRIT GO"]

These Indians are by no means idolaters, unless their puffing the tobacco smoke towards the sun, and rejoicing at the appearance of the new moon,[1] may be termed so. So far from idolatry are they, that they have no images amongst them, nor any religious rite or ceremony that I could perceive; but adore the Great Spirit, the giver and taker away of the breath of life, with the most profound and respectful homage. They believe in a future state, where the spirit exists, which they call the world of spirits, where they enjoy different degrees of tranquility or comforts, agreeable to their life spent here: a person who in this life has been an industrious hunter, provided well for his family, an intrepid and active warrior, just, upright, and done all the good he could, will, they say, in the world of spirits, live in a warm, pleasant country, where are expansive, green, flowery savannas[2] and high forests, watered with rivers of pure waters, replenished with deer, and every species of game; a serene, unclouded and peaceful sky; in short, where there is fulness of pleasure, uninterrupted.

They have many accounts of trances and visions of their people, who have been supposed to be dead, but afterwards reviving have related their visions, which tend to enforce the practice of virtue and the moral duties.

Before I went amongst the Indians I had often heard it reported that these people, when their parents, through extreme old age, become decrepit and helpless, in compassion for their miseries, send them to the other world, by a stroke of the tomahawk or bullet. Such a degree of depravity and species of impiety always appeared to me so incredibly inhuman and horrid, it was with the utmost difficulty that I assumed resolution sufficient to enquire into it.

The traders assured me they knew no instance of such barbarism, but that there had been instances of the communities performing such a deed at the earnest request of the victim.

---

[5]Revealed.

[6]Settled.

[1]"I have observed the young fellows very merry and jocose, at the appearance of the new moon, saying, how ashamed she looks under the veil, since sleeping with the sun these two or three nights, she is ashamed to show her face" (Bartram's note).

[2]Treeless plains.

When I was at Mucclasse[3] town, early one morning, at the invitation of the chief trader, we repaired to the public square, taking with us some presents for the Indian chiefs. On our arrival we took our seats in a circle of venerable men, round a fire in the center of the area; other citizens were continually coming in, and amongst them I was struck with awe and veneration at the appearance of a very aged man; his hair, what little he had, was as white as snow; he was conducted by three young men, one having hold of each arm, and the third behind to steady him. On his approach the whole circle saluted him, "welcome," and made way for him: he looked as smiling and cheerful as youth, yet stone-blind by extreme old age; he was the most ancient chief of the town, and they all seemed to reverence him. Soon after the old man had seated himself I distributed my presents, giving him a very fine handkerchief and a twist of choice tobacco; which passed through the hands of an elderly chief who sat next to him, telling him it was a present from one of their white brothers, lately arrived in the nation from Charleston: he received the present with a smile, and thanked me, returning the favor immediately with his own stone pipe and catskin of tobacco, and then complimented me with a long oration, the purport of which was the value he set on the friendship of the Carolinians. He said, that when he was a young man they had no iron hatchets, pots, hoes, knives, razors nor guns, but that they then made use of their own stone axes, clay pots, flint knives, bows and arrows; and that he was the first man who brought the white people's goods into his town, which he did on his back from Charleston, five hundred miles on foot, for they had no horses then amongst them.

The trader then related to me an anecdote concerning this ancient patriarch, which occurred not long since.

One morning after his attendants had led him to the council fire, before seating himself he addressed himself to the people after this manner—

"You yet love me; what can I do now to merit your regard? nothing; I am good for nothing; I cannot see to shoot the buck or hunt up the sturdy bear; I know I am but a burden to you; I have lived long enough; now let my spirit go; I want to see the warriors of my youth in the country of spirits; (baring his breast) here is the hatchet, take it and strike." They answered with one united voice, "We will not; we cannot; we want you here."

1791

---

[3]Muklasa, a former Upper Creek Indian town on the Tallapoosa River in Elmore County, Alabama.

POLITICS AND PHILOSOPHY

———

THOMAS PAINE
ALEXANDER HAMILTON

JAMES MADISON
THOMAS JEFFERSON

Whereas the Puritans thought and wrote most about their relationship to God, their descendants in the Age of Reason thought most deeply and wrote most eloquently about their relationship with each other in a social compact. Thomas Paine, Alexander Hamilton, James Madison, and Thomas Jefferson all differed in many ways, but they shared a passion for liberty under a government that derived its authority from the people's will. Rarely before or since have political pamphlets and governmental documents achieved classic literary status in the way their works did.

THOMAS PAINE
(1737–1809)

After confronting Great Britain with armed resistance at Lexington and Concord in 1775, the American colonists found themselves in early 1776 reading an anonymous pamphlet "Written by an Englishman": "In the following pages I offer nothing more than simple facts, plain arguments, and common sense. . . . The sun never shown on a cause of greater worth. . . . By referring the matter from argument to arms, a new era for politics is struck. . . . A government of our own is a natural right. . . . Nothing can settle our affairs so expeditiously as an open and determined Declaration of Independence." The sentences struck home, removed all hesitancy, and within five months inspired the delegates of the Continental Congress to issue the Declaration of Independence on July 4.

This Englishman whose words strongly influenced the stirring events of national birth was Thomas Paine. He had arrived in America only a little over a year before writing *Common Sense*. He was a thirty-nine-year-old failure in almost everything he had ever attempted, including two marriages—an unlikely leader to rally people to a cause.

Thomas Paine was born in Thetford, England, to a poor Quaker father and an Anglican mother. After a stint at Thetford Grammar School, he was brought home to work with his father as a maker of corsets and stays (close-fitting, stiff undergarments worn chiefly by women). In his early life, Paine was (at one time or another) a sailor, a schoolteacher, an excise man (tax collector), a tobacconist, and grocer. As an excise man, Paine was appointed to appeal to Parliament for an increase in wages. Dismissed from his position as excise man, Paine found himself forced to declare bankruptcy for his tobacco shop, a business he acquired with his second wife (his first having died after a year of marriage).

His financial affairs in chaos and his second marriage ending in separation, Paine's thoughts turned to the New World. He found his way to Benjamin Franklin, then in London representing the colonies, and received letters of introduction describing him as "this ingenious worthy young man." Armed with these letters, Paine sailed for America, arriving in November 1774. He was soon working and writing for *The Pennsylvania Magazine*.

Though *Common Sense* was published anonymously in early 1776, Paine's fame began to spread. Paine was appointed aide-de-camp to General Nathanael Greene in late 1776, and was serving in the Continental Army when it was pushed out of New York City and forced to retreat into New Jersey to the Delaware River, pursued by the invading British troops. Winter forced both sides to slow down, and the confident British forces relaxed and established winter quarters at Trenton, New Jersey.

It was at this moment, when the Continental Army's morale was at its lowest ebb, that Thomas Paine wrote the first number of *The American Crisis*, published December 19, 1776, in the *Pennsylvania Journal*. General Washington ordered it read to each regiment: "These are the times that try men's souls. The summer soldier and the sunshine patriot will, in this crisis, shrink from the service of his country; but he that stands it now, deserves the love and thanks of man and woman." General Washington crossed the Delaware on Christmas night, surprising the British and their Hessian mercenaries, and turned around the fortunes of the war.

Paine's *Crisis* papers became the voice of conscience of the colonists' cause, the last one appearing in December 1783, when American victory was assured. Paine by this time had become a worldwide celebrity. His temperament and spirit drew him toward political battle, wherever it broke out. He was in France at the beginning of the French Revolution and was given the key to the Bastille by Lafayette to be delivered to Washington.

In England when Edmund Burke published his condemnation of events taking place in France (*Reflections on the French Revolution*, 1790), Paine sprang to the Revolution's defense with *The Rights of Man* (1791). But because he in effect appealed to the British to overthrow their monarchy, his book was considered an act of treason and Paine was outlawed.

In France, Paine was made a French citizen and was elected to a seat in the Convention. He lost popularity when he proposed imprisonment rather than execution of Louis XVI. And when the Reign of Terror took over, Paine was arrested as an Englishman and imprisoned for almost a year (1793–94). In prison he was able to continue work on a new book attacking organized religions, especially Christianity. He was released from prison through the intervention of James Monroe, then the American minister to France. *The Age of Reason,* Part I, was published in 1794; Part II in 1796. It was in essence a Deistic, not atheistic, work: "I believe in one God, and no more; and I hope for happiness beyond this life. . . . The word of God is the creation we behold." But it was fiercely individualistic ("My own mind is my own church"). And it was relentless in its attacks on traditional religious myths. He concluded: "I have now gone through the Bible, as a man would go through a wood with an axe on his shoulder and fell trees." Little in the forest survived.

When Paine returned to America in 1802, he found himself poor, his health declining, and his friends few. He was in effect an outcast. On his death in 1809, he was buried on his farm in New Rochelle, New York. Attending his funeral were six people—a French woman and her two sons, two blacks, and a Quaker.

Paine believed keenly in the power of the word to change the world. But the word, he thought, must be carefully chosen. He would prune "ideas of all superfluous words, and consider them in their natural bareness and simplicity." Paine believed in frankness and boldness in language. And though he believed wit could "often defeat a whole regiment of heavy artillery," if "left to itself, it soon overflows its banks, mixes with common filth, and brings disrepute on the fountain." Above all he believed in combining "warm passion with a cool temper, and the full expansion of the imagination with the natural and necessary gravity of judgment, so as to be rightly balanced with themselves."

Thomas Jefferson once wrote of the pamphleteer of the American Revolution: "No writer has exceeded Paine in ease and familiarity of style, in perspicuity of expression, happiness of elucidation, and in simple and unassuming language." And in 1801 Jefferson wrote to Paine, recalling his pamphleteering for the American Revolution: "It will be your glory to have labored, and with as much effect as any living man."

ADDITIONAL READING

Thomas Paine: Representative Selections, with Introduction, Bibliography, and Notes, ed. Harry Hayden Clark, 1944, 1961.

M. D. Conway, *The Life of Thomas Paine,* 2 vols., 1892; Hesketh Pearson, *Tom Paine, Friend of Mankind,* 1937; John Dos Passos, *The Living Thought of Thomas Paine,* 1940; Leo Gurko, *Tom Paine, Freedom's Apostle,* 1957; I. M. Thompson, *The Religious Beliefs of Thomas Paine,* 1957; A. Owen Aldridge, *Man of Reason: The Life of Thomas Paine,* 1959; David F. Hawke, *Tom Paine,* 1974; Eric Foner, *Tom Paine and Revolutionary America,* 1976; A. Owen Aldridge, *Thomas Paine's American Ideology,* 1984; David Powell, *Tom Paine: The Greatest Exile,* 1985.

TEXT

The Writings of Thomas Paine, 4 vols., ed. Moncure Daniel Conway, 1894–96. Some changes in spelling and punctuation have been made to conform with modern English.

from Common Sense[1]

I. ON THE ORIGIN AND DESIGN OF GOVERNMENT IN GENERAL, WITH CONCISE REMARKS ON THE ENGLISH CONSTITUTION

SOME writers have so confounded society with government, as to leave little or no distinction between them; whereas they are not only different, but have different origins. Society is produced by our wants, and government by our wickedness; the former promotes our happiness *positively* by uniting our affections, the latter *negatively* by restraining our vices. The one encourages intercourse, the other creates distinctions. The first is a patron, the last a punisher.

Society in every state is a blessing, but government, even in its best state, is but a necessary evil; in its worst state an intolerable one: for when we suffer, or are exposed to the same miseries *by a government,* which we might expect in a country *without government,* our calamity is heightened by reflecting that we furnish the means by which we suffer. Government, like dress, is the badge of lost innocence; the palaces of kings are built upon the ruins of the bowers of paradise. For were the impulses of conscience clear, uniform and irresistibly obeyed, man would need no other law-giver; but that not being the case, he finds it necessary to surrender up a part of his property to furnish means for the protection of the rest; and this he is induced to do by the same prudence which in every other case advises him, out of two evils to choose the least. Wherefore, security being the true design and end of government, it unanswerably follows that whatever form thereof appears most likely to insure it to us, with the least expense and greatest benefit, is preferable to all others.

In order to gain a clear and just idea of the design and end of government, let us suppose a small number of persons settled in some sequestered part of the earth, unconnected with the rest; they will then represent the first peopling of any country, or of the world. In this state of natural liberty,[2] society will be their first thought. A thousand motives will excite them thereto; the strength of one man is so unequal to his wants, and his mind so unfitted for perpetual solitude, that he is soon obliged to seek assistance and relief of another, who in his turn requires the

---

[1]Published anonymously as a pamphlet in January, 1776, *Common Sense* was a runaway best-seller. Paine reported that it sold 120,000 copies in three months. In all, some 300,000 copies (perhaps more) were circulated. Parts I and III are presented or excerpted here. Part II is entitled "Of

Monarchy and Hereditary Succession;" Part IV: "Of the Present Ability of America; with some Miscellaneous Reflections."
[2]Cf., John Locke's idea in *Of Civil Government* (1690) that all men in a state of nature are free and equal.

same. Four or five united would be able to raise a tolerable dwelling in the midst of a wilderness, but one man might labour out the common period of life without accomplishing any thing; when he had felled his timber he could not remove it, nor erect it after it was removed; hunger in the mean time would urge him to quit his work, and every different want would call him a different way. Disease, nay even misfortune, would be death; for though neither might be mortal, yet either would disable him from living, and reduce him to a state in which he might rather be said to perish than to die.

Thus necessity, like a gravitating power, would soon form our newly arrived emigrants into society, the reciprocal blessings of which would supercede, and render the obligations of law and government unnecessary while they remained perfectly just to each other; but as nothing but Heaven is impregnable to vice, it will unavoidably happen that in proportion as they surmount the first difficulties of emigration, which bound them together in a common cause, they will begin to relax in their duty and attachment to each other: and this remissness will point out the necessity of establishing some form of government to supply the defect of moral virtue.

Some convenient tree will afford them a state house, under the branches of which the whole colony may assemble to deliberate on public matters. It is more than probable that their first laws will have the title only of regulations and be enforced by no other penalty than public disesteem. In this first parliament every man by natural right will have a seat.

But as the colony increases, the public concerns will increase likewise, and the distance at which the members may be separated, will render it too inconvenient for all of them to meet on every occasion as at first, when their number was small, their habitations near, and the public concerns few and trifling. This will point out the convenience of their consenting to leave the legislative part to be managed by a select number chosen from the whole body, who are supposed to have the same concerns at stake which those have who appointed them, and who will act in the same manner as the whole body would act were they present. If the colony continue increasing, it will become necessary to augment the number of representatives, and that the interest of every part of the colony may be attended to, it will be found best to divide the whole into convenient parts, each part sending its proper number: and that the *elected* might never form to themselves an interest separate from the *electors*, prudence will point out the propriety of having elections often: because as the *elected* might by that means return and mix again with the general body of the *electors* in a few months, their fidelity to the public will be secured by the prudent reflection of not making a rod for themselves. And as this frequent interchange will establish a common interest with every part of the community, they will mutually and naturally support each other, and on this, (not on the unmeaning name of king,) depends the *strength of government, and the happiness of the governed.*

Here then is the origin and rise of government; namely, a mode rendered necessary by the inability of moral virtue to govern the world; here too is the design and end of government, viz. freedom and security. And however our eyes may be dazzled with show, or our ears deceived by sound; however prejudice may warp our wills, or interest darken our understanding, the simple voice of nature and reason will say, 'tis right.

I draw my idea of the form of government from a principle in nature which no art can overturn, viz. that the more simple any thing is, the less liable it is to be disordered, and the easier repaired when disordered; and with this maxim in view I offer a few remarks on the so much boasted constitution of England. That it was noble for the dark and slavish times in which it was erected, is granted. When the world was overrun with tyranny the least remove therefrom was a glorious rescue.

But that it is imperfect, subject to convulsions, and incapable of producing what it seems to promise, is easily demonstrated.

Absolute governments, (though the disgrace of human nature) have this advantage with them, they are simple; if the people suffer, they know the head from which their suffering springs; know likewise the remedy; and are not bewildered by a variety of causes and cures. But the constitution of England is so exceedingly complex, that the nation may suffer for years together without being able to discover in which part the fault lies; some will say in one and some in another, and every political physician will advise a different medicine.

I know it is difficult to get over local or long standing prejudices, yet if we will suffer ourselves to examine the component parts of the English constitution, we shall find them to be the base remains of two ancient tyrannies, compounded with some new republican materials.

First.—The remains of monarchical tyranny in the person of the king.

Secondly.—The remains of aristocratical tyranny in the persons of the Peers.

Thirdly.—The new republican materials, in the persons of the Commons, on whose virtue depends the freedom of England.

The two first, by being hereditary, are independant of the People; wherefore in a *constitutional sense* they contribute nothing towards the freedom of the state.

To say that the constitution of England is an *union* of three powers, reciprocally *checking* each other, is farcical;[3] either the words have no meaning, or they are flat contradictions.

To say that the Commons is a check upon the king, presupposes two things.

First.—That the king is not to be trusted without being looked after; or in other words, that a thirst for absolute power is the natural disease of monarchy.

Secondly.—That the Commons, by being appointed for that purpose, are either wiser or more worthy of confidence than the crown.

But as the same constitution which gives the Commons a power to check the king by withholding the supplies, gives afterwards the king a power to check the Commons, by empowering him to reject their other bills; it again supposes that the king is wiser than those whom it has already supposed to be wiser than him. A mere absurdity!

There is something exceedingly ridiculous in the composition of monarchy; it first excludes a man from the means of information, yet empowers him to act in cases where the highest judgment is required. The state of a king shuts him from the world, yet the business of a king requires him to know it thoroughly; wherefore the different parts, by unnaturally opposing and destroying each other, prove the whole character to be absurd and useless.

Some writers have explained the English constitution thus: the king, say they, is one, the people another; the Peers are a house in behalf of the king, the Commons in behalf of the people; but this hath all the distinctions of a house divided against itself; and though the expressions be pleasantly arranged, yet when examined they appear idle and ambiguous; and it will always happen, that the nicest construction that words are capable of, when applied to the description of something which either cannot exist, or is too incomprehensible to be within the compass of description, will be words of sound only, and though they may amuse the ear, they cannot inform the mind: for this explanation includes a previous question, viz. *how came the king by a power which the people are afraid to trust, and always obliged to check?* Such a power could not be the gift of a wise people, neither can any power, *which needs checking,* be from God; yet the provision which the constitution makes supposes such a power to exist.

---

[3]Charles de Montesquieu, in *The Spirit of Laws* (1748), held this same view of the British system.

But the provision is unequal to the task; the means either cannot or will not accomplish the end, and the whole affair is a *Felo de se:*[4] for as the greater weight will always carry up the less, and as all the wheels of a machine are put in motion by one, it only remains to know which power in the constitution has the most weight, for that will govern: and though the others, or a part of them, may clog, or, as the phrase is, check the rapidity of its motion, yet so long as they cannot stop it, their endeavours will be ineffectual: the first moving power will at last have its way, and what it wants in speed is supplied by time.

That the crown is this overbearing part in the English constitution needs not be mentioned, and that it derives its whole consequence merely from being the giver of places and pensions is self-evident; wherefore, though we have been wise enough to shut and lock a door against absolute monarchy, we at the same time have been foolish enough to put the crown in possession of the key.

The prejudice of Englishmen, in favour of their own government, by king, Lords and Commons, arises as much or more from national pride than reason. Individuals are undoubtedly safer in England than in some other countries: but the will of the king is as much the law of the land in Britain as in France, with this difference, that instead of proceeding directly from his mouth, it is handed to the people under the formidable shape of an act of parliament. For the fate of Charles the First hath only made kings more subtle—not more just.

Wherefore, laying aside all national pride and prejudice in favour of modes and forms, the plain truth is that *it is wholly owing to the constitution of the people, and not to the constitution of the government* that the crown is not as oppressive in England as in Turkey.

An inquiry into the *constitutional errors* in the English form of government, is at this time highly necessary; for as we are never in a proper condition of doing justice to others, while we continue under the influence of some leading partiality, so neither are we capable of doing it to ourselves while we remain fettered by any obstinate prejudice. And as a man who is attached to a prostitute is unfitted to choose or judge of a wife, so any prepossession in favour of a rotten constitution of government will disable us from discerning a good one.

from III. THOUGHTS ON THE PRESENT STATE OF AMERICAN AFFAIRS

In the following pages I offer nothing more than simple facts, plain arguments, and common sense: and have no other preliminaries to settle with the reader, than that he will divest himself of prejudice and prepossession, and suffer his reason and his feelings to determine for themselves: that he will put on, or rather that he will not put off, the true character of a man, and generously enlarge his views beyond the present day.

Volumes have been written on the subject of the struggle between England and America. Men of all ranks have embarked in the controversy, from different motives, and with various designs; but all have been ineffectual, and the period of debate is closed. Arms as the last resource decide the contest; the appeal was the choice of the King, and the continent has accepted the challenge.

It hath been reported of the late Mr. Pelham[1] (who though an able minister was not without his faults) that on his being attacked in the House of Commons on the score that his measures were only of a temporary kind, replied, "*they will last my time.*" Should a thought so fatal and unmanly possess the colonies in the present contest, the name of ancestors will be remembered by future generations with detestation.

---

[4]"Murderers of itself" (Latin).
[1]Henry Pelham (1694–1754), prime minister of Great Britain (1743–54).

The sun never shined on a cause of greater worth. 'Tis not the affair of a city, a county, a province, or a kingdom; but of a continent—of at least one eighth part of the habitable globe. 'Tis not the concern of a day, a year, or an age; posterity are virtually involved in the contest, and will be more or less affected even to the end of time, by the proceedings now. Now is the seed-time of continental union, faith and honour. The least fracture now will be like a name engraved with the point of a pin on the tender rind of a young oak; the wound would enlarge with the tree, and posterity read it in full grown characters.

By referring the matter from argument to arms, a new era for politics is struck—a new method of thinking hath arisen. All plans, proposals, &c. prior to the nineteenth of April, *i.e.* to the commencement of hostilities,[2] are like the almanacs of the last year; which though proper then, are superceded and useless now. Whatever was advanced by the advocates on either side of the question then, terminated in one and the same point, viz. a union with Great Britain; the only difference between the parties was the method of effecting it; the one proposing force, the other friendship; but it hath so far happened that the first hath failed, and the second hath withdrawn her influence.

As much hath been said of the advantages of reconciliation, which, like an agreeable dream, hath passed away and left us as we were, it is but right that we should examine the contrary side of the argument, and enquire into some of the many material injuries which these colonies sustain, and always will sustain, by being connected with and dependent on Great-Britain. To examine that connection and dependence, on the principles of nature and common sense, to see what we have to trust to, if separated, and what we are to expect, if dependent.

I have heard it asserted by some, that as America has flourished under her former connection with Great-Britain, the same connection is necessary towards her future happiness, and will always have the same effect. Nothing can be more fallacious than this kind of argument. We may as well assert that because a child has thrived upon milk, that it is never to have meat, or that the first twenty years of our lives is to become a precedent for the next twenty. But even this is admitting more than is true; for I answer roundly, that America would have flourished as much, and probably much more, had no European power taken any notice of her. The commerce by which she hath enriched herself are the necessaries of life, and will always have a market while eating is the custom of Europe.

But she has protected us, say some. That she hath engrossed[3] us is true, and defended the continent at our expense as well as her own, is admitted; and she would have defended Turkey from the same motive, *viz.* for the sake of trade and dominion.

Alas! we have been long led away by ancient prejudices and made large sacrifices to superstition. We have boasted the protection of Great Britain, without considering, that her motive was *interest* not *attachment;* and that she did not protect us from *our enemies* on *our account;* but from *her enemies* on *her own account,* from those who had no quarrel with us on any *other account,* and who will always be our enemies on the *same account.* Let Britain waive her pretensions to the continent, or the continent throw off the dependence, and we should be at peace with France and Spain, were they at war with Britain. The miseries of Hanover's last war[4] ought to warn us against connections.

It hath lately been asserted in parliament, that the colonies have no relation to each other but through the parent country, *i.e.* that Pennsylvania and the Jerseys,[5] and so on for the rest, are sister colonies by the way of England; this is certainly a

---

[2]On April 19, 1775, Minutemen of Lexington, Mass., engaged the attacking British in the first battle of the American Revolution.
[3]Dominated.
[4]The Seven Years' War (1756–63), involving Britain's King

George III (descended from the Prussian House of Hanover); known in America as the French and Indian War, in which American losses were heavy.
[5]East Jersey and West Jersey (later New Jersey).

very roundabout way of proving relationship, but it is the nearest and only true way of proving enmity (or enemyship, if I may so call it). France and Spain never were, nor perhaps ever will be, our enemies as *Americans*, but as our being the *subjects of Great Britain.*

But Britain is the parent country, say some. Then the more shame upon her conduct. Even brutes do not devour their young, nor savages make war upon their families; wherefore, the assertion, if true, turns to her reproach; but it happens not to be true, or only partly so, and the phrase *parent* or *mother country* hath been jesuitically[6] adopted by the king and his parasites, with a low papistical design of gaining an unfair bias on the credulous weakness of our minds. Europe, and not England, is the parent country of America. This new world hath been the asylum for the persecuted lovers of civil and religious liberty from *every part* of Europe. Hither have they fled, not from the tender embraces of the mother, but from the cruelty of the monster; and it is so far true of England, that the same tyranny which drove the first emigrants from home, pursues their descendants still.

In this extensive quarter of the globe, we forget the narrow limits of three hundred and sixty miles (the extent of England) and carry our friendship on a larger scale; we claim brotherhood with every European Christian, and triumph in the generosity of the sentiment.

It is pleasant to observe by what regular gradations we surmount the force of local prejudices, as we enlarge our acquaintance with the world. A man born in any town in England divided into parishes, will naturally associate most with his fellow parishioners (because their interests in many cases will be common) and distinguish him by the name of *neighbour;* if he meet him but a few miles from home, he drops the narrow idea of a street, and salutes him by the name of *townsman;* if he travel out of the county and meet him in any other, he forgets the minor divisions of street and town, and calls him *countryman, i.e. countyman:* but if in their foreign excursions they should associate in France, or any other part of *Europe,* their local remembrance would be enlarged into that of *Englishmen.* And by a just parity of reasoning, all Europeans meeting in America, or any other quarter of the globe, are *countrymen;* for England, Holland, Germany, or Sweden, when compared with the whole, stand in the same places on the larger scale, which the divisions of street, town, and county do on the smaller ones; distinctions too limited for continental minds. Not one third of the inhabitants, even of this province,[7] are of English descent. Wherefore, I reprobate the phrase of parent or mother country applied to England only, as being false, selfish, narrow and ungenerous.

But, admitting that we were all of English descent, what does it amount to? Nothing. Britain, being now an open enemy, extinguishes every other name and title: and to say that reconciliation is our duty, is truly farcical. The first king of England, of the present line (William the Conqueror) was a Frenchman, and half the peers of England are descendants from the same country; wherefore, by the same method of reasoning, England ought to be governed by France.

Much hath been said of the united strength of Britain and the colonies, that in conjunction they might bid defiance to the world: But this is mere presumption; the fate of war is uncertain, neither do the expressions mean any thing; for this continent would never suffer itself to be drained of inhabitants, to support the British arms in either Asia, Africa, or Europe.

Besides, what have we to do with setting the world at defiance? Our plan is commerce, and that, well attended to, will secure us the peace and friendship of all Europe; because it is the interest of all Europe to have America a free port.

---

[6]Deviously.
[7]Pennsylvania.

Her trade will always be a protection, and her barrenness of gold and silver secure her from invaders.

I challenge the warmest advocate for reconciliation to show a single advantage that this continent can reap by being connected with Great Britain. I repeat the challenge; not a single advantage is derived. Our corn will fetch its price in any market in Europe, and our imported goods must be paid for buy them where we will.

But the injuries and disadvantages which we sustain by that connection, are without number; and our duty to mankind at large, as well as to ourselves, instruct us to renounce the alliance: because, any submission to, or dependence on, Great Britain, tends directly to involve this continent in European wars and quarrels, and set us at variance with nations who would otherwise seek our friendship, and against whom we have neither anger nor complaint. As Europe is our market for trade, we ought to form no partial connection with any part of it. It is the true interest of America to steer clear of European contentions, which she never can do, while, by her dependence on Britain, she is made the make-weight in the scale of British politics.

Europe is too thickly planted with kingdoms to be long at peace, and whenever a war breaks out between England and any foreign power, the trade of America goes to ruin, *because of her connection with Britain.* The next war may not turn out like the last,[8] and should it not, the advocates for reconciliation now will be wishing for separation then, because neutrality in that case would be a safer convoy than a man of war. Everything that is right or reasonable pleads for separation. The blood of the slain, the weeping voice of nature cries, "'Tis time to part." Even the distance at which the Almighty hath placed England and America is a strong and natural proof that the authority of the one over the other, was never the design of heaven. The time likewise at which the continent was discovered, adds weight to the argument, and the manner in which it was peopled, increases the force of it. The Reformation was preceded by the discovery of America: as if the Almighty graciously meant to open a sanctuary to the persecuted in future years, when home should afford neither friendship nor safety.

The authority of Great Britain over this continent, is a form of government, which sooner or later must have an end: and a serious mind can draw no true pleasure by looking forward, under the painful and positive conviction that what he calls "the present constitution" is merely temporary. As parents, we can have no joy, knowing that this government is not sufficiently lasting to ensure anything which we may bequeath to posterity: And by a plain method of argument, as we are running the next generation into debt, we ought to do the work of it, otherwise we use them meanly and pitifully. In order to discover the line of our duty rightly, we should take our children in our hand, and fix our station a few years farther into life; that eminence will present a prospect which a few present fears and prejudices conceal from our sight.

•   •   •   •   •

If there is any true cause of fear respecting independence, it is because no plan is yet laid down. Men do not see their way out. Wherefore, as an opening into that business I offer the following hints; at the same time modestly affirming, that I have no other opinion of them myself, than that they may be the means of giving rise to something better. Could the straggling thoughts of individuals be collected,

---

[8]The Seven Years' War (in America, the French and Indian War) ended in 1763 with England being given all of France's New World possessions in the Treaty of Paris.

they would frequently form materials for wise and able men to improve into useful matter.

Let the assemblies be annual, with a president only. The representation more equal, their business wholly domestic, and subject to the authority of a continental congress.

Let each colony be divided into six, eight, or ten, convenient districts, each district to send a proper number of delegates to congress, so that each colony send at least thirty. The whole number in congress will be at least 390. Each congress to sit and to choose a president by the following method. When the delegates are met, let a colony be taken from the whole thirteen colonies by lot, after which let the congress choose (by ballot) a president from out of the delegates of that province. In the next congress, let a colony be taken by lot from twelve only, omitting that colony from which the president was taken in the former congress, and so proceeding on till the whole thirteen shall have had their proper rotation. And in order that nothing may pass into a law but what is satisfactorily just, not less than three fifths of the congress to be called a majority. He that will promote discord, under a government so equally formed as this, would have joined Lucifer in his revolt.[9]

But as there is a peculiar delicacy from whom, or in what manner, this business must first arise, and as it seems most agreeable and consistent that it should come from some intermediate body between the governed and the governors, that is, between the congress and the people, let a continental conference be held in the following manner, and for the following purpose,

A committee of twenty-six members of congress, *viz.* two for each colony. Two members from each house of assembly, or provincial convention; and five representatives of the people at large, to be chosen in the capital city or town of each province, for, and in behalf of the whole province, by as many qualified voters as shall think proper to attend from all parts of the province for that purpose; or, if more convenient, the representatives may be chosen in two or three of the most populous parts thereof. In this conference, thus assembled, will be united the two grand principles of business, *knowledge* and *power*. The members of congress, assemblies, or conventions, by having had experience in national concerns, will be able and useful counsellors, and the whole, being empowered by the people, will have a truly legal authority.

The conferring members being met, let their business be to frame a continental charter, or Charter of the United Colonies; (answering to what is called the Magna Charta of England) fixing the number and manner of choosing members of congress, members of assembly, with their date of sitting; and drawing the line of business and jurisdiction between them: always remembering, that our strength is continental, not provincial. Securing freedom and property to all men, and above all things, the free exercise of religion, according to the dictates of conscience; with such other matter as it is necessary for a charter to contain. Immediately after which, the said conference to dissolve, and the bodies which shall be chosen conformable to the said charter, to be the legislators and governors of this continent for the time being: Whose peace and happiness, may GOD preserve. AMEN.

Should any body of men be hereafter delegated for this or some similar purpose, I offer them the following extracts from that wise observer on governments, Dragonetti. "The science," says he, "of the politician consists in fixing the true point of happiness and freedom. Those men would deserve the gratitude of ages, who should discover a mode of government that contained the greatest sum of

---

[9]Satan's name before rebelling against God; Isaiah 14:12: "How art thou fallen from heaven, O Lucifer, son of the morning!"

individual happiness, with the least national expense."[10] (Dragonetti on "Virtues and Reward.")

But where, say some, is the king of America? I'll tell you, friend, he reigns above, and doth not make havoc of mankind like the royal brute of Great Britain. Yet that we may not appear to be defective even in earthly honours, let a day be solemnly set apart for proclaiming the charter; let it be brought forth placed on the divine law, the Word of God; let a crown be placed thereon, by which the world may know, that so far as we approve of monarchy, that in America the law is king. For as in absolute governments the king is law, so in free countries the law ought to be king; and there ought to be no other. But lest any ill use should afterwards arise, let the crown at the conclusion of the ceremony be demolished, and scattered among the people whose right it is.

A government of our own is our natural right: and when a man seriously reflects on the precariousness of human affairs, he will become convinced, that it is infinitely wiser and safer, to form a constitution of our own in a cool deliberate manner, while we have it in our power, than to trust such an interesting event to time and chance. If we omit it now, some Massanello[11] may hereafter arise, who, laying hold of popular disquietudes, may collect together the desperate and the discontented, and by assuming to themselves the powers of government, finally sweep away the liberties of the continent like a deluge. Should the government of America return again into the hands of Britain, the tottering situation of things will be a temptation for some desperate adventurer to try his fortune; and in such a case, what relief can Britain give? Ere she could hear the news, the fatal business might be done; and ourselves suffering like the wretched Britons under the oppression of the conqueror. Ye that oppose independence now, ye know not what ye do: ye are opening a door to eternal tyranny, by keeping vacant the seat of government. There are thousands and tens of thousands, who would think it glorious to expel from the continent, that barbarous and hellish power, which hath stirred up the Indians and the Negroes to destroy us; the cruelty hath a double guilt, it is dealing brutally by us, and treacherously by them.

To talk of friendship with those in whom our reason forbids us to have faith, and our affections wounded through a thousand pores instruct us to detest, is madness and folly. Every day wears out the little remains of kindred between us and them; and can there be any reason to hope, that as the relationship expires, the affection will increase, or that we shall agree better when we have ten times more and greater concerns to quarrel over than ever?

Ye that tell us of harmony and reconciliation, can ye restore to us the time that is past? Can ye give to prostitution its former innocence? neither can ye reconcile Britain and America. The last cord now is broken, the people of England are presenting addresses against us. There are injuries which nature cannot forgive; she would cease to be nature if she did. As well can the lover forgive the ravisher of his mistress, as the continent forgive the murders of Britain. The Almighty hath implanted in us these unextinguishable feelings for good and wise purposes. They are the guardians of His image in our hearts. They distinguish us from the herd of common animals. The social compact would dissolve, and justice be extirpated from the earth, or have only a casual existence were we callous to the touches of affection. The robber and the murderer would often escape unpunished, did not the injuries which our tempers sustain, provoke us into justice.

O! ye that love mankind! Ye that dare oppose not only the tyranny but the ty-

---

[10]Giacinto Dragonetti (1738–1818), author of *Virtues and Rewards* (1767).
[11]"Thomas Anello, otherwise Massanello, a fisherman of Naples, who after spiriting up his countrymen in the public market place, against the oppression of the Spaniards, to whom the place was then subject, prompted them to revolt, and in the space of a day became King" (Paine's note).

rant, stand forth! Every spot of the old world is overrun with oppression. Freedom hath been hunted round the globe. Asia and Africa have long expelled her. Europe regards her like a stranger, and England hath given her warning to depart. O! receive the fugitive, and prepare in time an asylum for mankind.

1776

from The American Crisis

NUMBER ONE[1]

THESE are the times that try men's souls. The summer soldier and the sunshine patriot will, in this crisis, shrink from the service of their country; but he that stands it *now*, deserves the love and thanks of man and woman. Tyranny, like hell, is not easily conquered; yet we have this consolation with us, that the harder the conflict, the more glorious the triumph. What we obtain too cheap, we esteem too lightly: it is dearness only that gives every thing its value. Heaven knows how to put a proper price upon its goods; and it would be strange indeed if so celestial an article as FREEDOM should not be highly rated. Britain, with an army to enforce her tyranny, has declared that she has a right (*not only to* TAX) but "to BIND *us in* ALL CASES WHATSOEVER," and if being *bound in that manner*, is not slavery, then is there not such a thing as slavery upon earth. Even the expression is impious; for so unlimited a power can belong only to God.

Whether the independence of the continent was declared too soon, or delayed too long, I will not now enter into as an argument; my own simple opinion is, that had it been eight months earlier, it would have been much better. We did not make a proper use of last winter, neither could we, while we were in a dependent state. However, the fault, if it were one, was all our own;[2] we have none to blame but ourselves. But no great deal is lost yet. All that Howe[3] has been doing for this month past, is rather a ravage than a conquest, which the spirit of the Jerseys,[4] a year ago, would have quickly repulsed, and which time and a little resolution will soon recover.

I have as little superstition in me as any man living, but my secret opinion has ever been, and still is, that God Almighty will not give up a people to military destruction, or leave them unsupportedly to perish, who have so earnestly and so repeatedly sought to avoid the calamities of war, by every decent method which wisdom could invent. Neither have I so much of the infidel in me, as to suppose that He has relinquished the government of the world, and given us up to the care of devils; and as I do not, I cannot see on what grounds the king of Britain can look up to heaven for help against us: a common murderer, a highwayman, or a house-breaker, has as good a pretence as he.

'Tis surprising to see how rapidly a panic will sometimes run through a country. All nations and ages have been subject to them: Britain has trembled like an ague[5] at the report of a French fleet of flat bottomed boats;[6] and in the fourteenth

---

[1]The first in a series of sixteen, *Crisis* I appeared in the *Pennsylvania Journal*, December 19, 1776, and then in three pamphlet editions, one undated, the other two on December 19 and December 23. It was signed, Common Sense. Read to the troops and circulated widely among the people, it played an important part in rallying the populace at a low point in the fortunes of war.
[2]"The present winter is worth an age, if rightly employed; but, if lost or neglected, the whole continent will partake of the evil; and there is no punishment that man does not deserve, be he who, or what, or where he will, that may be the

means of sacrificing a season so precious and useful" (Paine's note, a quotation from his *Common Sense*).
[3]Lord William Howe (1729–1814), Commander of the British Army in America (1775–78).
[4]East Jersey (near New York City) and West Jersey (near Philadelphia).
[5]A fever accompanied by chills (causing shaking).
[6]In 1759, during the Seven Years' War, the French assembled an invasion fleet at Havre and other ports, but British naval victories caused abandonment of the plan.

century the whole English army, after ravaging the kingdom of France, was
driven back like men petrified with fear; and this brave exploit was performed by
a few broken forces collected and headed by a woman, Joan of Arc.[7] Would that
heaven might inspire some Jersey maid to spirit up her countrymen, and save her
fair fellow sufferers from ravage and ravishment! Yet panics, in some cases, have
their uses; they produce as much good as hurt. Their duration is always short; the
mind soon grows through them, and acquires a firmer habit than before. But
their peculiar advantage is, that they are the touchstones of sincerity and hypocrisy, and bring things and men to light, which might otherwise have lain forever
undiscovered. In fact, they have the same effect on secret traitors, which an imaginary apparition would have upon a private murderer. They sift out the hidden
thoughts of man, and hold them up in public to the world. Many a disguised tory[8]
has lately shown his head, that shall penitentially solemnize with curses the day on
which Howe arrived upon the Delaware.

As I was with the troops at Fort Lee, and marched with them to the edge of
Pennsylvania, I am well acquainted with many circumstances, which those who live
at a distance know but little or nothing of. Our situation there was exceedingly
cramped, the place being a narrow neck of land between the North River[9] and the
Hackensack. Our force was inconsiderable, being not one fourth so great as Howe
could bring against us. We had no army at hand to have relieved the garrison, had
we shut ourselves up and stood on our defence. Our ammunition, light artillery,
and the best part of our stores, had been removed, on the apprehension that
Howe would endeavor to penetrate the Jerseys, in which case fort Lee could be of
no use to us; for it must occur to every thinking man, whether in the army or not,
that these kind of field forts are only for temporary purposes, and last in use no
longer than the enemy directs his force against the particular object, which such
forts are raised to defend. Such was our situation and condition at fort Lee on the
morning of the 20th of November, when an officer arrived with information that
the enemy with 200 boats had landed about seven miles above: Major General
Green,[10] who commanded the garrison, immediately ordered them under arms,
and sent express to General Washington at the town of Hackensack, distant by the
way of the ferry, six miles. Our first object was to secure the bridge over the Hackensack, which laid up the river between the enemy and us, about six miles from
us, and three from them. General Washington arrived in about three quarters of
an hour, and marched at the head of the troops towards the bridge, which place I
expected we should have a brush for; however, they did not choose to dispute it
with us, and the greatest part of our troops went over the bridge, the rest over the
ferry, except some which passed at a mill on a small creek, between the bridge and
the ferry, and made their way through some marshy grounds up to the town of
Hackensack, and there passed the river. We brought off as much baggage as the
wagons could contain, the rest was lost. The simple object was to bring off the garrison, and march them on till they could be strengthened by the Jersey or Pennsylvania militia, so as to be enabled to make a stand. We staid four days at Newark,[11]
collected our out-posts with some of the Jersey militia, and marched out twice to
meet the enemy, on being informed that they were advancing, though our numbers were greatly inferior to theirs. Howe, in my little opinion, committed a great
error in generalship in not throwing a body of forces off from Staten Island
through Amboy, by which means he might have seized all our stores at Brunswick,
and intercepted our march into Pennsylvania; but if we believe the power of hell

---

[7]In the fifteenth century (in 1429), Joan of Arc led the
French to victory over the British.
[8]British sympathizer.
[9]Hudson River.
[10]Nathanael Greene (1742–1786); Paine was his aide-de-

camp. See "To the Memory of the Brave Americans," by
Philip Freneau.
[11]It was after this quick retreat from the forts on the Hudson that Paine, according to tradition, wrote *Crisis* I in
Newark on a drumhead.

to be limited, we must likewise believe that their agents are under some providential control.

I shall not now attempt to give all the particulars of our retreat to the Delaware; suffice it for the present to say, that both officers and men, though greatly harassed and fatigued, frequently without rest, covering, or provision, the inevitable consequences of a long retreat, bore it with a manly and martial spirit. All their wishes centred in one, which was, that the country would turn out and help them to drive the enemy back. Voltaire has remarked that king William never appeared to full advantage but in difficulties and in action;[12] the same remark may be made on General Washington, for the character fits him. There is a natural firmness in some minds which cannot be unlocked by trifles, but which, when unlocked, discovers a cabinet of fortitude; and I reckon it among those kind of public blessings, which we do not immediately see, that God hath blessed him with uninterrupted health, and given him a mind that can even flourish upon care.

I shall conclude this paper with some miscellaneous remarks on the state of our affairs; and shall begin with asking the following question, Why is it that the enemy have left the New-England provinces, and made these middle ones the seat of war? The answer is easy: New-England is not infested with tories, and we are. I have been tender in raising the cry against these men, and used numberless arguments to show them their danger, but it will not do to sacrifice a world either to their folly or their baseness. The period is now arrived, in which either they or we must change our sentiments, or one or both must fall. And what is a tory? Good God! what is he? I should not be afraid to go with a hundred whigs[13] against a thousand tories, were they to attempt to get into arms. Every tory is a coward; for servile, slavish, self-interested fear is the foundation of toryism; and a man under such influence, though he may be cruel, never can be brave.

But, before the line of irrecoverable separation be drawn between us, let us reason the matter together: your conduct is an invitation to the enemy, yet not one in a thousand of you has heart enough to join him. Howe is as much deceived by you as the American cause is injured by you. He expects you will all take up arms, and flock to his standard, with muskets on your shoulders. Your opinions are of no use to him, unless you support him personally, for 'tis soldiers, and not tories, that he wants.

I once felt all that kind of anger, which a man ought to feel, against the mean principles that are held by the tories: a noted one, who kept a tavern at Amboy,[14] was standing at his door, with as pretty a child in his hand, about eight or nine years old, as I ever saw, and after speaking his mind as freely as he thought was prudent, finished with this unfatherly expression, "Well! give me peace in my day." Not a man lives on the continent but fully believes that a separation must some time or other finally take place, and a generous parent should have said, "If there must be trouble, let it be in my day, that my child may have peace;" and this single reflection, well applied, is sufficient to awaken every man to duty. Not a place upon earth might be so happy as America. Her situation is remote from all the wrangling world, and she has nothing to do but to trade with them. A man can distinguish himself between temper and principle, and I am as confident, as I am that God governs the world, that America will never be happy till she gets clear of foreign dominion. Wars, without ceasing, will break out till that period arrives, and the continent must in the end be conqueror; for though the flame of liberty may sometimes cease to shine, the coal can never expire.

---

[12]Voltaire (1694–1778), author of *History of Louis the Fourteenth* (1751), directed this remark at England's King William III (1650–1702).

[13]Supporters of the Revolution.

[14]In August 1776, Paine enlisted in a Pennsylvania Division of the Continental Army and was stationed at Amboy, New Jersey.

America did not, nor does not want force; but she wanted a proper application of that force. Wisdom is not the purchase of a day, and it is no wonder that we should err at the first setting off. From an excess of tenderness, we were unwilling to raise an army, and trusted our cause to the temporary defence of a well-meaning militia. A summer's experience has now taught us better; yet with those troops, while they were collected, we were able to set bounds to the progress of the enemy, and, thank God! they are again assembling. I always considered militia as the best troops in the world for a sudden exertion, but they will not do for a long campaign. Howe, it is probable, will make an attempt on this city;[15] should he fail on this side the Delaware, he is ruined: if he succeeds, our cause is not ruined. He stakes all on his side against a part on ours; admitting he succeeds, the consequence will be, that armies from both ends of the continent will march to assist their suffering friends in the middle states; for he cannot go everywhere, it is impossible. I consider Howe as the greatest enemy the tories have; he is bringing a war into their country, which, had it not been for him and partly for themselves, they had been clear of. Should he now be expelled, I wish with all the devotion of a Christian, that the names of whig and tory may never more be mentioned; but should the tories give him encouragement to come, or assistance if he come, I as sincerely wish that our next year's arms may expel them from the continent, and the congress appropriate their possessions to the relief of those who have suffered in well-doing. A single successful battle next year will settle the whole. America could carry on a two years war by the confiscation of the property of disaffected persons, and be made happy by their expulsion. Say not that this is revenge, call it rather the soft resentment of a suffering people, who, having no object in view but the *good* of *all,* have staked their *own all* upon a seemingly doubtful event. Yet it is folly to argue against determined hardness; eloquence may strike the ear, and the language of sorrow draw forth the tear of compassion, but nothing can reach the heart that is steeled with prejudice.

Quitting this class of men, I turn with the warm ardor of a friend to those who have nobly stood, and are yet determined to stand the matter out: I call not upon a few, but upon all: not on *this* state or *that* state, but on *every* state: up and help us; lay your shoulders to the wheel; better have too much force than too little, when so great an object is at stake. Let it be told to the future world, that in the depth of winter, when nothing but hope and virtue could survive, that the city and the country, alarmed at one common danger, came forth to meet and to repulse it. Say not that thousands are gone, turn out your tens of thousands;[16] throw not the burden of the day upon Providence, but "show your faith by your works,"[17] that God may bless you. It matters not where you live, or what rank of life you hold, the evil or the blessing will reach you all. The far and the near, the home counties and the back,[18] the rich and the poor, will suffer or rejoice alike. The heart that feels not now, is dead: the blood of his children will curse his cowardice, who shrinks back at a time when a little might have saved the whole, and made *them* happy. I love the man that can smile in trouble, that can gather strength from distress, and grow brave by reflection. 'Tis the business of little minds to shrink; but he whose heart is firm, and whose conscience approves his conduct, will pursue his principles unto death. My own line of reasoning is to myself as straight and clear as a ray of light. Not all the treasures of the world, so far as I believe, could have induced me to support an offensive war, for I think it murder; but if a thief breaks into my house, burns and destroys my property, and kills or threatens to kill me, or those that are in it, and to "bind me in all cases

---

[15] Philadelphia.
[16] 1 Samuel 18:7: "Saul hath slain his thousands, and David his ten thousands."

[17] James 2:18.
[18] Backwoods, frontier.

whatsoever"[19] to his absolute will, am I to suffer it? What signifies it to me, whether he who does it is a king or a common man; my countryman or not my countryman; whether it be done by an individual villain, or an army of them? If we reason to the root of things we shall find no difference; neither can any just cause be assigned why we should punish in the one case and pardon in the other. Let them call me rebel, and welcome, I feel no concern from it; but I should suffer the misery of devils, were I to make a whore of my soul by swearing allegiance to one whose character is that of a sottish, stupid, stubborn, worthless, brutish man. I conceive likewise a horrid idea in receiving mercy from a being, who at the last day shall be shrieking to the rocks and mountains to cover him, and fleeing with terror from the orphan, the widow, and the slain of America.

There are cases which cannot be overdone by language, and this is one. There are persons, too, who see not the full extent of the evil which threatens them; they solace themselves with hopes that the enemy, if he succeed, will be merciful. It is the madness of folly, to expect mercy from those who have refused to do justice; and even mercy, where conquest is the object, is only a trick of war; the cunning of the fox is as murderous as the violence of the wolf, and we ought to guard equally against both. Howe's first object is, partly by threats and partly by promises, to terrify or seduce the people to deliver up their arms and receive mercy. The ministry recommended the same plan to Gage,[20] and this is what the tories call making their peace, "a peace which passeth all understanding"[21] *indeed!* A peace which would be the immediate forerunner of a worse ruin than any we have yet thought of. Ye men of Pennsylvania, do reason upon these things! Were the back counties to give up their arms, they would fall an easy prey to the Indians, who are all armed: this perhaps is what some tories would not be sorry for. Were the home counties to deliver up their arms, they would be exposed to the resentment of the back counties, who would then have it in their power to chastise their defection at pleasure. And were any one state to give up its arms, *that* state must be garrisoned by all Howe's army of Britons and Hessians[22] to preserve it from the anger of the rest. Mutual fear is the principal link in the chain of mutual love, and woe be to that state that breaks the compact. Howe is mercifully inviting you to barbarous destruction, and men must be either rogues or fools that will not see it. I dwell not upon the vapours of imagination: I bring reason to your ears, and, in language as plain as A, B, C, hold up truth to your eyes.

I thank God, that I fear not. I see no real cause for fear. I know our situation well, and can see the way out of it. While our army was collected, Howe dared not risk a battle; and it is no credit to him that he decamped from the White Plains,[23] and waited a mean opportunity to ravage the defenceless Jerseys; but it is great credit to us, that, with a handful of men, we sustained an orderly retreat for near an hundred miles, brought off our ammunition, all our field pieces, the greatest part of our stores, and had four rivers to pass. None can say that our retreat was precipitate, for we were near three weeks in performing it, that the country might have time to come in.[24] Twice we marched back to meet the enemy, and remained out till dark. The sign of fear was not seen in our camp, and had not some of the cowardly and disaffected inhabitants spread false alarms through the country, the Jerseys had never been ravaged. Once more we are again collected and collecting; our new army at both ends of the continent is recruiting fast, and we shall be able

---

[19]Declaratory Act of Parliament, February 24, 1766, asserting British authority over the colonies.
[20]General Thomas Gage (1721–1787) preceded Howe as Commander of British forces in America (1763–75).
[21]Philippians 4:7: "And the peace of God, which passeth all understanding, shall keep your hearts and minds through Christ Jesus."

[22]Mercenary soldiers from Hesse, Germany.
[23]On October 28, 1776, General Howe routed Washington's troops at White Plains but failed to follow up.
[24]Local volunteers, or militia, brought into the army.

to open the next campaign with sixty thousand men, well armed and clothed. This is our situation, and who will may know it. By perseverance and fortitude we have the prospect of a glorious issue; by cowardice and submission, the sad choice of a variety of evils—a ravaged country—a depopulated city—habitations without safety, and slavery without hope—our homes turned into barracks and bawdy-houses for Hessians, and a future race to provide for, whose fathers we shall doubt of. Look on this picture and weep over it! and if there yet remains one thoughtless wretch who believes it not, let him suffer it unlamented.

COMMON SENSE.

1776   *1776*

from The Age of Reason

PART I

CHAPTER I

THE AUTHOR'S PROFESSION OF FAITH

It has been my intention, for several years past, to publish my thoughts upon religion; I am well aware of the difficulties that attend the subject, and from that consideration, had reserved it to a more advanced period of life. I intended it to be the last offering I should make to my fellow-citizens of all nations, and that at a time when the purity of the motive that induced me to it could not admit of a question, even by those who might disapprove the work.

The circumstance that has now taken place in France, of the total abolition of the whole national order of priesthood, and of everything appertaining to compulsive systems of religion, and compulsive articles of faith,[1] has not only precipitated my intention, but rendered a work of this kind exceedingly necessary, lest, in the general wreck of superstition, of false systems of government, and false theology, we lose sight of morality, of humanity, and of the theology that is true.

As several of my colleagues, and others of my fellow-citizens of France, have given me the example of making their voluntary and individual profession of faith, I also will make mine; and I do this with all that sincerity and frankness with which the mind of man communicates with itself.

I believe in one God, and no more; and I hope for happiness beyond this life.

I believe the equality of man, and I believe that religious duties consist in doing justice, loving mercy, and endeavouring to make our fellow-creatures happy.

But, lest it should be supposed that I believe many other things in addition to these, I shall, in the progress of this work, declare the things I do not believe, and my reasons for not believing them.

I do not believe in the creed professed by the Jewish church, by the Roman church, by the Greek church, by the Turkish church, by the Protestant church, nor by any church that I know of. My own mind is my own church.

All national institutions of churches, whether Jewish, Christian, or Turkish, appear to me no other than human inventions set up to terrify and enslave mankind, and monopolize power and profit.

I do not mean by this declaration to condemn those who believe otherwise;

---

[1] The French Revolution had, by 1792, destroyed the privileged position of the Roman Catholic church in France and barred use of the churches.

they have the same right to their belief as I have to mine. But it is necessary to the happiness of man, that he be mentally faithful to himself. Infidelity does not consist in believing, or in disbelieving; it consists in professing to believe what he does not believe.

It is impossible to calculate the moral mischief, if I may so express it, that mental lying has produced in society. When a man has so far corrupted and prostituted the chastity of his mind, as to subscribe his professional belief to things he does not believe, he has prepared himself for the commission of every other crime. He takes up the trade of a priest for the sake of gain, and, in order to qualify himself for that trade, he begins with a perjury. Can we conceive anything more destructive to morality than this?

Soon after I had published the pamphlet *Common Sense,* in America, I saw the exceeding probability that a revolution in the system of government would be followed by a revolution in the system of religion. The adulterous connection of church and state, wherever it had taken place, whether Jewish, Christian, or Turkish, had so effectually prohibited, by pains and penalties, every discussion upon established creeds, and upon first principles of religion, that until the system of government should be changed, those subjects could not be brought fairly and openly before the world; but that whenever this should be done, a revolution in the system of religion would follow. Human inventions and priest-craft would be detected; and man would return to the pure, unmixed, and unadulterated belief of one God, and no more.

CHAPTER II
OF MISSIONS AND REVELATIONS

Every national church or religion has established itself by pretending some special mission from God, communicated to certain individuals. The Jews have their Moses; the Christians their Jesus Christ, their apostles and saints; and the Turks their Mahomet; as if the way to God was not open to every man alike.

Each of those churches shows certain books, which they call *revelation,* or the Word of God. The Jews say that their Word of God was given by God to Moses face to face; the Christians say, that their Word of God came by divine inspiration; and the Turks say, that their Word of God (the Koran) was brought by an angel from heaven. Each of those churches accuses the other of unbelief; and, for my own part, I disbelieve them all.

As it is necessary to affix right ideas to words, I will, before I proceed further into the subject, offer some observations on the word *revelation*. Revelation when applied to religion, means something communicated *immediately* from God to man.

No one will deny or dispute the power of the Almighty to make such a communication if he pleases. But admitting, for the sake of a case, that something has been revealed to a certain person, and not revealed to any other person, it is revelation to that person only. When he tells it to a second person, a second to a third, a third to a fourth, and so on, it ceases to be a revelation to all those persons. It is revelation to the first person only, and *hearsay* to every other, and, consequently, they are not obliged to believe it.

It is a contradiction in terms and ideas to call anything a revelation that comes to us at second hand, either verbally or in writing. Revelation is necessarily limited to the first communication. After this, it is only an account of something which that person says was a revelation made to him; and though he may find himself obliged to believe it, it cannot be incumbent on me to believe it in the same manner, for it was not a revelation made to *me,* and I have only his word for it that it was made to *him*.

When Moses told the children of Israel that he received the two tables of the commandments from the hand of God, they were not obliged to believe him, because they had no other authority for it than his telling them so; and I have no other authority for it than some historian telling me so, the commandments carrying no internal evidence of divinity with them. They contain some good moral precepts such as any man qualified to be a lawgiver or a legislator could produce himself, without having recourse to supernatural intervention.[1]

When I am told that the Koran was written in Heaven, and brought to Mahomet by an angel, the account comes to near the same kind of hearsay evidence and second hand authority as the former. I did not see the angel myself, and therefore I have a right not to believe it.

When also I am told that a woman, called the Virgin Mary, said, or gave out, that she was with child without any cohabitation with a man, and that her betrothed husband, Joseph, said that an angel told him so, I have a right to believe them or not: such a circumstance required a much stronger evidence than their bare word for it: but we have not even this; for neither Joseph nor Mary wrote any such matter themselves. It is only reported by others that *they said so*. It is hearsay upon hearsay, and I do not choose to rest my belief upon such evidence.

It is, however, not difficult to account for the credit that was given to the story of Jesus Christ being the Son of God. He was born when the heathen mythology had still some fashion and repute in the world, and that mythology had prepared the people for the belief of such a story. Almost all the extraordinary men that lived under the heathen mythology were reputed to be the sons of some of their gods. It was not a new thing at that time to believe a man to have been celestially begotten; the intercourse of gods with women was then a matter of familiar opinion. Their Jupiter,[2] according to their accounts, had cohabited with hundreds; the story therefore had nothing in it either new, wonderful, or obscene; it was conformable to the opinions that then prevailed among the people called Gentiles, or mythologists, and it was those people only that believed it. The Jews, who had kept strictly to the belief of one God, and no more, and who had always rejected the heathen mythology, never credited the story.

It is curious to observe how the theory of what is called the Christian Church, sprung out of the tail of the heathen mythology. A direct incorporation took place in the first instance, by making the reputed founder to be celestially begotten. The trinity of gods that then followed was no other than a reduction of the former plurality, which was about twenty or thirty thousand. The statue of Mary succeeded the statue of Diana of Ephesus.[3] The deification of heroes changed into the canonization of saints. The Mythologists had gods for everything; the Christian Mythologists had saints for everything. The church became as crowded with the one, as the pantheon[4] had been with the other; and Rome was the place of both. The Christian theory is little else than the idolatry of the ancient mythologists, accommodated to the purposes of power and revenue; and it yet remains to reason and philosophy to abolish the amphibious fraud.

CHAPTER III

CONCERNING THE CHARACTER OF JESUS CHRIST, AND HIS HISTORY

Nothing that is here said can apply, even with the most distant disrespect, to the *real* character of Jesus Christ. He was a virtuous and an amiable man. The morality that he preached and practised was of the most benevolent kind; and

---

[1]"It is, however, necessary to except the declaration which says that God *visits the sins of the fathers upon the children*. This is contrary to every principle of moral justice" (Paine's note).
[2]Principal Roman god (the Greek's Zeus).

[3]The temple at Ephesus in Asia Minor, one of the seven wonders of the world, contained the statue of Diana, worshipped as a fertility goddess.
[4]A temple in Rome dedicated to the Roman gods.

though similar systems of morality had been preached by Confucius,[1] and by some of the Greek philosophers, many years before, by the Quakers since, and by many good men in all ages, it has not been exceeded by any.

Jesus Christ wrote no account of himself, of his birth, parentage, or anything else. Not a line of what is called the New Testament is of his writing. The history of him is altogether the work of other people; and as to the account given of his resurrection and ascension, it was the necessary counterpart to the story of his birth. His historians, having brought him into the world in a supernatural manner, were obliged to take him out again in the same manner, or the first part of the story must have fallen to the ground.

The wretched contrivance with which this latter part is told, exceeds everything that went before it. The first part, that of the miraculous conception, was not a thing that admitted of publicity; and therefore the tellers of this part of the story had this advantage, that though they might not be credited, they could not be detected. They could not be expected to prove it, because it was not one of those things that admitted of proof, and it was impossible that the person of whom it was told could prove it himself.

But the resurrection of a dead person from the grave, and his ascension through the air, is a thing very different, as to the evidence it admits of, to the invisible conception of a child in the womb. The resurrection and ascension, supposing them to have taken place, admitted of public and ocular demonstration, like that of the ascension of a balloon, or the sun at noon day, to all Jerusalem at least. A thing which everybody is required to believe, requires that the proof and evidence of it should be equal to all, and universal; and as the public visibility of this last related act was the only evidence that could give sanction to the former part, the whole of it falls to the ground, because that evidence never was given. Instead of this, a small number of persons, not more than eight or nine, are introduced as proxies for the whole world, to say they saw it, and all the rest of the world are called upon to believe it. But it appears that Thomas did not believe the resurrection; and, as they say, would not believe without having ocular and manual demonstration himself.[2] *So neither will I;* and the reason is equally as good for me, and for every other person, as for Thomas.

It is in vain to attempt to palliate or disguise this matter. The story, so far as relates to the supernatural part, has every mark of fraud and imposition stamped upon the face of it. Who were the authors of it is as impossible for us now to know, as it is for us to be assured that the books in which the account is related were written by the persons whose names they bear. The best surviving evidence we now have respecting this affair is the Jews. They are regularly descended from the people who lived in the time this resurrection and ascension is said to have happened, and they say, *it is not true.* It has long appeared to me a strange inconsistency to cite the Jews as a proof of the truth of the story. It is just the same as if a man were to say, I will prove the truth of what I have told you, by producing the people who say it is false.

That such a person as Jesus Christ existed, and that he was crucified, which was the mode of execution at that day, are historical relations strictly within the limits of probability. He preached most excellent morality, and the equality of man; but he preached also against the corruptions and avarice of the Jewish priests, and this brought upon him the hatred and vengeance of the whole order of priesthood. The accusation which those priests brought against him was that of sedition and conspiracy against the Roman government, to which the Jews were then subject and tributary; and it is not improbable that the Roman government might

---

[1] Confucius (c. 557–479 B.C.), Chinese philosopher and teacher.

[2] Doubting Thomas, one of the twelve apostles who doubted at first the resurrection of Christ.

have some secret apprehension of the effects of his doctrine as well as the Jewish priests; neither is it improbable that Jesus Christ had in contemplation the delivery of the Jewish nation from the bondage of the Romans. Between the two, however, this virtuous reformer and revolutionist lost his life.

CHAPTER IV

OF THE BASES OF CHRISTIANITY

It is upon this plain narrative of facts, together with another case I am going to mention, that the Christian mythologists, calling themselves the Christian Church, have erected their fable, which for absurdity and extravagance is not exceeded by anything that is to be found in the mythology of the ancients.

The ancient mythologists tell us that the race of Giants made war against Jupiter, and that one of them threw a hundred rocks against him at one throw; that Jupiter defeated him with thunder, and confined him afterwards under Mount Etna; and that every time the Giant turns himself, Mount Etna belches fire. It is here easy to see that the circumstance of the mountain, that of its being a volcano, suggested the idea of the fable; and that the fable is made to fit and wind itself up with that circumstance.

The Christian mythologists tell that their Satan made war against the Almighty, who defeated him, and confined him afterwards, not under a mountain, but in a pit. It is here easy to see that the first fable suggested the idea of the second; for the fable of Jupiter and the Giants was told many hundred years before that of Satan.

Thus far the ancient and the Christian mythologists differ very little from each other. But the latter have contrived to carry the matter much farther. They have contrived to connect the fabulous part of the story of Jesus Christ with the fable originating from Mount Etna; and, in order to make all the parts of the story tye together, they have taken to their aid the traditions of the Jews; for the Christian mythology is made up partly from the ancient mythology, and partly from the Jewish traditions.

The Christian mythologists, after having confined Satan in a pit, were obliged to let him out again to bring on the sequel of the fable. He is then introduced into the garden of Eden in the shape of a snake, or a serpent, and in that shape he enters into familiar conversation with Eve, who is no ways surprised to hear a snake talk; and the issue of this tête-à-tête is, that he persuades her to eat an apple, and the eating of that apple damns all mankind.

After giving Satan this triumph over the whole creation, one would have supposed that the church mythologists would have been kind enough to send him back again to the pit, or, if they had not done this, that they would have put a mountain upon him, (for they say that their faith can remove a mountain) or have put him under a mountain, as the former mythologists had done, to prevent his getting again among the women, and doing more mischief. But instead of this, they leave him at large, without even obliging him to give his parole.[1] The secret of which is, that they could not do without him; and after being at the trouble of making him, they bribed him to stay. They promised him ALL the Jews, ALL the Turks by anticipation, nine-tenths of the world beside, and Mahomet into the bargain. After this, who can doubt the bountifulness of the Christian Mythology?

Having thus made an insurrection and a battle in heaven, in which none of the combatants could be either killed or wounded—put Satan into the pit—let him out again—given him a triumph over the whole creation—damned all mankind

---

[1]Word of honor.

by the eating of an apple, these Christian mythologists bring the two ends of their fable together. They represent this virtuous and amiable man, Jesus Christ, to be at once both God and man, and also the Son of God, celestially begotten, on purpose to be sacrificed, because they say that Eve in her longing had eaten an apple.

CHAPTER V

Examination in Detail of the Preceding Bases

Putting aside everything that might excite laughter by its absurdity, or detestation by its profaneness, and confining ourselves merely to an examination of the parts, it is impossible to conceive a story more derogatory to the Almighty, more inconsistent with his wisdom, more contradictory to his power, than this story is.

In order to make for it a foundation to rise upon, the inventors were under the necessity of giving to the being whom they call Satan a power equally as great, if not greater, than they attribute to the Almighty. They have not only given him the power of liberating himself from the pit, after what they call his fall, but they have made that power increase afterwards to infinity. Before this fall they represent him only as an angel of limited existence, as they represent the rest. After his fall, he becomes, by their account, omnipresent. He exists everywhere, and at the same time. He occupies the whole immensity of space.

Not content with this deification of Satan, they represent him as defeating by stratagem, in the shape of an animal of the creation, all the power and wisdom of the Almighty. They represent him as having compelled the Almighty to the *direct necessity* either of surrendering the whole of the creation to the government and sovereignty of this Satan, or of capitulating for its redemption by coming down upon earth, and exhibiting himself upon a cross in the shape of a man.

Had the inventors of this story told it the contrary way, that is, had they represented the Almighty as compelling Satan to exhibit *himself* on a cross in the shape of a snake, as a punishment for his new transgression, the story would have been less absurd, less contradictory. But, instead of this they make the transgressor triumph, and the Almighty fall.

That many good men have believed this strange fable, and lived very good lives under that belief (for credulity is not a crime) is what I have no doubt of. In the first place, they were educated to believe it, and they would have believed anything else in the same manner. There are also many who have been so enthusiastically enraptured by what they conceived to be the infinite love of God to man, in making a sacrifice of himself, that the vehemence of the idea has forbidden and deterred them from examining into the absurdity and profaneness of the story. The more unnatural anything is, the more is it capable of becoming the object of dismal admiration.

CHAPTER IX

In What the True Revelation Consists

But some perhaps will say—Are we to have no word of God—no revelation? I answer yes. There is a Word of God; there is a revelation.

THE WORD OF GOD IS THE CREATION WE BEHOLD: And it is in *this word,* which no human invention can counterfeit or alter, that God speaketh universally to man.

Human language is local and changeable, and is therefore incapable of being used as the means of unchangeable and universal information. The idea that God sent Jesus Christ to publish, as they say, the glad tidings to all nations, from one end of the earth unto the other, is consistent only with the ignorance of those who know nothing of the extent of the world, and who believed, as those world-saviours believed, and continued to believe for several centuries, (and that in contradiction to the discoveries of philosophers and the experience of navigators,) that the earth was flat like a trencher; and that a man might walk to the end of it.

But how was Jesus Christ to make anything known to all nations? He could speak but one language, which was Hebrew; and there are in the world several hundred languages. Scarcely any two nations speak the same language, or understand each other; and as to translations, every man who knows anything of languages, knows that it is impossible to translate from one language into another, not only without losing a great part of the original, but frequently of mistaking the sense; and besides all this, the art of printing was wholly unknown at the time Christ lived.

It is always necessary that the means that are to accomplish any end be equal to the accomplishment of that end, or the end cannot be accomplished. It is in this that the difference between finite and infinite power and wisdom discovers itself. Man frequently fails in accomplishing his end, from a natural inability of the power to the purpose; and frequently from the want of wisdom to apply power properly. But it is impossible for infinite power and wisdom to fail as man faileth. The means it useth are always equal to the end: but human language, more especially as there is not an universal language, is incapable of being used as an universal means of unchangeable and uniform information; and therefore it is not the means that God useth in manifesting himself universally to man.

It is only in the CREATION that all our ideas and conceptions of a *word of God* can unite. The Creation speaketh an universal language, independently of human speech or human language, multiplied and various as they be. It is an ever existing original, which every man can read. It cannot be forged; it cannot be counterfeited; it cannot be lost; it cannot be altered; it cannot be suppressed. It does not depend upon the will of man whether it shall be published or not; it publishes itself from one end of the earth to the other. It preaches to all nations and to all worlds; and this *word of God* reveals to man all that is necessary for man to know of God.

Do we want to contemplate his power? We see it in the immensity of the creation. Do we want to contemplate his wisdom? We see it in the unchangeable order by which the incomprehensible Whole is governed. Do we want to contemplate his munificence? We see it in the abundance with which he fills the earth. Do we want to contemplate his mercy? We see it in his not withholding that abundance even from the unthankful. In fine, do we want to know what God is? Search not the book called the scripture, which any human hand might make, but the scripture called the Creation.

1793   *1794*

THE FEDERALIST
(1787–88)

That same Continental Congress that issued the Declaration of Independence in 1776 also wrote the Articles of Confederation as a set of bylaws for a national government. As debate about the Articles went on for a year, it became clear that the "sovereign" states were willing to give up very little of their sovereignty to form a strong central government. The Articles that were ratified in 1781 barely succeeded in holding together the group of independent states. As the Revolutionary War progressed, the weakness of the Articles of Confederation became glaring. And after the war, as chaos in inter-state relations increased, the need for change was apparent to all if the union of states was to survive and endure.

Because of the fatal weakness of the Articles, the Constitutional Convention, which met in 1787 in Philadelphia, was able to fashion a document that would still be in force over two hundred years after it was written. Its durability was no accident. Those who drafted the Constitution were men of intelligence, classical education, and wide experience. They included George Washington, Alexander Hamilton, Benjamin Franklin, James Madison, Edmund Randolph, and Gouverneur Morris. Most had read deeply in the works of classical and modern philosophy, including John Locke's *Of Civil Government: The Second Treatise* (1690), with its focus on liberty, equality, natural law, and reason; and Charles de Montesquieu's *The Spirit of the Laws* (1748), with its emphasis on the balance of powers in governments among the legislative, executive, and judiciary functions.

Debate at the Constitutional Convention was vigorous, with sharp and energetic exchanges ending usually in compromise. No one was fully satisfied, nor anyone totally pleased. Benjamin Franklin spoke for all when, at the end, he expressed the wish that "every member of the Convention who may still have objections to [the Constitution] would with me on this occasion doubt a little of his own infallibility, and . . . make manifest our unanimity." His wish carried the day.

But there remained the necessity of obtaining the ratification by the several sovereign states that would have to give up some of their independence. There was strong and active opposition from those who feared that a strong presidency with no limits on reelectability would become hereditary, and from those who were incensed that no Bill of Rights specifically assured freedom of religion, of speech, of the press, or of assembly. There existed the real danger of rejection by several of the states.

Rallying support for the Constitution, *The Federalist Papers* began to appear in the press in October 1787. They presented the case for adopting the Constitution in calm, lucid, and persuasive prose. They were all signed by the name "Publius" (a common first name in ancient Rome) and they continued to appear through May 1788. It was soon known that the authors were three of the most eminent men of the day: Alexander Hamilton (1755–1804), aide-de-camp of General George Washington, and later the first Secretary of the Treasury (1789–95), a brilliant and forceful debater firmly committed to a strong federal government; James Madison (1751–1836), one of the most learned delegates to the Constitutional Convention, later Secretary of State (1801–09) and President (1809–17); and John Jay (1745–1829), member of the several continental congresses (beginning in 1774), later first Chief Justice of the United States Supreme Court (1789–95) and Governor of New York (1795–1801). Eighty-five papers were written in all: Hamilton wrote over half (some fifty-one), Madison at least fifteen, and Jay, who had become ill, five; the rest were written by Hamilton or Madison or by the two in collaboration. *The Federalist Papers* overcame the doubters, skeptics, cynics, and scrupulously cautious. One by one the states ratified the document, and by June 1788, the required nine states had given their approval; later the rest would approve it. The Constitution was declared in effect by the government in March 1789. Many of the states had given provisional approval, urgently recommending a Bill of Rights. Such a Bill was provided as the first ten amendments to the

Constitution. Thomas Jefferson had been minister to Paris during the Constitutional Convention, and had been shocked by the lack of a Bill of Rights in the original document. The correction of this flaw answered most of his doubts. He had no doubts about the value of *The Federalist Papers*. He wrote to Madison in 1788 that it was "the best commentary on the principles of government which was ever written."

ADDITIONAL READING

The Federalist, ed. Jacob E. Cooke, 1961; *The Federalist,* ed. Benjamin Fletcher Wright (with important introduction), 1961.

Bower Aly, *The Rhetoric of Alexander Hamilton,* 1941; Broadus Mitchell, *Alexander Hamilton: Youth to Maturity, 1755–1788,* 1957; and his *Alexander Hamilton: The National Adventure, 1788–1804,* 1962; Gottfried Dietze, *The Federalist: A Classic on Federalism and Free Government,* 1960; Robert Bain, "The Federalist," *American Literature, 1764–1789,* ed. Everett Emerson, 1977; Gary Wills, *Explaining America: The Federalist,* 1981; Albert Furtwangler, *The Authority of Publius, A Reading of the Federalist Papers,* 1984; Christopher Collier and James Lincoln Collier, *Decision in Philadelphia: The Constitutional Convention,* 1986.

TEXT

The Federalist, ed. Henry Cabot Lodge, 1904. Some changes in spelling and punctuation have been made to conform with contemporary English.

from The Federalist

NO. 1
[ESTABLISHING GOOD GOVERNMENT BY REFLECTION AND CHOICE]
ALEXANDER HAMILTON

To the People of the State of New York:

After an unequivocal experience of the inefficiency of the subsisting federal government, you are called upon to deliberate on a new Constitution for the United States of America. The subject speaks its own importance; comprehending in its consequences nothing less than the existence of the UNION, the safety and welfare of the parts of which it is composed, the fate of an empire in many respects the most interesting in the world. It has been frequently remarked that it seems to have been reserved to the people of this country, by their conduct and example, to decide the important question, whether societies of men are really capable or not of establishing good government from reflection and choice, or whether they are forever destined to depend for their political constitutions on accident and force. If there be any truth in the remark, the crisis at which we are arrived may with propriety be regarded as the era in which that decision is to be made; and a wrong election of the part we shall act may, in this view, deserve to be considered as the general misfortune of mankind.

This idea will add the inducements of philanthropy to those of patriotism to heighten the solicitude which all considerate and good men must feel for the event. Happy will it be if our choice should be directed by a judicious estimate of our true interests, unperplexed and unbiassed by considerations not connected with the public good. But this is a thing more ardently to be wished than seriously to be expected. The plan offered to our deliberations affects too many particular interests, innovates upon[1] too many local institutions, not to involve in its discussion a variety of objects foreign to its merits, and of views, passions and prejudices little favorable to the discovery of truth.

Among the most formidable of the obstacles which the new Constitution will have to encounter may readily be distinguished the obvious interest of a certain class of men in every State to resist all changes which may hazard a diminution of the power, emolument, and consequence of the offices they hold under the State establishments; and the perverted ambition of another class of men, who will either hope to aggrandize themselves by the confusions of their country, or will flatter themselves with fairer prospects of elevation from the subdivision of the empire into several partial confederacies than from its union under one government.

It is not, however, my design to dwell upon observations of this nature. I am well aware that it would be disingenuous to resolve indiscriminately the opposition of any set of men (merely because their situations might subject them to suspicion) into interested or ambitious views. Candor will oblige us to admit that even such men may be actuated by upright intentions; and it cannot be doubted that much of the opposition which has made its appearance, or may hereafter make its appearance, will spring from sources, blameless at least, if not respectable—the honest errors of minds led astray by preconceived jealousies and fears. So numerous indeed and so powerful are the causes which serve to give a false bias to the judgment, that we, upon many occasions, see wise and good men on the wrong as well as on the right side of questions of the first magnitude to society. This circumstance, if duly attended to, would furnish a lesson of moderation to those who are ever so much persuaded of their being in the right in any controversy. And a further reason for caution, in this respect, might be drawn from the reflection that we are not always sure that those who advocate the truth are influenced by purer principles than their antagonists. Ambition, avarice, personal animosity, party opposition, and many other motives not more laudable than these, are apt to operate as well upon those who support as those who oppose the right side of a question. Were there not even these inducements to moderation, nothing could be more ill-judged than that intolerant spirit which has, at all times, characterized political parties. For in politics, as in religion, it is equally absurd to aim at making proselytes by fire and sword. Heresies in either can rarely be cured by persecution.

And yet, however just these sentiments will be allowed to be, we have already sufficient indications that it will happen in this as in all former cases of great national discussion. A torrent of angry and malignant passions will be let loose. To judge from the conduct of the opposite parties, we shall be led to conclude that they will mutually hope to evince the justness of their opinions, and to increase the number of their converts by the loudness of their declamations and the bitterness of their invectives. An enlightened zeal for the energy and efficiency of government will be stigmatized as the offspring of a temper fond of despotic power and hostile to the principles of liberty. An over-scrupulous jealousy of danger to the rights of the people, which is more commonly the fault of the head than of the heart, will be represented as mere pretence and artifice, the stale bait for popularity at the expense of the public good. It will be forgotten, on the one hand, that jealousy is the usual concomitant of love, and that the noble enthusiasm of liberty is apt to be infected with a spirit of narrow and illiberal distrust. On the other hand, it will be equally forgotten that the vigor of government is essential to the security of liberty; that, in the contemplation of a sound and well-informed judgment, their interest can never be separated; and that a dangerous ambition more

---

[1] Brings new elements to.

often lurks behind the specious mask of zeal for the rights of the people than under the forbidding appearance of zeal for the firmness and efficiency of government. History will teach us that the former has been found a much more certain road to the introduction of despotism than the latter, and that of those men who have overturned the liberties of republics, the greatest number have begun their career by paying an obsequious court to the people; commencing demagogues, and ending tyrants.

In the course of the preceding observations, I have had an eye, my fellow-citizens, to putting you upon your guard against all attempts, from whatever quarter, to influence your decision in a matter of the utmost moment to your welfare, by any impressions other than those which may result from the evidence of truth. You will, no doubt, at the same time, have collected from the general scope of them, that they proceed from a source not unfriendly to the new Constitution. Yes, my countrymen, I own to you that, after having given it an attentive consideration, I am clearly of opinion it is your interest to adopt it. I am convinced that this is the safest course for your liberty, your dignity, and your happiness. I affect not reserves which I do not feel. I will not amuse you with an appearance of deliberation when I have decided. I frankly acknowledge to you my convictions, and I will freely lay before you the reasons on which they are founded. The consciousness of good intentions disdains ambiguity. I shall not, however, multiply professions on this head. My motives must remain in the depository of my own breast. My arguments will be open to all, and may be judged of by all. They shall at least be offered in a spirit which will not disgrace the cause of truth.

I propose, in a series of papers, to discuss the following interesting particulars:—*The utility of the UNION to your political prosperity*—*The insufficiency of the present Confederation to preserve that Union*—*The necessity of a government at least equally energetic with the one proposed, to the attainment of this object*—*The conformity of the proposed Constitution to the true principles of republican government*—*Its analogy to your own State constitution*—and lastly, *The additional security which its adoption will afford to the preservation of that species of government, to liberty, and to property.*

In the progress of this discussion I shall endeavor to give a satisfactory answer to all the objections which shall have made their appearance, that may seem to have any claim to your attention.

It may perhaps be thought superfluous to offer arguments to prove the utility of the UNION, a point, no doubt, deeply engraved on the hearts of the great body of the people in every State, and one, which it may be imagined, has no adversaries. But the fact is, that we already hear it whispered in the private circles of those who oppose the new Constitution, that the thirteen States are of too great extent for any general system, and that we must of necessity resort to separate confederacies of distinct portions of the whole. This doctrine will, in all probability, be gradually propagated, till it has votaries enough to countenance an open avowal of it. For nothing can be more evident, to those who are able to take an enlarged view of the subject, than the alternative of an adoption of the new Constitution or a dismemberment of the Union. It will therefore be of use to begin by examining the advantages of that Union, the certain evils, and the probable dangers, to which every State will be exposed from its dissolution. This shall accordingly constitute the subject of my next address.   Publius.[2]

1787

---

[2]A Roman first name adopted as a pseudonym by all three of the authors of *The Federalist Papers.*

NO. 10

[CONTROL OF FACTIONS IN A REPUBLIC[1]]

JAMES MADISON

To the People of the State of New York:

Among the numerous advantages promised by a well-constructed Union, none deserves to be more accurately developed than its tendency to break and control the violence of faction. The friend of popular governments never finds himself so much alarmed for their character and fate, as when he contemplates their propensity to this dangerous vice. He will not fail, therefore, to set a due value on any plan which, without violating the principles to which he is attached, provides a proper cure for it. The instability, injustice, and confusion introduced into the public councils, have, in truth, been the mortal diseases under which popular governments have everywhere perished; as they continue to be the favorite and fruitful topics from which the adversaries to liberty derive their most specious declamations. The valuable improvements made by the American constitutions on the popular models, both ancient and modern, cannot certainly be too much admired; but it would be an unwarrantable partiality, to contend that they have as effectually obviated the danger on this side, as was wished and expected. Complaints are everywhere heard from our most considerate and virtuous citizens, equally the friends of public and private faith, and of public and personal liberty, that our governments are too unstable, that the public good is disregarded in the conflicts of rival parties, and that measures are too often decided, not according to the rules of justice and the rights of the minor party, but by the superior force of an interested and overbearing majority. However anxiously we may wish that these complaints had no foundation, the evidence of known facts will not permit us to deny that they are in some degree true. It will be found, indeed, on a candid review of our situation, that some of the distresses under which we labor have been erroneously charged on the operation of our governments; but it will be found, at the same time, that other causes will not alone account for many of our heaviest misfortunes; and, particularly, for that prevailing and increasing distrust of public engagements, and alarm for private rights, which are echoed from one end of the continent to the other. These must be chiefly, if not wholly, effects of the unsteadiness and injustice with which a factious spirit has tainted our public administrations.

By a faction, I understand a number of citizens, whether amounting to a majority or minority of the whole, who are united and actuated by some common impulse of passion, or of interest, adverse to the rights of other citizens, or to the permanent and aggregate interests of the community.

There are two methods of curing the mischiefs of faction: the one, by removing its causes; the other, by controlling its effects.

There are again two methods of removing the causes of faction: the one, by destroying the liberty which is essential to its existence; the other, by giving to every citizen the same opinions, the same passions, and the same interests.

It could never be more truly said than of the first remedy, that it was worse than the disease. Liberty is to faction what air is to fire, an aliment[2] without which it instantly expires. But it could not be less folly to abolish liberty, which is essential to political life, because it nourishes faction, than it would be to wish the annihilation of air, which is essential to animal life, because it imparts to fire its destructive agency.

---

[1] Gary Wills, in *Explaining America* (1981), comments on *Federalist* No. 10: "The paper has a weightiness of language, an authoritative bearing, that awes the reader. It is a masterpiece of neoclassical prose. . . . Madison has 'concocted' his argument into a pure form. He recommends electoral distillation in words that have themselves been distilled, refined, enlarged."

[2] Sustenance, food.

The second expedient is as impracticable as the first would be unwise. As long as the reason of man continues fallible, and he is at liberty to exercise it, different opinions will be formed. As long as the connection subsists between his reason and his self-love, his opinions and his passions will have a reciprocal influence on each other; and the former will be objects to which the latter will attach themselves. The diversity in the faculties of men, from which the rights of property originate, is not less an insuperable obstacle to a uniformity of interests. The protection of these faculties is the first object of government. From the protection of different and unequal faculties of acquiring property, the possession of different degrees and kinds of property immediately results; and from the influence of these on the sentiments and views of the respective proprietors, ensues a division of the society into different interests and parties.

The latent causes of faction are thus sown in the nature of man; and we see them everywhere brought into different degrees of activity, according to the different circumstances of civil society. A zeal for different opinions concerning religion, concerning government, and many other points, as well of speculation as of practice; an attachment to different leaders ambitiously contending for pre-eminence and power; or to persons of other descriptions whose fortunes have been interesting to the human passions, have, in turn, divided mankind into parties, inflamed them with mutual animosity, and rendered them much more disposed to vex and oppress each other than to co-operate for their common good. So strong is this propensity of mankind to fall into mutual animosities, that where no substantial occasion presents itself, the most frivolous and fanciful distinctions have been sufficient to kindle their unfriendly passions and excite their most violent conflicts. But the most common and durable source of factions has been the various and unequal distribution of property. Those who hold and those who are without property have ever formed distinct interests in society. Those who are creditors, and those who are debtors, fall under a like discrimination. A landed interest, a manufacturing interest, a mercantile interest, a moneyed interest, with many lesser interests, grow up of necessity in civilized nations, and divide them into different classes, actuated by different sentiments and views. The regulation of these various and interfering interests forms the principal task of modern legislation, and involves the spirit of party and faction in the necessary and ordinary operations of the government.

No man is allowed to be a judge in his own cause, because his interest would certainly bias his judgment, and, not improbably, corrupt his integrity. With equal, nay with greater reason, a body of men are unfit to be both judges and parties at the same time; yet what are many of the most important acts of legislation, but so many judicial determinations, not indeed concerning the rights of single persons, but concerning the rights of large bodies of citizens? And what are the different classes of legislators but advocates and parties to the causes which they determine? Is a law proposed concerning private debts? It is a question to which the creditors are parties on one side and the debtors on the other. Justice ought to hold the balance between them. Yet the parties are, and must be, themselves the judges; and the most numerous party, or, in other words, the most powerful faction must be expected to prevail. Shall domestic manufactures be encouraged, and in what degree, by restrictions on foreign manufactures? are questions which would be differently decided by the landed and the manufacturing classes, and probably by neither with a sole regard to justice and the public good. The apportionment of taxes on the various descriptions of property is an act which seems to require the most exact impartiality; yet there is, perhaps, no legislative act in which greater opportunity and temptation are given to a predominant party to trample on the rules of justice. Every shilling with which they overburden the inferior number, is a shilling saved to their own pockets.

It is in vain to say that enlightened statesmen will be able to adjust these clashing interests, and render them all subservient to the public good. Enlightened statesmen will not always be at the helm. Nor, in many cases, can such an adjustment be made at all without taking into view indirect and remote considerations, which will rarely prevail over the immediate interest which one party may find in disregarding the rights of another or the good of the whole.

The inference to which we are brought is, that the *causes* of faction cannot be removed, and that relief is only to be sought in the means of controlling its *effects*.

If a faction consists of less than a majority, relief is supplied by the republican principle, which enables the majority to defeat its sinister views by regular vote. It may clog the administration, it may convulse the society; but it will be unable to execute and mask its violence under the forms of the Constitution. When a majority is included in a faction, the form of popular government, on the other hand, enables it to sacrifice to its ruling passion or interest both the public good and the rights of other citizens. To secure the public good and private rights against the danger of such a faction, and at the same time to preserve the spirit and the form of popular government, is then the great object to which our inquiries are directed. Let me add that it is the great desideratum[3] by which this form of government can be rescued from the opprobrium under which it has so long labored, and be recommended to the esteem and adoption of mankind.

By what means is this object attainable? Evidently by one of two only. Either the existence of the same passion or interest in a majority at the same time must be prevented, or the majority, having such coexistent passion or interest, must be rendered, by their number and local situation, unable to concert and carry into effect schemes of oppression. If the impulse and the opportunity be suffered to coincide, we well know that neither moral nor religious motives can be relied on as an adequate control. They are not found to be such on the injustice and violence of individuals, and lose their efficacy in proportion to the number combined together, that is, in proportion as their efficacy becomes needful.

From this view of the subject it may be concluded that a pure democracy, by which I mean a society consisting of a small number of citizens, who assemble and administer the government in person, can admit of no cure for the mischiefs of faction. A common passion or interest will, in almost every case, be felt by a majority of the whole; a communication and concert result from the form of government itself; and there is nothing to check the inducements to sacrifice the weaker party or an obnoxious individual. Hence it is that such democracies have ever been spectacles of turbulence and contention; have ever been found incompatible with personal security or the rights of property; and have in general been as short in their lives as they have been violent in their deaths. Theoretic politicians, who have patronized this species of government, have erroneously supposed that by reducing mankind to a perfect equality in their political rights, they would, at the same time, be perfectly equalized and assimilated in their possessions, their opinions, and their passions.

A republic, by which I mean a government in which the scheme of representation takes place, opens a different prospect, and promises the cure for which we are seeking. Let us examine the points in which it varies from pure democracy, and we shall comprehend both the nature of the cure and the efficacy which it must derive from the Union.

The two great points of difference between a democracy and a republic are: first, the delegation of the government, in the latter, to a small number of citizens elected by the rest; secondly, the greater number of citizens, and greater sphere of country, over which the latter may be extended.

---

[3]Something needed.

The effect of the first difference is, on the one hand, to refine and enlarge the public views, by passing them through the medium of a chosen body of citizens, whose wisdom may best discern the true interest of their country, and whose patriotism and love of justice will be least likely to sacrifice it to temporary or partial considerations. Under such a regulation, it may well happen that the public voice, pronounced by the representatives of the people, will be more consonant to the public good than if pronounced by the people themselves, convened for the purpose. On the other hand, the effect may be inverted. Men of factious tempers, of local prejudices, or of sinister designs, may, by intrigue, by corruption, or by other means, first obtain the suffrages,[4] and then betray the interests, of the people. The question resulting is, whether small or extensive republics are more favorable to the election of proper guardians of the public weal;[5] and it is clearly decided in favor of the latter by two obvious considerations:

In the first place, it is to be remarked that, however small the republic may be, the representatives must be raised to a certain number, in order to guard against the cabals[6] of a few; and that, however large it may be, they must be limited to a certain number, in order to guard against the confusion of a multitude. Hence, the number of representatives in the two cases not being in proportion to that of the two constituents, and being proportionally greater in the small republic, it follows that, if the proportion of fit characters be not less in the large than in the small republic, the former will present a greater option, and consequently a greater probability of a fit choice.

In the next place, as each representative will be chosen by a greater number of citizens in the large than in the small republic, it will be more difficult for unworthy candidates to practise with success the vicious arts by which elections are too often carried; and the suffrages of the people being more free, will be more likely to centre in men who possess the most attractive merit and the most diffusive and established characters.

It must be confessed that in this, as in most other cases, there is a mean, on both sides of which inconveniences will be found to lie. By enlarging too much the number of electors, you render the representative too little acquainted with all their local circumstances and lesser interests; as by reducing it too much, you render him unduly attached to these, and too little fit to comprehend and pursue great and national objects. The federal Constitution forms a happy combination in this respect; the great and aggregate interests being referred to the national, the local and particular to the State legislatures.

The other point of difference is, the greater number of citizens and extent of territory which may be brought within the compass of republican than of democratic government; and it is this circumstance principally which renders factious combinations less to be dreaded in the former than in the latter. The smaller the society, the fewer probably will be the distinct parties and interests composing it; the fewer the distinct parties and interests, the more frequently will a majority be found of the same party; and the smaller the number of individuals composing a majority, and the smaller the compass within which they are placed, the more easily will they concert and execute their plans of oppression. Extend the sphere, and you take in a greater variety of parties and interests; you make it less probable that a majority of the whole will have a common motive to invade the rights of other citizens; or if such a common motive exists, it will be more difficult for all who feel it to discover their own strength, and to act in unison with each other. Besides other impediments, it may be remarked that, where there is a conscious-

---

[4]Votes.
[5]Welfare, well-being.
[6]Conspiracies.

ness of unjust or dishonorable purposes, communication is always checked by distrust in proportion to the number whose concurrence is necessary.

Hence, it clearly appears, that the same advantage which a republic has over a democracy, in controlling the effects of faction, is enjoyed by a large over a small republic,—is enjoyed by the Union over the States composing it. Does the advantage consist in the substitution of representatives whose enlightened views and virtuous sentiments render them superior to local prejudices and to schemes of injustice? It will not be denied that the representation of the Union will be most likely to possess these requisite endowments. Does it consist in the greater security afforded by a greater variety of parties, against the event of any one party being able to outnumber and oppress the rest? In an equal degree does the increased variety of parties comprised within the Union, increase this security? Does it, in fine, consist in the greater obstacles opposed to the concert and accomplishment of the secret wishes of an unjust and interested majority? Here, again, the extent of the Union gives it the most palpable advantage.

The influence of factious leaders may kindle a flame within their particular States, but will be unable to spread a general conflagration through the other States. A religious sect may degenerate into a political faction in a part of the Confederacy; but the variety of sects dispersed over the entire face of it must secure the national councils against any danger from that source. A rage for paper money, for an abolition of debts, for an equal division of property, or for any other improper or wicked project, will be less apt to pervade the whole body of the Union than a particular member of it; in the same proportion as such a malady is more likely to taint a particular county or district, than an entire State.

In the extent and proper structure of the Union, therefore, we behold a republican remedy for the diseases most incident to republican government. And according to the degree of pleasure and pride we feel in being republicans, ought to be our zeal in cherishing the spirit and supporting the character of Federalists.

PUBLIUS.

1787

NO. 23

[POWERS NECESSARY FOR FEDERAL GOVERNMENT'S PURPOSES]

ALEXANDER HAMILTON

To the People of the State of New York:

The necessity of a Constitution, at least equally energetic with the one proposed, to the preservation of the Union, is the point at the examination of which we are now arrived.

This inquiry will naturally divide itself into three branches—the objects to be provided for by the federal government, the quantity of power necessary to the accomplishment of those objects, the persons upon whom that power ought to operate. Its distribution and organization will more properly claim our attention under the succeeding head.

The principal purposes to be answered by union are these—the common defence of the members; the preservation of the public peace, as well against internal convulsions as external attacks; the regulation of commerce with other nations and between the States; the superintendence of our intercourse, political and commercial, with foreign countries.

The authorities essential to the common defence are these: to raise armies; to build and equip fleets; to prescribe rules for the government of both; to direct their operations; to provide for their support. These powers ought to exist without limitation, *because it is impossible to foresee or define the extent and variety of national exigencies, or the correspondent extent and variety of the means which may be necessary to satisfy them.* The circumstances that endanger the safety of nations are infinite, and for this reason no constitutional shackles can wisely be imposed on the power to which the care of it is committed. This power ought to be co-extensive with all the possible combinations of such circumstances; and ought to be under the direction of the same councils which are appointed to preside over the common defence.

This is one of those truths which, to a correct and unprejudiced mind, carries its own evidence along with it; and may be obscured, but cannot be made plainer by argument or reasoning. It rests upon axioms as simple as they are universal; the *means* ought to be proportioned to the *end;* the persons, from whose agency the attainment of any *end* is expected, ought to possess the *means* by which it is to be attained.

Whether there ought to be a federal government intrusted with the care of the common defence, is a question in the first instance, open for discussion; but the moment it is decided in the affirmative, it will follow, that that government ought to be clothed with all the powers requisite to complete execution of its trust. And unless it can be shown that the circumstances which may affect the public safety are reducible within certain determinate limits; unless the contrary of this position can be fairly and rationally disputed, it must be admitted, as a necessary consequence, that there can be no limitation of that authority which is to provide for the defence and protection of the community, in any matter essential to its efficacy—that is, in any matter essential to the *formation, direction,* or *support* of the NATIONAL FORCES.

Defective as the present Confederation has been proved to be, this principle appears to have been fully recognized by the framers of it; though they have not made proper or adequate provision for its exercise. Congress have an unlimited discretion to make requisitions of men and money; to govern the army and navy; to direct their operations. As their requisitions are made constitutionally binding upon the States, who are in fact under the most solemn obligations to furnish the supplies required of them, the intention evidently was, that the United States should command whatever resources were by them judged requisite to the "common defence and general welfare." It was presumed that a sense of their true interests, and a regard to the dictates of good faith, would be found sufficient pledges for the punctual performance of the duty of the members to the federal head.

The experiment has, however, demonstrated that this expectation was ill-founded and illusory; and the observations, made under the last head,[1] will, I imagine, have sufficed to convince the impartial and discerning, that there is an absolute necessity for an entire change in the first principles of the system; that if we are in earnest about giving the Union energy and duration, we must abandon the vain project of legislating upon the States in their collective capacities; we must extend the laws of the federal government to the individual citizens of America; we must discard the fallacious scheme of quotas and requisitions, as equally impracticable and unjust. The result from all this is that the Union ought to be invested with full power to levy troops; to build and equip fleets; and to raise the revenues which will be required for the formation and support of an army and navy, in the customary and ordinary modes practised in other governments.

If the circumstances of our country are such as to demand a compound instead of a simple, a confederate instead of a sole, government, the essential point which will remain to be adjusted will be to discriminate the OBJECTS, as far as it can be done, which shall appertain to the different provinces or departments of power;

---

[1]*Federalists* Nos. 15–22 dealt with the defects and failure of the Articles of Confederation.

allowing to each the most ample authority for fulfilling the objects committed to its charge. Shall the Union be constituted the guardian of the common safety? Are fleets and armies and revenues necessary to this purpose? The government of the Union must be empowered to pass all laws, and to make all regulations which have relation to them. The same must be the case in respect to commerce, and to every other matter to which its jurisdiction is permitted to extend. Is the administration of justice between the citizens of the same State the proper department of the local governments? These must possess all the authorities which are connected with this object, and with every other that may be allotted to their particular cognizance and direction. Not to confer in each case a degree of power commensurate to the end, would be to violate the most obvious rules of prudence and propriety, and improvidently to trust the great interests of the nation to hands which are disabled from managing them with vigor and success.

Who so likely to make suitable provisions for the public defence, as that body to which the guardianship of the public safety is confided; which, as the centre of information, will best understand the extent and urgency of the dangers that threaten; as the representative of the WHOLE, will feel itself most deeply interested in the preservation of every part; which, from the responsibility implied in the duty assigned to it, will be most sensibly impressed with the necessity of proper exertions; and which, by the extension of its authority throughout the States, can alone establish uniformity and concert in the plans and measures by which the common safety is to be secured? Is there not a manifest inconsistency in devolving upon the federal government the care of the general defence, and leaving in the State governments the *effective* powers by which it is to be provided for? Is not a want of co-operation the infallible consequence of such a system? And will not weakness, disorder, an undue distribution of the burdens and calamities of war, an unnecessary and intolerable increase of expense, be its natural and inevitable concomitants? Have we not had unequivocal experience of its effects in the course of the revolution which we have just accomplished?

Every view we may take of the subject, as candid inquirers after truth, will serve to convince us, that it is both unwise and dangerous to deny the federal government an unconfined authority, as to all those objects which are intrusted to its management. It will indeed deserve the most vigilant and careful attention of the people, to see that it be modelled in such a manner as to admit of its being safely vested with the requisite powers. If any plan which has been, or may be, offered to our consideration, should not, upon a dispassionate inspection, be found to answer this description, it ought to be rejected. A government, the constitution of which renders it unfit to be trusted with all the powers which a free people *ought to delegate to any government*, would be an unsafe and improper depositary of the NATIONAL INTERESTS. Wherever THESE can with propriety be confided, the coincident powers may safely accompany them. This is the true result of all just reasoning upon the subject. And the adversaries of the plan promulgated by the convention ought to have confined themselves to showing, that the internal structure of the proposed government was such as to render it unworthy of the confidence of the people. They ought not to have wandered into inflammatory declamations and unmeaning cavils about the extent of the powers. The POWERS are not too extensive for the OBJECTS of federal administration, or, in other words, for the management of our NATIONAL INTERESTS; nor can any satisfactory argument be framed to show that they are chargeable with such an excess. If it be true, as has been insinuated by some of the writers on the other side, that the difficulty arises from the nature of the thing, and that the extent of the country will not permit us to form a government in which such ample powers can safely be reposed, it would prove that we ought to contract our views, and resort to the expedient of separate confederacies, which will move within more practicable spheres. For the absurdity must continually stare us in the face of confiding to a government the direction of the most essential national interests, without daring to trust it to the authorities which are indispensable to their proper and efficient management. Let us not attempt to reconcile contradictions, but firmly embrace a rational alternative.

I trust, however, that the impracticability of one general system cannot be shown. I am greatly mistaken, if any thing of weight has yet been advanced of this tendency; and I flatter myself, that the observations which have been made in the course of these papers have served to place the reverse of that position in as clear a light as any matter still in the womb of time and experience can be susceptible of. (This, at all events, must be evident, that the very difficulty itself, drawn from the extent of the country, is the strongest argument in favor of an energetic government; for any other can certainly never preserve the Union of so large an empire.) If we embrace the tenets of those who oppose the adoption of the proposed Constitution, as the standard of our political creed, we cannot fail to verify the gloomy doctrines which predict the impracticability of a national system pervading entire limits of the present Confederacy.   PUBLIUS.

1787

NO. 51
[SEPARATION OF POWERS][1]
JAMES MADISON[2]

To the People of the State of New York:

To what expedient, then, shall we finally resort, for maintaining in practice the necessary partition of power among the several departments, as laid down in the Constitution? The only answer that can be given is, that as all these exterior provisions are found to be inadequate, the defect must be supplied, by so contriving the interior structure of the government as that its several constituent parts may, by their mutual relations, be the means of keeping each other in their proper places. Without presuming to undertake a full development of this important idea, I will hazard a few general observations, which may perhaps place it in a clearer light, and enable us to form a more correct judgment of the principles and structure of the government planned by the convention.

In order to lay a due foundation for that separate and distinct exercise of the different powers of government, which to a certain extent is admitted on all hands to be essential to the preservation of liberty, it is evident that each department should have a will of its own; and consequently should be so constituted that the members of each should have as little agency as possible in the appointment of the members of the others. Were this principle rigorously adhered to, it would require that all the appointments for the supreme executive, legislative, and judiciary magistracies should be drawn from the same fountain of authority, the people, through channels having no communication whatever with one another. Perhaps such a plan of constructing the several departments would be less difficult in practice than it may in contemplation appear. Some difficulties, however, and some additional expense would attend the execution of it. Some deviations, therefore, from the principle must be admitted. In the constitution of the judiciary department in particular, it might be inexpedient to insist rigorously on the principle: first, because peculiar qualifications being essential in the members, the primary consideration ought to be to select that mode of choice which best secures

---

[1] For extensive commentary on *Federalist* No. 51, see Gary Wills, *Explaining America: The Federalist* (1981).
[2] Authorship of this essay has been disputed and sometimes ascribed to Hamilton; it is now generally agreed that the author of No. 51 was Madison.

these qualifications; secondly, because the permanent tenure by which the appointments are held in that department, must soon destroy all sense of dependence on the authority conferring them.

It is equally evident, that the members of each department should be as little dependent as possible on those of the others, for the emoluments annexed to their offices. Were the executive magistrate, or the judges, not independent of the legislature in this particular, their independence in every other would be merely nominal.

But the great security against a gradual concentration of the several powers in the same department, consists in giving to those who administer each department the necessary constitutional means and personal motives to resist encroachments of the others. The provision for defence must in this, as in all other cases, be made commensurate to the danger of attack. Ambition must be made to counteract ambition. The interest of the man must be connected with the constitutional rights of the place. It may be a reflection on human nature, that such devices should be necessary to control the abuses of government. But what is government itself, but the greatest of all reflections on human nature? If men were angels, no government would be necessary. If angels were to govern men, neither external nor internal controls on government would be necessary. In framing a government which is to be administered by men over men, the great difficulty lies in this: you must first enable the government to control the governed; and in the next place oblige it to control itself. A dependence on the people is, no doubt, the primary control on the government; but experience has taught mankind the necessity of auxiliary precautions.

This policy of supplying, by opposite and rival interests, the defect of better motives, might be traced through the whole system of human affairs, private as well as public. We see it particularly displayed in all the subordinate distributions of power, where the constant aim is to divide and arrange the several offices in such a manner as that each may be a check on the other—that the private interest of every individual may be a sentinel over the public rights. These inventions of prudence cannot be less requisite in the distribution of the supreme powers of the State.

But it is not possible to give to each department an equal power of self-defence. In republican government, the legislative authority necessarily predominates. The remedy for this inconveniency is to divide the legislature into different branches; and to render them, by different modes of election and different principles of action, as little connected with each other as the nature of their common functions and their common dependence on the society will admit. It may even be necessary to guard against dangerous encroachments by still further precautions. As the weight of the legislative authority requires that it should be thus divided, the weakness of the executive may require, on the other hand, that it should be fortified. An absolute negative on the legislature appears, at first view, to be the natural defence with which the executive magistrate should be armed. But perhaps it would be neither altogether safe nor alone sufficient. On ordinary occasions it might not be exerted with the requisite firmness, and on extraordinary occasions it might be perfidiously abused. May not this defect of an absolute negative be supplied by some qualified connection between this weaker department and the weaker branch of the stronger department, by which the latter may be led to support the constitutional rights of the former, without being too much detached from the rights of its own department?

If the principles on which these observations are founded be just, as I persuade myself they are, and they be applied as a criterion to the several State constitutions, and to the federal Constitution, it will be found that if the latter does not perfectly correspond with them, the former are infinitely less able to bear such a test.

There are, moreover, two considerations particularly applicable to the federal system of America, which place that system in a very interesting point of view.

First. In a single republic, all the power surrendered by the people is submitted to the administration of a single government; and the usurpations are guarded against by a division of the government into distinct and separate departments. In the compound republic of America, the power surrendered by the people is first divided between two distinct governments, and then the portion allotted to each subdivided among distinct and separate departments. Hence a double security arises to the rights of the people. The different governments will control each other, at the same time that each will be controlled by itself.

Second. It is of great importance in a republic not only to guard the society against the oppression of its rulers, but to guard one part of the society against the injustice of the other part. Different interests necessarily exist in different classes of citizens. If a majority be united by a common interest, the rights of the minority will be insecure. There are but two methods of providing against this evil: the one by creating a will in the community independent of the majority—that is, of the society itself; the other, by comprehending in the society so many separate descriptions of citizens as will render an unjust combination of a majority of the whole very improbable, if not impracticable. The first method prevails in all governments possessing an hereditary or self-appointed authority. This, at best, is but a precarious security; because a power independent of the society may as well espouse the unjust views of the major, as the rightful interests of the minor party, and may possibly be turned against both parties. The second method will be exemplified in the federal republic of the United States. Whilst all authority in it will be derived from and dependent on the society, the society itself will be broken into so many parts, interests, and classes of citizens, that the rights of individuals, or of the minority, will be in little danger from interested combinations of the majority. In a free government the security for civil rights must be the same as that for religious rights. It consists in the one case in the multiplicity of interests, and in the other in the multiplicity of sects. The degree of security in both cases will depend on the number of interests and sects; and this may be presumed to depend on the extent of country and number of people comprehended under the same government. This view of the subject must particularly recommend a proper federal system to all the sincere and considerate friends of republican government, since it shows that in exact proportion as the territory of the Union may be formed into more circumscribed Confederacies, or States, oppressive combinations of a majority will be facilitated; the best security, under the republican forms, for the rights of every class of citizens, will be diminished; and consequently the stability and independence of some member of the government, the only other security, must be proportionally increased. Justice is the end of government. It is the end of civil society. It ever has been and ever will be pursued until it be obtained, or until liberty be lost in the pursuit. In a society under the forms of which the stronger faction can readily unite and oppress the weaker, anarchy may as truly be said to reign as in a state of nature, where the weaker individual is not secured against the violence of the stronger; and as, in the latter state, even the stronger individuals are prompted, by the uncertainty of their condition, to submit to a government which may protect the weak as well as themselves; so, in the former state, will the more powerful factions or parties be gradually induced, by a like motive, to wish for a government which will protect all parties, the weaker as well as the more powerful. It can be little doubted that if the State of Rhode Island was separated from the Confederacy and left to itself, the insecurity of rights under the popular form of government within such narrow limits would be displayed by such reiterated oppressions of factious majorities that some power altogether independent of the people would soon be called for by the voice of the very factions whose misrule had proved the necessity of it. In the extended republic of the United States, and among the great variety of interests, parties, and sects which it embraces, a coalition of a majority of the whole society could seldom take place on any other principles than those of justice and the general good; whilst there being thus less danger to a minor from the will of a major party, there must be less pretext, also, to provide for the security of the former, by introducing into the government a will not dependent on the latter, or, in other words, a will independent of the society itself. It is no less certain than it is important, notwithstanding the contrary opinions which have been entertained, that the larger the society, provided it lie within a practical sphere, the more duly capable it will be of self-government. And happily for the *republican cause*, the practicable sphere may be carried to a very great extent, by a judicious modification and mixture of the *federal principle.*

PUBLIUS.

1788

THOMAS JEFFERSON
(1743–1826)

"America was conquered, and her settlements made and firmly established, at the expense of individuals. . . . Their own blood was spilt in acquiring lands for their settlement, their own fortunes expended in making that settlement effectual." "Kings are the servants, not the proprietors of the people." "The great principles of right and wrong are legible to every reader." "The God who gave us life, gave us liberty at the same time: the hand of force may destroy, but cannot disjoin them." These phrases appeared in a pamphlet entitled *A Summary View of the Rights of British America,* published in 1774. It was written by Thomas Jefferson, a thirty-one-year-old Virginian.

Jefferson had written his pamphlet hoping it would be adopted by a Virginia convention called to respond to England's repeated abrogation of colonists' rights. It was not adopted because it appeared too bold, but it was read widely throughout the colonies. In a few months, events and public sentiment would catch up with its views; and its ringing sentences would become the model for the call for independence approved by all the colonies. Jefferson would be its author.

At first glance, his origins and background make Jefferson an unlikely candidate to become the most eloquent spokesman for freedom at the founding of the nation. He was brought up in rural Albemarle County, Virginia. When his father died in 1757, the fourteen-year-old Jefferson (as the oldest son) inherited 2,750 acres of land and a large number of slaves. His mother was a Randolph, one of the wealthiest and most socially prominent families of Virginia.

All these ingredients might well have created in him an aristocratic and elitist outlook on life, but several leavening elements tended to make his views more radical. Jefferson obtained an early knowledge of Latin, Greek, and French and at seventeen entered William and Mary College in Williamsburg, the seat of colonial Virginia's capital. There he had a succession of teachers who sparked his interest in science and philosophy. He studied with George Wythe, the foremost teacher of law in Virginia, and was admitted to the bar in 1767. Some time along the way he began to question the historical reliability of the Bible and lost faith in conventional religion (but not in traditional morality). He read voraciously and his large library (later to become the nucleus collection of the Library of Congress) was a prized possession.

Jefferson married in 1772, moved into the unfinished Monticello, and began a family. Through marriage, his land holdings increased. In settled times, he could have lived out his life as a country squire, indulging his interests in philosophy and scientific experiment and managing his large estate. But the times were unsettled and unsettling, and his political genius was exposed to all in his *Summary View* (1774). He was called on to represent Virginia at the Continental Congress in Philadelphia, where he was assigned to the committee to draft the Declaration of Independence. On the committee, the other members (including John Adams and Benjamin Franklin) insisted that the thirty-three-year-old Jefferson write the draft. When Jefferson asked why he rather than Adams, Adams replied: "You can write ten times better than I can."

"We hold these truths to be self-evident: that all men are created equal; that they are endowed by their creator with certain unalienable rights; that among these are life, liberty, and the pursuit of happiness." These are perhaps the best known phrases ever written by an American. Although they were written for a specific situation long since passed into history, most citizens vaguely believe that they somehow have the force of an article of the Constitution. Such is the power of language to transcend its time and to transform a political position paper into a Founding document with quasi-legal force of permanent law.

Jefferson returned to Virginia, served in the House of Delegates, was elected governor in 1779 (succeeding Patrick Henry), and was near the end of his term when the British invaded Virginia, forcing the government to flee Richmond. In the confusion, Jefferson appeared to have abdicated his office. But an investigation cleared him, and he retired to his farm and books in 1781. There he began work on the one book he found the time in his life to write, *Notes on the State of Virginia,* started in response to a series of queries by a French diplomat put to Jefferson about Virginia (and also American) geography, government, religion, manners, industry, commerce, and culture. Jefferson used the opportunity to provide facts, descriptions, views, opinions, and ideas in essays filled with candid revelations, surprising asides, and venturesome thoughts—all in a style simple yet subtle, graceful yet vigorous.

Jefferson's wife died in 1782, a deep personal loss that made him more receptive than before to requests for his help in public service. He was elected to Congress in 1783, and then sent to France to assist John Adams and Benjamin Franklin in negotiating treaties of commerce. In 1785, he succeeded Franklin as minister to France, remaining there for the next four years. He witnessed with approval the beginnings of the French Revolution before his return to America in 1789.

In 1790 President George Washington persuaded him to serve as the first Secretary of State, but his tenure in office was marked by increasingly bitter conflict with Secretary of the Treasury Alexander Hamilton. In the presidential elections of 1796, he was defeated by John Adams and served as vice president. Finally, the Federalist rule of Washington and Adams was broken by the election of 1800. Jefferson and Aaron Burr (1756–1836), both of the Democratic-Republican party, tied in electoral votes for president, and the

House of Representatives decided in Jefferson's favor. He was the first president to be inaugurated in the new national capital, Washington, D.C. He held the office through two terms, and the major achievement of his administration was the Louisiana Purchase, for which Jefferson (with questionable authority) paid $15 million to Napoleon for the territory beyond the Mississippi River that doubled the land mass of the young country.

On his retirement from office in 1809, Jefferson returned to Monticello, seldom venturing far from his farm and books during the remaining seventeen years of his life. There is some evidence that Jefferson took as his mistress one of the Monticello quadroon slaves, Sally Hemings, who was the half-sister of his deceased wife. The rumor first circulated in the early nineteenth century, but the story was fully and responsibly explored in Fawn M. Brodie's book, *Thomas Jefferson, an Intimate History* (1974). Although the evidence is ambiguous, Jefferson's bachelorhood from about the age of forty renders the story plausible. Jefferson's biographers have been cognizant of the ironies of Jefferson's repeated condemnation of slavery in the light of his retaining his slaves and even perhaps having an intimate relationship with one of them. He was, indeed, a complicated—and very human—being.

Much of his time in retirement Jefferson spent in reading and writing a voluminous correspondence carried on with an incredible array of friends, philosophers, and intellectuals. Jefferson wrote over 18,000 letters, among them some of his most brilliant paragraphs; his collected works will run to sixty volumes when completed. It is interesting to note that the modern American poet Ezra Pound was so impressed by the correspondence of Thomas Jefferson and John Adams (continued until the death of both in 1826) that he culled from their letters to one another (and to others) quotations for many of his lines in clusters of his *Cantos* (1930–69). He said of Jefferson that he was "perhaps the last American official to have any general sense of civilization."

During his long career, Jefferson worked actively for separation of church and state and for freedom of conscience in religion. Although as an eldest son he benefitted from primogeniture (inheritance limited to the eldest son), he worked to abolish it in Virginia. His main complaint against the Constitution as first written was the absence of a Bill of Rights, subsequently supplied in the first ten amendments. Much of his time during his retirement years was spent in designing and building the University of Virginia, at Charlottesville, in view of Monticello.

No list of his achievements seems to exhaust the reality of his accomplishments. But he insisted on this simple epitaph: "Author of the Declaration of Independence, of the Statute of Virginia for Religious Freedom, and Father of the University of Virginia." His death occurred on July 4, 1826, just fifty years after the Declaration he wrote gave birth to the United States of America.

ADDITIONAL READING

The Papers of Thomas Jefferson, ed. Julian P. Boyd, in progress since 1950.

Carl Becker, *The Declaration of Independence*, 1922; Adrienne Koch, *The Philosophy of Thomas Jefferson*, 1943; Daniel Boorstin, *The Lost World of Thomas Jefferson*, 1948; Dumas Malone, *Jefferson and His Time*, 5 vols., 1948–74; John Dos Passos, *The Head and Heart of Thomas Jefferson*, 1954; James B. Conant, *Jefferson and the Development of American Public Education*,

1965; Fawn M. Brodie, *Thomas Jefferson, an Intimate History*, 1974; Gary Wills, *Inventing America: Jefferson's Declaration of Independence*, 1978; William K. Bottorff, *Thomas Jefferson*, 1979; Robert Ferguson, "Mysterious Obligation: Jefferson's *Notes on the State of Virginia*," *Law and Letters in American Culture*, 1984; Richard K. Matthews, *The Radical Politics of Thomas Jefferson: A Revisionist View*, 1984; Charles A. Miller, *Jefferson and Nature*, 1988.

TEXTS

"The Declaration of Independence" from *Autobiography of Thomas Jefferson, 1743–1790*, ed. Paul Leicester Ford, 1914; *Notes on the State of Virginia*, ed. William Peden, 1955; Letters (other than those to John Adams) and the First Inaugural Address, from *The Works of Thomas Jefferson*, 12 vols., ed. Paul Leicester Ford, 1904–05; *The Adams-Jefferson Letters*, ed. Lester J. Cappon, 1959. Some changes have been made in spelling and punctuation to conform with contemporary English.

from Autobiography

THE DECLARATION OF INDEPENDENCE
[COMPOSITION AND REVISION][1]

It appearing in the course of these debates that the colonies of N. York, New Jersey, Pennsylvania, Delaware, Maryland, and South Carolina were not yet matured for falling from the parent stem, but that they were fast advancing to that state, it was thought most prudent to wait a while for them, and to postpone the final decision to July 1, but that this might occasion as little delay as possible a committee was appointed to prepare a declaration of independence. The committee were J. Adams, Dr. Franklin, Roger Sherman, Robert R. Livingston and myself. Committees were also appointed at the same time to prepare a plan of confederation for the colonies, and to state the terms proper to be proposed for foreign alliance. The committee for drawing the Declaration of Independence desired me to do it. It was accordingly done, and being approved by them, I reported it to the house on Friday the 28th of June when it was read and ordered to lie on the table. On Monday, the 1st of July the house resolved itself into a committee of the whole and resumed the consideration of the original motion made by the delegates of Virginia, which being again debated through the day, was carried in the affirmative by the votes of N. Hampshire, Connecticut, Massachusetts, Rhode Island, N. Jersey, Maryland, Virginia, N. Carolina, and Georgia. S. Carolina and Pennsylvania voted against it. Delaware having but two members present, they were divided. The delegates for New York declared they were for it themselves and were assured their constituents were for it, but that their instructions having been drawn near a twelvemonth before, when reconciliation was still the general object, they were enjoined by them to do nothing which should impede that object. They therefore thought themselves not justifiable in voting on either side, and asked leave to withdraw from the question, which was given them. The committee rose and reported their resolution to the house. Mr. Edward Rutledge

---

[1]At the second Continental Congress, in June 1776, Richard Henry Lee, "the Cicero of America," moved that "these united Colonies are, and of a right ought to be, free and independent states." On June 11 the Congress approved a committee to "prepare a declaration" of independence. Committee members included Benjamin Franklin, John Adams, and Thomas Jefferson. Jefferson, thirty-three years old, was appointed to provide a draft, which was presented to the Congress on June 28. The Declaration was approved on July 4. Jefferson wrote this account in his *Autobiography*.

of S. Carolina then requested the determination might be put off to the next day, as he believed his colleagues, though they disapproved of the resolution, would then join in it for the sake of unanimity. The ultimate question whether the house would agree to the resolution of the committee was accordingly postponed to the next day, when it was again moved and S. Carolina concurred in voting for it. In the meantime a third member had come post[2] from the Delaware counties and turned the vote of that colony in favour of the resolution. Members of a different sentiment attending that morning from Pennsylvania also, their vote was changed, so that the whole twelve colonies who were authorized to vote at all, gave their voices for it; and within a few days, the convention of N. York approved of it and thus supplied the void occasioned by the withdrawing of her delegates from the vote.

Congress proceeded the same day to consider the Declaration of Independence which had been reported and lain on the table the Friday preceding, and on Monday referred to a committee of the whole. The pusillanimous idea that we had friends in England worth keeping terms with still haunted the minds of many. For this reason those passages which conveyed censures on the people of England were struck out, lest they should give them offense. The clause too, reprobating the enslaving the inhabitants of Africa, was struck out in complaisance to South Carolina and Georgia, who had never attempted to restrain the importation of slaves, and who on the contrary still wished to continue it. Our northern brethren also I believe felt a little tender under those censures; for though their people have very few slaves themselves; yet they had been pretty considerable carriers of them to others. The debates having taken up the greater parts of the 2d 3d and 4th days of July were, in the evening of the last, closed; the Declaration was reported by the committee, agreed to by the house and signed by every member present except Mr. Dickinson.[3] As the sentiments of men are known not only by what they receive, but what they reject also, I will state the form of the Declaration as originally reported. The parts struck out by Congress shall be distinguished by a black line drawn under them; and those inserted by them shall be placed in the margin or in a concurrent column.

A DECLARATION BY THE REPRESENTATIVES OF THE UNITED STATES OF AMERICA, IN GENERAL CONGRESS ASSEMBLED

When in the course of human events it becomes necessary for one people to dissolve the political bands which have connected them with another, and to assume among the powers of the earth the separate and equal station to which the laws of nature and of nature's God entitle them, a decent respect to the opinions of mankind requires that they should declare the causes which impel them to the separation.

We hold these truths to be self-evident: that all men are created equal;[1] that they are endowed by their Creator with inher-   certain
ent and inalienable rights; that among these are life, liberty, and the pursuit of happiness;[2] that to secure these rights, governments are instituted among men, deriving their just powers

---

[2]By postal stagecoach.
[3]John Dickinson, a Pennsylvania delegate who had opposed the Declaration.
[1]I.e., in endowment with the rights described in the following clauses, including the right to institute or change a form of government to assure these rights. Note: underlined passages were deleted or revised by the Congress; passages in the margin were substituted or added.

[2]Cf. John Wise (1652–1725), *A Vindication of the Government of New-England Churches* (1717): "And thus every man must be acknowledged equal to every man. . . . The end of all good government is to cultivate humanity, and promote the happiness of all, and the good of every man in all his rights, his life, liberty, estate, honor, etc. without injury or abuse done to any."

from the consent of the governed; that whenever any form of government becomes destructive of these ends, it is the right of the people to alter or abolish it, and to institute new government, laying its foundation on such principles, and organizing its powers in such form, as to them shall seem most likely to effect their safety and happiness. Prudence indeed will dictate that governments long established should not be changed for light and transient causes; and accordingly all experience hath shown that mankind are more disposed to suffer while evils are sufferable, then to right themselves by abolishing the forms to which they are accustomed. But when a long train of abuses and usurpations <u>begun at a distinguished[3] period and</u> pursuing invariably <u>the same object,</u> evinces a design to reduce them under absolute despotism, it is their right, it is their duty to throw off such government, and to provide new guards for their future security. Such has been the patient sufferance of these colonies; and such is now the necessity which constrains them to <u>expunge</u> their former systems of government. The history of the present king of Great Britain[4] is a history of <u>unremitting</u> injuries and usurpations, <u>among which appears no solitary fact to contradict the uniform tenor of the rest but all have</u> in direct object the establishment of an absolute tyranny over these states. To prove this let facts be submitted to a candid world <u>for the truth of which we pledge a faith yet unsullied by falsehood.</u>

alter

repeated
all having

He has refused his assent to laws the most wholesome and necessary for the public good.

He has forbidden his governors[5] to pass laws of immediate and pressing importance, unless suspended in their operation till his assent should be obtained; and when so suspended, he has utterly neglected to attend to them.

He has refused to pass other laws for the accommodation of large districts of people, unless those people would relinquish the right of representation in the legislature, a right inestimable to them, and formidable to tyrants only.

He has called together legislative bodies at places unusual, uncomfortable, and distant from the depository of their public records, for the sole purpose of fatiguing them into compliance with his measures.

He has dissolved representative houses repeatedly <u>and continually</u> for opposing with manly firmness his invasions on the rights of the people.

He has refused for a long time after such dissolutions to cause others to be elected, whereby the legislative powers, incapable of annihilation, have returned to the people at large for their exercise, the state remaining in the meantime exposed to all the dangers of invasion from without and convulsions within.

He has endeavored to prevent the population of these states; for that purpose obstructing the laws for naturalization of foreigners, refusing to pass others to encourage their migrations

---

[3]Determined.
[4]King Geoge III (r. 1760–1820).
[5]The royal governors of the colonies appointed by him.

hither, and raising the conditions of new appropriations of lands.

He has <u>suffered</u> the administration of justice totally to cease in some of these states refusing his assent to laws for establishing judiciary powers.   *obstructed by*

He has made <u>our</u> judges dependent on his will alone, for the tenure of their offices, and the amount and payment of their salaries.

He has erected a multitude of new offices <u>by a self-assumed power</u> and sent hither swarms of new officers to harass our people and eat out their substance.

He has kept among us in times of peace standing armies <u>and ships of war</u> without the consent of our legislatures.

He has affected to render the military independent of, and superior to, the civil power.

He has combined with others[6] to subject us to a jurisdiction foreign to our constitutions and unacknowledged by our laws, giving his assent to their acts of pretended legislation for quartering large bodies of armed troops among us; for protecting them by a mock-trial from punishment for any murders which they should commit on the inhabitants of these states; for cutting off our trade with all parts of the world; for imposing taxes on us without our consent; for depriving us [ ] of the benefits of trial by jury; for transporting us beyond seas to be tried for pretended offences; for abolishing the free system of English laws in a neighboring province, establishing therein an arbitrary government, and enlarging its boundaries, so as to render it at once an example and fit instrument for introducing the same absolute rule into these <u>states</u>;[7] for taking away our charters, abolishing our most valuable laws, and altering fundamentally the forms of our governments; for suspending our own legislatures, and declaring themselves invested with power to legislate for us in all cases whatsoever.   *in many cases* ... *colonies*

He has abdicated government here <u>withdrawing his governors, and declaring us out of his allegiance and protection.</u>   *by declaring us out of his protection, and waging war against us.*

He has plundered our seas, ravaged our coasts, burnt our towns, and destroyed the lives of our people.

He is at this time transporting large armies of foreign mercenaries[8] to complete the works of death, desolation and tyranny already begun with circumstances of cruelty and perfidy [ ] unworthy the head of a civilized nation.   *scarcely paralleled in the most barbarous ages, and totally*

He has constrained our fellow citizens taken captive on the high seas to bear arms against their country, to become the executioners of their friends and brethren, or to fall themselves by their hands.

He has [ ] endeavored to bring on the inhabitants of our frontiers the merciless Indian savages, whose known rule of warfare is an undistinguished destruction of all ages, sexes, and conditions <u>of existence.</u>   *excited domestic insurrection among us, and has*

---

[6]The British Parliament.
[7]After the Boston Tea Party of December 1773, the British Parliament in 1774 passed the five Intolerable Acts, one of which, the Quebec Act, extended Canada's boundaries to the Ohio River and recognized Roman Catholicism in Quebec.
[8]The German mercenaries.

He has incited treasonable insurrections of our fellow-citizens, with the allurements of forfeiture and confiscation of our property.

He has waged cruel war against human nature itself, violating its most sacred rights of life and liberty in the persons of a distant people who never offended him, captivating and carrying them into slavery in another hemisphere, or to incur miserable death in their transportation thither. This piratical warfare, the opprobrium of INFIDEL powers, is the warfare of the CHRISTIAN king of Great Britain. Determined to keep open a market where MEN should be bought and sold, he has prostituted his negative[9] for suppressing every legislative attempt to prohibit or to restrain this execrable commerce. And that this assemblage of horrors might want no fact of distinguished die, he is now exciting those very people to rise in arms among us, and to purchase that liberty of which he has deprived them, by murdering the people on whom he also obtruded them: thus paying off former crimes committed against the LIBERTIES of one people, with crimes which he urges them to commit against the LIVES of another.

In every stage of these oppressions we have petitioned for redress in the most humble terms: our repeated petitions have been answered only by repeated injuries.

A prince whose character is thus marked by every act which may define a tyrant is unfit to be the ruler of a [ ] people who   free
mean to be free. Future ages will scarcely believe that the hardiness of one man adventured, within the short compass of twelve years only, to lay a foundation so broad and so undisguised for tyranny over a people fostered and fixed in principles of freedom.

Nor have we been wanting in attention to our British brethren. We have warned them from time to time of attempts by   an unwarrantable
their legislature to extend a jurisdiction over these our states.   us
We have reminded them of the circumstances of our emigration and settlement here, no one of which could warrant so strange a pretension: that these were effected at the expense of our own blood and treasure, unassisted by the wealth or the strength of Great Britain: that in constituting indeed our several forms of government, we had adopted one common king, thereby laying a foundation for perpetual league and amity with them: but that submission to their parliament was no part of our constitution,   have
nor ever in idea, if history may be credited: and, we [ ] appealed   and we have
to their native justice and magnanimity as well as to the ties of   conjured them by
our common kindred to disavow these usurpations which were   would inevitably
likely to interrupt our connection and correspondence. They too have been deaf to the voice of justice and of consanguinity, and when occasions have been given them, by the regular course of their laws, of removing from their councils the disturbers of our harmony, they have, by their free election, re-established them in power. At this very time too they are permitting their chief magistrate to send over not only soldiers of our common blood,

---

[9]Vetoed.

but Scotch and foreign mercenaries to invade and destroy us. These facts have given the last stab to agonizing affection, and manly spirit bids us to renounce forever these unfeeling brethren. We must endeavor to forget our former love for them, and hold them as we hold the rest of mankind, enemies in war, in peace friends. We might have been a free and a great people together; but a communication of grandeur and of freedom it seems is below their dignity. Be it so, since they will have it. The road to happiness and to glory is open to us too. We will tread it apart from them, and acquiesce in the necessity which denounces[10] our eternal separation [ ]!

We must therefore and hold them as we hold the rest of mankind, enemies in war, in peace friends.

We therefore the representatives of the United States of America in General Congress assembled do in the name and by authority of the good people of these states reject and renounce all allegiance and subjection to the kings of Great Britain and all others who may hereafter claim by, through or under them: we utterly dissolve all political connection which may heretofore have subsisted between us and the people or parliament of Great Britain: and finally we do assert and declare these colonies to be free and independent states, and that as free and independent states, they have full power to levy war, conclude peace, contract alliances, establish commerce, and to do all other acts and things which independent states may of right do.

And for the support of this declaration we mutually pledge to each other our lives, our fortunes, and our sacred honor.

We therefore the representatives of the United States of America in General Congress assembled, appealing to the supreme judge of the world for the rectitude of our intentions, do in the name, and by the authority of the good people of these colonies, solemnly publish and declare that these united colonies are and of right ought to be free and independent states; that they are absolved from all allegiance to the British crown, and that all political connection between them and the state of Great Britain is, and ought to be, totally dissolved; and that as free and independent states they have full power to levy war, conclude peace, contract alliances, establish commerce and to do all other acts and things which independent states may of right do.

And for the support of this declaration, with a firm reliance on the protection of divine providence we mutually pledge to each other our lives, our fortunes, and our sacred honor.

The Declaration thus signed on the 4th, on paper was engrossed on parchment, and signed again on the 2d. of August.

1821　　　　　　　　　　　　　　　　　　　　　　　　　　　　*1829*

---

[10]Announces, gives formal notice.

from Notes on the State of Virginia[1]

from QUERY V: CASCADES
NATURAL BRIDGE[2]

The *Natural bridge*, the most sublime of Nature's works, though not compre-hended under the present head,[3] must not be pretermitted.[4] It is on the ascent of a hill, which seems to have been cloven through its length by some great convul-sion. The fissure, just at the bridge, is, by some admeasurements, 270 feet deep, by others only 205. It is about 45 feet wide at the bottom, and 90 feet at the top; this of course determines the length of the bridge, and its height from the water. Its breadth in the middle, is about 60 feet, but more at the ends, and the thickness of the mass at the summit of the arch, about 40 feet. A part of this thickness is constituted by a coat of earth, which gives growth to many large trees. The resi-due, with the hill on both sides, is one solid rock of limestone. The arch ap-proaches the Semi-elliptical form; but the larger axis of the ellipsis, which would be the cord of the arch, is many times longer than the ⟨semi-axis which gives it's height.⟩ Though the sides of this bridge are provided in some parts with a parapet of fixed rocks, yet few men have resolution to walk to them and look over into the abyss. You involuntarily fall on your hands and feet, creep to the parapet and peep over it. Looking down from this height about a minute, gave me a violent head ach. ⟨This painful sensation is relieved by a short, but pleasing view of the Blue ridge along the fissure downwards, and upwards by that of the Short hills, which, with the Purgatory mountain is a divergence from the North ridge; and, descending then to the valley below, the sensation becomes delightful in the ex-treme. It is impossible for the emotions, arising from the sublime, to be felt be-yond what they are here: so beautiful an arch, so elevated, so light, and springing, as it were, up to heaven, the rapture of the Spectator is really indiscribable! The fissure continues deep and narrow and, following the margin of the stream up-wards about three-eights of a mile you arrive at a limestone cavern, less remark-able, however, for height and extent than those before described. Its entrance into the hill is but a few feet above the bed of the stream.⟩ This bridge is in the county of Rockbridge, to which it has given name, and affords a public and commodious passage over a valley, which cannot be crossed elsewhere for a considerable dis-tance. The stream passing under it is called Cedar creek. It is a water of James river, and sufficient in the driest seasons to turn a grist-mill, though its fountain is not more than two miles above.

---

[1]As the colonies in the Revolutionary War (1775–83) struggled to free themselves from Britain, the desire for knowledge about this upstart country intensified, especially in France. In 1781, the Marquis de Barbe-Marbois, secre-tary of the French legation in Philadelphia, sent a series of twenty-three queries to Thomas Jefferson, who had just re-tired from the governorship of Virginia, concerning geog-raphy, ecology, customs, and history of the colony. Jeffer-son took the answering of the queries seriously and on the broadest possible terms, and he kept adding to his manu-script over the years. The *Notes* were published privately in 1784–85. In 1787, an edition was authorized in London when publication of an unauthorized French translation was rumored. The text here is based on the 1787 edition. Jefferson's later insertions are enclosed in angle brackets ⟨ ⟩.
[2]A bridge formed by nature itself, found on land near Lex-ington, Virginia, then owned by Jefferson.
[3]I.e., the bridge is not a "Cascade."
[4]Omitted.

from QUERY VI: PRODUCTIONS MINERAL, VEGETABLE,
AND ANIMAL

[THE SAVAGES OF THE NEW WORLD]

The opinion advanced by the Count de Buffon,[1] is 1. That the animals common both to the old and new world, are smaller in the latter. 2. That those peculiar to the new, are on a smaller scale. 3. That those which have been domesticated in both, have degenerated in America: and 4. That on the whole it exhibits fewer species. And the reason he thinks is, that the heats of America are less; that more waters are spread over its surface by nature, and fewer of these drained off by the hand of man. In other words, that *heat* is friendly, and *moisture* adverse to the production and development of large quadrupeds. I will not meet this hypothesis on its first doubtful ground, whether the climate of America be comparatively more humid? Because we are not furnished with observations sufficient to decide this question. And though, till it be decided, we are as free to deny, as others are to affirm the fact, yet for a moment let it be supposed. The hypothesis, after this supposition, proceeds to another; that *moisture* is unfriendly to animal growth. The truth of this is inscrutable to us by reasonings a priori.[2] Nature has hidden from us her modus agendi.[3] Our only appeal on such questions is to experience; and I think that experience is against the supposition. It is by the assistance of *heat* and *moisture* that vegetables are elaborated from the elements of earth, air, water, and fire. We accordingly see the more humid climates produce the greater quantity of vegetables. Vegetables are mediately or immediately the food of every animal: and in proportion to the quantity of food, we see animals not only multiplied in their numbers, but improved in their bulk, as far as the laws of their nature will admit. . . .

Hitherto I have considered this hypothesis as applied to brute animals only, and not in its extension to the man of America, whether aboriginal or transplanted. It is the opinion of Mons. de Buffon that the former furnishes no exception to it: "Although the savage of the new world is about the same height as man in our world, this does not suffice for him to constitute an exception to the general fact that all living nature has become smaller on that continent. The savage is feeble, and has small organs of generation; he has neither hair nor beard, and no ardor whatever for his female; although swifter than the European because he is better accustomed to running, he is, on the other hand, less strong in body; he is also less sensitive, and yet more timid and cowardly; he has no vivacity, no activity of mind; the activity of his body is less an exercise, a voluntary motion, than a necessary action caused by want; relieve him of hunger and thirst, and you deprive him of the active principle of all his movements; he will rest stupidly upon his legs or lying down entire days. There is no need for seeking further the cause of the isolated mode of life of these savages and their repugnance for society: the most precious spark of the fire of nature has been refused to them; they lack ardor for their females, and consequently have no love for their fellow men: not knowing this strongest and most tender of all affections, their other feelings are also cold and languid; they love their parents and children but little; the most intimate of all ties, the family connection, binds them therefore but loosely together; between family and family there is no tie at all; hence they have no communion, no commonwealth, no state of society. Physical love constitutes their only morality; their heart is icy, their society cold, and their rule harsh. They look upon their wives only as servants for all work, or as beasts of burden, which they load without con-

---

[1]George-Louis Leclerc Buffon (1707–1788), French naturalist who helped found zoology as a science; his *Natural History* (1749–88) indicated degeneration of species on the North American continent.

[2]Based on theory, not experience.
[3]Way of operating.

sideration with the burden of their hunting, and which they compel without mercy, without gratitude, to perform tasks which are often beyond their strength. They have only few children, and they take little care of them. Everywhere the original defect appears: they are indifferent because they have little sexual capacity, and this indifference to the other sex is the fundamental defect which weakens their nature, prevents its development, and—destroying the very germs of life— uproots society at the same time. Man is here no exception to the general rule. Nature, by refusing him the power of love, has treated him worse and lowered him deeper than any animal." An afflicting picture indeed, which, for the honor of human nature, I am glad to believe has no original. Of the Indian of South America I know nothing; for I would not honor with the appelation of knowledge, what I derive from the fables published of them. These I believe to be just as true as the fables of Æsop.[4] This belief is founded on what I have seen of man, white, red, and black, and what has been written of him by authors, enlightened themselves, and writing amidst an enlightened people. The Indian of North America being more within our reach, I can speak of him somewhat from my own knowledge, but more from the information of others better acquainted with him, and on whose truth and judgment I can rely. From these sources I am able to say, in contradiction to this representation, that he is neither more defective in ardor, nor more impotent with his female, than the white reduced to the same diet and exercise: that he is brave, when an enterprise depends on bravery; education with him making the point of honor consist in the destruction of an enemy by stratagem, and in the preservation of his own person free from injury; or perhaps this is nature; while it is education which teaches us to honor force more than finesse; that he will defend himself against an host of enemies, always choosing to be killed, rather than to surrender; though it be to the whites, who he knows will treat him well: that in other situations also he meets death with more deliberation, and endures tortures with a firmness unknown almost to religious enthusiasm with us: that he is affectionate to his children, careful of them, and indulgent in the extreme: that his affections comprehend his other connections, weakening, as with us, from circle to circle, as they recede from the center: that his friendships are strong and faithful to the uttermost extremity: that his sensibility is keen, even the warriors weeping most bitterly on the loss of their children, though in general they endeavour to appear superior to human events: that his vivacity and activity of mind is equal to ours in the same situation; hence his eagerness for hunting, and for games of chance. The women are submitted to unjust drudgery. This I believe is the case with every barbarous people. With such, force is law. The stronger sex therefore imposes on the weaker. It is civilization alone which replaces women in the enjoyment of their natural equality. That first teaches us to subdue the selfish passions, and to respect those rights in others which we value in ourselves. Were we in equal barbarism, our females would be equal drudges. The man with them is less strong than with us, but their woman stronger than ours; and both for the same obvious reason; because our man and their woman is habituated to labour, and formed by it. With both races the sex which is indulged with ease is least athletic. An Indian man is small in the hand and wrist for the same reason for which a sailor is large and strong in the arms and shoulders, and a porter in the legs and thighs.—They raise fewer children than we do. The causes of this are to be found, not in a difference of nature, but of circumstance. The women very frequently attending the men in their parties of war and of hunting, child-bearing becomes extremely inconvenient to them. It is said, therefore, that

---

[4]A Greek slave (sixth century B.C.), purported author of stories presenting a moral through fabulous action of animals or other creatures.

they have learnt the practice of procuring abortion by the use of some vegetable; and that it even extends to prevent conception for a considerable time after. During these parties they are exposed to numerous hazards, to excessive exertions, to the greatest extremities of hunger. Even at their homes the nation depends for food, through a certain part of every year, on the gleanings of the forest: that is, they experience a famine once in every year. With all animals, if the female be badly fed, or not fed at all, her young perish: and if both male and female be reduced to like want, generation becomes less active, less productive. To the obstacles then of want and hazard, which nature has opposed to the multiplication of wild animals, for the purpose of restraining their numbers within certain bounds, those of labour and of voluntary abortion are added with the Indian. No wonder then if they multiply less than we do. Where food is regularly supplied, a single farm will show more of cattle, than a whole country of forests can of buffaloes. The same Indian women, when married to white traders, who feed them and their children plentifully and regularly, who exempt them from excessive drudgery, who keep them stationary and unexposed to accident, produce and raise as many children as the white women. Instances are known, under these circumstances, of their rearing a dozen children. An inhuman practice once prevailed in this country of making slaves of the Indians. ⟨This practice commenced with the Spaniards with the first discovery of America⟩. It is a fact well known with us, that the Indian women so enslaved produced and raised as numerous families as either the whites or blacks among whom they lived.— It has been said, that Indians have less hair than the whites, except on the head. But this is a fact of which fair proof can scarcely be had. With them it is disgraceful to be hairy on the body. They say it likens them to hogs. They therefore pluck the hair as fast as it appears. But the traders who marry their women, and prevail on them to discontinue this practice, say, that nature is the same with them as with the whites. Nor, if the fact be true, is the consequence necessary which has been drawn from it. Negroes have notoriously less hair than the whites; yet they are more ardent. But if cold and moisture be the agents of nature for diminishing the races of animals, how comes she all at once to suspend their operation as to the physical man of the new world, whom the Count acknowledges to be "about the same size as the man of our hemisphere," and to let loose their influence on his moral faculties? How has this "combination of the elements and other physical causes, so contrary to the enlargement of animal nature in this new world, these obstacles to the development and formation of great germs," been arrested and suspended, so as to permit the human body to acquire its just dimensions, and by what inconceivable process has their action been directed on his mind alone? To judge of the truth of this, to form a just estimate of their genius and mental powers, more facts are wanting, and great allowance to be made for those circumstances of their situation which call for a display of particular talents only. This done, we shall probably find that they are formed in mind as well as in body, on the same module with the "Homo sapiens Europæus."[5] The principles of their society forbidding all compulsion, they are to be led to duty and to enterprize by personal influence and persuasion. Hence eloquence in council, bravery and address in war, become the foundations of all consequence with them. To these acquirements all their faculties are directed. Of their bravery and address in war we have multiplied proofs, because we have been the subjects on which they were exercised. Of their eminence in oratory we have fewer examples, because it is displayed chiefly in their own councils. Some, however, we have of very superior lustre. I may challenge the whole orations of Demosthenes and Cicero,[6] and of any more eminent orator, if

---

[5]European man.
[6]Demosthenes (*c.* 385–322 B.C.), Athenian orator; Cicero (106–43 B.C.), Roman orator.

Europe has furnished more eminent, to produce a single passage, superior to the speech of Logan, a Mingo chief, to Lord Dunmore, when governor of this state.[7] And, as a testimony of their talents in this line, I beg leave to introduce it, first stating the incidents necessary for understanding it. In the spring of the year 1774, a robbery was committed by some Indians on certain land-adventurers on the river Ohio. The whites in that quarter, according to their custom, undertook to punish this outrage in a summary way. Captain Michael Cresap,[8] and a certain Daniel Great-house, leading on these parties, surprised, at different times, travelling and hunting parties of the Indians, having their women and children with them, and murdered many. Among these were unfortunately the family of Logan, a chief celebrated in peace and war, and long distinguished as the friend of the whites. This unworthy return provoked his vengeance. He accordingly signalized himself in the war which ensued. In the autumn of the same year a decisive battle was fought at the mouth of the Great Kanhaway, between the collected forces of the Shawanese, Mingoes, and Delawares, and a detachment of the Virginia militia. The Indians were defeated, and sued for peace. Logan however disdained to be seen among the suppliants. But, lest the sincerity of a treaty should be distrusted, from which so distinguished a chief absented himself, he sent by a messenger the following speech to be delivered to Lord Dunmore.

"I appeal to any white man to say, if ever he entered Logan's cabin hungry, and he gave him not meat; if ever he came cold and naked, and he clothed him not. During the course of the last long and bloody war, Logan remained idle in his cabin, an advocate for peace. Such was my love for the whites, that my countrymen pointed as they passed, and said, 'Logan is the friend of white men.' I had even thought to have lived with you, but for the injuries of one man. Col. Cresap, the last spring, in cold blood, and unprovoked, murdered all the relations of Logan, not sparing even my women and children. There runs not a drop of my blood in the veins of any living creature. This called on me for revenge. I have sought it: I have killed many: I have fully glutted my vengeance. For my country, I rejoice at the beams of peace. But do not harbour a thought that mine is the joy of fear. Logan never felt fear. He will not turn on his heel to save his life. Who is there to mourn for Logan?—Not one."

Before we condemn the Indians of this continent as wanting genius,[9] we must consider that letters have not yet been introduced among them. Were we to compare them in their present state with the Europeans North of the Alps, when the Roman arms and arts first crossed those mountains, the comparison would be unequal, because, at that time, those parts of Europe were swarming with numbers; because numbers produce emulation, and multiply the chances of improvement, and one improvement begets another. Yet I may safely ask, How many good poets, how many able mathematicians, how many great inventors in arts or sciences, had Europe North of the Alps then produced? And it was sixteen centuries after this before a Newton[10] could be formed. I do not mean to deny, that there are varieties in the race of man, distinguished by their powers both of body and mind. I believe there are, as I see to be the case in the races of other animals. I only mean to suggest a doubt, whether the bulk and faculties of animals depend on the side of the Atlantic on which their food happens to grow, or which furnishes the elements of which they are compounded? Whether nature has enlisted herself as a Cis[11] or Trans-Atlantic partisan? I am induced to suspect, there has been more eloquence than sound reasoning displayed in support of this theory; that it is one of those cases where the judgment has been seduced by a glowing pen: and whilst

---

[7]Logan or Tahgahjute (*c.* 1725–1780), Mingo warrior and chief; John Murray, 4th Earl of Dunmore (1732–1809), colonial governor of Virginia (1772–76).
[8]Michael Cresap (1742–1775), Maryland soldier and frontiersman.

[9]Intellect.
[10]Sir Isaac Newton (1642–1727), British scientist and philosopher, noted for formulating laws of gravity and motion.
[11]Prefix, "on this side of."

I render every tribute of honor and esteem to the celebrated zoologist, who has added, and is still adding, so many precious things to the treasures of science, I must doubt whether in this instance he has not cherished error also, by lending her for a moment his vivid imagination and bewitching language.

[INTELLIGENCE OF WHITES TRANSPLANTED FROM EUROPE]

So far the Count de Buffon has carried this new theory of the tendency of nature to belittle her productions on this side of the Atlantic. Its application to the race of whites, transplanted from Europe, remained for the Abbé Raynal.[1] "One must be astonished (he says) that America has not yet produced one good poet, one able mathematician, one man of genius in a single art or a single science." "America has not yet produced one good poet." When we shall have existed as a people as long as the Greeks did before they produced a Homer, the Romans a Virgil, the French a Racine and Voltaire, the English a Shakespeare and Milton,[2] should this reproach be still true, we will enquire from what unfriendly causes it has proceeded, that the other countries of Europe and quarters of the earth shall not have inscribed any name in the roll of poets. But neither has America produced "one able mathematician, one man of genius in a single art or a single science." In war we have produced a Washington,[3] whose memory will be adored while liberty shall have votaries, whose name will triumph over time, and will in future ages assume its just station among the most celebrated worthies of the world, when that wretched philosophy shall be forgotten which would have arranged him among the degeneracies of nature. In physics we have produced a Franklin,[4] than whom no one of the present age has made more important discoveries, nor has enriched philosophy with more, or more ingenious solutions of the phænomena of nature. We have supposed Mr. Rittenhouse[5] second to no astronomer living: that in genius he must be the first, because he is self-taught. As an artist he has exhibited as great a proof of mechanical genius as the world has ever produced. He has not indeed made a world; but he has by imitation approached nearer its Maker than any man who has lived from the creation to this day. As in philosophy and war, so in government, in oratory, in painting, in the plastic art, we might show that America, though but a child of yesterday, has already given hopeful proofs of genius, as well of the nobler kinds, which arouse the best feelings of man, which call him into action, which substantiate his freedom, and conduct him to happiness, as of the subordinate, which serve to amuse him only. We therefore suppose, that this reproach is as unjust as it is unkind; and that, of the geniuses which adorn the present age, America contributes its full share. For comparing it with those countries, where genius is most cultivated, where are the most excellent models for art, and scaffoldings for the attainment of science, as France and England for instance, we calculate thus. The United States contain three millions of inhabitants; France twenty millions; and the British islands ten. We produce a Washington, a Franklin, a Rittenhouse. France then should have half a dozen in each of these lines, and Great-Britain half that number, equally eminent. It may be true, that France has: we are but just becoming acquainted with her, and our acquaintance so far gives us high ideas of the genius of her inhabitants. It

[1]Guillaume Thomas François Raynal (1713–1796), French historian, author of *Philosophical and Political History of the Establishment and of the Commerce of Europeans in the Two Indies* (1770).
[2]Homer (c. 850 B.C.), author of the *Iliad* and *Odyssey*; Virgil (70–19 B.C.), author of *The Aeneid*; Jean Baptiste Racine (1639–1699), author of tragedies (*Andromache*, 1667); Voltaire (1694–1778), author of satiric works (*Candide*, 1759); Shakespeare (1564–1616), dramatist (*Hamlet*, 1600–01); John Milton (1608–1674), poet (*Paradise Lost*, 1667).

[3]George Washington (1732–1799), Commander of American forces during the Revolutionary War, first president of the United States (1789–97).
[4]Benjamin Franklin (1706–1790), inventor, statesman, and author (*The Way to Wealth, Autobiography*).
[5]David Rittenhouse (1732–1796), American astronomer; built first telescope made in America.

would be injuring too many of them to name particularly a Voltaire, a Buffon, the constellation of Encyclopedists,[6] the Abbé Raynal himself, &c. &c. We therefore have reason to believe she can produce her full quota of genius. The present war having so long cut off all communication with Great-Britain, we are not able to make a fair estimate of the state of science in that country. The spirit in which she wages war is the only sample before our eyes, and that does not seem the legitimate offspring either of science or of civilization. The sun of her glory is fast descending to the horizon. Her philosophy has crossed the Channel, her freedom the Atlantic, and herself seems passing to that awful dissolution, whose issue is not given human foresight to scan.

QUERY XVII: RELIGION

[RIGHTS OF CONSCIENCE AS NATURAL RIGHTS]

The different religions received into that state?

The first settlers in this country were emigrants from England, of the English church, just at a point of time when it was flushed with complete victory over the religious of all other persuasions. Possessed, as they became, of the powers of making, administering, and executing the laws, they showed equal intolerance in this country with their Presbyterian brethren, who had emigrated to the northern government. The poor Quakers were flying from persecution in England. They cast their eyes on these new countries as asylums of civil and religious freedom; but they found them free only for the reigning sect. Several acts of the Virginia assembly of 1659, 1662, and 1693, had made it penal in parents to refuse to have their children baptized; had prohibited the unlawful assembling of Quakers; had made it penal for any master of a vessel to bring a Quaker into the state; had ordered those already here, and such as should come thereafter, to be imprisoned till they should abjure the country; provided a milder punishment for their first and second return, but death for their third; had inhibited all persons from suffering their meetings in or near their houses, entertaining them individually, or disposing of books which supported their tenets. If no capital execution took place here, as did in New England, it was not owing to the moderation of the church, or spirit of the legislature, as may be inferred from the law itself; but to historical circumstances which have not been handed down to us. The Anglicans retained full possession of the country about a century. Other opinions began then to creep in, and the great care of the government to support their own church, having begotten an equal degree of indolence in its clergy, two-thirds of the people had become dissenters at the commencement of the present revolution. The laws indeed were still oppressive on them, but the spirit of the one party had subsided into moderation, and of the other had risen to a degree of determination which commanded respect.

The present state of our laws on the subject of religion is this. The convention of May 1776, in their declaration of rights, declared it to be a truth, and a natural right, that the exercise of religion should be free; but when they proceeded to form on that declaration the ordinance of government, instead of taking up every principle declared in the bill of rights, and guarding it by legislative sanction, they passed over that which asserted our religious rights, leaving them as they found them.[1] The same convention, however, when they met as a member of the general assembly in October 1776, repealed all *acts of parliament* which had rendered crim-

---

[6]The Encyclopedists: Denis Diderot, d'Alembert and others whose *Encyclopedia* (28 vols., 1751–72) was a compendium of revolutionary and radical thought.

[1]Reference to the Virginia Declaration of Rights, Article 16.

inal the maintaining any opinions in matters of religion, the forbearing to repair to church, and the exercising any mode of worship; and suspended the laws giving salaries to the clergy, which suspension was made perpetual in October 1779. Statutory oppressions in religion being thus wiped away, we remain at present under those only imposed by the common law, or by our own acts of assembly. At the common law, *heresy* was a capital offence, punishable by burning. Its definition was left to the ecclesiastical judges, before whom the conviction was, till the statute of the I El. c. I.[2] circumscribed it, by declaring, that nothing should be deemed heresy, but what had been so determined by authority of the canonical scriptures, or by one of the four first general councils, or by some other council having for the grounds of their declaration the express and plain words of the scriptures. Heresy, thus circumscribed, being an offense at the common law, our act of assembly of October 1777, c. 17. gives cognizance of it to the general court, by declaring, that the jurisdiction of that court shall be general in all matters at the common law. The execution is by the writ *De hæretico comburendo*.[3] By our own act of assembly of 1705, c. 30, if a person brought up in the Christian religion denies the being of a God, or the Trinity, or asserts there are more Gods than one, or denies the Christian religion to be true, or the scriptures to be of divine authority, he is punishable on the first offence by incapacity to hold any office or employment ecclesiastical, civil, or military; on the second by disability to sue, to take any gift or legacy, to be guardian, executor, or administrator, and by three years imprisonment, without bail. A father's right to the custody of his own children being founded in law on his right of guardianship, this being taken away, they may of course be severed from him, and put, by the authority of a court, into more orthodox hands. This is a summary view of that religious slavery, under which a people have been willing to remain, who have lavished their lives and fortunes for the establishment of their civil freedom.

The error seems not sufficiently eradicated, that the operations of the mind, as well as the acts of the body, are subject to the coercion of the laws. But our rulers can have authority over such natural rights only as we have submitted to them. The rights of conscience we never submitted, we could not submit. We are answerable for them to our God. The legitimate powers of government extend to such acts only as are injurious to others. But it does me no injury for my neighbour to say there are twenty gods, or no god. It neither picks my pocket nor breaks my leg. If it be said, his testimony in a court of justice cannot be relied on, reject it then, and be the stigma on him. Constraint may make him worse by making him a hypocrite, but it will never make him a truer man. It may fix him obstinately in his errors, but will not cure them. Reason and free enquiry are the only effectual agents against error. Give a loose to them, they will support the true religion, by bringing every false one to their tribunal, to the test of their investigation. They are the natural enemies of error, and of error only. Had not the Roman government permitted free enquiry, Christianity could never have been introduced. Had not free enquiry been indulged, at the era of the reformation, the corruptions of Christianity could not have been purged away. If it be restrained now, the present corruptions will be protected, and new ones encouraged. Was the government to prescribe to us our medicine and diet, our bodies would be in such keeping as our souls are now. Thus in France the emetic was once forbidden as a medicine, and the potato as an article of food. Government is just as infallible too when it fixes systems in physics. Galileo[4] was sent to the inquisition for affirming that the earth was a sphere: the government had declared it to

---

[2] Chapter I of the first year of Queen Elizabeth's reign (1558–59).
[3] "For burning a heretic" (Latin).

[4] Galileo (1564–1642), Italian astronomer, tried by the Inquisition in 1632 and forced to recant, abandon his belief.

be as flat as a trencher, and Galileo was obliged to abjure his error. This error however at length prevailed, the earth became a globe, and Descartes[5] declared it was whirled round its axis by a vortex. The government in which he lived was wise enough to see that this was no question of civil jurisdiction, or we should all have been involved by authority in vortices. In fact, the vortices have been exploded, and the Newtonian principle of gravitation is now more firmly established, on the basis of reason, than it would be were the government to step in, and to make it an article of necessary faith. Reason and experiment have been indulged, and error has fled before them. It is error alone which needs the support of government. Truth can stand by itself. Subject opinion to coercion: whom will you make your inquisitors? Fallible men; men governed by bad passions, by private as well as public reasons. And why subject it to coercion? To produce uniformity. But is uniformity of opinion desirable? No more than of face and stature. Introduce the bed of Procrustes[6] then, and as there is danger that the large men may beat the small, make us all of a size, by lopping the former and stretching the latter. Difference of opinion is advantageous in religion. The several sects perform the office of a censor morum[7] over each other. Is uniformity attainable? Millions of innocent men, women, and children, since the introduction of Christianity, have been burnt, tortured, fined, imprisoned; yet we have not advanced one inch towards uniformity. What has been the effect of coercion? To make one half the world fools, and the other half hypocrites. To support roguery and error all over the earth. Let us reflect that it is inhabited by a thousand millions of people. That these profess probably a thousand different systems of religion. That ours is but one of that thousand. That if there be but one right, and ours that one, we should wish to see the 999 wandering sects gathered into the fold of truth. But against such a majority we cannot effect this by force. Reason and persuasion are the only practicable instruments. To make way for these, free enquiry must be indulged; and how can we wish others to indulge it while we refuse it ourselves. But every state, says an inquisitor, has established some religion. No two, say I, have established the same. Is this a proof of the infallibility of establishments? Our sister states of Pennsylvania and New York, however, have long subsisted without any establishment at all. The experiment was new and doubtful when they made it. It has answered beyond conception. They flourish infinitely. Religion is well supported; of various kinds, indeed, but all good enough; all sufficient to preserve peace and order: or if a sect arises, whose tenets would subvert morals, good sense has fair play, and reasons and laughs it out of doors, without suffering the state to be troubled with it. They do not hang more malefactors than we do. They are not more disturbed with religious dissensions. On the contrary, their harmony is unparalleled, and can be ascribed to nothing but their unbounded tolerance, because there is no other circumstance in which they differ from every nation on earth. They have made the happy discovery, that the way to silence religious disputes, is to take no notice of them. Let us too give this experiment fair play, and get rid, while we may, of those tyrannical laws. It is true, we are as yet secured against them by the spirit of the times. I doubt whether the people of this country would suffer an execution for heresy, or a three years imprisonment for not comprehending the mysteries of the Trinity. But is the spirit of the people an infallible, a permanent reliance? Is it government? Is this the kind of protection we receive in return for the rights we give up? Besides, the spirit of the times may alter, will alter. Our rulers will become corrupt, our people careless. A single zealot may

---

[5]René Descartes (1596–1650), French mathematician and philosopher.
[6]In Greek legend, Procrustes was a robber of Attica who stretched or cut the legs of his victims to fit his iron bed.
[7]Censor of morals or mores.

commence persecutor, and better men be his victims. It can never be too often repeated, that the time for fixing every essential right on a legal basis is while our rulers are honest, and ourselves united. From the conclusion of this war we shall be going down hill. It will not then be necessary to resort every moment to the people for support. They will be forgotten, therefore, and their rights disregarded. They will forget themselves, but in the sole faculty of making money, and will never think of uniting to effect a due respect for their rights. The shackles, therefore, which shall not be knocked off at the conclusion of this war, will remain on us long, will be made heavier and heavier, till our rights shall revive or expire in a convulsion.

QUERY XVIII: MANNERS

[DEGRADATION OF SLAVERY]

The particular customs and manners that may
happen to be received in that state?

It is difficult to determine on the standard by which the manners of a nation may be tried, whether *catholic,*[1] or *particular*. It is more difficult for a native to bring to that standard the manners of his own nation, familiarized to him by habit. There must doubtless be an unhappy influence on the manners of our people produced by the existence of slavery among us. The whole commerce between master and slave is a perpetual exercise of the most boisterous passions, the most unremitting despotism on the one part, and degrading submissions on the other. Our children see this, and learn to imitate it; for man is an imitative animal. This quality is the germ of all education in him. From his cradle to his grave he is learning to do what he sees others do. If a parent could find no motive either in his philanthropy or his self-love, for restraining the intemperance of passion towards his slave, it should always be a sufficient one that his child is present. But generally it is not sufficient. The parent storms, the child looks on, catches the lineaments of wrath, puts on the same airs in the circle of smaller slaves, gives a loose to his worst of passions, and thus nursed, educated, and daily exercised in tyranny, cannot but be stamped by it with odious peculiarities. The man must be a prodigy who can retain his manners and morals undepraved by such circumstances. And with what execration should the statesman be loaded, who permitting one half the citizens thus to trample on the rights of the other, transforms those into despots, and these into enemies, destroys the morals of the one part, and the amor patriæ[2] of the other. For if a slave can have a country in this world, it must be any other in preference to that in which he is born to live and labour for another: in which he must lock up the faculties of his nature, contribute as far as depends on his individual endeavours to the evanishment[3] of the human race, or entail[4] his own miserable condition on the endless generations proceeding from him. With the morals of the people, their industry also is destroyed. For in a warm climate, no man will labour for himself who can make another labour for him. This is so true, that of the proprietors of slaves a very small proportion indeed are ever seen to labour. And can the liberties of a nation be thought secure when we have removed their only firm basis, a conviction in the minds of the people that these liberties are of the gift of God? That they are not to be violated but with his wrath? Indeed I tremble for my country when I reflect that God is just: that his justice cannot sleep for ever: that considering numbers, nature and natural means only, a revolution of the wheel of fortune, an exchange of situation, is among pos-

---

[1]Universal.
[2]"Love of country" (Latin).

[3]Death.
[4]Force.

sible events: that it may become probable by supernatural interference! The Almighty has no attribute which can take side with us in such a contest.—But it is impossible to be temperate and to pursue this subject through the various considerations of policy, of morals, of history natural and civil. We must be contented to hope they will force their way into every one's mind. I think a change already perceptible, since the origin of the present revolution. The spirit of the master is abating, that of the slave rising from the dust, his condition mollifying, the way I hope preparing, under the auspices of heaven, for a total emancipation, and that this is disposed, in the order of events, to be with the consent of the masters, rather than by their extirpation.

QUERY XIX: MANUFACTURES

[HUSBANDMEN THE CHOSEN PEOPLE OF GOD]

The present state of manufactures, commerce,
interior and exterior trade?

We never had an interior trade of any importance. Our exterior commerce has suffered very much from the beginning of the present contest. During this time we have manufactured within our families the most necessary articles of clothing. Those of cotton will bear some comparison with the same kinds of manufacture in Europe; but those of wool, flax and hemp are very coarse, unsightly, and unpleasant: and such is our attachment to agriculture, and such our preference for foreign manufactures, that be it wise or unwise, our people will certainly return as soon as they can, to the raising raw materials, and exchanging them for finer manufactures than they are able to execute themselves.

The political economists of Europe have established it as a principle that every state should endeavour to manufacture for itself: and this principle, like many others, we transfer to America, without calculating the difference of circumstance which should often produce a difference of result. In Europe the lands are either cultivated, or locked up against the cultivator. Manufacture must therefore be resorted to of necessity not of choice, to support the surplus of their people. But we have an immensity of land courting the industry of the husbandman. Is it best then that all our citizens should be employed in its improvement, or that one half should be called off from that to exercise manufactures and handicraft arts for the other? Those who labour in the earth are the chosen people of God, if ever he had a chosen people, whose breasts he has made his peculiar deposit for substantial and genuine virtue. It is the focus in which he keeps alive that sacred fire, which otherwise might escape from the face of the earth. Corruption of morals in the mass of cultivators is a phenomenon of which no age nor nation has furnished an example. It is the mark set on those, who not looking up to heaven, to their own soil and industry, as does the husbandman, for their subsistance, depend for it on the casualties and caprice of customers. Dependence begets subservience and venality, suffocates the germ of virtue, and prepares fit tools for the designs of ambition. This, the natural progress and consequence of the arts, has sometimes perhaps been retarded by accidental circumstances: but, generally speaking, the proportion which the aggregate of the other classes of citizens bears in any state to that of its husbandmen, is the proportion of its unsound to its healthy parts, and is a good-enough barometer whereby to measure its degree of corruption. While we have land to labour then, let us never wish to see our citizens occupied at a workbench, or twirling a distaff.[1] Carpenters, masons, smiths, are wanting in husbandry: but, for the general operations of manufacture, let our work-shops re-

---

[1]A staff on which thread is wound for spinning.

main in Europe. It is better to carry provisions and materials to workmen there, than bring them to the provisions and materials, and with them their manners and principles. The loss by the transportation of commodities across the Atlantic will be made up in happiness and permanence of government. The mobs of great cities add just so much to the support of pure government, as sores do to the strength of the human body. It is the manners and spirit of a people which preserve a republic in vigour. A degeneracy in these is a canker which soon eats to the heart of its laws and constitution.[2]

1780–85   *1784–85*

POSTSCRIPT TO QUERY XIX: MANUFACTURES

[Views on Farming Revised in Letters of 1805 and 1816]

To J. Lithgow   Washington, January 4, 1805

My occupations by no means permit me at this time to revise the text,[1] and make those changes in it which I should now do. I should in that case certainly qualify several expressions in the nineteenth chapter, which have been construed differently from what they were intended. I had under my eye, when writing, the manufacturers of the great cities in the old countries, at the time present, with whom the want of food and clothing necessary to sustain life, has begotten a depravity of morals, a dependence and corruption, which renders them an undesirable accession to a country whose morals are sound. My expressions looked forward to the time when our own great cities would get into the same state. But they have been quoted as if meant for the present time here. As yet our manufacturers are as much at their ease, as independent and moral as our agricultural inhabitants, and they will continue so as long as there are vacant lands for them to resort to; because whenever it shall be attempted by the other classes to reduce them to the minimum of subsistence, they will quit their trades and go to laboring the earth. A first question is, whether it is desirable for us to receive at present the dissolute and demoralized handicraftsmen of the old cities of Europe? A second and more difficult one is, when even good handicraftsmen arrive here, is it better for them to set up their trade, or go to the culture of the earth? Whether their labor in their trade is worth more than their labor on the soil, increased by the creative energies of the earth? Had I time to revise that chapter, this question should be discussed, and other views of the subject taken, which are presented by the wonderful changes which have taken place here since 1781, when the *Notes on Virginia* were written. Perhaps when I retire, I may amuse myself with a serious review of this work; at present it is out of the question. Accept my salutations and good wishes.

To Benjamin Austin   Monticello, January 9, 1816

You tell me I am quoted by those who wish to continue our dependence on England for manufactures. There was a time when I might have been so quoted with more candor, but within the thirty years which have since elapsed, how are circumstances changed! We were then in peace. Our independent place among nations was acknowledged. A commerce which offered the raw material in exchange for the same material after receiving the last touch of industry, was worthy of welcome to all nations. It was expected that those especially to whom manufacturing industry was important, would cherish the friendship of such customers by every favor, by every inducement, and particularly cultivate their peace by every

---

[2]See the following letters by Jefferson, written January 4, 1805, and January 9, 1816, modifying his point of view in these paragraphs.
[1]*Notes on the State of Virginia.*

act of justice and friendship. Under this prospect the question seemed legitimate, whether, with such an immensity of unimproved land, courting the hand of husbandry, the industry of agriculture, or that of manufactures, would add most to the national wealth? And the doubt was entertained on this consideration chiefly, that to the labor of the husbandman a vast addition is made by the spontaneous energies of the earth on which it is employed: for one grain of wheat committed to the earth, she renders twenty, thirty, and even fifty fold, whereas to the labor of the manufacturer nothing is added. Pounds of flax, in his hands, yield, on the contrary, but pennyweights of lace. This exchange, too, laborious as it might seem, what a field did it promise for the occupations of the ocean; what a nursery for that class of citizens who were to exercise and maintain our equal rights on that element? This was the state of things in 1785, when the *Notes on Virginia* were first printed; when, the ocean being open to all nations, and their common right in it acknowledged and exercised under regulations sanctioned by the assent and usage of all, it was thought that the doubt might claim some consideration. But who in 1785 could foresee the rapid depravity which was to render the close of that century the disgrace of the history of man?[1] Who could have imagined that the two most distinguished in the rank of nations,[2] for science and civilization, would have suddenly descended from that honorable eminence, and setting at defiance all those moral laws established by the Author of nature between nation and nation, as between man and man, would cover earth and sea with robberies and piracies, merely because strong enough to do it with temporal impunity; and that under this disbandment of nations from social order, we should have been despoiled of a thousand ships, and have thousands of our citizens reduced to Algerine slavery.[3] Yet all this has taken place. One of these nations interdicted to our vessels all harbors of the globe without having first proceeded to some one of hers, there paid a tribute proportioned to the cargo, and obtained her license to proceed to the port of destination.[4] The other declared them to be lawful prize if they had touched at the port or been visited by a ship of the enemy nation.[5] Thus were we completely excluded from the ocean. Compare this state of things with that of '85, and say whether an opinion founded in the circumstances of that day can be fairly applied to those of the present. We have experienced what we did not then believe, that there exists both profligacy and power enough to exclude us from the field of interchange with other nations: that to be independent for the comforts of life we must fabricate them ourselves. We must now place the manufacturer by the side of the agriculturist. The former question is suppressed, or rather assumes a new form. Shall we make our own comforts, or go without them, at the will of a foreign nation? He, therefore, who is now against domestic manufacture, must be for reducing us either to dependence on that foreign nation, or to be clothed in skins, and to live like wild beasts in dens and caverns. I am not one of these; experience has taught me that manufactures are now as necessary to our independence as to our comfort; and if those who quote me as of a different opinion, will keep pace with me in purchasing nothing foreign where an equivalent of domestic fabric can be obtained, without regard to difference of price, it will not be our fault if we do not soon have a supply at home equal to our demand, and wrest that weapon of distress from the hand which has wielded it. If it shall be proposed to go beyond our own supply, the question of '85 will then recur, will our *surplus* labor be then most beneficially employed in the culture of the earth, or in the fabrications of art? We have time yet for consideration, before that

---

[1]The Reign of Terror (1793–94) of the French Revolution.
[2]England and France, at war with each other, England attempting to defeat Napoleon in his expansionary and predatory moves.
[3]Slavery in Algeria.
[4]England; these practices led America to declare war on England, resulting in the War of 1812.
[5]France.

question will press upon us; and the maxim to be applied will depend on the circumstances which shall then exist; for in so complicated a science as political economy, no one axiom can be laid down as wise and expedient for all times and circumstances, and for their contraries. Inattention to this is what has called for this explanation, which reflection would have rendered unnecessary with the candid, while nothing will do it with those who use the former opinion only as a stalking horse, to cover their disloyal propensities to keep us in eternal vassalage to a foreign and unfriendly people.

I salute you with assurances of great respect and esteem.

First Inaugural Address

["THE ESSENTIAL PRINCIPLES OF THIS GOVERNMENT"][1]

Friends and Fellow Citizens

Called upon to undertake the duties of the first Executive office of our country, I avail myself of the presence of that portion of my fellow citizens which is here assembled to express my grateful thanks for the favor with which they have been pleased to look towards me, to declare a sincere consciousness that the task is above my talents, and that I approach it with those anxious and awful presentiments, which the greatness of the charge, and the weakness of my powers so justly inspire.

A rising nation spread over a wide and fruitful land, traversing all the seas with the rich productions of their industry, engaged in commerce with nations who feel power and forget right, advancing rapidly to destinies beyond the reach of mortal eye; when I contemplate these transcendent objects, and see the honor, the happiness, and the hopes of this beloved country committed to the issue and the auspices of this day, I shrink from the contemplation, and humble myself before the magnitude of the undertaking.

Utterly indeed should I despair, did not the presence of many whom I here see, remind me, that in the other high authorities provided by our constitution, I shall find resources of wisdom, of virtue and of zeal, on which to rely under all difficulties.

To you then, gentlemen who are charged with the sovereign functions of legislation and to those associated with you, I look with encouragement for that guidance and support which may enable us to steer with safety, the vessel in which we are all embarked amidst the conflicting elements of a troubled sea.

During the contest of opinion through which we have passed, the animation of discussions and of exertions, has sometimes worn an aspect which might impose on strangers unused to think freely, and to speak and to write what they think.

But this being now decided by the voice of the nation, announced according to the rules of the constitution, all will of course arrange themselves under the will of the law, and unite in common efforts for the common good. All too will bear in mind this sacred principle that though the will of the Majority is in all cases to prevail, that will, to be rightful, must be reasonable: that the Minority possess their equal rights, which equal laws must protect, and to violate would be oppression.

Let us then, fellow citizens, unite with one heart and one mind; let us restore to

---

[1] Delivered March 4, 1801, before Congress in the yet unfinished Capitol. Jefferson and Aaron Burr were tied in the electoral vote and the House of Representatives voted for Jefferson. Burr became vice-president.

social intercourse that harmony and affection, without which Liberty, and even Life itself, are but dreary things.

And let us reflect that having banished from our land that religious intolerance under which mankind so long bled and suffered we have yet gained little, if we countenance a political intolerance, as despotic[,] as wicked[,] and capable of as bitter and bloody persecution.

During the throes and convulsions of the ancient world, during the agonised spasms of infuriated man, seeking through blood and slaughter his long lost liberty, it was not wonderful that the agitation of the billows should reach even this distant and peaceful shore[2] that this should be more felt and feared by some, and less by others, and should divide opinions as to measures of safety.

But every difference of opinion, is not a difference of principle. We have called, by different names, brethren of the same principle. We are all republicans: we are all federalists.[3]

If there be any among us who wish to dissolve this union, or to change its republican form, let them stand undisturbed, as monuments of the safety with which error of opinion may be tolerated where reason is left free to combat it.

I know indeed that some honest men have feared that a republican government cannot be strong; that this government is not strong enough. But would the honest patriot, in the full tide of successful experiment abandon a government which has so far kept us free and firm on the theoretic and visionary fear that this government, the world's best hope may, by possibility, want energy to preserve itself?

I trust not. I believe this, on the contrary, the strongest government on earth.

I believe it the only one where every man, at the call of the law, would fly to the standard of the law; would meet invasions of public order, as his own personal concern.

Some times it is said that man cannot be trusted with the government of himself.—Can he then be trusted with the government of others? Or have we found angels in the form of kings to govern him?—Let History answer this question.

Let us then pursue with courage and confidence our own federal and republican principles[,] our attachment to union and representative government.

Kindly separated by nature, and a wide ocean, from the exterminating havoc of one quarter of the globe,

Too high-minded to endure the degradations of the others;

Possessing a chosen country, with room enough for our descendants to the thousandth and thousandth generation;

Entertaining a due sense of our equal right, to the use of our own faculties, to the acquisitions of our own industry, to honor and confidence from our fellow citizens resulting not from birth, but from our actions and their sense of them, enlightened by a benign religion, professed indeed and practiced in various forms, yet all of them inculcating honesty, truth, temperance[,] gratitude, and the love of man, acknowledging and adoring an overruling providence, which by all its dispensations proves that it delights in the happiness of man here, and his greater happiness hereafter:

With all these blessings, what more is necessary to make us a happy and a prosperous people? Still one thing more, fellow citizens[,] a wise and frugal government, which shall restrain men from injuring one another, shall leave them otherwise free to regulate their own pursuits of industry and improvement, and shall not take from the mouth of labor the bread it has earned.

---

[2]The French Revolution's bloody Reign of Terror (1793–94), which polarized opinion in America.
[3]Jefferson is referring to these words in the common meaning. But the two political parties of the time were "Democratic-republicans," ancestors of today's Democrats; and the Federalists, ancestors of today's Republicans.

This is the sum of good government, and this is necessary to close the circle of our felicities.

About to enter[,] fellow citizens[,] on the exercise of duties, which comprehend everything dear and valuable to you, it is proper you should understand what I deem the essential principle of this government and consequently those which ought to shape its administration.

I will compress them in the narrowest compass they will bear, stating the general principle, but not all its limitations.

Equal and exact justice to all men, of whatever state or persuasion, religious or political:

Peace, commerce, and honest friendship with all nations, entangling alliances with none:

The support of the state governments in all their rights, as the most competent administrations for our domestic concerns, and the surest bulwarks against anti republican tendencies:

The preservation of the general government, in its whole constitutional vigor, as the sheet anchor of our peace at home, and safety abroad.

A jealous care of the right of election by the people, a mild and safe corrective of abuses, which are lopped by the sword of revolution, where peacable remedies are unprovided.

Absolute acquiescence in the decisions of the Majority[,] the vital principle of republics, from which is no appeal but to force, the vital principle and immediate parent of despotism.

A well disciplined militia, our best reliance in peace, and for the first moments of war, till regulars may relieve them: the supremacy of the civil over the military authority:

Economy in public expense, that labor may be lightly burdened:

The honest payment of our debts and sacred preservation of the public faith:

Encouragement of agriculture, and of commerce, as its handmaid:

The diffusion of information, and arraignment of all abuses at the bar of the public reason:

Freedom of religion, freedom of the press, and freedom of person under the protection of the habeas corpus:[4] And trial by juries, impartially selected.

These principles form the bright constellation which has gone before us, and guided our steps, through an age of revolution and reformation: The wisdom of our sages, and blood of our heroes, have been devoted to their attainment: they should be the creed of our political faith, the text of civic instruction, the touchstone by which to try the services of those we trust; and should we wander from them, in moments of error or alarm, let us hasten to retrace our steps and to regain the road which alone leads to peace, liberty and safety.

I repair then, fellow citizens[,] to the post which you have assigned me.

With experience enough in subordinate stations to know the difficulties of this the greatest of all, I have learnt to expect that it will rarely fall to the lot of imperfect man to retire from this station with the reputation and the favor which bring him into it.

Without pretensions to that high confidence you reposed in our first and greatest revolutionary character[5] whose preeminent services had entitled him to the first place in his country's love, and had destined for him the fairest page in the volume of faithful history, I ask so much confidence only as may give firmness and effect to the legal administration of your affairs.

---

[4] Guarantee of a court's early determination as to legality of detention or arrest.
[5] George Washington.

I shall often go wrong through defect of judgment: when right, I shall often be thought wrong by those whose positions will not command a view of the whole ground.

I ask your indulgence for my own errors, which will never be intentional: and your support against the errors of others who may condemn what they would not if seen in all its parts.

The approbation implied by your suffrage, is a great consolation to me for the past; and my future solicitude will be to retain the good opinion of those who have bestowed it in advance, to conciliate that of others, by doing them all the good in my power, and to be instrumental to the happiness and freedom of all.

Relying then on the patronage of your good will, I advance with obedience to the work, ready to retire from it whenever you become sensible how much better choice it is in your power to make.

And may that infinite power which rules the destinies of the universe lead our councils to what is best, and give them a favorable issue for your peace and prosperity.

1801   *1801*

from Letters

TO PETER CARR[1]
[ELEMENTS OF AN EDUCATION]

Paris, August 10, 1787

DEAR PETER,—I have received your two letters of December 30 and April 18, and am very happy to find by them, as well as by letters from Mr. Wythe,[2] that you have been so fortunate as to attract his notice and good will; I am sure you will find this to have been one of the most fortunate events of your life, as I have ever been sensible it was of mine. I enclose you a sketch of the sciences to which I would wish you to apply in such order as Mr. Wythe shall advise; I mention also the books in them worth your reading, which submit to his correction. Many of these are among your father's books, which you should have brought to you. As I do not recollect those of them not in his library, you must write to me for them, making out a catalogue of such as you think you shall have occasion for in eighteen months from the date of your letter, and consulting Mr. Wythe on the subject. To this sketch I will add a few particular observations:

1. Italian. I fear the learning this language will confound your French and Spanish. Being all of them degenerated dialects of the Latin, they are apt to mix in conversation. I have never seen a person speaking the three languages who did not mix them. It is a delightful language, but late events having rendered the Spanish more useful, lay it aside to prosecute that.

2. Spanish. Bestow great attention on this, and endeavor to acquire an accurate knowledge of it. Our future connections with Spain and Spanish America will render that language a valuable acquisition. The ancient history of a great part of America, too, is written in that language. I send you a dictionary.

3. Moral philosophy. I think it lost time to attend lectures in this branch. He who made us would have been a pitiful bungler if he had made the rules of our

---

[1]Son of Jefferson's sister Martha and Dabney Carr.
[2]George Wythe (1726–1806), a self-educated Virginia law- yer with whom Jefferson read law and prepared for practice.

moral conduct a matter of science. For one man of science, there are thousands who are not. What would have become of them? Man was destined for society. His morality therefore was to be formed to this object. He was endowed with a sense of right and wrong merely relative to this. This sense is as much a part of his nature as the sense of hearing, seeing, feeling; it is the true foundation of mortality, and not the το καλον,[3] truth, etc. as fanciful writers have imagined. The moral sense, or conscience, is as much a part of man as his leg or arm. It is given to all human beings in a stronger or weaker degree, as force of members is given them in a greater or less degree. It may be strengthened by exercise, as may any particular limb of the body. This sense is submitted indeed in some degree to the guidance of reason; but it is a small stock which is required for this: even a less one than what we call common sense. State a moral case to a ploughman and a professor. The former will decide it as well, and often better than the latter, because he has not been led astray by artificial rules. In this branch therefore read good books because they will encourage as well as direct your feelings. The writings of Sterne[4] particularly form the best course of morality that ever was written. Besides these read the books mentioned in the enclosed paper; and above all things lose no occasion of exercising your dispositions to be grateful, to be generous, to be charitable, to be humane, to be true, just, firm, orderly, courageous etc. Consider every act of this kind as an exercise which will strengthen your moral faculties, and increase your worth.

4. Religion. Your reason is now mature enough to examine this object. In the first place divest yourself of all bias in favour of novelty and singularity of opinion. Indulge them in any other subject rather than that of religion. It is too important, and the consequences of error may be too serious. On the other hand shake off all the fears and servile prejudices under which weak minds are servilely crouched. Fix reason firmly in her seat, and call to her tribunal every fact, every opinion. Question with boldness even the existence of a God; because, if there be one, He must more approve of the homage of reason, than that of blindfolded fear. You will naturally examine first the religion of your own country. Read the Bible then, as you would read Livy or Tacitus. The facts which are within the ordinary course of nature you will believe on the authority of the writer, as you do those of the same kind in Livy and Tacitus.[5] The testimony of the writer weighs in their favor in one scale, and their not being against the laws of nature does not weigh against them. But those facts in the Bible which contradict the laws of nature, must be examined with more care, and under a variety of faces. Here you must recur to the pretensions of the writer to inspiration from God. Examine upon what evidence his pretensions are founded, and whether that evidence is so strong as that its falsehood would be more improbable than a change in the laws of nature in the case he relates. For example in the book of Joshua we are told the sun stood still several hours.[6] Were we to read that fact in Livy or Tacitus we should class it with their showers of blood, speaking of statues, beasts, etc. But it is said that the writer of that book was inspired. Examine therefore candidly what evidence there is of his having been inspired. The pretension is entitled to your inquiry, because millions believe it. On the other hand you are astronomer enough to know how contrary it is to the law of nature that a body revolving on its axis as the earth does, should have stopped, should not by that sudden stoppage have prostrated animals, trees, buildings, and should after a certain time have resumed its revolution, and that without a second general prostration. Is this arrest

---

[3]"The beautiful" (Greek).
[4]Laurence Sterne (1713–1768), author of *Tristram Shandy* (1760–61).
[5]Livy (59 B.C.–A.D. 17), Roman historian; Cornelius Tacitus (A.D. 55?–after 117), Roman historian and orator.

[6]Joshua 10:13: "So the sun stood still in the midst of heaven and hasted not to go down about a whole day."

of the earth's motion, or the evidence which affirms it, most within the law of probabilities? You will next read the New Testament. It is the history of a personage called Jesus. Keep in your eye the opposite pretensions 1. of those who say he was begotten by God, born of a virgin, suspended and reversed the laws of nature at will, and ascended bodily into heaven: and 2. of those who say he was a man of illegitimate birth, of a benevolent heart, enthusiastic mind, who set out without pretensions to divinity, ended in believing them, and was punished capitally for sedition by being gibbeted according to the Roman law which punished the first commission of that offense by whipping, and the second by exile or death *in furcâ*.[7] See this law in the Digest Lib. 48. tit. 19. §. 28.3. and Lipsius Lib. 2. de cruce. cap. 2.[8] These questions are examined in the books I have mentioned under the head of religion, and several others. They will assist you in your inquiries, but keep your reason firmly on the watch in reading them all. Do not be frightened from this inquiry by any fear of its consequences. If it ends in a belief that there is no God, you will find incitements to virtue in the comfort and pleasantness you feel in its exercise, and the love of others which it will procure you. If you find reason to believe there is a God, a consciousness that you are acting under His eye, and that He approves you, will be a vast additional incitement; if that there be a future state, the hope of a happy existence in that increases the appetite to deserve it; if that Jesus was also a God, you will be comforted by a belief of His aid and love. In fine,[9] I repeat that you must lay aside all prejudice on both sides, and neither believe nor reject anything because any other persons, or description of persons have rejected or believed it. Your own reason is the only oracle given you by heaven, and you are answerable not for the rightness but uprightness of the decision. I forgot to observe when speaking of the New Testament that you should read all the histories of Christ, as well of those whom a council of ecclesiastics have decided for us to be Pseudo-evangelists,[10] as those they named Evangelists. Because these Pseudo-evangelists pretended to inspiration as much as the others, and you are to judge their pretensions by your own reason, and not by the reason of those ecclesiastics. Most of these are lost. There are some however still extant, collected by Fabricius[11] which I will endeavor to get and send you.

5. Travelling. This makes men wiser, but less happy. When men of sober age travel, they gather knowledge which they may apply usefully for their country, but they are subject ever after to recollections mixed with regret, their affections are weakened by being extended over more objects, and they learn new habits which cannot be gratified when they return home. Young men who travel are exposed to all these inconveniences in a higher degree, to others still more serious, and do not acquire that wisdom for which a previous foundation is requisite by repeated and just observations at home. The glare of pomp and pleasure is analogous to the motion of their blood, it absorbs all their affection and attention, they are torn from it as from the only good in this world, and return to their home as to a place of exile and condemnation. Their eyes are for ever turned back to the object they have lost, and its recollection poisons the residue of their lives. Their first and most delicate passions are hackneyed on unworthy objects here, and they carry home only the dregs, insufficient to make themselves or anybody else happy. Add to this that a habit of idleness, an inability to apply themselves to business is acquired and renders them useless to themselves and their country. These obser-

---

[7]By crucifixion.
[8]*Digest* (a body of laws collected by Tribonianus for Justin I, Roman emperor, 527–565), Book 48, Title 19, Section 28, Sentence 3; Justus Lipsius (1547–1606), Flemish scholar: Book 2, *De Cruce* ("*Of the Cross*," Latin), Head 2.
[9]To conclude.
[10]Nonapostolic writers, as Clement of Rome (fl. *c.* A.D. 96),

his epistle to Corinth; and the author of *The Shepherd of Hermas* (c. 139–154), containing Visions, Mandates and Similitudes. These works never achieved canonical status and were not included in the New Testament.
[11]Johann Albert Fabricius (1668–1736), German philologist, author/editor of *Codex Apocryphus* (1703), an important work on apocryphal Christian literature.

vations are founded in experience. There is no place where your pursuit of knowledge will be so little obstructed by foreign objects as in your own country, nor any wherein the virtues of the heart will be less exposed to be weakened. Be good, be learned, and be industrious, and you will not want the aid of travelling to render you precious to your country, dear to your friends, happy within yourself. I repeat my advice to take a great deal of exercise, and on foot. Health is the first requisite after morality. Write to me often and be assured of the interest I take in your success, as well as of the warmth of those sentiments of attachment with which I am, dear Peter, your affectionate friend.

P. S. Let me know your age in your next letter. Your cousins here are well and desire to be remembered to you.

TO BENJAMIN RUSH[1]

[THE COMPARATIVE MERITS OF CHRISTIANITY]

Washington, April 21, 1803

DEAR SIR,–In some of the delightful conversations with you, in the evenings of 1798–99, and which served as an anodyne to the afflictions of the crisis through which our country was then laboring, the Christian religion was sometimes our topic; and I then promised you, that one day or other, I would give you my views of it. They are the result of a life of inquiry and reflection, and very different from that anti-Christian system imputed to me by those who know nothing of my opinions. To the corruptions of Christianity I am indeed opposed; but not to the genuine precepts of Jesus himself. I am a Christian, in the only sense he wished any one to be; sincerely attached to his doctrines, in preference to all others; ascribing to himself every *human* excellence; and believing he never claimed any other. At the short intervals since these conversations, when I could justifiably abstract my mind from public affairs, the subject has been under my contemplation. But the more I considered it, the more it expanded beyond the measure of either my time or information. In the moment of my late departure from Monticello, I received from Dr. Priestley,[2] his little treatise of *Socrates and Jesus Compared*. This being a section of the general view I had taken of the field it became a subject of reflection while on the road, and unoccupied otherwise. The result was, to arrange in my mind a syllabus, or outline of such an estimate of the comparative merits of Christianity, as I wished to see executed by some one of more leisure and information for the task, than myself. This I now send you, as the only discharge of my promise I can probably ever execute. And in confiding it to you, I know it will not be exposed to the malignant perversions of those who make every word from me a text for new misrepresentations and calumnies. I am moreover averse to the communication of my religious tenets to the public; because it would countenance the presumption of those who have endeavored to draw them before that tribunal, and to seduce public opinion to erect itself into that inquisition over the rights of conscience, which the laws have so justly proscribed. It behooves every man who values liberty of conscience for himself, to resist invasions of it in the case of others; or their case may, by change of circumstances, become his own. It behooves him, too, in his own case, to give no example of concession, betraying the common right of independent opinion, by answering questions of faith, which the laws have left between God and himself. Accept my affectionate salutations.

---

[1]Benjamin Rush (c. 1745–1813), a scientist and physician, as well as political leader (signer of Declaration of Independence); a long time friend of Jefferson's.

[2]Joseph Priestley (1733–1804), British scientist and clergyman (Unitarian) who emigrated to Pennsylvania in 1794.

SYLLABUS OF AN ESTIMATE OF THE MERIT OF THE DOCTRINES OF JESUS, COMPARED WITH THOSE OF OTHERS

In a comparative view of the ethics of the enlightened nations of antiquity, of the Jews and of Jesus, no notice should be taken of the corruptions of reason among the ancients, to wit, the idolatry and superstition of the vulgar, nor of the corruptions of Christianity by the learned among its professors.

Let a just view be taken of the moral principles inculcated by the most esteemed of the sects of ancient philosophy, or of their individuals; particularly Pythagoras, Socrates, Epicurus, Cicero, Epictetus, Seneca, Antoninus.[3]

I. Philosophers. 1. Their precepts related chiefly to ourselves, and the government of those passions which, unrestrained, would disturb our tranquillity of mind. In this branch of philosophy they were really great.

2. In developing our duties to others, they were short and defective. They embraced, indeed, the circles of kindred and friends, and inculcated patriotism or the love of our country in the aggregate, as a primary obligation: toward our neighbors and countrymen they taught justice, but scarcely viewed them as within the circle of benevolence. Still less have they inculcated peace, charity and love to our fellow men, or embraced with benevolence the whole family of mankind.

II. Jews. 1. Their system was Deism; that is, the belief of one only God. But their ideas of him and of his attributes were degrading and injurious.

2. Their ethics were not only imperfect, but often irreconcilable with the sound dictates of reason and morality, as they respect intercourse with those around us; and repulsive and anti-social, as respecting other nations. They needed reformation, therefore, in an eminent degree.

III. Jesus. In this state of things among the Jews Jesus appeared. His parentage was obscure; his condition poor; his education null; his natural endowments great; his life correct and innocent: he was meek, benevolent, patient, firm, disinterested, and of the sublimest eloquence.

The disadvantages under which his doctrines appear are remarkable.

1. Like Socrates and Epictetus, he wrote nothing himself.

2. But he had not, like them, a Xenophon or an Arrian[4] to write for him. I name not Plato, who only used the name of Socrates to cover the whimsies of his own brain. On the contrary,[5] all the learned of his country, entrenched in its power and riches, were opposed to him, lest his labors should undermine their advantages; and the committing to writing his life and doctrines fell on the most unlettered and ignorant men; who wrote, too, from memory, and not till long after the transactions had passed.

3. According to the ordinary fate of those who attempt to enlighten and reform mankind, he fell an early victim to the jealousy and combination of the altar and the throne, at about thirty-three years of age, his reason having not yet attained the *maximum* of its energy, nor the course of his preaching, which was but of three years at most, presented occasions for developing a complete system of morals.

4. Hence the doctrines which he really delivered were defective as a whole, and

---

[3]Pythagoras (fl. *c.* 530 B.C.), Greek philosopher and mathematician; Socrates (470?–399 B.C.), Greek philosopher whose doctrines are the basis of idealistic philosophy (known only through the writings of Plato [427?–347 B.C.], his pupil; Epicurus (342?–270 B.C.), Greek philosopher and founder of Epicureanism—pleasure as the only good and the end of all morality; Cicero (106–43 B.C.), Roman orator and philosopher; Epictetus (fl. A.D. 90), Greek stoic philosopher (stoicism taught people to be calmly accepting and free from emotion); Seneca (4 B.C.–A.D. 65), Roman philosopher and dramatist, belonged to school of Stoicism; Antoninus (121–180), Roman emperor (r. 161–180), an eminent Stoic philosopher, author of *Meditations*.

[4]Xenophon (434?–?355 B.C.), Greek historian and essayist, disciple of Socrates, author of *Anabasis* and *Symposium;* Arrian (fl. second century A.D.), Greek historian, author of two books on Stoic philosophy of Epictetus.

[5]I.e., In Jesus' case . . . .

fragments only of what he did deliver have come to us mutilated, misstated, and often unintelligible.

5. They have been still more disfigured by the corruptions of schismatising followers, who have found an interest in sophisticating and perverting the simple doctrines he taught by engrafting on them the mysticisms of a Grecian sophist, frittering them into subtleties, and obscuring them with jargon, until they have caused good men to reject the whole in disgust, and to view Jesus himself as an impostor.

Notwithstanding these disadvantages, a system of morals is presented to us, which, if filled up in the true style and spirit of the rich fragments he left us, would be the most perfect and sublime that has ever been taught by man.

The question of his being a member of the Godhead, or in direct communication with it, claimed for him by some of his followers, and denied by others is foreign to the present view, which is merely an estimate of the intrinsic merit of his doctrines.

1. He corrected the Deism of the Jews, confirming them in their belief of one only God, and giving them juster notions of His attributes and government.

2. His moral doctrines, relating to kindred and friends, were more pure and perfect than those of the most correct of the philosophers, and greatly more so than those of the Jews; and they went far beyond both in inculcating universal philanthropy, not only to kindred and friends, to neighbors and countrymen, but to all mankind, gathering all into one family, under the bonds of love, charity, peace, common wants and common aids. A development of this head will evince the peculiar superiority of the system of Jesus over all others.

3. The precepts of philosophy, and of the Hebrew code, laid hold of actions only. He pushed his scrutinies into the heart of man; erected his tribunal in the region of his thoughts, and purified the waters at the fountain head.

4. He taught, emphatically, the doctrines of a future state, which was either doubted, or disbelieved by the Jews; and wielded it with efficacy, as an important incentive, supplementary to the other motives to moral conduct.

TO JOHN ADAMS[1]

[A NATURAL ARISTOCRACY]

Monticello, October 28, 1813

Dear Sir, . . . For I agree with you that there is a natural aristocracy among men. The grounds of this are virtue and talents. Formerly bodily powers gave place among the aristoi.[2] But since the invention of gunpowder has armed the weak as well as the strong with missile death, bodily strength, like beauty, good humor, politeness and other accomplishments, has become but an auxiliary ground of distinction. There is also an artificial aristocracy founded on wealth and birth, without either virtue or talents; for with these it would belong to the first class. The natural aristocracy I consider as the most precious gift of nature for the instruction, the trusts, and government of society. And indeed it would have been inconsistent in creation to have formed man for the social state, and not to have provided virtue and wisdom enough to manage the concerns of the society. May we not even say that that form of government is the best which provides the most effectually for a pure selection of these natural aristoi into the offices of government? The artificial aristocracy is a mischievous ingredient in government, and provision should be made to prevent its ascendancy. On the question, What is the

---

[1] John Adams served with Jefferson on the committee to write the Declaration of Independence; their friendship was strained when the Federalist Adams won the presidency in 1796, over the Republican Jefferson, the latter serving as vice president. After Jefferson's presidency (1800–08), the men resumed their friendship and corresponded frequently from 1812.
[2] The best.

best provision, you and I differ; but we differ as rational friends, using the free exercise of our own reason, and mutually indulging its errors. *You* think it best to put the pseudo-aristoi into a separate chamber of legislation where they may be hindered from doing mischief by their coordinate branches, and where also they may be a protection to wealth against the agrarian and plundering enterprises of the majority of the people. I think that to give them power in order to prevent them from doing mischief, is arming them for it, and increasing instead of remedying the evil. For if the coordinate branches can arrest their action, so may they that of the coordinates. Mischief may be done negatively as well as positively. Of this a cabal in the Senate of the U. S. has furnished many proofs. Nor do I believe them necessary to protect the wealthy; because enough of these will find their way into every branch of the legislation to protect themselves. From fifteen to twenty legislatures of our own, in action for thirty years past, have proved that no fears of an equalisation of property are to be apprehended from them.

I think the best remedy is exactly that provided by all our constitutions, to leave to the citizens the free election and separation of the aristoi from the pseudo-aristoi, of the wheat from the chaff. In general they will elect the real good and wise. In some instances, wealth may corrupt, and birth blind them; but not in sufficient degree to endanger the society.[3]

It is probable that our difference of opinion may in some measure be produced by a difference of character in those among whom we live. From what I have seen of Massachusetts and Connecticut myself, and still more from what I have heard, and the character given of the former by yourself, who know them so much better, there seems to be in those two states a traditionary reverence for certain families, which has rendered the offices of the government nearly hereditary in those families. I presume that from an early period of your history, members of these families happening to possess virtue and talents, have honestly exercised them for the good of the people, and by their services have endeared their names to them.

In coupling Connecticut with you, I mean it politically only, not morally. For having made the Bible the Common law of their land they seem to have modelled their morality on the story of Jacob and Laban.[4] But although this hereditary succession to office with you may in some degree be founded in real family merit, yet in a much higher degree it has proceeded from your strict alliance of church and state. These families are canonised in the eyes of the people on the common principle 'you tickle me, and I will tickle you.' In Virginia we have nothing of this. Our clergy, before the revolution, having been secured against rivalship by fixed salaries, did not give themselves the trouble of acquiring influence over the people. Of wealth, there were great accumulations in particular families, handed down from generation to generation under the English law of entails.[5] But the only object of ambition for the wealthy was a seat in the king's council.[6] All their court then was paid to the crown and its creatures; and they Philipised[7] in all collisions between the king and people. Hence they were unpopular; and that unpopularity continues attached to their names. A Randolph, a Carter, or a Burwell[8] must have great personal superiority over a common competitor to be elected by the people, even at this day.

At the first session of our legislature after the Declaration of Independence, we

---

[3]"Vol. 1 page 111" (Jefferson's note). Reference is to Adams's *Defense of the Constitutions of Government of the United States of America*, 3 vols. (1787, 1797).

[4]In Genesis 24–31, Jacob worked for Laban for seven years to win Laban's daughter Rachel but was tricked into marrying Laban's daughter Leah, and had to work an additional seven years to finally win Rachel. Jacob was, after wrestling with an angel, blessed with the name of Israel, thus establishing a family dynasty.

[5]Limiting inheritance to a specific line of heirs, as eldest sons.

[6]A Privy Council, appointed by the king.

[7]Compromised the rights of the people; from Philip II of Macedon, who bribed leaders to betray their people and support his policies destroying independence of the Greek city-states.

[8]John Randolph, Landon Carter, and Lewis Burwell were all from aristocratic, wealthy families.

passed a law abolishing entails.[9] And this was followed by one abolishing the privilege of primogeniture, and dividing the lands of intestates[10] equally among all their children, or other representatives. These laws, drawn by myself, laid the axe to the root of pseudo-aristocracy. And had another which I prepared been adopted by the legislature, our work would have been complete. It was a bill for the more general diffusion of learning. This proposed to divide every county into wards of five or six miles square, like your townships; to establish in each ward a free school for reading, writing and common arithmetic; to provide for the annual selection of the best subjects from these schools who might receive at the public expense a higher degree of education at a district school; and from these district schools to select a certain number of the most promising subjects to be completed at an university, where all the useful sciences should be taught. Worth and genius would thus have been sought out from every condition of life, and completely prepared by education for defeating the competition of wealth and birth for public trusts.

My proposition had for a further object to impart to these wards those portions of self-government for which they are best qualified, by confiding to them the care of their poor, their roads, police, elections, the nomination of jurors, administration of justice in small cases, elementary exercises of militia, in short, to have made them little republics, with a warden at the head of each, for all those concerns which, being under their eye, they would better manage than the larger republics of the county or state. A general call of ward-meetings by their wardens on the same day through the state would at any time produce the genuine sense of the people on any required point, and would enable the state to act in mass, as your people have so often done, and with so much effect, by their town meetings. The law for religious freedom,[11] which made a part of this system, having put down the aristocracy of the clergy, and restored to the citizen the freedom of the mind, and those of entails and descents nurturing an equality of condition among them, this on Education would have raised the mass of the people to the high ground of moral respectability necessary to their own safety, and to orderly government; and would have completed the great object of qualifying them to select the veritable aristoi, for the trusts of government, to the exclusion of the pseudalists: and the same Theognis who has furnished the epigraphs of your two letters assures us that Ουδεμιαν πω, κυρν' ἀγαθοι πολιν ὡλεσαν ἀνδρες.[12] Although this law has not yet been acted on but in a small and inefficient degree, it is still considered as before the legislature, with other bills of the revised code, not yet taken up, and I have great hope that some patriotic spirit will, at a favorable moment, call it up, and make it the key-stone of the arch of our government.

With respect to aristocracy, we should further consider that, before the establishment of the American states, nothing was known to history but the man of the old world, crowded within limits either small or overcharged, and steeped in the vices which that situation generates. A government adapted to such men would be one thing; but a very different one that for the man of these states. Here every one may have land to labor for himself if he chooses; or, preferring the exercise of any other industry, may exact for it such compensation as not only to afford a comfortable subsistence, but wherewith to provide for a cessation from labor in old age. Everyone, by his property, or by his satisfactory situation, is interested in the support of law and order. And such men may safely and advantageously reserve to themselves a wholesome control over their public affairs, and a degree of

---

[9]Jefferson had promoted legislation aimed against hereditary wealth in Virginia.
[10]Primogeniture left estates to eldest sons; intestates were those who died without writing wills.

[11]Passed in 1786.
[12]Theognis (fl. sixth century B.C.), Greek elegiac poet: "Curnis, good men have never harmed any city."

freedom, which in the hands of the Canaille[13] of the cities of Europe, would be instantly perverted to the demolition and destruction of every thing public and private. The history of the last twenty-five years of France,[14] and the last forty years in America, nay of its last two hundred years, proves the truth of both parts of this observation.

But even in Europe a change has sensibly taken place in the mind of man. Science had liberated the ideas of those who read and reflect, and the American example had kindled feelings of right in the people. An insurrection has consequently begun, of science, talents and courage against rank and birth, which have fallen into contempt. It has failed in its first effort, because the mobs of the cities, the instrument used for its accomplishment, debased by ignorance, poverty and vice, could not be restrained to rational action. But the world will recover from the panic of this first catastrophe. Science is progressive, and talents and enterprise on the alert. Resort may be had to the people of the country, a more governable power from their principles and subordination; and rank, and birth, and tinsel-aristocracy will finally shrink into insignificance, even there. This however we have no right to meddle with. It suffices for us, if the moral and physical condition of our own citizens qualifies them to select the able and good for the direction of their government, with a recurrence of elections at such short periods as will enable them to displace an unfaithful servant before the mischief he meditates may be irremediable.

I have thus stated my opinion on a point on which we differ, not with a view to controversy, for we are both too old to change opinions which are the result of a long life of inquiry and reflection; but on the suggestion of a former letter of yours, that we ought not to die before we have explained ourselves to each other. We acted in perfect harmony through a long and perilous contest for our liberty and independence. A constitution has been acquired which, though neither of us think perfect, yet both consider as competent to render our fellow-citizens the happiest and the securest on whom the sun has ever shone. If we do not think exactly alike as to its imperfections, it matters little to our country which, after devoting to it long lives of disinterested labor, we have delivered over to our successors in life, who will be able to take care of it, and of themselves.

Of the pamphlet on aristocracy which has been sent to you, or who may be its author, I have heard nothing but through your letter. If the person you suspect it may be known from the quaint, mystical and hyperbolical ideas, involved in affected, new-fangled and pedantic terms, which stamp his writings. Whatever it be, I hope your quiet is not to be affected at this day by the rudeness of intemperance of scribblers; but that you may continue in tranquility to live and to rejoice in the prosperity of our country until it shall be your own wish to take your seat among the aristoi who have gone before you. Ever and affectionately yours.

TH: JEFFERSON

TO JOHN ADAMS
[ON LIVING LIFE OVER]

Monticello, August 1, 1816

DEAR SIR

Your two philosophical letters of May 4 and 6 have been too long in my carton of "letters to be answered." To the question indeed on the utility of grief, no answer remains to be given. You have exhausted the subject. I see that, with the other evils of life, it is destined to temper the cup we are to drink.

---

[13]Rabble.
[14]Since the beginning of the French Revolution in 1789.

> Two urns by Jove's high throne have ever stood,
> The source of evil one, and one of good;
> From thence the cup of mortal man he fills,
> Blessings to these, to those distributes ills;
> To most he mingles both.[1]

Putting to myself your question, Would I agree to live my seventy-three years over again for ever? I hesitate to say. With Chew's limitations[2] from twenty-five to sixty, I would say yes; and might go further back, but not come lower down. For, at the latter period, with most of us, the powers of life are sensibly on the wane, sight becomes dim, hearing dull, memory constantly enlarging its frightful blank and parting with all we have ever seen or known, spirits evaporate, bodily debility creeps on palsying every limb, and so faculty after faculty quits us, and where then is life? If, in its full vigor, of good as well as evil, your friend Vassall[3] could doubt its value, it must be purely a negative quantity when its evils alone remain. Yet I do not go into his opinion entirely. I do not agree that an age of pleasure is no compensation for a moment of pain. I think, with you, that life is a fair matter of account, and the balance often, nay generally in its favor. It is not indeed easy, by calculation of intensity and time, to apply a common measure, or to fix the par between pleasure and pain: yet it exists, and is measurable. On the question, for example, whether to be cut for the stone? the young, with a longer prospect of years, think these overbalance the pain of the operation. Dr. Franklin, at the age of eighty, thought his residuum of life, not worth that price. I should have thought with him, even taking the stone out of the scale. There is a ripeness of time for death, regarding others as well as ourselves, when it is reasonable we should drop off, and make room for another growth. When we have lived our generation out, we should not wish to encroach on another. I enjoy good health; I am happy in what is around me. Yet I assure you I am ripe for leaving all, this year, this day, this hour. If it could be doubted whether we would go back to twenty-five how can it be, whether we would go forward from seventy-three? Bodily decay is gloomy in prospect; but of all human contemplations the most abhorrent is body without mind. Perhaps however I might accept of time to read Grimm[4] before I go. Fifteen volumes of anecdotes and incidents, within the compass of my own time and cognizance, written by a man of genius, of taste, of point, an acquaintance, the measure and traverses of whose mind I knew, could not fail to turn the scale in favor of life during their perusal. I must write to Ticknor[5] to add it to my catalogue, and hold on till it comes.

There is a Mr. Vanderkemp of N.Y.[6] a correspondent I believe of yours, with whom I have exchanged some letters, without knowing who he is. Will you tell me?

I know nothing of the history of the Jesuits you mention in four vols. Is it a good one? I dislike, with you, their restoration; because it marks a retrograde step from light towards darkness. We shall have our follies without doubt. Some one or more of them will always be afloat. But ours will be the follies of enthusiasm, not of bigotry, not of Jesuitism.[7] Bigotry is the disease of ignorance, of morbid minds;

---

[1]Alexander Pope (1688–1744), translator of Homer's *Iliad*, Book 24, ll. 663–67.
[2]In his letter to Jefferson, May 3, 1816, Adams refers to a statement by Benjamin Chew, a Philadelphia lawyer, that he would like "to go back to twenty-five, to all eternity."
[3]In his letter of May 3, Adams had quoted "a man of letters and virtues," William Vassall: "Pleasure is no compensation for pain."
[4]Friedrich Melchior von Grimm (1723–1807), journalist and critic, whose seventeen volumes of *Literary, Philosophic, and Critical Correspondence* appeared in 1812–14.

[5]George Ticknor (1791–1871), professor of French and Spanish at Harvard and founder of the Boston Public Library (1852).
[6]Francis Adrian Vanderkemp, an émigré to New York from Holland, where he had first been a soldier, and then a minister.
[7]Craftiness or trickiness, from the alleged habit of Jesuits to argue with more cunning than honesty.

enthusiasm of the free and buoyant. Education and free discussion are the antidotes of both. We are destined to be a barrier against the returns of ignorance and barbarism. Old Europe will have to lean on our shoulders, and to hobble along by our side, under the monkish trammels of priests and kings, as she can. What a Colossus shall we be when the southern continent comes up to our mark!

What a stand will it secure as a ralliance[8] for the reason and freedom of the globe. I like the dreams of the future better than the history of the past. So good night. I will dream on, always fancying that Mrs. Adams and yourself are by my side marking the progress and the obliquities of ages and countries.

TH: JEFFERSON

TO JOHN ADAMS
[THE BEING OF GOD]

Monticello, April 11, 1823

DEAR SIR

The wishes expressed, in your last favor, that I may continue in life and health until I become a Calvinist, at least in his exclamation of *"Mon Dieu! jusque à quand!"*[1] would make me immortal. I can never join Calvin in addressing *his God*. He was indeed an atheist, which I can never be; or rather his religion was demonism. If ever man worshipped a false god, he did. The being described in his five points is not the God whom you and I acknowledge and adore, the Creator and benevolent governor of the world; but a demon of malignant spirit. It would be more pardonable to believe in no god at all, than to blaspheme Him by the atrocious attributes of Calvin. Indeed I think that every Christian sect gives a great handle to atheism by their general dogma that, without a revelation, there would not be sufficient proof of the being of a god. Now one-sixth of mankind only are supposed to be Christians: the other five-sixths then, who do not believe in the Jewish and Christian revelation, are without a knowledge of the existence of a god! This gives completely a gain de cause[2] to the disciples of Ocellus, Timacus, Spinoza, Diderot and D'Holbach.[3] The argument which they rest on as triumphant and unanswerable is that, in every hypothesis of cosmogony you must admit an eternal preexistence of something; and according to the rule of sound philosophy, you are never to employ two principles to solve a difficulty when one will suffice. They say then that it is more simple to believe at once in the eternal pre-existence of the world, as it is now going on, and may for ever go on by the principle of reproduction which we see and witness, than to believe in the eternal pre-existence of an ulterior cause, or Creator of the world, a being whom we see not, and know not, of whose form substance and mode or place of existence, or of action no sense informs us, no power of the mind enables us to delineate or comprehend. On the contrary I hold (without appeal to revelation) that when we take a view of the universe, in its parts general or particular, it is impossible for the human mind not to perceive and feel a conviction of design, consummate skill, and indefinite power in every atom of its composition. The movements of the heavenly bodies, so exactly held in their course by the balance of centrifugal and centripetal forces, the structure of our earth itself, with its distribution of lands, waters and atmosphere, animal and vegetable bodies, examined in all their minutest particles, insects mere atoms of life, yet as perfectly organised as man or mammoth, the mineral sub-

---

[8]Ralliance, perhaps rally + alliance, a coming together.
[1]"Lord, how long!" (French).
[2]"For reason" (Latin).
[3]Ocellus Lucanus (fl. fifth century B.C.), Pythagorean philosopher, author of a treatise, *On the Nature of the Universe;* Timaeus (fl. *c.* 400 B.C.), whose name is attached to a Plato dialogue embodying a theory of the universe; Spinoza

(1632–1677), Dutch philosopher, proponent of pantheism; Diderot (1713–1784), French encyclopedist and philosopher; D'Holbach (1723–1789), French materialistic philosopher. Jefferson cites these philosophers as sharing a belief in a kind of pantheism, in which God is no more than the laws and forces of the self-existing universe.

stances, their generation and uses, it is impossible, I say, for the human mind not to believe that there is, in all this, design, cause and effect, up to an ultimate cause, a fabricator of all things from matter and motion, their preserver and regulator while permitted to exist in their present forms, and their regenerator into new and other forms. We see, too, evident proofs of the necessity of a superintending power to maintain the universe in its course and order. Stars, well known, have disappeared, new ones have come into view, comets, in their incalculable courses, may run foul of suns and planets and require renovation under other laws; certain races of animals are become extinct; and, were there no restoring power, all existences might extinguish successively, one by one, until all should be reduced to a shapeless chaos. So irresistible are these evidences of an intelligent and powerful Agent that, of the infinite numbers of men who have existed through all time, they have believed, in the proportion of a million at least to unit, in the hypothesis of an eternal pre-existence of a creator, rather than in that of a self-existent universe. Surely this unanimous sentiment renders this more probable than that of the few in the other hypothesis. Some early Christians indeed have believed in the coeternal pre-existence of both the Creator and the world, without changing their relation of cause and effect. That this was the opinion of St. Thomas,[4] we are informed by Cardinal Toledo,[5] in these words: "Deus ab æterno fuit jam omnipotens, sicut cum produxit mundum. Ab æterno potuit producere mundum.—Si sol ab æterno esset, lumen ab æterno esset; et si pes, similiter vestigium. At lumen et vestigium effectus sunt efficientis solis et pedis; potuit ergo cum causâ æterna effectus coæterna esse. Cujus sententiæ est S. Thomas Theologorum primus."[6]

• • • • •

So much for your quotation of Calvin's 'mon dieu! jusqu'a quand'[7] in which, when addressed to the God of Jesus, and our God, I join you cordially, and await his time and will with more readiness than reluctance. May we meet there again, in Congress, with our ancient Colleagues, and receive with them the seal of approbation "Well done, good and faithful servants."

Th: Jefferson

---

[4]St. Thomas Aquinas (c. 1225–1274), Italian philosopher and theologian, author of *Summa Theologiae*, a compendium of Catholic theology.
[5]Cardinal Francisco Toledo, Jesuit, Thomist scholar.
[6]"God has been omnipotent forever, just as when he made the world. He has had the power to make the world forever. If the sun were in existence forever, light would have been in existence forever; and if a foot then likewise a footprint. But light and footprint are the effects of an efficient sun and foot; therefore the effect has had the power to be co-eternal with the eternal cause. Of this opinion is St. Thomas, the first of the theologians" (Latin).
[7]"My God! how long" (French).

AN EMERGING AMERICAN POETRY: FROM CLASSIC TO ROMANTIC

PHILIP FRENEAU   JOEL BARLOW
PHILLIS WHEATLEY   WILLIAM CULLEN BRYANT

Philip Freneau, Phillis Wheatley, Joel Barlow, and William Cullen Bryant were the first voices—stammering as they sometimes were—of an American instead of a colonial poetry. The first three of these, all born in the 1750s, matured during the exciting period of the American Revolution and were shaped as writers by the political events of the time; Bryant, born after the Revolution, was shaped more by literary than political forces, and marked the beginning of a distinctively American romanticism. Yet all these poets set forth on the open road of literary independence. They travelled a long distance, far enough to see that the road stretched on and on to an ever receding horizon.

PHILIP FRENEAU
(1752–1832)

Philip Freneau has often been called the father of American poetry, but the epithet has always been ambiguous. President George Washington, frequently called the father of the country, once referred to the poet as "that rascal Freneau." Washington's label has stuck, calling into question the legitimacy of the other label. Many modern American poets, of course, would be delighted to trace their lineage back to an ancestor who was a "rascal" provoking the "establishment" to protest.

Vernon L. Parrington, with some justification, called Freneau the "poet of two revolutions." The first was the Revolutionary War (1775–83) in which America overthrew British rule. Freneau's poetry was constantly urging the colonies on in their rebellion, supplying determination in defeat, celebration in victory. Later, in the 1790s, when the young nation was beginning self-governance under Washington's presidency, and inchoate institutions were taking initial shape, Washington and Hamilton were striving to move the new country in the direction of a conservative Federalist—some called it "monarchical"—model. Jefferson and others like Madison mounted a secret resistance, pushing in the direction of a liberal Democratic-Republican model. Freneau was surreptitiously called into the fray, and through editing the newly established *National Gazette,* attacked the conservatives head-on. Jefferson later claimed that Freneau had "saved our Constitution, which was galloping fast into monarchy."

Whatever epithet we settle on Freneau, he deserves the position he won for himself at the beginning of American poetry, at a time when there were few rewards of any kind bestowed on poets. Freneau was born into a well-to-do New York family with a well-stocked library. The name was originally Fresneau, French, and the family had prospered as an importer of wines from France. He was tutored privately at home and then sent to Princeton (then called the College of New Jersey). Classmates included James Madison and Hugh Henry Brackenridge. While there, Freneau wrote "The Power of Fancy," a poem showing an early commitment to the life of poetry: "Fancy, to thy power I owe/Half my happiness below." Freneau also collaborated with Brackenridge in writing "The Rising Glory of America," which Brackenridge read at their graduation ceremony in 1771. Poetry and patriotism were to remain at the center of Freneau's life to the end of his eighty years.

For a time Freneau taught school and studied theology, but always he wrote poetry. With the outbreak of the Revolutionary War, he wrote and published a series of pamphlet satires attacking the British. Early in 1776 he was offered a position of secretaryship on a plantation in Santa Cruz in the West Indies (now St. Croix, Virgin Islands). He lived there for two and a half years witnessing an exotic culture, a leisure class supported by slavery, and flamboyantly brilliant subtropical land- and sea-scapes. There Freneau wrote some of his most innovative and original poetry, including "The House of Night."

Out of this experience emerged Freneau's love of the sea, to which he turned for a profession, signing on as supercargo (in charge of the cargo merchandise) on a ship sailing for the Azores. His sea adventures led to his capture by the British, who held him in a prison ship for six weeks, finally freeing him in a prisoner exchange. Freneau suffered brutal treatment at the hands of the British, which he described in *The British Prison Ship* in 1781. A new intensity entered his poetry vilifying the British and glorifying the Americans during the Revolution.

After the Revolution, Freneau continued to serve on merchant vessels, but marriage in 1789 brought him home from the sea. He settled with his wife in New Jersey. In 1791 his work supporting Jefferson's attack on the "monarchical" tendencies of the new U.S. government took him to Philadelphia where the capitol had just been moved. Editing the *National Gazette* came to an end in 1793, shortly after Thomas Jefferson's retirement from the post of Secretary of State. Freneau turned for a time to editing various journals, and then he returned to the sea, alternating between it and his farm in New Jersey.

Lewis Leary opened his biography of Freneau with the startling statement: "Philip Freneau failed in almost everything he attempted." Freneau's closing years dramatically demonstrated his genius for failure. No profession held him for long, no work paid him his worth. At the end he drifted into laboring as a handyman and tinkerer. In 1832, as he was returning home, perhaps from the tavern, he became confused and lost in a snow storm and died from exposure.

In "To an Author," Freneau lamented the fate of a poet doomed to live "where lovely Fancy has no sway": "An age employed in edging steel/Can no poetic raptures feel." It was Freneau's fate to live at a time when a revolution had to be fought and won, and a new nation created and shaped. There was little leisure for reading or appreciating poetry. Much of Freneau's poetic energy was poured into the causes and the battles of the day, and his poetry receded with history. The sobriquet, "Poet of the American Revolution," now has something of the ironic sound of a consolation prize. Perhaps Freneau's greatest achievement was in his casting off the neoclassical forms and subjects that dominated his imagination as a young poet, freeing himself to shape an American romantic poetry to which later poets could turn for models. He was in the true sense a *transitional* poet.

In spite of his failures and losses, Freneau's legacy remains a rich one. "The House of Night," still impressive, broke new ground as a romantic poem before the romantic movement began. Such polemical poems as "On Mr. Paine's Rights of Man," and such revolutionary elegies as "To the Memory of the Brave Americans" are enduring reminders of the nation's agony of birth. "To Sir Toby" offers eloquent (and early) testimony against slavery, and "The Indian Burying Ground" a poignant vision of the Indian's life in death—both poems examples of Freneau's sympathetic imagination and compassionate spirit. The Deistic poems, like "The Religion of Nature," are impressive in their simplicity, brevity, and honesty. Such deceptively whimsical lyrics as "The Wild Honeysuckle," "On a Bumble Bee," and "To a Caty-Did" continue to enchant or amuse while venturing modest but felt perceptions. This is an impressive list of achievements for a poet who, coming at the beginning, had to explore as a pioneer the American imagination, had, indeed, to invent the idea of an American poet.

ADDITIONAL READING

Poems of Freneau, ed. Harry Hayden Clark, 1929; *The Prose of Philip Freneau*, ed. Philip M. Marsh, 1955.

Fred Lewis Pattee, "Life of Philip Freneau, 1752–1832," *The Poems of Philip Freneau*, Vol. I, 1902; Lewis Leary, *That Rascal Freneau: A Study in Literary Failure*, 1941; Jacob M. Axelrod, *Philip Freneau: Champion of Democracy*, 1967; Philip M. Marsh, *Philip Freneau: Poet and Jour-*

nalist, 1967; Philip M. Marsh, *The Works of Philip Freneau: A Critical Study,* 1968; Mary Weatherspoon Bowden, *Philip Freneau,* 1976; Richard C. Vitzthum, *Land and Sea: The Lyric Poetry of Philip Freneau,* 1978.

TEXTS

"On Mr. Paine's Rights of Man," *Poems Written and Published During the American Revolutionary War, 1809,* ed. Lewis Leary, 1976; "On the Uniformity and Perfection of Nature," "On the Universality and Other Attributes of the God of Nature," "On the Religion of Nature," *A Collection of Poems on American Affairs and a Variety of Other Subjects Chiefly Moral and Political (1815),* ed. Lewis Leary, 1976; "On Observing a Large Red-streak Apple," *The Last Poems of Philip Freneau,* ed. Lewis Leary, 1945; all other poems from *The Poems of Philip Freneau: Poet of the American Revolution,* 3 vols., ed. Fred Lewis Pattee, 1902–07. Some changes in spelling and punctuation have been made to conform with modern English.

The Power of Fancy[1]

Wakeful, vagrant, restless thing,
Ever wandering on the wing,
Who thy wondrous source can find,
Fancy, regent of the mind;
A spark from Jove's[2] resplendent throne,   5
But thy nature all unknown.
  This spark of bright, celestial flame,
From Jove's seraphic altar came,
And hence alone in man we trace,
Resemblance to the immortal race.   10
Ah! what is all this mighty whole,
These suns and stars that round us roll!
What are they all, where'er they shine,
But Fancies of the Power Divine!
What is this globe, these lands, and seas,   15
And heat, and cold, and flowers, and trees,
And life, and death, and beast, and man,
And time—that with the sun began—
But thoughts on reason's scale combin'd,
Ideas of the Almighty mind!   20
  On the surface of the brain
Night after night she walks unseen,
Noble fabrics doth she raise
In the woods or on the seas,
On some high, steep, pointed rock,   25
Where the billows loudly knock
And the dreary tempests sweep
Clouds along the uncivil deep.
  Lo! she walks upon the moon,
Listens to the chimy tune   30
Of the bright, harmonious spheres,[3]

---

[1]In this early poem, written as an undergraduate at Princeton, Freneau draws upon the classics, Deism, Milton, and his own romantic inclinations. M. C. Tyler has noted that the poem, "in rhymed tetrameters—alert, elastic, full of music and motion—wholly discards the sing-song, the artificial phraseology, and the stilted movement then so common in English poetry."

[2]Another name for Jupiter, supreme Roman god.
[3]Ancient astronomers pictured the sun, moon, and planets revolving around the fixed earth on concentric crystal spheres whose movements created a harmonious music.

And the song of angels hears;
Sees this earth a distant star,[4]
Pendant, floating in the air;
Leads me to some lonely dome,   35
Where Religion loves to come,
Where the bride of Jesus[5] dwells,
And the deep ton'd organ swells
In notes with lofty anthems join'd,
Notes that half distract the mind.   40
    Now like lightning she descends
To the prison of the fiends,
Hears the rattling of their chains,
Feels their never ceasing pains—
But, O never may she tell   45
Half the frightfulness of hell.
    Now she views Arcadian[6] rocks,
Where the shepherds guard their flocks,
And, while yet her wings she spreads,
Sees chrystal streams and coral beds,   50
Wanders to some desert deep,
Or some dark, enchanted steep,
By the full moonlight doth shew
Forests of a dusky blue,
Where, upon some mossy bed,   55
Innocence reclines her head.
    Swift, she stretches o'er the seas
To the far off Hebrides,[7]
Canvas on the lofty mast
Could not travel half so fast—   60
Swifter than the eagle's flight
Or instantaneous rays of light!
Lo! contemplative she stands
On Norwegia's[8] rocky lands—
Fickle Goddess, set me down   65
Where the rugged winters frown
Upon Orca's[9] howling steep,
Nodding o'er the northern deep,
Where the winds tumultuous roar,
Vext that Ossian[10] sings no more.   70
Fancy, to that land repair,
Sweetest Ossian slumbers there;
Waft me far to southern isles
Where the soften'd winter smiles,
To Bermuda's orange shades,   75
Or Demarara's[11] lovely glades;
Bear me o'er the sounding cape,
Painting death in every shape,
Where daring Anson[12] spread the sail
Shatter'd by the stormy gale—   80
Lo! she leads me wide and far,

---

[4]"Milton's *Paradise Lost*, B. II, v. 1052" (Freneau's note).
[5]The heavenly city, the new Jerusalem (Revelation 21:2, 9–10).
[6]Pastoral; Arcadia, a mountainous region of ancient Greece, taken by poets to be the land of pastoral simplicity and happiness.
[7]Western Islands, off the coast of Scotland.
[8]Norway's.
[9]Orkneys, islands off the northeast coast of Scotland.
[10]Legendary Gaelic poet.
[11]Area in British Guiana, South America; now Guyana.
[12]George Anson (1697–1762), British Admiral in the Pacific, circumnavigated the world (1740–44).

Sense can never follow her—
Shape thy course o'er land and sea,
Help me to keep pace with thee,
Lead me to yon' chalky cliff,   85
Over rock and over reef,
Into Britain's fertile land,
Stretching far her proud command.
Look back and view, thro' many a year,
Cæsar, Julius Cæsar, there.[13]   90
       Now to Tempe's[14] verdant wood,
Over the mid-ocean flood
Lo! the islands of the sea—
Sappho, Lesbos mourns for thee:[15]
Greece, arouse thy humbled head,[16]   95
Where are all thy mighty dead,
Who states to endless ruin hurl'd
And carried vengeance through the world?—
Troy, thy vanish'd pomp resume,
Or, weeping at thy Hector's[17] tomb,   100
Yet those faded scenes renew,
Whose memory is to Homer due.
Fancy, lead me wandering still
Up to Ida's[18] cloud-topt hill;
Not a laurel there doth grow   105
But in vision thou shalt show,—
Every sprig on Virgil's[19] tomb
Shall in livelier colours bloom,
And every triumph Rome has seen
Flourish on the years between.   110
       Now she bears me far away
In the east to meet the day,
Leads me over Ganges'[20] streams,
Mother of the morning beams—
O'er the ocean hath she ran,   115
Places me on Tinian;[21]
Farther, farther in the east,
Till it almost meets the west,
Let us wandering both be lost
On Tahiti's[22] sea-beat coast,   120
Bear me from that distant strand,
Over ocean, over land,
To California's golden shore—
Fancy, stop, and rove no more.
       Now, tho' late, returning home,   125
Lead me to Belinda's[23] tomb;
Let me glide as well as you
Through the shroud and coffin too,
And behold, a moment, there,

---

[13]Caesar landed in Britain in 55 B.C.
[14]Valley in Thessaly, Greece.
[15]Sappho (seventh century B.C.), Greek lyric poet, lived on Lesbos, island in the Aegean off the coast of Turkey. So esteemed was her poetry that Plato called her the "tenth muse."
[16]Ruled by the Turks from the mid-fifteenth century until 1821, Greece was incited to revolt in 1770 by Russia.
[17]Trojan prince slain by Achilles during the seige of Troy in Homer's *Iliad*.

[18]Mount Ida, near Troy; from its peaks, Zeus watched the Trojan War.
[19]Roman poet (70–19 B.C.), author of the *Aeneid*.
[20]River in India.
[21]Island in the Pacific.
[22]Island in the Pacific.
[23]Common name in neoclassical literature.

All that once was good and fair—   130
Who doth here so soundly sleep?
Shall we break this prison deep?—
Thunders cannot wake the maid,
Lightnings cannot pierce the shade,
And tho' wintry tempests roar,   135
Tempests shall disturb no more.
   Yet must those eyes in darkness stay,
That once were rivals to the day?—
Like heaven's bright lamp beneath the main
They are but set to rise again.   140
   Fancy, thou the muses' pride,
In thy painted realms reside
Endless images of things,
Fluttering each on golden wings,
Ideal objects, such a store,   145
The universe could hold no more:
Fancy, to thy power I owe
Half my happiness below;
By thee Elysian groves²⁴ were made,
Thine were the notes that Orpheus²⁵ play'd;   150
By thee was Pluto charm'd so well
While rapture seiz'd the sons of hell—
Come, O come—perceiv'd by none,
You and I will walk alone.

1770   1786

A Political Litany¹

Libera Nos, Domine.—Deliver us, O Lord, not only
from British dependence, but also

From a junto² that labor with absolute power,
Whose schemes disappointed have made them look sour,
From the lords of the council, who fight against freedom,
Who still follow on where delusion shall lead them.

From the group at St. James's,³ who slight our petitions,   5
And fools that are waiting for further submissions—
From a nation whose manners are rough and severe,
From scoundrels and rascals,—do keep us all clear.

From pirates sent out by command of the king
To murder and plunder, but never to swing.   10
From Wallace and Greaves, and Vipers and Roses,⁴
Whom, if heaven pleases, we'll give bloody noses.

---

²⁴In Greek mythology, the land of spring and happiness
for the blessed dead.
²⁵In Greek mythology, Orpheus, son of Apollo and the
muse Calliope, famous poet and musician, freed his wife
Eurydice from Hades by enchanting Pluto, god of the underworld, with his song and lyre.
¹Freneau lived in New York from late spring through November 1775, during the early stages of the revolution and
published several satires against the British, including "A
Political Litany." Litany: a prayer of entreaty.
²Clique, ruling group.
³British royal court.
⁴"Captains and ships in the British navy, then employed on
the American coast" (Freneau's note).

From the valiant Dunmore,[5] with his crew of banditti,[6]
Who plunder Virginians at Williamsburg city,
From hot-headed Montague,[7] mighty to swear,   15
The little fat man with his pretty white hair.

From bishops in Britain, who butchers are grown,
From slaves that would die for a smile from the throne,
From assemblies that vote against Congress proceedings,
(Who now see the fruit of their stupid misleadings.)   20

From Tryon[8] the mighty, who flies from our city,
And swelled with importance disdains the committee:[9]
(But since he is pleased to proclaim us his foes,
What the devil care we where the devil he goes.)

From the caitiff,[10] lord North,[11] who would bind us in chains,   25
From a royal king Log,[12] with his tooth-full of brains,
Who dreams, and is certain (when taking a nap)
He has conquered our lands, as they lay on his map.

From a kingdom that bullies, and hectors, and swears,
We send up to heaven our wishes and prayers   30
That we, disunited, may freemen be still,
And Britain go on—to be damned if she will.

1775   *1775?, 1786*

from The House of Night[1]

A Vision

ADVERTISEMENT—This Poem is founded upon the authority of Scripture, inasmuch as these sacred books assert, that *the last enemy that shall be conquered is Death.*[2] For the purposes of poetry he is here personified, and represented as on his dying bed. The scene is laid at a solitary palace, (the time midnight) which, tho' before beautiful and joyous, is now become sad and gloomy, as being the abode and receptacle of Death. Its owner, an amiable, majestic youth, who had lately lost a beloved consort, nevertheless with a noble philosophical fortitude and humanity, entertains him in a friendly manner, and by employing Physicians, endeavours to restore him to health, altho' an enemy; convinced of the excellence and propriety of that divine precept, *If thine enemy hunger, feed him; if he thirst, give him drink.*[3] He nevertheless, as if by

---

[5]John Murray (1732–1809), Earl of Dunmore and last royal governor of Virginia. In April 1775, he removed the colony's gun powder, inciting the first armed uprising of Virginia.
[6]Bandits.
[7]John Montagu (1719–1795), British admiral.
[8]William Tryon (1725–1788), last royal governor of New York. In October 1775, he took refuge from the rebellion on a British warship in New York harbor.
[9]Committee of Safety, governing body established to protect colonial rights; in October 1775, the Continental Congress instructed the committees to arrest Loyalists.
[10]Coward.
[11]Frederick North (1732–1792), Earl of Guilford, and prime minister of Britain (1770–82).

[12]George III; in classic fable, Jupiter answers the frogs' request for a king by throwing down an inert log of wood.
[1]A romantic poem remarkably innovative for its time. It presents a view of death that contrasts sharply with the Puritan vision as dramatized in its most horrifying details in Wigglesworth's *Day of Doom*. Drawing elements from Gothic fiction as well as the "graveyard poets" of British literature, and developing them in a distinctively American moral frame, Freneau anticipates the romantic conceptions of Bryant, Poe, and Whitman.
[2]1 Corinthians 15:26.
[3]Romans 12:20.

a spirit of prophecy, informs this (fictitiously) wicked being of the certainty of his doom, and represents to him in a pathetic manner the vanity of his expectations, either of a reception into the abodes of the just, or continuing longer to make havock of mankind upon earth. The patient finding his end approaching, composes his epitaph, and orders it to be engraved on his tombstone, hinting to us thereby, that even Death and Distress have vanity; and would be remembered with honor after he is no more, altho' his whole life has been spent in deeds of devastation and murder. He dies at last in the utmost agonies of despair, after agreeing with an avaricious Undertaker to intomb his bones. This reflects upon the inhumanity of those men, who, not to mention an enemy, would scarcely cover a departed friend with a little dust, without certainty of reward for so doing. The circumstances of his funeral are then recited, and the visionary and fabulous part of the poem disappears. It concludes with a few reflections on the impropriety of a too great attachment to the present life, and incentives to such moral virtue as may assist in conducting us to a better.

1

Trembling I write my dream, and recollect
A fearful vision at the midnight hour;
So late, Death o'er me spread his sable wings,
Painted with fancies of malignant power!

. . . . .

3

Let others draw from smiling skies their theme,
And tell of climes that boast unfading light,   10
I draw a darker scene, replete with gloom,
I sing the horrors of the House of Night.

4

Stranger, believe the truth experience tells,
Poetic dreams are of a finer cast
Than those which o'er the sober brain diffus'd,   15
Are but a repetition of some action past.

. . . . .

6

By some sad means, when Reason holds no sway,
Lonely I rov'd at midnight o'er a plain
Where murmuring streams and mingling rivers flow
Far to their springs, or seek the sea again.

7

Sweet vernal May! tho' then thy woods in bloom   25
Flourish'd, yet nought of this could Fancy see,
No wild pinks bless'd the meads, no green the fields,
And naked seem'd to stand each lifeless tree:

8

Dark was the sky, and not one friendly star
Shone from the zenith or horizon, clear,   30
Mist sate upon the woods, and darkness rode
In her black chariot, with a wild career.

9

And from the woods the late resounding note
Issued of the loquacious Whip-poor-will,[4]
Hoarse, howling dogs, and nightly roving wolves   35
Clamor'd from far off cliffs invisible.

. . . .

11

At last, by chance and guardian fancy led,
I reach'd a noble dome, rais'd fair and high,
And saw the light from upper windows flame,
Presage of mirth and hospitality.

12

And by that light around the dome appear'd
A mournful garden of autumnal hue,   45
Its lately pleasing flowers all drooping stood
Amidst high weeds that in rank plenty grew.

13

The Primrose there, the violet darkly blue,
Daisies and fair Narcissus ceas'd to rise,
Gay spotted pinks their charming bloom withdrew,   50
And Polyanthus[5] quench'd its thousand dyes.

. . . . .

16

The poppy there, companion to repose,
Display'd her blossoms that began to fall,
And here the purple amaranthus[6] rose
With mint strong-scented, for the funeral.

17

And here and there with laurel shrubs between
A tombstone lay, inscrib'd with strains of woe,   65
And stanzas sad, throughout the dismal green,
Lamented for the dead that slept below.

18

Peace to this awful dome!—when strait I heard
The voice of men in a secluded room,
Much did they talk of death, and much of life,   70
Of coffins, shrouds, and horrors of a tomb.

. . . . .

23

Then up three winding stairs my feet were brought
To a high chamber, hung with mourning sad,   90

---

[4]"A bird peculiar to America, of a solitary nature, who
never sings but in the night. Her note resembles the name
given to her by the country people" (Freneau's note).

[5]Primrose with clusters of variously colored flowers.
[6]Imaginary flower that never fades.

The unsnuff'd candles glar'd with visage dim,
'Midst grief, in ecstasy of woe run mad.

24

A wide leaf'd table stood on either side,
Well fraught with phials, half their liquids spent,
And from a couch, behind the curtain's veil,   95
I heard a hollow voice of loud lament.

25

Turning to view the object whence it came,
My frighted eyes a horrid form survey'd;
Fancy, I own thy power—Death on the couch,
With fleshless limbs, at rueful length, was laid.   100

. . . . .

28

Sad was his countenance, if we can call
That countenance, where only bones were seen   110
And eyes sunk in their sockets, dark and low,
And teeth, that only show'd themselves to grin.

29

Reft was his scull of hair, and no fresh bloom
Of cheerful mirth sate[7] on his visage hoar:
Sometimes he rais'd his head, while deep-drawn groans   115
Were mixt with words that did his fate deplore.

. . . . .

47

But now this man of hell toward me turn'd,   185
And strait, in hideous tone, began to speak;
Long held he sage discourse, but I forebore
To answer him, much less his news to seek.

48

He talk'd of tomb-stones and of monuments,
Of Equinoctial climes[8] and India shores,   190
He talk'd of stars that shed their influence,
Fevers and plagues, and all their noxious stores.

. . . . .

50

Much spoke he of the myrtle and the yew,
Of ghosts that nightly walk the church-yard o'er,
Of storms that through the wint'ry ocean blow
And dash the well-mann'd galley on the shore,   200

---

[7]Sat.
[8]Places around the equator.

51

Of broad-mouth'd cannons, and the thunderbolt,
Of sieges and convulsions, dearth and fire,
Of poisonous weeds—but seem'd to sneer at these
Who by the laurel o'er him did aspire.

. . . . .

87

"Blame not on me the ravage to be made;   345
"Proclaim,—even Death abhors such woe to see;
"I'll quit the world, while decently I can,
"And leave the work to George my deputy."

88

Up rush'd a band, with compasses and scales
To measure his slim carcass, long and lean—   350
"Be sure," said he, "to frame my coffin strong,
"You, master workman, and your men, I mean:

. . . . .

90

"Of hardest ebon let the plank be found,
"With clamps and ponderous bars secur'd around,
"That if the box by Satan should be storm'd,
"It may be able for resistance found."   360

. . . . .

94

Strait they retir'd—when thus he gave me charge,
Pointing from the light window to the west,
"Go three miles o'er the plain, and you shall see   375
"A burying-yard of sinners dead, unblest.

95

"Amid the graves a spiry building stands
"Whose solemn knell resounding through the gloom
"Shall call thee o'er the circumjacent lands
"To the dull mansion destin'd for my tomb.   380

96

"There, since 'tis dark, I'll plant a glimmering light
"Just snatch'd from hell, by whose reflected beams
"Thou shalt behold a tomb-stone, full eight feet,
"Fast by a grave, replete with ghosts and dreams.

97

"And on that stone engrave this epitaph,   385
"Since Death, it seems, must die like mortal men;
"Yes—on that stone engrave this epitaph,
"Though all hell's fury aim to snatch the pen.

98

"Death in this tomb his weary bones hath laid,
"Sick of dominion o'er the human kind—   390
"Behold what devastations he hath made,
"Survey the millions by his arm confin'd.

99

"Six thousand years has sovereign sway been mine,
"None, but myself, can real glory claim;
"Great Regent of the world I reign'd alone,   395
"And princes trembled when my mandate came.

100

"Vast and unmatch'd throughout the world, my fame
"Takes place of gods, and asks no mortal date—
"No; by myself, and by the heavens, I swear,
"Not Alexander's name is half so great.   400

101

"Nor swords nor darts my prowess could withstand,
"All quit their arms, and bowed to my decree,
"Even mighty Julius died beneath my hand,
"For slaves and Cæsars were the same to me!

102

"Traveller, wouldst thou his noblest trophies seek,   405
"Search in no narrow spot obscure for those;
"The sea profound, the surface of all land
"Is moulded with the myriads of his foes."

103

Scarce had he spoke, when on the lofty dome
Rush'd from the clouds a hoarse resounding blast—   410
Round the four eaves so loud and sad it play'd
As though all music were to breathe its last.

· · · · ·

108

Yet, mindful of his dread command, I part
Glad from the magic dome—nor found relief;   430
Damps from the dead hung heavier round my heart,
While sad remembrance rous'd her stores of grief.

109

O'er a dark field I held my dubious way
Where Jack-a-lanthorn[9] walk'd his lonely round,
Beneath my feet substantial darkness lay,   435
And screams were heard from the distemper'd ground.

---

[9]An *ignis fatuus*, a phosphorescent light hovering over
swampy land at night; also called friar's lantern or will-o'-
the-wisp.

110

Nor look'd I back, till to a far off wood,
Trembling with fear, my weary feet had sped—
Dark was the night, but at the inchanted dome
I saw the infernal windows flaming red.   440

111

And from within the howls of Death I heard,
Cursing the dismal night that gave him birth,
Damning his ancient sire, and mother sin,
Who at the gates of hell, accursed, brought him forth.[10]

    .   .   .   .   .

117

Dim burnt the lamp, and now the phantom Death   465
Gave his last groans in horror and despair—
"All hell demands me hence,"—he said, and threw
The red lamp hissing through the midnight air.

118

Trembling, across the plain my course I held,
And found the grave-yard, loitering through the gloom,   470
And, in the midst, a hell-red, wandering light,
Walking in fiery circles round the tomb.

    .   .   .   .   .

125

At distance far approaching to the tomb,
By lamps and lanthorns guided through the shade,
A coal-black chariot hurried through the gloom,
Spectres attending, in black weeds array'd,   500

126

Whose woeful forms yet chill my soul with dread,
Each wore a vest in Stygian[11] chambers wove,
Death's kindred all—Death's horses they bestrode,
And gallop'd fiercely, as the chariot drove.

127

Each horrid face a grizly mask conceal'd,   505
Their busy eyes shot terror to my soul
As now and then, by the pale lanthorn's glare,
I saw them for their parted friend condole.

    .   .   .   .   .

130

That done, they plac'd the carcass in the tomb,
To dust and dull oblivion now resign'd,
Then turn'd the chariot tow'rd the House of Night,
Which soon flew off, and left no trace behind.   520

---

[10]The birth of death, son of Satan and sin, is described in
Milton's *Paradise Lost*, bk. II, 746–787.

[11]Infernal; from the River Styx, bordering Hades, in Greek
mythology.

131

But as I stoop'd to write the appointed verse,
Swifter than thought the airy scene decay'd;
Blushing the morn arose, and from the east
With her gay streams of light dispell'd the shade.

132

What is this Death, ye deep read sophists,[12] say?—   525
Death is no more than one unceasing change;
New forms arise while other forms decay,
Yet all is Life throughout creation's range.

133

The towering Alps, the haughty Appenine,[13]
The Andes, wrapt in everlasting snow,   530
The Apalachian and the Ararat[14]
Sooner or later must to ruin go.

134

Hills sink to plains, and man returns to dust,
That dust supports a reptile or a flower;
Each changeful atom by some other nurs'd   535
Takes some new form, to perish in an hour.

135

Too nearly join'd to sickness, toils, and pains,
(Perhaps for former crimes imprison'd here)
True to itself the immortal soul remains,
And seeks new mansions in the starry sphere.   540

136

When Nature bids thee from the world retire,
With joy thy lodging leave, a fated guest;
In Paradise, the land of thy desire,
Existing always, always to be blest.

1775–78   *1779, 1786*

The Vanity of Existence

To Thyrsis[1]

In youth, gay scenes attract our eyes,
    And not suspecting their decay
Life's flowery fields before us rise,
    Regardless of its winter day.

But vain pursuits, and joys as vain,   5
    Convince us life is but a dream.

---

[12]Philosophers.
[13]Mountains in Italy.

[14]Mountain in Turkey.
[1]Shepherd in classical pastoral poetry.

Death is to wake, to rise again
    To that true life you best esteem.

So nightly on some shallow tide,
    Oft have I seen a splendid show;   10
Reflected stars on either side,
    And glittering moons were seen below.

But when the tide had ebbed away,
    The scene fantastic with it fled,
A bank of mud around me lay,   15
    And sea-weed on the river's bed.

1781, 1795

To the Memory
of the Brave Americans[1]

Under General Greene, in South Carolina, who fell in the action of
September 8, 1781

At Eutaw Springs the valiant died;
    Their limbs with dust are covered o'er—
Weep on, ye springs, your tearful tide;
    How many heroes are no more!

If in this wreck of ruin, they   5
    Can yet be thought to claim a tear,
O smite your gentle breast, and say
    The friends of freedom slumber here!

Thou, who shalt trace this bloody plain,
    If goodness rules thy generous breast,   10
Sigh for the wasted rural reign;
    Sigh for the shepherds, sunk to rest!

Stranger, their humble graves adorn;
    You too may fall, and ask a tear;
'Tis not the beauty of the morn   15
    That proves the evening shall be clear.—

They saw their injured country's woe;
    The flaming town, the wasted field;
Then rushed to meet the insulting foe;
    They took the spear—but left the shield.   20

Led by the conquering genius, Greene,
    The Britons they compelled to fly;

---

[1]Over 500 Americans died at Eutaw Springs in what General Nathanael Greene (1742–1786) called "the most obstinate fight I ever saw." Crucial in forcing the British from South Carolina, the battle proved to be the last of the war in the South.

None distant viewed the fatal plain,
　　None grieved, in such a cause to die—

But, like the Parthian,[2] famed of old,　　　　25
　　Who, flying, still their arrows threw,
These routed Britons, full as bold,
　　Retreated, and retreating slew.

Now rest in peace, our patriot band;
　　Though far from nature's limits thrown,　　30
We trust they find a happier land,
　　A brighter sunshine of their own.

1781　　　　　　　　　　　　　　　*1781, 1786*

To Sir Toby

A Sugar Planter in the interior parts of Jamaica, near the City of San Jago
de la Vega, (Spanish Town) 1784

"The motions of his spirit are black as night,
　　And his affections dark as Erebus."
　　　　　　　　　　　　　—SHAKESPEARE.[1]

If there exists a hell—the case is clear—
Sir Toby's slaves enjoy that portion here:
Here are no blazing brimstone lakes—'tis true;
But kindled Rum too often burns as blue;
In which some fiend, whom nature must detest,　　5
Steeps Toby's brand, and marks poor Cudjoe's breast.[2]
　　Here whips on whips excite perpetual fears,
And mingled howlings vibrate on my ears:
Here nature's plagues abound, to fret and tease,
Snakes, scorpions, despots, lizards, centipees—　　10
No art, no care escapes the busy lash;
All have their dues—and all are paid in cash—
The eternal driver keeps a steady eye
On a black herd, who would his vengeance fly.
But chained, imprisoned, on a burning soil,　　15
For the mean avarice of a tyrant, toil!
The lengthy cart-whip guards this monster's reign—
And cracks, like pistols, from the fields of cane.
　　Ye powers! who formed these wretched tribes, relate,
What had they done, to merit such a fate!　　20
Why were they brought from Eboe's[3] sultry waste,

[2]The famous horsemen of Parthia, in ancient Persia, defeated their enemies by pretending retreat, then quickly turning to attack. The British, repulsed at first, retreated to a stone house.
[1]*The Merchant of Venice*, V., i, 79; there the words are "dull as night." Erebus: in Greek mythology, the dark region between earth and Hades.
[2]"This passage has a reference to the West India custom (sanctioned by law) of branding a newly imported slave on the breast, with a red-hot iron, as an evidence of the purchaser's property" (Freneau's note). Cudjoe or cudge, a common name for a slave.
[3]"A small Negro kingdom near the river Senegal" (Freneau's note).

To see that plenty which they must not taste—
Food, which they cannot buy, and dare not steal;
Yams and potatoes—many a scanty meal!—
One, with a gibbet[4] wakes his Negro's fears,   25
One to the windmill nails him by the ears;
One keeps his slave in darkened dens, unfed,
One puts the wretch in pickle ere he's dead:
This, from a tree suspends him by the thumbs,
That, from his table grudges even the crumbs!   30
O'er yond' rough hills a tribe of females go,
Each with her gourd, her infant, and her hoe;
Scorched by a sun that has no mercy here,
Driven by a devil, whom men call overseer—
In chains, twelve wretches to their labors haste;   35
Twice twelve I saw, with iron collars graced!—
Are such the fruits that spring from vast domains?
Is wealth, thus got, Sir Toby, worth your pains!—
Who would your wealth on terms, like these, possess,
Where all we see is pregnant with distress—   40
Angola's[5] natives scourged by ruffian hands,
And toil's hard product shipp'd to foreign lands.
Talk not of blossoms, and your endless spring;
What joy, what smile, can scenes of misery bring?—
Though Nature, here, has every blessing spread,   45
Poor is the laborer—and how meanly fed!—
Here Stygian[6] paintings light and shade renew,
Pictures of hell, that Virgil's[7] pencil drew:
Here, surly Charons[8] make their annual trip,
And ghosts arrive in every Guinea ship,[9]   50
To find what beasts these western isles afford,
Plutonian[10] scourges, and despotic lords:—
Here, they, of stuff determined to be free,
Must climb the rude cliffs of the Liguanee;[11]
Beyond the clouds, in skulking haste repair,   55
And hardly safe from brother traitors[12] there.—

1784   *1792, 1795, 1809*

The Wild Honey Suckle

Fair flower, that dost so comely grow,
Hid in this silent, dull retreat,
Untouched thy honied blossoms blow,
Unseen thy little branches greet:
    No roving foot shall crush thee here,   5
    No busy hand provoke a tear.

---

[4]Gallows.
[5]Portuguese colony in western Africa.
[6]Hellish; from the River Styx, bordering Hades, in Greek mythology.
[7]Virgil (70–19 B.C.), Roman poet, depicts the underworld in the *Aeneid*, Book VI.
[8]Ferryman who carried dead souls across the River Styx to Hades, in classical mythology.

[9]Slave ships from West Africa.
[10]In Greek mythology, Pluto was god of the underworld.
[11]"The mountains northward of Kingston" (Freneau's note).
[12]"Alluding to the *Independent* negroes in the blue mountains, who for a stipulated reward, deliver up every fugitive that falls into their hands, to the English Government" (Freneau's note).

By Nature's self in white arrayed,
She bade thee shun the vulgar eye,
And planted here the guardian shade,
And sent soft waters murmuring by;   10
 Thus quietly thy summer goes,
 Thy days declining to repose.

Smit with those charms, that must decay,
I grieve to see your future doom;
They died—nor were those flowers more gay,   15
The flowers that did in Eden bloom;
 Unpitying frosts, and Autumn's power
 Shall leave no vestige of this flower.

From morning suns and evening dews
At first thy little being came: 20
If nothing once, you nothing lose,
For when you die you are the same;
 The space between, is but an hour,
 The frail duration of a flower.

1786   1786

The Indian Burying Ground

In spite of all the learned have said,
 I still my old opinion keep;
The posture, that we give the dead,
 Points out the soul's eternal sleep.

Not so the ancients of these lands—   5
 The Indian, when from life released,
Again is seated with his friends,
 And shares again the joyous feast.[1]

His imaged birds, and painted bowl,
 And venison, for a journey dressed,   10
Bespeak the nature of the soul,
 Activity, that knows no rest.

His bow, for action ready bent,
 And arrows, with a head of stone,
Can only mean that life is spent,   15
 And not the old ideas gone.

Thou, stranger, that shalt come this way,
 No fraud upon the dead commit—
Observe the swelling turf, and say
 They do not lie, but here they sit.   20

---

[1]"The North American Indians bury their dead in a sitting posture; decorating the corpse with wampum, the images of birds, quadrupeds, etc. And (if that of a warrior) with bows, arrows, tomahawks, and other military weapons" (Freneau's note).

Here still a lofty rock remains,
    On which the curious eye may trace
(Now wasted, half, by wearing rains)
    The fancies of a ruder race.

Here still an aged elm aspires,   25
    Beneath whose far-projecting shade
(And which the shepherd still admires)
    The children of the forest played!

There oft a restless Indian queen
    (Pale Shebah,[2] with her braided hair)   30
And many a barbarous form is seen
    To chide the man that lingers there.

By midnight moons, o'er moistening dews;
    In habit for the chase arrayed,
The hunter still the deer pursues,   35
    The hunter and the deer, a shade![3]

And long shall timorous fancy see
    The painted chief, and painted spear,
And Reason's self shall bow the knee
    To shadows and delusions here.   40

                                            1787, 1795

To an Author

Your leaves bound up compact and fair,
In neat array at length prepare,
To pass their hour on learning's stage,
To meet the surly critic's rage;
The statesman's slight, the smatterer's sneer—   5
Were these, indeed, your only fear,
You might be tranquil and resigned:
What most should touch your fluttering mind;
Is that, few critics will be found
To sift your works, and deal the wound.   10

Thus, when one fleeting year is past
On some bye-shelf your book is cast—
Another comes, with something new,
And drives you fairly out of view:
With some to praise, but more to blame,   15
The mind returns to—whence it came;
And some alive, who scarce could read
Will publish satires on the dead.

---

[2]Sheba was the Arabian queen who tested Solomon's wisdom (1 Kings 10).
[3]Ghost.

Thrice happy Dryden,[1] who could meet
Some rival bard in every street! 20
When all were bent on writing well
It was some credit to excel:—

Thrice happy Dryden, who could find
A Milbourne[2] for his sport designed—
And Pope,[3] who saw the harmless rage 25
Of Dennis[4] bursting o'er his page
Might justly spurn the critic's aim,
Who only helped to swell his fame.

On these bleak climes by Fortune thrown,
Where rigid Reason reigns alone, 30
Where lovely Fancy has no sway,
Nor magic forms about us play—
Nor nature takes her summer hue
Tell me, what has the muse to do?—

An age employed in edging steel 35
Can no poetic raptures feel;
No solitude's attracting power,
No leisure of the noon day hour,
No shaded stream, no quiet grove
Can this fantastic century move; 40

The muse of love[5] in no request—
Go—try your fortune with the rest,
One of the nine[6] you should engage,
To meet the follies of the age:—

On one,[7] we fear, your choice must fall— 45
The least engaging of them all—
Her visage stern—an angry style—
A clouded brow—malicious smile—
A mind on murdered victims placed—
She, only she, can please the taste! 50

1788, 1809

---

[1]"See Johnson's lives of the English Poets" (Freneau's note). English poet John Dryden (1631–1700) appears in *Lives of the Poets* (1779–81) by English critic, author, and lexicographer Samuel Johnson (1709–1784).
[2]Luke Milbourne (1649–1720), whom Dryden called the "worst poet of the age."
[3]Alexander Pope (1688–1744), English poet.
[4]John Dennis (1657–1734), English critic and dramatist satirized by Pope.

[5]Erato, muse of love poetry.
[6]In Greek mythology, there were nine muses identified with individual arts and sciences.
[7]Probably Melpomene, muse of tragedy, pictured with a sword or the club of Hercules, with a stern or frowning countenance.

On Mr. Paine's
Rights of Man[1]

Thus briefly sketched the sacred RIGHTS OF MAN,
How inconsistent with the ROYAL PLAN!
Which for itself exclusive honor craves,
Where some are masters born, and millions slaves.
With what contempt must every eye look down   5
On that base, childish bauble called a *crown*,
The gilded bait, that lures the crowd, to come,
Bow down their necks, and meet a slavish doom;
The source of half the miseries men endure,
The quack that kills them, while it seems to cure.   10

   Roused by the REASON of his manly page,
Once more shall PAINE a listening world engage:
From Reason's source, a bold reform he brings,
In raising up *mankind*, he pulls down *kings*,
Who, source of discord, patrons of all wrong,   15
On blood and murder have been fed too long:
Hid from the world, and tutored to be base,
The curse, the scourge, the ruin of our race,
Theirs was the task, a dull designing few,
To shackle beings that they scarcely knew,   20
Who made this globe the residence of slaves,
And built their thrones on systems formed by knaves
—Advance, bright years, to work their final fall,
And haste the period that shall crush them all.

   Who, that has read and scanned the historic page   25
But glows, at every line, with kindling rage,
To see by them the rights of men aspersed,
Freedom restrained, and Nature's law reversed,
Man, ranked with beasts, by monarchs *willed* away,
And bound young fools, or madmen to obey: 30
Now driven to wars, and now oppressed at home,
Compelled in crowds o'er distant seas to roam,
From India's climes the plundered prize to bring
To glad the strumpet, or to glut the king.

   COLUMBIA, hail! immortal be thy reign: 35
Without a king, we till the smiling plain;
Without a king, we trace the unbounded sea,
And traffic round the globe, through each degree;
Each foreign clime our honored flag reveres,
Which asks no monarch, to support the STARS: 40
Without a *king*, the laws maintain their sway,
While honor bids each generous heart obey.
Be ours the task the ambitious to restrain,
And this great lesson teach—that kings are vain;
That warring realms to certain ruin haste,   45
That kings subsist by war, and wars are waste:
So shall our nation, formed on Virtue's plan,

[1]Thomas Paine (1737–1809), author of *The Rights of Man* (1791), argued that the rights of man derived not from a ruler but from nature (natural rights); and thus he encouraged the replacement of monarchies by democracies (or republics). His book made him a hero of the French Revolution, but it forced him to flee England, where it was considered seditious.

> Remain the guardian of the Rights of Man,
> A vast Republic, famed through every clime,
> Without a king, to see the end of time.   50

1791   *1791, 1809*

On a Honey Bee

DRINKING FROM A GLASS OF WINE AND DROWNED THEREIN

> Thou, born to sip the lake or spring,
> Or quaff the waters of the stream,
> Why hither come on vagrant wing?—
> Does Bacchus[1] tempting seem—
> Did he, for you, this glass prepare?—   5
> Will I admit you to a share?
>
> Did storms harass or foes perplex,
> Did wasps or king-birds bring dismay—
> Did wars distress, or labours vex,
> Or did you miss your way?—   10
> A better seat you could not take
> Than on the margin of this lake.
>
> Welcome!—I hail you to my glass:
> All welcome, here, you find;
> Here, let the cloud of trouble pass,   15
> Here, be all care resigned.—
> This fluid never fails to please,
> And drown the griefs of men or bees.
>
> What forced you here, we cannot know,
> And you will scarcely tell—   20
> But cheery we would have you go
> And bid a glad farewell:
> On lighter wings we bid you fly,
> Your dart will now all foes defy.
>
> Yet take not, oh! too deep a drink,   25
> And in this ocean die;
> Here bigger bees than you might sink,
> Even bees full six feet high.
> Like Pharoah, then, you would be said
> To perish in a sea of red.[2]   30
>
> Do as you please, your will is mine;
> Enjoy it without fear—
> And your grave will be this glass of wine,
> Your epitaph—a tear—

---

[1]Greek god of wine.
[2]The Egyptian army of Pharaoh in pursuit of the Israelites
drowned in the Red Sea (Exodus 14).

Go, take your seat in Charon's[3] boat,   35
We'll tell the hive, you died afloat.

1797, 1809

To a Caty-Did[1]

In a branch of willow hid
Sings the evening Caty-did:
From the lofty locust bough
Feeding on a drop of dew,
In her suit of green array'd   5
Hear her singing in the shade
    Caty-did, Caty-did, Caty-did!

While upon a leaf you tread,
Or repose your little head,
On your sheet of shadows laid,   10
All the day you nothing said:
Half the night your cheery tongue
Revell'd out its little song,
    Nothing else but Caty-did.

From your lodgings on the leaf   15
Did you utter joy or grief—?
Did you only mean to say,
I have had my summer's day,
And am passing, soon, away
To the grave of Caty-did:—   20
    Poor, unhappy Caty-did!

But you would have utter'd more
Had you known of nature's power—
From the world when you retreat,
And a leaf's your winding sheet,   25
Long before your spirit fled,
Who can tell but nature said.
Live again, my Caty-did!
    Live, and chatter Caty-did.

Tell me, what did Caty[2] do?   30
Did she mean to trouble you?—
Why was Caty not forbid
To trouble little Caty-did?—
Wrong, indeed at you to fling,
Hurting no one while you sing   35
    Caty-did! Caty-did! Caty-did!

---

[3]In Greek mythology, the ferryman conducting the dead across the River Styx.
[1]"A well-known insect, when full grown, about two inches in length, and of the exact color of a green leaf. It is of the genus cicada, or grasshopper kind, inhabiting the green foliage of trees and singing such a song as Caty-did in the evening, towards autumn" (Freneau's note).
[2]Freneau's third daughter, born in 1783, was Catherine.

Why continue to complain?
Caty tells me, she again
Will not give you plague or pain:—
Caty says you may be hid   40
Caty will not go to bed
While you sing us Caty-did.
    Caty-did! Caty-did! Caty-did!

But, while singing, you forgot
To tell us what did Caty not: 45
Caty-did not think of cold,
Flocks retiring to the fold,
Winter, with his wrinkles old,
Winter, that yourself foretold
    When you gave us Caty-did.   50

Stay securely in your nest;
Caty now, will do her best,
All she can, to make you blest;
But, you want no human aid—
Nature, when she form'd you, said,   55
"Independent you are made,
My dear little Caty-did:
Soon yourself must disappear
With the verdure of the year,"—
And to go, we know not where,   60
    With your song of Caty-did.

1815

On the Uniformity
and Perfection of Nature

On one fixed point all nature moves,
Nor deviates from the track she loves;
Her system, drawn from reason's source,
She scorns to change her wonted course.

Could she descend from that great plan   5
To work unusual things for man,
To suit the insect of an hour—
This would betray a want of power,

Unsettled in its first design
And erring, when it did combine   10
The parts that form the vast machine,
The figures sketched on nature's scene.

Perfections of the great first cause
Submit to no contracted laws,
But all-sufficient, all-supreme,   15
Include no trivial views in them.

Who looks through nature with an eye
That would the scheme of heaven descry,
Observes her constant, still the same,
In all her laws, through all her frame.   20

No imperfection can be found
In all that is, above, around,—
All, nature made, in reason's sight
Is order all, and *all is right*.

                                                            1815

On the Universality and Other Attributes of the God of Nature

ALL that we see, about, abroad,
What is it all, but nature's God?
In meaner works discovered here
No less than in the starry sphere.

In seas, on earth, this God is seen;   5
All that exist, upon him lean;
He lives in all, and never strayed
A moment from the works he made:

His system fixed on general laws
Bespeaks a wise creating cause;   10
Impartially he rules mankind
And all that on this globe we find.

Unchanged in all that seems to change,
Unbounded space is his great range;
To one vast purpose always true,   15
No time, with him, is old or new.

In all the attributes divine
Unlimited perfections shine;
In these enwrapt, in these complete,
All virtues in that center meet.   20

This power who doth all powers transcend,
To all intelligence a friend,
Exists, the *greatest and the best*[1]
Throughout all worlds, to make them blest.

All that he did he first approved   25
He all things into *being* loved;
O'er all he made he still presides,
For them in life, or death provides.

                                                            1815

---

[1] "Jupiter, optimus, maximus.—Cicero" (Freneau's note).

On the Religion of Nature

THE power, that gives with liberal hand
  The blessings man enjoys, while here,
And scatters through a smiling land
  Abundant products of the year;
     That power of nature, ever bless'd,   5
     Bestowed religion with the rest.

Born with ourselves, her early sway
  Inclines the tender mind to take
The path of right, fair virtue's way
  Its own felicity to make.   10
     This universally extends
     And leads to no mysterious ends.

Religion, such as nature taught,
  With all divine perfection suits;
Had all mankind this system sought   15
  Sophists would cease their vain disputes,
     And from this source would nations know
     All that can make their heaven below.

This deals not curses to mankind,
  Or dooms them to perpetual grief,   20
If from its aid no joys they find,
  It damns them not for unbelief;
     Upon a more exalted plan
     Creatress nature dealt with man—

Joy to the day, when all agree   25
  On such grand systems to proceed,
From fraud, design, and error free,
  And which to truth and goodness lead:
     Then persecution will retreat
     And man's religion be complete.   30

1815

On Observing a Large Red-Streak Apple

In spite of ice, in spite of snow,
In spite of all the winds that blow,
In spite of hail and biting frost,
Suspended here I see you tossed;
You still retain your wonted[1] hold   5
Though days are short and nights are cold.

Amidst this system of decay
How could you have one wish to stay?
If fate or fancy kept you there

---
[1]Accustomed.

They meant you for a solitaire.[2]   10
Were it not better to descend,
Or in the cider mill to end
Than thus to shiver in the storm
And not a leaf to keep you warm—
A moment, then, had buried all,   15
Nor you have doomed so late a fall.

But should the stem to which you cling
Uphold you to another spring,
Another race would round you rise
And view the stranger with surprise,   20
And, peeping from the blossoms say
Away, old dotard,[3] get away!

Alas! small pleasure can there be
To dwell, a hermit, on the tree—
Your old companions, all, are gone,   25
Have dropt, and perished, every one;
You only stay to face the blast,
A sad memento of the past.

Would fate or nature hear my prayer,
I would your bloom of youth repair   30
I would the wrongs of time restrain
And bring your blossom state again:
But fate and nature both say no;
And you, though late must perish too.

What can we say, what can we hope?   35
Ere from the branch I see you drop,
All I can do, all in my power
Will be to watch your parting hour:
When from the branch I see you fall,
A grave we dig a-south the wall.   40
There you shall sleep 'till from your core,
Of youngsters rises three or four;
These shall salute the coming spring
And red-streaks to perfection bring
When years have brought them to their prime   45
And they shall have their summer's time:
This, this is all you can attain,
And thus, I bid you, live again!

1822, 1945

---

[2]A single instance.
[3]Senile one.

PHILLIS WHEATLEY
(*c.* 1753–1784)

In July 1761, Mrs. Susanna Wheatley, wife of a wealthy merchant-tailor, selected from the slaves brought to Boston Harbor a frail, comely female of about seven ("shedding her front teeth"). No one could have predicted that twelve years later, in London, would appear *Poems on Various Subjects, Religious and Moral* (1773), dedicated to the Countess of Huntingdon, by Phillis Wheatley, "Negro Servant to Mr. John Wheatley." The volume could not have been published without the prefatory testimonial, signed by eighteen distinguished politicians, clergy, and citizens, including the governor and John Hancock, which assured the world that the poems "were written by Phillis . . . who was but a few years since, brought an uncultivated barbarian from Africa."

The poems, expressing Christian piety and using Biblical allusions, classical references, and neoclassical conventions, reflected Wheatley's precocious intelligence and poetic gift. It was Phillis's good fortune to have been brought under Susanna Wheatley's pious, zealous solicitude. Tutored by the Wheatley daughter Mary, Phillis was reading the "sacred writings" within sixteen months. She read the English poets, Pope, Gray, and Milton, and studied Latin to read Horace and Ovid. Treated as a member of the family, Phillis was encouraged to write from the age of thirteen. Mrs. Wheatley invited important intellectuals to hear Phillis recite and sent her first poem off to be published as a broadside in 1767. When her plan to publish a volume of poems failed to elicit Boston subscribers in 1772, Mrs. Wheatley arranged for London publication, having already acquainted her London friends such as the Countess of Huntingdon with the poems.

In 1773, Phillis became ill, and a physician recommended a sea voyage. Phillis accompanied the Wheatleys' son to London, where she saw her book appear and was introduced into British society, even meeting Benjamin Franklin. Her book of thirty-nine poems, widely noticed by the critics, created something of a literary sensation. She would have been presented at the court of George III, but was called back to America on Mrs. Wheatley's sickness.

Shortly after returning to Boston, Phillis was given her freedom. But her world began to change: Mrs. Wheatley died in 1774 and Mr. Wheatley in 1778. Phillis married a "free negro," John Peters, in 1778. Little is known of him, but in 1834 a Wheatley descendent published a memoir (perhaps not entirely reliable) noting that he "was a man of very handsome person and manners; wore a wig, carried a cane, and quite acted out 'the gentleman.' " But his grocery business failed shortly after the marriage and he was "too proud and too indolent to apply himself to any occupation below his fancied dignity."

Phillis's last years were lived out in poverty and obscurity. Like many Bostonians, she and her husband fled the city during the time of open conflict of the Revolutionary War, living for a time in Delaware, but returning when safety permitted. Phillis bore three children, but two preceded her in death. She herself, reduced to sickness and miserable living conditions, died in 1784, and her third child died shortly thereafter. They were buried together in an unmarked grave.

Phillis Wheatley's poetry is often passionately concerned with liberty. And though sometimes depicted as unconcerned with the loss of freedom in slavery, she made her feelings against slavery known—as in the poem in her

1773 volume addressed to the new British Secretary in charge of American colonies:

> Should you, my lord, while you peruse my song,
> Wonder from whence my love of freedom sprung,
> . . .
> I, young in life, by seeming cruel fate
> was snatched from Afric's fancied happy seat:
> What pangs excruciating must molest,
> What sorrows labour in my parents' breast?
> Steeled was that soul and by no misery moved
> That from a father seized his babe beloved;
> Such, such my case. And can I then but pray
> Others may never feel tyrannic sway?

Phillis Wheatley's book was reprinted in Boston in 1836, at a time when the Abolitionist movement was gaining strength in New England. And her poems have attracted keen interest in the twentieth century, beginning with the renewal of black consciousness in the civil rights movement. The critic William H. Robinson has written: "She proved herself a worthy black American poet-pioneer. She led the way."

ADDITIONAL READING

Phillis Wheatley and Her Writings, ed. William H. Robinson, 1984 (indispensable for bringing together all the poems and letters, plus the 1834 memoir of Phillis Wheatley by Margaretta Matilda Oddell, descendent of the Wheatleys; also presents Robinson's "On Phillis Wheatley and Her Boston," "On Phillis Wheatley's Poetry," and a bibliography); *The Collected Works of Phillis Wheatley,* ed. John C. Shields, 1988 (where possible, the materials included were "reproduced directly from original materials"; contains valuable essays by Henry Louis Gates, Jr., and John C. Shields).

Sidney Kaplan, *The Black Presence in the Era of the American Revolution, 1770–1800,* 1973; Merle A. Richmond, *Bid the Vassal Soar: Interpretive Essays on the Life and Poetry of Phillis Wheatley and George Moses Horton,* 1974; William H. Robinson, *Phillis Wheatley in Black American Beginnings,* 1975; Bernard W. Bell, "African-American Writers," *American Literature, 1764–1789: The Revolutionary Years,* ed. Everett Emerson, 1977; William H. Robinson, *Phillis Wheatley: A Bio-Bibliography,* 1981; William H. Robinson, ed., *Critical Essays on Phillis Wheatley,* 1982; Ann Allen Shockley, *Afro-American Women Writers, 1746–1933: An Anthology and Critical Guide,* 1988.

TEXTS

"America" from *Phillis Wheatley and Her Writings,* ed. William H. Robinson, 1984; all other poems from *The Poems of Phillis Wheatley,* ed. Julian D. Mason, Jr., 1966, rev. 1989.

On Virtue

> O thou bright jewel in my aim I strive
> To comprehend thee. Thine own words declare
> Wisdom is higher than a fool can reach.
> I cease to wonder, and no more attempt
> Thine height t'explore, or fathom thy profound. 5
> But, O my soul, sink not into despair,
> *Virtue* is near thee, and with gentle hand

Would now embrace thee, hovers o'er thine head.
Fain would the heav'n-born soul with her converse,
Then seek, then court her for her promis'd bliss.   10

    Auspicious queen, thine heav'nly pinions spread,
And lead celestial *Chastity* along;
Lo! now her sacred retinue descends,
Array'd in glory from the orbs above.
Attend me, *Virtue,* thro' my youthful years!   15
O leave me not to the false joys of time!
But guide my steps to endless life and bliss.
Greatness, or *Goodness,* say what I shall call thee,
To give an higher appellation still,
Teach me a better strain, a nobler lay,[1]   20
O Thou, enthroned with Cherubs in the realms of
    day!

1766   *1773*

America[1]

New England first a wilderness was found,
Till for a continent 'twas destined round;
From field to field the savage monsters run
Ere yet Britannia had her work begun.
Thy power, O liberty, makes strong the weak,   5
And (wondrous instinct) Ethiopians[2] speak:
Sometimes by simile, a victory's won.
A certain lady had an only son;
He grew up daily, virtuous as he grew.
Fearing his strength, which she undoubted knew,   10
She laid some taxes on her darling son,
And would have laid another act there on.
"Amend your manners I'll the task remove,"
Was said with seeming sympathy and love.
By many scourges she his goodness tried   15
Until at length the best of infants cried;
He wept, Britannia turned a senseless ear.
At last awakened by maternal fear:
"Why weeps Americus, why weeps my child?"
Thus spake Britannia, thus benign and mild.   20
"My dear mama," said he, "shall I repeat—"
Then prostrate fell, at her maternal feet.
"What ails the rebel," Great Britannia cried.
"Indeed," said he, "you have no cause to chide.
You see each day my fluent tears, my f[l]ood,   25
Without regard; what no more English blood?
Has length of time drove from our English veins?"

---

[1]Song.
[1]Written in 1768 in protest against Britain's repeated taxation of the colonies, this poem was included in a collection of poems proposed for publication in 1772 by Wheatley. The proposal was rejected, although other poems in the collection later saw print in the 1773 London publication. The manuscript of "America" was lost and not found until 1970, when it was first printed.
[2]The conventional name for people from Africa in Wheatley's time.

The kindred, he to Great Britannia deigns.
'Tis thus with thee, O Britain, keeping down
New English force; thou fear'st his tyranny and thou didst frown.   30
He weeps afresh to feel this iron chain.
Turn, O Britannia, claim thy child again.
Riech,[3] O love, drive by thy powerful charms
Indolence slumbering in forgetful arms.
See Agenoria[4] diligent employs   35
Her sons, and thus with rapture she replies,
"Arise my sons, with one consent arise."—
Lest distant continents with vult'ring eyes
Should charge America with negligence;
They praise industry but no pride commence   40
To raise their own profusion. O Britain, see:
By this, New England will increase like thee.

1768   1970

On Being Brought
from Africa to America

'Twas mercy brought me from my *Pagan* land,
Taught my benighted soul to understand
That there's a God, that there's a *Savior* too:
Once I redemption neither sought nor knew.
Some view our sable[1] race with scornful eye,   5
"Their color is a diabolic die."
Remember, *Christians*, *Negroes,* black as *Cain,*[2]
May be refined,[3] and join th' angelic train.

1768   1773

An Hymn to the Morning

Attend my lays, ye ever honored nine,[1]
Assist my labors, and my strains refine;
In smoothest numbers pour the notes along,
For bright *Aurora*[2] now demands my song.

Aurora hail, and all the thousand dyes,   5
Which deck thy progress through the vaulted skies:
The morn awakes, and wide extends her rays,
On ev'ry leaf the gentle zephyr plays;

---

[3]Reach; Wheatley's spelling and punctuation were erratic.
[4]England. May be feminization of Agenor, father of Europa, who sent his sons out to seek his lost daughter.
[1]Black.
[2]Genesis 4:1–15: After Cain slew his brother Abel, God condemned him to be a "fugitive and a vagabond in the earth." "And the Lord set a mark upon Cain, lest any finding him should kill him." This mark has been interpreted by some as the origin of the Negro.
[3]Purified; thus the pagans of Africa can become Christian.
[1]In classical mythology, the nine muses of art and science.
[2]In Roman mythology, goddess of the dawn.

Harmonious lays the feathered race resume,
Dart the bright eye, and shake the painted plume.   10

    Ye shady groves, your verdant gloom display
To shield your poet from the burning day:
Calliope[3] awake the sacred lyre,
While thy fair sisters fan the pleasing fire:
The bow'rs, the gales, the variegated skies   15
In all their pleasures in my bosom rise.

    See in the east th' illustrious king of day!
His rising radiance drives the shades away—
But Oh! I feel his fervid beams too strong,
And scarce begun, concludes th' abortive song.   20

1773

An Hymn to the Evening

Soon as the sun forsook the eastern main
The pealing thunder shook the heav'nly plain;
Majestic grandeur! From the zephyr's wing,
Exhales the incense of the blooming spring.
Soft purl[1] the streams, the birds renew their notes,   5
And through the air their mingled music floats.

    Through all the heav'ns what beauteous dyes are spread!
But the west glories in the deepest red:
So may our breasts with ev'ry virtue glow,
The living temples of our God below!   10

    Filled with the praise of him who gives the light;
And draws the sable curtains of the night,
Let placid slumbers sooth each weary mind,
At morn to wake more heav'nly, more refin'd;
So shall the labors of the day begin   15
More pure, more guarded from the snares of sin.

    Night's leaden sceptre seals my drowsy eyes,
Then cease, my song, till fair *Aurora* rise.

1773

On Imagination

Thy various works, imperial queen, we see,
How bright their forms! how decked with pomp by thee!

---

[3]Muse of epic poetry.
[1]Flow or ripple with a murmuring sound.

Thy wond'rous acts in beauteous order stand,
And all attest how potent is thine hand.

From *Helicon's*[1] refulgent heights attend,   5
Ye sacred choir, and my attempts befriend:
To tell her glories with a faithful tongue,
Ye blooming graces, triumph in my song.

Now here, now there, the roving *Fancy* flies,
Till some loved object strikes her wand'ring eyes,   10
Whose silken fetters all the senses bind,
And soft captivity involves the mind.

Imagination! who can sing thy force?
Or who describe the swiftness of thy course?
Soaring through air to find the bright abode,   15
Th' empyreal[2] palace of the thund'ring God,
We on thy pinions[3] can surpass the wind,
And leave the rolling universe behind:
From star to star the mental optics rove,
Measure the skies, and range the realms above.   20
There in one view we grasp the mighty whole,
Or with new worlds amaze th' unbounded soul.

Though *Winter* frowns to *Fancy's* raptured eyes
The fields may flourish, and gay scenes arise;
The frozen deep may break their iron bands,   25
And bid their waters murmur o'er the sands.
Fair *Flora*[4] may resume her fragrant reign,
And with her flow'ry riches deck the plain;
Sylvanus[5] may diffuse his honors round,
And all the forest may with leaves be crowned: 30
Show'rs may descend, and dews their gems disclose,
And nectar sparkle on the blooming rose.

Such is thy pow'r, nor are thine orders vain,
O thou the leader of the mental train:
In full perfection all thy works are wrought,   35
And thine the sceptre o'er the realms of thought.
Before thy throne the subject-passions bow,
Of subject-passions sov'reign ruler Thou,
At thy command joy rushes on the heart,
And through the glowing veins the spirits dart.   40

Fancy might now her silken pinions try
To rise from earth, and sweep th' expanse on high;

From *Tithon's*[6] bed now might *Aurora* rise,
Her cheeks all glowing with celestial dyes,
While a pure stream of light o'erflows the skies.   45
The monarch of the day I might behold,
And all the mountains tipt with radiant gold,

---

[1]Mount Helicon; in Greek mythology, home of the muses.
[2]Heavenly.
[3]Wings.
[4]Roman goddess of flowers.

[5]Roman god of forest glades.
[6]In Greek mythology, Tithonus was loved by the rosy-fingered goddess of the Dawn, Eos, called Aurora in Roman mythology.

But I reluctant leave the pleasing views,
Which *Fancy* dresses to delight the *Muse;*
Winter austere forbids me to aspire,   50
And northern tempests damp the rising fire;
They chill the tides of *Fancy's* flowing sea,
Cease then, my song, cease the unequal lay.[7]

1773

To S. M.[1] a Young African Painter, on Seeing His Works

To show the lab'ring bosom's deep intent,
And thought in living characters to paint,
When first thy pencil did those beauties give,
And breathing figures learnt from thee to live,
How did those prospects give my soul delight,   5
A new creation rushing on my sight?
Still, wond'rous youth! each noble path pursue,
On deathless glories fix thine ardent view:
Still may the painter's and the poet's fire
To aid thy pencil, and thy verse conspire!   10
And may the charms of each seraphic theme
Conduct thy footsteps to immortal fame!
High to the blissful wonders of the skies
Elate thy soul, and raise thy wishful eyes.
Thrice happy, when exalted to survey   15
That splendid city, crowned with endless day,
Whose twice six gates[2] on radiant hinges ring:
Celestial *Salem*[3] blooms in endless spring.

Calm and serene thy moments glide along,
And may the muse inspire each future song!   20
Still, with the sweets of contemplation bless'd,
May peace with balmy wings your soul invest!
But when these shades of time are chased away,
And darkness ends in everlasting day,
On what seraphic pinions shall we move,   25
And view the landscapes in the realms above?
There shall thy tongue in heav'nly murmurs flow,
And there my muse with heav'nly transport glow:
No more to tell of *Damon's*[4] tender sighs,
Or rising radiance of *Aurora's* eyes,   30
For nobler themes demand a nobler strain,
And purer language on th' ethereal plain.
Cease, gentle muse! the solemn gloom of night
Now seals the fair creation from my sight.

1773

---

[7]Melody, song.
[1]Scipio Moorhead, servant of the Reverend John Moorhead of Boston.
[2]Revelation 21:12: The wall of the heavenly city "had twelve gates, and at the gates twelve angels, and names

written thereon, which are the names of the twelve tribes of Israel."
[3]Jerusalem.
[4]Shepherd singer in Virgil's *Eclogues* 8; an ideal singer of love in pastoral poetry.

To His Excellency General Washington[1]

SIR.

I Have taken the freedom to address your Excellency in the enclosed poem, and entreat your acceptance, though I am not insensible to its inaccuracies. Your being appointed by the Grand Continental Congress to be Generalissimo of the armies of North America, together with the fame of your virtues, excite sensations not easy to suppress. Your generosity, therefore, I presume, will pardon the attempt. Wishing your Excellency all possible success in the great cause you are so generously engaged in, I am,

Your Excellency's most obedient humble servant,
PHILLIS WHEATLEY

Providence, Oct. 26, 1775.
His Excellency Gen. Washington.

> Celestial choir! enthroned in realms of light,
>   Columbia's scenes of glorious toils I write.
> While freedom's cause her anxious breast alarms,
> She flashes dreadful in refulgent arms.
> See mother earth her offspring's fate bemoan,   5
> And nations gaze at scenes before unknown!
> See the bright beams of heaven's revolving light
> Involved in sorrows and the veil of night!
>   The goddess comes, she moves divinely fair,
> Olive and laurel[2] bind her golden hair: 10
> Wherever shines this native of the skies,
> Unnumbered charms and recent graces rise.
>   Muse! bow propitious while my pen relates
> How pour her armies through a thousand gates,
> As when Eolus[3] heaven's fair face deforms,   15
> Enwrapped in tempest and a night of storms;
> Astonished ocean feels the wild uproar,
> The refluent surges beat the sounding shore;
> Or thick as leaves in Autumn's golden reign,
> Such, and so many, moves the warrior's train.   20
> In bright array they seek the work of war,
> Where high unfurled the ensign[4] waves in air.
> Shall I to Washington their praise recite?
> Enough thou know'st them in the fields of fight.
> Thee, first in peace and honors—we demand   25
> The grace and glory of thy martial band.
> Famed for thy valor, for thy virtues more,
> Hear every tongue thy guardian aid implore!
>   One century scarce performed its destined round,
> When Gallic powers Columbia's fury found;[5]   30

---

[1]The poem and accompanying letter were published in the *Virginia Gazette* in March 1776; in April 1776, they appeared in *The Pennsylvania Magazine*, then edited by Thomas Paine. Concerned about people's opinion of him, Washington had sent the Wheatley letter and poem on February 10, 1776, to his former secretary, who apparently sent them on to the magazines. Washington wrote to Wheatley on February 28, 1776, inviting her to visit him, and apologizing for not publishing the poem, for while wanting to "give the world this new instance of your genius, I might have incurred the imputation of vanity."
[2]The olive in ancient Greece symbolized peace and was given to victors in the Olympic Games and to distinguished citizens; the laurel honored poets, heroes, and victors.
[3]Aeolus, Greek god of the winds.
[4]Flag, banner.
[5]The struggle between France and England for control of North America extended over 74 years: King William's War (1689–97), Queen Anne's War (1702–13), King George's War (1744–48), the French and Indian War (1754–63). France ceded Canada and the upper Mississippi Valley to Britain at the end of the last war, which had begun with a skirmish between French regulars and Virginia militiamen commanded by Washington.

And so may you, whoever dares disgrace
The land of freedom's heaven-defended race!
Fixed are the eyes of nations on the scales,
For in their hopes Columbia's arm prevails.
Anon Britannia droops the pensive head,　　　　　　　35
While round increase the rising hills of dead.
Ah! cruel blindness to Columbia's state!
Lament thy thirst of boundless power too late.
　Proceed, great chief, with virtue on thy side,
Thy ev'ry action let the goddess guide.　　　　　　　40
A crown, a mansion, and a throne that shine,
With gold unfading, WASHINGTON! be thine.

1775　　　　　　　　　　　　　　　　　　　　　　　*1776*

JOEL BARLOW
(1754–1812)

Joel Barlow wanted desperately to be the epic poet of America. The obsession seized him early and held him all his life. By the time he was twenty-five, he had settled on Columbus as his pivotal, visionary figure and the sweeping history of the New World as his focus. He labored mightily, composing heroic couplet after heroic couplet, as—

Hail, holy Peace, from thy sublime abode
Mid circling saints that grace the throne of God.

When he was thirty-three, he published *The Vision of Columbus* (1787), and it brought him fame. But it is not clear that those who praised it had read all of its some 5,000 lines—or had felt the urgent cultural need of a monumental epic glorifying the newly born nation.

Barlow never ceased to tinker with his poem, publishing a patched up version in Paris in 1793. Then, in 1807, he published the completely overhauled version, called *The Columbiad,* now swollen to 3,675 heroic couplets (7,350 lines). Still he tinkered with the text, preparing it for inclusion in his collected works, until his sudden death in 1812 brought surcease from his obsession. Posterity's verdict has been close to that of William Cullen Bryant's made in 1818: "The plan of the work is utterly destitute of interest and that which was at first sufficiently wearisome has become doubly so by being drawn out to its present length."

It is a pity that Barlow's reputation has had to bear the ponderous weight of *The Columbiad.* He is a writer worthy of attention, and his turbulent career made him a witness at critical turning points in history—including the American Revolution, the French Revolution, and Napoleon's retreat from Moscow in 1812.

He was born on a farm in Connecticut, the eighth of nine children. He entered Dartmouth College in 1773, but following his father's death he used his small inheritance to switch to Yale in 1774. Yale was then a bastion of Calvinism and political conservatism. Most students of the time—including Noah Webster, Timothy Dwight, and John Trumbull—accepted these inherited views without question. Joel Barlow was to be different.

He served for a time (1780–82) as a chaplain in the Revolutionary War, taking time off to marry in 1781. After the war he founded and edited *The American Mercury,* but his partner in the enterprise took it over in 1785, and Barlow for a time ran a bookstore. In 1786, he was admitted to the bar and began the practice of law.

But Barlow's interest in writing never ceased. About this time he and three other writers (David Humphreys, John Trumbull, and Dr. Lemuel Hopkins) came together in a joint literary enterprise to write *The Anarchiad,* which appeared in twelve installments, October 1786–September 1787. The writers were concerned conservatives and Calvinists who were alarmed at the populistic tendencies of the time, as evidenced in the farmers' uprising in Massachusetts known as Shays's Rebellion. *The Anarchiad* cites Massachusetts:

> There Chaos, Anarch old, asserts his sway,
> And mobs in myriads blacken all the way.

The writers were the nucleus of a group to become known as the Connecticut Wits, the first "literary movement" in America. It is ironic that Joel Barlow is now remembered mainly in literary history as a Connecticut Wit when, in fact, he grew to oppose their fundamental beliefs with his egalitarianism and Deism.

With the publication and success of *The Vision of Columbus* in 1787, Barlow seemed on his way to a fulfilled career as an American poet. But as so often in his life, his career took an odd turn. He became involved with the Ohio Company and the Scioto Associates in a scheme to acquire huge tracts of frontier land that could then be sold in small farm-sized lots for settlement. Barlow was chosen as their European salesman and embarked for France in 1788. He would remain in Europe for seventeen years.

The Sciotio scheme turned out to be a disaster, and Barlow found himself the target of irate Frenchmen who lost money in it. A victim of unscrupulous adventurers back in America, Barlow dissociated himself from the company and turned to other interests in Europe. He met General Lafayette and Thomas Jefferson in Paris, and in London he visited Thomas Paine. He witnessed the fall of the Bastille on July 14, 1789. Caught up in the revolutionary fervor, he turned to pamphleteering, writing *Advice to the Privileged Orders,* which (like Paine's *Rights of Man*) was a response to Edmund Burke's 1790 attack on the course of events in France, *Reflections on the French Revolution.* Barlow followed his pamphlet with a satiric poem, "The Conspiracy of Kings."

These works were inflammatory enough for England to charge Barlow with sedition. France, on the other hand, made him an honorary citizen out of gratitude for *A Letter to the National Convention* (1792) in which Barlow attacked monarchy and encouraged creation of a government expressing the will of the people. At one point in 1793, in the midst of all his political involvement, Barlow found himself alone and lonely in Savoy, a province in southeastern France. He was served a dish of cornmeal mush, and a flood of memories carried him back to New England. He then wrote the mock epic poem, *The Hasty Pudding,* whose homely wit and charm ensured that it would outlast all his grandiose epics and political pamphlets.

Throughout his years abroad, Barlow was able through shrewd investment and the import business to accumulate something of a fortune. When he returned to America in 1804, the Democratic-Republican liberal Jefferson had displaced the Federalist conservative John Adams in the presidency, in a government now located in Washington, D.C. Finding the ruling party compatible with his revolutionary views, Barlow settled in a fine house in Georgetown to be near friends and turned once again to literature and his epic ambitions. *The Columbiad* (1807) Barlow thought of as a "patriotic legacy to my country."

But in the end his life took a bizarre twist. He was called out of retirement by President Madison (whose Secretary of State was James Monroe) to become minister to France in order to persuade Napoleon to sign a new trade treaty with America. He set off reluctantly in 1811, with eerie premonitions of death. When he arrived in France, Napoleon was off on his Russian campaign. He waited several months, and was then told he could meet Napoleon at Vilna, Lithuania. He set off on the difficult journey and waited there in the bleak winter.

Finally it became clear that Napoleon had been defeated and the remnants of his army were in retreat. Barlow started the journey back, shocked by the carnage, havoc, and suffering of war he witnessed. Somewhere on his return, he observed the death-covered landscape and wrote his most moving poem, "Advice to a Raven in Russia." He became ill of pneumonia on the freezing journey, and died in late December 1812. He was buried in the village of Zarnorwiec, Poland, near Cracow.

ADDITIONAL READING

The Works of Joel Barlow, ed. William K. Bottorff and Arthur L. Ford, 2 vols., 1970.

Charles Burr Todd, *The Life and Letters of Joel Barlow*, 1886; Leon Howard, *The Connecticut Wits*, 1943; James Woodress, *A Yankee's Odyssey: The Life of Joel Barlow*, 1958; Arthur L. Ford, *Joel Barlow*, 1971; Esther Morris Douty, *Hasty Pudding and Barbary Pirates, a Life of Joel Barlow*, 1975; Cecilia Tichi, "Joel Barlow and the Engineered Millennium," *New World, New Earth*, 1979.

TEXT

The Hasty Pudding from *New York Magazine* (January 1796); "Advice to a Raven in Russia" from Leon Howard, "Joel Barlow and Napoleon," *Huntington Library Quarterly*, II (1938). Some changes in spelling and punctuation have been made to conform with modern English.

The Hasty Pudding

A POEM, IN THREE CANTOS

WRITTEN AT CHAMBERY, IN SAVOY, JANUARY 1793

Omne tulit punctum qui miscuit utile dulci.[1]
He makes a good breakfast who mixes pudding
with molasses.

PREFACE

A simplicity in diet, whether it be considered with reference to the happiness of individuals or the prosperity of a nation, is of more consequence than we are apt

---

[1] Latin: "He has gained all approval who has mingled the useful with the pleasing" (Horace, *Ars Poetica*, line 343).

to imagine. In recommending so important an object to the rational part of mankind, I wish it were in my power to do it in such a manner as would be likely to gain their attention. I am sensible that it is one of those subjects in which example has infinitely more power than the most convincing arguments or the highest charms of poetry. Goldsmith's *Deserted Village*,[2] though possessing these two advantages in a greater degree than any other work of the kind, has not prevented villages in England from being deserted. The apparent interest of the rich individuals, who form the taste as well as the laws in that country, has been against him; and with that interest it has been vain to contend.

The vicious habits which in this little piece I endeavor to combat, seem to me not so difficult to cure. No class of people has any *interest* in supporting them; unless it be the interest which certain families may feel in vying with each other in sumptuous entertainments. There may indeed be some instances of depraved appetites, which no arguments will conquer; but these must be rare. There are very few persons but what would always prefer a plain dish for themselves, and would prefer it likewise for their guests, if there were no risk of reputation in the case. This difficulty can only be removed by example; and the example should proceed from those whose situation enables them to take the lead in forming the manners of a nation. Persons of this description in America, I should hope, are neither above nor below the influence of truth and reason, when conveyed in language suited to the subject.

Whether the manner I have chosen to address my arguments to them be such as to promise any success is what I cannot decide. But I certainly had hopes of doing some good, or I should not have taken the pains of putting so many rhymes together. The example of domestic virtues has doubtless a great effect. I only wish to rank *simplicity of diet* among the virtues. In that case I should hope it will be cherished and more esteemed by others than it is at present.

THE AUTHOR

CANTO I

Ye Alps audacious, through the heavens that rise,
To cramp the day and hide me from the skies;
Ye Gallic flags,[3] that o'er their heights unfurled,
Bear death to kings, and freedom to the world,
I sing not you. A softer theme I choose,   5
A virgin theme, unconscious of the muse,
But fruitful, rich, well suited to inspire
The purest frenzy of poetic fire.
   Despise it not, ye bards to terror steeled,
Who hurl your thunders round the epic field;   10
Nor ye who strain your midnight throats to sing
Joys that the vineyard and the stillhouse[4] bring;
Or on some distant fair your notes employ,
And speak of raptures that you ne'er enjoy.
I sing the sweets I know, the charms I feel,   15
My morning incense, and my evening meal,
The sweets of Hasty Pudding. Come, dear bowl,
Glide o'er my palate, and inspire my soul.
The milk beside thee, smoking from the kine,[5]
Its substance mingled, married in with thine,   20

---

[2]*The Deserted Village*, by Oliver Goldsmith (1728–1774), evokes the idyllic pleasures of English rural life doomed by growing commercialism.
[3]French flags. Savoy, part of the kingdom of Sardinia at the start of the French Revolution, was taken by France in 1792.
[4]Distillery.
[5]Cows.

Shall cool and temper thy superior heat,
And save the pains of blowing while I eat.
   Oh! could the smooth, the emblematic song
Flow like thy genial juices o'er my tongue,
Could those mild morsels in my numbers chime,   25
And, as they roll in substance, roll in rhyme,
No more thy awkward unpoetic name
Should shun the muse, or prejudice thy fame;
But rising grateful to the accustomed ear,
All bards should catch it, and all realms revere!   30
   Assist me first with pious toil to trace
Through wrecks of time thy lineage and thy race;
Declare what lovely squaw, in days of yore,
(Ere great Columbus sought thy native shore)
First gave thee to the world; her works of fame   35
Have lived indeed, but lived without a name.
Some tawny Ceres,[6] goddess of her days,
First learned with stones to crack the well-dried maize,
Through the rough sieve to shake the golden shower,
In boiling water stir the yellow flour: 40
The yellow flour, bestrewed and stirred with haste,
Swells in the flood and thickens to a paste,
Then puffs and wallops,[7] rises to the brim,
Drinks the dry knobs that on the surface swim;
The knobs at last the busy ladle breaks,   45
And the whole mass its true consistence takes.
   Could but her sacred name, unknown so long,
Rise, like her labors, to the son of song,
To her, to them, I'd consecrate my lays,
And blow her pudding with the breath of praise.   50
If 'twas Oella,[8] whom I sang before,
I here ascribe her one great virtue more.
Not through the rich Peruvian realms alone
The fame of Sol's sweet daughter should be known,
But o'er the world's wide climes should live secure,   55
Far as his rays extend, as long as they endure.
   Dear Hasty Pudding, what unpromised joy
Expands my heart, to meet thee in Savoy!
Doomed o'er the world through devious paths to roam,
Each clime my country, and each house my home,   60
My soul is soothed, my cares have found an end,
I greet my long-lost, unforgotten friend.
   For thee through Paris, that corrupted town,
How long in vain I wandered up and down,
Where shameless Bacchus,[9] with his drenching hoard,   65
Cold from his cave usurps the morning board.
London is lost in smoke and steeped in tea;
No Yankee there can lisp the name of thee;
The uncouth word, a libel on the town,
Would call a proclamation from the crown.[10]   70

[6]Roman goddess of agriculture.
[7]Bubbles.
[8]Legendary Incan princess, daughter of the sun and creator of spinning, appears in Barlow's *The Vision of Columbus* (1787).
[9]Roman god of wine.

[10]"A certain king, at the time when this was written, was publishing proclamations to prevent American principles from being propagated in his country" (Barlow's note). He refers to George III and the royal proclamation against seditious publications of May 1792.

For climes oblique, that fear the sun's full rays,
Chilled in their fogs, exclude the generous maize;
A grain whose rich luxuriant growth requires
Short gentle showers, and bright ethereal fires.
    But here, though distant from our native shore,   75
With mutual glee we meet and laugh once more.
The same! I know thee by that yellow face,
That strong complexion of true Indian race,
Which time can never change, nor soil impair,
Nor Alpine snows, nor Turkey's morbid air;   80
For endless years, through every mild domain,
Where grows the maize, there thou art sure to reign.
    But man, more fickle, the bold license claims,
In different realms to give thee different names.
Thee the soft nations round the warm Levant[11]   85
Polanta call, the French of course *polante;*[12]
Ev'n in thy native regions, how I blush
To hear the Pennsylvanians call thee *mush!*
On Hudson's banks, while men of Belgic spawn[13]
Insult and eat thee by the name *suppawn.*[14]   90
All spurious appellations, void of truth;
I've better known thee from my earliest youth,
Thy name is *Hasty Pudding!* thus our sires
Were wont to greet thee fuming from their fires;
And while they argued in thy just defence   95
With logic clear, they thus explained the sense:
"In *haste* the boiling cauldron, o'er the blaze,
Receives and cooks the ready-powdered maize;
In *haste* 'tis served, and then in equal *haste,*
With cooling milk, we make the sweet repast.   100
No carving to be done, no knife to grate
The tender ear, and wound the stony plate;
But the smooth spoon, just fitted to the lip,
And taught with art the yielding mass to dip,
By frequent journeys to the bowl well stored,   105
Performs the hasty honors of the board."
Such is thy name, significant and clear,
A name, a sound to every Yankee dear,
But most to me, whose heart and palate chaste
Preserve my pure hereditary taste.   110
    There are who strive to stamp with disrepute
The luscious food, because it feeds the brute;
In tropes[15] of high-strained wit, while gaudy prigs
Compare thy nursling, man, to pampered pigs;
With sovereign scorn I treat the vulgar jest,   115
Nor fear to share thy bounties with the beast.
What though the generous cow gives me to quaff
The milk nutritious; am I then a calf?
Or can the genius of the noisy swine,
Though nursed on pudding, thence lay claim to mine?   120
Sure the sweet song, I fashion to thy praise,
Runs more melodious than the notes they raise.

---

[11]Eastern Mediterranean countries.
[12]Variants of Italian *polènta* for corn meal pudding.
[13]The Dutch.
[14]Algonquian Indian for corn meal porridge.
[15]Figures of speech.

My song resounding in its grateful glee,
No merit claims; I praise myself in thee.
My father loved thee through his length of days;   125
For thee his fields were shaded o'er with maize;
From thee what health, what vigor he possessed,
Ten sturdy freemen from his loins attest;
Thy constellation ruled my natal morn,
And all my bones were made of Indian corn.   130
Delicious grain! whatever form it take,
To roast or boil, to smother or to bake,
In every dish 'tis welcome still to me,
But most, my Hasty Pudding, most in thee.
    Let the green succotash with thee contend,   135
Let beans and corn their sweetest juices blend,
Let butter drench them in its yellow tide,
And a long slice of bacon grace their side;
Not all the plate, how famed soe'er it be,
Can please my palate like a bowl of thee.   140
    Some talk of hoe-cake,[16] fair Virginia's pride,
Rich johnny-cake[17] this mouth has often tried;
Both please me well, their virtues much the same;
Alike their fabric, as allied their fame,
Except in dear New England, where the last   145
Receives a dash of pumpkin in the paste,
To give it sweetness and improve the taste.
But place them all before me, smoking hot,
The big round dumpling rolling from the pot;
The pudding of the bag, whose quivering breast,   150
With suet lined, leads on the Yankee feast;
The charlotte[18] brown, within whose crusty sides
A belly soft the pulpy apple hides;
The yellow bread, whose face like amber glows,
And all of Indian[19] that the bakepan knows—   155
You tempt me not—my favorite greets my eyes,
To that loved bowl my spoon by instinct flies.

CANTO II

    To mix the food by vicious rules of art,
To kill the stomach and to sink the heart,
To make mankind to social virtue sour,   160
Cram o'er each dish, and be what they devour;
For this the kitchen muse first framed her book,
Commanding sweat to stream from every cook;
Children no more their antic gambols tried,
And friends to physic wondered why they died.   165
    Not so the Yankee—his abundant feast,
With simples furnished, and with plainness dressed,
A numerous offspring gathers round the board,
And cheers alike the servant and the lord;
Whose well-bought hunger prompts the joyous taste,   170
And health attends them from the short repast.

---

[16]Cake of corn meal, water, and salt, baked before a fire on a board; slaves used their hoes for cooking them, thus the name.

[17]Corn bread cooked on a board, griddle, or in a pan.
[18]Cake or bread filled with custard or fruits.
[19]Short for Indian corn or meal.

While the full pail rewards the milkmaid's toil,
The mother sees the morning cauldron boil;
To stir the pudding next demands their care,
To spread the table and the bowls prepare;   175
To feed the children, as their portions cool,
And comb their heads, and send them off to school.
    Yet may the simplest dish some rules impart,
For nature scorns not all the aids of art.
Ev'n Hasty Pudding, purest of all food,   180
May still be bad, indifferent, or good,
As sage experience the short process guides,
Or want of skill, or want of care presides.
Whoe'er would form it on the surest plan,
To rear the child and long sustain the man;   185
To shield the morals while it mends the size,
And all the powers of every food supplies,
Attend the lessons that the muse shall bring.
Suspend your spoons, and listen while I sing.
    But since, O man! thy life and health demand   190
Not food alone, but labor from thy hand,
First in the field, beneath the sun's strong rays,
Ask of thy mother earth the needful maize;
She loves the race that courts her yielding soil,
And gives her bounties to the sons of toil.   195
    When now the ox, obedient to thy call,
Repays the loan that filled the winter stall,
Pursue his traces o'er the furrowed plain,
And plant in measured hills the golden grain.
But when the tender germ begins to shoot,   200
And the green spire declares the sprouting root,
Then guard your nursling from each greedy foe,
The insidious worm, the all-devouring crow.
A little ashes, sprinkled round the spire,
Soon steeped in rain, will bid the worm retire;   205
The feathered robber with his hungry maw
Swift flies the field before your man of straw,
A frightful image, such as schoolboys bring
When met to burn the Pope[1] or hang the King.
    Thrice in the season, through each verdant row   210
Wield the strong plowshare and the faithful hoe;
The faithful hoe, a double task that takes,
To till the summer corn, and roast the winter cakes.
    Slow springs the blade, while checked by chilling rains,
Ere yet the sun the seat of Cancer[2] gains;   215
But when his fiercest fires emblaze the land,
Then start the juices, then the roots expand;
Then, like a column of Corinthian mold,[3]
The stalk struts upward, and the leaves unfold;
The busy branches all the ridges fill,   220
Entwine their arms, and kiss from hill to hill.
Here cease to vex them, all your cares are done;

---

[1]May refer to the British celebration of Guy Fawkes Day, November 5, the anniversary of the discovery of the Gunpowder Plot in 1605, a Roman Catholic attempt to blow up Parliament and kill the king. Effigies of Guy Fawkes and the pope are burned.

[2]Sign of the zodiac that the sun enters on June 21, the summer solstice or longest day of the year.
[3]Most ornate of the three Greek column orders, with a slender fluted column topped by tiers of acanthus leaves on the capital.

Leave the last labors to the parent sun;
Beneath his genial smiles the well-dressed field,
When autumn calls, a plenteous crop shall yield.   225
　　Now the strong foliage bears the standards high,
And shoots the tall top-gallants[4] to the sky;
The suckling ears their silky fringes bend,
And pregnant grown, their swelling coats distend;
The loaded stalk, while still the burden grows,   230
O'erhangs the space that runs between the rows;
High as a hop-field waves the silent grove,
A safe retreat for little thefts of love,
When the pledged roasting-ears invite the maid,
To meet her swain beneath the new-formed shade;   235
His generous hand unloads the cumbrous hill,
And the green spoils her ready basket fill;
Small compensation for the two-fold bliss,
The promised wedding and the present kiss.
　　Slight depredations these; but now the moon   240
Calls from his hollow tree the sly raccoon;
And while by night he bears his prize away,
The bolder squirrel labors through the day.
Both thieves alike, but provident of time,
A virtue rare, that almost hides their crime.   245
Then let them steal the little stores they can,
And fill their granaries from the toils of man;
We've one advantage where they take no part,
With all their wiles they ne'er have found the art
To boil the Hasty Pudding; here we shine   250
Superior far to tenants of the pine;
This envied boon to man shall still belong,
Unshared by them in substance or in song.
　　At last the closing season browns the plain,
And ripe October gathers in the grain;   255
Deep loaded carts the spacious corn-house fill,
The sack distended marches to the mill;
The laboring mill beneath the burden groans,
And showers the future pudding from the stones;
Till the glad housewife greets the powdered gold,   260
And the new crop exterminates the old.[5]

CANTO III

　　The days grow short; but though the falling sun
To the glad swain proclaims his day's work done,
Night's pleasing shades his various task prolong,
And yield new subjects to my various song.   265
For now, the corn-house filled, the harvest home,
The invited neighbors to the *husking*[1] come;
A frolic scene, where work, and mirth, and play,
Unite their charms, to chase the hours away.
　　Where the huge heap lies centered in the hall,   270
The lamp suspended from the cheerful wall,
Brown corn-fed nymphs, and strong hard-handed beaux,

---

[4]Highest mast, sails or rigging on a ship.
[5]In a later edition Canto II concludes with these added lines: "Ah, who can sing what every wight must feel, / The joy that enters with the bag of meal, / A general jubilee per-

vades the house, / Wakes every child and gladdens every mouse."
[1]Party for husking corn, a husking bee.

Alternate ranged, extend in circling rows,
Assume their seats, the solid mass attack;
The dry husks rustle, and the corncobs crack;   275
The song, the laugh, alternate notes resound,
And the sweet cider trips in silence round.
    The laws of husking every wight can tell;
And sure no laws he ever keeps so well:
For each red ear a general kiss he gains,   280
With each smut ear[2] he smuts the luckless swains;
But when to some sweet maid a prize is cast,
Red as her lips, and taper as her waist,
She walks the round, and culls one favored beau,
Who leaps, the luscious tribute to bestow.   285
Various the sport, as are the wits and brains
Of well-pleased lasses and contending swains;
Till the vast mound of corn is swept away,
And he that gets the last ear wins the day.
    Meanwhile the housewife urges all her care,   290
The well-earned feast to hasten and prepare.
The sifted meal already waits her hand,
The milk is strained, the bowls in order stand,
The fire flames high; and, as a pool (that takes
The headlong stream that o'er the milldam breaks)   295
Foams, roars, and rages with incessant toils,
So the vexed cauldron rages, roars, and boils.
    First with clean salt she seasons well the food,
Then strews the flour, and thickens all the flood.
Long o'er the simmering fire she lets it stand;   300
To stir it well demands a stronger hand;
The husband takes his turn; and round and round
The ladle flies; at last the toil is crowned;
When to the board the thronging huskers pour,
And take their seats as at the corn before.   305
    I leave them to their feast. There still belong
More copious matters to my faithful song.
For rules there are, though ne'er unfolded yet,
Nice[3] rules and wise, how pudding should be ate.
    Some with molasses line the luscious treat,   310
And mix, like bards, the useful with the sweet.
A wholesome dish, and well deserving praise,
A great resource in those bleak wintry days,
When the chilled earth lies buried deep in snow,
And raging Boreas[4] drives the shivering cow.   315
    Blessed cow! thy praise shall still my notes employ,
Great source of health, the only source of joy;
Mother of Egypt's God[5]—but sure, for me,
Were I to leave my God, I'd worship thee.
How oft thy teats these pious hands have pressed!   320
How oft thy bounties proved my only feast!
How oft I've fed thee with my favorite grain!
And roared, like thee, to find thy children slain!
    Ye swains who know her various worth to prize,
Ah! house her well from winter's angry skies.   325

---

[2]Fungus-blackened ear.
[3]Precise, subtle.

[4]The north wind in Greek mythology.
[5]Nut, mother of Osiris, was often depicted as a cow.

Potatoes, pumpkins, should her sadness cheer,
Corn from your crib, and mashes[6] from your beer;
When spring returns she'll well acquaint the loan,
And nurse at once your infants and her own.

    Milk then with pudding I should always choose;   330
To this in future I confine my muse,
Till she in haste some further hints unfold,
Well for the young, nor useless to the old.
First in your bowl the milk abundant take,
Then drop with care along the silver lake   335
Your flakes of pudding; these at first will hide
Their little bulk beneath the swelling tide;
But when their growing mass no more can sink,
When the soft island looms above the brink,
Then check your hand; you've got the portion's due,   340
So taught our sires, and what they taught is true.

    There is a choice in spoons. Though small appear
The nice distinction, yet to me 'tis clear.
The deep-bowled Gallic spoon, contrived to scoop
In ample draughts the thin diluted soup,   345
Performs not well in those substantial things,
Whose mass adhesive to the metal clings;
Where the strong labial muscles must embrace,
The gentle curve, and sweep the hollow space.
With ease to enter and discharge the freight,   350
A bowl less concave but still more dilate,
Becomes the pudding best. The shape, the size,
A secret rests unknown to vulgar eyes.
Experienced feeders can alone impart
A rule so much above the lore of art.   355
These tuneful lips that thousand spoons have tried,
With just precision could the point decide,
Though not in song; the muse but poorly shines
In cones, and cubes, and geometric lines;
Yet the true form, as near as she can tell,   360
Is that small section of a goose-egg shell,
Which in two equal portions shall divide
The distance from the center to the side.

    Fear not to slaver; 'tis no deadly sin.
Like the free Frenchman, from your joyous chin   365
Suspend the ready napkin; or, like me,
Poise with one hand your bowl upon your knee;
Just in the zenith your wise head project,
Your full spoon, rising in a line direct,
Bold as a bucket, heeds no drops that fall,   370
The wide-mouthed bowl will surely catch them all.

1793   *1796*

---

[6]Grain mixture used in brewing beer.

Advice to
a Raven in Russia[1]

DECEMBER, 1812

Black fool, why winter here? These frozen skies,
Worn by your wings and deafened by your cries,
Should warn you hence, where milder suns invite,
And day alternates with his mother night.
You fear perhaps your food will fail you there,   5
Your human carnage, that delicious fare
That lured you hither, following still your friend
The great Napoleon to the world's bleak end.
You fear, because the southern climes poured forth
Their clustering nations to infest the north,   10
Bavarians, Austrians, those who drink the Po[2]
And those who skirt the Tuscan seas below,[3]
With all Germania, Neustria, Belgia, Gaul,[4]
Doomed here to wade through slaughter to their fall,
You fear he left behind no wars, to feed   15
His feathered cannibals and nurse the breed.

Fear not, my screamer, call your greedy train,
Sweep over Europe, hurry back to Spain,
You'll find his legions there; the valiant crew
Please best their master when they toil for you.   20
Abundant there they spread the country o'er.
And taint the breeze with every nation's gore,
Iberian, Lusian,[5] British widely strown,
But still more wide and copious flows their own.

Go where you will: Calabria,[6] Malta,[7] Greece,   25
Egypt and Syria still his fame increase,
Domingo's[8] fattened isle and India's plains
Glow deep with purple drawn from Gallic veins.
No raven's wing can stretch the flight so far
As the torn bandrols[9] of Napoleon's war.   30
Choose then your climate, fix your best abode,
He'll make you deserts and he'll bring you blood.

How could you fear a dearth? have not mankind,
Though slain by millions, millions left behind?
Has not conscription still the power to wield   35
Her annual falchion[10] o'er the human field?
A faithful harvester! or if a man

---

[1]This poem was found among Barlow's papers after his death, published in a corrupt version in 1843, and then forgotten; it did not appear in an authentic version until its recovery and publication in *The Huntington Library Quarterly* by Leon Howard in 1938.

On a mission to France in 1811–12 to negotiate a new treaty, Barlow waited for several months in Paris because Napoleon was away on his Russian campaign. Finally Barlow went to Vilna, Lithuania, in late 1812 to confer with Napoleon. He was forced to leave when word came on December 5 of Napoleon's retreat from Moscow. Barlow witnessed the "indescribable horrors of this campaign" and wrote this poem sometime before his death at the end of December in a village in Poland. Napoleon had invaded Russia in June 1812, with an army of 600,000, drawn from all the countries of Europe under his control. Finding Mos-

cow in flames, he ordered a retreat in early October. Over 400,000 died of wounds, sickness, starvation, or exposure.
[2]River in Italy flowing from the Alps in the northwest to the Adriatic Sea.
[3]Tuscany in central Italy bordering west on the Ligurian and Tyrrhenian seas.
[4]Germany, northern France, the Netherlands, and France, respectively.
[5]Lusitania, ancient name for Portugal; Iberian: Spanish. The British fought with Portuguese and Spanish guerillas against Napoleon in the Peninsular War (1808–14).
[6]In southwestern Italy.
[7]Mediterranean island south of Sicily.
[8]San Domingo, now Haiti, in the West Indies.
[9]Banderole: small battle flag.
[10]Sickle, sword.

Escape that gleaner, shall he scape the ban?[11]
The triple ban, that like the hound of hell[12]
Gripes with three joles,[13] to hold his victim well.   40
 Fear nothing then, hatch fast your ravenous brood,
Teach them to cry to Bonaparte for food;
They'll be like you, of all his suppliant train,
The only class that never cries in vain.
For see what mutual benefits you lend!   45
(The surest way to fix the mutual friend)
While on his slaughtered troops your tribes are fed,
You cleanse his camp and carry off his dead.
Imperial scavenger! but now you know
Your work is vain amid these hills of snow.   50
His tentless troops are marbled through with frost
And change to crystal when the breath is lost.
Mere trunks of ice, though limbed like human frames
And lately warmed with life's endearing flames,
They cannot taint the air, the world impest,[14]   55
Nor can you tear one fiber from their breast.
No! from their visual sockets, as they lie,
With beak and claws you cannot pluck an eye.
The frozen orb, preserving still its form,
Defies your talons as it braves the storm,   60
But stands and stares to God, as if to know
In what cursed hands He leaves His world below.
 Fly then, or starve; though all the dreadful road
From Minsk[15] to Moscow with their bodies strowed
May count some myriads, yet they can't suffice   65
To feed you more beneath these dreary skies.
Go back, and winter in the wilds of Spain;
Feast there awhile, and in the next campaign
Rejoin your master; for you'll find him then,
With his new million of the race of men,   70
Clothed in his thunders, all his flags unfurled,
Raging and storming o'er the prostrate world.
 War after war his hungry soul requires,
State after state shall sink beneath his fires,
Yet other Spains in victim smoke shall rise   75
And other Moscows suffocate the skies,
Each land lie reeking with its people's slain
And not a stream run bloodless to the main.
Till men resume their souls, and dare to shed
Earth's total vengeance on the monster's head,   80
Hurl from his blood-built throne this king of woes,
Dash him to dust, and let the world repose.

1812   *1938*

---

[11]Summons to arms. According to the 1798 French law of conscription, men of 20–25 years were assigned to five classes. The conscripts each year were drawn from the youngest class, each subsequent class to be called out if the first were not sufficient in number; the system provided Napoleon with 2,613,000 men over fourteen years.

[12]Three-headed Cerberus, mythical hound of hell that guards the gates of Hades.
[13]Jowls, jaws.
[14]Infect.
[15]City 400 miles southwest of Moscow.

WILLIAM CULLEN BRYANT
(1794–1878)

William Cullen Bryant has often been called a transitional poet, beginning to write, as he did, in the eighteenth-century neoclassical style with all its constraints but moving triumphantly to the nineteenth-century romantic style with all its freedom. He not only made this movement himself, but he encouraged American poets to give up imitation of outworn forms. In a piece on American poetry written in 1818, he observed that such an eighteenth-century form as the heroic couplet "allows just as much play and freedom to the faculties of the writer as a pair of stilts allows the body. The imagination is confined to one trodden circle, doomed to the chains of a perpetual mannerism, and condemned to tinkle the same eternal tune with its fetters."

Bryant has also been called the American Wordsworth. And there can be little doubt that Wordsworth played a key role in Bryant's poetic development. He remembered his first encounter with Wordsworth's *Lyrical Ballads* when he was around seventeen: "A thousand springs seemed to gush up at once into my heart and the face of nature, of a sudden, to change into a strange freshness and life." But Bryant understood from the beginning that as a poet he must engage the nature of America, not that of England. To his brother he once wrote: "I saw some lines by you to the skylark. Did you ever see such a bird? Let me counsel you to draw your own images, in describing nature, from what you observe around you. . . . The skylark is an English bird, and an American who has never visited Europe has no right to be in raptures about it."

Bryant started out as a conservative in every respect—a Federalist in politics, a Calvinist in religion, and a classicist in literary taste. He ended up at his death at eighty-four radically transformed—a Democrat, a Unitarian, and a romantic. The story of his life is largely the story of this transformation.

Bryant was born in Cummington in western Massachusetts. His father was a physician, a skilled surgeon, and a lover of books with a well-stocked library. Bryant attended elementary school and at the age of twelve he was sent to a minister-uncle to study Latin in preparation for college. After a year of Latin, he went to another minister for a year's study of Greek. In 1810, Bryant passed an examination which admitted him to the sophomore class of Williams College in Williamstown, Massachusetts.

After a year, Bryant withdrew from Williams to prepare himself to enter Yale for his junior year. When his father found that he did not have the means to send him there, Bryant decided on studying law instead. But by this time he had shown his precocity in the writing of poetry. In 1808, at age thirteen, he had written "The Embargo," a satire lambasting President Jefferson for the embargo he imposed on imported goods in retaliation for seizure of American ships and seamen by France and England. The Federalists were up in arms at Jefferson's interference with trade in New England. The young Bryant wrote—in heroic couplets—a scathing denunciation of Jefferson:

> And thou, the scorn of every patriot name,
> The country's ruin, and her council's shame.

The proud father saw that this 500-line poem was published as a pamphlet, to the later embarrassment of Bryant, who rejected his early poetry when publishing his collected poems.

Bryant continued to write poetry even as he studied for the bar. The year he was admitted (1815), he wrote two of his most famous poems—"To a Waterfowl" and "Thanatopsis," the latter published in a leading journal of the time, *North American Review,* in 1817. The editor had shown Bryant's poems to R. H. Dana, who remarked: "You have been imposed upon. No one this side of the Atlantic is capable of writing such verses." Upon the appearance of "Thanatopsis," Bryant was immediately recognized as an important writer and invited to submit other poems. In 1821 Bryant published a pamphlet containing twelve poems, including "Thanatopsis" in the form we now know it.

Bryant had by this time an established law practice in Great Barrington and had married. But his interest in writing poetry was increasing, and during the first half of the 1820s he wrote and published some of his best-loved poems, including "An Indian at the Burial Place of His Fathers" and "Forest Hymn." By 1825 he was recognized as America's finest poet and was offered the co-editorship of the *New York Review and Atheneum.* He accepted.

The magazine was failing within a year, and Bryant was desperately in need of money. When he was offered a position on the *New York Evening Post,* he accepted and soon worked his way up to editor and part owner. He edited the *Evening Post* until his death in 1878. It prospered, as did he. Bryant turned it into a highly influential newspaper in support of liberal causes. Bryant himself had abandoned the Federalists (who became the National-Republicans) for the Democratic-Republicans (the Jeffersonian party). He remained with the Democrats until the slavery issue caused him to switch. He was an enthusiastic supporter of Abraham Lincoln.

In the latter part of his career, Bryant found the leisure to travel, and in 1850 he published the first of several travel books, *Letters of a Traveller.* In his late years he turned to an early enthusiasm, translating Homer's *Iliad* (1870) and *Odyssey* (1872). He continued also to write poetry, but critics have tended to find his best poetry that which he wrote before 1830. His volume of *Poems* published in 1832 (including "To the Fringed Gentian") was called by the *North American Review* "the best volume of American verse that has ever appeared." Other collections appeared regularly and his *Poems* were published in three volumes in 1875.

In April 1878, Bryant delivered an oration at the unveiling of a statue honoring the Italian patriot Giuseppe Mazzini in Central Park. It was a hot day, and the eighty-four-year-old Bryant stumbled on some steps and suffered a brain concussion, fell into a coma, and died.

In *A Fable for Critics,* James Russell Lowell wrote: "There is Bryant, as quiet, as cool, and as dignified,/As a smooth, silent iceberg, that never is ignified." In pointing to Bryant's "supreme ice-olation," Lowell may have intuitively touched a theme in Bryant seldom emphasized—his melancholy verging on despair. There is something chilling in many of the poems as the reader senses life envisioned as a series of inescapable losses.

In many poems not often anthologized, such as "Midsummer," Bryant evokes a hostile or oppressive or indifferent Power in nature, without any attempt to find a balancing consolation. And even in poems that find their way to an often tenuous affirmation, the images of solitude, barrenness, and desolation seem to dominate and endure. In "To a Waterfowl," the bird, "swallowed up" in the "abyss" of heaven, brings the piercing awareness to the poet of the "long way" he must "tread alone." The final vision of the "Indian at the Burial-Place of His Fathers" is: "The realm our tribes are crushed to get/May be a barren desert yet." The sweeping vision of human history in "The Flood of Years" turns into a nightmare landscape telling of "blighted" hopes and "dreams of happiness/Dissolved in air." In these bleak moments Bryant resembles the twentieth century's Robert Frost, another poet whose shrewd geniality had its darker side.

ADDITIONAL READING

The Life and Works of William Cullen Bryant, ed. Parke Godwin, 6 vols., 1883–84; *William Cullen Bryant: Representative Selections, with Introduction, Bibliography, and Notes*, ed. Tremaine McDowell, 1935; *The Letters of William Cullen Bryant*, ed. William Cullen Bryant II and Thomas G. Voss, 1975–.

H. H. Peckham, *Gotham Yankee*, 1950; Curtiss S. Johnson, *Politics and a Belly-Full: Journalistic Career of William Cullen Bryant*, 1962; Albert F. McLean, Jr., *William Cullen Bryant*, 1964; Charles H. Brown, *William Cullen Bryant*, 1971; Stanley Brodwin et al., eds., *William Cullen Bryant and His America: Centennial Conference Proceedings 1878–1978*, 1983; Robert A. Ferguson, "William Cullen Bryant: The Creative Context of the Poet," *Law and Letters in American Culture*, 1984. Norbert Krapf, *Under Open Sky: Poets on William Cullen Bryant*, 1986.

TEXT

The Poetical Works of William Cullen Bryant, 2 vols., ed. Parke Godwin, 1883.

Thanatopsis[1]

To him who in the love of Nature holds
Communion with her visible forms, she speaks
A various language; for his gayer hours
She has a voice of gladness, and a smile
And eloquence of beauty, and she glides   5
Into his darker musings, with a mild
And healing sympathy, that steals away
Their sharpness, ere he is aware. When thoughts
Of the last bitter hour come like a blight
Over thy spirit, and sad images   10
Of the stern agony, and shroud, and pall,
And breathless darkness, and the narrow house,
Make thee to shudder, and grow sick at heart;—
Go forth, under the open sky, and list
To Nature's teachings, while from all around—   15
Earth and her waters, and the depths of air—
Comes a still voice.—

　　　　　Yet a few days, and thee
The all-beholding sun shall see no more
In all his course; nor yet in the cold ground,
Where thy pale form was laid, with many tears,   20

[1] "Thanatopsis" (Greek for "meditation on death") is Bryant's most popular poem. Because of Bryant's comments late in life, it was believed for a time that he wrote it when he was sixteen or seventeen. But scholarship has established that he wrote it in 1815, when he was around twenty-one. He added the first seventeen lines and the last sixteen lines on republication of the poem in 1821. "Thanatopsis" is remarkable in its use of blank verse, then unusual in American poetry. And the poem's expression of a view of death more stoic and Diestic than Christian is somewhat surprising, given Bryant's Puritan background.

Nor in the embrace of ocean, shall exist
Thy image. Earth, that nourished thee, shall claim
Thy growth, to be resolved to earth again,
And, lost each human trace, surrendering up
Thine individual being, shalt thou go   25
To mix for ever with the elements,
To be a brother to the insensible rock
And to the sluggish clod, which the rude swain
Turns with his share,[2] and treads upon. The oak
Shall send his roots abroad, and pierce thy mould.   30

   Yet not to thine eternal resting-place
Shalt thou retire alone, nor couldst thou wish
Couch more magnificent. Thou shalt lie down
With patriarchs of the infant world—with kings,
The powerful of the earth—the wise, the good,   35
Fair forms, and hoary seers of ages past,
All in one mighty sepulchre. The hills
Rock-ribbed and ancient as the sun,—the vales
Stretching in pensive quietness between;
The venerable woods—rivers that move   40
In majesty, and the complaining brooks
That make the meadows green; and, poured round all,
Old Ocean's gray and melancholy waste,—
Are but the solemn decorations all
Of the great tomb of man. The golden sun,   45
The planets, all the infinite host of heaven,
Are shining on the sad abodes of death,
Through the still lapse of ages. All that tread
The globe are but a handful to the tribes
That slumber in its bosom.—Take the wings   50
Of morning, pierce the Barcan wilderness,[3]
Or lose thyself in the continuous woods
Where rolls the Oregon,[4] and hears no sound,
Save his own dashings—yet the dead are there:
And millions in those solitudes, since first   55
The flight of years began, have laid them down
In their last sleep—the dead reign there alone.
So shalt thou rest, and what if thou withdraw
In silence from the living, and no friend
Take note of thy departure? All that breathe   60
Will share thy destiny. The gay will laugh
When thou art gone, the solemn brood of care
Plod on, and each one as before will chase
His favorite phantom; yet all these shall leave
Their mirth and their employments, and shall come   65
And make their bed with thee. As the long train
Of ages glides away, the sons of men,
The youth in life's fresh spring, and he who goes
In the full strength of years, matron and maid,
The speechless babe, and the gray-headed man—   70
Shall one by one be gathered to thy side,
By those, who in their turn shall follow them.

---

[2]Plowshare.
[3]Desert of Barca, ancient name for northeast Libya, North Africa. Numerous expeditions in the early nineteenth century described the Great Plains as the Great American Desert.
[4]Indian name for the Columbia River.

So live, that when thy summons comes to join
The innumerable caravan, which moves
To that mysterious realm, where each shall take   75
His chamber in the silent halls of death,
Thou go not, like the quarry-slave at night,
Scourged to his dungeon, but, sustained and soothed
By an unfaltering trust, approach thy grave,
Like one who wraps the drapery of his couch   80
About him, and lies down to pleasant dreams.

1815   *1817, 1821*

The Yellow Violet

When beechen buds begin to swell,
   And woods the blue-bird's warble know,
The yellow violet's modest bell
   Peeps from the last year's leaves below.

Ere russet fields their green resume,   5
   Sweet flower, I love, in forest bare,
To meet thee, when thy faint perfume
   Alone is in the virgin air.

Of all her train, the hands of Spring
   First plant thee in the watery mould,   10
And I have seen thee blossoming
   Beside the snow-bank's edges cold.

Thy parent sun, who bade thee view
   Pale skies, and chilling moisture sip,
Has bathed thee in his own bright hue,   15
   And streaked with jet[1] thy glowing lip.

Yet slight thy form, and low thy seat,
   And earthward bent thy gentle eye,
Unapt the passing view to meet,
   When loftier flowers are flaunting nigh.   20

Oft, in the sunless April day,
   Thy early smile has stayed my walk;
But midst the gorgeous blooms of May,
   I passed thee on thy humble stalk.

So they, who climb to wealth, forget   25
   The friends in darker fortunes tried.
I copied them—but I regret
   That I should ape the ways of pride.

---

[1]Deep, glossy black.

   And when again the genial hour
     Awakes the painted tribes of light.
   I'll not o'erlook the modest flower   30
     That made the woods of April bright.

1814   *1821*

Inscription for the
Entrance to a Wood

Stranger, if thou hast learned a truth which needs
No school of long experience, that the world
Is full of guilt and misery, and hast seen
Enough of all its sorrows, crimes, and cares,
To tire thee of it, enter this wild wood   5
And view the haunts of Nature. The calm shade
Shall bring a kindred calm, and the sweet breeze
That makes the green leaves dance, shall waft a balm
To thy sick heart. Thou wilt find nothing here
Of all that pained thee in the haunts of men,   10
And made thee loathe thy life. The primal curse[1]
Fell, it is true, upon the unsinning earth,
But not in vengeance. God hath yoked to guilt
Her pale tormentor, misery. Hence, these shades
Are still the abodes of gladness; the thick roof   15
Of green and stirring branches is alive
And musical with birds, that sing and sport
In wantonness of spirit; while below
The squirrel, with raised paws and form erect,
Chirps merrily. Throngs of insects in the shade   20
Try their thin wings and dance in the warm beam
That waked them into life. Even the green trees
Partake the deep contentment; as they bend
To the soft winds, the sun from the blue sky
Looks in and sheds a blessing on the scene.   25
Scarce less the cleft-born wild-flower seems to enjoy
Existence than the wingèd plunderer
That sucks its sweets. The mossy rocks themselves,
And the old and ponderous trunks of prostrate trees
That lead from knoll to knoll a causey[2] rude   30
Or bridge the sunken brook, and their dark roots,
With all their earth upon them, twisting high,
Breathe fixed tranquillity. The rivulet
Sends forth glad sounds, and tripping o'er its bed
Of pebbly sands, or leaping down the rocks,   35
Seems, with continuous laughter, to rejoice
In its own being. Softly tread the marge,[3]
Lest from her midway perch thou scare the wren

---

[1]After cursing the serpent and Eve, God said to Adam,   [2]Causeway.
"Cursed is the ground for thy sake" (Genesis 3:17).   [3]Margin, edge.

That dips her bill in water. The cool wind,
That stirs the stream in play, shall come to thee,   40
Like one that loves thee nor will let thee pass
Ungreeted, and shall give its light embrace.

1815   *1817, 1821*

To a Waterfowl

Whither, midst falling dew,
    While glow the heavens with the last steps of day,
Far, through their rosy depths, dost thou pursue
    Thy solitary way?

    Vainly the fowler's eye   5
Might mark thy distant flight to do thee wrong,
As, darkly painted on the crimson sky,
    Thy figure floats along.

    Seek'st thou the plashy[1] brink
Of weedy lake, or marge of river wide,   10
Or where the rocking billows rise and sink
    On the chafed ocean-side?

    There is a Power whose care
Teaches thy way along that pathless coast—
The desert and illimitable air—   15
    Lone wandering, but not lost.

    All day thy wings have fanned,
At that far height, the cold, thin atmosphere,
Yet stoop not, weary, to the welcome land,   20
    Though the dark night is near.

    And soon that toil shall end;
Soon shalt thou find a summer home, and rest,
And scream among thy fellows; reeds shall bend,
    Soon, o'er thy sheltered nest.

    Thou'rt gone, the abyss of heaven   25
Hath swallowed up thy form; yet, on my heart
Deeply has sunk the lesson thou hast given,
    And shall not soon depart.

    He who, from zone to zone,
Guides through the boundless sky thy certain flight,   30
In the long way that I must tread alone,
    Will lead my steps aright.

1815   *1818, 1821*

---

[1]Swampy, marshy.

Oh Fairest
of the Rural Maids

Oh fairest of the rural maids!
Thy birth was in the forest shades;
Green boughs and glimpses of the sky,
Were all that met thine infant eye.

Thy sports, thy wanderings, when a child,   5
Were ever in the sylvan[1] wild;
And all the beauty of the place
Is in thy heart and on thy face.

The twilight of the trees and rocks
Is in the light shade of thy locks;   10
Thy step is as the wind, that weaves
Its playful way among the leaves.

Thine eyes are springs, in whose serene
And silent waters heaven is seen;
Their lashes are the herbs that look   15
On their young figures in the brook.

The forest depths, by foot unpressed,
Are not more sinless than thy breast;
The holy peace, that fills the air
Of those calm solitudes, is there.   20

1820   1832

An Indian at the
Burial-Place of His Fathers

It is the spot I came to seek—
    My father's ancient burial-place,
Ere from these vales, ashamed and weak,
    Withdrew our wasted race.
It is the spot—I know it well—   5
Of which our old traditions tell.

For here the upland bank sends out
    A ridge toward the river-side;
I know the shaggy hills about,
    The meadows smooth and wide,   10
The plains, that, toward the southern sky,
Fenced east and west by mountains lie.

A white man, gazing on the scene,
    Would say a lovely spot was here,
And praise the lawns, so fresh and green,   15

---
[1]Wooded.

Between the hills so sheer.
I like it not—I would the plain
Lay in its tall old groves again.

The sheep are on the slopes around,
   The cattle in the meadows feed,
And laborers turn the crumbling ground,   20
   Or drop the yellow seed,
And prancing steeds, in trappings gay,
Whirl the bright chariot o'er the way.

Methinks it were a nobler sight   25
   To see these vales in woods arrayed,
Their summits in the golden light,
   Their trunks in grateful shade,
And herds of deer that bounding go
O'er hills and prostrate trees below.   30

And then to mark the lord of all,
   The forest hero, trained to wars,
Quivered and plumed, and lithe and tall,
   And seamed with glorious scars,
Walk forth, amid his reign, to dare   35
The wolf, and grapple with the bear.

This bank, in which the dead were laid,
   Was sacred when its soil was ours;
Hither the silent Indian maid
   Brought wreaths of beads and flowers,   40
And the gray chief and gifted seer
Worshipped the god of thunders here.

But now the wheat is green and high
   On clods that hid the warrior's breast,
And scattered in the furrows lie   45
   The weapons of his rest;
And there, in the loose sand, is thrown
Of his large arm the mouldering bone.

Ah, little thought the strong and brave
   Who bore their lifeless chieftain forth—   50
Or the young wife that weeping gave
   Her first-born to the earth,
That the pale race, who waste us now,
Among their bones should guide the plough.

They waste us—ay—like April snow   55
   In the warm noon, we shrink away;
And fast they follow, as we go
   Toward the setting day—
Till they shall fill the land, and we
Are driven into the Western sea.   60

But I behold a fearful sign,
   To which the white men's eyes are blind;
Their race may vanish hence, like mine,

And leave no trace behind,
Save ruins o'er the region spread,
And the white stones above the dead.   65

Before these fields were shorn and tilled,
    Full to the brim our rivers flowed;
The melody of waters filled
    The fresh and boundless wood;   70
And torrents dashed and rivulets played,
And fountains spouted in the shade.

Those grateful sounds are heard no more,
    The springs are silent in the sun;
The rivers, by the blackened shore,   75
    With lessening current run;
The realm our tribes are crushed to get
May be a barren desert yet.

1824   1824

A Forest Hymn

The groves were God's first temples. Ere man learned
To hew the shaft,[1] and lay the architrave,[2]
And spread the roof above them—ere he framed
The lofty vault,[3] to gather and roll back
The sound of anthems; in the darkling wood,   5
Amid the cool and silence, he knelt down,
And offered to the Mightiest solemn thanks
And supplication. For his simple heart
Might not resist the sacred influence
Which, from the stilly twilight of the place,   10
And from the gray old trunks that high in heaven
Mingled their mossy boughs, and from the sound
Of the invisible breath that swayed at once
All their green tops, stole over him, and bowed
His spirit with the thought of boundless power   15
And inaccessible majesty. Ah, why
Should we, in the world's riper years, neglect
God's ancient sanctuaries, and adore
Only among the crowd, and under roofs
That our frail hands have raised? Let me, at least,   20
Here, in the shadow of this aged wood,
Offer one hymn—thrice happy, if it find
Acceptance in His ear.

                    Father, thy hand
Hath reared these venerable columns, thou
Didst weave this verdant roof. Thou didst look down   25

---

[1]Column.
[2]In classical architecture, the lowest part of the entablature
resting on the column, with the frieze and cornice above.
[3]Arched ceiling of the Gothic cathedral.

Upon the naked earth, and, forthwith, rose
All these fair ranks of trees. They, in thy sun,
Budded, and shook their green leaves in thy breeze,
And shot toward heaven. The century-living crow   30
Whose birth was in their tops, grew old and died
Among their branches, till, at last, they stood,
As now they stand, massy, and tall, and dark,
Fit shrine for humble worshipper to hold
Communion with his Maker. These dim vaults,   35
These winding aisles, of human pomp or pride
Report not. No fantastic carvings show
The boast of our vain race to change the form
Of thy fair works. But thou are here—thou fill'st
The solitude. Thou art in the soft winds   40
That run along the summit of these trees
In music; thou art in the cooler breath
That from the inmost darkness of the place
Comes, scarcely felt; the barky trunks, the ground,
The fresh moist ground, are all instinct with thee.
Here is continual worship;—nature, here,   45
In the tranquillity that thou dost love,
Enjoys thy presence. Noiselessly, around,
From perch to perch, the solitary bird
Passes; and yon clear spring, that, midst its herbs,
Wells softly forth and wandering steeps the roots   50
Of half the mighty forest, tells no tale
Of all the good it does. Thou has not left
Thyself without a witness, in the shades,
Of thy perfections. Grandeur, strength, and grace
Are here to speak of thee. This mighty oak—   55
By whose immovable stem I stand and seem
Almost annihilated—not a prince,
In all that proud old world beyond the deep,
E'er wore his crown as loftily as he
Wears the green coronal[4] of leaves with which   60
Thy hand has graced him. Nestled at his root
Is beauty, such as blooms not in the glare
Of the broad sun. That delicate forest flower,
With scented breath and look so like a smile,
Seems, as it issues from the shapeless mould,   65
An emanation of the indwelling Life,
A visible token of the upholding Love,
That are the soul of this great universe.

My heart is awed within me when I think
Of the great miracle that still goes on,   70
In silence, round me—the perpetual work
Of thy creation, finished, yet renewed
Forever. Written on thy works I read
The lesson of thy own eternity.
Lo! all grow old and die—but see again,   75
How on the faltering footsteps of decay
Youth presses—ever gay and beautiful youth
In all its beautiful forms. These lofty trees

---

[4]Crown.

Wave not less proudly that their ancestors
Moulder beneath them. Oh, there is not lost   80
One of earth's charms: upon her bosom yet,
After the flight of untold centuries,
The freshness of her far beginning lies
And yet shall lie. Life mocks the idle hate
Of his arch-enemy Death—yea, seats himself   85
Upon the tyrant's throne—the sepulchre,
And of the triumphs of his ghastly foe
Makes his own nourishment. For he came forth
From thine own bosom, and shall have no end.

There have been holy men who hid themselves   90
Deep in the woody wilderness, and gave
Their lives to thought and prayer, till they outlived
The generation born with them, nor seemed
Less aged than the hoary trees and rocks
Around them;—and there have been holy men   95
Who deemed it were not well to pass life thus.
But let me often to these solitudes
Retire, and in thy presence reassure
My feeble virtue. Here its enemies,
The passions, at thy plainer footsteps shrink   100
And tremble and are still. O God! when thou
Dost scare the world with tempests, set on fire
The heavens with falling thunderbolts, or fill,
With all the waters of the firmament,
The swift dark whirlwind that uproots the woods   105
And drowns the villages; when, at thy call,
Uprises the great deep and throws himself
Upon the continent, and overwhelms
Its cities—who forgets not, at the sight
Of these tremendous tokens of thy power,   110
His pride, and lays his strifes and follies by?
Oh, from these sterner aspects of thy face
Spare me and mine, nor let us need the wrath
Of the mad unchained elements to teach
Who rules them. Be it ours to meditate,   115
In these calm shades, thy milder majesty,
And to the beautiful order of thy works
Learn to conform the order of our lives.

1825   *1825, 1832*

Midsummer

A power is on the earth and in the air
    From which the vital spirit shrinks afraid,
    And shelters him, in nooks of deepest shade,
From the hot steam and from the fiery glare,
Look forth upon the earth—her thousand plants   5
    Are smitten; even the dark sun-loving maize
    Faints in the field beneath the torrid blaze;

The herd beside the shaded fountain pants;
For life is driven from all the landscape brown;
  The bird has sought his tree, the snake his den,
  The trout floats dead in the hot stream, and men   10
Drop by the sun-stroke in the populous town;
  As if the Day of Fire had dawned, and sent
  Its deadly breath into the firmament.

1826   1826

To Cole, the Painter, Departing for Europe[1]

Thine eyes shall see the light of distant skies;
  Yet, COLE! thy heart shall bear to Europe's strand
  A living image of our own bright land,
Such as upon thy glorious canvas lies;
Lone lakes—savannas[2] where the bison roves—   5
  Rocks rich with summer garlands—solemn streams—
  Skies, where the desert eagle wheels and screams—
Spring bloom and autumn blaze of boundless groves.
Fair scenes shall greet thee where thou goest—fair,
  But different—everywhere the trace of men,   10
  Paths, homes, graves, ruins, from the lowest glen
To where life shrinks from the fierce Alpine air.
  Gaze on them, till the tears shall dim thy sight,
  But keep that earlier, wilder image bright.

1829   1830, 1832

To the Fringed Gentian

Thou blossom bright with autumn dew,
And colored with the heaven's own blue,
That openest when the quiet light
Succeeds the keen and frosty night.

Thou comest not when violets lean   5
O'er wandering brooks and springs unseen,
Or columbines, in purple dressed,
Nod o'er the ground-bird's hidden nest.

Thou waitest late and com'st alone,
When woods are bare and birds are flown,   10

[1]English-born Thomas Cole (1808–1848) became the leader of the Hudson River School of American landscape painters with his Hudson River scenes depicting the wild grandeur and sublimity of nature. "To walk with nature as a poet," Cole said, "is the necessary condition of the perfect artist." Cole often walked with Bryant in the Catskills, for their romantic affinities made poet and painter "Kindred Spirits," the title of a work by a member of the school. Ascher Durand, showing the two of them on a promontory overlooking a deep ravine in the Catskill forest setting. Cole left for Italy in 1829 for three years of study.
[2]Treeless plain.

And frosts and shortening days portend
The aged year is near his end.

Then doth thy sweet and quiet eye
Look through its fringes to the sky,
Blue—blue—as if that sky let fall   15
A flower from its cerulean wall.

I would that thus, when I shall see
The hour of death draw near to me,
Hope, blossoming within my heart,
May look to heaven as I depart.   20

1829   1832

The Prairies[1]

These are the gardens of the Desert,[2] these
The unshorn fields, boundless and beautiful,
For which the speech of England has no name—
The Prairies.[3] I behold them for the first,
And my heart swells, while the dilated sight   5
Takes in the encircling vastness. Lo! they stretch,
In airy undulations, far away,
As if the ocean, in his gentlest swell,
Stood still, with all his rounded billows fixed,
And motionless forever.—Motionless?—   10
No—they are all unchained again. The clouds
Sweep over with their shadows, and, beneath,
The surface rolls and fluctuates to the eye;
Dark hollows seem to glide along and chase
The sunny ridges. Breezes of the South!   15
Who toss the golden and the flame-like flowers,
And pass the prairie-hawk that, poised on high,
Flaps his broad wings, yet moves not—ye have played
Among the palms of Mexico and vines
Of Texas, and have crisped the limpid brooks   20
That from the fountains of Sonora[4] glide
Into the calm Pacific—have ye fanned
A nobler or a lovelier scene than this?
Man hath no power in all this glorious work:
The hand that built the firmament hath heaved   25
And smoothed these verdant swells, and sown their slopes
With herbage, planted them with island groves,
And hedged them round with forests. Fitting floor
For this magnificent temple of the sky—
With flowers whose glory and whose multitude   30

---

[1]While visiting his brothers in Illinois in 1832, Bryant toured the prairies and wrote to his wife: "What I have thought and felt amid these boundless wastes and awful solitudes I shall reserve for the only form of expression in which it can be properly uttered."
[2]The Great Plains region west of the Mississippi, then called the "Great American Desert."
[3]French for "meadows," adopted into the American language beginning in the late eighteenth and early nineteenth centuries.
[4]State in northwest Mexico.

Rival the constellations! The great heavens
Seem to stoop down upon the scene in love,—
A nearer vault, and of a tenderer blue,
Than that which bends above our eastern hills.

As o'er the verdant waste I guide my steed,   35
Among the high rank grass that sweeps his sides
The hollow beating of his footstep seems
A sacrilegious sound. I think of those
Upon whose rest he tramples. Are they here—
The dead of other days?—and did the dust   40
Of these fair solitudes once stir with life
And burn with passion? Let the mighty mounds[5]
That overlook the rivers, or that rise
In the dim forest crowded with old oaks,
Answer. A race, that long has passed away,   45
Built them;—a disciplined and populous race
Heaped, with long toil, the earth, while yet the Greek
Was hewing the Pentelicus[6] to forms
Of symmetry, and rearing on its rock
The glittering Parthenon. These ample fields   50
Nourished their harvests, here their herds were fed,
When haply by their stalls the bison lowed,[7]
And bowed his manèd shoulder to the yoke.
All day this desert murmured with their toils,
Till twilight blushed, and lovers walked, and wooed   55
In a forgotten language, and old tunes,
From instruments of unremembered form,
Gave the soft winds a voice. The red man came—
The roaming hunter tribes, warlike and fierce,
And the mound-builders vanished from the earth.   60
The solitude of centuries untold
Has settled where they dwelt. The prairie-wolf
Hunts in their meadows, and his fresh-dug den
Yawns by my path. The gopher mines the ground
Where stood their swarming cities. All is gone;   65
All—save the piles of earth that hold their bones,
The platforms where they worshipped unknown gods,
The barriers which they builded from the soil
To keep the foe at bay—till o'er the walls
The wild beleaguerers broke, and, one by one,   70
The strongholds of the plain were forced, and heaped
With corpses. The brown vultures of the wood
Flocked to those vast uncovered sepulchres,
And sat unscared and silent at their feast.
Haply some solitary fugitive,   75
Lurking in marsh and forest, till the sense
Of desolation and of fear became
Bitterer than death, yielded himself to die.
Man's better nature triumphed then. Kind words
Welcomed and soothed him; the rude conquerors   80

---

[5]Burial and effigy earthworks of the prehistoric Indian
Mound Builders. In Bryant's time they were believed to be
a highly civilized agricultural people distinct from the Indian.
[6]Mountain near Athens, where white marble was quarried

for the Parthenon, the temple of Athena on the Acropolis
in Athens.
[7]In his depiction of the unspoiled paradise of the Mound
Builders, Bryant imagines the bison, or buffalo, domesticated, not the prey of the "hunter tribes" to come.

Seated the captive with their chiefs; he chose
A bride among their maidens, and at length
Seemed to forget—yet ne'er forgot—the wife
Of his first love, and her sweet little ones,
Butchered, amid their shrieks, with all his race.   85

Thus change the forms of being. Thus arise
Races of living things, glorious in strength,
And perish, as the quickening breath of God
Fills them, or is withdrawn. The red man, too,
Has left the blooming wilds he ranged so long,   90
And, nearer to the Rocky Mountains, sought
A wilder hunting-ground. The beaver builds
No longer by these streams, but far away,
On waters whose blue surface ne'er gave back
The white man's face—among Missouri's springs,   95
And pools whose issues swell the Oregon[8]—
He rears his little Venice.[9] In these plains
The bison feeds no more. Twice twenty leagues
Beyond remotest smoke of hunter's camp,
Roams the majestic brute, in herds that shake   100
The earth with thundering steps—yet here I meet
His ancient footprints stamped beside the pool.

Still this great solitude is quick with life.
Myriads of insects, gaudy as the flowers
They flutter over, gentle quadrupeds,   105
And birds, that scarce have learned the fear of man,
Are here, and sliding reptiles of the ground,
Startlingly beautiful. The graceful deer
Bounds to the wood at my approach. The bee,
A more adventurous colonist than man,   110
With whom he came across the eastern deep,
Fills the savannas[10] with his murmurings,
And hides his sweets, as in the golden age,
Within the hollow oak. I listen long
To his domestic hum, and think I hear   115
The sound of that advancing multitude
Which soon shall fill these deserts. From the ground
Comes up the laugh of children, the soft voice
Of maidens, and the sweet and solemn hymn
Of Sabbath worshippers. The low of herds   120
Blends with the rustling of the heavy grain
Over the dark brown furrows. All at once
A fresher wind sweeps by, and breaks my dream,
And I am in the wilderness alone.

1832   1833

---

[8]Columbia River.
[9]I.e., the beaver's dams.
[10]Treeless plains.

The Poet

Thou, who wouldst wear the name
   Of poet mid thy brethren of mankind,
And clothe in words of flame
   Thoughts that shall live within the general mind!
Deem not the framing of a deathless lay   5
The pastime of a drowsy summer day.

But gather all thy powers,
   And wreak[1] them on the verse that thou dost weave,
And in thy lonely hours,
   At silent morning or at wakeful eve,   10
While the warm current tingles through thy veins,
Set forth the burning words in fluent strains.

No smooth array of phrase,
   Artfully sought and ordered though it be,
Which the cold rhymer lays   15
   Upon his page with languid industry,
Can wake the listless pulse to livelier speed,
Or fill with sudden tears the eyes that read.

The secret wouldst thou know
   To touch the heart or fire the blood at will?   20
Let thine own eyes o'erflow;
   Let thy lips quiver with the passionate thrill;
Seize the great thought, ere yet its power be past,
And bind, in words, the fleet emotion fast.

Then, should thy verse appear   25
   Halting and harsh, and all unaptly wrought,
Touch the crude line with fear,
   Save in the moment of impassioned thought;
Then summon back the original glow, and mend
The strain with rapture that with fire was penned.   30

Yet let no empty gust
   Of passion find an utterance in thy lay,
A blast that whirls the dust
   Along the howling street and dies away;
But feelings of calm power and mighty sweep,   35
Like currents journeying through the windless deep.

Seek'st thou, in living lays,
   To limn[2] the beauty of the earth and sky?
Before thine inner gaze
   Let all that beauty in clear vision lie;   40
Look on it with exceeding love, and write
The words inspired by wonder and delight.

Of tempests wouldst thou sing,
   Or tell of battles—make thyself a part

---

[1]Release.
[2]Depict.

Of the great tumult; cling 45
  To the tossed wreck with terror in thy heart;
Scale, with the assaulting host, the rampart's height,
And strike and struggle in the thickest fight.

So shalt thou frame a lay
  That haply may endure from age to age, 50
And they who read shall say:
  "What witchery hangs upon this poet's page!
What art is his the written spells to find
That sway from mood to mood the willing mind!"

1863   1864

The Flood of Years[1]

  A mighty Hand, from an exhaustless Urn,
Pours forth the never-ending Flood of Years,
Among the nations. How the rushing waves
Bear all before them! On their foremost edge,
And there alone, is Life. The Present there 5
Tosses and foams and fills the air with roar
Of mingled noises. There are they who toil,
And they who strive, and they who feast, and they
Who hurry to and fro. The sturdy swain—
Woodman and delver with the spade—is there, 10
And busy artisan beside his bench,
And pallid student with his written roll.
A moment on the mounting billow seen,
The flood sweeps over them and they are gone.
There groups of revellers whose brows are twined 15
With roses, ride the topmost swell awhile,
And as they raise their flowing cups and touch
The clinking brim to brim, are whirled beneath
The waves and disappear. I hear the jar
Of beaten drums, and thunders that break forth 20
From cannon, where the advancing billow sends
Up to the sight long files of armèd men,
That hurry to the charge through flame and smoke.
The torrent bears them under, whelmed and hid
Slayer and slain, in heaps of bloody foam. 25
Down go the steed and rider, the plumed chief
Sinks with his followers; the head that wears
The imperial diadem goes down beside
The felon's with cropped ear and branded cheek.
A funeral-train—the torrent sweeps away 30
Bearers and bier and mourners. By the bed

---

[1]Written when Bryant was eighty-one, "The Flood of Years" expresses a bleak view of the transience of life, but near the end turns to what the "wise and good have said" about life beyond death. One reader wrote to Bryant inquiring whether he really believed the last lines. Bryant answered: "Certainly I believe all that is said in the lines you have quoted: otherwise I could not have written them. I believe in the everlasting life of the soul, and it seems to me that immortality would be but an imperfect gift without the recognition in the life to come of those who are dear to us here."

Of one who dies men gather sorrowing,
And women weep aloud; the flood rolls on;
The wail is stilted and the sobbing group
Borne under. Hark to that shrill, sudden shout,   35
The cry of an applauding multitude,
Swayed by some loud-voiced orator who wields
The living mass as if he were its soul!
The waters choke the shout and all is still.
Lo! next a kneeling crowd, and one who spreads   40
The hands in prayer, the engulfing wave o'ertakes
And swallows them and him. A sculptor wields
The chisel, and the stricken marble grows
To beauty; at his easel, eager-eyed,
A painter stands, and sunshine at his touch   45
Gathers upon his canvas, and life glows;
A poet, as he paces to and fro,
Murmurs his sounding lines. Awhile they ride
The advancing billow, till its tossing crest
Strikes them and flings them under, while their tasks   50
Are yet unfinished. See a mother smile
On her young babe that smiles to her again;
The torrent wrests it from her arms; she shrieks
And weeps, and midst her tears is carried down.
A beam like that of moonlight turns the spray   55
To glistening pearls; two lovers, hand in hand,
Rise on the billowy swell and fondly look
Into each other's eyes. The rushing flood
Flings them apart: the youth goes down; the maid
With hands outstretched in vain, and streaming eyes,   60
Waits for the next high wave to follow him.
An aged man succeeds; his bending form
Sinks slowly. Mingling with the sullen stream
Gleam the white locks, and then are seen no more.
    Lo! wider grows the stream—a sea-like flood   65
Saps earth's walled cities; massive palaces
Crumble before it; fortresses and towers
Dissolve in the swift waters; populous realms
Swept by the torrent see their ancient tribes
Engulfed and lost; their very languages   70
Stifled, and never to be uttered more.
    I pause and turn my eyes, and looking back
Where that tumultuous flood has been, I see
The silent ocean of the Past, a waste
Of waters weltering over graves, its shores   75
Strewn with the wreck of fleets where mast and hull
Drop away piecemeal; battlemented walls
Frown idly, green with moss, and temples stand
Unroofed, forsaken by the worshipper.
There lie memorial stones, whence time has gnawed   80
The graven legends, thrones of kings o'erturned,
The broken altars of forgotten gods,
Foundations of old cities and long streets
Where never fall of human foot is heard,
On all the desolate pavement. I behold   85
Dim glimmerings of lost jewels, far within
The sleeping waters, diamond, sardonyx,
Ruby and topaz, pearl and chrysolite,

Once glittering at the banquet on fair brows
That long ago were dust, and all around   90
Strewn on the surface of that silent sea
Are withering bridal wreaths, and glossy locks
Shorn from dear brows, by loving hands, and scrolls
O'er written, haply with fond words of love
And vows of friendship, and fair pages flung   95
Fresh from the printer's engine. There they lie
A moment, and then sink away from sight.
 I look, and the quick tears are in my eyes,
For I behold in every one of these
A blighted hope, a separate history   100
Of human sorrows, telling of dear ties
Suddenly broken, dreams of happiness
Dissolved in air, and happy days too brief
That sorrowfully ended, and I think
How painfully must the poor heart have beat   105
In bosoms without number, as the blow
Was struck that slew their hope and broke their peace.
 Sadly I turn and look before, where yet
The Flood must pass, and I behold a mist
Where swarm dissolving forms, the brood of Hope,   110
Divinely fair, that rest on banks of flowers,
Or wander among rainbows, fading soon
And reappearing, haply giving place
To forms of grisly aspect such as Fear
Shapes from the idle air—where serpents lift   115
The head to strike, and skeletons stretch forth
The bony arm in menace. Further on
A belt of darkness seems to bar the way
Long, low, and distant, where the Life to come
Touches the Life that is. The Flood of Years   120
Rolls toward it near and nearer. It must pass
That dismal barrier. What is there beyond?
Hear what the wise and good have said. Beyond
That belt of darkness, still the Years roll on
More gently, but with not less mighty sweep.   125
They gather up again and softly bear
All the sweet lives that late were overwhelmed
And lost to sight, all that in them was good,
Noble, and truly great, and worthy of love—
The lives of infants and ingenuous youths,   130
Sages and saintly women who have made
Their households happy; all are raised and borne
By that great current in its onward sweep,
Wandering and rippling with caressing waves
Around green islands fragrant with the breath   135
Of flowers that never wither. So they pass,
From stage to stage along the shining course
Of that bright river, broadening like a sea.
As its smooth eddies curl along their way
They bring old friends together; hands are clasped   140
In joy unspeakable; the mother's arms
Again are folded round the child she loved
And lost. Old sorrows are forgotten now,
Or but remembered to make sweet the hour
That overpays them; wounded hearts that bled   145

Or broke are healed forever. In the room
Of this grief-shadowed present, there shall be
A Present in whose reign no grief shall gnaw
The heart, and never shall a tender tie
Be broken; in whose reign the eternal Change   150
That waits on growth and action shall proceed
With everlasting Concord hand in hand.

1876   1876

AN EMERGING AMERICAN DRAMA

ROYALL TYLER

"In justice to the Author . . . it may be proper to observe that this comedy has many claims to the public indulgence, independent of its intrinsic merit: It is the first essay of American genius in a difficult species of composition; it was written by one who never critically studied the rules of the drama, and, indeed, had seen but few of the exhibitions on the stage; it was undertaken and finished in the course of three weeks; and the profits of one night's performance were appropriated to the benefit of the sufferers by the fire at Boston."

From an advertisement published with *The Contrast* (1790)

693

ROYALL TYLER
(1757–1826)

The author of the first American play to be produced and win acclaim in America, Royall Tyler, was born in a city—Boston—in which drama was banned. The British Puritans, when they came to power in 1642, closed the theaters. Cotton Mather, writing in Boston in 1726 (in *Manductio ad Ministerium*), said the "powers of darkness" inspired the writing of plays. Dramas he described as "unclean spirits that came like frogs out of the mouth of the dragon and of the beast. . . those wretched scribbling of madmen." Before going to New York in 1787, the year *The Contrast* was produced, Royall Tyler had never seen a professionally produced play. His achievement is thus all the more remarkable.

Born William Clark Tyler in 1757, Tyler took his father's name of Royall Tyler on his father's death in 1771. His record at Harvard University was so outstanding that he was awarded degrees by both Harvard and Yale in recognition on his graduation in 1776. After a brief stint in the Revolutionary Army, Tyler was released because of his mother's widowhood. He studied at Harvard for the law, taking an M.A. in 1779, and was admitted to the bar of Massachusetts in 1780.

While practicing law in Braintree (now Quincy) Massachusetts, Tyler met and began to court Abigail Adams, daughter of John Adams, then in France to negotiate a peace treaty with England. Adams looked upon Tyler as an untrustworthy "reformed rake" ("I am not looking out for a poet"), and sent for his wife and daughter to join him abroad. The absence worked Adams's will and the engagement was broken off in 1785. Tyler retreated to brood. Abigail married Adams's secretary of legation, Col. William Stephen Smith. Ironically, Smith turned out to be a wastrel whose pay, Adams wrote later when president, "will not feed his dogs; and his dogs must be fed if his children starve. What a folly!"

In 1787, Tyler was appointed aide-de-camp to Major General Benjamin Lincoln, who was given the task by Massachusetts's governor to suppress Shays' Rebellion. Daniel Shays was leading a group of disgruntled western farmers, facing foreclosure on their farms in the middle of a depression and increased taxation, in a revolt against the state. On an excursion into Vermont, Tyler was involved mainly in an effort, somewhat successful, of dissuading Vermont from harboring the rebels and persuading the rebels to cease their rebellion.

Sent to New York on a similar mission later in 1787, Tyler took time out from his negotiating tasks to indulge an interest in the theater. Shortly after his arrival in March, he saw a production of Richard Brinsley Sheridan's *The School for Scandal* at the John Street Theater. Scarcely a month later, on April 16, 1787, he saw his own comedy *The Contrast* produced by the American Company. The play was a hit, performed five times in New York, and soon was produced in Baltimore, Philadelphia, Charleston, and Boston (where in 1792 it was advertised as "A Moral Lecture in Five Parts"). The Adamses were suspicious that the foppish villain of the play was modelled on their son-in-law.

Although Tyler tried his hand at writing other plays, some of them produced, he never again achieved the success of *The Contrast*. He married a young woman some eighteen years his junior in 1794 and settled into a law practice in Guilford, Vermont. He was appointed a judge on the Vermont supreme court in 1801 and chief justice in 1807, and he was a Professor of Jurisprudence at the University of Vermont (1811–14).

But he never gave up literature altogether. In 1794 he teamed up with another writer, Joseph Dennie, to write short commentaries on politics or manners, under the name of Colon and Spondee, published in various journals and papers. In 1797 he published an important novel *The Algerine Captive*, the first volume detailing the experience of growing up in Boston in the latter part of the eighteenth century, the second describing captivity into slavery in Algeria based on the actual experience of an uncle. Throughout his life, Tyler jotted down verses, but rarely polished them. The one exception was *The Chestnut Tree*, 756 lines long, consisting of a series of character sketches of simple village people, not published until 1931.

But Tyler's literary fame rests on *The Contrast*, whose title page on publication in 1790 did not carry his name but the cryptic information, by "a citizen of the United States." This emphasis seems appropriate, as the play does draw vitality from its relationship with the newly established, upstart nation. It introduced to the stage one Jonathan, a genuinely American innocent, whose naive honesty, natural shrewdness, and guileless simplicity amply balanced his lack of book-learning and European cultivation. *The Contrast* showed to audiences of Americans who they were—or ought to be. That the play has had successful revivals into the latter half of the twentieth century indicates that it can still bring to audiences refreshing awareness of what it meant in 1790—what it still means—to be an American.

ADDITIONAL READING

Four Plays by Royall Tyler, ed. Arthur W. Peach and George Floyd Newbrough, 1941 (Vol. 15 of *America's Lost Plays*, ed. Barrett H. Clark); *The Verse of Royall Tyler*, ed. Marius B. Péladeau, 1968; *The Prose of Royall Tyler*, ed. Marius B. Péladeau, 1972; *The Algerine Captive*, ed. Don L. Cook, 1970.

G. Thomas Tanselle, *Royall Tyler*, 1967; Ada Lou and Herbert L. Carson, *Royall Tyler*, 1979.

TEXT

The Contrast, A Comedy: in Five Acts: Written by a Citizen of the United States, 1790. Minor changes in spelling have been made in accord with modern English.

The Contrast[1]

CHARACTERS

Colonel Manly	Charlotte
Dimple	Maria
Van Rough	Letitia
Jessamy	Jenny
Jonathan	Servants

---

[1]*The Contrast* was produced in New York City in 1787 on April 16, April 18, May 2, May 5, and May 12. Publication in 1790 was by a "subscription printing"—individuals subscribed before actual appearance of the work. Heading the list of subscribers was George Washington, President of the United States.

SCENE, *NEW YORK*

Prologue

WRITTEN BY A YOUNG GENTLEMAN
OF NEW-YORK, AND SPOKEN BY MR. WIGNELL[2]

Exult each patriot heart!—this night is shown
A piece, which we may fairly call our own;
Where the proud titles of "My Lord! Your Grace!"
To humble *Mr.* and plain *Sir* give place.
Our Author pictures not from foreign climes   5
The fashions or the follies of the times;
But has confin'd the subject of his work
To the gay scenes—the circles of New-York.
On native themes his Muse displays her pow'rs;
If ours the faults, the virtues too are ours.   10
Why should our thoughts to distant countries roam,
When each refinement may be found at home?
Who travels now to ape the rich or great,
To deck an equipage and roll in state;
To court the graces, or to dance with ease,   15
Or by hypocrisy to strive to please?
Our free-born ancestors such arts despis'd;
Genuine sincerity alone they priz'd;
Their minds, with honest emulation fir'd;
To solid good—not ornament—aspir'd;   20
Or, if ambition rous'd a bolder flame,
Stern virtue throve, where indolence was shame.
    But modern youths, with imitative sense,
Deem taste in dress the proof of excellence;
And spurn the meanness of your homespun arts,   25
Since homespun habits would obscure their parts;
Whilst all, which aims at splendour and parade,
Must come from Europe, *and be ready made.*
Strange! we should thus our native worth disclaim,
And check the progress of our rising fame.   30
Yet *one,* whilst imitation bears the sway,
Aspires to nobler heights, and points the way,
Be rous'd, my friends! his bold example view;
Let your own Bards be proud to copy *you!*
Should rigid critics reprobate our play,   35
At least the patriotic heart will say,
"Glorious our fall, since in a noble cause.
"The bold *attempt alone* demands applause."
Still may the wisdom of the Comic Muse
Exalt your merits, or your faults accuse.   40
But think not, 'tis her aim to be severe;—
We all are mortals, and as mortals err.
If candour pleases, we are truly blest;
Vice trembles, when compell'd to stand confess'd.
Let not light Censure on your faults offend.   45

---

[2]Thomas Wignell (*c.* 1753–1803) was a comic actor of the
time and played Jonathan in the opening production. Most
critics believe that Tyler is the author of the "Prologue."

Which aims not to expose them, but amend.
Thus does our Author to your candour trust;
Conscious, the *free* are generous, as just.

ACT I

SCENE 1.

An Apartment at Charlotte's. CHARLOTTE *and* LETITIA *discovered.*

LETITIA. And so, Charlotte, you really think the pocket-hoop[1] unbecoming.

CHARLOTTE. No, I don't say so. It may be very becoming to saunter round the house of a rainy day; to visit my grand-mamma, or go to Quakers' meeting: but to swim in a minuet, with the eyes of fifty well-dressed beaux upon me, to trip it in the Mall,[2] or walk on the battery,[3] give me the luxurious, jaunty, flowing, bell-hoop. It would have delighted you to have seen me the last evening, my charming girl! I was dangling o'er the battery with Billy Dimple; a knot of young fellows were upon the platform; as I passed them I faultered with one of the most betwitching false steps you ever saw, and   10 then recovered myself with such a pretty confusion, flirting my hoop to discover a jet black shoe and brilliant buckle. Gad! how my little heart thrilled to hear the confused raptures of—"*Demme,*[4] *Jack, what a delicate foot!*" "*Ha! General, what a well-turn'd—*"

LETITIA. Fie! fie! Charlotte [*stopping her mouth*], I protest you are quite a libertine.

CHARLOTTE. Why, my dear little prude, are we not all such libertines? Do you think, when I sat tortured two hours under the hands of my friseur,[5] and an hour more at my toilet, that I had any thoughts of my aunt Susan, or my cousin Betsey? though they are both allowed to be critical judges of dress.   20

LETITIA. Why, who should we dress to please, but those who are judges of its merit?

CHARLOTTE. Why, a creature who does not know *Buffon* from *Souflée*[6]—Man!— my Letitia—Man! for whom we dress, walk, dance, talk, lisp, languish, and smile. Does not the grave Spectator[7] assure us that even our much bepraised diffidence, modesty, and blushes are all directed to make ourselves good wives and mothers as fast as we can? Why, I'll undertake with one flirt of this hoop to bring more beaux to my feet in one week than the grave Maria, and her sentimental circle, can do, by sighing sentiment till their hairs are grey.   30

LETITIA. Well, I won't argue with you; you always out-talk me; let us change the subject. I hear that Mr. Dimple and Maria are soon to be married.

CHARLOTTE. You hear true. I was consulted in the choice of the wedding clothes. She is to be married in a delicate white satin, and has a monstrous pretty brocaded lutestring[8] for the second day. It would have done you good to have seen with what an affected indifference the dear sentimentalist turned over a thousand pretty things, just as if her heart did not palpitate with her approaching happiness, and at last made her choice and arranged

---

[1]Hoopskirt with whalebone stiffening at the hips, smaller than the bell-hoop mentioned later.
[2]Fashionable place for strolling, such as Broadway or Bowling Green Park.
[3]A park at the southern tip of Manhattan, where the Dutch had built a fortification.
[4]Slang for "Damn me."
[5]Hairdresser.

[6]Buffon, variant of buffont, a piece of gauze or lace to cover a woman's breast; souflée, a baked dish made light by whipped egg white.
[7]English periodical published by Addison and Steele in the eighteenth century, with satiric pieces on manners, fashions, and morals.
[8]Variant of lustring, silk fabric.

her dress with such apathy as if she did not know that plain white satin and
a simple blond lace would shew her clear skin and dark hair to the greatest 40
advantage.

LETITIA. But they say her indifference to dress, and even to the gentleman himself, is not entirely affected.

CHARLOTTE. How?

LETITIA. It is whispered that if Maria gives her hand to Mr. Dimple, it will be
without her heart.

CHARLOTTE. Though the giving the heart is one of the last of all laughable considerations in the marriage of a girl of spirit, yet I should like to hear what
antiquated notions the dear little piece of old-fashioned prudery has got in
her head.   50

LETITIA. Why you know that old Mr. John-Richard-Robert-Jacob-Isaac-
Abraham-Cornelius Van Dumpling, Billy Dimple's father (for he has
thought fit to soften his name, as well as manners, during his English tour),
was the most intimate friend of Maria's father. The old folks, about a year
before Mr. Van Dumpling's death, proposed this match: the young folks
were accordingly introduced, and told they must love one another. Billy was
then a good-natured, decent-dressing young fellow, with a little dash of the
coxcomb, such as our young fellows of fortune usually have. At this time, I
really believe she thought she loved him; and had they then been married, I
doubt not they might have jogged on, to the end of the chapter, a good kind 60
of a sing-song lack-a-daysaical life, as other honest married folks do.

CHARLOTTE. Why did they not then marry?

LETITIA. Upon the death of his father, Billy went to England to see the world
and rub off a little of the patroon[9] rust. During his absence, Maria, like a
good girl, to keep herself constant to her *nown true-love,* avoided company,
and betook herself, for her amusement, to her books, and her dear Billy's
letters. But, alas! how many ways has the mischievous demon of inconstancy
of stealing into a woman's heart! Her love was destroyed by the very means
she took to support it.

CHARLOTTE. How?—Oh! I have it—some likely young beau found the way to 70
her study.

LETITIA. Be patient, Charlotte; your head so runs upon beaux. Why, she read
Sir Charles Grandison, Clarissa Harlow, Shenstone, and the Sentimental
Journey;[10] and between whiles, as I said, Billy's letters. But, as her taste improved, her love declined. The contrast was so striking betwixt the good
sense of her books and the flimsiness of her love-letters, that she discovered
she had unthinkingly engaged her hand without her heart; and then the
whole transaction, managed by the old folks, now appeared so unsentimental, and looked so like bargaining for a bale of goods, that she found she
ought to have rejected, according to every rule of romance, even the man of 80
her choice, if imposed upon her in that manner. Clary Harlow would have
scorned such a match.

CHARLOTTE. Well, how was it on Mr. Dimple's return? Did he meet a more favourable reception than his letters?

LETITIA. Much the same. She spoke of him with respect abroad, and with contempt in her closet.[11] She watched his conduct and conversation, and found
that he had by travelling acquired the wickedness of Lovelace[12] without his

---

[9]Dutch landholder in New York, here suggesting countri-
fied.
[10]*The History of Sir Charles Grandison* (1753–54) and *Clarissa,
or the History of a Young Lady* (1747–48), by English novelist
Samuel Richardson (1689–1761); William Shenstone

(1714–1763), British poet, author of *The Schoolmistress*
(1742); *A Sentimental Journey through France and Italy* (1768),
by British novelist Laurence Sterne (1713–1768).
[11]Private sitting room or study.
[12]Villain in Richardson's *Clarissa.*

wit, and the politeness of Sir Charles Grandison without his generosity. The ruddy youth, who washed his face at the cistern every morning, and swore and looked eternal love and constancy, was now metamorphosed into a flip- 90 pant, palid, polite beau, who devotes the morning to his toilet, reads a few pages of Chesterfield's letters,[13] and then minces out, to put the infamous principles in practice upon every woman he meets.

CHARLOTTE. But, if she is so apt at conjuring up these sentimental bugbears, why does she not discard him at once?

LETITIA. Why, she thinks her word too sacred to be trifled with. Besides, her father, who has a great respect for the memory of his deceased friend, is ever telling her how he shall renew his years in their union, and repeating the dying injunctions of old Van Dumpling.

CHARLOTTE. A mighty pretty story! And so you would make me believe that the 100 sensible Maria would give up Dumpling manor, and the all-accomplished Dimple as a husband, for the absurd, ridiculous reason, forsooth, because she despises and abhors him. Just as if a lady could not be privileged to spend a man's fortune, ride in his carriage, be called after his name, and call him her *nown dear lovee* when she wants money, without loving and respecting the great he-creature. Oh! my dear girl, you are a monstrous prude.

LETITIA. I don't say what I would do; I only intimate how I suppose she wishes to act.

CHARLOTTE. No, no, no! A fig for sentiment. If she breaks, or wishes to break, with Mr. Dimple, depend upon it, she has some other man in her eye. A 110 woman rarely discards one lover until she is sure of another.—Letitia little thinks what a clue I have to Dimple's conduct. The generous man submits to render himself disgusting to Maria, in order that she may leave him at liberty to address me. I must change the subject. [*Aside, and rings a bell.*]

[*Enter* SERVANT.]

Frank, order the horses to.—Talking of marriage, did you hear that Sally Bloomsbury is going to be married next week to Mr. Indigo, the rich Carolinian?

LETITIA. Sally Bloomsbury married!—why, she is not yet in her teens.

CHARLOTTE. I do not know how that is, but you may depend upon it, 'tis a done 120 affair. I have it from the best authority. There is my aunt Wyerly's Hannah. You know Hannah, though a black, she is a wench that was never caught in a lie in her life. Now, Hannah has a brother who courts Sarah, Mrs. Catgut the milliner's girl, and she told Hannah's brother, and Hannah, who, as I said before, is a girl of undoubted veracity, told it directly to me, that Mrs. Catgut was making a new cap for Miss Bloomsbury, which, as it was very dressy, it is very probable is designed for a wedding cap. Now, as she is to be married, who can it be to but to Mr. Indigo? Why, there is no other gentleman that visits at her papa's.

LETITIA. Say not a word more, Charlotte. Your intelligence is so direct and well 130 grounded, it is almost a pity that it is not a piece of scandal.

CHARLOTTE. Oh! I am the pink of prudence. Though I cannot charge myself with ever having discredited a tea-party by my silence, yet I take care never to report any thing of my acquaintance, especially if it is to their credit,— *discredit*, I mean,—until I have searched to the bottom of it. It is true, there is infinite pleasure in this charitable pursuit. Oh! how delicious to go and condole with the friends of some backsliding sister, or to retire with some old dowager or maiden aunt of the family, who love scandal so well that

---

[13]Philip Stanhope, Earl of Chesterfield (1694–1773), British diplomat, author of letters to his son (published 1774), which offer generally sensible advice, but also suggesting intrigue in affairs of dubious morality.

they cannot forbear gratifying their appetite at the expense of the reputation of their nearest relations! And then to return full fraught with a rich 140
collection of circumstances, to retail to the next circle of our acquaintance
under the strongest injunctions of secrecy,—ha, ha, ha!—interlarding the
melancholy tale with so many doleful shakes of the head, and more doleful
"Ah! who would have thought it! so amiable, so prudent a young lady, as we
all thought her, what a monstrous pity! well, I have nothing to charge myself with; I acted the part of a friend, I warned her of the principles of that
rake, I told her what would be the consequence; I told her so, I told her
so."—Ha, ha, ha!

LETITIA. Ha, ha, ha! Well, but, Charlotte, you don't tell me what you think of
Miss Bloomsbury's match.   150

CHARLOTTE. Think! why I think it is probable she cried for a plaything, and they
have given her a husband. Well, well, well, the puling chit[14] shall not be deprived of her plaything: 'tis only exchanging London dolls for American babies.—Apropos, of babies, have you heard what Mrs. Affable's high-flying
notions of delicacy have come to?

LETITIA. Who, she that was Miss Lovely?

CHARLOTTE. The same; she married Bob Affable of Schenectady. Don't you remember?

    [*Enter* SERVANT.]

SERVANT. Madam, the carriage is ready.   160

LETITIA. Shall we go to the stores first, or visiting?

CHARLOTTE. I should think it rather too early to visit, especially Mrs. Prim; you
know she is so particular.

LETITIA. Well, but what of Mrs. Affable?

CHARLOTTE. Oh, I'll tell you as we go; come, come, let us hasten. I hear Mrs.
Catgut has some of the prettiest caps arrived you ever saw. I shall die if I
have not the first sight of them.

    [*Exeunt.*]

SCENE 2.

A Room in Van Rough's House. MARIA *sitting disconsolate at a Table, with Books,
etc.*

SONG[1]

I.

The sun sets in night, and the stars shun the day;
But glory remains when their lights fade away!
Begin, ye tormentors! your threats are in vain,
For the son of Alknomook shall never complain.

II.

Remember the arrows he shot from his bow;
Remember your chiefs by his hatchet laid low:
Why so slow?—do you wait till I shrink from the pain?
No—the son of Alknomook will never complain.   10

---

[14] A child, here a childish woman.
[1] This song had been published in London in 1783 in Joseph Ritson's *Select Collection of English Song,* and in the
magazine *American Museum* in January 1787, under the title

"The Death Song of a Cherokee Indian." The poem was
once attributed to Philip Freneau, but there seems little
reason not to believe Tyler wrote it.

III.

Remember the wood where in ambush we lay,
And the scalps which we bore from your nation away:
Now the flame rises fast, you exult in my pain;
But the son of Alknomook can never complain.

IV.

I go to the land where my father is gone;
His ghost shall rejoice in the fame of his son:
Death comes like a friend, he relieves me from pain;
And my son, Oh Alknomook! has scorn'd to complain.   20

There is something in this song which ever calls forth my affections. The manly virtue of courage, that fortitude which steels the heart against the keenest misfortunes, which interweaves the laurel of glory amidst the instruments of torture and death, displays something so noble, so exalted, that in despite of the prejudices of education I cannot but admire it, even in a savage. The prepossession which our sex is supposed to entertain for the character of a soldier is, I know, a standing piece of raillery among the wits. A cockade, a lapell'd coat, and a feather,[2] they will tell you, are irresistible by a female heart. Let it be so. Who is it that considers the helpless situation of our sex, that does not see that we each moment stand in need of a protector,   30 and that a brave one too? Formed of the more delicate materials of nature, endowed only with the softer passions, incapable, from our ignorance of the world, to guard against the wiles of mankind, our security for happiness often depends upon their generosity and courage. Alas! how little of the former do we find! How inconsistent! that man should be leagued to destroy that honor upon which solely rests his respect and esteem. Ten thousand temptations allure us, ten thousand passions betray us; yet the smallest deviation from the path of rectitude is followed by the contempt and insult of man, and the more remorseless pity of woman; years of penitence and tears cannot wash away the stain, nor a life of virtue obliterate its remembrance.   40 Reputation is the life of woman; yet courage to protect it is masculine and disgusting; and the only safe asylum a woman of delicacy can find is in the arms of a man of honour. How naturally, then, should we love the brave and the generous; how gratefully should we bless the arm raised for our protection, when nerv'd by virtue and directed by honour! Heaven grant that the man with whom I may be connected—may be connected! Whither has my imagination transported me—whither does it now lead me? Am I not indissolubly engaged, "by every obligation of honour which my own consent and my father's approbation can give," to a man who can never share my affections, and whom a few days hence it will be criminal for me to   50 disapprove—to disapprove! would to heaven that were all—to despise. For, can the most frivolous manners, actuated by the most depraved heart, meet, or merit, anything but contempt from every woman of delicacy and sentiment?

    [VAN ROUGH, *without.* Mary!]
Ha! my father's voice—Sir!—
    [*Enter* VAN ROUGH.]

---

[2]Dress of a soldier: cockade, a knot of ribbon or something similar worn on the hat like a badge; feather, worn as a decoration.

VAN ROUGH. What, Mary, always singing doleful ditties, and moping over these plaguy[3] books.

MARIA. I hope, Sir, that it is not criminal to improve my mind with books, or to divert my melancholy with singing, at my leisure hours. 60

VAN ROUGH. Why, I don't know that, child; I don't know that. They us'd to say, when I was a young man, that if a woman knew how to make a pudding, and to keep herself out of fire and water, she knew enough for a wife. Now, what good have these books done you? have they not made you melancholy? as you call it. Pray, what right has a girl of your age to be in the dumps? haven't you everything your heart can wish; an't[4] you going to be married to a young man of great fortune; an't you going to have the quit-rent of twenty miles square?

MARIA. One-hundreth part of the land, and a lease for life of the heart of a man I could love, would satisfy me. 70

VAN ROUGH. Pho, pho, pho! child; nonsense, downright nonsense, child. This comes of your reading your story-books; your Charles Grandisons, your Sentimental Journals, and your Robinson Crusoes,[5] and such other trumpery. No, no, no! child; it is money makes the mare go; keep your eye upon the main chance,[6] Mary.

MARIA. Marriage, Sir, is, indeed, a very serious affair.

VAN ROUGH. You are right, child; you are right. I am sure I found it so, to my cost.

MARIA. I mean, Sir, that as marriage is a portion for life, and so intimately involves our happiness, we cannot be too considerate in the choice of our companion. 80

VAN ROUGH. Right, child; very right. A young woman should be very sober when she is making her choice, but when she has once made it, as you have done, I don't see why she should not be as merry as a grig;[7] I am sure she has reason enough to be so. Solomon says that "there is a time to laugh, and a time to weep."[8] Now, a time for a young woman to laugh is when she has made sure of a good rich husband. Now, a time to cry, according to you, Mary, is when she is making choice of him; but I should think that a young woman's time to cry was when she despaired of *getting* one. Why, there was your mother, now: to be sure, when I popp'd the question to her she did look a little silly; but when she had once looked down on her apron-strings, as all modest young women us'd to do, and drawled out ye-s, she was as brisk and as merry as a bee. 90

MARIA. My honoured mother, Sir, had no motive to melancholy; she married the man of her choice.

VAN ROUGH. The man of her choice! And pray, Mary, an't you going to marry the man of your choice—what trumpery notion is this? It is these vile books [*throwing them away*]. I'd have you to know, Mary, if you won't make young Van Dumpling the man of *your* choice, you shall marry him as the man of *my* choice. 100

MARIA. You terrify me, Sir. Indeed, Sir, I am all submission. My will is yours.

VAN ROUGH. Why, that is the way your mother us'd to talk, "My will is yours, my dear Mr. Van Rough, my will is yours"; but she took special care to have her own way, though, for all that.

MARIA. Do not reflect upon my mother's memory, Sir—

---

[3]Annoying.
[4]Early spelling of "ain't" (derived from contraction of "am not").
[5]Novel published in 1719 by Daniel Defoe (c. 1660–1731).

[6]Seize the big opportunity when it presents itself.
[7]A grasshopper or cricket.
[8]Ecclesiastes 3:4.

VAN ROUGH. Why not, Mary, why not? She kept me from speaking my mind all her *life*, and do you think she shall henpeck me now she is *dead* too? Come, come; don't go to sniveling; be a good girl, and mind the main chance. I'll see you well settled in the world. 110

MARIA. I do not doubt your love, Sir, and it is my duty to obey you. I will endeavour to make my duty and inclination go hand in hand.

VAN ROUGH. Well, well, Mary; do you be a good girl, mind the main chance, and never mind inclination. Why, do you know that I have been down in the cellar this very morning to examine a pipe[9] of Madeira which I purchased the week you were born, and mean to tap on your wedding day?—That pipe cost me fifty pounds sterling. It was well worth sixty pounds; but I overreach'd[10] Ben Bulkhead, the supercargo.[11] I'll tell you the whole story. You must know that—

[*Enter* SERVANT.] 120

SERVANT. Sir, Mr. Transfer, the broker, is below.

[*Exit.*]

VAN ROUGH. Well, Mary, I must go. Remember, and be a good girl, and mind the main chance.

[*Exit.*]

MARIA [*ALONE*]. How deplorable is my situation! How distressing for a daughter to find her heart militating with her filial duty! I know my father loves me tenderly; why then do I reluctantly obey him? Heaven knows! with what reluctance I should oppose the will of a parent, or set an example of filial disobedience; at a parent's command, I could wed awkwardness and deformity. 130 Were the heart of my husband good, I would so magnify his good qualities with the eye of conjugal affection, that the defects of his person and manners should be lost in the emanation of his virtues. At a father's command, I could embrace poverty. Were the poor man my husband, I would learn resignation to my lot; I would enliven our frugal meal with good humour, and chase away misfortune from our cottage with a smile. At a father's command, I could almost submit to what every female heart knows to be the most mortifying, to marry a weak man, and blush at my husband's folly in every company I visited. But to marry a depraved wretch, whose only virtue is a polished exterior; who is actuated by the unmanly ambition of conquer- 140 ing the defenseless; whose heart, insensible to the emotions of patriotism, dilates at the plaudits of every unthinking girl; whose laurels are the sighs and tears of the miserable victims of his specious behaviour,—can he, who has no regard for the peace and happiness of other families, ever have a due regard for the peace and happiness of his own? Would to heaven that my father were not so hasty in his temper! Surely, if I were to state my reasons for declining this match, he would not compel me to marry a man whom, though my lips may solemnly promise to honour, I find my heart must ever despise.

[*Exit.*] 150

---

[9]A large cask, usually 105 gallons.
[10]Got the better of.
[11]Officer on merchant vessel in charge of the cargo.

ACT II

Scene 1.

Enter Charlotte and Letitia.

Charlotte [*at entering*]. Betty, take those things out of the carriage and carry them to my chamber; see that you don't tumble them. My dear, I protest, I think it was the homeliest of the whole. I declare I was almost tempted to return and change it.

Letitia. Why would you take it?

Charlotte. Didn't Mrs. Catgut say it was the most fashionable?

Letitia. But, my dear, it will never fit becomingly on you.

Charlotte. I know that; but did not you hear Mrs. Catgut say it was fashionable? 10

Letitia. Did you see that sweet airy cap with the white sprig?

Charlotte. Yes, and I longed to take it; but, my dear, what could I do? Did not Mrs. Catgut say it was the most fashionable; and if I had not taken it, was not that awkward gawky, Sally Slender, ready to purchase it immediately?

Letitia. Did you observe how she tumbled over the things at the next shop, and then went off without purchasing any thing, nor even thanking the poor man for his trouble? But, of all the awkward creatures, did you see Miss Blouze endeavouring to thrust her unmerciful arm into those small kid gloves?

Charlotte. Ha, ha, ha, ha! 20

Letitia. Then did you take notice with what an affected warmth of friendship she and Miss Wasp met? when all their acquaintance know how much pleasure they take in abusing each other in every company.

Charlotte. Lud![1] Letitia, is that so extraordinary? Why, my dear, I hope you are not going to turn sentimentalist. Scandal, you know, is but amusing ourselves with the faults, foibles, follies, and reputations of our friends; indeed, I don't know why we should have friends, if we are not at liberty to make use of them. But no person is so ignorant of the world as to suppose, because I amuse myself with a lady's faults, that I am obliged to quarrel with her person every time we meet; believe me, my dear, we should have very 30 few acquaintance at that rate.

[servant *enters and delivers a letter to* Charlotte, *and—exit.*]

Charlotte. You'll excuse me, my dear. [*Opens and reads to herself.*]

Letitia. Oh, quite excusable.

Charlotte. As I hope to be married, my brother Henry is in the city.

Letitia. What, your brother, Colonel Manly?

Charlotte. Yes, my dear; the only brother I have in the world.

Letitia. Was he never in this city?

Charlotte. Never nearer than Harlem Heights,[2] where he lay with his regiment. 40

Letitia. What sort of a being is this brother of yours? If he is as chatty, as pretty, as sprightly as you, half the belles in the city will be pulling caps[3] for him.

Charlotte. My brother is the very counterpart and reverse of me: I am gay, he

---

[1]Lord.
[2]On northern end of Manhattan, scene of a Revolutionary War battle in 1776.
[3]Setting their caps.

is grave; I am airy, he is solid; I am ever selecting the most pleasing objects for my laughter, he has a tear for every pitiful one. And thus, whilst he is plucking the briars and thorns from the path of the unfortunate, I am strewing my own path with roses.

LETITIA. My sweet friend, not quite so poetical, and a little more particular.

CHARLOTTE. Hands off, Letitia. I feel the rage of simile upon me; I can't talk to you in any other way. My brother has a heart replete with the noblest sentiments, but then, it is like—it is like—Oh! you provoking girl, you have deranged all my ideas—it is like—Oh! I have it—his heart is like an old maiden lady's bandbox;[4] it contains many costly things, arranged with the most scrupulous nicety, yet the misfortune is that they are too delicate, costly, and antiquated for common use.

LETITIA. By what I can pick out of your flowery description, your brother is no beau.

CHARLOTTE. No, indeed; he makes no pretension to the character. He'd ride, or rather fly, an hundred miles to relieve a distressed object, or to do a gallant act in the service of his country; but should you drop your fan or bouquet in his presence, it is ten to one that some beau at the farther end of the room would have the honour of presenting it to you before he had observed that it fell. I'll tell you one of his antiquated anti-gallant notions. He said once in my presence, in a room full of company,—would you believe it?—in a large circle of ladies, that the best evidence a gentleman could give a young lady of his respect and affection was to endeavour in a friendly manner to rectify her foibles. I protest I was crimson to the eyes, upon reflecting that I was known as his sister.

LETITIA. Insupportable creature! tell a lady of her faults! if he is so grave, I fear I have no chance of captivating him.

CHARLOTTE. His conversation is like a rich, old-fashioned brocade,—it will stand alone; every sentence is a sentiment. Now you may judge what a time I had with him, in my twelve months' visit to my father. He read me such lectures, out of pure brotherly affection, against the extremes of fashion, dress, flirting, and coquetry, and all the other dear things which he knows I doat upon, that I protest his conversation made me as melancholy as if I had been at church; and heaven knows, though I never prayed to go there but on one occasion, yet I would have exchanged his conversation for a psalm and a sermon. Church is rather melancholy, to be sure; but then I can ogle the beaux, and be regaled with "here endeth the first lesson," but his brotherly *here*, you would think had no end. You captivate him! Why, my dear, he would as soon fall in love with a box of Italian flowers.[5] There is Maria, now, if she were not engaged, she might do something. Oh! how I should like to see that pair of penserosos[6] together, looking as grave as two sailors' wives of a stormy night, with a flow of sentiment meandering through their conversation like purling streams in modern poetry.

LETITIA. Oh! my dear fanciful—

CHARLOTTE. Hush! I hear some person coming through the entry.

[*Enter* SERVANT.]

SERVANT. Madam, there's a gentleman below who calls himself Colonel Manly; do you chuse to be at home?

CHARLOTTE. Show him in. [*Exit* SERVANT.] Now for a sober face.

[*Enter* COLONEL MANLY.]

MANLY. My dear Charlotte, I am happy that I once more enfold you within the

---

[4]Small box for holding various items of dress.
[5]Wax flowers.

[6]Serious, thoughtful persons, from "Il Penseroso" (1632) by John Milton (1608–1674).

arms of fraternal affection. I know you are going to ask (amiable impatience!) how our parents do,—the venerable pair transmit you their blessings by me. They totter on the verge of a well-spent life, and wish only to see their children settled in the world, to depart in peace.

CHARLOTTE. I am very happy to hear that they are well.   100
    [*Coolly.*] Brother, will you give me leave to introduce you to our uncle's ward, one of my most intimate friends?

MANLY. [*saluting* LETITIA]. I ought to regard your friends as my own.

CHARLOTTE. Come, Letitia, do give us a little dash of your vivacity; my brother is so sentimental and so grave, that I protest he'll give us the vapours.[7]

MANLY. Though sentiment and gravity, I know, are banished the polite world, yet I hoped they might find some countenance in the meeting of such near connections as brother and sister.

CHARLOTTE. Positively, brother, if you go one step further in this strain, you will   110
set me crying, and that, you know, would spoil my eyes; and then I should never get the husband which our good papa and mamma have so kindly wished me—never be established in the world.

MANLY. Forgive me, my sister,—I am no enemy to mirth; I love your sprightliness; and I hope it will one day enliven the hours of some worthy man; but when I mention the respectable authors of my existence,—the cherishers and protectors of my helpless infancy, whose hearts glow with such fondness and attachment that they would willingly lay down their lives for my welfare,—you will excuse me if I am so unfashionable as to speak of them with some degree of respect and reverence.   120

CHARLOTTE. Well, well, brother; if you won't be gay, we'll not differ; I will be as grave as you wish. [*Affects gravity.*] And so, brother, you have come to the city to exchange some of your commutation notes[8] for a little pleasure?

MANLY. Indeed you are mistaken; my errand is not of amusement, but business; and as I neither drink nor game, my expenses will be so trivial, I shall have no occasion to sell my notes.

CHARLOTTE. Then you won't have occasion to do a very good thing. Why, here was the Vermont General—he came down some time since, sold all his musty notes at one stroke, and then laid the cash out in trinkets for his dear Fanny.[9] I want a dozen pretty things myself; have you got the notes with   130
you?

MANLY. I shall be ever willing to contribute, as far as it is in my power, to adorn or in any way to please my sister; yet I hope I shall never be obliged for this to sell my notes. I may be romantic, but I preserve them as a sacred deposit. Their full amount is justly due to me, but as embarrassments, the natural consequences of a long war, disable my country from supporting its credit, I shall wait with patience until it is rich enough to discharge them. If that is not in my day, they shall be transmitted as an honourable certificate to posterity, that I have humbly imitated our illustrious WASHINGTON, in having exposed my health and life in the service of my country, without reaping any   140
other reward than the glory of conquering in so arduous a contest.

CHARLOTTE. Well said heroics. Why, my dear Henry, you have such a lofty way of saying things, that I protest I almost tremble at the thought of introducing you to the polite circles in the city. The belles would think you were a player[10] run mad, with your head filled with old scraps of tragedy; and as to

---

[7]Depressed spirits.
[8]Notes in lieu of money issued to those who fought in the Revolutionary Army, equivalent to several years' pay, discounted when cashed in before they were due.

[9]Probably Ethan Allen (1737–1789), Revolutionary War hero.
[10]Actor.

the beaux, they might admire, because they would not understand you. But, however, I must, I believe, introduce you to two or three ladies of my acquaintance.

LETITIA. And that will make him acquainted with thirty or forty beaux.

CHARLOTTE. Oh! brother, you don't know what a fund of happiness you have in store. 150

MANLY. I fear, sister, I have not refinement sufficient to enjoy it.

CHARLOTTE. Oh! you cannot fail being pleased.

LETITIA. Our ladies are so delicate and dressy.

CHARLOTTE. And our beaux are dressy and delicate.

LETITIA. Our ladies chat and flirt so agreeably.

CHARLOTTE. And our beaux simper and bow so gracefully.

LETITIA. With their hair so trim and neat.

CHARLOTTE. And their faces so soft and sleek.

LETITIA. Their buckles so tonish[11] and bright.   160

CHARLOTTE. And their hands so slender and white.

LETITIA. I vow, Charlotte, we are quite poetical.

CHARLOTTE. And then, brother, the faces of the beaux are of such a lily-white hue! None of that horrid robustness of constitution, that vulgar corn-fed glow of health, which can only serve to alarm an unmarried lady with apprehension, and prove a melancholy memento to a married one, that she can never hope for the happiness of being a widow. I will say this to the credit of our city beaux, that such is the delicacy of their complexion, dress, and address, that, even had I no reliance upon the honour of the dear Adonises,[12] I would trust myself in any possible situation with them, without the least 170 apprehensions of rudeness.

MANLY. Sister Charlotte!

CHARLOTTE. Now, now, now, brother [*interrupting him*], now don't go to spoil my mirth with a dash of your gravity; I am so glad to see you, I am in tiptop spirits. Oh! that you could be with us at a little snug party. There is Billy Simper, Jack Chaffé, and Colonel Van Titter, Miss Promonade, and the two Miss Tambours, sometimes make a party, with some other ladies, in a sidebox[13] at the play. Everything is conducted with such decorum. First we bow round to the company in general, then to each one in particular, then we have so many inquiries after each other's health, and we are so happy to 180 meet each other, and it is so many ages since we last had that pleasure, and if a married lady is in company, we have such a sweet dissertation upon her son Bobby's chin-cough;[14] then the curtain rises, then our sensibility is all awake, and then, by the mere force of apprehension, we torture some harmless expression into a double meaning, which the poor author never dreamt of, and then we have recourse to our fans, and then we blush, and then the gentlemen jog one another, peep under the fan, and make the prettiest remarks; and then we giggle and they simper, and they giggle and we simper, and then the curtain drops, and then for nuts and oranges, and then we bow, and it's pray, Ma'am, take it, and pray, Sir, keep it, and oh! not for the 190 world, Sir; and then the curtain rises again, and then we blush and giggle and simper and bow all over again. Oh! the sentimental charms of a sidebox conversation. [*All laugh.*]

MANLY. Well, sister, I join heartily with you in the laugh; for, in my opinion, it is as justifiable to laugh at folly as it is reprehensible to ridicule misfortune.

---

[11]Stylish.

[12]Adonis, a handsome young man loved by Aphrodite, goddess of love (Greek mythology).

[13]A box or enclosed area for seats at the side of the theater, a fashionable place to be seen.

[14]Whooping-cough.

CHARLOTTE. Well, but brother, positively I can't introduce you in these clothes: why, your coat looks as if it were calculated for the vulgar purpose of keeping yourself comfortable.

MANLY. This coat was my regimental coat in the late war. The public tumults of our state[15] have induced me to buckle on the sword in support of that gov- 200 ernment which I once fought to establish. I can only say, sister, that there was a time when this coat was respectable, and some people even thought that those men who had endured so many winter campaigns in the service of their country, without bread, clothing, or pay, at least deserved that the poverty of their appearance should not be ridiculed.

CHARLOTTE. We agree in opinion entirely, brother, though it would not have done for me to have said it: it is the coat makes the man respectable. In the time of the war, when we were almost frightened to death, why, your coat was respectable, that is, fashionable; now another kind of coat is fashionable, that is, respectable. And pray direct the tailor to make yours the height of 210 the fashion.

MANLY. Though it is of little consequence to me of what shape my coat is, yet, as to the height of the fashion, there you will please to excuse me, sister. You know my sentiments on that subject. I have often lamented the advantage which the French have over us in that particular. In Paris, the fashions have their dawnings, their routine, and declensions, and depend as much upon the caprice of the day as in other countries; but there every lady assumes a right to deviate from the general *ton*[16] as far as will be of advantage to her own appearance. In America, the cry is, what is the fashion? and we follow it indiscriminately, because it is so.   220

CHARLOTTE. Therefore it is, that when large hoops are in fashion, we often see many a plump girl lost in the immensity of a hoop-petticoat, whose want of height and *en-bon-point*[17] would never have been remarked in any other dress. When the high head-dress is the mode, how then do we see a lofty cushion, with a profusion of gauze, feathers, and ribband, supported by a face no bigger than an apple! whilst a broad full-faced lady, who really would have appeared tolerably handsome in a large head-dress, looks with her smart chapeau[18] as masculine as a soldier.

MANLY. But remember, my dear sister, and I wish all my fair country-women would recollect, that the only excuse a young lady can have for going extrav- 230 agantly into a fashion is because it makes her look extravagantly handsome.—Ladies, I must wish you a good morning.

CHARLOTTE. But, brother, you are going to make home with us.

MANLY. Indeed I cannot. I have seen my uncle and explained that matter.

CHARLOTTE. Come and dine with us, then. We have a family dinner about half-past four o'clock.

MANLY. I am engaged to dine with the Spanish ambassador. I was introduced to him by an old brother officer; and instead of freezing me with a cold card of compliment to dine with him ten days hence, he, with the true old Castilian[19] frankness in a friendly manner, asked me to dine with him to-day—an 240 honour I could not refuse. Sister, adieu—Madam, your most obedient—
    [*Exit.*]

---

[15]Refers to Shays's Rebellion (1786–87), which grew out of the belief of western Massachusetts's farmers, in the midst of a depression, that they were being taxed to the benefit of the Boston rich. Daniel Shays (1747–1825) led them in a revolt that required a large force to quell. Tyler took part in defusing the rebellion.

[16]Style.
[17]Chubbiness.
[18]Hat.
[19]From Castile, in central Spain, famed for its purity in language and manners.

CHARLOTTE. I will wait upon you to the door, brother; I have something particular to say to you.

[*Exit.*]

LETITIA [*alone*]. What a pair!—She the pink of flirtation, he the essence of everything that is *outré*[20] and gloomy.—I think I have completely deceived
Charlotte by my manner of speaking of Mr. Dimple; she's too much the
friend of Maria to be confided in. He is certainly rendering himself disagreeable to Maria, in order to break with her and proffer his hand to me. 250
This is what the delicate fellow hinted in our last conversation.

[*Exit.*]

SCENE 2.

The Mall.
[*Enter* JESSAMY.]

JESSAMY. Positively this Mall is a very pretty place. I hope the cits[1] won't ruin it
by repairs. To be sure, it won't do to speak of in the same day with Ranelagh
or Vauxhall;[2] however, it's a fine place for a young fellow to display his person to advantage. Indeed, nothing is lost here; the girls have taste, and I am
very happy to find they have adopted the elegant London fashion of looking
back, after a genteel fellow like me has passed them.— Ah! who comes here?
This, by his awkwardness, must be the Yankee colonel's servant. I'll accost
him. 10

[*Enter* JONATHAN.]

JESSAMY. Votre très—humble serviteur, Monsieur.[3] I understand Colonel
Manly, the Yankee officer, has the honour of your services.

JONATHAN. Sir!—

JESSAMY. I say, Sir, I understand that Colonel Manly has the honour of having
you for a servant.

JONATHAN. Servant! Sir, do you take me for a neger,—I am Colonel Manly's
waiter.[4]

JESSAMY. A true Yankee distinction, egad, without a difference. Why, Sir, do
you not perform all the offices of a servant? do you not even blacken his 20
boots?

JONATHAN. Yes; I do grease them a bit sometimes; but I am a true blue son of
liberty, for all that. Father said I should come as Colonel Manly's waiter, to
see the world, and all that; but no man shall master me. My father has a
good a farm as the colonel.

JESSAMY. Well, Sir, we will not quarrel about terms upon the eve of an acquaintance from which I promise myself so much satisfaction;—therefore, sans
ceremonie—[5]

JONATHAN. What?—

JESSAMY. I say I am extremely happy to see Colonel Manly's waiter. 30

JONATHAN. Well, and I vow, too, I am pretty considerably glad to see you; but
what the dogs need of all this outlandish lingo? Who may you be, Sir, if I
may be so bold?

---

[20]Unstylish.
[1]Citizens.
[2]Ranelagh Gardens and Vauxhall, popular eighteenth-
century pleasure resorts up the Thames River near London.

[3]"Your most humble servant, Sir" (French).
[4]Valet or orderly.
[5]"Without formality" (French).

JESSAMY. I have the honour to be Mr. Dimple's servant, or, if you please, waiter. We lodge under the same roof, and should be glad of the honour of your acquaintance.

JONATHAN. You a waiter! By the living jingo, you look so topping, I took you for one of the agents to Congress.[6]

JESSAMY. The brute has discernment, nothwithstanding his appearance.—Give me leave to say I wonder then at your familiarity.   40

JONATHAN. Why, as to the matter of that, Mr.—; pray, what's your name?

JESSAMY. Jessamy, at your service.

JONATHAN. Why, I swear we don't make any great matter of distinction in our state between quality and other folks.

JESSAMY. This is, indeed, a levelling principle.—I hope, Mr. Jonathan, you have not taken part with the insurgents.

JONATHAN. Why, since General Shays has sneaked off and given us the bag to hold, I don't care to give my opinion; but you'll promise not to tell—put your ear this way—you won't tell?—I vow I did think the sturgeons[7] were right.   50

JESSAMY. I thought, Mr. Jonathan, you Massachusetts men always argued with a gun in your hand. Why didn't you join them?

JONATHAN. Why, the colonel is one of those folks called the Shin—Shin[8]—dang it all, I can't speak them lignum vitae[9] words—you know who I mean— there is a company of them—they wear a china goose[10] at their button-hole—a kind of gilt thing.—Now the colonel told father and brother,—you must know there are, let me see—there is Elnathan, Silas, and Barnabas, Tabitha—no, no, she's a she—tarnation, now I have it—there's Elnathan, Silas, Barnabas, Jonathan, that's I—seven of us, six went into the wars, and I staid at home to take care of mother. Colonel said that it was a burning 60 shame for the true blue Bunker Hill sons of liberty, who had fought Gover-nor Hutchinson, Lord North[11] and the Devil, to have any hand in kicking up a cursed dust against a government which we had, every mother's son of us, a hand in making.

JESSAMY. Bravo!—Well, have you been abroad in the city since your arrival? What have you seen that is curious and entertaining?

JONATHAN. Oh! I have seen a power of fine sights. I went to see two marble-stone men and a leaden horse[12] that stands out in doors in all weathers; and when I came where they was, one had got no head, and t'other wern't there. They said as how the leaden man was a damn'd tory,[13] and that he took wit 70 in his anger and rode off in the time of the troubles.

JESSAMY. But this was not the end of your excursion?

JONATHAN. Oh, no; I went to a place they call Holy Ground. Now I counted this was a place where folks go to meeting; so I put my hymn-book in my pocket, and walked softly and grave as a minister; and when I came there, the dogs a bit of a meeting-house could I see. At last I spied a young gentlewoman standing by one of the seats which they have here at the doors. I took her to be the deacon's daughter, and she looked so kind, and so obliging, that I thought I would go and ask her the way to lecture, and—would you think

---

[6]Meeting in New York in 1785–88; in 1787, framing the new Constitution.

[7]Insurgents. Jonathan is siding with the rebels of Shays's Rebellion.

[8]Society of Cincinnati, formed by officers of Washington's army at the end of the Revolutionary War on May 13, 1783. Its hereditary membership made it suspect as un-democratic.

[9]"Wood of life" (Latin); i.e., very hard wood.

[10]The badge of the society of Cincinnati was a bald eagle.

[11]Thomas Hutchinson (1711–1780), royal governor (ap-pointed by the king) of Massachusetts (1771–74); Baron Frederick North (1732–1792), prime minister in England (1770–82).

[12]Statues.

[13]One who supported the British side in the Revolutionary War.

it?—she called me dear, and sweeting, and honey, just as if we were mar- 80
ried: by the living jingo, I had a month's mind to buss[14] her.

JESSAMY. Well, but how did it end?

JONATHAN. Why, as I was standing talking with her, a parcel of sailor men and
boys got round me, the snarl-headed curs fell a-kicking and cursing of me at
such a tarnal rate, that I vow I was glad to take my heels and split home,
right off, tail on end, like a stream of chalk.

JESSAMY. Why, my dear friend, you are not acquainted with the city; that girl
you saw was a—

　　[*Whispers.*]

JONATHAN. Mercy on my soul! was that young woman a harlot!—Well! if this is 90
New-York Holy Ground, what must the Holy-day Ground be!

JESSAMY. Well, you should not judge of the city too rashly. We have a number of
elegant, fine girls here that make a man's leisure hours pass very agreeably.
I would esteem it an honour to announce you to some of them.—Gad! that
announce is a select word; I wonder where I picked it up.

JONATHAN. I don't want to know them.

JESSAMY. Come, come, my dear friend, I see that I must assume the honour of
being the director of your amusements. Nature has given us passions, and
youth and opportunity stimulate to gratify them. It is no shame, my dear
Blueskin,[15] for a man to amuse himself with a little gallantry. 100

JONATHAN. Girl huntry! I don't altogether understand. I never played at that
game. I know how to play hunt the squirrel,[16] but I can't play anything with
the girls; I am as good as married.

JESSAMY. Vulgar, horrid brute! Married, and above a hundred miles from his
wife, and thinks that an objection to his making love to every woman he
meets! He never can have read, no, he never can have been in a room with a
volume of the divine Chesterfield.—So you are married?

JONATHAN. No, I don't say so; I said I was as good as married, a kind of promise.

JESSAMY. As good as married!— 110

JONATHAN. Why yes; there's Tabitha Wymen, the deacon's daughter, at home;
she and I have been courting a great while, and folks say as how we are to
be married; and so I broke a piece of money[17] with her when we parted,
and she promised not to spark it with Solomon Dyer while I am gone. You
wouldn't have me false to my true-love, would you?

JESSAMY. May be you have another reason for constancy; possibly the young
lady has a fortune? Ha! Mr. Jonathan, the solid charms: the chains of love
are never so binding as when the links are made of gold.

JONATHAN. Why, as to fortune, I must needs say her father is pretty dumb rich;
he went representative for our town last year. He will give her—let me 120
see—four times seven is—seven times four—nought and carry one,—he
will give her twenty acres of land—somewhat rocky though—a Bible, and a
cow.

JESSAMY. Twenty acres of rock, a Bible, and a cow! Why, my dear Mr. Jonathan,
we have servant-maids, or, as you would more elegantly express it, wait-
resses, in this city, who collect more in one year from their mistresses' cast[18]
clothes.

JONATHAN. You don't say so!—

---

[14]Kiss.
[15]A strong supporter of the American Revolution.
[16]Reference to *The Spectator*, No. 67: "Hunt the Squirrel, in
which while the Woman flies the man pursues her, but as

soon as she turns, he runs away, and she is obliged to follow."
[17]Sealing a pledge by breaking and dividing a coin.
[18]Discarded.

JESSAMY. Yes, and I'll introduce you to one of them. There is a little lump of flesh and delicacy that lives at next door, waitress to Miss Maria; we often 130 see her on the stoop.

JONATHAN. But are you sure she would be courted by me?

JESSAMY. Never doubt it; remember a faint heart never—blisters on my tongue—I was going to be guilty of a vile proverb; flat against the authority of Chesterfield. I say there can be no doubt that the brilliancy of your merit will secure you a favourable reception.

JONATHAN. Well, but what must I say to her?

JESSAMY. Say to her! why, my dear friend, though I admire your profound knowledge on every other subject, yet, you will pardon my saying that your want of opportunity has made the female heart escape the poignancy of 140 your penetration. Say to her! Why, when a man goes a-courting, and hopes for success, he must begin with doing, and not saying.

JONATHAN. Well, what must I do?

JESSAMY. Why, when you are introduced you must make five or six elegant bows.

JONATHAN. Six elegant bows! I understand that; six, you say? Well—

JESSAMY. Then you must press and kiss her hand; then press and kiss, and so on to her lips and cheeks; then talk as much as you can about hearts, darts, flames, nectar, and ambrosia—the more incoherent the better.

JONATHAN. Well, but suppose she should be angry with I?   150

JESSAMY. Why, if she should pretend—please to observe, Mr. Jonathan—if she should pretend to be offended, you must—But I'll tell you how my master acted in such a case: He was seated by a young lady of eighteen upon a sofa, plucking with a wanton hand the blooming sweets of youth and beauty. When the lady thought it necessary to check his ardour, she called up a frown upon her lovely face, so irresistably alluring, that it would have warmed the frozen bosom of age; remember, said she, putting her delicate arm upon his, remember your character and my honour. My master instantly dropped upon his knees, with eyes swimming with love, cheeks glowing with desire, and in the gentlest modulation of voice he said: My dear 160 Caroline, in a few months our hands will be indissolubly united at the altar; our hearts I feel are already so; the favours you now grant as evidence of your affection are favours indeed; yet, when the ceremony is once past, what will now be received with rapture will then be attributed to duty.

JONATHAN. Well, and what was the consequence?

JESSAMY. The consequence—Ah! forgive me, my dear friend, but you New England gentlemen have such a laudable curiosity of seeing the bottom of every thing;—why, to be honest, I confess I saw the blooming cherub of a consequence smiling in its angelic mother's arms, about ten months afterwards.

JONATHAN. Well, if I follow all your plans, make them six bows, and all that, 170 shall I have such little cherubim consequences?

JESSAMY. Undoubtedly.—What are you musing upon?

JONATHAN. You say you'll certainly make me acquainted?—Why, I was thinking then how I should contrive to pass this broken piece of silver—won't it buy a sugar-dram?[19]

JESSAMY. What is that, the love-token from the deacon's daughter?—You come on bravely. But I must hasten to my master. Adieu, my dear friend.

JONATHAN. Stay, Mr. Jessamy—must I buss her when I am introduced to her?

JESSAMY. I told you, you must kiss her.

---

[19]Drink of punch.

JONATHAN. Well, but must I buss her? 180

JESSAMY. Why kiss and buss, and buss and kiss, is all one.

JONATHAN. Oh! my dear friend, though you have a profound knowledge of all, a pugnency[20] of tribulation, you don't know everything.

[*Exit.*]

JESSAMY [*alone*]. Well, certainly I improve; my master could not have insinuated himself with more address into the heart of a man he despised. Now will this blundering dog sicken Jenny with his nauseous pawings, until she flies into my arms for very ease. How sweet will the contrast be between the blundering Jonathan and the courtly and accomplished Jessamy!

ACT III

SCENE 1.

Dimple's Room. DIMPLE *discovered at a Toilet,[1] Reading.*

DIMPLE. "Women have in general but one object, which is their beauty."[2] Very true, my lord; positively very true. "Nature has hardly formed a woman ugly enough to be insensible to flattery upon her person." Extremely just, my lord; every day's delightful experience confirms this. "If her face is so shocking that she must, in some degree, be conscious of it, her figure and air, she thinks, make ample amends for it." The sallow Miss Wan is a proof of this. Upon my telling the distasteful wretch, the other day, that her countenance spoke the pensive language of sentiment, and that Lady Wortley Montague[3] declared that if the ladies were arrayed in the garb of innocence, 10 the face would be the last part which would be admired, as Monsieur Milton expresses it, she grinn'd horribly a ghastly smile.[4] "If her figure is deformed, she thinks her face counterbalances it."

[*Enter* JESSAMY *with letters.*]

DIMPLE. Where got you these, Jessamy?

JESSAMY. Sir, the English packet[5] is arrived.

DIMPLE [*opens and reads a letter enclosing notes*]. "Sir,

"I have drawn bills on you in favour of Messrs. Van Cash and Co. as per margin. I have taken up your note to Col. Piquet, and discharged your debts to my Lord Lurcher and Sir Harry Rook. I herewith enclose you copies of the 20 bills, which I have no doubt will be immediately honoured. On failure, I shall empower some lawyer in your country to recover the amounts.

"I am, Sir,

"Your most humble servant,

"JOHN HAZARD."

Now, did not my lord expressly say that it was unbecoming a well-bred man to be in a passion, I confess I should be ruffled. [*Reads.*] "There is no accident so unfortunate, which a wise man may not turn to his advantage; nor any accident so fortunate, which a fool will not turn to his disadvantage." True, my lord; but how advantage can be derived from this I can't see. Chester- 30 field himself, who made, however, the worst practice of the most excellent precepts, was never in so embarrassing a situation. I love the person of

---

[20]Possibly *poignancy* (a word Jessamy has used), or *pugnancy* (pugnacious tendency).

[1]In a dressing room.

[2]See Chesterfield's letter to his son, October 16, 1747.

[3]Lady Mary Wortley Montague (1689–1762), British author of letters from Turkey and Italy (1763).

[4]John Milton (1608–1674), author of *Paradise Lost* (1667): Book II, ll. 845–46: "And death/ Grinn'd horrible a ghastly smile."

[5]Ship that carries mail and passengers.

Charlotte, and it is necessary I should command the fortune of Letitia. As to Maria!—I doubt not by my *sang-froid*[6] behaviour I shall compel her to decline the match; but the blame must not fall upon me. A prudent man, as my lord says, should take all the credit of a good action to himself, and throw the discredit of a bad one upon others. I must break with Maria, marry Letitia, and as for Charlotte—why, Charlotte must be a companion to my wife.—Here, Jessamy.

[*Enter* Jessamy. Dimple *folds and seals two letters.*]   40

Dimple. Here, Jessamy, take this letter to my love.

[*Gives one.*]

Jessamy. To which of your honour's loves?—Oh! [*reading*] to Miss Letitia, your honour's rich love.

Dimple. And this [*delivers another*] to Miss Charlotte Manly. See that you deliver them privately.

Jessamy. Yes, your honour.

[*Going.*]

Dimple. Jessamy, who are these strange lodgers that came to the house last night?   50

Jessamy. Why, the master is a Yankee colonel; I have not seen much of him; but the man is the most unpolished animal your honour ever disgraced your eyes by looking upon. I have had one of the most *outré* conversations with him!—He really has a most prodigious effect upon my risibility.

Dimple. I ought, according to every rule of Chesterfield, to wait on him and insinuate myself into his good graces.—Jessamy, wait on the colonel with my compliments, and if he is disengaged I will do myself the honour of paying him my respects.—Some ignorant unpolished boor—

[Jessamy *goes off and returns.*]

Jessamy. Sir, the colonel is gone out, and Jonathan his servant says that he is   60 gone to stretch his legs upon the Mall.—Stretch his legs! what an indelicacy of diction!

Dimple. Very well. Reach me my hat and sword. I'll accost him there, in my way to Letitia's, as by accident; pretend to be struck by his person and address, and endeavour to steal into his confidence. Jessamy, I have no business for you at present.

[*Exit.*]

Jessamy [*taking up the book*]. My master and I obtain our knowledge from the same source;—though, gad! I think myself much the prettier fellow of the two. [*Surveying himself in the glass.*] That was a brilliant thought, to insinuate   70 that I folded my master's letters for him; the folding is so neat, that it does honour to the operator. I once intended to have insinuated that I wrote his letters too; but that was before I saw them; it won't do now; no honour there, positively.—"Nothing looks more vulgar [*reading affectedly*], ordinary, and illiberal than ugly, uneven, and ragged nails; the ends of which should be kept even and clean, not tipped with black, and cut in small segments of circles."[7]—Segments of circles! surely my lord did not consider that he wrote for the beaux. Segments of circles; what a crabbed term! Now I dare answer that my master, with all his learning, does not know that this means, according to the present mode, to let the nails grow long, and then cut them   80 off even at top. [*Laughing without.*] Ha! that's Jenny's titter. I protest I despair of ever teaching that girl to laugh; she has something so execrably nat-

---

[6]"Cool, unpassionate" (French).
[7]Chesterfield's letter to his son, November 12, 1750.

ural in her laugh, that I declare it absolutely discomposes my nerves. How came she into our house! [*Calls.*] Jenny!

[*Enter* JENNY.]

JESSAMY. Prythee, Jenny, don't spoil your fine face with laughing.

JENNY. Why, mustn't I laugh, Mr. Jessamy?

JESSAMY. You may smile, but, as my lord says, nothing can authorise a laugh.[8]

JENNY. Well, but I can't help laughing.—Have you seen him, Mr. Jessamy? Ha, ha, ha!   90

JESSAMY. Seen whom?—

JENNY. Why, Jonathan, the New England colonel's servant. Do you know he was at the play last night, and the stupid creature don't know where he has been. He would not go to a play for the world; he thinks it was a show, as he calls it.

JESSAMY. As ignorant and unpolished as he is, do you know, Miss Jenny, that I propose to introduce him to the honour of your acquaintance?

JENNY. Introduce him to me! for what?

JESSAMY. Why, my lovely girl, that you may take him under your protection, as Madame Rambouilliet did young Stanhope;[9] that you may, by your plastic   100 hand, mould this uncouth cub into a gentleman. He is to make love to you.

JENNY. Make love to me!—

JESSAMY. Yes, Mistress Jenny, make love to you; and, I doubt not, when he shall become *domesticated* in your kitchen, that this boor, under your auspices, will soon become *un amiable petit Jonathan*.[10]

JENNY. I must say, Mr. Jessamy, if he copies after me, he will be vastly, monstrously polite.

JESSAMY. Stay here one moment, and I will call him.—Jonathan!—Mr. Jonathan!—

[*Calls.*]   110

JONATHAN [*within*]. Holla! there.—[*Enters.*] You promise to stand by me—six bows you say.

[*Bows.*]

JESSAMY. Mrs. Jenny. I have the honour of presenting Mr. Jonathan, Colonel Manly's waiter, to you. I am extremely happy that I have it in my power to make two worthy people acquainted with each other's merits.

JENNY. So, Mr. Jonathan, I hear you were at the play last night.

JONATHAN. At the play! why, did you think I went to the devil's drawing-room?

JENNY. The devil's drawing-room!

JONATHAN. Yes; why an't cards and dice the devil's device, and the play-house   120 the shop where the devil hangs out the vanities of the world upon the tenterhooks of temptation? I believe you have not heard how they were acting the old boy one night, and the wicked one came among them sure enough, and went right off in a storm, and carried one quarter of the play-house with him. Oh! no, no, no! you won't catch me at a play-house, I warrant you.

JENNY. Well, Mr. Jonathan, though I don't scruple your veracity, I have some reasons for believing you were there: pray, where were you about six o'clock?

JONATHAN. Why, I went to see one Mr. Morrison, the *hocus pocus* man;[11] they said as how he could eat a case knife.[12]   130

---

[8]Chesterfield's letters to his son, March 9 and October 19, 1748.
[9]The Marquise de Rambouillet (1588–1665) presided over a brilliant salon where the intellectuals and literati mingled. "Young Stanhope" may be an ancestor of Lord Chesterfield; or Jessamy may be mistaken.
[10]"A good-natured little Jonathan" (French).
[11]Magician.
[12]Long table knife (carried in a case). Jonathan expected to see a sword-swallowing act.

JENNY. Well, and how did you find the place?

JONATHAN. As I was going about here and there, to and again, to find it, I saw a great crowd of folks going into a long entry that had lanterns over the door; so I asked a man whether that was not the place where they played *hocus pocus?* He was a very civil, kind man, though he did speak like the Hessians;[13] he lifted up his eyes and said, "They play *hocus pocus* tricks enough there, Got knows, mine friend."

JENNY. Well—

JONATHAN. So I went right in, and they showed me away, clean up to the garret, just like meeting-house gallery. And so I saw a power of topping folks, all sitting round in little cabbins, "just like father's corncribs"; and then there was such a squeaking with the fiddles, and such a tarnal blaze with the lights, my head was near turned. At last the people that sat near me set up such a hissing—hiss—like so many mad cats; and then they went thump, thump, thump, just like our Peleg threshing wheat, and stamped away, just like the nation; and called out for one Mr. Langolee,—I suppose he helps act the tricks.

JENNY. Well, and what did you do all this time?

JONATHAN. Gor, I—I liked the fun, and so I thumped away, and hiss'd as lustily as the best of 'em. One sailor-looking man that sat by me, seeing me stamp, and knowing I was a cute[14] fellow, because I could make a roaring noise, clapt me on the shoulder and said, "you are a d—d hearty cock, smite my timbers!" I told him so I was, but I thought he need not swear so, and make use of such naughty words.

JESSAMY. The savage!—Well, and did you see the man with his tricks?

JONATHAN. Why, I vow, as I was looking for him, they lifted up a great green cloth and let us look right into the next neighbour's house. Have you a good many houses in New-York made so in that 'ere way?

JENNY. Not many: but did you see the family?

JONATHAN. Yes, swamp it; I see'd the family.

JENNY. Well, and how did you like them?

JONATHAN. Why, I vow they were pretty much like other families;—there was a poor, good-natured, curse of a husband, and a sad rantipole[15] of a wife.

JENNY. But did you see no other folks?

JONATHAN. Yes. There was one youngster; they called him Mr. Joseph;[16] he talked as sober and as pious as a minister; but, like some ministers that I know, he was a sly tike in his heart for all that. He was going to ask a young woman to spark it with him, and—the Lord have mercy on my soul!—she was another man's wife.

JESSAMY. The Wabash![17]

JENNY. And did you see any more folks?

JONATHAN. Why, they came on as thick as mustard. For my part, I thought the house was haunted. There was a soldier fellow, who talked about his row de dow, dow,[18] and courted a young woman; but, of all the cute folk I saw, I liked one little fellow—

JENNY. Aye! who was he?

JONATHAN. Why, he had red hair, and a little round plump face like mine, only not altogether so handsome. His name was—Darby;—that was his baptizing name; his other name I forgot. Oh! it was Wig—Wag—Wag-all, Darby

---

[13]Germans.
[14]Shrewd, acute.
[15]Scolding, unruly.
[16]Joseph Surface in *The School for Scandal* (1777), by Richard R. Sheridan (1751–1816).

[17]The cheat (slang).
[18]Disturbance. Also a song sung by a soldier in a comedy *The Poor Soldier* (1783) by John O'Keeffe (1747–1833).

Wag-all[19]—pray, do you know him?—I should like to take a sling[20] with 180 him, or a drap of cider with a pepper-pod in it, to make it warm and comfortable.

JENNY. I can't say I have that pleasure.

JONATHAN. I wish you did; he is a cute fellow. But there was one thing I didn't like in that Mr. Darby; and that was, he was afraid of some of them 'ere shooting irons,[21] such as your troopers wear on training days. Now, I'm a true born Yankee American son of liberty, and I never was afraid of a gun yet in all my life.

JENNY. Well, Mr. Jonathan, you were certainly at the play-house.

JONATHAN. I at the play-house!—Why didn't I see the play then? 190

JENNY. Why, the people you saw were players.

JONATHAN. Mercy on my soul! did I see the wicked players?—Mayhap that 'ere Darby that I liked so was the old serpent himself, and had his cloven foot in his pocket. Why, I vow, now I come to think on't, the candles seemed to burn blue, and I am sure where I sat it smelt tarnally of brimstone.

JESSAMY. Well, Mr. Jonathan, from your account, which I confess is very accurate, you must have been at the play-house.

JONATHAN. Why, I vow I began to smell a rat. When I came away, I went to the man for my money again; you want your money? says he; yes, says I; for what? says he; why, says I, no man shall jocky me out of my money; I paid 200 my money to see sights, and the dogs a bit of a sight have I seen, unless you call listening to people's private business a sight. Why, says he, it is the School for Scandalization.[22]—The School for Scandalization!—Oh! ho! no wonder you New York folks are so cute at it, when you go to school to learn it; and so I jogged off.

JESSAMY. My dear Jenny, my master's business drags me from you; would to heaven I knew no other servitude than to your charms.

JONATHAN. Well, but don't go; you won't leave me so—

JESSAMY. Excuse me.—Remember the cash.

    [*Aside to him, and—Exit.*] 210

JENNY. Mr. Jonathan, won't you please to sit down? Mr. Jessamy tells me you wanted to have some conversation with me.

    [*Having brought forward two chairs, they sit.*]

JONATHAN. Ma'am!—

JENNY. Sir!—

JONATHAN. Ma'am!—

JENNY. Pray, how do you like the city, Sir?

JONATHAN. Ma'am!—

JENNY. I say, Sir, how do you like New-York?

JONATHAN. Ma'am!— 220

JENNY. The stupid creature! but I must pass some little time with him, if it is only to endeavour to learn whether it was his master that made such an abrupt entrance into our house, and my young mistress's heart, this morning. [*Aside.*] As you don't seem to like to talk, Mr. Jonathan—do you sing?

JONATHAN. Gor, I—I am glad she asked that, for I forgot what Mr. Jessamy bid me say, and I dare as well be hanged as act what he bid me do, I'm so

[19]Refers to Thomas Wignell, who played Jonathan in *The Contrast;* one of his most popular roles was Darby in *The Poor Soldier.*

[20]A drink, often gin and water.

[21]In *The Poor Soldier,* Darby narrowly escapes getting involved in a duel.

[22]Richard Sheridan's *School for Scandal* and John O'Keeffe's *The Poor Soldier* played on a double bill in New York, on March 21, 1787; Tyler probably saw the plays then.

ashamed. [*Aside.*] Yes, Ma'am, I can sing—I can sing Mear, Old Hundred, and Bangor.[23]

JENNY. Oh! I don't mean psalm tunes. Have you no little song to please the ladies, such as Roslin Castle, or the Maid of the Mill?[24]   230

JONATHAN. Why, all my tunes are go to meeting tunes, save one, and I count
you won't altogether like that 'ere.

JENNY. What is it called?

JONATHAN. I am sure you have heard folks talk about it; it is called Yankee Doo-
dle.[25]

JENNY. Oh! it is the tune I am fond of; and if I know anything of my mistress,
she would be glad to dance to it. Pray, sing!

JONATHAN [*sings*].

> Father and I went up to camp,—
> Along with Captain Goodwin;
> And there we saw the men and boys,   240
> As thick as hasty-pudding.
> > Yankee doodle do, etc.
>
> And there we saw a swamping gun,
> Big as log of maple,
> On a little deuced cart,
> A load for father's cattle.
> > Yankee doodle do, etc.
>
> And every time they fired it off,
> It took a horn of powder,   250
> It made a noise—like father's gun,
> Only a nation louder.
> > Yankee doodle do, etc.
>
> There was a man in our town,
> His name was—

No, no, that won't do. Now, if I was with Tabitha Wymen and Jemima Cawley
down at father Chase's. I shouldn't mind singing this all out before them—
you would be affronted if I was to sing that, though that's a lucky thought;
if you should be affronted. I have something dang'd cute, which Jessamy
told me to say to you.   260

JENNY. Is that all! I assure you I like it of all things.

JONATHAN. No, no; I can sing more; some other time, when you and I are better
acquainted, I'll sing the whole of it—no, no—that's a fib—I can't sing but a
hundred and ninety verses; our Tabitha at home can sing it all.—[*Sings.*]

> Marblehead's a rocky place,
> And Cape-Cod is sandy;
> Charlestown is burnt down,
> Boston is the dandy.
> > Yankee doodle, doodle do, etc.

I vow, my own town song has put me into such topping spirits that I believe I'll   270
begin to do a little, as Jessamy says we must when we go a-courting.—[*Runs
and kisses her.*] Burning rivers! cooling flames! red-hot roses! pig-nuts! hasty-
pudding and ambrosia!

---

[23]Familiar New England psalm tunes.
[24]Popular songs of the time.

[25]Popular during the Revolutionary War, sung by the soldier in countless stanzas, some no doubt obscene.

JENNY. What means this freedom? you insulting wretch. [*Strikes him.*]

JONATHAN. Are you affronted?

JENNY. Affronted! with what looks shall I express my anger?

JONATHAN. Looks! why as to the matter of looks, you look as cross as a witch.

JENNY. Have you no feeling for the delicacy of my sex?

JONATHAN. Feeling! Gor, I—I feel the delicacy of your sex pretty smartly [*Rubbing his cheek*], though, I vow, I thought when you city ladies courted and 280 married, and all that, you put feeling out of the question. But I want to know whether you are really affronted, or only pretend to be so? 'Cause, if you are certainly right down affronted, I am at the end of my tether; Jessamy didn't tell me what to say to you.

JENNY. Pretend to be affronted!

JONATHAN. Aye, aye, if you only pretend, you shall hear how I'll go to work to make cherubim consequences.
    [*Runs up to her.*]

JENNY. Begone, you brute!

JONATHAN. That looks like mad; but I won't lose my speech. My dearest Jenny— 290 your name is Jenny, I think?—My dearest Jenny, though I have the highest esteem for the sweet favours you have just now granted me—Gor, that's a fib, though; but Jessamy says it is not wicked to tell lies to the women. [*Aside.*] I say, though I have the highest esteem for the favours you have just now granted me, yet you will consider that, as soon as the dissolvable knot is tied, they will no longer be favours, but only matters of duty and matters of course.

JENNY. Marry you! you audacious monster! get out of my sight, or, rather, let me fly from you. [*Exit hastily.*]

JONATHAN. Gor, she's gone off in a swinging passion, before I had time to think 300 of consequences. If this is the way with your city ladies, give me the twenty acres of rock, the Bible, the cow, and Tabitha, and a little peaceable bundling.[26]

SCENE 2.

The Mall. Enter MANLY.

MANLY. It must be so, Montague![1] and it is not all the tribe of Mandevilles[2] that shall convince me that a nation, to become great, must first become dissipated. Luxury is surely the bane of a nation: Luxury! which enervates both soul and body, by opening a thousand new sources of enjoyment, opens, also, a thousand new sources of contention and want: Luxury! which renders a people weak at home, and accessible to bribery, corruption, and force from abroad. When the Grecian states knew no other tools than the axe and the saw, the Grecians were a great, a free, and a happy people. The kings of Greece devoted their lives to the service of their country, and her senators 10 knew no other superiority over their fellow-citizens than a glorious preeminence in danger and virtue. They exhibited to the world a noble spectacle,—a number of independent states united by a similarity of language, sentiment, manners, common interest, and common consent, in one grand

---

[26]A custom of courtship in the country in winter—sitting in bed, fully dressed.
[1]Edward Montagu (1713–1776), author of *Reflections on the Rise and Fall of Ancient Republics* (1759).

[2]Bernard de Mandeville (1670?–1733), author of *The Fable of the Bees* (1714), contended that personal vices, purchased, benefit the public.

mutual league of protection. And, thus united, long might they have continued the cherishers of arts and sciences, the protectors of the oppressed, the
scourge of tyrants, and the safe asylum of liberty. But when foreign gold,
and still more pernicious foreign luxury, had crept among them, they
sapped the vitals of their virtue. The virtues of their ancestors were only
found in their writings. Envy and suspicion, the vices of little minds, pos- 20
sessed them. The various states engendered jealousies of each other; and,
more unfortunately, growing jealous of their great federal council, the
Amphictyons,[3] they forgot that their common safety had existed, and would
exist, in giving them an honourable extensive prerogative. The common
good was lost in the pursuit of private interest; and that people who, by
uniting, might have stood against the world in arms, by dividing, crumbled
into ruin;—their name is now only known in the page of the historian, and
what they once were is all we have left to admire. Oh! that America! Oh!
that my country, would, in this her day, learn the things which belong to her
peace!
30
    [*Enter* DIMPLE.]

DIMPLE. You are Colonel Manly, I presume?

MANLY. At your service, Sir.

DIMPLE. My name is Dimple, Sir. I have the honour to be a lodger in the same
house with you, and, hearing you were in the Mall, came hither to take the
liberty of joining you.

MANLY. You are very obliging, Sir.

DIMPLE. As I understand you are a stranger here, Sir, I have taken the liberty to
introduce myself to your acquaintance, as possibly I may have it in my
power to point out some things in this city worthy your notice. 40

MANLY. An attention to strangers is worthy a liberal mind, and must ever be
gratefully received. But to a soldier, who has no fixed abode, such attentions
are particularly pleasing.

DIMPLE. Sir, there is no character so respectable as that of a soldier. And, indeed, when we reflect how much we owe to those brave men who have suffered so much in the service of their country, and secured to us those inestimable blessings that we now enjoy, our liberty and independence, they
demand every attention which gratitude can pay. For my own part, I never
meet an officer, but I embrace him as my friend, nor a private in distress,
but I insensibly extend my charity to him.— I have hit the Bumkin off very 50
tolerably. [*Aside.*]

MANLY. Give me your hand, Sir! I do not proffer this hand to everybody; but
you steal into my heart. I hope I am as insensible to flattery as most men;
but I declare (it may be my weak side) that I never hear the name of soldier
mentioned with respect, but I experience a thrill of pleasure which I never
feel on any other occasion.

DIMPLE. Will you give me leave, my dear Colonel, to confer an obligation on
myself, by showing you some civilities during your stay here, and giving a
similar opportunity to some of my friends?

MANLY. Sir, I thank you; but I believe my stay in this city will be very short. 60

DIMPLE. I can introduce you to some men of excellent sense, in whose company
you will esteem yourself happy; and, by way of amusement, to some fine
girls, who will listen to your soft things with pleasure.

MANLY. Sir, I should be proud of the honour of being acquainted with those
gentlemen;—but, as for the ladies, I don't understand you.

---

[3]Assembly of the Greek city-states.

DIMPLE. Why, Sir, I need not tell you, that when a young gentleman is alone with a young lady he must say some soft things to her fair cheek—indeed, the lady will expect it. To be sure, there is not much pleasure when a man of the world and a finished coquette meet, who perfectly know each other; but how delicious is it to excite the emotions of joy, hope, expectation, and de- 70 light in the bosom of a lovely girl who believes every tittle of what you say to be serious!

MANLY. Serious, Sir! In my opinion, the man who, under pretensions of marriage, can plant thorns in the bosom of an innocent, unsuspecting girl is more detestable than a common robber, in the same proportion as private violence is more despicable than open force, and money of less value than happiness.

DIMPLE. How he awes me by the superiority of his sentiments. [*Aside.*] As you say, Sir, a gentleman should be cautious how he mentions marriage.

MANLY. Cautious, Sir! No person more approves of an intercourse between the 80 sexes than I do. Female conversation softens our manners, whilst our discourse, from the superiority of our literary advantages, improves their minds. But, in our young country, where there is no such thing as gallantry, when a gentleman speaks of love to a lady, whether he mentions marriage or not, she ought to conclude either that he meant to insult her or that his intentions are the most serious and honourable. How mean, how cruel, is it, by a thousand tender assiduities, to win the affections of an amiable girl, and, though you leave her virtue unspotted, to betray her into the appearance of so many tender partialities, that every man of delicacy would suppress his inclination towards her, by supposing her heart engaged! Can any 90 man, for the trivial gratification of his leisure hours, affect the happiness of a whole life! His not having spoken of marriage may add to his perfidy, but can be no excuse for his conduct.

DIMPLE. Sir, I admire your sentiments;—they are mine. The light observations that fell from me were only a principle of the tongue; they came not from the heart; my practice has ever disapproved these principles.

MANLY. I believe you, Sir. I should with reluctance suppose that those pernicious sentiments could find admittance into the heart of a gentleman.

DIMPLE. I am now, Sir, going to visit a family, where, if you please, I will have the honour of introducing you. Mr. Manly's ward, Miss Letitia, is a young 100 lady of immense fortune; and his niece, Miss Charlotte Manly, is a young lady of great sprightliness and beauty.

MANLY. That gentleman, Sir, is my uncle, and Miss Manly my sister.

DIMPLE. The devil she is! [*Aside.*] Miss Manly your sister, Sir? I rejoice to hear it, and feel a double pleasure in being known to you.—Plague on him! I wish he was at Boston again, with all my soul. [*Aside.*]

MANLY. Come, Sir, will you go?

DIMPLE. I will follow you in a moment, Sir. [*Exit* MANLY.] Plague on it! this is unlucky. A fighting brother is a cursed appendage to a fine girl. Egad! I just stopped in time; had he not discovered himself, in two minutes more I 110 should have told him how well I was with his sister. Indeed, I cannot see the satisfaction of an intrigue, if one can't have the pleasure of communicating it to our friends.

[*Exit.*]

ACT IV
Scene 1.

Charlotte's Apartment. CHARLOTTE *leading in* MARIA.

CHARLOTTE. This is so kind, my sweet friend, to come to see me at this moment. I declare, if I were going to be married in a few days, as you are, I should scarce have found time to visit my friends.

MARIA. Do you think, then, that there is an impropriety in it?—How should you dispose of your time?

CHARLOTTE. Why, I should be shut up in my chamber; and my head would so run upon—upon—upon the solemn ceremony that I was to pass through!—I declare, it would take me above two hours merely to learn that little monosyllable—*Yes.* Ah! my dear, your sentimental imagination does 10 not conceive what that little tiny word implies.

MARIA. Spare me your raillery, my sweet friend; I should love your agreeable vivacity at any other time.

CHARLOTTE. Why, this is the very time to amuse you. You grieve me to see you look so unhappy.

MARIA. Have I not reason to look so?

CHARLOTTE. What new grief distresses you?

MARIA. Oh! how sweet it is, when the heart is borne down with misfortune, to recline and repose on the bosom of friendship! Heaven knows that, although it is improper for a young lady to praise a gentleman, yet I have 20 ever concealed Mr. Dimple's foibles, and spoke of him as of one whose reputation I expected would be linked with mine; but his late conduct towards me has turned my coolness into contempt. He behaves as if he meant to insult and disgust me; whilst my father, in the last conversation on the subject of our marriage, spoke of it as a matter which laid near his heart, and in which he would not bear contradiction.

CHARLOTTE. This works well; oh! the generous Dimple. I'll endeavour to excite her to discharge him. [*Aside.*] But, my dear friend, your happiness depends on yourself. Why don't you discard him? Though the match has been of long standing, I would not be forced to make myself miserable: no parent in 30 the world should oblige me to marry the man I did not like.

MARIA. Oh! my dear, you never lived with your parents, and do not know what influence a father's frowns have upon a daughter's heart. Besides, what have I to allege against Mr. Dimple, to justify myself to the world? He carries himself so smoothly, that every one would impute the blame to me, and call me capricious.

CHARLOTTE. And call her capricious! Did ever such an objection start into the heart of woman? For my part, I wish I had fifty lovers to discard, for no other reason than because I did not fancy them. My dear Maria, you will forgive me; I know your candour and confidence in me; but I have at times, 40 I confess, been led to suppose that some other gentleman was the cause of your aversion to Mr. Dimple.

MARIA. No, my sweet friend, you may be assured, that though I have seen many gentleman I could prefer to Mr. Dimple, yet I never saw one that I thought I could give my hand to, until this morning.

CHARLOTTE. This morning!

MARIA. Yes; one of the strangest accidents in the world. The odious Dimple, after disgusting me with his conversation, had just left me, when a gentleman, who, it seems, boards in the same house with him, saw him coming out

of our door, and the houses looking very much alike, he came into our 50
house instead of his lodgings; nor did he discover his mistake until he got
into the parlour, where I was; he then bowed so gracefully, made such a
genteel apology, and looked so manly and noble!—

CHARLOTTE. I see some folks, though it is so great an impropriety, can praise a
gentleman, when he happens to be the man of their fancy. [*Aside.*]

MARIA. I don't know how it was,—I hope he did not think me indelicate,—but
I asked him, I believe, to sit down, or pointed to a chair. He sat down, and,
instead of having recourse to observations upon the weather, or hackneyed
criticisms upon the theatre, he entered readily into a conversation worthy of
a man of sense to speak, and a lady of delicacy and sentiment to hear. He 60
was not strictly handsome, but he spoke the language of sentiment, and his
eyes looked tenderness and honour.

CHARLOTTE. Oh! [*eagerly*] you sentimental, grave girls, when your hearts are
once touched, beat us rattles a bar's length. And so, you are quite in love
with this he-angel?

MARIA. In love with him! How can you rattle so, Charlotte? am I not going to
be miserable? [*Sighs.*] In love with a gentleman I never saw but one hour in
my life, and don't know his name! No; I only wished that the man I shall
marry may look, and talk, and act, just like him. Besides, my dear, he is a
married man. 70

CHARLOTTE. Why, that was good-natured—he told you so, I suppose, in mere
charity, to prevent you falling in love with him?

MARIA. He didn't tell me so; [*peevishly*] he looked as if he was married.

CHARLOTTE. How, my dear; did he look sheepish?

MARIA. I am sure he has a susceptible heart, and the ladies of his acquaintance
must be very stupid not to—

CHARLOTTE. Hush! I hear some person coming.

[*Enter* LETITIA.]

LETITIA. My dear Maria, I am happy to see you. Lud! what a pity it is that you
have purchased your wedding clothes. 80

MARIA. I think so. [*Sighing.*]

LETITIA. Why, my dear, there is the sweetest parcel of silks come over you ever
saw! Nancy Brilliant has a full suit come; she sent over her measure, and it
fits her to a hair; it is immensely dressy, and made for a court-hoop. I
thought they said the large hoops were going out of fashion.

CHARLOTTE. Did you see the hat? Is it a fact that the deep laces round the border is still the fashion?

DIMPLE [*within*]. Upon my honour, Sir.

MARIA. Ha! Dimple's voice! My dear, I must take leave of you. There are some
things necessary to be done at our house. Can't I go through the other 90
room?

[*Enter* DIMPLE *and* MANLY.]

DIMPLE. Ladies, your most obedient.

CHARLOTTE. Miss Van Rough, shall I present my brother Henry to you? Colonel
Manly, Maria,—Miss Van Rough, brother.

MARIA. Her brother! [*Turns and sees* MANLY.] Oh! my heart! the very gentleman I
have been praising.

MANLY. The same amiable girl I saw this morning!

CHARLOTTE. Why, you look as if you were acquainted.

MANLY. I unintentionally intruded into this lady's presence this morning, for 100
which she was so good as to promise me her forgiveness.

CHARLOTTE. Oh! ho! is that the case! Have these two penserosos been together?
Were they Henry's eyes that looked so tenderly? [*Aside.*] And so you prom-

ised to pardon him? and could you be so good-natured? have you really forgiven him? I beg you would do it for my sake [*whispering loud to* MARIA]. But,
my dear, as you are in such haste, it would be cruel to detain you; I can
show you the way through the other room.

MARIA. Spare me, my sprightly friend.

MANLY. The lady does not, I hope, intend to deprive us of the pleasure of her
company so soon.   110

CHARLOTTE. She has only a mantua-maker[1] who waits for her at home. But, as I
am to give my opinion of the dress, I think she cannot go yet. We were talking of the fashions when you came in, but I suppose the subject must be
changed to something of more importance now. Mr. Dimple, will you favour us with an account of the public entertainments?

DIMPLE. Why, really, Miss Manly, you could not have asked me a question more
mal-apropos.[2] For my part, I must confess that, to a man who has travelled,
there is nothing that is worthy the name of amusement to be found in this
city.

CHARLOTTE. Except visiting the ladies.   120

DIMPLE. Pardon me, Madam; that is the avocation of a man of taste. But for
amusement, I positively know of nothing that can be called so, unless you
dignify with that title the hopping once a fortnight to the sound of two or
three squeaking fiddles, and the clattering of the old tavern windows, or sitting to see the miserable mummers, whom you call actors, murder comedy
and make a farce of tragedy.

MANLY. Do you never attend the theatre, Sir?

DIMPLE. I was tortured there once.

CHARLOTTE. Pray, Mr. Dimple, was it a tragedy or a comedy?

DIMPLE. Faith, Madam, I cannot tell; for I sat with my back to the stage all the   130
time, admiring a much better actress than any there—a lady who played the
fine woman to perfection; though, by the laugh of the horrid creatures
round me, I suppose it was comedy. Yet, on second thoughts, it might be
some hero in a tragedy, dying so comically as to set the whole house in an
uproar. Colonel, I presume you have been in Europe?

MANLY. Indeed, Sir, I was never ten leagues from the continent.

DIMPLE. Believe me, Colonel, you have an immense pleasure to come; and when
you shall have seen the brilliant exhibitions of Europe, you will learn to despise the amusements of this country as much as I do.

MANLY. Therefore I do not wish to see them; for I can never esteem that   140
knowledge valuable which tends to give me a distaste for my native country.

DIMPLE. Well, Colonel, though you have not travelled, you have read.

MANLY. I have, a little; and by it have discovered that there is a laudable partiality which ignorant, untravelled men entertain for everything that belongs to
their native country. I call it laudable; it injures no one; adds to their own
happiness; and, when extended, becomes the noble principle of patriotism.
Travelled gentlemen rise superior, in their own opinion, to this; but if the
contempt which they contract for their country is the most valuable acquisition of their travels, I am far from thinking that their time and money are
well spent.   150

MARIA. What noble sentiments!

CHARLOTTE. Let my brother set out where he will in the fields of conversation,
he is sure to end his tour in the temple of gravity.

MANLY. Forgive me, my sister. I love my country; it has its foibles undoubt-

---

[1]Dressmaker.
[2]"Inappropriate" (French).

edly;—some foreigners will with pleasure remark them—but such remarks fall very ungracefully from the lips of her citizens.

DIMPLE. You are perfectly in the right, Colonel—America has her faults.

MANLY. Yes, Sir; and we, her children, should blush for them in private, and endeavour, as individuals, to reform them. But, if our country has its errors in common with other countries, I am proud to say America—I mean the 160 United States—has displayed virtues and achievements which modern nations may admire, but of which they have seldom set us the example.

CHARLOTTE. But, brother, we must introduce you to some of our gay folks, and let you see the city, such as it is. Mr. Dimple is known to almost every family in town; he will doubtless take a pleasure in introducing you.

DIMPLE. I shall esteem every service I can render your brother an honour.

MANLY. I fear the business I am upon will take up all my time, and my family will be anxious to hear from me.

MARIA. His family! but what is it to me that he is married! [*Aside.*] Pray, how did you leave your lady, Sir?   170

CHARLOTTE. My brother is not married [*observing her anxiety*]; it is only an odd way he has of expressing himself. Pray, brother, is this business, which you make your continual excuse, a secret?

MANLY. No, sister; I came hither to solicit the honourable Congress, that a number of my brave old soldiers may be put upon the pension-list, who were, at first, not judged to be so materially wounded as to need the public assistance. My sister says true [*to* MARIA]: I call my late soldiers my family. Those who were not in the field in the late glorious contest, and those who were, have their respective merits; but, I confess, my old brother-soldiers are dearer to me than the former description. Friendships made in adversity 180 are lasting; our countrymen may forget us, but that is no reason why we should forget one another. But I must leave you; my time of engagement approaches.

CHARLOTTE. Well, but, brother, if you will go, will you please to conduct my fair friend home? You live in the same street—I was to have gone with her myself—[*Aside.*] A lucky thought.

MARIA. I am obliged to your sister, Sir, and was just intending to go.
  [*Going.*]

MANLY. I shall attend her with pleasure.
  [*Exit with* MARIA, *followed by* DIMPLE *and* CHARLOTTE.]   190

MARIA. Now, pray, don't betray me to your brother.

CHARLOTTE [*Just as she sees him make a motion to take his leave*]. One word with you, brother, if you please.
  [*Follows them out.*]
  [*Manent,*[3] DIMPLE *and* LETITIA.]

DIMPLE. You received the billet[4] I sent you, I presume?

LETITIA. Hush!—Yes.

DIMPLE. When shall I pay my respects to you?

LETITIA. At eight I shall be unengaged.
  [*Reënter* CHARLOTTE.]   200

DIMPLE. Did my lovely angel receive my billet? [*to* CHARLOTTE.]

CHARLOTTE. Yes.

DIMPLE. What hour shall I expect with impatience?

CHARLOTTE. At eight I shall be at home unengaged.

---

[3]Remaining (stage direction).
[4]"Letter" (French).

DIMPLE. Unfortunate! I have a horrid engagement of business at that hour. Can't you finish your visit earlier and let six be the happy hour?

CHARLOTTE. You know your influence over me.

[*Exeunt severally.*]

SCENE 2.

Van Rough's House. VAN ROUGH, alone.

VAN ROUGH. It cannot possibly be true! The son of my old friend can't have acted so unadvisedly. Seventeen thousand pounds! in bills! Mr. Transfer must have been mistaken. He always appeared so prudent, and talked so well upon money matters, and even assured me that he intended to change his dress for a suit of clothes which would not cost so much, and look more substantial, as soon as he married. No, no, no! it can't be; it cannot be. But, however, I must look out sharp. I did not care what his principles or his actions were, so long as he minded the main chance. Seventeen thousand pounds! If he had lost it in trade, why the best men may have ill-luck; but to 10 game it away, as Transfer says—why, at this rate, his whole estate may go in one night, and, what is ten times worse, mine into the bargain. No, no, Mary is right. Leave women to look out in these matters; for all they look as if they didn't know a journal from a ledger, when their interest is concerned they know what's what; they mind the main chance as well as the best of us. I wonder Mary did not tell me she knew of his spending his money so foolishly. Seventeen thousand pounds! Why, if my daughter was standing up to be married, I would forbid the banns,[1] if I found it was to a man who did not mind the main chance.—Hush! I hear somebody coming. 'Tis Mary's voice; a man with her too! I shouldn't be surprised if this should be the 20 other string to her bow. Aye, aye, let them alone; women understand the main chance.—Though, i' faith, I'll listen a little.

[*Retires into a closet.*]

[MANLY *leading in* MARIA.]

MANLY. I hope you will excuse my speaking upon so important a subject so abruptly; but, the moment I entered your room, you struck me as the lady whom I had long loved in imagination, and never hoped to see.

MARIA. Indeed, Sir, I have been led to hear more upon this subject than I ought.

MANLY. Do you, then, disapprove my suit, Madam, or the abruptness of my in- 30 troducing it? If the latter, my peculiar situation, being obliged to leave the city in a few days, will, I hope, be my excuse; if the former, I will retire, for I am sure I would not give a moment's inquietude to her whom I could devote my life to please. I am not so indelicate as to seek your immediate approbation; permit me only to be near you, and by a thousand tender assiduities to endeavour to excite a grateful return.

MARIA. I have a father, whom I would die to make happy; he will disapprove—

MANLY. Do you think me so ungenerous as to seek a place in your esteem without his consent? You must—you ever ought to consider that man as unworthy of you who seeks an interest in your heart contrary to a father's appro- 40 bation. A young lady should reflect that the loss of a lover may be supplied, but nothing can compensate for the loss of a parent's affection. Yet, why do you suppose your father would disapprove? In our country, the affections

---

[1]Marriage announcements.

are not sacrificed to riches, or family aggrandizement: should you approve, my family is decent, and my rank honourable.

MARIA. You distress me, Sir.

MANLY. Then I will sincerely beg your excuse for obtruding so disagreeable a subject, and retire. [*Going.*]

MARIA. Stay, Sir! your generosity and good opinion of me deserve a return; but why must I declare what, for these few hours, I have scarce suffered myself 50 to think?—I am—

MANLY. What?

MARIA. Engaged, Sir; and, in a few days, to be married to the gentleman you saw at your sister's.

MANLY. Engaged to be married! And have I been basely invading the rights of another? Why have you permitted this? Is this the return for the partiality I declared for you?

MARIA. You distress me, Sir. What would you have me say? You are too gener- ous to wish the truth. Ought I to say that I dared not suffer myself to think of my engagement, and that I am going to give my hand without my heart? 60 Would you have me confess a partiality for you? If so, your triumph is com- plete, and you can be only more so when days of misery with the man I can- not love will make me think of him whom I could prefer.

MANLY [*after a pause*]. We are both unhappy; but it is your duty to obey your parent—mine to obey my honour. Let us, therefore, both follow the path of rectitude; and of this we may be assured, that if we are not happy, we shall, at least, deserve to be so. Adieu! I dare not trust myself longer with you.

[*Exeunt severally.*]

ACT V

SCENE 1.

Dimple's Lodgings. JESSAMY *meeting* JONATHAN.

JESSAMY. Well, Mr. Jonathan, what success with the fair?

JONATHAN. Why, such a tarnal cross tike you never saw. You would have counted she had lived upon crab-apples and vinegar for a fortnight. But what the rattle makes you look so tarnation glum?

JESSAMY. I was thinking, Mr. Jonathan, what could be the reason of her carrying herself so coolly to you.

JONATHAN. Coolly, do you call it? Why, I vow, she was fire-hot angry: may be it was because I buss'd her.

JESSAMY. No, no, Mr. Jonathan; there must be some other cause; I never yet 10 knew a lady angry at being kissed.

JONATHAN. Well, if it is not the young woman's bashfulness, I vow I can't con- ceive why she shouldn't like me.

JESSAMY. May be it is because you have not the Graces, Mr. Jonathan.

JONATHAN. Grace! Why, does the young woman expect I must be converted be- fore I court her?[1]

JESSAMY. I mean graces of person: for instance, my lord tells us that we must cut off our nails even at top, in small segments of circles—though you won't understand that; in the next place, you must regulate your laugh.

JONATHAN. Maple-log seize it! don't I laugh natural?   20

---

[1]Jonathan takes "grace" to mean the grace that brings sal- vation by God's covenant.

JESSAMY. That's the very fault, Mr. Jonathan. Besides, you absolutely misplace it. I was told by a friend of mine that you laughed outright at the play the other night, when you ought only to have tittered.

JONATHAN. Gor! I—what does one go to see fun for if they can't laugh?

JESSAMY. You may laugh; but you must laugh by rule.

JONATHAN. Swamp it—laugh by rule! Well, I should like that tarnally.

JESSAMY. Why, you know, Mr. Jonathan, that to dance, a lady to play with her fan, or a gentleman with his cane, and all other natural motions, are regulated by art. My master has composed an immensely pretty gamut, by which any lady or gentleman, with a few years' close application, may learn to laugh as gracefully as if they were born and bred to it.   30

JONATHAN. Mercy on my soul! A gamut for laughing—just like fa, la, sol?[2]

JESSAMY. Yes. It comprises every possible display of jocularity, from an *affettuoso* smile to a *piano* titter, or full chorus *fortissimo*[3] ha, ha, ha! My master employs his leisure hours in marking out the plays, like a cathedral chanting-book, that the ignorant may know where to laugh; and that pit, box, and gallery may keep time together, and not have a snigger in one part of the house, a broad grin in the other, and a d—d grum look in the third. How delightful to see the audience all smile together, then look on their books, then twist their mouths into an agreeable simper, then altogether shake the   40 house with a general ha, ha, ha! loud as a full chorus of Handel's[4] at an Abbey commemoration.

JONATHAN. Ha, ha, ha! that's dang'd cute, I swear.

JESSAMY. The gentlemen, you see, will laugh the tenor; the ladies will play the counter-tenor; the beaux will squeak the treble; and our jolly friends in the gallery a thorough bass, ho, ho, ho!

JONATHAN. Well, can't you let me see that gamut?

JESSAMY. Oh! yes, Mr. Jonathan, here it is. [*Takes out a book.*] Oh! no, this is only a titter with its variations. Ah, here it is. [*Takes out another.*] Now, you must know, Mr. Jonathan, this is a piece written by Ben Jonson,[5] which I have set   50 to my master's gamut. The places where you must smile, look grave, or laugh outright, are marked below the line. Now look over me. "There was a certain man"—now you must smile.

JONATHAN. Well, read it again; I warrant I'll mind my eye.

JESSAMY. "There was a certain man, who had a sad scolding wife,"—now you must laugh.

JONATHAN. Tarnation! That's no laughing matter though.

JESSAMY. "And she lay sick a-dying";—now you must titter.

JONATHAN. What, snigger when a good woman's a-dying! Gor, I—

JESSAMY. Yes, the notes say you must—"and she asked her husband leave to   60 make a will,"—now you must begin to look grave;—"and her husband said"—

JONATHAN. Ay, what did her husband say? Something dang'd cute, I reckon.

JESSAMY. "And her husband said, you have had your will all your life-time, and would you have it after you are dead, too?"

JONATHAN. Ho, ho, ho! There the old man was even with her! he was up to the notch—ha, ha, ha!

JESSAMY. But, Mr. Jonathan, you must not laugh so. Why, you ought to have tittered *piano*, and you have laughed *fortissimo*. Look here; you see these

---

[2]I.e., a scale for laughing like the scale for singing.
[3]All musical terms from Italian: *affettuoso*, tenderly expressive; *piano*, softly; *fortissimo*, very loudly.
[4]George Frederick Handel (1685–1759), English composer born in Germany.

[5]Ben Jonson (1572–1637), English dramatist noted for his satiric comedies.

marks, A, B, C, and so on; these are the references to the other part of the 70
book. Let us turn to it, and you will see the directions how to manage the
muscles. This [*turns over*] was note D you blundered at.—You must purse
the mouth into a smile, then titter, discovering the lower part of the three
front upper teeth.

JONATHAN. How? read it again.

JESSAMY. "There was a certain man"—very well!—"who had a sad scolding
wife,"—why don't you laugh?

JONATHAN. Now, that scolding wife sticks in my gizzard so pluckily that I can't
laugh for the blood and nowns[6] of me. Let me look grave here, and I'll
laugh your belly full, where the old creature's a-dying.— 80

JESSAMY. "And she asked her husband"—[*Bell rings.*] My master's bell! he's returned, I fear—Here Mr. Jonathan, take this gamut; and I make no doubt
but with a few years' application, you may be able to smile gracefully.

[*Exeunt severally.*]

SCENE 2.

Charlotte's Apartment. Enter MANLY.

MANLY. What, no one at home? How unfortunate to meet the only lady my
heart was ever moved by, to find her engaged to another, and confessing
her partiality for me! Yet engaged to a man who, by her intimation, and his
libertine conversation with me, I fear, does not merit her. Aye! there's the
sting; for, were I assured that Maria was happy, my heart is not so selfish
but that it would dilate in knowing it, even though it were with another. But
to know she is unhappy!—I must drive these thoughts from me. Charlotte
has some books; and this is what I believe she calls her little library.

[*Enters a closet.*] 10

[*Enter* DIMPLE *leading* LETITIA.]

LETITIA. And will you pretend to say now, Mr. Dimple, that you propose to
break with Maria? Are not the banns published? Are not the clothes purchased? Are not the friends invited? In short, is it not a done affair?

DIMPLE. Believe me, my dear Letitia, I would not marry her.

LETITIA. Why have you not broke with her before this, as you all along deluded
me by saying you would?

DIMPLE. Because I was in hopes she would, ere this, have broke with me.

LETITIA. You could not expect it.

DIMPLE. Nay, but be calm a moment; 'twas from my regard to you that I did not 20
discard her.

LETITIA. Regard to me!

DIMPLE. Yes; I have done everything in my power to break with her, but the
foolish girl is so fond of me that nothing can accomplish it. Besides, how can
I offer her my hand, when my heart is indissolubly engaged to you?

LETITIA. There may be reason in this; but why so attentive to Miss Manly?

DIMPLE. Attentive to Miss Manly! For heaven's sake, if you have no better opinion of my constancy, pay not so ill a compliment to my taste.

LETITIA. Did I not see you whisper her to-day?

DIMPLE. Possibly I might—but something of so very trifling a nature that I have 30
already forgot what it was.

LETITIA. I believe she has not forgot it.

[6]Variant of "wounds" (from "God's blood and wounds").

DIMPLE. My dear creature, how can you for a moment suppose I should have any serious thoughts of that trifling, gay, flighty coquette, that disagreeable—

[*Enter* CHARLOTTE.]

DIMPLE. My dear Miss Manly, I rejoice to see you; there is a charm in your conversation that always marks your entrance into company as fortunate.

LETITIA. Where have you been, my dear?

CHARLOTTE. Why, I have been about to twenty shops, turning over pretty 40 things, and so have left twenty visits unpaid. I wish you would step into the carriage and whisk round, make my apology, and leave my cards where our friends are not at home; that, you know, will serve as a visit. Come, do go.

LETITIA. So anxious to get me out! but I'll watch you. [*Aside.*] Oh! yes, I'll go; I want a little exercise. Positively [DIMPLE *offering to accompany her.*], Mr. Dimple, you shall not go; why, half my visits are cake and caudle[1] visits; it won't do, you know, for you to go.

[*Exit, but returns to the door in the back scene and listens.*]

DIMPLE. This attachment of your brother to Maria is fortunate.

CHARLOTTE. How did you come to the knowledge of it?   50

DIMPLE. I read it in their eyes.

CHARLOTTE. And I had it from her mouth. It would have amused you to have seen her! She, that thought it so great an impropriety to praise a gentleman that she could not bring out one word in your favour, found a redundancy to praise him.

DIMPLE. I have done everything in my power to assist his passion there: your delicacy, my dearest girl, would be shocked at half the instances of neglect and misbehaviour.

CHARLOTTE. I don't know how I should bear neglect; but Mr. Dimple must misbehave himself indeed, to forfeit my good opinion.   60

DIMPLE. Your good opinion, my angel, is the pride and pleasure of my heart; and if the most respectful tenderness for you, and an utter indifference for all your sex besides, can make me worthy of your esteem, I shall richly merit it.

CHARLOTTE. All my sex besides, Mr. Dimple!—you forgot your tête-à-tête with Letitia.

DIMPLE. How can you, my lovely angel, cast a thought on that insipid, wrymouthed, ugly creature!

CHARLOTTE. But her fortune may have charms?

DIMPLE. Not to a heart like mine. The man, who has been blessed with the good 70 opinion of my Charlotte, must despise the allurements of fortune.

CHARLOTTE. I am satisfied.

DIMPLE. Let us think no more on the odious subject, but devote the present hour to happiness.

CHARLOTTE. Can I be happy when I see the man I prefer going to be married to another?

DIMPLE. Have I not already satisfied my charming angel, that I can never think of marrying the puling Maria? But, even if it were so, could that be any bar to our happiness? for, as the poet sings,

"Love, free as air, at sight of human ties,   80
    Spreads his light wings, and in a moment flies."[2]

---

[1]Spiced wine or ale (a woman's drink).
[2]Alexander Pope (1688–1744), author of "Epistle from
Eloise to Abelard" (1717). See lines 75–76.

Come, then, my charming angel! why delay our bliss? The present moment is ours; the next is in the hand of fate. [*Kissing her.*]

CHARLOTTE. Begone, Sir! By your delusions you had almost lulled my honour asleep.

DIMPLE. Let me lull the demon to sleep again with kisses. [*He struggles with her; she screams.*]

    [*Enter* MANLY.]

MANLY. Turn, villain! and defend yourself.—[*Draws.* VAN ROUGH *enters and beats down their swords.*]

VAN ROUGH. Is the devil in you? are you going to murder one another? [*Holding* DIMPLE.]

DIMPLE. Hold him, hold him,—I can command my passion.

    [*Enter* JONATHAN.]

JONATHAN. What the rattle ails you? Is the old one in you? Let the colonel alone, can't you? I feel chock-full of fight,—do you want to kill the colonel?—

MANLY. Be still, Jonathan; the gentleman does not want to hurt me.

JONATHAN. Gor! I—I wish he did; I'd show him Yankee boys play, pretty quick—Don't you see you have frightened the young woman into the *hystrikes?*[3]

VAN ROUGH. Pray, some of you explain this; what has been the occasion of all this racket?

MANLY. That gentleman can explain it to you; it will be a very diverting story for an intended father-in-law to hear.

VAN ROUGH. How was this matter, Mr. Van Dumpling?

DIMPLE. Sir,—upon my honour,—all I know is, that I was talking to this young lady, and this gentleman broke in on us in a very extraordinary manner.

VAN ROUGH. Why, all this is nothing to the purpose; can you explain it, Miss? [*To* CHARLOTTE.]

    [*Enter* LETITIA *through the back scene.*]

LETITIA. I can explain it to that gentleman's confusion. Though long betrothed to your daughter [*to* VAN ROUGH], yet, allured by my fortune, it seems (with shame do I speak it) he has privately paid his addresses to me. I was drawn in to listen to him by his assuring me that the match was made by his father without his consent, and that he proposed to break with Maria, whether he married me or not. But, whatever were his intentions respecting your daughter, Sir, even to me he was false; for he has repeated the same story, with some cruel reflections upon my person, to Miss Manly.

JONATHAN. What a tarnal curse!

LETITIA. Nor is this all, Miss Manly. When he was with me this very morning, he made the same ungenerous reflections upon the weakness of your mind as he has so recently done upon the defects of my person.

JONATHAN. What a tarnal curse and damn, too!

DIMPLE. Ha! since I have lost Letitia, I believe I had as good make it up with Maria. [*Aside.*] Mr. Van Rough, at present I cannot enter into particulars; but, I believe, I can explain everything to your satisfaction in private.

VAN ROUGH. There is another matter, Mr. Van Dumpling, which I would have you explain. Pray, Sir, have Messrs. Van Cash and Co. presented you those bills for acceptance?

DIMPLE. The deuce! Has he heard of those bills! Nay, then, all's up with Maria, too; but an affair of this sort can never prejudice me among the ladies; they

---

[3]Hysterics.

will rather long to know what the dear creature possesses to make him so
agreeable. [*Aside.*] Sir, you'll hear from me. [*To* MANLY.]

MANLY. And you from me, Sir—

DIMPLE. Sir, you wear a sword—

MANLY. Yes, Sir. This sword was presented to me by that brave Gallic hero, the
Marquis De La Fayette.[4] I have drawn it in the service of my country, and in
private life, on the only occasion where a man is justified in drawing his 140
sword, in defence of a lady's honour. I have fought too many battles in the
service of my country to dread the imputation of cowardice. Death from a
man of honour would be a glory you do not merit; you shall live to bear the
insult of man and the contempt of that sex whose general smiles afforded
you all your happiness.

DIMPLE. You won't meet me, Sir? Then I'll post you for a coward.

MANLY. I'll venture that, Sir. The reputation of my life does not depend upon
the breath of a Mr. Dimple. I would have you to know, however, Sir, that I
have a cane to chastise the insolence of a scoundrel, and a sword and the
good laws of my country to protect me from the attempts of an assassin— 150

DIMPLE. Mighty well! Very fine, indeed! Ladies and gentlemen, I take my leave;
and you will please to observe in the case of my deportment, the contrast
between a gentleman who has read Chesterfield and received the polish of
Europe and an unpolished, untravelled American.

[*Exit.*]

[*Enter* MARIA.]

MARIA. Is he indeed gone?—

LETITIA. I hope, never to return.

VAN ROUGH. I am glad I heard of those bills; though it's plaguy unlucky: I
hoped to see Mary married before I died.   160

MANLY. Will you permit a gentleman, Sir, to offer himself as a suitor to your
daughter? Though a stranger to you, he is not altogether so to her, or unknown in this city. You may find a son-in-law of more fortune, but you can
never meet with one who is richer in love for her, or respect for you.

VAN ROUGH. Why, Mary, you have not let this gentleman make love to you without my leave?

MANLY. I did not say, Sir—

MARIA. Say, Sir!—I—the gentleman, to be sure, met me accidentally.

VAN ROUGH. Ha, ha, ha! Mark me, Mary; young folks think old folks to be
fools; but old folks know young folks to be fools. Why, I knew all about this 170
affair. This was only a cunning way I had to bring it about. Hark ye! I was
in the closet when you and he were at our house. [*Turns to the company.*] I
heard that little baggage say she loved her old father, and would die to
make him happy! Oh! how I loved the little baggage! And you talked very
prudently, young man. I have inquired into your character, and find you to
be a man of punctuality and mind the main chance. And so, as you love
Mary and Mary loves you, you shall have my consent immediately to be married. I'll settle my fortune on you, and go and live with you the remainder
of my life.

MANLY. Sir, I hope—   180

VAN ROUGH. Come, come, no fine speeches; mind the main chance, young man,
and you and I shall always agree.

---

[4]Marquis de Lafayette (1757–1834), fought on the American side in the Revolutionary War. He had revisited America in 1784.

LETITIA. I sincerely wish you joy [*advancing to* MARIA]; and hope your pardon for my conduct.

MARIA. I thank you for your congratulations, and hope we shall at once forget the wretch who has given us so much disquiet, and the trouble that he has occasioned.

CHARLOTTE. And I, my dear Maria,—how shall I look up to you for forgiveness? I, who, in the practice of the meanest arts, have violated the most sacred rights of friendship? I can never forgive myself, or hope charity from 190 the world; but, I confess, I have much to hope from such a brother; and I am happy that I may soon say, such a sister.

MARIA. My dear, you distress me; you have all my love.

MANLY. And mine.

CHARLOTTE. If repentance can entitle me to forgiveness, I have already much merit; for I despise the littleness of my past conduct. I now find that the heart of any worthy man cannot be gained by invidious attacks upon the rights and characters of others;—by countenancing the addresses of a thousand;—or that the finest assemblage of features, the greatest taste in dress, the genteelest address, or the most brilliant wit, cannot eventually secure a 200 coquette from contempt and ridicule.

MANLY. And I have learned that probity, virtue, honour, though they should not have received the polish of Europe, will secure to an honest American the good graces of his fair countrywomen, and, I hope, the applause of THE PUBLIC.

[*Curtain.*]

1787   *1790*

AN EMERGING AMERICAN FICTION

HUGH HENRY BRACKENRIDGE   WASHINGTON IRVING
CHARLES BROCKDEN BROWN   JAMES FENIMORE COOPER

An ironic novelist of comic picaresque adventures; a sensitive writer of lurid Gothic romances; a melancholy observer of life's poignant passing scenes; a dreamer of the archetypal American myths: such were Hugh Henry Brackenridge, Charles Brockden Brown, Washington Irving, and James Fenimore Cooper. They could not have been more disparate in temperament. In creating American fiction, they assured its continuing variety and diversity by the very measure of their remarkable differences.

HUGH HENRY BRACKENRIDGE
(1748–1816)

"Genius and virtue are independent of rank and fortune; and it is neither the opulent, nor the indigent, but the man of ability and integrity that ought to be called forth to serve his country. . . . The people are a sovereign, and greatly despotic; but in the main just." These are the opinions expressed by Hugh Henry Brackenridge in the reflective chapters of his great political satire *Modern Chivalry,* the first two volumes of which were published in 1792. Brackenridge's comic picaresque tale was an excellent antidote to the earnest, benumbing epic poems of the day, such as Timothy Dwight's *Conquest of Canaan* (1785) and Joel Barlow's *Vision of Columbus* (1787), the latter revised as *Columbiad* (1807).

All these works were responses of literary imaginations to the creation of the new, democratic American republic, all shaped by inherited traditions of form and style. Only Brackenridge was able to catch the complex reality in his Cervantean structure and Swiftean humor, both cloaking a serious purpose. *Modern Chivalry* seems constantly posing the question as to the best form of government and supplying the answer—"Democracy, alas."

This man that Vernon Louis Parrington called a "free-lance democrat," author of America's first "backcountry book," was born in Scotland and brought to America at the age of five in 1753. The family settled not in one of the major cities along the eastern seaboard but in the "Barrens" of York County, Peach Bottom Township, Pennsylvania. This frontier settlement of mainly Scotch immigrants seemed an unlikely place for a classical education, but, astonishingly, the young, farm-hardened Brackenridge mastered Greek and Latin—and developed a love of learning—from a local clergyman. At fifteen, he taught school in Gunpowder Falls, Maryland; and at twenty, he was ready to enter Princeton (then called the College of New Jersey). Fellow students were James Madison and Philip Freneau.

At the commencement exercises for awarding B.A. degrees in 1771, Brackenridge recited a poem, "The Rising Glory of America," written jointly by him and Freneau. It was a poem in the elevated, visionary style, describing America as mankind's greatest fulfillment:

> The final stage where time shall introduce
> Renowned characters, and glorious works
> Of high invention and of wond'rous art
> Which not the ravages of time shall waste
> Till he himself has run his long career.

Other poems by Brackenridge written at this same period were less elevated:

> I will declare, for all must know it,
> I long have strove to be a poet.
> Besides this sin, alas, God knows,
> I've wrote some dirty things in prose,
> Yes, I remember. T'was in Boston
> I put some tawdry rhymes a post-on
> About the Stamp Act they were written,
> How we were by Europeans bitten.

This comic streak in Brackenridge's imagination was at odds with the visionary strain from the very beginning. Out of this tension, no doubt, he was to find the perfect form—the comical, epical, satirical tradition of the picaresque tale—for his fictional masterpiece *Modern Chivalry.*

Brackenridge prepared for the ministry and in 1776 became a chaplain in Washington's Revolutionary Army. But he found over time that he could no longer believe in certain tenets of faith. In 1778, he left his chaplain post and settled in Philadelphia, which the British had just evacuated, and in 1779 established and edited a new periodical, *United States Magazine.* It ran for a year and then folded, a financial failure.

Brackenridge turned to the law and was admitted to the bar in 1780. In 1781, he settled in the frontier town of Pittsburgh, where he was to remain for the next two decades while practicing law. He served one term in the state assembly (1786–88), but was thrown out by constituents accusing him of not delivering on promises he had made. These and other experiences gave Brackenridge a first-hand knowledge of politics that would richly supply his imagination for his later writing. In 1886, Brackenridge helped found the first newspaper in Pittsburgh, and he opened the first bookstore. He was one of the founders of the Pittsburgh Academy (later, University of Pittsburgh). His first wife died in 1787 and he remarried in 1790.

When Brackenridge was passed over as his district's representative to the 1787 Constitutional Convention, he ridiculed the people's choice and wrote that, with such representatives, western Pennsylvania must "submit to stubborn fate/And be the backside of the state." He further decreased his popularity in 1787 by supporting the minority view in his area that the Constitution should be ratified. In 1798, Brackenridge worked as a leader in western Pennsylvania for Thomas Jefferson's Republican party. Jefferson's victory led to Brackenridge's appointment to the Pennsylvania supreme court in 1799, a position he filled until his death in 1816. There he became a frontier legend. Dishevelled, hair and beard unkempt, his "cravat twisted like a rope," his boots removed and his feet propped on a desk, he seemed to be playing a character out of his own fiction.

Some time in the late 1780s, Brackenridge began writing a long, satiric poem that he called "The Modern Chevalier," ridiculing a weaver named Traddle elected to an office for which he was not qualified. Some time in 1790, probably in frustration, he gave up the poem and turned to prose. Much of the rest of his life was given over to the writing of *Modern Chivalry,* published in parts in 1792, 1793, 1797, 1804, 1805, and 1815. His main character was Captain Farrago, a Don Quixote of the frontier, with his illiterate servant Teague O'Regan, an Irish Sancho Panza, Lawrence Sterne's *Tristram Shandy* and Henry Fielding's *Tom Jones* were important influences also. But Brackenridge himself supplied a dominant American voice for the narrator, and generously allowed that voice entire chapters for abundant moral reflection on the episodic action. A picaresque tale, it could be read and enjoyed in short segments. It demonstrated that citizens of the new democracy enjoyed laughing at themselves and the frequent gulf separating reality and the ideal in the working of their democratic institutions.

ADDITIONAL READING

Modern Chivalry, "Edited for the Modern Reader" by Lewis Leary (includes only Vols. I–IV; with useful introduction by editor), 1965.

Claude M. Newlin, *The Life and Writings of Hugh Henry Brackenridge*, 1932; Daniel Marder, *Hugh Henry Brackenridge*, 1967; William H. Hoffa, "The Language of Rogues and Fools in Brackenridge's *Modern Chivalry*," *Studies in the Novel*, Vol. 12 (1980), pp. 289–300.

TEXT

Modern Chivalry, ed. Claude M. Newlin, 1937; rpt. 1962. Minor changes in spelling and punctuation have been made in accordance with modern English.

from Modern Chivalry

from VOL. I

INTRODUCTION

[THE BEST MEANS TO FIX THE ENGLISH LANGUAGE]

It has been a question for some time past, what would be the best means to fix the English language. Some have thought of dictionaries, others of institutes, for that purpose. Swift,[1] I think it was, who proposed, in his letters to the Earl of Oxford, the forming an academy of learned men, in order by their observations and rules, to settle the true spelling, accentuation, and pronunciation, as well as the proper words, and the purest, most simple, and perfect phraseology of language. It has always appeared to me, that if some great master of style should arise, and without regarding sentiment, or subject, give an example of good language in his composition, which might serve as a model to future speakers and writers, it would do more to fix the orthography, choice of words, idiom of phrase, and structure of sentence, than all the dictionaries and institutes that have been ever made. For certainly, it is much more conducive to this end, to place before the eyes what is good writing, than to suggest it to the ear, which may forget in a short time all that has been said.

It is for this reason, that I have undertaken this work; and that it may attain the end the more perfectly, I shall consider language only, not in the least regarding the matter of the work; but as musicians, when they are about to give the most excellent melody, pay no attention to the words that are set to music; but take the most unmeaning phrases, such as sol, fa, la; so here, culling out the choicest flowers of diction, I shall pay no regard to the idea; for it is not in the power of human ingenuity to attain two things perfectly at once. Thus we see that they mistake greatly, who think to have a clock that can at once tell the hour of the day, the age of the moon, and the day of the week, month, or year; because the complexness of the machine hinders that perfection which the simplicity of the works and movements can alone give. For it is not in nature to have all things in one. If you are about to choose a wife, and expect beauty, you must give up family and fortune; or if you attain these, you must at least want good temper, health, or some other advantage: so to expect good language and good sense, at the same time, is absurd, and not in the compass of common nature to produce. Attempting only one thing, therefore, we may entertain the idea of hitting the point of perfection. It has been owing to an inattention to this principle, that so many fail in their attempts at good writing. A Jack of all Trades is proverbial of a bungler; and we scarcely ever find any one who excels in two parts of the same art; much

---

[1]Jonathan Swift (1667–1745), English satirist; Robert Harley, Earl of Oxford (1661–1724), English politician.

less in two arts at the same time. The smooth poet wants strength; and the orator of a good voice is destitute of logical reason and argument. How many have I heard speak, who, were they to attempt voice only, might be respectable; but undertaking, at the same time, to carry sense along with them, they utterly fail, and become contemptible. One thing at once is the best maxim that ever came into the mind of man. This might be illustrated by a thousand examples; but I shall not trouble myself with any; as it is not so much my object to convince others as to show the motives by which I myself am governed. Indeed, I could give authority which is superior to all examples; *viz.* that of the poet Horace;[2] who, speaking on this very subject of excellence in writing, says, *Quidvis,* that is, whatever you compose, let it be, *simplex duntaxit & unum:* that is, simple, and one thing only.

It will be needless for me to say any thing about the critics; for as this work is intended as a model or rule of good writing, it cannot be the subject of criticism. It is true, Homer has been criticised by a Zoilus and an Aristotle;[3] but the one contented himself with pointing out defects; the other, beauties. But Zoilus has been censured, Aristotle praised; because in a model there can be no defect; error consisting in a deviation from the truth, and faults, in an aberration from the original of beauty; so that where there are no faults there can be no food for criticism, taken in the unfavourable sense of finding fault with the productions of an author. I have no objections, therefore, to any praise that may be given to this work; but to censure or blame must appear absurd; because it cannot be doubted but that it will perfectly answer the end proposed.

Being a book without thought, or the smallest degree of sense, it will be useful to young minds, not fatiguing their understandings, and easily introducing a love of reading and study. Acquiring language at first by this means, they will afterwards gain knowledge. It will be useful especially to young men of light minds intended for the bar or pulpit. By heaping too much upon them, style and matter at once, you surfeit the stomach, and turn away the appetite from literary entertainment, to horse-racing and cock-fighting. I shall consider myself, therefore, as having performed an acceptable service, to all weak and visionary people, if I can give them something to read without the trouble of thinking. But these are collateral advantages of my work, the great object of which is, as I have said before, to give a model of perfect style in writing. If hereafter any author of supereminent abilities, should choose to give this style a body, and make it the covering to some work of sense, as you would wrap fine silk round a beautiful form, so that there may be, not only vestment, but life in the object, I have no objections; but shall be rather satisfied with having it put to so good a use.

CHAPTER I

[CAPTAIN FARRAGO AND HIS SERVANT TEAGUE]

John Farrago,[1] was a man of about fifty-three years of age, of good natural sense, and considerable reading; but in some things whimsical, owing perhaps to his greater knowledge of books than of the world; but, in some degree, also, to his having never married, being what they call an old bachelor, a characteristic of which is, usually, singularity and whim. He had the advantage of having had in early life, an academic education; but having never applied himself to any of the learned professions, he had lived the greater part of his life on a small farm, which he cultivated with servants or hired hands, as he could conveniently supply himself with either. The servant that he had at this time, was an Irishman, whose

---

[2]Roman poet (65–8 B.C.) whose *Ars Poetica* was adapted as a handbook on style in the sixteenth and seventeenth centuries.
[3]Zoilus (fourth century B.C.), Greek rhetorician and critic

known as the "scourge of Homer" because of his condemnation of Homer's works; Aristotle (384–322 B.C.), Greek philosopher who praised Homer in his *Poetics*.
[1]*Farrago* in Latin is a mixture, miscellany, or mess.

name was Teague O'Regan. I shall say nothing of the character of this man, because the very name imports what he was.[2]

A strange idea came into the head of Captain Farrago about this time; for, by the bye, I had forgot to mention that having been chosen captain of a company of militia in the neighbourhood, he had gone by the name of Captain ever since; for the rule is, once a captain, and always a captain; but, as I was observing, the idea had come in to his head, to saddle an old horse that he had, and ride about the world a little, with his man Teague at his heels, to see how things were going on here and there, and to observe human nature. For it is a mistake to suppose, that a man cannot learn man by reading him in a corner, as well as on the widest space of transaction. At any rate, it may yield amusement.

It was about a score of miles from his own house, that he fell in with what we call races. The jockeys seeing him advance, with Teague by his side, whom they took for his groom, conceived him to be some person who had brought his horse to enter for the purse. Coming up and accosting him, said they, "You seem to be for the races, Sir; and have a horse to enter." "Not at all," said the Captain; "this is but a common palfrey, and by no means remarkable for speed or bottom;[3] he is a common plough horse which I have used on my farm for several years, and can scarce go beyond a trot; much less match himself with your blooded horses that are going to take the field on this occasion."

The jockeys were of opinion, from the speech, that the horse was what they call a bite, and that under the appearance of leanness and stiffness, there was concealed some hidden quality of swiftness uncommon. For they had heard of instances, where the most knowing had been taken in by mean looking horses; so that having laid two, or more, to one, they were nevertheless bit by the bet; and the mean looking nags, proved to be horses of a more than common speed and bottom. So that there is no trusting appearances. Such was the reasoning of the jockeys. For they could have no idea, that a man could come there in so singular a manner, with a groom at his foot, unless he had some great object of making money by the adventure. Under this idea, they began to interrogate him with respect to the blood and pedigree of his horse: whether he was of the Dove, or the bay mare that took the purse; and was imported by such a one at such a time? whether his sire was Tamerlane or Bajazet?[4]

The Captain was irritated at the questions, and could not avoid answering.— "Gentlemen," said he, "it is a strange thing that you should suppose that it is of any consequence what may be the pedigree of a horse. For even in men it is of no avail. Do we not find that sages have had blockheads for their sons; and that blockheads have had sages? It is remarkable, that as estates have seldom lasted three generations, so understanding and ability have seldom been transmitted to the second. There never was a greater man, take him as an orator and philosopher, than Cicero:[5] and never was there a person who had greater opportunities than his son Marcus; and yet he proved of no account or reputation. This is an old instance, but there are a thousand others. Chesterfield[6] and his son are mentioned. It is true, Philip and Alexander[7] may be said to be exceptions: Philip of the strongest possible mind; capable of almost every thing we can conceive; the deepest policy and the most determined valour; his son Alexander not deficient in

---

[2]The generic name of the day for an ignorant Irishman (like Pat or Mike later).
[3]Staying power, endurance.
[4]The horse's names come from history: Tamerlane (1336?–1405), Mongol conqueror who invaded Turkey and captured the Sultan, Bajazet (1347–1403).
[5]Cicero (106–43 B.C.), Roman orator and statesman whose son is known only because he is Cicero's son.

[6]Philip Dormer Stanhope, Fourth Earl of Chesterfield (1694–1773), famous for his *Letters to His Son* (1774); the son, Philip (1732–1768), known for his father's letters to him.
[7]Philip II (382–336 B.C.) conquered Greece; his son, Alexander the Great (356–323 B.C.) conquered much of the world, including Persia.

the first, and before him in the last; if it is possible to be before a man than whom you can suppose nothing greater. It is possible, in modern times, that Tippo Saib may be equal to his father Hyder Ali.[8] Some talk of the two Pitts.[9] I have no idea that the son is, in any respect, equal to old Sir William. The one is a laboured artificial minister; the other spoke with the thunder, and acted with the lightning of the gods. I will venture to say, that when the present John Adamses, and Lees, and Jeffersons, and Jays, and Henrys,[10] and other great men, who figure upon the stage at this time, have gone to sleep with their fathers, it is an hundred to one if there is any of their descendents who can fill their places. Was I to lay a bet for a great man, I would sooner pick up the brat of a tinker, than go into the great houses to choose a piece of stuff for a man of genius. Even with respect to personal appearance, which is more in the power of natural production, we do not see that beauty always produces beauty; but on the contrary, the homeliest persons have oftentimes the best favoured offspring; so that there is no rule or reason in these things. With respect to this horse, therefore, it can be of no moment whether he is blooded or studed, or what he is. He is a good old horse, used to the plough, and carries my weight very well; and I have never yet made enquiry with respect to his ancestors, or affronted him so much as to cast up to him the defect of parentage. I bought him some years ago from Neil Thomas, who had him from a colt. As far as I can understand, he was of a brown mare that John M'Neis had; but of what horse I know no more than the horse himself. His gaits are good enough, as to riding a short journey of seven or eight miles, or the like; but he is rather a pacer than a trotter; and though his bottom may be good enough in carrying a bag to the mill, or going in the plough, or the sled, or the harrow, &c. yet his wind is not so good, nor his speed, as to be fit for the heats."[11]

The jockeys thought the man a fool, and gave themselves no more trouble about him.

The horses were now entered, and about to start for the purse. There was Black and all-Black, and Snip, John Duncan's Barbary Slim, and several others. The riders had been weighed, and when mounted, the word was given. It is needless to describe a race; everybody knows the circumstances of it. It is sufficient to say, that from the bets that were laid, there was much anxiety, and some passion in the minds of those concerned: so, that as two of the horses, Black and all-Black, and Slim, came out near together; there was dispute and confusion. It came to kicking and cuffing in some places. The Captain was a good deal hurt with such indecency amongst gentlemen, and advancing, addressed them in the following manner: "Gentlemen, this is an unequal and unfair proceeding. It is unbecoming modern manners, or even the ancient. For at the Olympic games of Greece, where were celebrated horse and chariot races, there was no such hurry scurry as this; and in times of chivalry itself, where men ate, drank, and slept on horseback, though there was a great deal of pell-meling, yet no such disorderly work as this. If men had a difference, they couched their lances, and ran full tilt at one another; but no such indecent expressions, as villain, scoundrel, liar, ever came out of their mouths. There was the most perfect courtesy in those days of heroism and honour; and this your horse-racing, which is a germ of the amusement of those times, ought to be conducted on the same principles of decorum, and good breeding."

[8]Haidar Ali (1722–1782), after taking power and anointing himself Maharajah in Hindu Mysore, defeated the British in 1767. His son, Tippoo Sahib (1753–1799), crowned Sultan in 1782, was defeated by the British in 1792.
[9]William Pitt (1708–1778), a great orator known as "the Great Commoner," had a distinguished career in Parliament and held various offices; his son, William Pitt (1759–1806), was considered England's greatest prime minister.
[10]John Adams, Henry Lee, Thomas Jefferson, John Jay, and Patrick Henry all played important roles in the Revolutionary War and the founding and running of the young American Republic during its first years. They were still alive when Brackenridge wrote.
[11]Preliminary rounds in a race.

As he was speaking, he was jostled by some one in the crowd, and thrown from his horse; and had it not been for Teague, who was at hand, and helped him on again, he would have suffered damage. As it was, he received a contusion in his head, of which he complained much; and having left the race-ground, and coming to a small cottage, he stopped a little, to alight and dress the wound. An old woman who was there, thought they ought to take a little of his water, and see how it was with him; but the Captain having no faith in telling disorders by the urine, thought proper to send for a surgeon who was hard by, to examine the bruise, and apply bandages. The surgeon attended, and examining the part, pronounced it a contusion of the cerebrum. But as there appeared but little laceration, and no fracture, simple or compound, the pia mater[12] could not be injured; nor even could there be more than a slight impression on the dura mater.[13] So that trepaning did not at all appear necessary. A most fortunate circumstance; for a wound in the head, is of all places the most dangerous; because there can be no amputation to save life. There being but one head to a man, and that being the residence of the five senses, it is impossible to live without it. Nevertheless, as the present case was highly dangerous, as it might lead to a subsultus tendinum, or lock-jaw, it was necessary to apply cataplasms[14] in order to reduce inflammation, and bring about a sanative disposition of the parts. Perhaps it might not be amiss, to take an anodyne[15] as a refrigerant. Many patients had been lost by the ignorance of empirics prescribing bracers; whereas, in the first stage of a contusion, relaxing and antifebrile medicines are proper. A little phlebotomy[16] was no doubt necessary, to prevent the bursting of the blood vessels.

The Captain hearing so many hard words, and bad accounts of this case, was much alarmed. Nevertheless he did not think it could be absolutely so dangerous. For it seemed to him that he was not sick at heart, or under any mortal pain. The surgeon observed, that in this case he could not himself be a judge. For the very part was affected by which he was to judge, *viz.* the head; that it was no uncommon thing for men in the extremest cases to imagine themselves out of danger; whereas in reality, they were in the greatest possible: that notwithstanding the symptoms were mild, yet from the contusion, a mortification might ensue. Hypocrates,[17] who might be styled an elementary physician, and has a treatise on this very subject, is of opinion, that the most dangerous symptom is a topical insensibility; but among the moderns, Sydenham[18] considers it in another point of view, and thinks that where there is no pain, there is as great reason to suppose that there is no hurt, as that there is a mortal one. Be this as it may, antiseptic medicines might be very proper.

The Captain hearing so much jargon, and conscious to himself that he was by no means in so bad a state as this son of Escalapius[19] would represent, broke out into some passion. "It is," said he, "the craft of your profession to make the case worse than it is, in order to increase the perquisites. But if there is any faith in you, make the same demand, and let me know your real judgment." The surgeon was irritated with his distrust, and took it into his head to fix some apprehension in the mind of his patient, if possible, that his case was not without danger. Looking steadfastly at him for some time, and feeling his pulse, "there is," said he, "an evident delirium approaching. This argues an affection of the brain, but it will be necessary, after some soporiferous draughts, to put the patient to sleep." Said the Captain, "If you will give me about a pint of whiskey and water, I will try to go to

---

[12]*Pia mater,* inner membrane enveloping brain and spinal cord; thus, one's wits.
[13]Outer membrane of the brain.
[14]Poultices.
[15]Pain reducer.
[16]Blood-letting.

[17]Hippocrates (460?–377 B.C.), Greek physician who devised a code of ethics now administered as an oath to those entering medicine.
[18]Thomas Sydenham (1624–1689), brilliant physician and scientist who was known as "the English Hippocrates."
[19]Asclepius, Greek god of healing and medicine.

sleep myself." "A deleterious mixture, in this case," said the surgeon, "cannot be proper; especially a distillation of that quality." The Captain would hear no more; but requesting the man of the cabin, to let him have the spirits proposed, drank a pint or two of grog, and having bound up his head with a handkerchief, went to bed.

CHAPTER II

CONTAINING SOME GENERAL REFLECTIONS

The first reflection that arises, is, the good sense of the Captain; who was unwilling to impose his horse for a racer; not being qualified for the course. Because, as an old lean beast, attempting a trot, he was respectable enough; but going out of his nature and affecting speed, he would have been contemptible. The great secret of preserving respect, is the cultivating and showing to the best advantage the powers that we possess, and the not going beyond them. Every thing in its element is good, and in their proper sphere all natures and capacities are excellent. This thought might be turned into a thousand different shapes, and clothed with various expressions; but after all, it comes to the old proverb at last, *Ne sutor ultra crepidam,* Let the cobler stick to his last; a sentiment we are about more to illustrate in the sequel of this work.

The second reflection that arises, is, the simplicity of the Captain; who was so unacquainted with the world, as to imagine that jockeys and men of the turf could be composed by reason and good sense; whereas there are no people who are by education of a less philosophic turn of mind. The company of horses is by no means favourable to good taste and genius. The rubbing and currying them, but little enlarges the faculties, or improves the mind; and even riding, by which a man is carried swiftly through the air, though it contributes to health, yet stores the mind with few or no ideas; and as men naturally consimilate with[1] their company, so it is observable that your jockeys are a class of people not far removed from the sagacity of a good horse. Hence most probably the fable of the centaur, among the ancients; by which they held out the moral of the jockey and the horse being one beast.

A third reflection is, that which he expressed; *viz.* the professional art of the surgeon to make the most of the case, and the technical terms used by him. I have to declare, that it is with no attempt at wit, that the terms are set down, or the art of the surgeon hinted at; because it is so common place a thing to ridicule the peculiarities of a profession, that it savours of mean parts to indulge it. For a man of real genius will never walk in the beaten track, because his object is what is new and uncommon. This surgeon does not appear to have been a man of very great ability; but the Captain was certainly wrong in declining his prescriptions; for the maxim is, *Unicuique in arte, sua perito, credendum est;* every one is to be trusted in his profession.

CHAPTER III

[THE ELECTION]

The Captain rising early next morning, and setting out on his way, had now arrived at a place where a number of people were convened, for the purpose of electing persons to represent them in the legislature of the state. There was a weaver who was a candidate for this appointment, and seemed to have a good deal of interest among the people. But another, who was a man of education, was his competitor. Relying on some talent of speaking which he thought he possessed, he addressed the multitude.

---

[1]Become like.

Said he, "Fellow citizens, I pretend not to any great abilities; but am conscious to myself that I have the best good will to serve you. But it is very astonishing to me, that this weaver should conceive himself qualified for the trust. For though my acquirements are not great, yet his are still less. The mechanical business which he pursues, must necessarily take up so much of his time, that he cannot apply himself to political studies. I should therefore think it would be more answerable to your dignity, and conducive to your interest, to be represented by a man at least of some letters, than by an illiterate handicraftsman like this. It will be more honourable for himself, to remain at his loom and knot threads, than to come forward in a legislative capacity: because, in the one case, he is in the sphere where God and nature has placed him; in the other, he is like a fish out of water, and must struggle for breath in a new element.

"Is it possible he can understand the affairs of government, whose mind has been concentered to the small object of weaving webs; to the price by the yard, the grist of the thread, and such like matters as concern a manufacturer of cloths? The feet of him who weaves, are more occupied than the head, or at least as much; and therefore the whole man must be, at least, but in half accustomed to exercise his mental powers. For these reasons, all other things set aside, the chance is in my favour, with respect to information. However, you will decide, and give your suffrages to him or to me, as you shall judge expedient."

The Captain hearing these observations, and looking at the weaver, could not help advancing, and undertaking to subjoin something in support of what had been just said. Said he, "I have no prejudice against a weaver more than another man. Nor do I know any harm in the trade; save that from the sedentary life in a damp place, there is usually a paleness of the countenance: but this is a physical, not a moral evil. Such usually occupy subterranean apartments; not for the purpose, like Demosthenes,[1] of shaving their heads, and writing over eight times the history of Thucydides,[2] and perfecting a style of oratory; but rather to keep the thread moist; or because this is considered but as an inglorious sort of trade, and is frequently thrust away into cellars, and damp outhouses, which are not occupied for a better use.

"But to rise from the cellar to the senate house, would be an unnatural hoist. To come from counting threads, and adjusting them to the splits of a reed, to regulate the finances of a government, would be preposterous; there being no congruity in the case. There is no analogy between knotting threads and framing laws. It would be a reversion of the order of things. Not that a manufacturer of linen or woolen, or other stuff, is an inferior character, but a different one, from that which ought to be employed in affairs of state. It is unnecessary to enlarge on this subject; for you must all be convinced of the truth and propriety of what I say. But if you will give me leave to take the manufacturer aside a little, I think I can explain to him my ideas on the subject; and very probably prevail with him to withdraw his pretensions." The people seeming to acquiesce, and beckoning to the weaver, they drew aside, and the Captain addressed him in the following words: "Mr. Traddle,"[3] said he, for that was the name of the manufacturer, "I have not the smallest idea of wounding your sensibility; but it would seem to me, it would be more your interest to pursue your occupation, than to launch out into that of which you have no knowledge. When you go to the senate house, the application to you will not be to warp a web;[4] but to make laws for the commonwealth. Now, suppose that the making these laws, requires a knowledge of commerce, or of the

---

[1]Demosthenes (384?–322 B.C.), great Greek orator.
[2]Thucydides (c. 460–400 B.C.), noted Greek historian of Peloponnesian War.
[3]Pun on treadle, the lower part of the loom operated by foot.

[4]The warp runs lengthwise, and with the vertical woof makes a web.

interests of agriculture, or those principles upon which the different manufactures depend, what service could you render. It is possible you might think justly enough; but could you speak? You are not in the habit of public speaking. You are not furnished with those common place ideas, with which even very ignorant men can pass for knowing something. There is nothing makes a man so ridiculous as to attempt what is above his sphere. You are no tumbler for instance; yet should you give out that you could vault upon a man's back; or turn head over heels, like the wheels of a cart; the stiffness of your joints would encumber you; and you would fall upon your backside to the ground. Such a squash as that would do you damage. The getting up to ride on the state is an unsafe thing to those who are not accustomed to such horsemanship. It is a disagreeable thing for a man to be laughed at, and there is no way of keeping one's self from it but by avoiding all affectation."

While they were thus discoursing, a bustle had taken place among the crowd. Teague hearing so much about elections, and serving the government, took it into his head, that he could be a legislator himself. The thing was not displeasing to the people, who seemed to favour his pretensions; owing, in some degree, to there being several of his countrymen among the crowd; but more especially to the fluctuation of the popular mind, and a disposition to what is new and ignoble. For though the weaver was not the most elevated object of choice, yet he was still preferable to this tatter-demalion,[5] who was but a menial servant, and had so much of what is called the brogue on his tongue, as to fall far short of an elegant speaker.

The Captain coming up, and finding what was on the carpet,[6] was greatly chagrined at not having been able to give the multitude a better idea of the importance of a legislative trust; alarmed also, from an apprehension of the loss of his servant. Under these impressions he resumed his address to the multitude. Said he, "This is making the matter still worse, gentlemen: this servant of mine is but a bog-trotter;[7] who can scarcely speak the dialect in which your laws ought to be written; but certainly has never read a single treatise on any political subject; for the truth is, he cannot read at all. The young people of the lower class, in Ireland, have seldom the advantage of a good education; especially the descendants of the ancient Irish, who have most of them a great assurance of countenance, but little information, or literature. This young man, whose family name is O'Regan, has been my servant for several years. And, except a too great fondness for women, which now and then brings him into scrapes, he has demeaned himself in a manner tolerable enough. But he is totally ignorant of the great principles of legislation; and more especially, the particular interests of the government. A free government is a noble possession to a people: and this freedom consists in an equal right to make laws, and to have the benefit of the laws when made. Though doubtless, in such a government, the lowest citizen may become chief magistrate; yet it is sufficient to possess the right; not absolutely necessary to exercise it. Or even if you should think proper, now and then, to show your privilege, and exert, in a signal manner, the democratic prerogative, yet is it not descending too low to filch away from me a hireling, which I cannot well spare, to serve your purpose. You are surely carrying the matter too far, in thinking to make a senator of this hostler;[8] to take him away from an employment to which he has been bred, and put him to another, to which he has served no apprenticeship: to set those hands which have been lately employed in currying my horse, to the drafting bills, and preparing business for the house."

---

[5]Person in ragged clothes.
[6]Under consideration.
[7]Contemptuous term for Irishman (one who trots among the bogs).
[8]Servant.

The people were tenacious of their choice, and insisted on giving Teague their suffrages; and by the frown upon their brows, seemed to indicate resentment at what has been said; as indirectly charging them with want of judgment; or calling in question their privilege to do what they thought proper. "It is a very strange thing," said one of them, who was a speaker for the rest, "that after having conquered Burgoyne and Cornwallis,[9] and got a government of our own, we cannot put in it whom we please. This young man may be your servant, or another man's servant; but if we chuse to make him a delegate, what is that to you. He may not be yet skilled in the matter, but there is a good day a-coming. We will empower him; and it is better to trust a plain man like him, than one of your high flyers, that will make laws to suit their own purposes."

Said the Captain, "I had much rather you would send the weaver, though I thought that improper, than to invade my household, and thus detract from me the very person that I have about me to brush my boots, and clean my spurs." The prolocutor[10] of the people gave him to understand that his surmises were useless, for the people had determined on the choice, and Teague they would have, for a representative.

Finding it answered no end to expostulate with the multitude, he requested to speak a word with Teague by himself. Stepping aside, he said to him, composing his voice, and addressing him in a soft manner: "Teague, you are quite wrong in this matter they have put into your head. Do you know what it is to be a member of a deliberate body? What qualifications are necessary? Do you understand any thing of geography? If a question should be, to make a law to dig a canal in some part of the state, can you describe the bearing of the mountains, and the course of the rivers? Or if commerce is to be pushed to some new quarter, by the force of regulations, are you competent to decide in such a case? There will be questions of law, and astronomy on the carpet. How you must gape and stare like a fool, when you come to be asked your opinion on these subjects? Are you acquainted with the abstract principles of finance; with the funding public securities; the ways and means of raising the revenue; providing for the discharge of the public debts, and all other things which respect the economy of the government? Even if you had knowledge, have you a facility of speaking. I would suppose you would have too much pride to go to the house just to say, Ay, or No. This is not the fault of your nature, but of your education; having been accustomed to dig turf in your early years, rather than instructing yourself in the classics, or common school books.

"When a man becomes a member of a public body, he is like a racoon, or other beast that climbs up the fork of a tree; the boys pushing at him with pitch-forks, or throwing stones, or shooting at him with an arrow, the dogs barking in the mean time. One will find fault with your not speaking; another with your speaking, if you speak at all. They will have you in the newspapers, and ridicule you as a perfect beast. There is what they call the caricatura; that is, representing you with a dog's head, or a cat's claw. As you have a red head, they will very probably make a fox of you, or a sorrel horse, or a brindled cow. It is the devil in hell to be exposed to the squibs and crackers[11] of the gazette wits and publications. You know no more about these matters than a goose; and yet you would undertake rashly, without advice, to enter on the office; nay, contrary to advice. For I would not for a thousand guineas,[12] though I have not the half of it to spare, that the breed of the O'Regans should come to this; bringing on them a worse stain than stealing sheep; to which they are addicted. You have nothing but your character, Teague, in a new country to depend upon. Let it never be said, that you quitted

---

[9]John Burgoyne (1722–1792) and Charles Cornwallis (1738–1805) were British Generals defeated by American forces in the Revolutionary War.

[10]Spokesman.

[11]Verbal jabs and insults.

[12]British gold coins.

an honest livelihood, the taking care of my horse, to follow the new fangled whims of the times, and to be a statesman."

Teague was moved chiefly with the last part of the address, and consented to give up the object.

The Captain, glad of this, took him back to the people, and announced his disposition to decline the honour which they had intended him.

Teague acknowledged that he had changed his mind, and was willing to remain in a private station.

The people did not seem well pleased with the Captain; but as nothing more could be said about the matter, they turned their attention to the weaver, and gave him their suffrages.

CHAPTER IV

[Capt. Farrago Visits a Conjuror]

Captain Farrago leaving this place, proceeded on his way; and at the distance of a mile or two, met a man with a bridle in his hand; who had lost a horse, and had been at a conjurer's to make enquiry, and recover his property.

It struck the mind of the Captain to go to this conjuring person, and make a demand of him, what was the cause that the multitude were so disposed to elevate the low to the highest station. He had rode but about a mile, when the habitation of the conjurer, by the direction and description of the man who had lost the horse had given, began to be in view. Coming up to the door, and enquiring if that was not where conjurer Kolt lived, they were answered Yes. Accordingly alighting, and entering the domicile, all those things took place which usually happen, or are described in cases of this nature, *viz.* there was the conjurer's assistant, who gave the Captain to understand that master had withdrawn a little, but would be in shortly.

In the mean time, the assistant endeavoured to draw from him some account of the occasion of his journey; which the other readily communicated; and the conjurer, who was listening through a crack in the partition, overheard. Finding it was not a horse or a cow, or a piece of linen that was lost, but an abstract question of political philosophy which was to be put, he came from his lurking place, and entered, as if not knowing that any person had been waiting for him.

After mutual salutations, the Captain gave him to understand the object which he had in view by calling on him.

Said the conjurer, "This lies not at all in my way. If it had been a dozen of spoons, or a stolen watch, that you had to look for, I could very readily, by the assistance of my art, have assisted you in the recovery; but as to this matter of man's imaginations and attachments in political affairs, I have no more understanding than another man."

"It is very strange," said the Captain, "that you who can tell by what means a thing is stolen, and the place where it is deposited, though at a thousand miles distance, should know so little of what is going on in the breast of man, as not to be able to develop his secret thoughts, and the motives of his actions."

"It is not of our business," said the other; "but should we undertake it, I do not see that it would be very difficult to explain all that puzzles you at present. There is no need of a conjurer to tell why it is that the common people are more disposed to trust one of their own class, than those who may affect to be superior. Besides, there is a certain pride in man, which leads him to elevate the low, and pull down the high. There is a kind of creating power exerted in making a senator of an unqualified person; which when the author has done, he exults over the work, and like the Creator himself when he made the world, sees that it is very good. Moreover, there is in every government a patrician class, against whom the spirit of the multitude naturally militates: And hence a perpetual war; the aristo-crats endeavouring to detrude[1] the people, and the people contending to obtrude[2] themselves. And it is right it should be so; for by this fermentation, the spirit of democracy is kept alive."

The Captain, thanking him for his information, asked him what was to pay; at the same time pulling out half a crown from a green silk purse which he had in his breeches pocket. The conjurer gave him to understand, that as the solution of these difficulties was not within his province, he took nothing for it. The Captain expressing his sense of his disinterested service, bade him adieu.

CHAPTER V
CONTAINING REFLECTIONS [ON DEMOCRACY]

A democracy is beyond all question the freest government: because under this, every man is equally protected by the laws, and has equally a voice in making them. But I do not say an equal voice; because some men have stronger lungs than others, and can express more forcibly their opinions of public affairs. Oth-ers, though they may not speak very loud, yet have a faculty of saying more in a short time; and even in the case of others, who speak little or none at all, yet what they do say containing good sense, comes with greater weight; so that all things considered, every citizen, has not, in this sense of the word, an equal voice. But the right being equal, what great harm if it is unequally exercised? is it necessary that every man should become a statesman? No more than that every man should become a poet or a painter. The sciences, are open to all; but let him only who has taste and genius pursue them. If any man covets the office of a bishop, says St. Paul, he covets a good work. But again, he adds this caution, Ordain not a novice, lest being lifted up with pride, he falls into the condemnation of the devil.[1] It is indeed making a devil of a man to lift him up to a state to which he is not suited. A ditcher is a respectable character, with his over-alls on, and a spade in his hand; but put the same man to those offices which require the head whereas he has been accustomed to impress with his foot, and there appears a contrast between the in-dividual and the occupation.

There are individuals in society, who prefer honour to wealth; or cultivate po-litical studies as a branch of literary pursuits; and offer themselves to serve public bodies, in order to have an opportunity of discovering their knowledge, and exer-cising their judgment. It must be chagrining to these, and hurtful to the public, to see those who have no talent this way, and ought to have no taste, preposterously obtrude themselves upon the government. It is the same as if a brick-layer should usurp the office of a tailor, and come with his square and perpendicular, to take the measure of a pair of breeches.

It is proper that those who cultivate oratory, should go to the house of orators. But for an Ay and No man to be ambitious of that place, is to sacrifice his credit to his vanity.

I would not mean to insinuate that legislators are to be selected from the more wealthy of the citizens, yet a man's circumstances ought to be such as afford him leisure for study and reflection. There is often wealth without taste or talent. I have no idea, that because a man lives in a great house and has a cluster of bricks or stones about his backside, that he is therefore fit for a legislator. There is so much pride and arrogance with those who consider themselves the first in a gov-ernment, that it deserves to be checked by the populace, and the evil most usually commences on this side. Men associate with their own persons, the adventitious

---

[1]Force down.
[2]Thrust forward.
[1]1 Timothy 3:1, 6: "This is a true saying. If a man desire the office of a bishop, he desireth a good work"; "Not a novice, lest being lifted up with pride he fall into the con-demnation of the devil."

circumstances of birth and fortune: So that a fellow blowing with fat and reple-
tion, conceives himself superior to the poor lean man, that lodges in an inferior
mansion. But as in all cases, so in this, there is a medium. Genius and virtue are
independent of rank and fortune; and it is neither the opulent, nor the indigent,
but the man of ability and integrity that ought to be called forth to serve his country: and while, on the one hand, the aristocratic part of the government, arrogates
a right to represent; on the other hand, the democratic contends the point; and
from this conjunction and opposition of forces, there is produced a compound
resolution, which carries the object in an intermediate direction. When we see
therefore, a Teague O'Regan lifted up, the philosopher will reflect, that it is to
balance some purse-proud fellow, equally as ignorant, that comes down from the
sphere of aristocratic interest.

But every man ought to consider for himself, whether it is his use to be this
draw-back, on either side. For as when good liquor is to be distilled, you throw in
some material useless in itself to correct the effervescence of the spirit; so it may
be his part to act as a sedative. For though we commend the effect, yet still the
material retains but its original value.

But as the nature of things is such, let no man who means well to the commonwealth, and offers to serve it, be hurt in his mind when some one of meaner talents is preferred. The people are a sovereign, and greatly despotic; but, in the
main, just.

I have a great mind, in order to elevate the composition, to make quotations
from the Greek and Roman history. And I am conscious to myself, that I have
read the writers on the government of Italy and Greece, in ancient, as well as in
modern times. But I have drawn a great deal more from reflection on the nature
of things, than from all the writings I have ever read. Nay, the history of the election, which I have just given, will afford a better lesson to the American mind,
than all that is to be found in other examples. We have seen here, a weaver a favoured candidate, and in the next instance, a bog-trotter superseding him. Now it
may be said, that this is fiction; but fiction, or no fiction, the nature of the thing
will make it a reality. But I return to the adventures of the Captain, whom I have
upon my hands; and who, as far as I can yet discover, is a good honest man; and
means what is benevolent and useful; though his ideas may not comport with the
ordinary manner of thinking, in every particular.

1790?   *1792*

CHARLES BROCKDEN BROWN
(1771–1810)

"A friend of mine lost his wife, after living ten years with her. Happily he
had no children, or rather perhaps, this was a want to be regretted. Filial regards might have precluded the consequences that took place. He shut himself up in that which had been their common chamber. He hung her picture
against the wall. He disposed various trinkets and parts of dress which had
belonged to her, in places where they continually solicited his notice. His
whole time was employed in ruminating on his loss. He never left the apartment longer than ten minutes at a time. He denied himself to all visitants. His
body was emaciated by grief, and this state of things terminated, at the end of
three years, in his death."

Brown included this vignette in a journalistic series he wrote for *The Weekly Magazine* in early 1798. It appears in an essay playfully considering love as a disease. In brief, it exemplifies the nature of Brown's imagination—its romantic inclination, its tendency to seize on the melancholy and morbid, its fascination with psychologically obsessive and bizarre behavior. This short-short story also makes clear why Brown is so often viewed as a forerunner of Edgar Allan Poe.

Brown has repeatedly been labelled the first writer in America to make authorship a profession. But it must hastily be added that it did not pay very well. Brown was born the son of a Philadelphia merchant, descendent of Pennsylvania Quakers. As a boy, he was prone to illness and, perhaps as a result, developed a voracious appetite for books. Early fascinated with the world of literature, and probably inspired by such poems as Joel Barlow's *The Vision of Columbus,* he made plans to write three epics based on Columbus's discovery of America, Pizarro's capture of Peru, and Cortez's conquest of Mexico.

Brown's family preferred him to prepare for law, and he was apprenticed to a Philadelphia lawyer. As he pursued his legal studies, he and his friends formed the Belles Lettres Club, a discussion group with strong interests in literature. By 1793, Brown abandoned law entirely to devote himself to literary pursuits. One of his fellow club members was Elihu Hubbard Smith, who had come from New York to Philadelphia to study medicine. Smith introduced Brown into the literary circles of New York, where Brown settled in 1796. He joined the Friendly Club, meeting William Dunlap, a dramatist of note who was later to become Brown's biographer.

Brown's omnivorous reading brought him under the spell of William Godwin's *Caleb Williams* (1794) and Godwin's wife Mary Wollstonecraft's *A Vindication of the Rights of Woman* (1792). Brown's Quaker background and romantic tendencies would have made him receptive to the radical doctrines of these two writers. Although Brown began to publish in the magazines as early as 1789, his first book to appear was *Alcuin: A Dialogue* (1798), later called *The Rights of Women* when it was published in *Weekly Magazine.*

It is a fiction in the form of a dialogue between a poor schoolmaster and a widow who holds open-house for the intellectual community. The drama lies in the venturesomeness of the ideas on women's oppression and rights in "conversation, careless, and unfettered, that is sometimes abrupt and sententious, sometimes fugitive and brilliant, and sometimes copious and declamatory." The fiction exists for the ideas, but the ideas are in dramatic play with each other and are serious and moving. Only half of the manuscript appeared in 1798. Probably because of its boldness in references to marriage, sexual intercourse, and divorce, the second half remained unpublished until after Brown's death in 1810. William Dunlap included it in his biography of Brown in 1815 (and it appears in part below).

From 1798 through 1801, Brown published novels with astonishing rapidity: *Wieland* (1798), *Ormond* (1799), *Edgar Huntly* (1799), *Arthur Mervyn* (1799–1800), *Clara Howard* (1801), and *Jane Talbot* (1801). Brown's novels are Gothic romances, full of incidents of violence and horror, with all the seeming supernatural elements rationally explained, and with characters obsessed or driven by strangely twisted psychological compulsions.

Wieland; or, The Transformation, in which a character is impelled by voices to murder his wife and children, is based on an actual event in which a religious fanatic killed his family in religious sacrifice. The plot is complicated by a sinister character practicing the then-new art of ventriloquism. In *Arthur Mervyn; or, Memoirs of the Year 1793,* Brown drew elements of his plot from terrible incidents he experienced during the plague of yellow fever in Philadelphia in 1793. Another epidemic in New York had killed his friend Elihu Hubbard Smith and had sent Brown himself to bed with the disease. In *Edgar Huntly; or, Memoirs of a Sleep-Walker,* Brown introduced the frontier and Indians into his plot, but they were not convincingly portrayed.

Throughout all his novels, Brown was, in accord with his beliefs, in process of exploring ideas. He held that all serious fiction had such responsibility: "The value of such works lies without doubt in their moral tendency. . . . The world is governed, not by the simpleton, but by the man of soaring passions and intellectual energy. By the display of such only can we hope to enchain the attention and ravish the souls of those who study and reflect. . . . A contexture of facts capable of suspending the faculties of every soul in curiosity, may be joined with depth of views into human nature and all the subtleties of reasoning."

After the concentrated period of remarkable creativity from 1798 to 1801, Brown never returned to the writing of novels. He earned very little from his fiction. In 1801, he went back to Philadelphia and became a partner with his brothers in a mercantile firm, but it went out of business in 1806. His marriage in 1804 and the subsequent birth of four children impelled him to undertake miscellaneous journalistic assignments to support his family. In 1810, at the age of thirty-nine, he died of tuberculosis.

For Brown, writing, whether fiction or journalism, was a necessity of life. He once remarked to a friend: "This employment was just as necessary to my mind as sustenance to my frame. It was synonymous with a vital function. . . . Had I been exiled in Kamschatka, I must have written as a mental necessity, and in it I have still found my highest enjoyment."

ADDITIONAL READING

Charles Brockden Brown's Novels, 6 vols., 1887; rpt. 1963, 1968; *Charles Brockden Brown: The Rhapsodist and Other Collected Writings,* ed. Harry R. Warfel, 1943; *The Novels and Related Works of Charles Brockden Brown* (Bicentennial Edition), ed. Sydney J. Krause, S.W. Reid, and Alexander Cowie, 1977– .

William Dunlap, *The Life of Charles Brockden Brown,* 2 vols., 1815; Harry R. Warfel, *Charles Brockden Brown: American Gothic Novelist,* 1949; David Lee Clark, *Charles Brockden Brown: Pioneer Voice of America,* 1952; Donald A. Ringe, *Charles Brockden Brown,* 1966; Patricia L. Parker, *Charles Brockden Brown: A Reference Guide,* 1980; Norman S. Grabo, *The Coincidental Art of Charles Brockden Brown,* 1981; Alan Axelrod, *Charles Brockden Brown, An American Tale,* 1983; Jane Tompkins, *Sensational Designs: The Cultural Work of American Fiction, 1790–1860,* 1985.

TEXT

Alcuin: A Dialogue, Parts III and IV, in William Dunlap's *The Life of Charles Brockden Brown,* 1815.

from Alcuin: A Dialogue
Parts III and IV

[THE PARADISE OF WOMEN]

In *Alcuin: A Dialogue*,[1] Parts I and II, Alcuin, a poor school teacher, is invited to one of Mrs. Carter's "evenings" in which intellectuals of advanced opinions gather to exchange conversation and views. Mrs. Carter is widowed and now lives as housekeeper and hostess with her brother, a "man of letters." In talking with Mrs. Carter,[2] Alcuin discovers that she has some strong opinions about the exclusion of women from the professions and politics, and about the inequality of women with men in marriage. In Parts III and IV, excerpted here, Alcuin returns a week later to Mrs. Carter's salon to continue their conversation about the oppression of women. In the meantime, he has visited the astonishing Paradise of Women.

ॐ

[MISTAKES AND CONJECTURES DELAY THE SUBSTANCE]

A week elapsed and I repeated my visit to Mrs. Carter. She greeted me in a friendly manner. "I have often," said she, "since I saw you, reflected on the subject of our former conversation. I have meditated more deeply than common, and I believe to more advantage. The hints that you gave me I have found useful guides."

"And I," said I, "have travelled farther than common, incited by a laudable desire of knowledge."

"Travelled?"

"Yes, I have visited since I saw you, the paradise of women; and I assure you have longed for an opportunity to communicate the information that I have collected."

"Well: you now enjoy the opportunity; you have engaged it every day in the week. Whenever you had thought proper to come, I could have promised you a welcome."

"I thank you. I should have claimed your welcome sooner, but only returned this evening."

"Returned! Whence, I pry'thee?"

"From the journey that I spoke of. Have I not told you that I have visited the paradise of women? The region, indeed is far distant, but a twinkling is sufficient for the longest of my journeys."

"You are somewhat mysterious, and mystery is one of the many things that abound in the world, for which I have an hearty aversion."

[Alcuin chatters on in what seem like endless descriptions and meaningless elaborations. Impatient to hear the details about this Paradise of Women, Mrs. Carter interrupts him.]

"Come, come," interrupted the lady, "this perhaps, may be poetry, but though pleasing it had better be dispensed with. I give you leave to pass over these incidents in silence: I desire merely to obtain the sum of your information, disembarrassed from details of the mode in which you acquired it, and of the mistakes and conjectures to which your ignorance subjected you."

---

[1] The original Alcuin (735–804), to whom Brown may be alluding, was a British writer and scholar who assisted Charlemagne in intellectual renewal and revival of learning at the court of the Franks.

[2] Some critics have suggested that Brown may have wanted to evoke someone like Elizabeth Carter (1717–1806), British poet and translator (*Epictetus*, 1758), and a friend of Dr. Johnson.

[No Distinctions of Dress]

"Well," said I, "these restraints it must be owned are a little hard, but since you are pleased to impose them I must conform to your pleasure. After my curiosity was sufficiently gratified by what was to be seen, I retired with my guide to his apartment. It was situated on a terrace which overlooked a mixed scene of groves and edifices, which the light of the moon that had now ascended the meridian, had rendered distinctly visible. After considerable discourse, in which satisfactory answers had been made to all the inquiries which I had thought proper to make, I ventured to ask, 'I pray thee my good friend, what is the condition of the female sex among you? In this evening's excursion I have met with those, whose faces and voices seemed to bespeak them women, though as far as I could discover they were distinguished by no peculiarities of manners or dress. In those assemblies to which you conducted me, I did not fail to observe that whatever was the business of the hour, both sexes seemed equally engaged in it. Was the spectacle theatrical? The stage was occupied sometimes by men, sometimes by women, and sometimes by a company of each. The tenor of the drama seemed to be followed as implicitly as if custom had enacted no laws upon this subject. Their voices were mingled in the choruses: I admired the order in which the spectators were arranged. Women were, to a certain degree, associated with women, and men with men; but it seemed as if magnificence and symmetry had been consulted, rather than a scrupulous decorum. Here no distinction in dress was observable, but I suppose the occasion dictated it. Was science or poetry, or art, the topic of discussion? The two sexes mingled their inquiries and opinions. The debate was managed with ardour and freedom, and all present were admitted to a share in the controversy, without particular exceptions or compliances of any sort. Were shadows and recesses sought by the studious few? As far as their faces were distinguishable, meditation had selected her votaries indiscriminately. I am not unaccustomed to some degree of this equality among my own countrymen, but it appears to be far more absolute and general among you; pray what are your customs and institutions on this head?'

"'Perhaps,' replied my friend, 'I do not see whither your question tends. What are our customs respecting women? You are doubtless apprised of the difference that subsists between the sexes. That physical constitution which entitles some of us to the appellation of male, and others to that of female you must know. You know its consequences. With these our customs and institutions have no concern; they result from the order of nature, which it is our business merely to investigate. I suppose there are physiologists or anatomists in your country. To them it belongs to explain this circumstance of animal existence.

"'The universe consists of individuals. They are perishable. Provision has been made that the place of those that perish should be supplied by new generations. The means by which this end is accomplished, are the same through every tribe of animals. Between contemporary beings the distinction of sex maintains; but the end of this distinction is that since each individual must perish, there may be a continual succession of individuals. If you seek to know more than this, I must refer you to books which contain the speculations of the anatomist, or to the hall where he publicly communicates his doctrines.'

"'It is evident,' answered I, 'that I have not made myself understood. I did not inquire into the structure of the human body, but into these moral or political maxims which are founded on the difference in this structure between the sexes.'

"'Need I repeat,' said my friend, 'what I have told you of the principles by which we are governed. I am aware that there are nations of men universally infected by error, or who at least entertain opinions different from ours. It is hard to trace all the effects of a particular belief, which chances to be current among a whole people. I have entered into a pretty copious explanation of the rules to which we conform in our intercourse with each other, but still perhaps have been deficient.'

"'No, I cannot complain of your brevity; perhaps my doubts would be solved by reflecting attentively on the information that I have already received. For that, leisure is requisite; meanwhile I cannot but confess my surprise that I find among you none of those exterior differences by which the sexes are distinguished by all other nations.'

"'Give me a specimen if you please, of those differences with which you have been familiar.'

"'One of them,' said I, 'is dress. Each sex has a garb peculiar to itself. The men and women of our country are more different from each other in this respect, than the natives of remotest countries.'

"'That is strange,' said my friend, 'why is it so?'

"'I know not. Each one dresses as custom prescribes. He has no other criterion. If he selects his garb because it is beautiful or convenient, it is beautiful and commodious in his eyes merely because it is customary.'

"'But wherefore does custom prescribe a different dress to each sex?'

"'I confess I cannot tell, but most certainly it is so. I must likewise acknowledge that nothing in your manners more excites my surprise than your uniformity in this particular.'

"'Why should it be inexplicable? For what end do we dress? Is it for the sake of ornament? Is it in compliance with our perceptions of the beautiful? These perceptions cannot be supposed to be the same in all. But since the standard of beauty whatever it be, must be one and the same: since our notions on this head are considerably affected by custom and example, and since all have nearly the same opportunities and materials of judgment, if beauty only were regarded, the differences among us would be trivial. Differences, perhaps, there would be. The garb of one being would, in some degree, however small, vary from that of another. But what causes there are that should make all women agree in their preference of one dress, and all men in that of another, is utterly incomprehensible; no less than that the difference resulting from this choice should be essential and conspicuous.

"'But ornament obtains no regard from us but in subservience to utility. We find it hard to distinguish between the useful and beautiful. When they appear to differ, we cannot hesitate to prefer the former. To us that instrument possesses an invincible superiority to every other which is best adapted to our purpose. Convince me that this garment is of more use than that, and you have determined my choice. We may afterwards inquire, which has the highest pretensions to beauty. Strange if utility and beauty fail to coincide. Stranger still, if having found them in any instance compatible, I sacrifice the former to the latter. But the elements of beauty, though perhaps they have a real existence, are fleeting and inconstant. Not so those principles which enable us to discover what is useful. These are uniform and permanent. So must be the results. Among us, what is useful to one, must be equally so to another. The condition of all is so much alike, that a stuff which deserves the preference of one, because it is obtained with least labour, because its texture is most durable, or most easily renewed or cleansed, is for similar reasons, preferable to all.'

"'But,' said I, 'you have various occupations. One kind of stuff or one fashion is not equally suitable to every employment. This must produce a variety among you, as it does among us.'

"'It does so. We find that our tools must vary with our designs. If the task requires a peculiar dress, we assume it. But as we take it up when we enter the workshop, we of course, lay it aside when we change the scene. It is not to be imagined that we wear the same garb at all times. No man enters society laden with the implements of his art. He does not visit the council hall or the theatre with his spade upon his shoulder. As little does he think of bringing thither the garb which he wore in the field. There are no such peculiarities of attitude or gesture among us, that the vesture that has proved most convenient to one in walking or sitting, should be found unsuitable to others. Do the differences of this kind prevalent among you, conform to these rules? Since every one has his stated employment, no doubt each one has a dress peculiar to himself or to those of his own profession.'

"'No. I cannot say that among us this principle has any extensive influence. The chief difference consists in degrees of expensiveness. By inspecting the garb of a passenger, we discover not so much the trade that he pursues, as the amount of his property. Few labour whose wealth allows them to disperse with it. The garb of each is far from varying with the hours of the day. He need only conform to the changes of the seasons, and model his appearance by the laws of ostentation, in public, and by those of ease in the intervals of solitude. These principles are common to both sexes. Small is the portion of morality or taste, that is displayed by either, but in this, as in most other cases, the conduct of the females is the least faulty. But of all infractions of decorum, we should deem the assuming of the dress of one sex by those of the other, as the most flagrant. It so rarely happens, that I do not remember to have witnessed a single metamorphosis, except perhaps on the stage, and even there a female cannot evince a more egregious negligence of reputation than by personating a man.'

"'All this,' replied my friend, 'is so strange as to be almost incredible. Why beings of the same nature, inhabiting the same spot, and accessible to the same influences, should exhibit such preposterous differences is wonderful. It is not possible that these modes should be equally commodious or graceful. Custom may account for the continuance, but not for the origin of manners.'"

[No Differences in Education]

"'The wonder that you express,' said I, 'is in its turn a subject of surprise to me. What you now say, induces me to expect that among you, women and men are more similarly treated than elsewhere. But this to me is so singular a spectacle, that I long to hear it more minutely described by you, and to witness it myself.'

"'If you remain long enough among us you will not want the opportunity. I hope you will find that every one receives that portion which is due to him, and since a diversity of sex cannot possibly make any essential difference in the claims and duties of reasonable beings, this difference will never be found. But you call upon me for descriptions. With what hues shall I delineate the scene? I have exhibited as distinctly as possible the equity that governs us. Its maxims are of various application. They regulate our conduct, not only to each other, but to the tribes of insects and birds. Every thing is to be treated as capable of happiness itself, or as instrumental to the happiness of others.'

"'But since the sexual differences is something,' said I, 'and since you are not guilty of the error of treating different things as if they were the same, doubtless in your conduct towards each other, the consideration of sex is of some weight.'

"'Undoubtedly. A species of conduct is incumbent upon men and women towards each other on certain occasions, that cannot take place between man and man; or between women and women. I may properly supply my son with a razor to remove superfluous hairs from his chin, but I may with no less propriety forbear to furnish my daughter with this impliment, because nature has denied her a beard; but all this is so evident that I cannot but indulge a smile at the formality with which you state it.'

"'But,' said I, 'it is the nature and extent of this difference of treatment that I want to know.'

"'Be explicit my good friend. Do you want a physiological dissertation on this subject or not? If you do, excuse me from performing the task, I am unequal to it.'

"'No. But I will try to explain myself, what for example is the difference which takes place in the education of the two sexes?'

"'There is no possible ground for difference. Nourishment is imparted and received in the same way. Their organs of digestion and secretion are the same. There is one diet, one regimen, one mode and degree of exercise, best adapted to unfold the powers of the human body, and maintain them for the longest time in full vigour. One individual may be affected by some casualty or disease, so as to claim to be treated in a manner different from another individual, but this difference is not necessarily connected with sex. Neither sex is exempt from injury, contracted through their own ignorance, or that of others. Doubtless the sound woman and the sick man it would be madness to subject to the same tasks, or the same regimen. But this is no less true if both be of the same sex. Diseases, on whichsoever they fall, are curable by the same means.

"'Human beings in their infancy,' continued my friend, 'require the same tendance and instruction: but does one sex require more or less, or a different sort of tendance or instruction than the other? Certainly not. If by any fatal delusion, one sex should imagine its interest to consist in the ill treatment of the other, time would soon detect their mistake. For how is the species to be continued? How is a woman, for example, to obtain a sound body, and impart it to her offspring, but, among other sources, from the perfect constitution of both her parents? But it is needless to argue on a supposition so incredible as that mankind can be benefitted by injustice and oppression.

"'Would we render the limbs supple, vigorous and active? And are there two modes equally efficacious of attaining this end? Must we suppose that one sex will find this end of less value than the other, or the means suitable to its attainment different? It cannot be supposed.

"'We are born with faculties that enable us to impart and receive happiness. There is one species of discipline, better adapted than any other to open and improve those faculties. This mode is to be practised. All are to be furnished with the means of instruction, whether these consist in the direct commerce of the senses with the material universe, or in intercourse with other intelligent beings. It is requisite to know the reasonings, actions and opinions of others, if we seek the improvement of our own understanding. For this end we must see them, and talk with them if present, or if distant or dead, we must consult these memorials which have been contrived by themselves or others. These are simple and intelligible maxims proper to regulate our treatment of rational beings. The only circumstance to which we are bound to attend is that the subjects of instruction be rational. If any one observe that the consideration of sex is of some moment, how must his remark be understood. Would he insinuate that because my sex is different from yours, one of us only can be treated as rational, or that though reason be a property of both, one of us possesses less of it than the other. I am not born among a people who can countenance so monstrous a doctrine.

"'No two persons are entitled in the strictest sense, to the same treatment, because no two can be precisely alike. All the possibilities and shades of difference, no human capacity can estimate. Observation will point out some of the more considerable sources of variety. Man is a progressive being, he is wise in proportion to the number of his ideas, and to the accuracy with which he compares and arranges them. These ideas are received through the inlets of his senses. They must be successively received. The objects which suggest them, must be present. There must be time for observation. Hence the difference is, in some degree, uniform between the old and the young. Between those, the sphere of whose observation has been limited, and those whose circle is extensive. Such causes as these of difference are no less incident to one sex than to the other. The career of both commences in childhood and ignorance. How far and how swiftly they may proceed before their steps are arrested by disease, or death, is to be inferred from a knowledge of their circumstances: such as betide them simply as individuals.

"'It would, perhaps, be unreasonable to affirm that the circumstance of sex affects in no degree the train of ideas in the mind. It is not possible that any circumstance, however trivial, should be totally without mental influence; but we may safely affirm that this circumstance is indeed trivial, and its consequences, therefore, unimportant. It is inferior to most other incidents of human existence, and to those which are necessarily incident to both sexes. He that resides among hills, is a different mortal from him that dwells on a plain. Subterranean darkness, or the seclusion of a valley, suggest ideas of a kind different from those that occur to us on the airy verge of a promontory, and in the neighbourhood of roaring waters. The influence on my character which flows from my age, from the number and quality of my associates, from the nature of my dwelling place, as sultry or cold, fertile or barren, level or diversified, the art that I cultivate, the extent or frequency of my excursions cannot be of small moment. In comparison with this, the qualities which are to be ascribed to my sex are unworthy of being mentioned. No doubt my character is in some degree tinged by it, but the tinge is inexpressibly small.'

"'You give me leave to conclude then,' said I, 'that the same method of education is pursued with regard to both sexes?'

"'Certainly,' returned my philosopher. 'Men possess powers that may be drawn forth and improved by exercise and discipline. Let them be so, says our system. It contents itself with prescribing certain general rules to all that bear the appellation of human. It permits all to refresh and invigorate their frames by frequenting the purest streams and the pleasantest fields, and by practising those gestures and evolutions that tend to make us robust and agile. It admits the young to the assemblies of their elders, and exhorts the elder to instruct the young. It multiplies the avenues, and facilitates the access to knowledge. Conversations, books, instruments, specimens of the productions of art and nature, haunts of meditation, and public halls, liberal propensities and leisure, it is the genius of our system to create, multiply, and place within the reach of all. It is far from creation, and debasing its views, by distinguishing those who dwell on the shore from those that inhabit the hills; the beings whom a cold temperature has bleached, from those that are embrowned by an hot.'"

[No Differences in Employment]

"'But different persons,' said I, 'have different employments. Skill cannot be obtained in them without a regular course of instruction. Each sex has, I doubt not, paths of its own into which the others must not intrude. Hence must arise a difference in their education.'

"'Who has taught you,' replied he, 'that each sex must have peculiar employments? Your doubts and your conjectures are equally amazing. One would imagine that among you, one sex had more arms, or legs, or senses than the other. Among us there is no such inequality. The principles that direct us in the choice of occupations are common to all.'

"'Pray tell me,' said I, 'what these principles are.'

"'They are abundantly obvious. There are some tasks which are equally incumbent upon all. These demand no more skill and strength than is possessed by all.

Men must provide themselves by their own efforts with food, clothing and shelter. As long as they live together there is a duty obliging them to join their skill and their exertions for the common benefit. A certain portion of labour will supply the needs of all. This portion then must be divided among all. Each one must acquire and exert the skill which this portion requires. But this skill and this strength are found by experience to be moderate and easily attained. To plant maize, to construct an arch, to weave a garment, are no such arduous employments but that all who have emerged from the infirmity and ignorance of childhood, may contribute their efforts to the performance.

"'But besides occupations which are thus of immediate and universal utility, there is an infinite variety of others. The most exquisite of all calamities, results from a vacant mind and unoccupied limbs. The highest pleasure demands the ceaseless activity of both. To enjoy this pleasure it is requisite to find some other occupation of our time, beside those which are enjoined by the physical necessities of our nature. Among these there is ample room for choice. The motives that may influence us in this choice, are endless. I shall not undertake to enumerate them. You can be at no loss to conceive them without my assistance: but whether they be solitary or social, whether speech or books, or observation, or experiment be the medium of instruction, there can be nothing in the distinction of sex to influence our determinations, or this influence is so inconsiderable as not to be worth mention.'

"'What,' cried I, 'are all obliged to partake of all the labours of tilling the ground, without distinction of rank and sex?'

"'Certainly. There are none that fail to consume some portion of the product of the ground. To exempt any from a share in the cultivation, would be an inexpiable injustice, both to those who are exempted and those who are not exempted. The exercise is cheerful and wholesome. Its purpose is just and necessary. Who shall dare to deny me a part in it? But we know full well that the task, which, if divided among many, is easy and salubrious, is converted into painful and unwholesome drudgery, by being confined to a sex, what phrenzy must that be which should prompt us to introduce a change in this respect? I cannot even imagine so great a perversion of the understanding. Common madness is unequal to so monstrous a conception. We must first not only cease to be reasonable, but cease to be men. Even that supposition is insufficient, for into what class of animals must we sink, before this injustice could be realized? Among beasts there are none who do not owe their accommodations to their own exertions.

"'Food is no less requisite to one sex than to the other. As the necessity of food, so the duty of providing it is common. But the reason why I am to share in the labour, is not merely because I am to share in the fruits. I am a being guided by reason and susceptible of happiness. So are other men. It is therefore a privilege that I cannot relinquish, to promote and contemplate the happiness of others. After the cravings of necessity are satisfied, it remains for me, by a new application of my powers, to enlarge the pleasures of existence. The inlets to this pleasure are numberless. What can prompt us to take from any the power of choosing among these, or to incapacitate him from choosing with judgment. The greater the number of those who are employed in administering to pleasure, the greater will be the product. Since both sexes partake of this capacity, what possible reasons can there be for limiting or precluding the efforts of either?

"'What I conceive to be unjust, may yet be otherwise; but my actions will conform to my opinions. If you would alter the former, you must previously introduce a change into the latter. I know the opinions of my countrymen. The tenor of their actions will conform to their notions of right. Can the time ever come, will the power ever arise, that shall teach them to endure the oppression of injustice themselves, or inflict it upon others? No.'

"'But in my opinion,' said I, 'the frame of women is too delicate, their limbs too minute for rough and toilsome occupations. I would rather confine them to employments more congenial to the female elements of softness and beauty.'

"'You would rather, would you? I will suppose you sincere, and inquire how you would expect to obtain their consent to your scheme.'

"'The sentiments,' said I, 'of a single individual, would avail nothing. But if all the males should agree to prescribe their employments to women—'

"'What then?' interrupted my friend. 'There are but two methods of effecting this end—by force or by persuasion. With respect to force we cannot suppose human beings capable of it, for any moral purpose; but supposing them capable, we would scarcely resort to force, while our opponents are equal in number, strength and skill to ourselves. The efficacy of persuasion is equally chimerical. That frailty of mind which should make a part of mankind willing to take upon themselves a double portion of the labour, and to convert what is pleasurable exercise to all, into a source of pain and misery to a few. But these are vain speculations, let us dismiss them from our notice.'"

[INTERLUDE ON WORDS SPOKEN AND WRITTEN]

"'Willingly,' said I, 'we will dismiss these topics for the sake of one more important.

"'I presume then,' said I, 'there is such a thing as marriage among you.'

"'I do not understand the term.'

"'I use it to express that relation which subsists between two human beings in consequence of difference of sex.'

"'You puzzle me exceedingly,' returned he. 'You question me as to the existence of that concerning which it is impossible for you to be ignorant. You cannot at this age be a stranger to the origin of human existence.'"

When I had gotten thus far in my narrative, I paused. Mrs. Carter still continued to favour me with her attention. On observing my silence she desired me to proceed.

"I presume," said she, "your supernatural conductor allowed you to finish the conversation. To snatch you away just now, in the very midst of your subject, would be doing you and me likewise a very unacceptable office. I beseech you go on with the discourse."

"It may not be proper," answered I. "This is a topic on which, strange to tell, we cannot discourse in the same terms before every audience. The remainder of our conversation decorum would not perhaps forbid you to read, but it prohibits you from hearing. If you wish it, I will give you the substance of the information I collected on this topic in writing."

"What is improper to be said in my hearing," said the lady, "it should seem was no less improper to be knowingly addressed to me by the pen."

"Then," said I, "you do not assent to my offer."

"Nay, I do not refuse my assent. I merely object to the distinction, that you have raised. There are many things improper to be uttered, or written, or to be read, or listened to, but the impropriety methinks must adhere to the sentiments themselves, and not result from the condition of the author or his audience."

"Are these your real sentiments?"

"Without doubt. But they appear not to be yours. However write what you please, I promise you to read it, and to inform you of my opinion respecting it. Your scheme, I suspect, will not be what is commonly called marriage, but something in your opinion, better. This footing is a dubious one. Take care, it is difficult to touch without overstepping the verge."

"Your caution is reasonable. I believe silence will be the safest. You will excuse me therefore from taking up the pen on this occasion. The ground you say, and I believe, is perilous. It will be most prudent to avoid it."

"As you please, but remember that though I may not approve of what you write, your silence I shall approve still less. If it be false, it will enable me at least to know you, and I shall thereby obtain an opportunity of correcting your mistakes. Neither of these purposes are trivial. Are you not aware that no future declaration of yours will be more unfavourable than what you have just said, that silence will be most safe. You are afraid no doubt, of shocking too greatly my prejudices; but you err. I am certainly prepossessed in favour of the system of marriage, but the strength of this prepossession will appear only in the ardour of my compassion for contrary opinions, and the eagerness of my endeavours to remove them."

"You would condescend then," said I, "to reason on the subject, as if it were possible that marriage was an erroneous institution; as if it were possible that any one could seriously maintain it to be, without entitling himself to the imputation of the lowest profligacy. Most women would think that the opponent of marriage, either assumed the character for the most odious and selfish purposes, and could therefore only deserve to be treated as an assassin: to be detested and shunned, or if he were sincere in his monstrous faith, that all efforts to correct his mistakes would avail nothing with respect to the patient, but might endanger the physician by exposing her to the illusions of sophistry or the contagion of passion."

"I am not one of these," said the lady. "The lowest stupidity only can seek its safety in shutting its ears. We may call that sophistry, which having previously heard, it fails to produce conviction. Yet sophistry perhaps implies not merely fallacious reasoning, but a fallaciousness of which the reasoner himself is apprised. If so, few charges ought to be made with more caution. But nothing can exceed the weakness that prevents us from attending to what is going to be urged against our opinions, merely from the persuasion that what is adverse to our preconceptions must be false. Yet there are examples of this folly among our acquaintance. 'You are wrong,' said I lately to one of these, 'if you will suffer me, I will convince you of your error.' 'You may save yourself the trouble,' she answered. 'You may torment me with doubts, but why, when I see the truth clearly already, should I risque the involving of it in obscurity?' I repeat, I am not of this class. Force is to be resisted by force, or eluded by flight: but he that argues, whatever be his motives, should be encountered with argument. He cannot commit a greater error than to urge topics, the insufficiency of which is known to himself. To demonstrate this error is as worthy of truth as any other province. To sophistry, in any sense of the term, the proper antidote is argument. Give me leave to take so much interest in your welfare, as to desire to see your errors corrected, and to contribute what is in my power to that end. If I know myself so well as sometimes to listen to others in the hope of profiting by their superior knowledge or sagacity, permit me likewise to be just to myself in other respects, and to believe myself capable sometimes of pointing out his mistakes to another."

"You seem," said I, "to think it certain that we differ in opinion upon this topic."

"No. I merely suspect that we do. A class of reasoners has lately arisen, who aim at the deepest foundation of civil society. Their addresses to the understanding have been urged with no despicable skill. But this was insufficient, it was necessary to subdue our incredulity, as to the effects of their new maxims, by exhibiting those effects in detail, and winning our assent to their truth by engrossing the fancy and charming the affections. The journey that you have lately made, I merely regard as an excursion into their visionary world. I can trace the argument of the parts which you have unfolded, with those which are yet to come, and can pretty well conjecture of what hues, and lines, and figures, the remainder of the picture is intended to consist."

"Then," said I, "the task that I enjoined on myself is superfluous. You are apprised of all that I mean to say on the topic of marriage, and have already laid in an ample stock of disapprobation for my service."

"I frankly confess that I expect not to approve the matter of your narrative, however pleased I may be with the manner. Nevertheless I wish you to execute your first design, that I may be able to unveil the fallacy of your opinions, and rescue one whom I have no reason to disrespect, from specious but fatal illusions."

"Your purpose is kind. It entitles you at least to my thanks. Yet to say truth, I did not at first despair of your confidence with me in some of my opinions. I imagined that some of the evils of marriage had not escaped you. I recollect that during our last conversation, you arraigned with great earnestness the injustice of condemning women to obey the will, and depend upon the bounty of father or husband."

"Come, come," interrupted the lady, with a severer aspect, "if you mean to preserve my good opinion, you must tread on this ground with more caution. Remember the atrociousness of the charge you would insinuate. What! Because a just indignation at the iniquities that are hourly committed on one half of the human species rises in my heart, because I vindicate the plainest dictates of justice, and am willing to rescue so large a portion of humankind, from so destructive a bondage: a bondage not only of the hands, but of the understanding; which divests them of all those energies which distinguish men from the basest animals, destroys all perception of moral rectitude, and reduces its subjects to so calamitous a state, that they adore the tyranny that rears its crest over them, and kiss the hand that loads them with ignominy! When I demand an equality of conditions among beings that equally partake of the same divine reason, would you rashly infer that I was an enemy to the institution of marriage itself? Where shall we look for human beings who surpass all others in depravity and wretchedness? Are they not to be found in the haunts of female licentiousness. If their vice admits of a darker hue, it would receive it from the circumstance of their being dissolute by theory; of their modelling voluptuousness into a speculative system. Yet this is the charge you would make upon me. You would brand me as an enemy to marriage, not in the sense that a vestal, or widow, or chaste, but deserted maid is an enemy; not even in that sense in which the abandoned victims of poverty and temptation are enemies, but in the sense of that detestable philosophy which scoffs at the matrimonial institution itself, which denies all its pretensions to sanctity, which consigns us to the guidance of a sensual impulse, and treats as fantastic or chimerical, the sacred charities of husband, son, and brother. Beware. Imputations of this kind are more fatal in the consequences than you may be able to conceive. They cannot be indifferent to me. In drawing such inferences, you would hardly be justified by the most disinterested intentions."

"Such inferences, my dear Madam, it is far from my intention to draw. I cannot but think your alarms unnecessary. If I am an enemy to marriage far be it from me to be the champion of sensuality. I know the sacredness of this word in the opinions of mankind; I know how liable to be misunderstood are the efforts of him who should labour to explode it. But still, is it not possible to define with so much perspicuity, and distinguish with so much accuracy as to preclude all possibility of mistake? I believe this possible. I deem it easy to justify the insinuation that you yourself are desirous of subverting the marriage state."

"Proceed," said the lady. "Men are at liberty to annex to words what meaning they think proper. What should hinder you, if you so please, from saying that snow is of the deepest black? Words are arbitrary. The idea that others annex to the word black, you are at liberty to transfer to the word white. But in the use of this privilege you must make your account in not being understood, and in reversing all the purposes of language."

[Marriage Is a Compact of Slavery]

"Well," said I, "that is yet to appear. Meanwhile, I pray you, what are *your* objections to the present system?"

"My objections are weighty ones. I disapprove of it, in the first place, because it renders the female a slave to the man. It enjoins and enforces submission on her part to the will of her husband. It includes a promise of implicit obedience and unalterable affection. Secondly, it leaves the woman destitute of property. Whatever she previously possesses, belongs absolutely to the man."

"This representation seems not to be a faithful one," said I. "Marriage leaves the wife without property, you say. How comes it then that she is able to subsist? You will answer, perhaps, that her sole dependence is placed upon the bounty of her husband. But this is surely an error. It is by virtue of express laws that all property subsists. But the same laws sanction the title of a wife to a subsistence proportioned to the estate of her husband. But if law were silent, custom would enforce this claim. The husband is in reality nothing but a steward. He is bound to make provision for his wife, proportionately to the extent of his own revenue. This is a practical truth, of which every woman is sensible. It is this that renders the riches of an husband a consideration of so much moment in the eye of a prudent woman. To select a wealthy partner is universally considered as the certain means of enriching ourselves, not less when the object of our choice is an husband than when it is a wife."

"Notwithstanding all this," said the lady, "you will not pretend to affirm that marriage renders the property common."

"May I not truly assert," rejoined I, "that the wife is legally entitled to her maintenance?"

"Yes, she is entitled to food, raiment, and shelter, if her husband can supply them. Suppose a man in possession of five thousand pounds a year: from this the wife is entitled to maintenance: but how shall the remainder be administered? Is not the power of the husband, over this, absolute? Cannot he reduce himself to poverty to-morrow? She may claim a certain portion of what she has, but he may, at his own pleasure, divest himself of all that he has. He may expend it on what purposes he pleases. It is his own, and, for the use of it, he is responsible to no tribunal; but in reality, this pompous claim of his wife amounts, in most cases, to nothing. It is the discretion of the husband that must decide, as to the kind and quantity of that provision. He may be niggardly or prodigal, according to the suggestions of his own caprice. He may hasten to poverty himself, or he may live, and compel his partner to live, in the midst of wealth as if he were labouring under extreme indigence. In neither case has the wife any remedy."

"But recollect, my good friend, the husband is commonly the original proprietor. Has the wife a just claim to that which, before marriage, belonged to her spouse?"

"Certainly not. Nor is it less true that the husband has no just claim to that which, previously to marriage, belonged to the wife. If property were, in all respects, justly administered, if patrimonies were equally divided among offspring, and if the various avenues that lead to the possession of property were equally accessible to both sexes, it would be found as frequently and extensively vested in one son as in the other. Marriage is productive of no consequences which justify the transfer of what either previously possessed to the other. The idea of common property is absurd and pernicious; but even this is better than poverty and dependence to which the present system subjects the female."

"But," said I, "it is not to be forgotten that the household is common. One dwelling, one table, one set of servants may justly be sustained by a single fund. This fund may be managed by common consent. No particle of expense may accrue without the concurrence of both parties, but if there be a difference of opinion, some one must ultimately decide. Why should not this be the husband? You will say that this would be unjust. I answer that, since it is necessary that power should be vested in one or the other the injustice is inevitable. An opposite procedure would not diminish it. If this necessary power of deciding in cases of disagreement were lodged in the wife, the injustice would remain."

"But a common fund and a common dwelling is superfluous. Why is marriage to condemn two human beings to dwell under the same roof and to eat at the same table, and to be served by the same domestics? This circumstance alone is the source of innumerable ills. Familiarity is the sure destroyer of reverence. All the bickerings and dissensions of a married life flow from no other source than that of too frequent communication. How difficult is it to introduce harmony of sentiment, even on topics of importance, between two persons? But this difficulty is increased in proportion to the number and frequency, and the connection with our private and personal deportment of these topics.

"If two persons are condemned to cohabitation, there must doubtless be mutual accommodation. But let us understand this term. No one can sacrifice his opinions. What is incumbent upon him, in certain cases, is only to forbear doing what he esteems to be right. Now that situation is most eligible in which we are at liberty to conform to the dictates of our judgment. Situations of a different kind will frequently occur in human life. Many of them exist without any necessity. Such, in its present state, is matrimony.

"Since an exact agreement of opinions is impossible, and since the intimate and constant intercourse of a married life requires either that the parties should agree in their opinions, or that one should forego his own resolutions, what is the consequence? Controversies will incessantly arise, and must be decided. If argument be insufficient, recourse must be had to legal authority, to brute force, or servile artifices, or to that superstition that has bound itself by a promise to obey. These might be endured if they were the necessary attendants of marriage; but they are spurious additions. Marriage is a sacred institution, but it would argue the most pitiful stupidity to imagine that all those circumstances which accident and custom have annexed to it are likewise sacred. Marriage is sacred, but iniquitous laws, by making it a compact of slavery, by imposing impracticable conditions and extorting impious promises have, in most countries, converted it into something flagitious and hateful."

[THE NATURE OF TRUE MARRIAGE]

"But what effects," said I, "may be expected from the removal of this restraint, upon the morals of the people? It seems to open a door to licentiousness and profligacy. If marriages can be dissolved and contracted at pleasure, will not every one deliver himself up to the impulse of a lawless appetite? Would not changes be incessant? All chastity of mind perhaps, would perish. A general corruption of manners would ensue, and this vice would pave the way for the admission of a thousand others, till the whole nation were sunk into a state of the lowest degeneracy."

"Pray thee," cried the lady, "leave this topic of declamation to the school boys— Liberty, in this respect, would eminently conduce to the happiness of mankind. A partial reformation would be insufficient. Set marriage on a right basis, and the pest that has hitherto made itself an inmate of every house, and ravaged every man's peace, will be exterminated. The servitude that has debased one half, and the tyranny that has depraved the other half of the human species will be at an end."

"And with all those objections to the present regulations on this subject, you will still maintain that you are an advocate of marriage?"

"Undoubtedly I retain the term, and am justified by common usage in retaining it. No one imagines that the forms which law or custom, in a particular age or nation, may happen to annex to marriage are essential to it, if lawgivers should enlarge the privilege of divorce, and new modify the rights of property, as they are affected by marriage. Should they ordain that henceforth the husband should vow obedience to the wife, in place of the former vow which the wife made to the husband, or entirely prohibit promises of any kind; should they expunge from the catalogue of conjugal duties that which confines them to the same dwelling, who would imagine that the institution itself were subverted? In the east, conjugal servitude has ever been more absolute than with us, and polygamy legally established. Yet, who will affirm that marriage is unknown in the east. Every one knows that regulations respecting property, domestic government, and the causes of divorce are incident to this state, and do not constitute its essence."

"I shall assent," said I, "to the truth of this statement. Perhaps I may be disposed to adventure a few steps further than you. It appears to me that marriage has no other criterion than custom. This term is descriptive of that mode of sexual intercourse, whatever it may be, which custom or law has established in any country. All the modifications of this intercourse that have ever existed, or can be supposed to exist, are so many species included in the general term. The question that we have been discussing is no other than this: what species of marriage is most agreeable to justice—Or, in other words, what are the principles that ought to regulate the sexual intercourse? It is not likely that any portion of mankind have reduced these principles to practice. Hence arises a second question of the highest moment: what conduct is incumbent upon me, when the species of marriage established among my countrymen, does not conform to my notions of duty."

"That indeed," returned she, "is going further than I am willing to accompany you. There are many conceivable modes of sexual intercourse on which I cannot bestow the appellation of marriage. There is something which inseparably belongs to it. It is not unallowable to call by this name a state which comprehends, together with these ingredients, any number of appendages. But to call a state which wants these ingredients marriage, appears to me a perversion of language."

"I pry'thee," said I, "what are these ingredients? You have largely expatiated on the non-essentials of matrimony: Be good enough to say what truly belongs to this state?"

"Willingly," answered she. "Marriage is an union founded on free and mutual consent. It cannot exist without friendship. It cannot exist without personal fidelity. As soon as the union ceases to be spontaneous it ceases to be just. This is the sum. If I were to talk for months, I could add nothing to the completeness of this definition."

1798 *1815*

WASHINGTON IRVING
(1783–1859)

"How the truth presses home upon us as we advance in life that every-thing around us is transient and uncertain. . . . We feel it withering at our hearts. . .in the funeral of our friends and written on the wrecks of our hopes and affections—when I look back for a few short years, what changes of all kinds have taken place, what wrecks of time and fortune are strewn around me." This entry in Washington Irving's notebook reveals in a way the essence of the man and the essence of his work. In his most famous story, "Rip Van Winkle," Rip returned from his long sleep to find "his house gone to decay. . . the windows shattered, and the doors off the hinges; he entered to find it "empty, forlorn, and apparently abandoned." He called for his wife and children: "the lonely chambers rang for a moment with his voice, and then all again was silence."

The melancholy mood is never far off in Irving's fiction, even when it ap-pears to be comic. At the heart is a kind of secret grieving for the tran-sience—or mutability—of all things. This theme may be accounted for in part by the age in which Irving lived. He was born in 1783, just at the end of the Revolutionary War. Change characterized all the institutions in America during his—and the nation's—childhood and youth. He lived to the edge of the Civil War, which would bring even deeper transfigurations in the social and political life of the United States.

Though a great deal is known about Washington Irving's life, his individ-ual personality remains elusive. It seems somehow significant that only after he was some fifty years old did he use his real name in his work. He was first, in letters to newspapers, "Jonathan Oldstyle." When he wrote pieces for the magazine *Salmagundi,* he was "Anthony Evergreen, Gent." His *History of New York* was written by "Diedrich Knickerbocker," and *The Sketch-Book* by "Geof-frey Crayon, Gent." Who was the real Washington Irving? The brief "Au-thor's Account of Himself" he placed at the beginning of *The Sketch-Book* em-phasizes his love of travelling, rambling, wandering, roving—a vagabond witness at "the scenes of life." This may give us a sense of the nature of the book's persona, but it reveals to us very little of the actual author.

Irving was the youngest of eleven children born to a well-to-do New York family. At the age of sixteen, he left school to enter a law office to "read law," a profession for which he had little taste. By the time he was nineteen, he had begun the writing that would occupy his life. His solicitous brothers, noting his frailty and ill health, sent him abroad, where he remained for two years, visiting France, Italy, Holland, and England. Throughout his travels he kept a notebook. On returning home in 1806, he joined with his brothers, James Kirke Paulding, and others in establishing *Salmagundi: or, the Whim-Wham and Opinions of Launcelot Langstaff, Esq. and Others,* a magazine that ran for a little over a year. As Anthony Evergreen, Gent., Irving expressed his opinions on the foibles and personalities of the day in a witty, casual, polished style that attracted attention.

That attention turned to wild enthusiasm with publication in 1809 of *A History of New York by Diedrich Knickerbocker.* A combination of comedy, hoax, burlesque, and satire, it seemed at its best a near-perfect marriage of style and wit, as in the description of Wouter Van Twiller: "He was exactly five feet six inches in height, and six feet five inches in circumference. . . . His body was oblong and particularly capacious at bottom; which was wisely ordered by Providence, seeing that he was a man of sedentary habits, and very averse to the idle labor of walking." The book gained for Irving something of an international reputation. Sir Walter Scott reported to Irving later that he had read it aloud at home to his family's delight.

Earlier in 1809, the young woman to whom Irving was betrothed, Matilda Hoffman, died suddenly of tuberculosis. This was the great tragedy of his life, if we are to believe Irving's later comments in his journals. It lay behind his restless wandering, and his staying a bachelor the remainder of his life. It might, of course, have been romantic self-dramatization by a lover of travel with a preference for the single state. Whatever the case, the incident figured large in Irving's imagination and surely contributed to his melancholy sense of life's impermanence.

Irving was an editor of Philadelphia's *Analectic Magazine* during 1813–14, moved to Washington on family business for a time, and in 1814–15 served in the New York militia as the War of 1812 was drawing to a close. Then in 1815 he was called on to go to Liverpool, England, to assist in a branch of the family business (importation of hardware). He was to remain abroad for seventeen years, from the age of thirty-two to forty-nine. Not long after he arrived in England, the family firm went bankrupt, and Irving turned to writing as a means of livelihood. The result was his best-known work, *The Sketch-Book* (1820), which established his reputation firmly both in America and England. William Makepeace Thackeray called Irving "the first ambassador whom the New World of letters sent to the Old."

During the next decade, Irving wandered through European countries with his notebook in hand, on the lookout for materials to use in his work. Germany was an especially rich source, France less so, but Spain turned out to offer the most abundant materials of all. In 1822 Irving published a collection of stories with English, French, and Spanish settings entitled *Bracebridge Hall;* and in 1824, another volume of sketches set mainly in Germany entitled *Tales of a Traveller.* Neither work enhanced Irving's reputation, and, indeed, the second received bad reviews.

Feeling that he had exhausted the materials congenial to his imagination in England, Germany, and France, Irving was relieved and pleased to receive an invitation to come to Madrid to be attached to the American Embassy and to engage himself on a literary enterprise involving Columbus. His Spanish phase brought a renewal of his imagination and resulted in a series of impressive books: *History of the Life and Voyages of Christopher Columbus* (1828), *A Chronicle of the Conquest of Granada* (1829), a partially fictionalized account of the Christian defeat of the Moors in Granada, *Voyages and Discoveries of the Companions of Columbus* (1831), and *Alhambra* (1832), a collection of stories written by Irving while living with peasants in the ancient Moorish palace in Granada (sometimes called Irving's Spanish *Sketch-Book*).

Irving returned to America in 1832, the first American "man of letters" with a truly international reputation. It was inevitable that his long period abroad would bring his Americanness into question. As though to prove it, Irving undertook an expedition into Indian country, writing the first of a series of impressive American books: *A Tour of the Prairies* (published in *The Crayon Miscellany,* 1835); *Astoria* (1836), a history of John Jacob Astor's fur trade in the Northwest; and *The Adventures of Captain Bonneville, U.S.A.* (1837), an account of a frontiersman's trapping expedition in the Rocky Mountains.

In these years Irving finally found a place to put down roots—an estate he called Sunnyside, near Tarrytown, on the Hudson. There he lived his remaining years except for the four he spent as Minister to Spain (1842–46). The last years were spent in writing three biographies—*Oliver Goldsmith* (1849), *Mahomet and His Successors* (1849–50), and the massive five-volume *Life of Washington* (1859). The biography of Washington had been conceived as early as 1825, and the writing occupied much of the time of Irving's last eleven years. He completed the fifth volume shortly before he died in November 1859. By this time, Irving's fame was fading in the shadow of other American writers claiming wide attention—Ralph Waldo Emerson, Nathaniel Hawthorne, and Edgar Allan Poe.

ADDITIONAL READING

Washington Irving: Representative Selections, ed. Henry A. Pochmann, 1934.

Pierre M. Irving, *The Life and Letters of Washington Irving*, 4 vols., 1862–64, 1967; Stanley T. Williams, *The Life of Washington Irving*, 2 vols., 1935–79; Van Wyck Brooks, *The World of Washington Irving*, 1944; Edward Wagenknecht, *Washington Irving: Moderation Displayed*, 1962; Lewis Leary, *Washington Irving*, 1963; William L. Hedges, *Washington Irving: An American Study: 1802–1832*, 1965; Donald Ringe, *The Pictorial Mode: Space & Time in the Art of Bryant, Irving, & Cooper*, 1971; Andrew B. Meyers, ed., *Washington Irving: A Tribute*, 1972; Martin Roth, *Comedy and America: The Lost World of Washington Irving*, 1976; Andrew B. Meyers, ed., *A Century of Commentary on the Works of Washington Irving*, 1976; Haskell Springer, *Washington Irving: A Reference Guide*, 1976; Philip McFarland, *Sojourners*, 1979; Mary Weatherspoon Bowden, *Washington Irving*, 1981; Stanley Brodwin, ed., *The Old and New World Romanticism of Washington Irving*, 1986; Jeffrey Rubin-Dorsky, *Adrift in the Old World: The Psychological Pilgrimage of Washington Irving*, 1988.

TEXTS

The Complete Works of Washington Irving, ed. Henry A. Pochmann, Herbert L. Kleinfeld, Richard Dilworth Rust et al.: Vol. VII, *A History of New York*, ed. Michael L. Black and Nancy B. Black, 1984; Vol. VIII, *The Sketch-Book of Geoffrey Crayon, Gent.*, ed. Haskell Springer, 1978; Vol. XXII, *The Crayon Miscellany*, ed. Dahlia Kirby Terrell, 1979.

from A History of New York, by Diedrich Knickerbocker[1]

BOOK III

In Which is Recorded the Golden Reign of Wouter Van Twiller

CHAPTER I

Of the renowned Wouter Van Twiller,[2] his unparalleled virtues—As likewise his unutterable wisdom in the law case of Wandle Schoonhoven and Barent Bleecker—And the great admiration of the public thereat

---

[1]The full title indicates the history is "From the Beginning of the World to the End of the Dutch Dynasty." It is, of course, a burlesque of history and makes fun of the pedantry, the heroic style, the adulation of past leaders, the elevation to epic significance of minor events that characterize much of history writing. Book I moves from creation of the world to discovery of America, Book II relates the Dutch colonization of the New World, and Books III–VII chronicle the reigns of Wouter Van Twiller, William the

Testy, and Peter the Headstrong. As in all satire, Irving feels free to invent or distort facts.

[2]Wouter Van Twiller (1580?–1656), governor of New Netherland (1633–37), established by Holland's grant to the Dutch West India Company in 1621. Dutch colonists settled along the Hudson River area, and particularly in New Amsterdam (later New York City). In 1664 the territory was taken over by the British and made into two colonies, New York and New Jersey.

Grievous and very much to be commiserated is the task of the feeling historian, who writes the history of his native land. If it fall to his lot to be the recorder of calamity or crime, the mournful page is watered with his tears—nor can he recall the most prosperous and blissful era, without a melancholy sigh at the reflection, that it has passed away for ever! I know not whether it be owing to an immoderate love for the simplicity of former times, or to that certain tenderness of heart inci- dent to all sentimental historians; but I candidly confess that I cannot look back on the happier days of our city, which I now describe, without great dejection of spirits. With faltering hand do I withdraw the curtain of oblivion, that veils the modest merit of our venerable ancestors, and as their figures rise to my mental vision, humble myself before their mighty shades.

Such are my feelings when I revisit the family mansion of the Knickerbockers, and spend a lonely hour in the chamber where hang the portraits of my forefa- thers, shrouded in dust, like the forms they represent. With pious reverence do I gaze on the countenances of those renowned burghers, who have preceded me in the steady march of existence—whose sober and temperate blood now meanders through my veins, flowing slower and slower in its feeble conduits, until its cur- rent shall soon be stopped for ever!

These, say I to myself, are but frail memorials of the mighty men who flour- ished in the days of the patriarchs; but who, alas, have long since mouldered in that tomb, towards which my steps are insensibly and irresistibly hastening! As I pace the darkened chamber and lose myself in melancholy musings, the shadowy images around me almost seem to steal once more into existence—their counte- nances to assume the animation of life—their eyes to pursue me in every move- ment! Carried away by the delusions of fancy, I almost imagine myself sur- rounded by the shades of the departed, and holding sweet converse with the worthies of antiquity! Ah, hapless Diedrich! born in degenerate age, abandoned to the buffetings of fortune—a stranger and a weary pilgrim in thy native land— blest with no weeping wife, nor family of helpless children; but doomed to wander neglected through those crowded streets, and elbowed by foreign upstarts from those fair abodes where once thine ancestors held sovereign empire!

Let me not, however, lose the historian in the man, nor suffer the doting rec- ollections of age to overcome me, while dwelling with fond garrulity on the virtu- ous days of the patriarchs—on those sweet days of simplicity and ease, which never more will dawn on the lovely island of Manna-hata![3]

These melancholy reflections have been forced from me by the growing wealth and importance of New Amsterdam, which I plainly perceive, are to involve it in all kinds of perils and disasters. Already, as I observed at the close of my last book, they had awakened the attention of the mother country. The usual mark of pro- tection shown by mother countries to wealthy colonies was forthwith manifested; a governor being sent out to rule over the province and squeeze out of it as much revenue as possible.

The arrival of a governor of course put an end to the protectorate of Oloffe the Dreamer.[4] He appears, however, to have dreamt to some purpose during his sway, as we find him afterwards living as a patroon on a great landed estate on the banks of the Hudson; having virtually forfeited all right to his ancient appellation of Kortlandt or Lackland.

It was in the year of our Lord 1629 that Mynheer Wouter Van Twiller was ap- pointed governor of the province of Nieuw Nederlandts, under the commission

---

[3]Indian name for Manhattan.
[4]Oloff Stevenszen Van Cortlandt (1600–1684) appears earlier in Irving's account. He was a mayor and merchant.

and control of their High Mightinesses the Lords States General of the United Netherlands, and the privileged West India Company.

This renowned old gentleman arrived at New Amsterdam in the merry month of June, the sweetest month in all the year; when dan Apollo seems to dance up the transparent firmament—when the robin, the thrush and a thousand other wanton songsters make the woods to resound with amorous ditties, and the luxurious little boblincon revels among the clover blossoms of the meadows—all which happy coincidence persuaded the old dames of New Amsterdam, who were skilled in the art of foretelling events, that this was to be a happy and prosperous administration.

The renowned Wouter (or Walter) Van Twiller, was descended from a long line of Dutch burgomasters, who had successively dozed away their lives, and grown fat upon the bench of magistracy in Rotterdam; and who had comported themselves with such singular wisdom and propriety, that they were never either heard or talked of—which, next to being universally applauded, should be the object of ambition of all magistrates and rulers. There are two opposite ways by which some men make a figure in the world; one by talking faster than they think; and the other by holding their tongues and not thinking at all. By the first many a smatterer acquires the reputation of a man of quick parts; by the other many a dunderpate, like the owl, the stupidest of birds, comes to be considered the very type of wisdom. This, by the way, is a casual remark, which I would not for the universe have it thought I apply to Governor Van Twiller. It is true he was a man shut up within himself, like an oyster, and rarely spoke except in monosyllables; but then it was allowed he seldom said a foolish thing. So invincible was his gravity that he was never known to laugh or even to smile through the whole course of a long and prosperous life. Nay if a joke were uttered in his presence, that set light-minded hearers in a roar, it was observed to throw him into a state of perplexity. Sometimes he would deign to inquire into the matter, and when, after much explanation, the joke was made as plain as a pike-staff, he would continue to smoke his pipe in silence, and at length, knocking out the ashes would exclaim, "Well! I see nothing in all that to laugh about."

With all his reflective habits, he never made up his mind on a subject. His adherents accounted for this by the astonishing magnitude of his ideas. He conceived every subject on so grand a scale that he had not room in his head to turn it over and examine both sides of it. Certain it is that if any matter were propounded to him on which ordinary mortals would rashly determine at first glance, he would put on a vague, mysterious look; shake his capacious head; smoke some time in profound silence and at length observe that "he had his doubts about the matter," which gained him the reputation of a man slow of belief and not easily imposed upon. What is more, it gained him a lasting name: for to this habit of the mind has been attributed his surname of Twiller; which is said to be a corruption of the original Twijfler, or, in plain English, *Doubter.*

The person of this illustrious old gentleman was formed, and proportioned, as though it had been moulded by the hands of some cunning Dutch statuary,[5] as a model of majesty and lordly grandeur. He was exactly five feet six inches in height, and six feet five inches in circumference. His head was a perfect sphere, and of such stupendous dimensions, that dame Nature with all her sex's ingenuity, would have been puzzled to construct a neck capable of supporting it; wherefore she wisely declined the attempt, and settled it firmly on the top of his backbone, just between the shoulders. His body was oblong and particularly capacious at bottom; which was wisely ordered by Providence, seeing that he was a man of

[5]Sculptor.

sedentary habits, and very averse to the idle labor of walking. His legs were short, but sturdy in proportion to the weight they had to sustain; so that when erect he had not a little the appearance of a beer barrel on skids. His face, that infallible index of the mind, presented a vast expanse, unfurrowed by any of those lines and angles which disfigure the human countenance with what is termed expression. Two small grey eyes twinkled feebly in the midst, like two stars of lesser magnitude in a hazy firmament; and his full-fed cheeks, which seemed to have taken toll of every thing that went into his mouth, were curiously mottled and streaked with dusky red, like a spitzenberg apple.

His habits were as regular as his person. He daily took his four stated meals, appropriating exactly an hour to each; he smoked and doubted eight hours, and he slept the remaining twelve of the four-and-twenty. Such was the renowned Wouter Van Twiller—a true philosopher, for his mind was either elevated above, or tranquilly settled below, the cares and perplexities of this world. He had lived in it for years, without feeling the least curiosity to know whether the sun revolved round it, or it round the sun; and he had watched, for at least half a century, the smoke curling from his pipe to the ceiling, without once troubling his head with any of those numerous theories, by which a philosopher would have perplexed his brain, in accounting for its rising above the surrounding atmosphere.

In his council he presided with great state and solemnity. He sat in a huge chair of solid oak, hewn in the celebrated forest of the Hague, fabricated by an experienced timmerman[6] of Amsterdam, and curiously carved about the arms and feet, into exact imitations of gigantic eagle's claws. Instead of a sceptre he swayed a long Turkish pipe, wrought with jasmin and amber, which had been presented to a stadtholder[7] of Holland, at the conclusion of a treaty with one of the petty Barbary powers.[8] In this stately chair would he sit, and this magnificent pipe would he smoke, shaking his right knee with a constant motion, and fixing his eye for hours together upon a little print of Amsterdam, which hung in a black frame against the opposite wall of the council-chamber. Nay, it has even been said, that when any deliberation of extraordinary length and intricacy was on the carpet, the renowned Wouter would shut his eyes for full two hours at a time, that he might not be disturbed by external objects—and at such times the internal commotion of his mind was evinced by certain regular guttural sounds, which his admirers declared were merely the noise of conflict, made by his contending doubts and opinions.

It is with infinite difficulty I have been enabled to collect these biographical anecdotes of the great man under consideration. The facts respecting him were so scattered and vague, and divers of them so questionable in point of authenticity, that I have had to give up the search after many, and decline the admission of still more, which would have tended to heighten the coloring of his portrait.

I have been the more anxious to delineate fully the person and habits of Wouter Van Twiller, from the consideration that he was not only the first, but also the best governor that ever presided over this ancient and respectable province; and so tranquil and benevolent was his reign, that I do not find throughout the whole of it, a single instance of any offender being brought to punishment—a most indubitable sign of a merciful governor, and a case unparalleled, excepting in the reign of the illustrious King Log,[9] from whom, it is hinted, the renowned Van Twiller was a lineal descendant.

---

[6]Carpenter (Dutch).
[7]Governor (Dutch).
[8]The Barbary States were Algeria, Tunisia, and Tripolitania, in northern Africa. The "Barbary pirates" preyed on Mediterranean shipping (including American vessels); they accepted tribute or kidnapped for ransom, enslaving the unransomed. From 1801 to 1805, there was sporadic conflict between the United States and the pirates, concluding with the Tripolitan Treaty of 1805.
[9]In Aesop's *Fables*, the frogs request a king from Zeus. He puts a log in the pond. The frogs complain that he does nothing. Zeus then changes the log for a water snake, which gobbles up frogs.

The very outset of the career of this excellent magistrate was distinguished by an example of legal acumen, that gave flattering presage of a wise and equitable administration. The morning after he had been installed in office, and at the moment that he was making his breakfast from a prodigious earthen dish, filled with milk and Indian pudding,[10] he was interrupted by the appearance of Wandle Schoonhoven, a very important old burgher of New Amsterdam, who complained bitterly of one Barent Bleecker, inasmuch as he refused to come to a settlement of accounts, seeing that there was a heavy balance in favor of the said Wandle. Governor Van Twiller, as I have already observed, was a man of few words; he was likewise a mortal enemy to multiplying writings—or being disturbed at his breakfast. Having listened attentively to the statement of Wandle Schoonhoven, giving an occasional grunt, as he shoveled a spoonful of Indian pudding into his mouth—either as a sign that he relished the dish, or comprehended the story—he called unto him his constable, and pulling out of his breeches pocket a huge jackknife, dispatched it after the defendant as a summons, accompanied by his tobacco box as a warrant.

This summary process was as effectual in those simple days as was the seal ring of the great Haroun Alraschid[11] among the true believers. The two parties being confronted before him, each produced a book of accounts, written in a language and character that would have puzzled any but a High Dutch commentator, or a learned decipherer of Egyptian obelisks. The sage Wouter took them one after the other, and having poised them in his hands, and attentively counted over the number of leaves, fell straightway into a very great doubt, and smoked for half an hour without saying a word; at length, laying his finger beside his nose, and shutting his eyes for a moment, with the air of a man who has just caught a subtle idea by the tail, he slowly took his pipe from his mouth, puffed forth a column of tobacco smoke and with marvellous gravity and solemnity pronounced—that having carefully counted over the leaves and weighed the books, it was found, that one was just as thick and as heavy as the other—therefore it was the final opinion of the court that the accounts were equally balanced—therefore Wandle should give Barent a receipt, and Barent should give Wandle a receipt—and the constable should pay the costs.

This decision being straightway made known, diffused general joy throughout New Amsterdam, for the people immediately perceived, that they had a very wise and equitable magistrate to rule over them. But its happiest effect was, that not another lawsuit took place throughout the whole of his administration—and the office of constable fell into such decay, that there was not one of those losel[12] scouts known in the province for many years. I am the more particular in dwelling on this transaction, not only because I deem it one of the most sage and righteous judgments on record, and well worthy the attention of modern magistrates, but because it was a miraculous event in the history of the renowned Wouter—being the only time he was ever known to come to a decision in the whole course of his life.

CHAPTER IV

Containing further particulars of the golden age, and what constituted a fine lady and gentleman in the days of Walter the Doubter

In this dulcet period of my history, when the beauteous island of Mannahata presented a scene, the very counterpart of those glowing pictures drawn of the

---

[10]A cornmeal mush, served with milk and molasses.
[11]Harun the Orthodox (763?–809), Caliph of Baghdad,
whose court was renowned for its art and learning.
[12]Worthless.

golden reign of Saturn,[1] there was, as I have before observed, a happy ignorance, an honest simplicity prevalent among its inhabitants, which, were I even able to depict, would be but little understood by the degenerate age for which I am doomed to write. Even the female sex, those arch innovators upon the tranquillity, the honesty and grey-beard customs of society, seemed for a while to conduct themselves with incredible sobriety and comeliness.

Their hair, untortured by the abominations of art, was scrupulously poma-tumed back from their foreheads with a candle, and covered with a little cap of quilted calico, which fitted exactly to their heads. Their petticoats of linsey-woolsey[2] were striped with a variety of gorgeous dyes—though I must confess these gallant garments were rather short, scarce reaching below the knee; but then they made up in the number, which generally equaled that of the gentle-men's small clothes;[3] and what is still more praiseworthy, they were all of their own manufacture—of which circumstance, as may well be supposed, they were not a little vain.

These were the honest days, in which every woman stayed at home, read the Bible and wore pockets—ay, and that too of a goodly size, fashioned with patch-work into many curious devices, and ostentatiously worn on the outside. These, in fact, were convenient receptacles, where all good housewives carefully stored away such things as they wished to have at hand; by which means they often came to be incredibly crammed—and I remember there was a story current when I was a boy, that the lady of Wouter Van Twiller once had occasion to empty her right pocket in search of a wooden ladle, when the contents filled a couple of corn bas-kets, and the utensil was discovered lying among some rubbish in one corner—but we must not give too much faith to all these stories; the anecdotes of those remote periods being very subject to exaggeration.

Besides these notable pockets, they likewise wore scissors and pincushions sus-pended from their girdles by red ribbands, or among the more opulent and showy classes, by brass, and even silver chains—indubitable tokens of thrifty housewives and industrious spinsters. I cannot say much in vindication of the shortness of the petticoats; it doubtless was introduced for the purpose of giving the stockings a chance to be seen, which were generally of blue worsted with mag-nificent red clocks—or perhaps to display a well-turned ankle, and a neat, though serviceable, foot, set off by a high-heeled leathern shoe, with a large and splendid silver buckle. Thus we find that the gentle sex in all ages have shown the same disposition to infringe a little upon the laws of decorum, in order to betray a lurk-ing beauty, or gratify an innocent love of finery.

From the sketch here given, it will be seen that our good grandmothers dif-fered considerably in their ideas of a fine figure from their scantily dressed de-scendants of the present day. A fine lady, in those times, waddled under more clothes, even on a fair summer's day, than would have clad the whole bevy of a modern ball-room. Nor were they the less admired by the gentlemen in conse-quence thereof. On the contrary, the greatness of a lover's passion seemed to in-crease in proportion to the magnitude of its object—and a voluminous damsel, arrayed in a dozen of petticoats, was declared by a Low Dutch[4] sonneteer of the province to be radiant as a sunflower, and luxuriant as a full-blown cabbage. Cer-tain it is, that in those days, the heart of a lover could not contain more than one lady at a time; whereas the heart of a modern gallant has often room enough to accommodate half a dozen. The reason of which I conclude to be, that either the

---

[1]According to classical mythology, the five ages of mankind were golden, silver, bronze, heroic, and iron. Irving indi-cates the age of Twiller was like the golden age in contrast with the degenerate age in which he wrote.
[2]Cloth made of linen and wool; in the original meaning, el-egant (now coarse).

[3]Knee-breeches.
[4]I.e., of Holland (one of the "Low Countries," which also include Belgium and Luxembourg).

hearts of the gentlemen have grown larger, or the persons of the ladies smaller—this, however, is a question for physiologists to determine.

But there was a secret charm in these petticoats, which no doubt entered into the consideration of the prudent gallants. The wardrobe of a lady was in those days her only fortune; and she who had a good stock of petticoats and stockings, was as absolutely an heiress as is a Kamschatka damsel with a store of bear skins, or a Lapland belle with a plenty of reindeer.[5] The ladies, therefore, were very anxious to display these powerful attractions to the greatest advantage; and the best rooms in the house, instead of being adorned with caricatures of dame Nature, in water-colors and needle-work, were always hung round with abundance of homespun garments, the manufacture and the property of the females—a piece of laudable ostentation that still prevails among the heiresses of our Dutch villages.

The gentlemen, in fact, who figured in the circles of the gay world in these ancient times, corresponded, in most particulars, with the beauteous damsels whose smiles they were ambitious to deserve. True it is, their merits would make but a very inconsiderable impression upon the heart of a modern fair; they neither drove their curricles nor sported their tandems,[6] for as yet those gaudy vehicles were not even dreamt of—neither did they distinguish themselves by their brilliancy at the table, and their consequent rencontres with watchmen, for our forefathers were of too pacific a disposition to need those guardians of the night, every soul throughout the town being sound asleep before nine o'clock. Neither did they establish their claims to gentility at the expense of their tailors—for as yet those offenders against the pockets of society, and the tranquillity of all aspiring young gentlemen, were unknown in New Amsterdam; every good housewife made the clothes of her husband and family, and even the goede vrouw[7] of Van Twiller himself thought it no disparagement to cut out her husband's linsey-woolsey galligaskins.[8]

Not but what there were some two or three youngsters who manifested the first dawnings of what is called fire and spirit; who held all labor in contempt; skulked about docks and market-places; loitered in the sunshine; squandered what little money they could procure at hustle-cap and chuck-farthing;[9] swore, boxed, fought cocks and raced their neighbor's horses—in short, who promised to be the wonder, the talk and abomination of the town, had not their stylish career been unfortunately cut short by an affair of honor with a whipping-post.

Far other, however, was the truly fashionable gentleman of those days—his dress, which served for both morning and evening, street and drawing-room, was a linsey-woolsey coat, made, perhaps, by the fair hands of the mistress of his affections, and gallantly bedecked with abundance of large brass buttons—half a score of breeches heightened the proportions of his figure—his shoes were decorated by enormous copper buckles—a low-crowned, broad-brimmed hat overshadowed his burly visage, and his hair dangled down his back in a prodigious queue of eelskin.

Thus equipped, he would manfully sally forth with pipe in mouth to besiege some fair damsel's obdurate heart—not such a pipe, good reader, as that which Acis did sweetly tune in praise of his Galatea,[10] but one of true Delft manufacture, and furnished with a charge of fragrant tobacco. With this would he resolutely set himself down before the fortress, and rarely failed, in the process of time, to smoke the fair enemy into a surrender, upon honorable terms.

---

[5]Kamschatka, region in extreme northeast of Russia; Lapland, area in northern Norway, Sweden, and Finland.
[6]Curricles were carriages drawn by horses abreast, tandems drawn by horses in file.
[7]Good frow (wife).
[8]Wide knee-breeches of that time.

[9]Games of chance of the time; in hustle-cap, the coins are shaken out of a cap; in chuck-farthing, coins are tossed toward a mark.
[10]In mythology, the river nymph Galatea loved Acis, killed by the Cyclops Polyphemus.

Such was the happy reign of Wouter Van Twiller, celebrated in many a long-forgotten song as the real golden age, the rest being nothing but counterfeit copper-washed coin. In that delightful period, a sweet and holy calm reigned over the whole province. The burgomaster smoked his pipe in peace—the substantial solace of his domestic cares, after her daily toils were done, sat soberly at the door, with her arms crossed over her apron of snowy white, without being insulted by ribald streetwalkers or vagabond boys—those unlucky urchins, who do so infest our streets, displaying under the roses of youth the thorns and briers of iniquity. Then it was that the lover with ten breeches, and the damsel with petticoats of half a score, indulged in all the innocent endearments of virtuous love without fear and without reproach; for what had that virtue to fear, which was defended by a shield of good linsey-woolseys, equal at least to the seven bull-hides of the invincible Ajax?[11]

Ah blissful, and never to be forgotten age! when every thing was better than it has ever been since, or ever will be again—when Buttermilk Channel[12] was quite dry at low water—when the shad in the Hudson were all salmon, and when the moon shone with a pure and resplendent whiteness, instead of that melancholy yellow light which is the consequence of her sickening at the abominations she every night witnesses in this degenerate city!

Happy would it have been for New Amsterdam could it always have existed in this state of blissful ignorance and lowly simplicity, but alas! the days of childhood are too sweet to last! Cities, like men, grow out of them in time, and are doomed alike to grow into the bustle, the cares and miseries of the world. Let no man congratulate himself, when he beholds the child of his bosom or the city of his birth increasing in magnitude and importance—let the history of his own life teach him the dangers of the one, and this excellent little history of Manna-hata convince him of the calamities of the other.

1809

from The Sketch-Book of Geoffrey Crayon, Gent.

THE AUTHOR'S ACCOUNT OF HIMSELF

I am of this mind with Homer, that as the snaile
that crept out of her shel was turned eftsoones into
a Toad, and thereby was forced to make a stoole to
sit on; so the traveller that stragleth from his owne
country is in a short time transformed into so
monstrous a shape that he is faine to alter his
mansion with his manners and to live where he can,
not where he would.

Lyly's Euphues.[1]

I was always fond of visiting new scenes and observing strange characters and manners. Even when a mere child I began my travels and made many tours of discovery into foreign parts and unknown regions of my native city; to the frequent alarm of my parents and the emolument of the town cryer. As I grew into

---

[11]Ajax, one of the strongest warriors in the siege of Troy (in Homer's *Iliad*), bore a huge shield of enormous strength.

[12]A body of water between Governor's Island and Long Island, originally very narrow and shallow.

[1]John Lyly (1554–1606), author of *Euphues: The Anatomy of Wit* (1578) and *Euphues and His England* (1580), both rambling romances short on plot but long on style, which sometimes sacrifices substance to elegant balance.

boyhood I extended the range of my observations. My holyday afternoons were spent in rambles about the surrounding country. I made myself familiar with all its places famous in history or fable. I knew every spot where a murder or robbery had been committed or a ghost seen. I visited the neighbouring villages and added greatly to my stock of knowledge, by noting their habits and customs, and conversing with their sages and great men. I even journeyed one long summer's day to the summit of the most distant hill, from whence I stretched my eye over many a mile of terra incognita,[2] and was astonished to find how vast a globe I inhabited.

This rambling propensity strengthened with my years. Books of voyages and travels became my passion, and in devouring their contents I neglected the regular exercises of the school. How wistfully would I wander about the pier heads in fine weather, and watch the parting ships, bound to distant climes. With what longing eyes would I gaze after their lessening sails, and waft myself in imagination to the ends of the earth.

Further reading and thinking, though they brought this vague inclination into more reasonable bounds, only served to make it more decided. I visited various parts of my own country, and had I been merely a lover of fine scenery, I should have felt little desire to seek elsewhere its gratification, for on no country have the charms of nature been more prodigally lavished. Her mighty lakes, like oceans of liquid silver; her mountains with their bright aerial tints; her valleys teeming with wild fertility; her tremendous cataracts thundering in their solitudes; her boundless plains waving with spontaneous verdure; her broad deep rivers, rolling in solemn silence to the ocean; her trackless forests, where vegetation puts forth all its magnificence; her skies kindling with the magic of summer clouds and glorious sunshine—no, never need an American look beyond his own country for the sublime and beautiful of natural scenery.

But Europe held forth the charms of storied and poetical association. There were to be seen the masterpieces of art, the refinements of highly cultivated society, the quaint peculiarities of ancient and local custom. My native country was full of youthful promise; Europe was rich in the accumulated treasures of age. Her very ruins told the history of times gone by, and every mouldering stone was a chronicle. I longed to wander over the scenes of renowned achievement—to tread as it were in the footsteps of antiquity—to loiter about the ruined castle—to meditate on the falling tower—to escape in short, from the commonplace realities of the present, and lose myself among the shadowy grandeurs of the past.

I had, beside all this, an earnest desire to see the great men of the earth. We have, it is true, our great men in America—not a city but has an ample share of them. I have mingled among them in my time, and been almost withered by the shade into which they cast me; for there is nothing so baleful to a small man as the shade of a great one, particularly the great man of a city. But I was anxious to see the great men of Europe; for I had read in the works of various philosophers, that all animals degenerated in America, and man among the number.[3] A great man of Europe, thought I, must therefore be as superior to a great man of America, as a peak of the Alps to a highland of the Hudson; and in this idea I was confirmed by observing the comparative importance and swelling magnitude of many English travellers among us; who, I was assured, were very little people in their own country.—I will visit this land of wonders, thought I, and see the gigantic race from which I am degenerated.

It has been either my good or evil lot to have my roving passion gratified. I

---

[2] "Unknown land" (Latin).
[3] A theory particularly of the French scientist-philosopher, Georges Louis Leclerc de Buffon (1707–1788).

have wandered through different countries and witnessed many of the shifting scenes of life. I cannot say that I have studied them with the eye of a philosopher, but rather with the sauntering gaze with which humble lovers of the picturesque stroll from the window of one print shop to another; caught sometimes by the delineations of beauty, sometimes by the distortions of caricature and sometimes by the loveliness of landscape. As it is the fashion for modern tourists to travel pencil in hand, and bring home their portfolios filled with sketches, I am disposed to get up a few for the entertainment of my friends. When I look over, however, the hints and memorandums I have taken down for the purpose, my heart almost fails me at finding how my idle humour has led me aside from the great objects studied by every regular traveller who would make a book. I fear I shall give equal disappointment with an unlucky landscape painter, who had travelled on the continent, but following the bent of his vagrant inclination, had sketched in nooks and corners and bye places. His sketch book was accordingly crowded with cottages, and landscapes, and obscure ruins; but he had neglected to paint St. Peter's or the Coliseum; the cascade of Terni[4] or the Bay of Naples; and had not a single Glacier or Volcano in his whole collection.

1819

RIP VAN WINKLE[1]

The following Tale was found among the papers of the late Diedrich Knickerbocker, an old gentleman of New York, who was very curious in the Dutch history of the province, and the manners of the descendants from its primitive settlers. His historical researches, however, did not lie so much among books, as among men; for the former are lamentably scanty on his favourite topics; whereas he found the old burghers, and still more, their wives, rich in that legendary lore so invaluable to true history. Whenever, therefore, he happened upon a genuine Dutch family, snugly shut up in its low roofed farm house, under a spreading sycamore, he looked upon it as a little clasped volume of black letter,[2] and studied it with the zeal of a bookworm.

The result of all these researches was a history of the province, during the reign of the Dutch governors, which he published some years since. There have been various opinions as to the literary character of his work and, to tell the truth, it is not a whit better than it should be. Its chief merit is its scrupulous accuracy, which indeed was a little questioned on its first appearance, but has since been completely established; and it is now admitted into all historical collections as a book of unquestionable authority.

The old gentleman died shortly after the publication of his work, and now that he is dead and gone, it cannot do much harm to his memory to say that his time might have been much better employed in weightier labours. He, however, was apt to ride his hobby his own way; and though it did now and then kick up the dust a little in the eyes of his neighbours, and grieve the spirit of some friends for whom he felt the truest deference and affection; yet his errors and follies are remembered "more in sorrow than in anger,"[3] and it begins to be suspected that he never intended to injure or offend. But however his memory may be appreciated by criticks, it is still held dear by many folk whose good opinion is well worth having; particularly by certain biscuit bakers, who have gone so far as to imprint his likeness on their new year cakes, and have thus given him a chance for immortal-

---

[4]Artificially created cascade near Terni in Italy's province of Perugia.
[1]Irving found his plot for "Rip Van Winkle" in German folk legend (particularly "Peter Klaus" in the *Volkssagen* of J. C. C. N. Otmar), but his experience of life in early New York shaped his imagination.
[2]A heavy-faced type used in the early book (Gothic).
[3]*Hamlet*, Act I, Scene ii.

ity, almost equal to being stamped on a Waterloo medal, or a Queen Anne's far-thing.[4]

RIP VAN WINKLE

A Posthumous Writing of Diedrich Knickerbocker

By Woden,[5] God of Saxons,
From whence comes Wensday, that is Wodensday,
Truth is a thing that ever I will keep
Unto thylke day in which I creep into
My sepulchre—

Cartwright.[6]

Whoever has made a voyage up the Hudson must remember the Kaatskill mountains. They are a dismembered branch of the great Appalachian family, and are seen away to the west of the river swelling up to noble height and lording it over the surrounding country. Every change of season, every change of weather, indeed every hour of the day, produces some change in the magical hues and shapes of these mountains, and they are regarded by all the good wives far and near as perfect barometers. When the weather is fair and settled they are clothed in blue and purple, and print their bold outlines on the clear evening sky; but sometimes, when the rest of the landscape is cloudless, they will gather a hood of grey vapours about their summits, which, in the last rays of the setting sun, will glow and light up like a crown of glory.

At the foot of these fairy mountains the voyager may have descried the light smoke curling up from a village, whose shingle roofs gleam among the trees, just where the blue tints of the upland melt away into the fresh green of the nearer landscape. It is a little village of great antiquity, having been founded by some of the Dutch colonists in the early times of the province, just about the beginning of the government of the good Peter Stuyvesant,[7] (may he rest in peace!) and there were some of the houses of the original settlers standing within a few years; built of small yellow bricks brought from Holland, having latticed windows and gable fronts, surmounted with weathercocks.

In that same village, and in one of these very houses (which to tell the precise truth was sadly time worn and weather beaten) there lived many years since, while the country was yet a province of Great Britain, a simple good natured fellow of the name of Rip Van Winkle. He was a descendant of the Van Winkles who figured so gallantly in the chivalrous days of Peter Stuyvesant, and accompanied him to the siege of Fort Christina. He inherited, however, but little of the martial character of his ancestors. I have observed that he was a simple good natured man; he was moreover a kind neighbour, and an obedient, henpecked husband. Indeed to the latter circumstance might be owing that meekness of spirit which gained him such universal popularity; for those men are most apt to be obsequious and conciliating abroad, who are under the discipline of shrews at home. Their tempers doubtless are rendered pliant and malleable in the fiery furnace of domestic tribulation, and a curtain lecture[8] is worth all the sermons in the world for teaching the virtues of patience and long suffering. A termagant wife may therefore in some respects be considered a tolerable blessing—and if so, Rip Van Winkle was thrice blessed.

---

[4]The Waterloo medal was issued to all the British soldiers who participated in the battle that defeated Napoleon in 1815; Queen Anne's farthings were small coins issued bearing her image during her reign (1702–14). Neither the medal nor the coin is rare.
[5]Norse god of war.

[6]William Cartwright (1611–1643), British playwright, author of the drama *The Ordinary*.
[7]Governor of New Netherland (1647–64).
[8]A scolding delivered by wife to husband after they have retreated behind the curtains of the old four-poster bed.

Certain it is that he was a great favourite among all the good wives of the village, who as usual with the amiable sex, took his part in all family squabbles, and never failed, whenever they talked those matters over in their evening gossippings, to lay all the blame on Dame Van Winkle. The children of the village too would shout with joy whenever he approached. He assisted at their sports, made their play things, taught them to fly kites and shoot marbles, and told them long stories of ghosts, witches and Indians. Whenever he went dodging about the village he was surrounded by a troop of them hanging on his skirts, clambering on his back and playing a thousand tricks on him with impunity; and not a dog would bark at him throughout the neighbourhood.

The great error in Rip's composition was an insuperable aversion to all kinds of profitable labour. It could not be from the want of assiduity or perseverance; for he would sit on a wet rock, with a rod as long and heavy as a Tartar's lance, and fish all day without a murmur, even though he should not be encouraged by a single nibble. He would carry a fowling piece on his shoulder for hours together, trudging through woods, and swamps and up hill and down dale, to shoot a few squirrels or wild pigeons; he would never refuse to assist a neighbour even in the roughest toil, and was a foremost man at all country frolicks for husking Indian corn, or building stone fences; the women of the village too used to employ him to run their errands and to do such little odd jobs as their less obliging husbands would not do for them—in a word Rip was ready to attend to any body's business but his own; but as to doing family duty, and keeping his farm in order, he found it impossible.

In fact he declared it was of no use to work on his farm; it was the most pestilent little piece of ground in the whole country; every thing about it went wrong and would go wrong in spite of him. His fences were continually falling to pieces; his cow would either go astray or get among the cabbages, weeds were sure to grow quicker in his fields than any where else; the rain always made a point of setting in just as he had some outdoor work to do. So that though his patrimonial estate had dwindled away under his management, acre by acre until there was little more left than a mere patch of Indian corn and potatoes, yet it was the worst conditioned farm in the neighbourhood.

His children too were as ragged and wild as if they belonged to nobody. His son Rip, an urchin begotten in his own likeness, promised to inherit the habits with the old clothes of his father. He was generally seen trooping like a colt at his mother's heels, equipped in a pair of his father's cast off galligaskins,[9] which he had much ado to hold up with one hand, as a fine lady does her train in bad weather.

Rip Van Winkle, however, was one of those happy mortals of foolish, well oiled dispositions, who take the world easy, eat white bread or brown, whichever can be got with least thought or trouble, and would rather starve on a penny than work for a pound. If left to himself, he would have whistled life away in perfect contentment, but his wife kept continually dinning in his ears about his idleness, his carelessness and the ruin he was bringing on his family. Morning noon and night her tongue was incessantly going, and every thing he said or did was sure to produce a torrent of household eloquence. Rip had but one way of replying to all lectures of the kind, and that by frequent use had grown into a habit. He shrugged his shoulders, shook his head, cast up his eyes, but said nothing. This, however, always provoked a fresh volley from his wife, so that he was fain to draw off his forces and take to the outside of the house—the only side which in truth belongs to a henpecked husband.

---

[9]Loose breeches.

Rip's sole domestic adherent was his dog Wolf who was as much henpecked as his master, for Dame Van Winkle regarded them as companions in idleness, and even looked upon Wolf with an evil eye as the cause of his master's going so often astray. True it is, in all points of spirit befitting an honourable dog, he was as courageous an animal as ever scoured the woods—but what courage can withstand the ever during and all besetting terrors of a woman's tongue? The moment Wolf entered the house his crest fell, his tail drooped to the ground or curled between his legs, he sneaked about with a gallows air, casting many a sidelong glance at Dame Van Winkle, and at the least flourish of a broomstick or ladle he would fly to the door with yelping precipitation.

Times grew worse and worse with Rip Van Winkle as years of matrimony rolled on; a tart temper never mellows with age, and a sharp tongue is the only edged tool that grows keener with constant use. For a long while he used to console himself when driven from home, by frequenting a kind of perpetual club of the sages, philosophers and other idle personages of the village which held its sessions on a bench before a small inn, designated by a rubicund portrait of his majesty George the Third. Here they used to sit in the shade, through a long lazy summer's day, talking listlessly over village gossip, or telling endless sleepy stories about nothing. But it would have been worth any statesman's money to have heard the profound discussions that sometimes took place, when by chance an old newspaper fell into their hands from some passing traveller. How solemnly they would listen to the contents as drawled out by Derrick Van Bummel the schoolmaster, a dapper, learned little man, who was not to be daunted by the most gigantic word in the dictionary; and how sagely they would deliberate upon public events some months after they had taken place.

The opinions of this junto[10] were completely controlled by Nicholaus Vedder, a patriarch of the village, and landlord of the inn, at the door of which he took his seat from morning till night, just moving sufficiently to avoid the sun and keep in the shade of a large tree; so that the neighbours could tell the hour by his movements as accurately as by a sun dial. It is true he was rarely heard to speak, but smoked his pipe incessantly. His adherents, however (for every great man has his adherents), perfectly understood him and knew how to gather his opinions. When any thing that was read or related displeased him, he was observed to smoke his pipe vehemently and to send forth short, frequent and angry puffs; but when pleased he would inhale the smoke slowly and tranquilly and emit it in light and placid clouds, and sometimes taking the pipe from his mouth and letting the fragrant vapour curl about his nose, would gravely nod his head in token of perfect approbation.

From even this strong hold the unlucky Rip was at length routed by his termagant wife who would suddenly break in upon the tranquility of the assemblage and call the members all to naught; nor was that august personage Nicholaus Vedder himself sacred from the daring tongue of this terrible virago, who charged him outright with encouraging her husband in habits of idleness.

Poor Rip was at last reduced almost to despair; and his only alternative to escape from the labour of the farm and the clamour of his wife, was to take gun in hand and stroll away into the woods. Here he would sometimes seat himself at the foot of a tree and share the contents of his wallet[11] with Wolf, with whom he sympathised as a fellow sufferer in persecution. "Poor Wolf," he would say, "thy mistress leads thee a dog's life of it, but never mind my lad, whilst I live thou shalt never want a friend to stand by thee!" Wolf would wag his tail, look wistfully in his master's face, and if dogs can feel pity I verily believe he reciprocated the sentiment with all his heart.

---

[10]Ruling group.
[11]Knapsack.

In a long ramble of the kind on a fine autumnal day, Rip had unconsciously scrambled to one of the highest parts of the Kaatskill mountains. He was after his favourite sport of squirrel shooting and the still solitudes had echoed and re-echoed with the reports of his gun. Panting and fatigued he threw himself, late in the afternoon, on a green knoll, covered with mountain herbage, that crowned the brow of a precipice. From an opening between the trees he could overlook all the lower country for many a mile of rich woodland. He saw at a distance the lordly Hudson, far, far below him, moving on its silent but majestic course, with the reflection of a purple cloud, or the sail of a lagging bark here and there sleeping on its glassy bosom, and at last losing itself in the blue highlands.

On the other side he looked down into a deep mountain glen, wild, lonely and shagged, the bottom filled with fragments from the impending cliffs and scarcely lighted by the reflected rays of the setting sun. For some time Rip lay musing on this scene, evening was gradually advancing, the mountains began to throw their long blue shadows over the valleys, he saw that it would be dark, long before he could reach the village, and he heaved a heavy sigh when he thought of encountering the terrors of Dame Van Winkle.

As he was about to descend he heard a voice from a distance hallooing "Rip Van Winkle! Rip Van Winkle!" He looked around, but could see nothing but a crow winging its solitary flight across the mountain. He thought his fancy must have deceived him and turned again to descend, which he heard the same cry ring through the still evening air: "Rip Van Winkle! Rip Van Winkle!"—at the same time Wolf bristled up his back and giving a low growl, skulked to his master's side, looking fearfully down into the glen. Rip now felt a vague apprehension stealing over him; he looked anxiously in the same direction and perceived a strange figure slowly toiling up the rocks and bending under the weight of something he carried on his back. He was surprised to see any human being in this lonely and unfrequented place, but supposing it to be some one of the neighbourhood in need of his assistance he hastened down to yield it.

On nearer approach he was still more surprised at the singularity of the stranger's appearance. He was a short, square built old fellow, with thick bushy hair and a grizzled beard. His dress was of the antique Dutch fashion, a cloth jerkin[12] strapped round the waist, several pair of breeches, the outer one of ample volume decorated with rows of buttons down the sides and bunches at the knees. He bore on his shoulder a stout keg that seemed full of liquor, and made signs for Rip to approach and assist him with the load. Though rather shy and distrustful of this new acquaintance Rip complied with his usual alacrity, and mutually relieving each other they clambered up a narrow gully apparently the dry bed of a mountain torrent. As they ascended Rip every now and then heard long rolling peals like distant thunder, that seemed to issue out of a deep ravine or rather cleft between lofty rocks, toward which their rugged path conducted. He paused for an instant, but supposing it to be the muttering of one of those transient thunder showers which often take place in mountain heights, he proceeded. Passing through the ravine they came to a hollow like a small amphitheatre, surrounded by perpendicular precipices, over the brinks of which impending trees shot their branches, so that you only caught glimpses of the azure sky and the bright evening cloud. During the whole time Rip and his companion had laboured on in silence, for though the former marvelled greatly what could be the object of carrying a keg of liquor up this wild mountain, yet there was something strange and incomprehensible about the unknown, that inspired awe and checked familiarity.

On entering the amphitheatre new objects of wonder presented themselves. On a level spot in the centre was a company of odd looking personages playing at ninepins. They were dressed in a quaint outlandish fashion—some wore short

---

[12]Jacket.

doublets,[13] others jerkins with long knives in their belts and most of them had enormous breeches of similar style with that of the guide's. Their visages too were peculiar. One had a large head, broad face and small piggish eyes. The face of another seemed to consist entirely of nose, and was surmounted by a white sugar-loaf hat, set off with a little red cock's tail. They all had beards of various shapes and colours. There was one who seemed to be the Commander. He was a stout old gentleman, with a weatherbeaten countenance. He wore a laced doublet, broad belt and hanger,[14] high crowned hat and feather, red stockings and high heel'd shoes with roses in them. The whole group reminded Rip of the figures in an old Flemish painting, in the parlour of Dominie[15] Van Schaick the village parson, and which had been brought over from Holland at the time of the settlement.

What seemed particularly odd to Rip was, that though these folks were evidently amusing themselves, yet they maintained the gravest faces, the most mysterious silence, and were, withal, the most melancholy party of pleasure he had ever witnessed. Nothing interrupted the stillness of the scene, but the noise of the balls, which, whenever they were rolled, echoed along the mountains like rumbling peals of thunder.

As Rip and his companion approached them they suddenly desisted from their play and stared at him with such fixed statue like gaze, and such strange uncouth, lack lustre countenances, that his heart turned within him, and his knees smote together. His companion now emptied the contents of the keg into large flagons and made signs to him to wait upon the company. He obeyed with fear and trembling; they quaffed the liquor in profound silence and then returned to their game.

By degrees Rip's awe and apprehension subsided. He even ventured, when no eye was fixed upon him, to taste the beverage, which he found had much of the flavour of excellent hollands.[16] He was naturally a thirsty soul and was soon tempted to repeat the draught. One taste provoked another, and he reiterated his visits to the flagon so often that at length his senses were overpowered, his eyes swam in his head—his head gradually declined and he fell into a deep sleep.

On awaking he found himself on the green knoll from whence he had first seen the old man of the glen. He rubbed his eyes—it was a bright, sunny morning. The birds were hopping and twittering among the bushes, and the eagle was wheeling aloft and breasting the pure mountain breeze. "Surely," thought Rip, "I have not slept here all night." He recalled the occurrences before he fell asleep. The strange man with a keg of liquor—the mountain ravine—the wild retreat among the rocks—the woe begone party at ninepins—the flagon—"ah! that flagon! that wicked flagon!" thought Rip—"what excuse shall I make to Dame Van Winkle?"

He looked round for his gun, but in place of the clean well oiled fowling piece he found an old firelock lying by him, the barrel encrusted with rust; the lock falling off and the stock worm eaten. He now suspected that the grave roysters of the mountain had put a trick upon him, and having dosed him with liquor, had robbed him of his gun. Wolf too had disappeared, but he might have strayed away after a squirrel or partridge. He whistled after him and shouted his name—but all in vain; the echoes repeated his whistle and shout, but no dog was to be seen.

He determined to revisit the scene of the last evening's gambol, and if he met with any of the party, to demand his dog and gun. As he arose to walk he found himself stiff in the joints and wanting in his usual activity. "These mountain beds do not agree with me," thought Rip, "and if this frolick should lay me up with a fit

---

[13]Man's close-fitting jacket.
[14]A short sword hung from the belt.

[15]Pastor.
[16]Gin made in Holland.

of the rheumatism, I shall have a blessed time with Dame Van Winkle." With some difficulty he got down into the glen; he found the gully up which he and his companion had ascended the preceding evening, but to his astonishment a mountain stream was now foaming down it; leaping from rock to rock, and filling the glen with babbling murmurs. He, however, made shift to scramble up its sides working his toilsome way through thickets of birch, sassafras and witch hazel, and sometimes tripped up or entangled by the wild grape vines that twisted their coils and tendrils from tree to tree, and spread a kind of net work in his path.

At length he reached to where the ravine had opened through the cliffs, to the amphitheatre—but no traces of such opening remained. The rocks presented a high impenetrable wall over which the torrent came tumbling in a sheet of feathery foam, and fell into a broad deep basin black from the shadows of the surrounding forest. Here then poor Rip was brought to a stand. He again called and whistled after his dog—he was only answered by the cawing of a flock of idle crows, sporting high in air about a dry tree that overhung a sunny precipice; and who, secure in their elevation seemed to look down and scoff at the poor man's perplexities.

What was to be done? The morning was passing away and Rip felt famished for want of his breakfast. He grieved to give up his dog and gun; he dreaded to meet his wife; but it would not do to starve among the mountains. He shook his head, shouldered the rusty fire lock and with a heart full of trouble and anxiety, turned his steps homeward.

As he approached the village he met a number of people, but none whom he knew, which somewhat surprised him, for he had thought himself acquainted with every one in the country round. Their dress too was of a different fashion from that to which he was accustomed. They all stared at him with equal marks of surprise, and whenever they cast their eyes upon him, invariably stroked their chins. The constant recurrence of this gesture induced Rip involuntarily to do the same, when to his astonishment he found his beard had grown a foot long!

He had now entered the skirts of the village. A troop of strange children ran at his heels, hooting after him and pointing at his grey beard. The dogs too, not one of which he recognized for an old acquaintance, barked at him as he passed. The very village was altered—it was larger and more populous. There were rows of houses which he had never seen before, and those which had been his familiar haunts had disappeared. Strange names were over the doors—strange faces at the windows—every thing was strange. His mind now misgave him; he began to doubt whether both he and the world around him were not bewitched. Surely this was his native village which he had left but the day before. There stood the Kaatskill mountains—there ran the silver Hudson at a distance—there was every hill and dale precisely as it had always been—Rip was sorely perplexed—"That flagon last night," thought he, "has addled my poor head sadly!"

It was with some difficulty that he found the way to his own house, which he approached with silent awe, expecting every moment to hear the shrill voice of Dame Van Winkle. He found the house gone to decay—the roof fallen in, the windows shattered and the doors off the hinges. A half-starved dog that looked like Wolf was skulking about it. Rip called him by name but the cur snarled, shewed his teeth and passed on. This was an unkind cut indeed—"My very dog," sighed poor Rip, "has forgotten me!"

He entered the house, which, to tell the truth, Dame Van Winkle had always kept in neat order. It was empty, forlorn and apparently abandoned. This desolateness overcame all his connubial fears—he called loudly for his wife and children—the lonely chambers rung for a moment with his voice, and then all again was silence.

He now hurried forth and hastened to his old resort, the village inn—but it too was gone. A large, ricketty wooden building stood in its place, with great gaping windows, some of them broken, and mended with old hats and petticoats, and over the door was printed "The Union Hotel, by Jonathan Doolittle." Instead of the great tree, that used to shelter the quiet little Dutch inn of yore, there now was reared a tall naked pole with something on top that looked like a red night cap,[17] and from it was fluttering a flag on which was a singular assemblage of stars and stripes—all this was strange and incomprehensible. He recognized on the sign, however, the ruby face of King George under which he had smoked so many a peaceful pipe, but even this was singularly metamorphosed. The red coat was changed for one of blue and buff;[18] a sword was held in the hand instead of a sceptre; the head was decorated with a cocked hat, and underneath was printed in large characters GENERAL WASHINGTON.

There was as usual a crowd of folk about the door; but none that Rip recollected. The very character of the people seemed changed. There was a busy, bustling disputatious tone about it, instead of the accustomed phlegm and drowsy tranquility. He looked in vain for the sage Nicholaus Vedder with his broad face, double chin and fair long pipe, uttering clouds of tobacco smoke instead of idle speeches. Or Van Bummel the schoolmaster doling forth the contents of an ancient newspaper. In place of these a lean bilious looking fellow with his pockets full of hand bills, was haranguing vehemently about rights of citizens—elections—members of Congress—liberty—Bunker's hill—heroes of seventy six—and other words which were a perfect babylonish jargon[19] to the bewildered Van Winkle.

The appearance of Rip with his long grizzled beard, his rusty fowling piece, his uncouth dress and an army of women and children at his heels soon attracted the attention of the tavern politicians. They crowded around him eying him from head to foot, with great curiosity. The orator bustled up to him, and drawing him partly aside, enquired "on which side he voted?"—Rip stared in vacant stupidity. Another short but busy little fellow, pulled him by the arm and rising on tiptoe, enquired in his ear "whether he was Federal or Democrat?"[20]—Rip was equally at a loss to comprehend the question—when a knowing, self important old gentleman, in a sharp cocked hat, made his way through the crowd, putting them to the right and left with his elbows as he passed, and planting himself before Van Winkle, with one arm akimbo, the other resting on his cane, his keen eyes and sharp hat penetrating as it were into his very soul, demanded in an austere tone—"what brought him to the election with a gun on his shoulder and a mob at his heels, and whether he meant to breed a riot in the village?"—"Alas gentlemen," cried Rip, somewhat dismayed, "I am a poor quiet man, a native of the place, and a loyal subject of the King—God bless him!"

Here a general shout burst from the byestanders—"A tory! a tory! a spy! a Refugee! hustle him! away with him!"—It was with great difficulty that the self important man in the cocked hat restored order; and having assumed a ten fold austerity of brow demanded again of the unknown culprit, what he came there for and whom he was seeking. The poor man humbly assured him that he meant no harm; but merely came there in search of some of his neighbours, who used to keep about the tavern.

"—Well—who are they?—name them."

Rip bethought himself a moment and enquired, "Where's Nicholaus Vedder?"

---

[17]A soft, visorless cap adopted by French Revolutionists as a symbol of liberty.
[18]Colors of the uniforms of American Revolutionary soldiers.
[19]Incomprehensible babble, as in the Tower of Babel, Genesis 11:1-9.

[20]Political parties established in the beginning of the United States, the Federalist, conservative and Hamiltonian, the Democratic-Republican, liberal and Jeffersonian.

There was a silence for a little while, when an old man replied, in a thin, piping voice, "Nicholaus Vedder? why he is dead and gone these eighteen years! There was a wooden tombstone in the church yard that used to tell all about him, but that's rotted and gone too."

"Where's Brom Dutcher?"

"Oh he went off to the army in the beginning of the war; some say he was killed at the storming of Stoney Point[21]—others say he was drowned in a squall at the foot of Antony's Nose[22]—I don't know—he never came back again."

"Where's Van Bummel the schoolmaster?"

"He went off to the wars too—was a great militia general, and is now in Congress."

Rip's heart died away at hearing of these sad changes in his home and friends, and finding himself thus alone in the world—every answer puzzled him too by treating of such enormous lapses of time and of matters which he could not understand—war—Congress, Stoney Point—he had no courage to ask after any more friends, but cried out in despair, "Does nobody here know Rip Van Winkle?"

"Oh. Rip Van Winkle?" exclaimed two or three—"oh to be sure!—that's Rip Van Winkle—yonder—leaning against the tree."

Rip looked and beheld a precise counterpart of himself, as he went up the mountain: apparently as lazy and certainly as ragged! The poor fellow was now completely confounded. He doubted his own identity, and whether he was himself or another man. In the midst of his bewilderment the man in the cocked hat demanded who he was,—what was his name?

"God knows," exclaimed he, at his wit's end. "I'm not myself.—I'm somebody else—that's me yonder—no—that's somebody else got into my shoes—I was myself last night; but I fell asleep on the mountain—and they've changed my gun—and every thing's changed—and I'm changed—and I can't tell what's my name, or who I am!"

The byestanders began now to look at each other, nod, wink significantly and tap their fingers against their foreheads. There was a whisper also about securing the gun, and keeping the old fellow from doing mischief—at the very suggestion of which, the self important man in the cocked hat retired with some precipitation. At this critical moment a fresh likely looking woman pressed through the throng to get a peep at the greybearded man. She had a chubby child in her arms, which frightened at his looks began to cry. "Hush Rip," cried she, "hush you little fool, the old man won't hurt you." The name of the child, the air of the mother, the tone of her voice all awakened a train of recollections in his mind. "What is your name my good woman?" asked he.

"Judith Gardenier."

"And your father's name?"

"Ah, poor man, Rip Van Winkle was his name, but it's twenty years since he went away from home with his gun and never has been heard of since—his dog came home without him—but whether he shot himself, or was carried away by the Indians no body can tell. I was then but a little girl."

Rip had but one question more to ask, but he put it with a faltering voice—

"Where's your mother?"—

Oh she too had died but a short time since—she broke a blood vessel in a fit of passion at a New England pedlar.—

There was a drop of comfort at least in this intelligence. The honest man could

---

[21]Location of British fort on the Hudson captured by Americans in 1779.
[22]Promontory near Stoney Point on the Hudson.

contain himself no longer—he caught his daughter and her child in his arms.—"I am your father!" cried he—"Young Rip Van Winkle once—old Rip Van Winkle now!—does nobody know poor Rip Van Winkle!"

All stood amazed, until an old woman tottering out from among the crowd put her hand to her brow and peering under it in his face for a moment exclaimed—"Sure enough!—it is Rip Van Winkle—it is himself—welcome home again old neighbour—why, where have you been these twenty long years?"

Rip's story was soon told, for the whole twenty years had been to him but as one night. The neighbours stared when they heard it; some were seen to wink at each other and put their tongues in their cheeks, and the self important man in the cocked hat, who when the alarm was over had returned to the field, screwed down the corners of his mouth and shook his head—upon which there was a general shaking of the head throughout the assemblage.

It was determined, however, to take the opinion of old Peter Vanderdonk, who was seen slowly advancing up the road. He was a descendant of the historian of that name,[23] who wrote one of the earliest accounts of the province. Peter was the most ancient inhabitant of the village and well versed in all the wonderful events and traditions of the neighbourhood. He recollected Rip at once, and corroborated his story in the most satisfactory manner. He assured the company that it was a fact handed down from his ancestor the historian, that the Kaatskill mountains had always been haunted by strange beings. That it was affirmed that the great Hendrick Hudson,[24] the first discoverer of the river and country, kept a kind of vigil there every twenty years, with his crew of the Half Moon—being permitted in this way to revisit the scenes of his enterprize and keep a guardian eye upon the river and the great city called by his name. That his father had once seen them in their old Dutch dresses playing at nine pins in a hollow of the mountain; and that he himself had heard one summer afternoon the sound of their balls, like distant peals of thunder.

To make a long story short—the company broke up, and returned to the more important concerns of the election. Rip's daughter took him home to live with her; she had a snug well furnished house, and a stout cheery farmer for a husband whom Rip recollected for one of the urchins that used to climb upon his back. As to Rip's son and heir, who was the ditto of himself seen leaning against the tree; he was employed to work on the farm; but evinced an hereditary disposition to attend to any thing else but his business.

Rip now resumed his old walks and habits; he soon found many of his former cronies, though all rather the worse for the wear and tear of time; and preferred making friends among the rising generation, with whom he soon grew into great favour. Having nothing to do at home, and being arrived at that happy age when a man can be idle, with impunity, he took his place once more on the bench at the inn door and was reverenced as one of the patriarchs of the village and a chronicle of the old times "before the war." It was some time before he could get into the regular track of gossip, or could be made to comprehend the strange events that had taken place during his torpor. How that there had been a revolutionary war—that the country had thrown off the yoke of Old England and that instead of being a subject of his majesty George the Third, he was now a free citizen of the United States. Rip in fact was no politician; the changes of states and empires made but little impression on him; but there was one species of despotism under which he had long groaned and that was petticoat government. Happily that was at an end—he had got his neck out of the yoke of matrimony, and could go in

[23]Adrian Van der Donck (1620–1655?), lawyer who wrote a history of New Netherland in 1655, published in English 1656.

[24]Henry Hudson (d. 1611), an English navigator and explorer in the service of the Dutch.

and out whenever he pleased without dreading the tyranny of Dame Van Winkle. Whenever her name was mentioned, however, he shook his head, shrugged his shoulders and cast up his eyes; which might pass either for an expression of resignation to his fate or joy at his deliverance.

He used to tell his story to every stranger that arrived at Mr. Doolittle's Hotel. He was observed at first to vary on some points, every time he told it, which was doubtless owing to his having so recently awaked. It at last settled down precisely to the tale I have related and not a man woman or child in the neighbourhood but knew it by heart. Some always pretended to doubt the reality of it, and insisted that Rip had been out of his head, and that this was one point on which he always remained flighty. The old Dutch inhabitants, however, almost universally gave it full credit—Even to this day they never hear a thunder storm of a summer afternoon about the Kaatskill, but they say Hendrick Hudson and his crew are at their game of nine pins; and it is a common wish of all henpecked husbands in the neighbourhood, when life hangs heavy on their hands, that they might have a quieting draught out of Rip Van Winkle's flagon.

NOTE

The foregoing tale one would suspect had been suggested to Mr. Knickerbocker by a little German superstition about the emperor Frederick *der Rothbart*[25] and the Kypphauser Mountain; the subjoined note, however, which he had appended to the tale, shews that it is an absolute fact, narrated with his usual fidelity.—

"The story of Rip Van Winkle may seem incredible to many, but nevertheless I give it my full belief, for I know the vicinity of our old Dutch settlements to have been very subject to marvellous events and appearances. Indeed I have heard many stranger stories than this, in the villages along the Hudson; all of which were too well authenticated to admit of a doubt. I have even talked with Rip Van Winkle myself, who when last I saw him was a very venerable old man and so perfectly rational and consistent on every other point, that I think no conscientious person could refuse to take this into the bargain—nay I have seen a certificate on the subject taken before a country justice and signed with a cross in the justice's own hand writing. The story therefore is beyond the possibility of doubt. D.K."

1819

THE LEGEND OF SLEEPY HOLLOW[1]

(FOUND AMONG THE PAPERS OF THE LATE DIEDRICH KNICKERBOCKER)

A pleasing land of drowsy head it was,
Of dreams that wave before the half-shut eye;
And of gay castles in the clouds that pass,
Forever flushing round a summer sky.

CASTLE OF INDOLENCE.[2]

In the bosom of one of those spacious coves which indent the eastern shore of the Hudson, at that broad expansion of the river denominated by the ancient Dutch navigators the Tappaan Zee, and where they always prudently shortened

---

[25]Frederick I, Holy Roman Emperor (1152–1190), sleeps according to legend in a cave in the Kyffhäusser mountain in Germany. Rothbart was also known as Barbarossa (both meaning Red Beard).
[1]For his "legend," Irving drew from various sources, including German folk tales, but he fashioned a work distinctively American in landscape, detail, and character.
[2]James Thomson (1700–1748), author of *Castle of Indolence* (1748).

sail, and implored the protection of St. Nicholas[3] when they crossed, there lies a small market town or rural port, which by some is called Greensburgh, but which is more generally and properly known by the name of Tarry Town.[4] This name was given, we are told, in former days, by the good housewives of the adjacent country, from the inveterate propensity of their husbands to linger about the village tavern on market days. Be that as it may, I do not vouch for the fact, but merely advert to it, for the sake of being precise and authentic. Not far from this village, perhaps about two miles, there is a little valley, or rather lap of land among high hills, which is one of the quietest places in the whole world. A small brook glides through it, with just murmur enough to lull one to repose, and the occasional whistle of a quail, or tapping of a woodpecker, is almost the only sound that ever breaks in upon the uniform tranquility.

I recollect that when a stripling, my first exploit in squirrel shooting was in a grove of tall walnut trees that shades one side of the valley. I had wandered into it at noon time, when all nature is peculiarly quiet, and was startled by the roar of my own gun, as it broke the sabbath stillness around, and was prolonged and reverberated by the angry echoes. If ever I should wish for a retreat, whither I might steal from the world and its distractions, and dream quietly away the remnant of a troubled life, I know of none more promising than this little valley.

From the listless repose of the place, and the peculiar character of its inhabitants, who are descendants from the original Dutch settlers, this sequestered glen has long been known by the name of SLEEPY HOLLOW, and its rustic lads are called the Sleepy Hollow Boys throughout all the neighbouring country. A drowsy, dreamy influence seems to hang over the land, and to pervade the very atmosphere. Some say that the place was bewitched by a high German doctor during the early days of the settlement; others, that an old Indian chief, the prophet or wizard of his tribe, held his powwows there before the country was discovered by Master Hendrick Hudson.[5] Certain it is, the place still continues under the sway of some witching power, that holds a spell over the minds of the good people, causing them to walk in a continual reverie. They are given to all kinds of marvellous beliefs; are subject to trances and visions, and frequently see strange sights, and hear music and voices in the air. The whole neighbourhood abounds with local tales, haunted spots, and twilight superstitions; stars shoot and meteors glare oftener across the valley than in any other part of the country, and the night mare, with her whole nine fold,[6] seems to make it the favourite scene of her gambols.

The dominant spirit, however, that haunts this enchanted region, and seems to be commander in chief of all the powers of the air, is the apparition of a figure on horseback without a head. It is said by some to be the ghost of a Hessian trooper,[7] whose head had been carried away by a cannon ball, in some nameless battle during the revolutionary war, and who is ever and anon seen by the country folk, hurrying along in the gloom of night, as if on the wings of the wind. His haunts are not confined to the valley, but extend at times to the adjacent roads, and especially to the vicinity of a church at no great distance. Indeed, certain of the most authentic historians of those parts, who have been careful in collecting and collating the floating facts concerning this spectre, allege, that the body of the trooper

---

[3]St. Nicholas was the protector of those in hazardous work, including sailors when shipwrecked.
[4]Tarrytown, some fifteen miles north of New York City. In 1835, Irving settled in the valley described here, building his home, Sunnyside.
[5]Henry Hudson (d. 1611), an Englishman who explored in the New World for the Dutch.

[6]*King Lear*, Act III, Scene iv, 1. 128: ". . .the nightmare and her nine fold"; in folklore, the demon nightmare had nine foals (mare's offspring) who were imps.
[7]German mercenary soldier who fought for the British in the Revolutionary War.

having been buried in the church yard, the ghost rides forth to the scene of battle in nightly quest of his head, and that the rushing speed with which he sometimes passes along the hollow, like a midnight blast, is owing to his being belated, and in a hurry to get back to the church yard before day break.

Such is the general purport of this legendary superstition, which has furnished materials for many a wild story in that region of shadows; and the spectre is known, at all the country firesides, by the name of The Headless Horseman of Sleepy Hollow.

It is remarkable, that the visionary propensity I have mentioned is not confined to the native inhabitants of the valley, but is unconsciously imbibed by every one who resides there for a time. However wide awake they may have been before they entered that sleepy region, they are sure, in a little time, to inhale the witching influence of the air, and begin to grow imaginative—to dream dreams, and see apparitions.

I mention this peaceful spot with all possible laud; for it is in such little retired Dutch valleys, found here and there embosomed in the great state of New York, that population, manners, and customs, remain fixed, while the great torrent of migration and improvement, which is making such incessant changes in other parts of this restless country, sweeps by them unobserved. They are like those little nooks of still water, which border a rapid stream, where we may see the straw and bubble riding quietly at anchor, or slowly revolving in their mimic harbour, undisturbed by the rush of the passing current. Though many years have elapsed since I trod the drowsy shades of Sleepy Hollow, yet I question whether I should not still find the same trees and the same families vegetating in its sheltered bosom.

In this by place of nature there abode, in a remote period of American history, that is to say, some thirty years since, a worthy wight of the name of Ichabod Crane, who sojourned, or, as he expressed it, "tarried," in Sleepy Hollow, for the purpose of instructing the children of the vicinity. He was a native of Connecticut, a state which supplies the Union with pioneers for the mind as well as for the forest, and sends forth yearly its legions of frontier woodmen and country schoolmasters. The cognomen of Crane was not inapplicable to his person. He was tall, but exceedingly lank, with narrow shoulders, long arms and legs, hands that dangled a mile out of his sleeves, feet that might have served for shovels, and his whole frame most loosely hung together. His head was small, and flat at top, with huge ears, large green glassy eyes, and a long snipe nose, so that it looked like a weathercock perched upon his spindle neck, to tell which way the wind blew. To see him striding along the profile of a hill on a windy day, with his clothes bagging and fluttering about him, one might have mistaken him for the genius of famine descending upon the earth, or some scarecrow eloped from a cornfield.

His school house was a low building of one large room, rudely constructed of logs; the windows partly glazed, and partly patched with leaves of old copy books. It was most ingeniously secured at vacant hours, by a withe twisted in the handle of the door, and stakes set against the window shutters; so that though a thief might get in with perfect ease, he would find some embarrassment in getting out; an idea most probably borrowed by the architect, Yost Van Houten, from the mystery of an eelpot. The school house stood in a rather lonely but pleasant situation, just at the foot of a woody hill, with a brook running close by, and a formidable birch tree growing at one end of it. From hence the low murmur of his pupils' voices conning over their lessons, might be heard of a drowsy summer's day, like the hum of a bee hive; interrupted now and then by the authoritative voice of the master, in the tone of menace or command, or peradventure, by the appalling sound of the birch, as he urged some tardy loiterer along the flowery path of knowledge. Truth to say, he was a conscientious man, and ever bore in mind the golden maxim, "spare the rod and spoil the child."[8]—Ichabod Crane's scholars certainly were not spoiled.

I would not have it imagined, however, that he was one of those cruel potentates of the school, who joy in the smart of their subjects; on the contrary, he administered justice with discrimination rather than severity; taking the burthen off the backs of the weak, and laying it on those of the strong. Your mere puny stripling, that winced at the least flourish of the rod, was passed by with indulgence; but the claims of justice were satisfied, by inflicting a double portion on some little, tough, wrong headed, broad skirted Dutch urchin, who sulked and swelled and grew dogged and sullen beneath the birch. All this he called "doing his duty by their parents;" and he never inflicted a chastisement without following it by the assurance, so consolatory to the smarting urchin, that "he would remember it and thank him for it the longest day he had to live."

When school hours were over, he was even the companion and playmate of the larger boys; and on holyday afternoons would convoy some of the smaller ones home, who happened to have pretty sisters, or good housewives for mothers, noted for the comforts of the cupboard. Indeed, it behooved him to keep on good terms with his pupils. The revenue arising from his school was small, and would have been scarcely sufficient to furnish him with daily bread, for he was a huge feeder, and though lank, had the dilating powers of an Anaconda; but to help out his maintenance, he was, according to country custom in those parts, boarded and lodged at the houses of the farmers, whose children he instructed. With these he lived successively a week at a time, thus going the rounds of the neighbourhood, with all his worldly effects tied up in a cotton handkerchief.

That all this might not be too onerous on the purses of his rustic patrons, who are apt to consider the costs of schooling a grievous burthen, and schoolmasters as mere drones, he had various ways of rendering himself both useful and agreeable. He assisted the farmers occasionally in the lighter labours of their farms, helped to make hay, mended the fences, took the horses to water, drove the cows from pasture, and cut wood for the winter fire. He laid aside, too, all the dominant dignity and absolute sway, with which he lorded it in his little empire, the school, and became wonderfully gentle and ingratiating. He found favour in the eyes of the mothers, by petting the children, particularly the youngest, and like the lion bold, which whilome so magnanimously the lamb did hold,[9] he would sit with a child on one knee, and rock a cradle with his foot, for whole hours together.

In addition to his other vocations, he was the singing master of the neighbourhood, and picked up many bright shillings by instructing the young folks in psalmody. It was a matter of no little vanity to him on Sundays, to take his station in front of the church gallery, with a band of chosen singers; where, in his own mind, he completely carried away the palm from the parson. Certain it is, his voice resounded far above all the rest of the congregation, and there are peculiar quavers still to be heard in that church, and which may even be heard half a mile off, quite to the opposite side of the mill pond, of a still Sunday morning, which are said to be legitimately descended from the nose of Ichabod Crane. Thus, by diverse little make shifts, in that ingenious way which is commonly denominated "by hook and by crook," the worthy pedagogue got on tolerably enough, and was thought, by all who understood nothing of the labour of headwork, to have a wonderfully easy life of it.

The schoolmaster is generally a man of some importance in the female circle of

---

[8]Proverbs 13:24: "He that spareth his rod hateth his son." Irving's phrasing is found in Samuel Butler's *Hudibras* (1663–78), Book 2, Canto 1, 1. 844.

[9]*New England Primer* (c. 1683). For the letter L: "The lion bold/The lamb doth hold."

a rural neighbourhood, being considered a kind of idle gentleman like personage, of vastly superior taste and accomplishments to the rough country swains, and, indeed, inferior in learning only to the parson. His appearance, therefore, is apt to occasion some little stir at the tea table of a farm house, and the addition of a supernumerary dish of cakes or sweetmeats, or, peradventure, the parade of a silver tea pot. Our man of letters, therefore, was peculiarly happy in the smiles of all the country damsels. How he would figure among them in the church yard, between services on Sundays; gathering grapes for them from the wild vines that overrun the surrounding trees; reciting for their amusement all the epitaphs on the tombstones, or sauntering, with a whole bevy of them, along the banks of the adjacent mill pond; while the more bashful country bumpkins hung sheepishly back, envying his superior elegance and address.

From his half itinerant life, also, he was a kind of travelling gazette, carrying the whole budget of local gossip from house to house; so that his appearance was always greeted with satisfaction. He was, moreover, esteemed by the women as a man of great erudition, for he had read several books quite through, and was a perfect master of Cotton Mather's History of New England Witchcraft,[10] in which, by the way, he most firmly and potently believed.

He was, in fact, an odd mixture of small shrewdness and simple credulity. His appetite for the marvellous, and his powers of digesting it, were equally extraordinary; and both had been increased by his residence in this spell bound region. No tale was too gross or monstrous for his capacious swallow. It was often his delight, after his school was dismissed of an afternoon, to stretch himself on the rich bed of clover, bordering the little brook that whimpered by his school house, and there con over old Mather's direful tales, until the gathering dusk of evening made the printed page a mere mist before his eyes. Then, as he wended his way, by swamp and stream and awful woodland, to the farm house where he happened to be quartered, every sound of nature, at that witching hour, fluttered his excited imagination: the moan of the whip-poor-will[11] from the hill side; the boding cry of the tree toad, that harbinger of storm; the dreary hooting of the screech owl; or the sudden rustling in the thicket, of birds frightened from their roost. The fire flies, too, which sparkled most vividly in the darkest places, now and then startled him, as one of uncommon brightness would stream across his path; and if, by chance, a huge blockhead of a beetle came winging his blundering flight against him, the poor varlet was ready to give up the ghost, with the idea that he was struck with a witch's token. His only resource on such occasions, either to drown thought, or drive away evil spirits, was to sing psalm tunes;—and the good people of Sleepy Hollow, as they sat by their doors of an evening, were often filled with awe, at hearing his nasal melody, "in linked sweetness long drawn out,"[12] floating from the distant hill, or along the dusky road.

Another of his sources of fearful pleasure was, to pass long winter evenings with the old Dutch wives, as they sat spinning by the fire, with a row of apples roasting and sputtering along the hearth, and listen to their marvellous tales of ghosts and goblins, and haunted fields and haunted brooks, and haunted bridges and haunted houses, and particularly of the headless horseman, or galloping Hessian of the Hollow, as they sometimes called him. He would delight them equally by his anecdotes of witchcraft, and of the direful omens and portentous sights and sounds in the air, which prevailed in the earlier times of Connecticut; and would frighten them wofully with speculations upon comets and shooting stars, and with

[10]Cotton Mather (1663–1728), New England Puritan minister, wrote on witchcraft in *Memorable Providences Relating to Witchcrafts and Possessions* (1689) and in *The Wonders of the Invisible World* (1693).

[11]"The whip-poor-will is a bird which is only heard at night. It receives its name from its note which is thought to resemble those words" (Irving's note).
[12]John Milton (1608–1674), "L'Allegro," line 140.

the alarming fact that the world did absolutely turn round, and that they were half the time topsy-turvy!

But if there was a pleasure in all this, while snugly cuddling in the chimney corner of a chamber that was all of a ruddy glow from the crackling wood fire, and where, of course, no spectre dared to show its face, it was dearly purchased by the terrors of his subsequent walk homewards. What fearful shapes and shadows beset his path, amidst the dim and ghastly glare of a snowy night!—With what wistful look did he eye every trembling ray of light streaming across the waste fields from some distant window!—How often was he appalled by some shrub covered with snow, which like a sheeted spectre beset his very path!—How often did he shrink with curdling awe at the sound of his own steps on the frosty crust beneath his feet; and dread to look over his shoulder, lest he should behold some uncouth being tramping close behind him!—and how often was he thrown into complete dismay by some rushing blast, howling among the trees, in the idea that it was the gallopping Hessian on one of his nightly scourings.

All these, however, were mere terrors of the night, phantoms of the mind, that walk in darkness; and though he had seen many spectres in his time, and been more than once beset by Satan in diverse shapes, in his lonely perambulations, yet daylight put an end to all these evils; and he would have passed a pleasant life of it, in despite of the Devil and all his works, if his path had not been crossed by a being that causes more perplexity to mortal man, than ghosts, goblins, and the whole race of witches put together, and that was—a woman.

Among the musical disciples who assembled, one evening in each week, to receive his instructions in psalmody, was Katrina Van Tassel, the daughter and only child of a substantial Dutch farmer. She was a blooming lass of fresh eighteen; plump as a partridge; ripe and melting and rosy cheeked as one of her father's peaches, and universally famed, not merely for her beauty, but her vast expectations. She was withal a little of a coquette, as might be perceived even in her dress, which was a mixture of ancient and modern fashions, as most suited to set off her charms. She wore the ornaments of pure yellow gold, which her great great grandmother had brought over from Saardam;[13] the tempting stomacher of the olden time, and withal a provokingly short petticoat, to display the prettiest foot and ankle in the country round.

Ichabod Crane had a soft and foolish heart toward the sex; and it is not to be wondered at, that so tempting a morsel soon found favour in his eyes, more especially after he had visited her in her paternal mansion. Old Baltus Van Tassel was a perfect picture of a thriving, contented, liberal hearted farmer. He seldom, it is true, sent either his eyes or his thoughts beyond the boundaries of his own farm; but within those every thing was snug, happy, and well conditioned. He was satisfied with his wealth, but not proud of it, and piqued himself upon the hearty abundance, rather than the style in which he lived. His strong hold was situated on the banks of the Hudson, in one of those green, sheltered, fertile nooks, in which the Dutch farmers are so fond of nestling. A great elm tree spread its broad branches over it, at the foot of which bubbled up a spring of the softest and sweetest water, in a little well, formed of a barrel, and then stole sparkling away through the grass, to a neighbouring brook, that babbled along among elders and dwarf willows. Hard by the farm house was a vast barn, that might have served for a church; every window and crevice of which seemed bursting forth with the treasures of the farm; the flail was busily resounding within it from morning to night; swallows and martins skimmed twittering about the eaves, and rows of pigeons, some with one eye turned up, as if watching the weather, some with their heads under their wings, or buried in their bosoms, and others, swelling, and cooing,

---

[13]A village some five miles northwest of Amsterdam (now Zaandam).

and bowing about their dames, were enjoying the sunshine on the roof. Sleek unwieldy porkers were grunting in the repose and abundance of their pens, from
whence sallied forth, now and then, troops of sucking pigs, as if to snuff the air. A
stately squadron of snowy geese were riding in an adjoining pond, convoying
whole fleets of ducks; regiments of turkeys were gobbling through the farm yard,
and guinea fowls fretting about it like ill tempered housewives, with their peevish
discontented cry. Before the barn door strutted the gallant cock, that pattern of a
husband, a warrior, and a fine gentleman, clapping his burnished wings, and
crowing in the pride and gladness of his heart—sometimes tearing up the earth
with his feet, and then generously calling his ever hungry family of wives and children to enjoy the rich morsel which he had discovered.

The pedagogue's mouth watered, as he looked upon this sumptuous promise
of luxurious winter fare. In his devouring mind's eye, he pictured to himself every
roasting pig running about with a pudding in his belly, and an apple in his mouth;
the pigeons were snugly put to bed in a comfortable pie, and tucked in with a cov-
erlet of crust; the geese were swimming in their own gravy; and the ducks pairing
cosily in dishes, like snug married couples, with a decent competency of onion
sauce; in the porkers he saw carved out the future sleek side of bacon, and juicy
relishing ham; not a turkey, but he beheld daintily trussed up, with its gizzard under its wing, and, peradventure, a necklace of savoury sausages; and even bright
chanticleer himself lay sprawling on his back, in a side dish, with uplifted claws, as
if craving that quarter, which his chivalrous spirit disdained to ask while living.

As the enraptured Ichabod fancied all this, and as he rolled his great green
eyes over the fat meadow lands, the rich fields of wheat, of rye, of buckwheat, and
Indian corn, and the orchards burthened with ruddy fruit, which surrounded the
warm tenement of Van Tassel, his heart yearned after the damsel who was to inherit these domains, and his imagination expanded with the idea, how they might
be readily turned into cash, and the money invested in immense tracts of wild
land, and shingle palaces in the wilderness. Nay, his busy fancy already realized
his hopes, and presented to him the blooming Katrina, with a whole family of children, mounted on the top of a waggon loaded with household trumpery, with
pots and kettles dangling beneath; and he beheld himself bestriding a pacing
mare, with a colt at her heels, setting out for Kentucky, Tennessee, or the Lord
knows where!

When he entered the house, the conquest of his heart was complete. It was one
of those spacious farm houses, with high ridged, but lowly sloping roofs, built in
the style handed down from the first Dutch settlers. The low, projecting eaves
formed a piazza along the front, capable of being closed up in bad weather. Under this were hung flails, harness, various utensils of husbandry, and nets for
fishing in the neighbouring river. Benches were built along the sides for summer
use; and a great spinning wheel at one end, and a churn at the other, showed the
various uses to which this important porch might be devoted. From this piazza the
wondering Ichabod entered the hall, which formed the centre of the mansion,
and the place of usual residence. Here, rows of resplendent pewter, ranged on a
long dresser, dazzled his eyes. In one corner stood a huge bag of wool ready to be
spun; in another a quantity of linsey-woolsey just from the loom; ears of Indian
corn, and strings of dried apples and peaches, hung in gay festoons along the
walls, mingled with the gaud of red peppers; and a door left ajar, gave him a peep
into the best parlour, where the claw footed chairs, and dark mahogany tables,
shone like mirrors; andirons, with their accompanying shovel and tongs, glistened
from their covert of asparagus tops; mock oranges and conch shells decorated the
mantlepiece; strings of various coloured birds' eggs were suspended above it; a
great ostrich egg was hung from the centre of the room, and a corner cupboard,
knowingly left open, displayed immense treasures of old silver and well mended
china.

From the moment Ichabod laid his eyes upon these regions of delight, the peace of his mind was at an end, and his only study was how to gain the affections of the peerless daughter of Van Tassel. In this enterprize, however, he had more real difficulties than generally fell to the lot of a knight errant of yore, who seldom had any thing but giants, enchanters, fiery dragons, and such like easily conquered adversaries, to contend with; and had to make his way merely through gates of iron and brass, and walls of adamant, to the castle keep, where the lady of his heart was confined; all which he achieved as easily as a man would carve his way to the centre of a Christmas pie, and then the lady gave him her hand as a matter of course. Ichabod, on the contrary, had to win his way to the heart of a country coquette, beset with a labyrinth of whims and caprices, which were for ever presenting new difficulties and impediments, and he had to encounter a host of fearful adversaries of real flesh and blood, the numerous rustic admirers, who beset every portal to her heart, keeping a watchful and angry eye upon each other, but ready to fly out in the common cause against any new competitor.

Among these, the most formidable, was a burly, roaring, roystering blade, of the name of Abraham, or, according to the Dutch abbreviation, Brom Van Brunt, the hero of the country round, which rung with his feats of strength and hardihood. He was broad shouldered and double jointed, with short curly black hair, and a bluff, but not unpleasant countenance, having a mingled air of fun and arrogance. From his Herculean frame and great powers of limb, he had received the nick name of BROM BONES, by which he was universally known. He was famed for great knowledge and skill in horsemanship, being as dexterous on horseback as a Tartar. He was foremost at all races and cock fights, and with the ascendancy which bodily strength acquires in rustic life, was the umpire in all disputes, setting his hat on one side, and giving his decisions with an air and tone admitting of no gainsay or appeal. He was always ready for either a fight or a frolick; but had more mischief than ill will in his composition; and with all his overbearing roughness, there was a strong dash of waggish good humour at bottom. He had three or four boon companions, who regarded him as their model, and at the head of whom he scoured the country, attending every scene of feud or merriment for miles round. In cold weather he was distinguished by a fur cap, surmounted with a flaunting fox's tail, and when the folks at a country gathering descried this well known crest at a distance, whisking about among a squad of hard riders, they always stood by for a squall. Sometimes his crew would be heard dashing along past the farm houses at midnight, with whoop and halloo, like a troop of Don Cossacks,[14] and the old dames, startled out of their sleep, would listen for a moment till the hurry scurry had clattered by, and then exclaim, "aye, there goes Brom Bones and his gang!" The neighbours looked upon him with a mixture of awe, admiration, and good will; and when any mad cap prank, or rustic brawl, occurred in the vicinity, always shook their heads, and warranted Brom Bones was at the bottom of it.

This rantipole[15] hero had for some time singled out the blooming Katrina for the object of his uncouth gallantries, and though his amorous toyings were something like the gentle caresses and endearments of a bear, yet it was whispered that she did not altogether discourage his hopes. Certain it is, his advances were signals for rival candidates to retire, who felt no inclination to cross a lion in his amours; insomuch, that when his horse was seen tied to Van Tassel's paling, of a Sunday night, (a sure sign that his master was courting, or, as it is termed, "sparking," within,) all other suitors passed by in despair, and carried the war into other quarters.

---

[14]Cossacks from the Don River valley in Russia; expert and spirited horsemen.
[15]Disorderly, reckless.

Such was the formidable rival with whom Ichabod Crane had to contend, and, considering all things, a stouter man than he would have shrunk from the competition, and a wiser man would have despaired. He had, however, a happy mixture of pliability and perseverance in his nature; he was in form and spirit like a supple jack[16]—yielding, but tough; though he bent, he never broke; and though he bowed beneath the slightest pressure, yet, the moment it was away—jerk!—he was as erect, and carried his head as high as ever.

To have taken the field openly against his rival, would have been madness; for he was not a man to be thwarted in his amours, any more than that stormy lover, Achilles.[17] Ichabod, therefore, made his advances in a quiet and gently insinuating manner. Under cover of his character of singing master, he made frequent visits at the farm house; not that he had any thing to apprehend from the meddlesome interference of parents, which is so often a stumbling block in the path of lovers. Balt Van Tassel was an easy indulgent soul; he loved his daughter better even than his pipe, and like a reasonable man, and an excellent father, let her have her way in every thing. His notable little wife too, had enough to do to attend to her housekeeping and manage her poultry, for, as she sagely observed, ducks and geese are foolish things, and must be looked after, but girls can take care of themselves. Thus while the busy dame bustled about the house, or plied her spinning wheel at one end of the piazza, honest Balt would sit smoking his evening pipe at the other, watching the achievements of a little wooden warrior, who, armed with a sword in each hand, was most valiantly fighting the wind on the pinnacle of the barn. In the mean time, Ichabod would carry on his suit with the daughter by the side of the spring under the great elm, or sauntering along in the twilight, that hour so favourable to the lover's eloquence.

I profess not to know how women's hearts are wooed and won. To me they have always been matters of riddle and admiration. Some seem to have but one vulnerable point, or door of access; while others have a thousand avenues, and may be captured in a thousand different ways. It is a great triumph of skill to gain the former, but a still greater proof of generalship to maintain possession of the latter, for a man must battle for his fortress at every door and window. He who wins a thousand common hearts, is therefore entitled to some renown; but he who keeps undisputed sway over the heart of a coquette, is indeed a hero. Certain it is, this was not the case with the redoutable Brom Bones; and from the moment Ichabod Crane made his advances, the interests of the former evidently declined; his horse was no longer seen tied at the palings on Sunday nights, and a deadly feud gradually arose between him and the preceptor of Sleepy Hollow.

Brom, who had a degree of rough chivalry in his nature, would fain have carried matters to open warfare, and have settled their pretensions to the lady, according to the mode of those most concise and simple reasoners, the knights errant of yore—by single combat; but Ichabod was too conscious of the superior might of his adversary to enter the lists against him; he had overheard a boast of Bones, that he would "double the schoolmaster up, and lay him on a shelf of his own school house;" and he was too wary to give him an opportunity. There was something extremely provoking in this obstinately pacific system, it left Brom no alternative but to draw upon the funds of rustic waggery in his disposition, and to play off boorish practical jokes upon his rival. Ichabod became the object of whimsical persecution to Bones, and his gang of rough riders. They harried his hitherto peaceful domains; smoked out his singing school, by stopping up the chimney; broke into the school house at night, in spite of its formidable fastenings of withe and window stakes, and turned every thing topsy-turvy, so that the poor schoolmaster began to think all the witches in the country held their meetings

---

[16]A vine whose pliant stems were often used as walking sticks.

[17]When deprived by Agamemnon of his captive maiden, Briseis, Achilles was outraged (see the *Iliad*).

there. But what was still more annoying, Brom took all opportunities of turning him into ridicule in presence of his mistress, and had a scoundrel dog, whom he taught to whine in the most ludicrous manner, and introduced as a rival of Ichabod's, to instruct her in psalmody.

In this way, matters went on for some time, without producing any material effect on the relative situations of the contending powers. On a fine autumnal afternoon, Ichabod, in pensive mood, sat enthroned on the lofty stool from whence he usually watched all the concerns of his little literary realm. In his hand he swayed a ferule, that sceptre of despotic power; the birch of justice reposed on three nails, behind the throne, a constant terror to evil doers; while on the desk before him might be seen sundry contraband articles and prohibited weapons, detected upon the persons of idle urchins, such as half munched apples, popguns, whirligigs, fly cages, and whole legions of rampant little paper game cocks. Apparently there had been some appalling act of justice recently inflicted, for his scholars were all busily intent upon their books, or slyly whispering behind them with one eye kept upon the master; and a kind of buzzing stillness reigned throughout the school room. It was suddenly interrupted by the appearance of a negro in tow cloth jacket and trowsers, a round crowned fragment of a hat, like the cap of Mercury,[18] and mounted on the back of a ragged, wild, half broken colt, which he managed with a rope by way of halter. He came clattering up to the school door with an invitation to Ichabod to attend a merry making, or "quilting frolick," to be held that evening at Mynheer Van Tassel's, and having delivered his message with that air of importance, and effort at fine language, which a negro is apt to display on petty embassies of the kind, he dashed over the brook, and was seen scampering away up the hollow, full of the importance and hurry of his mission.

All was now bustle and hubbub in the late quiet school room. The scholars were hurried through their lessons, without stopping at trifles; those who were nimble, skipped over half with impunity, and those who were tardy, had a smart application now and then in the rear, to quicken their speed, or help them over a tall word. Books were flung aside, without being put away on the shelves; inkstands were overturned, benches thrown down, and the whole school was turned loose an hour before the usual time; bursting forth like a legion of young imps, yelping and racketing about the green, in joy at their early emancipation.

The gallant Ichabod now spent at least an extra half hour at his toilet, brushing and furbishing up his best, and indeed only suit of rusty black, and arranging his looks by a bit of broken looking glass, that hung up in the school house. That he might make his appearance before his mistress in the true style of a cavalier, he borrowed a horse from the farmer with whom he was domiciliated, a choleric old Dutchman, of the name of Hans Van Ripper, and thus gallantly mounted, issued forth like a knight errant in quest of adventures. But it is meet I should, in the true spirit of romantic story, give some account of the looks and equipments of my hero and his steed. The animal he bestrode was a broken down plough horse, that had outlived almost every thing but his viciousness. He was gaunt and shagged, with a ewe neck and a head like a hammer; his rusty mane and tail were tangled and knotted with burrs; one eye had lost its pupil, and was glaring and spectral, but the other had the gleam of a genuine devil in it. Still he must have had fire and mettle in his day, if we may judge from the name he bore of Gunpowder. He had, in fact, been a favourite steed of his master's, the cholerick Van Ripper, who was a furious rider, and had infused, very probably, some of his own spirit into the animal, for, old and broken down as he looked, there was more of the lurking devil in him than in any young filly in the country.

---

[18]Winged cap, indicating speed.

Ichabod was a suitable figure for such a steed. He rode with short stirrups, which brought his knees nearly up to the pommel of the saddle; his sharp elbows stuck out like grasshoppers'; he carried his whip perpendicularly in his hand, like a sceptre, and as his horse jogged on, the motion of his arms was not unlike the flapping of a pair of wings. A small wool hat rested on the top of his nose, for so his scanty strip of forehead might be called, and the skirts of his black coat fluttered out almost to the horse's tail. Such was the appearance of Ichabod and his steed, as they shambled out of the gate of Hans Van Ripper, and it was altogether such an apparition as is seldom to be met with in broad day light.

It was, as I have said, a fine autumnal day, the sky was clear and serene, and nature wore that rich and golden livery which we always associate with the idea of abundance. The forests had put on their sober brown and yellow, while some trees of the tenderer kind had been nipped by the frosts into brilliant dyes of orange, purple, and scarlet. Streaming files of wild ducks began to make their appearance high in the air; the bark of the squirrel might be heard from the groves of beech and hickory nuts, and the pensive whistle of the quail at intervals from the neighbouring stubble field.

The small birds were taking their farewell banquets. In the fullness of their revelry, they fluttered, chirping and frolicking, from bush to bush, and tree to tree, capricious from the very profusion and variety around them. There was the honest cock robin, the favourite game of stripling sportsmen, with its loud querulous note; and the twittering blackbirds flying in sable clouds; and the golden winged woodpecker, with his crimson crest, his broad black gorget, and splendid plumage; and the cedar bird, with its red tipt wings and yellow tipt tail, and its little monteiro cap[19] of feathers; and the blue jay, that noisy coxcomb, in his gay light blue coat and white under clothes, screaming and chattering, nodding, and bobbing, and bowing, and pretending to be on good terms with every songster of the grove.

As Ichabod jogged slowly on his way, his eye, ever open to every symptom of culinary abundance, ranged with delight over the treasures of jolly autumn. On all sides he beheld vast store of apples, some hanging in oppressive opulence on the trees, some gathered into baskets and barrels for the market, others heaped up in rich piles for the cider press. Further on he beheld great fields of Indian corn, with its golden ears peeping from their leafy coverts, and holding out the promise of cakes and hasty pudding; and the yellow pumpkins lying beneath them, turning up their fair round bellies to the sun, and giving ample prospects of the most luxurious of pies; and anon he passed the fragrant buckwheat fields, breathing the odour of the bee hive, and as he beheld them, soft anticipations stole over his mind of dainty slap jacks, well buttered, and garnished with honey or treacle, by the delicate little dimpled hand of Katrina Van Tassel.

Thus feeding his mind with many sweet thoughts and "sugared suppositions," he journeyed along the sides of a range of hills which look out upon some of the goodliest scenes of the mighty Hudson. The sun gradually wheeled his broad disk down into the west. The wide bosom of the Tappaan Zee lay motionless and glassy, excepting that here and there a gentle undulation waved and prolonged the blue shadow of the distant mountain: a few amber clouds floated in the sky, without a breath of air to move them. The horizon was of a fine golden tint, changing gradually into a pure apple green, and from that into the deep blue of the mid-heaven. A slanting ray lingered on the woody crests of the precipices that overhung some parts of the river, giving greater depth to the dark grey and purple of their rocky sides. A sloop was loitering in the distance, dropping slowly

---

[19]Montero, hunter's cap, round with flaps.

down with the tide, her sail hanging uselessly against the mast, and as the reflection of the sky gleamed along the still water, it seemed as if the vessel was suspended in the air.

It was toward evening that Ichabod arrived at the castle of the Heer Van Tassel, which he found thronged with the pride and flower of the adjacent country. Old farmers, a spare, leathern faced race, in homespun coats and breeches, blue stockings, huge shoes and magnificent pewter buckles. Their brisk withered little dames in close crimped caps, long waisted short gowns, homespun petticoats, with scissors and pincushions, and gay calico pockets, hanging on the outside. Buxom lasses, almost as antiquated as their mothers, excepting where a straw hat, a fine ribband, or perhaps a white frock, gave symptoms of city innovation. The sons, in short square skirted coats with rows of stupendous brass buttons, and their hair generally queued in the fashion of the times, especially if they could procure an eel skin for the purpose, it being esteemed throughout the country as a potent nourisher and strengthener of the hair.

Brom Bones, however, was the hero of the scene, having come to the gathering on his favourite steed Daredevil, a creature, like himself, full of mettle and mischief, and which no one but himself could manage. He was in fact noted for preferring vicious animals, given to all kinds of tricks, which kept the rider in constant risk of his neck, for he held a tractable well broken horse as unworthy of a lad of spirit.

Fain would I pause to dwell upon the world of charms that burst upon the enraptured gaze of my hero, as he entered the state parlour of Van Tassel's mansion. Not those of the bevy of buxom lasses, with their luxurious display of red and white: but the ample charms of a genuine Dutch country tea table, in the sumptuous time of autumn. Such heaped up platters of cakes of various and almost indescribable kinds, known only to experienced Dutch housewives. There was the doughty dough nut, the tenderer oly koek, and the crisp and crumbling cruller;[20] sweet cakes and short cakes, ginger cakes and honey cakes, and the whole family of cakes. And then there were apple pies and peach pies and pumpkin pies; besides slices of ham and smoked beef; and moreover delectable dishes of preserved plums, and peaches, and pears, and quinces; not to mention broiled shad and roasted chickens; together with bowls of milk and cream, all mingled higgledy-piggledy, pretty much as I have enumerated them, with the motherly tea pot sending up its clouds of vapour from the midst—Heaven bless the mark! I want breath and time to discuss this banquet as it deserves, and am too eager to get on with my story. Happily, Ichabod Crane was not in so great a hurry as his historian, but did ample justice to every dainty.

He was a kind and thankful creature, whose heart dilated in proportion as his skin was filled with good cheer, and whose spirits rose with eating, as some men's do with drink. He could not help, too, rolling his large eyes round him as he ate, and chuckling with the possibility that he might one day be lord of all this scene of almost unimaginable luxury and splendour. Then, he thought, how soon he'd turn his back upon the old school house; snap his fingers in the face of Hans Van Ripper, and every other niggardly patron, and kick any itinerant pedagogue out of doors that should dare to call him comrade!

Old Baltus Van Tassel moved about among his guests with a face dilated with content and good humour, round and jolly as the harvest moon. His hospitable attentions were brief, but expressive, being confined to a shake of the hand, a slap on the shoulder, a loud laugh, and a pressing invitation to "fall to, and help themselves."

---

[20]Oil cake, a sweet cake deep-fried; cruller, dough shaped in twisted strips and deep-fried.

And now the sound of the music from the common room or hall, summoned to the dance. The musician was an old grey headed negro, who had been the itinerant orchestra of the neighbourhood for more than half a century. His instrument was as old and battered as himself. The greater part of the time he scraped away on two or three strings, accompanying every movement of the bow with a motion of the head; bowing almost to the ground, and stamping with his foot whenever a fresh couple were to start.

Ichabod prided himself upon his dancing as much as upon his vocal powers. Not a limb, not a fibre about him was idle, and to have seen his loosely hung frame in full motion, and clattering about the room, you would have thought Saint Vitus[21] himself, that blessed patron of the dance, was figuring before you in person. He was the admiration of all the negroes, who, having gathered, of all ages and sizes, from the farm and the neighbourhood, stood forming a pyramid of shining black faces at every door and window, gazing with delight at the scene, rolling their white eye balls, and showing grinning rows of ivory from ear to ear. How could the flogger of urchins be otherwise than animated and joyous; the lady of his heart was his partner in the dance; and smiling graciously in reply to all his amorous oglings, while Brom Bones, sorely smitten with love and jealousy, sat brooding by himself in one corner.

When the dance was at an end, Ichabod was attracted to a knot of the sager folks, who, with old Van Tassel, sat smoking at one end of the piazza, gossiping over former times, and drawling out long stories about the war.

This neighbourhood, at the time of which I am speaking, was one of those highly favoured places which abound with chronicle and great men. The British and American line had run near it during the war; it had, therefore, been the scene of marauding, and been infested with refugees, cow boys,[22] and all kinds of border chivalry. Just sufficient time had elapsed to enable each story teller to dress up his tale with a little becoming fiction, and in the indistinctness of his recollection, to make himself the hero of every exploit.

There was the story of Doffue Martling, a large, blue bearded Dutchman, who had nearly taken a British frigate with an old iron nine pounder from a mud breastwork, only that his gun burst at the sixth discharge. And there was an old gentleman who shall be nameless, being too rich a mynheer[23] to be lightly mentioned, who in the battle of Whiteplains,[24] being an excellent master of defence, parried a musket ball with a small sword, insomuch that he absolutely felt it whiz round the blade, and glance off at the hilt: in proof of which, he was ready at any time to show the sword, with the hilt a little bent. There were several more who had been equally great in the field, not one of whom but was persuaded that he had a considerable hand in bringing the war to a happy termination.

But all these were nothing to the tales of ghosts and apparitions that succeeded. The neighbourhood is rich in legendary treasures of the kind. Local tales and superstitions thrive best in these sheltered, long settled retreats; but are trampled under foot, by the shifting throng that forms the population of most of our country places. Besides, there is no encouragement for ghosts in most of our villages, for they have scarce had time to finish their first nap, and turn themselves in their graves, before their surviving friends have travelled away from the neighbourhood, so that when they turn out of a night to walk the rounds, they have no acquaintance left to call upon. This is perhaps the reason why we so seldom hear of ghosts except in our long established Dutch communities.

---

[21]St. Vitus Dance is a disease characterized by grotesque movements or "dancing."
[22]Name applied to Tory bands operating around New York during the Revolutionary War.
[23]Dutch title of address (as Mr.).

[24]General Howe forced the Americans to retreat from White Plains, October 28, 1776. The battle was indecisive, but Howe's hesitation enabled General Washington's troops to regroup and escape, and eventually to win.

The immediate cause, however, of the prevalence of supernatural stories in these parts, was doubtless owing to the vicinity of Sleepy Hollow. There was a contagion in the very air that blew from that haunted region; it breathed forth an atmosphere of dreams and fancies infecting all the land. Several of the Sleepy Hollow people were present at Van Tassel's, and, as usual, were doling out their wild and wonderful legends. Many dismal tales were told about funeral trains, and mournful cries and wailings heard and seen about the great tree where the unfortunate Major André[25] was taken, and which stood in the neighbourhood. Some mention was made also of the woman in white, that haunted the dark glen at Raven Rock, and was often heard to shriek on winter nights before a storm, having perished there in the snow. The chief part of the stories, however, turned upon the favourite spectre of Sleepy Hollow, the headless horseman, who had been heard several times of late, patroling the country; and it was said, tethered his horse nightly among the graves in the church yard.

The sequestered situation of this church seems always to have made it a favourite haunt of troubled spirits. It stands on a knoll, surrounded by locust trees and lofty elms, from among which its decent, whitewashed walls shine modestly forth, like Christian purity, beaming through the shades of retirement. A gentle slope descends from it to a silver sheet of water, bordered by high trees, between which, peeps may be caught at the blue hills of the Hudson. To look upon its grass grown yard, where the sunbeams seem to sleep so quietly, one would think that there at least the dead might rest in peace. On one side of the church extends a wide woody dell, along which raves a large brook among broken rocks and trunks of fallen trees. Over a deep black part of the stream, not far from the church, was formerly thrown a wooden bridge; the road that led to it, and the bridge itself, were thickly shaded by overhanging trees, which cast a gloom about it, even in the day time; but occasioned a fearful darkness at night. Such was one of the favourite haunts of the headless horseman, and the place where he was most frequently encountered. The tale was told of old Brouwer, a most heretical disbeliever in ghosts, how he met the horseman returning from his foray into Sleepy Hollow, and was obliged to get up behind him; how they galloped over bush and brake, over hill and swamp, until they reached the bridge, when the horseman suddenly turned into a skeleton, threw old Brouwer into the brook, and sprang away over the tree tops with a clap of thunder.

This story was immediately matched by a thrice marvellous adventure of Brom Bones, who made light of the galloping Hessian as an arrant jockey.[26] He affirmed, that on returning one night from the neighbouring village of Sing-Sing, he had been overtaken by this midnight trooper; that he had offered to race with him for a bowl of punch, and should have won it too, for Daredevil beat the goblin horse all hollow, but just as they came to the church bridge, the Hessian bolted, and vanished in a flash of fire.

All these tales, told in that drowsy under tone with which men talk in the dark, the countenances of the listeners only now and then receiving a casual gleam from the glare of a pipe, sunk deep in the mind of Ichabod. He repaid them in kind with large extracts from his invaluable author, Cotton Mather, and added many very marvellous events that had taken place in his native state of Connecticut, and fearful sights which he had seen in his nightly walks about Sleepy Hollow.

The revel now gradually broke up. The old farmers gathered together their families in their wagons, and were heard for some time rattling along the hollow roads, and over the distant hills. Some of the damsels, mounted on pillions behind

---

[25]Major John André, British officer (1751–1780), was involved in Benedict Arnold's treason, and executed as a spy.
[26]Con artist or trickster.

their favourite swains, and their light hearted laughter mingling with the clatter of hoofs, echoed along the silent woodlands, sounding fainter and fainter until they gradually died away—and the late scene of noise and frolick was all silent and deserted. Ichabod only lingered behind, according to the custom of country lovers, to have a tête-a-tête with the heiress; fully convinced that he was now on the high road to success. What passed at this interview I will not pretend to say, for in fact I do not know. Something, however, I fear me, must have gone wrong, for he certainly sallied forth, after no very great interval, with an air quite desolate and chopfallen—Oh these women! these women! Could that girl have been playing off any of her coquettish tricks?—Was her encouragement of the poor pedagogue all a mere sham to secure her conquest of his rival?—Heaven only knows, not I!— Let it suffice to say, Ichabod stole forth with the air of one who had been sacking a hen roost, rather than a fair lady's heart. Without looking to the right or left to notice the scene of rural wealth, on which he had so often gloated, he went straight to the stable, and with several hearty cuffs and kicks, roused his steed most uncourteously from the comfortable quarters in which he was soundly sleeping, dreaming of mountains of corn and oats, and whole valleys of timothy and clover.

It was the very witching time of night[27] that Ichabod, heavy hearted and crest fallen, pursued his travel homewards, along the sides of the lofty hills which rise above Tarry Town, and which he had traversed so cheerily in the afternoon. The hour was as dismal as himself. Far below him the Tappaan Zee spread its dusky and indistinct waste of waters, with here and there the tall mast of a sloop, riding quietly at anchor under the land. In the dead hush of midnight, he could even hear the barking of the watch dog from the opposite shore of the Hudson; but it was so vague and faint as only to give an idea of his distance from this faithful companion of man. Now and then, too, the long drawn crowing of a cock, accidentally awakened, would sound far, far off, from some farm house away among the hills—but it was like a dreaming sound in his ear. No signs of life occurred near him, but occasionally the melancholy chirp of a cricket, or perhaps the guttural twang of a bull frog, from a neighbouring marsh, as if sleeping uncomfortably, and turning suddenly in his bed.

All the stories of ghosts and goblins that he had heard in the afternoon, now came crowding upon his recollection. The night grew darker and darker; the stars seemed to sink deeper in the sky, and driving clouds occasionally hid them from his sight. He had never felt so lonely and dismal. He was, moreover, approaching the very place where many of the scenes of the ghost stories had been laid. In the centre of the road stood an enormous tulip tree, which towered like a giant above all the other trees of the neighbourhood, and formed a kind of land mark. Its limbs were gnarled, and fantastic, large enough to form trunks for ordinary trees, twisting down almost to the earth, and rising again into the air. It was connected with the tragical story of the unfortunate André, who had been taken prisoner hard by; and was universally known by the name of Major André's tree. The common people regarded it with a mixture of respect and superstition, partly out of sympathy for the fate of its ill starred namesake, and partly from the tales of strange sights, and doleful lamentations, told concerning it.

As Ichabod approached this fearful tree, he began to whistle; he thought his whistle was answered: it was but a blast sweeping sharply through the dry branches. As he approached a little nearer, he thought he saw something white, hanging in the midst of the tree: he paused and ceased whistling; but on looking more narrowly, perceived that it was a place where the tree had been scathed by

---

[27]*Hamlet*, Act III, Scene ii, 1. 406.

lightning, and the white wood laid bare. Suddenly he heard a groan—his teeth chattered, and his knees smote against the saddle: it was but the rubbing of one huge bough upon another, as they were swayed about by the breeze. He passed the tree in safety, but new perils lay before him.

About two hundred yards from the tree, a small brook crossed the road, and ran into a marshy and thickly wooded glen, known by the name of Wiley's Swamp. A few rough logs, laid side by side, served for a bridge over this stream. On that side of the road where the brook entered the wood, a group of oaks and chest-nuts, matted thick with wild grape vines, threw a cavernous gloom over it. To pass this bridge, was the severest trial. It was at this identical spot that the unfortunate André was captured, and under the covert of those chestnuts and vines were the sturdy yeomen concealed who surprised him. This has ever since been considered a haunted stream, and fearful are the feelings of the schoolboy who has to pass it alone after dark.

As he approached the stream, his heart began to thump; he, however, sum-moned up all his resolution, gave his horse half a score of kicks in the ribs, and attempted to dash briskly across the bridge; but instead of starting forward, the perverse old animal made a lateral movement, and ran broadside against the fence. Ichabod, whose fears increased with the delay, jerked the reins on the other side, and kicked lustily with the contrary foot: it was all in vain; his steed started, it is true, but it was only to plunge to the opposite side of the road into a thicket of brambles and alder bushes. The schoolmaster now bestowed both whip and heel upon the starvelling ribs of old Gunpowder, who dashed forward, snuffling and snorting, but came to a stand just by the bridge with a suddenness that had nearly sent his rider sprawling over his head. Just at this moment a plashy tramp by the side of the bridge caught the sensitive ear of Ichabod. In the dark shadow of the grove, on the margin of the brook, he beheld something huge, misshapen, black and towering. It stirred not, but seemed gathered up in the gloom, like some gi-gantic monster ready to spring upon the traveller.

The hair of the affrighted pedagogue rose upon his head with terror. What was to be done? To turn and fly was now too late; and besides, what chance was there of escaping ghost or goblin, if such it was, which could ride upon the wings of the wind? Summoning up, therefore, a show of courage, he demanded in stam-mering accents—"who are you?" He received no reply. He repeated his demand in a still more agitated voice.—Still there was no answer. Once more he cudgelled the sides of the inflexible Gunpowder, and shutting his eyes, broke forth with in-voluntary fervour into a psalm tune. Just then the shadowy object of alarm put itself in motion, and with a scramble and a bound, stood at once in the middle of the road. Though the night was dark and dismal, yet the form of the unknown might now in some degree be ascertained. He appeared to be a horseman of large dimensions, and mounted on a black horse of powerful frame. He made no offer of molestation or sociability, but kept aloof on one side of the road, jogging along on the blind side of old Gunpowder, who had now got over his fright and way-wardness.

Ichabod, who had no relish for this strange midnight companion, and be-thought himself of the adventure of Brom Bones with the galloping Hessian, now quickened his steed, in hopes of leaving him behind. The stranger, however, quickened his horse to an equal pace; Ichabod pulled up, and fell into a walk, thinking to lag behind—the other did the same. His heart began to sink within him; he endeavoured to resume his psalm tune, but his parched tongue clove to the roof of his mouth, and he could not utter a stave. There was something in the moody and dogged silence of this pertinacious companion, that was mysterious and appalling. It was soon fearfully accounted for. On mounting a rising ground, which brought the figure of his fellow traveller in relief against the sky, gigantic in height, and muffled in a cloak, Ichabod was horror struck, on perceiving that he was headless! but his horror was still more increased, on observing, that the head, which should have rested on his shoulders, was carried before him on the pommel of the saddle! His terror rose to desperation; he rained a shower of kicks and blows upon Gunpowder, hoping, by a sudden movement, to give his companion the slip—but the spectre started full jump with him. Away, then, they dashed, through thick and thin; stones flying, and sparks flashing, at every bound. Ichabod's flimsy garments fluttered in the air, as he stretched his long lank body away over his horse's head, in the eagerness of his flight.

They had now reached the road which turns off to Sleepy Hollow; but Gunpowder, who seemed possessed with a demon, instead of keeping up it, made an opposite turn, and plunged headlong down hill to the left. This road leads through a sandy hollow shaded by trees for about a quarter of a mile, where it crosses the bridge famous in goblin story, and just beyond swells the green knoll on which stands the whitewashed church.

As yet the panic of the steed had given his unskilful rider an apparent advantage in the chace, but just as he had got half way through the hollow, the girths of the saddle gave way, and he felt it slipping from under him; he seized it by the pommel, and endeavoured to hold it firm, but in vain; and had just time to save himself by clasping old Gunpowder round the neck, when the saddle fell to the earth, and he heard it trampled under foot by his pursuer. For a moment the terror of Hans Van Ripper's wrath passed across his mind—for it was his Sunday saddle; but this was no time for petty fears: the goblin was hard on his haunches; and (unskilful rider that he was!) he had much ado to maintain his seat; sometimes slipping on one side, sometimes on another, and sometimes jolted on the high ridge of his horse's back bone, with a violence that he verily feared would cleave him asunder.

An opening in the trees now cheered him with the hopes that the Church Bridge was at hand. The wavering reflection of a silver star in the bosom of the brook told him that he was not mistaken. He saw the walls of the church dimly glaring under the trees beyond. He recollected the place where Brom Bones' ghostly competitor had disappeared. "If I can but reach that bridge," thought Ichabod, "I am safe."[28] Just then he heard the black steed panting and blowing close behind him; he even fancied that he felt his hot breath. Another convulsive kick in the ribs, and old Gunpowder sprung upon the bridge; he thundered over the resounding planks; he gained the opposite side, and now Ichabod cast a look behind to see if his pursuer should vanish, according to rule, in a flash of fire and brimstone. Just then he saw the goblin rising in his stirrups, and in the very act of hurling his head at him. Ichabod endeavoured to dodge the horrible missile, but too late. It encountered his cranium with a tremendous crash—he was tumbled headlong into the dust, and Gunpowder, the black steed, and the goblin rider, passed by like a whirlwind.———

The next morning the old horse was found without his saddle, and with the bridle under his feet, soberly cropping the grass at his master's gate. Ichabod did not make his appearance at breakfast—dinner hour came, but no Ichabod. The boys assembled at the schoolhouse, and strolled idly about the banks of the brook; but no schoolmaster. Hans Van Ripper now began to feel some uneasiness about the fate of poor Ichabod, and his saddle. An inquiry was set on foot, and after diligent investigation they came upon his traces. In one part of the road leading to the church, was found the saddle trampled in the dirt; the tracks of horses' hoofs deeply dented in the road, and evidently at furious speed, were traced to the bridge, beyond which, on the bank of a broad part of the brook, where the water

---

[28] A common belief was that witches could not cross water.

ran deep and black, was found the hat of the unfortunate Ichabod, and close beside it a shattered pumpkin.

The brook was searched, but the body of the schoolmaster was not to be discovered. Hans Van Ripper, as executor of his estate, examined the bundle which contained all his worldly effects. They consisted of two shirts and a half; two stocks for the neck; a pair or two of worsted stockings; an old pair of corduroy small clothes; a rusty razor; a book of psalm tunes, full of dog's ears; and a broken pitch pipe. As to the books and furniture of the schoolhouse, they belonged to the community, excepting Cotton Mather's History of Witchcraft, a New England Almanack, and a book of dreams and fortune telling, in which last was a sheet of foolscap much scribbled and blotted, in several fruitless attempts to make a copy of verses in honour of the heiress of Van Tassel. These magic books and the poetic scrawl were forthwith consigned to the flames by Hans Van Ripper, who from that time forward determined to send his children no more to school, observing, that he never knew any good come of this same reading and writing. Whatever money the schoolmaster possessed, and he had received his quarter's pay but a day or two before, he must have had about his person at the time of his disappearance.

The mysterious event caused much speculation at the Church on the following Sunday. Knots of gazers and gossips were collected in the church yard, at the bridge, and at the spot where the hat and pumpkin had been found. The stories of Brouwer, of Bones, and a whole budget of others, were called to mind; and when they had diligently considered them all, and compared them with the symptoms of the present case, they shook their heads, and came to the conclusion, that Ichabod had been carried off by the gallopping Hessian. As he was a bachelor, and in nobody's debt, nobody troubled his head any more about him, the school was removed to a different quarter of the hollow, and another pedagogue reigned in his stead.

It is true, an old farmer, who had been down to New York on a visit several years after, and from whom this account of the ghostly adventure was received, brought home the intelligence that Ichabod Crane was still alive; that he had left the neighbourhood partly through fear of the goblin and Hans Van Ripper, and partly in mortification at having been suddenly dismissed by the heiress; that he had changed his quarters to a distant part of the country; had kept school and studied law at the same time; had been admitted to the bar, turned politician, electioneered, written for the newspapers, and finally had been made a Justice of the Ten Pound Court.[29] Brom Bones too, who, shortly after his rival's disappearance, conducted the blooming Katrina in triumph to the altar, was observed to look exceedingly knowing whenever the story of Ichabod was related, and always burst into a hearty laugh at the mention of the pumpkin; which led some to suspect that he knew more about the matter than he chose to tell.

The old country wives, however, who are the best judges of these matters, maintain to this day, that Ichabod was spirited away by supernatural means; and it is a favourite story often told about the neighbourhood round the winter evening fire. The bridge became more than ever an object of superstitious awe, and that may be the reason why the road has been altered of late years, so as to approach the church by the border of the millpond. The schoolhouse being deserted, soon fell to decay, and was reported to be haunted by the ghost of the unfortunate pedagogue; and the plough boy, loitering homeward of a still summer evening, has often fancied his voice at a distance, chanting a melancholy psalm tune among the tranquil solitudes of Sleepy Hollow.

---

[29]A small claims court.

POSTSCRIPT

Found in the Handwriting of Mr. Knickerbocker

The preceding Tale is given, almost in the precise words in which I heard it related at a corporation meeting of the ancient city of Manhattoes, at which were present many of its sagest and most illustrious burghers. The narrator was a pleasant, shabby, gentlemanly old fellow, in pepper and salt clothes, with a sadly humourous face, and one whom I strongly suspected of being poor, he made such efforts to be entertaining. When his story was concluded, there was much laughter and approbation, particularly from two or three deputy aldermen, who had been asleep the greater part of the time. There was, however, one tall, dry looking old gentleman, with beetling eye brows, who maintained a grave and rather severe face throughout; now and then folding his arms, inclining his head, and looking down upon the floor, as if turning a doubt over in his mind. He was one of your wary men, who never laugh but upon good grounds—when they have reason and the law on their side. When the mirth of the rest of the company had subsided, and silence was restored, he leaned one arm on the elbow of his chair, and sticking the other akimbo, demanded, with a slight, but exceedingly sage motion of the head, and contraction of the brow, what was the moral of the story, and what it went to prove.

The story teller, who was just putting a glass of wine to his lips, as a refreshment after his toils, paused for a moment, looked at his inquirer with an air of infinite deference, and lowering the glass slowly to the table, observed, that the story was intended most logically to prove,

"That there is no situation in life but has its advantages and pleasures, provided we will but take a joke as we find it:

"That, therefore, he that runs races with goblin troopers, is likely to have rough riding of it:

"Ergo, for a country schoolmaster to be refused the hand of a Dutch heiress, is a certain step to high preferment in the state."

The cautious old gentleman knit his brows tenfold closer after this explanation, being sorely puzzled by the ratiocination of the syllogism; while methought the one in pepper and salt eyed him with something of a triumphant leer. At length he observed, that all this was very well, but still he thought the story a little on the extravagant—there were one or two points on which he had his doubts.

"Faith, sir," replied the story teller, "as to that matter, I don't believe one half of it myself."

D.K.

1820

from A Tour on the Prairies[1]

CHAPTER V

FRONTIER SCENES—A LYCURGUS OF THE BORDER—LYNCH'S LAW—THE DANGER OF FINDING A HORSE—THE YOUNG OSAGE.

On the following morning (Oct. 11) we were on the march by half past seven o'clock, and rode through deep rich bottoms of alluvial soil, overgrown with redundant vegetation, and trees of an enormous size. Our route lay parallel to the west bank of the Arkansas, on the borders of which river, near the confluence of the Red Fork, we expected to overtake the main body of Rangers. For some miles the country was sprinkled with Creek villages and farm houses; the inhabitants of which appeared to have adopted, with considerable facility, the rudiments of civilization, and to have thriven in consequence. Their farms were well stocked and their houses had a look of comfort and abundance.

We met with numbers of them returning from one of their grand games of ball, for which their nation is celebrated. Some were on foot, some on horseback; the latter, occasionally, with gaily dressed females behind them. They are a well made race, muscular and closely knit, with well turned thighs and legs. They have a gipsey fondness for brilliant colours, and gay decorations, and are bright and fanciful objects when seen at a distance on the prairies. One had a scarlet handkerchief bound round his head surmounted with a tuft of black feathers like a cock's tail. Another had a white handkerchief, with red feathers; while a third, for want of a plume, had stuck in his turban a brilliant bunch of sumach.

On the verge of the wilderness we paused to enquire our way at a log house, owned by a white settler or squatter, a tall raw boned old fellow, with red hair, a lank lanthorn visage, and an inveterate habit of winking with one eye, as if every thing he said was of knowing import. He was in a towering passion. One of his horses was missing, he was sure it had been stolen in the night by a straggling party of Osages encamped in a neighboring swamp—but he would have satisfaction! He would make an example of the villains. He had accordingly caught down his rifle from the wall, that invariable enforcer of right or wrong upon the frontiers, and having saddled his steed was about to sally forth on a foray into the swamp; while a brother squatter, with rifle in hand, stood ready to accompany him.

We endeavored to calm the old campaigner of the prairies, by suggesting that his horse might have strayed into the neighboring woods; but he had the frontier propensity to charge every thing to the Indians, and nothing could dissuade him from carrying fire and sword into the swamp.

After riding a few miles further we lost the trail of the main body of rangers, and became perplexed by a variety of tracks made by the Indians and settlers. At length coming to a log house, inhabited by a white man, the very last on the frontier, we found that we had wandered from our true course. Taking us back for some distance he again brought us to the right trail; putting ourselves upon which, we took our final departure and launched into the broad wilderness.

The trail kept on like a straggling foot path, over hill and dale, through bush

---

[1]In 1832, Irving returned from seventeen years in Europe. Later that year, feeling the urge to know his country as well as he knew the foreign countries in which he lived, he set out from Ft. Gibson in what is now Oklahoma to visit the lands of the Osage and Pawnees. In his party was a U. S. Commissioner superintending resettlement of Indian tribes from east to west, an Englishman of a "thousand occupations," a young Swiss Count, and a French creole (Antoine, or Tonish) who was servant and cook. Irving wrote an account of his experience in *A Tour on the Prairies*, published in 1835.

and brake, and tangled thicket, and open prairie. In traversing the wilds it is customary for a party either of horse or foot to follow each other in single file like the Indians: so that the leaders break the way for those who follow and lessen their labour and fatigue. In this way, also, the number of a party is concealed, the whole leaving but one narrow well trampled track to mark their course.

We had not long regained the trail, when, on emerging from a forest, we beheld our raw boned, hard winking, hard riding knight errant of the frontier, descending the slope of a hill, followed by his companion in arms. As he drew near to us the gauntness of his figure and ruefulness of his aspect, reminded me of the descriptions of the hero of La Mancha,[2] and he was equally bent on affairs of doughty enterprise, being about to penetrate the thickets of the perilous swamp, within which the enemy lay ensconced.

While we were holding a parley with him on the slope of the hill, we descried an Osage on horseback, issuing out of a skirt of wood about half a mile off, and leading a horse by a halter. The latter was immediately recognized by our hard winking friend as the steed of which he was in quest. As the Osage drew near I was struck with his appearance. He was about nineteen or twenty years of age but well grown; with the fine Roman countenance common to his tribe, and as he rode with his blanket wrapped round his loins his naked bust would have furnished a model for a statuary. He was mounted on a beautiful pie bald horse, a mottled white and brown, of the wild breed of the prairies, decorated with a broad collar from which hung in front a tuft of horse hair dyed of a bright scarlet.

The youth rode slowly up to us with a frank open air, and signified, by means of our interpreter Beatte, that the horse he was leading had wandered to their camp and he was now on his way to conduct him back to his owner.

I had expected to witness an expression of gratitude on the part of our hard favoured cavalier, but to my surprize the old fellow broke out into a furious passion. He declared that the Indians had carried off his horse in the night, with the intention of bringing him home in the morning, and claiming a reward for finding him; a common practice, as he affirmed, among the Indians. He was, therefore, for tying the young Indian to a tree and giving him a sound lashing; and was quite surprized at the burst of indignation which this novel mode of requiting a service drew from us. Such, however, is too often the administration of law on the frontier, "Lynch's law,"[3] as it is technically termed, in which the plaintiff is apt to be witness, jury, judge and executioner, and the defendant to be convicted and punished on mere presumption: and in this way I am convinced, are occasioned many of those heart burnings and resentments among the Indians, which lead to retaliation, and end in Indian wars. When I compared the open, noble countenance and frank demeanour of the young Osage, with the sinister visage and high handed conduct of the frontiers-man, I felt little doubt on whose back a lash would be most meritoriously bestowed.

Being thus obliged to content himself with the recovery of his horse, without the pleasure of flogging the finder into the bargain, the old Lycurgus, or rather Draco,[4] of the frontier set off growling on his return homeward, followed by his brother squatter.

As for the youthful Osage, we were all prepossessed in his favour; the young count[5] especially, with the sympathies proper to his age and incident to his char-

---

[2]Don Quixote, hero of the novel of the same title, written by Miguel de Cervantes (1547–1616).
[3]I.e., immediate punishment without courts, judges, or trials; named after Captain William Lynch (1742–1820), member of a vigilante committee in Pittsylvania, Virginia.
[4]Lycurgus, Spartan lawgiver of ninth century B.C., whose code of laws was notorious for its harshness and cruelty;

Draco (c. 621 B.C.), Athenian lawgiver who prescribed death for most offenses.
[5]One of the party, described earlier by Irving as a "young Swiss Count, scarce twenty-one years of age, full of talent and spirit, but galliard [valiant] in the extreme, and prone to every kind of wild adventure."

acter, had taken quite a fancy to him. Nothing would suit but he must have the young Osage as a companion and squire in his expedition into the wilderness. The youth was easily tempted, and, with the prospect of a safe range over the buffalo prairies and the promise of a new blanket, he turned his bridle, left the swamp and the encampment of his friends behind him, and set off to follow the count in his wanderings in quest of the Osage hunters. Such is the glorious independence of man in a savage state. This youth with his rifle, his blanket and his horse was ready at a moments warning to rove the world; he carried all his worldly effects with him; and in the absence of artificial wants, possessed the great secret of personal freedom. We of society are slaves not so much to others, as to ourselves; our superfluities are the chains that bind us, impeding every movement of our bodies and thwarting every impulse of our souls. Such at least were my speculations at the time though I am not sure but that they took their tone from the enthusiasm of the young Count, who seemed more enchanted than ever with the wild chivalry of the prairies, and talked of putting on the Indian dress and adopting the Indian habits during the time he hoped to pass with the Osages.

CHAPTER VI

Trail of the Osage Hunters—Departure of the Count and His Party—A Deserted War Camp—A Vagrant Dog—The Encampment.

In the course of the morning the trail we were pursuing was crossed by another, which struck off through the forest to the west in a direct course for the Arkansas river. Beatte, our half breed,[1] after considering it for a moment, pronounced it the trail of the Osage Hunters; and that it must lead to the place where they had forded the river on their way to the hunting grounds.

Here then the young Count and his companion came to a halt and prepared to take leave of us. The most experienced frontiers men in the troop remonstrated on the hazard of the undertaking. They were about to throw themselves loose in the wilderness, with no other guides, guards or attendants than a young, ignorant half breed and a still younger Indian. They were embarrassed by a pack horse and two led horses, with which they would have to make their way through matted forests, and across rivers and morasses. The Osages and Pawnees were at war and they might fall in with some warrior party of the latter, who are ferocious foes; besides, their small number, and their valuable horses would form a great temptation to some of the straggling bands of Osages loitering about the frontier, who might rob them of their horses in the night, and leave them destitute and on foot in the midst of the prairies.

Nothing, however, could restrain the romantic ardour of the Count for a campaign of Buffalo hunting with the Osages, and he had a game spirit that seemed always stimulated by the idea of danger. His travelling companion, of discreeter age and calmer temperament, was convinced of the rashness of the enterprize, but he could not control the impetuous zeal of his youthful friend, and he was too loyal to leave him to pursue his hazardous scheme alone. To our great regret, therefore, we saw them abandon the protection of our escort, and strike off on their haphazard expedition. The old hunters of our party shook their heads, and our half breed Beatte predicted all kinds of trouble to them; my only hope, was that they would soon meet with perplexities enough to cool the impetuosity of the young count, and induce him to rejoin us. With this idea we travelled slowly and made a considerable halt at noon. After resuming our march we came in sight of

---

[1]Beatte was an experienced guide, half French and half Osage, hired to accompany the group.

the Arkansas. It presented a broad and rapid stream bordered by a beach of fine sand, overgrown with willows and cotton wood trees. Beyond the river the eye wandered over a beautiful champaign country, of flowery plains and sloping uplands, diversified by groves and clumps of trees, and long screens of woodland; the whole wearing the aspect of complete, and even ornamental cultivation, instead of native wildness. Not far from the river, on an open eminence, we passed through the recently deserted camping place of an Osage war party. The frames of the tents or wigwams remained, consisting of poles bent into an arch with each end stuck into the ground: these are intertwined with twigs and branches, and covered with bark, and skins. Those experienced in Indian lore can ascertain the tribe, and whether on a hunting, or a warlike expedition, by the shape and disposition of the wigwams. Beatte pointed out to us, in the present skeleton camp, the wigwam in which the chiefs had held their consultations round the council fire; and an open area, well trampled down, on which the grand war dance had been performed.

Pursuing our journey, as we were passing through a forest we were met by a forlorn half famished dog, who came rambling along the trail, with inflamed eyes, and bewildered look. Though nearly trampled upon by the foremost rangers he took notice of no one, but rambled heedlessly among the horses. The cry of "mad dog" was immediately raised, and one of the rangers levelled his rifle, but was stayed by the ever ready humanity of the Commissioner. "He is blind!" said he, "it is the dog of some poor Indian, following his master by the scent. It would be a shame to kill so faithful an animal." The ranger shouldered his rifle, the dog blundered blindly through the cavalcade unhurt; and, keeping his nose to the ground continued his course along the trail, affording a rare instance of a dog surviving a bad name.

About three o'clock we came to a recent camping place of the company of rangers: the brands of one of their fires were still smoking; so that, according to the opinion of Beatte, they could not have passed on above a day previously. As there was a fine stream of water close by, and plenty of pea vine for the horses, we encamped here for the night.

We had not been here long when we heard a halloo from a distance and beheld the young count and his party advancing through the forest. We welcomed them to the camp with heartfelt satisfaction; for their departure upon so hazardous an expedition had caused us great uneasiness. A short experiment had convinced them of the toil and difficulty of inexperienced travellers like themselves making their way through the wilderness with such a train of horses, and such slender attendance. Fortunately they determined to rejoin us before nightfall; one night's camping out might have cost them their horses. The Count had prevailed upon his protegee and esquire the young Osage to continue with him, and still calculated upon achieving great exploits with his assistance, on the Buffalo prairies.

CHAPTER VII

NEWS OF THE RANGERS—THE COUNT AND HIS INDIAN SQUIRE—HALT IN THE WOODS— WOODLAND SCENE—OSAGE VILLAGE—OSAGE VISITORS AT OUR EVENING CAMP.

In the morning early (Oct. 12) the two Creeks who had been sent express by the Commander of Fort Gibson, to stop the Company of rangers, arrived at our encampment on their return. They had left the company encamped about fifty miles distant in a fine place on the Arkansas abounding in game, where they intended to await our arrival. This news spread animation throughout our party and we set out on our march at sunrise, with renewed spirit.

In mounting our steeds the young Osage attempted to throw a blanket upon his wild horse. The fine, sensitive animal took fright, reared and recoiled. The attitudes of the wild horse and the almost naked savage would have formed studies for a painter or a statuary.[1]

I often pleased myself in the course of our march with noticing the appearance of the young count, and his newly enlisted follower, as they rode before me. Never was preux chevalier[2] better suited with an esquire. The count was well mounted, and, as I have before observed, was a bold and graceful rider. He was fond too of caracolling his horse, and dashing about in the buoyancy of youthful spirits. His dress was a gay Indian hunting frock of dressed deer skin, setting well to the shape, dyed of a beautiful purple and fancifully embroidered with silks of various colours; as if it had been the work of some Indian beauty to decorate a favorite chief. With this he wore leathern pantaloons and moccasins, a foraging cap, and a double barrelled gun slung by a bandaleer[3] athwart his back: so that he was quite a picturesque figure as he managed gracefully his spirited steed.

The young Osage would ride close behind him on his wild and beautifully mottled horse, which was decorated with crimson tufts of hair. He rode with his finely shaped head and bust naked; his blanket being girt round his waist. He carried his rifle in one hand and managed his horse with the other, and seemed ready to dash off at a moments warning, with his youthful leader on any mad cap foray or scamper. The count, with the sanguine anticipations of youth, promised himself many hardy adventures and exploits in company with his youthful "brave," when we should get among the buffaloes, in the Pawnee hunting grounds.

After riding some distance we crossed a narrow deep stream upon a solid bridge, the remains of an old beaver dam; the industrious community which had constructed it had all been destroyed. Above us a streaming flight of wild geese, high in air, and making a vociferous noise, gave note of the waning year.

About half past ten o'clock we made a halt in a forest where there was abundance of the pea vine. Here we turned the horses loose to graze. A fire was made, water procured from an adjacent spring, and in a short time our little Frenchman Tonish had a pot of coffee prepared, for our refreshment. While partaking of it we were joined by an old Osage, one of a small hunting party who had recently passed this way. He was in search of his horse which had wandered away or been stolen. Our half breed Beatte made a wry face on hearing of Osage hunters in this direction. "Until we pass those hunters," said he, "we shall see no buffaloes. They frighten away every thing, like a prairie on fire."

The morning repast being over the party amused themselves in various ways. Some shot with their rifles at a mark, others lay asleep half buried in the deep bed of foliage, with their heads resting on their saddles; others gossipped round the fire at the foot of a tree, which sent up wreaths of blue smoke among the branches. The horses banquetted luxuriously on the pea vine, and some lay down and rolled amongst them.

We were overshadowed by lofty trees, with straight smooth trunks, like stately columns, and as the glancing rays of the sun shone through the transparent leaves, tinted with the many coloured hues of autumn, I was reminded of the effect of sunshine among the stained windows and clustering columns of a Gothic cathedral. Indeed there is a grandeur and solemnity in some of our spacious forests of the West that awaken in me the same feeling I have experienced in those vast and venerable piles, and the sound of the wind sweeping through them, supplies occasionally the deep breathings of the organ.

---

[1] Sculptor.
[2] "Valiant knight" (French).

[3] Bandoleer (or bandolier): an ammunition belt worn over one shoulder and across the chest.

About noon the bugle sounded to horse, and we were again on the march, hoping to arrive at the encampment of the rangers before night, as the old Osage had assured us it was not above ten or twelve miles distant. In our course through a forest we passed by a lonely pool covered with the most magnificent water lilies that I had ever beheld; among which swam several wood ducks, one of the most beautiful of water fowl, remarkable for the gracefulness and brilliancy of its plumage.

After proceeding some distance farther we came down upon the banks of the Arkansas at a place where tracks of numerous horses all entering the water, shewed where a party of Osage hunters had recently crossed the river on their way to the buffalo range. After letting our horses drink in the river we continued along its bank for a space, and then across prairies where we saw a distant smoke, which we hoped might proceed from the encampment of the rangers. Following what we supposed to be their trail we came to a meadow in which were a number of horses grazing. They were not, however, the horses of the troop. A little further on, we reached a straggling Osage village on the banks of the Arkansas. Our arrival created quite a sensation. A number of old men came forward and shook hands with us all severally: while the women and children huddled together in groupes, staring at us wildly, chattering and laughing among themselves. We found that all the young men of the village had departed on a hunting expedition, leaving the women and children and old men behind. Here the Commissioner made a speech from horseback; informing his hearers of the purport of his mission to promote a general peace among the tribes of the West, and urging them to lay aside all warlike and bloodthirsty notions and not to make any wanton attacks upon the Pawnees. This speech being interpreted by Beatte, seemed to have a most pacifying effect upon the multitude who promised faithfully that as far as in them lay, the peace should not be disturbed; and indeed their age and sex gave some reason to hope that they would keep their word.

Still hoping to reach the encampment of the rangers before nightfall, we pushed on until twilight, when we were obliged to halt on the borders of a ravine. The rangers bivouacked under trees, at the bottom of the dell, while we pitched our tent on a rocky knoll near a running stream. The night came on dark and overcast, with flying clouds, and much appearance of rain. The fires of the rangers burnt brightly in the dell, and threw strong masses of light upon the robber looking groups that were cooking, eating and drinking around them. To add to the wildness of the scene, several Osage Indians, visitors from the village we had passed, were mingled among the men. Three of them came and seated themselves by our fire. They watched every thing that was going on round them in silence, and looked like figures of monumental bronze. We gave them food, and, what they most relished, coffee: for the Indians partake in the universal fondness for this beverage which pervades the West. When they had made their supper they stretched themselves, side by side, before the fire and began a low nasal chaunt,[4] drumming with their hands upon their breasts by way of accompanyment. Their chaunt seemed to consist of regular staves, every one terminating, not in a melodious cadence, but in the abrupt interjection huh! uttered almost like a hiccup. This chaunt, we were told by our interpreter Beatte related to ourselves; our appearance, our treatment of them, and all that they knew of our plans. In one part they spoke of the young count, whose animated character and eagerness for Indian enterprize had struck their fancy, and they indulged in some waggery about him and the young Indian beauties that produced great merryment among our half breeds.

---

[4]Variant of chant.

This mode of improvising is common throughout the savage tribes; and in this way with a few simple inflections of the voice, they chaunt all their exploits in war and hunting, and occasionally indulge in a vein of comic humour and dry satire, to which the Indians appear to me much more prone than is generally imagined.

In fact the Indians that I have had an opportunity of seeing in real life are quite different from those described in poetry. They are by no means the stoics that they are represented; taciturn, unbending, without a tear or a smile. Taciturn they are, it is true, when in company with white men, whose good will they distrust, and whose language they do not understand; but the white man is equally taciturn under like circumstances. When the Indians are among themselves, however, there cannot be greater gossips. Half their time is taken up in talking over their adventures in war and hunting, and in telling whimsical stories. They are great mimics and buffoons, also, and entertain themselves excessively at the expense of the whites, with whom they have associated, and who have supposed them impressed with profound respect for their grandeur and dignity. They are curious observers, noting every thing in silence, but with a keen and watchful eye; occasionally exchanging a glance or a grunt with each other, when any thing particularly strikes them: but reserving all comments until they are alone. Then it is that they give full scope to criticism, satire, mimicry and mirth.

In the course of my journey along the frontier I have had repeated opportunities of noticing their excitability and boisterous merryment at their games, and have occasionally noticed a groupe of Osages sitting round a fire until a late hour of the night, engaged in the most animated and lively conversation, and at times making the woods resound with peals of laughter.

As to tears, they have them in abundance both real and affected; for at times they make a merit of them. No one weeps more bitterly or profusely at the death of a relative or friend: and they have stated times when they repair to howl and lament at their graves. I have heard doleful wailings at daybreak in the neighborhood of Indian villages, made by some of the inhabitants, who go out at that hour into the fields, to mourn and weep for the dead: at such times, I am told, the tears will stream down their cheeks in torrents.

As far as I can judge, the Indian of poetical fiction is like the shepherd of pastoral romance, a mere personification of imaginary attributes.

The nasal chaunt of our Osage guests gradually died away, they covered their heads with their blankets and fell fast asleep and in a little while all was silent, excepting the pattering of scattered rain drops upon our tent.

In the morning our Indian visitors breakfasted with us, but the young Osage, who was to act as esquire to the Count in his knight errantry on the prairies, was no where to be found. His wild horse too was missing, and, after many conjectures we came to the conclusion that he had taken "Indian leave" of us in the night. We afterwards ascertained that he had been persuaded so to do by the Osages we had recently met with, who had represented to him the perils that would attend him on an expedition to the Pawnee hunting grounds, where he might fall into the hands of the implacable enemies of his tribe; and, what was scarcely less to be apprehended, the annoyances to which he would be subjected from the capricious and overbearing conduct of the white men; who, as I have witnessed in my own short experience, are prone to treat the poor Indians as little better than brute animals. Indeed he had had a specimen of it himself in the narrow escape he made from the infliction of Lynch's law, by the hard winking worthy of the frontier, for the flagitious crime of finding a stray horse.

The disappearance of the youth was generally regretted by our party, for we had all taken a great fancy to him from his handsome, frank and manly appearance, and the easy grace of his deportment. He was indeed a native born gentleman. By none, however, was he so much lamented as by the young count, who thus suddenly found himself deprived of his esquire. I regretted the departure of the Osage for his own sake, for we should have cherished him throughout the expedition, and I am convinced from the munificent spirit of his patron, he would have returned to his tribe laden with wealth of beads and trinkets and Indian blankets.

CHAPTER VIII

The Honey Camp.

The weather, which had been rainy in the night, having held up, we resumed our march at seven o'clock in the morning, in confident hope of soon arriving at the encampment of the rangers. We had not ridden above three or four miles when we came to a large tree, which had recently been felled by an axe, for the wild honey contained in the hollow of its trunk, several broken flakes of which still remained. We now felt sure that the camp could not be far distant. About a couple of miles further some of the rangers set up a shout and pointed to a number of horses grazing in a woody bottom. A few paces brought us to the brow of an elevated ridge whence we looked down upon the encampment. It was a wild bandit, or Robin Hood scene. In a beautiful open forest, traversed by a running stream, were booths of bark and branches, and tents of blankets, temporary shelters from the recent rain, for the rangers commonly bivouack in the open air. There were groupes of rangers in every kind of uncouth garb. Some were cooking at huge fires made at the feet of trees; some were stretching and dressing deer skins; some were shooting at a mark and some lying about on the grass. Venison jerked,[1] and hung on frames—was drying over the embers in one place; in another lay carcasses recently brought in by the hunters. Stacks of rifles were leaning against the trunks of the trees and saddles bridles and powder horns hanging above them, while horses were grazing here and there among the thickets.

Our arrival was greeted with acclamation. The rangers crowded about their comrades to enquire the news from the fort: for our own part, we were received in frank simple hunter's style by Capt. Bean the commander of the company; a man about forty years of age, vigorous and active.[2] His life had been chiefly passed on the frontier, occasionally in Indian warfare, so that he was a thorough woodsman, and a first rate hunter. He was equipped in character; in leathern hunting shirt and leggings, and a leathern foraging cap.

While we were conversing with the Captain a veteran huntsman approached whose whole appearance struck me. He was of the middle size, but tough and weather proved; a head partly bald and garnished with loose iron grey locks, and a fine black eye, beaming with youthful spirit. His dress was similar to that of the Captain, a rifle shirt and leggings of dressed deer skin, that had evidently seen service; a powder horn was slung by his side, a hunting knife stuck in his belt, and in his hand was an ancient and trusty rifle, doubtless as dear to him as a bosom friend. He asked permission to go hunting which was readily granted. "That's Old Ryan,"[3] said the captain, when he had gone. "There's not a better hunter in the camp. He's sure to bring in game."

In a little while our pack horses were unloaded and turned loose to revel among the pea vines. Our tent was pitched; our fire made; the half of a deer had been sent to us from the Captain's lodge; Beatte brought in a couple of wild turkeys; the spits were laden and the camp kettle crammed with meat, and to crown our luxuries, a basin filled with great flakes of delicious honey, the spoils of a plundered bee tree, was given us by one of the rangers. Our little Frenchman

---

[1]Preserved by being cut into strips and dried.
[2]Captain Jesse Bean, Tennessean who had taken part in the Indian wars in Florida before this assignment.

[3]John Ryan, a noted frontiersman; a Virginian who had settled in Arkansas, where Captain Bean had recruited him.

Tonish was in an extacy, and tucking up his sleeves to the elbows, set to work to make a display of his culinary skill, on which he prided himself almost as much as upon his hunting, his riding and his warlike prowess.

CHAPTER X

AMUSEMENTS IN THE CAMP—CONSULTATIONS— HUNTERS' FARE AND FEASTING—EVENING SCENES—CAMP MELODY—THE FATE OF AN AMATEUR OWL.

On returning to the camp[1] we found it a scene of the greatest hilarity. Some of the rangers were shooting at a mark, others were leaping, wrestling and playing at prison bars. They were mostly young men, on their first expedition, in high health and vigour, and buoyant with anticipations; and I can conceive nothing more likely to set the youthful blood into a flow than a wild wood life of the kind and the range of a magnificent wilderness abounding with game and fruitful of adventure. We send our youth abroad to grow luxurious and effeminate in Europe; it appears to me that a previous tour on the prairies would be more likely to produce that manliness, simplicity and self dependence most in unison with our political institutions.

While the young men were engaged in these boisterous amusements a graver set, composed of the Captain the Doctor and other sages and leaders of the camp were seated or stretched out on the grass, round a frontier map, holding a consultation about our position, and the course we were to pursue.

Our plan was to cross the Arkansas just above where the Red Fork[2] falls into it then to keep westerly, until we should pass through a grand belt of open forest, called the Cross Timber, which ranges nearly north and south from the Arkansas to Red river, after which we were to keep a southerly course towards the latter river.

Our half breed Beatte, being an experienced Osage hunter, was called into the consultation. "Have you ever hunted in this direction?" said the Captain.

"Yes," was the laconic reply.

"Perhaps then you can tell us in which direction lies the Red Fork."

"If you keep along yonder, by the edge of the prairie you will come to a bald hill, with a pile of stones upon it."

"I have noticed that hill as I was hunting," said the Captain.

"Well! those stones were set up by the Osages as a land mark: from that spot you may have a sight of the Red Fork."

"In that case," cried the Captain, "we shall reach the Red Fork tomorrow; then cross the Arkansas above it, into the Pawnee country, and then in two days we shall crack Buffalo bones!"

The idea of arriving at the adventurous hunting grounds of the Pawnees and of coming upon the traces of the buffaloes, made every eye sparkle with animation. Our further conversation was interrupted by the sharp report of a rifle at no great distance from the camp.

"That's Old Ryan's rifle," exclaimed the Captain, "there's a buck down I'll warrant." Nor was he mistaken, for, before long, the veteran made his appearance, calling upon one of the younger rangers to return with him and aid in bringing home the carcass.

The surrounding country in fact, abounded with game, so that the camp was overstocked with provisions, and, as no less than twenty bee trees had been cut

---

[1]After a bee hunt described in Chapter IX.
[2]The Cimarron River.

down in the vicinity every one revelled in luxury. With the wasteful prodigality of hunters there was a continual feasting, and scarce any one put by provision for the morrow. The cooking was conducted in hunters' style. The meat was stuck upon tapering spits of dog wood, which were thrust perpendicularly into the ground, so as to sustain the joint before the fire, where it was roasted or broiled with all its juices retained in it in a manner that would have tickled the palate of the most experienced gourmand. As much could not be said in favour of the bread. It was little more than a paste made of flour and water and fried like fritters, in lard; though some adopted a ruder style, twisting it round the ends of sticks and thus roasting it before the fire. In either way I have found it extremely palatable on the prairies. No one knows the true relish of food until he has a hunter's appetite.

Before sunset we were summoned by little Tonish to a sumptuous repast. Blankets had been spread on the ground near to the fire, upon which we took our seats. A large dish or bowl, made from the root of a maple tree, and which we had purchased at the Indian village, was placed on the ground before us, and into it were emptied the contents of one of the camp kettles, consisting of a wild turkey hashed, together with slips of bacon and lumps of dough. Beside it was placed another bowl of similar ware, containing an ample supply of fritters. After we had discussed the hash, two wooden spits, on which the ribs of a fat buck were broiling before the fire, were removed and planted in the ground before us, with a triumphant air, by little Tonish. Having no dishes we had to proceed in hunters' style, cutting off strips and slices with our hunting knives, and dipping them in salt and pepper. To do justice to Tonish's cookery, however, and to the keen sauce of the prairies, never have I tasted venison so delicious. With all this our beverage was coffee, boiled in a camp kettle sweetened with brown sugar, and drank out of tin cups: and such was the style of our banquetting throughout this expedition, whenever provisions were plenty, and as long as flour and coffee and sugar held out.

As the twilight thickened into night the centinels were marched forth to their stations around the camp, an indispensable precaution in a country infested by Indians. The encampment now presented a picturesque appearance. Camp fires were blazing and smouldering here and there among the trees, with groups of rangers around them; some seated or lying on the ground, others standing in the ruddy glare of the flames, or in shadowy relief.

At some of the fires there was much boisterous mirth, where peals of laughter were mingled with loud ribald jokes and uncouth exclamations, for the troop was evidently a raw undisciplined band; levied among the wild youngsters of the frontier, who had enlisted, some for the sake of roving adventure, and some for the purpose of getting a knowledge of the country. Many of them were the neighbors of their officers and accustomed to regard them with the familiarity of equals and companions. None of them had any idea of the restraint and decorum of a camp, or ambition to acquire a name for exactness in a profession in which they had no intention of continuing.

While this boisterous merriment prevailed at one of the fires, there suddenly rose a strain of nasal melody from another, at which a choir of "vocalists" were uniting their voices in a most lugubrious psalm tune. This was led by one of the lieutenants; a tall spare man, who we were informed had officiated as schoolmaster, singing master and occasionally as methodist preacher in one of the villages of the frontier. The chaunt rose solemnly and sadly in the night air, and reminded me of the description of similar canticles in the camps of the Covenanters;[3] and, indeed, the strange medley of figures and faces and uncouth garbs congregated

---

[3]Protestants who professed covenant theology, a belief that since Adam and Eve broke God's first covenant by disobe-   dience, He had made a second covenant promising salvation by faith through election.

together in our troop would not have disgraced the banners of Praise God Barebones.[4]

In one of the intervals of this nasal psalmody, an amateur owl, as if in competition, began his dreary hooting. Immediately there was a cry throughout the camp of "Charley's owl! Charley's owl!" It seems this "obscure bird" had visited the camp every night and had been fired at by one of the centinels, a half witted lad, named Charley, who on being called up for firing when on duty, excused himself by saying that he understood that owls made uncommonly good soup.

One of the young rangers mimicked the cry of this bird of wisdom, who, with a simplicity little consonant with his character, came hovering within sight and alighted on the naked branch of a tree lit up by the blaze of our fire. The young Count immediately seized his fowling piece, took fatal aim and in a twinkling the poor bird of ill omen came fluttering to the ground. Charley was now called upon to make and eat his dish of owl soup, but declined as he had not shot the bird.

In the course of the evening I paid a visit to the Captain's fire. It was composed of huge trunks of trees and of sufficient magnitude to roast a buffalo whole. Here were a number of the prime hunters and leaders of the camp, some sitting, some standing, and others lying on skins or blankets before the fire, telling old frontier stories about hunting and Indian warfare.

As the night advanced we perceived above the trees to the west, a ruddy glow flushing up the sky.

"That must be a prairie set on fire by the Osage hunters," said the Captain.

"It is at the Red Fork," said Beatte, regarding the sky. "It seems but three miles distant, yet it perhaps is twenty."

About half past eight o'clock a beautiful pale light gradually sprang up in the East, a precursor of the rising moon. Drawing off from the captain's lodge I now prepared for the nights repose. I had determined to abandon the shelter of the tent and henceforth to bivouack like the rangers. A bear skin spread at the foot of a tree was my bed, with a pair of saddle bags for a pillow. Wrapping myself in blankets I stretched myself on this hunter's couch, and soon fell into a sound and sweet sleep, from which I did not awake until the bugle sounded at day break.

1835

JAMES FENIMORE COOPER
(1789–1851)

In 1828 when James Fenimore Cooper tried to explain to Europeans why America had produced few works of literature, he sounded a theme that other writers from Hawthorne to James would echo, the "poverty of materials": "There are no annals for the historian; no follies (beyond the most vulgar and commonplace) for the satirist; no manners for the dramatist; no obscure fictions for the writer of romance; no gross and hardy offences against decorum for the moralist; nor any of the rich artificial auxiliaries of poetry. The weakest hand can extract a spark from the flint, but it would baffle the strength of a giant to attempt kindling a flame with a pudding-stone."

There is perhaps irony in the fact that when Cooper wrote these words in

---

[4]Praisegod Barbon, a British Anabaptist (against infant baptism), preacher of long sermons, served in Cromwell's Parliament of 1653.

Notions of the Americans, supposedly the words of a British bachelor travelling in America, Cooper was living in Paris, already internationally known for six novels, three of them part of *The Leather-Stocking* series, among the best he or any American would produce in the nineteenth century. The subtext of Cooper's comment is that the American writers had a doubly difficult time. They had not only to create the works, but they also had to create the materials out of which the works of art were to be wrought: *create,* not *find* ready at hand.

Cooper was born in Burlington, New Jersey, in 1789, the youngest of seven children. In 1790, when James was thirteen months old, his father moved the family by wagon train from the eastern city to the frontier area around Otsego Lake in central New York, where he owned over half a million acres of land acquired during the last days of the Revolution. Cooperstown, at the foot of Lake Otsego, had been named after him. Much of the Cooper family income came not from rent but the outright sale of land to settlers— over 40,000 of them. The old Dutch families who rented but refused to sell their huge land holdings would be the targets of the anti-rent war of the 1840s.

James Cooper (the Fenimore came later when, after his mother's death, he added her family name to his) grew up in an area in transition from frontier to rural settlement. He would have witnessed few frontiersmen and fewer Indians. But he roamed the woods where they had trod, hunted, and fought. And he would have heard stories. Life lived in the family mansion his father built was far from rude, and the education he received at an Albany preparatory school was infinitely more refined than that of a frontiersman in the forests. He entered Yale when he was thirteen and was expelled two years later for pranks, such as placing a donkey in the professor's chair.

It is not surprising that James Cooper was sent to sea in 1806 as a sailor on a merchant vessel. During the year's voyage the ship docked in London and at ports around the Mediterranean. By the time the excursion ended in New York, Cooper's love of the sea inspired him to enter the U.S. Navy as a midshipman (an officer-in-training). To his dismay, the Navy assigned him to shore duty as a recruiter. In New York, he met and fell in love with Susan De Lancey, from a wealthy Westchester County family. They were married in 1811. Cooper's father died in 1809, and he along with his five older brothers inherited $50,000 each. But the huge estate approaching a million dollars in value was willed to the eldest son, or succeeding sons in case of death. Between 1813 and 1819, his mother and all five of his older brothers died, leaving Cooper master of his father's large estate, now heavily in debt because of the neglect and lavish lifestyle of his brothers.

Legend has it that Cooper was reading a novel—perhaps by Jane Austen—to his wife one evening and threw it aside with the exclamation, "I could write you a better book than that myself." Challenged by his wife, he wrote a domestic or society novel, *Precaution* (1820), set in England. Cooper may well have been motivated by his wife's challenge, but there is no doubt that he was strongly motivated by the need for money. *Precaution* was a financial disaster, but, undaunted, Cooper next wrote *The Spy* (1821), a tale of intrigue set during the Revolutionary War. It was an immediate success, was translated into several languages, and made into a popular play. Cooper was embarked on his career.

Cooper was an indefatigable writer, turning out books with the regularity of clockwork, sometimes three in one year. By the time of his death, he had written thirty-two novels and some dozen other books of travel, social criticism, and history (including a two-volume *History of the Navy of the United States of America,* 1839). His writing career was compressed into a thirty-one-year period, during which few days could have passed without his taking pen in hand.

In 1823, Cooper published *The Pioneers,* the first of the *Leather-Stocking Tales,* set on the frontier and introducing the frontiersman Natty Bumppo and his Indian friend Chingachgook. It mined a vein of his imagination that would prove his richest resource and his most popular and enduring creation. In 1824, he published *The Pilot,* a sea story that drew on his experiences on the merchant vessel and in the Navy. It was the first of eleven such novels that he would write in the nautical novel genre that he is credited with inventing. These works proved astonishingly popular and saved Cooper from bankruptcy. They also earned him the epithet, "the American Sir Walter Scott," which irritated more than it pleased him.

In 1826, Cooper felt flush enough to take his family abroad on a trip that was to be in part a vacation, in part an educational experience, and in part a business trip to make arrangements with publishers. He was to be gone some seven years, living in Paris (where a friendship with Lafayette developed and he met Sir Walter Scott) and making the Grand Tour through England, France, Switzerland, Italy, and Germany. He left America an idolized writer. By the time he returned in 1833, he found himself attacked on all sides because of works he had published perceived to be critical of American democracy—particularly *Notions of the Americans* (1828).

Cooper, sometimes hot-tempered, was not adept in dealing with the press. He was never again to reach the heights of popularity he achieved with his first novels. He continued to pour forth books, including frontier novels, sea novels, and—more and more—polemical works that increased his unpopularity. Among the latter was the Littlepage trilogy, *Satanstoe, The Chainbearer,* and *The Redskins* (1845–46), which attacked the anti-rent agitators who were rebelling against a land system that doomed the tillers and toilers to perpetual poverty and the large landholders to a kind of perpetual aristocracy. Cooper was popularly seen as being on the side of wealth and privilege.

But instinctively, Cooper returned to the material most congenial to his imagination, the *Leather-Stocking* saga. Although he had described Leatherstocking's death in his eighties in *The Prairie,* published in 1827, he resurrected him for a period during his robust thirties in *The Pathfinder* (1840) and for his early twenties in *The Deerslayer* (1841). When the five parts were completed, Cooper wrote in a Preface: "If anything from the pen of the writer of these romances is at all to outlive himself, it is, unquestionably, the series of 'The Leather-Stocking Tales.'" And he advised readers to read the books not in the order of composition but in the order of the narrative's action; *The Deerslayer, The Last of the Mohicans, The Pathfinder, The Pioneers,* and *The Prairie.*

It is a commonplace of Cooper criticism that he did not know the frontier nor the American Indian, that he did not write out of firsthand experience. The observation is true, but not very profound. The sweeping epic movement over the American landscape of the *Leather-Stocking Tales,* the indelible portrait of the resourceful, creative, and compassionate frontiersman Natty Bumppo, and the mystically transfiguring, spiritually sustaining relationship between him and his Indian friend Chingachgook—these Cooper did not find but *created* out of the mythopoeic imagination lodged far down within his psyche, in those depths where it mingled with the collective American, or "civilized" imagination. It is as though Cooper created the answer to "What is an

American?" by creating an ideal frontiersman who combines the best of civilization and the wilderness, who embodies the genius of civilized and aboriginal man. He is an imaginative fulfillment of the American dream that reality was doomed never to match. It is thus that in reading Cooper's epic, we feel the shock of recognition of something longed for but long since gone—except in myth. D.H. Lawrence was near the mark when he called the *Leather-Stocking Tales* "a sort of American *Odyssey*, with Natty Bumppo as Odysseus."

ADDITIONAL READING

James Fenimore Cooper: Representative Selections, ed. Robert E. Spiller, 1936; *The Letters and Journals of James Fenimore Cooper*, 4 vols., ed. James Franklin Beard, 1960–64.

Thomas R. Lounsbury, *James Fenimore Cooper*, 1882; D.H. Lawrence, *Studies in Classic American Literature*, 1923; Henry W. Boynton, *James Fenimore Cooper*, 1931; Robert E. Spiller, *Fenimore Cooper: Critic of His Times*, 1931; Donald A. Ringe, *James Fenimore Cooper*, 1962; Warren Walker, *James Fenimore Cooper*, 1962; George Dekker, *James Fenimore Cooper: The Novelist*, 1967; Blake Nevius, *Cooper's Landscapes*, 1975; H. Daniel Peck, *A World by Itself: The Pastoral Moment in Cooper's Fiction*, 1977; Stephen Railton, *Fenimore Cooper: A Study of His Life and Imagination*, 1978; George A. Test, ed., *James Fenimore Cooper and His Country, or Getting Under Way*, 1979; George A. Test, ed., *James Fenimore Cooper: His Country and His Art*, 1980; Wayne Franklin, *The World of James Fenimore Cooper*, 1982; William P. Kelly, *Plotting America's Past: Fenimore Cooper and the Leatherstocking Tales*, 1984; Robert Clark, ed., *James Fenimore Cooper: New Critical Essays*, 1985; James D. Wallace, *Early Cooper and His Audience*, 1986.

TEXT

The Writings of James Fenimore Cooper, ed. James Franklin Beard, in progress from the 1960s: *The Pioneers*, ed. James Franklin Beard, Lance Schachterle, and Kenneth M. Anderson, Jr., 1980; *The Last of the Mohicans*, ed. James Franklin Beard, James A. Sappenfield, and E.N. Feltskog, 1983; [Literature and Arts of the United States], Letter XXIII, *Notions of the Americans: Picked up by a Travelling Bachelor*, 1828; "An Aristocrat and a Democrat," *The American Democrat*, 1838; "A Visit from Scott," *Gleanings in Europe: France*, ed. Robert E. Spiller, 1928.

from The Pioneers

[MASSACRE OF THE PIGEONS][1]

CHAPTER XXII

"Men, boys, and girls,
Desert th' unpeopled village; and wild crowds
Spread o'er the plain, by the sweet frenzy driven."
Somerville, *The Chace*, II.197-99.[2]

From this time to the close of April, the weather continued to be a succession of great and rapid changes. One day, the soft airs of spring seemed to be stealing along the valley, and, in unison with an invigorating sun, attempting, covertly, to rouse the dormant powers of the vegetable world; while on the next, the surly blasts from the north would sweep across the lake, and erase every impression left

---

[1]This self-contained episode appears in Chapter 22 (it was Chapter 3 in Vol. II of the first edition) of *The Pioneers, or The Sources of the Susquehanna*, the first written of the *Leather-Stocking Tales* but the fourth in narrative sequence.

The frontiersman Natty Bumppo is the hero of the entire series, but Cooper gives him many nicknames.
[2]William Somerville (1675–1742), author of *The Chace* (1735).

by their gentle adversaries. The snow, however, finally disappeared, and the green wheat fields were seen in every direction, spotted with the dark and charred stumps that had, the preceding season, supported some of the proudest trees of the forest. Ploughs were in motion, wherever those useful implements could be used, and the smokes of the sugar-camps[3] were no longer seen issuing from the woods of maple. The lake had lost the beauty of a field of ice, but still a dark and gloomy covering concealed its waters, for the absence of currents left them yet hid under a porous crust, which, saturated with the fluid, barely retained enough strength to preserve the contiguity of its parts. Large flocks of wild geese were seen passing over the country, which hovered, for a time, around the hidden sheet of water, apparently searching for a resting-place; and then, on finding themselves excluded by the chill covering, would soar away to the north, filling the air with discordant screams, as if venting their complaints at the tardy operations of nature.

For a week, the dark covering of the Otsego[4] was left to the undisturbed possession of two eagles, who alighted on the centre of its field, and sat eyeing their undisputed territory. During the presence of these monarchs of the air, the flocks of migrating birds avoided crossing the plain of ice, by turning into the hills, apparently seeking the protection of the forests, while the white and bald heads of the tenants of the lake were turned upward, with a look of contempt. But the time had come, when even these kings of birds were to be dispossessed. An opening had been gradually increasing, at the lower extremity of the lake, and around the dark spot where the current of the river prevented the formation of ice, during even the coldest weather; and the fresh southerly winds, that now breathed freely upon the valley, made an impression on the waters. Mimic waves begun to curl over the margin of the frozen field, which exhibited an outline of crystallizations, that slowly receded towards the north. At each step the power of the winds and the waves increased, until, after a struggle of a few hours, the turbulent little billows succeeded in setting the whole field in motion, when it was driven beyond the reach of the eye, with a rapidity, that was as magical as the change produced in the scene by this expulsion of the lingering remnant of winter. Just as the last sheet of agitated ice was disappearing in the distance, the eagles rose, and soared with a wide sweep above the clouds, while the waves tossed their little caps of snow into the air, as if rioting in their release from a thraldom of five months' duration.

The following morning Elizabeth[5] was awakened by the exhilarating sounds of the martins, who were quarreling and chattering around the little boxes suspended above her windows, and the cries of Richard,[6] who was calling, in tones animating as the signs of the season itself—

"Awake! awake! my fair lady! the gulls are hovering over the lake already, and the heavens are alive with pigeons. You may look an hour before you can find a hole, through which, to get a peep at the sun. Awake! awake! lazy ones! Benjamin[7] is overhauling the ammunition, and we only wait for our breakfasts, and away for the mountains and pigeon-shooting."

There was no resisting this animated appeal, and in a few minutes Miss Temple and her friend[8] descended to the parlour. The doors of the hall were thrown open, and the mild, balmy air of a clear spring morning was ventilating the apartment, where the vigilance of the ex-steward had been so long maintaining an artificial heat, with such unremitted diligence. The gentlemen were impatiently wait-

---

[3] Camps set up to turn sap of the maple tree into sugar.
[4] Lake at the headwaters of the Susquehanna River in central New York state. (Cooperstown is on this lake.)
[5] Elizabeth Temple, heroine of the novel; she has returned from school to her home in Templeton. Her father is Judge Marmaduke Temple.

[6] Richard Jones (called Dickon), a sheriff, is cousin to Judge Temple.
[7] "Ben" Penguillan, steward (or house servant) for Judge Temple.
[8] Louisa Grant, daughter of a minister.

ing for their morning's repast, each equipt in the garb of a sportsman. Mr. Jones made many visits to the southern door, and would cry—

"See, cousin Bess! see, 'duke![9] the pigeon-roosts of the south have broken up! They are growing more thick every instant. Here is a flock that the eye cannot see the end of. There is food enough in it to keep the army of Xerxes[10] for a month, and feathers enough to make beds for the whole country. Xerxes, Mr. Edwards,[11] was a Grecian king, who—no, he was a Turk, or a Persian, who wanted to conquer Greece, just the same as these rascals will overrun our wheat-fields, when they come back in the fall.—Away! away! Bess; I long to pepper them."

In this wish both Marmaduke and young Edwards seemed equally to participate, for the sight was exhilarating to a sportsman; and the ladies soon dismissed the party, after a hasty breakfast.

If the heavens were alive with pigeons, the whole village seemed equally in motion, with men, women, and children. Every species of fire-arms, from the French ducking-gun, with a barrel near six feet in length, to the common horseman's pistol, was to be seen in the hands of the men and boys; while bows and arrows, some made of the simple stick of a walnut sapling, and others in a rude imitation of the ancient cross-bows, were carried by many of the latter.

The houses, and the signs of life apparent in the village, drove the alarmed birds from the direct line of their flight, towards the mountains, along the sides and near the bases of which they were glancing in dense masses, equally wonderful by the rapidity of their motion, and their incredible numbers.

We have already said, that across the inclined plane which fell from the steep ascent of the mountain to the banks of the Susquehanna, ran the highway, on either side of which a clearing of many acres had been made, at a very early day. Over those clearings, and up the eastern mountain, and along the dangerous path that was cut into its side, the different individuals posted themselves, and in a few moments the attack commenced.

Amongst the sportsmen was the tall, gaunt form of Leather-stocking,[12] walking over the field, with his rifle hanging on his arm, his dogs at his heels; the latter now scenting the dead or wounded birds, that were beginning to tumble from the flocks, and then crouching under the legs of their master, as if they participated in his feelings, at this wasteful and unsportsman-like execution.

The reports of the fire-arms became rapid, whole volleys rising from the plain, as flocks of more than ordinary numbers darted over the opening, shadowing the field, like a cloud; and then the light smoke of a single piece would issue from among the leafless bushes on the mountain, as death was hurled on the retreat of the affrighted birds, who were rising from a volley, in a vain effort to escape. Arrows, and missiles of every kind, were in the midst of the flocks; and so numerous were the birds, and so low did they take their flight, that even long poles, in the hands of those on the sides of the mountain, were used to strike them to the earth.

During all this time, Mr. Jones, who disdained the humble and ordinary means of destruction used by his companions, was busily occupied, aided by Benjamin, in making arrangements for an assault of a more than ordinarily fatal character. Among the relics of the old military excursions, that occasionally are discovered throughout the different districts of the western part of New-York, there had been found in Templeton, at its settlement, a small swivel, which would carry a ball of a pound weight. It was thought to have been deserted by a war-party of the

---

[9]Marmaduke, the Judge.
[10]Xerxes (*c.* 519–*c.* 464 B.C.). Persian king whose army conquered Greece and was of legendary size.
[11]Oliver Edwards, a young guest whose background is unknown.

[12]One nickname of Natty Bumppo, after his characteristic dress of leather covering his legs, stocking-like protection against the various hazards of the wilderness.

whites, in one of their inroads into the Indian settlements, when, perhaps, convenience or their necessity induced them to leave such an encumbrance behind them in the woods. This miniature cannon had been released from the rust, and being mounted on little wheels, was now in a state for actual service. For several years, it was the sole organ for extraordinary rejoicings used in those mountains. On the mornings of the Fourths of July, it would be heard ringing among the hills, and even Captain Hollister,[13] who was the highest authority in that part of the country on all such occasions, affirmed that, considering its dimensions, it was no despicable gun for a salute. It was somewhat the worse for the service it had performed, it is true, there being but a trifling difference in size between the touch-hole and the muzzle. Still, the grand conceptions of Richard had suggested the importance of such an instrument, in hurling death at his nimble enemies. The swivel was dragged by a horse into a part of the open space, that the Sheriff thought most eligible for planting a battery of the kind, and Mr. Pump proceeded to load it. Several handfuls of duck-shot were placed on top of the powder, and the Major-domo announced that his piece was ready for service.

The sight of such an implement collected all the idle spectators to the spot, who, being mostly boys, filled the air with cries of exultation and delight. The gun was pointed high, and Richard, holding a coal of fire in a pair of tongs, patiently took his seat on a stump, awaiting the appearance of a flock worthy of his notice.

So prodigious was the number of the birds, that the scattering fire of the guns, with the hurling of missiles, and the cries of the boys, had no other effect than to break off small flocks from the immense masses that continued to dart along the valley, as if the whole of the feathered tribe were pouring through that one pass. None pretended to collect the game, which lay scattered over the fields in such profusion, as to cover the very ground with the fluttering victims.

Leather-stocking was a silent, but uneasy spectator of all these proceedings, but was able to keep his sentiments to himself until he saw the introduction of the swivel into the sports.

"This comes of settling a country!" he said—"here have I known the pigeons to fly for forty long years, and, till you made your clearings, there was nobody to skear or to hurt them. I loved to see them come into the woods, for they were company to a body; hurting nothing; being, as it was, as harmless as a garter-snake. But now it gives me sore thoughts when I hear the frighty things whizzing through the air, for I know it's only a motion to bring out all the brats in the village. Well! the Lord won't see the waste of his creaters for nothing, and right will be done to the pigeons, as well as others, by-and-by.—There's Mr. Oliver, as bad as the rest of them, firing into the flocks as if he was shooting down nothing but Mingo[14] warriors."

Among the sportsmen was Billy Kirby, who, armed with an old musket, was loading, and, without even looking into the air, was firing, and shouting as his victims fell even on his own person. He heard the speech of Natty, and took upon himself to reply—

"What! old Leather-stocking," he cried, "grumbling at the loss of a few pigeons! If you had to sow your wheat twice, and three times, as I have done, you wouldn't be so massyfully[15] feeling'd to'ards the divils.—Hurrah, boys! scatter the feathers. This is better than shooting at a turkey's head and neck, old fellow."

"It's better for you, maybe, Billy Kirby," replied the indignant old hunter, "and all them that don't know how to put a ball down a rifle-barrel, or how to bring it

---

[13]Proprietor of the local inn.
[14]In the novel, the Mingo Indians (a tribe of the Iroquois)
are the enemy, the Delaware Indians friends.
[15]Mercifully.

up ag'in with a true aim; but it's wicked to be shooting into flocks in this wastey manner; and none do it, who know how to knock over a single bird. If a body has a craving for pigeon's flesh, why! it's made the same as all other creater's, for man's eating, but not to kill twenty and eat one. When I want such a thing, I go into the woods till I find one to my liking, and then I shoot him off the branches without touching a feather of another, though there might be a hundred on the same tree. You couldn't do such a thing, Billy Kirby—you couldn't do it if you tried."

"What's that, old corn-stalk! you sapless stub!" cried the wood-chopper. "You've grown wordy, since the affair of the turkey; but if you're for a single shot, here goes at that bird which comes on by himself."

The fire from the distant part of the field had driven a single pigeon below the flock to which it belonged, and, frightened with the constant reports of the muskets, it was approaching the spot where the disputants stood, darting first from one side, and then to the other, cutting the air with the swiftness of lightning, and making a noise with its wings, not unlike the rushing of a bullet. Unfortunately for the wood-chopper, notwithstanding his vaunt, he did not see this bird until it was too late to fire as it approached, and he pulled his trigger at the unlucky moment when it was darting immediately over his head. The bird continued its course with the usual velocity.

Natty lowered the rifle from his arm, when the challenge was made, and, waiting a moment, until the terrified victim had got in a line with his eye, and had dropped near the bank of the lake, he raised it again with uncommon rapidity, and fired. It might have been chance, or it might have been skill, that produced the result; it was probably a union of both; but the pigeon whirled over in the air, and fell into the lake, with a broken wing. At the sound of his rifle, both his dogs started from his feet, and in a few minutes the "slut"[16] brought out the bird, still alive.

The wonderful exploit of Leather-stocking was noised through the field with great rapidity, and the sportsmen gathered in to learn the truth of the report.

"What," said young Edwards, "have you really killed a pigeon on the wing, Natty, with a single ball?"

"Haven't I killed loons before now, lad, that dive at the flash?" returned the hunter. "It's much better to kill only such as you want, without wasting your powder and lead, than to be firing into God's creaters in this wicked manner. But I come out for a bird, and you know the reason why I like small game, Mr. Oliver, and now I have got one I will go home, for I don't relish to see these wasty ways that you are all practysing, as if the least thing was not made for use, and not to destroy."

"Thou sayest well, Leather-stocking," cried Marmaduke, "and I begin to think it time to put an end to this work of destruction."

"Put an ind, Judge, to your clearings. An't the woods his work as well as the pigeons? Use, but don't waste. Wasn't the woods made for the beasts and birds to harbour in? and when man wanted their flesh, their skins, or their feathers, there's the place to seek them. But I'll go to the hut with my own game, for I wouldn't touch one of the harmless things that kiver the ground here, looking up with their eyes on me, as if they only wanted tongues to say their thoughts."

With this sentiment in his mouth, Leather-stocking threw his rifle over his arm, and, followed by his dogs, stepped across the clearing with great caution, taking care not to tread on one of the wounded birds in his path. He soon entered the bushes on the margin of the lake, and was hid from view.

Whatever impression the morality of Natty made on the Judge, it was utterly

---

[16]Female dog.

lost on Richard. He availed himself of the gathering of the sportsmen, to lay a plan for one "fell swoop" of destruction. The musketmen were drawn up in battle array, in a line extending on each side of his artillery, with orders to await the signal of firing from himself.

"Stand by, my lads," said Benjamin, who acted as an aide-de-camp, on this occasion, "stand by, my hearties, and when Squire Dickens heaves out the signal to begin the firing, d'ye see, you may open upon them in a broadside. Take care and fire low, boys, and you'll be sure to hull the flock."

"Fire low!" shouted Kirby—"hear the old fool! If we fire low, we may hit the stumps, but not ruffle a pigeon."

"How should you know, you lubber?"[17] cried Benjamin, with a very unbecoming heat, for an officer on the eve of battle—"how should you know, you grampus?[18] Havn't I sailed aboard of the Boadishy for five years? and wasn't it a standing order to fire low, and to hull your enemy? Keep silence at your guns, boys, and mind the order that is passed."

The loud laughs of the musketmen were silenced by the more authoritative voice of Richard, who called for attention and obedience to his signals.

Some millions of pigeons were supposed to have already passed, that morning, over the valley of Templeton; but nothing like the flock that was now approaching had been seen before. It extended from mountain to mountain in one solid blue mass, and the eye looked in vain over the southern hills to find its termination. The front of this living column was distinctly marked by a line, but very slightly indented, so regular and even was the flight. Even Marmaduke forgot the morality of Leather-stocking as it approached, and, in common with the rest, brought his musket to a poise.

"Fire!" cried the Sheriff, clapping a coal to the priming of the cannon. As half of Benjamin's charge escaped through the touch-hole, the whole volley of the musketry preceded the report of the swivel. On receiving this united discharge of small-arms, the front of the flock darted upward, while, at the same instant, myriads of those in the rear rushed with amazing rapidity into their places, so that when the column of white smoke gushed from the mouth of the little cannon, an accumulated mass of objects was gliding over its point of direction. The roar of the gun echoed along the mountains, and died away to the north, like distant thunder, while the whole flock of alarmed birds seemed, for a moment, thrown into one disorderly and agitated mass. The air was filled with their irregular flight, layer rising above layer, far above the tops of the highest pines, none daring to advance beyond the dangerous pass; when, suddenly, some of the leaders of the feathered tribe shot across the valley, taking their flight directly over the village, and hundreds of thousands in their rear followed the example, deserting the eastern side of the plain to their pe.secutors and the slain.

"Victory!" shouted Richard, "victory! we have driven the enemy from the field."

"Not so, Dickon," said Marmaduke; "the field is covered with them; and, like the Leather-stocking, I see nothing but eyes, in every direction, as the innocent sufferers turn their heads in terror. Full one half of those that have fallen are yet alive: and I think it is time to end the sport; if sport it be."

"Sport!" cried the Sheriff; "it is princely sport. There are some thousands of the blue-coated boys on the ground, so that every old woman in the village may have a pot-pie for the asking."

"Well, we have happily frightened the birds from this side of the valley," said Marmaduke, "and the carnage must of necessity end, for the present.——Boys, I

---

[17]Landlubber, clumsy oaf.
[18]Small variety of whale.

will give thee sixpence a hundred for the pigeons' heads only; so go to work, and bring them into the village."

This expedient produced the desired effect, for every urchin on the ground went industriously to work to wring the necks of the wounded birds. Judge Temple retired towards his dwelling with that kind of feeling, that many a man has experienced before him, who discovers, after the excitement of the moment has passed, that he has purchased pleasure at the price of misery to others. Horses were loaded with the dead; and, after this first burst of sporting, the shooting of pigeons became a business, with a few idlers, for the remainder of the season. Richard, however, boasted for many a year, of his shot with the "cricket;"[19] and Benjamin gravely asserted, that he thought they killed nearly as many pigeons on that day, as there were Frenchmen destroyed on the memorable occasion of Rodney's victory.[20]

1823

from The Last of the Mohicans

[INDIAN AND WHITE MAN: A DIALOGUE ON ORIGINS AND DESTINY][1]

CHAPTER III

> Before these fields were shorn and tilled,
>   Full to the brim our rivers flowed;
> The melody of waters filled
>   The fresh and boundless wood;
> And torrents dashed, and rivulets played,
> And fountains spouted in the shade.
>   Bryant,[2] "An Indian at the Burial-Place
>   of His Fathers," ll. 67–72.

*   *   *   *   *

On that day, two men were lingering on the banks of a small but rapid stream, . . . like those who awaited the appearance of an absent person, or the approach of some expected event. The vast canopy of woods spread itself to the margin of the river, overhanging the water, and shadowing its dark current with a deeper hue. The rays of the sun were beginning to grow less fierce, and the intense heat of the day was lessened, as the cooler vapours of the springs and fountains rose above their leafy beds, and rested in the atmosphere. Still that breathing silence, which marks the drowsy sultriness of an American landscape in July, pervaded the secluded spot, interrupted, only, by the low voices of the men, the occasional and lazy tap of a wood-pecker, the discordant cry of some gaudy jay, or a swelling on the ear, from the dull roar of a distant water-fall.

These feeble and broken sounds were, however, too familiar to the foresters, to draw their attention from the more interesting matter of their dialogue. While one of these loiterers showed the red skin and wild accoutrements of a native of

---

[19]Small cannon.
[20]Admiral George Brydges, Baron Rodney (1719–1792), won a decisive victory over the French in 1782 off Dominica (in the West Indies).
[1]Cooper's chapters in his novels are sometimes set pieces that may be read without regard to the novel's action. In Chapter III, Cooper's two main characters in the *Leather-*

Stocking Tales—the frontiersman, here called Hawkeye (Natty Bumppo), and his friend the Indian chief, Chingachgook—engage in a colloquy about the origins and destiny of the Indians.
[2]William Cullen Bryant (1794–1878); the poem quoted here is included in the volume.

the woods, the other exhibited, through the mask of his rude and nearly savage equipments, the brighter, though sunburnt and long-faded complexion of one who might claim descent from a European parentage. The former was seated on the end of a mossy log, in a posture that permitted him to heighten the effect of his earnest language, by the calm but expressive gestures of an Indian, engaged in debate. His body, which was nearly naked, presented a terrific emblem of death, drawn in intermingled colours of white and black. His closely shaved head, on which no other hair than the well known and chivalrous scalping tuft[3] was preserved, was without ornament of any kind, with the exception of a solitary eagle's plume, that crossed his crown, and depended over the left shoulder. A tomahawk and scalping-knife, of English manufacture, were in his girdle; while a short military rifle, of that sort with which the policy of the whites armed their savage allies, lay carelessly across his bare and sinewy knee. The expanded chest, full-formed limbs, and grave countenance of this warrior, would denote that he had reached the vigour of his days, though no symptoms of decay appeared to have yet weakened his manhood.

The frame of the white man, judging by such parts as were not concealed by his clothes, was like that of one who had known hardships and exertion from his earliest youth. His person, though muscular, was rather attenuated than full; but every nerve and muscle appeared strung and indurated,[4] by unremitted exposure and toil. He wore a hunting-shirt of forest-green, fringed with faded yellow,[5] and a summer cap, of skins which had been shorn of their fur. He also bore a knife in a girdle of wampum, like that which confined the scanty garments of the Indian, but no tomahawk. His moccasins were ornamented after the gay fashion of the natives, while the only part of his under dress which appeared below the hunting-frock, was a pair of buckskin leggings, that laced at the sides, and which were gartered above the knees, with the sinews of a deer. A pouch and horn completed his personal accoutrements, though a rifle of great length,[6] which the theory of the more ingenious whites had taught them, was the most dangerous of all fire-arms, leaned against a neighbouring sapling. The eye of the hunter, or scout, whichever he might be, was small, quick, keen, and restless, roving while he spoke, on every side of him, as if in que. of game, or distrusting the sudden approach of some lurking enemy. Notwithstanding these symptoms of habitual suspicion, his countenance was not only without guile, but at the moment at which he is introduced, it was charged with an expression of sturdy honesty.

"Even your traditions make the case in my favour, Chingachgook," he said, speaking in the tongue which was known to all the natives who formerly inhabited the country between the Hudson and the Potomack, and of which we shall give a free translation for the benefit of the reader; endeavouring, at the same time, to preserve some of the peculiarities, both of the individual and of the language. "Your fathers came from the setting sun, crossed the big river,[7] fought the people of the country, and took the land; and mine came from the red sky of the morning, over the salt lake, and did their work much after the fashion that had been set them by yours; then let God judge the matter between us, and friends spare their words!"

---

[3]"The North American warrior caused the hair to be plucked from his whole body; a small tuft, only, was left on the crown of his head, in order that his enemy might avail himself of it, in wrenching off the scalp in the event of his fall. The scalp was the only admissible trophy of victory. Thus, it was deemed more important to obtain the scalp than to kill the man. Some tribes lay great stress on the honour of striking a dead body. These practices have nearly disappeared among the Indians of the Atlantic states." (Cooper's note).

[4]Hardened.

[5]"The hunting-shirt is a picturesque smock-frock, being shorter, and ornamented with fringes and tassels. The colours are intended to imitate the hues of the wood, with a view to concealment. Many corps of American riflemen have been thus attired; and the dress is one of the most striking of modern times. The hunting shirt is frequently white" (Cooper's note).

[6]"The rifle of the army is short; that of the hunter is always long" (Cooper's note).

[7]"The Mississippi. The scout alludes to a tradition which is very popular among the tribes of the Atlantic states. Evidence of their Asiatic origin is deduced from the circumstance, though great uncertainty hangs over the whole history of the Indians" (Cooper's note).

"My fathers fought with the naked red-man!" returned the Indian, sternly, in the same language. "Is there no difference, Hawk-eye, between the stone-headed arrow of the warrior, and the leaden bullet with which you kill?"

"There is reason in an Indian, though nature has made him with a red skin!" said the white man, shaking his head, like one on whom such an appeal to his justice was not thrown away. For a moment he appeared to be conscious of having the worst of the argument, then rallying again, he answered the objection of his antagonist in the best manner his limited information would allow: "I am no scholar, and I care not who knows it; but judging from what I have seen at deer chaces, and squirrel hunts, of the sparks below, I should think a rifle in the hands of their grandfathers, was not so dangerous as a hickory bow, and a good flint-head might be, if drawn with Indian judgment, and sent by an Indian eye."

"You have the story told by your fathers," returned the other, coldly waving his hand. "What say your old men? do they tell the young warriors, that the pale-faces met the red-men, painted for war and armed with the stone hatchet or wooden gun?"

"I am not a prejudiced man, nor one who vaunts himself on his natural privileges, though the worst enemy I have on earth, and he is an Iroquois, daren't deny that I am genuine white," the scout replied, surveying, with secret satisfaction, the faded colour of his bony and sinewy hand; "and I am willing to own that my people have many ways, of which, as an honest man, I can't approve. It is one of their customs to write in books what they have done and seen, instead of telling them in their villages, where the lie can be given to the face of a cowardly boaster, and the brave soldier can call on his comrades to witness for the truth of his words. In consequence of this bad fashion, a man who is too conscientious to misspend his days among the women, in learning the names of black marks, may never hear of the deeds of his fathers, nor feel a pride in striving to outdo them. For myself, I conclude all the Bumppos could shoot; for I have a natural turn with a rifle, which must have been handed down from generation to generation, as our holy commandments tell us, all good and evil gifts are bestowed; though I should be loth to answer for other people in such a matter. But every story has its two sides; so I ask you, Chingachgook, what passed, according to the traditions of the red men, when our fathers first met?"

A silence of a minute succeeded, during which the Indian sat mute; then, full of the dignity of his office, he commenced his brief tale, with a solemnity that served to heighten its appearance of truth.

"Listen, Hawk-eye, and your ear shall drink no lie. 'Tis what my fathers have said, and what the Mohicans have done." He hesitated a single instant, and bending a cautious glance towards his companion, he continued in a manner that was divided between interrogation and assertion—"does not this stream at our feet, run towards the summer, until its waters grow salt, and the current flows upward!"

"It can't be denied, that your traditions tell you true in both these matters," said the white man; "for I have been there, and have seen them; though, why water, which is so sweet in the shade, should become bitter in the sun, is an alteration for which I have never been able to account."

"And the current!" demanded the Indian, who expected his reply with that sort of interest that a man feels in the confirmation of testimony, at which he marvels even while he respects it; "the fathers of Chingachgook have not lied!"

"The Holy Bible is not more true, and that is the truest thing in nature. They call this up-stream current the tide, which is a thing soon explained, and clear enough. Six hours the waters run in, and six hours they run out, and the reason is this; when there is higher water in the sea than in the river, they run in, until the river gets to be highest, and then it runs out again."

"The waters in the woods, and on the great lakes, run downward until they lie like my hand," said the Indian, stretching the limb horizontally before him, "and then they run no more."

"No honest man will deny it," said the scout, a little nettled at the implied distrust of his explanation of the mystery of the tides; "and I grant that it is true on the small scale, and where the land is level. But every thing depends on what scale you look at things. Now, on the small scale, the 'arth is level; but on the large scale it is round. In this manner, pools and ponds, and even the great fresh water lakes, may be stagnant, as you and I both know they are, having seen them; but when you come to spread water over a great tract, like the sea, where the earth is round, how in reason can the water be quiet? You might as well expect the river to lie still on the brink of those black rocks a mile above us, though your own ears tell you that it is tumbling over them at this very moment!"

If unsatisfied by the philosophy of his companion, the Indian was far too dignified to betray his unbelief. He listened like one who was convinced, and resumed his narrative in his former solemn manner.

"We came from the place where the sun is hid at night, over great plains where the buffaloes live, until we reached the big river. There we fought the Alligewi,[8] till the ground was red with their blood. From the banks of the big river to the shores of the salt lake, there was none to meet us. The Maquas[9] followed at a distance. We said the country should be ours from the place where the water runs up no longer, on this stream, to a river, twenty suns' journey toward the summer. The land we had taken like warriors, we kept like men. We drove the Maquas into the woods with the bears. They only tasted salt at the licks; they drew no fish from the great lake: we threw them the bones."

"All this I have heard and believe," said the white man, observing that the Indian paused; "but it was long before the English came into the country."

"A pine grew then, where this chestnut now stands. The first pale faces who came among us spoke no English. They came in a large canoe, when my fathers had buried the tomahawk with the red men around them. Then, Hawk-eye," he continued, betraying his deep emotion, only by permitting his voice to fall to those low, guttural tones, which render his language, as spoken at times, so very musical; "then, Hawk-eye, we were one people, and we were happy. The salt lake gave us its fish, the wood its deer, and the air its birds. We took wives who bore us children; we worshipped the Great Spirit; and we kept the Maquas beyond the sound of our songs of triumph!"

"Know you any thing of your own family, at that time?" demanded the white. "But you are a just man for an Indian! and as I suppose you hold their gifts, your fathers must have been brave warriors, and wise men at the council fire."

"My tribe is the grandfather of nations, but I am an unmixed man. The blood of chiefs is in my veins, where it must stay for ever. The Dutch landed, and gave my people the fire-water; they drank until the heavens and the earth seemed to meet, and they foolishly thought they had found the Great Spirit. Then they parted with their land. Foot by foot, they were driven back from the shores, until I, that am a chief and a Sagamore,[10] have never seen the sun shine but through the trees, and have never visited the graves of my fathers."

"Graves bring solemn feelings over the mind," returned the scout, a good deal touched at the calm suffering of his companion; "and they often aid a man in his good intentions, though, for myself, I expect to leave my own bones unburied, to bleach in the woods, or to be torn asunder by the wolves. But where are to be found those of your race who came to their kin in the Delaware country, so many summers since?"

---

[8]Probably the Alleghenies, a combination of the Delaware and Shawnee.

[9]Variant of Makwa, a Mohican branch.
[10]Chief of second rank; sachem.

"Where are the blossoms of those summers!—fallen, one by one: so all of my family departed, each in his turn, to the land of spirits. I am on the hill-top, and must go down into the valley; and when Uncas[11] follows in my footsteps, there will no longer be any of the blood of the Sagamores, for my boy is the last of the Mohicans."

"Uncas is here!" said another voice, in the same soft, guttural tones, near his elbow; "who speaks to Uncas?"

The white man loosened his knife in its leathern sheath, and made an involuntary movement of the hand towards his rifle, at this sudden interruption, but the Indian sat composed, and without turning his head at the unexpected sounds.

At the next instant, a youthful warrior passed between them, with a noiseless step, and seated himself on the bank of the rapid stream. No exclamation of surprise escaped the father, nor was any question asked or reply given for several minutes, each appearing to await the moment, when he might speak, without betraying womanish curiosity or childish impatience. The white man seemed to take counsel from their customs, and relinquishing his grasp of the rifle, he also remained silent and reserved. At length Chingachgook turned his eyes slowly towards his son, and demanded—

"Do the Maquas dare to leave the print of their moccasins in these woods?"

"I have been on their trail," replied the young Indian, "and know that they number as many as the fingers of my two hands; but they lie hid like cowards."

"The thieves are outlying for scalps and plunder!" said the white man, whom we shall call Hawk-eye, after the manner of his companions. "That busy Frenchman, Montcalm,[12] will send his spies into our very camp, but he will know what road we travel!"

" 'Tis enough!" returned the father, glancing his eye towards the setting sun; "they shall be driven like deer from their bushes. Hawk-eye, let us eat to-night, and show the Maquas that we are men tomorrow."

"I am as ready to do the one as the other; but to fight the Iroquois, 'tis necessary to find the skulkers; and to eat, 'tis necessary to get the game—talk of the devil and he will come; there is a pair of the biggest antlers I have seen this season, moving the bushes below the hill! Now, Uncas," he continued in a half whisper, and laughing with a kind of inward sound, like one who had learnt to be watchful, "I will bet my charger three times full of powder, against a foot of wampum, that I take him atwixt the eyes, and nearer to the right than to the left."

"It cannot be!" said the young Indian, springing to his feet with youthful eagerness; "all but the tips of his horns are hid!"

"He's a boy!" said the white man, shaking his head while he spoke, and addressing the father. "Does he think when a hunter sees a part of the creatur, he can't tell where the rest of him should be!"

Adjusting his rifle, he was about to make an exhibition of that skill, on which he so much valued himself, when the warrior struck up the piece with his hand, saying,

"Hawk-eye! will you fight the Maquas?"

"These Indians know the nature of the woods, as it might be by instinct!" returned the scout, dropping his rifle, and turning away like a man who was convinced of his error. "I must leave the buck to your arrow, Uncas, or we may kill a deer for them thieves, the Iroquois, to eat."

The instant the father seconded this intimation by an expressive gesture of the hand, Uncas threw himself on the ground, and approached the animal with wary movements. When, within a few yards of the cover, he fitted an arrow to his bow

---

[11]Chingachgook's son.
[12]Louis Joseph Montcalm (1712–1759), French general de-

feated by British General Wolfe in Battle of Quebec in 1759; Montcalm and Wolfe were killed in the battle.

with the utmost care, while the antlers moved, as if their owner snuffed an enemy in the tainted air. In another moment the twang of the cord was heard, a white streak was seen glancing into the bushes, and the wounded buck plunged from the cover, to the very feet of his hidden enemy. Avoiding the horns of the infuriated animal, Uncas darted to his side, and passed his knife across the throat, when bounding to the edge of the river, it fell, dying the waters with its blood.

" 'Twas done with Indian skill," said the scout, laughing inwardly, but with vast satisfaction; "and 'twas a pretty sight to behold! Though an arrow is a near shot, and needs a knife to finish the work."

"Hugh!" ejaculated his companion, turning quickly, like a hound who scented his game.

"By the Lord, there is a drove of them!" exclaimed the scout, whose eyes began to glisten with the ardour of his usual occupation; "if they come within range of a bullet, I will drop one, though the whole Six Nations[13] should be lurking within sound! What do you hear, Chingachgook? for to my ears the woods are dumb."

"There is but one deer, and he is dead," said the Indian, bending his body, till his ear nearly touched the earth. "I hear the sounds of feet!"

"Perhaps the wolves have driven the buck to shelter, and are following on his trail."

"No. The horses of white men are coming!" returned the other, raising himself with dignity, and resuming his seat on the log with his former composure. "Hawkeye, they are your brothers; speak to them."

"That will I, and in English that the king needn't be ashamed to answer," returned the hunter, speaking in the language of which he boasted; "but I see nothing, nor do I hear the sounds of man or beast; 'tis strange that an Indian should understand white sounds better than a man, who, his very enemies will own, has no cross in his blood, although he may have lived with the red skins long enough to be suspected! Ha! there goes something like the cracking of a dry stick, too— now I hear the bushes move—yes, yes, there is a trampling that I mistook for the falls—and—but here they come themselves; God keep them from the Iroquois!"

1826

from Notions of the Americans[1]

[Literature and Arts of the United States]

To the Abbate[2] Giromachi, &c. &c., Florence

Washington,_____

You ask me to write freely on the subject of the literature and the arts of the United States. The subjects are so meagre as to render it a task that would require no small portion of the talents necessary to figure in either, in order to render them of interest. Still, as the request has come in so urgent a form, I shall endeavour to oblige you.

The Americans have been placed, as respects moral and intellectual advancement, different from all other infant nations. They have never been without the wants of civilization, nor have they ever been entirely without the means of a sup-

---

[13]The Iroquois League, made up of the Seneca, Cayuga, Onondaga, Oneida, Mohawk, and Tuscarora tribes.
[1]*Notions of the Americans, Picked Up by a Travelling Bachelor* is written in the tradition of the British travel book. Cooper assumes the voice of a young English bachelor writing let-

ters from America to friends abroad. The work was written in Paris, in part at the urging of General Lafayette (who had toured America in 1824–25) and was first published in London.
[2]Priest.

ply. Thus pictures, and books, and statuary, and every thing else which appertains to elegant life, have always been known to them in an abundance, and of a quality exactly proportioned to their cost. Books, being the cheapest, and the nation having great leisure and prodigious zest for information, are not only the most common, as you will readily suppose, but they are probably more common than among any other people. I scarcely remember ever to have entered an American dwelling, however humble, without finding fewer or more books. As they form the most essential division of the subject, not only on account of their greater frequency, but on account of their far greater importance, I shall give them the first notice in this letter.

Unlike the progress of the two professions in the countries of our hemisphere, in America the printer came into existence before the author. Reprints of English works gave the first employment to the press. Then came almanacks, psalm-books, religious tracts, sermons, journals, political essays, and even rude attempts at poetry. All these preceded the revolution. The first journal was established in Boston at the commencement of the last century.[3] There are several original polemical works of great originality and power that belong to the same period. I do not know that more learning and talents existed at that early day in the states of New England than in Virginia, Maryland and the Carolinas, but there was certainly a stronger desire to exhibit them.

The colleges or universities, as they were somewhat prematurely called, date very far back in the brief history of the country. There is no stronger evidence of the intellectual character, or of the judicious ambition of these people, than what this simple fact furnishes. Harvard College, now the university of Cambridge—(it better deserves the title at this day)—was founded in 1638; within less than *twenty years* after the landing of the first settlers in New England! Yale (in Connecticut) was founded in 1701. Columbia (in the city of New York) was founded in 1754. Nassau Hall (in New Jersey) in 1738; and William and Mary (in Virginia) as far back as 1691.[4] These are the oldest literary institutions in the United States, and all but the last are in flourishing conditions to the present hour. The first has given degrees to about five thousand graduates, and rarely has less than three hundred and fifty or four hundred students. Yale is about as well attended. The others contain from a hundred and fifty to two hundred under-graduates. But these are not a moiety[5] of the present colleges, or universities, (as they all aspire to be called,) existing in the country. There is no state, except a few of the newest, without at least one, and several have two or three.

Less attention is paid to classical learning here than in Europe; and, as the term of residence rarely exceeds four years, profound scholars are by no means common. This country possesses neither the population nor the endowments to maintain a large class of learned idlers, in order that one man in a hundred may contribute a mite to the growing stock of general knowledge. There is a luxury in this expenditure of animal force, to which the Americans have not yet attained. The good is far too problematical and remote, and the expense of man too certain, to be prematurely sought. I have heard, I will confess, an American legislator quote Horace and Cicero;[6] but it is far from being the humour of the country. I thought the taste of the orator questionable. A learned quotation is rarely of any use in an argument, since few men are fools enough not to see that the application of any maxim to politics is liable to a thousand practical objections, and, nine times in

---

[3]The first American newspaper is considered to be *Publick Occurrences Both Foreign and Domestic,* published in Boston September 25, 1690. It was suppressed by the governor after one issue.

[4]Harvard was founded in 1636, Princeton (Nassau Hall) in 1746, and William and Mary in 1693.

[5]Half.

[6]Horace (65–8 B.C.), Roman satirist and poet; Cicero (106–43 B.C.), Roman orator.

ten, they are evidences of the want of a direct, natural, and vigorous train of thought. They are the affectations, but rarely the ebullitions of true talent. When a man feels strongly, or thinks strongly, or speaks strongly, he is just as apt to do it in his native tongue as he is to laugh when he is tickled, or to weep when in sorrow. The Americans are strong speakers and acute thinkers, but no great quoters of the morals and axioms of a heathen age, because they happen to be recorded in Latin.

The higher branches of learning are certainly on the advance in this country. The gentlemen of the middle and southern states, before the revolution, were very generally educated in Europe, and they were consequently, in this particular, like our own people. Those who came into life during the struggle, and shortly after, fared worse. Even the next generation had little to boast of in the way of instruction. I find that boys entered the colleges so late as the commencement of the present century, who had read a part of the Greek Testament, and a few books of Cicero and Virgil,[7] with perhaps a little of Horace. But great changes have been made, and are still making, in the degree of previous qualification.

Still, it would be premature to say that there is any one of the American universities where classical knowledge, or even science is profoundly attained, even at the present day. Some of the professors push their studies, for a life, certainly; and you well know, after all, that little short of a life, and a long one too, will make any man a good general scholar. In 1820, near eight thousand graduates of the twelve oldest colleges of this country (according to their catalogues) were then living. Of this number, 1,406 were clergymen. As some of the catalogues consulted were several years old, this number was, of necessity, greatly within the truth. Between the years 1800 and 1810, it is found that of 2,792 graduates, four hundred and fifty-three became clergymen. Here is pretty good evidence that religion is not neglected in America, and that its ministers are not, as a matter of course, absolutely ignorant.

But the effects of the literary institutions of the United States are somewhat peculiar. Few men devote their lives to scholarship. The knowledge that is actually acquired, is perhaps quite sufficient for the more practical and useful pursuits. Thousands of young men, who have read the more familiar classics, who have gone through enough of mathematics to obtain a sense of their own tastes, and of the value of precision, who have cultivated *belles lettres* to a reasonable extent, and who have been moderately instructed in the arts of composition, and in the rules of taste, are given forth to the country to mingle in its active employments. I am inclined to believe that a class of American graduates carries away with it quite as much general and diversified knowledge, as a class from one of our own universities. The excellence in particular branches is commonly wanting; but the deficiency is more than supplied by variety of information. The youth who has passed four years within the walls of a college, goes into the office of a lawyer for a few more. The profession of the law is not subdivided in America.[8] The same man is counsellor, attorney, and conveyancer.[9] Here the student gets a general insight into the principles, and a familiarity with the practice of the law, rather than an acquaintance with the study as a science. With this instruction he enters the world as a practitioner. Instead of existing in a state of dreaming retrospection, lost in a maze of theories, he is at once turned loose into the jostlings of the world. If perchance he encounters an antagonist a little more erudite than himself, he seizes the natural truth for his sheet anchor, and leaves precedent and quaint follies to him who has made them his study and delight. No doubt he often blunders, and is

---

[7]Virgil (70–19 B.C.), Roman poet, author of *The Aeneid*.
[8]As in England, with barristers appearing to plead cases in courts, and solicitors consulting with clients in their offices.

[9]Individual with legal training to draw up deeds for "conveying" property.

frequently, of necessity, defeated. But in the course of this irreverent treatment, usages and opinions, which are bottomed in no better foundation than antiquity, and which are as inapplicable to the present state of the world, as the present state of the world is, or ought to be, unfavourable to all feudal absurdities, come to receive their death warrants. In the mean time, by dint of sheer experience, and by the collision of intellects, the practitioner gets a stock of learning, that is acquired in the best possible school; and, what is of far more importance, the laws themselves get a dress which brings them within the fashions of the day. This same man becomes a legislator perhaps, and, if particularly clever, he is made to take an active part in the framing of laws that are not to harmonize with the other parts of an elaborate theory, but which are intended to make men comfortable and happy. Now, taken with more or less qualification, this is the history of thousands in this country, and it is also an important part of the history of the country itself.

In considering the course of instruction in the United States, you are always to commence at the foundation. The common schools, which so generally exist, have certainly elevated the population above that of any other country, and are still elevating it higher, as they improve and increase in numbers. Law is getting every day to be more of a science, but it is a science that is forming rules better adapted to the spirit of the age. Medicine is improving, and in the cities it is perhaps now, in point of practice, quite on a level with that of Europe. Indeed, the well-educated American physician very commonly enjoys an advantage that is little known in Europe. After obtaining a degree in his own country, he passes a few years in London, Edinburgh, Paris, and frequently in Germany, and returns with his gleanings from their several schools. This is not the case with one individual, but with many, annually. Indeed, there is so much of a fashion in it, and the custom is attended by so many positive advantages, that its neglect would be a serious obstacle to any very eminent success. Good operators are by no means scarce, and as surgery and medicine are united in the same person, there is great judgment in their practice. Human life is something more valuable in America than in Europe, and I think a critical attention to patients more common here than with us, especially when the sufferer belongs to an inferior condition in life. The profession is highly respectable; and in all parts of the country the better sort of its practitioners mingle, on terms of perfect equality, with the highest classes of society. There are several physicians in congress, and a great many in the different state legislatures.

Of the ministry it is unnecessary to speak. The clergy are of all denominations, and they are educated, or not, precisely as they belong to sects which consider the gift of human knowledge of any importance. You have already seen how large a proportion of the graduates of some of the colleges enter the desk.[10]

As respects authorship, there is not much to be said. Compared to the books that are printed and read, those of native origin are few indeed. The principal reason of this poverty of original writers, is owing to the circumstance that men are not yet driven to their wits for bread. The United States are the first nation that possessed institutions, and, of course, distinctive opinions of its own, that was ever dependent on a foreign people for its literature. Speaking the same language as the English, and long in the habit of importing their books from the mother country, the revolution effected no immediate change in the nature of their studies, or mental amusements. The works were reprinted, it is true, for the purposes of economy, but they still continued English. Had the latter nation used this powerful engine with tolerable address, I think they would have secured such an ally in this country as would have rendered their own decline not only more secure,

---

[10]Pulpits.

but as illustrious as had been their rise. There are many theories entertained as to the effect produced in this country by the falsehoods and jealous calumnies which have been undeniably uttered in the mother country, by means of the press, concerning her republican descendant. It is my own opinion that, like all other ridiculous absurdities, they have defeated themselves, and that they are now more laughed at and derided, even here, than resented. By all that I can learn, twenty years ago, the Americans were, perhaps, far too much disposed to receive the opinions and to adopt the prejudices of their relatives; whereas, I think it is very apparent that they are now beginning to receive them with singular distrust. It is not worth our while to enter further into this subject, except as it has had, or is likely to have, an influence on the national literature.[11]

It is quite obvious, that, so far as taste and forms alone are concerned, the literature of England and that of America must be fashioned after the same models. The authors, previously to the revolution, are common property, and it is quite idle to say that the American has not just as good a right to claim Milton, and Shakespeare, and all the old masters of the language, for his countrymen, as an Englishman. The Americans having continued to cultivate, and to cultivate extensively, an acquaintance with the writers of the mother country, since the separation, it is evident they must have kept pace with the trifling changes of the day. The only peculiarity that can, or ought to be expected in their literature, is that which is connected with the promulgation of their distinctive political opinions. They have not been remiss in this duty, as any one may see, who chooses to examine their books. But we will devote a few minutes to a more minute account of the actual condition of American literature.

The first, and the most important, though certainly the most familiar branch of this subject, is connected with the public journals. It is not easy to say how many newspapers are printed in the United States. The estimated number varies from six hundred to a thousand. In the State of New York there are more than fifty counties. Now, it is rare that a county, in a state as old as that of New York (especially in the more northern parts of the country), does not possess one paper at least. The cities have many. The smaller towns sometimes have three or four, and very many of the counties four or five. There cannot be many less than one hundred and fifty journals in the state of New York alone. Pennsylvania is said to possess eighty. But we will suppose that these two states publish two hundred journals. They contain about 3,000,000 of inhabitants. As the former is an enlightened state, and the latter rather below the scale of the general intelligence of the nation, it may not be a very bad average of the whole population. This rate would give eight hundred journals for the United States, which is probably something within the truth. I confess, however, this manner of equalizing estimates in America, is very uncertain in general, since a great deal, in such a question, must depend on the progress of society in each particular section of the country.

As might be expected, there is nearly every degree of merit to be found in these journals. No one of them has the benefit of that collected talent which is so often enlisted in the support of the more important journals of Europe. There is not often more than one editor to the best; but he is usually some man who has seen, in his own person, enough of men and things to enable him to speak with tolerable discretion on passing events. The usefulness of the American journals, however, does not consist in their giving the tone to the public mind, in politics and morals, but in imparting facts. It is certain that, could the journals agree, they

---

[11]"The writer might give, in proof of this opinion, one fact. He is led to believe that, so lately as within ten years, several English periodical works were reprinted, and much read in the United States, and that now they patronize their own, while the former are far less sought, though the demand, by means of the increased population, should have been nearly doubled. Some of the works are no longer even re-printed" (Cooper's note).

might, by their united efforts, give a powerful inclination to the common will. But, in point of fact, they do not agree on any one subject or set of subjects, except, perhaps, on those which directly affect their own interests. They, consequently, counteract, instead of aiding each other, on all points of disputed policy; and it is in the bold and sturdy discussions that follow, that men arrive at the truth. The occasional union in their own favour, is a thing too easily seen through to do either good or harm. So far, then, from the journals succeeding in leading the public opinion astray, they are invariably obliged to submit to it. They serve to keep it alive, by furnishing the means for its expression, but they rarely do more. Of course, the influence of each particular press is in proportion to the constancy and the ability with which it is found to support what is thought to be sound principles; but those principles must be in accordance with the private opinions of men, or most of their labour is lost.

The public press in America is rather more decent than that of England, and less decorous than that of France. The tone of the nation, and the respect for private feelings, which are, perhaps, in some measure, the consequence of a less artificial state of society, produce the former; and the liberty, which is a necessary attendant of fearless discussion, is, I think, the cause of the latter. The affairs of an individual are rarely touched upon in the journals of this country; never, unless it is thought they have a direct connection with the public interests, or from a wish to do him good. Still there is a habit, getting into use in America, no less than in France, that is borrowed from the English, which proves that the more unworthy feelings of our nature are common to men under all systems, and only need opportunity to find encouragement. I allude to the practice of repeating the proceedings of the courts of justice, in order to cater to a vicious appetite for amusement in the public.

It is pretended that, as a court of justice is open to the world, there can be no harm in giving the utmost publicity to its proceedings. It is strange the courts should act so rigidly on the principle, that it is better a dozen guilty men should go free, than that one innocent man should suffer, and yet permit the gross injustice that is daily done by means of this practice. One would think, that if a court of justice is so open to the world, that it should be the business of the people of the world to enter it, in order that they might be certain that the information they crave should be without colouring or exaggeration. It is idle to say that the reports are accurate, and that he who reads is enabled to do justice to the accused, by comparing the facts that are laid before him. A reporter may give the expression of the tongue; but can he convey that of the eye, of the countenance, or of the form?—without regarding all of which no man is perfectly master of the degree of credibility that is due to any witness of whose character he is necessarily ignorant. But every man has an infallible means of assuring himself of the value of these reports. Who has ever read a dozen of them without meeting with one (or perhaps more) in which the decision of the court and jury is to him a matter of surprise? It is true he assumes, that those who were present knew best, and as he has no great interest in the matter, he is commonly satisfied. But how is it with the unfortunate man who is wrongfully brought out of his retirement to repel an unjust attack against his person, his property, or his character? If he be a man of virtue, he is a man of sensibility; and not only he, but, what is far worse, those tender beings, whose existence is wrapped up in his own, are to be wounded daily and hourly, for weeks at a time, in order that a depraved appetite should be glutted. It is enough for justice that her proceedings should be so public as to prevent the danger of corruption; but we pervert a blessing to a curse, in making that which was intended for our protection, the means of so much individual misery. It is an unavoidable evil of the law that it necessarily works some wrong, in order to do much good; but it is cruel that even the acquittal of a man should be unnecessarily circulated, in a manner to make all men remember that he had been accused. We have proof of the consequences of this practice in England. Men daily shrink from resistance to base frauds, rather than expose themselves to the observations and comments of those who enliven their breakfasts by sporting with these exhibitions of their fellow creatures. There are, undoubtedly, cases of that magnitude which require some sacrifice of private feelings, in order that the community should reap the advantage; but the regular books are sufficient for authorities— the decisions of the courts are sufficient for justice—and the utmost possible oblivion should prove as nearly sufficient as may be to serve the ends of a prudent and a righteous humanity.

Nothing can be more free than the press of this country, on all subjects connected with politics. Treason cannot be written, unless by communicating with an open enemy. There is no other protection to a public man than that which is given by an independent jury, which punishes, of course, in proportion to the dignity and importance of the injured party. But the utmost lenity is always used in construing the right of the press to canvass the public acts of public men. Mere common place charges defeat themselves, and get into discredit so soon as to be lost, while graver accusations are met by grave replies. There is no doubt that the complacency of individuals is sometimes disturbed by these liberties; but they serve to keep the officers of the government to their work, while they rarely do any lasting, or even temporary injury. Serious and criminal accusations against a public man, if groundless, are, by the law of reason, a crime against the community, and, as such, they are punished. The general principle observed in these matters is very simple. If A. accuse B. of an act that is an offence against law, he may be called on for his proof, and if he fail he must take the consequences. But an editor of a paper, or any one else, who should bring a criminal charge, no matter how grave, against the president, and who could prove it, is just as certain of doing it with impunity, as if he held the whole power in his own hands. He would be protected by the invincible shield of public opinion, which is not only in consonance with the law, but which, in this country, makes law.

Actions for injuries done by the press, considering the number of journals, are astonishingly rare in America. When one remembers the usual difficulty of obtaining legal proof, which is a constant temptation, even to the guilty, to appeal to the courts; and, on the other hand, the great freedom of the press, which is a constant temptation to abuse the trust, this fact, in itself, furnishes irresistible evidence of the general tone of decency which predominates in this nation. The truth is, that public opinion, among its other laws, has imperiously prescribed that, amidst the utmost latitude of discussion, certain limits shall not be passed; and public opinion, which is so completely the offspring of a free press, must be obeyed in this, as well as in other matters.

Leaving the journals, we come to those publications which make their appearance periodically. Of these there are a good many, some few of which are well supported. There are several scientific works, that are printed monthly, or quarterly, of respectable merit, and four or five reviews. Magazines of a more general character are not much encouraged. England, which is teeming with educated men, who are glad to make their bread by writing for these works, still affords too strong a competition for the success of any American attempts, in this species of literature. Though few, perhaps no English magazine is actually republished in America, a vast number are imported and read in the towns, where the support for any similar original production must first be found.

The literature of the United States has, indeed, two powerful obstacles to conquer before (to use a mercantile expression) it can ever enter the markets of its own country on terms of perfect equality with that of England. Solitary and individual works of genius may, indeed, be occasionally brought to light, under the impulses of the high feeling which has conceived them; but, I fear, a good, whole-some, profitable, and continued pecuniary support is the applause that talent most craves. The fact, that an American publisher can get an English work without money,[12] must, for a few years longer (unless legislative protection shall be ex-tended to their own authors), have a tendency to repress a national literature. No man will pay a writer for an epic, a tragedy, a sonnet, a history, or a romance, when he can get a work of equal merit for nothing. I have conversed with those who are conversant on the subject, and, I confess, I have been astonished at the information they imparted.

A capital American publisher has assured me that there are not a dozen writers in this country, whose works he should feel confidence in publishing at all, while he reprints hundreds of English books without the least hesitation. This prefer-ence is by no means so much owing to any difference in merit, as to the fact that, when the price of the original author is to be added to the uniform hazard which accompanies all literary speculations, the risk becomes too great. The general taste of the reading world in this country is better than that of England.[13] The fact is both proved and explained by the circumstance that thousands of works that are printed and read in the mother country, are not printed and read here. The pub-lisher on this side of the Atlantic has the advantage of seeing the reviews of every book he wishes to print, and, what is of far more importance, he knows, with the exception of books that he is sure of selling, by means of a name, the decision of the English critics before he makes his choice. Nine times in ten, popularity, which is all he looks for, is a sufficient test of general merit. Thus, while you find every English work of character, or notoriety, on the shelves of an American book-store, you may ask in vain for most of the trash that is so greedily devoured in the cir-culating libraries of the mother country, and which would be just as eagerly de-voured here, had not a better taste been created by a compelled abstinence. That taste must now be overcome before such works could be sold at all.

When I say that books are not rejected here, from any want of talent in the writers, perhaps I ought to explain. I wish to express something a little different. Talent is sure of too many avenues to wealth and honours, in America, to seek, unnecessarily, an unknown and hazardous path. It is better paid in the ordinary pursuits of life, than it would be likely to be paid by an adventure in which an extraordinary and skilful, because practised, foreign competition is certain. Per-haps high talent does not often make the trial with the American bookseller; but it is precisely for the reason I have named.

The second obstacle against which American literature has to contend is in the poverty of materials. There is scarcely an ore which contributes to the wealth of the author, that is found, here, in veins as rich as in Europe. There are no annals for the historian; no follies (beyond the most vulgar and common place) for the satirist; no manners for the dramatist; no obscure fictions for the writer of ro-mance; no gross and hardy offences against decorum for the moralist; nor any of the rich artificial auxiliaries of poetry. The weakest hand can extract a spark from the flint, but it would baffle the strength of a giant to attempt kindling a flame with a pudding stone. I very well know there are theorists who assume that the society and institutions of this country are, or ought to be, particularly favourable to novelties and variety. But the experience of one month, in these states, is suffi-cient to show any observant man the falsity of their position. The effect of a pro-miscuous assemblage any where, is to create a standard of deportment; and great

---

[12]There was no protection of printed works by interna-tional copyright until the Bern Convention of 1887.

[13]"The writer does not mean that the best taste of America is better than that of England; perhaps it is not quite so good; but, as a whole, the American reading world requires better books than the whole of the English reading world" (Cooper's note).

liberty permits every one to aim at its attainment. I have never seen a nation so much alike in my life, as the people of the United States, and what is more, they are not only like each other, but they are remarkably like that which common sense tells them they ought to resemble. No doubt, traits of character that are a little peculiar, without, however, being either very poetical, or very rich, are to be found in remote districts; but they are rare, and not always happy exceptions. In short, it is not possible to conceive a state of society in which more of the attributes of plain good sense, or fewer of the artificial absurdities of life, are to be found, than here. There is no costume for the peasant, (there is scarcely a peasant at all,) no wig for the judge, no baton for the general, no diadem for the chief magistrate. The darkest ages of their history are illuminated by the light of truth; the utmost efforts of their chivalry are limited by the laws of God; and even the deeds of their sages and heroes are to be sung in a language that would differ but little from a version of the ten commandments. However useful and respectable all this may be in actual life, it indicates but one direction to the man of genius.

It is very true there are a few young poets now living in this country, who have known how to extract sweets from even these wholesome, but scentless native plants. They have, however, been compelled to seek their inspiration in the universal laws of nature, and they have succeeded, precisely in proportion as they have been most general in their application. Among these gifted young men, there is one (Halleck)[14] who is remarkable for an exquisite vein of ironical wit, mingled with a fine, poetical, and, frequently, a lofty expression. This gentleman commenced his career as a satirist in one of the journals of New York. Heaven knows, his materials were none of the richest; and yet the melody of his verse, the quaintness and force of his comparisons, and the exceeding humour of his strong points, brought him instantly into notice. He then attempted a general satire, by giving the history of the early days of a *belle.* He was again successful, though every body, at least every body of any talent, felt that he wrote in leading-strings.[15] But he happened, shortly after the appearance of the little volume just named *(Fanny),* to visit England. Here his spirit was properly excited, and, probably on a rainy day, he was induced to try his hand at a *jeu d'esprit,*[16] in the mother country. The result was one of the finest semi-heroic ironical descriptions to be found in the English language.[17] This simple fact, in itself, proves the truth of a great deal of what I have just been writing, since it shews the effect a superiority of material can produce on the efforts of a man of true genius.

Notwithstanding the difficulties of the subject, talent has even done more than in the instance of Mr. Halleck. I could mention several other young poets of this country of rare merit. By mentioning Bryant, Percival, and Sprague,[18] I shall direct your attention to the names of those whose works would be most likely to give you pleasure. Unfortunately they are not yet known in Italian, but I think even you would not turn in distaste from the task of translation which the best of their effusions will invite.

The next, though certainly an inferior branch of imaginative writing, is fictitious composition. From the facts just named, you cannot expect that the novelists, or romance writers of the United States, should be very successful. The same reason will be likely, for a long time to come, to repress the ardour of dramatic genius. Still, tales and plays are no novelties in the literature of this country. Of the former, there are many as old as soon after the revolution; and a vast number

---

[14]Fitz-Greene Halleck (1790–1867), author of *Fanny* (1819), satiric narrative of New York society.
[15]A kind of harness to lead or restrain children.
[16]Play of wits, a clever trifle.
[17]"This little *morceau* [morsel] of pleasant irony is called *Alnwick Castle*" (Cooper's note).

[18]William Cullen Bryant (1794–1878) was famous early with "Thanatopsis" (1821); James Gates Percival (1795–1856), author of *Poems* (1821); Charles Sprague (1791–1875), author of "The Funeral" and other popular "graveyard school" poems.

have been published within the last five years. One of their authors of romance, who curbed his talents by as few allusions as possible to actual society, is distinguished for power and comprehensiveness of thought. I remember to have read one of his books (Wieland) when a boy, and I take it to be a never-failing evidence of genius, that, amid a thousand similar pictures which have succeeded, the images it has left still stand distinct and prominent in my recollection. This author (Mr. Brockden Brown)[19] enjoys a high reputation among his countrymen, whose opinions are sufficiently impartial, since he flattered no particular prejudice of the nation in any of his works.

The reputation of Irving[20] is well known to you. He is an author distinguished for a quality (humour) that has been denied his countrymen; and his merit is the more rare, that it has been shewn in a state of society so cold and so restrained. Besides these writers, there are many others of a similar character, who enjoy a greater or less degree of favour in their own country. The works of two or three have even been translated (into French) in Europe, and a great many are reprinted in England. Though every writer of fiction in America has to contend against the difficulties I have named, there is a certain interest in the novelty of the subject, which is not without its charm. I think, however, it will be found that they have all been successful, or the reverse, just as they have drawn warily, or freely, on the distinctive habits of their own country. I now speak of their success purely as writers of romance. It certainly would be possible for an American to give a description of the manners of his own country, in a book that he might choose to call a romance, which should be read, because the world is curious on the subject, but which would certainly never be read for that nearly indefinable poetical interest which attaches itself to a description of manners less bald and uniform. All the attempts to blend history with romance in America, have been comparative failures, (and perhaps fortunately,) since the subjects are too familiar to be treated with the freedom that the imagination absolutely requires. Some of the descriptions of the progress of society on the borders,[21] have had a rather better success, since there is a positive, though no very poetical, novelty in the subject; but, on the whole, the books which have been best received, are those in which the authors have trusted most to their own conceptions of character, and to qualities that are common to the rest of the world and to human nature. This fact, if its truth be admitted, will serve to prove that the American writer must seek his renown in the exhibition of qualities that are general, while he is confessedly compelled to limit his observations to a state of society that has a wonderful tendency not only to repress passion, but to equalize humours.

The Americans have always been prolific writers on polemics and politics. Their sermons and fourth of July orations are numberless. Their historians, without being very classical or very profound, are remarkable for truth and good sense. There is not, perhaps, in the language a closer reasoner in metaphysics than Edwards;[22] and their theological writers find great favour among the sectarians of their respective schools.

The stage of the United States is decidedly English. Both plays and players, with few exceptions, are imported. Theatres are numerous, and they are to be found in places where a traveller would little expect to meet them. Of course they are of all sizes and of every degree of decoration and architectural beauty known in Europe, below the very highest. The facade of the principal theatre in Philadelphia is a chaste specimen in marble, of the Ionic, if my memory is correct. In New

---

[19]Charles Brockden Brown (1771–1810), author of *Wieland, or The Transformation* (1798).
[20]Washington Irving (1783–1859), author of the comic *A History of New York by Diedrich Knickerbocker* (1809).
[21]Frontier novels, like Cooper's own *The Pioneers* and *The Last of the Mohicans.*
[22]Jonathan Edwards (1703–1758), preeminent American Puritan theologian.

York, there are two theatres about as large as the Théatre Français[23] (in the interior), and not much inferior in embellishments. Besides these, there is a very pretty little theatre, where lighter pieces are performed, and another with a vast stage for melo-dramas. There are also one or two other places of dramatic representation in this city, in which horses and men contend for the bays.

The Americans pay well for dramatic talent. Cooke,[24] the greatest English tragedian of our age, died on this side of the Atlantic; and there are few players of eminence in the mother country who are not tempted, at some time or other, to cross the ocean. Shakespeare is, of course, the great author of America, as he is of England, and I think he is quite as well relished here as there. In point of taste, if all the rest of the world be any thing against England, that of America is the best, since it unquestionably approaches nearest to that of the continent of Europe. Nearly one half of the theatrical taste of the English is condemned by their own judgments, since the stage is not much supported by those who have had an opportunity of seeing any other. You will be apt to ask me how it happens, then, that the American taste is better? Because the people, being less exaggerated in their habits, are less disposed to tolerate caricatures, and because the theatres are not yet sufficiently numerous (though that hour is near) to admit of a representation that shall not be subject to the control of a certain degree of intelligence. I have heard an English player complain that he never saw such a dull audience as the one before which he had just been exhibiting; and I heard the same audience complain that they never listened to such dull jokes. Now, there was talent enough in both parties; but the one had formed his taste in a coarse school, and the others had formed theirs under the dominion of common sense. Independently of this peculiarity, there is a vast deal of acquired, travelled taste in this country. English tragedy, and high English comedy, both of which, you know, are excellent, never fail here, if well played; that is, they never fail under the usual limits of all amusement. One will cloy of sweets. But the fact of the taste and judgment of these people, in theatrical exhibitions, is proved by the number of their good theatres, compared to their population.

Of dramatic writers there are none, or next to none. The remarks I have made in respect to novels apply with double force to this species of composition. A witty and successful American comedy could only proceed from extraordinary talent. There would be less difficulty, certainly, with a tragedy; but still, there is rather too much foreign competition, and too much domestic employment in other pursuits, to invite genius to so doubtful an enterprise. The very baldness of ordinary American life is in deadly hostility to scenic representation. The character must be supported solely by its intrinsic power. The judge, the footman, the clown, the lawyer, the belle, or the beau, can receive no great assistance from dress. Melodramas, except the scene should be laid in the woods, are out of the question. It would be necessary to seek the great clock, which is to strike the portentous twelve blows, in the nearest church; a vaulted passage would degenerate into a cellar; and, as for ghosts, the country was discovered, since their visitations have ceased. The smallest departure from the incidents of ordinary life would do violence to every man's experience; and, as already mentioned, the passions which belong to human nature must be delineated, in America, subject to the influence of that despot—common sense.

Notwithstanding the overwhelming influence of British publications, and all the difficulties I have named, original books are getting to be numerous in the

---

[23]Famous national theater in Paris.
[24]George Frederick Cooke (1756–1811), British Shakespearean actor.

United States. The impulses of talent and intelligence are bearing down a thousand obstacles. I think the new works will increase rapidly, and that they are destined to produce a powerful influence on the world. We will pursue this subject another time.— Adieu.

1828

from The American Democrat

AN ARISTOCRAT AND A DEMOCRAT

We live in an age, when the words aristocrat and democrat are much used, without regard to the real significations. An aristocrat is one of a few, who possess the political power of a country; a democrat, one of the many. The words are also properly applied to those who entertain notions favorable to aristocratical or democratical forms of government. Such persons are not, necessarily, either aristocrats, or democrats in fact, but merely so in opinion. Thus a member of a democratical government may have an aristocratical bias, and *vice versa.*

To call a man who has the habits and opinions of a gentleman, an aristocrat, from that fact alone, is an abuse of terms, and betrays ignorance of the true principles of government, as well as of the world. It must be an equivocal freedom, under which every one is not the master of his own innocent acts and associations, and he is a sneaking democrat, indeed, who will submit to be dictated to, in those habits over which neither law nor morality assumes a right of control.

Some men fancy that a democrat can only be one who seeks the level, social, mental and moral, of the majority, a rule that would at once exclude all men of refinement, education and taste from the class. These persons are enemies of democracy, as they at once render it impracticable. They are usually great sticklers for their own associations and habits, too, though unable to comprehend any of a nature that are superior. They are, in truth, aristocrats in principle, though assuming a contrary pretension; the ground work of all their feelings and arguments being self. Such is not the intention of liberty, whose aim is to leave every man to be the master of his own acts; denying hereditary honors, it is true, as unjust and unnecessary, but not denying the inevitable consequences of civilization.

The law of God is the only rule of conduct, in this, as in other matters. Each man should do as he would be done by. Were the question put to the greatest advocate of indiscriminate association, whether he would submit to have his company and habits dictated to him, he would be one of the first to resist the tyranny; for they, who are the most rigid in maintaining their own claims, in such matters, are usually the loudest in decrying those whom they fancy to be better off than themselves. Indeed, it may be taken as a rule in social intercourse, that he who is the most apt to question the pretensions of others, is the most conscious of the doubtful position he himself occupies; thus establishing the very claims he affects to deny, by letting his jealousy of it be seen. Manners, education and refinement, are positive things, and they bring with them innocent tastes which are productive of high enjoyments; and it is as unjust to deny their possessors their indulgence, as it would be to insist on the less fortunate's passing the time they would rather devote to athletic amusements, in listening to operas for which they have no relish, sung in a language they do not understand.

All that democracy means, is as equal a participation in rights as is practicable; and to pretend that social equality is a condition of popular institutions, is to assume that the latter are destructive of civilization, for, as nothing is more self-evident than the impossibility of raising all men to the highest standard of tastes and refinement, the alternative would be to reduce the entire community to the lowest. The whole embarrassment on this point exists in the difficulty of making men comprehend qualities they do not themselves possess. We can all perceive the difference between ourselves and our inferiors, but when it comes to a question of the difference between us and our superiors, we fail to appreciate merits of which we have no proper conceptions. In face of this obvious difficulty, there is the safe and just governing rule, already mentioned, or that of permitting every one to be the undisturbed judge of his own habits and associations, so long as they are innocent, and do not impair the rights of others to be equally judges for themselves. It follows, that social intercourse must regulate itself, independently of institutions, with the exception that the latter, while they withhold no natural, bestow no factitious advantages beyond those which are inseparable from the rights of property, and general civilization.

In a democracy, men are just as free to aim at the highest attainable places in society, as to obtain the largest fortunes; and it would be clearly unworthy of all noble sentiment to say, that the grovelling competition for money shall alone be free, while that which enlists all the liberal acquirements and elevated sentiments of the race, is denied the democrat. Such an avowal would be at once, a declaration of the inferiority of the system, since nothing but ignorance and vulgarity could be its fruits.

The democratic gentleman must differ in many essential particulars, from the aristocratical gentleman, though in their ordinary habits and tastes they are virtually identical. Their principles vary; and, to a slight degree, their deportment accordingly. The democrat, recognizing the right of all to participate in power, will be more liberal in his general sentiments, a quality of superiority in itself; but, in conceding this much to his fellow man, he will proudly maintain his own independence of vulgar domination, as indispensable to his personal habits. The same principles and manliness that would induce him to depose a royal despot, would induce him to resist a vulgar tyrant.

There is no more capital, though more common error, than to suppose him an aristocrat who maintains his independence of habits; for democracy asserts the control of the majority, only, in matters of law, and not in matters of custom. The very object of the institution is the utmost practicable personal liberty, and to affirm the contrary, would be sacrificing the end to the means.

An aristocrat, therefore, is merely one who fortifies his exclusive privileges by positive institutions, and a democrat, one who is willing to admit of a free competition, in all things. To say, however, that the last supposes this competition will lead to nothing, is an assumption that means are employed without any reference to an end. He is the purest democrat who best maintains his rights, and no rights can be dearer to a man of cultivation, than exemptions from unseasonable invasions on his time, by the coarse-minded and ignorant.

1838

from Gleanings in Europe: France

from A VISIT FROM SCOTT[1]
(To James E. DeKay)

We have not only had Mr. Canning[2] in Paris, but Sir Walter Scott has suddenly appeared among us. The arrival of the *Great Unknown,* or, indeed, of any little unknown from England, would be an event to throw all the reading clubs at home into a state of high moral and poetical excitement. We are true village *lionizers.* As the professors of the Catholic religion are notoriously more addicted to yielding faith to miraculous interventions, in the remoter dioceses, than in Rome itself; as loyalty is always more zealous in a colony, than in a court; as fashions are more exaggerated in a province, than in a capital; and men are more prodigious to every one else, than their own valets; so do we throw the haloes of a vast ocean around the honoured heads of the celebrated men of this eastern hemisphere. This, perhaps, is the natural course of things, and is as unavoidable as that the sun shall hold the earth within the influence of its attraction, until matters shall be reversed by the earth's becoming the larger and more glorious orb of the two. Not so in Paris. Here men of every gradation of celebrity, from Napoleon down to the Psalmanazar[3] of the day, are so very common, that one scarcely turns round in the streets to look at them. Delicate and polite attentions, however, fall as much to the share of reputation, here, as in any other country, and perhaps more so, as respects literary men, though there is so little *wonder-mongering.* It would be quite impossible that the presence of Sir Walter Scott should not excite a sensation. He was frequently named in the journals, received a good deal of private, and some public notice, but, on the whole, much less of both, I think, than one would have a right to expect for him, in a place like Paris. I account for the fact, by the French distrusting the forthcoming work on Napoleon, and by a little dissatisfaction which prevails on the subject of the tone of "Paul's Letters to his Kinsfolk."[4] This feeling may surprise you, as coming from a nation as old and as great as France, but, alas! we are all human.

The King spoke to him, in going to his chapel, Sir Walter being in waiting for that purpose, but beyond this I believe he met with no civilities from the court.

As for myself, circumstances that it is needless to recount had brought me, to a slight degree, within the notice of Sir Walter Scott, though we had never met, nor had I ever seen him, even in public, so as to know his person. Still I was not without hopes of being more fortunate now, while I felt a delicacy about obtruding myself any further on his time and attention. Several days after his arrival went by, however, without my good luck bringing me in his way, and I began to give the matter up, though the Princesse _____,[5] with whom I had the advantage of being on friendly terms, flattered me with an opportunity of seeing the great writer at her house, for she had a fixed resolution of making his acquaintance before he left Paris, *coûte que coûte.*[6]

It might have been ten days after the arrival of Sir Walter Scott, that I had ordered a carriage, one morning, with an intention of driving over to the other side of the river, and had got as far as the lower flight of steps, on my way to enter it, when, by the tramping of horses in the court, I found that another coach was driving in. It was raining, and, as my own carriage drove from the door, to make

---

[1]Visit took place November 3, 1826.
[2]George Canning (1770–1827), English statesman.
[3]George Psalmanazar (1679?–1763), French literary impostor who, as a hoax, palmed himself off on Londoners as a pagan Formosan.

[4]By Sir Walter Scott. The volume is a record of his trip to Europe in 1815.
[5]Princess Galitzin (1748–1806), Russian émigrée.
[6]"Let it cost what it may" (French).

way for the new comer, I stopped where I was, until it could return. The carriage-steps rattled, and presently a large, heavy-moulded man appeared in the door of the hotel. He was gray, and limped a little, walking with a cane. His carriage immediately drove round, and was succeeded by mine, again; so I descended. We passed each other on the stairs, bowing as a matter of course. I had got to the door, and was about to enter the carriage, when it flashed on my mind that the visit might be to myself. The two lower floors of the hotel were occupied as a girl's boarding-school; the reason of our dwelling in it, for our own daughters were in the establishment; *au second,*[7] there was nothing but our own *appartement*, and above us, again, dwelt a family whose visitors never came in carriages. The door of the boarding-school was below, and men seldom came to it, at all. Strangers, moreover, sometimes did honour me with calls. Under these impressions I paused, to see if the visitor went as far as our flight of steps. All this time, I had not the slightest suspicion of who he was, though I fancied both the face and form were known to me.

The stranger got up the large stone steps slowly, leaning, with one hand, on the iron railing, and with the other, on his cane. He was on the first landing, as I stopped, and, turning towards the next flight, our eyes met. The idea that I might be the person he wanted seemed then to strike him for the first time. "*Est-ce Monsieur* _____, *que j'ai l'honneur de voir?*"[8] he asked, in French, and with but an indifferent accent. "*Monsieur, je m'appele* _____." "*Eh bien, donc—je suis Walter Scott.*"[9]

I ran up to the landing, shook him by the hand, which he stood holding out to me cordially, and expressed my sense of the honour he was conferring. He told me, in substance, that the Princesse _____ had been as good as her word, and having succeeded herself in getting hold of him, she had good-naturedly given him my address. By way of cutting short all ceremony he had driven from his hotel to my lodgings. All this time he was speaking French, while my answers and remarks were in English. Suddenly recollecting himself, he said—"Well, here have I been *parlez-vousing* to you, in a way to surprise you, no doubt; but these Frenchmen have got my tongue so set to their lingo, that I have half forgotten my own language." As we proceeded up the next flight of steps, he accepted my arm, and continued the conversation in English, walking with more difficulty than I had expected to see. You will excuse the vanity of my repeating the next observation he made, which I do in the hope that some of our own *exquisites*[10] in literature may learn in what manner a man of true sentiment and sound feeling regards a trait that they have seen fit to stigmatize as unbecoming. "I'll tell you what I most like," he added, abruptly; "and it is the manner in which you maintain the ascendancy of your own country on all proper occasions, without descending to vulgar abuse of ours. You are obliged to bring the two nations in collision, and I respect your liberal hostility." This will probably be esteemed treason in our own self-constituted mentors of the press, one of whom, I observe, has quite lately had to apologize to his readers for exposing some of the sins of the English writers in reference to ourselves! But these people are not worth our attention, for they have neither the independence which belongs to masculine reason, nor manhood even to prize the quality in others. "I am afraid the mother has not always treated the daughter well," he continued, "feeling a little jealous of her growth, perhaps; for, though we hope England has not yet begun to descend on the evil side, we have a presentiment that she has got to the top of the ladder."

---

[7]"On the second floor" (French); actually the third floor by American counting method.
[8]"Is it Mr. Cooper that I have the honor of seeing?" (French).

[9]"Sir, my name is Cooper." "Good, I am Walter Scott" (French).
[10]Those over-refined in manner.

There were two entrances to our apartments; one, the principal, leading by an ante-chamber and *salle à manger*[11] into the *salon,* and thence through other rooms to a terrace; and the other, by a private *corridor,* to the same spot. The door of my *cabinet*[12] opened on this *corridor,* and though it was dark, crooked, and any thing but savoury, as it led by the kitchen, I conducted Sir Walter through it, under an impression that he walked with pain, an idea, of which I could not divest myself, in the hurry of the moment. But for this awkwardness on my part, I believe I should have been the witness of a singular interview. General Lafayette had been with me a few minutes before, and he had gone away by the *salon,* in order to speak to Mrs. _____. Having a note to write, I had left him there, and I think his carriage could not have quitted the court when that of Sir Walter Scott entered. If so, the General must have passed out by the ante-chamber, about the time we came through the *corridor.*

There would be an impropriety in my relating all that passed in this interview; but we talked over a matter of business, and then the conversation was more general. You will remember that Sir Walter was still the *Unknown,*[13] and that he was believed to be in Paris, in search of facts for the life of Napoleon. Notwithstanding the former circumstance, he spoke of his works with great frankness and simplicity, and without the parade of asking any promises of secrecy. In short, as he commenced in this style, his authorship was alluded to by us both, just as if it had never been called in question. He asked me if I had a copy of the _____ by me, and on my confessing I did not own a single volume of any thing I had written, he laughed, and said he believed that most authors had the same feeling on the subject: as for himself, he cared not if he never saw a Waverly novel again, as long as he lived. Curious to know whether a writer as great and as practised as he, felt the occasional despondency which invariably attends all my own little efforts of this nature, I remarked that I found the mere composition of a tale a source of pleasure; so much so, that I always invented twice as much as was committed to paper, in my walks, or in bed, and, in my own judgment, much the best parts of the composition never saw the light; for, what was written was usually written at set hours, and was a good deal a matter of chance; and that going over and over the same subject, in proofs, disgusted me so thoroughly with the book, that I supposed every one else would be disposed to view it with the same eyes. To this he answered, that he was spared much of the labour of proof-reading, Scotland, he presumed, being better off than America, in this respect; but, still, he said he "would as soon see his dinner again, after a hearty meal, as to read one of his own tales when he was fairly rid of it."

He sat with me nearly an hour, and he manifested, during the time the conversation was not tied down to business, a strong propensity to humour. Having occasion to mention our common publisher in Paris, he quaintly termed him, with a sort of malicious fun, "our Gosling;"[14] adding, that he hoped he, at least, "laid golden eggs."

I hoped that he had found the facilities he desired, in obtaining facts for the forth-coming history. He rather hesitated about admitting this.—"One can hear as much as he pleases, in the way of anecdote," he said, "but then, as a gentleman, he is not always sure how much of it he can, with propriety, relate in a book;—besides," throwing all his latent humour into the expression of his small gray eyes, "one may even doubt how much of what he hears is fit for history, on another account." He paused, and his face assumed an exquisite air of confiding simplicity, as he continued with perfect *bonne foi*[15] and strong Scottish feeling, "I have been

---

[11]Dining room.
[12]Study.
[13]Scott's visit to Paris was not public knowledge.

[14]His name was Gasselin.
[15]"Good faith" (French).

to see *my countryman* M'Donald,[16] and I rather think that will be about as much as I can do here, now." This was uttered with so much *naïveté* that I could hardly believe it was the same man, who, a moment before, had shown so much shrewd distrust of oral relations of facts.

I inquired when we might expect the work. "Some time in the course of the winter," he replied, "though it is likely to prove larger than I, at first, intended. We have got several volumes printed, but I find I must add to the matter, considerably, in order to dispose of the subject. I thought I should get rid of it in seven volumes, which are already written, but it will reach, I think, to nine." "If you have two still to write, I shall not expect to see the book before spring." "You may. Let me once get back to Abbotsford, and I'll soon knock off those two fellows." To this I had nothing to say, although I thought such a *tour de force*[17] in writing might better suit invention than history.

When he rose to go, I begged him to step into the *salon*, that I might have the gratification of introducing my wife to him. To this he very good naturedly assented, and entering the room, after presenting Mrs. _____ and my nephew W _____,[18] he took a seat. He sat some little time, and his fit of pleasantry returned, for he illustrated his discourse by one or two apt anecdotes, related with a slightly Scottish accent, that he seemed to drop and assume at will. Mrs. _____ observed to him that the *bergère*[19] in which he was seated had been twice honoured that morning, for General Lafayette had not left it more than half an hour. Sir Walter Scott looked surprised at this, and said, inquiringly, "I thought he had gone to America to pass the rest of his days?" On my explaining the true state of the case, he merely observed, "He is a great man;" and yet, I thought the remark was made coldly, or in complaisance to us.

· · · · · ·

1837

---

[16]John MacDonald (1779–1849), Scottish clergyman.
[17]"Feat of strength" or "Clever technique" (French).

[18]William Cooper, Cooper's secretary.
[19]Arm chair.

PART III

FRUITION: THE COMING OF AGE (1830–1865)

GROWTH

The thirty-five-year period from the presidency of Andrew Jackson to the end of the Civil War represents an astonishing growth, in every sense, of the United States. If we can speak of the Declaration of Independence in 1776 as being the conception of the country and the Constitution in 1787 as its birth, followed by an infancy and childhood through the nurturing presidencies of the Founding Fathers—then the period beginning with Jacksonian democracy (1828–36) may be considered the onset of a swaggering adolescence, with eye-popping growth through the troublesome and even dangerous times of the Civil War to its end. That terrible trial, which at times threatened the very existence of the Union, brought an end to innocence and the beginning of maturity, with all the surprising and unsought responsibilities that maturation brings with it.

In this critical period, the United States almost tripled in population, from 12,800,000 to about 35,000,000. The states increased from twenty-four (one-half slave, the other half free) to thirty-six. The westward movement of the country is told by merely listing the twelve states added to the Union: Arkansas (1836), Michigan (1837), Florida (1845), Texas (1845), Iowa (1846), Wisconsin (1848), California (1850), Minnesota (1858), Oregon (1859), Kansas (1861), West Virginia (1863), Nevada (1864).

The population center of the United States moved from a point in West Virginia westward to a point near Cincinnati, Ohio. But most remarkable of all was the virtual doubling of the territory of the United States from 1,700,000 square miles in 1830 to over 3,000,000 in 1865—an area that would not increase again until well into the twentieth century and that would eventually become the forty-eight contiguous states of the Union. This increase in size was a result, some claimed, of "Manifest Destiny"—as inevitable as the growth of a child into strapping adulthood.

A LITERARY COMING OF AGE

Paralleling this physical growth was the intellectual and literary maturation of the country. In 1837, Ralph Waldo Emerson delivered his Phi Beta Kappa address at Harvard, entitled "The American Scholar": "We have listened too long to the courtly muses of Europe. . . . We will walk on our own feet; we will work with our own hands; we will speak our own minds." This eloquent summons to American self-reliance was justly called America's Declaration of Intellectual Independence. By the end of this period, American writers were forging a new *American* literature. America had found its own voice at last.

And what a voice—or chorus of voices! Critics have outdone themselves in thinking up metaphoric titles for the literary scene in America during the mid-nineteenth century. The Flowering of New England, the Golden Day, the American Renaissance: these tropes at first seem extravagant. But a consideration of the classic and near-classic works that cluster in the mid-century decade inspires awe:

1845: Poe's *Tales* and *The Raven and Other Poems*, Fuller's *Woman in the Nineteenth Century*, Douglass's *Narrative of the Life of Frederick Douglass*
1846: Hawthorne's *Mosses from an Old Manse*, Melville's *Typee*, Whittier's *Voices of Freedom*
1847: Emerson's *Poems*, Melville's *Omoo*, Longfellow's *Evangeline*
1848: Poe's *Eureka*, Lowell's *A Fable for Critics* and *The Biglow Papers: First Series*
1849: Thoreau's "Civil Disobedience" and *A Week on the Concord and Merrimack Rivers*, Emerson's *Nature, Addresses, and Lectures*, Melville's *Mardi* and *Redburn*
1850: Hawthorne's *The Scarlet Letter*, Melville's *White-Jacket*, Emerson's *Representative Men*
1851: Melville's *Moby-Dick*, Hawthorne's *The House of the Seven Gables*
1852: Stowe's *Uncle Tom's Cabin*, Melville's *Pierre*, Hawthorne's *The Blithedale Romance*
1853: Melville's "Bartleby the Scrivener" and "Cock-a-Doodle-Doo!"
1854: Thoreau's *Walden*, Melville's "The Encantadas"
1855: Whitman's *Leaves of Grass*, Longfellow's *Hiawatha*

This is an extraordinary list of extraordinary works. Had this list been compiled in the nineteenth century, it would have been quite different (there would have been little or no Melville, Thoreau, and Whitman; more Whittier, Lowell, and Longfellow); were it to be compiled a hundred years hence, it might not be familiar.

Yet it is hard to see how Emerson, Thoreau, and Whitman together with Poe, Hawthorne, and Melville, could fade into the shadows completely. They have not only major reputations at home but a strong standing abroad—Thoreau in India, Whitman in Russia and Japan, Poe in France, Melville worldwide (*Moby-Dick* ranks among the greatest novels of any country). Most ages misjudge their own literature, and subsequent ages sift, winnow, and reevaluate. After almost one hundred years of this process, these six writers seem most secure in their rank.

They are an interesting group because they are not like each other, and they are radically unlike the authors their time made most popular. They are all, in one way or another, in rebellion against the orthodoxies of the age. Emerson: "Society every-where is in conspiracy against the manhood of every one of its members." Thoreau: "The mass of men lead lives of quiet desperation." Whitman: "Through me forbidden voices,/Voices of sexes and lusts, voices veil'd and I remove the veil, voices indecent by me clarified and transfigur'd." Poe: "From childhood's hour I have not been/ As others were— I have not seen/ As others saw—I could not bring/ my passions from a common spring." Hawthorne: "At some brighter period, when the world should have grown ripe for it, in Heaven's own time, a new truth would be revealed, in order to establish the whole relation between man and woman on a surer ground of mutual happiness." Melville: "There are certain queer times and occasions in this strange affair we call life when a man takes this whole universe for a vast practical joke, though the wit thereof he but dimly discerns, and more than suspects that the joke is at nobody's expense but his own."

Popular literature tends to reflect popular—surface—values. These comments, on the other hand, are not calculated to be popular. Indeed, they can only be called subversive, troubling and challenging readers rather than reassuring them that all is well in the human world and God's universe.

What was it in American culture and American history that made possible what may justly be called America's classical literary period? The answer is not simple or easy, but some of the factors that contributed to this flourishing of American letters lie in the religious, philosophical, social, political, and economic controversies of the time. These were not abstract intellectual debates, but passionate encounters and confrontations deeply rooted in American history and in the turbulent society that had developed out of that history and persisted into the nineteenth century.

RELIGIOUS FERMENT AND TRANSCENDENTALISM

It is somehow appropriate that the figure most frequently cited as the father of American literature—Ralph Waldo Emerson—came from a long line of ministers and started out as a minister himself. But in 1832 he resigned from his pastorate of the Second Church of Boston because he could no longer with good conscience administer the sacrament of the Lord's Supper. The Second Church of Boston had been a stronghold of Calvinism under the ministry of the Mathers, Increase and Cotton. By the time Emerson took up his position there, it had become Unitarian. How had such a radical change come about? There was the gradual displacement of Calvinism during the eighteenth century, with most of the noted leaders of the American Revolution declaring themselves Deists, who believed that nature, not the Bible, was the true source of God's revelations.

There were, too, other beliefs spreading, like those of the Baptists, Methodists, and Cambellites (later the "Christian Church"), noted for their evangelical fervor. They popularized the camp meeting, in which itinerant preachers sought to convert sinners at mass community services. And there were other sects, like the Quakers, who believed in the existence of an Inner Light, which served as a source of divine guidance and spiritual sustenance for each individual. Noted for supporting unpopular moral positions, Quakers believed firmly that slavery was evil for both the slave and the master and that war was immoral. The diarist John Woolman was the chief eighteenth-century spokesman for Quakerism in America, and the poet John Greenleaf Whittier was the principal nineteenth-century Quaker writer.

Unitarianism grew out of the religious ferment of the period, clearly influenced by such beliefs as Deism and Quakerism. In 1794, Joseph Priestley emigrated from England to America to organize Unitarian churches. At Harvard the Divinity School was established as Unitarian in 1819. In Boston, also in 1819, the renowned minister William Ellery Channing declared for Unitarianism in an important sermon. By the 1830s, Unitarianism had taken over the old strongholds of Puritan Calvinism.

Unitarianism tended to demystify the older faith, denying the existence of a Holy Trinity. Christ was looked upon as a supreme human example—but not more divine than other men. God was no longer looked upon as an "angry" dispenser of punishment, but as a benevolent fountain of love. Human beings themselves were considered free, not predestined, and were not naturally depraved but innately good.

Emerson's resignation from the Second Church of Boston meant that he found even its quite liberal Unitarian beliefs too dogmatic for him. The distance he was to travel from the institutionalized religion of his day is suggested by the scandal he created in 1838 when he gave his "Divinity School Address" at Harvard. He told the graduating ministers that he shared the conviction of many "of the universal decay and now almost death of faith in society. The soul is not preached. The church seems to totter to its fall, almost all life extinct." His bleak view of the usefulness or efficacy of ministers and their churches offended his audience, and he was not invited back to Harvard for many decades.

But he was in the process, through his essays, of creating for himself, his friends, and disciples a new belief—part religion, part philosophy, part mysticism: transcendentalism. This uniquely American body of thought, or way of apprehending the world and cosmos, was eclectic in nature. It incorporated some aspects of Calvinism (a belief it opposed)—specifically Jonathan Edwards's "Divine and Supernatural Light, immediately imparted to the soul by the spirit of God." But it took from many sources: from Plato and the Neoplatonists; from the oriental religions and philosophies embodied in the Upanishads and the Bhagavad Gita; from Christian mystics, like Pascal and Swedenborg; and from the German transcendental philosophers like Immanuel Kant, particularly as they were reflected secondhand by such British authors as Samuel Taylor Coleridge and Thomas Carlyle.

The distinctive nature of American transcendentalism was suggested by James Russell Lowell in his characterization of Emerson in *A Fable for Critics:*

> A Greek head on right yankee shoulders, whose range
> Has Olympus for one pole, for t'other the Exchange. . . .

Consort with the gods on Olympus, participant in the bargaining at the stock exchange—such was the American transcendentalist, a practical mystic, a shrewd seer (or even an idealistic con man). Emerson had his head in the heavens, his feet on the ground. All of his essays were ignited by transcendental fire. Central to his belief was ultimate faith in divine intuition, available to all individuals through their common connection with the Oversoul. Because it was divine, this transcendent perception was superior to mere intellectual comprehension. The rational faculty (Emerson called it *Understanding*) could solve the riddles of society, the puzzles of nature; only the suprarational faculty (Emerson called it *Reason*) could penetrate to that divine unity that lies at the heart of the world's diversity and multiplicity. "Nothing is at last sacred but the integrity of your own mind," said Emerson.

With the formation of the Transcendental Club in 1836 in Concord, the informal meetings often held in Emerson's home, the belief became something of a movement. Members included Margaret Fuller, Henry David Thoreau, and Bronson Alcott. The Club sponsored a journal, *The Dial*, with Margaret Fuller serving as editor from 1840 to 1842, and then Emerson taking charge until the last issues in 1844.

REFORMS AND UTOPIAS

This period of religious ferment was, not suprisingly, also a time of many attempts to right wrongs, to eradicate injustices, and to perfect human nature and society. Certainly there were enough wrongs, injustices, and imperfections to inspire concern. Most notable of these movements was that against slavery, with the formation of the New England Anti-Slavery Society in 1831 and the American Anti-Slavery Society in 1833 (the Abolition Movement is dealt with in detail on pages 853–55). Concern for drunkenness brought into being the American Temperance Society in 1826, with the aim of instilling not temperance but total abstinence from drinking liquor. Both these movements had roots in religious beliefs and were led with evangelical fervor.

The woman suffrage movement began in 1848, with a convention in Seneca Falls, New York, sponsored and led by Elizabeth Cady Stanton and Lucretia Mott, which issued a "Declaration of Sentiments," modeled on the Declaration of Independence, calling for basic women's rights. Horace Mann opened the first American teachers' college for high school students (normal school) in Lexington, Massachusetts, in 1839 and became a crusader nationwide for free public education for all children.

The yearning for the establishment of a utopian society that had brought many of the first settlers to America manifested itself anew in the creation of many communities conceived as ideal social organizations. One of the most interesting was the brainchild of John Humphrey Noyes, whose philosophy of perfectionism was based on Matthew 5:48: "Be ye therefore perfect, even as your Father which is in heaven is perfect." Noyes believed that Christ's second coming, establishing the Millennium, occurred in A.D. 70 and brought into being the innate sinlessness of all humankind. On establishing a colony of Bible Communists at Putney, Vermont, in 1836, he instituted a system of "complex marriages" as a substitute for monogamy. But his colony came to an abrupt end in 1846 when an alarmed and incensed citizenry brought charges of adultery and he fled. He was more successful later in establishing his Oneida Community at Oneida, New York, in 1848.

The utopian community of greatest literary fame was Brook Farm, offspring of Unitarianism and transcendental idealism. Established in 1841 in Roxbury, Massachusetts, with the Boston Unitarian clergyman George Ripley as the principal leader, it was a communal settlement with the farm labor apportioned to all, and serious talk in the evenings. But the leading transcendentalists—Emerson, Thoreau, Margaret Fuller—observed it from the outside, sympathetic but reluctant to leave their woods and studies. Emerson described it as "a perpetual picnic, a French Revolution in small, an age of reason in a patty-pan." Nathaniel Hawthorne joined for a brief time and became disillusioned when he discovered the amount of energy sapped by digging in the dirt and milking the cows. He memorialized the community in his novel *The Blithedale Romance* (1852), satirizing Ripley and other participants and revealing his skepticism of the entire enterprise.

One of the most unusual utopian experiments was that established in 1843 by the transcendentalist Bronson Alcott and an English associate, Charles Lane. It was conceived by Alcott as a place where all participants would share in the farm labor and live as vegetarians, the communal working, eating, and living thus contributing to the "harmonic development of their physical, intellectual, and moral natures." The diet was worked out on moral grounds, with all commodities that were the product of slavery (cotton and sugar) forbidden, and foodstuffs and materials that were produced by exploiting animals (milk, wool, and leather) banned. Unconfirmed rumors spread that Alcott preferred "aspiring" vegetables (beans, corn, and peas) that grew above the ground rather than in the dirt. The experiment lasted seven months and collapsed. But Alcott's daughter, Louisa May Alcott, later wrote a delightful fictionalized account in "Transcendental Wild Oats" (1873).

The zeal with which good causes were pursued during this period may be suggested by the Chardon Street Convention in Boston. It was called through newspaper notices by the Friends of Universal Reform for three three-day sessions in 1840 and 1841. Participants included Bronson Alcott, Lloyd Garrison, Jones Very, and many more. Emerson wrote a short piece for *The Dial* describing the meetings:

> A great variety of dialect and of costume was noticed; a great deal of confusion, eccentricity, and freak appeared, as well as of zeal and enthusiasm. If the assembly was disorderly, it was picturesque. Madmen, madwomen, men with beards, Dunkers, Muggletonians, Come-outers, Groaners, Agrarians, Seventh-Day-Baptists, Quakers, Abolitionists, Calvinists, Unitarians and Philosophers,—all came successively to the top, and seized their moment, if not their hour, wherein to chide, or pray, or preach, or protest. The faces were a study. The most daring innovators and the champions-until-death of the old cause sat side by side.

Clearly the Friends of Universal Reform were sometimes enemies of each other, and found the possibilities of perfection in the imagined ideal more easily than in the concrete realities of actual experience.

WESTWARD EXPANSION AND MANIFEST DESTINY

Horace Greeley, editor of the *New York Tribune,* spoke to and for the nation when he said, "Go West, young man, go West!" From 1830 to 1865, there was an inexorable movement westward to the Pacific Ocean. During this period, the land area of the United States doubled and the population tripled. Under the term "Manifest Destiny," which gained currency in the 1840s, the westward movement was made to seem inevitable. And indeed, there was something of the inevitable in the movement of the frontier across the continent, under no restraint or control, as people moved to the edge of and beyond formal boundaries, seeking a new beginning, freedom, wealth, or adventure.

Little regard was given to the Indian tribes' communal ownership of the lands that settlers moved in to claim. The national policy pursued vigorously beginning with President Andrew Jackson was the removal of Indians from lands east of the Mississippi to Indian territory west of the great dividing river. The forced resettlement was largely accomplished by 1840, but the cost to the Indians in disease, hunger, and death was incalculable.

Black Hawk was the chief of one tribe—the Sauk—forced westward from Illinois in this great displacement. In a speech in 1832 counselling war, Black Hawk presented a view surely common to most of the tribes: "From the day when the pale faces landed upon our shores, they have been robbing us of our inheritance, and slowly, but surely, driving us back, back, back towards the setting sun, burning our villages, destroying our growing crops, ravishing our wives and daughters, beating our papooses with cruel sticks, and brutally murdering our people upon the most flimsy pretenses and trivial causes."

But nothing could or would stop the westward movement, whatever the expense to the Native Americans or to the great stretches of wilderness lands cleared for cultivation. One of the great engineering feats of the early nineteenth century was the building of the Erie Canal, linking the Atlantic Ocean through the Hudson River to the Great Lakes, thus enabling the westward-bound travellers to avoid crossing the formidable Appalachian Mountains. There were some four hundred miles of land through which the Canal had to be dug. It was begun in 1817 and finished in 1825, turning Buffalo, on Lake Erie, into an important port. This water route to the west was followed by the development of major cities along the Great Lakes—Cleveland, Detroit, and Chicago.

The search for religious freedom was one of the elements inspiring western settlement, just as it had been a force in the original move from Europe to America. The Mormon religion was founded as the Church of Jesus Christ of Latter-Day Saints in 1830 in New York state by Joseph Smith, who experienced a revelation of the Book of Mormon on Golden Tablets. A further divine revelation sanctioning polygamy earned the Mormons community hostility wherever they settled. Their movement was westward. They created a place for themselves at Nauvoo, Illinois, on the banks of the Mississippi, and Nauvoo became in 1842 the largest city in Illinois. But Smith was lynched by a mob in 1843, and the new leader, Brigham Young, led the Mormon band across the Great Plains to the valley of the Great Salt Lake, in what is now northern Utah, in 1846–47.

The Santa Fe Trail was opened for trade in the 1820s, leading from Independence, Missouri (on the Missouri River) to Santa Fe, then in Mexico. The journey was by horse or mule, and covered eight hundred miles of difficult terrain, much of it desert. But the profits in commerce with the Southwest could be high. In the 1840s, the Oregon Trail was established, beginning also at Independence and crossing the plains to the Rocky Mountains, across difficult mountain passes and rivers, to the Columbia River leading to the Pacific. The trail was some 2000 miles long, and on it moved the covered wagons bearing families and their belongings, their cattle driven alongside.

The peopling of the West was followed by large land acquisitions by the government. The Southwest from Texas to California belonged to Mexico, but Americans were gradually settling the area. There were enough such settlers in Texas by 1836 to rise up in rebellion and declare independence from Mexico. Although the defenders of the Alamo (in San Antonio) were wiped out, victory came for the Texans at San Jacinto, and Texas became a republic, immediately recognized by President Andrew Jackson. In 1845, Texas was admitted at its request as a state of the Union.

This annexation was a leading cause of the Mexican War (1846–48). Since southerners had largely settled Texas, it came into the Union as a slave state. The Mexican War was thus seen by many of the northerners who opposed slavery as an immoral war waged to extend slave-holding territory. This war caused Henry David Thoreau to withhold payment of his poll tax, spending the night in jail and providing the experience for writing "Civil Disobedience." And it was also this war that inspired James Russell Lowell to write the first series of his *Biglow Papers,* a satiric attack on the government's compromised morals and motives in attacking Mexico.

By the time a peace treaty was signed in 1848, the entire Southwest to the Pacific was flying the American flag. The area included what would become six states—Texas, New Mexico, Utah, Arizona, Nevada, and California. No sooner was the war over than gold was discovered in California, setting off one of the most exciting and colorful mass migrations in history, the gold rush of 1849. Added finally to all the other reasons to go West was now the lust for gold.

THE "PECULIAR INSTITUTION," ABOLITIONISM, AND THE FIERY TRIAL

By 1860, there were some 4,000,000 slaves in the southern states whose total population was 12,000,000. In South Carolina and Mississippi, blacks outnumbered whites. The positions of the proslavery forces in the South and the abolitionists in the North had hardened, and there were confrontations and clashes in every sphere of American life—economic, social, and political. The slavery issue seemed to be headed toward some kind of wrenching—or explosive—resolution. Abraham Lincoln voiced the feeling of the time in 1858 in a Senate campaign speech by quoting the Bible: "A house divided against itself cannot stand."

The 1776 Declaration of Independence, as revised from Jefferson's draft, had postponed the issue of slavery, and the Constitution in 1787 had skirted the issue (but provided that Congress could prohibit the importation of slaves in 1808). The Missouri Compromise of 1820, by admitting Missouri as a slave state and Maine as free and by forbidding slavery in the Louisiana Territory north of latitude 36° 30', again postponed a crisis for some decades. The Compromise of 1850 admitted California as free, left the territories of New Mexico and Utah to the future, and strengthened the fugitive slave law of 1793.

The strengthening of the fugitive slave law was aimed at the "underground railroad," which was organized by members of the American Anti-Slavery Society to help escaping slaves make their way to free states and to Canada. Frederick Douglass had published his *Narrative* in 1845 describing his escape from slavery in the South and his reception by abolitionists in the North, but he had withheld details of his means of escape so that others might follow. Harriet A. Jacobs published her *Incidents in the Life of a Slave Girl* in 1861 giving a vivid account of the humiliations she suffered as a slave and the hardships she underwent to escape. Harriet Beecher Stowe was inspired in part by the 1850 Compromise to write her *Uncle Tom's Cabin,* published in 1852, and include the story of Eliza escaping with her child across the frozen Ohio River. Incensed because of the great New England orator Daniel Webster's support of the Compromise of 1850, John Greenleaf Whittier penned one of his most powerful satiric poems attacking him in "Ichabod."

The Kansas-Nebraska Act of 1854 permitted residents of the two territories to decide for themselves the slavery question, thereby nullifying the Missouri Compromise of 1820 and establishing a precedent of congressional nonintervention on slavery in the territories. The result was an immediate migration to the area by those who favored and those who opposed slavery. There followed violence, with arson, lynchings, and pitched battles. John Brown and his sons were leaders on the antislavery side.

The 1857 Dred Scott decision by the Supreme Court further inflamed passions. The Court ruled against a slave who had contended that his four-year stay in free territory (he was taken to Illinois by his master) had made him legally free. The opinion held that since Scott was not a U.S. citizen, he could not sue in a federal court and that his temporary residence in free territory had not made him free. Contained in the opinion was the finding that Congress did not have the power to exclude slavery from the territories. The decision appeared to run rough-shod over the cause of the abolitionists and to render a peaceful solution to the slavery issue unlikely. John Brown resorted to violence in 1859 with his raid on the U.S. Arsenal at Harper's Ferry in Virginia. He was considered by many insane, but others found sense in his plan to lead an armed guerrilla movement in the mountains, making periodic raids into slave-holding states to rescue as many slaves as possible and thus build a freedom army.

Brown was captured, tried for treason, and hanged. His martyrdom probably did more for abolition than his bold schemes would have accomplished. Even Henry David Thoreau, apostle of nonviolent civil disobedience, was moved by the strong passions of the time to endorse Brown's actions: "It was his [Brown's] peculiar doctrine that a man has a perfect right to interfere by force with the slaveholder, in order to rescue the slave. I agree with him. . . . I shall not be forward to think him mistaken in his method who quickest succeeds to liberate the slave." Thoreau's approval of Brown's violence indicates how disillusioned he had become with alternative peaceful means to pursue the abolitionist cause. If Thoreau had become disillusioned, however briefly, others less thoughtful than he could only be more desperate—and ready for war.

By the time Abraham Lincoln, candidate for the presidency on the ticket of the Republican party (formed only three years before), won the election in 1860 and was inaugurated in March 1861, war was inevitable. Already the month before the inauguration, seven southern states had seceded from the Union and had formed the Confederate States of America, electing Jefferson Davis as its president. In April, Confederate guns fired on Fort Sumter in Charleston Harbor, South Carolina. The war was under way.

The first battle of Bull Run, fought in Virginia, in July 1861, was a sobering experience. Spectators flocked from Washington, D.C., to witness the defeat of the rebels, but observed instead the rout of the Union forces fleeing back to Washington. From that moment, the Union realized that the fighting would be hard, the war long, and victory uncertain. With an upsurge in Union fortunes on the battlefield in 1862, Lincoln issued his Emancipation Proclamation. And then, the victory in the Battle of Gettysburg in Pennsylvania in 1863, the major battle of the war, foretold the ultimate defeat of the Confederacy. It was not, however, until April 1865 that Lee surrendered his army to Grant at Appomattox Court House.

Lincoln's assassination in April 1865 was the closing tragic episode in the Civil War that had cost the Union over 364,000 dead, the Confederacy, over 133,000. Walt Whitman had witnessed much of the suffering and agony in the improvised hospitals on battlefields and in Washington, D.C. He concluded the account of his experiences as a wound-dresser during the war in his *Specimen Days* (1882) with a short piece entitled "The Real War Will Never Get in the Books": "Future years will never know the seething hell and black infernal background of countless minor scenes and interiors . . . of the Secession War. . . ."

That the Union survived was something of a miracle. But it had not only survived, it had been transformed from youthful innocence to sober, serious adulthood. The issue of slavery that had been set aside so often in the past was settled directly in 1865 by the Thirteenth Amendment to the Constitution: "Neither slavery nor involuntary servitude, except as a punishment for crime whereof the party shall have been duly convicted, shall exist within the United States, or any place subject to their jurisdiction." The southern conception of the United States as a confederation of sovereign states was permanently put to rest by the Fourteenth Amendment (1868), affirming the priority of U.S. citizenship over citizenship in the state of residence.

There was a general feeling of pride in the Union's winning the war, a feeling that America had come of age by proving itself to the world. James Russell Lowell gave words to this widespread feeling in his "Ode Recited at the Harvard Commemoration [of the War Dead]" when he asked:

> Who now shall sneer?
> Who dare again to say we trace
> Our lines to a plebeian race?

This feeling of pride was accompanied by a feeling of great relief that the horrors of war were over, captured by Whitman in a poem entitled "Reconciliation":

Beautiful that war and all its deeds of carnage must in time be utterly lost,
That the hands of the sisters Death and Night incessantly softly wash again, and
   ever again, this soil'd world.
For my enemy is dead, a man divine as myself is dead.

THE TRANSCENDENTAL SPIRIT: EMERSON AND THOREAU

It is too often assumed that Ralph Waldo Emerson may be equated with an abstract definition of transcendentalism, a movement over which he presided at its center. The truth is that encountering Emerson through reading his essays is radically different from encountering him as a composite of the various parts of a definition of a transcendentalist. "This one fact the world hates," he wrote, "that the soul *becomes*." This thought may be transferred to him: the only way to experience Emerson is to experience his *becoming* in reading his essays, which are explorations, not explanations. The best preparation for that experience is to abandon all preconceptions of him and transcendentalism and to let each of his sentences explode afresh in a receptive consciousness.

By so doing, we simply follow his advice. When we construct his intellectual model by bits and pieces of his thought, and then attempt to comprehend him through our intellectual construct of his philosophy, we run immediately into difficulties. We are trapped on the level of our *Understanding*. If we instead leap to the level he calls *Reason*, the intuitive faculty that derives more power from the soul than the mind, and open ourselves to the flow of his sentences, we discover deep within us a reciprocal flow of comprehension. That we later cannot intellectualize, encapsulate, and verbalize that experience should not in any way diminish our notion of its value.

"Speak your latent conviction, and it shall be the universal sense," Emerson said. And: "I do not wish to expiate, but to live. My life is for itself and not for a spectacle." And: "A foolish consistency is the hobgoblin of little minds, adored by little statesmen, philosophers, and divines." And: "An institution is the lengthened shadow of one man." And: "The Centuries are conspirators against the sanity and authority of the soul." And: "Life only avails, not the having lived." And: "Insist on yourself; never imitate." And: "The civilized man has built a coach, but has lost the use of his feet." These sentences are found sprinkled throughout "Self-Reliance." They gleam and flash in their contexts, and resonate as they pass into the deeper levels of consciousness as—and after—we read. This experience represents the Emerson we should try to come to terms with.

At the beginning of his essay "Fate," Emerson sets the question he wants to address—"a practical question of the conduct of life. How shall I live?" He might have set this question at the beginning of all his essays, the total body of his work. "How shall I live?" It is a *practical* question in that each individual must decide for himself or herself—or simply avoid any decision at all, leaving one's life to be shaped by others or by chance. But the question, explored repeatedly by Emerson throughout his life, is never mentioned in definitions of transcendentalism.

Emerson has drawn the enmity of several eminent twentieth-century critics—T. S. Eliot among them—for being oblivious to the very real presence of evil in the world. Such critics are fixated on such passages as the following from near the end of *Nature*, when Emerson is (after the exhortation, "Build therefore your own world") rising to an inspired climax:

> A correspondent revolution in things will attend the influx of the spirit. So fast will disagreeable appearances, swine, spiders, snakes, pests, mad-houses, prisons, enemies, vanish; they are temporary and shall be no more seen. The sordor and filths of nature, the sun shall dry up, and the wind exhale. As when the summer comes from the south, the snow-banks melt, and the face of the earth becomes green before it, so shall the advancing spirit create its ornaments along its path, and carry with it the beauty it visits, and the song which enchants it; it shall draw beautiful faces, and warm hearts, and wise discourse, and heroic acts, around its way, until evil is no more seen.

The rhetorical purpose of the passage is not to make evil disappear, but to suggest how it might be deflected from front and center, where it magnetizes all sight and subverts possibility with despair—deflected, that is, to its proper relational place.

Nature, in 1836, was Emerson's first published work, but a late essay, "Fate," developed in the 1850s as a lecture and published in 1860, finds Emerson determined to give evil its due: "No picture of life can have any veracity that does not admit the odious facts. A man's power is hooped in by a necessity which, by many experiments, he touches on every side until he learns its arc." In his attempt to confront the bleak condition of humankind, he hit upon the image of universal drowning: "I seemed in the height of a tempest to see men overboard struggling in the waves, and driven about here and there. They glanced intelligently at each other, but 'twas little they could do for one another; 'twas much if each could keep afloat alone. Well, they had a right to their eyebeams, and all the rest was Fate." It would be difficult to find, even in T. S. Eliot's *The Waste Land*, a more pessimistic image of the human condition than this of the drowning castaways. But it is characteristic of Emerson that this frightening image comes midway in his essay, climaxing the negative mood. The rest of the essay is spent in sifting through the wreckage, searching for scraps and shards of hope. Emerson does find some fragments (and even clues to unity) to shore against his ruins.

Transcendentalism, then, is best envisioned not as a fixed philosophical system but as a spirit of restless exploration in the optative mood. For a brief moment in our literary history in the 1830s and 1840s, it held sway in Concord, Massachusetts. Major talents by some chance gathered there—Henry

David Thoreau, Emerson's disciple; Margaret Fuller, his friend and critic; Nathaniel Hawthorne, his shrewd observer and satirist. Minor talents fell within transcendentalism's orbit—the orphic sayer, Bronson Alcott; the aspiring poet, Ellery Channing; the mad mystic, Jones Very. And even in New York, Walt Whitman felt the pull of Emerson's transcendental magnetism.

The cases of Thoreau and Whitman are particularly interesting, in that the two, long considered disciples or followers, have emerged from Emerson's shadow to cast substantial shadows of their own in the twentieth century. The outrageous suggestion used to be made that to find out what Thoreau or Whitman thought read Emerson. No longer. Although they imbibed the transcendental spirit, they created their own lives and works. Emerson does not contain *Walden* nor does he preempt *Leaves of Grass.*

It is now recognized generally, as Emerson himself recognized in his time, that Thoreau and Whitman did what he could not do—become the living embodiment in concrete actuality of principles that he could contemplate only in the abstract. Emerson and Thoreau lived close together, and for periods Thoreau lived in Emerson's house. It is no wonder that their friendship had its up and downs. Thoreau was often put off by Emerson's coolness. Emerson was often irritated by Thoreau's readiness with "some weary captious paradox to fight you with." But Thoreau's early death brought Emerson's honest evaluation in the privacy of his journal. He had been reading Thoreau's journal when he was moved to write about his "oaken strength": "In reading him, I find the same thought, the same spirit that is in me, but he takes a step beyond, and illustrates by excellent images that which I should have conveyed in a sleepy generality. 'Tis as if I went into a gymnasium, and saw youths leap, climb, and swing with a force unapproachable,—though their feats are only continuations of my initial grapplings and jumps."

Similarly Emerson saw Whitman as filling an outline that Emerson had sketched but could not himself fill. Emerson wrote in "The Poet" (1844), after describing the ideal poet as bard or seer and one of the "liberating gods":

> I look in vain for the poet whom I describe. . . . Dante's praise is, that he dared to write his autobiography in colossal cipher, or into universality. We have yet no genius in America, with tyrannous eye, which knew the value of our incomparable materials, and saw, in the barbarism and materialism of the times, another carnival of the same gods whose picture he so much admires in Homer. . . . Yet America is a poem in our eyes; its ample geography dazzles the imagination, and it will not wait long for metres.

A decade later, in 1855, when Whitman sent Emerson a copy of the first edition of *Leaves of Grass,* Emerson wrote a glowing letter to the unknown poet:

> I find [*Leaves of Grass*] the most extraordinary piece of wit and wisdom that America has yet contributed. I am very happy in reading it, as great power makes us happy. It meets the demand I am always making of what seemed the sterile and stingy nature, as if too much handiwork, or too much lymph in the temperament, were making our western wits fat and mean.

Though Emerson never reiterated this praise of Whitman, never did he repudiate it either, even when Whitman used it to advertise his second edition of *Leaves of Grass* in 1856. It can be taken for what it was, an immediate and honest reaction to the "free and brave thought" of *Leaves of Grass.* When Emerson cited it as the "most extraordinary piece of wit and wisdom that America has yet contributed," he no doubt meant just that. The best of his own work had already been published and included his *Poems* in 1847. Emerson would never have mistaken his own poetry as, like Dante's, writing "his auto-biography in colossal cipher, or into universality." Yet this is exactly what Whitman had done in *Leaves of Grass,* casting himself as his own hero in his modern lyric epic. On some level Emerson comprehended that extraordinary achievement.

Whatever the status of Emerson at home as the fountainhead of American literature, his reputation abroad has lagged far behind Thoreau's in the twentieth century. By the time of his death in 1862, Thoreau had published only two books, neither of which had caused much of a ripple. Gradually Thoreau's reputation spread, but it was one of his essays, "Civil Disobedience," that seems to have caught the imagination of the modern period. Mahatma Gandhi is said to have carried a copy of this essay with him through his years of agitation on behalf of the independence of India from Great Britain. After his death in 1948, the Indian government arranged for the translation of *Walden* into some fifteen Indian languages. In the 1960s civil rights movement in the United States, the black leader and apostle of nonviolent protest, Martin Luther King, Jr., drew inspiration from both Gandhi and Thoreau.

In "The Lake Isle of Innisfree" (1890), the Irish poet William Butler Yeats wrote:

> I will arise and go now, and go to Innisfree,
> And a small cabin build there, of clay and wattles made;
> Nine bean-rows will I have there, a hive for the honeybee,
> And live alone in the bee-loud glade.

Yeats commented on the inspiration for this famous poem: "My father had read to me some passages out of *Walden,* and I planned to live some day in a cottage on a little island called Innisfree." Yeats was not the first, and certainly not the last, to be moved by *Walden.* In an age of disappearing wildlands and encroaching pavements, overcrowded cities and imposed conformity, few readers fail to respond deeply to Thoreau's declaration for the right of individuality: "If a man does not keep pace with his companions, perhaps it is because he hears a different drummer. Let him step to the music which he hears, however measured or far away."

Walden and "Civil Disobedience," because they speak so directly to yearnings widespread today, have led to interest in Thoreau's other published book, *A Week on the Concord and Merrimack Rivers* (1849), and to other essays, especially "Life without Principle." But perhaps the greatest interest has developed in Thoreau's *Journal.* Begun in 1837, just after Thoreau graduated from Harvard, and continued to near his death in 1862, the *Journal* contains two million words. The so-called complete *Journal* published in 1906 in fourteen volumes is woefully inadequate in completeness and accuracy. Thoreau used his *Journal* as a source for his published works (as did Emerson), but it is clear that as time passed, Thoreau began to see the *Journal* as the central work of his life. In 1857, Thoreau wrote in it: "Is not the poet bound to write his own biography? Is there any work for him but a good journal? We do not wish to know how his imaginary hero, but how he, the actual hero, lived from day to day." Thoreau's books published during his lifetime, and shaped by his imagination, have become classics. It is their impact that has aroused interest in the life of Thoreau and turned attention to that life "lived from day to day" as recorded so vividly in his *Journal.*

Emerson thought of his *Journal* as his "savings bank." Like Thoreau's, it was indexed for quick reference, and it served as a source for Emerson's lectures and essays. The publication of his *Journals* in 1901–14 omitted much material and still filled ten volumes. The republication as *The Journals and Miscellaneous Notebooks* in 1960–82 fills sixteen large volumes. As with Thoreau, a higher valuation has been placed by recent criticism on Emerson's *Journal* than in the past. It has long been known that Emerson's work was a significant influence on the noted German philosopher Friederich Nietzsche (1844–1900). It is possible that a comprehensive reevaluation of Emerson will find him to be the American counterpart of Nietzsche. One critic, Michael Lopez, has said:

> To read through those forty-odd volumes [of Emerson] is to become gradually aware that in Emerson's books, letters, journals, lectures, and addresses there lies buried a 'philosophy of power' which, if not as deliberate, seems almost to rival Nietzsche's in its comprehensiveness. . . . The 'Aboriginal Power' which was his subject, the primitive force of language he hoped to unleash in his writing, the vitality of his constitution were all modes of the same energy.

THE BLACKNESS OF DARKNESS: POE, HAWTHORNE, MELVILLE

In "Hawthorne and His Mosses," Herman Melville noted that readers are often bewitched by the sunlight in Hawthorne's tales; but, said Melville, "there is the blackness of darkness beyond." This "mystical blackness" in Hawthorne, which may perhaps be "unknown to himself," is a "touch of the Puritanic gloom": "This great power of blackness in him derives its force from its appeals to that Calvinistic sense of Innate Depravity and Original Sin, from whose visitations, in some shape or other, no deeply thinking mind is always and wholly free. For, in certain moods, no man can weigh this world without throwing in something, somehow like Original Sin, to strike the uneven balance."

Poe, Hawthorne, and Melville created worlds in which there was always "the blackness of darkness beyond"—or within. Not one of them could be considered an orthodox Calvinist, yet they all portrayed human behavior that seemed to exhibit "Innate Depravity." They lived after the weakening of Puritan dogma and before the development of psychology as a field; in their profound explorations of the human psyche—conscious or unconscious—they discovered the psychological roots of pathological behavior that had previously been considered grounded solely in inexorable religious forces. Since a psychological vocabulary was not available to them, they often drafted metaphoric language from the familiar religious vocabulary (the devil, the serpent, witches, or wizards).

Poe's stories are often multilayered in their meaning. On the surface level there is frequently a supernatural interpretation possible. Beneath this level there is found a psychological explanation of the supernatural events. And at the deepest level there are occasional hints at allegorical meanings, not always coherent or fully elaborated. In "Ligeia," for example, the story on one level appears to be that of a dead wife who through strength of will comes back by taking over the body of her successor. On a lower level, it turns into the psychological story of a slightly mad opium addict who, in yearning for his dead wife, possibly kills her successor and hallucinates his wife's return. On a still lower level, it is the allegorical account of an artist transfiguring physical or earthly beauty (the second wife, Rowena) into abstract or ethereal beauty (the returning first wife, Ligeia) through a transcendent act of the imagination (inspiration symbolized by the opium).

Poe would probably have wanted his stories to work on all these three levels, attracting readers of a great variety of interests. Nevertheless, a primary focus of attention for writer and reader is the state of mind of the protagonist. Like so many characters in Poe's writings, he appears deranged and apparently engaged in serious violation of a fellow creature's soul. In "The Cask of Amontillado," the somewhat unbalanced narrator spills out the story of his long-ago act of vengeance in luring his victim into the remote depths of a wine cellar to be entombed alive. In "The Fall of the House of Usher," a veiled tale of incest, a brother entombs his twin sister alive, and she escapes and returns to carry him down in death with her. In "The Imp of the Perverse," an imprisoned murderer describes (but cannot explain) the compulsion that made him blurt out against his will a confession of his crime.

The world of Poe's stories is a nightmare world in which individuals are driven by wild passions and irrational compulsions. "William Wilson" shows a young man committed to an evil life of dissipation killing himself in attempting to kill his pursuer and apparent double (really his conscience). "The Man of the Crowd" portrays a city in which throngs are at the mercy of their own creation—an old man who is "the type and the genius of deep crime." "The Masque of the Red Death" demonstrates the futility of attempting to escape one's fate of horror—and concludes with one of the bleakest lines in all literature: "And Darkness and Decay and the Red Death held illimitable dominion over all."

The moment readers penetrate beneath the trivial supernatural level in a Poe story, they find themselves in a world filled with horrors distinctly modern. An irrational Kafkaesque world, it has affinities with T. S. Eliot's *The Waste Land* and Jorge Borges's fantasies and bafflements. When experienced in the fullness of their complexity, Poe's tales demonstrate the truth of Emily Dickinson's poem, "One Need Not Be a Chamber—To be haunted—":

> Far safer, through an Abbey gallop,
> The Stones a'chase—
> Than Unarmed, one's a'self encounter—
> In lonesome Place—
>
> Ourself behind ourself, concealed—
> Should startle most—
> Assassin hid in our Apartment
> Be Horror's least.

It is the horror within, not without, that takes us by surprise and swamps our self-assurance.

Nathaniel Hawthorne's tales, like Poe's, often offer the reader a supernatural reading of an event, but alongside it extend another choice of a realistic interpretation. The teasing tone determines our choice, but does not diminish the aura of ambiguity. Hawthorne also frequently sums up the lesson or moral of a tale, but again in a voice of self-mockery. Beware of such summations. Hawthorne himself observed in his Preface to *The House of the Seven Gables:* "When romances do really teach anything, or produce any effective operation, it is usually through a far more subtle process than the ostensible one."

There are moments in a Hawthorne story—perhaps they might be labelled startling shifts into the "blackness of darkness beyond"—that suddenly subvert an easy interpretation and throw the reader into a brown study. One example comes at the end of that brilliant story of initiation, "My Kinsman, Major Molineux," when young Robin, come from the country to the city in expectation of help from his distinguished kinsman, finds himself instead witnessing the despised leader tarred and feathered, the object of ridicule and mockery of the gathered mob. Loud, hysterical laughter at this disgraced, defenseless figure arises from the crowd—and Robin surprises himself when he too involuntarily sends forth "a shout of laughter that echoed through the street."

Another example occurs near the end of "'Roger Malvin's Burial," when frontiersman Reuben Bourne, haunted by his cowardice years before in not staying by his dying father-in-law-to-be and burying him, and further haunted by his letting his wife believe otherwise, half-accidentally, half-intentionally (we cannot know for sure) kills his son on the spot where he had abandoned the boy's grandfather—and suddenly feels his "sin . . . expiated," and a renewed ability to shed tears and to pray. The reader is likely to sit numbed by the horror of this ending, attempting to tease the text out of its mysteries.

Such ambiguities lurk in the dark corners of the best of Hawthorne's tales—"The Minister's Black Veil," "The Birthmark," "Rappaccini's Daughter," "Ethan Brand"—as the reader swings, often helplessly, between psychological and theological readings. The novels, too, especially *The Scarlet Letter* and *The House of the Seven Gables,* proliferate ambiguities, and alert readers are likely to have changed their minds about meaning enough times in the process of reading as to conclude that Hawthorne's fictional world bears strong resemblances to the real world we inhabit—in offering so many ethical puzzles and moral ambiguities.

It was his reading of *The House of the Seven Gables* that led Melville to write to Hawthorne an analysis of the novel, concluding:

> There is the grand truth about Nathaniel Hawthorne. He says No! in thunder; but the Devil himself cannot make him say *yes*. For all men who say *yes,* lie; and all men who say *no,*—why, they are in the happy condition of judicious, unincumbered travellers in Europe; they cross the frontiers into Eternity with nothing but a carpet-bag,—that is to say, the Ego. Whereas those *yes*-gentry, they travel with heaps of baggage, and, damn them! they will never get through the Custom House.

Though this comment hits home at the deepest meanings of Hawthorne's *House of the Seven Gables,* it also strikes home at Melville's own work. His *Moby-Dick* is dedicated to Hawthorne, and it is a book that thunders the No! of Ahab, shaking his fist at the fiery corposants on the masts of the *Pequod.* His is a woe that is madness. Ishmael's woe begins and ends in wisdom, the wisdom of human bonds and ties—but underneath is a No! as profound as Ahab's.

Hawthorne, then U.S. consul in Liverpool, wrote in his diary after seeing Melville for the last time on his 1856 visit: "He can neither believe, nor be comfortable in his unbelief; and he is too honest not to try to do one or the other." Melville travelled through life with very little of the baggage of belief, and his writing represented the struggle going on in him that Hawthorne so shrewdly summed up. In "Bartleby," the smug, self-contented narrator is nettled and then unsettled by Bartleby's quietly repeated "no" in the reiterated "I prefer not to" (preferring, finally, not to live). Captain Delano in "Benito Cereno" is similarly haunted by the retreat and final withdrawal of the sensitive Spanish captain who cannot recover from his shock at a world turned upside down when the slaves on his ship rebel and turn themselves into masters and the ship's officers into slaves. In that last work of fiction from his pen, *Billy Budd,* unpublished until the 1920s, Melville went over the familiar grounds of his previous fiction, pondering the absolute evil of the Master-of-Arms Claggart, the flawed innocence of Billy ("accidental" killer of Claggart), and the ambiguous actions of Captain Vere in executing Billy to prevent a threatened mutiny. As before, he found no easy, no final answers.

The party of Transcendence and the party of Darkness were at odds, even though they surreptitiously borrowed from each other. Emerson called Poe "the jingle man"; Poe called Emerson a "Frogpondian Euphuist." Poe's theory of the poem for the poem's sake (a variety of art for art's sake) was incompatible with Emerson's notions of the bardic profundity of great poetry. Yet Poe did not hesitate to incorporate transcendentalism in his long "prose poem" *Eureka* (1848), which is full of a melange of scientific and poetic ideas and truths. Hawthorne imbibed much of the transcendental spirit by his association with Emerson and others during his residence in Concord and his stay at Brook Farm, but he demonstrated his distance from transcendentalism by exaggerating and satirizing its traits in "The Celestial Railroad." Melville satirized both Thoreau and Emerson by turning them into versions of the con artist in his *Confidence-Man* (1857), in which the Emersonian figure Mark Winsome is described as "a kind of cross between a Yankee peddler and a Tartar priest." There is no indication that Emerson ever noticed the work of the obscure novelist Herman Melville.

Whatever the results of these minor literary skirmishes, the truth must be emphasized that the transcendentalists differed as much from each other as they differed from the party of Darkness. And indeed, Poe, Hawthorne, and Melville brought radically different artistic temperaments to the writing of radically different works. "Self-Reliance," *Walden,* "The Fall of the House of Usher," *The Scarlet Letter,* and *Moby-Dick* are classic texts bearing the individual stamp of genius of Emerson, Thoreau, Poe, Hawthorne, and Melville. Our literature is richer for having them all in all their welcome variety.

POETS OF THE TRADITION

The most popular and widely read writers of the period were the "poets of the tradition," including the Harvard Professor of Languages Henry Wadsworth Longfellow, the Quaker abolitionist John Greenleaf Whittier, the Harvard medical professor Oliver Wendell Holmes, and the language professor and (later) ambassador to England James Russell Lowell. Two other poets who were not given their due during their own time also belong in this group: the mystic transcendentalist Jones Very, and the wealthy recluse Frederick Goddard Tuckerman. All of these poets, though they were not great innovators, were writers of distinction and important achievement.

The popular writers were, as Newton Arvin said of Longfellow, poets of "acceptance, rather than rebellion and rejection." They provided readers with reassuring lines and images about the shared values of American life, and the shared memories of American experience, in such poems as Longfellow's "My Lost Youth":

> Often I think of the beautiful town
>   That is seated by the sea;
> Often in thought go up and down
> The pleasant streets of that dear old town,
>   And my youth comes back to me.

or Whittier's "Snow-Bound":

> Shut in from all the world without,
> We sat the clean-winged hearth about,
> Content to let the north-wind roar
> In baffled rage at pane and door
> While the red logs before us beat
> The frost-line back with tropic heat. . . .

or Holmes's "The Chambered Nautilus":

> Build thee more stately mansions, O my soul,
>   As the swift seasons roll!
>   Leave thy low-vaulted past!
> Let each new temple, nobler than the last,
> Shut thee from heaven with a dome more vast,
>   Till thou at length art free,
> Leaving thine outgrown shell by life's unresting sea!

All these poets were vulnerable to the charges Lowell levelled against himself in *A Fable for Critics:*

> There is Lowell, who's striving Parnassus to climb
> With a whole bale of *isms* tied together with rhyme,
> He might get on alone, spite of brambles and boulders,
> But he can't with that bundle he has on his shoulders,
> The top of the hill he will ne'er come nigh reaching
> Till he learns the distinction 'twixt singing and preaching. . . .

These popular poets have been variously called the "Fireside Poets" or the "Schoolroom Poets," titles that suggest (like a "G" rating for movies suitable for a "General" audience) that they are suitable for the whole family, whether read aloud at home or memorized for recitation at school.

Tuckerman and Very, generally unread in their time, wrote a more disturbing poetry. Tuckerman's vision was essentially tragic and stoic, his characteristic tone ironic and wistful:

> And change with hurried hand has swept these scenes:
> The woods have fallen, across the meadow-lot
> The hunter's trail and trap-path is forgot,
> And fire has drunk the swamps of evergreens. . . .

Very, on the other hand, assumed the voice of the Holy Ghost (which he claimed to hear), and wrote self-assured lines, apocalyptic and visionary:

> There is naught for thee by thy haste to gain;
> 'Tis not the swift with Me that win the race;
> Through long endurance of delaying pain,
> Thine opened eye shall see thy Father's face. . . .

Both these poets excelled in the arbitrary restraints of the traditional and familiar sonnet form.

All these poets achieve moments of brilliance in their poems, as Longfellow does in the "Divina Commedia" sonnet sequence, and Lowell in the "Ode Recited at the Harvard Commemoration." And even their work tied closely to the causes of their time, rewards careful attention—Whittier's abolitionist poetry, Lowell's antiwar *Biglow Papers,* or Holmes's anti-Calvinist "Wonderful One-Hoss Shay." Moreover, many of the lines of these poets, memorized as they were by successive generations of school children, are embedded so deeply in the national psyche, as to render criticism irrelevant or futile—like criticism of the Statue of Liberty as a mediocre work of art qua art.

CROSSCURRENTS AND UNDERTOWS

If the major writers of the period—Emerson, Thoreau, Whitman, Poe, Hawthorne, and Melville—are looked upon now as the main currents of the age's literary outpouring, and the poets of the tradition as minor currents in the main stream, then other clusters of writers and works may be seen as the cross currents and undertows, or the eddies and rapids, of the time. Among these clusters worthy of attention are writers of an emerging feminist perspective, American humorists, the anonymous authors of the literature of Native Americans, and writers speaking to the experience and issues of slavery and the Civil War.

EMERGING FEMINIST PERSPECTIVES

Contemporary interest in the writing of women has focused attention on neglected nineteenth-century women writers. The leading woman transcendentalist—Margaret Fuller—has particularly attracted attention, being the author of what might be called the founding document of American feminism: *Woman in the Nineteenth Century* (1845). It is remarkable in anticipating many contemporary women's issues, such as the importance of androgyny ("there is no wholly masculine man, no purely feminine woman") and the importance of feminine self-reliance ("I would have Woman lay aside all thought . . . . of being taught or led by men").

It was only some three years after the appearance of *Woman in the Nineteenth Century* that the first "Woman's Rights Convention" in the United States took place in Seneca Falls, New York, in 1848. It endorsed a revolutionary document drafted by the leader in the woman-suffrage movement, Elizabeth Cady Stanton, entitled "The Declaration of Sentiment." In its opening it copied—but "revised"—the Declaration of Independence: "We hold these truths to be self-evident: that all men and women are created equal." It may come as a surprise to many readers that several of the items on its long list of grievances against men have yet to be redressed.

A number of nineteenth-century women writers created powerful fictions addressing distinctively feminist issues. Elizabeth Barstow Stoddard depicts in her story "Lemorne *Versus* Huell" a protagonist who finally becomes aware of the ways she has been manipulated in courtship. After it is too late she confronts the terrible knowledge, "My husband is a scoundrel." Rose Terry Cooke in a deceptively comic story "How Celia Changed her Mind" portrays a savagely realistic picture of marriages in which men brow-beat and brutalize women. Rebecca Harding Davis in her remarkable account of "Life in the Iron-Mills" paints a sympathetic portrait of a deformed woman of the working class capable of enormous sacrifice in selfless love. And Louisa May Alcott in "Transcendental Wild Oats" presents a fictionalized account of the utopian community of Fruitlands in which her father Bronson Alcott is an ineffective, philosophizing simpleton-innocent, her mother the "drudge" who through sheer strength of spirit and body holds the family together by growing the crops, baking the bread, and insisting on the union of the family. All of these writings show a concern for the plight of women oppressed in open or subtle ways by men, often treated as servants, slaves, or commodities, not as fellow human beings or co-partners in a shared enterprise of living.

AMERICAN HUMORISTS

The long foreground of America's classic comic writer Mark Twain is to be found in a line of American humorists beginning early in the nineteenth century. These writers, usually journalists, deserve attention in their own right. They often invented characters, somewhat like alter egos, who became more famous than themselves. The horse-sense humorist of New England, Seba Smith, used his Jack Downing as a political commentator to increase interest in his newspaper. William Tappan Thompson, of Georgia, invented Major Jones as his cracker-barrel philosopher and storyteller. George Washington Harris invented one of the most famous characters of all, Tennessee mountaineer Sut Lovingood, who told his tales in his own vernacular. Thomas Bangs Thorpe set his narrator on a Mississippi steamboat to tell the tale of "The Big Bear of Arkansas," the archetypal tall tale of America. And Johnson Jones Hooper created a backwoods confidence man in Simon Suggs, who had no scruples about fleecing those experiencing religious ecstasy at a camp meeting held to save souls. Sugg's slogan—"It is good to be shifty in a new country"—became popular beyond his native Alabama. And many of the themes, techniques, and forms of these writers still have currency among American humorists writing today.

LITERATURE OF THE NATIVE AMERICANS

At the time Columbus first set eyes on the New World, he found the lands already occupied by large numbers of natives speaking strange languages. In fact, they had been living for centuries in what was to become the United States—some historians say for tens of thousands of years, having migrated in prehistoric times over a land bridge across the Bering Strait between what is now Alaska and Siberia. Some tribes were settled into communities and cultivated plants for food, while others were primarily hunters and led a nomadic life, following the migration of animals like the American buffalo on the Great Plains. They spoke several hundred dialects, and had no written languages. But they had a rich body of oral literature that was carefully preserved from generation to generation. Like land, literature was communally owned.

Although the Native Americans did not have written forms of language, they had an almost mystical attitude toward words. To them, language had magical properties that could control their environment, affect their lives, and shape their destiny. Words could be used to intercede with the spirit world, the world beyond death. In the oral tradition, according to a contemporary Kiowa, N. Scott Momaday, "Words are rare and therefore dear. They are jealously preserved in the ear and in the mind. Words are spoken with great care, and they are heard." Naming and saying, chanting and singing, telling and describing, are serious activities that involve the whole being and that command the alert respect of listeners.

The occasions for using language artfully were many. One scholar, A. Grove Day in *The Sky Clears,* has provided a catalogue of such occasions:

> The Indians made poems for many reasons: to praise their gods and ask their help in life; to speak to the gods through dramatic performances at seasonal celebrations or initiations or other rites; to work magical cures or enlist supernatural aid in hunting, plant-growing, or horsebreeding; to hymn the praises of the gods or pray to them; to chronicle tribal history; to explain the origins of the world; to teach right conduct; to mourn the dead; to arouse warlike feelings; to compel love; to arouse laughter; to ridicule a rival or bewitch an enemy; to praise famous men; to communicate the poet's private experience; to mark the beauties of nature; to boast of one's personal greatness; to record a vision scene; to characterize the actors in a folk tale; to quiet children; to lighten the burdens of work; to brighten up tribal games; and sometimes, to express simply joy and a spirit of fun.

The language in Native American literature as it has been written down and translated into English is characterized by rhythms and imaginative metaphoric passages that can only be described as poetic. Note, for example, this opening of Chief Seattle's reluctant acceptance of a "reservation," in what is now the state of Washington, in exchange for Indian lands claimed by the whites (1853): "Yonder sky that has wept tears of compassion upon my people for centuries untold, and which to us appears changeless and eternal, may change. My words are like the stars that never change."

A great body of myths, legends, tales, songs, poems, chants, orations, and speeches has accumutated. There has been much controversy about translation into English from the various Indian languages. Some translators prefer to render a literal translation, while others try to capture the spirit of the original. The literal translation often sacrifices the dynamic rhythm and emotional life of the work. A translation too free often violates or distorts the sense. Obviously a careful balance should be struck between the two. The attempt to achieve authenticity is worth the effort, as for example in the poet William Brandon's recreation of this delicately beautiful, haiku-like Quechuan poem:

> The water bug is drawing
> the shadows of evening
> toward him on the water.

SLAVERY AND THE CIVIL WAR

It is not commonly known that a black, David Walker, was one of the first militant abolitionists, publishing in 1829 his *Appeal . . . to the Colored Citizens of the World, But in Particular and Very Expressly to Those of the United States of America.* It was found so inflammatory as to inspire appeals from white southern leaders to the mayor of Boston (where Walker resided as a free black) to suppress it. In 1831, the militant white abolitionist William Lloyd Garrison began publishing in Boston *The Liberator,* calling for the immediate and complete freedom of slaves. The same year, he organized the New England Anti-Slavery Society. And in 1833, responding to a larger antislavery sentiment in the country, the abolitionists formed the American Anti-Slavery Society in Philadelphia, with the Quaker poet John Greenleaf Whittier a participant.

Sympathy for the oppressed slaves was fed by the publication of the slave-escape narratives, among the first and best of which was the *Narrative of the Life of Frederick Douglass,* published in 1845. Douglass fled from Baltimore to New York with false identity papers and sailor's garb, and there found his way to active abolitionists who helped him get to Massachusetts. He became a leader in the abolition movement and was extraordinarily successful as a lecturer. Black female slaves had their own trials and tribulations to bear. Harriet A. Jacobs gave a vivid account of her years as a slave and eventual escape to freedom in *Incidents in the Life of a Slave Girl,* first published in 1861. Another black woman, Frances E. W. Harper, although she had never been a slave, devoted her energies to the antislavery movement and became a popular lecturer dramatically reciting her own emotionally charged antislavery poems, such as "The Slave Mother." Her poetry was published in 1854 as *Poems on Miscellaneous Subjects.*

Perhaps the most inflammatory abolitionist document ever written was *Uncle Tom's Cabin,* published by Harriet Beecher Stowe in 1852. When Lincoln met her in 1862, he referred to her as "the little lady who wrote the book that made this big war." It is a forgivable exaggeration. There can be little doubt, however, that the book (and the extraordinarily popular play which quickly followed in 1853) fed the moral outrage at the degradation and brutalization of slavery and contributed to the ultimate defeat of a demoralized South.

Abraham Lincoln himself, one of the two or three greatest writers ever to hold the presidency, contributed to the cause by such addresses as the "House Divided" speech of 1858, delivered at the Republican State Convention in Illinois when he was nominated as Republican candidate for the U.S. Senate. His Gettysburg address, one of the most eloquent tributes to war dead ever written, quoted in its opening paragraph a predecessor president, Thomas Jefferson, whose style was equal to Lincoln's own. In commemorating the cause for which the soldiers had died at Gettysburg, Lincoln reached back to the Declaration of Independence for some of his phrasing to remind his listeners that the Founders "had brought forth . . . a new nation, conceived in Liberty, and dedicated to the proposition that all men are created equal."

Lincoln's assassination on April 14, 1865, inspired Walt Whitman to write the greatest elegy in American literature—and, indeed, one of the most powerful of any literature. Whitman had by then written most of his masterpieces, published in the first edition of *Leaves of Grass* in 1855 (and also in enlarged editions in 1856 and 1860). As nurse or wound-dresser in the makeshift hospitals on the Virginia battlefields and in the nation's capital, Whitman knew the war firsthand, and he had embodied his experiences of the tragedy of the war in a book of poems, *Drum-Taps* (1865). But the death of Lincoln, whom he had often seen pass in his carriage in the streets of Washington, stunned him as it shocked the country. In "When Lilacs Last in the Dooryard Bloom'd," Whitman expressed personal as well as national grief in an appropriate American measure—free verse.

Just as many came to consider Lincoln as the new western man, we now recognize Whitman as a new poetic voice who wrote a new kind of American poetry. It seems fitting—even fated—that these two great visionaries, passionately committed to liberty, should have their names forever linked through this elegy:

> When lilacs last in the dooryard bloom'd
> And the great star early droop'd in the western sky in the night,
> I mourn'd, and yet shall mourn with ever-returning spring.
>
> Ever-returning spring, trinity sure to me you bring,
> Lilac blooming perennial and drooping star in the west,
> And thought of him I love.

ADDITIONAL READING

D. H. Lawrence, *Studies in Classic American Literature*, 1923.

Lewis Mumford, *The Golden Day*, 1926.

Van Wyck Brooks, *The Flowering of New England, 1815–1865*, 1936.

F. O. Matthiessen, *American Renaissance*, 1941.

Van Wyck Brooks, *The Times of Melville and Whitman*, 1947.

Henry Nash Smith, *Virgin Land*, 1950.

Charles Feidelson, Jr., *Symbolism and American Literature*, 1953.

R. W. B. Lewis, *The American Adam*, 1955.

Perry Miller, *The Raven and the Whale . . . the Era of Poe and Melville*, 1956.

Harry Levin, *The Power of Blackness*, 1958.

Leslie Fiedler, *Love and Death in the American Novel*, 1960, 1966.

Edmund Wilson, *Patriotic Gore*, 1962.

Leo Marx, *The Machine in the Garden*, 1964.

Daniel Boorstin, *The Americans: The National Experience*, 1965.

Tony Tanner, *The Reign of Wonder*, 1965.

Richard Poirier, *A World Elsewhere*, 1966.

James E. Miller, Jr., *Quests Surd and Absurd: Essays in American Literature*, 1967.

James Woodress, *Eight American Authors: A Review of Research and Criticism*, 1971 (includes Emerson, Thoreau, Poe, Hawthorne, Melville, Whitman).

Lawrence Buell, *Literary Transcendentalism*, 1973.

Daniel Aaron, *The Unwritten War: American Writers and the Civil War*, 1973, 1987.

Russel B. Nye, *Society and Culture in America, 1830–1860*, 1974.

Annette Kolodny, *The Lay of the Land*, 1975.

Larzer Ziff, *Literary Democracy: The Declaration of Cultural Independence in America*, 1981.

John Carlos Rowe, *Through the Custom House: Nineteenth-Century American Fiction and Modern Theory*, 1982.

Joel Myerson, ed., *The Transcendentalists: A Review of Research and Criticism*, 1984.

Alfred Kazin, *An American Procession*, 1984.

Earl N. Harbert and Robert A. Rees, *Fifteen American Authors Before 1900: Bibliographic Essays on Research and Criticism*, 1984 (includes Longfellow, Whittier, Holmes, and Lowell).

Jane Tompkins, *Sensational Designs: The Cultural Work of American Fiction, 1790–1860*, 1985.

Albert J. Von Frank, *The Sacred Game: Provincialism and Frontier Consciousness in American Literature*, 1985.

Walter Benn Michaels and Donald E. Pease, eds., *The American Renaissance Reconsidered*, 1985.

Douglas Robinson, *American Apocalypses: The Image of the End of the World in American Literature*, 1985.

Roger O. Rock, *The Native American in American Literature: A Selectively Annotated Bibliography*, 1985.

Robert Weisbuch, *Atlantic Double-Cross: American Literature and British Influence in the Age of Emerson*, 1986.

Irvin Howe, *The American Newness: Culture and Politics in the Age of Emerson*, 1986.

Sacvan Bercovitch and Myra Jehlen, eds., *Ideology and Classic American Literature*, 1986.

Donald Pease, *Visionary Compacts: American Renaissance Writings in Cultural Context*, 1987.

David S. Reynolds, *Beneath the American Renaissance: The Subversive Imagination in the Age of Emerson and Melville*, 1988.

Ann Allen Shockley, ed., *Afro-American Women Writers, 1746–1933: An Anthology and Critical Guide*, 1988.

David Leverenz, *Manhood and the American Renaissance*, 1989.

THE TRANSCENDENTAL SPIRIT

RALPH WALDO EMERSON   HENRY DAVID THOREAU

"There is one animal, one plant, one matter, and one force. The laws of light and of heat translate each other—so do the laws of sound and of color; and so galvinism, electricity, and magnetism are varied forms of the selfsame energy. While the student ponders this immense unity, he observes that all things in Nature, the animals, the mountain, the river, the seasons, wood, iron, stone, vapor, have a mysterious relation to his thoughts and his life; their growths, decays, quality and use so curiously resemble himself, in parts and wholes, that he is compelled to speak by means of them. His words and his thoughts are framed by their help. Every noun is an image. Nature gives him, sometimes in a flattered likeness, sometimes in caricature, a copy of every humor and shade in his character and mind. The world is an immense picture-book of every passage in human life. Every object he beholds is the mask of a man."

Ralph Waldo Emerson, "Poetry and Imagination"

RALPH WALDO EMERSON
(1803–1882)

Ralph Waldo Emerson was the first major American writer to escape being labelled a British copy. Credited with writing the American Declaration of Intellectual Independence, he established his own "original relation with the universe." His reach was international. He was a life-long friend of the Scotsman Thomas Carlyle, the two influencing each other in subtle ways. And he was read closely by the German philosopher Friedrich Nietzsche, whose work reflected Emersonian ideas. He has been called the fountainhead of American literature because the currents of American literature carry his insights and attitudes down to the present day. In his own time, his literary personality became a magnet attracting other first-rate minds to Concord, Massachusetts—Margaret Fuller, Nathaniel Hawthorne, and Henry David Thoreau (who was born there and stayed on). American writers have been unable to ignore him. Some, like Walt Whitman and Wallace Stevens, took much but spoke with their own voices. Others, like Herman Melville and T. S. Eliot, rejected him and were shaped in part by their very rejection. He has been, in effect, enduring and inescapable.

Emerson was born in 1803 into a family whose ancestors had been ministers going back eight generations to the Puritan period. The Reverend William Emerson, minister of the First Church of Boston (originally Calvinist, but turned Unitarian) died when Emerson was eight years old, leaving a widow with six young children. Times were hard, but Emerson credits his Aunt Mary Moody Emerson as "the kind Aunt whose cares instructed my youth."

Despite the family's straitened circumstances, Emerson was able to attend the elite Boston Latin School and Harvard, which he entered at the age of fourteen, graduating in 1821. His career at school appears to have been undistinguished, perhaps in part because he worked, waiting at tables and tutoring. But it was there, in 1820, that he began keeping a journal which was to become the center of his inner life and the base and origin of his literary career. He very early saw it as his "savings bank" on which he would draw later for expressions and ideas incorporated in his lectures, which were still later to be refined into essays.

After a stint of teaching, which did not appeal to him, he attended Harvard's Divinity School and was ordained pastor at the Second Church of Boston in 1829. This same year he married Ellen Louisa Tucker, who died from tuberculosis some seventeen months later. Emerson found it difficult to reconcile himself to her death, as he found it difficult to adjust to his ministry. He resigned in 1832 and at a farewell sermon explained that he could no longer administer the sacrament of the Lord's Supper because he no longer believed in it. But Emerson's disenchantment with the ministry was more general and more profound.

Emerson travelled in Europe in 1832–33, meeting such literary figures as Samuel Taylor Coleridge, William Wordsworth, and Thomas Carlyle. On his return to Boston, Emerson gave his first lecture to the Natural History Society—and discovered his profession. The Lyceum system, offering lectures for self-improvement as well as entertainment, had only shortly before been established in America. Emerson was to become a familiar figure on the lyceum platform.

In 1834, Emerson bought property and settled in Concord, Massachusetts; the following year he married Lydia Jackson, a union that brought domestic comfort and happiness, as well as four children. Emerson settled in for his life's work of meditating, writing, lecturing, and publishing. By this time he was steeped in the literature that would shape his thinking—Plato, the Neoplatonists, the German idealists, the English romantics, the sacred texts of the orient, Montaigne, Swedenborg, and Thomas Carlyle.

In 1836, at the age of thirty-three, Emerson published his first book, *Nature*. In its most famous sentence, he quickly showed that in his personal engagement with nature he transcended his rational being and became a kind of mystic: "I become a transparent eyeball; I am nothing; the currents of the Universal Being circulate through me; I am part and parcel of God." After extensive examination of the way in which the individual apprehends nature, he asserted: "The best moments of life are these delicious awakenings of the higher powers."

In this first book Emerson touched again and again on an idea that would last his lifetime: of the two higher faculties (Understanding and Reason), Understanding was the inferior faculty that involved the intellect and logic in the analysis of nature in all its multiplicity; Reason, on the other hand, was the superior faculty that involved the intuition or higher imagination in perceiving directly into the heart of nature's unity. Thus in Emerson's view, what had been called an "Age of Reason" might better be characterized as an "Age of Understanding," its brightest stars of thought, such as John Locke, bound by the limitations of this latter faculty. To discover and delineate the higher faculty of genuinely intuitive Reason, Emerson put together a new constellation of stellar writers and texts, including Plato, Kant, Swedenborg, and the oriental religious works.

But it is misleading to suggest that Emerson's thought was all derivative. Had it been, he would have been in violation of every principle he enunciated in "The American Scholar"—his 1837 Phi Beta Kappa address at Harvard—and "Self-Reliance"—an essay made up of passages from his *Journal*, some dating back to the early and mid-1830s. The first has been called America's *intellectual* Declaration of Independence by Oliver Wendell Holmes; the latter might well have been styled the individual American's *spiritual* Declaration of Independence. They are filled with assertions that startle with their free, bold, and electrifying thought: "The one thing in the world, of value, is the active soul"; "We have listened too long to the courtly muses of Europe"; "Speak your latent conviction, and it shall be the universal sense"; "Nothing is at last sacred but the integrity of your own mind."

In 1838, Emerson was invited to address the graduating class at Harvard's Divinity School. In this lecture to those on the verge of entering the ministry, Emerson spoke of "the universal decay and now almost death of faith in society. . . . The church seems to totter to its fall, almost all life extinct." The creed of the Puritans, he observed, "is passing away, and none arises in its room. I think no man can go with his thoughts about him into one of our churches, without feeling that what hold the public worship had on men is gone, or going." Emerson's strong words scandalized the clergy, and there was a storm of protest. He was not invited to speak again at Harvard for thirty years.

Through his lectures and publications, Emerson's thought began to attract the attention of other free and brave spirits such as Margaret Fuller, Amos Bronson Alcott, and Henry David Thoreau. Concord became an intellectual center, with Emerson as a kind of nucleus. The Transcendental Club came into being, and with it a journal, *The Dial*. In 1840 Margaret Fuller became the first editor, with Emerson replacing her in 1842. Thoreau, who came to live as a handyman in the Emerson household in 1841, assisted Emerson in the editing. Alcott, father of Louisa May, published his transcendental "Orphic Sayings" in *The Dial*. Nathaniel Hawthorne, after having lived for a period in the transcendental utopian community of Brook Farm in West Roxbury, settled into Concord's Old Manse in 1842. Concord for a time was the center of vitality in American literature.

Emerson's reputation in America and England was enlarged and solidified with the publication of the First Series of *Essays* in 1841. It contained some of his most spirited, most tradition-shattering works—"Self-Reliance," "Love," "Friendship," "The Over-Soul," and "Circles." Thomas Carlyle provided a Preface for the English edition of *Essays*: "Sharp gleams of insight arrest us by their pure intellectuality; here and there, in heroic rusticism, a tone of modest manfulness, of mild invincibility, low-voiced but lion-strong, makes us too, thrill with a noble pride."

With this book, Emerson hit his stride as a writer. Other books followed. *Essays*, Second Series, appeared in 1844, containing "The Poet" and "Experience." On the insistence of his publisher, Emerson issued his *Poems* in 1846 (dated 1847). In 1849, he published two volumes: *Nature, Addresses, and Lectures*, containing "The American Scholar" and "Divinity School Address," and *Representative Men*, with important essays on "Plato, the Philosopher," "Swedenborg, the Mystic," and "Montaigne, the Skeptic," all writers of major influence on Emerson. By the end of this decade, Emerson's reputation as the preeminent writer of America was secure.

The professional triumph was not without personal cost, however. Emerson's son Waldo died in 1842 at the age of five. Emerson was shattered, and wrote in his *Journal* of his bitterness. He remarked to a friend, "I grieve that I cannot grieve," and attempted in the poem "Threnody" to come to terms with the loss. So devoted to the life of the mind, Emerson revealed in his *Journal* his haunting fear that he lacked human warmth, as Margaret Fuller had charged. It was as though the transcendental heights toward which he was constantly striving bestowed along with their purity a chilling of the common passions.

Although Emerson's personal relations with his close friends Margaret Fuller and Henry David Thoreau were sometimes strained, Emerson gave them their full due in the privacy of his *Journal*. His respect for Margaret Fuller's powers was set down on her tragic death by drowning in 1850: "Her heart, which few knew, was as great as her mind, which all knew. . . . I have lost in her my audience." On going through Thoreau's *Journal* after his death in 1862, Emerson wrote: "In reading him, I find the same thought, the same spirit that is in me, but he takes a step beyond, and illustrates by excellent images that which I should have conveyed in a sleepy generality."

Emerson's quick response to Walt Whitman on receiving a copy of Whitman's *Leaves of Grass* in July 1855 suggests the readiness with which he responded to new work out of his own deepest feelings: "I find it the most extraordinary piece of wit and wisdom that America has yet contributed." Although Whitman's public use of the letter no doubt cooled Emerson's ardency, he never repudiated his own extraordinary—and just—flash of appreciation of Whitman's genius.

Emerson continued to publish books that, more frequently than not, appeared first in embryo in the *Journal,* then were presented as lectures, and finally placed in print. *English Traits* was published in 1856, *The Conduct of Life* (which Carlyle hailed as his best book) in 1860, and *Society and Solitude* in 1870. But much of Emerson's time was taken up with the overpowering issues and events of the mid-nineteenth century. His reluctance to abandon his study to address contemporary moral issues receded as he became concerned with slavery and as the nation split apart during the Civil War. By the 1870s his major work was behind him, and when he died in 1882, his mind had faded to a serene and benevolent blank.

Much has been written about the defects of Emerson's prose and poetry. It is possible to see the defects not as weaknesses but as part of the strategy of his original form. The lack of logical sequentiality and rational structure in the essays may be attributed to Emerson's deliberate avoidance of intellectual coherence and his courting of intuitive form and mystical order. The lack of harmonious, mellifluous, and dulcet lines in his poems may be attributed to his deliberate smiting of the chords of the harp "rudely and hard" in order to convey "secrets of the solar track,/ Sparks of the supersolar blaze" (see "Merlin"). In any event, with Emerson it is a mistake to separate too deeply the prose and the poetry: the essays may be read on one level as imaginative poems; the poems on one level as distillations of the ideas gleaming in the prose.

ADDITIONAL READING

Selections from Ralph Waldo Emerson: An Organic Anthology, ed. Stephen E. Whicher, 1957; *Emerson in His Journals,* ed. Joel Porte, 1982.

Oliver Wendell Holmes, *Ralph Waldo Emerson,* 1898, rpt. 1980; Ralph L. Rusk, *Life of Ralph Waldo Emerson,* 1949; Vivian C. Hopkins, *Spires of Form: A Study of Emerson's Aesthetic Theory,* 1951; Sherman Paul, *Emerson's Angle of Vision: Man and Nature in American Experience,* 1952; Frederick Ives Carpenter, *Emerson Handbook,* 1953; Stephen E. Whicher, *Freedom and Fate: An Inner Life of Ralph Waldo Emerson,* 1953; Walter Harding, *Emerson's Library,* 1967; Joel Porte, *Emerson and Thoreau: Transcendentalists in Conflict,* 1967; Milton R. Konvitz, ed., *The Recognition of Ralph Waldo Emerson,* 1972; Lawrence Buell, *Literary Transcendentalism,* 1973; Hyatt Waggoner, *Emerson as Poet,* 1975; R. A. Yoder, *Emerson and the Orphic Poet in America,* 1978; David Porter, *Emerson and Literary Change,* 1978; Joel Porte, *Representative Man, Ralph Waldo Emerson in His Time,* 1979; Gay Wilson Allen, *Waldo Emerson: A Biography,* 1981; Donald Yannella, *Ralph Waldo Emerson,* 1982; B. L. Packer, *Emerson's Fall,* 1982; Joel Porte, ed., *Emerson: Prospect and Retrospect,* 1982; Jerome Loving, *Emerson, Whitman, and the American Muse,* 1982; Leonard Neufeldt, *The House of Emerson,* 1982; Joel Myerson, ed., *Emerson Centenary Essays,* 1982; David Robinson, *Apostle of Culture: Emerson as Preacher and Lecturer,* 1982; Robert E. Burkholder and Joel Myerson, eds., *Critical Essays on Ralph Waldo Emerson,* 1983; John McAleer, *Ralph Waldo Emerson: Days of Encounter,* 1984; Julie Ellison, *Emerson's Romantic Style,* 1984; Irving Howe, *The American Newness: Culture and Politics in the Age of Emerson,* 1987; Richard Poirier, *The Renewal of Literature,* 1987; Lawrence Rosenwald, *Emerson and the Art of the Diary,* 1988; John Michael, *Emerson and Skepticism: The Cipher of the World,* 1988.

TEXTS

The Collected Works of Ralph Waldo Emerson, ed. Alfred R. Ferguson, 1971–: Vol. I, *Nature, Addresses, and Lectures,* ed. Robert E. Spiller and Alfred R. Ferguson, 1971; Vol. II, *Essays: First Series,* ed. Joseph Slater, Alfred R. Ferguson, and Jean Ferguson Carr, 1979; Vol. III, *Essays: Second Series,* ed. Joseph Slater, Alfred R. Ferguson, and Jean Ferguson Carr, 1983. *The Complete Works of Ralph Waldo Emerson,* 12 vols. (Centenary Edition), ed. Edward Waldo Emerson, 1903–04: Vol. 6, *The Conduct of Life;* Vol. 9, *Poems. The Letters of Ralph Waldo Emerson,* 6 vols., ed. Ralph L. Rusk, 1939. *The Correspondence of Emerson and Carlyle,* ed. Joseph Slater, 1964. *The Journals of Ralph Waldo Emerson,* 10 vols., ed. Edward Waldo Emerson and

W. E. Forbes, 1909–14, provides the basic text, occasionally corrected in consultation with *The Journals and Miscellaneous Notebooks of Ralph Waldo Emerson*, 16 vols., ed. W. H. Gilman et al., 1960–82.

Nature[1]

A subtle chain of countless rings
The next unto the farthest brings;
The eye reads omens where it goes,
And speaks all languages the rose;
And, striving to be man, the worm
Mounts through all the spires of form.

INTRODUCTION

Our age is retrospective. It builds the sepulchres of the fathers. It writes biographies, histories, and criticism. The foregoing generations beheld God and nature face to face; we, through their eyes. Why should not we also enjoy an original relation to the universe? Why should not we have a poetry and philosophy of insight and not of tradition, and a religion by revelation to us, and not the history of theirs? Embosomed for a season in nature, whose floods of life stream around and through us, and invite us by the powers they supply, to action proportioned to nature, why should we grope among the dry bones of the past, or put the living generation into masquerade out of its faded wardrobe? The sun shines to-day also. There is more wool and flax in the fields. There are new lands, new men, new thoughts. Let us demand our own works and laws and worship.

Undoubtedly we have no questions to ask which are unanswerable. We must trust the perfection of the creation so far, as to believe that whatever curiosity the order of things has awakened in our minds, the order of things can satisfy. Every man's condition is a solution in hieroglyphic to those inquiries he would put. He acts it as life, before he apprehends it as truth. In like manner, nature is already, in its forms and tendencies, describing its own design. Let us interrogate the great apparition, that shines so peacefully around us. Let us inquire, to what end is nature?

All science has one aim, namely, to find a theory of nature. We have theories of races and of functions, but scarcely yet a remote approach to an idea of creation. We are now so far from the road to truth, that religious teachers dispute and hate each other, and speculative men are esteemed unsound and frivolous. But to a sound judgment, the most abstract truth is the most practical. Whenever a true theory appears, it will be its own evidence. Its test is, that it will explain all phenomena. Now many are thought not only unexplained but inexplicable; as language, sleep, madness, dreams, beasts, sex.

Philosophically considered, the universe is composed of Nature and the Soul. Strictly speaking, therefore, all that is separate from us, all which Philosophy distinguishes as the NOT ME, that is, both nature and art, all other men and my own body, must be ranked under this name, NATURE. In enumerating the values of nature and casting up their sum, I shall use the word in both senses; —in its common and in its philosophical import. In inquiries so general as our present one,

---

[1]*Nature*, Emerson's first book and the first major statement of American transcendentalism, appeared in 1836. Instead of the present epigraph, it contained a quotation from Plotinus: "Nature is but an image or imitation of wisdom, the last thing of the soul; nature being a thing which doth only do, but not know." The poem "Nature" replaced this epigraph when the work was included in Emerson's *Nature, Addresses, and Lectures* (1849).

the inaccuracy is not material; no confusion of thought will occur. *Nature,* in the common sense, refers to essences unchanged by man; space, the air, the river, the leaf. *Art* is applied to the mixture of his will with the same things, as in a house, a canal, a statue, a picture. But his operations taken together are so insignificant, a little chipping, baking, patching, and washing, that in an impression so grand as that of the world on the human mind, they do not vary the result.

CHAPTER I. NATURE

To go into solitude, a man needs to retire as much from his chamber as from society. I am not solitary whilst I read and write, though nobody is with me. But if a man would be alone, let him look at the stars. The rays that come from those heavenly worlds, will separate between him and vulgar things. One might think the atmosphere was made transparent with this design, to give man, in the heavenly bodies, the perpetual presence of the sublime. Seen in the streets of cities, how great they are! If the stars should appear one night in a thousand years, how would men believe and adore; and preserve for many generations the remembrance of the city of God which had been shown! But every night come out these envoys of beauty, and light the universe with their admonishing smile.

The stars awaken a certain reverence, because though always present, they are always inaccessible; but all natural objects make a kindred impression, when the mind is open to their influence. Nature never wears a mean appearance. Neither does the wisest man extort all her secret, and lose his curiosity by finding out all her perfection. Nature never became a toy to a wise spirit. The flowers, the animals, the mountains, reflected all the wisdom of his best hour, as much as they had delighted the simplicity of his childhood.

When we speak of nature in this manner, we have a distinct but most poetical sense in the mind. We mean the integrity of impression made by manifold natural objects. It is this which distinguishes the stick of timber of the wood-cutter, from the tree of the poet. The charming landscape which I saw this morning, is indubitably made up of some twenty or thirty farms. Miller owns this field, Locke that, and Manning the woodland beyond. But none of them owns the landscape. There is a property in the horizon which no man has but he whose eye can integrate all the parts, that is, the poet. This is the best part of these men's farms, yet to this their warranty-deeds give no title.

To speak truly, few adult persons can see nature. Most persons do not see the sun. At least they have a very superficial seeing. The sun illuminates only the eye of the man, but shines into the eye and the heart of the child. The lover of nature is he whose inward and outward senses are still truly adjusted to each other; who has retained the spirit of infancy even into the era of manhood. His intercourse with heaven and earth, becomes part of his daily food. In the presence of nature, a wild delight runs through the man, in spite of real sorrows. Nature says,—he is my creature, and maugre[2] all his impertinent griefs, he shall be glad with me. Not the sun or the summer alone, but every hour and season yields its tribute of delight; for every hour and change corresponds to and authorizes a different state of the mind, from breathless noon to grimmest midnight. Nature is a setting that fits equally well a comic or a mourning piece. In good health, the air is a cordial of incredible virtue. Crossing a bare common, in snow puddles, at twilight, under a clouded sky, without having in my thoughts any occurrence of special good fortune, I have enjoyed a perfect exhilaration. Almost I fear to think how glad I am. In the woods too, a man casts off his years, as the snake his slough, and at what period soever of life, is always a child. In the woods, is perpetual youth. Within

---

[2]In spite of.

these plantations of God, a decorum and sanctity reign, a perennial festival is dressed, and the guest sees not how he should tire of them in a thousand years. In the woods, we return to reason and faith. There I feel that nothing can befal me in life,—no disgrace, no calamity, (leaving me my eyes,) which nature cannot repair. Standing on the bare ground,—my head bathed by the blithe air, and uplifted into infinite space,—all mean egotism vanishes. I become a transparent eyeball. I am nothing. I see all. The currents of the Universal Being circulate through me; I am part or particle of God. The name of the nearest friend sounds then foreign and accidental. To be brothers, to be acquaintances,—master or servant, is then a trifle and a disturbance. I am the lover of uncontained and immortal beauty. In the wilderness, I find something more dear and connate[3] than in streets or villages. In the tranquil landscape, and especially in the distant line of the horizon, man beholds somewhat as beautiful as his own nature.

The greatest delight which the fields and woods minister, is the suggestion of an occult relation between man and the vegetable. I am not alone and unacknowledged. They nod to me and I to them. The waving of the boughs in the storm, is new to me and old. It takes me by surprise, and yet is not unknown. Its effect is like that of a higher thought or a better emotion coming over me, when I deemed I was thinking justly or doing right.

Yet it is certain that the power to produce this delight, does not reside in nature, but in man, or in a harmony of both. It is necessary to use these pleasures with great temperance. For, nature is not always tricked in holiday attire, but the same scene which yesterday breathed perfume and glittered as for the frolic of the nymphs, is overspread with melancholy today. Nature always wears the colors of the spirit. To a man laboring under calamity, the heat of his own fire hath sadness in it. Then, there is a kind of contempt of the landscape felt by him who has just lost by death a dear friend. The sky is less grand as it shuts down over less worth in the population.

CHAPTER II. COMMODITY

Whoever considers the final cause of the world, will discern a multitude of uses that enter as parts into that result. They all admit of being thrown into one of the following classes: Commodity; Beauty; Language; and Discipline.

Under the general name of Commodity, I rank all those advantages which our senses owe to nature. This, of course, is a benefit which is temporary and mediate, not ultimate, like its service to the soul. Yet although low, it is perfect in its kind, and is the only use of nature which all men apprehend. The misery of man appears like childish petulance, when we explore the steady and prodigal provision that has been made for his support and delight on this green ball which floats him through the heavens. What angels invented these splendid ornaments, these rich conveniences, this ocean of air above, this ocean of water beneath, this firmament of earth between? this zodiac of lights, this tent of dropping clouds, this striped coat of climates, this fourfold year? Beasts, fire, water, stones, and corn serve him. The field is at once his floor, his work-yard, his play-ground, his garden, and his bed.

> "More servants wait on man
> Than he'll take notice of."——[1]

Nature, in its ministry to man, is not only the material, but is also the process and the result. All the parts incessantly work into each other's hands for the profit of man. The wind sows the seed; the sun evaporates the sea; the wind blows the

---

[3]Inborn, innate.
[1]From "Man" by the English poet George Herbert (1593–1633); the poem is quoted at length in Chapter VIII, "Prospects."

vapor to the field; the ice, on the other side of the planet, condenses rain on this; the rain feeds the plant; the plant feeds the animal; and thus the endless circulations of the divine charity nourish man.

The useful arts are but reproductions or new combinations by the wit of man, of the same natural benefactors. He no longer waits for favoring gales, but by means of steam, he realizes the fable of Æolus's bag,[2] and carries the two and thirty winds in the boiler of his boat. To diminish friction, he paves the road with iron bars, and, mounting a coach with a ship-load of men, animals, and merchandise behind him, he darts through the country, from town to town, like an eagle or a swallow through the air. By the aggregate of these aids, how is the face of the world changed, from the era of Noah to that of Napoleon! The private poor man hath cities, ships, canals, bridges, built for him. He goes to the post-office, and the human race run on his errands; to the book-shop, and the human race read and write of all that happens, for him; to the court-house, and nations repair his wrongs. He sets his house upon the road, and the human race go forth every morning, and shovel out the snow, and cut a path for him.

But there is no need of specifying particulars in this class of uses. The catalogue is endless, and the examples so obvious, that I shall leave them to the reader's reflection, with the general remark, that this mercenary benefit is one which has respect to a farther good. A man is fed, not that he may be fed, but that he may work.

CHAPTER III. BEAUTY

A nobler want of man is served by nature, namely, the love of Beauty.

The ancient Greeks called the world κόσμος,[1] beauty. Such is the constitution of all things, or such the plastic[2] power of the human eye, that the primary forms, as the sky, the mountain, the tree, the animal, give us a delight *in and for themselves;* a pleasure arising from outline, color, motion, and grouping. This seems partly owing to the eye itself. The eye is the best of artists. By the mutual action of its structure and of the laws of light, perspective is produced, which integrates every mass of objects, of what character soever, into a well colored and shaded globe, so that where the particular objects are mean and unaffecting, the landscape which they compose, is round and symmetrical. And as the eye is the best composer, so light is the first of painters. There is no object so foul that intense light will not make beautiful. And the stimulus it affords to the sense, and a sort of infinitude which it hath, like space and time, make all matter gay. Even the corpse hath its own beauty. But beside this general grace diffused over nature, almost all the individual forms are agreeable to the eye, as is proved by our endless imitations of some of them, as the acorn, the grape, the pine-cone, the wheat-ear, the egg, the wings and forms of most birds, the lion's claw, the serpent, the butterfly, sea-shells, flames, clouds, buds, leaves, and the forms of many trees, as the palm.

For better consideration, we may distribute the aspects of Beauty in a threefold manner.

1. First, the simple perception of natural forms is a delight. The influence of the forms and actions in nature, is so needful to man, that, in its lowest functions, it seems to lie on the confines of commodity and beauty. To the body and mind which have been cramped by noxious work or company, nature is medicinal and restores their tone. The tradesman, the attorney comes out of the din and craft of the street, and sees the sky and the woods, and is a man again. In their eternal

---

[2]In the *Odyssey* (Book X), Odysseus receives from the god of the winds, Aeolus, a supply of winds in a bag. The sailors open the bag and the escaping winds cause a storm.

[1]Cosmos.
[2]Shaping.

calm, he finds himself. The health of the eye seems to demand a horizon. We are never tired, so long as we can see far enough.

But in other hours, Nature satisfies the soul purely by its loveliness, and without any mixture of corporeal benefit. I have seen the spectacle of morning from the hill-top over against my house, from day-break to sun-rise, with emotions which an angel might share. The long slender bars of cloud float like fishes in the sea of crimson light. From the earth, as a shore, I look out into that silent sea. I seem to partake its rapid transformations: the active enchantment reaches my dust, and I dilate and conspire with the morning wind. How does Nature deify us with a few and cheap elements! Give me health and a day, and I will make the pomp of emperors ridiculous. The dawn is my Assyria; the sun-set and moon-rise my Paphos,[3] and unimaginable realms of faerie; broad noon shall be my England of the senses and the understanding; the night shall be my Germany of mystic philosophy and dreams.[4]

Not less excellent, except for our less susceptibility in the afternoon, was the charm, last evening, of a January sunset. The western clouds divided and subdivided themselves into pink flakes modulated with tints of unspeakable softness; and the air had so much life and sweetness, that it was a pain to come within doors. What was it that nature would say? Was there no meaning in the live repose of the valley behind the mill, and which Homer or Shakspeare could not reform for me in words? The leafless trees become spires of flame in the sunset, with the blue east for their background, and the stars of the dead calices[5] of flowers, and every withered stem and stubble rimed with frost, contribute something to the mute music.

The inhabitants of cities suppose that the country landscape is pleasant only half the year. I please myself with observing the graces of the winter scenery, and believe that we are as much touched by it as by the genial influences of summer. To the attentive eye, each moment of the year has its own beauty, and in the same field, it beholds, every hour, a picture which was never seen before, and which shall never be seen again. The heavens change every moment, and reflect their glory or gloom on the plains beneath. The state of the crop in the surrounding farms alters the expression of the earth from week to week. The succession of native plants in the pastures and road-sides, which make the silent clock by which time tells the summer hours, will make even the divisions of the day sensible to a keen observer. The tribes of birds and insects, like the plants punctual to their time, follow each other, and the year has room for all. By water-courses, the variety is greater. In July, the blue pontederia or pickerel-weed blooms in large beds in the shallow parts of our pleasant river,[6] and swarms with yellow butterflies in continual motion. Art cannot rival this pomp of purple and gold. Indeed the river is a perpetual gala, and boasts each month a new ornament.

But this beauty of Nature which is seen and felt as beauty, is the least part. The shows of day, the dewy morning, the rainbow, mountains, orchards in blossom, stars, moonlight, shadows in still water, and the like, if too eagerly hunted, become shows merely, and mock us with their unreality. Go out of the house to see the moon, and 't is mere tinsel; it will not please as when its light shines upon your necessary journey. The beauty that shimmers in the yellow afternoons of October, who ever could clutch it? Go forth to find it, and it is gone: 't is only a mirage as you look from the windows of diligence.

2. The presence of a higher, namely, of the spiritual element is essential to its

---

[3] Assyria, an opulent and splendid Near East empire of antiquity; Paphos, an old city of Cyprus containing a temple to Aphrodite, goddess of love.
[4] Such rational English philosophers as Locke and Hume

are implicitly contrasted with German idealists such as Hegel and Kant.
[5] Calyx, the sepals or leaves cupping the flower at its base.
[6] The Concord River.

perfection. The high and divine beauty which can be loved without effeminacy, is that which is found in combination with the human will, and never separate. Beauty is the mark God sets upon virtue. Every natural action is graceful. Every heroic act is also decent, and causes the place and the bystanders to shine. We are taught by great actions that the universe is the property of every individual in it. Every rational creature has all nature for his dowry and estate. It is his, if he will. He may divest himself of it; he may creep into a corner, and abdicate his kingdom, as most men do, but he is entitled to the world by his constitution. In proportion to the energy of his thought and will, he takes up the world into himself. "All those things for which men plough, build, or sail, obey virtue;" said an ancient historian.[7] "The winds and waves," said Gibbon, "are always on the side of the ablest navigators."[8] So are the sun and moon and all the stars of heaven. When a noble act is done,—perchance in a scene of great natural beauty; when Leonidas and his three hundred martyrs consume one day in dying, and the sun and moon come each and look at them once in the steep defile of Thermopylæ;[9] when Arnold Winkelried, in the high Alps, under the shadow of the avalanche, gathers in his side a sheaf of Austrian spears to break the line for his comrades;[10] are not these heroes entitled to add the beauty of the scene to the beauty of the deed? When the bark of Columbus nears the shore of America;—before it, the beach lined with savages, fleeing out of all their huts of cane; the sea behind; and the purple mountains of the Indian Archipelago around, can we separate the man from the living picture? Does not the New World clothe his form with her palm-groves and savannahs as fit drapery? Ever does natural beauty steal in like air, and envelope great actions. When Sir Harry Vane was dragged up the Tower-hill, sitting on a sled, to suffer death, as the champion of the English laws, one of the multitude cried out to him, "You never sate on so glorious a seat." Charles II., to intimidate the citizens of London, caused the patriot Lord Russell to be drawn in an open coach, through the principal streets of the city, on his way to the scaffold. "But," to use the simple narrative of his biographer, "the multitude imagined they saw liberty and virtue sitting by his side."[11] In private places, among sordid objects, an act of truth or heroism seems at once to draw to itself the sky as its temple, the sun as its candle. Nature stretcheth out her arms to embrace man, only let his thoughts be of equal greatness. Willingly does she follow his steps with the rose and the violet, and bend her lines of grandeur and grace to the decoration of her darling child. Only let his thoughts be of equal scope, and the frame will suit the picture. A virtuous man is in unison with her works, and makes the central figure of the visible sphere. Homer, Pindar, Socrates, Phocion, associate themselves fully in our memory with the whole geography and climate of Greece.[12] The visible heavens and earth sympathize with Jesus. And in common life, whosoever has seen a person of powerful character and happy genius, will have remarked how easily he took all things along with him,—the persons, the opinions, and the day, and nature became ancillary to a man.

3. There is still another aspect under which the beauty of the world may be viewed, namely, as it becomes an object of the intellect. Beside the relation of

---

[7]Caius Sallustius Crispus, Roman historian of the first century B.C., author of *The Conspiracy of Catiline.* See Chapter II.

[8]Edward Gibbon (1737–1794), English historian, from *The Decline and Fall of the Roman Empire,* Vol. II, Chapter 68.

[9]King Leonidas of Sparta and his men died defending the pass at Thermopylae against the invading Persians in 480 B.C.

[10]Arnold Winkelried at the Battle of Sempach (1386) attracted all the Austrian spears and thus enabled his compatriots to defeat the disarmed enemy, assuring Swiss independence.

[11]Sir Harry Vane and Lord Russell were British leaders and patriots who were executed for treason during the reign of Charles II, Vane in 1662 on Tower-hill (location of the gallows) and Russell in 1683.

[12]Homer, ancient Greek poet and presumed author of the *Iliad* and the *Odyssey;* Pindar, Greek lyric poet (522?–443 B.C.); Socrates, Greek philosopher of the fifth century B.C. known through writings of his disciple, Plato; Phocion, Athenian political and military leader of the fourth century B.C.

things to virtue, they have a relation to thought. The intellect searches out the absolute order of things as they stand in the mind of God, and without the colors of affection.[13] The intellectual and the active powers seem to succeed each other in man, and the exclusive activity of the one, generates the exclusive activity of the other. There is something unfriendly in each to the other, but they are like the alternate periods of feeding and working in animals; each prepares and certainly will be followed by the other. Therefore does beauty, which, in relation to actions, as we have seen, comes unsought, and comes because it is unsought, remain for the apprehension and pursuit of the intellect; and then again, in its turn, of the active power. Nothing divine dies. All good is eternally reproductive. The beauty of nature reforms itself in the mind, and not for barren contemplation, but for new creation.

All men are in some degree impressed by the face of the world; some men even to delight. This love of beauty is Taste. Others have the same love in such excess, that, not content with admiring, they seek to embody it in new forms. The creation of beauty is Art.

The production of a work of art throws a light upon the mystery of humanity. A work of art is an abstract or epitome of the world. It is the result or expression of nature, in miniature. For although the works of nature are innumerable and all different, the result or the expression of them all is similar and single. Nature is a sea of forms radically alike and even unique. A leaf, a sun-beam, a landscape, the ocean, make an analogous impression on the mind. What is common to them all,—that perfectness and harmony, is beauty. Therefore the standard of beauty is the entire circuit of natural forms,—the totality of nature; which the Italians expressed by defining beauty "il piu nell' uno."[14] Nothing is quite beautiful alone: nothing but is beautiful in the whole. A single object is only so far beautiful as it suggests this universal grace. The poet, the painter, the sculptor, the musician, the architect, seek each to concentrate this radiance of the world on one point, and each in his several work to satisfy the love of beauty which stimulates him to produce. Thus is Art, a nature passed through the alembic[15] of man. Thus in art, does nature work through the will of a man filled with the beauty of her first works.

The world thus exists to the soul to satisfy the desire of beauty. Extend this element to the uttermost, and I call it an ultimate end. No reason can be asked or given why the soul seeks beauty. Beauty, in its largest and profoundest sense, is one expression for the universe. God is the all-fair. Truth, and goodness, and beauty, are but different faces of the same All. But beauty in nature is not ultimate. It is the herald of inward and eternal beauty, and is not alone a solid and satisfactory good. It must therefore stand as a part and not as yet the last or highest expression of the final cause of Nature.

CHAPTER IV. LANGUAGE

A third use which Nature subserves to man is that of Language. Nature is the vehicle of thought, and in a simple, double, and threefold degree.

1. Words are signs of natural facts.
2. Particular natural facts are symbols of particular spiritual facts.
3. Nature is the symbol of spirit.

1. Words are signs of natural facts. The use of natural history is to give us aid in supernatural history. The use of the outer creation is to give us language for the beings and changes of the inward creation. Every word which is used to ex-

---

[13]Feelings or emotions.
[14]"The many in one."
[15]Apparatus for distillation.

press a moral or intellectual fact, if traced to its root, is found to be borrowed from some material appearance. *Right* originally means *straight; wrong* means *twisted. Spirit* primarily means *wind; transgression,* the crossing of a *line; supercilious,* the *raising of the eye-brow.* We say the *heart* to express emotion, the *head* to denote thought; and *thought* and *emotion* are, in their turn, words borrowed from sensible things, and now appropriated to spiritual nature. Most of the process by which this transformation is made, is hidden from us in the remote time when language was framed; but the same tendency may be daily observed in children. Children and savages use only nouns or names of things, which they continually convert into verbs, and apply to analogous mental acts.

2. But this origin of all words that convey a spiritual import,— so conspicuous a fact in the history of language,— is our least debt to nature. It is not words only that are emblematic; it is things which are emblematic. Every natural fact is a symbol of some spiritual fact. Every appearance in nature corresponds to some state of the mind, and that state of the mind can only be described by presenting that natural appearance as its picture. An enraged man is a lion, a cunning man is a fox, a firm man is a rock, a learned man is a torch. A lamb is innocence; a snake is subtle spite; flowers express to us the delicate affections. Light and darkness are our familiar expression for knowledge and ignorance; and heat for love. Visible distance behind and before us, is respectively our image of memory and hope.

Who looks upon a river in a meditative hour, and is not reminded of the flux of all things? Throw a stone into the stream, and the circles that propagate themselves are the beautiful type of all influence. Man is conscious of a universal soul within or behind his individual life, wherein, as in a firmament, the natures of Justice, Truth, Love, Freedom, arise and shine. This universal soul, he calls Reason: it is not mine or thine or his, but we are its; we are its property and men. And the blue sky in which the private earth is buried, the sky with its eternal calm, and full of everlasting orbs, is the type of Reason. That which, intellectually considered, we call Reason, considered in relation to nature, we call Spirit. Spirit is the Creator. Spirit hath life in itself. And man in all ages and countries, embodies it in his language, as the FATHER.

It is easily seen that there is nothing lucky or capricious in these analogies, but that they are constant, and pervade nature. These are not the dreams of a few poets, here and there, but man is an analogist, and studies relations in all objects. He is placed in the centre of beings, and a ray of relation passes from every other being to him. And neither can man be understood without these objects, nor these objects without man. All the facts in natural history taken by themselves, have no value, but are barren like a single sex. But marry it to human history, and it is full of life. Whole Floras, all Linnæus' and Buffon's[1] volumes, are but dry catalogues of facts; but the most trivial of these facts, the habit of a plant, the organs, or work, or noise of an insect, applied to the illustration of a fact in intellectual philosophy, or, in any way associated to human nature, affects us in the most lively and agreeable manner. The seed of a plant,— to what affecting analogies in the nature of man, is that little fruit made use of, in all discourse, up to the voice of Paul, who calls the human corpse a seed,—"It is sown a natural body; it is raised a spiritual body."[2] The motion of the earth round its axis, and round the sun, makes the day, and the year. These are certain amounts of brute light and heat. But is there no intent of an analogy between man's life and the seasons? And do the seasons gain no grandeur or pathos from that analogy? The instincts of the

---

[1] Carl von Linné (1707–1778), Swedish botanist who developed the system for plant classification; Comte de Buffon (1707–1788), French naturalist who helped develop the biological sciences.
[2] 1 Corinthians 15:44.

ant are very unimportant considered as the ant's; but the moment a ray of relation is seen to extend from it to man, and the little drudge is seen to be a monitor, a little body with a mighty heart, then all its habits, even that said to be recently observed, that it never sleeps, become sublime.

Because of this radical[3] correspondence between visible things and human thoughts, savages, who have only what is necessary, converse in figures. As we go back in history, language becomes more picturesque, until its infancy, when it is all poetry; or, all spiritual facts are represented by natural symbols. The same symbols are found to make the original elements of all languages. It has moreover been observed, that the idioms of all languages approach each other in passages of the greatest eloquence and power. And as this is the first language, so is it the last. This immediate dependence of language upon nature, this conversion of an outward phenomenon into a type of somewhat in human life, never loses its power to affect us. It is this which gives that piquancy to the conversation of a strong-natured farmer or back-woodsman, which all men relish.

Thus is nature an interpreter, by whose means man converses with his fellow men. A man's power to connect his thought with its proper symbol, and so to utter it, depends on the simplicity of his character, that is, upon his love of truth and his desire to communicate it without loss. The corruption of man is followed by the corruption of language. When simplicity of character and the sovereignty of ideas is broken up by the prevalence of secondary desires, the desire of riches, the desire of pleasure, the desire of power, the desire of praise,—and duplicity and falsehood take place of simplicity and truth, the power over nature as an interpreter of the will, is in a degree lost; new imagery ceases to be created, and old words are perverted to stand for things which are not; a paper currency is employed when there is no bullion in the vaults. In due time, the fraud is manifest, and words lose all power to stimulate the understanding or the affections. Hundreds of writers may be found in every long-civilized nation, who for a short time believe, and make others believe, that they see and utter truths, who do not of themselves clothe one thought in its natural garment, but who feed unconsciously upon the language created by the primary writers of the country, those, namely, who hold primarily on nature.

But wise men pierce this rotten diction and fasten words again to visible things; so that picturesque language is at once a commanding certificate that he who employs it, is a man in alliance with truth and God. The moment our discourse rises above the ground line of familiar facts, and is inflamed with passion or exalted by thought, it clothes itself in images. A man conversing in earnest, if he watch his intellectual processes, will find that always a material image, more or less luminous, arises in his mind, cotemporaneous with every thought, which furnishes the vestment of the thought. Hence, good writing and brilliant discourse are perpetual allegories. This imagery is spontaneous. It is the blending of experience with the present action of the mind. It is proper creation. It is the working of the Original Cause through the instruments he has already made.

These facts may suggest the advantage which the country-life possesses for a powerful mind, over the artificial and curtailed life of cities. We know more from nature than we can at will communicate. Its light flows into the mind evermore, and we forget its presence. The poet, the orator, bred in the woods, whose senses have been nourished by their fair and appeasing changes, year after year, without design and without heed,—shall not lose their lesson altogether, in the roar of cities or the broil of politics. Long hereafter, amidst agitation and terror in national councils,—in the hour of revolution,—these solemn images shall reappear

---

[3]Basic (at the root).

in their morning lustre, as fit symbols and words of the thoughts which the passing events shall awaken. At the call of a noble sentiment, again the woods wave,
the pines murmur, the river rolls and shines, and the cattle low upon the mountains, as he saw and heard them in his infancy. And with these forms, the spells of
persuasion, the keys of power are put into his hands.

3. We are thus assisted by natural objects in the expression of particular meanings. But how great a language to convey such peppercorn informations! Did it
need such noble races of creatures, this profusion of forms, this host of orbs in
heaven, to furnish man with the dictionary and grammar of his municipal speech?
Whilst we use this grand cipher to expedite the affairs of our pot and kettle, we
feel that we have not yet put it to its use, neither are able. We are like travellers
using the cinders of a volcano to roast their eggs. Whilst we see that it always
stands ready to clothe what we would say, we cannot avoid the question, whether
the characters are not significant of themselves. Have mountains, and waves, and
skies, no significance but what we consciously give them, when we employ them as
emblems of our thoughts? The world is emblematic. Parts of speech are metaphors because the whole of nature is a metaphor of the human mind. The laws of
moral nature answer to those of matter as face to face in a glass. "The visible
world and the relation of its parts, is the dial plate of the invisible."[4] The axioms
of physics translate the laws of ethics. Thus, "the whole is greater than its part;"
"reaction is equal to action;" "the smallest weight may be made to lift the greatest,
the difference of weight being compensated by time;" and many the like propositions, which have an ethical as well as physical sense. These propositions have a
much more extensive and universal sense when applied to human life, than when
confined to technical use.

In like manner, the memorable words of history, and the proverbs of nations,
consist usually of a natural fact, selected as a picture or parable of a moral truth.
Thus; A rolling stone gathers no moss; A bird in the hand is worth two in the
bush; A cripple in the right way, will beat a racer in the wrong; Make hay whilst
the sun shines; 'T is hard to carry a full cup even; Vinegar is the son of wine; The
last ounce broke the camel's back; Long-lived trees make roots first;—and the like.
In their primary sense these are trivial facts, but we repeat them for the value of
their analogical import. What is true of proverbs, is true of all fables, parables,
and allegories.

This relation between the mind and matter is not fancied by some poet, but
stands in the will of God, and so is free to be known by all men. It appears to men,
or it does not appear. When in fortunate hours we ponder this miracle, the wise
man doubts, if, at all other times, he is not blind and deaf;

——"Can these things be,
And overcome us like a summer's cloud,
Without our special wonder?"[5]

for the universe becomes transparent, and the light of higher laws than its own,
shines through it. It is the standing problem which has exercised the wonder and
the study of every fine genius since the world began; from the era of the Egyptians and the Brahmins, to that of Pythagoras, of Plato, of Bacon, of Leibnitz, of
Swedenborg.[6] There sits the Sphinx at the road-side, and from age to age, as each
prophet comes by, he tries his fortune at reading her riddle.[7] There seems to be a
necessity in spirit to manifest itself in material forms; and day and night, river and

[4]Quoted from Emmanuel Swedenborg (1688–1772), Swedish philosopher and religious writer.
[5]*Macbeth*, III, iv, 110–112 ("Can *such* things be. . . .").
[6]Pythagoras and Plato, Greek philosophers of the fifth and fourth centuries B.C.; Bacon (1561–1626), British philosopher; Leibnitz (1646–1716), German philosopher and mathematician.
[7]In Greek mythology, the Sphinx posed riddles for all passers-by and killed those unable to answer.

storm, beast and bird, acid and alkali, preëxist in necessary Ideas in the mind of God, and are what they are by virtue of preceding affections, in the world of spirit. A Fact is the end or last issue of spirit. The visible creation is the terminus or the circumference of the invisible world. "Material objects," said a French philosopher, "are necessarily kinds of *scoriæ* of the substantial thoughts of the Creator, which must always preserve an exact relation to their first origin; in other words, visible nature must have a spiritual and moral side."[8]

This doctrine is abstruse, and though the images of "garment," "scoriæ," "mirror," &c., may stimulate the fancy, we must summon the aid of subtler and more vital expositors to make it plain. "Every scripture is to be interpreted by the same spirit which gave it forth,"[9]—is the fundamental law of criticism. A life in harmony with nature, the love of truth and of virtue, will purge the eyes to understand her text. By degrees we may come to know the primitive sense of the permanent objects of nature, so that the world shall be to us an open book, and every form significant of its hidden life and final cause.

A new interest surprises us, whilst, under the view now suggested, we contemplate the fearful extent and multitude of objects; since "every object rightly seen, unlocks a new faculty of the soul."[10] That which was unconscious truth, becomes, when interpreted and defined in an object, a part of the domain of knowledge,—a new weapon in the magazine of power.

CHAPTER V. DISCIPLINE

In view of this significance of nature, we arrive at once at a new fact, that nature is a discipline. This use of the world includes the preceding uses, as parts of itself.

Space, time, society, labor, climate, food, locomotion, the animals, the mechanical forces, give us sincerest lessons, day by day, whose meaning is unlimited. They educate both the Understanding and the Reason. Every property of matter is a school for the understanding,—its solidity or resistance, its inertia, its extension, its figure, its divisibility. The understanding adds, divides, combines, measures, and finds everlasting nutriment and room for its activity in this worthy scene. Meantime, Reason transfers all these lessons into its own world of thought, by perceiving the analogy that marries Matter and Mind.

1. Nature is a discipline of the understanding in intellectual truths. Our dealing with sensible objects is a constant exercise in the necessary lessons of difference, of likeness, of order, of being and seeming, of progressive arrangement; of ascent from particular to general; of combination to one end of manifold forces. Proportioned to the importance of the organ to be formed, is the extreme care with which its tuition[1] is provided,—a care pretermitted[2] in no single case. What tedious training, day after day, year after year, never ending, to form the common sense; what continual reproduction of annoyances, inconveniences, dilemmas; what rejoicing over us of little men; what disputing of prices, what reckonings of interest,—and all to form the Hand of the mind;—to instruct us that "good thoughts are no better than good dreams, unless they be executed!"[3]

The same good office is performed by Property and its filial systems of debt and credit. Debt, grinding debt, whose iron face the widow, the orphan, and the sons of genius fear and hate;—debt, which consumes so much time, which so cripples and disheartens a great spirit with cares that seem so base, is a preceptor

---

[8]Quoted from Guillaume Oegger's *The True Messiah* (1829); scoriae: slag left over from smelted ore.
[9]Quoted from the English founder of the Quakers, George Fox (1624–1691).
[10]From *Aids to Reflection* (1825), by Samuel Taylor Coleridge (1772–1834).

[1]Instruction (or guardianship).
[2]Overlooked.
[3]Paraphrased from "Of Great Place" in *Essays* (1625) by Sir Francis Bacon.

whose lessons cannot be foregone, and is needed most by those who suffer from it most. Moreover, property, which has been well compared to snow,—"if it fall level to-day, it will be blown into drifts to-morrow,"—is merely the surface action of internal machinery, like the index on the face of a clock. Whilst now it is the gymnastics of the understanding, it is hiving in the foresight of the spirit, experience in profounder laws.

The whole character and fortune of the individual are affected by the least inequalities in the culture of the understanding; for example, in the perception of differences. Therefore is Space, and therefore Time, that man may know that things are not huddled and lumped, but sundered and individual. A bell and a plough have each their use, and neither can do the office of the other. Water is good to drink, coal to burn, wool to wear; but wool cannot be drunk, nor water spun, nor coal eaten. The wise man shows his wisdom in separation, in gradation, and his scale of creatures and of merits, is as wide as nature. The foolish have no range in their scale, but suppose every man is as every other man. What is not good they call the worst, and what is not hateful, they call the best.

In like manner, what good heed, nature forms in us! She pardons no mistakes. Her yea is yea, and her nay, nay.

The first steps in Agriculture, Astronomy, Zoölogy, (those first steps which the farmer, the hunter, and the sailor take,) teach that nature's dice are always loaded; that in her heaps and rubbish are concealed sure and useful results.

How calmly and genially the mind apprehends one after another the laws of physics! What noble emotions dilate the mortal as he enters into the counsels of the creation, and feels by knowledge the privilege to BE! His insight refines him. The beauty of nature shines in his own breast. Man is greater that he can see this, and the universe less, because Time and Space relations vanish as laws are known.

Here again we are impressed and even daunted by the immense Universe to be explored. 'What we know, is a point to what we do not know.'[4] Open any recent journal of science, and weigh the problems suggested concerning Light, Heat, Electricity, Magnetism, Physiology, Geology, and judge whether the interest of natural science is likely to be soon exhausted.

Passing by many particulars of the discipline of nature we must not omit to specify two.

The exercise of the Will or the lesson of power is taught in every event. From the child's successive possession of his several senses up to the hour when he saith, "thy will be done!"[5] he is learning the secret, that he can reduce under his will, not only particular events, but great classes, nay the whole series of events, and so conform all facts to his character. Nature is thoroughly mediate. It is made to serve. It receives the dominion of man as meekly as the ass on which the Saviour rode.[6] It offers all its kingdoms to man as the raw material which he may mould into what is useful. Man is never weary of working it up. He forges the subtile and delicate air into wise and melodious words, and gives them wing as angels of persuasion and command. More and more, with every thought, does his kingdom stretch over things, until the world becomes, at last, only a realized will,—the double of the man.

2. Sensible objects conform to the premonitions of Reason and reflect the conscience. All things are moral; and in their boundless changes have an unceasing reference to spiritual nature. Therefore is nature glorious with form, color, and motion, that every globe in the remotest heaven; every chemical change from the rudest crystal up to the laws of life; every change of vegetation from the first principle of growth in the eye of a leaf, to the tropical forest and antediluvian coal-

---

[4]Ascribed to British Bishop Joseph Butler (1692–1752).
[5]From the Lord's Prayer, Matthew 6:9–13.

[6]Matthew 21:5: "Behold, thy King cometh unto thee, meek, and sitting upon an ass."

mine; every animal function from the sponge up to Hercules, shall hint or thunder to man the laws of right and wrong, and echo the Ten Commandments. Therefore is nature ever the ally of Religion: lends all her pomp and riches to the religious sentiment. Prophet and priest, David, Isaiah, Jesus, have drawn deeply from this source.

This ethical character so penetrates the bone and marrow of nature, as to seem the end for which it was made. Whatever private purpose is answered by any member or part, this is its public and universal function, and is never omitted. Nothing in nature is exhausted in its first use. When a thing has served an end to the uttermost, it is wholly new for an ulterior service. In God, every end is converted into a new means. Thus the use of Commodity, regarded by itself, is mean and squalid. But it is to the mind an education in the great doctrine of Use, namely, that a thing is good only so far as it serves; that a conspiring of parts and efforts to the production of an end, is essential to any being. The first and gross manifestation of this truth, is our inevitable and hated training in values and wants, in corn and meat.

It has already been illustrated, in treating of the significance of material things, that every natural process is but a version of a moral sentence. The moral law lies at the centre of nature and radiates to the circumference. It is the pith and marrow of every substance, every relation, and every process. All things with which we deal, preach to us. What is a farm but a mute gospel? The chaff and the wheat, weeds and plants, blight, rain, insects, sun,—it is a sacred emblem from the first furrow of spring to the last stack which the snow of winter overtakes in the fields. But the sailor, the shepherd, the miner, the merchant, in their several resorts, have each an experience precisely parallel and leading to the same conclusion: because all organizations are radically alike. Nor can it be doubted that this moral sentiment which thus scents the air, and grows in the grain, and impregnates the waters of the world, is caught by man and sinks into his soul. The moral influence of nature upon every individual is that amount of truth which it illustrates to him. Who can estimate this? Who can guess how much firmness the sea-beaten rock has taught the fisherman? how much tranquillity has been reflected to man from the azure sky, over whose unspotted deeps the winds forevermore drive flocks of stormy clouds, and leave no wrinkle or stain? how much industry and providence and affection we have caught from the pantomime of brutes? What a searching preacher of self-command is the varying phenomenon of Health!

Herein is especially apprehended the Unity of Nature,—the Unity in Variety,—which meets us everywhere. All the endless variety of things make a unique, an identical impression. Xenophanes[7] complained in his old age, that, look where he would, all things hastened back to Unity. He was weary of seeing the same entity in the tedious variety of forms. The fable of Proteus[8] has a cordial truth. Every particular in nature, a leaf, a drop, a crystal, a moment of time is related to the whole, and partakes of the perfection of the whole. Each particle is a microcosm, and faithfully renders the likeness of the world.

Not only resemblances exist in things whose analogy is obvious, as when we detect the type of the human hand in the flipper of the fossil saurus,[9] but also in objects wherein there is great superficial unlikeness. Thus architecture is called "frozen music," by De Stael and Goethe.[10] Vitruvius[11] thought an architect should be a musician. "A Gothic church," said Coleridge, "is a petrified religion."[12]

---

[7]Greek philosopher of the sixth century B.C. taught that plurality and change were illusions.
[8]Sea god who, when captured, could change shape and form.
[9]Lizard.
[10]Madame de Stael (1766–1817), French writer, in *Corinne*

(Bk. IV, Chap. III); Johann Wolfgang von Goethe (1749–1832), German poet, in *Conversations with Eckermann*.
[11]Roman architect of the first century B.C.
[12]In "Lecture on the General Character of the Gothic Mind in the Middle Ages," *Literary Remains* (1836).

Michael Angelo maintained, that, to an architect, a knowledge of anatomy is essential. In Haydn's oratorios,[13] the notes present to the imagination not only motions, as, of the snake, the stag, and the elephant, but colors also; as the green grass. The law of harmonic sounds reappears in the harmonic colors. The granite is differenced in its laws only by the more or less of heat, from the river that wears it away. The river, as it flows, resembles the air that flows over it; the air resembles the light which traverses it with more subtile currents; the light resembles the heat which rides with it through Space. Each creature is only a modification of the other; the likeness in them is more than the difference, and their radical law is one and the same. Hence it is, that a rule of one art, or a law of one organization, holds true throughout nature. So intimate is this Unity, that, it is easily seen, it lies under the undermost garment of nature, and betrays its source in universal Spirit. For, it pervades Thought also. Every universal truth which we express in words, implies or supposes every other truth. *Omne verum vero consonat.*[14] It is like a great circle on a sphere, comprising all possible circles; which, however, may be drawn, and comprise it, in like manner. Every such truth is the absolute Ens[15] seen from one side. But it has innumerable sides.

The same central Unity is still more conspicuous in actions. Words are finite organs of the infinite mind. They cannot cover the dimensions of what is in truth. They break, chop, and impoverish it. An action is the perfection and publication of thought. A right action seems to fill the eye, and to be related to all nature. "The wise man, in doing one thing, does all; or, in the one thing he does rightly, he sees the likeness of all which is done rightly."[16]

Words and actions are not the attributes of mute and brute nature. They introduce us to the human form, of which all other organizations appear to be degradations. When this organization appears among so many that surround it, the spirit prefers it to all others. It says, 'From such as this, have I drawn joy and knowledge. In such as this, have I found and beheld myself. I will speak to it. It can speak again. It can yield me thought already formed and alive.' In fact, the eye,—the mind,—is always accompanied by these forms, male and female; and these are incomparably the richest informations of the power and order that lie at the heart of things. Unfortunately, every one of them bears the marks as of some injury; is marred and superficially defective. Nevertheless, far different from the deaf and dumb nature around them, these all rest like fountain-pipes on the unfathomed sea of thought and virtue whereto they alone, of all organizations, are the entrances.

It were a pleasant inquiry to follow into detail their ministry to our education, but where would it stop? We are associated in adolescent and adult life with some friends, who, like skies and waters, are coextensive with our idea; who, answering each to a certain affection of the soul, satisfy our desire on that side; whom we lack power to put at such focal distance from us, that we can mend or even analyze them. We cannot chuse but love them. When much intercourse with a friend has supplied us with a standard of excellence, and has increased our respect for the resources of God who thus sends a real person to outgo our ideal; when he has, moreover, become an object of thought, and, whilst his character retains all its unconscious effect, is converted in the mind into solid and sweet wisdom,—it is a sign to us that his office is closing, and he is commonly withdrawn from our sight in a short time.

---

[13]Dramatic musical compositions by Joseph Haydn (1732–1809), Austrian composer.
[14]"Every truth agrees with every other truth" (Latin).

[15]Latin philosophical phrase: "abstract being."
[16]From Goethe's *Wilhelm Meister's Travels*, translated by British author Thomas Carlyle (1795–1881).

CHAPTER VI. IDEALISM

Thus is the unspeakable but intelligible and practicable meaning of the world conveyed to man, the immortal pupil, in every object of sense. To this one end of Discipline, all parts of nature conspire.

A noble doubt perpetually suggests itself, whether this end be not the Final Cause of the Universe; and whether nature outwardly exists. It is a sufficient account of that Appearance we call the World, that God will teach a human mind, and so makes it the receiver of a certain number of congruent sensations, which we call sun and moon, man and woman, house and trade. In my utter impotence to test the authenticity of the report of my senses, to know whether the impressions they make on me correspond with outlying objects, what difference does it make, whether Orion[1] is up there in heaven, or some god paints the image in the firmament of the soul? The relations of parts and the end of the whole remaining the same, what is the difference, whether land and sea interact, and worlds revolve and intermingle without number or end,—deep yawning under deep, and galaxy balancing galaxy, throughout absolute space, or, whether, without relations of time and space, the same appearances are inscribed in the constant faith of man? Whether nature enjoy a substantial existence without, or is only in the apocalypse of the mind, it is alike useful and alike venerable to me. Be it what it may, it is ideal to me, so long as I cannot try the accuracy of my senses.

The frivolous make themselves merry with the Ideal theory, as if its consequences were burlesque; as if it affected the stability of nature. It surely does not. God never jests with us, and will not compromise the end of nature, by permitting any inconsequence in its procession. Any distrust of the permanence of laws, would paralyze the faculties of man. Their permanence is sacredly respected, and his faith therein is perfect. The wheels and springs of man are all set to the hypothesis of the permanence of nature. We are not built like a ship to be tossed, but like a house to stand. It is a natural consequence of this structure, that, so long as the active powers predominate over the reflective, we resist with indignation any hint that nature is more short-lived or mutable than spirit. The broker, the wheelwright, the carpenter, the toll-man, are much displeased at the intimation.

But whilst we acquiesce entirely in the permanence of natural laws, the question of the absolute existence of nature, still remains open. It is the uniform effect of culture on the human mind, not to shake our faith in the stability of particular phenomena, as of heat, water, azote;[2] but to lead us to regard nature as a phenomenon, not a substance; to attribute necessary existence to spirit; to esteem nature as an accident and an effect.

To the senses and the unrenewed understanding, belongs a sort of instinctive belief in the absolute existence of nature. In their view, man and nature are indissolubly joined. Things are ultimates, and they never look beyond their sphere. The presence of Reason mars this faith. The first effort of thought tends to relax this despotism of the senses, which binds us to nature as if we were a part of it, and shows us nature aloof, and, as it were, afloat. Until this higher agency intervened, the animal eye sees, with wonderful accuracy, sharp outlines and colored surfaces. When the eye of Reason opens, to outline and surface are at once added, grace and expression. These proceed from imagination and affection, and abate somewhat of the angular distinctness of objects. If the Reason be stimulated to more earnest vision, outlines and surfaces become transparent, and are no longer seen; causes and spirits are seen through them. The best, the happiest moments of life, are these delicious awakenings of the higher powers, and the reverential withdrawing of nature before its God.

---

[1] An equatorial constellation.
[2] Nitrogen.

Let us proceed to indicate the effects of culture. 1. Our first institution in the Ideal philosophy is a hint from nature herself.

Nature is made to conspire with spirit to emancipate us. Certain mechanical changes, a small alteration in our local position apprizes us of a dualism. We are strangely affected by seeing the shore from a moving ship, from a balloon, or through the tints of an unusual sky. The least change in our point of view, gives the whole world a pictorial air. A man who seldom rides, needs only to get into a coach and traverse his own town, to turn the street into a puppet-show. The men, the women,—talking, running, bartering, fighting,—the earnest mechanic, the lounger, the beggar, the boys, the dogs, are unrealized at once, or, at least, wholly detached from all relation to the observer, and seen as apparent, not substantial beings. What new thoughts are suggested by seeing a face of country quite famil-iar, in the rapid movement of the rail-road car! Nay, the most wonted objects, (make a very slight change in the point of vision,) please us most. In a camera ob-scura,[3] the butcher's cart, and the figure of one of our own family amuse us. So a portrait of a well-known face gratifies us. Turn the eyes upside down, by looking at the landscape through your legs, and how agreeable is the picture, though you have seen it any time these twenty years!

In these cases, by mechanical means, is suggested the difference between the observer and the spectacle,—between man and nature. Hence arises a pleasure mixed with awe; I may say, a low degree of the sublime is felt from the fact, prob-ably, that man is hereby apprized, that, whilst the world is a spectacle, something in himself is stable.

2. In a higher manner, the poet communicates the same pleasure. By a few strokes he delineates, as on air, the sun, the mountain, the camp, the city, the hero, the maiden, not different from what we know them, but only lifted from the ground and afloat before the eye. He unfixes the land and the sea, makes them revolve around the axis of his primary thought, and disposes them anew. Pos-sessed himself by a heroic passion, he uses matter as symbols of it. The sensual man conforms thoughts to things; the poet conforms things to his thoughts. The one esteems nature as rooted and fast; the other, as fluid, and impresses his being thereon. To him, the refractory world is ductile and flexible; he invests dust and stones with humanity, and makes them the words of the Reason. The imagination may be defined to be, the use which the Reason makes of the material world. Shakspeare possesses the power of subordinating nature for the purposes of ex-pression, beyond all poets. His imperial muse tosses the creation like a bauble from hand to hand, and uses it to embody any capricious shade of thought that is uppermost in his mind. The remotest spaces of nature are visited, and the farthest sundered things are brought together, by a subtile spiritual connexion. We are made aware that magnitude of material things is merely relative, and all objects shrink and expand to serve the passion of the poet. Thus, in his sonnets, the lays of birds, the scents and dyes of flowers, he finds to be the *shadow* of his beloved; time, which keeps her from him, is his *chest;* the suspicion she has awakened, is her *ornament;*

> The ornament of beauty is Suspect,
> A crow which flies in heaven's sweetest air.[4]

His passion is not the fruit of chance; it swells, as he speaks, to a city, or a state.

> No, it was builded far from accident;
> It suffers not in smiling pomp, nor falls
> Under the brow of thralling discontent;

---

[3]Forerunner of the modern camera, consisting of a dark chamber with lens to project an image on a facing surface.
[4]From Shakespeare's Sonnet No. 70.

> It fears not policy, that heretic,
> That works on leases of short numbered hours,
> But all alone stands hugely politic.[5]

In the strength of his constancy, the Pyramids seem to him recent and transitory. And the freshness of youth and love dazzles him with its resemblance to morning.

> Take those lips away
> Which so sweetly were forsworn;
> And those eyes,—the break of day,
> Lights that do mislead the morn.[6]

The wild beauty of this hyperbole, I may say, in passing, it would not be easy to match in literature.

This transfiguration which all material objects undergo through the passion of the poet,—this power which he exerts, at any moment, to magnify the small, to micrify the great,—might be illustrated by a thousand examples from his Plays. I have before me the Tempest and will cite only these few lines.

> ARIEL. The strong based promontory
> Have I made shake, and by the spurs plucked up
> The pine and cedar.

Prospero calls for music to sooth the frantic Alonzo, and his companions;

> A solemn air, and the best comforter
> To an unsettled fancy, cure thy brains
> Now useless, boiled within thy skull.

Again;

> The charm dissolves apace
> And, as the morning steals upon the night,
> Melting the darkness, so their rising senses
> Begin to chase the ignorant fumes that mantle
> Their clearer reason.
>   Their understanding
> Begins to swell: and the approaching tide
> Will shortly fill the reasonable shores
> That now lie foul and muddy.[7]

The perception of real affinities between events, (that is to say, of *ideal* affinities, for those only are real,) enables the poet thus to make free with the most imposing forms and phenomena of the world, and to assert the predominance of the soul.

3. Whilst thus the poet delights us by animating nature like a creator, with his own thoughts, he differs from the philosopher only herein, that the one proposes Beauty as his main end; the other Truth. But, the philosopher, not less than the poet, postpones the apparent order and relations of things to the empire of thought. "The problem of philosophy," according to Plato, "is, for all that exists conditionally, to find a ground unconditioned and absolute."[8] It proceeds on the faith that a law determines all phenomena, which being known, the phenomena

---

[5]Shakespeare, Sonnet 124.
[6]Shakespeare, *Measure for Measure*, IV, i, 1–4.
[7]Shakespeare, *The Tempest*, V, i, 46–48 (the lines are spoken not by Ariel but by Prospero); V, i, 58–60; V, i, 64–68 and 79–82.

[8]From the *Republic*, Bk. V. Emerson takes the quotation from Coleridge's *The Friend* (1818).

can be predicted. That law, when in the mind, is an idea. Its beauty is infinite. The true philosopher and the true poet are one, and a beauty, which is truth, and a truth, which is beauty, is the aim of both. Is not the charm of one of Plato's or Aristotle's definitions, strictly like that of the Antigone of Sophocles? It is, in both cases, that a spiritual life has been imparted to nature; that the solid seeming block of matter has been pervaded and dissolved by a thought; that this feeble human being has penetrated the vast masses of nature with an informing soul, and recognised itself in their harmony, that is, seized their law. In physics, when this is attained, the memory disburthens itself of its cumbrous catalogues of particulars, and carries centuries of observation in a single formula.

Thus even in physics, the material is ever degraded before the spiritual. The astronomer, the geometer, rely on their irrefragable analysis, and disdain the results of observation. The sublime remark of Euler on his law of arches, "This will be found contrary to all experience, yet is true;"[9] had already transferred nature into the mind, and left matter like an outcast corpse.

4. Intellectual science has been observed to beget invariably a doubt of the existence of matter. Turgot said, "He that has never doubted the existence of matter, may be assured he has no aptitude for metaphysical inquiries."[10] It fastens the attention upon immortal necessary uncreated natures, that is, upon Ideas; and in their beautiful and majestic presence, we feel that our outward being is a dream and a shade. Whilst we wait in this Olympus of gods, we think of nature as an appendix to the soul. We ascend into their region, and know that these are the thoughts of the Supreme Being. "These are they who were set up from everlasting, from the beginning, or ever the earth was. When he prepared the heavens, they were there; when he established the clouds above, when he strengthened the fountains of the deep. Then they were by him, as one brought up with him. Of them took he counsel."[11]

Their influence is proportionate. As objects of science, they are accessible to few men. Yet all men are capable of being raised by piety or by passion, into their region. And no man touches these divine natures, without becoming, in some degree, himself divine. Like a new soul, they renew the body. We become physically nimble and lightsome; we tread on air; life is no longer irksome, and we think it will never be so. No man fears age or misfortune or death, in their serene company, for he is transported out of the district of change. Whilst we behold unveiled the nature of Justice and Truth, we learn the difference between the absolute and the conditional or relative. We apprehend the absolute. As it were, for the first time, *we exist*. We become immortal, for we learn that time and space are relations of matter; that, with a perception of truth, or a virtuous will, they have no affinity.

5. Finally, religion and ethics, which may be fitly called,—the practice of ideas, or the introduction of ideas into life,—have an analogous effect with all lower culture, in degrading nature and suggesting its dependence on spirit. Ethics and religion differ herein; that the one is the system of human duties commencing from man; the other, from God. Religion includes the personality of God; Ethics does not. They are one to our present design. They both put nature under foot. The first and last lesson of religion is, "The things that are seen, are temporal; the things that are unseen are eternal."[12] It puts an affront upon nature. It does that for the unschooled, which philosophy does for Berkeley and Viasa.[13] The uniform language that may be heard in the churches of the most ignorant sects, is,—

---

[9]Leonhard Euler, eighteenth-century Swiss mathematician. Emerson found the remarks in Coleridge's *Aids to Reflection* (1829).

[10]Anne Robert Jacques Turgot, eighteenth-century French statesman and economist.

[11]Variant version of Proverbs 8:23, 27, 28, 30.

[12]2 Corinthians 4:18.

[13]George Berkeley (1685–1753), British philosopher of idealism; Viasa, legendary Hindu mystic and seer.

'Contemn the unsubstantial shows of the world; they are vanities, dreams, shadows, unrealities; seek the realities of religion.' The devotee flouts nature. Some theosophists have arrived at a certain hostility and indignation towards matter, as the Manichean and Plotinus.[14] They distrusted in themselves any looking back to these flesh-pots of Egypt.[15] Plotinus was ashamed of his body. In short, they might all better say of matter, what Michael Angelo said of external beauty, "it is the frail and weary weed, in which God dresses the soul, which he has called into time."[16]

It appears that motion, poetry, physical and intellectual science, and religion, all tend to affect our convictions of the reality of the external world. But I own there is something ungrateful in expanding too curiously the particulars of the general proposition, that all culture tends to imbue us with idealism. I have no hostility to nature, but a child's love to it. I expand and live in the warm day like corn and melons. Let us speak her fair. I do not wish to fling stones at my beautiful mother, nor soil my gentle nest. I only wish to indicate the true position of nature in regard to man, wherein to establish man, all right education tends; as the ground which to attain is the object of human life, that is, of man's connexion with nature. Culture inverts the vulgar views of nature, and brings the mind to call that apparent, which it uses to call real, and that real, which it uses to call visionary. Children, it is true, believe in the external world. The belief that it appears only, is an afterthought, but with culture, this faith will as surely arise on the mind as did the first.

The advantage of the ideal theory over the popular faith, is this, that it presents the world in precisely that view which is most desirable to the mind. It is, in fact, the view which Reason, both speculative and practical, that is, philosophy and virtue, take. For, seen in the light of thought, the world always is phenomenal; and virtue subordinates it to the mind. Idealism sees the world in God. It beholds the whole circle of persons and things, of actions and events, of country and religion, not as painfully accumulated, atom after atom, act after act, in an aged creeping Past, but as one vast picture, which God paints on the instant eternity, for the contemplation of the soul. Therefore the soul holds itself off from a too trivial and microscopic study of the universal tablet. It respects the end too much, to immerse itself in the means. It sees something more important in Christianity, than the scandals of ecclesiastical history or the niceties of criticism; and, very incurious concerning persons or miracles, and not at all disturbed by chasms of historical evidence, it accepts from God the phenomenon, as it finds it, as the pure and awful form of religion in the world. It is not hot and passionate at the appearance of what it calls its own good or bad fortune, at the union or opposition of other persons. No man is its enemy. It accepts whatsoever befals, as part of its lesson. It is a watcher more than a doer, and it is a doer, only that it may the better watch.

CHAPTER VII. SPIRIT

It is essential to a true theory of nature and of man, that it should contain somewhat progressive. Uses that are exhausted or that may be, and facts that end in the statement, cannot be all that is true of this brave lodging wherein man is harbored, and wherein all his faculties find appropriate and endless exercise. And all the uses of nature admit of being summed in one, which yields the activity of man an infinite scope. Through all its kingdoms, to the suburbs and outskirts of things, it is faithful to the cause whence it had its origin. It always speaks of Spirit.

---

[14]Theosophists believe in direct apprehension of God through mystic meditation; Manicheans believe in a dual universe balanced between good and evil; Plotinus was a third-century Neoplatonist, combining Plato's philosophy with the ethics and mysticism of various religions.

[15]The wandering Israelites yearned to return to Egypt's "flesh pots" (Exodus 16:2–3).
[16]Michelangelo, Sonnet 51 (from *Rime di Michelangelo Buonarroti*).

It suggests the absolute. It is a perpetual effect. It is a great shadow pointing always to the sun behind us.

The aspect of nature is devout. Like the figure of Jesus, she stands with bended head, and hands folded upon the breast. The happiest man is he who learns from nature the lesson of worship.

Of that ineffable essence which we call Spirit, he that thinks most, will say least. We can foresee God in the course and, as it were, distant phenomena of matter; but when we try to define and describe himself, both language and thought desert us, and we are as helpless as fools and savages. That essence refuses to be recorded in propositions, but when man has worshipped him intellectually, the noblest ministry of nature is to stand as the apparition of God. It is the great organ through which the universal spirit speaks to the individual, and strives to lead back the individual to it.

When we consider Spirit, we see that the views already presented do not include the whole circumference of man. We must add some related thoughts.

Three problems are put by nature to the mind; What is matter? Whence is it? and Whereto? The first of these questions only, the ideal theory answers. Idealism saith: matter is a phenomenon, not a substance. Idealism acquaints us with the total disparity between the evidence of our own being, and the evidence of the world's being. The one is perfect; the other, incapable of any assurance; the mind is a part of the nature of things; the world is a divine dream, from which we may presently awake to the glories and certainties of day. Idealism is a hypothesis to account for nature by other principles than those of carpentry and chemistry. Yet, if it only deny the existence of matter, it does not satisfy the demands of the spirit. It leaves God out of me. It leaves me in the splendid labyrinth of my perceptions, to wander without end. Then the heart resists it, because it baulks the affections in denying substantive being to men and women. Nature is so pervaded with human life, that there is something of humanity in all, and in every particular. But this theory makes nature foreign to me, and does not account for that consanguinity which we acknowledge to it.

Let it stand then, in the present state of our knowledge, merely as a useful introductory hypothesis, serving to apprize us of the eternal distinction between the soul and the world.

But when, following the invisible steps of thought, we come to inquire, Whence is matter? and Whereto? many truths arise to us out of the recesses of consciousness. We learn that the highest is present to the soul of man, that the dread universal essence, which is not wisdom, or love, or beauty, or power, but all in one, and each entirely, is that for which all things exist, and that by which they are; that spirit creates; that behind nature, throughout nature, spirit is present; that spirit is one and not compound; that spirit does not act upon us from without, that is, in space and time, but spiritually, or through ourselves. Therefore, that spirit, that is, the Supreme Being, does not build up nature around us, but puts it forth through us, as the life of the tree puts forth new branches and leaves through the pores of the old. As a plant upon the earth, so a man rests upon the bosom of God; he is nourished by unfailing fountains, and draws, at his need, inexhaustible power. Who can set bounds to the possibilities of man? Once inhale the upper air, being admitted to behold the absolute natures of justice and truth, and we learn that man has access to the entire mind of the Creator, is himself the creator in the finite. This view, which admonishes me where the sources of wisdom and power lie, and points to virtue as to

> "The golden key
> Which opes the palace of eternity,"[1]

---

[1]From *Comus* (ll. 13–14), by John Milton (1608–1674).

carries upon its face the highest certificate of truth, because it animates me to create my own world through the purification of my soul.

The world proceeds from the same spirit as the body of man. It is a remoter and inferior incarnation of God, a projection of God in the unconscious. But it differs from the body in one important respect. It is not, like that, now subjected to the human will. Its serene order is inviolable by us. It is therefore, to us, the present expositor of the divine mind. It is a fixed point whereby we may measure our departure. As we degenerate, the contrast between us and our house is more evident. We are as much strangers in nature, as we are aliens from God. We do not understand the notes of birds. The fox and the deer run away from us; the bear and tiger rend us. We do not know the uses of more than a few plants, as corn and the apple, the potato and the vine. Is not the landscape, every glimpse of which hath a grandeur, a face of him? Yet this may show us what discord is between man and nature, for you cannot freely admire a noble landscape, if laborers are digging in the field hard by. The poet finds something ridiculous in his delight, until he is out of the sight of men.

CHAPTER VIII. PROSPECTS

In inquiries respecting the laws of the world and the frame of things, the highest reason is always the truest. That which seems faintly possible—it is so refined, is often faint and dim because it is deepest seated in the mind among the eternal verities. Empirical science is apt to cloud the sight, and, by the very knowledge of functions and processes, to bereave the student of the manly contemplation of the whole. The savant becomes unpoetic. But the best read naturalist who lends an entire and devout attention to truth, will see that there remains much to learn of his relation to the world, and that it is not to be learned by any addition or subtraction or other comparison of known quantities, but is arrived at by untaught sallies of the spirit, by a continual self-recovery, and by entire humility. He will perceive that there are far more excellent qualities in the student than preciseness and infallibility; that a guess is often more fruitful than an indisputable affirmation, and that a dream may let us deeper into the secret of nature than a hundred concerted experiments.

For, the problems to be solved are precisely those which the physiologist and the naturalist omit to state. It is not so pertinent to man to know all the individuals of the animal kingdom, as it is to know whence and whereto is this tyrannizing unity in his constitution, which evermore separates and classifies things, endeavoring to reduce the most diverse to one form. When I behold a rich landscape, it is less to my purpose to recite correctly the order and superposition of the strata, than to know why all thought of multitude is lost in a tranquil sense of unity. I cannot greatly honor minuteness in details, so long as there is no hint to explain the relation between things and thoughts; no ray upon the *metaphysics* of conchology,[1] of botany, of the arts, to show the relation of the forms of flowers, shells, animals, architecture, to the mind, and build science upon ideas. In a cabinet of natural history,[2] we become sensible of a certain occult recognition and sympathy in regard to the most unwieldy and eccentric forms of beast, fish, and insect. The American who has been confined, in his own country, to the sight of buildings designed after foreign models, is surprised on entering York Minster or St. Peter's at Rome,[3] by the feeling that these structures are imitations also,—faint copies of an invisible archetype. Nor has science sufficient humanity, so long as the naturalist overlooks that wonderful congruity which subsists between man and the world; of which he is lord, not because he is the most subtile inhabitant, but because he is its

---

[1] A branch of zoology, study of shells.
[2] Museum display cases showing artifacts of natural history.

[3] Cathedral of York in England; St. Peter's Cathedral, the center of Roman Catholicism in Italy.

head and heart, and finds something of himself in every great and small thing, in every mountain stratum, in every new law of color, fact of astronomy, or atmospheric influence which observation or analysis lay open. A perception of this mystery inspires the muse of George Herbert, the beautiful psalmist of the seventeenth century. The following lines are part of his little poem on Man.

> "Man is all symmetry,
> Full of proportions, one limb to another,
> And to all the world besides.
> Each part may call the farthest, brother;
> For head with foot hath private amity,
> And both with moons and tides.
>
> "Nothing hath got so far
> But man hath caught and kept it as his prey;
> His eyes dismount the highest star;
> He is in little all the sphere.
> Herbs gladly cure our flesh, because that they
> Find their acquaintance there.
>
> "For us, the winds do blow,
> The earth doth rest, heaven move, and fountains flow;
> Nothing we see, but means our good,
> As our delight, or as our treasure;
> The whole is either our cupboard of food,
> Or cabinet of pleasure.
>
> "The stars have us to bed:
> Night draws the curtain; which the sun withdraws.
> Music and light attend our head.
> All things unto our flesh are kind,
> In their descent and being; to our mind,
> In their ascent and cause.
>
> "More servants wait on man
> Than he'll take notice of. In every path,
> He treads down that which doth befriend him
> When sickness makes him pale and wan.
> Oh mighty love! Man is one world, and hath
> Another to attend him."[4]

The perception of this class of truths makes the eternal attraction which draws men to science, but the end is lost sight of in attention to the means. In view of this half-sight of science, we accept the sentence of Plato, that, "poetry comes nearer to vital truth than history."[5] Every surmise and vaticination of the mind is entitled to a certain respect, and we learn to prefer imperfect theories, and sentences, which contain glimpses of truth, to digested systems which have no one valuable suggestion. A wise writer will feel that the ends of study and composition are best answered by announcing undiscovered regions of thought, and so communicating, through hope, new activity to the torpid spirit.

I shall therefore conclude this essay with some traditions of man and nature, which a certain poet[6] sang to me; and which, as they have always been in the world, and perhaps reappear to every bard, may be both history and prophecy.

---

[4]From "Man" (1633), by George Herbert (1593–1633), British clergyman and poet.
[5]Aristotle, not Plato, is the source (see *Poetics*, section 9); "vaticination": inspired prediction.

[6]Speculation has centered on Bronson Alcott (1799–1888), Emerson's friend and author of *Orphic Sayings* (1840), but it is perhaps more likely Emerson's invention of another self.

'The foundations of man are not in matter, but in spirit. But the element of spirit is eternity. To it, therefore, the longest series of events, the oldest chronologies are young and recent. In the cycle of the universal man, from whom the known individuals proceed, centuries are points, and all history is but the epoch of one degradation.

'We distrust and deny inwardly our sympathy with nature. We own and disown our relation to it, by turns. We are, like Nebuchadnezzar, dethroned, bereft of reason, and eating grass like an ox.[7] But who can set limits to the remedial force of spirit?

'A man is a god in ruins. When men are innocent, life shall be longer, and shall pass into the immortal, as gently as we awake from dreams. Now, the world would be insane and rabid, if these disorganizations should last for hundreds of years. It is kept in check by death and infancy. Infancy is the perpetual Messiah, which comes into the arms of fallen men, and pleads with them to return to paradise.

'Man is the dwarf of himself. Once he was permeated and dissolved by spirit. He filled nature with his overflowing currents. Out from him sprang the sun and moon; from man, the sun; from woman, the moon. The laws of his mind, the periods of his actions externized themselves into day and night, into the year and the seasons. But, having made for himself this huge shell, his waters retired; he no longer fills the veins and veinlets; he is shrunk to a drop. He sees, that the structure still fits him, but fits him colossally. Say, rather, once it fitted him, now it corresponds to him from far and on high. He adores timidly his own work. Now is man the follower of the sun, and woman the follower of the moon. Yet sometimes he starts in his slumber, and wonders at himself and his house, and muses strangely at the resemblance betwixt him and it. He perceives that if his law is still paramount, if still he have elemental power, "if his word is sterling yet in nature," it is not conscious power, it is not inferior but superior to his will. It is Instinct.' Thus my Orphic[8] poet sang.

At present, man applies to nature but half his force. He works on the world with his understanding alone. He lives in it, and masters it by a penny-wisdom; and he that works most in it, is but a half-man, and whilst his arms are strong and his digestion good, his mind is imbruted and he is a selfish savage. His relation to nature, his power over it, is through the understanding; as by manure; the economic use of fire, wind, water, and the mariner's needle; steam, coal, chemical agriculture; the repairs of the human body by the dentist and the surgeon. This is such a resumption of power, as if a banished king should buy his territories inch by inch, instead of vaulting at once into his throne. Meantime, in the thick darkness, there are not wanting gleams of a better light,—occasional examples of the action of man upon nature with his entire force,—with reason as well as understanding. Such examples are; the traditions of miracles in the earliest antiquity of all nations; the history of Jesus Christ; the achievements of a principle, as in religious and political revolutions, and in the abolition of the Slave-trade; the miracles of enthusiasm,[9] as those reported of Swedenborg, Hohenlohe, and the Shakers;[10] many obscure and yet contested facts, now arranged under the name of Animal Magnetism;[11] prayer; eloquence; self-healing; and the wisdom of children. These are examples of Reason's momentary grasp of the sceptre; the exertions of a power which exists not in time or space, but an instantaneous in-streaming causing power. The difference between the actual and the ideal force of man is happily figured by the schoolmen, in saying, that the knowledge of man is an evening

---

[7]Daniel 4:33: Nebuchadnezzer went mad, "and he was driven from men, and did eat grass as oxen."
[8]Oracular.
[9]Inspired prophecy.
[10]Leopold Franz Emmerich, Prince of Hohenlohe-Waldenburg-Schillingsfurst (1794–1849), German Roman Catholic bishop and author; the Shakers, a visionary religious sect so named because of their frenzied rites of worship.
[11]Hypnotism.

knowledge, *vespertina cognitio,* but that of God is a morning knowledge, *matutina cognitio.*

The problem of restoring to the world original and eternal beauty, is solved by the redemption of the soul. The ruin or the blank, that we see when we look at nature, is in our own eye. The axis of vision is not coincident with the axis of things, and so they appear not transparent but opake. The reason why the world lacks unity, and lies broken and in heaps, is, because man is disunited with himself. He cannot be a naturalist, until he satisfies all the demands of the spirit. Love is as much its demand, as perception. Indeed, neither can be perfect without the other. In the uttermost meaning of the words, thought is devout, and devotion is thought. Deep calls unto deep.[12] But in actual life, the marriage is not celebrated. There are innocent men who worship God after the tradition of their fathers, but their sense of duty has not yet extended to the use of all their faculties. And there are patient naturalists, but they freeze their subject under the wintry light of the understanding. Is not prayer also a study of truth,—a sally of the soul into the unfound infinite? No man ever prayed heartily, without learning something. But when a faithful thinker, resolute to detach every object from personal relations, and see it in the light of thought, shall, at the same time, kindle science with the fire of the holiest affections, then will God go forth anew into the creation.

It will not need, when the mind is prepared for study, to search for objects. The invariable mark of wisdom is to see the miraculous in the common. What is a day? What is a year? What is summer? What is woman? What is a child? What is sleep? To our blindness, these things seem unaffecting. We make fables to hide the baldness of the fact and conform it, as we say, to the higher law of the mind. But when the fact is seen under the light of an idea, the gaudy fable fades and shrivels. We behold the real higher law. To the wise, therefore, a fact is true poetry, and the most beautiful of fables. These wonders are brought to our own door. You also are a man. Man and woman, and their social life, poverty, labor, sleep, fear, fortune, are known to you. Learn that none of these things is superficial, but that each phenomenon hath its roots in the faculties and affections of the mind. Whilst the abstract question occupies your intellect, nature brings it in the concrete to be solved by your hands. It were a wise inquiry for the closet, to compare, point by point, especially at remarkable crises in life, our daily history, with the rise and progress of ideas in the mind.

So shall we come to look at the world with new eyes. It shall answer the endless inquiry of the intellect,—What is truth? and of the affections,—What is good? by yielding itself passive to the educated Will. Then shall come to pass what my poet said; 'Nature is not fixed but fluid. Spirit alters, moulds, makes it. The immobility or bruteness of nature, is the absence of spirit; to pure spirit, it is fluid, it is volatile, it is obedient. Every spirit builds itself a house; and beyond its house, a world; and beyond its world, a heaven. Know then, that the world exists for you. For you is the phenomenon perfect. What we are, that only can we see. All that Adam had, all that Caesar could, you have and can do. Adam called his house, heaven and earth; Caesar called his house, Rome; you perhaps call yours, a cobler's trade; a hundred acres of ploughed land; or a scholar's garret. Yet line for line and point for point, your dominion is as great as theirs, though without fine names. Build, therefore, your own world. As fast as you conform your life to the pure idea in your mind, that will unfold its great proportions. A correspondent revolution in things will attend the influx of the spirit. So fast will disagreeable appearances, swine, spiders, snakes, pests, mad-houses, prisons, enemies, vanish; they are temporary and shall be no more seen. The sordor and filths of nature, the sun shall

---

[12]Psalm 42:7.

dry up, and the wind exhale. As when the summer comes from the south, the snow-banks melt, and the face of the earth becomes green before it, so shall the advancing spirit create its ornaments along its path, and carry with it the beauty it visits, and the song which enchants it; it shall draw beautiful faces, and warm hearts, and wise discourse, and heroic acts, around its way, until evil is no more seen. The kingdom of man over nature, which cometh not with observation,—a dominion such as now is beyond his dream of God,—he shall enter without more wonder than the blind man feels who is gradually restored to perfect sight.'

1836

The American Scholar[1]

AN ORATION

Delivered Before the Phi Beta Kappa Society, at Cambridge, August 31, 1837

Mr. President, and Gentlemen,

I greet you on the re-commencement of our literary year.[2] Our anniversary is one of hope, and, perhaps, not enough of labor. We do not meet for games of strength or skill, for the recitation of histories, tragedies and odes, like the ancient Greeks; for parliaments of love and poesy, like the Troubadours; nor for the advancement of science, like our cotemporaries in the British and European capitals. Thus far, our holiday has been simply a friendly sign of the survival of the love of letters amongst a people too busy to give to letters any more. As such, it is precious as the sign of an indestructible instinct. Perhaps the time is already come, when it ought to be, and will be something else; when the sluggard intellect of this continent will look from under its iron lids and fill the postponed expectation of the world with something better than the exertions of mechanical skill. Our day of dependence, our long apprenticeship to the learning of other lands, draws to a close. The millions that around us are rushing into life, cannot always be fed on the sere remains of foreign harvests. Events, actions arise, that must be sung, that will sing themselves. Who can doubt that poetry will revive and lead in a new age, as the star in the constellation Harp[3] which now flames in our zenith, astronomers announce, shall one day be the pole-star for a thousand years?

In the light of this hope, I accept the topic which not only usage, but the nature of our association, seem to prescribe to this day,—the AMERICAN SCHOLAR. Year by year, we come up hither to read one more chapter of his biography. Let us inquire what light new days and events have thrown on his character, his duties and his hopes.

It is one of those fables, which out of an unknown antiquity, convey an unlooked-for wisdom, that the gods, in the beginning, divided Man into men, that he might be more helpful to himself; just as the hand was divided into fingers, the better to answer its end.

The old fable covers a doctrine ever new and sublime; that there is One Man, —present to all particular men only partially, or through one faculty; and that

---

[1] Oliver Wendell Holmes's characterization of "The American Scholar" as America's "intellectual Declaration of Independence" has endured without challenge.
[2] I.e., the new academic year.

[3] The constellation Lyra, said to resemble the harp of Orpheus, containing the bright star Vega; in becoming the polestar, it would be the star toward which the earth's axis points.

you must take the whole society to find the whole man. Man is not a farmer, or a professor, or an engineer, but he is all. Man is priest, and scholar, and statesman, and producer, and soldier. In the *divided* or social state, these functions are parcelled out to individuals, each of whom aims to do his stint of the joint work, whilst each other performs his. The fable implies that the individual to possess himself, must sometimes return from his own labor to embrace all the other laborers. But unfortunately, this original unit, this fountain of power, has been so distributed to multitudes, has been so minutely subdivided and peddled out, that it is spilled into drops, and cannot be gathered. The state of society is one in which the members have suffered amputation from the trunk, and strut about so many walking monsters,—a good finger, a neck, a stomach, an elbow, but never a man.

Man is thus metamorphosed into a thing, into many things. The planter, who is Man sent out into the field to gather food, is seldom cheered by any idea of the true dignity of his ministry. He sees his bushel and his cart, and nothing beyond, and sinks into the farmer, instead of Man on the farm. The tradesman scarcely ever gives an ideal worth to his work, but is ridden by the routine of his craft, and the soul is subject to dollars. The priest becomes a form; the attorney, a statute-book; the mechanic, a machine; the sailor, a rope of a ship.

In this distribution of functions, the scholar is the delegated intellect. In the right state, he is, *Man Thinking*. In the degenerate state, when the victim of society, he tends to become a mere thinker, or, still worse, the parrot of other men's thinking.

In this view of him, as Man Thinking, the whole theory of his office is contained. Him nature solicits, with all her placid, all her monitory pictures. Him the past instructs. Him the future invites. Is not, indeed, every man a student, and do not all things exist for the student's behoof? And, finally, is not the true scholar the only true master? But, as the old oracle said, "All things have two handles. Beware of the wrong one." In life, too often, the scholar errs with mankind and forfeits his privilege. Let us see him in his school, and consider him in reference to the main influences he receives.

I. The first in time and the first in importance of the influences upon the mind is that of nature. Every day, the sun; and, after sunset, night and her stars. Ever the winds blow; ever the grass grows. Every day, men and women, conversing, beholding and beholden. The scholar must needs stand wistful and admiring before this great spectacle. He must settle its value in his mind. What is nature to him? There is never a beginning, there is never an end to the inexplicable continuity of this web of God, but always circular power returning into itself. Therein it resembles his own spirit, whose beginning, whose ending he never can find—so entire, so boundless. Far, too, as her splendors shine, system on system shooting like rays, upward, downward, without centre, without circumference,—in the mass and in the particle nature hastens to render account of herself to the mind. Classification begins. To the young mind, every thing is individual, stands by itself. By and by, it finds how to join two things, and see in them one nature; then three, then three thousand; and so, tyrannized over by its own unifying instinct, it goes on tying things together, diminishing anomalies, discovering roots running under ground, whereby contrary and remote things cohere, and flower out from one stem. It presently learns, that, since the dawn of history, there has been a constant accumulation and classifying of facts. But what is classification but the perceiving that these objects are not chaotic, and are not foreign, but have a law which is also a law of the human mind? The astronomer discovers that geometry, a pure abstraction of the human mind, is the measure of planetary motion. The chemist finds proportions and intelligible method throughout matter: and science is nothing but the finding of analogy, identity in the most remote parts. The ambitious soul sits down before each refractory fact; one after another, reduces all strange constitutions, all new powers, to their class and their law, and goes on forever to animate the last fibre of organization, the outskirts of nature, by insight.

Thus to him, to this school-boy under the bending dome of day, is suggested, that he and it proceed from one root; one is leaf and one is flower; relation, sympathy, stirring in every vein. And what is that Root? Is not that the soul of his soul?—A thought too bold—a dream too wild. Yet when this spiritual light shall have revealed the law of more earthly natures, when he has learned to worship the soul, and to see that the natural philosophy that now is, is only the first gropings of its gigantic hand, he shall look forward to an ever expanding knowledge as to a becoming creator. He shall see that nature is the opposite of the soul, answering to it part for part. One is seal, and one is print. Its beauty is the beauty of his own mind. Its laws are the laws of his own mind. Nature then becomes to him the measure of his attainments. So much of nature as he is ignorant of, so much of his own mind does he not yet possess. And, in fine, the ancient precept, "Know thyself," and the modern precept, "Study nature," become at last one maxim.

II. The next great influence into the spirit of the scholar, is, the mind of the Past,—in whatever form, whether of literature, of art, of institutions, that mind is inscribed. Books are the best type of the influence of the past, and perhaps we shall get at the truth—learn the amount of this influence more conveniently—by considering their value alone.

The theory of books is noble. The scholar of the first age received into him the world around; brooded thereon; gave it the new arrangement of his own mind, and uttered it again. It came into him—life; it went out from him—truth. It came to him—short-lived actions; it went out from him—immortal thoughts. It came to him—business; it went from him—poetry. It was—dead fact; now, it is quick[4] thought. It can stand, and it can go. It now endures, it now flies, it now inspires. Precisely in proportion to the depth of mind from which it issued, so high does it soar, so long does it sing.

Or, I might say, it depends on how far the process had gone, of transmuting life into truth. In proportion to the completeness of the distillation, so will the purity and imperishableness of the product be. But none is quite perfect. As no air-pump can by any means make a perfect vacuum, so neither can any artist entirely exclude the conventional, the local, the perishable from his book, or write a book of pure thought that shall be as efficient, in all respects, to a remote posterity, as to cotemporaries, or rather to the second age. Each age, it is found, must write its own books; or rather, each generation for the next succeeding. The books of an older period will not fit this.

Yet hence arises a grave mischief. The sacredness which attaches to the act of creation,—the act of thought,—is instantly transferred to the record. The poet chanting, was felt to be a divine man. Henceforth the chant is divine also. The writer was a just and wise spirit. Henceforward it is settled, the book is perfect; as love of the hero corrupts into worship of his statue. Instantly, the book becomes noxious. The guide is a tyrant. We sought a brother, and lo, a governor. The sluggish and perverted mind of the multitude, always slow to open to the incursions of Reason,[5] having once so opened, having once received this book, stands upon it, and makes an outcry, if it is disparaged. Colleges are built on it. Books are written on it by thinkers, not by Man Thinking; by men of talent, that is, who start wrong, who set out from accepted dogmas, not from their own sight of principles. Meek young men grow up in libraries, believing it their duty to accept the views which

---

[4]Living.
[5]In Emerson's vocabulary, "Reason" is the intuitional, mystical, suprarational and thus highest faculty of the mind, above "Understanding."

Cicero, which Locke, which Bacon have given, forgetful that Cicero, Locke and Bacon were only young men in libraries when they wrote these books.[6]

Hence, instead of Man Thinking, we have the bookworm. Hence, the book-learned class, who value books, as such; not as related to nature and the human constitution, but as making a sort of Third Estate with the world and the soul.[7] Hence, the restorers of readings, the emendators, the bibliomaniacs of all degrees.

This is bad; this is worse than it seems. Books are the best of things, well used; abused, among the worst. What is the right use? What is the one end which all means go to effect? They are for nothing but to inspire. I had better never see a book than to be warped by its attraction clean out of my own orbit, and made a satellite instead of a system. The one thing in the world of value, is, the active soul,—the soul, free, sovereign, active. This every man is entitled to; this every man contains within him, although in almost all men, obstructed, and as yet un-born. The soul active sees absolute truth; and utters truth, or creates. In this ac-tion, it is genius; not the privilege of here and there a favorite, but the sound es-tate of every man. In its essence, it is progressive. The book, the college, the school of art, the institution of any kind, stop with some past utterance of genius. This is good, say they, let us hold by this. They pin me down. They look backward and not forward. But genius always looks forward. The eyes of man are set in his forehead, not in his hindhead. Man hopes. Genius creates. To create,—to cre-ate,—is the proof of a divine presence. Whatever talents may be, if the man create not, the pure efflux[8] of the Deity is not his:—cinders and smoke, there may be, but not yet flame. There are creative manners, there are creative actions, and cre-ative words; manners, actions, words, that is, indicative of no custom or authority, but springing spontaneous from the mind's own sense of good and fair.

On the other part, instead of being its own seer, let it receive always from an-other mind its truth, though it were in torrents of light, without periods of soli-tude, inquest and self-recovery, and a fatal disservice is done. Genius is always suf-ficiently the enemy of genius by over-influence. The literature of every nation bear me witness. The English dramatic poets have Shakspearized now for two hundred years.

Undoubtedly there is a right way of reading,—so it be sternly subordinated. Man Thinking must not be subdued by his instruments. Books are for the schol-ar's idle times. When he can read God directly, the hour is too precious to be wasted in other men's transcripts of their readings. But when the intervals of darkness come, as come they must,—when the soul seeth not, when the sun is hid, and the stars withdraw their shining,—we repair to the lamps which were kindled by their ray to guide our steps to the East again, where the dawn is. We hear that we may speak. The Arabian proverb says, "A fig tree looking on a fig tree, be-cometh fruitful."

It is remarkable, the character of the pleasure we derive from the best books. They impress us ever with the conviction that one nature wrote and the same reads. We read the verses of one of the great English poets, of Chaucer, of Mar-vell, of Dryden, with the most modern joy,—with a pleasure, I mean, which is in great part caused by the abstraction of all *time* from their verses. There is some awe mixed with the joy of our surprise, when this poet, who lived in some past world, two or three hundred years ago, says that which lies close to my own soul, that which I also had wellnigh thought and said. But for the evidence thence af-

---

[6]Marcus Tullius Cicero (106–43 B.C.), Roman orator and philosopher; John Locke (1632–1704), British philoso-pher; Francis Bacon (1561–1626), British scientist and es-sayist. All are important thinkers and writers who were taught in the schools and read in the libraries.
[7]I.e., those who are merely book-learned, without relating their learning to living experience, constitute a third group or class separate from the world and the soul. In medieval Europe there were three estates or classes—the nobility, the clergy, and the common people.
[8]Outpouring.

forded to the philosophical doctrine of the identity of all minds, we should suppose some preestablished harmony, some foresight of souls that were to be, and some preparation of stores for their future wants, like the fact observed in insects, who lay up food before death for the young grub they shall never see.

I would not be hurried by any love of system, by any exaggeration of instincts, to underrate the Book. We all know, that as the human body can be nourished on any food, though it were boiled grass and the broth of shoes, so the human mind can be fed by any knowledge. And great and heroic men have existed, who had almost no other information than by the printed page. I only would say, that it needs a strong head to bear that diet. One must be an inventor to read well. As the proverb says, "He that would bring home the wealth of the Indies, must carry out the wealth of the Indies." There is then creative reading, as well as creative writing. When the mind is braced by labor and invention, the page of whatever book we read becomes luminous with manifold allusion. Every sentence is doubly significant, and the sense of our author is as broad as the world. We then see, what is always true, that as the seer's hour of vision is short and rare among heavy days and months, so is its record, perchance, the least part of his volume. The discerning will read in his Plato or Shakspeare, only that least part,— only the authentic utterances of the oracle,— and all the rest he rejects, were it never so many times Plato's and Shakspeare's.

Of course, there is a portion of reading quite indispensable to a wise man. History and exact science he must learn by laborious reading. Colleges, in like manner, have their indispensable office,— to teach elements. But they can only highly serve us, when they aim not to drill, but to create; when they gather from far every ray of various genius to their hospitable halls, and, by the concentrated fires, set the hearts of their youth on flame. Thought and knowledge are natures in which apparatus and pretension avail nothing. Gowns, and pecuniary foundations,[9] though of towns of gold, can never countervail the least sentence or syllable of wit.[10] Forget this, and our American colleges will recede in their public importance whilst they grow richer every year.

III. There goes in the world a notion that the scholar should be a recluse, a valetudinarian,[11] —as unfit for any handiwork or public labor, as a penknife for an axe. The so-called "practical men" sneer at speculative men, as if, because they speculate[12] or *see,* they could do nothing. I have heard it said that the clergy,— who are always more universally than any other class, the scholars of their day, —are addressed as women: that the rough, spontaneous conversation of men they do not hear, but only a mincing and diluted speech. They are often virtually disfranchised; and, indeed, there are advocates for their celibacy. As far as this is true of the studious classes, it is not just and wise. Action is with the scholar subordinate, but it is essential. Without it, he is not yet man. Without it, thought can never ripen into truth. Whilst the world hangs before the eye as a cloud of beauty, we cannot even see its beauty. Inaction is cowardice, but there can be no scholar without the heroic mind. The preamble of thought, the transition through which it passes from the unconscious to the conscious, is action. Only so much do I know, as I have lived. Instantly we know whose words are loaded with life, and whose not.

The world,— this shadow of the soul, or *other me,* lies wide around. Its attractions are the keys which unlock my thoughts and make me acquainted with myself. I run eagerly into this resounding tumult. I grasp the hands of those next me, and take my place in the ring to suffer and to work, taught by an instinct that so shall the dumb abyss be vocal with speech. I pierce its order; I dissipate its fear;

---

[9]Academic dress and financial foundations.
[10]Wisdom.

[11]Sickly person.
[12]From Latin, "observe."

I dispose of it within the circuit of my expanding life. So much only of life as I know by experience, so much of the wilderness have I vanquished and planted, or so far have I extended my being, my dominion. I do not see how any man can afford, for the sake of his nerves and his nap, to spare any action in which he can partake. It is pearls and rubies to his discourse. Drudgery, calamity, exasperation, want, are instructers in eloquence and wisdom. The true scholar grudges every opportunity of action past by, as a loss of power.

It is the raw material out of which the intellect moulds her splendid products. A strange process too, this, by which experience is converted into thought, as a mulberry leaf is converted into satin.[13] The manufacture goes forward at all hours.

The actions and events of our childhood and youth are now matters of calmest observation. They lie like fair pictures in the air. Not so with our recent actions,— with the business which we now have in hand. On this we are quite unable to speculate. Our affections as yet circulate through it. We no more feel or know it, than we feel the feet, or the hand, or the brain of our body. The new deed is yet a part of life,—remains for a time immersed in our unconscious life. In some contemplative hour, it detaches itself from the life like a ripe fruit, to become a thought of the mind. Instantly, it is raised, transfigured; the corruptible has put on incorruption.[14] Always now it is an object of beauty, however base its origin and neighborhood. Observe, too, the impossibility of antedating this act. In its grub state, it cannot fly, it cannot shine,—it is a dull grub. But suddenly, without observation, the selfsame thing unfurls beautiful wings, and is an angel of wisdom. So is there no fact, no event, in our private history, which shall not, sooner or later, lose its adhesive inert form, and astonish us by soaring from our body into the empyrean. Cradle and infancy, school and playground, the fear of boys, and dogs, and ferules,[15] the love of little maids and berries, and many another fact that once filled the whole sky, are gone already; friend and relative, profession and party, town and country, nation and world, must also soar and sing.

Of course, he who has put forth his total strength in fit actions, has the richest return of wisdom. I will not shut myself out of this globe of action and transplant an oak into a flower pot, there to hunger and pine; nor trust the revenue of some single faculty, and exhaust one vein of thought, much like those Savoyards,[16] who, getting their livelihood by carving shepherds, shepherdesses, and smoking Dutchmen, for all Europe, went out one day to the mountain to find stock, and discovered that they had whittled up the last of their pine trees. Authors we have in numbers, who have written out their vein, and who, moved by a commendable prudence, sail for Greece or Palestine, follow the trapper into the prairie, or ramble round Algiers to replenish their merchantable stock.

If it were only for a vocabulary the scholar would be covetous of action. Life is our dictionary. Years are well spent in country labors; in town—in the insight into trades and manufactures; in frank intercourse with many men and women; in science; in art; to the one end of mastering in all their facts a language, by which to illustrate and embody our perceptions. I learn immediately from any speaker how much he has already lived, through the poverty or the splendor of his speech. Life lies behind us as the quarry from whence we get tiles and copestones for the masonry of to-day. This is the way to learn grammar. Colleges and books only copy the language which the field and the work-yard made.

But the final value of action, like that of books, and better than books, is, that it is a resource. That great principle of Undulation in nature, that shows itself in the

[13]I.e., silk created by silkworms eating mulberry leaves.
[14]1 Corinthians 15:53: "For this corruptible must put on incorruption, and this mortal must put on immortality."
[15]A ruler or stick.
[16]People of Savoy, a province once in Italy, now in France.

inspiring and expiring of the breath; in desire and satiety; in the ebb and flow of the sea, in day and night, in heat and cold, and as yet more deeply ingrained in every atom and every fluid, is known to us under the name of Polarity,—these "fits of easy transmission and reflection,"[17] as Newton called them, are the law of nature because they are the law of spirit.

The mind now thinks; now acts; and each fit reproduces the other. When the artist has exhausted his materials, when the fancy no longer paints, when thoughts are no longer apprehended, and books are a weariness,—he has always the resource *to live*. Character is higher than intellect. Thinking is the function. Living is the functionary. The stream retreats to its source. A great soul will be strong to live, as well as strong to think. Does he lack organ or medium to impart his truths? He can still fall back on this elemental force of living them. This is a total act. Thinking is a partial act. Let the grandeur of justice shine in his affairs. Let the beauty of affection cheer his lowly roof. Those "far from fame" who dwell and act with him, will feel the force of his constitution in the doings and passages of the day better than it can be measured by any public and designed display. Time shall teach him that the scholar loses no hour which the man lives. Herein he unfolds the sacred germ of his instinct, screened from influence. What is lost in seemliness is gained in strength. Not out of those on whom systems of education have exhausted their culture, comes the helpful giant to destroy the old or to build the new, but out of unhandselled[18] savage nature, out of terrible Druids and Berserkirs,[19] come at last Alfred[20] and Shakspear.

I hear therefore with joy whatever is beginning to be said of the dignity and necessity of labor to every citizen. There is virtue yet in the hoe and the spade, for learned as well as for unlearned hands. And labor is every where welcome; always we are invited to work; only be this limitation observed, that a man shall not for the sake of wider activity sacrifice any opinion to the popular judgments and modes of action.

I have now spoken of the education of the scholar by nature, by books, and by action. It remains to say somewhat of his duties.

They are such as become Man Thinking. They may all be comprised in self-trust. The office of the scholar is to cheer, to raise, and to guide men by showing them facts amidst appearances. He plies the slow, unhonored, and unpaid task of observation. Flamsteed and Herschel,[21] in their glazed observatories, may catalogue the stars with the praise of all men, and, the results being splendid and useful, honor is sure. But he, in his private observatory, cataloguing obscure and nebulous stars of the human mind, which as yet no man has thought of as such,—watching days and months, sometimes, for a few facts; correcting still his old records;—must relinquish display and immediate fame. In the long period of his preparation, he must betray often an ignorance and shiftlessness in popular arts, incurring the disdain of the able who shoulder him aside. Long he must stammer in his speech; often forego the living for the dead. Worse yet, he must accept—how often! poverty and solitude. For the ease and pleasure of treading the old road, accepting the fashions, the education, the religion of society, he takes the cross of making his own, and, of course, the self-accusation, the faint heart, the frequent uncertainty and loss of time which are the nettles and tangling vines in the way of the self-relying and self-directed; and the state of virtual hostility in

---

[17]From *Optics* by Sir Isaac Newton (1642–1727), British scientist.

[18]I.e., without the gift of formal education; "handsel" is a gift or present.

[19]Druids were a Celtic religious order of priests in ancient Britain; Berserkers were frenzied warriors of Norse legend.

[20]King Alfred (849–899) ruled Wessex and, later, England, promoting English culture.

[21]John Flamsteed (1646–1719) and Sir William Herschel (1738–1822), noted early astronomers.

which he seems to stand to society, and especially to educated society. For all this loss and scorn, what offset? He is to find consolation in exercising the highest functions of human nature. He is one who raises himself from private considerations, and breathes and lives on public and illustrious thoughts. He is the world's eye. He is the world's heart. He is to resist the vulgar prosperity that retrogrades ever to barbarism, by preserving and communicating heroic sentiments, noble biographies, melodious verse, and the conclusions of history. Whatsoever oracles the human heart in all emergencies, in all solemn hours has uttered as its commentary on the world of actions,—these he shall receive and impart. And whatsoever new verdict Reason from her inviolable seat pronounces on the passing men and events of to-day,—this he shall hear and promulgate.

These being his functions, it becomes him to feel all confidence in himself, and to defer never to the popular cry. He and he only knows the world. The world of any moment is the merest appearance. Some great decorum,[22] some fetish of a government, some ephemeral trade, or war, or man, is cried up by half mankind and cried down by the other half, as if all depended on this particular up or down. The odds are that the whole question is not worth the poorest thought which the scholar has lost in listening to the controversy. Let him not quit his belief that a popgun is a popgun, though the ancient and honorable of the earth affirm it to be the crack of doom. In silence, in steadiness, in severe abstraction, let him hold by himself; add observation to observation, patient of neglect, patient of reproach; and bide his own time,—happy enough if he can satisfy himself alone that this day he has seen something truly. Success treads on every right step. For the instinct is sure that prompts him to tell his brother what he thinks. He then learns that in going down into the secrets of his own mind, he has descended into the secrets of all minds. He learns that he who has mastered any law in his private thoughts, is master to that extent of all men whose language he speaks, and of all into whose language his own can be translated. The poet in utter solitude remembering his spontaneous thoughts and recording them, is found to have recorded that which men in crowded cities find true for them also. The orator distrusts at first the fitness of his frank confessions,—his want of knowledge of the persons he addresses,—until he finds that he is the complement of his hearers;—that they drink his words because he fulfils for them their own nature; the deeper he dives into his privatest secretest presentiment,—to his wonder he finds, this is the most acceptable, most public, and universally true. The people delight in it; the better part of every man feels, This is my music: this is myself.

In self-trust, all the virtues are comprehended. Free should the scholar be,— free and brave. Free even to the definition of freedom, "without any hindrance that does not arise out of his own constitution." Brave; for fear is a thing which a scholar by his very function puts behind him. Fear always springs from ignorance. It is a shame to him if his tranquillity, amid dangerous times, arise from the presumption that like children and women, his is a protected class; or if he seek a temporary peace by the diversion of his thoughts from politics or vexed questions, hiding his head like an ostrich in the flowering bushes, peeping into microscopes, and turning rhymes, as a boy whistles to keep his courage up. So is the danger a danger still: so is the fear worse. Manlike let him turn and face it. Let him look into its eye and search its nature, inspect its origin,—see the whelping[23] of this lion,—which lies no great way back; he will then find in himself a perfect comprehension of its nature and extent; he will have made his hands meet on the other side, and can henceforth defy it, and pass on superior. The world is his who can see through its pretension. What deafness, what stone-blind custom, what over-

---

[22]Rule of conduct or behavior.
[23]Birth.

grown error you behold, is there only by sufferance,—by your sufferance. See it to be a lie, and you have already dealt it its mortal blow.

Yes, we are the cowed,—we the trustless. It is a mischievous notion that we are come late into nature; that the world was finished a long time ago. As the world was plastic and fluid in the hands of God, so it is ever to so much of his attributes as we bring to it. To ignorance and sin, it is flint. They adapt themselves to it as they may; but in proportion as a man has anything in him divine, the firmament flows before him, and takes his signet and form. Not he is great who can alter matter, but he who can alter my state of mind. They are the kings of the world who give the color of their present thought to all nature and all art, and persuade men by the cheerful serenity of their carrying the matter, that this thing which they do, is the apple which the ages have desired to pluck, now at last ripe, and inviting nations to the harvest. The great man makes the great thing. Wherever Macdonald sits, there is the head of the table.[24] Linnæus makes botany the most alluring of studies and wins it from the farmer and the herb-woman. Davy, chemistry: and Cuvier, fossils.[25] The day is always his, who works in it with serenity and great aims. The unstable estimates of men crowd to him whose mind is filled with a truth, as the heaped waves of the Atlantic follow the moon.

For this self-trust, the reason is deeper than can be fathomed,—darker than can be enlightened. I might not carry with me the feeling of my audience in stating my own belief. But I have already shown the ground of my hope, in adverting to the doctrine that man is one. I believe man has been wronged: he has wronged himself. He has almost lost the light that can lead him back to his prerogatives. Men are become of no account. Men in history, men in the world of to-day are bugs, are spawn, and are called "the mass," and "the herd." In a century, in a millenium, one or two men; that is to say—one or two approximations to the right state of every man. All the rest behold in the hero or the poet their own green and crude being—ripened; yes, and are content to be less, so *that* may attain to its full stature. What a testimony—full of grandeur, full of pity, is borne to the demands of his own nature, by the poor clansman, the poor partisan, who rejoices in the glory of his chief. The poor and the low find some amends to their immense moral capacity, for their acquiescence in a political and social inferiority. They are content to be brushed like flies from the path of a great person, so that justice shall be done by him to that common nature which it is the dearest desire of all to see enlarged and glorified. They sun themselves in the great man's light, and feel it to be their own element. They cast the dignity of man from their downtrod selves upon the shoulders of a hero, and will perish to add one drop of blood to make that great heart beat, those giant sinews combat and conquer. He lives for us, and we live in him.

Men such as they are, very naturally seek money or power; and power because it is as good as money,—the "spoils," so called, "of office." And why not? for they aspire to the highest, and this, in their sleep-walking, they dream is highest. Wake them, and they shall quit the false good and leap to the true, and leave governments to clerks and desks. This revolution is to be wrought by the gradual domestication of the idea of Culture. The main enterprise of the world for splendor, for extent, is the upbuilding of a man. Here are the materials strown along the ground. The private life of one man shall be a more illustrious monarchy,—more formidable to its enemy, more sweet and serene in its influence to its friend, than any kingdom in history. For a man, rightly viewed, comprehendeth the particular natures of all men. Each philosopher, each bard, each actor, has only done for

---

[24]A saying or proverb.
[25]Carolus Linnaeus (1707–1778), Swedish botanist; Sir Humphry Davy (1778–1829), British chemist; George Leopold Cuvier (1769–1832), French naturalist. All were innovators in their fields.

me, as by a delegate, what one day I can do for myself. The books which once we valued more than the apple of the eye, we have quite exhausted. What is that but saying that we have come up with the point of view which the universal mind took through the eyes of that one scribe; we have been that man, and have passed on. First, one; then, another; we drain all cisterns, and waxing[26] greater by all these supplies, we crave a better and more abundant food. The man has never lived that can feed us ever. The human mind cannot be enshrined in a person who shall set a barrier on any one side to this unbounded, unboundable empire. It is one central fire which flaming now out of the lips of Etna, lightens the capes of Sicily; and now out of the throat of Vesuvius, illuminates the towers and vineyards of Naples. It is one light which beams out of a thousand stars. It is one soul which animates all men.

But I have dwelt perhaps tediously upon this abstraction of the Scholar. I ought not to delay longer to add what I have to say, of nearer reference to the time and to this country.

Historically, there is thought to be a difference in the ideas which predominate over successive epochs, and there are data for marking the genius of the Classic, of the Romantic, and now of the Reflective or Philosophical age. With the views I have intimated of the oneness or the identity of the mind through all individuals, I do not much dwell on these differences. In fact, I believe each individual passes through all three. The boy is a Greek; the youth, romantic; the adult, reflective. I deny not, however, that a revolution in the leading idea may be distinctly enough traced.

Our age is bewailed as the age of Introversion. Must that needs be evil? We, it seems, are critical. We are embarrassed with second thoughts. We cannot enjoy any thing for hankering to know whereof the pleasure consists. We are lined with eyes. We see with our feet. The time is infected with Hamlet's unhappiness,—

"Sicklied o'er with the pale cast of thought."[27]

Is it so bad then? Sight is the last thing to be pitied. Would we be blind? Do we fear lest we should outsee nature and God, and drink truth dry? I look upon the discontent of the literary class as a mere announcement of the fact that they find themselves not in the state of mind of their fathers, and regret the coming state as untried; as a boy dreads the water before he has learned that he can swim. If there is any period one would desire to be born in,—is it not the age of Revolution; when the old and the new stand side by side, and admit of being compared; when the energies of all men are searched by fear and by hope; when the historic glories of the old, can be compensated by the rich possibilities of the new era? This time, like all times, is a very good one, if we but know what to do with it.

I read with joy some of the auspicious signs of the coming days as they glimmer already through poetry and art, through philosophy and science, through church and state.

One of these signs is the fact that the same movement which effected the elevation of what was called the lowest class in the state, assumed in literature a very marked and as benign an aspect. Instead of the sublime and beautiful, the near, the low, the common, was explored and poetized. That which had been negligently trodden under foot by those who were harnessing and provisioning themselves for long journeys into far countries, is suddenly found to be richer than all foreign parts. The literature of the poor, the feelings of the child, the philosophy of the street, the meaning of household life, are the topics of the time. It is a great stride. It is a sign—is it not? of new vigor, when the extremities are made active,

---

[26]Growing.
[27]*Hamlet*, III, i, 85.

when currents of warm life run into the hands and the feet. I ask not for the great, the remote, the romantic; what is doing in Italy or Arabia; what is Greek art, or Provencal Minstrelsy;[28] I embrace the common, I explore and sit at the feet of the familiar, the low. Give me insight into to-day, and you may have the antique and future worlds. What would we really know the meaning of? The meal in the firkin;[29] the milk in the pan; the ballad in the street; the news of the boat; the glance of the eye; the form and the gait of the body;—show me the ultimate reason of these matters;—show me the sublime presence of the highest spiritual cause lurking, as always it does lurk, in these suburbs and extremities of nature; let me see every trifle bristling with the polarity that ranges it instantly on an eternal law; and the shop, the plough, and the leger, referred to the like cause by which light undulates and poets sing;—and the world lies no longer a dull miscellany and lumber room,[30] but has form and order; there is no trifle; there is no puzzle; but one design unites and animates the farthest pinnacle and the lowest trench.

This idea has inspired the genius of Goldsmith, Burns, Cowper, and, in a newer time, of Goethe, Wordsworth, and Carlyle. This idea they have differently followed and with various success. In contrast with their writing, the style of Pope, of Johnson, of Gibbon, looks cold and pedantic.[31] This writing is blood-warm. Man is surprised to find that things near are not less beautiful and wondrous than things remote. The near explains the far. The drop is a small ocean. A man is related to all nature. This perception of the worth of the vulgar, is fruitful in discoveries. Goethe, in this very thing the most modern of the moderns, has shown us, as none ever did, the genius of the ancients.

There is one man of genius who has done much for this philosophy of life, whose literary value has never yet been rightly estimated;—I mean Emanuel Swedenborg.[32] The most imaginative of men, yet writing with the precision of a mathematician, he endeavored to engraft a purely philosophical Ethics on the popular Christianity of his time. Such an attempt, of course, must have difficulty which no genius could surmount. But he saw and showed the connexion between nature and the affections of the soul. He pierced the emblematic or spiritual character of the visible, audible, tangible world. Especially did his shade-loving muse hover over and interpret the lower parts of nature; he showed the mysterious bond that allies moral evil to the foul material forms, and has given in epical parables a theory of insanity, of beasts, of unclean and fearful things.

Another sign of our times, also marked by an analogous political movement is, the new importance given to the single person. Every thing that tends to insulate the individual,—to surround him with barriers of natural respect, so that each man shall feel the world is his, and man shall treat with man as a sovereign state with a sovereign state;—tends to true union as well as greatness. "I learned," said the melancholy Pestalozzi,[33] "that no man in God's wide earth is either willing or able to help any other man." Help must come from the bosom alone. The scholar is that man who must take up into himself all the ability of the time, all the contributions of the past, all the hopes of the future. He must be an university of knowledges. If there be one lesson more than another which should pierce his ear, it is, The world is nothing, the man is all; in yourself is the law of all nature, and you know not yet how a globule of sap ascends; in yourself slumbers the whole of Rea-

---

[28]Lyric poetry sung by the roaming troubadours of Provence (in southern France) during the medieval period.
[29]A container, about one-fourth of a barrel.
[30]Storeroom.
[31]Oliver Goldsmith, Robert Burns, and William Cowper were eighteenth-century forerunners of the great Romantic writers, Johann Wolfgang von Goethe, William Wordsworth, and Thomas Carlyle. Alexander Pope, Samuel

Johnson, and Edward Gibbon were the classical (distinctly un-Romantic) writers of the eighteenth century, the Age of Reason.
[32]Emmanuel Swedenborg (1688–1772), Swedish religious and mystical writer.
[33]Johann Heinrich Pestalozzi (1746–1827), Swiss educator, author of *Hints to Parents*.

son; it is for you to know all, it is for you to dare all. Mr. President and Gentlemen, this confidence in the unsearched might of man, belongs by all motives, by all prophecy, by all preparation, to the American Scholar. We have listened too long to the courtly muses of Europe. The spirit of the American freeman is already suspected to be timid, imitative, tame. Public and private avarice make the air we breathe thick and fat. The scholar is decent, indolent, complaisant. See already the tragic consequence. The mind of this country taught to aim at low objects, eats upon itself. There is no work for any but the decorous and the complaisant. Young men of the fairest promise, who begin life upon our shores, inflated by the mountain winds, shined upon by all the stars of God, find the earth below not in unison with these,—but are hindered from action by the disgust which the principles on which business is managed inspire, and turn drudges, or die of disgust,—some of them suicides. What is the remedy? They did not yet see, and thousands of young men as hopeful now crowding to the barriers for the career, do not yet see, that if the single man plant himself indomitably on his instincts, and there abide, the huge world will come round to him. Patience—patience;—with the shades of all the good and great for company; and for solace, the perspective of your own infinite life; and for work, the study and the communication of principles, the making those instincts prevalent, the conversion of the world. Is it not the chief disgrace in the world, not to be an unit;—not to be reckoned one character;—not to yield that peculiar fruit which each man was created to bear, but to be reckoned in the gross, in the hundred, or the thousand, of the party, the section, to which we belong; and our opinion predicted geographically, as the north, or the south. Not so, brothers and friends,—please God, ours shall not be so. We will walk on our own feet; we will work with our own hands; we will speak our own minds. The study of letters shall be no longer a name for pity, for doubt, and for sensual indulgence. The dread of man and the love of man shall be a wall of defence and a wreath of joy around all. A nation of men will for the first time exist, because each believes himself inspired by the Divine Soul which also inspires all men.

1837

The Divinity School Address[1]

AN ADDRESS

Delivered Before the Senior Class in Divinity College, Cambridge, Sunday Evening, 15 July, 1838

In this refulgent summer it has been a luxury to draw the breath of life. The grass grows, the buds burst, the meadow is spotted with fire and gold in the tint of flowers. The air is full of birds, and sweet with the breath of the pine, the balm-of-Gilead, and the new hay. Night brings no gloom to the heart with its welcome shade. Through the transparent darkness the stars pour their almost spiritual rays. Man under them seems a young child, and his huge globe a toy. The cool night bathes the world as with a river, and prepares his eyes again for the crimson

---

[1]As a result of this lecture placing individual spiritual intuition above traditional Christian revelation, Emerson was severely criticized by religious leaders. He wrote to Thomas Carlyle that his essay "has been the occasion of an outcry in all our leading newspapers against my 'infidelity,' 'pantheism,' and 'atheism.'" He was not invited to lecture at Harvard again until 1867.

dawn. The mystery of nature was never displayed more happily. The corn and the wine have been freely dealt to all creatures, and the never-broken silence with which the old bounty goes forward, has not yielded yet one word of explanation. One is constrained to respect the perfection of this world, in which our senses converse. How wide; how rich; what invitation from every property it gives to every faculty of man! In its fruitful soils; in its navigable sea; in its mountains of metal and stone; in its forests of all woods; in its animals; in its chemical ingredients; in the powers and path of light, heat, attraction, and life, it is well worth the pith and heart of great men to subdue and enjoy it. The planters, the mechanics, the inventors, the astronomers, the builders of cities, and the captains, history delights to honor.

But the moment the mind opens, and reveals the laws which traverse the universe, and make things what they are, then shrinks the great world at once into a mere illustration and fable of this mind. What am I? and What is? asks the human spirit with a curiosity new-kindled, but never to be quenched. Behold these outrunning laws, which our imperfect apprehension can see tend this way and that, but not come full circle. Behold these infinite relations, so like, so unlike; many, yet one. I would study, I would know, I would admire forever. These works of thought have been the entertainments of the human spirit in all ages.

A more secret, sweet, and overpowering beauty appears to man when his heart and mind open to the sentiment of virtue. Then instantly he is instructed in what is above him. He learns that his being is without bound; that, to the good, to the perfect, he is born, low as he now lies in evil and weakness. That which he venerates is still his own, though he has not realized it yet. *He ought.* He knows the sense of that grand word, though his analysis fails entirely to render account of it. When in innocency, or when by intellectual perception, he attains to say,—'I love the Right; Truth is beautiful within and without, forevermore. Virtue, I am thine: save me: use me: thee will I serve, day and night, in great, in small, that I may be not virtuous, but virtue;'—then is the end of the creation answered, and God is well pleased.

The sentiment of virtue is a reverence and delight in the presence of certain divine laws. It perceives that this homely game of life we play, covers, under what seem foolish details, principles that astonish. The child amidst his baubles, is learning the action of light, motion, gravity, muscular force; and in the game of human life, love, fear, justice, appetite, man, and God, interact. These laws refuse to be adequately stated. They will not by us or for us be written out on paper, or spoken by the tongue. They elude, evade our persevering thought, and yet we read them hourly in each other's faces, in each other's actions, in our own remorse. The moral traits which are all globed into every virtuous act and thought,—in speech, we must sever, and describe or suggest by painful enumeration of many particulars. Yet, as this sentiment is the essence of all religion, let me guide your eye to the precise objects of the sentiment, by an enumeration of some of those classes of facts in which this element is conspicuous.

The intuition of the moral sentiment is an insight of the perfection of the laws of the soul. These laws execute themselves. They are out of time, out of space, and not subject to circumstance. Thus; in the soul of man there is a justice whose retributions are instant and entire. He who does a good deed, is instantly ennobled himself. He who does a mean deed, is by the action itself contracted. He who puts off impurity, thereby puts on purity. If a man is at heart just, then in so far is he God; the safety of God, the immortality of God, the majesty of God do enter into that man with justice. If a man dissemble, deceive, he deceives himself, and goes out of acquaintance with his own being. A man in the view of absolute goodness, adores, with total humility. Every step so downward, is a step upward. The man who renounces himself, comes to himself by so doing.

See how this rapid intrinsic energy worketh everywhere, righting wrongs, correcting appearances, and bringing up facts to a harmony with thoughts. Its operation in life, though slow to the senses, is, at last, as sure as in the soul. By it, a man is made the Providence to himself, dispensing good to his goodness, and evil to his sin. Character is always known. Thefts never enrich; alms never impoverish; murder will speak out of stone walls. The least admixture of a lie,—for example, the smallest mixture of vanity, the least attempt to make a good impression, a favorable appearance,—will instantly vitiate the effect. But speak the truth, and all nature and all spirits help you with unexpected furtherance. Speak the truth, and all things alive or brute are vouchers, and the very roots of the grass underground there, do seem to stir and move to bear you witness. See again the perfection of the Law as it applies itself to the affections, and becomes the law of society. As we are, so we associate. The good, by affinity, seek the good; the vile, by affinity, the vile. Thus of their own volition, souls proceed into heaven, into hell.

These facts have always suggested to man the sublime creed, that the world is not the product of manifold power, but of one will, of one mind; and that one mind is everywhere active, in each ray of the star, in each wavelet of the pool; and whatever opposes that will, is everywhere baulked and baffled, because things are made so, and not otherwise. Good is positive. Evil is merely privative, not absolute. It is like cold, which is the privation of heat. All evil is so much death or nonentity. Benevolence is absolute and real. So much benevolence as a man hath, so much life hath he. For all things proceed out of this same spirit, which is differently named love, justice, temperance, in its different applications, just as the ocean receives different names on the several shores which it washes. All things proceed out of the same spirit, and all things conspire with it. Whilst a man seeks good ends, he is strong by the whole strength of nature. In so far as he roves from these ends, he bereaves himself of power, of auxiliaries; his being shrinks out of all remote channels, he becomes less and less, a mote, a point, until absolute badness is absolute death.

The perception of this law of laws always awakens in the mind a sentiment which we call the religious sentiment, and which makes our highest happiness. Wonderful is its power to charm and to command. It is a mountain air. It is the embalmer of the world. It is myrrh and storax, and chlorine and rosemary. It makes the sky and the hills sublime, and the silent song of the stars is it. By it, is the universe made safe and habitable, not by science or power. Thought may work cold and intransitive in things, and find no end or unity. But the dawn of the sentiment of virtue on the heart, gives and is the assurance that Law is sovereign over all natures; and the worlds, time, space, eternity, do seem to break out into joy.

This sentiment is divine and deifying. It is the beatitude of man. It makes him illimitable. Through it, the soul first knows itself. It corrects the capital mistake of the infant man, who seeks to be great by following the great, and hopes to derive advantages *from another*,—by showing the fountain of all good to be in himself, and that he, equally with every man, is an inlet into the deeps of Reason. When he says, "I ought;" when love warms him; when he chooses, warned from on high, the good and great deed; then, deep melodies wander through his soul from Supreme Wisdom. Then he can worship, and be enlarged by his worship; for he can never go behind this sentiment. In the sublimest flights of the soul, rectitude is never surmounted, love is never outgrown.

This sentiment lies at the foundation of society, and successively creates all forms of worship. The principle of veneration never dies out. Man fallen into superstition, into sensuality, is never wholly without the visions of the moral sentiment. In like manner, all the expressions of this sentiment are sacred and permanent in proportion to their purity. The expressions of this sentiment affect us deeper, greatlier, than all other compositions. The sentences of the oldest time, which ejaculate this piety, are still fresh and fragrant. This thought dwelled always deepest in the minds of men in the devout and contemplative East; not alone in Palestine, where it reached its purest expression, but in Egypt, in Persia, in India, in China. Europe has always owed to oriental genius, its divine impulses. What these holy bards said, all sane men found agreeable and true. And the unique impression of Jesus upon mankind, whose name is not so much written as ploughed into the history of this world, is proof of the subtle virtue of this infusion.

Meantime, whilst the doors of the temple stand open, night and day, before every man, and the oracles of this truth cease never, it is guarded by one stern condition; this, namely; It is an intuition. It cannot be received at second hand. Truly speaking, it is not instruction, but provocation, that I can receive from another soul. What he announces, I must find true in me, or wholly reject; and on his word, or as his second, be he who he may, I can accept nothing. On the contrary, the absence of this primary faith is the presence of degradation. As is the flood so is the ebb. Let this faith depart, and the very words it spake, and the things it made, become false and hurtful. Then falls the church, the state, art, letters, life. The doctrine of the divine nature being forgotten, a sickness infects and dwarfs the constitution. Once man was all; now he is an appendage, a nuisance. And because the indwelling Supreme Spirit cannot wholly be got rid of, the doctrine of it suffers this perversion, that the divine nature is attributed to one or two persons, and denied to all the rest, and denied with fury. The doctrine of inspiration is lost; the base doctrine of the majority of voices, usurps the place of the doctrine of the soul. Miracles, prophecy, poetry, the ideal life, the holy life, exist as ancient history merely; they are not in the belief, nor in the aspiration of society; but, when suggested, seem ridiculous. Life is comic or pitiful, as soon as the high ends of being fade out of sight, and man becomes near-sighted, and can only attend to what addresses the senses.

These general views, which, whilst they are general, none will contest, find abundant illustration in the history of religion, and especially in the history of the Christian church. In that, all of us have had our birth and nurture. The truth contained in that, you, my young friends, are now setting forth to teach. As the Cultus, or established worship of the civilized world, it has great historical interest for us. Of its blessed words, which have been the consolation of humanity, you need not that I should speak. I shall endeavor to discharge my duty to you, on this occasion, by pointing out two errors in its administration, which daily appear more gross from the point of view we have just now taken.

Jesus Christ belonged to the true race of prophets. He saw with open eye the mystery of the soul. Drawn by its severe harmony, ravished with its beauty, he lived in it, and had his being there. Alone in all history, he estimated the greatness of man. One man was true to what is in you and me. He saw that God incarnates himself in man, and evermore goes forth anew to take possession of his world. He said, in this jubilee of sublime emotion, 'I am divine. Through me, God acts; through me, speaks. Would you see God, see me; or, see thee, when thou also thinkest as I now think.'[2] But what a distortion did his doctrine and memory suffer in the same, in the next, and the following ages! There is no doctrine of the Reason which will bear to be taught by the Understanding.[3] The understanding caught this high chant from the poet's lips, and said, in the next age, 'This was Jehovah come down out of heaven. I will kill you, if you say he was a man.' The idioms of his language, and the figures of his rhetoric, have usurped the place of

---

[2] Not an exact quotation but Emerson's understanding of Christ's meaning.
[3] For Emerson, Reason is the intuitive and spiritual faculty, higher than Understanding, which is an intellectual, explaining faculty.

his truth; and churches are not built on his principles, but on his tropes. Christianity became a Mythus, as the poetic teaching of Greece and of Egypt, before. He spoke of miracles; for he felt that man's life was a miracle, and all that man doth, and he knew that this daily miracle shines, as the man is diviner. But the very word Miracle, as pronounced by Christian churches, gives a false impression; it is Monster. It is not one with the blowing clover and the falling rain.

He felt respect for Moses and the prophets; but no unfit tenderness at postponing their initial revelations, to the hour and the man that now is; to the eternal revelation in the heart. Thus was he a true man. Having seen that the law in us is commanding, he would not suffer it to be commanded. Boldly, with hand, and heart, and life, he declared it was God. Thus was he a true man. Thus is he, as I think, the only soul in history who has appreciated the worth of a man.

1. In thus contemplating Jesus, we become very sensible of the first defect of historical Christianity. Historical Christianity has fallen into the error that corrupts all attempts to communicate religion. As it appears to us, and as it has appeared for ages, it is not the doctrine of the soul, but an exaggeration of the personal, the positive, the ritual. It has dwelt, it dwells, with noxious exaggeration about the *person* of Jesus. The soul knows no persons. It invites every man to expand to the full circle of the universe, and will have no preferences but those of spontaneous love. But by this eastern monarchy of a Christianity, which indolence and fear have built, the friend of man is made the injurer of man. The manner in which his name is surrounded with expressions, which were once sallies of admiration and love, but are now petrified into official titles, kills all generous sympathy and liking. All who hear me, feel, that the language that describes Christ to Europe and America, is not the style of friendship and enthusiasm to a good and noble heart, but is appropriated and formal,—paints a demigod, as the Orientals or the Greeks would describe Osiris or Apollo. Accept the injurious impositions of our early catechetical instruction, and even honesty and self-denial were but splendid sins, if they did not wear the Christian name. One would rather be

'A pagan suckled in a creed outworn,'[4]

than to be defrauded of his manly right in coming into nature, and finding not names and places, not land and professions, but even virtue and truth foreclosed and monopolized. You shall not be a man even. You shall not own the world; you shall not dare, and live after the infinite Law that is in you, and in company with the infinite Beauty which heaven and earth reflect to you in all lovely forms; but you must subordinate your nature to Christ's nature; you must accept our interpretations; and take his portrait as the vulgar draw it.

That is always best which gives me to myself. The sublime is excited in me by the great stoical doctrine, Obey thyself. That which shows God in me, fortifies me. That which shows God out of me, makes me a wart and a wen. There is no longer a necessary reason for my being. Already the long shadows of untimely oblivion creep over me, and I shall decease forever.

The divine bards are the friends of my virtue, of my intellect, of my strength. They admonish me, that the gleams which flash across my mind, are not mine, but God's; that they had the like, and were not disobedient to the heavenly vision.[5] So I love them. Noble provocations go out from them, inviting me also to emancipate myself; to resist evil; to subdue the world; and to Be. And thus by his holy thoughts, Jesus serves us, and thus only. To aim to convert a man by miracles, is a profanation of the soul. A true conversion, a true Christ, is now, as always, to be made, by the reception of beautiful sentiments. It is true that a great and rich

---

[4]From the sonnet, "The World Is Too Much with Us," by William Wordsworth (1770–1850).

[5]Cf. Acts 26:19: "I was not disobedient unto the heavenly vision."

soul, like his, falling among the simple, does so preponderate, that, as his did, it names the world. The world seems to them to exist for him, and they have not yet drunk so deeply of his sense, as to see that only by coming again to themselves, or to God in themselves, can they grow forevermore. It is a low benefit to give me something; it is a high benefit to enable me to do somewhat of myself. The time is coming when all men will see, that the gift of God to the soul is not a vaunting, overpowering, excluding sanctity, but a sweet, natural goodness, a goodness like thine and mine, and that so invites thine and mine to be and to grow.

The injustice of the vulgar tone of preaching is not less flagrant to Jesus, than it is to the souls which it profanes. The preachers do not see that they make his gospel not glad, and shear him of the locks of beauty and the attributes of heaven. When I see a majestic Epaminondas,[6] or Washington; when I see among my contemporaries, a true orator, an upright judge, a dear friend; when I vibrate to the melody and fancy of a poem; I see beauty that is to be desired. And so lovely, and with yet more entire consent of my human being, sounds in my ear the severe music of the bards that have sung of the true God in all ages. Now do not degrade the life and dialogues of Christ out of the circle of this charm, by insulation and peculiarity. Let them lie as they befel, alive and warm, part of human life, and of the landscape, and of the cheerful day.

2. The second defect of the traditionary and limited way of using the mind of Christ is a consequence of the first; this, namely; that the Moral Nature, that Law of laws, whose revelations introduce greatness,—yea, God himself, into the open soul, is not explored as the fountain of the established teaching in society. Men have come to speak of the revelation as somewhat long ago given and done, as if God were dead. The injury to faith throttles the preacher; and the goodliest of institutions becomes an uncertain and inarticulate voice.

It is very certain that it is the effect of conversation with the beauty of the soul, to beget a desire and need to impart to others the same knowledge and love. If utterance is denied, the thought lies like a burden on the man. Always the seer is a sayer. Somehow his dream is told. Somehow he publishes it with solemn joy. Sometimes with pencil on canvas; sometimes with chisel on stone; sometimes in towers and aisles of granite, his soul's worship is builded; sometimes in anthems of indefinite music; but clearest and most permanent, in words.

The man enamored of this excellency, becomes its priest or poet. The office is coeval with the world. But observe the condition, the spiritual limitation of the office. The spirit only can teach. Not any profane man, not any sensual, not any liar, not any slave can teach, but only he can give, who has; he only can create, who is. The man on whom the soul descends, through whom the soul speaks, alone can teach. Courage, piety, love, wisdom, can teach; and every man can open his door to these angels, and they shall bring him the gift of tongues. But the man who aims to speak as books enable, as synods use, as the fashion guides, and as interest commands, babbles. Let him hush.

To this holy office, you propose to devote yourselves. I wish you may feel your call in throbs of desire and hope. The office is the first in the world. It is of that reality, that it cannot suffer the deduction of any falsehood. And it is my duty to say to you, that the need was never greater of new revelation than now. From the views I have already expressed, you will infer the sad conviction, which I share, I believe, with numbers, of the universal decay and now almost death of faith in society. The soul is not preached. The Church seems to totter to its fall, almost all life extinct. On this occasion, any complaisance, would be criminal, which told

---

[6]Theban statesman and general (died 362 B.C.) noted for his leadership and service to country.

you, whose hope and commission it is to preach the faith of Christ, that the faith of Christ is preached.

It is time that this ill-suppressed murmur of all thoughtful men against the famine of our churches; this moaning of the heart because it is bereaved of the consolation, the hope, the grandeur, that come alone out of the culture of the moral nature; should be heard through the sleep of indolence, and over the din of routine. This great and perpetual office of the preacher is not discharged. Preaching is the expression of the moral sentiment in application to the duties of life. In how many churches, by how many prophets, tell me, is man made sensible that he is an infinite Soul; that the earth and heavens are passing into his mind; that he is drinking forever the soul of God? Where now sounds the persuasion, that by its very melody imparadises my heart, and so affirms its own origin in heaven? Where shall I hear words such as in elder ages drew men to leave all and follow,—father and mother, house and land, wife and child? Where shall I hear these august laws of moral being so pronounced, as to fill my ear, and I feel ennobled by the offer of my uttermost action and passion? The test of the true faith, certainly, should be its power to charm and command the soul, as the laws of nature control the activity of the hands,—so commanding that we find pleasure and honor in obeying. The faith should blend with the light of rising and of setting suns, with the flying cloud, the singing bird, and the breath of flowers. But now the priest's Sabbath has lost the splendor of nature; it is unlovely; we are glad when it is done; we can make, we do make, even sitting in our pews, a far better, holier, sweeter, for ourselves.

Whenever the pulpit is usurped by a formalist, then is the worshipper defrauded and disconsolate. We shrink as soon as the prayers begin, which do not uplift, but smite and offend us. We are fain to wrap our cloaks about us, and secure, as best we can, a solitude that hears not. I once heard a preacher who sorely tempted me to say, I would go to church no more. Men go, thought I, where they are wont to go, else had no soul entered the temple in the afternoon. A snowstorm was falling around us. The snowstorm was real; the preacher merely spectral; and the eye felt the sad contrast in looking at him, and then out of the window behind him, into the beautiful meteor of the snow. He had lived in vain. He had no one word intimating that he had laughed or wept, was married or in love, had been commended, or cheated, or chagrined. If he had ever lived and acted, we were none the wiser for it. The capital secret of his profession, namely, to convert life into truth, he had not learned. Not one fact in all his experience, had he yet imported into his doctrine. This man had ploughed, and planted, and talked, and bought, and sold; he had read books; he had eaten and drunken; his head aches; his heart throbs; he smiles and suffers; yet was there not a surmise, a hint, in all the discourse, that he had ever lived at all. Not a line did he draw out of real history. The true preacher can always be known by this, that he deals out to the people his life,—life passed through the fire of thought. But of the bad preacher, it could not be told from his sermon, what age of the world he fell in; whether he had a father or a child; whether he was a freeholder or a pauper; whether he was a citizen or a countryman; or any other fact of his biography.

It seemed strange that the people should come to church. It seemed as if their houses were very unentertaining, that they should prefer this thoughtless clamor. It shows that there is a commanding attraction in the moral sentiment, that can lend a faint tint of light to dulness and ignorance, coming in its name and place. The good hearer is sure he has been touched sometimes; is sure there is somewhat to be reached, and some word that can reach it. When he listens to these vain words, he comforts himself by their relation to his remembrance of better hours, and so they clatter and echo unchallenged.

I am not ignorant that when we preach unworthily, it is not always quite in vain. There is a good ear, in some men, that draws supplies to virtue out of very indifferent nutriment. There is poetic truth concealed in all the common-places of prayer and of sermons, and though foolishly spoken, they may be wisely heard; for, each is some select expression that broke out in a moment of piety from some stricken or jubilant soul, and its excellency made it remembered. The prayers and even the dogmas of our church, are like the zodiac of Denderah,[7] and the astronomical monuments of the Hindoos, wholly insulated from anything now extant in the life and business of the people. They mark the height to which the waters once rose. But this docility is a check upon the mischief from the good and devout. In a large portion of the community, the religious service gives rise to quite other thoughts and emotions. We need not chide the negligent servant. We are struck with pity, rather, at the swift retribution of his sloth. Alas for the unhappy man that is called to stand in the pulpit, and *not* give bread of life. Everything that befals, accuses him. Would he ask contributions for the missions, foreign or domestic? Instantly his face is suffused with shame, to propose to his parish, that they should send money a hundred or a thousand miles, to furnish such poor fare as they have at home, and would do well to go the hundred or the thousand miles, to escape. Would he urge people to a godly way of living;—and can he ask a fellow creature to come to Sabbath meetings, when he and they all know what is the poor uttermost they can hope for therein? Will he invite them privately to the Lord's Supper?[8] He dares not. If no heart warm this rite, the hollow, dry, creaking formality is too plain, than that he can face a man of wit and energy, and put the invitation without terror. In the street, what has he to say to the bold village blasphemer? The village blasphemer sees fear in the face, form, and gait of the minister.

Let me not taint the sincerity of this plea by any oversight of the claims of good men. I know and honor the purity and strict conscience of numbers of the clergy. What life the public worship retains, it owes to the scattered company of pious men, who minister here and there in the churches, and who, sometimes accepting with too great tenderness the tenet of the elders, have not accepted from others, but from their own heart, the genuine impulses of virtue, and so still command our love and awe, to the sanctity of character. Moreover, the exceptions are not so much to be found in a few eminent preachers, as in the better hours, the truer inspirations of all,—nay, in the sincere moments of every man. But with whatever exception, it is still true, that tradition characterizes the preaching of this country; that it comes out of the memory, and not out of the soul; that it aims at what is usual, and not at what is necessary and eternal; that thus, historical Christianity destroys the power of preaching, by withdrawing it from the exploration of the moral nature of man, where the sublime is, where are the resources of astonishment and power. What a cruel injustice it is to that Law, the joy of the whole earth, which alone can make thought dear and rich; that Law whose fatal sureness the astronomical orbits poorly emulate, that it is travestied and depreciated, that it is behooted and behowled, and not a trait, not a word of it articulated. The pulpit in losing sight of this Law, loses all its inspiration, and gropes after it knows not what. And for want of this culture, the soul of the community is sick and faithless. It wants nothing so much as a stern, high, stoical, Christian discipline, to make it know itself and the divinity that speaks through it. Now man is ashamed of him-

---

[7]Ancient Egyptian village on the Nile, location of a temple for worship of cow-goddess Hathor, with signs of the zodiac represented on the ceiling.
[8]Emerson had resigned his ministry of the Second Church in Boston in 1832 because he could no longer believe in the special meaning associated with the sacrament of the Lord's Supper.

self; he skulks and sneaks through the world, to be tolerated, to be pitied, and scarcely in a thousand years does any man dare to be wise and good, and so draw after him the tears and blessings of his kind.

Certainly there have been periods when, from the inactivity of the intellect on certain truths, a greater faith was possible in names and persons. The Puritans in England and America, found in the Christ of the Catholic Church, and in the dogmas inherited from Rome, scope for their austere piety, and their longings for civil freedom. But their creed is passing away, and none arises in its room. I think no man can go with his thoughts about him, into one of our churches, without feeling that what hold the public worship had on men, is gone or going. It has lost its grasp on the affection of the good, and the fear of the bad. In the country,—neighborhoods, half parishes are *signing off*,—to use the local term. It is already beginning to indicate character and religion to withdraw from the religious meetings. I have heard a devout person, who prized the Sabbath, say in bitterness of heart, "On Sundays, it seems wicked to go to church." And the motive, that holds the best there, is now only a hope and a waiting. What was once a mere circumstance, that the best and the worst men in the parish, the poor and the rich, the learned and the ignorant, young and old, should meet one day as fellows in one house, in sign of an equal right in the soul, has come to be a paramount motive for going thither.

My friends, in these two errors, I think, I find the causes of that calamity of a decaying church and a wasting unbelief, which are casting malignant influences around us, and making the hearts of good men sad. And what greater calamity can fall upon a nation, than the loss of worship? Then all things go to decay. Genius leaves the temple, to haunt the senate, or the market. Literature becomes frivolous. Science is cold. The eye of youth is not lighted by the hope of other worlds, and age is without honor. Society lives to trifles, and when men die, we do not mention them.

And now, my brothers, you will ask, What in these desponding days can be done by us? The remedy is already declared in the ground of our complaint of the Church. We have contrasted the Church with the Soul. In the soul, then, let the redemption be sought. In one soul, in your soul, there are resources for the world. Wherever a man comes, there comes revolution. The old is for slaves. When a man comes, all books are legible, all things transparent, all religions are forms. He is religious. Man is the wonderworker. He is seen amid miracles. All men bless and curse. He saith yea and nay, only. The stationariness of religion; the assumption that the age of inspiration is past, that the Bible is closed; the fear of degrading the character of Jesus by representing him as a man; indicate with sufficient clearness the falsehood of our theology. It is the office of a true teacher to show us that God is, not was; that He speaketh, not spake. The true Christianity,—a faith like Christ's in the infinitude of man,—is lost. None believeth in the soul of man, but only in some man or person old and departed. Ah me! no man goeth alone. All men go in flocks to this saint or that poet, avoiding the God who seeth in secret. They cannot see in secret; they love to be blind in public. They think society wiser than their soul, and know not that one soul, and their soul, is wiser than the whole world. See how nations and races flit by on the sea of time, and leave no ripple to tell where they floated or sunk, and one good soul shall make the name of Moses, or of Zeno, or of Zoroaster,[9] reverend forever. None assayeth the stern ambition to be the Self of the nation, and of nature, but each

---

[9]Zeno (*c.* 334–*c.* 262 B.C.), Greek philosopher who founded the Stoic school; Zoroaster (fl. sixth century B.C.), Persian religious leader who founded Zoroastrianism.

would be an easy secondary to some Christian scheme, or sectarian connexion, or some eminent man. Once leave your own knowledge of God, your own sentiment, and take secondary knowledge, as St. Paul's, or George Fox's, or Swedenborg's,[10] and you get wide from God with every year this secondary form lasts, and if, as now, for centuries,—the chasm yawns to that breadth, that men can scarcely be convinced there is in them anything divine.

Let me admonish you, first of all, to go alone; to refuse the good models, even those most sacred in the imagination of men, and dare to love God without mediator or veil. Friends enough you shall find who will hold up to your emulation Wesleys and Oberlins,[11] Saints and Prophets. Thank God for these good men, but say, 'I also am a man.' Imitation cannot go above its model. The imitator dooms himself to hopeless mediocrity. The inventor did it, because it was natural to him, and so in him it has a charm. In the imitator, something else is natural, and he bereaves himself of his own beauty, to come short of another man's.

Yourself a newborn bard of the Holy Ghost,—cast behind you all conformity, and acquaint men at first hand with Deity. Be to them a man. Look to it first and only, that you are such; that fashion, custom, authority, pleasure, and money are nothing to you,—are not bandages over your eyes, that you cannot see,—but live with the privilege of the immeasurable mind. Not too anxious to visit periodically all families and each family in your parish connexion,—when you meet one of these men or women, be to them a divine man; be to them thought and virtue; let their timid aspirations find in you a friend; let their trampled instincts be genially tempted out in your atmosphere; let their doubts know that you have doubted, and their wonder feel that you have wondered. By trusting your own soul, you shall gain a greater confidence in other men. For all our penny-wisdom, for all our soul-destroying slavery to habit, it is not to be doubted, that all men have sublime thoughts; that all men do value the few real hours of life; they love to be heard; they love to be caught up into the vision of principles. We mark with light in the memory the few interviews, we have had in the dreary years of routine and of sin, with souls that made our souls wiser; that spoke what we thought; that told us what we knew; that gave us leave to be what we inly were. Discharge to men the priestly office, and, present or absent, you shall be followed with their love as by an angel.

And, to this end, let us not aim at common degrees of merit. Can we not leave, to such as love it, the virtue that glitters for the commendation of society, and ourselves pierce the deep solitudes of absolute ability and worth? We easily come up to the standard of goodness in society. Society's praise can be cheaply secured, and almost all men are content with those easy merits; but the instant effect of conversing with God, will be, to put them away. There are sublime merits; persons who are not actors, not speakers, but influences; persons too great for fame, for display; who disdain eloquence; to whom all we call art and artist, seems too nearly allied to show and by-ends, to the exaggeration of the finite and selfish, and loss of the universal. The orators, the poets, the commanders encroach on us only as fair women do, by our allowance and homage. Slight them by preoccupation of mind, slight them, as you can well afford to do, by high and universal aims, and they instantly feel that you have right, and that it is in lower places that they must shine. They also feel your right; for they with you are open to the influx of the all-knowing Spirit, which annihilates before its broad noon the little shades and gradations of intelligence in the compositions we call wiser and wisest.

In such high communion, let us study the grand strokes of rectitude: a bold

---

[10]George Fox (1624–1691), British founder of the Society of Friends (Quakers); Emmanuel Swedenborg (1688–1722), Swedish religious philosopher.

[11]John Wesley (1703–1791), British founder of Methodism; Jean Frédéric Oberlin (1740–1826), Lutheran clergyman and teacher.

benevolence, an independence of friends, so that not the unjust wishes of those who love us, shall impair our freedom, but we shall resist for truth's sake the freest flow of kindness, and appeal to sympathies far in advance; and,—what is the highest form in which we know this beautiful element,—a certain solidity of merit, that has nothing to do with opinion, and which is so essentially and manifestly virtue, that it is taken for granted, that the right, the brave, the generous step will be taken by it, and nobody thinks of commending it. You would compliment a coxcomb doing a good act, but you would not praise an angel. The silence that accepts merit as the most natural thing in the world, is the highest applause. Such souls, when they appear, are the Imperial Guard of Virtue, the perpetual reserve, the dictators of fortune. One needs not praise their courage,—they are the heart and soul of nature. O my friends, there are resources in us on which we have not drawn. There are men who rise refreshed on hearing a threat; men to whom a crisis which intimidates and paralyzes the majority—demanding not the faculties of prudence and thrift, but comprehension, immovableness, the readiness of sacrifice,—comes graceful and beloved as a bride. Napoleon said of Massena,[12] that he was not himself until the battle began to go against him; then, when the dead began to fall in ranks around him, awoke his powers of combination, and he put on terror and victory as a robe. So it is in rugged crises, in unweariable endurance, and in aims which put sympathy out of question, that the angel is shown. But these are heights that we can scarce remember and look up to, without contrition and shame. Let us thank God that such things exist.

And now let us do what we can to rekindle the smouldering, nigh quenched fire on the altar. The evils of the church that now is, are manifest. The question returns, What shall we do? I confess, all attempts to project and establish a Cultus with new rites and forms, seem to me vain. Faith makes us, and not we it, and faith makes its own forms. All attempts to contrive a system, are as cold as the new worship introduced by the French to the goddess of Reason,[13]—today, pasteboard and fillagree, and ending to-morrow in madness and murder. Rather let the breath of new life be breathed by you through the forms already existing. For, if once you are alive, you shall find they shall become plastic and new. The remedy to their deformity is, first, soul, and second, soul, and evermore, soul. A whole popedom of forms, one pulsation of virtue can uplift and vivify. Two inestimable advantages Christianity has given us; first; the Sabbath, the jubilee of the whole world; whose light dawns welcome alike into the closet of the philosopher, into the garret of toil, and into prison cells, and everywhere suggests, even to the vile, a thought of the dignity of spiritual being. Let it stand forevermore, a temple, which new love, new faith, new sight shall restore to more than its first splendor to mankind. And secondly, the institution of preaching,—the speech of man to men,—essentially the most flexible of all organs, of all forms. What hinders that now, everywhere, in pulpits, in lecture-rooms, in houses, in fields, wherever the invitation of men or your own occasions lead you, you speak the very truth, as your life and conscience teach it, and cheer the waiting, fainting hearts of men with new hope and new revelation?

I look for the hour when that supreme Beauty, which ravished the souls of those Eastern men, and chiefly of those Hebrews, and through their lips spoke oracles to all time, shall speak in the West also. The Hebrew and Greek Scriptures contain immortal sentences, that have been bread of life to millions. But they have no epical integrity; are fragmentary; are not shown in their order to the intellect. I look for the new Teacher, that shall follow so far those shining laws, that he shall

---

[12]André Messéna (1758–1817), one of Napoleon's military leaders.
[13]France in the middle of the Reign of Terror, in 1793, instituted the "worship of Reason" (that is, the intellectual, not the intuitive faculty).

see them come full circle; shall see their rounding complete grace; shall see the world to be the mirror of the soul; shall see the identity of the law of gravitation with purity of heart; and shall show that the Ought, that Duty, is one thing with Science, with Beauty, and with Joy.

1838   *1838*

Self-Reliance[1]

"Ne te quæsiveris extra."

"Man is his own star; and the soul that can
Render an honest and a perfect man,
Commands all light, all influence, all fate;
Nothing to him falls early or too late.
Our acts our angels are, or good or ill,
Our fatal shadows that walk by us still."

Epilogue to Beaumont and Fletcher's
Honest Man's Fortune.[2]

Cast the bantling[3] on the rocks,
Suckle him with the she-wolf's teat;
Wintered with the hawk and fox,
Power and speed be hands and feet.

I read the other day some verses written by an eminent painter[4] which were original and not conventional. The soul always hears an admonition in such lines, let the subject be what it may. The sentiment they instil is of more value than any thought they may contain. To believe your own thought, to believe that what is true for you in your private heart, is true for all men,—that is genius. Speak your latent conviction and it shall be the universal sense; for the inmost in due time becomes the outmost,—and our first thought is rendered back to us by the trumpets of the Last Judgment. Familiar as the voice of the mind is to each, the highest merit we ascribe to Moses, Plato, and Milton, is that they set at naught books and traditions, and spoke not what men but what they thought. A man should learn to detect and watch that gleam of light which flashes across his mind from within, more than the lustre of the firmament of bards and sages. Yet he dismisses without notice his thought, because it is his. In every work of genius we recognize our own rejected thoughts: they come back to us with a certain alienated majesty. Great works of art have no more affecting lesson for us than this. They teach us to abide by our spontaneous impression with good-humored inflexibility then most when the whole cry of voices is on the other side. Else, tomorrow a stranger will say with masterly good sense precisely what we have thought and felt all the time, and we shall be forced to take with shame our own opinion from another.

There is a time in every man's education when he arrives at the conviction that envy is ignorance; that imitation is suicide; that he must take himself for better, for worse, as his portion; that though the wide universe is full of good, no kernel

---

[1]Although "Self-Reliance" appeared first in *Essays* in 1841, it contained ideas and sentences from Emerson's *Journal* that dated as far back as 1832. The Latin epigraph: "Look to no one outside yourself."
[2]Beaumont and Fletcher were Elizabethan playwrights, co-authors of *The Honest Man's Fortune* (1647).

[3]Youngster. (Emerson is the author of this poem.)
[4]Washington Allston (1779–1843); in 1837 Emerson noted in his *Journal* reading Allston's "To the Author of 'The Diary of an Ennuyée.'"

of nourishing corn can come to him but through his toil bestowed on that plot of ground which is given to him to till. The power which resides in him is new in nature, and none but he knows what that is which he can do, nor does he know until he has tried. Not for nothing one face, one character, one fact makes much impression on him, and another none. This sculpture in the memory is not without preëstablished harmony. The eye was placed where one ray should fall, that it might testify of that particular ray. We but half express ourselves, and are ashamed of that divine idea which each of us represents. It may be safely trusted as proportionate and of good issues, so it be faithfully imparted, but God will not have his work made manifest by cowards. A man is relieved and gay when he has put his heart into his work and done his best; but what he has said or done otherwise, shall give him no peace. It is a deliverance which does not deliver. In the attempt his genius deserts him; no muse befriends; no invention, no hope.

Trust thyself: every heart vibrates to that iron string. Accept the place the divine Providence has found for you; the society of your contemporaries, the connexion of events. Great men have always done so and confided themselves childlike to the genius of their age, betraying their perception that the absolutely trustworthy was seated at their heart, working through their hands, predominating in all their being. And we are now men, and must accept in the highest mind the same transcendent destiny; and not minors and invalids in a protected corner, not cowards fleeing before a revolution, but guides, redeemers, and benefactors, obeying the Almighty effort, and advancing on Chaos and the Dark.

What pretty oracles nature yields us on this text in the face and behavior of children, babes and even brutes. That divided and rebel mind, that distrust of a sentiment because our arithmetic has computed the strength and means opposed to our purpose, these have not. Their mind being whole, their eye is as yet unconquered, and when we look in their faces, we are disconcerted. Infancy conforms to nobody: all conform to it, so that one babe commonly makes four or five out of the adults who prattle and play to it. So God has armed youth and puberty and manhood no less with its own piquancy and charm, and made it enviable and gracious and its claims not to be put by, if it will stand by itself. Do not think the youth has no force because he cannot speak to you and me. Hark! in the next room his voice is sufficiently clear and emphatic. It seems he knows how to speak to his contemporaries. Bashful or bold, then, he will know how to make us seniors very unnecessary.

The nonchalance of boys who are sure of a dinner, and would disdain as much as a lord to do or say aught to conciliate one, is the healthy attitude of human nature. A boy is in the parlour what the pit[5] is in the playhouse; independent, irresponsible, looking out from his corner on such people and facts as pass by, he tries and sentences them on their merits, in the swift summary way of boys, as good, bad, interesting, silly, eloquent, troublesome. He cumbers himself never about consequences, about interests: he gives an independent, genuine verdict. You must court him: he does not court you. But the man is, as it were, clapped into jail by his consciousness. As soon as he has once acted or spoken with eclat,[6] he is a committed person, watched by the sympathy or the hatred of hundreds whose affections must now enter into his account. There is no Lethe[7] for this. Ah, that he could pass again into his neutrality! Who can thus avoid all pledges, and having observed, observe again from the same unaffected, unbiassed, unbribable, unaffrighted innocence, must always be formidable. He would utter opinions on

---

[5]Location of the cheapest theater seats, in front of and below the stage—containing an uninhibited and demanding audience.

[6]Brilliance, acclaim.

[7]River of forgetfulness in Hades (Greek mythology).

all passing affairs, which being seen to be not private but necessary, would sink like darts into the ear of men, and put them in fear.

These are the voices which we hear in solitude, but they grow faint and inaudible as we enter into the world. Society everywhere is in conspiracy against the manhood of every one of its members. Society is a joint-stock company in which the members agree for the better securing of his bread to each shareholder, to surrender the liberty and culture of the eater. The virtue in most request is conformity. Self-reliance is its aversion. It loves not realities and creators, but names and customs.

Whoso would be a man must be a nonconformist. He who would gather immortal palms[8] must not be hindered by the name of goodness, but must explore if it be goodness. Nothing is at last sacred but the integrity of your own mind. Absolve you to yourself, and you shall have the suffrage of the world. I remember an answer which when quite young I was prompted to make to a valued adviser who was wont to importune me with the dear old doctrines of the church. On my saying, What have I to do with the sacredness of traditions, if I live wholly from within? my friend suggested—"But these impulses may be from below, not from above." I replied, "They do not seem to me to be such; but if I am the Devil's child, I will live then from the Devil." No law can be sacred to me but that of my nature. Good and bad are but names very readily transferable to that or this; the only right is what is after my constitution, the only wrong what is against it. A man is to carry himself in the presence of all opposition as if every thing were titular and ephemeral but he. I am ashamed to think how easily we capitulate to badges and names, to large societies and dead institutions. Every decent and well-spoken individual affects and sways me more than is right. I ought to go upright and vital, and speak the rude truth in all ways. If malice and vanity wear the coat of philanthropy, shall that pass? If an angry bigot assumes this bountiful cause of Abolition, and comes to me with his last news from Barbadoes,[9] why should I not say to him, 'Go love thy infant; love thy woodchopper: be good-natured and modest: have that grace; and never varnish your hard, uncharitable ambition with this incredible tenderness for black folk a thousand miles off. Thy love afar is spite at home.' Rough and graceless would be such greeting, but truth is handsomer than the affectation of love. Your goodness must have some edge to it—else it is none. The doctrine of hatred must be preached as the counteraction of the doctrine of love when that pules and whines. I shun father and mother and wife and brother, when my genius calls me. I would write on the lintels[10] of the door-post, *Whim*. I hope it is somewhat better than whim at last, but we cannot spend the day in explanation. Expect me not to show cause why I seek or why I exclude company. Then, again, do not tell me, as a good man did to-day, of my obligation to put all poor men in good situations. Are they *my* poor? I tell thee, thou foolish philanthropist, that I grudge the dollar, the dime, the cent I give to such men as do not belong to me and to whom I do not belong. There is a class of persons to whom by all spiritual affinity I am bought and sold; for them I will go to prison, if need be; but your miscellaneous popular charities; the education at college of fools; the building of meeting-houses to the vain end to which many now stand; alms to sots; and the thousandfold Relief Societies;—though I confess with shame I sometimes succumb and give the dollar, it is a wicked dollar which by and by I shall have the manhood to withhold.

Virtues are in the popular estimate rather the exception than the rule. There is

---

[8]Symbols of success or victory.
[9]Slavery was abolished in 1834 in this British West Indies island.
[10]The horizontal support above a door.

the man *and* his virtues. Men do what is called a good action, as some piece of courage or charity, much as they would pay a fine in expiation of daily non-appearance on parade. Their works are done as an apology or extenuation of their living in the world,—as invalids and the insane pay a high board. Their virtues are penances. I do not wish to expiate, but to live. My life is for itself and not for a spectacle. I much prefer that it should be of a lower strain, so it be genuine and equal, than that it should be glittering and unsteady. I wish it to be sound and sweet, and not to need diet and bleeding. I ask primary evidence that you are a man, and refuse this appeal from the man to his actions. I know that for myself it makes no difference whether I do or forbear those actions which are reckoned excellent. I cannot consent to pay for a privilege where I have intrinsic right. Few and mean as my gifts may be, I actually am, and do not need for my own assurance or the assurance of my fellows any secondary testimony.

What I must do, is all that concerns me, not what the people think. This rule, equally arduous in actual and in intellectual life, may serve for the whole distinction between greatness and meanness. It is the harder, because you will always find those who think they know what is your duty better than you know it. It is easy in the world to live after the world's opinion; it is easy in solitude to live after our own; but the great man is he who in the midst of the crowd keeps with perfect sweetness the independence of solitude.

The objection to conforming to usages that have become dead to you, is, that it scatters your force. It loses your time and blurs the impression of your character. If you maintain a dead church, contribute to a dead Bible-Society, vote with a great party either for the Government or against it, spread your table like base housekeepers,—under all these screens, I have difficulty to detect the precise man you are. And, of course, so much force is withdrawn from your proper life. But do your work, and I shall know you. Do your work, and you shall reinforce yourself. A man must consider what a blindman's-buff is this game of conformity. If I know your sect, I anticipate your argument. I hear a preacher announce for his text and topic the expediency of one of the institutions of his church. Do I not know beforehand that not possibly can he say a new and spontaneous word? Do I not know that with all this ostentation of examining the grounds of the institution, he will do no such thing? Do I not know that he is pledged to himself not to look but at one side,—the permitted side, not as a man, but as a parish minister? He is a retained attorney, and these airs of the bench[11] are the emptiest affectation. Well, most men have bound their eyes with one or another handkerchief, and attached themselves to some one of these communities of opinion. This conformity makes them not false in a few particulars, authors of a few lies, but false in all particulars. Their every truth is not quite true. Their two is not the real two, their four not the real four: so that every word they say chagrins us, and we know not where to begin to set them right. Meantime nature is not slow to equip us in the prison-uniform of the party to which we adhere. We come to wear one cut of face and figure, and acquire by degrees the gentlest asinine expression. There is a mortifying experience in particular which does not fail to wreak itself also in the general history; I mean "the foolish face of praise,"[12] the forced smile which we put on in company where we do not feel at ease in answer to conversation which does not interest us. The muscles, not spontaneously moved, but moved by a low usurping wilfulness, grow tight about the outline of the face with the most disagreeable sensation.

For nonconformity the world whips you with its displeasure. And therefore a

---

[11]Pretensions of authority (as a judge on the bench).
[12]From Alexander Pope's satire, "Epistle to Dr. Arbuthnot," 1. 212.

man must know how to estimate a sour face. The bystanders look askance on him in the public street or in the friend's parlor. If this aversation had its origin in contempt and resistance like his own, he might well go home with a sad countenance; but the sour faces of the multitude, like their sweet faces, have no deep cause, but are put on and off as the wind blows, and a newspaper directs. Yet is the discontent of the multitude more formidable than that of the senate and the college. It is easy enough for a firm man who knows the world to brook the rage of the cultivated classes. Their rage is decorous and prudent, for they are timid as being very vulnerable themselves. But when to their feminine rage the indignation of the people is added, when the ignorant and the poor are aroused, when the unintelligent brute force that lies at the bottom of society is made to growl and mow,[13] it needs the habit of magnanimity and religion to treat it godlike as a trifle of no concernment.

The other terror that scares us from self-trust is our consistency; a reverence for our past act or word, because the eyes of others have no other data for computing our orbit than our past acts, and we are loath to disappoint them.

But why should you keep your head over your shoulder? Why drag about this corpse of your memory, lest you contradict somewhat you have stated in this or that public place? Suppose you should contradict yourself; what then? It seems to be a rule of wisdom never to rely on your memory alone, scarcely even in acts of pure memory, but to bring the past for judgment into the thousand-eyed present, and live ever in a new day. In your metaphysics you have denied personality to the Deity: yet when the devout motions of the soul come, yield to them heart and life, though they should clothe God with shape and color. Leave your theory as Joseph his coat in the hand of the harlot, and flee.[14]

A foolish consistency is the hobgoblin of little minds, adored by little statesmen and philosophers and divines. With consistency a great soul has simply nothing to do. He may as well concern himself with his shadow on the wall. Speak what you think now in hard words, and to-morrow speak what to-morrow thinks in hard words again, though it contradict every thing you said to-day.—'Ah, so you shall be sure to be misunderstood.'—Is it so bad then to be misunderstood? Pythagoras was misunderstood, and Socrates, and Jesus, and Luther, and Copernicus, and Galileo, and Newton, and every pure and wise spirit that ever took flesh.[15] To be great is to be misunderstood.

I suppose no man can violate his nature. All the sallies of his will are rounded in by the law of his being as the inequalities of Andes and Himmaleh[16] are insignificant in the curve of the sphere. Nor does it matter how you gauge and try him. A character is like an acrostic or Alexandrian stanza;[17]—read it forward, backward, or across, it still spells the same thing. In this pleasing contrite wood-life which God allows me, let me record day by day my honest thought without prospect or retrospect, and, I cannot doubt, it will be found symmetrical, though I mean it not, and see it not. My book should smell of pines and resound with the hum of insects. The swallow over my window should interweave that thread or straw he carries in his bill into my web also. We pass for what we are. Character teaches above our wills. Men imagine that they communicate their virtue or vice only by overt actions and do not see that virtue or vice emit a breath every moment.

---

[13]Grimace.
[14]Genesis 39:12: Potiphar's wife seized Joseph "by his garment, saying, Lie with me; and he left his garment in her hand, and fled, and got him out."
[15]Greek philosopher (fl. 530 B.C.) whose strong adherence to reality as he saw it aroused resentment. Socrates, Jesus, and Luther were philosophers or religious leaders whose ideas or teachings disturbed their times. Copernicus (1473–1543), Galileo (1564–1642), and Newton (1642–1727) were scientists who demonstrated that the earth was not the center of the cosmos and the universe was governed not by deity but by fixed laws such as the law of gravity.
[16]Himalaya Mountains.
[17]A palindrome, reading the same backwards as forwards.

There will be an agreement in whatever variety of actions, so they be each honest and natural in their hour. For of one will, the actions will be harmonious, however unlike they seem. These varieties are lost sight of at a little distance, at a little height of thought. One tendency unites them all. The voyage of the best ship is a zigzag line of a hundred tacks. See the line from a sufficient distance, and it straightens itself to the average tendency. Your genuine action will explain itself and will explain your other genuine actions. Your conformity explains nothing. Act singly, and what you have already done singly, will justify you now. Greatness appeals to the future. If I can be firm enough to-day to do right and scorn eyes, I must have done so much right before, as to defend me now. Be it how it will, do right now. Always scorn appearances, and you always may. The force of character is cumulative. All the foregone days of virtue work their health into this. What makes the majesty of the heroes of the senate and the field, which so fills the imagination? The consciousness of a train of great days and victories behind. They shed an united light on the advancing actor. He is attended as by a visible escort of angels. That is it which throws thunder into Chatham's voice, and dignity into Washington's port, and America into Adams's eye.[18] Honor is venerable to us because it is no ephemeris. It is always ancient virtue. We worship it to-day, because it is not of to-day. We love it and pay it homage, because it is not a trap for our love and homage, but is self-dependent, self-derived, and therefore of an old immaculate pedigree, even if shown in a young person.

I hope in these days we have heard the last of conformity and consistency. Let the words be gazetted[19] and ridiculous henceforward. Instead of the gong for dinner, let us hear a whistle from the Spartan fife. Let us never bow and apologize more. A great man is coming to eat at my house. I do not wish to please him: I wish that he should wish to please me. I will stand here for humanity, and though I would make it kind, I would make it true. Let us affront and reprimand the smooth mediocrity and squalid contentment of the times, and hurl in the face of custom, and trade, and office, the fact which is the upshot of all history, that there is a great responsible Thinker and Actor working wherever a man works; that a true man belongs to no other time or place, but is the centre of things. Where he is, there is nature. He measures you, and all men, and all events. Ordinarily every body in society reminds us of somewhat else or of some other person. Character, reality, reminds you of nothing else; it takes place of the whole creation. The man must be so much that he must make all circumstances indifferent. Every true man is a cause, a country, and an age; requires infinite spaces and numbers and time fully to accomplish his design;—and posterity seem to follow his steps as a train of clients. A man Caesar is born, and for ages after, we have a Roman Empire. Christ is born, and millions of minds so grow and cleave to his genius, that he is confounded with virtue and the possible of man. An institution is the lengthened shadow of one man; as, Monachism, of the Hermit Antony; the Reformation, of Luther; Quakerism, of Fox; Methodism, of Wesley; Abolition, of Clarkson.[20] Scipio, Milton called "the height of Rome;"[21] and all history resolves itself very easily into the biography of a few stout and earnest persons.

Let a man then know his worth, and keep things under his feet. Let him not peep or steal, or skulk up and down with the air of a charity-boy, a bastard, or an interloper, in the world which exists for him. But the man in the street finding no

---

[18]William Pitt, Earl of Chatham (1708–1788), British statesman; George Washington (1732–1799), America's Revolutionary commander and first president; and (most likely) John Quincy Adams (1767–1848), sixth president and long-time member of the House of Representatives.
[19]Published in the gazette as dismissed.
[20]St. Anthony (c. 250–350), Egyptian founder of Christian monasticism; Martin Luther (1483–1546), German founder of Lutheranism, initiating the Reformation; George Fox (1624–1691), British founder of Quakerism (Society of Friends); John Wesley (1703–1791), British founder of Methodism; Thomas Clarkson (1760–1846), British leader against African slave trade.
[21]In *Paradise Lost*, IX, 510, John Milton so dubbed the Roman General Scipio (237–183 B.C.), who triumphed over Hannibal and sacked Carthage.

worth in himself which corresponds to the force which built a tower or sculptured a marble god, feels poor when he looks on these. To him a palace, a statue, or a costly book have an alien and forbidding air, much like a gay equipage, and seem to say like that, 'Who are you, sir?' Yet they all are his, suitors for his notice, petitioners to his faculties that they will come out and take possession. The picture waits for my verdict: it is not to command me, but I am to settle its claims to praise. That popular fable of the sot who was picked up dead drunk in the street, carried to the duke's house, washed and dressed and laid in the duke's bed, and, on his waking, treated with all obsequious ceremony like the duke, and assured that he had been insane, owes its popularity to the fact, that it symbolizes so well the state of man, who is in the world a sort of sot, but now and then wakes up, exercises his reason, and finds himself a true prince.

Our reading is mendicant and sycophantic. In history, our imagination plays us false. Kingdom and lordship, power and estate are a gaudier vocabulary than private John and Edward in a small house and common day's work: but the things of life are the same to both: the sum total of both is the same. Why all this deference to Alfred, and Scanderbeg, and Gustavus?[22] Suppose they were virtuous: did they wear out virtue? As great a stake depends on your private act to-day, as followed their public and renowned steps. When private men shall act with original views, the lustre will be transferred from the actions of kings to those of gentlemen.

The world has been instructed by its kings, who have so magnetized the eyes of nations. It has been taught by this colossal symbol the mutual reverence that is due from man to man. The joyful loyalty with which men have everywhere suffered the king, the noble, or the great proprietor to walk among them by a law of his own, make his own scale of men and things, and reverse theirs, pay for benefits not with money but with honor, and represent the Law in his person, was the hieroglyphic by which they obscurely signified their consciousness of their own right and comeliness, the right of every man.

The magnetism which all original action exerts is explained when we inquire the reason of self-trust. Who is the Trustee? What is the aboriginal Self on which a universal reliance may be grounded? What is the nature and power of that science-baffling star, without parallax,[23] without calculable elements, which shoots a ray of beauty even into trivial and impure actions, if the least mark of independence appear? The inquiry leads us to that source, at once the essence of genius, of virtue, and of life, which we call Spontaneity or Instinct. We denote this primary wisdom as Intuition, whilst all later teachings are tuitions. In that deep force, the last fact behind which analysis cannot go, all things find their common origin. For the sense of being which in calm hours rises, we know not how, in the soul, is not diverse from things, from space, from light, from time, from man, but one with them, and proceeds obviously from the same source whence their life and being also proceed. We first share the life by which things exist, and afterwards see them as appearances in nature, and forget that we have shared their cause. Here is the fountain of action and of thought. Here are the lungs of that inspiration which giveth man wisdom, and which cannot be denied without impiety and atheism. We lie in the lap of immense intelligence, which makes us receivers of its truth and organs of its activity. When we discern justice, when we discern truth, we do nothing of ourselves, but allow a passage to its beams. If we ask whence this comes, if we seek to pry into the soul that causes, all philosophy is at fault. Its presence or its absence is all we can affirm. Every man discriminates be-

---

[22]Alfred the Great (849–901), King of Wessex and England; Scanderbeg (*c.* 1403–1468), Albanian hero who fought the Turks; Gustavus Adolphus (1594–1632), Swedish king and brilliant general.

[23]I.e., uncalculable (impossible to determine a perspective on).

tween the voluntary acts of his mind, and his involuntary perceptions, and knows that to his involuntary perceptions a perfect faith is due. He may err in the expression of them, but he knows that these things are so, like day and night, not to be disputed. My wilful actions and acquisitions are but roving;—the idlest reverie, the faintest native emotion, command my curiosity and respect. Thoughtless people contradict as readily the statement of perceptions as of opinions, or rather much more readily; for, they do not distinguish between perception and notion. They fancy that I choose to see this or that thing. But perception is not whimsical, but fatal. If I see a trait, my children will see it after me, and in course of time, all mankind,—although it may chance that no one has seen it before me. For my perception of it is as much a fact as the sun.

The relations of the soul to the divine spirit are so pure that it is profane to seek to interpose helps. It must be that when God speaketh, he should communicate not one thing, but all things; should fill the world with his voice; should scatter forth light, nature, time, souls, from the centre of the present thought; and new date and new create the whole. Whenever a mind is simple, and receives a divine wisdom, old things pass away,—means, teachers, texts, temples fall; it lives now and absorbs past and future into the present hour. All things are made sacred by relation to it,—one as much as another. All things are dissolved to their centre by their cause, and in the universal miracle petty and particular miracles disappear. If, therefore, a man claims to know and speak of God, and carries you backward to the phraseology of some old mouldered nation in another country, in another world, believe him not. Is the acorn better than the oak which is its fulness and completion? Is the parent better than the child into whom he has cast his ripened being? Whence then this worship of the past? The centuries are conspirators against the sanity and authority of the soul. Time and space are but physiological colors which the eye makes, but the soul is light; where it is, is day; where it was, is night; and history is an impertinence and an injury, if it be anything more than a cheerful apologue or parable of my being and becoming.

Man is timid and apologetic; he is no longer upright; he dares not say 'I think,' 'I am,' but quotes some saint or sage. He is ashamed before the blade of grass or the blowing rose. These roses under my window make no reference to former roses or to better ones; they are for what they are; they exist with God to-day. There is no time to them. There is simply the rose; it is perfect in every moment of its existence. Before a leaf-bud has burst, its whole life acts; in the full-blown flower, there is no more; in the leafless root, there is no less. Its nature is satisfied, and it satisfies nature, in all moments alike. But man postpones or remembers; he does not live in the present, but with reverted eye laments the past, or, heedless of the riches that surround him, stands on tiptoe to foresee the future. He cannot be happy and strong until he too lives with nature in the present, above time.

This should be plain enough. Yet see what strong intellects dare not yet hear God himself, unless he speak the phraseology of I know not what David, or Jeremiah, or Paul. We shall not always set so great a price on a few texts, on a few lives. We are like children who repeat by rote the sentences of grandames and tutors, and, as they grow older, of the men of talents and character they chance to see,—painfully recollecting the exact words they spoke; afterwards, when they come into the point of view which those had who uttered these sayings, they understand them, and are willing to let the words go; for, at any time, they can use words as good, when occasion comes. If we live truly, we shall see truly. It is as easy for the strong man to be strong, as it is for the weak to be weak. When we have new perception, we shall gladly disburden the memory of its hoarded treasures as old rubbish. When a man lives with God, his voice shall be as sweet as the murmur of the brook and the rustle of the corn.

And now at last the highest truth on this subject remains unsaid; probably, cannot be said; for all that we say is the far off remembering of the intuition. That thought, by what I can now nearest approach to say it, is this. When good is near you, when you have life in yourself, it is not by any known or accustomed way; you shall not discern the foot-prints of any other; you shall not see the face of man; you shall not hear any name;—the way, the thought, the good shall be wholly strange and new. It shall exclude example and experience. You take the way from man, not to man. All persons that ever existed are its forgotten ministers. Fear and hope are alike beneath it. There is somewhat low even in hope. In the hour of vision, there is nothing that can be called gratitude, nor properly joy. The soul raised over passion beholds identity and eternal causation, perceives the self-existence of Truth and Right, and calms itself with knowing that all things go well. Vast spaces of nature, the Atlantic Ocean, the South Sea,—long intervals of time, years, centuries,—are of no account. This which I think and feel underlay every former state of life and circumstances, as it does underlie my present, and what is called life, and what is called death.

Life only avails, not the having lived. Power ceases in the instant of repose; it resides in the moment of transition from a past to a new state, in the shooting of the gulf, in the darting to an aim. This one fact the world hates, that the soul *becomes;* for, that forever degrades the past, turns all riches to poverty, all reputation to a shame, confounds the saint with the rogue, shoves Jesus and Judas equally aside. Why then do we prate of self-reliance? Inasmuch as the soul is present, there will be power not confident but agent. To talk of reliance, is a poor external way of speaking. Speak rather of that which relies, because it works and is. Who has more obedience than I, masters me, though he should not raise his finger. Round him I must revolve by the gravitation of spirits. We fancy it rhetoric when we speak of eminent virtue. We do not yet see that virtue is Height, and that a man or a company of men plastic and permeable to principles, by the law of nature must overpower and ride all cities, nations, kings, rich men, poets, who are not.

This is the ultimate fact which we so quickly reach on this as on every topic, the resolution of all into the ever blessed ONE. Self-existence is the attribute of the Supreme Cause, and it constitutes the measure of good by the degree in which it enters into all lower forms. All things real are so by so much virtue as they contain. Commerce, husbandry, hunting, whaling, war, eloquence, personal weight, are somewhat, and engage my respect as examples of its presence and impure action. I see the same law working in nature for conservation and growth. Power is in nature the essential measure of right. Nature suffers nothing to remain in her kingdoms which cannot help itself. The genesis and maturation of a planet, its poise and orbit, the bended tree recovering itself from the strong wind, the vital resources of every animal and vegetable, are demonstrations of the self-sufficing, and therefore self-relying soul.

Thus all concentrates; let us not rove; let us sit at home with the cause. Let us stun and astonish the intruding rabble of men and books and institutions by a simple declaration of the divine fact. Bid the invaders take the shoes from off their feet, for God is here within.[24] Let our simplicity judge them, and our docility to our own law demonstrate the poverty of nature and fortune beside our native riches.

But now we are a mob. Man does not stand in awe of man, nor is his genius admonished to stay at home, to put itself in communication with the internal

---

[24]Exodus 3:5: God to Moses: ". . .put off thy shoes from off thy feet, for the place whereon thou standest is holy ground."

ocean, but it goes abroad to beg a cup of water of the urns of other men. We must go alone. I like the silent church before the service begins, better than any preaching. How far off, how cool, how chaste the persons look, begirt each one with a precinct or sanctuary. So let us always sit. Why should we assume the faults of our friend, or wife, or father, or child, because they sit around our hearth, or are said to have the same blood? All men have my blood, and I have all men's. Not for that will I adopt their petulance or folly, even to the extent of being ashamed of it. But your isolation must not be mechanical, but spiritual, that is, must be elevation. At times the whole world seems to be in conspiracy to importune you with emphatic trifles. Friend, client, child, sickness, fear, want, charity, all knock at once at thy closet door and say,—'Come out unto us.' But keep thy state; come not into their confusion. The power men possess to annoy me, I give them by a weak curiosity. No man can come near me but through my act. "What we love that we have, but by desire we bereave ourselves of the love."

If we cannot at once rise to the sanctities of obedience and faith, let us at least resist our temptations; let us enter into the state of war, and wake Thor and Woden,[25] courage and constancy, in our Saxon breasts. This is to be done in our smooth times by speaking the truth. Check this lying hospitality and lying affection. Live no longer to the expectation of these deceived and deceiving people with whom we converse. Say to them, O father, O mother, O wife, O brother, O friend, I have lived with you after appearances hitherto. Henceforward I am the truth's. Be it known unto you that henceforward I obey no law less than the eternal law. I will have no covenants but proximities. I shall endeavor to nourish my parents, to support my family, to be the chaste husband of one wife,—but these relations I must fill after a new and unprecedented way. I appeal from your customs. I must be myself. I cannot break myself any longer for you, or you. If you can love me for what I am, we shall be the happier. If you cannot, I will still seek to deserve that you should. I will not hide my tastes or aversions. I will so trust that what is deep is holy, that I will do strongly before the sun and moon whatever inly rejoices me, and the heart appoints. If you are noble, I will love you; if you are not, I will not hurt you and myself by hypocritical attentions. If you are true, but not in the same truth with me, cleave to your companions; I will seek my own. I do this not selfishly, but humbly and truly. It is alike your interest and mine and all men's, however long we have dwelt in lies, to live in truth. Does this sound harsh to-day? You will soon love what is dictated by your nature as well as mine, and if we follow the truth, it will bring us out safe at last.—But so you may give these friends pain. Yes, but I cannot sell my liberty and my power, to save their sensibility. Besides, all persons have their moments of reason when they look out into the region of absolute truth; then will they justify me and do the same thing.

The populace think that your rejection of popular standards is a rejection of all standard, and mere antinomianism;[26] and the bold sensualist will use the name of philosophy to gild his crimes. But the law of consciousness abides. There are two confessionals, in one or the other of which we must be shriven. You may fulfil your round of duties by clearing yourself in the *direct*, or, in the *reflex* way. Consider whether you have satisfied your relations to father, mother, cousin, neighbor, town, cat, and dog; whether any of these can upbraid you. But I may also neglect this reflex standard, and absolve me to myself. I have my own stern claims and perfect circle. It denies the name of duty to many offices that are called duties. But if I can discharge its debts, it enables me to dispense with the popular

---

[25]War gods in Germanic or Norse mythology.
[26]Belief that faith alone, not the moral law, is the requisite for salvation.

code. If any one imagines that this law is lax, let him keep its commandment one day.

And truly it demands something godlike in him who has cast off the common motives of humanity, and has ventured to trust himself for a taskmaster. High be his heart, faithful his will, clear his sight, that he may in good earnest be doctrine, society, law to himself, that a simple purpose may be to him as strong as iron necessity is to others.

If any man consider the present aspects of what is called by distinction *society,* he will see the need of these ethics. The sinew and heart of man seem to be drawn out, and we are become timorous desponding whimperers. We are afraid of truth, afraid of fortune, afraid of death, and afraid of each other. Our age yields no great and perfect persons. We want men and women who shall renovate life and our social state, but we see that most natures are insolvent, cannot satisfy their own wants, have an ambition out of all proportion to their practical force, and do lean and beg day and night continually. Our housekeeping is mendicant, our arts, our occupations, our marriages, our religion we have not chosen, but society has chosen for us. We are parlor soldiers. We shun the rugged battle of fate, where strength is born.

If our young men miscarry in their first enterprizes, they lose all heart. If the young merchant fails, men say he is *ruined.* If the finest genius studies at one of our colleges, and is not installed in an office within one year afterwards in the cities or suburbs of Boston or New York, it seems to his friends and to himself that he is right in being disheartened and in complaining the rest of his life. A sturdy lad from New Hampshire or Vermont, who in turn tries all the professions, who *teams it, farms it, peddles,* keeps a school, preaches, edits a newspaper, goes to Congress, buys a township, and so forth, in successive years, and always, like a cat, falls on his feet, is worth a hundred of these city dolls. He walks abreast with his days, and feels no shame in not 'studying a profession,' for he does not postpone his life, but lives already. He has not one chance, but a hundred chances. Let a Stoic[27] open the resources of man, and tell men they are not leaning willows, but can and must detach themselves; that with the exercise of self-trust, new powers shall appear; that a man is the word made flesh,[28] born to shed healing to the nations, that he should be ashamed of our compassion, and that the moment he acts from himself, tossing the laws, the books, idolatries, and customs out of the window, we pity him no more but thank and revere him,—and that teacher shall restore the life of man to splendor, and make his name dear to all History.

It is easy to see that a greater self-reliance must work a revolution in all the offices and relations of men; in their religion; in their education; in their pursuits; their modes of living; their association; in their property; in their speculative views.

1. In what prayers do men allow themselves! That which they call a holy office, is not so much as brave and manly. Prayer looks abroad and asks for some foreign addition to come through some foreign virtue, and loses itself in endless mazes of natural and supernatural, and mediatorial and miraculous. Prayer that craves a particular commodity,—any thing less than all good,—is vicious. Prayer is the contemplation of the facts of life from the highest point of view. It is the soliloquy of a beholding and jubilant soul. It is the spirit of God pronouncing his works good.[29] But prayer as a means to effect a private end, is meanness and theft. It supposes dualism and not unity in nature and consciousness. As soon as the man

---

[27]One who believes that all that happens is inevitable and must be endured with calm acceptance, without passion.
[28]John 1:14: "And the word was made flesh, and dwelt among us. . . ."

[29]Genesis 1:31: "And God saw everything that he had made, and behold, it was very good."

is at one with God, he will not beg. He will then see prayer in all action. The prayer of the farmer kneeling in his field to weed it, the prayer of the rower kneeling with the stroke of his oar, are true prayers heard throughout nature, though for cheap ends. Caratach, in Fletcher's Bonduca, when admonished to inquire the mind of the god Audate, replies,—

> "His hidden meaning lies in our endeavors,
> Our valors are our best gods."[30]

Another sort of false prayers are our regrets. Discontent is the want of self-reliance: it is infirmity of will. Regret calamities, if you can thereby help the sufferer; if not, attend your own work, and already the evil begins to be repaired. Our sympathy is just as base. We come to them who weep foolishly, and sit down and cry for company, instead of imparting to them truth and health in rough electric shocks, putting them once more in communication with their own reason. The secret of fortune is joy in our hands. Welcome evermore to gods and men is the self-helping man. For him all doors are flung wide: him all tongues greet, all honors crown, all eyes follow with desire. Our love goes out to him and embraces him, because he did not need it. We solicitously and apologetically caress and celebrate him, because he held on his way and scorned our disapprobation. The gods love him because men hated him. "To the persevering mortal," said Zoroaster,[31] "the blessed Immortals are swift."

As men's prayers are a disease of the will, so are their creeds a disease of the intellect. They say with those foolish Israelites, 'Let not God speak to us, lest we die. Speak thou, speak any man with us, and we will obey.'[32] Everywhere I am hindered of meeting God in my brother, because he has shut his own temple doors, and recites fables merely of his brother's, or his brother's brother's God. Every new mind is a new classification. If it prove a mind of uncommon activity and power, a Locke, a Lavoisier, a Hutton, a Bentham, a Fourier,[33] it imposes its classification on other men, and lo! a new system. In proportion to the depth of the thought, and so to the number of the objects it touches and brings within reach of the pupil, is his complacency. But chiefly is this apparent in creeds and churches, which are also classifications of some powerful mind acting on the elemental thought of Duty, and man's relation to the Highest. Such is Calvinism, Quakerism, Swedenborgianism. The pupil takes the same delight in subordinating every thing to the new terminology, as a girl who has just learned botany in seeing a new earth and new seasons thereby. It will happen for a time, that the pupil will find his intellectual power has grown by the study of his master's mind. But in all unbalanced minds, the classification is idolized, passes for the end, and not for a speedily exhaustible means, so that the walls of the system blend to their eye in the remote horizon with the walls of the universe; the luminaries of heaven seem to them hung on the arch their master built. They cannot imagine how you aliens have any right to see,—how you can see; 'It must be somehow that you stole the light from us.' They do not yet perceive, that light, unsystematic, indomitable, will break into any cabin, even into theirs. Let them chirp awhile and call it their own. If they are honest and do well, presently their neat new pinfold[34] will be too strait and low, will crack, will lean, will rot and vanish, and the immortal light, all young

---

[30]From *Bonduca* (1647), III, i, 88–89, by John Fletcher (1579–1625).
[31]Founder of ancient Persian religion (fl. probably 600 B.C.).
[32]Inexactly quoted from Exodus 20:19; the Israelites' words to Moses after God had given him the Ten Commandments.

[33]John Locke (1632–1704), British philosopher; Antoine Lavoisier (1749–1794), French chemist; James Hutton (1726–1797), British geologist; Jeremy Bentham (1748–1832), British philosopher; François Fourier (1772–1837), French social scientist and reformer.
[34]Animal pound.

and joyful, million-orbed, million-colored, will beam over the universe as on the first morning.

2. It is for want of self-culture that the superstition of Travelling, whose idols are Italy, England, Egypt, retains its fascination for all educated Americans. They who made England, Italy, or Greece venerable in the imagination, did so by sticking fast where they were, like an axis of the earth. In manly hours, we feel that duty is our place. The soul is no traveller: the wise man stays at home, and when his necessities, his duties, on any occasion call him from his house, or into foreign lands, he is at home still, and shall make men sensible by the expression of his countenance, that he goes the missionary of wisdom and virtue, and visits cities and men like a sovereign, and not like an interloper or a valet.

I have no churlish objection to the circumnavigation of the globe, for the purposes of art, of study, and benevolence, so that the man is first domesticated, or does not go abroad with the hope of finding somewhat greater than he knows. He who travels to be amused, or to get somewhat which he does not carry, travels away from himself, and grows old even in youth among old things. In Thebes, in Palmyra,[35] his will and mind have become old and dilapidated as they. He carries ruins to ruins.

Travelling is a fool's paradise. Our first journeys discover to us the indifference of places. At home I dream that at Naples, at Rome, I can be intoxicated with beauty, and lose my sadness. I pack my trunk, embrace my friends, embark on the sea, and at last wake up in Naples, and there beside me is the stern Fact, the sad self, unrelenting, identical, that I fled from. I seek the Vatican, and the palaces. I affect to be intoxicated with sights and suggestions, but I am not intoxicated. My giant goes with me wherever I go.

3. But the rage of travelling is a symptom of a deeper unsoundness affecting the whole intellectual action. The intellect is vagabond, and our system of education fosters restlessness. Our minds travel when our bodies are forced to stay at home. We imitate; and what is imitation but the travelling of the mind? Our houses are built with foreign taste; our shelves are garnished with foreign ornaments; our opinions, our tastes, our faculties, lean, and follow the Past and the Distant. The soul created the arts wherever they have flourished. It was in his own mind that the artist sought his model. It was an application of his own thought to the thing to be done and the conditions to be observed. And why need we copy the Doric or the Gothic model?[36] Beauty, convenience, grandeur of thought, and quaint expression are as near to us as to any, and if the American artist will study with hope and love the precise thing to be done by him, considering the climate, the soil, the length of the day, the wants of the people, the habit and form of the government, he will create a house in which all these will find themselves fitted, and taste and sentiment will be satisfied also.

Insist on yourself; never imitate. Your own gift you can present every moment with the cumulative force of a whole life's cultivation; but of the adopted talent of another, you have only an extemporaneous, half possession. That which each can do best, none but his Maker can teach him. No man yet knows what it is, nor can, till that person has exhibited it. Where is the master who could have taught Shakspeare? Where is the master who could have instructed Franklin, or Washington, or Bacon, or Newton? Every great man is a unique. The Scipionism of Scipio is precisely that part he could not borrow. Shakspeare will never be made by the study of Shakspeare. Do that which is assigned you, and you cannot hope too much or dare too much. There is at this moment for you an utterance brave and

---

[35]Thebes in Egypt and Palmyra in Syria, ancient ruined cities.

[36]Doric is classic (or pagan Greek), Gothic, medieval (Christian).

grand as that of the colossal chisel of Phidias,[37] or trowel of the Egyptians,[38] or the pen of Moses, or Dante, but different from all these. Not possibly will the soul all rich, all eloquent, with thousand-cloven tongue, deign to repeat itself; but if you can hear what these patriarchs say, surely you can reply to them in the same pitch of voice: for the ear and the tongue are two organs of one nature. Abide in the simple and noble regions of thy life, obey thy heart, and thou shalt reproduce the Foreworld again.

4. As our Religion, our Education, our Art look abroad, so does our spirit of society. All men plume themselves on the improvement of society, and no man improves.

Society never advances. It recedes as fast on one side as it gains on the other. It undergoes continual changes: it is barbarous, it is civilized, it is christianized, it is rich, it is scientific; but this change is not amelioration. For every thing that is given, something is taken. Society acquires new arts and loses old instincts. What a contrast between the well-clad, reading, writing, thinking American, with a watch, a pencil, and a bill of exchange in his pocket, and the naked New Zealander, whose property is a club, a spear, a mat, and an undivided twentieth of a shed to sleep under. But compare the health of the two men, and you shall see that the white man has lost his aboriginal strength. If the traveller tell us truly, strike the savage with a broad axe, and in a day or two the flesh shall unite and heal as if you struck the blow into soft pitch, and the same blow shall send the white to his grave.

The civilized man has built a coach, but has lost the use of his feet. He is supported on crutches, but lacks so much support of muscle. He has a fine Geneva watch, but he fails of the skill to tell the hour by the sun. A Greenwich nautical almanac he has, and so being sure of the information when he wants it, the man in the street does not know a star in the sky. The solstice he does not observe; the equinox he knows as little; and the whole bright calendar of the year is without a dial in his mind. His note-books impair his memory; his libraries overload his wit; the insurance office increases the number of accidents; and it may be a question whether machinery does not encumber; whether we have not lost by refinement some energy, by a christianity entrenched in establishments and forms, some vigor of wild virtue. For every stoic was a stoic; but in Christendom where is the Christian?

There is no more deviation in the moral standard than in the standard of height or bulk. No greater men are now than ever were. A singular equality may be observed between the great men of the first and of the last ages; nor can all the science, art, religion and philosophy of the nineteenth century avail to educate greater men than Plutarch's heroes,[39] three or four and twenty centuries ago. Not in time is the race progressive. Phocion, Socrates, Anaxagoras, Diogenes,[40] are great men, but they leave no class. He who is really of their class will not be called by their name, but will be his own man, and, in his turn the founder of a sect. The arts and inventions of each period are only its costume, and do not invigorate men. The harm of the improved machinery may compensate its good. Hudson and Behring[41] accomplished so much in their fishing-boats, as to astonish Parry and Franklin,[42] whose equipment exhausted the resources of science and art. Galileo,[43] with an opera-glass, discovered a more splendid series of celestial phenom-

---

[37]Greek sculptor (fifth century B.C.).
[38]I.e., the pyramids.
[39]Great figures of Greece and Rome, the subject of biographies in the *Lives* by Plutarch (*c.* 46–*c.*120), Roman historian and biographer.
[40]All noted Greek philosophers of the fifth–third century B.C.

[41]Henry Hudson (d. 1611), English explorer; Vitus Jonassen Bering (1680–1741) Danish navigator.
[42]Sir William Edward Parry (1790–1855) and Sir John Franklin (1786–1847), British explorers of the Arctic.
[43]Italian astronomer (1564–1642) who, through the telescope, confirmed the Copernican theory that the earth revolved around the sun.

ena than any one since. Columbus found the New World in an undecked boat. It is curious to see the periodical disuse and perishing of means and machinery which were introduced with loud laudation, a few years or centuries before. The great genius returns to essential man. We reckoned the improvements of the art of war among the triumphs of science, and yet Napoleon conquered Europe by the Bivouac, which consisted of falling back on naked valor, and disencumbering it of all aids. The Emperor held it impossible to make a perfect army, says Las Cases,[44] "without abolishing our arms, magazines, commissaries, and carriages, until in imitation of the Roman custom, the soldier should receive his supply of corn, grind it in his hand-mill, and bake his bread himself."

Society is a wave. The wave moves onward, but the water of which it is composed, does not. The same particle does not rise from the valley to the ridge. Its unity is only phenomenal. The persons who make up a nation to-day, next year die, and their experience with them.

And so the reliance on Property, including the reliance on governments which protect it, is the want of self-reliance. Men have looked away from themselves and at things so long, that they have come to esteem the religious, learned, and civil institutions, as guards of property, and they deprecate assaults on these, because they feel them to be assaults on property. They measure their esteem of each other, by what each has, and not by what each is. But a cultivated man becomes ashamed of his property, out of new respect for his nature. Especially he hates what he has, if he see that it is accidental,—came to him by inheritance, or gift, or crime; then he feels that it is not having; it does not belong to him, has no root in him, and merely lies there, because no revolution or no robber takes it away. But that which a man is, does always by necessity acquire, and what the man acquires is living property, which does not wait the beck of rulers, or mobs, or revolutions, or fire, or storm, or bankruptcies, but perpetually renews itself wherever the man breathes. "Thy lot or portion of life," said the Caliph Ali,[45] "is seeking after thee; therefore be at rest from seeking after it." Our dependence on these foreign goods leads us to our slavish respect for numbers. The political parties meet in numerous conventions; the greater the concourse, and with each new uproar of announcement. The delegation from Essex![46] The Democrats from New Hampshire! The Whigs of Maine! the young patriot feels himself stronger than before by a new thousand of eyes and arms. In like manner the reformers summon conventions, and vote and resolve in multitude. Not so, O friends! will the God deign to enter and inhabit you, but by a method precisely the reverse. It is only as a man puts off all foreign support, and stands alone, that I see him to be strong and to prevail. He is weaker by every recruit to his banner. Is not a man better than a town? Ask nothing of men, and in the endless mutation, thou only firm column must presently appear the upholder of all that surrounds thee. He who knows that power is inborn, that he is weak because he has looked for good out of him and elsewhere, and so perceiving, throws himself unhesitatingly on his thought, instantly rights himself, stands in the erect position, commands his limbs, works miracles; just as a man who stands on his feet is stronger than a man who stands on his head.

So use all that is called Fortune. Most men gamble with her, and gain all, and lose all, as her wheel rolls. But do thou leave as unlawful these winnings, and deal with Cause and Effect, the chancellors of God. In the Will work and acquire, and thou hast chained the wheel of Chance, and shalt sit hereafter out of fear from her rotations. A political victory, a rise of rents, the recovery of your sick, or the

---

[44]Comte Emmanuel Augustin de Las Cases (1766–1842), French historian who published his conversations with Napoleon.

[45]Ali ibn-abi Talib (c. 602–661), fourth Caliph of Mecca.
[46]A Massachusetts county.

return of your absent friend, or some other favorable event, raises your spirits, and you think good days are preparing for you. Do not believe it. Nothing can bring you peace but yourself. Nothing can bring you peace but the triumph of principles.

1841

The Over-Soul[1]

"But souls that of his own good life partake,
He loves as his own self; dear as his eye
They are to Him: He'll never them forsake:
When they shall die, then God himself shall die:
They live, they live in blest eternity."

Henry More.[2]

Space is ample, east and west,
But two cannot go abreast,
Cannot travel in it two:
Yonder masterful cuckoo
Crowds every egg out of the nest,
Quick or dead, except its own;
A spell is laid on sod and stone,
Night and Day were tampered with,
Every quality and pith
Surcharged and sultry with a power
That works its will on age and hour.

There is a difference between one and another hour of life, in their authority and subsequent effect. Our faith comes in moments; our vice is habitual. Yet there is a depth in those brief moments, which constrains us to ascribe more reality to them than to all other experiences. For this reason, the argument, which is always forthcoming to silence those who conceive extraordinary hopes of man, namely, the appeal to experience, is forever invalid and vain. We give up the past to the objector, and yet we hope. He must explain this hope. We grant that human life is mean; but how did we find out that it was mean? What is the ground of this uneasiness of ours; of this old discontent? What is the universal sense of want and ignorance, but the fine innuendo by which the soul makes its enormous claim? Why do men feel that the natural history of man has never been written, but he is always leaving behind what you have said of him, and it becomes old, and books of metaphysics worthless? The philosophy of six thousand years has not searched the chambers and magazines of the soul. In its experiments there has always remained, in the last analysis, a residuum it could not resolve. Man is a stream whose source is hidden. Our being is descending into us from we know not whence. The most exact calculator has no prescience that somewhat incalculable may not baulk the very next moment. I am constrained every moment to acknowledge a higher origin for events than the will I call mine.

As with events, so is it with thoughts. When I watch that flowing river, which, out of regions I see not, pours for a season its streams into me, I see that I am a

---

[1]According to the *Oxford English Dictionary*, Emerson's own term for the "supreme spirit which animates the universe." [2]From "Psychozoia, or the Life of the Soul" (Canto II, Stanza 19), in *Philosophical Poems* (1647) by Henry More (1614–1687), a British religious writer; the second poem is Emerson's, published later as "Unity."

pensioner; not a cause, but a surprised spectator of this ethereal water; that I desire and look up, and put myself in the attitude of reception, but from some alien energy the visions come.

The Supreme Critic on the errors of the past and the present, and the only prophet of that which must be, is that great nature in which we rest, as the earth lies in the soft arms of the atmosphere; that Unity, that Over-Soul, within which every man's particular being is contained and made one with all other; that common heart, of which all sincere conversation is the worship, to which all right action is submission; that overpowering reality which confutes our tricks and talents, and constrains every one to pass for what he is, and to speak from his character and not from his tongue, and which evermore tends and aims to pass into our thought and hand, and become wisdom, and virtue, and power, and beauty. We live in succession, in division, in parts, in particles. Meantime within man is the soul of the whole; the wise silence; the universal beauty, to which every part and particle is equally related; the eternal ONE. And this deep power in which we exist, and whose beatitude is all accessible to us, is not only self-sufficing and perfect in every hour, but the act of seeing and the thing seen, the seer and the spectacle, the subject and the object, are one. We see the world piece by piece, as the sun, the moon, the animal, the tree; but the whole, of which these are the shining parts, is the soul. Only by the vision of that Wisdom can the horoscope of the ages be read, and by falling back on our better thoughts, by yielding to the spirit of prophecy which is innate in every man, we can know what it saith. Every man's words, who speaks from that life, must sound vain to those who do not dwell in the same thought on their own part. I dare not speak for it. My words do not carry its august sense; they fall short and cold. Only itself can inspire whom it will, and behold! their speech shall be lyrical, and sweet, and universal as the rising of the wind. Yet I desire, even by profane words, if I may not use sacred, to indicate the heaven of this deity, and to report what hints I have collected of the transcendent simplicity and energy of the Highest Law.

If we consider what happens in conversation, in reveries, in remorse, in times of passion, in surprises, in the instructions of dreams wherein often we see ourselves in masquerade,—the droll disguises only magnifying and enhancing a real element, and forcing it on our distinct notice,—we shall catch many hints that will broaden and lighten into knowledge of the secret of nature. All goes to show that the soul in man is not an organ, but animates and exercises all the organs; is not a function, like the power of memory, of calculation, of comparison, but uses these as hands and feet; is not a faculty, but a light; is not the intellect or the will, but the master of the intellect and the will; is the background of our being, in which they lie,—an immensity not possessed and that cannot be possessed. From within or from behind, a light shines through us upon things, and makes us aware that we are nothing, but the light is all. A man is the façade of a temple wherein all wisdom and all good abide. What we commonly call man, the eating, drinking, planting, counting man, does not, as we know him, represent himself, but misrepresents himself. Him we do not respect, but the soul, whose organ he is, would he let it appear through his action, would make our knees bend. When it breathes through his intellect, it is genius; when it breathes through his will, it is virtue; when it flows through his affection, it is love. And the blindness of the intellect begins, when it would be something of itself. The weakness of the will begins when the individual would be something of himself. All reform aims, in some one particular, to let the soul have its way through us; in other words, to engage us to obey.

Of this pure nature every man is at some time sensible. Language cannot paint it with his colors. It is too subtle. It is undefinable, unmeasurable, but we know that it pervades and contains us. We know that all spiritual being is in man. A wise old proverb says, "God comes to see us without bell:"[3] that is, as there is no screen or ceiling between our heads and the infinite heavens, so is there no bar or wall in the soul where man, the effect, ceases, and God, the cause, begins. The walls are taken away. We lie open on one side to the deeps of spiritual nature, to all the attributes of God. Justice we see and know, Love, Freedom, Power. These natures no man ever got above, but they tower over us, and most in the moment when our interests tempt us to wound them.

The sovereignty of this nature whereof we speak, is made known by its independency of those limitations which circumscribe us on every hand. The soul circumscribes all things. As I have said, it contradicts all experience. In like manner it abolishes time and space. The influence of the senses has, in most men, overpowered the mind to that degree, that the walls of time and space have come to look real and insurmountable; and to speak with levity of these limits, is, in the world, the sign of insanity. Yet time and space are but inverse measures of the force of the soul. The spirit sports with time—

> "Can crowd eternity into an hour,
> Or stretch an hour to eternity."[4]

We are often made to feel that there is another youth and age than that which is measured from the year of our natural birth. Some thoughts always find us young and keep us so. Such a thought is the love of the universal and eternal beauty. Every man parts from that contemplation with the feeling that it rather belongs to ages than to mortal life. The least activity of the intellectual powers redeems us in a degree from the conditions of time. In sickness, in languor, give us a strain of poetry or a profound sentence, and we are refreshed; or produce a volume of Plato, or Shakspeare, or remind us of their names, and instantly we come into a feeling of longevity. See how the deep, divine thought reduces centuries, and millenniums, and makes itself present through all ages. Is the teaching of Christ less effective now than it was when first his mouth was opened? The emphasis of facts and persons in my thought has nothing to do with time. And so, always, the soul's scale is one; the scale of the senses and the understanding is another. Before the revelations of the soul, Time, Space and Nature shrink away. In common speech, we refer all things to time, as we habitually refer the immensely sundered stars to one concave sphere. And so we say that the Judgment is distant or near, that the Millennium approaches, that a day of certain political, moral, social reforms is at hand, and the like, when we mean, that in the nature of things, one of the facts we contemplate is external and fugitive, and the other is permanent and connate with the soul. The things we now esteem fixed, shall, one by one, detach themselves, like ripe fruit, from our experience, and fall. The wind shall blow them none knows whither. The landscape, the figures, Boston, London, are facts as fugitive as any institution past, or any whiff of mist or smoke, and so is society, and so is the world. The soul looketh steadily forwards, creating a world before her, leaving worlds behind her. She has no dates, nor rites, nor persons, nor specialties, nor men. The soul knows only the soul; the web of events is the flowing robe in which she is clothed.

After its own law and not by arithmetic is the rate of its progress to be computed. The soul's advances are not made by gradation, such as can be represented by motion in a straight line; but rather by ascension of state, such as can be represented by metamorphosis,—from the egg to the worm, from the worm to the fly. The growths of genius are of a certain *total* character, that does not advance the

---

[3]One of the "Old Spanish Proverbs" in Vicesimus Knox, *Elegant Extracts . . . in Prose,* 7th. ed., 2 vols. (London, 1797), II, 1035.

[4]From Lucifer's speech in *Cain* (I, i, 536–537) by George Gordon, Lord Byron (1788–1824); preceding line: "With us acts are exempt from time, and we . . ."

elect individual first over John, then Adam, then Richard, and give to each the pain of discovered inferiority, but by every throe of growth, the man expands there where he works, passing, at each pulsation, classes, populations of men. With each divine impulse the mind rends the thin rinds of the visible and finite, and comes out into eternity, and inspires and expires its air. It converses with truths that have always been spoken in the world, and becomes conscious of a closer sympathy with Zeno and Arrian,[5] than with persons in the house.

This is the law of moral and of mental gain. The simple rise as by specific levity, not into a particular virtue, but into the region of all the virtues. They are in the spirit which contains them all. The soul requires purity, but purity is not it; requires justice, but justice is not that; requires beneficence, but is somewhat better: so that there is a kind of descent and accommodation felt when we leave speaking of moral nature, to urge a virtue which it enjoins. To the well-born child, all the virtues are natural, and not painfully acquired. Speak to his heart, and the man becomes suddenly virtuous.

Within the same sentiment is the germ of intellectual growth, which obeys the same law. Those who are capable of humility, of justice, of love, of aspiration, stand already on a platform that commands the sciences and arts, speech and poetry, action and grace. For whoso dwells in this moral beatitude already anticipates those special powers which men prize so highly. The lover has no talent, no skill, which passes for quite nothing with his enamored maiden, however little she may possess of related faculty; and the heart which abandons itself to the Supreme Mind finds itself related to all its works and will travel a royal road to particular knowledges and powers. In ascending to this primary and aboriginal sentiment, we have come from our remote station on the circumference instantaneously to the centre of the world, where, as in the closet of God, we see causes, and anticipate the universe, which is but a slow effect.

One mode of the divine teaching is the incarnation of the spirit in a form,—in forms, like my own. I live in society; with persons who answer to thoughts in my own mind, or express a certain obedience to the great instincts to which I live. I see its presence to them. I am certified of a common nature; and these other souls, these separated selves, draw me as nothing else can. They stir in me the new emotions we call passion; of love, hatred, fear, admiration, pity; thence comes conversation, competition, persuasion, cities, and war. Persons are supplementary to the primary teaching of the soul. In youth we are mad for persons. Childhood and youth see all the world in them. But the larger experience of man discovers the identical nature appearing through them all. Persons themselves acquaint us with the impersonal. In all conversation between two persons, tacit reference is made as to a third party, to a common nature. That third party or common nature is not social; it is impersonal; is God. And so in groups where debate is earnest, and especially on high questions, the company become aware that the thought rises to an equal level in all bosoms, that all have a spiritual property in what was said, as well as the sayer. They all become wiser than they were. It arches over them like a temple, this unity of thought, in which every heart beats with nobler sense of power and duty, and thinks and acts with unusual solemnity. All are conscious of attaining to a higher self-possession. It shines for all. There is a certain wisdom of humanity which is common to the greatest men with the lowest, and which our ordinary education often labors to silence and obstruct. The mind is one, and the best minds who love truth for its own sake, think much less of property in truth. They accept it thankfully everywhere, and do not label or

---

[5]Zeno (third–second century B.C.), Greek founder of Stoic school of philosophy; Arrian (d. A.D. 180), Greek historian, pupil of Epictetus, Roman Stoic philosopher.

stamp it with any man's name, for it is theirs long beforehand, and from eternity. The learned and the studious of thought have no monopoly of wisdom. Their violence of direction in some degree disqualifies them to think truly. We owe many valuable observations to people who are not very acute or profound, and who say the thing without effort, which we want and have long been hunting in vain. The action of the soul is oftener in that which is felt and left unsaid, than in that which is said in any conversation. It broods over every society, and they unconsciously seek for it in each other. We know better than we do. We do not yet possess ourselves, and we know at the same time that we are much more. I feel the same truth how often in my trivial conversation with my neighbors, that somewhat higher in each of us overlooks this by-play, and Jove nods to Jove from behind each of us.

Men descend to meet. In their habitual and mean service to the world, for which they forsake their native nobleness, they resemble those Arabian Sheikhs, who dwell in mean houses and affect an external poverty, to escape the rapacity of the Pacha,[6] and reserve all their display of wealth for their interior and guarded retirements.

As it is present in all persons, so it is in every period of life. It is adult already in the infant man. In my dealing with my child, my Latin and Greek, my accomplishments and my money, stead me nothing; but as much soul as I have avails. If I am wilful, he sets his will against mine, one for one, and leaves me, if I please, the degradation of beating him by my superiority of strength. But if I renounce my will, and act for the soul, setting that up as umpire between us two, out of his young eyes looks the same soul; he reveres and loves with me.

The soul is the perceiver and revealer of truth. We know truth when we see it, let skeptic and scoffer say what they choose. Foolish people ask you, when you have spoken what they do not wish to hear, 'How do you know it is truth, and not an error of your own?' We know truth when we see it, from opinion, as we know when we are awake that we are awake. It was a grand sentence of Emanuel Swedenborg,[7] which would alone indicate the greatness of that man's perception,—"It is no proof of a man's understanding to be able to confirm whatever he pleases; but to be able to discern that what is true is true, and that what is false is false, this is the mark and character of intelligence." In the book I read, the good thought returns to me, as every truth will, the image of the whole soul. To the bad thought which I find in it, the same soul becomes a discerning, separating sword and lops it away. We are wiser than we know. If we will not interfere with our thought, but will act entirely, or see how the thing stands in God, we know the particular thing, and every thing, and every man. For, the Maker of all things and all persons, stands behind us, and casts his dread omniscience through us over things.

But beyond this recognition of its own in particular passages of the individual's experience, it also reveals truth. And here we should seek to reinforce ourselves by its very presence, and to speak with a worthier, loftier strain of that advent.[8] For the soul's communication of truth is the highest event in nature, since it then does not give somewhat from itself, but it gives itself, or passes into and becomes that man whom it enlightens; or in proportion to that truth he receives, it takes him to itself.

We distinguish the announcements of the soul, its manifestations of its own nature, by the term *Revelation*. These are always attended by the emotion of the sublime. For this communication is an influx of the Divine mind into our mind. It is

---

[6]Variant of Pasha, Turkish civil or military authority.
[7]Swedenborg (1688–1772), Swedish religious and mystical writer.
[8]I.e., its coming.

an ebb of the individual rivulet before the flowing surges of the sea of life. Every distinct apprehension of this central commandment agitates men with awe and delight. A thrill passes through all men at the reception of new truth, or at the performance of a great action, which comes out of the heart of nature. In these communications, the power to see, is not separated from the will to do, but the insight proceeds from obedience, and the obedience proceeds from a joyful perception. Every moment when the individual feels himself invaded by it, is memorable. By the necessity of our constitution, a certain enthusiasm attends the individual's consciousness of that divine presence. The character and duration of this enthusiasm varies with the state of the individual, from an extasy and trance and prophetic inspiration,—which is its rarer appearance,—to the faintest glow of virtuous emotion, in which form it warms, like our household fires, all the families and associations of men, and makes society possible. A certain tendency to insanity has always attended the opening of the religious sense in men, as if they had been "blasted with excess of light."[9] The trances of Socrates, the "union" of Plotinus, the vision of Porphyry, the conversion of Paul, the aurora of Behmen, the convulsions of George Fox and his Quakers, the illumination of Swedenborg, are of this kind.[10] What was in the case of these remarkable persons a ravishment, has, in innumerable instances in common life, been exhibited in less striking manner. Everywhere the history of religion betrays a tendency to enthusiasm. The rapture of the Moravian and Quietist;[11] the opening of the internal sense of the Word, in the language of the New Jerusalem Church;[12] the *revival* of the Calvinistic churches; the *experiences* of the Methodists,[13] are varying forms of that shudder of awe and delight with which the individual soul always mingles with the universal soul.

The nature of these revelations is the same; they are perceptions of the absolute law. They are solutions of the soul's own questions. They do not answer the questions which the understanding asks. The soul answers never by words, but by the thing itself that is inquired after.

Revelation is the disclosure of the soul. The popular notion of a revelation, is, that it is a telling of fortunes. In past oracles of the soul, the understanding seeks to find answers to sensual questions, and undertakes to tell from God how long men shall exist, what their hands shall do, and who shall be their company, adding names, and dates, and places. But we must pick no locks. We must check this low curiosity. An answer in words is delusive; it is really no answer to the questions you ask. Do not require a description of the countries towards which you sail. The description does not describe them to you, and to-morrow you arrive there, and know them by inhabiting them. Men ask concerning the immortality of the soul, the employments of heaven, the state of the sinner, and so forth. They even dream that Jesus has left replies to precisely these interrogatories. Never a moment did that sublime spirit speak in their *patois*.[14] To truth, justice, love, the attributes of the soul, the idea of immutableness is essentially associated. Jesus, living in these moral sentiments, heedless of sensual fortunes, heeding only the manifestations of these, never made the separation of the idea of duration from the essence of these attributes, nor uttered a syllable concerning the duration of the soul. It was left to his disciples to sever duration from the moral elements and to teach the immortality of the soul as a doctrine, and maintain it by evidences. The moment the doctrine of the immortality is separately taught, man is already fallen. In the flowing of love, in the adoration of humility, there is no question of

[9]From *The Progress of Poesy*, III, ii, 7, by Thomas Gray (1716–1771), English poet; the line refers to John Milton.
[10]Socrates (470?–399 B.C.), Greek philosopher; Plotinus and Porphyry, Roman Neo-Platonic philosophers of the third century A.D.; St. Paul, converted to Christianity in the first century A.D.; Jakob Böhme (1575–1624), German mystic; George Fox, British founder of Quakers in seventeenth century.

[11]Moravian, an eighteenth-century sect founded in Moravia (or Bohemia) stressing peace of soul; Quietist, a seventeenth-century movement stressing passive preparation for revelation.
[12]The church of Swedenborg's followers.
[13]Methodists testified as to their conversion to faith for others' benefit.
[14]Dialect.

continuance. No inspired man ever asks this question, or condescends to these evidences. For the soul is true to itself, and the man in whom it is shed abroad, cannot wander from the present, which is infinite, to a future, which would be finite.

These questions which we lust to ask about the future, are a confession of sin. God has no answer for them. No answer in words can reply to a question of things. It is not in an arbitrary "decree of God," but in the nature of man that a veil shuts down on the facts of to-morrow: for the soul will not have us read any other cipher than that of cause and effect. By this veil, which curtains events, it instructs the children of men to live in to-day. The only mode of obtaining an answer to these questions of the senses, is, to forego all low curiosity, and, accepting the tide of being which floats us into the secret of nature, work and live, work and live, and all unawares, the advancing soul has built and forged for itself a new condition, and the question and the answer are one.

By the same fire, vital, consecrating, celestial, which burns until it shall dissolve all things into the waves and surges of an ocean of light, we see and know each other, and what spirit each is of. Who can tell the grounds of his knowledge of the character of the several individuals in his circle of friends? No man. Yet their acts and words do not disappoint him. In that man, though he knew no ill of him, he put no trust. In that other, though they had seldom met, authentic signs had yet passed, to signify that he might be trusted as one who had an interest in his own character. We know each other very well,—which of us has been just to himself, and whether that which we teach or behold, is only an aspiration, or is our honest effort also.

We are all discerners of spirits. That diagnosis lies aloft in our life or unconscious power. The intercourse of society,—its trade, its religion, its friendships, its quarrels,—is one wide, judicial investigation of character. In full court, or in small committee, or confronted face to face, accuser and accused, men offer themselves to be judged. Against their will they exhibit those decisive trifles by which character is read. But who judges? and what? Not our understanding. We do not read them by learning or craft. No; the wisdom of the wise man consists herein, that he does not judge them; he lets them judge themselves, and merely reads and records their own verdict.

By virtue of this inevitable nature, private will is overpowered, and, maugre[15] our efforts, or our imperfections, your genius will speak from you, and mine from me. That which we are, we shall teach, not voluntarily, but involuntarily. Thoughts come into our minds by avenues which we never left open, and thoughts go out of our minds through avenues which we never voluntarily opened. Character teaches over our head. The infallible index of true progress is found in the tone the man takes. Neither his age, nor his breeding, nor company, nor books, nor actions, nor talents, nor all together, can hinder him from being deferential to a higher spirit than his own. If he have not found his home in God, his manners, his forms of speech, the turn of his sentences, the build, shall I say, of all his opinions will involuntarily confess it, let him brave it out how he will. If he have found his centre, the Deity will shine through him, through all the disguises of ignorance, of ungenial temperament, of unfavorable circumstance. The tone of seeking, is one, and the tone of having is another.

The great distinction between teachers sacred or literary,—between poets like Herbert, and poets like Pope,[16]—between philosophers like Spinoza, Kant, and Coleridge, and philosophers like Locke, Paley, Mackintosh, and Stewart,[17]—be-

---

[15]In spite of.
[16]George Herbert (1593–1633), British religious poet; Alexander Pope (1688–1744), British "neoclassical" poet of the Age of Reason.
[17]The Dutch Baruch Spinoza (1632–1677), the German Immanuel Kant (1724–1804), and the British Samuel Taylor Coleridge (1772–1834)—all intuitive thinkers with a mystical bent; different from the more systematically logical thinkers: John Locke (1632–1704) and William Paley (1743–1805), British philosophers; and James Mackintosh (1765–1832) and Dugald Stewart (1753–1828), Scottish philosophers.

tween men of the world, who are reckoned accomplished talkers, and here and there a fervent mystic, prophesying, half-insane under the infinitude of his thought,—is, that one class speak *from within*, or from experience, as parties and possessors of the fact; and the other class, *from without*, as spectators merely, or perhaps as acquainted with the fact, on the evidence of third persons. It is of no use to preach to me from without. I can do that too easily myself. Jesus speaks always from within, and in a degree that transcends all others. In that, is the miracle. I believe beforehand that it ought so to be. All men stand continually in the expectation of the appearance of such a teacher. But if a man do not speak from within the veil, where the word is one with that it tells of, let him lowly confess it.

The same Omniscience flows into the intellect, and makes what we call genius. Much of the wisdom of the world is not wisdom, and the most illuminated class of men are no doubt superior to literary fame, and are not writers. Among the multitude of scholars and authors, we feel no hallowing presence; we are sensible of a knack and skill rather than of inspiration; they have a light, and know not whence it comes, and call it their own; their talent is some exaggerated faculty, some overgrown member, so that their strength is a disease. In these instances, the intellectual gifts do not make the impression of virtue, but almost of vice; and we feel that a man's talents stand in the way of his advancement in truth. But genius is religious. It is a larger imbibing of the common heart. It is not anomalous, but more like, and not less like other men. There is in all great poets, a wisdom of humanity, which is superior to any talents they exercise. The author, the wit, the partisan, the fine gentleman, does not take place of the man. Humanity shines in Homer, in Chaucer, in Spenser, in Shakspeare, in Milton. They are content with truth. They use the positive degree. They seem frigid and phlegmatic to those who have been spiced with the frantic passion and violent coloring of inferior, but popular writers. For, they are poets by the free course which they allow to the informing soul, which through their eyes beholds again, and blesses the things which it hath made. The soul is superior to its knowledge; wiser than any of its works. The great poet makes us feel our own wealth, and then we think less of his compositions. His best communication to our mind, is, to teach us to despise all he has done. Shakspeare carries us to such a lofty strain of intelligent activity, as to suggest a wealth which beggars his own; and we then feel that the splendid works which he has created, and which in other hours, we extol as a sort of self-existent poetry, take no stronger hold of real nature than the shadow of a passing traveller on the rock. The inspiration which uttered itself in Hamlet and Lear, could utter things as good from day to day, forever. Why then should I make account of Hamlet and Lear, as if we had not the soul from which they fell as syllables from the tongue?

This energy does not descend into individual life, on any other condition than entire possession. It comes to the lowly and simple; it comes to whomsoever will put off what is foreign and proud; it comes as insight; it comes as serenity and grandeur. When we see those whom it inhabits, we are apprized of new degrees of greatness. From that inspiration the man comes back with a changed tone. He does not talk with men, with an eye to their opinion. He tries them. It requires of us to be plain and true. The vain traveller attempts to embellish his life by quoting my Lord, and the Prince, and the Countess, who thus said or did to *him*. The ambitious vulgar,[18] show you their spoons, and brooches, and rings, and preserve their cards and compliments. The more cultivated, in their account of their own experience, cull out the pleasing poetic circumstance,—the visit to Rome, the man of genius they saw, the brilliant friend they know; still further on, perhaps, the

---

[18]Common people.

gorgeous landscape, the mountain lights, the mountain thoughts, they enjoyed yesterday,—and so seek to throw a romantic color over their life. But the soul that ascends to worship the great God, is plain and true; has no rose-color, no fine friends, no chivalry, no adventures; does not want admiration; dwells in the hour that now is, in the earnest experience of the common day,—by reason of the present moment and the mere trifle having become porous to thought, and bibulous of the sea of light.

Converse with a mind that is grandly simple, and literature looks like word-catching. The simplest utterances are worthiest to be written, yet are they so cheap, and so things of course, that in the infinite riches of the soul, it is like gathering a few pebbles off the ground, or bottling a little air in a phial, when the whole earth, and the whole atmosphere are ours. Nothing can pass there, or make you one of the circle, but the casting aside your trappings, and dealing man to man in naked truth, plain confession and omniscient affirmation.

Souls, such as these, treat you as gods would; walk as gods in the earth, accepting without any admiration, your wit, your bounty, your virtue even,—say rather your act of duty, for your virtue they own as their proper blood, royal as themselves, and over-royal, and the father of the gods. But what rebuke their plain fraternal bearing casts on the mutual flattery with which authors solace each other, and wound themselves! These flatter not. I do not wonder that these men go to see Cromwell, and Christina, and Charles II., and James I., and the Grand Turk.[19] For they are in their own elevation, the fellows of kings, and must feel the servile tone of conversation in the world. They must always be a godsend to princes, for they confront them, a king to a king, without ducking or concession, and give a high nature the refreshment and satisfaction of resistance, of plain humanity, of even companionship, and of new ideas. They leave them wiser and superior men. Souls like these make us feel that sincerity is more excellent than flattery. Deal so plainly with man and woman, as to constrain the utmost sincerity, and destroy all hope of trifling with you. It is the highest compliment you can pay. Their "highest praising," said Milton, "is not flattery, and their plainest advice is a kind of praising."[20]

Ineffable is the union of man and God in every act of the soul. The simplest person, who in his integrity worships God, becomes God; yet forever and ever the influx of this better and universal self is new and unsearchable. It inspires awe and astonishment. How dear, how soothing to man, arises the idea of God, peopling the lonely place, effacing the scars of our mistakes and disappointments! When we have broken our god of tradition, and ceased from our god of rhetoric, then may God fire the heart with his presence. It is the doubling of the heart itself, nay, the infinite enlargement of the heart with a power of growth to a new infinity on every side. It inspires in man an infallible trust. He has not the conviction, but the sight that the best is the true, and may in that thought easily dismiss all particular uncertainties and fears, and adjourn to the sure revelation of time, the solution of his private riddles. He is sure that his welfare is dear to the heart of being. In the presence of law to his mind, he is overflowed with a reliance so universal, that it sweeps away all cherished hopes and the most stable projects of mortal condition in its flood. He believes that he cannot escape from his good. The things that are really for thee, gravitate to thee. You are running to seek your friend. Let your feet run, but your mind need not. If you do not find him, will you not acquiesce that it is best you should not find him? for there is a power, which, as it is in you, is in him also, and could therefore very well bring you to-

---

[19]All heads of state: Oliver Cromwell (1599–1658), Lord Protector of the British Commonwealth; Queen Christina of Sweden (1626–1689); Charles II (1630–1685) and James I (1566–1625), kings of England; the Grand Turk, the Sultan of Turkey.
[20]From John Milton's *Areopagitica* (1644), paragraph 4.

gether, if it were for the best. You are preparing with eagerness to go and render a service to which your talent and your taste invite you, the love of men, and the hope of fame. Has it not occurred to you, that you have no right to go, unless you are equally willing to be prevented from going? O believe, as thou livest, that every sound that is spoken over the round world, which thou oughtest to hear, will vibrate on thine ear. Every proverb, every book, every byword that belongs to thee for aid or comfort, shall surely come home through open or winding passages. Every friend whom not thy fantastic will, but the great and tender heart in thee craveth, shall lock thee in his embrace. And this, because the heart in thee is the heart of all; not a valve, not a wall, not an intersection is there anywhere in nature, but one blood rolls uninterruptedly, an endless circulation through all men, as the water of the globe is all one sea, and, truly seen, its tide is one.

Let man then learn the revelation of all nature, and all thought to his heart; this, namely; that the Highest dwells with him; that the sources of nature are in his own mind, if the sentiment of duty is there. But if he would know what the great God speaketh, he must 'go into his closet and shut the door,' as Jesus said.[21] God will not make himself manifest to cowards. He must greatly listen to himself, withdrawing himself from all the accents of other men's devotion. Even their prayers are hurtful to him, until he have made his own. Our religion vulgarly stands on numbers of believers. Whenever the appeal is made,—no matter how indirectly,—to numbers, proclamation is then and there made, that religion is not. He that finds God a sweet, enveloping thought to him, never counts his company. When I sit in that presence, who shall dare to come in? When I rest in perfect humility, when I burn with pure love,—what can Calvin[22] or Swedenborg say?

It makes no difference whether the appeal is to numbers or to one. The faith that stands on authority is not faith. The reliance on authority, measures the decline of religion, the withdrawal of the soul. The position men have given to Jesus, now for many centuries of history, is a position of authority. It characterizes themselves. It cannot alter the eternal facts. Great is the soul, and plain. It is no flatterer, it is no follower; it never appeals from itself. It believes in itself. Before the immense possibilities of man, all mere experience, all past biography, however spotless and sainted, shrinks away. Before that heaven which our presentiments foreshow us, we cannot easily praise any form of life we have seen or read of. We not only affirm that we have few great men, but absolutely speaking, that we have none; that we have no history, no record of any character or mode of living, that entirely contents us. The saints and demigods whom history worships, we are constrained to accept with a grain of allowance. Though in our lonely hours, we draw a new strength out of their memory, yet pressed on our attention, as they are by the thoughtless and customary, they fatigue and invade. The soul gives itself alone, original, and pure, to the Lonely, Original and Pure, who, on that condition, gladly inhabits, leads, and speaks through it. Then is it glad, young, and nimble. It is not wise, but it sees through all things. It is not called religious, but it is innocent. It calls the light its own, and feels that the grass grows, and the stone falls by a law inferior to, and dependent on its nature. Behold, it saith, I am born into the great, the universal mind. I the imperfect, adore my own Perfect. I am somehow receptive of the great soul, and thereby I do overlook the sun and the stars, and feel them to be the fair accidents and effects which change and pass. More and more the surges of everlasting nature enter into me, and I become public and human in my regards and actions. So come I to live in thoughts, and act

---

[21]Matthew 6:6: "But thou, when thou prayest, enter into thy closet, and when thou hast shut thy door, pray to thy Father which is in secret; and thy Father which seeth in secret shall reward thee openly."

[22]John Calvin (1590–1664), French theologian (exiled in Switzerland), leader of the Reformation and founder of Calvinism.

with energies which are immortal. Thus revering the soul, and learning, as the ancient said, that "its beauty is immense," man will come to see that the world is the perennial miracle which the soul worketh, and be less astonished at particular wonders; he will learn that there is no profane history; that all history is sacred; that the universe is represented in an atom, in a moment of time. He will weave no longer a spotted life of shreds and patches, but he will live with a divine unity. He will cease from what is base and frivolous in his life, and be content with all places and with any service he can render. He will calmly front the morrow in the negligency of that trust which carries God with it, and so hath already the whole future in the bottom of the heart.

1841

Circles[1]

Nature centres into balls,
And her proud ephemerals,
Fast to surface and outside,
Scan the profile of the sphere;
Knew they what that signified,
A new genesis were here.

The eye is the first circle; the horizon which it forms is the second; and throughout nature this primary figure is repeated without end. It is the highest emblem in the cipher of the world. St. Augustine[2] described the nature of God as a circle whose centre was everywhere, and its circumference nowhere. We are all our lifetime reading the copious sense of this first of forms. One moral we have already deduced in considering the circular or compensatory character of every human action. Another analogy we shall now trace; that every action admits of being outdone. Our life is an apprenticeship to the truth, that around every circle another can be drawn; that there is no end in nature, but every end is a beginning; that there is always another dawn risen on mid-noon,[3] and under every deep a lower deep opens.

This fact, as far as it symbolizes the moral fact of the Unattainable, the flying Perfect, around which the hands of man can never meet, at once the inspirer and the condemner of every success, may conveniently serve us to connect many illustrations of human power in every department.

There are no fixtures in nature. The universe is fluid and volatile. Permanence is but a word of degrees. Our globe seen by God, is a transparent law, not a mass of facts. The law dissolves the fact and holds it fluid. Our culture is the predominance of an idea which draws after it this train of cities and institutions. Let us rise into another idea: they will disappear. The Greek sculpture is all melted away, as if it had been statues of ice: here and there a solitary figure or fragment remaining, as we see flecks and scraps of snow left in cold dells and mountain clefts, in June and July. For, the genius that created it, creates now somewhat else. The

---

[1] Written largely in 1840. "Circles" represents a side of Emerson that lives not so securely in the reassuring awareness of the Oversoul but that lives with the uneasy awareness of fluidity and contingency. The poetic epigraph is by Emerson.

[2] St. Augustine (A.D. 354–430) seems not to have made this statement. According to Joseph Slater, editor of *Essays: First Series* in the *Collected Works,* Emerson copied the quotation into his journal from John Norris's *An Essay Towards the Theory of the Ideal or Intelligible World* (1701–04), which referred not to God but to truth. It is next to some quotations in the journal from St. Augustine, and Emerson may thus have been misled.

[3] Cf. John Milton, *Paradise Lost,* V, 309–311; Adam calls to Eve to come and see the "glorious shape" that "comes this way moving; seems another morn/ Risen on mid-noon."

Greek letters last a little longer, but are already passing under the same sentence, and tumbling into the inevitable pit which the creation of new thought opens for all that is old. The new continents are built out of the ruins of an old planet: the new races fed out of the decomposition of the foregoing. New arts destroy the old. See the investment of capital in aqueducts, made useless by hydraulics; fortifications, by gunpowder; roads and canals, by railways; sails, by steam; steam by electricity.

You admire this tower of granite, weathering the hurts of so many ages. Yet a little waving hand built this huge wall, and that which builds, is better than that which is built. The hand that built, can topple it down much faster. Better than the hand, and nimbler, was the invisible thought which wrought through it, and thus ever behind the coarse effect, is a fine cause, which, being narrowly seen, is itself the effect of a finer cause. Every thing looks permanent until its secret is known. A rich estate appears to women a firm and lasting fact; to a merchant, one easily created out of any materials, and easily lost. An orchard, good tillage, good grounds, seem a fixture, like a gold mine, or a river, to a citizen; but to a large farmer, not much more fixed than the state of the crop. Nature looks provokingly stable and secular, but it has a cause like all the rest; and when once I comprehend that, will these fields stretch so immovably wide, these leaves hang so individually considerable? Permanence is a word of degrees. Every thing is medial. Moons are no more bounds to spiritual power than bat-balls.

The key to every man is his thought. Sturdy and defying though he look, he has a helm which he obeys, which is, the idea after which all his facts are classified. He can only be reformed by showing him a new idea which commands his own. The life of man is a self-evolving circle, which, from a ring imperceptibly small, rushes on all sides outwards to new and larger circles, and that without end. The extent to which this generation of circles, wheel without wheel will go, depends on the force or truth of the individual soul. For, it is the inert effort of each thought having formed itself into a circular wave of circumstance,—as, for instance, an empire, rules of an art, a local usage, a religious rite,—to heap itself on that ridge, and to solidify, and hem in the life. But if the soul is quick and strong, it bursts over that boundary on all sides, and expands another orbit on the great deep, which also runs up into a high wave, with attempt again to stop and to bind. But the heart refuses to be imprisoned; in its first and narrowest pulses, it already tends outward with a vast force, and to immense and innumerable expansions.

Every ultimate fact is only the first of a new series. Every general law only a particular fact of some more general law presently to disclose itself. There is no outside, no enclosing wall, no circumference to us. The man finishes his story,— how good! how final! how it puts a new face on all things! He fills the sky. Lo! on the other side rises also a man, and draws a circle around the circle we had just pronounced the outline of the sphere. Then already is our first speaker, not man, but only a first speaker. His only redress is forthwith to draw a circle outside of his antagonist. And so men do by themselves. The result of to-day which haunts the mind and cannot be escaped, will presently be abridged into a word, and the principle that seemed to explain nature, will itself be included as one example of a bolder generalization. In the thought of to-morrow there is a power to upheave all thy creed, all the creeds, all the literatures of the nations, and marshal thee to a heaven which no epic dream has yet depicted. Every man is not so much a workman in the world, as he is a suggestion of that he should be. Men walk as prophecies of the next age.

Step by step we scale this mysterious ladder: the steps are actions; the new prospect is power. Every several result is threatened and judged by that which follows. Every one seems to be contradicted by the new; it is only limited by the new. The new statement is always hated by the old, and, to those dwelling in the old, comes like an abyss of skepticism. But the eye soon gets wonted to it, for the eye and it are effects of one cause; then its innocency and benefit appear, and, presently, all its energy spent, it pales and dwindles before the revelation of the new hour.

Fear not the new generalization. Does the fact look crass and material, threatening to degrade thy theory of spirit? Resist it not; it goes to refine and raise thy theory of matter just as much.

There are no fixtures to men, if we appeal to consciousness. Every man supposes himself not to be fully understood; and if there is any truth in him, if he rests at last on the divine soul, I see not how it can be otherwise. The last chamber, the last closet, he must feel, was never opened; there is always a residuum unknown, unanalyzable. That is, every man believes that he has a greater possibility.

Our moods do not believe in each other. To-day, I am full of thoughts, and can write what I please. I see no reason why I should not have the same thought, the same power of expression to-morrow. What I write, whilst I write it, seems the most natural thing in the world: but, yesterday, I saw a dreary vacuity in this direction in which now I see so much; and a month hence, I doubt not, I shall wonder who he was that wrote so many continuous pages. Alas for this infirm faith, this will not strenuous, this vast ebb of a vast flow! I am God in nature; I am a weed by the wall.

The continual effort to raise himself above himself,[4] to work a pitch above his last height, betrays itself in a man's relations. We thirst for approbation, yet cannot forgive the approver. The sweet of nature is love; yet if I have a friend, I am tormented by my imperfections. The love of me accuses the other party. If he were high enough to slight me, then could I love him, and rise by my affection to new heights. A man's growth is seen in the successive choirs of his friends. For every friend whom he loses for truth, he gains a better. I thought, as I walked in the woods and mused on my friends, why should I play with them this game of idolatry? I know and see too well, when not voluntarily blind, the speedy limits of persons called high and worthy. Rich, noble, and great they are by the liberality of our speech, but truth is sad. O blessed Spirit, whom I forsake for these, they are not thou! Every personal consideration that we allow, costs us heavenly state. We sell the thrones of angels for a short and turbulent pleasure.

How often must we learn this lesson? Men cease to interest us when we find their limitations. The only sin is limitation. As soon as you once come up with a man's limitations, it is all over with him. Has he talents? has he enterprises? has he knowledge? it boots not. Infinitely alluring and attractive was he to you yesterday, a great hope, a sea to swim in; now, you have found his shores, found it a pond, and you care not if you never see it again.

Each new step we take in thought reconciles twenty seemingly discordant facts, as expressions of one law. Aristotle and Plato are reckoned the respective heads of two schools.[5] A wise man will see that Aristotle Platonizes. By going one step farther back in thought, discordant opinions are reconciled, by being seen to be two extremes of one principle, and we can never go so far back as to preclude a still higher vision.

Beware when the great God lets loose a thinker on this planet. Then all things are at risk. It is as when a conflagration has broken out in a great city, and no man knows what is safe, or where it will end. There is not a piece of science, but its flank may be turned to-morrow; there is not any literary reputation, not the so-

---

[4] Cf. Samuel Daniel's Epistle "To the Lady Margaret, Countess of Cumberland," 11. 98–99: "unless above himself he can/ Erect himself, how poor a thing is man!"
[5] Aristotle (384–322 B.C.) tended to be concrete and to rea-

son from facts to generalizations, or inductively; Plato (427–347 B.C.) tended to be idealistic and to reason from principles to specific instances, or deductively.

called eternal names of fame, that may not be revised and condemned. The very hopes of man, the thoughts of his heart, the religion of nations, the manners and morals of mankind, are all at the mercy of a new generalization. Generalization is always a new influx of the divinity into the mind. Hence the thrill that attends it.

Valor consists in the power of self-recovery, so that a man cannot have his flank turned, cannot be outgeneralled, but put him where you will, he stands. This can only be by his preferring truth to his past apprehension of truth; and his alert acceptance of it from whatever quarter; the intrepid conviction that his laws, his relations to society, his christianity, his world, may at any time be superseded and decease.

There are degrees in idealism. We learn first to play with it academically, as the magnet was once a toy. Then we see in the heyday of youth and poetry that it may be true, that it is true in gleams and fragments. Then, its countenance waxes stern and grand, and we see that it must be true. It now shows itself ethical and practical. We learn that God IS; that he is in me; and that all things are shadows of him. The idealism of Berkeley[6] is only a crude statement of the idealism of Jesus, and that, again, is a crude statement of the fact that all nature is the rapid efflux of goodness executing and organizing itself. Much more obviously is history and the state of the world at any one time, directly dependent on the intellectual classification then existing in the minds of men. The things which are dear to men at this hour, are so on account of the ideas which have emerged on their mental horizon, and which cause the present order of things as a tree bears its apples. A new degree of culture would instantly revolutionize the entire system of human pursuits.

Conversation is a game of circles. In conversation we pluck up the *termini*[7] which bound the common[8] of silence on every side. The parties are not to be judged by the spirit they partake and even express under this Pentecost. To-morrow they will have receded from this high-water mark. To-morrow you shall find them stooping under the old packsaddles. Yet let us enjoy the cloven flame whilst it glows on our walls.[9] When each new speaker strikes a new light, emancipates us from the oppression of the last speaker, to oppress us with the greatness and exclusiveness of his own thought, then yields us to another redeemer, we seem to recover our rights, to become men. O what truths profound and executable only in ages and orbs, are supposed in the announcement of every truth! In common hours, society sits cold and statuesque. We all stand waiting, empty,—knowing, possibly, that we can be full, surrounded by mighty symbols which are not symbols to us, but prose and trivial toys. Then cometh the god, and converts the statues into fiery men, and by a flash of his eye burns up the veil which shrouded all things, and the meaning of the very furniture, of cup and saucer, of chair and clock and tester, is manifest. The facts which loomed so large in the fogs of yesterday,—property, climate, breeding, personal beauty, and the like, have strangely changed their proportions. All that we reckoned settled, shakes and rattles; and literatures, cities, climates, religions, leave their foundations, and dance before our eyes. And yet here again see the swift circumscription. Good as is discourse, silence is better, and shames it. The length of the discourse indicates the distance of thought betwixt the speaker and the hearer. If they were at a perfect understanding in any part, no words would be necessary thereon. If at one in all parts, no words would be suffered.

Literature is a point outside of our hodiernal[10] circle, through which a new one

---

[6]Bishop George Berkeley (1685–1753), British philosopher, author of works (including *A Treatise Concerning the Principles of Human Knowledge*, 1710) setting forth his philosophy of subjective idealism (material things exist only in being perceived).

[7]"Ends" (Latin).

[8]Tract of publicly used land (here metaphorical).

[9]Cf. Acts 2:1–4: On the day of Pentecost (fifty days after the Resurrection), "suddenly there came a sound from heaven as of a rushing mighty wind, and it filled all the house where they were sitting. And there appeared unto them cloven tongues like as of fire, and it sat upon each of them."

[10]Of or belonging to the present day.

may be described. The use of literature is to afford us a platform whence we may command a view of our present life, a purchase by which we may move it. We fill ourselves with ancient learning; install ourselves the best we can in Greek, in Punic,[11] in Roman houses, only that we may wiselier see French, English, and American houses and modes of living. In like manner, we see literature best from the midst of wild nature, or from the din of affairs, or from a high religion. The field cannot be well seen from within the field. The astronomer must have his diameter of the earth's orbit as a base to find the parallax[12] of any star.

Therefore, we value the poet. All the argument, and all the wisdom, is not in the encyclopedia, or the treatise on metaphysics, or the Body of Divinity, but in the sonnet or the play. In my daily work I incline to repeat my old steps, and do not believe in remedial force, in the power of change and reform. But some Petrarch or Ariosto,[13] filled with the new wine of his imagination, writes me an ode, or a brisk romance, full of daring thought and action. He smites and arouses me with his shrill tones, breaks up my whole chain of habits, and I open my eye on my own possibilities. He claps wings to the sides of all the solid old lumber of the world, and I am capable once more of choosing a straight path in theory and practice.

We have the same need to command a view of the religion of the world. We can never see christianity from the catechism:[14]—from the pastures, from a boat in the pond, from amidst the songs of wood-birds, we possibly may. Cleansed by the elemental light and wind, steeped in the sea of beautiful forms which the field offers us, we may chance to cast a right glance back upon biography. Christianity is rightly dear to the best of mankind; yet was there never a young philosopher whose breeding had fallen into the christian church, by whom that brave text of Paul's, was not specially prized:—"Then shall also the Son be subject unto Him who put all things under him, that God may be all in all."[15] Let the claims and virtues of persons be never so great and welcome, the instinct of man presses eagerly onward to the impersonal and illimitable, and gladly arms itself against the dogmatism of bigots with this generous word, out of the book itself.

The natural world may be conceived of as a system of concentric circles, and we now and then detect in nature slight dislocations, which apprize us that this surface on which we now stand, is not fixed, but sliding. These manifold tenacious qualities, this chemistry and vegetation, these metals and animals, which seem to stand there for their own sake, are means and methods only,—are words of God, and as fugitive as other words. Has the naturalist or chemist learned his craft, who has explored the gravity of atoms and the elective affinities, who has not yet discerned the deeper law whereof this is only a partial or approximate statement, namely, that like draws to like; and that the goods which belong to you, gravitate to you, and need not be pursued with pains and cost? Yet is that statement approximate also, and not final. Omnipresence is a higher fact. Not through subtle, subterranean channels, need friend and fact be drawn to their counterpart, but, rightly considered, these things proceed from the eternal generation of the soul. Cause and effect are two sides of one fact.

The same law of eternal procession ranges all that we call the virtues, and extinguishes each in the light of a better. The great man will not be prudent in the popular sense; all his prudence will be so much deduction from his grandeur. But it behoves each to see when he sacrifices prudence, to what god he devotes it; if to ease and pleasure, he had better be prudent still: if to a great trust, he can well

---

[11]Of ancient Carthage (Carthaginian).
[12]Change in position of an object (star) caused by change in position from which it is viewed.
[13]Petrarch (1304–1374) and Ariosto (1474–1533), Italian classic and innovative poets.
[14]Questions and answers about a religion's principles.
[15]1 Corinthians 15:28.

spare his mule and panniers, who has a winged chariot instead. Geoffrey draws on his boots to go through the woods, that his feet may be safer from the bite of snakes; Aaron never thinks of such a peril. In many years, neither is harmed by such an accident. Yet it seems to me that with every precaution you take against such an evil, you put yourself into the power of the evil. I suppose that the highest prudence is the lowest prudence. Is this too sudden a rushing from the centre to the verge of our orbit? Think how many times we shall fall back into pitiful calculations, before we take up our rest in the great sentiment, or make the verge of to-day the new centre. Besides, your bravest sentiment is familiar to the humblest men. The poor and the low have their way of expressing the last facts of philosophy as well as you. "Blessed be nothing," and "the worse things are, the better they are," are proverbs which express the transcendentalism of common life.

One man's justice is another's injustice; one man's beauty, another's ugliness; one man's wisdom, another's folly; as one beholds the same objects from a higher point. One man thinks justice consists in paying debts, and has no measure in his abhorrence of another who is very remiss in this duty, and makes the creditor wait tediously. But that second man has his own way of looking at things; asks himself, which debt must I pay first, the debt to the rich, or the debt to the poor? the debt of money, or the debt of thought to mankind, of genius to nature? For you, O broker, there is no other principle but arithmetic. For me, commerce is of trivial import; love, faith, truth of character, the aspiration of man, these are sacred: nor can I detach one duty, like you, from all other duties, and concentrate my forces mechanically on the payment of moneys. Let me live onward: you shall find that, though slower, the progress of my character will liquidate all these debts without injustice to higher claims. If a man should dedicate himself to the payment of notes, would not this be injustice? Does he owe no debt but money? And are all claims on him to be postponed to a landlord's or a banker's?

There is no virtue which is final; all are initial. The virtues of society are vices of the saint. The terror of reform is the discovery that we must cast away our virtues, or what we have always esteemed such, into the same pit that has consumed our grosser vices.

> "Forgive his crimes, forgive his virtues too,
> Those smaller faults, half converts to the right."[16]

It is the highest power of divine moments that they abolish our contritions also. I accuse myself of sloth and unprofitableness, day by day; but when these waves of God flow into me, I no longer reckon lost time. I no longer poorly compute my possible achievement by what remains to me of the month or the year; for these moments confer a sort of omnipresence and omnipotence, which asks nothing of duration, but sees that the energy of the mind is commensurate with the work to be done, without time.

And thus, O circular philosopher, I hear some reader exclaim, you have arrived at a fine pyrrhonism,[17] at an equivalence and indifferency of all actions, and would fain teach us, that, *if we are true,* forsooth, our crimes may be lively stones out of which we shall construct the temple of the true God.[18]

I am not careful to justify myself. I own I am gladdened by seeing the predominance of the saccharine[19] principle throughout vegetable nature, and not less by beholding in morals that unrestrained inundation of the principle of good into every chink and hole that selfishness has left open, yea, into selfishness and sin itself;

---

[16]From *The Complaint; or, Night Thoughts,* IX, 2316–2317, by Edward Young (1683–1765), British poet.
[17]Extreme skepticism; derived from Pyrrho (*c.* 365–275 B.C.), Greek philosopher who taught that all knowledge was uncertain.
[18]Cf. 1 Peter 2:5 "Ye also, as lively stones, are built up a spiritual house, an holy priesthood, to offer up spiritual sacrifices, acceptable to God by Jesus Christ."
[19]Sweet (here not ironic).

so that no evil is pure, nor hell itself without its extreme satisfactions. But lest I should mislead any when I have my own head, and obey my whims, let me remind the reader that I am only an experimenter. Do not set the least value on what I do, or the least discredit on what I do not, as if I pretended to settle anything as true or false. I unsettle all things. No facts are to me sacred; none are profane; I simply experiment, an endless seeker, with no Past at my back.

Yet this incessant movement and progression, which all things partake, could never become sensible to us, but by contrast to some principle of fixture or stability in the soul. Whilst the eternal generation of circles proceeds, the eternal generator abides. That central life is somewhat superior to creation, superior to knowledge and thought, and contains all its circles. Forever it labors to create a life and thought as large and excellent as itself, suggesting to our thought a certain development, as if that which is made, instructs how to make a better.

Thus there is no sleep, no pause, no preservation, but all things renew, germinate, and spring. Why should we import rags and relics into the new hour? Nature abhors the old, and old age seems the only disease: all others run into this one. We call it by many names,—fever, intemperance, insanity, stupidity, and crime: they are all forms of old age: they are rest, conservatism, appropriation, inertia, not newness, not the way onward. We grizzle every day. I see no need of it. Whilst we converse with what is above us, we do not grow old, but grow young. Infancy, youth, receptive, aspiring, with religious eye looking upward, counts itself nothing, and abandons itself to the instruction flowing from all sides. But the man and woman of seventy assume to know all, they have outlived their hope, they renounce aspiration, accept the actual for the necessary, and talk down to the young. Let them then become organs of the Holy Ghost; let them be lovers; let them behold truth; and their eyes are uplifted, their wrinkles smoothed, they are perfumed again with hope and power. This old age ought not to creep on a human mind. In nature, every moment is new; the past is always swallowed and forgotten; the coming only is sacred. Nothing is secure but life, transition, the energizing spirit. No love can be bound by oath or covenant to secure it against a higher love. No truth so sublime but it may be trivial tomorrow in the light of new thoughts. People wish to be settled: only as far as they are unsettled, is there any hope for them.

Life is a series of surprises. We do not guess to-day the mood, the pleasure, the power of to-morrow, when we are building up our being. Of lower states,—of acts of routine and sense,—we can tell somewhat; but the masterpieces of God, the total growths and universal movements of the soul, he hideth; they are incalculable. I can know that truth is divine and helpful, but how it shall help me, I can have no guess, for, *so to be* is the sole inlet of *so to know*. The new position of the advancing man has all the powers of the old, yet has them all new. It carries in its bosom all the energies of the past, yet is itself an exhalation of the morning. I cast away in this new moment all my once hoarded knowledge, as vacant and vain. Now, for the first time, seem I to know any thing rightly. The simplest words,—we do not know what they mean, except when we love and aspire.

The difference between talents and character is adroitness to keep the old and trodden round, and power and courage to make a new road to new and better goals. Character makes an overpowering present, a cheerful, determined hour, which fortifies all the company, by making them see that much is possible and excellent, that was not thought of. Character dulls the impression of particular events. When we see the conqueror, we do not think much of any one battle or success. We see that we had exaggerated the difficulty. It was easy to him. The great man is not convulsible or tormentable; events pass over him without much impression. People say sometimes, 'See what I have overcome; see how cheerful I am; see how completely I have triumphed over these black events.' Not if they still remind me of the black event. True conquest is the causing the calamity to fade and disappear as an early cloud of insignificant result in a history so large and advancing.

The one thing which we seek with insatiable desire, is to forget ourselves, to be surprised out of our propriety, to lose our sempiternal memory, and to do something without knowing how or why; in short, to draw a new circle. Nothing great was ever achieved without enthusiasm.[20] The way of life is wonderful: it is by abandonment. The great moments of history are the facilities of performance through the strength of ideas, as the works of genius and religion. "A man," said Oliver Cromwell, "never rises so high as when he knows not whither he is going."[21] Dreams and drunkenness, the use of opium and alcohol are the semblance and counterfeit of this oracular genius, and hence their dangerous attraction for men. For the like reason, they ask the aid of wild passions, as in gaming and war, to ape in some manner these flames and generosities of the heart.

1841

The Poet[1]

A moody child and wildly wise
Pursued the game with joyful eyes,
Which chose, like meteors, their way,
And rived the dark with private ray:
They overleapt the horizon's edge,
Searched with Apollo's privilege;
Through man, and woman, and sea, and star,
Saw the dance of nature forward far;
Through worlds, and races, and terms, and times,
Saw musical order, and pairing rhymes.

Olympian bards who sung
Divine ideas below,
Which always find us young,
And always keep us so.

Those who are esteemed umpires of taste, are often persons who have acquired some knowledge of admired pictures or sculptures, and have an inclination for whatever is elegant; but if you inquire whether they are beautiful souls, and whether their own acts are like fair pictures, you learn that they are selfish and sensual. Their cultivation is local, as if you should rub a log of dry wood in one spot to produce fire, all the rest remaining cold. Their knowledge of the fine arts is some study of rules and particulars, or some limited judgment of color or form, which is exercised for amusement or for show. It is a proof of the shallowness of the doctrine of beauty, as it lies in the minds of our amateurs, that men seem to have lost the perception of the instant dependence of form upon soul. There is no

---

[20]Cf. Samuel Taylor Coleridge (1772–1834), *The Statesman's Manual* (Para. 18): ". . . the aphorism of ancient wisdom, that nothing great was ever achieved without enthusiasm. For what is enthusiasm but the oblivion and swallowing up of self in an object dearer than self, or in an idea more vivid?"

[21]Oliver Cromwell (1599–1628), English statesman, quoted in *History of the Rebellion and Civil Wars in England*, by Edward Hyde, First Earl of Clarendon (1609–1674).

[1]One of the important statements on poetic theory from the nineteenth century, comparable in significance to Walt Whitman's 1855 Preface to *Leaves of Grass*, about a decade later. The first epigraph is from one of Emerson's unfinished poems, "The Poet," the second from his "Ode to Beauty."

doctrine of forms in our philosophy. We were put into our bodies, as fire is put into a pan, to be carried about; but there is no accurate adjustment between the spirit and the organ, much less is the latter the germination of the former. So in regard to other forms, the intellectual men do not believe in any essential dependence of the material world on thought and volition. Theologians think it a pretty air-castle to talk of the spiritual meaning of a ship or a cloud, of a city or a contract, but they prefer to come again to the solid ground of historical evidence; and even the poets are contented with a civil and conformed manner of living, and to write poems from the fancy, at a safe distance from their own experience. But the highest minds of the world have never ceased to explore the double meaning, or, shall I say, the quadruple, or the centuple, or much more manifold meaning, of every sensuous fact: Orpheus, Empedocles, Heraclitus, Plato, Plutarch, Dante, Swedenborg,[2] and the masters of sculpture, picture, and poetry. For we are not pans and barrows, nor even porters of the fire and torch-bearers, but children of the fire, made of it, and only the same divinity transmuted, and at two or three removes, when we know least about it. And this hidden truth, that the fountains whence all this river of Time, and its creatures, floweth, are intrinsically ideal and beautiful, draws us to the consideration of the nature and functions of the Poet, or the man of Beauty, to the means and materials he uses, and to the general aspect of the art in the present time.

The breadth of the problem is great, for the poet is representative. He stands among partial men for the complete man, and apprises us not of his wealth, but of the commonwealth. The young man reveres men of genius, because, to speak truly, they are more himself than he is. They receive of the soul as he also receives, but they more. Nature enhances her beauty to the eye of loving men, from their belief that the poet is beholding her shows at the same time. He is isolated among his contemporaries, by truth and by his art, but with this consolation in his pursuits, that they will draw all men sooner or later. For all men live by truth, and stand in need of expression. In love, in art, in avarice, in politics, in labor, in games, we study to utter our painful secret. The man is only half himself, the other half is his expression.

Notwithstanding this necessity to be published, adequate expression is rare. I know not how it is that we need an interpreter; but the great majority of men seem to be minors, who have not yet come into possession of their own, or mutes, who cannot report the conversation they have had with nature. There is no man who does not anticipate a supersensual utility in the sun, and stars, earth, and water. These stand and wait to render him a peculiar service. But there is some obstruction, or some excess of phlegm in our constitution, which does not suffer them to yield the due effect. Too feeble fall the impressions of nature on us to make us artists. Every touch should thrill. Every man should be so much an artist, that he could report in conversation what had befallen him. Yet, in our experience, the rays or appulses have sufficient force to arrive at the senses, but not enough to reach the quick, and compel the reproduction of themselves in speech. The poet is the person in whom these powers are in balance, the man without impediment, who sees and handles that which others dream of, traverses the whole scale of experience, and is representative of man, in virtue of being the largest power to receive and to impart.

For the Universe has three children, born at one time, which reappear, under different names, in every system of thought, whether they be called cause, operation, and effect; or, more poetically, Jove, Pluto, Neptune; or, theologically, the

---

[2]Orpheus, the legendary poet of Greek mythology; Empedocles, Heraclitus, and Plato, Greek philosophers of sixth– fourth century B.C.; Plutarch, Greek biographer of first century A.D.; Dante, medieval Italian poet; Swedenborg, eighteenth-century Swedish mystic and scientist.

Father, the Spirit, and the Son; but which we will call here, the Knower, the Doer, and the Sayer.[3] These stand respectively for the love of truth, for the love of good, and for the love of beauty. These three are equal. Each is that which he is essentially, so that he cannot be surmounted or analyzed, and each of these three has the power of the others latent in him, and his own patent.

The poet is the sayer, the namer, and represents beauty. He is a sovereign, and stands on the centre. For the world is not painted, or adorned, but is from the beginning beautiful; and God has not made some beautiful things, but Beauty is the creator of the universe. Therefore the poet is not any permissive potentate, but is emperor in his own right. Criticism is infested with a cant of materialism, which assumes that manual skill and activity is the first merit of all men, and disparages such as say and do not, overlooking the fact, that some men, namely, poets, are natural sayers, sent into the world to the end of expression, and confounds them with those whose province is action, but who quit it to imitate the sayers. But Homer's words are as costly and admirable to Homer, as Agamemnon's victories are to Agamemnon. The poet does not wait for the hero or the sage, but, as they act and think primarily, so he writes primarily what will and must be spoken, reckoning the others, though primaries also, yet, in respect to him, secondaries and servants; as sitters or models in the studio of a painter, or as assistants who bring building materials to an architect.

For poetry was all written before time was, and whenever we are so finely organized that we can penetrate into that region where the air is music, we hear those primal warblings, and attempt to write them down, but we lose ever and anon a word, or a verse, and substitute something of our own, and thus miswrite the poem. The men of more delicate ear write down these cadences more faithfully, and these transcripts, though imperfect, become the songs of the nations. For nature is as truly beautiful as it is good, or as it is reasonable, and must as much appear, as it must be done, or be known. Words and deeds are quite indifferent[4] modes of the divine energy. Words are also actions, and actions are a kind of words.

The sign and credentials of the poet are, that he announces that which no man foretold. He is the true and only doctor;[5] he knows and tells; he is the only teller of news, for he was present and privy to the appearance which he describes. He is a beholder of ideas, and an utterer of the necessary and causal. For we do not speak now of men of poetical talents, or of industry and skill in metre, but of the true poet. I took part in a conversation the other day, concerning a recent writer of lyrics,[6] a man of subtle mind, whose head appeared to be a music-box of delicate tunes and rhythms, and whose skill, and command of language, we could not sufficiently praise. But when the question arose, whether he was not only a lyrist, but a poet, we were obliged to confess that he is plainly a contemporary, not an eternal man. He does not stand out of our low limitations, like a Chimborazo under the line, running up from the torrid base through all the climates of the globe, with belts of the herbage of every latitude on its high and mottled sides;[7] but this genius is the landscape-garden of a modern house, adorned with fountains and statues, with well-bred men and women standing and sitting in the walks and terraces. We hear, through all the varied music, the ground-tone of conventional life. Our poets are men of talents who sing, and not the children of music. The argument is secondary, the finish of the verses is primary.

---

[3]Critics (particularly Vivian C. Hopkins in *American Literature*, March 1951) have shown that Emerson was reading *The True Intellectual System of the Universe* by seventeenth-century Platonist Ralph Cudworth, who wrote: "Jupiter, who, together with Neptune and Pluto, is said to have been the son of Saturn, was not the supreme deity . . . but only the Aether, as Neptune was the sea, and Pluto the earth. . . . These three, Jupiter, Neptune, and Pluto were not three really distinct substantial beings, but only so many names for the Supreme God."

[4]I.e., not different; similar.

[5]I.e., learned man, teacher.

[6]Emerson's *Journal* indicates he was Tennyson.

[7]Mountain near the equator in Ecuador.

For it is not metres, but a metre-making argument, that makes a poem,—a thought so passionate and alive, that, like the spirit of a plant or an animal, it has an architecture of its own, and adorns nature with a new thing. The thought and the form are equal in the order of time, but in the order of genesis the thought is prior to the form. The poet has a new thought: he has a whole new experience to unfold; he will tell us how it was with him, and all men will be the richer in his fortune. For, the experience of each new age requires a new confession, and the world seems always waiting for its poet. I remember, when I was young, how much I was moved one morning by tidings that genius had appeared in a youth who sat near me at table. He had left his work, and gone rambling none knew whither, and had written hundreds of lines, but could not tell whether that which was in him was therein told: he could tell nothing but that all was changed,—man, beast, heaven, earth, and sea. How gladly we listened! how credulous! Society seemed to be compromised. We sat in the aurora of a sunrise which was to put out all the stars. Boston seemed to be at twice the distance it had the night before, or was much farther than that. Rome,—what was Rome? Plutarch and Shakspeare were in the yellow leaf,[8] and Homer no more should be heard of. It is much to know that poetry has been written this very day, under this very roof, by your side. What! that wonderful spirit has not expired! these stony moments are still sparkling and animated! I had fancied that the oracles were all silent, and nature had spent her fires, and behold! all night, from every pore, these fine auroras have been streaming. Every one has some interest in the advent of the poet, and no one knows how much it may concern him. We know that the secret of the world is profound, but who or what shall be our interpreter, we know not. A mountain ramble, a new style of face, a new person, may put the key into our hands. Of course, the value of genius to us is in the veracity of its report. Talent may frolic and juggle; genius realizes and adds. Mankind, in good earnest, have arrived so far in understanding themselves and their work, that the foremost watchman on the peak announces his news. It is the truest word ever spoken, and the phrase will be the fittest, most musical, and the unerring voice of the world for that time.

All that we call sacred history attests that the birth of a poet is the principal event in chronology. Man, never so often deceived, still watches for the arrival of a brother who can hold him steady to a truth, until he has made it his own. With what joy I begin to read a poem, which I confide in as an inspiration! And now my chains are to be broken; I shall mount above these clouds and opaque airs in which I live,—opaque, though they seem transparent,—and from the heaven of truth I shall see and comprehend my relations. That will reconcile me to life, and renovate nature, to see trifles animated by a tendency, and to know what I am doing. Life will no more be a noise; now I shall see men and women, and know the signs by which they may be discerned from fools and satans. This day shall be better than my birthday: then I became an animal: now I am invited into the science of the real. Such is the hope, but the fruition is postponed. Oftener it falls, that this winged man, who will carry me into the heaven, whirls me into mists, then leaps and frisks about with me as it were from cloud to cloud, still affirming that he is bound heavenward; and I, being myself a novice, am slow in perceiving that he does not know the way into the heavens, and is merely bent that I should admire his skill to rise, like a fowl or a flying fish, a little way from the ground or the water; but the all-piercing, all-feeding, and ocular air of heaven, that man shall never inhabit. I tumble down again soon into my old nooks, and lead the life of

---

[8]Cf. *Macbeth*, V, iii, 22–23: "I have lived long enough. My way of life is fallen into the sere, the yellow leaf."

exaggerations as before, and have lost some faith in the possibility of any guide who can lead me thither where I would be.

But leaving these victims of vanity, let us, with new hope, observe how nature, by worthier impulses, has ensured the poet's fidelity to his office of announcement and affirming, namely, by the beauty of things, which becomes a new, and higher beauty, when expressed. Nature offers all her creatures to him as a picture-language. Being used as a type, a second wonderful value appears in the object, far better than its old value, as the carpenter's stretched cord, if you hold your ear close enough, is musical in the breeze. "Things more excellent than every image," says Jamblichus,[9] "are expressed through images." Things admit of being used as symbols, because nature is a symbol, in the whole, and in every part. Every line we can draw in the sand, has expression; and there is no body without its spirit or genius. All form is an effect of character; all condition, of the quality of the life; all harmony, of health; (and, for this reason, a perception of beauty should be sympathetic, or proper only to the good.) The beautiful rests on the foundations of the necessary. The soul makes the body, as the wise Spenser teaches:—

> "So every spirit, as it is most pure,
> And hath in it the more of heavenly light,
> So it the fairer body doth procure
> To habit in, and it more fairly dight,
> With cheerful grace and amiable sight.
> For, of the soul, the body form doth take,
> For soul is form, and doth the body make."[10]

Here we find ourselves, suddenly, not in a critical speculation, but in a holy place, and should go very warily and reverently. We stand before the secret of the world, there where Being passes into Appearance, and Unity into Variety.

The Universe is the externization of the soul. Wherever the life is, that bursts into appearance around it. Our science is sensual, and therefore superficial. The earth, and the heavenly bodies, physics, and chemistry, we sensually treat, as if they were self-existent; but these are the retinue of that Being we have. "The mighty heaven," said Proclus,[11] "exhibits, in its transfigurations, clear images of the splendor of intellectual perceptions; being moved in conjunction with the un-apparent periods of intellectual natures." Therefore, science always goes abreast with the just elevation of the man, keeping step with religion and metaphysics; or, the state of science is an index of our self-knowledge. Since everything in nature answers to a moral power, if any phenomenon remains brute and dark, it is because the corresponding faculty in the observer is not yet active.

No wonder, then, if these waters be so deep, that we hover over them with a religious regard. The beauty of the fable proves the importance of the sense; to the poet, and to all others; or, if you please, every man is so far a poet as to be susceptible of these enchantments of nature: for all men have the thoughts whereof the universe is the celebration. I find that the fascination resides in the symbol. Who loves nature? Who does not? Is it only poets, and men of leisure and cultivation, who live with her? No; but also hunters, farmers, grooms, and butchers, though they express their affection in their choice of life, and not in their choice of words. The writer wonders what the coachman or the hunter values in riding, in horses, and dogs. It is not superficial qualities. When you talk with him, he holds these at as slight a rate as you. His worship is sympathetic; he has no

---

[9] Neoplatonist of fourth-century Alexandria.
[10] From "An Hymne in Honour of Beautie" (1596), 11.
127–133, by Edmund Spenser (1552?–1599), British poet.
[11] Greek Neoplatonist philosopher (410?–485).

definitions, but he is commanded in nature, by the living power which he feels to be there present. No imitation, or playing of these things, would content him; he loves the earnest of the north wind, of rain, of stone, and wood, and iron. A beauty not explicable, is dearer than a beauty which we can see to the end of. It is nature the symbol, nature certifying the supernatural, body overflowed by life, which he worships, with coarse, but sincere rites.

The inwardness, and mystery, of this attachment, drive men of every class to the use of emblems. The schools of poets, and philosophers, are not more intoxicated with their symbols, than the populace with theirs. In our political parties, compute the power of badges and emblems. See the huge wooden ball rolled by successive ardent crowds from Baltimore to Bunker hill![12] In the political processions, Lowell goes in a loom, and Lynn in a shoe, and Salem in a ship.[13] Witness the cider-barrel, the log-cabin, the hickory-stick, the palmetto,[14] and all the cognizances of party. See the power of national emblems. Some stars, lilies, leopards, a crescent, a lion, an eagle,[15] or other figure, which came into credit God knows how, on an old rag of bunting, blowing in the wind, on a fort, at the ends of the earth, shall make the blood tingle under the rudest, or the most conventional exterior. The people fancy they hate poetry, and they are all poets and mystics!

Beyond this universality of the symbolic language, we are apprised of the divineness of this superior use of things, whereby the world is a temple, whose walls are covered with emblems, pictures, and commandments of the Deity, in this, that there is no fact in nature which does not carry the whole sense of nature; and the distinctions which we make in events, and in affairs, of low and high, honest and base, disappear when nature is used as a symbol. Thought makes everything fit for use. The vocabulary of an omniscient man would embrace words and images excluded from polite conversation. What would be base, or even obscene, to the obscene, becomes illustrious, spoken in a new connexion of thought. The piety of the Hebrew prophets purges their grossness. The circumcision is an example of the power of poetry to raise the low and offensive. Small and mean things serve as well as great symbols. The meaner the type by which a law is expressed, the more pungent it is, and the more lasting in the memories of men: just as we choose the smallest box, or case, in which any needful utensil can be carried. Bare lists of words are found suggestive, to an imaginative and excited mind; as it is related of Lord Chatham,[16] that he was accustomed to read in Bailey's Dictionary, when he was preparing to speak in Parliament. The poorest experience is rich enough for all the purposes of expressing thought. Why covet a knowledge of new facts? Day and night, house and garden, a few books, a few actions, serve us as well as would all trades and all spectacles. We are far from having exhausted the significance of the few symbols we use. We can come to use them yet with a terrible simplicity. It does not need that a poem should be long. Every word was once a poem. Every new relation is a new word. Also, we use defects and deformities to a sacred purpose, so expressing our sense that the evils of the world are such only to the evil eye. In the old mythology, mythologists observe, defects are ascribed to divine natures, as lameness to Vulcan, blindness to Cupid, and the like, to signify exuberances.

For, as it is dislocation and detachment from the life of God, that makes things ugly, the poet, who re-attaches things to nature and the Whole,—re-attaching

---

[12]In the presidential campaign of 1840, William Henry Harrison (the winner) used the motto, "Keep the ball a-rolling," dramatized by the rolling of a large ball covered with slogans.
[13]These Massachusetts towns symbolized by their chief industries, weaving, shoemaking, and shipping.
[14]The cider-barrel and log-cabin were symbols of the Whig William Henry Harrison; the hickory-stick was the symbol of Democrat Andrew Jackson (Old Hickory), and the palmetto of South Carolina, which claimed him as native son.
[15]Lilies, France; leopards, Scotland; crescent, Turkey; lion, England; eagle, the United States.
[16]William Pitt, Earl of Chatham (1708–1778), English statesman.

even artificial things, and violations of nature, to nature, by a deeper insight,—disposes very easily of the most disagreeable facts. Readers of poetry see the factory-village, and the railway, and fancy that the poetry of the landscape is broken up by these; for these works of art are not yet consecrated in their reading; but the poet sees them fall within the great Order not less than the bee-hive, or the spider's geometrical web. Nature adopts them very fast into her vital circles, and the gliding train of cars she loves like her own. Besides, in a centred mind, it signifies nothing how many mechanical inventions you exhibit. Though you add millions, and never so surprising, the fact of mechanics has not gained a grain's weight. The spiritual fact remains unalterable, by many or by few particulars; as no mountain is of any appreciable height to break the curve of the sphere. A shrewd country-boy goes to the city for the first time, and the complacent citizen is not satisfied with his little wonder. It is not that he does not see all the fine houses, and know that he never saw such before, but he disposes of them as easily as the poet finds place for the railway. The chief value of the new fact, is to enhance the great and constant fact of Life, which can dwarf any and every circumstance, and to which the belt of wampum, and the commerce of America, are alike.

The world being thus put under the mind for verb and noun, the poet is he who can articulate it. For, though life is great, and fascinates, and absorbs,—and though all men are intelligent of the symbols through which it is named,—yet they cannot originally use them. We are symbols, and inhabit symbols; workmen, work, and tools, words and things, birth and death, all are emblems; but we sympathize with the symbols, and, being infatuated with the economical uses of things, we do not know that they are thoughts. The poet, by an ulterior intellectual perception, gives them a power which makes their old use forgotten, and puts eyes, and a tongue, into every dumb and inanimate object. He perceives the thought's independence of the symbol, the stability of the thought, the accidency and fugacity[17] of the symbol. As the eyes of Lyncæus[18] were said to see through the earth, so the poet turns the world to glass, and shows us all things in their right series and procession. For, through that better perception, he stands one step nearer to things, and sees the flowing or metamorphosis; perceives that thought is multiform: that within the form of every creature is a force impelling it to ascend into a higher form; and, following with his eyes the life, uses the forms which express that life, and so his speech flows with the flowing of nature. All the facts of the animal economy,—sex, nutriment, gestation, birth, growth—are symbols of the passage of the world into the soul of man, to suffer there a change, and reappear a new and higher fact. He uses forms according to the life, and not according to the form. This is true science. The poet alone knows astronomy, chemistry, vegetation, and animation, for he does not stop at these facts, but employs them as signs. He knows why the plain, or meadow of space, was strown with these flowers we call suns, and moons, and stars; why the great deep is adorned with animals, with men, and gods; for, in every word he speaks he rides on them as the horses of thought.

By virtue of this science the poet is the Namer, or Language-maker, naming things sometimes after their appearance, sometimes after their essence, and giving to every one its own name and not another's, thereby rejoicing the intellect, which delights in detachment or boundary. The poets made all the words, and therefore language is the archives of history, and, if we must say it, a sort of tomb of the muses. For, though the origin of most of our words is forgotten, each word was at first a stroke of genius, and obtained currency, because for the moment it symbol-

---

[17]Impermanence.
[18]In Greek mythology, the sharp-eyed member of the band who sought the Golden Fleece.

ized the world to the first speaker and to the hearer. The etymologist finds the deadest word to have been once a brilliant picture. Language is fossil poetry. As the limestone of the continent consists of infinite masses of the shells of animalcules, so language is made up of images, or tropes, which now, in their secondary use, have long ceased to remind us of their poetic origin. But the poet names the thing because he sees it, or comes one step nearer to it than any other. This expression, or naming, is not art, but a second nature, grown out of the first, as a leaf out of a tree. What we call nature, is a certain self-regulated motion, or change; and nature does all things by her own hands, and does not leave another to baptize her, but baptizes herself; and this through the metamorphosis again. I remember that a certain poet[19] described it to me thus:

Genius is the activity which repairs the decays of things, whether wholly or partly of a material and finite kind. Nature, through all her kingdoms, insures herself. Nobody cares for planting the poor fungus: so she shakes down from the gills of one agaric[20] countless spores, any one of which, being preserved, transmits new billions of spores to-morrow or next day. The new agaric of this hour has a chance which the old one had not. This atom of seed is thrown into a new place, not subject to the accidents which destroyed its parent two rods off. She makes a man; and having brought him to ripe age, she will no longer run the risk of losing this wonder at a blow, but she detaches from him a new self, that the kind may be safe from accidents to which the individual is exposed. So when the soul of the poet has come to ripeness of thought, she detaches and sends away from it its poems or songs,—a fearless, sleepless, deathless progeny, which is not exposed to the accidents of the weary kingdom of time: a fearless, vivacious offspring, clad with wings (such was the virtue of the soul out of which they came), which carry them fast and far, and infix them irrecoverably into the hearts of men. These wings are the beauty of the poet's soul. The songs, thus flying immortal from their mortal parent, are pursued by clamorous flights of censures, which swarm in far greater numbers, and threaten to devour them; but these last are not winged. At the end of a very short leap they fall plump down, and rot, having received from the souls out of which they came no beautiful wings. But the melodies of the poet ascend, and leap, and pierce into the deeps of infinite time.

So far the bard taught me, using his freer speech. But nature has a higher end, in the production of new individuals, than security, namely, *ascension,* or, the passage of the soul into higher forms. I knew, in my younger days, the sculptor who made the statue of the youth which stands in the public garden. He was, as I remember, unable to tell, directly, what made him happy, or unhappy, but by wonderful indirections he could tell. He rose one day, according to his habit, before the dawn, and saw the morning break, grand as the eternity out of which it came, and, for many days after, he strove to express this tranquillity, and, lo! his chisel had fashioned out of marble the form of a beautiful youth, Phosphor,[21] whose aspect is such, that, it is said, all persons who look on it become silent. The poet also resigns himself to his mood, and that thought which agitated him is expressed, but *alter idem,*[22] in a manner totally new. The expression is organic, or, the new type which things themselves take when liberated. As, in the sun, objects paint their images on the retina of the eye, so they, sharing the aspiration of the whole universe, tend to paint a far more delicate copy of their essence in his mind.

[19]Probably Emerson himself.
[20]Mushroom (or fungus).
[21]Phosphorus, or Lucifer, the morning star often portrayed as a beautiful youth.
[22]"The same yet another" (Latin).

Like the metamorphosis of things into higher organic forms, is their change into melodies. Over everything stands its dæmon, or soul, and, as the form of the thing is reflected by the eye, so the soul of the thing is reflected by a melody. The sea, the mountain-ridge, Niagara, and every flower-bed, pre-exist, or super-exist, in pre-cantations,[23] which sail like odors in the air, and when any man goes by with an ear sufficiently fine, he overhears them, and endeavors to write down the notes, without diluting or depraving them. And herein is the legitimation of criticism, in the mind's faith, that the poems are a corrupt version of some text in nature, with which they ought to be made to tally. A rhyme in one of our sonnets should not be less pleasing than the iterated nodes of a sea-shell, or the resembling difference of a group of flowers. The pairing[24] of the birds is an idyl, not tedious as our idyls are; a tempest is a rough ode without falsehood or rant; a summer, with its harvest sown, reaped, and stored, is an epic song, subordinating how many admirably executed parts. Why should not the symmetry and truth that modulate these, glide into our spirits, and we participate the invention of nature?

This insight, which expresses itself by what is called Imagination, is a very high sort of seeing, which does not come by study, but by the intellect being where and what it sees, by sharing the path, or circuit of things through forms, and so making them translucid to others. The path of things is silent. Will they suffer a speaker to go with them? A spy they will not suffer; a lover, a poet, is the transcendency of their own nature,—him they will suffer. The condition of true naming, on the poet's part, is his resigning himself to the divine *aura*[25] which breathes through forms, and accompanying that.

It is a secret which every intellectual man quickly learns, that, beyond the energy of his possessed and conscious intellect, he is capable of a new energy (as of an intellect doubled on itself), by abandonment to the nature of things; that, beside his privacy of power as an individual man, there is a great public power, on which he can draw, by unlocking, at all risks, his human doors, and suffering the ethereal tides to roll and circulate through him: then he is caught up into the life of the Universe, his speech is thunder, his thought is law, and his words are universally intelligible as the plants and animals. The poet knows that he speaks adequately, then only when he speaks somewhat wildly, or, "with the flower of the mind;"[26] not with the intellect, used as an organ, but with the intellect released from all service, and suffered to take its direction from its celestial life; or, as the ancients were wont to express themselves, not with intellect alone, but with the intellect inebriated by nectar. As the traveller who has lost his way, throws his reins on his horse's neck, and trusts to the instinct of the animal to find his road, so must we do with the divine animal who carries us through this world. For if in any manner we can stimulate this instinct, new passages are opened for us into nature, the mind flows into and through things hardest and highest, and the metamorphosis is possible.

This is the reason why bards love wine, mead, narcotics, coffee, tea, opium, the fumes of sandal-wood and tobacco, or whatever other procurers of animal exhilaration. All men avail themselves of such means as they can, to add this extraordinary power to their normal powers; and to this end they prize conversation, music, pictures, sculpture, dancing, theatres, travelling, war, mobs, fires, gaming, politics, or love, or science, or animal intoxication, which are several coarser or finer *quasi*-mechanical substitutes for the true nectar, which is the ravishment of the intellect by coming nearer to the fact. These are auxiliaries to the centrifugal tendency of a man, to his passage out into free space, and they help him to escape the custody of that body in which he is pent up, and of that jail-yard of individual

---

[23]Primordial incantations.
[24]Mating.
[25]Invisible emanation.

[26]Cf. Ralph Cudworth's *The True Intellectual System of the Universe:* "one supreme deity . . . that cannot be apprehended otherwise than by the flower of the mind."

relations in which he is enclosed. Hence a great number of such as were professionally expressors of Beauty, as painters, poets, musicians, and actors, have been more than others wont to lead a life of pleasure and indulgence; all but the few who received the true nectar; and, as it was a spurious mode of attaining freedom, as it was an emancipation not into the heavens, but into the freedom of baser places, they were punished for that advantage they won, by a dissipation and deterioration. But never can any advantage be taken of nature by a trick. The spirit of the world, the great calm presence of the creator, comes not forth to the sorceries of opium or of wine. The sublime vision comes to the pure and simple soul in a clean and chaste body. That is not an inspiration which we owe to narcotics, but some counterfeit excitement and fury. Milton says, that the lyric poet may drink wine and live generously, but the epic poet, he who shall sing of the gods, and their descent unto men, must drink water out of a wooden bowl.[27] For poetry is not 'Devil's wine,' but God's wine. It is with this as it is with toys. We fill the hands and nurseries of our children with all manner of dolls, drums, and horses, withdrawing their eyes from the plain face and sufficing objects of nature, the sun, and moon, the animals, the water, and stones, which should be their toys. So the poet's habit of living should be set on a key so low, that the common influences should delight him. His cheerfulness should be the gift of the sunlight; the air should suffice for his inspiration, and he should be tipsy with water. That spirit which suffices quiet hearts, which seems to come forth to such from every dry knoll of sere grass, from every pine-stump, and half-imbedded stone, on which the dull March sun shines, comes forth to the poor and hungry, and such as are of simple taste. If thou fill thy brain with Boston and New York, with fashion and covetousness, and wilt stimulate thy jaded senses with wine and French coffee, thou shalt find no radiance of wisdom in the lonely waste of the pinewoods.

If the imagination intoxicates the poet, it is not inactive in other men. The metamorphosis excites in the beholder an emotion of joy. The use of symbols has a certain power of emancipation and exhilaration for all men. We seem to be touched by a wand, which makes us dance and run about happily, like children. We are like persons who come out of a cave or cellar into the open air. This is the effect on us of tropes, fables, oracles, and all poetic forms. Poets are thus liberating gods. Men have really got a new sense, and found within their world, another world, or nest of worlds; for, the metamorphosis once seen, we divine that it does not stop. I will not now consider how much this makes the charm of algebra and the mathematics, which also have their tropes, but it is felt in every definition; as, when Aristotle defines *space* to be an immovable vessel, in which things are contained;[28]—or, when Plato defines a *line* to be a flowing point; or, *figure* to be a bound of solid; and many the like.[29] What a joyful sense of freedom we have, when Vitruvius[30] announces the old opinion of artists, that no architect can build any house well, who does not know something of anatomy. When Socrates, in Charmides,[31] tells us that the soul is cured of its maladies by certain incantations, and that these incantations are beautiful reasons, from which temperance is generated in souls; when Plato calls the world an animal; and Timæus[32] affirms that the plants also are animals; or affirms a man to be a heavenly tree, growing with his root, which is his head, upward; and, as George Chapman, following him, writes,—

> "So in our tree of man, whose nervie root
> Springs in his top;"[33]

---

[27]From "Elegia Sexta" (11. 51–64), a Latin poem by John Milton.

[28]See Aristotle's *Physics*.

[29]See Plato's *Meno*.

[30]Roman author (fl. 46 B.C.) of *On Architecture*.

[31]Dialogue by Plato.

[32]Speaker in Plato's dialogue, *Timaeus*.

[33]George Chapman (1559?–1634?), from his "Epistle Dedicatory" (11. 132–133) of his translation of Homer's *Iliad*.

when Orpheus speaks of hoariness as "that white flower which marks extreme old age;" when Proclus calls the universe the statue of the intellect; when Chaucer, in his praise of 'Gentilesse,' compares good blood in mean condition to fire, which, though carried to the darkest house betwixt this and the mount of Caucasus, will yet hold its natural office, and burn as bright as if twenty thousand men did it behold;[34] when John saw, in the apocalypse, the ruin of the world through evil, and the stars fall from heaven, as the figtree casteth her untimely fruit;[35] when Æsop[36] reports the whole catalogue of common daily relations through the masquerade of birds and beasts;—we take the cheerful hint of the immortality of our essence, and its versatile habit and escapes, as when the gypsies say of themselves, "it is in vain to hang them, they cannot die."[37]

The poets are thus liberating gods. The ancient British bards had for the title of their order, "Those who are free throughout the world." They are free, and they make free. An imaginative book renders us much more service at first, by stimulating us through its tropes, than afterward, when we arrive at the precise sense of the author. I think nothing is of any value in books, excepting the transcendental and extraordinary. If a man is inflamed and carried away by his thought, to that degree that he forgets the authors and the public, and heeds only this one dream, which holds him like an insanity, let me read his paper, and you may have all the arguments and histories and criticism. All the value which attaches to Pythagoras, Paracelsus, Cornelius Agrippa, Cardan, Kepler, Swedenborg, Schelling, Oken,[38] or any other who introduces questionable facts into his cosmogony, as angels, devils, magic, astrology, palmistry, mesmerism, and so on, is the certificate we have of departure from routine, and that here is a new witness. That also is the best success in conversation, the magic of liberty, which puts the world, like a ball, in our hands. How cheap even the liberty then seems; how mean to study, when an emotion communicates to the intellect the power to sap and upheave nature: how great the perspective! nations, times, systems, enter and disappear, like threads in tapestry of large figure and many colors; dream delivers us to dream, and, while the drunkenness lasts, we will sell our bed, our philosophy, our religion, in our opulence.

There is good reason why we should prize this liberation. The fate of the poor shepherd, who, blinded and lost in the snowstorm, perishes in a drift within a few feet of his cottage door, is an emblem of the state of man. On the brink of the waters of life and truth, we are miserably dying. The inaccessibleness of every thought but that we are in, is wonderful. What if you come near to it,—you are as remote, when you are nearest, as when you are farthest. Every thought is also a prison; every heaven is also a prison. Therefore we love the poet, the inventor, who in any form, whether in an ode, or in an action, or in looks and behavior, has yielded us a new thought. He unlocks our chains, and admits us to a new scene.

This emancipation is dear to all men, and the power to impart it, as it must come from greater depth and scope of thought, is a measure of intellect. Therefore all books of the imagination endure, all which ascend to that truth, that the writer sees nature beneath him, and uses it as his exponent. Every verse or sentence, possessing this virtue, will take care of its own immortality. The religions of the world are the ejaculations of a few imaginative men.

But the quality of the imagination is to flow, and not to freeze. The poet did

---

[34]In "The Wife of Bath's Tale," ll. 1132–1145.
[35]See Revelation 6:13.
[36]Sixth-century B.C. Greek author of *Fables*.
[37]Refers to the gypsies' belief in the transmigration of souls, quoted from George Borrow's *The Zincali; or, an Account of the Gypsies of Spain* (1842), in essay "Metempsychosis."
[38]All inspired writers: Pythagoras (sixth century B.C.), Greek philosopher; Philippus Paracelsus (1493–1541), Swiss alchemist; Cornelius Agrippa (1486?–1535), German physician; Jerome Cardan (1501–1576), Italian mathematician; Johannes Kepler (1571–1630), German astronomer; Emanuel Swedenborg (1688–1772), Swedish scientist and mystical writer; Friederich von Schelling (1775–1854), German philosopher; Lorenz Oken (1779–1851), German naturalist.

not stop at the color, or the form, but read their meaning; neither may he rest in this meaning, but he makes the same objects exponents of his new thought. Here is the difference betwixt the poet and the mystic, that the last nails a symbol to one sense, which was a true sense for a moment, but soon becomes old and false. For all symbols are fluxional;[39] all language is vehicular and transitive,[40] and is good, as ferries and horses are, for conveyance, not as farms and houses are, for homestead. Mysticism consists in the mistake of an accidental and individual symbol for an universal one. The morning-redness happens to be the favorite meteor to the eyes of Jacob Behmen,[41] and comes to stand to him for truth and faith; and he believes should stand for the same realities to every reader. But the first reader prefers as naturally the symbol of a mother and child, or a gardener and his bulb, or a jeweller polishing a gem. Either of these, or of a myriad more, are equally good to the person to whom they are significant. Only they must be held lightly, and be very willingly translated into the equivalent terms which others use. And the mystic must be steadily told,—All that you say is just as true without the tedious use of that symbol as with it. Let us have a little algebra, instead of this trite rhetoric,—universal signs, instead of these village symbols,—and we shall both be gainers. The history of hierarchies seems to show, that all religious error consisted in making the symbol too stark and solid, and, at last, nothing but an excess of the organ of language.

Swedenborg, of all men in the recent ages, stands eminently for the translator of nature into thought. I do not know the man in history to whom things stood so uniformly for words. Before him the metamorphosis continually plays. Everything on which his eye rests, obeys the impulses of moral nature. The figs become grapes whilst he eats them. When some of his angels affirmed a truth, the laurel twig which they held blossomed in their hands. The noise which, at a distance, appeared like gnashing and thumping, on coming nearer was found to be the voice of disputants. The men, in one of his visions, seen in heavenly light, appeared like dragons, and seemed in darkness; but, to each other, they appeared as men, and, when the light from heaven shone into their cabin, they complained of the darkness, and were compelled to shut the window that they might see.

There was this perception in him, which makes the poet or seer an object of awe and terror, namely, that the same man, or society of men, may wear one aspect to themselves and their companions, and a different aspect to higher intelligences. Certain priests, whom he describes as conversing very learnedly together, appeared to the children, who were at some distance, like dead horses; and many the like misappearances.[42] And instantly the mind inquires, whether these fishes under the bridge, yonder oxen in the pasture, those dogs in the yard, are immutably fishes, oxen, and dogs, or only so appear to me, and perchance to themselves appear upright men; and whether I appear as a man to all eyes. The Bramins and Pythagoras propounded the same question, and if any poet has witnessed the transformation, he doubtless found it in harmony with various experiences. We have all seen changes as considerable in wheat and caterpillars. He is the poet, and shall draw us with love and terror, who sees, through the flowing vest, the firm nature, and can declare it.

I look in vain for the poet whom I describe. We do not, with sufficient plainness, or sufficient profoundness, address ourselves to life, nor dare we chaunt our own times and social circumstance. If we filled the day with bravery, we should not shrink from celebrating it. Time and nature yield us many gifts, but not yet

---

[39]Continuously changing.
[40]Carries meaning from place to place and interconnects things.
[41]See *Aurora: The Day-Spring, or, Dawning of the Day in the*

East: or, Morning Redness in the Rising of the Sun, by Jakob Böhme (1575–1624), German mystic.
[42]See Swedenborg's *The Apocalypse Revealed* ("Memorable Revelations" conclude each chapter).

the timely man, the new religion, the reconciler, whom all things await. Dante's praise is, that he dared to write his autobiography in colossal cipher, or into universality.[43] We have yet had no genius in America, with tyrannous eye, which knew the value of our incomparable materials, and saw, in the barbarism and materialism of the times, another carnival of the same gods whose picture he so much admires in Homer; then in the middle age; then in Calvinism. Banks and tariffs, the newspaper and caucus, methodism and unitarianism, are flat and dull to dull people, but rest on the same foundations of wonder as the town of Troy, and the temple of Delphi,[44] and are as swiftly passing away. Our logrolling, our stumps[45] and their politics, our fisheries, our Negroes, and Indians, our boasts, and our repudiations, the wrath of rogues, and the pusillanimity of honest men, the northern trade, the southern planting, the western clearing, Oregon, and Texas,[46] are yet unsung. Yet America is a poem in our eyes; its ample geography dazzles the imagination, and it will not wait long for metres. If I have not found that excellent combination of gifts in my countrymen which I seek, neither could I aid myself to fix the idea of the poet by reading now and then in Chalmers's collection of five centuries of English poets.[47] These are wits, more than poets, though there have been poets among them. But when we adhere to the ideal of the poet, we have our difficulties even with Milton and Homer. Milton is too literary, and Homer too literal and historical.

But I am not wise enough for a national criticism, and must use the old largeness a little longer, to discharge my errand from the muse to the poet concerning his art.

Art is the path of the creator to his work. The paths, or methods, are ideal and eternal, though few men ever see them, not the artist himself for years, or for a lifetime, unless he come into the conditions. The painter, the sculptor, the composer, the epic rhapsodist, the orator, all partake one desire, namely, to express themselves symmetrically and abundantly, not dwarfishly and fragmentarily. They found or put themselves in certain conditions, as, the painter and sculptor before some impressive human figures; the orator, into the assembly of the people; and the others, in such scenes as each has found exciting to his intellect; and each presently feels the new desire. He hears a voice, he sees a beckoning. Then he is apprised, with wonder, what herds of dæmons hem him in. He can no more rest; he says, with the old painter, "By God, it is in me, and must go forth of me." He pursues a beauty, half seen, which flies before him. The poet pours out verses in every solitude. Most of the things he says are conventional, no doubt; but by and by he says something which is original and beautiful. That charms him. He would say nothing else but such things. In our way of talking, we say, 'That is yours, this is mine;' but the poet knows well that it is not his; that it is as strange and beautiful to him as to you; he would fain hear the like eloquence at length. Once having tasted this immortal ichor,[48] he cannot have enough of it, and, as an admirable creative power exists in these intellections, it is of the last importance that these things get spoken. What a little of all we know is said! What drops of all the sea of our science are baled[49] up! and by what accident it is that these are exposed, when so many secrets sleep in nature! Hence the necessity of speech and song; hence these throbs and heart-beatings in the orator, at the door of the assembly, to the end, namely, that thought may be ejaculated as Logos, or Word.[50]

---

[43]Dante Alighieri (1265–1321), Italian poet, author of *The Divine Comedy.*

[44]Town of Troy, setting of Homer's *Iliad;* temple of Delphi, seat of the oracles of Apollo.

[45]Logrolling: political wheeling and dealing; stumps: oratory (as on a tree stump).

[46]In 1844, both Texas and Oregon were much in the news as territories outside the United States but coveted. Texas

had won independence from Mexico in 1836; Oregon was under dispute with Great Britain. Americans were rapidly settling in both.

[47]*Works of the English Poets from Chaucer to Cowper* (1810), edited by Alexander Chalmers (1759–1834).

[48]Ethereal fluid of the veins of the gods.

[49]Variant spelling of "bailed" (as to *bail* water from a boat).

[50]Cf. John 1:1: "In the beginning was the Word."

Doubt not, O poet, but persist. Say, 'It is in me, and shall out.' Stand there, baulked and dumb, stuttering and stammering, hissed and hooted, stand and strive, until, at last, rage draw out of thee that *dream*-power which every night shows thee is thine own; a power transcending all limit and privacy, and by virtue of which a man is the conductor of the whole river of electricity. Nothing walks, or creeps, or grows, or exists, which must not in turn arise and walk before him as exponent of his meaning. Comes he to that power, his genius is no longer exhaustible. All the creatures, by pairs and by tribes, pour into his mind as into a Noah's ark, to come forth again to people a new world. This is like the stock of air for our respiration, or for the combustion of our fireplace, not a measure of gallons, but the entire atmosphere if wanted. And therefore the rich poets, as Homer, Chaucer, Shakspeare, and Raphael,[51] have obviously no limits to their works, except the limits of their lifetime, and resemble a mirror carried through the street, ready to render an image of every created thing.

O poet! a new nobility is conferred in groves and pastures, and not in castles, or by the sword-blade, any longer. The conditions are hard, but equal. Thou shalt leave the world, and know the muse only. Thou shalt not know any longer the times, customs, graces, politics, or opinions of men, but shalt take all from the muse. For the time of towns is tolled from the world by funereal chimes, but in nature the universal hours are counted by succeeding tribes of animals and plants, and by growth of joy on joy. God wills also that thou abdicate a duplex and manifold life, and that thou be content that others speak for thee. Others shall be thy gentlemen, and shall represent all courtesy and worldly life for thee; others shall do the great and resounding actions also. Thou shalt lie close hid with nature, and canst not be afforded to the Capitol or the Exchange.[52] The world is full of renunciations and apprenticeships, and this is thine; thou must pass for a fool and a churl for a long season. This is the screen and sheath in which Pan[53] has protected his well-beloved flower, and thou shalt be known only to thine own, and they shall console thee with tenderest love. And thou shalt not be able to rehearse the names of thy friends in thy verse, for an old shame before the holy ideal. And this is the reward: that the ideal shall be real to thee, and the impressions of the actual world shall fall like summer rain, copious, but not troublesome, to thy invulnerable essence. Thou shalt have the whole land for thy park and manor, the sea for thy bath and navigation, without tax and without envy; the woods and the rivers thou shalt own; and thou shalt possess that wherein others are only tenants and boarders. Thou true land-lord! sea-lord! air-lord! Wherever snow falls, or water flows, or birds fly, wherever day and night meet in twilight, wherever the blue heaven is hung by clouds, or sown with stars, wherever are forms with transparent boundaries, wherever are outlets into celestial space, wherever is danger, and awe, and love, there is Beauty, plenteous as rain, shed for thee, and though thou shouldst walk the world over, thou shalt not be able to find a condition inopportune or ignoble.

1844

---

[51]Emerson expands "rich poets" to embrace all inspired makers, so as to include a painter like Italy's Raphael (1483–1520).

[52]Stock exchange.
[53]Greek god of woods and fields.

Experience[1]

The lords of life, the lords of life,—
I saw them pass,
In their own guise,
Like and unlike,
Portly and grim,
Use and Surprise,
Surface and Dream,
Succession swift, and spectral Wrong,
Temperament without a tongue,
And the inventor of the game
Omnipresent without name;—
Some to see, some to be guessed,
They marched from east to west:
Little man, least of all,
Among the legs of his guardians tall,
Walked about with puzzled look:—
Him by the hand dear nature took;
Dearest nature, strong and kind,
Whispered, 'Darling, never mind!
Tomorrow they will wear another face,
The founder thou! these are thy race!'

Where do we find ourselves? In a series,[2] of which we do not know the extremes, and believe that it has none. We wake and find ourselves on a stair: there are stairs below us, which we seem to have ascended; there are stairs above us, many a one, which go upward and out of sight. But the Genius[3] which, according to the old belief, stands at the door by which we enter, and gives us the lethe to drink, that we may tell no tales, mixed the cup too strongly, and we cannot shake off the lethargy now at noonday. Sleep lingers all our lifetime about our eyes, as night hovers all day in the boughs of the fir-tree. All things swim and glimmer. Our life is not so much threatened as our perception. Ghostlike we glide through nature, and should not know our place again. Did our birth fall in some fit of indigence and frugality in nature, that she was so sparing of her fire and so liberal of her earth, that it appears to us that we lack the affirmative principle, and though we have health and reason, yet we have no superfluity of spirit for new creation? We have enough to live and bring the year about, but not an ounce to impart or to invest. Ah that our Genius were a little more of a genius! We are like millers on the lower levels of a stream, when the factories above them have exhausted the water. We too fancy that the upper people must have raised their dams.

If any of us knew what we were doing, or where we are going, then when we think we best know! We do not know today whether we are busy or idle. In times when we thought ourselves indolent, we have afterwards discovered, that much was accomplished, and much was begun in us. All our days are so unprofitable while they pass, that 'tis wonderful where or when we ever got anything of this which we call wisdom, poetry, virtue. We never got it on any dated calendar day. Some heavenly days must have been intercalated somewhere, like those that Her-

---

[1] "Experience" is unusual in that it did not develop out of a lecture; but much of it is traceable in Emerson's *Journal*. The epigraph is Emerson's.
[2] As in a mathematical or numerical series, without limits.

[3] The daimon or guardian spirit who conducts the souls of the dead to the river of forgetfulness, Lethe, so that they might drink and forget their previous incarnation before going on to the next. See the conclusion of Plato's *Republic*.

mes won with dice of the Moon, that Osiris might be born.[4] It is said, all martyr-
doms looked mean when they were suffered. Every ship is a romantic object, except that we sail in. Embark, and the romance quits our vessel, and hangs on every
other sail in the horizon. Our life looks trivial, and we shun to record it. Men seem
to have learned of the horizon the art of perpetual retreating and reference. 'Yonder uplands are rich pasturage, and my neighbor has fertile meadow, but my
field,' says the querulous farmer, 'only holds the world together.' I quote another
man's saying; unluckily, that other withdraws himself in the same way, and quotes
me. 'Tis the trick of nature thus to degrade today; a good deal of buzz, and somewhere a result slipped magically in. Every roof is agreeable to the eye, until it is
lifted; then we find tragedy and moaning women, and hard-eyed husbands, and
deluges of lethe, and the men ask, 'What's the news?' as if the old were so bad.
How many individuals can we count in society? how many actions? how many
opinions? So much of our time is preparation, so much is routine, and so much
retrospect, that the pith of each man's genius contracts itself to a very few hours.
The history of literature—take the net result of Tiraboschi, Warton, or Schlegel,[5]
—is a sum of very few ideas, and of very few original tales,—all the rest being
variation of these. So in this great society wide lying around us, a critical analysis
would find very few spontaneous actions. It is almost all custom and gross sense.
There are even few opinions, and these seem organic in the speakers, and do not
disturb the universal necessity.

What opium is instilled into all disaster! It shows formidable as we approach it,
but there is at last no rough rasping friction, but the most slippery sliding surfaces: we fall soft on a thought: *Ate Dea* is gentle,

> "Over men's heads walking aloft,
> With tender feet treading so soft."[6]

People grieve and bemoan themselves, but it is not half so bad with them as they
say. There are moods in which we court suffering, in the hope that here, at least,
we shall find reality, sharp peaks and edges of truth. But it turns out to be scene-
painting and counterfeit. The only thing grief has taught me, is to know how shallow it is. That, like all the rest, plays about the surface, and never introduces me
into the reality, for contact with which, we would even pay the costly price of sons
and lovers. Was it Boscovich[7] who found out that bodies never come in contact?
Well, souls never touch their objects. An innavigable sea washes with silent waves
between us and the things we aim at and converse with. Grief too will make us
idealists. In the death of my son,[8] now more than two years ago, I seem to have
lost a beautiful estate,—no more. I cannot get it nearer to me. If tomorrow I
should be informed of the bankruptcy of my principal debtors, the loss of my
property would be a great inconvenience to me, perhaps, for many years; but it
would leave me as it found me,—neither better nor worse. So is it with this calamity: it does not touch me: something which I fancied was a part of me, which could
not be torn away without tearing me, nor enlarged without enriching me, falls off
from me, and leaves no scar. It was caducous.[9] I grieve that grief can teach me
nothing, nor carry me one step into real nature. The Indian who was laid under a

[4]In ancient myth, the sun god, on finding Rhea unfaithful, pronounced that she could not give birth on any day of the year. Hermes interceded for her, and by winning at dice with the moon, gained five new days for the calendar, en-abling Rhea to bear Osiris, the major Egyptian god. See Plutarch's "Of Isis and Osiris," *Morals*. (The only interca-lary day of the modern calendar is February 29.)
[5]Girolamo Tiraboschi (1731–1794), Italian; Thomas War-ton (1728–1790), English; Friederich von Schlegel (1772–1829), or his brother August (1776–1845), German.

[6]Ate Dea is a goddess of mischief and moral blindness, de-scribed in Homer's *Iliad*, XIX, 92–93.
[7]Ruggiero Giuseppe Boscovich (1711–1787), an Italian physicist.
[8]Waldo, Emerson's first child, died at the age of five in 1842.
[9]Fleeting, unlasting.

curse, that the wind should not blow on him, nor water flow to him, nor fire burn him, is a type of us all.[10] The dearest events are summer-rain, and we the Para[11] coats that shed every drop. Nothing is left us now but death. We look to that with a grim satisfaction, saying, there at least is reality that will not dodge us.

I take this evanescence and lubricity[12] of all objects, which lets them slip through our fingers then when we clutch hardest, to be the most unhandsome part of our condition. Nature does not like to be observed, and likes that we should be her fools and playmates. We may have the sphere for our cricket-ball, but not a berry for our philosophy. Direct strokes she never gave us power to make; all our blows glance, all our hits are accidents. Our relations to each other are oblique and casual.

Dream delivers us to dream, and there is no end to illusion. Life is a train of moods like a string of beads, and, as we pass through them, they prove to be many-colored lenses which paint the world their own hue, and each shows only what lies in its focus. From the mountain you see the mountain. We animate what we can, and we see only what we animate. Nature and books belong to the eyes that see them. It depends on the mood of the man, whether he shall see the sunset or the fine poem. There are always sunsets, and there is always genius; but only a few hours so serene that we can relish nature or criticism. The more or less depends on structure or temperament. Temperament is the iron wire on which the beads are strung. Of what use is fortune or talent to a cold and defective nature? Who cares what sensibility or discrimination a man has at some time shown, if he falls asleep in his chair? or if he laugh and giggle? or if he apologize? or is infected with egotism? or thinks of his dollar? or cannot pass by food? or has gotten a child in his boyhood? Of what use is genius, if the organ is too convex or too concave, and cannot find a focal distance within the actual horizon of human life? Of what use, if the brain is too cold or too hot, and the man does not care enough for results, to stimulate him to experiment, and hold him up in it? or if the web is too finely woven, too irritable by pleasure and pain, so that life stagnates from too much reception, without due outlet? Of what use to make heroic vows of amendment, if the same old law-breaker is to keep them? What cheer can the religious sentiment yield, when that is suspected to be secretly dependent on the seasons of the year, and the state of the blood? I knew a witty physician who found the creed in the biliary duct,[13] and used to affirm that if there was disease in the liver, the man became a Calvinist, and if that organ was sound, he became a Unitarian. Very mortifying is the reluctant experience that some unfriendly excess or imbecility neutralizes the promise of genius. We see young men who owe us a new world, so readily and lavishly they promise, but they never acquit the debt; they die young and dodge the account: or if they live, they lose themselves in the crowd.

Temperament also enters fully into the system of illusions, and shuts us in a prison of glass which we cannot see. There is an optical illusion about every person we meet. In truth, they are all creatures of given temperament, which will appear in a given character, whose boundaries they will never pass: but we look at them, they seem alive, and we presume there is impulse in them. In the moment, it seems impulse; in the year, in the lifetime, it turns out to be a certain uniform tune which the revolving barrel of the music-box must play. Men resist the conclusion in the morning, but adopt it as the evening wears on, that temper prevails over everything of time, place, and condition, and is inconsumable in the flames

---

[10]Reference to *The Curse of Kehama* (1810), by Robert Southey (1774–1843), British poet.
[11]Rubber.
[12]Transitoriness and slipperiness.
[13]Bile-carrying duct.

of religion. Some modifications the moral sentiment avails to impose, but the individual texture holds its dominion, if not to bias the moral judgments, yet to fix the measure of activity and of enjoyment.

I thus express the law as it is read from the platform of ordinary life, but must not leave it without noticing the capital exception. For temperament is a power which no man willingly hears any one praise but himself. On the platform of physics, we cannot resist the contracting influences of so-called science. Temperament puts all divinity to rout. I know the mental proclivity of physicians. I hear the chuckle of the phrenologists.[14] Theoretic kidnappers and slave-drivers, they esteem each man the victim of another, who winds him round his finger by knowing the law of his being, and by such cheap signboards as the color of his beard, or the slope of his occiput,[15] reads the inventory of his fortunes and character. The grossest ignorance does not disgust like this impudent knowingness. The physicians say, they are not materialists; but they are:—Spirit is matter reduced to an extreme thinness: O *so* thin!—But the definition of *spiritual* should be, *that which is its own evidence.* What notions do they attach to love! what to religion! One would not willingly pronounce these words in their hearing, and give them the occasion to profane them. I saw a gracious gentleman who adapts his conversation to the form of the head of the man he talks with! I had fancied that the value of life lay in its inscrutable possibilities; in the fact that I never know, in addressing myself to a new individual, what may befall me. I carry the keys of my castle in my hand, ready to throw them at the feet of my lord, whenever and in what disguise soever he shall appear. I know he is in the neighborhood, hidden among vagabonds. Shall I preclude my future, by taking a high seat, and kindly adapting my conversation to the shape of heads? When I come to that, the doctors shall buy me for a cent.—'But, sir, medical history; the report to the Institute; the proven facts!'—I distrust the facts and the inferences. Temperament is the veto or limitation-power in the constitution, very justly applied to restrain an opposite excess in the constitution, but absurdly offered as a bar to original equity. When virtue is in presence, all subordinate powers sleep. On its own level, or in view of nature, temperament is final. I see not, if one be once caught in this trap of so-called sciences, any escape for the man from the links of the chain of physical necessity. Given such an embryo, such a history must follow. On this platform, one lives in a sty of sensualism, and would soon come to suicide. But it is impossible that the creative power should exclude itself. Into every intelligence there is a door which is never closed, through which the creator passes. The intellect, seeker of absolute truth, or the heart, lover of absolute good, intervenes for our succor, and at one whisper of these high powers, we awake from ineffectual struggles with this nightmare. We hurl it into its own hell, and cannot again contract ourselves to so base a state.

The secret of the illusoriness is in the necessity of a succession of moods or objects. Gladly we would anchor, but the anchorage is quicksand. This onward trick of nature is too strong for us: *Pero si muove.*[16] When, at night, I look at the moon and stars, I seem stationary, and they to hurry. Our love of the real draws us to permanence, but health of body consists in circulation, and sanity of mind in variety or facility of association. We need change of objects. Dedication to one thought is quickly odious. We house with the insane, and must humor them; then conversation dies out. Once I took such delight in Montaigne, that I thought I should not need any other book; before that, in Shakspeare; then in Plutarch; then in

---

[14]Early "psychologists" who found clues to personality traits by measuring bumps on the head.
[15]Back of the head.

[16]"Nevertheless it moves" (Italian), said to be Galileo's remark after being forced to retract his belief that the earth revolves around the sun.

Plotinus; at one time in Bacon; afterwards in Goethe; even in Bettine;[17] but now I turn the pages of either of them languidly, whilst I still cherish their genius. So with pictures; each will bear an emphasis of attention once, which it cannot retain, though we fain would continue to be pleased in that manner. How strongly I have felt of pictures, that when you have seen one well, you must take your leave of it; you shall never see it again. I have had good lessons from pictures, which I have since seen without emotion or remark. A deduction must be made from the opinion, which even the wise express of a new book or occurrence. Their opinion gives me tidings of their mood, and some vague guess at the new fact, but is nowise to be trusted as the lasting relation between that intellect and that thing. The child asks, 'Mamma, why don't I like the story as well as when you told it me yesterday?' Alas, child, it is even so with the oldest cherubim of knowledge. But will it answer thy question to say, Because thou wert born to a whole, and this story is a particular? The reason of the pain this discovery causes us (and we make it late in respect to works of art and intellect), is the plaint of tragedy which murmurs from it in regard to persons, to friendship and love.

That immobility and absence of elasticity which we find in the arts, we find with more pain in the artist. There is no power of expansion in men. Our friends early appear to us as representatives of certain ideas, which they never pass or exceed. They stand on the brink of the ocean of thought and power, but they never take the single step that would bring them there. A man is like a bit of Labrador spar,[18] which has no lustre as you turn it in your hand, until you come to a particular angle; then it shows deep and beautiful colors. There is no adaptation or universal applicability in men, but each has his special talent, and the mastery of successful men consists in adroitly keeping themselves where and when that turn shall be oftenest to be practised. We do what we must, and call it by the best names we can, and would fain have the praise of having intended the result which ensues. I cannot recall any form of man who is not superfluous sometimes. But is not this pitiful? Life is not worth the taking, to do tricks in.

Of course, it needs the whole society, to give the symmetry we seek. The particolored wheel must revolve very fast to appear white. Something is learned too by conversing with so much folly and defect. In fine, whoever loses, we are always of the gaining party. Divinity is behind our failures and follies also. The plays of children are nonsense, but very educative nonsense. So is it with the largest and solemnest things, with commerce, government, church, marriage, and so with the history of every man's bread, and the ways by which he is to come by it. Like a bird which alights nowhere, but hops perpetually from bough to bough, is the Power which abides in no man and in no woman, but for a moment speaks from this one, and for another moment from that one.

But what help from these fineries or pedantries? What help from thought? Life is not dialectics. We, I think, in these times, have had lessons enough of the futility of criticism. Our young people have thought and written much on labor and reform, and for all that they have written, neither the world nor themselves have got on a step. Intellectual tasting of life will not supersede muscular activity. If a man should consider the nicety of the passage of a piece of bread down his throat, he would starve. At Education-Farm,[19] the noblest theory of life sat on the noblest figures of young men and maidens, quite powerless and melancholy. It would not

---

[17]Michel de Montaigne (1533–1592), French essayist; Plutarch (46?–120?), Greek biographer; Plotinus (205?–270?), Roman Neoplatonist; Sir Francis Bacon (1561–1626), British essayist; Johann Wolfgang von Goethe (1749–1832), German poet; Elizabeth ("Bettine") von Arnim (1785–1859), German author.

[18]Crystalline rock found in Labrador.
[19]Brook Farm, a model Utopian community set up in West Roxbury, Massachusetts (1841–47). Many Transcendentalists and Unitarians were involved; but Emerson, Thoreau, and Margaret Fuller did not live there.

rake or pitch a ton of hay; it would not rub down a horse; and the men and maidens it left pale and hungry. A political orator wittily compared our party promises to western roads, which opened stately enough, with planted trees on either side, to tempt the traveller, but soon became narrow and narrower, and ended in a squirrel-track, and ran up a tree. So does culture with us; it ends in headache. Unspeakably sad and barren does life look to those, who a few months ago were dazzled with the splendor of the promise of the times. "There is now no longer any right course of action, nor any self-devotion left among the Iranis."[20] Objections and criticism we have had our fill of. There are objections to every course of life and action, and the practical wisdom infers an indifferency, from the omnipresence of objection. The whole frame of things preaches indifferency. Do not craze yourself with thinking, but go about your business anywhere. Life is not intellectual or critical, but sturdy. Its chief good is for well-mixed people who can enjoy what they find, without question. Nature hates peeping, and our mothers speak her very sense when they say, "Children, eat your victuals, and say no more of it." To fill the hour,—that is happiness; to fill the hour, and leave no crevice for a repentance or an approval. We live amid surfaces, and the true art of life is to skate well on them. Under the oldest mouldiest conventions, a man of native force prospers just as well as in the newest world, and that by skill of handling and treatment. He can take hold anywhere. Life itself is a mixture of power and form, and will not bear the least excess of either. To finish the moment, to find the journey's end in every step of the road, to live the greatest number of good hours, is wisdom. It is not the part of men, but of fanatics, or of mathematicians, if you will, to say, that, the shortness of life considered, it is not worth caring whether for so short a duration we were sprawling in want, or sitting high. Since our office is with moments, let us husband them. Five minutes of today are worth as much to me, as five minutes in the next millennium. Let us be poised, and wise, and our own, to-day. Let us treat the men and women well: treat them as if they were real: perhaps they are. Men live in their fancy, like drunkards whose hands are too soft and tremulous for successful labor. It is a tempest of fancies, and the only ballast I know, is a respect to the present hour. Without any shadow of doubt, amidst this vertigo of shows and politics, I settle myself ever the firmer in the creed, that we should not postpone and refer and wish, but do broad justice where we are, by whomsoever we deal with, accepting our actual companions and circumstances, however humble or odious, as the mystic officials to whom the universe has delegated its whole pleasure for us. If these are mean and malignant, their contentment, which is the last victory of justice, is a more satisfying echo to the heart, than the voice of poets and the casual sympathy of admirable persons. I think that however a thoughtful man may suffer from the defects and absurdities of his company, he cannot without affectation deny to any set of men and women, a sensibility to extraordinary merit. The coarse and frivolous have an instinct of superiority, if they have not a sympathy, and honor it in their blind capricious way with sincere homage.

The fine young people despise life, but in me, and in such as with me are free from dyspepsia, and to whom a day is a sound and solid good, it is a great excess of politeness to look scornful and to cry for company. I am grown by sympathy a little eager and sentimental, but leave me alone, and I should relish every hour and what it brought me, the potluck of the day, as heartily as the oldest gossip in the bar-room. I am thankful for small mercies. I compared notes with one of my friends who expects everything of the universe, and is disappointed when any-

[20]From *The Desatir, or Sacred Writings of the Ancient Persian Prophets*, translated by Jonathan Duncan and published in London in two volumes (1818).

thing is less than the best, and I found that I begin at the other extreme, expect-ing nothing, and am always full of thanks for moderate goods. I accept the clangor and jangle of contrary tendencies. I find my account in sots and bores also. They give a reality to the circumjacent picture, which such a vanishing mete-orous appearance can ill spare. In the morning I awake, and find the old world, wife, babes, and mother, Concord and Boston, the dear old spiritual world, and even the dear old devil not far off. If we will take the good we find, asking no questions, we shall have heaping measures. The great gifts are not got by analysis. Everything good is on the highway. The middle region of our being is the temper-ate zone. We may climb into the thin and cold realm of pure geometry and lifeless science, or sink into that of sensation. Between these extremes is the equator of life, of thought, of spirit, of poetry,—a narrow belt. Moreover, in popular experi-ence, everything good is on the highway. A collector peeps into all the picture-shops of Europe, for a landscape of Poussin, a crayon-sketch of Salvator; but the Transfiguration, the Last Judgment, the Communion of St. Jerome, and what are as transcendent as these, are on the walls of the Vatican, the Uffizi, or the Louvre, where every footman may see them;[21] to say nothing of nature's pictures in every street, of sunsets and sunrises every day, and the sculpture of the human body never absent. A collector recently bought at public auction, in London, for one hundred and fifty-seven guineas, an autograph of Shakspeare: but for nothing a schoolboy can read Hamlet, and can detect secrets of highest concernment yet un-published therein. I think I will never read any but the commonest books,—the Bible, Homer, Dante, Shakspeare, and Milton. Then we are impatient of so public a life and planet, and run hither and thither for nooks and secrets. The imagina-tion delights in the wood-craft of Indians, trappers, and bee-hunters. We fancy that we are strangers, and not so intimately domesticated in the planet as the wild man, and the wild beast and bird. But the exclusion reaches them also; reaches the climbing, flying, gliding, feathered and four-footed man. Fox and woodchuck, hawk and snipe, and bittern, when nearly seen, have no more root in the deep world than man, and are just such superficial tenants of the globe. Then the new molecular philosophy shows astronomical interspaces betwixt atom and atom, shows that the world is all outside: it has no inside.

The mid-world is best. Nature, as we know her, is no saint. The lights of the church, the ascetics, Gentoos[22] and corn-eaters,[23] she does not distinguish by any favor. She comes eating and drinking and sinning. Her darlings, the great, the strong, the beautiful, are not children of our law, do not come out of the Sunday School, nor weigh their food, nor punctually keep the commandments. If we will be strong with her strength, we must not harbor such disconsolate consciences, borrowed too from the consciences of other nations. We must set up the strong present tense against all the rumors of wrath, past or to come. So many things are unsettled which it is of the first importance to settle,—and, pending their settle-ment, we will do as we do. Whilst the debate goes forward on the equity of com-merce, and will not be closed for a century or two, New and Old England may keep shop. Law of copyright and international copyright is to be discussed, and, in the interim, we will sell our books for the most we can.[24] Expediency of literature, reason of literature, lawfulness of writing down a thought, is questioned; much is to say on both sides, and, while the fight waxes hot, thou, dearest scholar, stick to

---

[21]Nicholas Poussin (1594–1665), French historical and landscape painter; Salvator Rosa (1615–1673), Italian landscape artist; *Transfiguration, Last Judgment,* and *Com-munion of St. Jerome,* famous paintings by Raphael, Mich-elangelo, and Domenichino—all in the Vatican in Rome; the Vatican, the Uffizi, and the Louvre, famous art galler-ies in Rome (at St. Peter's), Florence, and Paris.

[22]Hindus.

[23]Vegetarians (Emerson had once written "Grahamites," a group that believed in vegetarianism).

[24]There was no effective international copyright law during this period.

thy foolish task, add a line every hour, and between whiles add a line. Right to hold land, right of property, is disputed, and the conventions convene, and before the vote is taken, dig away in your garden, and spend your earnings as a waif or godsend to all serene and beautiful purposes. Life itself is a bubble and a skepticism, and a sleep within a sleep. Grant it, and as much more as they will,—but thou, God's darling! heed thy private dream: thou wilt not be missed in the scorning and skepticism: there are enough of them: stay there in thy closet, and toil, until the rest are agreed what to do about it. Thy sickness, they say, and thy puny habit, require that thou do this or avoid that, but know that thy life is a flitting state, a tent for a night, and do thou, sick or well, finish that stint. Thou art sick, but shalt not be worse, and the universe, which holds thee dear, shall be the better.

Human life is made up of the two elements, power and form, and the proportion must be invariably kept, if we would have it sweet and sound. Each of these elements in excess makes a mischief as hurtful as its defect. Everything runs to excess: every good quality is noxious, if unmixed, and, to carry the danger to the edge of ruin, nature causes each man's peculiarity to super-abound. Here, among the farms, we adduce the scholars as examples of this treachery. They are nature's victims of expression. You who see the artist, the orator, the poet, too near, and find their life no more excellent than that of mechanics or farmers, and themselves victims of partiality, very hollow and haggard, and pronounce them failures,—not heroes, but quacks,—conclude very reasonably, that these arts are not for man, but are disease. Yet nature will not bear you out. Irresistible nature made men such, and makes legions more of such, every day. You love the boy reading in a book, gazing at a drawing, or a cast: yet what are these millions who read and behold, but incipient writers and sculptors? Add a little more of that quality which now reads and sees, and they will seize the pen and chisel. And if one remembers how innocently he began to be an artist, he perceives that nature joined with his enemy. A man is a golden impossibility. The line he must walk is a hair's breadth. The wise through excess of wisdom is made a fool.

How easily, if fate would suffer it, we might keep forever these beautiful limits, and adjust ourselves, once for all, to the perfect calculation of the kingdom of known cause and effect. In the street and in the newspapers, life appears so plain a business, that manly resolution and adherence to the multiplication-table through all weathers, will insure success. But ah! presently comes a day—or is it only a half-hour, with its angel-whispering—which discomfits the conclusions of nations and of years! Tomorrow again, everything looks real and angular, the habitual standards are reinstated, common sense is as rare as genius,—is the basis of genius, and experience is hands and feet to every enterprise;—and yet, he who should do his business on this understanding, would be quickly bankrupt. Power keeps quite another road than the turnpikes of choice and will, namely, the subterranean and invisible tunnels and channels of life. It is ridiculous that we are diplomatists, and doctors, and considerate people: there are no dupes like these. Life is a series of surprises, and would not be worth taking or keeping, if it were not. God delights to isolate us every day, and hide from us the past and the future. We would look about us, but with grand politeness he draws down before us an impenetrable screen of purest sky, and another behind us of purest sky. 'You will not remember,' he seems to say, 'and you will not expect.' All good conversation, manners, and action, come from a spontaneity which forgets usages, and makes the moment great. Nature hates calculators; her methods are saltatory[25]

---

[25]Subject to abrupt moving, jumpy.

and impulsive. Man lives by pulses; our organic movements are such; and the chemical and ethereal agents are undulatory and alternate; and the mind goes antagonizing on, and never prospers but by fits. We thrive by casualties.[26] Our chief experiences have been casual. The most attractive class of people are those who are powerful obliquely, and not by the direct stroke: men of genius, but not yet accredited: one gets the cheer of their light, without paying too great a tax. Theirs is the beauty of the bird, or the morning light, and not of art. In the thought of genius there is always a surprise; and the moral sentiment is well called "the newness," for it is never other; as new to the oldest intelligence as to the young child,—"the kingdom that cometh without observation."[27] In like manner, for practical success, there must not be too much design. A man will not be observed in doing that which he can do best. There is a certain magic about his properest action, which stupefies your powers of observation, so that though it is done before you, you wist not of it. The art of life has a pudency,[28] and will not be exposed. Every man is an impossibility, until he is born; every thing impossible, until we see a success. The ardors of piety agree at last with the coldest skepticism,—that nothing is of us or our works,—that all is of God. Nature will not spare us the smallest leaf of laurel. All writing comes by the grace of God, and all doing and having. I would gladly be moral, and keep due metes and bounds, which I dearly love, and allow the most to the will of man, but I have set my heart on honesty in this chapter, and I can see nothing at last, in success or failure, than more or less of vital force supplied from the Eternal. The results of life are uncalculated and uncalculable. The years teach much which the days never know. The persons who compose our company, converse, and come and go, and design and execute many things, and somewhat comes of it all, but an unlooked-for result. The individual is always mistaken. He designed many things, and drew in other persons as coadjutors, quarrelled with some or all, blundered much, and something is done; all are a little advanced, but the individual is always mistaken. It turns out somewhat new, and very unlike what he promised himself.

The ancients, struck with this irreducibleness of the elements of human life to calculation, exalted Chance into a divinity, but that is to stay too long at the spark,—which glitters truly at one point,—but the universe is warm with the latency of the same fire. The miracle of life which will not be expounded, but will remain a miracle, introduces a new element. In the growth of the embryo, Sir Everard Home,[29] I think, noticed that the evolution was not from one central point, but coactive from three or more points. Life has no memory. That which proceeds in succession might be remembered, but that which is coexistent, or ejaculated from a deeper cause, as yet far from being conscious, knows not its own tendency. So is it with us, now skeptical, or without unity, because immersed in forms and effects all seeming to be of equal yet hostile value, and now religious, whilst in the reception of spiritual law. Bear with these distractions, with this coetaneous[30] growth of the parts: they will one day be *members*, and obey one will. On that one will, on that secret cause, they nail our attention and hope. Life is hereby melted into an expectation or a religion. Underneath the inharmonious and trivial particulars, is a musical perfection, the Ideal journeying always with us, the heaven without rent or seam. Do but observe the mode of our illumination. When I converse with a profound mind, or if at any time being alone I have good thoughts, I do not at once arrive at satisfactions, as when, being thirsty, I drink

---

[26]Unpredictable happenings.
[27]Luke 17:20: "The kingdom of God cometh not with observation."
[28]Modesty.

[29]Scottish surgeon (1756–1832), author of *Lectures on Comparative Anatomy* (1814–28).
[30]Simultaneous.

water, or go to the fire, being cold: no! but I am at first apprised of my vicinity to a new and excellent region of life. By persisting to read or to think, this region gives further sign of itself, as it were in flashes of light, in sudden discoveries of its profound beauty and repose, as if the clouds that covered it parted at intervals, and showed the approaching traveller the inland mountains, with the tranquil eternal meadows spread at their base, whereon flocks graze, and shepherds pipe and dance. But every insight from this realm of thought is felt as initial, and promises a sequel. I do not make it; I arrive there, and behold what was there already. I make! O no! I clap my hands in infantine joy and amazement, before the first opening to me of this august magnificence, old with the love and homage of innumerable ages, young with the life of life, the sunbright Mecca of the desert. And what a future it opens! I feel a new heart beating with the love of the new beauty. I am ready to die out of nature, and be born again into this new yet un-approachable America I have found in the West.

> "Since neither now nor yesterday began
> These thoughts, which have been ever, nor yet can
> A man be found who their first entrance knew."[31]

If I have described life as a flux of moods, I must now add, that there is that in us which changes not, and which ranks all sensations and states of mind. The consciousness in each man is a sliding scale, which identifies him now with the First Cause, and now with the flesh of his body; life above life, in infinite degrees. The sentiment from which it sprung determines the dignity of any deed, and the question ever is, not, what you have done or forborne, but, at whose command you have done or forborne it.

Fortune, Minerva, Muse, Holy Ghost,—these are quaint names, too narrow to cover this unbounded substance. The baffled intellect must still kneel before this cause, which refuses to be named,—ineffable cause, which every fine genius has essayed to represent by some emphatic symbol, as, Thales by water, Anaximenes by air, Anaxagoras by (Νοῦς) thought, Zoroaster by fire, Jesus and the moderns by love:[32] and the metaphor of each has become a national religion. The Chinese Mencius has not been the least successful in his generalization. "I fully understand language," he said, "and nourish well my vast-flowing vigor."—"I beg to ask what you call vast-flowing vigor?" said his companion. "The explanation," replied Mencius, "is difficult. This vigor is supremely great, and in the highest degree unbend-ing. Nourish it correctly, and do it no injury, and it will fill up the vacancy be-tween heaven and earth. This vigor accords with and assists justice and reason, and leaves no hunger."[33] In our more correct writing, we give to this generaliza-tion the name of Being, and thereby confess that we have arrived as far as we can go. Suffice it for the joy of the universe, that we have not arrived at a wall, but at interminable oceans. Our life seems not present, so much as prospective; not for the affairs on which it is wasted, but as a hint of this vast-flowing vigor. Most of life seems to be mere advertisement of faculty: information is given us not to sell ourselves cheap; that we are very great. So, in particulars, our greatness is always in a tendency or direction, not in an action. It is for us to believe in the rule, not in the exception. The noble are thus known from the ignoble. So in accepting the leading of the sentiments, it is not what we believe concerning the immortality of the soul, or the like, but *the universal impulse to believe*, that is the material circum-stance, and is the principal fact in the history of the globe. Shall we describe this

---

[31]From *Antigone*, a tragedy by Sophocles (496?–406 B.C.), Greek playwright.
[32]Thales (seventh century B.C.), Greek philosopher who be-lieved in water as the central principle of the universe; Anaximenes (sixth century B.C.), in air; Anaxagoras (fifth century B.C.), in a supreme intelligence; Zoroaster (c. sixth century B.C.), in fire; Jesus, in love.
[33]*From the Chinese Classical Work Commonly Called the Four Books*, by Mencius (372?–289 B.C.), a philosopher of Confu-cianism.

cause as that which works directly? The spirit is not helpless or needful of mediate organs. It has plentiful powers and direct effects. I am explained without explaining, I am felt without acting, and where I am not. Therefore all just persons are satisfied with their own praise. They refuse to explain themselves, and are content that new actions should do them that office. They believe that we communicate without speech, and above speech, and that no right action of ours is quite unaffecting to our friends, at whatever distance; for the influence of action is not to be measured by miles. Why should I fret myself, because a circumstance has occurred, which hinders my presence where I was expected? If I am not at the meeting, my presence where I am should be as useful to the commonwealth of friendship and wisdom, as would be my presence in that place. I exert the same quality of power in all places. Thus journeys the mighty Ideal before us; it never was known to fall into the rear. No man ever came to an experience which was satiating, but his good is tidings of a better. Onward and onward! In liberated moments, we know that a new picture of life and duty is already possible; the elements already exist in many minds around you, of a doctrine of life which shall transcend any written record we have. The new statement will comprise the skepticisms, as well as the faiths of society, and out of unbeliefs a creed shall be formed. For, skepticisms are not gratuitous or lawless, but are limitations of the affirmative statement, and the new philosophy must take them in, and make affirmations outside of them, just as much as it must include the oldest beliefs.

It is very unhappy, but too late to be helped, the discovery we have made, that we exist. That discovery is called the Fall of Man. Ever afterwards, we suspect our instruments. We have learned that we do not see directly, but mediately, and that we have no means of correcting these colored and distorting lenses which we are, or of computing the amount of their errors. Perhaps these subject-lenses have a creative power; perhaps there are no objects. Once we lived in what we saw; now, the rapaciousness of this new power, which threatens to absorb all things, engages us. Nature, art, persons, letters, religions,—objects, successively tumble in, and God is but one of its ideas. Nature and literature are subjective phenomena; every evil and every good thing is a shadow which we cast. The street is full of humiliations to the proud. As the fop contrived to dress his bailiffs[34] in his livery, and make them wait on his guests at table, so the chagrins which the bad heart gives off as bubbles, at once take form as ladies and gentlemen in the street, shopmen or bar-keepers in hotels, and threaten or insult whatever is threatenable and insultable in us. 'Tis the same with our idolatries. People forget that it is the eye which makes the horizon, and the rounding mind's eye which makes this or that man a type or representative of humanity with the name of hero or saint. Jesus the "providential man,"[35] is a good man on whom many people are agreed that these optical laws shall take effect. By love on one part, and by forbearance to press objection on the other part, it is for a time settled, that we will look at him in the centre of the horizon, and ascribe to him the properties that will attach to any man so seen. But the longest love or aversion has a speedy term. The great and crescive[36] self, rooted in absolute nature, supplants all relative existence, and ruins the kingdom of mortal friendship and love. Marriage (in what is called the spiritual world) is impossible, because of the inequality between every subject and every object. The subject is the receiver of Godhead, and at every comparison must feel his being enhanced by that cryptic might. Though not in energy, yet by presence, this magazine[37] of substance cannot be otherwise than felt: nor can any force of intellect attribute to the object the proper deity which sleeps or wakes for-

---

[34]Managers or administrators.
[35]I.e., "divine man."

[36]Growing.
[37]I.e., storehouse.

ever in every subject. Never can love make consciousness and ascription[38] equal in force. There will be the same gulf between every me and thee, as between the original and the picture. The universe is the bride of the soul. All private sympathy is partial. Two human beings are like globes, which can touch only in a point, and, whilst they remain in contact, all other points of each of the spheres are inert; their turn must also come, and the longer a particular union lasts, the more energy of appetency[39] the parts not in union acquire.

Life will be imaged, but cannot be divided nor doubled. Any invasion of its unity would be chaos. The soul is not twin-born, but the only begotten, and though revealing itself as child in time, child in appearance, is of a fatal and universal power, admitting no co-life. Every day, every act betrays the ill-concealed deity. We believe in ourselves, as we do not believe in others. We permit all things to ourselves, and that which we call sin in others, is experiment for us. It is an instance of our faith in ourselves, that men never speak of crime as lightly as they think: or, every man thinks a latitude safe for himself, which is nowise to be indulged to another. The act looks very differently on the inside, and on the outside; in its quality, and in its consequences. Murder in the murderer is no such ruinous thought as poets and romancers will have it; it does not unsettle him, or fright him from his ordinary notice of trifles: it is an act quite easy to be contemplated, but in its sequel, it turns out to be a horrible jangle and confounding of all relations. Especially the crimes that spring from love, seem right and fair from the actor's point of view, but, when acted, are found destructive of society. No man at last believes that he can be lost, nor that the crime in him is as black as in the felon. Because the intellect qualifies in our own case the moral judgments. For there is no crime to the intellect. That is antinomian or hypernomian,[40] and judges law as well as fact. "It is worse than a crime, it is a blunder," said Napoleon,[41] speaking the language of the intellect. To it, the world is a problem in mathematics or the science of quantity, and it leaves out praise and blame, and all weak emotions. All stealing is comparative. If you come to absolutes, pray who does not steal? Saints are sad, because they behold sin, (even when they speculate,) from the point of view of the conscience, and not of the intellect; a confusion of thought. Sin seen from the thought, is a diminution or *less:* seen from the conscience or will, it is pravity or *bad.* The intellect names it shade, absence of light, and no essence. The conscience must feel it as essence, essential evil. This it is not: it has an objective existence, but no subjective.

Thus inevitably does the universe wear our color, and every object fall successively into the subject itself. The subject exists, the subject enlarges; all things sooner or later fall into place. As I am, so I see; use what language we will, we can never say anything but what we are; Hermes, Cadmus, Columbus, Newton, Bonaparte,[42] are the mind's ministers. Instead of feeling a poverty when we encounter a great man, let us treat the new comer like a travelling geologist, who passes through our estate, and shows us good slate, or limestone, or anthracite, in our brush pasture. The partial action of each strong mind in one direction, is a telescope for the objects on which it is pointed. But every other part of knowledge is to be pushed to the same extravagance, ere the soul attains her due sphericity. Do you see that kitten chasing so prettily her own tail? If you could look with her eyes, you might see her surrounded with hundreds of figures performing com-

---

[38]Ascribing, as in a prayer ascribing glory to God.
[39]Mutual attraction.
[40]Beyond the moral law.
[41]Reference to Napoleon's order for kidnapping and execution of the Duke D' Enghien, whom he believed to be in league with his enemies. The deed deepened hatred of and opposition to Napoleon.

[42]All discoverers or innovators: Hermes, Greek god, inventor of the lyre; Cadmus, legendary founder of Thebes and inventor of the alphabet; Columbus, discoverer of America; Newton, discoverer of the law of gravity; Bonaparte, conqueror of most of Europe.

plex dramas, with tragic and comic issues, long conversations, many characters, many ups and downs of fate,—and meantime it is only puss and her tail. How long before our masquerade will end its noise of tambourines, laughter, and shouting, and we shall find it was a solitary performance?—A subject and an object,—it takes so much to make the galvanic circuit complete, but magnitude adds nothing. What imports it whether it is Kepler[43] and the sphere; Columbus and America; a reader and his book; or puss with her tail?

It is true that all the muses and love and religion hate these developments, and will find a way to punish the chemist, who publishes in the parlor the secrets of the laboratory. And we cannot say too little of our constitutional necessity of seeing things under private aspects, or saturated with our humors. And yet is the God the native of these bleak rocks. That need makes in morals the capital virtue of self-trust. We must hold hard to this poverty, however scandalous, and by more vigorous self-recoveries, after the sallies of action, possess our axis more firmly. The life of truth is cold, and so far mournful; but it is not the slave of tears, contritions, and perturbations. It does not attempt another's work, nor adopt another's facts. It is a main lesson of wisdom to know your own from another's. I have learned that I cannot dispose of other people's facts; but I possess such a key to my own, as persuades me against all their denials, that they also have a key to theirs. A sympathetic person is placed in the dilemma of a swimmer among drowning men, who all catch at him, and if he give so much as a leg or a finger, they will drown him. They wish to be saved from the mischiefs of their vices, but not from their vices. Charity would be wasted on this poor waiting on the symptoms. A wise and hardy physician will say, *Come out of that*, as the first condition of advice.

In this our talking America, we are ruined by our good nature and listening on all sides. This compliance takes away the power of being greatly useful. A man should not be able to look other than directly and forthright. A preoccupied attention is the only answer to the importunate frivolity of other people: an attention, and to an aim which makes their wants frivolous. This is a divine answer, and leaves no appeal, and no hard thoughts. In Flaxman's drawing of the Eumenides of Æschylus, Orestes supplicates Apollo, whilst the Furies sleep on the threshold.[44] The face of the god expresses a shade of regret and compassion, but calm with the conviction of the irreconcilableness of the two spheres. He is born into other politics, into the eternal and beautiful. The man at his feet asks for his interest in turmoils of the earth, into which his nature cannot enter. And the Eumenides there lying express pictorially this disparity. The god is surcharged with his divine destiny.

Illusion, Temperament, Succession, Surface, Surprise, Reality, Subjectiveness,—these are threads on the loom of time, these are the lords of life. I dare not assume to give their order, but I name them as I find them in my way. I know better than to claim any completeness for my picture. I am a fragment, and this is a fragment of me. I can very confidently announce one or another law, which throws itself into relief and form, but I am too young yet by some ages to compile a code. I gossip for my hour concerning the eternal politics. I have seen many fair pictures not in vain. A wonderful time I have lived in. I am not the novice I was fourteen, nor yet seven years ago. Let who will ask, where is the fruit? I find a private fruit sufficient. This is a fruit,—that I should not ask for a rash effect

---

[43]Johannes Kepler (1571–1630), German astronomer who discovered in 1604 that Mars revolved about the sun in an elliptical orbit.
[44]John Flaxman (1755–1826), who illustrated Aeschylus's

The Eumenides, in which Orestes avenges his father's murder by killing his mother; he is then pursued by the Furies, or Eumenides.

from meditations, counsels, and the hiving of truths. I should feel it pitiful to demand a result on this town and county, an overt effect on the instant month and year. The effect is deep and secular[45] as the cause. It works on periods in which mortal lifetime is lost. All I know is reception; I am and I have: but I do not get, and when I have fancied I had gotten anything, I found I did not. I worship with wonder the great Fortune. My reception has been so large, that I am not annoyed by receiving this or that superabundantly. I say to the Genius, if he will pardon the proverb, *In for a mill, in for a million.* When I receive a new gift, I do not macerate[46] my body to make the account square, for, if I should die, I could not make the account square. The benefit overran the merit the first day, and has overran the merit ever since. The merit itself, so-called, I reckon part of the receiving.

Also, that hankering after an overt or practical effect seems to me an apostasy. In good earnest, I am willing to spare this most unnecessary deal of doing. Life wears to me a visionary face. Hardest, roughest action is visionary also. It is but a choice between soft and turbulent dreams. People disparage knowing and the intellectual life, and urge doing. I am very content with knowing, if only I could know. That is an august entertainment, and would suffice me a great while. To know a little, would be worth the expense of this world. I hear always the law of Adrastia, "that every soul which had acquired any truth, should be safe from harm until another period."[47]

I know that the world I converse with in the city and in the farms, is not the world I *think.* I observe that difference, and shall observe it. One day, I shall know the value and law of this discrepance. But I have not found that much was gained by manipular attempts to realize the world of thought. Many eager persons successively make an experiment in this way, and make themselves ridiculous. They acquire democratic manners, they foam at the mouth, they hate and deny. Worse, I observe, that, in the history of mankind, there is never a solitary example of success,—taking their own tests of success. I say this polemically, or in reply to the inquiry, why not realize your world? But far be from me the despair which prejudges the law by a paltry empiricism,—since there never was a right endeavor, but it succeeded. Patience and patience, we shall win at the last. We must be very suspicious of the deceptions of the element of time. It takes a good deal of time to eat or to sleep, or to earn a hundred dollars, and a very little time to entertain a hope and an insight which becomes the light of our life. We dress our garden, eat our dinners, discuss the household with our wives, and these things make no impression, are forgotten next week; but in the solitude to which every man is always returning, he has a sanity and revelations, which in his passage into new worlds he will carry with him. Never mind the ridicule, never mind the defeat: up again, old heart!—it seems to say,—there is victory yet for all justice; and the true romance which the world exists to realize, will be the transformation of genius into practical power.

1844

---

[45]Enduring.
[46]Torment.

[47]Adrastia was the goddess of justice or retribution. See Plato's *Phaedrus.*

Fate[1]

Delicate omens traced in air,
To the lone bard true witness bare;
Birds with auguries on their wings
Chanted undeceiving things,
Him to beckon, him to warn;
Well might then the poet scorn
To learn of scribe or courier
Hints writ in vaster character;
And on his mind, at dawn of day,
Soft shadows of the evening lay.
For the prevision is allied
Unto the thing so signified;
Or say, the foresight that awaits
Is the same Genius that creates.[2]

It chanced during one winter a few years ago, that our cities were bent on discussing the theory of the Age. By an odd coincidence, four or five noted men were each reading a discourse to the citizens of Boston or New York, on the Spirit of the Times. It so happened that the subject had the same prominence in some remarkable pamphlets and journals issued in London in the same season. To me, however, the question of the times resolved itself into a practical question of the conduct of life. How shall I live? We are incompetent to solve the times. Our geometry cannot span the huge orbits of the prevailing ideas, behold their return and reconcile their opposition. We can only obey our own polarity. 'T is fine for us to speculate and elect our course, if we must accept an irresistible dictation.

In our first steps to gain our wishes we come upon immovable limitations. We are fired with the hope to reform men. After many experiments we find that we must begin earlier,—at school. But the boys and girls are not docile; we can make nothing of them. We decide that they are not of good stock. We must begin our reform earlier still,—at generation: that is to say, there is Fate, or laws of the world.

But if there be irresistible dictation, this dictation understands itself. If we must accept Fate, we are not less compelled to affirm liberty, the significance of the individual, the grandeur of duty, the power of character. This is true, and that other is true. But our geometry cannot span these extreme points and reconcile them. What to do? By obeying each thought frankly, by harping, or, if you will, pounding on each string, we learn at last its power. By the same obedience to other thoughts we learn theirs, and then comes some reasonable hope of harmonizing them. We are sure that, though we know not how, necessity does comport with liberty, the individual with the world, my polarity with the spirit of the times. The riddle of the age has for each a private solution. If one would study his own time, it must be by this method of taking up in turn each of the leading topics which belong to our scheme of human life, and by firmly stating all that is agreeable to experience on one, and doing the same justice to the opposing facts in the others, the true limitations will appear. Any excess of emphasis on one part would be corrected, and a just balance would be made.

But let us honestly state the facts. Our America has a bad name for superficialness. Great men, great nations, have not been boasters and buffoons, but perceiv-

---

[1] "Fate" was presented as a lecture in 1851, and then was included as the first essay in *The Conduct of Life* (1860), the last of Emerson's major works.
[2] An earlier version of this poem, without the last four lines, appears in Emerson's *Poems*. It contains two opening lines that are somewhat elucidative: "The free winds told him what they knew,/Discoursed of fortune as they blew."

ers of the terror of life, and have manned themselves to face it. The Spartan, embodying his religion in his country, dies before its majesty without a question. The Turk, who believes his doom is written on the iron leaf in the moment when he entered the world, rushes on the enemy's sabre with undivided will. The Turk, the Arab, the Persian, accepts the foreordained fate:—

> On two days, it steads not to run from thy grave,
>   The appointed, and the unappointed day;
> On the first, neither balm nor physician can save,
>   Nor thee, on the second, the Universe slay.[3]

The Hindoo under the wheel is as firm. Our Calvinists in the last generation had something of the same dignity. They felt that the weight of the Universe held them down to their place. What could *they* do? Wise men feel that there is something which cannot be talked or voted away,—a strap or belt which girds the world:—

> The Destinee, ministre general,
> That executeth in the world over al,
> The purveiance that God hath seen beforne,
> So strong it is, that though the world had sworne
> The contrary of a thing by yea or nay,
> Yet sometime it shall fallen on a day
> That falleth not oft in a thousand yeer;
> For certainly, our appetités here,
> Be it of warre, or pees, or hate, or love,
> All this is ruled by the sight above.
>   CHAUCER: *The Knighte's Tale.*[4]

The Greek Tragedy expressed the same sense. "Whatever is fated that will take place. The great immense mind of Jove is not to be transgressed."

Savages cling to a local god of one tribe or town. The broad ethics of Jesus were quickly narrowed to village theologies, which preach an election or favoritism. And now and then an amiable parson, like Jung Stilling or Robert Huntington,[5] believes in a pistareen-Providence,[6] which, whenever the good man wants a dinner, makes that somebody shall knock at his door and leave a half-dollar. But Nature is no sentimentalist,—does not cosset or pamper us. We must see that the world is rough and surly, and will not mind drowning a man or a woman, but swallows your ship like a grain of dust. The cold, inconsiderate of persons, tingles your blood, benumbs your feet, freezes a man like an apple. The diseases, the elements, fortune, gravity, lightning, respect no persons. The way of Providence is a little rude. The habit of snake and spider, the snap of the tiger and other leapers and bloody jumpers, the crackle of the bones of his prey in the coil of the anaconda,—these are in the system, and our habits are like theirs. You have just dined, and however scrupulously the slaughter-house is concealed in the graceful distance of miles, there is complicity, expensive races,—race living at the expense of race. The planet is liable to shocks from comets, perturbations from planets, rendings from earthquake and volcano, alterations of climate, precessions of equinoxes.[7] Rivers dry up by opening of the forest. The sea changes its bed. Towns

---

[3]Emerson's translation of a German translation of a Persian poet.
[4]Lines 805–814, slightly modified. "The Greek Tragedy": Aeschylus, *The Suppliants*, ll. 1047–1049.
[5]Johann H. Jung-Stilling (1740–1817), German mystic and physician; Robert Huntington was probably William Huntington (1745–1813), an eccentric minister who believed in God's direct intervention in daily life.

[6]A God who involves Himself in the petty affairs of man. Pistareen: Spanish coin.
[7]The occurrence of the equinoxes earlier in each successive sidereal year (i.e., measured by the apparent motion of fixed stars).

and counties fall into it. At Lisbon an earthquake killed men like flies.[8] At Naples three years ago ten thousand persons were crushed in a few minutes.[9] The scurvy at sea, the sword of the climate in the west of Africa, at Cayenne, at Panama, at New Orleans, cut off men like a massacre. Our western prairie shakes with fever and ague. The cholera, the small-pox, have proved as mortal to some tribes as a frost to the crickets, which, having filled the summer with noise, are silenced by a fall of the temperature of one night. Without uncovering what does not concern us, or counting how many species of parasites hang on a bombyx,[10] or groping after intestinal parasites or infusory biters,[11] or the obscurities of alternate generation,—the forms of the shark, the *labrus*,[12] the jaw of the sea-wolf paved with crushing teeth, the weapons of the grampus,[13] and other warriors hidden in the sea, are hints of ferocity in the interiors of nature. Let us not deny it up and down. Providence has a wild, rough, incalculable road to its end, and it is of no use to try to whitewash its huge, mixed instrumentalities, or to dress up that terrific benefactor in a clean shirt and white neckcloth of a student in divinity.

Will you say, the disasters which threaten mankind are exceptional, and one need not lay his account for cataclysms every day? Aye, but what happens once may happen again, and so long as these strokes are not to be parried by us they must be feared.

But these shocks and ruins are less destructive to us than the stealthy power of other laws which act on us daily. An expense of ends to means is fate;—organization tyrannizing over character. The menagerie, or forms and powers of the spine, is a book of fate; the bill of the bird, the skull of the snake, determines tyrannically its limits. So is the scale of races, of temperaments;[14] so is sex; so is climate; so is the reaction of talents imprisoning the vital power in certain directions. Every spirit makes its house; but afterwards the house confines the spirit.

The gross lines are legible to the dull; the cabman is phrenologist so far, he looks in your face to see if his shilling is sure. A dome of brow denotes one thing, a pot-belly another; a squint, a pug-nose, mats of hair, the pigment of the epidermis, betray character. People seem sheathed in their tough organization. Ask Spurzheim, ask the doctors, ask Quetelet[15] if temperaments decide nothing?—or if there be anything they do not decide? Read the description in medical books of the four temperaments and you will think you are reading your own thoughts which you had not yet told. Find the part which black eyes and which blue eyes play severally in the company. How shall a man escape from his ancestors, or draw off from his veins the black drop which he drew from his father's or his mother's life? It often appears in a family as if all the qualities of the progenitors were potted in several jars,—some ruling quality in each son or daughter of the house; and sometimes the unmixed temperament, the rank unmitigated elixir, the family vice is drawn off in a separate individual and the others are proportionally relieved. We sometimes see a change of expression in our companion and say his father or his mother comes to the windows of his eyes, and sometimes a remote relative. In different hours a man represents each of several of his ancestors, as if there were seven or eight of us rolled up in each man's skin,—seven or eight ancestors at least; and they constitute the variety of notes for that new piece of music which his life is. At the corner of the street you read the possibility of each passenger in the facial angle, in the complexion, in the depth of his eye. His parentage

---

[8]The 1755 Lisbon earthquake killed 30,000 people and touched off discussions about fate and religion.
[9]December 17, 1857.
[10]Silkworm moth.
[11]Microscopic organisms.
[12]Predatory fish.
[13]The killer whale.
[14]In ancient and medieval physiology, human temperaments were believed to be shaped by a combination of the four cardinal humors: blood, phlegm, choler, and melancholy.
[15]Johann Spurzheim (1776–1832), German physician, popularizer of phrenology (analysis of character through study of the shape of the skull). Lambert Quetelet (1796–1874), Belgian mathematician who established the field of statistics.

determines it. Men are what their mothers made them. You may as well ask a loom which weaves huckabuck[16] why it does not make cashmere, as expect poetry from this engineer, or a chemical discovery from that jobber. Ask the digger in the ditch to explain Newton's laws[17]; the fine organs of his brain have been pinched by overwork and squalid poverty from father to son for a hundred years. When each comes forth from his mother's womb, the gate of gifts closes behind him. Let him value his hands and feet, he has but one pair. So he has but one future, and that is already predetermined in his lobes and described in that little fatty face, pig-eye, and squat form. All the privilege and all the legislation of the world cannot meddle or help to make a poet or a prince of him.

Jesus said, "When he looketh on her, he hath committed adultery."[18] But he is an adulterer before he has yet looked on the woman, by the superfluity of animal and the defect of thought in his constitution. Who meets him, or who meets her, in the street, sees that they are ripe to be each other's victim.

In certain men digestion and sex absorb the vital force, and the stronger these are, the individual is so much weaker. The more of these drones perish, the better for the hive. If, later, they give birth to some superior individual, with force enough to add to this animal a new aim and a complete apparatus to work it out, all the ancestors are gladly forgotten. Most men and most women are merely one couple more. Now and then one has a new cell or camarilla[19] opened in his brain,—an architectural, a musical, or a philological knack; some stray taste or talent for flowers, or chemistry, or pigments, or storytelling; a good hand for drawing, a good foot for dancing, an athletic frame for wide journeying, etc.—which skill nowise alters rank in the scale of nature, but serves to pass the time; the life of sensation going on as before. At last these hints and tendencies are fixed in one or in a succession. Each absorbs so much food and force as to become itself a new centre. The new talent draws off so rapidly the vital force that not enough remains for the animal functions, hardly enough for health; so that in the second generation, if the like genius appear, the health is visibly deteriorated and the generative force impaired.

People are born with the moral or with the material bias;—uterine brothers with this diverging destination; and I suppose, with high magnifiers, Mr. Frauenhofer or Dr. Carpenter[20] might come to distinguish in the embryo, at the fourth day,—this is a Whig, and that a Freesoiler.[21]

It was a poetic attempt to lift this mountain of Fate, to reconcile this despotism of race with liberty, which led the Hindoos to say, "Fate is nothing but the deeds committed in a prior state of existence." I find the coincidence of the extremes of Eastern and Western speculation in the daring statement of Schelling, "There is in every man a certain feeling that he has been what he is from all eternity, and by no means became such in time."[22] To say it less sublimely,—in the history of the individual is always an account of his condition, and he knows himself to be a party to his present estate.

A good deal of our politics is physiological. Now and then a man of wealth in the heyday of youth adopts the tenet of broadest freedom. In England there is always some man of wealth and large connection, planting himself, during all his years of health, on the side of progress, who, as soon as he begins to die, checks his forward play, calls in his troops and becomes conservative. All conservatives

---

[16]Coarse linen or cotton cloth.
[17]Sir Isaac Newton (1642–1727), English scientist who discovered the law of gravity and other physical laws operative in the universe.
[18]Cf. Matthew 5:28.
[19]Small chamber.
[20]Joseph von Frauenhofer (1787–1826), German astronomer who improved the telescope; Dr. William B. Carpenter (1813–1885), English biologist, authority on the microscope.
[21]Whig, one of the two major political parties of the time (the other, Democrat); Freesoilers belonged to an antislavery party.
[22]Friederich von Schelling (1775–1854), German philosopher.

are such from personal defects. They have been effeminated[23] by position or nature, born halt and blind, through luxury of their parents, and can only, like invalids, act on the defensive. But strong natures, backwoodsmen, New Hampshire giants, Napoleons, Burkes, Broughams, Websters, Kossuths,[24] are inevitable patriots, until their life ebbs and their defects and gout, palsy and money, warp them.

The strongest idea incarnates itself in majorities and nations, in the healthiest and strongest. Probably the election goes by avoirdupois weight, and if you could weigh bodily the tonnage of any hundred of the Whig and the Democratic party in a town on the Dearborn balance,[25] as they passed the hay-scales, you could predict with certainty which party would carry it. On the whole it would be rather the speediest way of deciding the vote, to put the selectmen or the mayor and aldermen at the hay-scales.

In science we have to consider two things: power and circumstance. All we know of the egg, from each successive discovery, is, *another vesicle;*[26] and if, after five hundred years you get a better observer or a better glass, he finds, within the last observed, another. In vegetable and animal tissue it is just alike, and all that the primary power or spasm operates is still vesicles, vesicles. Yes,—but the tyrannical Circumstance! A vesicle in new circumstances, a vesicle lodged in darkness, Oken[27] thought, became animal; in light, a plant. Lodged in the parent animal, it suffers changes which end in unsheathing miraculous capability in the unaltered vesicle, and it unlocks itself to fish, bird, or quadruped, head and foot, eye and claw. The Circumstance is Nature. Nature is what you may do. There is much you may not. We have two things,—the circumstance, and the life. Once we thought positive power was all. Now we learn that negative power, or circumstance, is half. Nature is the tyrannous circumstance, the thick skull, the sheathed snake, the ponderous, rock-like jaw; necessitated activity; violent direction; the conditions of a tool, like the locomotive, strong enough on its track, but which can do nothing but mischief off of it; or skates, which are wings on the ice but fetters on the ground.

The book of Nature is the book of Fate. She turns the gigantic pages,—leaf after leaf,—never re-turning one. One leaf she lays down, a floor of granite; then a thousand ages, and a bed of slate; a thousand ages, and a measure of coal; a thousand ages, and a layer of marl and mud: vegetable forms appear; her first misshapen animals, zoöphyte, trilobium, fish; then, saurians,—rude forms, in which she has only blocked her future statue, concealing under these unwieldy monsters the fine type of her coming king. The face of the planet cools and dries, the races meliorate, and man is born. But when a race has lived its term, it comes no more again.

The population of the world is a conditional population; not the best, but the best that could live now; and the scale of tribes, and the steadiness with which victory adheres to one tribe and defeat to another, is as uniform as the superposition of strata. We know in history what weight belongs to race. We see the English, French, and Germans planting themselves on every shore and market of America and Australia, and monopolizing the commerce of these countries. We like the nervous and victorious habit of our own branch of the family. We follow the step of the Jew, of the Indian, of the Negro. We see how much will has been expended to extinguish the Jew, in vain. Look at the unpalatable conclusions of Knox, in his

---

[23]Weakened, softened.
[24]Edmund Burke (1729–1797), Irish statesman and writer; Henry Brougham (1778–1868), English political leader; Daniel Webster (1782–1852), American political figure; Lajos Kossuth (1802–1894), Hungarian patriot, leader of movement for Hungarian independence.

[25]A spring balance named after its inventor, Henry Dearborn.
[26]Small fluid-filled sac.
[27]Lorenz Oken (1779–1851), German naturalist who, in *Procreation*, presented the theory that all organisms derived from cells (or vesicles).

Fragment of Races;[28]—a rash and unsatisfactory writer, but charged with pungent and unforgetable truths. "Nature respects race, and not hybrids." "Every race has its own *habitat*." "Detach a colony from the race, and it deteriorates to the crab." See the shades of the picture. The German and Irish millions, like the Negro, have a great deal of guano[29] in their destiny. They are ferried over the Atlantic and carted over America, to ditch and to drudge, to make corn cheap and then to lie down prematurely to make a spot of green grass on the prairie.

One more fagot of these adamantine bandages is the new science of Statistics. It is a rule that the most casual and extraordinary events, if the basis of population is broad enough, become matter of fixed calculation. It would not be safe to say when a captain like Bonaparte, a singer like Jenny Lind, or a navigator like Bowditch would be born in Boston; but, on a population of twenty or two hundred millions, something like accuracy may be had.[30]

'T is frivolous to fix pedantically the date of particular inventions. They have all been invented over and over fifty times. Man is the arch machine of which all these shifts drawn from himself are toy models. He helps himself on each emergency by copying or duplicating his own structure, just so far as the need is. 'T is hard to find the right Homer, Zoroaster, or Menu;[31] harder still to find the Tubal Cain, or Vulcan, or Cadmus, or Copernicus, or Fust, or Fulton;[32] the indisputable inventor. There are scores and centuries of them. "The air is full of men." This kind of talent so abounds, this constructive tool-making efficiency, as if it adhered to the chemic atoms; as if the air he breathes were made of Vaucansons, Franklins, and Watts.[33]

Doubtless in every million there will be an astronomer, a mathematician, a comic poet, a mystic. No one can read the history of astronomy without perceiving that Copernicus, Newton, Laplace,[34] are not new men, or a new kind of men, but that Thales, Anaximenes, Hipparchus, Empedocles, Aristarchus, Pythagoras, Œnipodes,[35] had anticipated them; each had the same tense geometrical brain, apt for the same vigorous computation and logic; a mind parallel to the movement of the world. The Roman mile probably rested on a measure of a degree of the meridian. Mahometan and Chinese know what we know of leap-year, of the Gregorian calendar,[36] and of the precession of the equinoxes. As in every barrel of cowries brought to New Bedford there shall be one *orangia*,[37] so there will, in a dozen millions of Malays and Mahometans, be one or two astronomical skulls.[38] In a

[28]Robert Knox (1791–1862), Scottish ethnologist, anatomist, and author of *The Races of Men, A Fragment* (1850) supporting an essentially racist theory of biologically distinct races; "Detach a colony. . . .": refers to apple trees degenerating to crabapples when left alone.

[29]Fertilizer made from bat or other dung.

[30]Jenny Lind (1820–1887), famous Swedish opera singer; Nathaniel Bowditch (1773–1838), American mathematician and author of *The New American Practical Navigator* (1802). Emerson adds in a footnote a quotation from Quetelet (see footnote 15): "Everything which pertains to the human species, considered as a whole, belongs to the order of physical facts. The greater the number of individuals, the more does the influence of the individual will disappear, leaving predominance to a series of general facts dependent on causes by which society exists, and is preserved."

[31]Homer (fl. *c.* 1000 B.C.), Greek epic poet, assumed author of the *Iliad* and the *Odyssey*; Zoroaster (sixth century B.C.), Persian prophet; Menu, reputed author of the Hindu *Laws of Manu*, written between 200 B.C. and 200 A.D.

[32]Tubal Cain, Biblical figure (Genesis 4:22), "instructor . . . in brass and iron"; Vulcan, Roman god of fire and metal work; Cadmus, legendary Phoenician prince who founded Thebes, helped by warriors who were created by his sowing the dragon's teeth; Nicolaus Copernicus (1473–

1543), Polish astronomer who demonstrated that the earth revolved about the sun; Johann Fust (1400?–1466?), German book dealer, partner of Gutenberg whom he financed in experiments leading to the invention of printing; Robert Fulton (1765–1815), inventor of the submarine and designer of early steamboats.

[33]Jacques de Vaucanson (1709–1782), French inventor of automata; Benjamin Franklin (1706–1790), American statesman and writer, inventor of the Franklin stove; James Watt (1736–1819), Scottish inventor of the modern steam engine.

[34]Pierre Simon, Marquis de Laplace (1749–1827), French astronomer and mathematician, who discovered many laws relating to movements of heavenly bodies.

[35]All Greek philosophers and scientists, ranging from the seventh to the second century B.C., who anticipated later "discoveries" that revolutionized modern thought (Aristarchus of Samos, for example, in the third century B.C. held that the earth turns on its axis and revolves about the sun).

[36]Corrected form of the Julian calendar, introduced by Pope Gregory XIII in 1582 and now used in most countries: a year of 365 days, with an extra day every four years.

[37]A specially beautiful kind of cowrie (tropical seashell, used for money in some countries).

[38]I.e., with minds capable of astronomical genius.

large city, the most casual things, and things whose beauty lies in their casualty, are produced as punctually and to order as the baker's muffin for breakfast. Punch makes exactly one capital joke a week; and the journals contrive to furnish one good piece of news every day.

And not less work the laws of repression, the penalities of violated functions. Famine, typhus, frost, war, suicide and effete races must be reckoned calculable parts of the system of the world.

These are pebbles from the mountain, hints of the terms by which our life is walled up, and which show a kind of mechanical exactness, as of a loom or mill in what we call casual or fortuitous events.

The force with which we resist these torrents of tendency looks so ridiculously inadequate that it amounts to little more than a criticism or protest made by a minority of one, under compulsion of millions. I seemed in the height of a tempest to see men overboard struggling in the waves, and driven about here and there. They glanced intelligently at each other, but 't was little they could do for one another; 't was much if each could keep afloat alone. Well, they had a right to their eye-beams, and all the rest was Fate.

We cannot trifle with this reality, this cropping-out in our planted gardens of the core of the world. No picture of life can have any veracity that does not admit the odious facts. A man's power is hooped in by a necessity which, by many experiments, he touches on every side until he learns its arc.

The element running through entire nature, which we popularly call Fate, is known to us as limitation. Whatever limits us we call Fate. If we are brute and barbarous, the fate takes a brute and dreadful shape. As we refine, our checks become finer. If we rise to spiritual culture, the antagonism takes a spiritual form. In the Hindoo fables, Vishnu follows Maya through all her ascending changes, from insect and crawfish up to elephant; whatever form she took, he took the male form of that kind, until she became at last woman and goddess, and he a man and a god.[39] The limitations refine as the soul purifies, but the ring of necessity is always perched at the top.

When the gods in the Norse heaven were unable to bind the Fenris Wolf[40] with steel or with weight of mountains,—the one he snapped and the other he spurned with his heel,—they put round his foot a limp band softer than silk or cobweb, and this held him; the more he spurned it the stiffer it drew. So soft and so stanch is the ring of Fate. Neither brandy, nor nectar, nor sulphuric ether, nor hell-fire, nor ichor,[41] nor poetry, nor genius, can get rid of this limp band. For if we give it the high sense in which the poets use it, even thought itself is not above Fate; that too must act according to eternal laws, and all that is wilful and fantastic in it is in opposition to its fundamental essence.

And last of all, high over thought, in the world of morals, Fate appears as vindicator, levelling the high, lifting the low, requiring justice in man, and always striking soon or late when justice is not done. What is useful will last, what is hurtful will sink. "The doer must suffer," said the Greeks; "you would soothe a Deity not to be soothed." "God himself cannot procure good for the wicked," said the Welsh triad.[42] "God may consent, but only for a time," said the bard of Spain. The limitation is impassable by any insight of man. In its last and loftiest ascensions, insight itself and the freedom of the will is one of its obedient members. But we must not run into generalizations too large, but show the natural bounds or essential distinctions, and seek to do justice to the other elements as well.

---

[39]The Hindu trinity consists of Brahma, Vishnu, and Siva; Vishnu is known as "the Preserver" and in one of his human incarnations he was Krishna. Maya: Hindu goddess of illusion.

[40]One of the evil brood of Loki, Norse god of discord.
[41]Pure fluid that runs through the veins of the gods.
[42]Welsh bards preserved the religion and laws and sayings of the people in three-fold groups, or triads.

Thus we trace Fate in matter, mind, and morals; in race, in retardations of strata, and in thought and character as well. It is everywhere bound or limitation. But Fate has its lord; limitation its limits,—is different seen from above and from below, from within and from without. For though Fate is immense, so is Power, which is the other fact in the dual world, immense. If Fate follows and limits Power, Power attends and antagonizes Fate. We must respect Fate as natural history, but there is more than natural history. For who and what is this criticism that pries into the matter? Man is not order of nature, sack and sack, belly and members, link in a chain, nor any ignominious baggage;[43] but a stupendous antagonism, a dragging together of the poles of the Universe. He betrays his relation to what is below him,—thick-skulled, small-brained, fishy, quadrumanous,[44] quadruped ill-disguised, hardly escaped into biped,—and has paid for the new powers by loss of some of the old ones. But the lightning which explodes and fashions planets, maker of planets and suns, is in him. On one side elemental order, sandstone and granite, rock-ledges, peat-bog, forest, sea and shore; and on the other part thought, the spirit which composes and decomposes nature,—here they are, side by side, god and devil, mind and matter, king and conspirator, belt and spasm, riding peacefully together in the eye and brain of every man.

Nor can he blink the freewill. To hazard the contradiction,—freedom is necessary. If you please to plant yourself on the side of Fate, and say, Fate is all; then we say, a part of Fate is the freedom of man. Forever wells up the impulse of choosing and acting in the soul. Intellect annuls Fate. So far as a man thinks, he is free. And though nothing is more disgusting than the crowing about liberty by slaves, as most men are, and the flippant mistaking for freedom of some paper preamble like a Declaration of Independence or the statute right to vote, by those who have never dared to think or to act,—yet it is wholesome to man to look not at Fate, but the other way: the practical view is the other. His sound relation to these facts is to use and command, not to cringe to them. "Look not on Nature, for her name is fatal," said the oracle. The too much contemplation of these limits induces meanness. They who talk much of destiny, their birth-star, etc., are in a lower dangerous plane, and invite the evils they fear.

I cited the instinctive and heroic races as proud believers in Destiny. They conspire with it; a loving resignation is with the event. But the dogma makes a different impression when it is held by the weak and lazy. 'T is weak and vicious people who cast the blame on Fate. The right use of Fate is to bring up our conduct to the loftiness of nature. Rude and invincible except by themselves are the elements. So let man be. Let him empty his breast of his windy conceits, and show his lordship by manners and deeds on the scale of nature. Let him hold his purpose as with the tug of gravitation. No power, no persuasion, no bribe shall make him give up his point. A man ought to compare advantageously with a river, an oak, or a mountain. He shall have not less the flow, the expansion, and the resistance of these.

'T is the best use of Fate to teach a fatal courage. Go face the fire at sea, or the cholera in your friend's house, or the burglar in your own, or what danger lies in the way of duty,—knowing you are guarded by the cherubim of Destiny. If you believe in Fate to your harm, believe it at least for your good.

For if Fate is so prevailing, man also is part of it, and can confront fate with fate. If the Universe have these savage accidents, our atoms are as savage in resistance. We should be crushed by the atmosphere, but for the reaction of the air within the body. A tube made of a film of glass can resist the shock of the ocean if

---

[43]I.e., material or physical, a belly plus its attachments or "members." See Shakespeare's *Coriolanus*, I, i, 99ff. for the "belly and members."

[44]Having all four feet adapted to function as hands (monkeys, for example).

filled with the same water. If there be omnipotence in the stroke, there is omnipotence of recoil.

1. But Fate against Fate is only parrying and defence: there are also the noble creative forces. The revelation of Thought takes man out of servitude into freedom. We rightly say of ourselves, we were born and afterward we were born again, and many times. We have successive experiences so important that the new forgets the old, and hence the mythology of the seven or the nine heavens. The day of days, the great day of the feast of life, is that in which the inward eye opens to the Unity in things, to the omnipresence of law:—sees that what is must be and ought to be, or is the best. This beatitude dips from on high down on us and we see. It is not in us so much as we are in it. If the air come to our lungs, we breathe and live; if not, we die. If the light come to our eyes, we see; else not. And if truth come to our mind we suddenly expand to its dimensions, as if we grew to worlds. We are as lawgivers; we speak for Nature; we prophesy and divine.

This insight throws us on the party and interest of the Universe, against all and sundry; against ourselves as much as others. A man speaking from insight affirms of himself what is true of the mind: seeing its immortality, he says, I am immortal; seeing its invincibility, he says, I am strong. It is not in us, but we are in it. It is of the maker, not of what is made. All things are touched and changed by it. This uses and is not used. It distances those who share it from those who share it not. Those who share it not are flocks and herds. It dates from itself; not from former men or better men, gospel, or constitution, or college, or custom. Where it shines, Nature is no longer intrusive, but all things make a musical or pictorial impression. The world of men show like a comedy without laughter: populations, interests, government, history; 't is all toy figures in a toy house. It does not overvalue particular truths. We hear eagerly every thought and word quoted from an intellectual man. But in his presence our own mind is roused to activity, and we forget very fast what he says, much more interested in the new play of our own thought than in any thought of his. 'T is the majesty into which we have suddenly mounted, the impersonality, the scorn of egotisms, the sphere of laws, that engage us. Once we were stepping a little this way and a little that way; now we are as men in a balloon, and do not think so much of the point we have left, or the point we would make, as of the liberty and glory of the way.

Just as much intellect as you add, so much organic power. He who sees through the design, presides over it, and must will that which must be. We sit and rule, and, though we sleep, our dream will come to pass. Our thought, though it were only an hour old, affirms an oldest necessity, not to be separated from thought, and not to be separated from will. They must always have coexisted. It apprises us of its sovereignty and godhead, which refuse to be severed from it. It is not mine or thine, but the will of all mind. It is poured into the souls of all men, as the soul itself which constitutes them men. I know not whether there be, as is alleged, in the upper region of our atmosphere, a permanent westerly current which carries with it all atoms which rise to that height, but I see that when souls reach a certain clearness of perception they accept a knowledge and motive above selfishness. A breath of will blows eternally through the universe of souls in the direction of the Right and Necessary. It is the air which all intellects inhale and exhale, and it is the wind which blows the worlds into order and orbit.

Thought dissolves the material universe by carrying the mind up into a sphere where all is plastic. Of two men, each obeying his own thought, he whose thought is deepest will be the strongest character. Always one man more than another represents the will of Divine Providence to the period.

2. If thought makes free, so does the moral sentiment. The mixtures of spiritual chemistry refuse to be analyzed. Yet we can see that with the perception of truth is joined the desire that it shall prevail; that affection is essential to will.

Moreover, when a strong will appears, it usually results from a certain unity of organization, as if the whole energy of body and mind flowed in one direction. All great force is real and elemental. There is no manufacturing a strong will. There must be a pound to balance a pound. Where power is shown in will, it must rest on the universal force. Alaric[45] and Bonaparte must believe they rest on a truth, or their will can be bought or bent. There is a bribe possible for any finite will. But the pure sympathy with universal ends is an infinite force, and cannot be bribed or bent. Whoever has had experience of the moral sentiment cannot choose but believe in unlimited power. Each pulse from that heart is an oath from the Most High. I know not what the word *sublime* means, if it be not the intimations, in this infant, of a terrific force. A text of heroism, a name and anecdote of courage, are not arguments but sallies of freedom. One of these is the verse of the Persian Hafiz,[46] "'T is written on the gate of Heaven, 'Woe unto him who suffers himself to be betrayed by Fate!' " Does the reading of history make us fatalists? What courage does not the opposite opinion show! A little whim of will to be free gallantly contending against the universe of chemistry.

But insight is not will, nor is affection will. Perception is cold, and goodness dies in wishes. As Voltaire[47] said, 't is the misfortune of worthy people that they are cowards; "un des plus grands malheurs des honnêtes gens c'est qu'ils sont des lâches." There must be a fusion of these two to generate the energy of will. There can be no driving force except through the conversion of the man into his will, making him the will, and the will him. And one may say boldly that no man has a right perception of any truth who has not been reacted on by it so as to be ready to be its martyr.

The one serious and formidable thing in nature is a will. Society is servile from want of will, and therefore the world wants saviours and religions. One way is right to go; the hero sees it, and moves on that aim, and has the world under him for root and support. He is to others as the world. His approbation is honor; his dissent, infamy. The glance of his eye has the force of sunbeams. A personal influence towers up in memory only worthy, and we gladly forget numbers, money, climate, gravitation, and the rest of Fate.

We can afford to allow the limitation, if we know it is the meter of the growing man. We stand against Fate, as children stand up against the wall in their father's house and notch their height from year to year. But when the boy grows to man, and is master of the house, he pulls down that wall and builds a new and bigger. 'T is only a question of time. Every brave youth is in training to ride and rule this dragon. His science is to make weapons and wings of these passions and retarding forces. Now whether, seeing these two things, fate and power, we are permitted to believe in unity? The bulk of mankind believe in two gods. They are under one dominion here in the house, as friend and parent, in social circles, in letters, in art, in love, in religion; but in mechanics, in dealing with steam and climate, in trade, in politics, they think they come under another; and that it would be a practical blunder to transfer the method and way of working of one sphere into the other. What good, honest, generous men at home, will be wolves and foxes on 'Change![48] What pious men in the parlor will vote for what reprobates at the polls! To a certain point, they believe themselves the care of a Providence. But in a steamboat, in an epidemic, in war, they believe a malignant energy rules.

But relation and connection are not somewhere and sometimes, but everywhere and always. The divine order does not stop where their sight stops. The

---

[45]Alaric (370?–410), Visigoth king who conquered Rome in 410.
[46]Fourteenth-century Persian poet.

[47]Voltaire (1694–1778), French writer, satirist, and freethinker.
[48]Stock exchange.

friendly power works on the same rules in the next farm and the next planet. But where they have not experience they run against it and hurt themselves. Fate then is a name for facts not yet passed under the fire of thought; for causes which are unpenetrated.

But every jet of chaos which threatens to exterminate us is convertible by intellect into wholesome force. Fate is unpenetrated causes. The water drowns ship and sailor like a grain of dust. But learn to swim, trim your bark, and the wave which drowned it will be cloven by it and carry it like its own foam, a plume and a power. The cold is inconsiderate of persons, tingles your blood, freezes a man like a dewdrop. But learn to skate, and the ice will give you a graceful, sweet, and poetic motion. The cold will brace your limbs and brain to genius, and make you foremost men of time. Cold and sea will train an imperial Saxon race, which nature cannot bear to lose, and after cooping it up for a thousand years in yonder England, gives a hundred Englands, a hundred Mexicos. All the bloods it shall absorb and domineer: and more than Mexicos, the secrets of water and steam, the spasms of electricity, the ductility of metals, the chariot of the air, the ruddered balloon are awaiting you.

The annual slaughter from typhus far exceeds that of war; but right drainage destroys typhus. The plague in the sea-service from scurvy is healed by lemon juice and other diets portable or procurable; the depopulation by cholera and small-pox is ended by drainage and vaccination; and every other pest is not less in the chain of cause and effect, and may be fought off. And whilst art draws out the venom, it commonly extorts some benefit from the vanquished enemy. The mischievous torrent is taught to drudge for man; the wild beasts he makes useful for food, or dress, or labor; the chemic explosions are controlled like his watch. These are now the steeds on which he rides. Man moves in all modes, by legs of horses, by wings of wind, by steam, by gas of balloon, by electricity, and stands on tiptoe threatening to hunt the eagle in his own element. There's nothing he will not make his carrier.

Steam was till the other day the devil which we dreaded. Every pot made by any human potter or brazier had a hole in its cover, to let off the enemy, lest he should lift pot and roof and carry the house away. But the Marquis of Worcester,[49] Watt, and Fulton bethought themselves that where was power was not devil, but was God; that it must be availed of, and not by any means let off and wasted. Could he lift pots and roofs and houses so handily? He was the workman they were in search of. He could be used to lift away, chain and compel other devils far more reluctant and dangerous, namely, cubic miles of earth, mountains, weight or resistance of water, machinery, and the labors of all men in the world; and time he shall lengthen, and shorten space.

It has not fared much otherwise with higher kinds of steam. The opinion of the million was the terror of the world, and it was attempted either to dissipate it, by amusing nations, or to pile it over with strata of society,—a layer of soldiers, over that a layer of lords, and a king on the top; with clamps and hoops of castles, garrisons, and police. But sometimes the religious principle would get in and burst the hoops and rive every mountain laid on top of it. The Fultons and Watts of politics, believing in unity, saw that it was a power, and by satisfying it (as justice satisfies everybody), through a different disposition of society,—grouping it on a level instead of piling it into a mountain,—they have contrived to make of this terror the most harmless and energetic form of a State.

Very odious, I confess, are the lessons of Fate. Who likes to have a dapper phrenologist pronouncing on his fortunes? Who likes to believe that he has, hid-

---

[49]Edward Somerset, Marquis of Worcester (1601–1667),
English inventor and early experimenter with steam power.

den in his skull, spine, and pelvis, all the vices of a Saxon or Celtic race, which will be sure to pull him down,—with what grandeur of hope and resolve he is fired,—into a selfish, huckstering, servile, dodging animal? A learned physician tells us the fact is invariable with the Neapolitan, that when mature he assumes the forms of the unmistakable scoundrel. That is a little overstated,—but may pass.

But these are magazines[50] and arsenals. A man must thank his defects, and stand in some terror of his talents. A transcendent talent draws so largely on his forces as to lame him; a defect pays him revenues on the other side. The sufferance which is the badge of the Jew, has made him, in these days, the ruler of the rulers of the earth. If Fate is ore and quarry, if evil is good in the making, if limitation is power that shall be, if calamities, oppositions, and weights are wings and means,—we are reconciled.

Fate involves the melioration. No statement of the Universe can have any soundness which does not admit its ascending effort. The direction of the whole and of the parts is toward benefit, and in proportion to the health. Behind every individual closes organization; before him opens liberty,—the Better, the Best. The first and worse races are dead. The second and imperfect races are dying out, or remain for the maturing of higher. In the latest race, in man, every generosity, every new perception, the love and praise he extorts from his fellows, are certificates of advance out of fate into freedom. Liberation of the will from the sheaths and clogs of organization which he has outgrown, is the end and aim of this world. Every calamity is a spur and valuable hint; and where his endeavors do not yet fully avail, they tell as tendency. The whole circle of animal life—tooth against tooth, devouring war, war for food, a yelp of pain and a grunt of triumph, until at last the whole menagerie, the whole chemical mass is mellowed and refined for higher use—pleases at a sufficient perspective.

But to see how fate slides into freedom and freedom into fate, observe how far the roots of every creature run, or find if you can a point where there is no thread of connection. Our life is consentaneous[51] and far-related. This knot of nature is so well tied that nobody was ever cunning enough to find the two ends. Nature is intricate, overlapped, interweaved and endless. Christopher Wren said of the beautiful King's College chapel,[52] that "if anybody would tell him where to lay the first stone, he would build such another." But where shall we find the first atom in this house of man, which is all consent, inosculation and balance of parts?

The web of relation is shown in *habitat,* shown in hibernation. When hibernation was observed, it was found that whilst some animals became torpid in winter, others were torpid in summer: hibernation then was a false name. The *long sleep* is not an effect of cold, but is regulated by the supply of food proper to the animal. It becomes torpid when the fruit or prey it lives on is not in season, and regains its activity when its food is ready.

Eyes are found in light; ears in auricular[53] air; feet on land; fins in water; wings in air; and each creature where it was meant to be, with a mutual fitness. Every zone has its own *Fauna.* There is adjustment between the animal and its food, its parasite, its enemy. Balances are kept. It is not allowed to diminish in numbers, nor to exceed. The like adjustments exist for man. His food is cooked when he arrives; his coal in the pit; the house ventilated; the mud of the deluge dried; his companions arrived at the same hour, and awaiting him with love, concert, laughter and tears. These are coarse adjustments, but the invisible are not

---

[50]Weaponry storehouses.
[51]Suited, consistent.
[52]Part of Cambridge University; Christopher Wren (1632–1723), renowned British architect.
[53]Related to hearing.

less. There are more belongings to every creature than his air and his food. His instincts must be met, and he has predisposing power that bends and fits what is near him to his use. He is not possible until the invisible things are right for him, as well as the visible. Of what changes then in sky and earth, and in finer skies and earths, does the appearance of some Dante or Columbus apprise us!

How is this effected? Nature is no spend-thrift, but takes the shortest way to her ends. As the general says to his soldiers, "If you want a fort, build a fort," so nature makes every creature do its own work and get its living,—is it planet, animal or tree. The planet makes itself. The animal cell makes itself;—then, what it wants. Every creature, wren or dragon, shall make its own lair. As soon as there is life, there is self-direction and absorbing and using of material. Life is freedom,— life in the direct ratio of its amount. You may be sure the new-born man is not inert. Life works both voluntarily and supernaturally in its neighborhood. Do you suppose he can be estimated by his weight in pounds, or that he is contained in his skin,—this reaching, radiating, jaculating[54] fellow? The smallest candle fills a mile with its rays, and the papillæ[55] of a man run out to every star.

When there is something to be done, the world knows how to get it done. The vegetable eye makes leaf, pericarp,[56] root, bark, or thorn, as the need is; the first cell converts itself into stomach, mouth, nose, or nail, according to the want; the world throws its life into a hero or a shepherd, and puts him where he is wanted. Dante and Columbus were Italians, in their time; they would be Russians or Americans to-day. Things ripen, new men come. The adaptation is not capricious. The ulterior aim, the purpose beyond itself, the correlation by which planets subside and crystallize, then animate beasts and men,—will not stop but will work into finer particulars, and from finer to finest.

The secret of the world is the tie between person and event. Person makes event, and event person. The "times," "the age," what is that but a few profound persons and a few active persons who epitomize the times?—Goethe, Hegel, Metternich, Adams, Calhoun, Guizot, Peel, Cobden, Kossuth, Rothschild, Astor, Brunel,[57] and the rest. The same fitness must be presumed between a man and the time and event, as between the sexes, or between a race of animals and the food it eats, or the inferior races it uses. He thinks his fate alien, because the copula is hidden. But the soul contains the event that shall befall it; for the event is only the actualization of its thoughts, and what we pray to ourselves for is always granted. The event is the print of your form. It fits you like your skin. What each does is proper to him. Events are the children of his body and mind. We learn that the soul of Fate is the soul of us, as Hafiz sings,—

> "Alas! till now I had not known,
> My guide and fortune's guide are one."

All the toys that infatuate men and which they play for,—houses, land, money, luxury, power, fame, are the selfsame thing, with a new gauze or two of illusion overlaid. And of all the drums and rattles by which men are made willing to have their heads broke, and are led out solemnly every morning to parade,—the most admirable is this by which we are brought to believe that events are arbitrary and independent of actions. At the conjuror's, we detect the hair by which he moves his puppet, but we have not eyes sharp enough to descry the thread that ties cause and effect.

---

[54]Darting, hurling.
[55]Nipple-like projections.
[56]Wall of ovary of a fruit, holding seed.
[57]All were individuals of eighteenth- and nineteenth-century Europe or America who put their stamp on the age: Goethe, German poet; Hegel, German philosopher; Metternich, Austrian leader; Adams, American president; Calhoun, American political leader; Guizot, French statesman and historian; Peel, British prime minister; Cobden, British political leader and economist; Kossuth, Hungarian patriot; Rothschild, German banker; Astor, American fur trader and financier; Brunel, English civil engineer of international renown (as builder of the Great Western Railway).

Nature magically suits the man to his fortunes, by making these the fruit of his character. Ducks take to the water, eagles to the sky, waders to the sea margin, hunters to the forest, clerks to counting-rooms, soldiers to the frontier. Thus events grow on the same stem with persons; are sub-persons. The pleasure of life is according to the man that lives it, and not according to the work or the place. Life is an ecstasy. We know what madness belongs to love,—what power to paint a vile object in hues of heaven. As insane persons are indifferent to their dress, diet, and other accommodations, and as we do in dreams, with equanimity, the most absurd acts, so a drop more of wine in our cup of life will reconcile us to strange company and work. Each creature puts forth from itself its own condition and sphere, as the slug sweats out its slimy house on the pear-leaf, and the woolly aphides on the apple perspire their own bed, and the fish its shell. In youth we clothe ourselves with rainbows and go as brave as the zodiac. In age we put out another sort of perspiration,—gout, fever, rheumatism, caprice, doubt, fretting and avarice.

A man's fortunes are the fruit of his character. A man's friends are his magnetisms. We go to Herodotus and Plutarch[58] for examples of Fate; but we are examples. "*Quisque suos patimur manes.*"[59] The tendency of every man to enact all that is in his constitution is expressed in the old belief that the efforts which we make to escape from our destiny only serve to lead us into it: and I have noticed a man likes better to be complimented on his position, as the proof of the last or total excellence, than on his merits.

A man will see his character emitted in the events that seem to meet, but which exude from and accompany him. Events expand with the character. As once he found himself among toys, so now he plays a part in colossal systems, and his growth is declared in his ambition, his companions and his performance. He looks like a piece of luck, but is a piece of causation; the mosaic, angulated[60] and ground to fit into the gap he fills. Hence in each town there is some man who is, in his brain and performance, an explanation of the tillage, production, factories, banks, churches, ways of living and society of that town. If you do not chance to meet him, all that you see will leave you a little puzzled; if you see him it will become plain. We know in Massachusetts who built New Bedford, who built Lynn, Lowell, Lawrence, Clinton, Fitchburg, Holyoke, Portland, and many another noisy mart. Each of these men, if they were transparent, would seem to you not so much men as walking cities, and wherever you put them they would build one.

History is the action and reaction of these two,—Nature and Thought; two boys pushing each other on the curbstone of the pavement. Everything is pusher or pushed; and matter and mind are in perpetual tilt and balance, so. Whilst the man is weak, the earth takes up him. He plants his brain and affections. By and by he will take up the earth, and have his gardens and vineyards in the beautiful order and productiveness of his thought. Every solid in the universe is ready to become fluid on the approach of the mind, and the power to flux it is the measure of the mind. If the wall remain adamant, it accuses the want of thought. To a subtle force it will stream into new forms, expressive of the character of the mind. What is the city in which we sit here, but an aggregate of incongruous materials which have obeyed the will of some man? The granite was reluctant, but his hands were stronger, and it came. Iron was deep in the ground and well combined with stone, but could not hide from his fires. Wood, lime, stuffs, fruits, gums, were dispersed over the earth and sea, in vain. Here they are, within reach of every man's day-labor,—what he wants of them. The whole world is the flux of matter over

---

[58]Herodotus (fifth century B.C.), Greek historian; Plutarch (first century A.D.), Greek biographer.
[59]"Each individual suffers his particular penalty" (Latin), from Virgil's *Aeneid*, VI, 743.
[60]Having angles or corners.

the wires of thought to the poles or points where it would build. The races of men rise out of the ground preoccupied with a thought which rules them, and divided into parties ready armed and angry to fight for this metaphysical abstraction. The quality of the thought differences the Egyptian and the Roman, the Austrian and the American. The men who come on the stage at one period are all found to be related to each other. Certain ideas are in the air. We are all impressionable, for we are made of them; all impressionable, but some more than others, and these first express them. This explains the curious contemporaneousness of inventions and discoveries. The truth is in the air, and the most impressionable brain will announce it first, but all will announce it a few minutes later. So women, as most susceptible, are the best index of the coming hour. So the great man, that is, the man most imbued with the spirit of the time, is the impressionable man;—of a fibre irritable and delicate, like iodine to light. He feels the infinitesimal attractions. His mind is righter than others because he yields to a current so feeble as can be felt only by a needle delicately poised.

The correlation is shown in defects. Möller,[61] in his Essay on Architecture, taught that the building which was fitted accurately to answer its end would turn out to be beautiful though beauty had not been intended. I find the like unity in human structures rather virulent and pervasive; that a crudity in the blood will appear in the argument; a hump in the shoulder will appear in the speech and handiwork. If his mind could be seen, the hump would be seen. If a man has a see-saw in his voice, it will run into his sentences, into his poem, into the structure of his fable, into his speculation, into his charity. And as every man is hunted by his own dæmon, vexed by his own disease, this checks all his activity.

So each man, like each plant, has his parasites. A strong, astringent, bilious nature has more truculent enemies than the slugs and moths that fret my leaves. Such an one has curculios, borers, knife-worms; a swindler ate him first, then a client, then a quack, then smooth, plausible gentlemen, bitter and selfish as Moloch.[62]

This correlation really existing can be divined. If the threads are there, thought can follow and show them. Especially when a soul is quick and docile, as Chaucer sings:—

> Or if the soule of proper kind
> Be so parfite as men find,
> That it wot what is to come,
> And that he warneth all and some
> Of everiche of hir aventures,
> By avisions or figures;
> But that our flesh hath no might
> To understand it aright
> For it is warned too derkely.[63]

Some people are made up of rhyme, coincidence, omen, periodicity, and presage: they meet the person they seek; what their companion prepares to say to them, they first say to him; and a hundred signs apprise them of what is about to befall.

Wonderful intricacy in the web, wonderful constancy in the design this vagabond life admits. We wonder how the fly finds its mate, and yet year after year, we find two men, two women, without legal or carnal tie, spend a great part of their best time within a few feet of each other. And the moral is that what we seek we shall find;[64] what we flee from flees from us; as Goethe said, "what we wish for in youth, comes in heaps on us in old age,"[65] too often cursed with the granting of

[61]Georg Moller (1784–1852), German architect, author of *Essay on the Origin and Progress of Gothic Architecture* (1825).
[62]In the Bible, the god of the ancient Phoenicians who demanded the sacrifice of children by burning.
[63]From *The House of Fame*, ll. 43–51.
[64]Matthew 7:7.
[65]From Goethe's *Poetry and Truth* (epigraph, Part II).

our prayer: and hence the high caution, that since we are sure of having what we wish, we beware to ask only for high things.

One key, one solution to the mysteries of human condition, one solution to the old knots of fate, freedom, and foreknowledge, exists; the propounding, namely, of the double consciousness. A man must ride alternately on the horses of his private and his public nature, as the equestrians in the circus throw themselves nimbly from horse to horse, or plant one foot on the back of one and the other foot on the back of the other. So when a man is the victim of his fate, has sciatica in his loins and cramp in his mind; a club-foot and a club in his wit; a sour face and a selfish temper; a strut in his gait and a conceit in his affection; or is ground to powder by the vice of his race;—he is to rally on his relation to the Universe, which his ruin benefits. Leaving the dæmon who suffers, he is to take sides with the Deity who secures universal benefit by his pain.

To offset the drag of temperament and race, which pulls down, learn this lesson, namely, that by the cunning co-presence of two elements, which is throughout nature, whatever lames or paralyzes you draws in with it the divinity, in some form, to repay. A good intention clothes itself with sudden power. When a god wishes to ride, any chip or pebble will bud and shoot out winged feet and serve him for a horse.

Let us build altars to the Blessed Unity which holds nature and souls in perfect solution, and compels every atom to serve an universal end. I do not wonder at a snow-flake, a shell, a summer landscape, or the glory of the stars; but at the necessity of beauty under which the universe lies; that all is and must be pictorial; that the rainbow and the curve of the horizon and the arch of the blue vault are only results from the organism of the eye. There is no need for foolish amateurs to fetch me to admire a garden of flowers, or a sun-gilt cloud, or a waterfall, when I cannot look without seeing splendor and grace. How idle to choose a random sparkle here or there, when the indwelling necessity plants the rose of beauty on the brow of chaos, and discloses the central intention of Nature to be harmony and joy.

Let us build altars to the Beautiful Necessity. If we thought men were free in the sense that in a single exception one fantastical will could prevail over the law of things, it were all one as if a child's hand could pull down the sun. If in the least particular one could derange the order of nature,—who would accept the gift of life?

Let us build altars to the Beautiful Necessity, which secures that all is made of one piece; that plaintiff and defendant, friend and enemy, animal and planet, food and eater are of one kind. In astronomy is vast space but no foreign system; in geology, vast time but the same laws as to-day. Why should we be afraid of Nature, which is no other than "philosophy and theology embodied"? Why should we fear to be crushed by savage elements, we who are made up of the same elements? Let us build to the Beautiful Necessity, which makes man brave in believing that he cannot shun a danger that is appointed, nor incur one that is not; to the Necessity which rudely or softly educates him to the perception that there are no contingencies; that Law rules throughout existence; a Law which is not intelligent but intelligence;—not personal nor impersonal—it disdains words and passes understanding; it dissolves persons; it vivifies nature; yet solicits the pure in heart to draw on all its omnipotence.

1851   *1860*

from **Poems**

Concord Hymn[1]

SUNG AT THE COMPLETION OF THE BATTLE MONUMENT, JULY 4, 1837

By the rude bridge that arched the flood,
    Their flag to April's breeze unfurled,
Here once the embattled farmers stood
    And fired the shot heard round the world.

The foe long since in silence slept;   5
    Alike the conqueror silent sleeps;
And Time the ruined bridge has swept
    Down the dark stream which seaward creeps.

On this green bank, by this soft stream,
    We set to-day a votive stone;   10
That memory may their deed redeem,
    When, like our sires, our sons are gone.

Spirit, that made those heroes dare
    To die, and leave their children free,
Bid Time and Nature gently spare   15
    The shaft we raise to them and thee.

                                                            1837

The Rhodora:[1]

ON BEING ASKED, WHENCE IS THE FLOWER?

In May, when sea-winds pierced our solitudes,
I found the fresh Rhodora in the woods,
Spreading its leafless blooms in a damp nook,
To please the desert and the sluggish brook.
The purple petals, fallen in the pool,   5
Made the black water with their beauty gay;
Here might the red-bird come his plumes to cool,
And court the flower that cheapens his array.
Rhodora! if the sages ask thee why
This charm is wasted on the earth and sky,   10
Tell them, dear, that if eyes were made for seeing,
Then Beauty is its own excuse for being:
Why thou wert there, O rival of the rose!
I never thought to ask, I never knew:
But, in my simple ignorance, suppose   15
The self-same Power that brought me there brought you.

1834   *1839*

---

[1]This poem was distributed on leaflets at the dedication of the monument in honor of the Minute Men who fought the British Redcoats at Lexington and Concord in 1775 in the opening battle of the American Revolution.

[1]A shrub with delicate pink flowers found in New England and Canada.

The Humble-Bee[1]

Burly, dozing humble-bee,
Where thou art is clime for me.
Let them sail for Porto Rique,[2]
Far-off heats through seas to seek;
I will follow thee alone,   5
Thou animated torrid-zone!
Zigzag steerer, desert cheerer,
Let me chase thy waving lines;
Keep me nearer, me thy hearer,
Singing over shrubs and vines.   10

Insect lover of the sun,
Joy of thy dominion!
Sailor of the atmosphere;
Swimmer through the waves of air;
Voyager of light and noon;   15
Epicurean of June;
Wait, I prithee, till I come
Within earshot of thy hum,—
All without is martyrdom.

When the south wind, in May days,   20
With a net of shining haze
Silvers the horizon wall,
And with softness touching all,
Tints the human countenance
With a color of romance,   25
And infusing subtle heats,
Turns the sod to violets,
Thou, in sunny solitudes,
Rover of the underwoods,
The green silence dost displace   30
With thy mellow, breezy bass.

Hot midsummer's petted crone,
Sweet to me thy drowsy tone
Tells of countless sunny hours,
Long days, and solid banks of flowers;   35
Of gulfs of sweetness without bound
In Indian wildernesses found;
Of Syrian peace, immortal leisure,
Firmest cheer, and bird-like pleasure.

Aught unsavory or unclean   40
Hath my insect never seen;
But violets and bilberry bells,
Maple-sap and daffodels,
Grass with green flag half-mast high,
Succory to match the sky,   45
Columbine with horn of honey,

---

[1]On May 9, 1837, Emerson wrote in his *Journal:* "Yesterday in the woods I followed the fine humble-bee with rhymes and fancies fine. . . . The humble-bee and pine-warbler seem to me the proper objects of attention in these disas- trous times." There was a depression and financial panic in America in 1837.
[2]Puerto Rico.

Scented fern, and agrimony,
Clover, catchfly, adder's-tongue
And brier-roses, dwelt among;
All beside was unknown waste,   50
All was picture as he passed.

Wiser far than human seer,
Yellow-breeched philosopher!
Seeing only what is fair,
Sipping only what is sweet,   55
Thou dost mock at fate and care,
Leave the chaff, and take the wheat.
When the fierce northwestern blast
Cools sea and land so far and fast,
Thou already slumberest deep;   60
Woe and want thou canst outsleep;
Want and woe, which torture us,
Thy sleep makes ridiculous.

1837   *1839*

Each and All

Little thinks, in the field, yon red-cloaked clown[1]
Of thee from the hill-top looking down;
The heifer that lows in the upland farm,
Far-heard, lows not thine ear to charm;
The sexton, tolling his bell at noon,   5
Deems not that great Napoleon
Stops his horse, and lists with delight,
Whilst his files sweep round yon Alpine height;
Nor knowest thou what argument
Thy life to thy neighbor's creed has lent.   10
All are needed by each one;
Nothing is fair or good alone.
I thought the sparrow's note from heaven,
Singing at dawn on the alder bough;
I brought him home, in his nest, at even;   15
He sings the song, but it cheers not now,
For I did not bring home the river and sky;—
He sang to my ear,—they sang to my eye.
The delicate shells lay on the shore;
The bubbles of the latest wave   20
Fresh pearls to their enamel gave,
And the bellowing of the savage sea
Greeted their safe escape to me.
I wiped away the weeds and foam,
I fetched my sea-born treasures home;   25
But the poor, unsightly, noisome things
Had left their beauty on the shore
With the sun and the sand and the wild uproar.

---

[1]Peasant.

The lover watched his graceful maid,
As 'mid the virgin train she strayed,   30
Nor knew her beauty's best attire
Was woven still by the snow-white choir.
At last she came to his hermitage,
Like the bird from the woodlands to the cage;—
The gay enchantment was undone,   35
A gentle wife, but fairy none.
Then I said, 'I covet truth;
Beauty is unripe childhood's cheat;
I leave it behind with the games of youth:'—
As I spoke, beneath my feet   40
The ground-pine curled its pretty wreath,
Running over the club-moss² burrs;
I inhaled the violet's breath;
Around me stood the oaks and firs;
Pine-cones and acorns lay on the ground;   45
Over me soared the eternal sky,
Full of light and of deity;
Again I saw, again I heard,
The rolling river, the morning bird;—
Beauty through my senses stole;   50
I yielded myself to the perfect whole.

1839

The Problem

I like a church; I like a cowl;
I love a prophet of the soul;
And on my heart monastic aisles
Fall like sweet strains, or pensive smiles;
Yet not for all his faith can see   5
Would I that cowled churchman be.

Why should the vest¹ on him allure,
Which I could not on me endure?

Not from a vain or shallow thought
His awful Jove young Phidias² brought;   10
Never from lips of cunning fell
The thrilling Delphic oracle;³
Out from the heart of nature rolled
The burdens of the Bible old;
The litanies of nations came,   15
Like the volcano's tongue of flame,
Up from the burning core below,—
The canticles of love and woe:
The hand that rounded Peter's dome

²Evergreen vines that creep along the ground.
¹Vestment, churchman's robes.
²The greatest sculptor of classical Greece (fl. fifth century B.C.). His masterpiece was the *Zeus* (Jove) *of Olympia*.

³In the temple of Apollo at Delphi, Greece, the priestesses gave out prophecies, often in puzzling symbolism.

And groined the aisles of Christian Rome   20
Wrought in a sad sincerity;[4]
Himself from God he could not free;
He builded better than he knew;—
The conscious stone to beauty grew.

Know'st thou what wove yon woodbird's nest   25
Of leaves, and feathers from her breast?
Or how the fish outbuilt her shell,
Painting with morn each annual cell?
Or how the sacred pine-tree adds
To her old leaves new myriads?   30
Such and so grew these holy piles,
Whilst love and terror laid the tiles.
Earth proudly wears the Parthenon,[5]
As the best gem upon her zone,
And Morning opes with haste her lids   35
To gaze upon the Pyramids;
O'er England's abbeys bends the sky,
As on its friends, with kindred eye;
For out of Thought's interior sphere
These wonders rose to upper air;   40
And Nature gladly gave them place,
Adopted them into her race,
And granted them an equal date
With Andes and with Ararat.[6]

These temples grew as grows the grass;   45
Art might obey, but not surpass.
The passive Master lent his hand
To the vast soul that o'er him planned;
And the same power that reared the shrine
Bestrode the tribes that knelt within.   50
Ever the fiery Pentecost[7]
Girds with one flame the countless host,
Trances the heart through chanting choirs,
And through the priest the mind inspires.
The word unto the prophet spoken   55
Was writ on tables yet unbroken;[8]
The word by seers or sibyls told,
In groves of oak, or fanes[9] of gold,
Still floats upon the morning wind,
Still whispers to the willing mind.   60
One accent of the Holy Ghost
The heedless world hath never lost.
I know what say the fathers wise,—
The Book itself before me lies,

---

[4]Michelangelo (1475–1564), Italian architect and sculptor who designed the dome of St. Peter's, the largest church in Christendom.
[5]Temple of Athena on the Acropolis of Athens (fifth century B.C.).
[6]Mountain in Asia Minor where Noah's Ark ended its voyage (Genesis 8:4).
[7]Fifty days after the Crucifixion, the Holy Spirit bestowed on the Apostles in "cloven tongues like as a fire" the ability to speak in unknown tongues to affirm the Resurrection to all (Acts 2).
[8]Exodus 32:1–19: When Moses came upon the Israelites worshipping the golden calf, he "cast the tables [of the Ten Commandments] out of his hands, and brake them beneath the mount." God later replaced the tables.
[9]Temples.

Old *Chrysostom*, best Augustine,[10]   65
And he who blent both in his line,
The younger *Golden Lips* or mines,
Taylor,[11] the Shakspeare of divines.
His words are music in my ear,
I see his cowlèd portrait dear;   70
And yet, for all his faith could see,
I would not the good bishop be.

1839   *1840*

The Sphinx[1]

The Sphinx is drowsy,
    Her wings are furled:
Her ear is heavy,
    She broods on the world.
"Who'll tell me my secret,   5
    The ages have kept?—
I awaited the seer
    While they slumbered and slept:—

"The fate of the man-child,
    The meaning of man;   10
Known fruit of the unknown;
    Dædalian[2] plan;
Out of sleeping a waking,
    Out of waking a sleep;
Life death overtaking;   15
    Deep underneath deep?

"Erect as a sunbeam,
    Upspringeth the palm;
The elephant browses,
    Undaunted and calm;   20
In beautiful motion
    The thrush plies his wings;
Kind leaves of his covert,
    Your silence he sings.

"The waves, unashamèd,   25
    In difference sweet,
Play glad with the breezes,

---

[10]St. John Chrysostom (345?–407), "golden mouthed," a father of the Greek church, Patriarch of Constantinople; St. Augustine (354–430), a church father and preeminent religious thinker, author of *Confessions* and *The City of God*.
[11]Jeremy Taylor (1613–1667), British clergyman and writer, author of *Holy Living* (1650) and *Holy Dying* (1651).
[1]In Greek mythology, a monster with the face of a woman, body of a lion, and wings of a bird, who propounded riddles, devouring those who could not answer. In 1859 Emerson wrote in his *Journal:* "I have often been asked the meaning of the 'Sphinx.' It is this,—The perception of

identity unites all things and explains one by another, and the most rare and strange is equally facile as the most common. But if the mind live only in particulars, and see only differences (wanting the power to see the whole—all in each), then the world addresses to this mind a question it cannot answer, and each new fact tears it to pieces, and it is vanquished by the distracting variety." For Henry David Thoreau's detailed analysis of the poem, see the entry in his *Journal* for March 7–10, 1841.
[2]From Daedalus, legendary creator of the Cretan labyrinth, and thus: puzzling, complicated.

Old playfellows meet;
The journeying atoms,
  Primordial wholes,   30
Firmly draw, firmly drive,
  By their animate poles.

"Sea, earth, air, sound, silence,
  Plant, quadruped, bird,
By one music enchanted,   35
  One deity stirred,—
Each the other adorning,
  Accompany still;
Night veileth the morning,
  The vapor the hill.   40

"The babe by its mother
  Lies bathèd in joy;
Glide its hours uncounted,—
  The sun is its toy;
Shines the peace of all being,   45
  Without cloud, in its eyes;
And the sum of the world
  In soft miniature lies.

"But man crouches and blushes,
  Absconds and conceals;   50
He creepeth and peepeth,
  He palters and steals;
Infirm, melancholy,
  Jealous glancing around,
An oaf, an accomplice,   55
  He poisons the ground.

"Out spoke the great mother,
  Beholding his fear;—
At the sound of her accents
  Cold shuddered the sphere:—   60
'Who has drugged my boy's cup?
  Who has mixed my boy's bread?
Who, with sadness and madness,
  Has turned my child's head?' "

I heard a poet answer   65
  Aloud and cheerfully,
"Say on, sweet Sphinx! thy dirges
  Are pleasant songs to me.
Deep love lieth under
  These pictures of time;   70
They fade in the light of
  Their meaning sublime.
"The fiend that man harries
  Is love of the Best;
Yawns the pit of the Dragon,[3]   75
  Lit by rays from the Blest.[4]

---

[3]Revelation 17:8; 19:20; 20:1–3.
[4]See Revelation 21.

The Lethe of Nature
  Can't trance him again,
Whose soul sees the perfect,
  Which his eyes seek in vain.   80

"To vision profounder,
  Man's spirit must dive;
His aye-rolling[5] orb
  At no goal will arrive;
The heavens that now draw him   85
  With sweetness untold,
Once found,—for new heavens
  He spurneth the old.

"Pride ruined the angels,
  Their shame them restores;   90
Lurks the joy that is sweetest
  In stings of remorse.
Have I a lover
  Who is noble and free?—
I would he were nobler   95
  Than to love me.

"Eterne alternation
  Now follows, now flies;
And under pain, pleasure,—
  Under pleasure, pain lies.   100
Love works at the centre,
  Heart-heaving alway;
Forth speed the strong pulses
  To the borders of day.

"Dull Sphinx, Jove keep thy five wits;   105
  Thy sight is growing blear;
Rue, myrrh and cummin[6] for the Sphinx,
  Her muddy eyes to clear!"
The old Sphinx bit her thick lip,—
  Said, "Who taught thee me to name?   110
I am thy spirit, yoke-fellow;
  Of thine eye I am eyebeam.

"Thou art the unanswered question;
  Couldst see thy proper eye,
Alway it asketh, asketh;   115
  And each answer is a lie.
So take thy quest through nature,
  It through thousand natures ply;
Ask on, thou clothed eternity;
  Time is the false reply."   120

Uprose the merry Sphinx,
  And crouched no more in stone;
She melted into purple cloud,
  She silvered in the moon;

---

[5]I.e., ever-rolling.
[6]Medicinal herbs.

She spired into a yellow flame;   125
   She flowered in blossoms red;
She flowed into a foaming wave:
   She stood Monadnoc's[7] head.

Thorough a thousand voices
   Spoke the universal dame;   130
"Who telleth one of my meanings
   Is master of all I am."

1841

The Snow-Storm

Announced by all the trumpets of the sky,
Arrives the snow, and, driving o'er the fields,
Seems nowhere to alight: the whited air
Hides hills and woods, the river, and the heaven,
And veils the farm-house at the garden's end.   5
The sled and traveller stopped, the courier's feet
Delayed, all friends shut out, the housemates sit
Around the radiant fireplace, enclosed
In a tumultuous privacy of storm.

   Come see the north wind's masonry.   10
Out of an unseen quarry evermore
Furnished with tile, the fierce artificer
Curves his white bastions with projected roof
Round every windward stake, or tree, or door.
Speeding, the myriad-handed, his wild work   15
So fanciful, so savage, nought cares he
For number or proportion. Mockingly,
On coop or kennel he hangs Parian[1] wreaths;
A swan-like form invests the hidden thorn;
Fills up the farmer's lane from wall to wall,   20
Maugre[2] the farmer's sighs; and at the gate
A tapering turret overtops the work.
And when his hours are numbered, and the world
Is all his own, retiring, as he were not,
Leaves, when the sun appears, astonished Art   25
To mimic in slow structures, stone by stone,
Built in an age, the mad wind's night-work,
The frolic architecture of the snow.

1835   *1841*

---

[7]New Hampshire mountain.
[1]I.e., like white marble from the Aegean island Paros, used
by Greek sculptors.
[2]In spite of.

Uriel[1]

It fell in the ancient periods
   Which the brooding soul surveys,
Or ever the wild Time coined itself
   Into calendar months and days.

This was the lapse of Uriel,   5
Which in Paradise befell.
Once, among the Pleiads[2] walking,
Seyd[3] overheard the young gods talking;
And the treason, too long pent,
To his ears was evident.   10
The young deities discussed
Laws of form, and metre just,
Orb, quintessence, and sunbeams,
What subsisteth, and what seems.
One, with low tones that decide,   15
And doubt and reverend use defied,
With a look that solved the sphere,
And stirred the devils everywhere,
Gave his sentiment divine
Against the being of a line.   20
'Line in nature is not found;
Unit and universe are round;
In vain produced, all rays return;
Evil will bless, and ice will burn.'
As Uriel spoke with piercing eye,   25
A shudder ran around the sky;
The stern old war-gods shook their heads,
The seraphs frowned from myrtle-beds;
Seemed to the holy festival
The rash word boded ill to all;   30
The balance-beam of Fate was bent;
The bounds of good and ill were rent;
Strong Hades[4] could not keep his own,
But all slid to confusion.

A sad self-knowledge, withering, fell   35
On the beauty of Uriel;
In heaven once eminent, the god
Withdrew, that hour, into his cloud;
Whether doomed to long gyration
In the sea of generation,   40
Or by knowledge grown too bright
To hit the nerve of feebler sight.
Straightway, a forgetting wind
Stole over the celestial kind,
And their lips the secret kept,   45
If in ashes the fire-seed slept.
But now and then, truth-speaking things

---

[1]Uriel was the bright archangel of the sun in Milton's *Paradise Lost* (1667) (see III, ll. 648–53).
[2]The Pleiades were the seven daughters of Atlas and Pleione, placed by Zeus among the stars in the constellation of Taurus.
[3]Variant of Saadi, thirteenth-century Persian poet whom Emerson considered the archetypal poet or bard.
[4]Prince of the underworld in classical mythology.

Shamed the angels' veiling wings;
And, shrilling from the solar course,
Or from fruit of chemic force,   50
Procession of a soul in matter,
Or the speeding change of water,
Or out of the good of evil born,
Came Uriel's voice of cherub scorn,
And a blush tinged the upper sky,   55
And the gods shook, they knew not why.

1847

Hamatreya[1]

Bulkeley, Hunt, Willard, Hosmer, Meriam, Flint,[2]
Possessed the land which rendered to their toil
Hay, corn, roots, hemp, flax, apples, wool and wood.
Each of these landlords walked amidst his farm,
Saying, "'Tis mine, my children's and my name's.   5
How sweet the west wind sounds in my own trees!
How graceful climb those shadows on my hill!
I fancy these pure waters and the flags[3]
Know me, as does my dog: we sympathize;
And, I affirm, my actions smack of the soil.'   10

Where are these men? Asleep beneath their grounds:
And strangers, fond[4] as they, their furrows plough.
Earth laughs in flowers, to see her boastful boys
Earth-proud, proud of the earth which is not theirs;
Who steer the plough, but cannot steer their feet   15
Clear of the grave.
They added ridge to valley, brook to pond,
And sighed for all that bounded their domain;
'This suits me for a pasture; that's my park;
We must have clay, lime, gravel, granite-ledge,   20
And misty lowland, where to go for peat.
The land is well,—lies fairly to the south.
'T is good, when you have crossed the sea and back,
To find the sitfast acres where you left them.'
Ah! the hot owner sees not Death, who adds   25
Him to his land, a lump of mould the more.
Hear what the Earth says:—

EARTH-SONG

'Mine and yours;
Mine, not yours.
Earth endures;   30
Stars abide—

---

[1] Emerson copied into his *Journal* in 1845 this passage from *Vishnu Purana*, sacred book of the Hindus: "These and other kings who with perishable frames have possessed this ever-luring world, and who . . . have indulged the feeling that suggests 'This earth is mine,—it is my son's . . .' have all passed away . . . Earth laughs. . . . I will repeat to you, Maitreya, the stanzas that were chanted by Earth. . . ." Hamatreya appears to be a variant of Maitreya, the Hindu god, or could derive from the Greek for "Earth-Mother."
[2] Early landowners in Concord, Massachusetts.
[3] Sweet flag, or calamus, a marsh plant.
[4] Foolish.

Shine down in the old sea;
Old are the shores;
But where are old men?
I who have seen much,
Such have I never seen.   35

'The lawyer's deed
Ran sure,
In tail,[5]
To them, and to their heirs   40
Who shall succeed,
Without fail,
Forevermore.

'Here is the land,
Shaggy with wood,   45
With its old valley,
Mound and flood.
But the heritors?—
Fled like the flood's foam.
The lawyer, and the laws,   50
And the kingdom,
Clean swept herefrom.

'They called me theirs,
Who so controlled me;
Yet every one   55
Wished to stay, and is gone,
How am I theirs,
If they cannot hold me,
But I hold them?'

When I heard the Earth-song   60
I was no longer brave;
My avarice cooled
Like lust in the chill of the grave.

1847

Give All to Love

Give all to love;
Obey thy heart;
Friends, kindred, days,
Estate, good-fame,
Plans, credit and the Muse,—   5
Nothing refuse.

'T is a brave master;
Let it have scope:
Follow it utterly,
Hope beyond hope: 10

---

[5]Inherited in perpetuity by succeeding, specified descendents (as eldest sons).

High and more high
It dives into noon,
With wing unspent,
Untold intent;
But it is a god,   15
Knows its own path
And the outlets of the sky.

It was never for the mean;
It requireth courage stout.
Souls above doubt,   20
Valor unbending,
It will reward,—
They shall return
More than they were,
And ever ascending.   25

Leave all for love;
Yet, hear me, yet,
One word more thy heart behoved,
One pulse more of firm endeavor,—
Keep thee to-day,   30
To-morrow, forever,
Free as an Arab
Of thy beloved.

Cling with life to the maid;
But when the surprise,   35
First vague shadow of surmise
Flits across her bosom young,
Of a joy apart from thee,
Free be she, fancy-free;
Nor thou detain her vesture's hem,   40
Nor the palest rose she flung
From her summer diadem.

Though thou loved her as thyself,
As a self of purer clay,
Though her parting dims the day,   45
Stealing grace from all alive;
Heartily know,
When half-gods go,
The gods arrive.

1847

Merlin[1]

I

Thy trivial harp will never please
Or fill my craving ear;

---

[1]The archetypal bard, free and liberating; not the magician
in the legends of King Arthur.

Its chords should ring as blows the breeze,
Free, peremptory, clear.
No jingling serenader's art,   5
Nor tinkle of piano strings,
Can make the wild blood start
In its mystic springs.
The kingly bard
Must smite the chords rudely and hard,   10
As with hammer or with mace;
That they may render back
Artful thunder, which conveys
Secrets of the solar track,
Sparks of the supersolar blaze.   15
Merlin's blows are strokes of fate,
Chiming with the forest tone,
When boughs buffet boughs in the wood;
Chiming with the gasp and moan
Of the ice-imprisoned flood;   20
With the pulse of manly hearts;
With the voice of orators;
With the din of city arts;
With the cannonade of wars;
With the marches of the brave;   25
And prayers of might from martyrs' cave.

Great is the art,
Great be the manners, of the bard.
He shall not his brain encumber
With the coil of rhythm and number;   30
But, leaving rule and pale forethought,
He shall aye² climb
For his rhyme.
"Pass in, pass in," the angels say,
"In to the upper doors,   35
Nor count compartments of the floors,
But mount to paradise
By the stairway of surprise."

Blameless master of the games,
King of sport that never shames,   40
He shall daily joy dispense
Hid in song's sweet influence.
Forms more cheerly live and go,
What time the subtle mind
Sings aloud the tune whereto   45
Their pulses beat,
And march their feet,
And their members are combined.

By Sybarites³ beguiled,
He shall no task decline;   50
Merlin's mighty line
Extremes of nature reconciled,—
Bereaved a tyrant of his will,

---

²Always.
³Those who indulge themselves in the pleasure of the
senses, deriving from Sybaris, the luxury-loving Greek city
in Italy.

And made the lion mild.
Songs can the tempest still,   55
Scattered on the stormy air,
Mould the year to fair increase,
And bring in poetic peace.

He shall not seek to weave,
In weak, unhappy times,   60
Efficacious rhymes;
Wait his returning strength.
Bird that from the nadir's floor
To the zenith's top can soar,—
The soaring orbit of the muse exceeds that
          journey's length.   65
Nor profane affect to hit
Or compass that, by meddling wit,
Which only the propitious mind
Publishes when 't is inclined.
There are open hours   70
When the God's will sallies free,
And the dull idiot might see
The flowing fortunes of a thousand years;—
Sudden, at unawares,
Self-moved, fly-to the doors,   75
Nor sword of angels could reveal
What they conceal.

II

The rhyme of the poet
Modulates the king's affairs;
Balance-loving Nature   80
Made all things in pairs.
To every foot its antipode;
Each color with its counter glowed;
To every tone beat answering tones,
Higher or graver;   85
Flavor gladly blends with flavor;
Leaf answers leaf upon the bough;
And match the paired cotyledons.[4]
Hands to hands, and feet to feet,
In one body grooms and brides;   90
Eldest rite, two married sides
In every mortal meet.
Light's far furnace shines,
Smelting balls and bars,
Forging double stars,   95
Glittering twins and trines.[5]
The animals are sick with love,
Lovesick with rhyme;
Each with all propitious Time
Into chorus wove.   100

---

[4]Earliest leaves.
[5]Triads.

Like the dancers' ordered band,
Thoughts come also hand in hand,
In equal couples mated,
Or else alternated;
Adding by their mutual gage,   105
One to other, health and age.
Solitary fancies go
Short-lived wandering to and fro,
Most like to bachelors,
Or an ungiven maid,   110
Not ancestors,
With no posterity to make the lie afraid,
Or keep truth undecayed.
Perfect-paired as eagle's wings,
Justice is the rhyme of things;   115
Trade and counting use
The self-same tuneful muse;
And Nemesis,[6]
Who with even matches odd,
Who athwart space redresses   120
The partial wrong,
Fills the just period,
And finishes the song.

Subtle rhymes, with ruin rife,
Murmur in the house of life,   125
Sung by the Sisters[7] as they spin;
In perfect time and measure they
Build and unbuild our echoing clay.
As the two twilights of the day
Fold us music-drunken in.   130

1846   1847

Bacchus[1]

Bring me wine, but wine which never grew
In the belly of the grape,
Or grew on vine whose tap-roots, reaching through
Under the Andes to the Cape,
Suffer no savor of the earth to scape.   5

Let its grapes the morn salute
From a nocturnal root,
Which feels the acrid juice
Of Styx and Erebus;[2]
And turns the woe of Night,   10
By its own craft, to a more rich delight.

---

[6]Goddess of just punishment.
[7]The three Fates in Greek mythology.
[1]Bacchus is the Greek god of wine. In his own copy of *Poems*, Emerson wrote an epigraph to "Bacchus" taken from Plato: "The man who is his own master knocks in vain at the doors of poetry."

[2]In Greek myth, the Styx was an underworld river; Erebus, an area of darkness in the underworld through which the dead passed to enter Hades.

We buy ashes for bread;
We buy diluted wine;
Give me of the true,—
Whose ample leaves and tendrils curled   15
Among the silver hills of heaven
Draw everlasting dew;
Wine of wine,
Blood of the world,
Form of forms, and mould of statures,   20
That I intoxicated,
And by the draught assimilated,
May float at pleasure through all natures;
The bird-language rightly spell,
And that which roses say so well.   25

Wine that is shed
Like the torrents of the sun
Up the horizon walls,
Or like the Atlantic streams, which run
When the South Sea calls.   30

Water and bread,
Food which needs no transmuting,
Rainbow-flowering, wisdom-fruiting,
Wine which is already man,
Food which teach and reason can.   35

Wine which Music is,—
Music and wine are one,—
That I, drinking this,
Shall hear far Chaos[3] talk with me;
Kings unborn shall walk with me;   40
And the poor grass shall plot and plan
What it will do when it is man.
Quickened so, will I unlock
Every crypt of every rock.

I thank the joyful juice   45
For all I know;—
Winds of remembering
Of the ancient being blow,
And seeming-solid walls of use
Open and flow.   50

Pour, Bacchus! the remembering wine;
Retrieve the loss of me and mine!
Vine for vine be antidote,
And the grape requite the lote![4]
Haste to cure the old despair,—   55
Reason[5] in Nature's lotus drenched,
The memory of ages quenched;
Give them again to shine;

---

[3]Primordial, unformed matter.
[4]Variant of lotus. In Homeric legend the lotus eaters forgot
the past and lived only for the pleasures of the present.
[5]Reason as the faculty of intuitive insight, not of logic.

Let wine repair what this undid;
And where the infection slid,   60
A dazzling memory revive;
Refresh the faded tints,
Recut the aged prints,
And write my old adventures with the pen
Which on the first day drew,   65
Upon the tablets blue,
The dancing Pleiads[6] and eternal men.

1846   *1847*

Threnody[1]

The South-wind brings
Life, sunshine and desire,
And on every mount and meadow
Breathes aromatic fire;
But over the dead he has no power,   5
The lost, the lost, he cannot restore;
And, looking over the hills, I mourn
The darling who shall not return.

I see my empty house,
I see my trees repair their boughs;   10
And he, the wondrous child,
Whose silver warble wild
Outvalued every pulsing sound
Within the air's cerulean[2] round,—
The hyacinthine boy,[3] for whom   15
Morn well might break and April bloom,
The gracious boy, who did adorn
The world whereinto he was born,
And by his countenance repay
The favor of the loving Day,—   20
Has disappeared from the Day's eye;
Far and wide she cannot find him;
My hopes pursue, they cannot bind him.
Returned this day, the South-wind searches,
And finds young pines and budding birches;   25
But finds not the budding man;
Nature, who lost, cannot remake him;
Fate let him fall, Fate can't retake him;
Nature, Fate, men, him seek in vain.

And whither now, my truant wise and sweet,   30
O, whither tend thy feet?

---

[6]The Pleiades were the seven daughters of Atlas and Pleione, placed by Zeus among the stars in the constellation Taurus.
[1]A funeral song. Emerson began this poem soon after his five-year-old son Waldo died in 1842. For Emerson's comments on death and on Waldo's death, see selections from the *Journal* under [Death].

[2]Sky-blue.
[3]Hyacinthus was the beautiful youth loved and accidentally killed by Apollo; the remorseful god created out of his blood a flower, whose return each spring recalls his fate.

I had the right, few days ago,
Thy steps to watch, thy place to know:
How have I forfeited the right?
Hast thou forgot me in a new delight?   35
I hearken for thy household cheer,
O eloquent child!
Whose voice, an equal messenger,
Conveyed thy meaning mild.
What though the pains and joys   40
Whereof it spoke were toys
Fitting his age and ken,
Yet fairest dames and bearded men,
Who heard the sweet request,
So gentle, wise and grave,   45
Bended with joy to his behest
And let the world's affairs go by,
A while to share his cordial game,
Or mend his wicker wagon-frame,
Still plotting how their hungry ear   50
That winsome voice again might hear;
For his lips could well pronounce
Words that were persuasions.

Gentlest guardians marked serene
His early hope, his liberal mien;   55
Took counsel from his guiding eyes
To make this wisdom earthly wise.
Ah, vainly do these eyes recall
The school-march, each day's festival,
When every morn my bosom glowed   60
To watch the convoy on the road;
The babe in willow wagon closed,
With rolling eyes and face composed;
With children forward and behind,
Like Cupids studiously inclined;   65
And he the chieftain paced beside,
The centre of the troop allied,
With sunny face of sweet repose,
To guard the babe from fancied foes.
The little captain innocent   70
Took the eye with him as he went;
Each village senior paused to scan
And speak the lovely caravan.
From the window I look out
To mark thy beautiful parade,   75
Stately marching in cap and coat
To some tune by fairies played;—
A music heard by thee alone
To works as noble led thee on.

Now Love and Pride, alas! in vain,   80
Up and down their glances strain.
The painted sled stands where it stood;
The kennel by the corded wood;
His gathered sticks to stanch the wall
Of the snow-tower, when snow should fall;   85
The ominous hole he dug in the sand,

And childhood's castles built or planned;
His daily haunts I well discern,—
The poultry-yard, the shed, the barn,—
And every inch of garden ground   90
Paced by the blessed feet around,
From the roadside to the brook
Whereinto he loved to look.
Step the meek fowls where erst they ranged;
The wintry garden lies unchanged;   95
The brook into the stream runs on;
But the deep-eyed boy is gone.

On that shaded day,
Dark with more clouds than tempests are,
When thou didst yield thy innocent breath   100
In birdlike heavings unto death,
Night came, and Nature had not thee;
I said, 'We are mates in misery.'
The morrow dawned with needless glow;
Each snowbird chirped, each fowl must crow;   105
Each tramper started; but the feet
Of the most beautiful and sweet
Of human youth had left the hill
And garden,—they were bound and still.
There's not a sparrow or a wren,   110
There's not a blade of autumn grain,
Which the four seasons do not tend
And tides of life and increase lend;
And every chick of every bird,
And weed and rock-moss is preferred.   115
O ostrich-like forgetfulness!
O loss of larger in the less!
Was there no star that could be sent,
No watcher in the firmament,
No angel from the countless host   120
That loiters round the crystal coast,
Could stoop to heal that only child,
Nature's sweet marvel undefiled,
And keep the blossom of the earth,
Which all her harvests were not worth?   125
Not mine,—I never called thee mine,
But Nature's heir,—if I repine,
And seeing rashly torn and moved
Not what I made, but what I loved,
Grow early old with grief that thou   130
Must to the wastes of Nature go,—
'T is because a general hope
Was quenched, and all must doubt and grope.
For flattering planets seemed to say
This child should ills of ages stay,   135
By wondrous tongue, and guided pen,
Bring the flown Muses back to men.
Perchance not he but Nature ailed,
The world and not the infant failed.
It was not ripe yet to sustain   140
A genius of so fine a strain,
Who gazed upon the sun and moon

As if he came unto his own,
And, pregnant with his grander thought,
Brought the old order into doubt.   145
His beauty once their beauty tried;
They could not feed him, and he died,
And wandered backward as in scorn,
To wait an æon to be born.
Ill day which made this beauty waste,   150
Plight broken, this high face defaced!
Some went and came about the dead;
And some in books of solace read;
Some to their friends the tidings say;
Some went to write, some went to pray;   155
One tarried here, there hurried one;
But their heart abode with none.
Covetous death bereaved us all,
To aggrandize one funeral.
The eager fate which carried thee   160
Took the largest part of me:
For this losing is true dying;
This is lordly man's down-lying,
This his slow but sure reclining,
Star by star his world resigning.   165

O child of paradise,
Boy who made dear his father's home,
In whose deep eyes
Men read the welfare of the times to come,
I am too much bereft.   170
The world dishonored thou hast left.
O truth's and nature's costly lie!
O trusted broken prophecy!
O richest fortune sourly crossed!
Born for the future, to the future lost!   175

The deep Heart answered, 'Weepest thou?
Worthier cause for passion wild
If I had not taken the child.
And deemest thou as those who pore,
With aged eyes, short way before,—   180
Think'st Beauty vanished from the coast
Of matter, and thy darling lost?
Taught he not thee—the man of eld,
Whose eyes within his eyes beheld
Heaven's numerous hierarchy span   185
The mystic gulf from God to man?
To be alone wilt thou begin
When worlds of lovers hem thee in?
To-morrow, when the masks shall fall
That dizen[4] Nature's carnival,   190
The pure shall see by their own will,
Which overflowing Love shall fill,
'T is not within the force of fate
The fate-conjoined to separate.

---

[4]Decorate.

But thou, my votary, weepest thou?   195
I gave thee sight—where is it now?
I taught thy heart beyond the reach
Of ritual, bible, or of speech;
Wrote in thy mind's transparent table,
As far as the incommunicable;   200
Taught thee each private sign to raise
Lit by the supersolar blaze.
Past utterance, and past belief,
And past the blasphemy of grief,
The mysteries of Nature's heart;   205
And though no Muse can these impart,
Throb thine with Nature's throbbing breast,
And all is clear from east to west.

'I came to thee as to a friend;
Dearest, to thee I did not send   210
Tutors, but a joyful eye,
Innocence that matched the sky,
Lovely locks, a form of wonder,
Laughter rich as woodland thunder,
That thou might'st entertain apart   215
The richest flowering of all art:
And, as the great all-loving Day
Through smallest chambers takes its way,
That thou might'st break thy daily bread
With prophet, savior and head;   220
That thou might'st cherish for thine own
The riches of sweet Mary's Son,
Boy-Rabbi, Israel's paragon.[5]
And thoughtest thou such guest
Would in thy hall take up his rest?   225
Would rushing life forget her laws,
Fate's glowing revolution pause?
High omens ask diviner guess;
Not to be conned to tediousness
And know my higher gifts unbind   230
The zone that girds the incarnate mind.
When the scanty shores are full
With Thought's perilous, whirling pool;
When frail Nature can no more,
Then the Spirit strikes the hour: 235
My servant Death, with solving rite,
Pours finite into infinite.
Wilt thou freeze love's tidal flow,
Whose streams through Nature circling go?
Nail the wild star to its track   240
On the half-climbed zodiac?
Light is light which radiates,
Blood is blood which circulates,
Life is life which generates,
And many-seeming life is one,—   245
Wilt thou transfix and make it none?

---

[5]Luke 2:41–52: Jesus, twelve years old, astonished the elders in the temple with his knowledge and wisdom.

Its onward force too starkly pent
In figure, bone and lineament?

Wilt thou, uncalled, interrogate,
Talker! the unreplying Fate?   250
Nor see the genius of the whole
Ascendant in the private soul,
Beckon it when to go and come,
Self-announced its hour of doom?
Fair the soul's recess and shrine,   255
Magic-built to last a season;
Masterpiece of love benign,
Fairer that expansive reason
Whose omen 't is, and sign.
Wilt thou not ope thy heart to know   260
What rainbows teach, and sunsets show?
Verdict which accumulates
From lengthening scroll of human fates,
Voice of earth to earth returned,
Prayers of saints that inly burned,—   265
Saying, *What is excellent,*
As God lives, is permanent;
Hearts are dust, hearts' loves remain;
Heart's love will meet thee again.
Revere the Maker; fetch thine eye   270
Up to his style, and manners of the sky.
Not of adamant and gold
Built he heaven stark and cold;
No, but a nest of bending reeds,
Flowering grass and scented weeds;   275
Or like a traveller's fleeing tent,
Or bow above the tempest bent;
Built of tears and sacred flames,
And virtue reaching to its aims;
Built of furtherance and pursuing,   280
Not of spent deeds, but of doing.
Silent rushes the swift Lord
Through ruined systems still restored,
Broadsowing, bleak and void to bless,
Plants with worlds the wilderness;   285
Waters with tears of ancient sorrow
Apples of Eden ripe to-morrow.
House and tenant go to ground,
Lost in God, in Godhead found.'

1842–46   *1847*

Days

Daughters of Time, the hypocritic Days,
Muffled and dumb like barefoot dervishes,[1]
And marching single in an endless file,

---

[1] Members of a Muslim sect devoted to poverty, some of
whom whirl in religious ecstasy.

Bring diadems and fagots[2] in their hands.
To each they offer gifts after his will,   5
Bread, kingdoms, stars, and sky that holds them all.
I, in my pleached[3] garden, watched the pomp,
Forgot my morning wishes, hastily
Took a few herbs and apples, and the Day
Turned and departed silent. I, too late,   10
Under her solemn fillet[4] saw the scorn.

c. 1852   *1857*

Brahma[1]

If the red slayer[2] think he slays,
 Or if the slain think he is slain,
They know not well the subtle ways
 I keep, and pass, and turn again.

Far or forgot to me is near;   5
 Shadow and sunlight are the same;
The vanished gods to me appear;
 And one to me are shame and fame.

They reckon ill who leave me out;
 When me they fly, I am the wings;   10
I am the doubter and the doubt,
 And I the hymn the Brahmin sings.

The strong gods[3] pine for my abode,
 And pine in vain the sacred Seven;[4]
But thou, meek lover of the good!   15
 Find me, and turn thy back on heaven.

1856   *1857*

Terminus[1]

It is time to be old,
To take in sail:—
The god of bounds,
Who sets to seas a shore,
Came to me in his fatal rounds,   5
And said: "No more!
No farther shoot

---

[2]Crowns and branches.
[3]Interlaced with light and shadow by overarching tree branches.
[4]Head band.
[1]Brahma is the eternal essence or spirit of the universe in Hindu theology. In discussing with his daughter the difficulty readers had with the poem, Emerson said: "If you tell them to say Jehovah instead of Brahma they will not feel any perplexity."
[2]Death.
[3]Agni, god of fire; Indra, god of the sky; Yama, god of death.
[4]The seven highest saints of Hinduism.
[1]Roman deity of boundaries and landmarks.

Thy broad ambitious branches, and thy root.
Fancy departs: no more invent;
Contract thy firmament   10
To compass of a tent.
There's not enough for this and that,
Make thy option which of two;
Economize the failing river,
Not the less revere the Giver,   15
Leave the many and hold the few.
Timely wise accept the terms,
Soften the fall with wary foot;
A little while
Still plan and smile,   20
And,—fault of² novel germs,—
Mature the unfallen fruit.
Curse, if thou wilt, thy sires,
Bad husbands of their fires,
Who, when they gave thee breath,   25
Failed to bequeath
The needful sinew stark as once,
The Baresark³ marrow to thy bones,
But left a legacy of ebbing veins,
Inconstant heat and nerveless reins,—   30
Amid the Muses, left thee deaf and dumb,
Amid the gladiators, halt and numb."

As the bird trims her to the gale,
I trim myself to the storm of time,
I man the rudder, reef the sail,   35
Obey the voice at eve obeyed at prime:
"Lowly faithful, banish fear,
Right onward drive unharmed;
The port, well worth the cruise, is near,
And every wave is charmed."   40

1866   *1867*

from The Journals

MYSELF

[EXAMINATION OF MY PAST AND PRESENT LIFE]

Sunday, *April* 18, 1824.

"Nil fuit unquam sic dispar sibi."

HORACE.¹

I am beginning my professional studies. In a month I shall be legally a man.
And I deliberately dedicate my time, my talents, and my hopes to the Church.
Man is an animal that looks before and after; and I should be loth to reflect at a

---

²Lacking (in default of).
³Literally, bare-shirt, as the berserkers, legendary Norse
warriors who were strong, fearless, and wild.

¹"Never was a creature so inconsistent" (Horace, *Satires*, I,
iii, 18).

remote period that I took so solemn a step in my existence without some careful examination of my past and present life. Since I cannot alter, I would not repent the resolution I have made, and this page must be witness to the latest year of my life whether I have good grounds to warrant my determination.

I cannot dissemble that my abilities are below my ambition. And I find that I judged by a false criterion when I measured my powers by my ability to understand and to criticize the intellectual character of another. For men graduate their respect, not by the secret wealth, but by the outward use; not by the power to understand, but by the power to act. I have, or had, a strong imagination, and consequently a keen relish for the beauties of poetry. The exercise which the practice of composition gives to this faculty is the cause of my immoderate fondness for writing, which has swelled these pages to a voluminous extent. My reasoning faculty is proportionably weak, nor can I ever hope to write a Butler's Analogy or an Essay of Hume.[2] Nor is it strange that with this confession I should choose theology, which is from everlasting to everlasting "debateable ground." For, the highest species of reasoning upon divine subjects is rather the fruit of a sort of moral imagination, than of the "Reasoning Machines," such as Locke and Clarke[3] and David Hume. Dr. Channing's Dudleian Lecture[4] is the model of what I mean, and the faculty which produced this is akin to the higher flights of the fancy. I may add that the preaching most in vogue at the present day depends chiefly on imagination for its success, and asks those accomplishments which I believe are most within my grasp. I have set down little which can gratify my vanity, and I must further say that every comparison of myself with my mates that six or seven, perhaps sixteen or seventeen, years have made, has convinced me that there exists a signal defect of character which neutralizes in great part the just influence my talents ought to have. Whether that defect be in the *address*, in the fault of good forms,—which, Queen Isabella said, were like perpetual letters-commendatory— or deeper seated in an absence of common *sympathies*, or even in a levity of the understanding, I cannot tell. But its bitter fruits are a sore uneasiness in the company of most men and women, a frigid fear of offending and jealousy of disrespect, an inability to lead and an unwillingness to follow the current conversation, which contrive to make me second with all those among whom chiefly I wish to be first.

Hence my bearing in the world is the direct opposite of that good-humoured independence and self-esteem which should mark the gentleman. Be it here remembered that there is a decent pride which is conspicuous in the perfect model of a Christian man. I am unfortunate also, as was Rienzi,[5] in a propensity to laugh, or rather, snicker. I am ill at ease, therefore, among men. I criticize with hardness; I lavishly applaud; I weakly argue; and I wonder with a "foolish face of praise."

Now the profession of law demands a good deal of personal address, an impregnable confidence in one's own powers, upon all occasions expected and unexpected, and a logical mode of thinking and speaking—which I do not possess, and may not reasonably hope to obtain. Medicine also makes large demands on the practitioner for a seducing mannerism. And I have no taste for the pestle and mortar, for Bell on the bones, or Hunter, or Celsus.[6]

---

[2]Joseph Butler (1692–1752), British theologian, author of *Analogy of Religion* (1736); David Hume (1711–1766), Scottish philosopher, author of *Philosophical Essays* (1748).
[3]John Locke (1632–1704), British philosopher, author of *An Essay Concerning Human Understanding* (1690); Samuel Clarke (1675–1729), British philosopher, author of *A Demonstration of the Being and Attributes of God* (1705).
[4]William Ellery Channing (1780–1842) delivered this Harvard lecture in 1821, "The Evidence of Revealed Religion."

[5]Cola di Rienzi (1313–1354), Italian patriot, became head of state but clashed with the people and the pope and was deposed.
[6]All are authors of medical treatises, the first two of the eighteenth and nineteenth centuries, the last of the first century A.D.

But in Divinity I hope to thrive. I inherit from my sire a formality of manner and speech, but I derive from him, or his patriotic parent, a passionate love for the strains of eloquence. I burn after the *"aliquid immensum infinitumque"*[7] which Cicero desired. What we ardently love we learn to imitate. My understanding venerates and my heart loves that cause which is dear to God and man—the laws of morals, the Revelations which sanction, and the blood of martyrs and triumphant suffering of the saints which seal them. In my better hours, I am the believer (if not the dupe) of brilliant promises, and can respect myself as the possessor of those powers which command the reason and passions of the multitude. The office of a clergyman is twofold: public preaching and private influence. Entire success in the first is the lot of few, but this I am encouraged to expect. If, however, the individual himself lack that moral worth which is to secure the last, his studies upon the first are idly spent. The most prodigious genius, a seraph's eloquence, will shamefully defeat its own end, if it has not first won the heart of the defender to the cause he defends. But the coolest reason cannot censure my choice when I oblige myself *professionally* to a life which all wise men freely and advisedly adopt. I put no great restraint on myself, and can therefore claim little merit in a manner of life which chimes with inclination and habit. But I would learn to love virtue for her own sake. I would have my pen so guided as was Milton's when a deep and enthusiastic love of goodness and of God dictated the *Comus* to the bard, or that prose rhapsody in the Third Book of Prelaty.[8] I would sacrifice inclination to the interest of mind and soul. I would remember that

"Spare Fast oft with Gods doth diet,"[9]

that Justinian[10] devoted but one out of twenty-four hours to sleep, and this week (for instance) I will remember to curtail my dinner and supper sensibly and rise from table each day with an appetite, till Tuesday evening next, and so see if it be a fact that I can understand more clearly.

I have mentioned a defect of character; perhaps it is not one, but many. Every wise man aims at an entire conquest of himself. We applaud, as possessed of extraordinary good sense, one who never makes the slightest mistake in speech or action; one in whom not only every important step of life, but every passage of conversation, every duty of the day, even every movement of every muscle—hands, feet, and tongue, are measured and dictated by deliberate reason. I am not assuredly that excellent creature. A score of words and deeds issue from me daily, of which I am not the master. They are begotten of weakness and born of shame. I cannot assume the elevation I ought,—but lose the influence I should exert among those of meaner or younger understanding, for want of sufficient *bottom* in my nature, for want of that confidence of manner which springs from an erect mind which is without fear and without reproach. In my frequent humiliation, even before women and children, I am compelled to remember the poor boy who cried, "I told you, Father, they would find me out." Even those feelings which are counted noble and generous take in me the taint of frailty. For my strong propensity to friendship, instead of working out its manly ends, degenerates to a fondness for particular casts of feature, perchance not unlike the doting of old King James.[11] Stateliness and silence hang very like Mokannah's suspicious silver veil, only concealing what is best not shewn.[12] What is called a warm heart, I have not.

---

[7]"Something great and unlimited." Cicero (106–43 B.C.), Roman orator and philosopher.

[8]John Milton (1608–1674), author of *Comus, a Mask* (1634) and *The Reason of Church Government Urged against Prelaty* (1642), an argument for abolition of prelates (high-ranking ecclesiastics).

[9]Milton's "Il Penseroso," 1. 46.

[10]Roman emperor, reigned 527–565.

[11]James I (1566–1625) of England wrote works on demonology.

[12]In Thomas Moore's *Lalla Rookh* (1817), Mokanna feigns wearing a veil to hide his countenance's supposed divine light.

The stern accuser Conscience cries that the catalogue of confessions is not yet full. I am a lover of indolence, and of the belly. And the good have a right to ask the neophyte who wears this garment of scarlet sin, why he comes where all are apparelled in white? Dares he hope that some patches of pure and generous feeling, some bright fragments of lofty thought, it may be of divine poesy, shall charm the eye away from all the particoloured shades of his character? And when he is clothed in the vestments of the priest, and has inscribed on his forehead "Holiness to the Lord," and wears on his breast the breastplate of the tribes, then can the Ethiopian change his skin, and the unclean be pure? Or how shall I strenuously enforce on men the duties and habits to which I am a stranger? Physician, heal thyself;[13] I need not go far for an answer to so natural a question. I am young in my everlasting existence. I already discern the deep dye of elementary errors, which threaten to colour its infinity of duration. And I judge that if I devote my nights and days *in form,* to the service of God and the War against Sin, I shall soon be prepared to do the same *in substance.*

I cannot accurately estimate my chances of success, in my profession, and in life. Were it just to judge the future from the past, they would be very low. In my case, I think it is not. I have never expected success in my present employment.[14] My scholars are carefully instructed, my money is faithfully earned, but the instructor is little wiser, and the duties were never congenial with my disposition. Thus far the dupe of Hope, I have trudged on with my bundle at my back, and my eye fixed on the distant hill where my burden would fall. It may be I shall write *dupe* a long time to come, and the end of life shall intervene betwixt me and the release. My trust is that my profession shall be my regeneration of mind, manners, inward and outward estate; or rather my starting-point, for I have hoped to put on eloquence as a robe, and by goodness and zeal and the awfulness of Virtue to press and prevail over the false judgments, the rebel passions and corrupt habits of men. We blame the past, we magnify and gild the future, and are not wiser for the multitude of days. Spin on, ye of the adamantine spindle,[15] spin on, my fragile thread.

WRITING
[THE RIGHT WORD; JULY 8, 1831]

No man can write well who thinks there is any choice of words for him. The laws of composition are as strict as those of sculpture and architecture. There is always one line that ought to be drawn, or one proportion that should be kept, and every other line or proportion is wrong, and so far wrong as it deviates from this. So in writing, there is always a right word, and every other than that is wrong. There is no beauty in words except in their collocation. The effect of a fanciful word misplaced, is like that of a horn of exquisite polish growing on a human head.

[LANGUAGE CLOTHES NATURE; NOVEMBER 10, 1836]

Language clothes Nature, as the air clothes the earth, taking the exact form and pressure of every object. Only words that are new fit exactly the thing, those that are old, like old *scoriæ*[1] that have been long exposed to the air and sunshine, have lost the sharpness of their mould and fit loosely. But in new objects and new names one is delighted with the plastic nature of man as much as in picture or sculpture. Thus Humboldt's[2] "volcanic paps," and "magnetic storms," are the very

---

13 Luke 4:23.
14 Teaching school.
15 Among the three Fates, Clotho spins the thread that determines human destiny.

1 The slag or refuse left over after the metal is smelted.
2 Alexander von Humboldt (1769–1859), German naturalist who studied tropical storms and volcanoes.

mnemonics of science, and so in general in books of modern science the vocabulary yields this poetic pleasure. "Veins inosculate."[3]

[FOLLOWING A NATURAL ORDER; OCTOBER 21, 1837]

Proportion. It is well and truly said that proportion is beauty; that no ornament in the details can compensate for want of this; nay, that ornamented details only make disproportion more unsightly; and that proportion charms us even more perhaps when the materials are coarse and unadorned.

I see these truths chiefly in that species of architecture which I study and practice, namely, Rhetoric, or the Building of Discourse. Profoundest thoughts, sublime images, dazzling figures are squandered and lost in an immethodical harangue. We are fatigued, and glad when it is done. We say of the writer, Nobody understood him: he does not understand himself. But let the same number of thoughts be dealt with by a natural rhetoric, let the question be asked—What is said? How many things? Which are they? Count and number them: put together those that belong together. Now say *what your subject is,* for now first you know: and now state your inference or peroration in what calm or inflammatory temper you must, and behold! out of the quarry you have erected a temple, soaring in due gradation, turret over tower, to heaven, cheerful with thorough-lights, majestic with strength, desired of all eyes. You will find the matter less cumbersome,—it even seems less when put in order,—and the discourse as fresh and agreeable at the conclusion as at the commencement. Moreover, if a natural order is obediently followed, the composition will have an abiding charm to yourself as well as to others; you will see that you were the scribe of a higher wisdom than your own, and it will remain to you, like one of Nature's works, pleasant and wholesome, and not, as our books so often are, a disagreeable remembrance to the author.

A man may find his words mean more than he thought when he uttered them, and be glad to employ them again in a new sense.

[A GOOD SENTENCE; NOVEMBER 13, 1839]

A good sentence, a noble verse which I meet in my reading, are an epoch in my life. From month to month, from year to year, they remain fresh and memorable. Yet when we once in our writing come out into the free air of thought, we seem to be assured that nothing is easier than to continue this communication at pleasure indefinitely. Up, down, around, the kingdom of thought has no enclosures, but the Muse makes us free of her city. Well, the world has a million writers. One would think then that thought would be as familiar as the air and water, and the gifts of each new hour exclude the repetition of those of the last. Yet I remember a beautiful verse for twenty years.

[WORDS MUST SPRING FROM LOVE; JULY 26, 1840]

Thy love must be thy art. Thy words must spring from love, and every thought be touched with love. Only such words fly and endure. There are two ways of speaking: one, when a man makes his discourse plausible and round by considering how it sounds to him who hears it, and the other mode when his own heart loves and so infuses grace into all that drops from him. Only this is living beauty. Nature also must teach thee rhetoric. She can teach thee, not only to speak truth, but to speak it truly. Only poets advance with every word. In most compositions there is one thought which was spontaneous, and many which were added and abutted: but, in the true, God writes every word.

---

[3]Veins joined together by openings at the end; also, intertwined.

[All Writing Should Be Selection; October–November 1869]

Good writing. All writing should be selection in order to drop every dead word. Why do you not save out of your speech or thinking only the vital things,—the spirited *mot*[4] which amused or warmed you when you spoke it,—because of its luck and newness? I have just been reading, in this careful book of a most intelligent and learned man, any number of flat conventional words and sentences. If a man would learn to read his own manuscript severely,—becoming really a third person, and search only for what interested him, he would blot to purpose,—and how every page would gain! Then all the words will be sprightly, and every sentence a surprise.

[The Writer Is an Explorer; October 2, 1870]

The writer is an explorer. Every step is an advance into new land.

LOVE

[Love Is a Holy Passion; December 1823]

Love is a holy passion, and is the instrument of our connexion with Deity; and when we drop the body, this, perhaps, will constitute the motive and impulse to all the acquisitions of an immortal education. As we are instinctively ashamed of selfishness, we venerate *love*, the noble and generous nature of which seeks another's good. . . . Embryo powers of which we were not hitherto conscious are nursed into the manhood of mind. A powerful motive is to the character what a skilful hypothesis is to the progress of science; it affords facility and room for the arrangement of the growing principles of our nature. What lay in chaos and barren before, is now adjusted in a beautiful and useful order, which exposes to the light numberless connexions and relations and fine issues of thought, not easily perceived until such a system is laid. A motive thus powerful and of such benignant fruits is *love*. . . . It bears many forms, but is *love*. It is the attachment to truth, to a sentiment, to our country, to a fellow being or to God, that has won and worn the crown of martyrdom, and that has stirred up in men's minds all the good which the earth has seen. Indeed pure love is too pure a principle for human bosoms; and, were it not mixed with the animal desires of our nature, would not meet that unqualified and universal honour it now finds among men. . . . What does the sensualist know of love? of such love as exists between God and man, and man and God; of such love as the pure mind conceives for moral grandeur, for the contemplation of which it was made?

[Man Is Insular and Cannot Be Touched; May 19, 1837]

Society an imperfect union. Is it not pathetic that the action of men on men is so partial? We never touch but at points. The most that I can have or be to my fellow man, is it the reading of his book, or the hearing of his project in conversation? I approach some Carlyle[1] with desire and joy. I am led on from month to month with an expectation of some total embrace and oneness with a noble mind, and learn at last that it is only so feeble and remote and hiant[2] action as reading a Mirabeau or Diderot paper,[3] and a few the like. This is all that can be looked for. More we shall not be to each other. Baulked soul! It is not that the sea and poverty and pursuit separate us. Here is Alcott[4] by my door, yet is the union more

---

[4]"Word" (French).
[1]Thomas Carlyle (1795–1881), Scottish essayist and longtime correspondent with Emerson.
[2]Gaping, empty.
[3]Comte de Mirabeau (1749–1791), French orator and revolutionary; Denis Diderot (1713–1784), French encyclopedist, wrote public or polemical rather than private or personal essays and treatises.
[4]Bronson Alcott (1799–1888), Emerson's friend and sometime neighbor.

profound? No, the sea, vocation, poverty, are seeming fences, but man is insular and cannot be touched. Every man is an infinitely repellent orb, and holds his individual being on that condition.

[TAME MAN TRANSFORMED BY LOVE; OCTOBER 20, 1837]

Wild man attracts. As the contemporaries of Columbus hungered to see the wild man, so undoubtedly we should have the liveliest interest in a wild man, but men in society do not interest us because they are tame. We know all they will do, and man is like man as one steamboat is like another. Tame men are inexpressibly tedious, like the talking with a young Southerner who says, "Yes, sir," indifferently to every sort of thing you say, thinking Yes, sir, to mean nothing. From every man, even from great men as the world goes, a large deduction is to be made on account of this taming, or Conventions. His going to church does not interest me because all men go to Church. His staying at home would, until I see why he stays at home, if from vulgar reasons,—it is dulness still. But he falls desperately in love. Ah, ha! does he? now I am wide-awake, this is not conventional, but the great epoch of the revelation of Beauty to his soul. Now let me see every line he writes, every step he makes, every kiss which makes him immortal; let those laugh who never were worthy to love; to me each act of his in these golden hours is holy and beautiful. The eternal beauty of this passion is sufficiently shown from the interest which attaches to every sort of love tale in verse or prose which the press spawns from January to December.

[YOU MUST LOVE ME AS I AM; FEBRUARY 9–10, 1838]

You must love me as I am. Do not tell me how much I should love you. I am content. I find my satisfactions in a calm, considerate reverence, measured by the virtues which provoke it. So love me as I am. When I am virtuous, love me; when I am vicious, hate me; when I am lukewarm, neither good nor bad, care not for me. But do not by your sorrow or your affection solicit me to be somewhat else than I by nature am.

[LOVE IS THAUMATURGIC; JUNE 6, 1839]

Love is thaumaturgic.[5] It converts a chair, a box, a scrap of paper, or a line carelessly drawn on it, a lock of hair, a faded weed, into amulets worth the world's fee. If we see out of what straws and nothings he builds his Elysium, we shall read nothing miraculous in the New Testament.

[THE INADEQUATENESS OF MY OLD ESSAY ON LOVE; JUNE 11, 1840]

I finish this morning transcribing my old essay on Love,[6] but I see well its inadequateness. I, cold because I am hot,—cold at the surface only as a sort of guard and compensation for the fluid tenderness of the core,—have much more experience than I have written there, more than I will, more than I can write. In silence we must wrap much of our life, because it is too fine for speech, because also we cannot explain it to others, and because somewhat we cannot yet understand. We do not live as angels, eager to introduce each other to new perfections in our brothers and sisters, and frankly avowing our delight in each new trait of character, in the magic of each new eyebeam, but that which passes for love in the world gets official, and instead of embracing, hates all the divine traits that dare to appear in other persons. A better and holier society will mend this selfish coward-

---

[5]Miraculous, magic.
[6]Prepared earlier as a lecture, "Love" appeared in *Essays: First Series* (1841).

ice, and we shall have brave ties of affection, not petrified by law, not dated or ordained by law to last for one year, for five years, or for life; but drawing their date, like all friendship, from itself only; brave as I said, because innocent, and religiously abstinent from the connubial endearments, being a higher league on a purely spiritual basis. This nobody believes possible who is not good. The good know it is possible. Cows and bulls and peacocks think it nonsense.

[SUPERSENSUOUS CHANNELS OF COMMUNICATION; SEPTEMBER 1, 1840]

One fact the fine conversations of the last week—now already fast fading into oblivion—revealed to me, not without a certain shudder of joy, that I must thank what I am, and not what I do, for the love my friends bear me. I, conscious all the time of the shortcoming of my hands, haunted ever with a sense of beauty which makes all I do and say pitiful to me, and the occasion of perpetual apologies, assure myself to disgust those whom I admire,—and now suddenly it comes out that they have been loving me all this time, not at all thinking of my hands or my words, but only of that love of something more beautiful than the world, which, it seems, being in my heart, overflowed through my eyes or the tones of my speech. Gladly I learn that we have these subterranean,—say rather, these supersensuous channels of communication, and that spirits can meet in their pure upper sky without the help of organs.

[LOVE LINKED TO UNIVERSALITIES; 1843]

The skeptic says: how can any man love any woman, except by delusion, and ignorance? Brothers do not wish to marry sisters because they see them too nearly, and all attractiveness, like fame, requires some distance. But the lover of nature loves nature in his mistress or his friend; he sees the faults and absurdities of the individual as well as you. No familiarity can exhaust the chasm. It is not personalities but universalities that draw him. The like is true of life. It seems to me that he has learned its lesson who has come to feel so assured of his well-being as to hold lightly all particulars of to-day and to-morrow, and to count death amongst the particulars. He must have such a grasp of the whole as to be willing to be ridiculous and unfortunate.

[INITIAL LOVE ALLOWED, CELESTIAL FOLLOWS; 1845]

Persons are a luxury and a convenience, like shops. Names are the only poems which loving maidens will hear. Nearness is the aim of all love. An exchange of nobleness is it also. But if you would sublimate it, I think you must keep it hard and cold, and with a Dantean leanness. We strangely stand—souls do—on the very edges of their own spheres, leaning tiptoe towards and into the adjoining sphere. The initial love must be allowed; then the celestial shall follow. The nuptial love releases each from that excess of influence which warped each from his own beauty, and gives each again to himself and herself, so that they acquire their own feature and proportion again, and a new beauty and dignity in each other's eyes. Healed of the fever, let them beware of a second fever. It is not for lovers (on a high degree of love) to sue. Great love has that temperance which asks for nothing which is not already in the moment granted. It is theirs only to be indulgent to the joyful necessity which, making them coexistent, has also made them contemporary. They are only to find each other and to be in each other.

DEATH

[IS IT GOOD TO DIE? MARCH 8, 1822]

. . . Life is the spark which kindles up a soul and opens its capacities to receive the great lessons which it is appointed to learn of the Universe—of Good—of

Evil—of accountability—of Eternity; of Beauty, of Happiness. The inestimable moment in which the history of past ages is opened, its own relations to the Universe explained, its dependence and independence shewn; the time to reach itself the affections, and to gratify them, to ally itself in kindly bonds with other beings of like destiny; the time to educate a citizen of unknown spheres; the time to serve the Lord.

And is it good to die? to exchange this precious consciousness capable of such sublime purposes for an unknown state (of which all that is seen is appalling); perhaps for a gloomy sleep? Is it good to be forced away against our will and through extreme suffering, from the vital body, and give up that organ of our enjoyment and sufferings to the worms, while what shall befall the soul we cannot tell? We shudder when the question is made, and terror, terror breaks down the vain refinements of philosophy, and the fences of affectation.

Reason bids us ask, who is the being that forces away the mind into this unknown state? Nature and Revelation have taught us something of this being. We are reduced to put our views of death entirely upon His character and will, and Death will become more or less terrible according to our notions of the Lord of Death.

[Fear of Death; November 3, 1830]

Is it possible for religious principle to overcome the fear of death? It is commonly overcome, as Bacon[1] observes, by every passion and humour in turn, love, honour, revenge, fun, &c. The instances are familiar of men habitually encountering the greatest risks,—sailor and soldier marching up to a battery for sixpence a day. And multitudes of the lower classes of mankind die continually with almost no exhibition of fear. In all these instances I apprehend it is not a conquest of the fear, but a setting it aside. It is want of thought. It is a dogged attention to the facts next them, and not a consideration of the event of death.

On the contrary, spiritual men exhibit not unfrequently strong apprehension, great gloom, as Dr. Johnson,[2] at the thought of dissolution. The more delicate the structure of the mind, the stronger this emotion, I suppose; and this for two reasons, first, because such persons have more to lose in losing life, and secondly, because they are not yet spiritual enough to overcome fear.

I suppose that he who . . . lives in the daily exercise of the purest and most expanded affections, especially has attained religious principles and loves to meditate on God and heaven,—I suppose that life is worth to him infinitely more than it is to a sensual wretch; life to him is a world of sweet and holy thought, and the idea of losing it is tremendous. I think therefore that Christianity has done much to increase the fear of death in the world by the general advance it has brought about in the cultivation of the moral powers, whilst it has yet failed to effect any large portion of society to that degree as to overcome this terror.

Secondly, I firmly believe that a fuller effect of Christian principles upon our hearts will be the disappearance of the fear of death. Men doubt their immortality because they doubt the real independent being of their moral nature. They fancy the thoughts of God, of goodness, of love, of ethics generally, may be visions of the mind, creations of the mind, and it and they may perish together.

I suppose that the reality, the independence of this part of our nature, can only appear to us by its use, that, in proportion as it is brought into exercise, its eternity will be felt. I have always noticed that when I had been occupied with diligence in

---

[1]Francis Bacon (1561–1626), British philosopher and essayist.

[2]Samuel Johnson (1709–1784), British dictionary maker, critic, famed conversationalist.

any ethical speculation, with the law of compensations, for example, with the great conclusions that come from the analysis of the affections or any kindred question,—if from the midst of such thoughts I glance at the question of immortality, I have at that time a clearer conviction of it.

I have heard moreover a great many anecdotes of people in the last and the former generation, quiet simple people of Malden and Concord who had no books but Bible and psalter,[3] and a less rational therefore, but far more fervid piety than is common now, who died without fear and with exaltation even, in the love of Christ. I suppose though they had neglected their minds, they had cultivated their moral power till it stood out to their minds a living soul, unaffected by any change of the body. This is true too of the apostles, who never speak of death as dreadful, to whom to die was gain. . . .

[I Do Not Fear Death; December 19, 1831]

When I talk with the sick they sometimes think I treat death with unbecoming indifference and do not make the case my own, or, if I do, err in my judgment. I do not fear death. I believe those who fear it have borrowed the terrors through which they see it from vulgar opinion, and not from their own minds. My own mind is the direct revelation which I have from God and far least liable to mistake in telling his will of any revelation. Following my own thoughts, especially as sometimes they have moved me in the country (as in the Gulf Road in Vermont), I should lie down in the lap of earth as trustingly as ever on my bed. But the terror to many persons is in the vague notions of what shall follow death. The judgment, an uncertain judgment to be passed upon them,—whether they shall be saved? It ought to be considered by them that there is no uncertainty about it. Already they may know exactly what is their spiritual condition. . . . He will not suffer his holy one to see corruption. . . . What are your sources of satisfaction? If they are meats and drinks, dress, gossip, revenge, hope of wealth, they must perish with the body. If they are contemplation, kind affections, admiration of what is admirable, self-command, self-improvement, then they survive death and will make you as happy then as now.

[Why Should We Dread to Die? August 17, 1832]

We are to act doubtless in our care of our own health as if there were no other world. We are to be punctilious in our care. No caution is unseemly. This is the design of Providence. But we are to recognize, in every instant of this creeping solicitude, that happy is the lot of those to whom the unspeakable secrets of the other state are disclosed. When our own hour comes, when every medicine and means has been exhausted, we are then to say to the angel, Hail! All Hail! and pass to whatever God has yet to reveal to the conscious spirit. Why should we dread to die, when all the good and the beautiful and the wise have died, and earth holds nothing so good as that which it has lost. But oh! let not life be valued, when that which makes the value of life is lost. It is only a clean conscience, the knowledge that we are beloved by our friends, and deserve to be beloved, that can persuade an honourable mind to pray that its being may be prolonged an hour; but to outlive your own respect, to live when your acquaintance shall shrug their shoulders, and count it a disgrace to you the breath that is yet in your nostrils,—I shall be glad to be told what is the pleasure, what is the profit that is worth buying at such a price.

---

[3]Book of Psalms.

[Where Shall I Be Then? October 21, 1837]

I said when I awoke, After some more sleepings and wakings I shall lie on this mattrass sick; then, dead; and through my gay entry they will carry these bones. Where shall I be then? I lifted my head and beheld the spotless orange light of the morning beaming up from the dark hills into the wide Universe.

[Death Is Always Astounding; October 28, 1837]

The event of death is always astounding; our philosophy never reaches, never possesses it; we are always at the beginning of our catechism; always the definition is yet to be made. What is death?

I see nothing to help beyond observing what the mind's habit is in regard to that crisis. Simply I have nothing to do with it. It is nothing to me. After I have made my will and set my house in order, I shall do in the immediate expectation of death the same things I should do without it.

But more difficult is it to know the death of another. Mrs. Ripley[4] says that her little Sophia told the mantua-maker this morning "that in Heaven she was going to ask Dod to let her sit by mother all the time," and if this little darling should die, Mrs. R. thinks she could not live. So with the expectation of the death of persons who are conveniently situated, who have all they desire, and to whom death is fearful, she looks in vain for a consolation. In us there ought to be remedy. There ought to be, there can be nothing to which the soul is called, to which the soul is not equal. And I suppose that the roots of my relation to every individual are in my own constitution, and not less the causes of his disappearance from me.

Why should we lie so? A question is asked of the Understanding which lies in the province of the Reason, and we foolishly try to make an answer. Our constructiveness overpowers our love of truth. How noble is it when the mourner looks for comfort in your face to give only sympathy and confession; confession that it is a great grief, and the greater because the apprehension of its nature still loiters. Who set you up for Professor of omniscience and *cicerone*[5] to the Universe? Why teach? Learn rather.

[Life and Death Are Apparitions; May 14, 1838]

Life and Death are apparitions.

Last night the teachers' Sunday School met here, and the theme was Judgment. I affirmed that we were spirits now incarnated, and should always be spirits incarnated. Our thought is the income of God. I taste therefore of eternity and pronounce of eternal law now, and not hereafter. Space and time are but forms of thought. I proceed from God now, and ever shall so proceed. Death is but an appearance. Yes, and life's circumstances are but an appearance through which the firm virtue of this God-law penetrates and which it moulds. The inertia of matter and of fortune and of our employment is the feebleness of our spirit.

[Waldo's Death; January 28 & 30, 1842]

Yesterday night, at fifteen minutes after eight, my little Waldo ended his life.[6]

What he looked upon is better; what he looked not upon is insignificant. The morning of Friday, I woke at three o'clock, and every cock in every barnyard was shrilling with the most unnecessary noise. The sun went up the morning sky with all his light, but the landscape was dishonored by this loss. For this boy, in whose

---

[4]Sarah Ripley, wife of Samuel Ripley (Emerson's half-uncle); "mantua-maker": dressmaker.
[5]Guide.
[6]Waldo was five years old and died of scarlatina.

remembrance I have both slept and awaked so oft, decorated for me the morning star, the evening cloud, how much more all the particulars of daily economy; for he had touched with his lively curiosity every trivial fact and circumstance in the household, the hard coal and the soft coal which I put into my stove; the wood, of which he brought his little quota for grandmother's fire; the hammer, the pincers and file he was so eager to use; the microscope, the magnet, the little globe, and every trinket and instrument in the study; the loads of gravel on the meadow, the nests in the hen-house, and many and many a little visit to the dog-house and to the barn.—For everything he had his own name and way of thinking, his own pronunciation and manner. And every word came mended from that tongue. A boy of early wisdom, of a grave and even majestic deportment, of a perfect gentleness.

Every tramper that ever tramped is abroad, but the little feet are still.

He gave up his little innocent breath like a bird.

He dictated a letter to his Cousin Willie on Monday night, to thank him for the magic lantern which he had sent him, and said, "I wish you would tell Cousin Willie that I have so many presents that I do not need that he should send me any more unless he wishes to very much."

The boy had his full swing in this world; never, I think, did a child enjoy more; he had been thoroughly respected by his parents and those around him, and not interfered with; and he had been the most fortunate in respect to the influences near him, for his Aunt Elizabeth had adopted him from his infancy and treated him ever with that plain and wise love which belongs to her and, as she boasted, had never given him sugarplums. So he was won to her, and always signalized her arrival as a visit to him, and left playmates, playthings, and all to go to her. Then Mary Russell[7] had been his friend and teacher for two summers, with true love and wisdom. Then Henry Thoreau had been one of the family for the last year, and charmed Waldo by the variety of toys,—whistles, boats, popguns,—and all kinds of instruments which he could make and mend; and possessed his love and respect by the gentle firmness with which he always treated him. Margaret Fuller and Caroline Sturgis[8] had also marked the boy and caressed and conversed with him whenever they were here.

Meantime every day his grandmother gave him his reading-lesson and had by patience taught him to read and spell; by patience and by love, for she loved him dearly.

Sorrow makes us all children again,—destroys all differences of intellect. The wisest knows nothing.

It seems as if I ought to call upon the winds to describe my boy, my fast receding boy, a child of so large and generous a nature that I cannot paint him by specialties, as I might another.

"Are there any other countries?" "Yes. I wish you to name the other countries"; so I went on to name London, Paris, Amsterdam, Cairo, etc. But Henry Thoreau well said, in allusion to his large way of speech, that "his questions did not admit of an answer; they were the same which you would ask yourself."

He named the parts of the toy house he was always building by fancy names which had a good sound, as "the interspeglium" and "the coridaga," which names, he told Margaret, "the children could not understand."

If I go down to the bottom of the garden it seems as if some one had fallen into the brook. Every place is handsome or tolerable where he has been. Once he sat in the pew.

---

[7] A friend of the Emersons who ran an infant school which Waldo attended.
[8] Long-time friends of Emerson.

His house he proposed to build in summer of burrs and in winter of snow.

"My music," he said, "makes the thunder dance," for it thundered when he was blowing his willow whistle.

"Mamma, may I have this bell which I have been making, to stand by the side of my bed?" "Yes, it may stand there." "But, Mamma, I am afraid it will alarm you. It may sound in the middle of the night, and it will be heard over the whole town; it will be louder than ten thousand hawks; it will be heard across the water, and in all the countries. It will be heard all over the world. It will sound like some great glass thing which falls down and breaks all to pieces."

[I COMPREHEND NOTHING; MARCH 23, 1842]

The least differences in intellect are immeasurable. This beloved and now departed Boy, this Image in every part beautiful, how he expands in his dimensions in this fond memory to the dimensions of Nature!

Ellen asks her grandmother "whether God can't stay alone with the angels a little while and let Waldo come down?"

The chrysalis[9] which he brought in with care and tenderness and gave to his mother to keep is still alive, and he, most beautiful of the children of men, is not here.

I comprehend nothing of this fact but its bitterness. Explanation I have none, consolation none that rises out of the fact itself; only diversion; only oblivion of this, and pursuit of new objects.

[THIS LATENT OMNISCIENCE COEXISTENT WITH OMNI-IGNORANCE; APRIL 6–12, 1842]

In short there ought to be no such thing as Fate. As long as we use this word, it is a sign of our impotence and that we are not yet ourselves. There is now a sublime revelation in each of us which makes us so strangely aware and certain of our riches that although I have never since I was born for so much as one moment expressed the truth, and although I have never heard the expression of it from any other, I know that the whole is here—the wealth of the Universe is for me. Every thing is explicable and practicable for me. And yet whilst I adore this ineffable life which is at my heart, it will not condescend to gossip with me, it will not announce to me any particulars of science, it will not enter into the details of my biography, and say to me why I have a son and daughters born to me, or why my son dies in his sixth year of joy. Herein then I have this latent omniscience coexistent with omnigorance. Moreover, whilst this Deity glows at the heart, and by his unlimited presentiments gives me all power, I know that tomorrow will be as this day, I am a dwarf, and I remain a dwarf. That is to say, I believe in Fate. As long as I am weak, I shall talk of Fate; whenever the God fills me with his fulness, I shall see the disappearance of Fate.

I am *Defeated* all the time; yet to Victory I am born.

[NO PROGRESS IN RECONCILIATION; JANUARY 30, 1844]

I wrote to M. F. that I had no experiences nor progress to reconcile me to the calamity whose anniversary returned the second time last Saturday.[10] The senses have a right to their method as well as the mind; there should be harmony in facts as well as in truths. Yet these ugly breaks happen there, which the continuity of

---

[9]The caterpillar or cocoon stage of a butterfly.
[10]The death of Waldo; M. F.: Margaret Fuller.

theory does not contemplate. The amends are of a different kind from the mischief.

But the astonishment of life is the absence of any appearances of reconciliation between the theory and practice of life. . . . .

THOREAU[1]

[HIS SIMPLICITY AND CLEAR PERCEPTION; FEBRUARY 17, 1838]

My good Henry Thoreau made this else solitary afternoon sunny with his simplicity and clear perception. How comic is simplicity in this double-dealing, quacking world. Everything that boy says makes merry with society, though nothing can be graver than his meaning. I told him he should write out the history of his college life, as Carlyle has his tutoring. We agreed that the seeing the stars through a telescope would be worth all the astronomical lectures. Then he described Mr. Quimby's electrical lecture here, and the experiment of the shock, and added that "college corporations are very blind to the fact that that twinge in the elbow is worth all the lecturing."

[A WALK TO THE CLIFF; APRIL 26–28, 1838]

Yesterday afternoon I went to the Cliff with Henry Thoreau. Warm, pleasant, misty weather, which the great mountain amphitheatre seemed to drink in with gladness. A crow's voice filled all the miles of air with sound. A bird's voice, even a piping frog, enlivens a solitude and makes world enough for us. At night I went out into the dark and saw a glimmering star and heard a frog, and Nature seemed to say, Well do not these suffice? Here is a new scene, a new experience. Ponder it, Emerson, and not like the foolish world, hanker after thunders and multitudes and vast landscapes, the sea or Niagara.

[FREE AND ERECT MIND; FEBRUARY 11, 1838]

At the "teachers' meeting"[2] last night, my good Edmund,[3] after disclaiming any wish to difference Jesus from a human mind, suddenly seemed to alter his tone, and said that Jesus made the world and was the Eternal God. Henry Thoreau merely remarked that "Mr. Hosmer had kicked the pail over." I delight much in my young friend [Thoreau], who seems to have as free and erect a mind as any I have ever met. He told as we walked this afternoon a good story about a boy who went to school with him, Wentworth, who resisted the school mistress's command that the children should bow to Dr. Heywood and other gentlemen as they went by, and when Dr. Heywood stood waiting and cleared his throat with a Hem, Wentworth said, "You need n't hem, Doctor. I shan't bow."

[A WALK TO WALDEN; NOVEMBER 10–11, 1838]

My brave Henry Thoreau walked with me to Walden this afternoon and complained of the proprietors who compelled him, to whom, as much as to any, the whole world belonged, to walk in a strip of road and crowded him out of all the rest of God's earth. He must not get over the fence: but to the building of that fence he was no party. Suppose, he said, some great proprietor, before he was born, had bought up the whole globe. So had he been hustled out of nature. Not having been privy to any of these arrangements, he does not feel called on to consent to them, and so cuts fishpoles in the woods without asking who has a better

---

[1]Thoreau was born in Concord and died there. He lived in Emerson's house for two years (1841–42) as a kind of handyman; and again later (1847–48) for a year, when Emerson was lecturing abroad.

[2]Sunday school teachers gathered in Emerson's house on Sunday evenings for serious talk.
[3]Edmund Hosmer, a neighboring farmer.

title to the wood than he. I defended, of course, the good institution as a scheme, not good, but the best that could be hit on for making the woods and waters and fields available to wit and worth, and for restraining the bold, bad man. At all events, I begged him, having this maggot of Freedom and Humanity in his brain, to write it out into good poetry and so clear himself of it. He replied, that he feared that that was not the best way, that in doing justice to the thought, the man did not always do justice to himself, the poem ought to sing itself: if the man took too much pains with the expression, he was not any longer the Idea himself. I acceded and confessed that this was the tragedy of Art that the artist was at the expense of the man; and hence, in the first age, as they tell, the sons of God printed no epics, carved no stone, painted no pictures, built no railroad; for the sculpture, the poetry, the music, and architecture, were in the man. And truly Bolts and Bars do not seem to me the most exalted or exalting of our institutions. And what other spirit reigns in our intellectual works? We have literary property. The very recording of a thought betrays a distrust that there is any more, or much more, as good for us. If we felt that the universe was ours, that we dwelled in eternity, and advance into all wisdom, we should be less covetous of these sparks and cinders. Why should we covetously build a Saint Peter's,[4] if we had the seeing Eye which beheld all the radiance of beauty and majesty in the matted grass and the overarching boughs? Why should a man spend years upon the carving an Apollo,[5] who looked Apollos into the landscape with every glance he threw?

[Verses of Rude Strength; November 1842]

Last night Henry Thoreau read me verses which pleased, if not by beauty of particular lines, yet by the honest truth, and by the length of flight and strength of wing; for most of our poets are only writers of lines or of epigrams. These of Henry's at least have rude strength, and we do not come to the bottom of the mine. Their fault is, that the gold does not yet flow pure, but is drossy and crude. The thyme and marjoram are not yet made into honey; the assimilation is imperfect. It seems as if the poetry was all written before time was. . . . But it is a great pleasure to have poetry of the second degree also, and mass here, as in other instances, is some compensation for superior quality, for I find myself stimulated and rejoiced like one who should see a cargo of sea-shells discharged on the wharf, whole boxes and crates of conchs, *cypræas*, cones, *neritas, cardiums, murexes*,[6] though there should be no pearl-oyster nor one shell of great rarity and value among them.

[The Trick of His Rhetoric; August 25, 1843]

Henry Thoreau sends me a paper with the old fault of unlimited contradiction. The trick of his rhetoric is soon learned: it consists in substituting for the obvious word and thought its diametrical antagonist. He praises wild mountains and winter forests for their domestic air; snow and ice for their warmth; villagers and wood-choppers for their urbanity, and the wilderness for resembling Rome and Paris. With the constant inclination to dispraise cities and civilization, he yet can find no way to know woods and woodmen except by paralleling them with towns and townsmen. Channing[7] declared the piece is excellent: but it makes me nervous and wretched to read it, with all its merits.

---

[4]Largest church in Christendom, at the Vatican City in Rome, home of the Catholic faith.
[5]Greek god identified with the sun, representing the type of manly beauty.
[6]Various kinds of shells.

[7]William Ellery Channing (1818–1901), nephew and namesake of the noted Boston Unitarian minister; a poet and writer, he came to live in Concord and became a close friend of Emerson.

[Secret of Doing One Thing at a Time; January–March 1844]

Otherness. Henry Thoreau said, he knew but one secret, which was to do one thing at a time, and though he has his evenings for study, if he was in the day inventing machines for sawing his plumbago,[8] he invents wheels all the evening and night also; and if this week he has some good reading and thoughts before him, his brain runs on that all day, whilst pencils pass through his hands. I find in me an opposite facility or perversity, that I never seem well to do a particular work until another is done. I cannot write the poem, though you give me a week, but if I promise to read a lecture day after tomorrow, at once the poem comes into my head and now the rhymes will flow. And let the proofs of the *Dial* be crowding on me from the printer, and I am full of faculty how to make the lecture.

[Continual Coining of the Present Moment; Spring 1844]

Henry Thoreau's conversation consisted of a continual coining of the present moment into a sentence and offering it to me. I compared it to a boy, who, from the universal snow lying on the earth, gathers up a little in his hand, rolls it into a ball, and flings it at me.

Henry said that the other world was all his art; that his pencils would draw no other; that his jackknife would cut nothing else. He does not use it as a means. Henry is a good substantial Childe,[9] not encumbered with himself. He has no troublesome memory, no wake, but lives *ex tempore*,[10] and brings to-day a new proposition as radical and revolutionary as that of yesterday, but different. The only man of leisure in the town. He is a good Abbot Samson:[11] and carries counsel in his breast. If I cannot show his performance much more manifest than that of the other grand promisers, at least I can see that, with his practical faculty, he has declined all the kingdoms of this world. Satan has no bribe for him.

[Like a Woodgod; July–August 1848]

Henry Thoreau is like the woodgod who solicits the wandering poet and draws him into antres[12] and desarts idle, and bereaves him of his memory, and leaves him naked, plaiting vines and with twigs in his hand. Very seductive are the first steps from the town to the woods, but the end is want and madness.

I spoke of friendship, but my friends and I are fishes in our habit. As for taking Thoreau's arm, I should as soon take the arm of an elm tree.

[Captain of Huckleberry Party; July 1851]

Is it not a convenience to have a person in town who knows where pennyroyal grows, or sassafras, or punk for a slow-match; or Celtis,—the false elm; or cats-o'-nine-tails; or wild cherries; or wild pears; where is the best apple tree, where is the Norway pine, where the beech, or epigæa, or Linnæa, or sanguinaria, or orchis pulcherrima, or drosera, or laurus benzoin, or pink huckleberry, or shag-barks; where is the best chestnut grove, hazelnuts; where are trout, where woodcocks, where wild bees, where pigeons; or who can tell where the stake-driver (bittern) can be heard; who has seen and can show you the Wilson's plover?

---

[8]Graphite (or carbon), used for lead pencils.
[9]Young man of noble birth.
[10]Offhand, on the spur of the moment.

[11]Abbott Samson, a strong, resourceful monk, is the hero of Carlyle's *Past and Present* (1843).
[12]Caves.

Thoreau wants a little ambition in his mixture. Fault of this, instead of being the head of American engineers, he is captain of huckleberry party.

[Gives Me My Own Ethics; July 1852]

A man avails much to us, like a point of departure to the seaman, or his stake and stones to the surveyor. I am my own man more than most men, yet the loss of a few persons would be most impoverishing;—a few persons who give flesh to what were, else, mere thoughts, and which now I am not at liberty to slight, or in any manner treat as fictions. It were too much to say that the Platonic world I might have learned to treat as cloud-land, had I not known Alcott,[13] who is a native of that country, yet I will say that he makes it as solid as Massachusetts to me; and Thoreau gives me, in flesh and blood and pertinacious Saxon belief, my own ethics. He is far more real, and daily practically obeying them, than I; and fortifies my memory at all times with an affirmative experience which refuses to be set aside.

[His Fancy for Walt Whitman; February 1862]

Thoreau. Perhaps his fancy for Walt Whitman grew out of his taste for wild nature, for an otter, a woodchuck, or a loon. He loved sufficiency, hated a sum that would not prove; loved Walt and hated Alcott.

[Some Weary Captious Paradox; February 29, 1856]

If I knew only Thoreau, I should think cooperation of good men impossible. Must we always talk for victory, and never once for truth, for comfort, and joy? Centrality he has, and penetration, strong understanding, and the higher gifts,— the insight of the real, or from the real, and the moral rectitude that belongs to it; but all this and all his resources of wit and invention are lost to me, in every experiment, year after year, that I make, to hold intercourse with his mind. Always some weary captious paradox to fight you with, and the time and temper wasted.

[Dying with Pleasure and Peace; March 24, 1862]

Sam Staples[14] yesterday had been to see Henry Thoreau. "Never spent an hour with more satisfaction. Never saw a man dying with so much pleasure and peace." Thinks that very few men in Concord know Mr. Thoreau; finds him serene and happy.

Henry praised to me lately the manners of an old-established, calm, well-behaved river, as perfectly distinguished from those of a new river. A new river is a torrent; an old one slow and steadily supplied. What happens in any part of the old river relates to what befals in every other part of it. 'T is full of compensations, resources, and reserve funds.

[How Near to the Old Monks; June–July 1862]

Henry Thoreau remains erect, calm, self-subsistent, before me,[15] and I read him not only truly in his Journal, but he is not long out of mind when I walk, and, as today, row upon the pond. He chose wisely no doubt for himself to be the bachelor of thought and nature that he was—how near to the old monks in their ascetic religion! He had no talent for wealth, and knew how to be poor without the least hint of squalor or inelegance.

---

[13]Bronson Alcott (1799–1888), friend and neighbor of Emerson; Transcendentalist and author, impractical and impecunious.
[14]A friend of Thoreau; constable and jailer of Concord who arrested and imprisoned Thoreau for nonpayment of taxes.
[15]Thoreau died on May 6, 1862.

Perhaps he fell, all of us do, into his way of living, without forecasting it much, but approved and confirmed it with later wisdom.

[THAT OAKEN STRENGTH; JUNE 1863]

In reading Henry Thoreau's journal, I am very sensible of the vigour of his constitution. That oaken strength which I noted whenever he walked, or worked, or surveyed wood-lots, the same unhesitating hand with which a field-labourer accosts a piece of work, which I should shun as a waste of strength, Henry shows in his literary task. He has muscle, and ventures on and performs feats which I am forced to decline. In reading him, I find the same thought, the same spirit that is in me, but he takes a step beyond, and illustrates by excellent images that which I should have conveyed in a sleepy generality. 'T is as if I went into a gymnasium, and saw youths leap, climb, and swing with a force unapproachable,—though their feats are only continuations of my initial grapplings and jumps.

[HEALTHY POWER IN HIS THOUGHTS; FEBRUARY 27, 1870]

How dangerous is criticism. My brilliant friend[16] cannot see any healthy power in Thoreau's thoughts. At first I suspect, of course, that he oversees me, who admire Thoreau's power. But when I meet again fine perceptions in Thoreau's papers, I see that there is defect in his critic that he should undervalue them. Thoreau writes, in his *Field Notes,* "I look back for the era of this creation not into the night, but to a dawn for which no man ever rose early enough." A fine example of his affirmative genius.

MARGARET FULLER

[EMERSON'S "INHOSPITALITY OF SOUL"; AUGUST 16, 1840]

After seeing Anna Barker[1] I rode with Margaret [Fuller] to the plains. She taxed me, as often before, so now more explicitly, with inhospitality of Soul. She and C.[2] would gladly be my friends, yet our intercourse is not friendship, but literary gossip. I count and weigh, but do not love. They make no progress with me, but however often we have met, we still meet as strangers. They feel wronged in such relation and do not wish to be catechised and criticised. I thought of my experience with several persons which resembled this: and confessed that I would not converse with the divinest person more than one week. M. insisted that it was no friendship which was thus so soon exhausted, and that I ought to know how to be silent and companionable at the same moment. She would surprise me,—she would have me say and do what surprised myself. I confess to all this charge with humility unfeigned. I can better converse with George Bradford[3] than with any other. Elizabeth Hoar[4] and I have a beautiful relation, not however quite free from the same hardness and fences. Yet would nothing be so grateful to me as to melt once for all these icy barriers, and unite with these lovers. But great is the law. I must do nothing to court their love which would lose my own. Unless that which I do to build up myself, endears me to them, our covenant would be injurious. Yet how joyfully would I form permanent relations with the three or four wise and beautiful whom I hold so dear, and dwell under the same roof or in a strict neighborhood. That would at once ennoble life. And it is practicable. It is easier than things which others do. It is easier than to go to Europe, or to subdue a forest farm in Illinois. But this survey of my experience taught me anew that no

---

[16]Probably James Russell Lowell.
[1]One of Margaret Fuller's friends (from New Orleans) whom she introduced to Emerson.
[2]Caroline Sturgis, friend of Margaret and the Emersons.

[3]Contemporary of Emerson's in his class at Divinity School, a distant relative (brother of Aunt Sarah Alden Ripley).
[4]A friend, one of Margaret Fuller's circle.

friend I have surprises, none exalts me. This then is to be set down, is it not? to the requirements we make of the friend, that he shall constrain us to sincerity, and put under contribution all our faculties.

[ATTRACTIVE-REPELLING CONVERSATIONS; OCTOBER 12, 1841]

I would that I could, I know afar off that I cannot give the lights and shades, the hopes and outlooks that come to me in these strange, cold-warm, attractive-repelling conversations with Margaret, whom I always admire, most revere when I nearest see, and sometimes love, yet whom I freeze, and who freezes me to silence, when we seem to promise to come nearest. Yet perhaps my old motto holds true here also: "And the more falls I get, move faster on."

[A BEING OF UNSETTLED RANK IN THE UNIVERSE; OCTOBER 22, 1841]

Margaret is "a being of unsettled rank in the universe." So proud and presumptuous, yet so meek; so worldly and artificial and with keenest sense and taste for all pleasures of luxurious society, yet living more than any other for long periods in a trance of religious sentiment; a person who, according to her own account of herself, expects everything for herself from the Universe.

[A PURE AND PURIFYING MIND; MARCH–APRIL 1843]

Margaret. A pure and purifying mind, self-purifying also, full of faith in men, and inspiring it. Unable to find any companion great enough to receive the rich effusions of her thought, so that her riches are still unknown and seem unknowable. It is a great joy to find that we have underrated our friend, that he or she is far more excellent than we had thought. All natures seem poor beside one so rich, which pours a stream of amber over all objects, clean and unclean, that lie in its path, and makes that comely and presentable which was mean in itself. We are taught by her plenty how lifeless and outward we were, what poor Laplanders[5] burrowing under the snows of prudence and pedantry. Beside her friendship, other friendships seem trade, and by the firmness with which she treads her upward path, all mortals are convinced that another road exists than that which their feet know. The wonderful generosity of her sentiments pours a contempt on books and writing at the very time when one asks how shall this fiery picture be kept in its glow and variety for other eyes. She excels other intellectual persons in this, that her sentiments are more blended with her life; so the expression of them has greater steadiness and greater clearness. I have never known any example of such steady progress from stage to stage of thought and of character. An inspirer of courage, the secret friend of all nobleness, the patient waiter for the realization of character, forgiver of injuries, gracefully waving aside folly, and elevating lowness,—in her presence all were apprised of their fettered estate and longed for liberation, of ugliness and longed for their beauty; of meanness and panted for grandeur.

Her growth is visible. All the persons whom we know have reached their height, or else their growth is so nearly at the same rate with ours, that it is imperceptible, but this child inspires always more faith in her. She rose before me at times into heroical and godlike regions, and I could remember no superior women, but thought of Ceres, Minerva, Proserpine,[6] and the august ideal forms of the foreworld. She said that no man gave such invitation to her mind as to tempt her to full expression; that she felt a power to enrich her thought with such

---

[5]Inhabitants of region in northern Norway.
[6]Goddesses of grain, wisdom, and earth in classical mythology.

wealth and variety of embellishment as would, no doubt, be tedious to such as she conversed with. And there is no form that does not seem to wait her beck,—dramatic, lyric, epic, passionate, pictorial, humorous.

She has great sincerity, force, and fluency as a writer, yet her powers of speech throw her writing into the shade. What method, what exquisite judgment, as well as energy, in the selection of her words; what character and wisdom they convey! You cannot predict her opinion. She sympathizes so fast with all forms of life, that she talks never narrowly or hostilely, nor betrays, like all the rest, under a thin garb of new words, the old droning cast-iron opinions or notions of many years' standing. What richness of experience, what newness of dress, and fast as Olympus to her principle. And a silver eloquence, which inmost Polymnia[7] taught. Meantime, all this pathos of sentiment and riches of literature, and of invention, and this march of character threatening to arrive presently at the shores and plunge into the sea of Buddhism and mystic trances, consists with a boundless fun and drollery, with light satire, and the most entertaining conversation in America.

Her experience contains, I know, golden moments, which, if they could be fitly narrated, would stand equally beside any histories of magnanimity which the world contains; and whilst Dante's *Nuova Vita*[8] is almost unique in the literature of Sentiment, I have called the imperfect record she gave me of two of her days, "Nuovissima Vita."

[I HAVE LOST IN HER MY AUDIENCE; JULY 21, 1850]

On Friday, July 19, Margaret dies on rocks of Fire Island Beach within sight of and within sixty rods of the shore. To the last her country proves inhospitable to her; brave, eloquent, subtle, accomplished, devoted, constant soul! If Nature availed in America to give birth to many such as she, freedom and honour and letters and art too were safe in this New World. She bound in the belt of her sympathy and friendship all whom I know and love,—Elizabeth, Caroline, Ward, the Channings, Ellen Hooper, Charles Newcomb, Hedge, and Sarah Clarke.

She knew more select people than any other person did, and her death will interest more. Yet her taste in music, painting, poetry, character would not be on universal but on idiosyncratic grounds, yet would be genuine.

She had a wonderful power of inspiring confidence and drawing out of people their last secret. The timorous said, "What shall we do? How shall she be received, now that she brings a husband and child home?" But she had only to open her mouth and a triumphant success awaited her. She would fast enough have disposed of the circumstances and the bystanders. For she had the impulse, and they wanted it. Here were already mothers waiting tediously for her coming, for the education of their daughters.

Mrs. Ripley[9] thinks that the marriage with Ossoli was like that of De Staël in her widowhood with the young *De Rocca*, who was enamoured of her.[10] And Mrs. Barlow[11] has an unshaken trust that what Margaret did she could well defend.

Her love of art, like that of many, was only a confession of sympathy with the artist in the mute condemnation which his work gave to the deformity of our daily life; her co-perception with him of the eloquence of Form; her aspiration with him to a life altogether beautiful.

Her heart, which few knew, was as great as her mind, which all knew (what

---

[7]Polyhymnia, the muse of sacred poetry.
[8]Dante Alighieri (1265–1321), Italian author of *The Divine Comedy* and *Nuova Vita* (*New Life*; contains love poems to Beatrice).
[9]A relative of Emerson (Ezra Ripley was his step-grandfather and Phebe Bliss Emerson Ripley, his paternal grandmother).

[10]Madame de Staël (1766–1817), French novelist who divorced the Baron de Staël-Holstein in 1797, had several love affairs, and married Albert de la Rocca in 1811.
[11]Mrs. Almira Penniman Barlow, friend and neighbor.

Jung Stilling said of Goethe)[12] Elizabeth Hoar says of Margaret; and that she was the largest woman; and not a woman who wished to be a man.

I have lost in her my audience. I hurry now to my work admonished that I have few days left. There should be a gathering of her friends and some Beethoven should play the dirge.

She poured a stream of amber over the endless store of private anecdotes, of bosom histories which her wonderful persuasion drew out of all to her. When I heard that a trunk of her correspondence had been found and opened, I felt what a panic would strike all her friends, for it was as if a clever reporter had got underneath a confessional and agreed to report all that transpired there in Wall Street.

Oh, yes, "Margaret and her Friends" must be written, but not post-haste. It is an essential line of American history.

"Yes, that is an example of a destiny springing from character."

"I see your destiny hovering before you, but it always escapes you."

"Nor custom stale her infinite variety."[13]

Elizabeth Hoar quotes Mrs. Barlow as saying that Margaret never disappointed you. To any one whose confidence she had once drawn out, she was always faithful. She could (and she was alone in this) talk of persons and never gossip, for she had a fine instinct that kept her from any reality and from any effect of treachery. The fact is she had large sympathies.

Mrs. Barlow has the superiority to say, of Margaret, death seems to her a fit and good conclusion to the life. Her life was romantic and exceptional: so let her death be; it sets the seal on her marriage, avoids all questions of society, all of employment, poverty, and old age, and besides was undoubtedly predetermined when the world was created.

Dr. W. E. Channing[14] said to her, "Miss Fuller, when I consider that you are all that Miss P.[15] wished to be, and that you despise her, and that she loves and honours you, I think her place in Heaven must be very high."

Lidian[16] says that in the fly-leaf of Margaret's Bible was written a hymn of Novalis.[17]

She had great tenderness and sympathy, as Aunt Mary[18] has none. If Aunt Mary finds out anything is dear and sacred to you, she instantly flings broken crockery at that.

Elizabeth Hoar says of Margaret,—Her friends were a necklace of diamonds about her neck. The confidences given her were their best, and she held them to them; that the honor of the Conversations was the high tone of sincerity and culture from so many consenting individuals, and that Margaret was the keystone of the whole. She was perhaps impatient of complacency in people who thought they had claims and stated their contrary opinion with an air. For such she had no mercy. But though not agreeable, it was just. And so her enemies were made.

[DID NOT OUTLIVE HER INFLUENCE; JULY–OCTOBER 1851]

Miss Peabody ransacks her memory for anecdotes of Margaret's youth, her self-devotion, her disappointments, which she tells with fervency, but I find myself

---

[12]Johann Heinrich Jung-Stilling (1740–1817), German mystic and writer; Johann Wolfgang von Goethe (1749–1832), German poet, edited Jung-Stilling's five-volume autobiography (1777–1804).
[13]Shakespeare, *Antony and Cleopatra*, II, ii, 241–42: "Age cannot wither, nor custom stale/Her infinite variety."
[14]Dr. William Ellery Channing (1780–1842), Transcendentalist and Unitarian minister in Boston.

[15]Elizabeth Peabody (1804–1894), social reformer, educator, and early feminist; her Boston home was the scene of the Conversation classes with Margaret Fuller.
[16]Emerson's second wife.
[17]Novalis (1772–1801), German lyric poet.
[18]Aunt Mary Moody Emerson, a paternal aunt.

always putting the previous question. These things have no value unless they lead somewhere. If a Burns,[19] if a De Staël, if an artist is the result, our attention is preengaged; but quantities of rectitude, mountains of merit, chaos of ruins are of no account without result;—'t is all mere nightmare; false instincts; wasted lives.

Now, unhappily, Margaret's writing does not justify any such research. All that can be said is that she represents an interesting hour and group in American cultivation; then that she was herself a fine, generous, inspiring, vinous, eloquent talker, who did not outlive her influence; and a kind of justice requires of us a monument, because crowds of vulgar people taunt her with want of position.

HAWTHORNE
[No Inside to It; 1838]

Elizabeth Peabody brought me yesterday Hawthorne's "Footprints on the Seashore"[1] to read. I complained that there was no inside to it. Alcott[2] and he together would make a man.

[A Long Walk; September 27, 1842]

September 27 was a fine day, and Hawthorne and I set forth on a walk. We went first to the Factory where Mr. Damon makes Domett cloths,[3] but his mills were standing still, his houses empty. Nothing so small but comes to honor and has its shining moment somewhere; and so was it here with our little Assabet or North Branch; it was falling over the rocks into silver, and above was expanded into this tranquil lake. After looking about us a few moments, we took the road to Stow. The day was full of sunshine, and it was a luxury to walk in the midst of all this warm and colored light. The days of September are so rich that it seems natural to walk to the end of one's strength, and then fall prostrate, saturated with the fine floods, and cry, *Nunc dimittis me.*[4] Fringed gentians, a thornbush with red fruit, wild apple trees whose fruit hung like berries, and grapevines were the decorations of the path. We scarcely encountered man or boy in our road nor saw any in the fields. This depopulation lasted all day. But the outlines of the landscape were so gentle that it seemed as if we were in a very cultivated country, and elegant persons must be living just over yonder hills. Three or four times, or oftener, we saw the entrance to their lordly park. But nothing in the farms or in the houses made this good. And it is to be considered that when any large brain is born in these towns, it is sent, at sixteen or twenty years, to Boston or New York, and the country is tilled only by the inferior class of the people, by the second crop or *rowan*[5] of the Men. Hence all these shiftless poverty-struck pig-farms. In Europe, where society has an aristocratic structure, the land is full of men of the best stock, and the best culture, whose interest and pride it is to remain half of the year at least on their estates and to fill these with every convenience and ornament. Of course these make model-farms and model-architecture, and are a constant education to the eye and hand of the surrounding population.

Our walk had no incidents. It needed none, for we were in excellent spirits, had much conversation, for we were both old collectors who had never had opportunity before to show each other our cabinets, so that we could have filled with matter much longer days. We agreed that it needed a little dash of humor or extravagance in the traveller to give occasion to incident in his journey. Here we sober men, easily pleased, kept on the outside of the land and did not by so much as

[19]Robert Burns (1759–1796), Scottish lyric poet.
[1]Published in the *United States Magazine and Democratic Review* in January 1838.
[2]Bronson Alcott (1799–1888), Transcendentalist, writer, and Emerson's friend and neighbor.

[3]Calvin Carver Damon (1803–1854), Concord fabric manufacturer, originator of Domett cloth, and founder of Damondale village.
[4]"Now let thy servant depart" (Latin).
[5]Variant of *rowen*, second growth of crop or hay.

a request for a cup of milk creep into any farmhouse. If want of pence in our pocket or some vagary in our brain drove us into these "huts where poor men lie," to crave dinner or night's lodging, it would be so easy to break into some mesh of domestic romance, learn so much pathetic private history, perchance see the first blush mantle on the cheeks of the young girl when the mail stage came or did not come, or even get entangled ourselves in some thread of gold or grey. Then again the opportunities which the taverns once offered the traveller, of witnessing and even sharing in the joke and the politics of the teamster and farmers on the road, are now no more. The Temperance Society emptied the bar-room. It is a cold place. Hawthorne tried to smoke a cigar, but I observed he was soon out on the piazza. After noon we reached Stow, and dined, and then continued our journey towards Harvard, making our day's walk, according to our best computation, about twenty miles. The last miles, however, we rode in a wagon, having been challenged by a friendly, fatherly gentleman, who knew my name, and my father's name and history, and who insisted on doing the honors of his town to us, and of us to his townsmen; for he fairly installed us at the tavern, introduced us to the Doctor, and to General——, and bespoke the landlord's best attention to our wants. We get the view of the Nashua River Valley from the top of Oak Hill, as we enter Harvard village. Next morning we began our walk at 6:30 o'clock for the Shaker Village,[6] distant three and a half miles. Whilst the good Sisters were getting ready our breakfast, we had a conversation with Seth Blanchard and Cloutman of the Brethren, who gave an honest account, by yea and by nay, of their faith and practice. They were not stupid, like some whom I have seen of their Society, and not worldly like others. The conversation on both parts was frank enough; with the downright I will be downright, thought I, and Seth showed some humor. I doubt not we should have had our own way with them to a good extent . . . if we could have stayed twenty-four hours; although my powers of persuasion were crippled by a disgraceful barking cold, and Hawthorne inclined to play Jove more than Mercurius.[7] After breakfast Cloutman showed us the farm, vineyard, orchard, barn, pressing-room, etc. The vineyard contained two noble arcades of grapes, both white and Isabella, full of fruit; the orchard, fine varieties of pears and peaches and apples.

They have fifteen hundred acres here, a tract of woodland in Ashburnham, and a sheep pasture somewhere else, enough to supply the wants of the two hundred souls in this family. They are in many ways an interesting Society, but at present have an additional importance as an experiment of Socialism which so falls in with the temper of the times. What improvement is made is made forever; this Capitalist is old and never dies, his subsistence was long ago secured, and he has gone on now for long scores of years in adding easily compound interests to his stock. Moreover, this settlement is of great value in the heart of the country as a model-farm, in the absence of that rural nobility we talked of yesterday. Here are improvements invented, or adopted from the other Shaker communities, which the neighboring farmers see and copy. From the Shaker Village we came to Littleton and thence to Acton, still in the same redundance of splendor. It was like a day of July, and from Acton we sauntered leisurely homeward, to finish the nineteen miles of our second day before four in the afternoon.

In a town which you enter for the first time at late sunset, the trees and houses look pictorial in the twilight, but you can never play tricks with old acquaintances.

There is something very agreeable in fatigue. I am willinger to die, having had my swing of the fair day; and seven times in his life, I suppose, every man sings, Now, Lord, let thy servant depart.

---

[6]The Shakers, or the Society of Believers in Christ's Second Coming, split from the Quakers in the eighteenth century and migrated to America, where they established colonies and put into practice their beliefs in celibacy, communal ownership of property, equality of the sexes, and pacifism.
[7]Chief deity rather than messenger-god.

[ON BROOK FARM; 1843]

We like the strong objectiveness of Homer and of the primitive poems of each country, ballads and the Chinese and Indian sentences, but that cannot be preserved in a large and civilized population. The scholar will inevitably be detached from the mechanic, and will not dwell in the same house, nor see his handiworks so near by, and must adopt new classification and a more metaphysical vocabulary. Hawthorne boasts that he lived at Brook Farm during its heroic age: then all were intimate and each knew the other's work: priest and cook conversed at night of the day's work. Now they complain that they are separated and such intimacy cannot be; there are a hundred souls.

[INVITES READERS INTO HIS STUDY; MAY 1846]

Hawthorne invites his readers too much into his study, opens the process before them. As if the confectioner should say to his customers, "Now, let us make the cake."

[WE BURIED HAWTHORNE; MAY 24, 1864]

Yesterday, May 23, we buried Hawthorne in Sleepy Hollow, in a pomp of sunshine and verdure, and gentle winds. James Freeman Clarke read the service in the church and at the grave. Longfellow, Lowell, Holmes, Agassiz, Hoar, Dwight, Whipple, Norton, Alcott, Hillard, Fields, Judge Thomas, and I attended the hearse as pallbearers. Franklin Pierce[8] was with the family. The church was copiously decorated with white flowers delicately arranged. The corpse was unwillingly shown,—only a few moments to this company of his friends. But it was noble and serene in its aspect,—nothing amiss,—a calm and powerful head. A large company filled the church and the grounds of the cemetery. All was so bright and quiet that pain or mourning was hardly suggested, and Holmes said to me that it looked like a happy meeting.

Clarke in the church said that Hawthorne had done more justice than any other to the shades of life, shown a sympathy with the crime in our nature, and, like Jesus, was the friend of sinners.

I thought there was a tragic element in the event, that might be more fully rendered,—in the painful solitude of the man, which, I suppose, could not longer be endured, and he died of it.

I have found in his death a surprise and disappointment. I thought him a greater man than any of his works betray, that there was still a great deal of work in him, and that he might one day show a purer power. Moreover, I have felt sure of him in his neighbourhood, and in his necessities of sympathy and intelligence,—that I could well wait his time,—his unwillingness and caprice,—and might one day conquer a friendship. It would have been a happiness, doubtless to both of us, to have come into habits of unreserved intercourse. It was easy to talk with him,—there were no barriers,—only, he said so little, that I talked too much, and stopped only because, as he gave no indications, I feared to exceed. He showed no egotism or self-assertion, rather a humility, and, at one time, a fear that he had written himself out. One day, when I found him on the top of his hill, in the woods, he paced back the path to his house, and said, "This path is the only remembrance of me that will remain." Now it appears that I waited too long.

Lately he had removed himself the more by the indignation his perverse politics and unfortunate friendship for that paltry Franklin Pierce awakened, though

---

[8]Franklin Pierce (1804–1869), classmate with Hawthorne at Bowdoin College, became the fourteenth U.S. president. Most of those named as attending the service were members of the Saturday Club, a discussion club to which Emerson belonged.

it rather moved pity for Hawthorne, and the assured belief that he would outlive it, and come right at last.

I have forgotten in what year [Sept. 27, 1842], but it was whilst he lived in the Manse, soon after his marriage, that I said to him, "I shall never see you in this hazardous way; we must take a long walk together. Will you go to Harvard and visit the Shakers?"

He agreed, and we took a June day, and walked the twelve miles, got our dinner from the Brethren, slept at the Harvard Inn, and returned home by another road, the next day. It was a satisfactory tramp, and we had good talk on the way, of which I set down some record in my journal.

from Letters

TO LYDIA JACKSON[1]
[Between Us the Most Permanent Ties]

Concord, February 1, 1835

One of my wise masters, Edmund Burke,[2] said, 'A wise man will speak the truth with temperance that he may speak it the longer.' In this new sentiment that you awaken in me, my Lydian Queen, what might scare others pleases me, its quietness, which I accept as a pledge of permanence. I delighted myself on Friday with my quite domesticated position & the good understanding that grew all the time, yet I went & came without one vehement word—or one passionate sign. In this was nothing of design, I merely surrendered myself to the hour & to the facts. I find a sort of grandeur in the modulated expressions of a love in which the individuals, & what might seem even reasonable personal expectations, are steadily postponed to a regard for truth & the universal love. Do not think me a metaphysical lover. I am a man & hate & suspect the over refiners, & do sympathize with the homeliest pleasures & attractions by which our good foster mother Nature draws her children together. Yet am I well pleased that between us the most permanent ties should be the first formed & thereon should grow whatever others human nature will.

My Mother rejoices very much & asks me all manner of questions about you, many of which I cannot answer. I dont know whether you sing, or read French, or Latin, or where you have lived, & much more. So you see there is nothing for it but that you should come here & on the Battle-Ground stand the fire of her catechism.

Under this morning's severe but beautiful light I thought dear friend that hardly should I get away from Concord. I must win you to love it. I am born a poet, of a low class without doubt yet a poet. That is my nature & vocation. My singing be sure is very 'husky,' & is for the most part in prose. Still am I a poet in the sense of a perceiver & dear lover of the harmonies that are in the soul & in matter, & specially of the correspondences between these & those. A sunset, a forest, a snow storm, a certain river-view, are more to me than many friends & do ordinarily divide my day with my books. Wherever I go therefore I guard & study my rambling propensities with a care that is ridiculous to people, but to me is the care of my high calling. Now Concord is only one of a hundred towns in which I

---

[1]Emerson's fiancée whom he would marry later in 1835.
[2]Edmund Burke (1729–1797), British philosopher, statesman, and writer.

could find these necessary objects but Plymouth I fear is not one. Plymouth is streets; I live in the wide champaign.[3]

Time enough for this however. If I succeed in preparing my lecture on Michel Angelo Buonaroti this week for Thursday,[4] I will come to Plymouth on Friday. If I do not succeed—do not attain unto the Idea of that man—I shall read of Luther, Thursday & then I know not when I shall steal a visit.—

Dearest forgive the egotism of all this letter Say they not 'The more love the more egotism.' Repay it by as much & more. Write, write to me. And please dear Lidian take that same low counsel & leave thinking for the present & let the winds of heaven blow away your dyspepsia.

Waldo E.

TO HENRY WARE, JR.[1]
[SUDDENLY RAISED INTO THE IMPORTANCE OF A HERETIC]

Concord, October 8, 1838

My dear Sir,

I ought sooner to have acknowledged your kind letter of last week & the sermon it accompanied.[2] The Letter was right manly & noble. The sermon I have read with attention. If it assails any statements of mine perhaps I am not as quick to see it as most writers. Certainly I felt no disposition to depart from my habitual contentment that you should speak your thought whilst I speak mine. I believe I must tell you what I think of my new position. It strikes me very oddly & even a little ludicrously that the good & great men of Cambridge should think of raising me into an object of criticism. I have always been from my very incapacity of methodical writing a chartered libertine free to worship & free to rail, lucky when I was understood but never esteemed near enough to the institutions & mind of society to deserve the notice of the masters of literature & religion. I have appreciated fully the advantage of my position for I well knew that there was no scholar less willing or less able to be a polemic. I could not give account of myself if challenged. I could not possibly give you one of the "arguments" on which as you cruelly hint any position of mine stands. For I do not know, I confess, what arguments mean in reference to any expression of a thought. I delight in telling what I think but if you ask me how I dare say so or why it is so I am the most helpless of mortal men; I see not even that either of these questions admit of an answer. So that in the present droll posture of my affairs when I see myself suddenly raised into the importance of a heretic, I am very uneasy if I advert to the supposed duties of such a personage who is expected to make good his thesis against all comers. I therefore tell you plainly I shall do no such thing. I shall read what you & other good men write as I have always done, glad when you speak my thought & skipping the page that has nothing for me. I shall go on just as before seeing whatever I can & telling what I see and I suppose with the same fortune as has hitherto attended me, the joy of finding that my abler & better brothers who work with the sympathy of society and love it, unexpectedly confirm my perceptions, & find my nonsense is only their own thought in motley.

---

[3]Plain.

[4]Emerson was delivering a series of lectures in Boston at the Society for the Diffusion of Useful Knowledge.

[1]Henry Ware (1764–1845), clergyman and professor of divinity at Harvard, was connected with the Unitarian branch of Congregationalists. The letter has been edited for presentation here, omitting the changes and deletions contained in the original publication.

[2]The sermon presumably was *The Personality of the Deity*, which was looked upon as a rejoinder to Emerson's "Divinity School Address," delivered in May 1838. Controversy over Emerson's lecture continued for some time, one periodical calling it "neither good divinity nor good sense." Clearly Ware wanted to lure Emerson into a theological debate.

TO CAROLINE STURGIS[1]

[I Chiefly Grieve that I Cannot Grieve]

Concord? February 4, 1842

Dear Caroline

The days of our mourning ought, no doubt, to be accomplished ere this, & the innocent & beautiful should not be sourly & gloomily lamented, but with music & fragrant thoughts & sportive recollections. Alas! I chiefly grieve that I cannot grieve; that this fact takes no more deep hold than other facts, is as dreamlike as they; a lambent flame that will not burn playing on the surface of my river. Must every experience—those that promised to be dearest & most penetrative,—only kiss my cheek like the wind & pass away? I think of Ixion & Tantalus & Kehama.[2] Dear Boy too precious & unique a creation to be huddled aside into the waste & prodigality of things! Yet his Image, so gentle, yet so rich in hopes, blends easily with every happy moment, every fair remembrance, every cherished friendship of my life. I delight in the regularity & symmetry of his nature. Calm & wise, calmly & wisely happy, the beautiful Creative power looked out from him & spoke of anything but chaos & interruption; signified strength & unity—& gladdening, all-uniting life. What was the moral of sun & moon, of roses & acorns, that was the moral of the sweet boy's life, softened only & humanized by blue eyes & infant eloquence. x x x

TO MARGARET FULLER[1]

[A Vagabond in this Universe of Pure Power]

Concord, June 7, 1843

Dear Margaret,

If the great sheet & little lines do not fright away thoughts, you shall have a letter though late. Yet I remember to have read that the human face seen through a magnifying glass, loses expression, and a little wit must needs seem less when gipsying it over so much white paper—But what to tell you? It is true—that which they say about our New England œstrum[2] which will never let us stand or sit but urges us like mad through the world. The calmest life, the most protected circumstance cannot save us. I want some intercalated days, as much as if I lived in State Street—to bethink me & to derive order to my life from the heart. That should be the use of a reasonable friend to check this headlong racing & put us in possession of ourselves once more for love or for shame. The life lived, the thing done is a paltry & drivelling affair, as far as I know it, though in the presence & consciousness of the magnificent, yea the unspeakably great. Yet I love life—never little,—and now, I think, more & more, entertained & puzzled though I be by this lubricity of it, & inaccessibleness of its pith & heart. The variety of our vital game delights me. I seem in the bosom of all possibility & have never tried but one or two trivial experiments. In happy hours it seems as if one could not lie too lightly on it and like a cloud it would buoy him up & convey him anywhither. But by infirm faith we lose our delicate balance, flounder about & come into the realms & under the laws of mud & stones. The depth of the notes which we accidentally sound on the strings of nature are out of all proportion to our taught & ascertained power and teach us what strangers & novices we are in nature, vagabond in this universe of pure power to which we

---

[1]Friend of Margaret Fuller and Emerson, and special friend to the five-year-old Waldo, who died in January 1842.
[2]The first two are sufferers from Greek mythology, the last from Hindu; Ixion was bound to a wheel that turned con-

tinuously; Tantalus was placed to be always out of reach of water and fruit he craved; Kehama was assigned in hell to be the fourth permanent support for the throne of Yamen.
[1]Margaret Fuller had written to Emerson from Niagara.
[2]Variant of *estrum*, frenzy or strong impulse.

have not the smallest key. I will at least be glad of my days—I who have so many of them,—and having been informed by God though in the casualest manner that my funds are inexhaustible I will believe it with all my heart. Let there be no œstrum for me. I think of sculpture & painting only so, that they shall teach us manners & abolish hurry. I have heard of Niagara that it falls without speed.—I was sorry that you should have cold weather for your journey & the Falls. You should have found them buried in floods of heat and under a warm moon. I only wish that so rare a spectacle should be set & circumstanced in the best of times & chances for so rare spectators. Whatever they gave you, you will one day give me, O most bountiful of friends. If it was cold & bad weather, will you not come back by the same road & see them in July?—I should shun to tell you of myself of my reading & writing but for my philosophical preface. What signifies that I write trifles & read trifles, if the spirit have these broad leisures & countless pipes & inlets communicating with the sphere and anywhere a great result shall be slipped in. I cannot recall anything that I delight to mention yet I have had several days of a creamy smoothness whose worth & sequel I cannot suspect, though no fruit appears. I have the best of Chinese Confucian books lately, an octavo published at Malacca, in English. Much of it is the old Confucius more fully rendered; but the book of *Mencius*[3] is wholly new to me, and in its quiet sunshine a dangerous foil to Carlyle's storm lights. . . .

TO WALT WHITMAN
[THE BEGINNING OF A GREAT CAREER]

Concord, July 21, 1855

Dear Sir—I am not blind to the worth of the wonderful gift of *Leaves of Grass*. I find it the most extraordinary piece of wit and wisdom that America has yet contributed. I am very happy in reading it, as great power makes us happy. It meets the demand I am always making of what seemed the sterile and stingy nature, as if too much handiwork, or too much lymph in the temperament, were making our western wits fat and mean.

I give you joy of your free and brave thought. I have great joy in it, I find incomparable things said incomparably well, as they must be. I find the courage of treatment which do delights us, and which large perception only can inspire.

I greet you at the beginning of a great career, which yet must have had a long foreground somewhere, for such a start. I rubbed my eyes a little, to see if this sunbeam were no illusion; but the solid sense of the book is a sober certainty. It has the best merits, namely, of fortifying and encouraging.

I did not know until I last night saw the book advertised in a newspaper that I could trust the name as real and available for a post-office. I wish to see my benefactor, and have felt much like striking my tasks, and visiting New York to pay you my respects.

R. W. Emerson

TO THOMAS CARLYLE
[ON *LEAVES OF GRASS*]

Concord, May 6, 1856

Dear Carlyle,

There is no escape from the forces of time & life, & we do not write letters to the gods or to our friends, but only to attorneys landlords & tenants. But the

---

[3]Confucius (*c.* 551–479 B.C.), Chinese philosopher, one of whose disciples was Mencius (*c.* 371–288 B.C.); the *Book of* *Mencius* is one of the *Four Books* of Chinese literature and an elaboration and application of Confucian philosophy.

planes or platforms on which all stand remain the same, & we are ever expecting the descent of the heavens, which is to put us into familiarity with the first named. When I ceased to write to you for a long time, I said to myself,—If any thing really good should happen here,—any stroke of good sense or virtue in our politics, or of great sense in a book,—I will send it on the instant to the formidable man; but I will not repeat to him every month, that there are no news. Thank me for my resolution, & for keeping it through the long night. One book, last summer, came out in New York, a nondescript monster which yet has terrible eyes & buffalo strength, & was indisputably American,—which I thought to send you; but the book throve so badly with the few to whom I showed it, & wanted good morals so much, that I never did. Yet I believe now again, I shall. It is called "Leaves of Grass,"—was written & printed by a journeyman printer in Brooklyn, N. Y. named Walter Whitman; and after you have looked into it, if you think, as you may, that it is only an auctioneer's inventory of a warehouse, you can light your pipe with it. . . .

HENRY DAVID THOREAU
(1817–1862)

In the remarkable opening pages of what is now recognized as a modern classic, *Walden; or, Life in the Woods,* Thoreau wrote: "I long ago lost a hound, a bay horse, and a turtledove, and am still on their trail." This famous line puzzled readers from the beginning, especially as Thoreau hinted that his losses may also have been his readers': "Many are the travellers I have spoken concerning them," he reported, "and they seemed as anxious to recover them as if they had lost them themselves." Emerson said of this enigmatic passage that Thoreau "knew well how to throw a poetic veil over his experience." He might have added that he knew how, by striking such a deeply personal note, to set in motion such hauntingly sympathetic vibrations. Are the losses, Thoreau's and ours, something primitive, something poetic, something sacred that modern life—given over to frenzied pursuit of wealth and power—no longer values, no longer misses? Few readers of Thoreau escape the longing to repair their losses, and ultimately to "front the essential facts of life" somehow in their own experience.

It is perhaps enough to know of Thoreau's life that he spent it in earnest pursuit of his hound, his bay horse, and his turtledove. But there are a few facts to flesh out this spare allegory. Of all America's writers connected with Concord, Thoreau was the only one born there. And he never ventured very far or for very long outside it. There were trips to Maine, a stay of a few months in New York tutoring, expeditions to Cape Cod, an excursion into New Hampshire to visit the White Mountains, and, finally, a year before he died, a journey to Minnesota in search of a cure for his tuberculosis. By and large, however, Thoreau lived his forty-four years in his place of birth and could say with honesty in *Walden:* "I have travelled a great deal in Concord."

Thoreau was sent to Concord Academy to prepare for college, and he attended Harvard from 1833 to 1837. His was an undistinguished record, but he was surely the best-read graduate of his class. No doubt the most important commitment he made during this time was to start his journal, probably at Emerson's suggestion. The first entry (when Thoreau was twenty) reads: "'What are you doing now,' he asked, 'Do you keep a journal?' So I make my first entry today." For the next twenty-five years he continued to keep his journal, and it became the center of his inner life and the source of much that he would publish. Thoreau never married, and he never found the ideal friend he sought: the journal filled the empty space of these "losses," and he gave to it "that of me which would else spill over and run to waste."

After leaving college, Thoreau tried his hand at a number of jobs, including that of assisting his father in his home industry of making lead pencils. He taught in the town school of Concord, but was criticized for not whipping students—whereupon in protest he whipped a number of startled students and resigned. Later he and his older brother opened their own school, first in the Thoreau house, later in the Academy building, with Henry teaching Latin, Greek, French, and mathematics. They took their students on "field trips" for nature study, an innovation in American schools. And they themselves, in 1839, went on a thirteen-day trip down the Concord River and up the Merrimack to Concord, New Hampshire, a journey that would provide the basis for Thoreau's first book some ten years later.

For a long time the myth has persisted that his solitude and celibacy grew out of his rejection by a pretty young woman that the two brothers fell in love with about this time. Ellen Sewall first turned down John, and then Henry (her father would not countenance a "radical" Transcendentalist in the family). Recent biographers have concluded that, whatever the feelings between Ellen and Henry, they were not so deep or enduring as to be a major determinant in his life. More enduring was the grief he felt at his brother's sudden death in 1842. By this time, Thoreau was living at the Emerson home as a handyman, and Emerson's five-year-old son Waldo died two weeks after the death of John Thoreau. The fourteen years that separated Thoreau and Emerson seemed to disappear as in their bitter grief, they found some solace in silent sharing.

While living with Emerson, Thoreau began to publish poems and essays in the organ of the Transcendental Club, *The Dial*, first edited by Margaret Fuller and later by Emerson. And he began to lecture at the Concord Lyceum and at other nearby towns. He spent some nine months in 1843 in Staten Island, New York, as a tutor to the children of William Emerson, Ralph Waldo's brother. There he met Horace Greeley, editor of the New York *Tribune*, who assisted him in getting his essays published.

On July 4, 1845, he moved into a cabin he had built himself on land owned by Emerson near Walden Pond, with the purpose of writing his book based on the river trip taken with his brother six years before. He did not live as a hermit, but often dined with Emerson, and he spent one night in the Concord jail in July 1846 for refusing to pay his poll tax as a protest against the war with Mexico. An aunt paid the tax, to his disappointment, and shortened his stay in jail. When after twenty-six months Thoreau left Walden Pond, he carried with him the first draft of his first book and the notes and ideas for his second, which would be based on his experiences at Walden Pond. In 1847, while Emerson was in Europe, he returned to live in the Emerson house, and the following year he went back to his family's home, where he remained until his death. Some of his time he spent as a professional surveyor.

In 1848 he delivered as a lecture the work later famous as "Civil Disobedience," describing his imprisonment for refusing to pay a tax that would support a war of which he disapproved. He continued to work on his growing manuscript, tapping his journal for much of the material. It was published at his expense in 1849 as *A Week on the Concord and Merrimack Rivers,* a title that was generally misleading inasmuch as the travel account was stuccoed all over with poems and essays about life and death, friendship and love, history, philosophy, and religion. Clearly it bewildered its few readers. In a four-year period, only a few more than two hundred copies were sold, and the remainder were sent to Thoreau. He wrote in his journal: "I have now a library of nearly nine hundred volumes, over seven hundred of which I wrote myself."

The failure of *A Week* postponed the publication of *Walden,* no doubt for the book's own good. Thoreau labored mightily in revising his manuscript, and it was published in 1854. Its title, *Walden; or, Life in the Woods,* was as misleading as the title of his first book. But in the work, Thoreau had struck a balance and hit his stride. The work was well proportioned, shorter than the first, and the action in the foreground more subtly integrated with the thoughts on living, being, and becoming.

He presented details on building his house, baking his bread, hoeing his beans. But the remarkable achievement in *Walden* was that the chapters were as well crafted as the cabin, the paragraphs as carefully nurtured as the beans. The sentences especially seemed held together with such tension that they were ready to snap: "The mass of men lead lives of quiet desperation"; "I would rather sit on a pumpkin and have it all to myself, than be crowded on a velvet cushion"; "Our life is frittered away by detail"; "Time is but a stream I go a-fishing in." Thoreau went to the woods "to drive life into a corner, and reduce it to its lowest terms," to discover whether "it proved to be mean" or "if it were sublime" and to "give a true account of it." He left the woods, he wrote, because "it seemed to me I had several more lives to live, and could not spare any more time for that one." The true account he gave was *Walden,* and no doubt that truth was a precious element in the book's vitality and endurance.

After the publication of *Walden,* Thoreau's horizon widened. He recognized a kindred free spirit in Walt Whitman, praised *Leaves of Grass,* and visited the poet in New York in 1856. He became more of an activist in causes, particularly coming to the defense of abolitionist leader John Brown after his raid at Harper's Ferry when he briefly took over the U.S. Armory there. He delivered his defense of Brown at the Concord Vestry over the protest of fellow townsmen, and was forced to ring the bell himself to announce his appearance. This defense was later published as "A Plea for Captain John Brown."

But more and more Thoreau turned to his journal as the place to explore his inner life. "A journal," he wrote, "is a record of experiences and growth." And in 1857 he asked, "Is not the poet bound to write his own biography? Is there any other work for him but a good journal?" As the journal grew, Thoreau clearly came to see it not as simply a source for his published essays and books, but as a work in its own right, having its own integrity as a structure. It fills fourteen of the twenty volumes of the 1906 Walden Edition. It contains over two million words. Thoreau's biographer, Henry Seidel Canby, called it "one of the most complete records extant of the inner life of the individual." One of Thoreau's couplets reads: "My life has been the poem I would have writ, / But I could not both live and utter it." Thoreau seems not only to have lived the poem of his life, but he came very close to having uttered it—in the words poured forth into his journal.

But his fame has been established on his published works, especially *Walden* and "Civil Disobedience." Few works have entered so directly into the consciousness and consciences of later generations as these two. It was their spirit that fired the independence movement led by Mahatma Gandhi in India and the civil rights movement led by Martin Luther King, Jr., in America.

Thoreau's health failed in 1861, and as he lay sick with tuberculosis in his room, one visitor reported: "Never saw a man dying with so much pleasure and peace." When asked by his Aunt Louisa whether he had made his peace with God, he said: "I did not know that we had ever quarreled." Although the relationship of Emerson and Thoreau had at times been quite strained, especially in the later years, Emerson spoke eloquently at the funeral. Later he confided his feelings to his *Journal*: "Henry Thoreau remains erect, calm, self-subsistent, before me, and I read him not only truly in his Journal, but he is not long out of mind when I walk, and, as today, row upon the pond. He chose wisely no doubt for himself to be the bachelor of thought and nature that he was—how near to the old monks in their ascetic religion!" Walt Whitman commented in his later years: "One thing about Thoreau keeps him very near to me: I refer to his lawless-ness—his dissent—his going his absolute own road let hell blaze all it chooses."

ADDITIONAL READING

The Heart of Thoreau's Journal, ed. Odell Shepard, 1927; *Consciousness in Concord: The Text of Thoreau's Hitherto "Lost Journal" (1840–41)*, ed. Perry Miller, 1958; *H. D. Thoreau: A Writer's Journal*, ed. Laurence Stapleton, 1960; *The Annotated Walden*, ed. Philip Van Doren Stern, 1970; *Thoreau's World: Miniatures from His Journal*, ed. Charles R. Anderson, 1971; *Thoreau in the Mountains*, ed. William Howarth, 1982.

Henry Seidel Canby, *Thoreau*, 1939; Joseph Wood Krutch, *Henry David Thoreau*, 1948; R. L. Cook, *Passage to Walden*, 1949; Walter Harding, ed., *Thoreau: A Century of Criticism*, 1954; J. Lyndon Shanley, *The Making of Walden*, 1957; Sherman Paul, *The Shores of America: Thoreau's Inward Exploration*, 1958; Sherman Paul, ed., *Thoreau: A Collection of Critical Essays*, 1962; Walter Harding, *The Days of Henry David Thoreau*, 1965; Joel Porte, *Emerson and Thoreau: Transcendentalists in Conflict*, 1966; Richard Ruling, ed., *Twentieth-Century Interpretations of Walden*, 1968; Charles R. Anderson, *The Magic Circle of Walden*, 1968; Walter Glick, ed., *The Recognition of Henry David Thoreau*, 1969; Robert Stowell, *A Thoreau Gazeteer*, 1970; Eugene F. Timpe, ed., *Thoreau Abroad*, 1971; Walter Harding, ed., *Henry David Thoreau: A Profile*, 1971; Stanley Cavell, *The Senses of Walden*, 1972; James McIntosh, *Thoreau as Romantic Naturalist*, 1974; Richard Tuerk, *Central Still*, 1975; Michael Meyer, *Several More Lives to Live*, 1977; Frederick Garber, *Thoreau's Redemptive Imagination*, 1977; Richard Lebeaux, *Young Man Thoreau*, 1977; Robert Sayre, *Thoreau and the American Indians*, 1977; Mary Elkins Moller, *Thoreau in the Human Community*, 1980; Walter Harding and Michael Meyer, *The New Thoreau Handbook*, 1980; Richard Bridgman, *Dark Thoreau*, 1982; William Howarth, *The Book of Concord: Thoreau's Life as a Writer*, 1982; Raymond R. Borst, *Henry David Thoreau: A Descriptive Bibliography*, 1982; Raymond D. Gozzi, ed., *Thoreau's Psychology: Eight Essays*, 1983; Richard Lebeaux, *Thoreau's Seasons*, 1984; Sharon Cameron, *Writing Nature*, 1986; Robert D. Richardson, Jr., *Henry David Thoreau: A Life of the Mind*, 1986; Richard Schneider, *Henry David Thoreau*, 1987.

TEXTS

The Writings of Henry David Thoreau, ed. Walter Harding, William L. Howarth et al. (The Princeton Edition), 1970– : *A Week on the Concord and Merrimack Rivers*, ed. Carl F. Hovde, et al., 1980; *Reform Papers*, ed. Wendell Glick, 1973. *The Writings of Henry David Thoreau*, 20 vols., the Walden Edition, 1906: Vol. II, *Walden*; Vols. VII–XX, *The Journal*, ed. Bradford Torrey, 1906. *The Collected Poems of Henry David Thoreau*, ed. Carl Bode, 1964. *The Correspondence of Henry David Thoreau*, ed. Walter Harding and Carl Bode, 1958.

from A Week on the Concord and Merrimack Rivers

[POETRY IS A NATURAL FRUIT]

What would we not give for some great poem to read now, which would be in harmony with the scenery,—for if men read aright, methinks they would never read anything but poems. No history nor philosophy can supply their place.

The wisest definition of poetry the poet will instantly prove false by setting aside its requisitions. We can, therefore, publish only our advertisement of it.

There is no doubt that the loftiest written wisdom is either rhymed, or in some way musically measured,—is, in form as well as substance, poetry; and a volume which should contain the condensed wisdom of mankind, need not have one rhythmless line.

Yet poetry, though the last and finest result, is a natural fruit. As naturally as the oak bears an acorn, and the vine a gourd, man bears a poem, either spoken or done. It is the chief and most memorable success, for history is but a prose narrative of poetic deeds. What else have the Hindoos, the Persians, the Babylonians, the Egyptians done, that can be told? It is the simplest relation of phenomena, and describes the commonest sensations with more truth than science does, and the latter at a distance slowly mimics its style and methods. The poet sings how the blood flows in his veins. He performs his functions, and is so well that he needs such stimulus to sing only as plants to put forth leaves and blossoms. He would strive in vain to modulate the remote and transient music which he sometimes hears, since his song is a vital function like breathing, and an integral result like weight. It is not the overflowing of life but its subsidence rather, and is drawn from under the feet of the poet. . . .

[POETRY IS THE MYSTICISM OF MANKIND]

Poetry is the mysticism of mankind.

The expressions of the poet cannot be analyzed; his sentence is one word, whose syllables are words. There are indeed no *words* quite worthy to be set to his music. But what matter if we do not hear the words always, if we hear the music?

Much verse fails of being poetry because it was not written exactly at the right crisis, though it may have been inconceivably near to it. It is only by a miracle that poetry is written at all. It is not recoverable thought, but a hue caught from a vaster receding thought.

A poem is one undivided unimpeded expression fallen ripe into literature, and it is undividedly and unimpededly received by those for whom it was matured.

If you can speak what you will never hear,—if you can write what you will never read, you have done rare things.

> The work we choose should be our own,
> God lets alone.

The unconsciousness of man is the consciousness of God.

Deep are the foundations of sincerity. Even stone walls have their foundation below the frost.

What is produced by a free stroke charms us, like the forms of lichens and leaves. There is a certain perfection in accident which we never consciously attain. Draw a blunt quill filled with ink over a sheet of paper, and fold the paper before the ink is dry transversely to this line, and a delicately shaded and regular figure will be produced, in some respects more pleasing than an elaborate drawing.

The talent of composition is very dangerous,—the striking out the heart of life at a blow, as the Indian takes off a scalp. I feel as if my life had grown more outward when I can express it. . . .

[THE POET IS NO TENDER SLIP]

The poet is no tender slip of fairy stock, who requires peculiar institutions and edicts for his defence, but the toughest son of earth and of Heaven, and by his greater strength and endurance his fainting companions will recognize the God in him. It is the worshippers of beauty, after all, who have done the real pioneer work of the world.

The poet will prevail to be popular in spite of his faults, and in spite of his beauties too. He will hit the nail on the head, and we shall not know the shape of his hammer. He makes us free of his hearth and heart, which is greater than to offer one the freedom of a city.

Great men, unknown to their generation, have their fame among the great who have preceded them, and all true worldly fame subsides from their high estimate beyond the stars.

Orpheus does not hear the strains which issue from his lyre, but only those which are breathed into it; for the original strain precedes the sound, by as much as the echo follows after; the rest is the perquisite of the rocks and trees and beasts.

When I stand in a library where is all the recorded wit of the world, but none of the recording, a mere accumulated, and not truly cumulative treasure, where immortal works stand side by side with anthologies which did not survive their month, and cobweb and mildew have already spread from these to the binding of those; and happily I am reminded of what poetry is, I perceive that Shakspeare and Milton did not foresee into what company they were to fall. Alas! that so soon the work of a true poet should be swept into such a dust-hole!

The poet will write for his peers alone. He will remember only that he saw truth and beauty from his position, and expect the time when a vision as broad shall overlook the same field as freely.

We are often prompted to speak our thoughts to our neighbors, or the single travellers whom we meet on the road, but poetry is a communication from our home and solitude addressed to all Intelligence. It never whispers in a private ear. Knowing this, we may understand those sonnets said to be addressed to particular persons, or "to a Mistress' Eyebrow." Let none feel flattered by them. For poetry write love, and it will be equally true.

No doubt it is an important difference between men of genius or poets, and men not of genius, that the latter are unable to grasp and confront the thought which visits them. But it is because it is too faint for expression, or even conscious impression. What merely quickens or retards the blood in their veins and fills their afternoons with pleasure they know not whence, conveys a distinct assurance to the finer organization of the poet.

We talk of genius as if it were a mere knack, and the poet could only express what other men conceived. But in comparison with his task, the poet is the least talented of any; the writer of prose has more skill. See what talent the smith has. His material is pliant in his hands. When the poet is most inspired, is stimulated by an *aura* which never even colors the afternoons of common men, then his talent is all gone, and he is no longer a poet. The gods do not grant him any skill more than another. They never put their gifts into his hands, but they encompass and sustain him with their breath.

To say that God has given a man many and great talents, frequently means, that he has brought his heavens down within reach of his hands.

When the poetic frenzy seizes us, we run and scratch with our pen, intent only on worms, calling our mates around us, like the cock, and delighting in the dust we make, but do not detect where the jewel lies, which, perhaps, we have in the mean time cast to a distance, or quite covered up again.

The poet's body even is not fed like other men's, but he sometimes tastes the genuine nectar and ambrosia of the gods, and lives a divine life. By the healthful and invigorating thrills of inspiration his life is preserved to a serene old age.

Some poems are for holidays only. They are polished and sweet, but it is the sweetness of sugar, and not such as toil gives to sour bread. The breath with which the poet utters his verse must be that by which he lives.

Great prose, of equal elevation, commands our respect more than great verse, since it implies a more permanent and level height, a life more pervaded with the grandeur of the thought. The poet often only makes an irruption, like a Parthian, and is off again, shooting while he retreats; but the prose writer has conquered like a Roman, and settled colonies.

The true poem is not that which the public read. There is always a poem not printed on paper, coincident with the production of this, stereotyped in the poet's life. It is *what he has become through his work*. Not how is the idea expressed in stone, or on canvas or paper, is the question, but how far it has obtained form and expression in the life of the artist. His true work will not stand in any prince's gallery.

> My life has been the poem I would have writ,
> But I could not both live and utter it.

1849

from Collected Poems

Within the Circuit
of This Plodding Life[1]

Within the circuit of this plodding life
There enter moments of an azure hue,
Untarnished fair as is the violet
Or anemone, when the spring strews them
By some meandering rivulet, which make   5
The best philosophy untrue that aims
But to console man for his grievances.
I have remembered when the winter came,
High in my chamber in the frosty nights,
When in the still light of the cheerful moon,   10
On every twig and rail and jutting spout,
The icy spears were adding to their length
Against the arrows of the coming sun,
How in the shimmering noon of summer past
Some unrecorded beam slanted across   15

---

[1]Entitled "Winter Memories" when published in 1895.

The upland pastures where the Johnswort[2] grew;
Or heard, amid the verdure of my mind,
The bee's long smothered hum, on the blue flag
Loitering amidst the mead; or busy rill,
Which now through all its course stands still and dumb   20
Its own memorial,—purling[3] at its play
Along the slopes, and through the meadows next,
Until its youthful sound was hushed at last
In the staid current of the lowland stream;
Or seen the furrows shine but late upturned,   25
And where the fieldfare[4] followed in the rear,
When all the fields around lay bound and hoar
Beneath a thick integument of snow.
So by God's cheap economy made rich
To go upon my winter's task again.   30

1841   1842

Conscience Is Instinct Bred in the House[1]

Conscience is instinct bred in the house,
Feeling and Thinking propagate the sin
By an unnatural breeding in and in.
I say, Turn it out doors,
Into the moors.   5
I love a life whose plot is simple,
And does not thicken with every pimple,
A soul so sound no sickly conscience binds it,
That makes the universe no worse than 't finds it.
I love an earnest soul,   10
Whose mighty joy and sorrow
Are not drowned in a bowl,
And brought to life to-morrow;
That lives one tragedy,
And not seventy;   15
A conscience worth keeping,
Laughing not weeping;
A conscience wise and steady,
And forever ready;
Not changing with events,   20
Dealing in compliments;
A conscience exercised about
Large things, where one *may* doubt.
I love a soul not all of wood,
Predestinated to be good,   25
But true to the backbone
Unto itself alone,

---

[2]St. Johnswort, or Klamath weed, a yellow-flowered perennial common in fields and waste places.
[3]Swirling.
[4]An American robin.
[1]In introducing this poem into the text of *A Week on the*

Concord and Merrimack Rivers, Thoreau wrote: "The conscience really does not, and ought not to, monopolize the whole of our lives, any more than the heart or the head. It is as liable to disease as any other part."

And false to none;
Born to its own affairs,
Its own joys and own cares;   30
By whom the work which God begun
Is finished, and not undone;
Taken up where he left off,
Whether to worship or to scoff;
If not good, why then evil,   35
If not good god, good devil.
Goodness! you hypocrite, come out of that,
Live your life, do your work, then take your hat.
I have no patience towards
Such conscientious cowards.   40
Give me simple laboring folk,
Who love their work,
Whose virtue is a song
To cheer God along.

1849

Lately, Alas, I
Knew a Gentle Boy[1]

Lately, alas, I knew a gentle boy,
  Whose features all were cast in Virtue's mould,
As one she had designed for Beauty's toy,
  But after manned him for her own strong-hold.

On every side he open was as day,   5
  That you might see no lack of strength within,
For walls and ports do only serve alway
  For a pretence to feebleness and sin.

Say not that Caesar was victorious,
  With toil and strife who stormed the House of Fame,   10
In other sense this youth was glorious,
  Himself a kingdom wheresoe'er he came.

No strength went out to get him victory,
  When all was income of its own accord;
For where he went none other was to see,   15
  But all were parcel of their noble lord.

He forayed like the subtile haze of summer,
  That stilly shows fresh landscapes to our eyes,
And revolutions works without a murmur,
  Or rustling of a leaf beneath the skies.   20

So was I taken unawares by this,
  I quite forgot my homage to confess;
Yet now am forced to know, though hard it is,
  I might have loved him had I loved him less.

---

[1]The early speculation that this poem was an expression of love for Ellen Sewall has been replaced by the assumption (particularly by Henry Seidel Canby in *Thoreau*, 1939) that it is about her younger brother Edmund Sewall, a pupil in Thoreau's school. Emerson said of this poem that it "reveals the tenderness under that triple steel of stoicism, and the intellectual subtlety it could animate." In *The Dial* (1840) it was entitled "Sympathy."

Each moment as we nearer drew to each,   25
  A stern respect withheld us farther yet,
So that we seemed beyond each other's reach,
  And less acquainted than when first we met.

We two were one while we did sympathize,
  So could we not the simplest bargain drive;   30
And what avails it now that we are wise,
  If absence doth this doubleness contrive?

Eternity may not the chance repeat,
  But I must tread my single way alone,
In sad remembrance that we once did meet,   35
  And know that bliss irrevocably gone.

The spheres henceforth my elegy shall sing,
  For elegy has other subject none;
Each strain of music in my ears shall ring
  Knell of departure from that other one.   40

Make haste and celebrate my tragedy;
  With fitting strain resound ye woods and fields;
Sorrow is dearer in such case to me
  Than all the joys other occasion yields.

———

Is't then too late the damage to repair?   45
  Distance, forsooth, from my weak grasp hath reft
The empty husk, and clutched the useless tare,
  But in my hands the wheat and kernel left.

If I but love that virtue which he is,
  Though it be scented in the morning air,   50
Still shall we be truest acquaintances,
  Nor mortals know a sympathy more rare.

1839   *1840*

My Love
Must Be as Free

My love must be as free
  As is the eagle's wing,
Hovering o'er land and sea
  And everything.

I must not dim my eye   5
  In thy saloon,
I must not leave my sky
  And nightly moon.

Be not the fowler's net
  Which stays my flight,
And craftily is set   10
  T' allure the sight.

But be the favoring gale
   That bears me on,
And still doth fill my sail   15
   When thou art gone.

I cannot leave my sky
   For thy caprice,
True love would soar as high
   As heaven is.   20

The eagle would not brook
   Her mate thus won,
Who trained his eye to look
   Beneath the sun.

1842

Friendship

I think awhile of Love, and while I think,
   Love is to me a world,
   Sole meat and sweetest drink,
   And close connecting link
     Tween heaven and earth.   5

I only know it is, not how or why,
   My greatest happiness;
   However hard I try,
   Not if I were to die,
     Can I explain.   10

I fain would ask my friend how it can be,
   But when the time arrives,
   Then Love is more lovely
   Than anything to me,
     And so I'm dumb.   15

For if the truth were known, Love cannot speak,
   But only thinks and does;
   Though surely out 'twill leak
   Without the help of Greek,
     Or any tongue.   20

A man may love the truth and practise it,
   Beauty he may admire,
   And goodness not omit,
   As much as may befit
     To reverence.   25

But only when these three together meet,
   As they always incline,
   And make one soul the seat,
   And favorite retreat
     Of loveliness;   30

When under kindred shape, like loves and hates
   And a kindred nature,

Proclaim us to be mates,
Exposed to equal fates
    Eternally;   35

And each may other help, and service do,
Drawing Love's bands more tight,
Service he ne'er shall rue
While one and one make two,
    And two are one;   40

In such case only doth man fully prove
Fully as man can do,
What power there is in Love
His inmost soul to move
    Resistlessly.   45

————

Two sturdy oaks I mean, which side by side,
Withstand the winter's storm,
And spite of wind and tide,
Grow up the meadow's pride,
    For both are strong.   50

Above they barely touch, but undermined
Down to their deepest source,
Admiring you shall find
Their roots are intertwined
    Insep'rably.   55

1838   *1906*

The Cliffs and Springs

When breathless noon hath paused on hill and vale,
And now no more the woodman plies his axe,
Nor mower whets his scythe,
Somewhat it is, sole sojourner on earth,
To hear the veery[1] on her oaken perch   5
Ringing her modest trill—
Sole sound of all the din that makes a world,
And I sole ear.
Fondly to nestle me in that sweet melody,
And own a kindred soul, speaking to me   10
From out the depths of universal being.
O'er birch and hazle, through the sultry air,
Comes that faint sound this way,
On Zephyr[2] borne, straight to my ear.
No longer time or place, nor faintest trace   15
Of earth, the landscape's shimmer is my only space,
Sole remnant of a world.
Anon that throat has done, and familiar sounds
Swell strangely on the breeze, the low of cattle,

---

[1] A thrush (or Wilson's thrush) of the eastern United States.
[2] The west wind, or any gentle breeze.

And the novel cries of sturdy swains   20
That plod the neighboring vale—
And I walk once more confounded a denizen[3] of earth.

1838   *1943*

I Knew
a Man by Sight

I knew a man by sight,
  A blameless wight,
Who, for a year or more,
Had daily passed my door,
Yet converse none had had with him.   5

I met him in a lane,
  Him and his cane,
About three miles from home,
Where I had chanced to roam,
And volumes stared at him, and he at me.   10

In a more distant place
  I glimpsed his face,
And bowed instinctively;
Starting he bowed to me,
Bowed simultaneously, and passed along.   15

Next, in a foreign land
  I grasped his hand,
And had a social chat,
About this thing and that,
As I had known him well a thousand years.   20

Late in a wilderness
  I shared his mess,
For he had hardships seen,
And I a wanderer been;
He was my bosom friend, and I was his.   25

And as, methinks, shall all,
  Both great and small,
That ever lived on earth,
Early or late their birth,
Stranger and foe, one day each other know.   30

1838   *1943*

Manhood

I love to see the man, a long-lived child,
As yet uninjured by all worldly taint

---

[3]Inhabitant.

As the fresh infant whose whole life is play.
'Tis a serene spectacle for a serene day;
But better still I love to contemplate   5
The mature soul of lesser innocence,
Who hath travelled far on life's dusty road
Far from the starting point of infancy
And proudly bears his small degen'racy
Blazon'd on his memorial standard high   10
Who from the sad experience of his fate
Since his bark struck on that unlucky rock
Has proudly steered his life with his own hands.
Though his face harbors less of innocence
Yet there do chiefly lurk within its depths   15
Furrowed by care, but yet all over spread
With the ripe bloom of a self-wrought content
Noble resolves which do reprove the gods
And it doth more assert man's eminence
Above the happy level of the brute   20
And more doth advertise me of the heights
To which no natural path doth ever lead
No natural light can ever light our steps,
—But the far-piercing ray that shines
From the recesses of a brave man's eye.   25

1943

Life

My life is like a stately warrior horse,
That walks with fluent pace along the way,
And I the upright horseman that bestrides
His flexuous[1] back, feeding my private thoughts.—
Alas, when will this rambling head and neck   5
Be welded to that firm and brawny breast?—
But still my steady steed goes proudly forth,
Mincing his stately steps along the road;
The sun may set, the silver moon may rise,
But my unresting steed holds on his way.   10
He is far gone ere this, you fain would say,
He is far going. Plants grow and rivers run;
You ne'er may look upon the ocean waves,
At morn or eventide, but you will see
Far in th' horizon with expanded sail,   15
Some solitary bark stand out to sea,
Far bound—well so my life sails far,
To double some far cape not yet explored.
A cloud ne'er standeth in the summer's sky,
The eagle sailing high, with outspread wings   20
Cleaving the silent air, resteth him not
A moment in his flight, the air is not his perch.
Nor doth my life fold its unwearied wings,

---

[1] Full of bends.

And hide its head within its downy breast,
But still it plows the shoreless seas of time,   25
Breasting the waves with an unsanded bow.

1864

Inspiration[1]

What'er we leave to God, God does,
    And blesses us;
The work we choose should be our own,
    God lets alone.

If with light head erect I sing,   5
    Though all the muses lend their force,
From my poor love of anything,
    The verse is weak and shallow as its source.

But if with bended neck I grope,
    Listening behind me for my wit,   10
With faith superior to hope,
    More anxious to keep back than forward it,

Making my soul accomplice there
    Unto the flame my heart hath lit,
Then will the verse forever wear,—   15
    Time cannot bend the line which God hath writ.

Always the general show of things
    Floats in review before my mind,
And such true love and reverence brings,
    That sometimes I forget that I am blind.   20

But now there comes unsought, unseen,
    Some clear, divine electuary,[2]
And I who had but sensual been,
    Grow sensible, and as God is, am wary.

I hearing get who had but ears,   25
    And sight, who had but eyes before,
I moments live who lived but years,
    And truth discern who knew but learning's lore.

I hear beyond the range of sound,
    I see beyond the range of sight,   30
New earths and skies and seas around,
    And in my day the sun doth pale his light.

A clear and ancient harmony
    Pierces my soul through all its din,
As through its utmost melody,—   35
    Farther behind than they—farther within.

---

[1]Although parts of this poem appeared scattered throughout *A Week* (1849), the poem in its entirety was not published until 1895 in *Poems of Nature*.
[2]Drugs and honey combined to form medicine.

More swift its bolt than lightning is,
  Its voice than thunder is more loud,
It doth expand my privacies
  To all, and leave me single in the crowd.   40

It speaks with such authority,
  With so serene and lofty tone,
That idle Time runs gadding by,
  And leaves me with Eternity alone.

Then chiefly is my natal hour,   45
  And only then my prime of life,
Of manhood's strength it is the flower,
  'Tis peace's end and war's beginning strife.

'T 'hath come in summer's broadest noon,
  By a grey wall or some chance place,
Unseasoned time, insulted June,   50
  And vexed the day with its presuming face.

Such fragrance round my couch it makes,
  More rich than are Arabian drugs,
That my soul scents its life and wakes   55
  The body up beneath its perfumed rugs.

Such is the Muse—the heavenly maid,
  The star that guides our mortal course,
Which shows where life's true kernel's laid,
  Its wheat's fine flower, and its undying force.   60

She with one breath attunes the spheres,
  And also my poor human heart,
With one impulse propels the years
  Around, and gives my throbbing pulse its start.

I will not doubt forever more,   65
  Nor falter from a steadfast faith,
For though the system be turned o'er,
  God takes not back the word which once he saith.

I will then trust the love untold
  Which not my worth nor want has bought,   70
Which wooed me young and woos me old,
  And to this evening hath me brought.

My memory I'll educate
  To know the one historic truth,
Remembering to the latest date   75
  The only true and sole immortal youth.

Be but thy inspiration given,
  No matter through what danger sought,
I'll fathom hell or climb to heaven,
  And yet esteem that cheap which love has bought.   80

———

    Fame cannot tempt the bard
      Who's famous with his God,
    Nor laurel him reward
      Who hath his Maker's nod.

1849, 1895

The Fall of the Leaf

Thank God who seasons thus the year,
   And sometimes kindly slants his rays;
For in his winter he's most near
   And plainest seen upon the shortest days.

Who gently tempers now his heats,   5
   And then his harsher cold, lest we
Should surfeit on the summer's sweets,
   Or pine upon the winter's crudity.

A sober mind will walk alone,
   Apart from nature, if need be,   10
And only its own seasons own;
   For nature leaving its humanity.

Sometimes a late autumnal thought
   Has crossed my mind in green July,
And to its early freshness brought   15
   Late ripened fruits, and an autumnal sky.

The evening of the year draws on,
   The fields a later aspect wear;
Since Summer's garishness is gone,
   Some grains of night tincture the noontide air.   20

Behold! the shadows of the trees
   Now circle wider 'bout their stem,
Like sentries that by slow degrees
   Perform their rounds, gently protecting them.

And as the year doth decline,   25
   The sun allows a scantier light;
Behind each needle of the pine
   There lurks a small auxiliar to the night.

I hear the cricket's slumbrous lay
   Around, beneath me, and on high;   30
It rocks the night, it soothes the day,
   And everywhere is Nature's lullaby.

But most he chirps beneath the sod,
   When he has made his winter bed;
His creak grown fainter but more broad,   35
   A film of autumn o'er the summer spread.

Small birds, in fleets migrating by,
   Now beat across some meadow's bay,
And as they tack and veer on high,
   With faint and hurried click beguile the way.   40

Far in the woods, these golden days,
   Some leaf obeys its Maker's call;
And through their hollow aisles it plays
   With delicate touch the prelude of the Fall.

Gently withdrawing from its stem,   45
   It lightly lays itself along
Where the same hand hath pillowed them,
   Resigned to sleep upon the old year's throng.

The loneliest birch is brown and sere,
  The furthest pool is strewn with leaves,   50
Which float upon their watery bier,
  Where is no eye that sees, no heart that grieves.

The jay screams through the chestnut wood;
  The crisped and yellow leaves around
Are hue and texture of my mood—   55
  And these rough burrs my heirlooms on the ground.

The threadbare trees, so poor and thin—
  They are no wealthier than I;
But with as brave a core within
  They rear their boughs to the October sky.   60

Poor knights they are which bravely wait
  The charge of Winter's cavalry,
Keeping a simple Roman state,
  Discumbered of their Persian luxury.

1863, 1895

Life Is a Summer's Day[1]

Life is a summer's day
When as it were for aye
  We sport and play.

Anon the night comes on,
The ploughman's work is done,   5
  And day is gone.

We read in this one page
Both Youth, Manhood, and Age
  That hoary Sage.

The morning is our prime,   10
That laughs to scorn old Time,
  And knows no crime.

The noon comes on apace,
And then with swel'tring face
  We run our race.   15

When eve comes stealing o'er
We ponder at our door
  On days of yore.

The patient kine, they say,
At dawn do frisk and play,   20
  And well they may.

By noon their sports abate,
For then, as bards relate,
  They vegetate.

---

[1]On the manuscript the title "Sic Vita," meaning "Thus is
life" (Latin), appears but has been fairly well erased.

When eventide hath come,   25
And grey flies cease their hum,
    And now are dumb,

They leave the tender bud,
That's cooling to the blood,
    And chew the cud.   30

———————

Let's make the most of morn,
Ere grey flies wind their horn,
    And it is gone.

1962

Resistance to Civil Government

[CIVIL DISOBEDIENCE][1]

I HEARTILY accept the motto,—"That government is best which governs least;"
and I should like to see it acted up to more rapidly and systematically. Carried
out, it finally amounts to this, which also I believe,—"That government is best
which governs not at all;" and when men are prepared for it, that will be the kind
of government which they will have. Government is at best but an expedient; but
most governments are usually, and all governments are sometimes, inexpedient.
The objections which have been brought against a standing army, and they are
many and weighty, and deserve to prevail, may also at last be brought against a
standing government. The standing army is only an arm of the standing government. The government itself, which is only the mode which the people have chosen to execute their will, is equally liable to be abused and perverted before the
people can act through it. Witness the present Mexican war,[2] the work of comparatively a few individuals using the standing government as their tool; for, in the
outset, the people would not have consented to this measure.

   This American government,—what is it but a tradition, though a recent one,
endeavoring to transmit itself unimpaired to posterity, but each instant losing
some of its integrity? It has not the vitality and force of a single living man; for a
single man can bend it to his will. It is a sort of wooden gun to the people themselves; and, if ever they should use it in earnest as a real one against each other, it
will surely split. But it is not the less necessary for this; for the people must have
some complicated machinery or other, and hear its din, to satisfy that idea of government which they have. Governments show thus how successfully men can be
imposed on, even impose on themselves, for their own advantage. It is excellent,
we must all allow; yet this government never of itself furthered any enterprise,
but by the alacrity with which it got out of its way. *It* does not keep the country
free. *It* does not settle the West. *It* does not educate. The character inherent in the
American people has done all that has been accomplished; and it would have

———————

[1]The title at first publication was "Resistance to Civil Government"; it was retitled "On the Duty of Civil Disobedience" on subsequent publication, and this title was shortened to "Civil Disobedience" as the work became widely
republished. The motto referred to in the opening sentence was used on the masthead of the New York monthly
Democratic Review and is a principle of Jeffersonian democracy as opposed to Hamiltonian federalism.

[2]The Mexican War (1846–48), following the annexation of
Texas in 1845, was inspired largely by U.S. ambitions to acquire California and New Mexico. Southerners hoped to
increase the number of slave states in the Union. Many opposed the war on moral grounds.

done somewhat more, if the government had not sometimes got in its way. For government is an expedient by which men would fain succeed in letting one another alone; and, as has been said, when it is most expedient, the governed are most let alone by it. Trade and commerce, if they were not made of India rubber, would never manage to bounce over the obstacles which legislators are continually putting in their way; and, if one were to judge these men wholly by the effects of their actions, and not partly by their intentions, they would deserve to be classed and punished with those mischievous persons who put obstructions on the railroads.

But, to speak practically and as a citizen, unlike those who call themselves no-government men, I ask for, not at once no government, but *at once* a better government. Let every man make known what kind of government would command his respect, and that will be one step toward obtaining it.

After all, the practical reason why, when the power is once in the hands of the people, a majority are permitted, and for a long period continue, to rule, is not because they are most likely to be in the right, nor because this seems fairest to the minority, but because they are physically the strongest. But a government in which the majority rule in all cases cannot be based on justice, even as far as men understand it. Can there not be a government in which majorities do not virtually decide right and wrong, but conscience?— in which majorities decide only those questions to which the rule of expediency is applicable? Must the citizen ever for a moment, or in the least degree, resign his conscience to the legislator? Why has every man a conscience, then? I think that we should be men first, and subjects afterward. It is not desirable to cultivate a respect for the law, so much as for the right. The only obligation which I have a right to assume, is to do at any time what I think right. It is truly enough said, that a corporation has no conscience;[3] but a corporation of conscientious men is a corporation *with* a conscience. Law never made men a whit more just; and, by means of their respect for it, even the well-disposed are daily made the agents of injustice. A common and natural result of an undue respect for law is, that you may see a file of soldiers, colonel, captain, corporal, privates, powder-monkeys and all, marching in admirable order over hill and dale to the wars, against their wills, aye, against their common sense and consciences, which makes it very steep marching indeed, and produces a palpitation of the heart. They have no doubt that it is a damnable business in which they are concerned; they are all peaceably inclined. Now, what are they? Men at all? or small moveable forts and magazines, at the service of some unscrupulous man in power? Visit the Navy Yard,[4] and behold a marine, such a man as an American government can make, or such as it can make a man with its black arts, a mere shadow and reminiscence of humanity, a man laid out alive and standing, and already, as one may say, buried under arms with funeral accompaniments, though it may be

> "Not a drum was heard, not a funeral note,
>   As his corse to the rampart we hurried;
> Not a soldier discharged his farewell shot
>   O'er the grave where our hero we buried."[5]

The mass of men serve the State thus, not as men mainly, but as machines, with their bodies. They are the standing army, and the militia, jailers, constables, *posse comitatus*,[6] &c. In most cases there is no free exercise whatever of the judgment or of the moral sense; but they put themselves on a level with wood and earth and

---

[3]From a legal decision by Sir Edward Coke (1612).
[4]Then at Charleston, Massachusetts, now incorporated into Boston.

[5]From Charles Wolfe's "The Burial of Sir John Moore" (1817), a favorite of Thoreau.
[6]"Sheriff's posse" (Latin).

stones, and wooden men can perhaps be manufactured that will serve the purpose as well. Such command no more respect than men of straw, or a lump of dirt. They have the same sort of worth only as horses and dogs. Yet such as these even are commonly esteemed good citizens. Others, as most legislators, politicians, lawyers, ministers, and officeholders, serve the State chiefly with their heads; and, as they rarely make any moral distinctions, they are as likely to serve the devil, without intending it, as God. A very few, as heroes, patriots, martyrs, reformers in the great sense, and *men,* serve the State with their consciences also, and so necessarily resist it for the most part; and they are commonly treated by it as enemies. A wise man will only be useful as a man, and will not submit to be "clay," and "stop a hole to keep the wind away,"[7] but leave that office to his dust at least:—

> "I am too high-born to be propertied,
> To be a secondary at control,
> Or useful serving-man and instrument
> To any sovereign state throughout the world."[8]

He who gives himself entirely to his fellow-men appears to them useless and selfish; but he who gives himself partially to them is pronounced a benefactor and philanthropist.

How does it become a man to behave toward this American government to-day?[9] I answer that he cannot without disgrace be associated with it. I cannot for an instant recognize that political organization as *my* government which is the *slave's* government also.

All men recognize the right of revolution; that is, the right to refuse allegiance to and to resist the government, when its tyranny or its inefficiency are great and unendurable. But almost all say that such is not the case now. But such was the case, they think, in the Revolution of '75. If one were to tell me that this was a bad government because it taxed certain foreign commodities brought to its ports, it is most probable that I should not make an ado about it, for I can do without them: all machines have their friction; and possibly this does enough good to counterbalance the evil. At any rate, it is a great evil to make a stir about it. But when the friction comes to have its machine, and oppression and robbery are organized, I say, let us not have such a machine any longer. In other words, when a sixth of the population of a nation which has undertaken to be the refuge of liberty are slaves, and a whole country is unjustly overrun and conquered by a foreign army, and subjected to military law, I think that it is not too soon for honest men to rebel and revolutionize. What makes this duty the more urgent is the fact, that the country so overrun is not our own, but ours is the invading army.

Paley, a common authority with many on moral questions, in his chapter on the "Duty of Submission to Civil Government," resolves all civil obligation into expediency; and he proceeds to say, "that so long as the interest of the whole society requires it, that is, so long as the established government cannot be resisted or changed without public inconveniency, it is the will of God that the established government be obeyed, and no longer." . . . "This principle being admitted, the justice of every particular case of resistance is reduced to a computation of the quantity of the danger and grievance on the one side, and of the probability and expense of redressing it on the other."[10] Of this, he says, every man shall judge for himself. But Paley appears never to have contemplated those cases to which the rule of expediency does not apply, in which a people, as well as an individual,

---

[7]From *Hamlet,* V, i, 236–37.
[8]From Shakespeare's *King John,* V, ii, 79–82.
[9]I.e., the administration of James K. Polk (president 1845–49), which promoted the war with Mexico.

[10]From *Principles of Moral and Political Philosophy* (1785), by William Paley (1743–1805), British moral philosopher.

must do justice, cost what it may. If I have unjustly wrested a plank from a drowning man, I must restore it to him though I drown myself. This, according to Paley, would be inconvenient. But he that would save his life, in such a case, shall lose it.[11] This people must cease to hold slaves, and to make war on Mexico, though it cost them their existence as a people.

In their practice, nations agree with Paley; but does any one think that Massachusetts does exactly what is right at the present crisis?

> "A drab of state, a cloth-o'-silver slut,
> To have her train borne up, and her soul trail in the dirt."[12]

Practically speaking, the opponents to a reform in Massachusetts are not a hundred thousand politicians at the South, but a hundred thousand merchants and farmers here, who are more interested in commerce and agriculture than they are in humanity, and are not prepared to do justice to the slave and to Mexico, *cost what it may.*[13] I quarrel not with far-off foes, but with those who, near at home, co-operate with, and do the bidding of those far away, and without whom the latter would be harmless. We are accustomed to say, that the mass of men are unprepared; but improvement is slow, because the few are not materially wiser or better than the many. It is not so important that many should be as good as you, as that there be some absolute goodness somewhere; for that will leaven the whole lump.[14] There are thousands who are *in opinion* opposed to slavery and to the war, who yet in effect do nothing to put an end to them; who, esteeming themselves children of Washington and Franklin,[15] sit down with their hands in their pockets, and say that they know not what to do, and do nothing; who even postpone the question of freedom to the question of free-trade, and quietly read the prices-current along with the latest advices from Mexico, after dinner, and, it may be, fall asleep over them both. What is the price-current of an honest man and patriot to-day? They hesitate, and they regret, and sometimes they petition; but they do nothing in earnest and with effect. They will wait, well-disposed, for others to remedy the evil, that they may no longer have it to regret. At most, they give only a cheap vote, and a feeble countenance and God-speed, to the right, as it goes by them. There are nine hundred and ninety-nine patrons of virtue to one virtuous man; but it is easier to deal with the real possessor of a thing than with the temporary guardian of it.

All voting is a sort of gaming, like chequers or backgammon, with a slight moral tinge to it, a playing with right and wrong, with moral questions; and betting naturally accompanies it. The character of the voters is not staked. I cast my vote, perchance, as I think right; but I am not vitally concerned that that right should prevail. I am willing to leave it to the majority. Its obligation, therefore, never exceeds that of expediency. Even voting *for the right* is *doing* nothing for it. It is only expressing to men feebly your desire that it should prevail. A wise man will not leave the right to the mercy of chance, nor wish it to prevail through the power of the majority. There is but little virtue in the action of masses of men. When the majority shall at length vote for the abolition of slavery, it will be because they are indifferent to slavery, or because there is but little slavery left to be abolished by their vote. *They* will then be the only slaves. Only *his* vote can hasten the abolition of slavery who asserts his own freedom by his vote.

I hear of a convention to be held at Baltimore, or elsewhere, for the selection

---

[11]Cf. Matthew 10:39, Luke 9:24.

[12]From *The Revenger's Tragedy* (1607), IV, iv, by Cyril Tourneur (1575?–1626), British dramatist.

[13]I.e., the Mexican War was supported by those who hoped to see slaveholding territory expanded; there was a financial alliance between the southern cotton growers and the northern manufacturing, agriculture, and shipping interests.

[14]1 Corinthians 5:6: "Know ye not that a little leaven leaveneth the whole lump."

[15]I.e., descendents of Revolutionary War heroes who overthrew their governments.

of a candidate for the Presidency, made up chiefly of editors, and men who are politicians by profession; but I think, what is it to any independent, intelligent, and respectable man what decision they may come to, shall we not have the advantage of his wisdom and honesty, nevertheless? Can we not count upon some independent votes? Are there not many individuals in the country who do not attend conventions? But no: I find that the respectable man, so called, has immediately drifted from his position, and despairs of his country, when his country has more reason to despair of him. He forthwith adopts one of the candidates thus selected as the only *available* one, thus proving that he is himself *available* for any purposes of the demagogue. His vote is of no more worth than that of any unprincipled foreigner or hireling native, who may have been bought. Oh for a man who is a *man,* and, as my neighbor says, has a bone in his back which you cannot pass your hand through! Our statistics are at fault: the population has been returned too large. How many *men* are there to a square thousand miles in this country? Hardly one. Does not America offer any inducement for men to settle here? The American has dwindled into an Odd Fellow,[16]—one who may be known by the development of his organ of gregariousness, and a manifest lack of intellect and cheerful self-reliance; whose first and chief concern, on coming into the world, is to see that the alms-houses are in good repair; and, before yet he has lawfully donned the virile garb,[17] to collect a fund for the support of the widows and orphans that may be; who, in short, ventures to live only by the aid of the mutual insurance company, which has promised to bury him decently.

It is not a man's duty, as a matter of course, to devote himself to the eradication of any, even the most enormous wrong; he may still properly have other concerns to engage him; but it is his duty, at least, to wash his hands of it, and, if he gives it no thought longer, not to give it practically his support. If I devote myself to other pursuits and contemplations, I must first see, at least, that I do not pursue them sitting upon another man's shoulders. I must get off him first, that he may pursue his contemplations too. See what gross inconsistency is tolerated. I have heard some of my townsmen say, "I should like to have them order me out to help put down an insurrection of the slaves, or to march to Mexico,—see if I would go;" and yet these very men have each, directly by their allegiance, and so indirectly, at least, by their money, furnished a substitute. The soldier is applauded who refuses to serve in an unjust war by those who do not refuse to sustain the unjust government which makes the war; is applauded by those whose own act and authority he disregards and sets at nought; as if the State were penitent to that degree that it hired one to scourge it while it sinned, but not to that degree that it left off sinning for a moment. Thus, under the name of order and civil government, we are all made at last to pay homage to and support our own meanness. After the first blush of sin, comes its indifference and from immoral it becomes, as it were, *un*moral, and not quite unnecessary to that life which we have made.

The broadest and most prevalent error requires the most disinterested virtue to sustain it. The slight reproach to which the virtue of patriotism is commonly liable, the noble are most likely to incur. Those who, while they disapprove of the character and measures of a government, yield to it their allegiance and support, are undoubtedly its most conscientious supporters, and so frequently the most serious obstacles to reform. Some are petitioning the State to dissolve the Union, to disregard the requisitions of the President.[18] Why do they not dissolve it them-

---

[16]The American branch of the Independent Order of Odd Fellows, a secret order dedicated to mutual support and moderate charity, was founded in 1806.

[17]I.e., the *toga virilis* which the Roman boy put on when reaching manhood at fourteen.

[18]I.e., President Polk's request for volunteers in the war with Mexico.

selves,—the union between themselves and the State,—and refuse to pay their quota into its treasury? Do not they stand in the same relation to the State, that the State does to the Union? And have not the same reasons prevented the State from resisting the Union, which have prevented them from resisting the State?

How can a man be satisfied to entertain an opinion merely, and enjoy *it?* Is there any enjoyment in it, if his opinion is that he is aggrieved? If you are cheated out of a single dollar by your neighbor, you do not rest satisfied with knowing that you are cheated, or with saying that you are cheated, or even with petitioning him to pay you your due; but you take effectual steps at once to obtain the full amount, and see that you are never cheated again. Action from principle,—the perception and the performance of right,—changes things and relations; it is essentially revolutionary, and does not consist wholly with any thing which was. It not only divides states and churches, it divides families; aye, it divides the *individual,* separating the diabolical in him from the divine.

Unjust laws exist: shall we be content to obey them, or shall we endeavor to amend them, and obey them until we have succeeded, or shall we transgress them at once? Men generally, under such a government as this, think that they ought to wait until they have persuaded the majority to alter them. They think that, if they should resist, the remedy would be worse than the evil. But it is the fault of the government itself that the remedy *is* worse than the evil. *It* makes it worse. Why is it not more apt to anticipate and provide for reform? Why does it not cherish its wise minority? Why does it cry and resist before it is hurt? Why does it not encourage its citizens to be on the alert to point out its faults, and *do* better than it would have them? Why does it always crucify Christ, and excommunicate Copernicus and Luther,[19] and pronounce Washington and Franklin rebels?

One would think, that a deliberate and practical denial of its authority was the only offence never contemplated by government; else, why has it not assigned its definite, its suitable and proportionate penalty? If a man who has no property refuses but once to earn nine shillings[20] for the State, he is put in prison for a period unlimited by any law that I know, and determined only by the discretion of those who placed him there; but if he should steal ninety times nine shillings from the State, he is soon permitted to go at large again.

If the injustice is part of the necessary friction of the machine of government, let it go, let it go: perchance it will wear smooth,—certainly the machine will wear out. If the injustice has a spring, or a pulley, or a rope, or a crank, exclusively for itself, then perhaps you may consider whether the remedy will not be worse than the evil; but if it is of such a nature that it requires you to be the agent of injustice to another, then, I say, break the law. Let your life be a counter friction to stop the machine. What I have to do is to see, at any rate, that I do not lend myself to the wrong which I condemn.

As for adopting the ways which the State has provided for remedying the evil, I know not of such ways. They take too much time, and a man's life will be gone. I have other affairs to attend to. I came into this world, not chiefly to make this a good place to live in, but to live in it, be it good or bad. A man has not every thing to do, but something; and because he cannot do *every thing,* it is not necessary that he should do *something* wrong. It is not my business to be petitioning the governor or the legislature any more than it is theirs to petition me; and, if they should not hear my petition, what should I do then? But in this case the State has provided no way: its very Constitution is the evil. This may seem to be harsh and stubborn and unconciliatory; but it is to treat with the utmost kindness and consideration

---

[19]Nicolaus Copernicus (1473–1543) was condemned by the Catholic Church for maintaining that the earth revolved about the sun; Martin Luther (1483–1546) was con-

demned for his attack on the corruption of the Church in selling indulgences.
[20]The amount of the poll tax which Thoreau did not pay.

the only spirit that can appreciate or deserves it. So is all change for the better, like birth and death which convulse the body.

I do not hesitate to say, that those who call themselves abolitionists should at once effectually withdraw their support, both in person and property, from the government of Massachusetts, and not wait till they constitute a majority of one, before they suffer the right to prevail through them. I think that it is enough if they have God on their side, without waiting for that other one. Moreover, any man more right than his neighbors, constitutes a majority of one already.

I meet this American government, or its representative the State government, directly, and face to face, once a year, no more, in the person of its tax-gatherer; this is the only mode in which a man situated as I am necessarily meets it; and it then says distinctly, Recognize me; and the simplest, the most effectual, and, in the present posture of affairs, the indispensablest mode of treating with it on this head, of expressing your little satisfaction with and love for it, is to deny it then. My civil neighbor, the tax-gatherer,[21] is the very man I have to deal with,—for it is, after all, with men and not with parchment that I quarrel,—and he has voluntarily chosen to be an agent of the government. How shall he ever know well what he is and does as an officer of the government, or as a man, until he is obliged to consider whether he shall treat me, his neighbor, for whom he has respect, as a neighbor and well-disposed man, or as a maniac and disturber of the peace, and see if he can get over this obstruction to his neighborliness without a ruder and more impetuous thought or speech corresponding with his action? I know this well, that if one thousand, if one hundred, if ten men whom I could name,—if ten *honest* men only,—aye, if *one* HONEST man, in this State of Massachusetts, *ceasing to hold slaves,* were actually to withdraw from this copartnership, and be locked up in the county jail therefor, it would be the abolition of slavery in America. For it matters not how small the beginning may seem to be: what is once well done is done for ever. But we love better to talk about it: that we say is our mission. Reform keeps many scores of newspapers in its service, but not one man. If my esteemed neighbor, the State's ambassador,[22] who will devote his days to the settlement of the question of human rights in the Council Chamber, instead of being threatened with the prisons of Carolina, were to sit down the prisoner of Massachusetts, that State which is so anxious to foist the sin of slavery upon her sister,— though at present she can discover only an act of inhospitality to be the ground of a quarrel with her,—the Legislature would not wholly waive the subject the following winter.

Under a government which imprisons any unjustly, the true place for a just man is also a prison. The proper place to-day, the only place which Massachusetts has provided for her freer and less desponding spirits, is in her prisons, to be put out and locked out of the State by her own act, as they have already put themselves out by their principles. It is there that the fugitive slave, and the Mexican prisoner on parole, and the Indian come to plead the wrongs of his race, should find them; on that separate, but more free and honorable ground, where the State places those who are not *with* her but *against* her,—the only house in a slave-state in which a free man can abide with honor. If any think that their influence would be lost there, and their voices no longer afflict the ear of the State, that they would not be as an enemy within its walls, they do not know by how much truth is stronger than error, nor how much more eloquently and effectively he can combat injustice who has experienced a little in his own person. Cast your whole vote, not a strip of paper merely, but your whole influence. A minority is powerless while it

---

[21]Sam Staples, Thoreau's friend and associate in surveying.
[22]Samuel Hoar (1778–1856) was sent in 1844 by Massachusetts to South Carolina to protest imprisonment there of Massachusetts's black sailors. He was expelled from the state.

conforms to the majority; it is not even a minority then; but it is irresistible when it clogs by its whole weight. If the alternative is to keep all just men in prison, or give up war and slavery, the State will not hesitate which to choose. If a thousand men were not to pay their tax-bills this year, that would not be a violent and bloody measure, as it would be to pay them, and enable the State to commit violence and shed innocent blood. This is, in fact, the definition of a peaceable revolution, if any such is possible. If the tax-gatherer, or any other public officer, asks me, as one has done, "But what shall I do?" my answer is, "If you really wish to do any thing, resign your office." When the subject has refused allegiance, and the officer has resigned his office, then the revolution is accomplished. But even suppose blood should flow. Is there not a sort of blood shed when the conscience is wounded? Through this wound a man's real manhood and immortality flow out, and he bleeds to an everlasting death. I see this blood flowing now.

I have contemplated the imprisonment of the offender, rather than the seizure of his goods,—though both will serve the same purpose,—because they who assert the purest right, and consequently are most dangerous to a corrupt State, commonly have not spent much time in accumulating property. To such the State renders comparatively small service, and a slight tax is wont to appear exorbitant, particularly if they are obliged to earn it by special labor with their hands. If there were one who lived wholly without the use of money, the State itself would hesitate to demand it of him. But the rich man—not to make any invidious comparison—is always sold to the institution which makes him rich. Absolutely speaking, the more money, the less virtue; for money comes between a man and his objects, and obtains them for him; and it was certainly no great virtue to obtain it. It puts to rest many questions which he would otherwise be taxed to answer; while the only new question which it puts is the hard but superfluous one, how to spend it. Thus his moral ground is taken from under his feet. The opportunities of living are diminished in proportion as what are called the "means" are increased. The best thing a man can do for his culture when he is rich is to endeavour to carry out those schemes which he entertained when he was poor. Christ answered the Herodians according to their condition. "Show me the tribute-money," said he;—and one took a penny out of his pocket;—If you use money which has the image of Cæsar on it, and which he has made current and valuable, that is, *if you are men of the State,* and gladly enjoy the advantages of Cæsar's government, then pay him back some of his own when he demands it; "Render therefore to Cæsar that which is Cæsar's, and to God those things which are God's,"[23]—leaving them no wiser than before as to which was which; for they did not wish to know.

When I converse with the freest of my neighbors, I perceive that, whatever they may say about the magnitude and seriousness of the question, and their regard for the public tranquillity, the long and the short of the matter is, that they cannot spare the protection of the existing government, and they dread the consequences of disobedience to it to their property and families. For my own part, I should not like to think that I ever rely on the protection of the State. But, if I deny the authority of the State when it presents its tax-bill, it will soon take and waste all my property, and so harass me and my children without end. This is hard. This makes it impossible for a man to live honestly and at the same time comfortably in outward respects. It will not be worth the while to accumulate property; that would be sure to go again. You must hire or squat somewhere, and raise but a small crop, and eat that soon. You must live within yourself, and depend upon yourself, always tucked up and ready for a start, and not have many affairs. A man may grow rich in Turkey even, if he will be in all respects a good

---

[23]Cf. Matthew 22:16–21.

subject of the Turkish government. Confucius said,—"If a State is governed by the principles of reason, poverty and misery are subjects of shame; if a State is not governed by the principles of reason, riches and honors are the subjects of shame."[24] No: until I want the protection of Massachusetts to be extended to me in some distant southern port, where my liberty is endangered, or until I am bent solely on building up an estate at home by peaceful enterprise, I can afford to refuse allegiance to Massachusetts, and her right to my property and life. It costs me less in every sense to incur the penalty of disobedience to the State, than it would to obey. I should feel as if I were worth less in that case.

Some years ago, the State met me in behalf of the church, and commanded me to pay a certain sum toward the support of a clergyman whose preaching my father attended, but never I myself. "Pay it," it said, "or be locked up in jail." I declined to pay. But, unfortunately, another man saw fit to pay it. I did not see why the schoolmaster should be taxed to support the priest, and not the priest the schoolmaster; for I was not the State's schoolmaster, but I supported myself by voluntary subscription. I did not see why the lyceum should not present its tax-bill, and have the State to back its demand, as well as the church. However, at the request of the selectmen, I condescended to make some such statement as this in writing:—"Know all men by these presents, that I, Henry Thoreau, do not wish to be regarded as a member of any incorporated society which I have not joined." This I gave to the town-clerk; and he has it. The State, having thus learned that I did not wish to be regarded as a member of that church, has never made a like demand on me since; though it said that it must adhere to its original presumption that time. If I had known how to name them, I should then have signed off in detail from all the societies which I never signed on to; but I did not know where to find a complete list.

I have paid no poll-tax for six years. I was put into a jail once on this account, for one night; and, as I stood considering the walls of solid stone, two or three feet thick, the door of wood and iron, a foot thick, and the iron grating which strained the light, I could not help being struck with the foolishness of that institution which treated me as if I were mere flesh and blood and bones, to be locked up. I wondered that it should have concluded at length that this was the best use it could put me to, and had never thought to avail itself of my services in some way. I saw that, if there was a wall of stone between me and my townsmen, there was a still more difficult one to climb or break through, before they could get to be as free as I was. I did not for a moment feel confined, and the walls seemed a great waste of stone and mortar. I felt as if I alone of all my townsmen had paid my tax. They plainly did not know how to treat me, but behaved like persons who are underbred. In every threat and in every compliment there was a blunder; for they thought that my chief desire was to stand the other side of that stone wall. I could not but smile to see how industriously they locked the door on my meditations, which followed them out again without let or hinderance, and *they* were really all that was dangerous. As they could not reach me, they had resolved to punish my body; just as boys, if they cannot come at some person against whom they have a spite, will abuse his dog. I saw that the State was half-witted, that it was timid as a lone woman with her silver spoons, and that it did not know its friends from its foes, and I lost all my remaining respect for it, and pitied it.

Thus the State never intentionally confronts a man's sense, intellectual or moral, but only his body, his senses. It is not armed with superior wit or honesty, but with superior physical strength. I was not born to be forced. I will breathe af-

---

[24]Cf. *Analects*, VIII, 13, by the Chinese philosopher Confucius (c. 551–479 B.C.).

ter my own fashion. Let us see who is the strongest. What force has a multitude? They only can force me who obey a higher law than I. They force me to become like themselves. I do not hear of *men* being *forced* to live this way or that by masses of men. What sort of life were that to live? When I meet a government which says to me, "Your money or your life," why should I be in haste to give it my money? It may be in a great strait, and not know what to do: I cannot help that. It must help itself; do as I do. It is not worth the while to snivel about it. I am not responsible for the successful working of the machinery of society. I am not the son of the engineer. I perceive that, when an acorn and a chestnut fall side by side, the one does not remain inert to make way for the other, but both obey their own laws, and spring and grow and flourish as best they can, till one, perchance, overshadows and destroys the other. If a plant cannot live according to its nature, it dies; and so a man.

The night in prison was novel and interesting enough. The prisoners in their shirt-sleeves were enjoying a chat and the evening air in the door-way, when I entered. But the jailer said, "Come, boys, it is time to lock up;" and so they dispersed, and I heard the sound of their steps returning into the hollow apartments. My roommate was introduced to me by the jailer, as "a first-rate fellow and a clever man." When the door was locked, he showed me where to hang my hat, and how he managed matters there. The rooms were whitewashed once a month; and this one, at least, was the whitest, most simply furnished, and probably the neatest apartment in the town. He naturally wanted to know where I came from, and what brought me there; and, when I had told him, I asked him in my turn how he came there, presuming him to be an honest man, of course; and, as the world goes, I believe he was. "Why," said he, "they accuse me of burning a barn; but I never did it." As near as I could discover, he had probably gone to bed in a barn when drunk, and smoked his pipe there; and so a barn was burnt. He had the reputation of being a clever man, had been there some three months waiting for his trial to come on, and would have to wait as much longer; but he was quite domesticated and contented, since he got his board for nothing, and thought that he was well treated.

He occupied one window, and I the other; and I saw, that, if one stayed there long, his principal business would be to look out the window. I had soon read all the tracts that were left there, and examined where former prisoners had broken out, and where a grate had been sawed off, and heard the history of the various occupants of that room; for I found that even here there was a history and a gossip which never circulated beyond the walls of the jail. Probably this is the only house in the town where verses are composed, which are afterward printed in a circular form, but not published. I was shown quite a long list of verses which were composed by some young men who had been detected in an attempt to escape, who avenged themselves by singing them.

I pumped my fellow-prisoner as dry as I could, for fear I should never see him again; but at length he showed me which was my bed, and left me to blow out the lamp.

It was like travelling into a far country, such as I had never expected to behold, to lie there for one night. It seemed to me that I never had heard the town-clock strike before, nor the evening sounds of the village; for we slept with the windows open, which were inside the grating. It was to see my native village in the light of the middle ages, and our Concord was turned into a Rhine stream, and visions of knights and castles passed before me. They were the voices of old burghers that I heard in the streets. I was an involuntary spectator and auditor of whatever was done and said in the kitchen of the adjacent village-inn,—a wholly new and rare experience to me. It was a closer view of my native town. I was fairly inside of it. I never had seen its institutions before. This is one of its peculiar institutions; for it is a shire town.[25] I began to comprehend what its inhabitants were about.

In the morning, our breakfasts were put through the hole in the door, in small oblong-square tin pans, made to fit, and holding a pint of chocolate, with brown bread, and an iron spoon. When they called for the vessels again, I was green enough to return what bread I had left; but my comrade seized it, and said that I should lay that up for lunch or dinner. Soon after, he was let out to work at haying in a neighboring field, whither he went every day, and would not be back till noon; so he bade me good-day, saying that he doubted if he should see me again.

When I came out of prison,—for some one interfered, and paid the tax,[26]—I did not perceive that great changes had taken place on the common, such as he observed who went in a youth, and emerged a tottering and gray-headed man; and yet a change had to my eyes come over the scene,—the town, and State, and country,—greater than any that mere time could effect. I saw yet more distinctly the State in which I lived. I saw to what extent the people among whom I lived could be trusted as good neighbors and friends; that their friendship was for summer weather only; that they did not greatly purpose to do right; that they were a distinct race from me by their prejudices and superstitions, as the Chinamen and Malays are; that, in their sacrifices to humanity, they ran no risks, not even to their property; that, after all, they were not so noble but they treated the thief as he had treated them, and hoped, by a certain outward observance and a few prayers, and by walking in a particular straight though useless path from time to time, to save their souls. This may be to judge my neighbors harshly; for I believe that most of them are not aware that they have such an institution as the jail in their village.

It was formerly the custom in our village, when a poor debtor came out of jail, for his acquaintances to salute him, looking through their fingers, which were crossed to represent the grating of a jail window, "How do ye do?" My neighbors did not thus salute me, but first looked at me, and then at one another, as if I had returned from a long journey. I was put into jail as I was going to the shoemaker's to get a shoe which was mended. When I was let out the next morning, I proceeded to finish my errand, and, having put on my mended shoe, joined a huckleberry party, who were impatient to put themselves under my conduct; and in half an hour,—for the horse was soon tackled,[27]—was in the midst of a huckleberry field, on one of our highest hills, two miles off; and then the State was nowhere to be seen.

This is the whole history of "My Prisons."[28]

I have never declined paying the highway tax, because I am as desirous of being a good neighbor as I am of being a bad subject; and, as for supporting schools, I am doing my part to educate my fellow-countrymen now. It is for no particular item in the tax-bill that I refuse to pay it. I simply wish to refuse allegiance to the State, to withdraw and stand aloof from it effectually. I do not care to trace the course of my dollar, if I could, till it buys a man, or a musket to shoot one with,—the dollar is innocent,—but I am concerned to trace the effects of my allegiance. In fact, I quietly declare war with the State, after my fashion, though I will still make what use and get what advantage of her I can, as is usual in such cases.

---

[25] Main town of a region (like a county seat).
[26] Thoreau's Aunt Maria, according to family testimony.
[27] I.e., harnessed.

[28] Ironic reference to *Le mie prigioni* (1832), by the Italian patriot, Silvio Pellico (1789–1854), who was put to hard labor in his Austrian imprisonment.

If others pay the tax which is demanded of me, from a sympathy with the State, they do but what they have already done in their own case, or rather they abet injustice to a greater extent than the State requires. If they pay the tax from a mistaken interest in the individual taxed, to save his property or prevent his going to jail, it is because they have not considered wisely how far they let their private feelings interfere with the public good.

This, then, is my position at present. But one cannot be too much on his guard in such a case, lest his action be biassed by obstinacy, or an undue regard for the opinions of men. Let him see that he does only what belongs to himself and to the hour.

I think sometimes, Why, this people mean well; they are only ignorant; they would do better if they knew how: why give your neighbors this pain to treat you as they are not inclined to? But I think, again, this is no reason why I should do as they do, or permit others to suffer much greater pain of a different kind. Again, I sometimes say to myself, When many millions of men, without heat, without ill-will, without personal feeling of any kind, demand of you a few shillings only, without the possibility, such is their constitution, of retracting or altering their present demand, and without the possibility, on your side, of appeal to any other millions, why expose yourself to this overwhelming brute force? You do not resist cold and hunger, the winds and the waves, thus obstinately; you quietly submit to a thousand similar necessities. You do not put your head into the fire. But just in proportion as I regard this as not wholly a brute force, but partly a human force, and consider that I have relations to those millions as to so many millions of men, and not of mere brute or inanimate things, I see that appeal is possible, first and instantaneously, from them to the Maker of them, and, secondly, from them to themselves. But, if I put my head deliberately into the fire, there is no appeal to fire or to the Maker of fire, and I have only myself to blame. If I could convince myself that I have any right to be satisfied with men as they are, and to treat them accordingly, and not according, in some respects, to my requisitions and expectations of what they and I ought to be, then, like a good Mussulman[29] and fatalist, I should endeavor to be satisfied with things as they are, and say it is the will of God. And, above all, there is this difference between resisting this and a purely brute or natural force, that I can resist this with some effect; but I cannot expect, like Orpheus, to change the nature of the rocks and trees and beasts.[30]

I do not wish to quarrel with any man or nation. I do not wish to split hairs, to make fine distinctions, or set myself up as better than my neighbors. I seek rather, I may say, even an excuse for conforming to the laws of the land. I am but too ready to conform to them. Indeed I have reason to suspect myself on this head; and each year, as the tax-gatherer comes round, I find myself disposed to review the acts and position of the general and state governments, and the spirit of the people, to discover a pretext for conformity. I believe that the State will soon be able to take all my work of this sort out of my hands, and then I shall be no better a patriot than my fellow-countrymen. Seen from a lower point of view, the Constitution, with all its faults, is very good; the law and the courts are very respectable; even this State and this American government are, in many respects, very admirable and rare things, to be thankful for, such as a great many have described them; but seen from a point of view a little higher, they are what I have described them; seen from a higher still, and the highest, who shall say what they are, or that they are worth looking at or thinking of at all?

However, the government does not concern me much, and I shall bestow the

---

[29]A Muslim.
[30]Orpheus, a figure in Greek mythology whose magic ability in playing the lyre affected beasts, rocks, and trees.

fewest possible thoughts on it. It is not many moments that I live under a government, even in this world. If a man is thought-free, fancy-free, imagination-free, that which *is not* never for a long time appearing *to be* to him, unwise rulers or reformers cannot fatally interrupt him.

I know that most men think differently from myself; but those whose lives are by profession devoted to the study of these or kindred subjects, content me as little as any. Statesmen and legislators, standing so completely within the institution, never distinctly and nakedly behold it. They speak of moving society, but have no resting-place without it. They may be men of a certain experience and discrimination, and have no doubt invented ingenious and even useful systems, for which we sincerely thank them; but all their wit and usefulness lie within certain not very wide limits. They are wont to forget that the world is not governed by policy and expediency. Webster[31] never goes behind government, and so cannot speak with authority about it. His words are wisdom to those legislators who contemplate no essential reform in the existing government; but for thinkers, and those who legislate for all time, he never once glances at the subject. I know of those whose serene and wise speculations on this theme would soon reveal the limits of his mind's range and hospitality. Yet, compared with the cheap professions of most reformers, and the still cheaper wisdom and eloquence of politicians in general, his are almost the only sensible and valuable words, and we thank Heaven for him. Comparatively, he is always strong, original, and, above all, practical. Still his quality is not wisdom, but prudence. The lawyer's truth is not Truth, but consistency, or a consistent expediency. Truth is always in harmony with herself, and is not concerned chiefly to reveal the justice that may consist with wrong-doing. He well deserves to be called, as he has been called, the Defender of the Constitution. There are really no blows to be given by him but defensive ones. He is not a leader, but a follower. His leaders are the men of '87.[32] "I have never made an effort," he says, "and never propose to make an effort; I have never countenanced an effort, and never mean to countenance an effort, to disturb the arrangement as originally made, by which the various States came into the Union."[33] Still thinking of the sanction which the Constitution gives to slavery, he says, "Because it was a part of the original compact,—let it stand." Notwithstanding his special acuteness and ability, he is unable to take a fact out of its merely political relations, and behold it as it lies absolutely to be disposed of by the intellect,—what, for instance, it behoves a man to do here in America to-day with regard to slavery,—but ventures, or is driven, to make some such desperate answer as the following, while professing to speak absolutely, and as a private man,—from which what new and singular code of social duties might be inferred?—"The manner," says he, "in which the governments of those States where slavery exists are to regulate it, is for their own consideration, under their responsibility to their constituents, to the general laws of propriety, humanity, and justice, and to God. Associations formed elsewhere, springing from a feeling of humanity, or any other cause, have nothing whatever to do with it. They have never received any encouragement from me, and they never will."[34]

They who know of no purer sources of truth, who have traced up its stream no higher, stand, and wisely stand, by the Bible and the Constitution, and drink at it there with reverence and humility; but they who behold where it comes trickling

---

[31]Daniel Webster (1782–1852), American politician who served in the Senate (1827–41), famed for his oratory.
[32]I.e., those like Washington, Madison, and Franklin who helped write the Constitution at the Constitutional Convention of 1787.
[33]From Webster's speech on the admission of Texas to the Union, December 22, 1845.

[34]"These extracts have been inserted since the Lecture was read" (Thoreau's note). The quotation is from Webster's speech on a bill to exclude slavery from the territories, delivered on August 12, 1848.

into this lake or that pool, gird up their loins once more, and continue their pilgrimage toward its fountain-head.

No man with a genius for legislation has appeared in America. They are rare in the history of the world. There are orators, politicians, and eloquent men, by the thousand; but the speaker has not yet opened his mouth to speak, who is capable of settling the much-vexed questions of the day. We love eloquence for its own sake, and not for any truth which it may utter, or any heroism it may inspire. Our legislators have not yet learned the comparative value of free-trade and of freedom, of union, and of rectitude, to a nation. They have no genius or talent for comparatively humble questions of taxation and finance, commerce and manufactures and agriculture. If we were left solely to the wordy wit of legislators in Congress for our guidance, uncorrected by the seasonable experience and the effectual complaints of the people, America would not long retain her rank among the nations. For eighteen hundred years, though perchance I have no right to say it, the New Testament has been written; yet where is the legislator who has wisdom and practical talent enough to avail himself of the light which it sheds on the science of legislation?

The authority of government, even such as I am willing to submit to,—for I will cheerfully obey those who know and can do better than I, and in many things even those who neither know nor can do so well,—is still an impure one: to be strictly just, it must have the sanction and consent of the governed. It can have no pure right over my person and property but what I concede to it. The progress from an absolute to a limited monarchy, from a limited monarchy to a democracy, is a progress toward a true respect for the individual. Is a democracy, such as we know it, the last improvement possible in government? Is it not possible to take a step further towards recognizing and organizing the rights of man? There will never be a really free and enlightened State, until the State comes to recognize the individual as a higher and independent power, from which all its own power and authority are derived, and treats him accordingly. I please myself with imagining a State at last which can afford to be just to all men, and to treat the individual with respect as a neighbor; which even would not think it inconsistent with its own repose, if a few were to live aloof from it, not meddling with it, nor embraced by it, who fulfilled all the duties of neighbors and fellow-men. A State which bore this kind of fruit, and suffered it to drop off as fast as it ripened, would prepare the way for a still more perfect and glorious State, which also I have imagined, but not yet anywhere seen.

1849

Life Without Principle[1]

At a lyceum, not long since, I felt that the lecturer had chosen a theme too foreign to himself, and so failed to interest me as much as he might have done. He described things not in or near to his heart, but toward his extremities and superficies. There was, in this sense, no truly central or centralizing thought in the lecture. I would have had him deal with his privatest experience, as the poet does. The greatest compliment that was ever paid me was when one asked me what *I*

---

[1]Although not published until after Thoreau's death, "Life without Principle" first appeared in embryonic form in his *Journal* (1851–55), and a version of it was presented as a lecture ("Getting a Living") as early as 1854. Just before his death in 1862, Thoreau approved the present title for publication in *The Atlantic Monthly*, where it appeared in October 1863.

thought, and attended to my answer. I am surprised, as well as delighted, when this happens, it is such a rare use he would make of me, as if he were acquainted with the tool. Commonly, if men want anything of me, it is only to know how many acres I make of their land,—since I am a surveyor,—or, at most, what trivial news I have burdened myself with. They never will go to law for my meat; they prefer the shell. A man once came a considerable distance to ask me to lecture on Slavery; but on conversing with him, I found that he and his clique expected seven-eighths of the lecture to be theirs, and only one-eighth mine; so I declined. I take it for granted, when I am invited to lecture anywhere,—for I have had a little experience in that business,—that there is a desire to hear what *I think* on some subject, though I may be the greatest fool in the country,—and not that I should say pleasant things merely, or such as the audience will assent to; and I resolve, accordingly, that I will give them a strong dose of myself. They have sent for me, and engaged to pay for me, and I am determined that they shall have me, though I bore them beyond all precedent.

So now I would say something similar to you, my readers. Since *you* are my readers, and I have not been much of a traveller, I will not talk about people a thousand miles off, but come as near home as I can. As the time is short, I will leave out all the flattery, and retain all the criticism.

Let us consider the way in which we spend our lives.

This world is a place of business. What an infinite bustle! I am awaked almost every night by the panting of the locomotive. It interrupts my dreams. There is no sabbath. It would be glorious to see mankind at leisure for once. It is nothing but work, work, work. I cannot easily buy a blank-book to write thoughts in; they are commonly ruled for dollars and cents. An Irishman, seeing me making a minute[2] in the fields, took it for granted that I was calculating my wages. If a man was tossed out of a window when an infant, and so made a cripple for life, or scared out of his wits by the Indians, it is regretted chiefly because he was thus incapacitated for—business! I think that there is nothing, not even crime, more opposed to poetry, to philosophy, ay, to life itself, than this incessant business.

There is a coarse and boisterous money-making fellow in the outskirts of our town, who is going to build a bank-wall under the hill along the edge of his meadow. The powers have put this into his head to keep him out of mischief, and he wishes me to spend three weeks digging there with him. The result will be that he will perhaps get some more money to hoard, and leave for his heirs to spend foolishly. If I do this, most will commend me as an industrious and hardworking man; but if I choose to devote myself to certain labors which yield more real profit, though but little money, they may be inclined to look on me as an idler. Nevertheless, as I do not need the police of meaningless labor to regulate me, and do not see anything absolutely praiseworthy in this fellow's undertaking, any more than in many an enterprise of our own or foreign governments, however amusing it may be to him or them, I prefer to finish my education at a different school.

If a man walk in the woods for love of them half of each day, he is in danger of being regarded as a loafer; but if he spends his whole day as a speculator, shearing off those woods and making earth bald before her time, he is esteemed an industrious and enterprising citizen. As if a town had no interest in its forests but to cut them down!

Most men would feel insulted, if it were proposed to employ them in throwing stones over a wall, and then in throwing them back, merely that they might earn their wages. But many are no more worthily employed now. For instance: just after sunrise, one summer morning, I noticed one of my neighbors walking beside

---

[2]I.e., making notes.

his team, which was slowly drawing a heavy hewn stone swung under the axle, surrounded by an atmosphere of industry,—his day's work begun,—his brow commenced to sweat,—a reproach to all sluggards and idlers,—pausing abreast the shoulders of his oxen, and half turning round with a flourish of his merciful whip, while they gained their length on him. And I thought, Such is the labor which the American Congress exists to protect,—honest, manly toil,—honest as the day is long,—that makes his bread taste sweet, and keeps society sweet,— which all men respect and have consecrated: one of the sacred band, doing the needful, but irksome drudgery. Indeed, I felt a slight reproach, because I observed this from the window, and was not abroad and stirring about a similar business. The day went by, and at evening I passed the yard of another neighbor, who keeps many servants, and spends much money foolishly, while he adds nothing to the common stock, and there I saw the stone of the morning lying beside a whimsical structure intended to adorn this Lord Timothy Dexter's[3] premises, and the dignity forthwith departed from the teamster's labor, in my eyes. In my opinion, the sun was made to light worthier toil than this. I may add, that his employer has since run off, in debt to a good part of the town, and, after passing through Chancery,[4] has settled somewhere else, there to become once more a patron of the arts.

The ways by which you may get money almost without exception lead downward. To have done anything by which you earned money *merely* is to have been truly idle or worse. If the laborer gets no more than the wages which his employer pays him, he is cheated, he cheats himself. If you would get money as a writer or lecturer, you must be popular, which is to go down perpendicularly. Those services which the community will most readily pay for it is most disagreeable to render. You are paid for being something less than a man. The State does not commonly reward a genius any more wisely. Even the poet-laureate would rather not have to celebrate the accidents of royalty. He must be bribed with a pipe of wine;[5] and perhaps another poet is called away from his muse to gauge that very pipe. As for my own business, even that kind of surveying which I could do with most satisfaction my employers do not want. They would prefer that I should do my work coarsely and not too well, ay, not well enough. When I observe that there are different ways of surveying, my employer commonly asks which will give him the most land, not which is most correct. I once invented a rule for measuring cordwood, and tried to introduce it in Boston; but the measurer there told me that the sellers did not wish to have their wood measured correctly,—that he was already too accurate for them, and therefore they commonly got their wood measured in Charlestown before crossing the bridge.

The aim of the laborer should be, not to get his living, to get "a good job," but to perform well a certain work; and, even in a pecuniary sense, it would be economy for a town to pay its laborers so well that they would not feel that they were working for low ends, as for a livelihood merely, but for scientific, or even moral ends. Do not hire a man who does your work for money, but him who does it for love of it.

It is remarkable that there are few men so well employed, so much to their minds, but that a little money or fame would commonly buy them off from their present pursuit. I see advertisements for *active* young men, as if activity were the whole of a young man's capital. Yet I have been surprised when one has with confidence proposed to me, a grown man, to embark in some enterprise of his, as if I had absolutely nothing to do, my life having been a complete failure hitherto.

---

[3]Timothy Dexter (1747–1806), dubbed "Lord" by his neighbors in Newburyport, Massachusetts, because of his eccentric behavior, including the decoration of his front yard with life-sized wooden statues of famous men.

[4]Court of equity, for filing bankruptcy.
[5]A large cask of about two hogsheads or 126 gallons—the traditional "earnings" of England's poet laureate.

What a doubtful compliment this is to pay me! As if he had met me half-way across the ocean beating up against the wind, but bound nowhere, and proposed to me to go along with him! If I did, what do you think the underwriters would say? No, no! I am not without employment at this stage of the voyage. To tell the truth, I saw an advertisement for able-bodied seamen, when I was a boy, saunter-ing in my native port, and as soon as I came of age I embarked.

The community has no bribe that will tempt a wise man. You may raise money enough to tunnel a mountain, but you cannot raise money enough to hire a man who is minding *his own* business. An efficient and valuable man does what he can, whether the community pay him for it or not. The inefficient offer their ineffi-ciency to the highest bidder, and are forever expecting to be put into office. One would suppose that they were rarely disappointed.

Perhaps I am more than usually jealous with respect to my freedom. I feel that my connection with and obligation to society are still very slight and transient. Those slight labors which afford me a livelihood, and by which it is allowed that I am to some extent serviceable to my contemporaries, are as yet commonly a plea-sure to me, and I am not often reminded that they are a necessity. So far I am successful. But I foresee, that, if my wants should be much increased, the labor required to supply them would become a drudgery. If I should sell both my fore-noons and afternoons to society, as most appear to do, I am sure, that, for me, there would be nothing left worth living for. I trust that I shall never thus sell my birthright for a mess of pottage.[6] I wish to suggest that a man may be very indus-trious, and yet not spend his time well. There is no more fatal blunderer than he who consumes the greater part of his life getting his living. All great enterprises are self-supporting. The poet, for instance, must sustain his body by his poetry, as a steam planing-mill feeds its boilers with the shavings it makes. You must get your living by loving. But as it is said of the merchants that ninety-seven in a hun-dred fail, so the life of men generally, tried by this standard, is a failure, and bankruptcy may be surely prophesied.

Merely to come into the world the heir of a fortune is not to be born, but to be still-born, rather. To be supported by the charity of friends, or a government-pension,—provided you continue to breathe,—by whatever fine synonymes you describe these relations, is to go into the almshouse. On Sundays the poor debtor goes to church to take an account of stock, and finds, of course, that his outgoes have been greater than his income. In the Catholic Church, especially, they go into Chancery, make a clean confession, give up all, and think to start again. Thus men will lie on their backs, talking about the fall of man, and never make an ef-fort to get up.

As for the comparative demand which men make on life, it is an important dif-ference between two, that the one is satisfied with a level success, that his marks can all be hit by point-blank shots, but the other, however low and unsuccessful his life may be, constantly elevates his aim, though at a very slight angle to the horizon. I should much rather be the last man,—though, as the Orientals say, "Greatness doth not approach him who is forever looking down; and all those who are looking high are growing poor."

It is remarkable that there is little or nothing to be remembered written on the subject of getting a living: how to make getting a living not merely honest and honorable, but altogether inviting and glorious; for if *getting* a living is not so, then living is not. One would think, from looking at literature, that this question had never disturbed a solitary individual's musings. Is it that men are too much disgusted with their experience to speak of it? The lesson of value which money

---

[6]Genesis 25:33–34. Pottage, a thick stew.

teaches, which the Author of the Universe has taken so much pains to teach us, we are inclined to skip altogether. As for the means of living, it is wonderful how indifferent men of all classes are about it, even reformers, so called,—whether they inherit, or earn, or steal it. I think that society has done nothing for us in this respect, or at least has undone what she has done. Cold and hunger seem more friendly to my nature than those methods which men have adopted and advise to ward them off.

The title *wise* is, for the most part, falsely applied. How can one be a wise man, if he does not know any better how to live than other men?—if he is only more cunning and intellectually subtle? Does Wisdom work in a tread-mill? or does she teach how to succeed *by her example?* Is there any such thing as wisdom not applied to life? Is she merely the miller who grinds the finest logic? It is pertinent to ask if Plato got his *living* in a better way or more successfully than his contemporaries,—or did he succumb to the difficulties of life like other men? Did he seem to prevail over some of them merely by indifference, or by assuming grand airs? or find it easier to live, because his aunt remembered him in her will? The ways in which most men get their living, that is, live, are mere make-shifts, and a shirking of the real business of life,—chiefly because they do not know, but partly because they do not mean, any better.

The rush to California,[7] for instance, and the attitude, not merely of merchants, but of philosophers and prophets, so called, in relation to it, reflect the greatest disgrace on mankind. That so many are ready to live by luck, and so get the means of commanding the labor of others less lucky, without contributing any value to society! And that is called enterprise! I know of no more startling development of the immorality of trade, and all the common modes of getting a living. The philosophy and poetry and religion of such a mankind are not worth the dust of a puff-ball. The hog that gets his living by rooting, stirring up the soil so, would be ashamed of such company. If I could command the wealth of all the worlds by lifting my finger, I would not pay *such* a price for it. Even Mahomet knew that God did not make this world in jest. It makes God to be a moneyed gentleman who scatters a handful of pennies in order to see mankind scramble for them. The world's raffle! A subsistence in the domains of Nature a thing to be raffled for! What a comment, what a satire on our institutions! The conclusion will be, that mankind will hang itself upon a tree. And have all the precepts in all the Bibles taught men only this? and is the last and most admirable invention of the human race only an improved muck-rake? Is this the ground on which Orientals and Occidentals meet? Did God direct us so to get our living, digging where we never planted,—and He would, perchance, reward us with lumps of gold?

God gave the righteous man a certificate entitling him to food and raiment, but the unrighteous man found a *facsimile* of the same in God's coffers, and appropriated it, and obtained food and raiment like the former. It is one of the most extensive systems of counterfeiting that the world has seen. I did not know that mankind were suffering for want of gold. I have seen a little of it. I know that it is very malleable, but not so malleable as wit. A grain of gold will gild a great surface, but not so much as a grain of wisdom.

The gold-digger in the ravines of the mountains is as much a gambler as his fellow in the saloons of San Francisco. What difference does it make, whether you shake dirt or shake dice? If you win, society is the loser. The gold-digger is the enemy of the honest laborer, whatever checks and compensations there may be. It is not enough to tell me that you worked hard to get your gold. So does the Devil work hard. The way of transgressors may be hard in many respects. The humblest

---

[7]In the gold rush, beginning in 1849.

observer who goes to the mines sees and says that gold-digging is of the character of a lottery; the gold thus obtained is not the same thing with the wages of honest toil. But, practically, he forgets what he has seen, for he has seen only the fact, not the principle, and goes into trade there, that is, buys a ticket in what commonly proves another lottery, where the fact is not so obvious.

After reading Howitt's account of the Australian gold-diggings[8] one evening, I had in my mind's eye, all night, the numerous valleys, with their streams, all cut up with foul pits, from ten to one hundred feet deep, and half a dozen feet across, as close as they can be dug, and partly filled with water,—the locality to which men furiously rush to probe for their fortunes,—uncertain where they shall break ground,—not knowing but the gold is under their camp itself,—sometimes digging one hundred and sixty feet before they strike the vein, or then missing it by a foot,—turned into demons, and regardless of each other's rights, in their thirst for riches,—whole valleys, for thirty miles, suddenly honey-combed by the pits of the miners,—so that even hundreds are drowned in them,—standing in water, and covered with mud and clay, they work night and day, dying of exposure and disease. Having read this, and partly forgotten it, I was thinking, accidentally, of my own unsatisfactory life, doing as others do; and with that vision of the diggings still before me, I asked myself, why I might not be washing some gold daily, though it were only the finest particles,—why I might not sink a shaft down to the gold within me, and work that mine. *There* is a Ballarat, a Bendigo[9] for you,—what though it were a Sulky Gully?[10] At any rate, I might pursue some path, however solitary and narrow and crooked, in which I could walk with love and reverence. Whereever a man separates from the multitude, and goes his own way in this mood, there indeed is a fork in the road, though ordinary travellers may see only a gap in the paling. His solitary path across-lots will turn out the *higher way* of the two.

Men rush to California and Australia as if the true gold were to be found in that direction; but that is to go to the very opposite extreme to where it lies. They go prospecting farther and farther away from the true lead, and are most unfortunate when they think themselves most successful. Is not our *native* soil auriferous?[11] Does not a stream from the golden mountains flow through our native valley? and has not this for more than geologic ages been bringing down the shining particles and forming the nuggets for us? Yet, strange to tell, if a digger steal away, prospecting for this true gold, into the unexplored solitudes around us, there is no danger that any will dog his steps, and endeavor to supplant him. He may claim and undermine the whole valley even, both the cultivated and the uncultivated portions, his whole life long in peace, for no one will ever dispute his claim. They will not mind his cradles or his toms.[12] He is not confined to a claim twelve feet square, as at Ballarat, but may mine anywhere, and wash the whole wide world in his tom.

Howitt says of the man who found the great nugget which weighed twenty-eight pounds, at the Bendigo diggings in Australia:—"He soon began to drink; got a horse and rode all about, generally at full gallop, and when he met people, called out to inquire if they knew who he was, and then kindly informed them that he was 'the bloody wretch that had found the nugget.' At last he rode full speed against a tree, and nearly knocked his brains out." I think, however, there was no danger of that, for he had already knocked his brains out against the nugget. Howitt adds, "He is a hopelessly ruined man." But he is a type of the class. They are all fast men. Hear some of the names of the places where they dig:—

---

[8]William Howitt (1792–1879), *Land, Labor and Gold, or, Two Years in Victoria* (1855).
[9]Mining centers in Australia.
[10]I.e., a mine that yields little gold.
[11]Gold-bearing.
[12]Containers for washing gold.

"Jackass Flat,"—"Sheep's-Head Gully,"—"Murderer's Bar," etc. Is there no satire in these names? Let them carry their ill-gotten wealth where they will, I am thinking it will still be "Jackass Flat," if not "Murderer's Bar," where they live.

The last resource of our energy has been the robbing of graveyards on the Isthmus of Darien,[13] an enterprise which appears to be but in its infancy; for, according to late accounts, an act has passed its second reading in the legislature of New Granada,[14] regulating this kind of mining; and a correspondent of the *Tribune* writes:—"In the dry season, when the weather will permit of the country being properly prospected, no doubt other rich *'guacas'* [that is, graveyards] will be found." To emigrants he says:—"Do not come before December; take the Isthmus route in preference to the Boca del Toro one; bring no useless baggage, and do not cumber yourself with a tent; but a good pair of blankets will be necessary; a pick, shovel, and axe of good material will be almost all that is required": advice which might have been taken from the "Burker's Guide."[15] And he concludes with this line in Italics and small capitals: *"If you are doing well at home,* STAY THERE," which may fairly be interpreted to mean, "If you are getting a good living by robbing graveyards at home, stay there."

But why go to California for a text? She is the child of New England, bred at her own school and church.

It is remarkable that among all the preachers there are so few moral teachers. The prophets are employed in excusing the ways of men. Most reverend seniors, the *illuminati* of the age, tell me, with a gracious, reminiscent smile, betwixt an aspiration and a shudder, not to be too tender about these things,—to lump all that, that is, make a lump of gold of it. The highest advice I have heard on these subjects was grovelling. The burden of it was,—It is not worth your while to undertake to reform the world in this particular. Do not ask how your bread is buttered; it will make you sick, if you do,—and the like. A man had better starve at once than lose his innocence in the process of getting his bread. If within the sophisticated man there is not an unsophisticated one, then he is but one of the Devil's angels. As we grow old, we live more coarsely, we relax a little in our disciplines, and, to some extent, cease to obey our finest instincts. But we should be fastidious to the extreme of sanity, disregarding the gibes of those who are more unfortunate than ourselves.

In our science and philosophy, even, there is commonly no true and absolute account of things. The spirit of sect and bigotry has planted its hoof amid the stars. You have only to discuss the problem, whether the stars are inhabited or not, in order to discover it. Why must we daub the heavens as well as the earth? It was an unfortunate discovery that Dr. Kane was a Mason, and that Sir John Franklin was another.[16] But it was a more cruel suggestion that possibly that was the reason why the former went in search of the latter. There is not a popular magazine in this country that would dare to print a child's thought on important subjects without comment. It must be submitted to the D. D.s.[17] I would it were the chickadee-dees.

You come from attending the funeral of mankind to attend to a natural phenomenon. A little thought is sexton[18] to all the world.

I hardly know an *intellectual* man, even, who is so broad and truly liberal that you can think aloud in his society. Most with whom you endeavor to talk soon

[13]I.e., Panama.
[14]I.e., Columbia.
[15]That is, a murderer's guide, referring to William Burke (1792–1829), Irish criminal who murdered in order to obtain bodies to sell for medical dissection.
[16]Sir John Franklin, a British explorer, died in 1847 on his expedition to the Arctic in search of the Northwest Passage; Elisha Kent Kane (1820–1857), an American explorer, not knowing of Franklin's death, headed rescue missions in 1850–51 and 1853–55.
[17]Doctors of Divinity, who were highly influential in all intellectual enterprises, including magazine publication.
[18]Caretaker of the graveyard, gravedigger.

come to a stand against some institution in which they appear to hold stock,—that is, some particular, not universal, way of viewing things. They will continually thrust their own low roof, with its narrow skylight, between you and the sky, when it is the unobstructed heavens you would view. Get out of the way with your cobwebs, wash your windows, I say! In some lyceums they tell me that they have voted to exclude the subject of religion. But how do I know what their religion is, and when I am near to or far from it? I have walked into such an arena and done my best to make a clean breast of what religion I have experienced, and the audience never suspected what I was about. The lecture was as harmless as moonshine to them. Whereas, if I had read to them the biography of the greatest scamps in history, they might have thought that I had written the lives of the deacons of their church. Ordinarily, the inquiry is, Where did you come from? or, Where are you going? That was a more pertinent question which I overheard one of my auditors put to another once,—"What does he lecture for?" It made me quake in my shoes.

To speak impartially, the best men that I know are not serene, a world in themselves. For the most part, they dwell in forms, and flatter and study effect only more finely than the rest. We select granite for the underpinning of our houses and barns; we build fences of stone; but we do not ourselves rest on an underpinning of granitic truth, the lowest primitive rock. Our sills are rotten. What stuff is the man made of who is not coexistent in our thought with the purest and subtilest truth? I often accuse my finest acquaintances of an immense frivolity; for, while there are manners and compliments we do not meet, we do not teach one another the lessons of honesty and sincerity that the brutes do, or of steadiness and solidity that the rocks do. The fault is commonly mutual, however; for we do not habitually demand any more of each other.

That excitement about Kossuth;[19] consider how characteristic, but superficial, it was!—only another kind of politics or dancing. Men were making speeches to him all over the country, but each expressed only the thought, or the want of thought, of the multitude. No man stood on truth. They were merely banded together, as usual, one leaning on another, and all together on nothing; as the Hindoos made the world rest on an elephant, the elephant on a tortoise, and the tortoise on a serpent, and had nothing to put under the serpent. For all fruit of that stir we have the Kossuth hat.

Just so hollow and ineffectual, for the most part, is our ordinary conversation. Surface meets surface. When our life ceases to be inward and private, conversation degenerates into mere gossip. We rarely meet a man who can tell us any news which he has not read in a newspaper, or been told by his neighbor; and, for the most part, the only difference between us and our fellow is, that he has seen the newspaper, or been out to tea, and we have not. In proportion as our inward life fails, we go more constantly and desperately to the post-office. You may depend on it, that the poor fellow who walks away with the greatest number of letters, proud of his extensive correspondence, has not heard from himself this long while.

I do not know but it is too much to read one newspaper a week. I have tried it recently, and for so long it seems to me that I have not dwelt in my native region. The sun, the clouds, the snow, the trees say not so much to me. You cannot serve two masters. It requires more than a day's devotion to know and to possess the wealth of a day.

We may well be ashamed to tell what things we have read or heard in our day.

---

[19]Lajos Kossuth (1802–1894), Hungarian patriot and revolutionary leader who toured the United States (1851–52), attended with much publicity.

I do not know why my news should be so trivial,—considering what one's dreams and expectations are, why the developments should be so paltry. The news we hear, for the most part, is not news to our genius. It is the stalest repetition. You are often tempted to ask, why such stress is laid on a particular experience which you have had,—that, after twenty-five years, you should meet Hobbins, Registrar of Deeds, again on the sidewalk.[20] Have you not budged an inch, then? Such is the daily news. Its facts appear to float in the atmosphere, insignificant as the sporules of fungi, and impinge on some neglected *thallus,* or surface of our minds, which affords a basis for them, and hence a parasitic growth. We should wash ourselves clean of such news. Of what consequence, though our planet explode, if there is no character involved in the explosion? In health we have not the least curiosity about such events. We do not live for idle amusement. I would not run round a corner to see the world blow up.

All summer, and far into the autumn, perchance, you unconsciously went by[21] the newspapers and the news, and now you find it was because the morning and the evening were full of news to you. Your walks were full of incidents. You attended, not to the affairs of Europe, but to your own affairs in Massachusetts fields. If you chance to live and move and have your being in that thin stratum in which the events that make the news transpire,—thinner than the paper on which it is printed,—then these things will fill the world for you; but if you soar above or dive below that plane, you cannot remember nor be reminded of them. Really to see the sun rise or go down every day, so to relate ourselves to a universal fact, would preserve us sane forever. Nations! What are nations? Tartars, and Huns, and Chinamen! Like insects, they swarm. The historian strives in vain to make them memorable. It is for want of a man that there are so many men. It is individuals that populate the world. Any man thinking may say with the Spirit of Lodin,—

> "I look down from my height on nations,
> And they become ashes before me;—
> Calm is my dwelling in the clouds;
> Pleasant are the great fields of my rest."[22]

Pray, let us live without being drawn by dogs, Esquimaux-fashion, tearing over hill and dale, and biting each other's ears.

Not without a slight shudder at the danger, I often perceive how near I had come to admitting into my mind the details of some trivial affair,—the news of the street; and I am astonished to observe how willing men are to lumber their minds with such rubbish,—to permit idle rumors and incidents of the most insignificant kind to intrude on ground which should be sacred to thought. Shall the mind be a public arena, where the affairs of the street and the gossip of the tea-table chiefly are discussed? Or shall it be a quarter of heaven itself,—an hypæthral[23] temple, consecrated to the service of the gods? I find it so difficult to dispose of the few facts which to me are significant, that I hesitate to burden my attention with those which are insignificant, which only a divine mind could illustrate. Such is, for the most part, the news in newspapers and conversation. It is important to preserve the mind's chastity in this respect. Think of admitting the details of a single case of the criminal court into our thoughts, to stalk profanely through their very *sanctum sanctorum*[24] for an hour, ay, for many hours! to make a very bar-room of the mind's inmost apartment, as if for so long the dust of the

---

[20]I.e., the imaginary Hobbins characterizes people by their external (and public) experiences or deeds, unaware of the more significant internal (and private) experiences and transfigurations.

[21]I.e., gave up.

[22]Variation of a speech by the Spirit of Loda in "Carric-Thura," from James Macpherson's *Poems of Ossian*.

[23]Open to the sky.

[24]Holy of holies, most sacred place.

street had occupied us,—the very street itself, with all its travel, its bustle, and filth had passed through our thoughts' shrine! Would it not be an intellectual and moral suicide? When I have been compelled to sit spectator and auditor in a court-room for some hours, and have seen my neighbors, who were not compelled, stealing in from time to time, and tiptoeing about with washed hands and faces, it has appeared to my mind's eye, that, when they took off their hats, their ears suddenly expanded into vast hoppers for sound, between which even their narrow heads were crowded. Like the vanes of windmills, they caught the broad, but shallow stream of sound, which, after a few titillating gyrations in their coggy brains, passed out the other side. I wondered if, when they got home, they were as careful to wash their ears as before their hands and faces. It has seemed to me, at such a time, that the auditors and the witnesses, the jury and the counsel, the judge and the criminal at the bar,—if I may presume him guilty before he is convicted,—were all equally criminal, and a thunderbolt might be expected to descend and consume them all together.

By all kinds of traps and sign-boards, threatening the extreme penalty of the divine law, exclude such trespassers from the only ground which can be sacred to you. It is so hard to forget what it is worse than useless to remember! If I am to be a thoroughfare, I prefer that it be of the mountain-brooks, the Parnassian streams,[25] and not the town-sewers. There is inspiration, that gossip which comes to the ear of the attentive mind from the courts of heaven. There is the profane and stale revelation of the bar-room and the police court. The same ear is fitted to receive both communications. Only the character of the hearer determines to which it shall be open, and to which closed. I believe that the mind can be permanently profaned by the habit of attending to trivial things, so that all our thoughts shall be tinged with triviality. Our very intellect shall be macadamized, as it were,—its foundation broken into fragments for the wheels of travel to roll over; and if you would know what will make the most durable pavement, surpassing rolled stones, spruce blocks, and asphaltum, you have only to look into some of our minds which have been subjected to this treatment so long.

If we have thus desecrated ourselves,—as who has not?—the remedy will be by wariness and devotion to reconsecrate ourselves, and make once more a fane[26] of the mind. We should treat our minds, that is, ourselves, as innocent and ingenuous children, whose guardians we are, and be careful what objects and what subjects we thrust on their attention. Read not the Times. Read the Eternities. Conventionalities are at length as bad as impurities. Even the facts of science may dust the mind by their dryness, unless they are in a sense effaced each morning, or rather rendered fertile by the dews of fresh and living truth. Knowledge does not come to us by details, but in flashes of light from heaven. Yes, every thought that passes through the mind helps to wear and tear it, and to deepen the ruts, which, as in the streets of Pompeii, evince how much it has been used. How many things there are concerning which we might well deliberate, whether we had better know them,—had better let their peddling-carts be driven, even at the slowest trot or walk, over that bridge of glorious span by which we trust to pass at last from the farthest brink of time to the nearest shore of eternity! Have we no culture, no refinement,—but skill only to live coarsely and serve the Devil?—to acquire a little worldly wealth, or fame, or liberty, and make a false show with it, as if we were all husk and shell, with no tender and living kernel to us? Shall our institutions be like those chestnut-burs which contain abortive nuts, perfect only to prick the fingers?

---

[25]Mount Parnassus was sacred to Apollo and the Muses, its streams thus inspirational and sacred.
[26]Sanctuary, temple.

America is said to be the arena on which the battle of freedom is to be fought; but surely it cannot be freedom in a merely political sense that is meant. Even if we grant that the American has freed himself from a political tyrant, he is still the slave of an economical and moral tyrant. Now that the republic—the *res-publica*—has been settled, it is time to look after the *res-privata,*—the private state,—to see, as the Roman senate charged its consuls, "*ne quid res-*PRIVATA *detrimenti caperet,*" that the *private* state receive no detriment.

Do we call this the land of the free? What is it to be free from King George and continue the slaves of King Prejudice? What is it to be born free and not to live free? What is the value of any political freedom, but as a means to moral freedom? Is it a freedom to be slaves, or a freedom to be free, of which we boast? We are a nation of politicians, concerned about the outmost defences only of freedom. It is our children's children who may perchance be really free. We tax ourselves unjustly. There is a part of us which is not represented. It is taxation without representation. We quarter troops, we quarter fools and cattle of all sorts upon ourselves. We quarter our gross bodies on our poor souls, till the former eat up all the latter's substance.

With respect to a true culture and manhood, we are essentially provincial still, not metropolitan,—mere Jonathans.[27] We are provincial, because we do not find at home our standards,—because we do not worship truth, but the reflection of truth,—because we are warped and narrowed by an exclusive devotion to trade and commerce and manufactures and agriculture and the like, which are but means, and not the end.

So is the English Parliament provincial. Mere country-bumpkins, they betray themselves, when any more important question arises for them to settle, the Irish question, for instance,—the English question why did I not say? Their natures are subdued to what they work in.[28] Their "good breeding" respects only secondary objects. The finest manners in the world are awkwardness and fatuity, when contrasted with a finer intelligence. They appear but as the fashions of past days,—mere courtliness, knee-buckles and small-clothes, out of date. It is the vice, but not the excellence of manners, that they are continually being deserted by the character; they are cast-off clothes or shells, claiming the respect which belonged to the living creature. You are presented with the shells instead of the meat, and it is no excuse generally, that, in the case of some fishes, the shells are of more worth than the meat. The man who thrusts his manners upon me does as if he were to insist on introducing me to his cabinet of curiosities, when I wished to see himself. It was not in this sense that the poet Decker called Christ "the first true gentleman that ever breathed."[29] I repeat that in this sense the most splendid court in Christendom is provincial, having authority to consult about Transalpine interests only, and not the affairs of Rome. A praetor or proconsul would suffice to settle the questions which absorb the attention of the English Parliament and the American Congress.

Government and legislation! these I thought were respectable professions. We have heard of heaven-born Numas, Lycurguses, and Solons,[30] in the history of the world, whose *names* at least may stand for ideal legislators; but think of legislating to *regulate* the breeding of slaves, or the exportation of tobacco! What have divine legislators to do with the exportation or the importation of tobacco? what humane ones with the breeding of slaves? Suppose you were to submit the question to any son of God,—and has He no children in the nineteenth century? is it a family

---

[27]Archetypal American as country bumpkin or provincial (see the character portrayed in Royall Tyler's *The Contrast*).
[28]See Shakespeare's Sonnet III, ll. 6–7: "And almost thence my nature is subdu'd/To what it works in, like the dyer's hand."

[29]From *The Honest Whore* (1604), I, xii, by Thomas Dekker (1572?–1632?).
[30]Legendary law-givers of Rome, Sparta, and Athens.

which is extinct?—in what condition would you get it again? What shall a State like Virginia say for itself at the last day, in which these have been the principal, the staple productions? What ground is there for patriotism in such a State? I derive my facts from statistical tables which the States themselves have published.

A commerce that whitens[31] every sea in quest of nuts and raisins, and makes slaves of its sailors for this purpose! I saw, the other day, a vessel which had been wrecked, and many lives lost, and her cargo of rags, juniper-berries, and bitter almonds were strewn along the shore. It seemed hardly worth the while to tempt the dangers of the sea between Leghorn and New York for the sake of a cargo of juniper-berries and bitter almonds. America sending to the Old World for her bitters! Is not the sea-brine, is not shipwreck, bitter enough to make the cup of life go down here? Yet such, to a great extent, is our boasted commerce; and there are those who style themselves statesmen and philosophers who are so blind as to think that progress and civilization depend on precisely this kind of interchange and activity,—the activity of flies about a molasses-hogshead. Very well, observes one, if men were oysters. And very well, answer I, if men were mosquitoes.

Lieutenant Herndon,[32] whom our Government sent to explore the Amazon, and, it is said, to extend the area of Slavery, observed that there was wanting there "an industrious and active population, who know what the comforts of life are, and who have artificial wants to draw out the great resources of the country." But what are the "artificial wants" to be encouraged? Not the love of luxuries, like the tobacco and slaves of, I believe, his native Virginia, nor the ice and granite and other material wealth of our native New England; nor are "the great resources of a country" that fertility or barrenness of soil which produces these. The chief want, in every State that I have been into, was a high and earnest purpose in its inhabitants. This alone draws out "the great resources" of Nature, and at last taxes her beyond her resources; for man naturally dies out of her. When we want culture more than potatoes, and illumination more than sugar-plums, then the great resources of a world are taxed and drawn out, and the result, or staple production, is, not slaves, nor operatives,[33] but men,—those rare fruits called heroes, saints, poets, philosophers, and redeemers.

In short, as a snow-drift is formed where there is a lull in the wind, so, one would say, where there is a lull of truth, an institution springs up. But the truth blows right on over it, nevertheless, and at length blows it down.

What is called politics is comparatively something so superficial and inhuman, that, practically, I have never fairly recognized that it concerns me at all. The newspapers, I perceive, devote some of their columns specially to politics or government without charge; and this, one would say, is all that saves it; but, as I love literature, and, to some extent, the truth also, I never read those columns at any rate. I do not wish to blunt my sense of right so much. I have not got to answer for having read a single President's Message. A strange age of the world this, when empires, kingdoms, and republics come a-begging to a private man's door, and utter their complaints at his elbow! I cannot take up a newspaper but I find that some wretched government or other, hard pushed, and on its last legs, is interceding with me, the reader, to vote for it,—more importunate than an Italian beggar; and if I have a mind to look at its certificate, made, perchance, by some benevolent merchant's clerk, or the skipper that brought it over, for it cannot speak a word of English itself, I shall probably read of the eruption of some Vesuvius, or the overflowing of some Po, true or forged, which brought it into this con-

---

[31]I.e., with sails of sailing ships.
[32]William Lewis Herndon (1813–1857), author of *Explorations of the Valley of the Amazon* (1854).
[33]Industrial workers.

dition. I do not hesitate, in such a case, to suggest work, or the almshouse; or why not keep its castle in silence, as I do commonly? The poor President, what with preserving his popularity and doing his duty, is completely bewildered. The newspapers are the ruling power. Any other government is reduced to a few marines at Fort Independence.[34] If a man neglects to read the Daily Times, Government will go down on its knees to him, for this is the only treason in these days.

Those things which now most engage the attention of men, as politics and the daily routine, are, it is true, vital functions of human society, but should be unconsciously performed, like the corresponding functions of the physical body. They are *infra*-human, a kind of vegetation. I sometimes awake to a half-consciousness of them going on about me, as a man may become conscious of some of the processes of digestion in a morbid state, and so have the dyspepsia, as it is called. It is as if a thinker submitted himself to be rasped by the great gizzard of creation. Politics is, as it were, the gizzard of society, full of grit and gravel, and the two political parties are its two opposite halves,—sometimes split into quarters, it may be, which grind on each other. Not only individuals, but States, have thus a confirmed dyspepsia, which expresses itself, you can imagine by what sort of eloquence. Thus our life is not altogether a forgetting,[35] but also, alas! to a great extent, a remembering of that which we should never have been conscious of, certainly not in our waking hours. Why should we not meet, not always as dyspeptics, to tell our bad dreams, but sometimes as *eu*peptics,[36] to congratulate each other on the ever glorious morning? I do not make an exorbitant demand, surely.

1863

from The Journal

ON KEEPING A JOURNAL
[THOUGHTS RESCUED FROM OBLIVION]

[February 8, 1841] My Journal is that of me which would else spill over and run to waste, gleanings from the field which in action I reap. I must not live for it, but in it for the gods. They are my correspondent, to whom daily I send off this sheet postpaid. I am clerk in their counting-room, and at evening transfer the account from day-book to ledger. It is as a leaf which hangs over my head in the path. I bend the twig and write my prayers on it; then letting it go, the bough springs up and shows the scrawl to heaven. As if it were not kept shut in my desk, but were as public a leaf as any in nature. It is papyrus by the riverside; it is vellum in the pastures; it is parchment on the hills. I find it everywhere as free as the leaves which troop along the lanes in autumn. The crow, the goose, the eagle carry my quill, and the wind blows the leaves as far as I go. Or, if my imagination does not soar, but gropes in slime and mud, then I write with a reed.

It is always a chance scrawl, and commemorates some accident,—as great as earthquake or eclipse. Like the sere leaves in yonder vase, these have been gathered far and wide. Upland and lowland, forest and field have been ransacked.

---

[34]In Boston Harbor.
[35]Cf. Wordsworth's "Intimations Ode," l. 58: "Our birth is but a sleep and a forgetting."
[36]Healthy, fully aware individuals.

[1845–47] From all points of the compass, from the earth beneath and the heavens above, have come these inspirations and been entered duly in the order of their arrival in the journal. Thereafter, when the time arrived, they were winnowed into lectures, and again, in due time, from lectures into essays. And at last they stand, like the cubes of Pythagoras,[1] firmly on either basis; like statues on their pedestals, but the statues rarely take hold of hands. There is only such connection and series as is attainable in the galleries. And this affects their immediate practical and popular influence.

[November 16, 1850] My Journal should be the record of my love. I would write in it only of the things I love, my affection for any aspect of the world, what I love to think of. I have no more distinctness or pointedness in my yearnings than an expanding bud, which does indeed point to flower and fruit, to summer and autumn, but is aware of the warm sun and spring influence only. I feel ripe for something, yet do nothing, can't discover what that thing is. I feel fertile merely. It is seedtime with me. I have lain fallow long enough.

[1851] It is something to know when you are addressed by Divinity and not by a common traveller. I went down cellar just now to get an armful of wood and, passing the brick piers with my wood and candle, I heard, methought, a commonplace suggestion, but when, as it were by accident, I reverently attended to the hint, I found that it was the voice of a god who had followed me down cellar to speak to me. How many communications may we not lose through inattention!

I would fain keep a journal which should contain those thoughts and impressions which I am most liable to forget that I have had; which would have in one sense the greatest remoteness, in another, the greatest nearness to me.

'T is healthy to be sick sometimes.

[January 22, 1852] To set down such choice experiences that my own writings may inspire me and at last I may make wholes of parts. Certainly it is a distinct profession to rescue from oblivion and to fix the sentiments and thoughts which visit all men more or less generally, that the contemplation of the unfinished picture may suggest its harmonious completion. Associate reverently and as much as you can with your loftiest thoughts. Each thought that is welcomed and recorded is a nest egg, by the side of which more will be laid. Thoughts accidentally thrown together become a frame in which more may be developed and exhibited. Perhaps this is the main value of a habit of writing, of keeping a journal,—that so we remember our best hours and stimulate ourselves. My thoughts are my company. They have a certain individuality and separate existence, aye, personality. Having by chance recorded a few disconnected thoughts and then brought them into juxtaposition, they suggest a whole new field in which it was possible to labor and to think. Thought begat thought.

[January 24, 1852] In thy journal let there never be a jest! To the earnest there is nothing ludicrous.

[January 27, 1852] I do not know but thoughts written down thus in a journal might be printed in the same form with greater advantage than if the related ones were brought together into separate essays. They are now allied to life, and are seen by the reader not to be far-fetched. It is more simple, less artful. I feel that in

---

[1]Greek mathematician and philosopher (fl. 530 B.C.). His contributions to geometry, including the study of various forms or cubes, were notable.

the other case I should have no proper frame for my sketches. Mere facts and names and dates communicate more than we suspect. Whether the flower looks better in the nosegay than in the meadow where it grew and we had to wet our feet to get it! Is the scholastic air any advantage?

[July 13, 1852] A journal, a book that shall contain a record of all your joy, your ecstasy.

[March 21, 1853] Might not my journal be called "Field Notes"?

[February 5, 1855] In a journal it is important in a few words to describe the weather, or character of the day, as it affects our feelings. That which was so important at the time cannot be unimportant to remember.

[December 26, 1855] In a true history or biography, of how little consequence those events of which so much is commonly made! For example, how difficult for a man to remember in what towns or houses he has lived, or when! Yet one of the first steps of his biographer will be to establish these facts, and he will thus give an undue importance to many of them. I find in my Journal that the most important events in my life, if recorded at all, are not dated.

[January 24, 1856] A journal is a record of experiences and growth, not a preserve of things well done or said. I am occasionally reminded of a statement which I have made in conversation and immediately forgotten, which would read much better than what I put in my journal. It is a ripe, dry fruit of long-past experience which falls from me easily, without giving pain or pleasure. The charm of the journal must consist in a certain greenness, though freshness, and not in maturity. Here I cannot afford to be remembering what I said or did, my scurf cast off, but what I am and aspire to become.

[March 27, 1857] I would fain make two reports in my Journal, first the incidents and observations of to-day; and by tomorrow I review the same and record what was omitted before, which will often be the most significant and poetic part. I do not know at first what it is that charms me. The men and things of to-day are wont to lie fairer and truer in to-morrow's memory.

[October 21, 1857] Is not the poet bound to write his own biography? Is there any other work for him but a good journal? We do not wish to know how his imaginary hero, but how he, the actual hero, lived from day to day.

WALKING

[WALKING, A RETURN TO THE SENSES]

[November 24, 1850] I feel a little alarmed when it happens that I have walked a mile into the woods bodily, without getting there in spirit. I would fain forget all my morning's occupation, my obligations to society. But sometimes it happens that I cannot easily shake off the village; the thought of some work, some surveying, will run in my head, and I am not where my body is, I am out of my senses. In my walks I would return to my senses like a bird or a beast. What business have I in the woods, if I am thinking of something out of the woods?

[WALK IN A WET SEASON]

[February 12, 1851] I find that it is an excellent walk for variety and novelty and wildness, to keep round the edge of the meadow,—the ice not being strong enough to bear and transparent as water,—on the bare ground or snow, just between the highest water mark and the present water line,—a narrow, meandering walk, rich in unexpected views and objects. The line of rubbish which marks the higher tides—withered flags and reeds and twigs and cranberries—is to my eyes a very agreeable and significant line, which Nature traces along the edge of the meadows. It is a strongly marked, enduring natural line, which in summer reminds me that the water has once stood over where I walk. Sometimes the grooved trees tell the same tale. The wrecks of the meadow, which fill a thousand coves, and tell a thousand tales to those who can read them. Our prairial, mediterranean shore. The gentle rise of water around the trees in the meadow, where oaks and maples stand far out in the sea, and young elms sometimes are seen standing close around some rock which lifts its head above the water, as if protecting it, preventing it from being washed away, though in truth they owe their origin and preservation to it. It first invited and detained their seed, and now preserves the soil in which they grow. A pleasant reminiscence of the rise of waters, to go up one side of the river and down the other, following this way, which meanders so much more than the river itself. If you cannot go on the ice, you are then gently compelled to take this course, which is on the whole more beautiful,—to follow the sinuosities of the meadow. Between the highest water mark and the present water line is a space generally from a few feet to a few rods in width. When the water comes over the road, then my spirits rise,—when the fences are carried away. A prairial walk. Saw a caterpillar crawling about on the snow.

The earth is so bare that it makes an impression on me as if it were catching cold.

[WALK ON A SUMMER NIGHT]

[June 11, 1851] Last night a beautiful summer night, not too warm, moon not quite full, after two or three rainy days. Walked to Fair Haven by railroad, returning by Potter's pasture and Sudbury road. I feared at first that there would be too much white light, like the pale remains of daylight, and not a yellow, gloomy, dreamier light; that it would be like a candlelight by day; but when I got away from the town and deeper into the night, it was better. I hear whip-poor-wills, and see a few fireflies in the meadow.

The woodland paths are never seen to such advantage as in a moonlight night, so embowered, still opening before you almost against expectation as you walk; you are so completely in the woods, and yet your feet meet no obstacles. It is as if it were not a path, but an open, winding passage through the bushes, which your feet find.

Now I go by the spring, and when I have risen to the same level as before, find myself in the warm stratum again.

The woods are about as destitute of inhabitants at night as the streets. In both there will be some nightwalkers. There are but few wild creatures to seek their prey. The greater part of its inhabitants have retired to rest.

Ah, that life that I have known! How hard it is to remember what is most memorable! We remember how we itched, not how our hearts beat. I can sometimes recall to mind the quality, the immortality, of my youthful life, but in memory is the only relation to it.

The very cows have now left their pastures and are driven home to their yards. I meet no creature in the fields.

I hear the night-warbler breaking out as in his dreams, made so from the first for some mysterious reason.

Our spiritual side takes a more distinct form, like our shadow which we see accompanying us.

I do not know but I feel less vigor at night; my legs will not carry me so far; as if the night were less favorable to muscular exertion,—weakened us, somewhat as darkness turns plants pale. But perhaps my experience is to be referred to being already exhausted by the day, and I have never tried the experiment fairly. Yet sometimes after a hard day's work I have found myself unexpectedly vigorous. It was so hot summer before last that the Irish laborers on the railroad worked by night instead of day for a while, several of them having been killed by the heat and cold water. I do not know but they did as much work as ever by day. Yet methinks Nature would not smile on such labors.

Only the Hunter's and Harvest moons are famous, but I think that each full moon deserves to be and has its own character well marked. One might be called the Midsummer-Night Moon.

The wind and water are still awake. At night you are sure to hear what wind there is stirring. The wind blows, the river flows, without resting. There lies Fair Haven Lake, undistinguishable from fallen sky. The pines seem forever foreign, at least to the civilized man,—not only their aspect but their scent, and their turpentine.

So still and moderate is the night! No scream is heard, whether of fear or joy. No great comedy nor tragedy is being enacted. The chirping of crickets is the most universal, if not the loudest, sound. There is no French Revolution in Nature, no excess. She is warmer or colder by a degree or two.

By night no flowers, at least no variety of colors. The pinks are no longer pink; they only shine faintly, reflecting more light. Instead of flowers underfoot, stars overhead.

My shadow has the distinctness of a second person, a certain black companion bordering on the imp, and I ask, "Who is this?" which I see dodging behind me as I am about to sit down on a rock.

No one, to my knowledge, has observed the minute differences in the seasons. Hardly two nights are alike. The rocks do not feel warm to-night, for the air is warmest; nor does the sand particularly. A book of the seasons, each page of which should be written in its own season and out-of-doors, or in its own locality wherever it may be.

When you get into the road, though far from the town, and feel the sand under your feet, it is as if you had reached your own gravel walk. You no longer hear the whip-poor-will, nor regard your shadow, for here you expect a fellow-traveller. You catch yourself walking merely. The road leads your steps and thoughts alike to the town. You see only the path, and your thoughts wander from the objects which are presented to your senses. You are no longer in place. It is like conformity,—walking in the ways of men.

[Walks on Old, Meandering, Uninhabited Roads]

July 21, [1851] 8 A.M.—The forenoon is fuller of light. The butterflies on the flowers look like other and frequently larger flowers themselves. Now I yearn for one of those old, meandering, dry, uninhabited roads, which lead away from towns, which lead us away from temptation, which conduct to the outside of earth, over its uppermost crust; where you may forget in what country you are travelling; where no farmer can complain that you are treading down his grass, no gentleman who has recently constructed a seat in the country that you are trespassing; on which you can go off at half-cock and wave adieu to the village; along which you may travel like a pilgrim, going nowhither; where travellers are not too often to be met; where my spirit is free; where the walls and fences are not cared for; where your head is more in heaven than your feet are on earth; which have long reaches where you can see the approaching traveller half a mile off and be prepared for him; not so luxuriant a soil as to attract men; some root and stump fences which do not need attention; where travellers have no occasion to stop, but pass along and leave you to your thoughts; where it makes no odds which way you face, whether you are going or coming, whether it is morning or evening, midnoon or midnight; where earth is cheap enough by being public; where you can walk and think with least obstruction, there being nothing to measure progress by; where you can pace when your breast is full, and cherish your moodiness; where you are not in false relations with men, are not dining nor conversing with them; by which you may go to the uttermost parts of the earth. It is wide enough, wide as the thoughts it allows to visit you. Sometimes it is some particular half-dozen rods which I wish to find myself pacing over, as where certain airs blow; then my life will come to me, methinks; like a hunter I walk in wait for it. When I am against this bare promontory of a huckleberry hill, then forsooth my thoughts will expand. Is it some influence, as a vapor which exhales from the ground, or something in the gales which blow there, or in all things there brought together agreeably to my spirit? The walls must not be too high, imprisoning me, but low, with numerous gaps. The trees must not be too numerous, nor the hills too near, bounding the view, nor the soil too rich, attracting the attention to the earth. It must simply be the way and the life,—a way that was never known to be repaired, nor to need repair, within the memory of the oldest inhabitant. I cannot walk habitually in those ways that are liable to be mended; for sure it was the devil only that wore them. Never by the heel of thinkers (of thought) were they worn; the zephyrs could repair that damage. The saunterer wears out no road, even though he travel on it, and therefore should pay no highway, or rather *low* way, tax. He may be taxed to construct a higher way than men travel. A way which no geese defile, nor hiss along it, but only sometimes their wild brethren fly far overhead; which the kingbird and the swallow twitter over, and the song sparrow sings on its rails; where the small red butterfly is at home on the yarrow, and no boys threaten it with imprisoning hat. There I can walk and stalk and pace and plod. Which nobody but Jonas Potter travels beside me; where no cow but his is tempted to linger for the herbage by its side; where the guide-board is fallen, and now the hand points to heaven significantly,—to a Sudbury and Marlborough in the skies. That's a road I can travel, that the particular Sudbury I am bound for, six miles an hour, or two, as you please; and few there be that enter thereon. There I can walk, and recover the lost child that I am without any ringing of a bell; where there was nothing ever discovered to detain a traveller, but all went through about their business; where I never passed the time of day with any,—indifferent to me were the arbitrary divisions of time; where Tullus Hostilius[1] might have disappeared,—at any rate has never been seen. The road to the Corner! the ninety and nine acres that you go through to get there! I would rather see it again, though I saw it this morning, than Gray's churchyard.[2] The road whence you may hear a stake-driver, a whip-poor-will, a quail in a midsummer day, a—yes, a quail comes nearest to the *gum-c*[3] bird heard there; where it would not be sport for a sportsman to go. And the mayweed looks up in my face,—not there; the pale lobelia, the Canada snapdragon, rather. A little hardhack and meadowsweet peep over the fence,—nothing more serious to obstruct the view,—and thimble-berries are the food of thought, before the drought, along by the walls.

It is they who go to Brighton and to market that wear out the roads, and they

---

[1] Third legendary king of the Romans (673–641 B.C.). He disappeared in a storm, struck dead by lightning.
[2] Thomas Gray (1716–1771), British poet, author of "Elegy Written in a Country Churchyard."

[3] "[William Ellery] Channing . . . calls it 'one of Thoreau's names for some bird, so named by the farmers.' The word as written is far from clear" (Editor's note).

should pay all the tax. The deliberate pace of a thinker never made a road the worse for travelling on.

There I have freedom in my thought, and in my soul am free. Excepting the omnipresent butcher with his calf-cart, followed by a distracted and anxious cow.

[A WALK IN WINTER]

[November 13, 1851] A cold and dark afternoon, the sun being behind clouds in the west. The landscape is barren of objects, the trees being leafless, and so little light in the sky for variety. Such a day as will almost oblige a man to eat his own heart. A day in which you must hold on to life by your teeth. You can hardly ruck up any skin on Nature's bones. The sap is down; she won't peel. Now is the time to cut timber for yokes and ox-bows, leaving the tough bark on,—yokes for your own neck. Finding yourself yoked to Matter and to Time. Truly a hard day, hard times these! Not a mosquito left. Not an insect to hum. Crickets gone into winter quarters. Friends long since gone there, and you left to walk on frozen ground, with your hands in your pockets. Ah, but is not this a glorious time for your deep inward fires? And will not your green hickory and white oak burn clear in this frosty air? Now is not your manhood taxed by the great Assessor? Taxed for having a soul, a ratable soul. A day when you cannot pluck a flower, cannot dig a parsnip, nor pull a turnip, for the frozen ground! What do the thoughts find to live on? What avails you now the fire you stole from heaven? Does not each thought become a vulture to gnaw your vitals? No Indian summer have we had this November. I see but few traces of the perennial spring. Now is there nothing, not even the cold beauty of ice crystals and snowy architecture, nothing but the echo of your steps over the frozen ground, no voice of birds nor frogs. You are dry as a farrow cow. The earth will not admit a spade. All fields lie fallow. Shall not your mind? True, the freezing ground is being prepared for immeasurable snows, but there are brave thoughts within you that shall remain to rustle the winter through like white oak leaves upon your boughs, or like scrub oaks that remind the traveller of a fire upon the hillsides; or evergreen thoughts, cold even in midsummer, by their nature shall contrast the more fairly with the snow. Some warm springs shall still tinkle and fume, and send their column of vapor to the skies.

The walker now fares like cows in the pastures, where is no grass but hay; he gets nothing but an appetite. If we must return to hay, pray let us have that which has been stored in barns, which has not lost its sweetness. The poet needs to have more stomachs than the cow, for for him no fodder is stored in barns. He relies upon his instinct, which teaches him to paw away the snow to come at the withered grass.

Methinks man came very near being made a dormant creature, just as some of these animals. The ground squirrel, for instance, which lays up vast stores, is yet found to be half dormant, if you dig him out. Now for the oily nuts of thought which you have stored up.

[WALKING AS SANATIVE]

[January 7, 1857] There is nothing so sanative, so poetic, as a walk in the woods and fields even now, when I meet none abroad for pleasure. Nothing so inspires me and excites such serene and profitable thought. The objects are elevating. In the street and in society I am almost invariably cheap and dissipated, my life is unspeakably mean. No amount of gold or respectability would in the least redeem it,—dining with the Governor or a member of Congress!! But alone in distant woods or fields, in unpretending sprout-lands or pastures tracked by rabbits, even in a bleak and, to most, cheerless day, like this, when a villager would be thinking of his inn, I come to myself, I once more feel myself grandly related, and that cold and solitude are friends of mine. I suppose that this value, in my case, is equivalent to what others get by churchgoing and prayer. I come to my solitary woodland walk as the homesick go home. I thus dispose of the superfluous and see things as they are, grand and beautiful. I have told many that I walk every day about half the daylight, but I think they do not believe it. I wish to get the Concord, the Massachusetts, the America, out of my head and be sane a part of every day. If there are missionaries for the heathen, why not send them to me? I wish to know something; I wish to be made better. I wish to forget, a considerable part of every day, all mean, narrow, trivial men (and this requires usually to forego and forget all personal relations so long), and therefore I come out to these solitudes, where the problem of existence is simplified. I get away a mile or two from the town into the stillness and solitude of nature, with rocks, trees, weeds, snow about me. I enter some glade in the woods, perchance, where a few weeds and dry leaves alone lift themselves above the surface of the snow, and it is as if I had come to an open window. I see out and around myself. Our *skylights* are thus far away from the ordinary resorts of men. I am not satisfied with ordinary windows. I must have a true *skylight*. My true skylight is on the outside of the village. I am not thus expanded, recreated, enlightened, when I meet a company of men. It chances that the sociable, the town and county, or the farmers' club does not prove a skylight to me. I do not invariably find myself translated under those circumstances. They bore me. The man I meet with is not often so instructive as the silence he breaks. This stillness, solitude, wildness of nature is a kind of thoroughwort, or boneset,[4] to my intellect. This is what I go out to seek. It is as if I always met in those places some grand, serene, immortal, infinitely encouraging, though invisible, companion, and walked with him. There at last my nerves are steadied, my senses and my mind do their office. I am aware that most of my neighbors would think it a hardship to be compelled to linger here one hour, especially this bleak day, and yet I receive this sweet and ineffable compensation for it. It is the most agreeable thing I do. Truly, my coins are uncurrent with them.

I love and celebrate nature, even in detail, merely because I love the scenery of these interviews and translations. I love to remember every creature that was at this *club*. I thus get off a certain social scurf and scaliness. I do not consider the other animals brutes in the common sense. I am attracted toward them undoubtedly because I never heard any nonsense from them. I have not convicted them of folly, or vanity, or pomposity, or stupidity, in dealing with me. Their vices, at any rate, do not interfere with me. My fairies invariably take to flight when a man appears upon the scene. In a caucus, a meeting-house, a lyceum, a clubroom, there is nothing like it in my experience. But away out of the town, on Brown's scrub oak lot, which was sold the other day for six dollars an acre, I have company such as England cannot buy, nor afford. This society is what I live, what I survey, for. I subscribe generously to *this*—all that I have and am.

There, in that Well Meadow Field, perhaps, I feel in my element again, as when a fish is put back into the water. I wash off all my chagrins. All things go smoothly as the axle of the universe. I can remember that when I was very young I used to have a dream night after night, over and over again, which might have been named Rough and Smooth. All existence, all satisfaction and dissatisfaction, all event was symbolized in this way. Now I seemed to be lying and tossing, per-

---

[4] Both names for a short plant with clusters of gray-white flowers.

chance, on a horrible, a fatal rough surface, which must soon, indeed, put an end to my existence, though even in the dream I knew it to be the symbol merely of my misery; and then again, suddenly, I was lying on a delicious smooth surface, as of a summer sea, as of gossamer or down or softest plush, and life was such a luxury to live. My waking experience *always* has been and is such an alternate Rough and Smooth. In other words it is Insanity and Sanity.

Might I aspire to praise the moderate nymph Nature! I must be like her, moderate.

SEEING

[WE ARE AS MUCH AS WE SEE]

[April 10, 1841] How much virtue there is in simply seeing! We may almost say that the hero has striven in vain for his preeminency, if the student oversees him. The woman who sits in the house and *sees* is a match for a stirring captain. Those still, piercing eyes, as faithfully exercised on their talent, will keep her even with Alexander or Shakespeare. They may go to Asia with parade, or to fairyland, but not beyond her ray. We are as much as we see. Faith is sight and knowledge. The hands only serve the eyes. The farthest blue streak in the horizon I can see, I may reach before many sunsets. What I saw alters not; in my night, when I wander, it is still steadfast as the star which the sailor steers by.

[SEEING BEYOND UNDERSTANDING]

[February 14, 1851] We shall see but little way if we require to understand what we see. How few things can a man measure with the tape of his understanding! How many greater things might he be seeing in the meanwhile!

One afternoon in the fall, November 21st, I saw Fair Haven Pond with its island and meadow; between the island and the shore, a strip of perfectly smooth water in the lee of the island; and two hawks sailing over it; and something more I saw which cannot easily be described, which made me say to myself that the landscape could not be improved. I did not see how it could be improved. Yet I do not know what these things can be; I begin to see such objects only when I leave off understanding them, and afterwards remember that I did not appreciate them before. But I get no further than this. How adapted these forms and colors to our eyes, a meadow and its islands! What are these things? Yet the hawks and the ducks keep so aloof, and nature is so reserved! We are made to love the river and the meadow, as the wind to ripple the water.

[BE NOT PREOCCUPIED WITH LOOKING]

[September 13, 1852] I must walk more with free senses. It is as bad to *study* stars and clouds as flowers and stones. I must let my senses wander as my thoughts, my eyes see without looking. Carlyle[1] said that how to observe was to look, but I say that it is rather to see, and the more you look the less you will observe. I have the habit of attention to such excess that my senses get no rest, but suffer from a constant strain. Be not preoccupied with looking. Go not to the object; let it come to you. When I have found myself ever looking down and confining my gaze to the flowers, I have thought it might be well to get into the habit of observing the clouds as a corrective; but no! that study would be just as bad. What I need is not to look at all, but a true sauntering of the eye.

---

[1]Thomas Carlyle (1795–1881), Scottish author and essayist, friend of Emerson.

[Looking Through and Beyond]

[March 23, 1853] Man cannot afford to be a naturalist, to look at Nature directly, but only with the side of his eye. He must look through and beyond her. To look at her is fatal as to look at the head of Medusa.[2] It turns the man of science to stone. I feel that I am dissipated by so many observations. I should be the magnet in the midst of all this dust and filings. I knock the back of my hand against a rock, and as I smooth back the skin, I find myself prepared to study lichens there. I look upon man but as a fungus. I have almost a slight, dry headache as the result of all this observing. How to observe is how to behave. O for a little Lethe![3] To crown all, lichens, which are so thin, are described in the *dry* state, as they are most commonly, not most truly, seen. Truly, they are *dryly* described.

[Observation Must Be Subjective]

[May 6, 1854] There is no such thing as pure *objective* observation. Your observation, to be interesting, *i. e.* to be significant, must be *subjective*. The sum of what the writer of whatever class has to report is simply some human experience, whether he be poet or philosopher or man of science. The man of most science is the man most alive, whose life is the greatest event. Senses that take cognizance of outward things merely are of no avail. It matters not where or how far you travel,—the farther commonly the worse,—but how much alive you are. If it is possible to conceive of an event outside to humanity, it is not of the slightest significance, though it were the explosion of a planet. Every important worker will report what life there is in him. It makes no odds into what seeming deserts the poet is born. Though all his neighbors pronounce it a Sahara, it will be a paradise to him; for the desert which we see is the result of the barrenness of our experience. No mere willful activity whatever, whether in writing verses or collecting statistics, will produce true poetry or science. If you are really a sick man, it is indeed to be regretted, for you cannot accomplish so much as if you were well. All that a man has to say or do that can possibly concern mankind, is in some shape or other to tell the story of his love,—to sing; and, if he is fortunate and keeps alive, he will be forever in love. This alone is to be alive to the extremities. It is a pity that this divine creature should ever suffer from cold feet; a still greater pity that the coldness so often reaches to his heart. I look over the report of the doings of a scientific association and am surprised that there is so little life to be reported; I am put off with a parcel of dry technical terms. Anything living is easily and naturally expressed in popular language. I cannot help suspecting that the life of these learned professors has been almost as inhuman and wooden as a rain-gauge or self-registering magnetic machine. They communicate no fact which rises to the temperature of blood-heat. It doesn't all amount to one rhyme.

[I Am Compelled to Look]

[November 7, 1855] I find it good to be out this still, dark, mizzling afternoon; my walk or voyage is more suggestive and profitable than in bright weather. The view is contracted by the misty rain, the water is perfectly smooth, and the stillness is favorable to reflection. I am more open to impressions, more sensitive (not calloused or indurated by sun and wind), as if in a chamber still. My thoughts are concentrated; I am all compact. The solitude is real, too, for the weather keeps other men at home. This mist is like a roof and walls over and around, and I walk

---

[2]In Greek mythology, Medusa was a Gorgon, a monstrous creature with serpents for hair; anyone who gazed at a Gorgon was turned to stone.
[3]In classical mythology, the river of oblivion in Hades.

with a domestic feeling. The sound of a wagon going over an unseen bridge is louder than ever, and so of other sounds. I am *compelled* to look at near objects. All things have a soothing effect; the very clouds and mists brood over me. My power of observation and contemplation is much increased. My attention does not wander. The world and my life are simplified. What now of Europe and Asia?

[SEEING WITH THE SIDE OF THE EYE]

[April 28, 1856] Again, as so many times, I [am] reminded of the advantage to the poet, and philosopher, and naturalist, and whomsoever, of pursuing from time to time some other business than his chosen one,—seeing with the side of the eye. The poet will so get visions which no deliberate abandonment can secure. The philosopher is so forced to recognize principles which long study might not detect. And the naturalist even will stumble upon some new and unexpected flower or animal.

[SEEING THE FAMILIAR AND HOMELY]

[November 20, 1857] In books, that which is most generally interesting is what comes home to the most cherished private experience of the greatest number. It is not the book of him who has travelled the farthest over the surface of the globe, but of him who has lived the deepest and been the most at home. If an equal emotion is excited by a familiar homely phenomenon as by the Pyramids, there is no advantage in seeing the Pyramids. It is on the whole better, as it is simpler, to use the common language. We require that the reporter be very permanently planted before the facts which he observes, not a mere passer-by; hence the facts cannot be too homely. A man is worth most to himself and to others, whether as an observer, or poet, or neighbor, or friend, where he is most himself, most contented and at home. There his life is the most intense and he loses the fewest moments. Familiar and surrounding objects are the best symbols and illustrations of his life. If a man who has had deep experiences should endeavor to describe them in a book of travels, it would be to use the language of a wandering tribe instead of a universal language. The poet has made the best roots in his native soil of any man, and is the hardest to transplant. The man who is often thinking that it is better to be somewhere else than where he is excommunicates himself. If a man is rich and strong anywhere, it must be on his native soil. Here I have been these forty years learning the language of these fields that I may the better express myself. If I should travel to the prairies, I should much less understand them, and my past life would serve me but ill to describe them. Many a weed here stands for more of life to me than the big trees of California would if I should go there. We only need travel enough to give our intellects an airing. In spite of Malthus[4] and the rest, there will be plenty of room in this world, if every man will mind his own business. I have not heard of any planet running against another yet.

[SEEING ONLY WHAT WE'RE PREPARED TO SEE]

[November 4, 1858] If, about the last of October, you ascend any hill in the outskirts of the town and look over the forest, you will see, amid the brown of other oaks, which are now withered, and the green of the pines, the bright-red tops or crescents of the scarlet oaks, very equally and thickly distributed on all sides, even to the horizon. Complete trees standing exposed on the edges of the forest, where you have never suspected them, or their tops only in the recesses of the forest sur-

---

[4]Thomas Robert Malthus (1766–1834), English economist whose *Essay on the Principle of Population* (1798) argued that world populations, when uncontrolled, tended to grow in a geometric ratio, while means of subsistence increased only in arithmetic ratio.

face, or perhaps towering above the surrounding trees, or reflecting a warm rose red from the very edge of the horizon in favorable lights. All this you will see, and much more, if you are prepared to see it,—if you *look* for it. Otherwise, regular and universal as this phenomenon is, you will think for threescore years and ten that all the wood is at this season sere and brown. Objects are concealed from our view not so much because they are out of the course of our visual ray (continued) as because there is no intention of the mind and eye toward them. We do not realize how far and widely, or how near and narrowly, we are to look. The greater part of the phenomena of nature are for this reason concealed to us all our lives. Here, too, as in political economy, the supply answers to the demand. Nature does not cast pearls before swine.[5] There is just as much beauty visible to us in the landscape as we are prepared to appreciate,—not a grain more. The actual objects which one person will see from a particular hilltop are just as different from those which another will see as the persons are different. The scarlet oak must, in a sense, be in your eye when you go forth. We cannot see anything until we are possessed with the idea of it, and then we can hardly see anything else. In my botanical rambles I find that first the idea, or image, of a plant occupies my thoughts, though it may at first seem very foreign to this locality, and for some weeks or months I go thinking of it and expecting it unconsciously, and at length I surely see it, and it is henceforth an actual neighbor of mine. This is the history of my finding a score or more of rare plants which I could name.

WRITING

[COMPOSITION ALLOWS OF NO TRICKS]

February 28, [1841] Nothing goes by luck in composition. It allows of no tricks. The best you can write will be the best you are. Every sentence is the result of a long probation. The author's character is read from title-page to end. Of this he never corrects the proofs. We read it as the essential character of a handwriting without regard to the flourishes. And so of the rest of our actions; it runs as straight as a ruled line through them all, no matter how many curvets about it. Our whole life is taxed for the least thing well done; it is its net result. How we eat, drink, sleep, and use our desultory hours, now in these indifferent days, with no eye to observe and no occasion [to] excite us, determines our authority and capacity for the time to come.

[SENTENCES CONCENTRATED AND NUTTY]

[August 22, 1851] It is the fault of some excellent writers—De Quincey's[1] first impressions on seeing London suggest it to me—that they express themselves with too great fullness and detail. They give the most faithful, natural, and lifelike account of their sensations, mental and physical, but they lack moderation and sententiousness. They do not affect us by an ineffectual earnestness and a reserve of meaning, like a stutterer; they say all they mean. Their sentences are not concentrated and nutty. Sentences which suggest far more than they say, which have an atmosphere about them, which do not merely report an old, but make a new, impression; sentences which suggest as many things and are as durable as a Roman aqueduct; to frame these, that is the *art* of writing. Sentences which are expensive, towards which so many volumes, so much life, went; which lie like boulders on the page, up and down or across; which contain the seed of other sentences, not mere repetition, but creation; which a man might sell his grounds and castles to build.

---

[5]Matthew 7:6.
[1]Thomas De Quincy (1785–1859), British writer, author of *Confessions of an English Opium Eater* (1821).

If De Quincey had suggested each of his pages in a sentence and passed on, it would have been far more excellent writing. His style is nowhere kinked and knotted up into something hard and significant, which you could swallow like a diamond, without digesting.

[WRITING WITH GUSTO]

[September 2, 1851] We cannot write well or truly but what we write with gusto. The body, the senses, must conspire with the mind. Expression is the act of the whole man, that our speech may be vascular. The intellect is powerless to express thought without the aid of the heart and liver and of every member. Often I feel that my head stands out too dry, when it should be immersed. A writer, a man writing, is the scribe of all nature; he is the corn and the grass and the atmosphere writing. It is always essential that we love to do what we are doing, do it with a heart. The maturity of the mind, however, may perchance consist with a certain dryness.

[PROBE THE UNIVERSE IN A MYRIAD POINTS]

[September 4, 1851] It is wise to write on many subjects, to try many themes, that so you may find the right and inspiring one. Be greedy of occasions to express your thought. Improve the opportunity to draw analogies. There are innumerable avenues to a perception of the truth. Improve the suggestion of each object however humble, however slight and transient the provocation. What else is there to be improved? Who knows what opportunities he may neglect? It is not in vain that the mind turns aside this way or that: follow its leading; apply it whither it inclines to go. Probe the universe in a myriad points. Be avaricious of these impulses. You must try a thousand themes before you find the right one, as nature makes a thousand acorns to get one oak. He is a wise man and experienced who has taken many views; to whom stones and plants and animals and a myriad objects have each suggested something, contributed something.

[BE NOT LONG ABSENT FROM THE GROUND]

November 12, [1851] Write often, write upon a thousand themes, rather than long at a time, not trying to turn too many feeble somersets in the air,—and so come down upon your head at last. Antæus-like,[2] be not long absent from the ground. Those sentences are good and well discharged which are like so many little resiliencies from the spring floor of our life,—a distinct fruit and kernel itself, springing from terra firma. Let there be as many distinct plants as the soil and the light can sustain. Take as many bounds in a day as possible. Sentences uttered with your back to the wall. Those are the admirable bounds when the performer has lately touched the springboard. A good bound into the air from the air [sic] is a good and wholesome experience, but what shall we say to a man's leaping off precipices in the attempt to fly? He comes down like lead. In the meanwhile, you have got your feet planted upon the rock, with the rock also at your back, and, as in the case of King James and Roderick Dhu, can say,—

> "Come one, come all! this rock shall fly
> From its firm base as soon as I."[3]

---

[2] In Greek mythology, one of the giants; he was always victorious in wrestling matches because, when he was thrown to the ground, his mother the earth would renew his strength, enabling him to rise again.
[3] From Canto V, Stanza 10 of *The Lady of the Lake* (1810), by Sir Walter Scott (1771–1832). The poem is set in sixteenth-century Scotland, and King James and Roderick Dhu (a rebel Highland chief) are principal characters who fight a duel.

Such, uttered or not, is the strength of your sentence. Sentences in which there is no strain. A fluttering and inconstant and *quasi* inspiration, and ever memorable Icarian[4] fall, in which your helpless wings are expanded merely by your swift descent into the *pelagos*[5] beneath.

[CLEAR A NEW FIELD INSTEAD OF MANURING THE OLD]

[December 25, 1851] It would be a truer discipline for the writer to take the least film of thought that floats in the twilight sky of his mind for his theme, about which he has scarcely one idea (that would be teaching his ideas how to shoot), faintest intimations, shadowiest subjects, make a lecture on this, by assiduity and attention get perchance two views of the same, increase a little the stock of knowledge, clear a new field instead of manuring the old; instead of making a lecture out of such obvious truths, hackneyed to the minds of all thinkers. We seek too soon to ally the perceptions of the mind to the experience of the hand, to prove our gossamer truths practical, to show their connection with our every-day life (better show their distance from our every-day life), to relate them to the cider-mill and the banking institution. Ah, give me pure mind, pure thought! Let me not be in haste to detect the *universal law;* let me see more clearly a particular instance of it! Much finer themes I aspire to, which will yield no satisfaction to the vulgar mind, not one sentence for them. Perchance it may convince such that there are more things in heaven and earth than are dreamed of in their philosophy.[6] Dissolve one nebula, and so destroy the nebular system and hypothesis. Do not seek expressions, seek thoughts to be expressed. By perseverance you get two views of the same rare truth.

That way of viewing things you know of, least insisted on by you, however, least remembered,—take that view, adhere to that, insist on that, see all things from that point of view. Will you let these intimations go unattended to and watch the door-bell or knocker? That is your text. Do not speak for other men; speak for yourself. They show you as in a vision the kingdoms of the world, and of all the worlds, but you prefer to look in upon a puppet-show. Though you should only speak to one kindred mind in all time, though you should not speak to one, but only utter aloud, that you may the more completely realize and live in the idea which contains the reason of your life, that you may build yourself up to the height of your conceptions, that you may remember your Creator in the days of your youth and justify His ways to man, that the end of life may not be its amusement, speak—though your thought presupposes the non-existence of your hearers—thoughts that transcend life and death. What though mortal ears are not fitted to hear absolute truth! Thoughts that blot out the earth are best conceived in the night, when darkness has already blotted it out from sight.

We look upward for inspiration.

[WRITE AS IF THY TIME WERE SHORT]

January 24, [1852] If thou art a writer, write as if thy time were short, for it is indeed short at the longest. Improve each occasion when thy soul is reached. Drain the cup of inspiration to its last dregs. Fear no intemperance in that, for the years will come when otherwise thou wilt regret opportunities unimproved. The spring will not last forever. These fertile and expanding seasons of thy life, when

---

[4]In Greek mythology, Icarus flew too near the sun with his wings (made by his father Daedalus) of wax and feathers, and fell from the sky.
[5]"Sea" (Greek).

[6]*Hamlet,* I, v, 166–167: "There are more things in heaven and earth, Horatio/Than are dreamt of in your philosophy."

the rain reaches thy root, when thy vigor shoots, when thy flower is budding, shall be fewer and farther between. Again I say, Remember thy Creator in the days of thy youth.[7] Use and commit to life what you cannot commit to memory. I hear the tones of my sister's piano below. It reminds me of strains which once I heard more frequently, when, possessed with the inaudible rhythm, I sought my chamber in the cold and communed with my own thoughts. I feel as if I then received the gifts of the gods with too much indifference. Why did I not cultivate those fields they introduced me to? Does nothing withstand the inevitable march of time? Why did I not use my eyes when I stood on Pisgah?[8] Now I hear those strains but seldom. My rhythmical mood does not endure. I cannot draw from it and return to it in my thought as to a well all the evening or the morning. I cannot dip my pen in it. I cannot work the vein, it is so fine and volatile. Ah, sweet, ineffable reminiscences!

[OBEY THE SPUR OF THE MOMENT]

[January 26, 1852] Obey the spur of the moment. These accumulated it is that make the impulse and the impetus of the life of genius. These are the spongioles or rootlets by which its trunk is fed. If you neglect the moments, if you cut off your fibrous roots, what but a languishing life is to be expected? Let the spurs of countless moments goad us incessantly into life. I feel the spur of the moment thrust deep into my side. The present is an inexorable rider. The moment always spurs either with a sharp or a blunt spur. Are my sides calloused? Let us trust the rider, that he knows the way, that he knows when speed and effort are required. What other impulse do we wait for? Let us preserve religiously, secure, protect the coincidence of our life with the life of nature. Else what are heat and cold, day and night, sun, moon, and stars to us? Was it not from sympathy with the present life of nature that we were born at this epoch rather than another?

[SIMPLE, CHEAP, AND HOMELY THEMES]

[October 18, 1856] Men commonly exaggerate the theme. Some themes they think are significant and others insignificant. I feel that my life is very homely, my pleasures very cheap. Joy and sorrow, success and failure, grandeur and meanness, and indeed most words in the English language do not mean for me what they do for my neighbors. I see that my neighbors look with compassion on me, that they think it is a mean and unfortunate destiny which makes me to walk in these fields and woods so much and sail on this river alone. But so long as I find here the only real elysium, I cannot hesitate in my choice. My work is writing, and I do not hesitate, though I know that no subject is too trivial for me, tried by ordinary standards; for, ye fools, the theme is nothing, the life is everything. All that interests the reader is the depth and intensity of the life excited. We touch our subject but by a point which has no breadth, but the pyramid of our experience, or our interest in it, rests on us by a broader or narrower base. That is, man is all in all, Nature nothing, but as she draws him out and reflects him. Give me simple, cheap, and homely themes.

[NO USE TO PLOW DEEPLY IN SHALLOW SOIL]

[November 9, 1858] It is of no use to plow deeper than the soil is, unless you mean to follow up that mode of cultivation persistently, manuring highly and cart-

---

[7]Ecclesiastes 12:1.
[8]Pisgah Mount, east of Jordan, from which Moses saw the Promised Land.

ing on muck at each plowing,—making a soil, in short. Yet many a man likes to tackle mighty themes, like immortality, but in his discourse he turns up nothing but yellow sand, under which what little fertile and available surface soil he may have is quite buried and lost. He should teach frugality rather,—how to postpone the fatal hour,—should plant a crop of beans. He might have raised enough of these to make a deacon of him, though never a preacher. Many a man runs his plow so deep in heavy or stony soil that it sticks fast in the furrow. It is a great art in the writer to improve from day to day just that soil and fertility which he has, to harvest that crop which his life yields, whatever it may be, not be straining as if to reach apples or oranges when he yields only ground-nuts. He should be digging, not soaring. Just as earnest as your life is, so deep is your soil. If strong and deep, you will sow wheat and raise bread of life in it.

[HYPERCRITICAL QUARRELLING ABOUT GRAMMAR AND STYLE]

[January 2, 1859] When I hear the hypercritical quarrelling about grammar and style, the position of the particles, etc., etc., stretching or contracting every speaker to certain rules of theirs,—Mr. Webster,[9] perhaps, not having spoken according to Mr. Kirkham's rule,—I see that they forget that the first requisite and rule is that expression shall be vital and natural, as much as the voice of a brute or an interjection: first of all, mother tongue; and last of all, artificial or father tongue. Essentially your truest poetic sentence is as free and lawless as a lamb's bleat. The grammarian is often one who can neither cry nor laugh, yet thinks that he can express human emotions. So the posture-masters tell you how you shall walk,—turning your toes out, perhaps, excessively,—but so the beautiful walkers are not made.

[WRITING AS GROPING AFTER THOUGHTS AND PERCEPTIONS]

[February 3, 1859] The writer must to some extent inspire himself. Most of his sentences may at first lie dead in his essay, but when all are arranged, some life and color will be reflected on them from the mature and successful lines; they will appear to pulsate with fresh life, and he will be enabled to eke out their slumbering sense, and make them worthy of their neighborhood. In his first essay on a given theme, he produces scarcely more than a frame and groundwork for his sentiment and poetry. Each clear thought that he attains to draws in its train many divided thoughts or perceptions. The writer has much to do even to create a theme for himself. Most that is first written on any subject is a mere groping after it, mere rubble-stone and foundation. It is only when many observations of different periods have been brought together that he begins to grasp his subject and can make one pertinent and just observation.

[AND THEN A LEAP IN THE DARK]

[March 11, 1859] There is always some accident in the best things, whether thoughts or expressions or deeds. The memorable thought, the happy expression, the admirable deed are only partly ours. The thought came to us because we were in a fit mood; also we were unconscious and did not know that we had said or done a good thing. We must walk consciously only part way toward our goal, and then leap in the dark to our success. What we do best or most perfectly is what we have most thoroughly learned by the longest practice, and at length it falls from us without our notice, as a leaf from a tree. It is the *last* time we shall do it,—our unconscious leavings.

---

[9]Daniel Webster (1782–1852), American political figure and famed orator. Samuel Kirkham, author of *A Compen-* *dium of English Grammar* (1823) and *An Essay on Elocution* (1833).

EMERSON AND FRIENDSHIP
[READING A FRIEND ARIGHT]

December 12, [1851] In regard to my friends, I feel that I know and have communion with a finer and subtler part of themselves which does not put me off when they put me off, which is not cold to me when they are cold, not till I am cold. I hold by a deeper and stronger tie than absence can sunder.

Ah, dear nature, the mere remembrance, after a short forgetfulness, of the pine woods! I come to it as a hungry man to a crust of bread.

I have been surveying for twenty or thirty days, living coarsely, even as respects my diet,—for I find that that will always alter to suit my employment,—indeed, leading a quite trivial life; and to-night, for the first time, had made a fire in my chamber and endeavored to return to myself. I wished to ally myself to the powers that rule the universe. I wished to dive into some deep stream of thoughtful and devoted life, which meandered through retired and fertile meadows far from towns. I wished to do again, or for once, things quite congenial to my highest inmost and most sacred nature, to lurk in crystalline thought like the trout under verdurous banks, where stray mankind should only see my bubble come to the surface. I wished to live, ah! as far away as a man can think. I wished for leisure and quiet to let my life flow in its proper channels, with its proper currents; when I might not waste the days, might establish daily prayer and thanksgiving in my family; might do my own work and not the work of Concord and Carlisle, which would yield me better than money. (How much forbearance, aye, sacrifice and loss, goes to every accomplishment! I am thinking by what long discipline and at what cost a man learns to speak simply at last.) I bethought myself, while my fire was kindling, to open one of Emerson's books, which it happens that I rarely look at, to try what a chance sentence out of that could do for me; thinking, at the same time, of a conversation I had with him the other night, I finding fault with him for the stress he had laid on some of Margaret Fuller's whims and superstitions, but he declaring gravely that she was one of those persons whose experience warranted her attaching importance to such things,—as the *Sortes Virgilianae*,[1] for instance, of which her numerous friends could tell remarkable instances. At any rate, I saw that he was disposed [to] regard such things more seriously than I. The first sentence which I opened upon in his book was this: "If, with a high trust, he can thus submit himself, he will find that ample returns are poured into his bosom out of what seemed hours of obstruction and loss. Let him not grieve too much on account of unfit associates. . . . In a society of perfect sympathy, no word, no act, no record, would be. He will learn that it is not much matter what he reads, what he does. Be a scholar, and he shall have the scholar's part of everything," etc., etc.[2]

Most of this responded well enough to my mood, and this would be as good an instance of the *Sortes Virgilianae* as most to quote. But what makes this coincidence very little if at all remarkable to me is the fact of the obviousness of the moral, so that I had, perhaps, *thought* the same thing myself twenty times during the day, and yet had not been *contented* with that account of it, leaving me thus to be amused by the coincidence, rather than impressed as by an intimation out of the deeps.

January 30, [1852] . . . I feel as if I were gradually parting company with certain friends, just as I perceive familiar objects successively disappear when I am leaving my native town in the cars.

· · · · ·

---

[1] "Virgilian lots" (Latin), a method of divination consisting of taking a passage from Virgil at random.

[2] From near the end of "Literary Ethics" in *Nature, Addresses, and Lectures* (1849).

One must not complain that his friend is cold, for heat is generated between them.

I doubt if Emerson could trundle a wheelbarrow through the streets, because it would be out of character. One needs to have a comprehensive character.

[January 31, 1852]———[*sic*] is too grand for me. He belongs to the nobility and wears their cloak and manners; is attracted to Plato, not to Socrates,[3] I fear partly because the latter's life and associates were too humble. I am a commoner. To me there is something devilish in manners. The best manners is nakedness of manners. I should value E.'s[4] praise more, which is always so discriminating, if there were not some alloy of patronage and hence of flattery about [it]. In that respect he is like———[*sic*]; they flatter you, but themselves more. Praise should be spoken as simply and naturally as a flower emits its fragrance.

[May 24, 1853] P. M.—Talked, or tried to talk, with R. W. E.[5] Lost my time—nay, almost my identity. He, assuming a false opposition where there was no difference of opinion, talked to the wind—told me what I knew—and I lost my time trying to imagine myself somebody else to oppose him.

March 4, [1856] To Carlisle, surveying.

I had two friends. The one offered me friendship on such terms that I could not accept it, without a sense of degradation. He would not meet me on equal terms, but only be to some extent my patron. He would not come to see me, but was hurt if I did not visit him. He would not readily accept a favor, but would gladly confer one. He treated me with ceremony occasionally, though he could be simple and downright sometimes; and from time to time acted a part, treating me as if I were a distinguished stranger; was on stilts, using made words. Our relation was one long tragedy, yet I did not directly speak of it. I do not believe in complaint, nor in explanation. The whole is but too plain, alas, already. We grieve that we do not love each other, that we cannot confide in each other. I could not bring myself to speak, and so recognize an obstacle to our affection.

I had another friend, who, through a slight obtuseness, perchance, did not recognize a fact which the dignity of friendship would by no means allow me to descend so far as to speak of, and yet the inevitable effect of that ignorance was to hold us apart forever.

[March 28, 1856] I think to say to my friend, There is but one interval between us. You are on one side of it, I on the other. You know as much about it as I,—how wide, how impassable it is. I will endeavor not to blame you. Do not blame me. There is nothing to be said about it. Recognize the truth, and pass over the intervals that are bridged.

Farewell, my friends, my path inclines to this side the mountain, yours to that. For a long time you have appeared further and further off to me. I see that you will at length disappear altogether. For a season my path seems lonely without you. The meadows are like barren ground. The memory of me is steadily passing away from you. My path grows narrower and steeper, and the night is approaching. Yet I have faith that, in the definite future, new suns will rise, and new plains expand before me, and I trust that I shall therein encounter pilgrims who bear that same virtue that I recognized in you, who will be that very virtue that was

---

[3]Plato (427?–347 B.C.) is the philosopher-writer whose works took the form of dialogues in which Socrates (c. 469–399 B.C.), the philosopher-teacher, engages students in subtle question-answer exchanges on complex philosophical and moral questions. Thus Plato is a philosopher of the study, Socrates a philosopher of the streets.
[4]Emerson's.
[5]Ralph Waldo Emerson.

you. I accept the everlasting and salutary law, which was promulgated as much that spring that I first knew you, as this that I seem to lose you.

My former friends, I visit you as one walks amid the columns of a ruined temple. You belong to an era, a civilization and glory, long past. I recognize still your fair proportions, notwithstanding the convulsions which we have felt, and the weeds and jackals that have sprung up around. I come here to be reminded of the past, to read your inscriptions, the hieroglyphics, the sacred writings. We are no longer the representatives of our former selves.

Love is a thirst that is never slaked. Under the coarsest rind, the sweetest meat. If you would read a friend aright, you must be able to read through something thicker and opaquer than horn. If you can read a friend, all languages will be easy to you. Enemies publish themselves. They declare war. The friend never declares his love.

from The Correspondence

LETTERS TO H. G. O. BLAKE[1]
[ILLUMINATIONS OF THE DARKNESS OF DAYLIGHT]

Concord, March 27, 1848

I am glad to hear that any words of mine, though spoken so long ago that I can hardly claim identity with their author, have reached you. It gives me pleasure, because I have therefore reason to suppose that I have uttered what concerns men, and that it is not in vain that man speaks to man. This is the value of literature. Yet those days are so distant, in every sense, that I have had to look at that page again, to learn what was the tenor of my thoughts then. I should value that article, however, if only because it was the occasion of your letter.

I do believe that the outward and the inward life correspond; that if any should succeed to live a higher life, others would not know of it; that difference and distance are one. To set about living a true life is to go a journey to a distant country, gradually to find ourselves surrounded by new scenes and men; and as long as the old are around me, I know that I am not in any true sense living a new or a better life. The outward is only the outside of that which is within. Men are not concealed under habits, but are revealed by them; they are their true clothes. I care not how curious a reason they may give for their abiding by them. Circumstances are not rigid and unyielding, but our habits are rigid. We are apt to speak vaguely sometimes, as if a divine life were to be grafted on to or built over this present as a suitable foundation. This might do if we could so build over our old life as to exclude from it all the warmth of our affection, and addle it, as the thrush builds over the cuckoo's egg, and lays her own atop, and hatches that only; but the fact is, we—so there is the partition—hatch them both, and the cuckoo's always by a day first, and that young bird crowds the young thrushes out of the nest. No. Destroy the cuckoo's egg, or build a new nest.

Change is change. No new life occupies the old bodies;—they decay. *It* is born, and grows, and flourishes. Men very pathetically inform the old, accept and wear it. Why put it up with the almshouse when you may go to heaven? It is embalm-

[1]Harrison Gray Otis Blake (1816?–1898) became a correspondent with Thoreau in 1848 after reading his work in *The Dial.* He taught school at Worcester, Massachusetts, and arranged for Thoreau to lecture there. The friendship lasted Thoreau's lifetime and inspired a large body of remarkable correspondence. Thoreau's sister willed his manuscripts to Blake, who edited a series of books out of the journal (1881–92), each volume named after one of the four seasons.

ing,—no more. Let alone your ointments and your linen swathes, and go into an infant's body. You see in the catacombs of Egypt the result of that experiment,—that is the end of it.

I do believe in simplicity. It is astonishing as well as sad, how many trivial affairs even the wisest man thinks he must attend to in a day; how singular an affair he thinks he must omit. When the mathematician would solve a difficult problem, he first frees the equation of all incumbrances, and reduces it to its simplest terms. So simplify the problem of life, distinguish the necessary and the real. Probe the earth to see where your main roots run. I would stand upon facts. Why not see,—use our eyes? Do men know nothing? I know many men who, in common things, are not to be deceived; who trust no moonshine; who count their money correctly, and know how to invest it; who are said to be prudent and knowing, who yet will stand at a desk the greater part of their lives, as cashiers in banks, and glimmer and rust and finally go out there. If they *know* anything, what under the sun do they do that for? Do they know what *bread* is? or what it is for? Do they know what life is? If they *knew* something, the places which know them now would know them no more forever.

This, our respectable daily life, in which the man of common sense, the Englishman of the world, stands so squarely, and on which our institutions are founded, is in fact the veriest illusion, and will vanish like the baseless fabric of a vision; but that faint glimmer of reality which sometimes illuminates the darkness of daylight for all men, reveals something more solid and enduring than adamant, which is in fact the corner-stone of the world.

Men cannot conceive of a state of things so fair that it cannot be realized. Can any man honestly consult his experience and say that it is so? Have we any facts to appeal to when we say that our dreams are premature? Did you ever hear of a man who had striven all his life faithfully and singly toward an object and in no measure obtained it? If a man constantly aspires, is he not elevated? Did ever a man try heroism, magnanimity, truth, sincerity, and find that there was no advantage in them? that it was a vain endeavor? Of course we do not expect that our paradise will be a garden. We know not what we ask. To look at literature;—how many fine thoughts has every man had! how few fine thoughts are expressed! Yet we never have a fantasy so subtile and ethereal, but that *talent merely*, with more resolution and faithful persistency, after a thousand failures, might fix and engrave it in distinct and enduring words, and we should see that our dreams are the solidest facts that we know. But I speak not of dreams.

What can be expressed in words can be expressed in life.

My actual life is a fact in view of which I have no occasion to congratulate myself, but for my faith and aspiration I have respect. It is from these that I speak. Every man's position is in fact too simple to be described. I have sworn no oath. I have no designs on society—or nature—or God. I am simply what I am, or I begin to be that. I *live* in the *present*. I only remember the past—and anticipate the future. I love to live, I love reform better than its modes. There is no history of how bad became better. I believe something, and there is nothing else but that. I know that I am—I know that [ano]ther is who knows more than I who takes interest in me, whose creature and yet [whose] kindred, in one sense, am I. I know that the enterprise is worthy—I know that things work well. I have heard no bad news.

As for positions—as for combinations and details—what are they? In clear weather when we look into the heavens, what do we see, but the sky and the sun?

If you would convince a man that he does wrong do right. But do not care to convince him.—Men will believe what they see. Let them see.

Pursue, keep up with, circle round and round your life as a dog does his master's chaise. Do what you love. Know your own bone; gnaw at it, bury it, unearth it, and gnaw it [still. Do not be too] moral. You may cheat yourself out of much life so. Aim above morality. Be not *simply* good—be good for something.—All fables indeed have their morals, but the innocent enjoy the story.

Let nothing come between you and the light. Respect men as brothers only. When you travel to the celestial city, carry no letter of introduction. When you knock ask to see God—none of the servants. In what concerns you much do not think that you have companions—know that you are alone in the world.

Thus I write at random. I need to see you, and I trust I shall, to correct my mistakes. Perhaps you have some oracles for me.

[Henry Thoreau]

[FOOD FOR THOSE FACULTIES YOU EXERCISE]

Concord, May 2, 1848

"We must have our bread." But what is our bread? Is it baker's bread? Methinks it should be very *home-made* bread. What is our meat? Is it butcher's meat? What is that which we *must* have? Is that bread which we are now earning sweet? Is it not bread which has been suffered to sour, and then been sweetened with an alkali, which has undergone the vinous, acetous, and sometimes the putrid fermentation, and then been whitened with vitriol? Is this the bread which we must have? Man must earn his bread by the sweat of his brow, truly, but also by the sweat of his brain within his brow. The body can feed the body only. I have tasted but little bread in my life. It has been mere grub and provender for the most part. Of bread that nourished the brain and the heart, scarcely any. There is absolutely none even on the tables of the rich.

There is not one kind of food for all men. You must and you will feed those faculties which you exercise. The laborer whose body is weary does not require the same food with the scholar whose brain is weary. Men should not labor foolishly like brutes, but the brain and the body should always, or as much as possible, work and rest together, and then the work will be of such a kind that when the body is hungry the brain will be hungry also, and the same food will suffice for both; otherwise the food which repairs the waste energy of the over-wrought body will oppress the sedentary brain, and the degenerate scholar will come to esteem all food vulgar, and all getting a living drudgery.

How shall we earn our bread is a grave question; yet it is a sweet and inviting question. Let us not shirk it, as is usually done. It is the most important and practical question which is put to man. Let us not answer it hastily. Let us not be content to get our bread in some gross, careless, and hasty manner. Some men go a-hunting, some a-fishing, some a-gaming, some to war; but none have so pleasant a time as they who in earnest seek to earn their bread. It is true actually as it is true really; it is true materially as it is true spiritually, that they who seek honestly and sincerely, with all their hearts and lives and strength, to earn their bread, do earn it, and it is sure to be very sweet to them. A very little bread,—a very few crumbs are enough, if it be of the right quality, for it is infinitely nutritious. Let each man, then, earn at least a crumb of bread for his body before he dies, and know the taste of it,—that it is identical with the bread of life, and that they both go down at one swallow.

Our bread need not ever be sour or hard to digest. What Nature is to the mind she is also to the body. As she feeds my imagination, she will feed my body; for what she says she means, and is ready to do. She is not simply beautiful to the poet's eye. Not only the rainbow and sunset are beautiful, but to be fed and clothed, sheltered and warmed aright, are equally beautiful and inspiring. There is not necessarily any gross and ugly fact which may not be eradicated from the life of man. We should endeavor practically in our lives to correct all the defects which our imagination detects. The heavens are as deep as our aspirations are high. So high as a tree aspires to grow, so high it will find an atmosphere suited to it. Every man should stand for a force which is perfectly irresistible. How can any man be weak who dares *to be* at all? Even the tenderest plants force their way up through the hardest earth, and the crevices of rocks; but a man no material power can resist. What a wedge, what a beetle, what a catapult, is an *earnest* man! What can resist him?

It is a momentous fact that a man may be *good,* or he may be *bad;* his life may be *true,* or it may be *false;* it may be either a shame or a glory to him. The good man builds himself up; the bad man destroys himself.

But whatever we do we must do confidently (if we are timid, let us, then, act timidly), not expecting more light, but having light enough. If we confidently expect more, then let us wait for it. But what is this which we have? Have we not already waited? Is this the beginning of time? Is there a man who does not see clearly beyond, though only a hair's breadth beyond where he at any time stands?

If one hesitates in his path, let him not proceed. Let him respect his doubts, for doubts, too, may have some divinity in them. That we have but little faith is not sad, but that we have but little faithfulness. By faithfulness faith is earned. When, in the progress of a life, a man swerves, though only by an angle infinitely small, from his proper and allotted path (and this is never done quite unconsciously even at first; in fact, that was his broad and scarlet sin,—ah, he knew of it more than he can tell), then the drama of his life turns to tragedy, and makes haste to its fifth act. When once we thus fall behind ourselves, there is no accounting for the obstacles which rise up in our path, and no one is so wise as to advise, and no one so powerful as to aid us while we abide on that ground. Such are cursed with *duties,* and the *neglect of their duties.* For such the decalogue[2] was made, and other far more voluminous and terrible codes.

These departures,—who have not made them?—for they are as faint as the parallax of a fixed star, and at the commencement we say they are nothing,—that is, they originate in a kind of sleep and forgetfulness of the soul when it is naught. A man cannot be too circumspect in order to keep in the straight road, and be sure that he sees all that he may at any time see, that so he may distinguish his true path.

You ask if there is no doctrine of sorrow in my philosophy. Of acute sorrow I suppose that I know comparatively little. My saddest and most genuine sorrows are apt to be but transient regrets. The place of sorrow is supplied, perchance, by a certain hard and proportionably barren indifference. I am of kin to the sod, and partake largely of its dull patience,—in winter expecting the sun of spring. In my cheapest moments I am apt to think that it is not my business to be "seeking the spirit," but as much its business to be seeking me. I know very well what Goethe[3] meant when he said that he never had a chagrin but he made a poem out of it. I have altogether too much patience of this kind. I am too easily contented with a slight and almost animal happiness. My happiness is a good deal like that of the woodchucks.

Methinks I am never quite committed, never wholly the creature of my moods, being always to some extent their critic. My only integral experience is in my vision. I see, perchance, with more integrity than I feel.

But I need not tell you what manner of man I am,—my virtues or my vices. You can guess if it is worth the while; and I do not discriminate them well.

I do not write this time at my hut in the woods. I am at present living with Mrs.

---

[2] The Ten Commandments (Exodus 20:1–17).
[3] Johann Wolfgang von Goethe (1749–1832), German poet and dramatist.

Emerson, whose house is an old home of mine, for company during Mr. Emerson's absence.

You will perceive that I am as often talking to myself, perhaps, as speaking to you.

[LET THE BEAUTIFUL LAWS PREVAIL]

Concord, April 3, 1850

Mr. Blake,—

I thank you for your letter, and I will endeavor to record some of the thoughts which it suggests, whether pertinent or not. You speak of poverty and dependence. Who are poor and dependent? Who are rich and independent? When was it that men agreed to respect the appearance and not the reality? Why should the appearance *appear?* Are we well acquainted, then, with the reality? There is none who does not lie hourly in the respect he pays to false appearance. How sweet it would be to treat men and things, for an hour, for just what they are! We wonder that the sinner does not confess his sin. When we are weary with travel, we lay down our load and rest by the wayside. So, when we are weary with the burden of life, why do we not lay down this load of falsehoods which we have volunteered to sustain, and be refreshed as never mortal was? Let the beautiful laws prevail. Let us not weary ourselves by resisting them. When we would rest our bodies we cease to support them; we recline on the lap of earth. So, when we would rest our spirits, we must recline on the Great Spirit. Let things alone; let them weigh what they will; let them soar or fall. To succeed in letting only one thing alone in a winter morning, if it be only one poor frozen-thawed apple that hangs on a tree, what a glorious achievement! Methinks it lightens through the dusky universe. What an infinite wealth we have discovered! God reigns, *i. e.,* when we take a liberal view,—when a liberal view is presented us.

Let God alone if need be. Methinks, if I loved him more, I should keep him,—I should keep myself rather,—at a more respectful distance. It is not when I am going to meet him, but when I am just turning away and leaving him alone, that I discover that God is. I say, God. I am not sure that that is the name. You will know whom I mean.

If for a moment we make way with our petty selves, wish no ill to anything, apprehend no ill, cease to be but as the crystal which reflects a ray,—what shall we not reflect! What a universe will appear crystallized and radiant around us!

I should say, let the Muse lead the Muse,—let the understanding lead the understanding, though in any case it is the farthest forward which leads them both. If the Muse accompany, she is no muse, but an amusement. The Muse should lead like a star which is very far off; but that does not imply that we are to follow foolishly, falling into sloughs and over precipices, for it is not foolishness, but understanding, which is to follow, which the Muse is appointed to lead, as a fit guide of a fit follower.

Will you live? or will you be embalmed? Will you live, though it be astride of a sunbeam; or will you repose safely in the catacombs for a thousand years? In the former case, the worst accident that can happen is that you may break your neck. Will you break your heart, your soul, to save your neck? Necks and pipe-stems are fated to be broken. Men make a great ado about the folly of demanding too much of life (or of eternity?), and of endeavoring to live according to that demand. It is much ado about nothing. No harm ever came from that quarter. I am not afraid that I shall exaggerate the value and significance of life, but that I shall not be up to the occasion which it is. I shall be sorry to remember that I was there, but noticed nothing remarkable,—not so much as a prince in disguise; lived in the golden age a hired man; visited Olympus even, but fell asleep after dinner, and did not hear the conversation of the gods. I lived in Judæa eighteen hundred years ago, but I never knew that there was such a one as Christ among my contemporaries! If there is anything more glorious than a congress of men a-framing or amending of a constitution going on, which I suspect there is, I desire to see the morning papers. I am greedy of the faintest rumor, though it were got by listening at the key-hole. I will dissipate myself in that direction.

I am glad to know that you find what I have said on Friendship[4] worthy of attention. I wish I could have the benefit of your criticism; it would be a rare help to me. Will you not communicate it?

[A Visit with Whitman]

Eaglewood, N.J., November 19, 1856

Mr. Blake,—

I have been here much longer than I expected, but have deferred answering you, because I could not foresee when I shall return. I do not know yet within three or four days. This uncertainty makes it impossible for me to appoint a day to meet you, until it shall be too late to hear from you again. I think, therefore, that I must go straight home. I feel some objection to reading that "What shall it profit"[5] lecture *again* in Worcester; but if you are quite sure that it will be worth the while (it is a grave consideration), I will even make an independent journey from Concord for that purpose. I have read three of my old lectures (that included) to the Eaglewood people, and, unexpectedly, with rare success—*i. e.*, I was aware that what I was saying was silently taken in by their ears.

You must excuse me if I write mainly a business letter now, for I am sold for the time,—am merely Thoreau the surveyor here,—and solitude is scarcely obtainable in these parts.

Alcott has been here three times, and, Saturday before last, I went with him and Greeley, by invitation of the last, to G.'s farm, thirty-six miles north of New York. The next day A. and I heard Beecher preach;[6] and what was more, we visited Whitman the next morning (A. had already seen him), and were much interested and provoked. He is apparently the greatest democrat the world has seen. Kings and aristocracy go by the board at once, as they have long deserved to. A remarkably strong though coarse nature, of a sweet disposition, and much prized by his friends. Though peculiar and rough in his exterior, his skin (all over (?)) red, he is essentially a gentleman. I am still somewhat in a quandary about him,— feel that he is essentially strange to me, at any rate; but I am surprised by the sight of him. He is very broad, but, as I have said, not fine. He said that I misapprehended him. I am not quite sure that I do. He told us that he loved to ride up and down Broadway all day on an omnibus, sitting beside the driver, listening to the roar of the carts, and sometimes gesticulating and declaiming Homer at the top of his voice. He has long been an editor and writer for the newspapers,—was editor of the "New Orleans Crescent" once; but now has no employment but to read and write in the forenoon, and walk in the afternoon, like all the rest of the scribbling gentry.[7]

I shall probably be in Concord next week; so you can direct to me there.

---

[4]The embedded essay on friendship in the Wednesday section of *A Week on the Concord and Merrimack Rivers* (1849).
[5]"Life without Principle."
[6]Amos Bronson Alcott (1799–1888), a neighbor in Concord, transcendentalist, author of "Orphic Sayings"; Horace Greeley (1811–1872), American journalist and political leader, founder of the New York *Tribune*, strongly antislavery; Henry Ward Beecher (1813–1887), congregational minister and famed preacher.
[7]"A penciled draft of the last part of this letter . . . includes an interesting addition to Thoreau's comments on Whitman . . . Whitman spoke to Thoreau about his having published Emerson's letter of endorsement of *Leaves of Grass*, an action that created a stir at the time and is still debated. Thoreau says: 'In his apologizing account of the matter he made the printing of E[merson']s letter seem a simple thing—and to some extent throws the burden of it—if there is any, on the writer,' that is, on Emerson—the sentence omitted from the published version" (Editor's note).

[WHITMAN: IT IS AS IF THE BEASTS SPOKE]

Concord, December 6, 1856

Mr Blake,

. . . Blake! Blake! Are you awake? Are you aware what an ever-glorious morning this is? What long expected never to be repeated opportunity is now offered to get life & knowledge?

For my part I am trying to wake up,—to wring slumber out of my pores;—For, generally, I take events as unconcernedly as a fence post,—absorb wet & cold like it, and am pleasantly tickled with lichens slowly spreading over me. Could I not be content then to be a cedar post, which lasts 25 years? Would I not rather be that than the farmer that set it? or he that preaches to that farmer?—& go to the heaven of posts at last? I think I should like that as well as any would like it. But I should not care if I sprouted into a living tree, put forth leaves & flowers, & have fruit.

I am grateful for what I am & have. My thanksgiving is perpetual. It is surprising how contented one can be with nothing definite—only a sense of existance. Well anything for variety. I am ready to try this for the next 1000 years, & exhaust it. How sweet to think of! My extremities well charred, and my intellectual part too, so that there is no danger of worm or rot for a long while. My breath is sweet to me. O how I laugh when I think of my vague indefinite riches. No run on my bank can drain it—for my wealth is not possession but enjoyment.

What are all these years made for? and now another winter comes, so much like the last? Cant we satisfy the beggars once for all? Have you got in your wood for this winter? What else have you got in? Of what use a great fire on the hearth & a confounded little fire in the heart? Are you prepared to make a decisive campaign—to pay for your costly tuition—to pay for the suns of past summers—for happiness & unhappiness lavished upon you?

Does not Time go by swifter than the swiftest equine trotter or racker?

December 7

That Walt Whitman, of whom I wrote to you, is the most interesting fact to me at present. I have just read his 2nd edition (which he gave me) and it has done me more good than any reading for a long time. Perhaps I remember best the poem of Walt Whitman an American & the Sun Down Poem.[8] There are 2 or 3 pieces in the book which are disagreeable to say the least, simply sensual. He does not celebrate love at all. It is as if the beasts spoke. I think that men have not been ashamed of themselves without reason. No doubt, there have always been dens where such deeds were unblushingly recited, and it is no merit to compete with their inhabitants. But even on this side, he has spoken more truth than any American or modern that I know. I have found his poem exhilirating encouraging. As for its sensuality,—& it may turn out to be less sensual than it appeared—I do not so much wish that those parts were not written, as that men & women were so pure that they could read them without harm, that is, without understanding them. One woman told me that no woman could read it as if a man could read what a woman could not. Of course Walt Whitman can communicate to us no experience, and if we are shocked, whose experience is it that we are reminded of?

On the whole it sounds to me very brave & American after whatever deductions. I do not believe that all the sermons so called that have been preached in this land put together are equal to it for preaching—

We ought to rejoice greatly in him. He occasionally suggests something a little more than human. You cant confound him with the other inhabitants of Brooklyn or New York. How they must shudder when they read him! He is awefully good.

---

[8]"Song of Myself" and "Crossing Brooklyn Ferry."

To be sure I sometimes feel a little imposed on. By his heartiness & broad generalities he puts me into a liberal frame of mind prepared to see wonders—as it were sets me upon a hill or in the midst of a plain—stirs me well up, and then—throws in a thousand of brick. Though rude & sometimes ineffectual, it is a great primitive poem,—an alarum or trumpet-note ringing through the American camp. Wonderfully like the Orientals, too, considering that when I asked him if he had read them, he answered, "No: tell me about them."

I did not get far in conversation with him,—two more being present,—and among the few things which I chanced to say, I remember that one was, in answer to him as representing America, that I did not think much of America or of politics, and so on, which may have been somewhat of a damper to him.

Since I have seen him; I find that I am not disturbed by any brag or egoism in his book. He may turn out the least of a braggart of all, having a better right to be confident.

He is a great fellow.

[My Own Destiny Made and Mended Here]

Concord, May 20, 1860

Mr Blake,

I must endeavor to pay some of my debts to you.

To begin where we left off then.

The presumption is that *we* are always the same; our opportunities & Nature herself fluctuating. Look at mankind. No great difference between two, apparently; perhaps the same height and breadth and weight; and yet to the man who sits most E. this life is a weariness, routine, dust and ashes, and he drowns his imaginary cares (!) (a sort of friction among his vital organs), in a bowl. But to the man who sits most W., his *contemporary* (!) it is a field for all noble endeavors, an elysium, the dwelling place of heroes & knights. The former complains that he has a thousand affairs to attend to; but he does not realize, that his affairs, (though they may be a thousand,) and he are one.

Men & boys are learning all kinds of trades but how to make *men* of themselves. They learn to make houses, but they are not so well housed, they are not so contented in their houses, as the woodchucks in their holes. What is the use of a house if you haven't got a tolerable planet to put it on? If you can not tolerate the planet it is on? Grade the ground first. If a man believes and expects great things of himself, it makes no odds where you put him, or what you show him, (of course, you cannot put him anywhere nor show him anything), he will be surrounded by grandeur. He's in the condition of a healthy & hungry man, who says to himself—How sweet this crust is!

If he despairs of himself, then Tophet[9] is his dwelling place, and he is in the condition of a sick man who is disgusted with the fruits of finest flavor.

Whether he sleeps or wakes, whether he runs or walks, whether he uses a microscope or a telescope, or his naked eye, a man never discovers anything, never overtakes anything or leaves anything behind, but himself. Whatever he says or does he merely reports himself. If he is in love, he *loves;* if he is in heaven he *enjoys,* if he is in hell he *suffers.* It is his condition that determines his locality.

The principal, the only thing a man makes is his condition, or fate. Though commonly he does not know it, nor put up a sign to this effect, "My own destiny made & mended here." [not *yours*] He is a masterworkman in this business. He works 24 hours a day at it and gets it done. Whatever else he neglects or botches, no man was ever known to neglect this work. A great many pretend to make *shoes*

---

[9]Hell; place where humans were sacrificed by fire to Moloch.

chiefly, and would scout the idea that they make the hard times which they experience.

Each reaching and aspiration is an instinct with which all nature consists & cooperates, and therefore it is not in vain. But alas! each relaxing and desperation is an instinct too. To be active, well, happy, implies rare courage. To be ready to fight in a duel or a battle implies desperation, or that you hold your life cheap.

If you take this life to be simply what old religious folks pretend, (I mean the effete, gone to seed in a drought, mere human galls stung by the Devil once), then all your joy & serenity is reduced to grinning and bearing it. The fact is, you have got to take the world on your shoulders like Atlas[10] and put along with it. You will do this for an idea's sake, and your success will be in proportion to your devotion to ideas. It may make your back ache occasionally, but you will have the satisfaction of hanging it or twirling it to suit yourself. Cowards suffer, heroes enjoy. After a long day's walk with it, pitch it into a hollow place, sit down and eat your luncheon. Unexpectedly, by some immortal thoughts, you will be compensated. The bank whereon you sit will be a fragrant and flowery one, and your world in the hollow a sleek and light gazelle.

Where is the "Unexplored land" but in our own untried enterprises? To an adventurous spirit any place,—London New York, Worcester, or his own yard, is "unexplored land," to seek which Freemont & Kane[11] travel so far. To a sluggish & defeated spirit even the Great Basin & the Polaris[12] are trivial places. If they ever get there (& indeed they are there now) they will want to sleep & give it up, just as they always do. These are the regions of the Known & of the Unknown. What is the use of going right over the old track again? There is an adder in the path which your own feet have worn. You must make tracks into the Unknown. That is what you have your board & clothes for. Why do you ever mend your clothes, unless that, wearing them, you may mend your ways?

Let us sing

H.D.T.

Walden[1]

> I do not propose to write an ode to dejection, but to
> brag as lustily as chanticleer in the morning, standing
> on his roost, if only to wake my neighbors up.

I

ECONOMY

When I wrote the following pages, or rather the bulk of them, I lived alone, in the woods, a mile from any neighbor, in a house which I had built myself, on the shore of Walden Pond, in Concord, Massachusetts, and earned my living by the labor of my hands only. I lived there two years and two months. At present I am a sojourner in civilized life again.

---

[10] In Greek legend, a giant forced to hold up the heavens on his shoulders.
[11] John Charles Fremont (1813–1890), Army officer and explorer, especially of Oregon territory; Elisha Kent Kane (1820–1857), American arctic explorer and author of books on his explorations.
[12] Great Basin, a plateau in the western United States between the Sierra Nevada and Wasatch Mountains; Polaris, the North Star which marks the position of the north pole.
[1] Thoreau went to live at Walden Pond on July 4, 1845, in the cabin that he was still building. A little over two years

later, on September 6, 1847, he moved back to Concord, by which time he had about half of *Walden* in draft. By the time the book was published in 1854, Thoreau had expanded the manuscript and had rigorously revised it several times. See J. Lyndon Shanley, *The Making of Walden* (1957). Other useful works: Walter Harding, ed., *The Variorum Walden* (1962) and Philip Van Doren Stern, ed., *The Annotated Walden* (1970).

The epigraph and Thoreau's map of Walden Pond (1846) are taken from the 1854 first edition of *Walden*.

I should not obtrude my affairs so much on the notice of my readers if very particular inquiries had not been made by my townsmen concerning my mode of life, which some would call impertinent, though they do not appear to me at all impertinent, but, considering the circumstances, very natural and pertinent. Some have asked what I got to eat; if I did not feel lonesome; if I was not afraid; and the like. Others have been curious to learn what portion of my income I devoted to charitable purposes; and some, who have large families, how many poor children I maintained. I will therefore ask those of my readers who feel no particular interest in me to pardon me if I undertake to answer some of these questions in this book. In most books, the *I*, or first person, is omitted; in this it will be retained; that, in respect to egotism, is the main difference. We commonly do not remember that it is, after all, always the first person that is speaking. I should not talk so much about myself if there were anybody else whom I knew as well. Unfortunately, I am confined to this theme by the narrowness of my experience. Moreover, I, on my side, require of every writer, first or last, a simple and sincere account of his own life, and not merely what he has heard of other men's lives; some such account as he would send to his kindred from a distant land; for if he has lived sincerely, it must have been in a distant land to me. Perhaps these pages are more particularly addressed to poor students. As for the rest of my readers, they will accept such portions as apply to them. I trust that none will stretch the seams in putting on the coat, for it may do good service to him whom it fits.

I would fain say something, not so much concerning the Chinese and Sandwich Islanders[2] as you who read these pages, who are said to live in New England; something about your condition, especially your outward condition or circumstances in this world, in this town, what it is, whether it is necessary that it be as bad as it is, whether it cannot be improved as well as not. I have travelled a good deal in Concord; and everywhere, in shops, and offices, and fields, the inhabitants have appeared to me to be doing penance in a thousand remarkable ways. What I have heard of Bramins[3] sitting exposed to four fires and looking in the face of the sun; or hanging suspended, with their heads downward, over flames; or looking at the heavens over their shoulders "until it becomes impossible for them to resume their natural position, while from the twist of the neck nothing but liquids can pass into the stomach;" or dwelling, chained for life, at the foot of a tree; or measuring with their bodies, like caterpillars, the breadth of vast empires; or standing on one leg on the tops of pillars,—even these forms of conscious penance are hardly more incredible and astonishing than the scenes which I daily witness. The twelve labors of Hercules[4] were trifling in comparison with those which my neighbors have undertaken; for they were only twelve, and had an end; but I could never see that these men slew or captured any monster or finished any labor. They have no friend Iolaus to burn with a hot iron the root of the hydra's head, but as soon as one head is crushed, two spring up.

I see young men, my townsmen, whose misfortune it is to have inherited farms, houses, barns, cattle, and farming tools; for these are more easily acquired than got rid of. Better if they had been born in the open pasture and suckled by a wolf, that they might have seen with clearer eyes what field they were called to labor in. Who made them serfs of the soil? Why should they eat their sixty acres, when man is condemned to eat only his peck of dirt? Why should they begin digging their graves as soon as they are born? They have got to live a man's life, pushing all these things before them, and get on as well as they can. How many a poor im-

---

[2] I.e., the Hawaiian Islanders.
[3] High-caste Hindus whose self-torture was religiously inspired.
[4] Son of the Greek god Zeus and a human, Hercules performed feats requiring superhuman strength. To earn immortality, he undertook twelve seemingly impossible labors. In his second labor, the killing of the multiheaded Lernean hydra, he was aided by Iolaus (who seared the stump as Hercules cut off each head).

mortal soul have I met well-nigh crushed and smothered under its load, creeping down the road of life, pushing before it a barn seventy-five feet by forty, its Augean stables[5] never cleansed, and one hundred acres of land, tillage, mowing, pasture, and wood-lot! The portionless, who struggle with no such unnecessary inherited encumbrances, find it labor enough to subdue and cultivate a few cubic feet of flesh.

But men labor under a mistake. The better part of the man is soon plowed into the soil for compost. By a seeming fate, commonly called necessity, they are employed, as it says in an old book, laying up treasures which moth and rust will corrupt and thieves break through and steal.[6] It is a fool's life, as they will find when they get to the end of it, if not before. It is said that Deucalion and Pyrrha created men by throwing stones over their heads behind them:—[7]

> Inde genus durum sumus, experiensque laborum,
> Et documenta damus quâ simus origine nati.

Or, as Raleigh rhymes it in his sonorous way,—

> "From thence our kind hard-hearted is, enduring pain and care,
> Approving that our bodies of a stony nature are."

So much for a blind obedience to a blundering oracle, throwing the stones over their heads behind them, and not seeing where they fell.

Most men, even in this comparatively free country, through mere ignorance and mistake, are so occupied with the factitious cares and superfluously coarse labors of life that its finer fruits cannot be plucked by them. Their fingers, from excessive toil, are too clumsy and tremble too much for that. Actually, the laboring man has not leisure for a true integrity day by day; he cannot afford to sustain the manliest relations to men; his labor would be depreciated in the market. He has no time to be anything but a machine. How can he remember well his ignorance—which his growth requires—who has so often to use his knowledge? We should feed and clothe him gratuitously sometimes, and recruit him with our cordials, before we judge of him. The finest qualities of our nature, like the bloom on fruits, can be preserved only by the most delicate handling. Yet we do not treat ourselves nor one another thus tenderly.

Some of you, we all know, are poor, find it hard to live, are sometimes, as it were, gasping for breath. I have no doubt that some of you who read this book are unable to pay for all the dinners which you have actually eaten, or for the coats and shoes which are fast wearing or are already worn out, and have come to this page to spend borrowed or stolen time, robbing your creditors of an hour. It is very evident what mean and sneaking lives many of you live, for my sight has been whetted by experience; always on the limits, trying to get into business and trying to get out of debt, a very ancient slough, called by the Latins *aes alienum*, another's brass, for some of their coins were made of brass; still living, and dying, and buried by this other's brass; always promising to pay, promising to pay, tomorrow, and dying to-day, insolvent; seeking to curry favor, to get custom, by how many modes, only not state-prison offences; lying, flattering, voting, contracting yourselves into a nutshell of civility or dilating into an atmosphere of thin and vaporous generosity, that you may persuade your neighbor to let you make his

---

[5]One of Hercules' labors was to cleanse King Augeas's stables, which housed 3,000 oxen and had not been cleaned for thirty years.
[6]Matthew 6:19–20.
[7]Deucalion and Pyrrha are the Noah and wife of Greek mythology, the only survivors (by raft) of a flood by which Zeus intended to destroy humankind. The raft landed on Mount Parnassus. After consulting the oracle of Themis, Deucalion and Pyrrha threw stones over their shoulders and the stones sprang up men and women, repeopling the world. The quotation is from Ovid's *Metamorphoses*, I, 414–415; the translation is from Sir Walter Raleigh's *The History of the World* (1614).

shoes, or his hat, or his coat, or his carriage, or import his groceries for him; making yourselves sick, that you may lay up something against a sick day, something to be tucked away in an old chest, or in a stocking behind the plastering, or, more safely, in the brick bank; no matter where, no matter how much or how little.

I sometimes wonder that we can be so frivolous, I may almost say, as to attend to the gross but somewhat foreign form of servitude called Negro Slavery, there are so many keen and subtle masters that enslave both North and South. It is hard to have a Southern overseer; it is worse to have a Northern one; but worst of all when you are the slave-driver of yourself. Talk of a divinity in man! Look at the teamster on the highway, wending to market by day or night; does any divinity stir within him? His highest duty to fodder and water his horses! What is his destiny to him compared with the shipping interests? Does not he drive for Squire Make-a-stir? How godlike, how immortal, is he? See how he cowers and sneaks, how vaguely all the day he fears, not being immortal nor divine, but the slave and prisoner of his own opinion of himself, a fame won by his own deeds. Public opinion is a weak tyrant compared with our own private opinion. What a man thinks of himself, that it is which determines, or rather indicates, his fate. Self-emancipation even in the West Indian provinces of the fancy and imagination,— what Wilberforce is there to bring that about?[8] Think, also, of the ladies of the land weaving toilet cushions against the last day, not to betray too green an interest in their fates! As if you could kill time without injuring eternity.

The mass of men lead lives of quiet desperation. What is called resignation is confirmed desperation. From the desperate city you go into the desperate country, and have to console yourself with the bravery of minks and muskrats. A stereotyped but unconscious despair is concealed even under what are called the games and amusements of mankind. There is no play in them, for this comes after work. But it is a characteristic of wisdom not to do desperate things.

When we consider what, to use the words of the catechism, is the chief end of man,[9] and what are the true necessaries and means of life, it appears as if men had deliberately chosen the common mode of living because they preferred it to any other. Yet they honestly think there is no choice left. But alert and healthy natures remember that the sun rose clear. It is never too late to give up our prejudices. No way of thinking or doing, however ancient, can be trusted without proof. What everybody echoes or in silence passes by as true to-day may turn out to be falsehood to-morrow, mere smoke of opinion, which some had trusted for a cloud that would sprinkle fertilizing rain on their fields. What old people say you cannot do, you try and find that you can. Old deeds for old people, and new deeds for new. Old people did not know enough once, perchance, to fetch fresh fuel to keep the fire a-going; new people put a little dry wood under a pot, and are whirled round the globe with the speed of birds, in a way to kill old people, as the phrase is. Age is no better, hardly so well, qualified for an instructor as youth, for it has not profited so much as it has lost. One may almost doubt if the wisest man has learned anything of absolute value by living. Practically, the old have no very important advice to give the young, their own experience has been so partial, and their lives have been such miserable failures, for private reasons, as they must believe; and it may be that they have some faith left which belies that experience, and they are only less young than they were. I have lived some thirty years on this planet, and I have yet to hear the first syllable of valuable or even earnest advice from my seniors. They have told me nothing, and probably cannot tell me any-

---

[8]William Wilberforce (1759–1833), British leader of the antislavery movement that led to the Emancipation Act of 1833 freeing all the slaves of the British Empire (including the British West Indies).

[9]The answer in the *Westminster Shorter Catechism*, printed in *The New England Primer*, to "what is the chief end of man?" is "to glorify God and to enjoy him forever."

thing to the purpose. Here is life, an experiment to a great extent untried by me; but it does not avail me that they have tried it. If I have any experience which I think valuable, I am sure to reflect that this my Mentors said nothing about.

One farmer says to me, "You cannot live on vegetable food solely, for it furnishes nothing to make bones with;" and so he religiously devotes a part of his day to supplying his system with the raw material of bones; walking all the while he talks behind his oxen, which, with vegetable-made bones, jerk him and his lumbering plow along in spite of every obstacle. Some things are really necessaries of life in some circles, the most helpless and diseased, which in others are luxuries merely, and in others still are entirely unknown.

The whole ground of human life seems to some to have been gone over by their predecessors, both the heights and the valleys, and all things to have been cared for. According to Evelyn, "the wise Solomon prescribed ordinances for the very distances of trees; and the Roman prætors have decided how often you may go into your neighbor's land to gather the acorns which fall on it without trespass, and what share belongs to that neighbor."[10] Hippocrates[11] has even left directions how we should cut our nails; that is, even with the ends of the fingers, neither shorter nor longer. Undoubtedly the very tedium and ennui which presume to have exhausted the variety and the joys of life are as old as Adam. But man's capacities have never been measured; nor are we to judge of what he can do by any precedents, so little has been tried. Whatever have been thy failures hitherto, "be not afflicted, my child, for who shall assign to thee what thou hast left undone?"[12]

We might try our lives by a thousand simple tests; as, for instance, that the same sun which ripens my beans illumines at once a system of earths like ours. If I had remembered this it would have prevented some mistakes. This was not the light in which I hoed them. The stars are the apexes of what wonderful triangles! What distant and different beings in the various mansions of the universe are contemplating the same one at the same moment! Nature and human life are as various as our several constitutions. Who shall say what prospect life offers to another? Could a greater miracle take place than for us to look through each other's eyes for an instant? We should live in all the ages of the world in an hour; ay, in all the worlds of the ages. History, Poetry, Mythology!—I know of no reading of another's experience so startling and informing as this would be.

The greater part of what my neighbors call good I believe in my soul to be bad, and if I repent of anything, it is very likely to be my good behavior. What demon possessed me that I behaved so well? You may say the wisest thing you can, old man,—you who have lived seventy years, not without honor of a kind,—I hear an irresistible voice which invites me away from all that. One generation abandons the enterprises of another like stranded vessels.

I think that we may safely trust a good deal more than we do. We may waive just so much care of ourselves as we honestly bestow elsewhere. Nature is as well adapted to our weakness as to our strength. The incessant anxiety and strain of some is a well-nigh incurable form of disease. We are made to exaggerate the importance of what work we do; and yet how much is not done by us! or, what if we had been taken sick? How vigilant we are! determined not to live by faith if we can avoid it; all the day long on the alert, at night we unwillingly say our prayers and commit ourselves to uncertainties. So thoroughly and sincerely are we compelled to live, reverencing our life, and denying the possibility of change. This is the only way, we say; but there are as many ways as there can be drawn radii from one

---

[10]From *Sylva; or a Discourse of Forest-Trees* (1664), by John Evelyn (1620–1706), British author and diarist.
[11]Greek physician (460?–377 B.C.), called the father of medicine.

[12]From the *Vishnu Purana*, a Hindu classic, translated into English by H. H. Wilson (1840).

centre. All change is a miracle to contemplate; but it is a miracle which is taking place every instant. Confucius said, "To know that we know what we know, and that we do not know what we do not know, that is true knowledge."[13] When one man has reduced a fact of the imagination to be a fact to his understanding, I foresee that all men will at length establish their lives on that basis.

Let us consider for a moment what most of the trouble and anxiety which I have referred to is about, and how much it is necessary that we be troubled, or at least careful. It would be some advantage to live a primitive and frontier life, though in the midst of an outward civilization, if only to learn what are the gross necessaries of life and what methods have been taken to obtain them; or even to look over the old day-books of the merchants, to see what it was that men most commonly bought at the stores, what they stored, that is, what are the grossest groceries. For the improvements of ages have had but little influence on the essential laws of man's existence: as our skeletons, probably, are not to be distinguished from those of our ancestors.

By the words, *necessary of life,* I mean whatever, of all that man obtains by his own exertions, has been from the first, or from long use has become, so important to human life that few, if any, whether from savageness, or poverty, or philosophy, ever attempt to do without it. To many creatures there is in this sense but one necessary of life, Food. To the bison of the prairie it is a few inches of palatable grass, with water to drink; unless he seeks the Shelter of the forest or the mountain's shadow. None of the brute creation requires more than Food and Shelter. The necessaries of life for man in this climate may, accurately enough, be distributed under the several heads of Food, Shelter, Clothing, and Fuel; for not till we have secured these are we prepared to entertain the true problems of life with freedom and a prospect of success. Man has invented, not only houses, but clothes and cooked food; and possibly from the accidental discovery of the warmth of fire, and the consequent use of it, at first a luxury, arose the present necessity to sit by it. We observe cats and dogs acquiring the same second nature. By proper Shelter and Clothing we legitimately retain our own internal heat; but with an excess of these, or of Fuel, that is, with an external heat greater than our own internal, may not cookery properly be said to begin? Darwin, the naturalist, says of the inhabitants of Tierra del Fuego, that while his own party, who were well clothed and sitting close to a fire, were far from too warm, these naked savages, who were farther off, were observed, to his great surprise, "to be streaming with perspiration at undergoing such a roasting."[14] So, we are told, the New Hollander[15] goes naked with impunity, while the European shivers in his clothes. Is it impossible to combine the hardiness of these savages with the intellectualness of the civilized man? According to Liebig,[16] man's body is a stove, and food the fuel which keeps up the internal combustion in the lungs. In cold weather we eat more, in warm less. The animal heat is the result of a slow combustion, and disease and death take place when this is too rapid; or for want of fuel, or from some defect in the draught, the fire goes out. Of course the vital heat is not to be confounded with fire; but so much for analogy. It appears, therefore, from the above list, that the expression, *animal life,* is nearly synonymous with the expression, *animal heat;* for while Food may be regarded as the Fuel which keeps up the fire within us,—and Fuel serves only to prepare that Food or to increase the warmth of our bodies by addition from without,—Shelter and Clothing also serve only to retain the *heat* thus generated and absorbed.

---

[13]Confucius (*c.* 551–479 B.C.), *The Analects,* II, Ch. 17.
[14]Charles Darwin (1809–1882), *Journal of Researches into the Geology and Natural History of the Various Countries Visited by H.M.S. Beagle* (1839).

[15]I.e., the Australian aborigine.
[16]Justus von Liebig (1803–1873), German organic chemist who proved that body heat results from combustion of foods in the body.

The grand necessity, then, for our bodies, is to keep warm, to keep the vital heat in us. What pains we accordingly take, not only with our Food, and Clothing, and Shelter, but with our beds, which are our nightclothes, robbing the nests and breasts of birds to prepare this shelter within a shelter, as the mole has its bed of grass and leaves at the end of its burrow! The poor man is wont to complain that this is a cold world; and to cold, no less physical than social, we refer directly a great part of our ails. The summer, in some climates, makes possible to man a sort of Elysian life.[17] Fuel, except to cook his Food, is then unnecessary; the sun is his fire, and many of the fruits are sufficiently cooked by its rays; while Food generally is more various, and more easily obtained, and Clothing and Shelter are wholly or half unnecessary. At the present day, and in this country, as I find by my own experience, a few implements, a knife, an axe, a spade, a wheelbarrow, etc., and for the studious, lamplight, stationery, and access to a few books, rank next to necessaries, and can all be obtained at a trifling cost. Yet some, not wise, go to the other side of the globe, to barbarous and unhealthy regions, and devote themselves to trade for ten or twenty years, in order that they may live,—that is, keep comfortably warm,—and die in New England at last. The luxuriously rich are not simply kept comfortably warm, but unnaturally hot; as I implied before, they are cooked, of course *à la mode*.

Most of the luxuries, and many of the so-called comforts of life, are not only not indispensable, but positive hindrances to the elevation of mankind. With respect to luxuries and comforts, the wisest have ever lived a more simple and meagre life than the poor. The ancient philosophers, Chinese, Hindoo, Persian, and Greek, were a class than which none has been poorer in outward riches, none so rich in inward. We know not much about them. It is remarkable that *we* know so much of them as we do. The same is true of the more modern reformers and benefactors of their race. None can be an impartial or wise observer of human life but from the vantage ground of what *we* should call voluntary poverty. Of a life of luxury the fruit is luxury, whether in agriculture, or commerce, or literature, or art. There are nowadays professors of philosophy, but not philosophers. Yet it is admirable to profess because it was once admirable to live. To be a philosopher is not merely to have subtle thoughts, nor even to found a school, but so to love wisdom as to live according to its dictates, a life of simplicity, independence, magnanimity, and trust. It is to solve some of the problems of life, not only theoretically, but practically. The success of great scholars and thinkers is commonly a courtier-like success, not kingly, not manly. They make shift to live merely by conformity, practically as their fathers did, and are in no sense the progenitors of a nobler race of men. But why do men degenerate ever? What makes families run out? What is the nature of the luxury which enervates and destroys nations? Are we sure that there is none of it in our own lives? The philosopher is in advance of his age even in the outward form of his life. He is not fed, sheltered, clothed, warmed, like his contemporaries. How can a man be a philosopher and not maintain his vital heat by better methods than other men?

When a man is warmed by the several modes which I have described, what does he want next? Surely not more warmth of the same kind, as more and richer food, larger and more splendid houses, finer and more abundant clothing, more numerous, incessant, and hotter fires, and the like. When he has obtained those things which are necessary to life, there is another alternative than to obtain the superfluities; and that is, to adventure on life now, his vacation from humbler toil having commenced. The soil, it appears, is suited to the seed, for it has sent its radicle downward, and it may now send its shoot upward also with confidence.

---

[17]Elysium was the place in Greek mythology where the virtuous went after death.

Why has man rooted himself thus firmly in the earth, but that he may rise in the same proportion into the heavens above?—for the nobler plants are valued for the fruit they bear at last in the air and light, far from the ground, and are not treated like the humbler esculents, which, though they may be biennials, are cultivated only till they have perfected their root, and often cut down at top for this purpose, so that most would not know them in their flowering season.

I do not mean to prescribe rules to strong and valiant natures, who will mind their own affairs whether in heaven or hell, and perchance build more magnificently and spend more lavishly than the richest, without ever impoverishing themselves, not knowing how they live,—if, indeed, there are any such, as has been dreamed; nor to those who find their encouragement and inspiration in precisely the present condition of things, and cherish it with the fondness and enthusiasm of lovers,—and, to some extent, I reckon myself in this number; I do not speak to those who are well employed, in whatever circumstances, and they know whether they are well employed or not;—but mainly to the mass of men who are discontented, and idly complaining of the hardness of their lot or of the times, when they might improve them. There are some who complain most energetically and inconsolably of any, because they are, as they say, doing their duty. I also have in my mind that seemingly wealthy, but most terribly impoverished class of all, who have accumulated dross, but know not how to use it, or get rid of it, and thus have forged their own golden or silver fetters.

If I should attempt to tell how I have desired to spend my life in years past, it would probably surprise those of my readers who are somewhat acquainted with its actual history; it would certainly astonish those who know nothing about it. I will only hint at some of the enterprises which I have cherished.

In any weather, at any hour of the day or night, I have been anxious to improve the nick of time, and notch it on my stick too; to stand on the meeting of two eternities, the past and future, which is precisely the present moment; to toe that line. You will pardon some obscurities, for there are more secrets in my trade than in most men's, and yet not voluntarily kept, but inseparable from its very nature. I would gladly tell all that I know about it, and never paint "No Admittance" on my gate.

I long ago lost a hound, a bay horse, and a turtledove, and am still on their trail.[18] Many are the travellers I have spoken concerning them, describing their tracks and what calls they answered to. I have met one or two who had heard the hound, and the tramp of the horse, and even seen the dove disappear behind a cloud, and they seemed as anxious to recover them as if they had lost them themselves.

To anticipate, not the sunrise and the dawn merely, but, if possible, Nature herself! How many mornings, summer and winter, before yet any neighbor was stirring about his business, have I been about mine! No doubt, many of my townsmen have met me returning from this enterprise, farmers starting for Boston in the twilight, or woodchoppers going to their work. It is true, I never assisted the sun materially in his rising, but, doubt not, it was of the last importance only to be present at it.

So many autumn, ay, and winter days, spent outside the town, trying to hear what was in the wind, to hear and carry it express! I well-nigh sunk all my capital

---

[18]When asked about the meaning of this enigmatic line, Thoreau replied (in a letter to B. B. Wiley, April 26, 1857): "We get the language with which to describe our various lives out of a common mint. If others have their losses, which they are busy repairing, so have I *mine*, and their hound and horse may *perhaps* be the symbols of some of them. But also I have lost, or am in danger of losing, a far finer and more etherial treasure, which commonly no loss of which they are conscious will symbolize—this I answer hastily and with some hesitation, according as I now understand my own words."

in it, and lost my own breath into the bargain, running in the face of it. If it had concerned either of the political parties, depend upon it, it would have appeared in the Gazette with the earliest intelligence. At other times watching from the observatory of some cliff or tree, to telegraph any new arrival; or waiting at evening on the hill-tops for the sky to fall, that I might catch something, though I never caught much, and that, manna-wise,[19] would dissolve again in the sun.

For a long time I was reporter to a journal,[20] of no very wide circulation, whose editor has never yet seen fit to print the bulk of my contributions, and, as is too common with writers, I got only my labor for my pains. However, in this case my pains were their own reward.

For many years I was self-appointed inspector of snow-storms and rain-storms, and did my duty faithfully; surveyor, if not of highways, then of forest paths and all across-lot routes, keeping them open, and ravines bridged and passable at all seasons, where the public heel had testified to their utility.

I have looked after the wild stock of the town, which give a faithful herdsman a good deal of trouble by leaping fences; and I have had an eye to the unfrequented nooks and corners of the farm; though I did not always know whether Jonas or Solomon worked in a particular field to-day; that was none of my business. I have watered the red huckleberry, the sand cherry and the nettletree, the red pine and the black ash, the white grape and the yellow violet, which might have withered else in dry seasons.

In short, I went on thus for a long time (I may say it without boasting), faithfully minding my business, till it became more and more evident that my townsmen would not after all admit me into the list of town officers, nor make my place a sinecure with a moderate allowance. My accounts, which I can swear to have kept faithfully, I have, indeed, never got audited, still less accepted, still less paid and settled. However, I have not set my heart on that.

Not long since, a strolling Indian went to sell baskets at the house of a well-known lawyer in my neighborhood. "Do you wish to buy any baskets?" he asked. "No, we do not want any," was the reply. "What!" exclaimed the Indian as he went out the gate, "do you mean to starve us?" Having seen his industrious white neighbors so well off,—that the lawyer had only to weave arguments, and, by some magic, wealth and standing followed,—he had said to himself: I will go into business; I will weave baskets; it is a thing which I can do. Thinking that when he had made the baskets he would have done his part, and then it would be the white man's to buy them. He had not discovered that it was necessary for him to make it worth the other's while to buy them, or at least make him think that it was so, or to make something else which it would be worth his while to buy. I too had woven a kind of basket of a delicate texture, but I had not made it worth any one's while to buy them. Yet not the less, in my case, did I think it worth my while to weave them, and instead of studying how to make it worth men's while to buy my baskets, I studied rather how to avoid the necessity of selling them. The life which men praise and regard as successful is but one kind. Why should we exaggerate any one kind at the expense of the others?

Finding that my fellow-citizens were not likely to offer me any room in the court house, or any curacy or living anywhere else, but I must shift for myself, I turned my face more exclusively than ever to the woods, where I was better known. I determined to go into business at once, and not wait to acquire the usual capital, using such slender means as I had already got. My purpose in going to Walden Pond was not to live cheaply nor to live dearly there, but to transact some

---

[19]Manna, the food miraculously sent from the heavens to the Israelites in the wilderness, melted in the sun (Exodus 16:14–36).

[20]A witty allusion to his own journal, which he began keeping in October 1837, when he was twenty.

private business with the fewest obstacles; to be hindered from accomplishing which for want of a little common sense, a little enterprise and business talent, appeared not so sad as foolish.

I have always endeavored to acquire strict business habits; they are indispensable to every man. If your trade is with the Celestial Empire,[21] then some small counting house on the coast, in some Salem harbor,[22] will be fixture enough. You will export such articles as the country affords, purely native products, much ice and pine timber and a little granite, always in native bottoms. These will be good ventures. To oversee all the details yourself in person; to be at once pilot and captain, and owner and underwriter; to buy and sell and keep the accounts; to read every letter received, and write or read every letter sent; to superintend the discharge of imports night and day; to be upon many parts of the coast almost at the same time,—often the richest freight will be discharged upon a Jersey shore;[23]—to be your own telegraph, unweariedly sweeping the horizon, speaking all passing vessels bound coastwise; to keep up a steady despatch of commodities, for the supply of such a distant and exorbitant market; to keep yourself informed of the state of the markets, prospects of war and peace everywhere, and anticipate the tendencies of trade and civilization,—taking advantage of the results of all exploring expeditions, using new passages and all improvements in navigation;—charts to be studied, the position of reefs and new lights and buoys to be ascertained, and ever, and ever, the logarithmic tables to be corrected, for by the error of some calculator the vessel often splits upon a rock that should have reached a friendly pier,—there is the untold fate of La Pérouse;[24]—universal science to be kept pace with, studying the lives of all great discoverers and navigators, great adventurers and merchants, from Hanno[25] and the Phœnicians down to our day; in fine, account of stock to be taken from time to time, to know how you stand. It is a labor to task the faculties of a man,—such problems of profit and loss, of interest, of tare and tret,[26] and gauging of all kinds in it, as demand a universal knowledge.

I have thought that Walden Pond would be a good place for business, not solely on account of the railroad and the ice trade; it offers advantages which it may not be good policy to divulge; it is a good port and a good foundation. No Neva marshes to be filled; though you must everywhere build on piles of your own driving. It is said that a flood-tide, with a westerly wind, and ice in the Neva, would sweep St. Petersburg[27] from the face of the earth.

As this business was to be entered into without the usual capital, it may not be easy to conjecture where those means, that will still be indispensable to every such undertaking, were to be obtained. As for Clothing, to come at once to the practical part of the question, perhaps we are led oftener by the love of novelty and a regard for the opinions of men, in procuring it, than by a true utility. Let him who has work to do recollect that the object of clothing is, first, to retain the vital heat, and secondly, in this state of society, to cover nakedness, and he may judge how much of any necessary or important work may be accomplished without adding to his wardrobe. Kings and queens who wear a suit but once, though made by some tailor or dressmaker to their majesties, cannot know the comfort of wearing a suit that fits. They are no better than wooden horses to hang the clean clothes on. Every day our garments become more assimilated to ourselves, receiving the impress

---

[21]Once a common name for China, deriving from the Chinese emperors' claims to be descendents of a line from Heaven.
[22]Salem, Massachusetts, was an important port in the nineteenth century.
[23]I.e., diverted because of shipwreck.
[24]Comte Jean François de Galaup de la Pérouse (1741–1788), apparently killed by natives when shipwrecked in the New Hebrides in the South Pacific.

[25]Carthaginian navigator of the sixth–fifth centuries B.C. who explored the west coast of Africa.
[26]*Tare* is the weight of a container deducted to determine the weight of contents of cargo; *tret* is an allowance made for waste or damage of goods in transit.
[27]Now Leningrad, U.S.S.R., on the Neva River.

of the wearer's character, until we hesitate to lay them aside without such delay and medical appliances and some such solemnity even as our bodies. No man ever stood the lower in my estimation for having a patch in his clothes; yet I am sure that there is greater anxiety, commonly, to have fashionable, or at least clean and unpatched clothes, than to have a sound conscience. But even if the rent is not mended, perhaps the worst vice betrayed is improvidence. I sometimes try my acquaintances by such tests as this,—Who could wear a patch, or two extra seams only, over the knee? Most behave as if they believed that their prospects for life would be ruined if they should do it. It would be easier for them to hobble to town with a broken leg than with a broken pantaloon. Often if an accident happens to a gentleman's legs, they can be mended; but if a similar accident happens to the legs of his pantaloons, there is no help for it; for he considers, not what is truly respectable, but what is respected. We know but few men, a great many coats and breeches. Dress a scarecrow in your last shift, you standing shiftless by, who would not soonest salute the scarecrow? Passing a cornfield the other day, close by a hat and coat on a stake, I recognized the owner of the farm. He was only a little more weather-beaten than when I saw him last. I have heard of a dog that barked at every stranger who approached his master's premises with clothes on, but was easily quieted by a naked thief. It is an interesting question how far men would retain their relative rank if they were divested of their clothes. Could you, in such a case, tell surely of any company of civilized men which belonged to the most respected class? When Madam Pfeiffer, in her adventurous travels round the world, from east to west, had got so near home as Asiatic Russia, she says that she felt the necessity of wearing other than a travelling dress, when she went to meet the authorities, for she "was now in a civilized country, where . . . people are judged of by their clothes."[28] Even in our democratic New England towns the accidental possession of wealth, and its manifestation in dress and equipage alone, obtain for the possessor almost universal respect. But they who yield such respect, numerous as they are, are so far heathen, and need to have a missionary sent to them. Beside, clothes introduced sewing, a kind of work which you may call endless; a woman's dress, at least, is never done.

A man who has at length found something to do will not need to get a new suit to do it in; for him the old will do, that has lain dusty in the garret for an indeterminate period. Old shoes will serve a hero longer than they have served his valet,—if a hero ever has a valet,—bare feet are older than shoes, and he can make them do. Only they who go to soirées and legislative halls must have new coats, coats to change as often as the man changes in them. But if my jacket and trousers, my hat and shoes, are fit to worship God in, they will do; will they not? Who ever saw his old clothes,—his old coat, actually worn out, resolved into its primitive elements, so that it was not a deed of charity to bestow it on some poor boy, by him perchance to be bestowed on some poorer still, or shall we say richer, who could do with less? I say, beware of all enterprises that require new clothes, and not rather a new wearer of clothes. If there is not a new man, how can the new clothes be made to fit? If you have any enterprise before you, try it in your old clothes. All men want, not something to *do with*, but something to *do*, or rather something to *be*. Perhaps we should never procure a new suit, however ragged or dirty the old, until we have so conducted, so enterprised or sailed in some way, that we feel like new men in the old, and that to retain it would be like keeping new wine in old bottles.[29] Our moulting season, like that of the fowls, must be a crisis in our lives. The loon retires to solitary ponds to spend it. Thus also the

---

[28]From *A Lady's Voyage Round the World* (1852), by Ida Laura Pfeiffer (1797–1858), an Austrian writer.
[29]Cf. Matthew 9:17.

snake casts its slough, and the caterpillar its wormy coat, by an internal industry and expansion; for clothes are but our outmost cuticle and mortal coil. Otherwise we shall be found sailing under false colors, and be inevitably cashiered at last by our own opinion, as well as that of mankind.

We don garment after garment, as if we grew like exogenous plants by addition without. Our outside and often thin and fanciful clothes are our epidermis, or false skin, which partakes not of our life, and may be stripped off here and there without fatal injury; our thicker garments, constantly worn, are our cellular integument, or cortex; but our shirts are our liber,[30] or true bark, which cannot be removed without girdling and so destroying the man. I believe that all races at some seasons wear something equivalent to the shirt. It is desirable that a man be clad so simply that he can lay his hands on himself in the dark, and that he live in all respects so compactly and preparedly that, if an enemy take the town, he can, like the old philosopher, walk out the gate empty-handed without anxiety. While one thick garment is, for most purposes, as good as three thin ones, and cheap clothing can be obtained at prices really to suit customers; while a thick coat can be bought for five dollars, which will last as many years, thick pantaloons for two dollars, cowhide boots for a dollar and a half a pair, a summer hat for a quarter of a dollar, and a winter cap for sixty-two and a half cents, or a better be made at home at a nominal cost, where is he so poor that, clad in such a suit, *of his own earning,* there will not be found wise men to do him reverence?

When I ask for a garment of a particular form, my tailoress tells me gravely, "They do not make them so now," not emphasizing the "They" at all, as if she quoted an authority as impersonal as the Fates, and I find it difficult to get made what I want, simply because she cannot believe that I mean what I say, that I am so rash. When I hear this oracular sentence, I am for a moment absorbed in thought, emphasizing to myself each word separately that I may come at the meaning of it, that I may find out by what degree of consanguinity *They* are related to *me,* and what authority they may have in an affair which affects me so nearly; and, finally, I am inclined to answer her with equal mystery, and without any more emphasis of the "they,"—"It is true, they did not make them so recently, but they do now." Of what use this measuring of me if she does not measure my character, but only the breadth of my shoulders, as it were a peg to hang the coat on? We worship not the Graces, nor the Parcæ,[31] but Fashion. She spins and weaves and cuts with full authority. The head monkey at Paris puts on a traveller's cap, and all the monkeys in America do the same. I sometimes despair of getting anything quite simple and honest done in this world by the help of men. They would have to be passed through a powerful press first, to squeeze their old notions out of them, so that they would not soon get upon their legs again; and then there would be some one in the company with a maggot in his head, hatched from an egg deposited there nobody knows when, for not even fire kills these things, and you would have lost your labor. Nevertheless, we will not forget that some Egyptian wheat was handed down to us by a mummy.

On the whole, I think that it cannot be maintained that dressing has in this or any country risen to the dignity of an art. At present men make shift to wear what they can get. Like shipwrecked sailors, they put on what they can find on the beach, and at a little distance, whether of space or time, laugh at each other's masquerade. Every generation laughs at the old fashions, but follows religiously the new. We are amused at beholding the costume of Henry VIII., or Queen Elizabeth, as much as if it was that of the King and Queen of the Cannibal Islands. All

---

[30]Strong woody fiber from the inner bark of plants such as hemp or flax.
[31]In classical mythology, the three Graces (Aglaia, Thalia, Euphrosyne) bestowed charm and beauty; the Parcae are the three fates (Clotho, Lachesis, Atropos) who in their weaving controlled the life and death of all.

costume off a man is pitiful or grotesque. It is only the serious eye peering from and the sincere life passed within it which restrain laughter and consecrate the costume of any people. Let Harlequin[32] be taken with a fit of the colic and his trappings will have to serve that mood too. When the soldier is hit by a cannon-ball, rags are as becoming as purple.

The childish and savage taste of men and women for new patterns keeps how many shaking and squinting through kaleidoscopes that they may discover the particular figure which this generation requires to-day. The manufacturers have learned that this taste is merely whimsical. Of two patterns which differ only by a few threads more or less of a particular color, the one will be sold readily, the other lie on the shelf, though it frequently happens that after the lapse of a season the latter becomes the most fashionable. Comparatively, tattooing is not the hideous custom which it is called. It is not barbarous merely because the printing is skin-deep and unalterable.

I cannot believe that our factory system is the best mode by which men may get clothing. The condition of the operatives is becoming every day more like that of the English; and it cannot be wondered at, since, as far as I have heard or observed, the principal object is, not that mankind may be well and honestly clad, but, unquestionably, that the corporations may be enriched. In the long run men hit only what they aim at. Therefore, though they should fail immediately, they had better aim at something high.

As for a Shelter, I will not deny that this is now a necessary of life, though there are instances of men having done without it for long periods in colder countries than this. Samuel Laing says that "the Laplander in his skin dress, and in a skin bag which he puts over his head and shoulders, will sleep night after night on the snow . . . in a degree of cold which would extinguish the life of one exposed to it in any woollen clothing." He had seen them asleep thus. Yet he adds, "They are not hardier than other people."[33] But, probably, man did not live long on the earth without discovering the convenience which there is in a house, the domestic comforts, which phrase may have originally signified the satisfactions of the house more than of the family; though these must be extremely partial and occasional in those climates where the house is associated in our thoughts with winter or the rainy season chiefly, and two thirds of the year, except for a parasol, is unnecessary. In our climate, in the summer, it was formerly almost solely a covering at night. In the Indian gazettes[34] a wigwam was the symbol of a day's march, and a row of them cut or painted on the bark of a tree signified that so many times they had camped. Man was not made so large limbed and robust but that he must seek to narrow his world, and wall in a space such as fitted him. He was at first bare and out of doors; but though this was pleasant enough in serene and warm weather, by daylight, the rainy season and the winter, to say nothing of the torrid sun, would perhaps have nipped his race in the bud if he had not made haste to clothe himself with the shelter of a house. Adam and Eve, according to the fable, wore the bower before other clothes. Man wanted a home, a place of warmth, or comfort, first of physical warmth, then the warmth of the affections.

We may imagine a time when, in the infancy of the human race, some enterprising mortal crept into a hollow in a rock for shelter. Every child begins the world again, to some extent, and loves to stay outdoors, even in wet and cold. It plays house, as well as horse, having an instinct for it. Who does not remember the interest with which, when young, he looked at shelving rocks, or any approach to a cave? It was the natural yearning of that portion of our most primitive ances-

---

[32]Traditional comic character in costume of many colors in the *commedia dell'arte*.
[33]From *Journal of a Residence in Norway* (1837), by Samuel

Laing (1780–1868), Scottish writer on Scandinavian social conditions.
[34]I.e., messages.

tor which still survived in us. From the cave we have advanced to roofs of palm leaves, of bark and boughs, of linen woven and stretched, of grass and straw, of boards and shingles, of stones and tiles. At last, we know not what it is to live in the open air, and our lives are domestic in more senses than we think. From the hearth the field is a great distance. It would be well, perhaps, if we were to spend more of our days and nights without any obstruction between us and the celestial bodies, if the poet did not speak so much from under a roof, or the saint dwell there so long. Birds do not sing in caves, nor do doves cherish their innocence in dovecots.

However, if one designs to construct a dwelling-house, it behooves him to exercise a little Yankee shrewdness, lest after all he find himself in a workhouse, a labyrinth without a clue, a museum, an almshouse, a prison, or a splendid mausoleum instead. Consider first how slight a shelter is absolutely necessary. I have seen Penobscot Indians, in this town, living in tents of thin cotton cloth, while the snow was nearly a foot deep around them, and I thought that they would be glad to have it deeper to keep out the wind. Formerly, when how to get my living honestly, with freedom left for my proper pursuits, was a question which vexed me even more than it does now, for unfortunately I am become somewhat callous, I used to see a large box by the railroad, six feet long by three wide, in which the laborers locked up their tools at night; and it suggested to me that every man who was hard pushed might get such a one for a dollar, and, having bored a few auger holes in it, to admit the air at least, get into it when it rained and at night, and hook down the lid, and so have freedom in his love, and in his soul be free. This did not appear the worst, nor by any means a despicable alternative. You could sit up as late as you pleased, and, whenever you got up, go abroad without any landlord or house-lord dogging you for rent. Many a man is harassed to death to pay the rent of a larger and more luxurious box who would not have frozen to death in such a box as this. I am far from jesting. Economy is a subject which admits of being treated with levity, but it cannot so be disposed of. A comfortable house for a rude and hardy race, that lived mostly out of doors, was once made here almost entirely of such materials as Nature furnished ready to their hands. Gookin, who was superintendent of the Indians subject to the Massachusetts Colony, writing in 1674, says, "The best of their houses are covered very neatly, tight and warm, with barks of trees, slipped from their bodies at those seasons when the sap is up, and made into great flakes, with pressure of weighty timber, when they are green. . . . The meaner sort are covered with mats which they make of a kind of bulrush, and are also indifferently tight and warm, but not so good as the former. . . . Some I have seen, sixty or a hundred feet long and thirty feet broad. . . . I have often lodged in their wigwams, and found them as warm as the best English houses."[35] He adds that they were commonly carpeted and lined within with well-wrought embroidered mats, and were furnished with various utensils. The Indians had advanced so far as to regulate the effect of the wind by a mat suspended over the hole in the roof and moved by a string. Such a lodge was in the first instance constructed in a day or two at most, and taken down and put up in a few hours; and every family owned one, or its apartment in one.

In the savage state every family owns a shelter as good as the best, and sufficient for its coarser and simpler wants; but I think that I speak within bounds when I say that, though the birds of the air have their nests, and the foxes their holes, and the savages their wigwams, in modern civilized society not more than one half the families own a shelter. In the large towns and cities, where civilization especially prevails, the number of those who own a shelter is a very small fraction

---

[35]From *Historical Collections of the Indians in New England* (1792), by Daniel Gookin (1612–1687).

of the whole. The rest pay an annual tax for this outside garment of all, become indispensable summer and winter, which would buy a village of Indian wigwams, but now helps to keep them poor as long as they live. I do not mean to insist here on the disadvantage of hiring compared with owning, but it is evident that the savage owns his shelter because it costs so little, while the civilized man hires his commonly because he cannot afford to own it; nor can he, in the long run, any better afford to hire. But, answers one, by merely paying this tax the poor civilized man secures an abode which is a palace compared with the savage's. An annual rent of from twenty-five to a hundred dollars (these are the country rates) entitles him to the benefit of the improvements of centuries, spacious apartments, clean paint and paper, Rumford fireplace,[36] back plastering, Venetian blinds, copper pump, spring lock, a commodious cellar, and many other things. But how happens it that he who is said to enjoy these things is so commonly a *poor* civilized man, while the savage, who has them not, is rich as a savage? If it is asserted that civilization is a real advance in the condition of man,—and I think that it is, though only the wise improve their advantages,—it must be shown that it has produced better dwellings without making them more costly; and the cost of a thing is the amount of what I will call life which is required to be exchanged for it, immediately or in the long run. An average house in this neighborhood costs perhaps eight hundred dollars, and to lay up this sum will take from ten to fifteen years of the laborer's life, even if he is not encumbered with a family,—estimating the pecuniary value of every man's labor at one dollar a day, for if some receive more, others receive less;—so that he must have spent more than half his life commonly before *his* wigwam will be earned. If we suppose him to pay a rent instead, this is but a doubtful choice of evils. Would the savage have been wise to exchange his wigwam for a palace on these terms?

It may be guessed that I reduce almost the whole advantage of holding this superfluous property as a fund in store against the future, so far as the individual is concerned, mainly to the defraying of funeral expenses. But perhaps a man is not required to bury himself. Nevertheless this points to an important distinction between the civilized man and the savage; and, no doubt, they have designs on us for our benefit, in making the life of a civilized people an *institution,* in which the life of the individual is to a great extent absorbed, in order to preserve and perfect that of the race. But I wish to show at what a sacrifice this advantage is at present obtained, and to suggest that we may possibly so live as to secure all the advantage without suffering any of the disadvantage. What mean ye by saying that the poor ye have always with you, or that the fathers have eaten sour grapes, and the children's teeth are set on edge?[37]

"As I live, saith the Lord God, ye shall not have occasion any more to use this proverb in Israel.

"Behold all souls are mine; as the soul of the father, so also the soul of the son is mine: the soul that sinneth, it shall die."[38]

When I consider my neighbors, the farmers of Concord, who are at least as well off as the other classes, I find that for the most part they have been toiling twenty, thirty, or forty years, that they may become the real owners of their farms, which commonly they have inherited with encumbrances, or else bought with hired money,—and we may regard one third of that toil as the cost of their houses,—but commonly they have not paid for them yet. It is true, the encumbrances sometimes outweigh the value of the farm, so that the farm itself becomes one great encumbrance, and still a man is found to inherit it, being well ac-

---

[36]Benjamin Thompson, Count Rumford (1753–1814) was the inventor of a fireplace with a shelf in the chimney to prevent downdrafts carrying smoke into the room.

[37]Biblical references to the poor, Matthew 26:11; sour grapes and children's teeth, Ezekiel 18:2.
[38]Ezekiel 18:3–4.

quainted with it, as he says. On applying to the assessors, I am surprised to learn that they cannot at once name a dozen in the town who own their farms free and clear. If you would know the history of these homesteads, inquire at the bank where they are mortgaged. The man who has actually paid for his farm with labor on it is so rare that every neighbor can point to him. I doubt if there are three such men in Concord. What has been said of the merchants, that a very large majority, even ninety-seven in a hundred, are sure to fail, is equally true of the farmers. With regard to the merchants, however, one of them says pertinently that a great part of their failures are not genuine pecuniary failures, but merely failures to fulfil their engagements, because it is inconvenient; that is, it is the moral character that breaks down. But this puts an infinitely worse face on the matter, and suggests, beside, that probably not even the other three succeed in saving their souls, but are perchance bankrupt in a worse sense than they who fail honestly. Bankruptcy and repudiation are the springboards from which much of our civilization vaults and turns its somersets, but the savage stands on the unelastic plank of famine. Yet the Middlesex Cattle Show goes off here with *éclat* annually, as if all the joints of the agricultural machine were suent.[39]

The farmer is endeavoring to solve the problem of a livelihood by a formula more complicated than the problem itself. To get his shoestrings he speculates in herds of cattle. With consummate skill he has set his trap with a hair springe to catch comfort and independence, and then, as he turned away, got his own leg into it. This is the reason he is poor; and for a similar reason we are all poor in respect to a thousand savage comforts, though surrounded by luxuries. As Chapman sings,—

> "The false society of men—
> —for earthly greatness
> All heavenly comforts rarefies to air."[40]

And when the farmer has got his house, he may not be the richer but the poorer for it, and it be the house that has got him. As I understand it, that was a valid objection urged by Momus[41] against the house which Minerva made, that she "had not made it movable, by which means a bad neighborhood might be avoided;" and it may still be urged, for our houses are such unwieldy property that we are often imprisoned rather than housed in them; and the bad neighborhood to be avoided is our own scurvy selves. I know one or two families, at least, in this town, who, for nearly a generation, have been wishing to sell their houses in the outskirts and move into the village, but have not been able to accomplish it, and only death will set them free.

Granted that the *majority* are able at last either to own or hire the modern house with all its improvements. While civilization has been improving our houses, it has not equally improved the men who are to inhabit them. It has created palaces, but it was not so easy to create noblemen and kings. And *if the civilized man's pursuits are no worthier than the savage's, if he is employed the greater part of his life in obtaining gross necessaries and comforts merely, why should he have a better dwelling than the former?*

But how do the poor *minority* fare? Perhaps it will be found that just in proportion as some have been placed in outward circumstances above the savage, others have been degraded below him. The luxury of one class is counterbalanced by the indigence of another. On the one side is the palace, on the other are the alms-

---

[39]Variant of "suant," in order or broken in.
[40]From *The Tragedy of Caesar and Pompey,* V, ii, by George Chapman (1559?–1634), British poet.

[41]In classical mythology, son of night and god of mockery and criticism. Minerva: goddess of wisdom and invention, handicrafts.

house and "silent poor."[42] The myriads who built the pyramids to be the tombs of the Pharaohs were fed on garlic, and it may be were not decently buried themselves. The mason who finishes the cornice of the palace returns at night perchance to a hut not so good as a wigwam. It is a mistake to suppose that, in a country where the usual evidences of civilization exist, the condition of a very large body of the inhabitants may not be as degraded as that of savages. I refer to the degraded poor, not now to the degraded rich. To know this I should not need to look farther than to the shanties which everywhere border our railroads, that last improvement in civilization; where I see in my daily walks human beings living in sties, and all winter with an open door, for the sake of light, without any visible, often imaginable, wood-pile, and the forms of both old and young are permanently contracted by the long habit of shrinking from cold and misery, and the development of all their limbs and faculties is checked. It certainly is fair to look at that class by whose labor the works which distinguish this generation are accomplished. Such too, to a greater or less extent, is the condition of the operatives of every denomination in England, which is the great workhouse of the world. Or I could refer you to Ireland, which is marked as one of the white or enlightened spots on the map.[43] Contrast the physical condition of the Irish with that of the North American Indian, or the South Sea Islander, or any other savage race before it was degraded by contact with the civilized man. Yet I have no doubt that that people's rulers are as wise as the average of civilized rulers. Their condition only proves what squalidness may consist with civilization. I hardly need refer now to the laborers in our Southern States who produce the staple exports of this country, and are themselves a staple production of the South. But to confine myself to those who are said to be in *moderate* circumstances.

Most men appear never to have considered what a house is, and are actually though needlessly poor all their lives because they think that they must have such a one as their neighbors have. As if one were to wear any sort of coat which the tailor might cut out for him, or, gradually leaving off palm-leaf hat or cap of woodchuck skin, complain of hard times because he could not afford to buy him a crown! It is possible to invent a house still more convenient and luxurious than we have, which yet all would admit that man could not afford to pay for. Shall we always study to obtain more of these things, and not sometimes to be content with less? Shall the respectable citizen thus gravely teach, by precept and example, the necessity of the young man's providing a certain number of superfluous glow-shoes,[44] and umbrellas, and empty guest chambers for empty guests, before he dies? Why should not our furniture be as simple as the Arab's or the Indian's? When I think of the benefactors of the race, whom we have apotheosized as messengers from heaven, bearers of divine gifts to man, I do not see in my mind any retinue at their heels, any carload of fashionable furniture. Or what if I were to allow—would it not be a singular allowance?—that our furniture should be more complex than the Arab's, in proportion as we are morally and intellectually his superiors! At present our houses are cluttered and defiled with it, and a good housewife would sweep out the greater part into the dust hole, and not leave her morning's work undone. Morning work! By the blushes of Aurora and the music of Memnon,[45] what should be man's *morning work* in this world? I had three pieces of limestone on my desk, but I was terrified to find that they required to be dusted daily, when the furniture of my mind was all undusted still, and I threw them out the window in disgust. How, then, could I have a furnished house? I would rather

---

[42]Those too proud to ask for aid.
[43]In the 1840s, with the potato famine in Ireland, about one million people died; many migrated to America. On the map, Ireland is white in contrast with unknown areas then indicated by black.

[44]Galoshes.
[45]Aurora was the goddess of dawn and mother of Memnon; his name is linked with the huge statue of an Egyptian king at Thebes which uttered a musical sound when touched by the rays of the rising sun.

sit in the open air, for no dust gathers on the grass, unless where man has broken ground.

It is the luxurious and dissipated who set the fashions which the herd so diligently follow. The traveller who stops at the best houses, so called, soon discovers this, for the publicans presume him to be a Sardanapalus,[46] and if he resigned himself to their tender mercies he would soon be completely emasculated. I think that in the railroad car we are inclined to spend more on luxury than on safety and convenience, and it threatens without attaining these to become no better than a modern drawing-room, with its divans, and ottomans, and sunshades, and a hundred other oriental things, which we are taking west with us, invented for the ladies of the harem and the effeminate natives of the Celestial Empire, which Jonathan[47] should be ashamed to know the names of. I would rather sit on a pumpkin and have it all to myself than be crowded on a velvet cushion. I would rather ride on earth in an ox cart, with a free circulation, than go to heaven in the fancy car of an excursion train and breathe a *malaria* all the way.

The very simplicity and nakedness of man's life in the primitive ages imply this advantage, at least, that they left him still but a sojourner in nature. When he was refreshed with food and sleep, he contemplated his journey again. He dwelt, as it were, in a tent in this world, and was either threading the valleys, or crossing the plains, or climbing the mountain-tops. But lo! men have become the tools of their tools. The man who independently plucked the fruits when he was hungry is become a farmer; and he who stood under a tree for shelter, a housekeeper. We now no longer camp as for a night, but have settled down on earth and forgotten heaven. We have adopted Christianity merely as an improved method of *agri-culture*. We have built for this world a family mansion, and for the next a family tomb. The best works of art are the expression of man's struggle to free himself from this condition, but the effect of our art is merely to make this low state comfortable and that higher state to be forgotten. There is actually no place in this village for a work of *fine* art, if any had come down to us, to stand, for our lives, our houses and streets, furnish no proper pedestal for it. There is not a nail to hang a picture on, nor a shelf to receive the bust of a hero or a saint. When I consider how our houses are built and paid for, or not paid for, and their internal economy managed and sustained, I wonder that the floor does not give way under the visitor while he is admiring the gewgaws upon the mantelpiece, and let him through into the cellar, to some solid and honest though earthy foundation. I cannot but perceive that this so-called rich and refined life is a thing jumped at, and I do not get on in the enjoyment of the *fine* arts which adorn it, my attention being wholly occupied with the jump; for I remember that the greatest genuine leap, due to human muscles alone, on record, is that of certain wandering Arabs, who are said to have cleared twenty-five feet on level ground. Without factitious support, man is sure to come to earth again beyond that distance. The first question which I am tempted to put to the proprietor of such great impropriety is, Who bolsters you? Are you one of the ninety-seven who fail, or the three who succeed? Answer me these questions, and then perhaps I may look at your bawbles and find them ornamental. The cart before the horse is neither beautiful nor useful. Before we can adorn our houses with beautiful objects the walls must be stripped, and our lives must be stripped, and beautiful housekeeping and beautiful living be laid for a foundation: now, a taste for the beautiful is most cultivated out of doors, where there is no house and no housekeeper.

Old Johnson, in his "Wonder-Working Providence,"[48] speaking of the first settlers of this town, with whom he was contemporary, tells us that "they burrow

---

[46]Cruel and effeminate Assyrian ruler (fl. 822 B.C.).
[47]General name for an American, characterized by both simplicity and shrewdness. See Royall Tyler's play, *The Contrast*.

[48]Edward Johnson (1598–1672), New England Puritan settler and historian, author of *Wonder-Working Providence of Sion's Saviour in New England* (1654).

themselves in the earth for their first shelter under some hillside, and, casting the soil aloft upon timber, they make a smoky fire against the earth, at the highest side." They did not "provide them houses," says he, "till the earth, by the Lord's blessing, brought forth bread to feed them," and the first year's crop was so light that "they were forced to cut their bread very thin for a long season." The secretary of the Province of New Netherland,[49] writing in Dutch, in 1650, for the information of those who wished to take up land there, states more particularly that "those in New Netherland, and especially in New England, who have no means to build farmhouses at first according to their wishes, dig a square pit in the ground, cellar fashion, six or seven feet deep, as long and as broad as they think proper, case the earth inside with wood all round the wall, and line the wood with the bark of trees or something else to prevent the caving in of the earth; floor this cellar with plank, and wainscot it overhead for a ceiling, raise a roof of spars clear up, and cover the spars with bark or green sods, so that they can live dry and warm in these houses with their entire families for two, three, and four years, it being understood that partitions are run through those cellars which are adapted to the size of the family. The wealthy and principal men in New England, in the beginning of the colonies, commenced their first dwelling-houses in this fashion for two reasons: firstly, in order not to waste time in building, and not to want food the next season; secondly, in order not to discourage poor laboring people whom they brought over in numbers from Fatherland. In the course of three or four years, when the country became adapted to agriculture, they built themselves handsome houses, spending on them several thousands."[50]

In this course which our ancestors took there was a show of prudence at least, as if their principle were to satisfy the more pressing wants first. But are the more pressing wants satisfied now? When I think of acquiring for myself one of our luxurious dwellings, I am deterred, for, so to speak, the country is not yet adapted to *human* culture, and we are still forced to cut our *spiritual* bread far thinner than our forefathers did their wheaten. Not that all architectural ornament is to be neglected even in the rudest periods; but let our houses first be lined with beauty, where they come in contact with our lives, like the tenement of the shellfish, and not overlaid with it. But, alas! I have been inside one or two of them, and know what they are lined with.

Though we are not so degenerate but that we might possibly live in a cave or a wigwam or wear skins to-day, it certainly is better to accept the advantages, though so dearly bought, which the invention and industry of mankind offer. In such a neighborhood as this, boards and shingles, lime and bricks, are cheaper and more easily obtained than suitable caves, or whole logs, or bark in sufficient quantities, or even well-tempered clay or flat stones. I speak understandingly on this subject, for I have made myself acquainted with it both theoretically and practically. With a little more wit we might use these materials so as to become richer than the richest now are, and make our civilization a blessing. The civilized man is a more experienced and wiser savage. But to make haste to my own experiment.

Near the end of March, 1845, I borrowed an axe and went down to the woods by Walden Pond, nearest to where I intended to build my house, and began to cut down some tall, arrowy white pines, still in their youth, for timber. It is difficult to begin without borrowing, but perhaps it is the most generous course thus to permit your fellow-men to have an interest in your enterprise. The owner of the axe, as he released his hold on it, said that it was the apple of his eye; but I returned it sharper than I received it. It was a pleasant hillside where I worked, covered with pine woods, through which I looked out on the pond, and a small open field in

---

[49] I.e., New York.
[50] From *The Documentary History of the State of New York* (1851), by Edmund Bailey O'Callaghan.

the woods where pines and hickories were springing up. The ice in the pond was not yet dissolved, though there were some open spaces, and it was all dark-colored and saturated with water. There were some slight flurries of snow during the days that I worked there; but for the most part when I came out on to the railroad, on my way home, its yellow sand-heap stretched away gleaming in the hazy atmosphere, and the rails shone in the spring sun, and I heard the lark and pewee and other birds already come to commence another year with us. They were pleasant spring days, in which the winter of man's discontent[51] was thawing as well as the earth, and the life that had lain torpid began to stretch itself. One day, when my axe had come off and I had cut a green hickory for a wedge, driving it with a stone, and had placed the whole to soak in a pond-hole in order to swell the wood, I saw a striped snake run into the water, and he lay on the bottom, apparently without inconvenience, as long as I stayed there, or more than a quarter of an hour; perhaps because he had not yet fairly come out of the torpid state. It appeared to me that for a like reason men remain in their present low and primitive condition; but if they should feel the influence of the spring of springs arousing them, they would of necessity rise to a higher and more ethereal life. I had previously seen the snakes in frosty mornings in my path with portions of their bodies still numb and inflexible, waiting for the sun to thaw them. On the 1st of April it rained and melted the ice, and in the early part of the day, which was very foggy, I heard a stray goose groping about over the pond and cackling as if lost, or like the spirit of the fog.

So I went on for some days cutting and hewing timber, and also studs and rafters, all with my narrow axe, not having many communicable or scholar-like thoughts, singing to myself,—

> Men say they know many things;
> But lo! they have taken wings,—
> The arts and sciences,
> And a thousand appliances;
> The wind that blows
> Is all that anybody knows.[52]

I hewed the main timbers six inches square, most of the studs on two sides only, and the rafters and floor timbers on one side, leaving the rest of the bark on, so that they were just as straight and much stronger than sawed ones. Each stick was carefully mortised or tenoned by its stump, for I had borrowed other tools by this time. My days in the woods were not very long ones; yet I usually carried my dinner of bread and butter, and read the newspaper in which it was wrapped, at noon, sitting amid the green pine boughs which I had cut off, and to my bread was imparted some of their fragrance, for my hands were covered with a thick coat of pitch. Before I had done I was more the friend than the foe of the pine tree, though I had cut down some of them, having become better acquainted with it. Sometimes a rambler in the wood was attracted by the sound of my axe, and we chatted pleasantly over the chips which I had made.

By the middle of April, for I made no haste in my work, but rather made the most of it, my house was framed and ready for the raising. I had already bought the shanty of James Collins, an Irishman who worked on the Fitchburg Railroad, for boards. James Collins' shanty was considered an uncommonly fine one. When I called to see it he was not at home. I walked about the outside, at first unobserved from within, the window was so deep and high. It was of small dimensions, with a peaked cottage roof, and not much else to be seen, the dirt being raised five

---

[51]See Shakespeare's *Richard III*, I, i, 1.
[52]This poem, like others in *Walden* without quotation marks, is by Thoreau.

feet all around as if it were a compost heap. The roof was the soundest part, though a good deal warped and made brittle by the sun. Door-sill there was none, but a perennial passage for the hens under the door-board. Mrs. C. came to the door and asked me to view it from the inside. The hens were driven in by my approach. It was dark, and had a dirt floor for the most part, dank, clammy, and aguish, only here a board and there a board which would not bear removal. She lighted a lamp to show me the inside of the roof and the walls, and also that the board floor extended under the bed, warning me not to step into the cellar, a sort of dust hole two feet deep. In her own words, they were "good boards overhead, good boards all around, and a good window,"—of two whole squares originally, only the cat had passed out that way lately. There was a stove, a bed, and a place to sit, an infant in the house where it was born, a silk parasol, gilt-framed looking-glass, and a patent new coffee-mill nailed to an oak sapling, all told. The bargain was soon concluded, for James had in the meanwhile returned. I to pay four dollars and twenty-five cents to-night, he to vacate at five to-morrow morning, selling to nobody else meanwhile: I to take possession at six. It were well, he said, to be there early, and anticipate certain indistinct but wholly unjust claims on the score of ground rent and fuel. This he assured me was the only encumbrance. At six I passed him and his family on the road. One large bundle held their all,—bed, coffee-mill, looking-glass, hens,—all but the cat; she took to the woods and became a wild cat, and, as I learned afterward, trod in a trap set for woodchucks, and so became a dead cat at last.

I took down this dwelling the same morning, drawing the nails, and removed it to the pond-side by small cartloads, spreading the boards on the grass there to bleach and warp back again in the sun. One early thrush gave me a note or two as I drove along the woodland path. I was informed treacherously by a young Patrick that neighbor Seeley, an Irishman, in the intervals of the carting, transferred the still tolerable, straight, and drivable nails, staples, and spikes to his pocket, and then stood when I came back to pass the time of day, and look freshly up, unconcerned, with spring thoughts, at the devastation; there being a dearth of work, as he said. He was there to represent spectatordom, and help make this seemingly insignificant event one with the removal of the gods of Troy.[53]

I dug my cellar in the side of a hill sloping to the south, where a woodchuck had formerly dug his burrow, down through sumach and blackberry roots, and the lowest stain of vegetation, six feet square by seven deep, to a fine sand where potatoes would not freeze in any winter. The sides were left shelving, and not stoned; but the sun having never shone on them, the sand still keeps its place. It was but two hours' work. I took particular pleasure in this breaking of ground, for in almost all latitudes men dig into the earth for an equable temperature. Under the most splendid house in the city is still to be found the cellar where they store their roots as of old, and long after the superstructure has disappeared posterity remark its dent in the earth. The house is still but a sort of porch at the entrance of a burrow.

At length, in the beginning of May, with the help of some of my acquaintances, rather to improve so good an occasion for neighborliness than from any necessity, I set up the frame of my house. No man was ever more honored in the character of his raisers[54] than I. They are destined, I trust, to assist at the raising of loftier structures one day. I began to occupy my house on the 4th of July, as soon as it was boarded and roofed, for the boards were carefully feather-edged and lapped, so that it was perfectly impervious to rain, but before boarding I laid the foundation of a chimney at one end, bringing two cartloads of stones up the hill from the pond in my arms. I built the chimney after my hoeing in the fall, before a fire

---

[53]When Troy fell (in Homer's *Iliad*), the conquering Greeks carried off the images of the gods.

[54]Those present for the ceremony included Emerson, Amos Bronson Alcott, and Ellery Channing.

became necessary for warmth, doing my cooking in the meanwhile out of doors on the ground, early in the morning: which mode I still think is in some respects more convenient and agreeable than the usual one. When it stormed before my bread was baked, I fixed a few boards over the fire, and sat under them to watch my loaf, and passed some pleasant hours in that way. In those days, when my hands were much employed, I read but little, but the least scraps of paper which lay on the ground, my holder, or tablecloth, afforded me as much entertainment, in fact answered the same purpose as the Iliad.

It would be worth the while to build still more deliberately than I did, considering, for instance, what foundation a door, a window, a cellar, a garret, have in the nature of man, and perchance never raising any superstructure until we found a better reason for it than our temporal necessities even. There is some of the same fitness in a man's building his own house that there is in a bird's building its own nest. Who knows but if men constructed their dwellings with their own hands, and provided food for themselves and families simply and honestly enough, the poetic faculty would be universally developed, as birds universally sing when they are so engaged? But alas! we do like cowbirds and cuckoos, which lay their eggs in nests which other birds have built, and cheer no traveller with their chattering and unmusical notes. Shall we forever resign the pleasure of construction to the carpenter? What does architecture amount to in the experience of the mass of men? I never in all my walks came across a man engaged in so simple and natural an occupation as building his house. We belong to the community. It is not the tailor alone who is the ninth part of a man; it is as much the preacher, and the merchant, and the farmer. Where is this division of labor to end? and what object does it finally serve? No doubt another *may* also think for me; but it is not therefore desirable that he should do so to the exclusion of my thinking for myself.

True, there are architects so called in this country, and I have heard of one at least possessed with the idea of making architectural ornaments have a core of truth, a necessity, and hence a beauty, as if it were a revelation to him.[55] All very well perhaps from his point of view, but only a little better than the common dilettantism. A sentimental reformer in architecture, he began at the cornice, not at the foundation. It was only how to put a core of truth within the ornaments, that every sugarplum, in fact, might have an almond or caraway seed in it,—though I hold that almonds are most wholesome without the sugar,—and not how the inhabitant, the indweller, might build truly within and without, and let the ornaments take care of themselves. What reasonable man ever supposed that ornaments were something outward and in the skin merely,—that the tortoise got his spotted shell, or the shell-fish its mother-o'-pearl tints, by such a contract as the inhabitants of Broadway their Trinity Church?[56] But a man has no more to do with the style of architecture of his house than a tortoise with that of its shell: nor need the soldier be so idle as to try to paint the precise *color* of his virtue on his standard. The enemy will find it out. He may turn pale when the trial comes. This man seemed to me to lean over the cornice, and timidly whisper his half truth to the rude occupants who really knew it better than he. What of architectural beauty I now see, I know has gradually grown from within outward, out of the necessities and character of the indweller, who is the only builder,—out of some unconscious truthfulness, and nobleness, without ever a thought for the appearance and whatever additional beauty of this kind is destined to be produced will be preceded by a like unconscious beauty of life. The most interesting dwellings in

---

[55]Horatio Greenough (1805–1852), American sculptor. Thoreau had seen a letter from Greenough to Emerson expressing these ideas.

[56]Trinity Church clearly did not represent an organic but a traditional style (the church Thoreau refers to burned down and has been replaced).

this country, as the painter knows, are the most unpretending, humble log huts and cottages of the poor commonly; it is the life of the inhabitants whose shells they are, and not any peculiarity in their surfaces merely, which makes them *picturesque;* and equally interesting will be the citizen's suburban box, when his life shall be as simple and as agreeable to the imagination, and there is as little straining after effect in the style of his dwelling. A great proportion of architectural ornaments are literally hollow, and a September gale would strip them off, like borrowed plumes, without injury to the substantials. They can do without *architecture* who have no olives nor wines in the cellar. What if an equal ado were made about the ornaments of style in literature, and the architects of our bibles spent as much time about their cornices as the architects of our churches do? So are made the *belles-lettres* and the *beaux-arts* and their professors. Much it concerns a man, forsooth, how a few sticks are slanted over him or under him, and what colors are daubed upon his box. It would signify somewhat, if, in any earnest sense, *he* slanted them and daubed it; but the spirit having departed out of the tenant, it is of a piece with constructing his own coffin—the architecture of the grave—and "carpenter" is but another name for "coffin-maker." One man says, in his despair or indifference to life, take up a handful of the earth at your feet, and paint your house that color. Is he thinking of his last and narrow house? Toss up a copper[57] for it as well. What an abundance of leisure he must have! Why do you take up a handful of dirt? Better paint your house your own complexion; let it turn pale or blush for you. An enterprise to improve the style of cottage architecture! When you have got my ornaments ready, I will wear them.

Before winter I built a chimney, and shingled the sides of my house, which were already impervious to rain, with imperfect and sappy shingles made of the first slice of the log, whose edges I was obliged to straighten with a plane.

I have thus a tight shingled and plastered house, ten feet wide by fifteen long, and eight-feet posts, with a garret and a closet, a large window on each side, two trap-doors, one door at the end, and a brick fireplace opposite. The exact cost of my house, paying the usual price for such materials as I used, but not counting the work, all of which was done by myself, was as follows; and I give the details because very few are able to tell exactly what their houses cost, and fewer still, if any, the separate cost of the various materials which compose them:—

Boards	$8 03½,	mostly shanty boards.
Refuse shingles for roof and sides	4 00	
Laths	1 25	
Two second-hand windows with glass	2 43	
One thousand old brick	4 00	
Two casks of lime	2 40	That was high.
Hair	0 31	More than I needed.
Mantle-tree iron	0 15	
Nails	3 90	
Hinges and screws	0 14	
Latch	0 10	
Chalk	0 01	
Transportation	1 40	I carried a good part on my back.
In all	$28 12½	

---

[57]Coin; requisite payment, in classic mythology, to the boatman who ferries the dead across the River Styx, provided their bodies have been buried in the world above.

These are all the materials, excepting the timber, stones, and sand, which I claimed by squatter's right. I have also a small woodshed adjoining, made chiefly of the stuff which was left after building the house.

I intend to build me a house which will surpass any on the main street in Concord in grandeur and luxury, as soon as it pleases me as much and will cost me no more than my present one.

I thus found that the student who wishes for a shelter can obtain one for a lifetime at an expense not greater than the rent which he now pays annually. If I seem to boast more than is becoming, my excuse is that I brag for humanity rather than for myself; and my shortcomings and inconsistencies do not affect the truth of my statement. Notwithstanding much cant and hypocrisy,—chaff which I find it difficult to separate from my wheat, but for which I am as sorry as any man,—I will breathe freely and stretch myself in this respect, it is such a relief to both the moral and physical system; and I am resolved that I will not through humility become the devil's attorney. I will endeavor to speak a good word for the truth. At Cambridge College[58] the mere rent of a student's room, which is only a little larger than my own, is thirty dollars each year, though the corporation had the advantage of building thirty-two side by side and under one roof, and the occupant suffers the inconvenience of many and noisy neighbors, and perhaps a residence in the fourth story. I cannot but think that if we had more true wisdom in these respects, not only less education would be needed, because, forsooth, more would already have been acquired, but the pecuniary expense of getting an education would in a great measure vanish. Those conveniences which the student requires at Cambridge or elsewhere cost him or somebody else ten times as great a sacrifice of life as they would with proper management on both sides. Those things for which the most money is demanded are never the things which the student most wants. Tuition, for instance, is an important item in the term bill, while for the far more valuable education which he gets by associating with the most cultivated of his contemporaries no charge is made. The mode of founding a college is, commonly, to get up a subscription of dollars and cents, and then, following blindly the principles of a division of labor to its extreme,—a principle which should never be followed but with circumspection,—to call in a contractor who makes this a subject of speculation, and he employs Irishmen or other operatives actually to lay the foundations, while the students that are to be are said to be fitting themselves for it; and for these oversights successive generations have to pay. I think that it would be *better than this,* for the students, or those who desire to be benefited by it, even to lay the foundation themselves. The student who secures his coveted leisure and retirement by systematically shirking any labor necessary to man obtains but an ignoble and unprofitable leisure, defrauding himself of the experience which alone can make leisure fruitful. "But," says one, "you do not mean that the students should go to work with their hands instead of their heads?" I do not mean that exactly, but I mean something which he might think a good deal like that; I mean that they should not *play* life, or *study* it merely, while the community supports them at this expensive game, but earnestly *live* it from beginning to end. How could youths better learn to live than by at once trying the experiment of living? Methinks this would exercise their minds as much as mathematics. If I wished a boy to know something about the arts and sciences, for instance, I would not pursue the common course, which is merely to send him into the neighborhood of some professor, where anything is professed and practised but the art of life;—to survey the world through a telescope or a microscope, and never with his natural eye; to study chemistry, and not learn how his bread is made, or mechanics, and not learn how it is earned; to discover new satellites to

---

[58]I.e., Harvard.

Neptune, and not detect the motes in his eyes, or to what vagabond he is a satellite himself; or to be devoured by the monsters that swarm all around him, while contemplating the monsters in a drop of vinegar. Which would have advanced the most at the end of a month,—the boy who had made his own jackknife from the ore which he had dug and smelted, reading as much as would be necessary for this—or the boy who had attended the lectures on metallurgy at the Institute in the meanwhile, and had received a Rodgers penknife[59] from his father? Which would be most likely to cut his fingers? . . . To my astonishment I was informed on leaving college that I had studied navigation!—why, if I had taken one turn down the harbor I should have known more about it. Even the *poor* student studies and is taught only *political* economy, while that economy of living which is synonymous with philosophy is not even sincerely professed in our colleges. The consequence is, that while he is reading Adam Smith, Ricardo, and Say,[60] he runs his father in debt irretrievably.

As with our colleges, so with a hundred "modern improvements;" there is an illusion about them; there is not always a positive advance. The devil goes on exacting compound interest to the last for his early share and numerous succeeding investments in them. Our inventions are wont to be pretty toys, which distract our attention from serious things. They are but improved means to an unimproved end, an end which it was already but too easy to arrive at; as railroads lead to Boston or New York. We are in great haste to construct a magnetic telegraph from Maine to Texas; but Maine and Texas, it may be, have nothing important to communicate. Either is in such a predicament as the man who was earnest to be introduced to a distinguished deaf woman, but when he was presented, and one end of her ear trumpet was put into his hand, had nothing to say. As if the main object were to talk fast and not to talk sensibly. We are eager to tunnel under the Atlantic and bring the Old World some weeks nearer to the New; but perchance the first news that will leak through into the broad, flapping American ear will be that the Princess Adelaide has the whooping cough. After all, the man whose horse trots a mile in a minute does not carry the most important messages; he is not an evangelist, nor does he come round eating locusts and wild honey.[61] I doubt if Flying Childers[62] ever carried a peck of corn to mill.

One says to me, "I wonder that you do not lay up money; you love to travel; you might take the cars and go to Fitchburg to-day and see the country." But I am wiser than that. I have learned that the swiftest traveller is he that goes afoot. I say to my friend, Suppose we try who will get there first. The distance is thirty miles; the fare ninety cents. That is almost a day's wages. I remember when wages were sixty cents a day for laborers on this very road. Well, I start now on foot, and get there before night; I have travelled at that rate by the week together. You will in the meanwhile have earned your fare, and arrive there some time to-morrow, or possibly this evening, if you are lucky enough to get a job in season. Instead of going to Fitchburg, you will be working here the greater part of the day. And so, if the railroad reached round the world, I think that I should keep ahead of you; and as for seeing the country and getting experience of that kind, I should have to cut your acquaintance altogether.

Such is the universal law, which no man can ever outwit, and with regard to the railroad even we may say it is as broad as it is long. To make a railroad round the world available to all mankind is equivalent to grading the whole surface of the planet. Men have an indistinct notion that if they keep up this activity of joint

---

[59]Knife made of fine Sheffield steel by the English Joseph Rodgers & Sons.
[60]The Scotsman Adam Smith (1723–1790), Englishman David Ricardo (1772–1823), and the Frenchman Jean-Baptiste Say (1767–1832) were all noted economists.

[61]Matthew 3:1–4: John the Baptist, "preaching in the wilderness of Judaea," whose "meat was locusts and wild honey."
[62]An English racehorse.

stocks and spades long enough all will at length ride somewhere, in next to no time, and for nothing; but though a crowd rushes to the depot, and the conductor shouts "All aboard!" when the smoke is blown away and the vapor condensed, it will be perceived that a few are riding, but the rest are run over,—and it will be called, and will be, "A melancholy accident." No doubt they can ride at last who shall have earned their fare, that is, if they survive so long, but they will probably have lost their elasticity and desire to travel by that time. This spending of the best part of one's life earning money in order to enjoy a questionable liberty during the least valuable part of it reminds me of the Englishman who went to India to make a fortune first, in order that he might return to England and live the life of a poet. He should have gone up garret at once. "What!" exclaim a million Irishmen starting up from all the shanties in the land, "is not this railroad which we have built a good thing?" Yes, I answer, *comparatively* good, that is, you might have done worse; but I wish, as you are brothers of mine, that you could have spent your time better than digging in this dirt.

Before I finished my house, wishing to earn ten or twelve dollars by some honest and agreeable method, in order to meet my unusual expenses, I planted about two acres and a half of light and sandy soil near it chiefly with beans, but also a small part with potatoes, corn, peas, and turnips. The whole lot contains eleven acres, mostly growing up to pines and hickories, and was sold the preceding season for eight dollars and eight cents an acre. One farmer said that it was "good for nothing but to raise cheeping squirrels on." I put no manure whatever on this land, not being the owner, but merely a squatter, and not expecting to cultivate so much again, and I did not quite hoe it all once. I got out several cords of stumps in plowing, which supplied me with fuel for a long time, and left small circles of virgin mould, easily distinguishable through the summer by the greater luxuriance of the beans there. The dead and for the most part unmerchantable wood behind my house, and the driftwood from the pond, have supplied the remainder of my fuel. I was obliged to hire a team and a man for the plowing, though I held the plow myself. My farm outgoes for the first season were, for implements, seed, work, etc., $14.72½. The seed corn was given me. This never costs anything to speak of, unless you plant more than enough. I got twelve bushels of beans, and eighteen bushels of potatoes, beside some peas and sweet corn. The yellow corn and turnips were too late to come to anything. My whole income from the farm was

$$\text{\$23 44}$$
Deducting the outgoes 14 72½
There are left $8 71½,

beside produce consumed and on hand at the time this estimate was made of the value of $4.50,—the amount on hand much more than balancing a little grass which I did not raise. All things considered, that is, considering the importance of a man's soul and of to-day, notwithstanding the short time occupied by my experiment, nay, partly even because of its transient character, I believe that that was doing better than any farmer in Concord did that year.

The next year I did better still, for I spaded up all the land which I required, about a third of an acre, and I learned from the experience of both years, not being in the least awed by many celebrated works on husbandry, Arthur Young[63]

---

[63]British agriculturist (1741–1820), author of works on agricultural economy and editor of *Annals of Agriculture* (1784–1809).

among the rest, that if one would live simply and eat only the crop which he raised, and raise no more than he ate, and not exchange it for an insufficient quantity of more luxurious and expensive things, he would need to cultivate only a few rods of ground, and that it would be cheaper to spade up that than to use oxen to plow it, and to select a fresh spot from time to time than to manure the old, and he could do all his necessary farm work as it were with his left hand at odd hours in the summer; and thus he would not be tied to an ox, or horse, or cow, or pig, as at present. I desire to speak impartially on this point, and as one not interested in the success or failure of the present economical and social arrangements. I was more independent than any farmer in Concord, for I was not anchored to a house or farm, but could follow the bent of my genius, which is a very crooked one, every moment. Beside being better off than they already, if my house had been burned or my crops had failed, I should have been nearly as well off as before.

I am wont to think that men are not so much the keepers of herds as herds are the keepers of men, the former are so much the freer. Men and oxen exchange work; but if we consider necessary work only, the oxen will be seen to have greatly the advantage, their farm is so much the larger. Man does some of his part of the exchange work in his six weeks of haying, and it is no boy's play. Certainly no nation that lived simply in all respects, that is, no nation of philosophers, would commit so great a blunder as to use the labor of animals. True, there never was and is not likely soon to be a nation of philosophers, nor am I certain it is desirable that there should be. However, *I* should never have broken a horse or bull and taken him to board for any work he might do for me, for fear I should become a horseman or a herds-man merely; and if society seems to be the gainer by so doing, are we certain that what is one man's gain is not another's loss, and that the stable-boy has equal cause with his master to be satisfied? Granted that some public works would not have been constructed without this aid, and let man share the glory of such with the ox and horse; does it follow that he could not have accomplished works yet more worthy of himself in that case? When men begin to do, not merely unnecessary or artistic, but luxurious and idle work, with their assistance, it is inevitable that a few do all the exchange work with the oxen, or, in other words, become the slaves of the strongest. Man thus not only works for the animal within him, but, for a symbol of this, he works for the animal without him. Though we have many substantial houses of brick or stone, the prosperity of the farmer is still measured by the degree to which the barn overshadows the house. This town is said to have the largest houses for oxen, cows, and horses hereabouts, and it is not behindhand in its public buildings; but there are very few halls for free worship or free speech in this county. It should not be by their architecture, but why not even by their power of abstract thought, that nations should seek to commemorate themselves? How much more admirable the Bhagvat-Geeta[64] than all the ruins of the East! Towers and temples are the luxury of princes. A simple and independent mind does not toil at the bidding of any prince. Genius is not a retainer to any emperor, nor is its material silver, or gold, or marble, except to a trifling extent. To what end, pray, is so much stone hammered? In Arcadia,[65] when I was there, I did not see any hammering stone. Nations are possessed with an insane ambition to perpetuate the memory of themselves by the amount of hammered stone they leave. What if equal pains were taken to smooth and polish their manners? One piece of good sense would be more memorable than a monument as high as the moon. I love better to see stones in place. The grandeur of Thebes[66]

---

[64]Variant of *Bhagavad Gita*, a Hindu religious text, *c.* 500 B.C.

[65]A place of pastoral or rural simplicity and peace, from the name of the agricultural area in Greece celebrated by Greek poets.

[66]Ancient capital of Egypt on the Nile, described in Homer's *Iliad* as a city of "a hundred gates"; a city of great splendor.

was a vulgar grandeur. More sensible is a rod of stone wall that bounds an honest man's field than a hundred-gated Thebes that has wandered farther from the true end of life. The religion and civilization which are barbaric and heathenish build splendid temples; but what you might call Christianity does not. Most of the stone a nation hammers goes toward its tomb only. It buries itself alive. As for the Pyramids, there is nothing to wonder at in them so much as the fact that so many men could be found degraded enough to spend their lives constructing a tomb for some ambitious booby, whom it would have been wiser and manlier to have drowned in the Nile, and then given his body to the dogs. I might possibly invent some excuse for them and him, but I have no time for it. As for the religion and love of art of the builders, it is much the same all the world over, whether the building be an Egyptian temple or the United States Bank. It costs more than it comes to. The mainspring is vanity, assisted by the love of garlic and bread and butter. Mr. Balcom, a promising young architect, designs it on the back of his Vitruvius,[67] with hard pencil and ruler, and the job is let out to Dobson & Sons, stonecutters. When the thirty centuries begin to look down on it, mankind begin to look up at it. As for your high towers and monuments, there was a crazy fellow once in this town who undertook to dig through to China, and he got so far that, as he said, he heard the Chinese pots and kettles rattle; but I think that I shall not go out of my way to admire the hole which he made. Many are concerned about the monuments of the West and the East,—to know who built them. For my part, I should like to know who in those days did not build them,—who were above such trifling. But to proceed with my statistics.

By surveying, carpentry, and day-labor of various other kinds in the village in the meanwhile, for I have as many trades as fingers, I had earned $13.34. The expense of food for eight months, namely, from July 4th to March 1st, the time when these estimates were made, though I lived there more than two years,— not counting potatoes, a little green corn, and some peas, which I had raised, nor considering the value of what was on hand at the last date,—was

Rice	$1 73$\frac{1}{2}$		
Molasses	1 73	Cheapest form of the saccharine.	
Rye meal	1 04$\frac{3}{4}$		
Indian meal	0 99$\frac{3}{4}$	Cheaper than rye.	
Pork	0 22		
Flour	0 88	Costs more than Indian meal, both money and trouble.	All experiments which failed.
Sugar	0 80		
Lard	0 65		
Apples	0 25		
Dried apple	0 22		
Sweet potatoes	0 10		
One pumpkin	0 6		
One watermelon	0 2		
Salt	0 3		

Yes, I did eat $8.74, all told; but I should not thus unblushingly publish my guilt, if I did not know that most of my readers were equally guilty with myself, and that their deeds would look no better in print. The next year I sometimes caught a

---

[67]Vitruvius Pollio, a noted Roman architect of the first century B.C., author of *De Architectura*, long a standard authority.

mess of fish for my dinner, and once I went so far as to slaughter a woodchuck which ravaged my bean-field,—effect his transmigration, as a Tartar[68] would say,—and devour him, partly for experiment's sake; but though it afforded me a momentary enjoyment, notwithstanding a musky flavor, I saw that the longest use would not make that a good practice, however it might seem to have your wood-chucks ready dressed by the village butcher.

Clothing and some incidental expenses within the same dates, though little can be inferred from this item, amounted to

$$\$8\ 40\tfrac{3}{4}$$

Oil and some household utensils . .   2 00

So that all the pecuniary outgoes, excepting for washing and mending, which for the most part were done out of the house, and their bills have not yet been received,—and these are all and more than all the ways by which money necessarily goes out in this part of the world,—were

House	$28 $12\tfrac{1}{2}$
Farm one year	14 $72\tfrac{1}{2}$
Food eight months	8 74
Clothing, etc., eight months . . .	8 $40\tfrac{3}{4}$
Oil, etc., eight months	2 00
In all	$61 $99\tfrac{3}{4}$

I address myself now to those of my readers who have a living to get. And to meet this I have for farm produce sold

	$23 44
Earned by day-labor	13 34
In all	$36 78,

which subtracted from the sum of the outgoes leaves a balance of 25.21\tfrac{3}{4}$ on the one side,—this being very nearly the means with which I started, and the measure of expenses to be incurred,—and on the other, beside the leisure and independence and health thus secured, a comfortable house for me as long as I choose to occupy it.

These statistics, however accidental and therefore uninstructive they may appear, as they have a certain completeness, have a certain value also. Nothing was given me of which I have not rendered some account. It appears from the above estimate, that my food alone cost me in money about twenty-seven cents a week. It was, for nearly two years after this, rye and Indian meal without yeast, potatoes, rice, a very little salt pork, molasses, and salt; and my drink, water. It was fit that I should live on rice, mainly, who loved so well the philosophy of India. To meet the objections of some inveterate cavillers, I may as well state, that if I dined out occasionally, as I always had done, and I trust shall have opportunities to do again, it was frequently to the detriment of my domestic arrangements. But the dining out, being, as I have stated, a constant element, does not in the least affect a comparative statement like this.

I learned from my two years' experience that it would cost incredibly little trouble to obtain one's necessary food, even in this latitude; that a man may use as simple a diet as the animals, and yet retain health and strength. I have made a

---

[68]Inhabitant of Tartary in Asia.

satisfactory dinner, satisfactory on several accounts, simply off a dish of purslane (*Portulaca oleracea*) which I gathered in my cornfield, boiled and salted. I give the Latin on account of the savoriness of the trivial name. And pray what more can a reasonable man desire, in peaceful times, in ordinary noons, than a sufficient number of ears of green sweet corn boiled, with the addition of salt? Even the little variety which I used was a yielding to the demands of appetite, and not of health. Yet men have come to such a pass that they frequently starve, not for want of necessaries, but for want of luxuries; and I know a good woman who thinks that her son lost his life because he took to drinking water only.

The reader will perceive that I am treating the subject rather from an economic than a dietetic point of view, and he will not venture to put my abstemiousness to the test unless he has a well-stocked larder.

Bread I at first made of pure Indian meal and salt, genuine hoe-cakes, which I baked before my fire out of doors on a shingle or the end of a stick of timber sawed off in building my house; but it was wont to get smoked and to have a piny flavor. I tried flour also; but have at last found a mixture of rye and Indian meal most convenient and agreeable. In cold weather it was no little amusement to bake several small loaves of this in succession, tending and turning them as carefully as an Egyptian his hatching eggs.[69] They were a real cereal fruit which I ripened, and they had to my senses a fragrance like that of other noble fruits, which I kept in as long as possible by wrapping them in cloths. I made a study of the ancient and indispensable art of breadmaking, consulting such authorities as offered, going back to the primitive days and first invention of the unleavened kind, when from the wildness of nuts and meats men first reached the mildness and refinement of this diet, and travelling gradually down in my studies through that accidental souring of the dough which, it is supposed, taught the leavening process, and through the various fermentations thereafter, till I came to "good, sweet, wholesome bread," the staff of life. Leaven, which some deem the soul of bread, the *spiritus*[70] which fills its cellular tissue, which is religiously preserved like the vestal fire,[71]—some precious bottleful, I suppose, first brought over in the Mayflower, did the business for America, and its influence is still rising, swelling, spreading, in cerealian[72] billows over the land,—this seed I regularly and faithfully procured from the village, till at length one morning I forgot the rules, and scalded my yeast; by which accident I discovered that even this was not indispensable,—for my discoveries were not by the synthetic but analytic process,—and I have gladly omitted it since, though most housewives earnestly assured me that safe and wholesome bread without yeast might not be, and elderly people prophesied a speedy decay of the vital forces. Yet I find it not to be an essential ingredient, and after going without it for a year am still in the land of the living; and I am glad to escape the trivialness of carrying a bottleful in my pocket, which would sometimes pop and discharge its contents to my discomfiture. It is simpler and more respectable to omit it. Man is an animal who more than any other can adapt himself to all climates and circumstances. Neither did I put any sal-soda, or other acid or alkali, into my bread. It would seem that I made it according to the recipe which Marcus Porcius Cato[73] gave about two centuries before Christ. "Panem depsticium sic facito. Manus mortariumque bene lavato. Farinam in mortarium indito, aquae paulatim addito, subigitoque pulchre. Ubi bene subegeris, defingito, coquitoque sub testu." Which I take to mean, "Make kneaded bread thus. Wash your hands and trough well. Put the meal into the trough, add water gradually, and

---

[69]The Egyptian had devised a method of artificial incubation.
[70]"Breath of life" (Latin).
[71]Sacred fire in the Roman temple of Vesta, goddess of the hearth.

[72]A pun on "cerulean" (sky-blue).
[73]Roman statesman (234–149 B.C.), author of *De Agri Cultura* (for the quotation see Chapter 74).

knead it thoroughly. When you have kneaded it well, mould it, and bake it under a cover," that is, in a baking-kettle. Not a word about leaven. But I did not always use this staff of life. At one time, owing to the emptiness of my purse, I saw none of it for more than a month.

Every New Englander might easily raise all his own breadstuffs in this land of rye and Indian corn, and not depend on distant and fluctuating markets for them. Yet so far are we from simplicity and independence that, in Concord, fresh and sweet meal is rarely sold in the shops, and hominy and corn in a still coarser form are hardly used by any. For the most part the farmer gives to his cattle and hogs the grain of his own producing, and buys flour, which is at least no more wholesome, at a greater cost, at the store. I saw that I could easily raise my bushel or two of rye and Indian corn, for the former will grow on the poorest land, and the latter does not require the best, and grind them in a hand-mill, and so do without rice and pork; and if I must have some concentrated sweet, I found by experiment that I could make a very good molasses either of pumpkins or beets, and I knew that I needed only to set out a few maples to obtain it more easily still, and while these were growing I could use various substitutes beside those which I have named. "For," as the Forefathers sang,—

> "we can make liquor to sweeten our lips
> Of pumpkins and parsnips and walnut-tree chips."[74]

Finally, as for salt, that grossest of groceries, to obtain this might be a fit occasion for a visit to the seashore, or, if I did without it altogether, I should probably drink the less water. I do not learn that the Indians ever troubled themselves to go after it.

Thus I could avoid all trade and barter, so far as my food was concerned, and having a shelter already, it would only remain to get clothing and fuel. The pantaloons which I now wear were woven in a farmer's family,—thank Heaven there is so much virtue still in man; for I think the fall from the farmer to the operative as great and memorable as that from the man to the farmer;—and in a new country, fuel is an encumbrance. As for a habitat, if I were not permitted still to squat, I might purchase one acre at the same price for which the land I cultivated was sold—namely, eight dollars and eight cents. But as it was, I considered that I enhanced the value of the land by squatting on it.

There is a certain class of unbelievers who sometimes ask me such questions as, if I think that I can live on vegetable food alone; and to strike at the root of the matter at once,—for the root is faith,—I am accustomed to answer such, that I can live on board nails. If they cannot understand that, they cannot understand much that I have to say. For my part, I am glad to hear of experiments of this kind being tried; as that a young man tried for a fortnight to live on hard, raw corn on the ear, using his teeth for all mortar. The squirrel tribe tried the same and succeeded. The human race is interested in these experiments, though a few old women who are incapacitated for them, or who own their thirds in mills,[75] may be alarmed.

My furniture, part of which I made myself,—and the rest cost me nothing of which I have not rendered an account,—consisted of a bed, a table, a desk, three chairs, a looking-glass three inches in diameter, a pair of tongs and andirons, a kettle, a skillet, and a frying-pan, a dipper, a wash-bowl, two knives and forks, three plates, one cup, one spoon, a jug for oil, a jug for molasses, and a japanned[76] lamp. None is so poor that he need sit on a pumpkin. That is shiftlessness. There

---

[74]From *Historical Collections* . . . *of* . . . *New England* (1839), compiled by John Warner Barber (1798–1885).

[75]A widow's share of her husband's estate was one-third.
[76]I.e., lacquered.

is a plenty of such chairs as I like best in the village garrets to be had for taking them away. Furniture! Thank God, I can sit and I can stand without the aid of a furniture warehouse. What man but a philosopher would not be ashamed to see his furniture packed in a cart and going up country exposed to the light of heaven and the eyes of men, a beggarly account of empty boxes? That is Spaulding's furniture. I could never tell from inspecting such a load whether it belonged to a so-called rich man or a poor one; the owner always seemed poverty-stricken. Indeed, the more you have of such things the poorer you are. Each load looks as if it contained the contents of a dozen shanties; and if one shanty is poor, this is a dozen times as poor. Pray, for what do we *move* ever but to get rid of our furniture, our *exuviæ*;[77] at last to go from this world to another newly furnished, and leave this to be burned? It is the same as if all these traps were buckled to a man's belt, and he could not move over the rough country where our lines are cast without dragging them,—dragging his trap. He was a lucky fox that left his tail in the trap. The muskrat will gnaw his third leg off to be free. No wonder man has lost his elasticity. How often he is at a dead set! "Sir, if I may be so bold, what do you mean by a dead set?" If you are a seer, whenever you meet a man you will see all that he owns, ay, and much that he pretends to disown, behind him, even to his kitchen furniture and all the trumpery which he saves and will not burn, and he will appear to be harnessed to it and making what headway he can. I think that the man is at a dead set who has got through a knot-hole or gateway where his sledge load of furniture cannot follow him. I cannot but feel compassion when I hear some trig,[78] compact-looking man, seemingly free, all girded and ready, speak of his "furniture," as whether it is insured or not. "But what shall I do with my furniture?" My gay butterfly is entangled in a spider's web then. Even those who seem for a long while not to have any, if you inquire more narrowly you will find have some stored in somebody's barn. I look upon England today as an old gentleman who is travelling with a great deal of baggage, trumpery which has accumulated from long housekeeping, which he has not the courage to burn; great trunk, little trunk, bandbox, and bundle. Throw away the first three at least. It would surpass the powers of a well man nowadays to take up his bed and walk, and I should certainly advise a sick one to lay down his bed and run. When I have met an immigrant tottering under a bundle which contained his all,—looking like an enormous wen which had grown out of the nape of his neck,—I have pitied him, not because that was his all, but because he had all *that* to carry. If I have got to drag my trap, I will take care that it be a light one and do not nip me in a vital part. But perchance it would be wisest never to put one's paw into it.

I would observe, by the way, that it costs me nothing for curtains, for I have no gazers to shut out but the sun and moon, and I am willing that they should look in. The moon will not sour milk nor taint meat of mine, nor will the sun injure my furniture or fade my carpet; and if he is sometimes too warm a friend, I find it still better economy to retreat behind some curtain which nature has provided, than to add a single item to the details of housekeeping. A lady once offered me a mat, but as I had no room to spare within the house, nor time to spare within or without to shake it, I declined it, preferring to wipe my feet on the sod before my door. It is best to avoid the beginnings of evil.

Not long since I was present at the auction of a deacon's effects, for his life had not been ineffectual:—

"The evil that men do lives after them."[79]

---

[77]"Discarded things" (Latin).
[78]Neat.
[79]From Shakespeare's *Julius Caesar*, III, ii, 81.

As usual, a great proportion was trumpery which had begun to accumulate in his father's day. Among the rest was a dried tapeworm. And now, after lying half a century in his garret and other dust holes, these things were not burned; instead of a *bonfire,* or purifying destruction of them, there was an *auction,*[80] or increasing of them. The neighbors eagerly collected to view them, bought them all, and carefully transported them to their garrets and dust holes, to lie there till their estates are settled, when they will start again. When a man dies he kicks the dust.

The customs of some savage nations might, perchance, be profitably imitated by us, for they at least go through the semblance of casting their slough annually; they have the idea of the thing, whether they have the reality or not. Would it not be well if we were to celebrate such a "busk," or "feast of first fruits," as Bartram[81] describes to have been the custom of the Mucclasse Indians? "When a town celebrates the busk," says he, "having previously provided themselves with new clothes, new pots, pans, and other household utensils and furniture, they collect all their worn out clothes and other despicable things, sweep and cleanse their houses, squares, and the whole town, of their filth, which with all the remaining grain and other old provisions they cast together into one common heap, and consume it with fire. After having taken medicine, and fasted for three days, all the fire in the town is extinguished. During this fast they abstain from the gratification of every appetite and passion whatever. A general amnesty is proclaimed; all malefactors may return to their town."

"On the fourth morning, the high priest, by rubbing dry wood together, produces new fire in the public square, from whence every habitation in the town is supplied with the new and pure flame."

They then feast on the new corn and fruits, and dance and sing for three days, "and the four following days they receive visits and rejoice with their friends from neighboring towns who have in like manner purified and prepared themselves."

The Mexicans also practised a similar purification at the end of every fifty-two years, in the belief that it was time for the world to come to an end.

I have scarcely heard of a truer sacrament, that is, as the dictionary defines it, "outward and visible sign of an inward and spiritual grace," than this, and I have no doubt that they were originally inspired directly from Heaven to do thus, though they have no Biblical record of the revelation.

For more than five years I maintained myself thus solely by the labor of my hands, and I found that, by working about six weeks in a year, I could meet all the expenses of living. The whole of my winters, as well as most of my summers, I had free and clear for study. I have thoroughly tried school-keeping, and found that my expenses were in proportion, or rather out of proportion, to my income, for I was obliged to dress and train, not to say think and believe, accordingly, and I lost my time into the bargain. As I did not teach for the good of my fellow-men, but simply for a livelihood, this was a failure. I have tried trade; but I found that it would take ten years to get under way in that, and that then I should probably be on my way to the devil. I was actually afraid that I might by that time be doing what is called a good business. When formerly I was looking about to see what I could do for a living, some sad experience in conforming to the wishes of friends being fresh in my mind to tax my ingenuity, I thought often and seriously of picking huckleberries; that surely I could do, and its small profits might suffice,—for my greatest skill has been to want but little,—so little capital it required, so little distraction from my wonted moods, I foolishly thought. While my acquaintances went unhesitatingly into trade or the professions, I contemplated this occupation

---

[80]From the Latin *auctio* (increase).
[81]William Bartram (1739–1823), American naturalist and author of *Travels through North and South Carolina, Georgia, East and West Florida. . .* (1791).

as most like theirs; ranging the hills all summer to pick the berries which came in my way, and thereafter carelessly dispose of them; so, to keep the flocks of Admetus.[82] I also dreamed that I might gather the wild herbs, or carry evergreens to such villagers as loved to be reminded of the woods, even to the city, by hay-cart loads. But I have since learned that trade curses everything it handles; and though you trade in messages from heaven, the whole curse of trade attaches to the business.

As I preferred some things to others, and especially valued my freedom, as I could fare hard and yet succeed well, I did not wish to spend my time in earning rich carpets or other fine furniture, or delicate cookery, or a house in the Grecian or the Gothic style just yet. If there are any to whom it is no interruption to acquire these things, and who know how to use them when acquired, I relinquish to them the pursuit. Some are "industrious," and appear to love labor for its own sake, or perhaps because it keeps them out of worse mischief; to such I have at present nothing to say. Those who would not know what to do with more leisure than they now enjoy, I might advise to work twice as hard as they do,—work till they pay for themselves, and get their free papers.[83] For myself I found that the occupation of a day-laborer was the most independent of any, especially as it required only thirty or forty days in a year to support one. The laborer's day ends with the going down of the sun, and he is then free to devote himself to his chosen pursuit, independent of his labor; but his employer, who speculates from month to month, has no respite from one end of the year to the other.

In short, I am convinced, both by faith and experience, that to maintain one's self on this earth is not a hardship but a pastime, if we will live simply and wisely; as the pursuits of the simpler nations are still the sports of the more artificial. It is not necessary that a man should earn his living by the sweat of his brow, unless he sweats easier than I do.

One young man of my acquaintance, who has inherited some acres, told me that he thought he should live as I did, *if he had the means.* I would not have any one adopt *my* mode of living on any account; for, beside that before he has fairly learned it I may have found out another for myself, I desire that there may be as many different persons in the world as possible; but I would have each one be very careful to find out and pursue *his own* way, and not his father's or his mother's or his neighbor's instead. The youth may build or plant or sail, only let him not be hindered from doing that which he tells me he would like to do. It is by a mathematical point only that we are wise, as the sailor or the fugitive slave keeps the polestar in his eye; but that is sufficient guidance for all our life. We may not arrive at our port within a calculable period, but we would preserve the true course.

Undoubtedly, in this case, what is true for one is truer still for a thousand, as a large house is not proportionally more expensive than a small one, since one roof may cover, one cellar underlie, and one wall separate several apartments. But for my part, I preferred the solitary dwelling. Moreover, it will commonly be cheaper to build the whole yourself than to convince another of the advantage of the common wall; and when you have done this, the common partition, to be much cheaper, must be a thin one, and that other may prove a bad neighbor, and also not keep his side in repair. The only coöperation which is commonly possible is exceedingly partial and superficial; and what little true coöperation there is, is as if it were not, being a harmony inaudible to men. If a man has faith, he will coöp-

---

[82]Zeus condemned Apollo, Greek god of the sun and poetry, to the menial task of tending the flocks of Admetus, King of Pherae; Apollo played his flute and charmed the wild beasts.

[83]I.e., having worked off their debts, they end their period as indentured servants.

erate with equal faith everywhere; if he has not faith, he will continue to live like the rest of the world, whatever company he is joined to. To coöperate in the highest as well as the lowest sense, means *to get our living together*. I heard it proposed lately that two young men should travel together over the world, the one without money, earning his means as he went, before the mast and behind the plow, the other carrying a bill of exchange in his pocket. It was easy to see that they could not long be companions or coöperate, since one would not *operate* at all. They would part at the first interesting crisis in their adventures. Above all, as I have implied, the man who goes alone can start to-day; but he who travels with another must wait till that other is ready, and it may be a long time before they get off.

But all this is very selfish, I have heard some of my townsmen say. I confess that I have hitherto indulged very little in philanthropic enterprises. I have made some sacrifices to a sense of duty, and among others have sacrificed this pleasure also. There are those who have used all their arts to persuade me to undertake the support of some poor family in the town; and if I had nothing to do—for the devil finds employment for the idle—I might try my hand at some such pastime as that. However, when I have thought to indulge myself in this respect, and lay their Heaven under an obligation by maintaining certain poor persons in all respects as comfortably as I maintain myself, and have even ventured so far as to make them the offer, they have one and all unhesitatingly preferred to remain poor. While my townsmen and women are devoted in so many ways to the good of their fellows, I trust that one at least may be spared to other and less humane pursuits. You must have a genius for charity as well as for anything else. As for Doing-good, that is one of the professions which are full. Moreover, I have tried it fairly, and, strange as it may seem, am satisfied that it does not agree with my constitution. Probably I should not consciously and deliberately forsake my particular calling to do the good which society demands of me, to save the universe from annihilation; and I believe that a like but infinitely greater steadfastness elsewhere is all that now preserves it. But I would not stand between any man and his genius; and to him who does this work, which I decline, with his whole heart and soul and life, I would say, Persevere, even if the world call it doing evil, as it is most likely they will.

I am far from supposing that my case is a peculiar one; no doubt many of my readers would make a similar defence. At doing something,—I will not engage that my neighbors shall pronounce it good,—I do not hesitate to say that I should be a capital fellow to hire; but what that is, it is for my employer to find out. What *good* I do, in the common sense of that word, must be aside from my main path, and for the most part wholly unintended. Men say, practically, Begin where you are and such as you are, without aiming mainly to become of more worth, and with kindness aforethought go about doing good. If I were to preach at all in this strain, I should say rather, Set about being good. As if the sun should stop when he had kindled his fires up to the splendor of a moon or a star of the sixth magnitude, and go about like a Robin Goodfellow,[84] peeping in at every cottage window, inspiring lunatics, and tainting meats, and making darkness visible, instead of steadily increasing his genial heat and beneficence till he is of such brightness that no mortal can look him in the face, and then, and in the meanwhile too, going about the world in his own orbit, doing it good, or rather, as a truer philosophy has discovered, the world going about him getting good. When Phaëton,[85] wishing to prove his heavenly birth by his beneficence, had the sun's chariot but

[84]Also called Puck, as in Shakespeare's *A Midsummer Night's Dream*.

[85]Variant of Phaethon, son of the sun god, killed when he attempted to drive his father's chariot, could not control the horses, and set the earth on fire.

one day, and drove out of the beaten track, he burned several blocks of houses in the lower streets of heaven, and scorched the surface of the earth, and dried up every spring, and made the great desert of Sahara, till at length Jupiter hurled him headlong to the earth with a thunderbolt, and the sun, through grief at his death, did not shine for a year.

There is no odor so bad as that which arises from goodness tainted. It is human, it is divine, carrion. If I knew for a certainty that a man was coming to my house with the conscious design of doing me good, I should run for my life, as from that dry and parching wind of the African deserts called the simoom, which fills the mouth and nose and ears and eyes with dust till you are suffocated, for fear that I should get some of his good done to me,—some of its virus mingled with my blood. No,—in this case I would rather suffer evil the natural way. A man is not a good *man* to me because he will feed me if I should be starving, or warm me if I should be freezing, or pull me out of a ditch if I should ever fall into one. I can find you a Newfoundland dog that will do as much. Philanthropy is not love for one's fellow-man in the broadest sense. Howard[86] was no doubt an exceedingly kind and worthy man in his way, and has his reward; but, comparatively speaking, what are a hundred Howards to *us*, if their philanthropy do not help *us* in our best estate, when we are most worthy to be helped? I never heard of a philanthropic meeting in which it was sincerely proposed to do any good to me, or the like of me.

The Jesuits were quite balked by those Indians who, being burned at the stake, suggested new modes of torture to their tormentors. Being superior to physical suffering, it sometimes chanced that they were superior to any consolation which the missionaries could offer; and the law to do as you would be done by fell with less persuasiveness on the ears of those who, for their part, did not care how they were done by, who loved their enemies after a new fashion, and came very near freely forgiving them all they did.

Be sure that you give the poor the aid they most need, though it be your example which leaves them far behind. If you give money, spend yourself with it, and do not merely abandon it to them. We make curious mistakes sometimes. Often the poor man is not so cold and hungry as he is dirty and ragged and gross. It is partly his taste, and not merely his misfortune. If you give him money, he will perhaps buy more rags with it. I was wont to pity the clumsy Irish laborers who cut ice on the pond, in such mean and ragged clothes, while I shivered in my more tidy and somewhat more fashionable garments, till, one bitter cold day, one who had slipped into the water came to my house to warm him, and I saw him strip off three pairs of pants and two pairs of stockings ere he got down to the skin, though they were dirty and ragged enough, it is true, and that he could afford to refuse the *extra* garments which I offered him, he had so many *intra* ones.[87] This ducking was the very thing he needed. Then I began to pity myself, and I saw that it would be a greater charity to bestow on me a flannel shirt than a whole slop-shop on him. There are a thousand hacking at the branches of evil to one who is striking at the root, and it may be that he who bestows the largest amount of time and money on the needy is doing the most by his mode of life to produce that misery which he strives in vain to relieve. It is the pious slave-breeder devoting the proceeds of every tenth slave to buy a Sunday's liberty for the rest. Some show their kindness to the poor by employing them in their kitchens. Would they not be kinder if they employed themselves there? You boast of spending a tenth part of

---

[86]John Howard (1726?–1790), a leader of prison reform in England.
[87]I.e., exterior *(extra)* and inner *(intra)* garments (Latin).

your income in charity;[88] maybe you should spend the nine tenths so, and done with it. Society recovers only a tenth part of the property then. Is this owing to the generosity of him in whose possession it is found, or to the remissness of the officers of justice?

Philanthropy is almost the only virtue which is sufficiently appreciated by mankind. Nay, it is greatly overrated; and it is our selfishness which overrates it. A robust poor man, one sunny day here in Concord, praised a fellow-townsman to me, because, as he said, he was kind to the poor; meaning himself. The kind uncles and aunts of the race are more esteemed than its true spiritual fathers and mothers. I once heard a reverend lecturer on England, a man of learning and intelligence, after enumerating her scientific, literary, and political worthies, Shakespeare, Bacon, Cromwell, Milton, Newton, and others, speak next of her Christian heroes, whom, as if his profession required it of him, he elevated to a place far above all the rest, as the greatest of the great. They were Penn, Howard, and Mrs. Fry.[89] Every one must feel the falsehood and cant of this. The last were not England's best men and women; only, perhaps, her best philanthropists.

I would not subtract anything from the praise that is due to philanthropy, but merely demand justice for all who by their lives and works are a blessing to mankind. I do not value chiefly a man's uprightness and benevolence, which are, as it were, his stem and leaves. Those plants of whose greenness withered we make herb tea for the sick serve but a humble use, and are most employed by quacks. I want the flower and fruit of a man; that some fragrance be wafted over from him to me, and some ripeness flavor our intercourse. His goodness must not be a partial and transitory act, but a constant superfluity, which costs him nothing and of which he is unconscious. This is a charity that hides a multitude of sins. The philanthropist too often surrounds mankind with the remembrance of his own cast-off griefs as an atmosphere, and calls it sympathy. We should impart our courage, and not our despair, our health and ease, and not our disease, and take care that this does not spread by contagion. From what southern plains comes up the voice of wailing? Under what latitudes reside the heathen to whom we would send light? Who is that intemperate and brutal man whom we would redeem? If anything ail a man, so that he does not perform his functions, if he have a pain in his bowels even,—for that is the seat of sympathy,[90]—he forthwith sets about reforming—the world. Being a microcosm himself, he discovers—and it is a true discovery, and he is the man to make it—that the world has been eating green apples; to his eyes, in fact, the globe itself is a great green apple, which there is danger awful to think of that the children of men will nibble before it is ripe; and straightway his drastic philanthropy seeks out the Esquimau and the Patagonian,[91] and embraces the populous Indian and Chinese villages; and thus, by a few years of philanthropic activity, the powers in the meanwhile using him for their own ends, no doubt, he cures himself of his dyspepsia, the globe acquires a faint blush on one or both of its cheeks, as if it were beginning to be ripe, and life loses its crudity and is once more sweet and wholesome to live. I never dreamed of any enormity greater than I have committed. I never knew, and never shall know, a worse man than myself.

I believe that what so saddens the reformer is not his sympathy with his fellows in distress, but, though he be the holiest son of God, is his private ail. Let this be

---

[88]In tithing, one pledges one tenth of one's income for charity or the support of the church.
[89]William Penn (1644–1718), Quaker and proprietor of Pennsylvania, which he established as a place of religious freedom; Elizabeth Fry (1780–1845), a Quaker and, like Howard, a prison reformer.

[90]A common belief.
[91]The eskimo and the Patagonian (who lives at the southern tip of South America).

righted, let the spring come to him, the morning rise over his couch, and he will
forsake his generous companions without apology. My excuse for not lecturing
against the use of tobacco is, that I never chewed it, that is a penalty which reformed tobacco-chewers have to pay; though there are things enough I have
chewed which I could lecture against. If you should ever be betrayed into any of
these philanthropies, do not let your left hand know what your right hand does,[92]
for it is not worth knowing. Rescue the drowning and tie your shoestrings. Take
your time, and set about some free labor.

Our manners have been corrupted by communication with the saints. Our
hymn-books resound with a melodious cursing of God and enduring Him forever.
One would say that even the prophets and redeemers had rather consoled the
fears than confirmed the hopes of man. There is nowhere recorded a simple and
irrepressible satisfaction with the gift of life, any memorable praise of God. All
health and success does me good, however far off and withdrawn it may appear;
all disease and failure helps to make me sad and does me evil, however much sympathy it may have with me or I with it. If, then, we would indeed restore mankind
by truly Indian, botanic, magnetic, or natural means, let us first be as simple and
well as Nature ourselves, dispel the clouds which hang over our own brows, and
take up a little life into our pores. Do not stay to be an overseer of the poor, but
endeavor to become one of the worthies of the world.

I read in the Gulistan, or Flower Garden, of Sheik Sadi of Shiraz,[93] that "they
asked a wise man, saying: Of the many celebrated trees which the Most High God
has created lofty and umbrageous, they call none azad, or free, excepting the cypress, which bears no fruit; what mystery is there in this? He replied: Each has its
appropriate produce, and appointed season, during the continuance of which it is
fresh and blooming, and during their absence dry and withered; to neither of
which states is the cypress exposed, being always flourishing; and of this nature
are the azads, or religious independents.— Fix not thy heart on that which is transitory; for the Dijlah, or Tigris, will continue to flow through Bagdad after the
race of caliphs is extinct: if thy hand has plenty, be liberal as the date tree; but if it
affords nothing to give away, be an azad, or free man, like the cypress."

COMPLEMENTAL VERSES
THE PRETENSIONS OF POVERTY[94]

Thou dost presume too much, poor needy wretch,
To claim a station in the firmament
Because thy humble cottage, or thy tub,
Nurses some lazy or pedantic virtue
In the cheap sunshine or by shady springs,
With roots and pot-herbs; where thy right hand,
Tearing those humane passions from the mind,
Upon whose stocks fair blooming virtues flourish,
Degradeth nature, and benumbeth sense,
And, Gorgon-like, turns active men to stone.
We not require the dull society
Of your necessitated temperance,
Or that unnatural stupidity
That knows nor joy nor sorrow; nor your forc'd
Falsely exalted passive fortitude

---

[92]See Matthew 6:3.
[93]Muslih-ud-Din Saadi (or Sadi) (1184?–1291), Persian
poet born in Shiraz and author of *The Gulistan* or *Rose Garden* (1258).

[94]A passage in which Mercury is speaking to Poverty in the
mosque, from *Coelum Britannicum* (1661) by the British
Cavalier poet, Thomas Carew (1595?–1645). Thoreau supplied this title.

Above the active. This low abject brood,
That fix their seats in mediocrity,
Become your servile minds; but we advance
Such virtues only as admit excess,
Brave, bounteous acts, regal magnificence,
All-seeing prudence, magnanimity
That knows no bound, and that heroic virtue
For which antiquity hath left no name,
But patterns only, such as Hercules,
Achilles, Theseus. Back to thy loath'd cell;
And when thou seest the new enlightened sphere,
Study to know but what those worthies were.

T. CAREW

II

WHERE I LIVED, AND WHAT I LIVED FOR

At a certain season of our life we are accustomed to consider every spot as the possible site of a house. I have thus surveyed the country on every side within a dozen miles of where I live. In imagination I have bought all the farms in succession, for all were to be bought, and I knew their price. I walked over each farmer's premises, tasted his wild apples, discoursed on husbandry with him, took his farm at his price, at any price, mortgaging it to him in my mind; even put a higher price on it,—took everything but a deed of it,—took his word for his deed, for I dearly love to talk,—cultivated it, and him too to some extent, I trust, and withdrew when I had enjoyed it long enough, leaving him to carry it on. This experience entitled me to be regarded as a sort of real-estate broker by my friends. Wherever I sat, there I might live, and the landscape radiated from me accordingly. What is a house but a *sedes*, a seat?—better if a country seat. I discovered many a site for a house not likely to be soon improved, which some might have thought too far from the village, but to my eyes the village was too far from it. Well, there I might live, I said; and there I did live, for an hour, a summer and a winter life; saw how I could let the years run off, buffet the winter through, and see the spring come in. The future inhabitants of this region, wherever they may place their houses, may be sure that they have been anticipated. An afternoon sufficed to lay out the land into orchard, wood-lot, and pasture, and to decide what fine oaks or pines should be left to stand before the door, and whence each blasted tree could be seen to the best advantage; and then I let it lie, fallow perchance, for a man is rich in proportion to the number of things which he can afford to let alone.

My imagination carried me so far that I even had the refusal of several farms,—the refusal was all I wanted,—but I never got my fingers burned by actual possession. The nearest that I came to actual possession was when I bought the Hollowell place, and had begun to sort my seeds, and collected materials with which to make a wheelbarrow to carry it on or off with; but before the owner gave me a deed of it, his wife—every man has such a wife—changed her mind and wished to keep it, and he offered me ten dollars to release him. Now, to speak the truth, I had but ten cents in the world, and it surpassed my arithmetic to tell, if I was that man who had ten cents, or who had a farm, or ten dollars, or all together. However, I let him keep the ten dollars and the farm too, for I had carried it far enough; or rather, to be generous, I sold him the farm for just what I gave for it, and, as he was not a rich man, made him a present of ten dollars, and still had my ten cents, and seeds, and materials for a wheelbarrow left. I found thus that I had been a rich man without any damage to my poverty. But I retained the landscape, and I have since annually carried off what it yielded without a wheelbarrow. With respect to landscapes,—

> "I am monarch of all I *survey,*
> My right there is none to dispute."[1]

I have frequently seen a poet withdraw, having enjoyed the most valuable part of a farm, while the crusty farmer supposed that he had got a few wild apples only. Why, the owner does not know it for many years when a poet has put his farm in rhyme, the most admirable kind of invisible fence, has fairly impounded it, milked it, skimmed it, and got all the cream, and left the farmer only the skimmed milk.

The real attractions of the Hollowell farm, to me, were: its complete retirement, being about two miles from the village, half a mile from the nearest neighbor, and separated from the highway by a broad field; its bounding on the river, which the owner said protected it by its fogs from frosts in the spring, though that was nothing to me; the gray color and ruinous state of the house and barn, and the dilapidated fences, which put such an interval between me and the last occupant; the hollow and lichen-covered apple trees, gnawed by rabbits, showing what kind of neighbors I should have; but above all, the recollection I had of it from my earliest voyages up the river, when the house was concealed behind a dense grove of red maples, through which I heard the house-dog bark. I was in haste to buy it, before the proprietor finished getting out some rocks, cutting down the hollow apple trees, and grubbing up some young birches which had sprung up in the pasture, or, in short, had made any more of his improvements. To enjoy these advantages I was ready to carry it on; like Atlas,[2] to take the world on my shoulders,—I never heard what compensation he received for that,—and do all those things which had no other motive or excuse but that I might pay for it and be unmolested in my possession of it; for I knew all the while that it would yield the most abundant crop of the kind I wanted, if I could only afford to let it alone. But it turned out as I have said.

All that I could say, then, with respect to farming on a large scale—I have always cultivated a garden—was, that I had had my seeds ready. Many think that seeds improve with age. I have no doubt that time discriminates between the good and the bad; and when at last I shall plant, I shall be less likely to be disappointed. But I would say to my fellows, once for all, As long as possible live free and uncommitted. It makes but little difference whether you are committed to a farm or the county jail.

Old Cato, whose "De Re Rusticâ"[3] is my "Cultivator," says,—and the only translation I have seen makes sheer nonsense of the passage,—"When you think of getting a farm turn it thus in your mind, not to buy greedily; nor spare your pains to look at it, and do not think it enough to go round it once. The oftener you go there the more it will please you, if it is good." I think I shall not buy greedily, but go round and round it as long as I live, and be buried in it first, that it may please me the more at last.

The present was my next experiment of this kind, which I purpose to describe more at length, for convenience putting the experience of two years into one. As I have said, I do not propose to write an ode to dejection, but to brag as lustily as

[1]From "Verses Supposed to Be Written by Alexander Selkirk," by William Cowper (1731–1800); Daniel Defoe modeled *Robinson Crusoe* (1719) on the experiences of Selkirk, who was stranded on an island off Chile for over four years. Thoreau, punning on his having been a surveyor, emphasizes "survey."

[2]One of the Titans directed by Zeus to hold up the world and sky for battling the gods of Olympus.
[3]Marcus Porcius Cato (234–149 B.C.), author of *De Agri Cultura,* also known as "De Re Rustica," "Concerning Country Life."

chanticleer in the morning, standing on his roost, if only to wake my neighbors up.

When first I took up my abode in the woods, that is, began to spend my nights as well as days there, which, by accident, was on Independence Day, or the Fourth of July, 1845, my house was not finished for winter, but was merely a defence against the rain, without plastering or chimney, the walls being of rough, weather-stained boards, with wide chinks, which made it cool at night. The upright white hewn studs and freshly planed door and window casings gave it a clean and airy look, especially in the morning, when its timbers were saturated with dew, so that I fancied that by noon some sweet gum would exude from them. To my imagination it retained throughout the day more or less of this auroral character, reminding me of a certain house on a mountain which I had visited a year before. This was an airy and unplastered cabin, fit to entertain a travelling god, and where a goddess might trail her garments. The winds which passed over my dwelling were such as sweep over the ridges of mountains, bearing the broken strains, or celestial parts only, of terrestrial music. The morning wind forever blows, the poem of creation is uninterrupted; but few are the ears that hear it. Olympus is but the outside of the earth everywhere.

The only house I had been the owner of before, if I except a boat, was a tent, which I used occasionally when making excursions in the summer, and this is still rolled up in my garret; but the boat, after passing from hand to hand, has gone down the stream of time. With this more substantial shelter about me, I had made some progress toward settling in the world. This frame, so slightly clad, was a sort of crystallization around me, and reacted on the builder. It was suggestive somewhat as a picture in outlines. I did not need to go outdoors to take the air, for the atmosphere within had lost none of its freshness. It was not so much within-doors as behind a door where I sat, even in the rainiest weather. The Harivansa[4] says, "An abode without birds is like a meat without seasoning." Such was not my abode, for I found myself suddenly neighbor to the birds; not by having imprisoned one, but having caged myself near them. I was not only nearer to some of those which commonly frequent the garden and the orchard, but to those wilder and more thrilling songsters of the forest which never, or rarely, serenade a villager,—the wood thrush, the veery, the scarlet tanager, the field sparrow, the whip-poor-will, and many others.

I was seated by the shore of a small pond, about a mile and a half south of the village of Concord and somewhat higher than it, in the midst of an extensive wood between that town and Lincoln, and about two miles south of that our only field known to fame, Concord Battle Ground;[5] but I was so low in the woods that the opposite shore, half a mile off, like the rest, covered with wood, was my most distant horizon. For the first week, whenever I looked out on the pond it impressed me like a tarn high up on the side of a mountain, its bottom far above the surface of other lakes, and, as the sun arose, I saw it throwing off its nightly clothing of mist, and here and there, by degrees, its soft ripples or its smooth reflecting surface was revealed, while the mists, like ghosts, were stealthily withdrawing in every direction into the woods, as at the breaking up of some nocturnal conventicle. The very dew seemed to hang upon the trees later into the day than usual, as on the sides of mountains.

This small lake was of most value as a neighbor in the intervals of a gentle rainstorm in August, when, both air and water being perfectly still, but the sky overcast, mid-afternoon had all the serenity of evening, and the wood thrush sang around, and was heard from shore to shore. A lake like this is never smoother

---

[4]A Hindu epic poem concerning Krishna, an incarnation of the Hindu god Vishnu.

[5]Scene of the opening battle of the American Revolution, April 19, 1775.

than at such a time; and the clear portion of the air above it being shallow and darkened by clouds, the water, full of light and reflections, becomes a lower heaven itself so much the more important. From a hill-top near by, where the wood had been recently cut off, there was a pleasing vista southward across the pond, through a wide indentation in the hills which form the shore there, where their opposite sides sloping toward each other suggested a stream flowing out in that direction through a wooded valley, but stream there was none. That way I looked between and over the near green hills to some distant and higher ones in the horizon, tinged with blue. Indeed, by standing on tiptoe I could catch a glimpse of some of the peaks of the still bluer and more distant mountain ranges in the northwest, those true-blue coins from heaven's own mint, and also of some portion of the village. But in other directions, even from this point, I could not see over or beyond the woods which surrounded me. It is well to have some water in your neighborhood, to give buoyancy to and float the earth. One value even of the smallest well is, that when you look into it you see that earth is not continent but insular. This is as important as that it keeps butter cool. When I looked across the pond from this peak toward the Sudbury meadows, which in time of flood I distinguished elevated perhaps by a mirage in their seething valley, like a coin in a basin, all the earth beyond the pond appeared like a thin crust insulated and floated even by this small sheet of intervening water, and I was reminded that this on which I dwelt was but *dry land.*

Though the view from my door was still more contracted, I did not feel crowded or confined in the least. There was pasture enough for my imagination. The low shrub oak plateau to which the opposite shore arose stretched away toward the prairies of the West and the steppes of Tartary,[6] affording ample room for all the roving families of men. "There are none happy in the world but beings who enjoy freely a vast horizon,"—said Damodara,[7] when his herds required new and larger pastures.

Both place and time were changed, and I dwelt nearer to those parts of the universe and to those eras in history which had most attracted me. Where I lived was as far off as many a region viewed nightly by astronomers. We are wont to imagine rare and delectable places in some remote and more celestial corner of the system, behind the constellation of Cassiopeia's Chair, far from noise and disturbance. I discovered that my house actually had its site in such a withdrawn, but forever new and unprofaned, part of the universe. If it were worth the while to settle in those parts near to the Pleiades or the Hyades, to Aldebaran or Altair,[8] then I was really there, or at an equal remoteness from the life which I had left behind, dwindled and twinkling with as fine a ray to my nearest neighbor, and to be seen only in moonless nights by him. Such was that part of creation where I had squatted;—

> "There was a shepherd that did live,
>   And held his thoughts as high
> As were the mounts whereon his flocks
>   Did hourly feed him by."[9]

What should we think of the shepherd's life if his flocks always wandered to higher pastures than his thoughts?

Every morning was a cheerful invitation to make my life of equal simplicity, and I may say innocence, with Nature herself. I have been as sincere a worshipper

---

[6]Vast plains of western Siberia and southern Russia.
[7]Another name for the Hindu deity Krishna.
[8]The Pleiades and the Hyades are clusters of stars within the constellation Taurus (the Bull), which also contains the bright red star Aldebaran; Altair is a first-magnitude star in the constellation Aquila.
[9]From "The Shepherd's Love for Philliday," an anonymous poem in Thomas Evans's *Old Ballads* (1810).

of Aurora[10] as the Greeks. I got up early and bathed in the pond; that was a religious exercise, and one of the best things which I did. They say that characters were engraven on the bathing tub of King Tching-thang to this effect: "Renew thyself completely each day; do it again, and again, and forever again."[11] I can understand that. Morning brings back the heroic ages. I was as much affected by the faint hum of a mosquito making its invisible and unimaginable tour through my apartment at earliest dawn, when I was sitting with door and windows open, as I could be by any trumpet that ever sang of fame. It was Homer's requiem; itself an Iliad and Odyssey in the air, singing its own wrath and wanderings. There was something cosmical about it; a standing advertisement, till forbidden,[12] of the everlasting vigor and fertility of the world. The morning, which is the most memorable season of the day, is the awakening hour. Then there is least somnolence in us; and for an hour, at least, some part of us awakes which slumbers all the rest of the day and night. Little is to be expected of that day, if it can be called a day, to which we are not awakened by our Genius, but by the mechanical nudgings of some servitor, are not awakened by our own newly acquired force and aspirations from within, accompanied by the undulations of celestial music, instead of factory bells, and a fragrance filling the air—to a higher life than we fell asleep from; and thus the darkness bear its fruit, and prove itself to be good, no less than the light. That man who does not believe that each day contains an earlier, more sacred, and auroral hour than he has yet profaned, has despaired of life, and is pursuing a descending and darkening way. After a partial cessation of his sensuous life, the soul of man, or its organs rather, are reinvigorated each day, and his Genius tries again what noble life it can make. All memorable events, I should say, transpire in morning time and in a morning atmosphere. The Vedas[13] say, "All intelligences awake with the morning." Poetry and art, and the fairest and most memorable of the actions of men, date from such an hour. All poets and heroes, like Memnon,[14] are the children of Aurora, and emit their music at sunrise. To him whose elastic and vigorous thought keeps pace with the sun, the day is a perpetual morning. It matters not what the clocks say or the attitudes and labors of men. Morning is when I am awake and there is a dawn in me. Moral reform is the effort to throw off sleep. Why is it that men give so poor an account of their day if they have not been slumbering? They are not such poor calculators. If they had not been overcome with drowsiness, they would have performed something. The millions are awake enough for physical labor; but only one in a million is awake enough for effective intellectual exertion, only one in a hundred millions to a poetic or divine life. To be awake is to be alive. I have never yet met a man who was quite awake. How could I have looked him in the face?

We must learn to reawaken and keep ourselves awake, not by mechanical aids, but by an infinite expectation of the dawn, which does not forsake us in our soundest sleep. I know of no more encouraging fact than the unquestionable ability of man to elevate his life by a conscious endeavor. It is something to be able to paint a particular picture, or to carve a statue, and so to make a few objects beautiful; but it is far more glorious to carve and paint the very atmosphere and medium through which we look, which morally we can do. To affect the quality of the day, that is the highest of arts. Every man is tasked to make his life, even in its details, worthy of the contemplation of his most elevated and critical hour. If we

[10]Roman goddess of the dawn identified with the Greek goddess Eos.
[11]A commentary on Confucius's *The Great Learning* engraved on the tub of the founder of the Shang dynasty (1766–1122 B.C.).
[12]In newspapers, advertisements marked TF (Till Forbidden) were to be repeated in each issue.
[13]Hindu sacred texts.
[14]Son of Aurora, goddess of dawn. Killed in the Trojan wars, his huge statue at Thebes emits strange musical sounds at dawn.

refused, or rather used up, such paltry information as we get, the oracles would distinctly inform us how this might be done.

I went to the woods because I wished to live deliberately, to front only the essential facts of life, and see if I could not learn what it had to teach, and not, when I came to die, discover that I had not lived. I did not wish to live what was not life, living is so dear; nor did I wish to practise resignation, unless it was quite necessary. I wanted to live deep and suck out all the marrow of life, to live so sturdily and Spartan-like as to put to rout all that was not life, to cut a broad swath and shave close, to drive life into a corner, and reduce it to its lowest terms, and, if it proved to be mean, why then to get the whole and genuine meanness of it, and publish its meanness to the world; or if it were sublime, to know it by experience, and be able to give a true account of it in my next excursion. For most men, it appears to me, are in a strange uncertainty about it, whether it is of the devil or of God, and have *somewhat hastily* concluded that it is the chief end of man here to "glorify God and enjoy him forever."[15]

Still we live meanly, like ants; though the fable tells us that we were long ago changed into men; like pygmies we fight with cranes;[16] it is error upon error, and clout upon clout, and our best virtue has for its occasion a superfluous and evitable wretchedness. Our life is frittered away by detail. An honest man has hardly need to count more than his ten fingers, or in extreme cases he may add his ten toes, and lump the rest. Simplicity, simplicity, simplicity! I say, let your affairs be as two or three, and not a hundred or a thousand; instead of a million count half a dozen, and keep your accounts on your thumb-nail. In the midst of this chopping sea of civilized life, such are the clouds and storms and quicksands and thousand-and-one items to be allowed for, that a man has to live, if he would not founder and go to the bottom and not make his port at all, by dead reckoning,[17] and he must be a great calculator indeed who succeeds. Simplify, simplify. Instead of three meals a day, if it be necessary eat but one; instead of a hundred dishes, five; and reduce other things in proportion. Our life is like a German Confederacy, made up of petty states,[18] with its boundary forever fluctuating, so that even a German cannot tell you how it is bounded at any moment. The nation itself, with all its so-called internal improvements, which, by the way are all external and superficial, is just such an unwieldy and overgrown establishment, cluttered with furniture and tripped up by its own traps, ruined by luxury and heedless expense, by want of calculation and a worthy aim, as the million households in the land; and the only cure for it, as for them, is in a rigid economy, a stern and more than Spartan simplicity of life and elevation of purpose. It lives too fast. Men think that it is essential that the *Nation* have commerce, and export ice, and talk through a telegraph, and ride thirty miles an hour, without a doubt, whether *they* do or not; but whether we should live like baboons or like men, is a little uncertain. If we do not get out sleepers,[19] and forge rails, and devote days and nights to the work, but go to tinkering upon our *lives* to improve *them*, who will build railroads? And if railroads are not built, how shall we get to heaven in season? But if we stay at home and mind our business, who will want railroads? We do not ride on the railroad; it rides upon us. Did you ever think what those sleepers are that underlie the railroad? Each one is a man, an Irishman, or a Yankee man. The rails are laid on them, and they are covered with sand, and the cars run smoothly over them. They are sound sleepers, I assure you. And every few years a new lot is laid down

---

[15]From the *Westminster Shorter Catechism* of 1643, used by the Puritans in the *New England Primer*.

[16]According to a Greek fable, Aeacus begged Zeus to turn ants into men to increase the population; in Homer's *Iliad* (III, 3), the Trojans are compared to cranes, their enemies to pygmies.

[17]Finding a ship's position through calculations based on previous positions without astronomical observations.

[18]I.e., before the unification of Germany under Prince Otto von Bismarck (1815–1898) later in the century (1871).

[19]British term for wooden railway ties (clearly a pun).

and run over; so that, if some have the pleasure of riding on a rail, others have the misfortune to be ridden upon. And when they run over a man that is walking in his sleep, a supernumerary sleeper in the wrong position, and wake him up, they suddenly stop the cars, and make a hue and cry about it, as if this were an exception. I am glad to know that it takes a gang of men for every five miles to keep the sleepers down and level in their beds as it is, for this is a sign that they may sometime get up again.

Why should we live with such hurry and waste of life? We are determined to be starved before we are hungry. Men say that a stitch in time saves nine, and so they take a thousand stitches to-day to save nine to-morrow. As for *work,* we have n't any of any consequence. We have the Saint Vitus' dance,[20] and cannot possibly keep our heads still. If I should only give a few pulls at the parish bell-rope, as for a fire, that is, without setting[21] the bell, there is hardly a man on his farm in the outskirts of Concord, notwithstanding that press of engagements which was his excuse so many times this morning, nor a boy, nor a woman, I might almost say, but would forsake all and follow that sound, not mainly to save property from the flames, but, if we will confess the truth, much more to see it burn, since burn it must, and we, be it known, did not set it on fire,—or to see it put out, and have a hand in it, if that is done as handsomely; yes, even if it were the parish church itself. Hardly a man takes a half-hour's nap after dinner, but when he wakes he holds up his head and asks, "What's the news?" as if the rest of mankind had stood his sentinels. Some give directions to be waked every half-hour, doubtless for no other purpose; and then, to pay for it, they tell what they have dreamed. After a night's sleep the news is as indispensable as the breakfast. "Pray tell me anything new that has happened to a man anywhere on this globe,"—and he reads it over his coffee and rolls, that a man has had his eyes gouged out this morning on the Wachito River;[22] never dreaming the while that he lives in the dark unfathomed mammoth cave of this world, and has but the rudiment of an eye himself.

For my part, I could easily do without the post-office. I think that there are very few important communications made through it. To speak critically, I never received more than one or two letters in my life—I wrote this some years ago—that were worth the postage. The penny-post is, commonly, an institution through which you seriously offer a man that penny for his thoughts which is so often safely offered in jest. And I am sure that I never read any memorable news in a newspaper. If we read of one man robbed, or murdered, or killed by accident, or one house burned, or one vessel wrecked, or one steamboat blown up, or one cow run over on the Western Railroad, or one mad dog killed, or one lot of grasshoppers in the winter,—we never need read of another. One is enough. If you are acquainted with the principle, what do you care for a myriad instances and applications? To a philosopher all *news,* as it is called, is gossip, and they who edit and read it are old women over their tea. Yet not a few are greedy after this gossip. There was such a rush, as I hear, the other day at one of the offices to learn the foreign news by the last arrival, that several large squares of plate glass belonging to the establishment were broken by the pressure,—news which I seriously think a ready wit might write a twelvemonth, or twelve years, beforehand with sufficient accuracy. As for Spain, for instance, if you know how to throw in Don Carlos and the Infanta, and Don Pedro[23] and Seville and Granada, from time to time in the right proportions,—they may have changed the names a little since I saw the pa-

---

[20]Spastic movements caused by Sydenham's chorea, a nervous disorder.
[21]Inverting.
[22]Variant spelling of Ouachito, a river in southern Arkansas (then frontier country).

[23]Don Carlos and Don Pedro attempted to succeed King Ferdinand of Spain on his death in 1839; Princess Isabella was made queen in 1843.

pers,—and serve up a bull-fight when other entertainments fail, it will be true to the letter, and give us as good an idea of the exact state or ruin of things in Spain as the most succinct and lucid reports under this head in the newspapers: and as for England, almost the last significant scrap of news from that quarter was the revolution of 1649;[24] and if you have learned the history of her crops for an average year, you never need attend to that thing again, unless your speculations are of a merely pecuniary character. If one may judge who rarely looks into the newspapers, nothing new does ever happen in foreign parts, a French revolution[25] not excepted.

What news! how much more important to know what that is which was never old! "Kieou-pe-yu (great dignitary of the state of Wei) sent a man to Khoung-tseu to know his news. Khoung-tseu caused the messenger to be seated near him, and questioned him in these terms: What is your master doing? The messenger answered with respect: My master desires to diminish the number of his faults, but he cannot come to the end of them. The messenger being gone, the philosopher remarked: What a worthy messenger! What a worthy messenger!"[26] The preacher, instead of vexing the ears of drowsy farmers on their day of rest at the end of the week,—for Sunday is the fit conclusion of an ill-spent week, and not the fresh and brave beginning of a new one,—with this one other draggle-tail of a sermon, should shout with thundering voice, "Pause! Avast! Why so seeming fast, but deadly slow?"[27]

Shams and delusions are esteemed for soundest truths, while reality is fabulous. If men would steadily observe realities only, and not allow themselves to be deluded, life, to compare it with such things as we know, would be like a fairy tale and the Arabian Nights' Entertainments. If we respected only what is inevitable and has a right to be, music and poetry would resound along the streets. When we are unhurried and wise, we perceive that only great and worthy things have any permanent and absolute existence, that petty fears and petty pleasures are but the shadow of the reality. This is always exhilarating and sublime. By closing the eyes and slumbering, and consenting to be deceived by shows, men establish and confirm their daily life of routine and habit everywhere, which still is built on purely illusory foundations. Children, who play life, discern its true law and relations more clearly than men, who fail to live it worthily, but who think that they are wiser by experience, that is, by failure. I have read in a Hindoo book, that "there was a king's son, who, being expelled in infancy from his native city, was brought up by a forester, and, growing up to maturity in that state, imagined himself to belong to the barbarous race with which he lived. One of his father's ministers having discovered him, revealed to him what he was, and the misconception of his character was removed, and he knew himself to be a prince. So soul," continues the Hindoo philosopher, "from the circumstances in which it is placed, mistakes its own character, until the truth is revealed to it by some holy teacher, and then it knows itself to be *Brahme*."[28] I perceive that we inhabitants of New England live this mean life that we do because our vision does not penetrate the surface of things. We think that that *is* which *appears* to be. If a man should walk through this town and see only the reality, where, think you, would the "Mill-dam"[29] go to? If he should give us an account of the realities he beheld there, we should not recognize the place in his description. Look at a meeting-house, or a court-house, or a jail, or a shop, or a dwelling-house, and say what that thing really is before a

---

[24]In 1649 Charles I of England was beheaded and the monarchy replaced by the Commonwealth, headed by Oliver Cromwell.

[25]The French Revolution of 1789 was the first of several upheavals in France, one of which was the French Revolution of 1848.

[26]Confucius, *Analects*, XIV, 26, 1–2.

[27]The nautical terminology has suggested to some readers that reference is to Father Taylor of Seamans Bethel (Boston), the original of Herman Melville's Father Mapple in *Moby-Dick*.

[28]Variant of Brahma, Hindu god who is the essence of all being. Cf. Emerson's "Over-Soul" and his poem "Brahma."

[29]The central or main street of Concord.

true gaze, and they would all go to pieces in your account of them. Men esteem truth remote, in the outskirts of the system, behind the farthest star, before Adam and after the last man. In eternity there is indeed something true and sublime. But all these times and places and occasions are now and here. God himself culminates in the present moment, and will never be more divine in the lapse of all the ages. And we are enabled to apprehend at all what is sublime and noble only by the perpetual instilling and drenching of the reality that surrounds us. The universe constantly and obediently answers to our conceptions; whether we travel fast or slow, the track is laid for us. Let us spend our lives in conceiving then. The poet or the artist never yet had so fair and noble a design but some of his posterity at least could accomplish it.

Let us spend one day as deliberately as Nature, and not be thrown off the track by every nutshell and mosquito's wing that falls on the rails. Let us rise early and fast, or break fast, gently and without perturbation; let company come and let company go, let the bells ring and the children cry,—determined to make a day of it. Why should we knock under and go with the stream? Let us not be upset and overwhelmed in that terrible rapid and whirlpool called a dinner, situated in the meridian shallows. Weather this danger and you are safe, for the rest of the way is down hill. With unrelaxed nerves, with morning vigor, sail by it, looking another way, tied to the mast like Ulysses.[30] If the engine whistles, let it whistle till it is hoarse for its pains. If the bell rings, why should we run? We will consider what kind of music they are like. Let us settle ourselves, and work and wedge our feet downward through the mud and slush of opinion, and prejudice, and tradition, and delusion, and appearance, that alluvion[31] which covers the globe, through Paris and London, through New York and Boston and Concord, through Church and State, through poetry and philosophy and religion, till we come to a hard bottom and rocks in place, which we can call *reality*, and say, This is, and no mistake; and then begin, having a *point d'appui*,[32] below freshet and frost and fire, a place where you might found a wall or a state, or set a lamp-post safely, or perhaps a gauge, not a Nilometer,[33] but a Realometer, that future ages might know how deep a freshet of shams and appearances had gathered from time to time. If you stand right fronting and face to face to a fact, you will see the sun glimmer on both its surfaces, as if it were a cimeter,[34] and feel its sweet edge dividing you through the heart and marrow, and so you will happily conclude your mortal career. Be it life or death, we crave only reality. If we are really dying, let us hear the rattle in our throats and feel cold in the extremities; if we are alive, let us go about our business.

Time is but the stream I go a-fishing in. I drink at it; but while I drink I see the sandy bottom and detect how shallow it is. Its thin current slides away, but eternity remains. I would drink deeper; fish in the sky, whose bottom is pebbly with stars. I cannot count one. I know not the first letter of the alphabet. I have always been regretting that I was not as wise as the day I was born. The intellect is a cleaver; it discerns and rifts its way into the secret of things. I do not wish to be any more busy with my hands than is necessary. My head is hands and feet. I feel all my best faculties concentrated in it. My instinct tells me that my head is an organ for burrowing, as some creatures use their snout and fore paws, and with it I would mine and burrow my way through these hills. I think that the richest vein is somewhere hereabouts; so by the divining-rod and thin rising vapors I judge; and here I will begin to mine.

---

[30]In Homer's *Odyssey*, Ulysses (or Odysseus) had himself bound to the mast so that, on passing the Sirens, he would not be bewitched by their songs and lured to jump into the sea.

[31]Sediment deposited on the banks by flowing rivers or streams.

[32]"Support," or "fulcrum" (French).

[33]A gauge used in ancient times on the Nile to indicate the level of the water at flood time.

[34]Variant of scimitar, a sword with a curved blade.

III

READING

With a little more deliberation in the choice of their pursuits, all men would perhaps become essentially students and observers, for certainly their nature and destiny are interesting to all alike. In accumulating property for ourselves or our posterity, in founding a family or a state, or acquiring fame even, we are mortal; but in dealing with truth we are immortal, and need fear no change nor accident. The oldest Egyptian or Hindoo philosopher raised a corner of the veil from the statue of the divinity; and still the trembling robe remains raised, and I gaze upon as fresh a glory as he did, since it was I in him that was then so bold, and it is he in me that now reviews the vision. No dust has settled on that robe; no time has elapsed since that divinity was revealed. That time which we really improve, or which is improvable, is neither past, present, nor future.

My residence was more favorable, not only to thought, but to serious reading, than a university; and though I was beyond the range of the ordinary circulating library, I had more than ever come within the influence of those books which circulate round the world, whose sentences were first written on bark, and are now merely copied from time to time on to linen paper. Says the poet Mîr Camar Uddîn Mast,[1] "Being seated, to run through the region of the spiritual world; I have had this advantage in books. To be intoxicated by a single glass of wine; I have experienced this pleasure when I have drunk the liquor of the esoteric doctrines." I kept Homer's Iliad on my table through the summer, though I looked at his page only now and then. Incessant labor with my hands, at first, for I had my house to finish and my beans to hoe at the same time, made more study impossible. Yet I sustained myself by the prospect of such reading in future. I read one or two shallow books of travel in the intervals of my work, till that employment made me ashamed of myself, and I asked where it was then that *I* lived.

The student may read Homer or Æschylus in the Greek without danger of dissipation or luxuriousness, for it implies that he in some measure emulate their heroes, and consecrate morning hours to their pages. The heroic books, even if printed in the character of our mother tongue, will always be in a language dead to degenerate times; and we must laboriously seek the meaning of each word and line, conjecturing a larger sense than common use permits out of what wisdom and valor and generosity we have. The modern cheap and fertile press, with all its translations, has done little to bring us nearer to the heroic writers of antiquity. They seem as solitary, and the letter in which they are printed as rare and curious, as ever. It is worth the expense of youthful days and costly hours, if you learn only some words of an ancient language, which are raised out of the trivialness of the street, to be perpetual suggestions and provocations. It is not in vain that the farmer remembers and repeats the few Latin words which he has heard. Men sometimes speak as if the study of the classics would at length make way for more modern and practical studies; but the adventurous student will always study classics, in whatever language they may be written and however ancient they may be. For what are the classics but the noblest recorded thoughts of man? They are the only oracles which are not decayed, and there are such answers to the most modern inquiry in them as Delphi and Dodona[2] never gave. We might as well omit to study Nature because she is old. To read well, that is, to read true books in a true spirit, is a noble exercise, and one that will task the reader more than any exercise which the customs of the day esteem. It requires a training such as the athletes

---

[1] Eighteenth-century Hindu poet; Thoreau translated this passage from a French history of Hindu literature.
[2] Delphi, the oracle of Apollo; Dodona, oracle of Zeus.

underwent, the steady intention almost of the whole life to this object. Books must be read as deliberately and reservedly as they were written. It is not enough even to be able to speak the language of that nation by which they are written, for there is a memorable interval between the spoken and the written language, the language heard and the language read. The one is commonly transitory, a sound, a tongue, a dialect merely, almost brutish, and we learn it unconsciously, like the brutes, of our mothers. The other is the maturity and experience of that; if that is our mother tongue, this is our father tongue, a reserved and select expression, too significant to be heard by the ear, which we must be born again in order to speak. The crowds of men who merely *spoke* the Greek and Latin tongues in the Middle Ages were not entitled by the accident of birth to *read* the works of genius written in those languages; for these were not written in that Greek or Latin which they knew, but in the select language of literature. They had not learned the nobler dialects of Greece and Rome, but the very materials on which they were written were waste paper to them, and they prized instead a cheap contemporary literature. But when the several nations of Europe had acquired distinct though rude written languages of their own, sufficient for the purposes of their rising literatures, then first learning revived, and scholars were enabled to discern from that remoteness the treasures of antiquity. What the Roman and Grecian multitude could not *hear,* after the lapse of ages a few scholars *read,* and a few scholars only are still reading it.

However much we may admire the orator's occasional bursts of eloquence, the noblest written words are commonly as far behind or above the fleeting spoken language as the firmament with its stars is behind the clouds. *There* are the stars, and they who can may read them. The astronomers forever comment on and observe them. They are not exhalations like our daily colloquies and vaporous breath. What is called eloquence in the forum is commonly found to be rhetoric in the study. The orator yields to the inspiration of a transient occasion, and speaks to the mob before him, to those who can *hear* him; but the writer, whose more equable life is his occasion, and who would be distracted by the event and the crowd which inspire the orator, speaks to the intellect and heart of mankind, to all in any age who can *understand* him.

No wonder that Alexander[3] carried the Iliad with him on his expeditions in a precious casket. A written word is the choicest of relics. It is something at once more intimate with us and more universal than any other work of art. It is the work of art nearest to life itself. It may be translated into every language, and not only be read but actually breathed from all human lips;—not be represented on canvas or in marble only, but be carved out of the breath of life itself. The symbol of an ancient man's thought becomes a modern man's speech. Two thousand summers have imparted to the monuments of Grecian literature, as to her marbles, only a maturer golden and autumnal tint, for they have carried their own serene and celestial atmosphere into all lands to protect them against the corrosion of time. Books are the treasured wealth of the world and the fit inheritance of generations and nations. Books, the oldest and the best, stand naturally and rightfully on the shelves of every cottage. They have no cause of their own to plead, but while they enlighten and sustain the reader his common sense will not refuse them. Their authors are a natural and irresistible aristocracy in every society, and, more than kings or emperors, exert an influence on mankind. When the illiterate and perhaps scornful trader has earned by enterprise and industry his coveted leisure and independence, and is admitted to the circles of wealth and fashion, he

---

[3]Alexander the Great (356–323 B.C.), according to Plutarch's *Lives,* carried the *Iliad* with him in a special box on his expeditions to conquer Greece and Persia.

turns inevitably at last to those still higher but yet inaccessible circles of intellect and genius, and is sensible only of the imperfection of his culture and the vanity and insufficiency of all his riches, and further proves his good sense by the pains which he takes to secure for his children that intellectual culture whose want he so keenly feels; and thus it is that he becomes the founder of a family.

Those who have not learned to read the ancient classics in the language in which they were written must have a very imperfect knowledge of the history of the human race; for it is remarkable that no transcript of them has ever been made into any modern tongue, unless our civilization itself may be regarded as such a transcript. Homer has never yet been printed in English, nor Æschylus, nor Virgil even,—works as refined, as solidly done, and as beautiful almost as the morning itself; for later writers, say what we will of their genius, have rarely, if ever, equalled the elaborate beauty and finish and the lifelong and heroic literary labors of the ancients. They only talk of forgetting them who never knew them. It will be soon enough to forget them when we have the learning and the genius which will enable us to attend to and appreciate them. That age will be rich indeed when those relics which we call Classics, and the still older and more than classic but even less known Scriptures of the nations, shall have still further accumulated, when the Vaticans[4] shall be filled with Vedas and Zendavestas and Bibles, with Homers and Dantes and Shakespeares, and all the centuries to come shall have successively deposited their trophies in the forum of the world. By such a pile we may hope to scale heaven at last.

The works of the great poets have never yet been read by mankind, for only great poets can read them. They have only been read as the multitude read the stars, at most astrologically, not astronomically. Most men have learned to read to serve a paltry convenience, as they have learned to cipher in order to keep accounts and not be cheated in trade; but of reading as a noble intellectual exercise they know little or nothing; yet this only is reading, in a high sense, not that which lulls us as a luxury and suffers the nobler faculties to sleep the while, but what we have to stand on tip-toe to read and devote our most alert and wakeful hours to.

I think that having learned our letters we should read the best that is in literature, and not be forever repeating our a-b-abs, and words of one syllable, in the fourth or fifth classes, sitting on the lowest and foremost form all our lives.[5] Most men are satisfied if they read or hear read, and perchance have been convicted by the wisdom of one good book, the Bible, and for the rest of their lives vegetate and dissipate their faculties in what is called easy reading. There is a work in several volumes in our Circulating Library entitled "Little Reading,"[6] which I thought referred to a town of that name which I had not been to. There are those who, like cormorants and ostriches, can digest all sorts of this, even after the fullest dinner of meats and vegetables, for they suffer nothing to be wasted. If others are the machines to provide this provender, they are the machines to read it. They read the nine thousandth tale about Zebulon and Sophronia,[7] and how they loved as none had ever loved before, and neither did the course of their true love run smooth,—at any rate, how it did run and stumble, and get up again and go on! how some poor unfortunate got up on to a steeple, who had better never have gone up as far as the belfry; and then, having needlessly got him up there, the happy novelist rings the bell for all the world to come together and hear, O dear! how he did get down again! For my part, I think that they had better metamor-

---

[4]I.e., libraries of the world's serious, especially religious, literature (after the Vatican, the home of the Catholic faith and popes in Rome, containing important archives and libraries). The Zendavestas are sacred Zoroastrian texts.
[5]I.e., in the one-room schoolhouse, the youngest children sat on the low seats up front.

[6]As Harding in *The Variorum Walden* points out, there was a book extant at the time called *Much Instruction from Little Reading*, listed in the 1836 *Catalogue* of the Concord Social Library.
[7]Apparently symbolic names for leading characters in popular sentimental fiction.

phose all such aspiring heroes of universal noveldom into man weather-cocks, as they used to put heroes among the constellations, and let them swing round there till they are rusty, and not come down at all to bother honest men with their pranks. The next time the novelist rings the bell I will not stir though the meeting-house burn down. "The Skip of the Tip-Toe-Hop, a Romance of the Middle Ages, by the celebrated author of 'Tittle-Tol-Tan,' to appear in monthly parts; a great rush; don't all come together."[8] All this they read with saucer eyes, and erect and primitive curiosity, and with unwearied gizzard, whose corrugations even yet need no sharpening, just as some little four-year-old bencher[9] his two-cent gilt-covered edition of Cinderella,—without any improvement, that I can see, in the pronunciation, or accent, or emphasis, or any more skill in extracting or inserting the moral. The result is dullness of sight, a stagnation of the vital circulations, and a general deliquium[10] and sloughing off of all the intellectual faculties. This sort of gingerbread is baked daily and more sedulously than pure wheat or rye-and-Indian in almost every oven, and finds a surer market.

The best books are not read even by those who are called good readers. What does our Concord culture amount to? There is in this town, with a very few exceptions, no taste for the best or for very good books even in English literature, whose words all can read and spell. Even the college-bred and so-called liberally educated men here and elsewhere have really little or no acquaintance with the English classics; and as for the recorded wisdom of mankind, the ancient classics and Bibles, which are accessible to all who will know of them, there are the feeblest efforts anywhere made to become acquainted with them. I know a wood-chopper, of middle age, who takes a French paper, not for news as he says, for he is above that, but to "keep himself in practice," he being a Canadian by birth; and when I ask him what he considers the best thing he can do in this world, he says, beside this, to keep up and add to his English. This is about as much as the college-bred generally do or aspire to do, and they take an English paper for the purpose. One who has just come from reading perhaps one of the best English books will find how many with whom he can converse about it? Or suppose he comes from reading a Greek or Latin classic in the original, whose praises are familiar even to the so-called illiterate; he will find nobody at all to speak to, but must keep silence about it. Indeed, there is hardly the professor in our colleges, who, if he has mastered the difficulties of the language, has proportionally mastered the difficulties of the wit and poetry of a Greek poet, and has any sympathy to impart to the alert and heroic reader; and as for the sacred Scriptures, or Bibles of mankind, who in this town can tell me even their titles? Most men do not know that any nation but the Hebrews have had a scripture. A man, any man, will go considerably out of his way to pick up a silver dollar; but here are golden words, which the wisest men of antiquity have uttered, and whose worth the wise of every succeeding age have assured us of;—and yet we learn to read only as far as Easy Reading, the primers and class-books, and when we leave school, the "Little Reading," and story-books, which are for boys and beginners; and our reading, our conversation and thinking, are all on a very low level, worthy only of pygmies and manikins.

I aspire to be acquainted with wiser men than this our Concord soil has produced, whose names are hardly known here. Or shall I hear the name of Plato and never read his book? As if Plato were my townsman and I never saw him,—my next neighbor and I never heard him speak or attended to the wisdom of his

---

[8]The titles seem to have been invented by Thoreau.
[9]Another reference to the youngest children in the one-room schoolhouse sitting on benches up front.
[10]A loss of vitality or energy.

words. But how actually is it? His Dialogues, which contain what was immortal in him, lie on the next shelf, and yet I never read them. We are underbred and low-lived and illiterate; and in this respect I confess I do not make any very broad distinction between the illiterateness of my townsman who cannot read at all and the illiterateness of him who has learned to read only what is for children and feeble intellects. We should be as good as the worthies of antiquity, but partly by first knowing how good they were. We are a race of tit-men,[11] and soar but little higher in our intellectual flights than the columns of the daily paper.

It is not all books that are as dull as their readers. There are probably words addressed to our condition exactly, which, if we could really hear and understand, would be more salutary than the morning or the spring to our lives, and possibly put a new aspect on the face of things for us. How many a man has dated a new era in his life from the reading of a book! The book exists for us, perchance, which will explain our miracles and reveal new ones. The at present unutterable things we may find somewhere uttered. These same questions that disturb and puzzle and confound us have in their turn occurred to all the wise men; not one has been omitted; and each has answered them, according to his ability, by his words and his life. Moreover, with wisdom we shall learn liberality. The solitary hired man on a farm in the outskirts of Concord, who has had his second birth and peculiar religious experience,[12] and is driven as he believes into silent gravity and exclusiveness by his faith, may think it is not true; but Zoroaster,[13] thousands of years ago, travelled the same road and had the same experience; but he, being wise, knew it to be universal, and treated his neighbors accordingly, and is even said to have invented and established worship among men. Let him humbly commune with Zoroaster then, and through the liberalizing influence of all the worthies, with Jesus Christ himself, and let "our church" go by the board.

We boast that we belong to the Nineteenth Century and are making the most rapid strides of any nation. But consider how little this village does for its own culture. I do not wish to flatter my townsmen, nor to be flattered by them, for that will not advance either of us. We need to be provoked,—goaded like oxen, as we are, into a trot. We have a comparatively decent system of common schools, schools for infants only; but excepting the half-starved Lyceum[14] in the winter, and latterly the puny beginning of a library suggested by the State, no school for ourselves. We spend more on almost any article of bodily aliment or ailment than on our mental aliment. It is time that we had uncommon schools, that we did not leave off our education when we begin to be men and women. It is time that villages were universities, and their elder inhabitants the fellows of universities, with leisure—if they are, indeed, so well off—to pursue liberal studies the rest of their lives. Shall the world be confined to one Paris[15] or one Oxford forever? Cannot students be boarded here and get a liberal education under the skies of Concord? Can we not hire some Abélard[16] to lecture to us? Alas! what with foddering the cattle and tending the store, we are kept from school too long, and our education is sadly neglected. In this country, the village should in some respects take the place of the nobleman of Europe. It should be the patron of the fine arts. It is rich enough. It wants only the magnanimity and refinement. It can spend money enough on such things as farmers and traders value, but it is thought Utopian to propose spending money for things which more intelligent men know to be of far

---

[11]Little, not in size, but in intellectual, spiritual, or moral growth; cf. tit-mice (small mice).

[12]I.e., conversion or spiritual rebirth.

[13]Variant of the name Zarathustra, a Persian religious leader (fl. about the sixth century B.C.); after experiencing a divine revelation, he founded the new religion of Zoroastrianism with its religious texts the *Zend Avesta.* In its origin, it was a religion of nature, with only outdoor altars.

[14]Named after the grove near Athens, where Aristotle taught, the nineteenth-century Lyceum was a lecture system that brought such figures as Emerson and Thoreau to a local public hall for lecturing on various topics.

[15]I.e., the Sorbonne University.

[16]Peter Abélard (1079–1142), one of the great philosophers and teachers of medieval France.

more worth. This town has spent seventeen thousand dollars on a town-house, thank fortune or politics, but probably it will not spend so much on living wit, the true meat to put into that shell, in a hundred years. The one hundred and twenty-five dollars annually subscribed for a Lyceum in the winter is better spent than any other equal sum raised in the town. If we live in the Nineteenth Century, why should we not enjoy the advantages which the Nineteenth Century offers? Why should our life be in any respect provincial? If we will read newspapers, why not skip the gossip of Boston and take the best newspaper in the world at once?—not be sucking the pap of "neutral family" papers, or browsing "Olive-Branches"[17] here in New England. Let the reports of all the learned societies come to us, and we will see if they know anything. Why should we leave it to Harper & Brothers and Redding & Co.[18] to select our reading? As the nobleman of cultivated taste surrounds himself with whatever conduces to his culture,—genius—learning—wit—books—paintings—statuary—music—philosophical instruments, and the like; so let the village do,—not stop short at a pedagogue, a parson, a sexton, a parish library, and three selectmen, because our Pilgrim forefathers got through a cold winter once on a bleak rock with these. To act collectively is according to the spirit of our institutions; and I am confident that, as our circumstances are more flourishing, our means are greater than the nobleman's. New England can hire all the wise men in the world to come and teach her, and board them round the while, and not be provincial at all. That is the *uncommon* school we want. Instead of noblemen, let us have noble villages of men. If it is necessary, omit one bridge over the river, go round a little there, and throw one arch at least over the darker gulf of ignorance which surrounds us.

IV

SOUNDS

But while we are confined to books, though the most select and classic, and read only particular written languages, which are themselves but dialects and provincial, we are in danger of forgetting the language which all things and events speak without metaphor, which alone is copious and standard. Much is published, but little printed. The rays which stream through the shutter will be no longer remembered when the shutter is wholly removed. No method nor discipline can supersede the necessity of being forever on the alert. What is a course of history or philosophy, or poetry, no matter how well selected, or the best society, or the most admirable routine of life, compared with the discipline of looking always at what is to be seen? Will you be a reader, a student merely, or a seer? Read your fate, see what is before you, and walk on into futurity.

I did not read books the first summer; I hoed beans. Nay, I often did better than this. There were times when I could not afford to sacrifice the bloom of the present moment to any work, whether of the head or hands. I love a broad margin to my life. Sometimes, in a summer morning, having taken my accustomed bath, I sat in my sunny doorway from sunrise till noon, rapt in a revery, amidst the pines and hickories and sumachs, in undisturbed solitude and stillness, while the birds sang around or flitted noiseless through the house, until by the sun falling in at my west window, or the noise of some traveller's wagon on the distant highway, I was reminded of the lapse of time. I grew in those seasons like corn in the night, and they were far better than any work of the hands would have been. They were not time subtracted from my life, but so much over and above my usual allowance. I realized what the Orientals mean by contemplation and the for-

---

[17]A Methodist weekly newspaper.
[18]New York publishing house and Boston bookseller, respectively.

saking of works. For the most part, I minded not how the hours went. The day advanced as if to light some work of mine; it was morning, and lo, now it is evening, and nothing memorable is accomplished. Instead of singing like the birds, I silently smiled at my incessant good fortune. As the sparrow had its trill, sitting on the hickory before my door, so had I my chuckle or suppressed warble which he might hear out of my nest. My days were not days of the week, bearing the stamp of any heathen deity,[1] nor were they minced into hours and fretted by the ticking of a clock; for I lived like the Puri Indians,[2] of whom it is said that "for yesterday, to-day, and to-morrow they have only one word, and they express the variety of meaning by pointing backward for yesterday, forward for to-morrow, and overhead for the passing day." This was sheer idleness to my fellow-townsmen, no doubt; but if the birds and flowers had tried me by their standard, I should not have been found wanting. A man must find his occasions in himself, it is true. The natural day is very calm, and will hardly reprove his indolence.

I had this advantage, at least, in my mode of life, over those who were obliged to look abroad for amusement, to society and the theatre, that my life itself was become my amusement and never ceased to be novel. It was a drama of many scenes and without an end. If we were always, indeed, getting our living, and reg-ulating our lives according to the last and best mode we had learned, we should never be troubled with ennui. Follow your genius closely enough, and it will not fail to show you a fresh prospect every hour. Housework was a pleasant pastime. When my floor was dirty, I rose early, and, setting all my furniture out of doors on the grass, bed and bedstead making but one budget,[3] dashed water on the floor, and sprinkled white sand from the pond on it, and then with a broom scrubbed it clean and white; and by the time the villagers had broken their fast the morning sun had dried my house sufficiently to allow me to move in again, and my meditations were almost uninterrupted. It was pleasant to see my whole household effects out on the grass, making a little pile like a gypsy's pack, and my three-legged table, from which I did not remove the books and pen and ink, standing amid the pines and hickories. They seemed glad to get out themselves, and as if unwilling to be brought in. I was sometimes tempted to stretch an aw-ning over them and take my seat there. It was worth the while to see the sun shine on these things, and hear the free wind blow on them; so much more interesting most familiar objects look out of doors than in the house. A bird sits on the next bough, life-everlasting grows under the table, and blackberry vines run round its legs; pine cones, chestnut burs, and strawberry leaves are strewn about. It looked as if this was the way these forms came to be transferred to our furniture, to ta-bles, chairs, and bedsteads,—because they once stood in their midst.

My house was on the side of a hill, immediately on the edge of the larger wood, in the midst of a young forest of pitch pines and hickories, and half a dozen rods[4] from the pond, to which a narrow footpath led down the hill. In my front yard grew the strawberry, blackberry, and life-everlasting, johnswort and goldenrod, shrub oaks and sand cherry, blueberry and groundnut. Near the end of May, the sand cherry (*Cerasus pumila*) adorned the sides of the path with its delicate flowers arranged in umbels cylindrically about its short stems, which last, in the fall, weighed down with good-sized and handsome cherries, fell over in wreaths like rays on every side. I tasted them out of compliment to Nature, though they were scarcely palatable. The sumach (*Rhus glabra*) grew luxuriantly about the house, pushing up through the embankment which I had made, and growing five or six

---

[1]The days in English are named after pagan gods, as, for example, Saturday after the Roman Saturn, god of agricul-ture.
[2]Brazilian tribe, described in the Austrian traveller Ida Pfeif-fer's *A Lady's Voyage Round the World* (1852).

[3]Collection of items.
[4]A rod equals 16½ feet.

feet the first season. Its broad pinnate tropical leaf was pleasant though strange to look on. The large buds, suddenly pushing out late in the spring from dry sticks which had seemed to be dead, developed themselves as by magic into graceful green and tender boughs, an inch in diameter; and sometimes, as I sat at my window, so heedlessly did they grow and tax their weak joints, I heard a fresh and tender bough suddenly fall like a fan to the ground, when there was not a breath of air stirring, broken off by its own weight. In August, the large masses of berries, which, when in flower, had attracted many wild bees, gradually assumed their bright velvety crimson hue, and by their weight again bent down and broke the tender limbs.

As I sit at my window this summer afternoon, hawks are circling about my clearing; the tantivy[5] of wild pigeons, flying by twos and threes athwart my view, or perching restless on the white pine boughs behind my house, gives a voice to the air; a fish hawk dimples the glassy surface of the pond and brings up a fish; a mink steals out of the marsh before my door and seizes a frog by the shore; the sedge is bending under the weight of the reed-birds flitting hither and thither; and for the last half-hour I have heard the rattle of railroad cars, now dying away and then reviving like the beat of a partridge, conveying travellers from Boston to the country. For I did not live so out of the world as that boy who, as I hear, was put out to a farmer in the east part of the town, but ere long ran away and came home again, quite down at the heel and homesick. He had never seen such a dull and out-of-the-way place; the folks were all gone off; why, you couldn't even hear the whistle! I doubt if there is such a place in Massachusetts now:—

> "In truth, our village has become a butt
> For one of those fleet railroad shafts, and o'er
> Our peaceful plain its soothing sound is—Concord."[6]

The Fitchburg Railroad touches the pond about a hundred rods south of where I dwell. I usually go to the village along its causeway, and am, as it were, related to society by this link. The men on the freight trains, who go over the whole length of the road, bow to me as to an old acquaintance, they pass me so often, and apparently they take me for an employee; and so I am. I too would fain be a track-repairer somewhere in the orbit of the earth.

The whistle of the locomotive penetrates my woods summer and winter, sounding like the scream of a hawk sailing over some farmer's yard, informing me that many restless city merchants are arriving within the circle of the town, or adventurous country traders from the other side. As they come under one horizon, they shout their warning to get off the track to the other, heard sometimes through the circles of two towns. Here come your groceries, country; your rations, countrymen! Nor is there any man so independent on his farm that he can say them nay. And here's your pay for them! screams the countryman's whistle; timber like long battering-rams going twenty miles an hour against the city's walls, and chairs enough to seat all the weary and heavy-laden that dwell within them. With such huge and lumbering civility the country hands a chair to the city. All the Indian huckleberry hills are stripped, all the cranberry meadows are raked into the city. Up comes the cotton, down goes the woven cloth; up comes the silk, down goes the woollen; up come the books, but down goes the wit that writes them.

When I meet the engine with its train of cars moving off with planetary motion,—or, rather, like a comet, for the beholder knows not if with that velocity and

---

[5]Rushing movement.
[6]From "Walden Spring" by Ellery Channing (1818–1901),
resident of Concord and friend of Thoreau.

with that direction it will ever revisit this system, since its orbit does not look like a returning curve,—with its steam cloud like a banner streaming behind in golden and silver wreaths, like many a downy cloud which I have seen, high in the heavens, unfolding its masses to the light,—as if this travelling demigod, this cloud-compeller, would ere long take the sunset sky for the livery of his train; when I hear the iron horse make the hills echo with his snort like thunder, shaking the earth with his feet, and breathing fire and smoke from his nostrils (what kind of winged horse or fiery dragon they will put into the new Mythology I don't know), it seems as if the earth had got a race now worthy to inhabit it. If all were as it seems, and men made the elements their servants for noble ends! If the cloud that hangs over the engine were the perspiration of heroic deeds, or as beneficent as that which floats over the farmer's fields, then the elements and Nature herself would cheerfully accompany men on their errands and be their escort.

I watch the passage of the morning cars with the same feeling that I do the rising of the sun, which is hardly more regular. Their train of clouds stretching far behind and rising higher and higher, going to heaven while the cars are going to Boston, conceals the sun for a minute and casts my distant field into the shade, a celestial train[7] beside which the petty train of cars which hugs the earth is but the barb of the spear. The stabler of the iron horse was up early this winter morning by the light of the stars amid the mountains, to fodder and harness his steed. Fire, too, was awakened thus early to put the vital heat in him and get him off. If the enterprise were as innocent as it is early! If the snow lies deep, they strap on his snowshoes, and, with the giant plow, plow a furrow from the mountains to the seaboard, in which the cars, like a following drill-barrow,[8] sprinkle all the restless men and floating merchandise in the country for seed. All day the fire-steed flies over the country, stopping only that his master may rest, and I am awakened by his tramp and defiant snort at midnight, when in some remote glen in the woods he fronts the elements incased in ice and snow; and he will reach his stall only with the morning star, to start once more on his travels without rest or slumber. Or perchance, at evening, I hear him in his stable blowing off the superfluous energy of the day, that he may calm his nerves and cool his liver and brain for a few hours of iron slumber. If the enterprise were as heroic and commanding as it is protracted and unwearied!

Far through unfrequented woods on the confines of towns, where once only the hunter penetrated by day, in the darkest night dart these bright saloons without the knowledge of their inhabitants; this moment stopping at some brilliant station-house in town or city, where a social crowd is gathered, the next in the Dismal Swamp,[9] scaring the owl and fox. The startings and arrivals of the cars are now the epochs in the village day. They go and come with such regularity and precision, and their whistle can be heard so far, that the farmers set their clocks by them, and thus one well-conducted institution regulates a whole country. Have not men improved somewhat in punctuality since the railroad was invented? Do they not talk and think faster in the depot than they did in the stage-office? There is something electrifying in the atmosphere of the former place. I have been astonished at the miracles it has wrought; that some of my neighbors, who, I should have prophesied, once for all, would never get to Boston by so prompt a conveyance, are on hand when the bell rings. To do things "railroad fashion" is now the byword; and it is worth the while to be warned so often and so sincerely by any power to get off its track. There is no stopping to read the riot act, no firing over

---

[7]Allusion to the short story "The Celestial Railroad," by Nathaniel Hawthorne.
[8]Agricultural machine that dug holes and dropped seeds, topping them with soil.

[9]An almost impassable marshy area in Virginia and North Carolina.

the heads of the mob, in this case. We have constructed a fate, an *Atropos*,[10] that never turns aside. (Let that be the name of your engine.) Men are advertised that at a certain hour and minute these bolts will be shot toward particular points of the compass; yet it interferes with no man's business, and the children go to school on the other track. We live the steadier for it. We are all educated thus to be sons of Tell.[11] The air is full of invisible bolts. Every path but your own is the path of fate. Keep on your own track, then.

What recommends commerce to me is its enterprise and bravery. It does not clasp its hands and pray to Jupiter. I see these men every day go about their business with more or less courage and content, doing more even than they suspect, and perchance better employed than they could have consciously devised. I am less affected by their heroism who stood up for half an hour in the front line at Buena Vista,[12] than by the steady and cheerful valor of the men who inhabit the snow-plow for their winter quarters; who have not merely the three-o'-clock-in-the-morning courage, which Bonaparte thought was the rarest, but whose courage does not go to rest so early, who go to sleep only when the storm sleeps or the sinews of their iron steed are frozen. On this morning of the Great Snow,[13] perchance, which is still raging and chilling men's blood, I hear the muffled tone of their engine bell from out the fog bank of their chilled breath, which announces that the cars *are coming*, without long delay, notwithstanding the veto of a New England northeast snow-storm, and I behold the plowmen covered with snow and rime,[14] their heads peering above the mould-board which is turning down other than daisies and the nests of field mice, like bowlders of the Sierra Nevada, that occupy an outside place in the universe.

Commerce is unexpectedly confident and serene, alert, adventurous, and unwearied. It is very natural in its methods withal, far more so than many fantastic enterprises and sentimental experiments, and hence its singular success. I am refreshed and expanded when the freight train rattles past me, and I smell the stores which go dispensing their odors all the way from Long Wharf to Lake Champlain,[15] reminding me of foreign parts, of coral reefs, and Indian oceans, and tropical climes, and the extent of the globe. I feel more like a citizen of the world at the sight of the palm-leaf which will cover so many flaxen New England heads the next summer, the Manilla hemp and cocoanut husks, the old junk, gunny bags, scrap iron, and rusty nails. This carload of torn sails is more legible and interesting now than if they should be wrought into paper and printed books. Who can write so graphically the history of the storms they have weathered as these rents have done? They are proof-sheets which need no correction. Here goes lumber from the Maine woods, which did not go out to sea in the last freshet, risen four dollars on the thousand because of what did go out or was split up; pine, spruce, cedar,—first, second, third, and fourth qualities, so lately all of one quality, to wave over the bear, and moose, and caribou. Next rolls Thomaston[16] lime, a prime lot, which will get far among the hills before it gets slacked. These rags in bales, of all hues and qualities, the lowest condition to which cotton and linen descend, the final result of dress,—of patterns which are now no longer cried up,[17] unless it be in Milwaukee, as those splendid articles, English, French, or American prints, ginghams, muslins, etc., gathered from all quarters both of

---

[10]One of the three Fates, Atropos cuts the thread of human life.
[11]William Tell, legendary Swiss hero, who was compelled to shoot an arrow into an apple placed on his son's head.
[12]In the War with Mexico (which Thoreau opposed), the battle at Buena Vista, Mexico, in 1847 resulted in the American defeat of Santa Anna and his Mexican Army.
[13]A snow storm in New England, February 20, 1717, which lived on in legend.

[14]Frost.
[15]Long wharf in Boston; Lake Champlain on the New York-Vermont border.
[16]Town in Maine producing good lime (*slacked* is variant of *slaked,* the bringing about of a chemical change in the lime).
[17]Touted.

fashion and poverty, going to become paper of one color or a few shades only, on which, forsooth, will be written tales of real life, high and low, and founded on fact! This closed car smells of salt fish, the strong New England and commercial scent, reminding me of the Grand Banks[18] and the fisheries. Who has not seen a salt fish, thoroughly cured for this world, so that nothing can spoil it, and putting the perseverance of the saints to the blush? with which you may sweep or pave the streets, and split your kindlings, and the teamster shelter himself and his lading against sun, wind, and rain behind it,—and the trader, as a Concord trader once did, hang it up by his door for a sign when he commences business, until at last his oldest customer cannot tell surely whether it be animal, vegetable, or mineral, and yet it shall be as pure as a snowflake, and if it be put into a pot and boiled, will come out an excellent dunfish[19] for a Saturday's dinner. Next Spanish hides, with the tails still preserving their twist and the angle of elevation they had when the oxen that wore them were careering over the pampas of the Spanish Main,—a type of all obstinacy, and evincing how almost hopeless and incurable are all constitutional vices. I confess, that practically speaking, when I have learned a man's real disposition, I have no hopes of changing it for the better or worse in this state of existence. As the Orientals say, "A cur's tail may be warmed, and pressed, and bound round with ligatures, and after a twelve years' labor bestowed upon it, still it will retain its natural form."[20] The only effectual cure for such inveteracies as these tails exhibit is to make glue of them, which I believe is what is usually done with them, and then they will stay put and stick. Here is a hogshead of molasses or of brandy directed to John Smith, Cuttingsville, Vermont, some trader among the Green Mountains, who imports for the farmers near his clearing, and now perchance stands over his bulkhead and thinks of the last arrivals on the coast, how they may affect the price for him, telling his customers this moment, as he has told them twenty times before this morning, that he expects some by the next train of prime quality. It is advertised in the Cuttingsville Times.

While these things go up other things come down. Warned by the whizzing sound, I look up from my book and see some tall pine, hewn on far northern hills, which has winged its way over the Green Mountains and the Connecticut, shot like an arrow through the township within ten minutes, and scarce another eye beholds it; going

> "to be the mast
> Of some great ammiral."[21]

And hark! here comes the cattle-train bearing the cattle of a thousand hills, sheepcots, stables, and cow-yards in the air, drovers with their sticks, and shepherd boys in the midst of their flocks, all but the mountain pastures, whirled along like leaves blown from the mountains by the September gales. The air is filled with the bleating of calves and sheep, and the hustling of oxen, as if a pastoral valley were going by. When the old bell-wether[22] at the head rattles his bell, the mountains do indeed skip like rams and the little hills like lambs. A carload of drovers, too, in the midst, on a level with their droves now, their vocation gone, but still clinging to their useless sticks as their badge of office. But their dogs, where are they? It is a stampede to them; they are quite thrown out; they have lost the scent. Methinks I hear them barking behind the Peterboro' Hills, or panting up the western slope of the Green Mountains. They will not be in at the death. Their vocation, too, is gone. Their fidelity and sagacity are below par now. They will slink back to their

---

[18]Fishing area off southeast Newfoundland.
[19]Dried codfish (note pun on "done").
[20]From "The Lion and the Rabbit," *Fables and Proverbs from the Sanskrit*, trans. Charles Wilkins.

[21]From Milton, *Paradise Lost*, I, 293–294. *Ammiral* is variant of *admiral*.
[22]Leader of the flock. Cf. Psalm 114:4.

kennels in disgrace, or perchance run wild and strike a league with the wolf and the fox. So is your pastoral life whirled past and away. But the bell rings, and I must get off the track and let the cars go by;—

> What's the railroad to me?
> I never go to see
> Where it ends.
> It fills a few hollows,
> And makes banks for the swallows,
> It sets the sand a-blowing,
> And the blackberries a-growing,

but I cross it like a cart-path in the woods. I will not have my eyes put out and my ears spoiled by its smoke and steam and hissing.

Now that the cars are gone by and all the restless world with them, and the fishes in the pond no longer feel their rumbling, I am more alone than ever. For the rest of the long afternoon, perhaps, my meditations are interrupted only by the faint rattle of a carriage or team along the distant highway.

Sometimes, on Sundays, I heard the bells, the Lincoln, Acton, Bedford, or Concord bell, when the wind was favorable, a faint, sweet, and, as it were, natural melody, worth importing into the wilderness. At a sufficient distance over the woods this sound acquires a certain vibratory hum, as if the pine needles in the horizon were the strings of a harp which it swept. All sound heard at the greatest possible distance produces one and the same effect, a vibration of the universal lyre, just as the intervening atmosphere makes a distant ridge of earth interesting to our eyes by the azure tint it imparts to it. There came to me in this case a melody which the air had strained, and which had conversed with every leaf and needle of the wood, that portion of the sound which the elements had taken up and modulated and echoed from vale to vale. The echo is, to some extent, an original sound, and therein is the magic and charm of it. It is not merely a repetition of what was worth repeating in the bell, but partly the voice of the wood; the same trivial words and notes sung by a wood-nymph.

At evening, the distant lowing of some cow in the horizon beyond the woods sounded sweet and melodious, and at first I would mistake it for the voices of certain minstrels by whom I was sometimes serenaded, who might be straying over hill and dale; but soon I was not unpleasantly disappointed when it was prolonged into the cheap and natural music of the cow. I do not mean to be satirical, but to express my appreciation of those youths' singing, when I state that I perceived clearly that it was akin to the music of the cow, and they were at length one articulation of Nature.

Regularly at half-past seven, in one part of the summer, after the evening train had gone by, the whip-poor-wills chanted their vespers for half an hour, sitting on a stump by my door, or upon the ridge-pole of the house. They would begin to sing almost with as much precision as a clock, within five minutes of a particular time, referred to the setting of the sun, every evening. I had a rare opportunity to become acquainted with their habits. Sometimes I heard four or five at once in different parts of the wood, by accident one a bar behind another, and so near me that I distinguished not only the cluck after each note, but often that singular buzzing sound like a fly in a spider's web, only proportionally louder. Sometimes one would circle round and round me in the woods a few feet distant as if tethered by a string, when probably I was near its eggs. They sang at intervals throughout the night, and were again as musical as ever just before and about dawn.

When other birds are still, the screech owls take up the strain, like mourning women their ancient u-lu-lu. Their dismal scream is truly Ben Jonsonian.[23] Wise midnight hags! It is no honest and blunt tu-whit tu-who[24] of the poets, but, without jesting, a most solemn graveyard ditty, the mutual consolations of suicide lovers remembering the pangs and the delights of supernal love in the infernal groves. Yet I love to hear their wailing, their doleful responses, trilled along the woodside; reminding me sometimes of music and singing birds; as if it were the dark and tearful side of music, the regrets and sighs that would fain be sung. They are the spirits, the low spirits and melancholy forebodings, of fallen souls that once in human shape night-walked the earth and did the deeds of darkness, now expiating their sins with their wailing hymns or threnodies[25] in the scenery of their transgressions. They give me a new sense of the variety and capacity of that nature which is our common dwelling. *Oh-o-o-o-o that I never had been bor-r-r-n!* sighs one on this side of the pond, and circles with the restlessness of despair to some new perch on the gray oaks. Then—*that I never had been bor-r-r-n!* echoes another on the farther side with tremulous sincerity, and—*bor-r-r-n!* comes faintly from far in the Lincoln woods.

I was also serenaded by a hooting owl. Near at hand you could fancy it the most melancholy sound in Nature, as if she meant by this to stereotype and make permanent in her choir the dying moans of a human being,—some poor weak relic of mortality who has left hope behind, and howls like an animal, yet with human sobs, on entering the dark valley, made more awful by a certain gurgling melodiousness,—I find myself beginning with the letters *gl* when I try to imitate it,— expressive of a mind which has reached the gelatinous, mildewy stage in the mortification of all healthy and courageous thought. It reminded me of ghouls and idiots and insane howlings. But now one answers from far woods in a strain made really melodious by distance,—*Hoo hoo hoo, hoorer hoo;* and indeed for the most part it suggested only pleasing associations, whether heard by day or night, summer or winter.

I rejoice that there are owls. Let them do the idiotic and maniacal hooting for men. It is a sound admirably suited to swamps and twilight woods which no day illustrates, suggesting a vast and undeveloped nature which men have not recognized. They represent the stark twilight and unsatisfied thoughts which all have. All day the sun has shone on the surface of some savage swamp, where the single spruce stands hung with usnea lichens, and small hawks circulate above, and the chickadee lisps amid the evergreens, and the partridge and rabbit skulk beneath; but now a more dismal and fitting day dawns, and a different race of creatures awakes to express the meaning of Nature there.

Late in the evening I heard the distant rumbling of wagons over bridges,—a sound heard farther than almost any other at night,—the baying of dogs, and sometimes again the lowing of some disconsolate cow in a distant barn-yard. In the meanwhile all the shore rang with the trump of bullfrogs, the sturdy spirits of ancient wine-bibbers and wassailers, still unrepentant, trying to sing a catch in their Stygian lake,[26]—if the Walden nymphs will pardon the comparison, for though there are almost no weeds, there are frogs there,—who would fain keep up the hilarious rules of their old festal tables, though their voices have waxed hoarse and solemnly grave, mocking at mirth, and the wine has lost its flavor, and become only liquor to distend their paunches, and sweet intoxication never comes to drown the memory of the past, but mere saturation and waterloggedness and distention. The most aldermanic, with his chin upon a heart-leaf, which serves for

---

[23]Melancholic or sad, as in the serious lyrics of Ben Jonson (1573–1637), Elizabethan playwright and poet.
[24]From Shakespeare's *Love's Labour's Lost,* V, 2, 936–937 ("Then nightly sings the staring owl, Tu-who;/ Tu-wit, to-who").

[25]Funeral songs.
[26]A lake resembling the River Styx, which in Greek mythology separates the world of the living from the world of the dead (Hades).

a napkin to his drooling chaps, under this northern shore quaffs a deep draught of the once scorned water, and passes round the cup with the ejaculation *tr-r-r-oonk, tr-r-r-oonk, tr-r-r-oonk!* and straightway comes over the water from some distant cove the same password repeated, where the next in seniority and girth has gulped down to his mark;[27] and when this observance has made the circuit of the shores, then ejaculates the master of ceremonies, with satisfaction, *tr-r-r-oonk!* and each in his turn repeats the same down to the least distended, leakiest, and flabbiest paunched, that there be no mistake; and then the bowl goes round again and again, until the sun disperses the morning mist, and only the patriarch is not under the pond,[28] but vainly bellowing *troonk* from time to time, and pausing for a reply.

I am not sure that I ever heard the sound of cockcrowing from my clearing, and I thought that it might be worth the while to keep a cockerel for his music merely, as a singing bird. The note of this once wild Indian pheasant is certainly the most remarkable of any bird's, and if they could be naturalized without being domesticated, it would soon become the most famous sound in our woods, surpassing the clangor of the goose and the hooting of the owl; and then imagine the cackling of the hens to fill the pauses when their lords' clarions rested! No wonder that man added this bird to his tame stock,—to say nothing of the eggs and drumsticks. To walk in a winter morning in a wood where these birds abounded, their native woods, and hear the wild cockerels crow on the trees, clear and shrill for miles over the resounding earth, drowning the feebler notes of other birds,— think of it! It would put nations on the alert. Who would not be early to rise, and rise earlier and earlier every successive day of his life, till he became unspeakably healthy, wealthy, and wise?[29] This foreign bird's note is celebrated by the poets of all countries along with the notes of their native songsters. All climates agree with brave Chanticleer. He is more indigenous even than the natives. His health is ever good, his lungs are sound, his spirits never flag. Even the sailor on the Atlantic and Pacific is awakened by his voice;[30] but its shrill sound never roused me from my slumbers. I kept neither dog, cat, cow, pig, nor hens, so that you would have said there was a deficiency of domestic sounds; neither the churn, nor the spinning-wheel, nor even the singing of the kettle, nor the hissing of the urn, nor children crying, to comfort one. An old-fashioned man would have lost his senses or died of ennui before this. Not even rats in the wall, for they were starved out, or rather were never baited in,—only squirrels on the roof and under the floor, a whip-poor-will on the ridge-pole, a blue jay screaming beneath the window, a hare or woodchuck under the house, a screech owl or a cat owl behind it, a flock of wild geese or a laughing loon on the pond, and a fox to bark in the night. Not even a lark or an oriole, those mild plantation birds, ever visited my clearing. No cockerels to crow nor hens to cackle in the yard. No yard! but unfenced nature reaching up to your very sills. A young forest growing up under your windows, and wild sumachs and blackberry vines breaking through into your cellar; sturdy pitch pines rubbing and creaking against the shingles for want of room, their roots reaching quite under the house. Instead of a scuttle or a blind blown off in the gale,—a pine tree snapped off or torn up by the roots behind your house for fuel. Instead of no path to the front-yard gate in the Great Snow,—no gate—no front-yard,—and no path to the civilized world.

---

[27]I.e., the mark in the cup indicating how much to drink before passing it along.
[28]Cf. "under the table."
[29]Cf. one of Benjamin Franklin's Poor Richard maxims:

"Early to bed and early to rise,/ Makes a man healthy, wealthy, and wise."
[30]Ships carried live chickens for a supply of eggs and meat.

V

SOLITUDE

This is a delicious evening, when the whole body is one sense, and imbibes delight through every pore. I go and come with a strange liberty in Nature, a part of herself. As I walk along the stony shore of the pond in my shirt-sleeves, though it is cool as well as cloudy and windy, and I see nothing special to attract me, all the elements are unusually congenial to me. The bullfrogs trump to usher in the night, and the note of the whip-poor-will is borne on the rippling wind from over the water. Sympathy with the fluttering alder and poplar leaves almost takes away my breath; yet, like the lake, my serenity is rippled but not ruffled. These small waves raised by the evening wind are as remote from storm as the smooth reflecting surface. Though it is now dark, the wind still blows and roars in the wood, the waves still dash, and some creatures lull the rest with their notes. The repose is never complete. The wildest animals do not repose, but seek their prey now; the fox, and skunk, and rabbit, now roam the fields and woods without fear. They are Nature's watchmen,—links which connect the days of animated life.

When I return to my house I find that visitors have been there and left their cards, either a bunch of flowers, or a wreath of evergreen, or a name in pencil on a yellow walnut leaf or a chip. They who come rarely to the woods take some little piece of the forest into their hands to play with by the way, which they leave, either intentionally or accidentally. One has peeled a willow wand, woven it into a ring, and dropped it on my table. I could always tell if visitors had called in my absence, either by the bended twigs or grass, or the print of their shoes, and generally of what sex or age or quality they were by some slight trace left, as a flower dropped, or a bunch of grass plucked and thrown away, even as far off as the railroad, half a mile distant, or by the lingering odor of a cigar or pipe. Nay, I was frequently notified of the passage of a traveller along the highway sixty rods off by the scent of his pipe.

There is commonly sufficient space about us. Our horizon is never quite at our elbows. The thick wood is not just at our door, nor the pond, but somewhat is always clearing, familiar and worn by us, appropriated and fenced in some way, and reclaimed from Nature. For what reason have I this vast range and circuit, some square miles of unfrequented forest, for my privacy, abandoned to me by men? My nearest neighbor is a mile distant, and no house is visible from any place but the hill-tops within half a mile of my own. I have my horizon bounded by woods all to myself; a distant view of the railroad where it touches the pond on the one hand, and of the fence which skirts the woodland road on the other. But for the most part it is as solitary where I live as on the prairies. It is as much Asia or Africa as New England. I have, as it were, my own sun and moon and stars, and a little world all to myself. At night there was never a traveller passed my house, or knocked at my door, more than if I were the first or last man; unless it were in the spring, when at long intervals some came from the village to fish for pouts,—they plainly fished much more in the Walden Pond of their own natures, and baited their hooks with darkness,—but they soon retreated, usually with light baskets, and left "the world to darkness and to me,"[1] and the black kernel of the night was never profaned by any human neighborhood. I believe that men are generally still a little afraid of the dark, though the witches are all hung, and Christianity and candles have been introduced.

Yet I experienced sometimes that the most sweet and tender, the most innocent and encouraging society may be found in any natural object, even for the

---

[1] From "Elegy Written in a Country Churchyard" (1751), by Thomas Gray (1716–1771), British poet.

poor misanthrope and most melancholy man. There can be no very black melancholy to him who lives in the midst of nature and has his senses still. There was never yet such a storm but it was Æolian music[2] to a healthy and innocent ear. Nothing can rightly compel a simple and brave man to a vulgar sadness. While I enjoy the friendship of the seasons I trust that nothing can make life a burden to me. The gentle rain which waters my beans and keeps me in the house to-day is not drear and melancholy, but good for me too. Though it prevents my hoeing them, it is of far more worth than my hoeing. If it should continue so long as to cause the seeds to rot in the ground and destroy the potatoes in the low lands, it would still be good for the grass on the uplands, and, being good for the grass, it would be good for me. Sometimes, when I compare myself with other men, it seems as if I were more favored by the gods than they, beyond any deserts that I am conscious of; as if I had a warrant and surety at their hands which my fellows have not, and were especially guided and guarded. I do not flatter myself, but if it be possible they flatter me. I have never felt lonesome, or in the least oppressed by a sense of solitude, but once, and that was a few weeks after I came to the woods, when, for an hour, I doubted if the near neighborhood of man was not essential to a serene and healthy life. To be alone was something unpleasant. But I was at the same time conscious of a slight insanity in my mood, and seemed to foresee my recovery. In the midst of a gentle rain while these thoughts prevailed, I was suddenly sensible of such sweet and beneficent society in Nature, in the very pattering of the drops, and in every sound and sight around my house, an infinite and unaccountable friendliness all at once like an atmosphere sustaining me, as made the fancied advantages of human neighborhood insignificant, and I have never thought of them since. Every little pine needle expanded and swelled with sympathy and befriended me. I was so distinctly made aware of the presence of something kindred to me, even in scenes which we are accustomed to call wild and dreary, and also that the nearest of blood to me and humanest was not a person nor a villager, that I thought no place could ever be strange to me again.—

> "Mourning untimely consumes the sad;
> Few are their days in the land of the living,
> Beautiful daughter of Toscar."[3]

Some of my pleasantest hours were during the long rain-storms in the spring or fall, which confined me to the house for the afternoon as well as the forenoon, soothed by their ceaseless roar and pelting; when an early twilight ushered in a long evening in which many thoughts had time to take root and unfold themselves. In those driving northeast rains which tried the village houses so, when the maids stood ready with mop and pail in front entries to keep the deluge out, I sat behind my door in my little house, which was all entry, and thoroughly enjoyed its protection. In one heavy thundershower the lightning struck a large pitch pine across the pond, making a very conspicuous and perfectly regular spiral groove from top to bottom, an inch or more deep, and four or five inches wide, as you would groove a walking-stick. I passed it again the other day, and was struck with awe on looking up and beholding that mark, now more distinct than ever, where a terrific and resistless bolt came down out of the harmless sky eight years ago. Men frequently say to me, "I should think you would feel lonesome down there, and want to be nearer to folks, rainy and snowy days and nights especially." I am tempted to reply to such,—This whole earth which we inhabit is but a point in space. How far apart, think you, dwell the two most distant inhabitants of yonder

---

[2]Created by winds passing over wires, etc., suggesting the sound of the Aeolian harp (Aeolus was keeper of the winds).

[3]From "Croma," *The Genuine Remains of Ossian* (1841), trans. Patrick MacGregor.

star, the breadth of whose disk cannot be appreciated by our instruments? Why should I feel lonely? is not our planet in the Milky Way? This which you put seems to me not to be the most important question. What sort of space is that which separates a man from his fellows and makes him solitary? I have found that no exertion of the legs can bring two minds much nearer to one another. What do we want most to dwell near to? Not to many men surely, the depot, the post-office, the bar-room, the meeting-house, the school-house, the grocery, Beacon Hill, or the Five Points,[4] where men most congregate, but to the perennial source of our life, whence in all our experience we have found that to issue, as the willow stands near the water and sends out its roots in that direction. This will vary with different natures, but this is the place where a wise man will dig his cellar. . . . I one evening overtook one of my townsmen, who has accumulated what is called "a handsome property,"—though I never got a *fair* view of it,—on the Walden road, driving a pair of cattle to market, who inquired of me how I could bring my mind to give up so many of the comforts of life. I answered that I was very sure I liked it passably well; I was not joking. And so I went home to my bed, and left him to pick his way through the darkness and the mud to Brighton,[5]—or Bright-town,— which place he would reach some time in the morning.

Any prospect of awakening or coming to life to a dead man makes indifferent all times and places. The place where that may occur is always the same, and indescribably pleasant to all our senses. For the most part we allow only outlying and transient circumstances to make our occasions. They are, in fact, the cause of our distraction. Nearest to all things is that power which fashions their being. *Next* to us the grandest laws are continually being executed. *Next* to us is not the workman whom we have hired, with whom we love so well to talk, but the workman whose work we are.

"How vast and profound is the influence of the subtile powers of Heaven and of Earth!"

"We seek to perceive them, and we do not see them; we seek to hear them, and we do not hear them; identified with the substance of things, they cannot be separated from them."

"They cause that in all the universe men purify and sanctify their hearts, and clothe themselves in their holiday garments to offer sacrifices and oblations to their ancestors. It is an ocean of subtile intelligences. They are everywhere, above us, on our left, on our right; they environ us on all sides."[6]

We are the subjects of an experiment which is not a little interesting to me. Can we not do without the society of our gossips a little while under these circumstances,—have our own thoughts to cheer us? Confucius says truly, "Virtue does not remain as an abandoned orphan; it must of necessity have neighbors."[7]

With thinking we may be beside ourselves in a sane sense. By a conscious effort of the mind we can stand aloof from actions and their consequences; and all things, good and bad, go by us like a torrent. We are not wholly involved in Nature. I may be either the driftwood in the stream, or Indra[8] in the sky looking down on it. I *may* be affected by a theatrical exhibition; on the other hand, I *may not* be affected by an actual event which appears to concern me much more. I only know myself as a human entity; the scene, so to speak, of thoughts and affections; and am sensible of a certain doubleness by which I can stand as remote from myself as from another. However intense my experience, I am conscious of the presence and criticism of a part of me, which, as it were, is not a part of me, but spec-

---

[4]Beacon Hill was (and is) a fashionable area of Boston; Five Points was one of the most corrupt and depressed areas of lower Manhattan.
[5]Then, a slaughterhouse area near Boston. "Bright" means "ox."

[6]From *The Doctrine of the Mean*, XVI, 1–3, by Confucius (c. 551–479 B.C.).
[7]From *The Analects*, IV, 25, by Confucius.
[8]Chief god in Hindu religion, associated with rain and thunderbolts.

tator, sharing no experience, but taking note of it, and that is no more I than it is you. When the play, it may be the tragedy, of life is over, the spectator goes his way. It was a kind of fiction, a work of the imagination only, so far as he was concerned. This doubleness may easily make us poor neighbors and friends sometimes.

I find it wholesome to be alone the greater part of the time. To be in company, even with the best, is soon wearisome and dissipating. I love to be alone. I never found the companion that was so companionable as solitude. We are for the most part more lonely when we go abroad among men than when we stay in our chambers. A man thinking or working is always alone, let him be where he will. Solitude is not measured by the miles of space that intervene between a man and his fellows. The really diligent student in one of the crowded hives of Cambridge College[9] is as solitary as a dervish in the desert. The farmer can work alone in the field or the woods all day, hoeing or chopping, and not feel lonesome, because he is employed; but when he comes home at night he cannot sit down in a room alone, at the mercy of his thoughts, but must be where he can "see the folks," and recreate, and, as he thinks, remunerate himself for his day's solitude; and hence he wonders how the student can sit alone in the house all night and most of the day without ennui and "the blues;" but he does not realize that the student, though in the house, is still at work in *his* field, and chopping in *his* woods, as the farmer in his, and in turn seeks the same recreation and society that the latter does, though it may be a more condensed form of it.

Society is commonly too cheap. We meet at very short intervals, not having had time to acquire any new value for each other. We meet at meals three times a day, and give each other a new taste of that old musty cheese that we are. We have had to agree on a certain set of rules, called etiquette and politeness, to make this frequent meeting tolerable and that we need not come to open war. We meet at the post-office, and at the sociable, and about the fireside every night; we live thick and are in each other's way, and stumble over one another, and I think that we thus lose some respect for one another. Certainly less frequency would suffice for all important and hearty communications. Consider the girls in a factory,—never alone, hardly in their dreams.[10] It would be better if there were but one inhabitant to a square mile, as where I live. The value of a man is not in his skin, that we should touch him.

I have heard of a man lost in the woods and dying of famine and exhaustion at the foot of a tree, whose loneliness was relieved by the grotesque visions with which, owing to bodily weakness, his diseased imagination surrounded him, and which he believed to be real. So also, owing to bodily and mental health and strength, we may be continually cheered by a like but more normal and natural society, and come to know that we are never alone.

I have a great deal of company in my house; especially in the morning, when nobody calls. Let me suggest a few comparisons, that some one may convey an idea of my situation. I am no more lonely than the loon in the pond that laughs so loud, or than Walden Pond itself. What company has that lonely lake, I pray? And yet it has not the blue devils, but the blue angels in it, in the azure tint of its waters. The sun is alone, except in thick weather, when there sometimes appear to be two, but one is a mock sun. God is alone,—but the devil, he is far from being alone; he sees a great deal of company; he is legion. I am no more lonely than a single mullein or dandelion in a pasture, or a bean leaf, or sorrel, or a horse-fly, or a humblebee. I am no more lonely than the Mill Brook,[11] or a weathercock, or

---

[9]I.e., Harvard College.
[10]In Lowell, the factory girls slept in dormitories near the mills.
[11]Small stream that runs through Concord.

the north star, or the south wind, or an April shower, or a January thaw, or the first spider in a new house.

I have occasional visits in the long winter evenings, when the snow falls fast and the wind howls in the wood, from an old settler and original proprietor, who is reported to have dug Walden Pond, and stoned it, and fringed it with pine woods; who tells me stories of old time and of new eternity; and between us we manage to pass a cheerful evening with social mirth and pleasant views of things, even without apples or cider,—a most wise and humorous friend, whom I love much, who keeps himself more secret than ever did Goffe or Whalley;[12] and though he is thought to be dead, none can show where he is buried. An elderly dame,[13] too, dwells in my neighborhood, invisible to most persons, in whose odorous herb garden I love to stroll sometimes, gathering simples and listening to her fables; for she has a genius of unequalled fertility, and her memory runs back farther than mythology, and she can tell me the original of every fable, and on what fact every one is founded, for the incidents occurred when she was young. A ruddy and lusty old dame, who delights in all weathers and seasons, and is likely to outlive all her children yet.

The indescribable innocence and beneficence of Nature,—of sun and wind and rain, of summer and winter,—such health, such cheer, they afford forever! and such sympathy have they ever with our race, that all Nature would be affected, and the sun's brightness fade, and the winds would sigh humanely, and the clouds rain tears, and the woods shed their leaves and put on mourning in midsummer, if any man should ever for a just cause grieve. Shall I not have intelligence with the earth? Am I not partly leaves and vegetable mould myself?

What is the pill which will keep us well, serene, contented? Not my or thy great-grandfather's, but our great-grandmother Nature's universal, vegetable, botanic medicines, by which she has kept herself young always, outlived so many old Parrs[14] in her day, and fed her health with their decaying fatness. For my panacea, instead of one of those quack vials[15] of a mixture dipped from Acheron[16] and the Dead Sea, which come out of those long shallow black-schooner looking wagons which we sometimes see made to carry bottles, let me have a draught of undiluted morning air. Morning air! If men will not drink of this at the fountainhead of the day, why, then, we must even bottle up some and sell it in the shops, for the benefit of those who have lost their subscription ticket to morning time in this world. But remember, it will not keep quite till noonday even in the coolest cellar, but drive out the stopples long ere that and follow westward the steps of Aurora. I am no worshipper of Hygeia,[17] who was the daughter of that old herb-doctor Æsculapius, and who is represented on monuments holding a serpent in one hand, and in the other a cup out of which the serpent sometimes drinks; but rather of Hebe,[18] cup-bearer to Jupiter, who was the daughter of Juno and wild lettuce, and who had the power of restoring gods and men to the vigor of youth. She was probably the only thoroughly sound-conditioned, healthy, and robust young lady that ever walked the globe, and wherever she came it was spring.

---

[12]William Goffe (d. 1679) and Edward Whalley (d. 1675?) signed the death warrant for Charles I in 1649. When the monarchy was restored in 1660, they escaped to New England.

[13]Mother Nature.

[14]Thomas Parr (1483?–1635), celebrated English centenarian who claimed to have lived during the reign of ten kings and queens.

[15]Patent medicines.

[16]In Greek mythology, the river over which Charon ferried the souls of the dead to Hades.

[17]In classical mythology, goddess of health and daughter of Aesculapius, god of medicine (whose emblem was the snake).

[18]Greek goddess of youth and cupbearer, she was borne by Juno, who conceived her on eating wild lettuce.

VI

VISITORS

I think that I love society as much as most, and am ready enough to fasten my-self like a bloodsucker for the time to any full-blooded man that comes in my way. I am naturally no hermit, but might possibly sit out the sturdiest frequenter of the bar-room, if my business called me thither.

I had three chairs in my house; one for solitude, two for friendship, three for society. When visitors came in larger and unexpected numbers there was but the third chair for them all, but they generally economized the room by standing up. It is surprising how many great men and women a small house will contain. I have had twenty-five or thirty souls, with their bodies, at once under my roof, and yet we often parted without being aware that we had come very near to one another. Many of our houses, both public and private, with their almost innumerable apartments, their huge halls and their cellars for the storage of wines and other munitions of peace, appear to me extravagantly large for their inhabitants. They are so vast and magnificent that the latter seem to be only vermin which infest them. I am surprised when the herald blows his summons before some Tremont or Astor or Middlesex House,[1] to see come creeping out over the piazza for all inhabitants a ridiculous mouse, which soon again slinks into some hole in the pavement.

One inconvenience I sometimes experienced in so small a house, the difficulty of getting to a sufficient distance from my guest when we began to utter the big thoughts in big words. You want room for your thoughts to get into sailing trim and run a course or two before they make their port. The bullet of your thought must have overcome its lateral and ricochet motion and fallen into its last and steady course before it reaches the ear of the hearer, else it may plow out again through the side of his head. Also, our sentences wanted room to unfold and form their columns in the interval. Individuals, like nations, must have suitable broad and natural boundaries, even a considerable neutral ground, between them. I have found it a singular luxury to talk across the pond to a companion on the opposite side. In my house we were so near that we could not begin to hear,— we could not speak low enough to be heard; as when you throw two stones into calm water so near that they break each other's undulations. If we are merely lo-quacious and loud talkers, then we can afford to stand very near together, cheek by jowl, and feel each other's breath; but if we speak reservedly and thoughtfully, we want to be farther apart, that all animal heat and moisture may have a chance to evaporate. If we would enjoy the most intimate society with that in each of us which is without, or above, being spoken to, we must not only be silent, but com-monly so far apart bodily that we cannot possibly hear each other's voice in any case. Referred to this standard, speech is for the convenience of those who are hard of hearing; but there are many fine things which we cannot say if we have to shout. As the conversation began to assume a loftier and grander tone, we gradu-ally shoved our chairs farther apart till they touched the wall in opposite corners, and then commonly there was not room enough.

My "best" room, however, my withdrawing room, always ready for company, on whose carpet the sun rarely fell, was the pine wood behind my house. Thither in summer days, when distinguished guests came, I took them, and a priceless do-mestic swept the floor and dusted the furniture and kept the things in order.

If one guest came he sometimes partook of my frugal meal, and it was no in-terruption to conversation to be stirring a hasty-pudding,[2] or watching the rising

---

[1]Hotels of Boston, New York, and Concord.
[2]Cornmeal mush.

and maturing of a loaf of bread in the ashes, in the meanwhile. But if twenty came and sat in my house there was nothing said about dinner, though there might be bread enough for two, more than if eating were a forsaken habit; but we naturally practised abstinence; and this was never felt to be an offence against hospitality, but the most proper and considerate course. The waste and decay of physical life, which so often needs repair, seemed miraculously retarded in such a case, and the vital vigor stood its ground. I could entertain thus a thousand as well as twenty; and if any ever went away disappointed or hungry from my house when they found me at home, they may depend upon it that I sympathized with them at least. So easy is it, though many housekeepers doubt it, to establish new and better customs in the place of the old. You need not rest your reputation on the dinners you give. For my own part, I was never so effectually deterred from frequenting a man's house, by any kind of Cerberus[3] whatever, as by the parade one made about dining me, which I took to be a very polite and roundabout hint never to trouble him so again. I think I shall never revisit those scenes. I should be proud to have for the motto of my cabin those lines of Spenser which one of my visitors inscribed on a yellow walnut leaf for a card:—

> "Arrivèd there, the little house they fill,
>   Ne looke for entertainment where none was;
> Rest is their feast, and all things at their will:
>   The noblest mind the best contentment has."[4]

When Winslow,[5] afterward governor of the Plymouth Colony, went with a companion on a visit of ceremony to Massasoit on foot through the woods, and arrived tired and hungry at his lodge, they were well received by the king, but nothing was said about eating that day. When the night arrived, to quote their own words,—"He laid us on the bed with himself and his wife, they at the one end and we at the other, it being only planks laid a foot from the ground and a thin mat upon them. Two more of his chief men, for want of room, pressed by and upon us; so that we were worse weary of our lodging than of our journey." At one o'clock the next day Massasoit "brought two fishes that he had shot," about thrice as big as a bream. "These being boiled, there were at least forty looked for a share in them; the most eat of them. This meal only we had in two nights and a day; and had not one of us bought a partridge, we had taken our journey fasting." Fearing that they would be light-headed for want of food and also sleep, owing to "the savages' barbarous singing, (for they use to sing themselves asleep,)" and that they might get home while they had strength to travel, they departed. As for lodging, it is true they were but poorly entertained, though what they found an inconvenience was no doubt intended for an honor; but as far as eating was concerned, I do not see how the Indians could have done better. They had nothing to eat themselves, and they were wiser than to think that apologies could supply the place of food to their guests; so they drew their belts tighter and said nothing about it. Another time when Winslow visited them, it being a season of plenty with them, there was no deficiency in this respect.

As for men, they will hardly fail one anywhere. I had more visitors while I lived in the woods than at any other period of my life; I mean that I had some. I met several there under more favorable circumstances than I could anywhere else. But fewer came to see me on trivial business. In this respect, my company was winnowed by my mere distance from town. I had withdrawn so far within the great

---

[3]In Greek mythology, a three-headed dog guarding the entrance to Hades.
[4]From *The Faerie Queen*, I, i, 35, by Edmund Spenser (1552?–1599).
[5]Edward Winslow (1595–1655), who arrived in America on the *Mayflower*, visited the Indian Chief Massasoit (c. 1580–1661), who helped the colonists survive in the New World wilderness. Winslow's *The English Plantation at Plymouth* was available to Thoreau in George B. Cheever, ed., *The Journal of the Pilgrims at Plymouth* (1848).

ocean of solitude, into which the rivers of society empty, that for the most part, so far as my needs were concerned, only the finest sediment was deposited around me. Beside, there were wafted to me evidences of unexplored and uncultivated continents on the other side.

Who should come to my lodge this morning but a true Homeric or Paphlagonian man,—he had so suitable and poetic a name that I am sorry I cannot print it here,—a Canadian, a woodchopper and post-maker, who can hole fifty posts in a day, who made his last supper on a woodchuck which his dog caught.[6] He, too, has heard of Homer, and, "if it were not for books," would "not know what to do rainy days," though perhaps he has not read one wholly through for many rainy seasons. Some priest who could pronounce the Greek itself taught him to read his verse in the Testament in his native parish far away; and now I must translate to him, while he holds the book, Achilles' reproof to Patroclus for his sad countenance.—"Why are you in tears, Patroclus, like a young girl?"—

> "Or have you alone heard some news from Phthia?
> They say that Menœtius lives yet, son of Actor,
> And Peleus lives, son of Æacus, among the Myrmidons,
> Either of whom having died, we should greatly grieve."[7]

He says, "That's good." He has a great bundle of white oak bark under his arm for a sick man, gathered this Sunday morning. "I suppose there's no harm in going after such a thing to-day," says he. To him Homer was a great writer, though what his writing was about he did not know. A more simple and natural man it would be hard to find. Vice and disease, which cast such a sombre moral hue over the world, seemed to have hardly any existence for him. He was about twenty-eight years old, and had left Canada and his father's house a dozen years before to work in the States, and earn money to buy a farm with at last, perhaps in his native country. He was cast in the coarsest mould; a stout but sluggish body, yet gracefully carried, with a thick sunburnt neck, dark bushy hair, and dull sleepy blue eyes, which were occasionally lit up with expression. He wore a flat gray cloth cap, a dingy wool-colored greatcoat, and cowhide boots. He was a great consumer of meat, usually carrying his dinner to his work a couple of miles past my house,— for he chopped all summer,—in a tin pail; cold meats, often cold woodchucks, and coffee in a stone bottle which dangled by a string from his belt; and sometimes he offered me a drink. He came along early, crossing my bean-field, though without anxiety or haste to get to his work, such as Yankees exhibit. He wasn't a-going to hurt himself. He didn't care if he only earned his board. Frequently he would leave his dinner in the bushes, when his dog had caught a woodchuck by the way, and go back a mile and a half to dress it and leave it in the cellar of the house where he boarded, after deliberating first for half an hour whether he could not sink it in the pond safely till nightfall,—loving to dwell long upon these themes. He would say, as he went by in the morning, "How thick the pigeons are! If working every day were not my trade, I could get all the meat I should want by hunting,—pigeons, woodchucks, rabbits, partridges,—by gosh! I could get all I should want for a week in one day."

He was a skilful chopper, and indulged in some flourishes and ornaments in his art. He cut his trees level and close to the ground, that the sprouts which came up afterward might be more vigorous and a sled might slide over the stumps; and

---

[6]Alex Therien, a fellow townsman and friend. Paphlagonia was a mountainous region in ancient Asia Minor. The Paphlagonians appear in Homer's *Iliad*.
[7]From the *Iliad*, Book 16.

instead of leaving a whole tree to support his corded wood, he would pare it away to a slender stake or splinter which you could break off with your hand at last.

He interested me because he was so quiet and solitary and so happy withal; a well of good humor and contentment which overflowed at his eyes. His mirth was without alloy. Sometimes I saw him at his work in the woods, felling trees, and he would greet me with a laugh of inexpressible satisfaction, and a salutation in Canadian French, though he spoke English as well. When I approached him he would suspend his work, and with half-suppressed mirth lie along the trunk of a pine which he had felled, and, peeling off the inner bark, roll it up into a ball and chew it while he laughed and talked. Such an exuberance of animal spirits had he that he sometimes tumbled down and rolled on the ground with laughter at anything which made him think and tickled him. Looking round upon the trees he would exclaim,—"By George! I can enjoy myself well enough here chopping; I want no better sport." Sometimes, when at leisure, he amused himself all day in the woods with a pocket pistol, firing salutes to himself at regular intervals as he walked. In the winter he had a fire by which at noon he warmed his coffee in a kettle; and as he sat on a log to eat his dinner the chickadees would sometimes come round and alight on his arm and peck at the potato in his fingers; and he said that he "liked to have the little *fellers* about him."

In him the animal man chiefly was developed. In physical endurance and contentment he was cousin to the pine and the rock. I asked him once if he was not sometimes tired at night, after working all day; and he answered, with a sincere and serious look, "Gorrappit, I never was tired in my life." But the intellectual and what is called spiritual man in him were slumbering as in an infant. He had been instructed only in that innocent and ineffectual way in which the Catholic priests teach the aborigines, by which the pupil is never educated to the degree of consciousness, but only to the degree of trust and reverence, and a child is not made a man, but kept a child. When Nature made him, she gave him a strong body and contentment for his portion, and propped him on every side with reverence and reliance, that he might live out his threescore years and ten a child. He was so genuine and unsophisticated that no introduction would serve to introduce him, more than if you introduced a woodchuck to your neighbor. He had got to find him out as you did. He would not play any part. Men paid him wages for work, and so helped to feed and clothe him; but he never exchanged opinions with them. He was so simply and naturally humble—if he can be called humble who never aspires—that humility was no distinct quality in him, nor could he conceive of it. Wiser men were demigods to him. If you told him that such a one was coming, he did as if he thought that anything so grand would expect nothing of himself, but take all the responsibility on itself, and let him be forgotten still. He never heard the sound of praise. He particularly reverenced the writer and the preacher. Their performances were miracles. When I told him that I wrote considerably, he thought for a long time that it was merely the handwriting which I meant, for he could write a remarkably good hand himself. I sometimes found the name of his native parish handsomely written in the snow by the highway, with the proper French accent, and knew that he had passed. I asked him if he ever wished to write his thoughts. He said that he had read and written letters for those who could not, but he never tried to write thoughts,—no, he could not, he could not tell what to put first, it would kill him, and then there was spelling to be attended to at the same time!

I heard that a distinguished wise man and reformer asked him if he did not want the world to be changed; but he answered with a chuckle of surprise in his Canadian accent, not knowing that the question had ever been entertained before, "No, I like it well enough." It would have suggested many things to a philosopher to have dealings with him. To a stranger he appeared to know nothing of things in general; yet I sometimes saw in him a man whom I had not seen before, and I did not know whether he was as wise as Shakespeare or as simply ignorant as a child, whether to suspect him of a fine poetic consciousness or of stupidity. A townsman told me that when he met him sauntering through the village in his small close-fitting cap, and whistling to himself, he reminded him of a prince in disguise.

His only books were an almanac and an arithmetic, in which last he was considerably expert. The former was a sort of cyclopædia to him, which he supposed to contain an abstract of human knowledge, as indeed it does to a considerable extent. I loved to sound him on the various reforms of the day, and he never failed to look at them in the most simple and practical light. He had never heard of such things before. Could he do without factories? I asked. He had worn the home-made Vermont gray, he said, and that was good. Could he dispense with tea and coffee? Did this country afford any beverage beside water? He had soaked hemlock leaves in water and drank it, and thought that was better than water in warm weather. When I asked him if he could do without money, he showed the convenience of money in such a way as to suggest and coincide with the most philosophical accounts of the origin of this institution, and the very derivation of the word *pecunia*.[8] If an ox were his property, and he wished to get needles and thread at the store, he thought it would be inconvenient and impossible soon to go on mortgaging some portion of the creature each time to that amount. He could defend many institutions better than any philosopher, because, in describing them as they concerned him, he gave the true reason for their prevalence, and speculation had not suggested to him any other. At another time, hearing Plato's definition of a man,—a biped without feathers,—and that one exhibited a cock plucked and called it Plato's man,[9] he thought it an important difference that the *knees* bent the wrong way. He would sometimes exclaim, "How I love to talk! By George, I could talk all day!" I asked him once, when I had not seen him for many months, if he had got a new idea this summer. "Good Lord," said he, "a man that has to work as I do, if he does not forget the ideas he has had, he will do well. May be the man you hoe with is inclined to race; then, by gorry, your mind must be there: you think of weeds." He would sometimes ask me first on such occasions, if I had made any improvement. One winter day I asked him if he was always satisfied with himself, wishing to suggest a substitute within him for the priest without, and some higher motive for living. "Satisfied!" said he; "some men are satisfied with one thing, and some with another. One man, perhaps, if he has got enough, will be satisfied to sit all day with his back to the fire and his belly to the table, by George!" Yet I never, by any manœuvring, could get him to take the spiritual view of things; the highest that he appeared to conceive of was a simple expediency, such as you might expect an animal to appreciate; and this, practically, is true of most men. If I suggested any improvement in his mode of life, he merely answered, without expressing any regret, that it was too late. Yet he thoroughly believed in honesty and the like virtues.

There was a certain positive originality, however slight, to be detected in him, and I occasionally observed that he was thinking for himself and expressing his own opinion, a phenomenon so rare that I would any day walk ten miles to observe it, and it amounted to the re-origination of many of the institutions of society. Though he hesitated, and perhaps failed to express himself distinctly, he always had a presentable thought behind. Yet his thinking was so primitive and immersed in his animal life, that, though more promising than a merely learned man's, it rarely ripened to anything which can be reported. He suggested that there might be men of genius in the lowest grades of life, however permanently humble and illiterate, who take their own view always, or do not pretend to see at

---

[8] Latin for "money," derived from *pecus*, cattle.
[9] Diogenes, on hearing Plato's definition of man as a "two-footed, featherless creature," plucked a cock and said, "This is Plato's man."

all; who are as bottomless even as Walden Pond was thought to be, though they may be dark and muddy.

Many a traveller came out of his way to see me and the inside of my house, and, as an excuse for calling, asked for a glass of water. I told them that I drank at the pond, and pointed thither, offering to lend them a dipper. Far off as I lived, I was not exempted from that annual visitation which occurs, methinks, about the first of April, when everybody is on the move; and I had my share of good luck, though there were some curious specimens among my visitors. Half-witted men from the almshouse and elsewhere came to see me; but I endeavored to make them exercise all the wit they had, and make their confessions to me; in such cases making wit the theme of our conversation; and so was compensated. Indeed, I found some of them to be wiser than the so-called *overseers* of the poor and select-men of the town, and thought it was time that the tables were turned. With respect to wit, I learned that there was not much difference between the half and the whole. One day, in particular, an inoffensive, simpleminded pauper, whom with others I had often seen used as fencing stuff, standing or sitting on a bushel in the fields to keep cattle and himself from straying, visited me, and expressed a wish to live as I did. He told me, with the utmost simplicity and truth, quite superior, or rather *inferior,* to anything that is called humility, that he was "deficient in intellect." These were his words. The Lord had made him so, yet he supposed the Lord cared as much for him as for another. "I have always been so," said he, "from my childhood; I never had much mind; I was not like other children; I am weak in the head. It was the Lord's will, I suppose." And there he was to prove the truth of his words. He was a metaphysical puzzle to me. I have rarely met a fellow-man on such promising ground,—it was so simple and sincere and so true all that he said. And, true enough, in proportion as he appeared to humble himself was he exalted. I did not know at first but it was the result of a wise policy. It seemed that from such a basis of truth and frankness as the poor weak-headed pauper had laid, our intercourse might go forward to something better than the intercourse of sages.

I had some guests from those not reckoned commonly among the town's poor, but who should be; who are among the world's poor, at any rate; guests who appeal, not to your hospitality, but to your *hospitalality;* who earnestly wish to be helped, and preface their appeal with the information that they are resolved, for one thing, never to help themselves. I require of a visitor that he be not actually starving, though he may have the very best appetite in the world, however he got it. Objects of charity are not guests. Men who did not know when their visit had terminated, though I went about my business again, answering them from greater and greater remoteness. Men of almost every degree of wit called on me in the migrating season. Some who had more wits than they knew what to do with; runaway slaves with plantation manners, who listened from time to time, like the fox in the fable, as if they heard the hounds a-baying on their track, and looked at me beseechingly, as much as to say,—

"O Christian, will you send me back?"

One real runaway slave, among the rest, whom I helped to forward toward the north star. Men of one idea, like a hen with one chicken, and that a duckling; men of a thousand ideas, and unkempt heads, like those hens which are made to take charge of a hundred chickens, all in pursuit of one bug, a score of them lost in every morning's dew,—and become frizzled and mangy in consequence; men of ideas instead of legs, a sort of intellectual centipede that made you crawl all over. One man proposed a book in which visitors should write their names, as at the White Mountains; but, alas! I have too good a memory to make that necessary.

I could not but notice some of the peculiarities of my visitors. Girls and boys and young women generally seemed glad to be in the woods. They looked in the pond and at the flowers, and improved their time. Men of business, even farmers, thought only of solitude and employment, and of the great distance at which I dwelt from something or other; and though they said that they loved a ramble in the woods occasionally, it was obvious that they did not. Restless committed men, whose time was all taken up in getting a living or keeping it; ministers who spoke of God as if they enjoyed a monopoly of the subject, who could not bear all kinds of opinions; doctors, lawyers, uneasy housekeepers who pried into my cupboard and bed when I was out,— how came Mrs. ——— to know that my sheets were not as clean as hers?— young men who had ceased to be young, and had concluded that it was safest to follow the beaten track of the professions,— all these generally said that it was not possible to do so much good in my position. Ay! there was the rub. The old and infirm and the timid, of whatever age or sex, thought most of sickness, and sudden accident and death; to them life seemed full of danger,— what danger is there if you don't think of any?— and they thought that a prudent man would carefully select the safest position, where Dr. B.[10] might be on hand at a moment's warning. To them the village was literally a *com-munity,* a league for mutual defence, and you would suppose that they would not go a-huckleberrying without a medicine chest. The amount of it is, if a man is alive, there is always *danger* that he may die, though the danger must be allowed to be less in propor- tion as he is dead-and-alive to begin with. A man sits as many risks as he runs. Finally, there were the self-styled reformers, the greatest bores of all, who thought that I was forever singing,—

> This is the house that I built;[11]
> This is the man that lives in the house that I built;

but they did not know that the third line was,—

> These are the folks that worry the man
> That lives in the house that I built.

I did not fear the hen-harriers,[12] for I kept no chickens; but I feared the men- harriers rather.

I had more cheering visitors than the last. Children come a-berrying, railroad men taking a Sunday morning walk in clean shirts, fishermen and hunters, poets and philosophers; in short, all honest pilgrims, who came out to the woods for freedom's sake, and really left the village behind, I was ready to greet with,— "Welcome, Englishmen! welcome, Englishmen!"[13] for I had had communication with that race.

VII

THE BEAN-FIELD

Meanwhile my beans, the length of whose rows, added together, was seven miles already planted, were impatient to be hoed, for the earliest had grown con- siderably before the latest were in the ground; indeed they were not easily to be put off. What was the meaning of this so steady and self-respecting, this small Herculean labor, I knew not. I came to love my rows, my beans, though so many more than I wanted. They attached me to the earth, and so I got strength like Antæus.[1] But why should I raise them? Only Heaven knows. This was my curious

---

[10]Dr. Josiah Bartlett, physician in Concord.
[11]Cf. the nursery rhyme, "This is the house that Jack built."
[12]Hawks.
[13]Supposedly spoken by the Indian Samoset when he walked into the new settlement of the Pilgrims.

[1]In Greek myth a giant, child of Earth, whose strength was renewed every time he landed on the ground; Hercules de- feated him by holding him aloft.

labor all summer,—to make this portion of the earth's surface, which had yielded only cinquefoil, blackberries, johnswort, and the like, before, sweet wild fruits and pleasant flowers, produce instead this pulse. What shall I learn of beans or beans of me? I cherish them, I hoe them, early and late I have an eye to them; and this is my day's work. It is a fine broad leaf to look on. My auxiliaries are the dews and rains which water this dry soil, and what fertility is in the soil itself, which for the most part is lean and effete. My enemies are worms, cool days, and most of all woodchucks. The last have nibbled for me a quarter of an acre clean. But what right had I to oust johnswort and the rest, and break up their ancient herb garden? Soon, however, the remaining beans will be too tough for them, and go forward to meet new foes.

When I was four years old, as I well remember, I was brought from Boston to this my native town, through these very woods and this field, to the pond. It is one of the oldest scenes stamped on my memory. And now to-night my flute has waked the echoes over that very water. The pines still stand here older than I; or, if some have fallen, I have cooked my supper with their stumps, and a new growth is rising all around, preparing another aspect for new infant eyes. Almost the same johnswort springs from the same perennial root in this pasture, and even I have at length helped to clothe that fabulous landscape of my infant dreams, and one of the results of my presence and influence is seen in these bean leaves, corn blades, and potato vines.

I planted about two acres and a half of upland; and as it was only about fifteen years since the land was cleared, and I myself had got out two or three cords of stumps, I did not give it any manure; but in the course of the summer it appeared by the arrowheads which I turned up in hoeing, that an extinct nation had anciently dwelt here and planted corn and beans ere white men came to clear the land, and so, to some extent, had exhausted the soil for this very crop.

Before yet any woodchuck or squirrel had run across the road, or the sun had got above the shrub oaks, while all the dew was on, though the farmers warned me against it,—I would advise you to do all your work if possible while the dew is on,—I began to level the ranks of haughty weeds in my bean-field and throw dust upon their heads. Early in the morning I worked barefooted, dabbling like a plastic artist in the dewy and crumbling sand, but later in the day the sun blistered my feet. There the sun lighted me to hoe beans, pacing slowly backward and forward over that yellow gravelly upland, between the long green rows, fifteen rods, the one end terminating in a shrub oak copse where I could rest in the shade, the other in a blackberry field where the green berries deepened their tints by the time I had made another bout. Removing the weeds, putting fresh soil about the bean stems, and encouraging this weed which I had sown, making the yellow soil express its summer thought in bean leaves and blossoms rather than in wormwood and piper and millet grass, making the earth say beans instead of grass,— this was my daily work. As I had little aid from horses or cattle, or hired men or boys, or improved implements of husbandry, I was much slower, and became much more intimate with my beans than usual. But labor of the hands, even when pursued to the verge of drudgery, is perhaps never the worst form of idleness. It has a constant and imperishable moral, and to the scholar it yields a classic result. A very *agricola laboriosus*[2] was I to travellers bound westward through Lincoln and Wayland to nobody knows where; they sitting at their ease in gigs,[3] with elbows on knees, and reins loosely hanging in festoons; I the home-staying, laborious native of the soil. But soon my homestead was out of their sight and thought. It was the only open and cultivated field for a great distance on either side of the road, so they made the most of it; and sometimes the man in the field heard more of trav-

---

[2]"Hard-working farmer" (Latin).
[3]Two-wheeled buggy.

ellers' gossip and comment than was meant for his ear: "Beans so late! peas so late!"—for I continued to plant when others had begun to hoe,—the ministerial husbandman had not suspected it. "Corn, my boy, for fodder; corn for fodder." "Does he *live* there?" asks the black bonnet of the gray coat; and the hard-featured farmer reins up his grateful dobbin to inquire what you are doing where he sees no manure in the furrow, and recommends a little chip dirt, or any little waste stuff, or it may be ashes or plaster. But here were two acres and a half of furrows, and only a hoe for cart and two hands to draw it,—there being an aversion to other carts and horses,—and chip dirt far away. Fellow-travellers as they rattled by compared it aloud with the fields which they had passed, so that I came to know how I stood in the agricultural world. This was one field not in Mr. Colman's report.[4] And, by the way, who estimates the value of the crop which nature yields in the still wilder fields unimproved by man? The crop of *English* hay is carefully weighed, the moisture calculated, the silicates and the potash; but in all dells and pond-holes in the woods and pastures and swamps grows a rich and various crop only unreaped by man. Mine was, as it were, the connecting link between wild and cultivated fields; as some states are civilized, and others half-civilized, and others savage or barbarous, so my field was, though not in a bad sense, a half-cultivated field. They were beans cheerfully returning to their wild and primitive state that I cultivated, and my hoe played the *Ranz des Vaches*[5] for them.

Near at hand, upon the topmost spray of a birch, sings the brown thrasher—or red mavis, as some love to call him—all the morning, glad of your society, that would find out another farmer's field if yours were not here. While you are planting the seed, he cries,—"Drop it, drop it,—cover it up, cover it up,—pull it up, pull it up, pull it up." But this was not corn, and so it was safe from such enemies as he. You may wonder what his rigmarole, his amateur Paganini[6] performances on one string or on twenty, have to do with your planting, and yet prefer it to leached ashes or plaster. It was a cheap sort of top dressing in which I had entire faith.

As I drew a still fresher soil about the rows with my hoe, I disturbed the ashes of unchronicled nations who in primeval years lived under these heavens, and their small implements of war and hunting were brought to the light of this modern day. They lay mingled with other natural stones, some of which bore the marks of having been burned by Indian fires, and some by the sun, and also bits of pottery and glass brought hither by the recent cultivators of the soil. When my hoe tinkled against the stones, that music echoed to the woods and the sky, and was an accompaniment to my labor which yielded an instant and immeasurable crop. It was no longer beans that I hoed, nor I that hoed beans; and I remembered with as much pity as pride, if I remembered at all, my acquaintances who had gone to the city to attend the oratorios. The nighthawk circled overhead in the sunny afternoons—for I sometimes made a day of it—like a mote in the eye, or in heaven's eye, falling from time to time with a swoop and a sound as if the heavens were rent, torn at last to very rags and tatters, and yet a seamless cope[7] remained; small imps that fill the air and lay their eggs on the ground on bare sand or rocks on the tops of hills, where few have found them; graceful and slender like ripples caught up from the pond, as leaves are raised by the wind to float in the heavens; such kindredship is in nature. The hawk is aerial brother of the wave which he sails over and surveys, those his perfect air-inflated wings answering to the elemental unfledged pinions of the sea. Or sometimes I watched a pair of hen-hawks circling high in the sky, alternately soaring and descending, ap-

---

[4]Henry Colman (1785–1849), author of several essays on the state of agriculture in Massachusetts.
[5]A Swiss song used for calling the cattle.

[6]Nicolò Paganini (1782–1840), Italian composer and violinist.
[7]Canopy or vault.

proaching and leaving one another, as if they were the embodiment of my own thoughts. Or I was attracted by the passage of wild pigeons from this wood to that, with a slight quivering winnowing sound and carrier haste; or from under a rotten stump my hoe turned up a sluggish portentous and outlandish spotted salamander, a trace of Egypt and the Nile, yet our contemporary. When I paused to lean on my hoe, these sounds and sights I heard and saw anywhere in the row, a part of the inexhaustible entertainment which the country offers.

On gala days the town fires its great guns, which echo like popguns to these woods, and some waifs of martial music occasionally penetrate thus far. To me, away there in my bean-field at the other end of the town, the big guns sounded as if a puffball[8] had burst; and when there was a military turnout of which I was ignorant, I have sometimes had a vague sense all the day of some sort of itching and disease in the horizon, as if some eruption would break out there soon, either scarlatina or canker-rash,[9] until at length some more favorable puff of wind, making haste over the fields and up the Wayland road, brought me information of the "trainers."[10] It seemed by the distant hum as if somebody's bees had swarmed, and that the neighbors, according to Virgil's advice, by a faint *tintinnabulum*[11] upon the most sonorous of their domestic utensils, were endeavoring to call them down into the hive again. And when the sound died quite away, and the hum had ceased, and the most favorable breezes told no tale, I knew that they had got the last drone of them all safely into the Middlesex hive, and that now their minds were bent on the honey with which it was smeared.

I felt proud to know that the liberties of Massachusetts and of our fatherland were in such safe keeping; and as I turned to my hoeing again I was filled with an inexpressible confidence, and pursued my labor cheerfully with a calm trust in the future.

When there were several bands of musicians, it sounded as if all the village was a vast bellows, and all the buildings expanded and collapsed alternately with a din. But sometimes it was a really noble and inspiring strain that reached these woods, and the trumpet that sings of fame, and I felt as if I could spit a Mexican[12] with a good relish,—for why should we always stand for trifles?—and looked round for a woodchuck or a skunk to exercise my chivalry upon. These martial strains seemed as far away as Palestine, and reminded me of a march of crusaders in the horizon, with a slight tantivy and tremulous motion of the elm tree tops which overhang the village. This was one of the *great* days; though the sky had from my clearing only the same everlastingly great look that it wears daily, and I saw no difference in it.

It was a singular experience that long acquaintance which I cultivated with beans, what with planting, and hoeing, and harvesting, and threshing, and picking over and selling them,—the last was the hardest of all,—I might add eating, for I did taste. I was determined to know beans. When they were growing, I used to hoe from five o'clock in the morning till noon, and commonly spent the rest of the day about other affairs. Consider the intimate and curious acquaintance one makes with various kinds of weeds,—it will bear some iteration in the account, for there was no little iteration in the labor,—disturbing their delicate organizations so ruthlessly, and making such invidious distinctions with his hoe, levelling whole ranks of one species, and sedulously cultivating another. That's Roman wormwood,—that's pigweed,—that's sorrel,—that's piper-grass,—have at him, chop him up, turn his roots upward to the sun, don't let him have a fibre in the shade, if you do he'll turn himself t'other side up and be as green as a leek in two days. A

---

[8]Ball-shaped mushroom-like plant or the tuft of the dandelion.
[9]Scarlet fever or sore throat (with ulcer-like sores).
[10]Members of state militia in uniform.
[11]Tinkling (as a bell).
[12]Ironic reference to the Mexican War, then going on.

long war, not with cranes, but with weeds, those Trojans who had sun and rain and dews on their side. Daily the beans saw me come to their rescue armed with a hoe, and thin the ranks of their enemies, filling up the trenches with weedy dead. Many a lusty crest-waving Hector,[13] that towered a whole foot above his crowding comrades, fell before my weapon and rolled in the dust.

Those summer days which some of my contemporaries devoted to the fine arts in Boston or Rome, and others to contemplation in India, and others to trade in London or New York, I thus, with the other farmers of New England, devoted to husbandry. Not that I wanted beans to eat, for I am by nature a Pythagorean,[14] so far as beans are concerned, whether they mean porridge or voting,[15] and exchanged them for rice; but, perchance, as some must work in fields if only for the sake of tropes and expression, to serve a parable-maker one day. It was on the whole a rare amusement, which, continued too long, might have become a dissipation. Though I gave them no manure, and did not hoe them all once, I hoed them unusually well as far as I went, and was paid for it in the end, "there being in truth," as Evelyn[16] says, "no compost or lætation whatsoever comparable to this continual motion, repastination, and turning of the mould with the spade." "The earth," he adds elsewhere, "especially if fresh, has a certain magnetism in it, by which it attracts the salt, power, or virtue (call it either) which gives it life, and is the logic of all the labor and stir we keep about it, to sustain us; all dungings and other sordid temperings being but the vicars succedaneous to this improvement." Moreover, this being one of those "worn-out and exhausted lay fields which enjoy their sabbath," had perchance, as Sir Kenelm Digby[17] thinks likely, attracted "vital spirits" from the air. I harvested twelve bushels of beans.

But to be more particular, for it is complained that Mr. Colman has reported chiefly the expensive experiments of gentlemen farmers, my outgoes were,—

For a hoe	$ 0 54	
Plowing, harrowing, and furrowing	7 50	Too much.
Beans for seed	3 12½	
Potatoes "	1 33	
Peas "	0 40	
Turnip seed	0 06	
White line for crow fence	0 02	
Horse cultivator and boy three hours	1 00	
Horse and cart to get crop	0 75	
In all	$14 72½	

My income was (patremfamilias vendacem, non emacem esse oportet),[18] from

Nine bushels and twelve quarts of beans sold	$16 94
Five " large potatoes	2 50
Nine " small "	2 25
Grass	1 00
Stalks	0 75
In all	$23 44
Leaving a pecuniary profit, as I have elsewhere said, of	$8 71½

---

[13]Valiant Trojan warrior slain by Achilles in a battle described in the *Iliad*.
[14]Pythagorus (*c.* 530 B.C.), Greek philosopher who forbade his followers to eat beans.
[15]In antiquity, beans were used in voting.

[16]John Evelyn (1620–1706), British diarist, author of *Terra: A Philosophical Discourse of Earth* (1729).
[17]Naval commander and author (1603–1665).
[18]"The head of the family should be the seller, not the buyer," Cato (234–149 B.C.). *De Agri Cultura*.

This is the result of my experience in raising beans: Plant the common small white bush bean about the first of June, in rows three feet by eighteen inches apart, being careful to select fresh round and unmixed seed. First look out for worms, and supply vacancies by planting anew. Then look out for woodchucks, if it is an exposed place, for they will nibble off the earliest tender leaves almost clean as they go; and again, when the young tendrils make their appearance, they have notice of it, and will shear them off with both buds and young pods, sitting erect like a squirrel. But above all harvest as early as possible, if you would escape frosts and have a fair and salable crop; you may save much loss by this means.

This further experience also I gained: I said to myself, I will not plant beans and corn with so much industry another summer, but such seeds, if the seed is not lost, as sincerity, truth, simplicity, faith, innocence, and the like, and see if they will not grow in this soil, even with less toil and manurance, and sustain me, for surely it has not been exhausted for these crops. Alas! I said this to myself; but now another summer is gone, and another, and another, and I am obliged to say to you, Reader, that the seeds which I planted, if indeed they *were* the seeds of those virtues, were wormeaten or had lost their vitality, and so did not come up. Commonly men will only be brave as their fathers were brave, or timid. This generation is very sure to plant corn and beans each new year precisely as the Indians did centuries ago and taught the first settlers to do, as if there were a fate in it. I saw an old man the other day, to my astonishment, making the holes with a hoe for the seventieth time at least, and not for himself to lie down in! But why should not the New Englander try new adventures, and not lay so much stress on his grain, his potato and grass crop, and his orchards,—raise other crops than these? Why concern ourselves so much about our beans for seed, and not be concerned at all about a new generation of men? We should really be fed and cheered if when we met a man we were sure to see that some of the qualities which I have named, which we all prize more than those other productions, but which are for the most part broadcast and floating in the air, had taken root and grown in him. Here comes such a subtle and ineffable quality, for instance, as truth or justice, though the slightest amount or new variety of it, along the road. Our ambassadors should be instructed to send home such seeds as these, and Congress help to distribute them over all the land. We should never stand upon ceremony with sincerity. We should never cheat and insult and banish one another by our meanness, if there were present the kernel of worth and friendliness. We should not meet thus in haste. Most men I do not meet at all, for they seem not to have time; they are busy about their beans. We would not deal with a man thus plodding ever, leaning on a hoe or a spade as a staff between his work, not as a mushroom, but partially risen out of the earth, something more than erect, like swallows alighted and walking on the ground:—

> "And as he spake, his wings would now and then
> Spread, as he meant to fly, then close again,—"[19]

so that we should suspect that we might be conversing with an angel. Bread may not always nourish us; but it always does us good, it even takes stiffness out of our joints, and makes us supple and buoyant, when we knew not what ailed us, to recognize any generosity in man or Nature, to share any unmixed and heroic joy.

Ancient poetry and mythology suggest, at least, that husbandry was once a sacred art; but it is pursued with irreverent haste and heedlessness by us, our object being to have large farms and large crops merely. We have no festival, nor procession, nor ceremony, not excepting our cattle-shows and so-called Thanksgiv-

---

[19]From *The Shepheard's Oracles* by Francis Quarles (1592–1644), British poet.

ings, by which the farmer expresses a sense of the sacredness of his calling, or is reminded of its sacred origin. It is the premium and the feast which tempt him. He sacrifices not to Ceres and the Terrestrial Jove, but to the infernal Plutus rather.[20] By avarice and selfishness, and a grovelling habit, from which none of us is free, of regarding the soil as property, or the means of acquiring property chiefly, the landscape is deformed, husbandry is degraded with us, and the farmer leads the meanest of lives. He knows Nature but as a robber. Cato says that the profits of agriculture are particularly pious or just (*maximeque pius quaestus*), and according to Varro the old Romans "called the same earth Mother and Ceres, and thought that they who cultivated it led a pious and useful life, and that they alone were left of the race of King Saturn."[21]

We are wont to forget that the sun looks on our cultivated fields and on the prairies and forests without distinction. They all reflect and absorb his rays alike, and the former make but a small part of the glorious picture which he beholds in his daily course. In his view the earth is all equally cultivated like a garden. Therefore we should receive the benefit of his light and heat with a corresponding trust and magnanimity. What though I value the seed of these beans, and harvest that in the fall of the year? This broad field which I have looked at so long looks not to me as the principal cultivator, but away from me to influences more genial to it, which water and make it green. These beans have results which are not harvested by me. Do they not grow for woodchucks partly? The ear of wheat (in Latin *spica*, obsoletely *speca*, from *spe*, hope) should not be the only hope of the husbandman; its kernel or grain (*granum*, from *gerendo*, bearing) is not all that it bears. How, then, can our harvest fail? Shall I not rejoice also at the abundance of the weeds whose seeds are the granary of the birds? It matters little comparatively whether the fields fill the farmer's barns. The true husbandman will cease from anxiety, as the squirrels manifest no concern whether the woods will bear chestnuts this year or not, and finish his labor with every day, relinquishing all claim to the produce of his fields, and sacrificing in his mind not only his first but his last fruits also.

VIII

THE VILLAGE

After hoeing, or perhaps reading and writing, in the forenoon, I usually bathed again in the pond, swimming across one of its coves for a stint, and washed the dust of labor from my person, or smoothed out the last wrinkle which study had made, and for the afternoon was absolutely free. Every day or two I strolled to the village to hear some of the gossip which is incessantly going on there, circulating either from mouth to mouth, or from newspaper to newspaper, and which, taken in homœopathic doses,[1] was really as refreshing in its way as the rustle of leaves and the peeping of frogs. As I walked in the woods to see the birds and squirrels, so I walked in the village to see the men and boys; instead of the wind among the pines I heard the carts rattle. In one direction from my house there was a colony of muskrats in the river meadows; under the grove of elms and buttonwoods in the other horizon was a village of busy men, as curious to me as if they had been prairie-dogs, each sitting at the mouth of its burrow, or running over to a neighbor's to gossip. I went there frequently to observe their habits. The village appeared to me a great news room; and on one side, to support it, as once at Redding & Company's on State Street,[2] they kept nuts and raisins, or salt and

---

[20]Ceres, Roman goddess of agriculture; Jove (also Jupiter), Roman chief deity; Plutus, Greek god of wealth.
[21]From *Rerum Rusticarum* (III, 1, 5), by Marcus Terentius Varro (116–27 B.C.). Saturn instructed humankind in the arts of agriculture.

[1]Minute amounts (homeotherapy treats a disease by giving small quantities of the substance that causes the disease).
[2]Boston booksellers.

meal and other groceries. Some have such a vast appetite for the former commodity, that is, the news, and such sound digestive organs, that they can sit forever in public avenues without stirring, and let it simmer and whisper through them like the Etesian winds,[3] or as if inhaling ether, it only producing numbness and insensibility to pain,—otherwise it would often be painful to hear,—without affecting the consciousness. I hardly ever failed, when I rambled through the village, to see a row of such worthies, either sitting on a ladder sunning themselves, with their bodies inclined forward and their eyes glancing along the line this way and that, from time to time, with a voluptuous expression, or else leaning against a barn with their hands in their pockets, like caryatides,[4] as if to prop it up. They, being commonly out of doors, heard whatever was in the wind. These are the coarsest mills, in which all gossip is first rudely digested or cracked up before it is emptied into finer and more delicate hoppers within doors. I observed that the vitals of the village were the grocery, the bar-room, the post-office, and the bank; and, as a necessary part of the machinery, they kept a bell, a big gun, and a fire-engine, at convenient places; and the houses were so arranged as to make the most of mankind, in lanes and fronting one another, so that every traveller had to run the gauntlet, and every man, woman, and child might get a lick at him. Of course, those who were stationed nearest to the head of the line, where they could most see and be seen, and have the first blow at him, paid the highest prices for their places; and the few straggling inhabitants in the outskirts, where long gaps in the line began to occur, and the traveller could get over walls or turn aside into cow-paths, and so escape, paid a very slight ground or window tax.[5] Signs were hung out on all sides to allure him; some to catch him by the appetite, as the tavern and victualling cellar; some by the fancy, as the dry goods store and the jeweller's; and others by the hair or the feet or the skirts, as the barber, the shoemaker, or the tailor. Besides, there was a still more terrible standing invitation to call at every one of these houses, and company expected about these times. For the most part I escaped wonderfully from these dangers, either by proceeding at once boldly and without deliberation to the goal, as is recommended to those who run the gauntlet, or by keeping my thoughts on high things, like Orpheus, who, "loudly singing the praises of the gods to his lyre, drowned the voices of the Sirens, and kept out of danger."[6] Sometimes I bolted suddenly, and nobody could tell my whereabouts, for I did not stand much about gracefulness, and never hesitated at a gap in a fence. I was even accustomed to make an irruption[7] into some houses, where I was well entertained, and after learning the kernels and very last sieveful of news,—what had subsided, the prospects of war and peace, and whether the world was likely to hold together much longer,—I was let out through the rear avenues, and so escaped to the woods again.

It was very pleasant, when I stayed late in town, to launch myself into the night, especially if it was dark and tempestuous, and set sail from some bright village parlor or lecture room, with a bag of rye or Indian meal upon my shoulder, for my snug harbor in the woods, having made all tight without and withdrawn under hatches with a merry crew of thoughts, leaving only my outer man at the helm, or even tying up the helm when it was plain sailing. I had many a genial thought by the cabin fire "as I sailed."[8] I was never cast away nor distressed in any weather, though I encountered some severe storms. It is darker in the woods, even in common nights, than most suppose. I frequently had to look up at the opening between the trees above the path in order to learn my route, and, where

---

[3]Mediterranean summer winds.
[4]Statuesque sculptured women used as supports and decoration in Greek architecture.
[5]Property tax based on number of windows.
[6]Identified by Harding as a translation (perhaps Thoreau's

own) from the *Argonautica*, by Apollonius Rhodius (c. 295—247 B.C.).
[7]Burst in.
[8]Harding identifies this phrase as a refrain from the American "Ballad of Captain Robert Kidd."

there was no cartpath, to feel with my feet the faint track which I had worn, or steer by the known relation of particular trees which I felt with my hands, passing between two pines for instance, not more than eighteen inches apart, in the midst of the woods, invariably, in the darkest night. Sometimes, after coming home thus late in a dark and muggy night, when my feet felt the path which my eyes could not see, dreaming and absent-minded all the way, until I was aroused by having to raise my hand to lift the latch, I have not been able to recall a single step of my walk, and I have thought that perhaps my body would find its way home if its master should forsake it, as the hand finds its way to the mouth without assistance. Several times, when a visitor chanced to stay into evening, and it proved a dark night, I was obliged to conduct him to the cart-path in the rear of the house, and then point out to him the direction he was to pursue, and in keeping which he was to be guided rather by his feet than his eyes. One very dark night I directed thus on their way two young men who had been fishing in the pond. They lived about a mile off through the woods, and were quite used to the route. A day or two after one of them told me that they wandered about the greater part of the night, close by their own premises, and did not get home till toward morning, by which time, as there had been several heavy showers in the meanwhile, and the leaves were very wet, they were drenched to their skins. I have heard of many going astray even in the village streets, when the darkness was so thick that you could cut it with a knife, as the saying is. Some who live in the outskirts, having come to town a-shopping in their wagons, have been obliged to put up for the night; and gentlemen and ladies making a call have gone half a mile out of their way, feeling the sidewalk only with their feet, and not knowing when they turned. It is a surprising and memorable, as well as valuable experience, to be lost in the woods any time. Often in a snow-storm, even by day, one will come out upon a well-known road and yet find it impossible to tell which way leads to the village. Though he knows that he has travelled it a thousand times, he cannot recognize a feature in it, but it is as strange to him as if it were a road in Siberia. By night, of course, the perplexity is infinitely greater. In our most trivial walks, we are constantly, though unconsciously, steering like pilots by certain well-known beacons and headlands, and if we go beyond our usual course we still carry in our minds the bearing of some neighboring cape; and not till we are completely lost, or turned round,—for a man needs only to be turned round once with his eyes shut in this world to be lost,—do we appreciate the vastness and strangeness of nature. Every man has to learn the points of compass again as often as he awakes, whether from sleep or any abstraction. Not till we are lost, in other words not till we have lost the world, do we begin to find ourselves, and realize where we are and the infinite extent of our relations.

One afternoon, near the end of the first summer, when I went to the village to get a shoe from the cobbler's, I was seized and put into jail, because, as I have elsewhere related,[9] I did not pay a tax to, or recognize the authority of, the State which buys and sells men, women, and children, like cattle, at the door of its senate-house. I had gone down to the woods for other purposes. But, wherever a man goes, men will pursue and paw him with their dirty institutions, and, if they can, constrain him to belong to their desperate odd-fellow society. It is true, I might have resisted forcibly with more or less effect, might have run "amok" against society; but I preferred that society should run "amok" against me, it being the desperate party. However, I was released the next day, obtained my mended shoe, and returned to the woods in season to get my dinner of huckleberries on Fair Haven Hill. I was never molested by any person but those who repre-

[9]In "Resistance to Civil Government."

sented the State. I had no lock nor bolt but for the desk which held my papers, not even a nail to put over my latch or windows. I never fastened my door night or day, though I was to be absent several days; not even when the next fall I spent a fortnight in the woods in Maine. And yet my house was more respected than if it had been surrounded by a file of soldiers. The tired rambler could rest and warm himself by my fire, the literary amuse himself with the few books on my table, or the curious, by opening my closet door, see what was left of my dinner, and what prospect I had of a supper. Yet, though many people of every class came this way to the pond, I suffered no serious inconvenience from these sources, and I never missed anything but one small book, a volume of Homer, which perhaps was improperly gilded, and this I trust a soldier of our camp has found by this time. I am convinced, that if all men were to live as simply as I then did, thieving and robbery would be unknown. These take place only in communities where some have got more than is sufficient while others have not enough. The Pope's Homers[10] would soon get properly distributed.

> "Nec bella fuerunt,
> Faginus astabat dum scyphus ante dapes."

> "Nor wars did men molest,
> When only beechen bowls were in request."[11]

"You who govern public affairs, what need have you to employ punishments? Love virtue, and the people will be virtuous. The virtues of a superior man are like the wind; the virtues of a common man are like the grass; the grass, when the wind passes over it, bends."[12]

IX

THE PONDS

Sometimes, having had a surfeit of human society and gossip, and worn out all my village friends, I rambled still farther westward than I habitually dwell, into yet more unfrequented parts of the town, "to fresh woods and pastures new,"[1] or, while the sun was setting, made my supper of huckleberries and blueberries on Fair Haven Hill, and laid up a store for several days. The fruits do not yield their true flavor to the purchaser of them, nor to him who raises them for the market. There is but one way to obtain it, yet few take that way. If you would know the flavor of huckleberries, ask the cow-boy or the partridge. It is a vulgar error[2] to suppose that you have tasted huckleberries who never plucked them. A huckleberry never reaches Boston; they have not been known there since they grew on her three hills. The ambrosial and essential part of the fruit is lost with the bloom which is rubbed off in the market cart, and they become mere provender. As long as Eternal Justice reigns, not one innocent huckleberry can be transported thither from the country's hills.

Occasionally, after my hoeing was done for the day, I joined some impatient companion who had been fishing on the pond since morning, as silent and motionless as a duck or a floating leaf, and, after practising various kinds of philosophy, had concluded commonly, by the time I arrived, that he belonged to the ancient sect of Cœnobites.[3] There was one older man, an excellent fisher and skilled in all kinds of woodcraft, who was pleased to look upon my house as a building

---

[10]Alexander Pope (1688–1744) translated the *Iliad* and *Odyssey* into heroic couplets.
[11]From *Elegies* (3, 11, 7–8), by Albius Tibullus (*c.* 48–19 B.C.), Roman poet.
[12]From the *Analects* (XII, 19), by Confucius (*c.* 551–479 B.C.).

[1]From the last line of the elegy "Lycidas," by John Milton.
[2]I.e., common mistake.
[3]A member of a religious order living in a community (opposite of *anchorite*). Note pun on fishing, "see, no bite."

erected for the convenience of fishermen; and I was equally pleased when he sat in my doorway to arrange his lines. Once in a while we sat together on the pond, he at one end of the boat, and I at the other; but not many words passed between us, for he had grown deaf in his later years, but he occasionally hummed a psalm, which harmonized well enough with my philosophy. Our intercourse was thus altogether one of unbroken harmony, far more pleasing to remember than if it had been carried on by speech. When, as was commonly the case, I had none to commune with, I used to raise the echoes by striking with a paddle on the side of my boat, filling the surrounding woods with circling and dilating sound, stirring them up as the keeper of a menagerie his wild beasts, until I elicited a growl from every wooded vale and hillside.

In warm evenings I frequently sat in the boat playing the flute, and saw the perch, which I seem to have charmed, hovering around me, and the moon travelling over the ribbed bottom, which was strewed with the wrecks of the forest. Formerly I had come to this pond adventurously, from time to time, in dark summer nights, with a companion, and, making a fire close to the water's edge, which we thought attracted the fishes, we caught pouts with a bunch of worms strung on a thread, and when we had done, far in the night, threw the burning brands high into the air like skyrockets, which, coming down into the pond, were quenched with a loud hissing, and we were suddenly groping in total darkness. Through this, whistling a tune, we took our way to the haunts of men again. But now I had made my home by the shore.

Sometimes, after staying in a village parlor till the family had all retired, I have returned to the woods, and, partly with a view to the next day's dinner, spent the hours of midnight fishing from a boat by moonlight, serenaded by owls and foxes, and hearing, from time to time, the creaking note of some unknown bird close at hand. These experiences were very memorable and valuable to me,—anchored in forty feet of water, and twenty or thirty rods from the shore, surrounded sometimes by thousands of small perch and shiners, dimpling the surface with their tails in the moonlight, and communicating by a long flaxen line with mysterious nocturnal fishes which had their dwelling forty feet below, or sometimes dragging sixty feet of line about the pond as I drifted in the gentle night breeze, now and then feeling a slight vibration along it, indicative of some life prowling about its extremity, of dull uncertain blundering purpose there, and slow to make up its mind. At length you slowly raise, pulling hand over hand, some horned pout squeaking and squirming to the upper air. It was very queer, especially in dark nights, when your thoughts had wandered to vast and cosmogonal themes in other spheres, to feel this faint jerk, which came to interrupt your dreams and link you to Nature again. It seemed as if I might next cast my line upward into the air, as well as downward into this element, which was scarcely more dense. Thus I caught two fishes as it were with one hook.

The scenery of Walden is on a humble scale, and, though very beautiful, does not approach to grandeur, nor can it much concern one who has not long frequented it or lived by its shore; yet this pond is so remarkable for its depth and purity as to merit a particular description. It is a clear and deep green well, half a mile long and a mile and three quarters in circumference, and contains about sixty-one and a half acres; a perennial spring in the midst of pine and oak woods, without any visible inlet or outlet except by the clouds and evaporation. The surrounding hills rise abruptly from the water to the height of forty to eighty feet, though on the southeast and east they attain to about one hundred and one hundred and fifty feet respectively, within a quarter and a third of a mile. They are exclusively woodland. All our Concord waters have two colors at least; one when viewed at a distance, and another, more proper, close at hand. The first depends more on the light, and follows the sky. In clear weather, in summer, they appear blue at a little distance, especially if agitated, and at a great distance all appear alike. In stormy weather they are sometimes of a dark slate-color. The sea, however, is said to be blue one day and green another without any perceptible change in the atmosphere. I have seen our river, when, the landscape being covered with snow, both water and ice were almost as green as grass. Some consider blue "to be the color of pure water, whether liquid or solid."[4] But, looking directly down into our waters from a boat, they are seen to be of very different colors. Walden is blue at one time and green at another, even from the same point of view. Lying between the earth and the heavens, it partakes of the color of both. Viewed from a hilltop it reflects the color of the sky; but near at hand it is of a yellowish tint next the shore where you can see the sand, then a light green, which gradually deepens to a uniform dark green in the body of the pond. In some lights, viewed even from a hilltop, it is of a vivid green next the shore. Some have referred this to the reflection of the verdure; but it is equally green there against the railroad sandbank, and in the spring, before the leaves are expanded, and it may be simply the result of the prevailing blue mixed with the yellow of the sand. Such is the color of its iris. This is that portion, also, where in the spring, the ice being warmed by the heat of the sun reflected from the bottom, and also transmitted through the earth, melts first and forms a narrow canal about the still frozen middle. Like the rest of our waters, when much agitated, in clear weather, so that the surface of the waves may reflect the sky at the right angle, or because there is more light mixed with it, it appears at a little distance of a darker blue than the sky itself; and at such a time, being on its surface, and looking with divided vision, so as to see the reflection, I have discerned a matchless and indescribable light blue, such as watered or changeable silks and sword blades suggest, more cerulean than the sky itself, alternating with the original dark green on the opposite sides of the waves, which last appeared but muddy in comparison. It is a vitreous greenish blue, as I remember it, like those patches of the winter sky seen through cloud vistas in the west before sundown. Yet a single glass of its water held up to the light is as colorless as an equal quantity of air. It is well known that a large plate of glass will have a green tint, owing, as the makers say, to its "body," but a small piece of the same will be colorless. How large a body of Walden water would be required to reflect a green tint I have never proved. The water of our river is black or a very dark brown to one looking directly down on it, and, like that of most ponds, imparts to the body of one bathing in it a yellowish tinge; but this water is of such crystalline purity that the body of the bather appears of an alabaster whiteness, still more unnatural, which, as the limbs are magnified and distorted withal, produces a monstrous effect, making fit studies for a Michael Angelo.[5]

The water is so transparent that the bottom can easily be discerned at the depth of twenty-five or thirty feet. Paddling over it, you may see, many feet beneath the surface, the schools of perch and shiners, perhaps only an inch long, yet the former easily distinguished by their transverse bars, and you think that they must be ascetic fish that find a subsistence there. Once, in the winter, many years ago, when I had been cutting holes through the ice in order to catch pickerel, as I stepped ashore I tossed my axe back on to the ice, but, as if some evil genius had directed it, it slid four or five rods directly into one of the holes, where the water was twenty-five feet deep. Out of curiosity, I lay down on the ice and looked through the hole, until I saw the axe a little on one side, standing on its head, with its helve erect and gently swaying to and fro with the pulse of the pond; and there

---

[4]From *Travels through the Alps of Savoy* (1843), by James D. Forbes (1809–1868), Scottish scientist.
[5]Michelangelo (1475–1564), Italian Renaissance artist and sculptor; his male figures are overpowering in their virile muscularity.

it might have stood erect and swaying till in the course of time the handle rotted off, if I had not disturbed it. Making another hole directly over it with an ice chisel which I had, and cutting down the longest birch which I could find in the neighborhood with my knife, I made a slip-noose, which I attached to its end, and, letting it down carefully, passed it over the knob of the handle, and drew it by a line along the birch, and so pulled the axe out again.

The shore is composed of a belt of smooth rounded white stones like paving-stones, excepting one or two short sand beaches, and is so steep that in many places a single leap will carry you into water over your head; and were it not for its remarkable transparency, that would be the last to be seen of its bottom till it rose on the opposite side. Some think it is bottomless. It is nowhere muddy, and a casual observer would say that there were no weeds at all in it; and of noticeable plants, except in the little meadows recently overflowed, which do not properly belong to it, a closer scrutiny does not detect a flag nor a bulrush, nor even a lily, yellow or white, but only a few small heart-leaves and potamogetons,[6] and perhaps a water-target[7] or two; all which however a bather might not perceive; and these plants are clean and bright like the element they grow in. The stones extend a rod or two into the water, and then the bottom is pure sand, except in the deepest parts, where there is usually a little sediment, probably from the decay of the leaves which have been wafted on to it so many successive falls, and a bright green weed is brought up on anchors even in midwinter.

We have one other pond just like this, White Pond, in Nine Acre Corner, about two and a half miles westerly; but, though I am acquainted with most of the ponds within a dozen miles of this centre, I do not know a third of this pure and well-like character. Successive nations perchance have drank at, admired, and fathomed it, and passed away, and still its water is green and pellucid as ever. Not an intermitting spring! Perhaps on that spring morning when Adam and Eve were driven out of Eden Walden Pond was already in existence, and even then breaking up in a gentle spring rain accompanied with mist and a southerly wind, and covered with myriads of ducks and geese, which had not heard of the fall, when still such pure lakes sufficed them. Even then it had commenced to rise and fall, and had clarified its waters and colored them of the hue they now wear, and obtained a patent of Heaven to be the only Walden Pond in the world and distiller of celestial dews. Who knows in how many unremembered nations' literatures this has been the Castalian Fountain?[8] or what nymphs presided over it in the Golden Age?[9] It is a gem of the first water which Concord wears in her coronet.

Yet perchance the first who came to this well have left some trace of their footsteps. I have been surprised to detect encircling the pond, even where a thick wood has just been cut down on the shore, a narrow shelf-like path in the steep hillside, alternately rising and falling, approaching and receding from the water's edge, as old probably as the race of man here, worn by the feet of aboriginal hunters, and still from time to time unwittingly trodden by the present occupants of the land. This is particularly distinct to one standing on the middle of the pond in winter, just after a light snow has fallen, appearing as a clear undulating white line, unobscured by weeds and twigs, and very obvious a quarter of a mile off in many places where in summer it is hardly distinguishable close at hand. The snow reprints it, as it were, in clear white type alto-relievo.[10] The ornamented grounds of villas which will one day be built here may still preserve some trace of this.

The pond rises and falls, but whether regularly or not, and within what period,

---

[6]Pond weeds or river plants.
[7]Aquatic plant.
[8]Spring sacred to Apollo and the muses, in classical mythology.

[9]In classical mythology, the earliest and ideal age of the world.
[10]I.e., in high relief (standing out against the background).

nobody knows, though, as usual, many pretend to know. It is commonly higher in the winter and lower in the summer, though not corresponding to the general wet and dryness. I can remember when it was a foot or two lower, and also when it was at least five feet higher, than when I lived by it. There is a narrow sand-bar running into it, with very deep water on one side, on which I helped boil a kettle of chowder, some six rods from the main shore, about the year 1824, which it has not been possible to do for twenty-five years; and, on the other hand, my friends used to listen with incredulity when I told them, that a few years later I was accustomed to fish from a boat in a secluded cove in the woods, fifteen rods from the only shore they knew, which place was long since converted into a meadow. But the pond has risen steadily for two years, and now, in the summer of '52, is just five feet higher than when I lived there, or as high as it was thirty years ago, and fishing goes on again in the meadow. This makes a difference of level, at the outside, of six or seven feet; and yet the water shed by the surrounding hills is insignificant in amount, and this overflow must be referred to causes which affect the deep springs. This same summer the pond has begun to fall again. It is remarkable that this fluctuation, whether periodical or not, appears thus to require many years for its accomplishment. I have observed one rise and a part of two falls, and I expect that a dozen or fifteen years hence the water will again be as low as I have ever known it. Flint's Pond, a mile eastward, allowing for the disturbance occasioned by its inlets and outlets, and the smaller intermediate ponds also, sympathize with Walden, and recently attained their greatest height at the same time with the latter. The same is true, as far as my observation goes, of White Pond.

This rise and fall of Walden at long intervals serves this use at least; the water standing at this great height for a year or more, though it makes it difficult to walk round it, kills the shrubs and trees which have sprung up about its edge since the last rise,—pitch pines, birches, alders, aspens, and others,—and, falling again, leaves an unobstructed shore; for, unlike many ponds and all waters which are subject to a daily tide, its shore is cleanest when the water is lowest. On the side of the pond next my house a row of pitch pines, fifteen feet high, has been killed and tipped over as if by a lever, and thus a stop put to their encroachments; and their size indicates how many years have elapsed since the last rise to this height. By this fluctuation the pond asserts its title to a shore, and thus the *shore* is *shorn*, and the trees cannot hold it by right of possession. These are the lips of the lake, on which no beard grows. It licks its chaps from time to time. When the water is at its height, the alders, willows, and maples send forth a mass of fibrous red roots several feet long from all sides of their stems in the water, and to the height of three or four feet from the ground, in the effort to maintain themselves; and I have known the high blueberry bushes about the shore, which commonly produce no fruit, bear an abundant crop under these circumstances.

Some have been puzzled to tell how the shore became so regularly paved. My townsmen have all heard the tradition—the oldest people tell me that they heard it in their youth—that anciently the Indians were holding a pow-wow upon a hill here, which rose as high into the heavens as the pond now sinks deep into the earth, and they used much profanity, as the story goes, though this vice is one of which the Indians were never guilty, and while they were thus engaged the hill shook and suddenly sank, and only one old squaw, named Walden, escaped, and from her the pond was named. It has been conjectured that when the hill shook these stones rolled down its side and became the present shore. It is very certain, at any rate, that once there was no pond here, and now there is one; and this Indian fable does not in any respect conflict with the account of that ancient settler whom I have mentioned, who remembers so well when he first came here with his divining-rod, saw a thin vapor rising from the sward, and the hazel pointed steadily downward, and he concluded to dig a well here. As for the stones, many still think that they are hardly to be accounted for by the action of the waves on these hills; but I observe that the surrounding hills are remarkably full of the same kind of stones, so that they have been obliged to pile them up in walls on both sides of the railroad cut nearest the pond; and, moreover, there are most stones where the shore is most abrupt; so that, unfortunately, it is no longer a mystery to me. I detect the paver.[11] If the name was not derived from that of some English locality,—Saffron Walden,[12] for instance,—one might suppose that it was called originally *Walled-in* Pond.

The pond was my well ready dug. For four months in the year its water is as cold as it is pure at all times; and I think that it is then as good as any, if not the best, in the town. In the winter, all water which is exposed to the air is colder than springs and wells which are protected from it. The temperature of the pond water which had stood in the room where I sat from five o'clock in the afternoon till noon the next day, the sixth of March, 1846, the thermometer having been up to 65° or 70° some of the time, owing partly to the sun on the roof, was 42°, or one degree colder than the water of one of the coldest wells in the village just drawn. The temperature of the Boiling Spring [13] the same day was 45°, or the warmest of any water tried, though it is the coldest that I know of in summer, when, beside, shallow and stagnant surface water is not mingled with it. Moreover, in summer, Walden never becomes so warm as most water which is exposed to the sun, on account of its depth. In the warmest weather I usually placed a pailful in my cellar, where it became cool in the night, and remained so during the day; though I also resorted to a spring in the neighborhood. It was as good when a week old as the day it was dipped, and had no taste of the pump. Whoever camps for a week in summer by the shore of a pond, needs only bury a pail of water a few feet deep in the shade of his camp to be independent of the luxury of ice.

There have been caught in Walden pickerel, one weighing seven pounds,—to say nothing of another which carried off a reel with great velocity, which the fisherman safely set down at eight pounds because he did not see him,—perch and pouts, some of each weighing over two pounds, shiners, chivins or roach (*Leuciscus pulchellus*), a very few breams, and a couple of eels, one weighing four pounds,—I am thus particular because the weight of a fish is commonly its only title to fame, and these are the only eels I have heard of here;—also, I have a faint recollection of a little fish some five inches long, with silvery sides and a greenish back, somewhat dace-like[14] in its character, which I mention here chiefly to link my facts to fable. Nevertheless, this pond is not very fertile in fish. Its pickerel, though not abundant, are its chief boast. I have seen at one time lying on the ice pickerel of at least three different kinds: a long and shallow one, steel-colored, most like those caught in the river; a bright golden kind, with greenish reflections and remarkably deep, which is the most common here; and another, golden-colored, and shaped like the last, but peppered on the sides with small dark brown or black spots, intermixed with a few faint blood-red ones, very much like a trout. The specific name *reticulatus* would not apply to this; it should be *guttatus* rather.[15] These are all very firm fish, and weigh more than their size promises. The shiners, pouts, and perch also, and indeed all the fishes which inhabit this pond, are much cleaner, handsomer, and firmer-fleshed than those in the river and most other ponds, as the water is purer, and they can easily be distinguished from them. Probably many ichthyologists[16] would make new varieties of some of them. There are also a clean race of frogs and tortoises, and a few mussels in it; muskrats and minks leave their traces about it, and occasionally a travelling mud-turtle visits it. Sometimes, when I pushed off my boat in the morning, I disturbed a great mud-turtle which had secreted himself under the boat in the night. Ducks and geese

---

[11]I.e., glacial action.
[12]English village (outside London).
[13]A bubbling (not really boiling) spring near Walden Pond.

[14]Dace—a small fresh-water fish of the carp family.
[15]Not "netlike" but "speckled."
[16]Scientists who specialize in the study of fish.

frequent it in the spring and fall, the white-bellied swallows (*Hirundo bicolor*) skim over it, and the peetweets (*Totanus macularius*) "teeter" along its stony shores all summer. I have sometimes disturbed a fish hawk sitting on a white pine over the water; but I doubt if it is ever profaned by the wing of a gull, like Fair Haven.[17] At most, it tolerates one annual loon. These are all the animals of consequence which frequent it now.

You may see from a boat, in calm weather, near the sandy eastern shore, where the water is eight or ten feet deep, and also in some other parts of the pond, some circular heaps half a dozen feet in diameter by a foot in height, consisting of small stones less than a hen's egg in size, where all around is bare sand. At first you wonder if the Indians could have formed them on the ice for any purpose, and so, when the ice melted, they sank to the bottom; but they are too regular and some of them plainly too fresh for that. They are similar to those found in rivers; but as there are no suckers nor lampreys here, I know not by what fish they could be made. Perhaps they are the nests of the chivin.[18] These lend a pleasing mystery to the bottom.

The shore is irregular enough not to be monotonous. I have in my mind's eye the western, indented with deep bays, the bolder northern, and the beautifully scalloped southern shore, where successive capes overlap each other and suggest unexplored coves between. The forest has never so good a setting, nor is so distinctly beautiful, as when seen from the middle of a small lake amid hills which rise from the water's edge; for the water in which it is reflected not only makes the best foreground in such a case, but, with its winding shore, the most natural and agreeable boundary to it. There is no rawness nor imperfection in its edge there, as where the axe has cleared a part, or a cultivated field abuts on it. The trees have ample room to expand on the water side, and each sends forth its most vigorous branch in that direction. There Nature has woven a natural selvage, and the eye rises by just gradations from the low shrubs of the shore to the highest trees. There are few traces of man's hand to be seen. The water laves the shore as it did a thousand years ago.

A lake is the landscape's most beautiful and expressive feature. It is earth's eye; looking into which the beholder measures the depth of his own nature. The fluviatile trees next the shore are the slender eyelashes which fringe it, and the wooded hills and cliffs around are its overhanging brows.

Standing on the smooth sandy beach at the east end of the pond, in a calm September afternoon, when a slight haze makes the opposite shore-line indistinct, I have seen whence came the expression, "the glassy surface of a lake." When you invert your head, it looks like a thread of finest gossamer stretched across the valley, and gleaming against the distant pine woods, separating one stratum of the atmosphere from another. You would think that you could walk dry under it to the opposite hills, and that the swallows which skim over might perch on it. Indeed, they sometimes dive below the line, as it were by mistake, and are undeceived. As you look over the pond westward you are obliged to employ both your hands to defend your eyes against the reflected as well as the true sun, for they are equally bright; and if, between the two, you survey its surface critically, it is literally as smooth as glass, except where the skater insects, at equal intervals scattered over its whole extent, by their motions in the sun produce the finest imaginable sparkle on it, or, perchance, a duck plumes itself, or, as I have said, a swallow skims so low as to touch it. It may be that in the distance a fish describes an arc of three or four feet in the air, and there is one bright flash where it emerges, and another where it strikes the water; sometimes the whole silvery arc is revealed; or here and there, perhaps, is a thistle-down floating on its surface, which the fishes

---

[17] Nearby bay on Sudbury River.
[18] Nest-building fish.

dart at and so dimple it again. It is like molten glass cooled but not congealed, and the few motes in it are pure and beautiful like the imperfections in glass. You may often detect a yet smoother and darker water, separated from the rest as if by an invisible cobweb, boom of the water nymphs, resting on it. From a hilltop you can see a fish leap in almost any part; for not a pickerel or shiner picks an insect from this smooth surface but it manifestly disturbs the equilibrium of the whole lake. It is wonderful with what elaborateness this simple fact is advertised,—this piscine murder will out,—and from my distant perch I distinguish the circling undulations when they are half a dozen rods in diameter. You can even detect a water-bug (*Gyrinus*) ceaselessly progressing over the smooth surface a quarter of a mile off; for they furrow the water slightly, making a conspicuous ripple bounded by two diverging lines, but the skaters glide over it without rippling it perceptibly. When the surface is considerably agitated there are no skaters nor waterbugs on it, but apparently, in calm days, they leave their havens and adventurously glide forth from the shore by short impulses till they completely cover it. It is a soothing employment, on one of those fine days in the fall when all the warmth of the sun is fully appreciated, to sit on a stump on such a height as this, overlooking the pond, and study the dimpling circles which are incessantly inscribed on its otherwise invisible surface amid the reflected skies and trees. Over this great expanse there is no disturbance but it is thus at once gently smoothed away and assuaged, as, when a vase of water is jarred, the trembling circles seek the shore and all is smooth again. Not a fish can leap or an insect fall on the pond but it is thus reported in circling dimples, in lines of beauty, as it were the constant welling up of its fountain, the gentle pulsing of its life, the heaving of its breast. The thrills of joy and thrills of pain are undistinguishable. How peaceful the phenomena of the lake! Again the works of man shine as in the spring. Ay, every leaf and twig and stone and cobweb sparkles now at mid-afternoon as when covered with dew in a spring morning. Every motion of an oar or an insect produces a flash of light; and if an oar falls, how sweet the echo!

In such a day, in September or October, Walden is a perfect forest mirror, set round with stones as precious to my eye as if fewer or rarer. Nothing so fair, so pure, and at the same time so large, as a lake, perchance, lies on the surface of the earth. Sky water. It needs no fence. Nations come and go without defiling it. It is a mirror which no stone can crack, whose quicksilver will never wear off, whose gilding Nature continually repairs; no storms, no dust, can dim its surface ever fresh;—a mirror in which all impurity presented to it sinks, swept and dusted by the sun's hazy brush,—this the light dust-cloth,—which retains no breath that is breathed on it, but sends its own to float as clouds high above its surface, and be reflected in its bosom still.

A field of water betrays the spirit that is in the air. It is continually receiving new life and motion from above. It is intermediate in its nature between land and sky. On land only the grass and trees wave, but the water itself is rippled by the wind. I see where the breeze dashes across it by the streaks or flakes of light. It is remarkable that we can look down on its surface. We shall, perhaps, look down thus on the surface of air at length, and mark where a still subtler spirit sweeps over it.

The skaters and water-bugs finally disappear in the latter part of October, when the severe frosts have come; and then and in November, usually, in a calm day, there is absolutely nothing to ripple the surface. One November afternoon, in the calm at the end of a rain-storm of several days' duration, when the sky was still completely overcast and the air was full of mist, I observed that the pond was remarkably smooth, so that it was difficult to distinguish its surface; though it no longer reflected the bright tints of October, but the sombre November colors of the surrounding hills. Though I passed over it as gently as possible, the slight undulations produced by my boat extended almost as far as I could see, and gave a ribbed appearance to the reflections. But, as I was looking over the surface, I saw here and there at a distance a faint glimmer, as if some skater insects which had escaped the frosts might be collected there, or, perchance, the surface, being so smooth, betrayed where a spring welled up from the bottom. Paddling gently to one of these places, I was surprised to find myself surrounded by myriads of small perch, about five inches long, of a rich bronze color in the green water, sporting there, and constantly rising to the surface and dimpling it, sometimes leaving bubbles on it. In such transparent and seemingly bottomless water, reflecting the clouds, I seemed to be floating through the air as in a balloon, and their swimming impressed me as a kind of flight or hovering, as if they were a compact flock of birds passing just beneath my level on the right or left, their fins, like sails, set all around them. There were many such schools in the pond, apparently improving the short season before winter would draw an icy shutter over their broad skylight, sometimes giving to the surface an appearance as if a slight breeze struck it, or a few rain-drops fell there. When I approached carelessly and alarmed them, they made a sudden plash and rippling with their tails, as if one had struck the water with a brushy bough, and instantly took refuge in the depths. At length the wind rose, the mist increased, and the waves began to run, and the perch leaped much higher than before, half out of water, a hundred black points, three inches long, at once above the surface. Even as late as the fifth of December, one year, I saw some dimples on the surface, and thinking it was going to rain hard immediately, the air being full of mist, I made haste to take my place at the oars and row homeward; already the rain seemed rapidly increasing, though I felt none on my cheek, and I anticipated a thorough soaking. But suddenly the dimples ceased, for they were produced by the perch, which the noise of my oars had scared into the depths, and I saw their schools dimly disappearing; so I spent a dry afternoon after all.

An old man who used to frequent this pond nearly sixty years ago, when it was dark with surrounding forests, tells me that in those days he sometimes saw it all alive with ducks and other water-fowl, and that there were many eagles about it. He came here a-fishing, and used an old log canoe which he found on the shore. It was made of two white pine logs dug out and pinned together, and was cut off square at the ends. It was very clumsy, but lasted a great many years before it became water-logged and perhaps sank to the bottom. He did not know whose it was; it belonged to the pond. He used to make a cable for his anchor of strips of hickory bark tied together. An old man, a potter, who lived by the pond before the Revolution, told him once that there was an iron chest at the bottom, and that he had seen it. Sometimes it would come floating up to the shore; but when you went toward it, it would go back into deep water and disappear. I was pleased to hear of the old log canoe, which took the place of an Indian one of the same material but more graceful construction, which perchance had first been a tree on the bank, and then, as it were, fell into the water, to float there for a generation, the most proper vessel for the lake. I remember that when I first looked into these depths there were many large trunks to be seen indistinctly lying on the bottom, which had either been blown over formerly, or left on the ice at the last cutting, when wood was cheaper; but now they have mostly disappeared.

When I first paddled a boat on Walden, it was completely surrounded by thick and lofty pine and oak woods, and in some of its coves grape-vines had run over the trees next the water and formed bowers under which a boat could pass. The hills which form its shores are so steep, and the woods on them were then so high, that, as you looked down from the west end, it had the appearance of an amphitheatre for some kind of sylvan spectacle. I have spent many an hour, when I was younger, floating over its surface as the zephyr[19] willed, having paddled my boat

---

[19] Gentle west wind.

to the middle, and lying on my back across the seats, in a summer forenoon, dreaming awake, until I was aroused by the boat touching the sand, and I arose to see what shore my fates had impelled me to; days when idleness was the most attractive and productive industry. Many a forenoon have I stolen away, preferring to spend thus the most valued part of the day; for I was rich, if not in money, in sunny hours and summer days, and spent them lavishly; nor do I regret that I did not waste more of them in the workshop or the teacher's desk. But since I left those shores the woodchoppers have still further laid them waste, and now for many a year there will be no more rambling through the aisles of the wood, with occasional vistas through which you see the water. My Muse may be excused if she is silent henceforth. How can you expect the birds to sing when their groves are cut down?

Now the trunks of trees on the bottom, and the old log canoe, and the dark surrounding woods, are gone, and the villagers, who scarcely know where it lies, instead of going to the pond to bathe or drink, are thinking to bring its water, which should be as sacred as the Ganges[20] at least, to the village in a pipe, to wash their dishes with!—to earn their Walden by the turning of a cock or drawing of a plug! That devilish Iron Horse, whose ear-rending neigh is heard throughout the town, has muddied the Boiling Spring with his foot, and he it is that has browsed off all the woods on Walden shore, that Trojan horse, with a thousand men in his belly, introduced by mercenary Greeks![21] Where is the country's champion, the Moore of Moore Hall,[22] to meet him at the Deep Cut[23] and thrust an avenging lance between the ribs of the bloated pest?

Nevertheless, of all the characters I have known, perhaps Walden wears best, and best preserves its purity. Many men have been likened to it, but few deserve that honor. Though the woodchoppers have laid bare first this shore and then that, and the Irish have built their sties by it, and the railroad has infringed on its border, and the ice-men have skimmed it once, it is itself unchanged, the same water which my youthful eyes fell on; all the change is in me. It has not acquired one permanent wrinkle after all its ripples. It is perennially young, and I may stand and see a swallow dip apparently to pick an insect from its surface as of yore. It struck me again to-night, as if I had not seen it almost daily for more than twenty years,—Why, here is Walden, the same woodland lake that I discovered so many years ago; where a forest was cut down last winter another is springing up by its shore as lustily as ever; the same thought is welling up to its surface that was then; it is the same liquid joy and happiness to itself and its Maker, ay, and it *may* be to me. It is the work of a brave man surely, in whom there was no guile! He rounded this water with his hand, deepened and clarified it in his thought, and in his will bequeathed it to Concord. I see by its face that it is visited by the same reflection; and I can almost say, Walden, is it you?

> It is no dream of mine,
> To ornament a line;
> I cannot come nearer to God and Heaven
> Than I live to Walden even.
> I am its stony shore,
> And the breeze that passes o'er;
> In the hollow of my hand
> Are its water and its sand,
> And its deepest resort
> Lies high in my thought.

---

[20]River in India, bathing in which is a religious ritual.
[21]By this device (hiding in the giant horse), the Greeks entered Troy and conquered it.
[22]See "The Dragon of Wantley" (in Bishop Thomas Percy's *Reliques of Ancient English Poetry*, 1765), a ballad about a dragon-slayer.
[23]A railroad cut near Walden.

The cars never pause to look at it; yet I fancy that the engineers and firemen and brakemen, and those passengers who have a season ticket and see it often, are better men for the sight. The engineer does not forget at night, or his nature does not, that he has beheld this vision of serenity and purity once at least during the day. Though seen but once, it helps to wash out State Street[24] and the engine's soot. One proposes that it be called "God's Drop."[25]

I have said that Walden has no visible inlet nor outlet, but it is on the one hand distantly and indirectly related to Flint's Pond, which is more elevated, by a chain of small ponds coming from that quarter, and on the other directly and manifestly to Concord River, which is lower, by a similar chain of ponds through which in some other geological period it may have flowed, and by a little digging, which God forbid, it can be made to flow thither again. If by living thus reserved and austere, like a hermit in the woods, so long, it has acquired such wonderful purity, who would not regret that the comparatively impure waters of Flint's Pond should be mingled with it, or itself should ever go to waste its sweetness in the ocean wave?

Flint's, or Sandy Pond, in Lincoln, our greatest lake and inland sea, lies about a mile east of Walden. It is much larger, being said to contain one hundred and ninety-seven acres, and is more fertile in fish; but it is comparatively shallow, and not remarkably pure. A walk through the woods thither was often my recreation. It was worth the while, if only to feel the wind blow on your cheek freely, and see the waves run, and remember the life of mariners. I went a-chestnutting there in the fall, on windy days, when the nuts were dropping into the water and were washed to my feet; and one day, as I crept along its sedgy shore, the fresh spray blowing in my face, I came upon the mouldering wreck of a boat, the sides gone, and hardly more than the impression of its flat bottom left amid the rushes; yet its model was sharply defined, as if it were a large decayed pad, with its veins. It was as impressive a wreck as one could imagine on the seashore, and had as good a moral. It is by this time mere vegetable mould and undistinguishable pond shore, through which rushes and flags have pushed up. I used to admire the ripple marks on the sandy bottom, at the north end of this pond, made firm and hard to the feet of the wader by the pressure of the water, and the rushes which grew in Indian file, in waving lines, corresponding to these marks, rank behind rank, as if the waves had planted them. There also I have found, in considerable quantities, curious balls, composed apparently of fine grass or roots, of pipewort perhaps, from half an inch to four inches in diameter, and perfectly spherical. These wash back and forth in shallow water on a sandy bottom, and are sometimes cast on the shore. They are either solid grass, or have a little sand in the middle. At first you would say that they were formed by the action of the waves, like a pebble; yet the smallest are made of equally coarse materials, half an inch long, and they are produced only at one season of the year. Moreover, the waves, I suspect, do not so much construct as wear down a material which has already acquired consistency. They preserve their form when dry for an indefinite period.

Flint's Pond! Such is the poverty of our nomenclature. What right had the unclean and stupid farmer, whose farm abutted on this sky water, whose shores he has ruthlessly laid bare, to give his name to it? Some skin-flint, who loved better the reflecting surface of a dollar, or a bright cent, in which he could see his own brazen face; who regarded even the wild ducks which settled in it as trespassers; his fingers grown into crooked and horny talons from the long habit of grasping harpy-like;—so it is not named for me. I go not there to see him nor to hear of

---

[24]Main financial street of Boston.
[25]I.e., an eye-drop.

him; who never *saw* it, who never bathed in it, who never loved it, who never protected it, who never spoke a good word for it, nor thanked God that He had made it. Rather let it be named from the fishes that swim in it, the wild fowl or quadrupeds which frequent it, the wild flowers which grow by its shores, or some wild man or child the thread of whose history is interwoven with its own; not from him who could show no title to it but the deed which a like-minded neighbor or legislature gave him,—him who thought only of its money value; whose presence perchance cursed all the shores; who exhausted the land around it, and would fain have exhausted the waters within it; who regretted only that it was not English hay or cranberry meadow,—there was nothing to redeem it, forsooth, in his eyes,— and would have drained and sold it for the mud at its bottom. It did not turn his mill, and it was no *privilege* to him to behold it. I respect not his labors, his farm where everything has its price, who would carry the landscape, who would carry his God, to market, if he could get anything for him; who goes to market *for* his god as it is; on whose farm nothing grows free, whose fields bear no crops, whose meadows no flowers, whose trees no fruits, but dollars; who loves not the beauty of his fruits, whose fruits are not ripe for him till they are turned to dollars. Give me the poverty that enjoys true wealth. Farmers are respectable and interesting to me in proportion as they are poor,—poor farmers. A model farm! where the house stands like a fungus in a muckheap, chambers for men, horses, oxen, and swine, cleansed and uncleansed, all contiguous to one another! Stocked with men! A great grease-spot, redolent of manures and buttermilk! Under a high state of cultivation, being manured with the hearts and brains of men! As if you were to raise your potatoes in the churchyard! Such is a model farm.

No, no; if the fairest features of the landscape are to be named after men, let them be the noblest and worthiest men alone. Let our lakes receive as true names at least as the Icarian Sea, where "still the shore" a "brave attempt resounds."[26]

Goose Pond, of small extent, is on my way to Flint's; Fair Haven, an expansion of Concord River, said to contain some seventy acres, is a mile southwest; and White Pond, of about forty acres, is a mile and a half beyond Fair Haven. This is my lake country.[27] These, with Concord River, are my water privileges; and night and day, year in year out, they grind such grist as I carry to them.

Since the wood-cutters, and the railroad, and I myself have profaned Walden, perhaps the most attractive, if not the most beautiful, of all our lakes, the gem of the woods, is White Pond;—a poor name from its commonness, whether derived from the remarkable purity of its waters or the color of its sands. In these as in other respects, however, it is a lesser twin of Walden. They are so much alike that you would say they must be connected under ground. It has the same stony shore, and its waters are of the same hue. As at Walden, in sultry dog-day weather, looking down through the woods on some of its bays which are not so deep but that the reflection from the bottom tinges them, its waters are of a misty bluish-green or glaucous color. Many years since I used to go there to collect the sand by cartloads, to make sandpaper with, and I have continued to visit it ever since. One who frequents it proposes to call it Virid[28] Lake. Perhaps it might be called Yellow Pine Lake, from the following circumstance. About fifteen years ago you could see the top of a pitch pine, of the kind called yellow pine hereabouts, though it is not a distinct species, projecting above the surface in deep water, many rods from the shore. It was even supposed by some that the pond had sunk, and this was one of

---

[26]From "Icarus," by William Drummond of Hawthornden (1585–1649), Scottish poet. The Icarian Sea is the part of the Aegean into which Icarus fell after flying too near the sun with his wings of wax and feathers.

[27]Cf. the lake country in England figuring in the works and lives of the British romantic poets (Wordsworth especially).
[28]Green.

the primitive forest that formerly stood there. I find that even so long ago as 1792, in a "Topographical Description of the Town of Concord," by one of its citizens,[29] in the Collections of the Massachusetts Historical Society, the author, after speaking of Walden and White Ponds, adds, "In the middle of the latter may be seen, when the water is very low, a tree which appears as if it grew in the place where it now stands, although the roots are fifty feet below the surface of the water; the top of this tree is broken off, and at that place measures fourteen inches in diameter." In the spring of '49 I talked with the man who lives nearest the pond in Sudbury, who told me that it was he who got out this tree ten or fifteen years before. As near as he could remember, it stood twelve or fifteen rods from the shore, where the water was thirty or forty feet deep. It was in the winter, and he had been getting out ice in the forenoon, and had resolved that in the afternoon, with the aid of his neighbors, he would take out the old yellow pine. He sawed a channel in the ice toward the shore, and hauled it over and along and out on to the ice with oxen; but, before he had gone far in his work, he was surprised to find that it was wrong end upward, with the stumps of the branches pointing down, and the small end firmly fastened in the sandy bottom. It was about a foot in diameter at the big end, and he had expected to get a good saw-log, but it was so rotten as to be fit only for fuel, if for that. He had some of it in his shed then. There were marks of an axe and of woodpeckers on the butt. He thought that it might have been a dead tree on the shore, but was finally blown over into the pond, and after the top had become water-logged, while the butt-end was still dry and light, had drifted out and sunk wrong end up. His father, eighty years old, could not remember when it was not there. Several pretty large logs may still be seen lying on the bottom, where, owing to the undulation of the surface, they look like huge water snakes in motion.

This pond has rarely been profaned by a boat, for there is little in it to tempt a fisherman. Instead of the white lily, which requires mud, or the common sweet flag, the blue flag (*Iris versicolor*) grows thinly in the pure water, rising from the stony bottom all around the shore, where it is visited by hummingbirds in June; and the color both of its bluish blades and its flowers and especially their reflections, is in singular harmony with the glaucous water.

White Pond and Walden are great crystals on the surface of the earth, Lakes of Light. If they were permanently congealed, and small enough to be clutched, they would, perchance, be carried off by slaves, like precious stones, to adorn the heads of emperors; but being liquid, and ample, and secured to us and our successors forever, we disregard them, and run after the diamond of Kohinoor.[30] They are too pure to have a market value; they contain no muck. How much more beautiful than our lives, how much more transparent than our characters, are they! We never learned meanness of them. How much fairer than the pool before the farmer's door, in which his ducks swim! Hither the clean wild ducks come. Nature has no human inhabitant who appreciates her. The birds with their plumage and their notes are in harmony with the flowers, but what youth or maiden conspires with the wild luxuriant beauty of Nature? She flourishes most alone, far from the towns where they reside. Talk of heaven! ye disgrace earth.

X

BAKER FARM

Sometimes I rambled to pine groves, standing like temples, or like fleets at sea, full-rigged, with wavy boughs, and rippling with light, so soft and green and

---

[29] William Jones.
[30] Legendary diamond from India, $186\frac{1}{2}$ carats, presented to Queen Victoria in 1850.

shady that the Druids[1] would have forsaken their oaks to worship in them; or to the cedar wood beyond Flint's Pond, where the trees, covered with hoary blue berries, spiring higher and higher, are fit to stand before Valhalla,[2] and the creeping juniper covers the ground with wreaths full of fruit; or to swamps where the usnea lichen[3] hangs in festoons from the white spruce trees, and toadstools, round tables of the swamp gods, cover the ground, and more beautiful fungi adorn the stumps, like butterflies or shells, vegetable winkles; where the swamp-pink and dogwood grow, the red alder berry glows like eyes of imps, the waxwork grooves and crushes the hardest woods in its folds, and the wild holly berries make the beholder forget his home with their beauty, and he is dazzled and tempted by nameless other wild forbidden fruits, too fair for mortal taste. Instead of calling on some scholar, I paid many a visit to particular trees, of kinds which are rare in this neighborhood, standing far away in the middle of some pasture, or in the depths of a wood or swamp, or on a hilltop; such as the black birch, of which we have some handsome specimens two feet in diameter; its cousin, the yellow birch, with its loose golden vest, perfumed like the first; the beech, which has so neat a bole[4] and beautifully lichen-painted, perfect in all its details, of which, excepting scattered specimens, I know but one small grove of sizable trees left in the township, supposed by some to have been planted by the pigeons that were once baited with beechnuts near by; it is worth the while to see the silver grain sparkle when you split this wood; the bass; the hornbeam; the *Celtis occidentalis,* or false elm, of which we have but one well-grown; some taller mast of a pine, a shingle tree, or a more perfect hemlock than usual, standing like a pagoda in the midst of the woods; and many others I could mention. These were the shrines I visited both summer and winter.

Once it chanced that I stood in the very abutment of a rainbow's arch, which filled the lower stratum of the atmosphere, tinging the grass and leaves around, and dazzling me as if I looked through colored crystal. It was a lake of rainbow light, in which, for a short while, I lived like a dolphin. If it had lasted longer it might have tinged my employments and life. As I walked on the railroad causeway, I used to wonder at the halo of light around my shadow, and would fain fancy myself one of the elect.[5] One who visited me declared that the shadows of some Irishmen before him had no halo about them, that it was only natives that were so distinguished. Benvenuto Cellini tells us in his memoirs, that, after a certain terrible dream or vision which he had during his confinement in the castle of St. Angelo a resplendent light appeared over the shadow of his head at morning and evening, whether he was in Italy or France, and it was particularly conspicuous when the grass was moist with dew.[6] This was probably the same phenomenon to which I have referred, which is especially observed in the morning, but also at other times, and even by moonlight. Though a constant one, it is not commonly noticed, and, in the case of an excitable imagination like Cellini's, it would be basis enough for superstition. Beside, he tells us that he showed it to very few. But are they not indeed distinguished who are conscious that they are regarded at all?

I set out one afternoon to go a-fishing to Fair Haven, through the woods, to eke out my scanty fare of vegetables. My way led through Pleasant Meadow, an

---

[1]Priests of ancient religion in Britain for whom oak groves were sacred retreats.
[2]In Norse mythology, the enormous hall where the souls of slain warriors gathered.
[3]Sometimes called beard lichen; a moss-like algae or fungi that grows on trees.

[4]Trunk.
[5]I.e., one selected by God to be saved (in accord with Calvinistic and Puritan theology).
[6]Cf. Chapter 26 of the *Autobiography* of Benvenuto Cellini (1500–1571), Italian sculptor.

adjunct of the Baker Farm, that retreat of which a poet has since sung, beginning,—

> "Thy entry is a pleasant field,
> Which some mossy fruit trees yield
> Partly to a ruddy brook,
> By gliding musquash undertook,
> And mercurial trout,
> Darting about."[7]

I thought of living there before I went to Walden. I "hooked" the apples, leaped the brook, and scared the musquash[8] and the trout. It was one of those afternoons which seem indefinitely long before one, in which many events may happen, a large portion of our natural life, though it was already half spent when I started. By the way there came up a shower, which compelled me to stand half an hour under a pine, piling boughs over my head, and wearing my handkerchief for a shed; and when at length I had made one cast over the pickerelweed, standing up to my middle in water, I found myself suddenly in the shadow of a cloud, and the thunder began to rumble with such emphasis that I could do no more than listen to it. The gods must be proud, thought I, with such forked flashes to rout a poor unarmed fisherman. So I made haste for shelter to the nearest hut, which stood half a mile from any road, but so much the nearer to the pond, and had long been uninhabited:—

> "And here a poet builded,
> In the completed years,
> For behold a trivial cabin
> That to destruction steers."

So the Muse fables. But therein, as I found, dwelt now John Field, an Irishman, and his wife, and several children, from the broad-faced boy who assisted his father at his work, and now came running by his side from the bog to escape the rain, to the wrinkled, sibyl-like,[9] cone-headed infant that sat upon its father's knee as in the palaces of nobles, and looked out from its home in the midst of wet and hunger inquisitively upon the stranger, with the privilege of infancy, not knowing but it was the last of a noble line, and the hope and cynosure of the world, instead of John Field's poor starveling brat. There we sat together under that part of the roof which leaked the least, while it showered and thundered without. I had sat there many times of old before the ship was built that floated this family to America. An honest, hard-working, but shiftless man plainly was John Field; and his wife, she too was brave to cook so many successive dinners in the recesses of that lofty stove; with round greasy face and bare breast,[10] still thinking to improve her condition one day; with the never absent mop in one hand, and yet no effects of it visible anywhere. The chickens, which had also taken shelter here from the rain, stalked about the room like members of the family, too humanized, methought, to roast well. They stood and looked in my eye or pecked at my shoe significantly. Meanwhile my host told me his story, how hard he worked "bogging" for a neighboring farmer, turning up a meadow with a spade or bog hoe at the rate of ten dollars an acre and the use of the land with manure for one year, and his little broad-faced son worked cheerfully at his father's side the while, not knowing how poor a bargain the latter had made. I tried to help him with my experience, telling

---

[7]These lines and other lines of poetry in this chapter are from the younger William Ellery Channing's "Baker Farm."

[8]Variant of muskrat.

[9]In classical mythology, the Sibyl (or prophetess), who was granted long life, forgot to ask for lasting youth, and thus became wrinkled.

[10]I.e., with more bosom visible than in the case of other New England ladies.

him that he was one of my nearest neighbors, and that I too, who came a-fishing here, and looked like a loafer, was getting my living like himself; that I lived in a tight, light, and clean house, which hardly cost more than the annual rent of such a ruin as his commonly amounts to; and how, if he chose, he might in a month or two build himself a palace of his own; that I did not use tea, nor coffee, nor butter, nor milk, nor fresh meat, and so did not have to work to get them; again, as I did not work hard, I did not have to eat hard, and it cost me but a trifle for my food; but as he began with tea, and coffee, and butter, and milk, and beef, he had to work hard to pay for them, and when he had worked hard he had to eat hard again to repair the waste of his system,—and so it was as broad as it was long, indeed it was broader than it was long, for he was discontented and wasted his life into the bargain; and yet he had rated it as a gain in coming to America, that here you could get tea, and coffee, and meat every day. But the only true America is that country where you are at liberty to pursue such a mode of life as may enable you to do without these, and where the state does not endeavor to compel you to sustain the slavery and war and other superfluous expenses which directly or indirectly result from the use of such things. For I purposely talked to him as if he were a philosopher, or desired to be one. I should be glad if all the meadows on the earth were left in a wild state, if that were the consequence of men's beginning to redeem themselves. A man will not need to study history to find out what is best for his own culture. But alas! the culture of an Irishman is an enterprise to be undertaken with a sort of moral bog hoe. I told him, that as he worked so hard at bogging, he required thick boots and stout clothing, which yet were soon soiled and worn out, but I wore light shoes and thin clothing, which cost not half so much, though he might think that I was dressed like a gentleman (which, however, was not the case), and in an hour or two, without labor, but as a recreation, I could, if I wished, catch as many fish as I should want for two days, or earn enough money to support me a week. If he and his family would live simply, they might all go a-huckleberrying in the summer for their amusement. John heaved a sigh at this, and his wife stared with arms a-kimbo, and both appeared to be wondering if they had capital enough to begin such a course with, or arithmetic enough to carry it through. It was sailing by dead reckoning[11] to them, and they saw not clearly how to make their port so; therefore I suppose they still take life bravely, after their fashion, face to face, giving it tooth and nail, not having skill to split its massive columns with any fine entering wedge, and rout it in detail;— thinking to deal with it roughly, as one should handle a thistle. But they fight at an overwhelming disadvantage,—living, John Field, alas! without arithmetic, and failing so.

"Do you ever fish?" I asked. "Oh yes, I catch a mess now and then when I am lying by; good perch I catch." "What's your bait?" "I catch shiners with fishworms, and bait the perch with them." "You'd better go now, John," said his wife, with glistening and hopeful face; but John demurred.

The shower was now over, and a rainbow above the eastern woods promised a fair evening; so I took my departure. When I had got without I asked for a drink, hoping to get a sight of the well bottom, to complete my survey of the premises; but there, alas! are shallows and quicksands, and rope broken withal, and bucket irrecoverable. Meanwhile the right culinary vessel was selected, water was seemingly distilled, and after consultation and long delay passed out to the thirsty one,—not yet suffered to cool, not yet to settle. Such gruel sustains life here, I thought; so, shutting my eyes, and excluding the motes by a skilfully directed un-

---

[11]I.e., without nautical devices, judging direction by some predetermined spot.

dercurrent, I drank to genuine hospitality the heartiest draught I could. I am not squeamish in such cases when manners are concerned.

As I was leaving the Irishman's roof after the rain, bending my steps again to the pond, my haste to catch pickerel, wading in retired meadows, in sloughs and bogholes, in forlorn and savage places, appeared for an instant trivial to me who had been sent to school and college; but as I ran down the hill toward the reddening west, with the rainbow over my shoulder, and some faint tinkling sounds borne to my ear through the cleansed air, from I know not what quarter, my Good Genius seemed to say,—Go fish and hunt far and wide day by day,—farther and wider,—and rest thee by many brooks and hearth-sides without misgiving. Remember thy Creator in the days of thy youth.[12] Rise free from care before the dawn, and seek adventures. Let the noon find thee by other lakes, and the night overtake thee everywhere at home. There are no larger fields than these, no worthier games than may here be played. Grow wild according to thy nature, like these sedges and brakes, which will never become English hay. Let the thunder rumble; what if it threaten ruin to farmers' crops? that is not its errand to thee. Take shelter under the cloud, while they flee to carts and sheds. Let not to get a living be thy trade, but thy sport. Enjoy the land, but own it not. Through want of enterprise and faith men are where they are, buying and selling, and spending their lives like serfs.

O Baker Farm!

> "Landscape where the richest element
> Is a little sunshine innocent." . . .

> "No one runs to revel
> On thy rail-fenced lea." . . .

> "Debate with no man hast thou,
>   With questions art never perplexed,
> As tame at the first sight as now,
>   In thy plain russet gabardine dressed." . . .

> "Come ye who love,
>   And ye who hate,
> Children of the Holy Dove,
>   And Guy Faux[13] of the state,
> And hang conspiracies
> From the tough rafters of the trees!"

Men come tamely home at night only from the next field or street, where their household echoes haunt, and their life pines because it breathes its own breath over again; their shadows, morning and evening, reach farther than their daily steps. We should come home from far, from adventures, and perils, and discoveries every day, with new experience and character.

Before I had reached the pond some fresh impulse had brought out John Field, with altered mind, letting go "bogging" ere this sunset. But he, poor man, disturbed only a couple of fins while I was catching a fair string, and he said it was his luck; but when we changed seats in the boat luck changed seats too. Poor John Field!—I trust he does not read this, unless he will improve by it,—thinking to live by some derivative old-country mode in this primitive new country,—to catch perch with shiners. It is good bait sometimes, I allow. With his horizon all his own,

---

[12]Ecclesiastes 12:1.
[13]Variant of Guy Fawkes (1570–1606), Catholic conspira-
tor and instigator of the Gunpowder Plot (1604–15) to blow up the House of Lords. He was executed in 1606.

yet he a poor man, born to be poor, with his inherited Irish poverty or poor life, his Adam's grandmother and boggy ways, not to rise in this world, he nor his posterity, till their wading webbed bog-trotting feet get *talaria* [14] to their heels.

XI

HIGHER LAWS

As I came home through the woods with my string of fish, trailing my pole, it being now quite dark, I caught a glimpse of a woodchuck stealing across my path, and felt a strange thrill of savage delight, and was strongly tempted to seize and devour him raw; not that I was hungry then, except for that wildness which he represented. Once or twice, however, while I lived at the pond, I found myself ranging the woods, like a half-starved hound, with a strange abandonment, seeking some kind of venison which I might devour, and no morsel could have been too savage for me. The wildest scenes had become unaccountably familiar. I found in myself, and still find, an instinct toward a higher, or, as it is named, spiritual life, as do most men, and another toward a primitive rank and savage one, and I reverence them both. I love the wild not less than the good. The wildness and adventure that are in fishing still recommended it to me. I like sometimes to take rank hold on life and spend my day more as the animals do. Perhaps I have owed to this employment and to hunting, when quite young, my closest acquaintance with Nature. They early introduce us to and detain us in scenery with which otherwise, at that age, we should have little acquaintance. Fisherman, hunters, woodchoppers, and others, spending their lives in the fields and woods, in a peculiar sense a part of Nature themselves, are often in a more favorable mood for observing her, in the intervals of their pursuits, than philosophers or poets even, who approach her with expectation. She is not afraid to exhibit herself to them. The traveller on the prairie is naturally a hunter, on the head waters of the Missouri and Columbia a trapper, and at the Falls of St. Mary[1] a fisherman. He who is only a traveller learns things at second-hand and by the halves, and is poor authority. We are most interested when science reports what those men already know practically or instinctively, for that alone is a true *humanity,* or account of human experience.

They mistake who assert that the Yankee has few amusements, because he has not so many public holidays, and men and boys do not play so many games as they do in England, for here the more primitive but solitary amusements of hunting, fishing, and the like have not yet given place to the former. Almost every New England boy among my contemporaries shouldered a fowling-piece between the ages of ten and fourteen; and his hunting and fishing grounds were not limited, like the preserves of an English nobleman, but were more boundless even than those of a savage. No wonder, then, that he did not oftener stay to play on the common. But already a change is taking place, owing, not to an increased humanity, but to an increased scarcity of game, for perhaps the hunter is the greatest friend of the animals hunted, not excepting the Humane Society.

Moreover, when at the pond, I wished sometimes to add fish to my fare for variety. I have actually fished from the same kind of necessity that the first fishers did. Whatever humanity I might conjure up against it was all factitious, and concerned my philosophy more than my feelings. I speak of fishing only now, for I had long felt differently about fowling, and sold my gun before I went to the woods. Not that I am less humane than others, but I did not perceive that my feel-

---

[14]Winged heels of certain Greek gods, such as Hermes and Perseus.

[1]Probably the rapids of St. Mary's River between Lakes Superior and Huron.

ings were much affected. I did not pity the fishes nor the worms. This was habit. As for fowling, during the last years that I carried a gun my excuse was that I was studying ornithology, and sought only new or rare birds. But I confess that I am now inclined to think that there is a finer way of studying ornithology than this. It requires so much closer attention to the habits of the birds, that, if for that reason only, I have been willing to omit the gun. Yet notwithstanding the objection on the score of humanity, I am compelled to doubt if equally valuable sports are ever substituted for these; and when some of my friends have asked me anxiously about their boys, whether they should let them hunt, I have answered, yes,— remembering that it was one of the best parts of my education,—*make* them hunters, though sportsmen only at first, if possible, mighty hunters at last, so that they shall not find game large enough for them in this or any vegetable wilderness,—hunters as well as fishers of men.[2] Thus far I am of the opinion of Chaucer's nun, who

> "yave not of the text a pulled hen
> That saith that hunters ben not holy men."[3]

There is a period in the history of the individual, as of the race, when the hunters are the "best men," as the Algonquins[4] called them. We cannot but pity the boy who has never fired a gun; he is no more humane, while his education has been sadly neglected. This was my answer with respect to those youths who were bent on this pursuit, trusting that they would soon outgrow it. No humane being, past the thoughtless age of boyhood, will wantonly murder any creature which holds its life by the same tenure that he does. The hare in its extremity cries like a child. I warn you, mothers, that my sympathies do not always make the usual philanthropic distinctions.

Such is oftenest the young man's introduction to the forest, and the most original part of himself. He goes thither at first as a hunter and fisher, until at last, if he has the seeds of a better life in him, he distinguishes his proper objects, as a poet or naturalist it may be, and leaves the gun and fish-pole behind. The mass of men are still and always young in this respect. In some countries a hunting parson is no uncommon sight. Such a one might make a good shepherd's dog, but is far from being the Good Shepherd. I have been surprised to consider that the only obvious employment, except wood-chopping, ice-cutting, or the like business, which ever to my knowledge detained at Walden Pond for a whole half-day any of my fellow-citizens; whether fathers or children of the town, with just one exception, was fishing. Commonly they did not think that they were lucky, or well paid for their time, unless they got a long string of fish, though they had the opportunity of seeing the pond all the while. They might go there a thousand times before the sediment of fishing would sink to the bottom and leave their purpose pure; but no doubt such a clarifying process would be going on all the while. The Governor and his Council faintly remember the pond, for they went a-fishing there when they were boys; but now they are too old and dignified to go a-fishing, and so they know it no more forever. Yet even they expect to go to heaven at last. If the legislature regards it, it is chiefly to regulate the number of hooks to be used there; but they know nothing about the hook of hooks with which to angle for the pond itself, impaling the legislature for a bait. Thus, even in civilized communities, the embryo man passes through the hunter stage of development.

I have found repeatedly, of late years, that I cannot fish without falling a little in self-respect. I have tried it again and again. I have skill at it, and, like many of

---

[2]Mark 1:17: "Come ye after me, and I will make you to become fishers of men."
[3]I.e., the nun (actually the monk) didn't give a plucked hen for the text that says hunters are not holy men; from "Pro-

logue" (11. 177–78) to *The Canterbury Tales* of Geoffrey Chaucer (1340?–1400).
[4]Indian tribe that lived in the area of the Ottawa River, in Canada and the northeastern United States.

my fellows, a certain instinct for it, which revives from time to time, but always when I have done I feel that it would have been better if I had not fished. I think that I do not mistake. It is a faint intimation, yet so are the first streaks of morning. There is unquestionably this instinct in me which belongs to the lower orders of creation; yet with every year I am less a fisherman, though without more humanity or even wisdom; at present I am no fisherman at all. But I see that if I were to live in a wilderness I should again be tempted to become a fisher and hunter in earnest. Beside, there is something essentially unclean about this diet and all flesh, and I began to see where housework commences, and whence the endeavor, which costs so much, to wear a tidy and respectable appearance each day, to keep the house sweet and free from all ill odors and sights. Having been my own butcher and scullion and cook, as well as the gentleman for whom the dishes were served up, I can speak from an unusually complete experience. The practical objection to animal food in my case was its uncleanness; and besides, when I had caught and cleaned and cooked and eaten my fish, they seemed not to have fed me essentially. It was insignificant and unnecessary, and cost more than it came to. A little bread or a few potatoes would have done as well, with less trouble and filth. Like many of my contemporaries, I had rarely for many years used animal food, or tea, or coffee, etc.; not so much because of any ill effects which I had traced to them, as because they were not agreeable to my imagination. The repugnance to animal food is not the effect of experience, but is an instinct. It appeared more beautiful to live low and fare hard in many respects; and though I never did so, I went far enough to please my imagination. I believe that every man who has ever been earnest to preserve his higher or poetic faculties in the best condition has been particularly inclined to abstain from animal food, and from much food of any kind. It is a significant fact, stated by entomologists,—I find it in Kirby and Spence,[5]—that "some insects in their perfect state, though furnished with organs of feeding, make no use of them;" and they lay it down as "a general rule, that almost all insects in this state eat much less than in that of larvæ. The voracious caterpillar when transformed into a butterfly . . . and the gluttonous maggot when become a fly" content themselves with a drop or two of honey or some other sweet liquid. The abdomen under the wings of the butterfly still represents the larva. This is the tidbit which tempts his insectivorous fate. The gross feeder is a man in the larva state; and there are whole nations in that condition, nations without fancy or imagination, whose vast abdomens betray them.

It is hard to provide and cook so simple and clean a diet as will not offend the imagination; but this, I think, is to be fed when we feed the body; they should both sit down at the same table. Yet perhaps this may be done. The fruits eaten temperately need not make us ashamed of our appetites, nor interrupt the worthiest pursuits. But put an extra condiment into your dish, and it will poison you. It is not worth the while to live by rich cookery. Most men would feel shame if caught preparing with their own hands precisely such a dinner, whether of animal or vegetable food, as is every day prepared for them by others. Yet till this is otherwise we are not civilized, and, if gentlemen and ladies, are not true men and women. This certainly suggests what change is to be made. It may be vain to ask why the imagination will not be reconciled to flesh and fat. I am satisfied that it is not. Is it not a reproach that man is a carnivorous animal? True, he can and does live, in a great measure, by preying on other animals; but this is a miserable way,—as any one who will go to snaring rabbits, or slaughtering lambs, may learn,—and he will be regarded as a benefactor of his race who shall teach man to confine himself to a more innocent and wholesome diet. Whatever my own prac-

---

[5] William Kirby and William Spence, authors of *An Introduction to Entomology* (1846).

tice may be, I have no doubt that it is a part of the destiny of the human race, in its gradual improvement, to leave off eating animals, as surely as the savage tribes have left off eating each other when they came in contact with the more civilized.

If one listens to the faintest but constant suggestions of his genius, which are certainly true, he sees not to what extremes, or even insanity, it may lead him; and yet that way, as he grows more resolute and faithful, his road lies. The faintest assured objection which one healthy man feels will at length prevail over the arguments and customs of mankind. No man ever followed his genius till it misled him. Though the result were bodily weakness, yet perhaps no one can say that the consequences were to be regretted, for these were a life in conformity to higher principles. If the day and the night are such that you greet them with joy, and life emits a fragrance like flowers and sweet-scented herbs, is more elastic, more starry, more immortal,—that is your success. All nature is your congratulation, and you have cause momentarily to bless yourself. The greatest gains and values are farthest from being appreciated. We easily come to doubt if they exist. We soon forget them. They are the highest reality. Perhaps the facts most astounding and most real are never communicated by man to man. The true harvest of my daily life is somewhat as intangible and indescribable as the tints of morning or evening. It is a little star-dust caught, a segment of the rainbow which I have clutched.

Yet, for my part, I was never unusually squeamish; I could sometimes eat a fried rat with a good relish, if it were necessary. I am glad to have drunk water so long, for the same reason that I prefer the natural sky to an opium-eater's heaven. I would fain keep sober always; and there are infinite degrees of drunkenness. I believe that water is the only drink for a wise man; wine is not so noble a liquor; and think of dashing the hopes of a morning with a cup of warm coffee, or of an evening with a dish of tea! Ah, how low I fall when I am tempted by them! Even music may be intoxicating. Such apparently slight causes destroyed Greece and Rome, and will destroy England and America. Of all ebriosity,[6] who does not prefer to be intoxicated by the air he breathes? I have found it to be the most serious objection to coarse labors long continued, that they compelled me to eat and drink coarsely also. But to tell the truth, I find myself at present somewhat less particular in these respects. I carry less religion to the table, ask no blessing; not because I am wiser than I was, but, I am obliged to confess, because, however much it is to be regretted, with years I have grown more coarse and indifferent. Perhaps these questions are entertained only in youth, as most believe of poetry. My practice is "nowhere," my opinion is here. Nevertheless I am far from regarding myself as one of those privileged ones to whom the Ved[7] refers when it says, that "he who has true faith in the Omnipresent Supreme Being may eat all that exists," that is, is not bound to inquire what is his food, or who prepares it; and even in their case it is to be observed, as a Hindoo commentator has remarked, that the Vedant limits this privilege to "the time of distress."[8]

Who has not sometimes derived an inexpressible satisfaction from his food in which appetite had no share? I have been thrilled to think that I owed a mental perception to the commonly gross sense of taste, that I have been inspired through the palate, that some berries which I had eaten on a hillside had fed my genius. "The soul not being mistress of herself," says Thseng-tseu, "one looks, and one does not see; one listens, and one does not hear; one eats, and one does not know the savor of food."[9] He who distinguishes the true savor of his food can

---

[6]Drunkenness.
[7]Vedas, sacred texts of the Hindus.
[8]From Rajah Rammohun Roy's translation of the *Vedas* (1832).

[9]From *The Great Learning* (VII), by Confucius, as compiled by his disciple, Thseng-tseu (Zhang Zi).

never be a glutton; he who does not cannot be otherwise. A puritan may go to his brown-bread crust with as gross an appetite as ever an alderman to his turtle. Not that food which entereth into the mouth defileth a man, but the appetite with which it is eaten.[10] It is neither the quality nor the quantity, but the devotion to sensual savors; when that which is eaten is not a viand to sustain our animal, or inspire our spiritual life, but food for the worms that possess us. If the hunter has a taste for mud-turtles, muskrats, and other such savage tidbits, the fine lady indulges a taste for jelly made of a calf's foot, or for sardines from over the sea, and they are even. He goes to the mill-pond, she to her preserve-pot. The wonder is how they, how you and I, can live this slimy, beastly life, eating and drinking.

Our whole life is startlingly moral. There is never an instant's truce between virtue and vice. Goodness is the only investment that never fails. In the music of the harp which trembles round the world it is the insisting on this which thrills us. The harp is the travelling patterer for the Universe's Insurance Company, recommending its laws, and our little goodness is all the assessment that we pay. Though the youth at last grows indifferent, the laws of the universe are not indifferent, but are forever on the side of the most sensitive. Listen to every zephyr for some reproof, for it is surely there, and he is unfortunate who does not hear it. We cannot touch a string or move a stop but the charming moral transfixes us. Many an irksome noise, go a long way off, is heard as music, a proud, sweet satire on the meanness of our lives.

We are conscious of an animal in us, which awakens in proportion as our higher nature slumbers. It is reptile and sensual, and perhaps cannot be wholly expelled; like the worms which, even in life and health, occupy our bodies. Possibly we may withdraw from it, but never change its nature. I fear that it may enjoy a certain health of its own; that we may be well, yet not pure. The other day I picked up the lower jaw of a hog, with white and sound teeth and tusks, which suggested that there was an animal health and vigor distinct from the spiritual. This creature succeeded by other means than temperance and purity. "That in which men differ from brute beasts," says Mencius, "is a thing very inconsiderable; the common herd lose it very soon; superior men preserve it carefully."[11] Who knows what sort of life would result if we had attained to purity? If I knew so wise a man as could teach me purity I would go to seek him forthwith. "A command over our passions, and over the external senses of the body, and good acts, are declared by the Ved to be indispensable in the mind's approximation to God."[12] Yet the spirit can for the time pervade and control every member and function of the body, and transmute what in form is the grossest sensuality into purity and devotion. The generative energy, which, when we are loose, dissipates and makes us unclean, when we are continent invigorates and inspires us. Chastity is the flowering of man; and what are called Genius, Heroism, Holiness, and the like, are but various fruits which succeed it. Man flows at once to God when the channel of purity is open. By turns our purity inspires and our impurity casts us down. He is blessed who is assured that the animal is dying out in him day by day, and the divine being established. Perhaps there is none but has cause for shame on account of the inferior and brutish nature to which he is allied. I fear that we are such gods or demigods only as fauns and satyrs,[13] the divine allied to beasts, the creatures of appetite, and that, to some extent, our very life is our disgrace.—

---

[10]Matthew 15:11: "Not that which goeth into the mouth defileth a man; but that which cometh out of the mouth, this defileth a man."
[11]From the *Works of Mencius* (Book IV, Chapter 19); Mencius (372?–289 B.C.) is regarded as second only to Confucius in Chinese philosophy.

[12]From Roy's translation of the *Vedas* (see footnote 8).
[13]In classical mythology, creatures who are half man, half beast.

"How happy's he who hath due place assigned
To his beasts and disafforested his mind!
. . . .
Can use his horse, goat, wolf, and ev'ry beast,
And is not ass himself to all the rest!
Else man not only is the herd of swine,
But he's those devils too which did incline
Them to a headlong rage, and made them worse."[14]

All sensuality is one, though it takes many forms; all purity is one. It is the same whether a man eat, or drink, or cohabit, or sleep sensually. They are but one appetite, and we only need to see a person do any one of these things to know how great a sensualist he is. The impure can neither stand nor sit with purity. When the reptile is attacked at one mouth of his burrow, he shows himself at another. If you would be chaste, you must be temperate. What is chastity? How shall a man know if he is chaste? He shall not know it. We have heard of this virtue, but we know not what it is. We speak conformably to the rumor which we have heard. From exertion come wisdom and purity; from sloth ignorance and sensuality. In the student sensuality is a sluggish habit of mind. An unclean person is universally a slothful one, one who sits by a stove, whom the sun shines on prostrate, who reposes without being fatigued. If you would avoid uncleanness, and all the sins, work earnestly, though it be at cleaning a stable. Nature is hard to be overcome, but she must be overcome. What avails it that you are Christian, if you are not purer than the heathen, if you deny yourself no more, if you are not more religious? I know of many systems of religion esteemed heathenish whose precepts fill the reader with shame, and provoke him to new endeavors, though it be to the performance of rites merely.

I hesitate to say these things, but it is not because of the subject,—I care not how obscene my *words* are,—but because I cannot speak of them without betraying my impurity. We discourse freely without shame of one form of sensuality, and are silent about another. We are so degraded that we cannot speak simply of the necessary functions of human nature. In earlier ages, in some countries, every function was reverently spoken of and regulated by law. Nothing was too trivial for the Hindoo lawgiver, however offensive it may be to modern taste. He teaches how to eat, drink, cohabit, void excrement and urine, and the like, elevating what is mean, and does not falsely excuse himself by calling these things trifles.

Every man is the builder of a temple, called his body, to the god he worships, after a style purely his own, nor can he get off by hammering marble instead. We are all sculptors and painters, and our material is our own flesh and blood and bones. Any nobleness begins at once to refine a man's features, any meanness or sensuality to imbrute them.

John Farmer sat at his door one September evening, after a hard day's work, his mind still running on his labor more or less. Having bathed, he sat down to re-create his intellectual man. It was a rather cool evening, and some of his neighbors were apprehending a frost. He had not attended to the train of his thoughts long when he heard some one playing on a flute,[15] and that sound harmonized with his mood. Still he thought of his work; but the burden of his thought was, that though this kept running in his head, and he found himself planning and contriving it against his will, yet it concerned him very little. It was no more than the scurf of his skin, which was constantly shuffled off. But the notes of the flute came home to his ears out of a different sphere from that he worked in, and sug-

---

[14]From "To Sir Edward Herbert, at Julyers" (ll. 9–17), by John Donne (1573–1631), British metaphysical poet.

[15]Thoreau played a flute; here he imagines the effect the music might have on a typical farmer-neighbor.

gested work for certain faculties which slumbered in him. They gently did away with the street, and the village, and the state in which he lived. A voice said to him,— Why do you stay here and live this mean moiling life, when a glorious existence is possible for you? Those same stars twinkle over other fields than these.— But how to come out of this condition and actually migrate thither? All that he could think of was to practise some new austerity, to let his mind descend into his body and redeem it, and treat himself with ever increasing respect.

XII

BRUTE NEIGHBORS

Sometimes I had a companion[1] in my fishing, who came through the village to my house from the other side of the town, and the catching of the dinner was as much a social exercise as the eating of it.

Hermit. I wonder what the world is doing now. I have not heard so much as a locust over the sweet-fern these three hours. The pigeons are all asleep upon their roosts,— no flutter from them. Was that a farmer's noon horn which sounded from beyond the woods just now? The hands are coming in to boiled salt beef and cider and Indian bread. Why will men worry themselves so? He that does not eat need not work. I wonder how much they have reaped. Who would live there where a body can never think for the barking of Bose?[2] And oh, the housekeeping! to keep bright the devil's door-knobs, and scour his tubs this bright day! Better not keep a house. Say, some hollow tree; and then for morning calls and dinner-parties! Only a woodpecker tapping. Oh, they swarm; the sun is too warm there; they are born too far into life for me. I have water from the spring, and a loaf of brown bread on the shelf.— Hark! I hear a rustling of the leaves. Is it some ill-fed village hound yielding to the instinct of the chase? or the lost pig which is said to be in these woods, whose tracks I saw after the rain? It comes on apace; my sumachs and sweetbriers tremble.— Eh, Mr. Poet, is it you? How do you like the world to-day?

Poet. See those clouds; how they hang! That's the greatest thing I have seen to-day. There's nothing like it in old paintings, nothing like it in foreign lands,— unless when we were off the coast of Spain. That's a true Mediterranean sky. I thought, as I have my living to get, and have not eaten to-day, that I might go a-fishing. That's the true industry for poets. It is the only trade I have learned. Come, let's along.

Hermit. I cannot resist. My brown bread will soon be gone. I will go with you gladly soon, but I am just concluding a serious meditation. I think that I am near the end of it. Leave me alone, then, for a while. But that we may not be delayed, you shall be digging the bait meanwhile. Angleworms are rarely to be met with in these parts, where the soil was never fattened with manure; the race is nearly extinct. The sport of digging the bait is nearly equal to that of catching the fish, when one's appetite is not too keen; and this you may have all to yourself to-day. I would advise you to set in the spade down yonder among the ground-nuts, where you see the johnswort waving. I think that I may warrant you one worm to every three sods you turn up, if you look well in among the roots of the grass, as if you were weeding. Or, if you choose to go farther, it will not be unwise, for I have found the increase of fair bait to be very nearly as the squares of the distances.

Hermit alone. Let me see; where was I? Methinks I was nearly in this frame of mind; the world lay about at this angle. Shall I go to heaven or a-fishing? If I should soon bring this meditation to an end, would another so sweet occasion be

---

[1] Ellery Channing (1818–1901), who dropped out of Harvard and came to Concord to devote his life to poetry.
[2] Generic name for a dog (like Fido).

likely to offer? I was as near being resolved into the essence of things as ever I was in my life. I fear my thoughts will not come back to me. If it would do any good, I would whistle for them. When they make us an offer, is it wise to say, We will think of it? My thoughts have left no track, and I cannot find the path again. What was it that I was thinking of? It was a very hazy day. I will just try these three sentences of Confut-see;[3] they may fetch that state about again. I know not whether it was the dumps or a budding ecstasy. Mem.[4] There never is but one opportunity of a kind.

Poet. How now, Hermit, is it too soon? I have got just thirteen whole ones, be-side several which are imperfect or undersized; but they will do for the smaller fry; they do not cover up the hook so much. Those village worms are quite too large; a shiner may make a meal off one without finding the skewer.

Hermit. Well, then, let's be off. Shall we to the Concord? There's good sport there if the water be not too high.

Why do precisely these objects which we behold make a world? Why has man just these species of animals for his neighbors; as if nothing but a mouse could have filled this crevice? I suspect that Pilpay & Co.[5] have put animals to their best use, for they are all beasts of burden, in a sense, made to carry some portion of our thoughts.

The mice which haunted my house were not the common ones, which are said to have been introduced into the country, but a wild native kind not found in the village. I sent one to a distinguished naturalist,[6] and it interested him much. When I was building, one of these had its nest underneath the house, and before I had laid the second floor, and swept out the shavings, would come out regularly at lunch time and pick up the crumbs at my feet. It probably had never seen a man before; and it soon became quite familiar, and would run over my shoes and up my clothes. It could readily ascend the sides of the room by short impulses, like a squirrel, which it resembled in its motions. At length, as I leaned with my elbow on the bench one day, it ran up my clothes, and along my sleeve, and round and round the paper which held my dinner, while I kept the latter close, and dodged and played at bopeep with it; and when at last I held still a piece of cheese be-tween my thumb and finger, it came and nibbled it, sitting in my hand, and after-ward cleaned its face and paws, like a fly, and walked away.

A phœbe soon built in my shed, and a robin for protection in a pine which grew against the house. In June the partridge (*Tetrao umbellus*), which is so shy a bird, led her brood past my windows, from the woods in the rear to the front of my house, clucking and calling to them like a hen, and in all her behavior proving herself the hen of the woods. The young suddenly disperse on your approach, at a signal from the mother, as if a whirlwind had swept them away, and they so ex-actly resemble the dried leaves and twigs that many a traveller has placed his foot in the midst of a brood, and heard the whir of the old bird as she flew off, and her anxious calls and mewing, or seen her trail her wings to attract his attention, with-out suspecting their neighborhood. The parent will sometimes roll and spin round before you in such a dishabille, that you cannot, for a few moments, detect what kind of creature it is. The young squat still and flat, often running their heads under a leaf, and mind only their mother's directions given from a distance, nor will your approach make them run again and betray themselves. You may even tread on them, or have your eyes on them for a minute, without discovering

---

[3]Confucius.
[4]Memorandum (as to the self).
[5]I.e., tellers of fables. Pilpay, variant of Bidpai, name given as author of ancient Sanskrit fables.

[6]Louis Agassiz (1807–1873), professor of natural history at Harvard and a leading intellectual of the time.

them. I have held them in my open hand at such a time, and still their only care, obedient to their mother and their instinct, was to squat there without fear or trembling. So perfect is this instinct, that once, when I had laid them on the leaves again, and one accidentally fell on its side, it was found with the rest in exactly the same position ten minutes afterward. They are not callow like the young of most birds, but more perfectly developed and precocious even than chickens. The remarkably adult yet innocent expression of their open and serene eyes is very memorable. All intelligence seems reflected in them. They suggest not merely the purity of infancy, but a wisdom clarified by experience. Such an eye was not born when the bird was, but is coeval with the sky it reflects. The woods do not yield another such a gem. The traveller does not often look into such a limpid well. The ignorant or reckless sportsman often shoots the parent at such a time, and leaves these innocents to fall a prey to some prowling beast or bird, or gradually mingle with the decaying leaves which they so much resemble. It is said that when hatched by a hen they will directly disperse on some alarm, and so are lost, for they never hear the mother's call which gathers them again. These were my hens and chickens.

It is remarkable how many creatures live wild and free though secret in the woods, and still sustain themselves in the neighborhood of towns, suspected by hunters only. How retired the otter manages to live here! He grows to be four feet long, as big as a small boy, perhaps without any human being getting a glimpse of him. I formerly saw the raccoon in the woods behind where my house is built, and probably still heard their whinnering[7] at night. Commonly I rested an hour or two in the shade at noon, after planting, and ate my lunch, and read a little by a spring which was the source of a swamp and of a brook, oozing from under Brister's Hill, half a mile from my field. The approach to this was through a succession of descending grassy hollows, full of young pitch pines, into a larger wood about the swamp. There, in a very secluded and shaded spot, under a spreading white pine, there was yet a clean, firm sward to sit on. I had dug out the spring and made a well of clear gray water, where I could dip up a pailful without roiling it, and thither I went for this purpose almost every day in midsummer, when the pond was warmest. Thither, too, the woodcock led her brood, to probe the mud for worms, flying but a foot above them down the bank, while they ran in a troop beneath; but at last, spying me, she would leave her young and circle round and round me, nearer and nearer till within four or five feet, pretending broken wings and legs, to attract my attention, and get off her young, who would already have taken up their march, with faint, wiry peep, single file through the swamp, as she directed. Or I heard the peep of the young when I could not see the parent bird. There too the turtle doves sat over the spring, or fluttered from bough to bough of the soft white pines over my head; or the red squirrel, coursing down the nearest bough, was particularly familiar and inquisitive. You only need sit still long enough in some attractive spot in the woods that all its inhabitants may exhibit themselves to you by turns.

I was witness to events of a less peaceful character. One day when I went out to my wood-pile, or rather my pile of stumps, I observed two large ants, the one red, the other much larger, nearly half an inch long, and black, fiercely contending with one another. Having once got hold they never let go, but struggled and wrestled and rolled on the chips incessantly. Looking farther, I was surprised to find that the chips were covered with such combatants, that it was not a *duellum*,[8] but a *bellum*, a war between two races of ants, the red always pitted against the black, and frequently two red ones to one black. The legions of these Myrmidons[9] cov-

---

[7]A feeble whine.
[8]"A duel" (Latin).

[9]The troops of Achilles in the Trojan War (Homer's *Iliad*). *Myrmex:* Greek for "ant."

ered all the hills and vales in my wood-yard, and the ground was already strewn with the dead and dying, both red and black. It was the only battle which I have ever witnessed, the only battle-field I ever trod while the battle was raging; internecine war; the red republicans on the one hand, and the black imperialists on the other. On every side they were engaged in deadly combat, yet without any noise that I could hear, and human soldiers never fought so resolutely. I watched a couple that were fast locked in each other's embraces, in a little sunny valley amid the chips, now at noonday prepared to fight till the sun went down, or life went out. The smaller red champion had fastened himself like a vice to his adversary's front, and through all the tumblings on that field never for an instant ceased to gnaw at one of his feelers near the root, having already caused the other to go by the board; while the stronger black one dashed him from side to side, and, as I saw on looking nearer, had already divested him of several of his members. They fought with more pertinacity than bulldogs. Neither manifested the least disposition to retreat. It was evident that their battle-cry was "Conquer or die." In the meanwhile there came along a single red ant on the hillside of this valley, evidently full of excitement, who either had despatched his foe, or had not yet taken part in the battle; probably the latter, for he had lost none of his limbs; whose mother had charged him to return with his shield or upon it.[10] Or perchance he was some Achilles, who had nourished his wrath apart, and had now come to avenge or rescue his Patroclus.[11] He saw this unequal combat from afar,—for the blacks were nearly twice the size of the red,—he drew near with rapid pace till he stood on his guard within half an inch of the combatants; then, watching his opportunity, he sprang upon the black warrior, and commenced his operations near the root of his right fore leg, leaving the foe to select among his own members; and so there were three united for life, as if a new kind of attraction had been invented which put all other locks and cements to shame. I should not have wondered by this time to find that they had their respective musical bands stationed on some eminent chip, and playing their national airs the while, to excite the slow and cheer the dying combatants. I was myself excited somewhat even as if they had been men. The more you think of it, the less the difference. And certainly there is not the fight recorded in Concord history, at least, if in the history of America, that will bear a moment's comparison with this, whether for the numbers engaged in it, or for the patriotism and heroism displayed. For numbers and for carnage it was an Austerlitz or Dresden.[12] Concord Fight! Two killed on the patriots' side, and Luther Blanchard wounded! Why here every ant was a Buttrick,—"Fire! for God's sake fire!"—and thousands shared the fate of Davis and Hosmer.[13] There was not one hireling there. I have no doubt that it was a principle they fought for, as much as our ancestors, and not to avoid a three-penny tax on their tea; and the results of this battle will be as important and memorable to those whom it concerns as those of the battle of Bunker Hill, at least.

I took up the chip on which the three I have particularly described were struggling, carried it into my house, and placed it under a tumbler on my window-sill, in order to see the issue. Holding a microscope[14] to the first-mentioned red ant, I saw that, though he was assiduously gnawing at the near fore leg of his enemy, having severed his remaining feeler, his own breast was all torn away, exposing what vitals he had there to the jaws of the black warrior, whose breastplate was apparently too thick for him to pierce; and the dark carbuncles of the sufferer's eyes shone with ferocity such as war only could excite. They struggled half an

---

[10]What Spartan mothers said to their sons, i.e., return still a fighter, or killed in battle.

[11]In Homer's *Iliad*, Achilles stayed in his tent until angered by the death of his friend Patroclus.

[12]Sites of battles during the Napoleonic wars.

[13]All these individuals took part in the Battle of Concord, in April 1775, the first battle of the Revolutionary War. Only two colonists (Davis and Hosmer) were killed.

[14]I.e., a magnifying glass.

hour longer under the tumbler, and when I looked again the black soldier had severed the heads of his foes from their bodies, and the still living heads were hanging on either side of him like ghastly trophies at his saddle-bow, still apparently as firmly fastened as ever, and he was endeavoring with feeble struggles, being without feelers and with only the remnant of a leg, and I know not how many other wounds, to divest himself of them; which at length, after half an hour more, he accomplished. I raised the glass, and he went off over the window-sill in that crippled state. Whether he finally survived that combat, and spent the remainder of his days in some Hôtel des Invalides,[15] I do not know; but I thought that his industry would not be worth much thereafter. I never learned which party was victorious, nor the cause of the war; but I felt for the rest of that day as if I had had my feelings excited and harrowed by witnessing the struggle, the ferocity and carnage, of a human battle before my door.

Kirby and Spence tell us that the battles of ants have long been celebrated and the date of them recorded, though they say that Huber[16] is the only modern author who appears to have witnessed them. "Æneas Sylvius,"[17] say they, "after giving a very circumstantial account of one contested with great obstinacy by a great and small species on the trunk of a pear tree," adds that "'this action was fought in the pontificate of Eugenius the Fourth, in the presence of Nicholas Pistoriensis, an eminent lawyer, who related the whole history of the battle with the greatest fidelity.' A similar engagement between great and small ants is recorded by Olaus Magnus,[18] in which the small ones, being victorious, are said to have buried the bodies of their own soldiers, but left those of their giant enemies a prey to the birds. This event happened previous to the expulsion of the tyrant Christiern the Second from Sweden."[19] The battle which I witnessed took place in the Presidency of Polk, five years before the passage of Webster's Fugitive-Slave Bill.[20]

Many a village Bose, fit only to course[21] a mud-turtle in a victualling cellar, sported his heavy quarters in the woods, without the knowledge of his master, and ineffectually smelled at old fox burrows and woodchucks' holes; led perchance by some slight cur which nimbly threaded the wood, and might still inspire a natural terror in its denizens;—now far behind his guide, barking like a canine bull toward some small squirrel which had treed itself for scrutiny, then, cantering off, bending the bushes with his weight, imagining that he is on the track of some stray member of the jerbilla[22] family. Once I was surprised to see a cat walking along the stony shore of the pond, for they rarely wander so far from home. The surprise was mutual. Nevertheless the most domestic cat, which has lain on a rug all her days, appears quite at home in the woods, and, by her sly and stealthy behavior, proves herself more native there than the regular inhabitants. Once, when berrying, I met with a cat with young kittens in the woods, quite wild, and they all, like their mother, had their backs up and were fiercely spitting at me. A few years before I lived in the woods there was what was called a "winged cat" in one of the farmhouses in Lincoln nearest the pond, Mr. Gilian Baker's. When I called to see her in June, 1842, she was gone a-hunting in the woods, as was her wont (I am not sure whether it was a male or female, and so use the more common pronoun), but her mistress told me that she came into the neighborhood a little more than a year before, in April, and was finally taken into their house; that she was of a dark brownish-gray color, with a white spot on her throat, and white feet, and had a

[15]Hospital for veterans in Paris, built in the 1670s. Napoleon's tomb has been there since 1840.
[16]Pierre Huber (1777–1840), Swiss entomologist, author of *The Natural History of Ants* (1810). His work was used by William Kirby and William Spence in their *Introduction to Entomology* (1846), quoted here.
[17]Pen name of Pope Pius II (1405–1464).
[18]Swedish ecclesiastic and historian (1490–1558).
[19]Christian II, called "the Cruel" (1481–1559).
[20]I.e., 1845. James K. Polk was president in 1845–49; and in 1850, Daniel Webster supported the pro-slavery Fugitive Slave Law.
[21]Race.
[22]Variant of gerbil, small rodent.

large bushy tail like a fox; that in the winter the fur grew thick and flatted out along her sides, forming strips ten or twelve inches long by two and a half wide, and under her chin like a muff, the upper side loose, the under matted like felt, and in the spring these appendages dropped off. They gave me a pair of her "wings," which I keep still. There is no appearance of a membrane about them. Some thought it was part flying squirrel or some other wild animal, which is not impossible, for, according to naturalists, prolific hybrids have been produced by the union of the marten and domestic cat. This would have been the right kind of cat for me to keep, if I had kept any; for why should not a poet's cat be winged as well as his horse?[23]

In the fall the loon (*Colymbus glacialis*) came, as usual, to moult and bathe in the pond, making the woods ring with his wild laughter before I had risen. At rumor of his arrival all the Mill-dam sportsmen are on the alert, in gigs and on foot, two by two and three by three, with patent rifles and conical balls and spy-glasses. They come rustling through the woods like autumn leaves, at least ten men to one loon. Some station themselves on this side of the pond, some on that, for the poor bird cannot be omnipresent; if he dive here he must come up there. But now the kind October wind rises, rustling the leaves and rippling the surface of the water, so that no loon can be heard or seen, though his foes sweep the pond with spy-glasses, and make the woods resound with their discharges. The waves generously rise and dash angrily, taking sides with all water-fowl, and our sportsmen must beat a retreat to town and shop and unfinished jobs. But they were too often successful. When I went to get a pail of water early in the morning I frequently saw this stately bird sailing out of my cove within a few rods. If I endeavored to overtake him in a boat, in order to see how he would manœuvre, he would dive and be completely lost, so that I did not discover him again, sometimes, till the latter part of the day. But I was more than a match for him on the surface. He commonly went off in a rain.

As I was paddling along the north shore one very calm October afternoon, for such days especially they settle on to the lakes, like the milkweed down, having looked in vain over the pond for a loon, suddenly one, sailing out from the shore toward the middle a few rods in front of me, set up his wild laugh and betrayed himself. I pursued with a paddle and he dived, but when he came up I was nearer than before. He dived again, but I miscalculated the direction he would take, and we were fifty rods apart when he came to the surface this time, for I had helped to widen the interval; and again he laughed long and loud, and with more reason than before. He manœuvred so cunningly that I could not get within half a dozen rods of him. Each time, when he came to the surface, turning his head this way and that, he coolly surveyed the water and the land, and apparently chose his course so that he might come up where there was the widest expanse of water and at the greatest distance from the boat. It was surprising how quickly he made up his mind and put his resolve into execution. He led me at once to the widest part of the pond, and could not be driven from it. While he was thinking one thing in his brain, I was endeavoring to divine his thought in mine. It was a pretty game, played on the smooth surface of the pond, a man against a loon. Suddenly your adversary's checker disappears beneath the board, and the problem is to place yours nearest to where his will appear again. Sometimes he would come up unexpectedly on the opposite side of me, having apparently passed directly under the boat. So long-winded was he and so unweariable, that when he had swum farthest he would immediately plunge again, nevertheless; and then no wit could divine

---

[23]Pegasus was the winged horse of classical mythology and, as the mount of poets, symbolized inspiration.

where in the deep pond, beneath the smooth surface, he might be speeding his way like a fish, for he had time and ability to visit the bottom of the pond in its deepest part. It is said that loons have been caught in the New York lakes eighty feet beneath the surface, with hooks set for trout,—though Walden is deeper than that. How surprised must the fishes be to see this ungainly visitor from another sphere speeding his way amid their schools! Yet he appeared to know his course as surely under water as on the surface, and swam much faster there. Once or twice I saw a ripple where he approached the surface, just put his head out to reconnoitre, and instantly dived again. I found that it was as well for me to rest on my oars and wait his reappearing as to endeavor to calculate where he would rise; for again and again, when I was straining my eyes over the surface one way, I would suddenly be startled by his unearthly laugh behind me. But why, after displaying so much cunning, did he invariably betray himself the moment he came up by that loud laugh? Did not his white breast enough betray him? He was indeed a silly loon, I thought. I could commonly hear the plash of the water when he came up, and so also detected him. But after an hour he seemed as fresh as ever, dived as willingly, and swam yet farther than at first. It was surprising to see how serenely he sailed off with unruffled breast when he came to the surface, doing all the work with his webbed feet beneath. His usual note was this demoniac laughter, yet somewhat like that of a water-fowl; but occasionally, when he had balked me most successfully and come up a long way off, he uttered a long-drawn unearthly howl, probably more like that of a wolf than any bird; as when a beast puts his muzzle to the ground and deliberately howls. This was his looning,—perhaps the wildest sound that is ever heard here, making the woods ring far and wide. I concluded that he laughed in derision of my efforts confident of his own resources. Though the sky was by this time overcast, the pond was so smooth that I could see where he broke the surface when I did not hear him. His white breast, the stillness of the air, and the smoothness of the water were all against him. At length, having come up fifty rods off, he uttered one of those prolonged howls, as if calling on the god of loons to aid him, and immediately there came a wind from the east and rippled the surface, and filled the whole air with misty rain, and I was impressed as if it were the prayer of the loon answered, and his god was angry with me; and so I left him disappearing far away on the tumultuous surface.

For hours, in fall days, I watched the ducks cunningly tack and veer and hold the middle of the pond, far from the sportsman; tricks which they will have less need to practise in Louisiana bayous. When compelled to rise they would sometimes circle round and round and over the pond at a considerable height, from which they could easily see to other ponds and the river, like black motes in the sky; and, when I thought they had gone off thither long since, they would settle down by a slanting flight of a quarter of a mile on to a distant part which was left free; but what beside safety they got by sailing in the middle of Walden I do not know, unless they love its water for the same reason that I do.

XIII

HOUSE-WARMING

In October I went a-graping to the river meadows, and loaded myself with clusters more precious for their beauty and fragrance than for food. There, too, I admired, though I did not gather, the cranberries, small waxen gems, pendants of the meadow grass, pearly and red, which the farmer plucks with an ugly rake, leaving the smooth meadow in a snarl, heedlessly measuring them by the bushel and the dollar only, and sells the spoils of the meads to Boston and New York; destined to be *jammed*, to satisfy the tastes of lovers of Nature there. So butchers rake the tongues of bison out of the prairie grass, regardless of the torn and drooping plant.[1] The barberry's brilliant fruit was likewise food for my eyes merely; but I collected a small store of wild apples for coddling, which the proprietor and travellers had overlooked. When chestnuts were ripe I laid up half a bushel for winter. It was very exciting at that season to roam the then boundless chestnut woods of Lincoln,—they now sleep their long sleep under the railroad,— with a bag on my shoulder, and a stick to open burs with in my hand, for I did not always wait for the frost, amid the rustling of leaves and the loud reproofs of the red squirrels and the jays, whose half-consumed nuts I sometimes stole, for the burs which they had selected were sure to contain sound ones. Occasionally I climbed and shook the trees. They grew also behind my house, and one large tree, which almost overshadowed it, was, when in flower, a bouquet which scented the whole neighborhood, but the squirrels and the jays got most of its fruit; the last coming in flocks early in the morning and picking the nuts out of the burs before they fell. I relinquished these trees to them and visited the more distant woods composed wholly of chestnut. These nuts, as far as they went, were a good substitute for bread. Many other substitutes might, perhaps, be found. Digging one day for fishworms, I discovered the groundnut (*Apios tuberosa*) on its string, the potato of the aborigines, a sort of fabulous fruit, which I had begun to doubt if I had ever dug and eaten in childhood, as I had told, and had not dreamed it. I had often since seen its crimpled red velvety blossom supported by the stems of other plants without knowing it to be the same. Cultivation has well-nigh exterminated it. It has a sweetish taste, much like that of a frost-bitten potato, and I found it better boiled than roasted. This tuber seemed like a faint promise of Nature to rear her own children and feed them simply here at some future period. In these days of fatted cattle and waving grain-fields this humble root, which was once the *totem* of an Indian tribe, is quite forgotten, or known only by its flowering vine; but let wild Nature reign here once more, and the tender and luxurious English grains will probably disappear before a myriad of foes, and without the care of man the crow may carry back even the last seed of corn to the great cornfield of the Indian's God in the southwest, whence he is said to have brought it; but the now almost exterminated ground-nut will perhaps revive and flourish in spite of frosts and wildness, prove itself indigenous, and resume its ancient importance and dignity as the diet of the hunter tribe. Some Indian Ceres or Minerva[2] must have been the inventor and bestower of it; and when the reign of poetry commences here, its leaves and string of nuts may be represented on our works of art.

Already, by the first of September, I had seen two or three small maples turned scarlet across the pond, beneath where the white stems of three aspens diverged, at the point of a promontory, next the water. Ah, many a tale their color told! And gradually from week to week the character of each tree came out, and it admired itself reflected in the smooth mirror of the lake. Each morning the manager of this gallery substituted some new picture, distinguished by more brilliant or harmonious coloring, for the old upon the walls.

The wasps came by thousands to my lodge in October, as to winter quarters, and settled on my windows within and on the walls overhead, sometimes deterring visitors from entering. Each morning, when they were numbed with cold, I swept some of them out, but I did not trouble myself much to get rid of them; I even felt complimented by their regarding my house as a desirable shelter. They never molested me seriously, though they bedded with me; and they gradually disappeared, into what crevices I do not know, avoiding winter and unspeakable cold.

---

[1] Reference to the wanton destruction of the buffalo on the American Great Plains for their skins and edible tongues.

[2] In classical mythology, goddess of agriculture and goddess of wisdom, respectively.

Like the wasps, before I finally went into winter quarters in November, I used to resort to the northeast side of Walden, which the sun, reflected from the pitch pine woods and the stony shore, made the fireside of the pond; it is so much pleasanter and wholesomer to be warmed by the sun while you can be, than by an artificial fire. I thus warmed myself by the still glowing embers which the summer, like a departed hunter, had left.

When I came to build my chimney I studied masonry. My bricks, being second-hand ones, required to be cleaned with a trowel, so that I learned more than usual of the qualities of bricks and trowels. The mortar on them was fifty years old, and was said to be still growing harder; but this is one of those sayings which men love to repeat whether they are true or not. Such sayings themselves grow harder and adhere more firmly with age, and it would take many blows with a trowel to clean an old wiseacre of them. Many of the villages of Mesopotamia are built of second-hand bricks of a very good quality, obtained from the ruins of Babylon, and the cement on them is older and probably harder still. However that may be, I was struck by the peculiar toughness of the steel which bore so many violent blows without being worn out. As my bricks had been in a chimney before, though I did not read the name of Nebuchadnezzar[3] on them, I picked out as many fireplace bricks as I could find, to save work and waste, and I filled the spaces between the bricks about the fireplace with stones from the pond shore, and also made my mortar with the white sand from the same place. I lingered most about the fireplace, as the most vital part of the house. Indeed, I worked so deliberately, that though I commenced at the ground in the morning, a course of bricks raised a few inches above the floor served for my pillow at night; yet I did not get a stiff neck for it that I remember; my stiff neck is of older date. I took a poet[4] to board for a fortnight about those times, which caused me to be put to it for room. He brought his own knife, though I had two, and we used to scour them by thrusting them into the earth. He shared with me the labors of cooking. I was pleased to see my work rising so square and solid by degrees, and reflected, that, if it proceeded slowly, it was calculated to endure a long time. The chimney is to some extent an independent structure, standing on the ground, and rising through the house to the heavens; even after the house is burned it still stands sometimes, and its importance and independence are apparent. This was toward the end of summer. It was now November.

The north wind had already begun to cool the pond, though it took many weeks of steady blowing to accomplish it, it is so deep. When I began to have a fire at evening, before I plastered my house, the chimney carried smoke particularly well, because of the numerous chinks between the boards. Yet I passed some cheerful evenings in that cool and airy apartment, surrounded by the rough brown boards full of knots, and rafters with the bark on high overhead. My house never pleased my eye so much after it was plastered, though I was obliged to confess that it was more comfortable. Should not every apartment in which man dwells be lofty enough to create some obscurity overhead, where flickering shadows may play at evening about the rafters? These forms are more agreeable to the fancy and imagination than fresco paintings or other the most expensive furniture. I now first began to inhabit my house, I may say, when I began to use it for warmth as well as shelter. I had got a couple of old fire-dogs[5] to keep the wood

---

[3]King of Babylon (605–562 B.C.) who (like other monarchs) had each brick used in royal building stamped with his name.

[4]Ellery Channing.
[5]I.e., andirons to hold the logs.

from the hearth, and it did me good to see the soot form on the back of the chimney which I had built, and I poked the fire with more right and more satisfaction than usual. My dwelling was small, and I could hardly entertain an echo in it; but it seemed larger for being a single apartment and remote from neighbors. All the attractions of a house were concentrated in one room; it was kitchen, chamber, parlor, and keepingroom;[6] and whatever satisfaction parent or child, master or servant, derive from living in a house, I enjoyed it all. Cato says, the master of a family (*patremfamilias*) must have in his rustic villa "cellam oleariam, vinariam, dolia multa, uti lubeat caritatem expectare, et rei, et virtuti, et gloriae erit," that is, "an oil and wine cellar, many casks, so that it may be pleasant to expect hard times; it will be for his advantage, and virtue, and glory."[7] I had in my cellar a firkin of potatoes, about two quarts of peas with the weevil in them, and on my shelf a little rice, a jug of molasses, and of rye and Indian meal a peck each.

I sometimes dream of a larger and more populous house, standing in a golden age, of enduring materials, and without gingerbread work, which shall still consist of only one room, a vast, rude, substantial, primitive hall, without ceiling or plastering, with bare rafters and purlins[8] supporting a sort of lower heaven over one's head,—useful to keep off rain and snow, where the king and queen posts[9] stand out to receive your homage, when you have done reverence to the prostrate Saturn[10] of an older dynasty on stepping over the sill; a cavernous house, wherein you must reach up a torch upon a pole to see the roof; where some may live in the fireplace, some in the recess of a window, and some on settles, some at one end of the hall, some at another, and some aloft on rafters with the spiders, if they choose; a house which you have got into when you have opened the outside door, and the ceremony is over; where the weary traveller may wash, and eat, and converse, and sleep, without further journey; such a shelter as you would be glad to reach in a tempestuous night, containing all the essentials of a house, and nothing for house-keeping; where you can see all the treasures of the house at one view, and everything hangs upon its peg that a man should use; at once kitchen, pantry, parlor, chamber, storehouse, and garret; where you can see so necessary a thing as a barrel or a ladder, so convenient a thing as a cupboard, and hear the pot boil, and pay your respects to the fire that cooks your dinner, and the oven that bakes your bread, and the necessary furniture and utensils are the chief ornaments; where the washing is not put out, nor the fire, nor the mistress, and perhaps you are sometimes requested to move from off the trap-door, when the cook would descend into the cellar, and so learn whether the ground is solid or hollow beneath you without stamping. A house whose inside is as open and manifest as a bird's nest, and you cannot go in at the front door and out at the back without seeing some of its inhabitants; where to be a guest is to be presented with the freedom of the house, and not to be carefully excluded from seven eighths of it, shut up in a particular cell, and told to make yourself at home there,—in solitary confinement. Nowadays the host does not admit you to *his* hearth, but has got the mason to build one for yourself somewhere in his alley, and hospitality is the art of *keeping* you at the greatest distance. There is as much secrecy about the cooking as if he had a design to poison you. I am aware that I have been on many a man's premises, and might have been legally ordered off, but I am not aware that I have been in many men's houses. I might visit in my old clothes a king and queen who lived simply in such a house as I have described, if I were going their way; but backing out of a modern palace will be all that I shall desire to learn, if ever I am caught in one.

---

[6]Sitting room.
[7]From *De Agri Cultura* (3, 2).
[8]Horizontal roof beams.

[9]Vertical roof beams.
[10]Literally, the door sill plank (Saturn was the Roman chief god until he was overthrown by Jupiter).

It would seem as if the very language of our parlors would lose all its nerve and degenerate into *palaver* wholly, our lives pass at such remoteness from its symbols, and its metaphors and tropes[11] are necessarily so far fetched, through slides and dumb-waiters, as it were; in other words, the parlor is so far from the kitchen and workshop. The dinner even is only the parable of a dinner, commonly. As if only the savage dwelt near enough to Nature and Truth to borrow a trope from them. How can the scholar, who dwells away in the North West Territory or the Isle of Man,[12] tell what is parliamentary in the kitchen?

However, only one or two of my guests were ever bold enough to stay and eat a hasty-pudding with me; but when they saw that crisis approaching they beat a hasty retreat rather, as if it would shake the house to its foundations. Nevertheless, it stood through a great many hasty-puddings.

I did not plaster till it was freezing weather. I brought over some whiter and cleaner sand for this purpose from the opposite shore of the pond in a boat, a sort of conveyance which would have tempted me to go much farther if necessary. My house had in the meanwhile been shingled down to the ground on every side. In lathing I was pleased to be able to send home each nail with a single blow of the hammer, and it was my ambition to transfer the plaster from the board to the wall neatly and rapidly. I remembered the story of a conceited fellow, who, in fine clothes, was wont to lounge about the village once, giving advice to workmen. Venturing one day to substitute deeds for words, he turned up his cuffs, seized a plasterer's board, and having loaded his trowel without mishap, with a complacent look toward the lathing overhead, made a bold gesture thitherward; and straightway, to his complete discomfiture, received the whole contents in his ruffled bosom. I admired anew the economy and convenience of plastering, which so effectually shuts out the cold and takes a handsome finish, and I learned the various casualties to which the plasterer is liable. I was surprised to see how thirsty the bricks were which drank up all the moisture in my plaster before I had smoothed it, and how many pailfuls of water it takes to christen a new hearth. I had the previous winter made a small quantity of lime by burning the shells of the *Unio fluviatilis*,[13] which our river affords, for the sake of the experiment; so that I knew where my materials came from. I might have got good limestone within a mile or two and burned it myself, if I had cared to do so.

The pond had in the meanwhile skimmed over[14] in the shadiest and shallowest coves, some days or even weeks before the general freezing. The first ice is especially interesting and perfect, being hard, dark, and transparent, and affords the best opportunity that ever offers for examining the bottom where it is shallow; for you can lie at your length on ice only an inch thick, like a skater insect on the surface of the water, and study the bottom at your leisure, only two or three inches distant, like a picture behind a glass, and the water is necessarily always smooth then. There are many furrows in the sand where some creature has travelled about and doubled on its tracks; and, for wrecks, it is strewn with the cases of caddis-worms made of minute grains of white quartz. Perhaps these have creased it, for you find some of their cases in the furrows, though they are deep and broad for them to make. But the ice itself is the object of most interest, though you must improve the earliest opportunity to study it. If you examine it closely the morning after it freezes, you find that the greater part of the bubbles, which at first appeared to be within it, are against its under surface, and that more

---

[11]Figures of speech.
[12]The Northwest Territory comprised the present states of Ohio, Indiana, Illinois, Michigan, Wisconsin, and Minnesota; the Isle of Man is in the Irish Sea.

[13]Fresh-water clams.
[14]I.e., with ice.

are continually rising from the bottom; while the ice is as yet comparatively solid and dark, that is, you see the water through it. These bubbles are from an eightieth to an eighth of an inch in diameter, very clear and beautiful, and you see your face reflected in them through the ice. There may be thirty or forty of them to a square inch. There are also already within the ice narrow oblong perpendicular bubbles about half an inch long, sharp cones with the apex upward; or oftener, if the ice is quite fresh, minute spherical bubbles one directly above another, like a string of beads. But these within the ice are not so numerous nor obvious as those beneath. I sometimes used to cast on stones to try the strength of the ice, and those which broke through carried in air with them, which formed very large and conspicuous white bubbles beneath. One day when I came to the same place forty-eight hours afterward, I found that those large bubbles were still perfect, though an inch more of ice had formed, as I could see distinctly by the seam in the edge of a cake. But as the last two days had been very warm, like an Indian summer, the ice was not now transparent, showing the dark green color of the water, and the bottom, but opaque and whitish or gray, and though twice as thick was hardly stronger than before, for the air bubbles had greatly expanded under this heat and run together, and lost their regularity; they were no longer one directly over another, but often like silvery coins poured from a bag, one overlapping another, or in thin flakes, as if occupying slight cleavages. The beauty of the ice was gone, and it was too late to study the bottom. Being curious to know what position my great bubbles occupied with regard to the new ice, I broke out a cake containing a middling sized one, and turned it bottom upward. The new ice had formed around and under the bubble, so that it was included between the two ices. It was wholly in the lower ice, but close against the upper, and was flattish, or perhaps slightly lenticular, with a rounded edge, a quarter of an inch deep by four inches in diameter; and I was surprised to find that directly under the bubble the ice was melted with great regularity in the form of a saucer reversed, to the height of five eighths of an inch in the middle, leaving a thin partition there between the water and the bubble, hardly an eighth of an inch thick; and in many places the small bubbles in this partition had burst out downward, and probably there was no ice at all under the largest bubbles, which were a foot in diameter. I inferred that the infinite number of minute bubbles which I had first seen against the under surface of the ice were now frozen in likewise, and that each, in its degree, had operated like a burning-glass on the ice beneath to melt and rot it. These are the little air-guns which contribute to make the ice crack and whoop.

At length the winter set in in good earnest, just as I had finished plastering, and the wind began to howl around the house as if it had not had permission to do so till then. Night after night the geese came lumbering in in the dark with a clangor and a whistling of wings, even after the ground was covered with snow, some to alight in Walden, and some flying low over the woods toward Fair Haven, bound for Mexico. Several times, when returning from the village at ten or eleven o'clock at night, I heard the tread of a flock of geese, or else ducks, on the dry leaves in the woods by a pond-hole behind my dwelling, where they had come up to feed, and the faint honk or quack of their leader as they hurried off. In 1845 Walden froze entirely over for the first time on the night of the 22d of December, Flint's and other shallower ponds and the river having been frozen ten days or more; in '46, the 16th; in '49, about the 31st; and in '50, about the 27th of December; in '52, the 5th of January; in '53, the 31st of December. The snow had already covered the ground since the 25th of November, and surrounded me suddenly with the scenery of winter. I withdrew yet farther into my shell, and endeavored to keep a bright fire both within my house and within my breast. My employment out of doors now was to collect the dead wood in the forest, bringing it in my hands or on my shoulders, or sometimes trailing a dead pine tree under each arm to my shed. An old forest fence which had seen its best days was a great haul for me. I sacrificed it to Vulcan, for it was past serving the god Terminus.[15] How much more interesting an event is that man's supper who has just been forth in the snow to hunt, nay, you might say, steal, the fuel to cook it with! His bread and meat are sweet. There are enough fagots and waste wood of all kinds in the forests of most of our towns to support many fires, but which at present warm none, and some think, hinder the growth of the young wood. There was also the driftwood of the pond. In the course of the summer I had discovered a raft of pitch pine logs with the bark on, pinned together by the Irish when the railroad was built. This I hauled up partly on the shore. After soaking two years and then lying high six months it was perfectly sound, though waterlogged past drying. I amused myself one winter day with sliding this piecemeal across the pond, nearly half a mile, skating behind with one end of a log fifteen feet long on my shoulder, and the other on the ice; or I tied several logs together with a birch withe, and then, with a longer birch or alder which had a hook at the end, dragged them across. Though completely waterlogged and almost as heavy as lead, they not only burned long, but made a very hot fire; nay, I thought that they burned better for the soaking, as if the pitch, being confined by the water, burned longer, as in a lamp.

Gilpin, in his account of the forest borderers of England, says that "the encroachments of trespassers, and the houses and fences thus raised on the borders of the forest," were "considered as great nuisances by the old forest law, and were severely punished under the name of *purprestures,* as tending *ad terrorem ferarum— ad nocumentum forestae,* etc.,"[16] to the frightening of the game and the detriment of the forest. But I was interested in the preservation of the venison and the vert[17] more than the hunters or woodchoppers, and as much as though I had been the Lord Warden[18] himself; and if any part was burned, though I burned it myself by accident, I grieved with a grief that lasted longer and was more inconsolable than that of the proprietors; nay, I grieved when it was cut down by the proprietors themselves. I would that our farmers when they cut down a forest felt some of that awe which the old Romans did when they came to thin, or let in the light to, a consecrated grove (*lucum conlucare*), that is, would believe that it is sacred to some god. The Roman made an expiatory offering, and prayed, Whatever god or goddess thou art to whom this grove is sacred, be propitious to me, my family, and children, etc.

It is remarkable what a value is still put upon wood even in this age and in this new country, a value more permanent and universal than that of gold. After all our discoveries and inventions no man will go by a pile of wood. It is as precious to us as it was to our Saxon and Norman ancestors. If they made their bows of it, we make our gun-stocks of it. Michaux, more than thirty years ago, says that the price of wood for fuel in New York and Philadelphia "nearly equals, and sometimes exceeds, that of the best wood in Paris, though this immense capital annually requires more than three hundred thousand cords, and is surrounded to the distance of three hundred miles by cultivated plains."[19] In this town the price of wood rises almost steadily, and the only question is, how much higher it is to be this year than it was the last. Mechanics and tradesmen who come in person to the forest on no other errand, are sure to attend the wood auction, and even pay a high price for the privilege of gleaning after the woodchopper. It is now many

---

[15]I.e., burned it (Vulcan was the god of fire, Terminus the god of boundaries).
[16]From *Remarks on Forest Scenery,* II, 122 (1834), by William Gilpen (1724–1804). *Purprestures:* "those who illogically take over the land" (Latin).

[17]Green vegetation.
[18]British official charged to protect the forests.
[19]From *North American Sylva* (1818), by French botanist François André Michaux (1746–1855).

years that men have resorted to the forest for fuel and the materials of the arts: the New Englander and the New Hollander, the Parisian and the Celt, the farmer and Robin Hood, Goody Blake and Harry Gill;[20] in most parts of the world the prince and the peasant, the scholar and the savage, equally require still a few sticks from the forest to warm them and cook their food. Neither could I do without them.

Every man looks at his wood-pile with a kind of affection. I loved to have mine before my window, and the more chips the better to remind me of my pleasing work. I had an old axe which nobody claimed, with which by spells in winter days, on the sunny side of the house, I played about the stumps which I had got out of my bean-field. As my driver prophesied when I was plowing, they warmed me twice,—once while I was splitting them, and again when they were on the fire, so that no fuel could give out more heat. As for the axe I was advised to get the village blacksmith to "jump" it;[21] but I jumped him, and, putting a hickory helve[22] from the woods into it, made it do. If it was dull, it was at least hung true.

A few pieces of fat pine were a great treasure. It is interesting to remember how much of this food for fire is still concealed in the bowels of the earth. In previous years I had often gone "prospecting" over some bare hillside, where a pitch pine wood had formerly stood, and got out the fat pine roots. They are almost indestructible. Stumps thirty or forty years old, at least, will still be sound at the core, though the sapwood has all become vegetable mould, as appears by the scales of the thick bark forming a ring level with the earth four or five inches distant from the heart. With axe and shovel you explore this mine, and follow the marrowy store, yellow as beef tallow, or as if you had struck on a vein of gold, deep into the earth. But commonly I kindled my fire with the dry leaves of the forest, which I had stored up in my shed before the snow came. Green hickory finely split makes the woodchopper's kindlings, when he has a camp in the woods. Once in a while I got a little of this. When the villagers were lighting their fires beyond the horizon, I too gave notice to the various wild inhabitants of Walden vale, by a smoky streamer from my chimney, that I was awake.—

> Light-winged Smoke, Icarian bird,
> Melting thy pinions in thy upward flight,
> Lark without song, and messenger of dawn,
> Circling above the hamlets as thy nest;
> Or else, departing dream, and shadowy form
> Of midnight vision, gathering up thy skirts;
> By night star-veiling, and by day
> Darkening the light and blotting out the sun;
> Go thou my incense upward from this hearth,
> And ask the gods to pardon this clear flame.

Hard green wood just cut, though I used but little of that, answered my purpose better than any other. I sometimes left a good fire when I went to take a walk in a winter afternoon; and when I returned, three or four hours afterward, it would be still alive and glowing. My house was not empty though I was gone. It was as if I had left a cheerful housekeeper behind. It was I and Fire that lived there; and commonly my housekeeper proved trustworthy. One day, however, as I was splitting wood, I thought that I would just look in at the window and see if the house was not on fire; it was the only time I remember to have been particu-

---

[20]In "Goody Blake and Harry Gill" (1798), by English poet William Wordsworth, a poor woman is caught stealing wood from a rich man's property and places a curse on him that he never be warm.

[21]To flatten and thicken the edge by hammering, prior to sharpening.
[22]Handle.

larly anxious on this score; so I looked and saw that a spark had caught my bed, and I went in and extinguished it when it had burned a place as big as my hand. But my house occupied so sunny and sheltered a position, and its roof was so low, that I could afford to let the fire go out in the middle of almost any winter day.

The moles nested in my cellar, nibbling every third potato, and making a snug bed even there of some hair left after plastering and of brown paper; for even the wildest animals love comfort and warmth as well as man, and they survive the winter only because they are so careful to secure them. Some of my friends spoke as if I was coming to the woods on purpose to freeze myself. The animal merely makes a bed, which he warms with his body, in a sheltered place; but man, having discovered fire, boxes up some air in a spacious apartment, and warms that, instead of robbing himself, makes that his bed, in which he can move about divested of more cumbrous clothing, maintain a kind of summer in the midst of winter, and by means of windows even admit the light, and with a lamp lengthen out the day. Thus he goes a step or two beyond instinct, and saves a little time for the fine arts. Though, when I had been exposed to the rudest blasts a long time, my whole body began to grow torpid, when I reached the genial atmosphere of my house I soon recovered my faculties and prolonged my life. But the most luxuriously housed has little to boast of in this respect, nor need we trouble ourselves to speculate how the human race may be at last destroyed. It would be easy to cut their threads any time with a little sharper blast from the north. We go on dating from Cold Fridays and Great Snows; but a little colder Friday, or greater snow would put a period to man's existence on the globe.

The next winter I used a small cooking-stove for economy, since I did not own the forest; but it did not keep fire so well as the open fireplace. Cooking was then, for the most part, no longer a poetic, but merely a chemic process. It will soon be forgotten, in these days of stoves, that we used to roast potatoes in the ashes, after the Indian fashion. The stove not only took up room and scented the house, but it concealed the fire, and I felt as if I had lost a companion. You can always see a face in the fire. The laborer, looking into it at evening, purifies his thoughts of the dross and earthiness which they have accumulated during the day. But I could no longer sit and look into the fire, and the pertinent words of a poet recurred to me with new force.—

> "Never, bright flame, may be denied to me
> Thy dear, life imaging, close sympathy.
> What but my hopes shot upward e'er so bright?
> What but my fortunes sunk so low in night?
> Why art thou banished from our hearth and hall,
> Thou who art welcomed and beloved by all?
> Was thy existence then too fanciful
> For our life's common light, who are so dull?
> Did thy bright gleam mysterious converse hold
> With our congenial souls? secrets too bold?
>
> Well, we are safe and strong, for now we sit
> Beside a hearth where no dim shadows flit,
> Where nothing cheers nor saddens, but a fire
> Warms feet and hands—nor does to more aspire;
> By whose compact utilitarian heap
> The present may sit down and go to sleep,
> Nor fear the ghosts who from the dim past walked,
> And with us by the unequal light of the old wood fire talked."[23]

---

[23]From "The Wood-fire" (published in *The Dial*, 1840), by Ellen Sturgis Hooper (1812–1848), American poet.

XIV

FORMER INHABITANTS; AND WINTER VISITORS

I weathered some merry snow-storms, and spent some cheerful winter eve-nings by my fireside, while the snow whirled wildly without, and even the hooting of the owl was hushed. For many weeks I met no one in my walks but those who came occasionally to cut wood and sled it to the village. The elements, however, abetted me in making a path through the deepest snow in the woods, for when I had once gone through the wind blew the oak leaves into my tracks, where they lodged, and by absorbing the rays of the sun melted the snow, and so not only made a dry bed for my feet, but in the night their dark line was my guide. For human society I was obliged to conjure up the former occupants of these woods. Within the memory of many of my townsmen the road near which my house stands resounded with the laugh and gossip of inhabitants, and the woods which border it were notched and dotted here and there with their little gardens and dwellings, though it was then much more shut in by the forest than now. In some places, within my own remembrance, the pines would scrape both sides of a chaise at once, and women and children who were compelled to go this way to Lincoln alone and on foot did it with fear, and often ran a good part of the distance. Though mainly but a humble route to neighboring villages, or for the woodman's team, it once amused the traveller more than now by its variety, and lingered longer in his memory. Where now firm open fields stretch from the village to the woods, it then ran through a maple swamp on a foundation of logs, the remnants of which, doubtless, still underlie the present dusty highway, from the Stratton, now the Alms-House, Farm, to Brister's Hill.

East of my bean-field, across the road, lived Cato Ingraham, slave of Duncan Ingraham, Esquire, gentleman, of Concord village, who built his slave a house, and gave him permission to live in Walden Woods;—Cato, not Uticensis, but Con-cordiensis.[1] Some say that he was a Guinea Negro. There are a few who remem-ber his little patch among the walnuts, which he let grow up till he should be old and need them; but a younger and whiter speculator got them at last. He too, however, occupies an equally narrow house[2] at present. Cato's half-obliterated cellar-hole still remains, though known to few, being concealed from the traveller by a fringe of pines. It is now filled with the smooth sumach (*Rhus glabra*), and one of the earliest species of goldenrod (*Solidago stricta*) grows there luxuriantly.

Here, by the very corner of my field, still nearer to town, Zilpha, a colored woman, had her little house, where she spun linen for the townsfolk, making the Walden Woods ring with her shrill singing, for she had a loud and notable voice. At length, in the war of 1812, her dwelling was set on fire by English soldiers, prisoners on parole, when she was away, and her cat and dog and hens were all burned up together. She led a hard life, and somewhat inhumane. One old fre-quenter of these woods remembers, that as he passed her house one noon he heard her muttering to herself over her gurgling pot,—"Ye are all bones, bones!" I have seen bricks amid the oak copse there.

Down the road, on the right hand, on Brister's Hill, lived Brister Freeman, "a handy Negro," slave of Squire Cummings once,—there where grow still the apple trees which Brister planted and tended; large old trees now, but their fruit still wild and ciderish to my taste. Not long since I read his epitaph in the old Lincoln burying-ground, a little on one side, near the unmarked graves of some British grenadiers who fell in the retreat from Concord,—where he is styled "Sippio Bris-ter,"—Scipio Africanus[3] he had some title to be called,—"a man of color," as if he

---

[1]Not the Roman Cato (95–46 B.C.), who died at Utica, but the American Cato of Concord.
[2]I.e., grave.

[3]Roman general (237–183 B.C.) who defeated the Carthaginian general Hannibal in Africa.

were discolored. It also told me, with staring emphasis, when he died; which was but an indirect way of informing me that he ever lived. With him dwelt Fenda, his hospitable wife, who told fortunes, yet pleasantly,—large, round, and black, blacker than any of the children of night, such a dusky orb as never rose on Concord before or since.

Farther down the hill, on the left, on the old road in the woods, are marks of some homestead of the Stratton family; whose orchard once covered all the slope of Brister's Hill, but was long since killed out by pitch pines, excepting a few stumps, whose old roots furnish still the wild stocks of many a thrifty village tree.

Nearer yet to town, you come to Breed's location, on the other side of the way, just on the edge of the wood; ground famous for the pranks of a demon not distinctly named in old mythology, who has acted a prominent and astounding part in our New England life, and deserves, as much as any mythological character, to have his biography written one day; who first comes in the guise of a friend or hired man, and then robs and murders the whole family,—New-England Rum. But history must not yet tell the tragedies enacted here; let time intervene in some measure to assuage and lend an azure tint to them. Here the most indistinct and dubious tradition says that once a tavern stood; the well the same, which tempered the traveller's beverage and refreshed his steed. Here then men saluted one another, and heard and told the news, and went their ways again.

Breed's hut was standing only a dozen years ago, though it had long been unoccupied. It was about the size of mine. It was set on fire by mischievous boys, one Election night, if I do not mistake. I lived on the edge of the village then, and had just lost myself over Davenant's "Gondibert,"[4] that winter that I labored with a lethargy,—which, by the way, I never knew whether to regard as a family complaint, having an uncle who goes to sleep shaving himself, and is obliged to sprout potatoes in a cellar Sundays, in order to keep awake and keep the Sabbath, or as the consequence of my attempt to read Chalmers' collection of English poetry[5] without skipping. It fairly overcame my Nervii.[6] I had just sunk my head on this when the bells rung fire, and in hot haste the engines rolled that way, led by a straggling troop of men and boys, and I among the foremost, for I had leaped the brook. We thought it was far south over the woods,—we who had run to fires before,—barn, shop, or dwelling-house, or all together. "It's Baker's barn," cried one. "It is the Codman place," affirmed another. And then fresh sparks went up above the wood, as if the roof fell in, and we all shouted "Concord to the rescue!" Wagons shot past with furious speed and crushing loads, bearing, perchance, among the rest, the agent of the Insurance Company, who was bound to go however far; and ever and anon the engine bell tinkled behind, more slow and sure; and rearmost of all, as it was afterward whispered, came they who set the fire and gave the alarm. Thus we kept on like true idealists, rejecting the evidence of our senses, until at a turn in the road we heard the crackling and actually felt the heat of the fire from over the wall, and realized, alas! that we were there. The very nearness of the fire but cooled our ardor. At first we thought to throw a frogpond on to it; but concluded to let it burn, it was so far gone and so worthless. So we stood round our engine, jostled one another, expressed our sentiments through speaking-trumpets, or in lower tone referred to the great conflagrations which the world has witnessed, including Bascom's shop, and, between ourselves, we thought that, were we there in season with our "tub,"[7] and a full frog-pond by, we could turn that threatened last and universal one into another flood. We finally retreated without doing any mischief,—returned to sleep and "Gondibert." But as

---

[4]*Gondibert: An Heroick Poem* (1672), by William Davenant (1606–1668), British dramatist.
[5]*The Works of the English Poets from Chaucer to Cowper* (1810), 21 volumes, edited by Alexander Chalmers (1759–1834).
[6]Barbaric tribe conquered by Caesar in 57 B.C. Note Thoreau's pun on "nerves."
[7]I.e., water pump.

for "Gondibert," I would except that passage in the preface about wit being the soul's powder,—"but most of mankind are strangers to wit, as Indians are to powder."

It chanced that I walked that way across the fields the following night, about the same hour, and hearing a low moaning at this spot, I drew near in the dark, and discovered the only survivor of the family that I know, the heir of both its virtues and its vices, who alone was interested in this burning, lying on his stomach and looking over the cellar wall at the still smouldering cinders beneath, muttering to himself, as is his wont. He had been working far off in the river meadows all day, and had improved the first moments that he could call his own to visit the home of his fathers and his youth. He gazed into the cellar from all sides and points of view by turns, always lying down to it, as if there was some treasure, which he remembered, concealed between the stones, where there was absolutely nothing but a heap of bricks and ashes. The house being gone, he looked at what there was left. He was soothed by the sympathy which my mere presence implied, and showed me, as well as the darkness permitted, where the well was covered up; which, thank Heaven, could never be burned; and he groped long about the wall to find the well-sweep[8] which his father had cut and mounted, feeling for the iron hook or staple by which a burden had been fastened to the heavy end,—all that he could now cling to;—to convince me that it was no common "rider."[9] I felt it, and still remark it almost daily in my walks, for by it hangs the history of a family.

Once more, on the left, where are seen the well and lilac bushes by the wall, in the now open field, lived Nutting and Le Grosse. But to return toward Lincoln.

Farther in the woods than any of these, where the road approaches nearest to the pond, Wyman the potter squatted, and furnished his townsmen with earthenware, and left descendants to succeed him. Neither were they rich in worldly goods, holding the land by sufferance while they lived; and there often the sheriff came in vain to collect the taxes, and "attached a chip,"[10] for form's sake, as I have read in his accounts, there being nothing else that he could lay his hands on. One day in midsummer, when I was hoeing, a man who was carrying a load of pottery to market stopped his horse against my field and inquired concerning Wyman the younger. He had long ago bought a potter's wheel of him, and wished to know what had become of him. I had read of the potter's clay and wheel in Scripture, but it had never occurred to me that the pots we use were not such as had come down unbroken from those days, or grown on trees like gourds somewhere, and I was pleased to hear that so fictile[11] an art was ever practiced in my neighborhood.

The last inhabitant of these woods before me was an Irishman, Hugh Quoil (if I have spelt his name with coil enough), who occupied Wyman's tenement,—Col. Quoil, he was called. Rumor said that he had been a soldier at Waterloo. If he had lived I should have made him fight his battles over again. His trade here was that of a ditcher. Napoleon went to St. Helena; Quoil came to Walden Woods. All I know of him is tragic. He was a man of manners, like one who had seen the world, and was capable of more civil speech than you could well attend to. He wore a greatcoat in midsummer, being affected with the trembling delirium, and his face was the color of carmine. He died in the road at the foot of Brister's Hill shortly after I came to the woods, so that I have not remembered him as a neighbor. Before his house was pulled down, when his comrades avoided it as "an unlucky castle," I visited it. There lay his old clothes curled up by use, as if they were himself, upon his raised plank bed. His pipe lay broken on the hearth, instead of a bowl

---

[8]Pole for raising the bucket in the well.
[9]Fence rail.
[10]A legal ploy, taking a worthless object to prove that an effort had been made to collect.

[11]That which can be molded, as clay to make pottery. For "potter's clay and wheel," see Jeremiah 18:1–6.

broken at the fountain. The last could never have been the symbol of his death, for he confessed to me that, though he had heard of Brister's Spring, he had never seen it; and soiled cards, kings of diamonds, spades, and hearts, were scattered over the floor. One black chicken which the administrator[12] could not catch, black as night and as silent, not even croaking, awaiting Reynard,[13] still went to roost in the next apartment. In the rear there was the dim outline of a garden, which had been planted but had never received its first hoeing, owing to those terrible shaking fits, though it was now harvest time. It was overrun with Roman wormwood and beggar-ticks, which last stuck to my clothes for all fruit. The skin of a woodchuck was freshly stretched upon the back of the house, a trophy of his last Waterloo; but no warm cap or mittens would he want more.

Now only a dent in the earth marks the site of these dwellings, with buried cellar stones, and strawberries, raspberries, thimble-berries, hazel-bushes, and sumachs growing in the sunny sward there; some pitch pine or gnarled oak occupies what was the chimney nook, and a sweet-scented black birch, perhaps, waves where the door-stone was. Sometimes the well dent is visible, where once a spring oozed; now dry and tearless grass; or it was covered deep,—not to be discovered till some late day,—with a flat stone under the sod, when the last of the race departed. What a sorrowful act must that be,—the covering up of wells! coincident with the opening of wells of tears. These cellar dents, like deserted fox burrows, old holes, are all that is left where once were the stir and bustle of human life, and "fate, free will, foreknowledge absolute,"[14] in some form and dialect or other were by turns discussed. But all I can learn of their conclusions amounts to just this, that "Cato and Brister pulled wool;"[15] which is about as edifying as the history of more famous schools of philosophy.

Still grows the vivacious lilac a generation after the door and lintel and the sill are gone, unfolding its sweet-scented flowers each spring, to be plucked by the musing traveller; planted and tended once by children's hands, in front-yard plots,—now standing by wallsides in retired pastures, and giving place to new-rising forests;—the last of that stirp, sole survivor of that family. Little did the dusky children think that the puny slip with its two eyes only, which they stuck in the ground in the shadow of the house and daily watered, would root itself so, and outlive them, and house itself in the rear that shaded it, and grown man's garden and orchard, and tell their story faintly to the lone wanderer a half-century after they had grown up and died,—blossoming as fair, and smelling as sweet, as in that first spring. I mark its still tender, civil, cheerful lilac colors.

But this small village, germ of something more, why did it fail while Concord keeps its ground? Were there no natural advantages,—no water privileges, forsooth? Ay, the deep Walden Pond and cool Brister's Spring,—privilege to drink long and healthy draughts at these, all unimproved by these men but to dilute their glass. They were universally a thirsty race. Might not the basket, stable-broom, mat-making, corn-parching, linen-spinning, and pottery business have thrived here, making the wilderness to blossom like the rose,[16] and a numerous posterity have inherited the land of their fathers? The sterile soil would at least have been proof against a lowland degeneracy. Alas! how little does the memory of these human inhabitants enhance the beauty of the landscape! Again, perhaps, Nature will try, with me for a first settler, and my house raised last spring to be the oldest in the hamlet.

I am not aware that any man has ever built on the spot which I occupy. Deliver me from a city built on the site of a more ancient city, whose materials are ruins,

---

[12]Executor of an estate.
[13]I.e., a fox.
[14]Milton, *Paradise Lost*, II. 560.

[15]I.e., worked at menial jobs.
[16]Cf. Isaiah 35:1.

whose gardens cemeteries. The soil is blanched and accursed there, and before that becomes necessary the earth itself will be destroyed. With such reminiscences I repeopled the woods and lulled myself asleep.

At this season I seldom had a visitor. When the snow lay deepest no wanderer ventured near my house for a week or fortnight at a time, but there I lived as snug as a meadow mouse, or as cattle and poultry which are said to have survived for a long time buried in drifts, even without food; or like that early settler's family in the town of Sutton, in this State, whose cottage was completely covered by the great snow of 1717 when he was absent, and an Indian found it only by the hole which the chimney's breath made in the drift, and so relieved the family. But no friendly Indian concerned himself about me; nor needed he, for the master of the house was at home. The Great Snow! How cheerful it is to hear of! When the farmers could not get to the woods and swamps with their teams, and were obliged to cut down the shade trees before their houses, and, when the crust was harder, cut off the trees in the swamps, ten feet from the ground, as it appeared the next spring.

In the deepest snows, the path which I used from the highway to my house, about half a mile long, might have been represented by a meandering dotted line, with wide intervals between the dots. For a week of even weather I took exactly the same number of steps, and of the same length, coming and going, stepping deliberately and with the precision of a pair of dividers in my own deep tracks,— to such routine the winter reduces us,—yet often they were filled with heaven's own blue. But no weather interfered fatally with my walks, or rather my going abroad, for I frequently tramped eight or ten miles through the deepest snow to keep an appointment with a beech tree, or a yellow birch, or an old acquaintance among the pines; when the ice and snow causing their limbs to droop, and so sharpening their tops, had changed the pines into fir trees; wading to the tops of the highest hills when the snow was nearly two feet deep on a level, and shaking down another snow-storm on my head at every step; or sometimes creeping and floundering thither on my hands and knees, when the hunters had gone into winter quarters. One afternoon I amused myself by watching a barred owl (*Strix nebulosa*) sitting on one of the lower dead limbs of a white pine, close to the trunk, in broad daylight, I standing within a rod of him. He could hear me when I moved and cronched the snow with my feet, but could not plainly see me. When I made most noise he would stretch out his neck, and erect his neck feathers, and open his eyes wide; but their lids soon fell again, and he began to nod. I too felt a slumberous influence after watching him half an hour, as he sat thus with his eyes half open, like a cat, winged brother of the cat. There was only a narrow slit left between their lids, by which he preserved a peninsular relation to me; thus, with half-shut eyes, looking out from the land of dreams, and endeavoring to realize me, vague object or mote that interrupted his visions. At length, on some louder noise or my nearer approach, he would grow uneasy and sluggishly turn about on his perch, as if impatient at having his dreams disturbed; and when he launched himself off and flapped through the pines, spreading his wings to unexpected breadth, I could not hear the slightest sound from them. Thus, guided amid the pine boughs rather by a delicate sense of their neighborhood than by sight, feeling his twilight way, as it were, with his sensitive pinions, he found a new perch, where he might in peace await the dawning of his day.

As I walked over the long causeway made for the railroad through the meadows, I encountered many a blustering and nipping wind, for nowhere has it freer play; and when the frost had smitten me on one cheek, heathen as I was, I turned to it the other also.[17] Nor was it much better by the carriage road from Brister's

---

[17]Cf. Matthew 5:39.

Hill. For I came to town still, like a friendly Indian, when the contents of the broad open fields were all piled up between the walls of the Walden road, and half an hour sufficed to obliterate the tracks of the last traveller. And when I returned new drifts would have formed, through which I floundered, where the busy northwest wind had been depositing the powdery snow round a sharp angle in the road, and not a rabbit's track, nor even the fine print, the small type, of a meadow mouse was to be seen. Yet I rarely failed to find, even in midwinter, some warm and springy swamp where the grass and the skunk-cabbage still put forth with perennial verdure, and some hardier bird occasionally awaited the return of spring.

Sometimes, notwithstanding the snow, when I returned from my walk at evening I crossed the deep tracks of a woodchopper leading from my door, and found his pile of whittlings on the hearth, and my house filled with the odor of his pipe. Or on a Sunday afternoon, if I chanced to be at home, I heard the cronching of the snow made by the step of a long-headed farmer, who from far through the woods sought my house, to have a social "crack;" one of the few of his vocation who are "men on their farms;"[18] who donned a frock instead of a professor's gown, and is as ready to extract the moral out of church or state as to haul a load of manure from his barn-yard. We talked of rude and simple times, when men sat about large fires in cold, bracing weather, with clear heads; and when other dessert failed, we tried our teeth on many a nut which wise squirrels have long since abandoned, for those which have the thickest shells are commonly empty.

The one who came from farthest to my lodge, through deepest snows and most dismal tempests, was a poet.[19] A farmer, a hunter, a soldier, a reporter, even a philosopher, may be daunted; but nothing can deter a poet, for he is actuated by pure love. Who can predict his comings and goings? His business calls him out at all hours, even when doctors sleep. We made that small house ring with boisterous mirth and resound with the murmur of much sober talk, making amends then to Walden vale for the long silences. Broadway was still and deserted in comparison. At suitable intervals there were regular salutes of laughter, which might have been referred indifferently to the last-uttered or the forth-coming jest. We made many a "bran new" theory of life over a thin dish of gruel, which combined the advantages of conviviality with the clear-headedness which philosophy requires.

I should not forget that during my last winter at the pond there was another welcome visitor, who at one time came through the village, through snow and rain and darkness, till he saw my lamp through the trees, and shared with me some long winter evenings.[20] One of the last of the philosophers,—Connecticut gave him to the world,—he peddled first her wares, afterwards, as he declares, his brains. These he peddles still, prompting God and disgracing man, bearing for fruit his brain only, like the nut its kernel. I think that he must be the man of the most faith of any alive. His words and attitude always suppose a better state of things than other men are acquainted with, and he will be the last man to be disappointed as the ages revolve. He has no venture in the present. But though comparatively disregarded now, when his day comes, laws unsuspected by most will take effect, and masters of families and rulers will come to him for advice.—

"How blind that cannot see serenity!"[21]

A true friend of man; almost the only friend of human progress. An Old Mortality,[22] say rather an Immortality, with unwearied patience and faith making plain

---

[18]Cf. Emerson on "The American Scholar": better to be a man on the farm than simply a farmer.
[19]Ellery Channing.
[20]Amos Bronson Alcott (1799–1888), transcendentalist and author of "Orphic Sayings," was once a peddler.

[21]From *The Life and Death of Thomas Wolsey, Cardinal* (1599), by Thomas Storer.
[22]Reference to the title character of *Old Mortality* (1816), a novel by Sir Walter Scott (1771–1832).

the image engraven in men's bodies, the God of whom they are but defaced and leaning monuments. With his hospitable intellect he embraces children, beggars, insane, and scholars, and entertains the thought of all, adding to it commonly some breadth and elegance. I think that he should keep a caravansary on the world's highway, where philosophers of all nations might put up, and on his sign should be printed, "Entertainment for man, but not for his beast. Enter ye that have leisure and a quiet mind, who earnestly seek the right road." He is perhaps the sanest man and has the fewest crotchets of any I chance to know; the same yesterday and to-morrow. Of yore we had sauntered and talked, and effectually put the world behind us; for he was pledged to no institution in it, freeborn, *ingenuus*. Whichever way we turned, it seemed that the heavens and the earth had met together, since he enhanced the beauty of the landscape. A blue-robed man, whose fittest roof is the overarching sky which reflects his serenity. I do not see how he can ever die; Nature cannot spare him.

Having each some shingles of thought well dried, we sat and whittled them, trying our knives, and admiring the clear yellowish grain of the pumpkin pine. We waded so gently and reverently, or we pulled together so smoothly, that the fishes of thought were not scared from the stream, nor feared any angler on the bank, but came and went grandly, like the clouds which float through the western sky, and the mother-o'-pearl flocks which sometimes form and dissolve there. There we worked, revising mythology, rounding a fable here and there, and building castles in the air for which earth offered no worthy foundation. Great Looker! Great Expecter! to converse with whom was a New England Night's Entertainment. Ah! such discourse we had, hermit and philosopher, and the old settler I have spoken of,—we three,—it expanded and racked my little house; I should not dare to say how many pounds' weight there was above the atmospheric pressure on every circular inch; it opened its seams so that they had to be calked with much dulness thereafter to stop the consequent leak;—but I had enough of that kind of oakum already picked.

There was one other[23] with whom I had "solid seasons," long to be remembered, at his house in the village, and who looked in upon me from time to time; but I had no more for society there.

There too, as everywhere, I sometimes expected the Visitor who never comes. The Vishnu Purana says, "The house-holder is to remain at eventide in his courtyard as long as it takes to milk a cow, or longer if he pleases, to await the arrival of a guest."[24] I often performed this duty of hospitality, waited long enough to milk a whole herd of cows, but did not see the man approaching from the town.[25]

XV

WINTER ANIMALS

When the ponds were firmly frozen, they afforded not only new and shorter routes to many points, but new views from their surfaces of the familiar landscape around them. When I crossed Flint's Pond, after it was covered with snow, though I had often paddled about and skated over it, it was so unexpectedly wide and so strange that I could think of nothing but Baffin's Bay.[1] The Lincoln hills rose up around me at the extremity of a snowy plain, in which I did not remember to have stood before; and the fishermen, at an indeterminable distance over the ice, moving slowly about with their wolfish dogs, passed for sealers or Esquimaux, or in misty weather loomed like fabulous creatures, and I did not know whether they

---

[23]Ralph Waldo Emerson.
[24]From the Hindu scripture *Vishnu Purana*, trans. H. H. Wilson (1840).
[25]From an Old English ballad, "The Children in the Wood"

("But never more could see the man/Approaching from the town").
[1]Between Greenland and Canada, a part of the northwest passage that joins the Atlantic and Arctic Oceans.

were giants or pygmies. I took this course when I went to lecture[2] in Lincoln in the evening, travelling in no road and passing no house between my own hut and the lecture room. In Goose Pond, which lay in my way, a colony of muskrats dwelt, and raised their cabins high above the ice, though none could be seen abroad when I crossed it. Walden, being like the rest usually bare of snow, or with only shallow and interrupted drifts on it, was my yard where I could walk freely when the snow was nearly two feet deep on a level elsewhere and the villagers were confined to their streets. There, far from the village street, and except at very long intervals, from the jingle of sleigh-bells, I slid and skated, as in a vast moose-yard well trodden, overhung by oak woods and solemn pines bent down with snow or bristling with icicles.

For sounds in winter nights, and often in winter days, I heard the forlorn but melodious note of a hooting owl indefinitely far; such a sound as the frozen earth would yield if struck with a suitable plectrum, the very *lingua vernacula*[3] of Walden Wood, and quite familiar to me at last, though I never saw the bird while it was making it. I seldom opened my door in a winter evening without hearing it; *Hoo hoo hoo, hoorer hoo,* sounded sonorously, and the first three syllables accented somewhat like *how der do;* or sometimes *hoo hoo* only. One night in the beginning of winter, before the pond froze over, about nine o'clock, I was startled by the loud honking of a goose, and, stepping to the door, heard the sound of their wings like a tempest in the woods as they flew low over my house. They passed over the pond toward Fair Haven, seemingly deterred from settling by my light, their commodore honking all the while with a regular beat. Suddenly an unmistakable cat owl from very near me, with the most harsh and tremendous voice I ever heard from any inhabitant of the woods, responded at regular intervals to the goose, as if determined to expose and disgrace this intruder from Hudson's Bay by exhibiting a greater compass and volume of voice in a native, and *boo-hoo* him out of Concord horizon. What do you mean by alarming the citadel at this time of night consecrated to me? Do you think I am ever caught napping at such an hour, and that I have not got lungs and a larynx as well as yourself? *Boo-hoo, boo-hoo, boo-hoo!* It was one of the most thrilling discords I ever heard. And yet, if you had a discriminating ear, there were in it the elements of a concord such as these plains never saw nor heard.

I also heard the whooping of the ice in the pond, my great bed-fellow in that part of Concord, as if it were restless in its bed and would fain turn over, were troubled with flatulency and bad dreams; or I was waked by the cracking of the ground by the frost, as if some one had driven a team against my door, and in the morning would find a crack in the earth a quarter of a mile long and a third of an inch wide.

Sometimes I heard the foxes as they ranged over the snow-crust, in moonlight nights, in search of a partridge or other game, barking raggedly and demoniacally like forest dogs, as if laboring with some anxiety, or seeking expression, struggling for light and to be dogs outright and run freely in the streets; for if we take the ages into our account, may there not be a civilization going on among brutes as well as men? They seemed to me to be rudimental, burrowing men, still standing on their defence, awaiting their transformation. Sometimes one came near to my window, attracted by my light, barked a vulpine curse at me, and then retreated.

Usually the red squirrel (*Sciurus Hudsonius*) waked me in the dawn, coursing over the roof and up and down the sides of the house, as if sent out of the woods for this purpose. In the course of the winter I threw out half a bushel of ears of

---

[2]Thoreau made some income by lecturing at various nearby towns such as Lincoln.
[3]"Local speech" or "everyday language" (Latin).

sweet corn, which had not got ripe, on to the snow-crust by my door, and was amused by watching the motions of the various animals which were baited by it. In the twilight and the night the rabbits came regularly and made a hearty meal. All day long the red squirrels came and went, and afforded me much entertainment by their manœuvres. One would approach at first warily through the shrub oaks, running over the snow-crust by fits and starts like a leaf blown by the wind, now a few paces this way, with wonderful speed and waste of energy, making inconceivable haste with his "trotters," as if it were for a wager, and now as many paces that way, but never getting on more than half a rod at a time; and then suddenly pausing with a ludicrous expression and a gratuitous somerset,[4] as if all the eyes in the universe were fixed on him,—for all the motions of a squirrel, even in the most solitary recesses of the forest, imply spectators as much as those of a dancing girl,—wasting more time in delay and circumspection than would have sufficed to walk the whole distance,—I never saw one walk,—and then suddenly, before you could say Jack Robinson, he would be in the top of a young pitch pine, winding up his clock and chiding all imaginary spectators, soliloquizing and talking to all the universe at the same time,—for no reason that I could ever detect, or he himself was aware of, I suspect. At length he would reach the corn, and selecting a suitable ear, frisk about in the same uncertain trigonometrical way to the topmost stick of my wood-pile, before my window, where he looked me in the face, and there sit for hours, supplying himself with a new ear from time to time, nibbling at first voraciously and throwing the half-naked cobs about; till at length he grew more dainty still and played with his food, tasting only the inside of the kernel, and the ear, which was held balanced over the stick by one paw, slipped from his careless grasp and fell to the ground, when he would look over at it with a ludicrous expression of uncertainty, as if suspecting that it had life, with a mind not made up whether to get it again, or a new one, or be off; now thinking of corn, then listening to hear what was in the wind. So the little impudent fellow would waste many an ear in a forenoon; till at last, seizing some longer and plumper one, considerably bigger than himself, and skilfully balancing it, he would set out with it to the woods, like a tiger with a buffalo, by the same zigzag course and frequent pauses, scratching along with it as if it were too heavy for him and falling all the while, making its fall a diagonal between a perpendicular and horizontal, being determined to put it through at any rate;—a singularly frivolous and whimsical fellow;—and so he would get off with it to where he lived, perhaps carry it to the top of a pine tree forty or fifty rods distant, and I would afterwards find the cobs strewn about the woods in various directions.

At length the jays arrive, whose discordant screams were heard long before, as they were warily making their approach an eighth of a mile off, and in a stealthy and sneaking manner they flit from tree to tree, nearer and nearer, and pick up the kernels which the squirrels have dropped. Then, sitting on a pitch pine bough, they attempt to swallow in their haste a kernel which is too big for their throats and chokes them; and after great labor they disgorge it, and spend an hour in the endeavor to crack it by repeated blows with their bills. They were manifestly thieves, and I had not much respect for them; but the squirrels, though at first shy, went to work as if they were taking what was their own.

Meanwhile also came the chickadees in flocks, which, picking up the crumbs the squirrels had dropped, flew to the nearest twig, and, placing them under their claws, hammered away at them with their little bills, as if it were an insect in the bark, till they were sufficiently reduced for their slender throats. A little flock of these titmice came daily to pick a dinner out of my wood-pile, or the crumbs at my

---

[4]Variant for somersault.

door, with faint flitting lisping notes, like the tinkling of icicles in the grass, or else with sprightly *day day day,* or more rarely, in springlike days, a wiry summery *phe-be* from the woodside. They were so familiar that at length one alighted on an armful of wood which I was carrying in, and pecked at the sticks without fear. I once had a sparrow alight upon my shoulder for a moment while I was hoeing in a village garden, and I felt that I was more distinguished by that circumstance than I should have been by any epaulet I could have worn. The squirrels also grew at last to be quite familiar, and occasionally stepped upon my shoe, when that was the nearest way.

When the ground was not yet quite covered, and again near the end of winter, when the snow was melted on my south hillside and about my wood-pile, the partridges came out of the woods morning and evening to feed there. Whichever side you walk in the woods the partridge bursts away on whirring wings, jarring the snow from the dry leaves and twigs on high, which comes sifting down in the sunbeams like golden dust, for this brave bird is not to be scared by winter. It is frequently covered up by drifts, and, it is said, "sometimes plunges from on wing into the soft snow, where it remains concealed for a day or two."[5] I used to start them in the open land also, where they had come out of the woods at sunset to "bud" the wild apple trees. They will come regularly every evening to particular trees, where the cunning sportsman lies in wait for them, and the distant orchards next the woods suffer thus not a little. I am glad that the partridge gets fed, at any rate. It is Nature's own bird which lives on buds and diet-drink.[6]

In dark winter mornings, or in short winter afternoons, I sometimes heard a pack of hounds threading all the woods with hounding cry and yelp, unable to resist the instinct of the chase, and the note of the hunting-horn at intervals, proving that man was in the rear. The woods ring again, and yet no fox bursts forth on to the open level of the pond, nor following pack pursuing their Actæon.[7] And perhaps at evening I see the hunters returning with a single brush trailing from their sleigh for a trophy, seeking their inn. They tell me that if the fox would remain in the bosom of the frozen earth he would be safe, or if he would run in a straight line away no foxhound could overtake him; but, having left his pursuers far behind, he stops to rest and listen till they come up, and when he runs he circles round to his old haunts, where the hunters await him. Sometimes, however, he will run upon a wall many rods, and then leap off far to one side, and he appears to know that water will not retain his scent. A hunter told me that he once saw a fox pursued by hounds burst out on to Walden when the ice was covered with shallow puddles, run part way across, and then return to the same shore. Ere long the hounds arrived, but here they lost the scent. Sometimes a pack hunting by themselves would pass my door, and circle round my house, and yelp and hound without regarding me, as if afflicted by a species of madness, so that nothing could divert them from the pursuit. Thus they circle until they fall upon the recent trail of a fox, for a wise hound will forsake everything else for this. One day a man came to my hut from Lexington to inquire after his hound that made a large track, and had been hunting for a week by himself. But I fear that he was not the wiser for all I told him, for every time I attempted to answer his questions he interrupted me by asking, "What do you do here?" He had lost a dog, but found a man.

One old hunter who has a dry tongue, who used to come to bathe in Walden once every year when the water was warmest, and at such times looked in upon

[5]According to J. Lyndon Shanley, Thoreau cites John James Audubon (1785–1851) for this quotation, but it has not been identified.
[6]I.e., water.
[7]In Greek legend, a hunter looked on the goddess Artemis bathing; he was turned into a stag for this transgression and devoured by his own dogs.

me, told me that many years ago he took his gun one afternoon and went out for a cruise in Walden Wood; and as he walked the Wayland road he heard the cry of hounds approaching, and ere long a fox leaped the wall into the road, and as quick as thought leaped the other wall out of the road, and his swift bullet had not touched him. Some way behind came an old hound and her three pups in full pursuit, hunting on their own account, and disappeared again in the woods. Late in the afternoon, as he was resting in the thick woods south of Walden, he heard the voice of the hounds far over toward Fair Haven still pursuing the fox; and on they came, their hounding cry which made all the woods ring sounding nearer and nearer, now from Well Meadow, now from the Baker Farm. For a long time he stood still and listened to their music, so sweet to a hunter's ear, when suddenly the fox appeared, threading the solemn aisles with an easy coursing pace, whose sound was concealed by a sympathetic rustle of the leaves, swift and still, keeping the ground, leaving his pursuers far behind; and, leaping upon a rock amid the woods, he sat erect and listening, with his back to the hunter. For a moment compassion restrained the latter's arm; but that was a short-lived mood, and as quick as thought can follow thought his piece was levelled, and *whang!*—the fox, rolling over the rock, lay dead on the ground. The hunter still kept his place and listened to the hounds. Still on they came, and now the near woods resounded through all their aisles with their demoniac cry. At length the old hound burst into view with muzzle to the ground, and snapping the air as if possessed, and ran directly to the rock; but, spying the dead fox, she suddenly ceased her hounding, as if struck dumb with amazement, and walked round and round him in silence; and one by one her pups arrived, and, like their mother, were sobered into silence by the mystery. Then the hunter came forward and stood in their midst, and the mystery was solved. They waited in silence while he skinned the fox, then followed the brush a while, and at length turned off into the woods again. That evening a Weston squire came to the Concord hunter's cottage to inquire for his hounds, and told how for a week they had been hunting on their own account from Weston woods. The Concord hunter told him what he knew and offered him the skin; but the other declined it and departed. He did not find his hounds that night, but the next day learned that they had crossed the river and put up at a farmhouse for the night, whence, having been well fed, they took their departure early in the morning.

The hunter who told me this could remember one Sam Nutting, who used to hunt bears on Fair Haven Ledges, and exchange their skins for rum in Concord village; who told him, even, that he had seen a moose there. Nutting had a famous foxhound named Burgoyne,—he pronounced it Bugine,—which my informant used to borrow. In the "Wast Book"[8] of an old trader of this town, who was also a captain, town-clerk, and representative, I find the following entry. Jan. 18th, 1742–3, "John Melven Cr. by 1 Grey Fox 0—2—3;" they are not now found here; and in his ledger, Feb. 7th, 1743, Hezekiah Stratton has credit "by ½ a Catt skin 0—1—4½;" of course, a wild-cat, for Stratton was a sergeant in the old French war, and would not have got credit for hunting less noble game. Credit is given for deerskins also, and they were daily sold. One man still preserves the horns of the last deer that was killed in this vicinity, and another has told me the particulars of the hunt in which his uncle was engaged. The hunters were formerly a numerous and merry crew here. I remember well one gaunt Nimrod[9] who would catch up a leaf by the roadside and play a strain on it wilder and more melodious, if my memory serves me, than any huntinghorn.

---

[8]Variant of "waste book," an informal account book where transactions are set down to be entered in regular account books later.

[9]Genesis 10:9: "He was a mighty hunter before the Lord: wherefore it is said, Even as Nimrod the mighty hunter before the Lord."

At midnight, when there was a moon, I sometimes met with hounds in my path prowling about the woods, which would skulk out of my way, as if afraid, and stand silent amid the bushes till I had passed.

Squirrels and wild mice disputed for my store of nuts. There were scores of pitch pines around my house, from one to four inches in diameter, which had been gnawed by mice the previous winter,—a Norwegian winter for them, for the snow lay long and deep, and they were obliged to mix a large proportion of pine bark with their other diet. These trees were alive and apparently flourishing at midsummer, and many of them had grown a foot, though completely girdled; but after another winter such were without exception dead. It is remarkable that a single mouse should thus be allowed a whole pine tree for its dinner, gnawing round instead of up and down it; but perhaps it is necessary in order to thin these trees, which are wont to grow up densely.

The hares (*Lepus Americanus*) were very familiar. One had her form under my house all winter, separated from me only by the flooring, and she startled me each morning by her hasty departure when I began to stir,—thump, thump, thump, striking her head against the floor timbers in her hurry. They used to come round my door at dusk to nibble the potato parings which I had thrown out, and were so nearly the color of the ground that they could hardly be distinguished when still. Sometimes in the twilight I alternately lost and recovered sight of one sitting motionless under my window. When I opened my door in the evening, off they would go with a squeak and a bounce. Near at hand they only excited my pity. One evening one sat by my door two paces from me, at first trembling with fear, yet unwilling to move; a poor wee thing, lean and bony, with ragged ears and sharp nose, scant tail and slender paws. It looked as if Nature no longer contained the breed of nobler bloods, but stood on her last toes. Its large eyes appeared young and unhealthy, almost dropsical. I took a step, and lo, away it scud with an elastic spring over the snow-crust, straightening its body and its limbs into graceful length, and soon put the forest between me and itself,—the wild free venison, asserting its vigor and the dignity of Nature. Not without reason was its slenderness. Such then was its nature. (*Lepus, levipes,* lightfoot, some think.)

What is a country without rabbits and partridges? They are among the most simple and indigenous animal products; ancient and venerable families known to antiquity as to modern times; of the very hue and substance of Nature, nearest allied to leaves and to the ground,—and to one another; it is either winged or it is legged. It is hardly as if you had seen a wild creature when a rabbit or a partridge bursts away, only a natural one, as much to be expected as rustling leaves. The partridge and the rabbit are still sure to thrive, like true natives of the soil, whatever revolutions occur. If the forest is cut off, the sprouts and bushes which spring up afford them concealment, and they become more numerous than ever. That must be a poor country indeed that does not support a hare. Our woods teem with them both, and around every swamp may be seen the partridge or rabbit walk, beset with twiggy fences[10] and horse-hair snares, which some cow-boy[11] tends.

XVI

THE POND IN WINTER

Ater a still winter night I awoke with the impression that some question had been put to me, which I had been endeavoring in vain to answer in my sleep, as what—how—when—where? But there was dawning Nature, in whom all crea-

---

[10]Small fences designed to propel game into traps.
[11]Cow herder.

tures live, looking in at my broad windows with serene and satisfied face, and no question on *her* lips. I awoke to an answered question, to Nature and daylight. The snow lying deep on the earth dotted with young pines, and the very slope of the hill on which my house is placed, seemed to say, Forward! Nature puts no question and answers none which we mortals ask. She has long ago taken her resolution. "O Prince, our eyes contemplate with admiration and transmit to the soul the wonderful and varied spectacle of this universe. The night veils without doubt a part of this glorious creation; but day comes to reveal to us this great work, which extends from earth even into the plains of the ether."[1]

Then to my morning work. First I take an axe and pail and go in search of water, if that be not a dream. After a cold and snowy night it needed a divining-rod to find it. Every winter the liquid and trembling surface of the pond, which was so sensitive to every breath, and reflected every light and shadow, becomes solid to the depth of a foot or a foot and a half, so that it will support the heaviest teams, and perchance the snow covers it to an equal depth, and it is not to be distinguished from any level field. Like the marmots in the surrounding hills, it closes its eyelids and becomes dormant for three months or more. Standing on the snow-covered plain, as if in a pasture amid the hills, I cut my way first through a foot of snow, and then a foot of ice, and open a window under my feet, where, kneeling to drink, I look down into the quiet parlor of the fishes, pervaded by a softened light as through a window of ground glass, with its bright sanded floor the same as in summer; there a perennial waveless serenity reigns as in the amber twilight sky, corresponding to the cool and even temperament of the inhabitants. Heaven is under our feet as well as over our heads.

Early in the morning, while all things are crisp with frost, men come with fishing-reels and slender lunch, and let down their fine lines through the snowy field to take pickerel and perch; wild men, who instinctively follow other fashions and trust other authorities than their townsmen, and by their goings and comings stitch towns together in parts where else they would be ripped. They sit and eat their luncheon in stout fear-naughts[2] on the dry oak leaves on the shore, as wise in natural lore as the citizen is in artificial. They never consulted with books, and know and can tell much less than they have done. The things which they practice are said not yet to be known. Here is one fishing for pickerel with grown perch for bait. You look into his pail with wonder as into a summer pond, as if he kept summer locked up at home, or knew where she had retreated. How, pray, did he get these in midwinter? Oh, he got worms out of rotten logs since the ground froze, and so he caught them. His life itself passes deeper in nature than the studies of the naturalist penetrate; himself a subject for the naturalist. The latter raises the moss and bark gently with his knife in search of insects; the former lays open logs to their core with his axe, and moss and bark fly far and wide. He gets his living by barking trees. Such a man has some right to fish, and I love to see nature carried out in him. The perch swallows the grub-worm, the pickerel swallows the perch, and the fisherman swallows the pickerel; and so all the chinks in the scale of being are filled.

When I strolled around the pond in misty weather I was sometimes amused by the primitive mode which some ruder fisherman had adopted. He would perhaps have placed alder branches over the narrow holes in the ice, which were four or five rods apart and an equal distance from the shore, and having fastened the end of the line to a stick to prevent its being pulled through, have passed the slack line

---

[1] From *The Harivansa*, appendix to *Mahabharata*, one of India's epic religious poems; Thoreau knew the work through a French translation.
[2] Warm winter coats made of thick cloth.

over a twig of the alder, a foot or more above the ice, and tied a dry oak leaf to it, which, being pulled down, would show when he had a bite. These alders loomed through the mist at regular intervals as you walked half way round the pond.

Ah, the pickerel of Walden! when I see them lying on the ice, or in the well which the fisherman cuts in the ice, making a little hole to admit the water, I am always surprised by their rare beauty, as if they were fabulous fishes, they are so foreign to the streets, even to the woods, foreign as Arabia to our Concord life. They possess a quite dazzling and transcendent beauty which separates them by a wide interval from the cadaverous cod and haddock whose fame is trumpeted in our streets. They are not green like the pines, nor gray like the stones, nor blue like the sky; but they have, to my eyes, if possible, yet rarer colors, like flowers and precious stones, as if they were the pearls, the animalized *nuclei* or crystals of the Walden water. They, of course, are Walden all over and all through; are themselves small Waldens in the animal kingdom, Waldenses.[3] It is surprising that they are caught here,—that in this deep and capacious spring, far beneath the rattling teams and chaises and tinkling sleighs that travel the Walden road, this great gold and emerald fish swims. I never chanced to see its kind in any market; it would be the cynosure of all eyes there. Easily, with a few convulsive quirks, they give up their watery ghosts, like a mortal translated before his time to the thin air of heaven.

As I was desirous to recover the long lost bottom of Walden Pond, I surveyed it carefully, before the ice broke up, early in '46, with compass and chain and sounding line. There have been many stories told about the bottom, or rather no bottom, of this pond, which certainly had no foundation for themselves. It is remarkable how long men will believe in the bottomlessness of a pond without taking the trouble to sound it. I have visited two such Bottomless Ponds in one walk in this neighborhood. Many have believed that Walden reached quite through to the other side of the globe. Some who have lain flat on the ice for a long time, looking down through the illusive medium, perchance with watery eyes into the bargain, and driven to hasty conclusions by the fear of catching cold in their breasts, have seen vast holes "into which a load of hay might be driven," if there were anybody to drive it, the undoubted source of the Styx and entrance to the Infernal Regions from these parts. Others have gone down from the village with a "fifty-six"[4] and a wagon load of inch rope, but yet have failed to find any bottom; for while the "fifty-six" was resting by the way, they were paying out the rope in the vain attempt to fathom their truly immeasurable capacity for marvellousness. But I can assure my readers that Walden has a reasonably tight bottom at a not unreasonable, though at an unusual, depth. I fathomed it easily with a cod-line and a stone weighing about a pound and a half, and could tell accurately when the stone left the bottom, by having to pull so much harder before the water got underneath to help me. The greatest depth was exactly one hundred and two feet; to which may be added the five feet which it has risen since, making one hundred and seven. This is a remarkable depth for so small an area; yet not an inch of it can be spared by the imagination. What if all ponds were shallow? Would it not react on the minds of men? I am thankful that this pond was made deep and pure for a symbol. While men believe in the infinite some ponds will be thought to be bottomless.

A factory-owner, hearing what depth I had found, thought that it could not be true, for, judging from his acquaintance with dams, sand would not lie at so steep an angle. But the deepest ponds are not so deep in proportion to their area as most suppose, and, if drained, would not leave very remarkable valleys. They are

[3] A persecuted protestant sect of twelfth-century France.
[4] A 56-pound weight.

not like cups between the hills; for this one, which is so unusually deep for its area, appears in a vertical section through its centre not deeper than a shallow plate. Most ponds, emptied, would leave a meadow no more hollow than we frequently see. William Gilpin,[5] who is so admirable in all that relates to landscapes, and usually so correct, standing at the head of Loch Fyne, in Scotland, which he describes as "a bay of salt water, sixty or seventy fathoms deep, four miles in breadth," and about fifty miles long, surrounded by mountains, observes, "If we could have seen it immediately after the diluvian crash, or whatever convulsion of nature occasioned it, before the waters gushed in, what a horrid chasm must it have appeared!

> "So high as heaved the tumid hills, so low
> Down sunk a hollow bottom broad and deep,
> Capacious bed of waters."[6]

But if, using the shortest diameter of Loch Fyne, we apply these proportions to Walden, which, as we have seen, appears already in a vertical section only like a shallow plate, it will appear four times as shallow. So much for the *increased* horrors of the chasm of Loch Fyne when emptied. No doubt many a smiling valley with its stretching cornfields occupies exactly such a "horrid chasm," from which the waters have receded, though it requires the insight and the far sight of the geologist to convince the unsuspecting inhabitants of this fact. Often an inquisitive eye may detect the shores of a primitive lake in the low horizon hills, and no subsequent elevation of the plain has been necessary to conceal their history. But it is easiest, as they who work on the highways know, to find the hollows by the puddles after a shower. The amount of it is, the imagination, give it the least license, dives deeper and soars higher than Nature goes. So, probably, the depth of the ocean will be found to be very inconsiderable compared with its breadth.

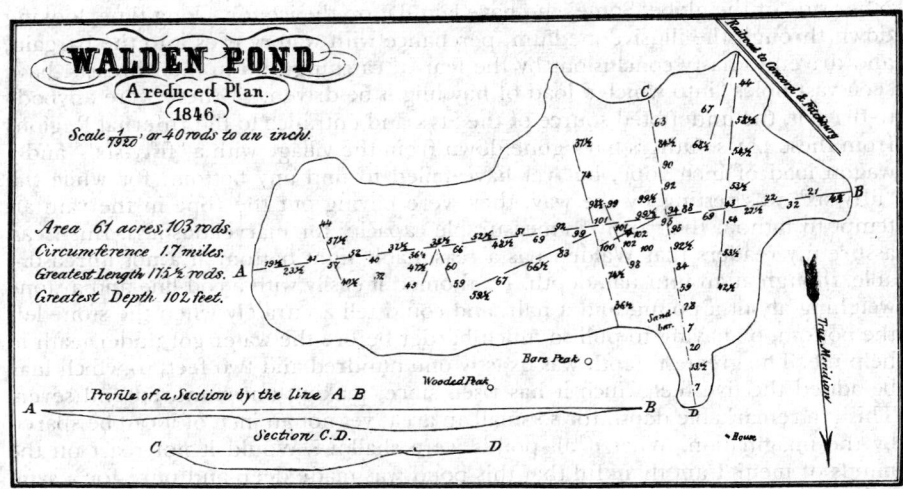

As I sounded through the ice I could determine the shape of the bottom with greater accuracy than is possible in surveying harbors which do not freeze over, and I was surprised at its general regularity. In the deepest part there are several

[5]William Gilpin (1724–1804), author of *Observations on the Highlands of Scotland* (1808).
[6]Milton, *Paradise Lost.* VII, 288–290.

acres more level than almost any field which is exposed to the sun, wind, and plow. In one instance, on a line arbitrarily chosen, the depth did not vary more than one foot in thirty rods; and generally, near the middle, I could calculate the variation for each one hundred feet in any direction beforehand within three or four inches. Some are accustomed to speak of deep and dangerous holes even in quiet sandy ponds like this, but the effect of water under these circumstances is to level all inequalities. The regularity of the bottom and its conformity to the shores and the range of the neighboring hills were so perfect that a distant promontory betrayed itself in the soundings quite across the pond, and its direction could be determined by observing the opposite shore. Cape becomes bar, and plain shoal, and valley and gorge deep water and channel.

When I had mapped the pond by the scale of ten rods to an inch, and put down the soundings, more than a hundred in all, I observed this remarkable co-incidence. Having noticed that the number indicating the greatest depth was apparently in the centre of the map, I laid a rule on the map lengthwise, and then breadthwise, and found, to my surprise, that the line of greatest length intersected the line of greatest breadth *exactly* at the point of greatest depth, notwithstanding that the middle is so nearly level, the outline of the pond far from regular, and the extreme length and breadth were got by measuring into the coves; and I said to myself, Who knows but this hint would conduct to the deepest part of the ocean as well as of a pond or puddle? Is not this the rule also for the height of mountains, regarded as the opposite of valleys? We know that a hill is not highest at its narrowest part.

Of five coves, three, or all which had been sounded, were observed to have a bar quite across their mouths and deeper water within, so that the bay tended to be an expansion of water within the land not only horizontally but vertically, and to form a basin or independent pond, the direction of the two capes showing the course of the bar. Every harbor on the sea-coast, also, has its bar at its entrance. In proportion as the mouth of the cove was wider compared with its length, the water over the bar was deeper compared with that in the basin. Given, then, the length and breadth of the cove, and the character of the surrounding shore, and you have almost elements enough to make out a formula for all cases.

In order to see how nearly I could guess, with this experience, at the deepest point in a pond, by observing the outlines of its surface and the character of its shores alone, I made a plan of White Pond, which contains about forty-one acres, and, like this, has no island in it, nor any visible inlet or outlet; and as the line of greatest breadth fell very near the line of least breadth, where two opposite capes approached each other and two opposite bays receded, I ventured to mark a point a short distance from the latter line, but still on the line of greatest length, as the deepest. The deepest part was found to be within one hundred feet of this, still farther in the direction to which I had inclined, and was only one foot deeper, namely, sixty feet. Of course, a stream running through, or an island in the pond, would make the problem much more complicated.

If we knew all the laws of Nature, we should need only one fact, or the description of one actual phenomenon, to infer all the particular results at that point. Now we know only a few laws, and our result is vitiated, not, of course, by any confusion or irregularity in Nature, but by our ignorance of essential elements in the calculation. Our notions of law and harmony are commonly confined to those instances which we detect; but the harmony which results from a far greater number of seemingly conflicting, but really concurring, laws, which we have not detected, is still more wonderful. The particular laws are as our points of view, as, to the traveller, a mountain outline varies with every step, and it has an infinite number of profiles, though absolutely but one form. Even when cleft or bored through it is not comprehended in its entirety.

What I have observed of the pond is no less true in ethics. It is the law of average. Such a rule of the two diameters not only guides us toward the sun in the system and the heart in man, but draw lines through the length and breadth of the aggregate of a man's particular daily behaviors and waves of life into his coves and inlets, and where they intersect will be the height or depth of his character. Perhaps we need only to know how his shores trend and his adjacent country or circumstances, to infer his depth and concealed bottom. If he is surrounded by mountainous circumstances, an Achillean shore,[7] whose peaks overshadow and are reflected in his bosom, they suggest a corresponding depth in him. But a low and smooth shore proves him shallow on that side. In our bodies, a bold projecting brow falls off to and indicates a corresponding depth of thought. Also there is a bar across the entrance of our every cove, or particular inclination; each is our harbor for a season, in which we are detained and partially land-locked. These inclinations are not whimsical usually, but their form, size, and direction are determined by the promontories of the shore, the ancient axes of elevation. When this bar is gradually increased by storms, tides, or currents, or there is a subsidence of the waters, so that it reaches to the surface, that which was at first but an inclination in the shore in which a thought was harbored becomes an individual lake, cut off from the ocean, wherein the thought secures its own conditions,— changes, perhaps, from salt to fresh, becomes a sweet sea, dead sea, or a marsh. At the advent of each individual into this life, may we not suppose that such a bar has risen to the surface somewhere? It is true, we are such poor navigators that our thoughts, for the most part, stand off and on upon a harborless coast, are conversant only with the bights[8] of the bays of poesy, or steer for the public ports of entry, and go into the dry docks of science, where they merely refit for this world, and no natural currents concur to individualize them.

As for the inlet or outlet of Walden, I have not discovered any but rain and snow and evaporation, though perhaps, with a thermometer and a line, such places may be found, for where the water flows into the pond it will probably be coldest in summer and warmest in winter. When the ice-men were at work here in '46–7, the cakes sent to the shore were one day rejected by those who were stacking them up there, not being thick enough to lie side by side with the rest; and the cutters thus discovered that the ice over a small space was two or three inches thinner than elsewhere, which made them think that there was an inlet there. They also showed me in another place what they thought was a "leach-hole," through which the pond leaked out under a hill into a neighboring meadow, pushing me out on a cake of ice to see it. It was a small cavity under ten feet of water; but I think that I can warrant the pond not to need soldering till they find a worse leak than that. One has suggested, that if such a "leach-hole" should be found, its connection with the meadow, if any existed, might be proved by conveying some colored powder or sawdust to the mouth of the hole, and then putting a strainer over the spring in the meadow, which would catch some of the particles carried through by the current.

While I was surveying, the ice, which was sixteen inches thick, undulated under a slight wind like water. It is well known that a level cannot be used on ice. At one rod from the shore its greatest fluctuation, when observed by means of a level on land directed toward a graduated staff on the ice, was three quarters of an inch, though the ice appeared firmly attached to the shore. It was probably greater in the middle. Who knows but if our instruments were delicate enough we might detect an undulation in the crust of the earth? When two legs of my level were on

---

[7]Achilles, Greek warrior in Homer's *Iliad*, was born on the mountainous shores of Thessaly in northeastern Greece.
[8]Curves, or loops, or bends.

the shore and the third on the ice, and the sights were directed over the latter, a rise or fall of the ice of an almost infinitesimal amount made a difference of several feet on a tree across the pond. When I began to cut holes for sounding there were three or four inches of water on the ice under a deep snow which had sunk it thus far; but the water began immediately to run into these holes, and continued to run for two days in deep streams, which wore away the ice on every side, and contributed essentially, if not mainly, to dry the surface of the pond; for, as the water ran in, it raised and floated the ice. This was somewhat like cutting a hole in the bottom of a ship to let the water out. When such holes freeze, and a rain succeeds, and finally a new freezing forms a fresh smooth ice over all, it is beautifully mottled internally by dark figures, shaped somewhat like a spider's web, what you may call ice rosettes, produced by the channels worn by the water flowing from all sides to a centre. Sometimes, also, when the ice was covered with shallow puddles, I saw a double shadow of myself, one standing on the head of the other, one on the ice, the other on the trees or hillside.

While yet it is cold January, and snow and ice are thick and solid, the prudent landlord comes from the village to get ice to cool his summer drink; impressively, even pathetically, wise, to foresee the heat and thirst of July now in January,— wearing a thick coat and mittens! when so many things are not provided for. It may be that he lays up no treasures in this world[9] which will cool his summer drink in the next. He cuts and saws the solid pond, unroofs the house of fishes, and carts off their very element and air, held fast by chains and stakes like corded wood, through the favoring winter air, to wintry cellars, to underlie the summer there. It looks like solidified azure, as, far off, it is drawn through the streets. These ice-cutters are a merry race, full of jest and sport, and when I went among them they were wont to invite me to saw pit-fashion with them, I standing underneath.

In the winter of '46–7 there came a hundred men of Hyperborean[10] extraction swoop down on to our pond one morning, with many carloads of ungainly-looking farming tools,—sleds, plows, drill-barrows, turf-knives, spades, saws, rakes, and each man was armed with a double-pointed pike-staff, such as is not described in the New-England Farmer or the Cultivator. I did not know whether they had come to sow a crop of winter rye, or some other kind of grain recently introduced from Iceland. As I saw no manure, I judged that they meant to skim the land, as I had done, thinking the soil was deep and had lain fallow long enough. They said that a gentleman farmer, who was behind the scenes, wanted to double his money, which, as I understood, amounted to half a million already; but in order to cover each one of his dollars with another, he took off the only coat, ay, the skin itself, of Walden Pond in the midst of a hard winter. They went to work at once, plowing, harrowing, rolling, furrowing, in admirable order, as if they were bent on making this a model farm; but when I was looking sharp to see what kind of seed they dropped into the furrow, a gang of fellows by my side suddenly began to hook up the virgin mould itself, with a peculiar jerk, clean down to the sand, or rather the water,—for it was a very springy soil,—indeed all the *terra firma* there was,—and haul it away on sleds, and then I guessed that they must be cutting peat in a bog. So they came and went every day, with a peculiar shriek from the locomotive, from and to some point of the polar regions, as it seemed to me, like a flock of arctic snowbirds. But sometimes Squaw Walden had her revenge, and a hired man, walking behind his team, slipped through a crack in the

---

[9]Matthew 6:19: "Lay not up for yourselves treasures upon earth. . . ."

[10]In classical mythology, those who lived in the far north. Thoreau's intruders are Irish.

ground down toward Tartarus,[11] and he who was so brave before suddenly became but the ninth part of a man, almost gave up his animal heat, and was glad to take refuge in my house, and acknowledged that there was some virtue in a stove; or sometimes the frozen soil took a piece of steel out of a plowshare, or a plow got set in the furrow and had to be cut out.

To speak literally, a hundred Irishmen, with Yankee overseers, came from Cambridge every day to get out the ice. They divided it into cakes by methods too well known to require description, and these, being sledded to the shore, were rapidly hauled off on to an ice platform, and raised by grappling irons and block and tackle, worked by horses, on to a stack, as surely as so many barrels of flour, and there placed evenly side by side, and row upon row, as if they formed the solid base of an obelisk designed to pierce the clouds. They told me that in a good day they could get out a thousand tons, which was the yield of about one acre. Deep ruts and "cradle-holes" were worn in the ice, as on *terra firma,* by the passage of the sleds over the same track, and the horses invariably ate their oats out of cakes of ice hollowed out like buckets. They stacked up the cakes thus in the open air in a pile thirty-five feet high on one side and six or seven rods square, putting hay between the outside layers to exclude the air; for when the wind, though never so cold, finds a passage through, it will wear large cavities, leaving slight supports or studs only here and there, and finally topple it down. At first it looked like a vast blue fort or Valhalla; but when they began to tuck the coarse meadow hay into the crevices, and this became covered with rime and icicles, it looked like a venerable moss-grown and hoary ruin, built of azure-tinted marble, the abode of Winter, that old man we see in the almanac,—his shanty, as if he had a design to estivate[12] with us. They calculated that not twenty-five per cent. of this would reach its destination, and that two or three per cent. would be wasted in the cars. However, a still greater part of this heap had a different destiny from what was intended; for, either because the ice was found not to keep so well as was expected, containing more air than usual, or for some other reason, it never got to market. This heap, made in the winter of '46–7 and estimated to contain ten thousand tons, was finally covered with hay and boards; and though it was unroofed the following July, and a part of it carried off, the rest remaining exposed to the sun, it stood over that summer and the next winter, and was not quite melted till September, 1848. Thus the pond recovered the greater part.

Like the water, the Walden ice, seen near at hand, has a green tint, but at a distance is beautifully blue, and you can easily tell it from the white ice of the river, or the merely greenish ice of some ponds, a quarter of a mile off. Sometimes one of those great cakes slips from the ice-man's sled into the village street, and lies there for a week like a great emerald, an object of interest to all passers. I have noticed that a portion of Walden which in the state of water was green will often, when frozen, appear from the same point of view blue. So the hollows about this pond will, sometimes, in the winter, be filled with a greenish water somewhat like its own, but the next day will have frozen blue. Perhaps the blue color of water and ice is due to the light and air they contain, and the most transparent is the bluest. Ice is an interesting subject for contemplation. They told me that they had some in the ice-houses at Fresh Pond five years old which was as good as ever. Why is it that a bucket of water soon becomes putrid, but frozen remains sweet forever? It is commonly said that this is the difference between the affections and the intellect.

Thus for sixteen days I saw from my window a hundred men at work like busy husbandmen, with teams and horses and apparently all the implements of farm-

---

[11]Hades, the Greek underworld.
[12]To spend the summer (especially in dormant condition).

ing, such a picture as we see on the first page of the almanac; and as often as I looked out I was reminded of the fable of the lark[13] and the reapers, or the parable of the sower,[14] and the like; and now they are all gone, and in thirty days more, probably, I shall look from the same window on the pure sea-green Walden water there, reflecting the clouds and the trees, and sending up its evaporations in solitude, and no traces will appear that a man has ever stood there. Perhaps I shall hear a solitary loon laugh as he dives and plumes himself, or shall see a lonely fisher in his boat, like a floating leaf, beholding his form reflected in the waves, where lately a hundred men securely labored.

Thus it appears that the sweltering inhabitants of Charleston and New Orleans, of Madras and Bombay and Calcutta, drink at my well. In the morning I bathe my intellect in the stupendous and cosmogonal philosophy of the Bhagvat-Geeta, since whose composition years of the gods have elapsed, and in comparison with which our modern world and its literature seem puny and trivial; and I doubt if that philosophy is not to be referred to a previous state of existence, so remote is its sublimity from our conceptions. I lay down the book and go to my well for water, and lo! there I meet the servant of the Bramin, priest of Brahma and Vishnu and Indra,[15] who still sits in his temple on the Ganges reading the Vedas, or dwells at the root of a tree with his crust and water jug. I meet his servant come to draw water for his master, and our buckets as it were grate together in the same well. The pure Walden water is mingled with the sacred water of the Ganges. With favoring winds it is wafted past the site of the fabulous islands of Atlantis and the Hesperides,[16] makes the periplus of Hanno,[17] and, floating by Ternate and Tidore[18] and the mouth of the Persian Gulf, melts in the tropic gales of the Indian seas, and is landed in ports of which Alexander [19] only heard the names.

XVII

SPRING

The opening of large tracts by the ice-cutters commonly causes a pond to break up earlier; for the water, agitated by the wind, even in cold weather, wears away the surrounding ice. But such was not the effect on Walden that year, for she had soon got a thick new garment to take the place of the old. This pond never breaks up so soon as the others in this neighborhood, on account both of its greater depth and its having no stream passing through it to melt or wear away the ice. I never knew it to open in the course of a winter, not excepting that of '52–3, which gave the ponds so severe a trial. It commonly opens about the first of April, a week or ten days later than Flint's Pond and Fair Haven, beginning to melt on the north side and in the shallower parts where it began to freeze. It indicates better than any water hereabouts the absolute progress of the season, being least affected by transient changes of temperature. A severe cold of a few days' duration in March may very much retard the opening of the former ponds, while the temperature of Walden increases almost uninterruptedly. A thermometer thrust into the middle of Walden on the 6th of March, 1847, stood at 32°, or freezing point; near the shore at 33°; in the middle of Flint's Pond, the same day, at 32½°; at a dozen rods from the shore, in shallow water, under ice a foot thick, at 36°. This difference of three and a half degrees between the temperature of the deep water and the shallow in the latter pond, and the fact that a great proportion of it is comparatively shallow, show why it should break up so much sooner than Walden.

---

[13]"The Lark and Her Young Ones," by La Fontaine, in J. Payne Colliers's *Old Ballads* (1843).
[14]Matthew 13:3–40.
[15]Hindu gods.
[16]In classical legend, mythical islands at the western edge of the world.

[17]Hanno, a Carthaginian navigator, made a voyage around Africa in 480 B.C.; "periplus": "circumnavigation" or "an account of circumnavigation."
[18]Spice Islands among the Dutch East Indies (mentioned in Milton's *Paradise Lost*).
[19]Alexander the Great (356–323 B.C.).

The ice in the shallowest part was at this time several inches thinner than in the middle. In midwinter the middle had been the warmest and the ice thinnest there. So, also, every one who has waded about the shores of a pond in summer must have perceived how much warmer the water is close to the shore, where only three or four inches deep, than a little distance out, and on the surface where it is deep, than near the bottom. In spring the sun not only exerts an influence through the increased temperature of the air and earth, but its heat passes through ice a foot or more thick, and is reflected from the bottom in shallow water, and so also warms the water and melts the under side of the ice, at the same time that it is melting it more directly above, making it uneven, and causing the air bubbles which it contains to extend themselves upward and downward until it is completely honeycombed, and at last disappears suddenly in a single spring rain. Ice has its grain as well as wood, and when a cake begins to rot or "comb," that is, assume the appearance of honeycomb, whatever may be its position, the air cells are at right angles with what was the water surface. Where there is a rock or a log rising near to the surface the ice over it is much thinner, and is frequently quite dissolved by this reflected heat; and I have been told that in the experiment at Cambridge to freeze water in a shallow wooden pond, though the cold air circulated underneath, and so had access to both sides, the reflection of the sun from the bottom more than counterbalanced this advantage. When a warm rain in the middle of the winter melts off the snow ice from Walden, and leaves a hard dark or transparent ice on the middle, there will be a strip of rotten though thicker white ice, a rod or more wide, about the shores, created by this reflected heat. Also, as I have said, the bubbles themselves within the ice operate as burning-glasses to melt the ice beneath.

The phenomena of the year take place every day in a pond on a small scale. Every morning, generally speaking, the shallow water is being warmed more rapidly than the deep, though it may not be made so warm after all, and every evening it is being cooled more rapidly until the morning. The day is an epitome of the year. The night is the winter, the morning and evening are the spring and fall, and the noon is the summer. The cracking and booming of the ice indicate a change of temperature. One pleasant morning after a cold night, February 24th, 1850, having gone to Flint's Pond to spend the day, I noticed with surprise, that when I struck the ice with the head of my axe, it resounded like a gong for many rods around, or as if I had struck on a tight drum-head. The pond began to boom about an hour after sunrise, when it felt the influence of the sun's rays slanted upon it from over the hills; it stretched itself and yawned like a waking man with a gradually increasing tumult, which was kept up three or four hours. It took a short siesta at noon, and boomed once more toward night, as the sun was withdrawing his influence. In the right stage of the weather a pond fires its evening gun with great regularity. But in the middle of the day, being full of cracks, and the air also being less elastic, it had completely lost its resonance, and probably fishes and muskrats could not then have been stunned by a blow on it. The fishermen say that the "thundering of the pond" scares the fishes and prevents their biting. The pond does not thunder every evening, and I cannot tell surely when to expect its thundering; but though I may perceive no difference in the weather, it does. Who would have suspected so large and cold and thick-skinned a thing to be so sensitive? Yet it has its law to which it thunders obedience when it should as surely as the buds expand in the spring. The earth is all alive and covered with papillæ. The largest pond is as sensitive to atmospheric changes as the globule of mercury in its tube.

One attraction in coming to the woods to live was that I should have leisure and opportunity to see the Spring come in. The ice in the pond at length begins to be honeycombed, and I can set my heel in it as I walk. Fogs and rains and warmer

suns are gradually melting the snow; the days have grown sensibly longer; and I
see how I shall get through the winter without adding to my wood-pile, for large
fires are no longer necessary. I am on the alert for the first signs of spring, to hear
the chance note of some arriving bird, or the striped squirrel's chirp, for his stores
must be now nearly exhausted, or see the woodchuck venture out of his winter
quarters. On the 13th of March, after I had heard the bluebird, song sparrow,
and red-wing, the ice was still nearly a foot thick. As the weather grew warmer it
was not sensibly worn away by the water, nor broken up and floated off as in rivers, but, though it was completely melted for half a rod in width about the shore,
the middle was merely honeycombed and saturated with water, so that you could
put your foot through it when six inches thick; but by the next day evening, perhaps, after a warm rain followed by fog, it would have wholly disappeared, all
gone off with the fog, spirited away. One year I went across the middle only five
days before it disappeared entirely. In 1845 Walden was first completely open on
the 1st of April; in '46, the 25th of March; in '47, the 8th of April; in '51, the 28th
of March; in '52, the 18th of April; in '53, the 23d of March; in '54, about the 7th
of April.

Every incident connected with the breaking up of the rivers and ponds and the
settling of the weather is particularly interesting to us who live in a climate of so
great extremes. When the warmer days come, they who dwell near the river hear
the ice crack at night with a startling whoop as loud as artillery, as if its icy fetters
were rent from end to end, and within a few days see it rapidly going out. So the
alligator comes out of the mud with quakings of the earth. One old man, who has
been a close observer of Nature, and seems as thoroughly wise in regard to all her
operations as if she had been put upon the stocks when he was a boy, and he had
helped to lay her keel,—who has come to his growth, and can hardly acquire
more of natural lore if he should live to the age of Methuselah,[1]—told me—and I
was surprised to hear him express wonder at any of Nature's operations, for I
thought that there were no secrets between them—that one spring day he took
his gun and boat, and thought that he would have a little sport with the ducks.
There was ice still on the meadows, but it was all gone out of the river, and he
dropped down without obstruction from Sudbury, where he lived, to Fair Haven
Pond, which he found, unexpectedly, covered for the most part with a firm field
of ice. It was a warm day, and he was surprised to see so great a body of ice remaining. Not seeing any ducks, he hid his boat on the north or back side of an
island in the pond, and then concealed himself in the bushes on the south side, to
await them. The ice was melted for three or four rods from the shore, and there
was a smooth and warm sheet of water, with a muddy bottom, such as the ducks
love, within, and he thought it likely that some would be along pretty soon. After
he had lain still there about an hour he heard a low and seemingly very distant
sound, but singularly grand and impressive, unlike anything he had ever heard,
gradually swelling and increasing as if it would have a universal and memorable
ending, a sullen rush and roar, which seemed to him all at once like the sound of
a vast body of fowl coming in to settle there, and, seizing his gun, he started up in
haste and excited; but he found, to his surprise, that the whole body of the ice had
started while he lay there, and drifted in to the shore, and the sound he had
heard was made by its edge grating on the shore,—at first gently nibbled and
crumbled off, but at length heaving up and scattering its wrecks along the island
to a considerable height before it came to a standstill.

At length the sun's rays have attained the right angle, and warm winds blow up
mist and rain and melt the snowbanks, and the sun, dispersing the mist, smiles on

---

[1]Genesis 5:27: "And the days of Methuselah were nine
hundred sixty and nine years: and he died."

a checkered landscape of russet and white smoking with incense, through which the traveller picks his way from islet to islet, cheered by the music of a thousand tinkling rills and rivulets whose veins are filled with the blood of winter which they are bearing off.

Few phenomena gave me more delight than to observe the forms which thawing sand and clay assume in flowing down the sides of a deep cut on the railroad through which I passed on my way to the village, a phenomenon not very common on so large a scale, though the number of freshly exposed banks of the right material must have been greatly multiplied since railroads were invented. The material was sand of every degree of fineness and of various rich colors, commonly mixed with a little clay. When the frost comes out in the spring, and even in a thawing day in the winter, the sand begins to flow down the slopes like lava, sometimes bursting out through the snow and overflowing it where no sand was to be seen before. Innumerable little streams overlap and interlace one with another, exhibiting a sort of hybrid product, which obeys half way the law of currents, and half way that of vegetation. As it flows it takes the forms of sappy leaves or vines, making heaps of pulpy sprays a foot or more in depth, and resembling, as you look down on them, the laciniated, lobed, and imbricated thalluses[2] of some lichens; or you are reminded of coral, of leopards' paws or birds' feet, of brains or lungs or bowels, and excrements of all kinds. It is a truly *grotesque* vegetation, whose forms and color we see imitated in bronze, a sort of architectural foliage more ancient and typical than acanthus, chiccory, ivy, vine, or any vegetable leaves; destined perhaps, under some circumstances, to become a puzzle to future geologists. The whole cut impressed me as if it were a cave with its stalactites laid open to the light. The various shades of the sand are singularly rich and agreeable, embracing the different iron colors, brown, gray, yellowish, and reddish. When the flowing mass reaches the drain at the foot of the bank it spreads out flatter into *strands,* the separate streams losing their semicylindrical form and gradually becoming more flat and broad, running together as they are more moist, till they form an almost flat *sand,* still variously and beautifully shaded, but in which you can trace the original forms of vegetation; till at length, in the water itself, they are converted into *banks,* like those formed off the mouths of rivers, and the forms of vegetation are lost in the ripple-marks on the bottom.

The whole bank, which is from twenty to forty feet high, is sometimes overlaid with a mass of this kind of foliage, or sandy rupture, for a quarter of a mile on one or both sides, the produce of one spring day. What makes this sand foliage remarkable is its springing into existence thus suddenly. When I see on the one side the inert bank,—for the sun acts on one side first,—and on the other this luxuriant foliage, the creation of an hour, I am affected as if in a peculiar sense I stood in the laboratory of the Artist who made the world and me,—had come to where he was still at work, sporting on this bank, and with excess of energy strewing his fresh designs about. I feel as if I were nearer to the vitals of the globe, for this sandy overflow is something such a foliaceous mass as the vitals of the animal body. You find thus in the very sands an anticipation of the vegetable leaf. No wonder that the earth expresses itself outwardly in leaves, it so labors with the idea inwardly. The atoms have already learned this law, and are pregnant by it. The overhanging leaf sees here its prototype. *Internally,* whether in the globe or animal body, it is a moist thick *lobe,* a word especially applicable to the liver and lungs and the *leaves* of fat ($\lambda\epsilon\acute{\iota}\beta\omega$, labor, lapsus, to flow or slip downward, a lapsing; $\lambda o\beta\acute{o}\varsigma$, globus, lobe, globe; also lap, flap, and many other words); *externally,* a dry

---

[2]Botanical terms: *laciniated* means the edges are fringed, cut into irregular lobes; *imbricated* means overlapping, as tiles; *thallus* is a plant without stem, roots, or leaves.

thin *leaf*, even as the *f* and *v* are a pressed and dried *b*. The radicals of *lobe* are *lb*, the soft mass of the *b* (single-lobed, or B, double-lobed), with the liquid *l* behind it pressing it forward. In globe, *glb*, the guttural *g* adds to the meaning the capacity of the throat. The feathers and wings of birds are still drier and thinner leaves. Thus, also, you pass from the lumpish grub in the earth to the airy and fluttering butterfly. The very globe continually transcends and translates itself, and becomes winged in its orbit. Even ice begins with delicate crystal leaves, as if it had flowed into moulds which the fronds of water-plants have impressed on the watery mirror. The whole tree itself is but one leaf, and rivers are still vaster leaves whose pulp is intervening earth, and towns and cities are the ova of insects in their axils.[3]

When the sun withdraws the sand ceases to flow, but in the morning the streams will start once more and branch and branch again into a myriad of others. You here see perchance how blood-vessels are formed. If you look closely you observe that first there pushes forward from the thawing mass a stream of softened sand with a drop-like point, like the ball of the finger, feeling its way slowly and blindly downward, until at last with more heat and moisture, as the sun gets higher, the most fluid portion, in its effort to obey the law to which the most inert also yields, separates from the latter and forms for itself a meandering channel or artery within that, in which is seen a little silvery stream glancing like lightning from one stage of pulpy leaves or branches to another, and ever and anon swallowed up in the sand. It is wonderful how rapidly yet perfectly the sand organizes itself as it flows, using the best material its mass affords to form the sharp edges of its channel. Such are the sources of rivers. In the silicious[4] matter which the water deposits is perhaps the bony system, and in the still finer soil and organic matter the fleshy fibre or cellular tissue. What is man but a mass of thawing clay? The ball of the human finger is but a drop congealed. The fingers and toes flow to their extent from the thawing mass of the body. Who knows what the human body would expand and flow out to under a more genial heaven? Is not the hand a spreading *palm* leaf with its lobes and veins? The ear may be regarded, fancifully, as a lichen, *Umbilicaria*, on the side of the head, with its lobe or drop. The lip— *labium*, from *labor* (?) —laps or lapses from the sides of the cavernous mouth. The nose is a manifest congealed drop or stalactite. The chin is a still larger drop, the confluent dripping of the face. The cheeks are a slide from the brows into the valley of the face, opposed and diffused by the cheek bones. Each rounded lobe of the vegetable leaf, too, is a thick and now loitering drop, larger or smaller; the lobes are the fingers of the leaf; and as many lobes as it has, in so many directions it tends to flow, and more heat or other genial influences would have caused it to flow yet farther.

Thus it seemed that this one hillside illustrated the principle of all the operations of Nature. The Maker of this earth but patented a leaf. What Champollion[5] will decipher this hieroglyphic for us, that we may turn over a new leaf at last? This phenomenon is more exhilarating to me than the luxuriance and fertility of vineyards. True, it is somewhat excrementitious in its character, and there is no end to the heaps of liver, lights,[6] and bowels, as if the globe were turned wrong side outward; but this suggests at least that Nature has some bowels, and there again is mother of humanity. This is the frost coming out of the ground; this is Spring. It precedes the green and flowery spring, as mythology precedes regular poetry. I know of nothing more purgative of winter fumes and indigestions. It

---

[3]Angle between a leaf or twig and the stem from which it grows.
[4]Sandy.
[5]Jean-François Champollion (1790–1832), French Egyptologist who deciphered the Rosetta Stone and founded the Egyptian Museum of the Louvre in Paris.
[6]Lungs.

convinces me that Earth is still in her swaddling-clothes, and stretches forth baby fingers on every side. Fresh curls spring from the baldest brow. There is nothing inorganic. These foliaceous heaps lie along the bank like the slag of a furnace, showing that Nature is "in full blast" within. The earth is not a mere fragment of dead history, stratum upon stratum like the leaves of a book, to be studied by geologists and antiquaries chiefly, but living poetry like the leaves of a tree, which precede flowers and fruit,—not a fossil earth, but a living earth; compared with whose great central life all animal and vegetable life is merely parasitic. Its throes will heave our exuviæ from their graves. You may melt your metals and cast them into the most beautiful moulds you can; they will never excite me like the forms which this molten earth flows out into. And not only it, but the institutions upon it are plastic like clay in the hands of the potter.

Ere long, not only on these banks, but on every hill and plain and in every hollow, the frost comes out of the ground like a dormant quadruped from its burrow, and seeks the sea with music, or migrates to other climes in clouds. Thaw with his gentle persuasion is more powerful than Thor with his hammer.[7] The one melts, the other but breaks in pieces.

When the ground was partially bare of snow, and a few warm days had dried its surface somewhat, it was pleasant to compare the first tender signs of the infant year just peeping forth with the stately beauty of the withered vegetation which had withstood the winter,—life-everlasting, goldenrods, pinweeds, and graceful wild grasses, more obvious and interesting frequently than in summer even, as if their beauty was not ripe till then; even cotton-grass, cat-tails, mulleins, johnswort, hardhack, meadow-sweet, and other strong-stemmed plants, those unexhausted granaries which entertain the earliest birds,—decent weeds,[8] at least, which widowed Nature wears. I am particularly attracted by the arching and sheaf-like top of the wool-grass; it brings back the summer to our winter memories, and is among the forms which art loves to copy, and which, in the vegetable kingdom, have the same relation to types already in the mind of man that astronomy has. It is an antique style, older than Greek or Egyptian. Many of the phenomena of Winter are suggestive of an inexpressible tenderness and fragile delicacy. We are accustomed to hear this king described as a rude and boisterous tyrant; but with the gentleness of a lover he adorns the tresses of Summer.

At the approach of spring the red squirrels got under my house, two at a time, directly under my feet as I sat reading or writing, and kept up the queerest chuckling and chirruping and vocal pirouetting and gurgling sounds that ever were heard; and when I stamped they only chirruped the louder, as if past all fear and respect in their mad pranks, defying humanity to stop them. No, you don't—chickaree—chickaree. They were wholly deaf to my arguments, or failed to perceive their force, and fell into a strain of invective that was irresistible.

The first sparrow of spring! The year beginning with younger hope than ever! The faint silvery warblings heard over the partially bare and moist fields from the bluebird, the song sparrow, and the red-wing, as if the last flakes of winter tinkled as they fell! What at such a time are histories, chronologies, traditions, and all written revelations? The brooks sing carols and glees to the spring. The marsh hawk, sailing low over the meadow, is already seeking the first slimy life that awakes. The sinking sound of melting snow is heard in all dells, and the ice dissolves apace in the ponds. The grass flames up on the hillsides like a spring fire,—"et primitus oritur herba imbribus primoribus evocata,"[9]—as if the earth sent forth an inward heat to greet the returning sun; not yellow but green is the color

---

[7]Norse god of thunder.
[8]Mourning dress.
[9]Marcus Terentius Varro (116–27 B.C.), Roman scholar, author of *Rerum rusticarum (On Agriculture)*, 2, 2, 14: "And the grass called forth by the early rains begins to grow."

of its flame;—the symbol of perpetual youth, the grass-blade, like a long green ribbon, streams from the sod into the summer, checked indeed by the frost, but anon pushing on again, lifting its spear of last year's hay with the fresh life below. It grows as steadily as the rill oozes out of the ground. It is almost identical with that, for in the growing days of June, when the rills are dry, the grass-blades are their channels, and from year to year the herds drink at this perennial green stream, and the mower draws from it betimes their winter supply. So our human life but dies down to its root, and still puts forth its green blade to eternity.

Walden is melting apace. There is a canal two rods wide along the northerly and westerly sides, and wider still at the east end. A great field of ice has cracked off from the main body. I hear a song sparrow singing from the bushes on the shore,—*olit, olit, olit,—chip, chip, chip, che char,—che wiss, wiss, wiss.* He too is helping to crack it. How handsome the great sweeping curves in the edge of the ice, answering somewhat to those of the shore, but more regular! It is unusually hard, owing to the recent severe but transient cold, and all watered or waved like a palace floor. But the wind slides eastward over its opaque surface in vain, till it reaches the living surface beyond. It is glorious to behold this ribbon of water sparkling in the sun, the bare face of the pond full of glee and youth, as if it spoke the joy of the fishes within it, and of the sands on its shore,—a silvery sheen as from the scales of a leuciscus,[10] as it were all one active fish. Such is the contrast between winter and spring. Walden was dead and is alive again. But this spring it broke up more steadily, as I have said.

The change from storm and winter to serene and mild weather, from dark and sluggish hours to bright and elastic ones, is a memorable crisis which all things proclaim. It is seemingly instantaneous at last. Suddenly an influx of light filled my house, though the evening was at hand, and the clouds of winter still overhung it, and the eaves were dripping with sleety rain. I looked out the window, and lo! where yesterday was cold gray ice there lay the transparent pond already calm and full of hope as on a summer evening, reflecting a summer evening sky in its bosom, though none was visible overhead, as if it had intelligence with some remote horizon. I heard a robin in the distance, the first I had heard for many a thousand years, methought, whose note I shall not forget for many a thousand more,—the same sweet and powerful song as of yore. O the evening robin, at the end of a New England summer day! If I could ever find the twig he sits upon! I mean *he;* I mean *the twig.* This at least is not the *Turdus migratorius.*[11] The pitch pines and shrub oaks about my house, which had so long drooped, suddenly resumed their several characters, looked brighter, greener, and more erect and alive, as if effectually cleansed and restored by the rain. I knew that it would not rain any more. You may tell by looking at any twig of the forest, ay, at your very wood-pile, whether its winter is past or not. As it grew darker, I was startled by the honking of geese flying low over the woods, like weary travellers getting in late from Southern lakes, and indulging at last in unrestrained complaint and mutual consolation. Standing at my door, I could hear the rush of their wings; when, driving toward my house, they suddenly spied my light, and with hushed clamor wheeled and settled in the pond. So I came in, and shut the door, and passed my first spring night in the woods.

In the morning I watched the geese from the door through the mist, sailing in the middle of the pond, fifty rods off, so large and tumultuous that Walden appeared like an artificial pond for their amusement. But when I stood on the shore they at once rose up with a great flapping of wings at the signal of their commander, and when they had got into rank circled about over my head, twenty-

---

[10]Fresh water fish.
[11]American thrush or robin.

nine of them, and then steered straight to Canada, with a regular *honk* from the leader at intervals, trusting to break their fast in muddier pools. A "plump"[12] of ducks rose at the same time and took the route to the north in the wake of their noisier cousins.

For a week I heard the circling, groping clangor of some solitary goose in the foggy mornings, seeking its companion, and still peopling the woods with the sound of a larger life than they could sustain. In April the pigeons were seen again flying express in small flocks, and in due time I heard the martins twittering over my clearing, though it had not seemed that the township contained so many that it could afford me any, and I fancied that they were peculiarly of the ancient race that dwelt in hollow trees ere white men came. In almost all climes the tortoise and the frog are among the precursors and heralds of this season, and birds fly with song and glancing plumage, and plants spring and bloom, and winds blow, to correct this slight oscillation of the poles and preserve the equilibrium of nature.

As every season seems best to us in its turn, so the coming in of spring is like the creation of Cosmos out of Chaos and the realization of the Golden Age.—

> "Eurus ad Auroram Nabathæaque regna recessit,
>   Persidaque, et radiis juga subdita matutinis."

> "The East-Wind withdrew to Aurora and the Nabathæan kingdom,
>   And the Persian, and the ridges placed under the morning rays.
>   . . . .
> Man was born. Whether that Artificer of things,
> The origin of a better world, made him from the divine seed;
> Or the earth, being recent and lately sundered from the high
> Ether, retained some seeds of cognate heaven."[13]

A single gentle rain makes the grass many shades greener. So our prospects brighten on the influx of better thoughts. We should be blessed if we lived in the present always, and took advantage of every accident that befell us, like the grass which confesses the influence of the slightest dew that falls on it; and did not spend our time in atoning for the neglect of past opportunities, which we call doing our duty. We loiter in winter while it is already spring. In a pleasant spring morning all men's sins are forgiven. Such a day is a truce to vice. While such a sun holds out to burn, the vilest sinner may return. Through our own recovered innocence we discern the innocence of our neighbors. You may have known your neighbor yesterday for a thief, a drunkard, or a sensualist, and merely pitied or despised him, and despaired of the world; but the sun shines bright and warm this first spring morning, re-creating the world, and you meet him at some serene work, and see how his exhausted and debauched veins expand with still joy and bless the new day, feel the spring influence with the innocence of infancy, and all his faults are forgotten. There is not only an atmosphere of good will about him, but even a savor of holiness groping for expression, blindly and ineffectually perhaps, like a new-born instinct, and for a short hour the south hillside echoes to no vulgar jest. You see some innocent fair shoots preparing to burst from his gnarled rind and try another year's life, tender and fresh as the youngest plant. Even he has entered into the joy of his Lord. Why the jailer does not leave open his prison doors,—why the judge does not dismiss his case,—why the preacher does not dismiss his congregation! It is because they do not obey the hint which God gives them, nor accept the pardon which he freely offers to all.

---

[12]Flock.
[13]From *Metamorphoses* (Book I), by Ovid (43 B.C.–A.D. 17?),
Roman poet.

"A return to goodness produced each day in the tranquil and beneficent breath of the morning, causes that in respect to the love of virtue and the hatred of vice, one approaches a little the primitive nature of man, as the sprouts of the forest which has been felled. In like manner the evil which one does in the interval of a day prevents the germs of virtues which began to spring up again from developing themselves and destroys them.

"After the germs of virtue have thus been prevented many times from developing themselves, then the beneficent breath of evening does not suffice to preserve them. As soon as the breath of evening does not suffice longer to preserve them, then the nature of man does not differ much from that of the brute. Men seeing the nature of this man like that of the brute, think that he has never possessed the innate faculty of reason. Are those the true and natural sentiments of man?"[14]

> "The Golden Age was first created, which without any avenger
> Spontaneously without law cherished fidelity and rectitude.
> Punishment and fear were not; nor were threatening words read
> On suspended brass; nor did the suppliant crowd fear
> The words of their judge; but were safe without an avenger.
> Not yet the pine felled on its mountains had descended
> To the liquid waves that it might see a foreign world,
> And mortals knew no shores but their own.
>   . . . .
> There was eternal spring, and placid zephyrs with warm
> Blasts soothed the flowers born without seed."[15]

On the 29th of April, as I was fishing from the bank of the river near the Nine-Acre-Corner bridge, standing on the quaking grass and willow roots, where the muskrats lurk, I heard a singular rattling sound, somewhat like that of the sticks which boys play with their fingers, when, looking up, I observed a very slight and graceful hawk, like a nighthawk, alternately soaring like a ripple and tumbling a rod or two over and over, showing the under side of its wings, which gleamed like a satin ribbon in the sun, or like the pearly inside of a shell. This sight reminded me of falconry and what nobleness and poetry are associated with that sport. The merlin[16] it seemed to me it might be called: but I care not for its name. It was the most ethereal flight I had ever witnessed. It did not simply flutter like a butterfly, nor soar like the larger hawks, but it sported with proud reliance in the fields of air; mounting again and again with its strange chuckle, it repeated its free and beautiful fall, turning over and over like a kite, and then recovering from its lofty tumbling, as if it had never set its foot on *terra firma*. It appeared to have no companion in the universe,—sporting there alone,—and to need none but the morning and the ether with which it played. It was not lonely, but made all the earth lonely beneath it. Where was the parent which hatched it, its kindred, and its father in the heavens? The tenant of the air, it seemed related to the earth but by an egg hatched some time in the crevice of a crag;—or was its native nest made in the angle of a cloud, woven of the rainbow's trimmings and the sunset sky, and lined with some soft midsummer haze caught up from earth? Its eyry[17] now some cliffy cloud.

Beside this I got a rare mess of golden and silver and bright cupreous[18] fishes, which looked like a string of jewels. Ah! I have penetrated to those meadows on the morning of many a first spring day, jumping from hummock to hummock,

---

[14]From *The Works of Mencius*, Book VI, Part 1, Chapter VIII.
[15]From Ovid's *Metamorphoses*, I.
[16]A small, bold falcon or pigeon hawk. Merlin in Arthurian legend was a magician, but Thoreau uses him here much as Emerson did in his poem "Merlin"—as the ideal bard.
[17]Bird's nest.
[18]Coppery.

from willow root to willow root, when the wild river valley and the woods were bathed in so pure and bright a light as would have waked the dead, if they had been slumbering in their graves, as some suppose. There needs no stronger proof of immortality. All things must live in such a light. O Death, where was thy sting? O Grave, where was thy victory, then?[19]

Our village life would stagnate if it were not for the unexplored forests and meadows which surround it. We need the tonic of wildness,—to wade sometimes in marshes where the bittern and the meadow-hen lurk, and hear the booming of the snipe; to smell the whispering sedge where only some wilder and more solitary fowl builds her nest, and the mink crawls with its belly close to the ground. At the same time that we are earnest to explore and learn all things, we require that all things be mysterious and unexplorable, that land and sea be infinitely wild, unsurveyed and unfathomed by us because unfathomable. We can never have enough of nature. We must be refreshed by the sight of inexhaustible vigor, vast and titanic features, the sea-coast with its wrecks, the wilderness with its living and its decaying trees, the thunder-cloud, and the rain which lasts three weeks and produces freshets. We need to witness our own limits transgressed, and some life pasturing freely where we never wander. We are cheered when we observe the vulture feeding on the carrion which disgusts and disheartens us, and deriving health and strength from the repast. There was a dead horse in the hollow by the path to my house, which compelled me sometimes to go out of my way, especially in the night when the air was heavy, but the assurance it gave me of the strong appetite and inviolable health of Nature was my compensation for this. I love to see that Nature is so rife with life that myriads can be afforded to be sacrificed and suffered to prey on one another; that tender organizations can be so serenely squashed out of existence like pulp,—tadpoles which herons gobble up, and tortoises and toads run over in the road; and that sometimes it has rained flesh and blood! With the liability to accident, we must see how little account is to be made of it. The impression made on a wise man is that of universal innocence. Poison is not poisonous after all, nor are any wounds fatal. Compassion is a very untenable ground. It must be expeditious. Its pleadings will not bear to be stereotyped.

Early in May, the oaks, hickories, maples, and other trees, just putting out amidst the pine woods around the pond, imparted a brightness like sunshine to the landscape, especially in cloudy days, as if the sun were breaking through mists and shining faintly on the hillsides here and there. On the third or fourth of May I saw a loon in the pond, and during the first week of the month I heard the whip-poor-will, the brown thrasher, the veery, the wood pewee, the chewink, and other birds. I had heard the wood thrush long before. The phœbe had already come once more and looked in at my door and window, to see if my house was cavern-like enough for her, sustaining herself on humming wings with clinched talons, as if she held by the air, while she surveyed the premises. The sulphur-like pollen of the pitch pine soon covered the pond and the stones and rotten wood along the shore, so that you could have collected a barrelful. This is the "sulphur showers" we hear of. Even in Calidas' drama of Sacontala, we read of "rills dyed yellow with the golden dust of the lotus."[20] And so the seasons went rolling on into summer, as one rambles into higher and higher grass.

Thus was my first year's life in the woods completed; and the second year was similar to it. I finally left Walden September 6th, 1847.

---

[19]Cf. 1 Corinthians 15:55.
[20]From *Sakuntalá* (Act V), by Hindu poet Kalidasa (fl. fifth century A.D.), translated from Sanskrit by Sir William Jones (1789).

XVIII

CONCLUSION

To the sick the doctors wisely recommend a change of air and scenery. Thank Heaven, here is not all the world. The buckeye does not grow in New England, and the mockingbird is rarely heard here. The wild goose is more of a cosmopolite than we; he breaks his fast in Canada, takes a luncheon in the Ohio, and plumes himself for the night in a southern bayou. Even the bison, to some extent, keeps pace with the seasons, cropping the pastures of the Colorado only till a greener and sweeter grass awaits him by the Yellowstone. Yet we think that if rail fences are pulled down, and stone walls piled up on our farms, bounds are henceforth set to our lives and our fates decided. If you are chosen town clerk, forsooth, you cannot go to Tierra del Fuego[1] this summer: but you may go to the land of infernal fire nevertheless. The universe is wider than our views of it.

Yet we should oftener look over the tafferel[2] of our craft, like curious passengers, and not make the voyage like stupid sailors picking oakum.[3] The other side of the globe is but the home of our correspondent. Our voyaging is only great-circle sailing, and the doctors prescribe for diseases of the skin merely. One hastens to southern Africa to chase the giraffe; but surely that is not the game he would be after. How long, pray, would a man hunt giraffes if he could? Snipes and woodcocks also may afford rare sport; but I trust it would be nobler game to shoot one's self.—

> "Direct your eye sight inward, and you'll find
> A thousand regions in your mind
> Yet undiscovered. Travel them, and be
> Expert in home-cosmography."[4]

What does Africa,—what does the West stand for? Is not our own interior white on the chart?[5] black though it may prove, like the coast, when discovered. Is it the source of the Nile, or the Niger, or the Mississippi, or a Northwest Passage around this continent, that we would find? Are these the problems which most concern mankind? Is Franklin[6] the only man who is lost, that his wife should be so earnest to find him? Does Mr. Grinnell[7] know where he himself is? Be rather the Mungo Park, the Lewis and Clark and Frobisher,[8] of your own streams and oceans; explore your own higher latitudes,—with shiploads of preserved meats to support you, if they be necessary; and pile the empty cans sky-high for a sign. Were preserved meats invented to preserve meat merely? Nay, be a Columbus to whole new continents and worlds within you, opening new channels, not of trade, but of thought. Every man is the lord of a realm beside which the earthly empire of the Czar[9] is but a petty state, a hummock left by the ice. Yet some can be patriotic who have no *self*-respect, and sacrifice the greater to the less. They love the soil which makes their graves, but have no sympathy with the spirit which may still animate their clay. Patriotism is a maggot in their heads. What was the meaning of that South-Sea Exploring Expedition,[10] with all its parade and expense, but an indirect recognition of the fact that there are continents and seas in the moral world to

---

[1]"Land of Fire" (Spanish), archipelago at the southern end of South America.
[2]Taffrail, guardrail at ship's stern.
[3]Hemp fiber picked from old ropes used for calking.
[4]From "To my Honored Friend, Sir Ed. P. Knight," by William Habington (1605–1654), British poet.
[5]I.e., unexplored territory.
[6]Sir John Franklin (1786–1847), British explorer lost in searching for the Northwest Passage in the Arctic.
[7]Henry Grinnell (1799–1874), an American, financed two expeditions (in 1850 and 1853) to find Sir John Franklin's party.
[8]Mungo Park (1771–1806), Scottish explorer of Africa (1799 and 1805); Merriwether Lewis (1774–1809) and William Clark (1770–1838), explorers of the lands of the Louisiana Purchase (1804–06); Sir Martin Frobisher (1535?–1594), British explorer of Canada.
[9]Ruler of Russia, the largest country imaginable to Thoreau.
[10]Made by Charles Wilkes, U.S. Navy (1838–42).

which every man is an isthmus or an inlet, yet unexplored by him, but that it is easier to sail many thousand miles through cold and storm and cannibals, in a government ship, with five hundred men and boys to assist one, than it is to explore the private sea, the Atlantic and Pacific Ocean of one's being alone.—

> "Erret, et extremos alter scrutetur Iberos.
> Plus habet hic vitæ, plus habet ille viæ."[11]

> Let them wander and scrutinize the outlandish Australians.
> I have more of God, they more of the road.

It is not worth the while to go round the world to count the cats in Zanzibar.[12] Yet do this even till you can do better, and you may perhaps find some "Symmes' Hole" [13] by which to get at the inside at last. England and France, Spain and Portugal, Gold Coast and Slave Coast, all front on this private sea; but no bark from them has ventured out of sight of land, though it is without doubt the direct way to India. If you would learn to speak all tongues and conform to the customs of all nations, if you would travel farther than all travellers, be naturalized in all climes, and cause the Sphinx to dash her head against a stone,[14] even obey the precept of the old philosopher, and Explore thyself. Herein are demanded the eye and the nerve. Only the defeated and deserters go to the wars, cowards that run away and enlist. Start now on that farthest western way, which does not pause at the Mississippi or the Pacific, nor conduct toward a wornout China or Japan, but leads on direct, a tangent to this sphere, summer and winter, day and night, sun down, moon down, and at last earth down too.

It is said that Mirabeau[15] took to highway robbery "to ascertain what degree of resolution was necessary in order to place one's self in formal opposition to the most sacred laws of society." He declared that "a soldier who fights in the ranks does not require half so much courage as a foot-pad,"—"that honor and religion have never stood in the way of a well-considered and a firm resolve."[16] This was manly, as the world goes; and yet it was idle, if not desperate. A saner man would have found himself often enough "in formal opposition" to what are deemed "the most sacred laws of society," through obedience to yet more sacred laws, and so have tested his resolution without going out of his way. It is not for a man to put himself in such an attitude to society, but to maintain himself in whatever attitude he find himself through obedience to the laws of his being, which will never be one of opposition to a just government, if he should chance to meet with such.

I left the woods for as good a reason as I went there. Perhaps it seemed to me that I had several more lives to live, and could not spare any more time for that one. It is remarkable how easily and insensibly we fall into a particular route, and make a beaten track for ourselves. I had not lived there a week before my feet wore a path from my door to the pond-side; and though it is five or six years since I trod it, it is still quite distinct. It is true, I fear, that others may have fallen into it, and so helped to keep it open. The surface of the earth is soft and impressible by the feet of men; and so with the paths which the mind travels. How worn and dusty, then, must be the highways of the world, how deep the ruts of tradition and conformity! I did not wish to take a cabin passage, but rather to go before the mast and on the deck of the world, for there I could best see the moonlight amid the mountains. I do not wish to go below now.

---

[11]From "Old Man of Verona," by Roman poet Claudian (fl. 395 A.D.). In his translation, Thoreau takes the liberty of changing "Spaniards" ("Iberos") to "Australians" and "of life" ("vitae") to "of God."
[12]Island in Indian Ocean, near east coast of Africa. Charles Pickering's *The Races of Men* (1851) reported on the cats in Zanzibar.
[13]John Symmes (1780–1829) published a pamphlet in 1818 proposing that the earth was hollow and open at both poles.
[14]When her riddle was answered by Oedipus, the Sphinx destroyed herself (see Emerson's poem "The Sphinx").
[15]Honoré-Gabriel Victor Riqueti, Comte de Mirabeau (1749–1791), French revolutionist.
[16]From an article on Mirabeau in *Harper's New Monthly*, I, 648 (1850); "foot-pad" is a thief.

I learned this, at least, by my experiment: that if one advances confidently in the direction of his dreams, and endeavors to live the life which he has imagined, he will meet with a success unexpected in common hours. He will put some things behind, will pass an invisible boundary; new, universal, and more liberal laws will begin to establish themselves around and within him; or the old laws be expanded, and interpreted in his favor in a more liberal sense, and he will live with the license of a higher order of beings. In proportion as he simplifies his life, the laws of the universe will appear less complex, and solitude will not be solitude, nor poverty poverty, nor weakness weakness. If you have built castles in the air, your work need not be lost; that is where they should be. Now put the foundations under them.

It is a ridiculous demand which England and America make, that you shall speak so that they can understand you. Neither men nor toadstools grow so. As if that were important, and there were not enough to understand you without them. As if Nature could support but one order of understandings, could not sustain birds as well as quadrupeds, flying as well as creeping things, and *hush* and *whoa*,[17] which Bright can understand, were the best English. As if there were safety in stupidity alone. I fear chiefly lest my expression may not be *extra-vagant* enough, may not wander far enough beyond the narrow limits of my daily experience, so as to be adequate to the truth of which I have been convinced. *Extra vagance!* it depends on how you are yarded. The migrating buffalo, which seeks new pastures in another latitude, is not extravagant like the cow which kicks over the pail, leaps the cowyard fence, and runs after her calf, in milking time. I desire to speak somewhere *without* bounds; like a man in a waking moment, to men in their waking moments; for I am convinced that I cannot exaggerate enough even to lay the foundation of a true expression. Who that has heard a strain of music feared then lest he should speak extravagantly any more forever? In view of the future or possible, we should live quite laxly and undefined in front, our outlines dim and misty on that side; as our shadows reveal an insensible perspiration toward the sun. The volatile truth of our words should continually betray the inadequacy of the residual statement. Their truth is instantly *translated;* its literal monument alone remains. The words which express our faith and piety are not definite; yet they are significant and fragrant like frankincense to superior natures.

Why level downward to our dullest perception always, and praise that as common sense? The commonest sense is the sense of men asleep, which they express by snoring. Sometimes we are inclined to class those who are once-and-a-half-witted with the half-witted, because we appreciate only a third part of their wit. Some would find fault with the morning red, if they ever got up early enough. "They pretend," as I hear, "that the verses of Kabir have four different senses; illusion, spirit, intellect, and the exoteric doctrine of the Vedas;"[18] but in this part of the world it is considered a ground for complaint if a man's writings admit of more than one interpretation. While England endeavors to cure the potato-rot, will not any endeavor to cure the brain-rot, which prevails so much more widely and fatally?

I do not suppose that I have attained to obscurity, but I should be proud if no more fatal fault were found with my pages on this score than was found with the Walden ice. Southern customers objected to its blue color, which is the evidence of its purity, as if it were muddy, and preferred the Cambridge ice, which is white, but tastes of weeds. The purity men love is like the mists which envelop the earth, and not like the azure ether beyond.

Some are dinning in our ears that we Americans, and moderns generally, are intellectual dwarfs compared with the ancients, or even the Elizabethan men. But

---

[17]Terms meaning "go" and "stop" to an ox ("Bright").
[18]A translation from Garcin de Tassy's *Histoire de la Littéra-* *ture Hindoue* (1839). Kabir is a variant for Kabar (1450?–1518), Hindu mystic.

what is that to the purpose? A living dog is better than a dead lion.[19] Shall a man go and hang himself because he belongs to the race of pygmies, and not be the biggest pygmy that he can? Let every one mind his own business, and endeavor to be what he was made.

Why should we be in such desperate haste to succeed and in such desperate enterprises? If a man does not keep pace with his companions, perhaps it is because he hears a different drummer. Let him step to the music which he hears, however measured or far away. It is not important that he should mature as soon as an apple tree or an oak. Shall he turn his spring into summer? If the condition of things which we were made for is not yet, what were any reality which we can substitute? We will not be shipwrecked on a vain reality. Shall we with pains erect a heaven of blue glass over ourselves, though when it is done we shall be sure to gaze still at the true ethereal heaven far above, as if the former were not?

There was an artist in the city of Kouroo[20] who was disposed to strive after perfection. One day it came into his mind to make a staff. Having considered that in an imperfect work time is an ingredient, but into a perfect work time does not enter, he said to himself, It shall be perfect in all respects, though I should do nothing else in my life. He proceeded instantly to the forest for wood, being resolved that it should not be made of unsuitable material; and as he searched for and rejected stick after stick, his friends gradually deserted him, for they grew old in their works and died, but he grew not older by a moment. His singleness of purpose and resolution, and his elevated piety, endowed him, without his knowledge, with perennial youth. As he made no compromise with Time, Time kept out of his way, and only sighed at a distance because he could not overcome him. Before he had found a stock in all respects suitable the city of Kouroo was a hoary ruin, and he sat on one of its mounds to peel the stick. Before he had given it the proper shape the dynasty of the Candahars was at an end, and with the point of the stick he wrote the name of the last of that race in the sand, and then resumed his work. By the time he had smoothed and polished the staff Kalpa was no longer the pole-star; and ere he had put on the ferule and the head adorned with precious stones, Brahma had awoke and slumbered many times. But why do I stay to mention these things? When the finishing stroke was put to his work, it suddenly expanded before the eyes of the astonished artist into the fairest of all the creations of Brahma. He had made a new system in making a staff, a world with full and fair proportions; in which, though the old cities and dynasties had passed away, fairer and more glorious ones had taken their places. And now he saw by the heap of shavings still fresh at his feet, that, for him and his work, the former lapse of time had been an illusion, and that no more time had elapsed than is required for a single scintillation from the brain of Brahma to fall on and inflame the tinder of a mortal brain. The material was pure, and his art was pure; how could the result be other than wonderful?

No face which we can give to a matter will stead us so well at last as the truth. This alone wears well. For the most part, we are not where we are, but in a false position. Through an infirmity of our natures, we suppose a case, and put ourselves into it, and hence are in two cases at the same time, and it is doubly difficult to get out. In sane moments we regard only the facts, the case that is. Say what you have to say, not what you ought. Any truth is better than make-believe. Tom Hyde, the tinker, standing on the gallows, was asked if he had anything to say. "Tell the tailors," said he, "to remember to make a knot in their thread before they take the first stitch."[21] His companion's prayer is forgotten.

---

[19]Cf. Ecclesiastes 9:4.
[20]This story or parable was probably invented by Thoreau and may obliquely refer to his own life.

[21]Presumably so the thread holding the shroud together will not come out.

However mean your life is, meet it and live it; do not shun it and call it hard names. It is not so bad as you are. It looks poorest when you are richest. The fault-finder will find faults even in paradise. Love your life, poor as it is. You may perhaps have some pleasant, thrilling, glorious hours, even in a poor-house. The setting sun is reflected from the windows of the alms-house as brightly as from the rich man's abode; the snow melts before its door as early in the spring. I do not see but a quiet mind may live as contentedly there, and have as cheering thoughts, as in a palace. The town's poor seem to me often to live the most independent lives of any. Maybe they are simply great enough to receive without misgiving. Most think that they are above being supported by the town; but it oftener happens that they are not above supporting themselves by dishonest means, which should be more disreputable. Cultivate poverty like a garden herb, like sage. Do not trouble yourself much to get new things, whether clothes or friends. Turn the old; return to them. Things do not change; we change. Sell your clothes and keep your thoughts. God will see that you do not want society. If I were confined to a corner of a garret all my days, like a spider, the world would be just as large to me while I had my thoughts about me. The philosopher said: "From an army of three divisions one can take away its general, and put it in disorder; from the man the most abject and vulgar one cannot take away his thought."[22] Do not seek so anxiously to be developed, to subject yourself to many influences to be played on; it is all dissipation. Humility like darkness reveals the heavenly lights. The shadows of poverty and meanness gather around us, "and lo! creation widens to our view."[23] We are often reminded that if there were bestowed on us the wealth of Crœsus,[24] our aims must still be the same, and our means essentially the same. Moreover, if you are restricted in your range by poverty, if you cannot buy books and newspapers, for instance, you are but confined to the most significant and vital experiences; you are compelled to deal with the material which yields the most sugar and the most starch. It is life near the bone where it is sweetest. You are defended from being a trifler. No man loses ever on a lower level by magnanimity on a higher. Superfluous wealth can buy superfluities only. Money is not required to buy one necessary of the soul.

I live in the angle of a leaden wall, into whose composition was poured a little alloy of bell-metal. Often, in the repose of my mid-day, there reaches my ears a confused *tintinnabulum*[25] from without. It is the noise of my contemporaries. My neighbors tell me of their adventures with famous gentlemen and ladies, what notabilities they met at the dinner-table; but I am no more interested in such things than in the contents of the Daily Times. The interest and the conversation are about costume and manners chiefly; but a goose is a goose still, dress it as you will. They tell me of California and Texas, of England and the Indies, of the Hon. Mr.———of Georgia or of Massachusetts, all transient and fleeting phenomena, till I am ready to leap from their court-yard like the Mameluke bey.[26] I delight to come to my bearings,—not walk in procession with pomp and parade, in a conspicuous place, but to walk even with the Builder of the universe, if I may,—not to live in this restless, nervous, bustling, trivial Nineteenth Century, but stand or sit thoughtfully while it goes by. What are men celebrating? They are all on a committee of arrangements, and hourly expect a speech from somebody. God is only the president of the day, and Webster is his orator.[27] I love to weigh, to settle, to

[22]Confucius, *Analects*, IX, 25.
[23]From "To Night," by Joseph Blanco White (1775–1841), English writer.
[24]A sixth-century B.C. ruler of Lydia, famed as the richest man in the world.
[25]Sound of the bell.
[26]In 1811, when the Mamelukes, a military caste of Egypt, were about to be assassinated, one bey (officer) jumped from the high wall to his horse to escape.
[27]Cf. "There is no other God than Allah, and Muhammed is his prophet"; Daniel Webster (1782–1852) was the most famous orator of the day, but his willingness to compromise on the issue of slavery drew Thoreau's contempt.

gravitate toward that which most strongly and rightfully attracts me;—not hang by the beam of the scale and try to weigh less,—not suppose a case, but take the case that is; to travel the only path I can, and that on which no power can resist me. It affords me no satisfaction to commence to spring an arch before I have got a solid foundation. Let us not play at kittly-benders.[28] There is a solid bottom everywhere. We read that the traveller asked the boy if the swamp before him had a hard bottom. The boy replied that it had. But presently the traveller's horse sank in up to the girths, and he observed to the boy, "I thought you said that this bog had a hard bottom." "So it has," answered the latter, "but you have not got half way to it yet." So it is with the bogs and quicksands of society; but he is an old boy that knows it. Only what is thought, said, or done at a certain rare coincidence is good. I would not be one of those who will foolishly drive a nail into mere lath and plastering; such a deed would keep me awake nights. Give me a hammer, and let me feel for the furring.[29] Do not depend on the putty. Drive a nail home and clinch it so faithfully that you can wake up in the night and think of your work with satisfaction,—a work at which you would not be ashamed to invoke the Muse. So will help you God, and so only. Every nail driven should be as another rivet in the machine of the universe, you carrying on the work.

Rather than love, than money, than fame, give me truth. I sat at a table where were rich food and wine in abundance, and obsequious attendance, but sincerity and truth were not; and I went away hungry from the inhospitable board. The hospitality was as cold as the ices. I thought that there was no need of ice to freeze them. They talked to me of the age of the wine and the fame of the vintage; but I thought of an older, a newer, and purer wine, of a more glorious vintage, which they had not got, and could not buy. The style, the house and grounds and "entertainment" pass for nothing with me. I called on the king, but he made me wait in his hall, and conducted like a man incapacitated for hospitality. There was a man in my neighborhood who lived in a hollow tree. His manners were truly regal. I should have done better had I called on him.

How long shall we sit in our porticoes practising idle and musty virtues, which any work would make impertinent? As if one were to begin the day with long-suffering, and hire a man to hoe his potatoes; and in the afternoon go forth to practise Christian meekness and charity with goodness aforethought! Consider the China[30] pride and stagnant self-complacency of mankind. This generation inclines a little to congratulate itself on being the last of an illustrious line; and in Boston and London and Paris and Rome, thinking of its long descent, it speaks of its progress in art and science and literature with satisfaction. There are the Records of the Philosophical Societies, and the public Eulogies of *Great Men!* It is the good Adam contemplating his own virtue. "Yes, we have done great deeds, and sung divine songs, which shall never die,"—that is, as long as *we* can remember them. The learned societies and great men of Assyria,—where are they? What youthful philosophers and experimentalists we are! There is not one of my readers who has yet lived a whole human life. These may be but the spring months in the life of the race. If we have had the seven-years' itch, we have not seen the seventeen-year locust yet in Concord. We are acquainted with a mere pellicle[31] of the globe on which we live. Most have not delved six feet beneath the surface, nor leaped as many above it. We know not where we are. Beside, we are sound asleep nearly half our time. Yet we esteem ourselves wise, and have an established order on the surface. Truly, we are deep thinkers, we are ambitious spirits! As I stand over the insect crawling amid the pine needles on the forest floor, and endeavor-

---

[28] Running over thin, bending ice.
[29] Wall studs to which covering is nailed.
[30] China-like in the sense of China's continuing isolation and stagnation after having produced in antiquity one of the greatest civilizations in world history.
[31] Skin.

ing to conceal itself from my sight, and ask myself why it will cherish those humble thoughts, and hide its head from me who might, perhaps, be its benefactor, and impart to its race some cheering information, I am reminded of the greater Benefactor and Intelligence that stands over me the human insect.

There is an incessant influx of novelty into the world, and yet we tolerate incredible dulness. I need only suggest what kind of sermons are still listened to in the most enlightened countries. There are such words as joy and sorrow, but they are only the burden of a psalm, sung with a nasal twang, while we believe in the ordinary and mean. We think that we can change our clothes only. It is said that the British Empire is very large and respectable, and that the United States are a first-rate power. We do not believe that a tide rises and falls behind every man which can float the British Empire like a chip, if he should ever harbor it in his mind. Who knows what sort of seventeen-year locust will next come out of the ground? The government of the world I live in was not framed, like that of Britain, in after-dinner conversations over the wine.

The life in us is like the water in the river. It may rise this year higher than man has ever known it, and flood the parched uplands; even this may be the eventful year, which will drown out all our muskrats. It was not always dry land where we dwell. I see far inland the banks which the stream anciently washed, before science began to record its freshets. Every one has heard the story which has gone the rounds of New England, of a strong and beautiful bug which came out of the dry leaf of an old table of apple-tree wood, which had stood in a farmer's kitchen for sixty years, first in Connecticut, and afterward in Massachusetts,— from an egg deposited in the living tree many years earlier still, as appeared by counting the annual layers beyond it; which was heard gnawing out for several weeks, hatched perchance by the heat of an urn.[32] Who does not feel his faith in a resurrection and immortality strengthened by hearing of this? Who knows what beautiful and winged life, whose egg has been buried for ages under many concentric layers of woodenness in the dead dry life of society, deposited at first in the alburnum of the green and living tree, which has been gradually converted into the semblance of its well-seasoned tomb,— heard perchance gnawing out now for years by the astonished family of man, as they sat round the festive board,— may unexpectedly come forth from amidst society's most trivial and handselled furniture, to enjoy its perfect summer life at last!

I do not say that John or Jonathan[33] will realize all this; but such is the character of that morrow which mere lapse of time can never make to dawn. The light which puts out our eyes is darkness to us. Only that day dawns to which we are awake. There is more day to dawn. The sun is but a morning star.

1846   *1854*

---

[32]This parable of rebirth has a long history and Thoreau could have heard it or read it in various places. Herman Melville used it in his short story "The Apple-Tree Table" (1856).

[33]John Bull and Brother Jonathan: the typical Englishman and the typical American.

THE BLACKNESS OF DARKNESS

EDGAR ALLAN POE   HERMAN MELVILLE
NATHANIEL HAWTHORNE

"For spite of all the Indian-summer sunlight on the hither side of Hawthorne's soul, the other side—like the dark half of the physical sphere—is shrouded in a blackness, ten times black. But this darkness but gives more effect to the ever-moving dawn, that for ever advances through it, and circumnavigates his world. Whether Hawthorne has simply availed himself of this mystical blackness as a means to the wondrous effects he makes it to produce in his lights and shades; or whether there really lurks in him, perhaps unknown to himself, a touch of Puritanic gloom,—this, I cannot altogether tell. Certain it is, however, that this great power of blackness in him derives its force from its appeal to that Calvinistic sense of Innate Depravity and Original Sin, from whose visitations, in some shape or other, no deeply thinking mind is always and wholly free. For, in certain moods, no man can weigh this world without throwing in something, somehow like Original Sin, to strike the uneven balance. At all events, perhaps no writer has ever wielded this terrific thought with greater terror than this same harmless Hawthorne. Still more: this black conceit pervades him through and through. You may be witched by his sunlight, transported by the bright gildings in the skies he builds over you; but there is the blackness of darkness beyond; and even his bright gildings but fringe and play upon the edges of thunderclouds."

Herman Melville, "Hawthorne and His Mosses"

EDGAR ALLAN POE
(1809–1849)

In one of his poems that sketches a metaphorical outline of his life, Poe wrote of himself as a youth, "I fell in love with melancholy." He confessed also, "I could not love except where Death / Was mingling his with Beauty's breath." In another poem he wrote the line, "One dwells in lonely places." When James Russell Lowell wrote to Poe asking for biographical data, Poe replied: "My life has been *whim*—impulse—passion—a longing for solitude—a scorn of all things present, in an earnest longing for the future."

These comments from the center of the lived life no doubt strike nearer the mark than the assembled exterior facts. A chronology of Poe's life seems always verging on the implausible, the incoherent. The beginning was not promising. His parents were itinerant actors. His American father, David Poe, deserted the family in Poe's first year of life; his British mother, Elizabeth Arnold Poe, died in his second.

Poe was taken in by well-to-do foster parents, the John Allans, in Richmond, Virginia, but was not adopted. He got along well with his foster mother, but from the beginning there was antagonism between son and foster father. In 1815 John Allan took his family to England to establish an English office of his tobacco export business. There Poe was placed in the Manor House School of the Reverend Mr. Bransby at Stoke Newington (described fictionally in "William Wilson").

After five years, having been unsuccessful in establishing the branch, John Allan brought his family back to Richmond, where Poe continued his education in a wealthy private school. By the time he was fourteen or fifteen, Poe was writing verses. He made the acquaintance of a schoolmate's mother, Jane Stith Stanard, for whom Poe developed a romantic, adolescent passion. She died suddenly in 1824, and Poe wrote one of his most popular poems to her—"To Helen." At the age of sixteen, Poe became engaged to a neighbor's daughter, Sarah Elmira Royster, but her family encouraged her to select someone else with better prospects than the tempestuous and unreliable Poe.

In 1826, Poe attended the newly opened University of Virginia, but remained only one semester. John Allan did not adequately support his foster son, and Poe compounded his problems by running up large gambling debts in an attempt to meet his expenses. And in despair, he turned to drink, which his system could not easily tolerate. Disgraced, Poe returned to the Allans. John Allan wanted Poe to read for the law, but Poe was determined to be a poet. They quarrelled, and Poe ran away from home.

Returning to Boston, the city of his birth, Poe arranged with the few funds he had for the publication of his first volume, *Tamerlane and Other Poems* (1827), "By a Bostonian." Poe was eighteen, penniless, and without a profession. He joined the army under the name Edgar A. Perry. From 1827 to 1829, Poe apparently worked efficiently in the Army and pleased his superiors, rising to the rank of regimental sergeant major. He applied to John Allan for help in being released from the army and sent to West Point, and Allan agreed. In February of 1829, Mrs. Allan died shortly after making a plea to her husband for her foster son. Poe arrived in Richmond after the burial and there was a formal reconciliation between him and Allan—not fated to last.

Poe had to await admission to West Point and went to stay with relatives in Baltimore. There he met his aunt, Mrs. Maria Clemm, and her young daughter, Virginia, who was to become Poe's bride a few years later. Poe set about finding a publisher for his second volume of poetry, *Al Aaraaf, Tamerlane, and Minor Poems* (1829). He was admitted to West Point in July 1830.

Poe had looked upon West Point as a means of getting an education and reconciling himself with Allan. But Allan's second marriage, together with the discovery of some derogatory remarks Poe had made about him, led to his disowning Poe. Convinced that there could never be a reconciliation, Poe deliberately began to miss roll calls and disobey orders to cause his dismissal from West Point. But before his ouster, Poe had persuaded fellow cadets to subscribe to his third volume of poetry, published in 1831 as *Poems of Edgar A. Poe.*

He took up residence with Mrs. Clemm and her daughter Virginia in Baltimore in 1831 and remained there until 1835, the year he married his cousin in secret (a public ceremony was held in 1836). She was thirteen. Some biographers have speculated that Poe was attracted to this frail, sickly child-bride because he was impotent. Whatever the case, Virginia's frequent illnesses, verging on death, made Poe's life into something of a recurrent nightmare.

During this period Poe began to publish his stories, winning a prize of fifty dollars in 1833 for "A Ms. Found in a Bottle." He came to the attention of the southern novelist John Pendleton Kennedy, who became a kind of patron, helping him become assistant editor of the *Southern Literary Messenger* in Richmond in 1835. Poe went to Richmond and entered into his duties with enthusiasm. Poe himself wrote an enormous number of reviews, essays, and stories for the *Literary Messenger,* and saw the circulation rise from 500 to 3,500 during his assistant-editorship. Part of Poe's *The Narrative of Arthur Gordon Pym* appeared in the magazine in two installments, January and February 1837 (and the whole book appeared in 1838). But there were tensions between Poe and the editor because of Poe's bouts of drinking and his low salary of $10 a week. In early 1837, Poe resigned and moved his household (Mrs. Clemm and Virginia) to New York, where he found the situation worsened because of the financial panic of that year. He moved on to Philadelphia in 1838 in desperate search of hack work or editing to make ends meet.

Poe was to remain in Philadelphia from 1838 to 1844, during which time he gained a national reputation. He became co-editor of *Burton's Gentleman's Magazine* in May 1839, but after several quarrels with the editor he left about a year later. Then he became literary editor of *Graham's Magazine,* a position he held from January 1841 to May 1842. While he was there, the subscriptions increased from 8,000 to 40,000, making it the most popular magazine in America. In the first of these magazines, Poe published "The Fall of the House of Usher" and "William Wilson"; in the latter, "The Oval Portrait" and "The Masque of the Red Death." In 1839 appeared the two-volume work, *Tales of the Grotesque and Arabesque,* Poe's first stories published in book form. During this period, Poe began to shape the genre he has been credited with inventing, the mystery story; "The Murders in the Rue Morgue" appeared in 1841, "The Purloined Letter" in 1844.

In spite of his growing fame, Poe's fortunes began to sink again after he parted from *Graham's Magazine.* Periods of dissipation played their part, with sprees that seemed to invite self-destruction. In 1844 he moved to New York, virtually penniless, and began to write for various publications. In 1845, Poe published the poem that he had begun in 1843—"The Raven." Its success was immediate and enormous, ultimately bringing Poe worldwide fame. Later that year, Poe brought out *The Raven and Other Poems*. A volume of his selected stories also appeared as *Tales*. But Poe's personal fortunes continued to decline. He became first editor and then owner of *The Broadway Journal* in 1845, but early in 1846 the enterprise collapsed, brought down by debt and Poe's ill health. In 1847, Virginia died after a last long illness, tuberculosis. Most readers find an oblique embodiment of Poe's grief in "Ulalume," written later that year. During all his misfortunes, Poe continued to produce, throwing himself into the writing of his prose-poem *Eureka*, outlining an astonishing cosmogony (containing elements of the Big Bang and Expanding Universe theories of creation), published in 1848.

Meantime, Poe became reacquainted with his childhood sweetheart in Richmond, Sarah Elmira Royster, now a rich widow. Poe proposed and she accepted. On a trip to bring Mrs. Clemm to the wedding, Poe passed through Baltimore, where he disappeared for five days. It was October, and an election was being held. One unreliable legend, often repeated, is that Poe went on a final drinking spree, was taken over by those who were organizing "repeater" voting, and was found unconscious in a tavern on October 3. Taken to a hospital, he died four days later without returning to full consciousness. The truth is more ambiguous, less romantic. It has been established that so much as a glass of wine would inebriate him. But beyond this fact, the circumstances surrounding his death are unknown.

Running through all of Poe's work is a curious tension between rational and irrational forces, with the latter often terrifyingly dominant in his Kafkaesque universe. In "Ligeia," for example, the protagonist reasons with meticulous care, but is at the same time at the mercy of inner passions or outer forces far beyond his control. A similar tension is seen between "The Raven," with all its hallucinatory brooding, and "The Philosophy of Composition," with its severely logical explanation of the poem's method of construction. The tension is seen also between the tales of the grotesque, portraying mad protagonists or narrators, and the tales of ratiocination, portraying masters of logic and reason unriddling baffling riddles. But the haunting and lasting impression of Poe's nightmare world is that human reason is but a frail faculty doomed to ultimate failure in confronting the irrational forces within and without.

Although Poe has always had a large popular following, he has not fared well with American critics. His literary executor and first editor, Rufus W. Griswold, appended a violent attack on Poe's character in his edition of Poe's work after his death. Ralph Waldo Emerson dismissed him as "the jingle man." Henry James remarked, "An enthusiasm for Poe is the mark of a decidedly primitive stage of reflection." T. S. Eliot observed that Poe's intellect was that of "a highly gifted young person before puberty."

But if American critics tended to look upon Poe as a minor, somewhat derivative writer (borrowing heavily from the British Gothic and romantic authors), French critics virtually turned Poe into a French writer. He was translated brilliantly by the poet Charles Baudelaire and written about with great enthusiasm by poets Stéphane Mallarmé and Paul Valéry. The French *Symbolistes* of the latter nineteenth century drew much of their theory from Poe's critical commentary and in turn influenced American modernists such as T. S. Eliot. Thus Eliot was ironically influenced by the French face of Poe. Now the post-structuralist criticism in France has elevated "The Purloined Letter" to rarefied heights by deeming it worthy to serve as the site for deconstructionist critical probes and raids. The avant-garde psychoanalytic French critic Jacques Lacan, in a long analysis in the 1960s, read Poe's story as a kind of psychoanalytic-linguistic allegory. The avant-garde French apostle of deconstruction, Jacques Derrida, in a famous essay in the 1970s, deconstructed Lacan's essay on "The Purloined Letter" by teasing out of his analysis its contradictions. Poe would no doubt be surprised and puzzled to find his simple tale of ratiocination the focus of so much learned—and at times obscure—debate (see John P. Muller and William J. Richardson, *The Purloined Poe; Lacan, Derrida, and Psychoanalytic Reading,* 1988).

Recent American criticism has been kinder to Poe, as critics have come to see the darker, more terrifying aspects of his work as relevant to the modern imagination trying to come to terms with the twentieth-century waste land and its wars, massacres, and holocausts. Most eloquent is the poet Richard Wilbur, who has in several essays reintroduced Poe to serious critical discussion. His deepest probing has been into the obscure corners of Poe's "major tales," which, he says, "are great and trail-blazing realizations of inner experience."

ADDITIONAL READING

The Poems of Edgar Allan Poe, ed. Killis Campbell, 1917; The Letters of Edgar Allan Poe, 2 vols., ed. John W. Ostrom, 1948, 1966; Literary Criticism of Edgar Allan Poe, ed. Robert L. Hough, 1965; The Poems of Edgar Allan Poe, ed. Floyd Stovall, 1965.

Joseph Wood Krutch, Edgar Allan Poe, 1926; Hervey Allan, Israfel—The Life and Times of Edgar Allan Poe, 1926; Killis Campbell, The Mind of Poe and Other Studies, 1933; Arthur Hobson Quinn, Edgar Allan Poe, 1941; Marie Bonaparte, The Life and Works of Edgar Allan Poe: A Psychoanalytic Interpretation, 1949; E. H. Davidson, Poe, a Critical Study, 1957; Patrick F. Quinn, The French Face of Edgar Allan Poe, 1957; Eric W. Carlson, ed., The Recognition of Edgar Allan Poe, 1966; Robert Regan, ed., Poe: A Collection of Critical Essays, 1967; Eric W. Carlson, ed., Introduction to Poe: A Thematic Reader, 1967; Robert D. Jacobs, Poe: Journalist and Critic, 1969; Robert L. Gale, Plots and Characters in the Fiction and Poetry of Edgar Allan Poe, 1970; Jean Alexander, Affidavits of Genius: Edgar Allan Poe and the French Critics, 1847–1924, 1971; William L. Howarth, Twentieth-Century Interpretations of Poe's Tales, 1971; Daniel Hoffman, An Edgar Allan Poe Companion, Poe, Poe, Poe, Poe, Poe, Poe, Poe, 1972; David Halliburton, Edgar Allan Poe: A Phenomenological View, 1973; G. R. Thompson, Poe's Fiction: Romantic Irony in the Gothic Tales, 1973; David B. Kesterson, ed., Critics on Poe, 1973; Richard Wilbur, Responses: Prose Pieces, 1953–1976, 1976 (contains several important pieces on Poe); David Sinclair, Edgar Allan Poe, 1977; Benjamin F. Fisher, ed., Poe at Work: Seven Textual Studies, 1978; Julian Symons, The Tell-Tale Heart: The Life and Works of Edgar Allan Poe, 1978; David Ketterer, The Rationale of Deception in Poe, 1979; Elizabeth Phillips, Edgar Allan Poe: An American Imagination, 1979; J. R. Hammond, An Edgar Allan Poe Companion, 1981; Burton R. Pollin, Word Index to Poe's Fiction, 1982; Harold Bloom, ed., Modern Critical Views: Edgar Allan Poe, 1985; I. M. Walker, ed., Edgar Allan Poe: The Critical Heritage, 1986; Benjamin Franklin Fisher, ed., Poe and Our Times, 1986; A. Robert Lee, ed., Edgar Allan Poe; The Design of Order, 1987; Dwight Thomas and David K. Jackson, The Poe Log, A Documentary Life, 1987; John P. Muller and William J. Richardson, eds., The Purloined Poe: Lacan, Derrida, and Psychoanalytic Reading, 1988.

TEXTS

Collected Works of Edgar Allan Poe, 3 vols., ed. Thomas Ollive Mabbott, 1969–78: The Poems, 1969; Tales and Sketches, 2 vols., 1978. Nonfiction prose selections from The Complete Works of Edgar Allan Poe (the Virginia Edition), 17 vols., ed. James A. Harrison, 1902.

from **Poems**

Introduction

["I Fell in Love with Melancholy"][1]

Romance, who loves to nod and sing,
With drowsy head and folded wing,
Among the green leaves as they shake
Far down within some shadowy lake,
To me a painted paroquet   5
Hath been—a most familiar bird—
Taught me my alphabet to say—
To lisp my very earliest word
While in the wild-wood I did lie
A child—with a most knowing eye.   10

Succeeding years, too wild for song,
Then roll'd like tropic storms along,
Where, tho' the garish lights that fly
Dying along the troubled sky,
Lay bare, thro' vistas thunder-riven,   15
The blackness of the general Heaven,
That very blackness yet doth fling
Light on the lightning's silver wing.

For, being an idle boy lang syne,[2]
Who read Anacreon,[3] and drank wine,   20
I early found Anacreon rhymes
Were almost passionate sometimes—
And by strange alchemy of brain
His pleasures always turn'd to pain—
His naivete to wild desire—   25
His wit to love—his wine to fire—
And so, being young and dipt in folly
I fell in love with melancholy,
And used to throw my earthly rest
And quiet all away in jest—   30
I could not love except where Death
Was mingling his with Beauty's breath—
Or Hymen,[4] Time, and Destiny
Were stalking between her and me.

O, then the eternal Condor[5] years   35
So shook the very Heavens on high,
With tumult as they thunder'd by;

---

[1]This poem appeared in Poe's volume *Poems,* published in 1831. It incorporated the entirety of a poem entitled "Preface" in Poe's 1829 volume, *Al Aaraaf, Tamerlane, and Minor Poems,* and called "Romance" in later volumes (included after this poem). The incorporated lines are 1–10 and 35–45. The poem as it was published in 1831 provides an important personal statement by Poe of the development of his romantic imagination.

[2]Long since (a long time ago).
[3]Greek lyric poet (563–478 B.C.) whose work praises love and wine.
[4]Classical Greek god of marriage.
[5]Vulture that preys on the dead.

I had no time for idle cares,
Thro' gazing on the unquiet sky!
Or if an hour with calmer wing   40
Its down did on my spirit fling,
That little hour with lyre and rhyme
To while away—forbidden thing!
My heart half fear'd to be a crime
Unless it trembled with the string.   45

But *now* my soul hath too much room—
Gone are the glory and the gloom—
The black hath mellow'd into grey,
And all the fires are fading away.

My draught of passion hath been deep—   50
I revell'd, and I now would sleep—
And after-drunkenness of soul
Succeeds the glories of the bowl—
An idle longing night and day
To dream my very life away.   55

But dreams—of those who dream as I,
Aspiringly, are damned, and die:
Yet should I swear I mean alone,
By notes so very shrilly blown,
To break upon Time's monotone,   60
While yet my vapid joy and grief
Are tintless of the yellow leaf—
Why not an imp the greybeard hath,
Will shake his shadow in my path—
And even the greybeard will o'erlook   65
Connivingly my dreaming-book.

                                        1831

Romance

Romance, who loves to nod and sing
With drowsy head and folded wing,
Among the green leaves as they shake
Far down within some shadowy lake,
To me a painted paroquet   5
Hath been—a most familiar bird—
Taught me my alphabet to say—
To lisp my very earliest word
While in the wild wood I did lie,
A child—with a most knowing eye.   10

Of late, eternal Condor years
So shake the very Heaven on high
With tumult as they thunder by,
I have no time for idle cares
Through gazing on the unquiet sky.   15
And when an hour with calmer wings

Its down upon my spirit flings—
That little time with lyre and rhyme
To while away—forbidden things!
My heart would feel to be a crime   20
Unless it trembled with the strings.

1829, 1845

[Alone]

From childhood's hour I have not been
As others were—I have not seen
As others saw—I could not bring
My passions from a common spring—
From the same source I have not taken   5
My sorrow—I could not awaken
My heart to joy at the same tone—
And all I lov'd—*I* lov'd alone—
Then—in my childhood—in the dawn
Of a most stormy life—was drawn   10
From ev'ry depth of good and ill
The mystery which binds me still—
From the torrent, or the fountain—
From the red cliff of the mountain—
From the sun that 'round me roll'd   15
In its autumn tint of gold—
From the lightning in the sky
As it pass'd me flying by—
From the thunder, and the storm—
And the cloud that took the form   20
(When the rest of Heaven was blue)
Of a demon in my view—

1829   *1875*

Sonnet—To Science

Science! true daughter of Old Time thou art!
  Who alterest all things with thy peering eyes.
Why preyest thou thus upon the poet's heart,
  Vulture, whose wings are dull realities?
How should he love thee? or how deem thee wise,   5
  Who wouldst not leave him in his wandering
To seek for treasure in the jewelled skies,
  Albeit he soared with an undaunted wing?
Hast thou not dragged Diana[1] from her car?
  And driven the Hamadryad[2] from the wood   10

---

[1] Roman goddess of the hunt, identified with the moon (her "car"), noted for her chastity.
[2] Tree nymph in classical mythology.

To seek a shelter in some happier star?
  Hast thou not torn the Naiad[3] from her flood,
The Elfin from the green grass, and from me
The summer dream beneath the tamarind tree?[4]

1829, 1843

To Helen[1]

Helen, thy beauty is to me
  Like those Nicéan[2] barks of yore,
That gently, o'er a perfumed sea,
  The weary, way-worn wanderer bore
  To his own native shore.   5

On desperate seas long wont to roam,
  Thy hyacinth hair,[3] thy classic face,
Thy Naiad airs[4] have brought me home
  To the glory that was Greece,
And the grandeur that was Rome.   10

Lo! in yon brilliant window-niche
  How statue-like I see thee stand,
The agate lamp within thy hand!
  Ah, Psyche,[5] from the regions which
  Are Holy-Land!   15

1831, 1843

The City in the Sea[1]

Lo! Death has reared himself a throne
In a strange city lying alone
Far down within the dim West,
Where the good and the bad and the worst and the best
Have gone to their eternal rest.   5
There shrines and palaces and towers
(Time-eaten towers that tremble not!)
Resemble nothing that is ours.
Around, by lifting winds forgot,
Resignedly beneath the sky   10
The melancholy waters lie.

---

[3]Fountain or stream nymph.
[4]Aromatic tropical tree with red-streaked yellow flowers.
[1]Helen of Troy, daughter of Zeus and Leda, symbolizes eternal female beauty; married to the Greek Menelaus, she eloped with Paris to Troy and thus was the cause of the Trojan War described by Homer in the *Iliad*. Poe's Helen was a boyhood idol, Mrs. Jane Stith Stanard, a Richmond neighbor who died in 1824.
[2]Nicéan has been variously defined; it may mean "victori-

ous" here, or may refer to one of several ancient cities of Nicea, one of which was linked to Dionysus.
[3]"Hyacinthine" is a common Homeric epithet for hair, suggesting black, glossy curls; Hyacinthus was the handsome youth loved and accidentally killed by Apollo.
[4]Manner or bearing of the fountain nymph.
[5]Greek goddess of the soul.
[1]When first published, called "The Doomed City."

No rays from the holy heaven come down
On the long night-time of that town;
But light from out the lurid sea
Streams up the turrets silently—   15
Gleams up the pinnacles far and free
Up domes—up spires—up kingly halls—
Up fanes[2]—up Babylon-like[3] walls—
Up shadowy long-forgotten bowers
Of sculptured ivy and stone flowers—   20
Up many and many a marvellous shrine
Whose wreathéd friezes intertwine
The viol, the violet, and the vine.

Resignedly beneath the sky
The melancholy waters lie.   25
So blend the turrets and shadows there
That all seem pendulous in air,
While from a proud tower in the town
Death looks gigantically down.

There open fanes and gaping graves   30
Yawn level with the luminous waves;
But not the riches there that lie
In each idol's diamond eye—
Not the gaily-jewelled dead
Tempt the waters from their bed;   35
For no ripples curl, alas!
Along that wilderness of glass—
No swellings tell that winds may be
Upon some far-off happier sea—
No heavings hint that winds have been   40
On seas less hideously serene.

But lo, a stir is in the air!
The wave—there is a movement there!
As if the towers had thrust aside,
In slightly sinking, the dull tide—   45
As if their tops had feebly given
A void within the filmy Heaven.
The waves have now a redder glow—
The hours are breathing faint and low—
And when, amid no earthly moans,   50
Down, down that town shall settle hence,
Hell, rising from a thousand thrones,
Shall do it reverence.

                                                  1831, 1845

---

[2]Temples.
[3]Biblical wicked and doomed city.

The Sleeper[1]

At midnight, in the month of June,
I stand beneath the mystic moon.
An opiate vapour, dewy, dim,
Exhales from out her golden rim,
And, softly dripping, drop by drop,   5
Upon the quiet mountain top,
Steals drowsily and musically
Into the universal valley.
The rosemary[2] nods upon the grave;
The lily lolls upon the wave;   10
Wrapping the fog about its breast,
The ruin moulders into rest;
Looking like Lethë,[3] see! the lake
A conscious slumber seems to take,
And would not, for the world, awake.   15
All Beauty sleeps!—and lo! where lies
Irenë, with her Destinies!

Oh, lady bright! can it be right—
This window open to the night?
The wanton airs, from the tree-top,   20
Laughingly through the lattice drop—
The bodiless airs, a wizard rout,
Flit through thy chamber in and out,
And wave the curtain canopy
So fitfully—so fearfully—   25
Above the closed and fringéd lid
'Neath which thy slumb'ring soul lies hid,
That, o'er the floor and down the wall,
Like ghosts the shadows rise and fall!
Oh, lady dear, hast thou no fear?   30
Why and what art thou dreaming here?
Sure thou art come o'er far-off seas,
A wonder to these garden trees!
Strange is thy pallor! strange thy dress!
Strange, above all, thy length of tress,[4]   35
And this all solemn silentness!

The lady sleeps! Oh, may her sleep,
Which is enduring, so be deep!
Heaven have her in its sacred keep!
This chamber changed for one more holy,   40
This bed for one more melancholy,
I pray to God that she may lie
Forever with unopened eye,
While the pale sheeted ghosts go by!

My love, she sleeps! Oh, may her sleep,   45
As it is lasting, so be deep!
Soft may the worms about her creep!

---

[1] In its earliest version, the poem was entitled "Irene."
[2] A flower symbolizing remembrance.
[3] A river in Hades bestowing forgetfulness.
[4] From the legend that hair grows quickly after death.

Far in the forest, dim and old,
For her may some tall vault unfold—
Some vault that oft hath flung its black   50
And wingéd pannels fluttering back,
Triumphant, o'er the crested palls,
Of her grand family funerals—
Some sepulchre, remote, alone,
Against whose portal she hath thrown,   55
In childhood, many an idle stone—
Some tomb from out whose sounding door
She ne'er shall force an echo more,
Thrilling to think, poor child of sin!
It was the dead who groaned within.   60

1831, 1845

Israfel

And the angel Israfel, whose heart-strings are a
lute, and who has the sweetest voice of all God's
creatures.— KORAN.[1]

In Heaven a spirit doth dwell
    "Whose heart-strings are a lute;"
None sing so wildly well
As the angel Israfel,
And the giddy stars (so legends tell)   5
Ceasing their hymns, attend the spell
    Of his voice, all mute.

Tottering above
    In her highest noon,
    The enamoured moon   10
Blushes with love,
    While, to listen, the red levin[2]
    (With the rapid Pleiads,[3] even,
    Which were seven,)
Pauses in Heaven.   15

And they say (the starry choir
    And the other listening things)
That Israfeli's fire
Is owing to that lyre
    By which he sits and sings—   20
The trembling living wire
Of those unusual strings.

But the skies that angel trod,
    Where deep thoughts are a duty—

---

[1]Poe's motto comes not from the Koran but from George Sale's "Preliminary Discourse" to his translation of the Koran (1734) quoted by Thomas Moore in a footnote to *Lalla Rookh* (1817).
[2]Lightning.

[3]Cluster of seven stars (seven daughters of Atlas) located in the constellation Taurus; one grew faint long ago and was thought to have disappeared, but later it became bright again.

Where Love's a grown-up God— 25
  Where the Houri[4] glances are
Imbued with all the beauty
  Which we worship in a star.

Therefore, thou art not wrong,
  Israfeli, who despisest 30
An unimpassioned song;
  To thee the laurels belong,
    Best bard, because the wisest!
Merrily live, and long!

The ecstasies above 35
  With thy burning measures suit—
Thy grief, thy joy, thy hate, thy love,
  With the fervour of thy lute—
    Well may the stars be mute!

Yes, Heaven is thine; but this 40
  Is a world of sweets and sours;
    Our flowers are merely—flowers,
And the shadow of thy perfect bliss
  Is the sunshine of ours.

If I could dwell 45
Where Israfel
  Hath dwelt, and he where I,
He might not sing so wildly well
  A mortal melody,
While a bolder note than this might swell 50
  From my lyre within the sky.

                                        1831, 1845

To One in Paradise[1]

Thou wast that all to me, love,
  For which my soul did pine—
A green isle in the sea, love,
  A fountain and a shrine,
All wreathed with fairy fruits and flowers, 5
  And all the flowers were mine.

Ah, dream too bright to last!
  Ah, starry Hope! that didst arise
But to be overcast!
  A voice from out the Future cries, 10
"On! on!"—but o'er the Past
  (Dim gulf!) my spirit hovering lies
Mute, motionless, aghast!

---

[4]Virgin beauty in Mohammedan paradise for the devout.
[1]Before appearing in Poe's last book of poetry, this poem appeared many times with several variants, including even a penultimate stanza which was discarded. The poem was clearly important to Poe.

For, alas! alas! with me
　　The light of Life is o'er!
　　No more—no more—no more—
(Such language holds the solemn sea
　　To the sands upon the shore)
Shall bloom the thunder-blasted tree,
　　Or the stricken eagle soar!　　　　　　　　　　　　20

And all my days are trances,
　　And all my nightly dreams
Are where thy grey eye glances,
　　And where thy footstep gleams—
In what ethereal dances,　　　　　　　　　　　　　25
By what eternal streams.

1833　　　　　　　　　　　　　　　　　　　1834, 1845, 1849

Sonnet—Silence

There are some qualities—some incorporate things,
　　That have a double life, which thus is made
A type of that twin entity which springs
　　From matter and light, evinced in solid and shade.
There is a two-fold *Silence*—sea and shore—　　　　5
　　Body and Soul. One dwells in lonely places,
　　Newly with grass o'ergrown; some solemn graces,
Some human memories and tearful lore,
Render him terrorless: his name's "No more."
He is the corporate Silence:[1] dread him not!　　　　10
　　No power hath he of evil in himself;
But should some urgent fate (untimely lot!)
　　Bring thee to meet his shadow[2] (nameless elf,
That haunteth the lone regions where hath trod
No foot of man,) commend thyself to God!　　　　　15

1839　　　　　　　　　　　　　　　　　　　　1840, 1845

The Raven[1]

Once upon a midnight dreary, while I pondered, weak and weary,
Over many a quaint and curious volume of forgotten lore—
While I nodded, nearly napping, suddenly there came a tapping,
As of some one gently rapping, rapping at my chamber door—
" 'Tis some visiter," I muttered, "tapping at my chamber door—　　5
　　Only this and nothing more."

---

[1] I.e., silence ensuing death of the body.
[2] I.e., death of the soul.
[1] See "The Philosophy of Composition" for Poe's account of how he wrote "The Raven"; most critics have expressed skepticism of some of his claims, but the account remains valuable for its theoretical implications.

Ah, distinctly I remember it was in the bleak December;
And each separate dying ember wrought its ghost upon the floor.
Eagerly I wished the morrow;—vainly I had sought to borrow
From my books surcease of sorrow—sorrow for the lost Lenore—   10
For the rare and radiant maiden whom the angels name Lenore—
        Nameless *here* for evermore.

And the silken, sad, uncertain rustling of each purple curtain
Thrilled me—filled me with fantastic terrors never felt before;
So that now, to still the beating of my heart, I stood repeating   15
" 'Tis some visiter entreating entrance at my chamber door—
Some late visiter entreating entrance at my chamber door;—
        This it is and nothing more."

Presently my soul grew stronger; hesitating then no longer,
"Sir," said I, "or Madam, truly your forgiveness I implore;   20
But the fact is I was napping, and so gently you came rapping,
And so faintly you came tapping, tapping at my chamber door,
That I scarce was sure I heard you"—here I opened wide the door;———
        Darkness there and nothing more.

Deep into that darkness peering, long I stood there wondering, fearing,   25
Doubting, dreaming dreams no mortal ever dared to dream before;
But the silence was unbroken, and the stillness gave no token,
And the only word there spoken was the whispered word, "Lenore?"
This I whispered, and an echo murmured back the word, "Lenore!"
        Merely this and nothing more.   30

Back into the chamber turning, all my soul within me burning,
Soon again I heard a tapping somewhat louder than before.
"Surely," said I, "surely that is something at my window lattice;
Let me see, then, what thereat is, and this mystery explore—
Let my heart be still a moment and this mystery explore;—   35
        'Tis the wind and nothing more!"

Open here I flung the shutter, when, with many a flirt and flutter,
In there stepped a stately Raven of the saintly days of yore;
Not the least obeisance made he; not a minute stopped or stayed he;
But, with mien of lord or lady, perched above my chamber door—   40
Perched upon a bust of Pallas[2] just above my chamber door—
        Perched, and sat, and nothing more.

Then this ebony bird beguiling my sad fancy into smiling,
By the grave and stern decorum of the countenance it wore,
"Though thy crest be shorn and shaven, thou," I said, "art sure no craven,   45
Ghastly grim and ancient Raven wandering from the Nightly shore—
Tell me what thy lordly name is on the Night's Plutonian shore!"[3]
        Quoth the Raven "Nevermore."

Much I marvelled this ungainly fowl to hear discourse so plainly,
Though its answer little meaning—little relevancy bore;   50

---

[2]Pallas Athena, Greek goddess of crafts, arts, and wisdom.
[3]The dark realm of death, ruled over by Pluto.

For we cannot help agreeing that no living human being
Ever yet was blessed with seeing bird above his chamber door—
Bird or beast upon the sculptured bust above his chamber door,
      With such name as "Nevermore."

But the Raven, sitting lonely on the placid bust, spoke only   55
That one word, as if his soul in that one word he did outpour.
Nothing farther then he uttered—not a feather then he fluttered—
Till I scarcely more than muttered "Other friends have flown before—
On the morrow *he* will leave me, as my Hopes have flown before."
      Then the bird said "Nevermore."   60

Startled at the stillness broken by reply so aptly spoken,
"Doubtless," said I, "what it utters is its only stock and store
Caught from some unhappy master whom unmerciful Disaster
Followed fast and followed faster till his songs one burden bore—
Till the dirges of his Hope that melancholy burden bore   65
      Of 'Never—nevermore.' "

But the Raven still beguiling my sad fancy into smiling,
Straight I wheeled a cushioned seat in front of bird, and bust and door;
Then, upon the velvet sinking, I betook myself to linking
Fancy unto fancy, thinking what this ominous bird of yore—   70
What this grim, ungainly, ghastly, gaunt, and ominous bird of yore
      Meant in croaking "Nevermore."

This I sat engaged in guessing, but no syllable expressing
To the fowl whose fiery eyes now burned into my bosom's core;
This and more I sat divining, with my head at ease reclining   75
On the cushion's velvet lining that the lamp-light gloated[4] o'er,
But whose velvet-violet lining with the lamp-light gloating o'er,
      She shall press, ah, nevermore!

Then, methought, the air grew denser, perfumed from an unseen censer
Swung by seraphim whose foot-falls tinkled on the tufted floor.   80
"Wretch," I cried, "thy God hath lent thee—by these angels he hath sent thee
Respite—respite and nepenthe[5] from thy memories of Lenore;
Quaff, oh quaff this kind nepenthe and forget this lost Lenore!"
      Quoth the Raven "Nevermore."

"Prophet!" said I, "thing of evil!—prophet still, if bird or devil!—   85
Whether Tempter sent, or whether tempest tossed thee here ashore,
Desolate yet all undaunted, on this desert land enchanted—
On this home by Horror haunted—tell me truly, I implore—
Is there—*is* there balm in Gilead?[6]—tell me—tell me, I implore!"
      Quoth the Raven "Nevermore."   90

"Prophet!" said I, "thing of evil!—prophet still, if bird or devil!
By that Heaven that bends above us—by that God we both adore—
Tell this soul with sorrow laden if, within the distant Aidenn,[7]

---

[4]Refracted light (rare meaning).
[5]Drink that obliterates memories.
[6]Cf. Jeremiah, 8:22: "Is there no balm in Gilead?" (*Balm* refers to medicinal herbs found in this mountainous region
between the sea of Galilee and the Dead Sea.)
[7]Variant of Eden.

It shall clasp a sainted maiden whom the angels name Lenore—
Clasp a rare and radiant maiden whom the angels name Lenore."   95
    Quoth the Raven "Nevermore."

"Be that word our sign of parting, bird or fiend!" I shrieked, upstarting—
"Get thee back into the tempest and the Night's Plutonian shore!
Leave no black plume as a token of that lie thy soul hath spoken!
Leave my loneliness unbroken!—quit the bust above my door!   100
Take thy beak from out my heart, and take thy form from off my door!"
    Quoth the Raven "Nevermore."

And the Raven, never flitting, still is sitting, *still* is sitting
On the pallid bust of Pallas just above my chamber door;
And his eyes have all the seeming of a demon's that is dreaming,   105
And the lamp-light o'er him streaming throws his shadow on the floor;
And my soul from out that shadow that lies floating on the floor
    Shall be lifted—nevermore!

1844   *1845, 1849*

Dream-Land

By a route obscure and lonely,
Haunted by ill angels only,
Where an Eidolon,[1] named Night,
On a black throne reigns upright,
I have reached these lands but newly   5
From an ultimate dim Thule—[2]
From a wild weird clime that lieth, sublime,
    Out of Space—out of Time.

Bottomless vales and boundless floods,
And chasms, and caves, and Titan[3] woods,   10
With forms that no man can discover
For the dews that drip all over;
Mountains toppling evermore
Into seas without a shore;
Seas that restlessly aspire,   15
Surging, unto skies of fire;
Lakes that endlessly outspread
Their lone waters—lone and dead,—
Their still waters—still and chilly
With the snows of the lolling lily.   20

By the lakes that thus outspread
Their lone waters, lone and dead,—
Their sad waters, sad and chilly
With the snows of the lolling lily,—
By the mountains—near the river   25
Murmuring lowly, murmuring ever,—

---
[1]Phantom or image.
[2]Greek name for an island north of England.
[3]Gigantic and ancient.

By the grey woods,—by the swamp
Where the toad and the newt encamp,—
By the dismal tarns and pools
   Where dwell the Ghouls,[4]—   30
By each spot the most unholy—
In each nook most melancholy,—
There the traveller meets aghast
Sheeted Memories of the Past—
Shrouded forms that start and sigh   35
As they pass the wanderer by—
White-robed forms of friends long given,
In agony, to the Earth—and Heaven.

For the heart whose woes are legion
'Tis a peaceful, soothing region—   40
For the spirit that walks in shadow
O! it is an Eldorado![5]
But the traveller, travelling through it,
May not—dare not openly view it;
Never its mysteries are exposed   45
To the weak human eye unclosed;
So wills its King, who hath forbid
The uplifting of the fringed lid;
And thus the sad Soul that here passes
Beholds it but through darkened glasses.   50

By a route obscure and lonely,
Haunted by ill angels only,
Where an Eidolon, name NIGHT,
On a black throne reigns upright,
I have wandered home but newly   55
From this ultimate dim Thule.

                                  1844, 1849

Ulalume[1]—A Ballad

The skies they were ashen and sober;
   The leaves they were crispéd and sere—
   The leaves they were withering and sere:
It was night, in the lonesome October
   Of my most immemorial[2] year: 5
It was hard by the dim lake of Auber,
   In the misty mid region of Weir:[3]—
It was down by the dank tarn[4] of Auber,
   In the ghoul-haunted woodland of Weir.

---

[4]Evil spirits that rob graves.
[5]Legendary golden place (or city) sought by Spanish explorers. Poe thought of Eldorado as "the place of heart's desire."
[1]The name was invented by Poe, and was pronounced "you-la-loom."
[2]Cannot be recalled; here the poet is unable to recall in detail something he recalls only in general.

[3]Auber and Weir may be poetic names invented by Poe. But the composer David François-Esprit Auber (1782–1871) wrote a ballet, *Le Lac des Fées* (1839); and Robert Walter Weir (1803–1889), a Hudson River School painter, depicted romantic haunting scenes in his paintings.
[4]Lake.

Here once, through an alley Titanic,   10
    Of cypress, I roamed with my Soul—
    Of cypress, with Psyche,[5] my Soul.
These were days when my heart was volcanic
    As the scoriac[6] rivers that roll—
    As the lavas that restlessly roll   15
Their sulphurous currents down Yaanek,[7]
    In the ultimate climes of the Pole—
That groan as they roll down Mount Yaanek,
    In the realms of the Boreal[8] Pole.

Our talk had been serious and sober,   20
    But our thoughts they were palsied and sere—
    Our memories were treacherous and sere;
For we knew not the month was October,
    And we marked not the night of the year—
    (Ah, night of all nights in the year!)   25
We noted not the dim lake of Auber,
    (Though once we had journeyed down here)
We remembered not the dank tarn of Auber,
    Nor the ghoul-haunted woodland of Weir.

And now, as the night was senescent,   30
    And star-dials pointed to morn—
    As the star-dials hinted of morn—
At the end of our path a liquescent
    And nebulous lustre was born,
Out of which a miraculous crescent   35
    Arose with a duplicate horn—
Astarte's[9] bediamonded crescent,
    Distinct with its duplicate horn.

And I said—"She is warmer than Dian;[10]
    She rolls through an ether of sighs—   40
    She revels in a region of sighs.
She has seen that the tears are not dry on
    These cheeks where the worm never dies,
And has come past the stars of the Lion,[11]
    To point us the path to the skies—   45
    To the Lethean[12] peace of the skies—
Come up, in despite of the Lion,
    To shine on us with her bright eyes—
Come up, through the lair of the Lion,
    With love in her luminous eyes."   50

But Psyche, uplifting her finger,
    Said—"Sadly this star I mistrust—
    Her pallor I strangely mistrust—
Ah, hasten!—ah, let us not linger!
    Ah, fly!—let us fly!—for we must."   55
In terror she spoke; letting sink her
    Wings till they trailed in the dust—

---

[5]Greek personification of the soul.
[6]Variant of scoriaceous, characterized by slag and cinder-like lava.
[7]Active volcano (invented by Poe).
[8]North Pole, generally, but Poe, following French terminology, refers to the South Pole.

[9]Phoenician goddess of love; cf. Venus.
[10]Diana, goddess of the moon and chastity.
[11]The constellation Leo (Lion), here suggested as a danger in the Zodiac.
[12]Oblivious (from Lethe, the river of forgetfulness in Hades).

In agony sobbed; letting sink her
  Plumes till they trailed in the dust—
  Till they sorrowfully trailed in the dust.   60

I replied—"This is nothing but dreaming.
  Let us on, by this tremulous light!
  Let us bathe in this crystalline light!
Its Sibyllic[13] splendor is beaming
  With Hope and in Beauty to-night—   65
  See!—it flickers up the sky through the night!
Ah, we safely may trust to its gleaming
  And be sure it will lead us aright—
We surely may trust to a gleaming
  That cannot but guide us aright   70
Since it flickers up to Heaven through the night."

Thus I pacified Psyche and kissed her,
  And tempted her out of her gloom—
  And conquered her scruples and gloom;
And we passed to the end of the vista—   75
  But were stopped by the door of a tomb—
  By the door of a legended tomb:—
And I said—"What is written, sweet sister,
  On the door of this legended tomb?"
  She replied—"Ulalume—Ulalume!—   80
  'T is the vault of thy lost Ulalume!"

Then my heart it grew ashen and sober
  As the leaves that were crispéd and sere—
  As the leaves that were withering and sere—
And I cried—"It was surely October,   85
  On *this* very night of last year,
  That I journeyed—I journeyed down here!—
  That I brought a dread burden down here—
  On this night, of all nights in the year,
  Ah, what demon hath tempted me here?   90
Well I know, now, this dim lake of Auber—
  This misty mid region of Weir:—
Well I know, now, this dank tarn of Auber—
  This ghoul-haunted woodland of Weir."

Said we, then—the two, then—"Ah, can it   95
  Have been that the woodlandish ghouls—
  The pitiful, the merciful ghouls,
To bar up our way and to ban it
  From the secret that lies in these wolds[14]—
  From the thing that lies hidden in these wolds—   100
Have drawn up the spectre of a planet
  From the limbo[15] of lunary souls—
This sinfully scintillant[16] planet
  From the Hell of the planetary souls?"

1847, 1849

---

[13]Oracular (from Greek Sibyl, a prophetess).
[14]Forests, woods.
[15]Abode of the unbaptized on the edge of hell.
[16]Glittering, sparkling.

Eldorado[1]

Gaily bedight,
A gallant knight,
In sunshine and in shadow,
Had journeyed long,
Singing a song,   5
In search of Eldorado.

But he grew old—
This knight so bold—
And o'er his heart a shadow
Fell, as he found   10
No spot of ground
That looked like Eldorado.

And, as his strength
Failed him at length
He met a pilgrim shadow—   15
"Shadow," said he,
"Where can it be—
This land of Eldorado?"

"Over the Mountains
Of the Moon,   20
Down the Valley of the Shadow,
Ride, boldly ride,"
The shade replied,—
"If you seek for Eldorado!"

1849

Sonnet to My Mother[1]

Because I feel that, in the Heavens above,
    The angels, whispering to one another,
Can find, among their burning terms of love,
    None so devotional as that of "Mother,"
Therefore by that dear name I long have called you—   5
    You who are more than mother unto me,
And fill my heart of hearts, where Death installed you
    In setting my Virginia's spirit free.
My mother—my own mother, who died early,
    Was but the mother of myself; but you   10
Are mother to the one I loved so dearly,
    And thus are dearer than the mother I knew
By that infinity with which my wife
    Was dearer to my soul than its soul-life.

1849, 1850

---

[1]El Dorado (Spanish for the golden place, or one) was the fabulous city of gold sought by the Spanish explorers. By Poe's day, it had come to be a common name for California because of the discovery of gold there. But of course Poe is using the word symbolically—as "the place of heart's desire."

[1]Poe's actress mother died in 1811, when Poe was an infant. In 1836, Poe married his thirteen-year-old cousin Virginia Clemm, who died in 1847. Her mother, Poe's aunt and mother-in-law, was Maria Poe Clemm.

A Dream
within a Dream[1]

Take this kiss upon the brow!
And, in parting from you now,
Thus much let me avow—
You are not wrong, who deem
That my days have been a dream;   5
Yet if hope has flown away
In a night, or in a day,
In a vision, or in none,
Is it therefore the less *gone*?
All that we see or seem   10
Is but a dream within a dream.

I stand amid the roar
Of a surf-tormented shore,
And I hold within my hand
Grains of the golden sand—   15
How few! yet how they creep
Through my fingers to the deep,
While I weep—while I weep!
O God! can I not grasp
Them with a tighter clasp?   20
O God! can I not save
One from the pitiless wave?
Is *all* that we see or seem
But a dream within a dream?

1849

Annabel Lee

It was many and many a year ago,
   In a kingdom by the sea,
That a maiden there lived whom you may know
   By the name of Annabel Lee;—
And this maiden she lived with no other thought   5
   Than to love and be loved by me.

She was a child and *I* was a child,
   In this kingdom by the sea,
But we loved with a love that was more than love—
   I and my Annabel Lee—   10
With a love that the wingéd seraphs of Heaven
   Coveted her and me.

And this was the reason that, long ago,
   In this kingdom by the sea,

---

[1]In his *Marginalia*, Poe wrote: "It is by no means an irrational fancy that, in a future existence, we shall look upon what we think our present existence, as a dream."

A wind blew out of a cloud by night   15
    Chilling my Annabel Lee;
So that her highborn kinsmen came
    And bore her away from me,
To shut her up, in a sepulchre
    In this kingdom by the sea.   20

The angels, not half so happy in Heaven,
    Went envying her and me:—
Yes! that was the reason (as all men know,
    In this kingdom by the sea)
That the wind came out of the cloud, chilling   25
    And killing my Annabel Lee.

But our love it was stronger by far than the love
    Of those who were older than we—
    Of many far wiser than we—
And neither the angels in Heaven above   30
    Nor the demons down under the sea
Can ever dissever my soul from the soul
    Of the beautiful Annabel Lee:—

For the moon never beams without bringing me dreams
    Of the beautiful Annabel Lee;   35
And the stars never rise but I see the bright eyes
    Of the beautiful Annabel Lee;
And so, all the night-tide, I lie down by the side
Of my darling, my darling, my life and my bride
    In her sepulchre there by the sea—   40
    In her tomb by the side of the sea.[1]

1849

from Tales and Sketches

Ligeia

And the will therein lieth, which dieth not. Who
knoweth the mysteries of the will, with its vigor?
For God is but a great will pervading all things by
nature of its intentness. Man doth not yield himself
to the angels, nor unto death utterly, save only
through the weakness of his feeble will.

JOSEPH GLANVILL[1]

I cannot, for my soul, remember how, when, or even precisely where, I first
became acquainted with the lady Ligeia. Long years have since elapsed, and my

---

[1] The last line originally read: "In her tomb by the sounding sea"; most critics prefer the original version.
[1] Joseph Glanvill (1636–1680), British clergyman and philosopher who believed in the preexistence of souls and in
witchcraft. The quotation appears to have been invented by
Poe.

memory is feeble through much suffering. Or, perhaps, I cannot *now* bring these points to mind, because, in truth, the character of my beloved, her rare learning, her singular yet placid cast of beauty, and the thrilling and enthralling eloquence of her low musical language, made their way into my heart by paces so steadily and stealthily progressive that they have been unnoticed and unknown. Yet I believe that I met her first and most frequently in some large, old, decaying city near the Rhine. Of her family—I have surely heard her speak. That it is of a remotely ancient date cannot be doubted. Ligeia! Ligeia! Buried in studies of a nature more than all else adapted to deaden impressions of the outward world, it is by that sweet word alone—by Ligeia—that I bring before mine eyes in fancy the image of her who is no more. And now, while I write, a recollection flashes upon me that I have *never known* the paternal name of her who was my friend and my betrothed, and who became the partner of my studies, and finally the wife of my bosom. Was it a playful charge on the part of my Ligeia? or was it a test of my strength of affection, that I should institute no inquiries upon this point? or was it rather a caprice of my own—a wildly romantic offering on the shrine of the most passionate devotion? I but indistinctly recall the fact itself—what wonder that I have utterly forgotten the circumstances which originated or attended it? And, indeed, if ever that spirit which is entitled *Romance*—if ever she, the wan and the misty-winged *Ashtophet*[2] of idolatrous Egypt, presided, as they tell, over marriages ill-omened, then most surely she presided over mine.

There is one dear topic, however, on which my memory fails me not. It is the *person* of Ligeia. In stature she was tall, somewhat slender, and, in her latter days, even emaciated. I would in vain attempt to portray the majesty, the quiet ease, of her demeanor, or the incomprehensible lightness and elasticity of her footfall. She came and departed as a shadow. I was never made aware of her entrance into my closed study save by the dear music of her low sweet voice, as she placed her marble hand upon my shoulder. In beauty of face no maiden ever equalled her. It was the radiance of an opium dream—an airy and spirit-lifting vision more wildly divine than the phantasies which hovered about the slumbering souls of the daughters of Delos.[3] Yet her features were not of that regular mould which we have been falsely taught to worship in the classical labors of the heathen. "There is no exquisite beauty," says Bacon, Lord Verulam, speaking truly of all the forms and *genera* of beauty, "without some *strangeness* in the proportion."[4] Yet, although I saw that the features of Ligeia were not of a classic regularity—although I perceived that her loveliness was indeed "exquisite," and felt that there was much of "strangeness" pervading it, yet I have tried in vain to detect the irregularity and to trace home my own perception of "the strange." I examined the contour of the lofty and pale forehead—it was faultless—how cold indeed that word when applied to a majesty so divine!—the skin rivalling the purest ivory, the commanding extent and repose, the gentle prominence of the regions above the temples; and then the raven-black, the glossy, the luxuriant and naturally-curling tresses, setting forth the full force of the Homeric epithet, "hyacinthine!"[5] I looked at the delicate outlines of the nose—and nowhere but in the graceful medallions of the Hebrews had I beheld a similar perfection. There were the same luxurious smoothness of surface, the same scarcely perceptible tendency to the aquiline, the same harmoniously curved nostrils speaking the free spirit. I regarded the sweet mouth. Here was indeed the triumph of all things heavenly—the magnificent

[2]Egyptian version of Ashtoreth, Syrian goddess of love (identified with Astarte and Aphrodite).
[3]An island regarded as the birthplace of Artemis and Apollo; the "Daughters of Delos" may refer to followers of Artemis, goddess of the hunt, fertility, childbirth, and the moon.

[4]From "Of Beauty," an essay by Francis Bacon, Baron Verulam (1561–1626); Bacon wrote *excellent* rather than *exquisite*.
[5]In the Odyssey (VI, 231), Homer compares Odysseus's hair to the hyacinth.

turn of the short upper lip—the soft, voluptuous slumber of the under—the dimples which sported, and the color which spoke—the teeth glancing back, with a brilliancy almost startling, every ray of the holy light which fell upon them in her serene and placid, yet most exultingly radiant of all smiles. I scrutinized the formation of the chin—and here, too, I found the gentleness of breadth, the softness and the majesty, the fullness and the spirituality, of the Greek—the contour which the God Apollo revealed but in a dream, to Cleomenes, the son of the Athenian.[6] And then I peered into the large eyes of Ligeia.

For eyes we have no models in the remotely antique. It might have been, too, that in these eyes of my beloved lay the secret to which Lord Verulam alludes. They were, I must believe, far larger than the ordinary eyes of our own race. They were even fuller than the fullest of the gazelle eyes of the tribe of the valley of Nourjahad.[7] Yet it was only at intervals—in moments of intense excitement— that this peculiarity became more than slightly noticeable in Ligeia. And at such moments was her beauty—in my heated fancy thus it appeared perhaps—the beauty of beings either above or apart from the earth—the beauty of the fabulous Houri[8] of the Turk. The hue of the orbs was the most brilliant of black, and, far over them, hung jetty lashes of great length. The brows, slightly irregular in outline, had the same tint. The "strangeness," however, which I found in the eyes, was of a nature distinct from the formation, or the color, or the brilliancy of the features, and must, after all, be referred to the *expression*. Ah, word of no meaning! behind whose vast latitude of mere sound we intrench our ignorance of so much of the spiritual. The expression of the eyes of Ligeia! How for long hours have I pondered upon it! How have I, through the whole of a midsummer night, struggled to fathom it! What was it—that something more profound than the well of Democritus[9]—which lay far within the pupils of my beloved? What *was* it? I was possessed with a passion to discover. Those eyes! those large, those shining, those divine orbs! they became to me twin stars of Leda,[10] and I to them devoutest of astrologers.

There is no point, among the many incomprehensible anomalies of the science of mind, more thrillingly exciting than the fact—never, I believe, noticed in the schools—that, in our endeavors to recall to memory something long forgotten, we often find ourselves *upon the very verge* of remembrance, without being able, in the end, to remember. And thus how frequently, in my intense scrutiny of Ligeia's eyes, have I felt approaching the full knowledge of their expression—felt it approaching—yet not quite be mine—and so at length entirely depart! And (strange, oh strangest mystery of all!) I found, in the commonest objects of the universe, a circle of analogies to that expression. I mean to say that, subsequently to the period when Ligeia's beauty passed into my spirit, there dwelling as in a shrine, I derived, from many existences in the material world, a sentiment such as I felt always aroused within me by her large and luminous orbs. Yet not the more could I define that sentiment, or analyze, or even steadily view it. I recognized it, let me repeat, sometimes in the survey of a rapidly-growing vine—in the contemplation of a moth, a butterfly, a chrysalis, a stream of running water. I have felt it in the ocean; in the falling of a meteor. I have felt it in the glances of unusually aged people. And there are one or two stars in heaven—(one especially, a star of the sixth magnitude, double and changeable, to be found near the large star in

---

[6]Greek sculptor whose name is on the Venus de Medici (presumably inspired by patron of the arts, Apollo); in fact, he may not have been the sculptor.

[7]See *The History of Nourjahad* (1767), by Mrs. Frances Sheridan (1724–1766); the hero searches the world over for the most beautiful women for his seraglio.

[8]Black-eyed virgin of Muhammadan paradise, endowed with perpetual beauty.

[9]Fifth-century B.C. Greek philosopher, who asserted that truth lies at the bottom of a well.

[10]The two bright stars, Castor and Pollux, in the constellation Gemini, are the twin offspring of Leda, whom Zeus seduced in the form of a swan.

Lyra)[11] in a telescopic scrutiny of which I have been made aware of the feeling. I have been filled with it by certain sounds from stringed instruments, and not unfrequently by passages from books. Among innumerable other instances, I well remember something in a volume of Joseph Glanvill, which (perhaps merely from its quaintness—who shall say?) never failed to inspire me with the sentiment;—"And the will therein lieth, which dieth not. Who knoweth the mysteries of the will, with its vigor? For God is but a great will pervading all things by nature of its intentness. Man doth not yield him to the angels, nor unto death utterly, save only through the weakness of his feeble will."

Length of years, and subsequent reflection, have enabled me to trace, indeed, some remote connection between this passage in the English moralist and a portion of the character of Ligeia. An *intensity* in thought, action, or speech, was possibly, in her, a result, or at least an index, of that gigantic volition which, during our long intercourse, failed to give other and more immediate evidence of its existence. Of all the women whom I have ever known, she, the outwardly calm, the ever-placid Ligeia, was the most violently a prey to the tumultuous vultures of stern passion. And of such passion I could form no estimate, save by the miraculous expansion of those eyes which at once so delighted and appalled me—by the almost magical melody, modulation, distinctness and placidity of her very low voice—and by the fierce energy (rendered doubly effective by contrast with her manner of utterance) of the wild words which she habitually uttered.

I have spoken of the learning of Ligeia: it was immense—such as I have never known in woman. In the classical tongues was she deeply proficient, and as far as my own acquaintance extended in regard to the modern dialects of Europe, I have never known her at fault. Indeed upon any theme of the most admired, because simply the most abstruse of the boasted erudition of the academy, have I *ever* found Ligeia at fault? How singularly—how thrillingly, this one point in the nature of my wife has forced itself, at this late period only, upon my attention! I said her knowledge was such as I have never known in woman—but where breathes the man who has traversed, and successfully, *all* the wide areas of moral, physical, and mathematical science? I saw not then what I now clearly perceive, that the acquisitions of Ligeia were gigantic, were astounding, yet I was sufficiently aware of her infinite supremacy to resign myself, with a child-like confidence, to her guidance through the chaotic world of metaphysical investigation at which I was most busily occupied during the earlier years of our marriage. With how vast a triumph—with how vivid a delight—with how much of all that is ethereal in hope—did I *feel*, as she bent over me in studies but little sought—but less known—that delicious vista by slow degrees expanding before me, down whose long, gorgeous, and all untrodden path, I might at length pass onward to the goal of a wisdom too divinely precious not to be forbidden!

How poignant, then, must have been the grief with which, after some years, I beheld my well-grounded expectations take wings to themselves and fly away! Without Ligeia I was but as a child groping benighted. Her presence, her readings alone, rendered vividly luminous the many mysteries of the transcendentalism in which we were immersed. Wanting the radiant lustre of her eyes, letters, lambent and golden, grew duller than Saturnian lead.[12] And now those eyes shone less and less frequently upon the pages over which I pored. Ligeia grew ill. The wild eyes blazed with a too—too glorious effulgence; the pale fingers became of the transparent waxen hue of the grave, and the blue veins upon the lofty forehead swelled and sank impetuously with the tides of the most gentle emotion. I saw that

---

[11]A constellation (the Harp) containing a bright star, Vega, and a "changeable" star, Epsilon Lyrae, which changes in brightness frequently during an hour.

[12] In alchemy, Saturn was a technical name for lead; hence to be "Saturnian" is to be dull or without sparkle.

she must die—and I struggled desperately in spirit with the grim Azrael.[13] And the struggles of the passionate wife were, to my astonishment, even more energetic than my own. There had been much in her stern nature to impress me with the belief that, to her, death would have come without its terrors;—but not so. Words are impotent to convey any just idea of the fierceness of resistance with which she wrestled with the Shadow. I groaned in anguish at the pitiable spectacle. I would have soothed—I would have reasoned; but, in the intensity of her wild desire for life,—for life—*but* for life—solace and reason were alike the uttermost of folly. Yet not until the last instance, amid the most convulsive writhings of her fierce spirit, was shaken the external placidity of her demeanor. Her voice grew more gentle—grew more low—yet I would not wish to dwell upon the wild meaning of the quietly uttered words. My brain reeled as I hearkened, entranced, to a melody more than mortal—to assumptions and aspirations which mortality had never before known.

That she loved me I should not have doubted; and I might have been easily aware that, in a bosom such as hers, love would have reigned no ordinary passion. But in death only, was I fully impressed with the strength of her affection. For long hours, detaining my hand, would she pour out before me the overflowing of a heart whose more than passionate devotion amounted to idolatry. How had I deserved to be so blessed by such confessions?—how had I deserved to be so cursed with the removal of my beloved in the hour of her making them? But upon this subject I cannot bear to dilate. Let me say only, that in Ligeia's more than womanly abandonment to a love, alas! all unmerited, all unworthily bestowed, I at length recognized the principle of her longing with so wildly earnest a desire for the life which was now fleeing so rapidly away. It is this wild longing—it is this eager vehemence of desire for life—*but* for life—that I have no power to portray—no utterance capable of expressing.

At high noon of the night in which she departed, beckoning me, peremptorily, to her side, she bade me repeat certain verses composed by herself not many days before. I obeyed her.—They were these:

> Lo! 'tis a gala night
>   Within the lonesome latter years!
> An angel throng, bewinged, bedight[14]
>   In veils, and drowned in tears,
> Sit in a theatre, to see
>   A play of hopes and fears,
> While the orchestra breathes fitfully
>   The music of the spheres.
>
> Mimes,[15] in the form of God on high,
>   Mutter and mumble low,
> And hither and thither fly—
>   Mere puppets they, who come and go
> At bidding of vast formless things
>   That shift the scenery to and fro,
> Flapping from out their Condor wings
>   Invisible Wo!
>
> That motley drama!—oh, be sure
>   It shall not be forgot!
> With its Phantom chased forevermore,
>   By a crowd that seize it not,

---

[13]Muhammadan angel of death.
[14]Bedecked.
[15]Pantomimists, mimes.

Through a circle that ever returneth in
  To the self-same spot,
And much of Madness and more of Sin,
  And Horror the soul of the plot.

But see, amid the mimic rout,
  A crawling shape intrude!
A blood-red thing that writhes from out
  The scenic solitude!
It writhes!—it writhes!—with mortal pangs
  The mimes become its food,
And the seraphs sob at vermin fangs
  In human gore imbued.

Out—out are the lights—out all!
  And over each quivering form,
The curtain, a funeral pall,
  Comes down with the rush of a storm,
And the angels, all pallid and wan,
  Uprising, unveiling, affirm
That the play is the tragedy, "Man,"
  And its hero the Conqueror Worm.

"O God!" half shrieked Ligeia, leaping to her feet and extending her arms aloft with a spasmodic movement, as I made an end of these lines—"O God! O Divine Father!—shall these things be undeviatingly so?—shall this Conqueror be not once conquered? Are we not part and parcel in Thee? Who—who knoweth the mysteries of the will with its vigor? Man doth not yield him to the angels, *nor unto death utterly,* save only through the weakness of his feeble will."

And now, as if exhausted with emotion, she suffered her white arms to fall, and returned solemnly to her bed of Death. And as she breathed her last sighs, there came mingled with them a low murmur from her lips. I bent to them my ear and distinguished, again, the concluding words of the passage in Glanvill—"*Man doth not yield him to the angels, nor unto death utterly, save only through the weakness of his feeble will.*"

She died;—and I, crushed into the very dust with sorrow, could no longer endure the lonely desolation of my dwelling in the dim and decaying city by the Rhine. I had no lack of what the world calls wealth. Ligeia had brought me far more, very far more than ordinarily falls to the lot of mortals. After a few months, therefore, of weary and aimless wandering, I purchased, and put in some repair, an abbey, which I shall not name, in one of the wildest and least frequented portions of fair England. The gloomy and dreary grandeur of the building, the almost savage aspect of the domain, the many melancholy and time-honored memories connected with both, had much in unison with the feelings of utter abandonment which had driven me into that remote and unsocial region of the country. Yet although the external abbey, with its verdant decay hanging about it, suffered but little alteration, I gave way, with a child-like perversity, and perchance with a faint hope of alleviating my sorrows, to a display of more than regal magnificence within. For such follies, even in childhood, I had imbibed a taste, and now they came back to me as if in the dotage of grief. Alas, I feel how much even of incipient madness might have been discovered in the gorgeous and fantastic draperies, in the solemn carvings of Egypt, in the wild cornices and furniture, in the Bedlam[16] patterns of the carpets of tufted gold! I had became a bounden

[16]Insane (after the London asylum).

slave in the trammels[17] of opium, and my labors and my orders had taken a coloring from my dreams. But these absurdities I must not pause to detail. Let me speak only of that one chamber, ever accursed, whither in a moment of mental alienation, I led from the altar as my bride—as the successor of the unforgotten Ligeia—the fair-haired and blue-eyed Lady Rowena Trevanion, of Tremaine.

There is no individual portion of the architecture and decoration of that bridal chamber which is not now visibly before me. Where were the souls of the haughty family of the bride, when, through thirst of gold, they permitted to pass the threshold of an apartment *so* bedecked, a maiden and a daughter so beloved? I have said that I minutely remember the details of the chamber—yet I am sadly forgetful on topics of deep moment—and here there was no system, no keeping, in the fantastic display, to take hold upon the memory. The room lay in a high turret of the castellated abbey, was pentagonal in shape, and of capacious size. Occupying the whole southern face of the pentagon was the sole window—an immense sheet of unbroken glass from Venice—a single pane, and tinted of a leaden hue, so that the rays of either the sun or moon, passing through it, fell with a ghastly lustre on the objects within. Over the upper portion of this huge window, extended the trellice-work of an aged vine, which clambered up the massy walls of the turret. The ceiling, of gloomy-looking oak, was excessively lofty, vaulted, and elaborately fretted with the wildest and most grotesque specimens of a semi-Gothic, semi-Druidical[18] device. From out the most central recess of this melancholy vaulting, depended, by a single chain of gold with long links, a huge censer of the same metal, Saracenic in pattern,[19] and with many perforations so contrived that there writhed in and out of them, as if endued with a serpent vitality, a continual succession of parti-colored fires.

Some few ottomans and golden candelabra, of Eastern figure, were in various stations about—and there was the couch, too—the bridal couch—of an Indian model, and low, and sculptured of solid ebony, with a pall-like canopy above. In each of the angles of the chamber stood on end a gigantic sarcophagus[20] of black granite, from the tombs of the kings over against Luxor,[21] with their aged lids full of immemorial sculpture. But in the draping of the apartment lay, alas! the chief phantasy of all. The lofty walls, gigantic in height—even unproportionably so— were hung from summit to foot, in vast folds, with a heavy and massive-looking tapestry—tapestry of a material which was found alike as a carpet on the floor, as a covering for the ottomans and the ebony bed, as a canopy for the bed, and as the gorgeous volutes[22] of the curtains which partially shaded the window. The material was the richest cloth of gold. It was spotted all over, at irregular intervals, with arabesque figures, about a foot in diameter, and wrought upon the cloth in patterns of the most jetty black. But these figures partook of the true character of the arabesque,[23] only when regarded from a single point of view. By a contrivance now common, and indeed traceable to a very remote period of antiquity, they were made changeable in aspect. To one entering the room, they bore the appearance of simple monstrosities; but upon a farther advance, this appearance gradually departed; and step by step, as the visiter moved his station in the chamber, he saw himself surrounded by an endless succession of the ghastly forms which belong to the superstition of the Norman,[24] or arise in the guilty slumbers of the monk. The phantasmagoric effect was vastly heightened by the artificial introduc-

---

[17]Shackles.

[18]I.e., half-Christian (as the soaring Gothic) and half-pagan (grotesque designs of the pre-Christian priest in England).

[19]Arabesque in design (complex intertwining of foliage, flowers, etc.).

[20]Tomb, usually elaborately carved.

[21]Ancient city in Egypt, site of important ruins.

[22]Whorls, or spiral; twisting form.

[23]Intricate interlinking and intertwining.

[24]The Normans were Viking seagoing conquerors whose surviving sagas indicate they imagined the existence of the most frightening beasts and dragons.

tion of a strong continual current of wind behind the draperies—giving a hideous and uneasy animation to the whole.

In halls such as these—in a bridal chamber such as this—I passed, with the Lady of Tremaine, the unhallowed hours of the first month of our marriage— passed them with but little disquietude. That my wife dreaded the fierce moodiness of my temper—that she shunned me and loved me but little—I could not help perceiving, but it gave me rather pleasure than otherwise. I loathed her with a hatred belonging more to demon than to man. My memory flew back, (oh, with what intensity of regret!) to Ligeia, the beloved, the august, the beautiful, the entombed. I revelled in recollections of her purity, of her wisdom, of her lofty, her ethereal nature, of her passionate, her idolatrous love. Now, then, did my spirit fully and freely burn with more than all the fires of her own. In the excitement of my opium dreams (for I was habitually fettered in the shackles of the drug) I would call aloud upon her name, during the silence of the night, or among the sheltered recesses of the glens by day, as if, through the wild eagerness, the solemn passion, the consuming ardor of my longing for the departed, I could restore her to the pathway she had abandoned—ah, *could* it be forever?—upon the earth.

About the commencement of the second month of the marriage, the Lady Rowena was attacked with sudden illness, from which her recovery was slow. The fever which consumed her rendered her nights uneasy; and in her perturbed state of half-slumber, she spoke of sounds, and of motions, in and about the chamber of the turret, which I concluded had no origin save in the distemper of her fancy, or perhaps in the phantasmagoric influences of the chamber itself. She became at length convalescent—finally well. Yet but a brief period elapsed, ere a second more violent disorder again threw her upon a bed of suffering; and from this attack her frame, at all times feeble, never altogether recovered. Her illnesses were, after this epoch, of alarming character, and of more alarming recurrence, defying alike the knowledge and the great exertions of her physicians. With the increase of the chronic disease which had thus, apparently, taken too sure hold upon her constitution to be eradicated by human means, I could not fail to observe a similar increase in the nervous irritation of her temperament, and in her excitability by trivial causes of fear. She spoke again, and now more frequently and pertinaciously, of the sounds—of the slight sounds—and of the unusual motions among the tapestries, to which she had formerly alluded.

One night, near the closing in of September, she pressed this distressing subject with more than usual emphasis upon my attention. She had just awakened from an unquiet slumber, and I had been watching, with feelings half of anxiety, half of a vague terror, the workings of her emaciated countenance. I sat by the side of her ebony bed, upon one of the ottomans of India. She partly arose, and spoke, in an earnest low whisper, of sounds which she *then* heard, but which I could not hear—of motions which she *then* saw, but which I could not perceive. The wind was rushing hurriedly behind the tapestries, and I wished to show her (what, let me confess it, I could not *all* believe) that those almost inarticulate breathings, and those very gentle variations of the figures upon the wall, were but the natural effects of that customary rushing of the wind. But a deadly pallor, over-spreading her face, had proved to me that my exertions to reassure her would be fruitless. She appeared to be fainting, and no attendants were within call. I remembered where was deposited a decanter of light wine which had been ordered by her physicians, and hastened across the chamber to procure it. But, as I stepped beneath the light of the censer, two circumstances of a startling nature attracted my attention. I had felt that some palpable although invisible object had passed lightly by my person; and I saw that there lay upon the golden carpet, in the very middle of the rich lustre thrown from the censer, a shadow—a faint, indefinite shadow of angelic aspect—such as might be fancied for the shadow of a shade. But I was wild with the excitement of an immoderate dose of opium, and heeded these things but little, nor spoke of them to Rowena. Having found the wine, I recrossed the chamber, and poured out a goblet-ful, which I held to the lips of the fainting lady. She had now partially recovered, however, and took the vessel herself, while I sank upon an ottoman near me, with my eyes fastened upon her person. It was then that I became distinctly aware of a gentle foot-fall upon the carpet, and near the couch; and in a second thereafter, as Rowena was in the act of raising the wine to her lips, I saw, or may have dreamed that I saw, fall within the goblet, as if from some invisible spring in the atmosphere of the room, three or four large drops of a brilliant and ruby colored fluid. If this I saw—not so Rowena. She swallowed the wine unhesitatingly, and I forbore to speak to her of a circumstance which must, after all, I considered, have been but the suggestion of a vivid imagination, rendered morbidly active by the terror of the lady, by the opium, and by the hour.

Yet I cannot conceal it from my own perception that, immediately subsequent to the fall of the ruby-drops, a rapid change for the worse took place in the disorder of my wife; so that, on the third subsequent night, the hands of her menials prepared her for the tomb, and on the fourth, I sat alone, with her shrouded body, in that fantastic chamber which had received her as my bride. Wild visions, opium-engendered, flitted, shadow-like, before me. I gazed with unquiet eye upon the sarcophagi in the angles of the room, upon the varying figures of the drapery, and upon the writhing of the parti-colored fires in the censer overhead. My eyes then fell, as I called to mind the circumstances of a former night, to the spot beneath the glare of the censer where I had seen the faint traces of the shadow. It was there, however, no longer; and breathing with greater freedom, I turned my glances to the pallid and rigid figure upon the bed. Then rushed upon me a thousand memories of Ligeia—and then came back upon my heart, with the turbulent violence of a flood, the whole of that unutterable wo with which I had regarded *her* thus enshrouded. The night waned; and still, with a bosom full of bitter thoughts of the one only and supremely beloved, I remained gazing upon the body of Rowena.

It might have been midnight, or perhaps earlier, or later, for I had taken no note of time, when a sob, low, gentle, but very distinct, startled me from my revery. I *felt* that it came from the bed of ebony—the bed of death. I listened in an agony of superstitious terror—but there was no repetition of the sound. I strained my vision to detect any motion in the corpse—but there was not the slightest perceptible. Yet I could not have been deceived. I *had* heard the noise, however faint, and my soul was awakened within me. I resolutely and perseveringly kept my attention riveted upon the body. Many minutes elapsed before any circumstance occurred tending to throw light upon the mystery. At length it became evident that a slight, a very feeble, and barely noticeable tinge of color had flushed up within the cheeks, and along the sunken small veins of the eyelids. Through a species of unutterable horror and awe, for which the language of mortality has no sufficiently energetic expression, I felt my heart cease to beat, my limbs grow rigid where I sat. Yet a sense of duty finally operated to restore my self-possession. I could no longer doubt that we had been precipitate in our preparations—that Rowena still lived. It was necessary that some immediate exertion be made; yet the turret was altogether apart from the portion of the abbey tenanted by the servants—there were none within call—I had no means of summoning them to my aid without leaving the room for many minutes—and this I could not venture to do. I therefore struggled alone in my endeavors to call back the spirit still hovering. In a short period it was certain, however, that a relapse had taken place; the color disappeared from both eyelid and cheek, leaving a wanness even more than that of marble; the lips became doubly shrivelled and pinched up in the ghastly expression of death; a repulsive clamminess and coldness overspread rapidly the surface of the body; and all the usual rigorous stiffness immediately supervened. I fell back with a shudder upon the couch from which I had been so startlingly aroused, and again gave myself up to passionate waking visions of Ligeia.

An hour thus elapsed when (could it be possible?) I was a second time aware of some vague sound issuing from the region of the bed. I listened—in extremity of horror. The sound came again—it was a sigh. Rushing to the corpse, I saw—distinctly saw—a tremor upon the lips. In a minute afterward they relaxed, disclosing a bright line of the pearly teeth. Amazement now struggled in my bosom with the profound awe which had hitherto reigned there alone. I felt that my vision grew dim, that my reason wandered, and it was only by a violent effort that I at length succeeded in nerving myself to the task which duty thus once more had pointed out. There was now a partial glow upon the forehead and upon the cheek and throat; a perceptible warmth pervaded the whole frame; there was even a slight pulsation at the heart. The lady *lived;* and with redoubled ardor I betook myself to the task of restoration. I chafed and bathed the temples and the hands, and used every exertion which experience, and no little medical reading, could suggest. But in vain. Suddenly, the color fled, the pulsation ceased, the lips resumed the expression of the dead, and, in an instant afterward, the whole body took upon itself the icy chilliness, the livid hue, the intense rigidity, the sunken outline, and all the loathsome peculiarities of that which has been, for many days, a tenant of the tomb.

And again I sunk into visions of Ligeia—and again, (what marvel that I shudder while I write?) *again* there reached my ears a low sob from the region of the ebony bed. But why shall I minutely detail the unspeakable horrors of that night? Why shall I pause to relate how, time after time, until near the period of the gray dawn, this hideous drama of revivification was repeated; how each terrific relapse was only into a sterner and apparently more irredeemable death; how each agony wore the aspect of a struggle with some invisible foe; and how each struggle was succeeded by I know not what of wild change in the personal appearance of the corpse? Let me hurry to a conclusion.

The greater part of the fearful night had worn away, and she who had been dead, once again stirred—and now more vigorously than hitherto, although arousing from a dissolution more appalling in its utter hopelessness than any. I had long ceased to struggle or to move, and remained sitting rigidly upon the ottoman, a helpless prey to a whirl of violent emotions, of which extreme awe was perhaps the least terrible, the least consuming. The corpse, I repeat, stirred, and now more vigorously than before. The hues of life flushed up with unwonted energy into the countenance—the limbs relaxed—and, save that the eyelids were yet pressed heavily together, and that the bandages and draperies of the grave still imparted their charnel[25] character to the figure, I might have dreamed that Rowena had indeed shaken off, utterly, the fetters of Death. But if this idea was not, even then, altogether adopted, I could at least doubt no longer, when, arising from the bed, tottering, with feeble steps, with closed eyes, and with the manner of one bewildered in a dream, the thing that was enshrouded advanced bodily and palpably into the middle of the apartment.

I trembled not—I stirred not—for a crowd of unutterable fancies connected with the air, the stature, the demeanor of the figure, rushing hurriedly through my brain, had paralyzed—had chilled me into stone. I stirred not—but gazed

---

[25]Deathlike.

upon the apparition. There was a mad disorder in my thoughts—a tumult unappeasable. Could it, indeed, be the *living* Rowena who confronted me? Could it indeed be Rowena *at all*—the fair-haired, the blue-eyed Lady Rowena Trevanion of Tremaine? Why, *why* should I doubt it? The bandage lay heavily about the mouth—but then might it not be the mouth of the breathing Lady of Tremaine? And the cheeks—there were the roses as in her noon of life—yes, these might indeed be the fair cheeks of the living Lady of Tremaine. And the chin, with its dimples, as in health, might it not be hers?—but *had she then grown taller since her malady?* What inexpressible madness seized me with that thought? One bound, and I had reached her feet! Shrinking from my touch, she let fall from her head the ghastly cerements[26] which had confined it, and there streamed forth, into the rushing atmosphere of the chamber, huge masses of long and dishevelled hair: *it was blacker than the wings of the midnight!* And now slowly opened *the eyes* of the figure which stood before me. "Here then, at least," I shrieked aloud, "can I never—can I never be mistaken—these are the full, and the black, and the wild eyes—of my lost love—of the lady—of the LADY LIGEIA!"

1838

The Fall of the House of Usher

Son cœur est un luth suspendu;
Sitôt qu'on le touche il résonne.
De Béranger[1]

During the whole of a dull, dark, and soundless day in the autumn of the year, when the clouds hung oppressively low in the heavens, I had been passing alone, on horseback, through a singularly dreary tract of country; and at length found myself, as the shades of the evening drew on, within view of the melancholy House of Usher. I know not how it was—but, with the first glimpse of the building, a sense of insufferable gloom pervaded my spirit. I say insufferable; for the feeling was unrelieved by any of that half-pleasurable, because poetic, sentiment, with which the mind usually receives even the sternest natural images of the desolate or terrible. I looked upon the scene before me—upon the mere house, and the simple landscape features of the domain—upon the bleak walls—upon the vacant eye-like windows—upon a few rank sedges—and upon a few white trunks of decayed trees—with an utter depression of soul which I can compare to no earthly sensation more properly than to the after-dream of the reveller upon opium—the bitter lapse into every-day life—the hideous dropping off of the veil. There was an iciness, a sinking, a sickening of the heart—an unredeemed dreariness of thought which no goading of the imagination could torture into aught of the sublime. What was it—I paused to think—what was it that so unnerved me in the contemplation of the House of Usher? It was a mystery all insoluble; nor could I grapple with the shadowy fancies that crowded upon me as I pondered. I was forced to fall back upon the unsatisfactory conclusion, that while, beyond doubt, there *are* combinations of very simple natural objects which have the power of thus affecting us, still the analysis of this power lies among considerations beyond our depth. It was possible, I reflected, that a mere different arrangement of

---

[26]Shrouds.
[1]"His heart is a suspended lute; as soon as it is touched, it resonates"; from "Le Refus" (1831) by Pierre-Jean de Bé- ranger (1780–1857), French poet. Poe changed "My heart" to "His heart."

the particulars of the scene, of the details of the picture, would be sufficient to modify, or perhaps to annihilate its capacity for sorrowful impression; and, acting upon this idea, I reined my horse to the precipitous brink of a black and lurid tarn[2] that lay in unruffled lustre by the dwelling, and gazed down—but with a shudder even more thrilling than before—upon the remodelled and inverted images of the gray sedge, and the ghastly tree-stems, and the vacant and eye-like windows.

Nevertheless, in this mansion of gloom I now proposed to myself a sojourn of some weeks. Its proprietor, Roderick Usher, had been one of my boon companions in boyhood; but many years had elapsed since our last meeting. A letter, however, had lately reached me in a distant part of the country—a letter from him—which, in its wildly importunate nature, had admitted of no other than a personal reply. The MS. gave evidence of nervous agitation. The writer spoke of acute bodily illness—of a mental disorder which oppressed him—and of an earnest desire to see me, as his best, and indeed his only personal friend, with a view of attempting, by the cheerfulness of my society, some alleviation of his malady. It was the manner in which all this, and much more, was said—it was the apparent *heart* that went with his request—which allowed me no room for hesitation; and I accordingly obeyed forthwith what I still considered a very singular summons.

Although, as boys, we had been even intimate associates, yet I really knew little of my friend. His reserve had been always excessive and habitual. I was aware, however, that his very ancient family had been noted, time out of mind, for a peculiar sensibility of temperament, displaying itself, through long ages, in many works of exalted art, and manifested, of late, in repeated deeds of munificent yet unobtrusive charity, as well as in a passionate devotion to the intricacies, perhaps even more than to the orthodox and easily recognisable beauties, of musical science. I had learned, too, the very remarkable fact, that the stem of the Usher race, all time-honored as it was, had put forth, at no period, any enduring branch; in other words, that the entire family lay in the direct line of descent, and had always, with very trifling and very temporary variation, so lain. It was this deficiency, I considered, while running over in thought the perfect keeping of the character of the premises with the accredited character of the people, and while speculating upon the possible influence which the one, in the long lapse of centuries, might have exercised upon the other—it was this deficiency, perhaps, of collateral issue, and the consequent undeviating transmission, from sire to son, of the patrimony with the name, which had, at length, so identified the two as to merge the original title of the estate in the quaint and equivocal appellation of the "House of Usher"—an appellation which seemed to include, in the minds of the peasantry who used it, both the family and the family mansion.

I have said that the sole effect of my somewhat childish experiment—that of looking down within the tarn—had been to deepen the first singular impression. There can be no doubt that the consciousness of the rapid increase of my superstition—for why should I not so term it?—served mainly to accelerate the increase itself. Such, I have long known, is the paradoxical law of all sentiments having terror as a basis. And it might have been for this reason only, that, when I again uplifted my eyes to the house itself, from its image in the pool, there grew in my mind a strange fancy—a fancy so ridiculous, indeed, that I but mention it to show the vivid force of the sensations which oppressed me. I had so worked upon my imagination as really to believe that about the whole mansion and domain there hung an atmosphere peculiar to themselves and their immediate vicinity—an atmosphere which had no affinity with the air of heaven, but which had

---

[2]Small pond or lake.

reeked up from the decayed trees, and the gray wall and the silent tarn—a pestilent and mystic vapor, dull, sluggish, faintly discernible, and leaden-hued.

Shaking off from my spirit what *must* have been a dream, I scanned more narrowly the real aspect of the building. Its principal feature seemed to be that of an excessive antiquity. The discoloration of ages had been great. Minute fungi overspread the whole exterior, hanging in a fine tangled web-work from the eaves. Yet all this was apart from any extraordinary dilapidation. No portion of the masonry had fallen; and there appeared to be a wild inconsistency between its still perfect adaptation of parts, and the crumbling condition of the individual stones. In this there was much that reminded me of the specious totality of old wood-work which has rotted for long years in some neglected vault, with no disturbance from the breath of the external air. Beyond this indication of extensive decay, however, the fabric gave little token of instability. Perhaps the eye of a scrutinizing observer might have discovered a barely perceptible fissure, which, extending from the roof of the building in front, made its way down the wall in a zigzag direction, until it became lost in the sullen waters of the tarn.

Noticing these things, I rode over a short causeway to the house. A servant in waiting took my horse, and I entered the Gothic archway of the hall. A valet, of stealthy step, thence conducted me, in silence, through many dark and intricate passages in my progress to the *studio* of his master. Much that I encountered on the way contributed, I know not how, to heighten the vague sentiments of which I have already spoken. While the objects around me—while the carvings of the ceilings, the sombre tapestries of the walls, the ebon blackness of the floors, and the phantasmagoric[3] armorial trophies which rattled as I strode, were but matters to which, or to such as which, I had been accustomed from my infancy—while I hesitated not to acknowledge how familiar was all this—I still wondered to find how unfamiliar were the fancies which ordinary images were stirring up. On one of the staircases, I met the physician of the family. His countenance, I thought, wore a mingled expression of low cunning and perplexity. He accosted me with trepidation and passed on. The valet now threw open a door and ushered me into the presence of his master.

The room in which I found myself was very large and lofty. The windows were long, narrow, and pointed, and at so vast a distance from the black oaken floor as to be altogether inaccessible from within. Feeble gleams of encrimsoned light made their way through the trellised panes, and served to render sufficiently distinct the more prominent objects around; the eye, however, struggled in vain to reach the remoter angles of the chamber, or the recesses of the vaulted and fretted ceiling. Dark draperies hung upon the walls. The general furniture was profuse, comfortless, antique, and tattered. Many books and musical instruments lay scattered about, but failed to give any vitality to the scene. I felt that I breathed an atmosphere of sorrow. An air of stern, deep, and irredeemable gloom hung over and pervaded all.

Upon my entrance, Usher arose from a sofa on which he had been lying at full length, and greeted me with a vivacious warmth which had much in it, I at first thought, of an overdone cordiality—of the constrained effort of the *ennuyé*[4] man of the world. A glance, however, at his countenance, convinced me of his perfect sincerity. We sat down; and for some moments, while he spoke not, I gazed upon him with a feeling half of pity, half of awe. Surely, man had never before so terribly altered, in so brief a period, as had Roderick Usher! It was with difficulty that I could bring myself to admit the identity of the wan being before me with the companion of my early boyhood. Yet the character of his face had been at all

---

[3]Evoking a series of rapidly changing bizarre images.
[4]"Bored" (French).

times remarkable. A cadaverousness of complexion; an eye large, liquid, and luminous beyond comparison; lips somewhat thin and very pallid, but of a surpassingly beautiful curve; a nose of a delicate Hebrew model, but with a breadth of nostril unusual in similar formations; a finely moulded chin, speaking, in its want of prominence, of a want of moral energy; hair of a more than web-like softness and tenuity; these features, with an inordinate expansion above the regions of the temple, made up altogether a countenance not easily to be forgotten. And now in the mere exaggeration of the prevailing character of these features, and of the expression they were wont to convey, lay so much of change that I doubted to whom I spoke. The now ghastly pallor of the skin, and the now miraculous lustre of the eye, above all things startled and even awed me. The silken hair, too, had been suffered to grow all unheeded, and as, in its wild gossamer texture, it floated rather than fell about the face, I could not, even with effort, connect its Arabesque expression with any idea of simple humanity.

In the manner of my friend I was at once struck with an incoherence—an inconsistency; and I soon found this to arise from a series of feeble and futile struggles to overcome an habitual trepidancy—an excessive nervous agitation. For something of this nature I had indeed been prepared, no less by his letter, than by reminiscences of certain boyish traits, and by conclusions deduced from his peculiar physical conformation and temperament. His action was alternately vivacious and sullen. His voice varied rapidly from a tremulous indecision (when the animal spirits seemed utterly in abeyance) to that species of energetic concision—that abrupt, weighty, unhurried, and hollow-sounding enunciation—that leaden, self-balanced and perfectly modulated guttural utterance, which may be observed in the lost drunkard, or the irreclaimable eater of opium, during the periods of his most intense excitement.

It was thus that he spoke of the object of my visit, of his earnest desire to see me, and of the solace he expected me to afford him. He entered, at some length, into what he conceived to be the nature of his malady. It was, he said, a constitutional and a family evil, and one for which he despaired to find a remedy—a mere nervous affection, he immediately added, which would undoubtedly soon pass. It displayed itself in a host of unnatural sensations. Some of these, as he detailed them, interested and bewildered me; although, perhaps, the terms, and the general manner of the narration had their weight. He suffered much from a morbid acuteness of the senses; the most insipid food was alone endurable; he could wear only garments of certain texture; the odors of all flowers were oppressive; his eyes were tortured by even a faint light; and there were but peculiar sounds, and these from stringed instruments, which did not inspire him with horror.

To an anomalous species of terror I found him a bounden slave. "I shall perish," said he, "I *must* perish in this deplorable folly. Thus, thus, and not otherwise, shall I be lost. I dread the events of the future, not in themselves, but in their results. I shudder at the thought of any, even the most trivial, incident, which may operate upon this intolerable agitation of soul. I have, indeed, no abhorrence of danger, except in its absolute effect—in terror. In this unnerved—in this pitiable condition—I feel that the period will sooner or later arrive when I must abandon life and reason together, in some struggle with the grim phantasm, FEAR."

I learned, moreover, at intervals, and through broken and equivocal hints, another singular feature of his mental condition. He was enchained by certain superstitious impressions in regard to the dwelling which he tenanted, and whence, for many years, he had never ventured forth—in regard to an influence whose supposititious force was conveyed in terms too shadowy here to be re-stated—an influence which some peculiarities in the mere form and substance of his family mansion, had, by dint of long sufferance, he said, obtained over his spirit—an effect which the *physique* of the gray walls and turrets, and of the dim tarn into which they all looked down, had, at length, brought about upon the *morale* of his existence.

He admitted, however, although with hesitation, that much of the peculiar gloom which thus afflicted him could be traced to a more natural and far more palpable origin—to the severe and long-continued illness—indeed to the evidently approaching dissolution—of a tenderly beloved sister—his sole companion for long years—his last and only relative on earth. "Her decease," he said, with a bitterness which I can never forget, "would leave him (him the hopeless and the frail) the last of the ancient race of the Ushers." While he spoke, the lady Madeline (for so was she called) passed slowly through a remote portion of the apartment, and, without having noticed my presence, disappeared. I regarded her with an utter astonishment not unmingled with dread—and yet I found it impossible to account for such feelings. A sensation of stupor oppressed me, as my eyes followed her retreating steps. When a door, at length, closed upon her, my glance sought instinctively and eagerly the countenance of the brother—but he had buried his face in his hands, and I could only perceive that a far more than ordinary wanness had overspread the emaciated fingers through which trickled many passionate tears.

The disease of the lady Madeline had long baffled the skill of her physicians. A settled apathy, a gradual wasting away of the person, and frequent although transient affections of a partially cataleptical[5] character, were the unusual diagnosis. Hitherto she had steadily borne up against the pressure of her malady, and had not betaken herself finally to bed; but, on the closing in of the evening of my arrival at the house, she succumbed (as her brother told me at night with inexpressible agitation) to the prostrating power of the destroyer; and I learned that the glimpse I had obtained of her person would thus probably be the last I should obtain—that the lady, at least while living, would be seen by me no more.

For several days ensuing, her name was unmentioned by either Usher or myself; and during this period I was busied in earnest endeavors to alleviate the melancholy of my friend. We painted and read together; or I listened, as if in a dream, to the wild improvisations of his speaking guitar. And thus, as a closer and still closer intimacy admitted me more unreservedly into the recesses of his spirit, the more bitterly did I perceive the futility of all attempt at cheering a mind from which darkness, as if an inherent positive quality, poured forth upon all objects of the moral and physical universe, in one unceasing radiation of gloom.

I shall ever bear about me a memory of the many solemn hours I thus spent alone with the master of the House of Usher. Yet I should fail in any attempt to convey an idea of the exact character of the studies, or of the occupations, in which he involved me, or led me the way. An excited and highly distempered ideality threw a sulphureous lustre over all. His long improvised dirges will ring forever in my ears. Among other things, I hold painfully in mind a certain singular perversion and amplification of the wild air of the last waltz of Von Weber.[6] From the paintings over which his elaborate fancy brooded, and which grew, touch by touch, into vaguenesses at which I shuddered the more thrillingly, because I shuddered knowing not why;—from these paintings (vivid as their images now are before me) I would in vain endeavor to educe more than a small portion which should lie within the compass of merely written words. By the utter simplicity, by the nakedness of his designs, he arrested and overawed attention. If ever mortal

---

[5]Characterized by muscular rigidity and loss of feelings and sensations.
[6]Actually written by Karl Gottlieb Reissiger (1798–1859), the waltz was copied out by Karl Maria, Baron von Weber (1786–1826). The music was believed his because on his sudden death, it was found in his handwriting; his was a highly romantic, often eerie and haunting music.

painted an idea, that mortal was Roderick Usher. For me at least—in the circumstances then surrounding me—there arose out of the pure abstractions which the hypochondriac contrived to throw upon his canvass, an intensity of intolerable awe, no shadow of which felt I ever yet in the contemplation of the certainly glowing yet too concrete reveries of Fuseli.[7]

One of the phantasmagoric conceptions of my friend, partaking not so rigidly of the spirit of abstraction, may be shadowed forth, although feebly, in words. A small picture presented the interior of an immensely long and rectangular vault or tunnel, with low walls, smooth, white, and without interruption or device. Certain accessory points of the design served well to convey the idea that this excavation lay at an exceeding depth below the surface of the earth. No outlet was observed in any portion of its vast extent, and no torch, or other artificial source of light was discernible; yet a flood of intense rays rolled throughout, and bathed the whole in a ghastly and inappropriate splendor.

I have just spoken of that morbid condition of the auditory nerve which rendered all music intolerable to the sufferer with the exception of certain effects of stringed instruments. It was, perhaps, the narrow limits to which he thus confined himself upon the guitar, which gave birth, in great measure, to the fantastic character of his performances. But the fervid *facility* of his *impromptus* could not be so accounted for. They must have been, and were, in the notes, as well as in the words of his wild fantasias (for he not unfrequently accompanied himself with rhymed verbal improvisations), the result of that intense mental collectedness and concentration to which I have previously alluded as observable only in particular moments of the highest artificial excitement. The words of one of these rhapsodies I have easily remembered. I was, perhaps, the more forcibly impressed with it, as he gave it, because, in the under or mystic current of its meaning, I fancied that I perceived, and for the first time, a full consciousness on the part of Usher, of the tottering of his lofty reason upon her throne. The verses, which were entitled "The Haunted Palace," ran very nearly, if not accurately, thus:

I

In the greenest of our valleys,
    By good angels tenanted,
Once a fair and stately palace—
    Radiant palace—reared its head.
In the monarch Thought's dominion—
    It stood there!
Never seraph spread a pinion
    Over fabric half so fair.

II

Banners yellow, glorious, golden,
    On its roof did float and flow;
(This—all this—was in the olden
    Time long ago)
And every gentle air that dallied,
    In that sweet day,
Along the ramparts plumed and pallid,
    A winged odor went away.

[7]Henry Fuseli (1741–1825), British painter (born in Switzerland) who specialized in strange or supernatural scenes, as his *The Nightmare*.

III

Wanderers in that happy valley
   Through two luminous windows saw
Spirits moving musically
   To a lute's well-tunéd law,
Round about a throne, where sitting
   (Porphyrogene!)[8]
In state his glory well befitting,
   The ruler of the realm was seen.

IV

And all with pearl and ruby glowing
   Was the fair palace door,
Through which came flowing, flowing, flowing,
   And sparkling evermore,
A troop of Echoes whose sweet duty
   Was but to sing,
In voices of surpassing beauty,
   The wit and wisdom of their king.

V

But evil things, in robes of sorrow,
   Assailed the monarch's high estate;
(Ah, let us mourn, for never morrow
   Shall dawn upon him, desolate!)
And, round about his home, the glory
   That blushed and bloomed
Is but a dim-remembered story
   Of the old time entombed.

VI

And travellers now within that valley,
   Through the red-litten windows, see
Vast forms that move fantastically
   To a discordant melody;
While, like a rapid ghastly river,
   Through the pale door,
A hideous throng rush out forever,
   And laugh—but smile no more.

    I well remember that suggestions arising from this ballad led us into a train of thought wherein there became manifest an opinion of Usher's which I mention not so much on account of its novelty, (for other men[9] have thought thus,) as on account of the pertinacity with which he maintained it. This opinion, in its general form, was that of the sentience of all vegetable things. But, in his disordered fancy, the idea had assumed a more daring character, and trespassed, under certain conditions, upon the kingdom of inorganization. I lack words to express the full extent, or the earnest *abandon* of his persuasion. The belief, however, was connected (as I have previously hinted) with the gray stones of the home of his forefathers. The conditions of the sentience had been here, he imagined, fulfilled in

---

8."Born to the purple," royalty (Latin).
9."Watson, Dr. Percival, Spallanzani, and especially the Bishop of Landaff.—See 'Chemical Essays,' vol. V" (Poe's note). Richard Watson (1737–1816) was a British chemist and theologian, becoming Bishop of Llandaff in Wales; he

was author of *Chemical Essays* (1787). In volume V, he refers to the Abbé Lazzaro Spallanzuni, eighteenth-century Italian naturalist, and Dr. Thomas Percival, eighteenth-century British scientist.

the method of collocation of these stones—in the order of their arrangement, as well as in that of the many *fungi* which overspread them, and of the decayed trees which stood around—above all, in the long undisturbed endurance of this arrangement, and in its reduplication in the still waters of the tarn. Its evidence—the evidence of the sentience—was to be seen, he said, (and I here started as he spoke,) in the gradual yet certain condensation of an atmosphere of their own about the waters and the walls. The result was discoverable, he added, in that silent, yet importunate and terrible influence which for centuries had moulded the destinies of his family, and which made *him* what I now saw him—what he was. Such opinions need no comment, and I will make none.

Our books—the books which, for years, had formed no small portion of the mental existence of the invalid—were, as might be supposed, in strict keeping with this character of phantasm. We pored together over such works[10] as the Ververt et Chartreuse of Gresset; the Belphegor of Machiavelli; the Heaven and Hell of Swedenborg; the Subterranean Voyage of Nicholas Klimm by Holberg; the Chiromancy of Robert Flud, of Jean D'Indaginé, and of De la Chambre; the Journey into the Blue Distance of Tieck; and the City of the Sun of Campanella. One favorite volume was a small octavo edition of the *Directorium Inquisitorum*, by the Dominican Eymeric de Gironne; and there were passages in Pomponius Mela, about the old African Satyrs and Œgipans, over which Usher would sit dreaming for hours. His chief delight, however, was found in the perusal of an exceedingly rare and curious book in quarto Gothic—the manual of a forgotten church—the *Vigiliae Mortuorum secundum Chorum Ecclesiae Maguntinae.*

I could not help thinking of the wild ritual of this work, and of its probable influence upon the hypochondriac, when, one evening, having informed me abruptly that the lady Madeline was no more, he stated his intention of preserving her corpse for a fortnight, (previously to its final interment,) in one of the numerous vaults within the main walls of the building. The worldly reason, however, assigned for this singular proceeding, was one which I did not feel at liberty to dispute. The brother had been led to his resolution (so he told me) by consideration of the unusual character of the malady of the deceased, of certain obtrusive and eager inquiries on the part of her medical men, and of the remote and exposed situation of the burial-ground of the family. I will not deny that when I called to mind the sinister countenance of the person whom I met upon the staircase, on the day of my arrival at the house, I had no desire to oppose what I regarded as at best but a harmless, and by no means an unnatural, precaution.[11]

At the request of Usher, I personally aided him in the arrangements for the temporary entombment. The body having been encoffined, we two alone bore it to its rest. The vault in which we placed it (and which had been so long unopened that our torches, half smothered in its oppressive atmosphere, gave us little opportunity for investigation) was small, damp, and entirely without means of admission for light; lying, at great depth, immediately beneath that portion of the building in which was my own sleeping apartment. It had been used, apparently, in remote feudal times, for the worst purposes of a donjon-keep,[12] and, in later

[10]The works listed are all real, and tend to treat the fantastic, supernatural, and diabolic. *Ver-Vert* and *La Chartreuse*, by Jean-Baptiste-Louis Gresset (1709–1777), French poet; *Belphegor, or The Demon Who Took a Wife*, by Niccolò Machiavelli (1469–1527), Italian philosopher; *Heaven and Hell*, by Emanuel Swedenborg (1688–1772), Swedish mystic; *Niels Klim's Underground Voyage*, by Ludvig Holberg (1684–1754), Danish author; books on chiromancy (palm reading) published in 1687 by Robert Fludd (British), in 1653 by Marin Cureau de la Chambre (French), and in 1522 by Joannes ab Indagine of Steinham (French); "A Journey into the Blue Distance" in *Das alte Buch und die Reise ins blaue hinein*, by Johann Ludwig Tieck (1773–1853), German novelist; *The City of the Sun*, by Tommaso Campanella (1568–1639), Italian poet and philosopher; *Directorium Inquisitorum* (*Procedures of the Inquisition*), by Nicholas Eymeric de Girone (1320?–1399), became Inquisitor-General for Castile in 1356; *Chorographia* by Pomponius Mela (first century A.D.), whose book on geography of the ancient world described strange beasts such as African goatmen ("Oegipans"); *Vigils for the dead according to the use of the church of Mainz* (c. 1500).
[11]I.e., corpses were often stolen for medical education.
[12]Dungeon or underground prison.

days, as a place of deposit for powder, or some other highly combustible substance, as a portion of its floor, and the whole interior of a long archway through which we reached it, were carefully sheathed with copper. The door, of massive iron, had been, also, similarly protected. Its immense weight caused an unusually sharp grating sound, as it moved upon its hinges.

Having deposited our mournful burden upon tressels within this region of horror, we partially turned aside the yet unscrewed lid of the coffin, and looked upon the face of the tenant. A striking similitude between the brother and sister now first arrested my attention; and Usher, divining, perhaps, my thoughts, murmured out some few words from which I learned that the deceased and himself had been twins, and that sympathies of a scarcely intelligible nature had always existed between them. Our glances, however, rested not long upon the dead—for we could not regard her unawed. The disease which had thus entombed the lady in the maturity of youth, had left, as usual in all maladies of a strictly cataleptical character, the mockery of a faint blush upon the bosom and the face, and that suspiciously lingering smile upon the lip which is so terrible in death. We replaced and screwed down the lid, and, having secured the door of iron, made our way, with toil, into the scarcely less gloomy apartments of the upper portion of the house.

And now, some days of bitter grief having elapsed, an observable change came over the features of the mental disorder of my friend. His ordinary manner had vanished. His ordinary occupations were neglected or forgotten. He roamed from chamber to chamber with hurried, unequal, and objectless step. The pallor of his countenance had assumed, if possible, a more ghastly hue—but the luminousness of his eye had utterly gone out. The once occasional huskiness of his tone was heard no more; and a tremulous quaver, as if of extreme terror, habitually characterized his utterance. There were times, indeed, when I thought his unceasingly agitated mind was laboring with some oppressive secret, to divulge which he struggled for the necessary courage. At times, again, I was obliged to resolve all into the mere inexplicable vagaries of madness, for I beheld him gazing upon vacancy for long hours, in an attitude of the profoundest attention, as if listening to some imaginary sound. It was no wonder that his condition terrified—that it infected me. I felt creeping upon me, by slow yet certain degrees, the wild influences of his own fantastic yet impressive superstitions.

It was, especially, upon retiring to bed late in the night of the seventh or eighth day after the placing of the lady Madeline within the donjon, that I experienced the full power of such feelings. Sleep came not near my couch—while the hours waned and waned away. I struggled to reason off the nervousness which had dominion over me. I endeavored to believe that much, if not all of what I felt, was due to the bewildering influence of the gloomy furniture of the room—of the dark and tattered draperies, which, tortured into motion by the breath of a rising tempest, swayed fitfully to and fro upon the walls, and rustled uneasily about the decorations of the bed. But my efforts were fruitless. An irrepressible tremor gradually pervaded my frame; and, at length, there sat upon my very heart an incubus[13] of utterly causeless alarm. Shaking this off with a gasp and a struggle, I uplifted myself upon the pillows, and, peering earnestly within the intense darkness of the chamber, harkened—I know not why, except that an instinctive spirit prompted me—to certain low and indefinite sounds which came, through the pauses of the storm, at long intervals, I knew not whence. Overpowered by an intense sentiment of horror, unaccountable yet unendurable, I threw on my clothes with haste (for I felt that I should sleep no more during the night), and endeav-

---

[13]Demon who was thought to sleep on top of people, especially women, attempting sexual intercourse.

ored to arouse myself from the pitiable condition into which I had fallen, by pacing rapidly to and fro through the apartment.

I had taken but few turns in this manner, when a light step on an adjoining staircase arrested my attention. I presently recognised it as that of Usher. In an instant afterward he rapped, with a gentle touch, at my door, and entered, bearing a lamp. His countenance was, as usual, cadaverously wan—but, moreover, there was a species of mad hilarity in his eyes—an evidently restrained *hysteria* in his whole demeanor. His air appalled me—but anything was preferable to the solitude which I had so long endured, and I even welcomed his presence as a relief.

"And you have not seen it?" he said abruptly, after having stared about him for some moments in silence—"you have not then seen it?—but, stay! you shall." Thus speaking, and having carefully shaded his lamp, he hurried to one of the casements, and threw it freely open to the storm.

The impetuous fury of the entering gust nearly lifted us from our feet. It was, indeed, a tempestuous yet sternly beautiful night, and one wildly singular in its terror and its beauty. A whirlwind had apparently collected its force in our vicinity: for there were frequent and violent alterations in the direction of the wind; and the exceeding density of the clouds (which hung so low as to press upon the turrets of the house) did not prevent our perceiving the life-like velocity with which they flew careering from all points against each other, without passing away into the distance. I say that even their exceeding density did not prevent our perceiving this—yet we had no glimpse of the moon or stars—nor was there any flashing forth of the lightning. But the under surfaces of the huge masses of agitated vapor, as well as all terrestrial objects immediately around us, were glowing in the unnatural light of a faintly luminous and distinctly visible gaseous exhalation which hung about and enshrouded the mansion.

"You must not—you shall not behold this!" said I, shudderingly, to Usher, as I led him, with a gentle violence, from the window to a seat. "These appearances, which bewilder you, are merely electrical phenomena not uncommon—or it may be that they have their ghastly origin in the rank miasma of the tarn. Let us close this casement;—the air is chilling and dangerous to your frame. Here is one of your favorite romances. I will read, and you shall listen;—and so we will pass away this terrible night together."

The antique volume which I had taken up was the "Mad Trist" of Sir Launcelot Canning;[14] but I had called it a favorite of Usher's more in sad jest than in earnest; for, in truth, there is little in its uncouth and unimaginative prolixity which could have had interest for the lofty and spiritual ideality of my friend. It was, however, the only book immediately at hand; and I indulged a vague hope that the excitement which now agitated the hypochondriac, might find relief (for the history of mental disorder is full of similar anomalies) even in the extremeness of the folly which I should read. Could I have judged, indeed, by the wild overstrained air of vivacity with which he harkened, or apparently harkened, to the words of the tale, I might well have congratulated myself upon the success of my design.

I had arrived at that well-known portion of the story where Ethelred, the hero of the Trist, having sought in vain for peaceable admission into the dwelling of the hermit, proceeds to make good an entrance by force. Here, it will be remembered, the words of the narrative run thus:

"And Ethelred, who was by nature of a doughty heart, and who was now mighty withal, on account of the powerfulness of the wine which he had drunken, waited no longer to hold parley with the hermit, who, in sooth, was of an obstinate

---

[14]Both title and author are products of Poe's imagination.

and maliceful turn, but, feeling the rain upon his shoulders, and fearing the rising of the tempest, uplifted his mace outright, and, with blows, made quickly room in the plankings of the door for his gauntleted hand; and now pulling therewith sturdily, he so cracked, and ripped, and tore all asunder, that the noise of the dry and hollow-sounding wood alarummed and reverberated throughout the forest."

At the termination of this sentence I started, and for a moment, paused; for it appeared to me (although I at once concluded that my excited fancy had deceived me)—it appeared to me that, from some very remote portion of the mansion, there came, indistinctly, to my ears, what might have been, in its exact similarity of character, the echo (but a stifled and dull one certainly) of the very cracking and ripping sound which Sir Launcelot had so particularly described. It was, beyond doubt, the coincidence alone which had arrested my attention; for, amid the rattling of the sashes of the casements, and the ordinary commingled noises of the still increasing storm, the sound, in itself, had nothing, surely, which should have interested or disturbed me. I continued the story:

"But the good champion Ethelred, now entering within the door, was sore enraged and amazed to perceive no signal of the maliceful hermit; but, in the stead thereof, a dragon of a scaly and prodigious demeanor, and of a fiery tongue, which sate in guard before a palace of gold, with a floor of silver; and upon the wall there hung a shield of shining brass with this legend enwritten—

> Who entereth herein, a conqueror hath bin;
> Who slayeth the dragon, the shield he shall win;

And Ethelred uplifted his mace, and struck upon the head of the dragon, which fell before him, and gave up his pesty breath, with a shriek so horrid and harsh, and withal so piercing, that Ethelred had fain to close his ears with his hands against the dreadful noise of it, the like whereof was never before heard."

Here again I paused abruptly, and now with a feeling of wild amazement—for there could be no doubt whatever that, in this instance, I did actually hear (although from what direction it proceeded I found it impossible to say) a low and apparently distant, but harsh, protracted, and most unusual screaming or grating sound—the exact counterpart of what my fancy had already conjured up for the dragon's unnatural shriek as described by the romancer.

Oppressed, as I certainly was, upon the occurrence of this second and most extraordinary coincidence, by a thousand conflicting sensations, in which wonder and extreme terror were predominant, I still retained sufficient presence of mind to avoid exciting, by any observation, the sensitive nervousness of my companion. I was by no means certain that he had noticed the sounds in question; although, assuredly, a strange alteration had, during the last few minutes, taken place in his demeanor. From a position fronting my own, he had gradually brought round his chair, so as to sit with his face to the door of the chamber; and thus I could but partially perceive his features, although I saw that his lips trembled as if he were murmuring inaudibly. His head had dropped upon his breast—yet I knew that he was not asleep, from the wide and rigid opening of the eye as I caught a glance of it in profile. The motion of his body, too, was at variance with this idea—for he rocked from side to side with a gentle yet constant and uniform sway. Having rapidly taken notice of all this, I resumed the narrative of Sir Launcelot, which thus proceeded:

"And now, the champion, having escaped from the terrible fury of the dragon, bethinking himself of the brazen shield, and of the breaking up of the enchantment which was upon it, removed the carcass from out of the way before him, and approached valorously over the silver pavement of the castle to where the shield was upon the wall; which in sooth tarried not for his full coming, but fell down at his feet upon the silver floor, with a mighty great and terrible ringing sound."

No sooner had these syllables passed my lips, than—as if a shield of brass had indeed, at the moment, fallen heavily upon a floor of silver—I became aware of a distinct, hollow, metallic, and clangorous, yet apparently muffled reverberation. Completely unnerved, I leaped to my feet; but the measured rocking movement of Usher was undisturbed. I rushed to the chair in which he sat. His eyes were bent fixedly before him, and throughout his whole countenance there reigned a stony rigidity. But, as I placed my hand upon his shoulder, there came a strong shudder over his whole person; a sickly smile quivered about his lips; and I saw that he spoke in a low, hurried, and gibbering murmur, as if unconscious of my presence. Bending closely over him, I at length drank in the hideous import of his words.

"Not hear it?—yes, I hear it, and *have* heard it. Long—long—long—many minutes, many hours, many days, have I heard it—yet I dared not—oh, pity me, miserable wretch that I am!—I dared not—I *dared* not speak! *We have put her living in the tomb!* Said I not that my senses were acute? I *now* tell you that I heard her first feeble movements in the hollow coffin. I heard them—many, many days ago—yet I dared not—*I dared not speak!* And now—to-night—Ethelred—ha! ha!—the breaking of the hermit's door, and the death-cry of the dragon, and the clangor of the shield!—say, rather, the rending of her coffin, and the grating of the iron hinges of her prison, and her struggles within the coppered archway of the vault! Oh whither shall I fly? Will she not be here anon? Is she not hurrying to upbraid me for my haste? Have I not heard her footstep on the stair? Do I not distinguish that heavy and horrible beating of her heart? Madman!"—here he sprang furiously to his feet, and shrieked out his syllables, as if in the effort he were giving up his soul—"*Madman! I tell you that she now stands without the door!*"

As if in the superhuman energy of his utterance there had been found the potency of a spell—the huge antique pannels to which the speaker pointed, threw slowly back, upon the instant, their ponderous and ebony jaws. It was the work of the rushing gust—but then without those doors there *did* stand the lofty and enshrouded figure of the lady Madeline of Usher. There was blood upon her white robes, and the evidence of some bitter struggle upon every portion of her emaciated frame. For a moment she remained trembling and reeling to and fro upon the threshold—then, with a low moaning cry, fell heavily inward upon the person of her brother, and in her violent and now final death-agonies, bore him to the floor a corpse, and a victim to the terrors he had anticipated.

From that chamber, and from that mansion, I fled aghast. The storm was still abroad in all its wrath as I found myself crossing the old causeway. Suddenly there shot along the path a wild light, and I turned to see whence a gleam so unusual could have issued; for the vast house and its shadows were alone behind me. The radiance was that of the full, setting, and blood-red moon, which now shone vividly through that once barely-discernible fissure, of which I have before spoken as extending from the roof of the building, in a zigzag direction, to the base. While I gazed, this fissure rapidly widened—there came a fierce breath of the whirlwind—the entire orb of the satellite burst at once upon my sight—my brain reeled as I saw the mighty walls rushing asunder—there was a long tumultuous shouting sound like the voice of a thousand waters—and the deep and dank tarn at my feet closed sullenly and silently over the fragments of the *"House of Usher."*

1839

William Wilson

> What say of it? what say of CONSCIENCE grim,
> That spectre in my path?
> Chamberlayne's *Pharonnida*[1]

Let me call myself, for the present, William Wilson. The fair page now lying before me need not be sullied with my real appellation. This has been already too much an object for the scorn—for the horror—for the detestation of my race. To the uttermost regions of the globe have not the indignant winds bruited its unparalleled infamy? Oh, outcast of all outcasts most abandoned!—to the earth art thou not forever dead? to its honors, to its flowers, to its golden aspirations?—and a cloud, dense, dismal, and limitless, does it not hang eternally between thy hopes and heaven?

I would not, if I could, here or to-day, embody a record of my later years of unspeakable misery, and unpardonable crime. This epoch—these later years—took unto themselves a sudden elevation in turpitude, whose origin alone it is my present purpose to assign. Men usually grow base by degrees. From me, in an instant, all virtue dropped bodily as a mantle. From comparatively trivial wickedness I passed, with the stride of a giant, into more than the enormities of an Elah-Gabalus.[2] What chance—what one event brought this evil thing to pass, bear with me while I relate. Death approaches; and the shadow which foreruns him has thrown a softening influence over my spirit. I long, in passing through the dim valley, for the sympathy—I had nearly said for the pity—of my fellow men. I would fain have them believe that I have been, in some measure, the slave of circumstances beyond human control. I would wish them to seek out for me, in the details I am about to give, some little oasis of *fatality* amid a wilderness of error. I would have them allow—what they cannot refrain from allowing—that, although temptation may have ere-while existed as great, man was never *thus*, at least, tempted before—certainly, never *thus* fell. And is it therefore that he has never thus suffered? Have I not indeed been living in a dream? And am I not now dying a victim to the horror and the mystery of the wildest of all sublunary visions?

I am the descendant of a race whose imaginative and easily excitable temperament has at all times rendered them remarkable; and, in my earliest infancy, I gave evidence of having fully inherited the family character. As I advanced in years it was more strongly developed; becoming, for many reasons, a cause of serious disquietude to my friends, and of positive injury to myself. I grew self-willed, addicted to the wildest caprices, and a prey to the most ungovernable passions. Weak-minded, and beset with constitutional infirmities akin to my own, my parents could do but little to check the evil propensities which distinguished me. Some feeble and ill-directed efforts resulted in complete failure on their part, and, of course, in total triumph on mine. Thenceforward my voice was a household law; and at an age when few children have abandoned their leading-strings, I was left to the guidance of my own will, and became, in all but name, the master of my own actions.

My earliest recollections of a school-life are connected with a large, rambling, Elizabethan house, in a misty-looking village of England, where were a vast num-

---

[1]The epigraph is not from *Pharonnida* (1659), by William Chamberlayne (1619–1689), British physician and poet, but may derive from his play, *Love's Victory* (1658): "Conscience waits on me like the frightening shades / Of ghosts when gastly[sic] messengers of death" (V, 2746f.).
[2]Variant of Heliogabalus (*c.* 205–222), reigned as Marcus Aurelius Antoninus from the age of thirteen (218) until his murder at age seventeen by the Imperial Guard. He imposed the worship of the sun god Baal, a cult in which he was a priest, and appointed to high position handsome youths to whom he was attracted.

ber of gigantic and gnarled trees, and where all the houses were excessively ancient. In truth, it was a dream-like and spirit-soothing place, that venerable old
town. At this moment, in fancy, I feel the refreshing chilliness of its deeply-
shadowed avenues, inhale the fragrance of its thousand shrubberies, and thrill
anew with undefinable delight, at the deep hollow note of the church-bell, breaking, each hour, with sullen and sudden roar, upon the stillness of the dusky atmosphere in which the fretted Gothic steeple lay imbedded and asleep.

It gives me, perhaps, as much of pleasure as I can now in any manner experience, to dwell upon minute recollections of the school and its concerns. Steeped in
misery as I am—misery, alas! only too real—I shall be pardoned for seeking relief, however slight and temporary, in the weakness of a few rambling details.
These, moreover, utterly trivial, and even ridiculous in themselves, assume, to my
fancy, adventitious importance, as connected with a period and a locality when
and where I recognise the first ambiguous monitions of the destiny which afterwards so fully overshadowed me. Let me then remember.

The house, I have said, was old and irregular. The grounds were extensive,
and a high and solid brick wall, topped with a bed of mortar and broken glass,
encompassed the whole. This prison-like rampart formed the limit of our domain;
beyond it we saw but thrice a week—once every Saturday afternoon, when, attended by two ushers,[3] we were permitted to take brief walks in a body through
some of the neighboring fields—and twice during Sunday, when we were paraded in the same formal manner to the morning and evening service in the one
church of the village. Of this church the principal of our school was pastor. With
how deep a spirit of wonder and perplexity was I wont to regard him from our
remote pew in the gallery, as, with step solemn and slow, he ascended the pulpit!
This reverend man, with countenance so demurely benign, with robes so glossy
and so clerically flowing, with wig so minutely powdered, so rigid and so vast,—
could this be he who, of late, with sour visage, and in snuffy habiliments, administered, ferule in hand, the Draconian Laws[4] of the academy? Oh, gigantic paradox, too utterly monstrous for solution!

At an angle of the ponderous wall frowned a more ponderous gate. It was riveted and studded with iron bolts, and surmounted with jagged iron spikes. What
impressions of deep awe did it inspire! It was never opened save for the three periodical egressions and ingressions already mentioned; then, in every creak of its
mighty hinges, we found a plenitude of mystery—a world of matter for solemn
remark, or for more solemn meditation.

The extensive enclosure was irregular in form, having many capacious recesses. Of these, three or four of the largest constituted the play-ground. It was
level, and covered with fine hard gravel. I well remember it had no trees, nor
benches, nor anything similar within it. Of course it was in the rear of the house.
In front lay a small parterre, planted with box and other shrubs; but through this
sacred division we passed only upon rare occasions indeed—such as a first advent
to school or final departure thence, or perhaps, when a parent or friend having
called for us, we joyfully took our way home for the Christmas or Midsummer
holydays.

But the house!—how quaint an old building was this!—to me how veritably a
palace of enchantment! There was really no end to its windings—to its incomprehensible subdivisions. It was difficult, at any given time, to say with certainty upon
which of its two stories one happened to be. From each room to every other there
were sure to be found three or four steps either in ascent or descent. Then the
lateral branches were innumerable—inconceivable—and so returning in upon

---

[3]I.e., assistant schoolmasters.
[4]Laws of great severity, named after Draco, Athenian lawgiver, whose code (*c.* 621 B.C.) prescribed the death penalty
for minor offenses.

themselves, that our most exact ideas in regard to the whole mansion were not very far different from those with which we pondered upon infinity. During the five years of my residence here, I was never able to ascertain with precision, in what remote locality lay the little sleeping apartment assigned to myself and some eighteen or twenty other scholars.

The school-room was the largest in the house—I could not help thinking, in the world. It was very long, narrow, and dismally low, with pointed Gothic windows and a ceiling of oak. In a remote and terror-inspiring angle was a square enclosure of eight or ten feet, comprising the *sanctum*, "during hours," of our principal, the Reverend Dr. Bransby.[5] It was a solid structure, with massy door, sooner than open which in the absence of the "Dominie,"[6] we would all have willingly perished by the *peine forte et dure*.[7] In other angles were two other similar boxes, far less reverenced, indeed, but still greatly matters of awe. One of these was the pulpit of the "classical" usher, one of the "English and mathematical." Interspersed about the room, crossing and recrossing in endless irregularity, were innumerable benches and desks, black, ancient, and time-worn, piled desperately with much-bethumbed books, and so beseamed with initial letters, names at full length, grotesque figures, and other multiplied efforts of the knife, as to have entirely lost what little of original form might have been their portion in days long departed. A huge bucket with water stood at one extremity of the room, and a clock of stupendous dimensions at the other.

Encompassed by the massy walls of this venerable academy, I passed, yet not in tedium or disgust, the years of the third lustrum[8] of my life. The teeming brain of childhood requires no external world of incident to occupy or amuse it; and the apparently dismal monotony of a school was replete with more intense excitement than my riper youth has derived from luxury, or my full manhood from crime. Yet I must believe that my first mental development had in it much of the uncommon—even much of the *outré*.[9] Upon mankind at large the events of very early existence rarely leave in mature age any definite impression. All is gray shadow—a weak and irregular remembrance—an indistinct regathering of feeble pleasures and phantasmagoric pains. With me this is not so. In childhood I must have felt with the energy of a man what I now find stamped upon memory in lines as vivid, as deep, and as durable as the *exergues* of the Carthaginian medals.[10]

Yet in fact—in the fact of the world's view—how little was there to remember! The morning's awakening, the nightly summons to bed; the connings,[11] the recitations; the periodical half-holidays, and perambulations; the play-ground, with its broils, its pastimes, its intrigues;—these, by a mental sorcery long forgotten, were made to involve a wilderness of sensation, a world of rich incident, an universe of varied emotion, of excitement the most passionate and spirit-stirring. "*Oh, le bon temps, que ce siecle de fer!*"[12]

In truth, the ardor, the enthusiasm, and the imperiousness of my disposition, soon rendered me a marked character among my schoolmates, and by slow, but natural gradations, gave me an ascendancy over all not greatly older than myself;—over all with a single exception. This exception was found in the person of a scholar, who, although no relation, bore the same Christian and surname as myself;—a circumstance, in fact, little remarkable; for, notwithstanding a noble de-

---

[5]Poe really attended in his youth the Manor House School of the Rev. John Bransby at Stoke Newington. The descriptions are based on his experience, but there are many departures from fact.
[6]A schoolmaster (in Scottish); also, pastor.
[7]Punishment by pressing to death, usually with rocks.
[8]I.e., 10 to 15 (a five year period).
[9]Eccentric, bizarre.
[10]*Exergues* were the spaces beneath the central figures por-

trayed in medals, containing inscriptions of various kinds; their position made exergues less likely to be worn from handling. Carthage was an ancient sea power in north Africa on the Mediterranean, defeated by Rome in the second century B.C.
[11]Memorizations.
[12]From *Le Mondain* (1736), by Voltaire (1694–1778), French philosopher: "Oh what a good time it was, the iron age."

scent, mine was one of those everyday appellations which seem, by prescriptive right, to have been, time out of mind, the common property of the mob. In this narrative I have therefore designated myself as William Wilson,—a fictitious title not very dissimilar to the real. My namesake alone, of those who in school-phraseology constituted "our set," presumed to compete with me in the studies of the class—in the sports and broils of the play-ground—to refuse implicit belief in my assertions, and submission to my will—indeed, to interfere with my arbitrary dictation in any respect whatsoever. If there is on earth a supreme and unqualified despotism, it is the despotism of a master-mind in boyhood over the less energetic spirits of its companions.

Wilson's rebellion was to me a source of the greatest embarrassment; the more so as, in spite of the bravado with which in public I made a point of treating him and his pretensions, I secretly felt that I feared him, and could not help thinking the equality which he maintained so easily with myself, a proof of his true superiority; since not to be overcome cost me a perpetual struggle. Yet this superiority—even this equality—was in truth acknowledged by no one but myself; our associates, by some unaccountable blindness, seemed not even to suspect it. Indeed, his competition, his resistance, and especially his impertinent and dogged interference with my purposes, were not more pointed than private. He apeared to be destitute alike of the ambition which urged, and of the passionate energy of mind which enabled me to excel. In his rivalry he might have been supposed actuated solely by a whimsical desire to thwart, astonish, or mortify myself; although there were times when I could not help observing, with a feeling made up of wonder, abasement, and pique, that he mingled with his injuries, his insults, or his contradictions, a certain most inappropriate, and assuredly most unwelcome *affectionateness* of manner. I could only conceive this singular behavior to arise from a consummate self-conceit assuming the vulgar airs of patronage and protection.

Perhaps it was this latter trait in Wilson's conduct, conjoined with our identity of name, and the mere accident of our having entered the school upon the same day, which set afloat the notion that we were brothers, among the senior classes in the academy. These do not usually inquire with much strictness into the affairs of their juniors. I have before said, or should have said, that Wilson was not, in the most remote degree, connected with my family. But assuredly if we *had* been brothers we must have been twins; for, after leaving Dr. Bransby's, I casually learned that my namesake was born on the nineteenth of January, 1813—and this is a somewhat remarkable coincidence; for the day is precisely that of my own nativity.[13]

It may seen strange that in spite of the continual anxiety occasioned me by the rivalry of Wilson, and his intolerable spirit of contradiction, I could not bring myself to hate him altogether. We had, to be sure, nearly every day a quarrel in which, yielding me publicly the palm of victory, he, in some manner, contrived to make me feel that it was he who had deserved it; yet a sense of pride on my part, and a veritable dignity on his own, kept us always upon what are called "speaking terms," while there were many points of strong congeniality in our tempers, operating to awake in me a sentiment which our position alone, perhaps, prevented from ripening into friendship. It is difficult, indeed, to define, or even to describe, my real feelings towards him. They formed a motley and heterogeneous admixture;—some petulant animosity, which was not yet hatred, some esteem, more respect, much fear, with a world of uneasy curiosity. To the moralist it will be un-

---

[13]Poe's birthday was January 19, 1809, but he often listed it as 1811 and 1813. (Variant texts of "William Wilson" also use all these variant dates.)

necessary to say, in addition, that Wilson and myself were the most inseparable of companions.

It was no doubt the anomalous state of affairs existing between us, which turned all my attacks upon him, (and they were many, either open or covert) into the channel of banter or practical joke (giving pain while assuming the aspect of mere fun) rather than into a more serious and determined hostility. But my endeavors on this head were by no means uniformly successful, even when my plans were the most wittily concocted; for my namesake had much about him, in character, of that unassuming and quiet austerity which, while enjoying the poignancy of its own jokes, has no heel of Achilles in itself,[14] and absolutely refuses to be laughed at. I could find, indeed, but one vulnerable point, and that, lying in a personal peculiarity, arising, perhaps, from constitutional disease, would have been spared by any antagonist less at his wit's end than myself;—my rival had a weakness in the faucial or guttural organs, which precluded him from raising his voice at any time *above a very low whisper.* Of this defect I did not fail to take what poor advantage lay in my power.

Wilson's retaliations in kind were many; and there was one form of his practical wit that disturbed me beyond measure. How his sagacity first discovered at all that so petty a thing would vex me, is a question I never could solve; but, having discovered, he habitually practised the annoyance. I had always felt aversion to my uncourtly patronymic, and its very common, if not plebeian prænomen. The words were venom in my ears; and when, upon the day of my arrival, a second William Wilson came also to the academy, I felt angry with him for bearing the name, and doubly disgusted with the name because a stranger bore it, who would be the cause of its twofold repetition, who would be constantly in my presence, and whose concerns, in the ordinary routine of the school business, must inevitably, on account of the detestable coincidence, be often confounded with my own.

The feeling of vexation thus engendered grew stronger with every circumstance tending to show resemblance, moral or physical, between my rival and myself. I had not then discovered the remarkable fact that we were of the same age; but I saw that we were of the same height, and I perceived that we were even singularly alike in general contour of person and outline of feature. I was galled, too, by the rumor touching a relationship, which had grown current in the upper forms. In a word, nothing could more seriously disturb me, (although I scrupulously concealed such disturbance,) than any allusion to a similarity of mind, person, or condition existing between us. But, in truth, I had no reason to believe that (with the exception of the matter of relationship, and in the case of Wilson himself,) this similarity had ever been made a subject of comment, or even observed at all by our schoolfellows. That *he* observed it in all its bearings, and as fixedly as I, was apparent; but that he could discover in such circumstances so fruitful a field of annoyance, can only be attributed, as I said before, to his more than ordinary penetration.

His cue, which was to perfect an imitation of myself, lay both in words and in actions; and most admirably did he play his part. My dress it was an easy matter to copy; my gait and general manner were, without difficulty, appropriated; in spite of his constitutional defect, even my voice did not escape him. My louder tones were, of course, unattempted, but then the key, it was identical; *and his singular whisper, it grew the very echo of my own.*

How greatly this most exquisite portraiture harassed me, (for it could not justly be termed a caricature,) I will not now venture to describe. I had but one consolation—in the fact that the imitation, apparently, was noticed by myself alone, and

---

[14]In Greek mythology, when Achilles' mother dipped her son in the River Styx to make him invulnerable, she held him by the heel; into that heel went the arrow that caused his death.

that I had to endure only the knowing and strangely sarcastic smiles of my name-sake himself. Satisfied with having produced in my bosom the intended effect, he seemed to chuckle in secret over the sting he had inflicted, and was characteristically disregardful of the public applause which the success of his witty endeavors might have so easily elicited. That the school, indeed, did not feel his design, perceive its accomplishment, and participate in his sneer, was, for many anxious months, a riddle I could not resolve. Perhaps the *gradation* of his copy rendered it not so readily perceptible; or, more possibly, I owed my security to the masterly air of the copyist, who, disdaining the letter, (which in a painting is all the obtuse can see,) gave but the full spirit of his original for my individual contemplation and chagrin.

I have already more than once spoken of the disgusting air of patronage which he assumed toward me, and of his frequent officious interference with my will. This interference often took the ungracious character of advice; advice not openly given, but hinted or insinuated. I received it with a repugnance which gained strength as I grew in years. Yet, at this distant day, let me do him the simple justice to acknowledge that I can recall no occasion when the suggestions of my rival were on the side of those errors or follies so usual to his immature age and seeming inexperience; that his moral sense, at least, if not his general talents and worldly wisdom, was far keener than my own; and that I might, to-day, have been a better, and thus a happier man, had I less frequently rejected the counsels embodied in those meaning whispers which I then but too cordially hated and too bitterly despised.

As it was, I at length grew restive in the extreme under his distasteful supervision, and daily resented more and more openly what I considered his intolerable arrogance. I have said that, in the first years of our connexion as schoolmates, my feelings in regard to him might have been easily ripened into friendship: but, in the latter months of my residence at the academy, although the intrusion of his ordinary manner had, beyond doubt, in some measure, abated, my sentiments, in nearly similar proportion, partook very much of positive hatred. Upon one occasion he saw this, I think, and afterwards avoided, or made a show of avoiding me.

It was about the same period, if I remember aright, that, in an altercation of violence with him, in which he was more than usually thrown off his guard, and spoke and acted with an openness of demeanor rather foreign to his nature, I discovered, or fancied I discovered, in his accent, his air, and general appearance, a something which first startled, and then deeply interested me, by bringing to mind dim visions of my earliest infancy—wild, confused and thronging memories of a time when memory herself was yet unborn. I cannot better describe the sensation which oppressed me, than by saying that I could with difficulty shake off the belief of my having been acquainted with the being who stood before me, at some epoch very long ago—some point of the past even infinitely remote. The delusion, however, faded rapidly as it came; and I mention it at all but to define the day of the last conversation I there held with my singular namesake.

The huge old house, with its countless subdivisions, had several large chambers communicating with each other, where slept the greater number of the students. There were, however, (as must necessarily happen in a building so awkwardly planned,) many little nooks or recesses, the odds and ends of the structure; and these the economic ingenuity of Dr. Bransby had also fitted up as dormitories; although, being the merest closets, they were capable of accommodating but a single individual. One of these small apartments was occupied by Wilson.

One night, about the close of my fifth year at the school, and immediately after the altercation just mentioned, finding every one wrapped in sleep, I arose from bed, and, lamp in hand, stole through a wilderness of narrow passages from my own bedroom to that of my rival. I had long been plotting one of those ill-natured pieces of practical wit at his expense in which I had hitherto been so uniformly unsuccessful. It was my intention, now, to put my scheme in operation, and I resolved to make him feel the whole extent of the malice with which I was imbued. Having reached his closet, I noiselessly entered, leaving the lamp, with a shade over it, on the outside. I advanced a step, and listened to the sound of his tranquil breathing. Assured of his being asleep, I returned, took the light, and with it again approached the bed. Close curtains were around it, which, in the prosecution of my plan, I slowly and quietly withdrew, when the bright rays fell vividly upon the sleeper, and my eyes, at the same moment, upon his countenance. I looked;—and a numbness, an iciness of feeling instantly pervaded my frame. My breast heaved, my knees tottered, my whole spirit became possessed with an objectless yet intolerable horror. Gasping for breath, I lowered the lamp in still nearer proximity to the face. Were these,—*these* the lineaments of William Wilson? I saw, indeed, that they were his, but I shook as if with a fit of the ague, in fancying they were not. What *was* there about them to confound me in this manner? I gazed;—while my brain reeled with a multitude of incoherent thoughts. Not thus he appeared—assuredly not *thus*—in the vivacity of his waking hours. The same name! the same contour of person! the same day of arrival at the academy! And then his dogged and meaningless imitation of my gait, my voice, my habits, and my manner! Was it, in truth, within the bounds of human possibility, that *what I now saw* was the result, merely, of the habitual practice of this sarcastic imitation? Awe-stricken, and with a creeping shudder, I extinguished the lamp, passed silently from the chamber, and left, at once, the halls of the old academy, never to enter them again.

After a lapse of some months, spent at home in mere idleness, I found myself a student at Eton. The brief interval had been sufficient to enfeeble my remembrance of the events at Dr. Bransby's, or at least to effect a material change in the nature of the feelings with which I remembered them. The truth—the tragedy—of the drama was no more. I could now find room to doubt the evidence of my senses; and seldom called up the subject at all but with wonder at the extent of human credulity, and a smile at the vivid force of the imagination which I hereditarily possessed. Neither was this species of skepticism likely to be diminished by the character of the life I led at Eton. The vortex of thoughtless folly into which I there so immediately and so recklessly plunged, washed away all but the froth of my past hours, ingulfed at once every solid or serious impression, and left to memory only the veriest levities of a former existence.

I do not wish, however, to trace the course of my miserable profligacy here—a profligacy which set at defiance the laws, while it eluded the vigilance of the institution. Three years of folly, passed without profit, had but given me rooted habits of vice, and added, in a somewhat unusual degree, to my bodily stature, when, after a week of soulless dissipation, I invited a small party of the most dissolute students to a secret carousal in my chambers. We met at a late hour of the night; for our debaucheries were to be faithfully protracted until morning. The wine flowed freely, and there were not wanting other and perhaps more dangerous seductions; so that the gray dawn had already faintly appeared in the east, while our delirious extravagance was at its height. Madly flushed with cards and intoxication, I was in the act of insisting upon a toast of more than wonted profanity, when my attention was suddenly diverted by the violent, although partial unclosing of the door of the apartment, and by the eager voice of a servant from without. He said that some person, apparently in great haste, demanded to speak with me in the hall.

Wildly excited with wine, the unexpected interruption rather delighted than surprised me. I staggered forward at once, and a few steps brought me to the vestibule of the building. In this low and small room there hung no lamp; and now no light at all was admitted, save that of the exceedingly feeble dawn which made its way through the semi-circular window. As I put my foot over the threshold, I became aware of the figure of a youth about my own height, and habited in a white kerseymere[15] morning frock, cut in the novel fashion of the one I myself wore at the moment. This the faint light enabled me to perceive; but the features of his face I could not distinguish. Upon my entering, he strode hurriedly up to me, and, seizing me by the arm with a gesture of petulant impatience, whispered the words "William Wilson!" in my ear.

I grew perfectly sober in an instant.

There was that in the manner of the stranger, and in the tremulous shake of his uplifted finger, as he held it between my eyes and the light, which filled me with unqualified amazement; but it was not this which had so violently moved me. It was the pregnancy of solemn admonition in the singular, low, hissing utterance; and, above all, it was the character, the tone, *the key*, of those few, simple, and familiar, yet *whispered* syllables, which came with a thousand thronging memories of by-gone days, and struck upon my soul with the shock of a galvanic battery. Ere I could recover the use of my senses he was gone.

Although this event failed not of a vivid effect upon my disordered imagination, yet was it evanescent as vivid. For some weeks, indeed, I busied myself in earnest inquiry, or was wrapped in a cloud of morbid speculation. I did not pretent to disguise from my perception the identity of the singular individual who thus perseveringly interfered with my affairs, and harassed me with his insinuated counsel. But who and what was this Wilson?—and whence came he?—and what were his purposes? Upon neither of these points could I be satisfied—merely ascertaining, in regard to him, that a sudden accident in his family had caused his removal from Dr. Bransby's academy on the afternoon of the day in which I myself had eloped. But in a brief period I ceased to think upon the subject, my attention being all absorbed in a contemplated departure for Oxford. Thither I soon went, the uncalculating vanity of my parents furnishing me with an outfit and annual establishment, which would enable me to indulge at will in the luxury already so dear to my heart—to vie in profuseness of expenditure with the haughtiest heirs of the wealthiest earldoms in Great Britain.

Excited by such appliances to vice, my constitutional temperament broke forth with redoubled ardor, and I spurned even the common restraints of decency in the mad infatuation of my revels. But it were absurd to pause in the detail of my extravagance. Let it suffice, that among spendthrifts I out-Heroded Herod,[16] and that, giving name to a multitude of novel follies, I added no brief appendix to the long catalogue of vices then usual in the most dissolute university of Europe.

It could hardly be credited, however, that I had, even here, so utterly fallen from the gentlemanly estate, as to seek acquaintance with the vilest arts of the gambler by profession, and, having become an adept in his despicable science, to practise it habitually as a means of increasing my already enormous income at the expense of the weak-minded among my fellow-collegians. Such, nevertheless, was the fact. And the very enormity of this offence against all manly and honorable sentiment proved, beyond doubt, the main if not the sole reason of the impunity with which it was committed. Who, indeed, among my most abandoned associates, would not rather have disputed the clearest evidence of his senses, than have suspected of such courses, the gay, the frank, the generous William Wilson—the noblest and most liberal commoner at Oxford—him whose follies (said his parasites)

[15]Variant of cashmere, a fine wool obtained from the goats of Kashmir.
[16]I.e., was wildly excessive; from Shakespeare's *Hamlet*, III, ii, 16. Herod (73–4 B.C.), the cruel tyrant of Judea, ordered the slaughter of all children in order to destroy Jesus.

were but the follies of youth and unbridled fancy—whose errors but inimitable whim—whose darkest vice but a careless and dashing extravagance?

I had been now two years successfully busied in this way, when there came to the university a young *parvenu*[17] nobleman, Glendinning—rich, said report, as Herodes Atticus—his riches, too, as easily acquired.[18] I soon found him of weak intellect, and, of course, marked him as a fitting subject for my skill. I frequently engaged him in play, and contrived, with the gambler's usual art, to let him win considerable sums, the more effectually to entangle him in my snares. At length, my schemes being ripe, I met him (with the full intention that this meeting should be final and decisive) at the chambers of a fellow-commoner, (Mr. Preston,) equally intimate with both, but who, to do him justice, entertained not even a remote suspicion of my design. To give to this a better coloring, I had contrived to have assembled a party of some eight or ten, and was solicitously careful that the introduction of cards should appear accidental, and originate in the proposal of my contemplated dupe himself. To be brief upon a vile topic, none of the low finesse was omitted, so customary upon similar occasions that it is a just matter for wonder how any are still found so besotted as to fall its victim.

We had protracted our sitting far into the night, and I had at length effected the manœuvre of getting Glendinning as my sole antagonist. The game, too, was my favorite *écarté*.[19] The rest of the company, interested in the extent of our play, had abandoned their own cards, and were standing around us as spectators. The *parvenu*, who had been induced by my artifices in the early part of the evening, to drink deeply, now shuffled, dealt, or played, with a wild nervousness of manner for which his intoxication, I thought, might partially, but could not altogether account. In a very short period he had became my debtor to a large amount, when, having taken a long draught of port, he did precisely what I had been coolly anticipating—he proposed to double our already extravagant stakes. With a well-feigned show of reluctance, and not until after my repeated refusal had seduced him into some angry words which gave a color of *pique* to my compliance, did I finally comply. The result, of course, did but prove how entirely the prey was in my toils: in less than an hour he had quadrupled his debt. For some time his countenance had been losing the florid tinge lent it by the wine; but now, to my astonishment, I perceived that it had grown to a pallor truly fearful. I say, to my astonishment. Glendinning had been represented to my eager inquiries as immeasurably wealthy; and the sums which he had as yet lost, although in themselves vast, could not, I supposed, very seriously annoy, much less so violently affect him. That he was overcome by the wine just swallowed, was the idea which most readily presented itself; and, rather with a view to the preservation of my own character in the eyes of my associates, than from any less interested motive, I was about to insist, peremptorily, upon a discontinuance of the play, when some expressions at my elbow from among the company, and an ejaculation evincing utter despair on the part of Glendinning, gave me to understand that I had effected his total ruin under circumstances which, rendering him an object for the pity of all, should have protected him from the ill offices even of a fiend.

What now might have been my conduct it is difficult to say. The pitiable condition of my dupe had thrown an air of embarrassed gloom over all; and, for some moments, a profound silence was maintained, during which I could not help feeling my cheeks tingle with the many burning glances of scorn or reproach cast upon me by the less abandoned of the party. I will even own that an intolerable

---

[17]New rich or powerful, often crude in manners.
[18]Tiberius Claudius Herodes (second-century A.D.), famed rhetorician of Athens, enormously wealthy through his father's discovery of a large treasure.
[19]Card game for two played with 32 cards.

weight of anxiety was for a brief instant lifted from my bosom by the sudden and extraordinary interruption which ensued. The wide, heavy folding doors of the apartment were all at once thrown open, to their full extent, with a vigorous and rushing impetuosity that extinguished, as if by magic, every candle in the room. Their light, in dying, enabled us just to perceive that a stranger had entered, about my own height, and closely muffled in a cloak. The darkness, however, was now total; and we could only *feel* that he was standing in our midst. Before any one of us could recover from the extreme astonishment into which this rudeness had thrown all, we heard the voice of the intruder.

"Gentlemen," he said, in a low, distinct, and never-to-be-forgotten *whisper* which thrilled to the very marrow of my bones, "Gentlemen, I make no apology for this behavior, because in thus behaving, I am but fulfilling a duty. You are, beyond doubt, uninformed of the true character of the person who has to-night won at *écarté* a large sum of money from Lord Glendinning. I will therefore put you upon an expeditious and decisive plan of obtaining this very necessary information. Please to examine, at your leisure, the inner linings of the cuff of his left sleeve, and the several little packages which may be found in the somewhat capacious pockets of his embroidered morning wrapper."

While he spoke, so profound was the stillness that one might have heard a pin drop upon the floor. In ceasing, he departed at once, and as abruptly as he had entered. Can I—shall I describe my sensations? Must I say that I felt all the horrors of the damned? Most assuredly I had little time for reflection. Many hands roughly seized me upon the spot, and lights were immediately re-procured. A search ensued. In the lining of my sleeve were found all the court cards essential in *écarté*, and, in the pockets of my wrapper, a number of packs, fac-similes of those used at our sittings, with the single exception that mine were of the species called, technically, *arrondées*,[20] the honors[21] being slightly convex at the ends, the lower cards slightly convex at the sides. In this disposition, the dupe who cuts, as customary, at the length of the pack, will invariably find that he cuts his antagonist an honor; while the gambler, cutting at the breadth, will, as certainly, cut nothing for his victim which may count in the records of the game.

Any burst of indignation upon this discovery would have affected me less than the silent contempt, or the sarcastic composure, with which it was received.

"Mr. Wilson," said our host, stooping to remove from beneath his feet an exceedingly luxurious cloak of rare furs, "Mr. Wilson, this is your property." (The weather was cold; and, upon quitting my own room, I had thrown a cloak over my dressing wrapper, putting it off upon reaching the scene of play.) "I presume it is supererogatory to seek here (eyeing the folds of the garment with a bitter smile) for any farther evidence of your skill. Indeed, we have had enough. You will see the necessity, I hope, of quitting Oxford—at all events, of quitting instantly my chambers."

Abased, humbled to the dust as I then was, it is probable that I should have resented this galling language by immediate personal violence, had not my whole attention been at the moment arrested by a fact of the most startling character. The cloak which I had worn was of a rare description of fur; how rare, how extravagantly costly, I shall not venture to say. Its fashion, too, was of my own fantastic invention; for I was fastidious to an absurd degree of coxcombry, in matters of this frivolous nature. When, therefore, Mr. Preston reached me that which he had picked up upon the floor, and near the folding-doors of the apartment, it was with an astonishment nearly bordering upon terror, that I perceived my own already hanging on my arm, (where I had no doubt unwittingly placed it,) and that

---

[20]"Made round, rounded" (French).
[21]Face or high value cards.

the one presented me was but its exact counterpart in every, in even the minutest possible particular. The singular being who had so disastrously exposed me, had been muffled, I remember, in a cloak; and none had been worn at all by any of the members of our party, with the exception of myself. Retaining some presence of mind, I took the one offered me by Preston; placed it, unnoticed, over my own; left the apartment with a resolute scowl of defiance; and, next morning ere dawn of day, commenced a hurried journey from Oxford to the continent, in a perfect agony of horror and of shame.

I fled in vain. My evil destiny pursued me as if in exultation, and proved, indeed, that the exercise of its mysterious dominion had as yet only begun. Scarcely had I set foot in Paris, ere I had fresh evidence of the detestable interest taken by this Wilson in my concerns. Years flew, while I experienced no relief. Villain!—at Rome, with how untimely, yet with how spectral an officiousness, stepped he in between me and my ambition! At Vienna, too—at Berlin—and at Moscow! Where, in truth, had I *not* bitter cause to curse him within my heart? From his inscrutable tyranny did I at length flee, panic-stricken, as from a pestilence; and to the very ends of the earth *I fled in vain.*

And again, and again, in secret communion with my own spirit, would I demand the questions "Who is he?—whence came he?—and what are his objects?" But no answer was there found. And now I scrutinized, with a minute scrutiny, the forms, and the methods, and the leading traits of his impertinent supervision. But even here there was very little upon which to base a conjecture. It was noticeable, indeed, that, in no one of the multiplied instances in which he had of late crossed my path, had he so crossed it except to frustrate those schemes, or to disturb those actions, which, if fully carried out, might have resulted in bitter mischief. Poor justification this, in truth, for an authority so imperiously assumed! Poor indemnity for natural rights of self-agency so pertinaciously, so insultingly denied!

I had also been forced to notice that my tormentor, for a very long period of time, (while scrupulously and with miraculous dexterity maintaining his whim of an identity of apparel with myself,) had so contrived it, in the execution of his varied interference with my will, that I saw not, at any moment, the features of his face. Be Wilson what he might, *this,* at least, was but the veriest of affectation, or of folly. Could he, for an instant, have supposed that, in my admonisher at Eton—in the destroyer of my honor at Oxford,—in him who thwarted my ambition at Rome, my revenge at Paris, my passionate love at Naples, or what he falsely termed my avarice in Egypt,—that in this, my arch-enemy and evil genius, I could fail to recognise the William Wilson of my school-boy days,—the namesake, the companion, the rival,—the hated and dreaded rival at Dr. Bransby's? Impossible!—But let me hasten to the last eventful scene of the drama.

Thus far I had succumbed supinely to this imperious domination. The sentiment of deep awe with which I habitually regarded the elevated character, the majestic wisdom, the apparent omnipresence and omnipotence of Wilson, added to a feeling of even terror, with which certain other traits in his nature and assumptions inspired me, had operated, hitherto, to impress me with an idea of my own utter weakness and helplessness, and to suggest an implicit, although bitterly reluctant submission to his arbitrary will. But, of late days, I had given myself up entirely to wine; and its maddening influence upon my hereditary temper rendered me more and more impatient of control. I began to murmur,—to hesitate,—to resist. And was it only fancy which induced me to believe that, with the increase of my own firmness, that of my tormentor underwent a proportional diminution? Be this as it may, I now began to feel the inspiration of a burning hope, and at length nurtured in my secret thoughts a stern and desperate resolution that I would submit no longer to be enslaved.

It was at Rome, during the Carnival of 18—, that I attended a masquerade in the palazzo of the Neapolitan Duke Di Broglio. I had indulged more freely than usual in the excesses of the wine-table; and now the suffocating atmosphere of the crowded rooms irritated me beyond endurance. The difficulty, too, of forcing my way through the mazes of the company contributed not a little to the ruffling of my temper; for I was anxiously seeking (let me not say with what unworthy motive) the young, the gay, the beautiful wife of the aged and doting Di Broglio. With a too unscrupulous confidence she had previously communicated to me the secret of the costume in which she would be habited, and now, having caught a glimpse of her person, I was hurrying to make my way into her presence. At this moment I felt a light hand placed upon my shoulder, and that ever-remembered, low, damnable *whisper* within my ear.

In an absolute frenzy of wrath, I turned at once upon him who had thus interrupted me, and seized him violently by the collar. He was attired, as I had expected, in a costume altogether similar to my own; wearing a Spanish cloak of blue velvet, begirt about the waist with a crimson belt sustaining a rapier. A mask of black silk entirely covered his face.

"Scoundrel!" I said, in a voice husky with rage, while every syllable I uttered seemed as new fuel to my fury; "scoundrel! impostor! accursed villain! you shall not—you *shall not* dog me unto death! Follow me, or I stab you where you stand!"—and I broke my way from the ball-room into a small ante-chamber adjoining, dragging him unresistingly with me as I went.

Upon entering, I thrust him furiously from me. He staggered against the wall, while I closed the door with an oath, and commanded him to draw. He hesitated but for an instant; then, with a slight sigh, drew in silence, and put himself upon his defence.

The contest was brief indeed. I was frantic with every species of wild excitement, and felt within my single arm the energy and power of a multitude. In a few seconds I forced him by sheer strength against the wainscoting, and thus, getting him at mercy, plunged my sword, with brute ferocity, repeatedly through and through his bosom.

At that instant some person tried the latch of the door. I hastened to prevent an intrusion, and then immediately returned to my dying antagonist. But what human language can adequately portray *that* astonishment, *that* horror which possessed me at the spectacle then presented to view? The brief moment in which I averted my eyes had been sufficient to produce, apparently, a material change in the arrangements at the upper or farther end of the room. A large mirror,—so at first it seemed to me in my confusion—now stood where none had been perceptible before; and, as I stepped up to it in extremity of terror, mine own image, but with features all pale and dabbled in blood, advanced to meet me with a feeble and tottering gait.

Thus it appeared, I say, but was not. It was my antagonist—it was Wilson, who then stood before me in the agonies of his dissolution. His mask and cloak lay, where he had thrown them, upon the floor. Not a thread in all his raiment—not a line in all the marked and singular lineaments of his face which was not, even in the most absolute identity, *mine own!*

It was Wilson; but he spoke no longer in a whisper, and I could have fancied that I myself was speaking while he said:

"*You have conquered, and I yield. Yet, henceforward art thou also dead—dead to the World, to Heaven and to Hope! In me didst thou exist—and, in my death, see by this image, which is thine own, how utterly thou hast murdered thyself.*"

1839

The Man of the Crowd

Ce grand malheur, de ne pouvoir être seul.
                                        La Bruyère[1]

It was well said of a certain German book that *"er lasst sich nicht lesen"*—it does not permit itself to be read. There are some secrets which do not permit themselves to be told. Men die nightly in their beds, wringing the hands of ghostly confessors, and looking them piteously in the eyes—die with despair of heart and convulsion of throat, on account of the hideousness of mysteries which will not *suffer themselves* to be revealed. Now and then, alas, the conscience of man takes up a burthen so heavy in horror that it can be thrown down only into the grave. And thus the essence of all crime is undivulged.

Not long ago, about the closing in of an evening in autumn, I sat at the large bow window of the D —— Coffee-House in London. For some months I had been ill in health, but was now convalescent, and, with returning strength, found myself in one of those happy moods which are so precisely the converse of *ennui*[2]— moods of the keenest appetency, when the film from the mental vision departs— the αχλυς ος πριν επηεν[3]—and the intellect, electrified, surpasses as greatly its every-day condition, as does the vivid yet candid reason of Leibnitz, the mad and flimsy rhetoric of Gorgias.[4] Merely to breathe was enjoyment; and I derived positive pleasure even from many of the legitimate sources of pain. I felt a calm but inquisitive interest in every thing. With a cigar in my mouth and a newspaper in my lap, I had been amusing myself for the greater part of the afternoon, now in poring over advertisements, now in observing the promiscuous company in the room, and now in peering through the smoky panes into the street.

This latter is one of the principal thoroughfares of the city, and had been very much crowded during the whole day. But, as the darkness came on, the throng momently increased; and, by the time the lamps were well lighted, two dense and continuous tides of population were rushing past the door. At this particular period of the evening I had never before been in a similar situation, and the tumultuous sea of human heads filled me, therefore, with a delicious novelty of emotion. I gave up, at length, all care of things within the hotel, and became absorbed in contemplation of the scene without.

At first my observations took an abstract and generalizing turn. I looked at the passengers in masses, and thought of them in their aggregate relations. Soon, however, I descended to details, and regarded with minute interest the innumerable varieties of figure, dress, air, gait, visage, and expression of countenance.

By far the greater number of those who went by had a satisfied business-like demeanor, and seemed to be thinking only of making their way through the press. Their brows were knit, and their eyes rolled quickly; when pushed against by fellow-wayfarers they evinced no symptom of impatience, but adjusted their clothes and hurried on. Others, still a numerous class, were restless in their movements, had flushed faces, and talked and gesticulated to themselves, as if feeling in solitude on account of the very denseness of the company around. When impeded in their progress, these people suddenly ceased muttering, but redoubled their gesticulations, and awaited, with an absent and overdone smile upon the lips,

---

[1]"That great misfortune, to be unable to be alone"; adapted from *Characters* by Jean de La Bruyère (1645–1696), French satirist and writer of maxims and character portraits.

[2]"Boredom" (French).

[3]"The mist that before was upon it" (from Homer's *Iliad,* Book V, 1, 127).

[4]Baron Gottfried Wilhelm von Leibnitz (1646–1716), German philosopher and mathematician; Gorgias, fourth-century B.C. Greek sophist whose name is given to one of Plato's Socratic dialogues on style as a means of flattery (and without substance).

the course of the persons impeding them. If jostled, they bowed profusely to the jostlers, and appeared overwhelmed with confusion.—There was nothing very distinctive about these two large classes beyond what I have noted. Their habiliments belonged to that order which is pointedly termed the decent. They were undoubtedly noblemen, merchants, attorneys, tradesmen, stock-jobbers—the Eupatrids[5] and the common-places of society—men of leisure and men actively engaged in affairs of their own—conducting business upon their own responsibility. They did not greatly excite my attention.

The tribe of clerks was an obvious one and here I discerned two remarkable divisions. There were the junior clerks of flash houses—young gentlemen with tight coats, bright boots, well-oiled hair, and supercilious lips. Setting aside a certain dapperness of carriage, which may be termed *deskism* for want of a better word, the manner of these persons seemed to me an exact facsimile of what had been the perfection of *bon ton*[6] about twelve or eighteen months before. They wore the cast-off graces of the gentry;—and this, I believe, involves the best definition of the class.

The division of the upper clerks of staunch firms, or of the "steady old fellows," it was not possible to mistake. These were known by their coats and pantaloons of black or brown, made to sit comfortably, with white cravats and waistcoats, broad solid-looking shoes, and thick hose or gaiters.—They had all slightly bald heads, from which the right ears, long used to pen-holding, had an odd habit of standing off on end. I observed that they always removed or settled their hats with both hands, and wore watches, with short gold chains of a substantial and ancient pattern. Theirs was the affectation of respectability;—if indeed there be an affectation so honorable.

There were many individuals of dashing appearance, whom I easily understood as belonging to the race of swell pick-pockets, with which all great cities are infested. I watched these gentry with much inquisitiveness, and found it difficult to imagine how they should ever be mistaken for gentlemen by gentlemen themselves. Their voluminousness of wristband, with an air of excessive frankness, should betray them at once.

The gamblers, of whom I descried not a few, were still more easily recognisable. They wore every variety of dress, from that of the desperate thimble-rig bully,[7] with velvet waistcoat, fancy neckerchief, gilt chains, and filagreed buttons, to that of the scrupulously inornate clergyman, than which nothing could be less liable to suspicion. Still all were distinguished by a certain sodden swarthiness of complexion, a filmy dimness of eye, and pallor and compression of lip. There were two other traits, moreover, by which I could always detect them;—a guarded lowness of tone in conversation, and a more than ordinary extension of the thumb in a direction at right angles with the fingers.— Very often, in company with these sharpers, I observed an order of men somewhat different in habits, but still birds of a kindred feather. They may be defined as the gentlemen who live by their wits. They seem to prey upon the public in two battalions—that of the dandies and that of the military men. Of the first grade the leading features are long locks and smiles; of the second frogged coats and frowns.

Descending in the scale of what is termed gentility, I found darker and deeper themes for speculation. I saw Jew pedlars, with hawk eyes flashing from countenances whose every other feature wore only an expression of abject humility; sturdy professional street beggars scowling upon mendicants of a better stamp, whom despair alone had driven forth into the night for charity; feeble and ghastly

---

[5] Sons of noble families (from the ancient nobility of Attica in Greece).
[6] Stylishness.

[7] Con man, swindler (from the game in which the cheat deftly switches a pea from under one thimble or cup to another).

invalids, upon whom death had placed a sure hand, and who sidled and tottered through the mob, looking every one beseechingly in the face, as if in search of some chance consolation, some lost hope; modest young girls returning from long and late labor to a cheerless home, and shrinking more tearfully than indignantly from the glances of ruffians, whose direct contact, even, could not be avoided; women of the town of all kinds and of all ages—the unequivocal beauty in the prime of her womanhood, putting one in mind of the statue in Lucian, with the surface of Parian marble, and the interior filled with filth[8]—the loathsome and utterly lost leper in rags—the wrinkled, bejewelled and paint-begrimed beldame, making a last effort at youth—the mere child of immature form, yet, from long association, an adept in the dreadful coquetries of her trade, and burning with a rabid ambition to be ranked the equal of her elders in vice; drunkards innumerable and indescribable—some in shreds and patches, reeling, inarticulate, with bruised visage and lack-lustre eyes—some in whole although filthy garments, with a slightly unsteady swagger, thick sensual lips, and hearty-looking rubicund faces—others clothed in materials which had once been good, and which even now were scrupulously well brushed—men who walked with a more than naturally firm and springy step, but whose countenances were fearfully pale, whose eyes hideously wild and red, and who clutched with quivering fingers, as they strode through the crowd, at every object which came within their reach; beside these, pie-men, porters, coal-heavers, sweeps; organ-grinders, monkey-exhibiters and ballad mongers, those who vended with those who sang; ragged artizans and exhausted laborers of every description, and all full of a noisy and inordinate vivacity which jarred discordantly upon the ear, and gave an aching sensation to the eye.

As the night deepened, so deepened to me the interest of the scene; for not only did the general character of the crowd materially alter (its gentler features retiring in the gradual withdrawal of the more orderly portion of the people, and its harsher ones coming out into bolder relief, as the late hour brought forth every species of infamy from its den,) but the rays of the gas-lamps, feeble at first in their struggle with the dying day, had now at length gained ascendancy, and threw over every thing a fitful and garish lustre. All was dark yet splendid—as that ebony to which has been likened the style of Tertullian.[9]

The wild effects of the light enchained me to an examination of individual faces; and although the rapidity with which the world of light flitted before the window, prevented me from casting more than a glance upon each visage, still it seemed that, in my then peculiar mental state, I could frequently read, even in that brief interval of a glance, the history of long years.

With my brow to the glass, I was thus occupied in scrutinizing the mob, when suddenly there came into view a countenance (that of a decrepid old man, some sixty-five or seventy years of age,)—a countenance which at once arrested and absorbed my whole attention, on account of the absolute idiosyncracy of its expression. Any thing even remotely resembling that expression I had never seen before. I well remember that my first thought, upon beholding it, was that Retzsch, had he viewed it, would have greatly preferred it to his own pictural incarnations of the fiend.[10] As I endeavored, during the brief minute of my original survey, to form some analysis of the meaning conveyed, there arose confusedly and paradoxically within my mind, the ideas of vast mental power, of caution, of penuriousness, of avarice, of coolness, of malice, of blood-thirstiness, of triumph, of mer-

---

[8]From *The Cock*, by Lucian of Samosata (125?–200?), Greek satirist. Parian marble (from the island of Paros) was the finest.
[9]Said by the French essayist Jean-Louis Guez de Balzac

(1594–1655) of the style of Quintus Septimus Florens Tertullianus (160?–230?), Latin ecclesiastical writer.
[10]Friederich August Moritz Retzsch (1779–1857), German engraver noted for his illustrations of Goethe's *Faust.*

riment, of excessive terror, of intense—of supreme despair. I felt singularly aroused, startled, fascinated. "How wild a history," I said to myself, "is written within that bosom!" Then came a craving desire to keep the man in view—to know more of him. Hurriedly putting on an overcoat, and seizing my hat and cane, I made my way into the street, and pushed through the crowd in the direction which I had seen him take; for he had already disappeared. With some little difficulty I at length came within sight of him, approached, and followed him closely, yet cautiously, so as not to attract his attention.

I had now a good opportunity of examining his person. He was short in stature, very thin, and apparently very feeble. His clothes, generally, were filthy and ragged; but as he came, now and then, within the strong glare of a lamp, I perceived that his linen, although dirty, was of beautiful texture; and my vision deceived me, or, through a rent in a closely-buttoned and evidently second-handed *roquelaire*[11] which enveloped him, I caught a glimpse both of a diamond and of a dagger. These observations heightened my curiosity, and I resolved to follow the stranger whithersoever he should go.

It was now fully night-fall, and a thick humid fog hung over the city, soon ending in a settled and heavy rain. This change of weather had an odd effect upon the crowd, the whole of which was at once put into new commotion, and overshadowed by a world of umbrellas. The waver, the jostle, and the hum increased in a tenfold degree. For my own part I did not much regard the rain—the lurking of an old fever in my system rendering the moisture somewhat too dangerously pleasant. Tying a handkerchief about my mouth, I kept on. For half an hour the old man held his way with difficulty along the great thoroughfare; and I here walked close at his elbow through fear of losing sight of him. Never once turning his head to look back, he did not observe me. By and bye he passed into a cross street, which, although densely filled with people, was not quite so much thronged as the main one he had quitted. Here a change in his demeanor became evident. He walked more slowly and with less object than before—more hesitatingly. He crossed and re-crossed the way repeatedly without apparent aim; and the press was still so thick that, at every such movement, I was obliged to follow him closely. The street was a narrow and long one, and his course lay within it for nearly an hour, during which the passengers had gradually diminished to about that number which is ordinarily seen at noon in Broadway near the Park—so vast a difference is there between a London populace and that of the most frequented American city. A second turn brought us into a square, brilliantly lighted, and overflowing with life. The old manner of the stranger re-appeared. His chin fell upon his breast, while his eyes rolled wildly from under his knit brows, in every direction, upon those who hemmed him in. He urged his way steadily and perseveringly. I was surprised, however, to find, upon his having made the circuit of the square, that he turned and retraced his steps. Still more was I astonished to see him repeat the same walk several times—once nearly detecting me as he came round with a sudden movement.

In this exercise he spent another hour, at the end of which we met with far less interruption from passengers than at first. The rain fell fast; the air grew cool; and the people were retiring to their homes. With a gesture of impatience, the wanderer passed into a bye-street comparatively deserted. Down this, some quarter of a mile long, he rushed with an activity I could not have dreamed of seeing in one so aged, and which put me to much trouble in pursuit. A few minutes brought us to a large and busy bazaar, with the localities of which the stranger appeared well acquainted, and where his original demeanor again became appar-

---

[11]Variant of *roquelaure*, knee-length cloak.

ent, as he forced his way to and fro, without aim, among the host of buyers and
sellers.

During the hour and a half, or thereabouts, which we passed in this place, it
required much caution on my part to keep him within reach without attracting his
observation. Luckily I wore a pair of caoutchouc[12] over-shoes, and could move
about in perfect silence. At no moment did he see that I watched him. He entered
shop after shop, priced nothing, spoke no word, and looked at all objects with a
wild and vacant stare. I was now utterly amazed at his behaviour, and firmly resolved that we should not part until I had satisfied myself in some measure respecting him.

A loud-toned clock struck eleven, and the company were fast deserting the bazaar. A shop-keeper, in putting up a shutter, jostled the old man, and at the instant I saw a strong shudder come over his frame. He hurried into the street,
looked anxiously around him for an instant, and then ran with incredible swiftness through many crooked and people-less lanes, until we emerged once more
upon the great thoroughfare whence we had started—the street of the D———
Hotel. It no longer wore, however, the same aspect. It was still brilliant with gas;
but the rain fell fiercely, and there were few persons to be seen. The stranger
grew pale. He walked moodily some paces up the once populous avenue, then,
with a heavy sigh, turned in the direction of the river, and, plunging through a
great variety of devious ways, came out, at length, in view of one of the principal
theatres. It was about being closed, and the audience were thronging from the
doors. I saw the old man gasp as if for breath while he threw himself amid the
crowd; but I thought that the intense agony of his countenance had, in some measure, abated. His head again fell upon his breast; he appeared as I had seen him
at first. I observed that he now took the course in which had gone the greater
number of the audience—but, upon the whole, I was at a loss to comprehend the
waywardness of his actions.

As he proceeded, the company grew more scattered, and his old uneasiness
and vacillation were resumed. For some time he followed closely a party of some
ten or twelve roisterers; but from this number one by one dropped off, until three
only remained together, in a narrow and gloomy lane little frequented. The
stranger paused, and, for a moment, seemed lost in thought; then, with every
mark of agitation, pursued rapidly a route which brought us to the verge of the
city, amid regions very different from those we had hitherto traversed. It was the
most noisome[13] quarter of London, where every thing wore the worst impress of
the most deplorable poverty, and of the most desperate crime. By the dim light of
an accidental lamp, tall, antique, worm-eaten, wooden tenements were seen tottering to their fall, in directions so many and capricious that scarce the semblance of
a passage was discernible between them. The paving-stones lay at random, displaced from their beds by the rankly-growing grass. Horrible filth festered in the
dammed-up gutters. The whole atmosphere teemed with desolation. Yet, as we
proceeded, the sounds of human life revived by sure degrees, and at length large
bands of the most abandoned of a London populace were seen reeling to and fro.
The spirits of the old man again flickered up, as a lamp which is near its death-
hour. Once more he strode onward with elastic tread. Suddenly a corner was
turned, a blaze of light burst upon our sight, and we stood before one of the huge
suburban temples of Intemperance—one of the palaces of the fiend, Gin.

It was now nearly day-break; but a number of wretched inebriates still pressed
in and out of the flaunting entrance. With a half shriek of joy the old man forced
a passage within, resumed at once his original bearing, and stalked backward and

---

[12]Rubber.
[13]Foul smelling.

forward, without apparent object, among the throng. He had not been thus long occupied, however, before a rush to the doors gave token that the host was closing them for the night. It was something even more intense than despair that I then observed upon the countenance of the singular being whom I had watched so pertinaciously. Yet he did not hesitate in his career, but, with a mad energy, retraced his steps at once, to the heart of the mighty London. Long and swiftly he fled, while I followed him in the wildest amazement, resolute not to abandon a scrutiny in which I now felt an interest all-absorbing. The sun arose while we proceeded, and, when we had once again reached that most thronged mart of the populous town, the street of the D——— Hotel, it presented an appearance of human bustle and activity scarcely inferior to what I had seen on the evening before. And here, long, amid the momently increasing confusion, did I persist in my pursuit of the stranger. But, as usual, he walked to and fro, and during the day did not pass from out the turmoil of that street. And, as the shades of the second evening came on, I grew wearied unto death, and, stopping fully in front of the wanderer, gazed at him steadfastly in the face. He noticed me not, but resumed his solemn walk, while I, ceasing to follow, remained absorbed in contemplation. "This old man," I said at length, "is the type and the genius of deep crime. He refuses to be alone. *He is the man of the crowd*. It will be in vain to follow; for I shall learn no more of him, nor of his deeds. The worst heart of the world is a grosser book than the 'Hortulus Animæ,'[14] and perhaps it is but one of the great mercies of God that *'er lasst sich nicht lesen.*' "[15]

1840

The Oval Portrait[1]

The chateau into which my valet had ventured to make forcible entrance, rather than permit me, in my desperately wounded condition, to pass a night in the open air, was one of those piles of commingled gloom and grandeur which have so long frowned among the Apennines, not less in fact than in the fancy of Mrs. Radcliffe.[2] To all appearance it had been temporarily and very lately abandoned. We established ourselves in one of the smallest and least sumptuously furnished apartments. It lay in a remote turret of the building. Its decorations were rich, yet tattered and antique. Its walls were hung with tapestry and bedecked with manifold and multiform armorial trophies, together with an unusually great number of very spirited modern paintings in frames of rich golden arabesque. In these paintings, which depended from the walls not only in their main surfaces, but in very many nooks which the bizarre architecture of the chateau rendered necessary—in these paintings my incipient delirium, perhaps, had caused me to take deep interest; so that I bade Pedro to close the heavy shutters of the room— since it was already night—to light the tongues of a tall candelabrum which stood by the head of my bed—and to throw open far and wide the fringed curtains of black velvet which enveloped the bed itself. I wished all this done that I might resign myself, if not to sleep, at least alternately to the contemplation of these pic-

[14]"The 'Hortulus Animae cum Oratiunculis Superadditis' of Grünninger" (Poe's note). *Little Garden of the Soul* (1500), published by the Strasbourg printer Johannes Grünninger, contained illustrations described as indecorous.
[15]"It does not permit itself to be read" (German), a repetition of the phrase in the first sentence of the story.

[1]In its first version, published in 1842, this story was much longer and carried the title "Life in Death."
[2]In *The Mysteries of Udolpho* (1794), by Ann Ward Radcliffe (1764–1823), terrifying episodes are set in an old castle in the Apennines, mountains of central Italy.

tures, and the perusal of a small volume which had been found upon the pillow, and which purported to criticise and describe them.

Long—long I read—and devoutly, devotedly I gazed. Rapidly and gloriously the hours flew by, and the deep midnight came. The position of the candelabrum displeased me, and outreaching my hand with difficulty, rather than disturb my slumbering valet, I placed it so as to throw its rays more fully upon the book.

But the action produced an effect altogether unanticipated. The rays of the numerous candles (for there were many) now fell within a niche of the room which had hitherto been thrown into deep shade by one of the bed-posts. I thus saw in vivid light a picture all unnoticed before. It was the portrait of a young girl just ripening into womanhood. I glanced at the painting hurriedly, and then closed my eyes. Why I did this was not at first apparent even to my own perception. But while my lids remained thus shut, I ran over in mind my reason for so shutting them. It was an impulsive movement to gain time for thought—to make sure that my vision had not deceived me—to calm and subdue my fancy for a more sober and more certain gaze. In a very few moments I again looked fixedly at the painting.

That I now saw aright I could not and would not doubt; for the first flashing of the candles upon that canvass had seemed to dissipate the dreamy stupor which was stealing over my senses, and to startle me at once into waking life.

The portrait, I have already said, was that of a young girl. It was a mere head and shoulders, done in what is technically termed a *vignette* manner; much in the style of the favorite heads of Sully.[3] The arms, the bosom and even the ends of the radiant hair, melted imperceptibly into the vague yet deep shadow which formed the back ground of the whole. The frame was oval, richly gilded and fila-greed in *Moresque*.[4] As a thing of art nothing could be more admirable than the painting itself. But it could have been neither the execution of the work, nor the immortal beauty of the countenance, which had so suddenly and so vehemently moved me. Least of all, could it have been that my fancy, shaken from its half slumber, had mistaken the head for that of a living person. I saw at once that the peculiarities of the design, of the *vignetting*, and of the frame, must have instantly dispelled such idea—must have prevented even its momentary entertainment. Thinking earnestly upon these points, I remained, for an hour perhaps, half sit-ting, half reclining, with my vision riveted upon the portrait. At length, satisfied with the true secret of its effect, I fell back within the bed. I had found the spell of the picture in an absolute *life-likeliness* of expression, which, at first startling, finally confounded, subdued and appalled me. With deep and reverent awe I replaced the candelabrum in its former position. The cause of my deep agitation being thus shut from view, I sought eagerly the volume which discussed the paintings and their histories. Turning to the number which designated the oval portrait, I there read the vague and quaint words which follow:

"She was a maiden of rarest beauty, and not more lovely than full of glee. And evil was the hour when she saw, and loved, and wedded the painter. He, passion-ate, studious, austere, and having already a bride in his Art; she a maiden of rar-est beauty, and not more lovely than full of glee: all light and smiles, and frolick-some as the young fawn: loving and cherishing all things: hating only the Art which was her rival: dreading only the pallet and brushes and other untoward in-struments which deprived her of the countenance of her lover. It was thus a ter-rible thing for this lady to hear the painter speak of his desire to portray even his

---

[3]A *vignette* in portraiture depicts head and shoulders with an indefinite border; Robert Sully, nephew of the re-nowned British painter Thomas Sully (1783–1872), was Poe's schoolmate in Richmond and a painter much after the style of his uncle; his painting is thought to have in-spired "The Oval Portrait."
[4]In the elaborate, fanciful Moorish style.

young bride. But she was humble and obedient, and sat meekly for many weeks in the dark high turret-chamber where the light dripped upon the pale canvass only from overhead. But he, the painter, took glory in his work, which went on from hour to hour, and from day to day. And he was a passionate, and wild, and moody man, who became lost in reveries; so that he *would* not see that the light which fell so ghastlily in that lone turret withered the health and the spirits of his bride, who pined visibly to all but him. Yet she smiled on and still on, uncomplainingly, because she saw that the painter, (who had high renown,) took a fervid and burning pleasure in his task, and wrought day and night to depict her who so loved him, yet who grew daily more dispirited and weak. And in sooth some who beheld the portrait spoke of its resemblance in low words, as of a mighty marvel, and a proof not less of the power of the painter than of his deep love for her whom he depicted so surpassingly well. But at length, as the labor drew nearer to its conclusion, there were admitted none into the turret; for the painter had grown wild with the ardor of his work, and turned his eyes from the canvass rarely, even to regard the countenance of his wife. And he *would* not see that the tints which he spread upon the canvass were drawn from the cheeks of her who sat beside him. And when many weeks had passed, and but little remained to do, save one brush upon the mouth and one tint upon the eye, the spirit of the lady again flickered up as the flame within the socket of the lamp. And then the brush was given, and then the tint was placed; and, for one moment, the painter stood entranced before the work which he had wrought; but in the next, while he yet gazed, he grew tremulous and very pallid, and aghast, and crying with a loud voice, 'This is indeed *Life* itself!' turned suddenly to regard his beloved:—*She was dead!*"

1842, 1845

The Masque of the Red Death

The "Red Death" had long devastated the country. No pestilence had ever been so fatal, or so hideous. Blood was its Avatar[1] and its seal—the redness and the horror of blood. There were sharp pains, and sudden dizziness, and then profuse bleeding at the pores, with dissolution. The scarlet stains upon the body and especially upon the face of the victim, were the pest ban which shut him out from the aid and from the sympathy of his fellowmen. And the whole seizure, progress and termination of the disease, were the incidents of half an hour.

But the Prince Prospero was happy and dauntless and sagacious. When his dominions were half depopulated, he summoned to his presence a thousand hale and light-hearted friends from among the knights and dames of his court, and with these retired to the deep seclusion of one of his castellated abbeys. This was an extensive and magnificent structure, the creation of the prince's own eccentric yet august taste. A strong and lofty wall girdled it in. This wall had gates of iron. The courtiers, having entered, brought furnaces and massy hammers and welded the bolts. They resolved to leave means neither of ingress or egress to the sudden impulses of despair or of frenzy from within. The abbey was amply provisioned. With such precautions the courtiers might bid defiance to contagion. The external world could take care of itself. In the meantime it was folly to grieve, or to think. The prince had provided all the appliances of pleasure. There were buffoons,

---

[1]Embodiment.

there were improvisatori,[2] there were ballet-dancers, there were musicians, there was Beauty, there was wine. All these and security were within. Without was the "Red Death."

It was toward the close of the fifth or sixth month of his seclusion, and while the pestilence raged most furiously abroad, that the Prince Prospero entertained his thousand friends at a masked ball of the most unusual magnificence.

It was a voluptuous scene, that masquerade. But first let me tell of the rooms in which it was held. There were seven—an imperial suite. In many palaces, however, such suites form a long and straight vista, while the folding doors slide back nearly to the walls on either hand, so that the view of the whole extent is scarcely impeded. Here the case was very different; as might have been expected from the duke's love of the *bizarre*. The apartments were so irregularly disposed that the vision embraced but little more than one at a time. There was a sharp turn at every twenty or thirty yards, and at each turn a novel effect. To the right and left, in the middle of each wall, a tall and narrow Gothic window looked out upon a closed corridor which pursued the windings of the suite. These windows were of stained glass whose color varied in accordance with the prevailing hue of the decorations of the chamber into which it opened. That at the eastern extremity was hung, for example, in blue—and vividly blue were its windows. The second chamber was purple in its ornaments and tapestries, and here the panes were purple. The third was green throughout, and so were the casements. The fourth was furnished and lighted with orange—the fifth with white—the sixth with violet. The seventh apartment was closely shrouded in black velvet tapestries that hung all over the ceiling and down the walls, falling in heavy folds upon a carpet of the same material and hue. But in this chamber only, the color of the windows failed to correspond with the decorations. The panes here were scarlet—a deep blood color. Now in no one of the seven apartments was there any lamp or candelabrum, amid the profusion of golden ornaments that lay scattered to and fro or depended from the roof. There was no light of any kind emanating from lamp or candle within the suite of chambers. But in the corridors that followed the suite, there stood, opposite to each window, a heavy tripod, bearing a brazier of fire that projected its rays through the tinted glass and so glaringly illumined the room. And thus were produced a multitude of gaudy and fantastic appearances. But in the western or black chamber the effect of the fire-light that streamed upon the dark hangings through the blood-tinted panes, was ghastly in the extreme, and produced so wild a look upon the countenances of those who entered, that there were few of the company bold enough to set foot within its precincts at all.

It was in this apartment, also, that there stood against the western wall, a gigantic clock of ebony. Its pendulum swung to and fro with a dull, heavy, monotonous clang; and when the minute-hand made the circuit of the face, and the hour was to be stricken, there came from the brazen lungs of the clock a sound which was clear and loud and deep and exceedingly musical, but of so peculiar a note and emphasis that, at each lapse of an hour, the musicians of the orchestra were constrained to pause, momentarily, in their performance, to harken to the sound; and thus the waltzers perforce ceased their evolutions; and there was a brief disconcert of the whole gay company; and, while the chimes of the clock yet rang, it was observed that the giddiest grew pale, and the more aged and sedate passed their hands over their brows as if in confused revery or meditation. But when the echoes had fully ceased, a light laughter at once pervaded the assembly; the musicians looked at each other and smiled as if at their own nervousness and folly, and made whispering vows, each to the other, that the next chiming of the clock

---

[2]Wandering musicians and composers, extemporaneously performing.

should produce in them no similar emotion; and then, after the lapse of sixty minutes, (which embrace three thousand and six hundred seconds of the Time that flies,) there came yet another chiming of the clock, and then were the same disconcert and tremulousness and meditation as before.

But, in spite of these things, it was a gay and magnificent revel. The tastes of the duke were peculiar. He had a fine eye for colors and effects. He disregarded the *decora*[3] of mere fashion. His plans were bold and fiery, and his conceptions glowed with barbaric lustre. There are some who would have thought him mad. His followers felt that he was not. It was necessary to hear and see and touch him to be *sure* that he was not.

He had directed, in great part, the moveable embellishments of the seven chambers, upon occasion of this great *fête;* and it was his own guiding taste which had given character to the masqueraders. Be sure they were grotesque. There were much glare and glitter and piquancy and phantasm—much of what has been since seen in "Hernani."[4] There were arabesque figures with unsuited limbs and appointments. There were delirious fancies such as the madman fashions. There were much of the beautiful, much of the wanton, much of the *bizarre,* something of the terrible, and not a little of that which might have excited disgust. To and fro in the seven chambers there stalked, in fact, a multitude of dreams. And these—the dreams—writhed in and about, taking hue from the rooms, and causing the wild music of the orchestra to seem as the echo of their steps. And, anon, there strikes the ebony clock which stands in the hall of the velvet. And then, for a moment, all is still, and all is silent save the voice of the clock. The dreams are stiff-frozen as they stand. But the echoes of the chime die away—they have endured but an instant—and a light, half-subdued laughter floats after them as they depart. And now again the music swells, and the dreams live, and writhe to and fro more merrily than ever, taking hue from the many tinted windows through which stream the rays from the tripods. But to the chamber which lies most westwardly of the seven, there are now none of the maskers who venture; for the night is waning away; and there flows a ruddier light through the blood-colored panes; and the blackness of the sable drapery appals; and to him whose foot falls upon the sable carpet, there comes from the near clock of ebony a muffled peal more solemnly emphatic than any which reaches *their* ears who indulge in the more remote gaieties of the other apartments.

But these other apartments were densely crowded, and in them beat feverishly the heart of life. And the revel went whirlingly on, until at length there commenced the sounding of midnight upon the clock. And then the music ceased, as I have told; and the evolutions of the waltzers were quieted; and there was an uneasy cessation of all things as before. But now there were twelve strokes to be sounded by the bell of the clock; and thus it happened, perhaps, that more of thought crept, with more of time, into the meditations of the thoughtful among those who revelled. And thus, too, it happened, perhaps, that before the last echoes of the last chime had utterly sunk into silence, there were many individuals in the crowd who had found leisure to become aware of the presence of a masked figure which had arrested the attention of no single individual before. And the rumor of this new presence having spread itself whisperingly around, there arose at length from the whole company a buzz, or murmur, expressive of disapprobation and surprise—then, finally, of terror, of horror, and of disgust.

In an assembly of phantasms such as I have painted, it may well be supposed that no ordinary appearance could have excited such sensation. In truth the mas-

---

[3]Rules or dictates.
[4]Elaborately costumed romantic play (1830) by Victor Hugo (1802–1885), French author.

querade license of the night was nearly unlimited; but the figure in question had out-Heroded Herod,[5] and gone beyond the bounds of even the prince's indefinite decorum. There are chords in the hearts of the most reckless which cannot be touched without emotion. Even with the utterly lost, to whom life and death are equally jests, there are matters of which no jest can be made. The whole company, indeed, seemed now deeply to feel that in the costume and bearing of the stranger neither wit nor propriety existed. The figure was tall and gaunt, and shrouded from head to foot in the habiliments of the grave. The mask which concealed the visage was made so nearly to resemble the countenance of a stiffened corpse that the closest scrutiny must have had difficulty in detecting the cheat. And yet all this might have been endured, if not approved, by the mad revellers around. But the mummer had gone so far as to assume the type of the Red Death. His vesture was dabbled in *blood*—and his broad brow, with all the features of the face, was besprinkled with the scarlet horror.

When the eyes of Prince Prospero fell upon this spectral image (which with a slow and solemn movement, as if more fully to sustain its *role,* stalked to and fro among the waltzers) he was seen to be convulsed, in the first moment with a strong shudder either of terror or distaste; but, in the next, his brow reddened with rage.

"Who dares?" he demanded hoarsely of the courtiers who stood near him— "who dares insult us with this blasphemous mockery? Seize him and unmask him—that we may know whom we have to hang at sunrise, from the battlements!"

It was in the eastern or blue chamber in which stood the Prince Prospero as he uttered these words. They rang throughout the seven rooms loudly and clearly— for the prince was a bold and robust man, and the music had became hushed at the waving of his hand.

It was in the blue room where stood the prince, with a group of pale courtiers by his side. At first, as he spoke, there was a slight rushing movement of this group in the direction of the intruder, who at the moment was also near at hand, and now, with deliberate and stately step, made closer approach to the speaker. But from a certain nameless awe with which the mad assumptions of the mummer had inspired the whole party, there were found none who put forth hand to seize him; so that, unimpeded, he passed within a yard of the prince's person; and, while the vast assembly, as if with one impulse, shrank from the centres of the rooms to the walls, he made his way uninterruptedly, but with the same solemn and measured step which had distinguished him from the first, through the blue chamber to the purple—through the purple to the green—through the green to the orange—through this again to the white—and even thence to the violet, ere a decided movement had been made to arrest him. It was then, however, that the Prince Prospero, maddening with rage and the shame of his own momentary cowardice, rushed hurriedly through the six chambers, while none followed him on account of a deadly terror that had seized upon all. He bore aloft a drawn dagger, and had approached, in rapid impetuosity, to within three or four feet of the retreating figure, when the latter, having attained the extremity of the velvet apartment, turned suddenly and confronted his pursuer. There was a sharp cry—and the dagger dropped gleaming upon the sable carpet, upon which, instantly afterwards, fell prostrate in death the Prince Prospero. Then, summoning the wild courage of despair, a throng of the revellers at once threw themselves into the black apartment, and, seizing the mummer, whose tall figure stood erect and motionless within the shadow of the ebony clock, gasped in unutterable horror at

---

[5]Gone beyond the limits of taste or sense, as did Herod, the king of Judea, in ordering the slaughter of all children in order to destroy Jesus; from Shakespeare's *Hamlet,* III, ii (Hamlet's speech to the players).

finding the grave cerements and corpse-like mask which they handled with so violent a rudeness, untenanted by any tangible form.

And now was acknowledged the presence of the Red Death. He had come like a thief in the night. And one by one dropped the revellers in the blood-bedewed halls of their revel, and died each in the despairing posture of his fall. And the life of the ebony clock went out with that of the last of the gay. And the flames of the tripods expired. And Darkness and Decay and the Red Death held illimitable dominion over all.

1842

The Purloined Letter

Nil sapientiae odiosius acumine nimio.

Seneca[1]

At Paris, just after dark one gusty evening in the autumn of 18—, I was enjoying the twofold luxury of meditation and a meerschaum,[2] in company with my friend C. Auguste Dupin, in his little back library, or book-closet, *au troisième*,[3] *No. 33, Rue Dunôt, Faubourg St. Germain*. For one hour at least we had maintained a profound silence; while each, to any casual observer, might have seemed intently and exclusively occupied with the curling eddies of smoke that oppressed the atmosphere of the chamber. For myself, however, I was mentally discussing certain topics which had formed matter for conversation between us at an earlier period of the evening; I mean the affair of the Rue Morgue, and the mystery attending the murder of Marie Rogêt.[4] I looked upon it, therefore, as something of a coincidence, when the door of our apartment was thrown open and admitted our old acquaintance, Monsieur G——, the Prefect[5] of the Parisian police.

We gave him a hearty welcome; for there was nearly half as much of the entertaining as of the contemptible about the man, and we had not seen him for several years. We had been sitting in the dark, and Dupin now arose for the purpose of lighting a lamp, but sat down again, without doing so, upon G.'s saying that he had called to consult us, or rather to ask the opinion of my friend, about some official business which had occasioned a great deal of trouble.

"If it is any point requiring reflection," observed Dupin, as he forebore to enkindle the wick, "we shall examine it to better purpose in the dark."

"That is another of your odd notions," said the Prefect, who had a fashion of calling every thing "odd" that was beyond his comprehension, and thus lived amid an absolute legion of "oddities."

"Very true," said Dupin, as he supplied his visiter with a pipe, and rolled towards him a comfortable chair.

"And what is the difficulty now?" I asked. "Nothing more in the assassination way, I hope?"

"Oh no; nothing of that nature. The fact is, the business is *very* simple indeed, and I make no doubt that we can manage it sufficiently well ourselves; but then I thought Dupin would like to hear the details of it, because it is so excessively *odd*."

"Simple and odd," said Dupin.

"Why, yes; and not exactly that, either. The fact is, we have all been a good deal puzzled because the affair *is* so simple, and yet baffles us altogether."

"Perhaps it is the very simplicity of the thing which puts you at fault," said my friend.

"What nonsense you *do* talk!" replied the Prefect, laughing heartily.

"Perhaps the mystery is a little *too* plain," said Dupin.

"Oh, good heavens! who ever heard of such an idea?"

"A little *too* self-evident."

"Ha! ha! ha!—ha! ha! ha!—ho! ho! ho!" roared our visiter, profoundly amused, "oh, Dupin, you will be the death of me yet!"

"And what, after all, *is* the matter on hand?" I asked.

"Why, I will tell you," replied the Prefect, as he gave a long, steady, and contemplative puff, and settled himself in his chair. "I will tell you in a few words; but, before I begin, let me caution you that this is an affair demanding the greatest secrecy, and that I should most probably lose the position I now hold, were it known that I confided it to any one."

"Proceed," said I.

"Or not," said Dupin.

"Well, then; I have received personal information, from a very high quarter, that a certain document of the last importance, has been purloined from the royal apartments. The individual who purloined it is known; this beyond a doubt; he was seen to take it. It is known, also, that it still remains in his possession."

"How is this known?" asked Dupin.

"It is clearly inferred," replied the Prefect, "from the nature of the document, and from the non-appearance of certain results which would at once arise from its passing *out* of the robber's possession;—that is to say, from his employing it as he must design in the end to employ it."

"Be a little more explicit," I said.

"Well, I may venture so far as to say that the paper gives its holder a certain power in a certain quarter where such power is immensely valuable." The Prefect was fond of the cant of diplomacy.

"Still I do not quite understand," said Dupin.

"No? Well; the disclosure of the document to a third person, who shall be nameless, would bring in question the honor of a personage of most exalted station; and this fact gives the holder of the document an ascendancy over the illustrious personage whose honor and peace are so jeopardized."

"But this ascendancy," I interposed, "would depend upon the robber's knowledge of the loser's knowledge of the robber. Who would dare—"

"The thief," said G., "is the Minister D——, who dares all things, those unbecoming as well as those becoming a man. The method of the theft was not less ingenious than bold. The document in question—a letter, to be frank—had been received by the personage robbed while alone in the royal *boudoir*. During its perusal she was suddenly interrupted by the entrance of the other exalted personage from whom especially it was her wish to conceal it. After a hurried and vain endeavor to thrust it in a drawer, she was forced to place it, open as it was, upon a table. The address, however, was uppermost, and, the contents thus unexposed, the letter escaped notice. At this juncture enters the Minister D——. His lynx eye immediately perceives the paper, recognises the handwriting of the address, observes the confusion of the personage addressed, and fathoms her secret. After some business transactions, hurried through in his ordinary manner, he produces a letter somewhat similar to the one in question, opens it, pretends to read it, and then places it in close juxtaposition to the other. Again he converses, for some fifteen minutes, upon the public affairs. At length, in taking leave, he takes also from the table the letter to which he had no claim. Its rightful owner saw, but, of course, dared not call attention to the act, in the presence of the third personage who stood at her elbow. The minister decamped; leaving his own letter—one of no importance—upon the table."

"Here, then," said Dupin to me, "you have precisely what you demand to make the ascendancy complete—the robber's knowledge of the loser's knowledge of the robber."

"Yes," replied the Prefect; "and the power thus attained has, for some months past, been wielded, for political purposes, to a very dangerous extent. The personage robbed is more thoroughly convinced, every day, of the necessity of reclaiming her letter. But this, of course, cannot be done openly. In fine, driven to despair, she has committed the matter to me."

"Than whom," said Dupin, amid a perfect whirlwind of smoke, "no more sagacious agent could, I suppose, be desired, or even imagined."

"You flatter me," replied the Prefect; "but it is possible that some such opinion may have been entertained."

"It is clear," said I, "as you observe, that the letter is still in possession of the minister; since it is this possession, and not any employment of the letter, which bestows the power. With the employment the power departs."

"True," said G.; "and upon this conviction I proceeded. My first care was to make thorough search of the minister's hotel;[6] and here my chief embarrassment lay in the necessity of searching without his knowledge. Beyond all things, I have been warned of the danger which would result from giving him reason to suspect our design."

"But," said I, "you are quite *au fait*[7] in these investigations. The Parisian police have done this thing often before."

"O yes; and for this reason I did not despair. The habits of the minister gave me, too, a great advantage. He is frequently absent from home all night. His servants are by no means numerous. They sleep at a distance from their master's apartment, and, being chiefly Neapolitans, are readily made drunk. I have keys, as you know, with which I can open any chamber or cabinet in Paris. For three months a night has not passed, during the greater part of which I have not been engaged, personally, in ransacking the D—— Hotel. My honor is interested, and, to mention a great secret, the reward is enormous. So I did not abandon the search until I had become fully satisfied that the thief is a more astute man than myself. I fancy that I have investigated every nook and corner of the premises in which it is possible that the paper can be concealed."

"But is it not possible," I suggested, "that although the letter may be in possession of the minister, as it unquestionably is, he may have concealed it elsewhere than upon his own premises?"

"This is barely possible," said Dupin. "The present peculiar condition of affairs at court, and especially of those intrigues in which D—— is known to be involved, would render the instant availability of the document—its susceptibility of being produced at a moment's notice—a point of nearly equal importance with its possession."

"Its susceptibility of being produced?" said I.

"That is to say, of being *destroyed*," said Dupin.

"True," I observed; "the paper is clearly then upon the premises. As for its being upon the person of the minister, we may consider that as out of the question."

"Entirely," said the Prefect. "He has been twice waylaid, as if by footpads, and his person rigorously searched under my own inspection."

---

[6]I.e., town residence.
[7]"Experienced," "expert" (French).

"You might have spared yourself this trouble," said Dupin. "D——, I presume, is not altogether a fool, and, if not, must have anticipated these waylayings, as a matter of course."

"Not *altogether* a fool," said G., "but then he's a poet, which I take to be only one remove from a fool."

"True," said Dupin, after a long and thoughtful whiff from his meerschaum, "although I have been guilty of certain doggrel myself."

"Suppose you detail," said I, "the particulars of your search."

"Why the fact is, we took our time, and we searched *every where*. I have had long experience in these affairs. I took the entire building, room by room; devoting the nights of a whole week to each. We examined, first, the furniture of each apartment. We opened every possible drawer; and I presume you know that, to a properly trained police agent, such a thing as a *secret* drawer is impossible. Any man is a dolt who permits a 'secret' drawer to escape him in a search of this kind. The thing is *so* plain. There is a certain amount of bulk—of space—to be accounted for in every cabinet. Then we have accurate rules. The fiftieth part of a line could not escape us. After the cabinets we took the chairs. The cushions we probed with the fine long needles you have seen me employ. From the tables we removed the tops."

"Why so?"

"Sometimes the top of a table, or other similarly arranged piece of furniture, is removed by the person wishing to conceal an article; then the leg is excavated, the article deposited within the cavity, and the top replaced. The bottoms and tops of bedposts are employed in the same way."

"But could not the cavity be detected by sounding?" I asked.

"By no means, if, when the article is deposited, a sufficient wadding of cotton be placed around it. Besides, in our case, we were obliged to proceed without noise."

"But you could not have removed—you could not have taken to pieces *all* articles of furniture in which it would have been possible to make a deposit in the manner you mention. A letter may be compressed into a thin spiral roll, not differing much in shape or bulk from a large knitting-needle, and in this form it might be inserted into the rung of a chair, for example. You did not take to pieces all the chairs?"

"Certainly not; but we did better—we examined the rungs of every chair in the hotel, and, indeed, the jointings of every description of furniture, by the aid of a most powerful microscope.[8] Had there been any traces of recent disturbance we should not have failed to detect it instantly. A single grain of gimlet-dust, for example, would have been as obvious as an apple. Any disorder in the glueing—any unusual gaping in the joints—would have sufficed to insure detection."

"I presume you looked to the mirrors, between the boards and the plates, and you probed the beds and the bed-clothes, as well as the curtains and carpets."

"That of course; and when we had absolutely completed every particle of the furniture in this way, then we examined the house itself. We divided its entire surface into compartments, which we numbered, so that none might be missed; then we scrutinized each individual square inch throughout the premises, including the two houses immediately adjoining, with the microscope, as before."

"The two houses adjoining!" I exclaimed; "you must have had a great deal of trouble."

"We had; but the reward offered is prodigious."

"You include the *grounds* about the houses?"

"All the grounds are paved with brick. They gave us comparatively little trouble. We examined the moss between the bricks, and found it undisturbed."

---

[8] I.e., magnifying glass.

"You looked among D——'s papers, of course, and into the books of the library?"

"Certainly; we opened every package and parcel; we not only opened every book, but we turned over every leaf in each volume, not contenting ourselves with a mere shake, according to the fashion of some of our police officers. We also measured the thickness of every book-*cover*, with the most accurate admeasurement, and applied to each the most jealous scrutiny of the microscope. Had any of the bindings been recently meddled with, it would have been utterly impossible that the fact should have escaped observation. Some five or six volumes, just from the hands of the binder, we carefully probed, longitudinally, with the needles."

"You explored the floors beneath the carpets?"

"Beyond doubt. We removed every carpet, and examined the boards with the microscope."

"And the paper on the walls?"

"Yes."

"You looked into the cellars?"

"We did."

"Then," I said, "you have been making a miscalculation, and the letter is *not* upon the premises, as you suppose."

"I fear you are right there," said the Prefect. "And now, Dupin, what would you advise me to do?"

"To make a thorough re-search of the premises."

"That is absolutely needless," replied G——. "I am not more sure that I breathe than I am that the letter is not at the Hotel."

"I have no better advice to give you," said Dupin. "You have, of course, an accurate description of the letter?"

"Oh yes!"—And here the Prefect, producing a memorandum-book, proceeded to read aloud a minute account of the internal, and especially of the external appearance of the missing document. Soon after finishing the perusal of this description, he took his departure, more entirely depressed in spirits than I had ever known the good gentleman before.

In about a month afterwards he paid us another visit, and found us occupied very nearly as before. He took a pipe and a chair and entered into some ordinary conversation. At length I said,—"Well, but G——, what of the purloined letter? I presume you have at last made up your mind that there is no such thing as overreaching the Minister?"

"Confound him, say I—yes; I made the re-examination, however, as Dupin suggested—but it was all labor lost, as I knew it would be."

"How much was the reward offered, did you say?" asked Dupin.

"Why, a very great deal—a *very* liberal reward—I don't like to say how much, precisely; but one thing I *will* say, that I wouldn't mind giving my individual check for fifty thousand francs to any one who could obtain me that letter. The fact is, it is becoming of more and more importance every day; and the reward has been lately doubled. If it were trebled, however, I could do no more than I have done."

"Why, yes," said Dupin, drawlingly, between the whiffs of his meerschaum, "I really—think, G——, you have not exerted yourself—to the utmost in this matter. You might—do a little more, I think, eh?"

"How?—in what way?"

"Why—puff, puff—you might—puff, puff—employ counsel in the matter, eh?—puff, puff, puff. Do you remember the story they tell of Abernethy?"[9]

"No; hang Abernethy!"

"To be sure! hang him and welcome. But, once upon a time, a certain rich mi-

---

[9]John Abernethy (1764–1831), renowned British surgeon.

ser conceived the design of spunging upon this Abernethy for a medical opinion. Getting up, for this purpose, an ordinary conversation in a private company, he insinuated his case to the physician, as that of an imaginary individual.

" 'We will suppose,' said the miser, 'that his symptoms are such and such; now, doctor, what would *you* have directed him to take?'

" 'Take!' said Abernethy, 'why, take *advice,* to be sure.' "

"But," said the Prefect, a little discomposed, "I am *perfectly* willing to take advice, and to pay for it. I would *really* give fifty thousand francs to any one who would aid me in the matter."

"In that case," replied Dupin, opening a drawer, and producing a check-book, "you may as well fill me up a check for the amount mentioned. When you have signed it, I will hand you the letter."

I was astounded. The Prefect appeared absolutely thunder-stricken. For some minutes he remained speechless and motionless, looking incredulously at my friend with open mouth, and eyes that seemed starting from their sockets; then, apparently recovering himself in some measure, he seized a pen, and after several pauses and vacant stares, finally filled up and signed a check for fifty thousand francs, and handed it across the table to Dupin. The latter examined it carefully and deposited it in his pocketbook; then, unlocking an *escritoire,*[10] took thence a letter and gave it to the Prefect. This functionary grasped it in a perfect agony of joy, opened it with a trembling hand, cast a rapid glance at its contents, and then, scrambling and struggling to the door, rushed at length unceremoniously from the room and from the house, without having uttered a syllable since Dupin had requested him to fill up the check.

When he had gone, my friend entered into some explanations.

"The Parisian police," he said, "are exceedingly able in their way. They are persevering, ingenious, cunning, and thoroughly versed in the knowledge which their duties seem chiefly to demand. Thus, when G—— detailed to us his mode of searching the premises at the Hotel D——, I felt entire confidence in his having made a satisfactory investigation—so far as his labors extended."

"So far as his labors extended?" said I.

"Yes," said Dupin. "The measures adopted were not only the best of their kind, but carried out to absolute perfection. Had the letter been deposited within the range of their search, these fellows would, beyond a question, have found it."

I merely laughed—but he seemed quite serious in all that he said.

"The measures, then," he continued, "were good in their kind and well executed; their defect lay in their being inapplicable to the case, and to the man. A certain set of highly ingenious resources are, with the Prefect, a sort of Procrustean bed,[11] to which he forcibly adapts his designs. But he perpetually errs by being too deep or too shallow, for the matter in hand; and many a school-boy is a better reasoner than he. I knew one about eight years of age, whose success at guessing in the game of 'even and odd' attracted universal admiration. This game is simple, and is played with marbles. One player holds in his hand a number of these toys, and demands of another whether that number is even or odd. If the guess is right, the guesser wins one; if wrong, he loses one. The boy to whom I allude won all the marbles of the school. Of course he had some principle of guessing; and this lay in mere observation and admeasurement of the astuteness of his opponents. For example, an arrant simpleton is his opponent, and, holding up his closed hand, asks, 'are they even or odd?' Our schoolboy replies, 'odd,' and loses; but upon the second trial he wins, for he then says to himself, "the simpleton had them even upon the first trial, and his amount of cunning is just sufficient

---

[10]"Writing desk" (French).
[11]Rigid, with arbitrary limits, from legendary Greek crimi-

nal Procrustes, who stretched or cut his victims to fit the bed on which he bound them.

to make him have them odd upon the second; I will therefore guess odd;—he guesses odd, and wins. Now, with a simpleton a degree above the first, he would have reasoned thus: 'This fellow finds that in the first instance I guessed odd, and, in the second, he will propose to himself, upon the first impulse, a simple variation from even to odd, as did the first simpleton; but then a second thought will suggest that this is too simple a variation, and finally he will decide upon putting it even as before. I will therefore guess even;'—he guesses even, and wins. Now this mode of reasoning in the schoolboy, whom his fellows termed 'lucky,'—what, in its last analysis, is it?"

"It is merely," I said, "an identification of the reasoner's intellect with that of his opponent."

"It is," said Dupin; "and, upon inquiring of the boy by what means he effected the *thorough* identification in which his success consisted, I received answer as follows: 'When I wish to find out how wise, or how stupid, or how good, or how wicked is any one, or what are his thoughts at the moment, I fashion the expression of my face, as accurately as possible, in accordance with the expression of his, and then wait to see what thoughts or sentiments arise in my mind or heart, as if to match or correspond with the expression.' This response of the schoolboy lies at the bottom of all the spurious profundity which has been attributed to Rochefoucault, to La Bruyère, to Machiavelli, and to Campanella."[12]

"And the identification," I said, "of the reasoner's intellect with that of his opponent, depends, if I understand you aright, upon the accuracy with which the opponent's intellect is admeasured."

"For its practical value it depends upon this," replied Dupin; "and the Prefect and his cohort fail so frequently, first, by default of this identification, and, secondly, by ill-admeasurement, or rather through non-admeasurement, of the intellect with which they are engaged. They consider only their *own* ideas of ingenuity; and, in searching for anything hidden, advert only to the modes in which *they* would have hidden it. They are right in this much—that their own ingenuity is a faithful representative of that of *the mass;* but when the cunning of the individual felon is diverse in character from their own, the felon foils them, of course. This always happens when it is above their own, and very usually when it is below. They have no variation of principle in their investigations; at best, when urged by some unusual emergency—by some extraordinary reward—they extend or exaggerate their old modes of *practice,* without touching their principles. What, for example, in this case of D——, has been done to vary the principle of action? What is all this boring, and probing, and sounding, and scrutinizing with the microscope, and dividing the surface of the building into registered square inches—what is it all but an exaggeration *of the application* of the one principle or set of principles of search, which are based upon the one set of notions regarding human ingenuity, to which the Prefect, in the long routine of his duty, has been accustomed? Do you not see he has taken it for granted that *all* men proceed to conceal a letter,—not exactly in a gimlet-hole bored in a chair-leg—but, at least, in *some* out-of-the-way hole or corner suggested by the same tenor of thought which would urge a man to secrete a letter in a gimlet-hole bored in a chair-leg? And do you not see also, that such *recherchés*[13] nooks for concealment are adapted only for ordinary occasions, and would be adopted only by ordinary intellects; for, in all cases of concealment, a disposal of the article concealed—a disposal of it in this *recherché* manner,—is, in the very first instance, presumable and presumed; and thus its discovery depends, not at all upon the acumen, but altogether upon the

---

[12]All French or Italian philosophers or moralists: La Rochefoucauld (1613–1680), La Bruyère (1645–1696), Machiavelli (1469–1527), Campanella (1568–1639).
[13]"Rare," "uncommon" (French).

mere care, patience, and determination of the seekers; and where the case is of importance—or, what amounts to the same thing in the policial eyes, when the reward is of magnitude,—the qualities in question have *never* been known to fail. You will now understand what I meant in suggesting that, had the purloined letter been hidden any where within the limits of the Prefect's examination—in other words, had the principle of its concealment been comprehended within the principles of the Prefect—its discovery would have been a matter altogether beyond question. This functionary, however, has been thoroughly mystified; and the remote source of his defeat lies in the supposition that the Minister is a fool, because he has acquired renown as a poet. All fools are poets; this the Prefect *feels;* and he is merely guilty of a *non distributio medii*[14] in thence inferring that all poets are fools."

"But is this really the poet?" I asked. "There are two brothers, I know; and both have attained reputation in letters. The Minister I believe has written learnedly on the Differential Calculus. He is a mathematician, and no poet."

"You are mistaken; I know him well; he is both. As poet *and* mathematician, he would reason well; as mere mathematician, he could not have reasoned at all, and thus would have been at the mercy of the Prefect."

"You surprise me," I said, "by these opinions, which have been contradicted by the voice of the world. You do not mean to set at naught the well-digested idea of centuries. The mathematical reason has long been regarded as *the* reason *par excellence.*"

" '*Il y a à parier,*' " replied Dupin, quoting from Chamfort, " '*que toute idée publique, toute convention reçue, est une sottise, car elle a convenu au plus grand nombre.*'[15] The mathematicians, I grant you, have done their best to promulgate the popular error to which you allude, and which is none the less an error for its promulgation as truth. With an art worthy a better cause, for example, they have insinuated the term 'analysis' into application to algebra. The French are the originators of this particular deception; but if a term is of any importance—if words derive any value from applicability—then 'analysis' conveys 'algebra' about as much as, in Latin, *'ambitus'* implies 'ambition,' *'religio'* 'religion,' or *'homines honesti,'* a set of *honorable* men."

"You have a quarrel on hand, I see," said I, "with some of the algebraists of Paris; but proceed."

"I dispute the availability, and thus the value, of that reason which is cultivated in any especial form other than the abstractly logical. I dispute, in particular, the reason educed by mathematical study. The mathematics are the science of form and quantity; mathematical reasoning is merely logic applied to observation upon form and quantity. The great error lies in supposing that even the truths of what is called *pure* algebra, are abstract or general truths. And this error is so egregious that I am confounded at the universality with which it has been received. Mathematical axioms are *not* axioms of general truth. What is true of *relation*—of form and quantity—is often grossly false in regard to morals, for example. In this latter science it is very usually *untrue* that the aggregated parts are equal to the whole. In chemistry also the axiom fails. In the consideration of motive it fails; for two motives, each of a given value, have not, necessarily, a value when united, equal to the sum of their values apart. There are numerous other mathematical truths which are only truths within the limits of *relation.* But the mathematician argues, from his *finite truths,* through habit, as if they were of an absolutely general applicability—as the world indeed imagines them to be. Bryant, in his very learned

---

[14]"Undistributed middle" (Latin); termed a "fallacy" (in logic) that leads to a wrong conclusion.
[15]"It is safe to bet that every common idea, every accepted

convention, is a stupidity, because it has been agreed to by the majority"; from *Maxims et Pensées,* by Sébastien-Roch Nicolas, known as Chamfort (1741–1794), French author.

'Mythology,' mentions an analogous source of error, when he says that 'although the Pagan fables are not believed, yet we forget ourselves continually, and make inferences from them as existing realities.'[16] With the algebraists, however, who are Pagans themselves, the 'Pagan fables' *are* believed, and the inferences are made, not so much through lapse of memory, as through an unaccountable addling of the brains. In short, I never yet encountered the mere mathematician who could be trusted out of equal roots, or one who did not clandestinely hold it as a point of his faith that $x^2 + px$ was absolutely and unconditionally equal to q. Say to one of these gentlemen, by way of experiment, if you please, that you believe occasions may occur where $x^2 + px$ is *not* altogether equal to q, and, having made him understand what you mean, get out of his reach as speedily as convenient, for, beyond doubt, he will endeavor to knock you down.

"I mean to say," continued Dupin, while I merely laughed at his last observations, "that if the Minister had been no more than a mathematician, the Prefect would have been under no necessity of giving me this check. I knew him, however, as both mathematician and poet, and my measures were adapted to his capacity, with reference to the circumstances by which he was surrounded. I knew him as a courtier, too, and as a bold *intriguant*.[17] Such a man, I considered, could not fail to be aware of the ordinary policial modes of action. He could not have failed to anticipate—and events have proved that he did not fail to anticipate—the waylayings to which he was subjected. He must have foreseen, I reflected, the secret investigations of his premises. His frequent absences from home at night, which were hailed by the Prefect as certain aids to his success, I regarded only as *ruses*, to afford opportunity for thorough search to the police, and thus the sooner to impress them with the conviction to which G——, in fact, did finally arrive—the conviction that the letter was not upon the premises. I felt, also, that the whole train of thought, which I was at some pains in detailing to you just now, concerning the invariable principle of policial action in searches for articles concealed—I felt that this whole train of thought would necessarily pass through the mind of the Minister. It would imperatively lead him to despise all the ordinary *nooks* of concealment. *He* could not, I reflected, be so weak as not to see that the most intricate and remote recess of his hotel would be as open as his commonest closets to the eyes, to the probes, to the gimlets, and to the microscopes of the Prefect. I saw, in fine, that he would be driven, as a matter of course, to *simplicity*, if not deliberately induced to it as a matter of choice. You will remember, perhaps, how desperately the Prefect laughed when I suggested, upon our first interview, that it was just possible this mystery troubled him so much on account of its being so *very* self-evident."

"Yes," said I, "I remember his merriment well. I really thought he would have fallen into convulsions."

"The material world," continued Dupin, "abounds with very strict analogies to the immaterial; and thus some color of truth has been given to the rhetorical dogma, that metaphor, or simile, may be made to strengthen an argument, as well as to embellish a description. The principle of the *vis inertiæ*,[18] for example, seems to be identical in physics and metaphysics. It is not more true in the former, that a large body is with more difficulty set in motion than a smaller one, and that its subsequent *momentum* is commensurate with this difficulty, than it is, in the latter, that intellects of the vaster capacity, while more forcible, more constant, and more eventful in their movements than those of inferior grade, are yet the less readily moved, and more embarrassed and full of hesitation in the first few steps of their

---

[16]From *A New System of Antient Mythology*, by Jacob Bryant (1715–1804), British classical scholar.

[17]"Adventurer" (French).
[18]"Force of inertia" (Latin).

progress. Again: have you ever noticed which of the street signs, over the shop-doors, are the most attractive of attention?"

"I have never given the matter a thought," I said.

"There is a game of puzzles," he resumed, "which is played upon a map. One party playing requires another to find a given word—the name of town, river, state or empire—any word, in short, upon the motley and perplexed surface of the chart. A novice in the game generally seeks to embarrass his opponents by giving them the most minutely lettered names; but the adept selects such words as stretch, in large characters, from one end of the chart to the other. These, like the over-largely lettered signs and placards of the street, escape observation by dint of being excessively obvious; and here the physical oversight is precisely analogous with the moral inapprehension by which the intellect suffers to pass unnoticed those considerations which are too obtrusively and too palpably self-evident. But this is a point, it appears, somewhat above or beneath the understanding of the Prefect. He never once thought it probable, or possible, that the Minister had deposited the letter immediately beneath the nose of the whole world, by way of best preventing any portion of that world from perceiving it.

"But the more I reflected upon the daring, dashing, and discriminating ingenuity of D——; upon the fact that the document must always have been *at hand,* if he intended to use it to good purpose; and upon the decisive evidence, obtained by the Prefect, that it was not hidden within the limits of that dignitary's ordinary search—the more satisfied I became that, to conceal this letter, the Minister had resorted to the comprehensive and sagacious expedient of not attempting to conceal it at all.

"Full of these ideas, I prepared myself with a pair of green spectacles, and called one fine morning, quite by accident, at the Ministerial hotel. I found D—— at home, yawning, lounging, and dawdling, as usual, and pretending to be in the last extremity of *ennui.*[19] He is, perhaps, the most really energetic human being now alive—but that is only when nobody sees him.

"To be even with him, I complained of my weak eyes, and lamented the necessity of the spectacles, under cover of which I cautiously and thoroughly surveyed the apartment, while seemingly intent only upon the conversation of my host.

"I paid especial attention to a large writing-table near which he sat, and upon which lay confusedly, some miscellaneous letters and other papers, with one or two musical instruments and a few books. Here, however, after a long and very deliberate scrutiny, I saw nothing to excite particular suspicion.

"At length my eyes, in going the circuit of the room, fell upon a trumpery filagree card-rack of pasteboard, that hung dangling by a dirty blue ribbon from a little brass knob just beneath the middle of the mantel-piece. In this rack, which had three or four compartments, were five or six visiting cards and a solitary letter. This last was much soiled and crumpled. It was torn nearly in two, across the middle—as if a design, in the first instance, to tear it entirely up as worthless, had been altered, or stayed, in the second. It had a large black seal, bearing the D—— cipher *very* conspicuously, and was addressed, in a diminutive female hand, to D——, the minister, himself. It was thrust carelessly, and even, as it seemed, contemptuously, into one of the upper divisions of the rack.

"No sooner had I glanced at this letter, than I concluded it to be that of which I was in search. To be sure, it was, to all appearance, radically different from the one of which the Prefect had read us so minute a description. Here the seal was large and black, with the D—— cipher; there it was small and red, with the ducal arms of the S—— family. Here, the address, to the Minister, was diminutive and

---

[19]"Boredom" (French).

feminine; there the superscription, to a certain royal personage, was markedly bold and decided; the size alone formed a point of correspondence. But, then, the *radicalness* of these differences, which was excessive; the dirt; the soiled and torn condition of the paper, so inconsistent with the *true* methodical habits of D——, and so suggestive of a design to delude the beholder into an idea of the worthlessness of the document; these things, together with the hyperobtrusive situation of this document, full in the view of every visiter, and thus exactly in accordance with the conclusions to which I had previously arrived; these things, I say, were strongly corroborative of suspicion, in one who came with the intention to suspect.

"I protracted my visit as long as possible, and, while I maintained a most animated discussion with the Minister, on a topic which I knew well had never failed to interest and excite him, I kept my attention really riveted upon the letter. In this examination, I committed to memory its external appearance and arrangement in the rack; and also fell, at length, upon a discovery which set at rest whatever trivial doubt I might have entertained. In scrutinizing the edges of the paper, I observed them to be more *chafed* than seemed necessary. They presented the *broken* appearance which is manifested when a stiff paper, having been once folded and pressed with a folder, is refolded in a reversed direction, in the same creases or edges which had formed the original fold. This discovery was sufficient. It was clear to me that the letter had been turned, as a glove, inside out, re-directed, and re-sealed. I bade the Minister good morning, and took my departure at once, leaving a gold snuff-box upon the table.

"The next morning I called for the snuff-box, when we resumed, quite eagerly, the conversation of the preceding day. While thus engaged, however, a loud report, as if of a pistol, was heard immediately beneath the windows of the hotel, and was succeeded by a series of fearful screams, and the shoutings of a mob. D—— rushed to a casement, threw it open, and looked out. In the meantime, I stepped to the card-rack, took the letter, put it in my pocket, and replaced it by a *fac-simile,* (so far as regards externals,) which I had carefully prepared at my lodgings; imitating the D—— cipher, very readily, by means of a seal formed of bread.

"The disturbance in the street had been occasioned by the frantic behavior of a man with a musket. He had fired it among a crowd of women and children. It proved, however, to have been without ball, and the fellow was suffered to go his way as a lunatic or a drunkard. When he had gone, D—— came from the window, whither I had followed him immediately upon securing the object in view. Soon afterwards I bade him farewell. The pretended lunatic was a man in my own pay."

"But what purpose had you," I asked, "in replacing the letter by a *fac-simile?* Would it not have been better, at the first visit, to have seized it openly, and departed?"

"D——," replied Dupin, "is a desperate man, and a man of nerve. His hotel, too, is not without attendants devoted to his interests. Had I made the wild attempt you suggest, I might never have left the Ministerial presence alive. The good people of Paris might have heard of me no more. But I had an object apart from these considerations. You know my political prepossessions. In this matter, I act as a partisan of the lady concerned. For eighteen months the Minister has had her in his power. She has now him in hers; since, being unaware that the letter is not in his possession, he will proceed with his exactions as if it was. Thus will he inevitably commit himself, at once, to his political destruction. His downfall, too, will not be more precipitate than awkward. It is all very well to talk about the *facilis descensus Averni;*[20] but in all kinds of climbing, as Catalani[21] said of singing, it is

---

[20]"Easy descent to Avernus [Hades]," from Virgil's *Aeneid,* Book VI.
[21]Angelica Catalani (1779–1849), Italian opera diva.

far more easy to get up than to come down. In the present instance I have no sympathy—at least no pity—for him who descends. He is that *monstrum horrendum*,[22] an unprincipled man of genius. I confess, however, that I should like very well to know the precise character of his thoughts, when, being defied by her whom the Prefect terms 'a certain personage,' he is reduced to opening the letter which I left for him in the card-rack."

"How? did you put any thing particular in it?"

"Why—it did not seem altogether right to leave the interior blank—that would have been insulting. D——, at Vienna once, did me an evil turn, which I told him, quite good-humoredly, that I should remember. So, as I knew he would feel some curiosity in regard to the identity of the person who had outwitted him, I thought it a pity not to give him a clue. He is well acquainted with my MS., and I just copied into the middle of the blank sheet the words—

——Un dessein si funeste,
S'il n'est digne d'Atrée, est digne de Thyeste.

They are to be found in Crébillon's 'Atrée.' "[23]

1844

The Imp of the Perverse

In the consideration of the faculties and impulses—of the *prima mobilia*[1] of the human soul, the phrenologists have failed to make room for a propensity which, although obviously existing as a radical, primitive, irreducible sentiment, has been equally overlooked by all the moralists who have preceded them. In the pure arrogance of the reason, we have all overlooked it. We have suffered its existence to escape our senses, solely through want of belief—of faith;—whether it be faith in Revelation, or faith in the Kabbala.[2] The idea of it has never occurred to us, simply because of its supererogation.[3] We saw no *need* of the impulse—for the propensity. We could not perceive its necessity. We could not understand, that is to say, we could not have understood, had the notion of this *primum mobile* ever obtruded itself;—we could not have understood in what manner it might be made to further the objects of humanity, either temporal or eternal. It cannot be denied that phrenology and, in great measure, all metaphysicianism have been concocted *à priori*.[4] The intellectual or logical man, rather than the understanding or observant man, set himself to imagine designs—to dictate purposes to God. Having thus fathomed, to his satisfaction, the intentions of Jehovah, out of these intentions he built his innumerable systems of mind. In the matter of phrenology,[5] for example, we first determined, naturally enough, that it was the design of the Deity that man should eat. We then assigned to man an organ of alimentiveness, and this organ is the scourge with which the Deity compels man, will-I nill-I, into eating. Secondly, having settled it to be God's will that man should continue his spe-

---

[22]"Terrifying monster," from Virgil's *Aeneid*, Book III.
[23]"So baleful a plan, if not worthy of Atreus, is worthy of Thyestes," from *Atrée et Thyeste* (1707), by Prosper-Jolyot de Crébillon (1674–1762); in the play, Thyestes seduces his brother Atreus's wife; in revenge, Atreus kills the children of Thyestes and serves them to him at a banquet.
[1]"First mover" (Latin). For "phrenologists," see note 5.
[2]A tradition of Jewish esoteric and occult theosophy based on the Talmud.
[3]Being beyond what is needed.

[4]Theory formulated first, followed by examination or selection of facts.
[5]A "science" of psychology based on reading or measuring the bumps on the head to discover an individual's character or personality traits. Among the organs of the brain (beneath the bumps) were alimentiveness (related to eating), amativeness (to love), combativeness (to conflict), ideality (to poetry), causality (to the metaphysical), and constructiveness (to the mechanical).

cies, we discovered an organ of amativeness, forthwith. And so with combative-ness, with ideality, with causality, with constructiveness,—so, in short, with every organ, whether representing a propensity, a moral sentiment, or a faculty of the pure intellect. And in these arrangements of the *principia*[6] of human action, the Spurzheimites,[7] whether right or wrong, in part, or upon the whole, have but fol-lowed, in principle, the footsteps of their predecessors; deducing and establishing every thing from the preconceived destiny of man, and upon the ground of the objects of his Creator.

It would have been wiser, it would have been safer to classify, (if classify we must,) upon the basis of what man usually or occasionally did, and was always oc-casionally doing, rather than upon the basis of what we took it for granted the Deity intended him to do. If we cannot comprehend God in his visible works, how then in his inconceivable thoughts, that call the works into being? If we cannot understand him in his objective creatures, how then in his substantive moods and phases of creation?

Induction, *à posteriori*,[8] would have brought phrenology to admit, as an innate and primitive principle of human action, a paradoxical something, which we may call *perverseness*, for want of a more characteristic term. In the sense I intend, it is, in fact, a *mobile*[9] without motive, a motive not *motivirt*.[10] Through its promptings we act without comprehensible object; or, if this shall be understood as a contra-diction in terms, we may so far modify the proposition as to say, that through its promptings we act, for the reason that we should *not*. In theory, no reason can be more unreasonable; but, in fact, there is none more strong. With certain minds, under certain conditions, it becomes absolutely irresistible. I am not more certain that I breathe, than that the assurance of the wrong or error of any action is often the one unconquerable *force* which impels us, and alone impels us to its prosecu-tion. Nor will this overwhelming tendency to do wrong for the wrong's sake, ad-mit of analysis, or resolution into ulterior elements. It is a radical, a primitive im-pulse—elementary. It will be said, I am aware, that when we persist in acts because we feel we should *not* persist in them, our conduct is but a modification of that which ordinarily springs from the *combativeness* of phrenology. But a glance will show the fallacy of this idea. The phrenological combativeness has for its es-sence, the necessity of self-defence. It is our safeguard against injury. Its principle regards our well-being; and thus the desire to be well is excited simultaneously with its development. It follows, that the desire to be well must be excited simul-taneously with any principle which shall be merely a modification of combative-ness, but in the case of that something which I term *perverseness*, the desire to be well is not only not aroused, but a strongly antagonistical sentiment exists.

An appeal to one's own heart is, after all, the best reply to the sophistry just noticed. No one who trustingly consults and thoroughly questions his own soul, will be disposed to deny the entire radicalness of the propensity in question. It is not more incomprehensible than distinctive. There lives no man who at some pe-riod has not been tormented, for example, by an earnest desire to tantalize a lis-tener by circumlocution. The speaker is aware that he displeases; he has every in-tention to please; he is usually curt, precise, and clear; the most laconic and luminous language is struggling for utterance upon his tongue; it is only with dif-ficulty that he restrains himself from giving it flow; he dreads and deprecates the anger of him whom he addresses; yet, the thought strikes him, that by certain in-volutions and parentheses, this anger may be engendered. That single thought is

---

[6]First principles.
[7]Followers of Dr. Johann Spurzheim (1776–1832), Ger-man scientist who (with Dr. Franz Josef Gall) propounded the fundamental principles of phrenology.

[8]Facts examined before theory is constructed (opposite to *à priori*).
[9]Movement.
[10]Motivated.

enough. The impulse increases to a wish, the wish to a desire, the desire to an uncontrollable longing, and the longing, (to the deep regret and mortification of the speaker, and in defiance of all consequences,) is indulged.

We have a task before us which must be speedily performed. We know that it will be ruinous to make delay. The most important crisis of our life calls, trumpet-tongued, for immediate energy and action. We glow, we are consumed with eagerness to commence the work, with the anticipation of whose glorious result our whole souls are on fire. It must, it shall be undertaken to-day, and yet we put it off until to-morrow; and why? There is no answer, except that we feel *perverse*, using the word with no comprehension of the principle. To-morrow arrives, and with it a more impatient anxiety to do our duty, but with this very increase of anxiety arrives, also, a nameless, a positively fearful because unfathomable, craving for delay. This craving gathers strength as the moments fly. The last hour for action is at hand. We tremble with the violence of the conflict within us,—of the definite with the indefinite—of the substance with the shadow. But, if the contest have proceeded thus far, it is the shadow which prevails,—we struggle in vain. The clock strikes, and is the knell of our welfare. At the same time, it is the chanticleer-note to the ghost that has so long overawed us. It flies—it disappears—we are free. The old energy returns. We will labor *now*. Alas, it is *too late!*

We stand upon the brink of a precipice. We peer into the abyss—we grow sick and dizzy. Our first impulse is to shrink from the danger. Unaccountably we remain. By slow degrees our sickness, and dizziness, and horror, become merged in a cloud of unnameable feeling. By gradations, still more imperceptible, this cloud assumes shape, as did the vapor from the bottle out of which arose the genius in the Arabian Nights.[11] But out of this *our* cloud upon the precipice's edge, there grows into palpability, a shape, far more terrible than any genius, or any demon of a tale, and yet it is but a thought, although a fearful one, and one which chills the very marrow of our bones with the fierceness of the delight of its horror. It is merely the idea of what would be our sensations during the sweeping precipitancy of a fall from such a height. And this fall—this rushing annihilation—for the very reason that it involves that one most ghastly and loathsome of all the most ghastly and loathsome images of death and suffering which have ever presented themselves to our imagination—for this very cause do we now the most vividly desire it. And because our reason violently deters us from the brink, *therefore*, do we the more impetuously approach it. There is no passion in nature so demoniacally impatient, as that of him, who shuddering upon the edge of a precipice, thus meditates a plunge. To indulge for a moment, in any attempt at *thought*, is to be inevitably lost; for reflection but urges us to forbear, and *therefore* it is, I say, that we *cannot*. If there be no friendly arm to check us, or if we fail in a sudden effort to prostrate ourselves backward from the abyss, we plunge, and are destroyed.

Examine these and similar actions as we will, we shall find them resulting solely from the spirit of the *Perverse*. We perpetrate them merely because we feel that we should *not*. Beyond or behind this, there is no intelligible principle: and we might, indeed, deem this perverseness a direct instigation of the arch-fiend,[12] were it not occasionally known to operate in furtherance of good.

I have said thus much, that in some measure I may answer your question—that I may explain to you why I am here—that I may assign to you something that shall have at least the faint aspect of a cause for my wearing these fetters, and for my tenanting this cell of the condemned. Had I not been thus prolix, you might either have misunderstood me altogether, or, with the rabble, have fancied

---

[11]In "Story of the Fisherman" from *The Arabian Nights*, a genie or spirit is released by a poor fisherman from a bottle.
[12]The devil.

me mad. As it is, you will easily perceive that I am one of the many uncounted victims of the Imp of the Perverse.

It is impossible that any deed could have been wrought with a more thorough deliberation. For weeks, for months, I pondered upon the means of the murder. I rejected a thousand schemes, because their accomplishment involved a *chance* of detection. At length, in reading some French memoirs, I found an account of a nearly fatal illness that occurred to Madame Pilau, through the agency of a candle accidentally poisoned.[13] The idea struck my fancy at once. I knew my victim's habit of reading in bed. I knew, too, that his apartment was narrow and ill-ventilated. But I need not vex you with impertinent details. I need not describe the easy artifices by which I substituted, in his bed-room candlestand, a wax-light of my own making, for the one which I there found. The next morning he was discovered dead in his bed, and the coroner's verdict was,—"Death by the visitation of God."

Having inherited his estate, all went well with me for years. The idea of detection never once entered my brain. Of the remains of the fatal taper, I had myself carefully disposed. I had left no shadow of a clue by which it would be possible to convict, or even to suspect me of the crime. It is inconceivable how rich a sentiment of satisfaction arose in my bosom as I reflected upon my absolute security. For a very long period of time, I was accustomed to revel in this sentiment. It afforded me more real delight than all the mere worldly advantages accruing from my sin. But there arrived at length an epoch, from which the pleasurable feeling grew, by scarcely perceptible gradations, into a haunting and harassing thought. It harassed because it haunted. I could scarcely get rid of it for an instant. It is quite a common thing to be thus annoyed with the ringing in our ears, or rather in our memories, of the burthen of some ordinary song, or some unimpressive snatches from an opera. Nor will we be less tormented if the song in itself be good, or the opera air meritorious. In this manner, at last, I would perpetually catch myself pondering upon my security, and repeating, in a low, under-tone, the phrase, "I am safe."

One day, whilst sauntering along the streets, I arrested myself in the act of murmuring, half aloud, these customary syllables. In a fit of petulance, I remodelled them thus:—"I am safe—I am safe—yes—if I be not fool enough to make open confession!"

No sooner had I spoken these words, than I felt an icy chill creep to my heart. I had had some experience in these fits of perversity, (whose nature I have been at some trouble to explain,) and I remembered well, that in no instance, I had successfully resisted their attacks. And now my own casual self-suggestion, that I might possibly be fool enough to confess the murder of which I had been guilty, confronted me, as if the very ghost of him whom I had murdered—and beckoned me on to death.

At first, I made an effort to shake off this nightmare of the soul. I walked vigorously—faster—still faster—at length I ran. I felt a maddening desire to shriek aloud. Every succeeding wave of thought overwhelmed me with new terror, for, alas! I well, too well understood that, to *think*, in my situation, was to be lost. I still quickened my pace. I bounded like a madman through the crowded thoroughfares. At length, the populace took the alarm, and pursued me. I felt *then* the consummation of my fate. Could I have torn out my tongue, I would have done it—but a rough voice resounded in my ears—a rougher grasp seized me by the shoulder. I turned—I gasped for breath. For a moment, I experienced all the pangs of suffocation; I became blind, and deaf, and giddy; and then, some invisi-

---

[13]The account appeared in "An Oddity of the Seventeenth Century," *New Monthly Magazine* (1839), by Mrs. Catherine Gore, English novelist.

ble fiend, I thought, struck me with his broad palm upon the back. The long-imprisoned secret burst forth from my soul.

They say that I spoke with a distinct enunciation, but with marked emphasis and passionate hurry, as if in dread of interruption before concluding the brief but pregnant sentences that consigned me to the hangman and to hell.

Having related all that was necessary for the fullest judicial conviction, I fell prostrate in a swoon.

But why shall I say more? To-day I wear these chains, and am *here*. To-morrow I shall be fetterless!—*but where?*

1845

The Cask of Amontillado

The thousand injuries of Fortunato I had borne as I best could; but when he ventured upon insult, I vowed revenge. You, who so well know the nature of my soul, will not suppose, however, that I gave utterance to a threat. *At length* I would be avenged; this was a point definitively settled—but the very definitiveness with which it was resolved precluded the idea of risk. I must not only punish, but punish with impunity. A wrong is unredressed when retribution overtakes its redresser. It is equally unredressed when the avenger fails to make himself felt as such to him who has done the wrong.

It must be understood that neither by word nor deed had I given Fortunato cause to doubt my good will. I continued, as was my wont, to smile in his face, and he did not perceive that my smile *now* was at the thought of his immolation.

He had a weak point—this Fortunato—although in other regards he was a man to be respected and even feared. He prided himself on his connoisseurship in wine. Few Italians have the true virtuoso spirit. For the most part their enthusiasm is adopted to suit the time and opportunity—to practise imposture upon the British and Austrian *millionaires*. In painting and gemmary Fortunato, like his countrymen, was a quack—but in the matter of old wines he was sincere. In this respect I did not differ from him materially; I was skilful in the Italian vintages myself, and bought largely whenever I could.

It was about dusk, one evening during the supreme madness of the carnival season,[1] that I encountered my friend. He accosted me with excessive warmth, for he had been drinking much. The man wore motley.[2] He had on a tight-fitting parti-striped dress, and his head was surmounted by the conical cap and bells. I was so pleased to see him that I thought I should never have done wringing his hand.

I said to him—"My dear Fortunato, you are luckily met. How remarkably well you are looking to-day! But I have received a pipe[3] of what passes for Amontillado,[4] and I have my doubts."

"How?" said he. "Amontillado? A pipe? Impossible! And in the middle of the carnival!"

"I have my doubts," I replied; "and I was silly enough to pay the full Amontillado price without consulting you in the matter. You were not to be found, and I was fearful of losing a bargain."

"Amontillado!"

---

[1] A celebration on Shrove Tuesday (confession and festivities), the day before Lent, the fasting period before Easter.
[2] Multicolored costume.
[3] Barrel.
[4] Spanish sherry, an amber wine.

"I have my doubts."

"Amontillado!"

"And I must satisfy them."

"Amontillado!"

"As you are engaged, I am on my way to Luchesi. If any one has a critical turn, it is he. He will tell me—"

"Luchesi cannot tell Amontillado from Sherry."

"And yet some fools will have it that his taste is a match for your own."

"Come, let us go."

"Whither?"

"To your vaults."

"My friend, no; I will not impose upon your good nature. I perceive you have an engagement. Luchesi—"

"I have no engagement;—come."

"My friend, no. It is not the engagement, but the severe cold with which I perceive you are afflicted. The vaults are insufferably damp. They are encrusted with nitre."[5]

"Let us go, nevertheless. The cold is merely nothing. Amontillado! You have been imposed upon. And as for Luchesi, he cannot distinguish Sherry from Amontillado."

Thus speaking, Fortunato possessed himself of my arm. Putting on a mask of black silk, and drawing a *roquelaire*[6] closely about my person, I suffered him to hurry me to my palazzo.

There were no attendants at home; they had absconded to make merry in honor of the time. I had told them that I should not return until the morning, and had given them explicit orders not to stir from the house. These orders were sufficient, I well knew, to insure their immediate disappearance, one and all, as soon as my back was turned.

I took from their sconces two flambeaux, and giving one to Fortunato, bowed him through several suites of rooms to the archway that led into the vaults. I passed down a long and winding staircase, requesting him to be cautious as he followed. We came at length to the foot of the descent, and stood together on the damp ground of the catacombs of the Montresors.

The gait of my friend was unsteady, and the bells upon his cap jingled as he strode.

"The pipe," said he.

"It is farther on," said I; "but observe the white web-work which gleams from these cavern walls."

He turned towards me, and looked into my eyes with two filmy orbs that distilled the rheum of intoxication.

"Nitre?" he asked, at length.

"Nitre," I replied. "How long have you had that cough?"

"Ugh! ugh! ugh!—ugh! ugh! ugh!—ugh! ugh! ugh!—ugh! ugh! ugh!—ugh! ugh! ugh!"

My poor friend found it impossible to reply for many minutes.

"It is nothing," he said, at last.

"Come," I said, with decision, "we will go back; your health is precious. You are rich, respected, admired, beloved; you are happy, as once I was. You are a man to be missed. For me it is no matter. We will go back; you will be ill, and I cannot be responsible. Besides, there is Luchesi—"

---

[5]A whitish, extruded mineral, saltpeter.
[6]Knee-length cloak.

"Enough," he said; "the cough is a mere nothing; it will not kill me. I shall not die of a cough."

"True—true," I replied; "and, indeed, I had no intention of alarming you unnecessarily—but you should use all proper caution. A draught of this Medoc[7] will defend us from the damps."

Here I knocked off the neck of a bottle which I drew from a long row of its fellows that lay upon the mould.

"Drink," I said, presenting him the wine.

He raised it to his lips with a leer. He paused and nodded to me familiarly, while his bells jingled.

"I drink," he said, "to the buried that repose around us."

"And I to your long life."

He again took my arm, and we proceeded.

"These vaults," he said, "are extensive."

"The Montresors," I replied, "were a great and numerous family."

"I forget your arms."

"A huge human foot d'or, in a field azure; the foot crushes a serpent rampant whose fangs are imbedded in the heel."[8]

"And the motto?"

"*Nemo me impune lacessit.*"[9]

"Good!" he said.

The wine sparkled in his eyes and the bells jingled. My own fancy grew warm with the Medoc. We had passed through walls of piled bones, with casks and puncheons intermingling, into the inmost recesses of the catacombs. I paused again, and this time I made bold to seize Fortunato by an arm above the elbow.

"The nitre!" I said; "see, it increases. It hangs like moss upon the vaults. We are below the river's bed. The drops of moisture trickle among the bones. Come, we will go back ere it is too late. Your cough—"

"It is nothing," he said; "let us go on. But first, another draught of the Medoc."

I broke and reached him a flaçon of De Grâve.[10] He emptied it at a breath. His eyes flashed with a fierce light. He laughed and threw the bottle upwards with a gesticulation I did not understand.

I looked at him in surprise. He repeated the movement—a grotesque one.

"You do not comprehend?" he said.

"Not I," I replied.

"Then you are not of the brotherhood."

"How?"

"You are not of the masons."[11]

"Yes, yes," I said, "yes, yes."

"You? Impossible! A mason?"

"A mason," I replied.

"A sign," he said.

"It is this," I answered, producing a trowel from beneath the folds of my *roquelaire.*

"You jest," he exclaimed, recoiling a few paces. "But let us proceed to the Amontillado."

"Be it so," I said, replacing the tool beneath the cloak, and again offering him my arm. He leaned upon it heavily. We continued our route in search of the Amontillado. We passed through a range of low arches, descended, passed on,

---

[7]French red wine.
[8]The Montresor coat-of-arms displays a large golden foot on a blue field crushing a serpent rearing up (rampant), stabbing the heel—emblematic of revenge.

[9]"No one assails me with impunity" (Latin).
[10]Bottle of De Grâve, a white French wine from Bordeaux.
[11]The Society of Freemasons, a secret society.

and descending again, arrived at a deep crypt, in which the foulness of the air caused our flambeaux rather to glow than flame.

At the most remote end of the crypt there appeared another less spacious. Its walls had been lined with human remains, piled to the vault overhead, in the fashion of the great catacombs of Paris. Three sides of this interior crypt were still ornamented in this manner. From the fourth the bones had been thrown down, and lay promiscuously upon the earth, forming at one point a mound of some size. Within the wall thus exposed by the displacing of the bones, we perceived a still interior recess, in depth about four feet, in width three, in height six or seven. It seemed to have been constructed for no especial use within itself, but formed merely the interval between two of the colossal supports of the roof of the catacombs, and was backed by one of their circumscribing walls of solid granite.

It was in vain that Fortunato, uplifting his dull torch, endeavored to pry into the depth of the recess. Its termination the feeble light did not enable us to see.

"Proceed," I said; "herein is the Amontillado. As for Luchesi—"

"He is an ignoramus," interrupted my friend, as he stepped unsteadily forward, while I followed immediately at his heels. In an instant he had reached the extremity of the niche, and finding his progress arrested by the rock, stood stupidly bewildered. A moment more and I had fettered him to the granite. In its surface were two iron staples, distant from each other about two feet, horizontally. From one of these depended a short chain, from the other a padlock. Throwing the links about his waist, it was but the work of a few seconds to secure it. He was too much astounded to resist. Withdrawing the key I stepped back from the recess.

"Pass your hand," I said, "over the wall; you cannot help feeling the nitre. Indeed it is *very* damp. Once more let me *implore* you to return. No? Then I must positively leave you. But I must first render you all the little attentions in my power."

"The Amontillado!" ejaculated my friend, not yet recovered from his astonishment.

"True," I replied; "the Amontillado."

As I said these words I busied myself among the pile of bones of which I have before spoken. Throwing them aside, I soon uncovered a quantity of building stone and mortar. With these materials and with the aid of my trowel, I began vigorously to wall up the entrance of the niche.

I had scarcely laid the first tier of the masonry when I discovered that the intoxication of Fortunato had in a great measure worn off. The earliest indication I had of this was a low moaning cry from the depth of the recess. It was *not* the cry of a drunken man. There was then a long and obstinate silence. I laid the second tier, and the third, and the fourth; and then I heard the furious vibrations of the chain. The noise lasted for several minutes, during which, that I might hearken to it with the more satisfaction, I ceased my labors and sat down upon the bones. When at last the clanking subsided, I resumed the trowel, and finished without interruption the fifth, the sixth, and the seventh tier. The wall was now nearly upon a level with my breast. I again paused, and holding the flambeaux over the mason-work, threw a few feeble rays upon the figure within.

A succession of loud and shrill screams, bursting suddenly from the throat of the chained form, seemed to thrust me violently back. For a brief moment I hesitated—I trembled. Unsheathing my rapier, I began to grope with it about the recess: but the thought of an instant reassured me. I placed my hand upon the solid fabric of the catacombs, and felt satisfied. I reapproached the wall. I replied to the yells of him who clamored. I re-echoed—I aided—I surpassed them in volume and in strength. I did this, and the clamorer grew still.

It was now midnight, and my task was drawing to a close. I had completed the eighth, the ninth, and the tenth tier. I had finished a portion of the last and the eleventh; there remained but a single stone to be fitted and plastered in. I struggled with its weight; I placed it partially in its destined position. But now there came from out the niche a low laugh that erected the hairs upon my head. It was succeeded by a sad voice, which I had difficulty in recognising as that of the noble Fortunato. The voice said—

"Ha! ha! ha!—he! he!—a very good joke indeed—an excellent jest. We will have many a rich laugh about it at the palazzo—he! he! he!—over our wine—he! he! he!"

"The Amontillado!" I said.

"He! he! he!—he! he! he!—yes, the Amontillado. But is it not getting late? Will not they be awaiting us at the palazzo, the Lady Fortunato and the rest? Let us be gone."

"Yes," I said, "let us be gone."

"*For the love of God, Montresor!*"

"Yes," I said, "for the love of God!"

But to these words I hearkened in vain for a reply. I grew impatient. I called aloud—

"Fortunato!"

No answer. I called again—

"Fortunato!"

No answer still. I thrust a torch through the remaining aperture and let it fall within. There came forth in return only a jingling of the bells. My heart grew sick—on account of the dampness of the catacombs. I hastened to make an end of my labor. I forced the last stone into its position; I plastered it up. Against the new masonry I re-erected the old rampart of bones. For the half of a century no mortal has disturbed them. *In pâce requiescat!*[12]

1846

Hop-Frog

I never knew any one so keenly alive to a joke as the king was. He seemed to live only for joking. To tell a good story of the joke kind, and to tell it well, was the surest road to his favor. Thus it happened that his seven ministers were all noted for their accomplishments as jokers. They all took after the king, too, in being large, corpulent, oily men, as well as inimitable jokers. Whether people grow fat by joking, or whether there is something in fat itself which predisposes to a joke, I have never been quite able to determine; but certain it is that a lean joker is a *rara avis in terris.*[1]

About the refinements, or, as he called them, the "ghosts" of wit, the king troubled himself very little. He had an especial admiration for *breadth* in a jest, and would often put up with *length,* for the sake of it. Over-niceties wearied him. He would have preferred Rabelais's "Gargantua," to the "Zadig" of Voltaire:[2] and, upon the whole, practical jokes suited his taste far better than verbal ones.

At the date of my narrative, professing jesters had not altogether gone out of fashion at court. Several of the great continental "powers" still retained their "fools," who were motley, with caps and bells, and who were expected to be always

[12]"May he rest in peace!" (Latin).

[1]"A rare bird in the world" (Latin), from Satires, VI, 165, by Juvenal (60?–140? A.D.), Roman poet.

[2]François Rabelais (1494?–1553), French author of *Gargan-* *tua and Pantagruel,* a satire on religion, politics, etc.; Voltaire (1694–1778), French author of *Zadig or Destiny,* a novel satirizing society's refusal to reform.

ready with sharp witticisms, at a moment's notice, in consideration of the crumbs that fell from the royal table.

Our king, as a matter of course, retained his "fool." The fact is, he *required* something in the way of folly—if only to counterbalance the heavy wisdom of the seven wise men who were his ministers—not to mention himself.

His fool, or professional jester, was not *only* a fool, however. His value was trebled in the eyes of the king, by the fact of his being also a dwarf and a cripple. Dwarfs were as common at court, in those days, as fools; and many monarchs would have found it difficult to get through their days (days are rather longer at court than elsewhere) without both a jester to laugh *with*, and a dwarf to laugh *at*. But, as I have already observed, your jesters, in ninety-nine cases out of a hundred, are fat, round and unwieldy—so that it was no small source of self-gratulation with our king that, in Hop-Frog (this was the fool's name,) he possessed a triplicate treasure in one person.

I believe the name "Hop-Frog" was *not* that given to the dwarf by his sponsors at baptism, but it was conferred upon him, by general consent of the seven ministers, on account of his inability to walk as other men do. In fact, Hop-Frog could only get along by a sort of interjectional gait—something between a leap and a wriggle—a movement that afforded illimitable amusement, and of course consolation, to the king, for (notwithstanding the protuberance of his stomach and a constitutional swelling of the head) the king, by his whole court, was accounted a capital figure.

But although Hop-Frog, through the distortion of his legs, could move only with great pain and difficulty along a road or floor, the prodigious muscular power which nature seemed to have bestowed upon his arms, by way of compensation for deficiency in the lower limbs, enabled him to perform many feats of wonderful dexterity, where trees or ropes were in question, or anything else to climb. At such exercises he certainly much more resembled a squirrel, or a small monkey, than a frog.

I am not able to say, with precision, from what country Hop-Frog originally came. It was from some barbarous region, however, that no person ever heard of—a vast distance from the court of our king. Hop-Frog, and a young girl very little less dwarfish than himself (although of exquisite proportions, and a marvellous dancer,) had been forcibly carried off from their respective homes in adjoining provinces, and sent as presents to the king, by one of his ever-victorious generals.

Under these circumstances, it is not to be wondered at that a close intimacy arose between the two little captives. Indeed, they soon became sworn friends. Hop-Frog, who, although he made a great deal of sport, was by no means popular, had it not in his power to render Trippetta many services; but *she*, on account of her grace and exquisite beauty (although a dwarf,) was universally admired and petted: so she possessed much influence; and never failed to use it, whenever she could, for the benefit of Hop-Frog.

On some grand state occasion—I forget what—the king determined to have a masquerade; and whenever a masquerade, or anything of that kind, occurred at our court, then the talents both of Hop-Frog and Trippetta were sure to be called in play. Hop-Frog, in especial, was so inventive in the way of getting up pageants, suggesting novel characters, and arranging costume, for masked balls, that nothing could be done, it seems, without his assistance.

The night appointed for the *fête* had arrived. A gorgeous hall had been fitted up, under Trippetta's eye, with every kind of device which could possibly give *éclat*[3] to a masquerade. The whole court was in a fever of expectation. As for costumes

---

[3]"Glitter," "pomp" (French).

and characters, it might well be supposed that everybody had come to a decision on such points. Many had made up their minds (as to what *rôles* they should assume) a week, or even a month, in advance; and, in fact, there was not a particle of indecision anywhere—except in the case of the king and his seven ministers. Why *they* hesitated I never could tell, unless they did it by way of a joke. More probably, they found it difficult, on account of being so fat, to make up their minds. At all events, time flew; and, as a last resource, they sent for Trippetta and Hop-Frog.

When the two little friends obeyed the summons of the king, they found him sitting at his wine with the seven members of his cabinet council; but the monarch appeared to be in a very ill humor. He knew that Hop-Frog was not fond of wine; for it excited the poor cripple almost to madness; and madness is no comfortable feeling. But the king loved his practical jokes, and took pleasure in forcing Hop-Frog to drink and (as the king called it) "to be merry."

"Come here, Hop-Frog," said he, as the jester and his friend entered the room: "swallow this bumper[4] to the health of your absent friends [here Hop-Frog sighed,] and then let us have the benefit of your invention. We want characters—*characters,* man—something novel—out of the way. We are wearied with this everlasting sameness. Come, drink! the wine will brighten your wits."

Hop-Frog endeavored, as usual, to get up a jest in reply to these advances from the king; but the effort was too much. It happened to be the poor dwarf's birthday, and the command to drink to his "absent friends" forced the tears to his eyes. Many large, bitter drops fell into the goblet as he took it, humbly, from the hand of the tyrant.

"Ah! ha! ha! ha!" roared the latter, as the dwarf reluctantly drained the beaker. "See what a glass of good wine can do! Why, your eyes are shining already!"

Poor fellow! his large eyes *gleamed,* rather than shone; for the effect of wine on his excitable brain was not more powerful than instantaneous. He placed the goblet nervously on the table, and looked round upon the company with a half-insane stare. They all seemed highly amused at the success of the king's "*joke.*"

"And now to business," said the prime minister, a *very* fat man.

"Yes," said the king; "come, Hop-Frog, lend us your assistance. Characters, my fine fellow; we stand in need of characters—all of us—ha! ha! ha!" and as this was seriously meant for a joke, his laugh was chorused by the seven.

Hop-Frog also laughed, although feebly and somewhat vacantly.

"Come, come," said the king, impatiently, "have you nothing to suggest?"

"I am endeavoring to think of something *novel,*" replied the dwarf, abstractedly, for he was quite bewildered by the wine.

"Endeavoring!" cried the tyrant, fiercely; "what do you mean by *that?* Ah, I perceive. You are sulky, and want more wine. Here, drink this!" and he poured out another goblet full and offered it to the cripple, who merely gazed at it, gasping for breath.

"Drink, I say!" shouted the monster, "or by the fiends—"

The dwarf hesitated. The king grew purple with rage. The courtiers smirked. Trippetta, pale as a corpse, advanced to the monarch's seat, and, falling on her knees before him, implored him to spare her friend.

The tyrant regarded her, for some moments, in evident wonder at her audacity. He seemed quite at a loss what to do or say—how most becomingly to express his indignation. At last, without uttering a syllable, he pushed her violently from him, and threw the contents of the brimming goblet in her face.

The poor girl got up as best she could, and, not daring even to sigh, resumed her position at the foot of the table.

---

[4]Goblet filled to the brim.

There was a dead silence for about a half a minute, during which the falling of a leaf, or of a feather, might have been heard. It was interrupted by a low, but harsh and protracted *grating* sound which seemed to come at once from every corner of the room.

"What—what—*what* are you making that noise for?" demanded the king, turning furiously to the dwarf.

The latter seemed to have recovered, in great measure, from his intoxication, and looking fixedly but quietly into the tyrant's face, merely ejaculated:

"I—I? How could it have been me?"

"The sound appeared to come from without," observed one of the courtiers. "I fancy it was the parrot at the window, whetting his bill upon his cage-wires."

"True," replied the monarch, as if much relieved by the suggestion; "but, on the honor of a knight, I could have sworn that it was the gritting of this vagabond's teeth."

Hereupon the dwarf laughed (the king was too confirmed a joker to object to any one's laughing), and displayed a set of large, powerful, and very repulsive teeth. Moreover, he avowed his perfect willingness to swallow as much wine as desired. The monarch was pacified; and having drained another bumper with no very perceptible ill effect, Hop-Frog entered at once, and with spirit, into the plans for the masquerade.

"I cannot tell what was the association of idea," observed he, very tranquilly, and as if he had never tasted wine in his life, "but *just after* your majesty had struck the girl and thrown the wine in her face—*just after* your majesty had done this, and while the parrot was making that odd noise outside the window, there came into my mind a capital diversion—one of my own country frolics—often enacted among us, at our masquerades: but here it will be new altogether. Unfortunately, however, it requires a company of eight persons, and—"

"Here we *are!*" cried the king, laughing at his acute discovery of the coincidence; "eight to a fraction—I and my seven ministers. Come! what is the diversion?"

"We call it," replied the cripple, "the Eight Chained Ourang-Outangs, and it really is excellent sport if well enacted."

"*We* will enact it," remarked the king, drawing himself up, and lowering his eyelids.

"The beauty of the game," continued Hop-Frog, "lies in the fright it occasions among the women."

"Capital!" roared in chorus the monarch and his ministry.

"*I* will equip you as ourang-outangs," proceeded the dwarf; "leave all that to me. The resemblance shall be so striking, that the company of masqueraders will take you for real beasts—and of course, they will be as much terrified as astonished."

"O, this is exquisite!" exclaimed the king. "Hop-Frog! I will make a man of you."

"The chains are for the purpose of increasing the confusion by their jangling. You are supposed to have escaped, *en masse*, from your keepers. Your majesty cannot conceive the *effect* produced, at a masquerade, by eight chained ourang-outangs, imagined to be real ones by most of the company; and rushing in with savage cries, among the crowd of delicately and gorgeously habited men and women. The *contrast* is inimitable."

"It *must* be," said the king: and the council arose hurriedly (as it was growing late), to put in execution the scheme of Hop-Frog.

His mode of equipping the party as ourang-outangs was very simple, but effective enough for his purposes. The animals in question had, at the epoch of my story, very rarely been seen in any part of the civilized world; and as the imitations made by the dwarf were sufficiently beast-like and more than sufficiently hideous, their truthfulness to nature was thus thought to be secured.

The king and his ministers were first encased in tight-fitting stockinet[5] shirts and drawers. They were then saturated with tar. At this stage of the process, some one of the party suggested feathers; but the suggestion was at once overruled by the dwarf, who soon convinced the eight, by ocular demonstration, that the hair of such a brute as the ourang-outang was much more efficiently represented by *flax*.[6] A thick coating of the latter was accordingly plastered upon the coating of tar. A long chain was now procured. First, it was passed about the waist of the king, *and tied;* then about another of the party, and also tied; then about all successively, in the same manner. When this chaining arrangement was complete, and the party stood as far apart from each other as possible, they formed a circle; and to make all things appear natural, Hop-Frog passed the residue of the chain, in two diameters, at right angles, across the circle, after the fashion adopted, at the present day, by those who capture Chimpanzees, or other large apes, in Borneo.

The grand saloon in which the masquerade was to take place, was a circular room, very lofty, and receiving the light of the sun only through a single window at top. At night (the season for which the apartment was especially designed,) it was illuminated principally by a large chandelier, depending by a chain from the centre of the sky-light, and lowered, or elevated, by means of a counter-balance as usual; but (in order not to look unsightly) this latter passed outside the cupola and over the roof.

The arrangements of the room had been left to Trippetta's superintendence; but, in some particulars, it seems, she had been guided by the calmer judgment of her friend the dwarf. At his suggestion it was that, on this occasion, the chandelier was removed. Its waxen drippings (which, in weather so warm, it was quite impossible to prevent,) would have been seriously detrimental to the rich dresses of the guests, who, on account of the crowded state of the saloon, could not *all* be expected to keep from out its centre—that is to say, from under the chandelier. Additional sconces[7] were set in various parts of the hall, out of the way; and a flambeau,[8] emitting sweet odor, was placed in the right hand of each of the Caryatides[9] that stood against the wall—some fifty or sixty altogether.

The eight ourang-outangs, taking Hop-Frog's advice, waited patiently until midnight (when the room was thoroughly filled with masqueraders) before making their appearance. No sooner had the clock ceased striking, however, than they rushed, or rather rolled in, all together—for the impediment of their chains caused most of the party to fall, and all to stumble as they entered.

The excitement among the masqueraders was prodigious, and filled the heart of the king with glee. As had been anticipated, there were not a few of the guests who supposed the ferocious-looking creatures to be beasts of *some* kind in reality, if not precisely ourang-outangs. Many of the women swooned with affright; and had not the king taken the precaution to exclude all weapons from the saloon, his party might soon have expiated their frolic in their blood. As it was, a general rush was made for the doors; but the king had ordered them to be locked immediately upon his entrance; and, at the dwarf's suggestion, the keys had been deposited with *him*.

While the tumult was at its height, and each masquerader attentive only to his own safety—(for, in fact, there was much *real* danger from the pressure of the

---

[5]An elastic knitted cloth used for making stockings, underwear, etc.
[6]The threadlike fibers of the flax plant, ready for spinning.
[7]Candle-holding brackets on the wall.
[8]Lighted torch.
[9]Supporting columns in the shape of women.

excited crowd,)—the chain by which the chandelier ordinarily hung, and which had been drawn up on its removal, might have been seen very gradually to descend, until its hooked extremity came within three feet of the floor.

Soon after this, the king and his seven friends, having reeled about the hall in all directions, found themselves, at length, in its centre, and, of course, in immediate contact with the chain. While they were thus situated, the dwarf, who had followed closely at their heels, inciting them to keep up the commotion, took hold of their own chain at the intersection of the two portions which crossed the circle diametrically and at right angles. Here, with the rapidity of thought, he inserted the hook from which the chandelier had been wont to depend; and, in an instant, by some unseen agency, the chandelier-chain was drawn so far upward as to take the hook out of reach, and, as an inevitable consequence, to drag the ourang-outangs together in close connection, and face to face.

The masqueraders, by this time, had recovered, in some measure, from their alarm; and, beginning to regard the whole matter as a well-contrived pleasantry, set up a loud shout of laughter at the predicament of the apes.

"Leave them to *me!*" now screamed Hop-Frog, his shrill voice making itself easily heard through all the din. "Leave them to *me.* I fancy *I* know them. If I can only get a good look at them, *I* can soon tell who they are."

Here, scrambling over the heads of the crowd, he managed to get to the wall; when, seizing a flambeau from one of the Caryatides, he returned, as he went, to the centre of the room—leaped, with the agility of a monkey, upon the king's head—and thence clambered a few feet up the chain—holding down the torch to examine the group of ourang-outangs, and still screaming, "*I* shall soon find out who they are!"

And now, while the whole assembly (the apes included) were convulsed with laughter, the jester suddenly uttered a shrill whistle; when the chain flew violently up for about thirty feet—dragging with it the dismayed and struggling ourang-outangs, and leaving them suspended in mid-air between the sky-light and the floor. Hop-Frog, clinging to the chain as it rose, still maintained his relative position in respect to the eight maskers, and still (as if nothing were the matter) continued to thrust his torch down towards them, as though endeavoring to discover who they were.

So thoroughly astonished were the whole company at this ascent, that a dead silence, of about a minute's duration, ensued. It was broken by just such a low, harsh, *grating* sound, as had before attracted the attention of the king and his councillors, when the former threw the wine in the face of Trippetta. But, on the present occasion, there could be no question as to *whence* the sound issued. It came from the fang-like teeth of the dwarf, who ground them and gnashed them as he foamed at the mouth, and glared, with an expression of maniacal rage, into the upturned countenances of the king and his seven companions.

"Ah, ha!" said at length the infuriated jester. "Ah, ha! I begin to see who these people *are,* now!" Here, pretending to scrutinize the king more closely, he held the flambeau to the flaxen coat which enveloped him, and which instantly burst into a sheet of vivid flame. In less than half a minute the whole eight ourang-outangs were blazing fiercely, amid the shrieks of the multitude who gazed at them from below, horror-stricken, and without the power to render them the slightest assistance.

At length the flames, suddenly increasing in virulence, forced the jester to climb higher up the chain, to be out of their reach; and, as he made this movement, the crowd again sank, for a brief instant, into silence. The dwarf seized his opportunity, and once more spoke:

"I now see *distinctly,*" he said, "what manner of people these maskers are. They are a great king and his seven privy-councillors—a king who does not scruple to strike a defenceless girl, and his seven councillors who abet him in the outrage. As for myself, I am simply Hop-Frog, the jester—and *this is my last jest.*"

Owing to the high combustibility of both the flax and the tar to which it adhered, the dwarf had scarcely made an end of his brief speech before the work of vengeance was complete. The eight corpses swung in their chains, a fetid, blackened, hideous, and indistinguishable mass. The cripple hurled his torch at them, clambered leisurely to the ceiling, and disappeared through the skylight.

It is supposed that Trippetta, stationed on the roof of the saloon, had been the accomplice of her friend in his fiery revenge, and that, together, they effected their escape to their own country: for neither was seen again.

1849

from Prose

from Undine: A Miniature Romance
[A Mystic or Undercurrent of Meaning]

This is an exceedingly meagre outline of the leading event of the story;[1] which, although brief, is crowded with incident. Beneath all, there runs a mystic or under current of meaning, of the simplest and most easily intelligible, yet of the most richly philosophical character. From internal evidence afforded by the book itself, we gather that the author has deeply suffered from the ills of an ill-assorted marriage—and to the bitter reflections induced by these ills, we owe the conception and peculiar execution of "Undine."

·　·　·　·　·

We have no hesitation in saying that this portion of the design of the romance—the portion which conveys an undercurrent of meaning—does not afford the fairest field to the romanticist—does not appertain to the higher regions of ideality. Although, in this case, the plan is essentially distinct from Allegory, yet it has too close an affinity to that most indefensible species of writing—a species whose gross demerits we cannot now pause to examine. That M. Fouqué was well aware of the disadvantage under which he laboured—that he well knew the field he traversed not to be the fairest—and that a personal object alone induced him to choose it—we cannot and shall not doubt. For the hand of the master is visible in every line of his beautiful fable. "Undine" is a model of models, in regard to the high artistical talent which it evinces. We could write volumes in a detailed commentary upon its various beauties in this respect. Its unity is absolute—its keeping unbroken. Yet every minute point of the picture fills and satisfies the eye. Everything is attended to, and nothing is out of time or out of place.

We say that some private and personal design to be fulfilled has thrown M. Fouqué upon that objectionable undercurrent of meaning which he has so elaborately managed. Yet his high genius has nearly succeeded in turning the blemish into a beauty. At all events he has succeeded, in spite of a radical defect, in pro-

---

[1] In his review of *Undine: A Miniature Romance: from the German of Baron De La Motte-Fouqué,* by Friederich Heinrich Karl de La Motte-Fouqué (1777–1843), Poe first presents a detailed summary, and then introduces his discussion of the undercurrent of meaning. Compare his comments here with those on allegory in his essay on Hawthorne.

ducing what we advisedly consider the finest romance in existence. We say this with a bitter kind of half-consciousness that only a very few will fully agree with us—yet these few are our all in such matters. They will stand by us in a just opinion.

1839

from Marginalia
[PSYCHAL IMPRESSIONS BETWEEN WAKING AND SLEEP][1]

Some Frenchman—possibly Montaigne[2]—says: "People talk about thinking, but for my part I never think, except when I sit down to write." It is this never thinking, unless when we sit down to write, which is the cause of so much indifferent composition. But perhaps there is something more involved in the Frenchman's observation than meets the eye. It is certain that the mere act of inditing, tends, in a great degree, to the logicalization of thought. Whenever, on account of its vagueness, I am dissatisfied with a conception of the brain, I resort forthwith to the pen, for the purpose of obtaining, through its aid, the necessary form, consequence and precision.

How very commonly we hear it remarked, that such and such thoughts are beyond the compass of words! I do not believe that any thought, properly so called, is out of the reach of language. I fancy, rather, that where difficulty in expression is experienced, there is, in the intellect which experiences it, a want either of deliberateness or of method. For my own part, I have never had a thought which I could not set down in words, with even more distinctness than that with which I conceived it:—as I have before observed, the thought is logicalized by the effort at (written) expression.

There is, however, a class of fancies, of exquisite delicacy, which are *not* thoughts, and to which, *as yet,* I have found it absolutely impossible to adapt language. I use the word *fancies* at random, and merely because I must use *some* word; but the idea commonly attached to the term is not even remotely applicable to the shadows of shadows in question. They seem to me rather psychal than intellectual. They arise in the soul (alas, how rarely!) only at its epochs of most intense tranquility—when the bodily and mental health are in perfection—and at those mere points of time where the confines of the waking world blend with those of the world of dreams. I am aware of these "fancies" only when I am upon the very brink of sleep, with the consciousness that I am so. I have satisfied myself that this condition exists but for an inappreciable *point* of time—yet it is crowded with these "shadows of shadows"; and for absolute *thought* there is demanded time's *endurance.*

These "fancies" have in them a pleasurable ecstasy as far beyond the most pleasurable of the world of wakefulness, or of dreams, as the Heaven of the Northman theology is beyond its Hell. I regard the visions, even as they arise, with an awe which, in some measure, moderates or tranquilizes the ecstasy—I so regard them, through a conviction (which seems a portion of the ecstasy itself) that this

---

[1] In this piece, Poe describes fancies—or "psychal impressions"—which come at the moment of tranquility before sleep, originating not in the intellect but in the soul. These impressions are extrasensory, supernal, or transcendental, and perhaps are a resource of imagination. In any event, the concept can prove useful in the reading of Poe's poems and stories. Richard Wilbur, for example, believes that "the typical Poe story is, in its action, an allegory of dream-experience; . . . the steps of the action correspond to the successive states of a mind moving into sleep; and the end of the action is the end of a dream."

[2] Michel Eyquem de Montaigne (1533–1592), French author of *Essays* (1571–80).

ecstasy, in itself, is of a character supernal to the Human Nature—is a glimpse of the spirit's outer world; and I arrive at this conclusion—if this term is at all applicable to instantaneous intuition—by a perception that the delight experienced has, as its element, but *the absoluteness of novelty.* I say the absoluteness—for in these fancies—let me now term them psychal impressions—there is really nothing even approximate in character to impressions ordinarily received. It is as if the five senses were supplanted by five myriad others alien to mortality.

Now, so entire is my faith in the *power of words,* that, at times, I have believed it possible to embody even the evanescence of fancies such as I have attempted to describe. In experiments with this end in view, I have proceeded so far as, first, to control (when the bodily and mental health are good) the existence of the condition:—that is to say, I can now (unless when ill) be sure that the condition will supervene, if I so wish it, at the point of time already described: of its supervention, until lately, I could never be certain, even under the most favorable circumstances. I mean to say, merely, that now I can be sure, when all circumstances are favorable, of the supervention of the condition, and feel even the capacity of inducing or compelling it:—the favorable circumstances, however, are not the less rare—else had I compelled, already, the Heaven into the Earth.

I have proceeded so far, secondly, as to prevent the lapse from *the point* of which I speak—the point of blending between wakefulness and sleep—as to prevent at will, I say, the lapse from this border-ground into the dominion of sleep. Not that I can *continue* the condition—not that I can render the point more than a point—but that I can startle myself from the point into wakefulness—*and thus transfer the point itself into the realm of Memory*—convey its impressions, or more properly their recollections, to a situation where (although still for a very brief period) I can survey them with the eye of analysis.

For these reasons—that is to say, because I have been enabled to accomplish thus much—I do not altogether despair of embodying in words at least enough of the fancies in question to convey, to certain classes of intellect, a shadowy conception of their character.

In saying this I am not to be understood as supposing that the fancies, or psychal impressions, to which I allude, are confined to my individual self—are not, in a word, common to all mankind—for on this point it is quite impossible that I should form an opinion—but nothing can be more certain than that even a partial record of the impressions would startle the universal intellect of mankind, by the *supremeness of the novelty* of the material employed, and of its consequent suggestions. In a word—should I ever write a paper on this topic, the world will be compelled to acknowledge that, at last, I have done an original thing.

1846

Tale-Writing—*Twice-Told Tales*—
Mosses from an Old Manse.
By Nathaniel Hawthorne[1]
[ON ORIGINALITY, ALLEGORY, UNITY OF EFFECT]

In the preface to my sketches of New York Literati,[2] while speaking of the broad distinction between the seeming public and real private opinion respecting our authors, I thus alluded to Nathaniel Hawthorne:

"For example, Mr. Hawthorne, the author of 'Twice-Told Tales,' is scarcely recognized by the press or by the public, and when noticed at all, is noticed merely to be damned by faint praise. Now, my opinion of him is, that although his walk is limited and he is fairly to be charged with mannerism, treating all subjects in a similar tone of dreamy *innuendo,* yet in this walk he evinces extraordinary genius, having no rival either in America or elsewhere; and this opinion I have never heard gainsaid by any one literary person in the country. That this opinion, however, is a spoken and not a written one, is referable to the facts, first, that Mr. Hawthorne is a poor man, and, secondly, that he *is not* an ubiquitous quack."

The reputation of the author of "Twice-Told Tales" has been confined, indeed, until very lately, to literary society; and I have not been wrong, perhaps, in citing him as *the* example, *par excellence,* in this country, of the privately-admired and publicly-unappreciated man of genius. Within the last year or two, it is true, an occasional critic has been urged, by honest indignation, into very warm approval. Mr. Webber,[3] for instance, (than whom no one has a keener relish for that kind of writing which Mr. Hawthorne has best illustrated,) gave us, in a late number of "The American Review," a cordial and certainly a full tribute to his talents; and since the issue of the "Mosses from an Old Manse," criticisms of similar tone have been by no means infrequent in our more authoritative journals. I can call to mind few reviews of Hawthorne published *before* the "Mosses." One I remember in "Arcturus" (edited by Mathews and Duyckinck) for May, 1841; another in the "American Monthly" (edited by Hoffman and Herbert) for March, 1838; a third in the ninety-sixth number of the "North American Review." These criticisms, however, seemed to have little effect on the popular taste—at least, if we are to form any idea of the popular taste by reference to its expression in the newspapers, or by the sale of the author's book. It was never the fashion (until lately) to speak of him in any summary of our best authors. The daily critics would say, on such occasions, "Is there not Irving and Cooper, and Bryant and Paulding, and—Smith?" or, "Have we not Halleck and Dana, and Longfellow and—Thompson?" or, "Can we not point triumphantly to our own Sprague, Willis, Channing, Bancroft, Prescott and—Jenkins?" but these unanswerable queries were never wound up by the name of Hawthorne.

Beyond doubt, this inappreciation of him on the part of the public arose chiefly from the two causes to which I have referred—from the facts that he is neither a man of wealth nor a quack;—but these are insufficient to account for the whole effect. No small portion of it is attributable to the very marked idiosyncrasy of Mr. Hawthorne himself. In one sense, and in great measure, to be peculiar is to be

---

[1]Poe published a highly favorable two-part review of Hawthorne's *Twice-Told Tales* in April and May 1842; by 1847, when he wrote this essay reviewing Hawthorne's two volumes of stories, he had become more critical of Hawthorne. He incorporated the significant theoretical passages of his previous reviews, but he elaborated on them and sharpened his points. This review-essay is Poe's most important commentary on fiction and the short story.

[2]*The Literati of New York City,* published in *Godey's Magazine and Lady's Book,* April–October 1846.
[3]Charles W. Webber (1819–1856), American adventurer and author of wild west tales and books of natural history; he served (as Poe later notes) as assistant editor of *The American Review.*

original, and than the true originality there is no higher literary virtue. This true or commendable originality, however, implies not the uniform, but the continuous peculiarity—a peculiarity springing from ever-active vigor of fancy—better still if from ever-present force of imagination, giving its own hue, its own character to everything it touches, and, especially, *self impelled to touch everything.*

It is often said, inconsiderately, that very original writers always fail in popularity—that such and such persons are too original to be comprehended by the mass. "Too peculiar," should be the phrase, "too idiosyncratic." It is, in fact, the excitable, undisciplined and childlike popular mind which most keenly feels the original. The criticism of the conservatives, of the hackneys, of the cultivated old clergymen of the "North American Review," is precisely the criticism which condemns and alone condemns it. "It becometh not a divine," saith Lord Coke,[4] "to be of a fiery and salamandrine spirit." Their conscience allowing them to move nothing themselves, these dignitaries have a holy horror of being moved. "Give us *quietude,*" they say. Opening their mouths with proper caution, they sigh forth the word "*Repose.*" And this is, indeed, the one thing they should be permitted to enjoy, if only upon the Christian principle of give and take.

The fact is, that if Mr. Hawthorne were really original, he could not fail of making himself felt by the public. But the fact is, he is *not* original in any sense. Those who speak of him as original, mean nothing more than that he differs in his manner of tone, and in his choice of subjects, from any author of their acquaintance—their acquaintance not extending to the German Tieck,[5] whose manner, in *some* of his works, is absolutely identical with that *habitual* to Hawthorne. But it is clear that the element of the literary originality is novelty. The element of its appreciation by the reader is the reader's sense of the new. Whatever gives him a new and insomuch a pleasurable emotion, he considers original, and whoever frequently gives him such emotion, he considers an original writer. In a word, it is by the sum total of these emotions that he decides upon the writer's claim to originality. I may observe here, however, that there is clearly a point at which even novelty itself would cease to produce the legitimate originality, if we judge this originality, as we should, by the effect designed; this point is that at which *novelty becomes nothing novel;* and here the artist, *to preserve his originality* will subside into the commonplace. No one, I think, has noticed that, merely through inattention to this matter, Moore has comparatively failed in his "Lalla Rookh."[6] Few readers, and indeed few critics, have commended this poem for originality—and, in fact, the effect, originality, is not produced by it—yet no work of equal size so abounds in the happiest originalities, individually considered. They are so excessive as, in the end, to deaden in the reader all capacity for their appreciation.

These points properly understood, it will be seen that the critic (unacquainted with Tieck) who reads a single tale or essay by Hawthorne, may be justified in thinking him original; but the tone, or manner, or choice of subject, which induces in this critic the sense of the new, will—if not in a second tale, at least in a third and all subsequent ones—not only fail of inducing it, but bring about an exactly antagonistic impression. In concluding a volume, and more especially in concluding all the volumes of the author, the critic will abandon his first design of calling him "original," and content himself with styling him "peculiar."

With the vague opinion that to be original is to be popular, I could, indeed, agree, were I to adopt an understanding of originality which, to my surprise, I have known adopted by many who have a right to be called critical. They have

---

[4]Sir Edward Coke (1552–1634), renowned English jurist and political leader.
[5]Ludwig Tieck (1773–1853), German poet, novelist, and dramatist of the Romantic period.

[6]Thomas Moore (1779–1852), British author of the romantic narrative poem set in the Orient, *Lalla Rookh* (1817).

limited, in a love for mere words, the literary to the metaphysical originality. They regard as original in letters, only such combinations of thought, of incident, and so forth, as are, in fact, absolutely novel. It is clear, however, not only that it is the novelty of *effect* alone which is worth consideration, but that this effect is *best* wrought, for the end of all fictitious composition, pleasure, by shunning rather than by seeking the absolute novelty of combination. Originality, thus understood, tasks and startles the intellect, and so brings into undue action the faculties to which, in the lighter literature, we least appeal. And thus understood, it cannot fail to prove unpopular with the masses, who, seeking in this literature amusement, are positively offended by instruction. But the true originality—true in respect of its purposes—is that which, in bringing out the half-formed, the reluctant, or the unexpressed fancies of mankind, or in exciting the more delicate pulses of the heart's passion, or in giving birth to some universal sentiment or instinct in embryo, thus combines with the pleasurable effect of *apparent* novelty, a real egoistic delight. The reader, in the case first supposed, (that of the absolute novelty,) is excited, but embarrassed, disturbed, in some degree even pained at his own want of perception, at his own folly in not having himself hit upon the idea. In the second case, his pleasure is doubled. He is filled with an intrinsic and extrinsic delight. He feels and intensely enjoys the seeming novelty of the thought, enjoys it as really novel, as absolutely original with the writer—*and himself*. They two, he fancies, have, alone of all men, thought thus. They two have, together, created this thing. Henceforward there is a bond of sympathy between them, a sympathy which irradiates every subsequent page of the book.

There is a species of writing which, with some difficulty, may be admitted as a lower degree of what I have called the true original. In its perusal, we say to ourselves, not "how original this is!" nor "here is an idea which I and the author have alone entertained," but "here is a charmingly obvious fancy," or sometimes even, "here is a thought which I am not sure has ever occurred to myself, but which, of course, has occurred to all the rest of the world." This kind of composition (which still appertains to a high order) is usually designated as "the natural." It has little external resemblance, but strong internal affinity to the true original, if, indeed, as I have suggested, it is not of this latter an inferior degree. It is best exemplified, among English writers, in Addison, Irving[7] and *Hawthorne*. The "ease" which is so often spoken of as its distinguishing feature, it has been the fashion to regard as ease in appearance alone, as a point of really difficult attainment. This idea, however, must be received with some reservation. The natural style is difficult only to those who should never intermeddle with it—to the unnatural. It is but the result of writing with the understanding, or with the instinct, that the *tone*, in composition, should be that which, at any given point or upon any given topic, would be the tone of the great mass of humanity. The author who, after the manner of the North Americans, is merely at *all* times *quiet*, is, of course, upon *most* occasions, merely silly or stupid, and has no more right to be thought "easy" or "natural" than has a cockney exquisite or the sleeping beauty in the wax-works.

The "peculiarity" or sameness, or monotone of Hawthorne, would, in its mere character of "peculiarity," and without reference to what *is* the peculiarity, suffice to deprive him of all chance of popular appreciation. But at his failure to be appreciated, we can, *of course*, no longer wonder, when we find him monotonous at decidedly the worst of all possible points—at that point which, having the least concern with Nature, is the farthest removed from the popular intellect, from the popular sentiment and from the popular taste. I allude to the strain of allegory

---

[7]The British writer, Joseph Addison (1672–1719), and the American, Washington Irving (1783–1859), were masters of the personal or informal essay.

which completely overwhelms the greater number of his subjects, and which in some measure interferes with the direct conduct of absolutely all.

In defence of allegory, (however, or for whatever object, employed,) there is scarcely one respectable word to be said. Its best appeals are made to the fancy— that is to say, to our sense of adaptation, not of matters proper, but of matters improper for the purpose, of the real with the unreal; having never more of intelligible connection than has something with nothing, never half so much of effective affinity as has the substance for the shadow. The deepest emotion aroused within us by the happiest allegory, *as* allegory, is a very, very imperfectly satisfied sense of the writer's ingenuity in overcoming a difficulty we should have preferred his not having attempted to overcome. The fallacy of the idea that allegory, in any of its moods, can be made to enforce a truth—that metaphor, for example, may illustrate as well as embellish an argument—could be promptly demonstrated: the converse of the supposed fact might be shown, indeed, with very little trouble—but these are topics foreign to my present purpose. One thing is clear, that if allegory ever establishes a fact, it is by dint of overturning a fiction. Where the suggested meaning runs through the obvious one in a *very* profound undercurrent so as never to interfere with the upper one without our own volition, so as never to show itself unless *called* to the surface, there only, for the proper uses of fictitious narrative, is it available at all. Under the best circumstances, it must always interfere with that unity of effect which to the artist, is worth all the allegory in the world. Its vital injury, however, is rendered to the most vitally important point in fiction—that of earnestness or verisimilitude. That "The Pilgrim's Progress"[8] is a ludicrously over-rated book, owing its seeming popularity to one or two of those accidents in critical literature which by the critical are sufficiently well under-stood, is a matter upon which no two thinking people disagree; but the pleasure derivable from it, in any sense, will be found in the direct ratio of the reader's capacity to smother its true purpose, in the direct ratio of his ability to keep the allegory out of sight, or of his *in*ability to comprehend it. Of allegory properly handled, judiciously subdued, seen only as a shadow or by suggestive glimpses, and making its nearest approach to truth in a not obtrusive and therefore not unpleasant *appositeness,* the "Undine" of De La Motte Fouqué[9] is the best, and undoubtedly a very remarkable specimen.

The obvious causes, however, which have prevented Mr. Hawthorne's *popularity,* do not suffice to condemn him in the eyes of the few who belong properly to books, and to whom books, perhaps, do not quite so properly belong. These few estimate an author, not as do the public, altogether by what he does, but in great measure—indeed, even in the greatest measure—by what he evinces a capability of doing. In this view, Hawthorne stands among literary people in America much in the same light as did Coleridge[10] in England. The few, also, through a certain warping of the taste, which long pondering upon books as books merely never fails to induce, are not in condition to view the errors of a scholar as errors altogether. At any time these gentlemen are prone to think the public not right rather than an educated author wrong. But the simple truth is that the writer who aims at impressing the people, is *always* wrong when he fails in forcing that people to receive the impression. How far Mr. Hawthorne has addressed the people at all, is, of course, not a question for me to decide. His books afford strong internal evidence of having been written to himself and his particular friends alone.

There has long existed in literature a fatal and unfounded prejudice, which it will be the office of this age to overthrow—the idea that the mere bulk of a work must enter largely into our estimate of its merit. I do not suppose even the weak-

---

[8]By John Bunyan (1628–1688), published in 1678.
[9]Friederich Heinrich Karl de La Motte-Fouqué (1777–1843), German romantic novelist, author of *Undine* (1811).

Poe reviewed an English translation in 1839 (see excerpt included in this volume).
[10]Samuel Taylor Coleridge (1772–1834).

est of the quarterly reviewers weak enough to maintain that in a book's size or mass, abstractly considered, there is anything which especially calls for our admiration. A mountain, simply through the sensation of physical magnitude which it conveys, does, indeed, affect us with a sense of the sublime, but we cannot admit any such influence in the contemplation even of "The Columbiad."[11] The Quarterlies themselves will not admit it. And yet, what else are we to understand by their continual prating about "sustained effort"? Granted that this sustained effort has accomplished an epic—let us then admire the effort, (if this be a thing admirable,) but certainly not the epic on the effort's account. Common sense, in the time to come, may possibly insist upon measuring a work of art rather by the object it fulfils, by the impression it makes, than by the time it took to fulfil the object, or by the extent of "sustained effort" which became necessary to produce the impression. The fact is, that perseverance is one thing and genius quite another; nor can all the transcendentalists in Heathendom confound them.

Full of its bulky ideas, the last number of the "North American Review," in what it imagines a criticism on Simms,[12] "honestly avows that it has little opinion of the mere tale;" and the honesty of the avowal is in no slight degree guaranteed by the fact that this Review has never yet been known to put forth an opinion which was *not* a very little one indeed.

The tale proper affords the fairest field which can be afforded by the wide domains of mere prose, for the exercise of the highest genius. Were I bidden to say how this genius could be most advantageously employed for the best display of its powers, I should answer, without hesitation, "in the composition of a rhymed poem not to exceed in length what might be perused in an hour." Within this limit alone can the noblest order of poetry exist. I have discussed this topic elsewhere,[13] and need here repeat only that the phrase "a long poem" embodies a paradox. A poem must intensely excite. Excitement is its province, its essentiality. Its value is in the ratio of its (elevating) excitement. But all excitement is, from a psychal necessity, transient. It cannot be sustained through a poem of great length. In the course of an hour's reading, at most, it flags, fails; and then the poem is, in effect, no longer such. Men admire, but are wearied with the "Paradise Lost;"[14] for platitude follows platitude, *inevitably*, at regular interspaces, (the depressions between the waves of excitement,) until the poem, (which, properly considered, is but a succession of brief poems,) having been brought to an end, we discover that the sums of our pleasure and of displeasure have been very nearly equal. The absolute, ultimate or aggregate effect of any epic under the sun is, for these reasons, a nullity. "The Iliad,"[15] in its form of epic, has but an imaginary existence; granting it real, however, I can only say of it that it is based on a primitive sense of Art. Of the modern epic nothing can be so well said as that it is a blindfold imitation of a "come-by-chance." By and by these propositions will be understood as self-evident, and in the meantime will not be essentially damaged as truths by being generally condemned as falsities.

A poem *too* brief, on the other hand, may produce a sharp or vivid, but never a profound or enduring impression. Without a certain continuity, without a certain duration or repetition of the cause, the soul is seldom moved to the effect. There must be the dropping of the water on the rock. There must be the pressing steadily down of the stamp upon the wax. De Béranger[16] has wrought brilliant things, pungent and spirit-stirring, but most of them are too immassive to have

---

[11]The long epic poem published in 1807 by Joel Barlow (1754–1812).
[12]William Gilmore Simms (1806–1870), American southern novelist of such works as *The Yemassee*, a tale of Indian warfare in South Carolina.
[13]See "The Philosophy of Composition" and "The Poetic Principle."

[14]Published in 1667 by John Milton (1608–1674).
[15]Ancient Greek epic of the Trojan War, by Homer (*c.* 1200 B.C.).
[16]Pierre-Jean de Béranger (1780–1857), French poet known as the poet of the people.

momentum, and, as so many feathers of fancy, have been blown aloft only to be whistled down the wind. Brevity, indeed, may degenerate into epigrammatism, but this danger does not prevent extreme length from being the one unpardonable sin.

Were I called upon, however, to designate that class of composition which, next to such a poem as I have suggested, should best fulfil the demands and serve the purposes of ambitious genius, should offer it the most advantageous field of exertion, and afford it the fairest opportunity of display, I should speak at once of the brief prose tale. History, philosophy, and other matters of that kind, we leave out of the question, of course. *Of course,* I say, and in spite of the gray-beards. These grave topics, to the end of time, will be best illustrated by what a discriminating world, turning up its nose at the drab pamphlets, has agreed to understand as *talent.* The ordinary novel is objectionable, from its length, for reasons analogous to those which render length objectionable in the poem. As the novel cannot be read at one sitting, it cannot avail itself of the immense benefit of *totality.* Worldly interests, intervening during the pauses of perusal, modify, counteract and annul the impressions intended. But simple cessation in reading would, of itself, be sufficient to destroy the true unity. In the brief tale, however, the author is enabled to carry out his full design without interruption. During the hour of perusal, the soul of the reader is at the writer's control.

A skilful artist has constructed a tale. He has not fashioned his thoughts to accommodate his incidents, but having deliberately conceived a certain *single effect* to be wrought, he then invents such incidents, he then combines such events, and discusses them in such tone as may best serve him in establishing this preconceived effect. If his very first sentence tend not to the out-bringing of this effect, then in his very first step has he committed a blunder. In the whole composition there should be no word written of which the tendency, direct or indirect, is not to the one pre-established design. And by such means, with such care and skill, a picture is at length painted which leaves in the mind of him who contemplates it with a kindred art, a sense of the fullest satisfaction. The idea of the tale, its thesis, has been presented unblemished, because undisturbed—an end absolutely demanded, yet, in the novel, altogether unattainable.

Of skilfully-constructed tales—I speak now without reference to other points, some of them more important than construction—there are very few American specimens. I am acquainted with no better one, upon the whole, than the "Murder Will Out" of Mr. Simms, and this has some glaring defects. The "Tales of a Traveler,"[17] by Irving, are graceful and impressive narratives—"The Young Italian" is especially good—but there is not one of the series which can be commended as a whole. In many of them the interest is subdivided and frittered away, and their conclusions are insufficiently *climacic.*[18] In the higher requisites of composition, John Neal's[19] magazine stories excel—I mean in vigor of thought, picturesque combination of incident, and so forth—but they ramble too much, and invariably break down just before coming to an end, as if the writer had received a sudden and irresistible summons to dinner, and thought it incumbent upon him to make a finish of his story before going. One of the happiest and best-sustained tales I have seen is "Jack Long; or, The Shot in the Eye," by Charles W. Webber, the assistant editor of Mr. Colton's "American Review." But in general skill of construction, the tales of Willis,[20] I think, surpass those of any American writer—with the exception of Mr. Hawthorne.

---

[17]Washington Irving's *Tales of a Traveller,* published in 1824.
[18]Variant of "climactic."
[19]John Neal (1793–1876), American author who produced novels, stories, and essays in large numbers and of great variety.

[20]Nathaniel Parker Willis (1806–1867), American author of stories, novels, travel sketches; he engaged Poe to become literary critic of the *Mirror.*

I must defer to the better opportunity of a volume now in hand, a full discussion of his individual pieces, and hasten to conclude this paper with a summary of his merits and demerits.

He is peculiar and *not* original—unless in those detailed fancies and detached thoughts which his want of general originality will deprive of the appreciation due to them, in preventing them forever reaching the *public eye*. He is infinitely too fond of allegory, and can never hope for popularity so long as he persists in it. This he will not do, for allegory is at war with the whole tone of his nature, which disports itself never so well as when escaping from the mysticism of his Goodman Browns and White Old Maids into the hearty, genial, but still Indian-summer sunshine of his Wakefields and Little Annie's Rambles. Indeed, *his* spirit of "metaphor run-mad" is clearly imbibed from the phalanx and phalanstery[21] atmosphere in which he has been so long struggling for breath. He has not half the material for the exclusiveness of authorship that he possesses for its universality. He has the purest style, the finest taste, the most available scholarship, the most delicate humor, the most touching pathos, the most radiant imagination, the most consummate ingenuity; and with these varied good qualities he has done *well* as a mystic. But is there any one of these qualities which should prevent his doing doubly as well in a career of honest, upright, sensible, prehensible[22] and comprehensible things? Let him mend his pen, get a bottle of visible ink, come out from the Old Manse, cut Mr. Alcott, hang (if possible) the editor of "The Dial," and throw out of the window to the pigs all his odd numbers of "The North American Review."[23]

1847

from Eureka: A Prose Poem
[Memories of a Destiny More Vast][1]

I have before said that "Attraction and Repulsion being undeniably the sole properties by which Matter is manifested to Mind, we are justified in assuming that Matter *exists* only as Attraction and Repulsion—in other words that Attraction and Repulsion *are* Matter; there being no conceivable case in which we may not employ the term Matter and the terms 'Attraction' and 'Repulsion' taken together, as equivalent, and therefore convertible, expressions of Logic."[2]

Now the very definition of Attraction implies particularity—the existence of parts, particles, or atoms; for we define it as the tendency of "each atom &c. to every other atom," &c. according to a certain law. Of course where there are *no* parts—where there is absolute Unity—where the tendency to oneness is satisfied—there can be no Attraction:—this has been fully shown, and all Philosophy admits it. When, on fulfilment of its purposes, then, Matter shall have returned

---

[21]Phalanx is a massed group, military or other; phalanstery is a communal group (like Brook Farm).
[22]Capable of being grasped.
[23]Transcendentalist Bronson Alcott (1799–1888); Margaret Fuller and then Ralph Waldo Emerson edited *The Dial* (1840–44), a transcendental journal; *The North American Review* published many pieces by transcendentalists.
[1]In *Eureka*, Poe draws on all his considerable knowledge of science in a work that leads to a mystical conclusion. In this prose poem, he has postulated that the universe is now expanding, but will one day contract, and that the repeated expansion and contraction of the universe may well be its eternal nature. In these closing paragraphs of his cosmo-

logical treatise, Poe argues that matter's only existence is, in fact, this attraction and repulsion, and this in turn is the throb of the "Heart Divine." And this "Heart Divine" is really our own! Thus we are coeval with the universe, and have existed and will exist forever; and moreover, we have memories, especially in youth, of this "Destiny more vast" than that of our mere "world existence." By the end of *Eureka*, Poe suggests that "Man" will come to "recognize his existence as that of Jehovah." Poe's critics have often turned to *Eureka* and these ideas for help in the interpretation of Poe's poems and stories.
[2]Poe quotes himself from an earlier page of Eureka.

into its original condition of *One*—a condition which presupposes the expulsion of the separative ether, whose province and whose capacity are limited to keeping the atoms apart until that great day when, this ether being no longer needed, the overwhelming pressure of the finally collective Attraction shall at length just sufficiently predominate and expel it:—when, I say, Matter, finally, expelling the Ether, shall have returned into absolute Unity,—it will then (to speak paradoxically for the moment) be Matter without Attraction and without Repulsion—in other words, Matter without Matter—in other words, again, *Matter no more.* In sinking into Unity, it will sink at once into that Nothingness which, to all Finite Perception, Unity must be—into that Material Nihility from which alone we can conceive it to have been evoked—to have been *created* by the Volition of God.

I repeat then—Let us endeavor to comprehend that the final globe of globes will instantaneously disappear, and that God will remain all in all.

But are we here to pause? Not so. On the Universal agglomeration and dissolution, we can readily conceive that a new and perhaps totally different series of conditions may ensue—another creation and irradiation, returning into itself—another action and rëaction of the Divine Will. Guiding our imaginations by that omniprevalent law of laws, the law of periodicity, are we not, indeed, more than justified in entertaining a belief—let us say, rather, in indulging a hope—that the processes we have here ventured to contemplate will be renewed forever, and forever, and forever; a novel Universe swelling into existence, and then subsiding into nothingness, at every throb of the Heart Divine?

And now—this Heart Divine—what is it? *It is our own.*

Let not the merely seeming irreverence of this idea frighten our souls from that cool exercise of consciousness—from that deep tranquility of self-inspection—through which alone we can hope to attain the presence of this, the most sublime of truths, and look it leisurely in the face.

The *phænomena* on which our conclusions must at this point depend, are merely spiritual shadows, but not the less thoroughly substantial.

We walk about, amid the destinies of our world-existence, encompassed by dim but ever present *Memories* of a Destiny more vast—very distant in the bygone time, and infinitely awful.

We live out a Youth peculiarly haunted by such dreams; yet never mistaking them for dreams. As Memories we *know* them. *During our Youth* the distinction is too clear to deceive us even for a moment.

So long as this Youth endures, the feeling *that we exist,* is the most natural of all feelings. We understand it *thoroughly.* That there was a period at which we did *not* exist—or, that it might so have happened that we never had existed at all—are the considerations, indeed, which *during this youth,* we find difficulty in understanding. Why we should *not* exist, is, *up to the epoch of our Manhood,* of all queries the most unanswerable. Existence—self-existence—existence from all Time and to all Eternity—seems, up to the epoch of Manhood, a normal and unquestionable condition:—*seems, because it is.*

But now comes the period at which a conventional World-Reason awakens us from the truth of our dream. Doubt, Surprise and Incomprehensibility arrive at the same moment. They say:—"You live and the time was when you lived not. You have been created. An Intelligence exists greater than your own; and it is only through this Intelligence you live at all." These things we struggle to comprehend and cannot:—*cannot,* because these things, being untrue, are thus, of necessity, incomprehensible.

No thinking being lives who, at some luminous point of his life of thought, has not felt himself lost amid the surges of futile efforts at understanding, or believing, that anything exists *greater than his own soul.* The utter impossibility of any one's soul feeling itself inferior to another; the intense, overwhelming dissatisfaction and rebellion at the thought;—these, with the omniprevalent aspirations at perfection, are but the spiritual, coincident with the material, struggles towards the original Unity—are, to my mind at least, a species of proof far surpassing what Man terms demonstration, that no one soul *is* inferior to another—that nothing is, or can be, superior to any one soul—that each soul is, in part, its own God—its own Creator:—in a word, that God—the material *and* spiritual God—*now* exists solely in the diffused Matter and Spirit of the Universe; and that the regathering of this diffused Matter and Spirit will be but the re-constitution of the *purely* Spiritual and Individual God.

In this view, and in this view alone, we comprehend the riddles of Divine Injustice—of Inexorable Fate. In this view alone the existence of Evil becomes intelligible; but in this view it becomes more—it becomes endurable. Our souls no longer rebel at a *Sorrow* which we ourselves have imposed upon ourselves, in furtherance of our own purposes—with a view—if even with a futile view—to the extension of our own *Joy.*

I have spoken of *Memories* that haunt us during our youth. They sometimes pursue us even in our Manhood:—assume gradually less and less indefinite shapes:—now and then speak to us with low voices, saying:

"There was an epoch in the Night of Time, when a still-existent Being existed—one of an absolutely infinite number of similar Beings that people the absolutely infinite domains of the absolutely infinite space. It was not and is not in the power of this Being—any more than it is in your own—to extend, by actual increase, the joy of his Existence; but just as it *is* in your power to expand or to concentrate your pleasures (the absolute amount of happiness remaining always the same) so did and does a similar capability appertain to this Divine Being, who thus passes his Eternity in perpetual variation of Concentrated Self and almost Infinite Self-Diffusion. What you call The Universe is but his present expansive existence. He now feels his life through an infinity of imperfect pleasures—the partial and pain-intertangled pleasures of those inconceivably numerous things which you designate as his creatures, but which are really but infinite individualizations of Himself. All these creatures—*all*—those which you term animate, as well as those to whom you deny life for no better reason than that you do not behold it in operation—*all* these creatures have, in a greater or less degree, a capacity for pleasure and for pain:—*but the general sum of their sensations is precisely that amount of Happiness which appertains by right to the Divine Being when concentrated within Himself.* These creatures are all too, more or less conscious Intelligences; conscious, first, of a proper identity; conscious, secondly and by faint indeterminate glimpses, of an identity with the Divine Being of whom we speak—of an identity with God. Of the two classes of consciousness, fancy that the former will grow weaker, the latter stronger, during the long succession of ages which must elapse before these myriads of individual Intelligences become blended—when the bright stars become blended—into One. Think that the sense of individual identity will be gradually merged in the general consciousness—that Man, for example, ceasing imperceptibly to feel himself Man, will at length attain that awfully triumphant epoch when he shall recognize his existence as that of Jehovah. In the meantime bear in mind that all is Life—Life—Life within Life—the less within the greater, and all within the *Spirit Divine.*

1848

The Philosophy of Composition[1]

CHARLES DICKENS, in a note now lying before me, alluding to an examination I once made of the mechanism of "Barnaby Rudge,"[2] says—"By the way, are you aware that Godwin wrote his 'Caleb Williams' backwards? He first involved his hero in a web of difficulties, forming the second volume, and then, for the first, cast about him for some mode of accounting for what had been done."[3]

I cannot think this the *precise* mode of procedure on the part of Godwin—and indeed what he himself acknowledges, is not altogether in accordance with Mr. Dickens' idea—but the author of "Caleb Williams" was too good an artist not to perceive the advantage derivable from at least a somewhat similar process. Nothing is more clear than that every plot, worth the name, must be elaborated to its *dénouement* before anything be attempted with the pen. It is only with the *dénouement* constantly in view that we can give a plot its indispensable air of consequence, or causation, by making the incidents, and especially the tone at all points, tend to the development of the intention.

There is a radical error, I think, in the usual mode of constructing a story. Either history affords a thesis—or one is suggested by an incident of the day—or, at best, the author sets himself to work in the combination of striking events to form merely the basis of his narrative—designing, generally, to fill in with description, dialogue, or autorial comment, whatever crevices of fact, or action, may, from page to page, render themselves apparent.

I prefer commencing with the consideration of an *effect*. Keeping originality *always* in view—for he is false to himself who ventures to dispense with so obvious and so easily attainable a source of interest—I say to myself, in the first place, "Of the innumerable effects, or impressions, of which the heart, the intellect, or (more generally) the soul is susceptible, what one shall I, on the present occasion, select?" Having chosen a novel, first, and secondly a vivid effect, I consider whether it can be best wrought by incident or tone—whether by ordinary incidents and peculiar tone, or the converse, or by peculiarity both of incident and tone—afterward looking about me (or rather within) for such combinations of event, or tone, as shall best aid me in the construction of the effect.

I have often thought how interesting a magazine paper might be written by any author who would—that is to say who could—detail, step by step, the processes by which any one of his compositions attained its ultimate point of completion. Why such a paper has never been given to the world, I am much at a loss to say— but, perhaps, the autorial vanity has had more to do with the omission than any one other cause. Most writers—poets in especial—prefer having it understood that they compose by a species of fine frenzy—an ecstatic intuition—and would positively shudder at letting the public take a peep behind the scenes, at the elaborate and vacillating crudities of thought—at the true purposes seized only at the last moment—at the innumerable glimpses of idea that arrived not at the maturity of full view—at the fully matured fancies discarded in despair as unmanageable—at the cautious selections and rejections—at the painful erasures and interpolations—in a word, at the wheels and pinions—the tackle for scene-shifting— the step-ladders and demon-traps—the cock's feathers, the red paint and the black patches, which, in ninety-nine cases out of the hundred, constitute the properties of the literary *histrio*.[4]

[1]Poe called this piece his "best specimen of analysis," but few critics believe that it describes, as it purports to do, the actual process of writing "The Raven." But taken as a kind of metaphorical account, the essay gives the reader fascinating glimpses into Poe's analytic-creative mind.
[2]In 1841, while reading Charles Dickens's murder mystery

Barnaby Rudge in serial form, Poe was able, before seeing the final installments, to name the murderer in a review.
[3]Revealed in William Godwin's Preface to *Caleb Williams* (1794).
[4]I.e., artist (actor).

I am aware, on the other hand, that the case is by no means common, in which an author is at all in condition to retrace the steps by which his conclusions have been attained. In general, suggestions, having arisen pell-mell, are pursued and forgotten in a similar manner.

For my own part, I have neither sympathy with the repugnance alluded to, nor, at any time the least difficulty in recalling to mind the progressive steps of any of my compositions; and, since the interest of an analysis, or reconstruction, such as I have considered a *desideratum,* is quite independent of any real or fancied interest in the thing analyzed, it will not be regarded as a breach of decorum on my part to show the *modus operandi*[5] by which some one of my own works was put together. I select "The Raven," as most generally known. It is my design to render it manifest that no one point in its composition is referable either to accident or intuition—that the work proceeded, step by step, to its completion with the precision and rigid consequence of a mathematical problem.

Let us dismiss, as irrelevant to the poem, *per se,* the circumstance—or say the necessity—which, in the first place, gave rise to the intention of composing *a* poem that should suit at once the popular and the critical taste.

We commence, then, with this intention.

The initial consideration was that of extent. If any literary work is too long to be read at one sitting, we must be content to dispense with the immensely important effect derivable from unity of impression—for, if two sittings be required, the affairs of the world interfere, and every thing like totality is at once destroyed. But since, *ceteris paribus,*[6] no poet can afford to dispense with *any thing* that may advance his design, it but remains to be seen whether there is, in extent, any advantage to counterbalance the loss of unity which attends it. Here I say no, at once. What we term a long poem is, in fact, merely a succession of brief ones— that is to say, of brief poetical effects. It is needless to demonstrate that a poem is such, only inasmuch as it intensely excites, by elevating, the soul; and all intense excitements are, through a psychal necessity, brief. For this reason, at least one half of the "Paradise Lost"[7] is essentially prose—a succession of poetical excitements interspersed, *inevitably,* with corresponding depressions—the whole being deprived, through the extremeness of its length, of the vastly important artistic element, totality, or unity, of effect.

It appears evident, then, that there is a distinct limit, as regards length, to all works of literary art—the limit of a single sitting—and that, although in certain classes of prose composition, such as "Robinson Crusoe,"[8] (demanding no unity,) this limit may be advantageously overpassed, it can never properly be overpassed in a poem. Within this limit, the extent of a poem may be made to bear mathematical relation to its merit—in other words, to the excitement or elevation—again in other words, to the degree of the true poetical effect which it is capable of inducing; for it is clear that the brevity must be in direct ratio of the intensity of the intended effect:—this, with one proviso—that a certain degree of duration is absolutely requisite for the production of any effect at all.

Holding in view these considerations, as well as that degree of excitement which I deemed not above the popular, while not below the critical, taste, I reached at once what I conceived the proper *length* for my intended poem—a length of about one hundred lines. It is, in fact, a hundred and eight.

My next thought concerned the choice of an impression, or effect, to be conveyed: and here I may as well observe that, throughout the construction, I kept steadily in view the design of rendering the work *universally* appreciable. I should

---

[5]"Method of proceeding (or operating)" (Latin).
[6]"Other things being equal" (Latin).
[7]John Milton's epic poem (1667) of over 10,000 lines.

[8]Daniel Defoe's account of shipwreck and living alone on an island (1719).

be carried too far out of my immediate topic were I to demonstrate a point upon which I have repeatedly insisted, and which, with the poetical, stands not in the slightest need of demonstration—the point, I mean, that Beauty is the sole legitimate province of the poem. A few words, however, in elucidation of my real meaning, which some of my friends have evinced a disposition to misrepresent. That pleasure which is at once the most intense, the most elevating, and the most pure, is, I believe, found in the contemplation of the beautiful. When, indeed, men speak of Beauty, they mean, precisely, not a quality, as is supposed, but an effect—they refer, in short, just to that intense and pure elevation of *soul*—*not* of intellect, or of heart—upon which I have commented, and which is experienced in consequence of contemplating "the beautiful." Now I designate Beauty as the province of the poem, merely because it is an obvious rule of Art that effects should be made to spring from direct causes—that objects should be attained through means best adapted for their attainment—no one as yet having been weak enough to deny that the peculiar elevation alluded to is *most readily* attained in the poem. Now the object, Truth, or the satisfaction of the intellect, and the object Passion, or the excitement of the heart, are, although attainable, to a certain extent, in poetry, far more readily attainable in prose. Truth, in fact, demands a precision, and Passion a *homeliness* (the truly passionate will comprehend me) which are absolutely antagonistic to that Beauty which, I maintain, is the excitement, or pleasurable elevation, of the soul. It by no means follows from any thing here said, that passion, or even truth, may not be introduced, and even profitably introduced, into a poem—for they may serve in elucidation, or aid the general effect, as do discords in music, by contrast—but the true artist will always contrive, first, to tone them into proper subservience to the predominant aim, and, secondly, to enveil them, as far as possible, in that Beauty which is the atmosphere and the essence of the poem.

Regarding, then, Beauty as my province, my next question referred to the *tone* of its highest manifestation—and all experience has shown that this tone is one of *sadness.* Beauty of whatever kind, in its supreme development, invariably excites the sensitive soul to tears. Melancholy is thus the most legitimate of all the poetical tones.

The length, the province, and the tone, being thus determined, I betook myself to ordinary induction, with the view of obtaining some artistic piquancy which might serve me as a key-note in the construction of the poem—some pivot upon which the whole structure might turn. In carefully thinking over all the usual artistic effects—or more properly *points,* in the theatrical sense—I did not fail to perceive immediately that no one had been so universally employed as that of the *refrain.* The universality of its employment sufficed to assure me of its intrinsic value, and spared me the necessity of submitting it to analysis. I considered it, however, with regard to its susceptibility of improvement, and soon saw it to be in a primitive condition. As commonly used, the *refrain,* or burden, not only is limited to lyric verse, but depends for its impression upon the force of monotone—both in sound and thought. The pleasure is deduced solely from the sense of identity—of repetition. I resolved to diversify, and so heighten, the effect, by adhering, in general, to the monotone of sound, while I continually varied that of thought: that is to say, I determined to produce continuously novel effects, by the variation *of the application* of the *refrain*—the *refrain* itself remaining, for the most part, unvaried.

These points being settled, I next bethought me of the *nature* of my *refrain.* Since its application was to be repeatedly varied, it was clear that the *refrain* itself must be brief, for there would have been an insurmountable difficulty in frequent variations of application in any sentence of length. In proportion to the brevity of the sentence, would, of course, be the facility of the variation. This led me at once to a single word as the best *refrain.*

The question now arose as to the *character* of the word. Having made up my mind to a *refrain*, the division of the poem into stanzas was, of course, a corollary: the *refrain* forming the close of each stanza. That such a close, to have force, must be sonorous and susceptible of protracted emphasis, admitted no doubt: and these considerations inevitably led me to the long *o* as the most sonorous vowel, in connection with *r* as the most producible consonant.

The sound of the *refrain* being thus determined, it became necessary to select a word embodying this sound, and at the same time in the fullest possible keeping with that melancholy which I had predetermined as the tone of the poem. In such a search it would have been absolutely impossible to overlook the word "Nevermore." In fact, it was the very first which presented itself.

The next *desideratum* was a pretext for the continuous use of the one word "nevermore." In observing the difficulty which I at once found in inventing a sufficiently plausible reason for its continuous repetition, I did not fail to perceive that this difficulty arose solely from the pre-assumption that the word was to be so continuously or monotonously spoken by *a human* being—I did not fail to perceive, in short, that the difficulty lay in the reconciliation of this monotony with the exercise of reason on the part of the creature repeating the word. Here, then, immediately arose the idea of a *non*-reasoning creature capable of speech; and, very naturally, a parrot, in the first instance, suggested itself, but was superseded forthwith by a Raven, as equally capable of speech, and infinitely more in keeping with the intended *tone.*

I had now gone so far as the conception of a Raven—the bird of ill omen—monotonously repeating the one word, "Nevermore," at the conclusion of each stanza, in a poem of melancholy tone, and in length about one hundred lines. Now, never losing sight of the object *supremeness,* or perfection, at all points, I asked myself—"Of all melancholy topics, what, according to the *universal* understanding of mankind, is the *most* melancholy?" Death—was the obvious reply. "And when," I said, "is this most melancholy of topics most poetical?" From what I have already explained at some length, the answer, here also, is obvious—"When it most closely allies itself to *Beauty:* the death, then, of a beautiful woman is, unquestionably, the most poetical topic in the world—and equally is it beyond doubt that the lips best suited for such topic are those of a bereaved lover."

I had now to combine the two ideas, of a lover lamenting his deceased mistress and a Raven continuously repeating the word "Nevermore."—I had to combine these, bearing in mind my design of varying, at every turn, the *application* of the word repeated; but the only intelligible mode of such combination is that of imagining the Raven employing the word in answer to the queries of the lover. And here it was that I saw at once the opportunity afforded for the effect on which I had been depending—that is to say, the effect of the *variation of application.* I saw that I could make the first query propounded by the lover—the first query to which the Raven should reply "Nevermore"—that I could make this first query a commonplace one—the second less so—the third still less, and so on—until at length the lover, startled from his original *nonchalance* by the melancholy character of the word itself—by its frequent repetition—and by a consideration of the ominous reputation of the fowl that uttered it—is at length excited to superstition, and wildly propounds queries of a far different character—queries whose solution he has passionately at heart—propounds them half in superstition and half in that species of despair which delights in self-torture—propounds them not altogether because he believes in the prophetic or demoniac character of the bird (which, reason assures him, is merely repeating a lesson learned by rote) but because he experiences a phrenzied pleasure in so modeling his questions as to receive from the *expected* "Nevermore" the most delicious because the most intolerable of sorrow. Perceiving the opportunity thus afforded me—or, more strictly, thus forced upon me in the progress of the construction—I first established in mind the climax, or concluding query—that query to which "Nevermore" should be in the last place an answer—that in reply to which this word "Nevermore" should involve the utmost conceivable amount of sorrow and despair.

Here then the poem may be said to have its beginning—at the end, where all works of art should begin—for it was here, at this point of my preconsiderations, that I first put pen to paper in the composition of the stanza:

> "Prophet," said I, "thing of evil! prophet still if bird or devil!
> By that heaven that bends above us—by that God we both adore,
> Tell this soul with sorrow laden, if within the distant Aidenn,
> It shall clasp a sainted maiden whom the angels name Lenore—
> Clasp a rare and radiant maiden whom the angels name Lenore."
>   Quoth the Raven "Nevermore."

I composed this stanza, at this point, first that, by establishing the climax, I might the better vary and graduate, as regards seriousness and importance, the preceding queries of the lover—and, secondly, that I might definitely settle the rhythm, the metre, and the length and general arrangement of the stanza—as well as graduate the stanzas which were to precede, so that none of them might surpass this in rhythmical effect. Had I been able, in the subsequent composition, to construct more vigorous stanzas, I should, without scruple, have purposely enfeebled them, so as not to interfere with the climacteric effect.

And here I may as well say a few words of the versification. My first object (as usual) was originality. The extent to which this has been neglected, in versification, is one of the most unaccountable things in the world. Admitting that there is little possibility of variety in mere *rhythm*, it is still clear that the possible varieties of metre and stanza are absolutely infinite—and yet, *for centuries, no man, in verse, has ever done, or ever seemed to think of doing, an original thing*. The fact is, that originality (unless in minds of very unusual force) is by no means a matter, as some suppose, of impulse or intuition. In general, to be found, it must be elaborately sought, and although a positive merit of the highest class, demands in its attainment less of invention than negation.

Of course, I pretend to no originality in either the rhythm or metre of the "Raven." The former is trochaic—the latter is octameter acatalectic, alternating with heptameter catalectic repeated in the *refrain* of the fifth verse, and terminating with tetrameter catalectic. Less pedantically—the feet employed throughout (trochees) consist of a long syllable followed by a short: the first line of the stanza consists of eight of these feet—the second of seven and a half (in effect two-thirds)—the third of eight—the fourth of seven and a half—the fifth the same—the sixth three and a half. Now, each of these lines, taken individually, has been employed before, and what originality the "Raven" has, is in their *combination into stanza;* nothing even remotely approaching this combination has ever been attempted. The effect of this originality of combination is aided by other unusual, and some altogether novel effects, arising from an extension of the application of the principles of rhyme and alliteration.

The next point to be considered was the mode of bringing together the lover and the Raven—and the first branch of this consideration was the *locale*. For this the most natural suggestion might seem to be a forest, or the fields—but it has always appeared to me that a close *circumscription of space* is absolutely necessary to the effect of insulated incident:—it has the force of a frame to a picture. It has an indisputable moral power in keeping concentrated the attention, and, of course, must not be confounded with mere unity of place.

I determined, then, to place the lover in his chamber—in a chamber rendered sacred to him by memories of her who had frequented it. The room is represented as richly furnished—this in mere pursuance of the ideas I have already explained on the subject of Beauty, as the sole true poetical thesis.

The *locale* being thus determined, I had now to introduce the bird—and the thought of introducing him through the window, was inevitable. The idea of making the lover suppose, in the first instance, that the flapping of the wings of the bird against the shutter, is a "tapping" at the door, originated in a wish to increase, by prolonging, the reader's curiosity, and in a desire to admit the incidental effect arising from the lover's throwing open the door, finding all dark, and thence adopting the half-fancy that it was the spirit of his mistress that knocked.

I made the night tempestuous, first, to account for the Raven's seeking admission, and secondly, for the effect of contrast with the (physical) serenity within the chamber.

I made the bird alight on the bust of Pallas,[9] also for the effect of contrast between the marble and the plumage—it being understood that the bust was absolutely *suggested* by the bird—the bust of *Pallas* being chosen, first, as most in keeping with the scholarship of the lover, and, secondly, for the sonorousness of the word, Pallas, itself.

About the middle of the poem, also, I have availed myself of the force of contrast, with a view of deepening the ultimate impression. For example, an air of the fantastic—approaching as nearly to the ludicrous as was admissible—is given to the Raven's entrance. He comes in "with many a flirt and flutter."

> Not the *least obeisance made he*—not a moment stopped or stayed he,
> *But with mien of lord or lady,* perched above my chamber door.

In the two stanzas which follow, the design is more obviously carried out:—

> Then this ebony bird beguiling my sad fancy into smiling
> By the *grave and stern decorum of the countenance it wore,*
> "Though thy *crest be shorn and shaven* thou," I said, "art sure no craven,
> Ghastly grim and ancient Raven wandering from the nightly shore—
> Tell me what thy lordly name is on the Night's Plutonian shore?"
> Quoth the Raven "Nevermore."

> Much I marvelled *this ungainly fowl* to hear discourse so plainly
> Though its answer little meaning—little relevancy bore;
> For we cannot help agreeing that no living human being
> *Ever yet was blessed with seeing bird above his chamber door—*
> *Bird or beast upon the sculptured bust above his chamber door,*
> With such name as "Nevermore."

The effect of the *dénouement* being thus provided for, I immediately drop the fantastic for a tone of the most profound seriousness:—this tone commencing in the stanza directly following the one last quoted, with the line,

> But the Raven, sitting lonely on that placid bust, spoke only, etc.

From this epoch the lover no longer jests—no longer sees any thing even of the fantastic in the Raven's demeanor. He speaks of him as a "grim, ungainly, ghastly, gaunt, and ominous bird of yore," and feels the "fiery eyes" burning into his "bosom's core." This revolution of thought, or fancy, on the lover's part, is intended to induce a similar one on the part of the reader—to bring the mind into a proper frame for the *dénouement*—which is now brought about as rapidly and as *directly* as possible.

With the *dénouement* proper—with the Raven's reply, "Nevermore," to the lover's final demand if he shall meet his mistress in another world—the poem, in its obvious phase, that of a simple narrative, may be said to have its completion. So far, every thing is within the limits of the accountable—of the real. A raven, hav-

[9]Pallas Athena, Greek goddess of wisdom, arts, and crafts.

ing learned by rote the single word "Nevermore," and having escaped from the custody of its owner, is driven at midnight, through the violence of a storm, to seek admission at a window from which a light still gleams—the chamber-window of a student, occupied half in poring over a volume, half in dreaming of a beloved mistress deceased. The casement being thrown open at the fluttering of the bird's wings, the bird itself perches on the most convenient seat out of the immediate reach of the student, who, amused by the incident and the oddity of the visitor's demeanor, demands of it, in jest and without looking for a reply, its name. The raven addressed, answers with its customary word, "Nevermore"—a word which finds immediate echo in the melancholy heart of the student, who, giving utterance aloud to certain thoughts suggested by the occasion, is again startled by the fowl's repetition of "Nevermore." The student now guesses the state of the case, but is impelled, as I have before explained, by the human thirst for self-torture, and in part by superstition, to propound such queries to the bird as will bring him, the lover, the most of the luxury of sorrow, through the anticipated answer "Nevermore." With the indulgence, to the extreme, of this self-torture, the narration, in what I have termed its first or obvious phase, has a natural termination, and so far there has been no overstepping of the limits of the real.

But in subjects so handled, however skilfully, or with however vivid an array of incident, there is always a certain hardness or nakedness, which repels the artistical eye. Two things are invariably required—first, some amount of complexity, or more properly, adaptation; and, secondly, some amount of suggestiveness—some under-current, however indefinite, of meaning. It is this latter, in especial, which imparts to a work of art so much of that *richness* (to borrow from colloquy a forcible term) which we are too fond of confounding with *the ideal*. It is the *excess* of the suggested meaning—it is the rendering this the upper instead of the under current of the theme—which turns into prose (and that of the very flattest kind) the so called poetry of the so called transcendentalists.

Holding these opinions, I added the two concluding stanzas of the poem—their suggestiveness being thus made to pervade all the narrative which has preceded them. The under-current of meaning is rendered first apparent in the lines—

> "Take thy beak from out *my heart,* and take thy form from off my door!"
> Quoth the Raven "Nevermore!"

It will be observed that the words, "from out my heart," involve the first metaphorical expression in the poem. They, with the answer, "Nevermore," dispose the mind to seek a moral in all that has been previously narrated. The reader begins now to regard the Raven as emblematical—but it is not until the very last line of the very last stanza, that the intention of making him emblematical of *Mournful and Never-ending Remembrance* is permitted distinctly to be seen:

> And the Raven, never flitting, still is sitting, still is sitting,
> On the pallid bust of Pallas, just above my chamber door;
> And his eyes have all the seeming of a demon's that is dreaming,
>
> And the lamplight o'er him streaming throws his shadow on the floor;
> And my soul *from out that shadow* that lies floating on the floor
> Shall be lifted—nevermore.

1846

from The Poetic Principle[1]
[LONG POEM: A CONTRADICTION IN TERMS]

In speaking of the Poetic Principle, I have no design to be either thorough or profound. While discussing, very much at random, the essentiality of what we call Poetry, my principal purpose will be to cite for consideration, some few of those minor English or American poems which best suit my own taste, or which, upon my own fancy, have left the most definite impression. By "minor poems" I mean, of course, poems of little length. And here, in the beginning, permit me to say a few words in regard to a somewhat peculiar principle, which, whether rightfully or wrongfully, has always had its influence in my own critical estimate of the poem. I hold that a long poem does not exist. I maintain that the phrase, "a long poem," is simply a flat contradiction in terms.

I need scarcely observe that a poem deserves its title only inasmuch as it excites, by elevating the soul. The value of the poem is in the ratio of this elevating excitement. But all excitements are, through a psychal necessity, transient. That degree of excitement which would entitle a poem to be so called at all, cannot be sustained throughout a composition of any great length. After the lapse of half an hour, at the very utmost, it flags—fails—a revulsion ensues—and then the poem is, in effect, and in fact, no longer such.

There are, no doubt, many who have found difficulty in reconciling the critical dictum that the "Paradise Lost" is to be devoutly admired throughout, with the absolute impossibility of maintaining for it, during perusal, the amount of enthusiasm which that critical dictum would demand. This great work, in fact, is to be regarded as poetical, only when, losing sight of that vital requisite in all works of Art, Unity, we view it merely as a series of minor poems. If, to preserve its Unity—its totality of effect or impression—we read it (as would be necessary) at a single sitting, the result is but a constant alternation of excitement and depression. After a passage of what we feel to be true poetry, there follows, inevitably, a passage of platitude which no critical pre-judgment can force us to admire; but if, upon completing the work, we read it again; omitting the first book—that is to say, commencing with the second—we shall be surprised at now finding that admirable which we before condemned—that damnable which we had previously so much admired. It follows from all this that the ultimate, aggregate, or absolute effect of even the best epic under the sun, is a nullity:—and this is precisely the fact.

In regard to the Iliad, we have, if not positive proof, at least very good reason, for believing it intended as a series of lyrics; but, granting the epic intention, I can say only that the work is based in an imperfect sense of art. The modern epic is, of the supposititious ancient model, but an inconsiderate and blindfold imitation. But the day of these artistic anomalies is over. If, at any time, any very long poem *were* popular in reality, which I doubt, it is at least clear that no very long poem will ever be popular again. . . .

[HERESY OF THE DIDACTIC]

While the epic mania—while the idea that, to merit in poetry, prolixity is indispensable—has, for some years past, been gradually dying out of the public mind, by mere dint of its own absurdity—we find it succeeded by a heresy too palpably

---

[1]Poe delivered this essay as a lecture during his final years. In it he incorporated the main theoretical portion of "Letter to B_____ ____" (which he had earlier used as the introductory commentary to his 1831 volume of po-etry). But he refined his points and gave them fuller treatment. "The Poetic Principle" was published in 1850, after his death.

false to be long tolerated, but one which, in the brief period it has already endured, may be said to have accomplished more in the corruption of our Poetical
Literature than all its other enemies combined. I allude to the heresy of *The Didactic*. It has been assumed, tacitly and avowedly, directly and indirectly, that the ultimate object of all Poetry is Truth. Every poem, it is said, should inculcate a
moral; and by this moral is the poetical merit of the work to be adjudged. We
Americans especially have patronised this happy idea; and we Bostonians,[2] very
especially, have developed it in full. We have taken it into our heads that to write a
poem simply for the poem's sake, and to acknowledge such to have been our design, would be to confess ourselves radically wanting in the true Poetic dignity and
force:—but the simple fact is, that, would we but permit ourselves to look into our
own souls, we should immediately there discover that under the sun there neither
exists nor *can* exist any work more thoroughly dignified—more supremely noble
than this very poem—this poem *per se*—this poem which is a poem and nothing
more—this poem written solely for the poem's sake.

With as deep a reverence for the True as ever inspired the bosom of man, I
would, nevertheless, limit, in some measure, its modes of inculcation. I would limit
to enforce them. I would not enfeeble them by dissipation. The demands of
Truth are severe. She has no sympathy with the myrtles.[3] All *that* which is so indispensable in Song, is precisely all *that* with which *she* has nothing whatever to do.
It is but making her a flaunting paradox, to wreathe her in gems and flowers. In
enforcing a truth, we need severity rather than efflorescence of language. We
must be simple, precise, terse. We must be cool, calm, unimpassioned. In a word,
we must be in that mood which, as nearly as possible, is the exact converse of the
poetical. *He* must be blind, indeed, who does not perceive the radical and chasmal
differences between the truthful and the poetical modes of inculcation. He must
be theory-mad beyond redemption who, in spite of these differences, shall still
persist in attempting to reconcile the obstinate oils and waters of Poetry and
Truth.

[POETRY: THE RHYTHMICAL CREATION OF BEAUTY]

Dividing the world of mind into its three most immediately obvious distinctions, we have the Pure Intellect, Taste, and the Moral Sense. I place Taste in the
middle, because it is just this position which, in the mind, it occupies. It holds intimate relations with either extreme; but from the Moral Sense is separated by so
faint a difference that Aristotle has not hesitated to place some of its operations
among the virtues themselves. Nevertheless, we find the *offices* of the trio marked
with a sufficient distinction. Just as the Intellect concerns itself with Truth, so
Taste informs us of the Beautiful while the Moral Sense is regardful of Duty. Of
this latter, while Conscience teaches the obligation, and Reason the expediency,
Taste contents herself with displaying the charms:—waging war upon Vice solely
on the ground of her deformity—her disproportion—her animosity to the fitting, to the appropriate, to the harmonious—in a word, to Beauty.

An immortal instinct, deep within the spirit of man, is thus, plainly, a sense of
the Beautiful. This it is which administers to his delight in the manifold forms,
and sounds, and odours, and sentiments amid which he exists. And just as the lily
is repeated in the lake, or the eyes of Amaryllis[4] in the mirror, so is the mere oral
or written repetition of these forms, and sounds, and colours, and odours, and
sentiments, a duplicate source of delight. But this mere repetition is not poetry.

---

[2] Poe was brought up in Richmond, Virginia, but he had
been born in Boston.
[3] I.e., beauty, pleasure; the myrtle was sacred to Venus,
classical goddess of love.
[4] Shepherdess beauty in classical pastoral poetry.

He who shall simply sing, with however glowing enthusiasm, or with however vivid a truth of description, of the sights, and sounds, and odours, and colours, and sentiments, which greet *him* in common with all mankind—he, I say, has yet failed to prove his divine title. There is still a something in the distance which he has been unable to attain. We have still a thirst unquenchable, to allay which he has not shown us the crystal springs. This thirst belongs to the immortality of Man. It is at once a consequence and an indication of his perennial existence. It is the desire of the moth for the star.[5] It is no mere appreciation of the Beauty before us—but a wild effort to reach the Beauty above. Inspired by an ecstatic prescience of the glories beyond the grave, we struggle, by multiform combinations among the things and thoughts of Time, to attain a portion of that Loveliness whose very elements, perhaps, appertain to eternity alone. And thus when by Poetry—or when by Music, the most entrancing of the Poetic moods—we find ourselves melted into tears—we weep them—not as the Abbate Gravina[6] supposes—through excess of pleasure, but through a certain, petulant, impatient sorrow at our inability to grasp *now*, wholly, here on earth, at once and for ever, those divine and rapturous joys, of which *through* the poem, or *through* the music, we attain to but brief and indeterminate glimpses.

The struggle to apprehend the supernal Loveliness—this struggle, on the part of souls fittingly constituted—has given to the world all *that* which it (the world) has ever been enabled at once to understand and *to feel* as poetic.

The Poetic Sentiment, of course, may develop itself in various modes—in Painting, in Sculpture, in Architecture, in the Dance—very especially in Music—and very peculiarly, and with a wide field, in the composition of the Landscape Garden. Our present theme, however, has regard only to its manifestation in words. And here let me speak briefly on the topic of rhythm. Contenting myself with the certainty that Music, in its various modes of metre, rhythm, and rhyme, is of so vast a moment in Poetry as never to be wisely rejected—is so vitally important an adjunct, that he is simply silly who declines its assistance, I will not now pause to maintain its absolute essentiality. It is in Music, perhaps, that the soul most nearly attains the great end for which, when inspired by the Poetic Sentiment, it struggles—the creation of supernal Beauty. It *may* be, indeed, that here this sublime end is, now and then, attained *in fact*. We are often made to feel, with a shivering delight, that from an earthly harp are stricken notes which *cannot* have been unfamiliar to the angels. And thus there can be little doubt that in the union of Poetry with Music in its popular sense, we shall find the widest field for the Poetic development. The old Bards and Minnesingers[7] had advantages which we do not possess—and Thomas Moore,[8] singing his own songs, was, in the most legitimate manner, perfecting them as poems.

To recapitulate, then:—I would define, in brief, the Poetry of words as *The Rhythmical Creation of Beauty*. Its sole arbiter is Taste. With the Intellect or with the Conscience, it has only collateral relations. Unless incidentally, it has no concern whatever either with Duty or with Truth.

A few words, however, in explanation. *That* pleasure which is at once the most pure, the most elevating, and the most intense, is derived, I maintain, from the contemplation of the Beautiful. In the contemplation of Beauty we alone find it possible to attain that pleasurable elevation, or excitement, *of the soul*, which we recognise as the Poetic Sentiment, and which is so easily distinguished from Truth, which is the satisfaction of the Reason, or from Passion, which is the excite-

---

[5]From "To———:One Word Is too Often Profaned," 1. 13, by Percy Bysshe Shelley (1792–1822), British romantic poet.

[6]Giovanni Vincenzo Gravina (1664–1718), Italian jurist and author of a book on verse.

[7]Poets of the Old English period and of the medieval period in Germany, comparable to wandering minstrels and troubadours.

[8]Irish romantic poet (1779–1852), one of Poe's favorite poets.

ment of the heart. I make Beauty, therefore—using the word as inclusive of the sublime—I make Beauty the province of the poem, simply because it is an obvious rule of Art that effects should be made to spring as directly as possible from their causes:—no one as yet having been weak enough to deny that the peculiar elevation in question is at least *most readily* attainable in the poem. It by no means follows, however, that the incitements of Passion, or the precepts of Duty, or even the lessons of Truth, may not be introduced into a poem, and with advantage; for they may subserve, incidentally, in various ways, the general purposes of the work:—but the true artist will always contrive to tone them down in proper subjection to that *Beauty* which is the atmosphere and the real essence of the poem. . . .

[LOVE: THE TRUEST OF ALL POETICAL THEMES]

Thus, although in a very cursory and imperfect manner, I have endeavoured to convey to you my conception of the Poetic Principle. It has been my purpose to suggest that, while this Principle itself is, strictly and simply, the Human Aspiration for Supernal Beauty, the manifestation of the Principle is always found in *an elevating excitement of the Soul*—quite independent of that passion which is the intoxication of the heart—or of that Truth which is the satisfaction of the Reason. For, in regard to Passion, alas! its tendency is to degrade, rather than to elevate the Soul. Love, on the contrary—Love—the true, the divine Eros—the Uranian, as distinguished from the Dionæan Venus[9]—is unquestionably the purest and truest of all poetical themes. And in regard to Truth—if, to be sure, through the attainment of a truth, we are led to perceive a harmony where none was apparent before, we experience, at once, the true poetical effect—but this effect is referable to the harmony alone, and not in the least degree to the truth which merely served to render the harmony manifest.

We shall reach, however, more immediately a distinct conception of what the true Poetry is, by mere reference to a few of the simple elements which induce in the Poet himself the true poetical effect. He recognises the ambrosia which nourishes his soul, in the bright orbs that shine in Heaven—in the volutes of the flower—in the clustering of low shrubberies—in the waving of the grain-fields—in the slanting of tall, Eastern trees—in the blue distance of mountains—in the grouping of clouds—in the twinkling of half-hidden brooks—in the gleaming of silver rivers—in the repose of sequestered lakes—in the star-mirroring depths of lonely wells. He perceives it in the songs of birds—in the harp of Æolus[10]—in the sighing of the night-wind—in the repining voice of the forest—in the surf that complains to the shore—in the fresh breath of the woods—in the scent of the violet—in the voluptuous perfume of the hyacinth—in the suggestive odour that comes to him, at eventide, from far-distant, undiscovered islands, over dim oceans, illimitable and unexplored. He owns it in all noble thoughts—in all unworldly motives—in all holy impulses—in all chivalrous, generous, and self-sacrificing deeds. He feels it in the beauty of woman—in the grace of her step—in the lustre of her eye—in the melody of her voice—in her soft laughter—in her sigh—in the harmony of the rustling of her robes. He deeply feels it in her winning endearments—in her burning enthusiasms—in her gentle charities—in her meek and devotional endurances—but above all—ah, far above all—he kneels to it—he worships it in the faith, in the purity, in the strength, in the altogether divine majesty—of her *love*. . . .

1850

---

[9]Ideal or spiritual love (Urania, muse of astronomy, was identified with the heavens) in contrast with sensual love (the Roman goddess of love, Venus, was the daughter of Zeus and his consort, Dione).

[10]Classical god of the winds, whose harp makes musical sounds when the wind blows across its strings.

NATHANIEL HAWTHORNE
(1804–1864)

When he was at Bowdoin College in Maine, Nathaniel Hathorne from Salem, Massachusetts, changed the family name for himself by inserting a "w" in Hathorne. It was a strange act, suggesting an unconscious disinheriting of himself, an ambiguous attempt to cut off an unsettling past. It is perhaps not surprising for a young man whose father had died at sea when the son was only four, and whose mother thereupon retreated to her room, a ghostly figure who ate her meals in seclusion.

But there was more in the past to worry about. Hawthorne's ancestor, John Hathorne, had served as one of the judges in the 1692 witchcraft trials in Salem. One of the convicted witches (according to tradition) placed a curse on the family. How deeply embedded this episode was in Hawthorne's psyche is suggested by the public apology he felt compelled to make in "The Custom House," his autobiographical essay introducing *The Scarlet Letter* (1850): "I . . . hereby take shame upon myself for their [his forbears] sakes, and pray that any curse incurred by them . . . may be now and henceforth removed."

And there was still more in the past that may have terrified Hawthorne. The Mannings, who were his mother's Puritan ancestors, had a family scandal to live down. A brother and sister had been caught in bed together, and in 1681 the two sisters in the family were convicted of "incestuous carriage." Their brother ran away, but the two girls were sentenced to sit before the entire town, their crime of incest emblazoned on them in capital letters. Hawthorne treated the theme of incest in what is probably his earliest story, "Alice Doane's Appeal." When collecting his stories for book publication he rejected this story, probably as much for reasons of its weakness of construction as for its theme.

When Hawthorne was near graduation at Bowdoin, he wrote, "I do not want to be a doctor and live by man's diseases, nor a minister and live by their sins, nor a lawyer and live by their quarrels. So I don't see that there is anything left but for me to be an author." He returned to Salem to serve twelve years in isolated apprenticeship as a writer. The older of his two sisters, Elizabeth, shared his literary interests and assisted him in research and obtaining books. They were extremely close. Elizabeth never married, and, later, could not abide the woman Hawthorne took as a bride. Hawthorne would come to see this long period of solitude as psychically unhealthy. When Henry Wadsworth Longfellow (a college friend) wrote to him appreciatively after the appearance of *Twice-Told Tales* in 1837, Hawthorne replied: "I have secluded myself from society. . . . I have made a captive of myself, and put me in a dungeon, and now I cannot find the key to let myself out."

Twice-Told Tales, containing many of Hawthorne's finest stories, was a critical but not a popular success. At the age of thirty-three, Hawthorne had to figure out how to make a living. He had in 1828 published a novel based on his college experiences, *Fanshawe*. But he was later so embarrassed by the work that he tracked down all the copies he could find to burn. He tried his hand at a number of things but ended up in 1839 in a patronage job of the Democrats—a weigher or measurer at the Boston Custom House. This same year he became engaged to Sophia Peabody.

Anticipating the loss of his job when the Whigs came to power, Hawthorne left the Custom House in 1841 and invested his entire savings, over $1,000, in

Brook Farm, which transcendental enthusiasts had established in West Roxbury, Massachusetts. It was the wrong move, because Hawthorne was supremely unhappy digging in the dirt and milking the cows. On the other hand, his unhappiness bore imaginative fruit in his 1852 novel *The Blithedale Romance*, based on the people and experiences of Brook Farm. On departing, however, Hawthorne thought of himself as freed from his "bondage": "Even my Custom House experience was not such a thralldom and weariness; my mind and heart were free."

Hawthorne was able to retrieve part of his investment, marry his beloved Sophia, and settle into the Old Manse in Concord, Massachusetts, in 1842, to live three of his happiest years. Ralph Waldo Emerson had written his first book, *Nature*, in the Old Manse, and now was a neighbor, as were Henry David Thoreau, Margaret Fuller (who, although she had not lived at Brook Farm, would figure in *The Blithedale Romance* as the basis for Zenobia), and other writers and intellectuals. Hawthorne was free to write, and in 1846 he brought out his second collection of stories, *Mosses from an Old Manse*.

In 1846, with the return of the Democrats to office, he was appointed surveyor in the Salem Custom House, a position he held until his dismissal in 1849 with another change in political power. But by the time of his dismissal, he had in progress what would turn out to be his masterpiece, *The Scarlet Letter*, published in 1850. In its prefatory essay, "The Custom House," Hawthorne satirized many of his fellow Custom House employees and described the house itself as cobwebbed, dingy, with an air of "general slovenliness" about the place. He also related finding in an attic there the scarlet letter "A," placing it on his own bosom, and feeling its "burning heat" before he learned the secrets of its meaning or its history. The scene has all the tension of an oblique or unconscious public confession.

With publication of *The Scarlet Letter*, Hawthorne's reputation was firmly established. In 1850 he moved with his family to Lenox, in the Berkshire Mountains in western Massachusetts, where he had rented a farmhouse; and he began work on his second novel, *The House of the Seven Gables*. Not far away, in Pittsfield, Herman Melville was living with his family in a heightened state of creative intensity, working on *Moby-Dick*. These two writers, at the peak of their artistic careers, had never met each other.

But Melville had been reading Hawthorne's work, discovering in it a sympathetic soul. He was inspired to write an appreciation, "Hawthorne and His Mosses," which remains one of the most perceptive accounts of Hawthorne (and revelations of Melville) that we have. What fascinated Melville was Hawthorne's "Puritanic gloom" or "mystical blackness": "This great power of blackness in him derives its force from its appeals to that Calvinistic sense of Innate Depravity and Original Sin, from whose visitations, in some shape or other, no deeply thinking mind is always and wholly free. . . . You may be witched by his sunlight . . . but there is the blackness of darkness beyond."

When Melville discovered this same Hawthorne living nearby, a friend with whom he might share his deepest thoughts, his creative and imaginative energies seemed suddenly to explode. He was thirty-one, Hawthorne forty-six. The conversations that they held must have roamed through the outer reaches of the universe, must indeed have risen to the heights of the heavens and plummeted more often to the darkest deeps of hell. Clearly both men were inspired, and their inspiration came in part from their mutual communion. Hawthorne published *The House of the Seven Gables* in 1851, and later the same year Melville followed with *Moby-Dick*, dedicated "in admiration for his genius" to Nathaniel Hawthorne.

Accident brought these two writers together for a few months, and as whimsically parted them. Hawthorne moved out of the Berkshires, finished his third novel in as many years (*The Blithedale Romance*), and then became enmeshed in presidential politics, writing the campaign biography for his Bowdoin classmate, Franklin Pierce. Pierce won the election in 1852 and appointed Hawthorne to serve as the United States Consul at Liverpool, England. There, in 1856, Melville turned up on his way to the Holy Land, and the two friends had their last encounter, their final deep-diving conversation. But Hawthorne was, by this time, burdened by his consulate duties and had little patience for speculative discussions of eternity. He was, in addition, more reserved than the younger man, and could not open himself with the same passionate intensity to the kind of intellectual-spiritual sharing Melville sought.

Hawthorne remained abroad for seven years (1853–60). On losing his position as consul after a shift in political fortunes in 1857, he went to Italy, living in Rome and Florence from 1857 to 1859. The encounter with Catholic and pagan Italy brought him around again to the serious literary career he had in a sense abandoned. He began to work on *The Marble Faun*, set in Catholic Rome with its central symbol the pagan sculpture of a handsome young faun, part man, part animal. Hawthorne had come across this startlingly attractive figure in Rome's Capitoline Museum. It would symbolize for him the strong appeal, but ultimate horror, of a life of the senses lived, like that of Adam and Eve before the Fall, without knowledge of good and evil, without, that is, possession of a soul.

Hawthorne finished *The Marble Faun* in England and published it in 1860, the year he returned to the United States. It immediately became popular, in part as a guidebook to Rome, so faithful was it to the Roman streets, museums, and galleries. It was Hawthorne's last completed work. He started several novels that seemed obsessively concerned with the themes of an American heir to a British estate, and an elixir or potion to bestow eternal life. All were abandoned.

Accompanied by his friend Franklin Pierce, Hawthorne set out in 1864 on a trip by carriage to New Hampshire in an attempt to regain his health. He died there in May and was taken back to Concord for burial in Sleepy Hollow Cemetery. Ralph Waldo Emerson, James Russell Lowell, and Oliver Wendell Holmes attended the services. Emerson recorded in his journal: "I thought there was a tragic element in the event . . . in the painful solitude of the man, which . . . could not longer be endured, and he died of it." Melville was shocked when he heard of Hawthorne's death, and wrote a farewell poem, "Monody":

> To have known him, to have loved him
>   After loneness long;
> And then to be estranged in life,
>   And neither in the wrong;
> And now for death to set his seal—
>   Ease me, a little ease, my song!

Hawthorne's rich literary legacy includes the four finished novels together with a number of stories and tales that are unsurpassed in their power to

evoke a sense of the "blackness of darkness." They are constructed with subtlety and filled with ambiguity. A first reading might well leave the reader
thinking the plot simple, the moral obvious. A second reading often under-
mines this sense of simplicity and begins to fill the reader's mind with wonder.
A third reading often brings revelations and reversals undreamed of in the
first. Whenever Hawthorne hands the reader his moral of a story neatly pack-
aged in a sentence, reader beware!

Whether Hawthorne should be called a religious writer or a psychological
writer is often debated. He was certainly steeped, through reading of his Calvinistic forbears, in the tenets, dogmas, and experiences of the Puritan settlers. And he used the inherited religious symbols and ideas in his stories, often becoming a noncommital narrator and leaving the problem of what to
believe up to the reader. Much of his strategy seems to have been directed to
the discovery of psychological roots of religious feelings and beliefs. To limit
Hawthorne to one or the other of religion or psychology diminishes his work;
to recognize the intertwining of the two in that work catches something of the
complexity at its heart.

ADDITIONAL READING

Nathaniel Hawthorne: Representative Selections, ed. Austin Warren, 1934; *The Portable Hawthorne*, ed. Malcolm Cowley, 1948; *Hawthorne's Selected Tales and Sketches*, ed. Hyatt H. Waggoner, 1970.

Henry James, *Hawthorne*, 1879; Randall Stewart, *Nathaniel Hawthorne*, 1948; Mark Van
Doren, *Nathaniel Hawthorne*, 1949; Hyatt H. Waggoner, *Hawthorne: A Critical Study*, 1955,
rev. 1963; Roy R. Male, *Hawthorne's Tragic Vision*, 1957, 1964; Arlin Turner, *Nathaniel Hawthorne: An Introduction and Interpretation*, 1961; Hubert H. Hoeltje, *Inward Sky: The Mind and
Heart of Nathaniel Hawthorne*, 1962; Roy Harvey Pearce, ed., *Hawthorne Centenary Essays*,
1964; Frederick Crews, *The Sins of the Fathers: Hawthorne's Psychological Themes*, 1966; A. N.
Kaul, ed., *Hawthorne: A Collection of Critical Essays*, 1966; James E. Miller, Jr., *Quests Surd and
Absurd*, 1967; Kenneth Cameron, *Hawthorne Among His Contemporaries*, 1968; B. Bernard Cohen, *The Recognition of Nathaniel Hawthorne: Selected Criticism Since 1828*, 1969; John Caldwell
Stubbs, *The Pursuit of Form: A Study of Hawthorne and the Romance*, 1970; Neal Frank Double-
day, *Hawthorne's Early Tales: A Critical Study*, 1972; Richard H. Brodhead, *Hawthorne, Melville,
and the Novel*, 1976; Nina Baym, *The Shape of Hawthorne's Career*, 1976; Kenneth Dauber, *Re-
discovering Hawthorne*, 1977; Edgar A. Dryden, *Nathaniel Hawthorne: The Poetics of Enchantment*, 1977; Lea V. Newman, *Reader's Guide to the Short Fiction of Nathaniel Hawthorne*, 1979;
Arlin Turner, *Nathaniel Hawthorne: A Biography*, 1980; James Mellow, *Nathaniel Hawthorne in
His Times*, 1980; Claudia D. Johnson, *The Productive Tension in Hawthorne's Art*, 1981; Terence
Martin, *Nathaniel Hawthorne*, 1983; Philip Young, *Hawthorne's Secret: An Untold Tale*, 1984;
Agnes McNeill Donohue, *Hawthorne: Calvin's Ironic Stepchild*, 1985; Samuel Coale, *In Haw-
thorne's Shadow: American Romance from Melville to Mailer*, 1985; Richard Brodhead, *The School
of Hawthorne*, 1986.

TEXTS

Centenary Edition of the Works of Nathaniel Hawthorne, ed. William Charvat, Roy Harvey
Pearce, Claude M. Simpson, Fredson Bowers et al., 1962–   : Vol. 2, *The House of the Seven
Gables*, 1965; Vol. 4, *The Marble Faun*, 1968; Vol. 8, *The American Notebooks*, ed. Claude M.
Simpson, 1972; Vol. 9, *Twice-Told Tales*, ed. J. Donald Crowley, 1974; Vol. 10, *Mosses from an
Old Manse*, ed. J. Donald Crowley, 1974; Vol. 11, *The Snow-Image*, ed. J. Donald Crowley,
1974; Vol. 14, *The French and Italian Notebooks*, ed. Thomas Woodson, 1980; Vol. 15, *The Let-
ters, 1813–1843*, ed. Thomas Woodson, L. Neal Smith, and Norman Holmes Pearson, 1984.
The Complete Works of Nathaniel Hawthorne, 12 vols., ed. George Lathrop, 1883: Vol. 12, *Tales,
Sketches, and Other Papers. The English Notebooks*, ed. Randall Stewart, 1941.

My Kinsman, Major Molineux

After the kings of Great Britain had assumed the right of appointing the colonial governors,[1] the measures of the latter seldom met with the ready and general approbation, which had been paid to those of their predecessors, under the original charters. The people looked with most jealous scrutiny to the exercise of power, which did not emanate from themselves, and they usually rewarded the rulers with slender gratitude, for the compliances, by which, in softening their instructions from beyond the sea, they had incurred the reprehension of those who gave them. The annals of Massachusetts Bay will inform us, that of six governors, in the space of about forty years from the surrender of the old charter, under James II., two were imprisoned by a popular insurrection; a third, as Hutchinson[2] inclines to believe, was driven from the province by the whizzing of a musket ball; a fourth, in the opinion of the same historian, was hastened to his grave by continual bickerings with the House of Representatives; and the remaining two, as well as their successors, till the Revolution, were favored with few and brief intervals of peaceful sway. The inferior members of the court party,[3] in times of high political excitement, led scarcely a more desirable life. These remarks may serve as preface to the following adventures, which chanced upon a summer night, not far from a hundred years ago. The reader, in order to avoid a long and dry detail of colonial affairs, is requested to dispense with an account of the train of circumstances, that had caused much temporary inflammation of the popular mind.

It was near nine o'clock of a moonlight evening, when a boat crossed the ferry with a single passenger, who had obtained his conveyance, at that unusual hour, by the promise of an extra fare. While he stood on the landing-place, searching in either pocket for the means of fulfilling his agreement, the ferryman lifted a lantern, by the aid of which, and the newly risen moon, he took a very accurate survey of the stranger's figure. He was a youth of barely eighteen years, evidently country-bred, and now, as it should seem, upon his first visit to town. He was clad in a coarse grey coat, well worn, but in excellent repair; his under garments were durably constructed of leather, and sat tight to a pair of serviceable and well-shaped limbs; his stockings of blue yarn, were the incontrovertible handiwork of a mother or a sister; and on his head was a three-cornered hat, which in its better days had perhaps sheltered the graver brow of the lad's father. Under his left arm was a heavy cudgel, formed of an oak sapling, and retaining a part of the hardened root; and his equipment was completed by a wallet,[4] not so abundantly stocked as to incommode the vigorous shoulders on which it hung. Brown, curly hair, well-shaped features, and bright, cheerful eyes, were nature's gifts, and worth all that art could have done for his adornment.

The youth, one of whose names was Robin, finally drew from his pocket the half of a little province-bill[5] of five shillings, which, in the depreciation of that sort of currency, did but satisfy the ferryman's demand, with the surplus of a sexangular piece of parchment valued at three pence. He then walked forward into the town, with as light a step, as if his day's journey had not already exceeded thirty miles, and with as eager an eye, as if he were entering London city, instead of the little metropolis of a New England colony. Before Robin had proceeded far, however, it occurred to him, that he knew not whither to direct his steps; so he

---

[1] The original Massachusetts Charter left the colonists to govern themselves. Charles II annulled it in 1684 and James II appointed the first royal governor in 1685.
[2] Thomas Hutchinson (1711–1780), author of *History of the Colony of Massachusetts Bay, from its First Settlement to the Year* *1750* (1764, 1767, 1828), and last royal governor (1771–74).
[3] I.e., the party that supported the king.
[4] Knapsack.
[5] I.e., paper money issued by the colony.

paused, and looked up and down the narrow street, scrutinizing the small and mean wooden buildings, that were scattered on either side.

'This low hovel cannot be my kinsman's dwelling,' thought he, 'nor yonder old house, where the moonlight enters at the broken casement; and truly I see none hereabouts that might be worthy of him. It would have been wise to inquire my way of the ferryman, and doubtless he would have gone with me, and earned a shilling from the Major for his pains. But the next man I meet will do as well.'

He resumed his walk, and was glad to perceive that the street now became wider, and the houses more respectable in their appearance. He soon discerned a figure moving on moderately in advance, and hastened his steps to overtake it. As Robin drew nigh, he saw that the passenger was a man in years, with a full periwig of grey hair, a wide-skirted coat of dark cloth, and silk stockings rolled about his knees. He carried a long and polished cane, which he struck down perpendicularly before him, at every step; and at regular intervals he uttered two successive hems, of a peculiarly solemn and sepulchral intonation. Having made these observations, Robin laid hold of the skirt of the old man's coat, just when the light from the open door and windows of a barber's shop, fell upon both their figures.

'Good evening to you, honored Sir,' said he, making a low bow, and still retaining his hold of the skirt. 'I pray you to tell me whereabouts is the dwelling of my kinsman, Major Molineux?'

The youth's question was uttered very loudly; and one of the barbers, whose razor was descending on a well-soaped chin, and another who was dressing a Ramillies wig,[6] left their occupations, and came to the door. The citizen, in the meantime, turned a long favored countenance upon Robin, and answered him in a tone of excessive anger and annoyance. His two sepulchral hems, however, broke into the very centre of his rebuke, with most singular effect, like a thought of the cold grave obtruding among wrathful passions.

'Let go my garment, fellow! I tell you, I know not the man you speak of. What! I have authority, I have—hem, hem—authority; and if this be the respect you show your betters, your feet shall be brought acquainted with the stocks,[7] by daylight, tomorrow morning!'

Robin released the old man's skirt, and hastened away, pursued by an ill-mannered roar of laughter from the barber's shop. He was at first considerably surprised by the result of his question, but, being a shrewd youth, soon thought himself able to account for the mystery.

'This is some country representative,' was his conclusion, 'who has never seen the inside of my kinsman's door, and lacks the breeding to answer a stranger civilly. The man is old, or verily—I might be tempted to turn back and smite him on the nose. Ah, Robin, Robin! even the barber's boys laugh at you, for choosing such a guide! You will be wiser in time, friend Robin.'

He now became entangled in a succession of crooked and narrow streets, which crossed each other, and meandered at no great distance from the water-side. The smell of tar was obvious to his nostrils, the masts of vessels pierced the moonlight above the tops of the buildings, and the numerous signs, which Robin paused to read, informed him that he was near the centre of business. But the streets were empty, the shops were closed, and lights were visible only in the second stories of a few dwelling-houses. At length, on the corner of a narrow lane, through which he was passing, he beheld the broad countenance of a British hero swinging before the door of an inn, whence proceeded the voices of many guests. The casement of one of the lower windows was thrown back, and a very thin curtain per-

---

[6]A plaited wig tied with ribbons, named after Ramillies, Belgium, in honor of a British victory over the French in 1706.

[7]A form of imprisonment consisting of a wooden frame containing holes for holding hands and feet.

mitted Robin to distinguish a party at supper, round a well-furnished table. The fragrance of the good cheer steamed forth into the outer air, and the youth could not fail to recollect, that the last remnant of his travelling stock of provision had yielded to his morning appetite, and that noon had found, and left him, dinnerless.

'Oh, that a parchment three-penny might give me a right to sit down at yonder table,' said Robin, with a sigh. 'But the Major will make me welcome to the best of his victuals; so I will even step boldly in, and inquire my way to his dwelling.'

He entered the tavern, and was guided by the murmur of voices, and fumes of tobacco, to the public room. It was a long and low apartment, with oaken walls, grown dark in the continual smoke, and a floor, which was thickly sanded, but of no immaculate purity. A number of persons, the larger part of whom appeared to be mariners, or in some way connected with the sea, occupied the wooden benches, or leather-bottomed chairs, conversing on various matters, and occasionally lending their attention to some topic of general interest. Three or four little groups were draining as many bowls of punch, which the great West India trade had long since made a familiar drink in the colony. Others, who had the aspect of men who lived by regular and laborious handicraft, preferred the insulated bliss of an unshared potation, and became more taciturn under its influence. Nearly all, in short, evinced a predilection for the Good Creature[8] in some of its various shapes, for this is a vice, to which, as the Fast-day[9] sermons of a hundred years ago will testify, we have a long hereditary claim. The only guests to whom Robin's sympathies inclined him, were two or three sheepish countrymen, who were using the inn somewhat after the fashion of a Turkish Caravansary;[10] they had gotten themselves into the darkest corner of the room, and, heedless of the Nicotian[11] atmosphere, were supping on the bread of their own ovens, and the bacon cured in their own chimney-smoke. But though Robin felt a sort of brotherhood with these strangers, his eyes were attracted from them, to a person who stood near the door, holding whispered conversation with a group of ill-dressed associates. His features were separately striking almost to grotesqueness, and the whole face left a deep impression in the memory. The forehead bulged out into a double prominence, with a vale between; the nose came boldly forth in an irregular curve, and its bridge was of more than a finger's breadth; the eyebrows were deep and shaggy, and the eyes glowed beneath them like fire in a cave.

While Robin deliberated of whom to inquire respecting his kinsman's dwelling, he was accosted by the innkeeper, a little man in a stained white apron, who had come to pay his professional welcome to the stranger. Being in the second generation from a French Protestant,[12] he seemed to have inherited the courtesy of his parent nation; but no variety of circumstance was ever known to change his voice from the one shrill note in which he now addressed Robin.

'From the country, I presume, Sir?' said he, with a profound bow. 'Beg to congratulate you on your arrival, and trust you intend a long stay with us. Fine town here, Sir, beautiful buildings, and much that may interest a stranger. May I hope for the honor of your commands in respect to supper?'

'The man sees a family likeness! the rogue has guessed that I am related to the Major!' thought Robin, who had hitherto experienced little superfluous civility.

All eyes were now turned on the country lad, standing at the door, in his worn

---

[8]Food, drink, etc., as described in 1 Timothy 4:4: "For every creature of God is good, and nothing to be refused, if it be received with thanksgiving."
[9]A holy day set aside for doing penance for sins committed.
[10]In the Orient, an inn with a large inner court where caravans stopped for the night.

[11]Smoke-filled; Jean Nicot (1530?–1600), French diplomat who introduced tobacco into France (hence "nicotine").
[12]Descendent of a Huguenot refugee from France.

three-cornered hat, grey coat, leather breeches, and blue yarn stockings, leaning on an oaken cudgel, and bearing a wallet on his back.

Robin replied to the courteous innkeeper, with such an assumption of consequence, as befitted the Major's relative.

'My honest friend,' he said, 'I shall make it a point to patronize your house on some occasion, when—' here he could not help lowering his voice—'I may have more than a parchment three-pence in my pocket. My present business,' continued he, speaking with lofty confidence, 'is merely to inquire the way to the dwelling of my kinsman, Major Molineux.'

There was a sudden and general movement in the room, which Robin interpreted as expressing the eagerness of each individual to become his guide. But the innkeeper turned his eyes to a written paper on the wall, which he read, or seemed to read, with occasional recurrences to the young man's figure.

'What have we here?' said he, breaking his speech into little dry fragments. ' "Left the house of the subscriber, bounden servant,[13] Hezekiah Mudge—had on, when he went away, grey coat, leather breeches, master's third best hat. One pound currency reward to whoever shall lodge him in any jail in the province." Better trudge, boy, better trudge!'

Robin had begun to draw his hand towards the lighter end of the oak cudgel, but a strange hostility in every countenance, induced him to relinquish his purpose of breaking the courteous innkeeper's head. As he turned to leave the room, he encountered a sneering glance from the bold-featured personage whom he had before noticed; and no sooner was he beyond the door, than he heard a general laugh, in which the innkeeper's voice might be distinguished, like the dropping of small stones into a kettle.

'Now is it not strange,' thought Robin, with his usual shrewdness, 'is it not strange, that the confession of an empty pocket, should outweigh the name of my kinsman, Major Molineux? Oh, if I had one of these grinning rascals in the woods, where I and my oak sapling grew up together, I would teach him that my arm is heavy, though my purse be light!'

On turning the corner of the narrow lane, Robin found himself in a spacious street, with an unbroken line of lofty houses on each side, and a steepled building at the upper end, whence the ringing of a bell announced the hour of nine. The light of the moon, and the lamps from numerous shop windows, discovered people promenading on the pavement, and amongst them, Robin hoped to recognize his hitherto inscrutable relative. The result of his former inquiries made him unwilling to hazard another, in a scene of such publicity, and he determined to walk slowly and silently up the street, thrusting his face close to that of every elderly gentleman, in search of the Major's lineaments. In his progress, Robin encountered many gay and gallant figures. Embroidered garments, of showy colors, enormous periwigs, gold-laced hats, and silver hilted swords, glided past him and dazzled his optics. Travelled youths, imitators of the European fine gentlemen of the period, trod jauntily along, half-dancing to the fashionable tunes which they hummed, and making poor Robin ashamed of his quiet and natural gait. At length, after many pauses to examine the gorgeous display of goods in the shop windows, and after suffering some rebukes for the impertinence of his scrutiny into people's faces, the Major's kinsman found himself near the steepled building, still unsuccessful in his search. As yet, however, he had seen only one side of the thronged street; so Robin crossed, and continued the same sort of inquisition down the opposite pavement, with stronger hopes than the philosopher seeking

---

[13]I.e., a servant who has signed a contract for a term of service, usually (at this time) as repayment for ship fare from England to America.

an honest man, but with no better fortune.[14] He had arrived about midway towards the lower end, from which his course began, when he overheard the approach of some one, who struck down a cane on the flag-stones at every step, uttering, at regular intervals, two sepulchral hems.

'Mercy on us!' quoth Robin, recognizing the sound.

Turning a corner, which chanced to be close at his right hand, he hastened to pursue his researches, in some other part of the town. His patience was now wearing low, and he seemed to feel more fatigue from his rambles since he crossed the ferry, than from his journey of several days on the other side. Hunger also pleaded loudly within him, and Robin began to balance the propriety of demanding, violently and with lifted cudgel, the necessary guidance from the first solitary passenger, whom he should meet. While a resolution to this effect was gaining strength, he entered a street of mean appearance, on either side of which, a row of ill-built houses was straggling towards the harbor. The moonlight fell upon no passenger along the whole extent, but in the third domicile which Robin passed, there was a half-opened door, and his keen glance detected a woman's garment within.

'My luck may be better here,' said he to himself.

Accordingly, he approached the door, and beheld it shut closer as he did so; yet an open space remained, sufficing for the fair occupant to observe the stranger, without a corresponding display on her part. All that Robin could discern was a strip of scarlet petticoat, and the occasional sparkle of an eye, as if the moonbeams were trembling on some bright thing.

'Pretty mistress,'—for I may call her so with a good conscience, thought the shrewd youth, since I know nothing to the contrary—'my sweet pretty mistress, will you be kind enough to tell me whereabouts I must seek the dwelling of my kinsman, Major Molineux?'

Robin's voice was plaintive and winning, and the female, seeing nothing to be shunned in the handsome country youth, thrust open the door, and came forth into the moonlight. She was a dainty little figure, with a white neck, round arms, and a slender waist, at the extremity of which her scarlet petticoat jutted out over a hoop, as if she were standing in a balloon. Moreover, her face was oval and pretty, her hair dark beneath the little cap, and her bright eyes possessed a sly freedom, which triumphed over those of Robin.

'Major Molineux dwells here,' said this fair woman.

Now her voice was the sweetest Robin had heard that night, the airy counterpart of a stream of melted silver; yet he could not help doubting whether that sweet voice spoke Gospel truth. He looked up and down the mean street, and then surveyed the house before which they stood. It was a small, dark edifice of two stories, the second of which projected over the lower floor; and the front apartment had the aspect of a shop for petty commodities.

'Now truly I am in luck,' replied Robin, cunningly, 'and so indeed is my kinsman, the Major, in having so pretty a housekeeper. But I prithee trouble him to step to the door; I will deliver him a message from his friends in the country, and then go back to my lodgings at the inn.'

'Nay, the Major has been a-bed this hour or more,' said the lady of the scarlet petticoat; 'and it would be to little purpose to disturb him to-night, seeing his evening draught was of the strongest. But he is a kind-hearted man, and it would be as much as my life's worth, to let a kinsman of his turn away from the door. You are the good old gentleman's very picture, and I could swear that was his

---

[14]Diogenes (*c.* 412–323 B.C.), Greek cynic philosopher, who went out by day bearing a lantern in search of an honest man.

rainy-weather hat. Also, he has garments very much resembling those leather—
But come in, I pray, for I bid you hearty welcome in his name.'

So saying, the fair and hospitable dame took our hero by the hand; and though
the touch was light, and the force was gentleness, and though Robin read in her
eyes what he did not hear in her words, yet the slender waisted woman, in the
scarlet petticoat, proved stronger than the athletic country youth. She had drawn
his half-willing footsteps nearly to the threshold, when the opening of a door in
the neighborhood, startled the Major's housekeeper, and, leaving the Major's
kinsman, she vanished speedily into her own domicile. A heavy yawn preceded
the appearance of a man, who, like the Moonshine of Pyramus and Thisbe,[15] carried a lantern, needlessly aiding his sister luminary in the heavens. As he walked
sleepily up the street, he turned his broad, dull face on Robin, and displayed a
long staff, spiked at the end.

'Home, vagabond, home!' said the watchman, in accents that seemed to fall
asleep as soon as they were uttered. 'Home, or we'll set you in the stocks by peep
of day!'

'This is the second hint of the kind,' thought Robin. 'I wish they would end my
difficulties, by setting me there to-night.'

Nevertheless, the youth felt an instinctive antipathy towards the guardian of
midnight order, which at first prevented him from asking his usual question. But
just when the man was about to vanish behind the corner, Robin resolved not to
lose the opportunity, and shouted lustily after him—

'I say, friend! will you guide me to the house of my kinsman, Major Molineux?'

The watchman made no reply, but turned the corner and was gone; yet Robin
seemed to hear the sound of drowsy laughter stealing along the solitary street. At
that moment, also, a pleasant titter saluted him from the open window above his
head; he looked up, and caught the sparkle of a saucy eye; a round arm beckoned
to him, and next he heard light footsteps descending the staircase within. But
Robin, being of the household of a New England clergyman, was a good youth, as
well as a shrewd one; so he resisted temptation, and fled away.

He now roamed desperately, and at random, through the town, almost ready
to believe that a spell was on him, like that, by which a wizard of his country, had
once kept three pursuers wandering, a whole winter night, within twenty paces of
the cottage which they sought. The streets lay before him, strange and desolate,
and the lights were extinguished in almost every house. Twice, however, little parties of men, among whom Robin distinguished individuals in outlandish attire,
came hurrying along, but though on both occasions they paused to address him,
such intercourse did not at all enlighten his perplexity. They did but utter a few
words in some language of which Robin knew nothing, and perceiving his inability
to answer, bestowed a curse upon him in plain English, and hastened away. Finally, the lad determined to knock at the door of every mansion that might appear worthy to be occupied by his kinsman, trusting that perseverance would
overcome the fatality which had hitherto thwarted him. Firm in this resolve, he
was passing beneath the walls of a church, which formed the corner of two streets,
when, as he turned into the shade of its steeple, he encountered a bulky stranger,
muffled in a cloak. The man was proceeding with the speed of earnest business,
but Robin planted himself full before him, holding the oak cudgel with both
hands across his body, as a bar to further passage.

'Halt, honest man, and answer me a question,' said he, very resolutely. 'Tell
me, this instant, whereabouts is the dwelling of my kinsman, Major Molineux?'

'Keep your tongue between your teeth, fool, and let me pass,' said a deep,

---

[15]See Shakespeare's *A Midsummer Night's Dream*, V, i; Moonshine is a character in the play within the play.

gruff voice, which Robin partly remembered. 'Let me pass, I say, or I'll strike you to the earth!'

'No, no, neighbor!' cried Robin, flourishing his cudgel, and then thrusting its larger end close to the man's muffled face. 'No, no, I'm not the fool you take me for, nor do you pass, till I have an answer to my question. Whereabouts is the dwelling of my kinsman, Major Molineux?'

The stranger, instead of attempting to force his passage, stept back into the moonlight, unmuffled his own face and stared full into that of Robin.

'Watch here an hour, and Major Molineux will pass by,' said he.

Robin gazed with dismay and astonishment, on the unprecedented physiognomy of the speaker. The forehead with its double prominence, the broad-hooked nose, the shaggy eyebrows, and fiery eyes, were those which he had noticed at the inn, but the man's complexion had undergone a singular, or, more properly, a two-fold change. One side of the face blazed of an intense red, while the other was black as midnight, the division line being in the broad bridge of the nose; and a mouth, which seemed to extend from ear to ear, was black or red, in contrast to the color of the cheek. The effect was as if two individual devils, a fiend of fire and a fiend of darkness, had united themselves to form this infernal visage. The stranger grinned in Robin's face, muffled his parti-colored features, and was out of sight in a moment.

'Strange things we travellers see!' ejaculated Robin.

He seated himself, however, upon the steps of the church-door, resolving to wait the appointed time for his kinsman's appearance. A few moments were consumed in philosophical speculations, upon the species of the *genus homo,* who had just left him, but having settled this point shrewdly, rationally, and satisfactorily, he was compelled to look elsewhere for amusement. And first he threw his eyes along the street; it was of more respectable appearance than most of those into which he had wandered, and the moon, 'creating, like the imaginative power, a beautiful strangeness in familiar objects,' gave something of romance to a scene, that might not have possessed it in the light of day. The irregular, and often quaint architecture of the houses, some of whose roofs were broken into numerous little peaks; while others ascended, steep and narrow, into a single point; and others again were square; the pure milk-white of some of their complexions, the aged darkness of others, and the thousand sparklings, reflected from bright substances in the plastered walls of many; these matters engaged Robin's attention for awhile, and then began to grow wearisome. Next he endeavored to define the forms of distant objects, starting away with almost ghostly indistinctness, just as his eye appeared to grasp them; and finally he took a minute survey of an edifice, which stood on the opposite side of the street, directly in front of the church-door, where he was stationed. It was a large square mansion, distinguished from its neighbors by a balcony, which rested on tall pillars, and by an elaborate Gothic window, communicating therewith.

'Perhaps this is the very house I have been seeking,' thought Robin.

Then he strove to speed away the time, by listening to a murmur, which swept continually along the street, yet was scarcely audible, except to an unaccustomed ear like his; it was a low, dull, dreamy sound, compounded of many noises, each of which was at too great a distance to be separately heard. Robin marvelled at this snore of a sleeping town, and marvelled more, whenever its continuity was broken, by now and then a distant shout, apparently loud where it originated. But altogether it was a sleep-inspiring sound, and to shake off its drowsy influence, Robin arose, and climbed a window-frame, that he might view the interior of the church. There the moonbeams came trembling in, and fell down upon the deserted pews, and extended along the quiet aisles. A fainter, yet more awful radiance, was hovering round the pulpit, and one solitary ray had dared to rest upon the opened page of the great Bible. Had Nature, in that deep hour, become a worshipper in the house, which man had builded? Or was that heavenly light the visible sanctity of the place, visible because no earthly and impure feet were within the walls? The scene made Robin's heart shiver with a sensation of loneliness, stronger than he had ever felt in the remotest depths of his native woods; so he turned away, and sat down again before the door. There were graves around the church, and now an uneasy thought obtruded into Robin's breast. What if the object of his search, which had been so often and so strangely thwarted, were all the time mouldering in his shroud? What if his kinsman should glide through yonder gate, and nod and smile to him in passing dimly by?

'Oh, that any breathing thing were here with me!' said Robin.

Recalling his thoughts from this uncomfortable track, he sent them over forest, hill, and stream, and attempted to imagine how that evening of ambiguity and weariness, had been spent by his father's household. He pictured them assembled at the door, beneath the tree, the great old tree, which had been spared for its huge twisted trunk, and venerable shade, when a thousand leafy brethren fell. There, at the going down of the summer sun, it was his father's custom to perform domestic worship, that the neighbors might come and join with him like brothers of the family, and that the wayfaring man might pause to drink at that fountain, and keep his heart pure by freshening the memory of home. Robin distinguished the seat of every individual of the little audience; he saw the good man in the midst, holding the Scriptures in the golden light that shone from the western clouds; he beheld him close the book, and all rise up to pray. He heard the old thanksgivings for daily mercies, the old supplications for their continuance, to which he had so often listened in weariness, but which were now among his dear remembrances. He perceived the slight inequality of his father's voice when he came to speak of the Absent One; he noted how his mother turned her face to the broad and knotted trunk; how his elder brother scorned, because the beard was rough upon his upper lip, to permit his features to be moved; how his younger sister drew down a low hanging branch before her eyes; and how the little one of all, whose sports had hitherto broken the decorum of the scene, understood the prayer for her playmate, and burst into clamorous grief. Then he saw them go in at the door; and when Robin would have entered also, the latch tinkled into its place, and he was excluded from his home.

'Am I here, or there?' cried Robin, starting; for all at once, when his thoughts had become visible and audible in a dream, the long, wide, solitary street shone out before him.

He aroused himself, and endeavored to fix his attention steadily upon the large edifice which he had surveyed before. But still his mind kept vibrating between fancy and reality; by turns, the pillars of the balcony lengthened into the tall, bare stems of pines, dwindled down to human figures, settled again in their true shape and size, and then commenced a new succession of changes. For a single moment, when he deemed himself awake, he could have sworn that a visage, one which he seemed to remember, yet could not absolutely name as his kinsman's, was looking towards him from the Gothic window. A deeper sleep wrestled with, and nearly overcame him, but fled at the sound of footsteps along the opposite pavement. Robin rubbed his eyes, discerned a man passing at the foot of the balcony, and addressed him in a loud, peevish, and lamentable cry.

'Halloo, friend! must I wait here all night for my kinsman, Major Molineux?'

The sleeping echoes awoke, and answered the voice; and the passenger, barely able to discern a figure sitting in the oblique shade of the steeple, traversed the street to obtain a nearer view. He was himself a gentleman in his prime, of open, intelligent, cheerful, and altogether prepossessing countenance. Perceiving a country youth, apparently homeless and without friends, he accosted him in a tone of real kindness, which had become strange to Robin's ears.

'Well, my good lad, why are you sitting here?' inquired he. 'Can I be of service to you in any way?'

'I am afraid not, Sir,' replied Robin, despondingly; 'yet I shall take it kindly, if you'll answer me a single question. I've been searching half the night for one Major Molineux; now, Sir, is there really such a person in these parts, or am I dreaming?'

'Major Molineux! The name is not altogether strange to me,' said the gentleman, smiling. 'Have you any objection to telling me the nature of your business with him?'

Then Robin briefly related that his father was a clergyman, settled on a small salary, at a long distance back in the country, and that he and Major Molineux were brothers' children. The Major, having inherited riches, and acquired civil and military rank, had visited his cousin in great pomp a year or two before; had manifested much interest in Robin and an elder brother, and, being childless himself, had thrown out hints respecting the future establishment of one of them in life. The elder brother was destined to succeed to the farm, which his father cultivated, in the interval of sacred duties; it was therefore determined that Robin should profit by his kinsman's generous intentions, especially as he had seemed to be rather the favorite, and was thought to possess other necessary endowments.

'For I have the name of being a shrewd youth,' observed Robin, in this part of his story.

'I doubt not you deserve it,' replied his new friend, good naturedly; 'but pray proceed.'

'Well, Sir, being nearly eighteen years old, and well grown, as you see,' continued Robin, raising himself to his full height, 'I thought it high time to begin the world. So my mother and sister put me in handsome trim, and my father gave me half the remnant of his last year's salary, and five days ago I started for this place, to pay the Major a visit. But would you believe it, Sir? I crossed the ferry a little after dusk, and have yet found nobody that would show me the way to his dwelling; only an hour or two since, I was told to wait here, and Major Molineux would pass by.'

'Can you describe the man who told you this?' inquired the gentleman.

'Oh, he was a very ill-favored fellow, Sir,' replied Robin, 'with two great bumps on his forehead, a hook nose, fiery eyes, and, what struck me as the strangest, his face was of two different colors. Do you happen to know such a man, Sir?'

'Not intimately,' answered the stranger, 'but I chanced to meet him a little time previous to your stopping me. I believe you may trust his word, and that the Major will very shortly pass through this street. In the mean time, as I have a singular curiosity to witness your meeting, I will sit down here upon the steps, and bear you company.'

He seated himself accordingly, and soon engaged his companion in animated discourse. It was but of brief continuance, however, for a noise of shouting, which had long been remotely audible, drew so much nearer, that Robin inquired its cause.

'What may be the meaning of this uproar?' asked he. 'Truly, if your town be always as noisy, I shall find little sleep, while I am an inhabitant.'

'Why, indeed, friend Robin, there do appear to be three or four riotous fellows abroad to-night,' replied the gentleman. 'You must not expect all the stillness of your native woods, here in our streets. But the watch will shortly be at the heels of these lads, and—'

'Aye, and set them in the stocks by peep of day,' interrupted Robin, recollecting his own encounter with the drowsy lantern-bearer. 'But, dear Sir, if I may trust my ears, an army of watchmen would never make head against such a multitude of rioters. There were at least a thousand voices went to make up that one shout.'

'May not one man have several voices, Robin, as well as two complexions?' said his friend.

'Perhaps a man may; but Heaven forbid that a woman should!' responded the shrewd youth, thinking of the seductive tones of the Major's housekeeper.

The sounds of a trumpet in some neighboring street now became so evident and continual, that Robin's curiosity was strongly excited. In addition to the shouts, he heard frequent bursts from many instruments of discord, and a wild and confused laughter filled up the intervals. Robin rose from the steps, and looked wistfully towards a point, whither several people seemed to be hastening.

'Surely some prodigious merrymaking is going on,' exclaimed he. 'I have laughed very little since I left home, Sir, and should be sorry to lose an opportunity. Shall we just step round the corner by that darkish house, and take our share of the fun?'

'Sit down again, sit down, good Robin,' replied the gentleman, laying his hand on the skirt of the grey coat. 'You forget that we must wait here for your kinsman; and there is reason to believe that he will pass by, in the course of a very few moments.'

The near approach of the uproar had now disturbed the neighborhood; windows flew open on all sides; and many heads, in the attire of the pillow, and confused by sleep suddenly broken, were protruded to the gaze of whoever had leisure to observe them. Eager voices hailed each other from house to house, all demanding the explanation, which not a soul could give. Half-dressed men hurried towards the unknown commotion, stumbling as they went over the stone steps, that thrust themselves into the narrow foot-walk. The shouts, the laughter, and the tuneless bray, the antipodes of music, came onward with increasing din, till scattered individuals, and then denser bodies, began to appear round a corner, at the distance of a hundred yards.

'Will you recognize your kinsman, Robin, if he passes in this crowd?' inquired the gentleman.

'Indeed, I can't warrant it, Sir; but I'll take my stand here, and keep a bright look out,' answered Robin, descending to the outer edge of the pavement.

A mighty stream of people now emptied into the street, and came rolling slowly towards the church. A single horseman wheeled the corner in the midst of them, and close behind him came a band of fearful wind-instruments, sending forth a fresher discord, now that no intervening buildings kept it from the ear. Then a redder light disturbed the moonbeams, and a dense multitude of torches shone along the street, concealing by their glare whatever object they illuminated. The single horseman, clad in a military dress, and bearing a drawn sword, rode onward as the leader, and, by his fierce and variegated countenance, appeared like war personified; the red of one cheek was an emblem of fire and sword; the blackness of the other betokened the mourning which attends them. In his train, were wild figures in the Indian dress, and many fantastic shapes without a model, giving the whole march a visionary air, as if a dream had broken forth from some feverish brain, and were sweeping visibly through the midnight streets. A mass of people, inactive, except as applauding spectators, hemmed the procession in, and several women ran along the sidewalks, piercing the confusion of heavier sounds, with their shrill voices of mirth or terror.

'The double-faced fellow has his eye upon me,' muttered Robin, with an indefinite but uncomfortable idea, that he was himself to bear a part in the pageantry.

The leader turned himself in the saddle, and fixed his glance full upon the country youth, as the steed went slowly by. When Robin had freed his eyes from those fiery ones, the musicians were passing before him, and the torches were close at hand; but the unsteady brightness of the latter formed a veil which he could not penetrate. The rattling of wheels over the stones sometimes found its way to his ear, and confused traces of a human form appeared at intervals, and then melted into the vivid light. A moment more, and the leader thundered a command to halt; the trumpets vomited a horrid breath, and held their peace; the shouts and laughter of the people died away, and there remained only a universal hum, nearly allied to silence. Right before Robin's eyes was an uncovered cart. There the torches blazed the brightest, there the moon shone out like day, and there, in tar-and-feathery dignity, sate his kinsman, Major Molineux!

He was an elderly man, of large and majestic person, and strong, square features, betokening a steady soul; but steady as it was, his enemies had found the means to shake it. His face was pale as death, and far more ghastly; the broad forehead was contracted in his agony, so that his eyebrows formed one grizzled line; his eyes were red and wild, and the foam hung white upon his quivering lip. His whole frame was agitated by a quick, and continual tremor, which his pride strove to quell, even in those circumstances of overwhelming humiliation. But perhaps the bitterest pang of all was when his eyes met those of Robin; for he evidently knew him on the instant, as the youth stood witnessing the foul disgrace of a head that had grown grey in honor. They stared at each other in silence, and Robin's knees shook, and his hair bristled, with a mixture of pity and terror. Soon, however, a bewildering excitement began to seize upon his mind; the preceding adventures of the night, the unexpected appearance of the crowd, the torches, the confused din, and the hush that followed, the spectre of his kinsman reviled by that great multitude, all this, and more than all, a perception of tremendous ridicule in the whole scene, affected him with a sort of mental inebriety. At that moment a voice of sluggish merriment saluted Robin's ears; he turned instinctively, and just behind the corner of the church stood the lantern-bearer, rubbing his eyes, and drowsily enjoying the lad's amazement. Then he heard a peal of laughter like the ringing of silvery bells; a woman twitched his arm, a saucy eye met his, and he saw the lady of the scarlet petticoat. A sharp, dry cachinnation appealed to his memory, and, standing on tiptoe in the crowd, with his white apron over his head, he beheld the courteous little innkeeper. And lastly, there sailed over the heads of the multitude a great, broad laugh, broken in the midst by two sepulchral hems; thus—

'Haw, haw, haw—hem, hem—haw, haw, haw, haw!'

The sound proceeded from the balcony of the opposite edifice, and thither Robin turned his eyes. In front of the Gothic window stood the old citizen, wrapped in a wide gown, his grey periwig exchanged for a nightcap, which was thrust back from his forehead, and his silk stockings hanging down about his legs. He supported himself on his polished cane in a fit of convulsive merriment, which manifested itself on his solemn old features, like a funny inscription on a tombstone. Then Robin seemed to hear the voices of the barbers; of the guests of the inn; and of all who had made sport of him that night. The contagion was spreading among the multitude, when, all at once, it seized upon Robin, and he sent forth a shout of laughter that echoed through the street; every man shook his sides, every man emptied his lungs, but Robin's shout was the loudest there. The cloud-spirits peeped from their silvery islands, as the congregated mirth went roaring up the sky! The Man in the Moon heard the far bellow; 'Oho,' quoth he, 'the old Earth is frolicsome to-night!'

When there was a momentary calm in that tempestuous sea of sound, the leader gave the sign, the procession resumed its march. On they went, like fiends that throng in mockery round some dead potentate, mighty no more, but majestic still in his agony. On they went, in counterfeited pomp, in senseless uproar, in frenzied merriment, trampling all on an old man's heart. On swept the tumult, and left a silent street behind.

'Well, Robin, are you dreaming?' inquired the gentleman, laying his hand on the youth's shoulder.

Robin started, and withdrew his arm from the stone post, to which he had instinctively clung, while the living stream rolled by him. His cheek was somewhat pale, and his eye not quite so lively as in the earlier part of the evening.

'Will you be kind enough to show me the way to the ferry?' said he, after a moment's pause.

'You have then adopted a new subject of inquiry?' observed his companion, with a smile.

'Why, yes, Sir,' replied Robin, rather dryly. 'Thanks to you, and to my other friends, I have at last met my kinsman, and he will scarce desire to see my face again. I begin to grow weary of a town life, Sir. Will you show me the way to the ferry?'

'No, my good friend Robin, not to-night, at least,' said the gentleman. 'Some few days hence, if you continue to wish it, I will speed you on your journey. Or, if you prefer to remain with us, perhaps, as you are a shrewd youth, you may rise in the world, without the help of your kinsman, Major Molineux.'

1832

Roger Malvin's Burial

One of the few incidents of Indian warfare, naturally susceptible of the moonlight of romance, was that expedition, undertaken, for the defence of the frontiers, in the year 1725, which resulted in the well-remembered 'Lovell's Fight.'[1] Imagination, by casting certain circumstances judiciously into the shade, may see much to admire in the heroism of a little band, who gave battle to twice their number in the heart of the enemy's country. The open bravery displayed by both parties was in accordance with civilized ideas of valor, and chivalry itself might not blush to record the deeds of one or two individuals. The battle, though so fatal to those who fought, was not unfortunate in its consequences to the country; for it broke the strength of a tribe, and conduced to the peace which subsisted during several ensuing years. History and tradition are unusually minute in their memorials of this affair; and the captain of a scouting party of frontier-men has acquired as actual a military renown, as many a victorious leader of thousands. Some of the incidents contained in the following pages will be recognized, notwithstanding the substitution of fictitious names, by such as have heard, from old men's lips, the fate of the few combatants who were in a condition to retreat, after 'Lovell's Fight.'

The early sunbeams hovered cheerfully upon the tree-tops, beneath which two weary and wounded men had stretched their limbs the night before. Their bed of withered oak-leaves was strewn upon the small level space, at the foot of a rock, situated near the summit of one of the gentle swells, by which the face of the country is there diversified. The mass of granite, rearing its smooth, flat surface, fifteen or twenty feet above their heads, was not unlike a gigantic grave-stone, upon which the veins seemed to form an inscription in forgotten characters. On a tract of several acres around this rock, oaks and other hard-wood trees had sup-

---

[1] A ballad about Captain John Lovewell's (1691–1725) last battle with Indians (the Pequawkets or Pigwackets) in Frye- burg, Maine, in 1725. His company was ambushed and he was killed near Lovewell's Pond.

plied the place of the pines, which were the usual growth of the land; and a young and vigorous sapling stood close beside the travellers.

The severe wound of the elder man had probably deprived him of sleep; for, so soon as the first ray of sunshine rested on the top of the highest tree, he reared himself painfully from his recumbent posture, and sat erect. The deep lines of his countenance, and the scattered grey of his hair, marked him as past the middle age; but his muscular frame would, but for the effects of his wound, have been as capable of sustaining fatigue, as in the early vigor of life. Languor and exhaustion now sat upon his haggard features, and the despairing glance which he sent forward through the depths of the forest, proved his own conviction that his pilgrimage was at an end. He next turned his eyes to the companion, who reclined by his side. The youth, for he had scarcely attained the years of manhood, lay, with his head upon his arm, in the embrace of an unquiet sleep, which a thrill of pain from his wounds seemed each moment on the point of breaking. His right hand grasped a musket, and, to judge from the violent action of his features, his slumbers were bringing back a vision of the conflict, of which he was one of the few survivors. A shout,—deep and loud to his dreaming fancy,—found its way in an imperfect murmur to his lips, and, starting even at the slight sound of his own voice, he suddenly awoke. The first act of reviving recollection, was to make anxious inquiries respecting the condition of his wounded fellow traveller. The latter shook his head.

'Reuben, my boy,' said he, 'this rock, beneath which we sit, will serve for an old hunter's grave-stone. There is many and many a long mile of howling wilderness before us yet; nor would it avail me anything, if the smoke of my own chimney were but on the other side of that swell of land. The Indian bullet was deadlier than I thought.'

'You are weary with our three days' travel,' replied the youth, 'and a little longer rest will recruit you. Sit you here, while I search the woods for the herbs and roots, that must be our sustenance; and having eaten, you shall lean on me, and we will turn our faces homeward. I doubt not, that, with my help, you can attain to some one of the frontier garrisons.'

'There is not two days' life in me, Reuben,' said the other, calmly, 'and I will no longer burthen you with my useless body, when you can scarcely support your own. Your wounds are deep, and your strength is failing fast; yet, if you hasten onward alone, you may be preserved. For me there is no hope; and I will await death here.'

'If it must be so, I will remain and watch by you,' said Reuben, resolutely.

'No, my son, no,' rejoined his companion. 'Let the wish of a dying man have weight with you; give me one grasp of your hand, and get you hence. Think you that my last moments will be eased by the thought, that I leave you to die a more lingering death? I have loved you like a father, Reuben, and, at a time like this, I should have something of a father's authority. I charge you to be gone, that I may die in peace.'

'And because you have been a father to me, should I therefore leave you to perish, and to lie unburied in the wilderness?' exclaimed the youth. 'No; if your end be in truth approaching, I will watch by you, and receive your parting words. I will dig a grave here by the rock, in which, if my weakness overcome me, we will rest together; or, if Heaven gives me strength, I will seek my way home.'

'In the cities, and wherever men dwell,' replied the other, 'they bury their dead in the earth; they hide them from the sight of the living; but here, where no step may pass, perhaps for a hundred years, wherefore should I not rest beneath the open sky, covered only by the oak-leaves, when the autumn winds shall strew them? And for a monument, here is this grey rock, on which my dying hand shall carve the name of Roger Malvin; and the traveller in days to come will know, that here sleeps a hunter and a warrior. Tarry not, then, for a folly like this, but hasten away, if not for your own sake, for hers who will else be desolate.'

Malvin spoke the last few words in a faultering voice, and their effect upon his companion was strongly visible. They reminded him that there were other, and less questionable duties, than that of sharing the fate of a man whom his death could not benefit. Nor can it be affirmed that no selfish feeling strove to enter Reuben's heart, though the consciousness made him more earnestly resist his companion's entreaties.

'How terrible, to wait the slow approach of death, in this solitude!' exclaimed he. 'A brave man does not shrink in the battle, and, when friends stand round the bed, even women may die composedly; but here—'

'I shall not shrink, even here, Reuben Bourne,' interrupted Malvin. 'I am a man of no weak heart; and, if I were, there is a surer support than that of earthly friends. You are young, and life is dear to you. Your last moments will need comfort far more than mine; and when you have laid me in the earth, and are alone, and night is settling on the forest, you will feel all the bitterness of the death that may now be escaped. But I will urge no selfish motive to your generous nature. Leave me for my sake; that, having said a prayer for your safety, I may have space to settle my account, undisturbed by worldly sorrows.'

'And your daughter! How shall I dare to meet her eye?' exclaimed Reuben. 'She will ask the fate of her father, whose life I vowed to defend with my own. Must I tell her, that he travelled three days' march with me from the field of battle, and that then I left him to perish in the wilderness? Were it not better to lie down and die by your side, than to return safe, and say this to Dorcas?'

'Tell my daughter,' said Roger Malvin, 'that, though yourself sore wounded, and weak, and weary, you led my tottering footsteps many a mile, and left me only at my earnest entreaty, because I would not have your blood upon my soul. Tell her, that through pain and danger you were faithful, and that, if your life-blood could have saved me, it would have flowed to its last drop. And tell her, that you will be something dearer than a father, and that my blessing is with you both, and that my dying eyes can see a long and pleasant path, in which you will journey together.'

As Malvin spoke, he almost raised himself from the ground, and the energy of his concluding words seemed to fill the wild and lonely forest with a vision of happiness. But when he sank exhausted upon his bed of oak-leaves, the light, which had kindled in Reuben's eye, was quenched. He felt as if it were both sin and folly to think of happiness at such a moment. His companion watched his changing countenance, and sought, with generous art, to wile him to his own good.

'Perhaps I deceive myself in regard to the time I have to live,' he resumed. 'It may be, that, with speedy assistance, I might recover of my wound. The foremost fugitives must, ere this, have carried tidings of our fatal battle to the frontiers, and parties will be out to succour those in like condition with ourselves. Should you meet one of these, and guide them hither, who can tell but that I may sit by my own fireside again?'

A mournful smile strayed across the features of the dying man, as he insinuated that unfounded hope; which, however, was not without its effect on Reuben. No merely selfish motive, nor even the desolate condition of Dorcas, could have induced him to desert his companion, at such a moment. But his wishes seized upon the thought, that Malvin's life might be preserved, and his sanguine nature heightened, almost to certainty, the remote possibility of procuring human aid.

'Surely there is reason, weighty reason, to hope that friends are not far distant,' he said, half aloud. 'There fled one coward, unwounded, in the beginning of the fight, and most probably he made good speed. Every true man on the frontier would shoulder his musket, at the news; and though no party may range so far into the woods as this, I shall perhaps encounter them in one day's march. Counsel me faithfully,' he added, turning to Malvin, in distrust of his own motives. 'Were your situation mine, would you desert me while life remained?'

'It is now twenty years,' replied Roger Malvin, sighing, however, as he secretly acknowledged the wide dissimilarity between the two cases,—'it is now twenty years, since I escaped, with one dear friend, from Indian captivity, near Montreal. We journeyed many days through the woods, till at length, overcome with hunger and weariness, my friend lay down, and besought me to leave him; for he knew, that, if I remained, we both must perish. And, with but little hope of obtaining succour, I heaped a pillow of dry leaves beneath his head, and hastened on.'

'And did you return in time to save him?' asked Reuben, hanging on Malvin's words, as if they were to be prophetic of his own success.

'I did,' answered the other. 'I came upon the camp of a hunting party, before sunset of the same day. I guided them to the spot where my comrade was expecting death; and he is now a hale and hearty man, upon his own farm, far within the frontiers, while I lie wounded here, in the depths of the wilderness.'

This example, powerful in effecting Reuben's decision, was aided, unconsciously to himself, by the hidden strength of many another motive. Roger Malvin perceived that the victory was nearly won.

'Now go, my son, and Heaven prosper you!' he said. 'Turn not back with our friends, when you meet them, lest your wounds and weariness overcome you; but send hitherward two or three, that may be spared, to search for me. And believe me, Reuben, my heart will be lighter with every step you take towards home.' Yet there was perhaps a change, both in his countenance and voice, as he spoke thus; for, after all, it was a ghastly fate, to be left expiring in the wilderness.

Reuben Bourne, but half convinced that he was acting rightly, at length raised himself from the ground, and prepared himself for his departure. And first, though contrary to Malvin's wishes, he collected a stock of roots and herbs, which had been their only food during the last two days. This useless supply he placed within reach of the dying man, for whom, also, he swept together a fresh bed of dry oak-leaves. Then, climbing to the summit of the rock, which on one side was rough and broken, he bent the oak-sapling downward, and bound his handkerchief to the topmost branch. This precaution was not unnecessary, to direct any who might come in search of Malvin; for every part of the rock, except its broad, smooth front, was concealed, at a little distance, by the dense undergrowth of the forest. The handkerchief had been the bandage of a wound upon Reuben's arm; and, as he bound it to the tree, he vowed, by the blood that stained it, that he would return, either to save his companion's life, or to lay his body in the grave. He then descended, and stood, with downcast eyes, to receive Roger Malvin's parting words.

The experience of the latter suggested much and minute advice, respecting the youth's journey through the trackless forest. Upon this subject he spoke with calm earnestness, as if he were sending Reuben to the battle or the chase, while he himself remained secure at home; and not as if the human countenance, that was about to leave him, were the last he would ever behold. But his firmness was shaken, before he concluded.

'Carry my blessing to Dorcas, and say that my last prayer shall be for her and you. Bid her have no hard thoughts because you left me here'—Reuben's heart smote him—'for that your life would not have weighed with you, if its sacrifice could have done me good. She will marry you, after she has mourned a little while for her father; and Heaven grant you long and happy days! and may your children's children stand round your death-bed! And, Reuben,' added he, as the weakness of mortality made its way at last, 'return, when your wounds are healed and your weariness refreshed, return to this wild rock, and lay my bones in the grave, and say a prayer over them.'

An almost superstitious regard, arising perhaps from the customs of the Indians, whose war was with the dead, as well as the living, was paid by the frontier inhabitants to the rites of sepulture; and there are many instances of the sacrifice of life, in the attempt to bury those who had fallen by the 'sword of the wilderness.' Reuben, therefore, felt the full importance of the promise, which he most solemnly made, to return, and perform Roger Malvin's obsequies. It was remarkable, that the latter, speaking his whole heart in his parting words, no longer endeavored to persuade the youth, that even the speediest succour might avail to the preservation of his life. Reuben was internally convinced, that he should see Malvin's living face no more. His generous nature would fain have delayed him, at whatever risk, till the dying scene were past; but the desire of existence, and the hope of happiness had strengthened in his heart, and he was unable to resist them.

'It is enough,' said Roger Malvin, having listened to Reuben's promise. 'Go, and God speed you!'

The youth pressed his hand in silence, turned, and was departing. His slow and faultering steps, however, had borne him but a little way, before Malvin's voice recalled him.

'Reuben, Reuben,' said he, faintly; and Reuben returned and knelt down by the dying man.

'Raise me, and let me lean against the rock,' was his last request. 'My face will be turned towards home, and I shall see you a moment longer, as you pass among the trees.'

Reuben, having made the desired alteration in his companion's posture, again began his solitary pilgrimage. He walked more hastily at first, than was consistent with his strength; for a sort of guilty feeling, which sometimes torments men in their most justifiable acts, caused him to seek concealment from Malvin's eyes. But, after he had trodden far upon the rustling forest-leaves, he crept back, impelled by a wild and painful curiosity, and, sheltered by the earthy roots of an up-torn tree, gazed earnestly at the desolate man. The morning sun was unclouded, and the trees and shrubs imbibed the sweet air of the month of May; yet there seemed a gloom on Nature's face, as if she sympathized with mortal pain and sorrow. Roger Malvin's hands were uplifted in a fervent prayer, some of the words of which stole through the stillness of the woods, and entered Reuben's heart, torturing it with an unutterable pang. They were the broken accents of a petition for his own happiness and that of Dorcas; and, as the youth listened, conscience, or something in its similitude, pleaded strongly with him to return, and lie down again by the rock. He felt how hard was the doom of the kind and generous being whom he had deserted in his extremity. Death would come, like the slow approach of a corpse, stealing gradually towards him through the forest, and showing its ghastly and motionless features from behind a nearer, and yet a nearer tree. But such must have been Reuben's own fate, had he tarried another sunset; and who shall impute blame to him, if he shrank from so useless a sacrifice? As he gave a parting look, a breeze waved the little banner upon the sapling-oak, and reminded Reuben of his vow.

Many circumstances contributed to retard the wounded traveller, in his way to the frontiers. On the second day, the clouds, gathering densely over the sky, precluded the possibility of regulating his course by the position of the sun; and he knew not but that every effort of his almost exhausted strength, was removing him farther from the home he sought. His scanty sustenance was supplied by the berries, and other spontaneous products of the forest. Herds of deer, it is true, sometimes bounded past him, and partridges frequently whirred up before his footsteps; but his ammunition had been expended in the fight, and he had no means of slaying them. His wounds, irritated by the constant exertion in which lay the only hope of life, wore away his strength, and at intervals confused his reason. But, even in the wanderings of intellect, Reuben's young heart clung strongly to existence, and it was only through absolute incapacity of motion, that he at last sank down beneath a tree, compelled there to await death. In this situation he was discovered by a party, who, upon the first intelligence of the fight, had been despatched to the relief of the survivors. They conveyed him to the nearest settlement, which chanced to be that of his own residence.

Dorcas, in the simplicity of the olden time, watched by the bed-side of her wounded lover, and administered all those comforts, that are in the sole gift of woman's heart and hand. During several days, Reuben's recollection strayed drowsily among the perils and hardships through which he had passed, and he was incapable of returning definite answers to the inquiries, with which many were eager to harass him. No authentic particulars of the battle had yet been circulated; nor could mothers, wives, and children tell, whether their loved ones were detained by captivity, or by the stronger chain of death. Dorcas nourished her apprehensions in silence, till one afternoon, when Reuben awoke from an unquiet sleep, and seemed to recognize her more perfectly than at any previous time. She saw that his intellect had become composed, and she could no longer restrain her filial anxiety.

'My father, Reuben?' she began; but the change in her lover's countenance made her pause.

The youth shrank, as if with a bitter pain, and the blood gushed vividly into his wan and hollow cheeks. His first impulse was to cover his face; but, apparently with a desperate effort, he half raised himself, and spoke vehemently, defending himself against an imaginary accusation.

'Your father was sore wounded in the battle, Dorcas, and he bade me not burthen myself with him, but only to lead him to the lake-side, that he might quench his thirst and die. But I would not desert the old man in his extremity, and, though bleeding myself, I supported him; I gave him half my strength, and led him away with me. For three days we journeyed on together, and your father was sustained beyond my hopes; but, awaking at sunrise on the fourth day, I found him faint and exhausted,—he was unable to proceed,—his life had ebbed away fast,—and—'

'He died!' exclaimed Dorcas, faintly.

Reuben felt it impossible to acknowledge, that his selfish love of life had hurried him away, before her father's fate was decided. He spoke not; he only bowed his head; and, between shame and exhaustion, sank back and hid his face in the pillow. Dorcas wept, when her fears were thus confirmed; but the shock, as it had been long anticipated, was on that account the less violent.

'You dug a grave for my poor father, in the wilderness, Reuben?' was the question by which her filial piety manifested itself.

'My hands were weak, but I did what I could,' replied the youth in a smothered tone. 'There stands a noble tomb-stone above his head, and I would to Heaven I slept as soundly as he!'

Dorcas, perceiving the wildness of his latter words, inquired no further at the time; but her heart found ease in the thought, that Roger Malvin had not lacked such funeral rites as it was possible to bestow. The tale of Reuben's courage and fidelity lost nothing, when she communicated it to her friends; and the poor youth, tottering from his sick chamber to breathe the sunny air, experienced from every tongue the miserable and humiliating torture of unmerited praise. All acknowledged that he might worthily demand the hand of the fair maiden, to whose father he had been 'faithful unto death'; and, as my tale is not of love, it shall suffice to say, that, in the space of a few months, Reuben became the husband of Dorcas Malvin. During the marriage ceremony, the bride was covered with blushes, but the bridegroom's face was pale.

There was now in the breast of Reuben Bourne an incommunicable thought; something which he was to conceal most heedfully from her whom he most loved and trusted. He regretted, deeply and bitterly, the moral cowardice that had restrained his words, when he was about to disclose the truth to Dorcas; but pride, the fear of losing her affection, the dread of universal scorn, forbade him to rectify this falsehood. He felt, that, for leaving Roger Malvin, he deserved no censure. His presence, the gratuitous sacrifice of his own life, would have added only another, and a needless agony to the last moments of the dying man. But concealment had imparted to a justifiable act, much of the secret effect of guilt; and Reuben, while reason told him that he had done right, experienced, in no small degree, the mental horrors, which punish the perpetrator of undiscovered crime. By a certain association of ideas, he at times almost imagined himself a murderer. For years, also, a thought would occasionally recur, which, though he perceived all its folly and extravagance, he had not power to banish from his mind; it was a haunting and torturing fancy, that his father-in-law was yet sitting at the foot of the rock, on the withered forest-leaves, alive, and awaiting his pledged assistance. These mental deceptions, however, came and went, nor did he ever mistake them for realities; but in the calmest and clearest moods of his mind, he was conscious that he had a deep vow unredeemed, and that an unburied corpse was calling to him, out of the wilderness. Yet, such was the consequence of his prevarication, that he could not obey the call. It was now too late to require the assistance of Roger Malvin's friends, in performing his long-deferred sepulture; and superstitious fears, of which none were more susceptible than the people of the outward settlements, forbade Reuben to go alone. Neither did he know where, in the pathless and illimitable forest, to seek that smooth and lettered rock, at the base of which the body lay; his remembrance of every portion of his travel thence was indistinct, and the latter part had left no impression upon his mind. There was, however, a continual impulse, a voice audible only to himself, commanding him to go forth and redeem his vow; and he had a strange impression, that, were he to make the trial, he would be led straight to Malvin's bones. But, year after year, that summons, unheard but felt, was disobeyed. His one secret thought, became like a chain, binding down his spirit, and, like a serpent, gnawing into his heart; and he was transformed into a sad and downcast, yet irritable man.

In the course of a few years after their marriage, changes began to be visible in the external prosperity of Reuben and Dorcas. The only riches of the former had been his stout heart and strong arm; but the latter, her father's sole heiress, had made her husband master of a farm, under older cultivation, larger, and better stocked than most of the frontier establishments. Reuben Bourne, however, was a neglectful husbandman; and while the lands of the other settlers became annually more fruitful, his deteriorated in the same proportion. The discouragements to agriculture were greatly lessened by the cessation of Indian war, during which men held the plough in one hand, and the musket in the other; and were fortunate if the products of their dangerous labor were not destroyed, either in the field or in the barn, by the savage enemy. But Reuben did not profit by the altered condition of the country; nor can it be denied, that his intervals of industrious attention to his affairs were but scantily rewarded with success. The irritability, by which he had recently become distinguished, was another cause of his declining prosperity, as it occasioned frequent quarrels, in his unavoidable intercourse with the neighboring settlers. The results of these were innumerable law-suits; for the people of New England, in the earliest stages and wildest circumstances of the country, adopted, whenever attainable, the legal mode of deciding their differences. To be brief, the world did not go well with Reuben Bourne, and, though not till many years after his marriage, he was finally a ruined man, with but one remaining expedient against the evil fate that had pursued him. He was to throw sunlight into some deep recess of the forest, and seek subsistence from the virgin bosom of the wilderness.

The only child of Reuben and Dorcas was a son, now arrived at the age of fifteen years, beautiful in youth, and giving promise of a glorious manhood. He was peculiarly qualified for, and already began to excel in, the wild accomplishments of frontier life. His foot was fleet, his aim true, his apprehension quick, his heart glad and high; and all, who anticipated the return of Indian war, spoke of Cyrus Bourne as a future leader in the land. The boy was loved by his father, with a deep and silent strength, as if whatever was good and happy in his own nature had been transferred to his child, carrying his affections with it. Even Dorcas, though loving and beloved, was far less dear to him; for Reuben's secret thoughts and insulated emotions had gradually made him a selfish man; and he could no longer love deeply, except where he saw, or imagined, some reflection or likeness of his own mind. In Cyrus he recognized what he had himself been in other days; and at intervals he seemed to partake of the boy's spirit, and to be revived with a fresh and happy life. Reuben was accompanied by his son in the expedition, for the purpose of selecting a tract of land, and felling and burning the timber, which necessarily preceded the removal of the household gods.[2] Two months of autumn were thus occupied; after which Reuben Bourne and his young hunter returned, to spend their last winter in the settlements.

It was early in the month of May, that the little family snapped asunder whatever tendrils of affection had clung to inanimate objects, and bade farewell to the few, who, in the blight of fortune, called themselves their friends. The sadness of the parting moment had, to each of the pilgrims, its peculiar alleviations. Reuben, a moody man, and misanthropic because unhappy, strode onward, with his usual stern brow and downcast eye, feeling few regrets, and disdaining to acknowledge any. Dorcas, while she wept abundantly over the broken ties by which her simple and affectionate nature had bound itself to everything, felt that the inhabitants of her inmost heart moved on with her, and that all else would be supplied wherever she might go. And the boy dashed one tear-drop from his eye, and thought of the adventurous pleasures of the untrodden forest. Oh! who, in the enthusiasm of a day-dream, has not wished that he were a wanderer in a world of summer wilderness, with one fair and gentle being hanging lightly on his arm? In youth, his free and exulting step would know no barrier but the rolling ocean or the snow-topt mountains; calmer manhood would choose a home, where Nature had strewn a double wealth, in the vale of some transparent stream; and when hoary age, after long, long years of that pure life, stole on and found him there, it would find him the father of a race, the patriarch of a people, the founder of a mighty nation yet to be. When death, like the sweet sleep which we welcome after a day of happiness, came over him, his far descendants would mourn over the venerated dust. Enveloped by tradition in mysterious attributes, the men of future generations would call him godlike; and remote posterity would see him standing, dimly glorious, far up the valley of a hundred centuries!

The tangled and gloomy forest, through which the personages of my tale were

---

[2]Essentials of home life, deriving from Roman divinities Lares and Penates, whose images were kept in the atrium or central room.

wandering, differed widely from the dreamer's Land of Fantasie; yet there was something in their way of life that Nature asserted as her own; and the gnawing cares, which went with them from the world, were all that now obstructed their happiness. One stout and shaggy steed, the bearer of all their wealth, did not shrink from the added weight of Dorcas; although her hardy breeding sustained her, during the latter part of each day's journey, by her husband's side. Reuben and his son, their muskets on their shoulders, and their axes slung behind them, kept an unwearied pace, each watching with a hunter's eye for the game that supplied their food. When hunger bade, they halted and prepared their meal on the bank of some unpolluted forest-brook, which, as they knelt down with thirsty lips to drink, murmured a sweet unwillingness, like a maiden, at love's first kiss. They slept beneath a hut of branches, and awoke at peep of light, refreshed for the toils of another day. Dorcas and the boy went on joyously, and even Reuben's spirit shone at intervals with an outward gladness; but inwardly there was a cold, cold sorrow, which he compared to the snow-drifts, lying deep in the glens and hollows of the rivulets, while the leaves were brightly green above.

Cyrus Bourne was sufficiently skilled in the travel of the woods, to observe, that his father did not adhere to the course they had pursued, in their expedition of the preceding autumn. They were now keeping farther to the north, striking out more directly from the settlements, and into a region, of which savage beasts and savage men were as yet the sole possessors. The boy sometimes hinted his opinions upon the subject, and Reuben listened attentively, and once or twice altered the direction of their march in accordance with his son's counsel. But having so done, he seemed ill at ease. His quick and wandering glances were sent forward, apparently in search of enemies lurking behind the tree-trunks; and seeing nothing there, he would cast his eyes backward, as if in fear of some pursuer. Cyrus, perceiving that his father gradually resumed the old direction, forbore to interfere; nor, though something began to weigh upon his heart, did his adventurous nature permit him to regret the increased length and the mystery of their way.

On the afternoon of the fifth day, they halted and made their simple encampment, nearly an hour before sunset. The face of the country, for the last few miles, had been diversified by swells of land, resembling huge waves of a petrified sea; and in one of the corresponding hollows, a wild and romantic spot, had the family reared their hut, and kindled their fire. There is something chilling, and yet heart-warming, in the thought of these three, united by strong bands of love, and insulated from all that breathe beside. The dark and gloomy pines looked down upon them, and, as the wind swept through their tops, a pitying sound was heard in the forest; or did those old trees groan, in fear that men were come to lay the axe to their roots at last? Reuben and his son, while Dorcas made ready their meal, proposed to wander out in search of game, of which that day's march had afforded no supply. The boy, promising not to quit the vicinity of the encampment, bounded off with a step as light and elastic as that of the deer he hoped to slay; while his father, feeling a transient happiness as he gazed after him, was about to pursue an opposite direction. Dorcas, in the meanwhile, had seated herself near their fire of fallen branches, upon the moss-grown and mouldering trunk of a tree, uprooted years before. Her employment, diversified by an occasional glance at the pot, now beginning to simmer over the blaze, was the perusal of the current year's Massachusetts Almanac, which, with the exception of an old black-letter Bible,[3] comprised all the literary wealth of the family. None pay a greater regard to arbitrary divisions of time, than those who are excluded from

---

[3]Bible printed by old type in the style used in lettering by medieval scribes.

society; and Dorcas mentioned, as if the information were of importance, that it was now the twelfth of May. Her husband started.

'The twelfth of May! I should remember it well,' muttered he, while many thoughts occasioned a momentary confusion in his mind. 'Where am I? Whither am I wandering? Where did I leave him?'

Dorcas, too well accustomed to her husband's wayward moods to note any peculiarity of demeanor, now laid aside the Almanac, and addressed him in that mournful tone, which the tender-hearted appropriate to griefs long cold and dead.

'It was near this time of the month, eighteen years ago, that my poor father left this world for a better. He had a kind arm to hold his head, and a kind voice to cheer him, Reuben, in his last moments; and the thought of the faithful care you took of him, has comforted me, many a time since. Oh! death would have been awful to a solitary man, in a wild place like this!'

'Pray Heaven, Dorcas,' said Reuben, in a broken voice, 'pray Heaven, that neither of us three die solitary, and lie unburied, in this howling wilderness!' And he hastened away, leaving her to watch the fire, beneath the gloomy pines.

Reuben Bourne's rapid pace gradually slackened, as the pang, unintentionally inflicted by the words of Dorcas, became less acute. Many strange reflections, however, thronged upon him; and, straying onward, rather like a sleep-walker than a hunter, it was attributable to no care of his own, that his devious course kept him in the vicinity of the encampment. His steps were imperceptibly led almost in a circle, nor did he observe that he was on the verge of a tract of land heavily timbered, but not with pine-trees. The place of the latter was here supplied by oaks, and other of the harder woods; and around their roots clustered a dense and bushy undergrowth, leaving, however, barren spaces between the trees, thick-strewn with withered leaves. Whenever the rustling of the branches, or the creaking of the trunks made a sound, as if the forest were waking from slumber, Reuben instinctively raised the musket that rested on his arm, and cast a quick, sharp glance on every side; but, convinced by a partial observation that no animal was near, he would again give himself up to his thoughts. He was musing on the strange influence, that had led him away from his premeditated course, and so far into the depths of the wilderness. Unable to penetrate to the secret place of his soul, where his motives lay hidden, he believed that a supernatural voice had called him onward, and that a supernatural power had obstructed his retreat. He trusted that it was Heaven's intent to afford him an opportunity of expiating his sin; he hoped that he might find the bones, so long unburied; and that, having laid the earth over them, peace would throw its sunlight into the sepulchre of his heart. From these thoughts he was aroused by a rustling in the forest, at some distance from the spot to which he had wandered. Perceiving the motion of some object behind a thick veil of undergrowth, he fired, with the instinct of a hunter, and the aim of a practised marksman. A low moan, which told his success, and by which even animals can express their dying agony, was unheeded by Reuben Bourne. What were the recollections now breaking upon him?

The thicket, into which Reuben had fired, was near the summit of a swell of land, and was clustered around the base of a rock, which, in the shape and smoothness of one of its surfaces, was not unlike a gigantic grave-stone. As if reflected in a mirror, its likeness was in Reuben's memory. He even recognized the veins which seemed to form an inscription in forgotten characters; everything remained the same, except that a thick covert of bushes shrouded the lower part of the rock, and would have hidden Roger Malvin, had he still been sitting there. Yet, in the next moment, Reuben's eye was caught by another change, that time had effected, since he last stood, where he was now standing again, behind the earthy roots of the uptorn tree. The sapling, to which he had bound the blood-stained symbol of his vow, had increased and strengthened into an oak, far indeed from its maturity, but with no mean spread of shadowy branches. There was one singularity, observable in this tree, which made Reuben tremble. The middle and lower branches were in luxuriant life, and an excess of vegetation had fringed the trunk, almost to the ground; but a blight had apparently stricken the upper part of the oak, and the very topmost bough was withered, sapless, and utterly dead. Reuben remembered how the little banner had fluttered on the topmost bough, when it was green and lovely, eighteen years before. Whose guilt had blasted it?

Dorcas, after the departure of the two hunters, continued her preparations for their evening repast. Her sylvan table was the moss-covered trunk of a large fallen tree, on the broadest part of which she had spread a snow-white cloth, and arranged what were left of the bright pewter vessels, that had been her pride in the settlements. It had a strange aspect—that one little spot of homely comfort, in the desolate heart of Nature. The sunshine yet lingered upon the higher branches of the trees that grew on rising ground; but the shades of evening had deepened into the hollow, where the encampment was made; and the fire-light began to redden as it gleamed up the tall trunks of the pines, or hovered on the dense and obscure mass of foliage, that circled round the spot. The heart of Dorcas was not sad; for she felt that it was better to journey in the wilderness, with two whom she loved, than to be a lonely woman in a crowd that cared not for her. As she busied herself in arranging seats of mouldering wood, covered with leaves, for Reuben and her son, her voice danced through the gloomy forest, in the measure of a song that she had learned in youth. The rude melody, the production of a bard who won no name, was descriptive of a winter evening in a frontier-cottage, when, secured from savage inroad by the high-piled snow-drifts, the family rejoiced by their own fireside. The whole song possessed that nameless charm, peculiar to un-borrowed thought; but four continually-recurring lines shone out from the rest, like the blaze of the hearth whose joys they celebrated. Into them, working magic with a few simple words, the poet had instilled the very essence of domestic love and household happiness, and they were poetry and picture joined in one. As Dorcas sang, the walls of her forsaken home seemed to encircle her; she no longer saw the gloomy pines, nor heard the wind, which still, as she began each verse, sent a heavy breath through the branches, and died away in a hollow moan, from the burthen of the song. She was aroused by the report of a gun, in the vicinity of the encampment; and either the sudden sound, or her loneliness by the glowing fire, caused her to tremble violently. The next moment, she laughed in the pride of a mother's heart.

'My beautiful young hunter! my boy has slain a deer!' she exclaimed, recollecting that, in the direction whence the shot proceeded, Cyrus had gone to the chase.

She waited a reasonable time, to hear her son's light step bounding over the rustling leaves, to tell of his success. But he did not immediately appear, and she sent her cheerful voice among the trees, in search of him.

'Cyrus! Cyrus!'

His coming was still delayed, and she determined, as the report had apparently been very near, to seek for him in person. Her assistance, also, might be necessary in bringing home the venison, which she flattered herself he had obtained. She therefore set forward, directing her steps by the long-past sound, and singing as she went, in order that the boy might be aware of her approach, and run to meet her. From behind the trunk of every tree, and from every hiding place in the thick foliage of the undergrowth, she hoped to discover the countenance of her son, laughing with the sportive mischief that is born of affection. The sun was now beneath the horizon, and the light that came down among the trees was sufficiently dim to create many illusions in her expecting fancy. Several times she seemed indistinctly to see his face gazing out from among the leaves; and once she imagined that he stood beckoning to her, at the base of a craggy rock. Keeping her eyes on this object, however, it proved to be no more than the trunk of an oak, fringed to the very ground with little branches, one of which, thrust out farther than the rest, was shaken by the breeze. Making her way round the foot of the rock, she suddenly found herself close to her husband, who had approached in another direction. Leaning upon the butt of his gun, the muzzle of which rested upon the withered leaves, he was apparently absorbed in the contemplation of some object at his feet.

'How is this, Reuben? Have you slain the deer, and fallen asleep over him?' exclaimed Dorcas, laughing cheerfully, on her first slight observation of his posture and appearance.

He stirred not, neither did he turn his eyes towards her; and a cold, shuddering fear, indefinite in its source and object, began to creep into her blood. She now perceived that her husband's face was ghastly pale, and his features were rigid, as if incapable of assuming any other expression than the strong despair which had hardened upon them. He gave not the slightest evidence that he was aware of her approach.

'For the love of Heaven, Reuben, speak to me!' cried Dorcas, and the strange sound of her own voice affrighted her even more than the dead silence.

Her husband started, stared into her face; drew her to the front of the rock, and pointed with his finger.

Oh! there lay the boy, asleep, but dreamless, upon the fallen forest-leaves! his cheek rested upon his arm, his curled locks were thrown back from his brow, his limbs were slightly relaxed. Had a sudden weariness overcome the youthful hunter? Would his mother's voice arouse him? She knew that it was death.

'This broad rock is the grave-stone of your near kindred, Dorcas,' said her husband. 'Your tears will fall at once over your father and your son.'

She heard him not. With one wild shriek, that seemed to force its way from the sufferer's inmost soul, she sank insensible by the side of her dead boy. At that moment, the withered topmost bough of the oak loosened itself, in the stilly air, and fell in soft, light fragments upon the rock, upon the leaves, upon Reuben, upon his wife and child, and upon Roger Malvin's bones. Then Reuben's heart was stricken, and the tears gushed out like water from a rock. The vow that the wounded youth had made, the blighted man had come to redeem. His sin was expiated, the curse was gone from him; and, in the hour, when he had shed blood dearer to him than his own, a prayer, the first for years, went up to Heaven from the lips of Reuben Bourne.

1832

Young Goodman Brown[1]

Young Goodman[2] Brown came forth, at sunset, into the street of Salem village, but put his head back, after crossing the threshold, to exchange a parting kiss with his young wife. And Faith, as the wife was aptly named, thrust her own pretty

---

[1]This story shows Hawthorne's familiarity with Cotton Mather's *Wonders of the Invisible World* (1693), which described such "Diabolical Sacraments" held in the dark woods, presided over by the devil in the form of a "dark" or "sable" figure like the one Brown encounters early in the story.
[2]Title equivalent to "Mr."

head into the street, letting the wind play with the pink ribbons of her cap, while she called to Goodman Brown.

'Dearest heart,' whispered she, softly and rather sadly, when her lips were close to his ear, 'pr'y thee, put off your journey until sunrise, and sleep in your own bed to-night. A lone woman is troubled with such dreams and such thoughts, that she's afeard of herself, sometimes. Pray, tarry with me this night, dear husband, of all nights in the year!'

'My love and my Faith,' replied young Goodman Brown, 'of all nights in the year, this one night must I tarry away from thee. My journey, as thou callest it, forth and back again, must needs be done 'twixt now and sunrise. What, my sweet, pretty wife, dost thou doubt me already, and we but three months married!'

'Then, God bless you!' said Faith, with the pink ribbons, 'and may you find all well, when you come back.'

'Amen!' cried Goodman Brown. 'Say thy prayers, dear Faith, and go to bed at dusk, and no harm will come to thee.'

So they parted; and the young man pursued his way, until, being about to turn the corner by the meeting-house, he looked back, and saw the head of Faith still peeping after him, with a melancholy air, in spite of her pink ribbons.

'Poor little Faith!' thought he, for his heart smote him. 'What a wretch am I, to leave her on such an errand! She talks of dreams, too. Methought, as she spoke, there was trouble in her face, as if a dream had warned her what work is to be done to-night. But, no, no! 'twould kill her to think it. Well; she's a blessed angel on earth; and after this one night, I'll cling to her skirts and follow her to Heaven.'

With this excellent resolve for the future, Goodman Brown felt himself justified in making more haste on his present evil purpose. He had taken a dreary road, darkened by all the gloomiest trees of the forest, which barely stood aside to let the narrow path creep through, and closed immediately behind. It was all as lonely as could be; and there is this peculiarity in such a solitude, that the traveller knows not who may be concealed by the innumerable trunks and the thick boughs overhead; so that, with lonely footsteps, he may yet be passing through an unseen multitude.

'There may be a devilish Indian behind every tree,' said Goodman Brown, to himself; and he glanced fearfully behind him, as he added, 'What if the devil himself should be at my very elbow!'

His head being turned back, he passed a crook of the road, and looking forward again, beheld the figure of a man, in grave and decent attire, seated at the foot of an old tree. He arose, at Goodman Brown's approach, and walked onward, side by side with him.

'You are late, Goodman Brown,' said he. 'The clock of the Old South was striking as I came through Boston; and that is full fifteen minutes agone.'

'Faith kept me back awhile,' replied the young man, with a tremor in his voice, caused by the sudden appearance of his companion, though not wholly unexpected.

It was now deep dusk in the forest, and deepest in that part of it where these two were journeying. As nearly as could be discerned, the second traveller was about fifty years old, apparently in the same rank of life as Goodman Brown, and bearing a considerable resemblance to him, though perhaps more in expression than features. Still, they might have been taken for father and son. And yet, though the elder person was as simply clad as the younger, and as simple in manner too, he had an indescribable air of one who knew the world, and would not have felt abashed at the governor's dinner-table, or in King William's court,[3] were

---

[3] William III (1650–1702), husband of Queen Mary II, who ruled England in 1689–1702.

it possible that his affairs should call him thither. But the only thing about him, that could be fixed upon as remarkable, was his staff, which bore the likeness of a great black snake, so curiously wrought, that it might almost be seen to twist and wriggle itself, like a living serpent. This, of course, must have been an ocular deception, assisted by the uncertain light.

'Come, Goodman Brown!' cried his fellow-traveller, 'this is a dull pace for the beginning of a journey. Take my staff, if you are so soon weary.'

'Friend,' said the other, exchanging his slow pace for a full stop, 'having kept covenant by meeting thee here, it is my purpose now to return whence I came. I have scruples, touching the matter thou wot'st of.'

'Sayest thou so?' replied he of the serpent, smiling apart. 'Let us walk on, nevertheless, reasoning as we go, and if I convince thee not, thou shalt turn back. We are but a little way in the forest, yet.'

'Too far, too far!' exclaimed the goodman, unconsciously resuming his walk. 'My father never went into the woods on such an errand, nor his father before him. We have been a race of honest men and good Christians, since the days of the martyrs.[4] And shall I be the first of the name of Brown, that ever took this path, and kept—'

'Such company, thou wouldst say,' observed the elder person, interpreting his pause. 'Well said, Goodman Brown! I have been as well acquainted with your family as with ever a one among the Puritans; and that's no trifle to say. I helped your grandfather, the constable, when he lashed the Quaker woman so smartly through the streets of Salem. And it was I that brought your father a pitch-pine knot, kindled at my own hearth, to set fire to an Indian village, in King Philip's war.[5] They were my good friends, both; and many a pleasant walk have we had along this path, and returned merrily after midnight. I would fain be friends with you, for their sake.'

'If it be as thou sayest,' replied Goodman Brown, 'I marvel they never spoke of these matters. Or, verily, I marvel not, seeing that the least rumor of the sort would have driven them from New-England. We are a people of prayer, and good works, to boot, and abide no such wickedness.'

'Wickedness or not,' said the traveller with the twisted staff, 'I have a very general acquaintance here in New-England. The deacons of many a church have drunk the communion wine with me; the selectmen,[6] of divers towns, make me their chairman; and a majority of the Great and General Court[7] are firm supporters of my interest. The governor and I, too—but these are state-secrets.'

'Can this be so!' cried Goodman Brown, with a stare of amazement at his undisturbed companion. 'Howbeit, I have nothing to do with the governor and council; they have their own ways, and are no rule for a simple husbandman, like me. But, were I to go on with thee, how should I meet the eye of that good old man, our minister, at Salem village? Oh, his voice would make me tremble, both Sabbath-day and lecture-day!'[8]

Thus far, the elder traveller had listened with due gravity, but now burst into a fit of irrepressible mirth, shaking himself so violently, that his snake-like staff actually seemed to wriggle in sympathy.

'Ha! ha! ha!' shouted he, again and again; then composing himself, 'Well, go on, Goodman Brown, go on; but pr'y thee, don't kill me with laughing!'

'Well, then, to end the matter at once,' said Goodman Brown, considerably net-

---

[4]During the reign of Mary Tudor (1553–1558), or "Bloody Mary," Protestants were persecuted.
[5]War of 1675–76 between the leader of the Wampanoag Indians (called King Philip) and the New England colonists.
[6]Board of officers elected in New England towns to handle municipal affairs.

[7]Legislature.
[8]Midweek day, Wednesday or Thursday, on which a sermon was preached.

tled, 'there is my wife, Faith. It would break her dear little heart; and I'd rather break my own!'

'Nay, if that be the case,' answered the other, 'e'en go thy ways, Goodman Brown. I would not, for twenty old women like the one hobbling before us, that Faith should come to any harm.'

As he spoke, he pointed his staff at a female figure on the path, in whom Goodman Brown recognized a very pious and exemplary dame, who had taught him his catechism, in youth, and was still his moral and spiritual adviser, jointly with the minister and Deacon Gookin.

'A marvel, truly, that Goody Cloyse[9] should be so far in the wilderness, at night-fall!' said he. 'But, with your leave, friend, I shall take a cut through the woods, until we have left this Christian woman behind. Being a stranger to you, she might ask whom I was consorting with, and whither I was going.'

'Be it so,' said his fellow-traveller. 'Betake you to the woods, and let me keep the path.'

Accordingly, the young man turned aside, but took care to watch his companion, who advanced softly along the road, until he had come within a staff's length of the old dame. She, meanwhile, was making the best of her way, with singular speed for so aged a woman, and mumbling some indistinct words, a prayer, doubtless, as she went. The traveller put forth his staff, and touched her withered neck with what seemed the serpent's tail.

'The devil!' screamed the pious old lady.

'Then Goody Cloyse knows her old friend?' observed the traveller, confronting her, and leaning on his writhing stick.

'Ah, forsooth, and is it your worship, indeed?' cried the good dame. 'Yea, truly is it, and in the very image of my old gossip, Goodman Brown, the grandfather of the silly fellow that now is. But—would your worship believe it?—my broomstick hath strangely disappeared, stolen, as I suspect, by that unhanged witch, Goody Cory, and that, too, when I was all anointed with the juice of smallage and cinque-foil and wolf's-bane—'[10]

'Mingled with fine wheat and the fat of a new-born babe,' said the shape of old Goodman Brown.

'Ah, your worship knows the receipt,' cried the old lady, cackling aloud. 'So, as I was saying, being all ready for the meeting, and no horse to ride on, I made up my mind to foot it; for they tell me, there is a nice young man to be taken into communion to-night. But now your good worship will lend me your arm, and we shall be there in a twinkling.'

'That can hardly be,' answered her friend. 'I may not spare you my arm, Goody Cloyse, but here is my staff, if you will.'

So saying, he threw it down at her feet, where, perhaps, it assumed life, being one of the rods which its owner had formerly lent to the Egyptian Magi.[11] Of this fact, however, Goodman Brown could not take cognizance. He had cast up his eyes in astonishment, and looking down again, beheld neither Goody Cloyse nor the serpentine staff, but his fellow-traveller alone, who waited for him as calmly as if nothing had happened.

'That old woman taught me my catechism!' said the young man; and there was a world of meaning in this simple comment.

They continued to walk onward, while the elder traveller exhorted his compan-

---

[9]"Goody" derives from "goodwife," a common title used for a housewife. Hawthorne here and elsewhere uses actual names of those who were tried for witchcraft and hanged in the New England trials of 1692.
[10]Plants commonly used by witches according to tradition: smallage, wild celery; cinque-foil, a plant with "five-fingered" leaves of the rose family; wolf's-bane, poisonous plant with large, showy flowers.
[11]Cf. Exodus 7:10–11: an Egyptian magician repeated Aaron's supernatural feat of changing his rod to a serpent before the Pharaoh.

ion to make good speed and persevere in the path, discoursing so aptly, that his arguments seemed rather to spring up in the bosom of his auditor, than to be suggested by himself. As they went, he plucked a branch of maple, to serve for a walking-stick, and began to strip it of the twigs and little boughs, which were wet with evening dew. The moment his fingers touched them, they became strangely withered and dried up, as with a week's sunshine. Thus the pair proceeded, at a good free pace, until suddenly, in a gloomy hollow of the road, Goodman Brown sat himself down on the stump of a tree, and refused to go any farther.

'Friend,' said he, stubbornly, 'my mind is made up. Not another step will I budge on this errand. What if a wretched old woman do choose to go to the devil, when I thought she was going to Heaven! Is that any reason why I should quit my dear Faith, and go after her?'

'You will think better of this, by-and-by,' said his acquaintance, composedly. 'Sit here and rest yourself awhile; and when you feel like moving again, there is my staff to help you along.'

Without more words, he threw his companion the maple stick, and was as speedily out of sight, as if he had vanished into the deepening gloom. The young man sat a few moments, by the road-side, applauding himself greatly, and thinking with how clear a conscience he should meet the minister, in his morning-walk, nor shrink from the eye of good old Deacon Gookin. And what calm sleep would be his, that very night, which was to have been spent so wickedly, but purely and sweetly now, in the arms of Faith! Amidst these pleasant and praiseworthy meditations, Goodman Brown heard the tramp of horses along the road, and deemed it advisable to conceal himself within the verge of the forest, conscious of the guilty purpose that had brought him thither, though now so happily turned from it.

On came the hoof-tramps and the voices of the riders, two grave old voices, conversing soberly as they drew near. These mingled sounds appeared to pass along the road, within a few yards of the young man's hiding-place; but owing, doubtless, to the depth of the gloom, at that particular spot, neither the travellers nor their steeds were visible. Though their figures brushed the small boughs by the way-side, it could not be seen that they intercepted, even for a moment, the faint gleam from the strip of bright sky, athwart which they must have passed. Goodman Brown alternately crouched and stood on tip-toe, pulling aside the branches, and thrusting forth his head as far as he durst, without discerning so much as a shadow. It vexed him the more, because he could have sworn, were such a thing possible, that he recognized the voices of the minister and Deacon Gookin, jogging along quietly, as they were wont to do, when bound to some ordination or ecclesiastical council. While yet within hearing, one of the riders stopped to pluck a switch.

'Of the two, reverend Sir,' said the voice like the deacon's, 'I had rather miss an ordination-dinner than to-night's meeting. They tell me that some of our community are to be here from Falmouth and beyond, and others from Connecticut and Rhode-Island; besides several of the Indian powows,[12] who, after their fashion, know almost as much deviltry as the best of us. Moreover, there is a goodly young woman to be taken into communion.'

'Mighty well, Deacon Gookin!' replied the solemn old tones of the minister. 'Spur up, or we shall be late. Nothing can be done, you know, until I get on the ground.'

The hoofs clattered again, and the voices, talking so strangely in the empty air, passed on through the forest, where no church had ever been gathered, nor soli-

---

[12]Medicine men (later "pow wow" came to mean a conference).

tary Christian prayed. Whither, then, could these holy men be journeying, so deep into the heathen wilderness? Young Goodman Brown caught hold of a tree, for support, being ready to sink down on the ground, faint and overburthened with the heavy sickness of his heart. He looked up to the sky, doubting whether there really was a Heaven above him. Yet, there was the blue arch, and the stars brightening in it.

'With Heaven above, and Faith below, I will yet stand firm against the devil!' cried Goodman Brown.

While he still gazed upward, into the deep arch of the firmament, and had lifted his hands to pray, a cloud, though no wind was stirring, hurried across the zenith, and hid the brightening stars. The blue sky was still visible, except directly overhead, where this black mass of cloud was sweeping swiftly northward. Aloft in the air, as if from the depths of the cloud, came a confused and doubtful sound of voices. Once, the listener fancied that he could distinguish the accents of town's-people of his own, men and women, both pious and ungodly, many of whom he had met at the communion-table, and had seen others rioting at the tavern. The next moment, so indistinct were the sounds, he doubted whether he had heard aught but the murmur of the old forest, whispering without a wind. Then came a stronger swell of those familiar tones, heard daily in the sunshine, at Salem village, but never, until now, from a cloud of night. There was one voice, of a young woman, uttering lamentations, yet with an uncertain sorrow, and entreating for some favor, which, perhaps, it would grieve her to obtain. And all the unseen multitude, both saints and sinners, seemed to encourage her onward.

'Faith!' shouted Goodman Brown, in a voice of agony and desperation; and the echoes of the forest mocked him, crying —'Faith! Faith!' as if bewildered wretches were seeking her, all through the wilderness.

The cry of grief, rage, and terror, was yet piercing the night, when the unhappy husband held his breath for a response. There was a scream, drowned immediately in a louder murmur of voices, fading into far-off laughter, as the dark cloud swept away, leaving the clear and silent sky above Goodman Brown. But something fluttered lightly down through the air, and caught on the branch of a tree. The young man seized it, and beheld a pink ribbon.

'My Faith is gone!' cried he, after one stupefied moment. 'There is no good on earth; and sin is but a name. Come, devil! for to thee is this world given.'

And maddened with despair, so that he laughed loud and long, did Goodman Brown grasp his staff and set forth again, at such a rate, that he seemed to fly along the forest-path, rather than to walk or run. The road grew wilder and drearier, and more faintly traced, and vanished at length, leaving him in the heart of the dark wilderness, still rushing onward, with the instinct that guides mortal man to evil. The whole forest was peopled with frightful sounds; the creaking of the trees, the howling of wild beasts, and the yell of Indians; while, sometimes, the wind tolled like a distant church-bell, and sometimes gave a broad roar around the traveller, as if all Nature were laughing him to scorn. But he was himself the chief horror of the scene, and shrank not from its other horrors.

'Ha! ha! ha!' roared Goodman Brown, when the wind laughed at him. 'Let us hear which will laugh loudest! Think not to frighten me with your deviltry! Come witch, come wizard, come Indian powow, come devil himself! and here comes Goodman Brown. You may as well fear him as he fear you!'

In truth, all through the haunted forest, there could be nothing more frightful than the figure of Goodman Brown. On he flew, among the black pines, brandishing his staff with frenzied gestures, now giving vent to an inspiration of horrid blasphemy, and now shouting forth such laughter, as set all the echoes of the forest laughing like demons around him. The fiend in his own shape is less hideous, than when he rages in the breast of man. Thus sped the demoniac on his course, until, quivering among the trees, he saw a red light before him, as when the felled trunks and branches of a clearing have been set on fire, and throw up their lurid blaze against the sky, at the hour of midnight. He paused, in a lull of the tempest that had driven him onward, and heard the swell of what seemed a hymn, rolling solemnly from a distance, with the weight of many voices. He knew the tune; it was a familiar one in the choir of the village meeting-house. The verse died heavily away, and was lengthened by a chorus, not of human voices, but of all the sounds of the benighted wilderness, pealing in awful harmony together. Goodman Brown cried out; and his cry was lost to his own ear, by its unison with the cry of the desert.

In the interval of silence, he stole forward, until the light glared full upon his eyes. At one extremity of an open space, hemmed in by the dark wall of the forest, arose a rock, bearing some rude, natural resemblance either to an altar or a pulpit, and surrounded by four blazing pines, their tops aflame, their stems untouched, like candles at an evening meeting. The mass of foliage, that had overgrown the summit of the rock, was all on fire, blazing high into the night, and fitfully illuminating the whole field. Each pendent twig and leafy festoon was in a blaze. As the red light arose and fell, a numerous congregation alternately shone forth, then disappeared in shadow, and again grew, as it were, out of the darkness, peopling the heart of the solitary woods at once.

'A grave and dark-clad company!' quoth Goodman Brown.

In truth, they were such. Among them, quivering to-and-fro, between gloom and splendor, appeared faces that would be seen, next day, at the council-board of the province, and others which, Sabbath after Sabbath, looked devoutly heavenward, and benignantly over the crowded pews, from the holiest pulpits in the land. Some affirm, that the lady of the governor was there. At least, there were high dames well known to her, and wives of honored husbands, and widows, a great multitude, and ancient maidens, all of excellent repute, and fair young girls, who trembled, lest their mothers should espy them. Either the sudden gleams of light, flashing over the obscure field, bedazzled Goodman Brown, or he recognized a score of the church-members of Salem village, famous for their especial sanctity. Good old Deacon Gookin had arrived, and waited at the skirts of that venerable saint, his revered pastor. But, irreverently consorting with these grave, reputable, and pious people, these elders of the church, these chaste dames and dewy virgins, there were men of dissolute lives and women of spotted fame, wretches given over to all mean and filthy vice, and suspected even of horrid crimes. It was strange to see, that the good shrank not from the wicked, nor were the sinners abashed by the saints. Scattered, also, among their pale-faced enemies, were the Indian priests, or powows, who had often scared their native forest with more hideous incantations than any known to English witchcraft.

'But, where is Faith?' thought Goodman Brown; and, as hope came into his heart, he trembled.

Another verse of the hymn arose, a slow and mournful strain, such as the pious love, but joined to words which expressed all that our nature can conceive of sin, and darkly hinted at far more. Unfathomable to mere mortals is the lore of fiends. Verse after verse was sung, and still the chorus of the desert swelled between, like the deepest tone of a mighty organ. And, with the final peal of that dreadful anthem, there came a sound, as if the roaring wind, the rushing streams, the howling beasts, and every other voice of the unconverted wilderness, were mingling and according with the voice of guilty man, in homage to the prince of all. The four blazing pines threw up a loftier flame, and obscurely discovered shapes and visages of horror on the smoke-wreaths, above the impious assembly. At the same moment, the fire on the rock shot redly forth, and formed a glowing arch above its base, where now appeared a figure. With reverence be it spoken, the figure bore no slight similitude, both in garb and manner, to some grave divine of the New-England churches.

'Bring forth the converts!' cried a voice, that echoed through the field and rolled into the forest.

At the word, Goodman Brown stept forth from the shadow of the trees, and approached the congregation, with whom he felt a loathful brotherhood, by the sympathy of all that was wicked in his heart. He could have well nigh sworn, that the shape of his own dead father beckoned him to advance, looking downward from a smoke-wreath, while a woman, with dim features of despair, threw out her hand to warn him back. Was it his mother? But he had no power to retreat one step, nor to resist, even in thought, when the minister and good old Deacon Gookin seized his arms, and led him to the blazing rock. Thither came also the slender form of a veiled female, led between Goody Cloyse, that pious teacher of the catechism, and Martha Carrier,[13] who had received the devil's promise to be queen of hell. A rampant hag was she! And there stood the proselytes, beneath the canopy of fire.

'Welcome, my children,' said the dark figure, 'to the communion of your race! Ye have found, thus young, your nature and your destiny. My children, look behind you!'

They turned; and flashing forth, as it were, in a sheet of flame, the fiend-worshippers were seen; the smile of welcome gleamed darkly on every visage.

'There,' resumed the sable form, 'are all whom ye have reverenced from youth. Ye deemed them holier than yourselves, and shrank from your own sin, contrasting it with their lives of righteousness, and prayerful aspirations heavenward. Yet, here are they all, in my worshipping assembly! This night it shall be granted you to know their secret deeds; how hoary-bearded elders of the church have whispered wanton words to the young maids of their households; how many a woman, eager for widow's weeds, has given her husband a drink at bed-time, and let him sleep his last sleep in her bosom; how beardless youths have made haste to inherit their fathers' wealth; and how fair damsels—blush not, sweet ones!—have dug little graves in the garden, and bidden me, the sole guest, to an infant's funeral. By the sympathy of your human hearts for sin, ye shall scent out all the places—whether in church, bed-chamber, street, field, or forest—where crime has been committed, and shall exult to behold the whole earth one stain of guilt, one mighty blood-spot. Far more than this! It shall be yours to penetrate, in every bosom, the deep mystery of sin, the fountain of all wicked arts, and which inexhaustibly supplies more evil impulses than human power—than my power, at its utmost!—can make manifest in deeds. And now, my children, look upon each other.'

They did so; and, by the blaze of the hell-kindled torches, the wretched man beheld his Faith, and the wife her husband, trembling before that unhallowed altar.

'Lo! there ye stand, my children,' said the figure, in a deep and solemn tone, almost sad, with its despairing awfulness, as if his once angelic nature could yet mourn for our miserable race. 'Depending upon one another's hearts, ye had still hoped, that virtue were not all a dream. Now are ye undeceived! Evil is the nature of mankind. Evil must be your only happiness. Welcome, again, my children, to the communion of your race!'

'Welcome!' repeated the fiend-worshippers, in one cry of despair and triumph.

And there they stood, the only pair, as it seemed, who were yet hesitating on

---

[13]Found guilty of witchcraft and hanged in the 1692 trials; her case is summarized in Cotton Mather's *Wonders of the Invisible World.*

the verge of wickedness, in this dark world. A basin was hollowed, naturally, in the rock. Did it contain water, reddened by the lurid light? or was it blood? or, perchance, a liquid flame? Herein did the Shape of Evil dip his hand, and prepare to lay the mark of baptism upon their foreheads, that they might be partakers of the mystery of sin, more conscious of the secret guilt of others, both in deed and thought, than they could now be of their own. The husband cast one look at his pale wife, and Faith at him. What polluted wretches would the next glance shew them to each other, shuddering alike at what they disclosed and what they saw!

'Faith! Faith!' cried the husband. 'Look up to Heaven, and resist the Wicked One!'

Whether Faith obeyed, he knew not. Hardly had he spoken, when he found himself amid calm night and solitude, listening to a roar of the wind, which died heavily away through the forest. He staggered against the rock and felt it chill and damp, while a hanging twig, that had been all on fire, besprinkled his cheek with the coldest dew.

The next morning, young Goodman Brown came slowly into the street of Salem village, staring around him like a bewildered man. The good old minister was taking a walk along the grave-yard, to get an appetite for breakfast and meditate his sermon, and bestowed a blessing, as he passed, on Goodman Brown. He shrank from the venerable saint, as if to avoid an anathema. Old Deacon Gookin was at domestic worship, and the holy words of his prayer were heard through the open window. 'What God doth the wizard pray to?' quoth Goodman Brown. Goody Cloyse, that excellent old Christian, stood in the early sunshine, at her own lattice, catechising a little girl, who had brought her a pint of morning's milk. Goodman Brown snatched away the child, as from the grasp of the fiend himself. Turning the corner by the meeting-house, he spied the head of Faith, with the pink ribbons, gazing anxiously forth, and bursting into such joy at sight of him, that she skipt along the street, and almost kissed her husband before the whole village. But, Goodman Brown looked sternly and sadly into her face, and passed on without a greeting.

Had Goodman Brown fallen asleep in the forest, and only dreamed a wild dream of a witch-meeting?

Be it so, if you will. But, alas! it was a dream of evil omen for young Goodman Brown. A stern, a sad, a darkly meditative, a distrustful, if not a desperate man, did he become, from the night of that fearful dream. On the Sabbath-day, when the congregation were singing a holy psalm, he could not listen, because an anthem of sin rushed loudly upon his ear, and drowned all the blessed strain. When the minister spoke from the pulpit, with power and fervid eloquence, and, with his hand on the open Bible, of the sacred truths of our religion, and of saint-like lives and triumphant deaths, and of future bliss or misery unutterable, then did Goodman Brown turn pale, dreading, lest the roof should thunder down upon the gray blasphemer and his hearers. Often, awakening suddenly at midnight, he shrank from the bosom of Faith, and at morning or eventide, when the family knelt down at prayer, he scowled, and muttered to himself, and gazed sternly at his wife, and turned away. And when he had lived long, and was borne to his grave, a hoary corpse, followed by Faith, an aged woman, and children and grandchildren, a goodly procession, besides neighbors, not a few, they carved no hopeful verse upon his tomb-stone; for his dying hour was gloom.

1835

Wakefield

In some old magazine or newspaper, I recollect a story, told as truth, of a man—let us call him Wakefield—who absented himself for a long time, from his wife. The fact, thus abstractedly stated, is not very uncommon, nor—without a proper distinction of circumstances—to be condemned either as naughty or nonsensical. Howbeit, this, though far from the most aggravated, is perhaps the strangest instance, on record, of marital delinquency; and, moreover, as remarkable a freak as may be found in the whole list of human oddities. The wedded couple lived in London. The man, under pretence of going a journey, took lodgings in the next street to his own house, and there, unheard of by his wife or friends, and without the shadow of a reason for such self-banishment, dwelt upwards of twenty years. During that period, he beheld his home every day, and frequently the forlorn Mrs. Wakefield. And after so great a gap in his matrimonial felicity—when his death was reckoned certain, his estate settled, his name dismissed from memory, and his wife, long, long ago, resigned to her autumnal widowhood—he entered the door one evening, quietly, as from a day's absence, and became a loving spouse till death.

This outline is all that I remember. But the incident, though of the purest originality, unexampled, and probably never to be repeated, is one, I think, which appeals to the general sympathies of mankind. We know, each for himself, that none of us would perpetrate such a folly, yet feel as if some other might. To my own contemplations, at least, it has often recurred, always exciting wonder, but with a sense that the story must be true, and a conception of its hero's character. Whenever any subject so forcibly affects the mind, time is well spent in thinking of it. If the reader choose, let him do his own meditation; or if he prefer to ramble with me through the twenty years of Wakefield's vagary, I bid him welcome; trusting that there will be a pervading spirit and a moral, even should we fail to find them, done up neatly, and condensed into the final sentence. Thought has always its efficacy, and every striking incident its moral.

What sort of a man was Wakefield? We are free to shape out our own idea, and call it by his name. He was now in the meridian of life; his matrimonial affections, never violent, were sobered into a calm, habitual sentiment; of all husbands, he was likely to be the most constant, because a certain sluggishness would keep his heart at rest, wherever it might be placed. He was intellectual, but not actively so; his mind occupied itself in long and lazy musings, that tended to no purpose, or had not vigor to attain it; his thoughts were seldom so energetic as to seize hold of words. Imagination, in the proper meaning of the term, made no part of Wakefield's gifts. With a cold, but not depraved nor wandering heart, and a mind never feverish with riotous thoughts, nor perplexed with originality, who could have anticipated, that our friend would entitle himself to a foremost place among the doers of eccentric deeds? Had his acquaintances been asked, who was the man in London, the surest to perform nothing to-day which should be remembered on the morrow, they would have thought of Wakefield. Only the wife of his bosom might have hesitated. She, without having analyzed his character, was partly aware of a quiet selfishness, that had rusted into his inactive mind—of a peculiar sort of vanity, the most uneasy attribute about him—of a disposition to craft, which had seldom produced more positive effects than the keeping of petty secrets, hardly worth revealing—and, lastly, of what she called a little strangeness, sometimes, in the good man. This latter quality is indefinable, and perhaps non-existent.

Let us now imagine Wakefield bidding adieu to his wife. It is the dusk of an October evening. His equipment is a drab great-coat, a hat covered with an oilcloth, top-boots, an umbrella in one hand and a small portmanteau in the other.

He has informed Mrs. Wakefield that he is to take the night-coach into the country. She would fain inquire the length of his journey, its object, and the probable time of his return; but, indulgent to his harmless love of mystery, interrogates him only by a look. He tells her not to expect him positively by the return coach, nor to be alarmed should he tarry three or four days; but, at all events, to look for him at supper on Friday evening. Wakefield himself, be it considered, has no suspicion of what is before him. He holds out his hand; she gives her own, and meets his parting kiss, in the matter-of-course way of a ten years matrimony; and forth goes the middle-aged Mr. Wakefield, almost resolved to perplex his good lady by a whole week's absence. After the door has closed behind him, she perceives it thrust partly open, and a vision of her husband's face, through the aperture, smiling on her, and gone in a moment. For the time, this little incident is dismissed without a thought. But, long afterwards, when she has been more years a widow than a wife, that smile recurs, and flickers across all her reminiscences of Wakefield's visage. In her many musings, she surrounds the original smile with a multitude of fantasies, which make it strange and awful; as, for instance, if she imagines him in a coffin, that parting look is frozen on his pale features; or, if she dreams of him in Heaven, still his blessed spirit wears a quiet and crafty smile. Yet, for its sake, when all others have given him up for dead, she sometimes doubts whether she is a widow.

But, our business is with the husband. We must hurry after him, along the street, ere he lose his individuality, and melt into the great mass of London life. It would be vain searching for him there. Let us follow close at his heels, therefore, until, after several superfluous turns and doublings, we find him comfortably established by the fireside of a small apartment, previously bespoken. He is in the next street to his own, and at his journey's end. He can scarcely trust his good fortune, in having got thither unperceived—recollecting that, at one time, he was delayed by the throng, in the very focus of a lighted lantern; and, again, there were footsteps, that seemed to tread behind his own, distinct from the multitudinous tramp around him; and, anon, he heard a voice shouting afar, and fancied that it called his name. Doubtless, a dozen busy-bodies had been watching him, and told his wife the whole affair. Poor Wakefield! Little knowest thou thine own insignificance in this great world! No mortal eye but mine has traced thee. Go quietly to thy bed, foolish man; and, on the morrow, if thou wilt be wise, get thee home to good Mrs. Wakefield, and tell her the truth. Remove not thyself, even for a little week, from thy place in her chaste bosom. Were she, for a single moment, to deem thee dead, or lost, or lastingly divided from her, thou wouldst be woefully conscious of a change in thy true wife, forever after. It is perilous to make a chasm in human affections; not that they gape so long and wide—but so quickly close again!

Almost repenting of his frolic, or whatever it may be termed, Wakefield lies down betimes, and starting from his first nap, spreads forth his arms into the wide and solitary waste of the unaccustomed bed. 'No'—thinks he, gathering the bed-clothes about him—'I will not sleep alone another night.'

In the morning, he rises earlier than usual, and sets himself to consider what he really means to do. Such are his loose and rambling modes of thought, that he has taken this very singular step, with the consciousness of a purpose, indeed, but without being able to define it sufficiently for his own contemplation. The vagueness of the project, and the convulsive effort with which he plunges into the execution of it, are equally characteristic of a feeble-minded man. Wakefield sifts his ideas, however, as minutely as he may, and finds himself curious to know the progress of matters at home—how his exemplary wife will endure her widowhood, of a week; and, briefly, how the little sphere of creatures and circumstances, in which he was a central object, will be affected by his removal. A morbid vanity, therefore, lies nearest the bottom of the affair. But, how is he to attain his ends? Not, certainly, by keeping close in this comfortable lodging, where, though he slept and awoke in the next street to his home, he is as effectually abroad, as if the stage-coach had been whirling him away all night. Yet, should he reappear, the whole project is knocked in the head. His poor brains being hopelessly puzzled with this dilemma, he at length ventures out, partly resolving to cross the head of the street, and send one hasty glance towards his forsaken domicile. Habit—for he is a man of habits—takes him by the hand, and guides him, wholly unaware, to his own door, where, just at the critical moment, he is aroused by the scraping of his foot upon the step. Wakefield! whither are you going?

At that instant, his fate was turning on the pivot. Little dreaming of the doom to which his first backward step devotes him, he hurries away, breathless with agitation hitherto unfelt, and hardly dares turn his head, at the distant corner. Can it be, that nobody caught sight of him? Will not the whole household—the decent Mrs. Wakefield, the smart maid-servant, and the dirty little foot-boy—raise a hue-and-cry, through London streets, in pursuit of their fugitive lord and master? Wonderful escape! He gathers courage to pause and look homeward, but is perplexed with a sense of change about the familiar edifice, such as affects us all, when, after a separation of months or years, we again see some hill or lake, or work of art, with which we were friends, of old. In ordinary cases, this indescribable impression is caused by the comparison and contrast between our imperfect reminiscences and the reality. In Wakefield, the magic of a single night has wrought a similar transformation, because, in that brief period, a great moral change has been effected. But this is a secret from himself. Before leaving the spot, he catches a far and momentary glimpse of his wife, passing athwart the front window, with her face turned towards the head of the street. The crafty nincompoop takes to his heels, scared with the idea, that, among a thousand such atoms of mortality, her eye must have detected him. Right glad is his heart, though his brain be somewhat dizzy, when he finds himself by the coal-fire of his lodgings.

So much for the commencement of this long whim-wham.[1] After the initial conception, and the stirring up of the man's sluggish temperament to put it in practice, the whole matter evolves itself in a natural train. We may suppose him, as the result of deep deliberation, buying a new wig, of reddish hair, and selecting sundry garments, in a fashion unlike his customary suit of brown, from a Jew's old-clothes bag. It is accomplished. Wakefield is another man. The new system being now established, a retrograde movement to the old would be almost as difficult as the step that placed him in his unparalleled position. Furthermore, he is rendered obstinate by a sulkiness, occasionally incident to his temper, and brought on, at present, by the inadequate sensation which he conceives to have been produced in the bosom of Mrs. Wakefield. He will not go back until she be frightened half to death. Well, twice or thrice has she passed before his sight, each time with a heavier step, a paler cheek, and more anxious brow; and, in the third week of his non-appearance, he detects a portent of evil entering the house, in the guise of an apothecary. Next day, the knocker is muffled. Towards night-fall, comes the chariot of a physician, and deposits its big-wigged and solemn burthen at Wakefield's door, whence, after a quarter of an hour's visit, he emerges, perchance the herald of a funeral. Dear woman! Will she die? By this time, Wakefield is excited to something like energy of feeling, but still lingers away from his wife's bedside, pleading with his conscience, that she must not be disturbed at such a juncture. If aught else restrains him, he does not know it. In the course of a few weeks, she gradually recovers; the crisis is over; her heart is sad, perhaps, but quiet; and, let him return soon or late, it will never be feverish for him again. Such ideas glim-

---

[1] Fantastic notion, odd fancy or whim.

mer through the mist of Wakefield's mind, and render him indistinctly conscious, that an almost impassable gulf divides his hired apartment from his former home. 'It is but in the next street!' he sometimes says. Fool! it is in another world. Hitherto, he has put off his return from one particular day to another; henceforward, he leaves the precise time undetermined. Not to-morrow—probably next week—pretty soon. Poor man! The dead have nearly as much chance of re-visiting their earthly homes, as the self-banished Wakefield.

Would that I had a folio to write, instead of an article of a dozen pages! Then might I exemplify how an influence, beyond our control, lays its strong hand on every deed which we do, and weaves its consequences into an iron tissue of necessity. Wakefield is spell-bound. We must leave him, for ten years or so, to haunt around his house, without once crossing the threshold, and to be faithful to his wife, with all the affection of which his heart is capable, while he is slowly fading out of hers. Long since, it must be remarked, he has lost the perception of singularity in his conduct.

Now for a scene! Amid the throng of a London street, we distinguish a man, now waxing elderly, with few characteristics to attract careless observers, yet bearing, in his whole aspect, the hand-writing of no common fate, for such as have the skill to read it. He is meagre; his low and narrow forehead is deeply wrinkled; his eyes, small and lustreless, sometimes wander apprehensively about him, but oftener seem to look inward. He bends his head, but moves with an indescribable obliquity of gait, as if unwilling to display his full front to the world. Watch him, long enough to see what we have described, and you will allow, that circumstances—which often produce remarkable men from nature's ordinary handiwork—have produced one such here. Next, leaving him to sidle along the footwalk, cast your eyes in the opposite direction, where a portly female, considerably in the wane of life, with a prayer-book in her hand, is proceeding to yonder church. She has the placid mien of settled widowhood. Her regrets have either died away, or have become so essential to her heart, that they would be poorly exchanged for joy. Just as the lean man and well conditioned woman are passing, a slight obstruction occurs, and brings these two figures directly in contact. Their hands touch; the pressure of the crowd forces her bosom against his shoulder; they stand, face to face, staring into each other's eyes. After a ten years' separation, thus Wakefield meets his wife!

The throng eddies away, and carries them asunder. The sober widow, resuming her former pace, proceeds to church, but pauses in the portal, and throws a perplexed glance along the street. She passes in, however, opening her prayer-book as she goes. And the man? With so wild a face, that busy and selfish London stands to gaze after him, he hurries to his lodgings, bolts the door, and throws himself upon the bed. The latent feelings of years break out; his feeble mind acquires a brief energy from their strength; all the miserable strangeness of his life is revealed to him at a glance; and he cries out, passionately—'Wakefield! Wakefield! You are mad!'

Perhaps he was so. The singularity of his situation must have so moulded him to itself, that, considered in regard to his fellow-creatures and the business of life, he could not be said to possess his right mind. He had contrived, or rather he had happened, to dissever himself from the world—to vanish—to give up his place and privileges with living men, without being admitted among the dead. The life of a hermit is nowise parallel to his. He was in the bustle of the city, as of old; but the crowd swept by, and saw him not; he was, we may figuratively say, always beside his wife, and at his hearth, yet must never feel the warmth of the one, nor the affection of the other. It was Wakefield's unprecedented fate, to retain his original share of human sympathies, and to be still involved in human interests, while he had lost his reciprocal influence on them. It would be a most curious speculation, to trace out the effect of such circumstances on his heart and intellect, separately, and in unison. Yet, changed as he was, he would seldom be conscious of it, but deem himself the same man as ever; glimpses of the truth, indeed, would come, but only for the moment; and still he would keep saying—'I shall soon go back!'—nor reflect, that he had been saying so for twenty years.

I conceive, also, that these twenty years would appear, in the retrospect, scarcely longer than the week to which Wakefield had at first limited his absence. He would look on the affair as no more than an interlude in the main business of his life. When, after a little while more, he should deem it time to re-enter his parlor, his wife would clap her hands for joy, on beholding the middle-aged Mr. Wakefield. Alas, what a mistake! Would Time but await the close of our favorite follies, we should be young men, all of us, and till Doom's Day.

One evening, in the twentieth year since he vanished, Wakefield is taking his customary walk towards the dwelling which he still calls his own. It is a gusty night of autumn, with frequent showers, that patter down upon the pavement, and are gone, before a man can put up his umbrella. Pausing near the house, Wakefield discerns, through the parlor-windows of the second floor, the red glow, and the glimmer and fitful flash, of a comfortable fire. On the ceiling, appears a grotesque shadow of good Mrs. Wakefield. The cap, the nose and chin, and the broad waist, form an admirable caricature, which dances, moreover, with the up-flickering and down-sinking blaze, almost too merrily for the shade of an elderly widow. At this instant, a shower chances to fall, and is driven, by the unmannerly gust, full into Wakefield's face and bosom. He is quite penetrated with its autumnal chill. Shall he stand, wet and shivering here, when his own hearth has a good fire to warm him, and his own wife will run to fetch the gray coat and small-clothes, which, doubtless, she has kept carefully in the closet of their bed-chamber? No! Wakefield is no such fool. He ascends the steps—heavily!—for twenty years have stiffened his legs, since he came down—but he knows it not. Stay, Wakefield! Would you go to the sole home that is left you? Then step into your grave! The door opens. As he passes in, we have a parting glimpse of his visage, and recognize the crafty smile, which was the precursor of the little joke, that he has ever since been playing off at his wife's expense. How unmercifully has he quizzed the poor woman! Well; a good night's rest to Wakefield!

This happy event—supposing it to be such—could only have occurred at an unpremeditated moment. We will not follow our friend across the threshold. He has left us much food for thought, a portion of which shall lend its wisdom to a moral; and be shaped into a figure. Amid the seeming confusion of our mysterious world, individuals are so nicely adjusted to a system, and systems to one another, and to a whole, that, by stepping aside for a moment, a man exposes himself to a fearful risk of losing his place forever. Like Wakefield, he may become, as it were, the Outcast of the Universe.

1835

The May-Pole of Merry Mount[1]

> There is an admirable foundation for a philosophic romance, in the curious history of the early settlement of Mount Wollaston, or Merry Mount. In the slight sketch here attempted, the facts, recorded on the grave pages of our New England annalists, have wrought themselves, almost spontaneously,

---

[1]See William Bradford's *Of Plymouth Plantation* and Thomas Morton's *The New English Canaan* in Part I of this volume for accounts of the incidents related here.

into a sort of allegory. The masques, mummeries, and festive customs, described in the text, are in accordance with the manners of the age. Authority on these points may be found in Strutt's Book of English Sports and Pastimes.[2]

Bright were the days at Merry Mount, when the May-Pole was the banner-staff of that gay colony! They who reared it, should their banner be triumphant, were to pour sunshine over New England's rugged hills, and scatter flower-seeds throughout the soil. Jollity and gloom were contending for an empire. Midsummer eve[3] had come, bringing deep verdure to the forest, and roses in her lap, of a more vivid hue than the tender buds of Spring. But May, or her mirthful spirit, dwelt all the year round at Merry Mount, sporting with the Summer months, and revelling with Autumn, and basking in the glow of Winter's fireside. Through a world of toil and care, she flitted with a dream-like smile, and came hither to find a home among the light-some hearts of Merry Mount.

Never had the May-Pole been so gaily decked as at sunset on midsummer eve. This venerated emblem was a pine tree, which had preserved the slender grace of youth, while it equalled the loftiest height of the old wood monarchs. From its top streamed a silken banner, colored like the rainbow. Down nearly to the ground, the pole was dressed with birchen boughs, and others of the liveliest green, and some with silvery leaves, fastened by ribbons that fluttered in fantastic knots of twenty different colors, but no sad ones. Garden flowers, and blossoms of the wilderness, laughed gladly forth amid the verdure, so fresh and dewy, that they must have grown by magic on that happy pine tree. Where this green and flowery splendor terminated, the shaft of the May-Pole was stained with the seven brilliant hues of the banner at its top. On the lowest green bough hung an abundant wreath of roses, some that had been gathered in the sunniest spots of the forest, and others, of still richer blush, which the colonists had reared from English seed. Oh, people of the Golden Age, the chief of your husbandry, was to raise flowers!

But what was the wild throng that stood hand in hand about the May-Pole? It could not be, that the Fauns and Nymphs, when driven from their classic groves and homes of ancient fable, had sought refuge, as all the persecuted did, in the fresh woods of the West. These were Gothic monsters, though perhaps of Grecian ancestry. On the shoulders of a comely youth, uprose the head and branching antlers of a stag; a second, human in all other points, had the grim visage of a wolf; a third, still with the trunk and limbs of a mortal man, showed the beard and horns of a venerable he-goat. There was the likeness of a bear erect, brute in all but his hind legs, which were adorned with pink silk stockings. And here again, almost as wondrous, stood a real bear of the dark forest, lending each of his fore paws to the grasp of a human hand, and as ready for the dance as any in that circle. His inferior nature rose half-way, to meet his companions as they stooped. Other faces wore the similitude of man or woman, but distorted or extravagant, with red noses pendulous before their mouths, which seemed of awful depth, and stretched from ear to ear in an eternal fit of laughter. Here might be seen the Salvage Man,[4] well known in heraldry, hairy as a baboon, and girdled with green leaves. By his side, a nobler figure, but still a counterfeit, appeared an Indian hunter, with feathery crest and wampum belt. Many of this strange company wore fools-caps, and had little bells appended to their garments, tinkling with a silvery sound, responsive to the inaudible music of their gleesome spirits. Some youths and maidens were of soberer garb, yet well maintained their places in the irregu-

---

[2]*The Sports and Pastimes of the People of England* (1801), by Joseph Strutt (1749–1802)
[3]The evening before Midsummer Day (June 24), the feast of St. John the Baptist; it occurs near the time of the summer solstice.

[4]Variant of "savage man," dressed in foliage (figure out of medieval pageantry).

lar throng, by the expression of wild revelry upon their features. Such were the colonists of Merry Mount, as they stood in the broad smile of sunset, round their venerated May-Pole.

Had a wanderer, bewildered in the melancholy forest, heard their mirth, and stolen a half-affrighted glance, he might have fancied them the crew of Comus,[5] some already transformed to brutes, some midway between man and beast, and the others rioting in the flow of tipsey jollity that foreran the change. But a band of Puritans, who watched the scene, invisible themselves, compared the masques to those devils and ruined souls, with whom their superstition peopled the black wilderness.

Within the ring of monsters, appeared the two airiest forms, that had ever trodden on any more solid footing than a purple and golden cloud. One was a youth, in glistening apparel, with a scarf of the rainbow pattern crosswise on his breast. His right hand held a gilded staff, the ensign[6] of high dignity among the revellers, and his left grasped the slender fingers of a fair maiden, not less gaily decorated than himself. Bright roses glowed in contrast with the dark and glossy curls of each, and were scattered round their feet, or had sprung up spontaneously there. Behind this lightsome couple, so close to the May-Pole that its boughs shaded his jovial face, stood the figure of an English priest, canonically dressed, yet decked with flowers, in heathen fashion, and wearing a chaplet[7] of the native vine leaves. By the riot of his rolling eye, and the pagan decorations of his holy garb, he seemed the wildest monster there, and the very Comus of the crew.

'Votaries of the May-Pole,' cried the flower-decked priest, 'merrily, all day long, have the woods echoed to your mirth. But be this your merriest hour, my hearts! Lo, here stand the Lord and Lady of the May, whom I, a clerk of Oxford,[8] and high priest of Merry Mount, am presently to join in holy matrimony. Up with your nimble spirits, ye morrice-dancers, green-men, and glee-maidens,[9] bears and wolves, and horned gentlemen! Come; a chorus now, rich with the old mirth of Merry England, and the wilder glee of this fresh forest; and then a dance, to show the youthful pair what life is made of, and how airily they should go through it! All ye that love the May-Pole, lend your voices to the nuptial song of the Lord and Lady of the May!'

This wedlock was more serious than most affairs of Merry Mount, where jest and delusion, trick and fantasy, kept up a continued carnival. The Lord and Lady of the May, though their titles must be laid down at sunset, were really and truly to be partners for the dance of life, beginning the measure that same bright eve. The wreath of roses, that hung from the lowest green bough of the May-Pole, had been twined for them, and would be thrown over both their heads, in symbol of their flowery union. When the priest had spoken, therefore, a riotous uproar burst from the rout of monstrous figures.

'Begin you the stave,[10] reverend Sir,' cried they all; 'and never did the woods ring to such a merry peal, as we of the May-Pole shall send up!'

Immediately a prelude of pipe, cittern, and viol,[11] touched with practised minstrelsy, began to play from a neighboring thicket, in such a mirthful cadence, that the boughs of the May-Pole quivered to the sound. But the May Lord, he of the gilded staff, chancing to look into his Lady's eyes, was wonderstruck at the almost pensive glance that met his own.

'Edith, sweet Lady of the May,' whispered he, reproachfully, 'is yon wreath of

---

[5] In classical myth, god of revelry; cf. John Milton's masque, *Comus* (1634), in which the title character is a sorcerer able to change people into animals.
[6] Flag or banner.
[7] Crown.
[8] Lay clergyman.

[9] Colorfully dressed folk dancers (originally "Moorish"), men dressed in green, and women minstrels or singers.
[10] Stanza, or set of verses.
[11] Musical instruments: a flute, a lute (cf. guitar), and a stringed instrument (cf. violin).

roses a garland to hang above our graves, that you look so sad? Oh, Edith, this is
our golden time! Tarnish it not by any pensive shadow of the mind; for it may be,
that nothing of futurity will be brighter than the mere remembrance of what is
now passing.'

'That was the very thought that saddened me! How came it in your mind too?'
said Edith, in a still lower tone than he; for it was high treason to be sad at Merry
Mount. 'Therefore do I sigh amid this festive music. And besides, dear Edgar, I
struggle as with a dream, and fancy that these shapes of our jovial friends are visionary, and their mirth unreal, and that we are no true Lord and Lady of the
May. What is the mystery in my heart?'

Just then, as if a spell had loosened them, down came a little shower of withering rose leaves from the May-Pole. Alas, for the young lovers! No sooner had
their hearts glowed with real passion, then they were sensible of something vague
and unsubstantial in their former pleasures, and felt a dreary presentiment of inevitable change. From the moment that they truly loved, they had subjected themselves to earth's doom of care, and sorrow, and troubled joy, and had no more a
home at Merry Mount. That was Edith's mystery. Now leave we the priest to
marry them, and the masquers to sport round the May-Pole, till the last sunbeam
be withdrawn from its summit, and the shadows of the forest mingle gloomily in
the dance. Meanwhile, we may discover who these gay people were.

Two hundred years ago, and more, the old world and its inhabitants became
mutually weary of each other. Men voyaged by thousands to the West; some to
barter glass beads, and such like jewels, for the furs of the Indian hunter; some to
conquer virgin empires; and one stern band to pray. But none of these motives
had much weight with the colonists of Merry Mount. Their leaders were men who
had sported so long with life, that when Thought and Wisdom came, even these
unwelcome guests were led astray, by the crowd of vanities which they should
have put to flight. Erring Thought and perverted Wisdom were made to put on
masques, and play the fool. The men of whom we speak, after losing the heart's
fresh gaiety, imagined a wild philosophy of pleasure, and came hither to act out
their latest day-dream. They gathered followers from all that giddy tribe, whose
whole life is like the festal[12] days of soberer men. In their train were minstrels, not
unknown in London streets; wandering players, whose theatres had been the halls
of noblemen; mummers,[13] rope-dancers, and mountebanks,[14] who would long be
missed at wakes, church-ales, and fairs; in a word, mirthmakers of every sort, such
as abounded in that age, but now began to be discountenanced by the rapid
growth of Puritanism. Light had their footsteps been on land, and as lightly they
came across the sea. Many had been maddened by their previous troubles into a
gay despair; others were as madly gay in the flush of youth, like the May Lord and
his Lady; but whatever might be the quality of their mirth, old and young were
gay at Merry Mount. The young deemed themselves happy. The elder spirits, if
they knew that mirth was but the counterfeit of happiness, yet followed the false
shadow wilfully, because at least her garments glittered brightest. Sworn triflers of
a lifetime, they would not venture among the sober truths of life, not even to be
truly blest.

All the hereditary pastimes of Old England were transplanted hither. The
King of Christmas was duly crowned, and the Lord of Misrule[15] bore potent sway.
On the eve of Saint John,[16] they felled whole acres of the forest to make bonfires,
and danced by the blaze all night, crowned with garlands, and throwing flowers
into the flame. At harvest time, though their crop was of the smallest, they made

---

[12]Feast or festive.
[13]Masked merrymakers.
[14]Charlatans, quacks, swindlers.

[15]The chosen leader of the revels.
[16]Midsummer Eve, June 23.

an image with the sheaves of Indian corn, and wreathed it with autumnal gar-lands, and bore it home triumphantly. But what chiefly characterized the colonists of Merry Mount, was their veneration for the May-Pole. It has made their true history a poet's tale. Spring decked the hallowed emblem with young blossoms and fresh green boughs; Summer brought roses of the deepest blush, and the perfected foliage of the forest; Autumn enriched it with that red and yellow gor-geousness, which converts each wild-wood leaf into a painted flower; and Winter silvered it with sleet, and hung it round with icicles, till it flashed in the cold sun-shine, itself a frozen sunbeam. Thus each alternate season did homage to the May-Pole, and paid it a tribute of its own richest splendor. Its votaries danced round it, once, at least, in every month; sometimes they called it their religion, or their altar; but always, it was the banner-staff of Merry Mount.

Unfortunately, there were men in the new world, of a sterner faith than these May-Pole worshippers. Not far from Merry Mount was a settlement of Puritans, most dismal wretches, who said their prayers before daylight, and then wrought in the forest or the cornfield, till evening made it prayer time again. Their weapons were always at hand, to shoot down the straggling savage. When they met in con-clave, it was never to keep up the old English mirth, but to hear sermons three hours long, or to proclaim bounties on the heads of wolves and the scalps of Indi-ans. Their festivals were fast-days, and their chief pastime the singing of psalms. Woe to the youth or maiden, who did but dream of a dance! The selectman nod-ded to the constable; and there sat the light-heeled reprobate in the stocks; or if he danced, it was round the whipping-post, which might be termed the Puritan May-Pole.

A party of these grim Puritans, toiling through the difficult woods, each with a horse-load of iron armor to burthen his footsteps, would sometimes draw near the sunny precincts of Merry Mount. There were the silken colonists, sporting round their May-Pole; perhaps teaching a bear to dance, or striving to communicate their mirth to the grave Indian; or masquerading in the skins of deer and wolves, which they had hunted for that especial purpose. Often, the whole colony were playing at blindman's buff, magistrates and all with their eyes bandaged, except a single scape-goat, whom the blinded sinners pursued by the tinkling of the bells at his garments. Once, it is said, they were seen following a flower-decked corpse, with merriment and festive music, to his grave. But did the dead man laugh? In their quietest times, they sang ballads and told tales, for the edification of their pious visiters; or perplexed them with juggling tricks; or grinned at them through horse-collars; and when sport itself grew wearisome, they made game of their own stupidity, and began a yawning match. At the very least of these enormities, the men of iron shook their heads and frowned so darkly, that the revellers looked up, imagining that a momentary cloud had overcast the sunshine, which was to be perpetual there. On the other hand, the Puritans affirmed, that, when a psalm was pealing from their place of worship, the echo, which the forest sent them back, seemed often like the chorus of a jolly catch, closing with a roar of laughter. Who but the fiend, and his bond-slaves, the crew of Merry Mount, had thus dis-turbed them! In due time, a feud arose, stern and bitter on one side, and as seri-ous on the other as any thing could be, among such light spirits as had sworn al-legiance to the May-Pole. The future complexion of New England was involved in this important quarrel. Should the grisly saints establish their jurisdiction over the gay sinners, then would their spirits darken all the clime, and make it a land of clouded visages, of hard toil, of sermon and psalm, forever. But should the banner-staff of Merry Mount be fortunate, sunshine would break upon the hills, and flowers would beautify the forest, and late posterity do homage to the May-Pole!

After these authentic passages from history, we return to the nuptials of the

Lord and Lady of the May. Alas! we have delayed too long, and must darken our tale too suddenly. As we glance again at the May-Pole, a solitary sunbeam is fading from the summit, and leaves only a faint golden tinge, blended with the hues of the rainbow banner. Even that dim light is now withdrawn, relinquishing the whole domain of Merry Mount to the evening gloom, which has rushed so instantaneously from the black surrounding woods. But some of these black shadows have rushed forth in human shape.

Yes: with the setting sun, the last day of mirth had passed from Merry Mount. The ring of gay masquers was disordered and broken; the stag lowered his antlers in dismay; the wolf grew weaker than a lamb; the bells of the morrice-dancers tinkled with tremulous affright. The Puritans had played a characteristic part in the May-Pole mummeries. Their dark-some figures were intermixed with the wild shapes of their foes, and made the scene a picture of the moment, when waking thoughts start up amid the scattered fantasies of a dream. The leader of the hostile party stood in the centre of the circle, while the rout of monsters cowered around him, like evil spirits in the presence of a dread magician. No fantastic foolery could look him in the face. So stern was the energy of his aspect, that the whole man, visage, frame, and soul, seemed wrought of iron, gifted with life and thought, yet all of one substance with his head-piece and breast-plate. It was the Puritan of Puritans; it was Endicott[17] himself!

'Stand off, priest of Baal!'[18] said he, with a grim frown, and laying no reverent hand upon the surplice. 'I know thee, Blackstone![19] Thou art the man, who couldst not abide the rule even of thine own corrupted church,[20] and hast come hither to preach iniquity, and to give example of it in thy life. But now shall it be seen that the Lord hath sanctified this wilderness for his peculiar people. Woe unto them that would defile it! And first for this flower-decked abomination, the altar of thy worship!'

And with his keen sword, Endicott assaulted the hallowed May-Pole. Nor long did it resist his arm. It groaned with a dismal sound; it showered leaves and rose-buds upon the remorseless enthusiast; and finally, with all its green boughs, and ribbons, and flowers, symbolic of departed pleasures, down fell the banner-staff of Merry Mount. As it sank, tradition says, the evening sky grew darker, and the woods threw forth a more sombre shadow.

'There,' cried Endicott, looking triumphantly on his work, 'there lies the only May-Pole in New England! The thought is strong within me, that, by its fall, is shadowed forth the fate of light and idle mirth-makers, amongst us and our posterity. Amen, saith John Endicott!'

'Amen!' echoed his followers.

But the votaries of the May-Pole gave one groan for their idol. At the sound, the Puritan leader glanced at the crew of Comus, each a figure of broad mirth, yet, at this moment, strangely expressive of sorrow and dismay.

'Valiant captain,' quoth Peter Palfrey, the Ancient[21] of the band, 'what order shall be taken with the prisoners?'

'I thought not to repent me of cutting down a May-Pole,' replied Endicott, 'yet now I could find in my heart to plant it again, and give each of these bestial pagans one other dance round their idol. It would have served rarely for a whipping-post!'

'But there are pine trees enow,' suggested the lieutenant.

---

[17]John Endicott (c. 1589–1665), served in several offices, including governor, of the Massachusetts Bay Colony.
[18]Considered sun god or god of fertility by ancient Semitic people; hence a false god, considered satanic by the Puritans.
[19]"Did Governor Endicott speak less positively, we should suspect a mistake here. The Rev. Mr. Blackstone, though an eccentric, is not known to have been an immoral man. We rather doubt his identity with the priest of Merry Mount" (Hawthorne's note).
[20]I.e., the Church of England.
[21]Ensign, or flag-bearer.

'True, good Ancient,' said the leader. 'Wherefore, bind the heathen crew, and bestow on them a small matter of stripes apiece, as earnest[22] of our future justice. Set some of the rogues in the stocks to rest themselves, so soon as Providence shall bring us to one of our own well-ordered settlements, where such accommodations may be found. Further penalties, such as branding and cropping of ears, shall be thought of hereafter.'

'How many stripes for the priest?' inquired Ancient Palfrey.

'None as yet,' answered Endicott, bending his iron frown upon the culprit. 'It must be for the Great and General Court[23] to determine, whether stripes and long imprisonment, and other grievous penalty, may atone for his transgressions. Let him look to himself! For such as violate our civil order, it may be permitted us to show mercy. But woe to the wretch that troubleth our religion!'

'And this dancing bear,' resumed the officer. 'Must he share the stripes of his fellows?'

'Shoot him through the head!' said the energetic Puritan. 'I suspect witchcraft in the beast.'

'Here be a couple of shining ones,' continued Peter Palfrey, pointing his weapon at the Lord and Lady of the May. 'They seem to be of high station among these mis-doers. Methinks their dignity will not be fitted with less than a double share of stripes.'

Endicott rested on his sword, and closely surveyed the dress and aspect of the hapless pair. There they stood, pale, downcast, and apprehensive. Yet there was an air of mutual support, and of pure affection, seeking aid and giving it, that showed them to be man and wife, with the sanction of a priest upon their love. The youth, in the peril of the moment, had dropped his gilded staff, and thrown his arm about the Lady of the May, who leaned against his breast, too lightly to burthen him, but with weight enough to express that their destinies were linked together, for good or evil. They looked first at each other, and then into the grim captain's face. There they stood, in the first hour of wedlock, while the idle plea-sures, of which their companions were the emblems, had given place to the ster-nest cares of life, personified by the dark Puritans. But never had their youthful beauty seemed so pure and high, as when its glow was chastened by adversity.

'Youth,' said Endicott, 'ye stand in an evil case, thou and thy maiden wife. Make ready presently; for I am minded that ye shall both have a token to remem-ber your wedding-day!'

'Stern man,' cried the May Lord, 'how can I move thee? Were the means at hand, I would resist to the death. Being powerless, I entreat! Do with me as thou wilt; but let Edith go untouched!'

'Not so,' replied the immitigable zealot. 'We are not wont to show an idle cour-tesy to that sex, which requireth the stricter discipline. What sayest thou, maid? Shall thy silken bridegroom suffer thy share of the penalty, besides his own?'

'Be it death,' said Edith, 'and lay it all on me!'

Truly, as Endicott had said, the poor lovers stood in a woeful case. Their foes were triumphant, their friends captive and abased, their home desolate, the be-nighted wilderness around them, and a rigorous destiny, in the shape of the Puri-tan leader, their only guide. Yet the deepening twilight could not altogether con-ceal, that the iron man was softened; he smiled, at the fair spectacle of early love; he almost sighed, for the inevitable blight of early hopes.

'The troubles of life have come hastily on this young couple,' observed Endi-cott. 'We will see how they comport themselves under their present trials, ere we burthen them with greater. If, among the spoil, there be any garments of a more

---

[22]Promise.
[23]Legislature.

decent fashion, let them be put upon this May Lord and his Lady, instead of their glistening vanities. Look to it, some of you.'

'And shall not the youth's hair be cut?' asked Peter Palfrey, looking with abhorrence at the love-lock and long glossy curls of the young man.

'Crop it forthwith, and that in the true pumpkin-shell fashion,'[24] answered the captain. 'Then bring them along with us, but more gently than their fellows. There be qualities in the youth, which may make him valiant to fight, and sober to toil, and pious to pray; and in the maiden, that may fit her to become a mother in our Israel,[25] bringing up babes in better nurture than her own hath been. Nor think ye, young ones, that they are the happiest, even in our lifetime of a moment, who misspend it in dancing round a May-Pole!'

And Endicott, the severest Puritan of all who laid the rock-foundation of New England, lifted the wreath of roses from the ruin of the May-Pole, and threw it, with his own gauntleted hand, over the heads of the Lord and Lady of the May. It was a deed of prophecy. As the moral gloom of the world overpowers all systematic gaiety, even so was their home of wild mirth made desolate amid the sad forest. They returned to it no more. But, as their flowery garland was wreathed of the brightest roses that had grown there, so, in the tie that united them, were intertwined all the purest and best of their early joys. They went heavenward, supporting each other along the difficult path which it was their lot to tread, and never wasted one regretful thought on the vanities of Merry Mount.

1836

The Minister's Black Veil

A PARABLE[1]

The Sexton stood in the porch of Milford meeting-house, pulling lustily at the bell-rope. The old people of the village came stooping along the street. Children, with bright faces, tript merrily beside their parents, or mimicked a graver gait, in the conscious dignity of their Sunday clothes. Spruce bachelors looked sidelong at the pretty maidens, and fancied that the Sabbath sunshine made them prettier than on week-days. When the throng had mostly streamed into the porch, the sexton began to toll the bell, keeping his eye on the Reverend Mr. Hooper's door. The first glimpse of the clergyman's figure was the signal for the bell to cease its summons.

'But what has good Parson Hooper got upon his face?' cried the sexton in astonishment.

All within hearing immediately turned about, and beheld the semblance of Mr. Hooper, pacing slowly his meditative way towards the meeting-house. With one accord they started, expressing more wonder than if some strange minister were coming to dust the cushions of Mr. Hooper's pulpit.

'Are you sure it is our parson?' inquired Goodman Gray of the sexton.

'Of a certainty it is good Mr. Hooper,' replied the sexton. 'He was to have exchanged pulpits with Parson Shute of Westbury; but Parson Shute sent to excuse himself yesterday, being to preach a funeral sermon.'

---

[24]I.e., "round-head" or close-cropped, after the Puritan style. The Puritans considered long hair a sign of sinful sensuousness.
[25]I.e., the New Jerusalem of the New World.
[1]"Another clergyman in New England, Mr. Joseph Moody, of York, Maine, who died about eighty years since, made himself remarkable by the same eccentricity that is here related of the Reverend Mr. Hooper. In his case, however, the symbol had a different import. In early life he had accidentally killed a beloved friend; and from that day till the hour of his own death, he hid his face from men" (Hawthorne's note).

The cause of so much amazement may appear sufficiently slight. Mr. Hooper, a gentlemanly person of about thirty, though still a bachelor, was dressed with due clerical neatness, as if a careful wife had starched his band, and brushed the weekly dust from his Sunday's garb. There was but one thing remarkable in his appearance. Swathed about his forehead, and hanging down over his face, so low as to be shaken by his breath, Mr. Hooper had on a black veil. On a nearer view, it seemed to consist of two folds of crape, which entirely concealed his features, except the mouth and chin, but probably did not intercept his sight, farther than to give a darkened aspect to all living and inanimate things. With this gloomy shade before him, good Mr. Hooper walked onward, at a slow and quiet pace, stooping somewhat and looking on the ground, as is customary with abstracted men, yet nodding kindly to those of his parishioners who still waited on the meeting-house steps. But so wonder-struck were they, that his greeting hardly met with a return.

'I can't really feel as if good Mr. Hooper's face was behind that piece of crape,' said the sexton.

'I don't like it,' muttered an old woman, as she hobbled into the meeting-house. 'He has changed himself into something awful, only by hiding his face.'

'Our parson has gone mad!' cried Goodman Gray, following him across the threshold.

A rumor of some unaccountable phenomenon had preceded Mr. Hooper into the meeting-house, and set all the congregation astir. Few could refrain from twisting their heads towards the door; many stood upright, and turned directly about; while several little boys clambered upon the seats, and came down again with a terrible racket. There was a general bustle, a rustling of the women's gowns and shuffling of the men's feet, greatly at variance with that hushed repose which should attend the entrance of the minister. But Mr. Hooper appeared not to notice the perturbation of his people. He entered with an almost noiseless step, bent his head mildly to the pews on each side, and bowed as he passed his oldest parishioner, a white-haired great-grandsire, who occupied an arm-chair in the centre of the aisle. It was strange to observe, how slowly this venerable man became conscious of something singular in the appearance of his pastor. He seemed not fully to partake of the prevailing wonder, till Mr. Hooper had ascended the stairs, and showed himself in the pulpit, face to face with his congregation, except for the black veil. That mysterious emblem was never once withdrawn. It shook with his measured breath as he gave out the psalm; it threw its obscurity between him and the holy page, as he read the Scriptures; and while he prayed, the veil lay heavily on his uplifted countenance. Did he seek to hide it from the dread Being whom he was addressing?

Such was the effect of this simple piece of crape, that more than one woman of delicate nerves was forced to leave the meeting-house. Yet perhaps the pale-faced congregation was almost as fearful a sight to the minister, as his black veil to them.

Mr. Hooper had the reputation of a good preacher, but not an energetic one: he strove to win his people heavenward, by mild persuasive influences, rather than to drive them thither, by the thunders of the Word. The sermon which he now delivered, was marked by the same characteristics of style and manner, as the general series of his pulpit oratory. But there was something, either in the sentiment of the discourse itself, or in the imagination of the auditors, which made it greatly the most powerful effort that they had ever heard from their pastor's lips. It was tinged, rather more darkly than usual, with the gentle gloom of Mr. Hooper's temperament. The subject had reference to secret sin, and those sad mysteries which we hide from our nearest and dearest, and would fain conceal from our own consciousness, even forgetting that the Omniscient can detect them. A subtle power was breathed into his words. Each member of the congregation, the most innocent girl, and the man of hardened breast, felt as if the preacher had crept upon them, behind his awful veil, and discovered their hoarded iniquity of deed or thought. Many spread their clasped hands on their bosoms. There was nothing terrible in what Mr. Hooper said; at least, no violence; and yet, with every tremor of his melancholy voice, the hearers quaked. An unsought pathos came hand in hand with awe. So sensible were the audience of some unwonted attribute in their minister, that they longed for a breath of wind to blow aside the veil, almost believing that a stranger's visage would be discovered, though the form, gesture, and voice were those of Mr. Hooper.

At the close of the services, the people hurried out with indecorous confusion, eager to communicate their pent-up amazement, and conscious of lighter spirits, the moment they lost sight of the black veil. Some gathered in little circles, huddled closely together, with their mouths all whispering in the centre; some went homeward alone, wrapt in silent meditation; some talked loudly, and profaned the Sabbath-day with ostentatious laughter. A few shook their sagacious heads, intimating that they could penetrate the mystery; while one or two affirmed that there was no mystery at all, but only that Mr. Hooper's eyes were so weakened by the midnight lamp, as to require a shade. After a brief interval, forth came good Mr. Hooper also, in the rear of his flock. Turning his veiled face from one group to another, he paid due reverence to the hoary heads, saluted the middle-aged with kind dignity, as their friend and spiritual guide, greeted the young with mingled authority and love, and laid his hands on the little children's heads to bless them. Such was always his custom on the Sabbath-day. Strange and bewildered looks repaid him for his courtesy. None, as on former occasions, aspired to the honor of walking by their pastor's side. Old Squire Saunders, doubtless by an accidental lapse of memory, neglected to invite Mr. Hooper to his table, where the good clergyman had been wont to bless the food, almost every Sunday since his settlement. He returned, therefore, to the parsonage, and, at the moment of closing the door, was observed to look back upon the people, all of whom had their eyes fixed upon the minister. A sad smile gleamed faintly from beneath the black veil, and flickered about his mouth, glimmering as he disappeared.

'How strange,' said a lady, 'that a simple black veil, such as any woman might wear on her bonnet, should become such a terrible thing on Mr. Hooper's face!'

'Something must surely be amiss with Mr. Hooper's intellects,' observed her husband, the physician of the village. 'But the strangest part of the affair is the effect of this vagary, even on a sober-minded man like myself. The black veil, though it covers only our pastor's face, throws its influence over his whole person, and makes him ghost-like from head to foot. Do you not feel it so?'

'Truly do I,' replied the lady; 'and I would not be alone with him for the world. I wonder he is not afraid to be alone with himself!'

'Men sometimes are so,' said her husband.

The afternoon service was attended with similar circumstances. At its conclusion, the bell tolled for the funeral of a young lady. The relatives and friends were assembled in the house, and the more distant acquaintances stood about the door, speaking of the good qualities of the deceased, when their talk was interrupted by the appearance of Mr. Hooper, still covered with his black veil. It was now an appropriate emblem. The clergyman stepped into the room where the corpse was laid, and bent over the coffin, to take a last farewell of his deceased parishioner. As he stooped, the veil hung straight down from his forehead, so that, if her eyelids had not been closed for ever, the dead maiden might have seen his face. Could Mr. Hooper be fearful of her glance, that he so hastily caught back the black veil? A person, who watched the interview between the dead and living, scrupled not to affirm, that, at the instant when the clergyman's features were disclosed, the corpse had slightly shuddered, rustling the shroud and muslin cap, though the countenance retained the composure of death. A superstitious old woman was the only witness of this prodigy. From the coffin, Mr. Hooper passed into the chamber of the mourners, and thence to the head of the staircase, to make the funeral prayer. It was a tender and heart-dissolving prayer, full of sorrow, yet so imbued with celestial hopes, that the music of a heavenly harp, swept by the fingers of the dead, seemed faintly to be heard among the saddest accents of the minister. The people trembled, though they but darkly understood him, when he prayed that they, and himself, and all of mortal race, might be ready, as he trusted this young maiden had been, for the dreadful hour that should snatch the veil from their faces. The bearers went heavily forth, and the mourners followed, saddening all the street, with the dead before them, and Mr. Hooper in his black veil behind.

'Why do you look back?' said one in the procession to his partner.

'I had a fancy,' replied she, 'that the minister and the maiden's spirit were walking hand in hand.'

'And so had I, at the same moment,' said the other.

That night, the handsomest couple in Milford village were to be joined in wedlock. Though reckoned a melancholy man, Mr. Hooper had a placid cheerfulness for such occasions, which often excited a sympathetic smile, where livelier merriment would have been thrown away. There was no quality of his disposition which made him more beloved than this. The company at the wedding awaited his arrival with impatience, trusting that the strange awe, which had gathered over him throughout the day, would now be dispelled. But such was not the result. When Mr. Hooper came, the first thing that their eyes rested on was the same horrible black veil, which had added deeper gloom to the funeral, and could portend nothing but evil to the wedding. Such was its immediate effect on the guests, that a cloud seemed to have rolled duskily from beneath the black crape, and dimmed the light of the candles. The bridal pair stood up before the minister. But the bride's cold fingers quivered in the tremulous hand of the bridegroom, and her death-like paleness caused a whisper, that the maiden who had been buried a few hours before, was come from her grave to be married. If ever another wedding were so dismal, it was that famous one, where they tolled the wedding-knell.[2] After performing the ceremony, Mr. Hooper raised a glass of wine to his lips, wishing happiness to the new-married couple, in a strain of mild pleasantry that ought to have brightened the features of the guests, like a cheerful gleam from the hearth. At that instant, catching a glimpse of his figure in the looking-glass, the black veil involved his own spirit in the horror with which it overwhelmed all others. His frame shuddered—his lips grew white—he spilt the untasted wine upon the carpet—and rushed forth into the darkness. For the Earth, too, had on her Black Veil.

The next day, the whole village of Milford talked of little else than Parson Hooper's black veil. That, and the mystery concealed behind it, supplied a topic for discussion between acquaintances meeting in the street, and good women gossiping at their open windows. It was the first item of news that the tavern-keeper told to his guests. The children babbled of it on their way to school. One imitative little imp covered his face with an old black handkerchief, thereby so affrighting his playmates, that the panic seized himself, and he well nigh lost his wits by his own waggery.

It was remarkable, that, of all the busy-bodies and impertinent people in the parish, not one ventured to put the plain question to Mr. Hooper, wherefore he did this thing. Hitherto, whenever there appeared the slightest call for such inter-

---

[2]Reference to Hawthorne's story, "The Wedding Knell," which appeared in *The Token* along with "The Minister's Black Veil" in 1836.

ference, he had never lacked advisers, not shown himself averse to be guided by their judgment. If he erred at all, it was by so painful a degree of self-distrust, that even the mildest censure would lead him to consider an indifferent action as a crime. Yet, though so well acquainted with this amiable weakness, no individual among his parishioners chose to make the black veil a subject of friendly remonstrance. There was a feeling of dread, neither plainly confessed nor carefully concealed, which caused each to shift the responsibility upon another, till at length it was found expedient to send a deputation of the church, in order to deal with Mr. Hooper about the mystery, before it should grow into a scandal. Never did an embassy so ill discharge its duties. The minister received them with friendly courtesy, but became silent, after they were seated, leaving to his visiters the whole burthen of introducing their important business. The topic, it might be supposed, was obvious enough. There was the black veil, swathed round Mr. Hooper's forehead, and concealing every feature above his placid mouth, on which, at times, they could perceive the glimmering of a melancholy smile. But that piece of crape, to their imagination, seemed to hang down before his heart, the symbol of a fearful secret between him and them. Were the veil but cast aside, they might speak freely of it, but not till then. Thus they sat a considerable time, speechless, confused, and shrinking uneasily from Mr. Hooper's eye, which they felt to be fixed upon them with an invisible glance. Finally, the deputies returned abashed to their constituents, pronouncing the matter too weighty to be handled, except by a council of the churches, if, indeed, it might not require a general synod.

But there was one person in the village, unappalled by the awe with which the black veil had impressed all beside herself. When the deputies returned without an explanation, or even venturing to demand one, she, with the calm energy of her character, determined to chase away the strange cloud that appeared to be settling round Mr. Hooper, every moment more darkly than before. As his plighted wife, it should be her privilege to know what the black veil concealed. At the minister's first visit, therefore, she entered upon the subject, with a direct simplicity, which made the task easier both for him and her. After he had seated himself, she fixed her eyes steadfastly upon the veil, but could discern nothing of the dreadful gloom that had so overawed the multitude: it was but a double fold of crape, hanging down from his forehead to his mouth, and slightly stirring with his breath.

'No,' said she aloud, and smiling, 'there is nothing terrible in this piece of crape, except that it hides a face which I am always glad to look upon. Come, good sir, let the sun shine from behind the cloud. First lay aside your black veil: then tell me why you put it on.'

Mr. Hooper's smile glimmered faintly.

'There is an hour to come,' said he, 'when all of us shall cast aside our veils. Take it not amiss, beloved friend, if I wear this piece of crape till then.'

'Your words are a mystery too,' returned the young lady. 'Take away the veil from them, at least.'

'Elizabeth, I will,' said he, 'so far as my vow may suffer me. Know, then, this veil is a type and a symbol, and I am bound to wear it ever, both in light and darkness, in solitude and before the gaze of multitudes, and as with strangers, so with my familiar friends. No mortal eye will see it withdrawn. This dismal shade must separate me from the world: even you, Elizabeth, can never come behind it!'

'What grievous affliction hath befallen you,' she earnestly inquired, 'that you should thus darken your eyes for ever?'

'If it be a sign of mourning,' replied Mr. Hooper, 'I, perhaps, like most other mortals, have sorrows dark enough to be typified by a black veil.'

'But what if the world will not believe that it is the type of an innocent sorrow?' urged Elizabeth. 'Beloved and respected as you are, there may be whispers, that you hide your face under the consciousness of secret sin. For the sake of your holy office, do away this scandal!'

The color rose into her cheeks, as she intimated the nature of the rumors that were already abroad in the village. But Mr. Hooper's mildness did not forsake him. He even smiled again—that same sad smile, which always appeared like a faint glimmering of light, proceeding from the obscurity beneath the veil.

'If I hide my face for sorrow, there is cause enough,' he merely replied; 'and if I cover it for secret sin, what mortal might not do the same?'

And with this gentle, but unconquerable obstinacy, did he resist all her entreaties. At length Elizabeth sat silent. For a few moments she appeared lost in thought, considering, probably, what new methods might be tried, to withdraw her lover from so dark a fantasy, which, if it had no other meaning, was perhaps a symptom of mental disease. Though of a firmer character than his own, the tears rolled down her cheeks. But, in an instant, as it were, a new feeling took the place of sorrow: her eyes were fixed insensibly on the black veil, when, like a sudden twilight in the air, its terrors fell around her. She arose, and stood trembling before him.

'And do you feel it then at last?' said he mournfully.

She made no reply, but covered her eyes with her hand, and turned to leave the room. He rushed forward and caught her arm.

'Have patience with me, Elizabeth!' cried he passionately. 'Do not desert me, though this veil must be between us here on earth. Be mine, and hereafter there shall be no veil over my face, no darkness between our souls! It is but a mortal veil—it is not for eternity! Oh! you know not how lonely I am, and how frightened to be alone behind my black veil. Do not leave me in this miserable obscurity for ever!'

'Lift the veil but once, and look me in the face,' said she.

'Never! It cannot be!' replied Mr. Hooper.

'Then, farewell!' said Elizabeth.

She withdrew her arm from his grasp, and slowly departed, pausing at the door, to give one long, shuddering gaze, that seemed almost to penetrate the mystery of the black veil. But, even amid his grief, Mr. Hooper smiled to think that only a material emblem had separated him from happiness, though the horrors which it shadowed forth, must be drawn darkly between the fondest of lovers.

From that time no attempts were made to remove Mr. Hooper's black veil, or, by a direct appeal, to discover the secret which it was supposed to hide. By persons who claimed a superiority to popular prejudice, it was reckoned merely an eccentric whim, such as often mingles with the sober actions of men otherwise rational, and tinges them all with its own semblance of insanity. But with the multitude, good Mr. Hooper was irreparably a bugbear. He could not walk the streets with any peace of mind, so conscious was he that the gentle and timid would turn aside to avoid him, and that others would make it a point of hardihood to throw themselves in his way. The impertinence of the latter class compelled him to give up his customary walk, at sunset, to the burial ground; for when he leaned pensively over the gate, there would always be faces behind the grave-stones, peeping at his black veil. A fable went the rounds, that the stare of the dead people drove him thence. It grieved him, to the very depth of his kind heart, to observe how the children fled from his approach, breaking up their merriest sports, while his melancholy figure was yet afar off. Their instinctive dread caused him to feel, more strongly than aught else, that a preternatural horror was interwoven with the threads of the black crape. In truth, his own antipathy to the veil was known to be so great, that he never willingly passed before a mirror, nor stooped to drink at a still fountain, lest, in its peaceful bosom, he should be affrighted by himself. This was what gave plausibility to the whispers, that Mr. Hooper's conscience tortured him for some great crime, too horrible to be entirely concealed, or otherwise than so obscurely intimated. Thus, from beneath the black veil, there rolled a cloud into the sunshine, an ambiguity of sin or sorrow, which enveloped the poor minister, so that love or sympathy could never reach him. It was said, that ghost and fiend consorted with him there. With self-shudderings and outward terrors, he walked continually in its shadow, groping darkly within his own soul, or gazing through a medium that saddened the whole world. Even the lawless wind, it was believed, respected his dreadful secret, and never blew aside the veil. But still good Mr. Hooper sadly smiled, at the pale visages of the worldly throng as he passed by.

Among all its bad influences, the black veil had the one desirable effect, of making its wearer a very efficient clergyman. By the aid of his mysterious emblem—for there was no other apparent cause—he became a man of awful power, over souls that were in agony for sin. His converts always regarded him with a dread peculiar to themselves, affirming, though but figuratively, that, before he brought them to celestial light, they had been with him behind the black veil. Its gloom, indeed, enabled him to sympathize with all dark affections. Dying sinners cried aloud for Mr. Hooper, and would not yield their breath till he appeared; though ever, as he stooped to whisper consolation, they shuddered at the veiled face so near their own. Such were the terrors of the black veil, even when Death had bared his visage! Strangers came long distances to attend service at his church, with the mere idle purpose of gazing at his figure, because it was forbidden them to behold his face. But many were made to quake ere they departed! Once, during Governor Belcher's[3] administration, Mr. Hooper was appointed to preach the election sermon. Covered with his black veil, he stood before the chief magistrate, the council, and the representatives, and wrought so deep an impression, that the legislative measures of that year, were characterized by all the gloom and piety of our earliest ancestral sway.

In this manner Mr. Hooper spent a long life, irreproachable in outward act, yet shrouded in dismal suspicions; kind and loving, though unloved, and dimly feared; a man apart from men, shunned in their health and joy, but ever summoned to their aid in mortal anguish. As years wore on, shedding their snows above his sable veil, he acquired a name throughout the New-England churches, and they called him Father Hooper. Nearly all his parishioners, who were of mature age when he was settled, had been borne away by many a funeral: he had one congregation in the church, and a more crowded one in the church-yard; and having wrought so late into the evening, and done his work so well, it was now good Father Hooper's turn to rest.

Several persons were visible by the shaded candlelight, in the death-chamber of the old clergyman. Natural connections he had none. But there was the decorously grave, though unmoved physician, seeking only to mitigate the last pangs of the patient whom he could not save. There were the deacons, and other eminently pious members of his church. There, also, was the Reverend Mr. Clark, of Westbury, a young and zealous divine, who had ridden in haste to pray by the bed-side of the expiring minister. There was the nurse, no hired handmaiden of death, but one whose calm affection had endured thus long, in secresy, in solitude, amid the chill of age, and would not perish, even at the dying hour. Who, but Elizabeth! And there lay the hoary head of good Father Hooper upon the death-pillow, with the black veil still swathed about his brow and reaching down over his face, so that each more difficult gasp of his faint breath caused it to stir. All through life that piece of crape had hung between him and the world: it had

---

[3]Jonathan Belcher (1682–1757), Royal Governor of the Massachusetts Bay Colony (1730–41). It was customary for an election sermon to be preached on installation of a new governor, and it was an honor to be chosen to preach it.

separated him from cheerful brotherhood and woman's love, and kept him in that saddest of all prisons, his own heart; and still it lay upon his face, as if to deepen the gloom of his darksome chamber, and shade him from the sunshine of eternity.

For some time previous, his mind had been confused, wavering doubtfully between the past and the present, and hovering forward, as it were, at intervals, into the indistinctness of the world to come. There had been feverish turns, which tossed him from side to side, and wore away what little strength he had. But in his most convulsive struggles, and in the wildest vagaries of his intellect, when no other thought retained its sober influence, he still showed an awful solicitude lest the black veil should slip aside. Even if his bewildered soul could have forgotten, there was a faithful woman at his pillow, who, with averted eyes, would have covered that aged face, which she had last beheld in the comeliness of manhood. At length the death-stricken old man lay quietly in the torpor of mental and bodily exhaustion, with an imperceptible pulse, and breath that grew fainter and fainter, except when a long, deep, and irregular inspiration seemed to prelude the flight of his spirit.

The minister of Westbury approached the bedside.

'Venerable Father Hooper,' said he, 'the moment of your release is at hand. Are you ready for the lifting of the veil, that shuts in time from eternity?'

Father Hooper at first replied merely by a feeble motion of his head; then, apprehensive, perhaps, that his meaning might be doubtful, he exerted himself to speak.

'Yea,' said he, in faint accents, 'my soul hath a patient weariness until that veil be lifted.'

'And is it fitting,' resumed the Reverend Mr. Clark, 'that a man so given to prayer, of such a blameless example, holy in deed and thought, so far as mortal judgment may pronounce; is it fitting that a father in the church should leave a shadow on his memory, that may seem to blacken a life so pure? I pray you, my venerable brother, let not this thing be! Suffer us to be gladdened by your triumphant aspect, as you go to your reward. Before the veil of eternity be lifted, let me cast aside this black veil from your face!'

And thus speaking, the Reverend Mr. Clark bent forward to reveal the mystery of so many years. But, exerting a sudden energy, that made all the beholders stand aghast, Father Hooper snatched both his hands from beneath the bedclothes, and pressed them strongly on the black veil, resolute to struggle, if the minister of Westbury would contend with a dying man.

'Never!' cried the veiled clergyman. 'On earth, never!'

'Dark old man!' exclaimed the affrighted minister, 'with what horrible crime upon your soul are you now passing to the judgment?'

Father Hooper's breath heaved; it rattled in his throat; but, with a mighty effort, grasping forward with his hands, he caught hold of life, and held it back till he should speak. He even raised himself in bed; and there he sat, shivering with the arms of death around him, while the black veil hung down, awful, at that last moment, in the gathered terrors of a life-time. And yet the faint, sad smile, so often there, now seemed to glimmer from its obscurity, and linger on Father Hooper's lips.

'Why do you tremble at me alone?' cried he, turning his veiled face round the circle of pale spectators. 'Tremble also at each other! Have men avoided me, and women shown no pity, and children screamed and fled, only for my black veil? What, but the mystery which it obscurely typifies, has made this piece of crape so awful? When the friend shows his inmost heart to his friend; the lover to his best-beloved; when man does not vainly shrink from the eye of his Creator, loathsomely treasuring up the secret of his sin; then deem me a monster, for the symbol beneath which I have lived, and die! I look around me, and, lo! on every visage a Black Veil!'

While his auditors shrank from one another, in mutual affright, Father Hooper fell back upon his pillow, a veiled corpse, with a faint smile lingering on the lips. Still veiled, they laid him in his coffin, and a veiled corpse they bore him to the grave. The grass of many years has sprung up and withered on that grave, the burial-stone is moss-grown, and good Mr. Hooper's face is dust; but awful is still the thought, that it mouldered beneath the Black Veil!

1836

The Birth-Mark

In the latter part of the last century, there lived a man of science—an eminent proficient in every branch of natural philosophy—who, not long before our story opens, had made experience of a spiritual affinity, more attractive than any chemical one. He had left his laboratory to the care of an assistant, cleared his fine countenance from the furnace-smoke, washed the stain of acids from his fingers, and persuaded a beautiful woman to become his wife. In those days, when the comparatively recent discovery of electricity, and other kindred mysteries of nature, seemed to open paths into the region of miracle, it was not unusual for the love of science to rival the love of woman, in its depth and absorbing energy. The higher intellect, the imagination, the spirit, and even the heart, might all find their congenial aliment in pursuits which, as some of their ardent votaries believed, would ascend from one step of powerful intelligence to another, until the philosopher should lay his hand on the secret of creative force, and perhaps make new worlds for himself. We know not whether Aylmer possessed this degree of faith in man's ultimate control over nature. He had devoted himself, however, too unreservedly to scientific studies, ever to be weaned from them by any second passion. His love for his young wife might prove the stronger of the two; but it could only be by intertwining itself with his love of science, and uniting the strength of the latter to its own.

Such a union accordingly took place, and was attended with truly remarkable consequences, and a deeply impressive moral. One day, very soon after their marriage, Aylmer sat gazing at his wife, with a trouble in his countenance that grew stronger, until he spoke.

"Georgiana," said he, "has it never occurred to you that the mark upon your cheek might be removed?"

"No, indeed," said she, smiling; but perceiving the seriousness of his manner, she blushed deeply. "To tell you the truth, it has been so often called a charm, that I was simple enough to imagine it might be so."

"Ah, upon another face, perhaps it might," replied her husband. "But never on yours! No, dearest Georgiana, you came so nearly perfect from the hand of Nature, that this slightest possible defect—which we hesitate whether to term a defect or a beauty—shocks me, as being the visible mark of earthly imperfection."

"Shocks you, my husband!" cried Georgiana, deeply hurt; at first reddening with momentary anger, but then bursting into tears. "Then why did you take me from my mother's side? You cannot love what shocks you!"

To explain this conversation, it must be mentioned, that, in the centre of Georgiana's left cheek, there was a singular mark, deeply interwoven, as it were, with the texture and substance of her face. In the usual state of her complexion,—a healthy, though delicate bloom,—the mark wore a tint of deeper crimson, which imperfectly defined its shape amid the surrounding rosiness. When she blushed, it gradually became more indistinct, and finally vanished amid the triumphant rush of blood, that bathed the whole cheek with its brilliant glow. But, if any shifting emotion caused her to turn pale, there was the mark again, a crimson stain upon the snow, in what Aylmer sometimes deemed an almost fearful distinctness. Its shape bore not a little similarity to the human hand, though of the smallest pigmy size. Georgiana's lovers were wont to say, that some fairy, at her birth-hour, had laid her tiny hand upon the infant's cheek, and left this impress there, in token of the magic endowments that were to give her such sway over all hearts. Many a desperate swain would have risked life for the privilege of pressing his lips to the mysterious hand. It must not be concealed, however, that the impression wrought by this fairy sign-manual varied exceedingly, according to the difference of temperament in the beholders. Some fastidious persons—but they were exclusively of her own sex—affirmed that the Bloody Hand, as they chose to call it, quite destroyed the effect of Georgiana's beauty, and rendered her countenance even hideous. But it would be as reasonable to say, that one of those small blue stains, which sometimes occur in the purest statuary marble, would convert the Eve of Powers[1] to a monster. Masculine observers, if the birth-mark did not heighten their admiration, contented themselves with wishing it away, that the world might possess one living specimen of ideal loveliness, without the semblance of a flaw. After his marriage—for he thought little or nothing of the matter before— Aylmer discovered that this was the case with himself.

Had she been less beautiful—if Envy's self could have found aught else to sneer at—he might have felt his affection heightened by the prettiness of this mimic hand, now vaguely portrayed, now lost, now stealing forth again, and glimmering to-and-fro with every pulse of emotion that throbbed within her heart. But, seeing her otherwise so perfect, he found this one defect grow more and more intolerable, with every moment of their united lives. It was the fatal flaw of humanity, which Nature, in one shape or another, stamps ineffaceably on all her productions, either to imply that they are temporary and finite, or that their perfection must be wrought by toil and pain. The Crimson Hand expressed the ineludible gripe, in which mortality clutches the highest and purest of earthly mould, degrading them into kindred with the lowest, and even with the very brutes, like whom their visible frames return to dust. In this manner, selecting it as the symbol of his wife's liability to sin, sorrow, decay, and death, Aylmer's sombre imagination was not long in rendering the birth-mark a frightful object, causing him more trouble and horror than ever Georgiana's beauty, whether of soul or sense, had given him delight.

At all the seasons which should have been their happiest, he invariably, and without intending it—nay, in spite of a purpose to the contrary—reverted to this one disastrous topic. Trifling as it at first appeared, it so connected itself with innumerable trains of thought, and modes of feeling, that it became the central point of all. With the morning twilight, Aylmer opened his eyes upon his wife's face, and recognized the symbol of imperfection; and when they sat together at the evening hearth, his eyes wandered stealthily to her cheek, and beheld, flickering with the blaze of the wood fire, the spectral Hand that wrote mortality, where he would fain have worshipped. Georgiana soon learned to shudder at his gaze. It needed but a glance, with the peculiar expression that his face often wore,

---

[1]Hiram Powers (1805–1873), American sculptor and creator of a life-sized work, "Eve Before the Fall."

to change the roses of her cheek into a deathlike paleness, amid which the Crimson Hand was brought strongly out, like a bas-relief of ruby on the whitest marble.

Late, one night, when the lights were growing dim, so as hardly to betray the stain on the poor wife's cheek, she herself, for the first time, voluntarily took up the subject.

"Do you remember, my dear Aylmer," said she, with a feeble attempt at a smile—"have you any recollection of a dream, last night, about this odious Hand?"

"None!—none whatever!" replied Aylmer, starting; but then he added in a dry, cold tone, affected for the sake of concealing the real depth of his emotion:— "I might well dream of it; for before I fell asleep, it had taken a pretty firm hold of my fancy."

"And you did dream of it," continued Georgiana, hastily; for she dreaded lest a gush of tears should interrupt what she had to say—"A terrible dream! I wonder that you can forget it. Is it possible to forget this one expression?—'It is in her heart now—we must have it out!'—Reflect, my husband; for by all means I would have you recall that dream."

The mind is in a sad note, when Sleep, the all-involving, cannot confine her spectres within the dim region of her sway, but suffers them to break forth, affrighting this actual life with secrets that perchance belong to a deeper one. Aylmer now remembered his dream. He had fancied himself, with his servant Aminadab, attempting an operation for the removal of the birth-mark. But the deeper went the knife, the deeper sank the Hand, until at length its tiny grasp appeared to have caught hold of Georgiana's heart; whence, however, her husband was inexorably resolved to cut or wrench it away.

When the dream had shaped itself perfectly in his memory, Aylmer sat in his wife's presence with a guilty feeling. Truth often finds its way to the mind close-muffled in robes of sleep, and then speaks with uncompromising directness of matters in regard to which we practise an unconscious self-deception, during our waking moments. Until now, he had not been aware of the tyrannizing influence acquired by one idea over his mind, and of the lengths which he might find in his heart to go, for the sake of giving himself peace.

"Aylmer," resumed Georgiana, solemnly, "I know not what may be the cost to both of us, to rid me of this fatal birth-mark. Perhaps its removal may cause cureless deformity. Or, it may be, the stain goes as deep as life itself. Again, do we know that there is a possibility, on any terms, of unclasping the firm gripe of this little Hand, which was laid upon me before I came into the world?"

"Dearest Georgiana, I have spent much thought upon the subject," hastily interrupted Aylmer—"I am convinced of the perfect practicability of its removal."

"If there be the remotest possibility of it," continued Georgiana, "let the attempt be made, at whatever risk. Danger is nothing to me; for life—while this hateful mark makes me the object of your horror and disgust—life is a burthen which I would fling down with joy. Either remove this dreadful Hand, or take my wretched life! You have deep science! All the world bears witness of it. You have achieved great wonders! Cannot you remove this little, little mark, which I cover with the tips of two small fingers? Is this beyond your power, for the sake of your own peace, and to save your poor wife from madness?"

"Noblest—dearest—tenderest wife!" cried Aylmer, rapturously. "Doubt not my power. I have already given this matter the deepest thought—thought which might almost have enlightened me to create a being less perfect than yourself. Georgiana, you have led me deeper than ever into the heart of science. I feel myself fully competent to render this dear cheek as faultless as its fellow; and then, most beloved, what will be my triumph, when I shall have corrected what Nature left imperfect, in her fairest work! Even Pygmalion,[2] when his sculptured woman assumed life, felt not greater ecstasy than mine will be."

"It is resolved, then," said Georgiana, faintly smiling,—"And, Aylmer, spare me not, though you should find the birth-mark take refuge in my heart at last."

Her husband tenderly kissed her cheek—her right cheek—not that which bore the impress of the Crimson Hand.

The next day, Aylmer apprized his wife of a plan that he had formed, whereby he might have opportunity for the intense thought and constant watchfulness, which the proposed operation would require; while Georgiana, likewise, would enjoy the perfect repose essential to its success. They were to seclude themselves in the extensive apartments occupied by Aylmer as a laboratory, and where, during his toilsome youth, he had made discoveries in the elemental powers of nature, that had roused the admiration of all the learned societies in Europe. Seated calmly in this laboratory, the pale philosopher had investigated the secrets of the highest cloud-region, and of the profoundest mines; he had satisfied himself of the causes that kindled and kept alive the fires of the volcano; and had explained the mystery of fountains, and how it is that they gush forth, some so bright and pure, and others with such rich medicinal virtues, from the dark bosom of the earth. Here, too, at an earlier period, he had studied the wonders of the human frame, and attempted to fathom the very process by which Nature assimilates all her precious influences from earth and air, and from the spiritual world, to create and foster Man, her masterpiece. The latter pursuit, however, Aylmer had long laid aside, in unwilling recognition of the truth, against which all seekers sooner or later stumble, that our great creative Mother, while she amuses us with apparently working in the broadest sunshine, is yet severely careful to keep her own secrets, and, in spite of her pretended openness, shows us nothing but results. She permits us indeed, to mar, but seldom to mend, and, like a jealous patentee, on no account to make. Now, however, Aylmer resumed these half-forgotten investigations; not, of course, with such hopes or wishes as first suggested them; but because they involved much physiological truth, and lay in the path of his proposed scheme for the treatment of Georgiana.

As he led her over the threshold of the laboratory, Georgiana was cold and tremulous. Aylmer looked cheerfully into her face, with intent to reassure her, but was so startled with the intense glow of the birth-mark upon the whiteness of her cheek, that he could not restrain a strong convulsive shudder. His wife fainted.

"Aminadab! Aminadab!" shouted Aylmer, stamping violently on the floor.

Forthwith, there issued from an inner apartment a man of low stature, but bulky frame, with shaggy hair hanging about his visage, which was grimed with the vapors of the furnace. This personage had been Aylmer's under-worker during his whole scientific career, and was admirably fitted for that office by his great mechanical readiness, and the skill with which, while incapable of comprehending a single principle, he executed all the practical details of his master's experiments. With his vast strength, his shaggy hair, his smoky aspect, and the indescribable earthiness that incrusted him, he seemed to represent man's physical nature; while Aylmer's slender figure, and pale, intellectual face, were no less apt a type of the spiritual element.

"Throw open the door of the boudoir, Aminadab," said Aylmer, "and burn a pastille."

"Yes, master," answered Aminadab, looking intently at the lifeless form of Georgiana; and then he muttered to himself:—"If she were my wife, I'd never part with that birth-mark."

---

[2]In Greek legend, king of Cyprus and sculptor who fell in love with his statue of Galatea, which was then brought to life by Aphrodite.

When Georgiana recovered consciousness, she found herself breathing an atmosphere of penetrating fragrance, the gentle potency of which had recalled her from her deathlike faintness. The scene around her looked like enchantment. Aylmer had converted those smoky, dingy, sombre rooms, where he had spent his brightest years in recondite pursuits, into a series of beautiful apartments, not unfit to be the secluded abode of a lovely woman. The walls were hung with gorgeous curtains, which imparted the combination of grandeur and grace, that no other species of adornment can achieve; and as they fell from the ceiling to the floor, their rich and ponderous folds, concealing all angles and straight lines, appeared to shut in the scene from infinite space. For aught Georgiana knew, it might be a pavilion among the clouds. And Aylmer, excluding the sunshine, which would have interfered with his chemical processes, had supplied its place with perfumed lamps, emitting flames of various hue, but all uniting in a soft, empurpled radiance. He now knelt by his wife's side, watching her earnestly, but without alarm; for he was confident in his science, and felt that he could draw a magic circle round her, within which no evil might intrude.

"Where am I?—Ah, I remember!" said Georgiana, faintly; and she placed her hand over her cheek, to hide the terrible mark from her husband's eyes.

"Fear not, dearest!" exclaimed he. "Do not shrink from me! Believe me, Georgiana, I even rejoice in this single imperfection, since it will be such rapture to remove it."

"Oh, spare me!" sadly replied his wife—"Pray do not look at it again. I never can forget that convulsive shudder."

In order to soothe Georgiana, and, as it were, to release her mind from the burthen of actual things, Aylmer now put in practice some of the light and playful secrets, which science had taught him among its profounder lore. Airy figures, absolutely bodiless ideas, and forms of unsubstantial beauty, came and danced before her, imprinting their momentary footsteps on beams of light. Though she had some indistinct idea of the method of these optical phenomena, still the illusion was almost perfect enough to warrant the belief, that her husband possessed sway over the spiritual world. Then again, when she felt a wish to look forth from her seclusion, immediately, as if her thoughts were answered, the procession of external existence flitted across a screen. The scenery and the figures of actual life were perfectly represented, but with that bewitching, yet indescribable difference, which always makes a picture, an image, or a shadow, so much more attractive than the original. When wearied of this, Aylmer bade her cast her eyes upon a vessel, containing a quantity of earth. She did so, with little interest at first, but was soon startled, to perceive the germ of a plant, shooting upward from the soil. Then came the slender stalk—the leaves gradually unfolded themselves—and amid them was a perfect and lovely flower.

"It is magical!" cried Georgianna, "I dare not touch it."

"Nay, pluck it," answered Aylmer, "pluck it, and inhale its brief perfume while you may. The flower will wither in a few moments, and leave nothing save its brown seed-vessels—but thence may be perpetuated a race as ephemeral as itself."

But Georgianna had no sooner touched the flower than the whole plant suffered a blight, its leaves turning coal-black, as if by the agency of fire.

"There was too powerful a stimulus," said Aylmer thoughtfully.

To make up for this abortive experiment, he proposed to take her portrait by a scientific process of his own invention. It was to be effected by rays of light striking upon a polished plate of metal. Georgiana assented—but, on looking at the result, was affrighted to find the features of the portrait blurred and indefinable; while the minute figure of a hand appeared where the cheek should have been. Aylmer snatched the metallic plate, and threw it into a jar of corrosive acid.

Soon, however, he forgot these mortifying failures. In the intervals of study and chemical experiment, he came to her, flushed and exhausted, but seemed invigorated by her presence, and spoke in glowing language of the resources of his art. He gave a history of the long dynasty of the Alchemists,[3] who spent so many ages in quest of the universal solvent, by which the Golden Principle might be elicited from all things vile and base. Aylmer appeared to believe, that, by the plainest scientific logic, it was altogether within the limits of possibility to discover this long-sought medium; but, he added, a philosopher who should go deep enough to acquire the power, would attain too lofty a wisdom to stoop to the exercise of it. Not less singular were his opinions in regard to the Elixir Vitæ.[4] He more than intimated, that it was his option to concoct a liquid that should prolong life for years—perhaps interminably—but that it would produce a discord in nature, which all the world, and chiefly the quaffer of the immortal nostrum, would find cause to curse.

"Aylmer, are you in earnest?" asked Georgiana, looking at him with amazement and fear; "it is terrible to possess such power, or even to dream of possessing it!"

"Oh, do not tremble, my love!" said her husband, "I would not wrong either you or myself by working such inharmonious effects upon our lives. But I would have you consider how trifling, in comparison, is the skill requisite to remove this little Hand."

At the mention of the birth-mark, Georgiana, as usual, shrank, as if a red-hot iron had touched her cheek.

Again Aylmer applied himself to his labors. She could hear his voice in the distant furnace-room, giving directions to Aminadab, whose harsh, uncouth, misshapen tones were audible in response, more like the grunt or growl of a brute than human speech. After hours of absence, Aylmer reappeared, and proposed that she should now examine his cabinet of chemical products, and natural treasures of the earth. Among the former he showed her a small vial, in which, he remarked, was contained a gentle yet most powerful fragrance, capable of impregnating all the breezes that blow across a kingdom. They were of inestimable value, the contents of that little vial; and, as he said so, he threw some of the perfume into the air, and filled the room with piercing and invigorating delight.

"And what is this?" asked Georgiana, pointing to a small crystal globe, containing a gold-colored liquid. "It is so beautiful to the eye, that I could imagine it the Elixir of Life."

"In one sense it is," replied Aylmer, "or rather the Elixir of Immortality. It is the most precious poison that ever was concocted in this world. By its aid, I could apportion the lifetime of any mortal at whom you might point your finger. The strength of the dose would determine whether he were to linger out years, or drop dead in the midst of a breath. No king, on his guarded throne, could keep his life, if I, in my private station, should deem that the welfare of millions justified me in depriving him of it."

"Why do you keep such a terrific drug?" inquired Georgiana in horror.

"Do not mistrust me, dearest!" said her husband, smiling; "its virtuous potency is yet greater than its harmful one. But, see! here is a powerful cosmetic. With a few drops of this, in a vase of water, freckles may be washed away as easily as the hands are cleansed. A stronger infusion would take the blood out of the cheek, and leave the rosiest beauty a pale ghost."

"Is it with this lotion that you intend to bathe my cheek?" asked Georgiana anxiously.

---

[3]Alchemy was the medieval science devoted to discovering methods of turning base metals into gold, universal cures for disease, and the elixir of longevity.
[4]"A potion that prolongs life" (Latin).

"Oh, no!" hastily replied her husband—"this is merely superficial. Your case demands a remedy that shall go deeper."

In his interviews with Georgiana, Aylmer generally made minute inquiries as to her sensations, and whether the confinement of the rooms, and the temperature of the atmosphere, agreed with her. These questions had such a particular drift, that Georgiana began to conjecture that she was already subjected to certain physical influences, either breathed in with the fragrant air, or taken with her food. She fancied, likewise—but it might be altogether fancy—that there was a stirring up of her system,—a strange indefinite sensation creeping through her veins, and tingling, half painfully, half pleasurably, at her heart. Still, whenever she dared to look into the mirror, there she beheld herself, pale as a white rose, and with the crimson birth-mark stamped upon her cheek. Not even Aylmer now hated it so much as she.

To dispel the tedium of the hours which her husband found it necessary to devote to the processes of combination and analysis, Georgiana turned over the volumes of his scientific library. In many dark old tomes, she met with chapters full of romance and poetry. They were the works of the philosophers of the middle ages, such as Albertus Magnus, Cornelius Agrippa, Paracelsus, and the famous friar who created the prophetic Brazen Head.[5] All these antique naturalists stood in advance of their centuries, yet were imbued with some of their credulity, and therefore were believed, and perhaps imagined themselves, to have acquired from the investigation of nature a power above nature, and from physics a sway over the spiritual world. Hardly less curious and imaginative were the early volumes of the Transactions of the Royal Society,[6] in which the members, knowing little of the limits of natural possibility, were continually recording wonders, or proposing methods whereby wonders might be wrought.

But, to Georgiana, the most engrossing volume was a large folio from her husband's own hand, in which he had recorded every experiment of his scientific career, with its original aim, the methods adopted for its development, and its final success or failure, with the circumstances to which either event was attributable. The book, in truth, was both the history and emblem of his ardent, ambitious, imaginative, yet practical and laborious, life. He handled physical details, as if there were nothing beyond them; yet spiritualized them all, and redeemed himself from materialism, by his strong and eager aspiration towards the infinite. In his grasp, the veriest clod of earth assumed a soul. Georgiana, as she read, reverenced Aylmer, and loved him more profoundly than ever, but with a less entire dependence on his judgment than heretofore. Much as he had accomplished, she could not but observe that his most splendid successes were almost invariably failures, if compared with the ideal at which he aimed. His brightest diamonds were the merest pebbles, and felt to be so by himself, in comparison with the inestimable gems which lay hidden beyond his reach. The volume, rich with achievements that had won renown for its author, was yet as melancholy a record as ever mortal hand had penned. It was the sad confession, and continual exemplification, of the short-comings of the composite man—the spirit burthened with clay and working in matter—and of the despair that assails the higher nature, at finding itself so miserably thwarted by the earthly part. Perhaps every man of genius, in whatever sphere, might recognize the image of his own experience in Aylmer's journal.

So deeply did these reflections affect Georgiana, that she laid her face upon the open volume, and burst into tears. In this situation she was found by her husband.

---

[5] Albertus Magnus (1193?–1280), German philosopher, alchemist and saint; Cornelius Agrippa (1486?–1535), German physician devoted to the occult; Paracelsus (1493–1541), Swiss-born alchemist and physician; Friar Roger Bacon (1214–1294), English philosopher and alchemist, was said to have made the legendary brass head that could speak.

[6] *Philosophical Transactions* of England's Royal Society for Improving Natural Knowledge, founded in 1660.

"It is dangerous to read in a sorcerer's books," said he, with a smile, though his countenance was uneasy and displeased. "Georgiana, there are pages in that volume, which I can scarcely glance over and keep my senses. Take heed lest it prove as detrimental to you!"

"It has made me worship you more than ever," said she.

"Ah! wait for this one success," rejoined he, "then worship me if you will. I shall deem myself hardly unworthy of it. But, come! I have sought you for the luxury of your voice. Sing to me, dearest!"

So she poured out the liquid music of her voice to quench the thirst of his spirit. He then took his leave, with a boyish exuberance of gaiety, assuring her that her seclusion would endure but a little longer, and that the result was already certain. Scarcely had he departed, when Georgiana felt irresistibly impelled to follow him. She had forgotten to inform Aylmer of a symptom, which, for two or three hours past, had begun to excite her attention. It was a sensation in the fatal birth-mark, not painful, but which induced a restlessness throughout her system. Hastening after her husband, she intruded, for the first time, into the laboratory.

The first thing that struck her eye was the furnace, that hot and feverish worker, with the intense glow of its fire, which, by the quantities of soot clustered above it, seemed to have been burning for ages. There was a distilling apparatus in full operation. Around the room were retorts, tubes, cylinders, crucibles, and other apparatus of chemical research. An electrical machine stood ready for immediate use. The atmosphere felt oppressively close, and was tainted with gaseous odors, which had been tormented forth by the processes of science. The severe and homely simplicity of the apartment, with its naked walls and brick pavement, looked strange, accustomed as Georgiana had become to the fantastic elegance of her boudoir. But what chiefly, indeed almost solely, drew her attention, was the aspect of Aylmer himself.

He was pale as death, anxious, and absorbed, and hung over the furnace as if it depended upon his utmost watchfulness whether the liquid, which it was distilling, should be the draught of immortal happiness or misery. How different from the sanguine and joyous mien that he had assumed for Georgiana's encouragement!

"Carefully now, Aminadab! Carefully, thou human machine! Carefully, thou man of clay!" muttered Aylmer, more to himself than his assistant. "Now, if there be a thought too much or too little, it is all over!"

"Hoh! hoh!" mumbled Aminadab—"look, master, look!"

Aylmer raised his eyes hastily, and at first reddened, then grew paler than ever, on beholding Georgiana. He rushed towards her, and seized her arm with a gripe that left the print of his fingers upon it.

"Why do you come hither? Have you no trust in your husband?" cried he impetuously. "Would you throw the blight of that fatal birth-mark over my labors? It is not well done. Go, prying woman, go!"

"Nay, Aylmer," said Georgiana, with the firmness of which she possessed no stinted endowment, "it is not you that have a right to complain. You mistrust your wife! You have concealed the anxiety with which you watch the development of this experiment. Think not so unworthily of me, my husband! Tell me all the risk we run; and fear not that I shall shrink, for my share in it is far less than your own!"

"No, no, Georgiana!" said Aylmer impatiently, "it must not be."

"I submit," replied she calmly. "And, Aylmer, I shall quaff whatever draught you bring me; but it will be on the same principle that would induce me to take a dose of poison, if offered by your hand."

"My noble wife," said Aylmer, deeply moved, "I knew not the height and depth of your nature, until now. Nothing shall be concealed. Know, then, that this Crimson Hand, superficial as it seems, has clutched its grasp into your being, with a strength of which I had no previous conception. I have already administered agents powerful enough to do aught except to change your entire physical system. Only one thing remains to be tried. If that fail us, we are ruined!"

"Why did you hesitate to tell me this?" asked she.

"Because, Georgiana," said Aylmer, in a low voice, "there is danger!"

"Danger? There is but one danger—that this horrible stigma shall be left upon my cheek!" cried Georgiana. "Remove it! remove it!—whatever be the cost—or we shall both go mad!"

"Heaven knows, your words are too true," said Aylmer, sadly. "And now, dearest, return to your boudoir. In a little while, all will be tested."

He conducted her back, and took leave of her with a solemn tenderness, which spoke far more than his words how much was now at stake. After his departure, Georgiana became wrapt in musings. She considered the character of Aylmer, and did it completer justice than at any previous moment. Her heart exulted, while it trembled, at his honorable love, so pure and lofty that it would accept nothing less than perfection, nor miserably make itself contented with an earthlier nature than he had dreamed of. She felt how much more precious was such a sentiment, than that meaner kind which would have borne with the imperfection for her sake, and have been guilty of treason to holy love, by degrading its perfect idea to the level of the actual. And, with her whole spirit, she prayed, that, for a single moment, she might satisfy his highest and deepest conception. Longer than one moment, she well knew, it could not be; for his spirit was ever on the march—ever ascending—and each instant required something that was beyond the scope of the instant before.

The sound of her husband's footsteps aroused her. He bore a crystal goblet, containing a liquor colorless as water, but bright enough to be the draught of immortality. Aylmer was pale; but it seemed rather the consequence of a highly wrought state of mind, and tension of spirit, than of fear or doubt.

"The concoction of the draught has been perfect," said he, in answer to Georgiana's look. "Unless all my science have deceived me, it cannot fail."

"Save on your account, my dearest Aylmer," observed his wife, "I might wish to put off this birth-mark of mortality by relinquishing mortality itself, in preference to any other mode. Life is but a sad possession to those who have attained precisely the degree of moral advancement at which I stand. Were I weaker and blinder, it might be happiness. Were I stronger, it might be endured hopefully. But, being what I find myself, methinks I am of all mortals the most fit to die."

"You are fit for heaven without tasting death!" replied her husband. "But why do we speak of dying? The draught cannot fail. Behold its effect upon this plant!"

On the window-seat there stood a geranium, diseased with yellow blotches, which had overspread all its leaves. Aylmer poured a small quantity of the liquid upon the soil in which it grew. In a little time, when the roots of the plant had taken up the moisture, the unsightly blotches began to be extinguished in a living verdure.

"There needed no proof," said Georgiana, quietly. "Give me the goblet. I joyfully stake all upon your word."

"Drink, then, thou lofty creature!" exclaimed Aylmer, with fervid admiration. "There is no taint of imperfection on thy spirit. Thy sensible frame, too, shall soon be all perfect!"

She quaffed the liquid, and returned the goblet to his hand.

"It is grateful," said she, with a placid smile. "Methinks it is like water from a heavenly fountain; for it contains I know not what of unobtrusive fragrance and deliciousness. It allays a feverish thirst, that had parched me for many days. Now, dearest, let me sleep. My earthly senses are closing over my spirit, like the leaves round the heart of a rose, at sunset."

She spoke the last words with a gentle reluctance, as if it required almost more energy than she could command to pronounce the faint and lingering syllables. Scarcely had they loitered through her lips, ere she was lost in slumber. Aylmer sat by her side, watching her aspect with the emotions proper to a man, the whole value of whose existence was involved in the process now to be tested. Mingled with this mood, however, was the philosophic investigation, characteristic of the man of science. Not the minutest symptom escaped him. A heightened flush of the cheek—a slight irregularity of breath—a quiver of the eyelid—a hardly perceptible tremor through the frame—such were the details which, as the moments passed, he wrote down in his folio volume. Intense thought had set its stamp upon every previous page of that volume; but the thoughts of years were all concentrated upon the last.

While thus employed, he failed not to gaze often at the fatal Hand, and not without a shudder. Yet once, by a strange and unaccountable impulse, he pressed it with his lips. His spirit recoiled, however, in the very act, and Georgiana, out of the midst of her deep sleep, moved uneasily and murmured, as if in remonstrance. Again, Aylmer resumed his watch. Nor was it without avail. The Crimson Hand, which at first had been strongly visible upon the marble paleness of Georgiana's cheek now grew more faintly outlined. She remained not less pale than ever; but the birth-mark, with every breath that came and went, lost somewhat of its former distinctness. Its presence had been awful; its departure was more awful still. Watch the stain of the rainbow fading out of the sky; and you will know how that mysterious symbol passed away.

"By Heaven, it is well nigh gone!" said Aylmer to himself, in almost irrepressible ecstasy. "I can scarcely trace it now. Success! Success! And now it is like the faintest rose-color. The slightest flush of blood across her cheek would overcome it. But she is so pale!"

He drew aside the window-curtain, and suffered the light of natural day to fall into the room, and rest upon her cheek. At the same time, he heard a gross, hoarse chuckle, which he had long known as his servant Aminadab's expression of delight.

"Ah, clod! Ah, earthly mass!" cried Aylmer, laughing in a sort of frenzy. "You have served me well! Matter and Spirit—Earth and Heaven—have both done their part in this! Laugh, thing of senses! You have earned the right to laugh."

These exclamations broke Georgiana's sleep. She slowly unclosed her eyes, and gazed into the mirror, which her husband had arranged for that purpose. A faint smile flitted over her lips, when she recognized how barely perceptible was now that Crimson Hand, which had once blazed forth with such disastrous brilliancy as to scare away all their happiness. But then her eyes sought Aylmer's face, with a trouble and anxiety that he could by no means account for.

"My poor Aylmer!" murmured she.

"Poor? Nay, richest! Happiest! Most favored!" exclaimed he. "My peerless bride, it is successful! You are perfect!"

"My poor Aylmer!" she repeated, with a more than human tenderness. "You have aimed loftily!—you have done nobly! Do not repent, that, with so high and pure a feeling, you have rejected the best that earth could offer. Aylmer—dearest Aylmer—I am dying!"

Alas, it was too true! The fatal Hand had grappled with the mystery of life, and was the bond by which an angelic spirit kept itself in union with a mortal frame. As the last crimson tint of the birth-mark—that sole token of human imperfection—faded from her cheek, the parting breath of the now perfect woman passed into the atmosphere, and her soul, lingering a moment near her husband, took its heavenward flight. Then a hoarse, chuckling laugh was heard again! Thus ever does the gross Fatality of Earth exult in its invariable triumph over the immortal essence, which, in this dim sphere of half-development, demands the completeness of a higher state. Yet, had Aylmer reached a profounder wisdom, he need not thus have flung away the happiness, which would have woven his mortal life of the self-same texture with the celestial. The momentary circumstance was too strong for him; he failed to look beyond the shadowy scope of Time, and living once for all in Eternity, to find the perfect Future in the present.

1843

The Celestial Rail-Road[1]

Not a great while ago, passing through the gate of dreams, I visited that region of the earth in which lies the famous city of Destruction. It interested me much to learn, that, by the public spirit of some of the inhabitants, a rail-road has recently been established between this populous and flourishing town, and the Celestial City. Having a little time upon my hands, I resolved to gratify a liberal curiosity by making a trip thither. Accordingly, one fine morning, after paying my bill at the hotel, and directing the porter to stow my luggage behind a coach, I took my seat in the vehicle, and set out for the Station House. It was my good fortune to enjoy the company of a gentleman—one Mr. Smooth-it-away—who, though he had never actually visited the Celestial City, yet seemed as well acquainted with its laws, customs, policy, and statistics, as with those of the city of Destruction, of which he was a native townsman. Being, moreover, a director of the rail-road corporation, and one of its largest stockholders, he had it in his power to give me all desirable information respecting that praiseworthy enterprise.

Our coach rattled out of the city, and, at a short distance from its outskirts, passed over a bridge, of elegant construction, but somewhat too slight, as I imagined, to sustain any considerable weight. On both sides lay an extensive quagmire, which could not have been more disagreeable either to sight or smell, had all the kennels of the earth emptied their pollution there.

"This," remarked Mr. Smooth-it-away, "is the famous Slough of Despond—a disgrace to all the neighborhood; and the greater, that it might so easily be converted into firm ground."

"I have understood," said I, "that efforts have been made for that purpose, from time immemorial. Bunyan mentions that above twenty thousand cart-loads of wholesome instructions had been thrown in here, without effect."

"Very probably!—and what effect could be anticipated from such unsubstantial stuff?" cried Mr. Smooth-it-away. "You observe this convenient bridge. We obtained a sufficient foundation for it by throwing into the slough some editions of books of morality, volumes of French philosophy and German rationalism, tracts, sermons, and essays of modern clergymen, extracts from Plato, Confucius, and various Hindoo sages, together with a few ingenious commentaries upon texts of Scripture—all of which, by some scientific process, have been converted into a mass like granite. The whole bog might be filled up with similar matter."

It really seemed to me, however, that the bridge vibrated and heaved up and

---

[1]This satiric story is a modern but debased version of John Bunyan's allegory, *Pilgrim's Progress* (1678), and at the same time a criticism of the facile Unitarian or transcendental doctrines of the time that portrayed salvation as simple and easy. Bunyan's hero Christian sets out from the City of Destruction with the burden of sin on his back, making his way through the Slough of Despond and many other threatening or tempting places (including the Valley of the Shadow of Death, Vanity Fair, Delectable Mountains), but refuses to be deflected from the road to his destination, the Celestial City. Significantly, the story was written in 1843, in Concord, when Hawthorne was frequently in the company of Emerson and other transcendentalists.

down, in a very formidable manner; and, spite of Mr. Smooth-it-away's testimony to the solidity of its foundation, I should be loth to cross it in a crowded omnibus; especially if each passenger were encumbered with as heavy luggage as that gentleman and myself. Nevertheless, we got over without accident, and soon found ourselves at the Station House. This very neat and spacious edifice is erected on the site of the little Wicket-Gate, which formerly, as all old pilgrims will recollect, stood directly across the highway, and, by its inconvenient narrowness, was a great obstruction to the traveller of liberal mind and expansive stomach. The reader of John Bunyan will be glad to know, that Christian's old friend Evangelist, who was accustomed to supply each pilgrim with a mystic roll,[2] now presides at the ticket-office. Some malicious persons, it is true, deny the identity of this reputable character with the Evangelist of old times, and even pretend to bring competent evidence of an imposture. Without involving myself in the dispute, I shall merely observe, that, so far as my experience goes, the square pieces of pasteboard, now delivered to passengers, are much more convenient and useful along the road, than the antique roll of parchment. Whether they will be as readily received at the gate of the Celestial City, I decline giving an opinion.

A large number of passengers were already at the Station House, awaiting the departure of the cars. By the aspect and demeanor of these persons, it was easy to judge that the feelings of the community had undergone a very favorable change, in reference to the Celestial pilgrimage. It would have done Bunyan's heart good to see it. Instead of a lonely and ragged man, with a huge burthen on his back, plodding along sorrowfully on foot, while the whole city hooted after him, here were parties of the first gentry and most respectable people in the neighborhood, setting forth towards the Celestial City, as cheerfully as if the pilgrimage were merely a summer tour. Among the gentlemen were characters of deserved eminence, magistrates, politicians, and men of wealth, by whose example religion could not but be greatly recommended to their meaner brethren. In the ladies' apartment, too, I rejoiced to distinguish some of those flowers of fashionable society, who are so well fitted to adorn the most elevated circles of the Celestial City. There was much pleasant conversation about the news of the day, topics of business, politics, or the lighter matters of amusement; while religion, though indubitably the main thing at heart, was thrown tastefully into the back-ground. Even an infidel would have heard little or nothing to shock his sensibility.

One great convenience of the new method of going on pilgrimage, I must not forget to mention. Our enormous burthens, instead of being carried on our shoulders, as had been the custom of old, were all snugly deposited in the baggage-car, and, as I was assured, would be delivered to their respective owners, at the journey's end. Another thing, likewise, the benevolent reader will be delighted to understand. It may be remembered that there was an ancient feud between Prince Beelzebub[3] and the keeper of the Wicket-Gate, and that the adherents of the former distinguished personage were accustomed to shoot deadly arrows at honest pilgrims, while knocking at the door. This dispute, much to the credit as well of the illustrious potentate above-mentioned as of the worthy and enlightened Directors of the rail-road, has been pacifically arranged, on the principle of mutual compromise. The prince's subjects are now pretty numerously employed about the Station House, some in taking care of the baggage, others in collecting fuel, feeding the engines, and such congenial occupations; and I can conscientiously affirm, that persons more attentive to their business, more willing to accommodate, or more generally agreeable to the passengers, are not to be found on any rail-

---

[2]The Evangelist's parchment roll in *Pilgrim's Progress* advises: "Fly from the wrath to come."
[3]In Matthew 12:24, Beelzebub is "the prince of darkness";

in Milton's *Paradise Lost*, he is just below Satan himself in rank; in *Pilgrim's Progress*, he is captain of the castle near Wicket-Gate.

road. Every good heart must surely exult at so satisfactory an arrangement of an immemorial difficulty.

"Where is Mr. Greatheart?"[4] inquired I. "Beyond a doubt, the Directors have engaged that famous old champion to be chief engineer on the rail-road?"

"Why, no," said Mr. Smooth-it-away, with a dry cough. "He was offered the situation of brake-man; but, to tell you the truth, our friend Greatheart has grown preposterously stiff and narrow, in his old age. He has so often guided pilgrims over the road, on foot, that he considers it a sin to travel in any other fashion. Besides, the old fellow had entered so heartily into the ancient feud with Prince Beelzebub, that he would have been perpetually at blows or ill language with some of the prince's subjects, and thus have embroiled us anew. So, on the whole, we were not sorry when honest Greatheart went off to the Celestial City in a huff, and left us at liberty to choose a more suitable and accommodating man. Yonder comes the engineer of the train. You will probably recognize him at once."

The engine at this moment took its station in advance of the cars, looking, I must confess, much more like a sort of mechanical demon, that would hurry us to the infernal regions, than a laudable contrivance for smoothing our way to the Celestial City. On its top sat a personage almost enveloped in smoke and flame, which—not to startle the reader—appeared to gush from his own mouth and stomach, as well as from the engine's brazen abdomen.

"Do my eyes deceive me? cried I. "What on earth is this! A living creature?—if so, he is own brother to the engine that he rides upon!"

"Poh, poh; you are obtuse!" said Mr. Smooth-it-away, with a hearty laugh. "Don't you know Apollyon,[5] Christian's old enemy, with whom he fought so fierce a battle in the Valley of Humiliation? He was the very fellow to manage the engine; and so we have reconciled him to the custom of going on pilgrimage, and engaged him as chief engineer."

"Bravo, bravo!" exclaimed I, with irrepressible enthusiasm, "This shows the liberality of the age; this proves, if anything can, that all musty prejudices are in a fair way to be obliterated. And how will Christian rejoice to hear of this happy transformation of his old antagonist! I promise myself great pleasure in informing him of it, when we reach the Celestial City."

The passengers being all comfortably seated, we now rattled away merrily, accomplishing a greater distance in ten minutes, than Christian probably trudged over, in a day. It was laughable, while we glanced along, as it were, at the tail of a thunder-bolt, to observe two dusty foot-travellers, in the old pilgrim-guise, with cockle-shell and staff, their mystic rolls of parchment in their hands, and their intolerable burthens on their backs. The preposterous obstinacy of these honest people, in persisting to groan and stumble along the difficult pathway, rather than take advantage of modern improvements, excited great mirth among our wiser brotherhood. We greeted the two pilgrims with many pleasant gibes and a roar of laughter; whereupon, they gazed at us with such woeful and absurdly compassionate visages, that our merriment grew tenfold more obstreperous. Apollyon, also, entered heartily into the fun, and contrived to flirt the smoke and flame of the engine, or of his own breath, into their faces, and enveloped them in an atmosphere of scalding steam. These little practical jokes amused us mightily, and doubtless afforded the pilgrims the gratification of considering themselves martyrs.

At some distance from the rail-road, Mr. Smooth-it-away pointed to a large, antique edifice, which, he observed, was a tavern of long standing, and had formerly

---

[4]Mr. Greatheart helps Christian's wife and children journey to Celestial City in the second part of *Pilgrim's Progress*.
[5]In *Pilgrim's Progress*, Apollyon "was clothed with scales like a fish," "had wings like a dragon, feet like a bear, and out of his belly came fire and smoke, and his mouth was as the mouth of a lion."

been a noted stopping-place for pilgrims. In Bunyan's road-book, it is mentioned as the Interpreter's House.

"I have long had a curiosity to visit that old mansion," remarked I.

"It is not one of our stations, as you perceive," said my companion. "The keeper was violently opposed to the rail-road; and well he might be, as the track left his house of entertainment on one side, and thus was pretty certain to deprive him of all his reputable customers. But the foot-path still passes his door; and the old gentleman now and then receives a call from some simple traveller, and entertains him with fare as old-fashioned as himself."

Before our talk on this subject came to a conclusion, we were rushing by the place where Christian's burthen fell from his shoulders, at the sight of the cross. This served as a theme for Mr. Smooth-it-away, Mr. Live-for-the-world, Mr. Hide-sin-in-the-heart, Mr. Scaly Conscience, and a knot of gentlemen from the town of Shun Repentance, to descant upon the inestimable advantages resulting from the safety of our baggage. Myself, and all the passengers indeed, joined with great unanimity in this view of the matter; for our burthens were rich in many things, esteemed precious throughout the world; and, especially, we each of us possessed a great variety of favorite Habits, which we trusted would not be out of fashion, even in the polite circles of the Celestial City. It would have been a sad spectacle, to see such an assortment of valuable articles tumbling into the sepulchre. Thus pleasantly conversing on the favorable circumstances of our position, as compared with those of past pilgrims, and of narrow-minded ones at the present day, we soon found ourselves at the foot of the Hill Difficulty. Through the very heart of this rocky mountain a tunnel has been constructed, of most admirable architecture, with a lofty arch and a spacious double-track; so that, unless the earth and rocks should chance to crumble down, it will remain an eternal monument of the builder's skill and enterprise. It is a great, though incidental advantage, that the materials from the heart of the Hill Difficulty have been employed in filling up the Valley of Humiliation; thus obviating the necessity of descending into that disagreeable and unwholesome hollow.

"This is a wonderful improvement, indeed," said I. "Yet I should have been glad of an opportunity to visit the Palace Beautiful, and be introduced to the charming young ladies—Miss Prudence, Miss Piety, Miss Charity, and the rest—who have the kindness to entertain pilgrims there."

"Young ladies!" cried Mr. Smooth-it-away, as soon as he could speak for laughing. "And charming young ladies! Why, my dear fellow, they are old maids, every soul of them—prim, starched, dry, and angular—and not one of them, I will venture to say, has altered so much as the fashion of her gown, since the days of Christian's pilgrimage."

"Ah, well," said I, much comforted. "Then I can very readily dispense with their acquaintance."

The respectable Apollyon was now putting on the steam at a prodigious rate, anxious, perhaps, to get rid of the unpleasant reminiscences, connected with the spot where he had so disastrously encountered Christian. Consulting Mr. Bunyan's road-book, I perceived that we must now be within a few miles of the Valley of the Shadow of Death; into which doleful region, at our present speed, we should plunge much sooner than seemed at all desirable. In truth, I expected nothing better than to find myself in the ditch on one side, or the quag on the other. But, on communicating my apprehensions to Mr. Smooth-it-away, he assured me that the difficulties of this passage, even in its worst condition, had been vastly exaggerated, and that, in its present state of improvement, I might consider myself as safe as on any rail-road in Christendom.

Even while we were speaking, the train shot into the entrance of this dreaded Valley. Though I plead guilty to some foolish palpitations of the heart, during our headlong rush over the causeway here constructed, yet it were unjust to withhold the highest encomiums on the boldness of its original conception, and the ingenuity of those who executed it. It was gratifying, likewise, to observe how much care had been taken to dispel the everlasting gloom, and supply the defect of cheerful sunshine; not a ray of which has ever penetrated among these awful shadows. For this purpose, the inflammable gas, which exudes plentifully from the soil, is collected by means of pipes, and thence communicated to a quadruple row of lamps, along the whole extent of the passage. Thus a radiance has been created, even out of the fiery and sulphurous curse that rests forever upon the Valley; a radiance hurtful, however, to the eyes, and somewhat bewildering, as I discovered by the changes which it wrought in the visages of my companions. In this respect, as compared with natural daylight, there is the same difference as between truth and falsehood; but, if the reader have ever travelled through the Dark Valley, he will have learned to be thankful for any light that he could get; if not from the sky above, then from the blasted soil beneath. Such was the red brilliancy of these lamps, that they appeared to build walls of fire on both sides of the track, between which we held our course at lightning-speed, while a reverberating thunder filled the Valley with its echoes. Had the engine run off the track—a catastrophe, it is whispered, by no means unprecedented—the bottomless pit, if there be any such place, would undoubtedly have received us. Just as some dismal fooleries of this nature had made my heart quake, there came a tremendous shriek, careering along the Valley as if a thousand devils had burst their lungs to utter it, but which proved to be merely the whistle of the engine, on arriving at a stopping-place.

The spot, where we had now paused, is the same that our friend Bunyan—a truthful man, but infected with many fantastic notions—has designated, in terms plainer than I like to repeat, as the mouth of the infernal region. This, however, must be a mistake; inasmuch as Mr. Smooth-it-away, while we remained in the smoky and lurid cavern, took occasion to prove that Tophet[6] has not even a metaphorical existence. The place, he assured us, is no other than the crater of a half-extinct volcano, in which the Directors had caused forges to be set up, for the manufacture of rail-road iron. Hence, also, is obtained a plentiful supply of fuel for the use of the engines. Whoever had gazed into the dismal obscurity of the broad cavern-mouth, whence, ever and anon, darted huge tongues of dusky flame,—and had seen the strange, half-shaped monsters, and visions of faces horribly grotesque, into which the smoke seemed to wreathe itself,—and had heard the awful murmurs, and shrieks, and deep shuddering whispers of the blast, sometimes forming itself into words almost articulate,—he would have seized upon Mr. Smooth-it-away's comfortable explanation, as greedily as we did. The inhabitants of the cavern, moreover, were unlovely personages, dark, smoke-begrimed, generally deformed, with misshapen feet, and a glow of dusky redness in their eyes; as if their hearts had caught fire, and were blazing out of the upper windows. It struck me as a peculiarity, that the laborers at the forge, and those who brought fuel to the engine, when they began to draw short breath, positively emitted smoke from their mouth and nostrils.

Among the idlers about the train, most of whom were puffing cigars which they had lighted at the flame of the crater, I was perplexed to notice several, who, to my certain knowledge, had heretofore set forth by rail-road for the Celestial City. They looked dark, wild, and smoky, with a singular resemblance, indeed, to the native inhabitants; like whom, also, they had a disagreeable propensity to ill-natured gibes and sneers; the habit of which had wrought a settled contortion of their visages. Having been on speaking terms with one of these persons—an in-

---

[6]I.e., hell.

dolent, good-for-nothing fellow, who went by the name of Take-it-easy—I called to him, and inquired what was his business there.

"Did you not start," said I, "for the Celestial City?"

"That's a fact," said Mr. Take-it-easy, carelessly puffing some smoke into my eyes. "But I heard such bad accounts, that I never took pains to climb the hill, on which the city stands. No business doing—no fun going on—nothing to drink, and no smoking allowed—and a thrumming of church-music from morning till night! I would not stay in such a place, if they offered me house-room and living free."

"But, my good Mr. Take-it-easy," cried I, "why take up your residence here, of all places in the world?"

"Oh," said the loafer, with a grin, "it is very warm hereabouts, and I meet with plenty of old acquaintances, and altogether the place suits me. I hope to see you back again, some day soon. A pleasant journey to you!"

While he was speaking, the bell of the engine rang, and we dashed away, after dropping a few passengers, but receiving no new ones. Rattling onward through the Valley, we were dazzled with the fiercely gleaming gas-lamps, as before. But sometimes, in the dark of intense brightness, grim faces, that bore the aspect and expression of individual sins, or evil passions, seemed to thrust themselves through the veil of light, glaring upon us, and stretching forth a great dusky hand, as if to impede our progress. I almost thought, that they were my own sins that appalled me there. These were freaks of imagination—nothing more, certainly,—mere delusions, which I ought to be heartily ashamed of—but, all through the Dark Valley, I was tormented, and pestered, and dolefully bewildered, with the same kind of waking dreams. The mephitic gasses of that region intoxicate the brain. As the light of natural day, however, began to struggle with the glow of the lanterns, these vain imaginations lost their vividness, and finally vanished with the first ray of sunshine that greeted our escape from the Valley of the Shadow of Death. Ere we had gone a mile beyond it, I could well nigh have taken my oath that this whole gloomy passage was a dream.

At the end of the Valley, as John Bunyan mentions, is a cavern, where, in his days, dwelt two cruel giants, Pope and Pagan, who had strewn the ground about their residence with the bones of slaughtered pilgrims. These vile old troglodytes are no longer there; but into their deserted cave another terrible giant has thrust himself, and makes it his business to seize upon honest travellers, and fat them for his table with plentiful meals of smoke, mist, moonshine, raw potatoes, and sawdust. He is a German by birth, and is called Giant Transcendentalist; but as to his form, his features, his substance, and his nature generally, it is the chief peculiarity of this huge miscreant, that neither he for himself, nor anybody for him, has ever been able to describe them. As we rushed by the cavern's mouth, we caught a hasty glimpse of him, looking somewhat like an ill-proportioned figure, but considerably more like a heap of fog and duskiness. He shouted after us, but in so strange a phraseology that we knew not what he meant, nor whether to be encouraged or affrighted.

It was late in the day, when the train thundered into the ancient city of Vanity, where Vanity Fair is still at the height of prosperity, and exhibits an epitome of whatever is brilliant, gay, and fascinating, beneath the sun. As I purposed to make a considerable stay here, it gratified me to learn that there is no longer the want of harmony between the townspeople and pilgrims, which impelled the former to such lamentably mistaken measures as the persecution of Christian, and the fiery martyrdom of Faithful. On the contrary, as the new rail-road brings with it great trade and a constant influx of strangers, the lord of Vanity Fair is its chief patron, and the capitalists of the city are among the largest stockholders. Many passengers stop to take their pleasure or make their profit in the Fair, instead of going onward to the Celestial City. Indeed, such are the charms of the place, that people often affirm it to be the true and only heaven; stoutly contending that there is no other, that those who seek further are mere dreamers, and that, if the fabled brightness of the Celestial City lay but a bare mile beyond the gates of Vanity, they would not be fools enough to go thither. Without subscribing to these, perhaps, exaggerated encomiums, I can truly say, that my abode in the city was mainly agreeable, and my intercourse with the inhabitants productive of much amusement and instruction.

Being naturally of a serious turn, my attention was directed to the solid advantages derivable from a residence here, rather than to the effervescent pleasures, which are the grand object with too many visitants. The Christian reader, if he have had no accounts of the city later than Bunyan's time, will be surprised to hear that almost every street has its church, and that the reverend clergy are nowhere held in higher respect than at Vanity Fair. And well do they deserve such honorable estimation; for the maxims of wisdom and virtue, which fall from their lips, come from as deep a spiritual source, and tend to us as lofty a religious aim, as those of the sagest philosophers of old. In justification of this high praise, I need only mention the names of the Rev. Mr. Shallow-deep; the Rev. Mr. Stumble-at-truth; that fine old clerical character, the Rev. Mr. This-to-day, who expects shortly to resign his pulpit to the Rev. Mr. That-to-morrow; together with the Rev. Mr. Bewilderment; the Rev. Mr. Clog-the-spirit; and, last and greatest, the Rev. Dr. Wind-of-doctrine. The labors of these eminent divines are aided by those of innumerable lecturers, who diffuse such a various profundity, in all subjects of human or celestial science, that any man may acquire an omnigenous[7] erudition, without the trouble of even learning to read. Thus literature is etherealized by assuming for its medium the human voice; and knowledge, depositing all its heavier particles—except, doubtless, its gold—becomes exhaled into a sound, which forthwith steals into the ever-open ear of the community. These ingenious methods constitute a sort of machinery, by which thought and study are done to every person's hand, without his putting himself to the slightest inconvenience in the matter. There is another species of machine for the wholesale manufacture of individual morality. This excellent result is effected by societies for all manner of virtuous purposes; with which a man has merely to connect himself, throwing, as it were, his quota of virtue into the common stock; and the president and directors will take care that the aggregate amount be well applied. All these, and other wonderful improvements in ethics, religion, and literature, being made plain to my comprehension by the ingenious Mr. Smooth-it-away, inspired me with a vast admiration of Vanity Fair.

It would fill a volume, in an age of pamphlets, were I to record all my observations in this great capital of human business and pleasure. There was an unlimited range of society—the powerful, the wise, the witty, and the famous in every walk of life—princes, presidents, poets, generals, artists, actors, and philanthropists, all making their own market at the Fair, and deeming no price too exorbitant for such commodities as hit their fancy. It was well worth one's while, even if he had no idea of buying or selling, to loiter through the bazaars, and observe the various sorts of traffic that were going forward.

Some of the purchasers, I thought, made very foolish bargains. For instance, a young man, having inherited a splendid fortune, laid out a considerable portion of it in the purchase of diseases, and finally spent all the rest for a heavy lot of repentance and a suit of rags. A very pretty girl bartered a heart as clear as crystal, and which seemed her most valuable possession, for another jewel of the same

[7]Of all kinds.

kind, but so worn and defaced as to be utterly worthless. In one shop, there were a great many crowns of laurel and myrtle, which soldiers, authors, statesmen, and various other people, pressed eagerly to buy; some purchased these paltry wreaths with their lives; others by a toilsome servitude of years; and many sacrificed whatever was most valuable, yet finally slunk away without the crown. There was a sort of stock or scrip, called Conscience, which seemed to be in great demand, and would purchase almost anything. Indeed, few rich commodities were to be obtained without paying a heavy sum in this particular stock; and a man's business was seldom very lucrative, unless he knew precisely when and how to throw his hoard of Conscience into the market. Yet, as this stock was the only thing of permanent value, whoever parted with it was sure to find himself a loser, in the long run. Several of the speculations were of a questionable character. Occasionally, a member of congress recruited his pocket by the sale of his constituents; and I was assured that public officers have often sold their country, at very moderate prices. Thousands sold their happiness for a whim. Gilded chains were in great demand, and purchased with almost any sacrifice. In truth, those who desired, according to the old adage, to sell anything valuable for a song, might find customers all over the Fair; and there were innumerable messes of pottage, piping hot, for such as chose to buy them with their birth-rights.[8] A few articles, however, could not be found genuine, at Vanity Fair. If a customer wished to renew his stock of youth, the dealers offered him a set of false teeth and an auburn wig; if he demanded peace of mind, they recommended opium or a brandy-bottle.

Tracts of land and golden mansions, situate in the Celestial City, were often exchanged, at very disadvantageous rates, for a few years lease of small, dismal, inconvenient tenements in Vanity Fair. Prince Beelzebub himself took great interest in this sort of traffic, and sometimes condescended to meddle with smaller matters. I once had the pleasure to see him bargaining with a miser for his soul, which, after much ingenious skirmishing on both sides, his Highness succeeded in obtaining at about the value of sixpence. The prince remarked, with a smile, that he was a loser by the transaction.

Day after day, as I walked the streets of Vanity, my manners and deportment became more and more like those of the inhabitants. The place began to seem like home; the idea of pursuing my travels to the Celestial City was almost obliterated from my mind. I was reminded of it, however, by the sight of the same pair of simple pilgrims at whom we had laughed so heartily, when Apollyon puffed smoke and steam into their faces, at the commencement of our journey. There they stood amid the densest bustle of Vanity—the dealers offering them their purple, and fine linen, and jewels; the men of wit and humor gibing at them; a pair of buxom ladies ogling them askance; while the benevolent Mr. Smooth-it-away whispered some of his wisdom at their elbows, and pointed to a newly erected temple—but there were these worthy simpletons, making the scene look wild and monstrous, merely by their sturdy repudiation of all part in its business or pleasures.

One of them—his name was Stick-to-the-right—perceived in my face, I suppose, a species of sympathy and almost admiration, which, to my own great surprise, I could not help feeling for this pragmatic couple. It prompted him to address me.

"Sir," inquired he, with a sad, yet mild and kindly voice, "do you call yourself a pilgrim?"

"Yes," I replied. "My right to that appellation is indubitable. I am merely a so-

---

[8] In Genesis 25:29–34, Esau sold his birthright to Jacob for a "mess of pottage."

journer here in Vanity Fair, being bound for the Celestial City, by the new rail-road."

"Alas, friend," rejoined Mr. Stick-to-the-right, "I do assure you, and beseech you to receive the truth of my words, that that whole concern is a bubble. You may travel on it all your life-time, were you to live thousands of years, and yet never get beyond the limits of Vanity Fair! Yea; though you should deem yourself entering the gates of the Blessed City, it will be nothing but a miserable delusion."

"The Lord of the Celestial City," began the other pilgrim, whose name was Mr. Foot-it-to-Heaven, "has refused, and will ever refuse, to grant an act of incorporation for this rail-road; and unless that be obtained, no passenger can ever hope to enter his dominions. Wherefore, every man, who buys a ticket, must lay his account with losing the purchase-money—which is the value of his own soul."

"Poh, nonsense!" said Mr. Smooth-it-away, taking my arm and leading me off. "These fellows ought to be indicted for a libel. If the law stood as it once did in Vanity Fair, we should see them grinning through the iron-bars of the prison-window."

This incident made a considerable impression on my mind, and contributed with other circumstances to indispose me to a permanent residence in the city of Vanity; although, of course, I was not simple enough to give up my original plan of gliding along easily and commodiously by rail-road. Still, I grew anxious to be gone. There was one strange thing that troubled me; amid the occupations or amusements of the Fair, nothing was more common than for a person—whether at a feast, theatre, or church, or trafficking for wealth and honors, or whatever he might be doing, and however unseasonable the interruption—suddenly to vanish like a soap-bubble, and be never more seen of his fellows; and so accustomed were the latter to such little accidents, that they went on with their business, as quietly as if nothing had happened. But it was otherwise with me.

Finally, after a pretty long residence at the Fair, I resumed my journey towards the Celestial City, still with Mr. Smooth-it-away at my side. At a short distance beyond the suburbs of Vanity, we passed the ancient silver-mine, of which Demas was the first discoverer, and which is now wrought to great advantage, supplying nearly all the coined currency of the world. A little further onward was the spot where Lot's wife had stood for ages, under the semblance of a pillar of salt.[9] Curious travellers have long since carried it away piece-meal. Had all regrets been punished as rigorously as this poor dame's were, my yearning for the relinquished delights of Vanity Fair might have produced a similar change in my own corporeal substance, and left me a warning to future pilgrims.

The next remarkable object was a large edifice, constructed of moss-grown stone, but in a modern and airy style of architecture. The engine came to a pause in its vicinity, with the usual tremendous shriek.

"This was formerly the castle of the redoubted giant Despair," observed Mr. Smooth-it-away; "but, since his death, Mr. Flimsy-faith has repaired it, and now keeps an excellent house of entertainment here. It is one of our stopping-places."

"It seems but slightly put together," remarked I, looking at the frail, yet ponderous walls. "I do not envy Mr. Flimsy-faith his habitation. Some day, it will thunder down upon the heads of the occupants."

"We shall escape, at all events," said Mr. Smooth-it-away; "for Apollyon is putting on the steam again."

The road now plunged into a gorge of the Delectable Mountains, and traversed the field where, in former ages, the blind men wandered and stumbled among the tombs. One of these ancient tomb-stones had been thrust across the

---

[9]Cf. Genesis 19:26: in fleeing Sodom, Lot's wife looked back and was turned into a pillar of salt.

track, by some malicious person, and gave the train of cars a terrible jolt. Far up the rugged side of a mountain, I perceived a rusty iron-door, half-overgrown with bushes and creeping-plants, but with smoke issuing from its crevices.

"Is that," inquired I, "the very door in the hill-side, which the shepherds assured Christian was a by-way to hell?"

"That was a joke on the part of the shepherds," said Mr. Smooth-it-away, with a smile. "It is neither more nor less than the door of a cavern, which they use as a smoke-house for the preparation of mutton-hams."

My recollections of the journey are now, for a little space, dim and confused; inasmuch as a singular drowsiness here overcame me, owing to the fact that we were passing over the Enchanted Ground, the air of which encourages a disposition to sleep. I awoke, however, as soon as we crossed the borders of the pleasant land of Beulah. All the passengers were rubbing their eyes, comparing watches, and congratulating one another on the prospect of arriving so seasonably at the journey's end. The sweet breezes of this happy clime came refreshingly to our nostrils; we beheld the glimmering gush of silver fountains, overhung by trees of beautiful foliage and delicious fruit, which were propagated by grafts from the Celestial gardens. Once, as we dashed onward like a hurricane, there was a flutter of wings, and the bright appearance of an angel in the air, speeding forth on some heavenly mission. The engine now announced the close vicinity of the final Station House, by one last and horrible scream, in which there seemed to be distinguishable every kind of wailing and woe, and bitter fierceness of wrath, all mixed up with the wild laughter of a devil or a madman. Throughout our journey, at every stopping-place, Apollyon had exercised his ingenuity in screwing the most abominable sounds out of the whistle of the steam-engine; but, in this closing effort, he outdid himself, and created an infernal uproar, which, besides disturbing the peaceful inhabitants of Beulah, must have sent its discord even through the Celestial gates.

While the horrid clamor was still ringing in our ears, we heard an exulting strain, as if a thousand instruments of music, with height, and depth, and sweetness in their tones, at once tender and triumphant, were struck in unison, to greet the approach of some illustrious hero, who had fought the good fight,[10] and won a glorious victory, and was come to lay aside his battered arms forever. Looking to ascertain what might be the occasion of this glad harmony, I perceived, on alighting from the cars, that a multitude of Shining Ones had assembled on the other side of the river, to welcome two poor pilgrims, who were just emerging from its depths. They were the same whom Apollyon and ourselves had persecuted with taunts and gibes, and scalding steam, at the commencement of our journey; the same whose unworldly aspect and impressive words had stirred my conscience, amid the wild revellers of Vanity Fair.

"How amazingly well those men have got on!" cried I to Mr. Smooth-it-away. "I wish we were secure of as good a reception."

"Never fear—never fear!" answered my friend. "Come!—make haste!—the ferry-boat will be off directly; and in three minutes you will be on the other side of the river. No doubt you will find coaches to carry you up to the city-gates."

A steam ferry-boat, the last improvement on this important route, lay at the river-side, puffing, snorting, and emitting all those other disagreeable utterances, which betoken the departure to be immediate. I hurried on board, with the rest of the passengers, most of whom were in great perturbation; some bawling out for their baggage; some tearing their hair, and exclaiming that the boat would explode or sink; some already pale with the heaving of the stream; some gazing af-

---

[10]2 Timothy 4:7: "I have fought a good fight, I have finished my course, I have kept the faith."

frighted at the ugly aspect of the steersman; and some still dizzy with the slumberous influences of the Enchanted Ground. Looking back to the shore, I was amazed to discern Mr. Smooth-it-away, waving his hand in token of farewell!

"Don't you go over to the Celestial City?" exclaimed I.

"Oh, no!" answered he with a queer smile, and that same disagreeable contortion of visage, which I had remarked in the inhabitants of the Dark Valley. "Oh, no! I have come thus far only for the sake of your pleasant company. Good bye! We shall meet again."

And then did my excellent friend, Mr. Smooth-it-away, laugh outright; in the midst of which cachinnation, a smoke-wreath issued from his mouth and nostrils; while a twinkle of lurid flame darted out of either eye, proving indubitably that his heart was all of a red blaze. The impudent Fiend! To deny the existence of Tophet, when he felt its fiery tortures raging within his breast! I rushed to the side of the boat, intending to fling myself on shore. But the wheels, as they began their revolutions, threw a dash of spray over me, so cold—so deadly cold, with the chill that will never leave those waters, until Death be drowned in his own river—that, with a shiver and a heart-quake, I awoke. Thank Heaven, it was a Dream!

1843   *1843*

The Artist of the Beautiful[1]

An elderly man, with his pretty daughter on his arm, was passing along the street, and emerged from the gloom of the cloudy evening into the light that fell across the pavement from the window of a small shop. It was a projecting window; and on the inside were suspended a variety of watches,—pinchbeck,[2] silver, and one or two of gold,—all with their faces turned from the street, as if churlishly disinclined to inform the wayfarers what o'clock it was. Seated within the shop, sidelong to the window, with his pale face bent earnestly over some delicate piece of mechanism, on which was thrown the concentrated lustre of a shade-lamp, appeared a young man.

"What can Owen Warland be about?" muttered old Peter Hovenden,—himself a retired watchmaker, and the former master of this same young man, whose occupation he was now wondering at. "What can the fellow be about? These six months past, I have never come by his shop without seeing him just as steadily at work as now. It would be a flight beyond his usual foolery to seek for the Perpetual Motion. And yet I know enough of my old business to be certain, that what he is now so busy with is no part of the machinery of a watch."

"Perhaps, father," said Annie, without showing much interest in the question, "Owen is inventing a new kind of time-keeper. I am sure he has ingenuity enough."

"Poh, child! he has not the sort of ingenuity to invent anything better than a Dutch toy," answered her father, who had formerly been put to much vexation by Owen Warland's irregular genius. "A plague on such ingenuity! All the effect that ever I knew of it, was to spoil the accuracy of some of the best watches in my shop. He would turn the sun out of its orbit, and derange the whole course of time, if, as I said before, his ingenuity could grasp anything bigger than a child's toy!"

"Hush, father! he hears you," whispered Annie, pressing the old man's arm.

---

[1]This story has generally been taken as Hawthorne's most extensive commentary on the nature of art.

[2]An alloy of copper and zinc, used in inexpensive jewelry as an imitation of gold.

"His ears are as delicate as his feelings, and you know how easily disturbed they are. Do let us move on."

So Peter Hovenden and his daughter Annie plodded on, without further conversation, until, in a by-street of the town, they found themselves passing the open door of a blacksmith's shop. Within was seen the forge, now blazing up, and illuminating the high and dusky roof, and now confining its lustre to a narrow precinct of the coal-strewn floor, according as the breath of the bellows was puffed forth, or again inhaled into its vast leathern lungs. In the intervals of brightness, it was easy to distinguish objects in remote corners of the shop, and the horse-shoes that hung upon the wall; in the momentary gloom, the fire seemed to be glimmering amidst the vagueness of unenclosed space. Moving about in this red glare and alternate dusk, was the figure of the blacksmith, well worthy to be viewed in so picturesque an aspect of light and shade, where the bright blaze struggled with the black night, as if each would have snatched his comely strength from the other. Anon, he drew a white-hot bar of iron from the coals, laid it on the anvil, uplifted his arm of might, and was soon enveloped in the myriads of sparks which the strokes of his hammer scattered into the surrounding gloom.

"Now, that is a pleasant sight," said the old watchmaker. "'I know what it is to work in gold, but give me the worker in iron, after all is said and done. He spends his labor upon a reality. What say you, daughter Annie?"

"Pray don't speak so loud, father," whispered Annie. "Robert Danforth will hear you."

"And what if he should hear me?" said Peter Hovenden; "I say again, it is a good and a wholesome thing to depend upon main strength and reality, and to earn one's bread with the bare and brawny arm of a blacksmith. A watchmaker gets his brain puzzled by his wheels within a wheel, or loses his health or the nicety of his eyesight, as was my case; and finds himself, at middle age, or a little after, past labor at his own trade, and fit for nothing else, yet too poor to live at his ease. So, I say once again, give me main strength for my money. And then, how it takes the nonsense out of a man! Did you ever hear of a blacksmith being such a fool as Owen Warland, yonder?"

"Well said, uncle Hovenden!" shouted Robert Danforth, from the forge, in a full, deep, merry voice, that made the roof re-echo. "And what says Miss Annie to that doctrine? She, I suppose, will think it a genteeler business to tinker up a lady's watch, than to forge a horse-shoe or make a gridiron!"

Annie drew her father onward, without giving him time for reply.

But we must return to Owen Warland's shop, and spend more meditation upon his history and character than either Peter Hovenden, or probably his daughter Annie, or Owen's old schoolfellow, Robert Danforth, would have thought due to so slight a subject. From the time that his little fingers could grasp a pen-knife, Owen had been remarkable for a delicate ingenuity, which sometimes produced pretty shapes in wood, principally figures of flowers and birds, and sometimes seemed to aim at the hidden mysteries of mechanism. But it was always for purposes of grace, and never with any mockery of the useful. He did not, like the crowd of schoolboy artizans, construct little windmills on the angle of a barn, or watermills across the neighboring brook. Those who discovered such peculiarity in the boy, as to think it worth their while to observe him closely, sometimes saw reason to suppose that he was attempting to imitate the beautiful movements of Nature, as exemplified in the flight of birds or the activity of little animals. It seemed, in fact, a new development of the love of the Beautiful, such as might have made him a poet, a painter, or a sculptor, and which was as completely refined from all utilitarian coarseness, as it could have been in either of the fine arts. He looked with singular distaste at the stiff and regular processes of ordinary machinery. Being once carried to see a steam-engine, in the expectation that his intuitive comprehension of mechanical principles would be gratified, he turned pale, and grew sick, as if something monstrous and unnatural had been presented to him. This horror was partly owing to the size and terrible energy of the Iron Laborer; for the character of Owen's mind was microscopic, and tended naturally to the minute, in accordance with his diminutive frame, and the marvellous smallness and delicate power of his fingers. Not that his sense of beauty was thereby diminished into a sense of prettiness. The Beautiful Idea has no relation to size, and may be as perfectly developed in a space too minute for any but microscopic investigation, as within the ample verge that is measured by the arc of the rainbow. But, at all events, this characteristic minuteness in his objects and accomplishments made the world even more incapable, than it might otherwise have been, of appreciating Owen Warland's genius. The boy's relatives saw nothing better to be done—as perhaps there was not—than to bind him apprentice to a watchmaker, hoping that his strange ingenuity might thus be regulated, and put to utilitarian purposes.

Peter Hovenden's opinion of his apprentice has already been expressed. He could make nothing of the lad. Owen's apprehension of the professional mysteries, it is true, was inconceivably quick. But he altogether forgot or despised the grand object of a watchmaker's business, and cared no more for the measurement of time than if it had been merged into eternity. So long, however, as he remained under his old master's care, Owen's lack of sturdiness made it possible, by strict injunctions and sharp oversight, to restrain his creative eccentricity within bounds. But when his apprenticeship was served out, and he had taken the little shop which Peter Hovenden's failing eyesight compelled him to relinquish, then did people recognize how unfit a person was Owen Warland to lead old blind Father Time along his daily course. One of his most rational projects was, to connect a musical operation with the machinery of his watches, so that all the harsh dissonances of life might be rendered tuneful, and each flitting moment fall into the abyss of the Past in golden drops of harmony. If a family-clock was entrusted to him for repair—one of those tall, ancient clocks that have grown nearly allied to human nature, by measuring out the lifetime of many generations—he would take upon himself to arrange a dance or funeral procession of figures, across its venerable face, representing twelve mirthful or melancholy hours. Several freaks of this kind quite destroyed the young watchmaker's credit with that steady and matter-of-fact class of people who hold the opinion that time is not to be trifled with, whether considered as the medium of advancement and prosperity in this world, or preparation for the next. His custom rapidly diminished—a misfortune, however, that was probably reckoned among his better accidents by Owen Warland, who was becoming more and more absorbed in a secret occupation, which drew all his science and manual dexterity into itself, and likewise gave full employment to the characteristic tendencies of his genius. This pursuit had already consumed many months.

After the old watchmaker and his pretty daughter had gazed at him, out of the obscurity of the street, Owen Warland was seized with a fluttering of the nerves, which made his hand tremble too violently to proceed with such delicate labor as he was now engaged upon.

"It was Annie herself!" murmured he. "I should have known it, by this throbbing of my heart, before I heard her father's voice. Ah, how it throbs! I shall scarcely be able to work again on this exquisite mechanism to-night. Annie—dearest Annie—thou shouldst give firmness to my heart and hand, and not shake them thus; for if I strive to put the very spirit of Beauty into form, and give it motion, it is for thy sake alone. Oh, throbbing heart, be quiet! If my labor be thus thwarted, there will come vague and unsatisfied dreams, which will leave me spiritless to-morrow."

As he was endeavoring to settle himself again to his task, the shop-door opened, and gave admittance to no other than the stalwart figure which Peter Hovenden had paused to admire, as seen amid the light and shadow of the black-smith's shop. Robert Danforth had brought a little anvil of his own manufacture, and peculiarly constructed, which the young artist had recently bespoken. Owen examined the article, and pronounced it fashioned according to his wish.

"Why, yes," said Robert Danforth, his strong voice filling the shop as with the sound of a bass-viol, "I consider myself equal to anything in the way of my own trade; though I should have made but a poor figure at yours, with such a fist as this,"—added he, laughing, as he laid his vast hand beside the delicate one of Owen. "But what then? I put more main strength into one blow of my sledge-hammer, than all that you have expended since you were a 'prentice. Is not that the truth?"

"Very probably," answered the low and slender voice of Owen. "Strength is an earthly monster. I make no pretensions to it. My force, whatever there may be of it, is altogether spiritual."

"Well; but, Owen, what are you about!" asked his old schoolfellow, still in such a hearty volume of tone that it made the artist shrink; especially as the question related to a subject so sacred as the absorbing dream of his imagination. "Folks do say, that you are trying to discover the Perpetual Motion."

"The Perpetual Motion?—nonsense!" replied Owen Warland, with a move-ment of disgust; for he was full of little petulances. "It can never be discovered! It is a dream that may delude men whose brains are mystified with matter, but not me. Besides, if such a discovery were possible, it would not be worth my while to make it, only to have the secret turned to such purposes as are now effected by steam and water-power. I am not ambitious to be honored with the paternity of a new kind of cotton-machine."

"That would be droll enough!" cried the blacksmith, breaking out into such an uproar of laughter, that Owen himself, and the bell-glasses on his work-board, quivered in unison. "No, no, Owen! No child of yours will have iron joints and sinews. Well, I won't hinder you any more. Good night, Owen, and success; and if you need any assistance, so far as a downright blow of hammer upon anvil will answer the purpose, I'm your man!"

And with another laugh, the man of main strength left the shop.

"How strange it is," whispered Owen Warland to himself, leaning his head upon his hand, "that all my musings, my purposes, my passion for the Beautiful, my consciousness of power to create it—a finer, more ethereal power, of which this earthly giant can have no conception—all, all, look so vain and idle, whenever my path is crossed by Robert Danforth! He would drive me mad, were I to meet him often. His hard, brute force darkens and confuses the spiritual element within me. But I, too, will be strong in my own way. I will not yield to him!"

He took from beneath a glass, a piece of minute machinery, which he set in the condensed light of his lamp, and, looking intently at it through a magnifying glass, proceeded to operate with a delicate instrument of steel. In an instant, how-ever, he fell back in his chair, and clasped his hands, with a look of horror on his face, that made its small features as impressive as those of a giant would have been.

"Heaven! What have I done!" exclaimed he. "The vapor!—the influence of that brute force!—it has bewildered me, and obscured my perception. I have made the very stroke—the fatal stroke—that I have dreaded from the first! It is all over—the toil of months—the object of my life! I am ruined!"

And there he sat, in strange despair, until his lamp flickered in the socket, and left the Artist of the Beautiful in darkness.

Thus it is, that ideas which grow up within the imagination, and appear so lovely to it, and of a value beyond whatever men call valuable, are exposed to be shattered and annihilated by contact with the Practical. It is requisite for the ideal artist to possess a force of character that seems hardly compatible with its delicacy; he must keep his faith in himself, while the incredulous world assails him with its utter disbelief; he must stand up against mankind and be his own sole disciple, both as respects his genius, and the objects to which it is directed.

For a time, Owen Warland succumbed to this severe, but inevitable test. He spent a few sluggish weeks, with his head so continually resting in his hands, that the townspeople had scarcely an opportunity to see his countenance. When, at last, it was again uplifted to the light of day, a cold, dull, nameless change was perceptible upon it. In the opinion of Peter Hovenden, however, and that order of sagacious understandings who think that life should be regulated, like clock-work, with leaden weights, the alteration was entirely for the better. Owen now indeed, applied himself to business with dogged industry. It was marvellous to witness the obtuse gravity with which he would inspect the wheels of a great, old silver watch; thereby delighting the owner, in whose fob it had been worn till he deemed it a portion of his own life, and was accordingly jealous of its treatment. In consequence of the good report thus acquired, Owen Warland was invited by the proper authorities to regulate the clock in the churchsteeple. He succeeded so admirably in this matter of public interest, that the merchants gruffly acknowl-edged his merits on 'Change;[3] the nurse whispered his praises, as she gave the potion in the sick-chamber; the lover blessed him at the hour of appointed inter-view; and the town in general thanked Owen for the punctuality of dinner-time. In a word, the heavy weight upon his spirits kept everything in order, not merely within his own system, but wheresoever the iron accents of the church-clock were audible. It was a circumstance, though minute, yet characteristic of his present state, that, when employed to engrave names or initials on silver spoons, he now wrote the requisite letters in the plainest possible style; omitting a variety of fanci-ful flourishes, that had heretofore distinguished his work in this kind.

One day, during the era of this happy transformation, old Peter Hovenden came to visit his former apprentice.

"Well, Owen," said he, "I am glad to hear such good accounts of you from all quarters; and especially from the town-clock yonder, which speaks in your com-mendation every hour of the twenty-four. Only get rid altogether of your nonsen-sical trash about the Beautiful—which I, nor nobody else, nor yourself to boot, could never understand—only free yourself of that, and your success in life is as sure as daylight. Why, if you go on in this way, I should even venture to let you doctor this precious old watch of mine; though, except my daughter Annie, I have nothing else so valuable in the world."

"I should hardly dare touch it, sir," replied Owen in a depressed tone; for he was weighed down by his old master's presence.

"In time," said the latter, "in time, you will be capable of it."

The old watchmaker, with the freedom naturally consequent on his former au-thority, went on inspecting the work which Owen had in hand at the moment, to-gether with other matters that were in progress. The artist, meanwhile, could scarcely lift his head. There was nothing so antipodal to his nature as this man's cold, unimaginative sagacity, by contact with which everything was converted into a dream, except the densest matter of the physical world. Owen groaned in spirit, and prayed fervently to be delivered from him.

"But what is this?" cried Peter Hovenden abruptly, taking up a dusty bell-glass, beneath which appeared a mechanical something, as delicate and minute as the

---

[3]I.e., exchange, a center where business is conducted.

system of a butterfly's anatomy. "What have we here! Owen, Owen! there is witch-craft in these little chains, and wheels, and paddles! See! with one pinch of my finger and thumb, I am going to deliver you from all future peril."

"For Heaven's sake," screamed Owen Warland, springing up with wonderful energy, "as you would not drive me mad—do not touch it! The slightest pressure of your finger would ruin me for ever."

"Aha, young man! And is it so?" said the old watchmaker, looking at him with just enough of penetration to torture Owen's soul with the bitterness of worldly criticism. "Well; take your own course. But I warn you again, that in this small piece of mechanism lives your evil spirit. Shall I exorcise him?"

"You are my Evil Spirit," answered Owen, much excited—"you, and the hard, coarse world! The leaden thoughts and the despondency that you fling upon me are my clogs. Else, I should long ago have achieved the task that I was created for."

Peter Hovenden shook his head, with the mixture of contempt and indignation which mankind, of whom he was partly a representative, deem themselves entitled to feel towards all simpletons who seek other prizes than the dusty ones along the highway. He then took his leave with an uplifted finger, and a sneer upon his face, that haunted the artist's dreams for many a night afterwards. At the time of his old master's visit, Owen was probably on the point of taking up the relin-quished task; but, by this sinister event, he was thrown back into the state whence he had been slowly emerging.

But the innate tendency of his soul had only been accumulating fresh vigor, during its apparent sluggishness. As the summer advanced, he almost totally relin-quished his business, and permitted Father Time, so far as the old gentleman was represented by the clocks and watches under his control, to stray at random through human life, making infinite confusion among the train of bewildered hours. He wasted the sunshine, as people said, in wandering through the woods and fields, and along the banks of streams. There, like a child, he found amuse-ment in chasing butterflies, or watching the motions of water-insects. There was something truly mysterious in the intentness with which he contemplated these living playthings, as they sported on the breeze; or examined the structure of an imperial insect whom he had imprisoned. The chase of butterflies was an apt em-blem of the ideal pursuit in which he had spent so many golden hours. But, would the Beautiful Idea ever be yielded to his hand, like the butterfly that symbolized it? Sweet, doubtless, were these days, and congenial to the artist's soul. They were full of bright conceptions, which gleamed through his intellectual world, as the butterflies gleamed through the outward atmosphere, and were real to him for the instant, without the toil, and perplexity, and many disappointments, of at-tempting to make them visible to the sensual eye. Alas, that the artist, whether in poetry or whatever other material, may not content himself with the inward enjoy-ment of the Beautiful, but must chase the flitting mystery beyond the verge of his ethereal domain, and crush its frail being in seizing it with a material grasp! Owen Warland felt the impulse to give external reality to his ideas, as irresistibly as any of the poets or painters, who have arrayed the world in a dimmer and fainter beauty, imperfectly copied from the richness of their visions.

The night was now his time for the slow process of recreating the one Idea, to which all his intellectual activity referred itself. Always at the approach of dusk, he stole into the town, locked himself within his shop, and wrought with patient del-icacy of touch, for many hours. Sometimes he was startled by the rap of the watch-man, who, when all the world should be asleep, had caught the gleam of lamp-light through the crevices of Owen Warland's shutters. Daylight, to the morbid sensibility of his mind, seemed to have an intrusiveness that interfered with his pursuits. On cloudy and inclement days, therefore, he sat with his head upon his hands, muffling, as it were, his sensitive brain in a mist of indefinite musings; for it was a relief to escape from the sharp distinctness with which he was compelled to shape out his thoughts, during his nightly toil.

From one of these fits of torpor, he was aroused by the entrance of Annie Hovenden, who came into the shop with the freedom of a customer, and also with something of the familiarity of a childish friend. She had worn a hole through her silver thimble, and wanted Owen to repair it.

"But I don't know whether you will condescend to such a task," said she, laughing, "now that you are so taken up with the notion of putting spirit into machinery."

"Where did you get that idea, Annie?" said Owen, starting in surprise.

"Oh, out of my own head," answered she, "and from something that I heard you say, long ago, when you were but a boy, and I a little child. But, come! will you mend this poor thimble of mine?"

"Anything for your sake, Annie," said Owen Warland—"anything; even were it to work at Robert Danforth's forge."

"And that would be a pretty sight!" retorted Annie, glancing with imperceptible slightness at the artist's small and slender frame. "Well; here is the thimble."

"But that is a strange idea of yours," said Owen, "about the spiritualization of matter!"

And then the thought stole into his mind, that this young girl possessed the gift to comprehend him, better than all the world beside. And what a help and strength would it be to him, in his lonely toil, if he could gain the sympathy of the only being whom he loved! To persons whose pursuits are insulated from the common business of life—who are either in advance of mankind, or apart from it—there often comes a sensation of moral cold, that makes the spirit shiver, as if it had reached the frozen solitudes around the pole. What the prophet, the poet, the reformer, the criminal, or any other man, with human yearnings, but separated from the multitude by a peculiar lot, might feel, poor Owen Warland felt.

"Annie," cried he, growing pale as death at the thought, "how gladly would I tell you the secret of my pursuit! You, methinks, would estimate it rightly. You, I know, would hear it with a reverence that I must not expect from the harsh, material world."

"Would I not? to be sure I would!" replied Annie Hovenden, lightly laughing. "Come; explain to me quickly what is the meaning of this little whirligig, so delicately wrought that it might be a plaything for Queen Mab.[4] See; I will put it in motion."

"Hold," exclaimed Owen, "hold!"

Annie had but given the slightest possible touch, with the point of a needle, to the same minute portion of complicated machinery which has been more than once mentioned, when the artist seized her by the wrist with a force that made her scream aloud. She was affrighted at the convulsion of intense rage and anguish that writhed across his features. The next instant he let his head sink upon his hands.

"Go, Annie," murmured he, "I have deceived myself, and must suffer for it. I yearned for sympathy—and thought—and fancied—and dreamed—that you might give it me. But you lack the talisman, Annie, that should admit you into my secrets. That touch has undone the toil of months, and the thought of a lifetime! It was not your fault, Annie—but you have ruined me!"

Poor Owen Warland! He had indeed erred, yet pardonably; for if any human spirit could have sufficiently reverenced the processes so sacred in his eyes, it must

---

[4]"The fairies' midwife," who helps humans to give birth to their dreams. See Shakespeare's *Romeo and Juliet*, I, iv, 53–94.

have been a woman's. Even Annie Hovenden, possibly, might not have disappointed him, had she been enlightened by the deep intelligence of love.

The artist spent the ensuing winter in a way that satisfied any persons, who had hitherto retained a hopeful opinion of him, that he was, in truth, irrevocably doomed to inutility as regarded the world, and to an evil destiny on his own part. The decease of a relative had put him in possession of a small inheritance. Thus freed from the necessity of toil, and having lost the steadfast influence of a great purpose—great, at least to him—he abandoned himself to habits from which, it might have been supposed, the mere delicacy of his organization would have availed to secure him. But when the ethereal portion of a man of genius is obscured, the earthly part assumes an influence the more uncontrollable, because the character is now thrown off the balance to which Providence had so nicely adjusted it, and which, in coarser natures, is adjusted by some other method. Owen Warland made proof of whatever show of bliss may be found in riot. He looked at the world through the golden medium of wine, and contemplated the visions that bubble up so gaily around the brim of the glass, and that people the air with shapes of pleasant madness, which so soon grow ghostly and forlorn. Even when this dismal and inevitable change had taken place, the young man might still have continued to quaff the cup of enchantments, though its vapor did but shroud life in gloom, and fill the gloom with spectres that mocked at him. There was a certain irksomeness of spirit, which, being real, and the deepest sensation of which the artist was now conscious, was more intolerable than any fantastic miseries and horrors that the abuse of wine could summon up. In the latter case, he could remember, even out of the midst of his trouble, that all was but a delusion; in the former, the heavy anguish was his actual life.

From this perilous state, he was redeemed by an incident which more than one person witnessed, but of which the shrewdest could not explain nor conjecture the operation on Owen Warland's mind. It was very simple. On a warm afternoon of spring, as the artist sat among his rioutous companions, with a glass of wine before him, a splendid butterfly flew in at the open window, and fluttered about his head.

"Ah!" exclaimed Owen, who had drank freely, "Are you alive again, child of the sun, and playmate of the summer breeze, after your dismal winter's nap! Then it is time for me to be at work!"

And leaving his unempted glass upon the table, he departed, and was never known to sip another drop of wine.

And now, again, he resumed his wanderings in the woods and fields. It might be fancied that the bright butterfly, which had come so spiritlike into the window, as Owen sat with the rude revellers, was indeed a spirit, commissioned to recall him to the pure, ideal life that had so etherealized him among men. It might be fancied, that he went forth to seek this spirit, in its sunny haunts; for still, as in the summer-time gone by, he was seen to steal gently up, wherever a butterfly had alighted, and lose himself in contemplation of it. When it took flight, his eyes followed the winged vision, as if its airy track would show the path to heaven. But what could be the purpose of the unseasonable toil, which was again resumed, as the watchman knew by the lines of lamp-light through the crevices of Owen Warland's shutters? The townspeople had one comprehensive explanation of all these singularities. Owen Warland had gone mad! How universally efficacious—how satisfactory, too, and soothing to the injured sensibility of narrowness and dullness—is this easy method of accounting for whatever lies beyond the world's most ordinary scope! From Saint Paul's days,[5] down to our poor little Artist of the

---

[5]Cf. Acts 26:24: "And as he thus spake for himself, Festus said with a loud voice, Paul, thou art beside thyself; much learning doeth make thee mad."

Beautiful, the same talisman has been applied to the elucidation of all mysteries in the words or deeds of men, who spoke or acted too wisely or too well. In Owen Warland's case, the judgment of his townspeople may have been correct. Perhaps he was mad. The lack of sympathy—that contrast between himself and his neighbors, which took away the restraint of example—was enough to make him so. Or, possibly, he had caught just so much of ethereal radiance as served to bewilder him, in an earthly sense, by its intermixture with the common daylight.

One evening, when the artist had returned from a customary ramble, and had just thrown the lustre of his lamp on the delicate piece of work, so often interrupted, but still taken up again, as if his fate were embodied in its mechanism, he was surprised by the entrance of old Peter Hovenden. Owen never met this man without a shrinking of the heart. Of all the world, he was most terrible, by reason of a keen understanding, which saw so distinctly what it did see, and disbelieved so uncompromisingly in what it could not see. On this occasion, the old watchmaker had merely a gracious word or two to say.

"Owen, my lad," said he, "we must see you at my house to-morrow night."

The artist began to mutter some excuse.

"Oh, but it must be so," quoth Peter Hovenden, "for the sake of the days when you were one of the household. What, my boy, don't you know that my daughter Annie is engaged to Robert Danforth? We are making an entertainment, in our humble way, to celebrate the event."

"Ah!" said Owen.

That little monosyllable was all he uttered; its tone seemed cold and unconcerned, to an ear like Peter Hovenden's; and yet there was in it the stifled outcry of the poor artist's heart, which he compressed within him like a man holding down an evil spirit. One slight outbreak, however, imperceptible to the old watchmaker, he allowed himself. Raising the instrument with which he was about to begin his work, he let it fall upon the little system of machinery that had, anew, cost him months of thought and toil. It was shattered by the stroke!

Owen Warland's story would have been no tolerable representation of the troubled life of those who strive to create the Beautiful, if, amid all other thwarting influences, love had not interposed to steal the cunning from his hand. Outwardly, he had been no ardent or enterprising lover; the career of his passion had confined its tumults and vicissitudes so entirely within the artist's imagination, that Annie herself had scarcely more than a woman's intuitive perception of it. But, in Owen's view, it covered the whole field of his life. Forgetful of the time when she had shown herself incapable of any deep response, he had persisted in connecting all his dreams of artistical success with Annie's image; she was the visible shape in which the spiritual power that he worshipped, and on whose altar he hoped to lay a not unworthy offering, was made manifest to him. Of course he had deceived himself; there were no such attributes in Annie Hovenden as his imagination had endowed her with. She, in the aspect which she wore to his inward vision, was as much a creation of his own, as the mysterious piece of mechanism would be were it ever realized. Had he become convinced of his mistake through the medium of successful love; had he won Annie to his bosom, and there beheld her fade from angel into ordinary woman, the disappointment might have driven him back, with concentrated energy, upon his sole remaining object. On the other hand, had he found Annie what he fancied, his lot would have been so rich in beauty, that, out of its mere redundancy, he might have wrought the Beautiful into many a worthier type than he had toiled for. But the guise in which his sorrow came to him, the sense that the angel of his life had been snatched away and given to a rude man of earth and iron, who could neither need nor appreciate her ministrations; this was the very perversity of fate, that makes human existence appear too absurd and contradictory to be the scene of one other hope or one other fear. There was nothing left for Owen Warland but to sit down like a man that had been stunned.

He went through a fit of illness. After his recovery, his small and slender frame assumed an obtuser garniture of flesh than it had ever before worn. His thin cheeks became round; his delicate little hand, so spiritually fashioned to achieve fairy task-work, grew plumper than the hand of a thriving infant. His aspect had a childishness, such as might have induced a stranger to pat him on the head—pausing, however, in the act, to wonder what manner of child was here. It was as if the spirit had gone out of him, leaving the body to flourish in a sort of vegetable existence. Not that Owen Warland was idiotic. He could talk, and not irrationally. Somewhat of a babbler, indeed, did people begin to think him; for he was apt to discourse at wearisome length, of marvels of mechanism that he had read about in books, but which he had learned to consider as absolutely fabulous. Among them he enumerated the Man of Brass, constructed by Albertus Magnus, and the Brazen Head of Friar Bacon;[6] and, coming down to later times, the automata of a little coach and horses, which, it was pretended, had been manufactured for the Dauphin of France;[7] together with an insect that buzzed about the ear like a living fly, and yet was but a contrivance of minute steel springs. There was a story, too, of a duck that waddled, and quacked, and ate; though, had any honest citizen purchased it for dinner, he would have found himself cheated with the mere mechanical apparition of a duck.

"But all these accounts," said Owen Warland, "I am now satisfied, are mere impositions."

Then, in a mysterious way, he would confess that he once thought differently. In his idle and dreamy days, he had considered it possible, in a certain sense, to spiritualize machinery; and to combine with the new species of life and motion, thus produced, a beauty that should attain to the ideal which Nature has proposed to herself, in all her creatures, but has never taken pains to realize. He seemed, however, to retain no very distinct perception either of the process of achieving this object, or of the design itself.

"I have thrown it all aside now," he would say. "It was a dream, such as young men are always mystifying themselves with. Now that I have acquired a little common sense, it makes me laugh to think of it."

Poor, poor, and fallen Owen Warland! These were the symptoms that he had ceased to be an inhabitant of the better sphere that lies unseen around us. He had lost his faith in the invisible, and now prided himself, as such unfortunates invariably do, in the wisdom which rejected much that even his eye could see, and trusted confidently in nothing but what his hand could touch. This is the calamity of men whose spiritual part dies out of them, and leaves the grosser understanding to assimilate them more and more to the things of which alone it can take cognizance. But, in Owen Warland, the spirit was not dead, nor past away; it only slept.

How it awoke again, is not recorded. Perhaps, the torpid slumber was broken by a convulsive pain. Perhaps, as in a former instance, the butterfly came and hovered about his head, and reinspired him—as, indeed, this creature of the sunshine had always a mysterious mission for the artist—reinspired him with the former purpose of his life. Whether it were pain or happiness that thrilled through his veins, his first impulse was to thank Heaven for rendering him again

---

[6]Albertus Magnus (1193?–1280), German scholastic philosopher, had the reputation of a magician; Friar Roger Bacon (1214–1294), English philosopher, who according to legend created a speaking head of brass.
[7]Title of the eldest son of the French king.

the being of thought, imagination, and keenest sensibility, that he had long ceased to be.

"Now for my task," said he. "Never did I feel such strength for it as now."

Yet, strong as he felt himself, he was incited to toil the more diligently, by an anxiety lest death should surprise him in the midst of his labors. This anxiety, perhaps, is common to all men who set their hearts upon anything so high, in their own view of it, that life becomes of importance only as conditional to its accomplishment. So long as we love life for itself, we seldom dread the losing it. When we desire life for the attainment of an object, we recognize the frailty of its texture. But, side by side with this sense of insecurity, there is a vital faith in our invulnerability to the shaft of death, while engaged in any task that seems assigned by Providence as our proper thing to do, and which the world would have cause to mourn for, should we leave it unaccomplished. Can the philosopher, big[8] with the inspiration of an idea that is to reform mankind, believe that he is to be beckoned from this sensible existence, at the very instant when he is mustering his breath to speak the word of light? Should he perish so, the weary ages may pass away—the world's whole life-sand[9] may fall, drop by drop—before another intellect is prepared to develope the truth that might have been uttered then. But history affords many an example, where the most precious spirit, at any particular epoch manifested in human shape, has gone hence untimely, without space alowed him, so far as mortal judgment could discern, to perform his mission on the earth. The prophet dies; and the man of torpid heart and sluggish brain lives on. The poet leaves his song half sung, or finishes it, beyond the scope of mortal ears, in a celestial choir. The painter—as Allston[10] did—leaves half his conception on the canvass, to sadden us with its imperfect beauty, and goes to picture forth the whole, if it be no irreverence to say so, in the hues of Heaven. But, rather, such incomplete designs of this life will be perfected nowhere. This so frequent abortion of man's dearest projects must be taken as a proof, that the deeds of earth, however etherealized by piety or genius, are without value, except as exercises and manifestations of the spirit. In Heaven, all ordinary thought is higher and more melodious than Milton's song. Then, would he add another verse to any strain that he had left unfinished here?

But to return to Owen Warland. It was his fortune, good or ill, to achieve the purpose of his life. Pass we over a long space of intense thought, yearning effort, minute toil, and wasting anxiety, succeeded by an instant of solitary triumph; let all this be imagined; and then behold the artist, on a winter evening, seeking admittance to Robert Danforth's fireside circle. There he found the Man of Iron, with his massive substance thoroughly warmed and attempered by domestic influences. And there was Annie, too, now transformed into a matron, with much of her husband's plain and sturdy nature, but imbued, as Owen Warland still believed, with a finer grace, that might enable her to be the interpreter between Strength and Beauty. It happened, likewise, that old Peter Hovenden was a guest, this evening, at his daughter's fireside; and it was his well-remembered expression of keen, cold criticism, that first encountered the artist's glance.

"My old friend Owen!" cried Robert Danforth, starting up, and compressing the artist's delicate fingers within a hand that was accustomed to gripe bars of iron. "This is kind and neighborly, to come to us at last! I was afraid your Perpetual Motion had bewitched you out of the remembrance of old times."

"We are glad to see you!" said Annie, while a blush reddened her matronly cheek. "It was not like a friend, to stay from us so long."

---

[8]Pregnant.
[9]Sand of the hourglass.
[10]Washington Allston (1779–1843), American painter who

spent the last decades of his life painting *Belshazzar's Feast*, which he left unfinished at his death.

"Well, Owen," inquired the old watchmaker, as his first greeting, "how comes on the Beautiful? Have you created it at last?"

The artist did not immediately reply, being startled by the apparition of a young child of strength, that was tumbling about on the carpet; a little personage who had come mysteriously out of the infinite, but with something so sturdy and real in his composition that he seemed moulded out of the densest substance which earth could supply. This hopeful infant crawled towards the new-comer, and setting himself on end—as Robert Danforth expressed the posture—stared at Owen with a look of such sagacious observation, that the mother could not help exchanging a proud glance with her husband. But the artist was disturbed by the child's look, as imagining a resemblance between it and Peter Hovenden's habitual expression. He could have fancied that the old watchmaker was compressed into this baby-shape, and was looking out of those baby-eyes, and repeating—as he now did—the malicious question:

"The Beautiful, Owen! How comes on the Beautiful? Have you succeeded in creating the Beautiful?"

"I have succeeded," replied the artist, with a momentary light of triumph in his eyes, and a smile of sunshine, yet steeped in such depth of thought that it was almost sadness. "Yes, my friends, it is the truth. I have succeeded!"

"Indeed!" cried Annie, a look of maiden mirthfulness peeping out of her face again. "And is it lawful, now, to inquire what the secret is?"

"Surely; it is to disclose it, that I have come," answered Owen Warland. "You shall know, and see, and touch, and possess, the secret! For Annie—if by that name I may still address the friend of my boyish years—Annie, it is for your bridal gift that I have wrought this spiritualized mechanism, this harmony of motion, this Mystery of Beauty! It comes late, indeed; but it is as we go onward in life, when objects begin to lose their freshness of hue, and our souls their delicacy of perception, that the spirit of Beauty is most needed. If—forgive me, Annie—if you know how to value this gift, it can never come too late!"

He produced, as he spoke, what seemed a jewel-box. It was carved richly out of ebony by his own hand, and inlaid with a fanciful tracery of pearl, representing a boy in pursuit of a butterfly, which, elsewhere, had become a winged spirit, and was flying heavenward; while the boy, or youth, had found such efficacy in his strong desire, that he ascended from earth to cloud, and from cloud to celestial atmosphere, to win the Beautiful. This case of ebony the artist opened, and bade Annie place her finger on its edge. She did so, but almost screamed, as a butterfly fluttered forth, and alighting on her finger's tip, sat waving the ample magnificence of its purple and gold-speckled wings, as if in prelude to a flight. It is impossible to express by words the glory, the splendor, the delicate gorgeousness, which were softened into the beauty of this object. Nature's ideal butterfly was here realized in all its perfection; not in the pattern of such faded insects as flit among earthly flowers, but of those which hover across the meads of Paradise, for child-angels and the spirits of departed infants to disport themselves with. The rich down was visible upon its wings; the lustre of its eyes seemed instinct with spirit. The firelight glimmered around this wonder—the candles gleamed upon it—but it glistened apparently by its own radiance, and illuminated the finger and outstretched hand on which it rested, with a white gleam like that of precious stones. In its perfect beauty, the consideration of size was entirely lost. Had its wings overarched the firmament, the mind could not have been more filled or satisfied.

"Beautiful! Beautiful!" exclaimed Annie. "Is it alive? Is it alive?"

"Alive? To be sure it is," answered her husband. "Do you suppose any mortal has skill enough to make a butterfly,—or would put himself to the trouble of making one, when any child may catch a score of them in a summer's afternoon?

Alive? Certainly! But this pretty box is undoubtedly of our friend Owen's manufacture; and really it does him credit."

At this moment, the butterfly waved its wings anew, with a motion so absolutely lifelike that Annie was startled, and even awe-stricken; for, in spite of her husband's opinion, she could not satisfy herself whether it was indeed a living creature, or a piece of wondrous mechanism.

"Is it alive?" she repeated, more earnestly than before.

"Judge for yourself," said Owen Warland, who stood gazing in her face with fixed attention.

The butterfly now flung itself upon the air, fluttered round Annie's head, and soared into a distant region of the parlor, still making itself perceptible to sight by the starry gleam in which the motion of its wings enveloped it. The infant on the floor, followed its course with his sagacious little eyes. After flying about the room, it returned, in a spiral curve, and settled again on Annie's finger.

"But is it alive?" exclaimed she again; and the finger, on which the gorgeous mystery had alighted, was so tremulous that the butterfly was forced to balance himself with his wings. "Tell me if it be alive, or whether you created it?"

"Wherefore ask who created it, so it be beautiful?" replied Owen Warland. "Alive? Yes, Annie; it may well be said to possess life, for it absorbed my own being into itself; and in the secret of that butterfly, and in its beauty—which is not merely outward, but deep as its whole system—is represented the intellect, the imagination, the sensibility, the soul, of an Artist of the Beautiful! Yes, I created it. But"—and here his countenance somewhat changed—"this butterfly is not now to me what it was when I beheld it afar off, in the daydreams of my youth."

"Be it what it may, it is a pretty plaything," said the blacksmith, grinning with childlike delight. "I wonder whether it would condescend to alight on such a great clumsy finger as mine? Hold it hither, Annie!"

By the artist's direction, Annie touched her finger's tip to that of her husband; and, after a momentary delay, the butterfly fluttered from one to the other. It preluded a second flight by a similar, yet not precisely the same waving of wings, as in the first experiment; then, ascending from the blacksmith's stalwart finger, it rose in a gradually enlarging curve to the ceiling, made one wide sweep around the room, and returned with an undulating movement to the point whence it had started.

"Well, that does beat all nature!" cried Robert Danforth, bestowing the heartiest praise that he could find expression for; and, indeed, had he paused there, a man of finer words and nicer perception, could not easily have said more. "That goes beyond me, I confess! But what then? There is more real use in one downright blow of my sledge-hammer, than in the whole five years' labor that our friend Owen has wasted on this butterfly!"

Here the child clapped his hands, and made a great babble of indistinct utterance, apparently demanding that the butterfly should be given him for a plaything.

Owen Warland, meanwhile, glanced sidelong at Annie, to discover whether she sympathized in her husband's estimate of the comparative value of the Beautiful and the Practical. There was, amid all her kindness towards himself, amid all the wonder and admiration with which she contemplated the marvelous work of his hands, and incarnation of his idea, a secret scorn; too secret, perhaps, for her own consciousness, and perceptible only to such intuitive discernment as that of the artist. But Owen, in the latter stages of his pursuit, had risen out of the region in which such a discovery might have been torture. He knew that the world, and Annie as the representative of the world, whatever praise might be bestowed, could never say the fitting word, nor feel the fitting sentiment which should be the perfect recompense of an artist who, symbolizing a lofty moral by a material trifle—

converting what was earthly, to spiritual gold—had won the Beautiful into his handiwork. Not at this latest moment, was he to learn that the reward of all high performance must be sought within itself, or sought in vain. There was, however, a view of the matter, which Annie, and her husband, and even Peter Hovenden, might fully have understood, and which would have satisfied them that the toil of years had here been worthily bestowed. Owen Warland might have told them, that this butterfly, this plaything, this bridal-gift of a poor watchmaker to a black-smith's wife, was, in truth, a gem of art that a monarch would have purchased with honors and abundant wealth, and have treasured it among the jewels of his kingdom, as the most unique and wondrous of them all! But the artist smiled, and kept the secret to himself.

"Father," said Annie, thinking that a word of praise from the old watchmaker might gratify his former apprentice, "do come and admire this pretty butterfly!"

"Let us see," said Peter Hovenden, rising from his chair, with the sneer upon his face that always made people doubt, as he himself did, in everything but a ma-terial existence. "Here is my finger for it to alight upon. I shall understand it bet-ter when once I have touched it."

But, to the increased astonishment of Annie, when the tip of her father's finger was pressed against that of her husband, on which the butterfly still rested, the insect drooped its wings, and seemed on the point of falling to the floor. Even the bright spots of gold upon its wings and body, unless her eyes deceived her, grew dim, and the glowing purple took a dusky hue, and the starry lustre that gleamed around the blacksmith's hand, became faint, and vanished.

"It is dying! it is dying!" cried Annie, in alarm.

"It has been delicately wrought," said the artist calmly. "As I told you, it has imbibed a spiritual essence—call it magnetism, or what you will. In an atmosphere of doubt and mockery, its exquisite susceptibility suffers torture, as does the soul of him who instilled his own life into it. It has already lost its beauty; in a few mo-ments more, its mechanism would be irreparably injured."

"Take away your hand, father!" entreated Annie, turning pale. "Here is my child; let it rest on his innocent hand. There, perhaps, its life will revive, and its colors grow brighter than ever."

Her father, with an acrid smile, withdrew his finger. The butterfly then ap-peared to recover the power of voluntary motion; while its hues assumed much of their original lustre, and the gleam of starlight, which was its most ethereal at-tribute, again formed a halo round about it. At first, when transferred from Rob-ert Danforth's hand to the small finger of the child, this radiance grew so power-ful that it positively threw the little fellow's shadow back against the wall. He, meanwhile, extended his plump hand as he had seen his father and mother do, and watched the waving of the insect's wings, with infantine delight. Nevertheless, there was a certain odd expression of sagacity, that made Owen Warland feel as if here were old Peter Hovenden, partially, and but partially, redeemed from his hard scepticism into childish faith.

"How wise the little monkey looks!" whispered Robert Danforth to his wife.

"I never saw such a look on a child's face," answered Annie, admiring her own infant, and with good reason, far more than the artistic butterfly. "The darling knows more of the mystery than we do."

As if the butterfly, like the artist, were conscious of something not entirely con-genial in the child's nature, it alternately sparkled and grew dim. At length, it arose from the small hand of the infant with an airy motion, that seemed to bear it upward without an effort; as if the ethereal instincts, with which its master's spirit had endowed it, impelled this fair vision involuntarily to a higher sphere. Had there been no obstruction, it might have soared into the sky, and grown immortal. But its lustre gleamed upon the ceiling; the exquisite texture of its wings brushed against that earthly medium; and a sparkle or two, as of star-dust, floated downward and lay glimmering on the carpet. Then the butterfly came fluttering down, and instead of returning to the infant, was apparently attracted towards the artist's hand.

"Not so, not so!" murmured Owen Warland, as if his handiwork could have understood him. "Thou hast gone forth out of thy master's heart. There is no return for thee!"

With a wavering movement, and emitting a tremulous radiance, the butterfly struggled, as it were, towards the infant, and was about to alight upon his finger. But, while it still hovered in the air, the little Child of Strength, with his grandsire's sharp and shrewd expression in his face, made a snatch at the marvellous insect, and compressed it in his hand. Annie screamed! Old Peter Hovendon burst into a cold and scornful laugh. The blacksmith, by main force, unclosed the infant's hand, and found within the palm a small heap of glittering fragments, whence the Mystery of Beauty had fled for ever. And as for Owen Warland, he looked placidly at what seemed the ruin of his life's labor, and which was yet no ruin. He had caught a far other butterfly than this. When the artist rose high enough to achieve the Beautiful, the symbol by which he made it perceptible to mortal senses became of little value in his eyes, while his spirit possessed itself in the enjoyment of the Reality.

1844

Rappaccini's Daughter

FROM THE WRITINGS OF AUBÉPINE[1]

We do not remember to have seen any translated specimens of the productions of M. de l'Aubépine; a fact the less to be wondered at, as his very name is unknown to many of his own countrymen, as well as to the student of foreign literature. As a writer, he seems to occupy an unfortunate position between the Transcendentalists (who, under one name or another, have their share in all the current literature of the world), and the great body of pen-and-ink men who address the intellect and sympathies of the multitude. If not too refined, at all events too remote, too shadowy and unsubstantial in his modes of development, to suit the taste of the latter class, and yet too popular to satisfy the spiritual or metaphysical requisitions of the former, he must necessarily find himself without an audience; except here and there an individual, or possibly an isolated clique. His writings, to do them justice, are not altogether destitute of fancy and originality; they might have won him greater reputation but for an inveterate love of allegory, which is apt to invest his plots and characters with the aspect of scenery and people in the clouds, and to steal away the human warmth out of his conceptions. His fictions are sometimes historical, sometimes of the present day, and sometimes, so far as can be discovered, have little or no reference either to time or space. In any case, he generally contents himself with a very slight embroidery of outward manners,—the faintest possible counterfeit of real life,—and endeavors to create an interest by some less obvious peculiarity of the subject. Occasionally, a breath of nature, a rain-drop of pathos and tenderness, or a gleam of humor, will find its way into the midst of his fantastic imagery, and make us feel as if, after all, we

---

[1]"Hawthorne" in French. The opening paragraphs present
a humorous account of his own career.

were yet within the limits of our native earth. We will only add to this very cursory notice, that M. de l'Aubépine's productions, if the reader chance to take them in precisely the proper point of view, may amuse a leisure hour as well as those of a brighter man; if otherwise, they can hardly fail to look excessively like nonsense.

Our author is voluminous; he continues to write and publish with as much praiseworthy and indefatigable prolixity, as if his efforts were crowned with the brilliant success that so justly attends those of Eugene Sue.[2] His first appearance was by a collection of stories, in a long series of volumes, entitled "*Contes deux fois racontées.*"[3] The titles of some of his more recent works (we quote from memory) are as follows:—"*Le Voyage Céleste à Chemin de Fer,*" 3 tom. 1838. "*Le nouveau Père Adam et la nouvelle Mère Eve,*" 2 tom. 1839. "*Roderic; ou le Serpent à l'estomac,*" 2 tom. 1840. "*Le Culte du Feu,*" a folio volume of ponderous research into the religion and ritual of the old Persian Ghebers, published in 1841. "*La Soirée du Chateau en Espagne,*" 1 tom. 8vo. 1842; and "*L'Artiste du Beau; ou le Papillon Mécanique,*" 5 tom. 4to. 1843.[4] Our somewhat wearisome perusal of this startling catalogue of volumes has left behind it a certain personal affection and sympathy, though by no means admiration, for M. de l'Aubépine; and we would fain do the little in our power towards introducing him favorably to the American public. The ensuing tale is a translation of his "*Beatrice; ou la Belle Empoisonneuse,*" recently published in "*La Revue Anti-Aristocratique.*"[5] This journal, edited by the Comte de Bearhaven,[6] has, for some years past, led the defence of liberal principles and popular rights, with a faithfulness and ability worthy of all praise.

A young man, named Giovanni Guasconti, came, very long ago, from the more southern region of Italy, to pursue his studies at the University of Padua. Giovanni, who had but a scanty supply of gold ducats in his pocket, took lodgings in a high and gloomy chamber of an old edifice, which looked not unworthy to have been the palace of a Paduan noble, and which, in fact, exhibited over its entrance the armorial bearings of a family long since extinct. The young stranger, who was not unstudied in the great poem of his country, recollected that one of the ancestors of this family, and perhaps an occupant of this very mansion, had been pictured by Dante as a partaker of the immortal agonies of his Inferno. These reminiscences and associations, together with the tendency to heart-break natural to a young man for the first time out of his native sphere, caused Giovanni to sigh heavily, as he looked around the desolate and ill-furnished apartment.

"Holy Virgin, Signor," cried old dame Lisabetta, who, won by the youth's remarkable beauty of person, was kindly endeavoring to give the chamber a habitable air, "what a sigh was that to come out of a young man's heart! Do you find this old mansion gloomy? For the love of heaven, then, put your head out of the window, and you will see as bright sunshine as you have left in Naples."

Guasconti mechanically did as the old woman advised, but could not quite agree with her that the Paduan sunshine was as cheerful as that of southern Italy. Such as it was, however, it fell upon a garden beneath the window, and expended its fostering influences on a variety of plants, which seemed to have been cultivated with exceeding care.

"Does this garden belong to the house?" asked Giovanni.

[2]French novelist (1804–1857), author of *The Wandering Jew* (1844–45).
[3]*Twice-Told Tales* (1837), Hawthorne's first volume of stories.
[4]The titles are all French versions of the titles of Hawthorne's stories (except for "Evening in a Castle in Spain"): "The Celestial Rail-Road," "The New Adam and Eve," "Egotism; or, the Bosom Serpent," "Fire-Worship," and "The Artist of the Beautiful." The bibliographical citations, "tom" (or "tome," French for "volume"), "8 vo." and "4 vo." ("octavo" and "quarto") are bogus; Hawthorne's stories were published in magazines (before they were collected), not in volumes.
[5]"Beatrice; or The Poisonous Belle," in *The Democratic Review.*
[6]John O'Sullivan, a friend of Hawthorne, edited *The Democratic Review.*

"Heaven forbid, Signor!—unless it were fruitful of better pot-herbs than any that grow there now," answered old Lisabetta. "No; that garden is cultivated by the own hands of Signor Giacomo Rappaccini, the famous Doctor, who, I warrant him, has been heard of as far as Naples. It is said that he distils these plants into medicines that are as potent as a charm. Oftentimes you may see the Signor Doctor at work, and perchance the Signora his daughter, too, gathering the strange flowers that grow in the garden."

The old woman had now done what she could for the aspect of the chamber, and, commending the young man to the protection of the saints, took her departure.

Giovanni still found no better occupation than to look down into the garden beneath his window. From its appearance, he judged it to be one of those botanic gardens, which were of earlier date in Padua than elsewhere in Italy, or in the world. Or, not improbably, it might once have been the pleasure-place of an opulent family; for there was the ruin of a marble fountain in the centre, sculptured with rare art, but so wofully shattered that it was impossible to trace the original design from the chaos of remaining fragments. The water, however, continued to gush and sparkle into the sunbeams as cheerfully as ever. A little gurgling sound ascended to the young man's window, and made him feel as if the fountain were an immortal spirit, that sung its song unceasingly, and without heeding the vicissitudes around it; while one century embodied it in marble, and another scattered the perishable garniture on the soil. All about the pool into which the water subsided, grew various plants, that seemed to require a plentiful supply of moisture for the nourishment of gigantic leaves, and, in some instances, flowers gorgeously magnificent. There was one shrub in particular, set in a marble vase in the midst of the pool, that bore a profusion of purple blossoms, each of which had the lustre and richness of a gem; and the whole together made a show so resplendent that it seemed enough to illuminate the garden, even had there been no sunshine. Every portion of the soil was peopled with plants and herbs, which, if less beautiful, still bore tokens of assiduous care; as if all had their individual virtues, known to the scientific mind that fostered them. Some were placed in urns, rich with old carving, and others in common garden-pots; some crept serpent-like along the ground, or climbed on high, using whatever means of ascent was offered them. One plant had wreathed itself round a statue of Vertumnus,[7] which was thus quite veiled and shrouded in a drapery of hanging foliage, so happily arranged that it might have served a sculptor for a study.

While Giovanni stood at the window, he heard a rustling behind a screen of leaves, and became aware that a person was at work in the garden. His figure soon emerged into view, and showed itself to be that of no common laborer, but a tall, emaciated, sallow, and sickly-looking man, dressed in a scholar's garb of black. He was beyond the middle term of life, with grey hair, a thin grey beard, and a face singularly marked with intellect and cultivation, but which could never, even in his more youthful days, have expressed much warmth of heart.

Nothing could exceed the intentness with which this scientific gardener examined every shrub which grew in his path; it seemed as if he was looking into their inmost nature, making observations in regard to their creative essence, and discovering why one leaf grew in this shape, and another in that, and wherefore such and such flowers differed among themselves in hue and perfume. Nevertheless, in spite of this deep intelligence on his part, there was no approach to intimacy between himself and these vegetable existences. On the contrary, he avoided their actual touch, or the direct inhaling of their odors, with a caution that impressed

---

[7]Roman god of gardens and the changing seasons.

Giovanni most disagreeably; for the man's demeanor was that of one walking among malignant influences, such as savage beasts, or deadly snakes, or evil spirits, which, should he allow them one moment of license, would wreak upon him some terrible fatality. It was strangely frightful to the young man's imagination, to see this air of insecurity in a person cultivating a garden, that most simple and innocent of human toils, and which had been alike the joy and labor of the unfallen parents of the race. Was this garden, then, the Eden of the present world?—and this man, with such a perception of harm in what his own hands caused to grow, was he the Adam?

The distrustful gardener, while plucking away the dead leaves or pruning the too luxuriant growth of the shrubs, defended his hands with a pair of thick gloves. Nor were these his only armor. When, in his walk through the garden, he came to the magnificent plant that hung its purple gems beside the marble fountain, he placed a kind of mask over his mouth and nostrils, as if all this beauty did but conceal a deadlier malice. But finding his task still too dangerous, he drew back, removed the mask, and called loudly, but in the infirm voice of a person affected with inward disease:

"Beatrice!—Beatrice!"

"Here am I, my father! What would you?" cried a rich and youthful voice from the window of the opposite house; a voice as rich as a tropical sunset, and which made Giovanni, though he knew not why, think of deep hues of purple or crimson, and of perfumes heavily delectable.—"Are you in the garden?"

"Yes, Beatrice," answered the gardener, "and I need your help."

Soon there emerged from under a sculptured portal the figure of a young girl, arrayed with as much richness of taste as the most splendid of the flowers, beautiful as the day, and with a bloom so deep and vivid that one shade more would have been too much. She looked redundant with life, health, and energy; all of which attributes were bound down and compressed, as it were, and girdled tensely, in their luxuriance, by her virgin zone.[8] Yet Giovanni's fancy must have grown morbid, while he looked down into the garden; for the impression which the fair stranger made upon him was as if here were another flower, the human sister of those vegetable ones, as beautiful as they—more beautiful than the richest of them—but still to be touched only with a glove, nor to be approached without a mask. As Beatrice came down the garden path, it was observable that she handled and inhaled the odor of several of the plants, which her father had most sedulously avoided.

"Here, Beatrice," said the latter,—"see how many needful offices require to be done to our chief treasure. Yet, shattered as I am, my life might pay the penalty of approaching it so closely as circumstances demand. Henceforth, I fear, this plant must be consigned to your sole charge."

"And gladly will I undertake it," cried again the rich tones of the young lady, as she bent towards the magnificent plant, and opened her arms as if to embrace it. "Yes, my sister, my splendor, it shall be Beatrice's task to nurse and serve thee; and thou shalt reward her with thy kisses and perfumed breath, which to her is as the breath of life!"

Then, with all the tenderness in her manner that was so strikingly expressed in her words, she busied herself with such attentions as the plant seemed to require; and Giovanni, at his lofty window, rubbed his eyes, and almost doubted whether it were a girl tending her favorite flower, or one sister performing the duties of affection to another. The scene soon terminated. Whether Doctor Rappaccini had

---

[8]A wide and distinctive belt, resembling a girdle, worn by unmarried women; thus, "virgin zone."

finished his labors in the garden, or that his watchful eye had caught the stranger's face, he now took his daughter's arm and retired. Night was already closing in; oppressive exhalations seemed to proceed from the plants, and steal upward past the open window; and Giovanni, closing the lattice, went to his couch, and dreamed of a rich flower and beautiful girl. Flower and maiden were different and yet the same, and fraught with some strange peril in either shape.

But there is an influence in the light of morning that tends to rectify whatever errors of fancy, or even of judgment, we may have incurred during the sun's decline, or among the shadows of the night, or in the less wholesome glow of moonshine. Giovanni's first movement on starting from sleep, was to throw open the window, and gaze down into the garden which his dreams had made so fertile of mysteries. He was surprised, and a little ashamed, to find how real and matter-of-fact an affair it proved to be, in the first rays of the sun, which gilded the dewdrops that hung upon leaf and blossom, and, while giving a brighter beauty to each rare flower, brought everything within the limits of ordinary experience. The young man rejoiced, that, in the heart of the barren city, he had the privilege of overlooking this spot of lovely and luxuriant vegetation. It would serve, he said to himself, as a symbolic language, to keep him in communion with Nature. Neither the sickly and thought-worn Doctor Giacomo Rappaccini, it is true, nor his brilliant daughter, were now visible; so that Giovanni could not determine how much of the singularity which he attributed to both, was due to their own qualities, and how much to his wonder-working fancy. But he was inclined to take a most rational view of the whole matter.

In the course of the day, he paid his respects to Signor Pietro Baglioni, professor of medicine in the University, a physician of eminent repute, to whom Giovanni had brought a letter of introduction. The Professor was an elderly personage, apparently of genial nature, and habits that might almost be called jovial; he kept the young man to dinner, and made himself very agreeable by the freedom and liveliness of his conversation, especially when warmed by a flask or two of Tuscan wine. Giovanni, conceiving that men of science, inhabitants of the same city, must needs be on familiar terms with one another, took an opportunity to mention the name of Doctor Rappaccini. But the Professor did not respond with so much cordiality as he had anticipated.

"Ill would it become a teacher of the divine art of medicine," said Professor Pietro Baglioni, in answer to a question of Giovanni, "to withhold due and well-considered praise of a physician so eminently skilled as Rappaccini. But, on the other hand, I should answer it but scantily to my conscience, were I to permit a worthy youth like yourself, Signor Giovanni, the son of an ancient friend, to imbibe erroneous ideas respecting a man who might hereafter chance to hold your life and death in his hands. The truth is, our worshipful Doctor Rappaccini has as much science as any member of the faculty—with perhaps one single exception—in Padua, or all Italy. But there are certain grave objections to his professional character."

"And what are they?" asked the young man.

"Has my friend Giovanni any disease of body or heart, that he is so inquisitive about physicians?" said the Professor, with a smile. "But as for Rappaccini, it is said of him—and I, who know the man well, can answer for its truth—that he cares infinitely more for science than for mankind. His patients are interesting to him only as subjects for some new experiment. He would sacrifice human life, his own among the rest, or whatever else was dearest to him, for the sake of adding so much as a grain of mustard-seed to the great heap of his accumulated knowledge."

"Methinks he is an awful man, indeed," remarked Guasconti, mentally recalling the cold and purely intellectual aspect of Rappaccini. "And yet, worshipful Professor, is it not a noble spirit? Are there many men capable of so spiritual a love of science?"

"God forbid," answered the Professor, somewhat testily—"at least, unless they take sounder views of the healing art than those adopted by Rappaccini. It is his theory, that all medicinal virtues are comprised within those substances which we term vegetable poisons. These he cultivates with his own hands, and is said even to have produced new varieties of poison, more horribly deleterious than Nature, without the assistance of this learned person, would ever have plagued the world withal. That the Signor Doctor does less mischief than might be expected, with such dangerous substances, is undeniable. Now and then, it must be owned, he has effected—or seemed to effect—a marvellous cure. But, to tell you my private mind, Signor Giovanni, he should receive little credit for such instances of success—they being probably the work of chance—but should be held strictly accountable for his failures, which may justly be considered his own work."

The youth might have taken Baglioni's opinions with many grains of allowance, had he known that there was a professional warfare of long continuance between him and Doctor Rappaccini, in which the latter was generally thought to have gained the advantage. If the reader be inclined to judge for himself, we refer him to certain black-letter tracts on both sides, preserved in the medical department of the University of Padua.

"I know not, most learned Professor," returned Giovanni, after musing on what had been said of Rappaccini's exclusive zeal for science—"I know not how dearly this physician may love his art; but surely there is one object more dear to him. He has a daughter."

"Aha!" cried the Professor with a laugh. "So now our friend Giovanni's secret is out. You have heard of this daughter, whom all the young men in Padua are wild about, though not half a dozen have ever had the good hap to see her face. I know little of the Signora Beatrice, save that Rappaccini is said to have instructed her deeply in his science, and that, young and beautiful as fame reports her, she is already qualified to fill a professor's chair. Perchance her father destines her for mine! Other absurd rumors there be, not worth talking about, or listening to. So now, Signor Giovanni, drink off your glass of Lacryma."[9]

Guasconti returned to his lodgings somewhat heated with the wine he had quaffed, and which caused his brain to swim with strange fantasies in reference to Doctor Rappaccini and the beautiful Beatrice. On his way, happening to pass by a florist's, he bought a fresh bouquet of flowers.

Ascending to his chamber, he seated himself near the window, but within the shadow thrown by the depth of the wall, so that he could look down into the garden with little risk of being discovered. All beneath his eye was a solitude. The strange plants were basking in the sunshine, and now and then nodding gently to one another, as if in acknowledgment of sympathy and kindred. In the midst, by the shattered fountain, grew the magnificent shrub, with its purple gems clustering all over it; they glowed in the air, and gleamed back again out of the depths of the pool, which thus seemed to overflow with colored radiance from the rich reflection that was steeped in it. At first, as we have said, the garden was a solitude. Soon, however,—as Giovanni had half-hoped, half-feared, would be the case,—a figure appeared beneath the antique sculptured portal, and came down between the rows of plants, inhaling their various perfumes, as if she were one of those

---

[9]Shortened form of "Lachryma Christi" (Tears of Christ), an Italian wine produced in southern Italy, around Naples and Vesuvius.

beings of old classic fable, that lived upon sweet odors. On again beholding Beatrice, the young man was even startled to perceive how much her beauty exceeded his recollection of it; so brilliant, so vivid was its character, that she glowed amid the sunlight, and, as Giovanni whispered to himself, positively illuminated the more shadowy intervals of the garden path. Her face being now more revealed than on the former occasion, he was struck by its expression of simplicity and sweetness; qualities that had not entered into his idea of her character, and which made him ask anew, what manner of mortal she might be. Nor did he fail again to observe, or imagine, an analogy between the beautiful girl and the gorgeous shrub that hung its gem-like flowers over the fountain; a resemblance which Beatrice seemed to have indulged a fantastic humor in heightening, both by the arrangement of her dress and the selection of its hues.

Approaching the shrub, she threw open her arms, as with a passionate ardor, and drew its branches into an intimate embrace; so intimate, that her features were hidden in its leafy bosom, and her glistening ringlets all intermingled with the flowers.

"Give me thy breath, my sister," exclaimed Beatrice; "for I am faint with common air! And give me this flower of thine, which I separate with gentlest fingers from the stem, and place it close beside my heart."

With these words, the beautiful daughter of Rappaccini plucked one of the richest blossoms of the shrub, and was about to fasten it in her bosom. But now, unless Giovanni's draughts of wine had bewildered his senses, a singular incident occurred. A small orange-colored reptile, of the lizard or chameleon species, chanced to be creeping along the path, just at the feet of Beatrice. It appeared to Giovanni—but, at the distance from which he gazed, he could scarcely have seen anything so minute—it appeared to him, however, that a drop or two of moisture from the broken stem of the flower descended upon the lizard's head. For an instant, the reptile contorted itself violently, and then lay motionless in the sunshine. Beatrice observed this remarkable phenomenon, and crossed herself, sadly, but without surprise; nor did she therefore hesitate to arrange the fatal flower in her bosom. There it blushed, and almost glimmered with the dazzling effect of a precious stone, adding to her dress and aspect the one appropriate charm, which nothing else in the world could have supplied. But Giovanni, out of the shadow of his window, bent forward and shrank back, and murmured and trembled.

"Am I awake? Have I my senses?" said he to himself. "What is this being?— beautiful, shall I call her?—or inexpressibly terrible?"

Beatrice now strayed carelessly through the garden, approaching closer beneath Giovanni's window, so that he was compelled to thrust his head quite out of its concealment in order to gratify the intense and painful curiosity which she excited. At this moment, there came a beautiful insect over the garden wall; it had perhaps wandered through the city and found no flowers nor verdure among those antique haunts of men, until the heavy perfumes of Doctor Rappaccini's shrubs had lured it from afar. Without alighting on the flowers, this winged brightness seemed to be attracted by Beatrice, and lingered in the air and fluttered about her head. Now, here it could not but that Giovanni Guasconti's eyes deceived him. Be that as it might, he fancied that while Beatrice was gazing at the insect with childish delight, it grew faint and fell at her feet;—its bright wings shivered; it was dead—from no cause that he could discern, unless it were the atmosphere of her breath. Again Beatrice crossed herself and sighed heavily, as she bent over the dead insect.

An impulsive movement of Giovanni drew her eyes to the window. There she beheld the beautiful head of the young man—rather a Grecian than an Italian head, with fair, regular features, and a glistening of gold among his ringlets—

gazing down upon her like a being that hovered in mid-air. Scarcely knowing what he did, Giovanni threw down the bouquet which he had hitherto held in his hand.

"Signora," said he, "there are pure and healthful flowers. Wear them for the sake of Giovanni Guasconti!"

"Thanks, Signor," replied Beatrice, with her rich voice, that came forth as it were like a gush of music; and with a mirthful expression half childish and half woman-like. "I accept your gift, and would fain recompense it with this precious purple flower; but if I toss it into the air, it will not reach you. So Signor Guasconti must even content himself with my thanks."

She lifted the bouquet from the ground, and then as if inwardly ashamed at having stepped aside from her maidenly reserve to respond to a stranger's greeting, passed swiftly homeward through the garden. But, few as the moments were, it seemed to Giovanni when she was on the point of vanishing beneath the sculptured portal, that his beautiful bouquet was already beginning to wither in her grasp. It was an idle thought; there could be no possibility of distinguishing a faded flower from a fresh one at so great a distance.

For many days after this incident, the young man avoided the window that looked into Doctor Rappaccini's garden, as if something ugly and monstrous would have blasted his eye-sight, had he been betrayed into a glance. He felt conscious of having put himself, to a certain extent, within the influence of an unintelligible power, by the communication which he had opened with Beatrice. The wisest course would have been, if his heart were in any real danger, to quit his lodgings and Padua itself, at once; the next wiser, to have accustomed himself, as far as possible, to the familiar and day-light view of Beatrice; thus bringing her rigidly and systematically within the limits of ordinary experience. Least of all, while avoiding her sight, ought Giovanni to have remained so near this extraordinary being, that the proximity and possibility even of intercourse, should give a kind of substance and reality to the wild vagaries which his imagination ran riot continually in producing. Guasconti had not a deep heart—or at all events, its depths were not sounded now—but he had a quick fancy, and an ardent southern temperament, which rose every instant to a higher fever-pitch. Whether or no Beatrice possessed those terrible attributes—that fatal breath—the affinity with those so beautiful and deadly flowers—which were indicated by what Giovanni had witnessed, she had at least instilled a fierce and subtle poison into his system. It was not love, although her rich beauty was a madness to him; nor horror, even while he fancied her spirit to be imbued with the same baneful essence that seemed to pervade her physical frame; but a wild offspring of both love and horror that had each parent in it, and burned like one and shivered like the other. Giovanni knew not what to dread; still less did he know what to hope; yet hope and dread kept a continual warfare in his breast, alternately vanquishing one another and starting up afresh to renew the contest. Blessed are all simple emotions, be they dark or bright! It is the lurid intermixture of the two that produces the illuminating blaze of the infernal regions.

Sometimes he endeavored to assuage the fever of his spirit by a rapid walk through the streets of Padua, or beyond its gates; his footsteps kept time with the throbbings of his brain, so that the walk was apt to accelerate itself to a race. One day, he found himself arrested; his arm was seized by a portly personage who had turned back on recognizing the young man, and expended much breath in overtaking him.

"Signor Giovanni!—stay, my young friend!" cried he. "Have you forgotten me? That might well be the case, if I were as much altered as yourself."

It was Baglioni, whom Giovanni had avoided, ever since their first meeting, from a doubt that the Professor's sagacity would look too deeply into his secrets. Endeavoring to recover himself, he stared forth wildly from his inner world into the outer one, and spoke like a man in a dream:

"Yes; I am Giovanni Guasconti. You are Professor Pietro Baglioni. Now let me pass!"

"Not yet—not yet, Signor Giovanni Guasconti," said the Professor, smiling, but at the same time scrutinizing the youth with an earnest glance.—"What; did I grow up side by side with your father, and shall his son pass me like a stranger, in these old streets of Padua? Stand still, Signor Giovanni; for we must have a word or two, before we part."

"Speedily, then, most worshipful Professor, speedily!" said Giovanni, with feverish impatience. "Does not your worship see that I am in haste?"

Now, while he was speaking, there came a man in black along the street, stooping and moving feebly, like a person in inferior health. His face was all overspread with a most sickly and sallow hue, but yet so pervaded with an expression of piercing and active intellect, that an observer might easily have overlooked the merely physical attributes, and have seen only this wonderful energy. As he passed, this person exchanged a cold and distant salutation with Baglioni, but fixed his eyes upon Giovanni with an intentness that seemed to bring out whatever was within him worthy of notice. Nevertheless, there was a peculiar quietness in the look, as if taking merely a speculative, not a human, interest in the young man.

"It is Doctor Rappaccini!" whispered the Professor, when the stranger had passed.—"Has he ever seen your face before?"

"Not that I know," answered Giovanni, starting at the name.

"He *has* seen you!—he must have seen you!" said Baglioni, hastily. "For some purpose or other, this man of science is making a study of you. I know that look of his! It is the same that coldly illuminates his face, as he bends over a bird, a mouse, or a butterfly, which, in pursuance of some experiment, he has killed by the perfume of a flower;—a look as deep as Nature itself, but without Nature's warmth of love. Signor Giovanni, I will stake my life upon it, you are the subject of one of Rappaccini's experiments!"

"Will you make a fool of me?" cried Giovanni, passionately. "*That,* Signor Professor, were an untoward experiment."

"Patience, patience!" replied the imperturbable Professor.—"I tell thee, my poor Giovanni, that Rappaccini has a scientific interest in thee. Thou hast fallen into fearful hands! And the Signora Beatrice? What part does she act in this mystery?"

But Guasconti, finding Baglioni's pertinacity intolerable, here broke away, and was gone before the Professor could again seize his arm. He looked after the young man intently, and shook his head.

"This must not be," said Baglioni to himself. "The youth is the son of my old friend, and shall not come to any harm from which the arcana of medical science can preserve him. Besides, it is too insufferable an impertinence in Rappaccini, thus to snatch the lad out of my own hands, as I may say, and make use of him for his infernal experiments. This daughter of his! It shall be looked to. Perchance, most learned Rappaccini, I may foil you where you little dream of it!"

Meanwhile, Giovanni had pursued a circuitous route, and at length found himself at the door of his lodgings. As he crossed the threshold, he was met by old Lisabetta, who smirked and smiled, and was evidently desirous to attract his attention; vainly, however, as the ebullition of his feelings had momentarily subsided into a cold and dull vacuity. He turned his eyes full upon the withered face that was puckering itself into a smile, but seemed to behold it not. The old dame, therefore, laid her grasp upon his cloak.

"Signor!—Signor!" whispered she, still with a smile over the whole breadth of her visage, so that it looked not unlike a grotesque carving in wood, darkened by centuries—"Listen, Signor! There is a private entrance into the garden!"

"What do you say?" exclaimed Giovanni, turning quickly about, as if an inanimate thing should start into feverish life.—"A private entrance into Doctor Rappaccini's garden!"

"Hush! hush!—not so loud!" whispered Lisabetta, putting her hand over his mouth. "Yes; into the worshipful Doctor's garden, where you may see all his fine shrubbery. Many a young man in Padua would give gold to be admitted among those flowers."

Giovanni put a piece of gold into her hand.

"Show me the way," said he.

A surmise, probably excited by his conversation with Baglioni, crossed his mind, that this interposition of old Lisabetta might perchance be connected with the intrigue, whatever were its nature, in which the Professor seemed to suppose that Doctor Rappaccini was involving him. But such a suspicion, though it disturbed Giovanni, was inadequate to restrain him. The instant that he was aware of the possibility of approaching Beatrice, it seemed an absolute necessity of his existence to do so. It mattered not whether she were angel or demon; he was irrevocably within her sphere, and must obey the law that whirled him onward, in ever lessening circles, towards a result which he did not attempt to foreshadow. And yet, strange to say, there came across him a sudden doubt, whether this intense interest on his part were not delusory—whether it were really of so deep and positive a nature as to justify him in now thrusting himself into an incalculable position—whether it were not merely the fantasy of a young man's brain, only slightly, or not at all, connected with his heart!

He paused—hesitated—turned half about—but again went on. His withered guide led him along several obscure passages, and finally undid a door, through which, as it was opened, there came the sight and sound of rustling leaves, with the broken sunshine glimmering among them. Giovanni stepped forth, and forcing himself through the entanglement of a shrub that wreathed its tendrils over the hidden entrance, he stood beneath his own window, in the open area of Doctor Rappaccini's garden.

How often is it the case, that, when impossibilities have come to pass, and dreams have condensed their misty substance into tangible realities, we find ourselves calm, and even coldly self-possessed, amid circumstances which it would have been a delirium of joy or agony to anticipate! Fate delights to thwart us thus. Passion will choose his own time to rush upon the scene, and lingers sluggishly behind, when an appropriate adjustment of events would seem to summon his appearance. So was it now with Giovanni. Day after day, his pulses had throbbed with feverish blood, at the improbable idea of an interview with Beatrice, and of standing with her, face to face, in this very garden, basking in the Oriental sunshine of her beauty, and snatching from her full gaze the mystery which he deemed the riddle of his own existence. But now there was a singular and untimely equanimity within his breast. He threw a glance around the garden to discover if Beatrice or her father were present, and perceiving that he was alone, began a critical observation of the plants.

The aspect of one and all of them dissatisfied him; their gorgeousness seemed fierce, passionate, and even unnatural. There was hardly an individual shrub which a wanderer, straying by himself through a forest, would not have been startled to find growing wild, as if an unearthly face had glared at him out of the thicket. Several, also, would have shocked a delicate instinct by an appearance of artificialness, indicating that there had been such commixture, and, as it were, adultery of various vegetable species, that the production was no longer of God's making, but the monstrous offspring of man's depraved fancy, glowing with only an evil mockery of beauty. They were probably the result of experiment, which, in one or two cases, had succeeded in mingling plants individually lovely into a compound possessing the questionable and ominous character that distinguished the whole growth of the garden. In fine, Giovanni recognized but two or three plants in the collection, and those of a kind that he well knew to be poisonous. While busy with these contemplations, he heard the rustling of a silken garment, and turning, beheld Beatrice emerging from beneath the sculptured portal.

Giovanni had not considered with himself what should be his deportment; whether he should apologize for his intrusion into the garden, or assume that he was there with the privity, at least, if not by the desire, of Doctor Rappaccini or his daughter. But Beatrice's manner placed him at his ease, though leaving him still in doubt by what agency he had gained admittance. She came lightly along the path, and met him near the broken fountain. There was surprise in her face, but brightened by a simple and kind expression of pleasure.

"You are a connoisseur in flowers, Signor," said Beatrice with a smile, alluding to the bouquet which he had flung her from the window. "It is no marvel, therefore, if the sight of my father's rare collection has tempted you to take a nearer view. If he were here, he could tell you many strange and interesting facts as to the nature and habits of these shrubs, for he has spent a life-time in such studies, and this garden is his world."

"And yourself, lady"—observed Giovanni—"if fame says true—you, likewise, are deeply skilled in the virtues indicated by these rich blossoms, and these spicy perfumes. Would you deign to be my instructress, I should prove an apter scholar than if taught by Signor Rappaccini himself."

"Are there such idle rumors?" asked Beatrice, with the music of a pleasant laugh. "Do people say that I am skilled in my father's science of plants? What a jest is there! No; though I have grown up among these flowers, I know no more of them than their hues and perfume; and sometimes, methinks I would fain rid myself of even that small knowledge. There are many flowers here, and those not the least brilliant, that shock and offend me, when they meet my eye. But, pray, Signor, do not believe these stories about my science. Believe nothing of me save what you see with your own eyes."

"And must I believe all that I have seen with my own eyes?" asked Giovanni pointedly, while the recollection of former scenes made him shrink. "No, Signora, you demand too little of me. Bid me believe nothing, save what comes from your own lips."

It would appear that Beatrice understood him. There came a deep flush to her cheek; but she looked full into Giovanni's eyes, and responded to his gaze of uneasy suspicion with a queen-like haughtiness.

"I do so bid you, Signor!" she replied. "Forget whatever you may have fancied in regard to me. If true to the outward senses, still it may be false in its essence. But the words of Beatrice Rappaccini's lips are true from the depths of the heart outward. Those you may believe!"

A fervor glowed in her whole aspect, and beamed upon Giovanni's consciousness like the light of truth itself. But while she spoke, there was a fragrance in the atmosphere around her, rich and delightful, though evanescent, yet which the young man, from an indefinable reluctance, scarcely dared to draw into his lungs. It might be the odor of the flowers. Could it be Beatrice's breath, which thus embalmed her words with a strange richness, as if by steeping them in her heart? A faintness passed like a shadow over Giovanni, and flitted away; he seemed to gaze through the beautiful girl's eyes into her transparent soul, and felt no more doubt or fear.

The tinge of passion that had colored Beatrice's manner vanished; she became gay, and appeared to derive a pure delight from her communion with the youth, not unlike what the maiden of a lonely island might have felt, conversing with a voyager from the civilized world. Evidently her experience of life had been confined within the limits of that garden. She talked now about matters as simple as the daylight or summer-clouds, and now asked questions in reference to the city, or Giovanni's distant home, his friends, his mother, and his sisters; questions indicating such seclusion, and such lack of familiarity with modes and forms, that Giovanni responded as if to an infant. Her spirit gushed out before him like a fresh rill, that was just catching its first glimpse of the sunlight, and wondering at the reflections of earth and sky which were flung into its bosom. There came thoughts, too, from a deep source, and fantasies of a gemlike brilliancy, as if diamonds and rubies sparkled upward among the bubbles of the fountain. Ever and anon, there gleamed across the young man's mind a sense of wonder, that he should be walking side by side with the being who had so wrought upon his imagination—whom he had idealized in such hues of terror—in whom he had positively witnessed such manifestations of dreadful attributes—that he should be conversing with Beatrice like a brother, and should find her so human and so maiden-like. But such reflections were only momentary; the effect of her character was too real, not to make itself familiar at once.

In this free intercourse, they had strayed through the garden, and now, after many turns among its avenues, were come to the shattered fountain, beside which grew the magnificent shrub with its treasury of glowing blossoms. A fragrance was diffused from it, which Giovanni recognized as identical with that which he had attributed to Beatrice's breath, but incomparably more powerful. As her eyes fell upon it, Giovanni beheld her press her hand to her bosom, as if her heart were throbbing suddenly and painfully.

"For the first time in my life," murmured she, addressing the shrub, "I had forgotten thee!"

"I remember, Signora," said Giovanni, "that you once promised to reward me with one of these living gems for the bouquet, which I had the happy boldness to fling to your feet. Permit me now to pluck it as a memorial of this interview."

He made a step towards the shrub, with extended hand. But Beatrice darted forward, uttering a shriek that went through his heart like a dagger. She caught his hand, and drew it back with the whole force of her slender figure. Giovanni felt her touch thrilling through his fibres.

"Touch it not!" exclaimed she, in a voice of agony. "Not for thy life! It is fatal!"

Then, hiding her face, she fled from him, and vanished beneath the sculptured portal. As Giovanni followed her with his eyes, he beheld the emaciated figure and pale intelligence of Doctor Rappaccini, who had been watching the scene, he knew not how long, within the shadow of the entrance.

No sooner was Guasconti alone in his chamber, than the image of Beatrice came back to his passionate musings, invested with all the witchery that had been gathering around it ever since his first glimpse of her, and now likewise imbued with a tender warmth of girlish womanhood. She was human: her nature was endowed with all gentle and feminine qualities; she was worthiest to be worshipped; she was capable, surely, on her part, of the height and heroism of love. Those tokens, which he had hitherto considered as proofs of a frightful peculiarity in her physical and moral system, were now either forgotten, or, by the subtle sophistry of passion, transmuted into a golden crown of enchantment, rendering Beatrice the more admirable, by so much as she was the more unique. Whatever had looked ugly, was now beautiful; or, if incapable of such a change, it stole away and hid itself among those shapeless half-ideas, which throng the dim region beyond the daylight of our perfect consciousness. Thus did he spend the night, nor fell asleep, until the dawn had begun to awake the slumbering flowers in Doctor Rappaccini's garden, whither Giovanni's dreams doubtless led him. Up rose the sun in

his due season, and flinging his beams upon the young man's eyelids, awoke him
to a sense of pain. When thoroughly aroused, he became sensible of a burning
and tingling agony in his hand—in his right hand—the very hand which Beatrice
had grasped in her own, when he was on the point of plucking one of the gem-
like flowers. On the back of that hand there was now a purple print, like that of
four small fingers, and the likeness of a slender thumb upon his wrist.

Oh, how stubbornly does love—or even that cunning semblance of love which
flourishes in the imagination, but strikes no depth of root into the heart—how
stubbornly does it hold its faith, until the moment come, when it is doomed to
vanish into thin mist! Giovanni wrapt a handkerchief about his hand, and wondered what evil thing had stung him, and soon forgot his pain in a reverie of Beatrice.

After the first interview, a second was in the inevitable course of what we call
fate. A third; a fourth; and a meeting with Beatrice in the garden was no longer
an incident in Giovanni's daily life, but the whole space in which he might be said
to live; for the anticipation and memory of that ecstatic hour made up the remainder. Nor was it otherwise with the daughter of Rappaccini. She watched for the
youth's appearance, and flew to his side with confidence as unreserved as if they
had been playmates from early infancy—as if they were such playmates still. If, by
any unwonted chance, he failed to come at the appointed moment, she stood beneath the window, and sent up the rich sweetness of her tones to float around him
in his chamber, and echo and reverberate throughout his heart—"Giovanni! Giovanni! Why tarriest thou? Come down!"—And down he hastened into that Eden
of poisonous flowers.

But, with all this intimate familiarity, there was still a reserve in Beatrice's demeanor, so rigidly and invariably sustained, that the idea of infringing it scarcely
occurred to his imagination. By all appreciable signs, they loved; they had looked
love, with eyes that conveyed the holy secret from the depths of one soul into the
depths of the other, as if it were too sacred to be whispered by the way; they had
even spoken love, in those gushes of passion when their spirits darted forth in articulated breath, like tongues of long-hidden flame; and yet there had been no
seal of lips, no clasp of hands, nor any slightest caress, such as love claims and
hallows. He had never touched one of the gleaming ringlets of her hair; her garment—so marked was the physical barrier between them—had never been waved
against him by a breeze. On the few occasions when Giovanni had seemed
tempted to overstep the limit, Beatrice grew so sad, so stern, and withal wore such
a look of desolate separation, shuddering at itself, that not a spoken word was requisite to repel him. At such times, he was startled at the horrible suspicions that
rose, monster-like, out of the caverns of his heart, and stared him in the face; his
love grew thin and faint as the morning-mist; his doubts alone had substance. But
when Beatrice's face brightened again, after the momentary shadow, she was
transformed at once from the mysterious, questionable being, whom he had
watched with so much awe and horror; she was now the beautiful and unsophisticated girl, whom he felt that his spirit knew with a certainty beyond all other
knowledge.

A considerable time had now passed since Giovanni's last meeting with Baglioni. One morning, however, he was disagreeably surprised by a visit from the Professor, whom he had scarcely thought of for whole weeks, and would willingly
have forgotten still longer. Given up, as he had long been, to a pervading excitement, he could tolerate no companions, except upon condition of their perfect
sympathy with his present state of feeling. Such sympathy was not to be expected
from Professor Baglioni.

The visitor chatted carelessly, for a few moments, about the gossip of the city
and the University, and then took up another topic.

"I have been reading an old classic author lately," said he, "and met with a story that strangely interested me.[10] Possibly you may remember it. It is of an Indian prince, who sent a beautiful woman as a present to Alexander the Great. She was as lovely as the dawn, and gorgeous as the sunset; but what especially distinguished her was a certain rich perfume in her breath—richer than a garden of Persian roses. Alexander, as was natural to a youthful conqueror, fell in love at first sight with this magnificent stranger. But a certain sage physician, happening to be present, discovered a terrible secret in regard to her."

"And what was that?" asked Giovanni, turning his eyes downward to avoid those of the Professor.

"That this lovely woman," continued Baglioni, with emphasis, "had been nourished with poisons from her birth upward, until her whole nature was so imbued with them, that she herself had become the deadliest poison in existence. Poison was her element of life. With that rich perfume of her breath, she blasted the very air. Her love would have been poison!—her embrace death! Is not this a marvellous tale?"

"A childish fable," answered Giovanni, nervously starting from his chair. "I marvel how your worship finds time to read such nonsense, among your graver studies."

"By the bye," said the Professor, looking uneasily about him, "what singular fragrance is this in your apartment? Is it the perfume of your gloves? It is faint, but delicious, and yet, after all, by no means agreeable. Were I to breathe it long, methinks it would make me ill. It is like the breath of a flower—but I see no flowers in the chamber."

"Nor are there any," replied Giovanni, who had turned pale as the Professor spoke; "nor, I think, is there any fragrance, except in your worship's imagination. Odors, being a sort of element combined of the sensual and the spiritual, are apt to deceive us in this manner. The recollection of a perfume—the bare idea of it—may easily be mistaken for a present reality."

"Aye; but my sober imagination does not often play such tricks," said Baglioni; "and were I to fancy any kind of odor, it would be that of some vile apothecary drug, wherewith my fingers are likely enough to be imbued. Our worshipful friend Rappaccini, as I have heard, tinctures his medicaments with odors richer than those of Araby. Doubtless, likewise, the fair and learned Signora Beatrice would minister to her patients with draughts as sweet as a maiden's breath. But wo to him that sips them!"

Giovanni's face evinced many contending emotions. The tone in which the Professor alluded to the pure and lovely daughter of Rappaccini was a torture to his soul; and yet, the intimation of a view of her character, opposite to his own, gave instantaneous distinctness to a thousand dim suspicions, which now grinned at him like so many demons. But he strove hard to quell them, and to respond to Baglioni with a true lover's perfect faith.

"Signor Professor," said he, "you were my father's friend—perchance, too, it is your purpose to act a friendly part towards his son. I would fain feel nothing towards you, save respect and deference. But I pray you to observe, Signor, that there is one subject on which we must not speak. You know not the Signora Beatrice. You cannot, therefore, estimate the wrong—the blasphemy, I may even say—that is offered to her character by a light or injurious word."

"Giovanni!—my poor Giovanni!" answered the Professor, with a calm expression of pity, "I know this wretched girl far better than yourself. You shall hear the

---

[10]The source Hawthorne had found in Sir Thomas Browne's *Vulgar Errors* (1646), Book VII, Caption 17; he had copied the passage into his *American Notebooks:* "A story there passeth of an Indian King, that sent unto Alexander a fair woman fed with aconite and other poisons, with this intent, either by converse or copulation complexionally to destroy him."

truth in respect to the poisoner Rappaccini, and his poisonous daughter. Yes; poisonous as she is beautiful! Listen; for even should you do violence to my grey hairs, it shall not silence me. That old fable of the Indian woman has become a truth, by the deep and deadly science of Rappaccini, and in the person of the lovely Beatrice!"

Giovanni groaned and hid his face.

"Her father," continued Baglioni, "was not restrained by natural affection from offering up his child, in this horrible manner, as the victim of his insane zeal for science. For—let us do him justice—he is as true a man of science as ever distilled his own heart in an alembic. What, then, will be your fate? Beyond a doubt, you are selected as the material of some new experiment. Perhaps the result is to be death—perhaps a fate more awful still! Rappaccini, with what he calls the interest of science before his eyes, will hesitate at nothing."

"It is a dream!" muttered Giovanni to himself, "surely it is a dream!"

"But," resumed the Professor, "be of good cheer, son of my friend! It is not yet too late for the rescue. Possibly, we may even succeed in bringing back this miserable child within the limits of ordinary nature, from which her father's madness has estranged her. Behold this little silver vase! It was wrought by the hands of the renowned Benvenuto Cellini,[11] and is well worthy to be a love-gift to the fairest dame in Italy. But its contents are invaluable. One little sip of this antidote would have rendered the most virulent poisons of the Borgias[12] innocuous. Doubt not that it will be as efficacious against those of Rappaccini. Bestow the vase, and the precious liquid within it, on your Beatrice, and hopefully await the result."

Baglioni laid a small, exquisitely wrought silver phial on the table, and withdrew, leaving what he had said to produce its effect upon the young man's mind.

"We will thwart Rappaccini yet!" thought he, chuckling to himself, as he descended the stairs. "But, let us confess the truth of him, he is a wonderful man!—a wonderful man indeed! A vile empiric, however, in his practice, and therefore not to be tolerated by those who respect the good old rules of the medical profession!"

Throughout Giovanni's whole acquaintance with Beatrice, he had occasionally, as we have said, been haunted by dark surmises as to her character. Yet, so thoroughly had she made herself felt by him as a simple, natural, most affectionate and guileless creature, that the image now held up by Professor Baglioni, looked as strange and incredible, as if it were not in accordance with his own original conception. True, there were ugly recollections connected with his first glimpses of the beautiful girl; he could not quite forget the bouquet that withered in her grasp, and the insect that perished amid the sunny air, by no ostensible agency, save the fragrance of her breath. These incidents, however, dissolving in the pure light of her character, had no longer the efficacy of facts, but were acknowledged as mistaken fantasies, by whatever testimony of the senses they might appear to be substantiated. There is something truer and more real, than what we can see with the eyes, and touch with the finger. On such better evidence, had Giovanni founded his confidence in Beatrice, though rather by the necessary force of her high attributes, than by any deep and generous faith, on his part. But, now, his spirit was incapable of sustaining itself at the height to which the early enthusiasm of passion had exalted it; he fell down, grovelling among earthly doubts, and defiled therewith the pure whiteness of Beatrice's image. Not that he gave her up; he did but distrust. He resolved to institute some decisive test that should satisfy him, once for all, whether there were those dreadful peculiarities in her physical nature, which could not be supposed to exist without some corresponding mon-

---

[11]Italian sculptor and goldsmith (1500–1571).
[12]Italian family highly influential during the Renaissance in church and government affairs and notorious for licentious behavior and cruelty in poisoning their enemies.

strosity of soul. His eyes, gazing down afar, might have deceived him as to the lizard, the insect, and the flowers. But if he could witness, at the distance of a few paces, the sudden blight of one fresh and healthful flower in Beatrice's hand, there would be room for no further question. With this idea, he hastened to the florist's, and purchased a bouquet that was still gemmed with the morning dewdrops.

It was now the customary hour of his daily interview with Beatrice. Before descending into the garden, Giovanni failed not to look at his figure in the mirror; a vanity to be expected in a beautiful young man, yet, as displaying itself at that troubled and feverish moment, the token of a certain shallowness of feeling and insincerity of character. He did gaze, however, and said to himself, that his features had never before possessed so rich a grace, nor his eyes such vivacity, nor his cheeks so warm a hue of superabundant life.

"At least," thought he, "her poison has not yet insinuated itself into my system. I am no flower to perish in her grasp!"

With that thought, he turned his eyes on the bouquet, which he had never once laid aside from his hand. A thrill of indefinable horror shot through his frame, on perceiving that those dewy flowers were already beginning to droop; they wore the aspect of things that had been fresh and lovely, yesterday. Giovanni grew white as marble, and stood motionless before the mirror, staring at his own reflection there, as at the likeness of something frightful. He remembered Baglioni's remark about the fragrance that seemed to pervade the chamber. It must have been the poison in his breath! Then he shuddered—shuddered at himself! Recovering from his stupor, he began to watch, with curious eye, a spider that was busily at work, hanging its web from the antique cornice of the apartment, crossing and re-crossing the artful system of interwoven lines, as vigorous and active a spider as ever dangled from an old ceiling. Giovanni bent towards the insect, and emitted a deep, long breath. The spider suddenly ceased its toil; the web vibrated with a tremor originating in the body of the small artizan. Again Giovanni sent forth a breath, deeper, longer, and imbued with a venomous feeling out of his heart; he knew not whether he were wicked or only desperate. The spider made a convulsive gripe with his limbs, and hung dead across the window.

"Accursed! Accursed!" muttered Giovanni, addressing himself. "Hast thou grown so poisonous, that this deadly insect perishes by thy breath?"

At that moment, a rich, sweet voice came floating up from the garden:—

"Giovanni! Giovanni! It is past the hour! Why tarriest thou! Come down!"

"Yes," muttered Giovanni again. "She is the only being whom my breath may not slay! Would that it might!"

He rushed down, and in an instant, was standing before the bright and loving eyes of Beatrice. A moment ago, his wrath and despair had been so fierce that he could have desired nothing so much as to wither her by a glance. But, with her actual presence, there came influences which had too real an existence to be at once shaken off; recollections of the delicate and benign power of her feminine nature, which had so often enveloped him in a religious calm; recollections of many a holy and passionate outgush of her heart, when the pure fountain had been unsealed from its depths, and made visible in its transparency to his mental eye; recollections which, had Giovanni known how to estimate them, would have assured him that all this ugly mystery was but an earthly illusion, and that, whatever mist of evil might seem to have gathered over her, the real Beatrice was a heavenly angel. Incapable as he was of such high faith, still her presence had not utterly lost its magic. Giovanni's rage was quelled into an aspect of sullen insensibility. Beatrice, with a quick spiritual sense, immediately felt that there was a gulf of blackness between them, which neither he nor she could pass. They walked on together, sad and silent, and came thus to the marble fountain, and to its pool of water on the ground, in the midst of which grew the shrub that bore gem-like blossoms. Giovanni was affrighted at the eager enjoyment—the appetite, as it were—with which he found himself inhaling the fragrance of the flowers.

"Beatrice," asked he abruptly, "whence came this shrub?"

"My father created it," answered she, with simplicity.

"Created it! created it!" repeated Giovanni. "What mean you, Beatrice?"

"He is a man fearfully acquainted with the secrets of nature," replied Beatrice; "and, at the hour when I first drew breath, this plant sprang from the soil, the offspring of his science, of his intellect, while I was but his earthly child. Approach it not!" continued she, observing with terror that Giovanni was drawing nearer to the shrub. "It has qualities that you little dream of. But I, dearest Giovanni,—I grew up and blossomed with the plant, and was nourished with its breath. It was my sister, and I loved it with a human affection: for—alas! hast thou not suspected it? there was an awful doom."

Here Giovanni frowned so darkly upon her that Beatrice paused and trembled. But her faith in his tenderness reassured her, and made her blush that she had doubted for an instant.

"There was an awful doom," she continued,—"the effect of my father's fatal love of science—which estranged me from all society of my kind. Until Heaven sent thee, dearest Giovanni, Oh! how lonely was thy poor Beatrice!"

"Was it a hard doom?" asked Giovanni, fixing his eyes upon her.

"Only of late have I known how hard it was," answered she tenderly. "Oh, yes; but my heart was torpid, and therefore quiet."

Giovanni's rage broke forth from his sullen gloom like a lightning-flash out of a dark cloud.

"Accursed one!" cried he, with venomous scorn and anger. "And finding thy solitude wearisome, thou hast severed me, likewise, from all the warmth of life, and enticed me into thy region of unspeakable horror!"

"Giovanni!" exclaimed Beatrice, turning her large bright eyes upon his face. The force of his words had not found its way into her mind; she was merely thunder-struck.

"Yes, poisonous thing!" repeated Giovanni, beside himself with passion. "Thou hast done it! Thou hast blasted me! Thou hast filled my veins with poison! Thou hast made me as hateful, as ugly, as loathsome and deadly a creature as thyself,— a world's wonder of hideous monstrosity! Now—if our breath be happily as fatal to ourselves as to all others—let us join our lips in one kiss of unutterable hatred, and so die!"

"What has befallen me?" murmured Beatrice, with a low moan out of her heart. "Holy Virgin pity me, a poor heartbroken child!"

"Thou! Dost thou pray?" cried Giovanni, still with the same fiendish scorn. "Thy very prayers, as they come from thy lips, taint the atmosphere with death. Yes, yes; let us pray! Let us to church, and dip our fingers in the holy water at the portal! They that come after us will perish as by a pestilence. Let us sign crosses in the air! It will be scattering curses abroad in the likeness of holy symbols!"

"Giovanni," said Beatrice calmly, for her grief was beyond passion, "why dost thou join thyself with me thus in those terrible words? I, it is true, am the horrible thing thou namest me. But thou!—what hast thou to do, save with one other shudder at my hideous misery, to go forth out of the garden and mingle with thy race, and forget that there ever crawled on earth such a monster as poor Beatrice?"

"Dost thou pretend ignorance?" asked Giovanni, scowling upon her. "Behold! This power have I gained from the pure daughter of Rappaccini!"

There was a swarm of summer-insects flitting through the air, in search of the food promised by the flower-odors of the fatal garden. They circled round Gio-

vanni's head, and were evidently attracted towards him by the same influence
which had drawn them, for an instant, within the sphere of several of the shrubs.
He sent forth a breath among them, and smiled bitterly at Beatrice, as at least a
score of the insects fell dead upon the ground.

"I see it! I see it!" shrieked Beatrice. "It is my father's fatal science! No, no,
Giovanni; it was not I! Never, never! I dreamed only to love thee, and be with
thee a little time, and so to let thee pass away, leaving but thine image in mine
heart. For, Giovanni—believe it—though my body be nourished with poison, my
spirit is God's creature, and craves love as its daily food. But my father!—he has
united us in this fearful sympathy. Yes; spurn me!—tread upon me!—kill me!
Oh, what is death, after such words as thine? But it was not I! Not for a world of
bliss would I have done it!"

Giovanni's passion had exhausted itself in its outburst from his lips. There now
came across him a sense, mournful, and not without tenderness, of the intimate
and peculiar relationship between Beatrice and himself. They stood, as it were, in
an utter solitude, which would be made none the less solitary by the densest
throng of human life. Ought not, then, the desert of humanity around them to
press this insulated pair closer together? If they should be cruel to one another,
who was there to be kind to them? Besides, thought Giovanni, might there not still
be a hope of his returning within the limits of ordinary nature, and leading Beatrice—the redeemed Beatrice—by the hand? Oh, weak, and selfish, and unworthy spirit, that could dream of an earthly union and earthly happiness as possible,
after such deep love had been so bitterly wronged as was Beatrice's love by Giovanni's blighting words! No, no; there could be no such hope. She must pass
heavily, with that broken heart, across the borders of Time—she must bathe her
hurts in some fount of Paradise, and forget her grief in the light of immortality—
and *there* be well!

But Giovanni did not know it.

"Dear Beatrice," said he, approaching her, while she shrank away, as always at
his approach, but now with a different impulse—"dearest Beatrice, our fate is not
yet so desperate. Behold! There is a medicine, potent, as a wise physician has assured me, and almost divine in its efficacy. It is composed of ingredients the most
opposite to those by which thy awful father has brought this calamity upon thee
and me. It is distilled of blessed herbs. Shall we not quaff it together, and thus be
purified from evil?"

"Give it me!" said Beatrice, extending her hand to receive the little silver phial
which Giovanni took from his bosom. She added, with a peculiar emphasis: "I will
drink—but do thou await the result."

She put Baglioni's antidote to her lips; and, at the same moment, the figure of
Rappaccini emerged from the portal, and came slowly towards the marble fountain. As he drew near, the pale man of science seemed to gaze with a triumphant
expression at the beautiful youth and maiden, as might an artist who should
spend his life in achieving a picture or a group of statuary, and finally be satisfied
with his success. He paused—his bent form grew erect with conscious power, he
spread out his hands over them, in the attitude of a father imploring a blessing
upon his children. But those were the same hands that had thrown poison into the
stream of their lives! Giovanni trembled. Beatrice shuddered nervously, and
pressed her hand upon her heart.

"My daughter," said Rappaccini, "thou art no longer lonely in the world! Pluck
one of those precious gems from thy sister shrub, and bid thy bridegroom wear it
in his bosom. It will not harm him now! My science, and the sympathy between
thee and him, have so wrought within his system, that he now stands apart from
common men, as thou dost, daughter of my pride and triumph, from ordinary
women. Pass on, then, through the world, most dear to one another, and dreadful
to all besides!"

"My father," said Beatrice, feebly—and still, as she spoke, she kept her hand upon her heart—"wherefore didst thou inflict this miserable doom upon thy child?"

"Miserable!" exclaimed Rappaccini. "What mean you, foolish girl? Dost thou deem it misery to be endowed with marvellous gifts, against which no power nor strength could avail an enemy? Misery, to be able to quell the mightiest with a breath? Misery, to be as terrible as thou art beautiful? Wouldst thou, then, have preferred the condition of a weak woman, exposed to all evil, and capable of none?"

"I would fain have been loved, not feared," murmured Beatrice, sinking down upon the ground.—"But now it matters not; I am going, father, where the evil, which thou hast striven to mingle with my being, will pass away like a dream—like the fragrance of these poisonous flowers, which will no longer taint my breath among the flowers of Eden. Farewell, Giovanni! Thy words of hatred are like lead within my heart—but they, too, will fall away as I ascend. Oh, was there not, from the first, more poison in thy nature than in mine?"

To Beatrice—so radically had her earthly part been wrought upon by Rappaccini's skill—as poison had been life, so the powerful antidote was death. And thus the poor victim of man's ingenuity and of thwarted nature, and of the fatality that attends all such efforts of perverted wisdom, perished there, at the feet of her father and Giovanni. Just at that moment, Professor Pietro Baglioni looked forth from the window, and called loudly, in a tone of triumph mixed with horror, to the thunder-stricken man of science:

"Rappaccini! Rappaccini! And is *this* the upshot of your experiment?"

1844

Ethan Brand[1]

A CHAPTER FROM AN ABORTIVE ROMANCE

Bartram, the lime-burner, a rough, heavy-looking man, begrimed with charcoal, sat watching his kiln, at nightfall, while his little son played at building houses with the scattered fragments of marble; when, on the hill-side below them, they heard a roar of laughter, not mirthful, but slow, and even solemn, like a wind shaking the boughs of the forest.

"Father, what is that?" asked the little boy, leaving his play, and pressing betwixt his father's knees.

"Oh, some drunken man, I suppose," answered the lime-burner;—"some merry fellow from the bar-room in the village, who dared not laugh loud enough within doors, lest he should blow the roof of the house off. So here he is, shaking his jolly sides, at the foot of Graylock."[2]

"But, father," said the child, more sensitive than the obtuse, middle-aged clown, "he does not laugh like a man that is glad. So the noise frightens me!"

"Don't be a fool, child!" cried his father, gruffly. "You will never make a man, I do believe; there is too much of your mother in you. I have known the rustling of a leaf startle you. Hark! Here comes the merry fellow now. You shall see that there is no harm in him."

Bartram and his little son, while they were talking thus, sat watching the same

---

[1] An 1844 notebook entry appears to be the germ of this story: "The search of an investigator for the Unpardonable Sin—he at last finds it in his own heart and practice."

[2] Mt. Graylock (Saddle Mountain) is the highest mountain in the Berkshires in Massachusetts.

lime-kiln that had been the scene of Ethan Brand's solitary and meditative life, before he began his search for the Unpardonable Sin. Many years, as we have seen, had now elapsed, since that portentous night when the IDEA was first developed. The kiln, however, on the mountainside, stood unimpaired, and was in nothing changed, since he had thrown his dark thoughts into the intense glow of its furnace, and melted them, as it were, into the one thought that took possession of his life. It was a rude, round, tower-like structure, about twenty feet high, heavily built of rough stones, and with a hillock of earth heaped about the larger part of its circumference; so that blocks and fragments of marble might be drawn by cart-loads, and thrown in at the top. There was an opening at the bottom of the tower, like an oven-mouth, but large enough to admit a man in a stooping posture, and provided with a massive iron door. With the smoke and jets of flame issuing from the chinks and crevices of this door, which seemed to give admittance into the hillside, it resembled nothing so much as the private entrance to the infernal regions, which the shepherds of the Delectable Mountains[3] were accustomed to show to pilgrims.

There are many such lime-kilns in that tract of country, for the purpose of burning the white marble which composes a large part of the substance of the hills. Some of them, built years ago, and long deserted, with weeds growing in the vacant round of the interior, which is open to the sky, and grass and wild flowers rooting themselves into the chinks of the stones, look already like relics of antiquity, and may yet be overspread with the lichens of centuries to come. Others, where the lime-burner still feeds his daily and night-long fire, afford points of interest to the wanderer among the hills, who seats himself on a log of wood or a fragment of marble, to hold chat with the solitary man. It is a lonesome, and, when the character is inclined to thought, may be an intensely thoughtful occupation; as it proved in the case of Ethan Brand, who had mused to such strange purpose, in days gone by, while the fire in this very kiln was burning.

The man, who now watched the fire, was of a different order, and troubled himself with no thoughts save the very few that were requisite to his business. At frequent intervals he flung back the clashing weight of the iron door, and, turning his face from the insufferable glare, thrust in huge logs of oak, or stirred the immense brands with a long pole. Within the furnace, was seen the curling and riotous flames, and the burning marble, almost molten with the intensity of heat; while, without, the reflection of the fire quivered on the dark intricacy of the surrounding forest, and showed, in the foreground, a bright and ruddy little picture of the hut, the spring beside its door, the athletic and coal-begrimed figure of the lime-burner, and the half-frightened child, shrinking into the protection of his father's shadow. And when, again, the iron door was closed, then re-appeared the tender light of the half-full moon, which vainly strove to trace out the indistinct shapes of the neighboring mountains; and, in the upper sky, there was a flitting congregation of clouds, still faintly tinged with the rosy sunset, though, thus far down into the valley, the sunshine had vanished long and long ago.

The little boy now crept still closer to his father, as footsteps were heard ascending the hill-side, and a human form thrust aside the bushes that clustered beneath the trees.

"Halloo! who is it?" cried the lime-burner, vexed at his son's timidity, yet half-infected by it. "Come forward, and show yourself, like a man; or I'll fling this chunk of marble at your head!"

---

[3]In John Bunyan's *Pilgrim's Progress* (Part I, 1678; Part II, 1684), Pilgrim is able from these mountains to also see the Celestial City.

"You offer me a rough welcome," said a gloomy voice, as the unknown man drew nigh. "Yet I neither claim nor desire a kinder one, even at my own fireside."

To obtain a distincter view, Bartram threw open the iron door of the kiln, whence immediately issued a gush of fierce light, that smote full upon the stranger's face and figure. To a careless eye, there appeared nothing very remarkable in his aspect, which was that of a man in a coarse, brown, country-made suit of clothes, tall and thin, with the staff and heavy shoes of a wayfarer. As he advanced, he fixed his eyes, which were very bright, intently upon the brightness of the furnace, as if he beheld, or expected to behold, some object worthy of note within it.

"Good evening, stranger," said the lime-burner, "whence come you, so late in the day?"

"I come from my search," answered the wayfarer; "for, at last, it is finished."

"Drunk, or crazy!" muttered Bartram to himself. "I shall have trouble with the fellow. The sooner I drive him away, the better."

The little boy, all in a tremble, whispered to his father, and begged him to shut the door of the kiln, so that there might not be so much light; for that there was something in the man's face which he was afraid to look at, yet could not look away from. And, indeed, even the lime-burner's dull and torpid sense began to be impressed by an indescribable something in that thin, rugged, thoughtful visage, with the grizzled hair hanging wildly about it, and those deeply sunken eyes, which gleamed like fires within the entrance of a mysterious cavern. But, as he closed the door, the stranger turned towards him, and spoke in a quiet, familiar way, that made Bartram feel as if he were a sane and sensible man, after all.

"Your task draws to an end, I see," said he. "This marble has already been burning three days. A few hours more will convert the stone to lime."

"Why, who are you?" exclaimed the lime-burner. "You seem as well acquainted with my business as I myself."

"And well I may be," said the stranger, "for I followed the same craft, many a long year; and here, too, on this very spot. But you are a new comer in these parts. Did you never hear of Ethan Brand?"

"The man that went in search of the Unpardonable Sin?" asked Bartram, with a laugh.

"The same," answered the stranger. "He has found what he sought, and therefore he comes back again."

"What! then you are Ethan Brand, himself?" cried the lime-burner in amazement. "I am a new comer here, as you say; and they call it eighteen years since you left the foot of Graylock. But, I can tell you, the good folks still talk about Ethan Brand, in the village yonder, and what a strange errand took him away from his lime-kiln. Well, and so you have found the Unpardonable Sin?"

"Even so!" said the stranger, calmly.

"If the question is a fair one," proceeded Bartram, "where might it be?"

Ethan Brand laid his finger on his own heart. "Here!" replied he.

And then, without mirth in his countenance, but as if moved by an involuntary recognition of the infinite absurdity of seeking throughout the world for what was the closest of all things to himself, and looking into every heart, save his own, for what was hidden in no other breast, he broke into a laugh of scorn. It was the same slow, heavy laugh, that had almost appalled the lime-burner, when it heralded the way-farer's approach.

The solitary mountain-side was made dismal by it. Laughter, when out of place, mistimed, or bursting forth from a disordered state of feeling, may be the most terrible modulation of the human voice. The laughter of one asleep, even if it be a little child—the madman's laugh—the wild, screaming laugh of a born idiot, are sounds that we sometimes tremble to hear, and would always willingly forget. Poets have imagined no utterance of fiends or hobgoblins so fearfully appropriate as a laugh. And even the obtuse lime-burner felt his nerves shaken, as this strange man looked inward at his own heart, and burst into laughter that rolled away into the night, and was indistinctly reverberated among the hills.

"Joe," said he to his little son, "scamper down to the tavern in the village, and tell the jolly fellows there that Ethan Brand has come back, and that he has found the Unpardonable Sin!"

The boy darted away on his errand, to which Ethan Brand made no objection, nor seemed hardly to notice it. He sat on a log of wood, looking steadfastly at the iron door of the kiln. When the child was out of sight, and his swift and light footsteps ceased to be heard, treading first on the fallen leaves, and then on the rocky mountain-path, the lime-burner began to regret his departure. He felt that the little fellow's presence had been a barrier between his guest and himself, and that he must now deal, heart to heart, with a man who, on his own confession, had committed the only crime for which Heaven could afford no mercy. That crime, in its indistinct blackness, seemed to overshadow him. The lime-burner's own sins rose up within him, and made his memory riotous with a throng of evil shapes that asserted their kindred with the Master Sin, whatever it might be, which it was within the scope of man's corrupted nature to conceive and cherish. They were all of one family; they went to and fro between his breast and Ethan Brand's, and carried dark greetings from one to the other.

Then Bartram remembered the stories which had grown traditionary in reference to this strange man, who had come upon him like a shadow of the night, and was making himself at home in his old place, after so long absence that the dead people, dead and buried for years, would have had more right to be at home, in any familiar spot, than he. Ethan Brand, it was said, had conversed with Satan himself, in the lurid blaze of this very kiln. The legend had been matter of mirth heretofore, but looked grisly now. According to this tale, before Ethan Brand departed on his search, he had been accustomed to evoke a fiend from the hot furnace of the lime-kiln, night after night, in order to confer with him about the Unpardonable Sin; the Man and the Fiend each laboring to frame the image of some mode of guilt, which could neither be atoned for, nor forgiven. And, with the first gleam of light upon the mountain-top, the fiend crept in at the iron door, there to abide in the intensest element of fire, until again summoned forth to share in the dreadful task of extending man's possible guilt beyond the scope of Heaven's else infinite mercy.

While the lime-burner was struggling with the horror of these thoughts, Ethan Brand rose from the log and flung open the door of the kiln. The action was in such accordance with the idea in Bartram's mind, that he almost expected to see the Evil One issue forth, red-hot from the raging furnace.

"Hold, hold!" cried he, with a tremulous attempt to laugh; for he was ashamed of his fears, although they overmastered him. "Don't, for mercy's sake, bring out your devil now!"

"Man!" sternly replied Ethan Brand, "what need have I of the devil? I have left him behind me on my track. It is with such half-way sinners as you that he busies himself. Fear not, because I open the door. I do but act by old custom, and am going to trim your fire, like a lime-burner, as I was once."

He stirred the vast coals, thrust in more wood, and bent forward to gaze into the hollow prison-house of the fire, regardless of the fierce glow that reddened upon his face. The lime-burner sat watching him, and half suspected his strange guest of a purpose, if not to evoke a fiend, at least to plunge bodily into the flames, and thus vanish from the sight of man. Ethan Brand, however, drew quietly back, and closed the door of the kiln.

"I have looked," said he, "into many a human heart that was seven times hotter with sinful passions than yonder furnace is with fire. But I found not there what I sought. No; not the Unpardonable Sin!"

"What is the Unpardonable Sin?" asked the lime-burner; and then he shrank farther from his companion, trembling lest his question should be answered.

"It is a sin that grew within my own breast," replied Ethan Brand, standing erect, with the pride that distinguishes all enthusiasts of his stamp. "A sin that grew nowhere else! The sin of an intellect that triumphed over the sense of brotherhood with man, and reverence for God, and sacrificed everything to its own mighty claims! The only sin that deserves a recompense of immortal agony! Freely, were it to do again, would I incur the guilt. Unshrinkingly, I accept the retribution!"

"The man's head is turned," muttered the lime-burner to himself. "He may be a sinner, like the rest of us—nothing more likely—but I'll be sworn, he is a madman, too."

Nevertheless, he felt uncomfortable at his situation, alone with Ethan Brand on the wild mountain-side, and was right glad to hear the rough murmur of tongues, and the footsteps of what seemed a pretty numerous party, stumbling over the stones, and rustling through the underbrush. Soon appeared the whole lazy regiment that was wont to infest the village tavern, comprehending three or four individuals who had drunk flip beside the bar-room fire, through all the winters, and smoked their pipes beneath the stoop, through all the summers since Ethan Brand's departure. Laughing boisterously, and mingling all their voices together in unceremonious talk, they now burst into the moonshine and narrow streaks of fire-light that illuminated the open space before the lime-kiln. Bartram set the door ajar again, flooding the spot with light, that the whole company might get a fair view of Ethan Brand, and he of them.

There, among other old acquaintances, was a once ubiquitous man, now almost extinct, but whom we were formerly sure to encounter at the hotel of every thriving village throughout the country. It was the stage-agent. The present specimen of the genus was a wilted and smoke-dried man, wrinkled and red-nosed, in a smartly cut, brown, bob-tailed coat, with brass buttons, who, for a length of time unknown, had kept his desk and corner in the bar-room, and was still puffing what seemed to be the same cigar that he had lighted twenty years before. He had great fame as a dry joker, though, perhaps, less on account of any intrinsic humor, than from a certain flavor of brandy-toddy and tobacco-smoke, which impregnated all his ideas and expressions, as well as his person. Another well-remembered, though strangely-altered face was that of Lawyer Giles, as people still called him in courtesy; an elderly ragamuffin, in his soiled shirt-sleeves and tow-cloth trowsers. This poor fellow had been an attorney, in what he called his better days, a sharp practitioner, and in great vogue among the village litigants; but flip, and sling, and toddy, and cocktails, imbibed at all hours, morning, noon, and night, had caused him to slide from intellectual, to various kinds and degrees of bodily labor, till, at last, to adopt his own phrase, he slid into a soap-vat. In other words, Giles was now a soap-boiler, in a small way. He had come to be but the fragment of a human being, a part of one foot having been chopped off by an axe, and an entire hand torn away by the devilish gripe of a steam-engine. Yet, though the corporeal hand was gone, a spiritual member remained; for, stretching forth the stump, Giles steadfastly averred, that he felt an invisible thumb and fingers, with as vivid a sensation as before the real ones were amputated. A maimed and miserable wretch he was; but one, nevertheless, whom the world could not trample on, and had no right to scorn, either in this or any previous stage of his misfortunes, since he had still kept up the courage and spirit of a man, asked nothing in charity, and, with his one hand—and that the left one—fought a stern battle against want and hostile circumstances.

Among the throng, too, came another personage, who, with certain points of similarity to Lawyer Giles, had more of difference. It was the village Doctor, a man of some fifty years, whom, at an earlier period of his life, we should have introduced as paying a professional visit to Ethan Brand, during the latter's supposed insanity. He was now a purple-visaged, rude, and brutal, yet half-gentlemanly figure, with something wild, ruined, and desperate in his talk, and in all the details of his gesture and manners. Brandy possessed this man like an evil spirit, and made him as surly and savage as a wild beast, and as miserable as a lost soul; but there was supposed to be in him such wonderful skill, such native gifts of healing, beyond any which medical science could impart, that society caught hold of him, and would not let him sink out of its reach. So, swaying to and fro upon his horse, and grumbling thick accents at the bedside, he visited all the sick chambers for miles about among the mountain towns; and sometimes raised a dying man, as it were, by miracle, or, quite as often, no doubt, sent his patient to a grave that was dug many a year too soon. The Doctor had an everlasting pipe in his mouth, and, as somebody said, in allusion to his habit of swearing, it was always alight with hell-fire.

These three worthies pressed forward, and greeted Ethan Brand, each after his own fashion, earnestly inviting him to partake of the contents of a certain black bottle; in which, as they averred, he would find something far better worth seeking for, than the Unpardonable Sin. No mind, which has wrought itself, by intense and solitary meditation, into a high state of enthusiasm, can endure the kind of contact with low and vulgar modes of thought and feeling, to which Ethan Brand was now subjected. It made him doubt—and, strange to say, it was a painful doubt—whether he had indeed found the Unpardonable Sin, and found it within himself. The whole question on which he had exhausted life, and more than life, looked like a delusion.

"Leave me," he said bitterly, "ye brute beasts, that have made yourselves so, shrivelling up your souls with fiery liquors! I have done with you. Years and years ago, I groped into your hearts and found nothing there for my purpose. Get ye gone!"

"Why, you uncivil scoundrel," cried the fierce Doctor, "is that the way you respond to the kindness of your best friends? Then let me tell you the truth. You have no more found the Unpardonable Sin than yonder boy Joe has. You are but a crazy fellow—I told you so, twenty years ago—neither better nor worse than a crazy fellow, and the fit companion of old Humphrey, here!"

He pointed to an old man, shabbily dressed, with long white hair, thin visage, and unsteady eyes. For some years past, this aged person had been wandering about among the hills, inquiring of all travellers whom he met, for his daughter. The girl, it seemed, had gone off with a company of circus-performers; and, occasionally, tidings of her came to the village, and fine stories were told of her glittering appearance, as she rode on horseback in the ring, or performed marvellous feats on the tight-rope.

The white-haired father now approached Ethan Brand, and gazed unsteadily into his face.

"They tell me you have been all over the earth," said he, wringing his hands with earnestness. "You must have seen my daughter; for she makes a grand figure in the world, and everybody goes to see her. Did she send any word to her old father, or say when she is coming back?"

Ethan Brand's eye quailed beneath the old man's. That daughter, from whom he so earnestly desired a word of greeting, was the Esther of our tale; the very girl whom, with such cold and remorseless purpose, Ethan Brand had made the subject of a psychological experiment, and wasted, absorbed, and perhaps annihilated her soul, in the process.

"Yes," murmured he, turning away from the hoary wanderer; "it is no delusion. There is an Unpardonable Sin!"

While these things were passing, a merry scene was going forward in the area of cheerful light, besides the spring and before the door of the hut. A number of the youth of the village, young men and girls, had hurried up the hill-side, impelled by curiosity to see Ethan Brand, the hero of so many a legend familiar to their childhood. Finding nothing, however, very remarkable in his aspect—nothing but a sunburnt wayfarer, in plain garb and dusty shoes, who sat looking into the fire, as if he fancied pictures among the coals—these young people speedily grew tired of observing him. As it happened, there was other amusement at hand. An old German Jew, travelling with a diorama[4] on his back, was passing down the mountain-road towards the village, just as the party turned aside from it; and, in hopes of eking out the profits of the day, the showman had kept them company to the lime-kiln.

"Come, old Dutchman," cried one of the young men, "let us see your pictures, if you can swear they are worth looking at!"

"Oh, yes, Captain," answered the Jew—whether as a matter of courtesy or craft, he styled everybody Captain—"I shall show you, indeed, some very superb pictures!"

So, placing his box in a proper position, he invited the young men and girls to look through the glass orifices of the machine, and proceeded to exhibit a series of the most outrageous scratchings and daubings, as specimens of the fine arts, that ever an itinerant showman had the face to impose upon his circle of spectators. The pictures were worn out, moreover, tattered, full of cracks and wrinkles, dingy with tobacco-smoke, and otherwise in a most pitiable condition. Some purported to be cities, public edifices, and ruined castles, in Europe; others represented Napoleon's battles, and Nelson's[5] sea-fights; and in the midst of these would be seen a gigantic, brown, hairy hand—which might have been mistaken for the Hand of Destiny, though, in truth, it was only the showman's—pointing its forefinger to various scenes of the conflict, while its owner gave historical illustrations. When, with much merriment at its abominable deficiency of merit, the exhibition was concluded, the German bade little Joe put his head into the box. Viewed through the magnifying glasses, the boy's round, rosy visage assumed the strangest imaginable aspect of an immense, Titanic child, the mouth grinning broadly, and the eyes, and every other feature, overflowing with fun at the joke. Suddenly, however, that merry face turned pale, and its expression changed to horror; for this easily impressed and excitable child had become sensible that the eye of Ethan Brand was fixed upon him through the glass.

"You make the little man to be afraid, Captain," said the German Jew, turning up the dark and strong outline of his visage, from his stooping posture. "But, look again; and, by chance, I shall cause you to see somewhat that is very fine, upon my word!"

Ethan Brand gazed into the box for an instant, and then starting back, looked fixedly at the German. What had he seen? Nothing, apparently; for a curious youth, who had peeped in, almost at the same moment, beheld only a vacant space of canvass.

"I remember you now," muttered Ethan Brand to the showman.

"Ah, Captain," whispered the Jew of Nuremberg, with a dark smile, "I find it to be a heavy matter in my show-box—this Unpardonable Sin! By my faith, Captain, it has wearied my shoulders, this long day, to carry it over the mountain."

---

[4]A box containing a lens through which the viewer sees enlarged or three-dimensional pictures.
[5]British admiral Horatio Nelson (1758–1805).

"Peace!" answered Ethan Brand, sternly, "or get thee into the furnace yonder!"

The Jew's exhibition had scarcely concluded, when a great, elderly dog—who seemed to be his own master, as no person in the company laid claim to him—saw fit to render himself the object of public notice. Hitherto, he had shown himself a very quiet, well-disposed old dog, going round from one to another, and, by way of being sociable, offering his rough head to be patted by any kindly hand that would take so much trouble. But, now, all of a sudden, this grave and venerable quadruped, of his own mere notion, and without the slightest suggestion from anybody else, began to run round after his tail, which, to heighten the absurdity of the proceeding, was a great deal shorter than it should have been. Never was seen such headlong eagerness in pursuit of an object that could not possibly be attained; never was heard such a tremendous outbreak of growling, snarling, barking, and snapping—as if one end of the ridiculous brute's body were at deadly and most unforgivable enmity with the other. Faster and faster, round-about went the cur; and faster and still faster fled the unapproachable brevity of his tail; and louder and fiercer grew his yells of rage and animosity; until, utterly exhausted, and as far from the goal as ever, the foolish old dog ceased his performance as suddenly as he had begun it. The next moment, he was as mild, quiet, sensible, and respectable in his deportment, as when he first scraped acquaintance with the company.

As may be supposed, the exhibition was greeted with universal laughter, clapping of hands, and shouts of encore; to which the canine performer responded by wagging all that there was to wag of his tail, but appeared totally unable to repeat his very successful effort to amuse the spectators.

Meanwhile, Ethan Brand had resumed his seat upon the log; and, moved, it might be, by a perception of some remote analogy between his own case and that of this self-pursuing cur, he broke into the awful laugh, which, more than any other token, expressed the condition of his inward being. From that moment, the merriment of the party was at an end; they stood aghast, dreading lest the inauspicious sound should be reverberated around the horizon, and that mountain would thunder it to mountain, and so the horror be prolonged upon their ears. Then, whispering one to another, that it was late—that the moon was almost down—that the August night was growing chill—they hurried homeward, leaving the lime-burner and little Joe to deal as they might with their unwelcome guest. Save for these three human beings, the open space on the hill-side was a solitude, set in a vast gloom of forest. Beyond that darksome verge, the fire-light glimmered on the stately trunks and almost black foliage of pines, intermixed with the lighter verdure of sapling oaks, maples, and poplars, while, here and there, lay the gigantic corpses of dead trees, decaying on the leaf-strewn soil. And it seemed to little Joe—a timorous and imaginative child—that the silent forest was holding its breath, until some fearful thing should happen.

Ethan Brand thrust more wood into the fire, and closed the door of the kiln; then looking over his shoulder at the lime-burner and his son, he bade, rather than advised, them to retire to rest.

"For myself I cannot sleep," said he. "I have matters that it concerns me to meditate upon. I will watch the fire, as I used to do in the old time."

"And call the devil out of the furnace to keep you company, I suppose," muttered Bartram, who had been making intimate acquaintance with the black bottle above-mentioned. "But watch, if you like, and call as many devils as you like! For my part, I shall be all the better for a snooze. Come, Joe!"

As the boy followed his father into the hut, he looked back to the wayfarer, and the tears came into his eyes; for his tender spirit had an intuition of the bleak and terrible loneliness in which this man had enveloped himself.

When they had gone, Ethan Brand sat listening to the crackling of the kindled wood, and looking at the little spirts of fire that issued through the chinks of the door. These trifles, however, once so familiar, had but the slightest hold of his attention; while deep within his mind, he was reviewing the gradual, but marvellous change, that had been wrought upon him by the search to which he had devoted himself. He remembered how the night-dew had fallen upon him—how the dark forest had whispered to him—how the stars had gleamed upon him—a simple and loving man, watching his fire in the years gone by, and ever musing as it burned. He remembered with what tenderness, with what love and sympathy for mankind, and what pity for human guilt and wo, he had first begun to contemplate those ideas which afterwards became the inspiration of his life; with what reverence he had then looked into the heart of man, viewing it as a temple originally divine, and however desecrated, still to be held sacred by a brother; with what awful fear he had deprecated the success of his pursuit, and prayed that the Unpardonable Sin might never be revealed to him. Then ensued that vast intellectual development, which, in its progress, disturbed the counterpoise between his mind and heart. The Idea that possessed his life had operated as a means of education; it had gone on cultivating his powers to the highest point of which they were susceptible; it had raised him from the level of an unlettered laborer, to stand on a star-light eminence, whither the philosophers of the earth, laden with the lore of universities, might vainly strive to clamber after him. So much for the intellect! But where was the heart? That, indeed, had withered—had contracted—had hardened—had perished! It had ceased to partake of the universal throb. He had lost his hold of the magnetic chain of humanity. He was no longer a brother-man, opening the chambers or the dungeons of our common nature by the key of holy sympathy, which gave him a right to share in all its secrets; he was now a cold observer, looking on mankind as the subject of his experiment, and, at length, converting man and woman to be his puppets, and pulling the wires that moved them to such degrees of crime as were demanded for his study.

Thus Ethan Brand became a fiend. He began to be so from the moment that his moral nature had ceased to keep the pace of improvement with his intellect. And now, as his highest effort and inevitable development—as the bright and gorgeous flower, and rich, delicious fruit of his life's labor—he had produced the Unpardonable Sin!

"What more have I to seek? What more to achieve?" said Ethan Brand to himself. "My task is done, and well done!"

Starting from the log with a certain alacrity in his gait, and ascending the hillock of earth that was raised against the stone circumference of the lime-kiln, he thus reached the top of the structure. It was a space of perhaps ten feet across, from edge to edge, presenting a view of the upper surface of the immense mass of broken marble with which the kiln was heaped. All these innumerable blocks and fragments of marble were red-hot, and vividly on fire, sending up great spouts of blue flame, which quivered aloft and danced madly, as within a magic circle, and sank and rose again, with continual and multitudinous activity. As the lonely man bent forward over this terrible body of fire, the blasting heat smote up against his person with a breath that, it might be supposed, would have scorched and shrivelled him up in a moment.

Ethan Brand stood erect and raised his arms on high. The blue flames played upon his face, and imparted the wild and ghastly light which alone could have suited its expression; it was that of a fiend on the verge of plunging into his gulf of intensest torment.

"Oh, Mother Earth," cried he, "who art no more my Mother, and into whose bosom this frame shall never be resolved! Oh, mankind, whose brotherhood I have cast off, and trampled thy great heart beneath my feet! Oh, stars of Heaven, that shone on me of old, as if to light me onward and upward!—farewell all, and forever! Come, deadly element of Fire—henceforth my familiar friend! Embrace me as I do thee!"

That night the sound of a fearful peal of laughter rolled heavily through the sleep of the lime-burner and his little son; dim shapes of horror and anguish haunted their dreams, and seemed still present in the rude hovel when they opened their eyes to the daylight.

"Up, boy, up!" cried the lime-burner, staring about him. "Thank Heaven, the night is gone at last; and rather than pass such another, I would watch my lime-kiln, wide awake, for a twelvemonth. This Ethan Brand, with his humbug of an Unpardonable Sin, has done me no such mighty favor in taking my place!"

He issued from the hut, followed by little Joe, who kept fast hold of his father's hand. The early sunshine was already pouring its gold upon the mountain-tops, and though the valleys were still in shadow, they smiled cheerfully in the promise of the bright day that was hastening onward. The village, completely shut in by hills, which swelled away gently about it, looked as if it had rested peacefully in the hollow of the great hand of Providence. Every dwelling was distinctly visible; the little spires of the two churches pointed upward, and caught a fore-glimmering of brightness from the sun-gilt skies upon their gilded weathercocks. The tavern was astir, and the figure of the old, smoke-dried stage-agent, cigar in mouth, was seen beneath the stoop. Old Graylock was glorified with a golden cloud upon his head. Scattered, likewise, over the breasts of the surrounding mountains, there were heaps of hoary mist, in fantastic shapes, some of them far down into the valley, others high up towards the summits, and still others, of the same family of mist or cloud, hovering in the gold radiance of the upper atmosphere. Stepping from one to another of the clouds that rested on the hills, and thence to the loftier brotherhood that sailed in air, it seemed almost as if a mortal man might thus ascend into the heavenly regions. Earth was so mingled with sky that it was a daydream to look at it.

To supply that charm of the familiar and homely, which Nature so readily adopts into a scene like this, the stagecoach was rattling down the mountain-road, and the driver sounded his horn; while echo caught up the notes and intertwined them into a rich, and varied, and elaborate harmony, of which the original performer could lay claim to little share. The great hills played a concert among themselves, each contributing a strain of airy sweetness.

Little Joe's face brightened at once.

"Dear father," cried he, skipping cheerily to and fro, "that strange man is gone, and the sky and the mountains all seem glad of it!"

"Yes," growled the lime-burner with an oath, "but he has let the fire go down, and no thanks to him, if five hundred bushels of lime are not spoilt. If I catch the fellow hereabouts again I shall feel like tossing him into the furnace!"

With his long pole in his hand he ascended to the top of the kiln. After a moment's pause he called to his son.

"Come up here, Joe!" said he.

So little Joe ran up the hillock and stood by his father's side. The marble was all burnt into perfect, snow-white lime. But on its surface, in the midst of the circle—snow-white too, and thoroughly converted into lime—lay a human skeleton, in the attitude of a person who, after long toil, lies down to long repose. Within the ribs—strange to say—was the shape of a human heart.

"Was the fellow's heart made of marble?" cried Bartram, in some perplexity at this phenomenon. "At any rate, it is burnt into what looks like special good lime; and, taking all the bones together, my kiln is half a bushel the richer for him."

So saying, the rude lime-burner lifted his pole, and letting it fall upon the skeleton, the relics of Ethan Brand were crumbled into fragments.

1851

from **Prefaces**

Preface to *The House of the Seven Gables*

[ROMANCE VS. NOVEL]

When a writer calls his work a Romance, it need hardly be observed that he wishes to claim a certain latitude, both as to its fashion and material, which he would not have felt himself entitled to assume, had he professed to be writing a Novel. The latter form of composition is presumed to aim at a very minute fidelity, not merely to the possible, but to the probable and ordinary course of man's experience. The former—while, as a work of art, it must rigidly subject itself to laws, and while it sins unpardonably, so far as it may swerve aside from the truth of the human heart—has fairly a right to present that truth under circumstances, to a great extent, of the writer's own choosing or creation. If he think fit, also, he may so manage his atmospherical medium as to bring out or mellow the lights and deepen and enrich the shadows of the picture. He will be wise, no doubt, to make a very moderate use of the privileges here stated, and, especially, to mingle the Marvellous rather as a slight, delicate, and evanescent flavor, than as any portion of the actual substance of the dish offered to the Public. He can hardly be said, however, to commit a literary crime, even if he disregard this caution.

In the present work, the Author has proposed to himself (but with what success, fortunately, it is not for him to judge) to keep undeviatingly within his immunities. The point of view in which this Tale comes under the Romantic definition, lies in the attempt to connect a by-gone time with the very Present that is flitting away from us. It is a Legend, prolonging itself, from an epoch now gray in the distance, down into our own broad daylight, and bringing along with it some of its legendary mist, which the Reader, according to his pleasure, may either disregard, or allow it to float almost imperceptibly about the characters and events, for the sake of a picturesque effect. The narrative, it may be, is woven of so humble a texture as to require this advantage, and, at the same time, to render it the more difficult of attainment.

Many writers lay very great stress upon some definite moral purpose, at which they profess to aim their works. Not to be deficient, in this particular, the Author has provided himself with a moral;—the truth, namely, that the wrong-doing of one generation lives into the successive ones, and, divesting itself of every temporary advantage, becomes a pure and uncontrollable mischief;—and he would feel it a singular gratification, if this Romance might effectually convince mankind (or, indeed, any one man) of the folly of tumbling down an avalanche of ill-gotten gold, or real estate, on the heads of an unfortunate posterity, thereby to maim and crush them, until the accumulated mass shall be scattered abroad in its original atoms. In good faith, however, he is not sufficiently imaginative to flatter himself with the slightest hope of this kind. When romances do really teach anything, or produce any effective operation, it is usually through a far more subtle process than the ostensible one. The Author has considered it hardly worth his while, therefore, relentlessly to impale the story with its moral, as with an iron rod—or rather, as by sticking a pin through a butterfly—thus at once depriving it of life, and causing it to stiffen in an ungainly and unnatural attitude. A high truth, indeed, fairly, finely, and skilfully wrought out, brightening at every step, and crowning the final development of a work of fiction, may add an artistic glory, but is never any truer, and seldom any more evident, at the last page than at the first.

The Reader may perhaps choose to assign an actual locality to the imaginary events of this narrative. If permitted by the historical connection, (which, though slight, was essential to his plan,) the Author would very willingly have avoided anything of this nature. Not to speak of other objections, it exposes the Romance to an inflexible and exceedingly dangerous species of criticism, by bringing his fancy-pictures almost into positive contact with the realities of the moment. It has been no part of his object, however, to describe local manners, nor in any way to meddle with the characteristics of a community for whom he cherishes a proper respect and a natural regard. He trusts not to be considered as unpardonably offending, by laying out a street that infringes upon nobody's private rights, and appropriating a lot of land which had no visible owner, and building a house, of materials long in use for constructing castles in the air. The personages of the Tale— though they give themselves out to be of ancient stability and considerable prominence—are really of the Author's own making, or, at all events, of his own mixing; their virtues can shed no lustre, nor their defects redound, in the remotest degree, to the discredit of the venerable town of which they profess to be inhabitants. He would be glad, therefore, if—especially in the quarter to which he alludes—the book may be read strictly as a Romance, having a great deal more to do with the clouds overhead, than with any portion of the actual soil of the County of Essex.

Lenox, January 27, 1851   *1851*

from Preface to *The Marble Faun*

[ROMANCE'S NEED FOR RUINS]

It is now seven or eight years (so many, at all events, that I cannot precisely remember the epoch) since the Author of this Romance last appeared before the Public.[1] It had grown to be a custom with him, to introduce each of his humble publications with a familiar kind of Preface, addressed nominally to the Public at large, but really to a character with whom he felt entitled to use far greater freedom. He meant it for that one congenial friend—more comprehensive of his purposes, more appreciative of his success, more indulgent of his short-comings, and, in all respects, closer and kinder than a brother—that all-sympathizing critic, in short, whom an author never actually meets, but to whom he implicitly makes his appeal, whenever he is conscious of having done his best.

The antique fashion of Prefaces recognized this genial personage as the 'Kind Reader,' the 'Gentle Reader,' the 'Beloved,' the 'Indulgent,' or, at coldest, the 'Honoured Reader,' to whom the prim old author was wont to make his preliminary explanations and apologies, with the certainty that they would be favourably received. I never personally encountered, nor corresponded through the Post, with this Representative Essence of all delightful and desirable qualities which a Reader can possess. But, fortunately for myself, I never therefore concluded him to be merely a mythic character. I had always a sturdy faith in his actual existence, and wrote for him, year after year, during which the great Eye of the Public (as well it might) almost utterly overlooked my small productions.

Unquestionably, this Gentle, Kind, Benevolent, Indulgent, and most Beloved and Honoured Reader, did once exist for me, and (in spite of the infinite chances against a letter's reaching its destination, without a definite address) duly received the scrolls which I flung upon whatever wind was blowing, in the faith that they would find him out. But, is he extant now? In these many years, since he last heard from me, may he not have deemed his earthly task accomplished, and have withdrawn to the Paradise of Gentle Readers, wherever it may be, to the enjoyments of which his kindly charity, on my behalf, must surely have entitled him? I have a sad foreboding that this may be the truth. The Gentle Reader, in the case

---

[1] *The Marble Faun* was published in 1860; *The Blithedale Romance* in 1852.

of any individual author, is apt to be extremely short-lived; he seldom outlasts a literary fashion, and, except in very rare instances, closes his weary eyes before the writer has half done with him. If I find him at all, it will probably be under some mossy grave-stone, inscribed with a half-obliterated name, which I shall never recognize.

Therefore, I have little heart or confidence (especially, writing, as I do, in a foreign land, and after a long, long absence from my own)[2] to presume upon the existence of that friend of friends, that unseen brother of the soul, whose apprehensive sympathy has so often encouraged me to be egotistical in my Prefaces, careless though unkindly eyes should skim over what was never meant for them. I stand upon ceremony, now, and, after stating a few particulars about the work which is here offered to the Public, must make my most reverential bow, and retire behind the curtain.

This Romance was sketched out during a residence of considerable length in Italy, and has been re-written and prepared for the press, in England. The author proposed to himself merely to write a fanciful story, evolving a thoughtful moral, and did not purpose attempting a portraiture of Italian manners and character. He has lived too long abroad, not to be aware that a foreigner seldom acquires that knowledge of a country, at once flexible and profound, which may justify him in endeavouring to idealize its traits.

Italy, as the site of his Romance, was chiefly valuable to him as affording a sort of poetic or fairy precinct, where actualities would not be so terribly insisted upon, as they are, and must needs be, in America. No author, without a trial, can conceive of the difficulty of writing a Romance about a country where there is no shadow, no antiquity, no mystery, no picturesque and gloomy wrong, nor anything but a common-place prosperity, in broad and simple daylight, as is happily the case with my dear native land. It will be very long, I trust, before romance-writers may find congenial and easily handled themes either in the annals of our stalwart Republic, or in any characteristic and probable events of our individual lives. Romance and poetry, like ivy, lichens, and wall-flowers, need Ruin to make them grow.

In re-writing these volumes, the Author was somewhat surprised to see the extent to which he had introduced descriptions of various Italian objects, antique, pictorial, and statuesque. Yet these things fill the mind, everywhere in Italy, and especially in Rome, and cannot easily be kept from flowing out upon the page, when one writes freely, and with self-enjoyment. And, again, while reproducing the book, on the broad and dreary sands of Redcar,[3] with the gray German Ocean tumbling in upon me, and the northern blast always howling in my ears, the complete change of scene made these Italian reminiscences shine out so vividly, that I could not find in my heart to cancel them.

· · · · · ·

1859   *1860*

---

[2]Hawthorne became United States Consul at Liverpool, England, in 1853, and in 1858, he went to Italy, where he began *The Marble Faun*. He finished it on his return to England in 1859. He came back to America in 1860.
[3]Seaside resort in northeast England on the North Sea.

from Letters, Notebooks, and Journalism

BROOK FARM[1]

TO SOPHIA PEABODY, BOSTON

Oak Hill,[2] April 13th, 1841

Ownest love,

Here is thy poor husband in a polar Paradise! I know not how to interpret this aspect of Nature—whether it be of good or evil omen to our enterprise. But I reflect that the Plymouth pilgrims arrived in the midst of storm and stept ashore upon mountain snow-drifts; and nevertheless they prospered, and became a great people—and doubtless it will be the same with us. I laud my stars, however, that thou wilt not have thy first impressions of our future home from such a day as this. Thou wouldst shiver all thy life afterwards, and never realize that there could be bright skies, and green hills and meadows, and trees heavy with foliage, where now the whole scene is a great snow-bank, and the sky full of snow likewise. Through faith, I persist in believing that spring and summer will come in their due season; but the unregenerated man shivers within me, and suggests a doubt whether I may not have wandered within the precincts of the Arctic circle, and chosen my heritage among everlasting snows. Dearest, provide thyself with a good stock of furs; and if thou canst obtain the skin of a polar bear, thou wilt find it a very suitable summer dress for this region. Thou must not hope ever to walk abroad, except upon snow-shoes, nor to find any warmth, save in thy husband's heart.

Belovedest, I have not yet taken my first lesson in agriculture, as thou mayst well suppose—except that I went to see our cows foddered, yesterday afternoon. We have eight of our own; and the number is now increased by a transcendental heifer, belonging to Miss Margaret Fuller.[3] She is very fractious, I believe, and apt to kick over the milk pail. Thou knowest best, whether, in these traits of character, she resembles her mistress. Thy husband intends to convert himself into a milk-maid, this evening; but I pray heaven that Mr. Ripley may be moved to assign him the kindliest cow in the herd—otherwise he will perform his duty with fear and trembling.

Ownest wife, I like my brethren in affliction very well; and couldst thou see us sitting round our table, at meal-times, before the great kitchen-fire, thou wouldst call it a cheerful sight. Mrs. Barker[4] is a most comfortable woman to behold; she looks as if her ample person were stuffed full of tenderness—indeed, as if she were all one great, kind heart. Wert thou but here, I should ask for nothing more—not even for sunshine and summer weather; for thou wouldst be both, to thy husband. And how is that cough of thine, my belovedest? Hast thou thought of me, in my perils and wanderings? Thou must not think how I longed for thee, when I crept into my cold bed last night,—my bosom remembered thee,—and refused to be comforted without thy caresses. I trust that thou dost muse upon me

---

[1]Brook Farm was established in 1841 under the auspices of the Transcendental Club and the leadership of George Ripley (1802–1880), Unitarian minister and editor of the fourteen-volume *Specimens of Foreign Standard Literature,* which contained texts important in shaping American Transcendentalism. Brook Farm was located in West Roxbury, about nine miles from Boston, and was dedicated to communal working and living, and aimed at promoting the moral and intellectual development of all participants. Hawthorne invested his savings (over $1,000) from his position at the Boston Custom House (1839–40) to participate, in the hopes that he would find a place where he could live quietly with his wife-to-be, Sophia Peabody, and

get on with the writing he wanted to do. He lived and worked there (with some absences) from April to November 1841. His letters to his affianced show his growing disillusionment (although he calls himself "husband" and Sophia "wife," they were not married until July 9, 1842). He would later satirize the Utopian experiment in *The Blithedale Romance* (1852).

[2]Place near Brook Farm.

[3]Margaret Fuller (1810–1850), editor of *The Dial* (1840–42).

[4]Elise Barker, a neighbor to Brook Farm who became a participant.

with hope and joy, not with repining. Think that I am gone before, to prepare a home for my Dove, and will return for her, all in good time.

Thy husband has the best chamber in the house, I believe; and though not quite so good as the apartment I have left, it will do very well. I have hung up thy two pictures; and they give me a glimpse of summer and of thee. The vase I intended to have brought in my arms, but could not very conveniently do it yesterday; so that it still remains at Mrs. Hillards,[5] together with my carpet. I shall bring them the next opportunity.

Now farewell, for the present, most beloved. I have been writing this in my chamber; but the fire is getting low, and the house is old and cold; so that the warmth of my whole person has retreated to my heart, which burns with love for thee. I must run down to the kitchen or parlor hearth, where thy image shall sit beside me—yea be pressed to my breast. At bed-time, thou shalt have a few lines more. Now I think of it, dearest, wilt thou give Mrs. Ripley[6] a copy of Grandfather's Chair and Liberty Tree; she wants them for some boys here. I have several vols of Famous Old People.[7]

April 14th. 10.A.M. Sweetest, I did not milk the cows last night, because Mr. Ripley was afraid to trust them to my hands, or me to their horns—I know not which. But this morning, I have done wonders. Before breakfast, I went out to the barn, and began to chop hay for the cattle; and with such "righteous vehemence" (as Mr. Ripley says) did I labor, that, in the space of ten minutes, I broke the machine. Then I brought wood and replenished the fires; and finally sat down to breakfast and ate up a huge mound of buckwheat cakes. After breakfast, Mr. Ripley put a four-pronged instrument into my hands, which he gave me to understand was called a pitch-fork; and he and Mr. Farley[8] being armed with similar weapons, we all three commenced a gallant attack upon a heap of manure. This affair being concluded, and thy husband having purified himself, he sits down to finish this letter to his most beloved wife. Dearest, I will never consent that thou come within half a mile of me, after such an encounter as that of this morning. Pray Heaven that this letter retain none of the fragrance with which the writer was imbued. As for thy husband himself, he is peculiarly partial to the odor; but that whimsical little nose of thine might chance to quarrel with it.

Belovedest, Miss Fuller's cow hooks the other cows, and has made herself ruler of the herd, and behaves in a very tyrannical manner. Sweetest, I know not when I shall see thee; but I trust it will not be longer than till the end of next week. I love thee! I love thee! I would thou wert with me; for then would my labor be joyful—and even now, it is not sorrowful. Dearest, I shall make an excellent husbandman. I feel the original Adam reviving within me.

TO SOPHIA PEABODY, BOSTON

Oak Hill, April 16th, 1/2 past 6 A.M. [1841]

Most beloved, I have a few moments to spare before breakfast; and perhaps thou wilt let me spend them in talking to thee. Thy two letters blessed me yesterday, having been brought by some private messenger of Mrs. Ripley's. Very joyful was I to hear from my Dove, and my heart gave a mighty heave and swell as thou hast sometimes felt it do while thou was resting upon it. That cough of thine—I do wish it would take its departure; for I cannot bear to think of thy tender little frame being shaken with it all night long. Thou dost need to be kissed, little Dove, every hour of thy life—that would be a sovereign remedy.

Dearest, since I last wrote thee, there has been an addition to our community

---

[5]Susan Howe Hillard, a friend of the Peabodys.
[6]Sophia Willard Dana Ripley (1803–1861), wife of the leader of Brook Farm.

[7]Hawthorne's children's books, *Grandfather's Chair, Famous Old People,* and *Liberty Tree,* were published in 1841.
[8]Francis D. Farley, a Brook Farm participant.

of four gentlemen in sables, who promise to be among our most useful and re-spectable members. They arrived yesterday, about noon. Mr. Ripley had proposed to them to join us, no longer ago than that very morning. I had some conversation with them in the afternoon, and was glad to hear them express much satisfaction with their new abode, and all the arrangements. They do not appear to be very communicative, however—or perhaps it may be merely an external reserve, like that of thy husband, to shield their delicacy. Several of their prominent character-istics, as well as their black attire, lead me to believe that they are members of the clerical profession; but I have not yet ascertained, from their own lips, what has been the nature of their past lives. I trust to have much pleasure in their society, and, sooner or later, that we shall all of us derive great strength from our inter-course with them. I cannot too highly applaud the readiness with which these four gentlemen in black have thrown aside all the fopperies and flummeries, which have their origin in a false state of society. When I last saw them, they looked as heroically regardless of the stains and soils incident to our profession, as thy hus-band did when he emerged from the gold mine.[9]

Ownest wife, thy husband has milked a cow!!!

Belovedest, the herd have rebelled against the usurpation of Miss Fuller's cow; and whenever they are turned out of the barn, she is compelled to take refuge under our protection. So much did she impede thy husband's labors, by keeping close to him, that he found it necessary to give her two or three gentle pats with a shovel; but still she preferred to trust herself to my tender mercies, rather than venture among the horns of the herd. She is not an amiable cow; but she has a very intelligent face, and seems to be of a reflective cast of character. I doubt not that she will soon perceive the expediency of being on good terms with the rest of the sisterhood.

I have not yet been twenty yards from our house and barn; but I begin to per-ceive that this is a beautiful place. The scenery is of a mild and placid character, with nothing bold in its character; but I think its beauties will grow upon us, and make us love it the more, the longer we live here. There is a brook, so near the house that we shall be able to hear its ripple, in the summer evenings; and when-ever we lie awake in the summer nights; but, for agricultural purposes, it has been made to flow in a straight and rectangular fashion, which does it infinite damage, as a picturesque object. . . .

TO SOPHIA PEABODY, BOSTON

Brook Farm, June 1st, 1841—nearly 6 A.M.

Very dearest,

I have been too busy to write thee a long letter by this opportunity; for I think this present life of mine gives me an antipathy to pen and ink, even more than my Custom House experience did. I could not live without the idea of thee, nor with-out spiritual communion with thee; but, in the midst of toil, or after a hard day's work in the gold mine, my soul obstinately refuses to be poured out on paper. That abominable gold mine! Thank God, we anticipate getting rid of its treasur-ers, in the course of two or three days. Of all hateful places, that is the worst; and I shall never comfort myself for having spent so many days of blessed sunshine there. It is my opinion, dearest, that a man's soul may be buried and perish under a dung-heap or in a furrow of the field, just as well as under a pile of money. Well; that giant, Mr. George Bradford,[10] will probably be here to-day; so that

---

[9]The manure pile, so-named by George Ripley.
[10]George Partridge Bradford (1807–1890), a graduate of

Harvard Divinity School, was in charge of the "department of belle-lettres" at Brook Farm.

there will be no danger of thy husband being under the necessity of laboring more than he likes, hereafter. Meantime, my health is perfect, and my spirits buoyant, even in the gold mine. . . .

TO SOPHIA PEABODY, LYNN

Brook Farm, August 12th, 1841

•   •   •   •   •

Belovedest, I am very well, and not at all weary; for yesterday's rain gave us a holyday; and moreover the labors of the farm are not so pressing as they have been. And—joyful thought!—in a little more than a fortnight, thy husband will be free from his bondage—free to think of his Dove—free to enjoy Nature—free to think and feel! I do think that a greater weight will then be removed from me, than when Christian's burthen fell off at the foot of the cross.[11] Even my Custom House experience was not such a thraldom and weariness; my mind and heart were freer. Oh; belovedest, labor is the curse of this world, and nobody can meddle with it, without becoming proportionably brutified. Dost thou think it a praiseworthy matter, that I have spent five golden months in providing food for cows and horses? Dearest, it is not so. Thank God, my soul is not utterly buried under a dung-heap. I shall yet rescue it, somewhat defiled, to be sure, but not utterly unsusceptible of purification. . . .

TO SOPHIA PEABODY, BOSTON

Brook Farm, September 22^d, 1841—P.M.

Dearest love, here is thy husband again, slowly adapting himself to the life of this queer community, whence he seems to have been absent half a life time—so utterly has he grown apart from the spirit and manners of the place.[12] Thou knowest not how much I wanted thee, to give me a home-feeling in the spot—to keep a feeling of coldness and strangeness from creeping into my heart and making me shiver. Nevertheless, I was most kindly received; and the fields and woods looked very pleasant, in the bright sunshine of the day before yesterday. I had a friendlier disposition towards the farm, now that I am no longer obliged to toil in its stubborn furrows. Yesterday and to-day, however, the weather has been intolerable—cold, chill, sullen, so that it is impossible to be on kindly terms with mother Nature. Would I were with thee, mine own warmest and truest-hearted wife! I never shiver, while encircled in thine arms.

Belovedest, I doubt whether I shall succeed in writing another volume of Grandfather's Library,[13] while I remain at the farm. I have not the sense of perfect seclusion, which has always been essential to my power of producing anything. It is true, nobody intrudes into my room; but still I cannot be quiet. Nothing here is settled—everything is but beginning to arrange itself—and though thy husband would seem to have little to do with aught beside his own thoughts, still he cannot but partake of the ferment around him. My mind will not be abstracted. I must observe, and think, and feel, and content myself with catching glimpses of things which may be wrought out hereafter. Perhaps it will be quite as well that I find myself unable to set seriously about literary occupation for the present. It will be good to have a longer interval between my labor of the body and that of the mind. I shall work to the better purpose, after the beginning of November. Mean-

---

[11]See John Bunyan (1628–1688), *Pilgrim's Progress* (1678); the leading character, Christian, bears the burden of sin on his back until it falls off at the Cross of Christ's Crucifixion.

[12]Hawthorne had been temporarily absent.

[13]I.e., the children's book series begun in 1841 with *Grandfather's Chair*.

time, I shall see these people and their enterprise under a new point of view, and perhaps be able to determine whether thou and I have any call to cast in our lot among them. . . .

TO SOPHIA PEABODY, BOSTON

Brook Farm, October 21st, 1841 — Noon

Ownest beloved, I know thou dost not care in the least about receiving a word from thy husband — thou lovest me not — in fact thou has quite forgotten that such a person exists. I do love thee so much, that I really think all the love is on my side; — there is no room for any more in the whole universe.

Sweetest, I have nothing at all to say to thee — nothing, I mean, that regards this external world; and as to matters of the heart and soul, they are not to be written about. What atrocious weather! In all this month, we have not had a single truly October day; it has been a real November month, and of the most disagreeable kind. I came to this place in one snow-storm, and shall probably leave it in another; so that my reminiscences of Brook Farm are like to be the coldest and dreariest imaginable. But next month,[14] thou, belovedest, will be my sunshine and my summer. No matter what weather it may be then.

Dearest, good bye. Dost thou love me, after all? Art thou magnificently well? God bless thee. Thou didst make me infinitely happiest, at our last meeting. Was it a pleasant season likewise to thee?

Thine Ownest,
Theodore de l'Aubépine[15]

RALPH WALDO EMERSON[1]

[EMERSON AND THE GOOD YEOMAN EDMUND HOSMER]

Monday, August 15th, [1842]

George Hillard[2] and his wife arrived from Boston, in the dusk of Saturday evening, to spend Sunday with us. It was a pleasant sensation when the coach rumbled up our avenue, and wheeled round at the door; for then I felt that I was regarded as a man with a wife and a household — a man having a tangible existence and locality in the world — when friends came to avail themselves of our hospitality. It was a sort of acknowledgement and reception of us into the corps of married people — a sanction by no means essential to our peace and well-being, but yet agreeable enough to receive. So my wife and I welcomed them cordially at the door, and ushered them into our parlor, and soon into the supper-room — and afterwards, in due season, to bed. Then came my dear little wife to her husband's bosom, and slept sweetly, I trust; for she is a beloved woman — which is more than can be said of every wife in the world. Pray Heaven that Mrs. Hillard had a good night's rest in our guest-chamber; but I hardly think that she slept so sweetly as my lily. However, the night flitted over us all, and passed away, and uprose a gray and sullen morning, which would have saddened me, only that my sunny wife shone into my heart, and made it warm and bright. We had a splendid breakfast of flapjacks — (or *slap*jacks, as my wife insists upon calling them) — of flapjacks or slap-jacks, and of whortle-berries, which we gathered on a neighboring hill, and of perch, bream, and pouts, which I hooked out of the river, the

---

[14]Hawthorne apparently planned to leave Brook Farm in November.
[15]Hawthorne in French.
[1]In 1842, the newly married Hawthorne moved into the "Old Manse" in Concord, Massachusetts, and became a neighbor of Emerson, Thoreau, and Margaret Fuller. The two selections here come from the *American Notebooks*.

[2]George Hillard (1808–1879), lawyer and author, took Hawthorne in as a lodger in 1839 when he was attached to the Boston Custom House; their friendship lasted for Hawthorne's lifetime.

evening before. About nine o'clock, Hillard and I set out for a walk to Walden Pond, calling by the way at Mr. Emerson's, to obtain his guidance or directions. He, from a scruple of his external conscience, detained us till after the people had got into church, and then accompanied us in his own illustrious person. We turned aside a little from our way to visit a Mr. Edmund Hosmer, a yeoman of whose homely and self-acquired wisdom Mr. Emerson has a very high opinion. We found him walking in his fields—a short, but stalwart and sturdy personage of middle age, somewhat uncouth and ugly to look at, but with a face of shrewd and kind expression, and manners of natural courtesy. He seemed to have a very free flow of talk, and not much diffidence about his own opinions; for, with a little induction from Mr. Emerson, he began to discourse about the state of the nation, agriculture, and business in general—uttering thoughts that had come to him at the plough, and which had a sort of flavor and smell of the fresh earth about them. I was not impressed with any remarkable originality in his views; but they were sensible and characteristic, and had grown in the soil where we found them. Methought, however, the good yeoman was not quite so natural as he may have been at a former period; the simplicity of his character has probably suffered, in some degree, by his detecting the impression which he makes on those around him. There is a circle, I suppose, who look up to him as an oracle; and so he inevitably assumes the oracular manner, and speaks as if truth and wisdom were uttering themselves by his voice. Mr. Emerson has risked the doing him much mischief, by putting him in print[3]—a trial which few persons can sustain, without losing their unconsciousness. But, after all, a man gifted with thought and expression, whatever his rank in life, and his mode of uttering himself, whether by pen or tongue, cannot be expected to go through the world, without finding himself out—and as all such self-discoveries are partial and imperfect, they do more harm than good to the character. Mr. Hosmer is more natural than ninety-nine men out of a hundred; and he is certainly a man of intellectual and moral substance, a sturdy fact, a reality, something to be felt and touched. It would be amusing to draw a parallel between him and his admirer, Mr. Emerson—the mystic, stretching his hand out of cloud-land, in vain search for something real; and the man of sturdy sense, all whose ideas seem to be dug out of his mind, hard and substantial, as he digs potatoes, beets, carrots, and turnips, out of the earth. Mr. Emerson is a great searcher for facts; but they seem to melt away and become unsubstantial in his grasp.

After leaving Mr. Hosmer, we proceeded through woodpaths to Walden Pond, picking blackberries of enormous size along the way. The pond itself was beautiful and refreshing to my soul, after such long and exclusive familiarity with our tawny and sluggish river. It lies embosomed among wooded hills, not very extensive, but large enough for waves to dance upon its surface, and to look like a piece of blue firmament, earth-encircled. The shore has a narrow, pebbly strand, which it was worth a day's journey to look at, for the sake of the contrast between it and the weedy, slimy, oozy margin of the river. Farther within its depths, you perceive a bottom of pure white sand, sparkling through the transparent water, which, methought, was the very purest liquid in the world. After Mr. Emerson left us, Hillard and I bathed in the pond; and it does really seem as if not only my corporeal person, but my moral self, had received a cleansing from that bath. A good deal of mud and river-slime had accumulated on my soul; but those bright waters washed it all away.

---

[3]Emerson had described and praised Hosmer (1798–1881) in "Agriculture in Massachusetts," published in *The Dial,* July 1842.

[MR. EMERSON WITH A SUNBEAM IN HIS FACE]

[April 9, 1843]

Mr. Emerson came, with a sunbeam in his face; and we had as good a talk as I ever remember experiencing with him. My little wife, I know, will demand to know every word that was spoken; but she knows me too well to anticipate anything of the kind. He seemed fullest of Margaret Fuller, who, he says, has risen perceptibly into a higher state, since their last meeting. He apotheosized her as the greatest woman, I believe, of ancient or modern times, and the one figure in the world worth considering. (There rings the supper-bell.) Then we spoke of Ellery Channing, a volume of whose poems is to be immediately published, with revisions by Mr. Emerson himself, and Mr. Sam Ward.[4] He seems to anticipate no very wide reception for them; he calls them "poetry for poets," and thinks that perhaps a hundred persons may admire them very much; while, to the rest of the world, they will be little or nothing. Next Mr. Thoreau was discussed, and his approaching departure; in respect to which we agreed pretty well; but Mr. Emerson appears to have suffered some inconveniency from his experience of Mr. Thoreau as an inmate.[5] It may well be that such a sturdy and uncompromising person is fitter to meet occasionally in the open air, than to have as a permanent guest at table and fireside. We talked of Brook Farm, and the singular moral aspects which it presents, and the great desirability that its progress and developements should be observed, and its history written. We talked of Charles Newcomb,[6] who, it appears, is now passing through a new moral phasis;[7] he is silent, inexpressive, talks little or none, and listens without response except a sardonic laugh; and some of his friends think that he is passing into permanent eclipse. Various other matters were discussed or glanced at; and finally, between five and six o'clock, Mr. Emerson took his leave, threatening to come again, unless I call on him very soon. I then went out to chop wood, my allotted space for which had been very much abridged by his visit; but, on the whole, I was not sorry. I went on with the journal for a few minutes before supper; and have finished the present record in the setting sunshine and gathering dusk. I would like to see my wife!

HENRY DAVID THOREAU[1]

["A KEEN AND DELICATE OBSERVER OF NATURE"]

Thursday, September 1st, [1842]

Mr. Thorow dined with us yesterday. He is a singular character—a young man with much of wild original nature still remaining in him; and so far as he is sophisticated, it is in a way and method of his own. He is as ugly as sin, long-nosed, queer-mouthed, and with uncouth and somewhat rustic, although courteous manners, corresponding very well with such an exterior. But his ugliness is of an honest and agreeable fashion, and becomes him much better than beauty. He was educated, I believe, at Cambridge, and formerly kept school in this town; but for two or three years back, he has repudiated all regular modes of getting a living, and seems inclined to lead a sort of Indian life among civilized men—an Indian life, I mean, as respects the absence of any systematic effort for a livelihood. He has been for sometime an inmate of Mr. Emerson's family; and, in requital, he labors in the garden, and performs such other offices as may suit him—being entertained by Mr. Emerson for the sake of what true manhood there is in him. Mr.

---

[4] Ellery Channing's *Poems* appeared in 1843. Samuel Ward, broker and dabbler in the arts, was a wealthy friend who financed publication of Channing's book.
[5] Thoreau was living as handyman in the Emerson household.
[6] Charles King Newcomb (1820–1894), a writer, contributor to *The Dial;* his *Journals* were published in 1946.

[7] Phase.
[1] Selection from the *American Notebooks.* Hawthorne's spelling of "Thorow" is indication that the first syllable of Thoreau's name should be stressed (cf. "thorough").

Thorow is a keen and delicate observer of nature—a genuine observer, which, I suspect, is almost as rare a character as even an original poet; and Nature, in return for his love, seems to adopt him as her especial child, and shows him secrets which few others are allowed to witness. He is familiar with beast, fish, fowl, and reptile, and has strange stories to tell of adventures, and friendly passages with these lower brethren of mortality. Herb and flower, likewise, wherever they grow, whether in garden or wild wood, are his familiar friends. He is also on intimate terms with the clouds, and can tell the portents of storms. It is a characteristic trait, that he has a great regard for the memory of the Indian tribes, whose wild life would have suited him so well; and strange to say, he seldom walks over a ploughed field without picking up an arrow-point, a spear-head, or other relic of the red men—as if their spirits willed him to be the inheritor of their simple wealth.

With all this he has more than a tincture of literature—a deep and true taste for poetry, especially the elder poets, although more exclusive than is desirable, like all other Transcendentalists, so far as I am acquainted with them. He is a good writer—at least, he has written one good article, a rambling disquisition on Natural History in the last Dial,—which, he says, was chiefly made up from journals of his own observations. Methinks this article gives a very fair image of his mind and character—so true, minute, and literal in observation, yet giving the spirit as well as letter of what he sees, even as a lake reflects its wooded banks, showing every leaf, yet giving the wild beauty of the whole scene;—then there are passages in the article of cloudy and dreamy metaphysics, partly affected, and partly the natural exhalations of his intellect;—and also passages where his thoughts seem to measure and attune themselves into spontaneous verse, as they rightfully may, since there is real poetry in him. There is a basis of good sense and moral truth, too, throughout the article, which also is a reflection of his character; for he is not unwise to think and feel, however imperfect in his own mode of action. On the whole, I find him a healthy and wholesome man to know.

After dinner (at which we cut the first water-melon and musk melon that our garden has ripened) Mr. Thorow and I walked up the bank of the river; and, at a certain point, he shouted for his boat. Forthwith, a young man paddled it across the river, and Mr. Thorow and I voyaged further up the stream, which soon became more beautiful than any picture, with its dark and quiet sheet of water, half shaded, half sunny, between high and wooded banks. The late rains have swollen the stream so much, that many trees are standing up to their knees, as it were, in the water; and boughs, which lately swung high in air, now dip and drink deep of the passing wave. As to the poor cardinals, which glowed upon the bank, a few days since, I could see only a few of their scarlet caps, peeping above the water. Mr. Thorow managed the boat so perfectly, either with two paddles or with one, that it seemed instinct with his own will, and to require no physical effort to guide it. He said that, when some Indians visited Concord a few years since, he found that he had acquired, without a teacher, their precise method of propelling and steering a canoe. Nevertheless, being in want of money, the poor fellow was desirous of selling the boat, of which he is so fit a pilot, and which was built by his own hands; so I agreed to give him his price (only seven dollars) and accordingly became possessor of the Musketaquid. I wish I could acquire the aquatic skill of its original owner at as reasonable a rate.

MARGARET FULLER[1]

["A Lady Reclining Near the Path"]

[Monday, August 22d, 1842]

I took a walk through the woods, yesterday afternoon, to Mr. Emerson's, with a book which Margaret Fuller had left behind her, after a call on Saturday eve.

After leaving the book at Mr. Emerson's, I returned through the woods, and entering Sleepy Hollow,[2] I perceived a lady reclining near the path which bends along its verge. It was Margaret herself. She had been there the whole afternoon, meditating or reading; for she had a book in her hand, with some strange title, which I did not understand and have forgotten. She said that nobody had broken her solitude, and was just giving utterance to a theory that no inhabitant of Concord ever visited Sleepy Hollow, when we saw a whole group of people entering the sacred precincts. Most of them followed a path that led them remote from us; but an old man passed near us, and smiled to see Margaret lying on the ground, and me sitting by her side. He made some remark about the beauty of the afternoon, and withdrew himself into the shadow of the wood. Then we talked about Autumn—and about the pleasures of getting lost in the woods—and about the crows, whose voices Margaret had heard—and about the experiences of early childhood, whose influence remains upon the character after the collection of them has passed away—and about the sight of mountains from a distance, and the view from their summits—and about other matters of high and low philosophy. In the midst of our talk, we heard footsteps above us, on the high bank; and while the intruder was still hidden among the trees, he called to Margaret, of whom he had gotten a glimpse. Then he emerged from the green shade; and, behold, it was Mr. Emerson, who, in spite of his clerical consecration, had found no better way of spending the Sabbath than to ramble among the woods. He appeared to have had a pleasant time; for he said that there were Muses in the woods to-day, and whispers to be heard in the breezes. It being now nearly six o'clock, we separated, Mr. Emerson and Margaret towards his house, and I towards mine, where my little wife was very busy getting tea. . . .

["I Like Her the Better for It"]

April 3[d], [1858] Saturday. Rome

A few days ago, my wife and I visited the studio of Mr. Mozier,[3] an American, who seems to have a good deal of vogue as a sculptor. We found a figure of Pocahontas, which he has repeated several times; another which he calls the "Wept of Wish-ton-Wish";[4] a figure of a smiling girl playing with a cat and dog; and a school-boy mending a pen. These two last were the only ones that gave me any pleasure, or that really had any merit; for his cleverness and ingenuity appear in homely subjects, but are quite lost in attempts at a higher ideality. Nevertheless, he has a groupe of the Prodigal Son,[5] possessing more merit than I should have expected from Mr. Mozier; the son reclining his head on his father's breast, with

---

[1]The first selection is from the *American Notebooks*, the second from the *French and Italian Notebooks*. The first was written when Hawthorne and Fuller were neighbors in Concord. The second was written sixteen years later, long after Margaret Fuller's death. The second somewhat harsh commentary evoked outrage when it was published in 1884 and the "facts" were disputed by Margaret Fuller's defenders. Hawthorne came to know Margaret Fuller at the transcendental experimental community, Brook Farm, when he went to live there in 1841. His novel *The Blithedale Romance* (1852) is believed to be based on his experiences there, with Blithedale representing Brook Farm, and Zenobia, the leading character, founded on Margaret Fuller. It is a complex, not unsympathetic portrayal.

[2]A park near Concord, now containing a cemetery where many literary figures (including Thoreau and Emerson) are buried.
[3]Joseph Mozier (1812–1870), a successful New York businessman turned sculptor when he settled in Rome in 1845; he acquired a modest celebrity.
[4]A novel by James Fenimore Cooper (1789–1851), published in 1829. Wish-ton-Wish is a Connecticut settlement attacked by Indians during King Philip's War. The "Wept of Wish-ton-Wish" depicts an Indian and his white wife, who are killed at the end of the novel.
[5]Cf. Luke 15:11–32: the younger son wastes his inheritance, but is forgiven by the father.

an expression of utter weariness, at length finding perfect rest, while the father bends his benign visage over him, and seems to receive him calmly into himself. This groupe (the plaster-cast standing beside it) is now taking shape out of an immense block of marble, and will be as indestructible as the Laocoon;[6] an idea at once awful and ludicrous, when we consider that it is at best but a respectable production. Miss Lander tells me that Mr Mozier has stolen—adopted, we will rather say—the attitude and general idea of this groupe from one executed by a student of the French Academy, and to be seen there in plaister.

Mr. Mozier has now been seventeen years in Italy; and, after all this time, he is still intensely American in everything but the most external surface of his manners; scarcely Europeanized, or much modified, even in that. He is a native of Ohio, but had his early breeding in New York, and might—for any polish or refinement that I can discern in him—still be a country shopkeeper in the interior of New York or New England. How strange! For one expects to find the polish, the close grain, and white purity of marble, in the artist who works in that noble material; but, after all, he handles clay, and, judging from the specimens I have seen here, is apt to be clay, not of the finest, himself. Mr. Mozier is sensible, shrewd, keen, clever; an ingenious workman, no doubt, with tact enough, and not destitute of taste; very agreeable and lively in his conversation, talking as fast and as naturally as a brook runs, without the slightest affectation. His naturalness is, in fact, a rather striking characteristic, in view of his lack of culture, while yet his life has been concerned with idealities, and a beautiful art. What degree of taste he pretends to, he seems really to possess; nor did I hear a single idea from him that struck me as otherwise than sensible.

He called to see us last night, and talked for about two hours in a very amusing and interesting style; his topics being taken from his own personal experience, and shrewdly treated. He spoke much of Greenough,[7] whom he described as an excellent critic of art, but possessed of not the slightest inventive genius. His statue of Washington, at the Capitol, is taken precisely from the Phidian Jupiter; his Chanting Cherubs are copied in marble from two figures in a picture by Raphael. He did nothing that was original with himself. From Greenough, Mr. Mozier passed to Margaret Fuller,[8] whom he knew well, she having been an inmate of his during a part of her residence in Italy. His developements about poor Margaret were very curious. He says that Ossoli's family, though technically noble, is really of no rank whatever; the elder brother, with the title of Marquis, being at this very time a working bricklayer, and the sisters walking the streets without bonnets—that is, being in the station of peasant girls, or the female populace of Rome.[9] Ossoli himself, to the best of his belief, was Margaret's servant, or had something to do with the care of her apartments. He was the handsomest man whom Mr. Mozier ever saw, but entirely ignorant even of his own language, scarcely able to read at all, destitute of manners; in short, half an idiot, and without any pretensions to be a gentleman.[10] At Margaret's request, Mr Mozier had taken him into his studio,

[6]Famous Roman sculpture now in the Vatican, discovered in 1506 but dating back to the second century B.C., representing Laocoön (son of the Trojan Priam) and his two sons being crushed to death by encircling serpents for having offended Apollo.
[7]Horatio Greenough (1805–1852), called "the first American sculptor" (because he was the first to devote his whole life to sculpture). He settled in Rome in 1825. His large, seated "George Washington," commissioned by the American Congress to be placed in the Capitol rotunda, was based (except for the head) on modern reproductions of Phidias's statue of Zeus. His "Chanting Cherubs" (1829–31), commissioned by James Fenimore Cooper, was based on two children's figures in Raphael's "Madonna del Baldacchino" ("Virgin of the Canopy").

[8]In 1846, Margaret Fuller went to Europe, ending up in Italy to write a history of the Roman Revolution of 1848–49. There she married the Marquis Angelo Ossoli and started on the voyage back to the United States with Ossoli and her child in 1850. The ship was wrecked in a storm near New York (off Fire Island), and she and her family died. Her manuscript on the Roman Revolution was lost.
[9]Modern scholarship has discovered the "facts" here are wrong. The family had been in service to the papacy for generations, filling important positions (such as secretary to the pope's privy council).
[10]Margaret Fuller had herself described Ossoli as "a person of no intellectual culture."

with a view to ascertain whether he was capable of instruction in sculpture; but, after four months' labor, Ossoli produced a thing intended to be a copy of a human foot; but the "big toe" was on the wrong side.[11] He could not possibly have had the least appreciation of Margaret; and the wonder is, what attraction she found in this boor, this hymen[12] without the intellectual spark—she that had always shown such a cruel and bitter scorn of intellectual deficiency. As from her towards him, I do not understand what feeling there could have been, except it were purely sensual; as from him towards her, there could hardly have been even this, for she had not the charm of womanhood. But she was a woman anxious to try all things, and fill up her experience in all directions; she had a strong and coarse nature, too, which she had done her utmost to refine, with infinite pains, but which of course could only be superficially changed. The solution of the riddle lies in this direction; nor does one's conscience revolt at the idea of thus solving it; for—at least, this is my own experience—Margaret has not left, in the hearts and minds of those who knew her, any deep witness for her integrity and purity. She was a great humbug; of course with much talent, and much moral reality, or else she could not have been so great a humbug. But she had stuck herself full of borrowed qualities, which she chose to provide herself with, but which had no root in her.

Mr. Mozier added, that Margaret had quite lost all power of literary production, before she left Rome, though occasionally the charm and power of her conversation would re-appear. To his certain knowledge, she had no important manuscripts with her when she sailed, (she having shown him all she had, with a view to his procuring their publication in America;) and the History of the Roman Revolution, about which there was so much lamentation, in the belief that it had been lost with her, never had existence.[13] Thus there appears to have been a total collapse in poor Margaret, morally and intellectually; and tragic as her catastrophe was, Providence was, after all, kind in putting her, and her clownish husband, and their child, on board that fated ship. There never was such a tragedy as her whole story; the sadder and sterner, because so much of the ridiculous was mixed up with it, and because she could bear anything better than to be ridiculous. It was such an awful joke, that she should have resolved—in all sincerity, no doubt—to make herself the greatest, wisest, best woman of the age; and, to that end, she set to work on her strong, heavy, unpliable, and, in many respects, defective and evil nature, and adorned it with a mosaic of admirable qualities, such as she chose to possess; putting in here a splendid talent, and there a moral excellence, and polishing each separate piece, and the whole together, till it seemed to shine afar and dazzle all who saw it. She took credit to herself for having been her own Redeemer, if not her own Creator; and, indeed, she was far more a work of art than any of Mr. Mozier's statues. But she was not working on an inanimate substance, like marble or clay; there was something within her that she could not possibly come at, to re-create and refine it; and, by and by, this rude old potency bestirred itself, and undid all her labor in the twinkling of an eye. On the whole, I do not know but I like her the better for it;—the better, because she proved herself a very woman, after all, and fell as the weakest of her sisters might.

---

[11]Mozier has (according to modern scholars) confused Ossoli with another Italian that Margaret Fuller had befriended.
[12]Marriage.

[13]Mozier again is wrong. Margaret Fuller had started the book in 1848 (at the outbreak of the revolution), and she worked on it in Florence (1849–50). One reason for her returning to America was to find a publisher.

HERMAN MELVILLE[1]
[TALKING OF TIME AND ETERNITY]

[Friday, August 1st, 1851]

We had, to-day, the first string beans of the season; the earliest product of our garden, indeed, except currants and lettuce. At three o'clock, came Julian[2] home. He said that he had tomatoes, beans, and asparagus, for dinner, and that he liked them very much, and had had a good time. I dressed him and myself for a walk to the village, and we set out at four. The mail not being in, at our arrival, we went to Mr. Farley's office (where we saw him and Mr. Sedgwick)[3] and afterwards to Mr. Farley's house, or rather to his hencoop, to see his splendid rooster and chickens. I gave Mr. Sedgwick to understand, by the by, that we should take Mrs. Kemble's house in the autumn. Returning to the Post office, I got Mr. Tappan's[4] mail and my own, and proceeded homeward, but clambered over the fence and sat down in Love Grove, to read the papers. While thus engaged, a cavalier on horseback came along the road, and saluted me in Spanish; to which I replied by touching my hat, and went on with the newspaper. But the cavalier renewing his salutation, I regarded him more attentively, and saw that it was Herman Melville! So, hereupon, Julian and I hastened to the road, where ensued a greeting, and we all went homeward together, talking as we went. Soon, Mr. Melville alighted, and put Julian into the saddle; and the little man was highly pleased, and sat on the horse with the freedom and fearlessness of an old equestrian, and had a ride of at least a mile homeward.

I asked Mrs. Peters to make some tea for Herman Melville; and so she did, and he drank a cup, but was afraid to drink much, because it would keep him awake. After supper, I put Julian to bed; and Melville and I had a talk about time and eternity, things of this world and of the next, and books, and publishers, and all possible and impossible matters, that lasted pretty deep into the night; and if truth must be told, we smoked cigars even within the sacred precincts of the sitting-room. At last, he arose, and saddled his horse (whom we had put into the barn) and rode off for his own domicile; and I hastened to make the most of what little sleeping-time remained for me.

[WANDERING TO AND FRO OVER THESE DESERTS]

November 20th, [1856] Thursday

A week ago last Monday, Herman Melville came to see me at the Consulate,[5] looking much as he used to do (a little paler, and perhaps a little sadder), in a rough outside coat, and with his characteristic gravity and reserve of manner. He had crossed from New York to Glasgow in a screw steamer,[6] about a fortnight before, and had since been seeing Edinburgh and other interesting places. I felt rather awkward at first; because this is the first time I have met him since my ineffectual attempt to get him a consular appointment from General Pierce. However, I failed only from real lack of power to serve him; so there was no reason to

---

[1]In 1850, Hawthorne moved his family to Lenox, Massachusetts, in the Berkshire Mountains. Melville was living on a farm nearby, at Pittsfield. They met and formed an intimate friendship, more fervent on the part of the younger Melville than on the part of the reserved, older Hawthorne. The first selection is from the *American Notebooks*, the second from the *English Notebooks*.
[2]Hawthorne's son.
[3]Probably Frank Farley and Charles Sedgwick, neighbors and friends.

[4]Owner of the house the Hawthornes were renting.
[5]At this time Hawthorne had been appointed United States Consul at Liverpool, England, by his college friend, then President of the United States, Franklin Pierce. Melville came by to see him on his way to the Holy Land, recovering from something in the nature of a nervous breakdown.
[6]Ship driven by a screw propeller.

be ashamed, and we soon found ourselves on pretty much our former terms of sociability and confidence. Melville has not been well, of late; he has been affected with neuralgic complaints in his head and limbs, and no doubt has suffered from too constant literary occupation, pursued without much success, latterly; and his writings, for a long while past, have indicated a morbid state of mind. So he left his place at Pittsfield, and has established his wife and family, I believe, with his father-in-law in Boston, and is thus far on his way to Constantinople. I do not wonder that he found it necessary to take an airing through the world, after so many years of toilsome pen-labor and domestic life, following upon so wild and adventurous a youth as his was. I invited him to come and stay with us at Southport, as long as he might remain in this vicinity; and, accordingly, he did come, the next day, taking with him, by way of baggage, the least little bit of a bundle, which, he told me, contained a night-shirt and a tooth-brush. He is a person of very gentlemanly instincts in every respect, save that he is a little heterodox in the matter of clean linen.

He stayed with us from Tuesday till Thursday; and, on the intervening day, we took a pretty long walk together, and sat down in a hollow among the sand hills (sheltering ourselves from the high, cool wind) and smoked a cigar. Melville, as he always does, began to reason of Providence and futurity, and of everything that lies beyond human ken, and informed me that he had "pretty much made up his mind to be annihilated"; but still he does not seem to rest in that anticipation; and, I think, will never rest until he gets hold of a definite belief. It is strange how he persists—and has persisted ever since I knew him, and probably long before—in wandering to-and-fro over these deserts, as dismal and monotonous as the sand hills amid which we were sitting. He can neither believe, nor be comfortable in his unbelief; and he is too honest and courageous not to try to do one or the other. If he were a religious man, he would be one of the most truly religious and reverential; he has a very high and noble nature, and better worth immortality than most of us.

He went back with me to Liverpool, on Thursday; and, the next day, Henry Bright met him at my office, and showed him whatever was worth seeing in town. On Saturday, Melville and I went to Chester together. I love to take every opportunity of going to Chester; it being the one only place, within easy reach of Liverpool, which possesses any old English interest. . . .

We left Chester at about four o'clock; and I took the rail for Southport at half-past six, parting from Melville at a street-corner in Liverpool, in the rainy evening. I saw him again on Monday, however. He said that he already felt much better than in America; but observed that he did not anticipate much pleasure in his rambles, for that the spirit of adventure is gone out of him. He certainly is much overshadowed since I saw him last; but I hope he will brighten as he goes onward. He sailed from Liverpool in a steamer on Tuesday, leaving his trunk behind him at my consulate, and taking only a carpetbag to hold all his travelling-gear. This is the next best thing to going naked; and as he wears his beard and moustache, and so needs no dressing-case—nothing but a tooth-brush—I do not know a more independent personage. He learned his travelling habits by drifting about, all over the South Sea, with no other clothes or equipage than a red flannel shirt and a pair of duck trowsers. Yet we seldom see men of less criticizable manners than he.

ABRAHAM LINCOLN[1]

[A Backwoods Humorist Transformed]

By and by there was a little stir on the staircase and in the passageway, and in lounged a tall, loose-jointed figure, of an exaggerated Yankee port and demeanor, whom (as being about the homeliest man I ever saw, yet by no means repulsive or disagreeable) it was impossible not to recognize as Uncle Abe.

Unquestionably, Western man though he be, and Kentuckian by birth, President Lincoln is the essential representative of all Yankees, and the veritable specimen, physically, of what the world seems determined to regard as our characteristic qualities. It is the strangest and yet the fittest thing in the jumble of human vicissitudes, that he, out of so many millions, unlooked for, unselected by any intelligible process that could be based upon his genuine qualities, unknown to those who chose him, and unsuspected of what endowments may adapt him for his tremendous responsibility, should have found the way open for him to fling his lank personality into the chair of state,—where, I presume, it was his first impulse to throw his legs on the council-table, and tell the Cabinet Ministers a story. There is no describing his lengthy awkwardness, nor the uncouthness of his movement; and yet it seemed as if I had been in the habit of seeing him daily, and had shaken hands with him a thousand times in some village street; so true was he to the aspect of the pattern American, though with a certain extravagance which, possibly, I exaggerated still further by the delighted eagerness with which I took it in. If I put to guess his calling and livelihood, I should have taken him for a country schoolmaster as soon as anything else. He was dressed in a rusty black frock coat and pantaloons, unbrushed, and worn so faithfully that the suit had adapted itself to the curves and angularities of his figure, and had grown to be an outer skin of the man. He had shabby slippers on his feet. His hair was black, still unmixed with gray, stiff, somewhat bushy, and had apparently been acquainted with neither brush nor comb that morning, after the disarrangement of the pillow; and as to a nightcap, Uncle Abe probably knows nothing of such effeminacies. His complexion is dark and sallow, betokening, I fear, an insalubrious atmosphere around the White House; he has thick black eyebrows and an impending brow; his nose is large, and the lines about his mouth are very strongly defined.

The whole physiognomy is as coarse a one as you would meet anywhere in the length and breadth of the States; but, withal, it is redeemed, illuminated, softened, and brightened by a kindly though serious look out of his eyes, and an expression of homely sagacity, that seems weighted with rich results of village experience. A great deal of native sense; no bookish cultivation, no refinement; honest at heart, and thoroughly so, and yet, in some sort, sly,—at least, endowed with a sort of tact and wisdom that are akin to craft, and would impel him, I think, to take an antagonist in flank, rather than to make a bull-run at him right in front. But, on the whole, I like this sallow, queer, sagacious visage, with the homely human sympathies that warmed it; and, for my small share in the matter, would as lief have Uncle Abe for a ruler as any man whom it would have been practicable to put in his place.

Immediately on his entrance the President accosted our member of Congress, who had us in charge, and, with a comical twist of his face, made some jocular remark about the length of his breakfast. He then greeted us all round, not wait-

---

[1] From "Chiefly about War Matters," as reprinted in the Riverside Edition of 1883; this portrait of Lincoln was omitted by James T. Fields when the essay was first published in *The Atlantic Monthly*, 1862. Fields did not think it "tasteful to print" this "portrait of a living man"; but he did publish it later in *The Atlantic Monthly* (1871) and in his own memoir *Yesterdays with Authors* (1872). Hawthorne went on to say in the published portion of the piece: "With whom is an American citizen entitled to take a liberty, if not with his own chief magistrate?. . .and if [Lincoln] came to Washington a backwoods humorist, he has already transformed himself into. . . a statesman." The excerpt begins with Hawthorne's party waiting to present a beautiful whip made in a Massachusetts whip factory to the president.

ing for an introduction, but shaking and squeezing everybody's hand with the utmost cordiality, whether the individual's name was announced to him or not. His manner towards us was wholly without pretence, but yet had a kind of natural dignity, quite sufficient to keep the forwardest of us from clapping him on the shoulder and asking him for a story. A mutual acquaintance being established, our leader took the whip out of its case, and began to read the address of presentation. The whip was an exceedingly long one, its handle wrought in ivory (by some artist in the Massachusetts State Prison, I believe), and ornamented with a medallion of the President, and other equally beautiful devices; and along its whole length there was a succession of golden bands and ferrules. The address was shorter than the whip, but equally well made, consisting chiefly of an explanatory description of these artistic designs, and closing with a hint that the gift was a suggestive and emblematic one, and that the President would recognize the use to which such an instrument should be put.

This suggestion gave Uncle Abe rather a delicate task in his reply, because, slight as the matter seemed, it apparently called for some declaration, or intimation, or faint foreshadowing of policy in reference to the conduct of the war, and the final treatment of the Rebels. But the President's Yankee aptness and not-to-be-caughtness stood him in good stead, and he jerked or wiggled himself out of the dilemma with an uncouth dexterity that was entirely in character; although, without his gesticulation of eye and mouth,—and especially the flourish of the whip, with which he imagined himself touching up a pair of fat horses,—I doubt whether his words would be worth recording, even if I could remember them. The gist of the reply was, that he accepted the whip as an emblem of peace, not punishment; and, this great affair over, we retired out of the presence in high good humor, only regretting that we could not have seen the President sit down and fold up his legs (which is said to be a most extraordinary spectacle), or have heard him tell one of those delectable stories for which he is so celebrated. A good many of them are afloat upon the common talk of Washington, and are certainly the aptest, pithiest, and funniest little things imaginable; though, to be sure, they smack of the frontier freedom, and would not always bear repetition in a drawing-room, or on the immaculate page of the Atlantic.

1862   *1871, 1872*

HERMAN MELVILLE
(1819–1891)

A whaling ship was his Yale and his Harvard, observed the orphaned seaman Ishmael, the narrator in *Moby-Dick*. He spoke for Melville, who grew up expecting a gentleman's education but was rudely awakened to poverty on his father's early death. Melville went to sea when other young men of his age went to college.

Later, when he was in his early thirties, he wrote to Nathaniel Hawthorne: "Until I was twenty-five, I had no development at all. From my twenty-fifth year I date my life. Three weeks have scarcely passed, at any time between then and now, that I have not unfolded within myself. But I feel that I am now come to the inmost leaf of the bulb, and that shortly the flower must fall to the mould."

The year that Melville says "dates" his life was 1844, when he was mustered out of the Navy in Boston, his life as a seaman ended. He turned to writing and reading, reading and writing. He had lived more life by then than most people his age, having been a vagabond in the world and having observed many of its remotest corners, both light and dark. But his inner life had lain dormant. He came to books late, but when he came, he devoured them in immense quantity, Plato, Spenser, Shakespeare, Milton, the Bible—the list could go on. They fired his imagination, moving him to the "inmost leaf of the bulb." When he wrote these words to Hawthorne, he was caught up in the compositional struggle with *Moby-Dick*, which would be his masterpiece, and a world classic.

Melville was born in New York, the second son (and third child) of eight children. Although a cultivated man and reader of books, Melville's father was not adept at commerce. His importing business went bankrupt in 1830, and two years later he died. Melville was twelve. The proud widow and her children were forced into a life of genteel poverty, dependent on relatives for help. Melville tried to become self-supporting by taking a series of jobs— clerking in a bank, farming, school-teaching.

Suddenly he decided to go to sea, shipping as a crew member in 1839 on a merchant vessel bound for Liverpool, England. He stayed about six weeks in Liverpool, the whole trip lasting about four months. This taste of life at sea whetted his appetite for adventure. In 1840, he travelled to Illinois to visit his Uncle Thomas, living in the then thriving lead-mining town of Galena, Illinois, on the Mississippi River. Melville rode a steamer down the great muddy river dividing the continent, but discovered no prospects for a livelihood.

In 1841, at the age of twenty-one, Melville answered the call of the sea and signed on as a common seaman aboard the whaler *Acushnet*, bound for the South Seas out of New Bedford Harbor. He would not see home again for almost four adventurous years. The eighteen months he spent whaling on the *Acushnet* would furnish his imagination the materials for *Moby-Dick*.

Melville jumped ship in 1842 and with his friend "Toby" Green set out to explore the Marquesas Islands in the South Pacific. They ended up for an idyllic interlude living with the natives in Typee valley, a spot then uncorrupted by civilization. A month later Melville sailed on an Australian whaler, but under charges of mutiny was put on shore at Tahiti for detention. Quickly released, he bummed around Tahiti and other islands, and ended up finally in Hawaii, where (after working for a time) he enlisted in the U.S. Navy as ordinary seaman in August 1843. He sailed for home on the frigate *United States*, arriving in Boston in October 1844.

Almost immediately Melville began trying his hand at writing about his experiences. In 1846 appeared his first book, *Typee*, and Melville found himself famous overnight. The book was sensational in its account of the "cannibalistic" natives, and it built suspense in the finally successful attempts at "escape." The readers were unaware of the large part Melville's imagination played in transferring his adventures from memory to page. Moreover, the blame Melville placed on the missionaries for bringing civilization's corruptions to the guileless societies of the Pacific islands precipitated a public controversy that aroused great interest in the book.

Melville set out on an author's career, systematically mining his experiences at sea for his writing. *Omoo*, published in 1847, was a kind of continuation of *Typee*, describing his vagabond life on Tahiti and the nearby island of Eimoo. By this time Melville thought his success at writing assured his future, and he married Elizabeth Shaw, daughter of Chief Justice Lemuel Shaw of Boston. They settled in New York where Melville became a part of the lively literary scene.

But on publication of *Mardi*, in 1849, Melville felt the sting of public indifference to his work. Readers had bought it expecting more adventures like those of the first two books. Instead they found the expected adventure turn quickly into what must have seemed an endless allegory, with long conversations by vaguely delineated characters about obscurely defined philosophical, religious, or political questions. Melville was clearly engaged, but he failed to engage his readers.

Disappointed, he quickly returned to the kind of tale he began with. *Redburn*, which followed *Mardi* in 1849, embodied his first voyage at sea. And *White-Jacket*, which was published in 1850, covered his last voyage from Honolulu to Boston as a sailor in the U.S. Navy. In addition to offering glimpses into life on a merchantman and on a warship, these works presented tales of initiation, or rites of passage, in their protagonists' movement from innocence to experience, or their *fall* into knowledge of evil.

With these two works behind him, Melville was ready once again for a major imaginative effort. He had been saving a segment of his experience for it, his voyage on the whaler *Acushnet*. He was soon launched on a book that would equal *Mardi* in length but far surpass it in achievement—*Moby-Dick*. In the meantime, he purchased a farm at Pittsfield in western Massachusetts, in the Berkshires, and settled his growing family there. He would live at Arrowhead for the next thirteen years.

To his delight, Melville discovered that a nearby neighbor living in Lenox was Nathaniel Hawthorne, then at work on *The House of the Seven Gables* (he had published *The Scarlet Letter* in 1850). Both writers were at the top of their form, and there is no doubt that both benefited imaginatively by their conversations on (according to Hawthorne's journal) "time and eternity, things of this world and the next, and books, and publishers, and all possible and impossible matters, that lasted pretty deep into the night." In 1851, Hawthorne published *The House of the Seven Gables*, and later in the year, Melville published *Moby-Dick*, dedicated to Hawthorne. It is likely that at their deepest levels, these two extraordinary works shared something also from those far-ranging conversations.

Moby-Dick's contemporary audience did not recognize it for the masterpiece we now acknowledge it to be. Again, Melville was disappointed, even embittered. He tried to recoup his reputation with a domestic novel, *Pierre; or The Ambiguities*, published in 1852. Writing to Sophia Hawthorne, he called it a "rural bowl of milk," hardly the right description for a novel that dealt with incest. *Pierre* was denounced as immoral, and Melville found his audience diminished further. That audience could not know that the twentieth century would praise *Pierre* for its depth of psychoanalytic insight.

To make money, Melville turned to publishing short fiction and sketches in the journals, including such major achievements in the form as *Bartleby, the Scrivener*, *Benito Cereno*, and *The Encantadas*. A volume of these was published as *The Piazza Tales* in 1856. This same year Melville finished his darkest work of fiction, published in 1857—*The Confidence-Man*, a work that was generally dismissed as incomprehensible at the time, but which the twentieth century numbers among his greatest books.

Exhausted, in debt, and on the verge of a nervous breakdown, Melville accepted his father-in-law's offer of funds for a trip to the Holy Land. He went by way of Liverpool, where Hawthorne had become the U.S. Consul. The two old friends took a walk along the seashore, sitting down in the sand hills for a conversation. Hawthorne recorded the event in his journal, giving probably the sharpest, deepest probing portrait of Melville that we have from those who knew him: "Melville, as he always does, began to reason of Providence and futurity, and of everything that lies beyond human ken, and informed me that he had 'pretty much made up his mind to be annihilated'; but still he does not seem to rest in that anticipation; and, I think, will never rest until he gets hold of a definite belief. It is strange how he persists—and has persisted ever since I knew him, and probably long before—in wandering to-and-fro over these deserts, as dismal and monotonous as the sand hills amid which we were sitting. He can neither believe, nor be comfortable in his unbelief; and he is too honest and couragious not to try to do one or the other."

For a time in 1857–60, Melville gave public lectures—on "The South Seas" and "Travelling"—but he was not very successful on the lecture platform. And he cast about for other employment. In 1863 he sold his farm to a younger brother and moved to New York. Finally in 1866 he was appointed a customs inspector at New York Harbor, a position he held for twenty years.

Melville would never get hold of "a definite belief." He turned from fiction to poetry and continued to write, no doubt out of his restlessness of spirit. He published three volumes of poems: *Battle-Pieces and Aspects of the War* (1866), *John Marr and Other Sailors* (1888), and *Timoleon* (1891). The last two volumes were published privately in small editions to distribute to friends.

In 1876, he published his long poem, *Clarel,* which was based on his visit to the Holy Land in 1856–57. Melville described it as a "metrical affair, a pilgrimage or whatnot, of several thousand lines, eminently adapted for unpopularity." But for the Melville enthusiast interested in Melville's intellectual-spiritual development, it is a vital text. Twentieth-century critics, including the poet-novelist Robert Penn Warren, have found Melville's poetry worthy of attention. Warren points to the poetry's "density of intellectual implication and immediate poetic impact" as linking it with the poetry of T. S. Eliot and other modernists.

Near the end of his life, Melville turned once more to prose, leaving at his death the manuscript of *Billy Budd.* This classic novella was rescued from oblivion and published for the first time in 1924. Its richness of thought and complexity of form show that Melville's talent was intact to the end, and that his struggle with belief was never completely resolved.

When Melville died in 1891, he was remembered in the few obituaries that appeared in America as the "man who had lived with the cannibals" (that is, the author of *Typee*). But in England there had always been an appreciative readership. The British poet-novelist Robert Buchanan wrote of his visit to America in 1885: "I sought everywhere for this Triton, who is still living somewhere in New York. No one seemed to know anything of the one great writer fit to stand shoulder to shoulder with Whitman on that continent."

The 1920s witnessed a new interest in Melville, fueled in part by Raymond Weaver's biography published in 1921. This interest intensified during the next decades, so that now Melville is viewed as one of the greatest writers America has yet produced, and *Moby-Dick* as a classic, inexhaustible in its meanings. Such works as *Pierre, The Confidence-Man, Bartleby,* "The Paradise of Bachelors and the Tartarus of Maids," and *Billy Budd* are seen as modern in temper and spirit. The blackness of darkness which Melville found in Hawthorne, and we find in him, suits in startling ways the contemporary outlook on personal and human destiny.

ADDITIONAL READING

The Writings of Herman Melville, ed. Harrison Hayford, Hershel Parker, and G. Thomas Tanselle, 1968–; *Complete Works of Herman Melville* (Hendricks House Edition), 7 vols., ed. Howard P. Vincent, 1947–1969; *The Works of Herman Melville*, 16 vols., 1922–1924; *Selected Poems of Herman Mellville*, ed. with intro. by Robert Penn Warren, 1970.

Raymond M. Weaver, *Herman Melville: Mariner and Mystic*, 1921; Lewis Mumford, *Herman Melville*, 1929, 1963; Charles R. Anderson, *Melville in the South Seas*, 1939; Charles Olson, *Call Me Ishmael*, 1947; Howard Vincent, *The Trying-Out of Moby-Dick*, 1949; Richard Chase, *Herman Melville: A Critical Study*, 1949; Newton Arvin, *Herman Melville*, 1950; Leon Howard, *Herman Melville: A Biography*, 1951; Jay Leyda, *The Melville Log: A Documentary Life of Herman Melville*, 1951, 1969; Edward H. Rosenberry, *Melville and the Comic Spirit*, 1955; Milton Stern, *The Fine Hammered Steel of Herman Melville*, 1957; Merlin Bowen, *The Long Encounter: Self and Experience in the Writings of Herman Melville*, 1960; James E. Miller, Jr., *A Reader's Guide to Herman Melville*, 1962, 1973; Warner Berthoff, *The Example of Melville*, 1962; Tyrus Hillway, *Herman Melville*, 1963, 1979; Herschel Parker, ed., *The Recognition of Herman Melville: Selected Criticism Since 1846*, 1967; Kingsley Widmer, *The Ways of Nihilism: A Study of Herman Melville's Short Novels*, 1970; John Seelye, *Melville: The Ironic Diagram*, 1970; Edwin Haviland Miller, *Melville*, 1975; Brian Higgins, *Herman Melville: An Annotated Bibliography, 1846–1930*, 1979; Jane Mushabac, *Melville's Humor*, 1981; Joyce Sparer Adler, *War in Melville's Imagination*, 1981; Merton M. Sealts, *Pursuing Melville, 1940–1980*, 1982; James Duban, *Melville's Major Fiction: Politics, Theology, and Imagination*, 1983; Michael Paul Rogin, *Subversive Genealogy: The Politics and Art of Herman Melville*, 1983; John Updike, "Melville's Withdrawal," *Hugging the Shore*, 1983; Robert K. Martin, *Hero, Captain, and Stranger*, 1986; John Bryant, ed., *A Companion to Melville Studies*, 1986; Walker Cowen, *Melville's Marginalia*, 2 vols., 1987; Brian Higgins, *Herman Melville: A Reference Guide, 1931–60*, 1987; Mary K. Bercaw, *Melville's Sources*, 1987; Merton M. Sealts, Jr., *Melville's Reading*, 1988; Neal L. Tolchin, *Mourning, Gender, and Creativity in the Art of Herman Melville*, 1988.

TEXTS

"Bartleby," First and Eighth Sketches of "The Encantadas, or Enchanted Isles," "Benito Cereno," *The Piazza Tales*, 1856; "The Paradise of Bachelors and the Tartarus of Maids," *Harper's New Monthly Magazine*, April, 1855; *Billy Budd*, ed. Harrison Hayford and Merton M. Sealts, Jr., 1962; *The Collected Poems of Herman Melville*, ed. Howard P. Vincent, 1947; "Hawthorne and His Mosses," *The Literary World*, August 17 and 24, 1850; *The Letters of Herman Melville*, ed., Merrell R. Davis and William H. Gilman, 1960.

Bartleby, the Scrivener

A STORY OF WALL STREET[1]

I am a rather elderly man. The nature of my avocations, for the last thirty years, has brought me into more than ordinary contact with what would seem an interesting and somewhat singular set of men, of whom, as yet, nothing, that I know of, has ever been written—I mean, the law-copyists, or scriveners. I have known very many of them, professionally and privately, and, if I pleased, could relate divers histories, at which good-natured gentlemen might smile, and senti-

---

[1]This title and subtitle was used on the story's first appearance in *Putnam's Monthly Magazine* (November–December 1853).

mental souls might weep. But I waive the biographies of all other scriveners, for a few passages in the life of Bartleby, who was a scrivener, the strangest I ever saw, or heard of. While, of other law-copyists, I might write the complete life, of Bartleby nothing of that sort can be done. I believe that no materials exist, for a full and satisfactory biography of this man. It is an irreparable loss to literature. Bartleby was one of those beings of whom nothing is ascertainable, except from the original sources, and, in his case, those are very small. What my own astonished eyes saw of Bartleby, *that* is all I know of him, except, indeed, one vague report, which will appear in the sequel.

Ere introducing the scrivener, as he first appeared to me, it is fit I make some mention of myself, my *employés*, my business, my chambers, and general surroundings; because some such description is indispensable to an adequate understanding of the chief character about to be presented. Imprimis: I am a man who, from his youth upwards, has been filled with a profound conviction that the easiest way of life is the best. Hence, though I belong to a profession proverbially energetic and nervous, even to turbulence, at times, yet nothing of that sort have I ever suffered to invade my peace. I am one of those unambitious lawyers who never address a jury, or in any way draw down public applause; but, in the cool tranquillity of a snug retreat, do a snug business among rich men's bonds, and mortgages, and title-deeds. All who know me, consider me an eminently *safe* man. The late John Jacob Astor,[2] a personage little given to poetic enthusiasm, had no hesitation in pronouncing my first grand point to be prudence; my next, method. I do not speak it in vanity, but simply record the fact, that I was not unemployed in my profession by the late John Jacob Astor; a name which, I admit, I love to repeat; for it hath a rounded and orbicular sound to it, and rings like unto bullion. I will freely add, that I was not insensible to the late John Jacob Astor's good opinion.

Some time prior to the period at which this little history begins, my avocations had been largely increased. The good old office, now extinct in the State of New York, of a Master in Chancery,[3] had been conferred upon me. It was not a very arduous office, but very pleasantly remunerative. I seldom lose my temper; much more seldom indulge in dangerous indignation at wrongs and outrages; but I must be permitted to be rash here and declare, that I consider the sudden and violent abrogation of the office of Master in Chancery, by the new Constitution, as a——premature act; inasmuch as I had counted upon a life-lease of the profits, whereas I only received those of a few short years. But this is by the way.

My chambers were up stairs, at No.——Wall Street. At one end, they looked upon the white wall of the interior of a spacious sky-light shaft, penetrating the building from top to bottom.

This view might have been considered rather tame than otherwise, deficient in what landscape painters call "life." But, if so, the view from the other end of my chambers offered, at least, a contrast, if nothing more. In that direction, my windows commanded an unobstructed view of a lofty brick wall, black by age and everlasting shade; which wall required no spy-glass to bring out its lurking beauties, but, for the benefit of all near-sighted spectators, was pushed up to within ten feet of my window-panes. Owing to the great height of the surrounding buildings, and my chambers being on the second floor, the interval between this wall and mine not a little resembled a huge square cistern.

At the period just preceding the advent of Bartleby, I had two persons as copyists in my employment, and a promising lad as an officeboy. First, Turkey; second, Nippers; third, Ginger Nut. These may seem names, the like of which are not

---

[2]John Jacob Astor (1763–1848), a poor German immigrant who made an enormous fortune in the fur trade.
[3]Chancery was a court of equity in which disputes over property and estates were settled; the Master always got his fees.

usually found in the Directory. In truth, they were nicknames, mutually conferred upon each other by my three clerks, and were deemed expressive of their respective persons or characters. Turkey was a short, pursy[4] Englishman, of about my own age—that is, somewhere not far from sixty. In the morning, one might say, his face was of a fine florid hue, but after twelve o'clock, meridian—his dinner hour—it blazed like a grate full of Christmas coals; and continued blazing—but, as it were, with a gradual wane—till six o'clock, P.M., or thereabouts; after which, I saw no more of the proprietor of the face, which, gaining its meridian with the sun, seemed to set with it, to rise, culminate, and decline the following day, with the like regularity and undiminished glory. There are many singular coincidences I have known in the course of my life, not the least among which was the fact, that, exactly when Turkey displayed his fullest beams from his red and radiant countenance, just then, too, at that critical moment, began the daily period when I considered his business capacities as seriously disturbed for the remainder of the twenty-four hours. Not that he was absolutely idle, or averse to business then; far from it. The difficulty was, he was apt to be altogether too energetic. There was a strange, inflamed, flurried, flighty recklessness of activity about him. He would be incautious in dipping his pen into his inkstand. All his blots upon my documents were dropped there after twelve o'clock, meridian. Indeed, not only would he be reckless, and sadly given to making blots in the afternoon, but, some days, he went further, and was rather noisy. At such times, too, his face flamed with augmented blazonry, as if cannel coal had been heaped on anthracite. He made an unpleasant racket with his chair; spilled his sand-box; in mending his pens, impatiently split them all to pieces, and threw them on the floor in a sudden passion; stood up, and leaned over his table, boxing his papers about in a most indecorous manner, very sad to behold in an elderly man like him. Nevertheless, as he was in many ways a most valuable person to me, and all the time before twelve o'clock, meridian, was the quickest, steadiest creature, too, accomplishing a great deal of work in a style not easily to be matched—for these reasons, I was willing to overlook his eccentricities, though, indeed, occasionally, I remonstrated with him. I did this very gently, however, because though the civilest, nay, the blandest and most reverential of men in the morning, yet, in the afternoon, he was disposed, upon provocation, to be slightly rash with his tongue—in fact, insolent. Now, valuing his morning services as I did, and resolved not to lose them—yet, at the same time, made uncomfortable by his inflamed ways after twelve o'clock—and being a man of peace, unwilling by my admonitions to call forth unseemly retorts from him, I took upon me, one Saturday noon (he was always worse on Saturdays) to hint to him, very kindly, that, perhaps, now that he was growing old, it might be well to abridge his labors; in short, he need not come to my chambers after twelve o'clock, but, dinner over, had best go home to his lodgings, and rest himself till tea-time. But no; he insisted upon his afternoon devotions. His countenance became intolerably fervid, as he oratorically assured me—gesticulating with a long ruler at the other end of the room—that if his services in the morning were useful, how indispensable, then, in the afternoon?

"With submission, sir," said Turkey, on this occasion, "I consider myself your right-hand man. In the morning I but marshal and deploy my columns; but in the afternoon I put myself at their head, and gallantly charge the foe, thus"—and he made a violent thrust with the ruler.

"But the blots, Turkey," intimated I.

"True; but, with submission, sir, behold these hairs! I am getting old. Surely, sir, a blot or two of a warm afternoon is not to be severely urged against gray hairs. Old age—even if it blot the page—is honorable. With submission, sir we *both* are getting old."

This appeal to my fellow-feeling was hardly to be resisted. At all events, I saw

---

[4]Fat, short-winded.

that go he would not. So, I made up my mind to let him stay, resolving, nevertheless, to see to it that, during the afternoon, he had to do with my less important papers.

Nippers, the second on my list, was a whiskered, sallow, and, upon the whole, rather piratical-looking young man, of about five-and-twenty. I always deemed him the victim of two evil powers—ambition and indigestion. The ambition was evinced by a certain impatience of the duties of a mere copyist, an unwarrantable usurpation of strictly professional affairs, such as the original drawing up of legal documents. The indigestion seemed betokened in an occasional nervous testiness and grinning irritability, causing the teeth to audibly grind together over mistakes committed in copying: unnecessary maledictions, hissed, rather than spoken, in the heat of business; and especially by a continual discontent with the height of the table where he worked. Though of a very ingenious mechanical turn, Nippers could never get this table to suit him. He put chips under it, blocks of various sorts, bits of pasteboard, and at last went so far as to attempt an exquisite adjustment, by final pieces of folded blotting-paper. But no invention would answer. If, for the sake of easing his back, he brought the table-lid at a sharp angle well up towards his chin, and wrote there like a man using the steep roof of a Dutch house for his desk, then he declared that it stopped the circulation in his arms. If now he lowered the table to his waistbands, and stooped over it in writing, then there was a sore aching in his back. In short, the truth of the matter was, Nippers knew not what he wanted. Or, if he wanted anything, it was to be rid of a scrivener's table altogether. Among the manifestations of his diseased ambition was a fondness he had for receiving visits from certain ambiguous-looking fellows in seedy coats, whom he called his clients. Indeed, I was aware that not only was he, at times, considerable of a ward-politician, but he occasionally did a little business at the Justices' courts, and was not unknown on the steps of the Tombs.[5] I have good reason to believe, however, that one individual who called upon him at my chambers, and who, with a grand air, he insisted was his client, was no other than a dun,[6] and the alleged title-deed, a bill. But, with all his failings, and the annoyances he caused me, Nippers, like his compatriot Turkey, was a very useful man to me; wrote a neat, swift hand; and, when he chose, was not deficient in a gentlemanly sort of deportment. Added to this, he always dressed in a gentlemanly sort of way; and so, incidentally, reflected credit upon my chambers. Whereas, with respect to Turkey, I had much ado to keep him from being a reproach to me. His clothes were apt to look oily, and smell of eating-houses. He wore his pantaloons very loose and baggy in summer. His coats were execrable; his hat not to be handled. But while the hat was a thing of indifference to me, inasmuch as his natural civility and deference, as a dependent Englishman, always led him to doff it the moment he entered the room, yet his coat was another matter. Concerning his coats, I reasoned with him; but with no effect. The truth was, I suppose, that a man with so small an income could not afford to sport such a lustrous face and a lustrous coat at one and the same time. As Nippers once observed, Turkey's money went chiefly for red ink. One winter day, I presented Turkey with a highly respectable-looking coat of my own—a padded gray coat, of a most comfortable warmth, and which buttoned straight up from the knee to the neck. I thought Turkey would appreciate the favor, and abate his rashness and obstreperousness of afternoons. But no; I verily believe that buttoning himself up in so downy and blanket-like a coat had a pernicious effect upon him—upon the same principle

---

[5]Maximum security prison, resembling Egyptian tombs, on the steps of which a hustler might make money in service to the entering prisoners.
[6]Bill collector.

that too much oats are bad for horses. In fact, precisely as a rash, restive horse is said to feel his oats, so Turkey felt his coat. It made him insolent. He was a man whom prosperity harmed.

Though, concerning the self-indulgent habits of Turkey, I had my own private surmises, yet, touching Nippers, I was well persuaded that, whatever might be his faults in other respects, he was, at least, a temperate young man. But, indeed, nature herself seemed to have been his vintner, and, at his birth, charged him so thoroughly with an irritable, brandy-like disposition, that all subsequent potations were needless. When I consider how, amid the stillness of my chambers, Nippers would sometimes impatiently rise from his seat, and stooping over his table, spread his arms wide apart, seize the whole desk, and move it, and jerk it, with a grim, grinding motion on the floor, as if the table were a perverse voluntary agent, intent on thwarting and vexing him, I plainly perceive that, for Nippers, brandy-and-water were altogether superfluous.

It was fortunate for me that, owing to its peculiar cause—indigestion—the irritability and consequent nervousness of Nippers were mainly observable in the morning, while in the afternoon he was comparatively mild. So that, Turkey's paroxysms only coming on about twelve o'clock, I never had to do with their eccentricities at one time. Their fits relieved each other, like guards. When Nipper's was on, Turkey's was off; and *vice versa*. This was a good natural arrangement, under the circumstances.

Ginger Nut, the third on my list, was a lad, some twelve years old. His father was a carman,[7] ambitious of seeing his son on the bench instead of a cart, before he died. So he sent him to my office, as student at law, errand-boy, cleaner and sweeper, at the rate of one dollar a week. He had a little desk to himself, but he did not use it much. Upon inspection, the drawer exhibited a great array of the shells of various sorts of nuts. Indeed, to this quick-witted youth, the whole noble science of the law was contained in a nutshell. Not the least among the employments of Ginger Nut, as well as one which he discharged with the most alacrity, was his duty as cake and apple purveyor for Turkey and Nippers. Copying law-papers being proverbially a dry, husky sort of business, my two scriveners were fain to moisten their mouths very often with Spitzenbergs,[8] to be had at the numerous stalls nigh the Custom House and Post office. Also, they sent Ginger Nut very frequently for that peculiar cake—small, flat, round, and very spicy—after which he had been named by them. Of a cold morning, when business was but dull, Turkey would gobble up scores of these cakes, as if they were mere wafers—indeed, they sell them at the rate of six or eight for a penny—the scrape of his pen blending with the crunching of the crisp particles in his mouth. Of all the fiery afternoon blunders and flurried rashnesses of Turkey, was his once moistening a ginger-cake between his lips, and clapping it on to a mortgage, for a seal.[9] I came within an ace of dismissing him then. But he mollified me by making an oriental bow, and saying—

"With submission, sir, it was generous of me to find you in stationery on my own account."

Now my original business—that of a conveyancer[10] and title hunter, and drawer-up of recondite documents of all sorts—was greatly increased by receiving the Master's office. There was now great work for scriveners. Not only must I push the clerks already with me, but I must have additional help.

In answer to my advertisement, a motionless young man one morning stood

---

[7]Streetcar conductor or motorman.
[8]A variety of winter apples with good flavor.
[9]I.e., a wax wafer used for seals on documents.

[10]Individual who "conveys" property from one owner to another by preparing legal documents. The title to the property must be searched to make sure it is clear.

upon my office threshold, the door being open, for it was summer. I can see that figure now—pallidly neat, pitiably respectable, incurably forlorn! It was Bartleby.

After a few words touching his qualifications, I engaged him, glad to have among my corps of copyists a man of so singularly sedate an aspect, which I thought might operate beneficially upon the flighty temper of Turkey, and the fiery one of Nippers.

I should have stated before that ground-glass folding-doors divided my premises into two parts, one of which was occupied by my scriveners, the other by myself. According to my humor, I threw open these doors, or closed them. I resolved to assign Bartleby a corner by the folding-doors, but on my side of them, so as to have this quiet man within easy call, in case any trifling thing was to be done. I placed his desk close up to a small side-window in that part of the room, a window which originally had afforded a lateral view of certain grimy backyards and bricks, but which, owing to subsequent erections, commanded at present no view at all, though it gave some light. Within three feet of the panes was a wall, and the light came down from far above, between two lofty buildings, as from a very small opening in a dome. Still further to a satisfactory arrangement, I procured a high green folding screen, which might entirely isolate Bartleby from my sight, though not remove him from my voice. And thus, in a manner, privacy and society were conjoined.

At first, Bartleby did an extraordinary quantity of writing. As if long famishing for something to copy, he seemed to gorge himself on my documents. There was no pause for digestion. He ran a day and night line, copying by sunlight and by candle-light. I should have been quite delighted with his application, had he been cheerfully industrious. But he wrote on silently, palely, mechanically.

It is, of course, an indispensable part of a scrivener's business to verify the accuracy of his copy, word by word. Where there are two or more scriveners in an office, they assist each other in this examination, one reading from the copy, the other holding the original. It is a very dull, wearisome, and lethargic affair. I can readily imagine that, to some sanguine temperaments, it would be altogether intolerable. For example, I cannot credit that the mettlesome poet, Byron, would have contentedly sat down with Bartleby to examine a law document of, say five hundred pages, closely written in a crimpy hand.

Now and then, in the haste of business, it had been my habit to assist in comparing some brief document myself, calling Turkey or Nippers for this purpose. One object I had, in placing Bartleby so handy to me behind the screen, was, to avail myself of his services on such trivial occasions. It was on the third day, I think, of his being with me, and before any necessity had arisen for having his own writing examined, that, being much hurried to complete a small affair I had in hand, I abruptly called to Bartleby. In my haste and natural expectancy of instant compliance, I sat with my head bent over the original on my desk, and my right hand sideways, and somewhat nervously extended with the copy, so that, immediately upon emerging from his retreat, Bartleby might snatch it and proceed to business without the least delay.

In this very attitude did I sit when I called to him, rapidly stating what it was I wanted him to do—namely, to examine a small paper with me. Imagine my surprise, nay, my consternation, when, without moving from his privacy, Bartleby, in a singularly mild, firm voice, replied, "I would prefer not to."

I sat awhile in perfect silence, rallying my stunned faculties. Immediately it occurred to me that my ears had deceived me, or Bartleby had entirely misunderstood my meaning. I repeated my request in the clearest tone I could assume; but in quite as clear a one came the previous reply, "I would prefer not to."

"Prefer not to," echoed I, rising in high excitement, and crossing the room with a stride. "What do you mean? Are you moon-struck? I want you to help me compare this sheet here—take it," and I thrust it towards him.

"I would prefer not to," said he.

I looked at him steadfastly. His face was leanly composed; his gray eye dimly calm. Not a wrinkle of agitation rippled him. Had there been the least uneasiness, anger, impatience or impertinence in his manner; in other words, had there been anything ordinarily human about him, doubtless I should have violently dismissed him from the premises. But as it was, I should have as soon thought of turning my pale plaster-of-paris bust of Cicero[11] out of doors. I stood gazing at him awhile, as he went on with his own writing, and then reseated myself at my desk. This is very strange, thought I. What had one best do? But my business hurried me. I concluded to forget the matter for the present, reserving it for my future leisure. So, calling Nippers from the other room, the paper was speedily examined.

A few days after this, Bartleby concluded four lengthy documents, being quadruplicates of a week's testimony taken before me in my High Court of Chancery. It became necessary to examine them. It was an important suit, and great accuracy was imperative. Having all things arranged, I called Turkey, Nippers and Ginger Nut, from the next room, meaning to place the four copies in the hands of my four clerks, while I should read from the original. Accordingly, Turkey, Nippers, and Ginger Nut had taken their seats in a row, each with his document in his hand, when I called to Bartleby to join this interesting group.

"Bartleby! quick, I am waiting."

I heard a slow scrape of his chair legs on the uncarpeted floor, and soon he appeared standing at the entrance of his hermitage.

"What is wanted?" said he, mildly.

"The copies, the copies," said I, hurriedly. "We are going to examine them. There"—and I held towards him the fourth quadruplicate.

"I would prefer not to," he said, and gently disappeared behind the screen.

For a few moments I was turned into a pillar of salt,[12] standing at the head of my seated column of clerks. Recovering myself, I advanced towards the screen, and demanded the reason for such extraordinary conduct.

"*Why* do you refuse?"

"I would prefer not to."

With any other man I should have flown outright into a dreadful passion, scorned all further words, and thrust him ignominiously from my presence. But there was something about Bartleby that not only strangely disarmed me, but, in a wonderful manner, touched and disconcerted me. I began to reason with him.

"These are your own copies we are about to examine. It is labor saving to you, because one examination will answer for your four papers. It is common usage. Every copyist is bound to help examine his copy. Is it not so? Will you not speak? Answer!"

"I prefer not to," he replied in a flute-like tone. It seemed to me that, while I had been addressing him, he carefully revolved every statement that I made; fully comprehended the meaning; could not gainsay the irresistible conclusion; but, at the same time, some paramount consideration prevailed with him to reply as he did.

"You are decided, then, not to comply with my request—a request made according to common usage and common sense?"

He briefly gave me to understand, that on that point my judgment was sound. Yes: his decision was irreversible.

---

[11]Roman philosopher and orator (106–43 B.C.).
[12]Like Lot's wife, punished for looking back as God destroyed Sodom and Gomorrah (Genesis 19:26).

It is not seldom the case that, when a man is browbeaten in some unprecedented and violently unreasonable way, he begins to stagger in his own plainest faith. He begins, as it were, vaguely to surmise that, wonderful as it may be, all the justice and all the reason is on the other side. Accordingly, if any disinterested persons are present, he turns to them for some reinforcement for his own faltering mind.

"Turkey," said I, "what do you think of this? Am I not right?"

"With submission, sir," said Turkey, in his blandest tone, "I think that you are."

"Nippers," said I, "what do *you* think of it?"

"I think I should kick him out of the office."

(The reader of nice[13] perceptions will here perceive that, it being morning, Turkey's answer is couched in polite and tranquil terms, but Nippers replies in ill-tempered ones. Or, to repeat a previous sentence, Nipper's ugly mood was on duty, and Turkey's off.)

"Ginger Nut," said I, willing to enlist the smallest suffrage in my behalf, "what do *you* think of it?"

"I think, sir, he's a little *luny*," replied Ginger Nut, with a grin.

"You hear what they say," said I, turning towards the screen, "come forth and do your duty."

But he vouchsafed no reply. I pondered a moment in sore perplexity. But once more business hurried me. I determined again to postpone the consideration of this dilemma to my future leisure. With a little trouble we made out to examine the papers without Bartleby, though at every page or two Turkey deferentially dropped his opinion, that this proceeding was quite out of the common; while Nippers, twitching in his chair with a dyspeptic nervousness, ground out, between his set teeth, occasional hissing maledictions against the stubborn oaf behind the screen. And for his (Nipper's) part, this was the first and the last time he would do another man's business without pay.

Meanwhile Bartleby sat in his hermitage, oblivious to everything but his own peculiar business there.

Some days passed, the scrivener being employed upon another lengthy work. His late remarkable conduct led me to regard his ways narrowly. I observed that he never went to dinner; indeed, that he never went anywhere. As yet I had never, of my personal knowledge, known him to be outside of my office. He was a perpetual sentry in the corner. At about eleven o'clock though, in the morning, I noticed that Ginger Nut would advance toward the opening in Bartleby's screen, as if silently beckoned thither by a gesture invisible to me where I sat. The boy would then leave the office, jingling a few pence, and reappear with a handful of ginger-nuts, which he delivered in the hermitage, receiving two of the cakes for his trouble.

He lives, then, on ginger-nuts, thought I; never eats a dinner, properly speaking; he must be a vegetarian, then; but no; he never eats even vegetables, he eats nothing but ginger-nuts. My mind then ran on in reveries concerning the probable effects upon the human constitution of living entirely on ginger-nuts. Ginger-nuts are so called, because they contain ginger as one of their peculiar constituents, and the final flavoring one. Now, what was ginger? A hot, spicy thing. Was Bartleby hot and spicy? Not at all. Ginger, then, had no effect upon Bartleby. Probably he preferred it should have none.

Nothing so aggravates an earnest person as a passive resistance. If the individual so resisted be of a not inhumane temper, and the resisting one perfectly harmless in his passivity, then, in the better moods of the former, he will endeavor

---

[13] I.e., discriminating.

charitably to construe to his imagination what proves impossible to be solved by his judgment. Even so, for the most part, I regarded Bartleby and his ways. Poor fellow! thought I, he means no mischief; it is plain he intends no insolence; his aspect sufficiently evinces that his eccentricities are involuntary. He is useful to me. I can get along with him. If I turn him away, the chances are he will fall in with some less indulgent employer, and then he will be rudely treated, and perhaps driven forth miserably to starve. Yes. Here I can cheaply purchase a delicious self-approval. To befriend Bartleby; to humor him in his strange wilfulness, will cost me little or nothing, while I lay up in my soul what will eventually prove a sweet morsel for my conscience. But this mood was not invariable with me. The passiveness of Bartleby sometimes irritated me. I felt strangely goaded on to encounter him in new opposition—to elicit some angry spark from him answerable to my own. But, indeed, I might as well have essayed to strike fire with my knuckles against a bit of Windsor soap.[14] But one afternoon the evil impulse in me mastered me, and the following little scene ensued:

"Bartleby," said I, "when those papers are all copied, I will compare them with you."

"I would prefer not to."

"How? Surely you do not mean to persist in that mulish vagary?"

No answer.

I threw open the folding-doors near by, and, turning upon Turkey and Nippers, exclaimed:

"Bartleby a second time says, he won't examine his papers. What do you think of it, Turkey?"

It was afternoon, be it remembered. Turkey sat glowing like a brass boiler; his bald head steaming; his hands reeling among his blotted papers.

"Think of it?" roared Turkey. "I think I'll just step behind his screen, and black his eyes for him!"

So saying, Turkey rose to his feet and threw his arms into a pugilistic position. He was hurrying away to make good his promise, when I detained him, alarmed at the effect of incautiously rousing Turkey's combativeness after dinner.

"Sit down, Turkey," said I, "and hear what Nippers has to say. What do you think of it, Nippers? Would I not be justified in immediately dismissing Bartleby?"

"Excuse me, that is for you to decide, sir. I think his conduct quite unusual, and, indeed, unjust, as regards Turkey and myself. But it may only be a passing whim."

"Ah," exclaimed I, "you have strangely changed your mind, then—you speak very gently of him now."

"All beer," cried Turkey; "gentleness is effects of beer—Nippers and I dined together to-day. You see how gentle *I* am, sir. Shall I go and black his eyes?"

"You refer to Bartleby, I suppose. No, not to-day, Turkey," I replied; "pray, put up your fists."

I closed the doors, and again advanced towards Bartleby. I felt additional incentives tempting me to my fate. I burned to be rebelled against again. I remembered that Bartleby never left the office.

"Bartleby," said I, "Ginger Nut is away; just step around to the Post Office, won't you?" (it was but a three minutes' walk) "and see if there is anything for me."

"I would prefer not to."

"You *will* not?"

"I *prefer* not."

I staggered to my desk, and sat there in a deep study. My blind inveteracy returned. Was there any other thing in which I could procure myself to be ignomin-

---

[14]Hand soap, scented, usually brown.

iously repulsed by this lean, penniless wight?—my hired clerk? What added thing is there, perfectly reasonable, that he will be sure to refuse to do?

"Bartleby!"

No answer.

"Bartleby," in a louder tone.

No answer.

"Bartleby," I roared.

Like a very ghost, agreeably to the laws of magical invocation, at the third summons, he appeared at the entrance of his hermitage.

"Go to the next room, and tell Nippers to come to me."

"I prefer not to," he respectfully and slowly said, and mildly disappeared.

"Very good, Bartleby," said I, in a quiet sort of serenely-severe self-possessed tone, intimating the unalterable purpose of some terrible retribution very close at hand. At the moment I half intended something of the kind. But upon the whole, as it was drawing towards my dinner-hour, I thought it best to put on my hat and walk home for the day, suffering much from perplexity and distress of mind.

Shall I acknowledge it? The conclusion of this whole business was, that it soon became a fixed fact of my chambers, that a pale young scrivener, by the name of Bartleby, had a desk there; that he copied for me at the usual rate of four cents a folio (one hundred words); but he was permanently exempt from examining the work done by him, that duty being transferred to Turkey and Nippers, out of compliment, doubtless, to their superior acuteness; moreover, said Bartleby was never, on any account, to be dispatched on the most trivial errand of any sort; and that even if entreated to take upon him such a matter, it was generally understood that he would "prefer not to"—in other words, that he would refuse point-blank.

As days passed on, I became considerably reconciled to Bartleby. His steadiness, his freedom from all dissipation, his incessant industry (except when he chose to throw himself into a standing revery behind his screen), his great stillness, his unalterableness of demeanor under all circumstances, made him a valuable acquisition. One prime thing was this—*he was always there*—first in the morning, continually through the day, and the last at night. I had a singular confidence in his honesty. I felt my most precious papers perfectly safe in his hands. Sometimes, to be sure, I could not, for the very soul of me, avoid falling into sudden spasmodic passions with him. For it was exceeding difficult to bear in mind all the time those strange peculiarities, privileges, and unheard-of exemptions, forming the tacit stipulations on Bartleby's part under which he remained in my office. Now and then, in the eagerness of dispatching pressing business, I would inadvertently summon Bartleby, in a short, rapid tone, to put his finger, say, on the incipient tie of a bit of red tape with which I was about compressing some papers. Of course, from behind the screen the usual answer, "I prefer not to," was sure to come; and then, how could a human creature, with the common infirmities of our nature, refrain from bitterly exclaiming upon such perverseness—such unreasonableness? However, every added repulse of this sort which I received only tended to lessen the probability of my repeating the inadvertence.

Here it must be said, that, according to the custom of most legal gentlemen occupying chambers in densely-populated law buildings, there were several keys to my door. One was kept by a woman residing in the attic, which person weekly scrubbed and daily swept and dusted my apartments. Another was kept by Turkey for convenience sake. The third I sometimes carried in my own pocket. The fourth I knew not who had.

Now, one Sunday morning I happened to go to Trinity Church,[15] to hear a celebrated preacher, and finding myself rather early on the ground I thought I

[15]Large Episcopal church near Wall Street, with bronze doors memorializing John Jacob Astor.

would walk round to my chambers for a while. Luckily I had my key with me; but upon applying it to the lock, I found it resisted by something inserted from the inside. Quite surprised, I called out; when to my consternation a key was turned from within; and thrusting his lean visage at me, and holding the door ajar, the apparition of Bartleby appeared, in his shirt-sleeves, and otherwise in a strangely tattered deshabille, saying quietly that he was sorry, but he was deeply engaged just then, and—preferred not admitting me at present. In a brief word or two, he moreover added, that perhaps I had better walk round the block two or three times, and by that time he would probably have concluded his affairs.

Now, the utterly unsurmised appearance of Bartleby, tenanting my law-chambers of a Sunday morning, with his cadaverously gentlemanly *nonchalance,* yet withal firm and self-possessed, had such a strange effect upon me, that incontinently I slunk away from my own door, and did as desired. But not without sundry twinges of impotent rebellion against the mild effrontery of this unaccountable scrivener. Indeed, it was his wonderful mildness chiefly, which not only disarmed me, but unmanned me, as it were. For I consider that one, for the time, is a sort of unmanned when he tranquilly permits his hired clerk to dictate to him, and order him away from his own premises. Furthermore, I was full of uneasiness as to what Bartleby could possibly be doing in my office in his shirt-sleeves, and in an otherwise dismantled condition of a Sunday morning. Was anything amiss going on? Nay, that was out of the question. It was not to be thought of for a moment that Bartleby was an immoral person. But what could he be doing there?—copying? Nay again, whatever might be his eccentricities, Bartleby was an eminently decorous person. He would be the last man to sit down to his desk in any state approaching to nudity. Besides, it was Sunday; and there was something about Bartleby that forbade the supposition that he would by any secular occupation violate the proprieties of the day.

Nevertheless, my mind was not pacified; and full of a restless curiosity, at last I returned to the door. Without hindrance I inserted my key, opened it, and entered. Bartleby was not to be seen. I looked round anxiously, peeped behind his screen; but it was very plain that he was gone. Upon more closely examining the place, I surmised that for an indefinite period Bartleby must have ate, dressed, and slept in my office, and that too without plate, mirror, or bed. The cushioned seat of a rickety old sofa in one corner bore the faint impress of a lean, reclining form. Rolled away under his desk, I found a blanket; under the empty grate, a blacking box and brush; on a chair, a tin basin, with soap and a ragged towel; in a newspaper a few crumbs of ginger-nuts and a morsel of cheese. Yes, thought I, it is evident enough that Bartleby has been making his home here, keeping bachelor's hall all by himself. Immediately then the thought came sweeping across me, what miserable friendlessness and loneliness are here revealed! His poverty is great; but his solitude, how horrible! Think of it. Of a Sunday, Wall Street is deserted as Petra;[16] and every night of every day it is an emptiness. This building, too, which of week-days hums with industry and life, at nightfall echoes with sheer vacancy, and all through Sunday is forlorn. And here Bartleby makes his home; sole spectator of a solitude which he has seen all populous—a sort of innocent and transformed Marius[17] brooding among the ruins of Carthage!

For the first time in my life a feeling of overpowering stinging melancholy seized me. Before, I had never experienced aught but a not unpleasing sadness. The bond of a common humanity now drew me irresistibly to gloom. A fraternal

---

[16]Ancient city in Jordan whose ruins were discovered in the early eighteenth century.

[17]Gaius Marius (155?–86 B.C.), Roman general and political leader who, after victories against enemies of Rome, was forced into exile by the patricians; but he returned to power and proscribed leaders of the aristocrats. He was a popular symbol in democratic thought and art.

melancholy! For both I and Bartleby were sons of Adam. I remembered the bright silks and sparkling faces I had seen that day, in gala trim, swan-like sailing down the Mississippi of Broadway; and I contrasted them with the pallid copyist, and thought to myself, Ah, happiness courts the light, so we deem the world is gay; but misery hides aloof, so we deem that misery there is none. These sad fancyings—chimeras, doubtless, of a sick and silly brain—led on to other and more special thoughts, concerning the eccentricities of Bartleby. Presentiments of strange discoveries hovered round me. The scrivener's pale form appeared to me laid out, among uncaring strangers, in its shivering winding-sheet.

Suddenly I was attracted by Bartleby's closed desk, the key in open sight left in the lock.

I mean no mischief, seek the gratification of no heartless curiosity, thought I; besides, the desk is mine, and its contents, too, so I will make bold to look within. Everything was methodically arranged, the papers smoothly placed. The pigeon-holes were deep, and removing the files of documents, I groped into their recesses. Presently I felt something there, and dragged it out. It was an old bandanna handkerchief, heavy and knotted. I opened it, and saw it was a saving's bank.

I now recalled all the quiet mysteries which I had noted in the man. I remembered that he never spoke but to answer; that, though at intervals he had considerable time to himself, yet I had never seen him reading—no, not even a newspaper; that for long periods he would stand looking out, at his pale window behind the screen, upon the dead brick wall; I was quite sure he never visited any refectory or eating-house; while his pale face clearly indicated that he never drank beer like Turkey, or tea and coffee even, like other men; that he never went anywhere in particular that I could learn; never went out for a walk, unless, indeed, that was the case at present; that he had declined telling who he was, or whence he came, or whether he had any relatives in the world; that though so thin and pale, he never complained of ill-health. And more than all, I remembered a certain unconscious air of pallid—how shall I call it?—of pallid haughtiness, say, or rather an austere reserve about him, which had positively awed me into my tame compliance with his eccentricities, when I had feared to ask him to do the slightest incidental thing for me, even though I might know, from his long-continued motionlessness, that behind his screen he must be standing in one of those dead-wall reveries of his.

Revolving all these things, and coupling them with the recently discovered fact, that he made my office his constant abiding place and home, and not forgetful of his morbid moodiness: revolving all these things, a prudential feeling began to steal over me. My first emotions had been those of pure melancholy and sincerest pity; but just in proportion as the forlornness of Bartleby grew and grew to my imagination, did that same melancholy merge into fear, that pity into repulsion. So true it is, and so terrible, too, that up to a certain point the thought or sight of misery enlists our best affections; but, in certain special cases, beyond that point it does not. They err who would assert that invariably this is owing to the inherent selfishness of the human heart. It rather proceeds from a certain hopelessness of remedying excessive and organic ill. To a sensitive being, pity is not seldom pain. And when at last it is perceived that such pity cannot lead to effectual succor, common sense bids the soul be rid of it. What I saw that morning persuaded me that the scrivener was the victim of innate and incurable disorder. I might give alms to his body; but his body did not pain him; it was his soul that suffered, and his soul I could not reach.

I did not accomplish the purpose of going to Trinity Church that morning. Somehow, the things I had seen disqualified me for the time from church-going. I walked homeward, thinking what I would do with Bartleby. Finally, I resolved upon this—I would put certain calm questions to him the next morning, touching his history, etc., and if he declined to answer them openly and unreservedly (and I supposed he would prefer not), then to give him a twenty dollar bill over and above whatever I might owe him, and tell him his services were no longer required; but that if in any other way I could assist him, I would be happy to do so, especially if he desired to return to his native place, wherever that might be, I would willingly help to defray the expenses. Morever, if, after reaching home, he found himself at any time in want of aid, a letter from him would be sure of a reply.

The next morning came.

"Bartleby," said I, gently calling to him behind his screen.

No reply.

"Bartleby," said I, in a still gentler tone, "come here; I am not going to ask you to do anything you would prefer not to do—I simply wish to speak to you."

Upon this he noiselessly slid into view.

"Will you tell me, Bartleby, where you were born?"

"I would prefer not to."

"Will you tell me *anything* about yourself?"

"I would prefer not to."

"But what reasonable objection can you have to speak to me? I feel friendly towards you."

He did not look at me while I spoke, but kept his glance fixed upon my bust of Cicero, which, as I then sat, was directly behind me, some six inches above my head.

"What is your answer, Bartleby?" said I, after waiting a considerable time for a reply, during which his countenance remained immovable, only there was the faintest conceivable tremor of the white attenuated mouth.

"At present I prefer to give no answer," he said, and retired into his hermitage.

It was rather weak in me I confess, but his manner, on this occasion, nettled me. Not only did there seem to lurk in it a certain calm disdain, but his perverseness seemed ungrateful, considering the undeniable good usage and indulgence he had received from me.

Again I sat ruminating what I should do. Mortified as I was at his behavior, and resolved as I had been to dismiss him when I entered my office, nevertheless I strangely felt something superstitious knocking at my heart, and forbidding me to carry out my purpose, and denouncing me for a villain if I dared to breathe one bitter word against this forlornest of mankind. At last, familiarly drawing my chair behind his screen, I sat down and said: "Bartleby, never mind, then, about revealing your history: but let me entreat you, as a friend, to comply as far as may be with the usages of this office. Say now, you will help to examine papers tomorrow or next day: in short, say now, that in a day or two you will begin to be a little reasonable:—say so, Bartleby."

"At present I would prefer not to be a little reasonable," was his mildly cadaverous reply.

Just then the folding-doors opened, and Nippers approached. He seemed suffering from an unusually bad night's rest, induced by severer indigestion than common. He overheard those final words of Bartleby.

"*Prefer not*, eh?" gritted Nippers—"I'd *prefer* him, if I were you, sir," addressing me—"I'd *prefer* him; I'd give him preferences, the stubborn mule! What is it, sir, pray, that he *prefers* not to do now?"

Bartleby moved not a limb.

"Mr. Nippers," said I, "I'd prefer that you would withdraw for the present."

Somehow, of late, I had got into the way of involuntarily using this word "prefer" upon all sorts of not exactly suitable occasions. And I trembled to think that my contact with the scrivener had already and seriously affected me in a mental way. And what further and deeper aberration might it not yet produce? This apprehension had not been without efficacy in determining me to summary measures.

As Nippers, looking very sour and sulky, was departing, Turkey blandly and deferentially approached.

"With submission, sir," said he, "yesterday I was thinking about Bartleby here, and I think that if he would but prefer to take a quart of good ale every day, it would do much towards mending him, and enabling him to assist in examining his papers."

"So you have got the word, too," said I, slightly excited.

"With submission, what word, sir?" asked Turkey, respectfully crowding himself into the contracted space behind the screen, and by so doing, making me jostle the scrivener. "What word, sir?"

"I would prefer to be left alone here," said Bartleby, as if offended at being mobbed in his privacy.

"*That's* the word, Turkey," said I—"*that's* it."

"Oh, *prefer?* oh yes—queer word. I never use it myself. But, sir, as I was saying, if he would but prefer—"

"Turkey," interrupted I, "you will please withdraw."

"Oh certainly, sir, if you prefer that I should."

As he opened the folding-door to retire, Nippers at his desk caught a glimpse of me, and asked whether I would prefer to have a certain paper copied on blue paper or white. He did not in the least roguishly accent the word "prefer." It was plain that it involuntarily rolled from his tongue. I thought to myself, surely I must get rid of a demented man, who already has in some degree turned the tongues, if not the heads of myself and clerks. But I thought it prudent not to break the dismission at once.

The next day I noticed that Bartleby did nothing but stand at his window in his dead-wall revery. Upon asking him why he did not write, he said that he had decided upon doing no more writing.

"Why, how now? what next?" exclaimed I, "do no more writing?"

"No more."

"And what is the reason?"

"Do you not see the reason for yourself?" he indifferently replied.

I looked steadfastly at him, and perceived that his eyes looked dull and glazed. Instantly it occurred to me, that his unexampled diligence in copying by his dim window for the first few weeks of his stay with me might have temporarily impaired his vision.

I was touched. I said something in condolence with him. I hinted that of course he did wisely in abstaining from writing for a while; and urged him to embrace that opportunity of taking wholesome exercise in the open air. This, however, he did not do. A few days after this, my other clerks being absent, and being in a great hurry to dispatch certain letters by the mail, I thought that, having nothing else earthly to do, Bartleby would surely be less inflexible than usual, and carry these letters to the post-office. But he blankly declined. So, much to my inconvenience, I went myself.

Still added days went by. Whether Bartleby's eyes improved or not, I could not say. To all appearance, I thought they did. But when I asked him if they did, he vouchsafed no answer. At all events, he would do no copying. At last, in reply to my urgings, he informed me that he had permanently given up copying.

"What!" exclaimed I; "suppose your eyes should get entirely well—better than ever before—would you not copy then?"

"I have given up copying," he answered, and slid aside.

He remained as ever, a fixture in my chamber. Nay—if that were possible—he became still more of a fixture than before. What was to be done? He would do nothing in the office; why should he stay there? In plain fact, he had now become a millstone to me, not only useless as a necklace, but afflictive to bear. Yet I was sorry for him. I speak less than truth when I say that, on his own account, he occasioned me uneasiness. If he would but have named a single relative or friend, I would instantly have written, and urged their taking the poor fellow away to some convenient retreat. But he seemed alone, absolutely alone in the universe. A bit of wreck in the mid-Atlantic. At length, necessities connected with my business tyrannized over all other considerations. Decently as I could, I told Bartleby that in six days' time he must unconditionally leave the office. I warned him to take measures, in the interval, for procuring some other abode. I offered to assist him in this endeavor, if he himself would but take the first step towards a removal. "And when you finally quit me, Bartleby," added I, "I shall see that you go not away entirely unprovided. Six days from this hour, remember."

At the expiration of that period, I peeped behind the screen and lo! Bartleby was there.

I buttoned up my coat, balanced myself; advanced slowly towards him, touched his shoulder, and said, "The time has come; you must quit this place; I am sorry for you; here is money; but you must go."

"I would prefer not," he replied, with his back still towards me.

"You *must*."

He remained silent.

Now I had an unbounded confidence in this man's common honesty. He had frequently restored to me sixpences and shillings carelessly dropped upon the floor, for I am apt to be very reckless in such shirt-button affairs. The proceeding, then, which followed will not be deemed extraordinary.

"Bartleby," said I, "I owe you twelve dollars on account; here are thirty-two; the odd twenty are yours—Will you take it?" and I handed the bills towards him.

But he made no motion.

"I will leave them here, then," putting them under a weight on the table. Then taking my hat and cane and going to the door, I tranquilly turned and added— "After you have removed your things from these offices, Bartleby, you will of course lock the door—since every one is now gone for the day but you—and if you please, slip your key underneath the mat, so that I may have it in the morning. I shall not see you again; so good-bye to you. If, hereafter, in your new place of abode, I can be of any service to you, do not fail to advise me by letter. Good-bye Bartleby, and fare you well."

But he answered not a word; like the last column of some ruined temple, he remained standing mute and solitary in the middle of the otherwise deserted room.

As I walked home in a pensive mood, my vanity got the better of my pity. I could not but highly plume myself on my masterly management in getting rid of Bartleby. Masterly I call it, and such it must appear to any dispassionate thinker. The beauty of my procedure seemed to consist in its perfect quietness. There was no vulgar bullying, no bravado of any sort, no choleric hectoring, and striding to and fro across the apartment, jerking out vehement commands for Bartleby to bundle himself off with his beggarly traps. Nothing of the kind. Without loudly bidding Bartleby depart—as an inferior genius might have done—I *assumed* the ground that depart he must; and upon that assumption built all I had to say. The more I thought over my procedure, the more I was charmed with it. Nevertheless, next morning, upon awakening, I had my doubts—I had somehow slept off the fumes of vanity. One of the coolest and wisest hours a man has, is just after he awakes in the morning. My procedure seemed as sagacious as ever—but only in theory. How it would prove in practice—there was the rub. It was truly a beautiful thought to have assumed Bartleby's departure; but, after all, that assumption was simply my own, and none of Bartleby's. The great point was, not whether I had assumed that he would quit me, but whether he would prefer so to do. He was more a man of preferences than assumptions.

After breakfast, I walked down town, arguing the probabilities *pro* and *con*. One moment I thought it would prove a miserable failure, and Bartleby would be found all alive at my office as usual; the next moment it seemed certain that I should find his chair empty. And so I kept veering about. At the corner of Broadway and Canal Street, I saw quite an excited group of people standing in earnest conversation.

"I'll take odds he doesn't," said a voice as I passed.

"Doesn't go?—done!" said I, "put up your money."

I was instinctively putting my hand in my pocket to produce my own, when I remembered that this was an election day. The words I had overheard bore no reference to Bartleby, but to the success or non-success of some candidate for the mayorality. In my intent frame of mind, I had, as it were, imagined that all Broadway shared in my excitement, and were debating the same question with me. I passed on, very thankful that the uproar of the street screened my momentary absent-mindedness.

As I had intended, I was earlier than usual at my office door. I stood listening for a moment. All was still. He must be gone. I tried the knob. The door was locked. Yes, my procedure had worked to a charm; he indeed must be vanished. Yet a certain melancholy mixed with this: I was almost sorry for my brilliant success. I was fumbling under the door mat for the key, which Bartleby was to have left there for me, when accidently my knee knocked against a panel, producing a summoning sound, and in response a voice came to me from within—"Not yet; I am occupied."

It was Bartleby.

I was thunderstruck. For an instant I stood like the man who, pipe in mouth, was killed one cloudless afternoon long ago in Virginia, by summer lightning; at his own warm open window he was killed, and remained leaning out there upon the dreamy afternoon, till some one touched him, when he fell.

"Not gone!" I murmured at last. But again obeying that wondrous ascendancy which the inscrutable scrivener had over me, and from which ascendancy, for all my chafing, I could not completely escape, I slowly went down stairs and out into the street, and while walking round the block, considered what I should next do in this unheard-of perplexity. Turn the man out by an actual thrusting I could not; to drive him away by calling him hard names would not do; calling in the police was an unpleasant idea; and yet, permit him to enjoy his cadaverous triumph over me—this, too, I could not think of. What was to be done? or, if nothing could be done, was there anything further that I could *assume* in the matter? Yes, as before I had prospectively assumed that Bartleby would depart, so now I might retrospectively assume that departed he was. In the legitimate carrying out of this assumption, I might enter my office in a great hurry, and pretending not to see Bartleby at all, walk straight against him as if he were air. Such a proceeding would in a singular degree have the appearance of a homethrust. It was hardly possible that Bartleby could withstand such an application of the doctrine of assumptions. But upon second thoughts the success of the plan seemed rather dubious. I resolved to argue the matter over with him again.

"Bartleby," said I, entering the office, with a quietly severe expression, "I am seriously displeased. I am pained, Bartleby. I had thought better of you. I had imagined you of such a gentlemanly organization, that in any delicate dilemma a slight hint would suffice—in short, an assumption. But it appears I am deceived.

Why," I added, unaffectedly starting, "you have not even touched that money yet," pointing to it, just where I had left it the evening previous.

He answered nothing.

"Will you, or will you not, quit me?" I now demanded in a sudden passion, advancing close to him.

"I would prefer *not* to quit you," he replied, gently emphasizing the *not*.

"What earthly right have you to stay here? Do you pay any rent? Do you pay any taxes? Or is this property yours?"

He answered nothing.

"Are you ready to go and write now? Are your eyes recovered? Could you copy a small paper for me this morning? or help examine a few lines? or step round to the post-office? In a word, will you do anything at all, to give a coloring to your refusal to depart the premises?"

He silently retired into his hermitage.

I was now in such a state of nervous resentment that I thought it but prudent to check myself at present from further demonstrations. Bartleby and I were alone. I remembered the tragedy of the unfortunate Adams and the still more unfortunate Colt in the solitary office of the latter; and how poor Colt, being dreadfully incensed by Adams, and imprudently permitting himself to get wildly excited, was at unawares hurried into his fatal act[18]—an act which certainly no man could possibly deplore more than the actor himself. Often it had occurred to me in my ponderings upon the subject that had that altercation taken place in the public street, or at a private residence, it would not have terminated as it did. It was the circumstance of being alone in a solitary office, up stairs, of a building entirely unhallowed by humanizing domestic associations—an uncarpeted office, doubtless, of a dusty haggard sort of appearance—this it must have been, which greatly helped to enhance the irritable desperation of the hapless Colt.

But when this old Adam of resentment rose in me and tempted me concerning Bartleby, I grappled him and threw him. How? Why, simply by recalling the divine injunction: "A new commandment give I unto you, that ye love one another."[19] Yes, this it was that saved me. Aside from higher considerations, charity often operates as a vastly wise and prudent principle—a great safeguard to its possessor. Men have committed murder for jealousy's sake, and anger's sake, and hatred's sake, and selfishness' sake, and spiritual pride's sake; but no man, that ever I heard of, ever committed a diabolical murder for sweet charity's sake. Mere self-interest, then, if no better motive can be enlisted, should, especially with high-tempered men, prompt all beings to charity and philanthropy. At any rate, upon the occasion in question, I strove to drown my exasperated feelings towards the scrivener by benevolently construing his conduct. Poor fellow, poor fellow! thought I, he don't mean anything; and besides, he has seen hard times, and ought to be indulged.

I endeavored, also, immediately to occupy myself, and at the same time to comfort my despondency. I tried to fancy, that in the course of the morning, at such time as might prove agreeable to him, Bartleby, of his own free accord, would emerge from his hermitage and take up some decided line of march in the direction of the door. But no. Half-past twelve o'clock came; Turkey began to glow in the face, overturn his inkstand, and become generally obstreperous; Nippers abated down into quietude and courtesy; Ginger Nut munched his noon apple; and Bartleby remained standing at his window in one of his profoundest dead-

---

[18]In famous murder case of 1841–42: Samuel Adams went to collect a debt from John C. Colt in his office in New York City, whereupon Colt killed Adams with a hatchet and attempted to ship the corpse to New Orleans. The corpse was discovered and Colt convicted and sentenced to be hanged. He committed suicide shortly before the hanging was to take place.
[19]Cf. John 13:34.

wall reveries. Will it be credited? Ought I to acknowledge it? That afternoon I left the office without saying one further word to him.

Some days now passed, during which, at leisure intervals I looked a little into "Edwards on the Will," and "Priestly on Necessity."[20] Under the circumstances, those books induced a salutary feeling. Gradually I slid into the persuasion that these troubles of mine, touching the scrivener, had been all predestinated from eternity, and Bartleby was billeted upon me for some mysterious purpose of an all-wise Providence, which it was not for a mere mortal like me to fathom. Yes, Bartleby, stay there behind your screen, thought I; I shall persecute you no more; you are harmless and noiseless as any of these old chairs; in short, I never feel so private as when I know you are here. At last I see it, I feel it; I penetrate to the predestinated purpose of my life. I am content. Others may have loftier parts to enact; but my mission in this world, Bartleby, is to furnish you with office-room for such period as you may see fit to remain.

I believe that this wise and blessed frame of mind would have continued with me, had it not been for the unsolicited and uncharitable remarks obtruded upon me by my professional friends who visited the rooms. But thus it often is, that the constant friction of illiberal minds wears out at last the best resolves of the more generous. Though to be sure, when I reflected upon it, it was not strange that people entering my office should be struck by the peculiar aspect of the unaccountable Bartleby, and so be tempted to throw out some sinister observations concerning him. Sometimes an attorney, having business with me, and calling at my office, and finding no one but the scrivener there, would undertake to obtain some sort of precise information from him touching my whereabouts; but without heeding his idle talk, Bartleby would remain standing immovable in the middle of the room. So after contemplating him in that position for a time, the attorney would depart, no wiser than he came.

Also, when a reference[21] was going on, and the room full of lawyers and witnesses, and business driving fast, some deeply-occupied legal gentleman present, seeing Bartleby wholly unemployed, would request him to run round to his (the legal gentleman's) office and fetch some papers for him. Thereupon, Bartleby would tranquilly decline, and yet remain idle as before. Then the lawyer would give a great stare, and turn to me. And what could I say? At last I was made aware that all through the circle of my professional acquaintance, a whisper of wonder was running round, having reference to the strange creature I kept at my office. This worried me very much. And as the idea came upon me of his possibly turning out a long-lived man, and keep occupying my chambers, and denying my authority; and perplexing my visitors; and scandalizing my professional reputation; and casting a general gloom over the premises; keeping soul and body together to the last upon his savings (for doubtless he spent but half a dime a day), and in the end perhaps outlive me, and claim possession of my office by right of his perpetual occupancy: as all these dark anticipations crowded upon me more and more, and my friends continually intruded their relentless remarks upon the apparition in my room; a great change was wrought in me. I resolved to gather all my faculties together, and forever rid me of this intolerable incubus.

Ere revolving any complicated project, however, adapted to this end, I first simply suggested to Bartleby the propriety of his permanent departure. In a calm and serious tone, I commended the idea to his careful and mature consideration. But, having taken three days to meditate upon it, he apprised me, that his original

---

[20]Jonathan Edwards (1703–1758), the great Puritan defender of the Calvinistic Puritan dogma, author of a defense of divine predestination in his *Freedom of the Will* (1754); Joseph Priestley (1733–1804), English Unitarian clergyman and chemist, author of a defense of natural or causal determinism in *The Doctrine of Philosophical Necessity Illustrated* (1777).

[21]Referral of a dispute to referees.

determination remained the same; in short, that he still preferred to abide with me.

What shall I do? I now said to myself, buttoning up my coat to the last button. What shall I do? what ought I to do? what does conscience say I *should* do with this man, or, rather, ghost. Rid myself of him, I must; go, he shall. But how? You will not thrust him, the poor, pale, passive mortal—you will not thrust such a helpless creature out of your door? you will not dishonor yourself by such cruelty? No, I will not, I cannot do that. Rather would I let him live and die here, and then mason up his remains in the wall. What, then, will you do? For all your coaxing, he will not budge. Bribes he leaves under your own paperweight on your table; in short, it is quite plain that he prefers to cling to you.

Then something severe, something unusual must be done. What! surely you will not have him collared by a constable, and commit his innocent pallor to the common jail? And upon what ground could you procure such a thing to be done?—a vagrant, is he? What! he a vagrant, a wanderer, who refuses to budge? It is because he will *not* be a vagrant, then, that you seek to count him *as* a vagrant. That is too absurd. No visible means of support: there I have him. Wrong again: for indubitably he *does* support himself, and that is the only unanswerable proof that any man can show of his possessing the means so to do. No more, then. Since he will not quit me, I must quit him. I will change my offices; I will move elsewhere, and give him fair notice, that if I find him on my new premises I will then proceed against him as a common trespasser.

Acting accordingly, next day I thus addressed him: "I find these chambers too far from the City Hall; the air is unwholesome. In a word, I propose to remove my offices next week, and shall no longer require your services. I tell you this now, in order that you may seek another place."

He made no reply, and nothing more was said.

On the appointed day I engaged carts and men, proceeded to my chambers, and, having but little furniture, everything was removed in a few hours. Throughout, the scrivener remained standing behind the screen, which I directed to be removed the last thing. It was withdrawn: and, being folded up like a huge folio, left him the motionless occupant of a naked room. I stood in the entry watching him a moment, while something from within me upbraided me.

I re-entered, with my hand in my pocket—and—and my heart in my mouth.

"Good-bye, Bartleby; I am going—good-bye, and God some way bless you; and take that," slipping something in his hand. But it dropped upon the floor, and then—strange to say—I tore myself from him whom I had so longed to be rid of.

Established in my new quarters, for a day or two I kept the door locked, and started at every footfall in the passages. When I returned to my rooms, after any little absence, I would pause at the threshold for an instant, and attentively listen, ere applying my key. But these fears were needless. Bartleby never came nigh me.

I thought all was going well, when a perturbed-looking stranger visited me, inquiring whether I was the person who had recently occupied rooms at No.—Wall Street.

Full of forebodings, I replied that I was.

"Then, sir," said the stranger, who proved a lawyer, "you are responsible for the man you left there. He refuses to do any copying; he refuses to do anything; he says he prefers not to; and he refuses to quit the premises."

"I am very sorry, sir," said I, with assumed tranquillity, but an inward tremor, "but, really, the man you allude to is nothing to me—he is no relation or apprentice of mine, that you should hold me responsible for him."

"In mercy's name, who is he?"

"I certainly cannot inform you. I know nothing about him. Formerly I employed him as a copyist; but he has done nothing for me now for some time past."

"I shall settle him, then—good morning, sir."

Several days passed, and I heard nothing more; and, though I often felt a charitable prompting to call at the place and see poor Bartleby, yet a certain squeamishness, of I know not what, withheld me.

All is over with him, by this time, thought I, at last, when, through another week, no further intelligence reached me. But, coming to my room the day after, I found several persons waiting at my door in a high state of nervous excitement.

"That's the man—here he comes," cried the foremost one, whom I recognized as the lawyer who had previously called upon me alone.

"You must take him away, sir, at once," cried a portly person among them, advancing upon me, and whom I knew to be the landlord of No.—Wall Street. "These gentlemen, my tenants, cannot stand it any longer; Mr. B——," pointing to the lawyer, "has turned him out of his room, and he now persists in haunting the building generally, sitting upon the banisters of the stairs by day, and sleeping in the entry by night. Everybody is concerned; clients are leaving the offices; some fears are entertained of a mob; something you must do, and that without delay."

Aghast at this torrent, I fell back before it, and would fain have locked myself in my new quarters. In vain I persisted that Bartleby was nothing to me—no more than to any one else. In vain—I was the last person known to have anything to do with him, and they held me to the terrible account. Fearful, then, of being exposed in the papers (as one person present obscurely threatened), I considered the matter, and, at length, said, that if the lawyer would give me a confidential interview with the scrivener, in his (the lawyer's) own room, I would, that afternoon, strive my best to rid them of the nuisance they complained of.

Going up stairs to my old haunt, there was Bartleby silently sitting upon the banister at the landing.

"What are you doing here, Bartleby?" said I.

"Sitting upon the banister," he mildly replied.

I motioned him into the lawyer's room, who then left us.

"Bartleby," said I, "are you aware that you are the cause of great tribulation to me, by persisting in occupying the entry after being dismissed from the office?"

No answer.

"Now one of two things must take place. Either you must do something, or something must be done to you. Now what sort of business would you like to engage in? Would you like to re-engage in copying for some one?"

"No; I would prefer not to make any change."

"Would you like a clerkship in a dry-goods store?"

"There is too much confinement about that. No, I would not like a clerkship; but I am not particular."

"Too much confinement," I cried, "why, you keep yourself confined all the time!"

"I would prefer not to take a clerkship," he rejoined, as if to settle that little item at once.

"How would a bar-tender's business suit you? There is no trying of the eyesight in that."

"I would not like it at all; though, as I said before, I am not particular."

His unwonted wordiness inspirited me. I returned to the charge.

"Well, then, would you like to travel through the country collecting bills for the merchants? That would improve your health."

"No, I would prefer to be doing something else."

"How, then, would going as a companion to Europe, to entertain some young gentleman with your conversation—how would that suit you?"

"Not at all. It does not strike me that there is anything definite about that. I like to be stationary. But I am not particular."

"Stationary you shall be, then," I cried, now losing all patience, and, for the first time in all my exasperating connection with him, fairly flying into a passion.

"If you do not go away from these premises before night, I shall feel bound—indeed, I *am* bound—to—to—to quit the premises myself!" I rather absurdly concluded, knowing not with what possible threat to try to frighten his immobility into compliance. Despairing of all further efforts, I was precipitately leaving him, when a final thought occurred to me—one which had not been wholly unindulged before.

"Bartleby," said I, in the kindest tone I could assume under such exciting circumstances, "will you go home with me now—not to my office, but my dwelling—and remain there till we can conclude upon some convenient arrangement for you at our leisure? Come, let us start now, right away."

"No: at present I would prefer not to make any change at all."

I answered nothing; but, effectually dodging every one by the suddenness and rapidity of my flight, rushed from the building, ran up Wall Street towards Broadway, and, jumping into the first omnibus, was soon removed from pursuit. As soon as tranquillity returned, I distinctly perceived that I had now done all that I possibly could, both in respect to the demands of the landlord and his tenants, and with regard to my own desire and sense of duty, to benefit Bartleby, and shield him from rude persecution. I now strove to be entirely care-free and quiescent; and my conscience justified me in the attempt; though, indeed, it was not so successful as I could have wished. So fearful was I of being again hunted out by the incensed landlord and his exasperated tenants, that, surrendering my business to Nippers, for a few days, I drove about the upper part of the town and through the suburbs, in my rockaway;[22] crossed over to Jersey City and Hoboken, and paid fugitive visits to Manhattanville and Astoria. In fact, I almost lived in my rockaway for the time.

When again I entered my office, lo, a note from the landlord lay upon the desk. I opened it with trembling hands. It informed me that the writer had sent to the police, and had Bartleby removed to the Tombs as a vagrant. Moreover, since I knew more about him than any one else, he wished me to appear at that place, and make a suitable statement of the facts. These tidings had a conflicting effect upon me. At first I was indignant; but, at last, almost approved. The landlord's energetic, summary disposition, had led him to adopt a procedure which I do not think I would have decided upon myself; and yet, as a last resort, under such peculiar circumstances, it seemed the only plan.

As I afterwards learned, the poor scrivener, when told that he must be conducted to the Tombs, offered not the slightest obstacle, but, in his pale, unmoving way, silently acquiesced.

Some of the compassionate and curious by-standers joined the party; and headed by one of the constables arm-in-arm with Bartleby, the silent procession filed its way through all the noise, and heat, and joy of the roaring thoroughfares at noon.

The same day I received the note, I went to the Tombs, or, to speak more properly, the Halls of Justice. Seeking the right officer, I stated the purpose of my call, and was informed that the individual I described was, indeed, within. I then assured the functionary that Bartleby was a perfectly honest man, and greatly to be compassionated, however unaccountably eccentric. I narrated all I knew, and closed by suggesting the idea of letting him remain in as indulgent confinement as possible, till something less harsh might be done—though, indeed, I hardly knew what. At all events, if nothing else could be decided upon, the alms-house must receive him. I then begged to have an interview.

Being under no disgraceful charge, and quite serene and harmless in all his ways, they had permitted him freely to wander about the prison, and, especially, in the inclosed grass-platted yards thereof. And so I found him there, standing all

---

[22]Light horse-drawn, open-sided carriage.

alone in the quietest of the yards, his face towards a high wall, while all around, from the narrow slits of the jail windows, I thought I saw peering out upon him the eyes of murderers and thieves.

"Bartleby!"

"I know you," he said, without looking round—"and I want nothing to say to you."

"It was not I that brought you here, Bartleby," said I, keenly pained at his implied suspicion. "And to you, this should not be so vile a place. Nothing reproachful attaches to you by being here. And see, it is not so sad a place as one might think. Look, there is the sky, and here is the grass."

"I know where I am," he replied, but would say nothing more, and so I left him.

As I entered the corridor again, a broad meat-like man, in an apron, accosted me, and, jerking his thumb over his shoulder, said—"Is that your friend?"

"Yes."

"Does he want to starve? If he does, let him live on the prison fare, that's all."

"Who are you?" asked I, not knowing what to make of such an unofficially speaking person in such a place.

"I am the grub-man. Such gentlemen as have friends here, hire me to provide them with something good to eat."

"Is this so?" said I, turning to the turnkey.

He said it was.

"Well, then," said I, slipping some silver into the grub-man's hands (for so they called him), "I want you to give particular attention to my friend there; let him have the best dinner you can get. And you must be as polite to him as possible."

"Introduce me, will you?" said the grub-man, looking at me with an expression which seemed to say he was all impatience for an opportunity to give a specimen of his breeding.

Thinking it would prove of benefit to the scrivener, I acquiesced; and, asking the grub-man his name, went up with him to Bartleby.

"Bartleby, this is a friend; you will find him very useful to you."

"Your sarvant, sir, your sarvant," said the grub-man, making a low salutation behind his apron. "Hope you find it pleasant here, sir; nice grounds—cool apartments—hope you'll stay with us some time—try to make it agreeable. What will you have for dinner to-day?"

"I prefer not to dine to-day," said Bartleby, turning away. "It would disagree with me; I am unused to dinners." So saying, he slowly moved to the other side of the inclosure, and took up a position fronting the dead-wall.

"How's this?" said the grub-man, addressing me with a stare of astonishment. "He's odd, ain't he?"

"I think he is a little deranged," said I, sadly.

"Deranged? deranged is it? Well, now, upon my word, I thought that friend of yourn was a gentleman forger; they are always pale and genteel-like, them forgers. I can't help pity 'em—can't help it, sir. Did you know Monroe Edwards?"[23] he added, touchingly, and paused. Then, laying his hand piteously on my shoulder, sighed, "he died of consumption at Sing-Sing.[24] So you weren't acquainted with Monroe?"

"No, I was never socially acquainted with any forgers. But I cannot stop longer. Look to my friend yonder. You will not lose by it. I will see you again."

Some few days after this, I again obtained admission to the Tombs, and went through the corridors in quest of Bartleby; but without finding him.

---

[23]Col. Monroe Edwards (1808–1847), eminent financier convicted in 1842 of swindling firms out of many thousands of dollars through the use of forged documents.
[24]New York state prison in Ossining.

"I saw him coming from his cell not long ago," said a turnkey, "may be he's gone to loiter in the yards."

So I went in that direction.

"Are you looking for the silent man?" said another turnkey, passing me. "Yonder he lies—sleeping in the yard there. 'Tis not twenty minutes since I saw him lie down."

The yard was entirely quiet. It was not accessible to the common prisoners. The surrounding walls, of amazing thickness, kept off all sounds behind them. The Egyptian character of the masonry weighed upon me with its gloom. But a soft imprisoned turf grew under foot. The heart of the eternal pyramids, it seemed, wherein, by some strange magic, through the clefts, grass-seed, dropped by birds, had sprung.

Strangely huddled at the base of the wall, his knees drawn up and lying on his side, his head touching the cold stones, I saw the wasted Bartleby. But nothing stirred. I paused; then went close up to him; stooped over, and saw that his dim eyes were open; otherwise he seemed profoundly sleeping. Something prompted me to touch him. I felt his hand, when a tingling shiver ran up my arm and down my spine to my feet.

The round face of the grub-man peered upon me now. "His dinner is ready. Won't he dine to-day either? Or does he live without dining?"

"Lives without dining," said I, and closed the eyes.

"Eh!—He's asleep, ain't he?"

"With kings and counselors,"[25] murmured I.

• • • • •

There would seem little need for proceeding further in this history. Imagination will readily supply the meagre recital of poor Bartleby's interment. But, ere parting with the reader, let me say, that if this little narrative has sufficiently interested him, to awaken curiosity as to who Bartleby was, and what manner of life he led prior to the present narrator's making his acquaintance, I can only reply, that in such curiosity I fully share, but am wholly unable to gratify it. Yet here I hardly know whether I should divulge one little item of rumor, which came to my ear a few months after the scrivener's decease. Upon what basis it rested, I could never ascertain; and hence, how true it is I cannot now tell. But, inasmuch as this vague report has not been without a certain suggestive interest to me, however sad, it may prove the same with some others; and so I will briefly mention it. The report was this: that Bartleby had been a subordinate clerk in the Dead Letter Office at Washington, from which he had been suddenly removed by a change in the administration. When I think over this rumor, hardly can I express the emotions which seize me. Dead letters! does it not sound like dead men? Conceive a man by nature and misfortune prone to a pallid hopelessness, can any business seem more fitted to heighten it than that of continually handling these dead letters, and assorting them for the flames? For by the cart-load they are annually burned. Sometimes from out the folded paper the pale clerk takes a ring—the finger it was meant for, perhaps, moulders in the grave; a bank-note sent in swiftest charity—he whom it would relieve, nor eats nor hungers any more; pardon for those who died despairing; hope for those who died unhoping; good tidings for those who died stifled by unrelieved calamities. On errands of life, these letters speed to death.

Ah, Bartleby! Ah, humanity!

1853, 1856

---

[25] Job 3:14: "with kings and counsellors of the earth, which built desolate places for themselves."

from The Encantadas, or Enchanted Isles[1]

SKETCH FIRST
THE ISLES AT LARGE

—"That may not be, said then the ferryman,
Least we unweeting hap to be fordonne;
For those same islands seeming now and than,
Are not firme land, nor any certein wonne,
But stragling plots which to and fro do ronne
In the wide waters; therefore are they hight
The Wandering Islands; therefore do them shonne;
For they have oft drawne many a wandring wight
Into most deadly daunger and distressed plight;
For whosoever once hath fastened
His foot thereon may never it secure
But wandreth evermore uncertein and unsure."

. . . . .

"Darke, dolefull, dreary, like a greedy grave,
That still for carrion carcasses doth crave;
On top whereof ay dwelt the ghastly owl,
Shrieking his balefull note, which ever drave
Far from that haunt all other cheerful fowl,
And all about it wandring ghosts did wayle and howl."[2]

Take five-and-twenty heaps of cinders dumped here and there in an outside city lot; imagine some of them magnified into mountains, and the vacant lot the sea; and you will have a fit idea of the general aspect of the Encantadas, or Enchanted Isles. A group rather of extinct volcanoes than of isles; looking much as the world at large might, after a penal conflagration.

It is to be doubted whether any spot of earth can, in desolateness, furnish a parallel to this group. Abandoned cemeteries of long ago, old cities by piecemeal tumbling to their ruin, these are melancholy enough; but, like all else which has but once been associated with humanity, they still awaken in us some thoughts of sympathy, however sad. Hence, even the Dead Sea, along with whatever other emotions it may at times inspire, does not fail to touch in the pilgrim some of his less unpleasurable feelings.

And as for solitariness; the great forests of the north, the expanses of unnavigated waters, the Greenland ice-fields, are the profoundest of solitudes to a human observer; still the magic of their changeable tides and seasons mitigates their terror; because, though unvisited by men, those forests are visited by the May; the remotest seas reflect familiar stars even as Lake Erie does; and in the clear air of a fine Polar day, the irradiated, azure ice shows beautifully as malachite.[3]

But the special curse, as one may call it, of the Encantadas, that which exalts

---

[1] In 1841, when he was a sailor on the whaler *Acushnet*, Melville visited the Galapagos Islands, or the Encantadas. Charles Darwin had explored these islands just six years before, in 1835, and found there in the unique animal and bird species much important evidence for his theory of evolution, not to be published until 1859 as *The Origin of Species and Natural Selection*. Melville first published his series of ten sketches in March, April, and May 1854, in *Putnam's Monthly Magazine* and then put them in his *Piazza Tales* (1856).
[2] From Edmund Spenser's *The Faerie Queene* (1589–96); the first excerpt, Book II, Canto 12, Stanzas 11 and 12; second excerpt, Book I, Canto 9, Stanza 33.
[3] Green mineral that takes a high polish and is used for ornamental objects.

them in desolation above Idumea[4] and the Pole, is, that to them change never comes; neither the change of seasons nor of sorrows. Cut by the Equator, they know not autumn, and they know not spring; while already reduced to the lees of fire, ruin itself can work little more upon them. The showers refresh the deserts; but in these isles, rain never falls. Like split Syrian gourds left withering in the sun, they are cracked by an everlasting drought beneath a torrid sky. "Have mercy upon me," the wailing spirit of the Encantadas seems to cry, "and send Lazarus that he may dip the tip of his finger in water and cool my tongue, for I am tormented in this flame."[5]

Another feature in these isles is their emphatic uninhabitableness. It is deemed a fit type of all-forsaken overthrow, that the jackal should den in the wastes of weedy Babylon;[6] but the Encantadas refuse to harbor even the outcasts of the beasts. Man and wolf alike disown them. Little but reptile life is here found: tortoises, lizards, immense spiders, snakes, and that strangest anomaly of outlandish nature, the *aguano*.[7] No voice, no low, no howl is heard; the chief sound of life here is a hiss.

On most of the isles where vegetation is found at all, it is more ungrateful than the blankness of Aracama.[8] Tangled thickets of wiry bushes, without fruit and without a name, springing up among deep fissures of calcined rock, and treacherously masking them; or a parched growth of distorted cactus trees.

In many places the coast is rock-bound, or, more properly, clinker-bound; tumbled masses of blackish or greenish stuff like the dross of an iron-furnace, forming dark clefts and caves here and there, into which a ceaseless sea pours a fury of foam; overhanging them with a swirl of gray, haggard mist, amidst which sail screaming flights of unearthly birds heightening the dismal din. However calm the sea without, there is no rest for these swells and those rocks; they lash and are lashed, even when the outer ocean is most at peace with itself. On the oppressive, clouded days, such as are peculiar to this part of the watery Equator, the dark, vitrified masses, many of which raise themselves among white whirlpools and breakers in detached and perilous places off the shore, present a most Plutonian[9] sight. In no world but a fallen one could such lands exist.

Those parts of the strand free from the marks of fire, stretch away in wide level beaches of multitudinous dead shells, with here and there decayed bits of sugar-cane, bamboos, and cocoanuts, washed upon this other and darker world from the charming palm isles to the westward and southward; all the way from Paradise to Tartarus;[10] while mixed with the relics of distant beauty you will sometimes see fragments of charred wood and moldering ribs of wrecks. Neither will any one be surprised at meeting these last, after observing the conflicting currents which eddy throughout nearly all the wide channels of the entire group. The capriciousness of the tides of air sympathizes with those of the sea. Nowhere is the wind so light, baffling, and every way unreliable, and so given to perplexing calms, as at the Encantadas. Nigh a month has been spent by a ship going from one isle to another, though but ninety miles between; for owing to the force of the current, the boats employed to tow barely suffice to keep the craft from sweeping upon the cliffs, but do nothing towards accelerating her voyage. Sometimes it is impossible for a vessel from afar to fetch up with the group itself, unless large allowances for prospective lee-way[11] have been made ere its coming in sight. And

---

[4]Variant of Edom, barren area where the Israelites wandered in their search for the Promised Land.
[5]Cf. Luke 16:24 (the words of the rich man in hell on seeing Lazarus, the beggar he had refused, in heaven).
[6]Jeremiah 51:37: The Lord's judgment: "And Babylon shall become heaps, a dwelling place for dragons, an astonishment, and an hissing, without an inhabitant."
[7]Giant tropical lizard.

[8]Variant of Atacama, a desert, one of the driest areas on earth, centering in Chile and Ecuador.
[9]Hell-like (in classical mythology, Pluto ruled the underworld).
[10]Hell (abyss below Hades).
[11]The drift from the true course, in the direction toward which the wind blows.

yet, at other times, there is a mysterious indraft, which irresistibly draws a passing vessel among the isles, though not bound to them.

True, at one period, as to some extent at the present day, large fleets of whale-men cruised for spermaceti[12] upon what some seamen call the Enchanted Ground. But this, as in due place will be described, was off the great outer isle of Albemarle, away from the intricacies of the smaller isles, where there is plenty of sea-room; and hence, to that vicinity, the above remarks do not altogether apply; though even there the current runs at times with singular force, shifting, too, with as singular a caprice.

Indeed, there are seasons when currents quite unaccountable prevail for a great distance round about the total group, and are so strong and irregular as to change a vessel's course against the helm, though sailing at the rate of four or five miles the hour. The difference in the reckonings of navigators, produced by these causes, along with the light and variable winds, long nourished a persuasion, that there existed two distinct clusters of isles in the parallel of the Encantadas, about a hundred leagues apart. Such was the idea of their earlier visitors, the Buccaneers; and as late as 1750, the charts of that part of the Pacific accorded with the strange delusion. And this apparent fleetingness and unreality of the locality of the isles was most probably one reason for the Spaniards calling them the Encantada, or Enchanted Group.

But not uninfluenced by their character, as they now confessedly exist, the modern voyager will be inclined to fancy that the bestowal of this name might have in part originated in that air of spell-bound desertness which so significantly invests the isles. Nothing can better suggest the aspect of once living things ma-lignly crumbled from ruddiness into ashes. Apples of Sodom,[13] after touching, seem these isles.

However wavering their place may seem by reason of the currents, they them-selves, at least to one upon the shore, appear invariably the same: fixed, cast, glued into the very body of cadaverous death.

Nor would the appellation, enchanted, seem misapplied in still another sense. For concerning the peculiar reptile inhabitant of these wilds—whose presence gives the group its second Spanish name, Gallipagos—concerning the tortoises found here, most mariners have long cherished a superstition, not more frightful than grotesque. They earnestly believe that all wicked sea-officers, more especially commodores and captains, are at death (and, in some cases, before death) trans-formed into tortoises; thenceforth dwelling upon these hot aridities, sole solitary lords of Asphaltum.[14]

Doubtless, so quaintly dolorous a thought was originally inspired by the woe-begone landscape itself; but more particularly, perhaps, by the tortoises. For, apart from their strictly physical features, there is something strangely self-condemned in the appearance of these creatures. Lasting sorrow and penal hope-lessness are in no animal form so suppliantly expressed as in theirs; while the thought of their wonderful longevity does not fail to enhance the impression.

Nor even at the risk of meriting the charge of absurdly believing in enchant-ments, can I restrain the admission that sometimes, even now, when leaving the crowded city to wander out July and August among the Adirondack Mountains, far from the influences of towns and proportionally nigh to the mysterious ones of nature; when at such times I sit me down in the mossy head of some deep-

---

[12]I.e., the Sperm Whale, valuable for its oil (from the blub-ber) and its spermaceti (a waxy substance found in the head, used for making perfumes).
[13]Legendary apples from the Dead Sea area, beautiful on sight, but only ashes within.

[14]Variant of asphalt, a dark tarlike substance, found in na-ture or made by evaporating petroleum; mixed with gravel and used for paving.

wooded gorge, surrounded by prostrate trunks of blasted pines and recall, as in a dream, my other and far-distant rovings in the baked heart of the charmed isles; and remember the sudden glimpses of dusky shells, and long languid necks protruded from the leafless thickets; and again have beheld the vitreous inland rocks worn down and grooved into deep ruts by ages and ages of the slow draggings of tortoises in quest of pools of scanty water; I can hardly resist the feeling that in my time I have indeed slept upon evilly enchanted ground.

Nay, such is the vividness of my memory, or the magic of my fancy, that I know not whether I am not the occasional victim of optical delusion concerning the Gallipagos. For, often in scenes of social merriment, and especially at revels held by candle-light in old-fashioned mansions, so that shadows are thrown into the further recesses of an angular and spacious room, making them put on a look of haunted undergrowth of lonely woods, I have drawn the attention of my comrades by my fixed gaze and sudden change of air, as I have seemed to see, slowly emerging from those imagined solitudes, and heavily crawling along the floor, the ghost of a gigantic tortoise, with "Memento* * * * *"[15] burning in live letters upon his back.

SKETCH EIGHTH

NORFOLK ISLE AND THE CHOLA WIDOW

"At last they in an island did espy
A seemly woman sitting by the shore,
That with great sorrow and sad agony
Seemed some great misfortune to deplore,
And loud to them for succor called evermore."

"Black his eye as the midnight sky,
White his neck as the driven snow,
Red his cheek as the morning light;—
Cold he lies in the ground below.
      My love is dead,
      Gone to his death-bed ys,
All under the cactus tree."

"Each lonely scene shall thee restore,
For thee the tear be duly shed;
Belov'd till life can charm no more,
And mourned till Pity's self be dead."[1]

Far to the northeast of Charles's Isle, sequestered from the rest, lies Norfolk Isle; and, however insignificant to most voyagers, to me, through sympathy, that lone island has become a spot made sacred by the strangest trials of humanity.

It was my first visit to the Encantadas. Two days had been spent ashore in hunting tortoises. There was not time to capture many; so on the third afternoon we loosed our sails. We were just in the act of getting under way, the uprooted anchor yet suspended and invisibly swaying beneath the wave, as the good ship gradually turned her heel to leave the isle behind, when the seaman who heaved with me at the windlass[2] paused suddenly, and directed my attention to something moving on the land, not along the beach, but somewhat back, fluttering from a height.

---

[15]I.e., "Memento Mori," remember that you must die.
[1]Three epigraphs adapted from *The Faerie Queene* (1589, 1596), Book II, Canto 12, Stanza 27; from "The Mystelle's Songe" (Stanza 2) from *Aella: A Tragycal Enterlude* (1777), by Thomas Chatterton; from William Collins's "Dirge in Cymbeline" (1744).
[2]Apparatus consisting of cylinder and cable for hoisting anchor.

In view of the sequel of this little story, be it here narrated how it came to pass, that an object which partly from its being so small was quite lost to every other man on board, still caught the eye of my handspike[3] companion. The rest of the crew, myself included, merely stood up to our spikes in heaving, whereas, unwontedly exhilarated, at every turn of the ponderous windlass, my belted comrade leaped atop of it, with might and main giving a downward, thewey, perpendicular heave, his raised eye bent in cheery animation upon the slowly receding shore. Being high lifted above all others was the reason he perceived the object, otherwise unperceivable; and this elevation of his eye was owing to the elevation of his spirits; and this again—for truth must out—to a dram of Peruvian pisco,[4] in guerdon for some kindness done, secretly administered to him that morning by our mulatto steward. Now, certainly, pisco does a deal of michief in the world; yet seeing that, in the present case, it was the means, though indirect, of rescuing a human being from the most dreadful fate, must we not also needs admit that sometimes pisco does a deal of good?

Glancing across the water in the direction pointed out, I saw some white thing hanging from an inland rock, perhaps half a mile from the sea.

"It is a bird; a white-winged bird; perhaps a——no; it is——it is a handkerchief!"

"Ay, a handkerchief!" echoed my comrade, and with a louder shout apprised the captain.

Quickly now—like the running out and training of a great gun—the long cabin spy-glass was thrust through the mizzen rigging from the high platform of the poop; whereupon a human figure was plainly seen upon the inland rock, eagerly waving towards us what seemed to be the handkerchief.

Our captain was a prompt, good fellow. Dropping the glass, he lustily ran forward, ordering the anchor to be dropped again; hands to stand by a boat, and lower away.

In a half-hour's time the swift boat returned. It went with six and came with seven; and the seventh was a woman.

It is not artistic heartlessness, but I wish I could but draw in crayons; for this woman was a most touching sight; and crayons, tracing softly melancholy lines, would best depict the mournful image of the dark-damasked Chola widow.

Her story was soon told, and though given in her own strange language was as quickly understood; for our captain, from long trading on the Chilian coast, was well versed in the Spanish. A Cholo, or half-breed Indian woman of Payta in Peru, three years gone by, with her young new-wedded husband Felipe, of pure Castilian blood, and her one only Indian brother, Truxill, Hunilla had taken passage on the main[5] in a French whaler, commanded by a joyous man; which vessel, bound to the cruising grounds beyond the Enchanted Isles, proposed passing close by their vicinity. The object of the little party was to procure tortoise oil, a fluid which for its great purity and delicacy is held in high estimation wherever known; and it is well known all along this part of the Pacific coast. With a chest of clothes, tools, cooking utensils, a rude apparatus for trying out[6] the oil, some casks of biscuit, and other things, not omitting two favorite dogs, of which faithful animal all the Cholos are very fond, Hunilla and her companions were safely landed at their chosen place; the Frenchman, according to the contract made ere sailing, engaged to take them off upon returning from a four months' cruise in the westward seas; which interval the three adventurers deemed quite sufficient for their purposes.

---

[3]Lever for operating the windlass.
[4]Strong grape brandy made in Chile and Peru.
[5]Spanish Main, here referring to the region of South America's west coast.
[6]Rendering.

On the isle's lone beach they paid him in silver for their passage out, the stranger having declined to carry them at all except upon that condition; though willing to take every means to insure the due fulfillment of his promise. Felipe had striven hard to have this payment put off to the period of the ship's return. But in vain. Still they thought they had, in another way, ample pledge of the good faith of the Frenchman. It was arranged that the expenses of the passage home should not be payable in silver, but in tortoises; one hundred tortoises ready captured to the returning captain's hand. These the Cholos meant to secure after their own work was done, against the probable time of the Frenchman's coming back; and no doubt in prospect already felt, that in those hundred tortoises—now somewhere ranging the isle's interior—they possessed one hundred hostages. Enough: the vessel sailed; the gazing three on shore answered the loud glee of the singing crew; and ere evening, the French craft was hull down in the distant sea, its masts three faintest lines which quickly faded from Hunilla's eye.

The stranger had given a blithesome promise, and anchored it with oaths; but oaths and anchors equally will drag; naught else abides on fickle earth but unkept promises of joy. Contrary winds from out unstable skies, or contrary moods of his more varying mind, or shipwreck and sudden death in solitary waves; whatever was the cause, the blithe stranger never was seen again.

Yet, however dire a calamity was here in store, misgivings of it ere due time never disturbed the Cholos' busy mind, now all intent upon the toilsome matter which had brought them hither. Nay, by swift doom coming like the thief at night, ere seven weeks went by, two of the little party were removed from all anxieties of land or sea. No more they sought to gaze with feverish fear, or still more feverish hope, beyond the present's horizon line; but into the furthest future their own silent spirits sailed. By persevering labor beneath that burning sun, Felipe and Truxill had brought down to their hut many scores of tortoises, and tried out the oil, when, elated with their good success, and to reward themselves for such hard work, they, too hastily, made a catamaran, or Indian raft, much used on the Spanish main, and merrily started on a fishing trip, just without a long reef with many jagged gaps, running parallel with the shore, about half a mile from it. By some bad tide or hap, or natural negligence of joyfulness (for though they could not be heard, yet by their gestures they seemed singing at the time) forced in deep water against that iron bar, the ill-made catamaran was overset, and came all to pieces; when dashed by broad-chested swells between their broken logs and the sharp teeth of the reef, both adventurers perished before Hunilla's eyes.

Before Hunilla's eyes they sank. The real woe of this event passed before her sight as some sham tragedy on the stage. She was seated on a rude bower among the withered thickets, crowning a lofty cliff, a little back from the beach. The thickets were so disposed, that in looking upon the sea at large she peered out from among the branches as from the lattice of a high balcony. But upon the day we speak of here, the better to watch the adventure of those two hearts she loved, Hunilla had withdrawn the branches to one side, and held them so. They formed an oval frame, through which the bluely boundless sea rolled like a painted one. And there, the invisible painter painted to her view the wave-tossed and disjointed raft, its once level logs slantingly upheaved, as raking masts, and the four struggling arms undistinguishable among them; and then all subsided into smooth-flowing creamy waters, slowly drifting the splintered wreck; while first and last, no sound of any sort was heard. Death in a silent picture; a dream of the eye; such vanishing shapes as the mirage shows.

So instant was the scene, so trance-like its mild pictorial effect, so distant from her blasted bower and her common sense of things, that Hunilla gazed and gazed, nor raised a finger or a wail. But as good to sit thus dumb, in stupor staring on that dumb show, for all that otherwise might be done. With half a mile of sea between, how could her two enchanted arms aid those four fated ones? The distance long, the time one sand. After the lightning is beheld, what fool shall stay the thunder-bolt? Felipe's body was washed ashore, but Truxill's never came; only his gay, braided hat of golden straw—that same sunflower thing he waved to her, pushing from the strand—and now, to the last gallant, it still saluted her. But Felipe's body floated to the marge, with one arm encirclingly outstretched. Lock-jawed in grim death, the lover-husband softly clasped his bride, true to her even in death's dream. Ah, heaven, when man thus keeps his faith, wilt thou be faithless who created the faithful one? But they cannot break faith who never plighted it.

It needs not to be said what nameless misery now wrapped the lonely widow. In telling her own story she passed this almost entirely over, simply recounting the event. Construe the comment of her features as you might, from her mere words little would you have weened that Hunilla was herself the heroine of her tale. But not thus did she defraud us of our tears. All hearts bled that grief could be so brave.

She but showed us her soul's lid, and the strange ciphers thereon engraved; all within, with pride's timidity, was withheld. Yet was there one exception. Holding out her small olive hand before her captain, she said in mild and slowest Spanish, "Señor, I buried him;" then paused, struggled as against the writhed coilings of a snake, and cringing suddenly, leaped up, repeating in impassioned pain, "I buried him, my life, my soul!"

Doubtless, it was by half-unconscious, automatic motions of her hands, that this heavy-hearted one performed the final office for Felipe, and planted a rude cross of withered sticks—no green ones might be had—at the head of that lonely grave, where rested now in lasting uncomplaint and quiet haven he whom untranquil seas had overthrown.

But some dull sense of another body that should be interred, of another cross that should hallow another grave—unmade as yet—some dull anxiety and pain touching her undiscovered brother, now haunted the oppressed Hunilla. Her hands fresh from the burial earth, she slowly went back to the beach, with unshaped purposes wandering there, her spell-bound eye bent upon the incessant waves. But they bore nothing to her but a dirge, which maddened her to think that murderers should mourn. As time went by, and these things came less dreamingly to her mind, the strong persuasions of her Romish faith, which sets peculiar store by consecrated urns, prompted her to resume in waking earnest that pious search which had but been begun as in somnambulism. Day after day, week after week, she trod the cindery beach, till at length a double motive edged every eager glance. With equal longing she now looked for the living and the dead; the brother and the captain; alike vanished, never to return. Little accurate note of time had Hunilla taken under such emotions as were hers, and little, outside herself, served for calendar or dial. As to poor Crusoe in the self-same sea,[7] no saint's bell pealed forth the lapse of week or month; each day went by unchallenged; no chanticleer announced those sultry dawns, no lowing herds those poisonous nights. All wonted and steadily recurring sounds, human, or humanized by sweet fellowship with man, but one stirred that torrid trance—the cry of dogs; save which naught but the rolling sea invaded it, an all-pervading monotone; and to the widow that was the least loved voice she could have heard.

No wonder, that as her thoughts now wandered to the unreturning ship, and were beaten back again, the hope against hope so struggled in her soul, that at length she desperately said, "Not yet, not yet; my foolish heart runs on too fast."

---

[7]Actually, the protagonist of Daniel Defoe's *Robinson Crusoe* (1719) was left on an island in the Caribbean; his model and Defoe's source, Alexander Selkirk, had been left on one of the Juan Fernández islets, near the Encantadas.

So she forced patience for some further weeks. But to those whom earth's sure indraft[8] draws, patience or impatience is still the same.

Hunilla now sought to settle precisely in her mind, to an hour, how long it was since the ship had sailed; and then, with the same precision, how long a space remained to pass. But this proved impossible. What present day or month it was she could not say. Time was her labyrinth, in which Hunilla was entirely lost.

And now follows——

Against my own purposes a pause descends upon me here. One knows not whether nature doth not impose some secrecy upon him who has been privy to certain things. At least, it is to be doubted whether it be good to blazon such. If some books are deemed most baneful and their sale forbid, how, then, with deadlier facts, not dreams of doting men? Those whom books will hurt will not be proof against events. Events, not books, should be forbid. But in all things man sows upon the wind, which bloweth just there whither it listeth; for ill or good, man cannot know.[9] Often ill comes from the good, as good from ill.

When Hunilla——

Dire sight it is to see some silken beast long dally with a golden lizard ere she devour. More terrible, to see how feline Fate will sometimes dally with a human soul, and by a nameless magic make it repulse a sane despair with a hope which is but mad. Unwittingly I imp this cat-like thing, sporting with the heart of him who reads; for if he feel not he reads in vain.

—"The ship sails this day, to-day," at last said Hunilla to herself; "this gives me certain time to stand on; without certainty I go mad. In loose ignorance I have hoped and hoped; now in firm knowledge I will but wait. Now I live and no longer perish in bewilderings. Holy Virgin, aid me! Thou wilt waft back the ship. Oh, past length of weary weeks—all to be dragged over—to buy the certainty of to-day, I freely give ye, though I tear ye from me!"

As mariners, tost in tempest on some desolate ledge, patch them a boat out of the remnants of their vessel's wreck, and launch it in the self-same waves, see here Hunilla, this lone shipwrecked soul, out of treachery invoking trust. Humanity, thou strong thing, I worship thee, not in the laureled victor, but in this vanquished one.

Truly Hunilla leaned upon a reed, a real one; no metaphor; a real Eastern reed. A piece of hollow cane, drifted from unknown isles, and found upon the beach, its once jagged ends rubbed smoothly even as by sand-paper; its golden glazing gone. Long ground between the sea and land, upper and nether stone, the unvarnished substance was filed bare, and wore another polish now, one with itself, the polish of its agony. Circular lines at intervals cut all round this surface, divided it into six panels of unequal length. In the first were scored the days, each tenth one marked by a longer and deeper notch; the second was scored for the number of sea-fowl eggs for sustenance, picked out from the rocky nests; the third, how many fish had been caught from the shore; the fourth, how many small tortoises found inland; the fifth, how many days of sun; the sixth, of clouds; which last, of the two, was the greater one. Long night of busy numbering, misery's mathematics, to weary her too-wakeful soul to sleep; yet sleep for that was none.

The panel of the days was deeply worn—the long tenth notches half effaced, as alphabets of the blind. Ten thousand times the longing widow had traced her finger over the bamboo—dull flute, which played on, gave no sound—as if counting birds flown by in air would hasten tortoises creeping through the woods.

---

[8]Inward pull or attraction (as a current).
[9]Cf. John 3:8: "The wind bloweth where it listeth, and thou hearest the sound thereof, but canst not tell whence it cometh, and whither it goeth: so is every one that is born of the spirit."

After the one hundred and eightieth day no further mark was seen; that last one was the faintest, as the first the deepest.

"There were more days," said our Captain; "many, many more; why did you not go on and notch them, too, Hunilla?"

"Señor, ask me not."

"And meantime, did no other vessel pass the isle?"

"Nay, Señor;—but——"

"You do not speak; but *what*, Hunilla?"

"Ask me not, Señor."

"You saw ships pass, far away; you waved to them; they passed on;—was that it, Hunilla?"

"Señor, be it as you say."

Braced against her woe, Hunilla would not, durst not trust the weakness of her tongue. Then when our Captain asked whether any whale-boats had ——

But no, I will not file this thing complete for scoffing souls to quote, and call it firm proof upon their side. The half shall here remain untold. Those two un-named events which befell Hunilla on this isle, let them abide between her and her God. In nature, as in law, it may be libelous to speak some truths.

Still, how it was that, although our vessel had lain three days anchored nigh the isle, its one human tenant should not have discovered us till just upon the point of sailing, never to revisit so lone and far a spot, this needs explaining ere the sequel come.

The place where the French captain had landed the little party was on the fur-ther and opposite end of the isle. There, too, it was that they had afterwards built their hut. Nor did the widow in her solitude desert the spot where her loved ones had dwelt with her, and where the dearest of the twain now slept his last long sleep, and all her plaints awaked him not, and he of husbands the most faithful during life.

Now, high broken land rises between the opposite extremities of the isle. A ship anchored at one side is invisible from the other. Neither is the isle so small, but a considerable company might wander for days through the wilderness of one side, and never be seen, or their halloos heard, by any stranger holding aloof on the other. Hence Hunilla, who naturally associated the possible coming of ships with her own part of the isle, might to the end have remained quite ignorant of the presence of our vessel, were it not for a mysterious presentiment, borne to her, so our mariners averred, by this isle's enchanted air. Nor did the widow's an-swer undo the thought.

"How did you come to cross the isle this morning, then, Hunilla?" said our Captain.

"Señor, something came flitting by me. It touched my cheek, my heart, Señor."

"What do you say, Hunilla?"

"I have said, Señor, something came through the air."

It was a narrow chance. For when in crossing the isle Hunilla gained the high land in the centre, she must then for the first have perceived our masts, and also marked that their sails were being loosed, perhaps even heard the echoing chorus of the windlass song. The strange ship was about to sail, and she behind. With all haste she now descends the height on the hither side, but soon loses sight of the ship among the sunken jungles at the mountain's base. She struggles on through the withered branches, which seek at every step to bar her path, till she comes to the isolated rock, still some way from the water. This she climbs, to reassure her-self. The ship is still in plainest sight. But now, worn out with over-tension, Hu-nilla all but faints; she fears to step down from her giddy perch; she is fain[10] to

---

[10]Compelled by circumstances.

pause, there where she is, and as a last resort catches the turban from her head, unfurls and waves it over the jungles towards us.

During the telling of her story the mariners formed a voiceless circle round Hunilla and the Captain; and when at length the word was given to man the fastest boat, and pull round to the isle's thither side, to bring away Hunilla's chest and the tortoise-oil, such alacrity of both cheery and sad obedience seldom before was seen. Little ado was made. Already the anchor had been recommitted to the bottom, and the ship swung calmly to it.

But Hunilla insisted upon accompanying the boat as indispensable pilot to her hidden hut. So being refreshed with the best the steward could supply, she started with us. Nor did ever any wife of the most famous admiral, in her husband's barge, receive more silent reverence of respect than poor Hunilla from this boat's crew.

Rounding many a vitreous cape and bluff, in two hours' time we shot inside the fatal reef; wound into a secret cove, looked up along a green many-gabled lava wall, and saw the island's solitary dwelling.

It hung upon an impending cliff, sheltered on two sides by tangled thickets, and half-screened from view in front by juttings of the rude stairway, which climbed the precipice from the sea. Built of canes, it was thatched with long, mildewed grass. It seemed an abandoned hay-rick, whose haymakers were now no more. The roof inclined but one way; the eaves coming to within two feet of the ground. And here was a simple apparatus to collect the dews, or rather doubly-distilled and finest winnowed rains, which, in mercy or in mockery, the night-skies sometimes drop upon these blighted Encantadas. All along beneath the eaves, a spotted sheet, quite weather-stained, was spread, pinned to short, upright stakes, set in the shallow sand. A small clinker, thrown into the cloth, weighed its middle down, thereby straining all moisture into a calabash[11] placed below. This vessel supplied each drop of water ever drunk upon the isle by the Cholos. Hunilla told us the calabash would sometimes, but not often, be half filled overnight. It held six quarts, perhaps. "But," said she, "we were used to thirst. At sandy Payta, where I live, no shower from heaven ever fell; all the water there is brought on mules from the inland vales."

Tied among the thickets were some twenty moaning tortoises, supplying Hunilla's lonely larder; while hundreds of vast tableted black bucklers, like displaced, shattered tombstones of dark slate, were also scattered round. These were the skeleton backs of those great tortoises from which Felipe and Truxill had made their precious oil. Several large calabashes and two goodly kegs were filled with it. In a pot near by were the caked crusts of a quantity which had been permitted to evaporate. "They meant to have strained it off next day," said Hunilla, as she turned aside.

I forgot to mention the most singular sight of all, though the first that greeted us after landing.

Some ten small, soft-haired, ringleted dogs, of a beautiful breed, peculiar to Peru, set up a concert of glad welcomings when we gained the beach, which was responded to by Hunilla. Some of these dogs had, since her widowhood, been born upon the isle, the progeny of the two brought from Payta. Owing to the jagged steeps and pitfalls, tortuous thickets, sunken clefts and perilous intricacies of all sorts in the interior, Hunilla, admonished by the loss of one favorite among them, never allowed these delicate creatures to follow her in her occasional birds'-nests climbs and other wanderings; so that, through long habituation, they offered not to follow, when that morning she crossed the land, and her own soul

---

[11]Dish made from a hollow gourd.

was then too full of other things to heed their lingering behind. Yet, all along she had so clung to them, that, besides what moisture they lapped up at early day-break from the small scoop-holes among the adjacent rocks, she had shared the dew of her calabash among them; never laying by any considerable store against those prolonged and utter droughts which, in some disastrous seasons, warp these isles.

Having pointed out, at our desire, what few things she would like transported to the ship—her chest, the oil, not omitting the live tortoises which she intended for a grateful present to our Captain—we immediately set to work, carrying them to the boat down the long, sloping stair of deeply-shadowed rock. While my comrades were thus employed, I looked and Hunilla had disappeared.

It was not curiosity alone, but, it seems to me, something different mingled with it, which prompted me to drop my tortoise, and once more gaze slowly around. I remembered the husband buried by Hunilla's hands. A narrow pathway led into a dense part of the thickets. Following it through many mazes, I came out upon a small, round, open space, deeply chambered there.

The mound rose in the middle; a bare heap of finest sand, like that unver-dured heap found at the bottom of an hour-glass run out. At its head stood the cross of withered sticks; the dry, peeled bark still fraying from it; its transverse limb tied up with rope, and forlornly adroop in the silent air.

Hunilla was partly prostrate upon the grave; her dark head bowed, and lost in her long, loosened Indian hair; her hands extended to the cross-foot, with a little brass crucifix clasped between; a crucifix worn featureless, like an ancient graven knocker long plied in vain. She did not see me, and I made no noise, but slid aside, and left the spot.

A few moments ere all was ready for our going, she reappeared among us. I looked into her eyes, but saw no tear. There was something which seemed strangely haughty in her air, and yet it was the air of woe. A Spanish and an In-dian grief, which would not visibly lament. Pride's height in vain abased to prone-ness on the rack; nature's pride subduing nature's torture.

Like pages the small and silken dogs surrounded her, as she slowly descended towards the beach. She caught the two most eager creatures in her arms:—"Mia Teeta! Mia Tomoteeta!" and fondling them, inquired how many could we take on board.

The mate commanded the boat's crew; not a hard-hearted man, but his way of life had been such that in most things, even in the smallest, simple utility was his leading motive.

"We cannot take them all, Hunilla; our supplies are short; the winds are unreliable; we may be a good many days going to Tombez. So take those you have, Hunilla; but no more."

She was in the boat; the oarsmen, too, were seated; all save one, who stood ready to push off and then spring himself. With the sagacity of their race, the dogs now seemed aware that they were in the very instant of being deserted upon a barren strand. The gunwales of the boat were high; its prow—presented in-land—was lifted; so owing to the water, which they seem instinctively to shun, the dogs could not well leap into the little craft. But their busy paws hard scraped the prow, as it had been some farmer's door shutting them out from shelter in a win-ter storm. A clamorous agony of alarm. They did not howl, or whine; they all but spoke.

"Push off! Give way!" cried the mate. The boat gave one heavy drag and lurch, and next moment shot swiftly from the beach, turned on her heel, and sped. The dogs ran howling along the water's marge; now pausing to gaze at the flying boat, then motioning as if to leap in chase, but mysteriously withheld themselves; and again ran howling along the beach. Had they been human beings, hardly would they have more vividly inspired the sense of desolation. The oars were plied as confederate feathers of two wings. No one spoke. I looked back upon the beach, and then upon Hunilla, but her face was set in a stern dusky calm. The dogs crouching in her lap vainly licked her rigid hands. She never looked behind her; but sat motionless, till we turned a promontory of the coast and lost all sights and sounds astern. She seemed as one who, having experienced the sharpest of mortal pangs, was henceforth content to have all lesser heartstrings riven, one by one. To Hunilla, pain seemed so necessary, that pain in other beings, though by love and sympathy made her own, was unrepiningly to be borne. A heart of yearning in a frame of steel. A heart of earthly yearning, frozen by the frost which falleth from the sky.

The sequel is soon told. After a long passage, vexed by calms and baffling winds, we made the little port of Tombez in Peru, there to recruit the ship. Payta was not very distant. Our captain sold the tortoise oil to a Tombez merchant; and adding to the silver a contribution from all hands, gave it to our silent passenger, who knew not what the mariners had done.

The last seen of lone Hunilla she was passing into Payta town, riding upon a small gray ass; and before her on the ass's shoulders, she eyed the jointed workings of the beast's armorial cross.[12]

1854, 1856

The Paradise of Bachelors and the Tartarus of Maids[1]

I. THE PARADISE OF BACHELORS

It lies not far from Temple-Bar.[2]

Going to it, by the usual way, is like stealing from a heated plain into some cool, deep glen, shady among harboring hills.

Sick with the din and soiled with the mud of Fleet Street—where the Benedick[3] tradesmen are hurrying by, with ledger-lines ruled along their brows, thinking upon rise of bread and fall of babies—you adroitly turn a mystic corner—not a street—glide down a dim, monastic way, flanked by dark, sedate, and solemn piles, and still wending on, give the whole care-worn world the slip, and, disentangled, stand beneath the quiet cloisters of the Paradise of Bachelors.[4]

Sweet are the oases in Sahara; charming the isle-groves of August prairies; delectable pure faith amidst a thousand perfidies: but sweeter, still more charming, most delectable, the dreamy Paradise of Bachelors, found in the stony heart of stunning London.

---

[12]Cf. Matthew 21:1–10 and Mark 11:7–11. Jesus enters Jerusalem triumphantly, seated on an ass. Melville could have taken the legend of the armorial cross embedded on the ass's shoulders from William Wordsworth's "Peter Bell" (1819), who is portrayed riding an ass and noticing the cross on the "shoulder scored," and taking it as a "Memorial of his [Christ's] touch—that day/ When Jesus humbly deigned to ride,/ Entering the proud Jerusalem. . . ."

[1]These paired stories are meant to be read together, the second completing the meaning of the first. Melville draws on his visit in 1849 to a private club in London and his trip in 1851 out from Pittsfield to buy paper at a nearby mill. But Melville's imagination radically transfigures these episodes into a commentary on bachelorhood, male bonding, maidenhood, and the female fate in bearing children. Melville's second child, Stanwix, was born in October 1851.

Melville's growing family responsibilities together with his inability to make his writing pay significantly certainly must have figured into that remarkable imaginative transmutation of the mundane facts of his experience. Tartarus: hell, in Greek mythology the region below Hades.

[2]Elegant London gateway standing between Fleet Street and the Strand, designed by noted architect Christopher Wren in 1670.

[3]I.e., married (from Benedick in Shakespeare's *Much Ado about Nothing*, who gives up his bachelorhood for marriage at the end).

[4]These "cloisters" in central London constitute England's legal district, made up of the four Inns of Court used by lawyers and students. The library and chapel (described below) are part of the complex.

In mild meditation pace the cloisters; take your pleasure, sip your leisure, in the garden waterward; go linger in the ancient library; go worship in the sculptured chapel: but little have you seen, just nothing do you know, not the sweet kernel have you tasted, till you dine among the banded Bachelors, and see their convivial eyes and glasses sparkle. Not dine in bustling commons, during term-time, in the hall; but tranquilly, by private hint, at a private table; some fine Templar's[5] hospitably invited guest.

Templar? That's a romantic name. Let me see. Brian de Bois Gilbert[6] was a Templar, I believe. Do we understand you to insinuate that those famous Templars still survive in modern London? May the ring of their armed heels be heard, and the rattle of their shields, as in mailed prayer the monk-knights kneel before the consecrated Host? Surely a monk-knight were a curious sight picking his way along the Strand,[7] his gleaming corselet[8] and snowy surcoat spattered by an omnibus. Long-bearded, too, according to his order's rule; his face fuzzy as a pard's;[9] how would the grim ghost look among the crop-haired, close-shaven citizens? We know indeed—sad history recounts it—that a moral blight tainted at last this sacred Brotherhood. Though no sworded foe might outskill them in the fence, yet the worm of luxury crawled beneath their guard, gnawing the core of knightly troth, nibbling the monastic vow, till at last the monk's austerity relaxed to wassailing, and the sworn knights-bachelors grew to be but hypocrites and rakes.

But for all this, quite unprepared were we to learn that Knights-Templars (if at all in being) were so entirely secularized as to be reduced from carving out immortal fame in glorious battling for the Holy Land, to the carving of roast-mutton at a dinner-board. Like Anacreon,[10] do these degenerate Templars now think it sweeter far to fall in banquet than in war? Or, indeed, how can there be any survival of that famous order? Templars in modern London! Templars in their red-cross mantles smoking cigars at the Divan![11] Templars crowded in a railway train, till, stacked with steel helmet, spear, and shield, the whole train looks like one elongated locomotive!

No. The genuine Templar is long since departed. Go view the wondrous tombs in the Temple Church;[12] see there the rigidly-haughty forms stretched out, with crossed arms upon their stilly hearts, in everlasting and undreaming rest. Like the years before the flood, the bold Knights-Templars are no more. Nevertheless, the name remains, and the nominal society, and the ancient grounds, and some of the ancient edifices. But the iron heel is changed to a boot of patent-leather: the long two-handed sword to a one-handed quill; the monk-giver of gratuitous ghostly counsel now counsels for a fee; the defender of the sarcophagus (if in good practice with his weapon) now has more than one case to defend; the vowed opener and clearer of all highways leading to the Holy Sepulchre,[13] now has it in particular charge to check, to clog, to hinder, and embarrass all the courts and avenues of Law; the knight-combatant of the Saracen, breasting spear-points at Acre,[14] now fights law-points in Westminster Hall.[15] The helmet is a wig. Struck by Time's enchanter's wand, the Templar is to-day a Lawyer.

---

[5]The Temple district, part of the Inns of Court, was once owned by the Knights Templars (Order of the Poor Knights of Christ), formed to go on crusades to the Temple of Solomon in Jerusalem at the beginning of the twelfth century. They adopted the Benedictine rule of poverty and their symbol was the red cross. The order later became wealthy and licentious, and members were persecuted and the order suppressed in the fourteenth century.
[6]Actually, Brian de Bois-Guilbert in Sir Walter Scott's *Ivanhoe* (1819).
[7]Street running along the Thames.
[8]Armor for the body; the surcoat was an outer coat worn by the knight.

[9]I.e., leopard.
[10]Greek lyric poet (572?–488? B.C.), whose "Anacreontics" celebrated wine and love.
[11]Council room (in the Orient).
[12]In the Inns of Court Temple area.
[13]Christ's tomb.
[14]City, now in Israel, the site of battles between crusaders and Muslims (or Saracens) in the twelfth and thirteenth centuries.
[15]This huge entrance hall to Westminster Palace, housing the British Parliament, was used in Melville's day as a law court.

But, like many others tumbled from proud glory's height—like the apple, hard on the bough but mellow on the ground—the Templar's fall has but made him all the finer fellow.

I dare say those old warrior-priests were but gruff and grouty at the best; cased in Birmingham[16] hardware, how could their crimped arms give yours or mine a hearty shake? Their proud, ambitious, monkish souls clasped shut, like horn-book missals;[17] their very faces clapped in bomb-shells; what sort of genial men were these? But best of comrades, most affable of hosts, capital diner is the modern Templar. His wit and wine are both of sparkling brands.

The church and cloisters, courts and vaults, lanes and passages, banquet-halls, refectories, libraries, terraces, gardens, broad walks, domicils, and dessert-rooms, covering a very large space of ground, and all grouped in central neighborhood, and quite sequestered from the old city's surrounding din; and every thing about the place being kept in most bachelor-like particularity, no part of London offers to a quiet wight so agreeable a refuge.

The Temple is, indeed, a city by itself. A city with all the best appurtenances, as the above enumeration shows. A city with a park to it, and flower-beds, and a river-side—the Thames flowing by as openly, in one part, as by Eden's primal garden flowed the mild Euphrates. In what is now the Temple Garden the old Crusaders used to exercise their steeds and lances; the modern Templars now lounge on the benches beneath the trees, and, switching their patent-leather boots, in gay discourse exercise at repartee.

Long lines of stately portraits in the banquet-halls, show what great men of mark—famous nobles, judges, and Lord Chancellors—have in their time been Templars. But all Templars are not known to universal fame; though, if the having warm hearts and warmer welcomes, full minds and fuller cellars, and giving good advice and glorious dinners, spiced with rare divertisements of fun and fancy, merit immortal mention, set down, ye muses, the names of R. F. C.[18] and his imperial brother.

Though to be a Templar, in the one true sense, you must needs be a lawyer, or a student at the law, and be ceremoniously enrolled as member of the order, yet as many such, though Templars, do not reside within the Temple's precincts, though they may have their offices there, just so, on the other hand, there are many residents of the hoary old domicils who are not admitted Templars. If being, say, a lounging gentleman and bachelor, or a quiet, unmarried, literary man, charmed with the soft seclusion of the spot, you much desire to pitch your shady tent among the rest in this serene encampment, then you must make some special friend among the order, and procure him to rent, in his name but at your charge, whatever vacant chamber you may find to suit.

Thus, I suppose, did Dr. Johnson,[19] that nominal Benedick and widower but virtual bachelor, when for a space he resided here. So, too, did that undoubted bachelor and rare good soul, Charles Lamb.[20] And hundreds more, of sterling spirits, Brethren of the Order of Celibacy, from time to time have dined, and slept, and tabernacled here. Indeed, the place is all a honeycomb of offices and domicils. Like any cheese, it is quite perforated through and through in all directions with the snug cells of bachelors. Dear, delightful spot! Ah! when I bethink me of the sweet hours there passed, enjoying such genial hospitalities beneath

---

[16]British center of manufacturing.

[17]Book of prayers, here with covers of protective horn held shut with a clasp.

[18]Robert Francis Cooke and his brother entertained Melville in the Temple area of the Inns of Court in December 1849.

[19]Dr. Samuel Johnson (1709–1784), British critic, lexicographer, and conversationalist.

[20]Renowned British personal essayist (1775–1834).

those time-honored roofs, my heart only finds due utterance through poetry; and, with a sigh, I softly sing, "Carry me back to old Virginny!"[21]

Such then, at large, is the Paradise of Bachelors. And such I found it one pleasant afternoon in the smiling month of May, when, sallying from my hotel in Trafalgar Square, I went to keep my dinner-appointment with that fine Barrister, Bachelor, and Bencher, R. F. C. (he *is* the first and second, and *should be* the third; I hereby nominate him), whose card I kept fast pinched between my gloved forefinger and thumb and every now and then snatched still another look at the pleasant address inscribed beneath the name, "No.—, Elm Court, Temple."

At the core he was a right bluff, care-free, right comfortable, and most companionable Englishman. If on a first acquaintance he seemed reserved, quite icy in his air—patience; this Champagne will thaw. And if it never do, better frozen Champagne than liquid vinegar.

There were nine gentlemen, all bachelors, at the dinner. One was from "No.—, King's Bench Walk, Temple;" a second, third, and fourth, and fifth, from various courts or passages christened with some similarly rich resounding syllables. It was indeed a sort of Senate of the Bachelors, sent to this dinner from widely-scattered districts, to represent the general celibacy of the Temple. Nay it was, by representation, a Grand Parliament of the best Bachelors in universal London; several of those present being from distant quarters of the town, noted immemorial seats of lawyers and unmarried men—Lincoln's Inn, Furnival's Inn;[22] and one gentleman, upon whom I looked with a sort of collateral awe, hailed from the spot where Lord Verulam[23] once abode a bachelor—Gray's Inn.

The apartment was well up toward heaven. I know not how many strange old stairs I climbed to get to it. But a good dinner, with famous company, should be well earned. No doubt our host had his dining-room so high with a view to secure the prior exercise necessary to the due relishing and digesting of it.

The furniture was wonderfully unpretending, old, and snug. No new shining mahogany, sticky with undried varnish; no uncomfortably luxurious ottomans, and sofas too fine to use, vexed you in this sedate apartment. It is a thing which every sensible American should learn from every sensible Englishman, that glare and glitter, gimcracks and gewgaws, are not indispensable to domestic solacement. The American Benedick snatches, down-town, a tough chop in a gilded show-box; the English bachelor leisurely dines at home on that incomparable South Down[24] of his, off a plain deal board.

The ceiling of the room was low. Who wants to dine under the dome of St. Peter's?[25] High ceilings! If that is your demand, and the higher the better, and you be so very tall, then go dine out with the topping giraffe in the open air.

In good time the nine gentlemen sat down to nine covers, and soon were fairly under way.

If I remember right, ox-tail soup inaugurated the affair. Of a rich russet hue, its agreeable flavor dissipated my first confounding of its main ingredient with teamster's gads[26] and the rawhides of ushers.[27] (By way of interlude, we here drank a little claret.) Neptune's[28] was the next tribute rendered—turbot coming

---

[21]By Edwin P. Christy (1815–1862) of "Christy Minstrel Show." The refrain in the song is, "Then carry me back to old Virginny,/To old Virginny's shore." The song of the same title (with the second line, "There's where the cotton and the corn and taters grow") was written by James Bland (1854–1911) and published in 1878.
[22]The four Inns of Court are Lincoln's Inn, Gray's Inn, Inner Temple, and Middle Temple. Furnival's Inn was an Inn of Chancery (equity or property court) in Melville's day, but has since been destroyed.
[23]Francis Bacon, Baron Verulam, Viscount St. Albans (1561–1626), British philosopher, statesman, and essayist.

[24]Variant of Southdown, mutton, from an English breed of sheep.
[25]The cathedral in Rome, center of Catholic faith where the pope presides; the magnificent dome was designed by Michelangelo.
[26]A goad, or switch.
[27]Assistant teachers.
[28]I.e., the sea furnished the turbot, a large European flatfish.

second; snow-white, flaky, and just gelatinous enough, not too turtleish in its unctuousness.

(At this point we refreshed ourselves with a glass of sherry.) After these light skirmishers had vanished, the heavy artillery of the feast marched in, led by that well-known English generalissimo, roast beef. For aids-de-camp we had a saddle of mutton, a fat turkey, a chicken-pie, and endless other savory things; while for avant-couriers came nine silver flagons of humming ale. This heavy ordnance having departed on the track of the light skirmishers, a picked brigade of game-fowl encamped upon the board, their camp-fires lit by the ruddiest of decanters.

Tarts and puddings followed, with innumerable niceties; then cheese and crackers. (By way of ceremony, simply, only to keep up good old fashions, we here each drank a glass of good old port.)

The cloth was now removed; and like Blucher's[29] army coming in at the death on the field of Waterloo, in marched a fresh detachment of bottles, dusty with their hurried march.

All these manœuvrings of the forces were superintended by a surprising old field-marshal (I can not school myself to call him by the inglorious name of waiter), with snowy hair and napkin, and a head like Socrates.[30] Amidst all the hilarity of the feast, intent on important business, he disdained to smile. Venerable man!

I have above endeavored to give some slight schedule of the general plan of operations. But any one knows that a good, genial dinner is a sort of pell-mell, indiscriminate affair, quite baffling to detail in all particulars. Thus, I spoke of taking a glass of claret, and a glass of sherry, and a glass of port, and a mug of ale—all at certain specific periods and times. But those were merely the state bumpers,[31] so to speak. Innumerable impromptu glasses were drained between the periods of those grand imposing ones.

The nine bachelors seemed to have the most tender concern for each other's health. All the time, in flowing wine, they most earnestly expressed their sincerest wishes for the entire well-being and lasting hygiene of the gentlemen on the right and on the left. I noticed that when one of these kind bachelors desired a little more wine (just for his stomach's sake, like Timothy),[32] he would not help himself to it unless some other bachelor would join him. It seemed held something indelicate, selfish, and unfraternal, to be seen taking a lonely, unparticipated glass. Meantime, as the wine ran apace, the spirits of the company grew more and more to perfect genialness and unconstraint. They related all sorts of pleasant stories. Choice experiences in their private lives were now brought out, like choice brands of Moselle or Rhenish, only kept for particular company. One told us how mellowly he lived when a student at Oxford; with various spicy anecdotes of most frank-hearted noble lords, his liberal companions. Another bachelor, a gray-headed man, with a sunny face, who, by his own account, embraced every opportunity of leisure to cross over into the Low Countries,[33] on sudden tours of inspection of the fine old Flemish architecture there—this learned, white-haired, sunny-faced old bachelor, excelled in his descriptions of the elaborate splendors of those old guild-halls, town-halls, and stadthold-houses, to be seen in the land of the ancient Flemings. A third was a great frequenter of the British Museum,[34] and knew all about scores of wonderful antiquities, of Oriental manuscripts, and costly books without a duplicate. A fourth had lately returned from a trip to Old Gra-

---

[29] Gebhard von Blucher (1742–1819), Prussian General who aided Wellington in defeating Napoleon near the end of the Battle of Waterloo (1815).
[30] Greek philosopher (470?–399 B.C.), known through his disciple Plato's "dialogues."
[31] Glass or goblet filled to the brim.

[32] 1 Timothy 5:23: "Drink no longer water, but use a little wine for thy stomach's sake and thine often infirmities."
[33] Belgium, Holland, and Luxembourg.
[34] Now the British Library, rich in its collection of books and manuscripts.

nada, and, of course, was full of Saracenic scenery. A fifth had a funny case in law to tell. A sixth was erudite in wines. A seventh had a strange characteristic anecdote of the private life of the Iron Duke,[35] never printed, and never before announced in any public or private company. An eighth had lately been amusing his evenings, now and then, with translating a comic poem of Pulci's.[36] He quoted for us the more amusing passages.

And so the evening slipped along, the hours told, not by a water-clock, like King Alfred's,[37] but a wine-chronometer. Meantime the table seemed a sort of Epsom Heath;[38] a regular ring, where the decanters galloped round. For fear one decanter should not with sufficient speed reach his destination, another was sent express after him to hurry him; and then a third to hurry the second; and so on with a fourth and fifth. And throughout all this nothing loud, nothing unmannerly, nothing turbulent. I am quite sure, from the scrupulous gravity and austerity of his air, that had Socrates, the field-marshal, perceived aught of indecorum in the company he served, he would have forthwith departed without giving warning. I afterward learned that, during the repast, an invalid bachelor in an adjoining chamber enjoyed his first sound refreshing slumber in three long, weary weeks.

It was the very perfection of quiet absorption of good living, good drinking, good feeling, and good talk. We were a band of brothers. Comfort—fraternal, household comfort, was the grand trait of the affair. Also, you could plainly see that these easy-hearted men had no wives or children to give an anxious thought. Almost all of them were travelers, too; for bachelors alone can travel freely, and without any twinges of their consciences touching desertion of the fireside.

The thing called pain, the bugbear styled trouble—those two legends seemed preposterous to their bachelor imaginations. How could men of liberal sense, ripe scholarship in the world, and capacious philosophical and convivial understandings—how could they suffer themselves to be imposed upon by such monkish fables? Pain! Trouble! As well talk of Catholic miracles. No such thing.—Pass the sherry, Sir.—Pooh, pooh! Can't be!—The port, Sir, if you please. Nonsense; don't tell me so.—The decanter stops with you, Sir, I believe.

And so it went.

Not long after the cloth was drawn our host glanced significantly upon Socrates, who, solemnly stepping to a stand, returned with an immense convolved horn, a regular Jericho horn,[39] mounted with polished silver, and otherwise chased and curiously enriched; not omitting two life-like goat's heads, with four more horns of solid silver, projecting from opposite sides of the mouth of the noble main horn.

Not having heard that our host was a performer on the bugle, I was surprised to see him lift this horn from the table, as if he were about to blow an inspiring blast. But I was relieved from this, and set quite right as touching the purposes of the horn, by his now inserting his thumb and forefinger into its mouth; whereupon a slight aroma was stirred up, and my nostrils were greeted with the smell of some choice Rappee. It was a mull[40] of snuff. It went the rounds. Capital idea this, thought I, of taking snuff about this juncture. This goodly fashion must be introduced among my countrymen at home, further ruminated I.

The remarkable decorum of the nine bachelors—a decorum not to be affected by any quantity of wine—a decorum unassailable by any degree of mirthfulness—this was again set in a forcible light to me, by now observing that, though they

---

[35]The Duke of Wellington (1769–1852), who defeated Napoleon at Waterloo (1815).
[36]Luigi Pulci (1432–1484), Italian poet, author of *Morgante Maggiore*, a serio-comic romantic poem.
[37]Alfred the Great (849–899), King of the West Saxons.

[38]British race track at Epsom, Surrey.
[39]Named after the rams horns used to tumble the walls of Jericho, enabling Joshua to take the city (Joshua 6:13–20).
[40]Small container; Rappee is a strong, fragrant snuff.

took snuff very freely, yet not a man so far violated the proprieties, or so far molested the invalid bachelor in the adjoining room as to indulge himself in a sneeze. The snuff was snuffed silently, as if it had been some fine innoxious[41] powder brushed off the wings of butterflies.

But fine though they be, bachelors' dinners, like bachelors' lives, can not endure forever. The time came for breaking up. One by one the bachelors took their hats, and two by two, and arm-in-arm they descended, still conversing, to the flagging of the court; some going to their neighboring chambers to turn over the *Decameron*[42] ere retiring for the night; some to smoke a cigar, promenading in the garden on the cool river-side; some to make for the street, call a hack, and be driven snugly to their distant lodgings.

I was the last lingerer.

"Well," said my smiling host, "what do you think of the Temple here, and the sort of life we bachelors make out to live in it?"

"Sir," said I, with a burst of admiring candor—"Sir, this is the very Paradise of Bachelors!"

II. THE TARTURUS OF MAIDS

It lies not far from Woedolor[1] Mountain in New England. Turning to the east, right out from among bright farms and sunny meadows, nodding in early June with odorous grasses, you enter ascendingly among bleak hills. These gradually close in upon a dusky pass, which, from the violent Gulf Stream of air unceasingly driving between its cloven walls of haggard rock, as well as from the tradition of a crazy spinster's hut having long ago stood somewhere hereabouts, is called the Mad Maid's Bellows'-pipe.

Winding along at the bottom of the gorge is a dangerously narrow wheel-road, occupying the bed of a former torrent. Following this road to its highest point, you stand as within a Dantean gateway.[2] From the steepness of the walls here, their strangely ebon hue, and the sudden contraction of the gorge, this particular point is called the Black Notch. The ravine now expandingly descends into a great, purple, hopper-shaped[3] hollow, far sunk among many Plutonian,[4] shaggy-wooded mountains. By the country people this hollow is called the Devil's Dungeon. Sounds of torrents fall on all sides upon the ear. These rapid waters unite at last in one turbid brick-colored stream, boiling through a flume among enormous boulders. They call this strange-colored torrent Blood River. Gaining a dark precipice it wheels suddenly to the west, and makes one maniac spring of sixty feet into the arms of a stunted wood of gray-haired pines, between which it thence eddies on its further way down to the invisible lowlands.

Conspicuously crowning a rocky bluff high to one side, at the cataract's verge, is the ruin of an old saw-mill, built in those primitive times when vast pines and hemlocks superabounded throughout the neighboring region. The black-mossed bulk of those immense, rough-hewn, and spike-knotted logs, here and there tumbled all together, in long abandonment and decay, or left in solitary, perilous projection over the cataract's gloomy brink, impart to this rude wooden ruin not only much of the aspect of one of rough-quarried stone, but also a sort of feudal, Rhineland, and Thurmberg look,[5] derived from the pinnacled wildness of the neighboring scenery.

---

[41]Harmless.
[42]By Giovanni Boccaccio (1313–1375), containing tales of intrigue and romance.
[1]Invented by Melville out of *woe* (misery) plus *dolor* (grief).
[2]I.e., gateway to hell; Dante Alighieri (1265–1321), Italian poet and author of the *Inferno* (first part of *The Divine Comedy*), described the inscription on the entrance to hell: "Abandon hope, all ye who enter here."

[3]Shaped like a hopper designed to pass on whatever is taken in.
[4]In classical mythology, Pluto ruled the underworld.
[5]I.e., a medieval lookout somewhat like the old castles and other antique structures found along the Rhine, a river in west Germany.

Not far from the bottom of the Dungeon stands a large white-washed building, relieved, like some great whited sepulchre,[6] against the sullen background of mountain-side firs, and other hardy evergreens, inaccessibly rising in grim terraces for some two thousand feet.

The building is a paper-mill.

Having embarked on a large scale in the seedsman's business (so extensively and broadcast, indeed, that at length my seeds were distributed through all the Eastern and Northern States, and even fell into the far soil of Missouri and the Carolinas), the demand for paper at my place became so great, that the expenditure soon amounted to a most important item in the general account. It need hardly be hinted how paper comes into use with seedsmen, as envelopes. These are mostly made of yellowish paper, folded square; and when filled, are all but flat, and being stamped, and superscribed with the nature of the seeds contained, assume not a little the appearance of business-letters ready for the mail. Of these small envelopes I used an incredible quantity—several hundreds of thousands in a year. For a time I had purchased my paper from the wholesale dealers in a neighboring town. For economy's sake, and partly for the adventure of the trip, I now resolved to cross the mountains, some sixty miles, and order my future paper at the Devil's Dungeon paper-mill.

The sleighing being uncommonly fine toward the end of January, and promising to hold so for no small period, in spite of the bitter cold I started one gray Friday noon in my pung,[7] well fitted with buffalo and wolf robes; and, spending one night on the road, next noon came in sight of Woedolor Mountain.

The far summit fairly smoked with frost; white vapors curled up from its white-wooded top, as from a chimney. The intense congelation made the whole country look like one petrifaction. The steel shoes of my pung craunched and gritted over the vitreous, chippy snow, as if it had been broken glass. The forests here and there skirting the route, feeling the same all-stiffening influence, their inmost fibres penetrated with the cold, strangely groaned—not in the swaying branches merely, but likewise in the vertical trunk—as the fitful gusts remorselessly swept through them. Brittle with excessive frost, many colossal tough-grained maples, snapped in twain like pipe-stems, cumbered the unfeeling earth.

Flaked all over with frozen sweat, white as a milky ram, his nostrils at each breath sending forth two horn-shaped shoots of heated respiration, Black, my good horse, but six years old, started at a sudden turn, where, right across the track—not ten minutes fallen—an old distorted hemlock lay, darkly undulatory as an anaconda.

Gaining the Bellows'-pipe, the violent blast, dead from behind, all but shoved my high-backed pung up-hill. The gust shrieked through the shivered pass, as if laden with lost spirits bound to the unhappy world. Ere gaining the summit, Black, my horse, as if exasperated by the cutting wind, slung out with his strong hind legs, tore the light pung straight up-hill, and sweeping grazingly through the narrow notch, sped downward madly past the ruined saw-mill. Into the Devil's Dungeon horse and cataract rushed together.

With might and main, quitting my seat and robes, and standing backward, with one foot braced against the dash-board, I rasped and churned the bit, and stopped him just in time to avoid collision, at a turn, with the bleak nozzle of a rock, couchant like a lion in the way—a road-side rock.

At first I could not discover the paper-mill.

---

[6]Cf. Matthew 23:27: "Woe unto you, scribes and Pharisees, hypocrites! for ye are like unto whited sepulchres, which indeed appear beautiful outward, but are within full of dead men's bones, and of all uncleanness."

[7]A box-like sleigh pulled by one horse.

The whole hollow gleamed with the white, except, here and there, where a pinnacle of granite showed one wind-swept angle bare. The mountains stood pinned in shrouds—a pass of Alpine corpses. Where stands the mill? Suddenly a whirling, humming sound broke upon my ear. I looked, and there, like an arrested avalanche, lay the large whitewashed factory. It was subordinately surrounded by a cluster of other and smaller buildings, some of which, from their cheap, blank air, great length, gregarious windows, and comfortless expression, no doubt were boarding-houses of the operatives.[8] A snow-white hamlet amidst the snows. Various rude, irregular squares and courts resulted from the somewhat picturesque clusterings of these buildings, owing to the broken, rocky nature of the ground, which forbade all method in their relative arrangement. Several narrow lanes and alleys, too, partly blocked with snow fallen from the roof, cut up the hamlet in all directions.

When, turning from the traveled highway, jingling with bells of numerous farmers—who, availing themselves of the fine sleighing, were dragging their wood to market—and frequently diversified with swift cutters dashing from inn to inn of the scattered villages—when, I say, turning from that bustling main-road, I by degrees wound into the Mad Maid's Bellows'-pipe, and saw the grim Black Notch beyond, then something latent, as well as something obvious in the time and scene, strangely brought back to my mind my first sight of dark and grimy Temple-Bar. And when Black, my horse, went darting through the Notch, perilously grazing its rocky wall, I remembered being in a runaway London omnibus, which in much the same sort of style, though by no means at an equal rate, dashed through the ancient arch of Wren.[9] Though the two objects did by no means completely correspond, yet this partial inadequacy but served to tinge the similitude not less with the vividness than the disorder of a dream. So that, when upon reining up at the protruding rock I at last caught sight of the quaint groupings of the factory-buildings, and with the traveled highway and the Notch behind, found myself all alone, silently and privily stealing through deep-cloven passages into this sequestered spot, and saw the long, high-gabled main factory edifice, with a rude tower—for hoisting heavy boxes—at one end, standing among its crowded outbuildings and boarding-houses, as the Temple Church amidst the surrounding offices and dormitories, and when the marvelous retirement of this mysterious mountain nook fastened its whole spell upon me, then, what memory lacked, all tributary imagination furnished, and I said to myself, "This is the very counterpart of the Paradise of Bachelors, but snowed upon, and frost-painted to a sepulchre."[10]

Dismounting, and warily picking my way down the dangerous declivity—horse and man both sliding now and then upon the icy ledges—at length I drove, or the blast drove me, into the largest square, before one side of the main edifice. Piercingly and shrilly the shotted blast blew by the corner; and redly and demoniacally boiled Blood River at one side. A long woodpile, of many scores of cords, all glittering in mail of crusted ice, stood crosswise in the square. A row of horse-posts, their north sides plastered with adhesive snow, flanked the factory wall. The bleak frost packed and paved the square as with some ringing metal.

The inverted similitude recurred—"The sweet, tranquil Temple garden, with the Thames bordering its green beds," strangely meditated I.

But where are the gay bachelors?

Then, as I and my horse stood shivering in the wind-spray, a girl ran from a neighboring dormitory door, and throwing her thin apron over her bare head, made for the opposite building.

---

[8] Workers.

[9] I.e., Temple Bar, London gateway.

[10] This is but one of several indications that Melville thought of the two stories as inseparably linked in meaning not explicitly presented in the text.

"One moment, my girl; is there no shed hereabouts which I may drive into?"

Pausing, she turned upon me a face pale with work, and blue with cold; an eye supernatural with unrelated misery.

"Nay," faltered I, "I mistook you. Go on; I want nothing."

Leading my horse close to the door from which she had come, I knocked. Another pale, blue girl appeared, shivering in the doorway as, to prevent the blast, she jealously held the door ajar.

"Nay, I mistake again. In God's name shut the door. But hold, is there no man about?"

That moment a dark-complexioned well-wrapped personage passed, making for the factory door, and spying him coming, the girl rapidly closed the other one.

"Is there no horse-shed here, Sir?"

"Yonder, to the wood-shed," he replied, and disappeared inside the factory.

With much ado I managed to wedge in horse and pung between the scattered piles of wood all sawn and split. Then, blanketing my horse, and piling my buffalo on the blanket's top, and tucking in its edges well around the breast-band and breeching, so that the wind might not strip him bare, I tied him fast, and ran lamely for the factory door, stiff with frost, and cumbered with my driver's dreadnaught.[11]

Immediately I found myself standing in a spacious place, intolerably lighted by long rows of windows, focusing inward the snowy scene without.

At rows of blank-looking counters sat rows of blank-looking girls, with blank, white folders in their blank hands, all blankly folding blank paper.

In one corner stood some huge frame of ponderous iron, with a vertical thing like a piston periodically rising and falling upon a heavy wooden block. Before it—its tame minister—stood a tall girl, feeding the iron animal with half-quires of rose-hued note paper, which, at every downward dab of the piston-like machine, received in the corner the impress of a wreath of roses. I looked from the rosy paper to the pallid cheek, but said nothing.

Seated before a long apparatus, strung with long, slender strings like any harp, another girl was feeding it with foolscap sheets, which, so soon as they curiously traveled from her on the cords, were withdrawn at the opposite end of the machine by a second girl. They came to the first girl blank; they went to the second girl ruled.

I looked upon the first girl's brow, and saw it was young and fair; I looked upon the second girl's brow, and saw it was ruled and wrinkled. Then, as I still looked, the two—for some small variety to the monotony—changed places; and where had stood the young, fair brow, now stood the ruled and wrinkled one.

Perched high upon a narrow platform, and still higher upon a high stool crowning it, sat another figure serving some other iron animal; while below the platform sat her mate in some sort of reciprocal attendance.

Not a syllable was breathed. Nothing was heard but the low, steady, overruling hum of the iron animals. The human voice was banished from the spot. Machinery—that vaunted slave of humanity—here stood menially served by human beings, who served mutely and cringingly as the slave serves the Sultan. The girls did not so much seem accessory wheels to the general machinery as mere cogs to the wheels.

All this scene around me was instantaneously taken in at one sweeping glance—even before I had proceeded to unwind the heavy fur tippet[12] from around my neck. But as soon as this fell from me the dark-complexioned man, standing close by, raised a sudden cry, and seizing my arm, dragged me out into

[11]Coat of thick woolen cloth.
[12]Long scarf.

the open air, and without pausing for a word instantly caught up some congealed snow and began rubbing both my cheeks.

"Two white spots like the whites of your eyes," he said; "man, your cheeks are frozen."

"That may well be," muttered I; "'tis some wonder the frost of the Devil's Dungeon strikes in no deeper. Rub away."

Soon a horrible, tearing pain caught at my reviving cheeks. Two gaunt bloodhounds, one on each side, seemed mumbling them. I seemed Actæon.[13]

Presently, when all was over, I re-entered the factory, made known my business, concluded it satisfactorily, and then begged to be conducted throughout the place to view it.

"Cupid is the boy for that," said the dark-complexioned man. "Cupid!" and by this odd fancy-name calling a dimpled, red-cheeked, spirited-looking, forward little fellow, who was rather impudently, I thought, gliding about among the passive-looking girls—like a gold fish through hueless waves—yet doing nothing in particular that I could see, the man bade him lead the stranger through the edifice.

"Come first and see the water-wheel," said this lively lad, with the air of boyishly-brisk importance.

Quitting the folding-room, we crossed some damp, cold boards, and stood beneath a great wet shed, incessantly showering with foam, like the green barnacled bow of some East India-man[14] in a gale. Round and round here went the enormous revolutions of the dark colossal waterwheel, grim with its one immutable purpose.

"This sets our whole machinery a-going, Sir; in every part of all these buildings; where the girls work and all."

I looked, and saw that the turbid waters of Blood River had not changed their hue by coming under the use of man.

"You make only blank paper; no printing of any sort, I suppose? All blank paper, don't you?"

"Certainly; what else should a paper-factory make?"

The lad here looked at me as if suspicious of my common-sense.

"Oh, to be sure!" said I, confused and stammering; "it only struck me as so strange that red waters should turn out pale chee—paper, I mean."

He took me up a wet and rickety stair to a great light room, furnished with no visible thing but rude, manger-like receptacles running all round its sides; and up to these mangers, like so many mares haltered to the rack, stood rows of girls. Before each was vertically thrust up a long, glittering scythe, immovably fixed at bottom to the manger-edge. The curve of the scythe, and its having no snath[15] to it, made it look exactly like a sword. To and fro, across the sharp edge, the girls forever dragged long strips of rags, washed white, picked from baskets at one side; thus ripping asunder every seam, and converting the tatters almost into lint. The air swam with the fine, poisonous particles, which from all sides darted, subtilely, as motes in sunbeams, into the lungs.

"This is the rag-room," coughed the boy.

"You find it rather stifling here," coughed I, in answer; "but the girls don't cough."

"Oh, they are used to it."

"Where do you get such hosts of rags?" picking up a handful from a basket.

---

[13]In classical mythology, the hunter was turned into a stag and killed by his own dogs for watching Diana (virgin goddess of the hunt) as she bathed.

[14]Large ship in the service of the East India Company, the large, prosperous British trading firm (1600–1858).
[15]Curved shaft or handle.

"Some from the country round about; some from far over sea—Leghorn[16] and London."

"'Tis not unlikely, then," murmured I, "that among these heaps of rags there may be some old shirts, gathered from the dormitories of the Paradise of Bachelors. But the buttons are all dropped off. Pray, my lad, do you ever find any bachelor's buttons hereabouts?"

"None grow in this part of the country. The Devil's Dungeon is no place for flowers."

"Oh! you mean the *flowers* so called—the Bachelor's Buttons?"

"And was not that what you asked about? Or did you mean the gold bosom-buttons of our boss, Old Bach, as our whispering girls all call him?"

"The man, then, I saw below is a bachelor, is he?"

"Oh, yes, he's a Bach."

"The edges of those swords, they are turned outward from the girls, if I see right; but their rags and fingers fly so, I can not distinctly see."

"Turned outward."

Yes, murmured I to myself; I see it now; turned outward; and each erected sword is so borne, edge-outward, before each girl. If my reading fails me not, just so, of old, condemned state-prisoners went from the hall of judgment to their doom: an officer before, bearing a sword, its edge turned outward, in significance of their fatal sentence. So, through consumptive[17] pallors of this blank, raggy life, go these white girls to death.

"Those scythes look very sharp," again turning toward the boy.

"Yes; they have to keep them so. Look!"

That moment two of the girls, dropping their rags, plied each a whet-stone up and down the sword-blade. My unaccustomed blood curdled at the sharp shriek of the tormented steel.

Their own executioners; themselves whetting the very swords that slay them; meditated I.

"What makes those girls so sheet-white, my lad?"

"Why"—with a roguish twinkle, pure ignorant drollery, not knowing heartlessness—"I suppose the handling of such white bits of sheets all the time makes them so sheety."

"Let us leave the rag-room now, my lad."

More tragical and more inscrutably mysterious than any mystic sight, human or machine, throughout the factory, was the strange innocence of cruel-heartedness in this usage-hardened boy.

"And now," said he, cheerily, "I suppose you want to see our great machine, which cost us twelve thousand dollars only last autumn. That's the machine that makes the paper, too. This way, Sir."

Following him, I crossed a large, bespattered place, with two great round vats in it, full of a white, wet, woolly-looking stuff, not unlike the albuminous part of an egg, soft-boiled.

"There," said Cupid, tapping the vats carelessly, "these are the first beginnings of the paper; this white pulp you see. Look how it swims bubbling round and round, moved by the paddle here. From hence it pours from both vats into that one common channel yonder; and so goes, mixed up and leisurely, to the great machine. And now for that."

He led me into a room, stifling with a strange, blood-like, abdominal heat, as if here, true enough, were being finally developed the germinous particles lately seen.

---

[16]Seaport in western Italy.
[17]Tubercular-like.

Before me, rolled out like some long Eastern manuscript, lay stretched one continuous length of iron frame-work—multitudinous and mystical, with all sorts of rollers, wheels, and cylinders, in slowly-measured and unceasing motion.

"Here first comes the pulp now," said Cupid, pointing to the nighest end of the machine. "See; first it pours out and spreads itself upon this wide, sloping board; and then—look—slides, thin and quivering, beneath the first roller there. Follow on now, and see it as it slides from under that to the next cylinder. There; see how it has become just a very little less pulpy now. One step more, and it grows still more to some slight consistence. Still another cylinder, and it is so knitted— though as yet mere dragon-fly wing—that it forms an air-bridge here, like a suspended cobweb, between two more separated rollers; and flowing over the last one, and under again, and doubling about there out of sight for a minute among all those mixed cylinders you indistinctly see, it reappears here, looking now at last a little less like pulp and more like paper, but still quite delicate and defective yet awhile. But—a little further onward, Sir, if you please—here now, at this further point, it puts on something of a real look, as if it might turn out to be something you might possibly handle in the end. But it's not yet done, Sir. Good way to travel yet, and plenty more of cylinders must roll it."

"Bless my soul!" said I, amazed at the elongation, interminable convolutions, and deliberate slowness of the machine; "it must take a long time for the pulp to pass from end to end, and come out paper."

"Oh! not so long," smiled the precocious lad, with a superior and patronizing air; "only nine minutes. But look; you may try it for yourself. Have you a bit of paper? Ah! here's a bit on the floor. Now mark that with any word you please, and let me dab it on here, and we'll see how long before it comes out at the other end."

"Well, let me see," said I, taking out my pencil; "come, I'll mark it with your name."

Bidding me take out my watch, Cupid adroitly dropped the inscribed slip on an exposed part of the incipient mass.

Instantly my eye marked the second-hand on my dial-plate.

Slowly I followed the slip, inch by inch; sometimes pausing for full half a minute as it disappeared beneath inscrutable groups of the lower cylinders, but only gradually to emerge again; and so, on, and on, and on—inch by inch; now in open sight, sliding along like a freckle on the quivering sheet; and then again wholly vanished; and so, on, and on, and on—inch by inch; all the time the main sheet growing more and more to final firmness—when, suddenly, I saw a sort of paper-fall, not wholly unlike a water-fall; a scissory sound smote my ear, as of some cord being snapped; and down dropped an unfolded sheet of perfect foolscap,[18] with my "Cupid" half faded out of it, and still moist and warm.

My travels were at an end, for here was the end of the machine.

"Well, how long was it?" said Cupid.

"Nine minutes to a second," replied I, watch in hand.

"I told you so."

For a moment a curious emotion filled me, not wholly unlike that which one might experience at the fulfillment of some mysterious prophecy. But how absurd, thought I again; the thing is a mere machine, the essence of which is unvarying punctuality and precision.

Previously absorbed by the wheels and cylinders, my attention was now directed to a sad-looking woman standing by.

"That is rather an elderly person so silently tending the machine-end here. She would not seem wholly used to it either."

---

[18]Writing paper of large size, 12 × 15 inches to 13 × 17 inches.

"Oh," knowingly whispered Cupid, through the din, "she only came last week. She was a nurse formerly. But the business is poor in these parts, and she's left it. But look at the paper she is piling there."

"Ay, foolscap," handling the piles of moist, warm sheets, which continually were being delivered into the woman's waiting hands. "Don't you turn out any thing but foolscap at this machine?"

"Oh, sometimes, but not often, we turn out finer work—cream-laid and royal sheets, we call them. But foolscap being in chief demand, we turn out foolscap most."

It was very curious. Looking at that blank paper continually dropping, dropping, dropping, my mind ran on in wonderings of those strange uses to which those thousand sheets eventually would be put. All sorts of writings would be writ on those now vacant things—sermons, lawyers' briefs, physicians' prescriptions, love-letters, marriage certificates, bills of divorce, registers of births, death-warrants, and so on, without end. Then, recurring back to them as they here lay all blank, I could not but bethink me of that celebrated comparison of John Locke, who, in demonstration of his theory that man had no innate ideas, compared the human mind at birth to a sheet of blank paper; something destined to be scribbled on, but what sort of characters no soul might tell.[19]

Pacing slowly to and fro along the involved machine, still humming with its play, I was struck as well by the inevitability as the evolvement-power in all its motions.

"Does that thin cobweb there," said I, pointing to the sheet in its more imperfect stage, "does that never tear or break? It is marvelous fragile, and yet this machine it passes through is so mighty."

"It never is known to tear a hair's point."

"Does it never stop—get clogged?"

"No. It *must* go. The machinery makes it go just *so;* just that very way, and at that very pace you there plainly *see* it go. The pulp can't help going."

Something of awe now stole over me, as I gazed upon this inflexible iron animal. Always, more or less, machinery of this ponderous, elaborate sort strikes, in some moods, strange dread into the human heart, as some living, panting Behemoth might. But what made the thing I saw so specially terrible to me was the metallic necessity, the unbudging fatality which governed it. Though, here and there, I could not follow the thin, gauzy vail of pulp in the course of its more mysterious or entirely invisible advance, yet it was indubitable that, at those points where it eluded me, it still marched on in unvarying docility to the autocratic cunning of the machine. A fascination fastened on me. I stood spell-bound and wandering in my soul. Before my eyes—there, passing in slow procession along the wheeling cylinders, I seemed to see, glued to the pallid incipience of the pulp, the yet more pallid faces of all the pallid girls I had eyed that heavy day. Slowly, mournfully, beseechingly, yet unresistingly, they gleamed along, their agony dimly outlined on the imperfect paper, like the print of the tormented face on the handkerchief of Saint Veronica.[20]

"Halloa! the heat of the room is too much for you," cried Cupid, staring at me.

"No—I am rather chill, if any thing."

"Come out, Sir—out—out," and, with the protecting air of a careful father, the precocious lad hurried me outside.

In a few moments, feeling revived a little, I went into the folding-room—the

---

[19]John Locke (1632–1704), in his *Essay Concerning Human Understanding* (1690), described the mind of a newly born child as a *tabula rasa*, a blank tablet.

[20]St. Veronica was said to have wiped the bleeding face of Jesus on his way to Calvary; an imprint of his face miraculously remained on her handkerchief.

first room I had entered, and where the desk for transacting business stood, surrounded by the blank counters and blank girls engaged at them.

"Cupid here has led me a strange tour," said I to the dark-complexioned man before mentioned, whom I had ere this discovered not only to be an old bachelor, but also the principal proprietor. "Yours is a most wonderful factory. Your great machine is a miracle of inscrutable intricacy."

"Yes, all our visitors think it so. But we don't have many. We are in a very out-of-the-way corner here. Few inhabitants, too. Most of our girls come from far-off villages."

"The girls," echoed I, glancing round at their silent forms. "Why is it, Sir, that in most factories, female operatives, of whatever age, are indiscriminately called girls, never women?"

"Oh! as to that—why, I suppose, the fact of their being generally unmarried—that's the reason, I should think. But it never struck me before. For our factory here, we will not have married women; they are apt to be off-and-on too much. We want none but steady workers: twelve hours to the day, day after day, through the three hundred and sixty-five days, excepting Sundays, Thanksgiving, and Fastdays. That's our rule. And so, having no married women, what females we have are rightly enough called girls."

"Then these are all maids," said I, while some pained homage to their pale virginity made me involuntarily bow.

"All maids."

Again the strange emotion filled me.

"Your cheeks look whitish yet, Sir," said the man, gazing at me narrowly. "You must be careful going home. Do they pain you at all now? It's a bad sign, if they do."

"No doubt, Sir," answered I, "when once I have got out of the Devil's Dungeon, I shall feel them mending."

"Ah, yes; the winter air in valleys, or gorges, or any sunken place, is far colder and more bitter than elsewhere. You would hardly believe it now, but it is colder here than at the top of Woedolor Mountain."

"I dare say it is, Sir. But time presses me; I must depart."

With that, remuffling myself in dread-naught and tippet, thrusting my hands into my huge seal-skin mittens, I sallied out into the nipping air, and found poor Black, my horse, all cringing and doubled up with the cold.

Soon, wrapped in furs and meditations, I ascended from the Devil's Dungeon.

At the Black Notch I paused, and once more bethought me of Temple-Bar. Then, shooting through the pass, all alone with inscrutable nature, I exclaimed— Oh! Paradise of Bachelors! and oh! Tartarus of Maids!

1855

Benito Cereno[1]

In the year 1799, Captain Amasa Delano, of Duxbury, in Massachusetts, commanding a large sealer[2] and general trader, lay at anchor with a valuable cargo, in the harbor of Santa Maria—a small, desert, uninhabited island toward the southern extremity of the long coast of Chile. There he had touched for water.

On the second day, not long after dawn, while lying in his berth, his mate came

---

[1] Melville's main source for this story is Amasa Delano's *Narrative of Voyages and Travels in the Northern and Southern Hemispheres* (1817).
[2] A ship hunting seals.

below, informing him that a strange sail was coming into the bay. Ships were then not so plenty in those waters as now. He rose, dressed, and went on deck.

The morning was one peculiar to that coast. Everything was mute and calm; everything gray. The sea, though undulated into long roods of swells, seemed fixed, and was sleeked at the surface like waved lead that has cooled and set in the smelter's mold. The sky seemed a gray surtout. Flights of troubled gray fowl, kith and kin with flights of troubled gray vapors among which they were mixed, skimmed low and fitfully over the waters, as swallows over meadows before storms. Shadows present, foreshadowing deeper shadows to come.

To Captain Delano's surprise, the stranger, viewed through the glass, showed no colors; though to do so upon entering a haven, however uninhabited in its shores, where but a single other ship might be lying, was the custom among peaceful seamen of all nations. Considering the lawlessness and loneliness of the spot, and the sort of stories, at that day, associated with those seas, Captain Delano's surprise might have deepened into some uneasiness had he not been a person of a singularly undistrustful good-nature, not liable, except on extraordinary and repeated incentives, and hardly then, to indulge in personal alarms, any way involving the imputation of malign evil in man. Whether, in view of what humanity is capable, such a trait implies, along with a benevolent heart, more than ordinary quickness and accuracy of intellectual perception, may be left to the wise to determine.

But whatever misgivings might have obtruded on first seeing the stranger, would almost, in any seaman's mind, have been dissipated by observing that, the ship, in navigating into the harbor, was drawing too near the land; a sunken reef making out off her bow. This seemed to prove her a stranger, indeed, not only to the sealer, but the island; consequently, she could be no wonted freebooter on that ocean. With no small interest, Captain Delano continued to watch her—a proceeding not much facilitated by the vapors partly mantling the hull, through which the far matin[3] light from her cabin streamed equivocally enough; much like the sun—by this time hemisphered on the rim of the horizon, and, apparently, in company with the strange ship entering the harbor—which, wimpled by the same low, creeping clouds, showed not unlike a Lima intriguante's one sinister eye peering across the Plaza from the Indian loop-hole of her dusk *saya-y-manto*.[4]

It might have been but a deception of the vapors, but, the longer the stranger was watched the more singular appeared her manœuvres. Ere long it seemed hard to decide whether she meant to come in or no—what she wanted, or what she was about. The wind, which had breezed up a little during the night, was not extremely light and baffling, which the more increased the apparent uncertainty of her movements.

Surmising, at last, that it might be a ship in distress, Captain Delano ordered his whale-boat to be dropped, and, much to the wary opposition of his mate, prepared to board her, and, at the least, pilot her in. On the night previous, a fishing party of the seamen had gone a long distance to some detached rocks out of sight from the sealer, and, an hour or two before daybreak, had returned, having met with no small success. Presuming that the stranger might have been long off soundings, the good captain put several baskets of the fish, for presents, into his boat, and so pulled away. From her continuing too near the sunken reef, deeming her in danger, calling to his men, he made all haste to apprise those on board of their situation. But, some time ere the boat came up, the wind, light though it was,

---

[3]Early morning.
[4]"Skirt and mantle" (Spanish); in the scene imagined, the shawl is arranged around the face to let only one eye peer out.

having shifted, had headed the vessel off, as well as partly broken the vapors from about her.

Upon gaining a less remote view, the ship, when made signally visible on the verge of the leaden-hued swells, with the shreds of fog here and there raggedly furring her, appeared like a whitewashed monastery after a thunder-storm, seen perched upon some dun cliff among the Pyrenees. But it was no purely fanciful resemblance which now, for a moment, almost led Captain Delano to think that nothing less than a ship-load of monks was before him. Peering over the bulwarks were what really seemed, in the hazy distance, throngs of dark cowls; while, fitfully revealed through the open port-holes, other dark moving figures were dimly descried, as of Black Friars[5] pacing the cloisters.

Upon a still nigher approach, this appearance was modified, and the true character of the vessel was plain—a Spanish merchantman of the first class, carrying negro slaves, amongst other valuable freight, from one colonial port to another. A very large, and, in its time, a very fine vessel, such as in those days were at intervals encountered along that main; sometimes superseded Acapulco treasure-ships, or retired frigates of the Spanish king's navy, which, like superannuated Italian palaces, still, under a decline of masters, preserved signs of former state.

As the whale-boat drew more and more nigh, the cause of the peculiar pipe-clayed aspect of the stranger was seen in the slovenly neglect pervading her. The spars, ropes, and great part of the bulwarks, looked woolly, from long unacquaintance with the scraper, tar, and the brush. Her keel seemed laid, her ribs put together, and she launched, from Ezekiel's Valley of Dry Bones.[6]

In the present business in which she was engaged, the ship's general model and rig appeared to have undergone no material change from their original warlike and Froissart[7] pattern. However, no guns were seen.

The tops[8] were large, and were railed about with what had once been octagonal net-work, all now in sad disrepair. These tops hung overhead like three ruinous aviaries, in one of which was seen perched, on a ratlin,[9] a white noddy, a strange fowl, so called from its lethargic, somnambulistic character, being frequently caught by hand at sea. Battered and mouldy, the castellated forecastle seemed some ancient turret, long ago taken by assault, and then left to decay. Toward the stern, two high-raised quarter galleries—the balustrades here and there covered with dry, tindery seamoss—opening out from the unoccupied state-cabin, whose dead-lights,[10] for all the mild weather, were hermetically closed and calked—these tenantless balconies hung over the sea as if it were the grand Venetian canal. But the principal relic of faded grandeur was the ample oval of the shield-like stern-piece, intricately carved with the arms of Castile and Leon,[11] medallioned about by groups of mythological or symbolical devices; uppermost and central of which was a dark satyr in a mask, holding his foot on the prostrate neck of a writhing figure, likewise masked.

Whether the ship had a figure-head, or only a plain beak, was not quite certain, owing to canvas wrapped about that part, either to protect it while undergoing a refurbishing, or else decently to hide its decay. Rudely painted or chalked, as in a sailor freak, along the forward side of a sort of pedestal below the canvas, was the sentence, "*Seguid vuestro jefe,*" (follow your leader); while upon the tarnished headboards, near by, appeared, in stately capitals, once gilt, the ship's name, "San Dom-

---

[5]Dominicans, an order of mendicant, preaching friars who wore black mantles.

[6]Ezekiel 37:1–14: Ezekiel tells of God placing him in a valley of dry bones and bidding him to prophesy to the bones the word of the Lord; Ezekiel obeyed, and the bones came together with life restored.

[7]Jean Froissart (1333?–1400?), French historian and chronicler (thus, an antique ship as described by Froissart).

[8]Platforms at the top of the masts.

[9]Ratlines were small pieces of rope joining the ship's shrouds, thus forming a ladder.

[10]Covers for the portholes or cabin windows.

[11]Old kingdoms of Spain.

INICK," each letter streakingly corroded with tricklings of copper-spike rust; while, like mourning weeds, dark festoons of sea-grass slimily swept to and fro over the name, with every hearse-like roll of the hull.

As, at last, the boat was hooked from the bow along toward the gangway amidship, its keel, while yet some inches separated from the hull, harshly grated as on a sunken coral reef. It proved a huge bunch of conglobated[12] barnacles adhering below the water to the side like a wen—a token of baffling airs and long calms passed somewhere in those seas.

Climbing the side, the visitor was at once surrounded by a clamorous throng of whites and blacks, but the latter outnumbering the former more than could have been expected, negro transportation-ship as the stranger in port was. But, in one language, and as with one voice, all poured out a common tale of suffering; in which the negresses, of whom there were not a few, exceeded the others in their dolorous vehemence. The scurvy, together with the fever, had swept off a great part of their number, more especially the Spaniards. Off Cape Horn they had narrowly escaped shipwreck; then, for days together, they had lain tranced without wind; their provisions were low; their water next to none; their lips that moment were baked.

While Captain Delano was thus made the mark of all eager tongues, his one eager glance took in all faces, with every other object about him.

Always upon first boarding a large and populous ship at sea, especially a foreign one, with a nondescript crew such as Lascars or Manila men,[13] the impression varies in a peculiar way from that produced by first entering a strange house with strange inmates in a strange land. Both house and ship—the one by its walls and blinds, the other by its high bulwarks like ramparts—hoard from view their interiors till the last moment; but in the case of the ship there is this addition: that the living spectacle it contains, upon its sudden and complete disclosure, has, in contrast with the blank ocean which zones it, something of the effect of enchantment. The ship seems unreal; these strange costumes, gestures, and faces, but a shadowy tableau just emerged from the deep, which directly must receive back what it gave.

Perhaps it was some such influence, as above is attempted to be described, which, in Captain Delano's mind, heightened whatever, upon a staid scrutiny, might have seemed unusual; especially the conspicuous figures of four elderly grizzled negroes, their heads like black, doddered willow tops, who, in venerable contrast to the tumult below them, were couched, sphynx-like, one on the starboard cat-head,[14] another on the larboard, and the remaining pair face to face on the opposite bulwarks above the main-chains. They each had bits of unstranded old junk in their hands, and, with a sort of stoical self-content, were picking the junk into oakum,[15] a small heap of which lay by their sides. They accompanied the task with a continuous, low, monotonous chant; droning and drooling away like so many gray-headed bag-pipers playing a funeral march.

The quarter-deck rose into an ample elevated poop, upon the forward verge of which, lifted, like the oakum-pickers, some eight feet above the general throng, sat along in a row, separated by regular spaces, the cross-legged figures of six other blacks; each with a rusty hatchet in his hand, which, with a bit of brick and a rag, he was engaged like a scullion in scouring; while between each two was a small stack of hatchets, their rusted edges turned forward awaiting a like operation. Though occasionally the four oakum-pickers would briefly address some

---

[12]Collected into a rounded mass.
[13]East Indian (or Malaysian) and Filipino sailors.
[14]A projecting beam at the bow of the ship used for raising or lowering the anchor.

[15]Hemp fibers used to caulk the ship's seams, picked from old tar-soaked ropes (junk).

person or persons in the crowd below, yet the six hatchet-polishers neither spoke to others, nor breathed a whisper among themselves, but sat intent upon their task, except at intervals, when, with the peculiar love in negroes of uniting industry with pastime, two and two they sideways clashed their hatchets together, like cymbals, with a barbarous din. All six, unlike the generality, had the raw aspect of unsophisticated Africans.

But that first comprehensive glance which took in those ten figures, with scores less conspicuous, rested but an instant upon them, as, impatient of the hubbub of voices, the visitor turned in quest of whomsoever it might be that commanded the ship.

But as if not unwilling to let nature make known her own case among his suffering charge, or else in despair of restraining it for the time, the Spanish captain, a gentlemanly, reserved-looking, and rather young man to a stranger's eye, dressed with singular richness, but bearing plain traces of recent sleepless cares and disquietudes, stood passively by, leaning against the main-mast, at one moment casting a dreary, spiritless look upon his excited people, at the next an unhappy glance toward his visitor. By his side stood a black of small stature, in whose rude face, as occasionally, like a shepherd's dog, he mutely turned it up into the Spaniard's, sorrow and affection were equally blended.

Struggling through the throng, the American advanced to the Spaniard, assuring him of his sympathies, and offering to render whatever assistance might be in his power. To which the Spaniard returned for the present but grave and ceremonious acknowledgments, his national formality dusked by the saturnine mood of ill-health.

But losing no time in mere compliments, Captain Delano, returning to the gangway, had his baskets of fish brought up; and as the wind still continued light, so that some hours at least must elapse ere the ship could be brought to the anchorage, he bade his men return to the sealer, and fetch back as much water as the whale-boat could carry, with whatever soft bread the steward might have, all the remaining pumpkins on board, with a box of sugar, and a dozen of his private bottles of cider.

Not many minutes after the boat's pushing off, to the vexation of all, the wind entirely died away, and the tide turning, began drifting back the ship helplessly seaward. But trusting this would not long last, Captain Delano sought, with good hopes, to cheer up the strangers, feeling no small satisfaction that, with persons in their condition, he could—thanks to his frequent voyages along the Spanish main[16]—converse with some freedom in their native tongue.

While left alone with them, he was not long in observing somethings tending to heighten his first impressions; but surprise was lost in pity, both for the Spaniards and blacks, alike evidently reduced from scarcity of water and provisions; while long-continued suffering seemed to have brought out the less good-natured qualities of the negroes, besides, at the same time, impairing the Spaniard's authority over them. But, under the circumstances, precisely this condition of things was to have been anticipated. In armies, navies, cities, or families, in nature herself, nothing more relaxes good order than misery. Still, Captain Delano was not without the idea, that had Benito Cereno been a man of greater energy, misrule would hardly have come to the present pass. But the debility, constitutional or induced by hardships, bodily and mental, of the Spanish captain, was too obvious to be overlooked. A prey to settled dejection, as if long mocked with hope he would not now indulge it, even when it had ceased to be a mock, the prospect of that day, or

[16]Areas in which Spanish ships travelled, here the coastal waters of South America, on both the Atlantic and Pacific sides.

evening at furthest, lying at anchor, with plenty of water for his people, and a brother captain to counsel and befriend, seemed in no perceptible degree to encourage him. His mind appeared unstrung, if not still more seriously affected. Shut up in these oaken walls, chained to one dull round of command, whose unconditionality cloyed him, like some hypochondriac abbot he moved slowly about, at times suddenly pausing, starting, or staring, biting his lip, biting his finger-nail, flushing, paling, twitching his beard, with other symptoms of an absent or moody mind. This distempered spirit was lodged, as before hinted, in as distempered a frame. He was rather tall, but seemed never to have been robust, and now with nervous suffering was almost worn to a skeleton. A tendency to some pulmonary complaint appeared to have been lately confirmed. His voice was like that of one with lungs half gone—hoarsely suppressed, a husky whisper. No wonder that, as in this state he tottered about, his private servant apprehensively followed him. Sometimes the negro gave his master his arm, or took his handkerchief out of his pocket for him; performing these and similar offices with that affectionate zeal which transmutes into something filial or fraternal acts in themselves but menial; and which has gained for the negro the repute of making the most pleasing body-servant in the world; one, too, whom a master need be on no stiffly superior terms with, but may treat with familiar trust; less a servant than a devoted companion.

Marking the noisy indocility of the blacks in general, as well as what seemed the sullen inefficiency of the whites it was not without humane satisfaction that Captain Delano witnessed the steady good conduct of Babo.

But the good conduct of Babo, hardly more than the ill-behavior of others, seemed to withdraw the half-lunatic Don Benito from his cloudy languor. Not that such precisely was the impression made by the Spaniard on the mind of his visitor. The Spaniard's individual unrest was, for the present, but noted as a conspicuous feature in the ship's general affliction. Still, Captain Delano was not a little concerned at what he could not help taking for the time to be Don Benito's unfriendly indifference towards himself. The Spaniard's manner, too, conveyed a sort of sour and gloomy disdain, which he seemed at no pains to disguise. But this the American in charity ascribed to the harassing effects of sickness, since, in former instances, he had noted that there are peculiar natures on whom prolonged physical suffering seems to cancel every social instinct of kindness; as if, forced to black bread themselves, they deemed it but equity that each person coming nigh them should, indirectly, by some slight or affront, be made to partake of their fare.

But ere long Captain Delano bethought him that, indulgent as he was at the first, in judging the Spaniard, he might not, after all, have exercised charity enough. At bottom it was Don Benito's reserve which displeased him; but the same reserve was shown towards all but his faithful personal attendant. Even the formal reports which, according to sea-usage, were, at stated times, made to him by some petty underling, either a white, mulatto or black, he hardly had patience enough to listen to, without betraying contemptuous aversion. His manner upon such occasions was, in its degree, not unlike that which might be supposed to have been his imperial countryman's, Charles V,[17] just previous to the anchoritish retirement of that monarch from the throne.

This splenetic disrelish of his place was evinced in almost every function pertaining to it. Proud as he was moody, he condescended to no personal mandate. Whatever special orders were necessary, their delivery was delegated to his body-servant, who in turn transferred them to their ultimate destination, through runners, alert Spanish boys or slave boys, like pages or pilot-fish[18] within easy call

---

[17]Holy Roman Emperor and King of Spain (1500–1558); he abdicated and retired to a monastery in 1557.

[18]Small fish swimming alongside sharks, thus seeming to pilot them.

continually hovering round Don Benito. So that to have beheld this undemonstrative invalid gliding about, apathetic and mute, no landsman could have dreamed that in him was lodged a dictatorship beyond which, while at sea, there was no earthly appeal.

Thus, the Spaniard, regarded in his reserve, seemed the involuntary victim of mental disorder. But, in fact, his reserve might, in some degree, have proceeded from design. If so, then here was evinced the unhealthy climax of that icy though conscientious policy, more or less adopted by all commanders of large ships, which, except in signal emergencies, obliterates alike the manifestation of sway with every trace of sociality; transforming the man into a block, or rather into a loaded cannon, which, until there is call for thunder, has nothing to say.

Viewing him in this light, it seemed but a natural token of the perverse habit induced by a long course of such hard self-restraint, that, notwithstanding the present condition of his ship, the Spaniard should still persist in a demeanor, which, however harmless, or, it may be, appropriate, in a well-appointed vessel, such as the *San Dominick* might have been at the outset of the voyage, was anything but judicious now. But the Spaniard, perhaps, thought that it was with captains as with gods: reserve, under all events, must still be their cue. But probably this appearance of slumbering dominion might have been but an attempted disguise to conscious imbecility—not deep policy, but shallow device. But be all this as it might, whether Don Benito's manner was designed or not, the more Captain Delano noted its pervading reserve, the less he felt uneasiness at any particular manifestation of that reserve towards himself.

Neither were his thoughts taken up by the captain alone. Wonted to the quiet orderliness of the sealer's comfortable family of a crew, the noisy confusion of the *San Dominick's* suffering host repeatedly challenged his eye. Some prominent breaches, not only of discipline but of decency, were observed. These Captain Delano could not but ascribe, in the main, to the absence of those subordinate deck-officers to whom, along with higher duties, is intrusted what may be styled the police department of a populous ship. True, the old oakum-pickers appeared at times to act the part of monitorial constables to their countrymen, the blacks; but though occasionally succeeding in allaying trifling outbreaks now and then between man and man, they could do little or nothing toward establishing general quiet. The *San Dominick* was in the condition of a transatlantic emigrant ship, among whose multitude of living freight are some individuals, doubtless, as little troublesome as crates and bales; but the friendly remonstrances of such with their ruder companions are of not so much avail as the unfriendly arm of the mate. What the *San Dominick* wanted was, what the emigrant ship has, stern superior officers. But on these decks not so much as a fourth-mate was to be seen.

The visitor's curiosity was roused to learn the particulars of those mishaps which had brought about such absenteeism, with its consequences; because, though deriving some inkling of the voyage from the wails which at the first moment had greeted him, yet of the details no clear understanding had been had. The best account would, doubtless, be given by the captain. Yet at first the visitor was loth to ask it, unwilling to provoke some distant rebuff. But plucking up courage, he at last accosted Don Benito, renewing the expression of his benevolent interest, adding, that did he (Captain Delano) but know the particulars of the ship's misfortunes, he would, perhaps, be better able in the end to relieve them. Would Don Benito favor him with the whole story?

Don Benito faltered; then, like some somnambulist suddenly interfered with, vacantly stared at his visitor, and ended by looking down on the deck. He maintained this posture so long, that Captain Delano, almost equally disconcerted, and involuntarily almost as rude, turned suddenly from him, walking forward to accost one of the Spanish seamen for the desired information. But he had hardly gone five paces, when, with a sort of eagerness, Don Benito invited him back, regretting his momentary absence of mind, and professing readiness to gratify him.

While most part of the story was being given, the two captains stood on the after part of the main-deck, a privileged spot, no one being near but the servant.

"It is now a hundred and ninety days," began the Spaniard, in his husky whisper, "that this ship, well officered and well manned, with several cabin passengers—some fifty Spaniards in all—sailed from Buenos Ayres bound to Lima, with a general cargo, hardware, Paraguay tea and the like—and," pointing forward, "that parcel of negroes, now not more than a hundred and fifty, as you see, but then numbering over three hundred souls. Off Cape Horn we had heavy gales. In one moment, by night, three of my best officers, with fifteen sailors, were lost, with the main-yard;[19] the spar snapping under them in the slings,[20] as they sought, with heavers,[21] to beat down the icy sail. To lighten the hull, the heavier sacks of maté[22] were thrown into the sea, with most of the water-pipes[23] lashed on deck at the time. And this last necessity it was, combined with the prolonged detentions afterwards experienced, which eventually brought about our chief causes of suffering. When——"

Here there was a sudden fainting attack of his cough, brought on, no doubt, by his mental distress. His servant sustained him, and drawing a cordial from his pocket placed it to his lips. He a little revived. But unwilling to leave him unsupported while yet imperfectly restored, the black with one arm still encircled his master, at the same time keeping his eye fixed on his face, as if to watch for the first sign of complete restoration, or relapse, as the event might prove.

The Spaniard proceeded, but brokenly and obscurely, as one in a dream.

—"Oh, my God! rather than pass through what I have, with joy I would have hailed the most terrible gales; but——"

His cough returned and with increased violence; this subsiding, with reddened lips and closed eyes he fell heavily against his supporter.

"His mind wanders. He was thinking of the plague that followed the gales," plaintively sighed the servant; "my poor, poor master!" wringing one hand, and with the other wiping the mouth. "But be patient, Señor," again turning to Captain Delano, "these fits do not last long; master will soon be himself."

Don Benito reviving, went on; but as this portion of the story was very brokenly delivered, the substance only will here be set down.

It appeared that after the ship had been many days tossed in storms off the Cape, the scurvy broke out, carrying off numbers of the whites and blacks. When at last they had worked round into the Pacific, their spars and sails were so damaged, and so inadequately handled by the surviving mariners, most of whom were become invalids, that, unable to lay her northerly course by the wind, which was powerful, the unmanageable ship, for successive days and nights, was blown northwestward, where the breeze suddenly deserted her, in unknown waters, to sultry calms. The absence of the water-pipes now proved as fatal to life as before their presence had menaced it. Induced, or at least aggravated, by the more than scanty allowance of water, a malignant fever followed the scurvy; with the excessive heat of the lengthened calm, making such short work of it as to sweep away, as by billows, whole families of the Africans, and a yet larger number, proportionably, of the Spaniards, including, by a luckless fatality, every remaining officer on board. Consequently, in the smart west winds eventually following the calm, the already rent sails, having to be simply dropped, not furled, at need, had been

---

[19]Rod or spar at right angles to the mainmast to support the sail.
[20]Slings are ropes or chains attached to the lower yard and passing around the mast near the masthead for support.

[21]Short lever for twisting or prying.
[22]Tea (Spanish American).
[23]Kegs of water.

gradually reduced to the beggars' rags they were now. To procure substitutes for his lost sailors, as well as supplies of water and sails, the captain, at the earliest opportunity, had made for Valdivia, the southernmost civilized port of Chile and South America; but upon nearing the coast the thick weather had prevented him from so much as sighting that harbor. Since which period, almost without a crew, and almost without canvas and almost without water, and, at intervals, giving its added dead to the sea, the *San Dominick* had been battledored[24] about by contrary winds, inveigled by currents, or grown weedy in calms. Like a man lost in woods, more than once she had doubled upon her own track.

"But throughout these calamities," huskily continued Don Benito, painfully turning in the half embrace of his servant, "I have to thank those negroes you see, who, though to your inexperienced eyes appearing unruly, have, indeed, conducted themselves with less of restlessness than even their owner could have thought possible under such circumstances."

Here he again fell faintly back. Again his mind wandered; but he rallied, and less obscurely proceeded.

"Yes, their owner was quite right in assuring me that no fetters would be needed with his blacks; so that while, as is wont in this transportation, those negroes have always remained upon deck—not thrust below, as in the Guineamen[25]—they have, also, from the beginning, been freely permitted to range within given bounds at their pleasure."

Once more the faintness returned—his mind roved—but, recovering, he resumed:

"But it is Babo here to whom, under God, I owe not only my own preservation, but likewise to him, chiefly, the merit is due, of pacifying his more ignorant brethren, when at intervals tempted to murmurings."

"Ah, master," sighed the black, bowing his face, "don't speak of me; Babo is nothing; what Babo has done was but duty."

"Faithful fellow!" cried Captain Delano. "Don Benito, I envy you such a friend; slave I cannot call him."

As master and man stood before him, the black upholding the white, Captain Delano could not but bethink him of the beauty of that relationship which could present such a spectacle of fidelity on the one hand and confidence on the other. The scene was heightened by the contrast in dress, denoting their relative positions. The Spaniard wore a loose Chile jacket of dark velvet; white small-clothes and stockings, with silver buckles at the knee and instep; a high-crowned sombrero, of fine grass, a slender sword, silver mounted, hung from a knot in his sash—the last being an almost invariable adjunct, more for utility than ornament, of a South American gentleman's dress to this hour. Excepting when his occasional nervous contortions brought about disarray, there was a certain precision in his attire curiously at variance with the unsightly disorder around; especially in the belittered Ghetto, forward of the mainmast, wholly occupied by the blacks.

The servant wore nothing but wide trowsers, apparently, from their coarseness and patches, made out of some old topsail; they were clean, and confined at the waist by a bit of unstranded rope which, with his composed, deprecatory air at times, made him look something like a begging friar of St. Francis.[26]

However unsuitable for the time and place, at least in the blunt-thinking American's eyes, and however strangely surviving in the midst of all his afflictions, the toilette of Don Benito might not, in fashion at least, have gone beyond the style of the day among South Americans of his class. Though on the present voyage sail-

---

[24]From "battledore," the wooden paddle used in the game to hit the shuttlecock.
[25]Slaveships that traded with Guinea in west Africa.

[26]I.e., a member of the order established by St. Francis of Assisi (1182–1226), dedicated to poverty.

ing from Buenos Ayres, he had avowed himself a native and resident of Chile, whose inhabitants had not so generally adopted the plain coat and once plebeian pantaloons; but, with a becoming modification, adhered to their provincial costume, picturesque as any in the world. Still, relatively to the pale history of the voyage, and his own pale face, there seemed something so incongruous in the Spaniard's apparel, as almost to suggest the image of an invalid courtier tottering about London streets in the time of the plague.

The portion of the narrative which, perhaps, most excited interest, as well as some surprise, considering the latitudes in question, was the long calms spoken of, and more particularly the ship's so long drifting about. Without communicating the opinion, of course, the American could not but impute at least part of the detentions both to clumsy seamanship and faulty navigation. Eying Don Benito's small, yellow hands, he easily inferred that the young captain had not got into command at the hawse-hole, but the cabin-window;[27] and if so, why wonder at incompetence, in youth, sickness, and gentility united?

But drowning criticism in compassion, after a fresh repetition of his sympathies, Captain Delano, having heard out his story, not only engaged, as in the first place, to see Don Benito and his people supplied in their immediate bodily needs, but, also, now further promised to assist him in procuring a large permanent supply of water, as well as some sails and rigging; and, though it would involve no small embarrassment to himself, yet he would spare three of his best seamen for temporary deck-officers; so that without delay the ship might proceed to Concepcion, there fully to refit for Lima, her destined port.

Such generosity was not without its effect, even upon the invalid. His face lighted up; eager and hectic, he met the honest glance of his visitor. With gratitude he seemed overcome.

"This excitement is bad for master," whispered the servant, taking his arm, and with soothing words gently drawing him aside.

When Don Benito returned, the American was pained to observe that his hopefulness, like the sudden kindling in his cheek, was but febrile and transient.

Ere long, with a joyless mien, looking up towards the poop, the host invited his guest to accompany him there, for the benefit of what little breath of wind might be stirring.

As during the telling of the story, Captain Delano had once or twice started at the occasional cymballing of the hatchet-polishers, wondering why such an interruption should be allowed, especially in that part of the ship, and in the ears of an invalid; and moreover, as the hatchets had anything but an attractive look, and the handlers of them still less so, it was, therefore, to tell the truth, not without some lurking reluctance, or even shrinking, it may be, that Captain Delano, with apparent complaisance, acquiesced in his host's invitation. The more so, since, with an untimely caprice of punctilio, rendered distressing by his cadaverous aspect, Don Benito, with Castilian[28] bows, solemnly insisted upon his guest's preceding him up the ladder leading to the elevation; where, one on each side of the last step, sat for armorial supporters and sentries two of the ominous file. Gingerly enough stepped good Captain Delano between them, and in the instant of leaving them behind, like one running the gauntlet, he felt an apprehensive twitch in the calves of his legs.

But when, facing about, he saw the whole file, like so many organ-grinders, still

---

[27]I.e., Don Benito's hands show he did not work his way up (as, for example, tending the metal-lined hole through which cables pass), but began as an officer in his seagoing profession.
[28]Graceful, deferential.

stupidly intent on their work, unmindful of everything beside, he could not but smile at his late fidgety panic.

Presently, while standing with his host, looking forward upon the decks below, he was struck by one of those instances of insubordination previously alluded to. Three black boys, with two Spanish boys, were sitting together on the hatches, scraping a rude wooden platter, in which some scanty mess had recently been cooked. Suddenly, one of the black boys, enraged at a word dropped by one of his white companions, seized a knife, and, though called to forbear by one of the oakum-pickers, struck the lad over the head, inflicting a gash from which blood flowed.

In amazement, Captain Delano inquired what this meant. To which the pale Don Benito dully muttered, that it was merely the sport of the lad.

"Pretty serious sport, truly," rejoined Captain Delano. "Had such a thing happened on board the *Bachelor's Delight,* instant punishment would have followed."

At these words the Spaniard turned upon the American one of his sudden, staring, half-lunatic looks; then, relapsing into his torpor, answered, "Doubtless, doubtless, Señor."

Is it, thought Captain Delano, that this hapless man is one of those paper captains I've known, who by policy wink at what by power they cannot put down? I know no sadder sight than a commander who has little of command but the name.

"I should think, Don Benito," he now said, glancing towards the oakum-picker who had sought to interfere with the boys, "that you would find it advantageous to keep all your blacks employed, especially the younger ones, no matter at what useless task, and no matter what happens to the ship. Why, even with my little band, I find such a course indispensable. I once kept a crew on my quarter-deck thrumming[29] mats for my cabin, when, for three days, I had given up my ship—mats, men, and all—for a speedy loss, owing to the violence of a gale, in which we could do nothing but helplessly drive before it."

"Doubtless, doubtless," muttered Don Benito.

"But," continued Captain Delano, again glancing upon the oakum-pickers and then at the hatchet-polishers, near by, "I see you keep some, at least, of your host employed."

"Yes," was again the vacant response.

"Those old men there, shaking their pows[30] from their pulpits," continued Captain Delano, pointing to the oakum-pickers, "seem to act the part of old dominies[31] to the rest, little heeded as their admonitions are at times. Is this voluntary on their part, Don Benito, or have you appointed them shepherds to your flock of black sheep?"

"What posts they fill, I appointed them," rejoined the Spaniard, in an acrid tone, as if resenting some supposed satiric reflection.

And these others, these Ashantee[32] conjurors here," continued Captain Delano, rather uneasily eying the brandished steel of the hatchet-polishers, where, in spots, it had been brought to a shine, "this seems a curious business they are at, Don Benito?"

"In the gales we met," answered the Spaniard, "what of our general cargo was not thrown overboard was much damaged by the brine. Since coming into calm weather, I have had several cases of knives and hatchets daily brought up for overhauling and cleaning."

"A prudent idea, Don Benito. You are part owner of ship and cargo, I presume; but none of the slaves, perhaps?"

---

[29]Weaving ropes into canvas to create a mat with a rough surface, used to prevent chafing.
[30]Heads.

[31]Pastors or clergymen.
[32]West African people.

"I am owner of all you see," impatiently returned Don Benito, "except the main company of blacks, who belonged to my late friend, Alexandro Aranda."

As he mentioned this name, his air was heart-broken; his knees shook; his servant supported him.

Thinking he divined the cause of such unusual emotion, to confirm his surmise, Captain Delano, after a pause, said: "And may I ask, Don Benito, whether—since a while ago you spoke of some cabin passengers—the friend, whose loss so afflicts you, at the outset of the voyage accompanied his blacks?"

"Yes."

"But died of the fever?"

"Died of the fever. Oh, could I but——" Again quivering, the Spaniard paused.

"Pardon me," said Captain Delano, lowly, "but I think that, by a sympathetic experience, I conjecture, Don Benito, what it is that gives the keener edge to your grief. It was once my hard fortune to lose, at sea, a dear friend, my own brother, then supercargo. Assured of the welfare of his spirit, its departure I could have borne like a man; but that honest eye, that honest hand—both of which had so often met mine—and that warm heart; all, all—like scraps to the dogs—to throw all to the sharks! It was then I vowed never to have for fellow-voyager a man I loved, unless, unbeknown to him, I had provided every requisite, in case of a fatality, for embalming his mortal part for interment on shore. Were your friend's remains now on board this ship, Don Benito, not thus strangely would the mention of his name affect you."

"On board this ship?" echoed the Spaniard. Then, with horrified gestures, as directed against some spectre, he unconsciously fell into the ready arms of his attendant, who, with a silent appeal toward Captain Delano, seemed beseeching him not again to broach a theme so unspeakably distressing to his master.

This poor fellow now, thought the pained American, is the victim of that sad superstition which associates goblins with the deserted body of man, as ghosts with an abandoned house. How unlike are we made! What to me, in like case, would have been a solemn satisfaction, the bare suggestion, even, terrifies the Spaniard into this trance. Poor Alexandro Aranda! what would you say could you here see your friend—who, on former voyages, when you, for months, were left behind, has, I dare say, often longed, and longed, for one peep at you—now transported with terror at the least thought of having you anyway nigh him.

At this moment, with a dreary grave-yard toll, betokening a flaw, the ship's forecastle bell, smote by one of the grizzled oakum-pickers, proclaimed ten o'clock, through the leaden calm; when Captain Delano's attention was caught by the moving figure of a gigantic black, emerging from the general crowd below, and slowly advancing towards the elevated poop. An iron collar was about his neck, from which depended a chain, thrice wound round his body; the terminating links padlocked together at a broad band of iron, his girdle.

"How like a mute Atufal moves," murmured the servant.

The black mounted the steps of the poop, and, like a brave prisoner, brought up to receive sentence, stood in unquailing muteness before Don Benito, now recovered from his attack.

At the first glimpse of his approach, Don Benito had started, a resentful shadow swept over his face; and, as with the sudden memory of bootless[33] rage, his white lips glued together.

This is some mulish mutineer, thought Captain Delano, surveying, not without a mixture of admiration, the colossal form of the negro.

---

[33]Useless.

"See, he waits your question, master," said the servant.

Thus reminded, Don Benito, nervously averting his glance, as if shunning, by anticipation, some rebellious response, in a disconcerted voice, thus spoke:—

"Atufal, will you ask my pardon, now?"

The black was silent.

"Again, master," murmured the servant, with bitter upbraiding eying his countryman, "Again, master; he will bend to master yet."

"Answer," said Don Benito, still averting his glance, "say but the one word, *pardon,* and your chains shall be off."

Upon this, the black, slowly raising both arms, let them lifelessly fall, his links clanking, his head bowed; as much as to say, "No, I am content."

"Go," said Don Benito, with inkept and unknown emotion.

Deliberately as he had come, the black obeyed.

"Excuse me, Don Benito," said Captain Delano, "but this scene surprises me; what means it, pray?"

"It means that that negro alone, of all the band, has given me peculiar cause of offense. I have put him in chains; I——"

Here he paused; his hand to his head, as if there were a swimming there, or a sudden bewilderment of memory had come over him; but meeting his servant's kindly glance seemed reassured, and proceeded:—

"I could not scourge such a form. But I told him he must ask my pardon. As yet he has not. At my command, every two hours he stands before me."

"And how long has this been?"

"Some sixty days."

"And obedient in all else? And respectful?"

"Yes."

"Upon my conscience, then," exclaimed Captain Delano, impulsively, "he has a royal spirit in him, this fellow."

"He may have some right to it," bitterly returned Don Benito, "he says he was king in his own land."

"Yes," said the servant, entering a word, "those slits in Atufal's ears once held wedges of gold; but poor Babo here, in his own land, was only a poor slave; a black man's slave was Babo, who now is the white's."

Somewhat annoyed by these conversational familiarities, Captain Delano turned curiously upon the attendant, then glanced inquiringly at his master; but, as if long wonted to these little informalities, neither master nor man seemed to understand him.

"What, pray, was Atufal's offense, Don Benito?" asked Captain Delano; "if it was not something very serious, take a fool's advice, and, in view of his general docility, as well as in some natural respect for his spirit, remit him his penalty."

"No, no, master never will do that," here murmured the servant to himself, "proud Atufal must first ask master's pardon. The slave there carries the padlock, but master here carries the key."

His attention thus directed, Captain Delano now noticed for the first, that, suspended by a slender silken cord, from Don Benito's neck, hung a key. At once, from the servant's muttered syllables, divining the key's purpose, he smiled and said:—"So, Don Benito—padlock and key—significant symbols, truly."

Biting his lip, Don Benito faltered.

Though the remark of Captain Delano, a man of such native simplicity as to be incapable of satire or irony, had been dropped in playful allusion to the Spaniard's singularly evidenced lordship over the black; yet the hypochondriac seemed some way to have taken it as a malicious reflection upon his confessed inability thus far to break down, at least, on a verbal summons, the entrenched will of the slave. Deploring this supposed misconception, yet despairing of correcting it, Captain Delano shifted the subject; but finding his companion more than ever withdrawn, as if still sourly digesting the lees of the presumed affront above-mentioned, by and by Captain Delano likewise became less talkative, oppressed, against his own will, by what seemed the secret vindictiveness of the morbidly sensitive Spaniard. But the good sailor, himself of a quite contrary disposition, refrained, on his part, alike from the appearance as from the feeling of resentment, and if silent, was only so from contagion.

Presently the Spaniard, assisted by his servant, somewhat discourteously crossed over from his guest; a procedure which, sensibly enough, might have been allowed to pass for idle caprice of ill-humor, had not master and man, lingering round the corner of the elevated skylight, begun whispering together in low voices. This was unpleasing. And more: the moody air of the Spaniard, which at times had not been without a sort of valetudinarian stateliness, now seemed anything but dignified; while the menial familiarity of the servant lost its original charm of simplehearted attachment.

In his embarrassment, the visitor turned his face to the other side of the ship. By so doing, his glance accidentally fell on a young Spanish sailor, a coil of rope in his hand, just stepped from the deck to the first round of the mizzenrigging. Perhaps the man would not have been particularly noticed, were it not that, during his ascent to one of the yards, he, with a sort of covert intentness, kept his eye fixed on Captain Delano, from whom, presently, it passed, as if by a natural sequence, to the two whisperers.

His own attention thus redirected to that quarter, Captain Delano gave a slight start. From something in Don Benito's manner just then, it seemed as if the visitor had, at least partly, been the subject of the withdrawn consultation going on—a conjecture as little agreeable to the guest as it was little flattering to the host.

The singular alternations of courtesy and ill-breeding in the Spanish captain were unaccountable, except on one of two suppositions—innocent lunacy, or wicked imposture.

But the first idea, though it might naturally have occurred to an indifferent observer, and, in some respect, had not hitherto been wholly a stranger to Captain Delano's mind, yet, now that, in an incipient way, he began to regard the stranger's conduct something in the light of an intentional affront, of course the idea of lunacy was virtually vacated. But if not a lunatic, what then? Under the circumstances, would a gentleman, nay, any honest boor, act the part now acted by his host? The man was an imposter. Some low-born adventurer, masquerading as an oceanic grandee; yet so ignorant of the first requisites of mere gentlemanhood as to be betrayed into the present remarkable indecorum. That strange ceremoniousness, too, at other times evinced, seemed not uncharacteristic of one playing a part above his real level. Benito Cereno—Don Benito Cereno—a sounding name. One, too, at that period, not unknown, in the surname, to super-cargoes and sea captains trading along the Spanish Main, as belonging to one of the most enterprising and extensive mercantile families in all those provinces; several members of it having titles; a sort of Castilian Rothschild,[34] with a noble brother, or cousin, in every great trading town of South America. The alleged Don Benito was in early manhood, about twenty-nine or thirty. To assume a sort of roving cadetship in the maritime affairs of such a house, what more likely scheme for a young knave of talent and spirit? But the Spaniard was a pale invalid. Never mind. For even to the degree of simulating mortal disease, the craft of some tricksters had been known to attain. To think that, under the aspect of infantile weakness, the most savage energies might be couched—those velvets of the Spaniard but the silky paw to his fangs.

---

[34]A great German banking family.

From no train of thought did these fancies come; not from within, but from without; suddenly, too, and in one throng, like hoar frost; yet as soon to vanish as the mild sun of Captain Delano's good-nature regained its meridian.

Glancing over once more towards his host—whose sideface, revealed above the skylight, was now turned towards him—he was struck by the profile, whose clearness of cut was refined by the thinness, incident to ill-health, as well as ennobled about the chin by the beard. Away with suspicion. He was a true off-shoot of a true hidalgo[35] Cereno.

Relieved by these and other better thoughts, the visitor, lightly humming a tune, now began indifferently pacing the poop, so as not to betray to Don Benito that he had at all mistrusted incivility, much less duplicity; for such mistrust would yet be proved illusory, and by the event; though, for the present, the circumstance which had provoked that distrust remained unexplained. But when that little mystery should have been cleared up, Captain Delano thought he might extremely regret it, did he allow Don Benito to become aware that he had indulged in ungenerous surmises. In short, to the Spaniard's black-letter[36] text, it was best, for a while, to leave open margin.

Presently, his pale face twitching and overcast, the Spaniard, still supported by his attendant, moved over towards his guest, when, with even more than his usual embarrassment, and a strange sort of intriguing intonation in his husky whisper, the following conversation began:—

"Señor, may I ask how long you have lain at this isle?"

"Oh, but a day or two, Don Benito."

"And from what port are you last?"

"Canton."

"And there, Señor, you exchanged your sealskins for teas and silks, I think you said?"

"Yes. Silks, mostly."

"And the balance you took in specie, perhaps?"

Captain Delano, fidgeting a little, answered—

"Yes; some silver; not a very great deal, though."

"Ah—well. May I ask how many men have you, Señor?"

Captain Delano slightly started, but answered—

"About five-and-twenty, all told."

"And at present, Señor, all on board, I suppose?"

"All on board, Don Benito," replied the Captain, now with satisfaction.

"And will be to-night, Señor?"

At this last question, following so many pertinacious ones, for the soul of him Captain Delano could not but look very earnestly at the questioner, who, instead of meeting the glance, with every token of craven discomposure dropped his eyes to the deck; presenting an unworthy contrast to his servant, who, just then, was kneeling at his feet, adjusting a loose shoe-buckle; his disengaged face meantime, with humble curiosity, turned openly up into his master's downcast one.

The Spaniard, still with a guilty shuffle, repeated his question:

"And—and will be to-night, Señor?"

"Yes, for aught I know," returned Captain Delano—"but nay," rallying himself into fearless truth, "some of them talked of going off on another fishing party about midnight."

"Your ships generally go—go more or less armed, I believe, Señor?"

"Oh, a six-pounder or two, in case of emergency," was the intrepidly indifferent reply, "with a small stock of muskets, sealing-spears, and cutlasses, you know."

[35]Nobleman.
[36]A type face similar to medieval script; in leaving "open margin," Delano avoids any attempt at explanation for the time being.

As he thus responded, Captain Delano again glanced at Don Benito, but the latter's eyes were averted; while abruptly and awkwardly shifting the subject, he made some peevish allusion to the calm, and then, without apology, once more, with his attendant, withdrew to the opposite bulwarks, where the whispering was resumed.

At this moment, and ere Captain Delano could cast a cool thought upon what had just passed, the young Spanish sailor, before mentioned, was seen descending from the rigging. In act of stooping over to spring inboard to the deck, his voluminous, unconfined frock, or shirt, of coarse woolen, much spotted with tar, opened out far down the chest, revealing a soiled under-garment of what seemed the finest linen, edged, about the neck, with a narrow blue ribbon, sadly faded and worn. At this moment the young sailor's eye was again fixed on the whisperers, and Captain Delano thought he observed a lurking significance in it, as if silent signs, of some Freemason[37] sort, had that instant been interchanged.

This once more impelled his own glance in the direction of Don Benito, and, as before, he could not but infer that himself formed the subject of the conference. He paused. The sound of the hatchet-polishing fell on his ears. He cast another swift side-look at the two. They had the air of conspirators. In connection with the late questionings, and the incident of the young sailor, these things now begat such return of involuntary suspicion, that the singular guilelessness of the American could not endure it. Plucking up a gay and humorous expression, he crossed over to the two rapidly, saying:—"Ha, Don Benito, your black here seems high in your trust; a sort of privy-counselor, in fact."

Upon this, the servant looked up with a good-natured grin, but the master started as from a venomous bite. It was a moment or two before the Spaniard sufficiently recovered himself to reply; which he did, at last, with cold constraint:— "Yes, Señor, I have trust in Babo."

Here Babo, changing his previous grin of mere animal humor into an intelligent smile, not ungratefully eyed his master.

Finding that the Spaniard now stood silent and reserved, as if involuntarily, or purposely giving hint that his guest's proximity was inconvenient just then, Captain Delano, unwilling to appear uncivil even to incivility itself made some trivial remark and moved off; again and again turning over in his mind the mysterious demeanor of Don Benito Cereno.

He had descended from the poop, and, wrapped in thought, was passing near a dark hatchway, leading down into the steerage, when, perceiving motion there, he looked to see what moved. The same instant there was a sparkle in the shadowy hatchway, and he saw one of the Spanish sailors, prowling there, hurriedly placing his hand in the bosom of his frock, as if hiding something. Before the man could have been certain who it was that was passing, he slunk below out of sight. But enough was seen of him to make it sure that he was the same young sailor before noticed in the rigging.

What was that which so sparkled? thought Captain Delano. It was no lamp— no match—no live coal. Could it have been a jewel? But how come sailors with jewels?—or with silk-trimmed under-shirts either? Has he been robbing the trunks of the dead cabin-passengers? But if so, he would hardly wear one of the stolen articles on board ship here. Ah, ah—if, now, that was, indeed, a secret sign I saw passing between this suspicious fellow and his captain awhile since; if I could only be certain that, in my uneasiness, my senses did not deceive me, then——

Here, passing from one suspicious thing to another, his mind revolved the strange questions put to him concerning his ship.

---

[37] A secret society dedicated to brotherliness and mutual aid; members used secret signs to recognize each other.

By a curious coincidence, as each point was recalled, the black wizards of Ashantee would strike up with their hatchets, as in ominous comment on the white stranger's thoughts. Pressed by such enigmas and portents, it would have been almost against nature, had not, even into the least distrustful heart, some ugly misgivings obtruded.

Observing the ship, now helplessly fallen into a current, with enchanted sails, drifting with increased rapidity seaward; and noting that, from a lately intercepted projection of the land, the sealer was hidden, the stout mariner began to quake at thoughts which he barely durst confess to himself. Above all, he began to feel a ghostly dread of Don Benito. And yet, when he roused himself, dilated his chest, felt himself strong on his legs, and coolly considered it—what did all these phantoms amount to?

Had the Spaniard any sinister scheme, it must have reference not so much to him (Captain Delano) as to his ship (the *Bachelor's Delight*). Hence the present drifting away of the one ship from the other, instead of favoring any such possible scheme, was, for the time, at least, opposed to it. Clearly any suspicion, combining such contradictions, must need be delusive. Besides, was it not absurd to think of a vessel in distress—a vessel by sickness almost dismanned of her crew—a vessel whose inmates were parched for water—was it not a thousand times absurd that such a craft should, at present, be of a piratical character; or her commander, either for himself or those under him, cherish any desire but for speedy relief and refreshment? But then, might not general distress, and thirst in particular, be affected? And might not that same undiminished Spanish crew, alleged to have perished off to a remnant, be at that very moment lurking in the hold? On heartbroken pretense of entreating a cup of cold water, fiends in human form had got into lonely dwellings, nor retired until a dark deed had been done. And among the Malay pirates, it was no unusual thing to lure ships after them into their treacherous harbors, or entice boarders from a declared enemy at sea, by the spectacle of thinly manned or vacant decks, beneath which prowled a hundred spears with yellow arms ready to upthrust them through the mats. Not that Captain Delano had entirely credited such things. He had heard of them—and now, as stories, they recurred. The present destination of the ship was the anchorage. There she would be near his own vessel. Upon gaining that vicinity, might not the *San Dominick*, like a slumbering volcano, suddenly let loose energies now hid?

He recalled the Spaniard's manner while telling his story. There was a gloomy hesitancy and subterfuge about it. It was just the manner of one making up his tale for evil purposes, as he goes. But if that story was not true, what was the truth? That the ship had unlawfully come into the Spaniard's possession? But in many of its details, especially in reference to the more calamitous parts, such as the fatalities among the seamen, the consequent prolonged beating about, the past sufferings from obstinate calms, and still continued suffering from thirst; in all these points, as well as others, Don Benito's story had corroborated not only the wailing ejaculations of the indiscriminate multitude, white and black, but likewise—what seemed impossible to be counterfeit—by the very expression and play of every human feature, which Captain Delano saw. If Don Benito's story was, throughout, an invention, then every soul on board, down to the youngest negress, was his carefully drilled recruit in the plot: an incredible inference. And yet, if there was ground for mistrusting his veracity, that inference was a legitimate one.

But those questions of the Spaniard. There, indeed, one might pause. Did they not seem put with much the same object with which the burglar or assassin, by day-time, reconnoitres the walls of a house? But, with ill purposes, to solicit such information openly of the chief person endangered, and so, in effect, setting him on his guard; how unlikely a procedure was that? Absurd, then, to suppose that those questions had been prompted by evil designs. Thus, the same conduct, which, in this instance, had raised the alarm, served to dispel it. In short, scarce any suspicion or uneasiness, however apparently reasonable at the time, which was not now, with equally apparent reason, dismissed.

At last he began to laugh at his former forebodings; and laugh at the strange ship for, in its aspect, someway siding with them, as it were; and laugh, too, at the odd looking blacks, particularly those old scissors-grinders, the Ashantees; and those bed-ridden old knitting women, the oakum-pickers; and almost at the dark Spaniard himself, the central hobgoblin of all.

For the rest, whatever in a serious way seemed enigmatical, was now good-naturedly explained away by the thought that, for the most part, the poor invalid scarcely knew what he was about; either sulking in black vapors, or putting idle questions without sense or object. Evidently, for the present, the man was not fit to be intrusted with the ship. On some benevolent plea withdrawing the command from him, Captain Delano would yet have to send her to Concepcion, in charge of his second mate, a worthy person and good navigator—a plan not more convenient for the *San Dominick* than for Don Benito; for, relieved from all anxiety, keeping wholly to his cabin, the sick man, under the good nursing of his servant, would, probably, by the end of the passage, be in a measure restored to health, and with that he should also be restored to authority.

Such were the American's thoughts. They were tranquillizing. There was a difference between the idea of Don Benito's darkly preordaining Captain Delano's fate, and Captain Delano's lightly arranging Don Benito's. Nevertheless, it was not without something of relief that the good seaman presently perceived his whale-boat in the distance. Its absence had been prolonged by unexpected detention at the sealer's side, as well as its returning trip lengthened by the continual recession of the goal.

The advancing speck was observed by the blacks. Their shouts attracted the attention of Don Benito, who, with a return of courtesy, approaching Captain Delano, expressed satisfaction at the coming of some supplies, slight and temporary as they must necessarily prove.

Captain Delano responded; but while doing so, his attention was drawn to something passing on the deck below: among the crowd climbing the landward bulwarks, anxiously watching the coming boat, two blacks, to all appearances accidentally incommoded by one of the sailors, violently pushed him aside, which the sailor someway resenting, they dashed him to the deck, despite the earnest cries of the oakum-pickers.

"Don Benito," said Captain Delano quickly, "do you see what is going on there? Look!"

But, seized by his cough, the Spaniard staggered, with both hands to his face, on the point of falling. Captain Delano would have supported him, but the servant was more alert, who, with one hand sustaining his master, with the other applied the cordial. Don Benito restored, the black withdrew his support, slipping aside a little, but dutifully remaining within call of a whisper. Such discretion was here evinced as quite wiped away, in the visitor's eyes, any blemish of impropriety which might have attached to the attendant, from the indecorous conferences before mentioned; showing, too, that if the servant were to blame, it might be more the master's fault than his own, since, when left to himself, he could conduct thus well.

His glance called away from the spectacle of disorder to the more pleasing one before him, Captain Delano could not avoid again congratulating his host upon possessing such a servant, who, though perhaps a little too forward now and then, must upon the whole be invaluable to one in the invalid's situation.

"Tell me, Don Benito," he added, with a smile—"I should like to have your man here, myself—what will you take for him? Would fifty doubloons be any object?"

"Master wouldn't part with Babo for a thousand doubloons," murmured the black, overhearing the offer, and taking it in earnest, and, with the strange vanity of a faithful slave, appreciated by his master, scorning to hear so paltry a valuation put upon him by a stranger. But Don Benito, apparently hardly yet completely restored, and again interrupted by his cough, made but some broken reply.

Soon his physical distress became so great, affecting his mind, too, apparently, that, as if to screen the sad spectacle, the servant gently conducted his master below.

Left to himself, the American, to while away the time till his boat should arrive, would have pleasantly accosted some one of the few Spanish seamen he saw; but recalling something that Don Benito had said touching their ill conduct, he refrained; as a shipmaster indisposed to countenance cowardice or unfaithfulness in seamen.

While, with these thoughts, standing with eye directed forward towards that handful of sailors, suddenly he thought that one or two of them returned the glance and with a sort of meaning. He rubbed his eyes, and looked again; but again seemed to see the same thing. Under a new form, but more obscure than any previous one, the old suspicions recurred, but, in the absence of Don Benito, with less of panic than before. Despite the bad account given of the sailors, Captain Delano resolved forthwith to accost one of them. Descending the poop, he made his way through blacks, his movement drawing a queer cry from the oakum-pickers, prompted by whom, the negroes, twitching each other aside, divided before him; but, as if curious to see what was the object of this deliberate visit to their Ghetto, closing in behind, in tolerable order, followed the white stranger up. His progress thus proclaimed as by mounted kings-at-arms, and escorted as by a Kaffir[38] guard of honor, Captain Delano, assuming a good-humored, off-handed air, continued to advance; now and then saying a blithe word to the negroes, and his eye curiously surveying the white faces, here and there sparsely mixed in with the blacks, like stray white pawns venturously involved in the ranks of the chessmen opposed.

While thinking which of them to select for his purpose, he chanced to observe a sailor seated on the deck engaged in tarring the strap of a large block, a circle of blacks squatted round him inquisitively eying the process.

The mean employment of the man was in contrast with something superior in his figure. His hand, black with continually thrusting it into the tar-pot held for him by a negro, seemed not naturally allied to his face, a face which would have been a very fine one but for its haggardness. Whether this haggardness had aught to do with criminality, could not be determined; since, as intense heat and cold, though unlike, produce like sensations, so innocence and guilt, when, through casual association with mental pain, stamping any visible impress, use one seal—a hacked one.

Not again that this reflection occurred to Captain Delano at the time, charitable man as he was. Rather another idea. Because observing so singular a haggardness combined with a dark eye, averted as in trouble and shame, and then again recalling Don Benito's confessed ill opinion of his crew, insensibly he was operated upon by certain general notions which, while disconnecting pain and abashment from virtue, invariably link them with vice.

If, indeed, there be any wickedness on board this ship, thought Captain Delano, be sure that man there has fouled his hand in it, even as now he fouls it in

---

[38]South African Bantu tribe.

the pitch. I don't like to accost him. I will speak to this other, this old Jack here on the windlass.

He advanced to an old Barcelona tar, in ragged red breeches and dirty night-cap, cheeks trenched and bronzed, whiskers dense as thorn hedges. Seated between two sleepy-looking Africans, this mariner, like his younger shipmate, was employed upon some rigging—splicing a cable—the sleepy-looking blacks performing the inferior function of holding the outer parts of the ropes for him.

Upon Captain Delano's approach, the man at once hung his head below its previous level; the one necessary for business. It appeared as if he desired to be thought absorbed, with more than common fidelity, in his task. Being addressed, he glanced up, but with what seemed a furtive, diffident air, which sat strangely enough on his weatherbeaten visage, much as if a grizzly bear, instead of growling and biting, should simper and cast sheep's eyes. He was asked several questions concerning the voyage—questions purposely referring to several particulars in Don Benito's narrative, not previously corroborated by those impulsive cries greeting the visitor on first coming on board. The questions were briefly answered, confirming all that remained to be confirmed of the story. The negroes about the windlass joined in with the old sailor; but, as they became talkative, he by degrees became mute, and at length quite glum, seemed morosely unwilling to answer more questions, and yet, all the while, this ursine[39] air was somehow mixed with his sheepish one.

Despairing of getting into unembarrassed talk with such a centaur, Captain Delano, after glancing round for a more promising countenance, but seeing none, spoke pleasantly to the blacks to make way for him; and so, amid various grins and grimaces, returned to the poop, feeling a little strange at first, he could hardly tell why, but upon the whole with regained confidence in Benito Cereno.

How plainly, thought he, did that old whiskerando yonder betray a consciousness of ill desert. No doubt, when he saw me coming, he dreaded lest I, apprised by his captain of the crew's general misbehavior, came with sharp words for him, and so down with his head. And yet—and yet, now that I think of it, that very old fellow, if I err not, was one of those who seemed so earnestly eying me here awhile since. Ah, these currents spin one's head round almost as much as they do the ship. Ha, there now's a pleasant sort of sunny sight; quite sociable, too.

His attention had been drawn to a slumbering negress, partly disclosed through the lacework of some rigging, lying, with youthful limbs carelessly disposed, under the lee of the bulwarks, like a doe in the shade of a woodland rock. Sprawling at her lapped breasts, was her wide-awake fawn, stark naked, its black little body half lifted from the deck, crosswise with its dam's; its hands, like two paws, clambering upon her; its mouth and nose ineffectually rooting to get at the mark; and meantime giving a vexatious half-grunt, blending with the composed snore of the negress.

The uncommon vigor of the child at length roused the mother. She started up, at a distance facing Captain Delano. But as if not at all concerned at the attitude in which she had been caught, delightedly she caught the child up, with maternal transports, covering it with kisses.

There's naked nature, now; pure tenderness and love, thought Captain Delano, well pleased.

This incident prompted him to remark the other negresses more particularly than before. He was gratified with their manners; like most uncivilized women, they seemed at once tender of heart and tough of constitution; equally ready to die for their infants or fight for them. Unsophisticated as leopardesses; loving as

---

[39]Bearlike.

doves. Ah! thought Captain Delano, these, perhaps, are some of the very women whom Ledyard[40] saw in Africa, and gave such a noble account of.

These natural sights somehow insensibly deepened his confidence and ease. At last he looked to see how his boat was getting on; but it was still pretty remote. He turned to see if Don Benito had returned; but he had not.

To change the scene, as well as to please himself with a leisurely observation of the coming boat, stepping over into the mizzen-chains, he clambered his way into the starboard quarter-gallery—one of those abandoned Venetian-looking water-balconies previously mentioned—retreats cut off from the deck. As his foot pressed the half-damp, half-dry seamosses matting the place, and a chance phantom cats-paw—an islet of breeze, unheralded, unfollowed—as this ghostly cats-paw came fanning his cheek; as his glance fell upon the row of small, round dead-lights—all closed like coppered eyes of the coffined—and the state-cabin door, once connecting with the gallery, even as the dead-lights had once looked out upon it, but now calked fast like a sarcophagus lid; and to a purple-black, tarred-over panel, threshold, and post; and he bethought him of the time, when that state-cabin and this state-balcony had heard the voices of the Spanish king's officers, and the forms of the Lima viceroy's daughters had perhaps leaned where he stood—as these and other images flitted through his mind, as the cats-paw through the calm, gradually he felt rising a dreamy inquietude, like that of one who alone on the prairie feels unrest from the repose of the noon.

He leaned against the carved balustrade, again looking off toward his boat; but found his eye falling upon the ribbon grass, trailing along the ship's water-line, straight as a border of green box; and parterres of sea-weed, broad ovals and crescents, floating nigh and far, with what seemed long formal alleys between, crossing the terraces of swells, and sweeping round as if leading to the grottoes below. And overhanging all was the balustrade by his arm, which, partly stained with pitch and partly embossed with moss, seemed the charred ruin of some summer-house in a grand garden long running to waste.

Trying to break one charm, he was but becharmed anew. Though upon the wide sea, he seemed in some far inland country; prisoner in some deserted château, left to stare at empty grounds, and peer out at vague roads, where never wagon or wayfarer passed.

But these enchantments were a little disenchanted as his eye fell on the corroded main-chains. Of an ancient style, massy and rusty in link, shackle and bolt, they seemed even more fit for the ship's present business than the one for which she had been built.

Presently he thought something moved nigh the chains. He rubbed his eyes, and looked hard. Groves of rigging were about the chains; and there, peering from behind a great stay, like an Indian from behind a hemlock, a Spanish sailor, a marlingspike in his hand, was seen, who made what seemed an imperfect gesture towards the balcony, but immediately, as if alarmed by some advancing step along the deck within, vanished into the recesses of the hempen forest, like a poacher.

What meant this? Something the man had sought to communicate, unbeknown to any one, even to his captain. Did the secret involve aught unfavorable to his captain? Were those previous misgivings of Captain Delano's about to be verified? Or, in his haunted mood at the moment, had some random, unintentional motion of the man, while busy with the stay, as if repairing it, been mistaken for a significant beckoning?

---

[40]John Ledyard (1751–1789), American traveller and author of *Proceedings of the Association for Promoting the Discovery of the Interior Parts of Africa* (1790).

Not unbewildered, again he gazed off for his boat. But it was temporarily hidden by a rocky spur of the isle. As with some eagerness he bent forward, watching for the first shooting view of its beak, the balustrade gave way before him like charcoal. Had he not clutched an outreaching rope he would have fallen into the sea. The crash, though feeble, and the fall, though hollow, of the rotten fragments, must have been overheard. He glanced up. With sober curiosity peering down upon him was one of the old oakum-pickers, slipped from his perch to an outside boom; while below the old negro, and, invisible to him, reconnoitering from a port-hole like a fox from the mouth of its den, crouched the Spanish sailor again. From something suddenly suggested by the man's air, the mad idea now darted into Captain Delano's mind, that Don Benito's plea of indisposition, in withdrawing below, was but a pretense; that he was engaged there maturing his plot, of which the sailor, by some means gaining an inkling, had a mind to warn the stranger against; incited, it may be, by gratitude for a kind word on first boarding the ship. Was it from foreseeing some possible interference like this, that Don Benito had, beforehand, given such a bad character of his sailors, while praising the negroes; though indeed, the former seemed as docile as the latter the contrary? The whites, too, by nature, were the shrewder race. A man with some evil design, would he not be likely to speak well of that stupidity which was blind to his depravity, and malign that intelligence from which it might not be hidden? Not unlikely, perhaps. But if the whites had dark secrets concerning Don Benito, could then Don Benito be any way in complicity with the blacks? But they were too stupid. Besides, who ever heard of a white so far a renegade as to apostatize from his very species almost, by leaguing in against it with negroes? These difficulties recalled former ones. Lost in their mazes, Captain Delano, who had now regained the deck, was uneasily advancing along it, when he observed a new face; an aged sailor seated cross-legged near the main hatchway. His skin was shrunk up with wrinkles like a pelican's empty pouch; his hair frosted; his countenance grave and composed. His hands were full of ropes, which he was working into a large knot. Some blacks were about him obligingly dipping the strands for him, here and there, as the exigencies of the operation demanded.

Captain Delano crossed over to him, and stood in silence surveying the knot; his mind, by a not uncongenial transition, passing from its own entanglements to those of the hemp. For intricacy, such a knot he had never seen in an American ship, nor indeed any other. The old man looked like an Egyptian priest, making Gordian knots for the temple of Ammon.[41] The knot seemed a combination of double-bowline-knot, treble-crown-knot, back-handed-well-knot, knot-in-and-out-knot, and jamming-knot.

At last, puzzled to comprehend the meaning of such a knot, Captain Delano addressed the knotter:—

"What are you knotting there, my man?"

"The knot," was the brief reply, without looking up.

"So it seems; but what is it for?"

"For some one else to undo," muttered back the old man, plying his fingers harder than ever, the knot being now nearly completed.

While Captain Delano stood watching him, suddenly the old man threw the knot towards him, saying in broken English—the first heard in the ship—something to this effect: "Undo it, cut it, quick." It was said lowly, but with such condensation of rapidity, that the long, slow words in Spanish, which had preceded and followed, almost operated as covers to the brief English between.

---

[41]Egyptian Oracle; according to legend, the Ammon, when consulted by Alexander the Great (356–323 B.C.), proclaimed him a god. Later, Alexander cut the Gordian knot in Phrygia with his sword and became master of Asia.

For a moment, knot in hand, and knot in head, Captain Delano stood mute; while, without further heeding him, the old man was now intent upon other ropes. Presently there was a slight stir behind Captain Delano. Turning, he saw the chained negro, Atufal, standing quietly there. The next moment the old sailor rose, muttering, and, followed by his subordinate negroes, removed to the forward part of the ship, where in the crowd he disappeared.

An elderly negro, in a clout like an infant's, and with a pepper and salt head, and a kind of attorney air, now approached Captain Delano. In tolerable Spanish, and with a good-natured, knowing wink, he informed him that the old knotter was simple-witted, but harmless; often playing his odd tricks. The negro concluded by begging the knot, for of course the stranger would not care to be troubled with it. Unconsciously, it was handed to him. With a sort of congé,[42] the negro received it, and, turning his back, ferreted into it like a detective custom-house officer after smuggled laces. Soon, with some African word, equivalent to pshaw, he tossed the knot overboard.

All this is very queer now, thought Captain Delano, with a qualmish sort of emotion; but, as one feeling incipient sea-sickness, he strove, by ignoring the symptoms, to get rid of the malady. Once more he looked off for his boat. To his delight, it was now again in view, leaving the rocky spur astern.

The sensation here experienced, after at first relieving his uneasiness, with unforeseen efficacy soon began to remove it. The less distant sight of that well-known boat—showing it, not as before, half blended with the haze, but with outline defined, so that its individuality, like a man's, was manifest; that boat, *Rover* by name, which, though now in strange seas, had often pressed the beach of Captain Delano's home, and brought to its threshold for repairs, had familiarly lain there, as a Newfoundland dog; the sight of that household boat evoked a thousand trustful associations, which, contrasted with previous suspicions, filled him not only with lightsome confidence, but somehow with half humorous self-reproaches at his former lack of it.

"What, I, Amasa Delano—Jack of the Beach, as they called me when a lad—I, Amasa; the same that, duck-satchel in hand, used to paddle along the water-side to the school-house made from the old hulk—I, little Jack of the Beach, that used to go berrying with cousin Nat and the rest; I to be murdered here at the ends of the earth, on board a haunted pirate-ship by a horrible Spaniard? Too nonsensical to think of! Who would murder Amasa Delano? His conscience is clean. There is some one above. Fie, fie, Jack of the Beach! you are a child indeed; a child of the second childhood, old boy; you are beginning to dote and drool, I'm afraid."

Light of heart and foot, he stepped aft, and there was met by Don Benito's servant, who, with a pleasing expression, responsive to his own present feelings, informed him that his master had recovered from the effects of his coughing fit, and had just ordered him to go present his compliments to his good guest, Don Amasa, and say that he (Don Benito) would soon have the happiness to rejoin him.

There now, do you mark that? again thought Captain Delano, walking the poop. What a donkey I was. This kind gentleman who here sends me his kind compliments, he, but ten minutes ago, dark-lantern in hand, was dodging round some old grindstone in the hold, sharpening a hatchet for me, I thought. Well, well; these long calms have a morbid effect on the mind, I've often heard, though I never believed it before. Ha! glancing towards the boat; there's *Rover;* good dog; a white bone in her mouth. A pretty big bone though, seems to me.— What? Yes, she has fallen afoul of the bubbling tide-rip there. It sets her the other way, too, for the time. Patience.

---

[42] A bow, especially of leave-taking.

It was now about noon, though, from the grayness of everything, it seemed to be getting towards dusk.

The calm was confirmed. In the far distance, away from the influence of land, the leaden ocean seemed laid out and leaded up, its course finished, soul gone, defunct. But the current from landward, where the ship was, increased; silently sweeping her further and further towards the tranced waters beyond.

Still, from his knowledge of those latitudes, cherishing hopes of a breeze, and a fair and fresh one, at any moment, Captain Delano, despite present prospects, buoyantly counted upon bringing the *San Dominick* safely to anchor ere night. The distance swept over was nothing; since, with a good wind, ten minutes' sailing would retrace more than sixty minutes' drifting. Meantime, one moment turning to mark *Rover* fighting the tide-rip, and the next to see Don Benito approaching, he continued walking the poop.

Gradually he felt a vexation arising from the delay of his boat; this soon merged into uneasiness; and at last—his eye falling continually, as from a stage-box into the pit, upon the strange crowd before and below him, and, by and by, recognizing there the face—now composed to indifference—of the Spanish sailor who had seemed to beckon from the main-chains—something of his old trepidations returned.

Ah, thought he—gravely enough—this is like the ague: because it went off, it follows not that it won't come back.

Though ashamed of the relapse, he could not altogether subdue it; and so, exerting his good-nature to the utmost, insensibly he came to a compromise.

Yes, this is a strange craft; a strange history, too, and strange folks on board. But—nothing more.

By way of keeping his mind out of mischief till the boat should arrive, he tried to occupy it with turning over and over, in a purely speculative sort of way, some lesser peculiarities of the captain and crew. Among others, four curious points recurred:

First, the affair of the Spanish lad assailed with a knife by the slave boy; an act winked at by Don Benito. Second, the tyranny in Don Benito's treatment of Atufal, the black; as if a child should lead a bull of the Nile by the ring in his nose. Third, the trampling of the sailor by the two negroes; a piece of insolence passed over without so much as a reprimand. Fourth, the cringing submission to their master, of all the ship's underlings, mostly blacks; as if by the least inadvertence they feared to draw down his despotic displeasure.

Coupling these points, they seemed somewhat contradictory. But what then, thought Captain Delano, glancing towards his now nearing boat—what then? Why, Don Benito is a very capricious commander. But he is not the first of the sort I have seen; though it's true he rather exceeds any other. But as a nation—continued he in his reveries—these Spaniards are all an odd set; the very word Spaniard has a curious, conspirator, Guy-Fawkish[43] twang to it. And yet, I dare say, Spaniards in the main are as good folks as any in Duxbury, Massachusetts. Ah good! At last *Rover* has come.

As, with its welcome freight, the boat touched the side, the oakum-pickers, with venerable gestures, sought to restrain the blacks, who at the sight of three gurried[44] water-casks in its bottom, and a pile of wilted pumpkins in its bow, hung over the bulwarks in disorderly raptures.

Don Benito, with his servant, now appeared; his coming, perhaps, hastened by hearing the noise. Of him Captain Delano sought permission to serve out the wa-

[43]Guy Fawkes (1570–1606), executed for his part in the Gunpowder Plot to blow up the Parliament in England.
[44]Slimy from fish offal.

ter, so that all might share alike, and none injure themselves by unfair excess. But sensible, and, on Don Benito's account, kind as this offer was, it was received with what seemed impatience; as if aware that he lacked energy as a commander, Don Benito, with the true jealousy of weakness, resented as an affront any interference. So, at least, Captain Delano inferred.

In another moment the casks were being hoisted in, when some of the eager negroes accidentally jostled Captain Delano, where he stood by the gangway; so that, unmindful of Don Benito, yielding to the impulse of the moment, with good-natured authority he bade the blacks stand back; to enforce his words making use of a half-mirthful, half-menacing gesture. Instantly the blacks paused, just where they were, each negro and negress suspended in his or her posture, exactly as the word had found them—for a few seconds continuing so—while, as between the responsive posts of a telegraph, an unknown syllable ran from man to man among the perched oakum-pickers. While the visitor's attention was fixed by this scene, suddenly the hatchet-polishers half rose, and a rapid cry came from Don Benito.

Thinking that at the signal of the Spaniard he was about to be massacred, Captain Delano would have sprung for his boat, but paused, as the oakum-pickers, dropping down into the crowd with earnest exclamations, forced every white and every negro back, at the same moment, with gestures friendly and familiar, almost jocose, bidding him, in substance, not be a fool. Simultaneously the hatchet-polishers resumed their seats, quietly as so many tailors, and at once, as if nothing had happened, the work of hoisting in the casks was resumed, whites and blacks singing at the tackle.

Captain Delano glanced towards Don Benito. As he saw his meagre form in the act of recovering itself from reclining in the servant's arms, into which the agitated invalid had fallen, he could not but marvel at the panic by which himself had been surprised, on the darting supposition that such a commander, who, upon a legitimate occasion, so trivial, too, as it now appeared, could lose all self-command, was, with energetic iniquity, going to bring about his murder.

The casks being on deck, Captain Delano was handed a number of jars and cups by one of the steward's aids, who, in the name of his captain, entreated him to do as he had proposed—dole out the water. He complied, with republican impartiality as to this republican element, which always seeks one level, serving the oldest white no better than the youngest black; excepting, indeed, poor Don Benito, whose condition, if not rank, demanded extra allowance. To him, in the first place, Captain Delano presented a fair pitcher of the fluid; but, thirsting as he was for it, the Spaniard quaffed not a drop until after several grave bows and salutes. A reciprocation of courtesies which the sight-loving Africans hailed with clapping of hands.

Two of the less wilted pumpkins being reserved for the cabin table, the residue were minced up on the spot for the general regalement. But the soft bread, sugar, and bottled cider, Captain Delano would have given the whites alone, and in chief Don Benito; but the latter objected; which disinterestedness not a little pleased the American; and so mouthfuls all around were given alike to whites and blacks; excepting one bottle of cider, which Babo insisted upon setting aside for his master.

Here it may be observed that as, on the first visit of the boat, the American had not permitted his men to board the ship, neither did he now; being unwilling to add to the confusion of the decks.

Not uninfluenced by the peculiar good-humor at present prevailing, and for the time oblivious of any but benevolent thoughts, Captain Delano, who, from recent indications, counted upon a breeze within an hour or two at furthest, dispatched the boat back to the sealer, with orders for all the hands that could be spared immediately to set about rafting casks to the watering-place and filling them. Likewise he bade word be carried to his chief officer, that if, against present expectation, the ship was not brought to anchor by sunset, he need be under no concern; for as there was to be a full moon that night, he (Captain Delano) would remain on board ready to play the pilot, come the wind soon or late.

As the two Captains stood together, observing the departing boat—the servant, as it happened, having just spied a spot on his master's velvet sleeve, and silently engaged rubbing it out—the American expressed his regrets that the *San Dominick* had no boats; none, at least, but the unseaworthy old hulk of the long-boat, which, warped as a camel's skeleton in the desert, and almost as bleached, lay pot-wise inverted amid-ships, one side a little tipped, furnishing a subterraneous sort of den for family groups of the blacks, mostly women and small children; who, squatting on old mats below, or perched above in the dark dome, on the elevated seats, were descried, some distance within, like a social circle of bats, sheltering in some friendly cave; at intervals, ebon flights of naked boys and girls, three or four years old, darting in and out of the den's mouth.

"Had you three or four boats now, Don Benito," said Captain Delano, "I think that, by tugging at the oars, your negroes here might help along matters some. Did you sail from port without boats, Don Benito?"

"They were stove in the gales, Señor."

"That was bad. Many men, too, you lost then. Boats and men. Those must have been hard gales, Don Benito."

"Past all speech," cringed the Spaniard.

"Tell me, Don Benito," continued his companion with increased interest, "tell me, were these gales immediately off the pitch of Cape Horn?"

"Cape Horn?—who spoke of Cape Horn?"

"Yourself did, when giving me an account of your voyage," answered Captain Delano, with almost equal astonishment at this eating of his own words, even as he ever seemed eating his own heart, on the part of the Spaniard. "You yourself, Don Benito, spoke of Cape Horn," he emphatically repeated.

The Spaniard turned, in a sort of stooping posture, pausing an instant, as one about to make a plunging exchange of elements, as from air to water.

At this moment a messenger-boy, a white, hurried by, in the regular performance of his function carrying the last expired half-hour forward to the forecastle, from the cabin time-piece, to have it struck at the ship's large bell.

"Master," said the servant, discontinuing his work on the coat sleeve, and addressing the rapt Spaniard with a sort of timid apprehensiveness, as one charged with a duty, the discharge of which, it was foreseen, would prove irksome to the very person who had imposed it, and for whose benefit it was intended, "master told me never mind where he was, or how engaged, always to remind him, to a minute, when shaving-time comes. Miguel has gone to strike the half-hour afternoon. It is *now*, master. Will master go into the cuddy?"

"Ah—yes," answered the Spaniard, starting, as from dreams into realities; then turning upon Captain Delano, he said that ere long he would resume the conversation.

"Then if master means to talk more to Don Amasa," said the servant, "why not let Don Amasa sit by master in the cuddy, and master can talk, and Don Amasa can listen, while Babo here lathers and strops."

"Yes," said Captain Delano, not unpleased with this sociable plan, "yes, Don Benito, unless you had rather not, I will go with you."

"Be it so, Señor."

As the three passed aft, the American could not but think it another strange instance of his host's capriciousness, this being shaved with such uncommon punctuality in the middle of the day. But he deemed it more than likely that the servant's anxious fidelity had something to do with the matter; inasmuch as the timely interruption served to rally his master from the mood which had evidently been coming upon him.

The place called the cuddy was a light deck-cabin formed by the poop, a sort of attic to the large cabin below. Part of it had formerly been the quarters of the officers; but since their death all the partitionings had been thrown down, and the whole interior converted into one spacious and airy marine hall; for absence of fine furniture and picturesque disarray of odd appurtenances, somewhat answering to the wide, cluttered hall of some eccentric bachelor-squire in the country, who hangs his shooting-jacket and tobacco-pouch on deer antlers, and keeps his fishing-rod, tongs, and walking-stick in the same corner.

The similitude was heightened, if not originally suggested, by glimpses of the surrounding sea; since, in one aspect, the country and the ocean seem cousins-german.

The floor of the cuddy was matted. Overhead, four or five old muskets were stuck into horizontal holes along the beams. On one side was a claw-footed old table lashed to the deck; a thumbed missal[45] on it, and over it a small, meagre crucifix attached to the bulk-head. Under the table lay a dented cutlass or two, with a hacked harpoon, among some melancholy old rigging, like a heap of poor friars' girdles. There were also two long, sharp-ribbed settees of Malacca cane, black with age, and uncomfortable to look at as inquisitors' racks, with a large, misshapen arm-chair, which, furnished with a rude barber's crotch[46] at the back, working with a screw, seemed some grotesque engine of torment. A flag-locker was in one corner, open, exposing various colored bunting, some rolled up, others half unrolled, still others tumbled. Opposite was a cumbrous washstand, of black mahogany, all of one block, with a pedestal, like a font, and over it a railed shelf, containing combs, brushes, and other implements of the toilet. A torn hammock of stained grass swung near; the sheets tossed, and the pillow wrinkled up like a brow, as if whoever slept here slept but illy, with alternate visitations of sad thoughts and bad dreams.

The further extremity of the cuddy, overhanging the ship's stern, was pierced with three openings, windows or port-holes, according as men or cannon might peer, socially or unsocially, out of them. At present neither men nor cannon were seen, though huge ring-bolts and other rusty iron fixtures of the wood-work hinted of twenty-four-pounders.

Glancing towards the hammock as he entered, Captain Delano said, "You sleep here, Don Benito?"

"Yes, Señor, since we got into mild weather."

"This seems a sort of dormitory, sitting-room, sail-loft, chapel, armory, and private closet all together, Don Benito," added Captain Delano, looking round.

"Yes, Señor; events have not been favorable to much order in my arrangements."

Here the servant, napkin on arm, made a motion as if waiting his master's good pleasure. Don Benito signified his readiness, when, seating him in the Malacca arm-chair, and for the guest's convenience drawing opposite one of the settees, the servant commenced operations by throwing back his master's collar and loosening his cravat.

There is something in the negro which, in a peculiar way, fits him for avocations about one's person. Most negroes are natural valets and hair-dressers; taking to the comb and brush congenially as to the castanets, and flourishing them apparently with almost equal satisfaction. There is, too, a smooth tact about them in this employment, with a marvelous, noiseless, gliding briskness, not ungraceful in its way, singularly pleasing to behold, and still more so to be the manipulated subject of. And above all is the great gift of good-humor. Not the mere grin or laugh is here meant. Those were unsuitable. But a certain easy cheerfulness, harmoni-

---

[45]Prayer book.
[46]Head rest.

ous in every glance and gesture; as though God had set the whole negro to some pleasant tune.

When to this is added the docility arising from the unaspiring contentment of a limited mind, and that susceptibility of blind attachment sometimes inhering in indisputable inferiors, one readily perceives why those hypochondriacs, Johnson and Byron[47]—it may be, something like the hypochondriac Benito Cereno—took to their hearts, almost to the exclusion of the entire white race, their serving men, the negroes, Barber and Fletcher. But if there be that in the negro which exempts him from the inflicted sourness of the morbid or cynical mind, how, in his most prepossessing aspects, must he appear to a benevolent one? When at ease with respect to exterior things, Captain Delano's nature was not only benign, but familiarly and humorously so: At home, he had often taken rare satisfaction in sitting in his door, watching some free man of color at his work or play. If on a voyage he chanced to have a black sailor, invariably he was on chatty and half-gamesome terms with him. In fact, like most men of a good, blithe heart, Captain Delano took to negroes, not philanthropically, but genially, just as other men to Newfoundland dogs.

Hitherto, the circumstances in which he found the *San Dominick* had repressed the tendency. But in the cuddy, relieved from his former uneasiness, and, for various reasons, more sociably inclined than at any previous period of the day, and seeing the colored servant, napkin on arm, so debonair about his master, in a business so familiar as that of shaving, too, all his old weakness for negroes returned.

Among other things, he was amused with an odd instance of the African love of bright colors and fine shows, in the black's informally taking from the flag-locker a great piece of bunting of all hues, and lavishingly tucking it under his master's chin for an apron.

The mode of shaving among the Spaniards is a little different from what it is with other nations. They have a basin, specifically called a barber's basin, which on one side is scooped out, so as accurately to receive the chin, against which it is closely held in lathering; which is done, not with a brush, but with soap dipped in the water of the basin and rubbed on the face.

In the present instance salt-water was used for lack of better; and the parts lathered were only the upper lip, and low down under the throat, all the rest being cultivated beard.

The preliminaries being somewhat novel to Captain Delano, he sat curiously eying them, so that no conversation took place, nor, for the present, did Don Benito appear disposed to renew any.

Setting down his basin, the negro searched among the razors, as for the sharpest, and having found it, gave it an additional edge by expertly stropping it on the firm, smooth, oily skin of his open palm; he then made a gesture as if to begin, but midway stood suspended for an instant, one hand elevating the razor, the other professionally dabbling among the bubbling suds on the Spaniard's lank neck. Not unaffected by the close sight of the gleaming steel, Don Benito nervously shuddered; his usual ghastliness was heightened by the lather, which lather, again, was intensified in its hue by the contrasting sootiness of the negro's body. Altogether the scene was somewhat peculiar, at least to Captain Delano, nor, as he saw the two thus postured, could he resist the vagary, that in the black he saw a headsman, and in the white a man at the block. But this was one of those antic conceits, appearing and vanishing in a breath, from which, perhaps, the best regulated mind is not always free.

---

[47]Dr. Samuel Johnson (1709–1784) had Frank Barber (a black) as a servant for a long period and remembered him in his will; George Gordon Byron (1788–1824) had William Fletcher (a white) as his servant (Melville seems to confuse him with a friend's black servant that sometimes accompanied Byron).

Meantime the agitation of the Spaniard had a little loosened the bunting from around him, so that one broad fold swept curtain-like over the chair-arm to the floor, revealing, amid a profusion of armorial bars and ground-colors—black, blue, and yellow—a closed castle in a blood-red field diagonal with a lion rampant in a white.

"The castle and the lion," exclaimed Captain Delano—"why Don Benito, this is the flag of Spain you use here. It's well it's only I, and not the King, that sees this," he added, with a smile, "but"—turning towards the black—"it's all one, I suppose, so the colors be gay," which playful remark did not fail somewhat to tickle the negro.

"Now, master," he said, readjusting the flag, and pressing the head gently further back into the crotch of the chair; "now, master," and the steel glanced nigh the throat.

Again Don Benito faintly shuddered.

"You must not shake so, master. See, Don Amasa, master always shakes when I shave him. And yet master knows I never yet have drawn blood, though it's true, if master will shake so, I may some of these times. Now, master," he continued. "And now, Don Amasa, please go on with your talk about the gale, and all that; master can hear, and, between times, master can answer."

"Ah yes, these gales," said Captain Delano; "but the more I think of your voyage, Don Benito, the more I wonder, not at the gales, terrible as they must have been, but at the disastrous interval following them. For here, by your account, have you been these two months and more getting from Cape Horn to Santa Maria, a distance which I myself, with a good wind, have sailed in a few days. True, you had calms, and long ones, but to be becalmed for two months, that is, at least, unusual. Why, Don Benito, had almost any other gentleman told me such a story, I should have been half disposed to a little incredulity."

Here an involuntary expression came over the Spaniard, similar to that just before on the deck, and whether it was the start he gave, or a sudden gawky roll of the hull in the calm, or a momentary unsteadiness of the servant's hand, however it was, just then the razor drew blood, spots of which stained the creamy lather under the throat; immediately the black barber drew back his steel, and, remaining in his professional attitude, back to Captain Delano, and face to Don Benito, held up the trickling razor, saying, with a sort of half humorous sorrow, "See, master—you shook so—here's Babo's first blood."

No sword drawn before James the First of England, no assassination in that timid King's presence,[48] could have produced a more terrified aspect than was now presented by Don Benito.

Poor fellow, thought Captain Delano, so nervous he can't even bear the sight of barber's blood; and this unstrung, sick man, is it credible that I should have imagined he meant to spill all my blood, who can't endure the sight of one little drop of his own? Surely, Amasa Delano, you have been beside yourself this day. Tell it not when you get home, sappy Amasa. Well, well, he looks like a murderer, doesn't he? More like as if himself were to be done for. Well, well, this day's experience shall be a good lesson.

Meantime, while these things were running through the honest seaman's mind, the servant had taken the napkin from his arm, and to Don Benito had said—"But answer Don Amasa, please, master, while I wipe this ugly stuff off the razor, and strop it again."

As he said the words, his face was turned half round, so as to be alike visible to the Spaniard and the American, and seemed, by its expression, to hint, that he

---

[48]James I (1566–1625) lived in great fear of assassination, especially after the Gunpowder Plot of 1605.

was desirous, by getting his master to go on with the conversation, considerately to withdraw his attention from the recent annoying accident. As if glad to snatch the offered relief, Don Benito resumed, rehearsing to Captain Delano, that not only were the calms of unusual duration, but the ship had fallen in with obstinate currents; and other things he added, some of which were but repetitions of former statements, to explain how it came to pass that the passage from Cape Horn to Santa Maria had been so exceedingly long; now and then mingling with his words, incidental praises, less qualified than before, to the blacks, for their general good conduct. These particulars were not given consecutively, the servant, at convenient times, using his razor, and so, between the intervals of shaving, the story and panegyric went on with more than usual huskiness.

To Captain Delano's imagination, now again not wholly at rest, there was something so hollow in the Spaniard's manner, with apparently some reciprocal hollowness in the servant's dusky comment of silence, that the idea flashed across him, that possibly master and man, for some unknown purpose, were acting out, both in word and deed, nay, to the very tremor of Don Benito's limbs, some juggling play before him. Neither did the suspicion of collusion lack apparent support, from the fact of those whispered conferences before mentioned. But then, what could be the object of enacting this play of the barber before him? At last, regarding the notion as a whimsy, insensibly suggested, perhaps, by the theatrical aspect of Don Benito in his harlequin ensign, Captain Delano speedily banished it.

The shaving over, the servant bestirred himself with a small bottle of scented waters, pouring a few drops on the head, and then diligently rubbing: the vehemence of the exercise causing the muscles of his face to twitch rather strangely.

His next operation was with comb, scissors, and brush; going round and round, smoothing a curl here, clipping an unruly whisker-hair there, giving a graceful sweep to the temple-lock, with other impromptu touches evincing the hand of a master; while, like any resigned gentleman in barber's hands, Don Benito bore all, much less uneasily, at least, than he had done the razoring; indeed, he sat so pale and rigid now, that the negro seemed a Nubian sculptor finishing off a white statue-head.

All being over at last, the standard of Spain removed, tumbled up, and tossed back into the flag-locker, the negro's warm breath blowing away any stray hair which might have lodged down his master's neck; collar and cravat readjusted; a speck of lint whisked off the velvet lapel; all this being done, backing off a little space, and pausing with an expression of subdued self-complacency, the servant for a moment surveyed his master, as, in toilet at least, the creature of his own tasteful hands.

Captain Delano playfully complimented him upon his achievement; at the same time congratulating Don Benito.

But neither sweet waters, nor shampooing, nor fidelity, nor sociality, delighted the Spaniard. Seeing him relapsing into forbidding gloom, and still remaining seated, Captain Delano, thinking that his presence was undesired just then, withdrew, on pretense of seeing whether, as he had prophesied, any signs of a breeze were visible.

Walking forward to the main-mast, he stood awhile thinking over the scene, and not without some undefined misgivings, when he heard a noise near the cuddy, and turning, saw the negro, his hand to his cheek. Advancing, Captain Delano perceived that the cheek was bleeding. He was about to ask the cause, when the negro's wailing soliloquy enlightened him.

"Ah, when will master get better from his sickness; only the sour heart that sour sickness breeds made him serve Babo so; cutting Babo with the razor, because, only by accident, Babo had given master one little scratch; and for the first time in so many a day, too. Ah, ah, ah," holding his hand to his face.

Is it possible, thought Captain Delano; was it to wreak in private his Spanish spite against this poor friend of his, that Don Benito, by his sullen manner, impelled me to withdraw? Ah, this slavery breeds ugly passions in man.—Poor fellow!

He was about to speak in sympathy to the negro, but with a timid reluctance he now re-entered the cuddy.

Presently master and man came forth; Don Benito leaning on his servant as if nothing had happened.

But a sort of love-quarrel, after all, thought Captain Delano.

He accosted Don Benito, and they slowly walked together. They had gone but a few paces, when the steward—a tall, rajah-looking mulatto, orientally set off with a pagoda turban formed by three or four Madras handkerchiefs wound about his head, tier on tier—approaching with a salaam, announced lunch in the cabin.

On their way thither, the two captains were preceded by the mulatto, who, turning round as he advanced, with continual smiles and bows, ushered them on, a display of elegance which quite completed the insignificance of the small bareheaded Babo, who, as if not unconscious of inferiority, eyed askance the graceful steward. But in part, Captain Delano imputed his jealous watchfulness to that peculiar feeling which the full-blooded African entertains for the adulterated one. As for the steward, his manner, if not bespeaking much dignity of self-respect, yet evidenced his extreme desire to please; which is doubly meritorious, as at once Christian and Chesterfieldian.[49]

Captain Delano observed with interest that while the complexion of the mulatto was hybrid, his physiognomy was European—classically so.

"Don Benito," whispered he, "I am glad to see this usher-of-the-golden-rod[50] of yours; the sight refutes an ugly remark once made to me by a Barbados planter; that when a mulatto has a regular European face, look out for him; he is a devil. But see, your steward here has features more regular than King George's of England; and yet there he nods, and bows, and smiles; a king, indeed—the king of kind hearts and polite fellows. What a pleasant voice he has, too."

"He has, señor".

"But tell me, has he not, so far as you have known him, always proved a good, worthy fellow?" said Captain Delano, pausing, while with a final genuflexion the steward disappeared into the cabin; "come, for the reason just mentioned, I am curious to know."

"Francesco is a good man," sort of sluggishly responded Don Benito, like a phlegmatic appreciator, who would neither find fault nor flatter.

"Ah, I thought so. For it were strange, indeed, and not very creditable to us white-skins, if a little of our blood mixed with the African's, should, far from improving the latter's quality, have the sad effect of pouring vitriolic acid into black broth; improving the hue, perhaps, but not the wholesomeness."

"Doubtless, doubtless, Señor, but"—glancing at Babo—"not to speak of negroes, your planter's remark I have heard applied to the Spanish and Indian intermixtures in our provinces. But I know nothing about the matter," he listlessly added.

And here they entered the cabin.

The lunch was a frugal one. Some of Captain Delano's fresh fish and pumpkins, biscuit and salt beef, the reserved bottle of cider, and the *San Dominick's* last bottle of Canary.[51]

---

[49]The fourth Earl of Chesterfield, Philip Stanhope (1694–1773), in his letters of advice to his son advocated not a strictly religious but a worldly way of behavior.

[50]An attendant carrying a sceptor walking ahead of a dignitary.

[51]Wine from the Canary Islands.

As they entered, Francesco, with two or three colored aids, was hovering over the table giving the last adjustments. Upon perceiving their master they withdrew, Francesco making a smiling congé, and the Spaniard, without condescending to notice it, fastidiously remarking to his companion that he relished not superfluous attendance.

Without companions, host and guest sat down, like a childless married couple, at opposite ends of the table, Don Benito waving Captain Delano to his place, and, weak as he was, insisting upon that gentleman being seated before himself.

The negro placed a rug under Don Benito's feet, and a cushion behind his back, and then stood behind, not his master's chair, but Captain Delano's. At first, this a little surprised the latter. But it was soon evident that, in taking his position, the black was still true to his master; since by facing him he could the more readily anticipate his slightest want.

"This is an uncommonly intelligent fellow of yours, Don Benito," whispered Captain Delano across the table.

"You say true, Señor."

During the repast, the guest again reverted to parts of Don Benito's story, begging further particulars here and there. He inquired how it was that the scurvy and fever should have committed such wholesale havoc upon the whites, while destroying less than half of the blacks. As if this question reproduced the whole scene of plague before the Spaniard's eyes, miserably reminding him of his solitude in a cabin where before he had had so many friends and officers round him, his hand shook, his face became hueless, broken words escaped; but directly the sane memory of the past seemed replaced by insane terrors of the present. With starting eyes he stared before him at vacancy. For nothing was to be seen but the hand of his servant pushing the Canary over towards him. At length a few sips served partially to restore him. He made random reference to the different constitution of races, enabling one to offer more resistance to certain maladies than another. The thought was new to his companion.

Presently Captain Delano, intending to say something to his host concerning the pecuniary part of the business he had undertaken for him, especially—since he was strictly accountable to his owners—with reference to the new suit of sails, and other things of that sort; and naturally preferring to conduct such affairs in private, was desirous that the servant should withdraw; imagining that Don Benito for a few minutes could dispense with his attendance. He, however, waited awhile; thinking that, as the conversation proceeded, Don Benito, without being prompted, would perceive the propriety of the step.

But it was otherwise. At last catching his host's eye, Captain Delano, with a slight backward gesture of his thumb, whispered, "Don Benito, pardon me, but there is an interference with the full expression of what I have to say to you."

Upon this the Spaniard changed countenance; which was imputed to his resenting the hint, as in some way a reflection upon his servant. After a moment's pause, he assured his guest that the black's remaining with them could be of no disservice; because since losing his officers he had made Babo (whose original office, it now appeared, had been captain of the slaves) not only his constant attendant and companion, but in all things his confidant.

After this, nothing more could be said; though, indeed, Captain Delano could hardly avoid some little tinge of irritation upon being left ungratified in so inconsiderable a wish, by one, too, for whom he intended such solid services. But it is only his querulousness, thought he; and so filling his glass he proceeded to business.

The price of the sails and other matters was fixed upon. But while this was being done, the American observed that, though his original offer of assistance had been hailed with hectic animation, yet now, when it was reduced to a business transaction, indifference and apathy were betrayed. Don Benito, in fact, appeared to submit to hearing the details more out of regard to common propriety, than from any impression that weighty benefit to himself and his voyage was involved.

Soon, his manner became still more reserved. The effort was vain to seek to draw him into social talk. Gnawed by his splenetic mood, he sat twitching his beard, while to little purpose the hand of his servant, mute as that on the wall, slowly pushed over the Canary.

Lunch being over, they sat down on the cushioned transom; the servant placing a pillow behind his master. The long continuance of the calm had now affected the atmosphere. Don Benito sighed heavily, as if for breath.

"Why not adjourn to the cuddy?" said Captain Delano. "There is more air there." But the host sat silent and motionless.

Meantime his servant knelt before him, with a large fan of feathers. And Francesco coming in on tiptoes, handed the negro a little cup of aromatic waters, with which at intervals he chafed his master's brow; smoothing the hair along the temples as a nurse does a child's. He spoke no word. He only rested his eye on his master's, as if, amid all Don Benito's distress, a little to refresh his spirit by the silent sight of fidelity.

Presently the ship's bell sounded two o'clock; and through the cabin windows a slight rippling of the sea was discerned; and from the desired direction.

"There," exclaimed Captain Delano, "I told you so, Don Benito, look!"

He had risen to his feet, speaking in a very animated tone, with a view the more to rouse his companion. But though the crimson curtain of the stern-window near him that moment fluttered against his pale cheek, Don Benito seemed to have even less welcome for the breeze than the calm.

Poor fellow, thought Captain Delano, bitter experience has taught him that one ripple does not make a wind, any more than one swallow a summer. But he is mistaken for once. I will get his ship in for him, and prove it.

Briefly alluding to his weak condition, he urged his host to remain quietly where he was, since he (Captain Delano) would with pleasure take upon himself the responsibility of making the best use of the wind.

Upon gaining the deck, Captain Delano started at the unexpected figure of Atufal, monumentally fixed at the threshold, like one of those sculptured porters of black marble guarding the porches of Egyptian tombs.

But this time the start was, perhaps, purely physical. Atufal's presence, singularly attesting docility even in sullenness, was contrasted with that of the hatchet-polishers, who in patience evinced their industry; while both spectacles showed, that lax as Don Benito's general authority might be, still, whenever he chose to exert it, no man so savage or colossal but must, more or less, bow.

Snatching a trumpet which hung from the bulwarks, with a free step Captain Delano advanced to the forward edge of the poop, issuing his orders in his best Spanish. The few sailors and many negroes, all equally pleased, obediently set about heading the ship towards the harbor.

While giving some directions about setting a lower stu'n-sail, suddenly Captain Delano heard a voice faithfully repeating his orders. Turning, he saw Babo, now for the time acting, under the pilot, his original part of captain of the slaves. This assistance proved valuable. Tattered sails and warped yards were soon brought into some trim. And no brace or halyard was pulled but to blithe songs of the inspirited negroes.

Good fellows, thought Captain Delano, a little training would make fine sailors of them. Why see, the very women pull and sing too. These must be some of those Ashantee negresses that make such capital soldiers, I've heard. But who's at the helm? I must have a good hand there.

He went to see.

The *San Dominick* steered with a cumbrous tiller, with large horizontal pulleys attached. At each pulley-end stood a subordinate black, and between them, at the tiller-head, the responsible post, a Spanish seaman, whose countenance evinced his due share in the general hopefulness and confidence at the coming of the breeze.

He proved the same man who had behaved with so shame-faced an air on the windlass.

"Ah,—it is you, my man," exclaimed Captain Delano—"well, no more sheep's eyes now;—look straight forward and keep the ship so. Good hand, I trust? And want to get into the harbor, don't you?

The man assented with an inward chuckle, grasping the tillerhead firmly. Upon this, unperceived by the American, the two blacks eyed the sailor intently.

Finding all right at the helm, the pilot went forward to the forecastle, to see how matters stood there.

The ship now had way enough to breast the current. With the approach of evening, the breeze would be sure to freshen.

Having done all that was needed for the present, Captain Delano, giving his last orders to the sailors, turned aft to report affairs to Don Benito in the cabin; perhaps additionally incited to rejoin him by the hope of snatching a moment's private chat while the servant was engaged upon deck.

From opposite sides, there were, beneath the poop, two approaches to the cabin; one further forward than the other, and consequently communicating with a longer passage. Marking the servant still above, Captain Delano, taking the nighest entrance—the one last named, and at whose porch Atufal still stood—hurried on his way, till, arrived at the cabin threshold, he paused an instant, a little to recover from his eagerness. Then, with the words of his intended business upon his lips, he entered. As he advanced toward the seated Spaniard, he heard another footstep, keeping time with his. From the opposite door, a salver in hand, the servant was likewise advancing.

"Confound the faithful fellow," thought Captain Delano; "what a vexatious coincidence."

Possibly, the vexation might have been something different, were it not for the brisk confidence inspired by the breeze. But even as it was, he felt a slight twinge, from a sudden indefinite association in his mind of Babo with Atufal.

"Don Benito," said he, "I give you joy; the breeze will hold, and will increase. By the way, your tall man and time-piece, Atufal, stands without. By your order, of course?"

Don Benito recoiled, as if at some bland satirical touch, delivered with such adroit garnish of apparent good breeding as to present no handle for retort.

He is like one flayed alive, thought Captain Delano; where may one touch him without causing a shrink?

The servant moved before his master, adjusting a cushion; recalled to civility, the Spaniard stiffly replied: "You are right. The slave appears where you saw him, according to my command; which is, that if at the given hour I am below, he must take his stand and abide my coming."

"Ah now, pardon me, but that is treating the poor fellow like an ex-king indeed. Ah, Don Benito," smiling, "for all the license you permit in some things, I fear lest, at bottom, you are a bitter hard master."

Again Don Benito shrank; and this time, as the good sailor thought, from a genuine twinge of his conscience.

Again conversation became constrained. In vain Captain Delano called attention to the now perceptible motion of the keel gently cleaving the sea; with lacklustre eye, Don Benito returned words few and reserved.

By and by, the wind having steadily risen, and still blowing right into the harbor, bore the *San Dominick* swiftly on. Rounding a point of land, the sealer at distance came into open view.

Meantime Captain Delano had again repaired to the deck, remaining there some time. Having at last altered the ship's course, so as to give the reef a wide berth, he returned for a few moments below.

I will cheer up my poor friend, this time, thought he.

"Better and better, Don Benito," he cried as he blithely re-entered: "there will soon be an end to your cares, at least for a while. For when, after a long, sad voyage, you know, the anchor drops into the haven, all its vast weight seems lifted from the captain's heart. We are getting on famously, Don Benito. My ship is in sight. Look through this side-light here; there she is; all a-taunt-o! The *Bachelor's Delight*, my good friend. Ah, how this wind braces one up. Come, you must take a cup of coffee with me this evening. My old steward will give you as fine a cup as ever any sultan tasted. What say you, Don Benito, will you?"

At first, the Spaniard glanced feverishly up, casting a longing look towards the sealer, while with mute concern his servant gazed into his face. Suddenly the old ague of coldness returned, and dropping back to his cushions he was silent.

"You do not answer. Come, all day you have been my host; would you have hospitality all on one side?"

"I cannot go," was the response.

"What? It will not fatigue you. The ships will lie together as near as they can, without swinging foul. It will be little more than stepping from deck to deck; which is but as from room to room. Come, come, you must not refuse me."

"I cannot go," decisively and repulsively repeated Don Benito.

Renouncing all but the last appearance of courtesy, with a sort of cadaverous sullenness, and biting his thin nails to the quick, he glanced, almost glared, at his guest, as if impatient that a stranger's presence should interfere with the full indulgence of his morbid hour. Meantime the sound of the parted waters came more and more gurglingly and merrily in at the windows; as reproaching him for his dark spleen; as telling him that, sulk as he might, and go mad with it, nature cared not a jot; since, whose fault was it, pray?

But the foul mood was now at its depth, as the fair wind at its height.

There was something in the man so far beyond any mere unsociality or sourness previously evinced, that even the forbearing good-nature of his guest could no longer endure it. Wholly at a loss to account for such demeanor, and deeming sickness with eccentricity, however extreme, no adequate excuse, well satisfied, too, that nothing in his own conduct could justify it, Captain Delano's pride began to be roused. Himself became reserved. But all seemed one to the Spaniard. Quitting him, therefore, Captain Delano once more went to the deck.

The ship was now within less than two miles of the sealer. The whale-boat was seen darting over the interval.

To be brief, the two vessels, thanks to the pilot's skill, ere long in neighborly style lay anchored together.

Before returning to his own vessel, Captain Delano had intended communicating to Don Benito the smaller details of the proposed services to be rendered. But, as it was, unwilling anew to subject himself to rebuffs, he resolved, now that he had seen the *San Dominick* safely moored, immediately to quit her, without further allusion to hospitality or business. Indefinitely postponing his ulterior plans, he would regulate his future actions according to future circumstances. His boat was ready to receive him; but his host still tarried below. Well, thought Captain Delano, if he has little breeding, the more need to show mine. He descended to the cabin to bid a ceremonious, and, it may be, tacitly rebukeful adieu. But to his great satisfaction, Don Benito, as if he began to feel the weight of that treatment with which his slighted guest had, not indecorously, retaliated upon him, now supported by his servant, rose to his feet, and grasping Captain Delano's hand, stood tremulous; too much agitated to speak. But the good augury hence drawn was suddenly dashed, by his resuming all his previous reserve, with augmented gloom, as, with half-averted eyes, he silently reseated himself on his cushions. With a corresponding return of his own chilled feelings, Captain Delano bowed and withdrew.

He was hardly midway in the narrow corridor, dim as a tunnel, leading from the cabin to the stairs, when a sound, as of the tolling for execution in some jail-yard, fell on his ears. It was the echo of the ship's flawed bell, striking the hour, drearily reverberated in this subterranean vault. Instantly, by a fatality not to be withstood, his mind, responsive to the portent, swarmed with superstitious suspicions. He paused. In images far swifter than these sentences, the minutest details of all his former distrusts swept through him.

Hitherto, credulous good-nature had been too ready to furnish excuses for reasonable fears. Why was the Spaniard, so superfluously punctilious at times, now heedless of common propriety in not accompanying to the side his departing guest? Did indisposition forbid? Indisposition had not forbidden more irksome exertion that day. His last equivocal demeanor recurred. He had risen to his feet, grasped his guest's hand, motioned toward his hat; then, in an instant, all was eclipsed in sinister muteness and gloom. Did this imply one brief, repentant relenting at the final moment, from some iniquitous plot, followed by remorseless return to it? His last glance seemed to express a calamitous, yet acquiescent farewell to Captain Delano forever. Why decline the invitation to visit the sealer that evening? Or was the Spaniard less hardened than the Jew, who refrained not from supping at the board of him whom the same night he meant to betray?[52] What imported all those day-long enigmas and contradictions, except they were intended to mystify, preliminary to some stealthy blow? Atufal, the pretended rebel, but punctual shadow, that moment lurked by the threshold without. He seemed a sentry, and more. Who, by his own confession, had stationed him there? Was the negro now lying in wait?

The Spaniard behind—his creature before: to rush from darkness to light was the involuntary choice.

The next moment, with clenched jaw and hand, he passed Atufal, and stood unharmed in the light. As he saw his trim ship lying peacefully at anchor, and almost within ordinary call; as he saw his household boat, with familiar faces in it, patiently rising and falling on the short waves by the *San Dominick's* side; and then, glancing about the decks where he stood, saw the oakum-pickers still gravely plying their fingers; and heard the low, buzzing whistle and industrious hum of the hatchet-polishers, still bestirring themselves over their endless occupation; and more than all, as he saw the benign aspect of nature, taking her innocent repose in the evening; the screened sun in the quiet camp of the west shining out like the mild light from Abraham's[53] tent; as charmed eye and ear took in all these, with the chained figure of the black, clenched jaw and hand relaxed. Once again he smiled at the phantoms which had mocked him, and felt something like a tinge of remorse, that, by harboring them even for a moment, he should, by implication, have betrayed an atheist doubt of the ever-watchful Providence above.

There was a few minutes' delay, while, in obedience to his orders, the boat was being hooked along to the gangway. During this interval, a sort of saddened satisfaction stole over Captain Delano, at thinking of the kindly offices he had that day discharged for a stranger. Ah, thought he, after good actions one's conscience is never ungrateful, however much so the benefited party may be.

---

[52]Judas. See Matthew 26.
[53]Hebrew patriarch, the father of many nations, is the subject of Genesis 11–25; God bestows his blessing in Genesis 22:17–18.

Presently, his foot, at the first act of descent into the boat, pressed the first round of the side-ladder, his face presented inward upon the deck. In the same moment, he heard his name courteously sounded; and, to his pleased surprise, saw Don Benito advancing—an unwonted energy in his air, as if, at the last moment, intent upon making amends for his recent discourtesy. With instinctive good feeling, Captain Delano, withdrawing his foot, turned and reciprocally advanced. As he did so, the Spaniard's nervous eagerness increased, but his vital energy failed; so that, the better to support him, the servant, placing his master's hand on his naked shoulder, and gently holding it there, formed himself into a sort of crutch.

When the two captains met, the Spaniard again fervently took the hand of the American, at the same time casting an earnest glance into his eyes, but, as before, too much overcome to speak.

I have done him wrong, self-reproachfully thought Captain Delano; his apparent coldness has deceived me; in no instance has he meant to offend.

Meantime, as if fearful that the continuance of the scene might too much unstring his master, the servant seemed anxious to terminate it. And so still presenting himself as a crutch, and walking between the two captains, he advanced with them towards the gangway; while still, as if full of kindly contrition, Don Benito would not let go the hand of Captain Delano, but retained it in his, across the black's body.

Soon they were standing by the side, looking over into the boat, whose crew turned up their curious eyes. Waiting a moment for the Spaniard to relinquish his hold, the now embarrassed Captain Delano lifted his foot, to overstep the threshold of the open gangway; but still Don Benito would not let go his hand. And yet, with an agitated tone, he said, "I can go no further; here I must bid you adieu. Adieu, my dear, dear Don Amasa. Go—go!" suddenly tearing his hand loose, "go, and God guard you better than me, my best friend."

Not unaffected, Captain Delano would now have lingered; but catching the meekly admonitory eye of the servant, with a hasty farewell he descended into his boat, followed by the continual adieus of Don Benito, standing rooted in the gangway.

Seating himself in the stern, Captain Delano, making a last salute, ordered the boat shoved off. The crew had their oars on end. The bowsmen pushed the boat a sufficient distance for the oars to be lengthwise dropped. The instant that was done, Don Benito sprang over the bulwarks, falling at the feet of Captain Delano; at the same time calling towards his ship, but in tones so frenzied, that none in the boat could understand him. But, as if not equally obtuse, three sailors, from three different and distant parts of the ship, splashed into the sea, swimming after their captain, as if intent upon his rescue.

The dismayed officer of the boat eagerly asked what this meant. To which, Captain Delano, turning a disdainful smile upon the unaccountable Spaniard, answered, that, for his part, he neither knew nor cared; but it seemed as if Don Benito had taken it into his head to produce the impression among his people that the boat wanted to kidnap him. "Or else—give way for your lives," he wildly added, starting at a clattering hubbub in the ship, above which rang the tocsin[54] of the hatchet-polishers; and seizing Don Benito by the throat he added, "this plotting pirate means murder!" Here, in apparent verification of the words, the servant, a dagger in his hand, was seen on the rail overhead, poised, in the act of leaping, as if with desperate fidelity to befriend his master to the last; while, seem-

---

[54]Alarm bell.

ingly to aid the black, the three white sailors were trying to clamber into the hampered bow. Meantime, the whole host of negroes, as if inflamed at the sight of their jeopardized captain, impended in one sooty avalanche over the bulwarks.

All this, with what preceded, and what followed, occurred with such involutions of rapidity, that past, present, and future seemed one.

Seeing the negro coming, Captain Delano had flung the Spaniard aside, almost in the very act of clutching him, and, by the unconscious recoil, shifting his place, with arms thrown up, so promptly grappled the servant in his descent, that with dagger presented at Captain Delano's heart, the black seemed of purpose to have leaped there as to his mark. But the weapon was wrenched away, and the assailant dashed down into the bottom of the boat, which now, with disentangled oars, began to speed through the sea.

At this juncture, the left hand of Captain Delano, on one side, again clutched the half-reclining Don Benito, heedless that he was in a speechless faint, while his right foot, on the other side, ground the prostrate negro; and his right arm pressed for added speed on the after oar, his eye bent forward, encouraging his men to their utmost.

But here, the officer of the boat, who had at last succeeded in beating off the towing sailors, and was now, with face turned aft, assisting the bowsman at his oar, suddenly called to Captain Delano, to see what the black was about; while a Portuguese oarsman shouted to him to give heed to what the Spaniard was saying.

Glancing down at his feet, Captain Delano saw the freed hand of the servant aiming with a second dagger—a small one, before concealed in his wool—with this he was snakishly writhing up from the boat's bottom, at the heart of his master, his countenance lividly vindictive, expressing the centred purpose of his soul; while the Spaniard, half-choked, was vainly shrinking away, with husky words, incoherent to all but the Portuguese.

That moment, across the long-benighted mind of Captain Delano, a flash of revelation swept, illuminating, in unanticipated clearness, his host's whole mysterious demeanor, with every enigmatic event of the day, as well as the entire past voyage of the *San Dominick*. He smote Babo's hand down, but his own heart smote him harder. With infinite pity he withdrew his hold from Don Benito. Not Captain Delano, but Don Benito, the black, in leaping into the boat, had intended to stab.

Both the black's hands were held, as, glancing up towards the *San Dominick*, Captain Delano, now with scales dropped from his eyes, saw the negroes, not in misrule, not in tumult, not as if frantically concerned for Don Benito, but with mask torn away, flourishing hatchets, and knives, in ferocious piratical revolt. Like delirious black dervishes, the six Ashantees danced on the poop. Prevented by their foes from springing into the water, the Spanish boys were hurrying up to the topmost spars, while such of the few Spanish sailors, not already in the sea, less alert, were descried, helplessly mixed in, on deck, with the blacks.

Meantime Captain Delano hailed his own vessel, ordering the ports up, and the guns run out. But by this time the cable of the *San Dominick* had been cut; and the fag-end, in lashing out, whipped away the canvas shroud about the beak, suddenly revealing, as the bleached hull swung round towards the open ocean, death for the figurehead, in a human skeleton; chalky comment on the chalked words below, *"Follow your leader."*

At the sight, Don Benito, covering his face, wailed out: "Tis he, Aranda! my murdered, unburied friend!"

Upon reaching the sealer, calling for ropes, Captain Delano bound the negro, who made no resistance, and had him hoisted to the deck. He would then have assisted the now almost helpless Don Benito up the side; but Don Benito, wan as he was, refused to move, or be moved, until the negro should have been first put below out of view. When, presently assured that it was done, he no more shrank from the ascent.

The boat was immediately dispatched back to pick up the three swimming sailors. Meantime, the guns were in readiness, though, owing to the *San Dominick* having glided somewhat astern of the sealer, only the aftermost one could be brought to bear. With this, they fired six times; thinking to cripple the fugitive ship by bringing down her spars. But only a few inconsiderable ropes were shot away. Soon the ship was beyond the gun's range, steering broad out of the bay; the blacks thickly clustering round the bowsprit, one moment with taunting cries towards the whites, the next with upthrown gestures hailing the now dusky moors of ocean—cawing crows escaped from the hand of the fowler.

The first impulse was to slip the cables and give chase. But, upon second thoughts, to pursue with whale-boat and yawl seemed more promising.

Upon inquiring of Don Benito what fire-arms they had on board the *San Dominick,* Captain Delano was answered that they had none that could be used; because, in the earlier stages of the mutiny, a cabin-passenger, since dead, had secretly put out of order the locks of what few muskets there were. But with all his remaining strength, Don Benito entreated the American not to give chase, either with ship or boat; for the negroes had already proved themselves such desperadoes, that, in case of a present assault, nothing but a total massacre of the whites could be looked for. But, regarding this warning as coming from one whose spirit had been crushed by misery, the American did not give up his design.

The boats were got ready and armed. Captain Delano ordered his men into them. He was going himself when Don Benito grasped his arm.

"What! have you saved my life, Señor, and are you now going to throw away your own?"

The Officers also, for reasons connected with their interests and those of the voyage, and a duty owing to the owners, strongly objected against their commander's going. Weighing their remonstrances a moment, Captain Delano felt bound to remain; appointing his chief mate—an athletic and resolute man, who had been a privateer's-man[55]—to head the party. The more to encourage the sailors, they were told, that the Spanish captain considered his ship good as lost; that she and her cargo, including some gold and silver, were worth more than a thousand doubloons. Take her, and no small part should be theirs. The sailors replied with a shout.

The fugitives had now almost gained an offing. It was nearly night; but the moon was rising. After hard, prolonged pulling, the boats came up on the ship's quarters, at a suitable distance laying upon their oars to discharge their muskets. Having no bullets to return, the negroes sent their yells. But, upon the second volley, Indian-like, they hurled their hatchets. One took off a sailor's fingers. Another struck the whale-boat's bow, cutting off the rope there, and remaining stuck in the gunwale like a woodman's axe. Snatching it, quivering from its lodgment, the mate hurled it back. The returned gauntlet now stuck in the ship's broken quarter-gallery, and so remained.

The negroes giving too hot a reception, the whites kept a more respectful distance. Hovering now just out of reach of the hurtling hatchets, they, with a view of the close encounter which must soon come, sought to decoy the blacks into entirely disarming themselves of their most murderous weapons in a hand-to-hand fight, by foolishly flinging them, as missiles, short of the mark, into the sea. But, ere long, perceiving the stratagem, the negroes desisted, though not before many

---

[55]Served on a ship licensed by a country to engage in piracy against the ships of other countries.

of them had to replace their lost hatchets with handspikes; an exchange which, as counted upon, proved, in the end, favorable to the assailants.

Meantime, with a strong wind, the ship still clove the water; the boats alternately falling behind, and pulling up, to discharge fresh volleys.

The fire was mostly directed towards the stern, since there, chiefly, the negroes, at present, were clustering. But to kill or maim the negroes was not the object. To take them, with the ship, was the object. To do it, the ship must be boarded; which could not be done by boats while she was sailing so fast.

A thought now struck the mate. Observing the Spanish boys still aloft, high as they could get, he called to them to descend to the yards, and cut adrift the sails. It was done. About this time, owing to causes hereafter to be shown, two Spaniards, in the dress of sailors, and conspicuously showing themselves, were killed; not by volleys, but by deliberate marksman's shots; while, as it afterward appeared, by one of the general discharges, Atufal, the black, and the Spaniard at the helm likewise were killed. What now, with the loss of the sails, and loss of leaders, the ship became unmanageable to the negroes.

With creaking masts, she came heavily round to the wind; the prow slowly swinging into view of the boats, its skeleton gleaming in the horizontal moonlight, and casting a gigantic ribbed shadow upon the water. One extended arm of the ghost seemed beckoning the whites to avenge it.

"Follow your leader!" cried the mate; and, one on each bow, the boats boarded. Sealing-spears and cutlasses crossed hatchets and hand-spikes. Huddled upon the long-boat amidships, the negresses raised a wailing chant, whose chorus was the clash of the steel.

For a time, the attack wavered; the negroes wedging themselves to beat it back; the half-repelled sailors, as yet unable to gain a footing, fighting as troopers in the saddle, one leg sideways flung over the bulwarks, and one without, plying their cutlasses like carters' whips. But in vain. They were almost overborne, when, rallying themselves into a squad as one man, with a huzza, they sprang inboard, where, entangled, they involuntarily separated again. For a few breaths' space, there was a vague, muffled, inner sound, as of submerged sword-fish rushing hither and thither through shoals of black-fish. Soon, in a reunited band, and joined by the Spanish seamen, the whites came to the surface, irresistibly driving the negroes toward the stern. But a barricade of casks and sacks, from side to side, had been thrown up by the main-mast. Here the negroes faced about, and though scorning peace or truce, yet fain would have had respite. But, without pause, overleaping the barrier, the unflagging sailors again closed. Exhausted, the blacks now fought in despair. Their red tongues lolled, wolf-like, from their black mouths. But the pale sailors' teeth were set; not a word was spoken; and in five minutes more, the ship was won.

Nearly a score of the negroes were killed. Exclusive of those by the balls,[56] many were mangled; their wounds—mostly inflicted by the long-edged sealing-spears, resembling those shaven ones of the English at Preston Pans, made by the poled scythes of the Highlanders.[57] On the other side, none were killed, though several were wounded; some severely, including the mate. The surviving negroes were temporarily secured, and the ship, towed back into the harbor at midnight, once more lay anchored.

Omitting the incidents and arrangements ensuing, suffice it that, after two days spent in refitting, the ships sailed in company for Concepcion, in Chile, and thence for Lima, in Peru; where, before the vice-regal courts, the whole affair, from the beginning, underwent investigation.

---

[56]I.e., musket balls.
[57]At the Battle of Prestonpans (1745), the Scottish Prince   Charles Edward defeated the English forces by using poles with scythes fastened at the end.

Though, midway on the passage, the ill-fated Spaniard, relaxed from constraint, showed some signs of regaining health with free-will; yet, agreeably to his own foreboding, shortly before arriving at Lima, he relapsed, finally becoming so reduced as to be carried ashore in arms. Hearing of his story and plight, one of the many religious institutions of the City of Kings opened an hospitable refuge to him, where both physician and priest were his nurses, and a member of the order volunteered to be his one special guardian and consoler, by night and by day.

The following extracts, translated from one of the official Spanish documents, will, it is hoped, shed light on the preceding narrative, as well as, in the first place, reveal the true port of departure and true history of the *San Dominick's* voyage, down to the time of her touching at the island of Santa Maria.

But, ere the extracts come, it may be well to preface them with a remark.

The document selected, from among many others, for partial translation, contains the deposition of Benito Cereno; the first taken in the case. Some disclosures therein were, at the time, held dubious for both learned and natural reasons. The tribunal inclined to the opinion that the deponent, not undisturbed in his mind by recent events, raved of some things which could never have happened. But subsequent depositions of the surviving sailors, bearing out the revelations of their captain in several of the strangest particulars, gave credence to the rest. So that the tribunal, in its final decision, rested its capital sentences upon statements which, had they lacked confirmation, it would have deemed it but duty to reject.

I, DON JOSE DE ABOS AND PADILLA, *His Majesty's Notary for the Royal Revenue, and Register of this Province, and Notary Public of the Holy Crusade of this Bishoprick, &c.*

Do certify and declare, as much as is requisite in law, that, in the criminal cause commenced the twenty-fourth of the month of September, in the year seventeen hundred and ninety-nine, against the negroes of the ship San Dominick, *the following declaration before me was made:*

Declaration of the first Witness, DON BENITO CERENO.

The same day and month and year, His Honor, Doctor Juan Martinez de Rozas, Councilor of the Royal Audience of this Kingdom, and learned in the law of this Intendency,[58] ordered the captain of the ship San Dominick, *Don Benito Cereno, to appear; which he did in his litter, attended by the monk Infelez; of whom he received the oath, which he took by God, our Lord, and a Sign of the Cross; under which he promised to tell the truth of whatever he should know and should be asked;—and being interrogated agreeably to the tenor of the act, commencing the process, he said, that on the twentieth of May last, he set sail with his ship from the port of Valparaiso, bound to that of Callao; loaded with the produce of the country beside thirty cases of hardware and one hundred and sixty blacks, of both sexes, mostly belonging to Don Alexandro Aranda, gentleman, of the City of Mendoza; that the crew of the ship consisted of thirty-six men, beside the persons who went as passengers; that the negroes were in part as follows:*

[Here, in the original, follows a list of some fifty names, descriptions, and ages compiled from certain recovered documents of Aranda's and also from recollections of the deponent, from which portions only are extracted.][59]

—One, from about eighteen to nineteen years, named José, and this was the man that waited upon his master, Don Alexandro, and who speaks well the Spanish, having served

---

[58]District.
[59]Brackets and ellipses throughout this passage are Melville's.

*him four or five years;*** *a mulatto, named Francesco, the cabin steward, of a good person and voice, having sung in the Valparaiso churches, native of the province of Buenos Ayres, aged about thirty-five years. ***A smart negro, named Dago, who had been for many years a gravedigger among the Spaniards, aged forty-six years. *** Four old negroes, born in Africa, from sixty to seventy, but sound, calkers by trade, whose names are as follows:—the first was named Mure, and he was killed (as was also his son named Diamelo); the second, Nacta; the third, Yola, likewise killed; the fourth, Ghofan; and six full-grown negroes, aged from thirty to forty-five, all raw, and born among the Ashantees—Matinqui, Yau, Leche, Mapenda, Yambaio, Akim; four of whom were killed; *** a powerful negro named Atufal, who being supposed to have been a chief in Africa, his owner set great store by him. *** And a small negro of Senegal, but some years among the Spaniards, aged about thirty, which negro's name was Babo; *** that he does not remember the names of the others, but that still expecting the residue of Don Alexandro's papers will be found, will then take due account of them all, and remit to the court; *** and thirty-nine women and children of all ages.*

[The catalogue over, the deposition goes on:]

*** *That all the negroes slept upon deck, as is customary in this navigation, and none wore fetters, because the owner, his friend Aranda, told him that they were all tractable; *** that on the seventh day after leaving port, at three o'clock in the morning, all the Spaniards being asleep except the two officers on the watch, who were the boatswain, Juan Robles, and the carpenter, Juan Bautista Gayete, and the helmsman and his boy, the negroes revolted suddenly, wounded dangerously the boatswain and the carpenter, and successively killed eighteen men of those who were sleeping upon deck, some with hand-spikes and hatchets, and others by throwing them alive overboard, after tying them; that of the Spaniards upon deck, they left about seven, as he thinks, alive and tied, to manœuvre the ship, and three or four more, who hid themselves, remained also alive. Although in the act of revolt the negroes made themselves masters of the hatchway, six or seven wounded went through it to the cock-pit, without any hindrance on their part; that during the act of revolt, the mate and another person, whose name he does not recollect, attempted to come up through the hatchway, but being quickly wounded, were obliged to return to the cabin; that the deponent resolved at break of day to come up the companionway, where the negro Babo was, being the ringleader, and Atufal, who assisted him, and having spoken to them, exhorted them to cease committing such atrocities, asking them, at the same time, what they wanted and intended to do, offering, himself, to obey their commands; that notwithstanding this, they threw, in his presence, three men, alive and tied, overboard; that they told the deponent to come up, and that they would not kill him; which having done, the negro Babo asked him whether there were in those seas any negro countries where they might be carried, and he answered them, No; that the negro Babo afterwards told him to carry them to Senegal, or to the neighboring islands of St. Nicholas; and he answered, that this was impossible, on account of the great distance, the necessity involved of rounding Cape Horn, the bad condition of the vessel, the want of provisions, sails, and water; but that the negro Babo replied to him he must carry them in any way; that they would do and conform themselves to everything the deponent should require as to eating and drinking; that after a long conference, being absolutely compelled to please them, for they threatened to kill all the whites if they were not, at all events, carried to Senegal, he told them that what was most wanting for the voyage was water; that they would go near the coast to take it, and thence they would proceed on their course; that the negro Babo agreed to it; and the deponent steered towards the intermediate ports, hoping to meet some Spanish or foreign vessel that would save them; that within ten or eleven days they saw the land, and continued their course by it in the vicinity of Nasca; that the deponent observed that the negroes were now restless and mutinous, because he did not effect the taking in of water, the negro Babo having required, with threats, that it should be done, without fail, the following day; he* told him he saw plainly that the coast was steep, and the rivers designated in the maps were not to be found, with other reasons suitable to the circumstances; that the best way would be to go to the island of Santa Maria, where they might water easily, it being a solitary island, as the foreigners did; that the deponent did not go to Pisco, that was near, nor make any other port of the coast, because the negro Babo had intimated to him several times, that he would kill all the whites the very moment he should perceive any city, town, or settlement of any kind on the shores to which they should be carried; that having determined to go to the island of Santa Maria, as the deponent had planned, for the purpose of trying whether, on the passage or near the island itself, they could find any vessel that should favor them, or whether he could escape from it in a boat to the neighboring coast of Arauco, to adopt the necessary means he immediately changed his course, steering for the island; that the negroes Babo and Atufal held daily conferences, in which they discussed what was necessary for their design of returning to Senegal, whether they were to kill all the Spaniards, and particularly the deponent; that eight days after parting from the coast of Nasca, the deponent being on the watch a little after day-break, and soon after the negroes had their meeting, the negro Babo came to the place where the deponent was, and told him that he had determined to kill his master, Don Alexandro Aranda, both because he and his companions could not otherwise be sure of their liberty, and that to keep the seamen in subjection, he wanted to prepare a warning of what road they should be made to take did they or any of them oppose him; and that, by means of the death of Don Alexandro, that warning would best be given; but, that what this last meant, the deponent did not at the time comprehend, nor could not, further than that the death of Don Alexandro was intended; and moreover the negro Babo proposed to the deponent to call the mate Raneds, who was sleeping in the cabin, before the thing was done, for fear, as the deponent understood it that the mate, who was a good navigator, should not be killed with Don Alexandro and the rest; that the deponent, who was the friend, from youth, of Don Alexandro, prayed and conjured, but all was useless; for the negro Babo answered him that the thing could not be prevented, and that all the Spaniards risked their death if they should attempt to frustrate his will in this matter, or any other; that, in this conflict, the deponent called the mate, Raneds, who was forced to go apart, and immediately the negro Babo commanded the Ashantee Matinqui and the Ashantee Leche to go and commit the murder; that those two went down with hatchets to the berth of Don Alexandro; that, yet half alive and mangled, they dragged him on deck; that they were going to throw him overboard in that state, but the negro Babo stopped them, bidding the murder be completed on the deck before him, which was done, when, by his orders, the body was carried below, forward; that nothing more was seen of it by the deponent for three days; *** that Don Alonzo Sidonia, an old man, long resident at Valparaiso, and lately appointed to a civil office in Peru, whither he had taken passage, was at the time sleeping in the berth opposite Don Alexandro's; that awakening at his cries, surprised by them, and at the sight of the negroes with their bloody hatchets in their hands, he threw himself into the sea through a window which was near him, and was drowned, without it being in the power of the deponent to assist or take him up; *** that a short time after killing Aranda, they brought upon deck his cousin-german, of middle-age, Don Francisco Masa, of Mendoza, and the young Don Joaquin, Marques de Aramboalaza, then lately from Spain, with his Spanish servant Ponce, and the three young clerks of Aranda, José Morairi, Lorenzo Bargas, and Hermenegildo Gandix, all of Cadiz; that Don Joaquin and Hermenegildo Gandix, the negro Babo, for purposes hereafter to appear, preserved alive; but Don Francisco Masa, José Morairi, and Lorenzo Bargas, with Ponce the servant, beside the boatswain, Juan Robles, the boatswain's mates, Manuel Viscaya and Roderigo Hurta, and four of the sailors, the negro Babo ordered to be thrown alive into the sea, although they made no resistance, nor begged for anything else but mercy; that the boatswain, Juan Robles, who knew how to swim, kept the longest above water, making acts of contrition, and, in the last words he uttered, charged this deponent to cause mass to be said for his soul to our Lady of Succor; *** that, during the three days which followed, the deponent, uncertain what fate *had befallen the remains of Don Alexandro, frequently asked the negro Babo where they were, and, if still on board, whether they were to be preserved for interment ashore, entreating him so to order it; that the negro Babo answered nothing till the fourth day, when at sunrise, the deponent coming on deck, the negro Babo showed him a skeleton, which had been substituted for the ship's proper figure-head—the image of Cristobal Colon, the discoverer of the New World; that the negro Babo asked him whose skeleton that was, and whether, from its whiteness, he should not think it a white's; that, upon discovering his face, the negro Babo, coming close, said words to this effect: "Keep faith with the blacks from here to Senegal, or you shall in spirit, as now in body, follow your leader," pointing to the prow; *** that the same morning the negro Babo took by succession each Spaniard forward, and asked him whose skeleton that was, and whether, from its whiteness, he should not think it a white's; that each Spaniard covered his face; that then to each the negro Babo repeated the words in the first place said to the deponent; *** that they (the Spaniards), being then assembled aft, the negro Babo harangued them, saying that he had now done all; that the deponent (as navigator for the negroes) might pursue his course, warning him and all of them that they should, soul and body, go the way of Don Alexandro, if he saw them (the Spaniards) speak or plot anything against them (the negroes)—a threat which was repeated every day; that, before the events last mentioned, they had tied the cook to throw him overboard, for it is not known what thing they heard him speak, but finally the negro Babo spared his life, at the request of the deponent; that a few days after, the deponent, endeavoring not to omit any means to preserve the lives of the remaining whites, spoke to the negroes peace and tranquillity, and agreed to draw up a paper, signed by the deponent and the sailors who could write, as also by the negro Babo, for himself and all the blacks, in which the deponent obliged himself to carry them to Senegal, and they not to kill any more, and he formally to make over to them the ship, with the cargo, with which they were for that time satisfied and quieted. *** But the next day, the more surely to guard against the sailors' escape, the negro Babo commanded all the boats to be destroyed but the long-boat, which was unseaworthy, and another, a cutter in good condition, which knowing it would yet be wanted for towing the water casks, he had it lowered down into the hold. ****

[Various particulars of the prolonged and perplexed navigation ensuing here follow, with incidents of a calamitous calm, from which portion one passage is extracted, to wit:]

—*That on the fifth day of the calm, all on board suffering much from the heat, and want of water, and five having died in fits, and mad, the negroes became irritable, and for a chance gesture, which they deemed suspicious—though it was harmless—made by the mate, Raneds, to the deponent in the act of handing a quadrant, they killed him; but that for this they afterwards were sorry, the mate being the only remaining navigator on board, except the deponent.*

. . . . .

—*That omitting other events, which daily happened, and which can only serve uselessly to recall past misfortunes and conflicts, after seventy-three days' navigation, reckoned from the time they sailed from Nasca, during which they navigated under a scanty allowance of water, and were afflicted with the calms before mentioned, they at last arrived at the island of Santa Maria, on the seventeenth of the month of August, at about six o'clock in the afternoon, at which hour they cast anchor very near the American ship,* Bachelor's Delight, *which lay in the same bay, commanded by the generous Captain Amasa Delano; but at six o'clock in the morning, they had already descried the port, and the negroes became uneasy, as soon as at distance they saw the ship, not having expected to see one there; that the negro Babo pacified them, assuring them that no fear need be had; that straightway he ordered the figure on the bow to be covered with canvas, as for repairs, and*

*had the decks a little set in order; that for a time the negro Babo and the negro Atufal
conferred; that the negro Atufal was for sailing away, but the negro Babo would not, and,
by himself, cast about what to do; that at last he came to the deponent, proposing to him to
say and do all that the deponent declares to have said and done to the American captain;
*** that the negro Babo warned him that if he varied in the least, or uttered any word, or
gave any look that should give the least intimation of the past events or present state, he
would instantly kill him, with all his companions, showing a dagger, which he carried hid,
saying something which, as he understood it, meant that that dagger would be alert as his
eye; that the negro Babo then announced the plan to all his companions, which pleased
them; that he then, the better to disguise the truth, devised many expedients, in some of
them uniting deceit and defense; that of this sort was the device of the six Ashantees before
named, who were his bravoes;[60] that them he stationed on the break of the poop, as if to
clean certain hatchets (in cases, which were part of the cargo), but in reality to use them,
and distribute them at need, and at a given word he told them; that, among other devices,
was the device of presenting Atufal, his right hand man, as chained, though in a moment
the chains could be dropped; that in every particular he informed the deponent what part
he was expected to enact in every device, and what story he was to tell on every occasion,
always threatening him with instant death if he varied in the least; that, conscious that
many of the negroes would be turbulent, the negro Babo appointed the four aged negroes,
who were calkers, to keep what domestic order they could on the decks; that again and
again he harangued the Spaniards and his companions, informing them of his intent, and
of his devices, and of the invented story that this deponent was to tell; charging them lest
any of them varied from that story; that these arrangements were made and matured
during the interval of two or three hours, between their first sighting the ship and the
arrival on board of Captain Amasa Delano; that this happened about half-past seven
o'clock in the morning, Captain Amasa Delano coming in his boat, and all gladly
receiving him; that the deponent, as well as he could force himself, acting then the part of
principal owner, and a free captain of the ship, told Captain Amasa Delano, when called
upon, that he came from Buenos Ayres, bound to Lima, with three hundred negroes; that
off Cape Horn, and in a subsequent fever, many negroes had died; that also, by similar
casualties, all the sea-officers and the greatest part of the crew had died.*

· · · · · · ·

[And so the deposition goes on, circumstantially recounting the fictitious story
dictated to the deponent by Babo, and through the deponent imposed upon Captain Delano; and also recounting the friendly offers of Captain Delano, with other
things, but all of which is here omitted. After the fictitious story, etc., the deposition proceeds:]

*—that the generous Captain Amasa Delano remained on board all the day, till he left the
ship anchored at six o'clock in the evening, deponent speaking to him always of his pretended
misfortunes, under the forementioned principles, without having had it in his power to tell a
single word, or give him the least hint, that he might know the truth and state of things;
because the negro Babo, performing the office of an officious servant with all the appearance
of submission of the humble slave, did not leave the deponent one moment; that this was in
order to observe the deponent's actions and words, for the negro Babo understands well the
Spanish; and besides, there were thereabout some others who were constantly on the watch,
and likewise understood the Spanish; *** that upon one occasion, while deponent was standing on the deck conversing with Amasa Delano, by a secret sign the negro Babo drew him
(the deponent) aside, the act appearing as if originating with the deponent; that then, he
being drawn aside, the negro Babo proposed to him to gain from Amasa Delano full particulars about his ship, and crew, and arms; that the deponent asked "For what?" that the negro Babo answered he might conceive; that, grieved at the prospect of what might overtake*

---

[60]Assassins, desperadoes.

the generous Captain Amasa Delano, the deponent at first refused to ask the desired questions, and used every argument to induce the negro Babo to give up this new design; that the negro Babo showed the point of his dagger; that, after the information had been obtained, the negro Babo again drew him aside, telling him that that very night he (the deponent) would be captain of two ships, instead of one, for that, great part of the American's ship's crew being to be absent fishing, the six Ashantees, without any one else, would easily take it; that at this time he said other things to the same purpose; that no entreaties availed; that, before Amasa Delano's coming on board, no hint had been given touching the capture of the American ship; that to prevent this project the deponent was powerless; *** —*that in some things his memory is confused, he cannot distinctly recall every event,* *** —*that as soon as they had cast anchor at six o'clock in the evening, as has before been stated, the American Captain took leave, to return to his vessel; that upon a sudden impulse, which the deponent believes to have come from God and his angels, he, after the farewell had been said, followed the generous Captain Amasa Delano as far as the gunwale, where he stayed, under pretense of taking leave, until Amasa Delano should have been seated in his boat; that on shoving off, the deponent sprang from the gunwale into the boat, and fell into it, he knows not how, God guarding him; that—*

[Here, in the original, follows the account of what further happened at the escape, and how the *San Dominick* was retaken, and of the passage to the coast; including in the recital many expressions of "eternal gratitude" to the "generous Captain Amasa Delano." The deposition then proceeds with recapitulatory remarks, and a partial renumeration of the negroes, making record of their individual part in the past events, with a view to furnishing, according to command of the court, the data whereon to found the criminal sentences to be pronounced. From this portion is the following:]

—*That he believes that all the negroes, though not in the first place knowing to the design of revolt, when it was accomplished, approved it.* *** *That the negro, José, eighteen years old, and in the personal service of Don Alexandro, was the one who communicated the information to the negro Babo about the state of things in the cabin, before the revolt; that this is known, because, in the preceding nights, he used to come from his berth, which was under his master's, in the cabin, to the deck where the ringleader and his associates were, and had secret conversations with the negro Babo, in which he was several times seen by the mate; that, one night, the mate drove him away twice;* *** *that this same negro José was the one who, without being commanded to do so by the negro Babo, as Leche and Matinqui were, stabbed his master, Don Alexandro, after he had been dragged half-lifeless to the deck;* *** *that the mulatto steward, Francesco, was of the first band of revolters, that he was, in all things, the creature and tool of the negro Babo; that, to make his court, he, just before a repast in the cabin, proposed, to the negro Babo, poisoning a dish for the generous Captain Amasa Delano; this is known and believed, because the negroes have said it; but that the negro Babo, having another design, forbade Francesco;* *** *that the Ashantee Leche was one of the worst of them; for that, on the day the ship was retaken, he assisted in the defense of her, with a hatchet in each hand, with one of which he wounded, in the breast, the chief mate of Amasa Delano, in the first act of boarding; this all knew; that, in sight of the deponent, Leche struck with a hatchet, Don Francisco Masa, when, by the negro Babo's orders, he was carrying him to throw him overboard alive, beside participating in the murder, before mentioned, of Don Alexandro Aranda, and others of the cabin-passengers; that, owing to the fury with which the Ashantees fought in the engagement with the boats, but this Leche and Yau survived; that Yau was bad as Leche; that Yau was the man who, by Babo's command, willingly prepared the skeleton of Don Alexandro, in a way the negroes afterwards told the deponent, but which he, so long as reason is left him, can never divulge; that Yau and Leche were the two who, in a calm by night, riveted the skeleton to the bow; this also the negroes told him; that the negro Babo was he who traced the inscription below it; that the negro Babo was the plot-*

*ter from first to last; he ordered every murder, and was the helm and keel of the revolt; that Atufal was his lieutenant in all; but Atufal, with his own hand, committed no murder; nor did the negro Babo; *** that Atufal was shot, being killed in the fight with the boats, ere boarding; *** that the negresses of age, were knowing to the revolt, and testified themselves satisfied at the death of their master, Don Alexandro; that, had the negroes not restrained them, they would have tortured to death, instead of simply killing, the Spaniards slain by command of the negro Babo; that the negresses used their utmost influence to have the deponent made away with; that in the various acts of murder, they sang songs and danced—not gaily, but solemnly; and before the engagement with the boats, as well as during the action, they sang melancholy songs to the negroes, and that this melancholy tone was more inflaming than a different one would have been, and was so intended; that all this is believed, because the negroes have said it;—that of the thirty-six men of the crew, exclusive of the passengers (all of whom are now dead), which the deponent had knowledge of, six only remained alive, with four cabin-boys and ship-boys, not included with the crew; ***—that the negroes broke an arm of one of the cabin-boys and gave him strokes with hatchets.*

[Then follow various random disclosures referring to various periods of time. The following are extracted:]

*—That during the presence of Captain Amasa Delano on board, some attempts were made by the sailors, and one by Hermenegildo Gandix, to convey hints to him of the true state of affairs; but that these attempts were ineffectual, owing to fear of incurring death, and, furthermore, owing to the devices which offered contradictions to the true state of affairs, as well as owing to the generosity and piety of Amasa Delano incapable of sounding such wickedness; *** that Luys Galgo, a sailor about sixty years of age, and formerly of the King's navy, was one of those who sought to convey tokens to Captain Amasa Delano; but his intent, though undiscovered, being suspected, he was, on a pretense, made to retire out of sight, and at last into the hold, and there was made away with. This the negroes have since said; *** that one of the ship-boys feeling, from Captain Amasa Delano's presence, some hopes of release, and not having enough prudence, dropped some chance word respecting his expectations, which being overheard and understood by a slave-boy with whom he was eating at the time, the latter struck him on the head with a knife, inflicting a bad wound, but of which the boy is now healing; that likewise, not long before the ship was brought to anchor, one of the seamen, steering at the time, endangered himself by letting the blacks remark some expression in his countenance, arising from a cause similar to the above; but this sailor, by his heedful after conduct, escaped; *** that these statements are made to show the court that from the beginning to the end of the revolt, it was impossible for the deponent and his men to act otherwise than they did; ***—that the third clerk, Hermenegildo Gandix, who before had been forced to live among the seamen, wearing a seaman's habit, and in all respects appearing to be one for the time, he, Gandix was killed by a musket ball fired through mistake from the boats before boarding; having in his fright run up the mizzen-rigging, calling to the boats—"don't board," lest upon their boarding the negroes should kill him; that this inducing the Americans to believe he some way favored the cause of the negroes, they fired two balls at him, so that he fell wounded from the rigging, and was drowned in the sea; ***— that the young Don Joaquin, Marques de Aramboalaza, like Hermenegildo Gandix, the third clerk, was degraded to the office and appearance of a common seaman; that upon one occasion when Don Joaquin shrank, the negro Babo commanded the Ashantee Leche to take tar and heat it, and pour it upon Don Joaquin's hands; ***— that Don Joaquin was killed owing to another mistake of the Americans, but one impossible to be avoided, as upon the approach of the boats, Don Joaquin, with a hatchet tied edge out and upright to his hand, was made by the negroes to appear on the bulwarks; whereupon, seen with arms in his hands and in a questionable attitude, he was shot for a renegade seaman; ***—that on the person of Don Joaquin was found secreted a jewel, which, by papers that were discovered, proved to*

have been meant for the shrine of our Lady of Mercy in Lima; a votive offering, beforehand prepared and guarded, to attest his gratitude, when he should have landed in Peru, his last destination, for the safe conclusion of his entire voyage from Spain; ***—*that the jewel, with the other effects of the late Don Joaquin, is in the custody of the brethren of the Hospital de Sacerdotes, awaiting the disposition of the honorable court;* ***—*that, owing to the condition of the deponent, as well as the haste in which the boats departed for the attack, the Americans were not fore-warned that there were, among the apparent crew, a passenger and one of the clerks disguised by the negro Babo;* ***—*that, beside the negroes killed in the action, some were killed after the capture and re-anchoring at night, were shackled to the ring-bolts on deck; that these deaths were committed by the sailors, ere they could be prevented. That so soon as informed of it, Captain Amasa Delano used all his authority, and, in particular with his own hand, struck down Martinez Gola, who, having found a razor in the pocket of an old jacket of his, which one of the shackled negroes had on, was aiming it at the negro's throat; that the noble Captain Amasa Delano also wrenched from the hand of Bartholomew Barlo a dagger, secreted at the time of the massacre of the whites, with which he was in the act of stabbing a shackled negro, who, the same day, with another negro, had thrown him down and jumped upon him;* ***—*that, for all the events, befalling through so long a time, during which the ship was in the hands of the negro Babo, he cannot here give account; but that, what he has said is the most substantial of what occurs to him at present, and is the truth under the oath which he has taken; which declaration he affirmed and ratified, after hearing it read to him.*

He said that he is twenty-nine years of age, and broken in body and mind; that when finally dismissed by the court, he shall not return home to Chile, but betake himself to the monastery on Mount Agonia without; and signed with his honor, and crossed himself, and, for the time, departed as he came, in his litter, with the monk Infelez, to the Hospital de Sacerdotes.   BENITO CERENO.
DOCTOR ROZAS.

If the Deposition have served as the key to fit into the lock of the complications which precede it, then, as a vault whose door has been flung back, the *San Dominick's* hull lies open to-day.

Hitherto the nature of this narrative, besides rendering the intricacies in the beginning unavoidable, has more or less required that many things, instead of being set down in the order of occurrence, should be retrospectively, or irregularly given; this last is the case with the following passages, which will conclude the account:

During the long, mild voyage to Lima, there was, as before hinted, a period during which the sufferer a little recovered his health, or, at least in some degree, his tranquillity. Ere the decided relapse which came, the two captains had many cordial conversations—their fraternal unreserve in singular contrast with former withdrawments.

Again and again it was repeated, how hard it had been to enact the part forced on the Spaniard by Babo.

"Ah, my dear friend," Don Benito once said, "at those very times when you thought me so morose and ungrateful, nay, when, as you now admit, you have thought me plotting your murder, at those very times my heart was frozen; I could not look at you, thinking of what, both on board this ship and your own, hung, from other hands, over my kind benefactor. And as God lives, Don Amasa, I know not whether desire for my own safety alone could have nerved me to that leap into your boat, had it not been for the thought that, did you, unenlightened, return to your ship, you, my best friend, with all who might be with you, stolen upon, that night, in your hammocks, would never in this world have wakened again. Do but think how you walked this deck, how you sat in this cabin, every inch of ground mined into honey-combs under you. Had I dropped the least hint, made the least advance towards an understanding between us, death, explosive death—yours as mine—would have ended the scene."

"True, true," cried Captain Delano, starting, "you have saved my life, Don Benito, more than I yours; saved it, too, against my knowledge and will."

"Nay, my friend," rejoined the Spaniard, courteous even to the point of religion, "God charmed your life, but you saved mine. To think of some things you did—those smilings and chattings, rash pointings and gesturings. For less than these, they slew my mate, Raneds; but you had the Prince of Heaven's safe-conduct through all ambuscades."

"Yes, all is owing to Providence, I know; but the temper of my mind that morning was more than commonly pleasant, while the sight of so much suffering, more apparent than real, added to my good-nature, compassion, and charity, happily interweaving the three. Had it been otherwise, doubtless, as you hint, some of my interferences might have ended unhappily enough. Besides, those feelings I spoke of enabled me to get the better of momentary distrust, at times when acuteness might have cost me my life, without saving another's. Only at the end did my suspicions get the better of me, and you know how wide of the mark they then proved."

"Wide, indeed," said Don Benito, sadly; "you were with me all day; stood with me, sat with me, talked with me, looked at me, ate with me, drank with me; and yet, your last act was to clutch for a monster, not only an innocent man, but the most pitiable of all men. To such degree may malign machinations and deceptions impose. So far may even the best man err, in judging the conduct of one with the recesses of whose condition he is not acquainted. But you were forced to it; and you were in time undeceived. Would that, in both respects, it was so ever, and with all men."

"You generalize, Don Benito; and mournfully enough. But the past is passed; why moralize upon it? Forget it. See, yon bright sun has forgotten it all, and the blue sea, and the blue sky; these have turned over new leaves."

"Because they have no memory," he dejectedly replied; "because they are not human."

"But these mild trades[61] that now fan your cheek, do they not come with a human-like healing to you? Warm friends, steadfast friends are the trades."

"With their steadfastness they but waft me to my tomb, Señor," was the foreboding response.

"You are saved," cried Captain Delano, more and more astonished and pained; "you are saved; what has cast such a shadow upon you?"

"The negro."

There was silence, while the moody man sat, slowly and unconsciously gathering his mantle about him, as if it were a pall.

There was no more conversation that day.

But if the Spaniard's melancholy sometimes ended in muteness upon topics like the above, there were others upon which he never spoke at all; on which, indeed, all his old reserves were piled. Pass over the worst, and, only to elucidate, let an item or two of these be cited. The dress, so precise and costly, worn by him on the day whose events have been narrated, had not willingly been put on. And that silver-mounted sword, apparent symbol of despotic command, was not, indeed, a sword, but the ghost of one. The scabbard, artificially stiffened, was empty.

As for the black—whose brain, not body, had schemed and led the revolt, with the plot—his slight frame, inadequate to that which it held, had at once yielded to the superior muscular strength of his captor, in the boat. Seeing all was over, he

---

[61]Trade winds.

uttered no sound, and could not be forced to. His aspect seemed to say, since I cannot do deeds, I will not speak words. Put in irons in the hold, with the rest, he was carried to Lima. During the passage, Don Benito did not visit him. Nor then, nor at any time after, would he look at him. Before the tribunal he refused. When pressed by the judges he fainted. On the testimony of the sailors alone rested the legal identity of Babo.

Some months after, dragged to the gibbet at the tail of a mule, the black met his voiceless end. The body was burned to ashes; but for many days, the head, that hive of subtlety, fixed on a pole in the Plaza, met, unabashed, the gaze of the whites; and across the Plaza looked towards St. Bartholomew's church, in whose vaults slept then, as now, the recovered bones of Aranda: and across the Rimac bridge looked towards the monastery, on Mount Agonia without; where, three months after being dismissed by the court, Benito Cereno, borne on the bier, did, indeed, follow his leader.

1855

Billy Budd, Sailor[1]

(AN INSIDE NARRATIVE)

DEDICATED

TO

JACK CHASE

ENGLISHMAN

Wherever that great heart may now be
Here on Earth or harbored in Paradise
Captain of the Maintop
in the year 1843
in the U.S. Frigate
United States

1

In the time before steamships, or then more frequently than now, a stroller along the docks of any considerable seaport would occasionally have his attention arrested by a group of bronzed mariners, man-of-war's men or merchant sailors in holiday attire, ashore on liberty. In certain instances they would flank, or like a bodyguard quite surround, some superior figure of their own class, moving along with them like Aldebaran[2] among the lesser lights of his constellation. That signal object was the "Handsome Sailor" of the less prosaic time alike of the military and merchant navies. With no perceptible trace of the vainglorious about him, rather with the offhand unaffectedness of natural regality, he seemed to accept the spontaneous homage of his shipmates.

A somewhat remarkable instance recurs to me. In Liverpool, now half a century ago, I saw under the shadow of the great dingy street-wall of Prince's Dock (an obstruction long since removed) a common sailor so intensely black that he must needs have been a native African of the unadulterate blood of Ham[3]—a

---

[1]Melville began work on *Billy Budd* in the 1880s; he had given up fiction and turned to poetry in the late 1850s. *Billy Budd* remained unpublished until the twentieth century, when it was found among Melville's papers and published in 1924. Since Melville did not prepare the work for publication, there has been considerable dispute over the text,

especially given the confusing state of the manuscripts. This version, edited by Harrison Hayford and Merton M. Sealts, Jr., is generally regarded as the best edition.
[2]The "eye" star in the constellation Taurus, the Bull.
[3]A common belief was that the black race derived from Noah's curse placed on Ham's son in Genesis 9:25.

symmetric figure much above the average height. The two ends of a gay silk handkerchief thrown loose about the neck danced upon the displayed ebony of his chest, in his ears were big hoops of gold, and a Highland bonnet with a tartan band set off his shapely head. It was a hot noon in July; and his face, lustrous with perspiration, beamed with barbaric good humor. In jovial sallies right and left, his white teeth flashing into view, he rollicked along, the center of a company of his shipmates. These were made up of such an assortment of tribes and complexions as would have well fitted them to be marched up by Anacharsis Cloots[4] before the bar of the first French Assembly as Representatives of the Human Race. At each spontaneous tribute rendered by the wayfarers to this black pagod[5] of a fellow—the tribute of a pause and stare, and less frequently an exclamation—the motley retinue showed that they took that sort of pride in the evoker of it which the Assyrian priests doubtless showed for their grand sculptured Bull when the faithful prostrated themselves.

To return. If in some cases a bit of a nautical Murat[6] in setting forth his person ashore, the Handsome Sailor of the period in question evinced nothing of the dandified Billy-be-Dam, an amusing character all but extinct now, but occasionally to be encountered, and in a form yet more amusing than the original, at the tiller of the boats on the tempestuous Erie Canal or, more likely, vaporing in the groggeries along the towpath.[7] Invariably a proficient in his perilous calling, he was also more or less of a mighty boxer or wrestler. It was strength and beauty. Tales of his prowess were recited. Ashore he was the champion; afloat the spokesman; on every suitable occasion always foremost. Close-reefing topsails in a gale, there he was, astride the weather yardarm-end, foot in the Flemish horse as stirrup, both hands tugging at the earing as at a bridle, in very much the attitude of young Alexander curbing the fiery Bucephalus.[8] A superb figure, tossed up as by the horns of Taurus against the thunderous sky, cheerily hallooing to the strenuous file along the spar.

The moral nature was seldom out of keeping with the physical make. Indeed, except as toned by the former, the comeliness and power, always attractive in masculine conjunction, hardly could have drawn the sort of honest homage the Handsome Sailor in some examples received from his less gifted associates.

Such a cynosure, at least in aspect, and something such too in nature, though with important variations made apparent as the story proceeds, was welkin-eyed[9] Billy Budd—or Baby Budd, as more familiarly, under circumstances hereafter to be given, he at last came to be called—aged twenty-one, a foretopman of the British fleet toward the close of the last decade of the eighteenth century. It was not very long prior to the time of the narration that follows that he had entered the King's service, having been impressed on the Narrow Seas[10] from a homeward-bound English merchantman into a seventy-four[11] outward bound, H.M.S. *Bellipotent;* which ship, as was not unusual in those hurried days, having been obliged to put to sea short of her proper complement of men. Plump upon Billy at first sight in the gangway the boarding officer, Lieutenant Ratcliffe, pounced, even before the merchantman's crew was formally mustered on the quarter-deck for his deliberate inspection. And him only he elected. For whether it was because the other men when ranged before him showed to ill advantage after Billy, or

[4]A Prussian revolutionary (1755–1794), Cloots presented an assortment of representative racial types to the Assembly during the French Revolution.

[5]Idol (from pagoda).

[6]A dandy; Joachim Murat (1767?–1815), appointed King of Naples (1808), known as the "Dandy King."

[7]Path alongside a canal used by men or animals to tow canalboats.

[8]Greece's Alexander the Great (356–323 B.C.) broke in the wild horse Bucephalus by positioning it so it could not see its own shadow, fulfilling a prophecy; Taurus is the constellation (the Bull).

[9]Sky blue.

[10]I.e., Billy had been forced into naval service on the English Channel and St. George's Channel (separating England and Ireland).

[11]A war ship carrying seventy-four guns; "Bellipotent" means "powerful in war."

whether he had some scruples in view of the merchantman's being rather short-handed, however it might be, the officer contented himself with his first spontaneous choice. To the surprise of the ship's company, though much to the lieutenant's satisfaction, Billy made no demur. But, indeed, any demur would have been as idle as the protest of a goldfinch popped into a cage.

Noting this uncomplaining acquiescence, all but cheerful, one might say, the shipmaster turned a surprised glance of silent reproach at the sailor. The shipmaster was one of those worthy mortals found in every vocation, even the humbler ones—the sort of person whom everybody agrees in calling "a respectable man." And—nor so strange to report as it may appear to be though a ploughman of the troubled waters, lifelong contending with the intractable elements, there was nothing this honest soul at heart loved better than simple peace and quiet. For the rest, he was fifty or thereabouts, a little inclined to corpulence, a prepossessing face, unwhiskered, and of an agreeable color—a rather full face, humanely intelligent in expression. On a fair day with a fair wind and all going well, a certain musical chime in his voice seemed to be the veritable unobstructed outcome of the innermost man. He had much prudence, much conscientiousness, and there were occasions when these virtues were the cause of overmuch disquietude in him. On a passage, so long as his craft was in any proximity to land, no sleep for Captain Graveling. He took to heart those serious responsibilities not so heavily borne by some shipmasters.

Now while Billy Budd was down in the forecastle getting his kit together, the *Bellipotent's* lieutenant, burly and bluff, nowise disconcerted by Captain Graveling's omitting to proffer the customary hospitalities on an occasion so unwelcome to him, an omission simply caused by preoccupation of thought, unceremoniously invited himself into the cabin, and also to a flask from the spirit locker, a receptacle which his experienced eye instantly discovered. In fact he was one of those sea dogs in whom all the hardship and peril of naval life in the great prolonged wars of his time never impaired the natural instinct for sensuous enjoyment. His duty he always faithfully did; but duty is sometimes a dry obligation, and he was for irrigating its aridity, whensoever possible, with a fertilizing decoction of strong waters. For the cabin's proprietor there was nothing left but to play the part of the enforced host with whatever grace and alacrity were practicable. As necessary adjuncts to the flask, he silently placed tumbler and water jug before the irrepressible guest. But excusing himself from partaking just then, he dismally watched the unembarrassed officer deliberately diluting his grog a little, then tossing it off in three swallows, pushing the empty tumbler away, yet not so far as to be beyond easy reach, at the same time settling himself in his seat and smacking his lips with high satisfaction, looking straight at the host.

These proceedings over, the master broke the silence; and there lurked a rueful reproach in the tone of his voice: "Lieutenant, you are going to take my best man from me, the jewel of 'em."

"Yes, I know," rejoined the other, immediately drawing back the tumbler preliminary to a replenishing. "Yes, I know. Sorry."

"Beg pardon, but you don't understand, Lieutenant. See here, now. Before I shipped that young fellow, my forecastle was a rat-pit of quarrels. It was black times, I tell you, aboard the *Rights* here. I was worried to that degree my pipe had no comfort for me. But Billy came; and it was like a Catholic priest striking peace in an Irish shindy.[12] Not that he preached to them or said or did anything in particular; but a virtue went out of him, sugaring the sour ones. They took to him like hornets to treacle; all but the buffer of the gang, the big shaggy chap with the

---

[12]Row, noisy disturbance.

fire-red whiskers. He indeed, out of envy, perhaps, of the newcomer, and thinking such a "sweet and pleasant fellow," as he mockingly designated him to the others, could hardly have the spirit of a gamecock, must needs bestir himself in trying
to get up an ugly row with him. Billy forebore with him and reasoned with him in
a pleasant way—he is something like myself, Lieutenant, to whom aught like a
quarrel is hateful—but nothing served. So, in the second dogwatch one day, the
Red Whiskers in presence of the others, under pretense of showing Billy just
whence a sirloin steak was cut—for the fellow had once been a butcher—insultingly gave him a dig under the ribs. Quick as lightning Billy let fly his arm. I dare
say he never meant to do quite as much as he did, but anyhow he gave the burly
fool a terrible drubbing. It took about half a minute, I should think. And, lord
bless you, the lubber was astonished at the celerity. And will you believe it, Lieutenant, the Red Whiskers now really loves Billy—loves him, or is the biggest hypocrite that ever I heard of. But they all love him. Some of 'em do his washing,
darn his old trousers for him; the carpenter is at odd times making a pretty little
chest of drawers for him. Anybody will do anything for Billy Budd; and it's the
happy family here. But now, Lieutenant, if that young fellow goes—I know how it
will be aboard the *Rights*. Not again very soon shall I, coming up from dinner,
lean over the capstan smoking a quiet pipe—no, not very soon again, I think. Ay,
Lieutenant, you are going to take away the jewel of 'em; you are going to take
away my peacemaker!" And with that the good soul had really some ado in checking a rising sob.

"Well," said the lieutenant, who had listened with amused interest to all this
and now was waxing merry with his tipple; "well, blessed are the peacemakers, especially the fighting peacemakers. And such are the seventy-four beauties some of
which you see poking their noses out of the portholes of yonder warship lying to
for me," pointing through the cabin window at the *Bellipotent*. "But courage! Don't
look so downhearted, man. Why, I pledge you in advance the royal approbation.
Rest assured that His Majesty will be delighted to know that in a time when his
hardtack is not sought for by sailors with such avidity as should be, a time also
when some shipmasters privily resent the borrowing from them a tar or two for
the service; His Majesty, I say, will be delighted to learn that *one* shipmaster at
least cheerfully surrenders to the King the flower of his flock, a sailor who with
equal loyalty makes no dissent.—But where's my beauty? Ah," looking through
the cabin's open door, "here he comes; and, by Jove, lugging along his chest—
Apollo with his portmanteau!—My man," stepping out to him, "you can't take
that big box aboard a warship. The boxes there are mostly shot boxes. Put your
duds in a bag, lad. Boot and saddle for the cavalryman, bag and hammock for the
man-of-war's man."

The transfer from chest to bag was made. And, after seeing his man into the
cutter and then following him down, the lieutenant pushed off from the *Rights-of-
Man*.[13] That was the merchant ship's name, though by her master and crew abbreviated in sailor fashion into the *Rights*. The hardheaded Dundee owner was a
staunch admirer of Thomas Paine, whose book in rejoinder to Burke's arraignment of the French Revolution had then been published for some time and had
gone everywhere. In christening his vessel after the title of Paine's volume the man
of Dundee was something like his contemporary shipowner, Stephen Girard[14] of
Philadelphia, whose sympathies, alike with his native land and its liberal philosophers, he evinced by naming his ships after Voltaire, Diderot,[15] and so forth.

---

[13]Also the title of a work by Thomas Paine (1737–1809), published in 1791–92 (during the French Revolution).
[14]Philadelphia businessman, philanthropist, banker, and shipbuilder; born in France, he was a supporter of the revolutionary cause in France.

[15]Voltaire (1694–1778), author of *Candide*, and Diderot (1713–1784), an encyclopedist, were liberal philosophers and writers who fueled the spirit of the French Revolution.

But now, when the boat swept under the merchantman's stern, and officer and oarsmen were noting—some bitterly and others with a grin—the name emblazoned there; just then it was that the new recruit jumped up from the bow where the coxswain[16] had directed him to sit, and waving hat to his silent shipmates sorrowfully looking over at him from the taffrail, bade the lads a genial good-bye. Then, making a salutation as to the ship herself, "And good-bye to you too, old *Rights-of-Man.*"

"Down, sir!" roared the lieutenant, instantly assuming all the rigor of his rank, though with difficulty repressing a smile.

To be sure, Billy's action was a terrible breach of naval decorum. But in that decorum he had never been instructed; in consideration of which the lieutenant would hardly have been so energetic in reproof but for the concluding farewell to the ship. This he rather took as meant to convey a covert sally on the new recruit's part, a sly slur at impressment in general, and that of himself in especial. And yet, more likely, if satire it was in effect, it was hardly so by intention, for Billy, though happily endowed with the gaiety of high health, youth, and a free heart, was yet by no means of a satirical turn. The will to it and the sinister dexterity were alike wanting. To deal in double meanings and insinuations of any sort was quite foreign to his nature.

As to his enforced enlistment, that he seemed to take pretty much as he was wont to take any vicissitude of weather. Like the animals, though no philosopher, he was, without knowing it, practically a fatalist. And it may be that he rather liked this adventurous turn in his affairs, which promised an opening into novel scenes and martial excitements.

Aboard the *Bellipotent* our merchant sailor was forthwith rated as an able seaman and assigned to the starboard watch of the foretop.[17] He was soon at home in the service, not at all disliked for his unpretentious good looks and a sort of genial happy-go-lucky air. No merrier man in his mess:[18] in marked contrast to certain other individuals included like himself among the impressed portion of the ship's company; for these when not actively employed were sometimes, and more particularly in the last dogwatch[19] when the drawing near of twilight induced revery, apt to fall into a saddish mood which in some partook of sullenness. But they were not so young as our foretopman, and no few of them must have known a hearth of some sort, others may have had wives and children left, too probably, in uncertain circumstances, and hardly any but must have had acknowledged kith and kin, while for Billy, as will shortly be seen, his entire family was practically invested in himself.

2

Though our new-made foretopman was well received in the top and on the gun decks, hardly here was he that cynosure he had previously been among those minor ship's companies of the merchant marine, with which companies only had he hitherto consorted.

He was young; and despite his all but fully developed frame, in aspect looked even younger than he really was, owing to a lingering adolescent expression in the as yet smooth face all but feminine in purity of natural complexion but where, thanks to his seagoing, the lily was quite suppressed and the rose had some ado visibly to flush through the tan.

To one essentially such a novice in the complexities of factitious life, the abrupt transition from his former and simpler sphere to the ampler and more knowing

---

[16]Boat steersman.
[17]Platform at the top of the foremast (the mast nearest the bow, or front, of the ship).

[18]Dining hall.
[19]I.e., 6 to 8 P.M. (half of the length of the usual watch).

world of a great warship; this might well have abashed him had there been any
conceit or vanity in his composition. Among her miscellaneous multitude, the *Bellipotent* mustered several individuals who however inferior in grade were of no
common natural stamp, sailors more signally susceptive of that air which continuous martial discipline and repeated presence in battle can in some degree impart
even to the average man. As the Handsome Sailor, Billy Budd's position aboard
the seventy-four was something analogous to that of a rustic beauty transplanted
from the provinces and brought into competition with the highborn dames of the
court. But this change of circumstances he scarce noted. As little did he observe
that something about him provoked an ambiguous smile in one or two harder
faces among the bluejackets. Nor less unaware was he of the peculiar favorable
effect his person and demeanor had upon the more intelligent gentlemen of the
quarter-deck. Nor could this well have been otherwise. Cast in a mold peculiar to
the finest physical examples of those Englishmen in whom the Saxon strain would
seem not at all to partake of any Norman or other admixture, he showed in face
that humane look of reposeful good nature which the Greek sculptor in some instances gave to his heroic strong man, Hercules. But this again was subtly modified by another and pervasive quality. The ear, small and shapely, the arch of the
foot, the curve in mouth and nostril, even the indurated hand dyed to the orange-
tawny of the toucan's bill,[1] a hand telling alike of the halyards and tar bucket; but,
above all, something in the mobile expression, and every chance attitude and
movement, something suggestive of a mother eminently favored by Love and the
Graces; all this strangely indicated a lineage in direct contradiction to his lot. The
mysteriousness here became less mysterious through a matter of fact elicited when
Billy at the capstan was being formally mustered into the service. Asked by the
officer, a small, brisk little gentleman as it chanced, among other questions, his
place of birth, he replied, "Please, sir, I don't know."

"Don't know where you were born? Who was your father?"

"God knows, sir."

Struck by the straightforward simplicity of these replies, the officer next asked,
"Do you know anything about your beginning?"

"No, sir. But I have heard that I was found in a pretty silk-lined basket hanging
one morning from the knocker of a good man's door in Bristol."

"*Found,* say you? Well," throwing back his head and looking up and down the
new recruit; "well, it turns out to have been a pretty good find. Hope they'll find
some more like you, my man; the fleet sadly needs them."

Yes, Billy Budd was a foundling, a presumable by-blow,[2] and, evidently, no ignoble one. Noble descent was as evident in him as in a blood horse.

For the rest, with little or no sharpness of faculty or any trace of the wisdom of
the serpent, nor yet quite a dove, he possessed that kind and degree of intelligence going along with the unconventional rectitude of a sound human creature,
one to whom not yet has been proffered the questionable apple of knowledge. He
was illiterate; he could not read, but he could sing, and like the illiterate nightingale was sometimes the composer of his own song.

Of self-consciousness he seemed to have little or none, or about as much as we
may reasonably impute to a dog of Saint Bernard's breed.

Habitually living with the elements and knowing little more of the land than as
a beach, or, rather, that portion of the terraqueous globe providentially set apart
for dance-houses, doxies, and tapsters,[3] in short what sailors call a "fiddler's
green," his simple nature remained unsophisticated by those moral obliquities

[1] Brightly colored bird of tropical America.
[2] Illegitimate child.
[3] Doxies, whores; tapsters, barmaids.

which are not in every case incompatible with that manufacturable thing known as respectability. But are sailors, frequenters of fiddlers' greens, without vices? No; but less often than with landsmen do their vices, so called, partake of crookedness of heart, seeming less to proceed from viciousness than exuberance of vitality after long constraint: frank manifestations in accordance with natural law. By his original constitution aided by the co-operating influences of his lot, Billy in many respects was little more than a sort of upright barbarian, much such perhaps as Adam presumably might have been ere the urbane Serpent wriggled himself into his company.

And here be it submitted that apparently going to corroborate the doctrine of man's Fall, a doctrine now popularly ignored, it is observable that where certain virtues pristine and unadulterate peculiarly characterize anybody in the external uniform of civilization, they will upon scrutiny seem not to be derived from custom or convention, but rather to be out of keeping with these, as if indeed exceptionally transmitted from a period prior to Cain's city[4] and citified man. The character marked by such qualities has to an unvitiated taste an untampered-with flavor like that of berries, while the man thoroughly civilized, even in a fair specimen of the breed, has to the same moral palate a questionable smack as of a compounded wine. To any stray inheritor of these primitive qualities found, like Caspar Hauser,[5] wandering dazed in any Christian capital of our time, the good-natured poet's famous invocation, near two thousand years ago, of the good rustic out of his latitude in the Rome of the Caesars, still appropriately holds:

> Honest and poor, faithful in word and thought,
> What hath thee, Fabian, to the city brought?[6]

Though our Handsome Sailor had as much of masculine beauty as one can expect anywhere to see; nevertheless, like the beautiful woman in one of Hawthorne's minor tales,[7] there was just one thing amiss in him. No visible blemish indeed, as with the lady; no, but an occasional liability to a vocal defect. Though in the hour of elemental uproar or peril he was everything that a sailor should be, yet under sudden provocation of strong heart-feeling his voice, otherwise singularly musical, as if expressive of the harmony within, was apt to develop an organic hesitancy, in fact more or less of a stutter or even worse. In this particular Billy was a striking instance that the arch interferer, the envious marplot of Eden,[8] still has more or less to do with every human consignment to this planet of Earth. In every case, one way or another he is sure to slip in his little card, as much as to remind us—I too have a hand here.

The avowal of such an imperfection in the Handsome Sailor should be evidence not alone that he is not presented as a conventional hero, but also that the story in which he is the main figure is no romance.

3

At the time of Billy Budd's arbitrary enlistment into the *Bellipotent* that ship was on her way to join the Mediterranean fleet. No long time elapsed before the junction was effected. As one of that fleet the seventy-four participated in its movements, though at times on account of her superior sailing qualities, in the absence of frigates, dispatched on separate duty as a scout and at times on less temporary

---

[4]See Genesis 4:8–17: after Cain killed Abel, he was banished by God; he went to the land of Nod, took a wife and "builded a city" named after his son Enoch.
[5]A foundling (1812?–1833) who was discovered in 1828 in Nuremberg, thought to be of noble lineage, and mysteriously killed.

[6]From *Epigrams* (I, iv, 1–2), by Martial, Roman poet of the first century A.D.
[7]"The Birthmark."
[8]I.e., Satan.

service. But with all this the story has little concernment, restricted as it is to the inner life of one particular ship and the career of an individual sailor.

It was the summer of 1797. In the April of that year had occurred the commotion at Spithead[1] followed in May by a second and yet more serious outbreak in the fleet at the Nore. The latter is known, and without exaggeration in the epithet, as "the Great Mutiny." It was indeed a demonstration more menacing to England than the contemporary manifestoes and conquering and proselyting armies of the French Directory.[2] To the British Empire the Nore Mutiny was what a strike in the fire brigade would be to London threatened by general arson. In a crisis when the kingdom might well have anticipated the famous signal that some years later published along the naval line of battle what it was that upon occasion England expected of Englishmen;[3] *that* was the time when at the mastheads of the three-deckers and seventy-fours moored in her own roadstead[4]—a fleet the right arm of a Power then all but the sole free conservative one of the Old World—the bluejackets, to be numbered by thousands, ran up with huzzas the British colors with the union and cross wiped out; by that cancellation transmuting the flag of founded law and freedom defined, into the enemy's red meteor of unbridled and unbounded revolt. Reasonable discontent growing out of practical grievances in the fleet had been ignited into irrational combustion as by live cinders blown across the Channel from France in flames.[5]

The event converted into irony for a time those spirited strains of Dibdin[6]—as a song-writer no mean auxiliary to the English government at that European conjuncture—strains celebrating, among other things, the patriotic devotion of the British tar: "And as for my life, 'tis the King's!"

Such an episode in the Island's grand naval story her naval historians naturally abridge, one of them (William James)[7] candidly acknowledging that fain would he pass it over did not "impartiality forbid fastidiousness." And yet his mention is less a narration than a reference, having to do hardly at all with details. Nor are these readily to be found in the libraries. Like some other events in every age befalling states everywhere, including America, the Great Mutiny was of such character that national pride along with views of policy would fain shade it off into the historical background. Such events cannot be ignored, but there is a considerate way of historically treating them. If a well-constituted individual refrains from blazoning aught amiss or calamitous in his family, a nation in the like circumstance may without reproach be equally discreet.

Though after parleyings between government and the ringleaders, and concessions by the former as to some glaring abuses, the first uprising—that at Spithead—with difficulty was put down, or matters for the time pacified; yet at the Nore the unforeseen renewal of insurrection on a yet larger scale, and emphasized in the conferences that ensued by demands deemed by the authorities not only inadmissible but aggressively insolent, indicated—if the Red Flag[8] did not sufficiently do so—what was the spirit animating the men. Final suppression, however, there was; but only made possible perhaps by the unswerving loyalty of the marine corps and a voluntary resumption of loyalty among influential sections of the crews.

To some extent the Nore Mutiny may be regarded as analogous to the distempering irruption of contagious fever in a frame constitutionally sound, and which anon throws it off.

---

[1]Between Portsmouth and the Isle of Wight, south of England; Nore is at the mouth of the Thames.
[2]Ruling group of five governing France (1795–99).
[3]Admiral Nelson's message to his fleet before the battle of Trafalgar (1805): "England expects that every man will do his duty."
[4]I.e., in her own, not enemy, territory.
[5]The Reign of Terror (1793–94) and the execution of the French king (Louis XVI) raised fears throughout the world.
[6]Charles Dibden (1745–1814), English playwright and ballad writer ("Poor Jack" is quoted).
[7]British naval historian (d. 1827), author of *Naval History of Great Britain from the Declaration of War by France in 1793 to the Accession of George IV* (1822–24).
[8]Revolutionary symbol.

At all events, of these thousands of mutineers were some of the tars who not so very long afterwards—whether wholly prompted thereto by patriotism, or pugnacious instinct, or by both—helped to win a coronet for Nelson at the Nile, and the naval crown of crowns for him at Trafalgar.[9] To the mutineers, those battles and especially Trafalgar were a plenary absolution and a grand one. For all that goes to make up scenic naval display and heroic magnificence in arms, those battles, especially Trafalgar, stand unmatched in human annals.

4

In this matter of writing, resolve as one may to keep to the main road, some bypaths have an enticement not readily to be withstood. I am going to err into such a bypath. If the reader will keep me company I shall be glad. At the least, we can promise ourselves that pleasure which is wickedly said to be in sinning, for a literary sin the divergence will be.

Very likely it is no new remark that the inventions of our time have at last brought about a change in sea warfare in degree corresponding to the revolution in all warfare effected by the original introduction from China into Europe of gunpowder. The first European firearm, a clumsy contrivance, was, as is well known, scouted by no few of the knights as a base implement, good enough peradventure for weavers too craven to stand up crossing steel with steel in frank fight. But as ashore knightly valor, though shorn of its blazonry, did not cease with the knights, neither on the seas—though nowadays in encounters there a certain kind of displayed gallantry be fallen out of date as hardly applicable under changed circumstances—did the nobler qualities of such naval magnates as Don John of Austria, Doria, Van Tromp, Jean Bart, the long line of British admirals, and the American Decaturs of 1812 become obsolete with their wooden walls.[1]

Nevertheless, to anybody who can hold the Present at its worth without being inappreciative of the Past, it may be forgiven, if to such an one the solitary old hulk at Portsmouth, Nelson's *Victory,* seems to float there, not alone as the decaying monument of a fame incorruptible, but also as a poetic reproach, softened by its picturesqueness, to the *Monitors*[2] and yet mightier hulls of the European ironclads. And this not altogether because such craft are unsightly, unavoidably lacking the symmetry and grand lines of the old battleships, but equally for other reasons.

There are some, perhaps, who while not altogether inaccessible to that poetic reproach just alluded to, may yet on behalf of the new order be disposed to parry it; and this to the extent of iconoclasm, if need be. For example, prompted by the sight of the star inserted in the *Victory's* quarter-deck designating the spot where the Great Sailor fell, these martial utilitarians may suggest considerations implying that Nelson's ornate publication of his person in battle was not only unnecessary, but not military, nay, savored of foolhardiness and vanity. They may add, too, that at Trafalgar it was in effect nothing less than a challenge to death; and death came; and that but for his bravado the victorious admiral might possibly have survived the battle, and so, instead of having his sagacious dying injunctions overruled by his immediate successor in command, he himself when the contest was decided might have brought his shattered fleet to anchor, a proceeding which might have averted the deplorable loss of life by shipwreck in the elemental tempest that followed the martial one.

<hr>

[9]Admiral Nelson's first great victory at the Nile (1798) won him a title; his second at Trafalgar (1805) brought his death.
[1]All admirals of wooden ships: Don John of Austria (1547?–1578), Commander of the Holy League fleet that defeated the Turks in 1571 at Lepanto; Andrea Doria (1468?–1560), admiral of Genoese fleet helping Spain fight the Turks and Barbarossa pirates; Maarten Tromp (1597–

1653), admiral of Dutch fleet fighting against England, Spain, and Portugal for independence; Jean Bart (1650–1702), French soldier of fortune and commander of privateers against the Dutch; Stephen Decatur (1779–1820), American naval officer who fought the Tripoli pirates (1803–04) and England in the War of 1812.
[2]An ironclad Union ship that defeated the Confederate's ironclad *Merrimack* (1862) during the American Civil War.

Well, should we set aside the more than disputable point whether for various reasons it was possible to anchor the fleet, then plausibly enough the Benthamites of war[3] may urge the above. But the *might-have-been* is but boggy ground to build on. And, certainly, in foresight as to the larger issue of an encounter, and anxious preparations for it—buoying the deadly way and mapping it out, as at Copenhagen[4]—few commanders have been so painstakingly circumspect as this same reckless declarer of his person in fight.

Personal prudence, even when dictated by quite other than selfish considerations, surely is no special virtue in a military man; while an excessive love of glory, impassioning a less burning impulse, the honest sense of duty, is the first. If the name *Wellington*[5] is not so much of a trumpet to the blood as the simpler name *Nelson,* the reason for this may perhaps be inferred from the above. Alfred in his funeral ode on the victor of Waterloo ventures not to call him the greatest soldier of all time, though in the same ode he invokes Nelson as "the greatest sailor since our world began."[6]

At Trafalgar Nelson on the brink of opening the fight sat down and wrote his last brief will and testament. If under the presentiment of the most magnificent of all victories to be crowned by his own glorious death, a sort of priestly motive led him to dress his person in the jewelled vouchers of his own shining deeds; if thus to have adorned himself for the altar and the sacrifice were indeed vainglory, then affectation and fustian is each more heroic line in the great epics and dramas, since in such lines the poet but embodies in verse those exaltations of sentiment that a nature like Nelson, the opportunity being given, vitalizes into acts.

5

Yes, the outbreak at the Nore was put down. But not every grievance was redressed. If the contractors, for example, were no longer permitted to ply some practices peculiar to their tribe everywhere, such as providing shoddy cloth, rations not sound, or false in the measure; not the less impressment, for one thing, went on. By custom sanctioned for centuries, and judicially maintained by a Lord Chancellor as late as Mansfield,[1] that mode of manning the fleet, a mode now fallen into a sort of abeyance but never formally renounced, it was not practicable to give up in those years. Its abrogation would have crippled the indispensable fleet, one wholly under canvas, no steam power, its innumerable sails and thousands of cannon, everything in short, worked, by muscle alone; a fleet the more insatiate in demand for men, because then multiplying its ships of all grades against contingencies present and to come of the convulsed Continent.

Discontent foreran the Two Mutinies,[2] and more or less it lurkingly survived them. Hence it was not unreasonable to apprehend some return of trouble sporadic or general. One instance of such apprehensions: In the same year with this story, Nelson, then Rear Admiral Sir Horatio, being with the fleet off the Spanish coast, was directed by the admiral in command to shift his pennant from the *Captain* to the *Theseus;*[3] and for this reason: that the latter ship having newly arrived on the station from home, where it had taken part in the Great Mutiny, danger was apprehended from the temper of the men; and it was thought that an officer like Nelson was the one, not indeed to terrorize the crew into base subjection, but to win them, by force of his mere presence and heroic personality, back to an allegiance if not as enthusiastic as his own yet as true.

---

[3]I.e., Utilitarians, after the philosophy of Jeremy Bentham (1748–1832), who believed the worth of anything was in its usefulness or utility.
[4]Nelson was extremely careful in working out his plans that led to his victory against the Danes at Copenhagen in 1801.
[5]The Duke of Wellington (1769–1852) defeated Napoleon at Waterloo (1815).

[6]Alfred, Lord Tennyson (1809–1892), English poet laureate (1850–92), wrote "Ode on the Death of the Duke of Wellington" (1852).
[1]William Murray, Earl of Mansfield (1705–1793), was Lord Chief Justice (1756–88).
[2]Those at Spithead and Nore, described in Chapter 3.
[3]I.e., to move his command post to the *Theseus.*

So it was that for a time, on more than one quarter-deck, anxiety did exist. At sea, precautionary vigilance was strained against relapse. At short notice an engagement might come on. When it did, the lieutenants assigned to batteries felt it incumbent on them, in some instances, to stand with drawn swords behind the men working the guns.

6

But on board the seventy-four in which Billy now swung his hammock, very little in the manner of the men and nothing obvious in the demeanor of the officers would have suggested to an ordinary observer that the Great Mutiny was a recent event. In their general bearing and conduct the commissioned officers of a warship naturally take their tone from the commander, that is if he have that ascendancy of character that ought to be his.

Captain the Honorable Edward Fairfax Vere, to give his full title, was a bachelor of forty or thereabouts, a sailor of distinction even in a time prolific of renowned seamen. Though allied to the higher nobility, his advancement had not been altogether owing to influences connected with that circumstance. He had seen much service, been in various engagements, always acquitting himself as an officer mindful of the welfare of his men, but never tolerating an infraction of discipline; thoroughly versed in the science of his profession, and intrepid to the verge of temerity, though never injudiciously so. For his gallantry in the West Indian waters as flag lieutenant under Rodney in that admiral's crowning victory over De Grasse,[1] he was made a post captain.

Ashore, in the garb of a civilian, scarce anyone would have taken him for a sailor, more especially that he never garnished unprofessional talk with nautical terms, and grave in his bearing, evinced little appreciation of mere humor. It was not out of keeping with these traits that on a passage when nothing demanded his paramount action, he was the most undemonstrative of men. Any landsman observing this gentleman not conspicuous by his stature and wearing no pronounced insignia, emerging from his cabin to the open deck, and noting the silent deference of the officers retiring to leeward, might have taken him for the King's guest, a civilian aboard the King's ship, some highly honorable discreet envoy on his way to an important post. But in fact this unobtrusiveness of demeanor may have proceeded from a certain unaffected modesty of manhood sometimes accompanying a resolute nature, a modesty evinced at all times not calling for pronounced action, which shown in any rank of life suggests a virtue aristocratic in kind. As with some others engaged in various departments of the world's more heroic activities, Captain Vere though practical enough upon occasion would at times betray a certain dreaminess of mood. Standing alone on the weather side of the quarter-deck, one hand holding by the rigging, he would absently gaze off at the blank sea. At the presentation to him then of some minor matter interrupting the current of his thoughts, he would show more or less irascibility; but instantly he would control it.

In the navy he was popularly known by the appellation "Starry Vere." How such a designation happened to fall upon one who whatever his sterling qualities was without any brilliant ones, was in this wise: A favorite kinsman, Lord Denton, a freehearted fellow, had been the first to meet and congratulate him upon his return to England from his West Indian cruise; and but the day previous turning over a copy of Andrew Marvell's[2] poems had lighted, not for the first time, however, upon the lines entitled "Appleton House," the name of one of the seats of

---

[1]British Admiral George Brydges Rodney, Baron Rodney (1719–1792) defeated French Admiral François Joseph Paul de Grasse (1723–1788), off Dominica in the West Indies (1782).
[2]British poet (1621–1678).

their common ancestor, a hero in the German wars of the seventeenth century, in which poem occur the lines:

> This 'tis to have been from the first
> In a domestic heaven nursed,
> Under the discipline severe
> Of Fairfax and the starry Vere.

And so, upon embracing his cousin fresh from Rodney's great victory wherein he had played so gallant a part, brimming over with just family pride in the sailor of their house, he exuberantly exclaimed, "Give ye joy, Ed; give ye joy, my starry Vere!" This got currency, and the novel prefix serving in familiar parlance readily to distinguish the *Bellipotent's* captain from another Vere his senior, a distant relative, an officer of like rank in the navy, it remained permanently attached to the surname.

7

In view of the part that the commander of the *Bellipotent* plays in scenes shortly to follow, it may be well to fill out that sketch of him outlined in the previous chapter.

Aside from his qualities as a sea officer Captain Vere was an exceptional character. Unlike no few of England's renowned sailors, "long and arduous service with signal devotion to it had not resulted in absorbing and *salting* the entire man." He had a marked leaning toward everything intellectual. He loved books, never going to sea without a newly replenished library, compact but of the best. The isolated leisure, in some cases so wearisome, falling at intervals to commanders even during a war cruise, never was tedious to Captain Vere. With nothing of that literary taste which less heeds the thing conveyed than the vehicle, his bias was toward those books to which every serious mind of superior order occupying any active post of authority in the world naturally inclines: books treating of actual men and events no matter of what era—history, biography, and unconventional writers like Montaigne,[1] who, free from cant and convention, honestly and in the spirit of common sense philosophize upon realities. In this line of reading he found confirmation of his own more reserved thoughts—confirmation which he had vainly sought in social converse, so that as touching most fundamental topics, there had got to be established in him some positive convictions which he forefelt would abide in him essentially unmodified so long as his intelligent part remained unimpaired. In view of the troubled period in which his lot was cast, this was well for him. His settled convictions were as a dike against those invading waters of novel opinion social, political, and otherwise, which carried away as in a torrent no few minds in those days, minds by nature not inferior to his own. While other members of that aristocracy to which by birth he belonged were incensed at the innovators mainly because their theories were inimical to the privileged classes, Captain Vere disinterestedly opposed them not alone because they seemed to him insusceptible of embodiment in lasting institutions, but at war with the peace of the world and the true welfare of mankind.

With minds less stored than his and less earnest, some officers of his rank, with whom at times he would necessarily consort, found him lacking in the companionable quality, a dry and bookish gentleman, as they deemed. Upon any chance withdrawal from their company one would be apt to say to another something like this: "Vere is a noble fellow, Starry Vere. 'Spite the gazettes,[2] Sir Horatio" (meaning him who became Lord Nelson) "is at bottom scarce a better seaman or fighter.

---

[1]Michel de Montaigne (1533–1592), French essayist.
[2]I.e., newspapers.

But between you and me now, don't you think there is a queer streak of the pedantic running through him? Yes, like the King's yarn in a coil of navy rope?"

Some apparent ground there was for this sort of confidential criticism; since not only did the captain's discourse never fall into the jocosely familiar, but in illustrating of any point touching the stirring personages and events of the time he would be as apt to cite some historic character or incident of antiquity as he would be to cite from the moderns. He seemed unmindful of the circumstance that to his bluff company such remote allusions, however pertinent they might really be, were altogether alien to men whose reading was mainly confined to the journals.[3] But considerateness in such matters is not easy to natures constituted like Captain Vere's. Their honesty prescribes to them directness, sometimes far-reaching like that of a migratory fowl that in its flight never heeds when it crosses a frontier.

8

The lieutenants and other commissioned gentlemen forming Captain Vere's staff it is not necessary here to particularize, nor needs it to make any mention of any of the warrant officers. But among the petty officers was one who, having much to do with the story, may as well be forthwith introduced. His portrait I essay, but shall never hit it. This was John Claggart, the master-at-arms. But that sea title may to landsmen seem somewhat equivocal. Originally, doubtless, that petty officer's function was the instruction of the men in the use of arms, sword or cutlass. But very long ago, owing to the advance in gunnery making hand-to-hand encounters less frequent and giving to niter and sulphur the pre-eminence over steel, that function ceased; the master-at-arms of a great warship becoming a sort of chief of police charged among other matters with the duty of preserving order on the populous lower gun decks.

Claggart was a man about five-and-thirty, somewhat spare and tall, yet of no ill figure upon the whole. His hand was too small and shapely to have been accustomed to hard toil. The face was a notable one, the features all except the chin cleanly cut as those on a Greek medallion; yet the chin, beardless as Tecumseh's,[1] had something of strange protuberant broadness in its make that recalled the prints of the Reverend Dr. Titus Oates, the historic deponent with the clerical drawl in the time of Charles II and the fraud of the alleged Popish Plot.[2] It served Claggart in his office that his eye could cast a tutoring glance. His brow was of the sort phrenologically[3] associated with more than average intellect; silken jet curls partly clustering over it, making a foil to the pallor below, a pallor tinged with a faint shade of amber akin to the hue of time-tinted marbles of old. This complexion, singularly contrasting with the red or deeply bronzed visages of the sailors, and in part the result of his official seclusion from the sunlight, though it was not exactly displeasing, nevertheless seemed to hint of something defective or abnormal in the constitution and blood. But his general aspect and manner were so suggestive of an education and career incongruous with his naval function that when not actively engaged in it he looked like a man of high quality, social and moral, who for reasons of his own was keeping incog.[4] Nothing was known of his former life. It might be that he was an Englishman; and yet there lurked a bit of accent in his speech suggesting that possibly he was not such by birth, but through naturalization in early childhood. Among certain grizzled sea gossips of the gun decks and forecastle went a rumor perdue[5] that the master-at-arms was a *chevalier*[6] who

[3]Newspapers.
[1]A Shawnee Indian Chief (1768?–1813); he joined the British in the War of 1812 and was killed in battle in 1813.
[2]Titus Oates (1649–1705) pretended conversion to Catholicism and in 1678 claimed to uncover plots whereby Catholics were to kill Protestants, set fire to London, and assassinate Charles II. He was widely believed but ultimately discredited.

[3]From phrenology, a primitive form of psychology that attempted to discover personality traits from measuring the bumps on the head.
[4]Incognito.
[5]Obscure, concealed.
[6]A gallant, cavalier.

had volunteered into the King's navy by way of compounding for some mysterious swindle whereof he had been arraigned at the King's Bench.[7] The fact that nobody could substantiate this report was, of course, nothing against its secret currency. Such a rumor once started on the gun decks in reference to almost anyone below the rank of a commissioned officer would, during the period assigned to this narrative, have seemed not altogether wanting in credibility to the tarry old wiseacres of a man-of-war crew. And indeed a man of Claggart's accomplishments, without prior nautical experience entering the navy at mature life, as he did, and necessarily allotted at the start to the lowest grade in it; a man too who never made allusion to his previous life ashore; these were circumstances which in the dearth of exact knowledge as to his true antecedents opened to the invidious a vague field for unfavorable surmise.

But the sailors' dogwatch gossip concerning him derived a vague plausibility from the fact that now for some period the British navy could so little afford to be squeamish in the matter of keeping up the muster rolls,[8] that not only were press gangs[9] notoriously abroad both afloat and ashore, but there was little or no secret about another matter, namely, that the London police were at liberty to capture any able-bodied suspect, any questionable fellow at large, and summarily ship him to the dockyard or fleet. Furthermore, even among voluntary enlistments there were instances where the motive thereto partook neither of patriotic impulse nor yet of a random desire to experience a bit of sea life and martial adventure. Insolvent debtors of minor grade, together with the promiscuous lame ducks of morality, found in the navy a convenient and secure refuge, secure because, once enlisted aboard a King's ship, they were as much in sanctuary as the transgressor of the Middle Ages harboring himself under the shadow of the altar. Such sanctioned irregularities, which for obvious reasons the government would hardly think to parade at the time and which consequently, and as affecting the least influential class of mankind, have all but dropped into oblivion, lend color to something for the truth whereof I do not vouch, and hence have some scruple in stating; something I remember having seen in print though the book I cannot recall; but the same thing was personally communicated to me now more than forty years ago by an old pensioner in a cocked hat with whom I had a most interesting talk on the terrace at Greenwich, a Baltimore Negro, a Trafalgar man.[10] It was to this effect: In the case of a warship short of hands whose speedy sailing was imperative, the deficient quota, in lack of any other way of making it good, would be eked out by drafts culled direct from the jails. For reasons previously suggested it would not perhaps be easy at the present day directly to prove or disprove the allegation. But allowed as a verity, how significant would it be of England's straits at the time confronted by those wars which like a flight of harpies rose shrieking from the din and dust of the fallen Bastille.[11] That era appears measurably clear to us who look back at it, and but read of it. But to the grandfathers of us graybeards, the more thoughtful of them, the genius of it presented an aspect like that of Camoëns'[12] Spirit of the Cape, an eclipsing menace mysterious and prodigious. Not America was exempt from apprehension. At the height of Napoleon's unexampled conquests, there were Americans who had fought at Bunker Hill[13] who looked forward to the possibility that the Atlantic might prove no barrier against

---

[7]I.e., in court.

[8]I.e., full complement of recruits.

[9]Groups licensed to shanghai (virtually kidnap) men for the service, especially from low or criminal classes.

[10]One who had fought with Nelson at Trafalgar.

[11]The storming of the notorious French prison, the Bastille, on July 14, 1789, signalled the beginning of the French Revolution, sending shock-waves ("flight of harpies," hideous monsters) throughout European countries.

[12]Luiz Vaz de Camoëns (1524–1580), Portuguese poet, author of the epic *The Lusiads* (1572), in which a violent Spirit off the Cape of Good Hope attacks Vasco da Gama as he sails for India.

[13]Scene of the first important battle of the American Revolutionary War in 1775, in which the British defeated the Americans, but demonstrated their vulnerability in spite of the size of their force.

the ultimate schemes of this French portentous upstart from the revolutionary chaos who seemed in act of fulfilling judgment prefigured in the Apocalypse.[14]

But the less credence was to be given to the gun-deck talk touching Claggart, seeing that no man holding his office in a man-of-war can ever hope to be popular with the crew. Besides, in derogatory comments upon anyone against whom they have a grudge, or for any reason or no reason mislike, sailors are much like landsmen: they are apt to exaggerate or romance it.

About as much was really known to the *Bellipotent's* tars of the master-at-arms' career before entering the service as an astronomer knows about a comet's travels prior to its first observable appearance in the sky. The verdict of the sea quidnuncs[15] has been cited only by way of showing what sort of moral impression the man made upon rude uncultivated natures whose conceptions of human wickedness were necessarily of the narrowest, limited to ideas of vulgar rascality—a thief among the swinging hammocks during a night watch, or the man-brokers and land-sharks[16] of the seaports.

It was no gossip, however, but fact that though, as before hinted, Claggart upon his entrance into the navy was, as a novice, assigned to the least honorable section[17] of a man-of-war's crew, embracing the drudgery, he did not long remain there. The superior capacity he immediately evinced, his constitutional sobriety, an ingratiating deference to superiors, together with a peculiar ferreting genius manifested on a singular occasion; all this, capped by a certain austere patriotism, abruptly advanced him to the position of master-at-arms.

Of this maritime chief of police the ship's corporals, so called, were the immediate subordinates, and compliant ones; and this, as is to be noted in some business departments ashore, almost to a degree inconsistent with entire moral volition. His place put various converging wires of underground influence under the chief's control, capable when astutely worked through his understrappers of operating to the mysterious discomfort, if nothing worse, of any of the sea commonalty.

9

Life in the foretop well agreed with Billy Budd. There, when not actually engaged on the yards yet higher aloft, the topmen, who as such had been picked out for youth and activity, constituted an aerial club lounging at ease against the smaller stun'sails rolled up into cushions, spinning yarns like the lazy gods, and frequently amused with what was going on in the busy world of the decks below. No wonder then that a young fellow of Billy's disposition was well content in such society. Giving no cause of offense to anybody, he was always alert at a call. So in the merchant service it had been with him. But now such a punctiliousness in duty was shown that his topmates would sometimes good-naturedly laugh at him for it. This heightened alacrity had its cause, namely, the impression made upon him by the first formal gangway-punishment he had ever witnessed, which befell the day following his impressment. It had been incurred by a little fellow, young, a novice after-guardsman[1] absent from his assigned post when the ship was being put about; a dereliction resulting in a rather serious hitch to that maneuver, one demanding instantaneous promptitude in letting go and making fast. When Billy saw the culprit's naked back under the scourge, gridironed with red welts and worse, when he marked the dire expression in the liberated man's face as with his woolen shirt flung over him by the executioner he rushed forward from the spot

---

[14]The devastations and destruction described in the Bible's Book of Revelation.
[15]Gossips, busybodies.
[16]Those who engaged in the business of luring or shanghaiing men for the service.

[17]I.e., a kind of latrine duty, disposing of wastes.
[1]A low-ranking seaman whose tasks require neither great strength nor seamanship, and thus often a landsman.

to bury himself in the crowd, Billy was horrified. He resolved that never through remissness would he make himself liable to such a visitation or do or omit aught that might merit even verbal reproof. What then was his surprise and concern when ultimately he found himself getting into petty trouble occasionally about such matters as the stowage of his bag or something amiss in his hammock, matters under the police oversight of the ship's corporals of the lower decks, and which brought down on him a vague threat from one of them.

So heedful in all things as he was, how could this be? He could not understand it, and it more than vexed him. When he spoke to his young topmates about it they were either lightly incredulous or found something comical in his unconcealed anxiety. "Is it your bag, Billy?" said one. "Well, sew yourself up in it, bully boy, and then you'll be sure to know if anybody meddles with it."

Now there was a veteran aboard who because his years began to disqualify him for more active work had been recently assigned duty as mainmastman in his watch, looking to the gear belayed at the rail roundabout that great spar near the deck. At off-times the foretopman had picked up some acquaintance with him, and now in his trouble it occurred to him that he might be the sort of person to go to for wise counsel. He was an old Dansker[2] long anglicized in the service, of few words, many wrinkles, and some honorable scars. His wizened face, time-tinted and weather-stained to the complexion of an antique parchment, was here and there peppered blue by the chance explosion of a gun cartridge in action.

He was an *Agamemnon* man, some two years prior to the time of this story having served under Nelson when still captain in that ship immortal in naval memory, which dismantled and in part broken up to her bare ribs is seen a grand skeleton in Haden's etching.[3] As one of a boarding party from the *Agamemnon* he had received a cut slantwise along one temple and cheek leaving a long pale scar like a streak of dawn's light falling athwart the dark visage. It was on account of that scar and the affair in which it was known that he had received it, as well as from his blue-peppered complexion, that the Dansker went among the *Bellipotent's* crew by the name of "Board-Her-in-the-Smoke."

Now the first time that his small weasel eyes happened to light on Billy Budd, a certain grim internal merriment set all his ancient wrinkles into antic play. Was it that his eccentric unsentimental old sapience, primitive in its kind, saw or thought it saw something which in contrast with the warship's environment looked oddly incongruous in the Handsome Sailor? But after slyly studying him at intervals, the old Merlin's[4] equivocal merriment was modified; for now when the twain would meet, it would start in his face a quizzing sort of look, but it would be but momentary and sometimes replaced by an expression of speculative query as to what might eventually befall a nature like that, dropped into a world not without some mantraps and against whose subtleties simple courage lacking experience and address, and without any touch of defensive ugliness, is of little avail; and where such innocence as man is capable of does yet in a moral emergency not always sharpen the faculties or enlighten the will.

However it was, the Dansker in his ascetic way rather took to Billy. Nor was this only because of a certain philosophic interest in such a character. There was another cause. While the old man's eccentricities, sometimes bordering on the ursine,[5] repelled the juniors, Billy, undeterred thereby, revering him as a salt hero, would make advances, never passing the old *Agamemnon* man without a salutation marked by that respect which is seldom lost on the aged, however crabbed at times or whatever their station in life.

---

[2]A Dane.
[3]"Breaking Up of the *Agamemnon*," masterpiece of Sir Francis Seymour Haden (1818–1910).

[4]Legendary magician, wizard, and seer of the court of King Arthur (supposed to have existed *c.* sixth century A.D.).
[5]Bear-like.

There was a vein of dry humor, or what not, in the mastman; and, whether in freak of patriarchal irony touching Billy's youth and athletic frame, or for some other and more recondite reason, from the first in addressing him he always substituted *Baby* for Billy, the Dansker in fact being the originator of the name by which the foretopman eventually became known aboard ship.

Well then, in his mysterious little difficulty going in quest of the wrinkled one, Billy found him off duty in a dogwatch ruminating by himself, seated on a shot box of the upper gun deck, now and then surveying with a somewhat cynical regard certain of the more swaggering promenaders there. Billy recounted his trouble, again wondering how it all happened. The salt seer attentively listened, accompanying the foretopman's recital with queer twitchings of his wrinkles and problematical little sparkles of his small ferret eyes. Making an end of his story, the foretopman asked, "And now, Dansker, do tell me what you think of it."

The old man, shoving up the front of his tarpaulin and deliberately rubbing the long slant scar at the point where it entered the thin hair, laconically said, "Baby Budd, *Jemmy Legs*"[6] (meaning the master-at-arms) "is down on you."

"*Jemmy Legs!*" ejaculated Billy, his welkin eyes expanding. "What for? Why, he calls me 'the sweet and pleasant young fellow,' they tell me."

"Does he so?" grinned the grizzled one; then said, "Ay, Baby lad, a sweet voice has Jemmy Legs."

"No, not always. But to me he has. I seldom pass him but there comes a pleasant word."

"And that's because he's down upon you, Baby Budd."

Such reiteration, along with the manner of it, incomprehensible to a novice, disturbed Billy almost as much as the mystery for which he had sought explanation. Something less unpleasingly oracular he tried to extract; but the old sea Chiron,[7] thinking perhaps that for the nonce he had sufficiently instructed his young Achilles, pursed his lips, gathered all his wrinkles together, and would commit himself to nothing further.

Years, and those experiences which befall certain shrewder men subordinated lifelong to the will of superiors, all this had developed in the Dansker the pithy guarded cynicism that was his leading characteristic.

10

The next day an incident served to confirm Billy Budd in his incredulity as to the Dansker's strange summing up of the case submitted. The ship at noon, going large before the wind, was rolling on her course, and he below at dinner and engaged in some sportful talk with the members of his mess, chanced in a sudden lurch to spill the entire contents of his soup pan upon the new-scrubbed deck. Claggart, the master-at-arms, official rattan[1] in hand, happened to be passing along the battery in a bay of which the mess was lodged, and the greasy liquid streamed just across his path. Stepping over it, he was proceeding on his way without comment, since the matter was nothing to take notice of under the circumstances, when he happened to observe who it was that had done the spilling. His countenance changed. Pausing, he was about to ejaculate something hasty at the sailor, but checked himself, and pointing down to the streaming soup, playfully tapped him from behind with his rattan, saying in a low musical voice peculiar to him at times, "Handsomely done, my lad! And handsome is as handsome did it, too!" And with that passed on. Not noted by Billy as not coming within his view was the involuntary smile, or rather grimace, that accompanied Claggart's equivo-

[6]Variant of "Jimmy Legs," a traditional familiar term for a master-at-arms.
[7]In Greek myth, a centaur (part horse, part man) who was wise in music and medicine and who tutored Achilles, Greek hero in the Trojan War.
[1]A cane, or switch.

cal words. Aridly it drew down the thin corners of his shapely mouth. But everybody taking his remark as meant for humorous, and at which therefore as coming from a superior they were bound to laugh "with counterfeited glee,"[2] acted accordingly; and Billy, tickled, it may be, by the allusion to his being the Handsome Sailor, merrily joined in; then addressing his messmates exclaimed, "There now, who says that Jemmy Legs is down on me!"

"And who said he was, Beauty?" demanded one Donald with some surprise. Whereat the foretopman looked a little foolish, recalling that it was only one person, Board-Her-in-the-Smoke, who had suggested what to him was the smoky idea that this master-at-arms was in any peculiar way hostile to him. Meantime that functionary, resuming his path, must have momentarily worn some expression less guarded than that of the bitter smile, usurping the face from the heart— some distorting expression perhaps, for a drummer-boy heedlessly frolicking along from the opposite direction and chancing to come into light collision with his person was strangely disconcerted by his aspect. Nor was the impression lessened when the official, impetuously giving him a sharp cut with the rattan, vehemently exclaimed, "Look where you go!"

11

What was the matter with the master-at-arms? And, be the matter what it might, how could it have direct relation to Billy Budd, with whom prior to the affair of the spilled soup he had never come into any special contact official or otherwise? What indeed could the trouble have to do with one so little inclined to give offense as the merchant-ship's "peacemaker," even him who in Claggart's own phrase was "the sweet and pleasant young fellow"? Yes, why should Jemmy Legs, to borrow the Dansker's expression, be "down" on the Handsome Sailor? But, at heart and not for nothing, as the late chance encounter may indicate to the discerning, down on him, secretly down on him, he assuredly was.

Now to invent something touching the more private career of Claggart, something involving Billy Budd, of which something the latter should be wholly ignorant, some romantic incident implying that Claggart's knowledge of the young blue-jacket began at some period anterior to catching sight of him on board the seventy-four—all this, not so difficult to do, might avail in a way more or less interesting to account for whatever of enigma may appear to lurk in the case. But in fact there was nothing of the sort. And yet the cause necessarily to be assumed as the sole one assignable is in its very realism as much charged with that prime element of Radcliffian romance,[1] the mysterious, as any that the ingenuity of the author of *The Mysteries of Udolpho* could devise. For what can more partake of the mysterious than an antipathy spontaneous and profound such as is evoked in certain exceptional mortals by the mere aspect of some other mortal, however harmless he may be, if not called forth by this very harmlessness itself?

Now there can exist no irritating juxtaposition of dissimilar personalities comparable to that which is possible aboard a great warship fully manned and at sea. There, every day among all ranks, almost every man comes into more or less of contact with almost every other man. Wholly there to avoid even the sight of an aggravating object one must needs give it Jonah's toss[2] or jump overboard himself. Imagine how all this might eventually operate on some peculiar human creature the direct reverse of a saint!

But for the adequate comprehending of Claggart by a normal nature these

---

[2]Echo from *The Deserted Village* by Oliver Goldsmith (1728–1774), in which students feel compelled to laugh at the jokes of the severe schoolmaster.
[1]Ann Radcliffe (1764–1823) was the British author of

many Gothic romances, including *The Mysteries of Udolpho* (1794).
[2]Cf. Jonah 1:15: "So they took up Jonah, and cast him forth into the sea: and the sea ceased from her raging."

hints are insufficient. To pass from a normal nature to him one must cross "the deadly space between." And this is best done by indirection.

Long ago an honest scholar, my senior,[3] said to me in reference to one who like himself is now no more, a man so unimpeachably respectable that against him nothing was ever openly said though among the few something was whispered, "Yes, X——is a nut not to be cracked by the tap of a lady's fan. You are aware that I am the adherent of no organized religion, much less of any philosophy built into a system. Well, for all that, I think that to try and get into X——, enter his labyrinth and get out again, without a clue derived from some source other that what is known as 'knowledge of the world'—that were hardly possible, at least for me."

"Why," said I, "X——, however singular a study to some, is yet human, and knowledge of the world assuredly implies the knowledge of human nature, and in most of its varieties."

"Yes, but a superficial knowledge of it, serving ordinary purposes. But for anything deeper, I am not certain whether to know the world and to know human nature be not two distinct branches of knowledge, which while they may coexist in the same heart, yet either may exist with little or nothing of the other. Nay, in an average man of the world, his constant rubbing with it blunts that finer spiritual insight indispensable to the understanding of the essential in certain exceptional characters, whether evil ones or good. In a matter of some importance I have seen a girl wind an old lawyer about her little finger. Nor was it the dotage of senile love. Nothing of the sort. But he knew law better than he knew the girl's heart. Coke and Blackstone[4] hardly shed so much light into obscure spiritual places as the Hebrew prophets. And who were they? Mostly recluses."

At the time, my inexperience was such that I did not quite see the drift of all this. It may be that I see it now. And, indeed, if that lexicon which is based on Holy Writ were any longer popular, one might with less difficulty define and denominate certain phenomenal men. As it is, one must turn to some authority not liable to the charge of being tinctured with the biblical element.

In a list of definitions included in the authentic translation of Plato, a list attributed to him, occurs this: "Natural Depravity: a depravity according to nature,"[5] a definition which, though savoring of Calvinism, by no means involves Calvin's dogma as to total mankind.[6] Evidently its intent makes it applicable but to individuals. Not many are the examples of this depravity which the gallows and jail supply. At any rate, for notable instances, since these have no vulgar alloy of the brute in them, but invariably are dominated by intellectuality, one must go elsewhere. Civilization, especially if of the austerer sort, is auspicious to it. It folds itself in the mantle of respectability. It has its certain negative virtues serving as silent auxiliaries. It never allows wine to get within its guard. It is not going too far to say that it is without vices or small sins. There is a phenomenal pride in it that excludes them. It is never mercenary or avaricious. In short, the depravity here meant partakes nothing of the sordid or sensual. It is serious, but free from acerbity. Though no flatterer of mankind it never speaks ill of it.

But the thing which in eminent instances signalizes so exceptional a nature is this: Though the man's even temper and discreet bearing would seem to intimate a mind peculiarly subject to the law of reason, not the less in heart he would seem to riot in complete exemption from that law, having apparently little to do with

---

[3] Actually, Melville himself.
[4] Sir Edward Coke (1552–1634) and Sir William Blackstone (1723–1780), British authorities and writers on the law.
[5] Found in the Bohn edition of Plato, vol. 6 (1854), under "Definitions": the entire quotation: "Natural Depravity–a badness by nature, and a sinning in that which is according to nature: a disease of that, which is according to nature."

[6] John Calvin (1509–1564), French Protestant theologian who was a leader of the Reformation and major influence on the American Puritans; a leading tenet of Calvinistic belief was that "natural depravity" was the lot of all humankind.

reason further than to employ it as an ambidexter implement for effecting the irrational. That is to say: Toward the accomplishment of an aim which in wantonness of atrocity would seem to partake of the insane, he will direct a cool judgment sagacious and sound. These men are madmen, and of the most dangerous
sort, for their lunacy is not continuous, but occasional, evoked by some special object; it is protectively secretive, which is as much as to say it is self-contained, so
that when, moreover, most active it is to the average mind not distinguishable
from sanity, and for the reason above suggested: that whatever its aims may be—
and the aim is never declared—the method and the outward proceeding are always perfectly rational.

Now something such an one was Claggart, in whom was the mania of an evil
nature, not engendered by vicious training or corrupting books or licentious living, but born with him and innate, in short "a depravity according to nature."

Dark sayings are these, some will say. But why? Is it because they somewhat
savor of Holy Writ in its phrase "mystery of iniquity"?[7] If they do, such savor was
far enough from being intended, for little will it commend these pages to many a
reader of today.

The point of the present story turning on the hidden nature of the master-at-
arms has necessitated this chapter. With an added hint or two in connection with
the incident at the mess, the resumed narrative must be left to vindicate, as it may,
its own credibility.

12

That Claggart's figure was not amiss, and his face, save the chin, well molded, has
already been said. Of these favorable points he seemed not insensible, for he was
not only neat but careful in his dress. But the form of Billy Budd was heroic; and
if his face was without the intellectual look of the pallid Claggart's, not the less was
it lit, like his, from within, though from a different source. The bonfire in his
heart made luminous the rose-tan in his cheek.

In view of the marked contrast between the persons of the twain, it is more
than probable that when the master-at-arms in the scene last given applied to the
sailor the proverb "Handsome is as handsome does," he there let escape an ironic
inkling, not caught by the young sailors who heard it, as to what it was that had
first moved him against Billy, namely, his significant personal beauty.

Now envy and antipathy, passions irreconcilable in reason, nevertheless in fact
may spring conjoined like Chang and Eng[1] in one birth. Is Envy then such a monster? Well, though many an arraigned mortal has in hopes of mitigated penalty
pleaded guilty to horrible actions, did ever anybody seriously confess to envy?
Something there is in it universally felt to be more shameful than even felonious
crime. And not only does everybody disown it, but the better sort are inclined to
incredulity when it is in earnest imputed to an intelligent man. But since its lodgment is in the heart not the brain, no degree of intellect supplies a guarantee
against it. But Claggart's was no vulgar form of the passion. Nor, as directed toward Billy Budd, did it partake of that streak of apprehensive jealousy that
marred Saul's visage[2] perturbedly brooding on the comely young David. Claggart's envy struck deeper. If askance he eyed the good looks, cheery health, and
frank enjoyment of young life in Billy Budd, it was because these went along with
a nature that, as Claggart magnetically felt, had in its simplicity never willed malice or experienced the reactionary bite of that serpent. To him, the spirit lodged
within Billy, and looking out from his welkin eyes as from windows, that ineffabil-

---

[7] Cf. 2 Thessalonians 2:7.
[1] Siamese twins (1811–1874), widely known because of
their exhibition in P. T. Barnum's travelling show.

[2] See 1 Samuel 16:18, 18:8. Saul, King of Israel, became
jealous of David, destined to be his successor.

ity it was which made the dimple in his dyed cheek, suppled his joints, and dancing in his yellow curls made him pre-eminently the Handsome Sailor. One person excepted, the master-at-arms was perhaps the only man in the ship intellectually capable of adequately appreciating the moral phenomenon presented in Billy Budd. And the insight but intensified his passion, which assuming various secret forms within him, at times assumed that of cynic disdain, disdain of innocence—to be nothing more than innocent! Yet in an aesthetic way he saw the charm of it, the courageous free-and-easy temper of it, and fain would have shared it, but he despaired of it.

With no power to annul the elemental evil in him, though readily enough he could hide it; apprehending the good, but powerless to be it; a nature like Claggart's, surcharged with energy as such natures almost invariably are, what recourse is left to it but to recoil upon itself and, like the scorpion for which the Creator alone is responsible, act out to the end the part allotted it.

13

Passion, and passion in its profoundest, is not a thing demanding a palatial stage whereon to play its part. Down among the groundlings,[1] among the beggars and rakers of the garbage, profound passion is enacted. And the circumstances that provoke it, however trivial or mean, are no measure of its power. In the present instance the stage is a scrubbed gun deck, and one of the external provocations a man-of-war's man's spilled soup.

Now when the master-at-arms noticed whence came that greasy fluid streaming before his feet, he must have taken it to some extent wilfully, perhaps—not for the mere accident it assuredly was, but for the sly escape of a spontaneous feeling on Billy's part more or less answering to the antipathy on his own. In effect a foolish demonstration, he must have thought, and very harmless, like the futile kick of a heifer, which yet were the heifer a shod stallion would not be so harmless. Even so was it that into the gall of Claggart's envy he infused the vitriol of his contempt. But the incident confirmed to him certain telltale reports purveyed to his ear by "Squeak," one of his more cunning corporals, a grizzled little man, so nicknamed by the sailors on account of his squeaky voice and sharp visage ferreting about the dark corners of the lower decks after interlopers, satirically suggesting to them the idea of a rat in a cellar.

From his chief's employing him as an implicit tool in laying little traps for the worriment of the foretopman—for it was from the master-at-arms that the petty persecutions heretofore adverted to had proceeded—the corporal, having naturally enough concluded that his master could have no love for the sailor, made it his business, faithful understrapper that he was, to foment the ill blood by perverting to his chief certain innocent frolics of the good-natured foretopman, besides inventing for his mouth sundry contumelious epithets he claimed to have overheard him let fall. The master-at-arms never suspected the veracity of these reports, more especially as to the epithets, for he well knew how secretly unpopular may become a master-at-arms, at least a master-at-arms of those days, zealous in his function, and how the bluejackets shoot at him in private their raillery and wit; the nickname by which he goes among them (Jemmy Legs) implying under the form of merriment their cherished disrespect and dislike. But in view of the greediness of hate for pabulum it hardly needed a purveyor to feed Claggart's passion.

An uncommon prudence is habitual with the subtler depravity, for it has everything to hide. And in case of an injury but suspected, its secretiveness voluntarily

---

[1]Spectators at a theater occupying the pit (on the ground), the cheapest space.

cuts it off from enlightenment or disillusion; and, not unreluctantly, action is taken upon surmise as upon certainty. And the retaliation is apt to be in monstrous disproportion to the supposed offense; for when in anybody was revenge in its exactions aught else but an inordinate usurer? But how with Claggart's conscience? For though consciences are unlike as foreheads, every intelligence, not excluding the scriptural devils who "believe and tremble,"[2] has one. But Claggart's conscience being but the lawyer to his will, made ogres of trifles, probably arguing that the motive imputed to Billy in spilling the soup just when he did, together with the epithets alleged, these, if nothing more, made a strong case against him; nay, justified animosity into a sort of retributive righteousness. The Pharisee is the Guy Fawkes[3] prowling in the hid chambers underlying some natures like Claggart's. And they can really form no conception of an unreciprocated malice. Probably the master-at-arms' clandestine persecution of Billy was started to try the temper of the man; but it had not developed any quality in him that enmity could make official use of or even pervert into plausible self-justification; so that the occurrence at the mess, petty if it were, was a welcome one to that peculiar conscience assigned to be the private mentor of Claggart; and, for the rest, not improbably it put him upon new experiments.

14

Not many days after the last incident narrated, something befell Billy Budd that more graveled him than aught that had previously occurred.

It was a warm night for the latitude; and the foretopman, whose watch at the time was properly below, was dozing on the uppermost deck whither he had ascended from his hot hammock, one of hundreds suspended so closely wedged together over a lower gun deck that there was little or no swing to them. He lay as in the shadow of a hillside, stretched under the lee[1] of the booms, a piled ridge of spare spars amidships between foremast and mainmast among which the ship's largest boat, the launch, was stowed. Alongside of three other slumberers from below, he lay near that end of the booms which approaches the foremast; his station aloft on duty as a foretopman being just over the deck-station of the forecastlemen, entitling him according to usage to make himself more or less at home in that neighborhood.

Presently he was stirred into semiconsciousness by somebody, who must have previously sounded the sleep of the others, touching his shoulder, and then, as the foretopman raised his head, breathing into his ear in a quick whisper, "Slip into the lee forechains,[2] Billy; there is something in the wind. Don't speak. Quick, I will meet you there," and disappearing.

Now Billy, like sundry other essentially good-natured ones, had some of the weaknesses inseparable from essential good nature; and among these was a reluctance, almost an incapacity of plumply saying *no* to an abrupt proposition not obviously absurd on the face of it, nor obviously unfriendly, nor iniquitous. And being of warm blood, he had not the phlegm tacitly to negative any proposition by unresponsive inaction. Like his sense of fear, his apprehension as to aught outside of the honest and natural was seldom very quick. Besides, upon the present occasion, the drowse from his sleep still hung upon him.

However it was, he mechanically rose and, sleepily wondering what could be in the wind, betook himself to the designated place, a narrow platform, one of six, outside of the high bulwarks and screened by the great deadeyes and multiple col-

---

[2]Cf. James 2:19.
[3]Chief conspirator in the Gunpowder Plot to blow up Parliament in 1605; thus likened to the Pharisees, Christ's opponents in the New Testament, described as self-righteous and hypocritical.

[1]Shelter.
[2]A platform (described in second paragraph below).

umned lanyards of the shrouds and backstays;[3] and, in a great warship of that time, of dimensions commensurate to the hull's magnitude; a tarry balcony in short, overhanging the sea, and so secluded that one mariner of the *Bellipotent,* a Nonconformist old tar of a serious turn, made it even in daytime his private oratory.[4]

In this retired nook the stranger soon joined Billy Budd. There was no moon as yet; a haze obscured the starlight. He could not distinctly see the stranger's face. Yet from something in the outline and carriage, Billy took him, and correctly, for one of the afterguard.

"Hist! Billy," said the man, in the same quick cautionary whisper as before. "You were impressed, weren't you? Well, so was I"; and he paused, as to mark the effect. But Billy, not knowing exactly what to make of this, said nothing. Then the other: "We are not the only impressed ones, Billy. There's a gang of us.— Couldn't you—help—at a pinch?"

"What do you mean?" demanded Billy, here thoroughly shaking off his drowse.

"Hist, hist!" the hurried whisper now growing husky. "See here," and the man held up two small objects faintly twinkling in the night-light; "see, they are yours, Billy, if you'll only—"

But Billy broke in, and in his resentful eagerness to deliver himself his vocal infirmity somewhat intruded. "D—d—damme, I don't know what you are d— d—driving at, or what you mean, but you had better g—g—go where you belong!" For the moment the fellow, as confounded, did not stir; and Billy, springing to his feet, said, "If you d—don't start, I'll t—t—toss you back over the r— rail!" There was no mistaking this, and the mysterious emissary decamped, disappearing in the direction of the mainmast in the shadow of the booms.

"Hallo, what's the matter?" here came growling from a forecastleman awakened from his deck-doze by Billy's raised voice. And as the foretopman reappeared and was recognized by him: "Ah, Beauty, is it you? Well, something must have been the matter, for you st—st—stuttered."

"Oh," rejoined Billy, now mastering the impediment, "I found an afterguardsman in our part of the ship here, and I bid him be off where he belongs."

"And is that all you did about it, Foretopman?" gruffly demanded another, an irascible old fellow of brick-colored visage and hair who was known to his associate forecastlemen as "Red Pepper." "Such sneaks I should like to marry to the gunner's daughter!"—by that expression meaning that he would like to subject them to disciplinary castigation over a gun.

However, Billy's rendering of the matter satisfactorily accounted to these inquirers for the brief commotion, since of all the sections of a ship's company the forecastlemen, veterans for the most part and bigoted in their sea prejudices, are the most jealous in resenting territorial encroachments, especially on the part of any of the afterguard, of whom they have but a sorry opinion—chiefly landsmen, never going aloft except to reef or furl the mainsail, and in no wise competent to handle a marlinspike or turn in a deadeye, say.

15

This incident sorely puzzled Billy Budd. It was an entirely new experience, the first time in his life that he had ever been personally approached in underhand

---

[3]"Bulwark" is the ship's side above deck; "deadeyes," round, flat blocks of wood containing three holes through which ropes run; "lanyards" are short ropes to hold the "shrouds," which in turn are longer ropes attached to and supporting the masts; "backstays" are supporting ropes running from the top of the masts aft.

[4]Nonconformists were English Protestants who refused to conform to Church of England practices; an oratory is a small chapel.

intriguing fashion. Prior to this encounter he had known nothing of the after-guardsman, the two men being stationed wide apart, one forward and aloft during his watch, the other on deck and aft.

What could it mean? And could they really be guineas,[1] those two glittering objects the interloper had held up to his (Billy's) eyes? Where could the fellow get guineas? Why, even spare buttons are not so plentiful at sea. The more he turned the matter over, the more he was nonplussed, and made uneasy and discomfited. In his disgustful recoil from an overture which, though he but ill comprehended, he instinctively knew must involve evil of some sort, Billy Budd was like a young horse fresh from the pasture suddenly inhaling a vile whiff from some chemical factory, and by repeated snortings trying to get it out of his nostrils and lungs. This frame of mind barred all desire of holding further parley with the fellow, even were it but for the purpose of gaining some enlightenment as to his design in approaching him. And yet he was not without natural curiosity to see how such a visitor in the dark would look in broad day.

He espied him the following afternoon in his first dogwatch below, one of the smokers on that forward part of the upper gun deck allotted to the pipe.[2] He recognized him by his general cut and build more than by his round freckled face and glassy eyes of pale blue, veiled with lashes all but white. And yet Billy was a bit uncertain whether indeed it were he—yonder chap about his own age chatting and laughing in freehearted way, leaning against a gun; a genial young fellow enough to look at, and something of a rattlebrain, to all appearance. Rather chubby too for a sailor, even an afterguardsman. In short, the last man in the world, one would think, to be overburdened with thoughts, especially those perilous thoughts that must needs belong to a conspirator in any serious project, or even to the underling of such a conspirator.

Although Billy was not aware of it, the fellow, with a sidelong watchful glance, had perceived Billy first, and then noting that Billy was looking at him, thereupon nodded a familiar sort of friendly recognition as to an old acquaintance, without interrupting the talk he was engaged in with the group of smokers. A day or two afterwards, chancing in the evening promenade on a gun deck to pass Billy, he offered a flying word of good-fellowship, as it were, which by its unexpectedness, and equivocalness under the circumstances, so embarrassed Billy that he knew not how to respond to it, and let it go unnoticed.

Billy was now left more at a loss than before. The ineffectual speculations into which he was led were so disturbingly alien to him that he did his best to smother them. It never entered his mind that here was a matter which, from its extreme questionableness, it was his duty as a loyal bluejacket to report in the proper quarter. And, probably, had such a step been suggested to him, he would have been deterred from taking it by the thought, one of novice magnanimity, that it would savor overmuch of the dirty work of a telltale. He kept the thing to himself. Yet upon one occasion he could not forbear a little disburdening himself to the old Dansker, tempted thereto perhaps by the influence of a balmy night when the ship lay becalmed; the twain, silent for the most part, sitting together on deck, their heads propped against the bulwarks. But it was only a partial and anonymous account that Billy gave, the unfounded scruples above referred to preventing full disclosure to anybody. Upon hearing Billy's version, the sage Dansker seemed to divine more than he was told; and after a little meditation, during which his wrinkles were pursed as into a point, quite effacing for the time that quizzing expression his face sometimes wore: "Didn't I say so, Baby Budd?"

"Say what?" demanded Billy.

---

[1] Gold coins worth twenty-one shillings (last minted in 1813).
[2] Designated place for smoking.

"Why, *Jemmy Legs* is *down* on you."

"And what," rejoined Billy in amazement, "has *Jemmy Legs* to do with that cracked afterguardsman?"

"Ho, it was an afterguardsman, then. A cat's-paw, a cat's-paw!" And with that exclamation, whether it had reference to a light puff of air just then coming over the calm sea, or a subtler relation to the afterguardsman, there is no telling, the old Merlin gave a twisting wrench with his black teeth at his plug of tobacco, vouchsafing no reply to Billy's impetuous question, though now repeated, for it was his wont to relapse into grim silence when interrogated in skeptical sort as to any of his sententious oracles, not always very clear ones, rather partaking of that obscurity which invests most Delphic deliverances[3] from any quarter.

Long experience had very likely brought this old man to that bitter prudence which never interferes in aught and never gives advice.

16

Yes, despite the Dansker's pithy insistence as to the master-at-arms being at the bottom of these strange experiences of Billy on board the *Bellipotent*, the young sailor was ready to ascribe them to almost anybody but the man who, to use Billy's own expression, "always had a pleasant word for him." This is to be wondered at. Yet not so much to be wondered at. In certain matters, some sailors even in mature life remain unsophisticated enough. But a young seafarer of the disposition of our athletic foretopman is much of a child-man. And yet a child's utter innocence is but its blank ignorance, and the innocence more or less wanes as intelligence waxes. But in Billy Budd intelligence, such as it was, had advanced while yet his simple-mindedness remained for the most part unaffected. Experience is a teacher indeed; yet did Billy's years make his experience small. Besides, he had none of that intuitive knowledge of the bad which in natures not good or incompletely so foreruns experience, and therefore may pertain, as in some instances it too clearly does pertain, even to youth.

And what could Billy know of man except of man as a mere sailor? And the old-fashioned sailor, the veritable man before the mast, the sailor from boyhood up, he, though indeed of the same species as a landsman, is in some respects singularly distinct from him. The sailor is frankness, the landsman is finesse. Life is not a game with the sailor, demanding the long head[1]—no intricate game of chess where few moves are made in straight-forwardness and ends are attained by indirection, an oblique, tedious, barren game hardly worth that poor candle burnt out in playing it.[2]

Yes, as a class, sailors are in character a juvenile race. Even their deviations are marked by juvenility, this more especially holding true with the sailors of Billy's time. Then too, certain things which apply to all sailors do more pointedly operate here and there upon the junior one. Every sailor, too, is accustomed to obey orders without debating them; his life afloat is externally ruled for him; he is not brought into that promiscuous commerce with mankind where unobstructed free agency on equal terms—equal superficially, at least—soon teaches one that unless upon occasion he exercise a distrust keen in proportion to the fairness of the appearance, some foul turn may be served him. A ruled undemonstrative distrustfulness is so habitual, not with businessmen so much as with men who know their kind in less shallow relations than business, namely, certain men of the world, that they come at last to employ it all but unconsciously; and some of them would very likely feel real surprise at being charged with it as one of their general characteristics.

---

[3]Oracular, prophetic statements.
[1]Shrewdness, foresight.

[2]Cf. Shakespeare's *Macbeth* (V, v): Macbeth, on hearing of his wife's death, cries out: "Out, out, brief candle."

17

But after the little matter at the mess Billy Budd no more found himself in strange trouble at times about his hammock or his clothes bag or what not. As to that smile that occasionally sunned him, and the pleasant passing word, these were, if not more frequent, yet if anything more pronounced than before.

But for all that, there were certain other demonstrations now. When Claggart's unobserved glance happened to light on belted Billy rolling along the upper gun deck in the leisure of the second dogwatch, exchanging passing broadsides of fun with other young promenaders in the crowd, that glance would follow the cheerful sea Hyperion[1] with a settled meditative and melancholy expression, his eyes strangely suffused with incipient feverish tears. Then would Claggart look like the man of sorrows. Yes, and sometimes the melancholy expression would have in it a touch of soft yearning, as if Claggart could even have loved Billy but for fate and ban. But this was an evanescence, and quickly repented of, as it were, by an immitigable look, pinching and shriveling the visage into the momentary semblance of a wrinkled walnut. But sometimes catching sight in advance of the foretopman coming in his direction, he would, upon their nearing, step aside a little to let him pass, dwelling upon Billy for the moment with the glittering dental satire of a Guise.[2] But upon any abrupt unforeseen encounter a red light would flash forth from his eye like a spark from an anvil in a dusk smithy. That quick, fierce light was a strange one, darted from orbs which in repose were of a color nearest approaching a deeper violet, the softest of shades.

Though some of these caprices of the pit could not but be observed by their object, yet were they beyond the construing of such a nature. And the thews[3] of Billy were hardly compatible with that sort of sensitive spiritual organization which in some cases instinctively conveys to ignorant innocence an admonition of the proximity of the malign. He thought the master-at-arms acted in a manner rather queer at times. That was all. But the occasional frank air and pleasant word went for what they purported to be, the young sailor never having heard as yet of the "too fair-spoken man."

Had the foretopman been conscious of having done or said anything to provoke the ill will of the official, it would have been different with him, and his sight might have been purged if not sharpened. As it was, innocence was his blinder.

So was it with him in yet another matter. Two minor officers, the armorer and captain of the hold,[4] with whom he had never exchanged a word, his position in the ship not bringing him into contact with them, these men now for the first began to cast upon Billy, when they chanced to encounter him, that peculiar glance which evidences that the man from whom it comes has been some way tampered with, and to the prejudice of him upon whom the glance lights. Never did it occur to Billy as a thing to be noted or a thing suspicious, though he well knew the fact, that the armorer and captain of the hold, with the ship's yeoman, apothecary, and others of that grade, were by naval usage messmates of the master-at-arms, men with ears convenient to his confidential tongue.

But the general popularity that came from our Handsome Sailor's manly forwardness upon occasion and irresistible good nature, indicating no mental superiority tending to excite an invidious feeling, this good will on the part of most of his shipmates made him the less to concern himself about such mute aspects toward him as those whereto allusion has just been made, aspects he could not so fathom as to infer their whole import.

---

[1] In Greek mythology, one of the Titans, son of Uranus, and father of the sun god Helios.
[2] A smile that conceals treachery; the Guise family of sixteenth-century France was a ducal family noted for its involvement in intrigue and conspiratorial plotting.
[3] I.e., muscles.
[4] Minor officers whose responsibilities were the care of munitions and of the area of the vessel below decks.

As to the afterguardsman, though Billy for reasons already given necessarily saw little of him, yet when the two did happen to meet, invariably came the fellow's offhand cheerful recognition, sometimes accompanied by a passing pleasant word or two. Whatever that equivocal young person's original design may really have been, or the design of which he might have been the deputy, certain it was from his manner upon these occasions that he had wholly dropped it.

It was as if his precocity of crookedness (and every vulgar villain is precocious) had for once deceived him, and the man he had sought to entrap as a simpleton had through his very simplicity ignominiously baffled him.

But shrewd ones may opine that it was hardly possible for Billy to refrain from going up to the afterguardsman and bluntly demanding to know his purpose in the initial interview so abruptly closed in the forechains. Shrewd ones may also think it but natural in Billy to set about sounding some of the other impressed men of the ship in order to discover what basis, if any, there was for the emissary's obscure suggestions as to plotting disaffection aboard. Yes, shrewd ones may so think. But something more, or rather something else than mere shrewdness is perhaps needful for the due understanding of such a character as Billy Budd's.

As to Claggart, the monomania in the man—if that indeed it were—as involuntarily disclosed by starts in the manifestations detailed, yet in general covered over by his self-contained and rational demeanor; this, like a subterranean fire, was eating its way deeper and deeper in him. Something decisive must come of it.

18

After the mysterious interview in the forechains, the one so abruptly ended there by Billy, nothing especially germane to the story occurred until the events now about to be narrated.

Elsewhere it has been said that in the lack of frigates (of course better sailers than line-of-battle ships) in the English squadron up the Straits at that period, the *Bellipotent 74* was occasionally employed not only as an available substitute for a scout, but at times on detached service of more important kind. This was not alone because of her sailing qualities, not common in a ship of her rate, but quite as much, probably, that the character of her commander, it was thought, specially adapted him for any duty where under unforeseen difficulties a prompt initiative might have to be taken in some matter demanding knowledge and ability in addition to those qualities implied in good seamanship. It was on an expedition of the latter sort, a somewhat distant one, and when the *Bellipotent* was almost at her furthest remove from the fleet, that in the latter part of an afternoon watch she unexpectedly came in sight of a ship of the enemy. It proved to be a frigate. The latter, perceiving through the glass that the weight of men and metal would be heavily against her, invoking her light heels crowded sail to get away. After a chase urged almost against hope and lasting until about the middle of the first dogwatch, she signally succeeded in effecting her escape.

Not long after the pursuit had been given up, and ere the excitement incident thereto had altogether waned away, the master-at-arms, ascending from his cavernous sphere, made his appearance cap in hand by the mainmast respectfully waiting the notice of Captain Vere, then solitary walking the weather side of the quarter-deck, doubtless somewhat chafed at the failure of the pursuit. The spot where Claggart stood was the place allotted to men of lesser grades seeking some more particular interview either with the officer of the deck or the captain himself. But from the latter it was not often that a sailor or petty officer of those days would seek a hearing; only some exceptional cause would, according to established custom, have warranted that.

Presently, just as the commander, absorbed in his reflections, was on the point of turning aft in his promenade, he became sensible of Claggart's presence, and saw the doffed cap held in deferential expectancy. Here be it said that Captain

Vere's personal knowledge of this petty officer had only begun at the time of the ship's last sailing from home, Claggart then for the first, in transfer from a ship detained for repairs, supplying on board the *Bellipotent* the place of a previous master-at-arms disabled and ashore.

No sooner did the commander observe who it was that now deferentially stood awaiting his notice than a peculiar expression came over him. It was not unlike that which uncontrollably will flit across the countenance of one at unawares encountering a person who, though known to him indeed, has hardly been long enough known for thorough knowledge, but something in whose aspect nevertheless now for the first provokes a vaguely repellent distaste. But coming to a stand and resuming much of his wonted official manner, save that a sort of impatience lurked in the intonation of the opening word, he said "Well? What is it, Master-at-arms?"

With the air of a subordinate grieved at the necessity of being a messenger of ill tidings, and while conscientiously determined to be frank yet equally resolved upon shunning overstatement, Claggart at this invitation, or rather summons to disburden, spoke up. What he said, conveyed in the language of no uneducated man, was to the effect following, if not altogether in these words, namely, that during the chase and preparations for the possible encounter he had seen enough to convince him that at least one sailor aboard was a dangerous character in a ship mustering some who not only had taken a guilty part in the late serious troubles, but others also who, like the man in question, had entered His Majesty's service under another form than enlistment.

At this point Captain Vere with some impatience interrupted him: "Be direct, man; say *impressed men.*"

Claggart made a gesture of subservience, and proceeded. Quite lately he (Claggart) had begun to suspect that on the gun decks some sort of movement prompted by the sailor in question was covertly going on, but he had not thought himself warranted in reporting the suspicion so long as it remained indistinct. But from what he had that afternoon observed in the man referred to, the suspicion of something clandestine going on had advanced to a point less removed from certainty. He deeply felt, he added, the serious responsibility assumed in making a report involving such possible consequences to the individual mainly concerned, besides tending to augment those natural anxieties which every naval commander must feel in view of extraordinary outbreaks so recent as those which, he sorrowfully said it, it needed not to name.

Now at the first broaching of the matter Captain Vere, taken by surprise, could not wholly dissemble his disquietude. But as Claggart went on, the former's aspect changed into restiveness under something in the testifier's manner in giving his testimony. However, he refrained from interrupting him. And Claggart, continuing, concluded with this: "God forbid, your honor, that the *Bellipotent's* should be the experience of the——"

"Never mind that!" here peremptorily broke in the superior, his face altering with anger, instinctively divining the ship that the other was about to name, one in which the Nore Mutiny had assumed a singularly tragical character that for a time jeopardized the life of its commander. Under the circumstances he was indignant at the purposed allusion. When the commissioned officers themselves were on all occasions very heedful how they referred to the recent events in the fleet, for a petty officer unnecessarily to allude to them in the presence of his captain, this struck him as a most immodest presumption. Besides, to his quick sense of self-respect it even looked under the circumstances something like an attempt to alarm him. Nor at first was he without some surprise that one who so far as he had hitherto come under his notice had shown considerable tact in his function should in this particular evince such lack of it.

But these thoughts and kindred dubious ones flitting across his mind were suddenly replaced by an intuitional surmise which, though as yet obscure in form, served practically to affect his reception of the ill tidings. Certain it is that, long versed in everything pertaining to the complicated gun-deck life, which like every other form of life has its secret mines and dubious side, the side popularly disclaimed, Captain Vere did not permit himself to be unduly disturbed by the general tenor of his subordinate's report.

Furthermore, if in view of recent events prompt action should be taken at the first palpable sign of recurring insubordination, for all that, not judicious would it be, he thought, to keep the idea of lingering disaffection alive by undue forwardness in crediting an informer, even if his own subordinate and charged among other things with police surveillance of the crew. This feeling would not perhaps have so prevailed with him were it not that upon a prior occasion the patriotic zeal officially evinced by Claggart had somewhat irritated him as appearing rather supersensible and strained. Furthermore, something even in the official's self-possessed and somewhat ostentatious manner in making his specifications strangely reminded him of a bandsman,[1] a perjurious witness in a capital case before a courtmartial ashore of which when a lieutenant he (Captain Vere) had been a member.

Now the peremptory check given to Claggart in the matter of the arrested allusion was quickly followed up by this: "You say that there is at least one dangerous man aboard. Name him."

"William Budd, a foretopman, your honor."

"William Budd!" repeated Captain Vere with unfeigned astonishment. "And mean you the man that Lieutenant Ratcliffe took from the merchantman not very long ago, the young fellow who seems to be so popular with the men—Billy, the Handsome Sailor, as they call him?"

"The same, your honor; but for all his youth and good looks, a deep one. Not for nothing does he insinuate himself into the good will of his shipmates, since at the least they will at a pinch say—all hands will—a good word for him, and at all hazards. Did Lieutenant Ratcliffe happen to tell your honor of that adroit fling of Budd's, jumping up in the cutter's bow under the merchantman's stern when he was being taken off? It is even masked by that sort of good-humored air that at heart he resents his impressment. You have but noted his fair cheek. A mantrap may be under the ruddy-tipped daisies."

Now the Handsome Sailor as a signal figure among the crew had naturally enough attracted the captain's attention from the first. Though in general not very demonstrative to his officers, he had congratulated Lieutenant Ratcliffe upon his good fortune in lighting on such a fine specimen of the *genus homo*,[2] who in the nude might have posed for a statue of young Adam before the Fall. As to Billy's adieu to the ship *Rights-of-Man*, which the boarding lieutenant had indeed reported to him, but, in a deferential way, more as a good story than aught else, Captain Vere, though mistakenly understanding it as a satiric sally, had but thought so much the better of the impressed man for it; as a military sailor, admiring the spirit that could take an arbitrary enlistment so merrily and sensibly. The foretopman's conduct, too, so far as it had fallen under the captain's notice, had confirmed the first happy augury, while the new recruit's qualities as a "sailorman" seemed to be such that he had thought of recommending him to the executive officer for promotion to a place that would more frequently bring him under his own observation, namely, the captaincy of the mizzentop,[3] replacing there in the starboard watch a man not so young whom partly for that reason he deemed

---

[1]One who operates the hoist.
[2]Classification of man (human race).

[3]The platform at the top of the mast at the stern (back) of the ship.

less fitted for the post. Be it parenthesized here that since the mizzentopmen have not to handle such breadths of heavy canvas as the lower sails on the mainmast and foremast, a young man if of the right stuff not only seems best adapted to duty there, but in fact is generally selected for the captaincy of that top, and the company under him are light hands and often but striplings. In sum, Captain Vere had from the beginning deemed Billy Budd to be what in the naval parlance of the time was called a "King's bargain": that is to say, for His Britannic Majesty's navy a capital investment at small outlay or none at all.

After a brief pause, during which the reminiscences above mentioned passed vividly through his mind and he weighed the import of Claggart's last suggestion conveyed in the phrase "mantrap under the daisies," and the more he weighed it the less reliance he felt in the informer's good faith, suddenly he turned upon him and in a low voice demanded: "Do you come to me, Master-at-arms, with so foggy a tale? As to Budd, cite me an act or spoken word of his confirmatory of what you in general charge against him. Stay," drawing nearer to him; "heed what you speak. Just now, and in a case like this, there is a yardarm-end[4] for the false witness."

"Ah, your honor!" sighed Claggart, mildly shaking his shapely head as in sad deprecation of such unmerited severity of tone. Then, bridling—erecting himself as in virtuous self-assertion—he circumstantially alleged certain words and acts which collectively, if credited, led to presumptions mortally inculpating Budd. And for some of these averments, he added, substantiating proof was not far.

With gray eyes impatient and distrustful essaying to fathom to the bottom Claggart's calm violet ones, Captain Vere again heard him out; then for the moment stood ruminating. The mood he evinced, Claggart—himself for the time liberated from the other's scrutiny—steadily regarded with a look difficult to render: a look curious of the operation of his tactics, a look such as might have been that of the spokesman of the envious children of Jacob deceptively imposing upon the troubled patriarch the blood-dyed coat of young Joseph.[5]

Though something exceptional in the moral quality of Captain Vere made him, in earnest encounter with a fellow man, a veritable touchstone of that man's essential nature, yet now as to Claggart and what was really going on in him his feeling partook less of intuitional conviction than of strong suspicion clogged by strange dubieties. The perplexity he evinced proceeded less from aught touching the man informed against—as Claggart doubtless opined—than from considerations how best to act in regard to the informer. At first, indeed, he was naturally for summoning that substantiation of his allegations which Claggart said was at hand. But such a proceeding would result in the matter at once getting abroad, which in the present stage of it, he thought, might undesirably affect the ship's company. If Claggart was a false witness—that closed the affair. And therefore, before trying the accusation, he would first practically test the accuser; and he thought this could be done in a quiet, undemonstrative way.

The measure he determined upon involved a shifting of the scene, a transfer to a place less exposed to observation than the broad quarter-deck. For although the few gun-room officers there at the time had, in due observance of naval etiquette, withdrawn to leeward the moment Captain Vere had begun his promenade on the deck's weather side; and though during the colloquy with Claggart they of course ventured not to diminish the distance; and though throughout the interview Captain Vere's voice was far from high, and Claggart's silvery and low; and the wind in the cordage and the wash of the sea helped the more to put them

---

[4]Place for hangings.
[5]Genesis 37:31–32: after selling Joseph, his brothers made his father think he was murdered.

beyond earshot; nevertheless, the interview's continuance already had attracted observation from some topmen aloft and other sailors in the waist or further forward.

Having determined upon his measures, Captain Vere forthwith took action. Abruptly turning to Claggart, he asked, "Master-at-arms, is it now Budd's watch aloft?"

"No, your honor."

Whereupon, "Mr. Wilkes!" summoning the nearest midshipman. "Tell Albert to come to me." Albert was the captain's hammock-boy, a sort of sea valet in whose discretion and fidelity his master had much confidence. The lad appeared.

"You know Budd, the foretopman?"

"I do, sir."

"Go find him. It is his watch off. Manage to tell him out of earshot that he is wanted aft. Contrive it that he speaks to nobody. Keep him in talk yourself. And not till you get well aft here, not till then let him know that the place where he is wanted is my cabin. You understand. Go.— Master-at-arms, show yourself on the decks below, and when you think it time for Albert to be coming with his man, stand by quietly to follow the sailor in."

19

Now when the foretopman found himself in the cabin, closeted there, as it were, with the captain and Claggart, he was surprised enough. But it was a surprise unaccompanied by apprehension or distrust. To an immature nature essentially honest and humane, forewarning intimations of subtler danger from one's kind come tardily if at all. The only thing that took shape in the young sailor's mind was this: Yes, the captain, I have always thought, looks kindly upon me. Wonder if he's going to make me his coxswain. I should like that. And may be now he is going to ask the master-at-arms about me.

"Shut the door there, sentry," said the commander; "stand without, and let nobody come in.— Now, Master-at-arms, tell this man to his face what you told of him to me," and stood prepared to scrutinize the mutually confronting visages.

With the measured step and calm collected air of an asylum physician approaching in the public hall some patient beginning to show indications of a coming paroxysm, Claggart deliberately advanced within short range of Billy and, mesmerically looking him in the eye, briefly recapitulated the accusation.

Not at first did Billy take it in. When he did, the rose-tan of his cheek looked struck as by white leprosy. He stood like one impaled and gagged. Meanwhile the accuser's eyes, removing not as yet from the blue dilated ones, underwent a phenomenal change, their wonted rich violet color blurring into a muddy purple. Those lights of human intelligence, losing human expression, were gelidly protruding like the alien eyes of certain uncatalogued creatures of the deep. The first mesmeristic glance was one of serpent fascination; the last was as the paralyzing lurch of the torpedo fish.[1]

"Speak, man!" said Captain Vere to the transfixed one, struck by his aspect even more than by Claggart's. "Speak! Defend yourself!" Which appeal caused but a strange dumb gesturing and gurgling in Billy; amazement at such an accusation so suddenly sprung on inexperienced nonage; this, and, it may be, horror of the accuser's eyes, serving to bring out his lurking defect and in this instance for the time intensifying it into a convulsed tongue-tie; while the intent head and entire form straining forward in an agony of ineffectual eagerness to obey the injunction to speak and defend himself, gave an expression to the face like that of a con-

---

[1] Fish charged with electricity to shock its prey.

demned vestal priestess in the moment of being buried alive, and in the first struggle against suffocation.[2]

Though at the time Captain Vere was quite ignorant of Billy's liability to vocal impediment, he now immediately divined it, since vividly Billy's aspect recalled to him that of a bright young schoolmate of his whom he had once seen struck by much the same startling impotence in the act of eagerly rising in the class to be foremost in response to a testing question put to it by the master. Going close up to the young sailor, and laying a soothing hand on his shoulder, he said, "There is no hurry, my boy. Take your time, take your time." Contrary to the effect intended, these words so fatherly in tone, doubtless touching Billy's heart to the quick, prompted yet more violent efforts at utterance—efforts soon ending for the time in confirming the paralysis, and bringing to his face an expression which was as a crucifixion to behold. The next instant, quick as the flame from a discharged cannon at night, his right arm shot out, and Claggart dropped to the deck. Whether intentionally or but owing to the young athlete's superior height, the blow had taken effect full upon the forehead, so shapely and intellectual-looking a feature in the master-at-arms; so that the body fell over lengthwise, like a heavy plank tilted from erectness. A gasp or two, and he lay motionless.

"Fated boy," breathed Captain Vere in tone so low as to be almost a whisper, "what have you done! But here, help me."

The twain raised the felled one from the loins up into a sitting position. The spare form flexibly acquiesced, but inertly. It was like handling a dead snake. They lowered it back. Regaining erectness, Captain Vere with one hand covering his face stood to all appearance as impassive as the object at his feet. Was he absorbed in taking in all the bearings of the event and what was best not only now at once to be done, but also in the sequel? Slowly he uncovered his face; and the effect was as if the moon emerging from eclipse should reappear with quite another aspect than that which had gone into hiding. The father in him, manifested towards Billy thus far in the scene, was replaced by the military disciplinarian. In his official tone he bade the foretopman retire to a stateroom aft (pointing it out), and there remain till thence summoned. This order Billy in silence mechanically obeyed. Then going to the cabin door where it opened on the quarter-deck, Captain Vere said to the sentry without, "Tell somebody to send Albert here." When the lad appeared, his master so contrived it that he should not catch sight of the prone one. "Albert," he said to him, "tell the surgeon I wish to see him. You need not come back till called."

When the surgeon entered—a self-poised character of that grave sense and experience that hardly anything could take him aback—Captain Vere advanced to meet him, thus unconsciously intercepting his view of Claggart, and, interrupting the other's wonted ceremonious salutation, said, "Nay. Tell me how it is with yonder man," directing his attention to the prostrate one.

The surgeon looked, and for all his self-command somewhat started at the abrupt revelation. On Claggart's always pallid complexion, thick black blood was now oozing from nostril and ear. To the gazer's professional eye it was unmistakably no living man that he saw.

"Is it so, then?" said Captain Vere, intently watching him. "I thought it. But verify it." Whereupon the customary tests confirmed the surgeon's first glance, who now, looking up in unfeigned concern, cast a look of intense inquisitiveness upon his superior. But Captain Vere, with one hand to his brow, was standing motionless. Suddenly, catching the surgeon's arm convulsively, he exclaimed, pointing down to the body, "It is the divine judgment on Ananias![3] Look!"

---

[2]Vestal virgins were priestesses of Vesta sworn to chastity; violation of the oath brought horrible punishment.
[3]Cf. Acts 5:3–5: Peter says to Ananias, "Thou hast not lied unto men, but unto God"; whereupon Ananias "fell down, and gave up the ghost."

Disturbed by the excited manner he had never before observed in the *Bellipotent's* captain, and as yet wholly ignorant of the affair, the prudent surgeon nevertheless held his peace, only again looking an earnest interrogatory as to what it was that had resulted in such a tragedy.

But Captain Vere was now again motionless, standing absorbed in thought. Again starting, he vehemently exclaimed, "Struck dead by an angel of God! Yet the angel must hang!"

At these passionate interjections, mere incoherences to the listener as yet unapprised of the antecedents, the surgeon was profoundly discomposed. But now, as recollecting himself, Captain Vere in less passionate tone briefly related the circumstances leading up to the event. "But come; we must dispatch," he added. "Help me to remove him" (meaning the body) "to yonder compartment," designating one opposite that where the foretopman remained immured. Anew disturbed by a request that, as implying a desire for secrecy, seemed unaccountably strange to him, there was nothing for the subordinate to do but comply.

"Go now," said Captain Vere with something of his wonted manner. "Go now. I presently shall call a drumhead court.[4] Tell the lieutenants what has happened, and tell Mr. Mordant" (meaning the captain of marines), "and charge them to keep the matter to themselves."

20

Full of disquietude and misgiving, the surgeon left the cabin. Was Captain Vere suddenly affected in his mind, or was it but a transient excitement, brought about by so strange and extraordinary a tragedy? As to the drumhead court, it struck the surgeon as impolitic, if nothing more. The thing to do, he thought, was to place Billy Budd in confinement, and in a way dictated by usage, and postpone further action in so extraordinary a case to such time as they should rejoin the squadron, and then refer it to the admiral. He recalled the unwonted agitation of Captain Vere and his excited exclamations, so at variance with his normal manner. Was he unhinged?

But assuming that he is, it is not so susceptible of proof. What then can the surgeon do? No more trying situation is conceivable than that of an officer subordinate under a captain whom he suspects to be not mad, indeed, but yet not quite unaffected in his intellects. To argue his order to him would be insolence. To resist him would be mutiny.

In obedience to Captain Vere, he communicated what had happened to the lieutenants and captain of marines, saying nothing as to the captain's state. They fully shared his own surprise and concern. Like him too, they seemed to think that such a matter should be referred to the admiral.

21

Who in the rainbow can draw the line where the violet tint ends and the orange tint begins? Distinctly we see the difference of the colors, but where exactly does the one first blendingly enter into the other? So with sanity and insanity. In pronounced cases there is no question about them. But in some supposed cases, in various degrees supposedly less pronounced, to draw the exact line of demarcation few will undertake, though for a fee becoming considerate some professional experts will. There is nothing namable but that some men will, or undertake to, do it for pay.

Whether Captain Vere, as the surgeon professionally and privately surmised,

---

[4]Immediate courtmartial held in the field or on board ship
during war (so called from the drum used as a table).

was really the sudden victim of any degree of aberration, every one must determine for himself by such light as this narrative may afford.

That the unhappy event which has been narrated could not have happened at a worse juncture was but too true. For it was close on the heel of the suppressed insurrections, an aftertime very critical to naval authority, demanding from every English sea commander two qualities not readily interfusable—prudence and rigor. Moreover, there was something crucial in the case.

In the jugglery of circumstances preceding and attending the event on board the *Bellipotent,* and in the light of that martial code whereby it was formally to be judged, innocence and guilt personified in Claggart and Budd in effect changed places. In a legal view the apparent victim of the tragedy was he who had sought to victimize a man blameless; and the indisputable deed of the latter, navally regarded, constituted the most heinous of military crimes. Yet more. The essential right and wrong involved in the matter, the clearer that might be, so much the worse for the responsibility of a loyal sea commander, inasmuch as he was not authorized to determine the matter on that primitive basis.

Small wonder then that the *Bellipotent's* captain, though in general a man of rapid decision, felt that circumspectness not less than promptitude was necessary. Until he could decide upon his course, and in each detail; and not only so, but until the concluding measure was upon the point of being enacted, he deemed it advisable, in view of all the circumstances, to guard as much as possible against publicity. Here he may or may not have erred. Certain it is, however, that subsequently in the confidential talk of more than one or two gun rooms and cabins he was not a little criticized by some officers, a fact imputed by his friends and vehemently by his cousin Jack Denton to professional jealousy of Starry Vere. Some imaginative ground for invidious comment there was. The maintenance of secrecy in the matter, the confining all knowledge of it for a time to the place where the homicide occurred, the quarter-deck cabin; in these particulars lurked some resemblance to the policy adopted in those tragedies of the palace which have occurred more than once in the capital founded by Peter the Barbarian.[1]

The case indeed was such that fain would the *Bellipotent's* captain have deferred taking any action whatever respecting it further than to keep the foretopman a close prisoner till the ship rejoined the squadron and then submitting the matter to the judgment of his admiral.

But a true military officer is in one particular like a true monk. Not with more of self-abnegation will the latter keep his vows of monastic obedience than the former his vows of allegiance to martial duty.

Feeling that unless quick action was taken on it, the deed of the foretopman, so soon as it should be known on the gun decks, would tend to awaken any slumbering embers of the Nore among the crew, a sense of the urgency of the case overruled in Captain Vere every other consideration. But though a conscientious disciplinarian, he was no lover of authority for mere authority's sake. Very far was he from embracing opportunities for monopolizing to himself the perils of moral responsibility, none at least that could properly be referred to an official superior or shared with him by his official equals or even subordinates. So thinking, he was glad it would not be at variance with usage to turn the matter over to a summary court of his own officers, reserving to himself, as the one on whom the ultimate accountability would rest, the right of maintaining a supervision of it, or formally or informally interposing at need. Accordingly a drumhead court was summarily convened, he electing the individuals composing it: the first lieutenant, the captain of marines, and the sailing master.[2]

---

[1] Czar of Russia, Peter the Great (1672–1725).
[2] Chief navigator of the ship.

In associating an officer of marines with the sea lieutenant and the sailing master in a case having to do with a sailor, the commander perhaps deviated from general custom. He was prompted thereto by the circumstance that he took that soldier to be a judicious person, thoughtful, and not altogether incapable of grappling with a difficult case unprecedented in his prior experience. Yet even as to him he was not without some latent misgiving, for withal he was an extremely good-natured man, an enjoyer of his dinner, a sound sleeper, and inclined to obesity—a man who though he would always maintain his manhood in battle might not prove altogether reliable in a moral dilemma involving aught of the tragic. As to the first lieutenant and the sailing master, Captain Vere could not but be aware that though honest natures, of approved gallantry upon occasion, their intelligence was mostly confined to the matter of active seamanship and the fighting demands of their profession.

The court was held in the same cabin where the unfortunate affair had taken place. This cabin, the commander's, embraced the entire area under the poop deck. Aft, and on either side, was a small stateroom, the one now temporarily a jail and the other a dead-house, and a yet smaller compartment, leaving a space between expanding forward into a goodly oblong of length coinciding with the ship's beam.[3] A skylight of moderate dimension was overhead, and at each end of the oblong space were two sashed porthole windows easily convertible back into embrasures for short carronades.[4]

All being quickly in readiness, Billy Budd was arraigned, Captain Vere necessarily appearing as the sole witness in the case, and as such temporarily sinking his rank, though singularly maintaining it in a matter apparently trivial, namely, that he testified from the ship's weather side, with that object having caused the court to sit on the lee side.[5] Concisely he narrated all that had led up to the catastrophe, omitting nothing in Claggart's accusation and deposing as to the manner in which the prisoner had received it. At this testimony the three officers glanced with no little surprise at Billy Budd, the last man they would have suspected either of the mutinous design alleged by Claggart or the undeniable deed he himself had done. The first lieutenant, taking judicial primacy and turning toward the prisoner, said, "Captain Vere has spoken. Is it or is it not as Captain Vere says?"

In response came syllables not so much impeded in the utterance as might have been anticipated. They were these: "Captain Vere tells the truth. It is just as Captain Vere says, but it is not as the master-at-arms said. I have eaten the King's bread and I am true to the King."

"I believe you, my man," said the witness, his voice indicating a suppressed emotion not otherwise betrayed.

"God will bless you for that, your honor!" not without stammering said Billy, and all but broke down. But immediately he was recalled to self-control by another question, to which with the same emotional difficulty of utterance he said, "No, there was no malice between us. I never bore malice against the master-at-arms. I am sorry that he is dead. I did not mean to kill him. Could I have used my tongue I would not have struck him. But he foully lied to my face and in presence of my captain, and I had to say something, and I could only say it with a blow, God help me!"

In the impulsive aboveboard manner of the frank one the court saw confirmed all that was implied in words that just previously had perplexed them, coming as they did from the testifier to the tragedy and promptly following Billy's impas-

---

[3]Beam running the full width of the ship at its widest.
[4]Openings suitable for short, light, large-bore cannon.
[5]Side furthest from the side from which the wind blows (thus Capt. Vere speaks from the wind side, which raises the ship and elevates him).

sioned disclaimer of mutinous intent—Captain Vere's words, "I believe you, my man."

Next it was asked of him whether he knew of or suspected aught savoring of incipient trouble (meaning mutiny, though the explicit term was avoided) going on in any section of the ship's company.

The reply lingered. This was naturally imputed by the court to the same vocal embarrassment which had retarded or obstructed previous answers. But in main it was otherwise here, the question immediately recalling to Billy's mind the interview with the afterguardsman in the forechains. But an innate repugnance to playing a part at all approaching that of an informer against one's own shipmates—the same erring sense of uninstructed honor which had stood in the way of his reporting the matter at the time, though as a loyal man-of-war's man it was incumbent on him, and failure so to do, if charged against him and proven, would have subjected him to the heaviest of penalties; this, with the blind feeling now his that nothing really was being hatched, prevailed with him. When the answer came it was a negative.

"One question more," said the officer of marines, now first speaking and with a troubled earnestness. "You tell us that what the master-at-arms said against you was a lie. Now why should he have so lied, so maliciously lied, since you declare there was no malice between you?"

At that question, unintentionally touching on a spiritual sphere wholly obscure to Billy's thoughts, he was nonplussed, evincing a confusion indeed that some observers, such as can readily be imagined, would have construed into involuntary evidence of hidden guilt. Nevertheless, he strove some way to answer, but all at once relinquished the vain endeavor, at the same time turning an appealing glance towards Captain Vere as deeming him his best helper and friend. Captain Vere, who had been seated for a time, rose to his feet, addressing the interrogator. "The question you put to him comes naturally enough. But how can he rightly answer it?—or anybody else, unless indeed it be he who lies within there," designating the compartment where lay the corpse. "But the prone one there will not rise to our summons. In effect, though, as it seems to me, the point you make is hardly material. Quite aside from any conceivable motive actuating the master-at-arms, and irrespective of the provocation to the blow, a martial court must needs in the present case confine its attention to the blow's consequence, which consequence justly is to be deemed not otherwise than as the striker's deed."

This utterance, the full significance of which it was not at all likely that Billy took in, nevertheless caused him to turn a wistful interrogative look toward the speaker, a look in its dumb expressiveness not unlike that which a dog of generous breed might turn upon his master, seeking in his face some elucidation of a previous gesture ambiguous to the canine intelligence. Nor was the same utterance without marked effect upon the three officers, more especially the soldier. Couched in it seemed to them a meaning unanticipated, involving a prejudgment on the speaker's part. It served to augment a mental disturbance previously evident enough.

The soldier once more spoke, in a tone of suggestive dubiety addressing at once his associates and Captain Vere: "Nobody is present—none of the ship's company, I mean—who might shed lateral light, if any is to be had, upon what remains mysterious in this matter."

"That is thoughtfully put," said Captain Vere; "I see your drift. Ay, there is a mystery; but, to use a scriptural phrase, it is a 'mystery of iniquity,'[6] a matter for psychologic theologians to discuss. But what has a military court to do with it? Not to add that for us any possible investigation of it is cut off by the lasting tongue-tie

[6] 2 Thessalonians 2:7.

of—him—in yonder," again designating the mortuary stateroom. "The prisoner's deed—with that alone we have to do."

To this, and particularly the closing reiteration, the marine soldier, knowing not how aptly to reply, sadly abstained from saying aught. The first lieutenant, who at the outset had not unnaturally assumed primacy in the court, now overrulingly instructed by a glance from Captain Vere, a glance more effective than words, resumed that primacy. Turning to the prisoner, "Budd," he said, and scarce in equable tones, "Budd, if you have aught further to say for yourself, say it now."

Upon this the young sailor turned another quick glance toward Captain Vere; then, as taking a hint from that aspect, a hint confirming his own instinct that silence was now best, replied to the lieutenant, "I have said all, sir."

The marine—the same who had been the sentinel without the cabin door at the time that the foretopman, followed by the master-at-arms, entered it—he, standing by the sailor throughout these judicial proceedings, was now directed to take him back to the after compartment originally assigned to the prisoner and his custodian. As the twain disappeared from view, the three officers, as partially liberated from some inward constraint associated with Billy's mere presence, simultaneously stirred in their seats. They exchanged looks of troubled indecision, yet feeling that decide they must and without long delay. For Captain Vere, he for the time stood—unconsciously with his back toward them, apparently in one of his absent fits—gazing out from a sashed porthole to windward upon the monotonous blank of the twilight sea. But the court's silence continuing, broken only at moments by brief consultations, in low earnest tones, this served to arouse him and energize him. Turning, he to-and-fro paced the cabin athwart; in the returning ascent to windward climbing the slant deck in the ship's lee roll,[7] without knowing it symbolizing thus in his action a mind resolute to surmount difficulties even if against primitive instincts strong as the wind and the sea. Presently he came to a stand before the three. After scanning their faces he stood less as mustering his thoughts for expression than as one inly deliberating how best to put them to well-meaning men not intellectually mature, men with whom it was necessary to demonstrate certain principles that were axioms to himself. Similar impatience as to talking is perhaps one reason that deters some minds from addressing any popular assemblies.

When speak he did, something, both in the substance of what he said and his manner of saying it, showed the influence of unshared studies modifying and tempering the practical training of an active career. This, along with his phraseology, now and then was suggestive of the grounds whereon rested that imputation of a certain pedantry socially alleged against him by certain naval men of wholly practical cast, captains who nevertheless would frankly concede that His Majesty's navy mustered no more efficient officer of their grade than Starry Vere.

What he said was to this effect: "Hitherto I have been but the witness, little more; and I should hardly think now to take another tone, that of your coadjutor for the time, did I not perceive in you—at the crisis too—a troubled hesitancy, proceeding, I doubt not, from the clash of military duty with moral scruple—scruple vitalized by compassion. For the compassion, how can I otherwise than share it? But, mindful of paramount obligations, I strive against scruples that may tend to enervate decision. Not, gentlemen, that I hide from myself that the case is an exceptional one. Speculatively regarded, it well might be referred to a jury of casuists.[8] But for us here, acting not as casuists or moralists, it is a case practical, and under martial law practically to be dealt with.

---

[7] Moving up as the ship was tipped by the wind.
[8] A quibbler, one using nit-picking or hair-splitting arguments.

"But your scruples: do they move as in a dusk? Challenge them. Make them advance and declare themselves. Come now; do they import something like this: If, mindless of palliating circumstances, we are bound to regard the death of the master-at-arms as the prisoner's deed, then does that deed constitute a capital crime whereof the penalty is a mortal one. But in natural justice is nothing but the prisoner's overt act to be considered? How can we adjudge to summary and shameful death a fellow creature innocent before God, and whom we feel to be so?—Does that state it aright? You sign sad assent. Well, I too feel that, the full force of that. It is Nature. But do these buttons that we wear attest that our allegiance is to Nature? No, to the King. Though the ocean, which is inviolate Nature primeval, though this be the element where we move and have our being as sailors, yet as the King's officers lies our duty in a sphere correspondingly natural? So little is that true, that in receiving our commissions we in the most important regards ceased to be natural free agents. When war is declared are we the commissioned fighters previously consulted? We fight at command. If our judgments approve the war, that is but coincidence. So in other particulars. So now. For suppose condemnation to follow these present proceedings. Would it be so much we ourselves that would condemn as it would be martial law operating through us? For that law and the rigor of it, we are not responsible. Our vowed responsibility is in this: That however pitilessly that law may operate in any instances, we nevertheless adhere to it and administer it.

"But the exceptional in the matter moves the hearts within you. Even so too is mine moved. But let not warm hearts betray heads that should be cool. Ashore in a criminal case, will an upright judge allow himself off the bench to be waylaid by some tender kinswoman of the accused seeking to touch him with her tearful plea? Well, the heart here, sometimes the feminine in man, is as that piteous woman, and hard though it be, she must here be ruled out."

He paused, earnestly studying them for a moment; then resumed.

"But something in your aspect seems to urge that it is not solely the heart that moves in you, but also the conscience, the private conscience. But tell me whether or not, occupying the position we do, private conscience should not yield to that imperial one formulated in the code under which alone we officially proceed?"

Here the three men moved in their seats, less convinced than agitated by the course of an argument troubling but the more the spontaneous conflict within.

Perceiving which, the speaker paused for a moment; then abruptly changing his tone, went on.

"To steady us a bit, let us recur to the facts.—In wartime at sea a man-of-war's man strikes his superior in grade, and the blow kills. Apart from its effect the blow itself is, according to the Articles of War, a capital crime. Furthermore——"

"Ay, sir," emotionally broke in the officer of marines, "in one sense it was. But surely Budd purposed neither mutiny nor homicide."

"Surely not, my good man. And before a court less arbitrary and more merciful than a martial one, that plea would largely extenuate. At the Last Assizes[9] it shall acquit. But how here? We proceed under the law of the Mutiny Act. In feature no child can resemble his father more than that Act resembles in spirit the thing from which it derives—War. In His Majesty's service—in this ship, indeed—there are Englishmen forced to fight for the King against their will. Against their conscience, for aught we know. Though as their fellow creatures some of us may appreciate their position, yet as navy officers what reck we of it? Still less recks the enemy. Our impressed men he would fain cut down in the same swath with our volunteers. As regards the enemy's naval conscripts, some of whom may even share our own abhorrence of the regicidal French Directory,[10] it

---

[9] The Biblical Last Judgment.
[10] The ruling body in France, regicidal in that it was implicated in the execution of the king; now the head of government of England's enemy.

is the same on our side. War looks but to the frontage, the appearance. And the Mutiny Act, War's child, takes after the father. Budd's intent or non-intent is nothing to the purpose.

"But while, put to it by those anxieties in you which I cannot but respect, I only repeat myself—while thus strangely we prolong proceedings that should be summary—the enemy may be sighted and an engagement result. We must do; and one of two things must we do—condemn or let go."

"Can we not convict and yet mitigate the penalty?" asked the sailing master, here speaking, and falteringly, for the first.

"Gentlemen, were that clearly lawful for us under the circumstances, consider the consequences of such clemency. The people" (meaning the ship's company) "have native sense; most of them are familiar with our naval usage and tradition; and how would they take it? Even could you explain to them—which our official position forbids—they, long molded by arbitrary discipline, have not that kind of intelligent responsiveness that might qualify them to comprehend and discriminate. No, to the people the foretopman's deed, however it be worded in the announcement, will be plain homicide committed in a flagrant act of mutiny. What penalty for that should follow, they know. But it does not follow. *Why?* they will ruminate. You know what sailors are. Will they not revert to the recent outbreak at the Nore? Ay. They know the well-founded alarm—the panic it struck throughout England. Your clement sentence they would account pusillanimous. They would think that we flinch, that we are afraid of them—afraid of practicing a lawful rigor singularly demanded at this juncture, lest it should provoke new troubles. What shame to us such a conjecture on their part, and how deadly to discipline. You see then, whither, prompted by duty and the law, I steadfastly drive. But I beseech you, my friends, do not take me amiss. I feel as you do for this unfortunate boy. But did he know our hearts, I take him to be of that generous nature that he would feel even for us on whom in this military necessity so heavy a compulsion is laid."

With that, crossing the deck he resumed his place by the sashed porthole, tacitly leaving the three to come to a decision. On the cabin's opposite side the troubled court sat silent. Loyal lieges, plain and practical, though at bottom they dissented from some points Captain Vere had put to them, they were without the faculty, hardly had the inclination, to gainsay one whom they felt to be an earnest man, one too not less their superior in mind than in naval rank. But it is not improbable that even such of his words as were not without influence over them, less came home to them than his closing appeal to their instinct as sea officers: in the forethought he threw out as to the practical consequences to discipline, considering the unconfirmed tone of the fleet at the time, should a man-of-war's man's violent killing at sea of a superior in grade be allowed to pass for aught else than a capital crime demanding prompt infliction of the penalty.

Not unlikely they were brought to something more or less akin to that harassed frame of mind which in the year 1842 actuated the commander of the U.S. brig-of-war *Somers* to resolve, under the so-called Articles of War, Articles modeled upon the English Mutiny Act, to resolve upon the execution at sea of a midshipman and two sailors as mutineers designing the seizure of the brig.[11] Which resolution was carried out though in a time of peace and within not many days' sail of home. An act vindicated by a naval court of inquiry subsequently convened ashore. History, and here cited without comment. True, the circumstances on board the *Somers* were different from those on board the *Bellipotent*. But the urgency felt, well-warranted or otherwise, was much the same.

---

[11]This well-known case of mutiny, trial, and execution of those found guilty involved Melville's cousin Guert Gan- sevoort, who presided at the drumhead court. The harsh sentences (hanging) were a matter of heated controversy.

Says a writer[12] whom few know, "Forty years after a battle it is easy for a non-combatant to reason about how it ought to have been fought. It is another thing personally and under fire to have to direct the fighting while involved in the obscuring smoke of it. Much so with respect to other emergencies involving considerations both practical and moral, and when it is imperative promptly to act. The greater the fog the more it imperils the steamer, and speed is put on though at the hazard of running somebody down. Little ween the snug card players in the cabin of the responsibilities of the sleepless man on the bridge."

In brief, Billy Budd was formally convicted and sentenced to be hung at the yardarm in the early morning watch, it being now night. Otherwise, as is customary in such cases, the sentence would forthwith have been carried out. In wartime on the field or in the fleet, a mortal punishment decreed by a drumhead court—on the field sometimes decreed by but a nod from the general—follows without delay on the heel of conviction, without appeal.

22

It was Captain Vere himself who of his own motion communicated the finding of the court to the prisoner, for that purpose going to the compartment where he was in custody and bidding the marine there to withdraw for the time.

Beyond the communication of the sentence, what took place at this interview was never known. But in view of the character of the twain briefly closeted in that stateroom, each radically sharing in the rarer qualities of our nature—so rare indeed as to be all but incredible to average minds however much cultivated—some conjectures may be ventured.

It would have been in consonance with the spirit of Captain Vere should he on this occasion have concealed nothing from the condemned one—should he indeed have frankly disclosed to him the part he himself had played in bringing about the decision, at the same time revealing his actuating motives. On Billy's side it is not improbable that such a confession would have been received in much the same spirit that prompted it. Not without a sort of joy, indeed, he might have appreciated the brave opinion of him implied in his captain's making such a confidant of him. Nor, as to the sentence itself, could he have been insensible that it was imparted to him as to one not afraid to die. Even more may have been. Captain Vere in end may have developed the passion sometimes latent under an exterior stoical or indifferent. He was old enough to have been Billy's father. The austere devotee of military duty, letting himself melt back into what remains primeval in our formalized humanity, may in end have caught Billy to his heart, even as Abraham may have caught young Isaac on the brink of resolutely offering him up in obedience to the exacting behest.[1] But there is no telling the sacrament, seldom if in any case revealed to the gadding world, wherever under circumstances at all akin to those here attempted to be set forth two of great Nature's nobler order embrace. There is privacy at the time, inviolable to the survivor; and holy oblivion, the sequel to each diviner magnanimity, providentially covers all at last.

The first to encounter Captain Vere in act of leaving the compartment was the senior lieutenant. The face he beheld, for the moment one expressive of the agony of the strong, was to that officer, though a man of fifty, a startling revelation. That the condemned one suffered less than he who mainly had effected the condemnation was apparently indicated by the former's exclamation in the scene soon perforce to be touched upon.

---

[12]Melville himself.
[1]Cf. Genesis 22:1–18: God commanded Abraham to sacrifice his son; as Abraham prepared to do so, God withdrew the command.

23

Of a series of incidents within a brief term rapidly following each other, the adequate narration may take up a term less brief, especially if explanation or comment here and there seem requisite to the better understanding of such incidents. Between the entrance into the cabin of him who never left it alive, and him who when he did leave it left it as one condemned to die; between this and the closeted interview just given, less than an hour and a half had elapsed. It was an interval long enough, however, to awaken speculations among no few of the ship's company as to what it was that could be detaining in the cabin the master-at-arms and the sailor; for a rumor that both of them had been seen to enter it and neither of them had been seen to emerge, this rumor had got abroad upon the gun decks and in the tops, the people of a great warship being in one respect like villagers, taking microscopic note of every outward movement or non-movement going on. When therefore, in weather not at all tempestuous, all hands were called in the second dogwatch, a summons under such circumstances not usual in those hours, the crew were not wholly unprepared for some announcement extraordinary, one having connection too with the continued absence of the two men from their wonted haunts.

There was a moderate sea at the time; and the moon, newly risen and near to being at its full, silvered the white spar deck wherever not blotted by the clear-cut shadows horizontally thrown of fixtures and moving men. On either side the quarter-deck the marine guard under arms was drawn up; and Captain Vere, standing in his place surrounded by all the wardroom officers,[1] addressed his men. In so doing, his manner showed neither more nor less than that properly pertaining to his supreme position aboard his own ship. In clear terms and concise he told them what had taken place in the cabin: that the master-at-arms was dead, that he who had killed him had been already tried by a summary court and condemned to death, and that the execution would take place in the early morning watch. The word *mutiny* was not named in what he said. He refrained too from making the occasion an opportunity for any preachment as to the maintenance of discipline, thinking perhaps that under existing circumstances in the navy the consequence of violating discipline should be made to speak for itself.

Their captain's announcement was listened to by the throng of standing sailors in a dumbness like that of a seated congregation of believers in hell listening to the clergyman's announcement of his Calvinistic text.

At the close, however, a confused murmur went up. It began to wax. All but instantly, then, at a sign, it was pierced and suppressed by shrill whistles of the boatswain and his mates. The word was given to about ship.

To be prepared for burial Claggart's body was delivered to certain petty officers of his mess. And here, not to clog the sequel with lateral matters, it may be added that at a suitable hour, the master-at-arms was committed to the sea with every funeral honor properly belonging to his naval grade.

In this proceeding as in every public one growing out of the tragedy strict adherence to usage was observed. Nor in any point could it have been at all deviated from, either with respect to Claggart or Billy Budd, without begetting undesirable speculations in the ship's company, sailors, and more particularly men-of-war's men, being of all men the greatest sticklers for usage. For similar cause, all communication between Captain Vere and the condemned one ended with the closeted interview already given, the latter being now surrendered to the ordinary routine preliminary to the end. His transfer under guard from the captain's quarters was effected without unusual precautions—at least no visible ones. If possi-

---

[1]Those above rank of ensign.

ble, not to let the men so much as surmise that their officers anticipate aught amiss from them is the tacit rule in a military ship. And the more that some sort of trouble should really be apprehended, the more do the officers keep that apprehension to themselves, though not the less unostentatious vigilance may be augmented. In the present instance, the sentry placed over the prisoner had strict orders to let no one have communication with him but the chaplain. And certain unobtrusive measures were taken absolutely to insure this point.

24

In a seventy-four of the old order the deck known as the upper gun deck was the one covered over by the spar deck, which last, though not without its armament, was for the most part exposed to the weather. In general it was at all hours free from hammocks; those of the crew swinging on the lower gun deck and berth deck, the latter being not only a dormitory but also the place for the stowing of the sailors' bags, and on both sides lined with the large chests or movable pantries of the many messes of the men.

On the starboard side of the *Bellipotent's* upper gun deck, behold Billy Budd under sentry lying prone in irons in one of the bays formed by the regular spacing of the guns comprising the batteries on either side. All these pieces were of the heavier caliber of that period. Mounted on lumbering wooden carriages, they were hampered with cumbersome harness of breeching and strong side-tackles for running them out. Guns and carriages, together with the long rammers and shorter linstocks[1] lodged in loops overhead—all these, as customary, were painted black; and the heavy hempen breechings, tarred to the same tint, wore the like livery of the undertakers. In contrast with the funereal hue of these surroundings, the prone sailor's exterior apparel, white jumper and white duck trousers, each more or less soiled, dimly glimmered in the obscure light of the bay like a patch of discolored snow in early April lingering at some upland cave's black mouth. In effect he is already in his shroud, or the garments that shall serve him in lieu of one. Over him but scarce illuminating him, two battle lanterns swing from two massive beams of the deck above. Fed with the oil supplied by the war contractors (whose gains, honest or otherwise, are in every land an anticipated portion of the harvest of death), with flickering splashes of dirty yellow light they pollute the pale moonshine all but ineffectually struggling in obstructed flecks through the open ports from which the tampioned[2] cannon protrude. Other lanterns at intervals serve but to bring out somewhat the obscurer bays which, like small confessionals or side-chapels in a cathedral, branch from the long dim-vistaed broad aisle between the two batteries of that covered tier.

Such was the deck where now lay the Handsome Sailor. Through the rose-tan of his complexion no pallor could have shown. It would have taken days of sequestration from the winds and the sun to have brought about the effacement of that. But the skeleton in the cheekbone at the point of its angle was just beginning delicately to be defined under the warm-tinted skin. In fervid hearts self-contained, some brief experiences devour our human tissue as secret fire in a ship's hold consumes cotton in the bale.

But now lying between the two guns, as nipped in the vice of fate, Billy's agony, mainly proceeding from a generous young heart's virgin experience of the diabolical incarnate and effective in some men—the tension of that agony was over now. It survived not the something healing in the closeted interview with Captain Vere.

---

[1] Rods for ramming the charge down the barrel of the cannon and long stick to extend a lighted match to fire a cannon.
[2] Plugged up with a stopper called a tampion.

Without movement, he lay as in a trance, that adolescent expression previously noted as his taking on something akin to the look of a slumbering child in the cradle when the warm hearth-glow of the still chamber at night plays on the dimples that at whiles mysteriously form in the cheek, silently coming and going there. For now and then in the gyved[3] one's trance a serene happy light born of some wandering reminiscence or dream would diffuse itself over his face, and then wane away only anew to return.

The chaplain, coming to see him and finding him thus, and perceiving no sign that he was conscious of his presence, attentively regarded him for a space, then slipping aside, withdrew for the time, peradventure feeling that even he, the minister of Christ though receiving his stipend from Mars,[4] had no consolation to proffer which could result in a peace transcending that which he beheld. But in the small hours he came again. And the prisoner, now awake to his surroundings, noticed his approach, and civilly, all but cheerfully, welcomed him. But it was to little purpose that in the interview following, the good man sought to bring Billy Budd to some godly understanding that he must die, and at dawn. True, Billy himself freely referred to his death as a thing close at hand; but it was something in the way that children will refer to death in general, who yet among their other sports will play a funeral with hearse and mourners.

Not that like children Billy was incapable of conceiving what death really is. No, but he was wholly without irrational fear of it, a fear more prevalent in highly civilized communities than those so-called barbarous ones which in all respects stand nearer to unadulterate Nature. And, as elsewhere said, a barbarian Billy radically was—as much so, for all the costume, as his countrymen the British captives, living trophies, made to march in the Roman triumph of Germanicus.[5] Quite as much so as those later barbarians, young men probably, and picked specimens among the earlier British converts to Christianity, at least nominally such, taken to Rome (as today converts from lesser isles of the sea may be taken to London), of whom the Pope of that time,[6] admiring the strangeness of their personal beauty so unlike the Italian stamp, their clear ruddy complexion and curled flaxen locks, exclaimed, "Angles" (meaning *English*, the modern derivative), "Angles, do you call them? And is it because they look so like angels?" Had it been later in time, one would think that the Pope had in mind Fra Angelico's[7] seraphs, some of whom, plucking apples in gardens of the Hesperides,[8] have the faint rosebud complexion of the more beautiful English girls.

If in vain the good chaplain sought to impress the young barbarian with ideas of death akin to those conveyed in the skull, dial, and crossbones on old tombstones, equally futile to all appearance were his efforts to bring home to him the thought of salvation and a Savior. Billy listened, but less out of awe or reverence, perhaps, than from a certain natural politeness, doubtless at bottom regarding all that in much the same way that most mariners of his class take any discourse abstract or out of the common tone of the workaday world. And this sailor way of taking clerical discourse is not wholly unlike the way in which the primer of Christianity, full of transcendent miracles, was received long ago on tropic isles by any superior *savage*, so called—a Tahitian, say, of Captain Cook's time or shortly after that time.[9] Out of natural courtesy he received, but did not appropriate. It was like a gift placed in the palm of an outreached hand upon which the fingers do not close.

---

[3]Fettered, shackled.
[4]God of war.
[5]Roman general (15 B.C.–A.D. 19) who fought German tribes and returned triumphantly to Rome (A.D. 17).
[6]Gregory I (Pope 590–604).
[7]Giovanni da Fiesole, or Fra Angelico (1387–1455), Italian Renaissance painter.

[8]In Greek mythology, fabled gardens in the far west where grew golden apples.
[9]Captain James Cook (1728–1779), British explorer who visited Tahiti first in 1769.

But the *Bellipotent's* chaplain was a discreet man possessing the good sense of a good heart. So he insisted not in his vocation here. At the instance of Captain Vere, a lieutenant had apprised him of pretty much everything as to Billy; and since he felt that innocence was even a better thing than religion wherewith to go to Judgment, he reluctantly withdrew; but in his emotion not without first performing an act strange enough in an Englishman, and under the circumstances yet more so in any regular priest. Stooping over, he kissed on the fair cheek his fellow man, a felon in martial law, one whom though on the confines of death he felt he could never convert to a dogma; nor for all that did he fear for his future.

Marvel not that having been made acquainted with the young sailor's essential innocence the worthy man lifted not a finger to avert the doom of such a martyr to martial discipline. So to do would not only have been as idle as invoking the desert, but would also have been an audacious transgression of the bounds of his function, one as exactly prescribed to him by military law as that of the boatswain or any other naval officer. Bluntly put, a chaplain is the minister of the Prince of Peace serving in the host of the God of War—Mars. As such, he is as incongruous as a musket would be on the altar at Christmas. Why, then, is he there? Because he indirectly subserves the purpose attested by the cannon; because too he lends the sanction of the religion of the meek to that which practically is the abrogation of everything but brute Force.

25

The night so luminous on the spar deck, but otherwise on the cavernous ones below, levels so like the tiered galleries in a coal mine—the luminous night passed away. But like the prophet in the chariot disappearing in heaven and dropping his mantle to Elisha,[1] the withdrawing night transferred its pale robe to the breaking day. A meek, shy light appeared in the East, where stretched a diaphanous fleece of white furrowed vapor. That light slowly waxed. Suddenly *eight bells* was struck aft, responded to by one louder metallic stroke from forward. It was four o'clock in the morning. Instantly the silver whistles were heard summoning all hands to witness punishment. Up through the great hatchways rimmed with racks of heavy shot the watch below came pouring, overspreading with the watch already on deck the space between the mainmast and foremast including that occupied by the capacious launch and the black booms tiered on either side of it, boat and booms making a summit of observation for the powder-boys and younger tars. A different group comprising one watch of topmen leaned over the rail of that sea balcony, no small one in a seventy-four, looking down on the crowd below. Man or boy, none spake but in whisper, and few spake at all. Captain Vere—as before, the central figure among the assembled commissioned officers—stood nigh the break of the poop deck facing forward. Just below him on the quarter-deck the marines in full equipment were drawn up much as at the scene of the promulgated sentence.

At sea in the old time, the execution by halter of a military sailor was generally from the foreyard. In the present instance, for special reasons the mainyard was assigned. Under an arm of that yard the prisoner was presently brought up, the chaplain attending him. It was noted at the time, and remarked upon afterwards, that in this final scene the good man evinced little or nothing of the perfunctory. Brief speech indeed he had with the condemned one, but the genuine Gospel was less on his tongue than in his aspect and manner towards him. The final prepara-

---

[1]Cf. 2 Kings 2:11–13: When Elijah "went up by a whirl-wind into heaven," his disciple Elisha "took up the mantle of Elijah that fell from him."

tions personal to the latter being speedily brought to an end by two boatswain's mates, the consummation impended. Billy stood facing aft. At the penultimate moment, his words, his only ones, words wholly unobstructed in the utterance, were these: "God bless Captain Vere!" Syllables so unanticipated coming from one with the ignominious hemp about his neck—a conventional felon's benediction directed aft towards the quarters of honor; syllables too delivered in the clear melody of a singing bird on the point of launching from the twig—had a phenomenal effect, not unenhanced by the rare personal beauty of the young sailor, spiritualized now through late experiences so poignantly profound.

Without volition, as it were, as if indeed the ship's populace were but the vehicles of some vocal current electric, with one voice from alow and aloft came a resonant sympathetic echo: "God bless Captain Vere!" And yet at that instant Billy alone must have been in their hearts, even as in their eyes.

At the pronounced words and the spontaneous echo that voluminously rebounded them, Captain Vere, either through stoic self-control or a sort of momentary paralysis induced by emotional shock, stood erectly rigid as a musket in the ship-armorer's rack.

The hull, deliberately recovering from the periodic roll to leeward, was just regaining an even keel when the last signal, a preconcerted dumb one, was given. At the same moment it chanced that the vapory fleece hanging low in the East was shot through with a soft glory as of the fleece of the Lamb of God seen in mystical vision,[2] and simultaneously therewith, watched by the wedged mass of upturned faces, Billy ascended; and, ascending, took the full rose of the dawn.

In the pinioned figure arrived at the yard-end, to the wonder of all no motion was apparent, none save that created by the slow roll of the hull in moderate weather, so majestic in a great ship ponderously cannoned.

26

When some days afterwards, in reference to the singularity just mentioned, the purser,[1] a rather ruddy, rotund person more accurate as an accountant than profound as a philosopher, said at mess to the surgeon, "What testimony to the force lodged in will power," the latter, saturnine, spare, and tall, one in whom a discreet causticity went along with a manner less genial than polite, replied, "Your pardon, Mr. Purser. In a hanging scientifically conducted—and under special orders I myself directed how Budd's was to be effected—any movement following the completed suspension and originating in the body suspended, such movement indicates mechanical spasm in the muscular system. Hence the absence of that is no more attributable to will power, as you call it, than to horsepower—begging your pardon."

"But this muscular spasm you speak of, is not that in a degree more or less invariable in these cases?"

"Assuredly so, Mr. Purser."

"How then, my good sir, do you account for its absence in this instance?"

"Mr. Purser, it is clear that your sense of the singularity in this matter equals not mine. You account for it by what you call will power—a term not yet included in the lexicon of science. For me, I do not, with my present knowledge, pretend to account for it at all. Even should we assume the hypothesis that at the first touch of the halyards the action of Budd's heart, intensified by extraordinary emotion at its climax, abruptly stopped—much like a watch when in carelessly winding it up

---

[2]Cf. Revelation 1:14: John describes his vision of Jesus: "His head and his hairs were white like wool, as white as snow; and his eyes were as a flame of fire."
[1]Paymaster.

you strain at the finish, thus snapping the chain—even under that hypothesis how account for the phenomenon that followed?"

"You admit, then, that the absence of spasmodic movement was phenomenal."

"It was phenomenal, Mr. Purser, in the sense that it was an appearance the cause of which is not immediately to be assigned."

"But tell me, my dear sir," pertinaciously continued the other, "was the man's death effected by the halter, or was it a species of euthanasia?"[2]

"*Euthanasia,* Mr. Purser, is something like your *will power:* I doubt its authenticity as a scientific term—begging your pardon again. It is at once imaginative and metaphysical—in short, Greek.—But," abruptly changing his tone, "there is a case in the sick bay that I do not care to leave to my assistants. Beg your pardon, but excuse me." And rising from the mess he formally withdrew.

27

The silence at the moment of execution and for a moment or two continuing thereafter, a silence but emphasized by the regular wash of the sea against the hull or the flutter of a sail caused by the helmsman's eyes being tempted astray, this emphasized silence was gradually disturbed by a sound not easily to be verbally rendered. Whoever has heard the freshet-wave of a torrent suddenly swelled by pouring showers in tropical mountains, showers not shared by the plain; whoever has heard the first muffled murmur of its sloping advance through precipitous woods may form some conception of the sound now heard. The seeming remoteness of its source was because of its murmurous indistinctness, since it came from close by, even from the men massed on the ship's open deck. Being inarticulate, it was dubious in significance further than it seemed to indicate some capricious revulsion of thought or feeling such as mobs ashore are liable to, in the present instance possibly implying a sullen revocation on the men's part of their involuntary echoing of Billy's benediction. But ere the murmur had time to wax into clamor it was met by a strategic command, the more telling that it came with abrupt unexpectedness: "Pipe down the starboard watch, Boatswain, and see that they go."

Shrill as the shriek of the sea hawk, the silver whistles of the boatswain and his mates pierced that ominous low sound, dissipating it; and yielding to the mechanism of discipline the throng was thinned by one-half. For the remainder, most of them were set to temporary employments connected with trimming the yards and so forth, business readily to be got up to serve occasion by any officer of the deck.

Now each proceeding that follows a mortal sentence pronounced at sea by a drumhead court is characterized by promptitude not perceptibly merging into hurry, though bordering that. The hammock, the one which had been Billy's bed when alive, having already been ballasted with shot and otherwise prepared to serve for his canvas coffin, the last offices of the sea undertakers, the sailmaker's mates, were now speedily completed. When everything was in readiness a second call for all hands, made necessary by the strategic movement before mentioned, was sounded, now to witness burial.

The details of this closing formality it needs not to give. But when the tilted plank let slide its freight into the sea, a second strange human murmur was heard, blended now with another inarticulate sound proceeding from certain larger seafowl who, their attention having been attracted by the peculiar commotion in the water resulting from the heavy sloped dive of the shotted hammock into the sea, flew screaming to the spot. So near the hull did they come, that the stridor or bony creak of their gaunt double-jointed pinions was audible. As the ship under light airs passed on, leaving the burial spot astern, they still kept circling it low

---

[2] I.e., an easy and painless death (not the common meaning of a death to ease pain).

down with the moving shadow of their outstretched wings and the croaked requiem of their cries.

Upon sailors as superstitious as those of the age preceding ours, men-of-war's men too who had just beheld the prodigy of repose in the form suspended in air, and now foundering in the deeps; to such mariners the action of the seafowl, though dictated by mere animal greed for prey, was big with no prosaic significance. An uncertain movement began among them, in which some encroachment was made. It was tolerated but for a moment. For suddenly the drum beat to quarters, which familiar sound happening at least twice every day, had upon the present occasion a signal peremptoriness in it. True martial discipline long continued superinduces in average man a sort of impulse whose operation at the official word of command much resembles in its promptitude the effect of an instinct.

The drumbeat dissolved the multitude, distributing most of them along the batteries of the two covered gun decks. There, as wonted, the guns' crews stood by their respective cannon erect and silent. In due course the first officer, sword under arm and standing in his place on the quarter-deck, formally received the successive reports of the sworded lieutenants commanding the sections of batteries below; the last of which reports being made, the summed report he delivered with the customary salute to the commander. All this occupied time, which in the present case was the object in beating to quarters at an hour prior to the customary one. That such variance from usage was authorized by an officer like Captain Vere, a martinet as some deemed him, was evidence of the necessity for unusual action implied in what he deemed to be temporarily the mood of his men. "With mankind," he would say, "forms, measured forms, are everything; and that is the import couched in the story of Orpheus with his lyre spellbinding the wild denizens of the wood."[1] And this he once applied to the disruption of forms going on across the Channel and the consequences thereof.

At this unwonted muster at quarters, all proceeded as at the regular hour. The band on the quarter-deck played a sacred air, after which the chaplain went through the customary morning service. That done, the drum beat the retreat; and toned by music and religious rites subserving the discipline and purposes of war, the men in their wonted orderly manner dispersed to the places allotted them when not at the guns.

And now it was full day. The fleece of low-hanging vapor had vanished, licked up by the sun that late had so glorified it. And the circumambient air in the clearness of its serenity was like smooth white marble in the polished block not yet removed from the marble-dealer's yard.

28

The symmetry of form attainable in pure fiction cannot so readily be achieved in a narration essentially having less to do with fable than with fact. Truth uncompromisingly told will always have its ragged edges; hence the conclusion of such a narration is apt to be less finished than an architectural finial.[1]

How it fared with the Handsome Sailor during the year of the Great Mutiny has been faithfully given. But though properly the story ends with his life, something in way of sequel will not be amiss. Three brief chapters will suffice.

In the general rechristening under the Directory of the craft originally forming the navy of the French monarchy, the *St. Louis* line-of-battle ship was named the *Athée* (the *Atheist*). Such a name, like some other substituted ones in the Revolutionary fleet, while proclaiming the infidel audacity of the ruling power, was yet,

---

[1] In Greek mythology, a musician whose magic ability with his lyre affected beasts and even rocks and trees.
[1] Ornament topping a spire, gable, or pillar.

though not so intended to be, the aptest name, if one consider it, ever given to a warship; far more so indeed than the *Devastation*, the *Erebus* (the *Hell*), and similar names bestowed upon fighting ships.

On the return passage to the English fleet from the detached cruise during which occurred the events already recorded, the *Bellipotent* fell in with the *Athée*. An engagement ensued, during which Captain Vere, in the act of putting his ship alongside the enemy with a view of throwing his boarders across her bulwarks, was hit by a musket ball from a porthole of the enemy's main cabin. More than disabled, he dropped to the deck and was carried below to the same cockpit where some of his men already lay. The senior lieutenant took command. Under him the enemy was finally captured, and though much crippled was by rare good fortune successfully taken into Gibraltar, an English port not very distant from the scene of the fight. There, Captain Vere with the rest of the wounded was put ashore. He lingered for some days, but the end came. Unhappily he was cut off too early for the Nile and Trafalgar.[2] The spirit that 'spite its philosophic austerity may yet have indulged in the most secret of all passions, ambition, never attained to the fulness of fame.

Not long before death, while lying under the influence of that magical drug[3] which, soothing the physical frame, mysteriously operates on the subtler element in man, he was heard to murmur words inexplicable to his attendant: "Billy Budd, Billy Budd." That these were not the accents of remorse would seem clear from what the attendant said to the *Bellipotent's* senior officer of marines, who, as the most reluctant to condemn of the members of the drumhead court, too well knew, though here he kept the knowledge to himself, who Billy Budd was.

29

Some few weeks after the execution, among other matters under the head of "News from the Mediterranean," there appeared in a naval chronicle of the time, an authorized weekly publication, an account of the affair. It was doubtless for the most part written in good faith, though the medium, partly rumor, through which the facts must have reached the writer served to deflect and in part falsify them. The account was as follows:

"On the tenth of the last month a deplorable occurrence took place on board H.M.S. *Bellipotent*. John Claggart, the ship's master-at-arms, discovering that some sort of plot was incipient among an inferior section of the ship's company, and that the ringleader was one William Budd; he, Claggart, in the act of arraigning the man before the captain, was vindictively stabbed to the heart by the suddenly drawn sheath knife of Budd.

"The deed and the implement employed sufficiently suggest that though mustered into the service under an English name the assassin was no Englishman, but one of those aliens adopting English cognomens whom the present extraordinary necessities of the service have caused to be admitted into it in considerable numbers.

"The enormity of the crime and the extreme depravity of the criminal appear the greater in view of the character of the victim, a middle-aged man respectable and discreet, belonging to that minor official grade, the petty officers, upon whom, as none know better than the commissioned gentlemen, the efficiency of His Majesty's navy so largely depends. His function was a responsible one, at once onerous and thankless; and his fidelity in it the greater because of his strong patriotic impulse. In this instance as in so many other instances in these days, the

---

[2] In the sea battle of the Nile (1798), Admiral Nelson destroyed Napoleon's fleet; in the battle at Trafalgar (1805), he ended France's ability to fight on the sea and was himself killed.

[3] Possibly opium, used in the past in medical treatment to ease pain.

character of this unfortunate man signally refutes, if refutation were needed, that peevish saying attributed to the late Dr. Johnson, that patriotism is the last refuge of a scoundrel.[1]

"The criminal paid the penalty of his crime. The promptitude of the punishment has proved salutary. Nothing amiss is now apprehended aboard H.M.S. *Bellipotent.*"

The above, appearing in a publication now long ago superannuated and forgotten, is all that hitherto has stood in human record to attest what manner of men respectively were John Claggart and Billy Budd.

30

Everything is for a term venerated in navies. Any tangible object associated with some striking incident of the service is converted into a monument. The spar from which the foretopman was suspended was for some few years kept trace of by the bluejackets. Their knowledges followed it from ship to dockyard and again from dockyard to ship, still pursuing it even when at last reduced to a mere dockyard boom. To them a chip of it was as a piece of the Cross. Ignorant though they were of the secret facts of the tragedy, and not thinking but that the penalty was somehow unavoidably inflicted from the naval point of view, for all that, they instinctively felt that Billy was a sort of man as incapable of mutiny as of wilful murder. They recalled the fresh young image of the Handsome Sailor, that face never deformed by a sneer or subtler vile freak of the heart within. This impression of him was doubtless deepened by the fact that he was gone, and in a measure mysteriously gone. On the gun decks of the *Bellipotent* the general estimate of his nature and its unconscious simplicity eventually found rude utterance from another foretopman, one of his own watch, gifted, as some sailors are, with an artless *poetic* temperament. The tarry hand made some lines which, after circulating among the shipboard crews for a while, finally got rudely printed at Portsmouth as a ballad. The title given to it was the sailor's.

BILLY IN THE DARBIES[1]

> Good of the chaplain to enter Lone Bay
> And down on his marrowbones here and pray
> For the likes just o' me, Billy Budd.—But, look:
> Through the port comes the moonshine astray!
> It tips the guard's cutlass and silvers this nook;
> But 'twill die in the dawning of Billy's last day.
> A jewel-block they'll make of me tomorrow,
> Pendant pearl from the yardarm-end
> Like the eardrop I gave to Bristol Molly—
> O, 'tis me, not the sentence they'll suspend.
> Ay, ay, all is up; and I must up too,
> Early in the morning, aloft from alow.
> On an empty stomach now never it would do.
> They'll give me a nibble—bit o' biscuit ere I go.
> Sure, a messmate will reach me the last parting cup;
> But, turning heads away from the hoist and the belay,
> Heaven knows who will have the running of me up!
> No pipe to those halyards.—But aren't it all sham?
> A blur's in my eyes; it is dreaming that I am.
> A hatchet to my hawser? All adrift to go?

---

[1]Preserved in the *Life of Johnson* (1791), by James Boswell (1740–1795), constant companion, from 1763, of Dr. Samuel Johnson (1709–1784).
[1]Fetters, manacles, or handcuffs.

The drum roll to grog, and Billy never know?
But Donald he has promised to stand by the plank;
So I'll shake a friendly hand ere I sink.
But—no! It is dead then I'll be, come to think.
I remember Taff the Welshman when he sank.
And his cheek it was like the budding pink.
But me they'll lash in hammock, drop me deep.
Fathoms down, fathoms down, how I'll dream fast asleep.
I feel it stealing now. Sentry, are you there?
Just ease these darbies at the wrist,
And roll me over fair!
I am sleepy, and the oozy weeds about me twist.

1886–91   *1924, 1962*

from Collected Poems

from MARDI

Gold-Hunters[1]

We rovers bold,
  To the land of Gold,
Over the bowling billows are gliding:
    Eager to toil,
    For the golden spoil,   5
And every hardship biding.[2]
    See! See!
Before our prows' resistless dashes
The gold-fish fly in golden flashes!
    'Neath a sun of gold,   10
    We rovers bold,
On the golden land are gaining;
    And every night,
    We steer aright,
By golden stars unwaning!   15
All fires burn a golden glare:
No locks so bright as golden hair!
All orange groves have golden gushings:
All mornings dawn with golden flushings!
In a shower of gold, say fables old,   20
A maiden was won by the god of gold![3]
    In golden goblets wine is beaming:
    On golden couches kings are dreaming!

---

[1]From Melville's 1849 allegorical novel, *Mardi*, "Gold-Hunters" is different in its spirited, even rollicking, pace from the more meditative later poetry. The poem was inspired by the California gold rush, which began in 1848 and was at its height in 1849. There was a kind of mania in the quest for gold as 80,000 people rushed by land or by sea to California to seek their fortune.

[2]Abiding, enduring.

[3]Zeus; in Greek mythology, Danaë was imprisoned in a tower because an oracle had told her father he would be killed by his daughter's son. There Zeus visited her in a shower of gold.

The Golden Rule[4] dries many tears!
  The Golden Number[5] rules the spheres! 25
Gold, gold it is, that sways the nations:
Gold! gold! the center of all rotations!
  On golden axles worlds are turning:
  With phosphorescence seas are burning!
All fire-flies flame with golden gleamings: 30
  Gold-hunters' hearts with golden dreamings!
  With golden arrows kings are slain:
  With gold we'll buy a freeman's name!
In toilsome trades, for scanty earnings,
At home we've slaved, with stifled yearnings: 35
No light! no hope! Oh, heavy woe!
When nights fled fast, and days dragged slow.
  But joyful now, with eager eye,
Fast to the Promised Land we fly:
    Where in deep mines, 40
    The treasure shines;
Or down in beds of golden streams,
The gold-flakes glance in golden gleams!
    How we long to sift,
    That yellow drift! 45
Rivers! Rivers! cease your going!
  Sand-bars! rise, and stay the tide!
'Till we've gained the golden flowing;
  And in the golden haven ride!

1849

from BATTLE PIECES AND ASPECTS OF THE WAR[1]

The Portent[2]

(1859)

Hanging from the beam,
  Slowly swaying (such the law),
Gaunt the shadow on your green,
  Shenandoah!
The cut is on the crown 5
  (Lo, John Brown),
And the stabs shall heal no more.

Hidden in the cap
  Is the anguish none can draw;
So your future veils its face, 10

---

[4]Luke 6:31: in paraphrase, do unto others as you would have them do unto you.
[5]So-called from its importance in calculating the date of Easter, it is the number of any year in the Metonic lunar cycle of nineteen years (during which there are 235 lunar revolutions, at the end of which the new moon reappears on the same day as at the beginning).
[1]Melville's first volume of poems was published in 1866 and dedicated "to the memory of the Three Hundred Thousand who in the war for the maintenance of the Union fell devotedly under the flag of their fathers." The poems are topical and arranged chronologically, and thus form a poetic history of the Civil War.
[2]John Brown made his raid to seize the U.S. Arsenal at Harper's Ferry, Virginia (now West Virginia), at the juncture of the Shenandoah and Potomac Rivers, on October 16, 1859. He was captured, convicted of treason, and hanged.

Shenandoah!
But the streaming beard is shown
(Weird John Brown),
The meteor of the war.

1866

Misgivings[1]

(1860)

When ocean-clouds over inland hills
    Sweep storming in late autumn brown,
And horror the sodden valley fills,
    And the spire falls crashing in the town,
I muse upon my country's ills—   5
The tempest bursting from the waste of Time
On the world's fairest hope linked with man's foulest crime.

Nature's dark side is heeded now—
    (Ah! optimist-cheer disheartened flown)—
A child may read the moody brow   10
    Of yon black mountain lone.
With shouts the torrents down the gorges go,
And storms are formed behind the storm we feel:
The hemlock shakes in the rafter, the oak in the driving keel.

1866

Shiloh[1]

A Requiem
(April, 1862)

Skimming lightly, wheeling still,
    The swallows fly low
Over the field in clouded days,
    The forest-field of Shiloh—
Over the field where April rain   5
Solaced the parched ones stretched in pain
Through the pause of night
That followed the Sunday fight
    Around the church of Shiloh—
The church so lone, the log-built one,   10
That echoed to many a parting groan
    And natural prayer
    Of dying foemen mingled there—

---

[1]First shots of the Civil War were fired on April 12, 1861, by the Confederates against Fort Sumter in South Carolina. Melville's poem is written out of the ominous, brooding quiet before the storm.

[1]Shiloh in western Tennessee was the scene of one of the bloodiest Civil War battles in April 1862. There were 13,047 Union dead, and 10,694 Confederate dead.

Foemen at morn, but friends at eve—
  Fame or country least their care: 15
(What like a bullet can undeceive!)
  But now they lie low,
  While over them the swallows skim,
    And all is hushed at Shiloh.

                                      1866

The House-Top[1]

A Night Piece
(July, 1863)

No sleep. The sultriness pervades the air
And binds the brain—a dense oppression, such
As tawny tigers feel in matted shades,
Vexing their blood and making apt for ravage.
Beneath the stars the roofy desert spreads   5
Vacant as Libya. All is hushed near by.
Yet fitfully from far breaks a mixed surf
Of muffled sound, the Atheist roar of riot.
Yonder, where parching Sirius[2] set in drought,
Balefully glares red Arson—there—and there.   10
The Town is taken by its rats—ship-rats
And rats of the wharves. All civil charms
And priestly spells which late held hearts in awe—
Fear-bound, subjected to a better sway
Than sway of self; these like a dream dissolve,   15
And man rebounds whole æons back in nature.
Hail to the low dull rumble, dull and dead,
And ponderous drag that jars the wall.
Wise Draco[3] comes, deep in the midnight roll
Of black artillery; he comes, though late;   20
In code corroborating Calvin's[4] creed
And cynic tyrannies of honest kings;
He comes, nor parlies; and the Town, redeemed,
Gives thanks devout; nor, being thankful, heeds
The grimy slur on the Republic's faith implied,   25
Which holds that Man is naturally good,
And—more—is Nature's Roman, never to be scourged.[5]

                                        1866

---

[1]This poem was inspired by the New York draft riots of July 11–13, 1863, against the Conscription Act, which permitted men to escape the draft by a payment of $300, thus putting the main burden of the war on the poor. Order was restored after three days by suspension of the act. Melville added this note: " 'I dare not write the horrible and inconceivable atrocities committed'; says Froissart, in alluding to the remarkable sedition in France during his time. The like may be hinted of some proceedings of the draft-rioters."
[2]Brightest star in heaven, found in the constellation Canis Major (also called the Dog Star).

[3]Athenian lawgiver (seventh century B.C.), whose code was harsh, levelling the death penalty for minor crimes.
[4]John Calvin (1509–1564) believed (as did the Calvinistic American Puritans) in the innate depravity of man.
[5]Cf. Acts 22:25: "And as they bound him with thongs, Paul said unto the centurion that stood by, Is it lawful for you to scourge a man that is a Roman, and uncondemned?" Scourging (such as flogging) was considered a degrading punishment.

The Martyr[1]

INDICATIVE OF THE PASSION OF THE PEOPLE ON THE 15TH DAY OF APRIL, 1865

Good Friday was the day
 Of the prodigy and crime,
When they killed him in his pity,
 When they killed him in his prime
Of clemency and calm—   5
     When with yearning he was filled
     To redeem the evil-willed,
And, though conqueror, be kind;
     But they killed him in his kindness,
     In their madness and their blindness,   10
And they killed him from behind.

     There is sobbing of the strong,
        And a pall upon the land;
     But the people in their weeping
           Bare the iron hand;   15
        Beware the People weeping
           When they bare the iron hand.

He lieth in his blood—
     The father in his face;
They have killed him, the Forgiver—   20
     The Avenger takes his place,[2]
The Avenger wisely stern,
        Who in righteousness shall do
        What the heavens call him to,
And the parricides remand;[3]   25
     For they killed him in his kindness,
     In their madness and their blindness,
And his blood is on their hand.

     There is sobbing of the strong,
        And a pall upon the land;   30
     But the People in their weeping
           Bare the iron hand:
        Beware the People weeping
           When they bare the iron hand.

                                                            1866

---

[1]President Abraham Lincoln was shot by John Wilkes Booth in the Ford Theater on April 14, but died the next day, April 15.
[2]Vice President Andrew Johnson became president when Lincoln died; although he was from the South, he was not from the dominant class there and "had been hardly treated by the Secessionists" (as Melville remarked in a note). It was therefore thought that he would become the Avenger, in contrast with the Forgiver which Lincoln appeared to be.
[3]The Southerners, as the collective assassins of Lincoln (parricides are "parent killers"), will be "remanded," or sent to prison.

from JOHN MARR AND OTHER SAILORS

The Aeolian Harp[1]

AT THE SURF INN

List the harp in window wailing
   Stirred by fitful gales from sea:
Shrieking up in mad crescendo—
   Dying down in plaintive key!

Listen: less a strain ideal   5
   Than Ariel's[2] rendering of the Real.
What that Real is, let hint
   A picture stamped in memory's mint.

Braced well up, with beams aslant,
Betwixt the continents sails the *Phocion*,   10
To Baltimore bound from Alicant.[3]
Blue breezy skies white fleeces fleck
Over the chill blue white-capped ocean:
From yard-arm comes—"Wreck ho, a wreck!"

Dismasted and adrift,   15
Long time a thing forsaken;
Overwashed by every wave
Like the slumbering kraken;[4]
Heedless if the billow roar,
Oblivious of the lull,   20
Leagues and leagues from shoal or shore,
It swims—a levelled hull:
Bulwarks gone—a shaven wreck,
Nameless, and a grass-green deck.
A lumberman: perchance, in hold   25
Prostrate pines with hemlocks rolled.

It has drifted, waterlogged,
Till by trailing weeds beclogged:
   Drifted, drifted, day by day,
   Pilotless on pathless way.
It has drifted till each plank   30
Is oozy as the oyster-bank:
   Drifted, drifted, night by night,
   Craft that never shows a light;
Nor ever, to prevent worse knell,   35
Tolls in fog the warning bell.

---

[1] A box with a hole in it over which strings are stretched so that they make musical sounds when the wind blows over them.
[2] The airy spirit who served as Prospero's servant in Shakespeare's *The Tempest.*
[3] Spanish seaport.
[4] Fabulous sea monster of the northern seas.

From collision never shrinking,
Drive what may through darksome smother;
Saturate, but never sinking,
Fatal only to the *other!*   40
    Deadlier than the sunken reef
Since still the snare it shifteth,
    Torpid in dumb ambuscade
Waylayingly it drifteth.

    O, the sailors—O, the sails!   45
    O, the lost crews never heard of!
    Well the harp of Ariel wails
    Thoughts that tongue can tell no word of!

1888

The Tuft of Kelp[1]

All dripping in tangles green,
    Cast up by a lonely sea
If purer for that, O Weed,
    Bitterer, too, are ye?

1888

The Maldive Shark[1]

About the Shark, phlegmatical one,
Pale sot[2] of the Maldive sea,
The sleek little pilot-fish, azure and slim,
How alert in attendance be.
From his saw-pit of mouth, from his charnel of maw   5
They have nothing of harm to dread,
But liquidly glide on his ghastly flank
Or before his Gorgonian[3] head;
Or lurk in the port of serrated teeth
In white triple tiers of glittering gates,   10
And there find a haven when peril's abroad,
An asylum in jaws of the Fates!
They are friends; and friendly they guide him to prey,
Yet never partake of the treat—
Eyes and brains to the dotard lethargic and dull,   15
Pale ravener of horrible meat.

1888

---

[1]Seaweed.

[1]In *Mardi*, Melville wrote, "There is a fish in the sea that ever more, like a surly lord, only goes abroad attended by his suite. It is the shovel-nosed shark." The "suite" is made up of the attendant pilot-fish. The Maldive Sea is off the Maldive Islands, west of India.

[2]Scourge, or whip (obsolete).

[3]Ugly, repulsive (in Greek mythology, the Gorgons were three ugly sisters with snakes for hair).

The Berg

(A DREAM)

I saw a ship of martial build
(Her standards[1] set, her brave apparel on)
Directed as by madness mere
Against a stolid iceberg steer,
Nor budge it, though the infatuate[2] ship went down.   5
The impact made huge ice-cubes fall
Sullen, in tons that crashed the deck;
But that one avalanche was all—
No other movement save the foundering wreck.

Along the spurs of ridges pale,   10
Not any slenderest shaft and frail,
A prism over glass-green gorges lone,
Toppled; or lace of traceries fine,
Nor pendant drops in grot[3] or mine
Were jarred, when the stunned ship went down.   15
Nor sole the gulls in cloud that wheeled
Circling one snow-flanked peak afar,
But nearer fowl the floes that skimmed
And crystal beaches, felt no jar.
No thrill transmitted stirred the lock   20
Of jack-straw needle-ice at base;
Towers undermined by waves—the block
Atilt impending—kept their place.
Seals, dozing sleek on sliddery ledges
Slipt never, when by loftier edges   25
Through very inertia overthrown,
The impetuous ship in bafflement went down.

Hard Berg (methought), so cold, so vast,
With mortal damps self-overcast;
Exhaling still thy dankish breath—   30
Adrift dissolving, bound for death;
Though lumpish thou, a lumbering one—
A lumbering lubbard[4] loitering slow,
Impingers rue thee and go down,
Sounding thy precipice below,   35
Nor stir the slimy slug that sprawls
Along thy dead indifference of walls.

1888

---

[1]Pennants or flags.
[2]Foolish.
[3]Grotto.
[4]Variant of lubber, a stupid, clumsy person.

from TIMOLEON

After the Pleasure Party[1]

LINES TRACED UNDER AN IMAGE OF AMOR THREATENING[2]

Fear me, virgin whosoever
Taking pride from love exempt,
Fear me, slighted. Never, never
Brave me, nor my fury tempt:
Downy wings, but wroth they beat   5
Tempest even in reason's seat.

Behind the house the upland falls
With many an odorous tree—
White marbles gleaming through green halls,
Terrace by terrace, down and down,   10
And meets the starlit Mediterranean Sea.

 'Tis Paradise. In such an hour
Some pangs that rend might take release.
Nor less perturbed who keeps this bower
Of balm, nor finds balsamic peace?   15
From whom the passionate words in vent
After long revery's discontent?

 Tired of the homeless deep,
Look how their flight yon hurrying billows urge,
Hitherward but to reap   20
Passive repulse from the iron-bound verge!
Insensate, can they never know
'Tis mad to wreck the impulsion so?

 An art of memory is, they tell:
But to forget! forget the glade   25
Wherein Fate sprung Love's ambuscade,
To flout pale years of cloistral life
And flush me in this sensuous strife.
'Tis Vesta struck with Sappho's smart.[3]
No fable her delirious leap: 30
With more of cause in desperate heart,
Myself could take it—but to sleep!

 Now first I feel, what all may ween,
That soon or late, if faded e'en,
One's sex asserts itself. Desire,   35
The dear desire through love to sway,

---

[1]A dramatic monologue, beginning after the first six lines, spoken by an unmarried woman who is an astronomer dedicated to the life of the intellect and who discovers to her sorrow that "sex asserts itself." The poet's voice as narrator enters at line 111.
[2]Amor is cupid, his weapon the bow and arrow. He is in a painting or sketch, underneath which the first six lines rep-

resent his warning to virgins who think they are "from love exempt."
[3]Vesta was the Roman goddess of the hearth, attended in mythology by the Vestal Virgins who had to be chaste. Vesta is seized with the same desire that struck the heart of Sappho, a seventh-century B.C. Greek lyric poet whose poems speak of a longing for love.

Is like the Geysers that aspire—
Through cold obstruction win their fervid way.
But baffled here—to take disdain,
To feel rule's instinct, yet not reign;   40
To dote, to come to this drear shame—
Hence the winged blaze that sweeps my soul
Like prairie fires that spurn control,
Where withering weeds incense the flame.

   And kept I long heaven's watch for this,   45
Contemning love, for this, even this?
O terrace chill in Northern air,
O reaching ranging tube I placed
Against yon skies, and fable chased
Till, fool, I hailed for sister there   50
Starred Cassiopea in Golden Chair.[4]
In dream I throned me, nor I saw
In cell the idiot crowned with straw.

   And yet, ah yet scarce ill I reigned,
Through self-illusion self- sustained,   55
When now—enlightened, undeceived—
What gain I barrenly bereaved!
Than this can be yet lower decline—
Envy and spleen, can these be mine?

   The pleasant girl demure that trod   60
Beside our wheels that climbed the way,
And bore along a blossoming rod
That looked the sceptre of May-day—
On her—to fire this petty hell,
His softened glance how moistly fell!   65
The cheat! on briars her buds were strung;
And wiles peeped forth from mien how meek.
The innocent bare-foot! young, so young!
To girls, strong man's a novice weak.
To tell such beads! And more remain,   70
Sad rosary of belittling pain.

   When after lunch and sallies gay,
Like the Decameron folk[5] we lay
In sylvan groups; and I—let be!
O, dreams he, can he dream that one   75
Because not roseate feels no sun?
The plain lone bramble thrills with Spring
As much as vines that grapes shall bring.

   Me now fair studies charm no more.
Shall great thoughts writ, or high themes sung   80
Damask wan cheeks—unlock his arm
About some radiant ninny flung?
How glad with all my starry lore,

---

[4]Cassiopea was an Ethiopian queen overly proud of her beauty who for punishment was made into the constellation resembling her chair; at certain times her chair turns her upside down.

[5]Those who gathered together to escape the plague and whiled away the time, telling amusing stories (often risqué), the subject of the *Decameron* (1353) by Giovanni Boccaccio (1313–1375), Italian writer.

I'd buy the veriest wanton's rose
Would but my bee therein repose.   85

Could I remake me! or set free
This sexless bound in sex, then plunge
Deeper than Sappho, in a lunge
Piercing Pan's[6] paramount mystery!
For, Nature, in no shallow surge   90
Against thee either sex may urge,
Why hast thou made us but in halves—
Co-relatives?[7] This makes us slaves.
If these co-relatives never meet
Self-hood itself seems incomplete.   95
And such the dicing of blind fate
Few matching halves here meet and mate.
What Cosmic jest or Anarch blunder
The human integral clove asunder
And shied the fractions through life's gate?   100

Ye stars that long your votary knew
Rapt in her vigil, see me here!
Whither is gone the spell ye threw
When rose before me Cassiopea?
Usurped on by love's stronger reign—   105
But lo, your very selves do wane:
Light breaks—truth breaks! Silvered no more,
But chilled by dawn that brings the gale
Shivers yon bramble above the vale,
And disillusion opens all the shore.   110

One knows not if Urania[8] yet
The pleasure-party may forget;
Or whether she lived down the strain
Of turbulent heart and rebel brain;
For Amor so resents a slight,   115
And her's had been such haught disdain,
He long may wreak his boyish spite,
And boy-like, little reck the pain.

One knows not, no. But late in Rome
(For queens discrowned a congruous home)   120
Entering Albani's porch[9] she stood
Fixed by an antique pagan stone
Colossal carved. No anchorite seer,
Not Thomas a Kempis,[10] monk austere,
Religious more are in their tone;   125
Yet far, how far from Christian heart
That form august of heathen Art.
Swayed by its influence, long she stood,
Till surged emotion seething down,
She rallied and this mood she won: 130

---

[6]Greek god of fields and forests, with a torso of a human but legs of a goat (often with tail and horns).
[7]Allusion to the legend related in Plato's *Symposium* that in the beginning man was a four-legged creature composed of both sexes, later split in two, with the two halves forever trying to reunite.

[8]Greek muse of astronomy.
[9]The Villa Albani, close to Rome, contains a great collection of classical sculpture.
[10]German monk (1380?–1471), the reputed author of *Imitation of Christ*.

Languid in frame for me,
To-day by Mary's convent shrine,
Touched by her picture's moving plea
In that poor nerveless hour of mine,
I mused—A wanderer still must grieve.   135
Half I resolved to kneel and believe,
Believe and submit, the veil take on.
But thee, armed Virgin! less benign,
Thee now I invoke, thou mightier one.
Helmeted woman—if such term   140
Befit thee, far from strife
Of that which makes the sexual feud
And clogs the aspirant life—
O self-reliant, strong and free,
Thou in whom power and peace unite,   145
Transcender! raise me up to thee,
Raise me and arm me!

                              Fond appeal.
For never passion peace shall bring,
Nor Art inanimate for long   150
Inspire. Nothing may help or heal
While Amor incensed remembers wrong.
Vindictive, not himself he'll spare;
For scope to give his vengeance play
Himself he'll blaspheme and betray.   155

    Then for Urania, virgins everywhere,
O pray! Example take too, and have care.

                                1891

The Ravaged Villa

In shards the sylvan vases lie,
    Their links of dance undone,
And brambles wither by thy brim,
    Choked fountain of the sun!
The spider in the laurel spins,   5
    The weed exiles the flower:
And, flung to kiln, Apollo's[1] bust
    Makes lime for Mammon's[2] tower.

                                1891

---

[1] In classical mythology, god of music, poetry, and the sun.
[2] The god of this world; Matthew 6:24: "Ye cannot serve God and mammon."

In a Garret

Gems and jewels let them heap—
    Wax sumptuous as the Sophi:[1]
For me, to grapple from Art's deep
    One dripping trophy!

           1891

Monody[1]

To have known him, to have loved him
    After loneness long;
And then to be estranged in life,
    And neither in the wrong;
And now for death to set his seal—   5
    Ease me, a little ease, my song!

By wintry hills his hermit-mound
    The sheeted snow-drifts drape,
And houseless there the snow-bird flits
    Beneath the fir-trees' crape: 10
Glazed now with ice the cloistral vine
    That hid the shyest grape.

           1891

Lone Founts

Though fast youth's glorious fable flies,
View not the world with worldling's[1] eyes;
Nor turn with weather of the time.
Foreclose the coming of surprise:
Stand where Posterity shall stand;   5
Stand where the Ancients stood before,
And, dipping in lone founts thy hand,
Drink of the never-varying lore:
Wise once, and wise thence evermore.

           1891

Art

In placid hours well-pleased we dream
Of many a brave unbodied scheme.

---

[1]Title previously given to the Persian rulers or shahs.

[1]"Monody": a poem expressing grief for another's death. This poem is about Nathaniel Hawthorne, who died in 1864. In his long poem *Clarel*. Melville uses Hawthorne as the basis of his character Vine, incorporating in him many of Hawthorne's shy, "cloistral" traits.

[1]One devoted to the affairs of this world.

But form to lend, pulsed life create,
What unlike things must meet and mate:
A flame to melt—a wind to freeze;   5
Sad patience—joyous energies;
Humility—yet pride and scorn;
Instinct and study; love and hate;
Audacity—reverence. These must mate,
And fuse with Jacob's[1] mystic heart,   10
To wrestle with the angel—Art.

                                        1891

Buddha

"FOR WHAT IS YOUR LIFE? IT IS EVEN A VAPOR THAT APPEARETH FOR A
LITTLE TIME AND THEN VANISHETH AWAY."[1]

Swooning swim to less and less,
    Aspirant to nothingness!
Sobs of the worlds, and dole of kinds
    That dumb endurers be—
Nirvana![2] absorb us in your skies,   5
    Annul us into thee.

                                        1891

from MISCELLANEOUS POEMS

The New
Ancient of Days[1]

THE MAN OF THE CAVE OF ENGIHOUL[2]

The man of bone confirms his throne
    In cave where fossils be;
Outdating every mummy known,
Not older Cuvier's[3] mastodon,
    Nor older much the sea: 5

---

[1]Cf. Genesis 32:24–30: after wrestling with an angel, Jacob received a divine blessing.

[1]Cf. James 4:14.

[2]In Buddhism, the blessed state in which the soul is absorbed into the supreme spirit.

[1]In "The New Ancient of Days," Melville shows an ingenious playfulness in the use of language that links him with the poets of nonsense verse Lewis Carroll (1832–1898) and Edward Lear (1812–1888) and that also anticipates the verbal fireworks of a James Joyce (1882–1941). Melville noted on the manuscript; "See Lyell's [*The Geological Evidence of the*] *Antiquities of Man* and Darwin's *Descent of the Species* [*Origin of Species*, 1859; *The Descent of Man*, 1871]." William Bysshe Stein, in an article on the poem, writes that it "monkeys around with the skeletons in the closets of mythology, religion, and science. While transparently a *reductio ad absurdum* of the contradictory legendary, biblical, and evolutionary pictures of human origins, the poem generates its fullest meaning in the freakishness of its language. . . ." (See William Bysshe Stein, "The New Ancient of Days: The Poetics of Logocracy," *Essays in Arts and Sciences*, University of New Haven, July 1976).

[2]Melville invents the new discovery of an ancient man.

[3]Baron Cuvier (1769–1832), French naturalist and founder of comparative anatomy and paleontology; he believed in "catastrophism," a doctrine that taught that periodically in the earth's history all living creatures were destroyed by cataclysms and replaced by different life forms.

Old as the Glacial Period,[4] he;
And claims he calls to mind the day
When Thule's[5] king, by reindeer drawn,
His sleigh-bells jingling in icy morn,
Slid clean from the Pole to the Wetterhorn[6]   10
Over frozen waters in May!
   Oh, the man of the cave of Engihoul,
   With Eld[7] doth he dote and drule?

A wizard one, his lore is none
   Ye spell with A. B. C.;   15
But *do-do* tracks, all up and down
That slate he poreth much upon,
   His algebra may be:—
Yea, there he cyphers and sums it free;
To ages ere Indus[8] met ocean's swell   20
Addeth æons ere Satan or Saturn[9] fell.
His totals of time make an awful schism,
And old Chronos[10] he pitches adown the abysm
Like a pebble down Carisbrook well.[11]
   Yea, the man of the cave of Engihoul   25
   From Moses knocks under the stool.

In *bas-relief*[12] he late has shown
   A horrible show, agree—
Megalosaurus, iguanodon,
Palæotherium Glypthæcon,[13]   30
   A Barnum-show[14] raree;
   The vomit of slimy and sludgey sea:
Purposeless creatures, odd inchoate things
Which splashed thro' morasses on fleshly wings;
The cubs of Chaos, with eyes askance,   35
Preposterous griffins[15] that squint at Chance
And Anarch's cracked decree!
   Oh the showman who dens in Engihoul,
   Would he fright us, or quit us, or fool?

But, needs to own, he takes a tone,   40
   Satiric on nobs,[16] pardee!
"Though in ages whose term is yet to run,
Old Adam a seraph may have for son,
   His gran'ther's a crab, d'y'see!
And why cut your kinsman the ape?" adds he: 45
"Your trick of scratching is borrowed from him,
Grimace and cunning, with many a whim,

---

[4]Ancient periods when a large part of the earth was covered with glaciers.
[5]The northernmost part of the world.
[6]Mountain in the Alps in Switzerland.
[7]Antiquity.
[8]River in northwestern India.
[9]Satan (or Lucifer) was the chief of the fallen angels cast out of heaven by Michael; Saturn was an Italian deity (later identified with Cronus) and a legendary king of Rome during a golden age, celebrated by the festival Saturnalia.
[10]Cronus was a Titan who overthrew his father Uranus to become ruler of the universe, and in turn was overthrown by his son Zeus.

[11]A village on the Isle of Wight, England, where are found Roman ruins and the remains of a castle with a keep.
[12]Sculpture in which figures are only slightly raised.
[13]Megalosaurus: huge, flesh-eating dinosaurs (extinct); iguanodon: large, two-footed lizards (extinct); Palaeotherium: a perissodactyl mammal, with tapir-like or hog-like form (extinct); Glypthaecon: "Glyptic," pertaining to carving or engraving (the look and sound of the syllables are becoming more important than the meaning).
[14]A famous travelling circus of the nineteenth century.
[15]Mythical animals with body and hind legs of a lion and the head and wings of an eagle.
[16]Persons of wealth.

Your fidgets and hypoes, and each megrim[17]—
All's traced in the family tree!"
    Ha, the wag of the cave of Engihoul:
    Buss me, gorilla and ghoul!   50

Obstreperous grown he'd fain dethrone
Joe Smith, and e'en Jones Three;[18]
Against even Jos and great Mahone
He flings his fossiliffer's stone[19]   55
    And rattles his shanks for glee.
    I'll settle these parvenu fellows, he-he!
Diluvian Jove of Ducalion's day[20]—
A parting take to the Phocene[21] clay!
He swears no Ens[22] that takes a name   60
Commensurate is with the vasty claim
Of the protoplastic Fegee.[23]
    O, the spook of the cave of Engihoul
    He flogs us and sends us to school.

Hyena of bone![24] Ah, beat him down,   65
    Great Pope, with Peter's key,[25]
Ere the Grand Pan-Jam[26] be overthrown
With Joe and Jos and great Mahone,
    And the firmament mix with the sea;
And then, my masters, where should we be?   70
But the ogre of bone he snickers alone,
    He grins for his godless glee:
"I have flung my stone, my fossil stone,
And your gods, how they scamper," saith he.
    Imp! imp of the cave of Engihoul,   75
    Shall he grin like the Gorgon[27] and rule?

                                                          1924

Pontoosuce[1]

Crowning a bluff where gleams the lake below,
Some pillared pines in well-spaced order stand
And like an open temple show.
And here in best of seasons bland,

---

[17]Severe headache.
[18]Eagerly dethrone Joseph Smith, founder of Mormonism, and "Jones Three" (Jones III, royalty? or an ordinary name plus a mystic number).
[19]He flings the "philosopher's stone" at " 'jos[s],' pidgin English for the Portuguese *deos* and a Chinese god, along with 'Mahoun,' the deified Mohammed of the Middle Ages" (W. B. Stein).
[20]Jove (Roman name for Zeus) is called "diluvian" because he decided to destroy the world by a flood; Deucalion, warned by his father Prometheus, built a boat which saved him and his wife Pyrrha, and after the flood they repeopled the earth by throwing stones (Mother Earth's bones) over their shoulders, from which sprang a new race of people.
[21]Perhaps "phocine," relating to seals; or "phocenic," relat-

ing to oil in porpoises; whatever its nature, ancient clay is the source of archeological speculation.
[22]Abstract being.
[23]Protoplastic, having the characteristics of a thing or being the first of its kind; Feegee, variant of Fiji, a native of the Fiji Islands, in the South Pacific.
[24]I.e., the man of the cave of Engihoul, who is just a bone, after all.
[25]Roman Catholic Pope; Saint Peter, to whom Jesus gave the keys to the kingdom of heaven.
[26]Variant of "panjandrum," pompous official.
[27]In Greek mythology, any of three ugly sisters with snakes for hair.
[1]A lake in western Massachusetts, north of Pittsfield and Melville's home at Arrowhead. Melville did not adopt the real Indian name of the lake, "Schoon-keek-mon-keek."

Autumnal noon-tide, I look out   5
From dusk arcades on sunshine all about.

Beyond the Lake, in upland cheer
Fields, pastoral fields and barns appear,
They skirt the hills where lonely roads
Revealed in links thro' tiers of woods   10
Wind up to indistinct abodes
And faery-peopled neighborhoods;
While further fainter mountains keep
Hazed in romance impenetrably deep.

Look, corn in stacks, on many a farm,   15
And orchards ripe in languorous charm,
As dreamy Nature, feeling sure
Of all her genial labor done,
And the last mellow fruitage won,
Would idle out her term mature;   20
Reposing like a thing reclined
In kinship with man's meditative mind.

For me, within the brown arcade—
Rich life, methought; sweet here in shade
And pleasant abroad in air!—But, nay,   25
A counter thought intrusive played,
A thought as old as thought itself,
And who shall lay it on the shelf!—
I felt the beauty bless the day
In opulence of autumn's dower;   30
But evanescence will not stay!
A year ago was such an hour,
As this, which but foreruns the blast
Shall sweep these live leaves to the dead leaves past.

All dies!—   35

            I stood in revery long.
Then, to forget death's ancient wrong,
I turned me in the deep arcade,
And there by chance in lateral glade
I saw low tawny mounds in lines   40
Relics of trunks of stately pines
Ranked erst in colonnades where, lo!
Erect succeeding pillars show!

            All dies! and not alone
The aspiring trees and men and grass;   45
The poet's forms of beauty pass,
And noblest deeds they are undone
Even truth itself decays, and lo,
From truth's sad ashes fraud and falsehood grow.

All dies!   50

The workman dies, and after him, the work;
Like to these pines whose graves I trace,
Statue and statuary fall upon their face:
In very amaranths[2] the worm doth lurk,

---

[2]Imaginary flowers that never fade or die (poetic).

Even stars, Chaldæans say,[3] have left their place.   55
Andes and Apalachee tell
Of havoc ere our Adam fell,
And present Nature as a moss doth show
On the ruins of the Nature of the æons of long ago.

But look—and hark!   60

       Adown the glade,
Where light and shadow sport at will,
Who cometh vocal, and arrayed
As in the first pale tints of morn—
So pure, rose-clear, and fresh and chill!   65
Some ground-pine sprigs her brow adorn,
The earthy rootlets tangled clinging.
Over tufts of moss which dead things made,
Under vital twigs which danced or swayed,
Along she floats, and lightly singing: 70

"Dies, all dies!
The grass it dies, but in vernal rain
Up it springs and it lives again;
Over and over, again and again
It lives, it dies and it lives again.   75
Who sighs that all dies?
Summer and winter, and pleasure and pain
And everything everywhere in God's reign,
They end, and anon they begin again:
Wane and wax, wax and wane: 80
Over and over and over amain
End, ever end, and begin again—
End, ever end, and forever and ever begin again!"

She ceased, and nearer slid, and hung
In dewy guise; then softlier sung: 85
"Since light and shade are equal set
And all revolves, nor more ye know;
Ah, why should tears the pale cheek fret
For aught that waneth here below.
Let go, let go!"   90

With that, her warm lips thrilled me through,
She kissed me, while her chaplet[4] cold
Its rootlets brushed against my brow,
With all their humid clinging mould.
She vanished, leaving fragrant breath   95
And warmth and chill of wedded life and death.

1924

---

[3]Ancient people of antique region in southwestern Asia,
among whom astrology flourished.
[4]Garland around the head.

Hawthorne and His Mosses[1]

A papered chamber in a fine old farm-house—a mile from any other dwelling, and dipped to the eaves in foliage—surrounded by mountains, old woods, and Indian ponds—this, surely, is the place to write of Hawthorne. Some charm is in this northern air, for love and duty seem both impelling to the task. A man of a deep and noble nature has seized me in this seclusion. His wild, witch voice rings through me; or, in softer cadences, I seem to hear it in the songs of the hillside birds that sing in the larch trees at my window.

Would that all excellent books were foundlings, without father or mother, that so it might be, we could glorify them, without including their ostensible authors! Nor would any true men take exception to this—least of all, he who writes: "When the Artist rises high enough to achieve the Beautiful, the symbol by which he makes it perceptible to mortal senses becomes of little value in his eyes, while his spirit possesses itself in the enjoyment of the reality."[2]

But more than this, I know not what would be the right name to put on the title page of an excellent book; but this I feel, that the names of all fine authors are fictitious ones, far more so than that of Junius[3]—simply standing, as they do, for the mystical, ever-eluding Spirit of all Beauty, which ubiquitously possesses men of genius. Purely imaginative as this fancy may appear, it nevertheless seems to receive some warranty from the fact that on a personal interview no great author has ever come up to the idea of his reader. But that dust of which our bodies are composed, how can it fitly express the nobler intelligence among us? With reverence be it spoken, that not even in the case of one deemed more than man, not even in our Savior, did his visible frame betoken anything of the augustness of the nature within. Else, how could those Jewish eye-witnesses fail to see heaven in his glance?

It is curious, how a man may travel along a country road, and yet miss the grandest or sweetest of prospects, by reason of an intervening hedge so like all other hedges as in no way to hint of the wide landscape beyond. So has it been with me concerning the enchanting landscape in the soul of this Hawthorne, this most excellent Man of Mosses. His *Old Manse* has been written now four years, but I never read it till a day or two since. I had seen it in the bookstores—heard of it often—even had it recommended to me by a tasteful friend,[4] as a rare, quiet book, perhaps too deserving of popularity to be popular. But there are so many books called "excellent," and so much unpopular merit, that amid the thick stir of other things, the hint of my tasteful friend was disregarded; and for four years the Mosses on the Old Manse never refreshed me with their perennial green. It may be, however, that all this while, the book, like wine, was only improving in flavor and body. At any rate, it so chanced that this long procrastination eventuated in a happy result. At breakfast the other day, a mountain girl, a cousin of mine, who for the last two weeks has every morning helped me to strawberries and raspberries—which, like the roses and pearls in the fairy-tale, seemed to fall into the saucer from those strawberry-beds, her cheeks—this delightful creature, this charming Cherry, says to me—"I see you spent your mornings in the hay-mow; and yesterday I found there Dwight's *Travels in New England*.[5] Now I have

---

[1]Published in *The Literary World*, August 17 and 24, 1850, this essay appeared as "By a Virginian spending July in Vermont." Melville had met Hawthorne on August 5, in a group of authors that went on a walk in the Berkshires to climb Monument Mountain.
[2]Closing line of "The Artist of the Beautiful."
[3]Pseudonym for author of *The Letters of Junius* (1769–72), which criticized leading British political figures.

[4]Perhaps Evert A. Duyckinck (1816–1878), editor of *The Literary World* and a friend of both Melville and Hawthorne.
[5]A four-volume work (1821–22) by Timothy Dwight (1752–1817), president of Yale and a dedicated Calvinist and Federalist.

something far better than that—something more congenial to our summer on these hills. Take these raspberries, and then I will give you some moss."—"Moss!" said I.—"Yes, and you must take it to the barn with you, and good-by to 'Dwight.' "

With that she left me, and soon returned with a volume, verdantly bound, and garnished with a curious frontispiece in green—nothing less than a fragment of real moss cunningly pressed to a flyleaf.—"Why this," said I, spilling my raspberries, "this is the *Mosses from an Old Manse*." "Yes," said cousin Cherry, "yes, it is that flowering Hawthorne."—"Hawthorne and Mosses," said I, "no more: it is morning: it is July in the country: and I am off for the barn."

Stretched on that new-mown clover, the hillside breeze blowing over me through the wide barn door, and soothed by the hum of the bees in the meadows around, how magically stole over me this Mossy Man! And how amply, how bountifully, did he redeem that delicious promise to his guests in the Old Manse, of whom it is written: "Others could give them pleasure and amusement, or instruction—these could be picked up anywhere—but it was for me to give them rest. Rest, in a life of trouble! What better could be done for those weary and world-worn spirits? . . . what better could be done for anybody, who came within our magic circle, than to throw the spell of a magic spirit over him?"[6]— So all that day, half-buried in the new clover, I watched this Hawthorne's "Assyrian dawn and Paphian sunset and moonrise, from the summit of our eastern hill."[7]

The soft ravishments of the man spun me round about in a web of dreams, and when the book was closed, when the spell was over, this wizard "dismissed me, with but misty reminiscences, as if I had been dreaming of him."

What a wild moonlight of contemplative humor bathes that Old Manse!—the rich and rare distillment of a spicy and slowly oozing heart. No rollicking rudeness, no gross fun fed on fat dinners, and bred in the lees of wine—but a humor so spiritually gentle, so high, so deep, and yet so richly relishable, that it were hardly inappropriate in an angel. It is the very religion of mirth; for nothing so human but it may be advanced to that. The orchard of the Old Manse seems the visible type of the fine mind that has described it. Those twisted and contorted old trees that "stretch out their crooked branches, and take such hold of the imagination, that we remember them as humorists and odd fellows." And then, as surrounded by these grotesque forms, and hushed in the noonday repose of this Hawthorne's spell, how aptly might the still fall of his ruddy thoughts into your soul be symbolized by "the thump of a great apple, in the stillest afternoon, falling without a breath of wind, from the mere necessity of perfect ripeness!" For no less ripe than ruddy are the apples of the thoughts and fancies in this sweet Man of Mosses.

"Buds and Bird-Voices"[8]—What a delicious thing is that!—"Will the world ever be so decayed, that spring may not renew its greenness?"—And the "Fire-Worship." Was ever the hearth so glorified into an altar before? The mere title of that piece is better than any common work in fifty folio volumes. How exquisite is this:

> Nor did it lessen the charm of his soft, familiar courtesy and helpfulness, that the mighty spirit, were opportunity offered him, would run riot through the peaceful house, wrap its inmates in his terrible embrace, and leave nothing of them save their whitened bones. This possibility of mad de-

---

struction only made his domestic kindness the more beautiful and touching. It was so sweet of him, being endowed with such power, to dwell, day after day, and one long, lonesome night after another, on the dusky hearth, only now and then betraying his wild nature, by thrusting his red tongue out of the chimney-top! True, he had done much mischief in the world, and was pretty certain to do more; but his warm heart atoned for all. He was kindly to the race of man. . . .

But he has still other apples, not quite so ruddy, though full as ripe—apples that have been left to wither on the tree, after the pleasant autumn gathering is past. The sketch of "The Old Apple-Dealer" is conceived in the subtlest spirit of sadness; he whose "subdued and nerveless boyhood prefigured his abortive prime, which, likewise, contained within itself the prophecy and image of his lean and torpid age." Such touches as are in this piece cannot proceed from any common heart. They argue such a depth of tenderness, such a boundless sympathy with all forms of being, such an omnipresent love, that we must needs say that this Hawthorne is here almost alone—in his generation at least—in the artistic manifestation of these things. Still more. Such touches as these—and many, very many similar ones, all through his chapters—furnish clues, whereby we enter a little way into the intricate, profound heart where they originated. And we see that suffering, some time or other and in some shape or other—this only can enable any man to depict it in others. All over him, Hawthorne's melancholy rests like an Indian summer, which, though bathing a whole country in one softness, still reveals the distinctive hue of every towering hill, and each far-winding vale.

But it is the least part of genius that attracts admiration. Where Hawthorne is known, he seems to be deemed a pleasant writer, with a pleasant style—a sequestered, harmless man, from whom any deep and weighty thing would hardly be anticipated: a man who means no meanings. But there is no man, in whom humor and love, like mountain peaks, soar to such a rapt height, as to receive the irradiations of the upper skies; there is no man in whom humor and love are developed in that high form called genius—no such man can exist without also possessing, as the indispensable complement of these, a great, deep intellect, which drops down into the universe like a plummet. Or, love and humor are only the eyes, through which such an intellect views this world. The great beauty in such a mind is but the product of its strength. What, to all readers, can be more charming than the piece entitled "Monsieur du Miroir"; and to a reader at all capable of fully fathoming it, what, at the same time, can possess more mystical depth of meaning?— Yes, there he sits, and looks at me—this "shape of mystery," this "identical Monsieur du Miroir."—"Methinks I should tremble now, were his wizard power, of gliding through all impediments in search of me, to place him suddenly before my eyes."

How profound, nay, appalling, is the moral evolved by the "Earth's Holocaust," where—beginning with the hollow follies and affectations of the world—all vanities and empty theories and forms are, one after another, and by an admirably graduated, growing comprehensiveness, thrown into the allegorical fire, till, at length, nothing is left but the all-engendering heart of man; which remaining still unconsumed, the great conflagration is naught.

Of a piece with this is "The Intelligence Office," a wondrous symbolizing of the secret workings in men's souls. There are other sketches, still more charged with ponderous import.

"The Christmas Banquet" and "The Bosom Serpent" would be fine subjects for a curious and elaborate analysis, touching the conjectural parts of the mind that produced them. For spite of all the Indian-summer sunlight on the hither side of Hawthorne's soul, the other side—like the dark half of the physical sphere—is shrouded in a blackness, ten times black. But this darkness but gives more effect to the ever-moving dawn, that forever advances through it, and circumnavigates his world. Whether Hawthorne has simply availed himself of this mystical blackness as a means to the wondrous effects he makes it to produce in his lights and shades; or whether there really lurks in him, perhaps unknown to himself, a touch of Puritanic gloom—this, I cannot altogether tell. Certain it is, however, that this great power of blackness in him derives its force from its appeals to that Calvinistic sense of Innate Depravity and Original Sin, from whose visitations, in some shape or other, no deeply thinking mind is always and wholly free. For, in certain moods, no man can weigh this world, without throwing in something, somehow like Original Sin, to strike the uneven balance. At all events, perhaps no writer has ever wielded this terrific thought with greater terror than this same harmless Hawthorne. Still more: this black conceit pervades him, through and through. You may be witched by his sunlight, transported by the bright gildings in the skies he builds over you, but there is the blackness of darkness beyond; and even his bright gildings but fringe and play upon the edges of thunder-clouds.—In one word, the world is mistaken in this Nathaniel Hawthorne. He himself must often have smiled at its absurd misconception of him. He is immeasurably deeper than the plummet of the mere critic. For it is not the brain that can test such a man; it is only the heart. You cannot come to know greatness by inspecting it; there is no glimpse to be caught of it, except by intuition; you need not ring it, you but touch it, and you find it is gold.

Now it is that blackness in Hawthorne, of which I have spoken, that so fixes and fascinates me. It may be, nevertheless, that it is too largely developed in him. Perhaps he does not give us a ray of his light for every shade of his dark. But however this may be, this blackness it is that furnishes the infinite obscure of his background—that background, against which Shakespeare plays his grandest conceits, the things that have made for Shakespeare his loftiest but most circumscribed renown, as the profoundest of thinkers. For by philosophers Shakespeare is not adored as the great man of tragedy and comedy.—"Off with his head! so much for Buckingham!"[9] This sort of rant, interlined by another hand, brings down the house—those mistaken souls, who dream of Shakespeare as a mere man of Richard-the-Third humps, and Macbeth daggers. But it is those deep far-away things in him; those occasional flashings-forth of the intuitive Truth in him; those short, quick probings at the very axis of reality;—these are the things that make Shakespeare Shakespeare. Through the mouths of the dark characters of Hamlet, Timon, Lear, and Iago, he craftily says, or sometimes insinuates, the things which we feel to be so terrifically true that it were all but madness for any good man, in his own proper character, to utter, or even hint of them. Tormented into desperation, Lear the frantic king tears off the mask, and speaks the sane madness of vital truth. But, as I before said, it is the least part of genius that attracts admiration. And so, much of the blind, unbridled admiration that has been heaped upon Shakespeare has been lavished upon the least part of him. And few of his endless commentators and critics seem to have remembered, or even perceived, that the immediate products of a great mind are not so great as that undeveloped, and sometimes undevelopable yet dimly discernible greatness, to which these immediate products are but the infallible indices. In Shakespeare's tomb lies infinitely more than Shakespeare ever wrote. And if I magnify Shakespeare, it is not so much for what he did do, as for what he did not do, or refrained from doing. For in this world of lies, Truth is forced to fly like a scared white doe in the woodlands; and only by cunning glimpses will she reveal herself, as in Shakespeare and

---

[9] By Colley Cibber (1671–1757), an inferior writer; he revised Shakespeare's *Richard III* and interpolated this line.

other masters of the great Art of Telling the Truth—even though it be covertly, and by snatches.

But if this view of the all-popular Shakespeare be seldom taken by his readers, and if very few who extol him have ever read him deeply, or, perhaps, only have seen him on the tricky stage (which alone made, and is still making, him his mere mob renown)—if few men have time, or patience, or palate, for the spiritual truth as it is in that great genius—it is, then, no matter of surprise that in a contemporaneous age, Nathaniel Hawthorne is a man as yet almost utterly mistaken among men. Here and there, in some quiet armchair in the noisy town, or some deep nook among the noiseless mountains, he may be appreciated for something of what he is. But unlike Shakespeare, who was forced to the contrary course by circumstances, Hawthorne (either from simple disinclination, or else from inaptitude) refrains from all the popularizing noise and show of broad farce, and blood-besmeared tragedy; content with the still, rich utterances of a great intellect in repose, and which sends few thoughts into circulation, except they be arterialized at his large warm lungs, and expanded in his honest heart.

Nor need you fix upon that blackness in him, if it suit you not. Nor, indeed, will all readers discern it, for it is, mostly, insinuated to those who may best understand it, and account for it; it is not obtruded upon every one alike.

Some may start to read of Shakespeare and Hawthorne on the same page. They may say, that if an illustration were needed, a lesser light might have sufficed to elucidate this Hawthorne, this small man of yesterday. But I am not, willingly, one of those who, as touching Shakespeare at least, exemplify the maxim of Rochefoucauld,[10] that "we exalt the reputation of some, in order to depress that of others"; who, to teach all noble-souled aspirants that there is no hope for them, pronounce Shakespeare absolutely unapproachable. But Shakespeare has been approached. There are minds that have gone as far as Shakespeare into the universe. And hardly a mortal man, who, at some time or other, has not felt as great thoughts in him as any you will find in *Hamlet*. We must not inferentially malign mankind for the sake of any one man, whoever he may be. This is too cheap a purchase of contentment for conscious mediocrity to make. Besides, this absolute and unconditional adoration of Shakespeare has grown to be a part of our Anglo-Saxon superstitions. The Thirty-Nine Articles[11] are now Forty. Intolerance has come to exist in this matter. You must believe in Shakespeare's unapproachability, or quit the country. But what sort of a belief is this for an American, a man who is bound to carry republican progressiveness into Literature, as well as into Life? Believe me, my friends, that men not very much inferior to Shakespeare are this day being born on the banks of the Ohio. And the day will come when you shall say; who reads a book by an Englishman that is a modern?[12] The great mistake seems to be that even with those Americans who look forward to the coming of a great literary genius among us, they somehow fancy he will come in the costume of Queen Elizabeth's day, be a writer of dramas founded upon old English history, or the tales of Boccaccio. Whereas great geniuses are parts of the times; they themselves are the times, and possess a correspondent coloring. It is of a piece with the Jews, who, while their Shiloh[13] was meekly walking in their streets, were still praying for his magnificent coming: looking for him in a chariot, who was already among them on an ass.[14] Nor must we forget that, in his own lifetime, Shakespeare was not Shakespeare, but only Master William Shakespeare of the shrewd, thriving business firm of Condell, Shakespeare & Co., proprietors of the

[10]François de la Rochefoucauld (1613–1680), French writer, especially of *Moral Maxims*.
[11]The basic doctrines or articles of faith of the Church of England.
[12]Adaptation of "Who reads an American book?" asked by the Englishman Sydney Smith (1771–1845) in 1820.
[13]A name for the Messiah, Christ (see Genesis 49:10).
[14]Jesus entered Jerusalem triumphantly on an ass.

Globe Theatre in London, and by a courtly author, of the name of Chettle,[15] was looked at as an "upstart crow" beautified "with other birds' feathers." For, mark it well, imitation is often the first charge brought against real originality. Why this is so, there is not space to set forth here. You must have plenty of sea-room to tell the Truth in; especially when it seems to have an aspect of newness, as America did in 1492, though it was then just as old, and perhaps older than Asia, only those sagacious philosophers, the common sailors, had never seen it before, swearing it was all water and moonshine there.

Now, I do not say that Nathaniel of Salem is a greater than William of Avon, or as great. But the difference between the two men is by no means immeasurable. Not a very great deal more, and Nathaniel were verily William.

This, too, I mean—that if Shakespeare has not been equaled, give the world time, and he is sure to be surpassed, in one hemisphere or the other. Nor will it at all do to say that the world is getting gray and grizzled now, and has lost that fresh charm which she wore of old, and by virtue of which the great poets of past times made themselves what we esteem them to be. Not so. The world is as young today as when it was created and this Vermont morning dew is as wet to my feet as Eden's dew to Adam's. Nor has Nature been all over ransacked by our progenitors, so that no new charms and mysteries remain for this latter generation to find. Far from it. The trillionth part has not yet been said, and all that has been said but multiplies the avenues to what remains to be said. It is not so much paucity as superabundance of material that seems to incapacitate modern authors.

Let America then prize and cherish her writers; yea, let her glorify them. They are not so many in number as to exhaust her good will. And while she has good kith and kin of her own, to take to her bosom, let her not lavish her embraces upon the household of an alien. For believe it or not, England, after all, is, in many things, an alien to us. China has more bowels of real love for us than she. But even were[16] there no strong literary individualities among us, as there are some dozen at least, nevertheless, let America first praise mediocrity even, in her own children, before she praises (for everywhere, merit demands acknowledgment from every one) the best excellence in the children of any other land. Let her own authors, I say, have the priority of appreciation. I was much pleased with a hot-headed Carolina cousin of mine, who once said, "If there were no other American to stand by, in Literature—why, then, I would stand by Pop Emmons and his *Fredoniad*,[17] and till a better epic came along, swear it was not very far behind the *Iliad*." Take away the words, and in spirit he was sound.

Not that American genius needs patronage in order to expand. For that explosive sort of stuff will expand though screwed up in a vise, and burst it, though it were triple steel. It is for the nation's sake, and not for her authors' sake, that I would have America be heedful of the increasing greatness among her writers. For how great the shame, if other nations should be before her, in crowning her heroes of the pen! But this is almost the case now. American authors have received more just and discriminating praise (however loftily and ridiculously given, in certain cases) even from some Englishmen, than from their own countrymen. There are hardly five critics in America; and several of them are asleep. As for patronage, it is the American author who now patronizes his country, and not his country him. And if at times some among them appeal to the people for more recognition, it is not always with selfish motives, but patriotic ones.

---

[15]Actually made by Robert Greene (1560?–1592) in *A Groatsworth of Wit Bought with a Million of Repentance* (1592).
[16]At this point, the editor of *The Literary World*, Duyckinck, changed Melville's text. Melville originally wrote: "But even were there no Hawthorne, no Emerson, no Whittier, no Irving, no Bryant, no Dana, no Cooper, no Willis (not the author of the 'Darter,' but the author of the 'Belfry Pigeon')—were there none of these, and others of like calibre, nevertheless, let America first praise mediocrity even. . . ."
[17]Richard Emmons (1788–1840) is the author of *Fredoniad, or Independence Preserved—An Epic Poem of the War of 1812*, a work extraordinarily difficult to praise.

It is true that but few of them as yet have evinced that decided originality which merits great praise. But that graceful writer,[18] who perhaps of all Americans has received the most plaudits from his own country for his productions—that very popular and amiable writer, however good, and self-reliant in many things, perhaps owes his chief reputation to the self-acknowledged imitation of a foreign model, and to the studied avoidance of all topics but smooth ones. But it is better to fail in originality than to succeed in imitation. He who has never failed somewhere, that man can not be great. Failure is the true test of greatness. And if it be said that continual success is a proof that a man wisely knows his powers, it is only to be added that, in that case, he knows them to be small. Let us believe it, then, once for all, that there is no hope for us in these smooth, pleasing writers that know their powers. Without malice, but to speak the plain fact, they but furnish an appendix to Goldsmith, and other English authors. And we want no American Goldsmiths; nay, we want no American Miltons. It were the vilest thing you could say of a true American author, that he were an American Tompkins.[19] Call him an American, and have done; for you cannot say a nobler thing of him.—But it is not meant that all American writers should studiously cleave to nationality in their writings; only this, no American writer should write like an Englishman, or a Frenchman; let him write like a man, for then he will be sure to write like an American. Let us away with this leaven of literary flunkyism towards England. If either must play the flunky in this thing, let England do it, not us. While we are rapidly preparing for that political supremacy among the nations, which prophetically awaits us at the close of the present century, in a literary point of view we are deplorably unprepared for it, and we seem studious to remain so. Hitherto, reasons might have existed why this should be; but no good reason exists now. And all that is requisite to amendment in this matter is simply this: that, while freely acknowledging all excellence, everywhere, we should refrain from unduly lauding foreign writers and, at the same time, duly recognize the meritorious writers that are our own; those writers who breathe that unshackled, democratic spirit of Christianity in all things, which now takes the practical lead in this world, though at the same time led by ourselves—us Americans. Let us boldly contemn all imitation, though it comes to us graceful and fragrant as the morning, and foster all originality, though, at first, it be crabbed and ugly as our own pine knots. And if any of our authors fail, or seem to fail, then, in the words of my enthusiastic Carolina cousin, let us clap him on the shoulder, and back him against all Europe for his second round. The truth is that, in our point of view, this matter of a national literature has come to such a pass with us that in some sense we must turn bullies, else the day is lost, or superiority so far beyond us, that we can hardly say it will ever be ours.

And now, my countrymen, as an excellent author, of your own flesh and blood—an unimitating, and, perhaps, in his way, an inimitable man—whom better can I commend to you, in the first place, than Nathaniel Hawthorne. He is one of the new and far better generation of your writers. The smell of your beeches and hemlocks is upon him; your own broad prairies are in his soul; and if you travel away inland into his deep and noble nature, you will hear the far roar of his Niagara. Give not over to future generations the glad duty of acknowledging him for what he is. Take that joy to yourself, in your own generation; and so shall he feel those grateful impulses in him that may possibly prompt him to the full flower of some still greater achievement in your eyes. And by confessing him, you thereby confess others; you brace the whole brotherhood. For genius, all over the

---

[18]Washington Irving.
[19]A kind of generic name for an English butler; flunky.

world, stands hand in hand, and one shock of recognition runs the whole circle round.

In treating of Hawthorne, or rather of Hawthorne in his writings (for I never saw the man, and in the chances of a quiet plantation life, remote from his haunts, perhaps never shall); in treating of his works, I say, I have thus far omitted all mention of his *Twice-Told Tales,* and *The Scarlet Letter.* Both are excellent, but full of such manifold, strange, and diffusive beauties, that time would all but fail me to point the half of them out. But there are things in those two books which, had they been written in England a century ago, Nathaniel Hawthorne had utterly displaced many of the bright names we now revere on authority. But I am content to leave Hawthorne to himself, and to the infallible finding of posterity; and however great may be the praise I have bestowed upon him, I feel, that in so doing, I have more served and honored myself than him. For, at bottom, great excellence is praise enough to itself; but the feeling of a sincere and appreciative love and admiration towards it—this is relieved by utterance; and warm, honest praise ever leaves a pleasant flavor in the mouth; and it is an honorable thing to confess to what is honorable in others.

But I cannot leave my subject yet. No man can read a fine author, and relish him to his very bones, while he reads, without subsequently fancying to himself some ideal image of the man and his mind. And if you rightly look for it, you will almost always find that the author himself has somewhere furnished you with his own picture. For poets (whether in prose or verse), being painters of Nature, are like their brethren of the pencil, the true portrait painters, who, in the multitude of likenesses to be sketched, do not invariably omit their own; and in all high instances, they paint them without any vanity, though, at times, with a lurking something, that would take several pages to properly define.

I submit it, then, to those best acquainted with the man personally, whether the following is not Nathaniel Hawthorne; and to himself, whether something involved in it does not express the temper of his mind—that lasting temper of all true, candid men—a seeker, not a finder yet:

> A man now entered, in neglected attire, with the aspect of a thinker, but somewhat too rough-hewn and brawny for a scholar. His face was full of sturdy vigor, with some finer and keener attribute beneath; though harsh at first, it was tempered with the glow of a large, warm heart, which had force enough to heat his powerful intellect through and through. He advanced to the Intelligencer, and looked at him with a glance of such stern sincerity, that perhaps few secrets were beyond its scope.
> "I seek for Truth," said he.[20]

Twenty-four hours have elapsed since writing the foregoing. I have just returned from the haymow, charged more and more with love and admiration of Hawthorne. For I have just been gleaning through the *Mosses,* picking up many things here and there that had previously escaped me. And I found that but to glean after this man is better than to be in at the harvest of others. To be frank (though, perhaps, rather foolish), notwithstanding what I wrote yesterday of these Mosses, I had not then culled them all; but had, nevertheless, been sufficiently sensible of the subtle essences in them as to write as I did. To what infinite height of loving wonder and admiration I may yet be borne, when by repeatedly banqueting on their Mosses, I shall have thoroughly incorporated their whole stuff into my being—that, I can not tell. But already I feel that this Hawthorne has dropped germinous seeds into my soul. He expands and deepens down, the more

---

[20]From "The Intelligence Office" (in *Mosses*).

I contemplate him; and further, and further, shoots his strong New England roots into the hot soil of my Southern soul.

By careful reference to the "Table of Contents," I now find that I have gone through all the sketches, but that when I yesterday wrote I had not at all read two particular pieces to which I now desire to call special attention—"A Select Party," and "Young Goodman Brown." Here be it said to all those whom this poor fugitive scrawl of mine may tempt to the perusal of the *Mosses* that they must on no account suffer themselves to be trifled with, disappointed, or deceived by the triviality of many of the titles of these Sketches. For in more than one instance the title utterly belies the piece. It is as if rustic demijohns containing the very best and costliest of Falernian and Tokay were labeled "Cider," "Perry," and "Elderberry Wine." The truth seems to be that, like many other geniuses, this Man of Mosses takes great delight in hoodwinking the world—at least with respect to himself. Personally, I doubt not that he rather prefers to be generally esteemed but a so-so sort of author; being willing to reserve the thorough and acute appreciation of what he is to that party most qualified to judge—that is, to himself. Besides, at the bottom of their natures, men like Hawthorne, in many things, deem the plaudits of the public such strong presumptive evidence of mediocrity in the object of them, that it would in some degree render them doubtful of their own powers, did they hear much and vociferous braying concerning them in the public pastures. True, I have been braying myself (if you please to be witty enough to have it so), but then I claim to be the first that has so brayed in this particular matter; and therefore, while pleading guilty to the charge, still claim all the merit due to originality.

But with whatever motive, playful or profound, Nathaniel Hawthorne has chosen to entitle his pieces in the manner he has, it is certain that some of them are directly calculated to deceive—egregiously deceive—the superficial skimmer of pages. To be downright and candid once more, let me cheerfully say that two of these titles did dolefully dupe no less an eagle-eyed reader than myself; and that, too, after I had been impressed with a sense of the great depth and breadth of this American man. "Who in the name of thunder" (as the country people say in this neighborhood), "who in the name of thunder," would anticipate any marvel in a piece entitled "Young Goodman Brown"? You would of course suppose that it was a simple little tale, intended as a supplement to "Goody Two-Shoes." Whereas it is deep as Dante; nor can you finish it, without addressing the author in his own words: "It is yours to penetrate, in every bosom, the deep mystery of sin." And with Young Goodman, too, in allegorical pursuit of his Puritan wife, you cry out in your anguish:

> "Faith!" shouted Goodman Brown, in a voice of agony and desperation; and the echoes of the forest mocked him, crying—"Faith! Faith!" as if bewildered wretches were seeking her, all through the wilderness.

Now this same piece, entitled "Young Goodman Brown," is one of the two that I had not at all read yesterday; and I allude to it now, because it is, in itself, such a strong positive illustration of that blackness in Hawthorne which I had assumed from the mere occasional shadows of it, as revealed in several of the other sketches. But had I previously perused "Young Goodman Brown," I should have been at no pains to draw the conclusion which I came to at a time when I was ignorant that the book contained one such direct and unqualified manifestation of it.

The other piece of the two referred to is entitled "A Select Party," which, in my first simplicity upon originally taking hold of the book, I fancied must treat of some pumpkin-pie party in Old Salem, or some chowder party on Cape Cod.

Whereas, by all the gods of Peedee![21] it is the sweetest and sublimest thing that has been written since Spenser wrote. Nay, there is nothing in Spenser that surpasses it, perhaps, nothing that equals it. And the test is this: read any canto in *The Faery Queen,* and then read "A Select Party," and decide which pleases you the most—that is, if you are qualified to judge. Do not be frightened at this; for when Spenser was alive, he was thought of very much as Hawthorne is now, was generally accounted just such a "gentle" harmless man. It may be that, to common eyes, the sublimity of Hawthorne seems lost in his sweetness—as perhaps in this same "Select Party" of his, for whom he has builded so august a dome of sunset clouds, and served them on richer plate than Belshazzar's when he banqueted his lords in Babylon.[22]

But my chief business now is to point out a particular page in this piece, having reference to an honored guest, who, under the name of "The Master Genius" but in the guise "of a young man of poor attire, with no insignia of rank or acknowledged eminence," is introduced to the Man of Fancy, who is the giver of the feast. Now the page having reference to this "Master Genius" so happily expresses much of what I yesterday wrote, touching the coming of the literary Shiloh of America, that I cannot but be charmed by the coincidence; especially, when it shows such a parity of ideas, at least in this one point, between a man like Hawthorne and a man like me.

And here, let me throw out another conceit of mine touching this American Shiloh, or "Master Genius," as Hawthorne calls him. May it not be, that this commanding mind has not been, is not, and never will be, individually developed in any one man? And would it, indeed, appear so unreasonable to suppose that this great fullness and overflowing may be, or may be destined to be, shared by a plurality of men of genius? Surely, to take the very greatest example on record, Shakespeare cannot be regarded as in himself the concretion of all the genius of his time, nor as so immeasurably beyond Marlowe, Webster, Ford, Beaumont, Jonson, that those great men can be said to share none of his power? For one, I conceive that there were dramatists in Elizabeth's day, between whom and Shakespeare the distance was by no means great. Let anyone, hitherto little acquainted with those neglected old authors, for the first time read them thoroughly, or even read Charles Lamb's *Specimens*[23] of them, and he will be amazed at the wondrous ability of those Anaks[24] of men, and shocked at this renewed example of the fact that Fortune has more to do with fame than merit—though, without merit, lasting fame there can be none.

The words are his—in "A Select Party"; and they are a magnificent setting to a coincident sentiment of my own, but ramblingly expressed yesterday, in reference to himself. Gainsay it who will, as I now write, I am Posterity speaking by proxy—and after times will make it more than good, when I declare that the American, who up to the present day, has evinced, in Literature, the largest brain with the largest heart—that man is Nathaniel Hawthorne. Moreover, that whatever Nathaniel Hawthorne may hereafter write, the *Mosses from an Old Manse* will be ultimately accounted his masterpiece. For there is a sure though a secret sign in some works which proves the culmination of the powers (only the developable ones, however) that produced them. But I am by no means desirous of the glory of a prophet. I pray Heaven that Hawthorne may *yet* prove me an impostor in this prediction. Especially, as I somehow cling to the strange fancy that, in all men, hiddenly reside certain wondrous, occult properties—as in some plants and miner-

---

[21]A river in North and South Carolina.
[22]Cf. Daniel 5:1: "Belshazzar the king made a great feast to a thousand of his lords, and drank wine before the thousand."

[23]Charles Lamb edited *Specimens of the English Dramatic Poets Who Lived about the Time of Shakespeare* (1808).
[24]Anakims, a Canaanite tribe feared to be giants, destroyed by Joshua (see Joshua 11:21).

als—which by some happy but very rare accident (as bronze was discovered by the melting of the iron and brass in the burning of Corinth) may chance to be called forth here on earth, not entirely waiting for their better discovery in the more congenial, blessed atmosphere of heaven.

Once more—for it is hard to be finite upon an infinite subject, and all subjects are infinite. By some people, this entire scrawl of mine may be esteemed altogether unnecessary, inasmuch, "as years ago" (they may say) "we found out the rich and rare stuff in this Hawthorne, whom you now parade forth as if only *yourself* were the discoverer of this Portuguese diamond in our Literature."—But even granting all this—and adding to it, the assumption that the books of Hawthorne have sold by the five thousand—what does that signify? They should be sold by the hundred thousand, and read by the million, and admired by every one who is capable of admiration.

1850

from Letters

TO NATHANIEL HAWTHORNE
[HAWTHORNE: "HE SAYS NO! IN THUNDER"]

Pittsfield, Wednesday morning. [April 16? 1851]
My Dear Hawthorne,—Concerning the young gentleman's shoes, I desire to say that a pair to fit him, of the desired pattern, cannot be had in all Pittsfield,[1]—a fact which sadly impairs that metropolitan pride I formerly took in the capital of Berkshire. Henceforth Pittsfield must hide its head. However, if a pair of *bootees* will at all answer, Pittsfield will be very happy to provide them. Pray mention all this to Mrs. Hawthorne, and command me.

"The House of the Seven Gables: A Romance. By Nathaniel Hawthorne. One vol. 16mo, pp. 344."[2] The contents of this book do not belie its rich, clustering, romantic title. With great enjoyment we spent almost an hour in each separate gable. This book is like a fine old chamber, abundantly, but still judiciously, furnished with precisely that sort of furniture best fitted to furnish it. There are rich hangings, wherein are braided scenes from tragedies! There is old china with rare devices, set out on the carved buffet; there are long and indolent lounges to throw yourself upon; there is an admirable sideboard, plentifully stored with good viands; there is a smell as of old wine in the pantry; and finally, in one corner, there is a dark little black-letter volume in golden clasps, entitled "Hawthorne: A Problem." It has delighted us; it has piqued a re-perusal; it has robbed us of a day, and made us a present of a whole year of thoughtfulness; it has bred great exhilaration and exultation with the remembrance that the architect of the Gables resides only six miles off, and not three thousand miles away, in England, say. We think the book, for pleasantness of running interest, surpasses the other works of the author. The curtains are more drawn; the sun comes in more; genialities peep out more. Were we to particularize what most struck us in the deeper passages, we would point out the scene where Clifford, for a moment, would fain throw himself forth from the window to join the procession; or the scene where the judge is left seated in his ancestral chair. Clifford is full of an awful truth throughout. He

---

[1] Melville had been asked to look in Pittsfield for shoes for Hawthorne's young son, Julian.

[2] Newly published; Hawthorne had brought a copy over a few days before.

is conceived in the finest, truest spirit. He is no caricature. He is Clifford. And here we would say that, did circumstances permit, we should like nothing better than to devote an elaborate and careful paper to the full consideration and analysis of the purport and significance of what so strongly characterizes all of this author's writings. There is a certain tragic phase of humanity which, in our opinion, was never more powerfully embodied than by Hawthorne. We mean the tragicalness of human thought in its own unbiassed, native, and profounder workings. We think that into no recorded mind has the intense feeling of the visable truth ever entered more deeply than into this man's. By visable truth, we mean the apprehension of the absolute condition of present things as they strike the eye of the man who fears them not, though they do their worst to him,—the man who, like Russia or the British Empire, declares himself a sovereign nature (in himself) amid the powers of heaven, hell, and earth. He may perish; but so long as he exists he insists upon treating with all Powers upon an equal basis. If any of those other Powers choose to withhold certain secrets, let them; that does not impair my sovereignty in myself; that does not make me tributary. And perhaps, after all, there is *no* secret. We incline to think that the Problem of the Universe is like the Freemason's mighty secret, so terrible to all children. It turns out, at last, to consist in a triangle, a mallet, and an apron,—nothing more! We incline to think that God cannot explain His own secrets, and that He would like a little information upon certain points Himself. We mortals astonish Him as much as He us. But it is this *Being* of the matter; there lies the knot with which we choke ourselves. As soon as you say *Me*, a *God*, a *Nature*, so soon you jump off from your stool and hang from the beam. Yes, that word is the hangman. Take God out of the dictionary, and you would have Him in the street.

There is the grand truth about Nathaniel Hawthorne. He says NO! in thunder; but the Devil himself cannot make him say *yes*. For all men who say *yes*, lie; and all men who say *no*,—why, they are in the happy condition of judicious, unincumbered travellers in Europe; they cross the frontiers into Eternity with nothing but a carpet-bag,—that is to say, the Ego. Whereas those *yes*-gentry, they travel with heaps of baggage, and, damn them! they will never get through the Custom House. What's the reason, Mr. Hawthorne, that in the last stages of metaphysics a fellow always falls to *swearing* so? I could rip an hour. You see, I began with a little criticism extracted for your benefit from the "Pittsfield Secret Review," and here I have landed in Africa.

Walk down one of these mornings and see me. No nonsense; come. Remember me to Mrs. Hawthorne and the children.

H. Melville.

P.S. The marriage of Phoebe with the daguerreotypist is a fine stroke, because of his turning out to be a *Maule*. If you pass Hepzibah's cent-shop, buy me a Jim Crow (fresh) and send it to me by Ned Higgins.

["DOLLARS DAMN ME"; THE WHALE "IN HIS FLURRY"]

[Pittsfield, June 1? 1851]

My Dear Hawthorne,—I should have been rumbling down to you in my pineboard chariot a long time ago, were it not that for some weeks past I have been more busy than you can well imagine,—out of doors,—building and patching and tinkering away in all directions. Besides, I had my crops to get in,—corn and potatoes (I hope to show you some famous ones by and by),—and many other things to attend to, all accumulating upon this one particular season. I work myself; and at night my bodily sensations are akin to those I have so often felt before, when a hired man, doing my day's work from sun to sun. But I mean to continue visiting you until you tell me that my visits are both supererogatory and superfluous. With no son of man do I stand upon any etiquette or ceremony, except the Christian ones of charity and honesty. I am told, my fellow-man, that there is an aristocracy of the brain. Some men have boldly advocated and asserted it. Schiller[1] seems to have done so, though I don't know much about him. At any rate, it is true that there have been those who, while earnest in behalf of political equality, still accept the intellectual estates. And I can well perceive, I think, how a man of superior mind can, by its intense cultivation, bring himself, as it were, into a certain spontaneous aristocracy of feeling,—exceedingly nice and fastidious,—similar to that which, in an English Howard,[2] conveys a torpedo-fish thrill at the slightest contact with a social plebeian. So, when you see or hear of my ruthless democracy on all sides, you may possibly feel a touch of a shrink, or something of that sort. It is but nature to be shy of a mortal who boldly declares that a thief in jail is as honorable a personage as Gen. George Washington. This is ludicrous. But Truth is the silliest thing under the sun. Try to get a living by the Truth—and go to the Soup Societies. Heavens! Let any clergyman try to preach the Truth from its very stronghold, the pulpit, and they would ride him out of his church on his own pulpit bannister. It can hardly be doubted that all Reformers are bottomed upon the truth, more or less; and to the world at large are not reformers almost universally laughingstocks? Why so? Truth is ridiculous to men. Thus easily in my room here do I, conceited and garrulous, reverse the test of my Lord Shaftesbury.[3]

It seems an inconsistency to assert unconditional democracy in all things, and yet confess a dislike to all mankind—in the mass. But not so.—But it's an endless sermon,—no more of it. I began by saying that the reason I have not been to Lenox is this,—in the evening I feel completely done up, as the phrase is, and incapable of the long jolting to get to your house and back. In a week or so, I go to New York, to bury myself in a third-story room, and work and slave on my "Whale" while it is driving through the press. *That* is the only way I can finish it now,—I am so pulled hither and thither by circumstances. The calm, the coolness, the silent grass-growing mood in which a man *ought* always to compose,—that, I fear, can seldom be mine. Dollars damn me; and the malicious Devil is forever grinning in upon me, holding the door ajar. My dear Sir, a presentiment is on me,—I shall at last be worn out and perish, like an old nutmeg-grater, grated to pieces by the constant attrition of the wood, that is, the nutmeg. What I feel most moved to write, that is banned,—it will not pay. Yet, altogether, write the *other* way I cannot. So the product is a final hash, and all my books are botches. I'm rather sore, perhaps, in this letter; but see my hand!—four blisters on this palm, made by hoes and hammers within the last few days. It is a rainy morning; so I am indoors, and all work suspended. I feel cheerfully disposed, and therefore I write a little bluely. Would the Gin were here! If ever, my dear Hawthorne, in the eternal times that are to come, you and I shall sit down in Paradise, in some little shady corner by ourselves; and if we shall by any means be able to smuggle a basket of champagne there (I won't believe in a Temperance Heaven), and if we shall then cross our celestial legs in the celestial grass that is forever tropical, and strike our glasses and our heads together, till both musically ring in concert,—then, O my dear fellow-mortal, how shall we pleasantly discourse of all the things manifold which now so distress us,—when all the earth shall be but a reminiscence, yea, its final dissolution an antiquity. Then shall songs be composed as when wars are over; humorous, comic songs,—"Oh, when I lived in that queer little hole called the world," or, "Oh, when I toiled and sweated below," or, "Oh, when I

---

[1] Johann Christoph Friedrich von Schiller (1759–1805), German poet and playwright.

[2] Could be any one of a number of notable people of a distinguished British family.

[3] Anthony Ashley Cooper, Lord Shaftesbury (1671–1713) argued that a thing is true if it can survive ridicule (in *Characteristics of Men, Manners, Opinions, Times*, 1711). Melville revised the observation.

knocked and was knocked in the fight"—yes, let us look forward to such things. Let us swear that, though now we sweat, yet it is because of the dry heat which is indispensable to the nourishment of the vine which is to bear the grapes that are to give us the champagne hereafter.

But I was talking about the "Whale." As the fishermen say, "he's in his flurry"[4] when I left him some three weeks ago. I'm going to take him by his jaw, however, before long, and finish him up in some fashion or other. What's the use of elaborating what, in its very essence, is so short-lived as a modern book? Though I wrote the Gospels in this century, I should die in the gutter.—I talk all about myself, and this is selfishness and egotism. Granted. But how help it? I am writing to you; I know little about you, but something about myself. So I write about myself,—at least, to you. Don't trouble yourself, though, about writing; and don't trouble yourself about visiting; and when you *do* visit, don't trouble yourself about talking. I will do all the writing and visiting and talking myself.—By the way, in the last "Dollar Magazine" I read "The Unpardonable Sin."[5] He was a sad fellow, that Ethan Brand. I have no doubt you are by this time responsible for many a shake and tremor of the tribe of "general readers." It is a frightful poetical creed that the cultivation of the brain eats out the heart. But it's my *prose* opinion that in most cases, in those men who have fine brains and work them well, the heart extends down to hams. And though you smoke them with the fire of tribulation, yet, like veritable hams, the head only gives the richer and the better flavor. I stand for the heart. To the dogs with the head! I had rather be a fool with a heart, than Jupiter Olympus with his head. The reason the mass of men fear God, and *at bottom dislike* Him, is because they rather distrust His heart, and fancy Him all brain like a watch. (You perceive I employ a capital initial in the pronoun referring to the Deity; don't you think there is a slight dash of flunkeyism in that usage?) Another thing. I was in New York for four-and-twenty hours the other day, and saw a portrait of N.H. And I have seen and heard many flattering (in a publisher's point of view) allusions to the "Seven Gables." And I have seen "Tales," and "A New Volume" announced, by N.H. So upon the whole, I say to myself, this N.H. is in the ascendant. My dear Sir, they begin to patronize. All Fame is patronage. Let me be infamous: there is no patronage in *that*. What "reputation" H.M. has is horrible. Think of it! To go down to posterity is bad enough, any way; but to go down as a "man who lived among the cannibals"! When I speak of posterity, in reference to myself, I only mean the babies who will probably be born in the moment immediately ensuing upon my giving up the ghost. I shall go down to some of them, in all likelihood. "Typee" will be given to them, perhaps, with their gingerbread. I have come to regard this matter of Fame as the most transparent of all vanities. I read Solomon more and more, and every time see deeper and deeper and unspeakable meanings in him.[6] I did not think of Fame, a year ago, as I do now. My development has been all within a few years past. I am like one of those seeds taken out of the Egyptian Pyramids, which, after being three thousand years a seed and nothing but a seed, being planted in English soil, it developed itself, grew to greenness, and then fell to mould. So I. Until I was twenty-five, I had no development at all. From my twenty-fifth year I date my life. Three weeks have scarcely passed, at any time between then and now, that I have not unfolded within myself. But I feel that I am now come to the inmost leaf of the bulb, and that shortly the flower must fall to the mould. It seems to me now that Solomon was the truest man who ever spoke, and yet that he a little *managed* the truth with

---

[4]I.e., in his death agitation or agony.
[5]Now known as "Ethan Brand"; Melville had read it in *Holden's Dollar Magazine*, (May 1851).
[6]Cf. *Moby-Dick:* "The truest of all men was the Man of Sorrows, and the truest of all books is Solomon's, and Ecclesiastes is the fine hammered steel of woe. All is vanity. ALL. This wilful world hath not got hold of unchristian Solomon's wisdom yet."

a view to popular conservatism; or else there have been many corruptions and in-terpolations of the text.— In reading some of Goethe's sayings, so worshipped by his votaries, I came across this, *"Live in the all."*[7] That is to say, your separate iden-tity is but a wretched one,— good; but get out of yourself, spread and expand yourself, and bring to yourself the tinglings of life that are felt in the flowers and the woods, that are felt in the planets Saturn and Venus, and the Fixed Stars. What nonsense! Here is a fellow with a raging toothache. "My dear boy," Goethe says to him, "you are sorely afflicted with that tooth; but you must *live in the all,* and then you will be happy!" As with all great genius, there is an immense deal of flummery in Goethe, and in proportion to my own contact with him, a monstrous deal of it in me.

H. Melville.

P.S. "Amen!" saith Hawthorne.

N.B. This "all" feeling, though, there is some truth in. You must often have felt it, lying on the grass on a warm summer's day. Your legs seem to send out shoots into the earth. Your hair feels like leaves upon your head. This is the *all* feeling. But what plays the mischief with the truth is that men will insist upon the univer-sal application of a temporary feeling or opinion.

P.S. You must not fail to admire my discretion in paying the postage on this letter.

["Shall I Send You a Fin of the *Whale*?"]

Pittsfield June 29th 185[1]

My dear Hawthorne— The clear air and open window invite me to write to you. For some time past I have been so busy with a thousand things that I have almost forgotten when I wrote you last, and whether I received an answer. This most persuasive season has now for weeks recalled me from certain crotchetty and over doleful chimearas, the like of which men like you and me and some others, form-ing a chain of God's posts round the world, must be content to encounter now and then, and fight them the best way we can. But come they will,— for, in the bound-less, trackless, but still glorious wild wilderness through which these outposts run, the Indians do sorely abound, as well as the insignificant but still stinging mosqui-toes. Since you have been here, I have been building some shanties of houses (connected with the old one) and likewise some shanties of chapters and essays. I have been plowing and sowing and raising and painting and printing and pray-ing,— and now begin to come out upon a less bustling time, and to enjoy the calm prospect of things from a fair piazza at the north of the old farm house here.

Not entirely yet, though, am I without something to be urgent with. The "Whale" is only half through the press; for, wearied with the long delay of the printers, and disgusted with the heat and dust of the babylonish[1] brick-kiln of New York, I came back to the country to feel the grass— and end the book reclin-ing on it, if I may.— I am sure you will pardon this speaking all about myself,— for if I *say* so much on that head, be sure all the rest of the world are thinking about themselves ten times as much. Let us speak, though we show all our faults and weaknesses,— for it is a sign of strength to be weak, to know it, and out with it,— not in [a] set way and ostentatiously, though, but incidentally and without premeditation.— But I am falling into my old foible— preaching. I am busy, but shall not be very long. Come and spend a day here, if you can and want to; if not, stay in Lenox, and God give you long life. When I am quite free of my present engagements, I am going to treat myself to a ride and a visit to you. Have ready a bottle of brandy, because I always feel like drinking that heroic drink when we

---

[7]Johann Wolfgang von Goethe (1749–1832), German poet; the exact source of the quotation is not known.

[1]Ancient city on the Euphrates, famous for wealth, luxury, and wickedness.

talk ontological heroics together. This is rather a crazy letter in some respects, I apprehend. If so, ascribe it to the intoxicating effects of the latter end of June operating upon a very susceptible and peradventure feeble temperament.

Shall I send you a fin of the *Whale* by way of a specimen mouthful? The tail is not yet cooked—though the hell-fire in which the whole book is broiled might not unreasonably have cooked it all ere this. This is the book's motto (the secret one),—Ego non baptiso te in nomine—but make out the rest yourself.[2]

H.M.

["I Have Written a Wicked Book, and Feel Spotless as the Lamb"]

Pittsfield, Monday afternoon. [November 17? 1851]

My Dear Hawthorne,—People think that if a man has undergone any hardship, he should have a reward; but for my part, if I have done the hardest possible day's work, and then come to sit down in a corner and eat my supper comfortably—why, then I don't think I deserve any reward for my hard day's work—for am I not now at peace? Is not my supper good? My peace and my supper are my reward, my dear Hawthorne. So your joy-giving and exultation-breeding letter is not my reward for my ditcher's[1] work with that book, but is the good goddess's bonus over and above what was stipulated for—for not one man in five cycles, who is wise, will expect appreciative recognition from his fellows, or any one of them. Appreciation! Recognition! Is love appreciated? Why, ever since Adam, who has got to the meaning of this great allegory—the world? Then we pygmies must be content to have our paper allegories but ill comprehended. I say your appreciation is my glorious gratuity. In my proud, humble way,—a shepherd-king,—I was lord of a little vale in the solitary Crimea; but you have now given me the crown of India. But on trying it on my head, I found it fell down on my ears, notwithstanding their asinine length—for it's only such ears that sustain such crowns.

Your letter was handed me last night on the road going to Mr. Morewood's, and I read it there. Had I been at home, I would have sat down at once and answered it. In me divine maganimities are spontaneous and instantaneous—catch them while you can. The world goes round, and the other side comes up. So now I can't write what I felt. But I felt pantheistic then—your heart beat in my ribs and mine in yours, and both in God's. A sense of unspeakable security is in me this moment, on account of your having understood the book. I have written a wicked book, and feel spotless as the lamb. Ineffable socialities are in me. I would sit down and dine with you and all the gods in old Rome's Pantheon. It is a strange feeling—no hopefulness is in it, no despair. Content—that is it; and irresponsibility; but without licentious inclination. I speak now of my profoundest sense of being, not of an incidental feeling.

Whence come you, Hawthorne? By what right do you drink from my flagon of life? And when I put it to my lips—lo, they are yours and not mine. I feel that the Godhead is broken up like the bread at the Supper,[2] and that we are the pieces. Hence this infinite fraternity of feeling. Now, sympathizing with the paper, my angel turns over another page. You did not care a penny for the book. But, now and then as you read, you understood the pervading thought that impelled the book—and that you praised. Was it not so? You were archangel enough to despise the imperfect body, and embrace the soul. Once you hugged the ugly Socrates[3] because you saw the flame in the mouth, and heard the rushing of the

---

[2]"I do not baptise thee in the name [of God]. . . ." The ending appears in *Moby-Dick*, as Ahab baptizes the harpoons of the pagan harpooneers with their own blood; ". . .*sed in nomine diaboli* [but in the name of the devil]."

[1]Ditchdigger's.
[2]Cf. John 13–15.
[3]Greek philosopher (470?–399 B.C.), known through his disciple Plato's dialogues.

demon,—the familiar,—and recognized the sound; for you have heard it in your own solitudes.

My dear Hawthorne, the atmospheric skepticisms steal into me now, and make me doubtful of my sanity in writing you thus. But, believe me, I am not mad, most noble Festus![4] But truth is ever incoherent, and when the big hearts strike together, the concussion is a little stunning. Farewell. Don't write a word about the book. That would be robbing me of my miserly delight. I am heartily sorry I ever wrote anything about you—it was paltry.[5] Lord, when shall we be done growing? As long as we have anything more to do, we have done nothing. So, now, let us add Moby Dick to our blessing, and step from that. Leviathan is not the biggest fish;—I have heard of Krakens.[6]

This is a long letter, but you are not at all bound to answer it. Possibly, if you do answer it, and direct it to Herman Melville, you will missend it—for the very fingers that now guide this pen are not precisely the same that just took it up and put it on this paper. Lord, when shall we be done changing? Ah! it's a long stage, and no inn in sight, and night coming, and the body cold. But with you for a passenger, I am content and can be happy. I shall leave the world, I feel, with more satisfaction for having come to know you. Knowing you persuades me more than the Bible of our immortality.

What a pity, that, for your plain, bluff letter, you should get such gibberish! Mention me to Mrs. Hawthorne and to the children, and so, good-by to you, with my blessing.

                                                                                    Herman.

P.S. I can't stop yet. If the world was entirely made up of Magians,[7] I'll tell you what I should do. I should have a paper-mill established at one end of the house, and so have an endless riband of foolscap rolling in upon my desk; and upon that endless riband I should write a thousand—a million—billion thoughts, all under the form of a letter to you. The divine magnet is on you, and my magnet responds. Which is the biggest? A foolish question—they are *One*.   H.

P.P.S. Don't think that by writing me a letter, you shall always be bored with an immediate reply to it—and so keep both of us delving over a writing-desk eternally. No such thing! I sh'n't always answer your letters, and you may do just as you please.

[THE STORY OF THE DISAPPEARING HUSBAND[1]]

                                                           Pittsfield Aug: 13th 1852

[*Salutation torn off*]—While visiting Nantucket some four weeks ago, I made the acquaintance of a gentleman from New Bedford, a lawyer, who gave me considerable information upon several matters concerning which I was curious.—One night we were talking, I think, of the great patience, & endurance, & resignedness of the women of the island in submitting so uncomplainingly to the long, long absences of their sailor husbands, when, by way of anecdote, this lawyer gave me a leaf from his professional experience. Altho' his memory was a little confused with regard to some of the items of the story, yet he told me enough to awaken the most lively interest in me; and I begged him to be sure and send me a more full account so soon as he arrived home—he having previously told me that at the

---

[4]See Acts 26:24–25. Words of St. Paul in making his "appeal unto Caesar" to the Roman procurator of Judea, Porcius Festus.
[5]"Hawthorne and His Mosses," *Literary World* (August 17 and 24, 1850).
[6]Legendary sea monster of northern seas.
[7]Variant of Magi, priestly caste or wise men in ancient Media and Persia.

[1]In this letter, Melville urgently offers a "plot" he has heard (from John H. Clifford, a New Bedford lawyer) to Hawthorne for a tale: the daughter of a lighthouse keeper marries a ship-wrecked sailor, and is deserted by him; he turns up many years later to reestablish the relationship. Melville's letter offers many clues as to the operation of his artistic imagination on the raw material of life.

time of the affair he had made a record in his books.—I heard nothing more, till a few days after arriving here at Pittsfield I received thro' the Post Office the enclosed document.[2]—You will perceive by the gentleman's note to me that he assumed that I purposed making literary use of the story; but I had not hinted anything of the kind to him, & my first spontaneous interest in it arose from very different considerations. I confess, however, that since then I have a little turned the subject over in my mind with a view to a regular story to be founded on these striking incidents. But, thinking again, it has occurred to me that this thing lies very much in a vein, with which you are peculiarly familiar. To be plump, I think that in this matter you would make a better hand at it than I would.—Besides the thing seems naturally to gravitate towards you (to spea[k] . . . [*half a line torn*] should of right belong to you. I cou[ld] . . . [*half a line torn*] the Steward to deliver it to you.—

The very great interest I felt in this story while narrating to me, was heightened by the emotion of the gentleman who told it, who evinced the most unaffected sympathy in it, tho' now a matter of his past.—But perhaps this great interest of mine may have been largely helped by some accidental circumstance or other; so that, possibly, to you the story may not seem to possess so much of pathos, & so much of depth. But you will see how it is.————

In estimating the character of Robinson[3] Charity should be allowed a liberal play. I take exception to that passage from the Diary which says that "*he must have received a portion of his punishment in this life*"—thus hinting of a future supplemental castigation.—I do not at all suppose that his desertion of his wife was a premeditated thing. If it had been so, he would have changed his name, probably, after quitting her.—No: he was a weak man, & his temptations (tho' we know little of them) were strong. The whole sin stole upon him insensibly—so that it would perhaps have been hard for him to settle upon the exact day when he could say to himself, "*Now* I have deserted my wife["]; unless, indeed upon the day he wedded the Alexandran lady.—And here I am reminded of your *London husband;*[4] tho' the cases so rudely contrast.—Many more things might be mentioned; but I forbear; you will find out the suggestiveness for yourself; & all the better perhaps, for my not intermeddling.—

If you should be sufficiently interested, to engage upon a regular story founded on this narration [narrative?]; then I consider you but fairly entitled to the following tributary items, collected by me, by chance, during my strolls thro the islands; & which—as you will perceive—seem legitimately to belong to the story, in its rounded & beautified & thoroughly developed state;—but of all this you must of course be your own judge—I but submit matter to you—I don't decide.

Supposing the story to open with the wreck—then there must be a storm; & it were well if some faint shadow of the preceding *calm* were thrown forth to lead the whole.—Now imagine a high cliff overhanging the sea & crowned with a pasture for sheep; a little way off—higher up,—a light-house, where resides the father of the future Mrs Robinson the First. The afternoon is mild & warm. The sea with an air of solemn deliberation, with an elaborate deliberation, ceremoniously rolls upon the beach. The air is suppressedly charged with the sound of long lines of surf. There is no land over against this cliff short of Europe & the West Indies. Young Agatha (but you must give her some other name) comes wandering along the cliff. She marks how the continual assaults of the sea have undermined it; so that the fences fall over, & have need of many shiftings inland. The sea has en-

---

[2]See below, at the end of this letter.
[3]Actually Robertson, in the Clifford account.
[4]I.e., Hawthorne's story, "Wakefield," a story in which a husband deserts his wife for twenty years, living in a nearby street.

croached also upon that part where their dwelling-house stands near the light-house.— Filled with meditations, she reclines along the edge of the cliff & gazes out seaward. She marks a handful of cloud on the horizon, presaging a storm tho' [thro'?] all this quietude. (Of a maratime family & always dwelling on the coast, she is learned in these matters) This again gives food for thought. Suddenly she catches the long shadow of the cliff cast upon the beach 100 feet beneath her; and now she notes a shadow moving along the shadow. It is cast by a sheep from the pasture. It has advanced to the very edge of the cliff, & is sending a mild innocent glance far out upon the water. Here [There?], in strange & beautiful contrast, we have the innocence of the land placidly eyeing the malignity of the sea. (All this having poetic reference to Agatha & her sea-lover, who is coming in the storm: the storm carries her lover to her; she catches a dim distant glimpse of his ship ere quitting the cliff)————

P.S. It were well, if from her knowledge of the deep miseries produced to wives by marrying seafaring men, Agatha should have formed a young determination never to marry a sailor; which resolve in her, however, is afterwards overborne by the omnipotence of Love.— P.S. No 2. Agatha should be active during the wreck, & should, in some way, be made the saviour of young Robinson. He should be the only survivor. He should be ministered to by Agatha at the house during the ill-ness ensuing upon his injuries from the wreck.— Now this wrecked ship was driven over the shoals, & driven upon the beach where she goes to pieces, all but her stem-part. This in course of time becomes embedded in the sand—after the lapse of some years showing nothing but the sturdy stem (or, prow-bone) project-ing some two feet at low water. All the rest is filled & packed down with the sand.— So that after her husband has disappeared the sad Agatha every day sees this melancholy monument, with all its remindings.————

After a sufficient lapse of time—when Agatha has become alarmed about the protracted abscence of her young husband & is feverishly expecting a letter from him—then we must introduce the mail-post—no, that phrase wont' do, but here is the *thing*. —Owing to the remoteness of the lighthouse from any settled place no regular mail reaches it. But some mile or so distant there is a road leading be-tween two post-towns. And at the junction of what we shall call the Light-House road with this Post Rode, there stands a post surmounted with a little rude wood box with a lid to it & a leather hinge. Into this box the Post boy drops all letters for the people of the light house & that vicinity of fishermen. To this *post* they must come for their letters. And, of course, daily young Agatha goes—for seven-teen years she [?] goes thither daily [.] As her hopes gradually decay in her, so does the post itself & the little box decay. The post rots in the ground at last. Ow-ing to its being little used—hardly used at all—grass grows rankly about it. At last a little bird nests in it. At last the post falls.

The father of Agatha must be an old widower—a man of the sea, but early driven away from it by repeated disasters. Hence, is he subdued & quiet & wise in his life. And now he tends a light house, to warn people from those very perils, from which he himself has suffered.

Some few other items occur to me—but nothing material—and I fear to weary you, if not, make you smile at my strange impertinent officiousness.— And it would be so, were it not that these things do, in my mind, seem legitimately to belong to the story; for they were visably suggested to me by scenes I actually be-held while on the very coast where the story of Agatha occurred.— I do not there-fore, My Dear Hawthorne, at all imagine that you will think that I am so silly as to flatter myself I am giving you anything of my own. I am but restoring to you your own property—which you would quickly enough have identified for yourself—had you but been on the spot as I happened to be.

Let me conclude by saying that it seems to me that with your great power in these things, you can construct a story of remarkable interest out of this material furnished by the New Bedford lawyer.—You have a skeleton of actual reality to build about with fulness & veins & beauty. And if I thought I could do it as well as you, why, I should not let you have it.—The narrative [narration?] from the Diary is instinct with significance.—Consider the mention of the *shawls*—& the inference derived from it. Ponder the conduct of this Robinson throughout.—Mark his trepidation & suspicion when any one called upon him.—But why prate so—you will mark it all & mark it deeper than I would, perhaps.

I have written all this in a great hurry; so you must spell it out the best way you may.

P.S. The business was settled in a few weeks afterwards, in a most amicable & honorable manner, by a division of the property. I think Mrs. Robinson & her family refused to claim or receive anything that really belonged to Mrs. Irwin, or which Robinson had derived through her.—

[*Enclosure:* Mr. Clifford's story of Agatha]

May 28th 1842 Saturday. I have just returned from a visit to Falmouth with a Mr Janney of M^o on one of the most interesting and romantic cases I ever expect to be engaged in.—The gentleman from Missouri Mr Janney came to my house last Sunday evening and related to myself and partner that he had married the daughter of a Mrs Irvin formerly of Pittsburgh Pa. and that Mrs Irvin had married a second husband by the name of Robertson. The latter deceased about two years since. He was appointed Adm^r to his Estate which amounted to $20 000—about 15 months afterwards Mrs Robertson also died and in the meantime the Adm^r had been engaged in looking up heirs to the Estate—He learned that Robertson was an Englishman whose original name was Shinn—that he resided at Alexandria D.C. where he had two nephews—He also wrote to England and had ascertained the history and genealogy of the family with much accuracy, when on going to the Post Office one day he found a letter directed to James Robertson the deceased, post marked Falmouth Mass^{tts}—On opening it he found it from a person signing herself Rebecca A. Gifford and addressing him as "Father." The existence of this girl had been known before by Mrs Robertson and her husband had pronounced her to be illegitimate The Adm^r then addressed a letter to Mrs Gifford informing her of the decease of her father. He was surprised soon after by the appearance in St Louis of a shrewd Quaker from Falmouth named Dillingham with full powers and fortified by letters and affidavits shewing the existence of a wife in Falmouth whom Robertson married in 1807 at Pembroke M[a]ss & the legitimacy of the daughter who had married a Mr Gifford and laying strong claims to the entire property.

The Adm^r and heirs having strong doubts arising from the declarations of Robertson during his lifetime & the peculiar expressions contained in the letters exhibited, as to the validity of the marriage & the claim based upon it, determined to resist and legal proceedings were at once commenced. The object of the visit of Mr Janney was to attend the taking of depositions, upon a notice from the claimants—The Minister Town Clerk and Witnesses present at the ceremony established the fact of a legal marriage and the birth of a child in wedlock, beyond all cavil or controversy all of the witnesses were of the highest respectability and the widow and daughter interested me very much.

It appeared that Robertson was wrecked on the coast of Pembroke where this girl, then Miss Agatha Hatch was living—that he was hospitably entertained and cared for, and that within a year after, he married her, in due form of law—that he went two short voyages to sea. About two years after the marriage, leaving his wife *enciente* [*sic*] he started off in search of employment and from that time until *Seventeen* years afterwards she never heard from him in any way whatsoever, directly or indirectly, not even a word. Being poor she went out nursing for her daily bread and yet contrived out of her small earnings to give her daughter a first rate education. Having become connected with the Society of Friends she sent her to their most celebrated boarding school and when I saw her I found she had profited by all her advantages beyond most females. In the meantime Robertson had gone to Alexandria D.C. where he had entered into a successful and profitable business and married a second wife. At the expiration of this long period of 17 years which for the poor forsaken wife, had glided wearily away, while she was engaged away from home, her Father rode up in a gig and informed her that her husband had returned and wished to see her and her child — but if she would not see him, to see her child at all events — They all returned together and encountered him on the way coming to meet them about half a mile from her father's house. This meeting was described to me by the mother and daughter — Every incident seemed branded upon the memories of both. He excused himself as well as he could for his long absence and silence, appeard very affectionate refused to tell where he was living and persuaded them not to make any inquiries, gave them a handsome sum of money, promised to return for good and left the next day — He appeared again in about a year, just on the eve of his daughter's marriage & gave her a bridal present. It was not long after this that his wife in Alexandria died — He then wrote to his son-in-law to come there — He did so — remained 2 days and brought back a gold watch and three handsome shawls which had been previously worn by some person — They all admitted that they had suspicions then & from this circumstance that he had been a second time married.

Soon after this he visited Falmouth again & as it proved for the last time — He announced his intention of removing to Missouri & urged the whole family to go with him, promising money land and other assistance to his son-in-law. The offer was not accepted He shed tears when he bade them farewell — From the time of his return to Missouri till the time of his death a constant correspondence was kept up money was remitted by him annually and he announced to them his marriage with Mrs Irvin — He had no children by either of his last two wives.

Mr Janney was entirely disappointed in the character of the evidence and the character of the claimants. He considered them, when he first came, as parties to the imposition practised upon Mrs Irvin & her children. But I was satisfied and I think he was, that their motives in keeping silence were high and pure, creditable in every way to the true Mrs Robertson. She stated the causes with a simplicity & pathos which carried that conviction irresistibly to my mind. The only good(?) it could have done to expose him would have been to drive Robertson away and forever disgrace him & it would certainly have made Mrs Irvin & her children wretched for the rest of their days — "I had no wish" said the wife "to make either of them unhappy, notwithstanding all I had suffered on his account" — It was to me a most striking instance of long continued & uncomplaining submission to wrong and anguish on the part of a wife, wch made her in my eyes a heroine.

Janney informed me that R. and his last wife did not live very happily together and particularly that he seemed to be a very jealous suspicious man — that when a person called at his house he would never enter the room till he knew who it was & "all about him.["] He must have received a portion of his punishment in this life. The fact came out in the course of examination that they had agreed to give Dillingham one half of what he might obtain deducting the expenses from his half — After the strength of the evidence became known Mr Janney commenced the making of serious efforts to effect a compromise of the claim. What the result will be time will shew—This is, I suspect, the end of my connexion with the case—

[THE DESERTING SAILOR-HUSBAND AND THE MARRIAGE VOW]

[Pittsfield] Monday Morning 25th Oct: 1852

My Dear Hawthorne—

If you thought it worth while to write the story of Agatha,[1] and should you be engaged upon it; then I have a little idea touching it, which however trifling, may not be entirely out of place. Perhaps, tho', the idea has occurred to yourself.— The probable facility with which Robinson first leaves his wife & then takes another, may, possibly, be ascribed to the peculiarly latitudinarian notions, which most sailors have of all tender obligations of that sort. In his previous sailor life Robinson had found a wife (for a night) in every port. The sense of the obligation of the marriage-vow to Agatha had little weight with him at first. *It* was only when some years of life ashore had passed that his moral sense on that point became developed. And hence his subsequent conduct—Remorse &c. Turn this over in your mind & see if it is right. If not—make it so yourself.

If you come across a little book called "Taughconic"—look into it and divert yourself with it. Among others, you figure in it, & I also. But you are the most honored, being the most abused, and having the greatest space allotted you.— It is a "Guide Book" to Berkshire.[2]

I dont know when I shall see you. I shall lay eyes on you one of these days however. Keep some Champagne or Gin for me.

My respects and best remembrances to Mrs: Hawthorne & a reminder to the children.

H Melville

If you find any *sand* in this letter, regard it as so many sands of my life, which run out as I was writing it.

---

[1]In this letter, Melville continued to urge Hawthorne to accept his "Agatha" plot (see previous letter). But Hawthorne turned down the offer and urged Melville to write the story. Melville tried his hand, but apparently could not finish the work.

[2]*Taghonic: or Letters and Legends about Our Summer Home* (1852), by Godfrey Greylock (J. E. A. Smith); a guide book, it contains pieces by various writers.

POETS OF THE TRADITION

———

HENRY WADSWORTH LONGFELLOW   JAMES RUSSELL LOWELL
JOHN GREENLEAF WHITTIER   JONES VERY
OLIVER WENDELL HOLMES   FREDERICK GODDARD TUCKERMAN

They broke no bonds, shaped no new forms, invented no new measures, these poets of the tradition. But they poured forth a flood of poems that served their time, and they crafted numerous poems of high achievement within that tradition they never challenged. James Russell Lowell spoke for them all when he said: "The poet's office is to be a Voice, not of one crying in the wilderness to a knot of already magnetized acolytes, but singing amid the throng of men, and lifting their common aspirations and sympathies (so first clearly revealed to themselves) on the wings of his song to a purer ether and a wider reach of view." "A Psalm of Life," "Snow-Bound," "The Chambered Nautilus," "To the Dandelion" lie so deeply lodged in the American imagination as to be virtually beyond criticism. Some of these poets—Longfellow, Whittier, Holmes, and Lowell—were extraordinarily popular. Others—the sonneteers Very and Tuckerman—were scarcely read. But they all chose to accommodate the tradition, and the tradition accommodated them.

HENRY WADSWORTH
LONGFELLOW
(1807–1882)

When Henry Wadsworth Longfellow died in 1882, he was the best-known and best-loved American poet throughout the world. In America, his fame was immediate on the publication of his first book of poems, *Voices of the Night*, in 1839, and particularly with one poem universally admired, "A Psalm of Life" ("Life is real! Life is earnest!/And the grave is not its goal"). His birthday in 1881 was celebrated by school children throughout the land. Nathaniel Hawthorne wrote him from England in 1855, "No other poet has anything like your vogue." On its first day of sale in London, "The Courtship of Miles Standish" (1858) sold 10,000 copies. By the end of the nineteenth century, Longfellow's poems had been translated into a dozen languages, including Dutch, Swedish, Polish, Hungarian, and Russian. In 1884, Longfellow was enshrined in Westminster Abbey in London by the unveiling of a bust of him in the Poet's Corner. His place among the immortal English poets seemed assured for all time.

But alas, fate played Longfellow a cruel joke in the twentieth century. His reputation sank so low that one literary historian, Ludwig Lewisohn, exclaimed in the 1930s, "Who, except wretched schoolchildren, now read Longfellow?" In recognition of their affirmations of the values of family, home, and hearth, Longfellow and other poets of the tradition are often grouped in anthologies under such titles as "The Schoolroom Poets" or "The Fireside Poets." The one grouping indicates that the poets have achieved a minor immortality by being recited by school children under the poets' somber gaze from their bearded portraits on the schoolroom walls. The other suggests poets read aloud by the entire family before the fireplace. As the twentieth century has worn on, and pictures of literary figures have disappeared from schools, and fireplaces vanished from homes and apartments, these categories have come to seem nostalgic memorializations of a past that no longer exists—and perhaps never did.

Longfellow never deserved the unqualified adulation he once had, nor does he deserve the widespread neglect he now suffers. His was a remarkable life of achievement. Born in Portland, Maine, he attended Maine's Bowdoin College, where one classmate was Nathaniel Hawthorne. Longfellow was so good at languages that he was offered a position at Bowdoin if he would spend time abroad perfecting his ability. He spent time in France, Spain, Italy, and Germany from 1826 to 1829, and then returned to his professorship at Bowdoin.

In 1835, Longfellow accepted a professorship at Harvard, a post he held until 1854, when he retired and devoted his full time to writing. There were two tragedies in his life, the death of his first wife by miscarriage in 1835, and the death of a second wife (married in 1843) by fire in 1861. From that time until his death in 1882, Longfellow lived on alone in the large historic Craigie House in Cambridge that had been a wedding gift of his second wife's father, a prosperous Boston merchant.

Throughout his life he issued a steady stream of volumes, including *Ballads and Other Poems* (1841), *Poems on Slavery* (1842), *The Belfry of Bruges and Other Poems* (1845), *Evangeline* (1847), and *The Song of Hiawatha* (1855). After his second wife's death in 1861, he devoted much creative effort to the translation of Dante's *Divine Comedy*. The sonnets ("Divina Commedia") written to introduce the three books are now considered to be among his best poems.

Longfellow deserves considerable credit for introducing elements of European civilization and culture to Americans through his poetry. He was clearly a learned and sophisticated man, at home in Europe as much as in America, but he did not overwhelm his poems with his learning. When he turned to native American subjects, he often introduced European forms or elements. For example, he adapted the meter of the Finnish folk epic *Kalvela* for use in his *Song of Hiawatha,* based on American Indian legends.

The overriding emotion evoked by Longfellow's poems is melancholy, his recurrent theme, perseverance in the face of adversity: "Tell me not, in mournful numbers, / Life is but an empty dream!" Anyone who begins a poem ("A Psalm of Life") with these lines could well have been haunted on the lower levels of consciousness by the lurking thought that life was, indeed, but an empty dream. His poetry is filled with a piercing sense of the transience of all things—vanished scenes, lost youth, unfulfilled years. One of his most moving poems begins, "All things must have an end; the world itself," and envisions the earth, like a sinking ship, slipping into "the dark abyss." This melancholy vision is the dimension of his poetry most likely to appeal to the imagination of modern readers.

ADDITIONAL READING

The Letters of Henry Wadsworth Longfellow, 6 vols., ed. Andrew Hilen, Jr., 1967–82.

Samuel Longfellow, *The Life of Henry Wadsworth Longfellow,* 3 vols., 1891; Lawrence Thompson, *Young Longfellow,* 1938; George Arms, "Longfellow," *The Fields Were Green,* 1948; Edward Wagenknecht, *Longfellow: A Full-Length Portrait,* 1955, rev. as *Henry Wadsworth Longfellow: Portrait of an American Humanist,* 1966; Newton Arvin, *Longfellow: His Life and Works,* 1963; Cecil B. Williams, *Henry Wadsworth Longfellow,* 1964; Edward L. Hirsh, *Henry Wadsworth Longfellow,* 1964; J. Chesley Mathews, ed., *Henry W. Longfellow Reconsidered: A Symposium,* 1970; *Papers Presented at the Longfellow Memorial Conference,* 1982; Edward Wagenknecht, *Henry Wadsworth Longfellow: His Poetry and Prose,* 1986.

TEXT

The Complete Poetical Works of Henry Wadsworth Longfellow, ed. Horace E. Scudder, 1893.

A Psalm of Life

WHAT THE HEART OF THE YOUNG MAN SAID TO THE PSALMIST

Tell me not, in mournful numbers,
　　Life is but an empty dream!—
For the soul is dead that slumbers,
　　And things are not what they seem.

Life is real! Life is earnest!　　　　　　　　　　　5
　　And the grave is not its goal;
Dust thou art, to dust returnest,
　　Was not spoken of the soul.

Not enjoyment, and not sorrow,
   Is our destined end or way;
But to act, that each to-morrow
   Find us farther than to-day.   10

Art is long, and Time is fleeting,[1]
   And our hearts, though stout and brave,
Still, like muffled drums, are beating   15
   Funeral marches to the grave.

In the world's broad field of battle,
   In the bivouac of Life,
Be not like dumb, driven cattle!
   Be a hero in the strife!   20

Trust no Future, howe'er pleasant!
   Let the dead Past bury its dead!
Act,—act in the living Present!
   Heart within, and God o'erhead!

Lives of great men all remind us   25
   We can make our lives sublime,
And, departing, leave behind us
   Footprints on the sands of time;

Footprints, that perhaps another,
   Sailing o'er life's solemn main,   30
A forlorn and shipwrecked brother,
   Seeing, shall take heart again.

Let us, then, be up and doing,
   With a heart for any fate;
Still achieving, still pursuing,   35
   Learn to labor and to wait.

1838   1838

Hymn to the Night

'Ασπασίη, τρίλλιστος[1]

I heard the trailing garments of the Night
   Sweep through her marble halls!
I saw her sable skirts all fringed with light
   From the celestial walls!

I felt her presence, by its spell of might,   5
   Stoop o'er me from above;
The calm, majestic presence of the Night,
   As of the one I love.

---

[1]From *Aphorisms*, I, 1, of the Greek physician Hippocrates (c. 460–400 B.C.); rendered by the Roman philosopher Seneca (8 B.C.–A.D. 65) in *De Brevitate vitae* I, 1, as *Vita brevis est, ars longa* and by the English poet Chaucer in *The Parlia-* *ment of Fowls* as "The lyfe so short, the craft so long to lerne."
[1]"Welcome three times prayed for" from Greek poet Homer's *Iliad*, VIII, 488.

I heard the sounds of sorrow and delight,
   The manifold, soft chimes,   10
That fill the haunted chambers of the Night,
   Like some old poet's rhymes.

From the cool cisterns of the midnight air
   My spirit drank repose;
The fountain of perpetual peace flows there,—   15
   From those deep cisterns flows.

O holy Night! from thee I learn to bear
   What man has borne before!
Thou layest thy finger on the lips of Care,
   And they complain no more.   20

Peace! Peace! Orestes[2]-like I breathe this prayer!
   Descend with broad-winged flight,
The welcome, the thrice-prayed for, the most fair,
   The best-beloved Night!

1839   *1839*

Mezzo Cammin[1]

Written at Boppard on the Rhine, August 25, 1842, just before leaving for home.

Half of my life is gone, and I have let
   The years slip from me and have not fulfilled
   The aspiration of my youth, to build
   Some tower of song with lofty parapet.
Not indolence, nor pleasure, nor the fret   5
   Of restless passions that would not be stilled,
   But sorrow, and a care that almost killed,[2]
   Kept me from what I may accomplish yet;
Though, half-way up the hill, I see the Past
   Lying beneath me with its sounds and sights,—   10
   A city in the twilight dim and vast,
With smoking roofs, soft bells, and gleaming lights,—
   And hear above me on the autumnal blast
   The cataract of Death far thundering from the heights.

1842   *1886*

---

[2]Orestes, tormented by the Furies, prays for and finds peace in the tragedy *The Eumenides* by the Greek poet Aeschylus (525–456 B.C.).
[1]From the first line of Dante's *Inferno: Nel mezzo del cammin di nostra vita*, "Midway in the journey of our life." Longfellow was 35, the mid-point of his life according to the Bible, Psalm 90:10: "The days of our years are threescore years and ten."
[2]His first wife died after a miscarrage in 1835.

The Arsenal at Springfield[1]

This is the Arsenal. From floor to ceiling,
   Like a huge organ, rise the burnished arms;
But from their silent pipes no anthem pealing
   Startles the villages with strange alarms.

Ah! what a sound will rise, how wild and dreary,   5
   When the death-angel touches those swift keys!
What loud lament and dismal Miserere[2]
   Will mingle with their awful symphonies!

I hear even now the infinite fierce chorus,
   The cries of agony, the endless groan,   10
Which, through the ages that have gone before us,
   In long reverberations reach our own.

On helm and harness rings the Saxon hammer,
   Through Cimbric forest roars the Norseman's song,[3]
And loud, amid the universal clamor,   15
   O'er distant deserts sounds the Tartar gong.

I hear the Florentine, who from his palace
   Wheels out his battle-bell with dreadful din,
And Aztec priests upon their teocallis[4]
   Beat the wild war-drums made of serpent's skin;   20

The tumult of each sacked and burning village;
   The shout that every prayer for mercy drowns;
The soldiers' revels in the midst of pillage;
   The wail of famine in beleaguered towns;

The bursting shell, the gateway wrenched asunder,   25
   The rattling musketry, the clashing blade;
And ever and anon, in tones of thunder
   The diapason[5] of the cannonade.

Is it, O man, with such discordant noises,
   With such accursed instruments as these,   30
Thou drownest Nature's sweet and kindly voices,
   And jarrest the celestial harmonies?

Were half the power, that fills the world with terror,
   Were half the wealth bestowed on camps and courts,
Given to redeem the human mind from error,   35
   There were no need of arsenals or forts:

The warrior's name would be a·name abhorred!
   And every nation, that should lift again

---

[1] In 1843, Longfellow visited the arsenal at Springfield, Massachusetts, with his newly wed second wife, who likened the gun barrels to the organ, remarked on the mournful music death would bring from them, and urged him to write a peace poem.
[2] From the Latin *Miserere mei Domine*, "Have mercy upon me, O Lord" (Psalm 50 in the Catholic Latin Vulgate Bible, 51 in the King James).
[3] The Cimbri, a Germanic tribe in Denmark.
[4] Temples on top of pyramids.
[5] Swelling sound (from organ stops).

Its hand against a brother, on its forehead
    Would wear forevermore the curse of Cain!   40

Down the dark future, through long generations,
    The echoing sounds grow fainter and then cease;
And like a bell, with solemn, sweet vibrations,
    I hear once more the voice of Christ say, "Peace!"

Peace! and no longer from its brazen portals   45
    The blast of War's great organ shakes the skies!
But beautiful as songs of the immortals,
    The holy melodies of love arise.

1844   1844

The Fire of Drift-Wood

Devereux Farm, Near Marblehead[1]

We sat within the farm-house old,
    Whose windows, looking o'er the bay,
Gave to the sea-breeze damp and cold,
    An easy entrance, night and day.

Not far away we saw the port,   5
    The strange, old-fashioned, silent town,
The lighthouse, the dismantled fort,
    The wooden houses, quaint and brown.

We sat and talked until the night,
    Descending, filled the little room;   10
Our faces faded from the sight,
    Our voices only broke the gloom.

We spake of many a vanished scene,
    Of what we once had thought and said,
Of what had been and might have been,   15
    And who was changed, and who was dead;

And all that fills the hearts of friends,
    When first they feel, with secret pain,
Their lives thenceforth have separate ends,
    And never can be one again;   20

The first slight swerving of the heart,
    That words are powerless to express,
And leave it still unsaid in part,
    Or say it in too great excess.

The very tones in which we spake   25
    Had something strange, I could but mark;

---

[1]A harbor town on the Atlantic in Massachusetts near
Salem.

The leaves of memory seemed to make
  A mournful rustling in the dark.

Oft died the words upon our lips,
  As suddenly, from out the fire   30
Built of the wreck of stranded ships,
  The flames would leap and then expire.

And, as their splendor flashed and failed,
  We thought of wrecks upon the main,
Of ships dismasted, that were hailed   35
  And sent no answer back again.

The windows, rattling in their frames,
  The ocean, roaring up the beach,
The gusty blast, the bickering flames,
  All mingled vaguely in our speech;   40

Until they made themselves a part
  Of fancies floating through the brain,
The long-lost ventures of the heart,
  That send no answers back again.

O flames that glowed! O hearts that yearned!   45
  They were indeed too much akin,
The drift-wood fire without that burned,
  The thoughts that burned and glowed within.

1848   1849

"All Things Must Have
An End; The World Itself"[1]
from Michael Angelo: A Fragment

All things must have an end; the world itself
Must have an end, as in a dream I saw it.
There came a great hand out of heaven, and touched
The earth, and stopped it in its course. The seas
Leaped, a vast cataract, into the abyss;   5
The forests and the fields slid off, and floated
Like wooded islands in the air. The dead
Were hurled forth from their sepulchres; the living
Were mingled with them, and themselves were dead,—
All being dead; and the fair, shining cities   10
Dropped out like jewels from a broken crown.
Naught but the core of the great globe remained,
A skeleton of stone. And over it
The wrack of matter drifted like a cloud,
And then recoiled upon itself, and fell   15

---

[1]These lines are spoken by the aged artist Michaelangelo as he stands in the ruins of the Colosseum in Rome, from part III, section IV ("In the Coliseum") of the dramatic poem *Michael Angelo: A Fragment*, found in Longfellow's desk after his death.

Back on the empty world, that with the weight
Reeled, staggered, righted, and then headlong plunged
Into the darkness, as a ship, when struck
By a great sea, throws off the waves at first
On either side, then settles and goes down   20
Into the dark abyss, with her dead crew.

1850   *1883*

The Jewish Cemetery at Newport[1]

How strange it seems! These Hebrews in their graves,
    Close by the street of this fair seaport town,
Silent beside the never-silent waves,
    At rest in all this moving up and down!

The trees are white with dust, that o'er their sleep   5
    Wave their broad curtains in the south-wind's breath,
While underneath these leafy tents they keep
    The long, mysterious Exodus[2] of Death.

And these sepulchral stones, so old and brown,
    That pave with level flags their burial-place,   10
Seem like the tablets of the Law, thrown down
    And broken by Moses at the mountain's base.[3]

The very names recorded here are strange,
    Of foreign accent, and of different climes;
Alvares and Rivera[4] interchange   15
    With Abraham and Jacob of old times.

"Blessed be God! for he created Death!"
    The mourners said, "and Death is rest and peace;"
Then added, in the certainty of faith,
    "And giveth Life that nevermore shall cease."   20

Closed are the portals of their Synagogue,
    No Psalms of David now the silence break,
No Rabbi reads the ancient Decalogue[5]
    In the grand dialect the Prophets spake.

Gone are the living, but the dead remain,   25
    And not neglected; for a hand unseen,
Scattering its bounty, like a summer rain,
    Still keeps their graves and their remembrance green.

How came they here? What burst of Christian hate,
    What persecution, merciless and blind,   30

---

[1]Rhode Island.
[2]Departure; the book of Exodus recounts the departure of the Israelites from Egypt under Moses.
[3]Angered that the Israelites were worshipping a golden calf, Moses broke the stone tablets inscribed with the Ten Commandments (Exodus 32:1–19).
[4]Portuguese and Spanish Jews settled in New England.
[5]The Ten Commandments.

Drove o'er the sea—that desert desolate—
   These Ishmaels and Hagars[6] of mankind?

They lived in narrow streets and lanes obscure,
   Ghetto and Judenstrass,[7] in mirk and mire;
Taught in the school of patience to endure   35
   The life of anguish and the death of fire.

All their lives long, with the unleavened bread
   And bitter herbs of exile and its fears,
The wasting famine of the heart they fed,
   And slaked its thirst with marah[8] of their tears.   40

Anathema maranatha![9] was the cry
   That rang from town to town, from street to street;
At every gate the accursed Mordecai[10]
   Was mocked and jeered, and spurned by Christian feet.

Pride and humiliation hand in hand   45
   Walked with them through the world where'er they went;
Trampled and beaten were they as the sand,
   And yet unshaken as the continent.

For in the background figures vague and vast
   Of patriarchs and of prophets rose sublime,   50
And all the great traditions of the Past
   They saw reflected in the coming time.

And thus forever with reverted look
   The mystic volume of the world they read,
Spelling it backward, like a Hebrew book,[11]   55
   Till life became a Legend of the Dead.

But ah! what once has been shall be no more!
   The groaning earth in travail and in pain
Brings forth its races, but does not restore,
   And the dead nations never rise again.   60

1852   1854

The Ropewalk[1]

In that building, long and low,
With its windows all a-row,
   Like the port-holes of a hulk,
Human spiders spin and spin,

---

[6]Hagar, concubine of Abraham, was cast out into the desert with Ishmael, her son by him (Genesis 16, 21).
[7]German: Jew's Street; ghetto: segregated quarter.
[8]Hebrew: bitter; a reference to the bitter waters of Marah in Exodus 15:23.
[9]"Let him be cursed; the Lord has come," a curse given to non-Christians (1 Corinthians 16:22).

[10]In the Book of Esther, Mordecai, in the face of Persian threats to destroy the Jews, remains faithful to his people and their welfare.
[11]Hebrew is printed to be read from right to left.
[1]A long, narrow mill factory for rope weaving or spinning.

Backward down their threads so thin   5
  Dropping, each a hempen bulk.

At the end, an open door;
Squares of sunshine on the floor
  Light the long and dusky lane;
And the whirring of a wheel,   10
Dull and drowsy, makes me feel
  All its spokes are in my brain.

As the spinners to the end
Downward go and reascend,
  Gleam the long threads in the sun;   15
While within this brain of mine
Cobwebs brighter and more fine
  By the busy wheel are spun.

Two fair maidens in a swing,
Like white doves upon the wing,   20
  First before my vision pass;
Laughing, as their gentle hands
Closely clasp the twisted strands,
  At their shadow on the grass.

Then a booth of mountebanks,[2]   25
With its smell of tan[3] and planks,
  And a girl poised high in air
On a cord, in spangled dress,
With a faded loveliness,
  And a weary look of care.   30

Then a homestead among farms,
And a woman with bare arms
  Drawing water from a well;
As the bucket mounts apace,
With it mounts her own fair face,   35
  As at some magician's spell.

Then an old man in a tower,
Ringing loud the noontide hour,
  While the rope coils round and round
Like a serpent at his feet,   40
And again, in swift retreat,
  Nearly lifts him from the ground.

Then within a prison-yard,
Faces fixed, and stern, and hard,
  Laughter and indecent mirth;   45
Ah! it is the gallows-tree!
Breath of Christian charity,
  Blow, and sweep it from the earth!

---

[2]Itinerant quacks who would mount shows on elevated
platforms in order to sell medicine to the audience.
[3]Tree bark.

Then a school-boy, with his kite
Gleaming in a sky of light,
   And an eager, upward look;   50
Steeds pursued through land and field;
Fowlers with their snares concealed;
   And an angler by a brook.

Ships rejoicing in the breeze,   55
Wrecks that float o'er unknown seas,
   Anchors dragged through faithless sand;
Sea-fog drifting overhead,
And, with lessening line and lead,
   Sailors feeling for the land.   60

All these scenes do I behold,
These, and many left untold,
   In that building long and low;
While the wheel goes round and round,
With a drowsy, dreamy sound,   65
   And the spinners backward go.

1854   *1854*

My Lost Youth

Often I think of the beautiful town[1]
   That is seated by the sea;
Often in thought go up and down
The pleasant streets of that dear old town,
   And my youth comes back to me.   5
     And a verse of a Lapland song
     Is haunting my memory still:
     "A boy's will is the wind's will,
And the thoughts of youth are long, long thoughts."[2]

I can see the shadowy lines of its trees,   10
   And catch, in sudden gleams,
The sheen of the far-surrounding seas,
And islands that were the Hesperides[3]
   Of all my boyish dreams.
     And the burden of that old song,   15
     It murmurs and whispers still:
     "A boy's will is the wind's will,
And the thoughts of youth are long, long thoughts."

I remember the black wharves and the slips,
   And the sea-tides tossing free;
And Spanish sailors with bearded lips,   20

---

[1]Portland, Maine, his birthplace.
[2]Longfellow's English version of two lines from a Lapland folksong that had been translated into German by Johann Gottfried von Herder (1744–1803) for his anthology of folk poetry, *Die Stimmen der Völker in Liedern* (1778–79).

[3]Islands of the Blest on the western seas, in Greek mythology.

And the beauty and mystery of the ships,
   And the magic of the sea.
      And the voice of that wayward song
      Is singing and saying still: 25
      "A boy's will is the wind's will,
And the thoughts of youth are long, long thoughts."

I remember the bulwarks by the shore,
   And the fort upon the hill;
The sunrise gun, with its hollow roar,   30
The drum-beat repeated o'er and o'er,
   And the bugle wild and shrill.
      And the music of that old song
      Throbs in my memory still:
      "A boy's will is the wind's will,   35
And the thoughts of youth are long, long thoughts."

I remember the sea-fight far away,
   How it thundered o'er the tide!
And the dead captains, as they lay
In their graves, o'erlooking the tranquil bay   40
   Where they in battle died.[4]
      And the sound of that mournful song
      Goes through me with a thrill:
      "A boy's will is the wind's will,
And the thoughts of youth are long, long thoughts."   45

I can see the breezy dome of groves,
   The shadows of Deering's Woods;[5]
And the friendships old and the early loves
Come back with a Sabbath sound, as of doves
   In quiet neighborhoods.   50
      And the verse of that sweet old song,
      It flutters and murmurs still:
      "A boy's will is the wind's will,
And the thoughts of youth are long, long thoughts."

I remember the gleams and glooms that dart   55
   Across the school-boy's brain;
The song and the silence in the heart,
That in part are prophecies, and in part
   Are longings wild and vain.
      And the voice of that fitful song   60
      Sings on, and is never still:
      "A boy's will is the wind's will,
And the thoughts of youth are long, long thoughts."

There are things of which I may not speak;
   There are dreams that cannot die;   65
There are thoughts that make the strong heart weak,
And bring a pallor into the cheek,

---

[4]In September 1813, the British brig *Boxer* was captured
off the Maine coast by the American *Enterprise* and brought
into Portland harbor; the two captains, killed in the battle,
were buried in the cemetery at Munjoy's Hill.
[5]Then on the edge of Portland.

And a mist before the eye.
    And the words of that fatal song
    Come over me like a chill: 70
    "A boy's will is the wind's will,
And the thoughts of youth are long, long thoughts."

Strange to me now are the forms I meet
    When I visit the dear old town;
But the native air is pure and sweet,   75
And the trees that o'ershadow each well-known street,
    As they balance up and down,
        Are singing the beautiful song,
        Are sighing and whispering still:
        "A boy's will is the wind's will,   80
And the thoughts of youth are long, long thoughts."

And Deering's Woods are fresh and fair,
    And with joy that is almost pain
My heart goes back to wander there,
And among the dreams of the days that were,   85
    I find my lost youth again.
        And the strange and beautiful song,
        The groves are repeating it still:
        "A boy's will is the wind's will,
And the thoughts of youth are long, long thoughts."   90

1855   1855

Snow-Flakes

Out of the bosom of the Air,
    Out of the cloud-folds of her garments shaken,
Over the woodlands brown and bare,
    Over the harvest-fields forsaken,
        Silent, and soft, and slow   5
        Descends the snow.

Even as our cloudy fancies take
    Suddenly shape in some divine expression,
Even as the troubled heart doth make
    In the white countenance confession,   10
        The troubled sky reveals
        The grief it feels.

This is the poem of the air,
    Slowly in silent syllables recorded;
This is the secret of despair,   15
    Long in its cloudy bosom hoarded,
        Now whispered and revealed
        To wood and field.

1859   1863

Divina Commedia[1]

I

Oft have I seen at some cathedral door
    A laborer, pausing in the dust and heat,
    Lay down his burden, and with reverent feet
Enter, and cross himself, and on the floor
Kneel to repeat his paternoster[2] o'er;   5
    Far off the noises of the world retreat;
    The loud vociferations of the street
Become an undistinguishable roar.
So, as I enter here from day to day,
    And leave my burden at this minster gate,[3]   10
    Kneeling in prayer, and not ashamed to pray,
The tumult of the time disconsolate[4]
    To inarticulate murmurs dies away,
    While the eternal ages watch and wait.

II

How strange the sculptures that adorn these towers!   15
    This crowd of statues, in whose folded sleeves
    Birds build their nests; while canopied with leaves
Parvis[5] and portal blood like trellised bowers,
And the vast minster seems a cross of flowers!
    But fiends and dragons on the gargoyled eaves   20
    Watch the dead Christ between the living thieves,[6]
And, underneath, the traitor Judas lowers![7]
Ah! from what agonies of heart and brain,
    What exultations trampling on despair,
    What tenderness, what tears, what hate of wrong,   25
What passionate outcry of a soul in pain,
    Uprose this poem of the earth and air,
    This mediæval miracle of song!

III

I enter, and I see thee in the gloom
    Of the long aisles, O poet saturnine![8]   30
    And strive to make my steps keep pace with thine.
The air is filled with some unknown perfume;
    The congregation of the dead make room
    For thee to pass; the votive tapers[9] shine;
Like rooks that haunt Ravenna's[10] groves of pine   35
    The hovering echoes fly from tomb to tomb.
From the confessionals I hear arise
    Rehearsals of forgotten tragedies,
    And lamentations from the crypts below;

---

[1] *The Divine Comedy*, by Dante Alighieri (1265–1321), the great epic poem of the Middle Ages. After his second wife died from burns when her dress caught on fire in 1861, Longfellow resumed his translation of the *Comedy*, begun in 1843. He wrote these sonnets to preface the three parts of the translation: I and II precede the *Inferno;* III and IV, the *Purgatorio;* and V and VI, the *Paradiso.*
[2] Latin: Our Father; The Lord's Prayer.
[3] Cathedral door.
[4] The time of the Civil War.

[5] Church porch.
[6] Christ died before the two thieves hanging on either side of him. John 19:33.
[7] Looks sullen. Judas Iscariot, who betrayed Christ, hanged himself when he found that Christ was condemned to death: Matthew 27:3–5.
[8] Dante.
[9] Candles lit by individuals for particular prayers, promises, or worship.
[10] City in Italy, where Dante is buried.

And then a voice celestial that begins   40
   With the pathetic words, "Although your sins
   As scarlet be," and ends with "as the snow."[11]

IV

With snow-white veil and garments as of flame,
   She stands before thee, who so long ago
   Filled thy young heart with passion and the woe   45
   From which thy song and all its splendors came;[12]
And while with stern rebuke she speaks thy name,
   The ice about thy heart melts as the snow
   On mountain heights, and in swift overflow
   Comes gushing from thy lips in sobs of shame.   50
Thou makest full confession; and a gleam,
   As of the dawn on some dark forest cast,
   Seems on thy lifted forehead to increase;
Lethe and Eunoë[13]—the remembered dream
   And the forgotten sorrow—bring at last   55
   That perfect pardon which is perfect peace.

V

I lift mine eyes, and all the windows blaze
   With forms of Saints and holy men who died,
   Here martyred and hereafter glorified;
   And the great Rose[14] upon its leaves displays   60
Christ's Triumph, and the angelic roundelays,
   With splendor upon splendor multiplied;
   And Beatrice again at Dante's side
No more rebukes, but smiles her words of praise.
And then the organ sounds, and unseen choirs   65
   Sing the old Latin hymns of peace and love
   And benedictions of the Holy Ghost;
And the melodious bells among the spires
   O'er all the house-tops and through heaven above
   Proclaim the elevation of the Host![15]   70

VI

O star of morning and of liberty![16]
   O bringer of the light, whose splendor shines
   Above the darkness of the Apennines,[17]
   Forerunner of the day that is to be!
The voices of the city and the sea,   75
   The voices of the mountains and the pines,
   Repeat thy song, till the familiar lines
   Are footpaths for the thought of Italy!
Thy fame is blown abroad from all the heights,
   Through all the nations, and a sound is heard,   80
   As of a mighty wind, and men devout,

---

[11]Isaiah 1:18: "Though your sins be as scarlet, they shall be as white as snow."

[12]At the top of the Mount of Purgatory, Dante meets the dead Beatrice, whom he has loved from afar since he first saw her when he was nine. She rebukes him for the wayward life he has led following her death, for which he must repent and be purified before he can enter paradise, where she will be his guide.

[13]Dante drinks from the waters of Lethe, the river of for-getfulness, and Eunoë, the river of the memory of the good.

[14]The cathedral's stained glass rose window and also Dante's vision in the *Paradiso* of the Trinity and the re-deemed in the shape of a great white rose.

[15]At the climax of the Mass, the bread is lifted high at the consecration, the change into the body of Christ.

[16]Dante.

[17]Mountains in Italy.

Strangers of Rome,[18] and the new proselytes,
   In their own language hear thy wondrous word,
   And many are amazed and many doubt.

1864–67   *1865–67*

Aftermath

When the summer fields are mown,
When the birds are fledged and flown,
   And the dry leaves strew the path;
With the falling of the snow,
With the cawing of the crow,   5
Once again the fields we mow
   And gather in the aftermath.

Not the sweet, new grass with flowers
Is this harvesting of ours;
   Not the upland clover bloom;   10
But the rowen[1] mixed with weeds,
Tangled tufts from marsh and meads,
Where the poppy drops its seeds
   In the silence and the gloom.

                                                   1873

Chaucer

An old man in a lodge within a park;
   The chamber walls depicted all around
   With portraitures of huntsman, hawk, and hound,
   And the hurt deer. He listeneth to the lark,
Whose song comes with the sunshine through the dark   5
   Of painted glass in leaden lattice bound;
   He listeneth and he laugheth at the sound,
   Then writeth in a book like any clerk.[1]
He is the poet of the dawn, who wrote
   The Canterbury Tales, and his old age   10
   Made beautiful with song; and as I read
I hear the crowing cock, I hear the note
   Of lark and linnet, and from every page
   Rise odors of ploughed field or flowery mead.

1873   *1875*

---

[18]Non-Roman Catholics.
[1]Second crop in a season.
[1]Scholar.

Milton

I pace the sounding sea-beach and behold
  How the voluminous billows roll and run,
  Upheaving and subsiding, while the sun
  Shines through their sheeted emerald far unrolled,
And the ninth wave,[1] slow gathering fold by fold   5
  All its loose-flowing garments into one,
  Plunges upon the shore, and floods the dun
  Pale reach of sands, and changes them to gold.
So in majestic cadence rise and fall
  The mighty undulations of thy song,   10
  O sightless bard, England's Mæonides![2]
And ever and anon, high over all
  Uplifted, a ninth wave superb and strong,
  Floods all the soul with its melodious seas.

1873   1875

Keats

The young Endymion sleeps Endymion's sleep;[1]
  The shepherd-boy whose tale was left half told!
  The solemn grove uplifts its shield of gold
  To the red rising moon, and loud and deep
The nightingale is singing from the steep;   5
  It is midsummer, but the air is cold;
  Can it be death? Alas, beside the fold
  A shepherd's pipe lies shattered near his sheep.
Lo! in the moonlight gleams a marble white,
  On which I read: "Here lieth one whose name   10
  Was writ in water."[2] And was this the meed[3]
Of his sweet singing? Rather let me write:
  "The smoking flax before it burst to flame
  Was quenched by death, and broken the bruised reed."[4]

1873   1875

Nature

As a fond mother, when the day is o'er,
  Leads by the hand her little child to bed,
  Half willing, half reluctant to be led,

---

[1]The mightiest of a series, according to legend.
[2]Homer; like Milton, he was blind and the author of great epic poems.
[1]Longfellow compares the English romantic poet John Keats (1795–1821) to Endymion, the shepherd in Greek myth, loved by the goddess of the moon and granted perpetual youth united with perpetual sleep. In Keats's poetic romance "Endymion" (1818), the youth searches for eternal beauty and ideal love amidst the beauties of nature and human sexuality.
[2]Keats composed the inscription on his tombstone: "Here lies one whose name was writ in water."
[3]Reward.
[4]In Isaiah 42:3, the Lord says of His servant, "A bruised reed shall he not break, and the smoking flax shall he not quench: he shall bring forth judgment unto truth."

And leave his broken playthings on the floor,
Still gazing at them through the open door,   5
    Nor wholly reassured and comforted
    By promises of others in their stead,
    Which, though more splendid, may not please him more;
So nature deals with us, and takes away
    Our playthings one by one, and by the hand   10
    Leads us to rest so gently, that we go
Scarce knowing if we wish to go or stay,
    Being too full of sleep to understand
    How far the unknown transcends the what we know.

                                                              1875

The Cross of Snow

In the long, sleepless watches of the night,
    A gentle face—the face of one long dead[1]—
    Looks at me from the wall, where round its head
    The night-lamp casts a halo of pale light.
Here in this room she died; and soul more white   5
    Never through martyrdom of fire was led
    To its repose; nor can in books be read
    The legend of a life more benedight[2]
There is a mountain in the distant West
    That, sun-defying, in its deep ravines   10
    Displays a cross of snow upon its side.
Such is the cross I wear upon by breast
    These eighteen years, through all the changing scenes
    And seasons, changeless since the day she died.

1879   *1886*

The Tide
Rises, the Tide Falls

The tide rises, the tide falls,
The twilight darkens, the curlew calls;
Along the sea-sands damp and brown
The traveller hastens toward the town,
    And the tide rises, the tide falls.   5

Darkness settles on roofs and walls,
But the sea, the sea in the darkness calls;
The little waves, with their soft, white hands,
Efface the footprints in the sands,
    And the tide rises, the tide falls.   10

---

[1]Longfellow's second wife, Frances Appleton, who died of
burns in 1861.
[2]Blessed.

The morning breaks; the steeds in their stalls
Stamp and neigh, as the hostler calls;
The day returns, but nevermore
Returns the traveller to the shore,
   And the tide rises, the tide falls.   15

1879   *1880*

Ultima Thule[1]

DEDICATION
TO G. W. G.

With favoring winds, o'er sunlit seas,
We sailed for the Hesperides,[2]
The land where golden apples grow;
But that, ah! that was long ago.

How far since then the ocean streams   5
Have swept us from that land of dreams,
That land of fiction and of truth,
The lost Atlantis[3] of our youth!

Whither, ah, whither? Are not these
The tempest-haunted Orcades,[4]   10
Where sea-gulls scream, and breakers roar,
And wreak and sea-weed line the shore?

Ultima Thule! Utmost Isle!
Here in thy harbors for a while
We lower our sails; a while we rest   15
From the unending, endless quest.

1880   *1880*

JOHN GREENLEAF WHITTIER
(1807–1892)

John Greenleaf Whittier was born in Haverhill, Massachusetts, in a house made of hand-hewn logs built by his great-great-grandfather. He grew up as a farm boy, in a Quaker household, pretty much like the "barefoot boy" he would write about later, with "Health that mocks the doctor's rules,/Knowledge never learned of schools." His rural experiences would furnish the substance of much of his poetry later. Although he was to celebrate country life,

[1]In 1880, Longfellow published his last volume of poetry, *Ultima Thule,* which means the farthest limits of travel or discovery, and dedicated the volume, in this poem, to a lifelong friend, George Washington Greene, with whom, as a young man, he had confided his aspirations in life.

[2]In Greek mythology, the distant western Islands of the Blest, where the golden apples of the sunset grow.
[3]Legendary island of bliss said to have sunk into the sea.
[4]Classical name for the bleak, treeless Orkney Islands off the north coast of Scotland.

he was not blind to the sometimes brutalizing labor of farming. And, indeed, he did everything he could to escape the lifetime drudgery of a marginal farmer. He wrote in a youthful poem:

> And must I always swing the flail,
> And help to fill the milking pail?
> I wish to go away to school;
> I do not wish to be a fool.

Going to school was an issue in the Whittier household, as it would normally be for an eldest son, especially one so precocious as Whittier. Around the age of fourteen, he came upon a volume of poems by Robert Burns, the Scottish poet who wrote about simple life in the country, even addressing one poem to a mouse encountered while plowing a field. Whittier immediately began to write poems in Scottish dialect—quite skilled ones, actually. His older sister sent one of his poems to the *Free Press,* edited by William Lloyd Garrison, who was to be famous later as the editor of the first abolitionist newspaper, the *Liberator.* Garrison was so impressed with the poem that he published it on June 8, 1826, and he visited the Whittier household to urge Whittier's father to send his nineteen-year-old son to school. The father replied, "Sir, poetry will not give him bread." Whittier for a time took up shoemaking. He saved his money and entered Haverhill Academy in 1827. But his money ran out after one term, and he turned to teaching in a country school. This teaching experience was an unhappy one and Whittier returned briefly to school.

Garrison lured Whittier into journalism in Boston, and he served as editor of a succession of papers, usually published in support of radical causes, throughout the rest of his life. But the illness of his father in 1829 (and his death a year later) necessitated his return to the farm, interrupting both his journalistic and literary careers. Whittier was happy to escape the farm again when, in 1830, he was asked to become editor of the *New England Weekly Review,* in Hartford, Connecticut, a position he held for nearly two years. Whittier threw himself into the job, writing reviews, essays, poems, and participating in the considerable literary life of Hartford. In 1831, he brought out his first book, *Legends of New England,* consisting of both prose and poetry. It is said that he later became so embarrassed about this book that he offered five dollars for any copy brought to him to be burned.

Illness and depression forced him once again to return to Haverhill. There he continued to write, gradually becoming known through his contributions to various newspapers. With the publication of *Justice and Expediency* (1833), he became intensely involved in the abolitionist movement, and was elected a delegate to the National Anti-Slavery Convention in Philadelphia that same year. And in 1835, he was elected to the Massachusetts legislature for one term.

The pattern of his life was set: politics, causes, poetry, and journalism. His Quaker faith was a determining factor in all that he did. It meant for him a spiritual life of plainness and simplicity, with clear-cut humanitarian positions—anti-slavery, anti-war, pro-worker, and pro-poor. His life was so full, he had no time for the domestic demands of marriage. In 1836, he sold the Haverhill farm and moved to nearby Amesbury, where he would live the rest of his life. Whittier settled down to publishing books regularly, year after year, including *Poems Written during the Progress of the Abolition Question in the United States* (1837), *Lays of My Home and Other Poems* (1843), *Voices of Freedom* (1846), *Songs of Labor and Other Poems* (1850), *Literary Recreations and Miscella-*

nies (1854), *Home Ballads, Poems and Lyrics* (1860). For the subject matter of his poetry, he alternated between his causes of conscience and the simple country life and legends remembered from his past.

In 1866, he published *Snow-Bound,* his masterpiece inspired by recollections of his boyhood on the farm, and celebrating the simple pleasures of warmth, love, and companionship in the isolation imposed by New England's severe winter snowstorms. This poem and others of similar appeal made Whittier immensely popular until his death in 1892. As time passed, however, and the causes that Whittier championed in his poetry diminished in importance because of political, economic, or social change, his popularity decreased. The bulk of his topical or didactic poetry remains unread today. But *Snow-Bound* and a number of lyrics and ballads such as "Skipper Ireson's Ride," "Telling the Bees," and "The Pressed Gentian" are likely to endure because of their imaginative embodiment of an earlier, simpler rural life in an idyllic America now passed into history.

ADDITIONAL READING

Whittier on Writers and Writings, ed. Edwin H. Cady and Harry Hayden Clark, 1950; *Memorabilia of John Greenleaf Whittier,* ed. John B. Pickard, 1968; *Letters of John Greenleaf Whittier,* 3 vols., ed. John B. Pickard, 1975.

Samuel T. Pickard, *Life and Letters of John Greenleaf Whittier,* 2 vols., 1894, 1907; Albert Mordell, *Quaker Militant: John Greenleaf Whittier,* 1933; Whitman Bennet, *Whittier: Bard of Freedom,* 1941; John A. Pollard, *John Greenleaf Whittier: Friend of Man,* 1949; George Arms, *The Fields Were Green,* 1953; John B. Pickard, *John Greenleaf Whittier: An Introduction and Interpretation,* 1961; Lewis Leary, *John Greenleaf Whittier,* 1961; Edward Wagenknecht, *John Greenleaf Whittier: A Portrait in Paradox,* 1967; Robert Penn Warren, *John Greenleaf Whittier's Poetry: An Appraisal and a Selection,* 1971; Donald C. Freeman, John B. Pickard, and Robert H. Woodwell, *Whittier and Whittierland: Portrait of a Poet and His World,* 1976; Jane K. Kribbs, ed., *Critical Essays on John Greenleaf Whittier,* 1980.

TEXT

The Writings of John Greenleaf Whittier, 7 vols., ed. Horace E. Scudder, 1894.

Proem[1]

I love the old melodious lays
Which softly melt the ages through,
   The songs of Spenser's golden days,
   Arcadian Sidney's silvery phrase,[2]
Sprinkling our noon of time with freshest morning dew.   5

   Yet, vainly in my quiet hours
To breathe their marvellous notes I try;
   I feel them, as the leaves and flowers
   In silence feel the dewy showers,
And drink with glad, still lips the blessing of the sky.   10

---

[1]Preface. This poem was written to introduce the first general collection of Whittier's poetry.
[2]English poets Edmond Spenser (*c.* 1552–1599), author of *The Faerie Queene,* and Sir Philip Sidney (1554–1586), whose prose romance *The Arcadia,* including songs and pastoral eclogues, derives its name from the idealized pastoral world of classical and Renaissance poetry.

The rigor of a frozen clime,
The harshness of an untaught ear,
   The jarring words of one whose rhyme
   Beat often Labor's hurried time,
Or Duty's rugged march through storm and strife, are here.   15

   Of mystic beauty, dreamy grace,
No rounded art the lack supplies;
   Unskilled the subtle lines to trace,
   Or softer shades of Nature's face,
I view her common forms with unanointed eyes.   20

   Nor mine the seer-like power to show
The secrets of the heart and mind;
   To drop the plummet-line below
   Our common world of joy and woe,
A more intense despair or brighter hope to find.   25

   Yet here at least an earnest sense
Of human right and weal[3] is shown;
   A hate of tyranny intense,
   And hearty in its vehemence,
As if my brother's pain and sorrow were my own.   30

   O Freedom! if to me belong
Nor mighty Milton's gift divine,
   Nor Marvell's wit and graceful song,[4]
   Still with a love as deep and strong
As theirs, I lay, like them, my best gifts on thy shrine!   35

1847   *1849*

Ichabod[1]

So fallen! so lost! the light withdrawn
   Which once he wore!
The glory from his gray hairs gone
   Forevermore!

Revile him not, the Tempter hath   5
   A snare for all;
And pitying tears, not scorn and wrath,
   Befit his fall!

Oh, dumb be passion's stormy rage,
   When he who might   10

---

[3]Happiness.
[4]English poets John Milton (1608–1674), author of the epic *Paradise Lost*, and Andrew Marvell (1621–1678).
[1]"This poem was the outcome of the surprise and grief and forecast of evil consequences which I felt on reading the seventh of March speech of Daniel Webster in support of the 'compromise,' and the Fugitive Slave Law. No partisan or personal enmity dictated it. On the contrary my admiration of the splendid personality and intellectual power of

the great Senator was never stronger than when I laid down his speech, and, in one of the saddest moments of my life, penned my protest" (Whittier's note). The law, which required the northern states to return runaway slaves, enflamed the abolitionists. This poem was published on May 2, 1850, in the abolitionist paper *National Era*, which Whittier helped edit. The title is from 1 Samuel 4:21: "And she named the child Ichabod, saying, The glory is departed from Israel."

Have lighted up and led his age,
    Falls back in night.

Scorn! would the angels laugh, to mark
    A bright soul driven,
Fiend-goaded, down the endless dark,   15
    From hope and heaven!

Let not the land once proud of him
    Insult him now,
Nor brand with deeper shame his dim,
    Dishonored brow.   20

But let its humbled sons, instead,
    From sea to lake,
A long lament, as for the dead,
    In sadness make.

Of all we loved and honored, naught   25
    Save power remains;
A fallen angel's pride of thought,
    Still strong in chains.

All else is gone; from those great eyes
    The soul has fled;   30
When faith is lost, when honor dies,
    The man is dead!

Then, pay the reverence of old days
    To his dead fame;
Walk backward, with averted gaze,   35
    And hide the shame![2]

                                    1850

The Fruit-Gift

Last night, just as the tints of autumn's sky
    Of sunset faded from our hills and streams,
    I sat, vague listening, lapped in twilight dreams,
To the leaf's rustle, and the cricket's cry.
Then, like that basket, flush with summer fruit,   5
Dropped by the angels at the Prophet's foot,[1]
Came, unannounced, a gift of clustered sweetness,
    Full-orbed, and glowing with the prisoned beams
Of summery suns, and rounded to completeness
By kisses of the south-wind and the dew.   10
Thrilled with a glad surprise, methought I knew
The pleasure of the homeward-turning Jew,

---

[2]As the sons of Noah did when he lay drunken and naked in his tent and they covered him (Genesis 9:20–24).

[1]In a vision the prophet Amos beholds a basket of summer fruit (Amos 8:1).

When Eshcol's clusters on his shoulders lay,
Dropping their sweetness on his desert way.[2]

I said, "This fruit beseems no world of sin.   15
    Its parent vine, rooted in Paradise,
    O'ercrept the wall, and never paid the price
    Of the great mischief,—an ambrosial tree,
Eden's exotic, somehow smuggled in,
    To keep the thorns and thistles company."[3]   20
Perchance our frail, sad mother plucked in haste
    A single vine-slip as she passed the gate,
Where the dread sword alternate paled and burned,[4]
    And the stern angel, pitying her fate,
Forgave the lovely trespasser, and turned   25
Aside his face of fire; and thus the waste
And fallen world hath yet its annual taste
Of primal good, to prove of sin the cost,
And show by one gleaned ear the mighty harvest lost.

1854

Skipper Ireson's Ride[1]

Of all the rides since the birth of time,
Told in story or sung in rhyme,—
On Apuleius's Golden Ass,[2]
Or one-eyed Calendar's horse of brass,[3]
Witch astride of a human back,   5
Islam's prophet on Al-Borák,[4]—
The strangest ride that ever was sped
Was Ireson's, out from Marblehead!
    Old Floyd Ireson, for his hard heart,
    Tarred and feathered and carried in a cart   10
    By the women of Marblehead!

Body of turkey, head of owl,
Wings a-droop like a rained-on fowl,
Feathered and ruffled in every part,
Skipper Ireson stood in the cart.   15
Scores of women, old and young,
Strong of muscle, and glib of tongue,
Pushed and pulled up the rocky lane,

---

[2]As the Israelites neared the Promised Land, Moses sent out spies, who returned from Eshcol, a valley in Judea, bearing on a staff a cluster of grapes, some pomegranates, and figs, and saying; the land "floweth with milk and honey; and this is the fruit of it" (Numbers 13:23–27).
[3]After Adam and Eve sinned ("the great mischief"), God cursed the serpent, each of them, and the land, saying to Adam: "cursed is the ground for thy sake; in sorrow shalt though eat of it all the days of thy life; Thorns also and thistles shall it bring forth to thee" (Genesis 3:1–18).
[4]Genesis 3:24: "So he drove out the man; and he placed at the east of the garden of Eden Cherubims, and a flaming sword which turned every way."
[1]In 1828 Whittier wrote a draft of this ballad based on a schoolmate's song, but he did not finish it for nearly thirty years. When it was published in the *Atlantic Monthly*, the editor James Russell Lowell suggested that Whittier phrase the quoted refrain in the dialect of Marblehead, the sea-coast town on Massachusetts Bay.
[2]*The Golden Ass* (or *Metamorphoses*), the satirical romance by Lucius Apuleius (second century A.D.) recounts the adventures of a young man transformed into an ass.
[3]In a tale from *The Arabian Nights*, a king kills the rider of the brass horse, later rides a winged horse who gouges out his eye, and then becomes a calender, a mendicant dervish, or friar.
[4]Muhammad, according to legend, was lifted to seventh heaven on a winged animal called Al-Borák.

Shouting and singing the shrill refrain:
  "Here's Flud Oirson, fur his horrd horrt,
  Torr'd an' futherr'd an' corr'd in a corrt
    By the women o' Morble'ead!"

Wrinkled scolds with hands on hips,
Girls in bloom of cheek and lips,
Wild-eyed, free-limbed, such as chase   25
Bacchus[5] round some antique vase,
Brief of skirt, with ankles bare,
Loose of kerchief and loose of hair,
With conch-shells blowing and fish-horns' twang,
Over and over the Mænads[6] sang: 30
  "Here's Flud Oirson, fur his horrd horrt,
  Torr'd an' futherr'd an' corr'd in a corrt
    By the women o' Morble'ead!"

Small pity for him!—He sailed away
From a leaking ship, in Chaleur Bay,[7]—   35
Sailed away from a sinking wreck,
With his own town's-people on her deck!
"Lay by! lay by!" they called to him.
Back he answered, "Sink or swim!
Brag of your catch of fish again!"   40
And off he sailed through the fog and rain!
  Old Floyd Ireson, for his hard heart,
  Tarred and feathered and carried in a cart
    By the women of Marblehead!

Fathoms deep in dark Chaleur   45
That wreck shall lie forevermore.
Mother and sister, wife and maid,
Looked from the rocks of Marblehead
Over the moaning and rainy sea,—
Looked for the coming that might not be!   50
What did the winds and the sea-birds say
Of the cruel captain who sailed away?—
  Old Floyd Ireson, for his hard heart,
  Tarred and feathered and carried in a cart
    By the women of Marblehead!   55

Through the street, on either side,
Up flew windows, doors swung wide;
Sharp-tongued spinsters, old wives gray,
Treble lent the fish-horn's bray.
Sea-worn grandsires, cripple-bound,   60
Hulks of old sailors run aground,
Shook head, and fist, and hat, and cane,
And cracked with curses the hoarse refrain:
  "Here's Flud Oirson, fur his horrd horrt,
  Torr'd an' futherr'd an' corr'd in a corrt   65
    By the women o' Morble'ead!"

---

[5] Roman god of wine.
[6] The female members of the cult of Bacchus, also called Bacchantes.
[7] In the Gulf of St. Lawrence.

Sweetly along the Salem road
Bloom of orchard and lilac showed.
Little the wicked skipper knew
Of the fields so green and the sky so blue.   70
Riding there in his sorry trim,
Like an Indian idol glum and grim,
Scarcely he seemed the sound to hear
Of voices shouting, far and near:
   "Here's Flud Oirson, fur his horrd horrt,   75
    Torr'd an' futherr'd an' corr'd in a corrt
     By the women o' Morble'ead!"

"Hear me, neighbors!" at last he cried,—
"What to me is this noisy ride?
What is the shame that clothes the skin   80
To the nameless horror that lives within?
Waking or sleeping, I see a wreck,
And hear a cry from a reeling deck!
Hate me and curse me,—I only dread
The hand of God and the face of the dead!"   85
   Said old Floyd Ireson, for his hard heart,
    Tarred and feathered and carried in a cart
     By the women of Marblehead!

Then the wife of the skipper lost at sea
Said, "God has touched him! why should we?"   90
Said an old wife mourning her only son,
"Cut the rogue's tether and let him run!"
So with soft relentings and rude excuse,
Half scorn, half pity, they cut him loose,
And gave him a cloak to hide him in,   95
And left him alone with his shame and sin.
   Poor Floyd Ireson, for his hard heart,
    Tarred and feathered and carried in a cart
     By the women of Marblehead!

1857

Telling the Bees[1]

Here is the place; right over the hill
  Runs the path I took;
You can see the gap in the old wall still,
  And the stepping-stones in the shallow brook.

There is the house, with the gate red-barred,   5
  And the poplars tall;
And the barn's brown length, and the cattle-yard,
  And the white horns tossing above the wall.

---

[1]"A remarkable custom, brought from the Old Country, formerly prevailed in the rural districts of New England. On the death of a member of the family, the bees were at once informed of the event, and their hives dressed in mourning. This ceremonial was supposed to be necessary to prevent the swarms from leaving their hives and seeking a new home" (Whittier's note).

There are the beehives ranged in the sun;
 And down by the brink   10
Of the brook are her poor flowers, weed-o'errun,
 Pansy and daffodil, rose and pink.

A year has gone, as the tortoise goes,
 Heavy and slow;
And the same rose blows, and the same sun glows, 15
 And the same brook sings of a year ago.

There's the same sweet clover-smell in the breeze;
 And the June sun warm
Tangles his wings of fire in the trees,
 Setting, as then, over Fernside farm.   20

I mind me how with a lover's care
 From my Sunday coat
I brushed off the burrs, and smoothed my hair,
 And cooled at the brookside my brow and throat.

Since we parted, a month had passed,—   25
 To love, a year;
Down through the beeches I looked at last
 On the little red gate and the well-sweep near.

I can see it all now,—the slantwise rain
 Of light through the leaves,   30
The sundown's blaze on her window-pane,
 The bloom of her roses under the eaves.

Just the same as a month before,—
 The house and the trees,
The barn's brown gable, the vine by the door,— 35
 Nothing changed but the hives of bees.

Before them, under the garden wall,
 Forward and back,
Went drearily singing the chore-girl small,
 Draping each hive with a shred of black.   40

Trembling, I listened: the summer sun
 Had the chill of snow;
For I knew she was telling the bees of one
 Gone on the journey we all must go!

Then I said to myself, "My Mary weeps   45
 For the dead to-day:
Haply her blind old grandsire sleeps
 The fret and the pain of his age away."

But her dog whined low; on the doorway sill,
 With his cane to his chin,   50
The old man sat; and the chore-girl still
 Sung to the bees stealing out and in.

And the song she was singing ever since
 In my ear sounds on:—

"Stay at home, pretty bees, fly not hence!   55
   Mistress Mary is dead and gone!"

1858

The Waiting[1]

I wait and watch: before my eyes
   Methinks the night grows thin and gray;
I wait and watch the eastern skies
To see the golden spears uprise
   Beneath the oriflamme[2] of day!   5

Like one whose limbs are bound in trance
   I hear the day-sounds swell and grow,
And see across the twilight glance,
Troop after troop, in swift advance,
   The shining ones with plumes of snow!   10

I know the errand of their feet,
   I know what mighty work is theirs;
I can but lift up hands unmeet[3]
The threshing-floors of God to beat,
   And speed them with unworthy prayers.   15

I will not dream in vain despair
   The steps of progress wait for me:
The puny leverage of a hair
The planet's impulse well may spare,
   A drop of dew the tided sea.   20

The loss if loss there be, is mine,
   And yet not mine if understood;
For one shall grasp and one resign,
One drink life's rue,[4] and one its wine,
   And God shall make the balance good.   25

Oh power to do! Oh baffled will!
   Oh prayer and action! ye are one.
Who may not strive, may yet fulfill
The harder task of standing still,
   And good but wished with God is done!   30

1862, 1864

---

[1]Published in 1864; the last three stanzas, with the title "Patience," appeared in 1862. As a pacifist Quaker, Whittier could not condone the Civil War; yet he knew that victory for the North would put an end to slavery, which he passionately desired; he had worked for that end for more than thirty years.

[2]Gold-flame banner.
[3]Unseemly.
[4]A plant yielding bitter oil once used in medicine; sorrow.

Snow-Bound

A Winter Idyl

TO THE MEMORY OF THE HOUSEHOLD IT DESCRIBES, THIS POEM IS DEDICATED BY THE AUTHOR

The inmates of the family at the Whittier homestead who are referred to in the poem were my father, mother, my brother and two sisters, and my uncle and aunt both unmarried. In addition, there was the district school-master who boarded with us. The "not unfeared, half-welcome guest" was Harriet Livermore, daughter of Judge Livermore, of New Hampshire, a young woman of fine natural ability, enthusiastic, eccentric, with slight control over her violent temper, which sometimes made her religious profession doubtful. She was equally ready to exhort in schoolhouse prayer-meetings and dance in a Washington ball-room, while her father was a member of Congress. She early embraced the doctrine of the Second Advent, and felt it her duty to proclaim the Lord's speedy coming. With this message she crossed the Atlantic and spent the greater part of a long life in travelling over Europe and Asia. She lived some time with Lady Hester Stanhope,[1] a woman as fantastic and mentally strained as herself, on the slope of Mt. Lebanon, but finally quarrelled with her in regard to two white horses with red marks on their backs which suggested the idea of saddles, on which her titled hostess expected to ride into Jerusalem with the Lord. A friend of mine found her, when quite an old woman, wandering in Syria with a tribe of Arabs, who with the Oriental notion that madness is inspiration, accepted her as their prophetess and leader. At the time referred to in *Snow-Bound* she was boarding at the Rocks Village about two miles from us.

In my boyhood, in our lonely farm-house, we had scanty sources of information; few books and only a small weekly newspaper. Our only annual was the Almanac. Under such circumstances story-telling was a necessary resource in the long winter evenings. My father when a young man had traversed the wilderness to Canada, and could tell us of his adventures with Indians and wild beasts, and of his sojourn in the French villages. My uncle was ready with his record of hunting and fishing and, it must be confessed, with stories which he at least half believed, of witchcraft and apparitions. My mother, who was born in the Indian-haunted region of Somersworth, New Hampshire, between Dover and Portsmouth, told us of the inroads of the savages, and the narrow escape of her ancestors. She described strange people who lived on the Piscataqua and Cocheco,[2] among whom was Bantam the sorcerer. I have in my possession the wizard's "conjuring book," which he solemnly opened when consulted. It is a copy of Cornelius Agrippa's *Magic* printed in 1651, dedicated to Dr. Robert Child, who, like Michael Scott, had learned

> "the art of glammorie
> In Padua beyond the sea,"

and who is famous in the annals of Massachusetts, where he was at one time a resident, as the first man who dared petition the General Court for liberty of con-

---

[1] Lady Hester Stanhope (1776–1839), English religious eccentric, settled in 1814 on Mt. Lebanon among the Druses as dictator and prophetess.
[2] New Hampshire rivers.

science.[3] The full title of the book is *Three Books of Occult Philosophy, by Henry Cornelius Agrippa, Knight, Doctor of both Laws, Counsellor to Cæsar's Sacred Majesty and Judge of the Prerogative Court.*

> "As the Spirits of Darkness be stronger in the dark,
> so Good Spirits, which be Angels of Light, are
> augmented not only by the Divine light of the Sun,
> but also by our common VVood Fire: and as the
> Celestial Fire drives away dark spirits, so also this
> our Fire of VVood doth the same."—COR. AGRIPPA,
> *Occult Philosophy*, Book I. ch. v.

> "Announced by all the trumpets of the sky,
> Arrives the snow, and, driving o'er the fields,
> Seems nowhere to alight: the whited air
> Hides hills and woods, the river and the heaven,
> And veils the farm-house at the garden's end.
> The sled and traveller stopped, the courier's feet
> Delayed, all friends shut out, the housemates sit
> Around the radiant fireplace, enclosed
> In a tumultuous privacy of storm."
>   EMERSON. *The Snow Storm.*

The sun that brief December day
Rose cheerless over hills of gray,
And, darkly circled, gave at noon
A sadder light than waning moon.
Slow tracing down the thickening sky   5
Its mute and ominous prophecy,
A portent seeming less than threat,
It sank from sight before it set.
A chill no coat, however stout,
Of homespun stuff could quite shut out,   10
A hard, dull bitterness of cold,
That checked, mid-vein, the circling race
Of life-blood in the sharpened face,
The coming of the snow-storm told.
The wind blew east;[4] we heard the roar   15
Of Ocean on his wintry shore,
And felt the strong pulse throbbing there
Beat with low rhythm our inland air.
Meanwhile we did our nightly chores,—
Brought in the wood from out of doors,   20
Littered the stalls, and from the mows
Raked down the herd's-grass for the cows:
Heard the horse whinnying for his corn;
And, sharply clashing horn on horn,

---

[3]Robert Child (1613–1654) placed his name first on a Remonstrance (1646) petitioning the General Court of the Massachusetts Bay Colony to extend suffrage and toleration to non-Puritans. Because he studied at Padua, thought of as a center of magic, Whittier likens him to Michael Scott (1175?–1234?), Scottish scholar, whose fame was such that legend transformed him from scientist to magician. Scott appears so in much European literature, including *The Lay of the Last Minstrel* (1805) by Scottish poet Sir Walter Scott

(1771–1832). Whittier adapts two lines (I.11) from that poem here, changing "the art that none may name" to "the art of glammorie," or magic. The magic or "conjuring" book that Bantram the "wizard" consulted is a later English edition of that first published in 1531 by Heinrich Cornelius Agrippa von Nettesheim (1486–1535), German physician, considered to be a magician.
[4]From the East.

Impatient down the stanchion rows   25
The cattle shake their walnut bows;[5]
While, peering from his early perch
Upon the scaffold's[6] pole of birch,
The cock his crested helmet bent
And down his querulous challenge sent.   30

Unwarmed by any sunset light
The gray day darkened into night,
A night made hoary with the swarm,
And whirl-dance of the blinding storm,
As zigzag, wavering to and fro,   35
Crossed and recrossed the wingèd snow:
And ere the early bedtime came
The white drift piled the window-frame.
And through the glass the clothes-line posts
Looked in like tall and sheeted ghosts.   40

So all night long the storm roared on:
The morning broke without a sun;
In tiny spherule traced with lines
Of Nature's geometric signs,
In starry flake, and pellicle,[7]   45
All day the hoary meteor fell;
And, when the second morning shone,
We looked upon a world unknown,
On nothing we could call our own.
Around the glistening wonder bent   50
The blue walls of the firmament,
No cloud above, no earth below,—
A universe of sky and snow!
The old familiar sights of ours
Took marvellous shapes; strange domes and towers   55
Rose up where sty or corn-crib stood,
Or garden-wall, or belt of wood;
A smooth white mound the brush-pile showed,
A fenceless drift what once was road;
The bridle-post an old man sat   60
With loose-flung coat and high cocked hat;
The well-curb had a Chinese roof;
And even the long sweep,[8] high aloof,
In its slant splendor, seemed to tell
Of Pisa's leaning miracle.[9]   65

A prompt, decisive man, no breath
Our father wasted: "Boys, a path!"
Well pleased, (for when did farmer boy
Count such a summons less than joy?)
Our buskins[10] on our feet we drew;   70
With mittened hands, and caps drawn low,
To guard our necks and ears from snow,
We cut the solid whiteness through.

---

[5]Walnut bows, or yokes, were fastened around the cows'
necks and affixed to upright posts, or stanchions.
[6]Grain loft.
[7]Thin crust.

[8]Pole attached to a pivot, with a bucket at one end to raise
water.
[9]The leaning tower of Pisa, Italy.
[10]Boots.

And, where the drift was deepest, made
A tunnel walled and overlaid   75
With dazzling crystal: we had read
Of rare Aladdin's wondrous cave,[11]
And to our own his name we gave,
With many a wish the luck were ours
To test his lamp's supernal powers.   80
We reached the barn with merry din,
And roused the prisoned brutes within.
The old horse thrust his long head out,
And grave with wonder gazed about;
The cock his lusty greeting said,   85
And forth his speckled harem led;
The oxen lashed their tails, and hooked,
And mild reproach of hunger looked;
The hornëd patriarch of the sheep,
Like Egypt's Amun[12] roused from sleep,   90
Shook his sage head with gesture mute,
And emphasized with stamp of foot.

All day the gusty north-wind bore
The loosening drift its breath before;
Low circling round its southern zone,   95
The sun through dazzling snow-mist shone.
No church-bell lent its Christian tone
To the savage air, no social smoke
Curled over woods of snow-hung oak.
A solitude made more intense   100
By dreary-voicëd elements,
The shrieking of the mindless wind,
The moaning tree-boughs swaying blind,
And on the glass the unmeaning beat
Of ghostly finger-tips of sleet.   105
Beyond the circle of our hearth
No welcome sound of toil or mirth
Unbound the spell, and testified
Of human life and thought outside.
We minded that the sharpest ear   110
The buried brooklet could not hear,
The music of whose liquid lip
Had been to us companionship,
And, in our lonely life, had grown
To have an almost human tone.   115

As night drew on, and, from the crest
Of wooded knolls that ridged the west,
The sun, a snow-blown traveller, sank
From sight beneath the smothering bank,
We piled, with care, our nightly stack   120
Of wood against the chimney-back,—
The oaken log, green, huge, and thick,
And on its top the stout back-stick;

---

[11]The cave where Aladdin, a character in *The Arabian
Nights*, found the magic lamp, source of wealth and good
fortune.
[12]Egyptian god with the head of a ram.

The knotty forestick laid apart,
And filled between with curious art
The ragged brush; then, hovering near,   125
We watched the first red blaze appear,
Heard the sharp crackle, caught the gleam
On whitewashed wall and sagging beam,
Until the old, rude-furnished room   130
Burst, flower-like, into rosy bloom;
While radiant with a mimic flame
Outside the sparkling drift became,
And through the bare-boughed lilac-tree
Our own warm hearth seemed blazing free: 135
The crane and pendent trammels showed,
The Turks' heads on the andirons glowed;[13]
While childish fancy, prompt to tell
The meaning of the miracle,
Whispered the old rhyme: "*Under the tree,*   140
When fire outdoors burns merrily,
There the witches are making tea."

The moon above the eastern wood
Shone at its full; the hill-range stood
Transfigured in the silver flood,   145
Its blown snows flashing cold and keen,
Dead white, save where some sharp ravine
Took shadow, or the sombre green
Of hemlocks turned to pitchy black
Against the whiteness at their back.   150
For such a world and such a night
Most fitting that unwarming light,
Which only seemed where'er it fell
To make the coldness visible.

Shut in from all the world without,   155
We sat the clean-winged hearth about,
Content to let the north-wind roar
In baffled rage at pane and door,
While the red logs before us beat
The frost-line back with tropic heat;   160
And ever, when a louder blast
Shook beam and rafter as it passed,
The merrier up its roaring draught
The great throat of the chimney laughed;
The house-dog on his paws outspread   165
Laid to the fire his drowsy head,
The cat's dark silhouette on the wall
A couchant[14] tiger's seemed to fall;
And, for the winter fireside meet,
Between the andirons' straddling feet,   170
The mug of cider simmered slow,

---

[13]In the fireplace, the cooking pot was hung from the crane, or swinging arm, by trammels, or links and hooks. The andirons, or metal supports for the logs, had ornamented cone-shaped tops like Turkish fezzes.
[14]Lying down with the head raised (a term from heraldry).

The apples sputtered in a row,
And, close at hand, the basket stood
With nuts from brown October's wood.

What matter how the night behaved?   175
What matter how the north-wind raved?
Blow high, blow low, not all its snow
Could quench our hearth-fire's ruddy glow.
O Time and Change!—with hair as gray
As was my sire's that winter day,   180
How strange it seems, with so much gone
Of life and love, to still live on!
Ah, brother![15] only I and thou
Are left of all that circle now,—
The dear home faces whereupon   185
That fitful firelight paled and shone.
Henceforward, listen as we will,
The voices of that hearth are still;
Look where we may, the wide earth o'er
Those lighted faces smile no more.   190
We tread the paths their feet have worn,
    We sit beneath their orchard trees,
    We hear, like them, the hum of bees
And rustle of the bladed corn;
We turn the pages that they read,   195
    Their written words we linger o'er,
But in the sun they cast no shade,
No voice is heard, no sign is made,
    No step is on the conscious floor!
Yet Love will dream, and Faith will trust,   200
(Since He who knows our need is just,)
That somehow, somewhere, meet we must.
Alas for him who never sees
The stars shine through his cypress-trees!
Who, hopeless, lays his dead away,   205
Nor looks to see the breaking day
Across the mournful marbles[16] play!
Who hath not learned, in hours of faith,
    The truth to flesh and sense unknown,
That Life is ever lord of Death,   210
    And Love can never lose its own!

We sped the time with stories old,
Wrought puzzles out, and riddles told,
Or stammered from our school-book lore
"The Chief of Gambia's golden shore."[17]   215
How often since, when all the land
Was clay in Slavery's shaping hand,
As if a far-blown trumpet stirred
The languorous sin-sick air, I heard:
"*Does not the voice of reason cry,*   220
    Claim the first right which Nature gave,

---

[15]Matthew Franklin Whittier (1812–1883).
[16]Tombstones.
[17]Quotations in this stanza are from "The African Chief,"

an antislavery poem by Sarah Wentworth Morton (1759–1846).

From the red scourge of bondage fly,
    Nor deign to live a burdened slave!"
Our father rode again his ride[18]
On Memphremagog's[19] wooded side;   225
Sat down again to moose and samp[20]
In trapper's hut and Indian camp;
Lived o'er the old idyllic ease
Beneath St. François'[21] hemlock-trees;
Again for him the moonlight shone   230
On Norman cap and bodiced zone;[22]
Again he heard the violin play
Which led the village dance away,
And mingled in its merry whirl
The grandam and the laughing girl.   235
Or, nearer home, our steps he led
Where Salisbury's[23] level marshes spread
    Mile-wide as flies the laden bee;
Where merry mowers, hale and strong,
Swept, scythe on scythe, their swaths along   240
    The low green prairies of the sea.
We shared the fishing off Boar's Head,[24]
    And round the rocky Isles of Shoals[25]
    The hake-broil[26] on the drift-wood coals;
The chowder on the sand-beach made,   245
Dipped by the hungry, steaming hot,
With spoons of clam-shell from the pot.
We heard the tales of witchcraft old,
And dream and sign and marvel told
To sleepy listeners as they lay   250
Stretched idly on the salted hay,
Adrift along the winding shores,
When favoring breezes deigned to blow
The square sail of the gundelow[27]
And idle lay the useless oars.   255

Our mother,[28] while she turned her wheel
Or run the new-knit stocking-heel,
Told how the Indian hordes came down
At midnight on Cocheco town,[29]
And how her own great-uncle bore   260
His cruel scalp-mark to fourscore.
Recalling, in her fitting phrase,
    So rich and picturesque and free,
    (The common unrhymed poetry
Of simple life and country ways,)   265
The story of her early days,—
She made us welcome to her home;
Old hearths grew wide to give us room;

---

[18]John Whittier (1760–1830) recalls a trip made in his youth.
[19]Lake between Canada and Vermont.
[20]Cornmeal mush.
[21]Quebec village.
[22]The women in the French-Canadian province dressed in the costume of Normandy in France.
[23]Town near the Whittier farm in northeastern Massachusetts.

[24]Promontory on the New Hampshire coast.
[25]Near Boar's Head.
[26]A fish.
[27]Flat-bottomed boat.
[28]Abigail Hussey Whittier (1781–1857).
[29]Near Dover, New Hampshire, on the Cocheco River.

We stole with her a frightened look
At the gray wizard's conjuring-book,[30]   270
The fame whereof went far and wide
Through all the simple country side;
We heard the hawks at twilight play,
The boat-horn on Piscataqua,[31]
The loon's weird laughter far away;   275
We fished her little trout-brook, knew
What flowers in wood and meadow grew,
What sunny hillsides autumn-brown
She climbed to shake the ripe nuts down,
Saw where in sheltered cove and bay   280
The ducks' black squadron anchored lay,
And heard the wild-geese calling loud
Beneath the gray November cloud.

Then, haply, with a look more grave,
And soberer tone, some tale she gave   285
From painful Sewel's ancient tome,[32]
Beloved in every Quaker home,
Of faith fire-winged by martyrdom,
Or Chalkley's Journal,[33] old and quaint,—
Gentlest of skippers, rare sea-saint!—   290
Who, when the dreary calms prevailed,
And water-butt and bread-cask failed,
And cruel, hungry eyes pursued
His portly presence mad for food,
With dark hints muttered under breath   295
Of casting lots for life or death,
Offered, if Heaven withheld supplies,
To be himself the sacrifice.
Then, suddenly, as if to save
The good man from his living grave,   300
A ripple on the water grew,
A school of porpoise flashed in view.
"Take, eat,"[34] he said, "and be content;
These fishes in my stead are sent
By Him who gave the tangled ram   305
To spare the child of Abraham."[35]

Our uncle,[36] innocent of books,
Was rich in lore of fields and brooks,
The ancient teachers never dumb
Of Nature's unhoused lyceum.[37]   310
In moons and tides and weather wise,
He read the clouds as prophecies,
And foul or fair could well divine,
By many an occult hint and sign,
Holding the cunning-warded[38] keys   315

---

[30]Agrippa's *Occult Philosophy*, described in the Introduction; a quotation from it precedes the poem.
[31]Foghorn on the Piscataqua River.
[32]The *History of the Christian People Called Quakers* (1717 in Dutch; 1725 in English) by Willem Sewel (1650–1725). Whittier read the American edition of 1823.
[33]Thomas Chalkley (1675–1741), Quaker sea captain and preacher, published his *Journal* in 1747.

[34]At the Last Supper, Jesus said, "Take, eat; this is my body" (Matthew 26:26).
[35]Seeing that Abraham was willing to sacrifice his own son Isaac in obedience, God sent a ram to be offered instead (Genesis 22:1–13).
[36]Moses Whittier (d. 1824).
[37]Lecture hall.
[38]Skillfully notched.

To all the woodcraft mysteries;
Himself to Nature's heart so near
That all her voices in his ear
Of beast or bird had meanings clear,
Like Apollonius[39] of old,   320
Who knew the tales the sparrows told,
Or Hermes[40] who interpreted
What the sage cranes of Nilus[41] said;
Content to live where life began;
A simple, guileless, childlike man,   325
Strong only on his native grounds,
The little world of sights and sounds
Whose girdle was the parish bounds,
Whereof his fondly partial pride
The common features magnified,   330
As Surrey hills to mountains grew
In White of Selborne's[42] loving view,—
He told how teal and loon he shot,
And how the eagle's eggs he got,
The feats on pond and river done,   335
The prodigies of rod and gun;
Till, warming with the tales he told,
Forgotten was the outside cold,
The bitter wind unheeded blew,
From ripening corn the pigeons flew,   340
The partridge drummed i' the wood, the mink
Went fishing down the river-brink.
In fields with bean or clover gay,
The woodchuck, like a hermit gray,
    Peered from the doorway of his cell;   345
The muskrat plied the mason's trade,
And tier by tier his mud-walls laid;
And from the shagbark overhead
    The grizzled squirrel dropped his shell.

Next, the dear aunt,[43] whose smile of cheer   350
And voice in dreams I see and hear,—
The sweetest woman ever Fate
Perverse denied a household mate,
Who, lonely, homeless, not the less
Found peace in love's unselfishness,   355
And welcome wheresoe'er she went,
A calm and gracious element,
Whose presence seemed the sweet income
And womanly atmosphere of home,—
Called up her girlhood memories,   360
The huskings and the apple-bees,
The sleigh-rides and the summer sails,
Weaving through all the poor details
And homespun warp of circumstance
A golden woof-thread of romance.   365

---

[39]Greek mystic of Tyana (first century A.D.), said to possess miraculous powers.
[40]Hermes Trismegistus, Egyptian god said to have written third-century books on medicine, ritual, and magic.
[41]Nile River.

[42]English naturalist Gilbert White (1720–1793) lived in the village of Selborne (near the county of Surry, England), which he describes in *The Natural History and Antiquities of Selborne* (1789).
[43]Mercy Evans Hussey (d. 1846).

For well she kept her genial mood
And simple faith of maidenhood;
Before her still a cloud-land lay,
The mirage loomed across her way;
The morning dew, that dries so soon   370
With others, glistened at her noon;
Through years of toil and soil and care,
From glossy tress to thin gray hair,
All unprofaned she held apart
The virgin fancies of the heart.   375
Be shame to him of woman born
Who hath for such but thought of scorn.

There, too, our elder sister[44] plied
Her evening task the stand beside;
A full, rich nature, free to trust,   380
Truthful and almost sternly just,
Impulsive, earnest, prompt to act,
And make her generous thought a fact,
Keeping with many a light disguise
The secret of self-sacrifice.   385
O heart sore-tried! thou hast the best
That Heaven itself could give thee,—rest,
Rest from all bitter thoughts and things!
    How many a poor one's blessing went
    With thee beneath the low green tent   390
Whose curtain never outward swings!

As one who held herself a part
Of all she saw, and let her heart
    Against the household bosom lean,
Upon the motley-braided mat   395
Our youngest and our dearest[45] sat,
Lifting her large, sweet, asking eyes,
    Now bathed in the unfading green
And holy peace of Paradise.
Oh, looking from some heavenly hill,   400
    Or from the shade of saintly palms,
    Or silver reach of river calms,
Do those large eyes behold me still?
With me one little year ago:—
The chill weight of the winter snow   405
    For months upon her grave has lain;
And now, when summer south-winds blow
    And brier and harebell bloom again,
I tread the pleasant paths we trod,
I see the violet-sprinkled sod   410
Whereon she leaned, too frail and weak
The hillside flowers she loved to seek,
Yet following me where'er I went
With dark eyes full of love's content.
The birds are glad; the brier-rose fills   415
The air with sweetness; all the hills

---

[44]Mary Whittier Caldwell (1806–1861).
[45]Elizabeth Hussey Whittier (1815–1864).

Stretch green to June's unclouded sky;
But still I wait with ear and eye
For something gone which should be nigh,
A loss in all familiar things,   420
In flower that blooms, and bird that sings.
And yet, dear heart! remembering thee,
    Am I not richer than of old?
Safe in thy immortality,
    What change can reach the wealth I hold?   425
    What chance can mar the pearl and gold
Thy love hath left in trust with me?
And while in life's late afternoon,
    Where cool and long the shadows grow,
I walk to meet the night that soon   430
    Shall shape and shadow overflow,
I cannot feel that thou art far,
Since near at need the angels are;
And when the sunset gates unbar,
    Shall I not see thee waiting stand,   435
And, white against the evening star,
    The welcome of thy beckoning hand?

Brisk wielder of the birch and rule,
The master of the district school[46]
Held at the fire his favored place,   440
Its warm glow lit a laughing face
Fresh-hued and fair, where scarce appeared
The uncertain prophecy of beard.
He teased the mitten-blinded cat,
Played cross-pins on my uncle's hat,   445
Sang songs, and told us what befalls
In classic Dartmouth's college halls.
Born the wild Northern hills among,
From whence his yeoman father wrung
By patient toil subsistence scant,   450
Not competence and yet not want,
He early gained the power to pay
His cheerful, self-reliant way;
Could doff at ease his scholar's gown
To peddle wares from town to town;   455
Or through the long vacation's reach
In lonely lowland districts teach,
Where all the droll experience found
At stranger hearths in boarding round,
The moonlit skater's keen delight,   460
The sleigh-drive through the frosty night,
The rustic party, with its rough
Accompaniment of blind-man's-buff,
And whirling plate, and forfeits paid,
His winter task a pastime made.   465
Happy the snow-locked homes wherein
He tuned his merry violin,
Or played the athlete in the barn,
Or held the good dame's winding-yarn,

---

[46]George Haskell (1799–1876).

Or mirth-provoking versions told   470
Of classic legends rare and old,
Wherein the scenes of Greece and Rome
Had all the commonplace of home,
And little seemed at best the odds
'Twixt Yankee pedlers and old gods;   475
Where Pindus-born Arachthus[47] took
The guise of any grist-mill brook,
And dread Olympus[48] at his will
Became a huckleberry hill.

A careless boy that night he seemed;   480
  But at his desk he had the look
And air of one who wisely schemed,
  And hostage from the future took
  In trainëd thought and lore of book.
Large-brained, clear-eyed, of such as he   485
Shall Freedom's young apostles be,
Who, following in War's bloody trail,
Shall every lingering wrong assail;
All chains from limb and spirit strike,
Uplift the black and white alike;   490
Scatter before their swift advance
The darkness and the ignorance,
The pride, the lust, the squalid sloth,
Which nurtured Treason's monstrous growth,
Made murder pastime, and the hell   495
Of prison-torture possible;
The cruel lie of caste refute,
Old forms remould, and substitute
For Slavery's lash the freeman's will,
For blind routine, wise-handed skill;   500
A school-house plant on every hill,
Stretching in radiate nerve-lines thence
The quick wires of intelligence;[49]
Till North and South together brought
Shall own the same electric thought,   505
In peace a common flag salute,
And, side by side in labor's free
And unresentful rivalry,
Harvest the fields wherein they fought.

Another guest[50] that winter night   510
Flashed back from lustrous eyes the light.
Unmarked by time, and yet not young,
The honeyed music of her tongue
And words of meekness scarcely told
A nature passionate and bold,   515
Strong, self-concentred, spurning guide,
Its milder features dwarfed beside
Her unbent will's majestic pride.
She sat among us, at the best,
A not unfeared, half-welcome guest,   520

---

[47]Greek river whose source is in the Pindus Mountains.
[48]Mount Olympus, home of the gods in Greek mythology.
[49]The telegraph.

[50]Harriet Livermore (1788–1867), described in the Introduction.

Rebuking with her cultured phrase
Our homeliness of words and ways.
A certain pard-like,[51] treacherous grace
  Swayed the lithe limbs and dropped the lash,
  Lent the white teeth their dazzling flash;   525
  And under low brows, black with night,
  Rayed out at times a dangerous light;
The sharp heat-lightnings of her face
Presaging ill to him whom Fate
Condemned to share her love or hate.   530
A woman tropical, intense
In thought and act, in soul and sense,
She blended in a like degree
The vixen and the devotee,
Revealing with each freak or feint   535
  The temper of Petruchio's Kate,[52]
The raptures of Siena's saint.[53]
Her tapering hand and rounded wrist
Had facile power to form a fist;
The warm, dark languish of her eyes   540
Was never safe from wrath's surprise.
Brows saintly calm and lips devout
Knew every change of scowl and pout;
And the sweet voice had notes more high
And shrill for social battle-cry.   545

Since then what old cathedral town
Has missed her pilgrim staff and gown,
What convent-gate has held its lock
Against the challenge of her knock!
Through Smyrna's plague-hushed thoroughfares,   550
Up sea-set Malta's rocky stairs,
Gray olive slopes of hills that hem
  Thy tombs and shrines, Jerusalem,
Or startling on her desert throne
The crazy Queen of Lebanon[54]   555
With claims fantastic as her own,
Her tireless feet have held their way;
And still, unrestful, bowed, and gray,
She watches under Eastern skies,
  With hope each day renewed and fresh,   560
  The Lord's quick coming in the flesh,
Whereof she dreams and prophesies!

Where'er her troubled path may be,
  The Lord's sweet pity with her go!
The outward wayward life we see,   565
  The hidden springs we may not know.
Nor is it given us to discern
  What threads the fatal sisters spun,[55]
  Through what ancestral years has run
The sorrow with the woman born,   570

---

[51]Leopard-like.
[52]Ill-tempered heroine subdued by Petruchio in Shakespeare's *The Taming of the Shrew.*
[53]St. Catherine (1347–1380) experienced ecstatic visions.

[54]Lady Hester Stanhope (see footnote 1).
[55]The three Fates of Greek mythology who spin, measure, and cut the thread of human destiny.

What forged her cruel chain of moods,
What set her feet in solitudes,
   And held the love within her mute,
What mingled madness in the blood,
   A life-long discord and annoy,   575
   Water of tears with oil of joy,
And hid within the folded bud
   Perversities of flower and fruit.
It is not ours to separate
   The tangled skein of will and fate,   580
To show what metes and bounds should stand
Upon the soul's debatable land,
And between choice and Providence
Divide the circle of events;
But He who knows our frame is just,   585
Merciful and compassionate,
And full of sweet assurances
And hope for all the language is,
That He remembereth we are dust![56]

At last the great logs, crumbling low,   590
Sent out a dull and duller glow,
The bull's-eye watch that hung in view,
Ticking its weary circuit through,
Pointed with mutely warning sign
Its black hand to the hour of nine.   595
That sign the pleasant circle broke:
My uncle ceased his pipe to smoke,
Knocked from its bowl the refuse gray,
And laid it tenderly away,
Then roused himself to safely cover   600
The dull red brands with ashes over.
And while, with care, our mother laid
The work aside, her steps she stayed
One moment, seeking to express
Her grateful sense of happiness   605
For food and shelter, warmth and health,
And love's contentment more than wealth,
With simple wishes (not the weak,
Vain prayers which no fulfilment seek,
But such as warm the generous heart,   610
O'er-prompt to do with Heaven its part)
That none might lack, that bitter night,
For bread and clothing, warmth and light.

Within our beds awhile we heard
The wind that round the gables roared,   615
With now and then a ruder shock,
Which made our very bedsteads rock.
We heard the loosened clapboards tost,
The board-nails snapping in the frost;
And on us, through the unplastered wall,   620
Felt the light sifted snow-flakes fall.

---

[56] Psalm 103:14: "'For he knoweth our frame; he remembereth that we are dust."

But sleep stole on, as sleep will do
When hearts are light and life is new;
Faint and more faint the murmurs grew,
Till in the summer-land of dreams   625
They softened to the sound of streams,
Low stir of leaves, and dip of oars,
And lapsing waves on quiet shores.

Next morn we wakened with the shout
Of merry voices high and clear;   630
And saw the teamsters drawing near
To break the drifted highways out.
Down the long hillside treading slow
We saw the half-buried oxen go,
Shaking the snow from heads uptost,   635
Their straining nostrils white with frost.
Before our door the straggling train
Drew up, an added team to gain.
The elders threshed their hands a-cold,
    Passed, with the cider-mug, their jokes   640
    From lip to lip; the younger folks
Down the loose snow-banks, wrestling, rolled,
Then toiled again the cavalcade
    O'er windy hill, through clogged ravine,
    And woodland paths that wound between   645
Low drooping pine-boughs winter-weighed.
From every barn a team afoot,
At every house a new recruit,
Where, drawn by Nature's subtlest law
Haply the watchful young men saw   650
Sweet doorway pictures of the curls
And curious eyes of merry girls,
Lifting their hands in mock defence
Against the snow-ball's compliments,
And reading in each missive tost   655
The charm with Eden never lost.

We heard once more the sleigh-bells' sound;
    And, following where the teamsters led,
The wise old Doctor[57] went his round,
Just pausing at our door to say,   660
In the brief autocratic way
Of one who, prompt at Duty's call,
Was free to urge her claim on all,
    That some poor neighbor sick abed
At night our mother's aid would need.   665
For, one in generous thought and deed,
    What mattered in the sufferer's sight
    The Quaker matron's inward light,
The Doctor's mail of Calvin's creed?[58]
All hearts confess the saints elect   670
    Who, twain in faith, in love agree,

---

[57]Dr. Elias Weld, of whom Whittier wrote, "He was the one cultivated man in the neighborhood. His small but well-chosen library was placed at my disposal."
[58]The armor of Calvin's rigid moral code, belief in man's sinfulness, predestination, and Scripture as the source of divine revelation, is contrasted with the Quaker belief in God's revelation from within, the "inward light."

And melt not in an acid sect
  The Christian pearl of charity!

So days went on: a week had passed
Since the great world was heard from last.   675
The Almanac we studied o'er,
Read and reread our little store,
Of books and pamphlets, scarce a score;
One harmless novel, mostly hid
From younger eyes, a book forbid,   680
And poetry, (or good or bad,
A single book was all we had,)
Where Ellwood's meek, drab-skirted Muse,
  A stranger to the heathen Nine,
  Sang, with a somewhat nasal whine,   685
The wars of David and the Jews.[59]
At last the floundering carrier bore
The village paper to our door.
Lo! broadening outward as we read,
To warmer zones the horizon spread;   690
In panoramic length unrolled
We saw the marvels that it told.
Before us passed the painted Creeks,[60]
  And daft McGregor on his raids
  In Costa Rica's everglades.[61]   695
And up Taygetos winding slow
Rode Ypsilanti's Mainote Greeks,
A Turk's head at each saddle-bow![62]
Welcome to us its week-old news,
Its corner for the rustic Muse,   700
  Its monthly gauge of snow and rain,
Its record, mingling in a breath
The wedding bell and dirge of death:
Jest, anecdote, and love-lorn tale,
The latest culprit sent to jail;   705
Its hue and cry of stolen and lost,
Its vendue[63] sales and goods at cost,
  And traffic calling loud for gain.
We felt the stir of hall and street,
The pulse of life that round us beat;   710
The chill embargo of the snow
Was melted in the genial glow;
Wide swung again our ice-locked door,
And all the world was ours once more!

Clasp, Angel of the backward look   715
  And folded wings of ashen gray
  And voice of echoes far away,

---

[59]The *Davideis* (1712), Biblical epic by English Quaker Thomas Ellwood (1639–1714), uninspired by the nine Greek muses who preside over the arts and sciences.
[60]Indians of Georgia and Alabama, defeated in 1814 by Andrew Jackson and moved to Indian Territory, now Oklahoma, in the 1830s.
[61]Adventurer Sir Gregor MacGregor, who called himself Highness, took possession of a Florida Island in 1817. He settled among Indians in Central America in 1821, taking the title Cacique (chief) of the Payais, but failed to establish a colony.
[62]The Mainote Greeks, who lived in the province Maina, encompassing the mountain range of Taygetus on the Peloponnese, were among the first to rise against the Turks in 1821 at the outbreak of the War of Independence. Demetrios Ypsilanti (1793–1832), brother of Alexander (1792–1828), was in command of the Peloponnese forces.
[63]Auction.

The brazen covers of thy book;
The weird palimpsest[64] old and vast,
Wherein thou hid'st the spectral past;   720
Where, closely mingling, pale and glow
The characters of joy and woe;
The monographs of outlived years,
Or smile-illumed or dim with tears,
   Green hills of life that slope to death,   725
And haunts of home, whose vistaed trees
Shade off to mournful cypresses
   With the white amaranths[65] underneath.
Even while I look, I can but heed
   The restless sands' incessant fall,   730
Importunate hours that hours succeed,
Each clamorous with its own sharp need,
   And duty keeping pace with all.
Shut down and clasp the heavy lids;
I hear again the voice that bids   735
The dreamer leave his dream midway
For larger hopes and graver fears:
Life greatens in these later years,
The century's aloe[66] flowers to-day!

Yet, haply, in some lull of life,   740
Some Truce of God which breaks its strife,
The worldling's eyes shall gather dew,
   Dreaming in throngful city ways
Of winter joys his boyhood knew;
And dear and early friends—the few   745
Who yet remain—shall pause to view
   These Flemish pictures[67] of old days;
Sit with me by the homestead hearth,
And stretch the hands of memory forth
   To warm them at the wood-fire's blaze!   750
And thanks untraced to lips unknown
Shall greet me like the odors blown
From unseen meadows newly mown,
Or lilies floating in some pond,
Wood-fringed, the wayside gaze beyond;   755
The traveller owns the grateful sense
Of sweetness near, he knows not whence,
And, pausing, takes with forehead bare
The benediction of the air.

                  1866

---

[64]Document with imperfectly erased writings visible beneath later writings.
[65]Undying imaginary flowers.
[66]The "American Aloe," or century plant, blooms, with flower stems sometimes 40 feet high, once at maturity—said to be every hundred years—and then dies.

[67]The realistic *genre* paintings of familiar scenes from daily life excelled at by the Flemish and Dutch masters of the seventeenth century.

Prelude to *Among the Hills*[1]

Along the roadside, like the flowers of gold
That tawny Incas[2] for their gardens wrought,
Heavy with sunshine droops the golden-rod,
And the red pennons[3] of the cardinal-flowers
Hang motionless upon their upright staves.   5
The sky is hot and hazy, and the wind,
Wing-weary with its long flight from the south,
Unfelt; yet, closely scanned, yon maple leaf
With faintest motion, as one stirs in dreams,
Confesses it. The locust by the wall   10
Stabs the noon-silence with his sharp alarm.
A single hay-cart down the dusty road
Creaks slowly, with its driver fast asleep
On the load's top. Against the neighboring hill,
Huddled along the stone wall's shady side,   15
The sheep show white, as if a snowdrift still
Defied the dog-star.[4] Through the open door
A drowsy smell of flowers—gray heliotrope,
And white sweet clover, and shy mignonette—
Comes faintly in, and silent chorus lends   20
To the pervading symphony of peace.

No time is this for hands long overworn
To task their strength: and (unto Him be praise
Who giveth quietness!) the stress and strain
Of years that did the work of centuries   25
Have ceased, and we can draw our breath once more
Freely and full. So, as yon harvesters
Make glad their nooning underneath the elms
With tale and riddle and old snatch of song,
I lay aside grave themes, and idly turn   30
The leaves of memory's sketch-book, dreaming o'er
Old summer pictures of the quiet hills,
And human life, as quiet, at their feet.

And yet not idly all. A farmer's son,
Proud of field-lore and harvest craft, and feeling   35
All their fine possibilities, how rich
And restful even poverty and toil
Become when beauty, harmony, and love
Sit at their humble hearth as angels sat
At evening in the patriarch's tent, when man   40
Makes labor noble, and his farmer's frock
The symbol of a Christian chivalry
Tender and just and generous to her

---

[1]The Prelude introduces a narrative poem, *Among the Hills*, which presents an idealized portrait of a marriage between a strong, manly farmer and a cultured, charming city girl, living the "simple life" at the "homely hearth," with "beauty's sphere surrounding." In the Prelude, the poet meditates on the writing of his simple story, protesting that he knows "another side"—"How wearily the grind of toil goes on / Where love is wanting." There follow some of Whittier's most sordidly realistic lines, describing the run-down, slovenly farmers' households where "querulous women" and "sullen men" endure without affection. Whittier then returns to the rural home where love dwells, invoking the "Golden Age" and "all the old virtues" to introduce his narrative.
[2]Peruvian Indians, famed goldsmiths, fashioned gardens of gold.
[3]Streamers.
[4]Sirius, the brightest star in the sky, chief of the constellation Canis Major or Great Dog, which is visible near the sun at dawn during the hottest "dog days" of August.

Who clothes with grace all duty; still, I know
Too well the picture has another side,—   45
How wearily the grind of toil goes on
Where love is wanting, how the eye and ear
And heart are starved amidst the plenitude
Of nature, and how hard and colorless
Is life without an atmosphere. I look   50
Across the lapse of half a century,
And call to mind old homesteads, where no flower
Told that the spring had come, but evil weeds,
Nightshade and rough-leaved burdock in the place
Of the sweet doorway greeting of the rose   55
And honeysuckle, where the house walls seemed
Blistering in sun, without a tree or vine
To cast the tremulous shadow of its leaves
Across the curtainless windows from whose panes
Fluttered the signal rags of shiftlessness;   60
Within, the cluttered kitchen-floor, unwashed
(Broom-clean I think they called it); the best room
Stifling with cellar damp, shut from the air
In hot midsummer, bookless, pictureless
Save the inevitable sampler hung   65
Over the fireplace, or a mourning piece,[5]
A green-haired woman, peony-cheeked, beneath
Impossible willows; the wide-throated hearth
Bristling with faded pine-boughs half concealing
The piled-up rubbish at the chimney's back;   70
And, in sad keeping with all things about them,
Shrill, querulous women, sour and sullen men,
Untidy, loveless, old before their time,
With scarce a human interest save their own
Monotonous round of small economies,   75
Or the poor scandal of the neighborhood;
Blind to the beauty everywhere revealed,
Treading the May-flowers with regardless feet;
For them the song-sparrow and the bobolink
Sang not, nor winds made music in the leaves;   80
For them in vain October's holocaust
Burned, gold and crimson, over all the hills,
The sacramental mystery of the woods.
Church-goers, fearful of the unseen Powers,
But grumbling over pulpit-tax and pew-rent,   85
Saving, as shrewd economists, their souls
And winter pork with the least possible outlay
Of salt and sanctity; in daily life
Showing as little actual comprehension
Of Christian charity and love and duty,   90
As if the Sermon on the Mount[6] had been
Out dated like a last year's almanac:
Rich in broad woodlands and in half-tilled fields,
And yet so pinched and bare and comfortless,
The veriest straggler limping on his rounds,   95
The sun and air his sole inheritance,

---

[5]Artwork, often with verse, to honor the dead.
[6]Christ's sermon, given in Matthew 5–7.

Laughed at a poverty that paid its taxes,
And hugged his rags in self-complacency!

Not such should be the homesteads of a land
Where whoso wisely wills and acts may dwell   100
As king and lawgiver, in broad-acred state,
With beauty, art, taste, culture, books, to make
His hours of leisure richer than a life
Of fourscore to the barons of old time,
Our yeoman[7] should be equal to his home   105
Set in the fair, green valleys, purple walled,
A man to match his mountains, not to creep
Dwarfed and abased below them. I would fain
In this light way (of which I needs must own
With the knife-grinder of whom Canning sings,   110
"Story, God bless you! I have none to tell you!")[8]
Invite the eye to see and the heart to feel
The beauty and the joy within their reach,—
Home, and home loves, and the beatitudes
Of nature free to all. Haply in years   115
That wait to take the places of our own,
Heard where some breezy balcony looks down
On happy homes, or where the lake in the moon
Sleeps dreaming of the mountains, fair as Ruth,
In the old Hebrew pastoral, at the feet   120
Of Boaz,[9] even this simple lay of mine
May seem the burden of a prophecy,
Finding its late fulfillment in a change
Slow as the oak's growth lifting manhood up
Through broader culture, finer manners, love,   125
And reverence, to the level of the hills.

O Golden Age, whose light is of the dawn,
And not of sunset, forward, not behind,
Flood the new heavens and earth, and with thee bring
All the old virtues, whatsoever things   130
Are pure and honest and of good repute,
But add thereto whatever bard has sung
Or seer has told of when in trance and dream
They saw the Happy Isles of prophecy!
Let Justice hold her scale, and Truth divide   135
Between the right and wrong; but give the heart
The freedom of its fair inheritance;
Let the poor prisoner, cramped and starved so long,
At Nature's table feast his ear and eye
With joy and wonder, let all harmonies   140
Of sound, form, color, motion, wait upon
The princely guest, whether in soft attire
Of leisure clad, or the coarse frock of toil,
And, lending life to the dead form of faith,
Give human nature reverence for the sake   145

---

[7] Independent farmer.
[8] The knife-grinder's reply to the do-gooder's request to hear the "pitiful story" of wrongs suffered, in "The Friend of Humanity and the Knife-Grinder" (1797), a parody of "Republican enthusiasm and universal philanthropy" by British statesman George Canning (1770–1827).

[9] The young widow Ruth, faithful daughter-in-law of Naomi, found favor in the eyes of kinsman Boaz, and from their marriage was descended King David and Jesus (Ruth 3, 4).

Of One who bore it, making it divine
With the ineffable tenderness of God;
Let common need, the brotherhood of prayer,
The heirship of an unknown destiny,
The unsolved mystery round about us, make   150
A man more precious than the gold of Ophir.[10]
Sacred, inviolate, unto whom all things
Should minister, as outward types and signs
Of the eternal beauty which fulfils
The one great purpose of creation, Love,   155
The sole necessity of Earth and Heaven!

1869

The Pressed Gentian

The time of gifts has come again,
And, on my northern window-pane,
Outlined against the day's brief light,
A Christmas token hangs in sight.
The wayside travellers, as they pass,   5
Mark the gray disk of clouded glass;
And the dull blankness seems, perchance,
Folly to their wise ignorance.

They cannot from their outlook see
The perfect grace it hath for me;   10
For there the flower, whose fringes through
The frosty breath of autumn blew,
Turns from without its face of bloom
To the warm tropic of my room,
As fair as when beside its brook   15
The hue of bending skies it took.

So from the trodden ways of earth,
Seem some sweet souls who veil their worth,
And offer to the careless glance
The clouding gray of circumstance.   20
They blossom best where hearth-fires burn,
To loving eyes alone they turn
The flowers of inward grace, that hide
Their beauty from the world outside.

But deeper meanings come to me,   25
My half-immortal flower, from thee!
Man judges from a partial view,
None ever yet his brother knew;
The Eternal Eye that sees the whole
May better read the darkened soul,   30
And find, to outward sense denied,
The flower upon its inmost side!

1876

---

[10]Old Testament land, source of gold (1 Kings 9:28).

The Trailing Arbutus[1]

I wandered lonely where the pine-trees made
Against the bitter East their barricade,
    And, guided by its sweet
Perfume, I found, within a narrow dell,
The trailing spring flower tinted like a shell   5
    Amid dry leaves and mosses at my feet.

From under dead boughs, for whose loss the pines
Moaned ceaseless overhead, the blossoming vines
    Lifted their glad surprise,
While yet the bluebird smoothed in leafless trees   10
His feathers ruffled by the chill sea-breeze,
    And snow-drifts lingered under April skies.

As, pausing, o'er the lonely flower I bent,
I thought of lives thus lowly, clogged and pent,
    Which yet find room,   15
Through care and cumber,[2] coldness and decay,
To lend a sweetness to the ungenial day
    And make the sad earth happier for their bloom.

1880   *1880*

OLIVER WENDELL HOLMES
(1809–1894)

One school of modern criticism has held that "poetry makes nothing happen." Oliver Wendell Holmes would have been hard to convince. After reading a news item about the imminent destruction of the historic frigate *Constitution,* the twenty-one-year-old Holmes, freshly out of Harvard, penned the three stanzas "Old Ironsides" and published the poem in the *Boston Daily Advertiser.* It was picked up and published all over the country—and saved the ship that had become a "hero" in the War of 1812.

Holmes came from a family of Boston "Brahmins" (a term he invented for the intellectual aristocracy), his father the Calvinistic minister of the renowned First Church. He was educated at Phillips-Andover Academy and Harvard, where the Unitarian influence had become strong. He graduated in 1829 and began the study of law, but switched to medicine, going to the then world center for medical education, Paris, in 1833. While abroad he travelled extensively in Europe, returning to Boston in 1835 to take his medical degree at Harvard in 1836.

He discovered he preferred teaching to practice and accepted appointment in the Harvard Medical School, serving as Dean from 1847 to 1853, and continuing as Professor of Anatomy until retirement in 1882. Throughout his medical career, he published scholarly papers on scientific subjects, bringing

[1]Also called "mayflower."
[2]Encumbrance, hindrance.

to bear his wide knowledge of European research. In one important paper, written in a day before modern bacteriology, he assembled the evidence for "The Contagiousness of Puerperal [Childbed] Fever." And he was right, though many of his contemporaries were skeptical.

Although he was committed to the medical profession, Holmes never gave up his literary career. He published volumes of poems in 1836, 1846, 1849, and his *Poetical Works* in 1852. He was elected Class Poet by his Harvard classmates, and continued to write a class poem annually, bringing out in 1854 *Songs of the Class of 1829*.

Holmes belonged to the Saturday Club in Boston, which undertook sponsorship of a magazine in 1857. Holmes supplied the name—*The Atlantic Monthly*—and, at the insistence of its first editor, James Russell Lowell, became a regular contributor. He picked up a series he had begun a quarter of a century before in the *New England Magazine,* entitled "The Autocrat of the Breakfast Table." His opening line was, "I was just going to say, when I was interrupted. . . ." The series of conversations, presumably taking place regularly at the dining table of a boarding house—a melange of serious and witty prose and verse—appeared as a book in 1858 and was an immediate and popular success.

Other "Breakfast Table" books appeared in 1860 and 1872. Much of Holmes's important poetry was introduced in these volumes, including "The Chambered Nautilus," which he considered his best poem, and "The Deacon's Masterpiece, or the Wonderful 'One-Horse Shay,' " his greatest achievement in light verse with an undercurrent of serious meaning. There were many other books, most notably three works of fiction which he called "medicated novels"—*Elsie Venner* (1861), *The Guardian Angel* (1867), and *A Mortal Antipathy* (1885). These works all deal with characters whose behavior is determined by physiological or psychological elements beyond their control, raising serious questions about assessing moral responsibility. Thus these works, like his "Deacon's Masterpiece," are challenges to the Calvinism of his father.

Holmes has been described as Boston's Dr. Johnson who had to become his own Boswell (as in the "Breakfast Table" series). He would not have minded the characterization. As he said in one of his books, "I have always been good company for myself."

ADDITIONAL READING

The Riverside Edition of *The Writings of Oliver Wendell Holmes,* 13 vols., 1891; reproduced as the Standard Library Edition, *The Works of Oliver Wendell Holmes,* 13 vols., 1892; increased to 15 vols. by the addition of J. T. Morse, *Life and Letters of Oliver Wendell Holmes,* 2 vols., 1896; *Oliver Wendell Holmes: Representative Selections,* ed. S. I. Hayakawa and Howard Mumford Jones, 1939.

M. A. DeWolfe Howe, *Holmes of the Breakfast-Table,* 1939; Clarence P. Oberndorf, *The Psychiatric Novels of Oliver Wendell Holmes,* 1943; Eleanor M. Tilton, *Amiable Autocrat: A Biography of Dr. Oliver Wendell Holmes,* 1947; George Arms, "Holmes," *The Fields Were Green,* 1953; Miriam Rossiter Small, *Oliver Wendell Holmes,* 1962; Edwin P. Hoyt, *The Improper Bostonian: Dr. Oliver Wendell Holmes,* 1979.

TEXT

The Complete Poetical Works of Oliver Wendell Holmes, ed. Horace E. Scudder, 1895.

Old Ironsides[1]

Ay, tear her tattered ensign down!
  Long has it waved on high,
And many an eye has danced to see
  That banner in the sky;
Beneath it rung the battle shout,   5
  And burst the cannon's roar;—
The meteor of the ocean air
  Shall sweep the clouds no more.

Her deck, once red with heroes' blood,
  Where knelt the vanquished foe,   10
When winds were hurrying o'er the flood,
  And waves were white below,
No more shall feel the victor's tread,
  Or know the conquered knee;—
The harpies[2] of the shore shall pluck   15
  The eagle of the sea!

Oh, better that her shattered hulk
  Should sink beneath the wave;
Her thunder shook the mighty deep,
  And there should be her grave;   20
Nail to the mast her holy flag,
  Set every threadbare sail,
And give her to the god of storms,
  The lightning and the gale!

1830

The Last Leaf[1]

I saw him once before,
As he passed by the door,
  And again
The pavement stones resound,
As he totters o'er the ground   5
  With his cane.

They say that in his prime,
Ere the pruning-knife of Time
  Cut him down,
Not a better man was found   10
By the Crier[2] on his round
  Through the town.

---

[1]Holmes said that this "poem was an impromptu outburst of feeling" written in 1830 after reading in the *Boston Daily Advertiser* that "Old Ironsides," the unseaworthy frigate *Constitution*, conqueror of the British *Guerrière* in the War of 1812, was to be destroyed. Printed two days later in the same paper, and widely reprinted, the poem aroused the people and saved the ship.
[2]Voracious monsters, in Greek mythology.

[1]"The poem was suggested by the sight of a figure well known to Bostonians [in 1831 or 1832], that of Major Thomas Melville, 'the last of the cocked hats,' as he was sometimes called. . . . He was often pointed out as one of the 'Indians' of the famous 'Boston Tea-Party' of 1774" (Holmes's note). Thomas Melville (1751–1832) was the grandfather of Herman Melville.
[2]Person appointed to shout out public announcements.

But now he walks the streets,
And he looks at all he meets
   Sad and wan,   15
And he shakes his feeble head,
That it seems as if he said,
   "They are gone."

The mossy marbles rest
On the lips that he has prest   20
   In their bloom,
And the names he loved to hear
Have been carved for many a year
   On the tomb.

My grandmamma has said—   25
Poor old lady, she is dead
   Long ago—
That he had a Roman nose,
And his cheek was like a rose
   In the snow;   30

But now his nose is thin,
And it rests upon his chin
   Like a staff,
And a crook is in his back,
And a melancholy crack   35
   In his laugh.

I know it is a sin
For me to sit and grin
   At him here;
But the old three-cornered hat,   40
And the breeches, and all that,
   Are so queer!

And if I should live to be
The last leaf upon the tree
   In the spring,   45
Let them smile, as I do now,
At the old forsaken bough
   Where I cling.

                      1831

My Aunt

My aunt! my dear unmarried aunt!
   Long years have o'er her flown;
Yet still she strains the aching clasp
   That binds her virgin zone;[1]
I know it hurts her,—though she looks   5

---

[1] Belt.

As cheerful as she can;
  Her waist is ampler than her life,
For life is but a span.

My aunt! my poor deluded aunt!
  Her hair is almost gray;   10
Why will she train that winter curl
  In such a spring-like way?
How can she lay her glasses down,
  And say she reads as well,
When through a double convex lens   15
  She just makes out to spell?

Her father—grandpapa! forgive
  This erring lip its smiles—
Vowed she should make the finest girl
  Within a hundred miles;   20
He sent her to a stylish school;
  'Twas in her thirteenth June;
And with her, as the rules required,
  "Two towels and a spoon."

They braced my aunt against a board,   25
  To make her straight and tall;
They laced her up, they starved her down,
  To make her light and small;
They pinched her feet, they singed her hair,
  They screwed it up with pins;—   30
Oh, never mortal suffered more
  In penance for her sins.

So, when my precious aunt was done,
  My grandsire brought her back;
(By daylight, lest some rabid youth   35
  Might follow on the track;)
"Ah!" said my grandsire, as he shook
  Some powder in his pan,[2]
"What could this lovely creature do
  Against a desperate man!"   40

Alas! nor chariot, nor barouche,[3]
  Nor bandit cavalcade,
Tore from the trembling father's arms
  His all-accomplished maid.
For her how happy had it been!   45
  And Heaven had spared to me
To see one sad, ungathered rose
  On my ancestral tree.

1831

---

[2]The hollow in the loading part of a musket.
[3]Four-wheeled carriage with collapsible top.

The Chambered Nautilus[1]

This is the ship of pearl, which, poets feign,
    Sails the unshadowed main,—
    The venturous bark that flings
On the sweet summer wind its purpled wings
In gulfs enchanted, where the Siren sings,   5
    And coral reefs lie bare,
Where the cold sea-maids rise to sun their streaming hair.

Its webs of living gauze no more unfurl;
    Wrecked is the ship of pearl!
    And every chambered cell,   10
Where its dim dreaming life was wont to dwell,
As the frail tenant shaped his growing shell,
    Before thee lies revealed,—
Its irised[2] ceiling rent, its sunless crypt unsealed!

Year after year beheld the silent toil   15
    That spread his lustrous coil;
    Still, as the spiral grew,
He left the past year's dwelling for the new,
Stole with soft step its shining archway through,
    Built up its idle door,   20
Stretched in his last-found home, and knew the old no more.

Thanks for the heavenly message brought by thee,
    Child of the wandering sea,
    Cast from her lap, forlorn!
From thy dead lips a clearer note is born   25
Than ever Triton blew from wreathèd horn![3]
    While on mine ear it rings,
Through the deep caves of thought I hear a voice that sings:—

Build thee more stately mansions, O my soul,
    As the swift seasons roll!   30
    Leave thy low-vaulted past!
Let each new temple, nobler than the last,
Shut thee from heaven with a dome more vast,
    Till thou at length art free,
Leaving thine outgrown shell by life's unresting sea!   35

1858

---

[1] The pearly nautilus, a mollusk of the Indian and South Pacific Oceans, long compared to a ship because of the air-filled chambers of the shell enabling it to float and a membrane once thought to serve as a sail; hence "nautilus," Greek for sailor. "If you will look into Roget's *Bridgewater Treatise*, you will find a figure of one of these shells, and a section of it. The last will show you the series of enlarging compartments successively dwelt in by the animal that inhabits the shell, which is built in a widening spiral. Can you find no lesson in this?" (Holmes's note).

[2] Rainbow colored, as is pearl.

[3] In Greek mythology, Triton is the trumpeter of the ocean, stirring or soothing the waves by blowing a conch shell.

The Deacon's Masterpiece

OR, THE WONDERFUL "ONE-HOSS SHAY"
A LOGICAL STORY[1]

Have you heard of the wonderful one-hoss shay,[2]
That was built in such a logical way
It ran a hundred years to a day,
And then, of a sudden, it—ah, but stay,
I'll tell you what happened without delay,   5
Scaring the parson into fits,
Frightening people out of their wits,—
Have you ever heard of that, I say?

Seventeen hundred and fifty-five.
Georgius Secundus[3] was then alive,—   10
Snuffy old drone from the German hive.
That was the year when Lisbon-town
Saw the earth open and gulp her down,
And Braddock's army was done so brown,
Left without a scalp to its crown.[4]   15
It was on the terrible Earthquake-day
That the Deacon finished the one-hoss shay.

Now in building of chaises, I tell you what,
There is always *somewhere* a weakest spot,—
In hub, tire, felloe,[5] in spring or thill,[6]   20
In panel, or crossbar, or floor, or sill,
In screw, bolt, thoroughbrace,[7]—lurking still,
Find it somewhere you must and will,—
Above or below, or within or without,—
And that's the reason, beyond a doubt,   25
That a chaise *breaks down*, but doesn't *wear out*.

But the Deacon swore (as Deacons do,
With an "I dew vum," or an "I tell *yeou*")
He would build one shay to beat the taown
'N' the keounty 'n' all the kentry raoun';   30
It should be so built that it *could n'* break daown;
"Fur," said the Deacon, " 't's mighty plain
Thut the weakes' place mus' stan' the strain;
'N' the way t' fix it, uz I maintain,
    Is only jest   35
T' make that place uz strong uz the rest."

[1] A satirical allegory on the limitations and ultimate collapse of logical systems, this poem is generally thought to be an attack on the great logical system of Calvinist theology, the faith of the early Puritans, especially as it was elaborated in the work of Jonathan Edwards, whose defense of predestination, in *The Freedom of the Will*, appeared in 1754. One year later, on November 1, 1755, the catastrophic Lisbon earthquake inspired widespread theological debate and disillusionment in religious dogma.
[2] A chaise, a light two-wheeled, horse-drawn carriage.
[3] George II (1683–1760), German-born king of England (r. 1727–60).

[4] Edward Braddock (1695–1755), commander of the British, and many of his men were killed near Fort Duquesne (Pittsburgh) when ambushed by the French and Indians on July 9, 1755.
[5] Wheel rim.
[6] One of two shafts extending from the carriage between which the horse is harnessed.
[7] One of two leather bands connected to front and back springs and supporting the body of the carriage.

So the Deacon inquired of the village folk
Where he could find the strongest oak,
That could n't be split nor bent nor broke,—
That was for spokes and floors and sills;   40
He sent for lancewood to make the thills;
The crossbars were ash, from the straightest trees,
The panels of white-wood, that cuts like cheese,
But lasts like iron for things like these;
The hubs of logs from the "Settler's ellum,"—[8]   45
Last of its timber,—they could n't sell 'em,
Never an axe had seen their chips,
And the wedges flew from between their lips,
Their blunt ends frizzled like celery-tips;
Step and prop-iron, bolt and screw,   50
Spring, tire, axle, and linchpin[9] too,
Steel of the finest, bright and blue;
Thoroughbrace bison-skin, thick and wide;
Boot, top, dasher,[10] from tough old hide
Found in the pit when the tanner died.   55
That was the way he "put her through."
"There!" said the Deacon, "naow she'll dew!"

Do! I tell you, I rather guess
She was a wonder, and nothing less!
Colts grew horses, beards turned gray,   60
Deacon and deaconess dropped away,
Children and grandchildren—where were they?
But there stood the stout old one-hoss shay
As fresh as on Lisbon-earthquake-day!

EIGHTEEN HUNDRED;—it came and found   65
The Deacon's masterpiece strong and sound.
Eighteen hundred increased by ten;—
"Hahnsum kerridge" they called it then.
Eighteen hundred and twenty came;—
Running as usual; much the same.   70
Thirty and forty at last arrive,
And then come fifty, and FIFTY-FIVE.

Little of all we value here
Wakes on the morn of its hundredth year
Without both feeling and looking queer.   75
In fact, there's nothing that keeps its youth,
So far as I know, but a tree and truth.
(This is a moral that runs at large;
Take it.—You're welcome.—No extra charge.)

FIRST OF NOVEMBER,—the Earthquake-day,—   80
There are traces of age in the one-hoss shay,
A general flavor of mild decay,
But nothing local, as one may say.
There could n't be,—for the Deacon's art

---

[8]Elm dating from the time of the first settler.
[9]Pin locking the wheel to the axle.
[10]Dashboard.

Had made it so like in every part   85
That there wasn't a chance for one to start.
For the wheels were just as strong as the thills,
And the floor was just as strong as the sills,
And the panels just as strong as the floor,
And the whipple-tree[11] neither less nor more,   90
And the back crossbar as strong as the fore,
And spring and axle and hub *encore*.
And yet, *as a whole*, it is past a doubt
In another hour it will be *worn out!*

First of November, 'Fifty-five!   95
This morning the parson takes a drive.
Now, small boys, get out of the way!
Here comes the wonderful one-hoss shay,
Drawn by a rat-tailed, ewe-necked bay.[12]
"Huddup!" said the parson.—Off went they.   100
The parson was working his Sunday's text,—
Had got to *fifthly*, and stopped perplexed
At what the—Moses—was coming next.
All at once the horse stood still,
Close by the meet'n'-house on the hill.   105
First a shiver, and then a thrill,
Then something decidedly like a spill,—
And the parson was sitting upon a rock,
At half past nine by the meet'n'-house clock—
Just the hour of the Earthquake shock!   110
What do you think the parson found,
When he got up and stared around?
The poor old chaise in a heap or mound,
As if it had been to the mill and ground!
You see, of course, if you're not a dunce,   115
How it went to pieces all at once,—
All at once, and nothing first,—
Just as bubbles do when they burst.

End of the wonderful one-hoss shay.
Logic is logic. That 's all I say.   120

                                              1858

Nearing the Snow-Line

Slow toiling upward from the misty vale,
   I leave the bright enamelled zones below;
   No more for me their beauteous bloom shall glow,
Their lingering sweetness load the morning gale;
Few are the slender flowerets, scentless, pale,   5
   That on their ice-clad stems all trembling blow
   Along the margin of unmelting snow;

---

[11]Pivoted bar to which the harness is attached.
[12]Long, hollow-necked, reddish-brown horse.

Yet with unsaddened voice thy verge I hail,
   White realm of peace above the flowering line;
Welcome thy frozen domes, thy rocky spires!   10
   O'er thee undimmed the moon-girt planets shine,
On thy majestic altars fade the fires
That filled the air with smoke of vain desires,
   And all the unclouded blue of heaven is thine!

1870

JAMES RUSSELL LOWELL
(1819–1891)

The year 1848 was a signal year for the twenty-nine-year-old James Russell Lowell. That year he published *Poems: Second Series, The Biglow Papers: First Series, A Fable for Critics,* and *The Vision of Sir Launfal.* These books represented Lowell's range of subjects, styles, and abilities. The first contained such moralistic lyrics as "To a Dandelion"; the second was a comic work in dialect, prose and poetry, attacking the Mexican War and the South's passion to extend slave territory; the third was a survey of contemporary American poets in comic rhymed couplets full of critical capers and linguistic fireworks; and the fourth was a narrative poem in rhymed iambic tetrameter, based on the legendary search for the holy grail, and constituting a parable in Christian charity.

In a letter to a friend written in December 1848, Lowell wrote: "I believe that I have done better than the world knows yet. . . . I am the first poet who has endeavored to express the American idea, and I shall be popular by and by." There is irony in the private self-valuation. It is true that when Lowell died in 1891, he was generally considered America's most distinguished man of letters. But the twentieth century has not been so kind in its judgment, and has relegated Lowell to the rank of the "schoolroom poets."

Margaret Fuller's judgment of 1846 has been closer to the mark: "[Lowell's] interest in the moral questions of the day has supplied the want of vitality in himself; his great facility at versification has enabled him to fill the ear with a copious stream of pleasant sound. But his verse is stereotyped; his thought sounds no depth, and posterity will not remember him." Lowell was clearly stung by these words and responded with his severe (but witty) strictures on Fuller in *A Fable for Critics.*

Few other writers began careers with such promise. After graduating from Harvard in 1838, and taking a law degree in 1840, Lowell issued his first volume of poems, *A Year's Life,* in 1841 when he was twenty-two. A second volume appeared in 1844, the same year in which he published *Conversations on Some of the Old Poets.* There was a steady stream of poems, reviews, critical essays, and political satire from Lowell's pen from this time forward. He followed Longfellow at Harvard in 1856 as Professor of French and Spanish Language and Literatures. He began editing *The Atlantic Monthly* at its founding in 1857, and he became coeditor of the *North American Review* in 1864. As a reward for services to the Republican party he was appointed Minister to Spain (1877–80) and Minister to England (1880–85).

By every outward count, Lowell could look upon his career as a success. Even the tragic deaths of his two wives (the first in 1854 after nine years of marriage, the second in 1885 after twenty-eight) did not deflect him from his steady flow of publications. In 1890, the year before his death, his collected *Writings* were published in ten volumes.

And yet, he must have been aware that his ambitions and dreams of youth had been compromised. As one critic, Leon Howard, suggested, he seems to have "accepted his limitations, and wrote safely within them." He had described those limitations as early as 1848, in *A Fable for Critics,* seeing himself as striving to climb Parnassus "with a whole bale of *isms*":

> The top of the hill he will ne'er come nigh reaching
> Till he learns the distinction 'twixt singing and preaching.

The wit of *A Fable for Critics* endures, however, as does, to a large extent, the humor of *The Biglow Papers.* Moreover, "To a Dandelion," the "Ode Recited at the Harvard Commemoration" (on the Civil War dead), and "Auspex" are among those few lyric poems that transcend Lowell's usual self-acknowledged weaknesses. These poems represent no small poetic achievement.

ADDITIONAL READING

Letters of James Russell Lowell, 3 vols., ed. C. E. Norton, 1904; *New Letters of James Russell Lowell,* ed. M. A. DeW. Howe, 1932; *James Russell Lowell: Representative Selections,* ed. Harry Hayden Clark and Norman Foerster, 1947; *James Russell Lowell's The Biglow Papers* [*First Series*]: *A Critical Edition,* ed. Thomas Wortham, 1977.

Horace E. Scudder, *James Russell Lowell: A Biography,* 2 vols., 1901; Richmond C. Beatty, *James Russell Lowell,* 1942; Leon Howard, *Victorian Knight-Errant: A Study of the Early Literary Career of James Russell Lowell,* 1952; George Arms, "Lowell," *The Fields Were Green,* 1953; Martin Duberman, *James Russell Lowell,* 1966; Claire McGlinchee, *James Russell Lowell,* 1967; Edward Wagenknecht, *James Russell Lowell,* 1971; C. David Heymann, *American Aristocracy: The Lives and Times of James Russell, Amy, and Robert Lowell,* 1980.

TEXT

The Writings of James Russell Lowell, 10 vols., 1890.

To the Dandelion

Dear common flower, that grow'st beside the way,
　Fringing the dusty road with harmless gold,
　　First pledge of blithesome May,
　Which children pluck, and, full of pride uphold,
　　High-hearted buccaneers, o'erjoyed that they   5
An Eldorado[1] in the grass have found,
　　Which not the rich earth's ample round
　May match in wealth, thou art more dear to me
　Than all the prouder summer-blooms may be.

Gold such as thine ne'er drew the Spanish prow   10
　Through the primeval hush of Indian seas,

---

[1]Legendary city of gold.

Nor wrinkled the lean brow
Of age, to rob the lover's heart of ease;
  'Tis the Spring's largess, which she scatters now
To rich and poor alike, with lavish hand,   15
    Though most hearts never understand
  To take it at God's value, but pass by
  The offered wealth with unrewarded eye.

Thou art my tropics and mine Italy;
To look at thee unlocks a warmer clime;   20
    The eyes thou givest me
Are in the heart, and heed not space or time:
  Not in mid June the golden-cuirassed² bee
Feels a more summer-like warm ravishment
    In the white lily's breezy tent,   25
  His fragrant Sybaris,³ than I, when first
  From the dark green thy yellow circles burst.

Then think I of deep shadows on the grass,
Of meadows where in sun the cattle graze,
    Where, as the breezes pass,   30
The gleaming rushes lean a thousand ways,
  Of leaves that slumber in a cloudy mass,
Or whiten in the wind, of waters blue
    That from the distance sparkle through
  Some woodland gap, and of a sky above,   35
  Where one white cloud like a stray lamb doth move.

My childhood's earliest thoughts are linked with thee;
The sight of thee calls back the robin's song,
    Who, from the dark old tree
Beside the door, sang clearly all day long,   40
  And I, secure in childish piety,
Listened as if I heard an angel sing
    With news from heaven, which he could bring
  Fresh every day to my untainted ears
  When birds and flowers and I were happy peers.   45

How like a prodigal doth nature seem,
When thou, for all thy gold, so common art!
    Thou teachest me to deem
More sacredly of every human heart,
  Since each reflects in joy its scanty gleam   50
Of heaven, and could some wondrous secret show,
    Did we but pay the love we owe,
  And with a child's undoubting wisdom look
  On all these living pages of God's book.

1845

---

²Armored.
³Ancient Greek city in southern Italy famed for luxury and
voluptuousness.

from The Biglow Papers, First Series[1]

NO. I
A LETTER

FROM MR. EZEKIEL BIGLOW OF JAALAM TO THE
HON. JOSEPH T. BUCKINGHAM, EDITOR OF THE BOSTON COURIER,
INCLOSING A POEM OF HIS SON, MR. HOSEA BIGLOW.

JAYLEM, june 1846.

MISTER EDDYTER:—Our Hosea wuz down to Boston last week, and he see a cruetin Sarjunt[2] a struttin round as popler as a hen with 1 chicking, with 2 fellers a drumming and fifin arter him like all nater.[3] the sarjunt he thout Hosea hed n't gut his i teeth cut cos he looked a kindo 's though he'd jest com down,[4] so he cal'lated to hook him in, but Hosy wood n't take none o' his sarse[5] for all he hed much as 20 Rooster's tales stuck onto his hat and eenamost enuf brass a bobbin up and down on his shoulders and figureed onto his coat and trousis, let alone wut nater hed sot in his featers, to make a 6 pounder[6] out on.

wal, Hosea he com home considerabal riled, and arter I'd gone to bed I heern Him a thrashin round like a short-tailed Bull in fli-time. The old Woman ses she to me ses she, Zekle, ses she, our Hosee's gut the chollery[7] or suthin anuther ses she, don't you Bee skeered, ses I, he's oney amakin pottery[8] ses i, he's ollers on hand at that ere busynes like Da & martin,[9] and shure enuf, cum mornin, Hosy he cum down stares full chizzle,[10] hare on eend and cote tales flyin, and sot rite of to go reed his varses to Parson Wilbur bein he haint aney grate shows o' book larnin himself, bimeby he cum back and sed the parson wuz dreffle tickled with 'em as i hoop you will Be, and said they wuz True grit.[11]

Hosea ses taint hardly fair to call 'em hisn now, cos the parson kind o' slicked off sum o' the last varses, but he told Hosee he did n't want to put his ore in to tetch to the Rest on 'em, bein they wuz verry well As thay wuz, and then Hosy ses he sed suthin a nuther about Simplex Mundishes[12] or sum sech feller, but I guess Hosea kind o' did n't hear him, for I never hearn o' nobody o' that name in this villadge, and I've lived here man and boy 76 year cum next tater diggin, and thair aint no wheres a kitting spryer 'n I be.

If you print 'em I wish you'd jest let folks know who hosy's father is, cos my ant Keziah used to say it 's nater to be curus ses she, she aint livin though and he's a likely kind o' lad.

EZEKIEL BIGLOW.

---

[1]Written in protest against the Mexican War (1846–48), which Lowell considered "a national crime committed in behoof of Slavery, our common sin," the first Biglow Papers appeared anonymously from 1846 through 1848, their popularity astonishing the then almost unread author. For his satiric "little puppet show," Lowell created the versifying rustic, Hosea Biglow, embodying New England's "homely common-sense vivified and heated by conscience, speaking the native Yankee idiom, "racy with life and vigor and originality, bucksome . . . to our new occasions." The "more cautious element of the New England character and its pedantry" is expressed by the Reverend Homer Wilbur, "H. W.," Hosea's parson and editor of his poems.
[2]Recruiting sergeant. President Polk called for 50,000 volunteers after war was declared on May 13, 1846. On May 26, Massachusetts Governor Briggs called for the enrollment of a regiment.
[3]Nature.
[4]I.e., come down from the country.
[5]"Abuse, impertinence" (Lowell's note in the glossary of the 1848 edition).
[6]Brass cannon.
[7]Choleric, bad-tempered.
[8]"*Aut insanit, aut versus facit.*—H. W." (Lowell's note). Homer Wilbur misquotes the Latin of Roman poet Horace, *Satires* 2.7.117: "He is either mad or is making verses." Pottery: poetry.
[9]Day and Martin advertised their shoe blacking in verse.
[10]Full chisel, at full speed.
[11]"Grit: spirit, energy, pluck" (Lowell's note).
[12]Hosea's mispronunciation of the Parson's *simplex munditiis* ("simple in neatness") from Horace, *Odes* 1.5.5.

Thrash away, you'll *hev* to rattle
  On them kittle-drums o' yourn,—
'Taint a knowin' kind o' cattle
  Thet is ketched with mouldy corn;
Put in stiff, you fifer feller,   5
  Let folks see how spry you be,—
Guess you 'll toot till you are yeller
  'Fore you git ahold o' me!

Thet air flag's a leetle rotten,
  Hope it aint your Sunday's best;—   10
Fact! it takes a sight o' cotton[13]
  To stuff out a soger's[14] chest:
Sence we farmers hev to pay fer 't,
  Ef you must wear humps like these,
S'posin' you should try salt hay fer 't,   15
  It would du ez slick ez grease.

'T would n't suit them Southun fellers,
  They 're a dreffle graspin' set,
We must ollers blow the bellers
  Wen they want their irons het;   20
May be it 's all right ez preachin',
  But *my* narves it kind o' grates,
Wen I see the overreachin'
  O' them nigger-drivin' States.

Them thet rule us, them slave-traders,   25
  Haint they cut a thunderin' swarth
(Helped by Yankee renegaders),
  Thru the vartu o' the North!
We begin to think it 's nater
  To take sarse an' not be riled;—   30
Who 'd expect to see a tater
  All on eend at bein' biled?

Ez fer war, I call it murder,—
  There you hev it plain an' flat;
I don't want to go no furder   35
  Than my Testyment fer that;
God hez sed so plump an' fairly,
  It 's ez long ez it is broad,
An' you 've gut to git up airly
  Ef you want to take in God.   40

'Taint your eppyletts an' feathers
  Make the thing a grain more right;
'Taint afollerin' your bell-wethers[15]
  Will excuse ye in His sight;
Ef you take a sword an' dror it,   45
  An' go stick a feller thru,
Guv'ment aint to answer for it,
  God 'll send the bill to you.

---

[13]The abolitionists held that the Mexican War was caused
by the need to acquire new land for the South's cotton crop
and slave labor.

[14]Soldier's.
[15]Male sheep, with a bell on its neck, that leads the flock.

Wut's the use o' meetin'-goin'
　　Every Sabbath, wet or dry, 50
Ef it 's right to go amowin'
　　Feller-men like oats an' rye?
I dunno but wut it's pooty
　　Trainin' round in bobtail coats,—
But it's curus Christian dooty 55
　　This 'ere cuttin' folks's throats.

They may talk o' Freedom's airy[16]
　　Tell they're pupple in the face,—
It 's a grand gret cemetary
　　Fer the barthrights of our race; 60
They jest want this Californy
　　So 's to lug new slave-states in
To abuse ye, an' to scorn ye,
　　An' to plunder ye like sin.

Aint it cute to see a Yankee 65
　　Take sech everlastin' pains,
All to git the Devil's thankee
　　Helpin' on 'em weld their chains?
Wy, it 's jest ez clear ez figgers,
　　Clear ez one an' one make two, 70
Chaps thet make black slaves o' niggers
　　Want to make wite slaves o' you.

Tell ye jest the eend I 've come to
　　Arter cipherin' plaguy smart,
An' it makes a handy sum, tu, 75
　　Any gump[17] could larn by heart;
Laborin' man an' laborin' woman
　　Hev one glory an' one shame.
Ev'y thin' thet 's done inhuman
　　Injers all on 'em the same. 80

'Taint by turnin' out to hack folks
　　You 're agoin' to git your right,
Nor by lookin' down on black folks
　　Coz you 're put upon by wite;
Slavery aint o' nary color, 85
　　'Taint the hide thet makes it wus,
All it keers fer in a feller
　　'S jest to make him fill its pus.[18]

Want to tackle *me* in, du ye?
　　I expect you 'll hev to wait; 90
Wen cold lead puts daylight thru ye
　　You 'll begin to kal'late;[19]
S'pose the crows wun't fall to pickin'
　　All the carkiss from your bones,
Coz you helped to give a lickin' 95
　　To them poor half-Spanish drones?[20]

---

[16]"Area" (Lowell's note).
[17]"A foolish fellow, a dullard" (Lowell's note).
[18]"Purse" (Lowell's note).

[19]Calculate.
[20]The Mexicans.

Jest go home an' ask our Nancy
    Wether I 'd be sech a goose
Ez to jine ye,—guess you 'd fancy
    The etarnal bung[21] wuz loose!
She wants me fer home consumption,   100
    Let alone the hay 's to mow,—
Ef you 're arter folks o' gumption,
    You 've a darned long row to hoe.

Take them editors thet 's crowin'   105
    Like a cockerel three months old,—
Don't ketch any on 'em goin',
    Though they *be* so blasted bold;
Aint they a prime lot o' fellers?
    'Fore they think on 't guess they'll sprout   110
(Like a peach thet's got the yellers),[22]
    With the meanness bustin' out.

Wal, go 'long to help 'em stealin'
    Bigger pens to cram with slaves,
Help the men thet 's ollers dealin'   115
    Insults on your fathers' graves;
Help the strong to grind the feeble,
    Help the many agin the few,
Help the men thet call your people
    Witewashed slaves an' peddlin' crew!   120

Massachusetts, God forgive her,
    She 's akneelin' with the rest,[23]
She, thet ough' to ha' clung ferever
    In her grand old eagle-nest;
She thet ough' to stand so fearless   125
    W'ile the wracks are round her hurled,
Holdin' up a beacon peerless
    To the oppressed of all the world!—

Ha'n't they sold your colored seamen?
    Ha'n't they made your env'ys w'iz?[24]   130
Wut 'll make ye act like freemen?
    Wut 'll git your dander riz?
Come, I 'll tell ye wut I 'm thinkin'
    Is our dooty in this fix,
They 'd ha' done 't ez quick ez winkin'   135
    In the days o' seventy-six.

Clang the bells in every steeple,
    Call all true men to disown
The tradoocers of our people,
    The enslavers o' their own;   140
Let our dear old Bay State proudly
    Put the trumpet to her mouth,

[21]Plug.
[22]"A disease of peach trees" (Lowell's note).
[23]The governor had called for troops and some Massachusetts congressmen had voted to declare war.

[24]Envoys sent to southern states to protest the capture of free colored citizens of Massachusetts, especially seamen, were made to whiz, that is, were forced to flee.

Let her ring this messidge loudly
  In the ears of all the South:—

"I'll return ye good fer evil   145
  Much ez we frail mortils can,
But I wun't go help the Devil
  Makin' man the cus o' man;
Call me coward, call me traiter,
  Jest ez suits your mean idees,—   150
Here I stand a tyrant-hater,
  An' the friend o' God an' Peace!"

Ef I 'd *my* way I hed ruther
  We should go to work an' part,
They take one way, we take t' other,   155
  Guess it would n't break my heart;
Man hed ough' to put asunder
  Them thet God has noways jined;[25]
An' I should n't gretly wonder
  Ef there 's thousands o' my mind.   160

[The first recruiting sergeant on record I conceive to have been that individual who is mentioned in the Book of Job as *going to and fro in the earth, and walking up and down in it.*[26] Bishop Latimer will have him to have been a bishop,[27] but to me that other calling would appear more congenial. The sect of Cainites[28] is not yet extinct, who esteemed the first-born of Adam to be the most worthy, not only because of that privilege of primogeniture, but inasmuch as he was able to overcome and slay his younger brother. That was a wise saying of the famous Marquis Pescara[29] to the Papal Legate, that *it was impossible for men to serve Mars and Christ at the same time.* Yet in time past the profession of arms was judged to be κατ' εξοχήν[30] that of a gentleman, nor does this opinion want for strenuous upholders even in our day. Must we suppose, then, that the profession of Christianity was only intended for losels, or, at best, to afford an opening for plebeian ambition? Or shall we hold with that nicely metaphysical Pomeranian, Captain Vratz, who was Count Königsmark's chief instrument in the murder of Mr. Thynne, that the Scheme of Salvation has been arranged with an especial eye to the necessities of the upper classes, and that "God would consider a *gentleman* and deal with him suitably to the condition and profession he had placed him in"?[31] It may be said of us all, *Exemplo plus quam ratione vivimus.*[32]—H. W.]

1846   1846

---

[25]Cf. Matthew 19:6: "What therefore God hath joined together, let not man put asunder."

[26]The "individual" is Satan (Job 1:7 and 2:2). This long note is Parson Wilbur's commentary on Hosea's poem.

[27]Bishop Hugh Latimer (1485?–1555), English Reformation leader, in his sermon "Of the Plough" (January 18, 1548) called the devil a bishop.

[28]Second-century sect worshipping Cain and other evil characters in the Bible.

[29]Fernando Francesco de Ávalos, Marqués de Pescara

(1489–1525), Spanish commander in chief serving the Emperor Charles V.

[30]"Especially" (Greek).

[31]Captain Vratz is reported to have said approximately this as he walked to his execution for having killed Thomas Thynne at the instigation of Count Königsmark, in love with Thynne's wife. The story is told by English diarist John Evelyn (1620–1706) in his *Diary* for March 10, 1682, the day of the execution.

[32]"We live more by example than by reason" (Latin).

from **A Fable for Critics**[1]

Reader! walk up at once (it will soon be too late),
and buy at a perfectly ruinous rate

A FABLE FOR CRITICS:

OR, BETTER,

(I like, as a thing that the reader's first fancy may strike,
an old-fashioned title-page,
such as presents a tabular view of the volume's contents),

A GLANCE AT A FEW OF OUR LITERARY PROGENIES

(MRS. MALAPROP'S WORD)[2]

FROM THE TUB OF DIOGENES;[3]

A VOCAL AND MUSICAL MEDLEY,

THAT IS,

A SERIES OF JOKES

By A Wonderful Quiz,

WHO ACCOMPANIES HIMSELF WITH A RUB-A-DUB-DUB, FULL OF SPIRIT AND GRACE, ON THE TOP OF THE TUB.

Set forth in October, the 31st day,
In the year '48, G. P. Putnam, Broadway.

. . . . . .

One word to such readers (judicious and wise) as read books with something behind the mere eyes, of whom in the country, perhaps, there are two, including myself, gentle reader, and you. All the characters sketched in this slight *jeu d' esprit*,[4] though, it may be, they seem, here and there, rather free, and drawn from a somewhat too cynical standpoint, are *meant* to be faithful, for that is the grand point, and none but an owl would feel sore at a rub from a jester who tells you, without any subterfuge, that he sits in Diogenes' tub.

. . . . . .

---

[1]The elaborate title page and the prefatory remarks to the reader are composed in the same rhymed rollicking meter as the *Fable*, which Lowell describes as "a frail, slender thing, rhyme-ywinged, with a sting in its tail."
[2]Mrs. Malaprop, a character in Sheridan's *The Rivals*

(1775), gets her words mixed up: "progenies" for "prodigies."
[3]Diogenes (412?–323 B.C.), Greek Cynic philosopher who rejected social conventions, reputedly lived in a tub.
[4]"Witty display" (French).

[APOLLO SKETCHES THE POETS OF AMERICA]

[Phoebus Apollo, Greek god of poetry, distractedly glances at the poems sent to him by the pestering poets. Finding it "convenient sometimes/ To get his court clear of the makers of rhymes," he keeps a critic at hand, "who, by means of a bray," or a review, drives "the rabble away." Two aggressively nationalistic New York editors come up, one complaining about English attacks on American letters, who nevertheless admits "'t is/The whole aim of our lives to get one English notice." The other, denouncing the "hack/Who thinks every national author a poor one,/That isn't a copy of something that's foreign," gives Apollo another book by an American for his review. In answer, Apollo speaks of "these desperate books" as so bad as to be fit punishment for criminals, and, seeing the first of a long line of visitors approaching, he continues:]

"But stay, here come Tityrus Griswold,[5] and leads on
The flocks whom he first plucks alive, and then feeds on,—   525
A loud-cackling swarm, in whose feathers warm-drest,
He goes for as perfect a—swan as the rest.

[EMERSON]

"There comes Emerson first, whose rich words, every one,
Are like gold nails[6] in temples to hang trophies on,
Whose prose is grand verse, while his verse, the Lord knows,   530
Is some of it pr— No, 't is not even prose;
I 'm speaking of metres; some poems have welled
From those rare depths of soul that have ne'er been excelled;
They 're not epics, but that does n't matter a pin,
In creating, the only hard thing 's to begin;   535
A glass-blade 's no easier to make than an oak;
If you 've once found the way, you 've achieved the grand stroke;
In the worst of his poems are mines of rich matter,
But thrown in a heap with a crash and a clatter;
Now it is not one thing nor another alone   540
Makes a poem, but rather the general tone,
The something pervading, uniting the whole,
The before unconceived, unconceivable soul,
So that just in removing this trifle or that, you
Take away, as it were, a chief limb of the statue;   545
Roots, wood, bark, and leaves singly perfect may be,
But, clapt hodge-podge together, they don't make a tree.

"But, to come back to Emerson (whom, by the way,
I believe we left waiting),—his is, we may say,
A Greek head on right Yankee shoulders, whose range   550
Has Olympus for one pole, for t'other the Exchange;[7]
He seems, to my thinking (although I 'm afraid
The comparison must, long ere this, have been made),
A Plotinus-Montaigne, where the Egyptian's gold mist
And the Gascon's shrewd wit cheek-by-jowl co-exist;[8]   555
All admire, and yet scarcely six converts he 's got

---

[5]Rufus Griswold (1815–1857), critic and editor of numerous anthologies, including *The Poet and Poetry of America* (1842). Tityrus is the name of an ideal goatherd in Greek and Latin pastoral poetry.
[6]Ecclesiastes 12:11: "The words of the wise are as goads, and as nails fastened by the masters of assemblies, which are given from one shepherd."

[7]Olympus: mountain home of the Greek gods; Exchange: stock market.
[8]Plotinus (205?–270?), neoplatonic (idealist) philosopher, born in Egypt; Michel Eyquem de Montaigne (1533–1592), French ("Gascon") essayist and skeptic.

To I don't (nor they either) exactly know what;
For though he builds glorious temples, 't is odd
He leaves never a doorway to get in a god.
'T is refreshing to old-fashioned people like me   560
To meet such a primitive Pagan as he,
In whose mind all creation is duly respected
As parts of himself—just a little projected;
And who 's willing to worship the stars and the sun,
A convert to—nothing but Emerson.   565
So perfect a balance there is in his head,
That he talks of things sometimes as if they were dead;
Life, nature, love, God, and affairs of that sort,
He looks at as merely ideas; in short,
As if they were fossils stuck round in a cabinet,   570
Of such vast extent that our earth 's a mere dab in it;
Composed just as he is inclined to conjecture her,
Namely, one part pure earth, ninety-nine parts pure lecturer;
You are filled with delight at his clear demonstration,
Each figure, word, gesture, just fits the occasion,   575
With the quiet precision of science he 'll sort 'em,
But you can't help suspecting the whole a *post mortem*.

   "There are persons, mole-blind to the soul's make and style,
Who insist on a likeness 'twixt him and Carlyle;[9]
To compare him with Plato[10] would be vastly fairer,   580
Carlyle 's the more burly, but E. is the rarer;
He sees fewer objects, but clearlier, truelier,
If C. 's as original, E. 's more peculiar;
That he 's more of a man you might say of the one,
Of the other he 's more of an Emerson;   585
C. 's the Titan, as shaggy of mind as of limb,—
E. the clear-eyed Olympian, rapid and slim;[11]
The one 's two thirds Norseman, the other half Greek,[12]
Where the one 's most abounding, the other 's to seek;
C.'s generals require to be seen in the mass,—   590
E.'s specialties gain if enlarged by the glass;
C. gives Nature and God his own fits of the blues,
And rims common-sense things with mystical hues,—
E. sits in a mystery calm and intense,
And looks coolly around him with sharp common sense;   595
C. shows you how every-day matters unite
With the dim transdiurnal recesses of night,—
While E., in a plain, preternatural way,
Makes mysteries matters of mere every day;
C. draws all his characters quite *à la* Fuseli,[13]—   600
Not sketching their bundles of muscles and thews illy,
He paints with a brush so untamed and profuse,
They seem nothing but bundles of muscles and thews;
E. is rather like Flaxman,[14] lines strait and severe,
And a colorless outline, but full, round, and clear;—   605

---

[9]Thomas Carlyle (1795–1881), Scottish essayist and historian, friend of Emerson.
[10]Plato (427–347 B.C.), Greek philosopher.
[11]Titan, one of the primitive gods, born of heaven and earth, overthrown by the Olympians, the gods of heaven.
[12]Carlyle is like the Norseman or pillaging Viking because he took over the Germanic idealistic thought of Kant and Hegel, whereas Emerson is half practical Yankee and half Platonic idealist.
[13]Heinrich Fuseli (1741–1825), Anglo-Swiss painter of exotic, dreamlike paintings and elongated, distorted figures.
[14]John Flaxman (1755–1826), English neoclassical sculptor.

To the men he thinks worthy he frankly accords
The design of a white marble statue in words
C. labors to get at the centre, and then
Take a reckoning from there of his actions and men;
E. calmly assumes the said centre as granted,   610
And, given himself, has whatever is wanted.

"He has imitators in scores, who omit
No part of the man but his wisdom and wit,—
Who go carefully o'er the sky-blue of his brain,
And when he has skimmed it once, skim it again;   615
If at all they resemble him, you may be sure it is
Because their shoals mirror his mists and obscurities,
As a mud-puddle seems deep as heaven for a minute,
While a cloud that floats o'er is reflected within it.

"There comes——,[15] for instance; to see him's rare sport,   620
Tread in Emerson's tracks with legs painfully short;
How he jumps, how he strains, and gets red in the face,
To keep step with the mystagogue's natural pace!
He follows as close as a stick to a rocket,
His fingers exploring the prophet's each pocket.   625
Fie, for shame, brother bard; with good fruit of your own,
Can't you let Neighbor Emerson's orchards alone?
Besides, 't is no use, you 'll not find e'en a core,—
——[16] has picked up all the windfalls before.
They might strip every tree, and E. never would catch 'em,   630
His Hesperides have no rude dragon to watch 'em;[17]
When they send him a dishful, and ask him to try 'em,
He never suspects how the sly rogues came by 'em;
He wonders why 't is there are none such his trees on,
And thinks 'em the best he has tasted this season.   635

• • • • •

[BRYANT]

"There is Bryant, as quiet, as cool, and as dignified,   815
As a smooth, silent iceberg, that never is ignified,
Save when by reflection 't is kindled o' nights
With a semblance of flame by the chill Northern Lights.
He may rank (Griswold says so) first bard of your nation
(There 's no doubt that he stands in supreme ice-olation),   820
Your topmost Parnassus[18] he may set his heel on,
But no warm applauses come, peal following peal on,—
He 's too smooth and too polished to hang any zeal on:
Unqualified merits, I 'll grant, if you choose, he has 'em,
But he lacks the one merit of kindling enthusiasm;   825
If he stir you at all, it is just, on my soul,
Like being stirred up with the very North Pole.

"He is very nice reading in summer, but *inter
Nos*,[19] we don't want *extra* freezing in winter;

---

[15]William Ellery Channing (1818–1901), minor poet who moved to Concord to be near Emerson.
[16]Thoreau.
[17]In classical mythology, the garden of golden apples in the western Isles of the Blest, the Hesperides, were guarded by the daughters of Hesper, the Evening Star, and a sleepless dragon.
[18]Greek mountain sacred to Apollo and the Muses.
[19]"Between us" (Latin).

Take him up in the depth of July, my advice is, 830
When you feel an Egyptian devotion to ices.[20]
But, deduct all you can, there 's enough that 's right good in him,
He has a true soul for field, river, and wood in him;
And his heart, in the midst of brick walls, or where'er it is,
Glows, softens, and thrills with the tenderest charities— 835
To you mortals that delve in this trade-ridden planet?
No, to old Berkshire's hills, with their limestone and granite.
If you 're one who *in loco* (add *foco* here) *desipis*,[21]
You will get of his outermost heart (as I guess) a piece;
But you'd get deeper down if you came as a precipice, 840
And would break the last seal of its inwardest fountain,
If you only could palm yourself off for a mountain.
Mr. Quivis,[22] or somebody quite as discerning,
Some scholar who 's hourly expecting his learning,
Calls B. the American Wordsworth; but Wordworth 845
May be rated at more than your whole tuneful herd 's worth.
No, don't be absurd, he 's an excellent Bryant;
But, my friends, you 'll endanger the life of your client,
By attempting to stretch him up into a giant:
If you choose to compare him, I think there are two per- 850
-sons fit for a parallel—Thompson and Cowper;[23]
I don't mean exactly,—there's something of each,
There 's T.'s love of nature, C.'s penchant to preach;
Just mix up their minds so that C.'s spice of craziness
Shall balance and neutralize T.'s turn for laziness, 855
And it gives you a brain cool, quite frictionless, quiet,
Whose internal police nips the buds of all riot,—
A brain like a permanent strait-jacket put on
The heart that strives vainly to burst off a button,—
A brain which, without being slow or mechanic, 860
Does more than a larger less drilled, more volcanic;
He 's a Cowper condensed, with no craziness bitten,
And the advantage that Wordsworth before him had written.

"But, my dear little bardlings, don't prick up your ears
Nor suppose I would rank you and Bryant as peers; 865
If I call him an iceberg, I don't mean to say
There is nothing in that which is grand in its way;
He is almost the one of your poets that knows
How much grace, strength, and dignity lie in Repose;
If he sometimes fall short, he is too wise to mar 870
His thought's modest fulness by going too far;
'T would be well if your authors should all make a trial
Of what virtue there is in severe self-denial,
And measure their writings by Hesiod's staff,
Which teaches that all has less value than half.[24] 875

---

[20]Pun on Isis, Egyptian goddess of fertility.
[21]*In loco desipis:* "can be foolish in a particular place" (Latin). *Foco:* "fireplace" (Latin). *Loco:* "crazy" (Spanish). Locofoco is the name given to the radical Democrats who foiled a plot to put the lights out at their meeting in 1835 by buying stores of locofoco matches, newly invented.
[22]"Mr. Anyone" (Latin).
[23]"To demonstrate quickly and easily how per- / -versely absurd 'tis to sound this name *Cowper*, / As people in gen-

eral call him named *super*, / I remark that he rhymes it himself with horse-trooper "(Lowell's note). James Thomson (1700–1748), Scottish nature poet, author of *The Seasons* (1726–30) and *The Castle of Indolence* (1748); William Cowper (1731–1800), English poet, author of *The Task* (1785), and subject to fits of insanity.
[24]"Fools, they do not know how much more is the half than the whole" (*Works and Days,* 1. 40), the staff, or measure, of Greek didactic poet Hesiod (fl. 766 B.C.).

[WHITTIER]

"There is Whittier, whose swelling and vehement heart
Strains the strait-breasted drab of the Quaker apart,
And reveals the live Man, still supreme and erect,
Underneath the bemummying wrappers of sect;
There was ne'er a man born who had more of the swing   880
Of the true lyric bard and all that kind of thing;
And his failures arise (though he seem not to know it)
From the very same cause that has made him a poet,—
A fervor of mind which knows no separation
'Twixt simple excitement and pure inspiration,   885
As my Pythoness erst sometimes erred from not knowing
If 't were I or mere wind through her tripod was blowing;[25]
Let his mind once get head in its favorite direction
And the torrent of verse bursts the dams of reflection,
While, borne with the rush of the metre along,   890
The poet may chance to go right or go wrong,
Content with the whirl and delirium of song;
Then his grammar's not always correct, nor his rhymes,
And he 's prone to repeat his own lyrics sometimes,
Not his best, though, for those are struck off at white-heats   895
When the heart in his breast like a trip-hammer beats,
And can ne'er be repeated again any more
Than they could have been carefully plotted before:
Like old what 's-his-name there at the battle of Hastings
(Who, however, gave more than mere rhythmical bastings),[26]   900
Our Quaker leads off metaphorical fights
For reform and whatever they call human rights,
Both singing and striking in front of the war,
And hitting his foes with the mallet of Thor;[27]
Anne haec, one exclaims, on beholding his knocks,   905
Vestis filii tui,[28] O leather-clad Fox?[29]
Can that be thy son, in the battle's mid din,
Preaching brotherly love and then driving it in
To the brain of the tough old Goliath[30] of sin,
With the smoothest of pebbles from Castaly's spring[31]   910
Impressed on his hard moral sense with a sling?

"All honor and praise to the right-hearted bard
Who was true to The Voice when such service was hard,
Who himself was so free he dared sing for the slave
When to look but a protest in silence was brave;   915
All honor and praise to the women and men
Who spoke out for the dumb and the down-trodden then!
It needs not to name them, already for each
I see History preparing the statue and niche;
They were harsh, but shall *you* be so shocked at hard words   920
Who have beaten your pruning-hooks up into swords,[32]

---

[25]The Pythia or Delphic oracle, priestess of Apollo, uttered the god's words while inhaling vapors from a chasm over which she was seated on a tripod.
[26]Taillefer, a Norman minstrel, singing the *Song of Roland*, led the cavalry charge of William the Conqueror at the Battle of Hastings (1066) in southwest England.
[27]Norse god of war and thunder.
[28]"Is this the coat of thy son?" (Latin version of Genesis 37:32. Asked of Jacob by Joseph's brothers about the coat of many colors).

[29]George Fox (1624–1691), English founder of the Society of Friends, the Quakers, who wore leather breeches.
[30]The Philistine giant Goliath was slain by the young David with a stone from his slingshot. See 1 Samuel 17:39–50.
[31]The Castalian Spring, at the foot of Mt. Parnassus, sacred to Apollo, source of poetic inspiration.
[32]Joel 3:10: "Beat your plowshares into swords, and your pruninghooks into spears." I.e., why should those who supported the Mexican War (a proslavery war) be shocked at the harsh antislavery words of Whittier?

Whose rewards and hurrahs men are surer to gain
By the reaping of men and of women than grain?
Why should *you* stand aghast at their fierce wordy war, if
You scalp one another for Bank or for Tariff?[33]   925
Your calling them cut-throats and knaves all day long
Does n't prove that the use of hard language is wrong;
While the World's heart beats quicker to think of such men
As signed Tyranny's doom with a bloody steel-pen,
While on Fourth-of-Julys beardless orators fright one   930
With hints at Harmodius and Aristogeiton,[34]
You need not look shy at your sisters and brothers
Who stab with sharp words for the freedom of others;—
No, a wreath, twine a wreath for the loyal and true
Who, for sake of the many, dared stand with the few,   935
Not of blood-spattered laurel for enemies braved,
But of broad, peaceful oak-leaves for citizens saved!

· · · · ·

[HAWTHORNE]

"There is Hawthorne, with genius so shrinking and rare
That you hardly at first see the strength that is there;
A frame so robust, with a nature so sweet,   1000
So earnest, so graceful, so lithe and so fleet,
Is worth a descent from Olympus to meet;
'T is as if a rough oak that for ages had stood,
With his gnarled bony branches like ribs of the wood,
Should bloom, after cycles of struggle and scathe,   1005
With a single anemone trembly and rathe;[35]
His strength is so tender, his wildness so meek,
That a suitable parallel sets one to seek,—
He 's a John Bunyan Fouqué,[36] a Puritan Tieck;[37]
When Nature was shaping him, clay was not granted   1010
For making so full-sized a man as she wanted,
So, to fill out her model, a little she spared
From some finer-grained stuff for a woman prepared,
And she could not have hit a more excellent plan
For making him fully and perfectly man.   1015

· · · · ·

[COOPER]

"Here 's Cooper, who 's written six volumes to show
He 's as good as a lord: well, let 's grant that he 's so;
If a person prefer that description of praise,
Why, a coronet 's certainly cheaper than bays;   1025
But he need take no pains to convince us he 's not
(As his enemies say) the American Scott.[38]
Choose any twelve men, and let C. read aloud
That one of his novels of which he 's most proud,
And I'd lay any bet that, without ever quitting   1030
Their box, they 'd be all, to a man, for acquitting.

---

[33]A United States Bank and the protective tariff were two heated issues of the time.
[34]Sixth-century B.C. Greeks who killed Hipparchus, tyrant of Athens.
[35]Early in the season.
[36]John Bunyan (1628–1688), English preacher, author of the allegorical *Pilgrim's Progress;* Baron Friedrich de La Motte-Fouqué (1777–1843), German romantic novelist and poet.
[37]Ludwig Tieck (1773–1853), German romantic writer.
[38]Sir Walter Scott (1771–1832), Scotch novelist and poet.

He has drawn you one character, though, that is new,
One wildflower he 's plucked that is wet with the dew
Of this fresh Western world, and, the thing not to mince,
He has done naught but copy it ill ever since;   1035
His Indians, with proper respect be it said,
Are just Natty Bumppo,[39] daubed over with red,
And his very Long Toms[40] are the same useful Nat,
Rigged up in duck pants and a sou'wester hat
(Though once in a Coffin, a good chance was found   1040
To have slipped the old fellow away under ground).
All his other men-figures are clothes upon sticks,
The *dernière chemise*[41] of a man in a fix
(As a captain besieged, when his garrison 's small,
Sets up caps upon poles to be seen o'er the wall);   1045
And the women he draws from one model don't vary,
All sappy as maples and flat as a prairie.
When a character 's wanted, he goes to the task
As a cooper would do in composing a cask;
He picks out the staves, of their qualities heedful,   1050
Just hoops them together as tight as is needful,
And, if the best fortune should crown the attempt, he
Has made at the most something wooden and empty.

"Don't suppose I would underrate Cooper's abilities;
If I thought you 'd do that, I should feel very ill at ease;   1055
The men who have given to *one* character life
And objective existence are not very rife;
You may number them all, both prose-writers and singers,
Without overrunning the bounds of your fingers,
And Natty won't go to oblivion quicker   1060
Than Adams the parson or Primrose the vicar.[42]

"There is one thing in Cooper I like, too, and that is
That on manners he lectures his countrymen gratis;
Not precisely so either, because, for a rarity,
He is paid for his tickets in unpopularity.[43]   1065
Now he may overcharge his American pictures,
But you 'll grant there 's a good deal of truth in his strictures;
And I honor the man who is willing to sink
Half his present repute for the freedom to think,
And when he has thought, be his cause strong or weak,   1070
Will risk t'other half for the freedom to speak,
Caring naught for what vengeance the mob has in store,
Let that mob be the upper ten thousand or lower.

[APOLLO DIGRESSES ON OLD WORLD AND NEW]

"There are truths you Americans need to be told,
And it never 'll refute them to swagger and scold;   1075
John Bull,[44] looking o'er the Atlantic, in choler[45]

---

[39]Hero whose leggings gave the title to Cooper's five-novel *Leather-Stocking Tales.*
[40]Long Tom Coffin, the American sailor in *The Pilot* (1823).
[41]"Last shirt" (French).
[42]Two characters in English novels: Parson Adams in Henry Fielding's *Joseph Andrews* (1742) and Dr. Primrose in Oliver Goldsmith's *The Vicar of Wakefield* (1766).

[43]Cooper had become unpopular by such works as *Notions of the Americans* (1828) in which he was thought to be critical of American democracy.
[44]England.
[45]Anger.

At your aptness for trade, says you worship the dollar;
But to scorn such eye-dollar-try 's what very few do,
And John goes to that church as often as you do.
No matter what John says, don't try to outcrow him,   1080
'T is enough to go quietly on and outgrow him;
Like most fathers, Bull hates to see Number One
Displacing himself in the mind of his son,
And detests the same faults in himself he 'd neglected
When he sees them again in his child's glass reflected;   1085
To love one another you 're too like by half;
If he is a bull, you 're a pretty stout calf,
And tear your own pasture for naught but to show
What a nice pair of horns you 're beginning to grow.

   "There are one or two things I should just like to hint,   1090
For you don't often get the truth told you in print;
The most of you (this is what strikes all beholders)
Have a mental and physical stoop in the shoulders;
Though you ought to be free as the winds and the waves,
You 've the gait and the manners of runaway slaves;   1095
Though you brag of your New World, you don't half believe in it;
And as much of the Old as is possible weave in it;
Your goddess of freedom, a tight, buxom girl,
With lips like a cherry and teeth like a pearl,
With eyes bold as Herë's,[46] and hair floating free,   1100
And full of the sun as the spray of the sea,
Who can sing at a husking or romp at a shearing,
Who can trip through the forests alone without fearing,
Who can drive home the cows with a song through the grass,
Keeps glancing aside into Europe's cracked glass,   1105
Hides her red hands in gloves, pinches up her lithe waist,
And makes herself wretched with transmarine taste;
She loses her fresh country charm when she takes
Any mirror except her own rivers and lakes.

   "You steal Englishmen's books[47] and think Englishmen's thought,   1110
With their salt on her tail your wild eagle is caught;
Your literature suits its each whisper and motion
To what will be thought of it over the ocean;
The cast clothes of Europe your statesmanship tries
And mumbles again the old blarneys and lies;—   1115
Forget Europe wholly, your veins throb with blood,
To which the dull current in hers is but mud;
Let her sneer, let her say your experiment fails,
In her voice there 's a tremble e'en now while she rails,
And your shore will soon be in the nature of things   1120
Covered thick with gilt driftwood of castaway kings,
Where alone, as it were in a Longfellow's Waif,[48]
Her fugitive pieces will find themselves safe.
O my friends, thank your god, if you have one, that he
'Twixt the Old World and you set the gulf of a sea;   1125
Be strong-backed, brown-handed, upright as your pines,
By the scale of a hemisphere shape your designs,

---

[46]Hera, wife of Zeus, king of the gods; called ox-eyed by Homer.
[47]The International Copyright Act, protecting the works of foreign authors, was not passed until 1891.

[48]Longfellow edited a collection of fugitive verse called *The Waif* (1845).

Be true to yourselves and this new nineteenth age,
As a statue by Powers, or a picture by Page,[49]
Plough, sail, forge, build, carve, paint, make all over new,   1130
To your own New-World instincts contrive to be true,
Keep your ears open wide to the Future's first call,
Be whatever you will, but yourselves first of all,
Stand fronting the dawn on Toil's heaven-scaling peaks,
And become my new race of more practical Greeks.—   1135
Hem! your likeness at present, I shudder to tell o't,
Is that you have your slaves, and the Greek had his helot."[50]

．　．　．　．　．　．

[MARGARET FULLER]

"But there comes Miranda,[51] Zeus! where shall I flee to?
She has such a penchant for bothering me too!   1160
She always keeps asking if I don't observe a
Particular likeness 'twixt her and Minerva;[52]
She tells me my efforts in verse are quite clever;—
She 's been travelling now, and will be worse than ever;
One would think, though, a sharp-sighted noter she 'd be
Of all that 's worth mentioning over the sea,   1165
For a woman must surely see well, if she try,
The whole of whose being 's a capital I:
She will take an old notion, and make it her own,
By saying it o'er in her Sibylline[53] tone,
Or persuade you 't is something tremendously deep,   1170
By repeating it so as to put you to sleep;
And she well may defy any mortal to see through it,
When once she has mixed up her infinite *me* through it.
There is one thing she owns in her own single right,
It is native and genuine—namely, her spite;   1175
Though, when acting as censor, she privately blows
A censer of vanity 'neath her own nose."

Here Miranda came up, and said, "Phœbus![54] you know
That the Infinite Soul has its infinite woe,
As I ought to know, having lived cheek-by-jowl,   1180
Since the day I was born, with the Infinite Soul;
I myself introduced, I myself, I alone,
To my Land's better life authors solely my own,
Who the sad heart of earth on their shoulders have taken,
Whose works sound a depth by Life's quiet unshaken,   1185
Such as Shakespeare, for instance, the Bible, and Bacon,[55]

---

[49]Hiram Powers (1805–1873), American sculptor of portrait busts of Van Buren, Adams, Jackson, Webster, Calhoun; William Page (1811–1885), American portrait painter to whom Lowell dedicated his first book of poems (1843).

[50]A serf or bondsman in ancient Sparta, neither slave nor free.

[51]Margaret Fuller, named Miranda after the autobiographical character in her *Woman in the Nineteenth Century* (1845). Editor of the transcendental organ, the *Dial* (1840–42), she became literary critic for the New York *Tribune* in 1844 and was currently travelling in Europe. In her essay "American Literature" (1846), she criticized Lowell as "wanting in the true spirit and tone of poesy. His interest in the moral questions of the day has supplied the want of vitality in

himself; his great facility at versification has enabled him to fill the ear with a copious stream of pleasant sound. But his verse is stereotyped; his thought sounds no depth; and posterity will not remember him."

[52]Roman goddess of wisdom (Athena in Greek mythology), sprung from the brain of Jupiter (Zeus). Fuller had written in *Woman in the Nineteenth Century:* "Man partakes of the feminine in the Apollo; Woman of the masculine as Minerva."

[53]Prophetic; sibyls were women regarded as oracles in ancient Greece and Rome.

[54]Apollo.

[55]Francis Bacon (1561–1626), English philosopher, statesman, and essayist.

Not to mention my own works; Time's nadir is fleet,
And, as for myself, I'm quite out of conceit[56]—"

"Quite out of conceit! I 'm enchanted to hear it,"
Cried Apollo aside. "Who 'd have thought she was near it?   1190
To be sure, one is apt to exhaust those commodities
One uses too fast, yet in this case as odd it is
As if Neptune should say to his turbots and whitings,
'I 'm as much out of salt as Miranda's own writings'
(Which, as she in her own happy manner has said,   1195
Sound a depth, for 't is one of the functions of lead).
She often has asked me if I could not find
A place somewhere near me that suited her mind;
I know but a single one vacant, which she,
With her rare talent that way, would fit to a T.   1200
And it would not imply any pause or cessation
In the work she esteems her peculiar vocation,—
She may enter on duty to-day, if she chooses,
And remain Tiring-woman[57] for life to the Muses."

Miranda meanwhile has succeeded in driving   1205
Up into a corner, in spite of their striving,
A small flock of terrified victims, and there,
With an I-turn-the-crank-of-the-Universe air
And a tone which, at least to *my* fancy, appears
Not so much to be entering as boxing your ears,   1210
Is unfolding a tale (of herself, I surmise,
For 't is dotted as thick as a peacock's with I's).

∙ ∙ ∙ ∙ ∙

But 't is time now with pen phonographic[58] to follow
Through some more of his sketches our laughing Apollo:—

∙ ∙ ∙ ∙ ∙

[POE]

"There comes Poe, with his raven, like Barnaby Rudge,[59]
Three fifths of him genius and two fifths sheer fudge,
Who talks like a book of iambs and pentameters,   1300
In a way to make people of common sense damn metres,
Who has written some things quite the best of their kind,
But the heart somehow seems all squeezed out by the mind,
Who— But hey-day! What 's this? Messieurs Mathews and Poe,
You must n't fling mud-balls at Longfellow so,[60]   1305
Does it make a man worse that his character 's such
As to make his friends love him (as you think) too much?
Why, there is not a bard at this moment alive
More willing than he that his fellows should thrive;
While you are abusing him thus, even now   1310
He would help either one of you out of a slough;

---

[56]Ingenious or witty thought; Lowell plays with its other
meaning, vanity.
[57]Lady's maid, dressing assistant.
[58]I.e., with his pen the author transcribes the speech of
Apollo.
[59]Half-witted hero of Charles Dickens's *Barnaby Rudge*
(1841), whose pet is a talking raven that cries, "I'm a devil."

The novel came out serially, and Poe guessed the murderer
in a review.
[60]Cornelius Mathews (1817–1889), New York editor and
writer who called for a national literature, attacked
Longfellow's poetry, and Poe accused Longfellow of plagia-
rism.

You may say that he 's smooth and all that till you 're hoarse,
But remember that elegance also is force;
After polishing granite as much as you will,
The heart keeps its tough old persistency still;   1315
Deduct all you can, *that* still keeps you at bay;
Why, he 'll live till men weary of Collins and Gray.[61]
I'm not over-fond of Greek metres in English,[62]
To me rhyme's a gain, so it be not too jinglish,
And your modern hexameter verses are no more   1320
Like Greek ones than sleek Mr. Pope is like Homer;[63]
As the roar of the sea to the coo of a pigeon is,
So, compared to your moderns, sounds old Melesigenes;[64]
I may be too partial, the reason, perhaps, o't is
That I've heard the old blind man recite his own rhapsodies,   1325
And my ear with that music impregnate may be,
Like the poor exiled shell with the soul of the sea,
Or as one can't bear Strauss[65] when his nature is cloven
To its deeps within deeps by the stroke of Beethoven;[66]
But, set that aside, and 't is truth that I speak,   1330
Had Theocritus[67] written in English, not Greek,
I believe that his exquisite sense would scarce change a line
In that rare, tender, virgin-like pastoral Evangeline.
That's not ancient nor modern, its place is apart
Where time has no sway, in the realm of pure Art,   1335
'T is a shrine of retreat from Earth's hubbub and strife
As quiet and chaste as the author's own life.

· · · · · ·

[IRVING]

"What! Irving? thrice welcome, warm heart and fine brain,   1440
You bring back the happiest spirit from Spain,[68]
And the gravest sweet humor, that ever were there
Since Cervantes met death in his gentle despair;[69]
Nay, don't be embarrassed, nor look so beseeching,
I shan't run directly against my own preaching,   1445
And, having just laughed at their Raphaels and Dantes,[70]
Go to setting you up beside matchless Cervantes;
But allow me to speak what I honestly feel,—
To a true poet-heart add the fun of Dick Steele,
Throw in all of Addison,[71] *minus* the chill,   1450
With the whole of that partnership's stock and goodwill,
Mix well, and while stirring, hum o'er, as a spell,

---

[61]English poets William Collins (1721–1759) and Thomas Gray (1716–1771), author of the famous "Elegy Written in a Country Churchyard" (1751).
[62]Longfellow used the hexameter of Greek poetry in his *Evangeline* (1847).
[63]English poet Alexander Pope (1688–1744) used the heroic couplet in his translation of Homer's *Iliad* and *Odyssey*.
[64]Homer, Melos-born, said to be blind.
[65]Johann Strauss the Elder (1804–1849) composed and promoted Viennese waltzes.
[66]Ludwig van Beethoven (1770–1827), German romantic composer.
[67]Greek poet of the third century B.C., regarded as the founder of pastoral poetry.

[68]Washington Irving had written *A Chronicle of the Conquest of Granada* (1829) and a "Spanish *Sketch-Book*," *The Alhambra* (1832). He served as minister to Spain (1842–45) and returned to New York in 1846.
[69]Miguel de Cervantes Saavedra (1547–1616), author of *Don Quixote* (1605, 1615), wrote a moving farewell in the dedication of his last work four days before he died.
[70]The overvalued American authors pushed upon Apollo by the nationalistic critic-editors.
[71]Richard Steele (1672–1729) and Joseph Addison (1672–1719), English essayists who collaborated on the witty, urbane periodical *The Spectator*.

The fine *old* English Gentleman,[72] simmer it well,
Sweeten just to your own private liking, then strain,
That only the finest and clearest remain,   1455
Let it stand out of doors till a soul it receives
From the warm lazy sun loitering down through green leaves,
And you 'll find a choice nature, not wholly deserving
A name either English or Yankee,—just Irving.

· · · · ·

[HOLMES]

"There 's Holmes, who is matchless among you for wit;
A Leyden-jar[73] always full-charged, from which flit
The electrical tingles of hit after hit;   1560
In long poems 't is painful sometimes, and invites
A thought of the way the new Telegraph[74] writes,
Which pricks down its little sharp sentences spitefully
As if you got more than you 'd title to rightfully,
And you find yourself hoping its wild father Lightning   1565
Would flame in for a second and give you a fright'ning.
He has perfect sway of what *I* call a sham metre,
But many admire it, the English pentameter,
And Campbell,[75] I think, wrote most commonly worse,
With less nerve, swing, and fire in the same kind of verse,   1570
Nor e'er achieved aught in 't so worthy of praise
As the tribute of Holmes to the grand *Marseillaise*.[76]
You went crazy last year over Bulwer's New Timon;[77]—
Why, if B., to the day of his dying, should rhyme on,
Heaping verses on verses and tomes upon tomes,   1575
He could ne'er reach the best point and vigor of Holmes.
His are just the fine hands, too, to weave you a lyric
Full of fancy, fun, feeling, or spiced with satiric
In a measure so kindly, you doubt if the toes
That are trodden upon are your own or your foes'.   1580

[LOWELL]

"There is Lowell, who 's striving Parnassus to climb
With a whole bale of *isms* tied together with rhyme,
He might get on alone, spite of brambles and boulders,
But he can't with that bundle he has on his shoulders,
The top of the hill he will ne'er come nigh reaching   1585
Till he learns the distinction 'twixt singing and preaching;
His lyre has some chords that would ring pretty well,
But he'd rather by half make a drum of the shell,
And rattle away till he 's old as Methusalem,[78]
At the head of a march to the last new Jerusalem."   1590

· · · · ·

---

[72]"The English Country Gentleman," an essay by Irving in *Bracebridge Hall* (1822).
[73]Glass jar used as an electrical condenser.
[74]The Morse code invented in 1844 by Samuel F. B. Morse (1791–1872).
[75]Thomas Campbell (1777–1844), British poet.
[76]The French national anthem. The tribute occurs in Holmes's *Poetry: A Metrical Essay* (1836).

[77]*The New Timon: A Romance of London*, a poem in which Edward Bulwer-Lytton (1803–1873) satirizes other poets, including Tennyson, was published anonymously in 1846. Lowell's *Fable* also appeared anonymously.
[78]Methuselah lived 969 years (Genesis 5:27).

Here Miranda came up and began, "As to that—"   1805
Apollo at once seized his gloves, cane, and hat,
And, seeing the place getting rapidly cleared,
I too snatched my notes and forthwith disappeared.

1847–48   1848

Ode Recited
at the Harvard Commemoration[1]

JULY 21, 1865

I

Weak-winged is song,
Nor aims at that clear-ethered height
Whither the brave deed climbs for light:
    We seem to do them wrong,
Bringing our robin's-leaf to deck their hearse   5
Who in warm life-blood wrote their nobler verse;
Our trivial song to honor those who come
With ears attuned to strenuous trump and drum,
And shaped in squadron-strophes their desire,
Live battle-odes whose lines were steel and fire: 10
    Yet sometimes feathered words are strong,
A gracious memory to buoy up and save
From Lethe's[2] dreamless ooze, the common grave
    Of the unventurous throng.

II

To-day our Reverend Mother[3] welcomes back   15
    Her wisest Scholars, those who understood
The deeper teaching of her mystic tome,
    And offered their fresh lives to make it good:
        No lore of Greece or Rome,
No science peddling with the names of things,   20
Or reading stars to find inglorious fates,
        Can lift our life with wings
Far from Death's idle gulf that for the many waits,
        And lengthen out our dates
With that clear fame whose memory sings   25
In manly hearts to come, and nerves them and dilates:
Nor such thy teaching, Mother of us all!
        Not such the trumpet-call
        Of thy diviner mood,
        That could thy sons entice   30
From happy homes and toils, the fruitful nest

---

[1]The commemoration honored Harvard students who had fought in the Civil War. Among the speakers were Major General Meade, hero of Gettysburg, and Lowell. Keeping in mind that the poem was to be read aloud, Lowell experimented with a variety of verse forms, noting that his "problem was to contrive a measure which should not be tedious by uniformity, which should vary with varying moods, in which the transitions (including those of the voice) should be managed without jar."
[2]Mythological river of forgetfulness in the underworld.
[3]Harvard College, their alma mater.

Of those half-virtues which the world calls best,
   Into War's tumult rude;
   But rather far that stern device
The sponsors chose that round thy cradle stood   35
   In the dim, unventured wood,
   The VERITAS[4] that lurks beneath
   The letter's unprolific sheath,
  Life of whate'er makes life worth living,
Seed-grain of high emprise, immortal food,   40
  One heavenly thing whereof earth hath the giving.

III

Many loved Truth, and lavished life's best oil
  Amid the dust of books to find her,
Content at last, for guerdon[5] of their toil,
   With the cast mantle she hath left behind her.   45
    Many in sad faith sought for her,
    Many with crossed hands sighed for her;
    But these, our brothers, fought for her;
    At life's dear peril wrought for her,
    So loved her that they died for her,   50
    Tasting the raptured fleetness
    Of her divine completeness:
     Their higher instinct knew
Those love her best who to themselves are true,
And what they dare to dream of, dare to do;   55
    They followed her and found her
    Where all may hope to find,
Not in the ashes of the burnt-out mind,
But beautiful, with danger's sweetness round her.
    Where faith made whole with deed   60
    Breathes its awakening breath
    Into the lifeless creed,
    They saw her plumed and mailed,
    With sweet, stern face unveiled,
And all-repaying eyes, look proud on them in death.   65

IV

Our slender life runs rippling by, and glides
  Into the silent hollow of the past;
   What is there that abides
To make the next age better for the last?
   Is earth too poor to give us   70
Something to live for here that shall outlive us?
   Some more substantial boon
Than such as flows and ebbs with Fortune's fickle moon?
    The little that we see
    From doubt is never free;   75
    The little that we do
    Is but half-nobly true;
    With our laborious hiving
What men call treasure, and the gods call dross,

---

[4]Latin for "Truth," Harvard's motto, chosen by the founders.
[5]Reward.

Life seems a jest of Fate's contriving,   80
   Only secure in every one's conniving,
A long account of nothings paid with loss,
Where we poor puppets, jerked by unseen wires,
   After our little hour of strut and rave,
With all our pasteboard passions and desires,   85
Loves, hates, ambitions, and immortal fires,
   Are tossed pell-mell together in the grave.
   But stay! no age was e'er degenerate,
   Unless men held it at too cheap a rate,
   For in our likeness still we shape our fate.   90
      Ah, there is something here
   Unfathomed by the cynic's sneer,
   Something that gives our feeble light
   A high immunity from Night,
   Something that leaps life's narrow bars   95
To claim its birthright with the hosts of heaven;
   A seed of sunshine that can leaven
   Our earthly dulness with the beams of stars,
      And glorify our clay
With light from fountains elder than the Day;   100
   A conscience more divine than we,
   A gladness fed with secret tears,
   A vexing, forward-reaching sense
   Of some more noble permanence;
      A light across the sea,   105
Which haunts the soul and will not let it be,
Still beaconing from the heights of undegenerate years.

V

   Whither leads the path
   To ampler fates that leads?
   Not down through flowery meads,   110
   To reap an aftermath
  Of youth's vainglorious weeds,
  But up the steep, amid the wrath
And shock of deadly-hostile creeds,
   Where the world's best hope and stay   115
By battle's flashes gropes a desperate way,
And every turf the fierce foot clings to bleeds.
   Peace hath her not ignoble wreath,
   Ere yet the sharp, decisive word
Light the black lips of cannon, and the sword   120
   Dreams in its easeful sheath;
But some day the live coal behind the thought,
   Whether from Baäl's[6] stone obscene,
   Or from the shrine serene
   Of God's pure altar brought,   125
Burst up in flame; the war of tongue and pen
Learns with what deadly purpose it was fraught,
And, helpless in the fiery passion caught,
Shakes all the pillared state with shock of men;
Some day the soft Ideal that we wooed   130

---

[6]Nature god condemned by the Hebrews as a blasphemous
idol.

Confronts us fiercely, foe-beset, pursued,
And cries reproachful: "Was it, then, my praise,
And not myself was loved? Prove now thy truth;
I claim of thee the promise of thy youth;
Give me thy life, or cower in empty phrase,   135
The victim of thy genius, not its mate!"
   Life may be given in many ways,
   And loyalty to Truth be sealed
As bravely in the closet as the field,
      So bountiful is Fate;   140
      But then to stand beside her,
      When craven churls deride her,
To front a lie in arms and not to yield,
      This shows, methinks, God's plan
      And measure of a stalwart man,   145
      Limbed like the old heroic breeds,
      Who stands self-poised on manhood's solid earth,
      Not forced to frame excuses for his birth,
Fed from within with all the strength he needs.

VI

Such was he, our Martyr-Chief,[7]   150
      Whom late the Nation he had led,
      With ashes on her head,
Wept with the passion of an angry grief:
Forgive me, if from present things I turn
To speak what in my heart will beat and burn.   155
And hang my wreath on his world-honored urn.
      Nature, they say, doth dote,
      And cannot make a man
      Save on some worn-out plan,
      Repeating us by rote: 160
For him her Old-World moulds aside she threw,
      And, choosing sweet clay from the breast
      Of the unexhausted West,
With stuff untainted shaped a hero new,
Wise, steadfast in the strength of God, and true.   165
      How beautiful to see
Once more a shepherd of mankind indeed,
Who loved his charge, but never loved to lead;
One whose meek flock the people joyed to be,
      Not lured by any cheat of birth,   170
      But by his clear-grained human worth,
And brave old wisdom of sincerity!
      They knew that outward grace is dust;
      They could not choose but trust
In that sure-footed mind's unfaltering skill,   175
      And supple-tempered will
That bent like perfect steel to spring again and thrust.
      His was no lonely mountain-peak of mind,
      Thrusting to thin air o'er our cloudy bars,
      A sea-mark now, now lost in vapors blind;   180
      Broad prairie rather, genial, level-lined,

---

[7]The assassinated Lincoln. This sixth section was added after the public recital.

Fruitful and friendly for all human kind,
Yet also nigh to heaven and loved of loftiest stars.
    Nothing of Europe here,
Or, then, of Europe fronting mornward still,   185
    Ere any names of Serf and Peer
    Could Nature's equal scheme deface
    And thwart her genial will;
    Here was a type of the true elder race,
And one of Plutarch's men[8] talked with us face to face.   190
    I praise him not; it were too late;
And some innative weakness there must be
In him who condescends to victory
Such as the Present gives, and cannot wait,
    Safe in himself as in a fate.   195
    So always firmly he:
    He knew to bide his time,
    And can his fame abide,
Still patient in his simple faith sublime,
    Till the wise years decide.   200
    Great captains, with their guns and drums,
    Disturb our judgment for the hour,
    But at last silence comes;
These all are gone, and, standing like a tower,
    Our children shall behold his fame,   205
    The kindly-earnest, brave, foreseeing man,
Sagacious, patient, dreading praise, not blame,
    New birth of our new soil, the first American.

VII

Long as man's hope insatiate can discern
    Or only guess some more inspiring goal   210
    Outside of Self, enduring as the pole,
Along whose course the flying axles burn
Of spirits bravely-pitched, earth's manlier brood;
    Long as below we cannot find
The meed[9] that stills the inexorable mind;   215
So long this faith to some ideal Good,
    Under whatever mortal names it masks,
    Freedom, Law, Country, this ethereal mood
That thanks the Fates for their severer tasks,
    Feeling its challenged pulses leap,   220
    While others skulk in subterfuges cheap,
And, set in Danger's van, has all the boon it asks,
    Shall win man's praise and woman's love,
    Shall be a wisdom that we set above
All other skills and gifts to culture dear,   225
    A virtue round whose forehead we inwreathe
    Laurels that with a living passion breathe
When other crowns grow, while we twine them, sear.[10]
    What brings us thronging these high rites to pay,
And seal these hours the noblest of our year,   230
    Save that our brothers found this better way?

---

[8]Plutarch (46?–120) memorialized heroic Greeks and Romans in his *Parallel Lives.*

[9]The merited gift.
[10]Withered.

VIII

We sit here in the Promised Land
That flows with Freedom's honey and milk:[11]
But 't was they won it, sword in hand,
Making the nettle danger soft for us as silk.   235
    We welcome back our bravest and our best;—
    Ah me! not all! some come not with the rest,
Who went forth brave and bright as any here!
I strive to mix some gladness with my strain,
        But the sad strings complain,   240
        And will not please the ear:
I sweep them for a pæan, but they wane
        Again and yet again
Into a dirge, and die away, in pain.
In these brave ranks I only see the gaps,   245
Thinking of dear ones whom the dumb turf wraps,
Dark to the triumph which they died to gain:
    Fitlier may others greet the living,
    For me the past is unforgiving;
        I with uncovered head   250
        Salute the sacred dead,
Who went, and who return not.—Say not so!
'T is not the grapes of Canaan[12] that repay,
But the high faith that failed not by the way;
Virtue treads paths that end not in the grave;   255
No ban of endless night exiles the brave;
        And to the saner mind
We rather seem the dead that stayed behind.
Blow, trumpets, all your exultations blow!
For never shall their aureoled[13] presence lack: 260
I see them muster in a gleaming row,
With ever-youthful brows that nobler show;
We find in our dull road their shining track;
        In every nobler mood
We feel the orient of their spirit glow,   265
Part of our life's unalterable good,
Of all our saintlier aspiration;
        They come transfigured back,
Secure from change in their high-hearted ways,
Beautiful evermore, and with the rays   270
Of morn on their white Shields of Expectation!

IX

    But is there hope to save
    Even this ethereal essence from the grave?
What ever 'scaped Oblivion's subtle wrong
Save a few clarion names, or golden threads of song?   275
        Before my musing eye
    The mighty ones of old sweep by,
    Disvoicèd now and insubstantial things,

---

[11]God delivered His chosen people, the Israelites, from the hands of the Egyptians, and led them to the Promised Land, flowing with milk and honey (Exodus 3:8 and 13:5; Numbers 13).

[12]Canaan, a section of Palestine between the Jordan River and the Mediterranean Sea, was the Promised Land.
[13]Haloed.

As noisy once as we; poor ghosts of kings,
Shadows of empire wholly gone to dust,   280
And many races, nameless long ago,
To darkness driven by that imperious gust
Of ever-rushing Time that here doth blow:
O visionary world, condition strange,
Where naught abiding is but only Change,   285
Where the deep-bolted stars themselves still shift and range!
    Shall we to more continuance make pretence?
Renown builds tombs; a life-estate is Wit;
        And, bit by bit,
The cunning years steal all from us but woe;   290
    Leaves are we, whose decays no harvest sow.
        But, when we vanish hence,
Shall they lie forceless in the dark below,
Save to make green their little length of sods,
Or deepen pansies for a year or two,   295
Who now to us are shining-sweet as gods?
Was dying all they had the skill to do?
That were not fruitless: but the Soul resents
Such short-lived service, as if blind events
Ruled without her, or earth could so endure;   300
She claims a more divine investiture
Of longer tenure than Fame's airy rents;
Whate'er she touches doth her nature share;
Her inspiration haunts the ennobled air,
        Gives eyes to mountains blind,   305
Ears to the deaf earth, voices to the wind,
And her clear trump sings succor everywhere
By lonely bivouacs to the wakeful mind;
For soul inherits all that soul could dare:
        Yea, Manhood hath a wider span   310
And larger privilege of life than man.
The single deed, the private sacrifice,
So radiant now through proudly-hidden tears,
Is covered up ere long from mortal eyes
With thoughtless drift of the deciduous years;   315
But that high privilege that makes all men peers,
That leap of heart whereby a people rise
        Up to a noble anger's height,
And, flamed on by the Fates, not shrink, but grow more bright,
    That swift validity in noble veins,   320
        Of choosing danger and disdaining shame,
            Of being set on flame
By the pure fire that flies all contact base,
But wraps its chosen with angelic might,
        These are imperishable gains,   325
Sure as the sun, medicinal as light,
These hold great futures in their lusty reins
And certify to earth a new imperial race.

                        X

        Who now shall sneer?
        Who dare again to say we trace   330
        Our lines to a plebeian race?

Roundhead and Cavalier![14]
Dumb are those names erewhile in battle loud;
Dream-footed as the shadow of a cloud,
    They flit across the ear: 335
That is best blood that hath most iron in 't,
To edge resolve with, pouring without stint
    For what makes manhood dear.
    Tell us not of Plantagenets,
Hapsburgs, and Guelfs,[15] whose thin bloods crawl   340
Down from some victor in a border-brawl!
    How poor their outworn coronets,
Matched with one leaf of that plain civic wreath
Our brave for honor's blazon shall bequeath,
    Through whose desert a rescued Nation sets   345
Her heel on treason, and the trumpet hears
Shout victory, tingling Europe's sullen ears
    With vain resentments and more vain regrets!

XI

    Not in anger, not in pride,
    Pure from passion's mixture rude   350
    Ever to base earth allied,
    But with far-heard gratitude,
    Still with heart and voice renewed,
To heroes living and dear martyrs dead,
The strain should close that consecrates our brave.   355
    Lift the heart and lift the head!
    Lofty be its mood and grave,
    Not without a martial ring,
    Not without a prouder tread
    And a peal of exultation: 360
    Little right has he to sing
    Through whose heart in such an hour
    Beats no march of conscious power,
    Sweeps no tumult of elation!
    'T is no Man we celebrate,   365
    By his country's victories great,
A hero half, and half the whim of Fate,
    But the pith and marrow of a Nation
    Drawing force from all her men,
    Highest, humblest, weakest, all,   370
    For her time of need, and then
    Pulsing it again through them,
Till the basest can no longer cower,
Feeling his soul spring up divinely tall,
Touched but in passing by her mantle-hem.   375
Come back, then, noble pride, for 't is her dower!
    How could poet ever tower,
    In his passions, hopes, and fears,
    If his triumphs and his tears,
    Kept not measure with his people?   380

---

[14]The Puritan supporters of Cromwell and the Royalist supporters of Charles I in the English Civil War of the 1640s, here representing the New Englanders and the Southerners.

[15]Plantagenets, family name of English Kings (1154–1485); Hapsburgs, German princely family, rulers of the Holy Roman Empire (fifteenth to eighteenth centuries); Guelphs, papal party in medieval Italy.

Boom, cannon, boom to all the winds and waves!
Clash out, glad bells, from every rocking steeple!
Banners, a-dance with triumph, bend your staves!
 And from every mountain-peak
 Let beacon-fire to answering beacon speak,   385
 Katahdin tell Monadnock, Whiteface[16] he,
And so leap on in light from sea to sea,
  Till the glad news be sent
  Across a kindling continent,
Making earth feel more firm and air breathe braver: 390
"Be proud! for she is saved, and all have helped to save her!
 She that lifts up the manhood of the poor,
 She of the open soul and open door,
 With room about her hearth for all mankind!
 The fire is dreadful in her eyes no more;   395
 From her bold front the helm she doth unbind,
 Sends all her handmaid armies back to spin,
 And bids her navies, that so lately hurled
 Their crashing battle, hold their thunders in,
 Swimming like birds of calm along the unharmful shore. 400
 No challenge sends she to the elder world,
 That looked askance and hated; a light scorn
 Plays o'er her mouth, as round her mighty knees
 She calls her children back, and waits the morn
Of nobler day, enthroned between her subject seas."   405

XII

Bow down, dear Land, for thou hast found release!
 Thy God, in these distempered days,
 Hath taught thee the sure wisdom of His ways,
And through thine enemies hath wrought thy peace!
  Bow down in prayer and praise!   410
No poorest in thy borders but may now
Lift to the juster skies a man's enfranchised brow.
O Beautiful! my Country! ours once more!
Smoothing thy gold of war-dishevelled hair
O'er such sweet brows as never other wore,   415
  And letting thy set lips,
  Freed from wrath's pale eclipse,
The rosy edges of their smile lay bare,
What words divine of lover or of poet
Could tell our love and make thee know it,   420
Among the Nations bright beyond compare?
  What were our lives without thee?
  What all our lives to save thee?
  We reck not what we gave thee;
  We will not dare to doubt thee,   425
But ask whatever else, and we will dare!

1865   *1865*

---

[16]Mountains in Maine, New Hampshire, and New York.

Auspex[1]

My heart, I cannot still it,
Nest that had song-birds in it;
And when the last shall go,
The dreary days, to fill it,
Instead of lark or linnet,[2]   5
Shall whirl dead leaves and snow.

Had they been swallows only,
Without the passion stronger
That skyward longs and sings,—[3]
Woe's me, I shall be lonely   10
When I can feel no longer
The impatience of their wings!

A moment, sweet delusion,
Like birds the brown leaves hover,
But it will not be long   15
Before their wild confusion
Fall wavering down to cover
The poet and his song.

1878

JONES VERY
(1813–1880)

Nathaniel Hawthorne described Jones Very in 1842 as "a poet whose voice is scarcely heard among us by reason of its depth." Certain it is that Very's poetry had a quite small audience when Ralph Waldo Emerson helped him publish a book of prose and verse, *Essays and Poems,* in 1839. But some of the book's admirers were extravagant in their praise. James Russell Lowell wrote in the margins of his copy, "some of the sonnets . . . [are] better poetry than has yet been published in America." Richard Dana, Sr., thought that it would be impossible to find "anything in this country to compare with these sonnets." And William Cullen Bryant thought that Very's poems exhibited "outstanding grace and originality."

But Hawthorne's ambiguous judgment of Very was the one that prevailed. His quiet voice distanced itself in its depth and was no longer heard. When he died in 1880, he was one of the forgotten Transcendentalists. In the four-volume *Cambridge History of American Literature* (1917–21), the discussion of the Transcendentalists contained a single reference to Very as "the extreme mystic of the whole group, a victim for a time of religious mania."

It was left to Yvor Winters to "rediscover" Jones Very in 1936, in an essay included in *Maule's Curse* (1938) as "Jones Very and R. W. Emerson." In Win-

---

[1]Prophet or soothsayer who interprets omens taken from the actions of birds. The first line served as the title for the poem's first publication in 1878.

[2]European songbirds.

[3]The swallow is contrasted with the skylark, noted for the heights it attains and for its singing while in flight.

ters's comparison of these two writers, Emerson was too severely diminished. But the comparison was valuable in defining and distinguishing Very's poetry: "[Emerson's] poetry deals not with the [mystical] experience, but with his own theory of the experience; it is not mystical poetry but gnomic, or didactic, poetry. . . . [Whereas] Very speaks with the authority of [the mystical] experience—and this holds true, even if we feel less certain than Very as to the origin of the experience. . . ."

Since Winters provided Very with a poetic rebirth, the poet has found other critical champions and his poetry has appeared in modern editions. Having spent the last forty years of his life in relaxed obscurity, Very would be surprised at this new life. His early life had been lived with notorious intensity. He was born the son of a sea captain in Salem, Massachusetts, and accompanied his father to Russia and elsewhere, even attending school briefly in New Orleans. On his father's death in 1824, Very was thrown back on his own resources to obtain an education. He earned tuition expenses and entered Harvard in 1834, graduating with honors in 1836.

He entered Harvard Divinity School and went through an extraordinary religious experience in which he began to write sonnets at great speed under direct instructions from the Holy Ghost. Some acquaintances were skeptical, others sympathetic. He withdrew from school in 1838 at the faculty's request and entered an asylum for about a month.

Emerson became his sponsor and other Transcendentalists rallied around. They denied that he was insane, as had been charged. Emerson declared him "profoundly sane." After the publication of his book, and with the passing of time, Emerson's enthusiasm flagged. Without a Divinity degree, Very's career was limited. But he was licensed to preach and held some temporary pastorates. He was not, however, a gifted preacher. He lived his last years as a virtual recluse, under the protective care of a sister.

At the center of Very's mystic doctrine was the "will-less existence," an existence directed from without by the divine will. This doctrine clearly had connections with Calvinistic predestination, with the Quaker inner light, and the transcendental oversoul. But through his startling commitment to the interior voice of the Holy Ghost, Very made this mystic doctrine uniquely his in his poetry. It is a poetry of total spiritual self-confidence, at ease, in harmony with a knowing nature:

> The flowers I pass have eyes that look at me,
> The birds have ears that hear my spirit's voice,
> And I am glad the leaping brook to see,
> Because it does at my light step rejoice.

ADDITIONAL READING

Jones Very: Selected Poems, ed. Nathan Lyons, 1966.

Yvor Winters, "Jones Very: A New England Mystic," *The American Review*, VII (May, 1936), pp. 159–78, rpt. as "Jones Very and R. W. Emerson: Aspects of New England Mysticism" in *Maule's Curse* (1938); William Irving Bartlett, *Jones Very: Emerson's "Brave Saint,"* 1942; Edward Gittleman, *Jones Very: The Effective Years, 1833–1840*, 1967.

TEXTS

"The New Birth," "The Song," and "To the Pure All Things Are Pure" from *Essays and Poems by Jones Very*, 1839. "The Columbine," "The Lost," "The Dead," "The Hand and Foot," and "The Created" from *Poems by Jones Very*, ed. William P. Andrews, 1883. "The

Presence" and "The Absent" from *Poems and Essays by Jones Very*, ed. James Freeman Clarke, 1886. "The Eagles" from *Jones Very: Emerson's "Brave Saint,"* ed. William Irving Bartlett, 1942.

The Columbine

Still, still my eye will gaze long fixed on thee,
Till I forget that I am called a man,
And at thy side fast-rooted seem to be,
And the breeze comes my cheek with thine to fan.
Upon this craggy hill our life shall pass,— 5
A life of summer days and summer joys,—
Nodding our honey-bells mid pliant grass
In which the bee, half-hid, his time employs;
And here we'll drink with thirsty pores the rain,
And turn dew-sprinkled to the rising sun, 10
And look when in the flaming west again
His orb across the heaven its path has run;
Here left in darkness on the rocky steep,
My weary eyes shall close like folding flowers in sleep.

1838, 1839

The New Birth

'Tis a new life;—thoughts move not as they did
With slow uncertain steps across my mind,
In thronging haste fast pressing on they bid
The portals open to the viewless wind
That comes not save when in the dust is laid 5
The crown of pride that gilds each mortal brow,
And from before man's vision melting fade
The heavens and earth;—their walls are falling now.—
Fast crowding on, each thought asks utterance strong;
Storm-lifted waves swift rushing to the shore, 10
On from the sea they send their shouts along,
Back through the cave-worn rocks their thunders roar;
And I a child of God by Christ made free
Start from death's slumbers to Eternity.

1838, 1839

The Presence

I sit within my room, and joy to find
That Thou who always lov'st art with me here,
That I am never left by Thee behind,
But by Thyself Thou keep'st me ever near;

The fire burns brighter when with Thee I look,   5
And seems a kinder servant sent to me;
With gladder heart I read Thy holy book,
Because Thou art the eyes by which I see;
This aged chair, that table, watch and door
Around in ready service ever wait;   10
Nor can I ask of Thee a menial more
To fill the measure of my large estate,
For Thou Thyself, with all a Father's care,
Where'er I turn, art ever with me there.

                                                                        1839

The Lost

The fairest day that ever yet has shone,
Will be when thou the day within shalt see;
The fairest rose that ever yet has blown,
When thou the flower thou lookest on shalt be.
But thou art far away among Time's toys;   5
Thyself the day thou lookest for in them,
Thyself the flower that now thine eye enjoys,
But wilted now thou hang'st upon thy stem.
The bird thou hearest on the budding tree,
Thou hast made sing with thy forgotten voice;   10
But when it swells again to melody,
The song is thine in which thou wilt rejoice;
And thou new risen 'midst these wonders live,
That now to them dost all thy substance give.

                                                                  1839, 1883

The Dead

I see them,—crowd on crowd they walk the earth,
Dry leafless trees no autumn wind laid bare;
And in their nakedness find cause for mirth,
And all unclad would winter's rudeness dare;
No sap doth through their clattering branches flow,   5
Whence springing leaves and blossoms bright appear;
Their hearts the living God have ceased to know
Who gives the spring-time to th' expectant year.
They mimic life, as if from Him to steal
His glow of health to paint the livid cheek;   10
They borrow words for thoughts they cannot feel,
That with a seeming heart their tongue may speak;
And in their show of life more dead they live
Than those that to the earth with many tears they give.

                                                                        1839

The Song

When I would sing of crooked streams and fields,
On, on from me they stretch too far and wide,
And at their look my song all powerless yields,
And down the river bears me with its tide;
Amid the fields I am a child again,   5
The spots that then I loved I love the more,
My fingers drop the strangely-scrawling pen,
And I remember nought but nature's lore;
I plunge me in the river's cooling wave,
Or on the embroidered bank admiring lean,   10
Now some endangered insect life to save,
Now watch the pictured flowers and grasses green;
Forever playing where a boy I played,
By hill and grove, by field and stream delayed.

1839

To the Pure
All Things Are Pure

The flowers I pass have eyes that look at me,
The birds have ears that hear my spirit's voice,
And I am glad the leaping brook to see,
Because it does at my light step rejoice.
Come, brothers, all who tread the grassy hill,   5
Or wander thoughtless o'er the blooming fields,
Come learn the sweet obedience of the will;
Thence every sight and sound new pleasure yields.
Nature shall seem another house of thine,
When he who formed thee, bids it live and play,   10
And in thy rambles e'en the creeping vine
Shall keep with thee a jocund holiday,
And every plant, and bird, and insect, be
Thine own companions born for harmony.

1839

The Absent

Thou art not yet at home in thine own house,
But to one room I see thee now confined;
Having one hole like rat or skulking mouse,
And as a mole to all the others blind;
Does the great Day find preference when he shines   5
In at each window, lighting every room?
No selfish wish the moon's bright glance confines,
And each in turn the stars' faint rays illume;
Within thy sleeping room thou dost abide,

And thou the social parlor dost prefer;   10
All other thou wilt in the cupboard hide,
And this or that's the room for him or her;
But the same sun, and moon with silver face,
Look in on all, and lighten every place.

1838?   1841, 1886

The Hand and Foot

The hand and foot that stir not, they shall find
Sooner than all the rightful place to go:
Now in their motion free as roving wind,
Though first no snail so limited and slow;
I mark them full of labor all the day,   5
Each active motion made in perfect rest;
They cannot from their path mistaken stray,
Though 't is not theirs, yet in it they are blest;
The bird has not their hidden track found out,
The cunning fox though full of art he be;   10
It is the way unseen, the certain route,
Where ever bound, yet thou art ever free;
The path of Him, whose perfect law of love
Bids spheres and atoms in just order move.

1883

The Created

There is naught for thee by thy haste to gain;
'T is not the swift with Me that win the race;
Through long endurance of delaying pain,
Thine opened eye shall see thy Father's face;
Nor here nor there, where now thy feet would turn,   5
Thou wilt find Him who ever seeks for thee;
But let obedience quench desires that burn,
And where thou art thy Father, too, will be.
Behold! as day by day the spirit grows,
Thou see'st by inward light things hid before;   10
Till what God is, thyself, His image, shows;
And thou wilt wear the robe that first thou wore.
When bright with radiance from his forming hand,
He saw the lord of all His creatures stand.

1838?   1883

The Eagles[1]

The eagles gather on the place of death
So thick the ground is spotted with their wings,
The air is tainted with the noisome breath
The wind from off the field of slaughter brings;
Alas! no mourners weep them for the slain,   5
But all unburied lies the naked soul;
The whitening bones of thousands strew the plain,
Yet none can now the pestilence control;
The eagles gathering on the carcass feed,
In every heart behold their half-formed prey;   10
The battened wills beneath their talons bleed,
Their iron beaks without remorse must slay;
Till by the sun no more the place is seen,
Where they who worshiped idol gods have been.

1838?   *1942*

FREDERICK GODDARD
TUCKERMAN
(1821–1873)

Early in the twentieth century, one Louis How put together a collection of American poetry. As it circulated in search of a publisher, it came to the attention of Walter Prichard Eaton, a critic who paused over two sonnets by Frederick Goddard Tuckerman in the manuscript. He was curious and searched out Tuckerman's published volume of poems, last issued in 1869. Eaton liked what he saw. He penned a critical appreciation and published it in the *Forum* in 1909, expressing astonishment that "this introspective, withdrawing, contemplative man . . . was so absolutely unknown in the history of American letters."

By such fragile threads are literary reputations rescued from oblivion. The poet Witter Bynner read Eaton's essay and got in touch with Tuckerman's descendents. He discovered a cache of unpublished poems, and in 1931 he edited *The Sonnets of Frederick Goddard Tuckerman*. In his Introduction, he made his case for reading Tuckerman's work: "Not only are the sonnets the fine thoughts of a devout stoic, they are the subtly fine craft of a devout poet"; he concluded, "Tuckerman's sonnets rank with the noblest in the language." Critics noticed, read the poems, and were converted, among them Yvor Winters, Samuel A. Golden, and N. Scott Momaday.

Little appears to be known about Tuckerman's life that proves helpful in understanding his role or fate as a poet. He was born in a well-to-do family, went to Harvard (he dropped out for a year because of eye problems), and took a law degree in 1842. He was admitted to the bar in 1844, but decided against law as a career. As a gentleman of independent means, he could de-

---

[1]Matthew 24:28: "For wheresoever the carcass is, there will the eagles be gathered together."

vote himself to his real interests—poetry, botany, and astronomy—the last two informing and embracing the first.

In 1847 he married Hannah Lucinda Jones and settled in Greenfield, Massachusetts, where he lived the remainder of his life. He made two trips abroad, in 1851 and 1854, and on the second of these was entertained over several days by Tennyson, whose letters indicate a lasting friendship. Hannah died a few days after the birth of a third child in 1857. Tuckerman's grief, as expressed in his poems, was deep and prolonged.

There was the impulse of a recluse in Tuckerman. His son wrote to Walter Prichard Eaton in 1909: "My father lived much in seclusion from the world. His life was passed in the society of his books and close communions with Nature." He did, however, send out his poems to the magazines (several were published) and his privately printed volume *Poems* (1860), praised by Emerson and Hawthorne, was reprinted in London in 1863 and in Boston in 1864 and 1869. But after his death in 1873—the long silence.

Tuckerman's sardonic comment about himself, that his was "a life well-lost," suggests the ironic pessimism that dominates many of his poems. His darkness may have intensified after his wife's death, but it existed in the poetry before that. The melancholy, however, is redeemed from sentimentality by a stoic will to endure, as in these lines from "The Cricket":

> Even while we stop to wrangle or repine
>   Our lives are gone—
>   Like thinnest mist,
> Like yon escaping color in the tree;
> Rejoice! rejoice! whilest yet the hours exist. . . .

ADDITIONAL READING

The Sonnets of Frederick Goddard Tuckerman, ed. Witter Bynner, 1931.

Walter Prichard Eaton, "A Forgotten American Poet," *The Forum,* XLI (Jan., 1909); Samuel A. Golden, *Frederick Goddard Tuckerman: An American Sonneteer,* 1952; Samuel A. Golden, *Frederick Goddard Tuckerman,* 1966.

TEXT

The Complete Poems of Frederick Goddard Tuckerman, ed. N. Scott Momaday, 1965.

from Sonnets, First Series

VII

Dank fens of cedar, hemlock branches gray
With trees and trail of mosses, wringing-wet,
Beds of the black pitchpine in dead leaves set
Whose wasted red has wasted to white away,
Remnants of rain and droppings of decay,   5
Why hold ye so my heart, nor dimly let
Through your deep leaves the light of yesterday,
The faded glimmer of a sunshine set?
Is it that in your darkness, shut from strife,
The bread of tears becomes the bread of life?   10

Far from the roar of day, beneath your boughs
Fresh griefs beat tranquilly, and loves and vows
Grow green in your gray shadows, dearer far
Even than all lovely lights and roses are?

1860

VIII

As when down some broad river dropping, we
Day after day behold the assuming shores
Sink and grow dim, as the great watercourse
Pushes his banks apart and seeks the sea:
Benches of pines, high shelf and balcony,   5
To flats of willow and low sycamores
Subsiding, till where'er the wave we see,
Himself is his horizon utterly.
So fades the portion of our early world,
Still on the ambit[1] hangs the purple air;   10
Yet while we lean to read the secret there,
The stream that by green shoresides plashed and purled
Expands: the mountains melt to vapors rare,
And life alone circles out flat and bare.

1860

X

An upper chamber in a darkened house,
Where, ere his footsteps reached ripe manhood's brink,
Terror and anguish were his lot to drink;
I cannot rid the thought nor hold it close
But dimly dream upon that man alone: 5
Now though the autumn clouds most softly pass,
The cricket chides beneath the doorstep stone
And greener than the season grows the grass.
Nor can I drop my lids nor shade my brows,
But there he stands beside the lifted sash;   10
And with a swooning of the heart, I think
Where the black shingles slope to meet the boughs
And, shattered on the roof like smallest snows,
The tiny petals of the mountain ash.

1860

XXIII

Shall I not see her? yes: for one has seen
Her in her beauty since we called her dead,
One like herself, a fair young mother led
By her own lot to feel compassion keen;
And unto her last night my Anna[1] came   5
And sat within her arms and spoke her name
While the old smile, she said, like starlight gleamed,
And like herself in fair young bloom, she said,
Only the white more white, the red more red,

---

[1]Circumference.
[1]Tuckerman's wife Hannah died in 1857 after giving birth
to their third child.

And fainter than the mist her pressure seemed.   10
And words there were, though vague yet beautiful,
Which she who heard them could not tell to me;
It is enough: my Anna did not flee
To grief or fear, nor lies in slumber dull.

                                                        1860

from Sonnets, Second Series

I

That boy, the farmer said, with hazel wand
Pointing him out, half by the haycock[1] hid,
Though bare sixteen, can work at what he's bid
From sun till set, to cradle,[2] reap, or band.
I heard the words, but scarce could understand   5
Whether they claimed a smile or gave me pain:
Or was it aught to me, in that green lane,
That all day yesterday, the briars amid,
He held the plough against the jarring land
Steady, or kept his place among the mowers   10
Whilst other fingers, sweeping for the flowers,
Brought from the forest back a crimson stain?
Was it a thorn that touched the flesh, or did
The pokeberry spit purple on my hand?

                                                        1860

XVI

Under the mountain, as when first I knew
Its low dark roof and chimney creeper-twined,
The red house stands; and yet my footsteps find,
Vague in the walks, waste balm and feverfew.[1]
But they are gone: no soft-eyed sisters[2] trip   5
Across the porch or lintels; where, behind,
The mother sat, sat knitting with pursed lip.
The house stands vacant in its green recess,
Absent of beauty as a broken heart.
The wild rain enters, and the sunset wind   10
Sighs in the chambers of their loveliness
Or shakes the pane—and in the silent noons
The glass falls from the window, part by part,
And ringeth faintly in the grassy stones.

                                                        1860

XVIII

And change with hurried hand has swept these scenes:
The woods have fallen, across the meadow-lot
The hunter's trail and trap-path is forgot,

---

[1]Conical mound of hay, haystack.
[2]To cut with a cradle scythe.
[1]Balm: fragrant garden herb; feverfew: aromatic plant
with clusters of white-rayed, button flowers.

[2]The twin sisters Gertrude and Gulielma, once Tuckerman's neighbors, now dead.

And fire has drunk the swamps of evergreens;
Yet for a moment let my fancy plant   5
These autumn hills again: the wild dove's haunt,
The wild deer's walk. In golden umbrage[1] shut,
The Indian river runs, Quonecktacut![2]
Here, but a lifetime back, where falls tonight
Behind the curtained pane a sheltered light   10
On buds of rose or vase of violet
Aloft upon the marble mantle set,
Here in the forest-heart, hung blackening
The wolfbait on the bush beside the spring.

                                                            1860

XXXIII

One still dark night I sat alone and wrote:
So still it was that distant Chanticleer[1]
Seemed to cry out his warning at my ear,
Save for the brooding echo in his throat.
Sullen I sat, when like the nightwind's note   5
A voice said, "Wherefore doth he weep and fear?
Doth he not know no cry to God is dumb?"
Another spoke: "His heart is dimmed and drowned
With grief." I knew the shape that bended then[2]
To kiss me, when suddenly I once again   10
Across the watches of the starless gloom
Heard the cock scream and pause: the morning bell
Into the gulfs of night dropped One! The vision fell
And left me listening to the sinking sound.

                                                            1860

from Sonnets, Fifth Series

XVI

Let me give something!—as the years unfold,
Some faint fruition, though not much, my most:
Perhaps a monument of labor lost.
But thou, who givest all things, give not me
To sink in silence, seared with early cold,   5
Frost-burnt and blackened, but quick fire for frost!
As once I saw at a houseside, a tree
Struck scarlet by the lightning, utterly
To its last limb and twig: so strange it seemed,
I stopped to think if this indeed were May,   10
And were those windflowers? or had I dreamed?
But there it stood, close by the cottage eaves,
Red-ripened to the heart: shedding its leaves
And autumn sadness on the dim spring day.

                                                            1931

---

[1]Shade-giving foliage.
[2]The Connecticut River.
[1]Rooster or cock.

[2]His wife Hannah, who had died in 1857 after their third child was born.

The Cricket

I

The humming bee purrs softly o'er his flower;
  From lawn and thicket
The dogday[1] locust singeth in the sun
  From hour to hour:
Each has his bard, and thou, ere day be done,   5
  Shalt have no wrong.
So bright that murmur mid the insect crowd,
Muffled and lost in bottom-grass, or loud
  By pale and picket:
Shall I not take to help me in my song   10
  A little cooing cricket?

II

The afternoon is sleepy; let us lie
Beneath these branches whilst the burdened brook,
Muttering and moaning to himself, goes by;
And mark our minstrel's carol whilst we look   15
Toward the faint horizon swooning blue.
  Or in a garden bower,
Trellised and trammeled with deep drapery
  Of hanging green,
  Light glimmering through—   20
There let the dull hop be,
Let bloom, with poppy's dark refreshing flower:
Let the dead fragrance round our temples beat,
Stunning the sense to slumber, whilst between
The falling water and fluttering wind   25
  Mingle and meet,
  Murmur and mix,
No few faint pipings from the glades behind,
  Or alder-thicks:
But louder as the day declines,   30
From tingling tassel, blade, and sheath,
Rising from nets of river vines,
  Winrows and ricks,[2]
  Above, beneath,
  At every breath,   35
At hand, around, illimitably
Rising and falling like the sea,
  Acres of cricks!

III

Dear to the child who hears thy rustling voice
Cease at his footstep, though he hears thee still, 40
Cease and resume with vibrance crisp and shrill,
Thou sittest in the sunshine to rejoice.
Night lover too; bringer of all things dark
And rest and silence; yet thou bringest to me
Always that burthen of the unresting Sea,   45
The moaning cliffs, the low rocks blackly stark;

---

[1]Summer.
[2]Rows and stacks of hay.

These upland inland fields no more I view,
But the long flat seaside beach, the wild seamew,[3]
   And the overturning wave!
Thou bringest too, dim accents from the grave   50
To him who walketh when the day is dim,
Dreaming of those who dream no more of him,
With edged remembrances of joy and pain;
And heyday looks and laughter come again:
Forms that in happy sunshine lie and leap,   55
With faces where but now a gap must be,
Renunciations, and partitions deep
And perfect tears, and crowning vacancy!
And to thy poet at the twilight's hush,
No chirping touch of lips with laugh and blush,   60
But wringing arms, hearts wild with love and woe,
Closed eyes, and kisses that would not let go!

IV

So wert thou loved in that old graceful time
   When Greece was fair,
While god and hero hearkened to thy chime;   65
   Softly astir
Where the long grasses fringed Caÿster's lip;[4]
Long-drawn, with glimmering sails of swan and ship,
   And ship and swan;
   Or where   70
   Reedy Eurotas[5] ran.
Did that low warble teach thy tender flute
   Xenaphyle?[6]
Its breathings mild? say! did the grasshopper
Sit golden in thy purple hair   75
   O Psammathe?[7]
   Or wert thou mute,
Grieving for Pan[8] amid the alders there?
And by the water and along the hill
That thirsty tinkle in the herbage still,   80
Though the lost forest wailed to horns of Arcady?

V

Like the Enchanter old—[9]
Who sought mid the dead water's weeds and scum
For evil growths beneath the moonbeam cold,
   Or mandrake or dorcynium;[10]   85
And touched the leaf that opened both his ears,

---

[3]Sea gull.
[4]The mouth of the Cayster River in Asia Minor (now Turkey), near the port of the ancient Ionian city of Ephesus on the Aegean Sea. The river was noted for its melodious swans according to Greek poet Ovid (*Metamorphoses* 2:251–52).
[5]River in ancient Laconia in the Peloponnesus in southern Greece.
[6]Xenophilus, Pythagorean philosopher and musician of ancient Greece.
[7]Mother of Apollo's son, Linus (Greek: "woe is me"), who, in fear of her father, exposed the child to devouring dogs and was driven away. To appease the wrathful god, mournful songs were sung in their honor during the scorching crop-killing summer heat or, later, at the harvesting (death) of the grapes.

[8]Half-goatish, amorous Greek god of woods and fields, flocks and shepherds, inventor of the shepherd's pipe. Pan was native to the mountainous region of Greece, Arcadia. Taken as symbolic of the universe and as a personification of nature, he later came to represent the Greek gods and paganism. In Christian tradition, when Christ's birth is announced by the angels, a groan is heard throughout Greece, a signal that the great Pan is dead.
[9]Melampus, a prophet in Greek myth who interpreted the cries and actions of birds and other animate beings.
[10]Mandrake: poisonous plant, yielding a narcotic, with fleshy forked roots resembling the human body, and believed to have magical powers; dorcynium, misspelling of dorcynium: a genus of plants, probably thought to have magical powers.

So that articulate voices now he hears
In cry of beast, or bird, or insect's hum,—
Might I but find thy knowledge in thy song!
   That twittering tongue,   90
Ancient as light, returning like the years.
   So might I be,
Unwise to sing, thy true interpreter
Through denser stillness and in sounder dark,
Than ere thy notes have pierced to harrow me.   95
   So might I stir
   The world to hark
   To thee my lord and lawgiver,
   And cease my quest:
Content to bring thy wisdom to the world;   100
Content to gain at last some low applause,
   Now low, now lost
Like thine from mossy stone, amid the stems and straws,
   Or garden gravemound tricked and dressed—
   Powdered and pearled   105
   By stealing frost—
In dusky rainbow beauty of euphorbias![11]
For larger would be less indeed, and like
The ceaseless simmer in the summer grass
To him who toileth in the windy field,   110
   Or where the sunbeams strike,
Naught in innumerable numerousness.
   So might I much possess,
   So much must yield;
But failing this, the dell and grassy dike,   115
The water and the waste shall still be dear,
And all the pleasant plots and places
   Where thou hast sung, and I have hung
   To ignorantly hear.
Then Cricket, sing thy song! or answer mine!   120
Thine whispers blame, but mine has naught but praises.
It matters not. Behold! the autumn goes,
   The shadow grows,
The moments take hold of eternity;
Even while we stop to wrangle or repine   125
   Our lives are gone—
   Like thinnest mist,
Like yon escaping color in the tree;
Rejoice! rejoice! whilst yet the hours exist—
Rejoice or mourn, and let the world swing on   130
Unmoved by cricket song of thee or me.

1950

---

[11]Medicinal plants.

EMERGING FEMINIST PERSPECTIVES

MARGARET FULLER
ELIZABETH CADY STANTON
ELIZABETH BARSTOW STODDARD

ROSE TERRY COOKE
REBECCA HARDING DAVIS
LOUISA MAY ALCOTT

"Every relation, every gradation of nature is incalculably precious, but only to the soul which is poised upon itself, and to whom no loss, no change, can bring dull discord, for it is in harmony with the central soul.

If any individual live too much in relations, so that he becomes a stranger to the resources of his own nature, he falls, after a while, into a distraction, or imbecility, from which he can only be cured by a time of isolation, which gives the renovating fountains time to rise up. . . .

It is therefore that I would have woman lay aside all thought, such as she habitually cherishes, of being taught and led by men. I would have her, like the Indian girl, dedicate herself to the Sun, the Sun of Truth, and go nowhere if his beams did not make clear the path. I would have her free from compromise, from complaisance, from helplessness, because I would have her good enough and strong enough to love one and all beings, from the fulness, not the poverty of being."

Margaret Fuller, *Woman in the Nineteenth Century*

MARGARET FULLER
(1810–1850)

"We would have every arbitrary barrier thrown down. We would have every path laid open to woman as freely as to man"; "If the negro be a soul, if the woman be a soul, . . . to one Master only are they accountable"; "There is no wholly masculine man, no purely feminine woman"; "Only . . . the soul which is poised upon itself . . . is in harmony with the central soul"; "I do not care what case you put; let them be sea-captains, if you will"; "It is a vulgar error that love, *a* love to woman is her whole existence; she also is born for Truth and Love in their universal energy." These sentences all come from a work by Margaret Fuller published in 1845—*Woman in the Nineteenth Century*. It is a pioneering work in the history of the women's movement, serving as a kind of founding document for the Women's Rights Convention held in 1848 in Seneca Falls, New York, at which the women's suffrage movement was born.

Ever since her tragic death in 1850, Margaret Fuller has been a controversial figure in American literature. The image of Fuller passed on to posterity was largely shaped by males. We find glimpses of her in Emerson's and Hawthorne's journals, and in Lowell's *A Fable for Critics*. When Emerson, William Henry Channing, and James Freeman Clarke (all friends of Fuller) edited *Memoirs of Margaret Fuller Ossoli* in 1852, little was made of her *Woman in the Nineteenth Century* or any other of Fuller's writing. And source material was mutilated or suppressed, presumably to protect her reputation. Most students of literature have formed notions of her character and career through reading satiric portraits of her in Hawthorne's *The Blithedale Romance* or Henry James's *The Bostonians*. Only recently has a thorough-going reassessment of her and her work been initiated.

Sarah Margaret Fuller was born in Cambridgeport, near Boston, the eldest of nine children, into the household of a lawyer-politician. Her father served in the Massachusetts senate and the U.S. Congress, was an admirer of Jefferson and a supporter of John Quincy Adams (U.S. president, 1825–29). He had wanted a boy, but adapted himself to his daughter to the extent of taking over her education completely.

A Harvard graduate and a reader of books, Timothy Fuller taught her English and Latin grammar at the age of six and started her reading of Horace and Virgil. In addition, she was set free in the large Fuller library and encouraged to read at random. She early discovered the delights of England's Shakespeare, Spain's Cervantes, and France's Molière. Sent for two years to the Prescott School in Groton, Massachusetts, she found the discipline distasteful. She was relieved to return home and devoted herself to long hours of studying philosophy, French, Italian, German, and Greek. Later, in *Woman in the Nineteenth Century*, she would describe her education directed by her father as ideal for a young girl.

Whatever else it did, Fuller's education prepared her to scorn the traditional role expected of a nineteenth-century woman. She later wrote: "From a very early age I have felt that I was not born to the common womanly lot. I knew I should never find a being who could keep the key of my character; that there would be none on whom I could always lean; from whom I could always learn; that I should be a pilgrim, a sojourner on earth, and that the birds and foxes would be surer of a place to lay the head than I."

She began to attend meetings of the Transcendental Club and became acquainted with literary figures of Concord and Boston. Her interest in the German poet Goethe, a lifelong passion, led to her translation of Johann Eckermann's *Conversations with Goethe*, published in 1839 and highly praised. And in 1839 she began her famous Conversations with a course of thirteen sessions, two hours each, in Elizabeth Peabody's home in Boston, with twenty-five women in attendance. The first course was on mythology, and later ones devoted to the fine arts, ethics, creeds, and the ideal. The Conversations continued to 1844, with Margaret Fuller leading and encouraging discussions, which were remarkably successful in enticing women trained to be silent into speech on serious subjects.

In 1840, Fuller was asked to become editor of the Transcendental Club's new journal, *The Dial*. She threw herself into the duties of editor, soliciting manuscripts and meeting deadlines, and often writing a large amount of material to fill the magazine. It is doubtful that she received all of the $300 annual salary she had been promised. She brought the magazine into being and held it together, dealing tactfully with such sensitive writers as Thoreau, Ellery Channing, and Bronson Alcott. But she decided after two years that she no longer had the energy to lead her Conversations and edit *The Dial*. She convinced Emerson to succeed her in the editorship.

Fuller's Conversations functioned as a kind of laboratory for her in finding out how women viewed themselves, their lives, and their role in society. Drawing on material from them, from her own experience as an intellectual, and from her reading, she wrote "The Great Lawsuit: Man *versus* Men; Woman *versus* Women," which appeared in *The Dial* in 1843. She later revised this essay and published it as a book under the title *Woman in the Nineteenth Century*. After finishing this work, Fuller sensed instinctively its importance and wrote: "Then I felt a delightful glow as if I had put a good deal of my true life in it, as if, suppose I went away now, the measure of my footprint would be left on the earth."

A trip with friends out west to Chicago, via the Great Lakes, gave Fuller a sense of the possibilities and promise of the undeveloped frontier areas of America that she had not seen before. She showed her journal to Thoreau, who encouraged her to publish it. The result, *Summer on the Lakes, in 1843*, was published in 1844. It was much admired by Horace Greeley, the New York newspaperman, who said: "I still consider 'Summer on the Lakes' unequalled, especially in its picture of the Prairies and of the sunnier aspects of pioneer life."

This book and her other work led Greeley to offer Fuller a position as regular contributor on his newspaper, the *New York Tribune*. For two years she supplied articles and reviews, passing judgment on such literary figures as Thomas Carlyle, Alfred, Lord Tennyson, and Robert Browning. Her comments on James Russell Lowell ("his thought sounds no depths") was so stinging that he answered in kind with the satiric portrait in *A Fable for Critics*.

But her restless spirit would not permit her to settle in, put down roots. She once wrote in her journal: "With intellect I always have, always shall, overcome; but that is not half of the work. The life, the life! O, my God! shall the life never be sweet?" An opportunity to go to Europe in 1846 led to a stay abroad that lasted four years—the rest of her life, as it turned out. In England she visited Carlyle and Wordsworth. In Paris she was much taken by George Sand, who had achieved fulfillment both intellectually as a novelist and emotionally as a woman in her liaisons with a succession of lovers.

In Italy, Fuller became acquainted with a poor but handsome marchese,

Giovanni Angelo Ossoli, ten years her junior. A child was born, a marriage took place—the details are uncertain and disputed. But a revolution was in progress in Rome, a part of the 1848 revolutionary spirit sweeping Europe. The Italian patriot Giuseppe Garibaldi was leading forces to establish a republic, and French troops intervened on behalf of Pope Pius IX. Ossoli fought with the republican rebels, while Fuller helped organize hospitals.

When Rome fell to the French, Ossoli and Fuller fled to Florence, and then, with their child, sailed for America in 1850. Fuller carried with her in manuscript a history of the Roman Revolution. As they neared America, there was a violent storm and the ship went down off Fire Island, near New York. Ossoli, Fuller, and her manuscript were lost; the child's body washed up on shore. Opinion about her was extreme in death, as even in life. There were those who believed that her violent end was just punishment for her defiance of the moral code. Others—including Emerson and Thoreau—came to her defense.

With all her considerable achievements, Margaret Fuller's death at the age of forty left (and still leaves) an impression of immense promise unfulfilled. So fixed was this view that for a long time the works she did leave behind her remained on the shelves, unregarded. It was said that her genius was in her Conversations, which could not survive her.

More recently, however, her literary importance has been quietly reinstated. Some decades ago, Vernon L. Parrington made the case in his *Main Currents in American Thought*: "Misunderstood in her own time, caricatured by unfriendly critics, and with significant facts of her life suppressed by her friends out of a chivalrous sense of loyalty, the real woman has been lost in a Margaret Fuller myth and later generations have come to underestimate her powers and undervalue her work. Yet no other woman of her generation in America is so well worth recalling."

ADDITIONAL READING

Memoirs of Margaret Fuller Ossoli, ed. W. H. Channing, James Freeman Clarke, and Ralph Waldo Emerson, 1852; *Margaret Fuller, American Romantic: A Selection from Her Writings and Correspondence*, ed. Perry Miller, 1963; *The Woman and the Myth: Margaret Fuller's Life and Writings*, ed. Bell Gale Chevigny, 1976; *The Letters of Margaret Fuller*, ed. Robert N. Hudspeth, 1983—.

Kate Sanborn, "Margaret Fuller," *Our Famous Women; An Authorized and Complete Record of the Lives and Deeds of Eminent Women of Our Times*, 1888; Mason Wade, *Margaret Fuller, Whetstone of Genius*, 1940; Madeleine B. Stern, *The Life of Margaret Fuller*, 1942; Arthur W. Brown, *Margaret Fuller*, 1964; Joseph Jay Deiss, *The Roman Years of Margaret Fuller*, 1969; Joel Myerson, *Margaret Fuller: An Annotated Secondary Bibliography*, 1977; Paula Blanchard, *Margaret Fuller: From Transcendentalism to Revolution*, 1978; Margaret Vanderhaar Allen, *The Achievement of Margaret Fuller*, 1979; Marie Mitchell Olesen Urbanski, *Margaret Fuller's "Woman in the Nineteenth Century": A Literary Study of Form and Content, of Sources and Influences*, 1980; Joel Myerson, ed., *Critical Essays on Margaret Fuller*, 1980; Elizabeth Hardwick, "The Genius of Margaret Fuller," *The New York Review of Books*, April 10, 1986.

TEXT

"Woman in the Nineteenth Century," *Margaret Fuller: Essays on American Life and Letters*, ed. Joel Myerson, 1978.

from Woman in the Nineteenth Century[1]

[A TRULY HUMAN LIFE AT HAND]

"Frailty, thy name is WOMAN."[2]
"The Earth waits for her Queen."[3]

The connection between these quotations may not be obvious, but it is strict. Yet would any contradict us, if we made them applicable to the other side, and began also

Frailty, thy name is MAN.
The Earth waits for its King.

Yet man, if not yet fully installed in his powers, has given much earnest[4] of his claims. Frail he is indeed, how frail! how impure! Yet often has the vein of gold displayed itself amid the baser ores, and Man has appeared before us in princely promise worthy of his future.

If, oftentimes, we see the prodigal son feeding on the husks in the fair field no more his own,[5] anon, we raise the eyelids, heavy from bitter tears, to behold in him the radiant apparition of genius and love, demanding not less than the all of goodness, power and beauty. We see that in him the largest claim finds a due foundation. That claim is for no partial sway, no exclusive possession. He cannot be satisfied with any one gift of life, any one department of knowledge or tele-scopic peep at the heavens. He feels himself called to understand and aid nature, that she may, through his intelligence, be raised and interpreted; to be a student of, and servant to, the universe-spirit;[6] and king of his planet, that as an angelic minister, he may bring it into conscious harmony with the law of that spirit.

. . . . .

Such marks have been made by the footsteps of *man*, (still alas! to be spoken of as the *ideal* man,) wherever he has passed through the wilderness of *men*, and whenever the pigmies stepped in one of those they felt dilate within the breast somewhat that promised nobler stature and purer blood. They were impelled to forsake their evil ways of decrepit scepticism, and covetousness of corruptible pos-sessions. Conviction flowed in upon them. They, too, raised the cry; God is living, now, to-day; and all beings are brothers, for they are his children. Simple words enough, yet which only angelic nature, can use or hear in their full free sense.

These were the triumphant moments, but soon the lower nature took its turn, and the era of a truly human life was postponed.

. . . . .

[1]The first version of this work appeared in the July 1843 *Dial* as "The Great Lawsuit: Man *versus* Men; Woman *versus* Women." Urged to expand it into a book, Fuller revised the essay, providing more examples, much new material, and, because of objections, a new title. In the preface to the 1845 edition, Fuller explained why she preferred the orig-inal title: "It requires some thought to see what it means, and might thus prepare the reader to meet me on my own ground. Besides, it offers a larger scope, and is, in that way, more just to my desire. I meant by that title to inti-mate the fact that, while it is the destiny of Man, in the course of the ages, to ascertain and fulfil the law of his be-ing, so that his life shall be seen, as a whole, to be that of an angel or messenger, the action of prejudices and passions which attend, in the day, the growth of the individual, is continually obstructing the holy work that is to make the earth a part of heaven. By Man I mean both man and woman; these are the two halves of one thought. I lay no especial stress on the welfare of either. I believe that the development of the one cannot be effected without that of the other. My highest wish is that this truth should be dis-tinctly and rationally apprehended, and the conditions of life and freedom recognized as the same for the daughters and the sons of time; twin exponents of a divine thought."
[2]*Hamlet* 1.2.146.
[3]Unidentified; perhaps by Fuller.
[4]Promise.
[5]Luke 15:11–16: The younger son who wasted his inheri-tance "would fain have filled his belly with the husks that the swine did eat."
[6]Cf. Emerson's "The Over-Soul."

Yet, no doubt, a new manifestation is at hand, a new hour in the day of man. We cannot expect to see any one sample of completed being, when the mass of men still lie engaged in the sod, or use the freedom of their limbs only with wolfish energy. The tree cannot come to flower till its root be free from the cankering worm, and its whole growth open to air and light. While any one is base, none can be entirely free and noble. Yet something new shall presently be shown of the life of man, for hearts crave, if minds do not know how to ask it.

· · · · · ·

[WHAT WOMAN NEEDS]

. . . Many women are considering within themselves, what they need that they have not, and what they can have, if they find they need it. Many men are considering whether women are capable of being and having more than they are and have, *and,* whether, if so, it will be best to consent to improvement in their condition. . . .

Knowing that there exists in the minds of men a tone of feeling towards women as towards slaves, such as is expressed in the common phrase, "Tell that to women and children," that the infinite soul[1] can only work through them in already ascertained limits; that the gift of reason, man's highest prerogative, is allotted to them in much lower degree; that they must be kept from mischief and melancholy by being constantly engaged in active labor, which is to be furnished and directed by those better able to think, &c. &c.; we need not multiply instances, for who can review the experience of last week without recalling words which imply, whether in jest or earnest, these views or views like these; knowing this, can we wonder that many reformers think that measures are not likely to be taken in behalf of women, unless their wishes could be publicly represented by women?

That can never be necessary, cry the other side. All men are privately influenced by women; each has his wife, sister, or female friends, and is too much biased by these relations to fail of representing their interests, and, if this is not enough, let them propose and enforce their wishes with the pen. The beauty of home would be destroyed, the delicacy of the sex be violated, the dignity of halls of legislation degraded by an attempt to introduce them there. Such duties are inconsistent with those of a mother; and then we have ludicrous pictures of ladies in hysterics at the polls, and senate chambers filled with cradles.

But if, in reply, we admit as truth that woman seems destined by nature rather for the inner circle, we must add that the arrangements of civilized life have not been, as yet, such as to secure it to her. Her circle, if the duller, is not the quieter. If kept from "excitement," she is not from drudgery. Not only the Indian squaw carries the burdens of the camp, but the favorites of Louis the Fourteenth accompany him in his journeys,[2] and the washerwoman stands at her tub and carries home her work at all seasons, and in all states of health. Those who think the physical circumstances of woman would make a part of the affairs of national government unsuitable, are by no means those who think it impossible for the negresses to endure field work, even during pregnancy, or the semptstresses[3] to go through their killing labors.

As to the use of the pen, there was quite as much opposition to woman's possessing herself of that help to free agency, as there is now to her seizing on the rostrum or the desk; and she is likely to draw, from a permission to plead her cause that way, opposite inferences to what might be wished by those who now grant it.

---

[1] Cf. Emerson's essay, "The Over-Soul."
[2] The favored women in attendance at the elaborate court of French King Louis XIV (1638–1715).
[3] Seamstresses.

As to the possibility of her filling with grace and dignity, any such position, we should think those who had seen the great actresses, and heard the Quaker preachers of modern times,[4] would not doubt, that woman can express publicly the fulness of thought and creation, without losing any of the peculiar beauty of her sex. What can pollute and tarnish is to act thus from any motive except that something needs to be said or done. Women could take part in the processions, the songs, the dances of old religion; no one fancied their delicacy was impaired by appearing in public for such a cause.

As to her home, she is not likely to leave it more than she now does for balls, theatres, meetings for promoting missions, revival meetings, and others to which she flies, in hope of an animation for her existence, commensurate with what she sees enjoyed by men. Governors of ladies' fairs[5] are no less engrossed by such a change, than the Governor of the state by his; presidents of Washingtonian societies no less away from home than presidents of conventions. If men look straitly to it, they will find that, unless their lives are domestic, those of the women will not be. A house is no home unless it contain food and fire for the mind as well as for the body. The female Greek, of our day, is as much in the street as the male to cry. What news? We doubt not it was the same in Athens of old. The women, shut out from the market place, made up for it at the religious festivals. For human beings are not so constituted that they can live without expansion. If they do not get it one way, they must another, or perish.

As to men's representing women fairly at present, while we hear from men who owe to their wives not only all that is comfortable or graceful, but all that is wise in the arrangement of their lives, the frequent remark, "You cannot reason with a woman," when from those of delicacy, nobleness, and poetic culture, the contemptuous phrase "women and children," and that in no light sally of the hour, but in works intended to give a permanent statement of the best experiences, when not one man, in the million, shall I say? no, not in the hundred million, can rise above the belief that woman was made *for man,* when such traits as these are daily forced upon the attention, can we feel that man will always do justice to the interests of woman? Can we think that he takes a sufficiently discerning and religious view of her office and destiny, *ever* to do her justice, except when prompted by sentiment, accidentally or transiently, that is, for the sentiment will vary according to the relations in which he is placed. The lover, the poet, the artist, are likely to view her nobly. The father and the philosopher have some chance of liberality; the man of the world, the legislator for expediency, none.

Under these circumstances, without attaching importance, in themselves, to the changes demanded by the champions of woman, we hail them as signs of the times. We would have every arbitrary barrier thrown down. We would have every path laid open to woman as freely as to man. Were this done and a slight temporary fermentation allowed to subside, we should see crystallizations more pure and of more various beauty. We believe the divine energy would pervade nature to a degree unknown in the history of former ages, and that no discordant collision, but a ravishing harmony of the spheres[6] would ensue.

Yet, then and only then, will mankind be ripe for this, when inward and outward freedom for woman as much as for man shall be acknowledged as a right,

---

[4]Among the famous women actresses of the time were Charlotte Cushman (1816–1876), America's first great tragedienne, who created a memorable Lady Macbeth and had a penchant for male roles, causing a stir with her Romeo in 1837; and Fanny Kemble (1809–1893), English actress, who gave up the stage in 1834 to marry an American. Fuller praised Quakers for making men and women equal in speech, whether at worship or in daily life. Famous Quaker preachers were the antislavery crusaders Sarah Grimké (1792–1873), her sister Angelina (1805–1879),

and Abby Kelley (1811–1887), who addressed large crowds of men and women, scandalizing many as "women preachers."
[5]Charitable bazaars run by women.
[6]In ancient astronomy, harmony resulted from a just adaptation of the parts of creation to each other, the distances of the planets from one another corresponding to the proportions of the musical scale. Fuller also has in mind male platitudes about woman's "proper sphere."

not yielded as a concession. As the friend of the negro assumes that one man cannot by right, hold another in bondage, so should the friend of woman assume that man cannot, by right, lay even well-meant restrictions on woman. If the negro be a soul, if the woman be a soul, appareled in flesh, to one Master only are they accountable. There is but one law for souls, and if there is to be an interpreter of it, he must come not as man, or son of man, but as son of God.

Were thought and feeling once so far elevated that man should esteem himself the brother and friend, but nowise the lord and tutor of woman, were he really bound with her in equal worship, arrangements as to function and employment would be of no consequence. What woman needs is not as a woman to act or rule, but as a nature to grow, as an intellect to discern, as a soul to live freely and unimpeded, to unfold such powers as were given her when we left our common home. If fewer talents were given her, yet if allowed the free and full employment of these, so that she may render back to the giver his own with usury,[7] she will not complain; nay I dare to say she will bless and rejoice in her earthly birth-place, her earthly lot. Let us consider what obstructions impede this good era, and what signs give reason to hope that it draws near.

[MIRANDA: EDUCATION IN SELF-RELIANCE]

I was talking on this subject with Miranda, a woman, who, if any in the world could, might speak without heat and bitterness of the position of her sex.[1] Her father was a man who cherished no sentimental reverence for woman, but a firm belief in the equality of the sexes. She was his eldest child, and came to him at an age when he needed a companion. From the time she could speak and go alone, he addressed her not as a plaything, but as a living mind. Among the few verses he ever wrote was a copy addressed to this child, when the first locks were cut from her head, and the reverence expressed on this occasion for that cherished head, he never belied. It was to him the temple of immortal intellect. He respected his child, however, too much to be an indulgent parent. He called on her for clear judgment, for courage, for honor and fidelity; in short, for such virtues as he knew. In so far as he possessed the keys to the wonders of this universe, he allowed free use of them to her, and by the incentive of a high expectation, he forbade, as far as possible, that she should let the privilege lie idle.

Thus this child was early led to feel herself a child of the spirit. She took her place easily, not only in the world of organized being, but in the world of mind. A dignified sense of self-dependence was given as all her portion, and she found it a sure anchor. Herself securely anchored, her relations with others were established with equal security. She was fortunate in a total absence of those charms which might have drawn to her bewildering flatteries, and in a strong electric nature, which repelled those who did not belong to her, and attracted those who did. With men and women her relations were noble, affectionate without passion, intellectual without coldness. The world was free to her, and she lived freely in it. Outward adversity came, and inward conflict, but that faith and self-respect had early been awakened which must always lead at last, to an outward serenity and an inward peace.

Of Miranda I had always thought as an example, that the restraints upon the sex were insuperable only to those who think them so, or who noisily strive to break them. She had taken a course of her own, and no man stood in her way. Many of her acts had been unusual, but excited no uproar. Few helped, but none checked her, and the many men, who knew her mind and her life, showed to her

---

[7]Interest.
[1]Through the persona of "Miranda," Fuller presents her own educational upbringing and beliefs.

confidence, as to a brother, gentleness as to a sister. And not only refined, but very coarse men approved and aided one in whom they saw resolution and clearness of design. Her mind was often the leading one, always effective.

When I talked with her upon these matters, and had said very much what I have written, she smilingly replied: "and yet we must admit that I have been fortunate, and this should not be. My good father's early trust gave the first bias, and the rest followed of course. It is true that I have had less outward aid, in after years, than most women, but that is of little consequence. Religion was early awakened in my soul, a sense that what the soul is capable to ask it must attain, and that, though I might be aided and instructed by others, I must depend on myself as the only constant friend. This self dependence, which was honored in me, is deprecated as a fault in most women. They are taught to learn their rule from without, not to unfold it from within."

"This is the fault of man, who is still vain, and wishes to be more important to woman than, by right, he should be."

"Men have not shown this disposition toward you," I said.

"No! because the position I early was enabled to take was one of self-reliance.[2] And were all women as sure of their wants as I was, the result would be the same. But they are so overloaded with precepts by guardians, who think that nothing is so much to be dreaded for a woman as originality of thought or character, that their minds are impeded by doubts till they lose their chance of fair free proportions. The difficulty is to get them to the point from which they shall naturally develope self-respect, and learn self-help.

"Once I thought that men would help to forward this state of things more than I do now. I saw so many of them wretched in the connections they had formed in weakness and vanity. They seemed so glad to esteem women whenever they could.

"The soft arms of affection," said one of the most discerning spirits, "will not suffice for me, unless on them I see the steel bracelets of strength."

But early I perceived that men never, in any extreme of despair, wished to be women. On the contrary they were ever ready to taunt one another at any sign of weakness, with,

> "Art thou not like the women, who"—

The passage ends various ways, according to the occasion and rhetoric of the speaker. When they admired any woman they were inclined to speak of her as "above her sex." Silently I observed this, and feared it argued a rooted scepticism, which for ages had been fastening on the heart, and which only an age of miracles could eradicate. Ever I have been treated with great sincerity; and I look upon it as a signal instance of this, that an intimate friend of the other sex said, in a fervent moment, that I "deserved in some star to be a man." He was much surprised when I disclosed my view of my position and hopes, when I declared my faith that the feminine side, the side of love, of beauty, of holiness, was now to have its full chance, and that, if either were better, it was better now to be a woman, for even the slightest achievement of good was furthering an especial work of our time. He smiled incredulous. "She makes the best she can of it," thought he. "Let Jews believe the pride of Jewry, but I am of the better sort, and know better."

Another used as highest praise, in speaking of a character in literature, the words "a manly woman."

So in the noble passage of Ben Jonson:

> "I meant the day-star should not brighter ride,
>   Nor shed like influence from its lucent seat;

---

[2]Cf. Emerson's essay, "Self-Reliance."

> I meant she should be courteous, facile, sweet,
>   Free from that solemn vice of greatness, pride;
> I meant each softest virtue there should meet,
>   Fit in that softer bosom to abide,
> Only a learned and a *manly* soul,
>   I purposed her, that should with even powers,
> The rock, the spindle, and the shears control
>   Of destiny, and spin her own free hours."[3]

"Methinks," said I, "you are too fastidious in objecting to this. Jonson in using the word 'manly' only meant to heighten the picture of this, the true, the intelligent fate, with one of the deeper colors." 'And yet,' said she, 'so invariable is the use of this word where a heroic quality is to be described, and I feel so sure that persistence and courage are the most womanly no less than the most manly qualities, that I would exchange these words for others of a larger sense at the risk of marring the fine tissue of the verse. Read, 'a heavenward and instructed soul,' and I should be satisfied. Let it not be said, wherever there is energy or creative genius, 'She has a masculine mind.' '

•   •   •   •   •   •

[THE BIRTHRIGHT OF EVERY BEING]

It is not the transient breath of poetic incense that women want; each can receive that from a lover. It is not life-long sway; it needs but to become a coquette, a shrew, or a good cook, to be sure of that. It is not money, nor notoriety, nor the badges of authority that men have appropriated to themselves. If demands, made in their behalf, lay stress on any of these particulars, those who make them have not searched deeply into the need. It is for that which at once includes these and precludes them; which would not be forbidden power, lest there be temptation to steal and misuse it; which would not have the mind perverted by flattery from a worthiness of esteem. It is for that which is the birthright of every being capable to receive it,—the freedom, the religious, the intelligent freedom of the universe, to use its means; to learn its secret as far as nature has enabled them, with God alone for their guide and their judge.

Ye cannot believe it, men; but the only reason why women ever assume what is more appropriate to you, is because you prevent them from finding out what is fit for themselves. Were they free, were they wise fully to develop the strength and beauty of woman; they would never wish to be men, or manlike. The well-instructed moon flies not from her orbit to seize on the glories of her partner. No; for she knows that one law rules, one heaven contains, one universe replies to them alike. It is with women as with the slave.

> "Vor dem Sklaven, wenn er die Kette bricht,
> Vor dem freien Menschen erzittert nicht."[1]

Tremble not before the free man, but before the slave who has chains to break.

•   •   •   •   •

[FULNESS OF BEING]

Another sign of the times is furnished by the triumphs of female authorship. These have been great and constantly increasing. Women have taken possession

---

[3]From Epigram LXXVI, "On Lucy, Countess of Bedford," by English poet Ben Jonson (*c.* 1573–1637). Fuller's emphasis.

[1]From "Die Worte des Glaubens" ("The Word of the Faithful"), str. 2, by German poet Johann Christoph Friedrich von Schiller (1759–1805). Fuller's translation follows.

of so many provinces for which men had pronounced them unfit, that though these still declare there are some inaccessible to them, it is difficult to say just *where* they must stop. . . .

Whether much or little has been done or will be done, whether women will add to the talent of narration, the power of systematizing, whether they will carve marble, as well as draw and paint, is not important. But that it should be acknowledged that they have intellect which needs developing, that they should not be considered complete, if beings of affection and habit alone, is important.

Yet even this acknowledgement, rather conquered by woman than proffered by man, has been sullied by the usual selfishness. So much is said of women being better educated, that they may become better companions and mothers *for men.* They should be fit for such companionship, and we have mentioned, with satisfaction, instances where it has been established. Earth knows no fairer, holier relation than that of a mother. It is one which, rightly understood, must both promote and require the highest attainments. But a being of infinite scope must not be treated with an exclusive view to any one relation. Give the soul free course, let the organization, both of body and mind, be freely developed, and the being will be fit for any and every relation to which it may be called. The intellect, no more than the sense of hearing, is to be cultivated [not] merely that she may be a more valuable companion to man, but because the Power who gave a power, by its mere existence, signifies that it must be brought out towards perfection.

[OLD BACHELORS, OLD MAIDS, OLD AGE]

In this regard of self-dependence, and a greater simplicity and fulness of being, we must hail as a preliminary the increase of the class contemptuously designated as old maids.

We cannot wonder at the aversion with which old bachelors and old maids have been regarded. Marriage is the natural means of forming a sphere, of taking root on the earth; it requires more strength to do this without such an opening; very many have failed, and their imperfections have been in every one's way. They have been more partial, more harsh, more officious and impertinent than those compelled by severer friction to render themselves endurable. Those, who have a more full experience of the instincts, have a distrust, as to whether they can be thoroughly human and humane, such as is hinted in the saying, "Old maids' and bachelors' children are well cared for," which derides at once their ignorance and their presumption.

Yet the business of society has become so complex, that it could now scarcely be carried on without the presence of these despised auxiliaries; and detachments from the army of aunts and uncles are wanted to stop gaps in every hedge. They rove about, mental and moral Ishmaelites,[1] pitching their tents amid the fixed and ornamented homes of men.

In a striking variety of forms, genius of late, both at home and abroad, has paid its tribute to the character of the Aunt, and the Uncle, recognizing in these personages the spiritual parents, who had supplied defects in the treatment of the busy or careless actual parents.

They also gain a wider, if not so deep experience. Those who are not intimately and permanently linked with others, are thrown upon themselves, and, if they do not there find peace and incessant life, there is none to flatter them that they are not very poor and very mean.

A position which so constantly admonishes, may be of inestimable benefit. The

---

[1]Outcasts. Ishmael, illegitimate son of Abraham, was cast out of Abraham's tent with his mother Hagar into the wilderness (Genesis 16; 17; 21:1–21).

person may gain, undistracted by other relationships, a closer communion with the one. Such a use is made of it by saints and sibyls.[2] Or she may be one of the lay sisters of charity, a Canoness, bound by an inward vow! Or the useful drudge of all men, the Martha,[3] much sought, little prized! Or the intellectual interpreter of the varied life she sees; the Urania[4] of a half-formed world's twilight.

Or she may combine all these. Not "needing to care that she may please a husband," a frail and limited being, her thoughts may turn to the centre, and she may, by steadfast contemplation entering into the secret of truth and love, use it for the use of all men, instead of a chosen few, and interpret through it all the forms of life. It is possible, perhaps, to be at once a priestly servant, and a loving muse.

Saints and geniuses have often chosen a lonely position in the faith that if, undisturbed by the pressure of near ties, they would give themselves up to the inspiring spirit, it would enable them to understand and reproduce life better than actual experience could.

How many old maids take this high stand, we cannot say: it is an unhappy fact, that too many who have come before the eye are gossips rather, and not always good-natured gossips. But if these abuse, and none make the best of their vocation, yet it has not failed to produce some good results. It has been seen by others, if not by themselves, that beings, likely to be left alone, need to be fortified and furnished within themselves, and education and thought have tended more and more to regard these beings as related to absolute Being, as well as to other men. It has been seen that, as the breaking of no bond ought to destroy a man, so ought the missing of none to hinder him from growing. And thus a circumstance of the time, which springs rather from its luxury than its purity, has helped to place women on the true platform.

Perhaps the next generation, looking deeper into this matter, will find that contempt is put upon old maids, or old women at all, merely because they do not use the elixir[5] which would keep them always young. Under its influence a gem brightens yearly which is only seen to more advantage through the fissures Time makes in the casket.[6] No one thinks of Michael Angelo's Persican Sibyl, or St. Theresa, or Tasso's Leonora, or the Greek Electra, as an old maid, more than of Michael Angelo or Canova as old bachelors, though all had reached the period in life's course appointed to take that degree.[7]

See a common woman at forty; scarcely has she the remains of beauty, of any soft poetic grace which gave her attraction as woman, which kindled the hearts of those who looked on her to sparkling thoughts, or diffused round her a roseate air of gentle love. See her, who was, indeed, a lovely girl, in the coarse full-blown dahlia flower of what is commonly called matron-beauty, fat, fair, and forty, showily dressed, and with manners as broad and full as her frill or satin cloak. People observe, "how well she is preserved;" "she is a fine woman still," they say. This

---

[2]Prophetic oracles of ancient Greece and Rome.

[3]The patron saint of good housewives, the sister of Lazarus and Mary, who did not sit at the feet of Jesus to hear his words, but rather "was cumbered about much serving" (Luke 10:38–40).

[4]Muse of astronomy in Greek mythology.

[5]Essence believed by the alchemists to prolong life; also used to refer to the "Philosopher's stone," the substance believed capable of changing base metals into gold. For Fuller, the elixir to keep one always young is not a matter of dress or make-up, but is a matter of wisdom, as the following note by her suggests.

[6]"Appendix F" (Fuller's note). Casket: jewel case, a metaphor for the body. In Appendix F, Fuller quotes from memory an extract from *Memoirs of an American Lady* (1808) by Scottish writer Anne Grant, known as Mrs. Grant of Laggan (1755–1838): "Observing of how little consequence the Indian women are in youth, and how much in age, be-

cause in that trying life, good counsel and sagacity are more prized than charms, Mrs. Grant expresses a wish that Reformers would take a hint from observation of this circumstance. In another place she says: 'The misfortune of our sex is, that young women are not regarded as the material from which old women must be made.'"

[7]The Persian Sibyl painted on the ceiling of the Sistine Chapel in Rome by Italian sculptor, painter, architect Michaelangelo (1475–1564); Saint Terésa (1515–1582), Spanish Carmelite nun, mystic, and author; Italian poet Torquato Tasso (1544–1595) and his legendary passion for Leonora d'Este which led to his imprisonment (now discredited) are the subject of Goethe's drama *Tasso* (1789) and Byron's poem "The Lament of Tasso" (1817); Electra, in classic myth, is the daughter of Agamemnon and Clytemnestra, who helps her brother Orestes avenge their father's death by killing their mother; Antonio Canova (1757–1822), Italian sculptor.

woman, whether as a duchess in diamonds, or one of our city dames in mosaics,[8] charms the poet's heart no more, and would look much out of place kneeling before the Madonna. She "does well the honors of her house," "leads society," is, in short, always spoken and thought of upholstery-wise.[9]

Or see that care-worn face, from which every soft line is blotted, those faded eyes from which lonely tears have driven the flashes of fancy, the mild white beam of a tender enthusiasm. This woman is not so ornamental to a tea party; yet she would please better, in picture. Yet surely she, no more than the other, looks as a human being should at the end of forty years. Forty years! have they bound those brows with no garland? shed in the lamp no drop of ambrosial oil?[10]

Not so looked the Iphigenia in Aulis.[11] Her forty years had seen her in anguish, in sacrifice, in utter loneliness. But those pains were borne for her father and her country; the sacrifice she had made pure for herself and those around her. Wandering alone at night in the vestal solitude of her imprisoning grove, she has looked up through its "living summits" to the stars, which shed down into her aspect their own lofty melody. At forty she would not misbecome the marble.

Not so looks the Persica.[12] She is withered, she is faded; the drapery that enfolds her has, in its dignity an angularity, too, that tells of age, of sorrow, of a stern composure to the *must*. But her eye, that torch of the soul, is untamed, and in the intensity of her reading, we see a soul invincibly young in faith and hope. Her age is her charm, for it is the night of the Past that gives this beacon fire leave to shine. Wither more and more, black Chrysalid![13] thou dost but give the winged beauty time to mature its splendors.

Not so looked Vittoria Colonna,[14] after her life of a great hope, and of true conjugal fidelity. She had been, not merely a bride, but a wife, and each hour had helped to plume the noble bird. A coronet of pearls will not shame her brow; it is white and ample, a worthy altar for love and thought.

Even among the North American Indians, a race of men as completely engaged in mere instinctive life as almost any in the world, and where each chief, keeping many wives as useful servants, of course looks with no kind eye on celibacy in woman, it was excused in the following instance mentioned by Mrs. Jameson.[15] A woman dreamt in youth that she was betrothed to the Sun. She built her a wigwam apart, filled it with emblems of her alliance, and means of an independent life. There she passed her days, sustained by her own exertions, and true to her supposed engagement.

In any tribe, we believe, a woman, who lived as if she was betrothed to the Sun, would be tolerated, and the rays which made her youth blossom sweetly, would crown her with a halo in age.

·　·　·　·　·

---

[8]Decorations made of small pieces of inlaid glass or stone.
[9]Reference, perhaps, to her role as hostess, presiding in salons, parlors, and other "upholstered" areas.
[10]I.e., one who reaches forty is deserving of the victor's crowning laurel wreath and the tribute of the lamp, lit with oil fit for the gods ("ambrosial").
[11]When the Greek fleet sailing against Troy was becalmed at Aulis, Agamemnon agreed to sacrifice his daughter Iphigenia and sent for her under the pretense that she would be wed to Achilles. When the ruse was discovered, Iphigenia at first protested, but then accepted the need to sacrifice herself to save her country. At the moment of the sacrifice, unbeknownst to the onlookers, the goddess Artemis substituted a hind for Iphigenia and conveyed her to Tauris, making her a priestess of her temple. In Appendix G, Fuller states that she has "borrowed from the papers of Miranda" her notes on the women of the Greek dramatists, quoting at length from Euripides' *Iphigenia at Aulis*, which ends at the moment of sacrifice, and referring to "Goethe's Iphigenia, the mature woman." In a courageous defense of German poet Goethe, considered immoral by Americans at the time, Fuller wrote of his *Iphigenie auf Tauris* (1787): "Goethe has unfolded a part of the life of this being, unknown elsewhere. . . the priestess, the full beauty of virgin womanhood. . . ." (*Dial*, July 1841).
[12]The Persica or Persian sibyl, one of the oldest sibyls, is portrayed by Michaelangelo as an elderly woman, bent with age, face half turned, with eyes gazing down at an open book.
[13]Chrysalis, developmental stage in the life of the insect, enclosed in a cocoon; hence the butterfly-like soul encased in the aging body.
[14]Vittoria Colonna (1490–1547), Italian poet and devoted wife, although early widowed, was noted for her goodness and admired by friends such as Michaelangelo and Tasso.
[15]Anna Brownell Jameson (1794–1860), British author, tells this story of a Chippewa woman in *Winter Studies and Summer Rambles in Canada* (1838).

[MUSE AND MINERVA]

There are two aspects of woman's nature, represented by the ancients as Muse and Minerva.[1] It is the former to which the writer in the Pathfinder[2] looks. It is the latter which Wordsworth has in mind, when he says—

> "With a placid brow,
> Which woman ne'er should forfeit, keep thy vow."[3]

The especial genius of woman I believe to be electrical[4] in movement, intuitive in function, spiritual in tendency. She excels not so easily in classification, or recreation, as in an instinctive seizure of causes, and a simple breathing out of what she receives that has the singleness of life, rather than the selecting and energizing of art.

More native is it to her to be the living model of the artist than to set apart from herself any one form in objective reality; more native to inspire and receive the poem, than to create it. In so far as soul is in her completely developed, all soul is the same; but as far as it is modified in her as woman, it flows, it breathes, it sings, rather than deposits soil, or finishes work, and that which is especially feminine flushes, in blossom, the face of earth, and pervades, like air and water, all this seeming solid globe, daily renewing and purifying its life. Such may be the especially feminine element, spoken of as Femality. But it is no more the order of nature that it should be incarnated pure in any form, than that the masculine energy should exist unmingled with it in any form.

Male and female represent the two sides of the great radical dualism. But, in fact, they are perpetually passing into one another. Fluid hardens to solid, solid rushes to fluid. There is no wholly masculine man, no purely feminine woman.

History jeers at the attempts of physiologists to bind great original laws by the forms which flow from them. They make a rule; they say from observation, what can and cannot be. In vain! Nature provides exceptions to every rule. She sends women to battle, and sets Hercules spinning; she enables women to bear immense burdens, cold, and frost; she enables the man, who feels maternal love, to nourish his infant like a mother. Of late she plays still gayer pranks. Not only she deprives organizations, but organs, of a necessary end. She enables people to read with the top of the head, and see with the pit of the stomach. Presently she will make a female Newton, and a male Syren.[5]

Man partakes of the feminine in the Apollo,[6] woman of the masculine as Minerva.

What I mean by the Muse is the unimpeded clearness of the intuitive powers which a perfectly truthful adherence to every admonition of the higher instincts would bring to a finely organized human being. It may appear as prophecy or as poesy. It enabled Cassandra to foresee the results of actions passing round her; the Seeress to behold the true character of the person through the mask of his customary life.[7] (Sometimes she saw a feminine form behind the man, sometimes the reverse.) It enabled the daughter of Linnæus to see the soul of the flower ex-

---

[1]The nine muses of Greek mythology presided over song and prompted the memory, each inspiring a department of literature, art, or science; Minerva, Roman name for the Greek virgin goddess Athena, is the goddess of war and of wisdom.

[2]Two articles headed "Femality" appeared in the March 1843 *New York Pathfinder*, described earlier by Fuller as expressive of "the lyrical, the inspiring" aspects of woman's being.

[3]From "Liberty: Sequel to the Preceding" (1835) by English poet William Wordsworth (1770–1850).

[4]Defined earlier in the essay as "the electrical, the magnetic element [which is] commonly expressed by saying that her intuitions are more rapid and correct."

[5]Sir Isaac Newton (1642–1727), great English scientist; sirens: Greek sea nymphs whose song lures sailors to destruction on the rocks.

[6]Greek god of the sun and of poetry.

[7]Cassandra, given the gift of prophecy by Apollo, foretold the events of the Trojan War; seeress: woman clairvoyant.

haling from the flower.[8] It gave a man, but a poet man, the power of which he thus speaks: "Often in my contemplation of nature, radiant intimations, and as it were sheaves of light appear before me as to the facts of cosmogony in which my mind has, perhaps, taken especial part." He wisely adds, "but it is necessary with earnestness to verify the knowledge we gain by these flashes of light."[9] And none should forget this. Sight must be verified by life before it can deserve the honors of piety and genius. Yet sight comes first, and of this sight of the world of causes, this approximation to the region of primitive motions, women I hold to be especially capable. Even without equal freedom with the other sex, they have already shown themselves so, and should these faculties have free play, I believe they will open new, deeper and purer sources of joyous inspiration than have as yet refreshed the earth.

Let us be wise and not impede the soul. Let her work as she will. Let us have one creative energy, one incessant revelation. Let it take what form it will, and let us not bind it by the past to man or woman, black or white. Jove sprang from Rhea, Pallas from Jove.[10] So let it be.

If it has been the tendency of these remarks to call woman rather to the Minerva side,—if I, unlike the more generous writer, have spoken from society no less than the soul,—let it be pardoned! It is love that has caused this, love for many incarcerated souls, that might be freed, could the idea of religious self-dependence be established in them, could the weakening habit of dependence on others be broken up.

Proclus[11] teaches that every life has, in its sphere, a totality or wholeness of the animating powers of the other spheres; having only, as its own characteristic, a predominance of some one power. Thus Jupiter comprises, within himself, the other twelve powers, which stand thus: The first triad is *demiurgic or fabricative*, i.e., Jupiter, Neptune, Vulcan; the second, *defensive*, Vesta, Minerva, Mars; the third, *vivific*, Ceres, Juno, Diana; and the fourth, Mercury, Venus, Apollo, *elevating and harmonic*.[12] In the sphere of Jupiter, energy is predominant—with Venus, beauty; but each comprehends and apprehends all the others.

When the same community of life and consciousness of mind begins among men, humanity will have, positively and finally, subjugated its brute elements and Titanic[13] childhood; criticism will have perished; arbitrary limits and ignorant censure be impossible; all will have entered upon the liberty of law, and the harmony of common growth.

Then Apollo will sing to his lyre what Vulcan forges on the anvil, and the Muse weave anew the tapestries of Minerva.

It is, therefore, only in the present crisis that the preference is given to Minerva. The power of continence must establish the legitimacy of freedom, the power of self-poise the perfection of motion.

---

[8]"The daughter of Linnæus [1707–1778, Swedish botanist] states, that, while looking steadfastly at the red lily, she saw its spirit hovering above it, as a red flame. It is true, this, like many fair spirit-stories, may be explained away as an optical illusion, but its poetic beauty and meaning would, even than, make it valuable, as an illustration of the spiritual fact" (Fuller's note).

[9]Unidentified.

[10]Jove or Jupiter, Roman name for Zeus, king of the Greek gods, whose mother was Rhea, the great mother of the gods; Pallas Athena, Greek name for Minerva, Roman goddess of wisdom who sprang fully armed from the brain of Jove.

[11]Proclus (*c.* 410–485), Greek Neoplatonist philosopher.

[12]The *demiurgic* (creative) powers: Jupiter, Supreme Ruler of the Universe; Neptune, god of the sea; Vulcan, god of earthly fire—volcanic eruptions, the forge, the hearth. The *defensive* powers: Vesta, virgin goddess of the hearth; Minerva, goddess of war and wisdom; Mars, god of war. The *vivific* (enlivening) powers: Ceres, goddess of agriculture; Juno, wife of Jupiter and goddess of women; Diana, feminine counterpart of Apollo, goddess of the moon. The *elevating and harmonic* powers: Mercury, messenger of the gods, inventor of the lyre, patron of industry; Venus, goddess of love and beauty; Apollo, god of the sun and poetry.

[13]Titans were the primordial, lawless giants overthrown by the Olympian gods.

[The Soul Poised upon Itself]

Every relation, every gradation of nature is incalculably precious, but only to the soul which is poised upon itself, and to whom no loss, no change, can bring dull discord, for it is in harmony with the central soul.[1]

If any individual live too much in relations, so that he becomes a stranger to the resources of his own nature, he falls, after a while, into a distraction, or imbecility, from which he can only be cured by a time of isolation, which gives the renovating fountains time to rise up. With a society it is the same. Many minds, deprived of the traditionary or instinctive means of passing a cheerful existence, must find help in self-impulse, or perish. It is therefore that, while any elevation, in the view of union, is to be hailed with joy, we shall not decline celibacy as the great fact of the time. It is one from which no vow, no arrangement, can at present save a thinking mind. For now the rowers are pausing on their oars; they wait a change before they can pull together. All tends to illustrate the thought of a wise co[n]temporary. Union is only possible to those who are units.[2] To be fit for relations in time, souls, whether of man or woman, must be able to do without them in the spirit.

It is therefore that I would have woman lay aside all thought, such as she habitually cherishes, of being taught and led by men. I would have her, like the Indian girl,[3] dedicate herself to the Sun, the Sun of Truth, and go no where if his beams did not make clear the path. I would have her free from compromise, from complaisance, from helplessness, because I would have her good enough and strong enough to love one and all beings, from the fulness, not the poverty of being.

Men, as at present instructed, will not help this work, because they also are under the slavery of habit. . . .

Men do *not* look at both sides, and women must leave off asking them and being influenced by them, but retire within themselves, and explore the groundwork of life till they find their peculiar secret. Then, when they come forth again, renovated and baptized, they will know how to turn all dross to gold, and will be rich and free though they live in a hut, tranquil, if in a crowd. Then their sweet singing shall not be from passionate impulse, but the lyrical over-flow of a devine rapture, and a new music shall be evolved from this many-chorded world.

Grant her, then, for a while, the armor and the javelin.[4] Let her put from her the press of other minds and meditate in virgin loneliness. The same idea shall re-appear in due time as Muse, or Ceres,[5] the all-kindly patient Earth-Spirit.

．　　．　　．　　．　　．

[Summary: History and Prophecy]

And now I have designated in outline, if not in fulness, the stream which is ever flowing from the heights of my thought.

In the earlier tract,[1] I was told, I did not make my meaning sufficiently clear. In this I have consequently tried to illustrate it in various ways, and may have been guilty of much repetition. Yet, as I am anxious to leave no room for doubt, I shall venture to retrace, once more, the scope of my design in points, as was done in old-fashioned sermons.

Man is a being of two-fold relations, to nature beneath, and intelligences above

---

[1]Cf. Emerson's "Over-Soul."
[2]Unidentified.
[3]The Indian girl, mentioned above, who chose a celibate life and married the Sun.
[4]The weapons of Minerva.

[5]Roman goddess of agriculture.
[1]"The Great Lawsuit: Man *versus* Men; Woman *versus* Women," published in the *Dial* in April 1843, the earlier version of this essay.

him. The earth is his school, if not his birth-place: God his object: life and thought, his means of interpreting nature, and aspiring to God.

Only a fraction of this purpose is accomplished in the life of any one man. Its entire accomplishment is to be hoped only from the sum of the lives of men, or man considered as a whole.

As this whole has one soul and one body, any injury or obstruction to a part, or to the meanest member, affects the whole. Man can never be perfectly happy or virtuous, till all men are so.

To address[2] man wisely, you must not forget that his life is partly animal, subject to the same laws with nature.

But you cannot address him wisely unless you consider him still more as soul, and appreciate the conditions and destiny of soul.

The growth of man is two-fold, masculine and feminine.

As far as these two methods can be distinguished they are so as

Energy and Harmony.

Power and Beauty.

Intellect and Love.

Or by some such rude classification, for we have not language primitive and pure enough to express such ideas with precision.

These two sides are supposed to be expressed in man and woman, that is, as the more and less, for the faculties have not been given pure to either, but only in preponderance. There are also exceptions in great number, such as men of far more beauty than power, and the reverse. But as a general rule, it seems to have been the intention to give a preponderance on the one side, that is called masculine, and on the other, one that is called feminine.

There cannot be a doubt that, if these two developments were in perfect harmony, they would correspond to and fulfil one another, like hemispheres, or the tenor and bass in music.

But there is no perfect harmony in human nature; and the two parts answer one another only now and then, or, if there be a persistent consonance, it can only be traced, at long intervals, instead of discoursing an obvious melody.

What is the cause of this?

Man, in the order of time, was developed first; as energy comes before harmony; power before beauty.

Woman was therefore under his care as an elder. He might have been her guardian and teacher.

But as human nature goes not straight forward, but by excessive action and then reaction in an undulated course, he misunderstood and abused his advantages, and became her temporal master instead of her spiritual sire.

On himself came the punishment. He educated woman more as a servant than a daughter, and found himself a king without a queen.

The children of this unequal union showed unequal natures, and, more and more, men seemed sons of the handmaid, rather than princes.

At last there were so many Ishmaelites that the rest grew frightened and indignant. They laid the blame on Hagar, and drove her forth into the wilderness.[3]

But there were none the fewer Ishmaelites for that.

At last men became a little wiser, and saw that the infant Moses was, in every case, saved by the pure instincts of woman's breast.[4] For, as too much adversity is

---

[2]Consider.

[3]Hagar, the Egyptian handmaid of the barren Sarah, was given to Abraham as a concubine and bore Ishmael. After Sarah gave birth to Isaac, she drove Hagar and Ishmael into the wilderness (Genesis 16; 17; 21:1–21).

[4]Because of the Egyptian decree to kill newborn Hebrew males, his mother cast Moses adrift in a basket on the Nile River, from which he was rescued by Pharaoh's daughter (Exodus 2:1–10).

better for the moral nature than too much prosperity, woman, in this respect, dwindled less than man, though in other respects, still a child in leading strings.[5]

So man did her more and more justice, and grew more and more kind.

But yet, his habits and his will corrupted by the past, he did not clearly see that woman was half himself, that her interests were identical with his, and that, by the law of their common being, he could never reach his true proportions while she remained in any wise shorn[6] of hers.

And so it has gone on to our day; both ideas developing, but more slowly than they would under a clearer recognition of truth and justice, which would have permitted the sexes their due influence on one another, and mutual improvement from more dignified relations.

Wherever there was pure love, the natural influences were, for the time, restored.

Wherever the poet or artist gave free course to his genius, he saw the truth, and expressed it in worthy forms, for these men especially share and need the feminine principle. The divine birds need to be brooded[7] into life and song by mothers.

Wherever religion (I mean the thirst for truth and good, not the love of sect and dogma,) had its course, the original design was apprehended in its simplicity, and the dove presaged sweetly from Dodona's oak.[8]

I have aimed to show that no age was left entirely without a witness of the equality of the sexes in function, duty and hope.

Also that, when there was unwillingness or ignorance, which prevented this being acted upon, women had not the less power for their want of light and noble freedom. But it was power which hurt alike them and those against whom they made use of the arms of the servile; cunning, blandishment, and unreasonable emotion.

That now the time has come when a clearer vision and better action are possible. When man and woman may regard one another as brother and sister, the pillars of one porch, the priests of one worship.

I have believed and intimated that this hope would receive an ampler fruition, than ever before, in our own land.

And it will do so if this land carry out the principles from which sprang our national life.

I believe that, at present, women are the best helpers of one another.

Let them think; let them act; till they know what they need.

We only ask of men to remove arbitrary barriers. Some would like to do more. But I believe it needs for woman to show herself in her native dignity, to teach them how to aid her; their minds are so encumbered by tradition.

When Lord Edward Fitzgerald travelled with the Indians,[9] his manly heart obliged him at once, to take the packs from the squaws and carry them. But we do not read that the red men followed his example, though they are ready enough to carry the pack of the white woman, because she seems to them a superior being.

Let woman appear in the mild majesty of Ceres,[10] and rudest churls[11] will be willing to learn from her.

You ask, what use will she make of liberty, when she has so long been sustained and restrained?

I answer; in the first place, this will not be suddenly given. I read yesterday a

---

[5]Strings used to support and guide a child learning to walk.
[6]In any way deprived.
[7]Hatched.
[8]Site of an oracle of Zeus in Greece, whose sanctity was revealed by a dove's spoken words.
[9]Lord Edward Fitzgerald (1763–1798), Irish patriot, jour-

neyed in 1789 from New Brunswick to Quebec and to New Orleans, fraternizing with Indians along the way; at Detroit he was formally adopted and made a chief of the Hurons.
[10]Roman goddess of agriculture.
[11]Low-bred men.

debate of this year on the subject of enlarging women's rights over property.[12] It was a leaf from the class-book that is preparing for the needed instruction. The men learned visibly as they spoke. The champions of woman saw the fallacy of arguments, on the opposite side, and were startled by their own convictions. With their wives at home, and the readers of the paper, it was the same. And so the stream flows on; thought urging action, and action leading to the evolution of still better thought.

But, were this freedom to come suddenly, I have no fear of the consequences. Individuals might commit excesses, but there is not only in the sex a reverence for decorums and limits inherited and enhanced from generation to generation, which many years of other life could not efface, but a native love, in woman as woman, of proportion, of "the simple art of not too much," a Greek moderation,[13] which would create immediately a restraining party, the natural legislators and instructors of the rest, and would gradually establish such rules as are needed to guard, without impeding, life.

The Graces[14] would lead the choral dance, and teach the rest to regulate their steps to the measure of beauty.

But if you ask me what offices they may fill; I reply—any. I do not care what case you put; let them be sea-captains, if you will. I do not doubt there are women well fitted for such an office, and, if so, I should be glad to see them in it, as to welcome the maid of Saragossa, or the maid of Missolonghi, or the Suliote heroine, or Emily Plater.[15]

I think women need, especially at this juncture, a much greater range of occupation than they have, to rouse their latent powers. A party of travellers lately visited a lonely hut on a mountain. There they found an old woman that told them she and her husband had lived there forty years. "Why," they said, "did you choose so barren a spot?" She "did not know; *it was the man's notion.*"

And, during forty years, she had been content to act, without knowing why, upon "the man's notion." I would not have it so.

In families that I know, some little girls like to saw wood, others to use carpenters' tools. Where these tastes are indulged, cheerfulness and good humor are promoted. Where they are forbidden, because "such things are not proper for girls," they grow sullen and mischievous.

Fourier[16] had observed these wants of women, as no one can fail to do who watches the desires of little girls, or knows the ennui that haunts grown women, except where they make to themselves a serene little world by art of some kind. He, therefore, in proposing a great variety of employments, in manufactures or the care of plants and animals, allows for one third of woman, as likely to have a taste for masculine pursuits, one third of men for feminine.

Who does not observe the immediate glow and serenity that is diffused over the life of women, before restless or fretful, by engaging in gardening, building, or the lowest department of art. Here is something that is not routine, something that draws forth life toward the infinite.

I have no doubt, however, that a large proportion of women would give them-

[12]In 1844, the legislature of Rhode Island was considering a bill, subsequently passed, that would secure to married women their property rights "under certain regulations." In the next few years several states passed similar bills, the most liberal being New York's of 1848; not until the 1860 act in New York were equal property rights secured.
[13]The classical golden mean.
[14]Euphrosyne (merriment), Aglaia (festivity), and Thalia (good cheer), sister goddesses in Greek mythology who preside over the banquet, the dance, social pleasures, and accomplishments.
[15]Maria Augustín, one of the defenders of Saragossa, Spain, during a French seige (1808–09) and described in Byron's *Childe Harold* (I.LIV) as one who "stalks with Minerva's step where Mars might quake to tread"; the Greek town Missolonghi, where Byron died (1824) during the Greek War of Independence (1821–33), sustained several Turkish sieges; after a prolonged seige, the Greek people, Suliotes, yielded to the Albanians in 1803; Emily Plater led a regiment in the Polish army against the Russians (1831).
[16]Charles Fourier (1772–1837), French social scientist and reformer, whose theories served as a model for the utopian Brook Farm community.

selves to the same employments as now, because there are circumstances that must lead them. Mothers will delight to make the nest soft and warm. Nature would take care of that; no need to clip the wings of any bird that wants to soar and sing, or finds in itself the strength of pinion[17] for a migratory flight unusual to its kind. The difference would be that *all* need not be constrained to employments, for which *some* are unfit.

I have urged upon the sex self-subsistence in its two forms of self-reliance and self-impulse, because I believe them to be the needed means of the present juncture.

I have urged on woman independence of man, not that I do not think the sexes mutually needed by one another, but because in woman this fact has led to an excessive devotion, which has cooled love, degraded marriage, and prevented either sex from being what it should be to itself or the other.

I wish woman to live, *first* for God's sake. Then she will not make an imperfect man her god, and thus sink to idolatry. Then she will not take what is not fit for her from a sense of weakness and poverty. Then, if she finds what she needs in man embodied, she will know how to love, and be worthy of being loved.

By being more a soul, she will not be less woman, for nature is perfected through spirit.

Now there is no woman, only an overgrown child.

That her hand may be given with dignity, she must be able to stand alone. I wish to see men and women capable of such relations as are depicted by Landor in his Pericles and Aspasia,[18] where grace is the natural garb of strength, and the affections are calm, because deep. The softness is that of a firm tissue, as when

> "The gods approve
> The depth, but not the tumult of the soul,
> A fervent, not ungovernable love."[19]

A profound thinker has said, "no married woman can represent the female world, for she belongs to her husband. The idea of woman must be represented by a virgin."[20]

But that is the very fault of marriage, and of the present relation between the sexes, that the woman does belong to the man, instead of forming a whole with him. Were it otherwise, there would be no such limitation to the thought.

Woman, self-centred, would never be absorbed by any relation; it would be only an experience to her as to man. It is a vulgar error that love, *a* love to woman is her whole existence; she also is born for Truth and Love in their universal energy. Would she but assume her inheritance, Mary would not be the only virgin mother. Not Manzoni alone would celebrate in his wife the virgin mind with the maternal wisdom and conjugal affections.[21] The soul is ever young, ever virgin.

And will not she soon appear? The woman who shall vindicate their birthright for all women; who shall teach them what to claim, and how to use what they obtain? Shall not her name be for her era Victoria, for her country and life Virginia?[22] Yet predictions are rash; she herself must teach us to give her the fitting name.

An idea not unknown to ancient times has of late been revived, that, in the

---

[17]Wing.
[18]English poet Walter Savage Landor (1775–1864), author of *Pericles and Aspasia* (1836), imaginary letters including discussions of art, literature, philosophy, religion, and politics.
[19]From stanza 13 of *Laodamia* (1814) by English poet William Wordsworth (1770–1850).
[20]Unidentified.
[21]Alessandro Manzoni (1785–1873), Italian writer, dedi-

cated his *Adelchi* (1822) to his wife "who, with conjugal affection and maternal wisdom, has preserved a virgin mind."
[22]Victoria: like the Queen of England who took the throne in 1837 and meaning "Triumphant victor" (Minerva-like); Virginia: referring to the virgin land, America, where woman will become worthy of her potential, and to the virgin self described in this work.

metamorphoses of life, the soul assumes the form, first of man, then of woman,[23] and takes the chances, and reaps the benefits of either lot. Why then, say some, lay such emphasis on the rights or needs of woman? What she wins not, as woman, will come to her as man.

That makes no difference. It is not woman, but the law of right, the law of growth, that speaks in us, and demands the perfection of each being in its kind, apple as apple, woman as woman. Without adopting your theory I know that I, a daughter, live through the life of man; but what concerns me now is, that my life be a beautiful, powerful, in a word, a complete life in its kind. Had I but one more moment to live, I must wish the same.

Suppose, at the end of your cycle, your great world-year, all will be completed, whether I exert myself or not (and the supposition is *false*,) but suppose it true, am I to be indifferent about it? Not so! I must beat my own pulse true in the heart of the world; for *that* is virtue, excellence, health.

Thou, Lord of Day! didst leave us to-night so calmly glorious, not dismayed that cold winter is coming, not postponing thy beneficence to the fruitful summer! Thou didst smile on thy day's work when it was done, and adorn thy down-going as thy up-rising, for thou art loyal, and it is thy nature to give life, if thou canst, and shine at all events!

I stand in the sunny noon of life. Objects no longer glitter in the dews of morning, neither are yet softened by the shadows of evening. Every spot is seen, every chasm revealed. Climbing the dusty hill, some fair effigies that once stood for symbols of human destiny have been broken; those I still have with me, show defects in this broad light. Yet enough is left, even by experience, to point distinctly to the glories of that destiny; faint, but not to be mistaken streaks of the future day. I can say with the bard,

"Though many have suffered shipwreck, still beat noble hearts."[24]

Always the soul says to us all: Cherish your best hopes as a faith, and abide by them in action. Such shall be the effectual fervent means to their fulfilment,

> For the Power to whom we bow
> Has given its pledge that, if not now,
> They of pure and stedfast mind,
> By faith exalted, truth refined,
> *Shall* hear all music loud and clear,
> Whose first notes they ventured here.
> Then fear not thou to wind[25] the horn,
> Though elf and gnome thy courage scorn;
> Ask for the Castle's King and Queen;
> Though rabble rout may rush between,
> Beat thee senseless to the ground,
> In the dark beset thee round;
> Persist to ask and it will come,
> Seek not for rest in humbler home;
> So shalt thou see what few have seen,
> The palace home of King and Queen.[26]

15th November, 1844   *1845*

---

[23]A reference to metempsychosis, or the transmigration of souls. Some ancients believed that the immortal soul underwent a fixed cycle of incarnations, being born into a lower or higher form of life according to how one had lived. In the *Timaeus* (42), Plato describes the hierarchy: if man failed to live well, he would pass into a woman at the second birth, and into brute forms thereafter.
[24]Unidentified.
[25]Blow.
[26]Poem by Fuller.

ELIZABETH CADY STANTON
(1815–1902)

Elizabeth Cady Stanton was one of the two most important leaders of the women's rights movement in the nineteenth century; the other was Susan B. Anthony (1820–1906), a long time friend and associate. Stanton was the primary mover in bringing about the first Woman's Rights Convention in America in Seneca Falls, New York, July 19–20, 1848. And it was she who drafted the "Declaration of Sentiments" adopted (with revisions and resolutions) at the convention.

She was born Elizabeth Cady in 1815 in Johnstown, New York, to a lawyer father who served in Congress and a politically involved mother who was active in her husband's compaigns. In 1840 she married Henry B. Stanton, and they went on their honeymoon to England in order to attend a World Anti-Slavery Convention in London. To Elizabeth Stanton's surprise, women were barred as delegates. She wrote later in her autobiography: "Though women were members of the National Anti-Slavery Society, accustomed to speak and vote in all its conventions, and to take an equally active part with men in the whole anti-slavery struggle, and were there as delegates from associations of men and women, as well as those distinctively of their own sex, yet all alike were rejected because they were women." Thus as it would in the twentieth century, the women's movement in the nineteenth century gained impetus by the discrimination practiced against women in a movement against racism (or slavery).

Throughout her long career, Stanton served the cause of women's rights, especially in collaboration with Susan B. Anthony. She served as the first president of the National Woman Suffrage Association (1869–90). She was author and compiler (together with Susan B. Anthony and Matilda Joslyn Gage) of the three-volume *History of Woman Suffrage* (1881–86). Disturbed by the sexism of the Bible, she published *The Woman's Bible* in two volumes, 1895 and 1898. Her autobiography, *Eighty Years & More: Reminiscences 1815–1897*, was published in 1898.

Perhaps Stanton's most radical act was to call, organize, and see through to the end the first American Woman's Rights Convention in Seneca Falls in 1848. Her draft of the "Declaration of Sentiments," approved at the convention, was ingeniously designed to follow the rhetoric of Jefferson's "Declaration of Independence," but with significant changes to include women. The charges against King George in the original were changed to charges against "all men." The number of the charges remained the same—eighteen—and the language also remained the same, wherever possible. But in spite of following so closely the form and substance of such a revered founding document, the response to the "Declaration of Sentiments" was hostile. In her account, Stanton reported that the "proceedings were extensively published, unsparingly ridiculed by the press, and denounced by the pulpit, much to the surprise and chagrin of the leaders."

The Seneca Falls Convention gradually stimulated the holding of women's rights conventions in other states. Stanton's focus in the declaration was on political equality for women and she worked for it until her death in 1902. She saw it as "the stronghold of the fortress—*the one* woman will find the most difficult to take, *the one* man will most reluctantly give up." In 1920, with the adoption of the Nineteenth Amendment to the Constitution, women finally were granted the right to vote.

ADDITIONAL READING

Elizabeth Cady Stanton as Revealed in her Letters, Diary and Reminiscences, 2 vols., ed. Theodore Stanton and Harriet Stanton Blatch, 1922; *Elizabeth Cady Stanton, Susan B. Anthony: Correspondence, Writing, Speeches*, ed. Ellen Carol DuBois, 1981.

Alma Lutz, *Created Equal: A Biography of Elizabeth Cady Stanton, 1815–1902*, 1940; Mary Ann B. Oakley, *Elizabeth Cady Stanton*, 1972; Lois W. Banner, *Elizabeth Cady Stanton: A Radical for Women's Rights*, 1980; Elisabeth Griffith, *In Her Own Right: The Life of Elizabeth Cady Stanton*, 1982.

TEXT

History of Woman Suffrage, Vol. 1, ed. Elizabeth Cady Stanton, Susan B. Anthony, and Matilda Joslyn Gage, 1881.

"Declaration of Sentiments" of the Seneca Falls Woman's Rights Convention, 1848

When, in the course of human events, it becomes necessary for one portion of the family of man to assume among the people of the earth a position different from that which they have hitherto occupied, but one to which the laws of nature and of nature's God entitle them, a decent respect to the opinions of mankind requires that they should declare the causes that impel them to such a course.

We hold these truths to be self-evident: that all men and women are created equal; that they are endowed by their Creator with certain inalienable rights; that among these are life, liberty, and the pursuit of happiness; that to secure these rights governments are instituted, deriving their just powers from the consent of the governed. Whenever any form of government becomes destructive of these ends, it is the right of those who suffer from it to refuse allegiance to it, and to insist upon the institution of a new government, laying its foundation on such principles, and organizing its powers in such form, as to them shall seem most likely to effect their safety and happiness. Prudence, indeed, will dictate that governments long established should not be changed for light and transient causes; and accordingly all experience hath shown that mankind are more disposed to suffer, while evils are sufferable, than to right themselves by abolishing the forms to which they were accustomed. But when a long train of abuses and usurpations, pursuing invariably the same object evinces a design to reduce them under absolute despotism, it is their duty to throw off such government, and to provide new guards for their future security. Such has been the patient sufferance of the women under this government, and such is now the necessity which constrains them to demand the equal station to which they are entitled.

The history of mankind is a history of repeated injuries and usurpations on the part of man toward woman, having in direct object the establishment of an absolute tyranny over her. To prove this, let facts be submitted to a candid world.

He has never permitted her to exercise her inalienable right to the elective franchise.

He has compelled her to submit to laws, in the formation of which she had no voice.

He has withheld from her rights which are given to the most ignorant and degraded men—both natives and foreigners.

Having deprived her of this first right of a citizen, the elective franchise, thereby leaving her without representation in the halls of legislation, he has oppressed her on all sides.

He has made her, if married, in the eye of the law, civilly dead.

He has taken from her all right in property, even to the wages she earns.

He has made her, morally, an irresponsible being, as she can commit many crimes with impunity, provided they be done in the presence of her husband. In the covenant of marriage, she is compelled to promise obedience to her husband, he becoming, to all intents and purposes, her master—the law giving him power to deprive her of her liberty, and to administer chastisement.

He has so framed the laws of divorce, as to what shall be the proper causes, and in case of separation, to whom the guardianship of the children shall be given, as to be wholly regardless of the happiness of women—the law, in all cases, going upon a false supposition of the supremacy of man, and giving all power into his hands.

After depriving her of all rights as a married woman, if single, and the owner of property, he has taxed her to support a government which recognizes her only when her property can be made profitable to it.

He has monopolized nearly all the profitable employments, and from those she is permitted to follow, she receives but a scanty remuneration. He closes against her all the avenues to wealth and distinction which he considers most honorable to himself. As a teacher of theology, medicine, or law, she is not known.

He has denied her the facilities for obtaining a thorough education, all colleges being closed against her.

He allows her in Church, as well as State, but a subordinate position, claiming Apostolic authority for her exclusion from the ministry, and, with some exceptions, from any public participation in the affairs of the Church.

He has created a false public sentiment by giving to the world a different code of morals for men and women, by which moral delinquencies which exclude women from society, are not only tolerated, but deemed of little account in man.

He has usurped the prerogative of Jehovah himself, claiming it as his right to assign for her a sphere of action, when that belongs to her conscience and to her God.

He has endeavored, in every way that he could, to destroy her confidence in her own powers, to lessen her self-respect, and to make her willing to lead a dependent and abject life.

Now, in view of this entire disfranchisement of one-half the people of this country, their social and religious degradation—in view of the unjust laws above mentioned, and because women do feel themselves aggrieved, oppressed, and fraudulently deprived of their most sacred rights, we insist that they have immediate admission to all the rights and privileges which belong to them as citizens of the United States.

In entering upon the great work before us, we anticipate no small amount of misconception, misrepresentation, and ridicule; but we shall use every instrumentality within our power to effect our object. We shall employ agents, circulate tracts, petition the State and National legislatures, and endeavor to enlist the pulpit and the press in our behalf. We hope this Convention will be followed by a series of Conventions embracing every part of the country.

RESOLUTIONS:

WHEREAS, The great precept of nature is conceded to be, that "man shall pursue his own true and substantial happiness." Blackstone in his Commentaries[1] remarks, that this law of Nature being coeval with mankind, and dictated by God himself, is of course superior in obligation to any other. It is binding over all the globe, in all countries and at all times; no human laws are of any validity if contrary to this, and such of them as are valid, derive all their force, and all their validity, and all their authority, mediately and immediately, from this original; therefore,

Resolved, That such laws as conflict, in any way, with the true and substantial happiness of woman, are contrary to the great precept of nature and of no validity, for this is "superior in obligation to any other."

Resolved, That all laws which prevent woman from occupying such a station in society as her conscience shall dictate, or which place her in a position inferior to that of man, are contrary to the great precept of nature, and therefore of no force or authority.

Resolved, That woman is man's equal—was intended to be so by the Creator, and the highest good of the race demands that she should be recognized as such.

Resolved, That the women of this country ought to be enlightened in regard to the laws under which they live, that they may no longer publish their degradation by declaring themselves satisfied with their present position, nor their ignorance, by asserting that they have all the rights they want.

Resolved, That inasmuch as man, while claiming for himself intellectual superiority, does accord to woman moral superiority, it is pre-eminently his duty to encourage her to speak and teach, as she has an opportunity, in all religious assemblies.

Resolved, That the same amount of virtue, delicacy, and refinement of behavior that is required of woman in the social state, should also be required of man, and the same transgressions should be visited with equal severity on both man and woman.

Resolved, That the objection of indelicacy and impropriety, which is so often brought against woman when she addresses a public audience, comes with a very ill-grace from those who encourage, by their attendance, her appearance on the stage, in the concert, or in feats of the circus.

Resolved, That woman has too long rested satisfied in the circumscribed limits which corrupt customs and a perverted application of the Scriptures have marked out for her, and that it is time she should move in the enlarged sphere which her great Creator has assigned her.

Resolved, That it is the duty of the women of this country to secure to themselves their sacred right to the elective franchise.

Resolved, That the equality of human rights results necessarily from the fact of the identity of the race in capabilities and responsibilities.

Resolved, therefore, That, being invested by the Creator with the same capabilities, and the same consciousness of responsibility for their exercise, it is demonstrably the right and duty of woman, equally with man, to promote every righteous cause by every righteous means; and especially in regard to the great subjects of morals and religion, it is self-evidently her right to participate with her brother in teaching them, both in private and in public, by writing and by speak-

[1]Sir William Blackstone (1723–1780), British jurist and author of *Commentaries on the Laws of England* (1765–69), a work which exerted great influence on American jurisprudence.

ing, by any instrumentalities proper to be used, and in any assemblies proper to be held; and this being a self-evident truth growing out of the divinely implanted principles of human nature, any custom or authority adverse to it, whether modern or wearing the hoary sanction of antiquity, is to be regarded as a self-evident falsehood, and at war with mankind.

Resolved, That the speedy success of our cause depends upon the zealous and untiring efforts of both men and women, for the overthrow of the monopoly of the pulpit, and for the securing to woman an equal participation with men in the various trades, professions, and commerce.

1848

ELIZABETH BARSTOW STODDARD
(1823–1902)

During her lifetime, Elizabeth Barstow Stoddard's works of fiction were highly praised by Nathaniel Hawthorne, Leslie Stephen, and William Dean Howells as they appeared, but sales were modest. Like few other writers, Elizabeth Stoddard was given a second chance. In the late 1880s, her novels were reprinted because of the critical esteem of such literary figures as Howells. The interest they generated was slight, and after her death, she and her work were forgotten.

In 1900, Howells wrote of her, "she has failed of the recognition which her work merits. Her tales have in them a foretaste of realism, which was too strong for the palate of their day, and is now too familiar, perhaps. . . . But in whatever she did she left the stamp of a talent like no other, and of personality disdainful of literary environment. In a time when most of us had to write like Tennyson or Longfellow, or Browning, she never would write like anyone but herself."

Elizabeth Barstow was born in the seacoast town of Mattapoisett, on Buzzard's Bay, Massachusetts. Her father was a prosperous shipbuilder, and his firm had built the whaler *Acushnet* (in *Moby-Dick*, the *Pequod*) on which Herman Melville sailed in 1841 to the South Seas. Elizabeth was educated at Wheaton Female Seminary in Norton, Massachusetts. From the beginning, she was an avid reader, and found in the library of her friend, the Rev. Thomas Robbins, the works of the classic eighteenth-century English writers Addison and Steele, Dr. Johnson, Fielding, Smollett, and Sterne. She remarked of Robbins, "his library was the only lion in our neighborhood." Later, a character in one of her stories was to be endowed with a passion like hers: "Happily she was fond of reading. No one about her ever dreamed what channels of thought were opened by an indiscriminate, incessant course of reading."

Some time in her late twenties, Elizabeth Barstow met an impecunious poet, Richard Stoddard, a New Yorker with a Connecticut background. They married and settled in New York. Since neither was able to manage money well, the rest of their life was spent precariously on the brink of poverty but dedicated to intellectual and literary pursuits. Of the three children of the marriage, two died in infancy. Through Nathaniel Hawthorne, a distant cousin of Elizabeth's, Richard obtained a Custom House job in New York, where he came to know Herman Melville.

Richard Stoddard spent most of his life at various journalistic enterprises and literary hackwork. And he wrote poetry. But the truth was, his poetry was mediocre at best—banal sentiments expressed in an undistinguished style. His greatest contribution to literature was the encouragement he gave his wife to write. He may have touched a vein of truth when he observed of her: "She had a great passion for reading, but a great disinclination for study."

She was clearly a woman of unconventional, always interesting, and sometimes arresting opinions, as witness her comments on women in a letter of 1852: "I am glad to speak of the excessive prudery of American women. . . . Women seem to be on the alert for something improper in conversation or manners; feeling it to be their mission to shrink, and blush, or to keep in arms, in case anybody should venture into some sin against convention." As for herself, she declared (in a kind of anticipation of Henry James), "All my aim is to live intensely."

From 1854 to 1858, she became a regular contributor to the *Daily Alta California* newspaper, forcing her to a schedule which challenged and sharpened her fluency and skill in writing. In a column in 1855 she wrote: "You can form no idea of the balderdash in our bookstores. . . . One of our publishers has the run of three lunatic asylums, another collects 'compositions' of seventeen female boarding schools." Clearly someone with these views would tend to contradict received opinion and violate convention in her art. She began to publish poems, stories, and sketches in various magazines, including *Harper's*, *Atlantic Monthly*, *Saturday Press*, and *Vanity Fair*.

In 1862 she published her first novel, which has come to be considered her masterpiece: *The Morgesons*. The novel was autobiographical, portraying herself, her family, and her New England home life in fictionalized form. Her central character, Cassandra, based on herself, was a strong-willed, passionate individual in rebellion against the conventions and interdictions that stultified or diminished life, especially a woman's life. Other novels of unusual power followed—*Two Men*, in 1865, and *Temple House*, in 1867. They brought praise, but little money.

The financial failure of her novels brought a kind of resignation to Elizabeth Stoddard in the latter part of her life, a resignation that deepened to bitterness when the reissue of her work in the 1880s failed to spark a lasting revival of her reputation. Given the repeated setbacks in her personal and professional life, there is little reason for surprise at her developing talent for losing friends and alienating people. Even she was aware of this knack, and wrote to one friend, "I should both hurt and offend you I know, if I saw you very often."

Neither her disagreeable temperament nor her unjust neglect can diminish her very real contribution to American literature, however. A full-dress dissertation in 1968 by James H. Matlack, "The Literary Career of Elizabeth Barstow Stoddard," did all that dissertations can do to call attention to a neglected writer. And the appearance in 1984 of *The Morgesons and Other Writings, Published and Unpublished, by Elizabeth Stoddard*, edited by Lawrence Buell and Sandra A. Zagarell, offers a third chance for the revival of her reputation. There are some signs now that this neglected writer is getting the attention her achievement merits.

ADDITIONAL READING

Richard Henry Stoddard, *Recollections, Personal and Literary*, ed. Ripley Hitchcock, 1903; James H. Matlack, "The Literary Career of Elizabeth Barstow Stoddard," Ph.D. Dissertation, Yale University, 1968.

TEXT

The Morgesons and Other Writings, Published and Unpublished, by *Elizabeth Stoddard*, ed. Lawrence Buell and Sandra A. Zagarell, 1984.

Lemorne *versus* Huell

The two months I spent at Newport[1] with Aunt Eliza Huell, who had been ordered to the sea-side for the benefit of her health, were the months that created all that is dramatic in my destiny. My aunt was troublesome, for she was not only out of health, but in a lawsuit. She wrote to me, for we lived apart, asking me to accompany her—not because she was fond of me, or wished to give me pleasure, but because I was useful in various ways. Mother insisted upon my accepting her invitation, not because she loved her late husband's sister, but because she thought it wise to cotton to her in every particular, for Aunt Eliza was rich, and we—two lone women—were poor.

I gave my music-pupils a longer and earlier vacation than usual, took a week to arrange my wardrobe—for I made my own dresses—and then started for New York, with the five dollars which Aunt Eliza had sent for my fare thither. I arrived at her house in Bond Street at 7 a.m., and found her man James in conversation with the milkman. He informed me that Miss Huell was very bad, and that the housekeeper was still in bed. I supposed that Aunt Eliza was in bed also, but I had hardly entered the house when I heard her bell ring as she only could ring it—with an impatient jerk.

"She wants hot milk," said James, "and the man has just come."

I laid my bonnet down, and went to the kitchen. Saluting the cook, who was an old acquaintance, and who told me that the "divil" had been in the range that morning, I took a pan, into which I poured some milk, and held it over the gaslight till it was hot; then I carried it up to Aunt Eliza.

"Here is your milk, Aunt Eliza. You have sent for me to help you, and I begin with the earliest opportunity."

"I looked for you an hour ago. Ring the bell."

I rang it.

"Your mother is well, I suppose. She would have sent you, though, had she been sick in bed."

"She has done so. She thinks better of my coming than I do."

The housekeeper, Mrs. Roll, came in, and Aunt Eliza politely requested her to have breakfast for her niece as soon as possible.

"I do not go down of mornings yet," said Aunt Eliza, "but Mrs. Roll presides. See that the coffee is good, Roll."

"It is good generally, Miss Huell."

"You see that Margaret brought me my milk."

"Ahem!" said Mrs. Roll, marching out.

At the beginning of each visit to Aunt Eliza I was in the habit of dwelling on

---

[1]Newport, Rhode Island, a seaside resort.

the contrast between her way of living and ours. We lived from "hand to mouth." Every thing about her wore a hereditary air; for she lived in my grandfather's house, and it was the same as in his day. If I was at home when these contrasts occurred to me I should have felt angry; as it was, I felt them as in a dream—the china, the silver, the old furniture, and the excellent fare soothed me.

In the middle of the day Aunt Eliza came down stairs, and after she had received a visit from her doctor, decided to go to Newport on Saturday. It was Wednesday; and I could, if I chose, make any addition to my wardrobe. I had none to make, I informed her. What were my dresses?—had I a black silk? she asked. I had no black silk, and thought one would be unnecessary for hot weather.

"Who ever heard of a girl of twenty-four having no black silk! You have slimsy[2] muslins, I dare say?"

"Yes."

"And you like them?"

"For present wear."

That afternoon she sent Mrs. Roll out, who returned with a splendid heavy silk for me, which Aunt Eliza said should be made before Saturday, and it was. I went to a fashionable dress-maker of her recommending, and on Friday it came home, beautifully made and trimmed with real lace.

"Even the Pushers could find no fault with this," said Aunt Eliza, turning over the sleeves and smoothing the lace. Somehow she smuggled into the house a white straw-bonnet, with white roses; also a handsome mantilla. She held the bonnet before me with a nod, and deposited it again in the box, which made a part of the luggage for Newport.

On Sunday morning we arrived in Newport, and went to a quiet hotel in the town. James was with us, but Mrs. Roll was left in Bond Street, in charge of the household. Monday was spent in an endeavor to make an arrangement regarding the hire of a coach and coachman. Several livery-stable keepers were in attendance, but nothing was settled, till I suggested that Aunt Eliza should send for her own carriage. James was sent back the next day, and returned on Thursday with coach, horses, and William her coachman. That matter being finished, and the trunks being unpacked, she decided to take her first bath in the sea, expecting me to support her through the trying ordeal of the surf. As we were returning from the beach we met a carriage containing a number of persons with a family resemblance.

When Aunt Eliza saw them she angrily exclaimed, "Am I to see those Uxbridges every day?"

Of the Uxbridges this much I knew—that the two brothers Uxbridge were the lawyers of her opponents in the lawsuit which had existed three or four years. I had never felt any interest in it, though I knew that it was concerning a tract of ground in the city which had belonged to my grandfather, and which had, since his day, become very valuable. Litigation was a habit of the Huell family. So the sight of the Uxbridge family did not agitate me as it did Aunt Eliza.

"The sly, methodical dogs! but I shall beat Lemorne yet!"

"How will you amuse yourself then, aunt?"

"I'll adopt some boys to inherit what I shall save from his clutches."

The bath fatigued her so she remained in her room for the rest of the day; but she kept me busy with a hundred trifles. I wrote for her, computed interest, studied out bills of fare, till four o'clock came, and with it a fog. Nevertheless I must ride on the Avenue, and the carriage was ordered.

"Wear your silk, Margaret; it will just about last your visit through—the fog will use it up."

---

[2]Flimsy.

"I am glad of it," I answered.

"You will ride every day. Wear the bonnet I bought for you also."

"Certainly; but won't that go quicker in the fog than the dress?"

"Maybe; but wear it."

I rode every day afterward, from four to six, in the black silk, the mantilla, and the white straw. When Aunt Eliza went she was so on the alert for the Uxbridge family carriage that she could have had little enjoyment of the ride. Rocks never were a passion with her, she said, nor promontories, chasms, or sand. She came to Newport to be washed with salt-water; when she had washed up to the doctor's prescription she should leave, as ignorant of the peculiar pleasures of Newport as when she arrived. She had no fancy for its conglomerate societies, its literary cottages, its parvenue suits of rooms,[3] its saloon[4] habits, and its bathing herds.

I considered the rides a part of the contract of what was expected in my two months' performance. I did not dream that I was enjoying them, any more than I supposed myself to be enjoying a sea-bath while pulling Aunt Eliza to and fro in the surf. Nothing in the life around me stirred me, nothing in nature attracted me. I liked the fog; somehow it seemed to emanate from me instead of rolling up from the ocean, and to represent me. Whether I went alone or not, the coachman was ordered to drive a certain round; after that I could extend the ride in whatever direction I pleased, but I always said, "Any where, William." One afternoon, which happened to be a bright one, I was riding on the road which led to the glen, when I heard the screaming of a flock of geese which were waddling across the path in front of the horses. I started, for I was asleep probably, and, looking forward, saw the Uxbridge carriage, filled with ladies and children, coming toward me; and by it rode a gentleman on horseback. His horse was rearing among the hissing geese, but neither horse nor geese appeared to engage him; his eyes were fixed upon me. The horse swerved so near that its long mane almost brushed against me. By an irresistible impulse I laid my ungloved hand upon it, but did not look at the rider. Carriage and horseman passed on, and William resumed his pace. A vague idea took possession of me that I had seen the horseman before on my various drives. I had a vision of a man galloping on a black horse out of the fog, and into it again. I was very sure, however, that I had never seen him on so pleasant a day as this! William did not bring his horses to time; it was after six when I went into Aunt Eliza's parlor, and found her impatient for her tea and toast. She was crosser than the occasion warranted; but I understood it when she gave me the outlines of a letter she desired me to write to her lawyer in New York. Something had turned up, he had written her; the Uxbridges believed that they had ferreted out what would go against her. I told her that I had met the Uxbridge carriage.

"One of them is in New York; how else could they be giving me trouble just now?"

"There was a gentleman on horseback beside the carriage."

"Did he look mean and cunning?"

"He did not wear his legal beaver[5] up, I think; but he rode a fine horse and sat it well."

"A lawyer on horseback should, like the beggar of the adage, ride to the devil."[6]

"Your business now is the 'Lemorne?'"

---

[3]Suites of rooms rented by persons suddenly risen to a new social and economic class with little background or training for their new status.

[4]Variant of salon: large reception rooms for entertainments or meetings.

[5]Moveable face guard for a helmet. When Hamlet asked if the face of his father's ghost was seen, he was told: "O yes, my lord! He wore his beaver up." *Hamlet* (I.ii.230).

[6]"Our own old saying, 'Set a beggar on horse-back, and he'll ride to the devil,'" from the 1809 weekly *Political Register* (XV.xii.429) edited by English journalist William Cobbett (1763–1835). A variant appears in Hawthorne's "Old News" in *The Snow Image* (1851) and Bohn's *Foreign Proverbs, German* (1855).

"You know it is."

"I did not know but that you had found something besides to litigate."

"It must have been Edward Uxbridge that you saw. He is the brain of the firm."

"You expect Mr. Van Horn?"

"Oh, he must come; I can not be writing letters."

We had been in Newport two weeks when Mr. Van Horn, Aunt Eliza's lawyer, came. He said that he would see Mr. Edward Uxbridge. Between them they might delay a term, which he thought would be best. "Would Miss Huell ever be ready for a compromise?" he jestingly asked.

"Are you suspicious?" she inquired.

"No; but the Uxbridge chaps are clever."

He dined with us; and at four o'clock Aunt Eliza graciously asked him to take a seat in the carriage with me, making some excuse for not going herself.

"Hullo!" said Mr. Van Horn when we had reached the country road; "there's Uxbridge now." And he waved his hand to him.

It was indeed the black horse and the same rider that I had met. He reined up beside us, and shook hands with Mr. Van Horn.

"We are required to answer this new complaint?" said Mr. Van Horn.

Mr. Uxbridge nodded.

"And after that the judgment?"

Mr. Uxbridge laughed.

"I wish that certain gore[7] of land had been sunk instead of being mapped in 1835."

"The surveyor did his business well enough, I am sure."

They talked together in a low voice for a few minutes, and then Mr. Van Horn leaned back in his seat again. "Allow me," he said, "to introduce you, Uxbridge, to Miss Margaret Huell, Miss Huell's niece. Huell *vs.* Brown, you know," he added, in an explanatory tone; for I was Huell *vs.* Brown's daughter.

"Oh!" said Mr. Uxbridge bowing, and looking at me gravely. I looked at him also; he was a pale, stern-looking man, and forty years old certainly. I derived the impression at once that he had a domineering disposition, perhaps from the way in which he controlled his horse.

"Nice beast that," said Mr. Van Horn.

"Yes," he answered, laying his hand on its mane, so that the action brought immediately to my mind the recollection that I had done so too. I would not meet his eye again, however.

"How long shall you remain, Uxbridge?"

"I don't know. You are not interested in the lawsuit, Miss Huell?" he said, putting on his hat.

"Not in the least; nothing of mine is involved."

"We'll gain it for your portion yet, Miss Margaret," said Mr. Van Horn, nodding to Mr. Uxbridge, and bidding William drive on. He returned the next day, and we settled into the routine of hotel life. A few mornings after, she sent me to a matinée, which was given by some of the Opera people, who were in Newport strengthening the larynx with applications of brine. When the concert was half over, and the audience were making the usual hum and stir, I saw Mr. Uxbridge against a pillar, with his hands incased in pearl-colored gloves, and holding a shiny hat. He turned half away when he caught my eye, and then darted toward me.

"You have not been much more interested in the music than you are in the lawsuit," he said, seating himself beside me.

---

[7]Small triangular plot of land.

"The *tutoyer*[8] of the Italian voice is agreeable, however."

"It makes one dreamy."

"A child."

"Yes, a child; not a man nor a woman."

"I teach music. I can not dream over 'one, two, three.'"

"*You*—a music teacher!"

"For six years."

I was aware that he looked at me from head to foot, and I picked at the lace of my invariable black silk; but what did it matter whether I owned that I was a genteel pauper, representing my aunt's position for two months, or not?

"Where?"

"In Waterbury."[9]

"Waterbury differs from Newport."

"I suppose so."

"You suppose!"

A young gentleman sauntered by us, and Mr. Uxbridge called to him to look up the Misses Uxbridge, his nieces, on the other side of the hall.

"Paterfamilias Uxbridge has left his brood in my charge," he said. "I try to do my duty," and he held out a twisted pearl-colored glove, which he pulled off while talking. What white nervous fingers he had! I thought they might pinch like steel.

"You suppose," he repeated.

"I do not look at Newport."

"Have you observed Waterbury?"

"I observe what is in my sphere."

"Oh!"

He was silent then. The second part of the concert began; but I could not compose myself to appreciation. Either the music or I grew chaotic. So many tumultuous sounds I heard—of hope, doubt, inquiry, melancholy, and desire; or did I feel the emotions which these words express? Or was there magnetism stealing into me from the quiet man beside me? He left me with a bow before the concert was over, and I saw him making his way out of the hall when it was finished.

I had been sent in the carriage, of course; but several carriages were in advance of it before the walk, and I waited there for William to drive up. When he did so, I saw by the oscillatory motion of his head, though his arms and whiphand were perfectly correct, that he was inebriated. It was his first occasion of meeting fellow-coachmen in full dress, and the occasion had proved too much for him. My hand, however, was on the coach door, when I heard Mr. Uxbridge say, at my elbow.

"It is not safe for you."

"Oh, Sir, it is in the programme that I ride home from the concert." And I prepared to step in.

"I shall sit on the box, then."

"But your nieces?"

"They are walking home, squired by a younger knight."

Aunt Eliza would say, I thought, "Needs must when a lawyer drives"; and I concluded to allow him to have his way, telling him that he was taking a great deal of trouble. He thought it would be less if he were allowed to sit inside; both ways were unsafe.

Nothing happened. William drove well from habit; but James was obliged to assist him to dismount. Mr. Uxbridge waited a moment at the door, and so there

---

[8]French: "to address familiarly." Here, descriptive of the tone of the singer's voice.

[9]Waterbury, Connecticut, at the time of the story, was the center of the brass industry and manufactured clocks.

was quite a little sensation, which spread its ripples till Aunt Eliza was reached. She sent for William, whose only excuse was "dampness."

"Uxbridge knew my carriage, of course," she said, with a complacent voice.

"He knew me," I replied.

"You do not look like the Huells."

"I look precisely like the young woman to whom he was introduced by Mr. Van Horn."

"Oh ho!"

"He thought it unsafe for me to come alone under William's charge."

"Ah ha!"

No more was said on the subject of his coming home with me. Aunt Eliza had several fits of musing in the course of the evening while I read aloud to her, which had no connection with the subject of the book. As I put it down she said that it would be well for me to go to church the next day. I acquiesced, but remarked that my piety would not require the carriage, and that I preferred to walk. Besides, it would be well for William and James to attend divine service. She could not spare James, and thought William had better clean the harness, by way of penance.

The morning proved to be warm and sunny. I donned a muslin dress of home manufacture and my own bonnet, and started for church. I had walked but a few paces when the consciousness of being *free* and *alone* struck me. I halted, looked about me, and concluded that I would not go to church, but walk into the fields. I had no knowledge of the whereabouts of the fields; but I walked straight forward, and after a while came upon some barren fields, cropping with coarse rocks, along which ran a narrow road. I turned into it, and soon saw beyond the rough coast the blue ring of the ocean—vast, silent, and splendid in the sunshine. I found a seat on the ruins of an old stone-wall, among some tangled bushes and briers. There being no Aunt Eliza to pull through the surf, and no animated bathers near, I discovered the beauty of the sea, and that I loved it.

Presently I heard the steps of a horse, and, to my astonishment, Mr. Uxbridge rode past. I was glad he did not know me. I watched him as he rode slowly down the road, deep in thought. He let drop the bridle, and the horse stopped, as if accustomed to the circumstance, and pawed the ground gently, or yawed his neck for pastime. Mr. Uxbridge folded his arms and raised his head to look seaward. It seemed to me as if he were about to address the jury. I had dropped so entirely from my observance of the landscape that I jumped when he resumed the bridle and turned his horse to come back. I slipped from my seat to look among the bushes, determined that he should not recognize me; but my attempt was a failure—he did not ride by the second time.

"Miss Huell!" And he jumped from his saddle, slipping his arm through the bridle.

"I am a runaway. What do you think of the Fugitive Slave Bill?"[10]

"I approve of returning property to its owners."

"The sea must have been God's temple first, instead of the groves."[11]

"I believe the Saurians[12] were an Orthodox tribe."

"Did you stop yonder to ponder the sea?"

"I was pondering 'Lemorne vs. Huell.'"

He looked at me earnestly, and then gave a tug at the bridle, for his steed was inclined to make a crude repast from the bushes.

"How was it that I did not detect you at once?" he continued.

---

[10]The Fugitive Slave Bill, requiring the return of runaway slaves, became law on September 18, 1850.
[11]An allusion to "The groves were God's first temples," from "A Forest Hymn" by American poet William Cullen Bryant.
[12]Lizards.

"My apparel is Waterbury apparel."

"Ah!"

We walked up the road slowly till we came to the end of it; then I stopped for him to understand that I thought it time for him to leave me. He sprang into the saddle.

"Give us good-by!" he said, bringing his horse close to me.

"We are not on equal terms; I feel too humble afoot to salute you."

"Put your foot on the stirrup then."

A leaf stuck in the horse's forelock, and I pulled it off and waved it in token of farewell. A powerful light shot into his eyes when he saw my hand close on the leaf.

"May I come and see you?" he asked, abruptly. "I will."

"I shall say neither 'No' nor 'Yes.'"

He rode on at a quick pace, and I walked homeward forgetting the sense of liberty I had started with, and proceeded straightway to Aunt Eliza.

"I have not been to church, aunt, but to walk beyond the town; it was not so nominated in the bond,[13] but I went. The taste of freedom was so pleasant that I warn you there is danger of my 'striking.'[14] When will you have done with Newport?"

"I am pleased with Newport now," she answered, with a curious intonation. "I like it."

"I do also."

Her keen eyes sparkled.

"Did you ever like anything when you were with me before?"

"Never. I will tell you why I like it: because I have met, and shall probably meet, Mr. Uxbridge. I saw him to-day. He asked permission to visit me."

"Let him come."

"He will come."

But we did not see him either at the hotel or when we went abroad. Aunt Eliza rode with me each afternoon, and each morning we went to the beach. She engaged me every moment when at home, and I faithfully performed all my tasks. I clapped to the door on self-investigation—locked it against any analysis or reasoning upon any circumstance connected with Mr. Uxbridge. The only piece of treachery to my code that I was guilty of was the putting of the leaf which I brought home on Sunday between the leaves of that poem whose motto is,

"Mariana in the moated grange."[15]

On Saturday morning, nearly a week after I saw him on my walk, Aunt Eliza proposed that we should go to Turo Street on a shopping excursion; she wanted a cap, and various articles besides. As we went into a large shop I saw Mr. Uxbridge at a counter buying gloves; her quick eye caught sight of him, and she edged away, saying she would look at some goods on the other side; I might wait where I was. As he turned to go out he saw me and stopped.

"I have been in New York since I saw you," he said. "Mr. Lemorne sent for me."

"There is my aunt," I said.

He shrugged his shoulders.

"I shall not go away soon again," he remarked. "I missed Newport greatly."

I made some foolish reply, and kept my eyes on Aunt Eliza, who dawdled unaccountably. He appeared amused, and after a little talk went away.

---

[13]The agreement or contract between them whereby she would assist her Aunt during the Newport stay.
[14]Ceasing to work for her aunt.
[15]The motto of "Mariana" (1830) by English poet Alfred,

Lord Tennyson (1809–1892) is taken from Shakespeare's *Measure for Measure* (III.i.277): "There at the moated grange [solitary farm house] resides this dejected Mariana." Both Marianas wait for lovers who have deserted them.

Aunt Eliza's purchase was a rose-colored moire[16] antique, which she said was to be made for me; for Mrs. Bliss, one of our hotel acquaintances, had offered to chaperon me to the great ball which would come off in a few days, and she had accepted the offer for me.

"There will be no chance for you to take a walk instead," she finished with.

"I can not dance, you know."

"But you will be *there*."

I was sent to a dress-maker of Mrs. Bliss's recommending; but I ordered the dress to be made after my own design, long plain sleeves, and high plain corsage,[17] and requested that it should not be sent home till the evening of the ball. Before it came off Mr. Uxbridge called, and was graciously received by Aunt Eliza, who could be gracious to all except her relatives. I could not but perceive, however, that they watched each other in spite of their lively conversation. To me he was deferential, but went over the ground of our acquaintance as if it had been the most natural thing in the world. But for my life-long habit of never calling in question the behavior of those I came in contact with, and of never expecting any thing different from that I received, I might have wondered over his visit. Every person's individuality was sacred to me, from the fact, perhaps, that my own individuality had never been respected by any person with whom I had any relation— not even by my own mother.

After Mr. Uxbridge went, I asked Aunt Eliza if she thought he looked mean and cunning? She laughed, and replied that she was bound to think that Mr. Lemorne's lawyer could not look otherwise.

When, on the night of the ball, I presented myself in the rose-colored moire antique for her inspection, she raised her eyebrows, but said nothing about it.

"I need not be careful of it, I suppose, aunt?"

"Spill as much wine and ice-cream on it as you like."

In the dressing room Mrs. Bliss surveyed me.

"I think I like this mass of rose-color," she said. "Your hair comes out in contrast so brilliantly. Why, you have not a single ornament on!"

"It is so easy to dress without."

This was all the conversation we had together during the evening, except when she introduced some acquaintance to fulfill her matronizing duties. As I was no dancer I was left alone most of the time, and amused myself by gliding from window to window along the wall, that it might not be observed that I was a fixed flower. Still I suffered the annoyance of being stared at by wandering squads of young gentlemen, the "curled darlings"[18] of the ballroom. I borrowed Mrs. Bliss's fan in one of her visits for a protection. With that, and the embrasure of a remote window where I finally stationed myself, I hoped to escape further notice. The music of the celebrated band which played between the dances recalled the chorus of spirits which charmed Faust:

> "And the fluttering
> Ribbons of drapery
> Cover the plains,
> Cover the bowers,
> Where lovers,
> Deep in thought,
> Give themselves for life."[19]

---

[16]Silk with a watered or wavy pattern.
[17]Bodice of dress extending from the waist to the shoulder.
[18]Desdemona's father, hearing that she has married the Moor Othello, believes her bewitched for she had always been "a maid so tender, fair, and happy,/So opposite to marriage that she shunn'd/The wealthy curled darlings of our nation." Shakespeare's *Othello* (I.ii.66–68).
[19]*Faust*, Part I (1808) by Johann Wolfgang von Goethe (1749–1832). In this excerpt (lines 1463–69), Faust is lulled to sleep by the spirits summoned by Mephistopheles.

The voice of Mrs. Bliss broke its spell.

"I bring an old friend, Miss Huell, and he tells me an acquaintance of yours."

It was Mr. Uxbridge.

"I had no thought of meeting you, Miss Huell."

And he coolly took the seat beside me in the window, leaving to Mrs. Bliss the alternative of standing or of going away; she chose the latter.

"I saw you as soon as I came in," he said, "gliding from window to window, like a vessel hugging the shore in a storm."

"With colors at half-mast; I have no dancing partner."

"How many have observed you?"

"Several young gentlemen."

"Moths."

"Oh no, butterflies."

"They must keep away now."

"Are you Rhadamanthus?"[20]

"And Charon, too. I would have you row in the same boat with me."

"Now you are fishing."

"Won't you compliment me. Did I ever look better?"

His evening costume *was* becoming, but he looked pale, and weary, and disturbed. But if we were engaged for a tournament, as his behavior indicated, I must do my best at telling. So I told him that he never looked better, and asked him how I looked. He would look at me presently, he said, and decide. Mrs. Bliss skimmed by us with nods and smiles; as she vanished our eyes followed her, and we talked vaguely on various matters, sounding ourselves and each other. When a furious redowa[21] set in which cut our conversation into rhythm he pushed up the window and said, "Look out."

I turned my face to him to do so, and saw the moon at the full, riding through the strip of sky which our vision commanded. From the moon our eyes fell on each other. After a moment's silence, during which I returned his steadfast gaze, for I could not help it, he said:

"If we understand the impression we make upon each other, what must be said?"

I made no reply, but fanned myself, neither looking at the moon, nor upon the redowa, nor upon any thing.

He took the fan from me.

"Speak of yourself," he said.

"Speak you."

"I am what I seem, a man within your sphere. By all the accidents of position and circumstance suited to it. Have you not learned it?"

"I am not what I seem. I never wore so splendid a dress as this till tonight, and shall not again."

He gave the fan such a twirl that its slender sticks snapped, and it dropped like the broken wing of a bird.

"Mr. Uxbridge, that fan belongs to Mrs. Bliss."

He threw it out of the window.

"You have courage, fidelity, and patience—this character with a passionate soul. I am sure that you have such a soul?"

"I do not know."

"I have fallen in love with you. It happened on the very day when I passed you

---

[20]In classical mythology, one of the three judges of the underworld who sentence the dead, rowed over the River Styx by ferryman Charon.
[21]Bohemian waltz.

on the way to the Glen. I never got away from the remembrance of seeing your hand on the mane of my horse."

He waited for me to speak, but I could not; the balance of my mind was gone. Why should this have happened to me—a slave? As it had happened, why did I not feel exultant in the sense of power which the chance for freedom with him should give?

"What is it, Margaret? your face is as sad as death."

"How do you call me 'Margaret?'"

"As I would call my wife—Margaret."

He rose and stood before me to screen my face from observation. I supposed so, and endeavored to stifle my agitation.

"You are better," he said, presently. "Come go with me and get some refreshment." And he beckoned to Mrs. Bliss, who was down the hall with an unwieldly gentleman.

"Will you go to supper now?" she asked.

"We are only waiting for you," Mr. Uxbridge answered, offering me his arm.

When we emerged into the blaze and glitter of the supper-room I sought refuge in the shadow of Mrs. Bliss's companion, for it seemed to me that I had lost my own.

"Drink this Champagne," said Mr. Uxbridge. "Pay no attention to the Colonel on your left; he won't expect it."

"Neither must you."

"Drink."

The Champagne did not prevent me from reflecting on the fact that he had not yet asked whether I loved him.

The spirit chorus again floated through my mind:

> "Where lovers,
> Deep in thought,
> *Give* themselves for life."

I was not allowed to *give* myself—I was *taken*.

"No heel-taps,"[22] he whispered, "to the bottom quaff."

"Take me home, will you?"

"Mrs. Bliss is not ready."

"Tell her that I must go."

He went behind her chair and whispered something, and she nodded to me to go without her.

When her carriage came up, I think he gave the coachman an order to drive home in a round-about way, for we were a long time reaching it. I kept my face to the window, and he made no effort to divert my attention. When we came to a street whose thick rows of trees shut out the moonlight my eager soul longed to leap out into the dark and demand of him his heart, soul, life, for *me*.

I struck him lightly on the shoulder; he seized my hand.

"Oh, I know you, Margaret; you are mine!"

"We are at the hotel."

He sent the carriage back, and said that he would leave me at my aunt's door. He wished that he could see her then. Was it magic that made her open the door before I reached it?

"Have you come on legal business?" she asked him.

"You have divined what I come for."

---

[22]Liquor left in a glass after drinking.

"Step in, step in; it's very late. I should have been in bed but for neuralgia. Did Mr. Uxbridge come home with you, Margaret?"

"Yes, in Mrs. Bliss's carriage; I wished to come before she was ready to leave."

"Well, Mr. Uxbridge is old enough for your protector, certainly."

"I *am* forty, ma'am."

"Do you want Margaret?"

"I do."

"You know exactly how much is involved in your client's suit?"

"Exactly."

"You also know that his claim is an unjust one."

"Do I?"

"I shall not be poor if I lose; if I gain, Margaret will be rich."

"'Margaret will be rich,'" he repeated, absently.

"What! have you changed your mind respecting the orphans, aunt?"

"She has, and is—nothing," she went on, not heeding my remark. "Her father married below his station; when he died his wife fell back to her place—for he spent his fortune—and there she and Margaret must remain, unless Lemorne is defeated."

"Aunt, for your succinct biography of my position many thanks."

"Sixty thousand dollars," she continued. "Van Horn tells me that, as yet, the firm of Uxbridge Brothers have only an income—no capital."

"It is true," he answered, musingly.

The clock on the mantle struck two.

"A thousand dollars for every year of my life," she said. "You and I, Uxbridge, know the value and beauty of money."

"Yes, there is beauty in money, and"—looking at me—"beauty without it."

"The striking of the clock," I soliloquized, "proves that this scene is not a phantasm."

"Margaret is fatigued," he said, rising. "May I come to-morrow?"

"It is my part only," replied Aunt Eliza, "to see that she is, or is not, Cinderella."

"If you have ever thought of me, aunt, as an individual, you must have seen that I am not averse to ashes."

He held my hand a moment, and then kissed me with a kiss of appropriation.

"He is in love with you," she said, after he had gone. "I think I know him. He has found beauty ignorant of itself; he will teach you to develop it."

The next morning Mr. Uxbridge had an interview with Aunt Eliza before he saw me.

When we were alone I asked him how her eccentricities affected him; he could not but consider her violent, prejudiced, warped, and whimsical. I told him that I had been taught to accept all that she did on this basis. Would this explain to him my silence in regard to her?

"Can you endure to live with her in Bond Street for the present, or would you rather return to Waterbury?"

"She desires my company while she is in Newport only. I have never been with her so long before."

"I understand her. Law is a game, in her estimation, in which cheating can as easily be carried on as at cards."

"Her soul is in this case."

"Her soul is not too large for it. Will you ride this afternoon?"

I promised, of course. From that time till he left Newport we saw each other every day, and though I found little opportunity to express my own peculiar feelings, he comprehended many of my wishes, and all my tastes. I grew fond of him hourly. Had I not reason? Never was friend so considerate, never was lover more devoted.

When he had been gone a few days, Aunt Eliza declared that she was ready to depart from Newport. The rose-colored days were ended! In two days we were on the Sound,[23] coach, horses, servants, and ourselves.

It was the 1st of September when we arrived in Bond Street. A week from that date Samuel Uxbridge, the senior partner of Uxbridge Brothers, went to Europe with his family, and I went to Waterbury, accompanied by Mr. Uxbridge. He consulted mother in regard to our marriage, and appointed it in November. In October Aunt Eliza sent for me to come back to Bond Street and spend a week. She had some fine marking[24] to do, she wrote. While there I noticed a restlessness in her which I had never before observed, and conferred with Mrs. Roll on the matter. "She do be awake nights a deal, and that's the reason," Mrs. Roll said. Her manner was the same in other respects. She said she would not give me any thing for my wedding outfit, but she paid my fare from Waterbury and back.

She could not spare me to go out, she told Mr. Uxbridge, and in consequence I saw little of him while there.

In November we were married. Aunt Eliza was not at the wedding, which was a quiet one. Mr. Uxbridge desired me to remain in Waterbury till spring. He would not decide about taking a house in New York till then; by that time his brother might return, and if possible we would go to Europe for a few months. I acquiesced in all his plans. Indeed I was not consulted; but I was happy—happy in him, and happy in every thing.

The winter passed in waiting for him to come to Waterbury every Saturday; and in the enjoyment of the two days he passed with me. In March Aunt Eliza wrote me that Lemorne was beaten! Van Horn had taken up the whole contents of his snuff-box in her house the evening before in amazement at the turn things had taken.

That night I dreamed of the scene in the hotel at Newport. I heard Aunt Eliza saying, "If I gain, Margaret will be rich." And I heard also the clock strike two. As it struck I said, *"My husband is a scoundrel,"* and woke with a start.

1863

ROSE TERRY COOKE
(1827–1892)

Admitted into the freemasonry of married women, [Celia] discovered how few among them were more than household drudges, the servants of their families, worked to the verge of exhaustion, and neither thanked nor rewarded for their pains. She saw here a woman whose children were careless of, and ungrateful to her, and her husband coldly indifferent; there was one on whom the man she had married wreaked all his fiendish temper in daily small injuries, little vexatious acts, petty tyrannies, a "street-angel, house-devil" of a man, of all sorts the most hateful. There were many whose lives had no other outlook than hard work until the end should come, who rose up to labor and lay down in sleepless exhaustion, and some whose days were a constant terror to them from the intemperate brutes to whom they had intrusted their happiness, and indeed their whole existence.

---

[23]Long Island Sound.
[24]Of dress patterns for Eliza.

This bleak view of marriage was written by Rose Terry Cooke in her story, "How Celia Changed Her Mind," published in 1891. By and large it is a comic story, with quaint characters and touches of local color. But it is a story full of surprises, the most astonishing being the undercurrent of bitterness about men's treatment of women that flashes to the surface here and there as the authorial voice seems carried away by strong indignation at male brutality and female victimization. The story seems to confirm a line from Thoreau's *Walden*, with only a variation of gender: "The mass of women lead lives of quiet desperation."

Rose Terry grew up as the eldest of two daughters in an established and well-to-do New England family in Hartford, Connecticut. She attended Hartford Female Seminary (founded by Catherine Beecher, Harriet Beecher Stowe's sister), graduating at the age of sixteen. Because of her father's financial reverses, she apparently began to support herself shortly after graduation. She remarked later, "I have taken care of myself ever since I left school, and hope to do so as long as I live." She taught for a time and then served as a governess. However, the death of her sister required her presence at home to help take care of her sister's children. At home with domestic concerns, she turned to literature and especially the writing of poetry. She published poetry in various journals, and collected her poems in volumes which appeared in 1861 and 1888. But poetry did not pay and she turned more and more to the writing of fiction. She had published her first story at the age of eighteen and she soon had a position on the contributing staff of *Putnam's Monthly Magazine*.

Her success was extraordinary. She placed a story in the first issue of *The Atlantic Monthly* in 1857 and seven more in the next ten issues of the magazine (then edited by James Russell Lowell). She wrote with great rapidity, publishing several collections during her lifetime, including *Somebody's Neighbors* (1881) and *Huckleberries Gathered from New England Hills* (1891). Her best stories dealt with New England country or small town characters, shrewd, determined, close-mouthed, coping with genteel poverty, and most often leading diminished, thwarted lives. She wrote with passion but not with sentimentality; her pen flowed with wit tinged with sympathy, never malice. "Hers was that subtlest of all humor, the humor that is natively inherent in the material used," Fred Lewis Pattee has justly said.

In 1873, Rose Terry married a widower, Rollin H. Cooke, a bank clerk and sometime author, who was sixteen years her junior. The evidence seems to be that, although the marriage was a happy one, Rollin Cooke squandered his wife's savings, forcing her to work even harder to regain the economic security she had once achieved at considerable cost in time and effort.

Rose Terry Cooke grew to resent the economic discrimination which she encountered against women writers. She observed in 1879, in "A Letter to Mary Ann": "If a man has a reputation as a writer, it does him great service; there are a few men in America who might write the wildest nonsense, and in their script and under their name no editor would dare to refuse it; but it is not so with women." She concluded with resignation: "I only say that as a rule men are paid more than women. . . . It is the thing that is, and being a woman you will have to submit to it."

"I always write impulsively—very fast and without much plan," she once said. The magazines remain filled with her fiction that has never been collected. Yet one critic, Jay Martin, wrote in *Harvests of Change* (1967): "Mrs. Cooke has been unjustly ignored by historians of American literature. . . .

Her analysis of the tragedy of New England character was shrewd and decisive, establishing the conventions to be followed by Sarah Orne Jewett, Mary E. Wilkins, and even Edwin Arlington Robinson and Robert Frost."

ADDITIONAL READING

"*How Celia Changed Her Mind*" *and Selected Stories by Rose Terry Cooke*, ed. with an Introduction by Elizabeth Ammons, 1986.

Harriet Prescott Spofford, "Rose Terry Cooke," *Our Famous Women: An Authorized and Complex Record of the Lives and Deeds of Eminent Women of Our Times*, 1888; Harriet Prescott Spofford, *A Little Book of Friends*, 1916; Fred Lewis Pattee, *The Development of the American Short Story*, 1923; Jay Martin, *Harvests of Change, American Literature, 1865–1914*, 1967; Katherine Kleitz, "Essence of New England: The Portraits of Rose Terry Cooke," *American Transcendental Quarterly*, 47–48 (Summer–Fall, 1980).

TEXT

Huckleberries Gathered from New England Hills, 1891.

How Celia Changed Her Mind

"If there's anything on the face of the earth I *do* hate, it's an old maid!"

Mrs. Stearns looked up from her sewing in astonishment.

"Why, Miss Celia!"

"Oh, yes! I know it. I'm one myself, but all the same, I hate 'em worse than p'ison. They ain't nothing nor nobody; they're cumberers of the ground." And Celia Barnes laid down her scissors with a bang, as if she might be Atropos[1] herself, ready to cut the thread of life for all the despised class of which she was a notable member.

The minister's wife was genuinely surprised at this outburst; she herself had been well along in life before she married, and though she had been fairly happy in the uncertain relationship to which she had attained, she was, on the whole, inclined to agree with St. Paul, that the woman who did not marry "doeth better."[2] "I don't agree with you, Miss Celia," she said gently. "Many, indeed, most of my best friends are maiden ladies, and I respect and love them just as much as if they were married women."

"Well, I don't. A woman that's married is somebody; she's got a place in the world; she ain't everybody's tag;[3] folks don't say, 'Oh, it's nobody but that old maid Celye Barnes;' it's 'Mis' Price,' and 'Mis' Simms,' or 'Thomas Smith's wife,' as though you was somebody. I don't know how 't is elsewheres, but here in Bassett you might as well be a dog as an old maid. I allow it might be better if they all had means or eddication: money's 'a dreadful good thing to have in the house,' as I see in a book once, and learning is sort of comp'ny to you if you're lonesome; but then lonesome you be, and you've got to be, if you're an old maid, and it can't be helped noway."

Mrs. Stearns smiled a little sadly, thinking that even married life had its own loneliness when your husband was shut up in his study, or gone off on a long drive to see some sick parishioner or conduct a neighborhood prayer-meeting, or even when he was the other side of the fireplace absorbed in a religious paper or a

---

[1] One of the three Fates in charge of human destiny in Greek mythology.

[2] 1 Corinthians 7:38: "So then he that giveth her in marriage doeth well; but he that giveth her not in marriage doeth better."

[3] Rabble.

New York daily, or meditating on his next sermon, while the silent wife sat unnoticed at her mending or knitting. "But married women have more troubles and responsibilities than the unmarried, Miss Celia," she said. "You have no children to bring up and be anxious about, no daily dread of not doing your duty by the family whom you preside over, and no fear of the supplies giving out that are really needed. Nobody but your own self to look out for."

"That's jest it," snapped Celia, laying down the boy's coat she was sewing with a vicious jerk of her thread. "There 't is! Nobody to home to care if you live or die; nobody to peek out of the winder to see if you're comin', or to make a mess of gruel or a cup of tea for you, or to throw ye a feelin' word if you're sick nigh unto death. And old maids is just as li'ble to up and die as them that's married. And as to responsibility, I ain't afraid to tackle that. Never! I don't hold with them that cringe and crawl and are skeert at a shadder, and won't do a living thing that they had ought to do because they're 'afraid to take the responsibility.' Why, there's Mrs. Deacon Trimble, she durst n't so much as set up a prayer-meetin' for missions or the temp'rance cause, because 't was 'sech a responsibility to take the lead in them matters.' I suppose it's somethin' of a responsible chore to preach the gospel to the heathen, or grab a drinkin' feller by the scruff of his neck and haul him out of the horrible pit anyway, but if it's dooty it's got to be done, whether or no; and I ain't afraid of pitchin' into anything the Lord sets me to do!"

"Except being an old maid," said Mrs. Stearns.

Celia darted a sharp glance at her over her silver-rimmed spectacles, and pulled her needle through and through the seams of Willy's jacket with fresh vigor, while a thoughtful shadow came across her fine old face. Celia was a candid woman, for all her prejudices, a combination peculiarly characteristic of New England, for she was a typical Yankee. Presently she said abruptly, "I had n't thought on 't in that light." But then the minister opened the door, and the conversation stopped.

Parson Stearns was tired and hungry and cross, and his wife knew all that as soon as she saw his face. She had learned long ago that ministers, however good they may be, are still men; so to-day she had kept her husband's dinner warm in the under-oven, and had the kettle boiling to make him a cup of tea on the spot to assuage his irritation in the shortest and surest way; but though the odor of a savory stew and the cheerful warmth of the cooking-stove greeted him as he preceded her through the door into the kitchen, he snapped out, sharply enough for Celia to hear him through the half-closed door, "What do you have that old maid here for so often?"

"There!" said Celia to herself,—"there 't is! *He* don't look upon 't as a dispensation,[4] if she doos. Men-folks run the world, and they know it. There ain't one of the hull caboodle but what despises an onmarried woman! Well, 't ain't altogether my fault. I would n't marry them that I could; I could n't—not and be honest; and them that I would hev had did n't ask me. I don't know as I'm to blame, after all, when you look into 't."

And she went on sewing Willy's jacket, contrived with pains and skill out of an old coat of his father's, while Mrs. Stearns poured out her husband's tea in the kitchen, replenished his plate with stew, and cut for him more than one segment of the crisp, fresh apple-pie, and urged upon him the squares of new cheese that legitimately accompany this deleterious viand[5] of the race and country, the sempiternal,[6] insistent, flagrant, and alas! also fragrant pie.

Celia Barnes was the tailoress of the little scattered country town of Bassett.

---

[4] Arranged by God.
[5] Harmful food.
[6] Eternal.

Early left an orphan, without near relatives or money, she had received the scant-iest measure of education that our town authorities deal to the pauper children of such organizations. She was ten years old when her mother, a widow for almost all those ten years, left her to the tender mercies of the selectmen[7] of Bassett. The selectmen of our country towns are almost irresponsible governors of their petty spheres, and gratify the instinct of oligarchy[8] peculiar to, and conservative of, the human race. Men must be governed and tyrannized over,—it is an inborn neces-sity of their nature; and while a republic is a beautiful theory, eminently fitted for a race who are "non Angli, sed Angeli,"[9] it has in practice the effect of producing more than Russian tyranny, but on smaller scales and in far and scattered locali-ties. Nowhere are there more despots than among village selectmen in New Eng-land. Those who have wrestled with their absolute monarchism in behalf of some charity that might abstract a few of the almighty dollars made out of poverty and distress from their official pockets know how positive and dogmatic is their use of power—*experto crede.*[10] The Bassett "first selectman" promptly bound out little Ce-lia Barnes to a hard, imperious woman, who made a white slave of the child, and only dealt out to her the smallest measure of schooling demanded by law, because the good old minister, Father Perkins, interfered in the child's behalf.

As she was strong and hardy and resolute, Celia lived through her bondage, and at the "free" age of eighteen apprenticed herself to old Miss Polly Mariner, the Bassett tailoress, and being deft with her fingers and quick of brain, soon out-ran her teacher, and when Polly died, succeeded to her business.

She was a bright girl, not particularly noticeable among others, for she had none of that delicate flower-like New England beauty which is so peculiar, so charming, and so evanescent; her features were tolerably regular, her forehead broad and calm, her gray eyes keen and perceptive, and she had abundant hair of an uncertain brown; but forty other girls in Bassett might have been described in the same way; Celia's face was one to improve with age; its strong sense, capacity for humor, fine outlines of a rugged sort, were always more the style of fifty than fifteen, and what she said of herself was true.

She had been asked to marry an old farmer with five uproarious boys, a man notorious in East Bassett for his stinginess and bad temper, and she had promptly declined the offer. Once more fate had given her a chance. A young fellow of no character, poor, "shiftless," and given to cider as a beverage, had considered it a good idea to marry some one who would make a home for him and earn his liv-ing. Looking about him for a proper person to fill this pleasant situation, he pounced on Celia—and she returned the attention!

"Marry *you*? I wonder you've got the sass to ask any decent girl to marry ye, Alfred Hatch! What be you good for, anyway? I don't know what under the can-opy the Lord spares you for,—only He doos let the tares[11] grow amongst the wheat, Scripter says, and I'm free to suppose He knows why, but I don't. No, *sir!* Ef you was the last man in the livin' universe I would n't tech ye with the tongs. If you'd got a speck of grit into you, you'd be ashamed to ask a woman to take ye in and support ye, for that's what it comes to. You go 'long! I can make my hands save my head so long as I hev the use of 'em, and I have n't no call to set up a private poor-house!"

So Alfred Hatch sneaked off, much like a cur that has sought to share the ken-nel of a mastiff, and been shortly and sharply convinced of his presumption.

Here ended Celia's "chances," as she phrased it. Young men were few in Bas-

---

[7]New England town officials elected annually.
[8]Government by a small group.
[9]"Not Angles, but angels" (Latin). Said by Pope Gregory (c. 540–604) when he saw English (Angles) slaves.

[10]"Believe one who speaks from experience" (Latin, Virgil's *Aeneid* 11.283).
[11]Poisonous weeds resembling wheat. Matthew 13:30: "Let both grow together until the harvest."

sett; the West had drawn them away with its subtle attraction of unknown possibilities, just as it does to-day, and Celia grew old in the service of those established matrons who always want clothes cut over for their children, carpet rags sewed, quilts quilted, and comfortables tacked. She was industrious and frugal, and in time laid up some money in the Dartford Savings' Bank; but she did not, like many spinsters, invest her hard-earned dollars in a small house. Often she was urged to do so, but her reasons were good for refusing.

"I should be so independent? Well, I'm as independent now as the law allows. I've got two good rooms to myself, south winders, stairs of my own and outside door, and some privileges. If I had a house there'd be taxes, and insurance, and cleanin' off snow come winter-time, and hoein' paths; and likely enough I should be so fur left to myself that I should set up a garden, and make my succotash cost a dollar a pint a-hirin' of a man to dig it up and hoe it down. Like enough, too, I should be gettin' flower seeds and things; I'm kinder fond of blows[12] in the time of 'em. My old fish-geran'um[13] is a sight of comfort to me as 't is, and there would be a bill of expense again. Then you can't noway build a house with only two rooms in 't, it would be all outside; and you might as well try to heat the universe with a cookin'-stove as such a house. Besides, how lonesome I should be! It's forlorn enough to be an old maid anyway, but to have it sort of ground into you, as you may say, by livin' all alone in a hull house, that ain't necessary nor agreeable. Now, if I'm sick or sorry, I can just step downstairs and have aunt Nabby to help or hearten me. Deacon Everts he did set to work one time to persuade me to buy a house; he said 't was a good thing to be able to give somebody shelter 't was poorer 'n I was. Says I, 'Deacon, I've worked for my livin' ever sence I remember, and I know there's no use in anybody bein' poorer than I be. I have n't no call to take any sech in and do for 'em. I give what I can to missions,—home ones,—and I'm willin', cheerfully willin', to do a day's work now and again for somebody that is strivin' with too heavy burdens; but as for keepin' free lodgin' and board, I sha'n't do it.' 'Well, well, well,' says he, kinder as if I was a fractious[14] young one, and a-sawin' his fat hand up and down in the air till I wanted to slap him, 'just as you'd ruther, Celye,—just as you'd ruther. I don't mean to drive ye a mite, only, as Scripter says, "Provoke one another to love and good works." '[15]

"That did rile me! Says I: 'Well, you've provoked me full enough, though I don't know as you've done it in the Scripter sense; and mabbe I should n't have got so fur provoked if I had n't have known that little red house your grandsir' lived and died in was throwed back on your hands just now, and advertised for sellin'. I see the "Mounting County Herald," Deacon Everts.' He shut up, I tell ye. But I sha'n't never buy no house so long as aunt Nabby lets me have her two south chambers, and use the back stairway and the north door continual."

So Miss Celia had kept on in her way till now she was fifty, and to-day making over old clothes at the minister's. The minister's wife had, as we have seen, little romance or wild happiness in her life; it is not often the portion of country ministers' wives; and, moreover, she had two step-daughters who were girls of sixteen and twelve when she married their father. Katy was married herself now, this ten years, and doing her hard duty by an annual baby and a struggling parish in Dakota; but Rosabel, whose fine name had been the only legacy her dying mother left the day-old child she had scarce had time to kiss and christen before she went to take her own "new name" above, was now a girl of twenty-two, pretty, headstrong, and rebellious. Nature had endowed her with keen dark eyes, crisp dark curls, a long chin, and a very obstinate mouth, which only her red lips and white

---

[12]Blossoms.
[13]Fish geranium, ancestor of the garden geranium.
[14]Troublesome.

[15]Hebrews 10:24: "And let us consider one another to provoke unto love and to good works."

even teeth redeemed from ugliness; her bright color and her sense of fun made her attractive to young men wherever she encountered one of that rare species. Just now she was engaged in a serious flirtation with the station-master at Bassett Centre,—an impecunious youth of no special interest to other people and quite unable to maintain a wife. But out of the "strong necessity of loving," as it is called, and the want of young society or settled occupation, Rosa Stearns chose to fall in love with Amos Barker, and her father considered it a "fall" indeed. So, with the natural clumsiness of a man and a father, Parson Stearns set himself to prevent the matter, and began by forbidding Rosabel to see or speak or write to the youth in question, and thereby inspired in her mind a burning desire to do all three. Up to this time she had rather languidly amused herself by mild and gentle flirtations with him, such as looking at him sidewise in church on Sunday, meeting him accidentally on his way to and from the station, for she spent at least half her time at her aunt's in Bassett Centre, and had even taught the small school there during the last six months. She had also sent him her tintype,[16] and his own was secreted in her bureau drawer. He had invited her to go with him to two sleigh-rides and one sugaring-off,[17] and always came home with her from prayer-meeting and singing-school; but like a wise youth he had never yet proposed to marry her in due form, not so much because he was wise as because he was thoughtless and lazy; and while he enjoyed the society of a bright girl, and liked to dangle after the prettiest one in Bassett, and the minister's daughter too, he did not love work well enough to shoulder the responsibility of providing for another those material but necessary supplies that imply labor of an incessant sort.

Rosabel, in her first inconsiderate anger at her father's command, sat down and wrote a note to Amos, eminently calculated to call out his sympathy with her own wrath, and promptly mailed it as soon as it was written. It ran as follows:—

> DEAR FRIEND,—Pa has forbidden me to speak to you any more, or to corre-spond with you. I suppose I must submit so far; but he did not say I must return your picture [the parson had not an idea that she possessed that pre-cious thing], so I shall keep it to remind me of the pleasant hours we have passed together.
>
> > "Fare thee well, and if forever,
> > Still forever fare thee well!"[18]
>
> Your true friend,   ROSABEL STEARNS.
>
> P.S.—I think pa is *horrid!*

So did Amos as he read this heart-rending missive, in which the postscript, ac-cording to the established sneer at woman's postscripts, carried the whole force of the epistle.

Now Amos had made a friend of Miss Celia by once telegraphing for her trunk, which she had lost on her way home from the only journey of her life, a trip to Boston, whither she had gone, on the strength of the one share of B. & A. R. R.[19] stock she held, to spend the allotted three days granted to stockholders on their annual excursions, presumably to attend the annual meeting. Amos had put himself to the immense trouble of sending two messages for Miss Celia, and asked her nothing for the civility, so that ever after, in the fashion of solitary women,

---

[16]Photograph made on an iron plate.
[17]A social gathering where guests help make maple sugar.
[18]"Fare Thee Well" (1816), st. 1, by English romantic poet Lord Byron (1788–1824).
[19]Boston and Albany Railroad, completed in 1842.

she held herself deeply in his debt. He knew that she was at work for Mrs. Stearns when he received Rosa's epistle, for he had just been over to Bassett on the train—there was but a mile to traverse—to get her to repair his Sunday coat, and not found her at home, but had no time to look her up at the parson's, as he must walk back to his station. Now he resolved to take his answer to Rosa to Miss Celia in the evening, and so be sure that his abused sweetheart received it, for he had read too many dime novels to doubt that her tyrannic father would intercept their letters, and drive them both to madness and despair. That well-meaning but rather dull divine never would have thought of such a thing; he was a puffy, absent-minded, fat little man, with a weak, squeaky voice, and a sudden temper that blazed up like a bunch of dry weeds at a passing spark, and went out at once in flattest ashes. It had been Mrs. Stearns's step-motherly interference that drove him into his harshness to Rosa. She meant well and he meant well, but we all know what good intentions with no further sequel of act are good for, and nobody did more of that "paving" than these two excellent but futile people.

Miss Celia was ready to do anything for Amos Barker, and she considered it little less than a mortal sin to stand in the way of any marriage that was really desired by two parties. That Amos was poor did not daunt her at all; she had the curious faith that possesses some women, that any man can be prosperous if he has the will so to be; and she had a high opinion of this youth, based on his civility to her. It may be said of men, as of elephants, that it is lucky they do not know their own power; for how many more women would become their worshipers and slaves than are so to-day if they knew the abject gratitude the average woman feels for the least attention, the smallest kindness, the faintest expression of affection or good will. We are all, like the Syrophenician woman,[20] glad and ready to eat of the crumbs which fall from the children's table, so great is our faith—in men.

Miss Celia took the note in her big basket over to the minister's the very next day after that on which we introduced her to our readers. She was perhaps more rejoiced to contravene that reverend gentleman's orders than if she had not heard his querulous and contemptuous remark about her through the crack of the door on the previous afternoon; and it was with a sense of joy that, after all, an old maid could do something, that she slipped the envelope into Rosa's hands, and told her to put it quickly into her pocket, the very first moment she found herself alone with that young woman.

Many a hasty word had Parson Stearns spoken in the suddenness of his petulant temper, but never one that bore direr fruit than that when he called Celia Barnes "that old maid."

For of course Amos and Rosabel found in her an ardent friend. They had the instinct of distressed lovers to cajole her with all their confidences, caresses, and eager gratitude, and for once she felt herself dear and of importance. Amos consulted her on his plans for the future, which of course pointed westward, where he had a brother editing and owning a newspaper. This brother had before offered him a place in his office, but Amos had liked better the easy work of a station-master in a tiny village. Now his ambition was aroused, for the time at least. He wanted to make a home for Rosabel, but, alack! he had not one cent to pay their united expenses to Peoria, and a lion stood in the way. Here again Celia stepped in: she had some money laid up; she would lend it to them.

I do not say that at this stage she had no misgivings, but even these were set at rest by a conversation she had with Mrs. Stearns some six weeks after the day on

---

[20]This gentile woman showed her faith in Jesus and thus got Him to cast out the devil from her daughter by noting that even as the dogs eat the crumbs of the bread He feeds the children so she would be content with the smallest token of His powers to help her daughter; Mark 7:26–30.

which Celia had so fully expressed her scorn of spinsters. She was there again to tack a comfortable[21] for Rosabel's bed, and bethought herself that it was a good time to feel her way a little concerning Mrs. Stearns's opinion of things.

"They do say," she remarked, stopping to snip off her thread and twist the end of it through her needle's eye, "that your Rosy don't go with Amos Barker no more. Is that so?"

"Yes," said Mrs. Stearns, with a half sigh. "Husband was rather prompt about it; he don't think Amos Barker ever'll amount to much, and he thinks his people are not just what they should be. You know his father never was very much of a man, and his grandfather is a real old reprobate. Husband says he never knew anything but crows come out of a crow's nest, and so he told Rosa to break acquaintance with him."

"Who does he like to hev come to see her?" asked Celia, with a grim set of her lips, stabbing her needle fiercely through the unoffending calico.

Mrs. Stearns laughed rather feebly. "I don't think he has anybody on his mind, Miss Celia. I don't think there are any young men in Bassett. I dare say Rosa will never marry. I wish she would, for she is n't happy here, and I can't do much to help her, with all my cares."

"And you can't feel for her as though she was your own, if you try ever so," confidently asserted Celia.

"No, I suppose not. I try to do my duty by her, and I am sorry for her; but I know all the time an own mother would understand her better and make it easier for her. Mr. Stearns is peculiar, and men don't know just how to manage girls."

It was a cautious admission, but Miss Celia had sharp eyes, and knew very well that Rosabel neither loved nor respected her father, and that they were now on terms of real if unavowed hostility.

"Well," said she, "I don' know but you will have to have one of them onpleasant creturs, an old maid, in your fam'ly. I declare for 't, I'd hold a Thanksgiving Day all to myself ef I'd escaped that marcy."

"You may not always think so, Celia."

"I don't know what'll change me. 'T will be something I don't look forrard to now," answered Celia obstinately.

Mrs. Stearns sighed. "I hope Rosa will do nothing worse than to live unmarried," she said; but she could not help wishing silently that some worthy man would carry the perverse and annoying girl out of the parsonage for good.

After this Celia felt a certain freedom to help Rosabel; she encouraged the lovers to meet at her house, helped plan their elopement, sewed for the girl, and at last went with them as far as Brimfield when they stole away one evening, saw them safely married at the Methodist parsonage there, and bidding them godspeed, returned to Bassett Centre on the midnight train, and walked over to her own dwelling in the full moonshine of the October night, quite fearless and entirely exultant.

But she was not to come off unscathed. There was a scene of wild commotion at the parsonage next day, when Rosa's letter, modeled on that of the last novel heroine she had become acquainted with, was found on her bureau, as per novel aforesaid.

With her natural thoughtlessness she assured her parents that she "fled not uncompanioned," that her "kind and all but maternal friend, Miss Celia Barnes, would accompany her to the altar, and give her support and her countenance to the solemn ceremony that should make Rosabel Stearns the blessed wife of Amos Barker!"

---

[21]To stitch loosely a comforter or bed cover.

It was all the minister could do not to swear as he read this astounding letter. His flabby face grew purple; his fat, sallow hands shook with rage; he dared not speak, he only sputtered, for he knew that profane and unbecoming words would surely leap from his tongue if he set it free; but he must—he really must—do or say something! So he clapped on his old hat, and with coat tails flying in the breeze, and rage in every step, set out to find Celia Barnes; and find her he did.

It would be unpleasant, and it is needless, to depict this encounter; language both unjust and unsavory smote the air and reverberated along the highway, for he met the spinster on her road to an engagement at Deacon Stiles's. Suffice it to say that both freed their minds with great enlargement of opinion, and the parson wound up with,—

"And I never want to see you again inside of my house, you confounded old maid!"

"There! that's it!" retorted Celia. "Ef I was n't an old maid, you would n't no more have darst to 'a' talked to me this way than nothin'. Ef I'd had a man to stand up to ye you'd have been dumber'n Balaam's ass a great sight,—afore it seen the angel, I mean.[22] I swow to man, I b'lieve I'd marry a hitchin'-post if 't was big enough to trounce ye. You great lummox, if I could knock ye over you would n't peep nor mutter agin, if I be a woman!"

And with a burst of furious tears that asserted her womanhood Miss Celia went her way. Her hands were clinched under her blanket-shawl, her eyes red with angry rain, and as she walked on she soliloquized aloud:—

"I declare for 't, I b'lieve I'd marry the Old Boy[23] himself if he'd ask me. I'm sicker'n ever of bein' an old maid!"

"Be ye?" queried a voice at her elbow. "P'r'aps, then, you might hear to me if I was to speak my mind, Celye."

Celia jumped. As she said afterward, "I vum[24] I thought 't was the Enemy, for certain; and to think 't was only Deacon Everts!"

"Mercy me!" she said now; "is 't you, deacon?"

"Yes, it's me; and I think 't is a real providence I come up behind ye just in the nick of time. I've sold my farm only last week, and I've come to live on the street in that old red house of grandsir's, that you mistrusted once I wanted you to buy. I'm real lonesome sence I lost my partner" (he meant his wife), "and I've been a-hangin' on by the edges the past two year; hired help is worse than nothing onto a farm, and hard to get at that; so I sold out, and I'm a-movin' yet, but the old house looks forlorn enough, and I was intendin' to look about for a second; so if you'll have me, Celye, here I be."

Celia looked at him sharply; he was an apple-faced little man, with shrewd, twinkling eyes, a hard, dull red still lingering on his round cheeks in spite of the deep wrinkles about his pursed-up lips and around his eyelids; his mouth gave him a consequential and self-important air, to which the short stubbly hair, brushed up "like a blaze" above his forehead, added; and his old blue coat with brass buttons, his homespun trousers, the old-fashioned aspect of his unbleached cotton shirt, all attested his frugality. Indeed, everybody knew that Deacon Everts was "near,"[25] and also that he had plenty of money, that is to say, far more than he could spend. He had no children, no near relations; his first wife had died two years since, after long invalidism, and all her relations had moved far west. All this Celia knew and now recalled; her wrath against Parson Stearns was yet fresh and vivid; she remembered that Simeon Everts was senior deacon of the church, and

---

[22]When the angel appeared to Balaam on his dumb ass, it was the ass and not Balaam who saw and carried out the Lord's wishes, thus proving wiser than the man; Numbers 22:21–35.

[23]The devil.
[24]Vow. Enemy: devil.
[25]Stingy.

had it in his power to make the minister extremely uncomfortable if he chose. I have never said Celia was a very good woman; her religion was of the dormant type not uncommon nowadays; she kept up its observances properly, and said her prayers every day, bestowed a part of her savings on each church collection, and was rated as a church-member "in good and regular standing;" but the vital trans-forming power of that Christianity which means to "love the Lord thy God with all thy heart, and mind, and soul, and strength, and thy neighbor as thyself,"[26] had no more entered into her soul than it had into Deacon Everts's; and while she would have honestly admitted that revenge was a very wrong sentiment, and en-tirely improper for any other person to cherish, she felt that she did well to be angry with Parson Stearns, and had a perfect right to "pay him off" in any way she could.

Now here was her opportunity. If she said "Yes" to Deacon Everts, he would no doubt take her part. Her objections to housekeeping were set aside by the fact that the house-owner himself would have to do those heavy labors about the house which she must otherwise have hired a man to do; and the cooking and the indoor work for two people could not be so hard as to sew from house to house for her daily bread. In short, her mind was slowly turning favorably toward this sudden project, but she did not want this wooer to be too sure; so she said: "W-e-ll, 't is a life sentence, as you may say, deacon, and I want to think on 't a spell. Let's see,—to-day's Tuesday; I'll let ye know Thursday night, after prayer-meetin'."

"Well," answered the deacon.

Blessed Yankee monosyllable that means so much and so little; that has such shades of phrase and intention in its myriad inflections; that is "yes," or "no," or "perhaps," just as you accent it; that is at once preface and peroration, evasion and definition! What would all New England speech be without "well"? Even as salt without any savor, or pepper with no pungency.

Now it meant to Miss Celia assent to her proposition; and in accordance the deacon escorted her home from meeting Thursday night, and received for re-ward a consenting answer. This was no love affair, but a matter of mere business. Deacon Everts needed a housekeeper, and did not want to pay out wages for one; and Miss Celia's position she expressed herself as she put out her tallow candle on that memorable night, and breathed out on the darkness the audible aspiration, "Thank goodness, I sha'n't hev to die an old maid!"

There was no touch of sanctifying love or consoling affection, or even friendly comradeship, in this arrangement; it was as truly a *mariage de convenance*[27] as was ever contracted in Paris itself, and when the wedding day came, a short month afterward, the sourest aspect of November skies threatening a drenching pour, the dead and sodden leaves that strewed the earth, the wailing northeast wind, even the draggled and bony old horse behind which they jogged over to Bassett Centre, seemed fit accompaniments to the degraded ceremony performed by a justice of the peace, who concluded this merely legal compact, for Miss Celia stoutly refused to be married by Parson Stearns; she would not be accessory to putting one dollar in his pocket, even as her own wedding fee. So she went home to the little red house on Bassett Street, and begun her married life by scrubbing the dust and dirt of years from the kitchen table, making biscuit for tea, washing up the dishes, and at last falling asleep during the deacon's long nasal prayer, wherein he wandered to the ends of the earth, and prayed fervently for the hea-then, piteously unconscious that he was little better than a heathen himself.

It did not take many weeks to discover to Celia what is meant by "the curse of a

---

[26]Matthew 22:35–40.
[27]"Marriage for practical reasons" (French).

granted prayer." She could not at first accept the situation at all; she was accustomed to enough food, if it was plain and simple, when she herself provided it; but now it was hard to get such viands as would satisfy a healthy appetite.

"You've used a sight of pork, Celye," the deacon would remonstrate. "My first never cooked half what you do. We shall come to want certain, if you're so free-handed."

"Well, Mr. Everts, there was n't a mite left to set by. We eat it all, and I did n't have no more'n I wanted, if you did."

"We must mortify the flesh, Celye. It's hullsome to get up from your victuals hungry. Ye know what Scripter says, 'Jeshurun waxed fat an' kicked.' "[28]

"Well, I ain't Jeshurun, but I expect I shall be more likely to kick if I don't have enough to eat, when it's only pork 'n' potatoes."

"My first used to say them was the best, for steady victuals, of anything, and she never used but two codfish and two quarts of m'lasses the year round; and as for butter, she was real sparin'; she'd fry our bread along with the salt pork, and 't was just as good."

"Look here!" snapped Celia. "I don't want to hear no more about your 'first.' I'm ready to say I wish 't she'd ha' been your last too."

"Well, well, well! this is onseemly contention, Celye," sputtered the alarmed deacon. "Le' 's dwell together in unity so fur as we can, Mis' Everts. I have n't no intention to starve ye, none whatever. I only want to be keerful, so as we sha'n't have to fetch up in the poor-us."

"No need to have a poor-house to home," muttered Celia.

But this is only a mild specimen of poor Celia's life as a married woman. She did not find the honor and glory of "Mrs." before her name a compensation for the thousand evils that she "knew not of" when she fled to them as a desirable change from her single blessedness. Deacon Everts entirely refused to enter into any of her devices against Parson Stearns; he did not care a penny about Celia's wrongs, and he knew very well that no other man than dreamy, unpractical Mr. Stearns, who eked out his minute pittance by writing schoolbooks of a primary sort, would put up with four hundred dollars a year from his parish; yet that was all Bassett people would pay. If they must have the gospel, they must have it at the lowest living rates, and everybody would not assent to that.

So Celia found her revenge no more feasible after her marriage than before, and, gradually absorbed in her own wrongs and sufferings, her desire to reward Mr. Stearns in kind for his treatment of her vanished; she thought less of his futile wrath and more of her present distresses every day.

For Celia, like everybody who profanes the sacrament of marriage, was beginning to suffer the consequences of her misstep. As her husband's mean, querulous, loveless character unveiled itself in the terrible intimacy of constant and inevitable companionship, she began to look woefully back to the freedom and peace of her maiden days. She learned that a husband is by no means his wife's defender always, not even against reviling tongues. It did not suit Deacon Everts to quarrel with any one, whatever they said to him, or of him and his; he "did n't want no enemies," and Celia bitterly felt that she must fight her own battles; she had not even an ally in her husband. She became not only defiant, but also depressed; the consciousness of a vital and life-long mistake is not productive of cheer or content; and now, admitted into the free-masonry[29] of married women, she discovered how few among them were more than household drudges, the servants of their families, worked to the verge of exhaustion, and neither thanked

---

[28]Jeshurun, a poetic name for Israel (God's people), became vicious after good living and kind treatment; Deuteronomy 32:15.
[29]Fellowship and sympathy.

nor rewarded for their pains. She saw here a woman whose children were careless of, and ungrateful to her, and her husband coldly indifferent; there was one on whom the man she had married wreaked all his fiendish temper in daily small injuries, little vexatious acts, petty tyrannies, a "street-angel, house-devil" of a man, of all sorts the most hateful. There were many whose lives had no other outlook than hard work until the end should come, who rose up to labor and lay down in sleepless exhaustion, and some whose days were a constant terror to them from the intemperate brutes to whom they had intrusted their happiness, and indeed their whole existence.

It was no worse with Celia than with most of her sex in Bassett; here and there, there were of course exceptions, but so rare as to be shining examples and objects of envy. Then, too, after two years, there came forlorn accounts of poor Rosabel's situation at the west. Amos Barker had done his best at first to make his wife comfortable, but change of place or new motives do not at once, if ever, transform an indolent man into an active and efficient one. He found work in his brother's office, but it was the hard work of collecting bills all about the country; the roads were bad, the weather as fluctuating as weather always is, the climate did not agree with him, and he got woefully tired of driving about from dawn till after dark, to dun unwilling debtors. Rosa had chills and fever and babies with persistent alacrity; she had indeed enough to eat, with no appetite, and a house, with no strength to keep it. She grew untidy, listless, hysterical; and her father, getting worried by her despondent and infrequent letters, actually so far roused himself as to sell his horse, and with this sacrificial money betook himself to Mound Village, where he found Rosabel with two babies in her arms, dust an inch deep on all her possessions, nothing but pork, potatoes, and corn bread in the pantry, and a slatternly negress washing some clothes in a kitchen that made the parson shudder.

The little man's heart was bigger than his soul. He put his arms about Rosa and the dingy babies, and forgave her all; but he had to say, even while he held them closely and fondly to his breast, "Oh, Rosy, I told you what would happen if you married that fellow."

Of course Rosa resented the speech, for, after all, she had loved Amos; perhaps could love him still if the poverty and malaria and babies could have all been eliminated from her daily life.

Fortunately the parson's horse had sold well, for it was strong and young, and the rack of venerable bones with which he replaced it was bought very cheap at a farmer's auction, so he had money enough to carry Rosa and the two children home to Bassett, where two months after she added another feeble, howling cipher to the miserable sum of humanity.

Miss—no, Mrs.—Celia's conscience stung her to the quick when she encountered this ghastly wreck of pretty Rosabel Stearns, now called Mrs. Barker. She remembered with deep regret how she had given aid and comfort to the girl who had defied and disobeyed parental counsel and authority, and so brought on herself all this misery. She fancied that Parson Stearns glared at her with eyes of bitter accusation and reproach, and not improbably he did, for beside his pity and affection for his daughter, it was no slight burden to take into his house a feeble woman with two children helpless as babies, and to look forward to the expense and anxiety of another soon to come. And Mrs. Stearns had never loved Rosa well enough to be complacent at this addition to her family cares. She gave the parson no sympathy. It would have been her way to let Rosabel lie on the bed she had made, and die there if need be. But the poor worn-out creature died at home, after all, and the third baby lay on its mother's breast in her coffin: they had gone together.

Celia felt almost like a murderess when she heard that Rosabel Barker was dead. She did not reflect that in all human probability the girl would have married

Amos if she, Celia, had refused to help or encourage her. It began to be an importunate question in our friend's mind whether she herself had not made a mistake too; whether the phrase "single blessedness" was not an expression of a vital truth rather than a scoff. Celia was changing her mind no doubt, surely if slowly.

Meantime Deacon Everts did not find all the satisfaction with his "second" that he had anticipated. Celia had a will of her own, quite undisciplined, and it was too often asserted to suit her lord and master. Secretly he planned devices to circumvent her purposes, and sometimes succeeded. In prayer-meeting and in Sunday-school the idea haunted him; his malice lay down and rose up with him. Even when he propounded to his Bible class the important question, "How fur be the heathen *ree*-sponsible for what they dun know?" and asked them "to ponder on 't through the comin' week," he chuckled inwardly at the thought that Celia could not evade *her* responsibility; she knew enough, and would be judged accordingly: the deacon was not a merciful man.

At last he hit upon that great legal engine whereby men do inflict the last deadly kick upon their wives: he would remodel his will. Yes, he would leave those gathered thousands to foreign missions; he would leave behind him the indisputable testimony and taunt that he considered the wife of his bosom less than the savages and heathen afar off. He forgot conveniently that the man "who provideth not for his own household hath denied the faith, and is worse than an infidel."[30] And in his delight of revenge he also forgot that the law of the land provides for a man's wife and children[31] in spite of his wicked will. Nor did he remember that his life-insurance policy for five thousand dollars was made out in his wife's name, simply as his wife, her own name not being specified. He had paid the premium always from his "first's" small annual income, and agreed that it should be written for her benefit, but he supposed that at her death it had reverted to him. He forgot that he still had a wife when he mentioned that policy in his assets recorded in the will, and to save money he drew that evil document up himself, and had it signed down at "the store" by three witnesses.[32]

Celia had borne her self-imposed yoke for four years, when it was suddenly broken. A late crop of grass was to be mowed in mid-July on the meadow which appertained to the old house, and the deacon, now some seventy years old, to save hiring help, determined to do it by himself. The grass was heavy and over-ripe, the day extremely hot and breathless, and the grim Mower of Man trod side by side with Simeon Everts, and laid him too, all along by the rough heads of timothy and the purpled feather-tops of the blue-grass. He did not come home at noon or at night, and when Celia went down to the lot to call him he heard no summons of hers; he had answered a call far more imperative and final.

After the funeral Celia found his will pushed back in the deep drawer of an old secretary, where he kept his one quill pen, a bottle of dried ink, a lump of chalk, some rat-poison, and various other odds and ends.

She was indignant enough at its tenor; but it was easily broken, and she not only had her "thirds,"[33] but the life policy reverted to her also, as it was made out to Simeon Everts's wife, and surely she had occupied that position for four wretched years. Then, also, she had a right to her support for one year out of the estate, and the use of the house for that time.

Oh, how sweet was her freedom! With her characteristic honesty she refused to put on mourning, and even went to the funeral in her usual gray Sunday gown and bonnet. "I won't lie, anyhow!" she answered to Mrs. Stiles's remonstrance. "I

---

[30]1 Timothy 5:8.
[31]Dower, the life-use portion of the deceased man's real estate allotted by law to the widow, amounted to one-third the value.

[32]In New England, a witnessed will had to be attested to by three witnesses.
[33]That percentage of the estate allotted to her by law.

ain't a mite sorry nor mournful. I could ha' wished he'd had time to repent of his sins, but sence the Lord saw fit to cut him short, I don't feel to rebel ag'inst it. I wish 't I'd never married him, that's all!"

"But, Celye, you got a good livin'."

"I earned it."

"And he's left ye with means too."

"He done his best not to. I don't owe him nothing for that; and I earned that too,—the hull on 't. It's poor pay for what I've lived through; and I'm a'most a mind to call it the wages of sin, for I done wrong, ondeniably wrong, in marryin' of him; but the Lord knows I've repented, and said my lesson, if I did get it by the hardest."

Yet all Bassett opened eyes and mouth both when on the next Thanksgiving Day Celia invited every old maid in town—seven all told—to take dinner with her. Never before had she celebrated this old New England day of solemn revel. A woman living in two small rooms could not "keep the feast," and rarely had she been asked to any family conclave. We Yankees are conservative at Thanksgiving if nowhere else, and like to gather our own people only about the family hearth; so Celia had but once or twice shared the turkeys of her more fortunate neighbors.

Now she called in Nabby Hyde and Sarah Gillett, Ann Smith, Celestia Potter, Delia Hills, Sophronia Ann Jenkins and her sister Adelia Ann, ancient twins, who lived together on next to nothing, and were happy.

Celia bloomed at the head of the board, not with beauty, but with gratification. "Well," she said, as soon as they were seated, "I sent for ye all to come because I wanted to have a good time, for one thing, and because it seems as though I'd ought to take back all the sassy and disagreeable things I used to be forever flingin' at old maids. 'I spoke in my haste,'[34] as Scripter says, and also in my ignorance, I'm free to confess. I feel as though I could keep Thanksgivin' to-day with my hull soul. I'm so thankful to be an old maid ag'in!"

"I thought you was a widder," snapped Sally Gillett.

Celia flung a glance of wrath at her, but scorned to reply.

"And I'm thankful too that I'm spared to help ondo somethin' done in that ignorance. I've got means, and, as I've said before, I earned 'em. I don't feel noway obleeged to him for 'em; he did n't mean it. But now I can I'm goin' to adopt Rosy Barker's two children, and fetch 'em up to be dyed-in-the-wool old maids; and every year, so long as I live, I'm goin' to keep an old maids' Thanksgivin' for a kind of a burnt-offering, sech as the Bible tells about,[35] for I've changed my mind clear down to the bottom, and I go the hull figure with the 'postle Paul when he speaks about the onmarried, 'It is better if she so abide.'[36] Now let's go to work at the victuals."

1891

---

[34]Psalm 31:22: "For I said in my haste, I am cut off from before thine eyes; nevertheless thou heardest the voice of my supplications when I cried unto thee."
[35]The burnt offering was the commonest sacrifice for atonement or thanksgiving, and the animal offered had to be male; Leviticus 1.
[36]1 Corinthians 7:40: "But she is happier if she so abide."

REBECCA HARDING DAVIS
(1831–1910)

When Rebecca Harding Davis died in 1910, the obituary in the *New York Times* was headlined: "Mother of Richard Harding Davis Dies at Son's Home in Mt. Kisco, age 79." Richard Harding Davis (1864–1916) was at the time a celebrated journalist and short story writer whose name had come to over-shadow his mother's. But in a queer act of fate, a new reversal has taken place: the son is now forgotten and the mother remembered. This resurrec-tion has been brought about by the passionate efforts of the contemporary novelist, Tillie Olsen, who edited the Feminist Press reissue of *Life in the Iron-Mills and Other Stories* in 1972, reprinted in 1985.

"Life in the Iron-Mills" had first appeared anonymously in *The Atlantic Monthly* in 1861 and had created a sensation. Before the advent of American realism or naturalism, before the appearance of Émile Zola in France, the au-thor in the opening pages challenged the reader with a bold, direct address: "Stop a moment. I am going to be honest. This is what I want you to do. I want you to hide your disgust, take no heed to your clean clothes, and come right down with me,—here, into the thickest of the fog and mud and foul effluvia. I want you to hear this story. There is a secret down here, in this nightmare fog, that has lain dumb for centuries: I want to make it a real thing to you."

In this astonishing passage and others like it, the author is working out for herself a theory of realism that would justify using the downtrodden mill workers as subject matter for fiction. She depicts them not for comic purposes or picturesque background but for the human values they themselves repre-sent, however debased and dehumanized they are by an industrial-economic system that exploits and brutalizes them.

The author so much in advance of her time was born in Washington, Pennsylvania, taken briefly to live in Alabama, and, at the age of five, moved with her middle-class family to the industrial town of Wheeling, Virginia (now West Virginia). Her schooling was at the nearby Washington Female Semi-nary, where she graduated in 1848 as valedictorian at age seventeen. Her fa-ther, an Englishman, was a reader of books, particularly Shakespeare and other Elizabethan writers.

Rebecca Harding must have sensed a radical difference between the ro-mantic literature she found in the magazines she read and the grime, de-bauchery, and brutish behavior she witnessed in the soot-blackened streets of Wheeling. She touched on this difference in a passage in a later work: "You want something, in fact, to lift you out of this crowded, tobacco-stained com-monplace, to kindle and chafe, and glow in you. I want you to dig into this commonplace, this vulgar American life, and see what is in it. Sometimes I think it has a new and awful significance that we do not see."

There was no intellectual or literary life in the isolated town on the border between North and South. What she achieved in literary development had to be achieved in isolation from the American centers of culture—Boston, New York, Philadelphia. From age seventeen to age thirty, when Rebecca Harding sent "Life in the Iron-Mills" to *The Atlantic Monthly*, little is known of her life. Certain it is, however, that she read widely—the British writers such as John Bunyan and Elizabeth Gaskell, American writers such as Margaret Fuller and Nathaniel Hawthorne. When "Life in the Iron-Mills" appeared in 1861, it drew the astonished attention of, among others, Louisa May Alcott, Ralph Waldo Emerson, and Nathaniel Hawthorne (who wrote an appreciative letter).

On a visit to Boston in 1862, when her novel *Margaret Howth* was being serialized in *The Atlantic Monthly,* Rebecca Harding met the editor, James T. Fields and became a lifelong friend of his wife Annie Fields. She met, too, the leading literary lights of the day—Hawthorne, Emerson, Thoreau, and others.

"Life in the Iron-Mills" had also inspired a young journalist studying for the bar in Philadelphia to write a letter, which led to a meeting. The meeting led to marriage in 1863 to Lemuel Clarke Davis, some three to four years her junior. He persuaded her to write for a journal with which he was connected, *Peterson's Magazine.* Thus she soon found herself with a growing family and multiplying deadlines. She wrote hastily—and never again so well as she had written in her first story. Her work was popular, and some of the books have a continuing appeal—*Waiting for the Verdict* (1868), *A Law unto Herself* (1878), *Silhouettes of American Life* (1892).

Although Rebecca Harding Davis has been largely neglected until recently, "Life in the Iron-Mills" had not been entirely overlooked. Earlier in the century, in *The Development of the American Short Story* (1923), Fred Lewis Pattee wrote that her story "has a convincingness and a sharpness of outline that were its author's own and that place her among the pioneers of American fiction. . . . A tale by Gogol could not be more hauntingly depressing. Shuddering realism at every point, and yet nothing too much: the reader cannot shake the effect of the thing from him for hours."

ADDITIONAL READING

Life in the Iron-Mills and Other Stories, by Rebecca Harding Davis, ed. with a Biographical Interpretation by Tillie Olsen, 1972, 1985.

Charles Belmont Davis, ed., *The Adventures and Letters of Richard Harding Davis,* 1917; Helen Woodward Sheaffer, "Rebecca Harding Davis, Pioneer Realist," Ph.D. Dissertation, University of Pennsylvania, 1947; Gerald Langford, *The Richard Harding Davis Years: A Biography of a Mother and Son,* 1961.

TEXT

"Life in the Iron-Mills," *The Atlantic Monthly,* April 7, 1861.

Life in the Iron-Mills

> "Is this the end?
> O Life, as futile, then, as frail!
> What hope of answer or redress?"[1]

A cloudy day: do you know what that is in a town of iron-works? The sky sank down before dawn, muddy, flat, immovable. The air is thick, clammy with the breath of crowded human beings. It stifles me. I open the window, and, looking out, can scarcely see through the rain the grocer's shop opposite, where a crowd

---

[1] *In Memoriam* (1850), 12.16, 56.25, 27, by English poet Alfred, Lord Tennyson (1850–1892).

of drunken Irishmen are puffing Lynchburg tobacco[2] in their pipes. I can detect the scent through all the foul smells ranging loose in the air.

The idiosyncrasy of this town is smoke. It rolls sullenly in slow folds from the great chimneys of the iron-foundries, and settles down in black, slimy pools on the muddy streets. Smoke on the wharves, smoke on the dingy boats, on the yellow river,—clinging in a coating of greasy soot to the house-front, the two faded poplars, the faces of the passers-by. The long train of mules, dragging masses of pig-iron[3] through the narrow street, have a foul vapor hanging to their reeking sides. Here, inside, is a little broken figure of an angel pointing upward from the mantel-shelf; but even its wings are covered with smoke, clotted and black. Smoke everywhere! A dirty canary chirps desolately in a cage beside me. Its dream of green fields and sunshine is a very old dream,—almost worn out, I think.

From the back-window I can see a narrow brick-yard sloping down to the river-side, strewed with rain-butts[4] and tubs. The river, dull and tawny-colored, *(la belle rivière!)*[5] drags itself sluggishly along, tired of the heavy weight of boats and coal-barges. What wonder? When I was a child, I used to fancy a look of weary, dumb appeal upon the face of the negro-like river slavishly bearing its burden day after day. Something of the same idle notion comes to me to-day, when from the street-window I look on the slow stream of human life creeping past, night and morning, to the great mills. Masses of men, with dull, besotted faces bent to the ground, sharpened here and there by pain or cunning; skin and muscle and flesh begrimed with smoke and ashes; stooping all night over boiling caldrons of metal, laired by day in dens of drunkenness and infamy; breathing from infancy to death an air saturated with fog and grease and soot, vileness for soul and body. What do you make of a case like that, amateur psychologist? You call it an altogether serious thing to be alive: to these men it is a drunken jest, a joke,—horrible to angels perhaps, to them commonplace enough. My fancy about the river was an idle one: it is no type of such a life. What if it be stagnant and slimy here? It knows that beyond there waits for it odorous sunlight,—quaint old gardens, dusky with soft, green foliage of apple-trees, and flushing crimson with roses,—air, and fields, and mountains. The future of the Welsh puddler[6] passing just now is not so pleasant. To be stowed away, after his grimy work is done, in a hole in the muddy graveyard, and after that,——*not* air, nor green fields, nor curious roses.

Can you see how foggy the day is? As I stand here, idly tapping the window-pane, and looking out through the rain at the dirty back-yard and the coal-boats below, fragments of an old story float up before me,—a story of this old house into which I happened to come today. You may think it a tiresome story enough, as foggy as the day, sharpened by no sudden flashes of pain or pleasure.—I know: only the outline of a dull life, that long since, with thousands of dull lives like its own, was vainly lived and lost: thousands of them,—massed, vile, slimy lives, like those of the torpid lizards in yonder stagnant water-butt.—Lost? There is a curious point for you to settle, my friend, who study psychology in a lazy, *dilettante*[7] way. Stop a moment. I am going to be honest. This is what I want you to do. I want you to hide your disgust, take no heed to your clean clothes, and come right down with me,—here, into the thickest of the fog and mud and foul effluvia.[8] I want you to hear this story. There is a secret down here, in this nightmare fog, that has lain dumb for centuries: I want to make it a real thing to you. You, Ego-

[2]Cheap tobacco from Virginia.
[3]Crude iron cast in oblong blocks (pigs).
[4]Large casks to catch rainwater.
[5]"The beautiful river" (French), an ironic allusion to the pristine quality of the Ohio River when the French first discovered it.

[6]One who purifies the impure molten pig iron by stirring (puddling) it in an oxidizing atmosphere. Welsh: from Wales, principality of the United Kingdom west of England, noted for its coal mines.
[7]Amateurish.
[8]Vapors.

ist, or Pantheist, or Arminian,[9] busy in making straight paths for your feet[10] on the hills, do not see it clearly,—this terrible question which men here have gone mad and died trying to answer. I dare not put this secret into words. I told you it was dumb. These men, going by with drunken faces and brains full of unawakened power, do not ask it of Society or of God. Their lives ask it; their deaths ask it. There is no reply. I will tell you plainly that I have a great hope; and I bring it to you to be tested. It is this: that this terrible dumb question is its own reply; that it is not the sentence of death we think it, but, from the very extremity of its darkness, the most solemn prophecy which the world has known of the Hope to come. I dare make my meaning no clearer, but will only tell my story. It will, perhaps, seem to you as foul and dark as this thick vapor about us, and as pregnant with death; but if your eyes are free as mine are to look deeper, no perfume-tinted dawn will be so fair with promise of the day that shall surely come.

My story is very simple,—only what I remember of the life of one of these men,—a furnace-tender in one of Kirby & John's rolling-mills,[11]—Hugh Wolfe. You know the mills? They took the great order for the Lower Virginia railroads there last winter; run usually with about a thousand men. I cannot tell why I choose the half-forgotten story of this Wolfe more than that of myriads of these furnace-hands. Perhaps because there is a secret underlying sympathy between that story and this day with its impure fog and thwarted sunshine,—or perhaps simply for the reason that this house is the one where the Wolfes lived. There were the father and son,—both hands, as I said, in one of Kirby & John's mills for making railroad-iron,—and Deborah, their cousin, a picker[12] in some of the cotton-mills. The house was rented then to half a dozen families. The Wolfes had two of the cellar-rooms. The old man, like many of the puddlers and feeders[13] of the mills, was Welsh,—had spent half of his life in the Cornish[14] tin-mines. You may pick the Welsh emigrants, Cornish miners, out of the throng passing the windows, any day. They are a trifle more filthy; their muscles are not so brawny; they stoop more. When they are drunk, they neither yell, nor shout, nor stagger, but skulk along like beaten hounds. A pure, unmixed blood, I fancy: shows itself in the slight angular bodies and sharply-cut facial lines. It is nearly thirty years since the Wolfes lived here. Their lives were like those of their class: incessant labor, sleeping in kennel-like rooms, eating rank pork and molasses, drinking—God and the distillers only know what; with an occasional night in jail, to atone for some drunken excess. Is that all of their lives?—of the portion given to them and these their duplicates swarming the streets to-day?—nothing beneath?—all? So many a political reformer will tell you,—and many a private reformer, too, who has gone among them with a heart tender with Christ's charity, and come out outraged, hardened.

One rainy night, about eleven o'clock, a crowd of half-clothed women stopped outside of the cellar-door. They were going home from the cotton-mill.

"Good-night, Deb," said one, a mulatto, steadying herself against the gas-post. She needed the post to steady her. So did more than one of them.

"Dah's a ball to Miss Potts' to-night. Ye'd best come."

"Inteet, Deb, if hur'll come, hur'll hef fun,"[15] said a shrill Welsh voice in the crowd.

---

[9]One devoted to self-interest; one who identifies God with nature; and one opposing the Calvinistic tenets of predestination, of a powerless human will, and of an "elect," as did Dutch theologian Jacobus Arminius (1560–1609).
[10]Hebrews 12:13: "And make straight paths for your feet, lest that which is lame be turned out of the way; but let it rather be healed."

[11]Mills in which metal is rolled out, flattened.
[12]One who operates the machine that separates and cleans cotton fibers.
[13]One who feeds molten metal into the casts.
[14]Cornwall, county in southwest England with important tin mines.
[15]"Indeed, Deb, if you'll come, you'll have fun."

Two or three dirty hands were thrust out to catch the gown of the woman, who was groping for the latch of the door.

"No."

"No? Where's Kit Small, then?"

"Begorra! on the spools.[16] Alleys behint, though we helped her, we dud. An wid ye! Let Deb alone! It's ondacent frettin' a quite body. Be the powers, an' we'll have a night of it! there 'll be lashin's[17] o' drink,—the Vargent[18] be blessed and praised for 't!"

They went on, the mulatto inclining for a moment to show fight, and drag the woman Wolfe off with them; but, being pacified, she staggered away.

Deborah groped her way into the cellar, and, after considerable stumbling, kindled a match, and lighted a tallow dip, that sent a yellow glimmer over the room. It was low, damp,—the earthen floor covered with a green, slimy moss,—a fetid air smothering the breath. Old Wolfe lay asleep on a heap of straw, wrapped in a torn horse-blanket. He was a pale, meek little man, with a white face and red rabbit-eyes. The woman Deborah was like him; only her face was even more ghastly, her lips bluer, her eyes more watery. She wore a faded cotton gown and a slouching bonnet. When she walked, one could see that she was deformed, almost a hunchback. She trod softly, so as not to waken him, and went through into the room beyond. There she found by the half-extinguished fire an iron saucepan filled with cold boiled potatoes, which she put upon a broken chair with a pint-cup of ale. Placing the old candlestick beside this dainty repast, she untied her bonnet, which hung limp and wet over her face, and prepared to eat her supper. It was the first food that had touched her lips since morning. There was enough of it, however: there is not always. She was hungry,—one could see that easily enough,—and not drunk, as most of her companions would have been found at this hour. She did not drink, this woman,—her face told that, too,—nothing stronger than ale. Perhaps the weak, flaccid wretch had some stimulant in her pale life to keep her up,—some love or hope, it might be, or urgent need. When that stimulant was gone, she would take to whiskey. Man cannot live by work alone.[19] While she was skinning the potatoes, and munching them, a noise behind her made her stop.

"Janey!" she called, lifting the candle and peering into the darkness. "Janey, are you there?"

A heap of ragged coats was heaved up, and the face of a young girl emerged, staring sleepily at the woman.

"Deborah," she said, at last, "I'm here the night."

"Yes, child. Hur's[20] welcome," she said, quietly eating on.

The girl's face was haggard and sickly; her eyes were heavy with sleep and hunger: real Milesian[21] eyes they were, dark, delicate blue, glooming out from black shadows with a pitiful fright.

"I was alone," she said, timidly.

"Where's the father?" asked Deborah, holding out a potato, which the girl greedily seized.

"He's beyant,—wid Haley,—in the stone house." (Did you ever hear the word *jail* from an Irish mouth?) "I came here. Hugh told me never to stay me-lone."

"Hugh?"

---

[16]Begorra: a mild oath (Irish for "By God"). Spools: the spindles on which the cotton is wound.
[17]Lavish quantities.
[18]Virgin Mary.
[19]Cf. Deuteronomy 8:3: ". . . man doth not live by bread only, but by every word that proceedeth out of the mouth of the Lord doth man live."

[20]You're. In the rest of the story, "Hur" or "hur's" can in most cases be read as "you," "your," "you're," or "yours," depending on the context.
[21]Irish.

"Yes."

A vexed frown crossed her face. The girl saw it, and added quickly,—

"I have not seen Hugh the day, Deb. The old man says his watch[22] lasts till the mornin'."

The woman sprang up, and hastily began to arrange some bread and flitch[23] in a tin pail, and to pour her own measure of ale into a bottle. Tying on her bonnet, she blew out the candle.

"Lay ye down, Janey dear," she said, gently, covering her with the old rags. "Hur can eat the potatoes, if hur's hungry."

"Where are ye goin', Deb? The rain's sharp."

"To the mill, with Hugh's supper."

"Let him bide till th' morn. Sit ye down."

"No, no,"—sharply pushing her off. "The boy'll starve."

She hurried from the cellar, while the child wearily coiled herself up for sleep. The rain was falling heavily, as the woman, pail in hand, emerged from the mouth of the alley, and turned down the narrow street, that stretched out, long and black, miles before her. Here and there a flicker of gas lighted an uncertain space of muddy footwalk and gutter; the long rows of houses, except an occasional lager-bier shop, were closed; now and then she met a band of mill-hands skulking to or from their work.

Not many even of the inhabitants of a manufacturing town know the vast machinery of system by which the bodies of workmen are governed, that goes on unceasingly from year to year. The hands of each mill are divided into watches that relieve each other as regularly as the sentinels of an army. By night and day the work goes on, the unsleeping engines groan and shriek, the fiery pools of metal boil and surge. Only for a day in the week, in half-courtesy to public censure, the fires are partially veiled; but as soon as the clock strikes midnight, the great furnaces break forth with renewed fury, the clamor begins with fresh, breathless vigor, the engines sob and shriek like "gods in pain."

As Deborah hurried down through the heavy rain, the noise of these thousand engines sounded through the sleep and shadow of the city like far-off thunder. The mill to which she was going lay on the river, a mile below the city-limits. It was far, and she was weak, aching from standing twelve hours at the spools. Yet it was her almost nightly walk to take this man his supper, though at every square she sat down to rest, and she knew she should receive small word of thanks.

Perhaps, if she had possessed an artist's eye, the picturesque oddity of the scene might have made her step stagger less, and the path seem shorter; but to her the mills were only "summat deilish[24] to look at by night."

The road leading to the mills had been quarried from the solid rock, which rose abrupt and bare on one side of the cinder-covered road, while the river, sluggish and black, crept past on the other. The mills for rolling iron are simply immense tent-like roofs, covering acres of ground, open on every side. Beneath these roofs Deborah looked in on a city of fires, that burned hot and fiercely in the night. Fire in every horrible form: pits of flame waving in the wind; liquid metal-flames writhing in tortuous streams through the sand; wide caldrons filled with boiling fire, over which bent ghastly wretches stirring the strange brewing; and through all, crowds of half-clad men, looking like revengeful ghosts in the red light, hurried, throwing masses of glittering fire. It was like a street in Hell. Even Deborah muttered, as she crept through, "'T looks like t' Devil's place!" It did,—in more ways than one.

---

[22]Shift at work.
[23]Side of cured pork.
[24]Somewhat devilish.

She found the man she was looking for, at last, heaping coal on a furnace. He had not time to eat his supper; so she went behind the furnace, and waited. Only a few men were with him, and they noticed her only by a "Hyur comes t' hunchback, Wolfe."

Deborah was stupid with sleep; her back pained her sharply; and her teeth chattered with cold, with the rain that soaked her clothes and dripped from her at every step. She stood, however, patiently holding the pail, and waiting.

"Hout, woman! ye look like a drowned cat. Come near to the fire,"—said one of the men, approaching to scrape away the ashes.

She shook her head. Wolfe had forgotten her. He turned, hearing the man, and came closer.

"I did no' think; gi' me my supper, woman."

She watched him eat with a painful eagerness. With a woman's quick instinct, she saw that he was not hungry,—was eating to please her. Her pale, watery eyes began to gather a strange light.

"Is't good, Hugh? T' ale was a bit sour, I feared."

"No, good enough." He hesitated a moment. "Ye're tired, poor lass! Bide here till I go. Lay down there on that heap of ash, and go to sleep."

He threw her an old coat for a pillow, and turned to his work. The heap was the refuse of the burnt iron, and was not a hard bed; the half-smothered warmth, too, penetrated her limbs, dulling their pain and cold shiver.

Miserable enough she looked, lying there on the ashes like a limp, dirty rag,— yet not an unfitting figure to crown the scene of hopeless discomfort and veiled crime: more fitting, if one looked deeper into the heart of things,—at her thwarted woman's form, her colorless life, her waking stupor that smothered pain and hunger,—even more fit to be a type of her class. Deeper yet if one could look, was there nothing worth reading in this wet, faded thing, half-covered with ashes? no story of a soul filled with groping passionate love, heroic unselfishness, fierce jealousy? of years of weary trying to please the one human being whom she loved, to gain one look of real heart-kindness from him? If anything like this were hidden beneath the pale, bleared eyes, and dull, washed-out-looking face, no one had ever taken the trouble to read its faint signs: not the half-clothed furnace-tender, Wolfe, certainly. Yet he was kind to her: it was his nature to be kind, even to the very rats that swarmed in the cellar: kind to her in just the same way. She knew that. And it might be that very knowledge had given to her face its apathy and vacancy more than her low, torpid life. One sees that dead, vacant look steal sometimes over the rarest, finest of women's faces,—in the very midst, it may be, of their warmest summer's day; and then one can guess at the secret of intolerable solitude that lies hid beneath the delicate laces and brilliant smile. There was no warmth, no brilliancy, no summer for this woman; so the stupor and vacancy had time to gnaw into her face perpetually. She was young, too, though no one guessed it; so the gnawing was the fiercer.

She lay quiet in the dark corner, listening, through the monotonous din and uncertain glare of the works, to the dull plash of the rain in the far distance,— shrinking back whenever the man Wolfe happened to look towards her. She knew, in spite of all his kindness, that there was that in her face and form which made him loathe the sight of her. She felt by instinct, although she could not comprehend it, the finer nature of the man, which made him among his fellow-workmen something unique, set apart. She knew, that, down under all the vileness and coarseness of his life, there was a groping passion for whatever was beautiful and pure,—that his soul sickened with disgust at her deformity, even when his words were kindest. Through this dull consciousness, which never left her, came, like a sting, the recollection of the dark blue eyes and lithe figure of the little Irish girl she had left in the cellar. The recollection struck through even her stupid in-

tellect with a vivid glow of beauty and of grace. Little Janey, timid, helpless, clinging to Hugh as her only friend: that was the sharp thought, the bitter thought,
that drove into the glazed eyes a fierce light of pain. You laugh at it? Are pain and
jealousy less savage realities down here in this place I am taking you to than in
your own house or your own heart,—your heart, which they clutch at sometimes?
The note is the same, I fancy, be the octave high or low.

If you could go into this mill where Deborah lay, and drag out from the hearts
of these men the terrible tragedy of their lives, taking it as a symptom of the disease of their class, no ghost Horror would terrify you more. A reality of soul-
starvation, of living death, that meets you every day under the besotted faces on
the street,—I can paint nothing of this, only give you the outside outlines of a
night, a crisis in the life of one man: whatever muddy depth of soul-history lies
beneath you can read according to the eyes God has given you.

Wolfe, while Deborah watched him as a spaniel its master, bent over the furnace with his iron pole, unconscious of her scrutiny, only stopping to receive orders. Physically, Nature had promised the man but little. He had already lost the
strength and instinct vigor of a man, his muscles were thin, his nerves weak, his
face (a meek, woman's face) haggard, yellow with consumption. In the mill he was
known as one of the girl-men: "Molly Wolfe" was his *sobriquet*.[25] He was never
seen in the cockpit, did not own a terrier,[26] drank but seldom; when he did, desperately. He fought sometimes, but was always thrashed, pommelled to a jelly.
The man was game enough, when his blood was up: but he was no favorite in the
mill; he had the taint of school-learning on him,—not to a dangerous extent, only
a quarter or so in the free-school in fact, but enough to ruin him as a good hand
in a fight.

For other reasons, too, he was not popular. Not one of themselves, they felt
that, though outwardly as filthy and ash-covered; silent, with foreign thoughts and
longings breaking out through his quietness in innumerable curious ways: this
one, for instance. In the neighboring furnace-buildings lay great heaps of the
refuse from the ore after the pig-metal is run. *Korl* we call it here: a light, porous
substance, of a delicate, waxen, flesh-colored tinge. Out of the blocks of this korl,
Wolfe, in his off-hours from the furnace, had a habit of chipping and moulding
figures,—hideous, fantastic enough, but sometimes strangely beautiful: even the
mill-men saw that, while they jeered at him. It was a curious fancy in the man,
almost a passion. The few hours for rest he spent hewing and hacking with his
blunt knife, never speaking, until his watch came again,—working at one figure
for months, and, when it was finished, breaking it to pieces perhaps, in a fit of
disappointment. A morbid, gloomy man, untaught, unled, left to feed his soul in
grossness and crime, and hard, grinding labor.

I want you to come down and look at this Wolfe, standing there among the
lowest of his kind, and see him just as he is, that you may judge him justly when
you hear the story of this night. I want you to look back, as he does every day, at
his birth in vice, his starved infancy; to remember the heavy years he has groped
through as boy and man,—the slow, heavy years of constant, hot work. So long
ago he began, that he thinks sometimes he has worked there for ages. There is no
hope that it will ever end. Think that God put into this man's soul a fierce thirst
for beauty,—to know it, to create it; to *be*—something, he knows not what,—other
than he is. There are moments when a passing cloud, the sun glinting on the purple thistles, a kindly smile, a child's face, will rouse him to a passion of pain,—
when his nature starts up with a mad cry of rage against God, man, whoever it is

---

[25]Humorous nickname.
[26]He never attended violent cockfights, nor did he own a
terrier, which was a hunting dog.

that has forced this vile, slimy life upon him. With all this groping, this mad desire, a great blind intellect stumbling through wrong, a loving poet's heart, the man was by habit only a coarse, vulgar laborer, familiar with sights and words you would blush to name. Be just: when I tell you about this night, see him as he is. Be just,—not like man's law, which seizes on one isolated fact, but like God's judging angel, whose clear, sad eye saw all the countless cankering days of this man's life, all the countless nights, when, sick with starving, his soul fainted in him, before it judged him for this night, the saddest of all.

I called this night the crisis of his life. If it was, it stole on him unawares. These great turning-days of life cast no shadow before, slip by unconsciously. Only a trifle, a little turn of the rudder, and the ship goes to heaven or hell.

Wolfe, while Deborah watched him, dug into the furnace of melting iron with his pole, dully thinking only how many rails the lump would yield. It was late, — nearly Sunday morning; another hour, and the heavy work would be done,—only the furnaces to replenish and cover for the next day. The workmen were growing more noisy, shouting, as they had to do, to be heard over the deep clamor of the mills. Suddenly they grew less boisterous,—at the far end, entirely silent. Something unusual had happened. After a moment, the silence came nearer; the men stopped their jeers and drunken choruses. Deborah, stupidly lifting up her head, saw the cause of the quiet. A group of five or six men were slowly approaching, stopping to examine each furnace as they came. Visitors often came to see the mills after night: except by growing less noisy, the men took no notice of them. The furnace where Wolfe worked was near the bounds of the works; they halted there hot and tired: a walk over one of these great foundries is no trifling task. The woman, drawing out of sight, turned over to sleep. Wolfe, seeing them stop, suddenly roused from his indifferent stupor, and watched them keenly. He knew some of them: the overseer, Clarke,—a son of Kirby, one of the mill-owners,— and a Doctor May, one of the town-physicians. The other two were strangers. Wolfe came closer. He seized eagerly every chance that brought him into contact with this mysterious class that shone down on him perpetually with the glamour of another order of being. What made the difference between them? That was the mystery of his life. He had a vague notion that perhaps to-night he could find it out. One of the strangers sat down on a pile of bricks, and beckoned young Kirby to his side.

"This *is* hot, with a vengeance. A match, please?"—lighting his cigar. "But the walk is worth the trouble. If it were not that you must have heard it so often, Kirby, I would tell you that your works look like Dante's Inferno."[27]

Kirby laughed.

"Yes. Yonder is Farinata himself in the burning tomb,"[28]—pointing to some figure in the shimmering shadows.

"Judging from some of the faces of your men," said the other, "they bid fair to try the reality of Dante's vision, some day."

Young Kirby looked curiously around, as if seeing the faces of his hands for the first time.

"They're bad enough, that's true. A desperate set, I fancy. Eh, Clarke?"

The overseer did not hear him. He was talking of net profits just then,—giving, in fact, a schedule of the annual business of the firm to a sharp peering little Yankee, who jotted down notes on a paper laid on the crown of his hat: a reporter for one of the city-papers, getting up a series of reviews of the leading manufactories. The other gentlemen had accompanied them merely for amusement. They

---

[27] Hell is vividly portrayed in the first part of Dante's *Divine Comedy* entitled *The Inferno.*
[28] The heretic Farinata degli Uberti is lying in a fiery open tomb, not to be closed until judgment day (*Inferno*, Canto 10).

were silent until the notes were finished, drying their feet at the furnaces, and sheltering their faces from the intolerable heat. At last the overseer concluded with—

"I believe that is a pretty fair estimate, Captain."

"Here, some of you men!" said Kirby, "bring up those boards. We may as well sit down, gentlemen, until the rain is over. It cannot last much longer at this rate."

"Pig-metal,"—mumbled the reporter,—"um!—coal facilities,—um!—hands employed, twelve hundred,—bitumen,—um!—all right, I believe, Mr. Clarke;—sinking-fund,[29]—what did you say was your sinking-fund?"

"Twelve hundred hands?" said the stranger, the young man who had first spoken. "Do you control their votes, Kirby?"

"Control? No." The young man smiled complacently. "But my father brought seven hundred votes to the polls for his candidate last November. No force-work, you understand,—only a speech or two, a hint to form themselves into a society, and a bit of red and blue bunting to make them a flag. The Invincible Roughs,—I believe that is their name. I forget the motto: 'Our country's hope,' I think."

There was a laugh. The young man talking to Kirby sat with an amused light in his cool gray eye, surveying critically the half-clothed figures of the puddlers, and the slow swing of their brawny muscles. He was a stranger in the city,—spending a couple of months in the borders of a Slave State, to study the institutions of the South,[30]—a brother-in-law of Kirby's,—Mitchell. He was an amateur gymnast,—hence his anatomical eye; a patron, in a *blasé* way, of the prize-ring; a man who sucked the essence out of a science or philosophy in an indifferent, gentlemanly way; who took Kant, Novalis, Humboldt,[31] for what they were worth in his own scales; accepting all, despising nothing, in heaven, earth, or hell, but one-idead men; with a temper yielding and brilliant as summer water, until his Self was touched, when it was ice, though brilliant still. Such men are not rare in the States.

As he knocked the ashes from his cigar, Wolfe caught with a quick pleasure the contour of the white hand, the blood-glow of a red ring he wore. His voice, too, and that of Kirby's, touched him like music,—low, even, with chording cadences. About this man Mitchell hung the impalpable atmosphere belonging to the thorough-bred gentleman. Wolfe, scraping away the ashes beside him, was conscious of it, did obeisance to it with his artist sense, unconscious that he did so.

The rain did not cease. Clarke and the reporter left the mills; the others, comfortably seated near the furnace, lingered, smoking and talking in a desultory way. Greek would not have been more unintelligible to the furnace-tenders, whose presence they soon forgot entirely. Kirby drew out a newspaper from his pocket and read aloud some article, which they discussed eagerly. At every sentence, Wolfe listened more and more like a dumb, hopeless animal, with a duller, more stolid look creeping over his face, glancing now and then at Mitchell, marking acutely every smallest sign of refinement, then back to himself, seeing as in a mirror his filthy body, his more stained soul.

Never! He had no words for such a thought, but he knew now, in all the sharpness of the bitter certainty, that between them there was a great gulf never to be passed.[32] Never!

The bell of the mills rang for midnight. Sunday morning had dawned. Whatever hidden message lay in the tolling bells floated past these men unknown. Yet it was there. Veiled in the solemn music ushering the risen Saviour was a key-note to

---

[29]Fund accumulated to pay a corporate debt.
[30]I.e., slavery.
[31]Influential Germans: Immanuel Kant (1724–1804), idealist philosopher; Novalis, pseudonym of Frederick von Hardenberg (1772–1801), Romantic poet; Wilhelm von Humboldt (1767–1835), philologist, statesman, and brother of Alexander von Humboldt (1769–1854), naturalist, traveller, and statesman.
[32]An allusion to the great gulf between the beggar Lazarus in heaven and the rich man (Dives in the Latin *Vulgate*) in hell, described in Luke 16:26.

solve the darkest secrets of a world gone wrong,—even this social riddle which the brain of the grimy puddler grappled with madly to-night.

The men began to withdraw the metal from the caldrons. The mills were deserted on Sundays, except by the hands who fed the fires, and those who had no lodgings and slept usually on the ash-heaps. The three strangers sat still during the next hour, watching the men cover the furnaces, laughing now and then at some jest of Kirby's.

"Do you know," said Mitchell, "I like this view of the works better than when the glare was fiercest? These heavy shadows and the amphitheatre of smothered fires are ghostly, unreal. One could fancy these red smouldering lights to be the half-shut eyes of wild beasts, and the spectral figures their victims in the den."

Kirby laughed. "You are fanciful. Come, let us get out of the den. The spectral figures, as you call them, are a little too real for me to fancy a close proximity in the darkness,—unarmed, too."

The others rose, buttoning their overcoats, and lighting cigars.

"Raining, still," said Doctor May, "and hard. Where did we leave the coach, Mitchell?"

"At the other side of the works.— Kirby, what's that?"

Mitchell started back, half-frightened, as, suddenly turning a corner, the white figure of a woman faced him in the darkness,—a woman, white, of giant proportions, crouching on the ground, her arms flung out in some wild gesture of warning.

"Stop! Make that fire burn there!" cried Kirby, stopping short.

The flame burst out, flashing the gaunt figure into bold relief.

Mitchell drew a long breath.

"I thought it was alive," he said, going up curiously.

The others followed.

"Not marble, eh?" asked Kirby, touching it.

One of the lower overseers stopped.

"Korl, Sir."

"Who did it?"

"Can't say. Some of the hands; chipped it out in off-hours."

"Chipped to some purpose, I should say. What a flesh-tint the stuff has! Do you see, Mitchell?"

"I see."

He had stepped aside where the light fell boldest on the figure, looking at it in silence. There was not one line of beauty or grace in it: a nude woman's form, muscular, grown coarse with labor, the powerful limbs instinct with some one poignant longing. One idea: there it was in the tense, rigid muscles, the clutching hands, the wild, eager face, like that of a starving wolf's. Kirby and Doctor May walked around it, critical, curious. Mitchell stood aloof, silent. The figure touched him strangely.

"Not badly done," said Doctor May. "Where did the fellow learn that sweep of the muscles in the arm and hand? Look at them! They are groping,—do you see?—clutching: the peculiar action of a man dying of thirst."

"They have ample facilities for studying anatomy," sneered Kirby, glancing at the half-naked figures.

"Look," continued the Doctor, "at this bony wrist, and the strained sinews of the instep! A working-woman,—the very type of her class."

"God forbid!" muttered Mitchell.

"Why?" demanded May. "What does the fellow intend by the figure? I cannot catch the meaning."

"Ask him," said the other, dryly. "There he stands,"—pointing to Wolfe, who stood with a group of men, leaning on his ash-rake.

The Doctor beckoned him with the affable smile which kind-hearted men put on, when talking to these people.

"Mr. Mitchell has picked you out as the man who did this,—I'm sure I don't know why. But what did you mean by it?"

"She be hungry."

Wolfe's eyes answered Mitchell, not the Doctor.

"Oh-h! But what a mistake you have made, my fine fellow! You have given no sign of starvation to the body. It is strong,—terribly strong. It has the mad, half-despairing gesture of drowning."

Wolfe stammered, glanced appealingly at Mitchell, who saw the soul of the thing, he knew. But the cool, probing eyes were turned on himself now,—mocking, cruel, relentless.

"Not hungry for meat," the furnace-tender said at last.

"What then? Whiskey?" jeered Kirby, with a coarse laugh.

Wolfe was silent a moment, thinking.

"I dunno," he said, with a bewildered look. "It mebbe. Summet to make her live, I think,—like you. Whiskey ull do it, in a way."

The young man laughed again. Mitchell flashed a look of disgust somewhere,—not at Wolfe.

"May," he broke out impatiently, "are you blind? Look at that woman's face! It asks questions of God, and says, 'I have a right to know.' Good God, how hungry it is!"

They looked a moment; then May turned to the mill-owner:—

"Have you many such hands as this? What are you going to do with them? Keep them at puddling iron?"

Kirby shrugged his shoulders. Mitchell's look had irritated him.

"*Ce n'est pas mon affaire.*[33] I have no fancy for nursing infant geniuses. I suppose there are some stray gleams of mind and soul among these wretches. The Lord will take care of his own; or else they can work out their own salvation. I have heard you call our American system a ladder which any man can scale. Do you doubt it? Or perhaps you want to banish all social ladders, and put us all on a flat table-land,—eh, May?"

The Doctor looked vexed, puzzled. Some terrible problem lay hid in this woman's face, and troubled these men. Kirby waited for an answer, and, receiving none, went on, warming with his subject.

"I tell you, there's something wrong that no talk of '*Liberté*' or '*Égalité*'[34] will do away. If I had the making of men, these men who do the lowest part of the world's work should be machines,—nothing more,—hands. It would be kindness. God help them! What are taste, reason, to creatures who must live such lives as that?" He pointed to Deborah, sleeping on the ash-heap. "So many nerves to sting them to pain. What if God had put your brain, with all its agony of touch, into your fingers, and bid you work and strike with that?"

"You think you could govern the world better?" laughed the Doctor.

"I do not think at all."

"That is true philosophy. Drift with the stream, because you cannot dive deep enough to find bottom, eh?"

"Exactly," rejoined Kirby. "I do not think. I wash my hands of all social problems,—slavery, caste, white or black. My duty to my operatives[35] has a narrow limit,—the pay-hour on Saturday night. Outside of that, if they cut korl, or cut

---

[33]"It's not my business" (French).
[34]The slogan of the French Revolution: *Liberté, Égalité, Fraternité* (Liberty, Equality, Brotherhood).
[35]Workers.

each other's throats, (the more popular amusement of the two,) I am not responsible."

The Doctor sighed,—a good honest sigh, from the depths of his stomach.

"God help us! Who is responsible?"

"Not I, I tell you," said Kirby, testily. "What has the man who pays them money to do with their souls' concerns, more than the grocer or butcher who takes it?"

"And yet," said Mitchell's cynical voice, "look at her! How hungry she is!"

Kirby tapped his boot with his cane. No one spoke. Only the dumb face of the rough image looking into their faces with the awful question, "What shall we do to be saved?"[36] Only Wolfe's face, with its heavy weight of brain, its weak, uncertain mouth, its desperate eyes, out of which looked the soul of his class,—only Wolfe's face turned towards Kirby's. Mitchell laughed,—a cool, musical laugh.

"Money has spoken!" he said, seating himself lightly on a stone with the air of an amused spectator at a play. "Are you answered?"—turning to Wolfe his clear, magnetic face.

Bright and deep and cold Arctic air, the soul of the man lay tranquil beneath. He looked at the furnace-tender as he had looked at a rare mosaic in the morning; only the man was the more amusing study of the two.

"Are you answered? Why, May, look at him! *'De profundis clamavi.'*[37] Or, to quote in English, 'Hungry and thirsty, his soul faints in him.'[38] And so Money sends back its answer into the depths through you, Kirby! Very clear the answer, too!—I think I remember reading the same words somewhere:—washing your hands in Eau de Cologne, and saying, 'I am innocent of the blood of this man. See ye to it!' "[39]

Kirby flushed angrily.

"You quote Scripture freely."

"Do I not quote correctly? I think I remember another line, which may amend my meaning: 'Inasmuch as ye did it unto one of the least of these, ye did it unto me.'[40] Deist? Bless you, man, I was raised on the milk of the Word. Now, Doctor, the pocket of the world having uttered its voice, what has the heart to say? You are a philanthropist, in a small way,—*n'est ce pas?*[41] Here, boy, this gentleman can show you how to cut korl better,—or your destiny. Go on, May!"

"I think a mocking devil possesses you to-night," rejoined the Doctor, seriously.

He went to Wolfe and put his hand kindly on his arm. Something of a vague idea possessed the Doctor's brain that much good was to be done here by a friendly word or two: a latent genius to be warmed into life by a waited-for sunbeam. Here it was: he had brought it. So he went on complacently:—

"Do you know, boy, you have it in you to be a great sculptor, a great man?—do you understand?" (talking down to the capacity of his hearer: it is a way people have with children, and men like Wolfe,)—"to live a better, stronger life than I, or Mr. Kirby here? A man may make himself anything he chooses. God has given you stronger powers than many men,—me, for instance."

May stopped, heated, glowing with his own magnanimity. And it was magnanimous. The puddler had drunk in every word, looking through the Doctor's flurry, and generous heat, and self-approval, into his will, with those slow, absorbing eyes of his.

"Make yourself what you will. It is your right."

---

[36]Spoken by Paul's prison-keeper after an earthquake opens the doors and frees the prisoners' bonds (Acts 16:30).
[37]"Out of the depths have I cried unto thee, O Lord" (Latin of Psalm 130:1).
[38]Psalm 107:5: "Hungry and thirsty, their soul fainted in them."
[39]When he delivered Jesus to the mob to be crucified, Roman governor Pontius Pilate spoke these words as he washed his hands in water (Matthew 27:24).
[40]Words of Jesus in Matthew 25:40. Deist: one who believes, on the evidence of reason alone, in an impersonal God who created the universe and its laws, but who does not intervene in its functioning, and who gave no supernatural revelation; nature, not the Word, is the bible.
[41]"Aren't you?" (French).

"I know," quietly. "Will you help me?"

Mitchell laughed again. The Doctor turned now, in a passion,—

"You know, Mitchell, I have not the means. You know, if I had, it is in my heart to take this boy and educate him for"—

"The glory of God, and the glory of John May."

May did not speak for a moment; then, controlled, he said,—

"Why should one be raised, when myriads are left?—I have not the money, boy," to Wolfe, shortly.

"Money?" He said it over slowly, as one repeats the guessed answer to a riddle, doubtfully. "That is it? Money?"

"Yes, money,—that is it," said Mitchell, rising, and drawing his furred coat about him. "You've found the cure for all the world's diseases.—Come, May, find your good-humor, and come home. This damp wind chills my very bones. Come and preach your Saint-Simonian[42] doctrines to-morrow to Kirby's hands. Let them have a clear idea of the rights of the soul, and I'll venture next week they'll strike for higher wages. That will be the end of it."

"Will you send the coach-driver to this side of the mills?" asked Kirby, turning to Wolfe.

He spoke kindly: it was his habit to do so. Deborah, seeing the puddler go, crept after him. The three men waited outside. Doctor May walked up and down, chafed. Suddenly he stopped.

"Go back, Mitchell! You say the pocket and the heart of the world speak without meaning to these people. What has its head to say? Taste, culture, refinement? Go!"

Mitchell was leaning against a brick wall. He turned his head indolently, and looked into the mills. There hung about the place a thick, unclean odor. The slightest motion of his hand marked that he perceived it, and his insufferable disgust. That was all. May said nothing, only quickened his angry tramp.

"Besides," added Mitchell, giving a corollary to his answer, "it would be of no use. I am not one of them."

"You do not mean"—said May, facing him.

"Yes, I mean just that. Reform is born of need, not pity. No vital movement of the people's has worked down, for good or evil; fermented, instead, carried up the heaving, cloggy mass. Think back through history, and you will know it. What will this lowest deep—thieves, Magdalens,[43] negroes—do with the light filtered through ponderous Church creeds, Baconian theories, Goethe schemes?[44] Some day, out of their bitter need will be thrown up their own light-bringer,—their Jean Paul, their Cromwell, their Messiah."[45]

"Bah!" was the Doctor's inward criticism. However, in practice, he adopted the theory; for, when, night and morning, afterwards, he prayed that power might be given these degraded souls to rise, he glowed at heart, recognizing an accomplished duty.

Wolfe and the woman had stood in the shadow of the works as the coach drove

---

[42]Socialist doctrines developed by the followers of French social reformer Claude Henri de Rouvroy, Comte de Saint-Simon (1760–1825).

[43]Prostitutes, after the repentant prostitute in Luke 7:36–50, considered to be Mary Magdalene, "out of whom went seven devils" (Luke 8:2).

[44]All powerful forces in directing individuals and shaping society: the church, through its beliefs as revealed by God; the English philosopher Francis Bacon (1561–1624), who attempted a "Great Renewal" (*Instauratio Magna*) in science and civilization and described a scientific utopia in *New Atlantis* (1627); and the great German writer Johann Wolfgang von Goethe (1749–1832), who embodied modern man's strivings in *Faust* (1808, 1832) and celebrated social

and technological progress in *Wilhelm Meister's Travels* (1821–29), suggesting there a resettlement plan for immigrants in the land of the future, America.

[45]Johann Paul Richter, called Jean Paul (1763–1825), German Romantic novelist, who rose above his humble background to exert a great influence on his contemporaries, expressed revolutionary ideas in his *Titan* (1800–03; English translation, 1862); the English Puritan leader Oliver Cromwell (1599–1658) defeated the royalist forces and established a protectorate characterized by religious toleration; "their Messiah": any liberator of the people, such as that waited for by the Jews, and Jesus, Savior of the Christians.

off. The Doctor had held out his hand in a frank, generous way, telling him to "take care of himself, and to remember it was his right to rise." Mitchell had simply touched his hat, as to an equal, with a quiet look of thorough recognition. Kirby had thrown Deborah some money, which she found, and clutched eagerly enough. They were gone now, all of them. The man sat down on the cinder-road, looking up into the murky sky.

"'T be late, Hugh. Wunnot hur come?"

He shook his head doggedly, and the woman crouched out of his sight against the wall. Do you remember rare moments when a sudden light flashed over yourself, your world, God? when you stood on a mountain-peak, seeing your life as it might have been, as it is? one quick instant, when custom lost its force and everyday usage? when your friend, wife, brother, stood in a new light? your soul was bared, and the grave,—a foretaste of the nakedness of the Judgment-Day? So it came before him, his life, that night. The slow tides of pain he had borne gathered themselves up and surged against his soul. His squalid daily life, the brutal coarseness eating into his brain, as the ashes into his skin: before, these things had been a dull aching into his consciousness; to-night, they were reality. He griped the filthy red shirt that clung, stiff with soot, about him, and tore it savagely from his arm. The flesh beneath was muddy with grease and ashes,—and the heart beneath that! And the soul? God knows.

Then flashed before his vivid poetic sense the man who had left him,—the pure face, the delicate, sinewy limbs, in harmony with all he knew of beauty or truth. In his cloudy fancy he had pictured a Something like this. He had found it in this Mitchell, even when he idly scoffed at his pain: a Man all-knowing, allseeing, crowned by Nature, reigning,—the keen glance of his eye falling like a sceptre on other men. And yet his instinct taught him that he too—He! He looked at himself with sudden loathing, sick, wrung his hands with a cry, and then was silent. With all the phantoms of his heated, ignorant fancy, Wolfe had not been vague in his ambitions. They were practical, slowly built up before him out of his knowledge of what he could do. Through years he had day by day made this hope a real thing to himself,—a clear, projected figure of himself, as he might become.

Able to speak, to know what was best, to raise these men and women working at his side up with him: sometimes he forgot this defined hope in the frantic anguish to escape,—only to escape,—out of the wet, the pain, the ashes, somewhere, anywhere,—only for one moment of free air on a hill-side, to lie down and let his sick soul throb itself out in the sunshine. But to-night he panted for life. The savage strength of his nature was roused; his cry was fierce to God for justice.

"Look at me!" he said to Deborah, with a low, bitter laugh, striking his puny chest savagely. "What am I worth, Deb? Is it my fault that I am no better? My fault? My fault?"

He stopped, stung with a sudden remorse, seeing her hunchback shape writhing with sobs. For Deborah was crying thankless tears, according to the fashion of women.

"God forgi' me, woman! Things go harder wi' you nor me. It's a worse share."

He got up and helped her to rise; and they went doggedly down the muddy street, side by side.

"It's all wrong," he muttered, slowly,—"all wrong! I dunnot understan'. But it'll end some day."

"Come home, Hugh!" she said, coaxingly; for he had stopped, looking around bewildered.

"Home,—and back to the mill!" He went on saying this over to himself, as if he would mutter down every pain in this dull despair.

She followed him through the fog, her blue lips chattering with cold. They reached the cellar at last. Old Wolfe had been drinking since she went out, and had crept nearer the door. The girl Janey slept heavily in the corner. He went up to her, touching softly the worn white arm with his fingers. Some bitterer thought stung him, as he stood there. He wiped the drops from his forehead, and went into the room beyond, livid, trembling. A hope, trifling, perhaps, but very dear, had died just then out of the poor puddler's life, as he looked at the sleeping, innocent girl,—some plan for the future, in which she had borne a part. He gave it up that moment, then and forever. Only a trifle, perhaps, to us: his face grew a shade paler,—that was all. But, somehow, the man's soul, as God and the angels looked down on it, never was the same afterwards.

Deborah followed him into the inner room. She carried a candle, which she placed on the floor, closing the door after her. She had seen the look on his face, as he turned away: her own grew deadly. Yet, as she came up to him, her eyes glowed. He was seated on an old chest, quiet, holding his face in his hands.

"Hugh!" she said, softly.

He did not speak.

"Hugh, did hur hear what the man said,—him with the clear voice? Did hur hear? Money, money,—that it wud do all?"

He pushed her away,—gently, but he was worn out; her rasping tone fretted him.

"Hugh!"

The candle flared a pale yellow light over the cobwebbed brick walls, and the woman standing there. He looked at her. She was young, in deadly earnest; her faded eyes, and wet, ragged figure caught from their frantic eagerness a power akin to beauty.

"Hugh, it is true! Money ull do it! Oh, Hugh, boy, listen till me! He said it true! It is money!"

"I know. Go back! I do not want you here."

"Hugh, it is t' last time. I'll never worrit[46] hur again."

There were tears in her voice now, but she choked them back.

"Hear till me only to-night! If one of t' witch people wud come, them we heard of t' home,[47] and gif hur all hur wants, what then? Say, Hugh!"

"What do you mean?"

"I mean money."

Her whisper shrilled through his brain.

"If one of t' witch dwarfs wud come from t' lane moors to-night, and gif hur money, to go out,—*out*, I say,—out, lad, where t' sun shines, and t' heath grows, and t' ladies walk in silken gownds, and God stays all t' time,—where t' man lives that talked to us to-night,—Hugh knows,—Hugh could walk there like a king!"

He thought the woman mad, tried to check her, but she went on, fierce in her eager haste.

"If *I* were t' witch dwarf, if I had t' money, wud hur thank me? Wud hur take me out o' this place wid hur and Janey? I wud not come into the gran' house hur wud build, to vex hur wid t' hunch,—only at night, when t' shadows were dark, stand far off to see hur."

Mad? Yes! Are many of us mad in this way?

"Poor Deb! poor Deb!" he said, soothingly.

"It is here," she said, suddenly jerking into his hand a small roll. "I took it! I did it! Me, me!—not hur! I shall be hanged, I shall be burnt in hell, if anybody knows I took it! Out of his pocket, as he leaned against t' bricks. Hur knows?"

---

[46]Worry.
[47]The witch people of Welsh folklore.

She thrust it into his hand, and then, her errand done, began to gather chips together to make a fire, choking down hysteric sobs.

"Has it come to this?"

That was all he said. The Welsh Wolfe blood was honest. The roll was a small green pocket-book containing one or two gold pieces, and a check for an incredible amount, as it seemed to the poor puddler. He laid it down, hiding his face again in his hands.

"Hugh, don't be angry wud me! It's only poor Deb,—hur knows?"

He took the long skinny fingers kindly in his.

"Angry? God help me, no! Let me sleep. I am tired."

He threw himself heavily down on the wooden bench, stunned with pain and weariness. She brought some old rags to cover him.

It was late on Sunday evening before he awoke. I tell God's truth, when I say he had then no thought of keeping this money. Deborah had hid it in his pocket. He found it there. She watched him eagerly, as he took it out.

"I must gif it to him," he said, reading her face.

"Hur knows," she said with a bitter sigh of disappointment. "But it is hur right to keep it."

His right! The word struck him. Doctor May had used the same. He washed himself, and went out to find this man Mitchell. His right! Why did this chance word cling to him so obstinately? Do you hear the fierce devils whisper in his ear, as he went slowly down the darkening street?

The evening came on, slow and calm. He seated himself at the end of an alley leading into one of the larger streets. His brain was clear to-night, keen, intent, mastering. It would not start back, cowardly, from any hellish temptation, but meet it face to face. Therefore the great temptation of his life came to him veiled by no sophistry, but bold, defiant, owning its own vile name, trusting to one bold blow for victory.

He did not deceive himself. Theft! That was it. At first the word sickened him; then he grappled with it. Sitting there on a broken cart-wheel, the fading day, the noisy groups, the church-bells' tolling passed before him like a panorama,[48] while the sharp struggle went on within. This money! He took it out, and looked at it. If he gave it back, what then? He was going to be cool about it.

People going by to church saw only a sickly mill-boy watching them quietly at the alley's mouth. They did not know that he was mad, or they would not have gone by so quietly: mad with hunger; stretching out his hands to the world, that had given so much to them, for leave to live the life God meant him to live. His soul within him was smothering to death; he wanted so much, thought so much, and *knew*—nothing. There was nothing of which he was certain, except the mill and things there. Of God and heaven he had heard so little, that they were to him what fairy-land is to a child: something real, but not here; very far off. His brain, greedy, dwarfed, full of thwarted energy and unused powers, questioned these men and women going by, coldly, bitterly, that night. Was it not his right to live as they,—a pure life, a good, true-hearted life, full of beauty and kind words? He only wanted to know how to use the strength within him. His heart warmed, as he thought of it. He suffered himself to think of it longer. If he took the money?

Then he saw himself as he might be, strong, helpful, kindly. The night crept on, as this one image slowly evolved itself from the crowd of other thoughts and stood triumphant. He looked at it. As he might be! What wonder, if it blinded him to delirium,—the madness that underlies all revolution, all progress, and all fall?

---

[48]A continuous passing scene like those painted on a cylindrical surface or on a canvas and unrolled before spectators, as was common in the nineteenth century.

You laugh at the shallow temptation. You see the error underlying its argument so clearly,—that to him a true life was one of full development rather than self-restraint? that he was deaf to the higher tone in a cry of voluntary suffering for truth's sake than in the fullest flow of spontaneous harmony? I do not plead his cause. I only want to show you the mote in my brother's eye: then you can see clearly to take it out.[49]

The money,—there it lay on his knee, a little blotted slip of paper, nothing in itself; used to raise him out of the pit; something straight from God's hand. A thief! Well, what was it to be a thief? He met the question at last, face to face, wiping the clammy drops of sweat from his forehead. God made this money—the fresh air, too—for his children's use. He never made the difference between poor and rich. The Something who looked down on him that moment through the cool gray sky had a kindly face, he knew,—loved his children alike. Oh, he knew that!

There were times when the soft floods of color in the crimson and purple flames, or the clear depth of amber in the water below the bridge, had somehow given him a glimpse of another world than this,—of an infinite depth of beauty and of quiet somewhere,—somewhere,—a depth of quiet and rest and love. Looking up now, it became strangely real. The sun had sunk quite below the hill but his last rays struck upward, touching the zenith. The fog had risen, and the town and river were steeped in its thick, gray damp; but overhead, the sun-touched smoke-clouds opened like a cleft ocean,—shifting, rolling seas of crimson mist, waves of billowy silver veined with blood-scarlet, inner depths unfathomable of glancing light. Wolfe's artist-eye grew drunk with color. The gates of that other world! Fading, flashing before him now! What, in that world of Beauty, Content, and Right, were the petty laws, the mine and thine, of mill-owners and mill-hands?

A consciousness of power stirred within him. He stood up. A man,—he thought, stretching out his hands,—free to work, to live, to love! Free! His right! He folded the scrap of paper in his hand. As his nervous fingers took it in, limp and blotted, so his soul took in the mean temptation, lapped it in fancied rights, in dreams of improved existences, drifting and endless as the cloud-seas of color. Clutching it, as if the tightness of his hold would strengthen his sense of possession, he went aimlessly down the street. It was his watch at the mill. He need not go, need never go again, thank God!—shaking off the thought with unspeakable loathing.

Shall I go over the history of the hours of that night? how the man wandered from one to another of his old haunts, with a half-consciousness of bidding them farewell,—lanes and alleys and backyards where the mill-hands lodged,—noting, with a new eagerness, the filth and drunkenness, the pig-pens, the ash-heaps covered with potato-skins, the bloated, pimpled women at the doors,—with a new disgust, a new sense of sudden triumph, and, under all, a new, vague dread, unknown before, smothered down, kept under, but still there? It left him but once during the night, when, for the second time in his life, he entered a church. It was a sombre Gothic pile, where the stained light lost itself in far-retreating arches; built to meet the requirements and sympathies of a far other class than Wolfe's. Yet it touched, moved him uncontrollably. The distances, the shadows, the still, marble figures, the mass of silent kneeling worshippers, the mysterious music, thrilled, lifted his soul with a wonderful pain. Wolfe forgot himself, forgot the new life he was going to live, the mean terror gnawing underneath. The voice of the speaker strengthened the charm; it was clear, feeling, full, strong. An old

---

[49]Matthew 7:3–5: "And why beholdest thou the mote [speck] that is in thy brother's eye, but considerest not the beam [log] that is in thine own eye? . . . Thou hypocrite, first cast out the beam out of thine own eye; and then shalt thou see clearly to cast out the mote out of thy brother's eye?"

man, who had lived much, suffered much; whose brain was keenly alive, dominant; whose heart was summer-warm with charity. He taught it to-night. He held up Humanity in its grand total; showed the great world-cancer to his people. Who could show it better? He was a Christian reformer; he had studied the age thoroughly; his outlook at man had been free, world-wide, over all time. His faith stood sublime upon the Rock of Ages;[50] his fiery zeal guided vast schemes by which the gospel was to be preached to all nations. How did he preach it to-night? In burning, light-laden words he painted the incarnate Life, Love, the universal Man: words that became reality in the lives of these people,—that lived again in beautiful words and actions, trifling, but heroic. Sin, as he defied it, was a real foe to them; their trials, temptations, were his. His words passed far over the furnace-tender's grasp, toned to suit another class of culture; they sounded in his ears a very pleasant song in an unknown tongue. He meant to cure this world-cancer with a steady eye that had never glared with hunger, and a hand that neither poverty nor strychnine-whiskey[51] had taught to shake. In this morbid, distorted heart of the Welsh puddler he had failed.

Wolfe rose at last, and turned from the church down the street. He looked up; the night had come on foggy, damp; the golden mists had vanished, and the sky lay dull and ash-colored. He wandered again aimlessly down the street, idly wondering what had become of the cloud-sea of crimson and scarlet. The trial-day of this man's life was over, and he had lost the victory. What followed was mere drifting circumstance,—a quicker walking over the path,—that was all. Do you want to hear the end of it? You wish me to make a tragic story out of it? Why, in the police-reports of the morning paper you can find a dozen such tragedies: hints of shipwrecks unlike any that ever befell on the high seas; hints that here a power was lost to heaven,—that there a soul went down where no tide can ebb or flow. Commonplace enough the hints are,—jocose sometimes, done up in rhyme.

Doctor May, a month after the night I have told you of, was reading to his wife at breakfast from this fourth column of the morning-paper: an unusual thing,— these police-reports not being, in general, choice reading for ladies; but it was only one item he read.

"Oh, my dear! You remember that man I told you of, that we saw at Kirby's mill?—that was arrested for robbing Mitchell? Here he is; just listen:—'Circuit Court. Judge Day. Hugh Wolfe, operative in Kirby & John's Loudon Mills. Charge, grand larceny. Sentence, nineteen years hard labor in penitentiary.'— Scoundrel! Serves him right! After all our kindness that night! Picking Mitchell's pocket at the very time!"

His wife said something about the ingratitude of that kind of people, and then they began to talk of something else.

Nineteen years! How easy that was to read! What a simple word for Judge Day to utter! Nineteen years! Half a lifetime!

Hugh Wolfe sat on the window-ledge of his cell, looking out. His ankles were ironed. Not usual in such cases; but he had made two desperate efforts to escape. "Well," as Haley, the jailer, said, "small blame to him! Nineteen years' imprisonment was not a pleasant thing to look forward to." Haley was very good-natured about it, though Wolfe had fought him savagely.

"When he was first caught," the jailer said afterwards, in telling the story, "before the trial, the fellow was cut down at once,—laid there on that pallet like a dead man, with his hands over his eyes. Never saw a man so cut down in my life. Time of the trial, too, came the queerest dodge of any customer I ever had.

---

[50]Christ and His church; one of the most popular hymns was "Rock of Ages" (1775) by Anglican Divine turned Calvinist, Augustus Montague Toplady (1740–48).
[51]Cheap, dangerous (often lethal) type of whiskey.

Would choose no lawyer. Judge gave him one, of course. Gibson it was. He tried to prove the fellow crazy; but it wouldn't go. Thing was plain as daylight: money found on him. 'Twas a hard sentence,— all the law allows; but it was for 'xample's sake. These mill-hands are gettin' onbearable. When the sentence was read, he just looked up, and said the money was his by rights, and that all the world had gone wrong. That night, after the trial, a gentleman came to see him here, name of Mitchell,— him as he stole from. Talked to him for an hour. Thought he came for curiosity, like. After he was gone, thought Wolfe was remarkable quiet, and went into his cell. Found him very low; bed all bloody. Doctor said he had been bleeding at the lungs. He was as weak as a cat; yet, if ye'll b'lieve me, he tried to get a-past me and get out. I just carried him like a baby, and threw him on the pallet. Three days after, he tried it again: that time reached the wall. Lord help you! he fought like a tiger,— giv' some terrible blows. Fightin' for life, you see; for he can't live long, shut up in the stone crib down yonder. Got a death-cough now. 'T took two of us to bring him down that day; so I just put the irons on his feet. There he sits, in there. Goin' to-morrow,[52] with a batch more of 'em. That woman, hunchback, tried with him,— you remember?— she's only got three years. 'Complice. But *she's* a woman, you know. He's been quiet ever since I put on irons: giv' up, I suppose. Looks white, sick-lookin'. It acts different on 'em, bein' sentenced. Most of 'em gets reckless, devilish-like. Some prays awful, and sings them vile songs of the mills, all in a breath. That woman, now, she's desper't'. Been beggin' to see Hugh, as she calls him, for three days. I'm a-goin' to let her in. She don't go with him. Here she is in this next cell. I'm a-goin' now to let her in."

He let her in. Wolfe did not see her. She crept into a corner of the cell, and stood watching him. He was scratching the iron bars of the window with a piece of tin which he had picked up, with an idle, uncertain, vacant stare, just as a child or idiot would do.

"Tryin' to get out, old boy?" laughed Haley. "Them irons will need a crowbar beside your tin, before you can open 'em."

Wolfe laughed, too, in a senseless way.

"I think I'll get out," he said.

"I believe his brain's touched," said Haley, when he came out.

The puddler scraped away with the tin for half an hour. Still Deborah did not speak. At last she ventured nearer, and touched his arm.

"Blood?" she said, looking at some spots on his coat with a shudder.

He looked up at her. "Why, Deb!" he said, smiling,— such a bright, boyish smile, that it went to poor Deborah's heart directly, and she sobbed and cried out loud.

"Oh, Hugh, lad! Hugh! dunnot look at me, when it wur my fault! To think I brought hur to it! And I loved hur so! Oh, lad, I dud!"

The confession, even in this wretch, came with the woman's blush through the sharp cry.

He did not seem to hear her,— scraping away diligently at the bars with the bit of tin.

Was he going mad? She peered closely into his face. Something she saw there made her draw suddenly back,— something which Haley had not seen, that lay beneath the pinched, vacant look it had caught since the trial, or the curious gray shadow that rested on it. That gray shadow,— yes, she knew what that meant. She had often seen it creeping over women's faces for months, who died at last of slow hunger or consumption. That meant death, distant, lingering: but this— Whatever it was the woman saw, or thought she saw, used as she was to crime and misery, seemed to make her sick with a new horror. Forgetting her fear of him, she caught his shoulders, and looked keenly, steadily, into his eyes.

---

[52]To the penitentiary.

"Hugh!" she cried, in a desperate whisper,—"oh, boy, not that! for God's sake, not *that!*"

The vacant laugh went off his face, and he answered her in a muttered word or two that drove her away. Yet the words were kindly enough. Sitting there on his pallet, she cried silently a hopeless sort of tears, but did not speak again. The man looked up furtively at her now and then. Whatever his own trouble was, her distress vexed him with a momentary sting.

It was market-day. The narrow window of the jail looked down directly on the carts and wagons drawn up in a long line, where they had unloaded. He could see, too, and hear distinctly the clink of money as it changed hands, the busy crowd of whites and blacks shoving, pushing one another, and the chaffering[53] and swearing at the stalls. Somehow, the sound, more than anything else had done, wakened him up,—made the whole real to him. He was done with the world and the business of it. He let the tin fall, and looked out, pressing his face close to the rusty bars. How they crowded and pushed! And he,—he should never walk that pavement again! There came Neff Sanders, one of the feeders at the mill, with a basket on his arm. Sure enough, Neff was married the other week. He whistled, hoping he would look up; but he did not. He wondered if Neff remembered he was there,—if any of the boys thought of him up there, and thought that he never was to go down that old cinder-road again. Never again! He had not quite understood it before; but now he did. Not for days or years, but never!— that was it.

How clear the light fell on that stall in front of the market! and how like a picture it was, the dark-green heaps of corn, and the crimson beets, and golden melons! There was another with game: how the light flickered on that pheasant's breast, with the purplish blood dripping over the brown feathers! He could see the red shining of the drops, it was so near. In one minute he could be down there. It was just a step. So easy, as it seemed, so natural to go! Yet it could never be—not in all the thousands of years to come—that he should put his foot on that street again! He thought of himself with a sorrowful pity, as of some one else. There was a dog down in the market, walking after his master with such a stately, grave look!—only a dog, yet he could go backwards and forwards just as he pleased: he had good luck! Why, the very vilest cur, yelping there in the gutter, had not lived his life, had been free to act out whatever thought God had put into his brain; while he—No, he would not think of that! He tried to put the thought away, and to listen to a dispute between a countryman and a woman about some meat; but it would come back. He, what had he done to bear this?

Then came the sudden picture of what might have been, and now. He knew what it was to be in the penitentiary,—how it went with men there. He knew how in these long years he should slowly die, but not until soul and body had become corrupt and rotten,—how, when he came out, if he lived to come, even the lowest of the mill-hands would jeer him,—how his hands would be weak, and his brain senseless and stupid. He believed he was almost that now. He put his hand to his head, with a puzzled, weary look. It ached, his head, with thinking. He tried to quiet himself. It was only right, perhaps; he had done wrong. But was there right or wrong for such as he? What was right? And who had ever taught him? He thrust the whole matter away. A dark, cold quiet crept through his brain. It was all wrong; but let it be! It was nothing to him more than the others. Let it be!

The door grated, as Haley opened it.

"Come, my woman! Must lock up for t' night. Come, stir yerself!"

She went up and took Hugh's hand.

---

[53]Bargaining.

"Good-night, Deb," he said, carelessly.

She had not hoped he would say more; but the tired pain on her mouth just then was bitterer than death. She took his passive hand and kissed it.

"Hur'll never see Deb again!" she ventured, her lips growing colder and more bloodless.

What did she say that for? Did he not know it? Yet he would not be impatient with poor old Deb. She had trouble of her own, as well as he.

"No, never again," he said, trying to be cheerful.

She stood just a moment, looking at him. Do you laugh at her, standing there, with her hunchback, her rags, her bleared, withered face, and the great despised love tugging at her heart?

"Come, you!" called Haley, impatiently.

She did not move.

"Hugh!" she whispered.

It was to be her last word. What was it?

"Hugh, boy, not THAT!"

He did not answer. She wrung her hands, trying to be silent, looking in his face in an agony of entreaty. He smiled again, kindly.

"It is best, Deb. I cannot bear to be hurted any more."

"Hur knows," she said, humbly.

"Tell my father good-bye; and—and kiss little Janey."

She nodded, saying nothing, looked in his face again, and went out of the door. As she went, she staggered.

"Drinkin' to-day?" broke out Haley, pushing her before him. "Where the Devil did you get it? Here, in with ye!" and he shoved her into her cell, next to Wolfe's, and shut the door.

Along the wall of her cell there was a crack low down by the floor, through which she could see the light from Wolfe's. She had discovered it days before. She hurried in now, and, kneeling down by it, listened, hoping to hear some sound. Nothing but the rasping of the tin on the bars. He was at his old amusement again. Something in the noise jarred on her ear, for she shivered as she heard it. Hugh rasped away at the bars. A dull old bit of tin, not fit to cut korl with.

He looked out of the window again. People were leaving the market now. A tall mulatto girl, following her mistress, her basket on her head, crossed the street just below, and looked up. She was laughing; but, when she caught sight of the haggard face peering out through the bars, suddenly grew grave, and hurried by. A free, firm step, a clear-cut olive face, with a scarlet turban tied on one side, dark, shining eyes, and on the head the basket poised, filled with fruit and flowers, under which the scarlet turban and bright eyes looked out half-shadowed. The picture caught his eye. It was good to see a face like that. He would try to-morrow, and cut one like it. *To-morrow!* He threw down the tin, trembling, and covered his face with his hands. When he looked up again, the daylight was gone.

Deborah, crouching near by on the other side of the wall, heard no noise. He sat on the side of the low pallet, thinking. Whatever was the mystery which the woman had seen on his face, it came out now slowly, in the dark there, and became fixed,—a something never seen on his face before. The evening was darkening fast. The market had been over for an hour; the rumbling of the carts over the pavement grew more infrequent: he listened to each, as it passed, because he thought it was to be for the last time. For the same reason, it was, I suppose, that he strained his eyes to catch a glimpse of each passer-by, wondering who they were, what kind of homes they were going to, if they had children,—listening eagerly to every chance word in the street, as if—(God be merciful to the man! what strange fancy was this?)—as if he never should hear human voices again.

It was quite dark at last. The street was a lonely one. The last passenger, he thought, was gone. No,—there was a quick step: Joe Hill, lighting the lamps. Joe was a good old chap; never passed a fellow without some joke or other. He remembered once seeing the place where he lived with his wife. "Granny Hill" the boys called her. Bedridden she was; but so kind as Joe was to her! kept the room so clean!—and the old woman, when he was there, was laughing at "some of t' lad's foolishness." The step was far down the street; but he could see him place the ladder, run up, and light the gas. A longing seized him to be spoken to once more.

"Joe!" he called, out of the grating. "Good-bye, Joe!"

The old man stopped a moment, listening uncertainly; then hurried on. The prisoner thrust his hand out of the window, and called again, louder; but Joe was too far down the street. It was a little thing; but it hurt him,—this disappointment.

"Good-bye, Joe!" he called, sorrowfully enough.

"Be quiet!" said one of the jailers, passing the door, striking on it with his club. Oh, that was the last, was it?

There was an inexpressible bitterness on his face, as he lay down on the bed, taking the bit of tin, which he had rasped to a tolerable degree of sharpness, in his hand,—to play with, it may be. He bared his arms, looking intently at their corded veins and sinews. Deborah, listening in the next cell, heard a slight clicking sound, often repeated. She shut her lips tightly, that she might not scream; the cold drops of sweat broke over her, in her dumb agony.

"Hur knows best," she muttered at last, fiercely clutching the boards where she lay.

If she could have seen Wolfe, there was nothing about him to frighten her. He lay quite still, his arms outstretched, looking at the pearly stream of moonlight coming into the window. I think in that one hour that came then he lived back over all the years that had gone before. I think that all the low, vile life, all his wrongs, all his starved hopes, came then, and stung him with a farewell poison that made him sick unto death. He made neither moan nor cry, only turned his worn face now and then to the pure light, that seemed so far off, as one that said, "How long, O Lord? how long?"[54]

The hour was over at last. The moon, passing over her nightly path, slowly came nearer, and threw the light across his bed on his feet. He watched it steadily, as it crept up, inch by inch, slowly. It seemed to him to carry with it a great silence. He had been so hot and tired there always in the mills! The years had been so fierce and cruel! There was coming now quiet and coolness and sleep. His tense limbs relaxed, and settled in a calm languor. The blood ran fainter and slow from his heart. He did not think now with a savage anger of what might be and was not; he was conscious only of deep stillness creeping over him. At first he saw a sea of faces: the mill-men,—women he had known, drunken and bloated,—Janeys timid and pitiful,—poor old Debs: then they floated together like a mist, and faded away, leaving only the clear, pearly moonlight.

Whether, as the pure light crept up the stretched-out figure, it brought with it calm and peace, who shall say? His dumb soul was alone with God in judgment. A Voice may have spoken for it from far-off Calvary, "Father, forgive them, for they know not what they do!"[55] Who dare say? Fainter and fainter the heart rose and fell, slower and slower the moon floated from behind a cloud, until, when at last its full tide of white splendor swept over the cell, it seemed to wrap and fold into a deeper stillness the dead figure that never should move again. Silence deeper than the Night! Nothing that moved, save the black, nauseous stream of blood dripping slowly from the pallet to the floor!

---

[54]Psalm 13:1–2: "How long wilt thou forget me, O Lord? for ever? how long wilt thou hide thy face from me? How long shall I take counsel in my soul, having sorrow in my heart daily? How long shall mine enemy be exalted over me?"

[55]The words of Jesus on the cross (Luke:23:34).

There was outcry and crowd enough in the cell the next day. The coroner and his jury, the local editors, Kirby himself, and boys with their hands thrust knowingly into their pockets and heads on one side, jammed into the corners. Coming and going all day. Only one woman. She came late, and outstayed them all. A Quaker, or Friend, as they call themselves. I think this woman was known by that name in heaven. A homely body, coarsely dressed in gray and white. Deborah (for Haley had let her in) took notice of her. She watched them all—sitting on the end of the pallet, holding his head in her arms—with the ferocity of a watch-dog, if any of them touched the body. There was no meekness, no sorrow, in her face; the stuff out of which murderers are made, instead. All the time Haley and the woman were laying straight the limbs and cleaning the cell, Deborah sat still, keenly watching the Quaker's face. Of all the crowd there that day, this woman alone had not spoken to her,—only once or twice had put some cordial to her lips. After they all were gone, the woman, in the same still, gentle way, brought a vase of wood-leaves and berries, and placed it by the pallet, then opened the narrow window. The fresh air blew in, and swept the woody fragrance over the dead face. Deborah looked up with a quick wonder.

"Did hur know my boy wud like it? Did hur know Hugh?"

"I know Hugh now."

The white fingers passed in a slow, pitiful way over the dead, worn face. There was a heavy shadow in the quiet eyes.

"Did hur know where they'll bury Hugh?" said Deborah in a shrill tone, catching her arm.

This had been the question hanging on her lips all day.

"In t' town-yard? Under t' mud and ash? T' lad 'll smother, woman! He wur born on t' lane moor, where t' air is frick[56] and strong. Take hur[57] out, for God's sake, take hur out where t' air blows!"

The Quaker hesitated, but only for a moment. She put her strong arm around Deborah and led her to the window.

"Thee sees the hills, friend, over the river? Thee sees how the light lies warm there, and the winds of God blow all the day? I live there,—where the blue smoke is, by the trees. Look at me." She turned Deborah's face to her own, clear and earnest. "Thee will believe me? I will take Hugh and bury him there to-morrow."

Deborah did not doubt her. As the evening wore on, she leaned against the iron bars, looking at the hills that rose far off, through the thick sodden clouds, like a bright, unattainable calm. As she looked, a shadow of their solemn repose fell on her face: its fierce discontent faded into a pitiful, humble quiet. Slow, solemn tears gathered in her eyes: the poor weak eyes turned so hopelessly to the place where Hugh was to rest, the grave heights looking higher and brighter and more solemn than ever before. The Quaker watched her keenly. She came to her at last, and touched her arm.

"When thee comes back," she said, in a low, sorrowful tone, like one who speaks from a strong heart deeply moved with remorse or pity, "thee shall begin thy life again,—there on the hills. I came too late; but not for thee,—by God's help, it may be."

Not too late. Three years after, the Quaker began her work. I end my story here. At evening-time it was light. There is no need to tire you with the long years of sunshine, and fresh air, and slow, patient Christ-love, needed to make healthy and hopeful this impure body and soul. There is a homely pine house, on one of these hills, whose windows overlook broad, wooded slopes and clover-crimsoned meadows,—niched into the very place where the light is warmest, the air freest. It

---

[56]Fresh; moor: extensive area of open uncultivated land of rock and peat covered with heather and coarse grasses.
[57]Him.

is the Friends' meeting-house. Once a week they sit there, in their grave, earnest way, waiting for the Spirit of Love to speak, opening their simple hearts to receive His words. There is a woman, old, deformed, who takes a humble place among them: waiting like them: in her gray dress, her worn face, pure and meek, turned now and then to the sky. A woman much loved by these silent, restful people; more silent than they, more humble, more loving. Waiting: with her eyes turned to hills higher and purer than these on which she lives,—dim and far off now, but to be reached some day. There may be in her heart some latent hope to meet there the love denied her here,—that she shall find him whom she lost, and that then she will not be all-unworthy. Who blames her? Something is lost in the passage of every soul from one eternity to the other,—something pure and beautiful, which might have been and was not: a hope, a talent, a love, over which the soul mourns, like Esau deprived of his birthright.[58] What blame to the meek Quaker, if she took her lost hope to make the hills of heaven more fair?

Nothing remains to tell that the poor Welsh puddler once lived, but this figure of the mill-woman cut in korl. I have it here in a corner of my library. I keep it hid behind a curtain,—it is such a rough, ungainly thing. Yet there are about it touches, grand sweeps of outline, that show a master's hand. Sometimes,—to-night, for instance,—the curtain is accidentally drawn back, and I see a bare arm stretched out imploringly in the darkness, and an eager, wolfish face watching mine: a wan, woful face, through which the spirit of the dead korl-cutter looks out, with its thwarted life, its mighty hunger, its unfinished work. Its pale, vague lips seem to tremble with a terrible question. "Is this the End?" they say,—"nothing beyond?—no more?"[59] Why, you tell me you have seen that look in the eyes of dumb brutes,—horses dying under the lash. I know.

The deep of the night is passing while I write. The gas-light wakens from the shadows here and there the objects which lie scattered through the room: only faintly, though; for they belong to the open sunlight. As I glance at them, they each recall some task or pleasure of the coming day. A half-moulded child's head; Aphrodite;[60] a bough of forest-leaves; music; work; homely fragments, in which lie the secrets of all eternal truth and beauty. Prophetic all! Only this dumb, woful face seems to belong to and end with the night. I turn to look at it. Has the power of its desperate need commanded the darkness away? While the room is yet steeped in heavy shadow, a cool, gray light suddenly touches its head like a blessing hand, and its groping arm points through the broken cloud to the far East, where, in the flickering, nebulous crimson, God has set the promise of the Dawn.

1861

---

[58]Esau, the oldest son of Isaac and Rebecca, was displaced by his younger twin brother Jacob (Genesis 25–27).

[59]The outstretched imploring arm and the terrible question ("Is this [life on earth] the end? . . . nothing beyond?—no more?) allude to Tennyson's *In Memoriam* again, to the passage immediately preceding the opening epigraph of this story. His friend dead, the bereaved poet "stretch[es] lame hands of faith, and grope[s]," trusting that there is life "beyond the grave" (55.18,2). Nature answers: "From scarpéd cliff and quarried stone/ . . . A thousand types are gone;

. . . I bring to life, I bring to death;/The spirit does but mean the breath:/I know no more" (56. 2, 3, 6–8). The poet persists: "Man, her last work," who "trusted God was love . . ./And love Creation's final law—/Though Nature, red in truth and claw/ . . . shrieked against" it, shall man "who loved/who suffered countless ills,/Who battled for the True, the Just,/Be blown about the desert dust,/Or sealed within the iron hills?/No more?" (56.9, 13–21).

[60]The goddess of love and beauty in Greek mythology; Venus in Roman.

LOUISA MAY ALCOTT
(1832–1888)

Bronson Alcott was a dreamy transcendentalist whose fate in literary history was to be identified as the father of a famous daughter, Louisa May Alcott, author of *Little Women.* One critic, Austin Warren, commented in 1956, "Bronson Alcott . . . does not deserve to reach posterity as the impractical parent of a story-teller for girls." Today's critic is likely to say, "On the contrary, Louisa May Alcott does not deserve to reach posterity as the daughter of the most impractical of the Transcendentalists." Since the 1950s, the Louisa May Alcott who wrote for adults has been rediscovered. Her life and her work have been cast in a new light with the renewed interest in the curious and instructive fate of women writers of the past. Whatever the characterization of father or daughter, the linking of their names seems inevitable in view of their intertwined lives and careers. By a strange quirk of fate, they died within two days of each other in 1888, as though there were an interdependency that death itself could not interrupt.

Louisa May was born in 1832, the second of four daughters, all of whom would become famous later as the originals for characters in Louisa May Alcott's *Little Women* (1868). But the road to that novel, which would save the Alcott family and delight and inspire successive generations of youths, was a long and torturous one, with many difficult detours and melancholy delays. Her education was largely informal, imparted by her father but with some instruction or guidance from Henry David Thoreau, Ralph Waldo Emerson, and other transcendentalists.

Alcott must have intuited early—as the family moved frequently and the father failed in successive enterprises—that life for her and her family would never be conventionally stable and secure. Certain it is that an unsettling awareness came to her at the tender age of eleven or twelve, when she witnessed her family caught up in the utopian experiment of Fruitlands.

Bronson Alcott's progressive school in Boston failed because of its frank conversations about pregnancy and its acceptance for admission of a young black girl. But in England, Alcott's ideas about education flourished, to the extent of the establishment of a school near London called "Alcott House." Ralph Waldo Emerson, sympathetic with Alcott after the collapse of his Boston school, financed a trip to England where he could meet his admirers. He went, and after a few months returned with a British partner, accompanied by his young son, bent on creating a community devoted to vegetarian principles, with no exploitation of animals: no meat, milk, eggs, cheese, butter, leather; no use of horses or manure.

Thus was Fruitlands established in 1843, attracting the peculiar, the eccentric, and the bizarre. The British partner, Charles Lane, whose money had acquired the property for Fruitlands, inspired Alcott with the virtues of celibacy and independence. There followed family discussion, in which the open and saintly Alcott posed the question of separation to his wife and children.

The experience was traumatic for the young Louisa May. She wrote in her diary for December 10th, 1843: "In the eve father and mother and Anna and I had a long talk. I was very unhappy, and we all cried. Anna and I cried in bed, and I prayed God to keep us all together." The older Louisa May, looking at this entry many years later, was moved to add a note, "Little Lu [her family name] began early to feel the family cares and peculiar trials. . . .She never forgot this experience, and her little cross began to grow heavier from this hour."

The cross was nothing less than the budding realization that she must become her mother's helper, her father's keeper—which is precisely what she became. At Fruitlands, her mother through hard work held things together for the short time the "experiment" lasted. The men went off on journeys holding "conversations," leaving the family and other participants to carry on the farm labor. The crops, erratically planted and tended, yielded little to eat.

After the failure of Fruitlands, Bronson Alcott fell into despondency for a time. Mrs. Alcott took charge, made decisions, earned money through sewing to keep the family afloat. And Louisa helped. She also began to write—poems, stories, sketches. She produced her first book at sixteen—*Flower Fables*, a series of fairy tales published in 1854. In scrambling to help the family finances, she worked at a variety of jobs—as a seamstress, servant, teacher, travelling companion. During the Civil War she worked as a nurse in Washington for a brief period, but returned home in ill health. Her *Hospital Sketches*, valuable glimpses of care for the wounded in the Civil War, appeared in 1863, and her first novel, *Moods*, said to be based in part on her early infatuation with Thoreau, was published in 1864. Beginning about this time she began publishing under pseudonyms a long series of thrillers and Gothic romances in the popular magazines, later collected as *Behind a Mask* (1975) and *Plots and Counterplots* (1976).

But the sensational success of *Little Women* in 1868 brought the security to herself and her family which she had longed for as a child. The book was a barely fictionalized account of the Alcott family, with a cheerful but hardworking mother, a father away as a chaplain in the Civil War, the four girls growing up with laughter, love, and tears, the latter especially on the death of Beth (based on the death of Elizabeth Alcott in 1858). The book had an enormous sale and was translated into many languages.

Alcott continued to write and publish books in large numbers, some of them sequels to *Little Women*—*Little Men* in 1871, *Jo's Boys* in 1886. She showed her concern for the plight of working women in *Work: A Story of Experience* (1873). And in "Transcendental Wild Oats," published first in a magazine in 1873 and collected in *Silver Pitchers and Independence* (1876), she ventured to treat the experiences at Fruitlands of over thirty years before. By this time she could see the comic dimension of the episode and could treat it satirically. It is one of her finest pieces of writing.

In effect, Louisa May Alcott sacrificed herself to her family. She never married. And after her mother's death in 1877, she drew closer to her father. Both were beset by a series of illnesses. Bronson Alcott died March 4, 1888. Two days later, Louisa May Alcott followed her father in death.

A generation that has grown up familiar with women's liberation (and one of its central texts by the British novelist Virginia Woolf, *A Room of One's Own*) might find food for thought in the following entry from Alcott's *Journal*:

> I never had a study. Any pen and paper do, and an old atlas on my knee is all I want. . . .
> Used to sit fourteen hours a day at one time, eating little, and unable to stir till a certain amount was done.
> Very few stories written in Concord [at home]; no inspiration in that dull place. Go to Boston, hire a quiet room and shut myself up in it.

A reader cannot but contemplate what Louisa May Alcott might have written had she had, at the critical moment in her life, a room of her own.

ADDITIONAL READING

Louisa May Alcott, Her Life, Letters, and Journals, ed. Ednah D. Cheney, 1900; *Transcendental Wild Oats and Excerpts from the Fruitlands Diary,* with an Introduction by William Henry Harrison, 1975; *The Selected Letters of Louisa May Alcott,* ed. Joel Myerson and Daniel Shealy, 1987; *A Double Life: Newly Discovered Thrillers of Louisa May Alcott,* ed. Madeleine B. Stern, 1988; *Alternative Alcott: Louisa May Alcott,* ed. Elaine Showalter, 1988.

Louise Chandler Moulton, "Louisa May Alcott," *Our Famous Women: An Authorized and Complete Record of the Lives and Deeds of Eminent Women of Our Times,* 1888; Cornelia Lynde Meigs, *The Story of the Author of Little Women: Invincible Louisa,* 1933; Katherine Susan Anthony, *Louisa May Alcott,* 1939; Madeleine B. Stern, *Louisa May Alcott,* 1950, rev. 1971; Marjorie Worthington, *Miss Alcott of Concord: A Biography,* 1958; Cornelia Lynde Meigs, *Louisa May Alcott and the American Family Story,* 1970; Martha Saxton, *Louisa May: A Modern Biography of Louisa May Alcott,* 1978; Nina Auerbach, *Communities of Women,* 1979; Alma J. Payne, *Louisa May Alcott, A Reference Guide,* 1980; Madelon Bedell, *The Alcotts: Biography of a Family,* 1980; Carolyn Heilbrun, "Louisa May Alcott: The Influence of *Little Women,*" in *Women, the Arts, and the 1920s in Paris and New York,* ed. Kenneth Wheeler and Virginia Lee Dussier, 1982; Ruth K. MacDonald, *Louisa May Alcott,* 1983; Madeleine B. Stern, ed., *Critical Essays on Louisa May Alcott,* 1984; Charles Strickland, *Victorian Domesticity: Families in the Life and Art of Louisa May Alcott,* 1985.

TEXT

Bronson Alcott's Fruitlands, with Transcendental Wild Oats, compiled by Clara Endicott Sears, 1915.

Transcendental Wild Oats

A CHAPTER FROM AN UNWRITTEN ROMANCE[1]

On the first day of June, 184–, a large wagon, drawn by a small horse and containing a motley load, went lumbering over certain New England hills, with the pleasing accompaniments of wind, rain, and hail. A serene man[2] with a serene child upon his knee was driving, or rather being driven, for the small horse had it all his own way. A brown boy with a William Penn style of countenance[3] sat beside him, firmly embracing a bust of Socrates. Behind them was an energetic-looking woman,[4] with a benevolent brow, satirical mouth, and eyes brimful of hope and courage. A baby[5] reposed upon her lap, a mirror leaned against her knee, and a

---

[1] Wild oats: youthful indiscretions. This piece was published in the *Independent,* December 18, 1873, thirty years after the failure of Fruitlands, the experiment in utopian living founded by her father Bronson Alcott (1799–1888). He later said that in this satiric account of the venture, "Louisa has given the comic side . . .; but Mrs. Alcott could give you the tragic side." The mystical Alcott, called the most transcendental of the transcendentalists, advocated a radical, progressive "infant education," which finally scandalized Boston—forcing the closing of his Temple School—but which won support in England. There, in May of 1842, he visited a community/school renamed Alcott House and returned in October with the English transcendentalist Charles Lane and his son William Lane to establish an ideal community in New England. Lane bought a farmhouse and land in Harvard, Massachusetts, about fifteen miles northwest of Concord, and on June 1, 1843, the members

of the "consociate family" (united in spirit rather than blood) set out from Concord to the "New Eden."
[2] Abel Lamb (Bronson Alcott). Since the four Alcott children are depicted below, the "serene child" is imaginary, an allusion to Alcott's educational theories, found in his *The Record of a School, Exemplifying the General Principles of Spiritual Culture* (1835) and *Conversations with Children on the Gospels* (1836, 1837). With Jesus and Socrates as models, Alcott created a pleasing environment, avoided punishment, and used the dialogue method, believing that children were innately good and in possession of knowledge which needed only to be drawn out.
[3] The young William Lane, looking sober and pious like the Quaker William Penn.
[4] Sister Hope Lamb (Mrs. Abigail Alcott).
[5] May Alcott.

basket of provisions danced about at her feet, as she struggled with a large, unruly umbrella. Two blue-eyed little girls,[6] with hands full of childish treasures, sat under one old shawl, chatting happily together.

In front of this lively party stalked a tall, sharp-featured man,[7] in a long blue cloak; and a fourth small girl[8] trudged along beside him through the mud as if she rather enjoyed it.

The wind whistled over the bleak hills; the rain fell in a despondent drizzle, and twilight began to fall. But the calm man gazed as tranquilly into the fog as if he beheld a radiant bow of promise spanning the gray sky.[9] The cheery woman tried to cover every one but herself with the big umbrella. The brown boy pillowed his head on the bald pate of Socrates and slumbered peacefully. The little girls sang lullabies to their dolls in soft, maternal murmurs. The sharp-nosed pedestrian marched steadily on, with the blue cloak streaming out behind him like a banner; and the lively infant splashed through the puddles with a duck-like satisfaction pleasant to behold.

Thus these modern pilgrims journeyed hopefully out of the old world, to found a new one in the wilderness.

The editors of *The Transcendental Tripod* had received from Messrs. Lion & Lamb (two of the aforesaid pilgrims) a communication from which the following statement is an extract:[10]

"We have made arrangements with the proprietor of an estate of about a hundred acres which liberates this tract from human ownership. Here we shall prosecute our effort to initiate a Family in harmony with the primitive instincts of man.

"Ordinary secular farming is not our object. Fruit, grain, pulse,[11] herbs, flax, and other vegetable products, receiving assiduous attention, will afford ample manual occupation, and chaste supplies for the bodily needs. It is intended to adorn the pastures with orchards, and to supersede the labor of cattle by the spade and the pruning-knife.

"Consecrated to human freedom, the land awaits the sober culture of devoted men. Beginning with small pecuniary means, this enterprise must be rooted in a reliance on the succors[12] of an ever-bounteous Providence, whose vital affinities being secured by this union with uncorrupted field and unworldly persons, the cares and injuries of a life of gain are avoided.

"The inner nature of each member of the Family is at no time neglected. Our plan contemplates all such disciplines, cultures, and habits as evidently conduce to the purifying of the inmates.

"Pledged to the spirit alone, the founders anticipate no hasty or numerous addition to their numbers. The kingdom of peace is entered only through the gates of self-denial; and felicity is the test and the reward of loyalty to the unswerving law of Love."

This prospective Eden at present consisted of an old red farm-house, a dilapidated barn, many acres of meadow-land, and a grove. Ten ancient apple-trees were all the "chaste supply" which the place offered as yet; but, in the firm belief that plenteous orchards were soon to be evoked from their inner consciousness, these sanguine founders had christened their domain Fruitlands.

Here Timon Lion intended to found a colony of Latter Day Saints,[13] who, un-

---

[6]Anna, age twelve, and Elizabeth Alcott, age eight.
[7]Timon Lion (Charles Lane).
[8]Louisa May Alcott, age ten.
[9]The rainbow, sign of God's covenant promise to Noah not to destroy the earth by flood again (Genesis 9:12–13).
[10]The letter, dated June 10, 1843, Fruitlands, from Lane and Alcott, appeared in the July 1843 *Dial,* the chief periodical of the transcendentalists. Alcott calls it the *Transcendental Tripod,* alluding to the tripod on which the Delphic

oracle sat as she uttered the words of Apollo. Bronson Alcott had contributed to the first two issues of the *Dial* (July and October 1840) his "Orphic Sayings," imitations of the oracular sayings of the Greek philosopher Pythagoras (sixth century B.C.), whose school at Crotona, Italy, served as a model for Fruitlands.
[11]Edible seeds from peas and beans.
[12]Help.
[13]I.e., a modern spiritual community, not Mormon.

der his patriarchal sway, should regenerate the world and glorify his name for ever. Here Abel Lamb, with the devoutest faith in the high ideal which was to him a living truth, desired to plant a Paradise, where Beauty, Virtue, Justice, and Love might live happily together, without the possibility of a serpent entering in. And here his wife, unconverted but faithful to the end, hoped, after many wanderings over the face of the earth, to find rest for herself and a home for her children.

"There is our new abode," announced the enthusiast, smiling with a satisfaction quite undamped by the drops dripping from his hat-brim, as they turned at length into a cart-path that wound along a steep hillside into a barren-looking valley.

"A little difficult of access," observed his practical wife, as she endeavored to keep her various household gods from going overboard with every lurch of the laden ark.

"Like all good things. But those who earnestly desire and patiently seek will soon find us," placidly responded the philosopher from the mud, through which he was now endeavoring to pilot the much-enduring horse.

"Truth lies at the bottom of a well,[14] Sister Hope," said Brother Timon, pausing to detach his small comrade from a gate, whereon she was perched for a clearer gaze into futurity.

"That's the reason we so seldom get at it, I suppose," replied Mrs. Hope, making a vain clutch at the mirror, which a sudden jolt sent flying out of her hands.

"We want no false reflections here," said Timon, with a grim smile, as he crunched the fragments under foot in his onward march.

Sister Hope held her peace, and looked wistfully through the mist at her promised home. The old red house with a hospitable glimmer at its windows cheered her eyes; and, considering the weather, was a fitter refuge than the sylvan bowers some of the more ardent souls might have preferred.

The newcomers were welcomed by one of the elect precious—a regenerate farmer,[15] whose idea of reform consisted chiefly in wearing white cotten raiment and shoes of untanned leather. This costume, with a snowy beard, gave him a venerable, and at the same time a somewhat bridal appearance.

The goods and chattels of the Society not having arrived, the weary family reposed before the fire on blocks of wood, while Brother Moses White regaled them with roasted potatoes, brown bread and water, in two plates, a tin pan, and one mug—his table service being limited. But, having cast the forms and vanities of a depraved world behind them, the elders welcomed hardship with the enthusiasm of new pioneers, and the children heartily enjoyed this foretaste of what they believed was to be a sort of perpetual picnic.

During the progress of this frugal meal, two more brothers appeared. One a dark, melancholy man, clad in homespun, whose peculiar mission was to turn his name hind part before and use as few words as possible.[16] The other was a bland, bearded Englishman, who expected to be saved by eating uncooked food and going without clothes.[17] He had not yet adopted the primitive costume, however; but contented himself with meditatively chewing dry beans out of a basket.

"Every meal should be a sacrament, and the vessels used beautiful and symbolical," observed Brother Lamb, mildly, righting the tin pan slipping about on his

---

[14]"Of truth we know nothing, for truth is in a well," Democritus, Greek philosopher of the fifth century B.C. (Diogenes Laertius, *Pyrrho*, Bk. IX, sec. 72).
[15]Moses White (Joseph Palmer of No Town, Massachusetts, was persecuted for wearing a beard, then considered unchristian. He had just spent a year in jail for refusing to pay a fine incurred defending himself).

[16]Alcott conflates two people here. The melancholy man was Forest Absalom (the real-life Abraham Everett, once put in an insane asylum by his family). Abram Wood was the man who called himself Wood Abram.
[17]John Pease (the Englishman Samuel Bower, nudist. Another Fruitlands member, Samuel Larned, lived one year on crackers and another year on apples).

knees. "I priced a silver service when in town, but it was too costly; so I got some graceful cups and vases of Britannia ware."[18]

"Hardest things in the world to keep bright. Will whiting[19] be allowed in the community?" inquired Sister Hope, with a housewife's interest in labor-saving institutions.

"Such trivial questions will be discussed at a more fitting time," answered Brother Timon, sharply, as he burnt his fingers with a very hot potato. "Neither sugar, molasses, milk, butter, cheese, nor flesh are to be used among us, for nothing is to be admitted which has caused wrong or death to man or beast."

"Our garments are to be linen till we learn to raise our own cotton or some substitute for woollen fabrics," added Brother Abel, blissfully basking in an imaginary future as warm and brilliant as the generous fire before him.

"Haou abaout shoes?" asked Brother Moses, surveying his own with interest.

"We must yield that point till we can manufacture an innocent substitute for leather. Bark, wood, or some durable fabric will be invented in time. Meanwhile, those who desire to carry out our idea to the fullest extent can go barefooted," said Lion, who liked extreme measures.

"I never will, nor let my girls," murmured rebellious Sister Hope, under her breath.

"Haou do you cattle'ate[20] to treat the ten-acre lot? Ef things ain't 'tended to right smart, we shan't hev no crops," observed the practical patriarch in cotton.

"We shall spade it," replied Abel, in such perfect good faith that Moses said no more, though he indulged in a shake of the head as he glanced at hands that had held nothing heavier than a pen for years. He was a paternal old soul and regarded the younger men as promising boys on a new sort of lark.

"What shall we do for lamps, if we cannot use any animal substance? I do hope light of some sort is to be thrown upon the enterprise," said Mrs. Lamb, with anxiety, for in those days kerosene and camphene were not, and gas unknown in the wilderness.[21]

"We shall go without till we have discovered some vegetable oil or wax to serve us," replied Brother Timon, in a decided tone, which caused Sister Hope to resolve that her private lamp should be always trimmed, if not burning.

"Each member is to perform the work for which experience, strength, and taste best fit him," continued Dictator Lion. "Thus drudgery and disorder will be avoided and harmony prevail. We shall arise at dawn, begin the day by bathing, followed by music, and then a chaste repast of fruit and bread. Each one finds congenial occupation till the meridian[22] meal; when some deep-searching conversation gives rest to the body and development to the mind. Healthful labor again engages us till the last meal, when we assemble in social communion, prolonged till sunset, when we retire to sweet repose, ready for the next day's activity."

"What part of the work do you incline to yourself?" asked Sister Hope, with a humorous glimmer in her keen eyes.

"I shall wait till it is made clear to me. Being in preference to doing is the great aim,[23] and this comes to us rather by a resigned willingness than a willful activity, which is a check to all divine growth," responded Brother Timon.

"I thought so." And Mrs. Lamb sighed audibly, for during the year he had spent in her family Brother Timon had so faithfully carried out his idea of "being, not doing," that she had found his "divine growth" both an expensive and unsatisfactory process.

---

[18]White alloy of tin resembling silver.
[19]Finely powdered chalk used to polish silver or to whiten.
[20]Calculate.
[21]Without these non-animal fuels, lamps would be lit by means of whale oil or candles made with animal tallow.

[22]Noon.
[23]Lane, with others in England had written of their master, educator James P. Greaves, and his "peculiar practical doctrine," "the eminent superiority of Being to all knowing and doing."

Here her husband struck into the conversation, his face shining with the light and joy of the splendid dreams and high ideals hovering before him.

"In these steps of reform, we do not rely so much on scientific reasoning or physiological skill as on the spirit's dictates. The greater part of man's duty consists in leaving alone much that he now does. Shall I stimulate with tea, coffee, or wine? No. Shall I consume flesh? Not if I value health. Shall I subjugate cattle? Shall I claim property in any created thing? Shall I trade? Shall I adopt a form of religion? Shall I interest myself in politics? To how many of these questions— could we ask them deeply enough and could they be heard as having relation to our eternal welfare—would the response be 'Abstain'?"[24]

A mild snore seemed to echo the last word of Abel's rhapsody, for Brother Moses had succumbed to mundane slumber and sat nodding like a massive ghost. Forest Absalom, the silent man, and John Pease, the English member, now departed to the barn; and Mrs. Lamb led her flock to a temporary fold, leaving the founders of the "Consociate Family" to build castles in the air till the fire went out and the symposium ended in smoke.

The furniture arrived next day, and was soon bestowed; for the principal property of the community consisted in books.[25] To this rare library was devoted the best room in the house, and the few busts and pictures that still survived many flittings were added to beautify the sanctuary, for here the family was to meet for amusement, instruction, and worship.

Any housewife can imagine the emotions of Sister Hope, when she took possession of a large, dilapidated kitchen, containing an old stove and the peculiar stores out of which food was to be evolved for her little family of eleven. Cakes of maple sugar, dried peas and beans, barley and hominy, meal of all sorts, potatoes, and dried fruit. No milk, butter, cheese, tea, or meat, appeared. Even salt was considered a useless luxury and spice entirely forbidden by these lovers of Spartan simplicity. A ten years' experience of vegetarian vagaries[26] had been good training for this new freak, and her sense of the ludicrous supported her through many trying scenes.

Unleavened bread, porridge, and water for breakfast; bread, vegetables, and water for dinner; bread, fruit, and water for supper was the bill of fare ordained by the elders. No teapot profaned that sacred stove, no gory steak cried aloud for vengeance from her chaste gridiron; and only a brave woman's taste, time, and temper were sacrificed on that domestic altar.

The vexed question of light was settled by buying a quantity of bayberry wax for candles; and, on discovering that no one knew how to make them, pine knots were introduced, to be used when absolutely necessary. Being summer, the evenings were not long, and the weary fraternity found it no great hardship to retire with the birds. The inner light[27] was sufficient for most of them. But Mrs. Lamb rebelled. Evening was the only time she had to herself, and while the tired feet rested the skilful hands mended torn frocks and little stockings, or anxious heart forgot its burden in a book.

So "mother's lamp" burned steadily, while the philosophers built a new heaven and earth by moonlight; and through all the metaphysical mists and philanthropic pyrotechnics of that period Sister Hope played her own little game of "throwing light," and none but the moths were the worse for it.

Such farming probably was never seen before since Adam delved. The band of

---

[24]Taken from a letter written by Lane and Alcott and published in the *Herald of Freedom*, September 8, 1843.
[25]The Fruitlands library, composed of books brought from England, was described by Emerson as "a cabalistic [occult] collection" of "rare & valuable mystical" titles. A "catalogue" of the books appeared in the April 1843 *Dial*.

[26]Bronson had long ago given up animal food, and in 1836, the family adopted the vegetarian diet of the reformer Sylvester Graham (1794–1851), for whom the cracker was named.
[27]The divine light within.

brothers began by spading garden and field; but a few days of it lessened their ardor amazingly. Blistered hands and aching backs suggested the expediency of permitting the use of cattle till the workers were better fitted for noble toil by a summer of the new life.

Brother Moses brought a yoke of oxen from his farm—at least, the philosophers thought so till it was discovered that one of the animals was a cow; and Moses confessed that he "must be let down easy, for he couldn't live on garden sarse[28] entirely."

Great was Dictator Lion's indignation at this lapse from virtue. But time pressed, the work must be done; so the meek cow was permitted to wear the yoke and the recreant[29] brother continued to enjoy forbidden draughts in the barn, which dark proceeding caused the children to regard him as one set apart for destruction.

The sowing was equally peculiar, for, owing to some mistake, the three brethren, who devoted themselves to this graceful task, found when about half through the job that each had been sowing a different sort of grain in the same field; a mistake which caused much perplexity, as it could not be remedied; but, after a long consultation and a good deal of laughter, it was decided to say nothing and see what would come of it.

The garden was planted with a generous supply of useful roots and herbs; but, as manure was not allowed to profane the virgin soil, few of these vegetable treasures ever came up. Purslane[30] reigned supreme, and the disappointed planters ate it philosophically, deciding that Nature knew what was best for them, and would generously supply their needs, if they could only learn to digest her "sallets" and wild roots.

The orchard was laid out, a little grafting done, new trees and vines set, regardless of the unfit season and entire ignorance of the husbandmen, who honestly believed that in the autumn they would reap a bounteous harvest.

Slowly things got into order, and rapidly rumors of the new experiment went abroad, causing many strange spirits to flock thither, for in those days communities were the fashion[31] and transcendentalism raged wildly. Some came to look on and laugh, some to be supported in poetic idleness, a few to believe sincerely and work heartily. Each member was allowed to mount his favorite hobby and ride it to his heart's content. Very queer were some of the riders, and very rampant some of the hobbies.

One youth, believing that language was of little consequence if the spirit was only right, startled newcomers by blandly greeting them with "good morning, damn you,"[32] and other remarks of an equally mixed order. A second irrepressible being held that all the emotions of the soul should be freely expressed, and illustrated his theory by antics that would have sent him to a lunatic asylum, if, as an unregenerate wag said, he had not already been in one. When his spirit soared, he climbed trees and shouted; when doubt assailed him, he lay upon the floor and groaned lamentably. At joyful periods, he raced, leaped, and sang; when sad, he wept aloud; and when a great thought burst upon him in the watches of the night, he crowed like a jocund cockerel, to the great delight of the children and the great annoyance of the elders. One musical brother fiddled whenever so moved, sang

---

[28]Sarsaparilla, a drink flavored with the dried roots of the sarsaparilla plant. He secretly milked the cow.
[29]Unfaithful.
[30]Trailing weed with fleshy leaves sometimes used in salads ("sallets").
[31]Among them were John Humphrey Noyes's Bible Communists at Putney, Vermont (1836–46), and his Oneida Community, central New York (1848–79); Adin Ballou's

Hopedale, Milford, Massachusetts (1842–56); Albert Brisbane's North American Phalanx, Red Bank, New Jersey (1843–54); Robert Owens's New Harmony, Indiana (1825–28); and one of the most famous, George Ripley's Brook Farm, West Roxbury, Massachusetts (1841–47).
[32]In its first periodical publication, the sentence was changed by the editors to "greeting them with 'Good-morning,' appending an anathema.'"

sentimentally to the four little girls, and put a music-box on the wall when he hoed corn.

Brother Pease ground away at his uncooked food, or browsed over the farm on sorrel, mint, green fruit, and new vegetables. Occasionally he took his walks abroad, airily attired in an unbleached cotton *poncho,* which was the nearest approach to the primeval costume he was allowed to indulge in. At midsummer he retired to the wilderness, to try his plan where the woodchucks were without prejudices and huckleberry bushes were hospitably full. A sunstroke unfortunately spoilt his plan, and he returned to semi-civilization a sadder and wiser man.

Forest Absalom preserved his Pythagorean silence,[33] cultivated his fine dark locks, and worked like a beaver, setting an excellent example of brotherly love, justice, and fidelity by his upright life. He it was who helped overworked Sister Hope with her heavy washes, kneaded the endless succession of batches of bread, watched over the children, and did the many tasks left undone by the brethren, who were so busy discussing and defining great duties that they forgot to perform the small ones.

Moses White placidly plodded about, "chorin' raound," as he called it, looking like an old-time patriarch, with his silver hair and flowing beard, and saving the community from many a mishap by his thrift and Yankee shrewdness.

Brother Lion domineered over the whole concern; for, having put the most money into the speculation, he was resolved to make it pay—as if anything founded on an ideal basis could be expected to do so by any but enthusiasts.

Abel Lamb simply revelled in the Newness,[34] firmly believing that his dream was to be beautifully realized and in time not only little Fruitlands, but the whole earth, be turned into a Happy Valley.[35] He worked with every muscle of his body, for *he* was in deadly earnest. He taught with his whole head and heart; planned and sacrificed, preached and prophesied, with a soul full of the purest aspirations, most unselfish purposes, and desires for a life devoted to God and man, too high and tender to bear the rough usage of this world.

It was a little remarkable that only one woman ever joined this community. Mrs. Lamb merely followed wheresoever her husband led—"as ballast[36] for his balloon," as she said, in her bright way.

Miss Jane Gage[37] was a stout lady of mature years, sentimental, amiable, and lazy. She wrote verses copiously, and had vague yearnings and graspings after the unknown, which led her to believe herself fitted for a higher sphere than any she had yet adorned.

Having been a teacher, she was set to instructing the children in the common branches. Each adult member took a turn at the infants; and, as each taught in his own way, the result was a chronic state of chaos in the minds of these much-afflicted innocents.

Sleep, food, and poetic musings were the desires of dear Jane's life, and she shirked all duties as clogs upon her spirit's wings. Any thought of lending a hand with the domestic drudgery never occurred to her; and when to the question, "Are there any beasts of burden on the place?" Mrs. Lamb answered, with a face that told its own tale, "Only one woman!" the buxom Jane took no shame to herself, but laughed at the joke, and let the stout-hearted sister tug on alone.

Unfortunately, the poor lady hankered after the fleshpots,[38] and endeavored

---

[33]Vows of silence were part of the Pythagorean regime.
[34]Term used by some to refer to transcendentalism.
[35]Home of the Prince of Abyssinia in English writer Samuel Johnson's *Rasselas* (1759), an isolated Garden of Peace and luxury, which is so monotonous that Prince Rasselas and the philosopher Imlac are happy to escape.
[36]Stabilizer.
[37]Anne Page, of Providence, arrived in August.
[38]Pots in which meat is cooked (Exodus 16:3).

to stay herself with private sips of milk, crackers, and cheese, and on one dire occasion she partook of fish at a neighbor's table.

One of the children reported this sad lapse from virtue, and poor Jane was publicly reprimanded by Timon.

"I only took a little bit of the tail," sobbed the penitent poetess.

"Yes, but the whole fish had to be tortured and slain that you might tempt your carnal appetite with that one taste of the tail. Know ye not, consumers of flesh meat, that ye are nourishing the wolf and tiger in your bosoms?"[39]

At this awful question and the peal of laughter which arose from some of the younger brethren, tickled by the ludicrous contrast between the stout sinner, the stern judge, and the naughty satisfaction of the young detective, poor Jane fled from the room to pack her trunk and return to a world where fishes' tails were not forbidden fruit.

Transcendental wild oats were sown broadcast that year, and the fame thereof has not yet ceased in the land; for, futile as this crop seemed to outsiders, it bore an invisible harvest, worth much to those who planted in earnest. As none of the members of this particular community have ever recounted their experiences before, a few of them may not be amiss, since the interest in these attempts has never died out and Fuitlands was the most ideal of all these castles in Spain.

A new dress was invented, since cotton, silk, and wool were forbidden as the product of slave-labor, worm-slaughter, and sheep-robbery. Tunics and trowsers of brown linen were the only wear. The women's skirts were longer, and their straw hat-brims wider than the men's, and this was the only difference. Some persecution lent a charm to the costume, and the long-haired, linen-clad reformers quite enjoyed the mild martyrdom they endured when they left home.

Money was abjured, as the root of all evil.[40] The produce of the land was to supply most of their wants, or be exchanged for the few things they could not grow. This idea had its inconveniences; but self-denial was the fashion, and it was surprising how many things one can do without. When they desired to travel, they walked, if possible, begged the loan of a vehicle, or boldly entered car or coach, and, stating their principles to the officials, took the consequences. Usually their dress, their earnest frankness, and gentle resolution won them a passage; but now and then they met with hard usage, and had the satisfaction of suffering for their principles.

On one of these penniless pilgrimages they took passage on a boat, and, when fare was demanded, artlessly offered to talk, instead of pay. As the boat was well under way and they actually had not a cent, there was no help for it. So Brothers Lion and Lamb held forth to the assembled passengers in their most eloquent style. There must have been something effective in this conversation, for the listeners were moved to take up a contribution for these inspired lunatics, who preached peace on earth and goodwill to man so earnestly, with empty pockets. A goodly sum was collected; but when the captain presented it the reformers proved that they were consistent even in their madness, for not a penny would they accept, saying, with a look at the group about them, whose indifference or contempt had changed to interest and respect, "You see how well we get on without money;" and so went serenely on their way, with their linen blouses flapping airily in the cold October wind.

They preached vegetarianism everywhere and resisted all temptations of the flesh, contentedly eating apples and bread at well-spread tables, and much afflicting hospitable hostesses by denouncing their food and taking away their appetites,

---

[39]They believed that you are what you eat, that if you eat an animal, you become one. In her Fruitlands diary for November 2, Louisa wrote: "Without flesh diet/there could be no/blood-shedding war" and "Pluck your body/from the orchard;/do not snatch it/from the shamble [meat market]."
[40]1 Timothy 6:10.

discussing the "horrors of shambles,"[41] the "incorporation of the brute in man," and "on elegant abstinence the sign of a pure soul." But, when the perplexed or offended ladies asked what they should eat, they got in reply a bill of fare consisting of "bowls of sunrise for breakfast," "solar seeds of the sphere," "dishes from Plutarch's[42] chaste table," and other viands equally hard to find in any modern market.

Reform conventions of all sorts were haunted by these brethren, who said many wise things and did many foolish ones. Unfortunately, these wanderings interfered with their harvest at home; but the rule was to do what the spirit moved, so they left their crops to Providence and went a-reaping in wider and, let us hope, more fruitful fields than their own.

Luckily, the earthly providence who watched over Abel Lamb was at hand to glean the scanty crop yielded by the "uncorrupted land," which, "consecrated to human freedom," had received "the sober culture of devout men."

About the time the grain was ready to house, some call of the Oversoul[43] wafted all the men away. An easterly storm was coming up and the yellow stacks were sure to be ruined. Then Sister Hope gathered her forces. Three little girls, one boy (Timon's son), and herself, harnessed to clothes-baskets and Russia-linen[44] sheets, were the only teams she could command; but with these poor appliances the indomitable woman got in the grain and saved food for her young, with the instinct and energy of a mother-bird with a brood of hungry nestlings to feed.

This attempt at regeneration had its tragic as well as comic side, though the world only saw the former.

With the first frosts, the butterflies, who had sunned themselves in the new light through the summer, took flight, leaving the few bees to see what honey they had stored for winter use. Precious little appeared beyond the satisfaction of a few months of holy living.

At first it seemed as if a chance to try holy dying also was to be offered them. Timon, much disgusted with the failure of the scheme, decided to retire to the Shakers,[45] who seemed to be the only successful community going.

"What is to become of us?" asked Mrs. Hope, for Abel was heartbroken at the bursting of his lovely bubble.

"You can stay here, if you like, till a tenant is found. No more wood must be cut, however, and no more corn ground. All I have must be sold to pay the debts of the concern, as the responsibility is mine," was the cheering reply.

"Who is to pay us for what we have lost? I gave all I had—furniture, time, strength, six months of my children's lives—and all are wasted. Abel gave himself body and soul, and is almost wrecked by hard work and disappointment. Are we to have no return for this, but leave to starve and freeze in an old house, with winter at hand, no money, and hardly a friend left, for this wild scheme has alienated nearly all we had. You talk much about justice. Let us have a little, since there is nothing else left."

But the woman's appeal met with no reply but the old one: "It was an experiment. We all risked something, and must bear our losses as we can."

With this cold comfort, Timon departed with his son, and was absorbed into the Shaker brotherhood,[46] where he soon found that the order of things was reversed, and it was all work and no play.

---

[41]The meat market, or slaughterhouse.
[42]Greek moral philosopher of the first century, whose *Morals* and *Lives* were in the Fruitlands library.
[43]The spiritual force in the universe, transcending the individual, in which all souls participate.
[44]Russian duck: a strong linen cloth.

[45]"The United Society of Believer's in Christ's Second Appearing," called Shakers because of their contortions during religious services. A settlement of this celibate sect was nearby.
[46]Lane and his son left Fruitlands on January 6, 1844.

Then the tragedy began for the forsaken little family. Desolation and despair fell upon Abel. As his wife said, his new beliefs had alienated many friends. Some thought him mad, some unprincipled. Even the most kindly thought him a visionary, whom it was useless to help till he took more practical views of life. All stood aloof, saying: "Let him work out his own ideas, and see what they are worth."

He had tried, but it was a failure. The world was not ready for Utopia yet, and those who attempted to found it only got laughed at for their pains. In other days, men could sell all and give to the poor, lead lives devoted to holiness and high thought, and, after the persecution was over, find themselves honored as saints or martyrs. But in modern times these things are out of fashion. To live for one's principles, at all costs, is a dangerous speculation; and the failure of an ideal, no matter how humane and noble, is harder for the world to forgive and forget than bank robbery or the grand swindles of corrupt politicians.

Deep waters now for Abel, and for a time there seemed no passage through. Strength and spirits were exhausted by hard work and too much thought. Courage failed when, looking about for help, he saw no sympathizing face, no hand outstretched to help him, no voice to say cheerily:

"We all make mistakes, and it takes many experiences to shape a life. Try again, and let us help you."

Every door was closed, every eye averted, every heart cold, and no way open whereby he might earn bread for his children. His principles would not permit him to do many things that others did; and in the few fields where conscience would allow him to work, who would employ a man who had flown in the face of society, as he had done?

Then this dreamer, whose dream was the life of his life, resolved to carry out his idea to the bitter end. There seemed no place for him here—no work, no friend. To go begging conditions was as ignoble as to go begging money. Better perish of want than sell one's soul for the sustenance of his body. Silently he lay down upon his bed, turned his face to the wall, and waited with pathetic patience for death to cut the knot which he could not untie. Days and nights went by, and neither food nor water passed his lips. Soul and body were dumbly struggling together, and no word of complaint betrayed what either suffered.

His wife, when tears and prayers were unavailing, sat down to wait the end with a mysterious awe and submission; for in this entire resignation of all things there was an eloquent significance to her who knew him as no other human being did.

"Leave all to God," was his belief; and in this crisis the loving soul clung to this faith, sure that the All-wise Father would not desert this child who tried to live so near to Him. Gathering her children about her, she waited the issue of the tragedy that was being enacted in that solitary room, while the first snow fell outside, untrodden by the footprints of a single friend.

But the strong angels who sustain and teach perplexed and troubled souls came and went, leaving no trace without, but working miracles within. For, when all other sentiments had faded into dimness, all other hopes died utterly; when the bitterness of death was nearly over, when body was past any pang of hunger or thirst, and soul stood ready to depart, the love that outlives all else refused to die. Head had bowed to defeat, hand had grown weary with too heavy tasks, but heart could not grow cold to those who lived in its tender depths, even when death touched it.

"My faithful wife, my little girls—they have not forsaken me, they are mine by ties that none can break. What right have I to leave them alone? What right to escape from the burden and the sorrow I have helped to bring? This duty remains to me, and I must do it manfully. For their sakes, the world will forgive me in time; for their sakes, God will sustain me now."

Too feeble to rise, Abel groped for the food that always lay within his reach, and in the darkness and solitude of that memorable night ate and drank what was to him the bread and wine of a new communion, a new dedication of heart and life to the duties that were left him when the dreams fled.

In the early dawn, when that sad wife crept fearfully to see what change had come to the patient face on the pillow, she found it smiling at her, saw a wasted hand outstretched to her, and heard a feeble voice cry bravely, "Hope!"

What passed in that little room is not to be recorded except in the hearts of those who suffered and endured much for love's sake. Enough for us to know that soon the wan shadow of a man came forth, leaning on the arm that never failed him, to be welcomed and cherished by the children, who never forgot the experiences of that time.

"Hope" was the watchword now; and, while the last logs blazed on the hearth, the last bread and apples covered the table, the new commander, with recovered courage, said to her husband:

"Leave all to God—and me. He has done his part; now I will do mine."

"But we have no money, dear."

"Yes, we have. I sold all we could spare, and have enough to take us away from this snowbank."

"Where can we go?"

"I have engaged four rooms at our good neighbor, Lovejoy's. There we can live cheaply till spring. Then for new plans and a home of our own, please God."

"But, Hope, your little store won't last long, and we have no friends."

"I can sew and you can chop wood. Lovejoy offers you the same pay as he gives his other men; my old friend, Mrs. Truman, will send me all the work I want; and my blessed brother stands by us to the end. Cheer up, dear heart, for while there is work and love in the world we shall not suffer."[47]

"And while I have my good angel Hope, I shall not despair, even if I wait another thirty years before I step beyond the circle of the sacred little world in which I still have a place to fill."[48]

So one bleak December day,[49] with their few possessions piled on an ox-sled, the rosy children perched atop, and the parents trudging arm in arm behind, the exiles left their Eden and faced the world again.

"Ah, me! my happy dream. How much I leave behind that never can be mine again," said Abel, looking back at the lost Paradise, lying white and chill in its shroud of snow.

"Yes, dear; but how much we bring away," answered brave-hearted Hope, glancing from husband to children.

"Poor Fruitlands! The name was as great a failure as the rest!" continued Abel, with a sigh, as a frost-bitten apple fell from a leafless bough at his feet.

But the sigh changed to a smile as his wife added, in a half-tender, half-satirical tone:

"Don't you think Apple Slump would be a better name for it, dear?"

1873, 1876

---

[47]The family was supported through Mrs. Alcott's sewing and social work, Louisa's teaching, domestic service, and writing, and assistance from family and friends. With the publication of *Little Women* in 1868, Louisa May Alcott assured her family's financial security.
[48]Bronson Alcott left the family circle periodically for his series of tours during which he would hold "conversations" for little pay. In 1859, his educational contributions were recognized when he was made superintendent of schools in Concord.
[49]The day was actually January 16, 1844.

AMERICAN HUMORISTS

SEBA SMITH
WILLIAM TAPPAN THOMPSON
GEORGE WASHINGTON HARRIS

THOMAS BANGS THORPE
JOHNSON JONES HOOPER

"'Out West' is certainly a great country . . . there is one little town in 'them diggins' which . . . is 'all sorts of a stirring place.' In one day, they recently had two street fights, hung a man, rode three men out of town on a rail, got up a quarter race, a turkey shooting, a gander pulling, a match dog fight, had preaching by a circus rider, who afterwards ran a footrace for apple jack all round, and, as if this was not enough, the judge of the court, after losing his year's salary at single-handed poker, and licking a person who said he didn't understand the game, went out and helped to lynch his grandfather for hog stealing."

Anonymous, *The Spirit of the Times*, 1851

AMERICAN HUMORISTS

In his book on Nathaniel Hawthorne (1879), Henry James imagined growing to maturity in Salem, Massachusetts, in the early nineteenth century, and compiled a long list of the items so richly present in Europe that were absent from American life. The list of "absences"—no aristocracy, no palaces, no ivied ruins—was so long and comprehensive that a reader might conclude that "everything is left out." But James quickly added: "The American knows that a good deal remains; what it is that remains—that is his secret, his joke, as one may say. It would be cruel, in this terrible denudation, to deny him the consolation of his natural gift, that 'American humor' of which of late years we have heard so much."

This natural gift, "American humor," had come to literary climax in the celebrated American writer, Mark Twain (1835–1910). But there was a long foreground for Twain, filled with "rustic yankees," "frontier storytellers," "funny fellows," and "local colorists" (these categories are those used by Walter Blair, distinguished scholar of American humor). Many of these writers wrote minor masterpieces, pioneering in such American techniques as the use of an illiterate but shrewd, hilarious but poker-faced narrator, and in such American forms as the ornately elaborated and grotesquely exaggerated tall tale.

A New York magazine called *Spirit of the Times,* established by William T. Porter (1809–1858), published many of these writers and promoted their work. Porter also gathered many of the stories he had published in his magazine into a series of anthologies. One of the most influential of these collections, *The Big Bear of Arkansas, and Other Tales,* appeared in 1843 and included the title story, William Tappan Thompson's popular tall tale. Porter wrote that these backwoods humorists had discovered "a new vein of literature, as original as it is inexhaustible in its source."

Here is a rich sampling of the work of five of the most significant of the early American humorists—Seba Smith, William Tappan Thompson, George Washington Harris, Thomas Bangs Thorpe, and Johnson Jones Hooper.

ADDITIONAL READING

Constance Rourke, *American Humor: A Study of the National Character,* 1931, 1965; Franklin J. Meine, *Tall Tales of the Southwest,* 1930; Walter Blair, ed., *Native American Humor (1800–1900),* 1937, 1960 (contains book-length introduction); Walter Blair, *Horse Sense in American Humor,* 1942, 1962; Norris W. Yates, *William T. Porter and "The Spirit of the Times": A Study of the "Big Bear" School of Humor,* 1957; Elton Miles, *Southwest Humorists,* 1969; L. D. Rubin et al., *The Comic Imagination in American Literature,* 1973; Hennig Cohen and William B. Dillingham, eds., *Humor of the Old Southwest,* 1975; M. Thomas Inge, ed., *The Frontier Humorists: Critical Views,* 1975; Walter Blair and Hamlin Hill, *America's Humor: From Poor Richard to Doonesbury,* 1978; Neil Schmitz, *Of Huck and Alice: Humorous Writing in American Literature,* 1983; Walter Blair, "Introduction," *The Mirth of a Nation,* ed. Walter Blair and Raven I. McDavid, Jr., 1983; W. Bedford Clark and W. Craig Turner, eds., *Critical Essays on American Humor,* 1984; Carolyn S. Brown, *The Tall Tale in American Folklore and Literature,* 1987.

Works on and collections of individual authors: Patricia and Milton Rickels, *Seba Smith,* 1977; Milton Rickels, *George Washington Harris,* 1965; *Sut Lovingood,* ed. Brom Weber, 1954; *The Lovingood Papers,* ed. Ben Harris McClary, 1962–; *Sut Lovingood's Yarns,* ed. M. Thomas Inge, 1966; *High Times and Hard Times: Sketches and Tales by George Washington Harris,* ed. M. Thomas Inge, 1967; Milton Rickels, *Thomas Bangs Thorpe: Humorist of the Old Southwest,* 1962; W. Stanley Hoole, *Alias Simon Suggs: The Life and Times of Johnson Jones Hooper,* 1952.

TEXTS

All texts come from *The Mirth of a Nation: America's Great Dialect Humor,* ed. Walter Blair and Raven I. McDavid, Jr., 1983. Texts of the nineteenth-century American humorists have been so densely dialectical and rife with misspellings as to render them inaccessible to twentieth-century readers. Walter Blair, scholar and critic of American humor, and Raven McDavid, linguist and authority on American dialects, have provided readable, authentic texts.

SEBA SMITH

(1792–1868)

The cracker-barrel philosopher and horse-sense humorist has been a part of American culture for a very long time. The original or archetype was Jack Downing, invented by a New Englander in Maine, Seba Smith. Jack Downing came into being because Smith was looking for a way to boost the circulation of Maine's *Portland Courier,* which he founded and edited. Downing's home-spun letters began to appear in 1830 and continued to evoke laughter until the Civil War. Illiterate but shrewd, Downing was willing to comment on any-thing and everything. His comments were funny, and he emerged through them as a distinctive character, as familiar as an old shoe. Seba Smith sent him out on the road, to the state legislature and then to Congress in Washington, D.C. Downing proved an acute observer of the political scene, pointing out hilarious incongruities with a poker face. So successful was he that many writ-ers imitated his style, some even using Downing's name in pirated editions. Collections of his pieces appeared in *The Life and Writings of Major Jack Down-ing* (1833) and *My Thirty Years Out of the Senate* (1859), both very popular. His basic character was reincarnated by such comic writers or talkers as Davy Crockett, Mark Twain, and Will Rogers. And something of his personality and physique have endured in that strangely awkward symbol for the United States, Uncle Sam.

Jack's Grandfather

As I said afore, my grandfather, old Mr. Zebedee Downing, was the first settler in Downingville. Bless his old heart, he's living yet; and although he is eighty-six years old, he attended a public caucus for the good of his country about two years ago, and made a speech, as you will find somewhere before you get through this book, where it tells about my being nominated for Governor of the State of Maine.

As it is the fashion, in writing the lives of great folks, to go back and tell some-thing about their posterity, I s'pose I ought to give some account of my good old grandfather, for he was a true patriot, and as strong a republican as ever Uncle Joshua was. He was born somewhere in the old Bay State away back of Boston, and when the Revolutionary War come on, he went a-soldierin. Many and many a time, when I was a little boy, I've sot on the dye-pot in the corner till most midnight, to hear him tell over his going through the *fatigue of Burgoyne*.[1] If one of the neighbors came in to chat awhile in the evening, my grandfather was always sure to go through with the fatigue of Burgoyne, and if a stranger was traveling through Downingville and stopped at my grandfather's in a warm afternoon to get a drink of water, it was ten chances to one if he could get away till my grandfather had been through the whole story of the fatigue of Burgoyne.

He used to tell it the best to old Mr. Johnson, who used to come in regularly about once a week to spend an evening and drink a mug of my grandfather's cider. And he would set so patiently and hear my grandfather through from beginning to end, that I never could tell which took the most comfort, Mr. Johnson in drinking the cider, or my grandfather in going through the fatigue of Burgoyne. After Mr. Johnson had taken about two or three drinks, he would smack his lips and, says he, "I guess, Mr. Downing, you would have been glad to get such a mug of cider as this in the battle of Burgoyne."

"Why, yes," said my grandfather, "or when we was on the march from Cambridge to Peekskill, either, or from Peekskill to Albany, or from Albany to Saratogue, where we went through the fatigue of Burgoyne.

"Old Schuyler was our general," said my grandfather, bracing himself back in his chair, "and he turned out to be a traitor, and was sent for, to go to General Washington to be court-martialed! Then General Gates was sent to us to take the command, and he was a most capital officer, every inch of him. He had his cocked hat on, and his regimentals, and his furbelows[2] on his shoulders, and he looked nobly," said my grandfather.

"I can see him now as plain as if 'twas yesterday. He wore a plaguy great stub queue,[3] as big as my wrist, sticking out at the back of his neck as straight as a handspike. Well, when Gates came, we were all reviewed, and everything was put in complete order, and he led us on, ye see, to take Burgoyne. By daylight in the morning we were called out by the sound of the drum, and drawn up in regiments, and the word was, 'On your posts,[4] march!' And there we stood, marching on our posts without moving forward an inch, heads up, looking to the right. We didn't dare to move an eye, or hardly to wink.

"By and by along comes the old General to inspect us, riding along so stately, and that old stub queue sticking out behind his head so straight, it seems as though I can see him right here before me. And then he addressed us, like a father talking to his children.

"'Fellow soldiers,' says he, 'this day we are going to try the strength of Burgoyne's forces. Now let every man keep a stiff upper lip, go forward boldly and attack them with courage, and you've nothing to fear.' Oh, he addressed us completely; and then we marched off to meet the enemy.

"By and by we begun to hear the balls whizzing over our heads, and the enemy's guns begun to roar like thunder. I felt terribly for a minute or two, but we kept marching up, marching up," said my grandfather, rising and marching across the floor, "for we had orders not to fire a gun till we got up so near we could almost reach 'em with our bayonets. And there was a hundred drums in a bunch, rattling enough to craze a nation, and the fifes and bugles," continued my grandfather, still marching across the floor, "went 'tootle, tootle, tootle, tootle!'— Oh, I can hear that very tune ringing in my ears now, as plain as if 'twas yesterday, and I shall never forget it to my dying day.

---

[1]The British General John Burgoyne (1722–1792) was, through a series of blunders, forced to surrender all his forces to the American Revolutionary Army at Saratoga, New York, in 1777—the turning point in the war, assuring American victory; Burgoyne was sent home in disgrace and deprived of his rank. "Fatigue" is used in the military as a term for punishment, usually in the form of menial labor.
[2]Showy ornamentation.
[3]Pigtail.
[4]I.e., in position.

"When we got up so near the enemy that we could fairly see the whites of their eyes, the word was 'Halt!'" said my grandfather, suddenly halting in the middle of the floor, and sticking his head back straight as a soldier, " 'Make ready!'

" 'Twas did in a moment," continued my grandfather, throwing his staff up against his shoulder, " 'Take aim!'

" 'Twas did in a moment," fetching his staff down straight before his eyes. " 'Fire!' Then, O mercy, what a roar," said my grandfather, striking his staff down on the floor, "and such a smother and smoke you couldn't hardly see your hand afore you.

"Well, in an instant the word was 'Prime and load!' And as fast as we fired we fell back in the rear to let others come up and take their turn, so by the time we were loaded we were in front and ready to fire again, for we kept marching all the time," said my grandfather, beginning to march again across the floor.

"But the enemy stood their ground and kept pouring in upon us tremendously, and we kept marching up and firing, marching up and firing, but didn't gain forward an inch. I felt streaked enough, for the balls were whistling over our heads, and sometimes a man would drop down on one side of me and sometimes on t'other; but it wouldn't do to flinch a hair; we must march up and fire and wheel to the right and left, and keep it going.

"By and by the word was 'advance columns!' Then, heavens and earth, how light I felt," said my grandfather, quickening his march across the floor. "I knew in a moment the enemy was retreating, and it seemed to me I could have jumped over the moon. Well, we marched forward, but still kept firing, and presently we came to the enemy's ground. And then, O mercy! such a sight I never see before and never want to again: stepping over the dead bodies, and the poor wounded wretches wallowing in their blood, mangled all to pieces, and such screeches and groans—some crying out, 'Don't kill me! don't kill me!' and others begging us to kill 'em to put 'em out of misery. Oh, it was enough to melt the very heart of a stone," said my grandfather, wiping the tears from his eyes.

"But they needn't have been afraid of being hurt, for our General was one of the best men that ever lived. He had the carts brought up immediately and all the poor wounded souls carried off as fast as possible where they would be taken good care of. He wouldn't let one of 'em be hurt more than he would one of his own men. But it was a dreadful hot battle; we fit and skirmished all the afternoon and took a good many prisoners, and some cannon and ammunition. When it come night, the enemy retreated to their fortifications, and we camped all night on the ground with our guns in our hands, ready at a moment's warning to pitch battle again.

"As soon as it was daylight, we were all mustered and paraded again, and round come the old General to see how we looked. He held up his head like a soldier, and the old stub queue stuck out as straight as ever. I can see it now as plain as I can see my staff," said my grandfather. "And O my stars, how he addressed us; it made our hearts jump to hear him. 'Fellow soldiers,' says he, 'this day we shall make Burgoyne tremble. If you are only as brave as you were yesterday, we shall have him and his army before night.'

"But Burgoyne had slipped away in the night and got into a place stronger fortified. But he couldn't get away; he was hemmed in all round, so we got him before it was over. We were five or six days skirmishing about it; but I can't tell you all, nor a quarter part on't."

"But how was it you took Burgoyne at last?" said Mr. Johnson, taking another drink of cider.

"O, he had to give up at last," said my grandfather. "After we had skirmished a day or two longer, General Gates sent word to Burgoyne, that if he had a mind to march his army back into Canada and leave everything this side unmolested, he'd let him go peaceably. But Burgoyne would not accept it; he sent word back that he was going to winter with his troops in Boston. Well, after we had skirmished round two or three days longer, and Burgoyne got into such close quarters that he couldn't get away anyhow, he sent word to General Gates that he'd accept the offer and march back to Canada. But Gates sent word back to him again, 'You said you meant to winter in Boston, and I mean to make you as good as your word.'

"At last Burgoyne see it was no use for him to hold out any longer, so he give all of his men up prisoners of war. Then we were all paraded in lines a little ways apart to see them surrender. And they marched right out and marched along towards us; and it was a most noble sight to see them all dressed out in their regimentals, and their bayonets glistening in the sun enough to dazzle anybody's eyes. And they marched along and stacked their arms, and they all marched through between our lines, looking homesick enough. I guess we felt as well as they did, if our clothes wa'n't so good.

"Well, that was the end of the war in the northern states. There was a little skirmishing away off to the South afterwards, but nothing to be compared to that. The battle of Burgoyne was what achieved our independence; it was the capstone of the war; there never was such a glorious battle as that since the days of Caesar, nor Methusaleh, no, nor clear back to Adam."

"I don't think there ever was," said Mr. Johnson, handing me the quart mug and telling me to run and get another mug of cider; for before my grandfather could get through the fatigue of Burgoyne, Mr. Johnson would most always get to the bottom of the mug.

When I brought in the second mug, Mr. Johnson took another sip and smacked his lips, and says he, "Mr. Downing, I should like to drink a toast with you; so here's health and prosperity to the apple trees of Downingville. Mr. Downing, what will you drink to us?" said he, handing the mug to my grandfather.

"Why, I don't care about any cider," said my grandfather (for he is a very temperate man, and so are all the Downings remarkably temperate), "but I will just drink a little to the memory of the greatest and the bravest general that this world ever see yet. So here's my respects to old General Gates's stub queue." By this time my grandfather having poured out of him the whole fatigue of Burgoyne, and Mr. Johnson having poured into him about three pints of cider, they would both of them feel pretty considerably relieved, and Mr. Johnson would bid us good night and go home.

I take it that it was hearing these stories of my grandfather's bravery told over so often in my younger days that made me such a military character as to induce the President to appoint me to the command at Madawaska,[5] and also to go to South Carolina to put down the Nullifiers.[6] But I'm getting a little before my story, for I haven't got through with my grandfather yet, and my father comes before I do, too.

As I said afore, my grandfather was the first settler in Downingville. When he got through soldiering in the Revolutionary War, he took a notion he'd go and pick him out a good lot of land away down East to settle on, where there was land enough to be had just for whistling for it, and where his boys would have a chance to do something in the world. So he took grandmother and the two boys, for father and Uncle Joshua were all the boys he had then, and packed them into a horse-wagon, and took an axe and a hoe and a shovel, and some victuals, and a bed tick to put some straw in, and a gun and some blankets and one thing and another, and started off down East.

[5]Town in northern Maine.
[6]South Carolina adopted the "Ordinance of Nullification" in 1833, aimed at the protective tariff passed by Congress in 1828; declaring the tariff act "null and void," South Carolina threatened armed resistance.

He drove away into Maine till he got clear to the end of the road, and then he picked his way along through the woods and round the pond five miles further, till he got to the very spot where Downingville now is, and there he stopped and baited his horse, and while grandmother and the boys sot down and took a bit of a luncheon, grandfather went up top of one of the hills to take a view of the country. And when he come down again, says he, "I guess we may as well untackle, for I don't believe we shall find a better place if we travel all summer."

So he untackled the old horse, and took the wagon and turned it over against a great oak tree, and put some bushes up round it and made a pretty comfortable sort of a house for 'em to sleep in a few nights, and then he took his axe and slashed away amongst the trees. But that old oak tree never was cut down; it's the very same one that stands out a little ways in front of grandfather's house now.

And poor old grandmother, long as she lived—for she's been dead about five years—always made it a practice once a year, when the day come round that they first camped under the old oak, to have the table carried out and set under the tree. And all hands, children and grandchildren, had to go and eat supper there, and the good old lady always used to tell over the whole story—how she slept eight nights under the wagon, and how they were the sweetest nights' rest she ever had.

1833

WILLIAM TAPPAN THOMPSON
(1812–1882)

As Shakespeare wrote in *Hamlet,* "brevity is the soul of wit." "A Coon Hunt in a Fency Country" is extraordinarily short, but it fulfills its comic purpose. One critic, Henry Prentice Miller, analyzed the formula of such humorous pieces: "A single paragraph of general moralizing or crackerbox philosophizing; a quick sketching of the characters; a few statements about background; a single incident, and finally the point or nub which ties up the initial paragraph." Mark Twain was later to take over the technique in the creation of some of America's most enduring comic tales. Like so many of America's comic storytellers, the Ohio-born William Tappan Thompson became a newspaperman, editing Georgia's *Southern Miscellany.* Casting about to spice up his paper, he began a series of pieces involving a Major Jones, an uneducated storyteller and cracker-barrel philosopher. These sketches were collected as *Major Jones's Courtship* (1843), *Chronicles of Pineville* (1845), and *Major Jones's Sketches of Travel* (1848). They proved extremely popular until later in the century.

A Coon Hunt in a Fency Country

It is really astonishin what a monstrous sight of mischief there is in a bottle of rum. If one of 'em was to be submitted to a analization, as the doctors call it, it would be found to contain all manner of devilment that ever entered the head of man, from cussin and stealin up to murder and whippin his own mother, and nonsense enough to turn all the men in the world out of their senses. If a man's got any badness in him, let him drink whiskey, and it will bring it out just as sassafras tea does the measles; and if he's a good-for-nothin sort of a fellow, without no bad traits in particular, it'll bring out all his foolishness. It affects different people in different ways—it makes some men monstrous brave and full of fight, and some it makes cowards—some it makes rich and happy, and some poor and miserable. And it has different effects on different peoples's eyes—some it makes see double, and some it makes so blind that they can't tell themselves from a side of bacon. One of the worst cases of rum-foolery that I've heard of for a long time tuck place in Pineville last fall.

Bill Sweeney and Tom Culpepper is the two greatest old coveys[1] in our settlement for coon-huntin.[2] The fact is, they don't do much of anything else, and when *they* can't catch coons, it's a sure sign that coons is scarce. Well, one night they had everything ready for a regular hunt, but owin to some extra good fortun, Tom had got a pocket-pistol, as he called it, of genuine old Jamaica rum. After takin a good startin horn, they went out on their hunt, with their lightwood torch a-blazin, and the dogs a-barkin and yelpin like they was crazy.

They struck out into the woods, gwine in the direction of old Starlin Jones's new-ground, a great place for coons. Every now and then they would stop to wait for the dogs, and then they would drink one another's health, until they begun to feel first-rate. On they went, chattin away about one thing and another, takin a nip now and then from Tom's bottle, not mindin much where they was gwine. By and by they come to a fence. Well, over they got without much difficulty.

"Whose fence is this?" says Bill.

"'T ain't no matter," says Tom. "Let's take a drink."

After takin a pull at the bottle, they went on again, wonderin what upon yea'th had come of the dogs. The next thing they come to was a terrible muddy branch. After gropin their way through the bushes and briars and gittin on t'other side, they tuck another drink. Fixing up their torch and startin on agin, they didn't go but a little ways before they come to another branch, as bad as the first one, and a little further they come to another fence—a monstrous high one this time.

"Where upon yea'th[3] is we got to, Culpepper?" says Bill. "I never seed such a heap of fences and branches in these parts."

"Why," says Tom, "It's old Starlin's doins. You know, he's always building fences and makin infernal improvements, as he calls 'em. But never mind, we's through 'em now."

"The devil we is," says Bill. "Why, here's the all-firedest high fence yit."

Sure enough, there they was right ag'in another fence. By this time they begun to be considerable tired and limber in their j'ints; and it was such a terrible high fence. Tom dropped the last piece of the torch, and there they was in the dark.

"Now you *is* done it!" says Bill.

Tom knowed he had, but he thought it was no use to grieve over what couldn't be helped, so, says he,

"Never mind, old hoss—come ahead, and I'll take you out," and the next minute, kerslash! he went into the water up to his neck.

Bill heard the splash, and he clung to the fence with both hands, like he thought it was slewin round to throw him off.

"Hello, Tom!" says he. "Where in creation has you got to?"

"Here I is!" says Tom, spittin the water out of his mouth, and coughin like he'd swallowed something. "Look out, there's another dratted branch here."

---

[1]Small group of people.
[2]Raccoon, a small, tree-climbing mammal, with yellow-black fur, and a long, black-ringed tail.
[3]I.e., the earth.

"Name o'sense, where is we?" says Bill. "If this isn't a fency country, dad fetch my buttons!"

"Yes, and a branchy one, too!" says Tom, "and they is the thickest and deepest that I ever seed in all my born days."

After a good deal of cussin and gruntin, Bill got himself loose from the fence. "Which way is you?" says he.

"Here, right over the branch," says Tom.

The next minute in Bill went, up to his middle in the branch.

"Come ahead," says Tom, "and let's go home."

"Come thunder!" says Bill, "in such a place as this, where a fellow hain't more'n got his coattail unhitched from a fence before he's head and ears in a cussed branch."

Bill made a terrible job of gittin across the branch, which he swore was the deepest one yit. They managed to git together agin after feelin about in the dark a while, and, takin another drink, they sot out for home, cussin the fences and the branches, and helpin one another up now and then when they got their legs tangled in the brush. But they hadn't gone more'n twenty yards before they found themselves in the middle of another branch. After gittin through the branch and gwine about twenty yards they was brung up all standin agin by another everlastin fence.

"Dad blame my pictur," says Bill, "if I don't think we's bewitched. Who upon yea'th would go and build fences all over outdoors this way?"

It tuck 'em a long time to climb the fence, but when they got on top of it they found the ground on t'other side without much trouble. This time the bottle was broke, and they come monstrous nigh havin a fight about the catastrophe. But it was a very good thing the liquor was spilt, for after crossin three or four more branches and climbin as many fences, it got to be daylight, when to their great astonishment they found out that they had been climbin the same fence and wadin the same branch all night, not more'n a hundred yards from the place where they first come to 'em.

Bill Sweeney says he can't account for it no other way but that the liquor sorta turned their heads; and he says he really does believe if it hadn't gin out,[4] they'd been climbin that same fence and wadin that same branch till now.

1847, 1872

GEORGE WASHINGTON HARRIS
(1814–1869)

In "Rare Ripe Garden Seed," George Washington Harris followed the practice of other comic writers in using an invented character to narrate the story, thus creating a frame (the tale-teller and the listeners) for the narrated action itself. Readers of Harris would have been more familiar with Sut Lovingood's name than with Harris's, and would have read the story because they were drawn to Sut Lovingood's voice. One critic, Walter Blair, has pointed out that from the Lovingood tales "emerges a character, coarser and earthier, perhaps, than any other in our literature during the nineteenth century, but at the same time, understandably true to life, an ingratiating mischief-maker. . . ."

---

[4]Given out.

   Though born in Pennsylvania, Harris migrated to Tennessee as a boy. He knocked about a lot, trying his hand at many trades—metalsmith, steamboat captain, farmer, manager in a glassworks, sawmill and mine, postmaster, and railway conductor. But he gravitated to newspaper editing, which led to his writing. His invention of the Tennessee mountaineer Sut Lovingood was ingenious. A lover of corn whisky and crude pranks, Lovingood delighted readers with his earthy language. The stories narrated by him were collected in 1867 as *Sut Lovingood. Yarns Spun by a "Nat'ral Born Durn'd Fool."* Among those he influenced are Mark Twain and Flannery O'Connor. William Faulkner once commented: "I like Sut Lovingood from a book written by George Harris about 1840 or '50 in the Tennessee mountains. He had no illusions about himself, did the best he could; at certain times he was a coward and knew it and wasn't ashamed; he never blamed his misfortunes on anyone and never cursed God for them."

Rare Ripe Garden Seed

   "I tell you now, I minds my first big scare just as well as rich boys minds their first boots, or seeing the first spotted horse circus. The red top of them boots is still a rich red stripe in their minds, and the burnin red of my first scare has left as deep a scar onto my thinking works.

   "Mam had me a-standin atwixt her knees. I can feel the knobs of her j'ints a-rattlin a-past my ribs yet. She didn't have much petticoats to speak of, and I had but one, and hit were calico slit from the nape of my neck to the tail, hilt together at the top with a drawstring, and at the bottom by the hem. Hit were the handiest clothes I ever seed, and would be pow'ful comfortin in summer if hit warn't for the flies. If they was good to run in, I'd wear one yet. They beats pasted shirts, and britches, as bad as a feather bed beats a bag of warnut shells for sleepin on.

   "Say, George, wouldn't you like to see me into one, 'bout half faded, slit and a-walkin just so, up the middle street of your city church, a-aimin for your pew pen, and it chock full of your fine city gal friends, just a'ter the people had sot down from the first prayer, and the organ beginnin to groan. What would you do in such a 'mergency? Say, hoss?"

   "Why, I'd shoot you dead, Monday morning before eight o'clock," was my reply.

   "Well I 'spect you would. But you'd take a real old maid faint first, right among them-ere gals. Lordy! wouldn't you be 'shamed of me! Yet, why not to church in such a suit, when you hasn't got no store clothes?

   "Well, as I were sayin, mam were feedin us brats onto mush and milk, without the milk, and as I were the baby then, she hilt me so as to see that I got my share. When there ain't enough food, big childer roots little childer out'n the trough, and gobbles up their part. Just so the yearth over: bishops eats elders,[1] elders eats common people. They eats such cattle as me; I eats possums; possums eats chickens; chickens swallows worms, and worms am content to eat dust, and the dust am the end of hit all. Hit am all as regular as the sounds from the treble down to the bull bass of a fiddle in good chune. And I 'spect hit am right, or hit wouldn't be 'lowed.

   " '*The sheriff!* ' hissed mam in a keen tremblin whisper. Hit sounded to me like

---

[1]I.e., elders or leaders of the church.

the screech of a hen when she says 'hawk!' to her little round-shouldered, fuzzy, bead-eyed striped-backs.

"I acted just adzackly as they does. I darted on all fours under mam's petticoat-tails, and there I met, face to face, the wooden bowl, and the mush, and the spoon what she slid under from t'other side. I's mad at myself yet, for right there I showed the first flush of the nat'ral born durn fool what I now is. I oughta et hit all up, in justice to my stomach and my growin, while the sheriff was levyin onto the bed and the chairs. To this day, if anybody says 'sheriff,' I feels scare, and if I hears 'constable' mentioned, my legs goes through runnin motions, even if I is asleep. Did you ever watch a dog dreamin of rabbit huntin? Them's the motions, and the feelin am the rabbit's.

"Sheriffs am awful 'spectable people; everybody looks up to 'em. I never adzackly seed the 'spectable part myself. I's too feared of 'em, I reckon, to 'zamine for hit much. One thing I know; no country atwixt here and Tophet[2] can ever 'lect me to sell out widows' plunder or poor men's corn, and the thoughts of hit gins me a good feelin. Hit sort of flashes through my heart when I thinks of hit.

"I axed[3] a parson once, what hit could be, and he pronounced hit to be unre-generate pride, what I ought to squelch in prayer, and in 'tendin church on collection days. I were in hopes it mout be 'ligion, or sense, a-soakin into me. Hit feels good, anyhow, and I don't care if every circuitrider out'n jail knows hit.

"Sheriffs' shirts alluz has nettle dust or fleas inside of 'em when they lies down to sleep, and I's glad of hit, for they's alluz discomfortin me, durn 'em. I scarcely ever get to drink a horn,[4] or eat a mess[5] in peace. I'll hurt one some day, see if I don't. Show me a sheriff a-steppin softly round, and a-sorta sightin at me, and I'll show you the speed of a express engine, fired up with rich, dry rosiny[6] scares. They don't catch me much, usin only human legs as weapons.

"Old John Dobbin were a 'spectable sheriff, mons'ously so, and had the best scent for poor fugitive devils and women I ever seed. He were sure fire. He toted a warrant for this here skinful of durned fool 'bout that-ere misfortunate nigger meetin business, until he wore hit into six separate square bits, and had wore out much shoe leather a-chasin of me. I'd found a doggery[7] in full milk, and hated pow'ful bad to leave that settlement while hit sucked free. So I sot into sort of try and wean him off from botherin me so much. I succeeded so well that he not only quit racin of me, and women, but he were teetotally sp'iled as a sheriff, and lost the 'spectable section of his character.[8] To make you fool fellows understand how hit were done, I must introduce your minds to one Wat Mastin, a bullet-headed young blacksmith.

"Well, last year—no, hit were the year afore last—in struttin and gobblin time[9]—Wat felt his keepin right warm; so he sot into bellowin and pawin up dust in the neighborhood round the old widow McKildrin's. The more dust he flung up, the worse he got, until at last he just couldn't stand the ticklin sensations an-other minute. So he put for the county clerk's office, with his hands socked down deep in his britches pockets, like he was feared of pickpockets, his back roached round, and a-chompin his teeth until he splotched his whiskers with foam. Oh! he were yearnest hot, and as restless as a cockroach in a hot skillet."

"What was the matter with this Mr. Mastin? I cannot understand you, Mr. Lov-ingood. Had he hydrophobia?" remarked a man in a square-tail coat and cloth

---

[2] In the Bible, a place where human sacrifices were made to Moloch (a hell).
[3] Asked.
[4] I.e., drinking horn.
[5] Meal.
[6] Resiny; i.e., wood filled with resin, which burns with great intensity.

[7] Saloon.
[8] I.e., Sut Lovingood through a scheme got the sheriff to drink whisky.
[9] I.e., springtime, when a young man's fancy turns to thoughts of love.

gaiters, who was obtaining subscribers for some forthcoming Encyclopedia of Useful Knowledge, who had quartered at our camp, uninvited and really unwanted.

"What do you mean by hy-dry-foby?" and Sut looked puzzled.

"A madness produced by being bit by some rabid animal," explained Squaretail, in a pompous manner.

"Yes, hoss, he had hy-dry-foby *awful,* and Mary McKildrin, the widow McKildrin's only daughter, had gin him the complaint. I don't know whether she bit him or not. He might have cotch hit[10] from her breath, and he were now in the roach back chompin stage of the sickness. So he were a'ter the clerk for a ticket to the hospital. Well, the clerk sold him a piece of paper, part printin and part writin, with a picture of two pigs' hearts, what some boy had shot a arrow through and left hit stickin, printed at the top. That paper were a splicin pass—some calls hit a pair of license—and that very night he tuck Mary, for better, for worse, to have and to hold to him, his heirs and—"

"Allow me to interrupt you," said our guest. "You do not quote the marriage ceremony correctly."

"You go to *hell,* mistofer; you bothers me."

This outrageous remark took the stranger all aback, and he sat down.

"Where were I? Oh, yes, he married Mary tight and fast, and next day he were able to be about. His coat, though, and his trousers looked just a scrimption too big and heavy to tote. I axed him if he felt sound. He said yes, but he'd welded a steamboat shafts the day before, and were sort of tired like. There he told a durn lie, for he'd been a-hornin up dirt most of the day, round the widow's garden, and bellowin in the orchard.

"Mary and him sot square into housekeepin, and 'mong other things he bought a lot of *rare ripe garden seed,* from a Yankee peddler. Rare ripe corn, rare ripe peas, rare ripe 'taters, rare ripe everything, and the two young durned fools were dreadfully exercised 'bout hit. Wat said he meant to get him a rare ripe hammer and anvil, and Mary vowed to gracious that she'd have a rare ripe wheel and loom, if money could get 'em.

"Pretty soon a'ter he had made the garden, he tuck a notion to work a spell down to Atlanty, in the railroad shop, as he said he had a sort of ailin in his back, and he thought weldin rail car-tire and engine axletrees were lighter work nor sharpenin plows and puttin lap-links in trace-chains.

"So down he went, and found hit agreed with him, for he didn't come back until the middle of August. The first thing he seed when he landed into his cabin door were a shoe box with rockers under hit. And the next thing he seed were Mary herself, propped up in bed. And the next thing he seed a'ter that were a pair of little rat-eyes a-shinin above the end of the quilt. And the next and last thing he seed were the two little rat-eyes aforesaid, a-turnin into two hundred thousand big green stars, and a-swingin round and round the room, faster and faster, until they mixed into one awful green flash. He drapped into a limber pile on the floor. The durned fool what had welded the steamboat shafts had fainted safe and sound as a gal scared at a mad bull.

"Mary fotch[11] a weak cat-scream, and covered her head, and sot into work on a whifflin dry cry, while little Rat-eyes gin hitself[12] up to suckin. Cryin and suckin both at once ain't fair; must come pow'ful strainin on the wet section of a woman's constitution; yet hit am often done, and more too.

"Old Missis McKildrin, what were a-nursin Mary, just got up from knittin, and flung a big gourd of water square into Wat's face. Then she fotch a glass bottle of

---

[10]I.e., "caught it."
[11]Fetched, or made.
[12]I.e., "gave itself."

swell-skull whiskey out'n the three-cornered cupboard, and stood fornint[13] Wat, a-holdin hit in one hand and the tin cup in t' other, waitin for Wat to come to. She were the piousest lookin old 'oman just then, you ever seed outside of a prayer meetin. After a spell, Wat begun to move, twitchin his fingers and battin his eyes, sorta 'stonished like. That pious-lookin statue said to him:

" 'My son, just take a drap of spirits, honey. You's very sick, dumplin. Don't take on, darlin, if you can help it, ducky, for poor Margaret-Jane am mons'ous ailin, and the least n'ise[14] or takin on will kill the poor sufferin dear, and you'll lose your turkle ducky dove of a sweet wifey, a'ter all she's done gone through for you. My dear son Watty, you must consider her feelins a little.' "

"Says Wat, a-turnin up his eyes at that virtuous old relic sorta sick like—'I is a-considerin 'em a heap, right now.'

" 'Oh, that's right, my good kind child.'

"Oh damned if old mother-in-laws can't plaster humbug over a fellow, just as soft and easy as they spreads a cambric[15] handkerchief over a three-hour-old baby's face. You don't feel hit at all, but hit am there, a plumb inch thick, and stickin fast as court plaster.

"She raised Wat's head, and sot the edge of the tin cup agin his lower teeth, and turned up the bottom slow and careful, a-winkin at Mary, who were a-peepin over the edge of the coverlid, to see if Wat *tuck the prescription,*[16] for a heap of family comfort depended on that-ere horn of spirits. *One* horn alluz softens a man, the yearth over.

"Wat keep a-battin his eyes, worse nor a owl in daylight. At last he raised hisself onto one elbow, and rested his head in that hand, sort of weak like.

"Says he, mons'ous tremblin and slow: 'Aprile—May—June—July—and 'most—half—of—August,' a-countin the months onto the fingers of t'other hand, with the thumb, a-shakin of his head and lookin at his spread fingers like they warn't hisn, or they were nastied with somethin.

"Then he counted 'em agin, slower: 'Aprile—May—June—July, and 'most half-of-August.' And he run his thumb atwixt his fingers, as meanin 'most half of August, and looked at the p'int of hit, like hit mout be a snake's head. He raised his eyes to the widow's face, who were standin just as steady as a hitchin post, and still a-wearin that pious expression onto her personal featurs, and a flood of soft love for Wat, a-shinin straight from her eyes into hisn.

"Says he, 'That just makes four months, and most a half, don't hit, Missis McKildrin?'

"She never said one word.

"Wat reached for the hearth, and got a dead fire-coal; then he made a mark clean across a floor-plank.

"Says he, 'Aprile,' a-holdin down the coal onto the end of the mark, like he were feared hit mout blow away afore he got hit christened Aprile.

"Says he, 'May'—and he marked across the board agin. Then he counted the marks, one, two, a-dottin at 'em with the coal.

" 'June,' and he marked agin, one, two, three, counted with the p'int of the coal. He scratched his head with the little finger of the hand holdin the charcoal, and he drawed hit slowly across the board agin, peepin under his wrist to see when hit reached the crack, and says he, 'July,' as he lifted the coal; 'one, two, three, four,' countin from left to right and then from right to left.

" 'That hain't but four, no way I can fix hit. Old Pike[17] hisself couldn't make hit five, if he were to cipher onto hit until his legs turned into figure eights.'

---

[13]Variant of "fornent," directly opposite to, facing.
[14]Noise.
[15]Fine linen.
[16]I.e., fell for the trick and drank the whisky.

[17]Named after a person from Pike County, Missouri, Pike became in fiction of the time the prototype of the unschooled westerner, often characterized by his shrewdness.

"Then he made a mark, half acrost a plank, spit on his finger, and rubbed off a half inch of the end, and says he, "Most half of August.' He looked up at the widow, and there she were, same as ever, still a-holdin her flask agin her bosom, and says he, 'Four months, and 'most a half. *Hain't enough, is hit, mammy?* Hit's just 'bout (lackin a little) *half enough,* hain't it, mammy?'

"Missis McKildrin shuck her head sort of uncertain like, and says she, 'Take a drap more spirits, Watty, my dear pet. Does you mind buyin that-ere rare ripe seed from the peddler?'

"Wat nodded his head, and looked 'what of hit?' but didn't say hit.

"This is what comes of hit, and four months and a half am rare ripe time for babies, adzackly. To be sure, hit lacks a day or two, but Margaret-Jane were alluz a pow'ful enterprisin gal, and a early riser."

"Says Wat, 'How 'bout the 'taters?'

" 'Oh, *we* et 'taters as big as goose-eggs afore old Missis Collins's blossomed.'

" 'How 'bout corn?'

" 'Oh, we shaved down roas'in-ears afore hern tassled.'

" 'And peas?'

" 'Yes, son, we had gobs and lots in three weeks. Everything comes in adzackly half the time that hit takes the old sort, and you *knows,* my darlin son, you planted hit wasteful. I thought then you'd rare ripe everything on the place. You planted *often,* too, didn't you, love, for fear hit wouldn't come up.'

" 'Ye-ye-s-s he-he did,' said Mary, a-cryin.

"Wat studied pow'ful deep a spell, and the widow just waited. Widows alluz wait and alluz win.

"At last, says he, 'Mammy.'

"She looked at Mary and winked these-here words at her, as plain as she could a-talked 'em:

" 'You hearn him call me *mammy twiste.* I's *got him* now. His backbone's a-limberin fast; he'll own the baby yet; see if he don't. Just hold still, my daughter, and let your mammy knead this dough; then you may bake hit as brown as you please.'

" 'Mammy, when I married on the first day of Aprile—'

"The widow looked uneasy. She thought he mout be a-couplin that day, his weddin, and the idea, damn fool, together.

"But he warn't, for he said, 'That day I gin old man Collins my note of hand for a hundred dollars, due in one year a'ter date, the balance on this land. Do you think that seed will change the *time* any, or will hit alter the *amount?*' And Wat looked at her, powerful anxious.

"She raised the whiskey bottle way above her head, with the hand on the mouth, and fotch the bottom down onto her hand, spat!

"Says she, 'Watty, my dear b'loved son, prepare to pay *two* hundred dollars 'bout the first of October. For hit'll be due then, *as* sure as that little black-eyed angel in the bed there am your daughter.'

"Wat dropped his head, and said, *'Then hit's a damn sure thing.'*

"Right here, the baby fotch a rattlin loud squall. (I 'spect Mary were sort of fidgety just then, and hurt hit).

" 'Yes,' says Wat, a-wallin a red eye towards the bed. 'My little she—what were hit you called her name, mammy?'

" 'I called her a sweet little angel, and she is one, as sure as you're her daddy, my b'loved son.'

" 'Well,' says Wat. 'My little sweet, patent rare ripe she angel, if you lives to marryin time, you'll 'stonish some man body out'n his shirt, if you don't rare ripe lose hits virtue a'ter the first plantin, that's all.'

"He reared up on end, with his mouth pouched out. He had a pow'ful fore-head, far-reachin, bread-funnel, anyhow—could a-bit the eggs out'n a catfish, in two foot water, without wettin his eyebrows. 'Dod durn rare ripe seed, and rare ripe peddlers, and rare ripe notes to the hottest corner of—'

" 'Stop, Watty, darlin. Don't swear. 'Member you belongs to meeting.'

" 'My blacksmith's fire,' ended Wat, and he studied a long spell.

"Says he, 'Did you save any of that infernal double-trigger seed?'

" 'Yes,' says the widow. 'There in that bag by the cupboard.'

"Wat got up off'n the floor, took a countin sorta look at the charcoal marks, and reached down the bag. He went to the door and called, 'Sook, muley! Sook, sook, cow! Chick, chick, chickie, chick!'

" 'What's you gwine to do now, my dear son?' said Missis McKildrin.

" 'I's just gwine to feed this active *smart* trick to the cow and the hens; that's what I's gwine to do. Old muley hain't had a calf in two years, and I'll eat some rare ripe eggs.'

"Mary now ventered to speak. 'Husband, I ain't sure hit'll work on hens. Come and kiss me, my love.'

" 'I hain't sure hit'll work on hens, either,' said Wat. 'They's pow'ful uncertain in their ways, well as women,' And he flung out another handful, spiteful like.

" 'Takin the rare ripe invention all together, from 'taters and peas to notes of hand, and childer, I can't say I likes hit much.' And he flung out another handful.

" 'Your mam had thirteen the old way, and if this truck stays 'bout the house, you's good for twenty-six, maybe thirty, for you's a pow'ful enterprisin gal, your mam says.' And he flung out another handful, overhanded, as hard as if he were flingin rocks at a stealin sow.

" 'Make your mind easy,' said the widow. 'Hit never works on married folks only the first time.'

" 'Say them words agin,' said Wat. 'I's glad to hear 'em. Is hit the same way with notes of hand?'

" 'I 'spect hit am, answered the widow, with just a taste of strong vinegar in the words, as she sot the flask in the cupboard with a push."

1867

THOMAS BANGS THORPE
(1815–1878)

"The Big Bear of Arkansas," published in *The Spirit of the Times* in 1841, is the archetypal tall tale of America. How big was the bear? "'Twould astonish you to know how big he was: I made a *bedspread of his skin,* and the way it used to cover my bear mattress, and leave several feet on each side to tuck up, would have delighted you." The mythical gigantic bear was a part of early American lore, and was to reach its classic embodiment in the twentieth century in William Faulkner's "The Bear." It is ironic that the author whose masterpiece is "The Big Bear of Arkansas," a great example of Old Southwest humor, was born in New England. But he left his native Boston in 1837 to go to Louisiana to recover from ill health. He painted landscapes and portraits with some success but more and more turned to journalism and editing newspapers. Two of his collections of stories are *The Mysteries of the Backwoods* (1846) and *The Hive of the Bee Hunter* (1854). He wrote and illustrated a book on the Mexican War, *Our Army on the Rio Grande* (1846), and published *The Taylor Anecdote Book* (1848). In 1854 he returned to New York and from 1859 to 1861 was part owner and editor of *The Spirit of the Times*. He served as a Union officer in New Orleans during the Civil War and spent his last years in the New York City customs house.

But Thorpe is remembered mainly as the author of "The Big Bear of Arkansas." The title of the story has even been given to the genre it represented and developed—the "Big Bear School of Humor." When asked once about the relation of the Thorpe tale to his own story "The Bear," William Faulkner replied: "That's a fine story. A writer is afraid of a story like that. He's afraid he'll try to rewrite it. A writer has to learn when to run from a story."

The Big Bear of Arkansas

A steamboat on the Mississippi frequently, in making her regular trips, carries between places varying from one to two thousand miles apart. And as these boats advertise to land passengers and freight at "all intermediate landings," the heterogeneous character of the passengers of one of these up-country boats can scarcely be imagined by one who has never seen it with his own eyes. Starting from New Orleans in one of these boats, you will find yourself associated with men from every state in the Union, and from every portion of the globe; and a man of observation need not lack for amusement or instruction in such a crowd, if he will take the trouble to read the great book of character so favorably opened before him.

Here may be seen jostling together the wealthy Southern planter and the peddler of tinware from New England—the Northern merchant, and the Southern jockey—a venerable bishop, and a desperate gambler—the land speculator, and the honest farmer—professional men of all creeds and characters—Wolverines, Suckers, Hoosiers, Buckeyes, and Corncrackers,[1] besides a plentiful sprinkling of the half-horse and half-alligator species of men, who are peculiar to old Mississippi, and who appear to gain a livelihood simply by going up and down the river. In the pursuit of pleasure or business, I have frequently found myself in such a crowd.

On one occasion, when in New Orleans, I had occasion to take a trip of a few miles up the Mississippi, and I hurried on board the well-known "high-pressure-and-beat-everything" steamboat *Invincible,* just as the last note of the last bell was sounding. And when the confusion and bustle that is natural to a boat's getting under way had subsided, I discovered that I was associated in as heterogeneous a crowd as was ever got together. As my trip was to be of a few hours' duration only, I made no endeavors to become acquainted with my fellow passengers, most of whom would be together many days. Instead of this, I took out of my pocket the latest paper, and more critically than usual, examined its contents; my fellow passengers at the same time disposed themselves in little groups.

While I was thus busily employed in reading, and my companions were more busily employed in discussing such subjects as suited their humors best, we were startled most unexpectedly by a loud Indian whoop, uttered in the "social hall," that part of the cabin fitted off for a bar. Then was to be heard a loud crowing, which would not have continued to have interested us—such sounds being quite common in that place of spirits—had not the hero of these windy accomplishments stuck his head into the cabin and hallooed out, "Hurrah for the Big Bear of

---

[1]Nicknames for people from Michigan, Illinois, Indiana, Ohio, and Kentucky.

Arkansas!" And then might be heard a confused hum of voices, unintelligible, save in such broken sentences as "horse," "screamer,"[2] "lightning is slow," etc.

As might have been expected, this continued interruption attracted the attention of everyone in the cabin. All conversation dropped, and in the midst of this surprise the "Big Bear" walked into the cabin, took a chair, put his feet on the stove, and looking back over his shoulder, passed the general familiar salute of "Strangers, how are you?" He then expressed himself as much at home as if he had been at the Forks of Cypress, and perhaps a little more so.

Some of the company at this familiarity looked a little angry, and some astonished; but in a moment every face was wreathed in a smile. There was something about the intruder that won the heart on sight. He appeared to be a man enjoying perfect health and contentment; his eyes were as sparkling as diamonds, and good natured to simplicity. Then his perfect confidence in himself was irresistibly droll.

"Perhaps," said he, "gentlemen," running on without a person speaking, "perhaps you have been to New Orleans often. I never made *the first visit before,* and I don't intend to make another in a crow's life. I am thrown away in that-ere place, and useless, that are a fact. Some of the gentlemen there called me *green*—well, perhaps I am, said I, *but I aren't so at home.* And if I ain't off my trail much, the heads of them polite chaps themselves weren't much the hardest. For according to my notion, they were real *know-nothings,* as green as a pumpkin vine—couldn't, in farming, I'll bet, raise a crop of turnips; and as for shooting, they'd miss a barn if the door was swinging, and that, too, with the best rifle in the country.

"And then they talked to me 'bout hunting, and laughed at my calling the principal game in Arkansas poker, and high-low jack. 'Perhaps,' said I, 'you prefer chickens and roulette.'[3] At this they laughed harder than ever, and asked me if I lived in the woods and didn't know what *game* was?

"At this I rather think I laughed. 'Yes,' I roared, and says, 'Strangers, if you'd asked me *how we got our meat* in Arkansas, I'd a-told you at once, and given you a list of varmints that would make a caravan, beginning with the bear and ending off with the cat. That's *meat,* though, not game.'

"Game indeed, that's what city folks call it, and with them it means chippenbirds and shite-pokes.[4] Maybe such trash live in my diggins, but I aren't noticed them yet; a bird anyway is too trifling. I never did shoot at but one, and I'd never forgiven myself for that, had it weighed less than forty pounds. I wouldn't draw a rifle on anything less than that, and when I meet with another wild turkey of the same weight I will drop him."

"A wild turkey weighing forty pounds!" exclaimed twenty voices in the cabin at once.

"Yes, strangers, and wasn't it a whopper? You see, the thing was so fat that it couldn't fly far. And when he fell out of the tree, after I shot him, on striking the ground he bust open behind, and the way the pound gobs of tallow rolled out of the opening was perfectly beautiful."

"Where did all this happen?" asked a cynical-looking Hoosier.

"Happen! happened in Arkansas! Where else could it have happened but in the creation state, the finishing up country—a state where the *sile* runs down to the center of the earth, and government gives you title to every inch of it? Then its airs—just breathe them, and they will make you snort like a horse. It's a state without a fault, it is."

"Excepting mosquitoes," cried the Hoosier.

"Well, stranger, except them; for it are a fact that they are rather *enormous,* and do push themselves in somewhat troublesome. But, stranger, they never stick

---

[2]A thing or creature extraordinary in size, strength, or swiftness.

[3]Chicken hazard (a game at low stakes) and roulette.
[4]Chipping sparrows and green herons.

twice in the same place; and give them a fair chance for a few months, and you will get as much above noticing them as an alligator. They can't hurt my feelings, for they lay under the skin; and I never knew but one case of injury resulting from them, and that was a Yankee. And they take worse to foreigners, anyhow, than they do to natives.

"But the way they used that fellow up! First they punched him until he swelled up and busted. Then he su-per-a-ted, as the doctor called it, until he was as raw as beef. Then he took the aguer,[5] owing to the warm weather, and finally he took a steamboat and left the country. He was the only man that ever took mosquitoes to heart that I know of. But mosquitoes is natur, and I never find fault with her. If they are large, Arkansas is large, her varmints are large, her trees are large, her rivers are large, and a small mosquito would be no more use in Arkansas than preaching in a cane-brake."

This knock-down argument in favor of big mosquitoes used the Hoosier up, and the logician started on a new track, to explain how numerous bear were in his "diggins," where he represented them to be "about as plenty as blackberries, and a little plentifuler."

Upon the utterance of this assertion, a timid little man near me inquired if the bear in Arkansas ever attacked the settlers in numbers.

"No," said our hero, warming with the subject, "no, stranger, for you see it ain't the natur of bear to go in droves; but the way they squander about in pairs and single ones is edifying. And then the way I hunt them the old black rascals know the crack of my gun as well as they know a pig's squealing. They grow thin in our parts, it frightens them so, and they do take the noise dreadfully, poor things. That gun of mine is *perfect epidemic among bear*. If not watched closely, it will go off as quick on a warm scent as my dog Bowie-knife will. And then that dog—whew! Why the fellow thinks that the world is full of bear, he finds them so easy.

"It's lucky he don't talk as well as think, for with his natural modesty, if he should suddenly learn how much he is acknowledged to be ahead of all other dogs in the universe, he would be astonished to death in two minutes. Strangers, the dog knows a bear's way as well as a horse-jockey knows a woman's. He always barks at the right time, bites at the exact place, and whips without getting a scratch. I never could tell whether he was made expressly to hunt bear, or whether bear was made expressly for him to hunt. Anyway, I believe they were ordained to go together as naturally as Squire Jones says a man and a woman is, when he moralizes in marrying a couple. In fact, Jones once said, said he, 'Marriage according to the law is a civil contract of divine origin; it's common to all countries as well as Arkansas, and people take to it as naturally as Jim Doggett's Bowie-knife takes to bear.'"

"What season of the year do your hunts take place?" inquired a gentlemanly foreigner, who, from some peculiarities of his baggage I suspected to be an Englishman, on some hunting expedition, probably at the foot of the Rocky Mountains.

"The season for bear hunting, stranger," said the man of Arkansas, "is generally all the year round, and the hunts take place about as regular. I read in history that varmints have their fat season, and their lean season. That is not the case in Arkansas, feeding as they do upon the *spontenacious* production of the *sile*, they have one continued fat season the year round, though in winter things in this way is rather more greasy than in summer, I admit. For that reason, bear with us run in warm weather, but in winter, they only waddle.

"Fat! fat! it's an enemy to speed; it tames everything that has plenty of it. I have

---

[5]Ague: chills and fevers.

seen wild turkeys, from its influence, as gentle as chickens. Run a bear in this fat condition, and the way it improves the critter is amazing; it sort of mixes the ile up with the meat, until you can't tell t'other from which. I've done this often. I recollect one pretty morning in particular, of putting an old fellow on the stretch, and considering the weight he carried, he ran well. But the dogs soon tired him down, and when I come up with him, wasn't he in a beautiful sweat—I might say fever; and then to see his tongue sticking out of his mouth a foot, and his sides sinking and opening like a bellows, and his cheeks so fat he couldn't look cross. In this fix I blazed at him, and pitch me naked into a briar patch if the steam didn't come out of the bullet hole ten feet in a straight line. The fellow, I reckon, was made on the high-pressure system, and the lead sort of bust his b'iler."

"That column of steam was rather curious, or else the bear must have been *warm*," observed the foreigner, with a laugh.

"Stranger, as you observe, that bear was WARM, and the blowing off of the steam showed it, and also how much the varmint had been run. I have no doubt that if he had kept on two miles further his insides would have been stewed. And I expect to meet with a varmint yet of extra bottom, who will run himself into a skinful of bear's grease. It is possible, much unlikelier things have happened."

"Whereabouts are these bears so abundant?" inquired the foreigner, with increasing interest.

"Why, stranger, they inhabit the neighborhood of my settlement, one of the prettiest places on old Mississippi—a perfect location, and no mistake; a place that had some defects until the river made the cut-off at Shirt-Tail Bend and that remedied the evil, as it brought my cabin on the edge of the river—a great advantage in wet weather, I assure you, as you can now roll a barrel of whiskey into my yard in high water from a boat, as easy as falling off a log. It's a great improvement, as toting it by hand in a jug, as I used to do, *evaporated* it too fast, and it became expensive. Just stop with me, stranger, a month or two, or a year if you like, and you will appreciate my place. I can give you plenty to eat; for beside hog and hominy, you can have bear ham, and bear sausages, and a mattress of bear skins to sleep on, and a wildcat skin, pulled off whole, stuffed with corn shucks, for a pillow. That bed would put you to sleep if you had the rheumatics in every joint in your body. I call that-ere bed a *quietus*.[6]

"Then look at my land—the government ain't got another such a piece to dispose of. Such timber and such bottom land, only you can't preserve anything natural you plant in it unless you pick it young, things you there will grow out of shape so quick. I once planted in those diggins a few potatoes and beets; they took a fine start, and after that an ox team couldn't have kept them from growing. I went off to old Kentuck on business, and did not hear from them things in three months, when I accidentally stumbled on a fellow who had stopped at my place with an idea of buying me out.

" 'How did you like things?' said I.

" 'Pretty well,' said he. 'The cabin is convenient, and the timber land is good; but that bottom land ain't worth the first red cent.'

" 'Why?' said I.

" ''Cause,' said he.

" ''Cause what?' said I.

" ''Cause it's full of cedar stumps and Indian mounds,' said he, *'and it can't be cleared.'*

" 'Lord!' said I, 'Them-ere "cedar stumps" is beets, and them-ere "Indian mounds" are tater hills.' As I expected, the crop was overgrown and useless; the

---

[6]Release from life; i.e., death.

sile is too rich, *and planting in Arkansas is dangerous.* I had a good-sized sow killed in that same bottom land. The old thief stole an ear of corn, and took it down where she slept at night to eat. Well, she left a grain or two on the ground, and lay down on them; before morning the corn shot up, and the percussion killed her dead. I don't plant anymore; natur intended Arkansas for a hunting ground, and I go according to natur."

The questioner who thus elicited the description of our hero's settlement seemed to be perfectly satisfied and said no more. But the "Big Bear of Arkansas" rambled on from one thing to another, with a volubility perfectly astonishing, occasionally disputing with those around him, particularly with a "live Sucker" from Illinois, who had the daring to say that our Arkansas friend's stories "smelt rather tall."

In this manner the evening was spent, but conscious that my own association with so singular a person would probably end before morning, I asked him if he would not give me a description of some particular bear hunt, adding that I took great interest in such things, though I was no sportsman. The desire seemed to please him, and he squared himself round towards me, saying that he could give me an idea of a bear hunt that was never beat in this world, or in any other. His manner was so singular, that half of his story consisted in his excellent way of telling it, the great peculiarity of which was the happy manner he had of emphasizing the prominent parts of his conversation. As near as I can recollect, I have italicized them, and give you the story in his own words.

"Stranger," said he, "in bear hunts *I am numerous,* and which particular one, as you say, I shall tell, puzzles me. There was the old she devil I shot at the Harricane last fall—then there was the old hog thief I popped over at the Bloody Crossing, and then, Yes, I have it! I will give you an idea of a hunt, in which the greatest bear was killed that ever lived, *none excepted;* about an old fellow that I hunted, more or less, for two or three years, and if that ain't a particular bear hunt, I ain't got one to tell. But in the first place, stranger, let me say, I am pleased with you, because you ain't ashamed to go in for information by asking, and listening. And that's what I say to Countess's pups every day when I'm home, and I have great hopes of them-ere pups, because they are continually *nosing* about; and although they stick it sometimes in the wrong place, they gain experience anyhow, and may learn something useful to boot.

"Well, as I was saying about this big bear, you see when I and some more first settled in our region, we were driven to hunting naturally. We soon liked it, and after that we found it an easy matter to make the thing our business. One old chap who had pioneered afore us, gave us to understand that we had settled in the right place. He dwelt upon its merits until it was affecting, and showed us, to prove his assertion, more marks on the sassafras trees than I ever saw on a tavern door 'lection time.[7]

" 'Who keeps that-ere reckoning?' said I.

" 'The bear,' said he.

" 'What for?' said I.

" 'Can't tell,' said he; 'but so it is. The bear bite the bark and wood too, at the highest point from the ground they can reach, and you can tell, by the mark,' said he, 'the length of the bear to an inch.'

" 'Enough,' said I; 'I've learned something here a'ready, and I'll put it in practice.'

"Well, stranger, just one month from that time I killed a bear and told its exact length before I measured it, by those very marks. And when I did that, I swelled

---

[7]Whisky bills tacked to the tavern door; at election time, taverns were very busy.

up considerable—I've been a prouder man ever since. So I went on, larning something every day, until I was reckoned a buster,[8] and allowed to be decidedly the best bear hunter in my district. And that is a reputation as much harder to earn than to be reckoned first man in Congress, as an iron ramrod is harder than a toadstool.

"Did the varmints grow over-cunning by being fooled with by greenhorn hunters, and by this means get troublesome, they send for me as a matter of course; and thus I do my own hunting and most of my neighbors'. I walk into the varmints though, and it has become about as much the same to me as drinking. It is told in two sentences—a bear is started, and he is killed. The thing is somewhat monotonous now—I know just how much they will run, where they will tire, how much they will growl, and what a thundering time I will have in getting them home. I could give you this history of the chase with all particulars at the commencement. I know the signs so well—*stranger*, I'm certain. Once I met with a match, though, and I will tell you about it; for a common hunt would not be worth relating.

"One fine fall day, long time ago, I was trailing about for bear, and what should I see but fresh marks on the sassafras trees, about eight inches above any in the forests that I know of. Says I, 'Them marks is a hoax, or it indicates the damnedest bear that was ever grown.' In fact, stranger, I couldn't believe it was real, and I went on. Again I saw the same marks, at the same height, and *I knew the thing lived.* That conviction came back to my soul like an earthquake. Says I, 'Here is something a-purpose for me. That bear is mine, or I give up the hunting business.' The very next morning what should I see but a number of buzzards hovering over my cornfield. 'The rascal has been there,' said I, 'for that sign is certain.' And sure enough, on examining, I found the bones of what had been as beautiful a hog the day before as was ever raised by a Buckeye. Then I tracked the critter out of the woods, and all the marks he left behind, showed me that he was *the bear.*

"Well, stranger, the first fair chase I had with that big critter, I saw him no less than three distinct times at a distance. The dogs run him over eighteen miles and broke down, my horse gave out, and I was as nearly used up as a man can be, made on *my* principle, *which is patent.* Before this adventure, such things were unknown to me as possible; but, strange as it was, that bear got me used to it before I was done with him. For he got so at last that he would leave me on a long chase *quite easy.* How he did it, I never could understand. That a bear runs at all is puzzling; but how this once could tire down and bust up a pack of hounds and a horse, that were used to overhauling everything they started after, in no time, was past my understanding. Well, stranger, that bear finally got so sassy that he used to help himself to a hog off my premises whenever he wanted one. The buzzards followed after what he left, and so between *bear and buzzard,* I rather think I was *out of pork.*

"Well, missing that bear so often took hold of my vitals, and I wasted away. The thing had been carried too far, and it reduced me in flesh faster than an aguer. I would see that bear in everything I did; *he haunted me,* and that, too, like a devil, which I began to think he was. While in this fix, I made preparations to give him a last brush, and be done with it. Having completed everything to my satisfaction, I started at sunrise, and to my great joy, I discovered from the way the dogs run, that they were near him. Finding his trail was nothing, for that had become as plain to the pack as a turnpike road. On we went, and coming to an open country, what should I see but the bear very leisurely ascending a hill, and the dogs

---

[8]A prodigy.

close at his heels, either a match for him in speed, or else he did not care to get out of their way—I don't know which. But wasn't he a beauty, though? I loved him like a brother.

"On he went, until he came to a tree, the limbs of which formed a crotch about six feet from the ground. Into this crotch he got and seated himself, the dogs yelling all around it, and there he sat eyeing them as quiet as a pond in low water. A greenhorn friend of mine, in company, reached shooting distance before me, and blazed away, hitting the critter in the center of his forehead. The bear shook his head as the ball struck it, and then walked down from that tree as gently as a lady would from a carriage. 'Twas a beautiful sight to see him do that—he was in such a rage that he seemed to be as little afraid of the dogs as if they had been sucking pigs. And the dogs warn't slow in making a ring around him at a respectful distance; even Bowie-knife, himself, stood off. Then the way his eyes flashed—why the fire of them would have singed a cat's hair; in fact, that bear was in a *wrath all over*.

"Only one pup came near him, and he was brushed out so totally with the bear's left paw that he entirely disappeared; and that made the old dogs more cautious still. In the meantime, I came up, and taking deliberate aim as a man should do, at his side, just back of his foreleg, *if my gun did not snap*,[9] call me a coward, and I won't take it personal. Yes, stranger, *it snapped*, and I could not find a cap about my person. While in this predicament, I turned round to my fool friend—says I, 'Bill,' says I, 'your're an ass—you're a fool—you might as well have tried to kill that bear by barking the tree under his belly, as to have done it by hitting him in the head. Your shot has made a tiger of him, and blast me, if a dog gets wounded when they come to blows, I will stick my knife into your liver, I will—'My wrath was up. I had lost my caps, my gun had snapped, the fellow with me had fired at the bear's head, and I expected every moment to see him close in with the dogs, and kill a dozen of them at least.

"In this thing I was mistaken, for the bear leaped over the ring formed by the dogs, and giving a fierce growl was off—the pack, of course, in full cry after him. The run this time was short, for coming to the edge of a lake the varmint jumped in, and swam to a little island in the lake, which it reached just a moment before the dogs.

" 'I'll have him now,' said I, for I had found my caps in the *lining of my coat*. So, rolling a log into the lake, I paddled myself across to the island, just as the dogs had cornered the bear in a thicket. I rushed up and fired. At the same time the critter leaped over the dogs and came within three feet of me, running like mad. He jumped into the lake, and tried to mount the log I had just deserted, but every time he got half his body on it, it would roll over and send him under. The dogs, too, got around him and pulled him about, and finally Bowie-knife clenched with him, and they sank into the lake together. Stranger, about this time I was excited, and I stripped off my coat, drew my knife, and intended to have taken a part with Bowie-knife myself, when the bear rose to the surface. But the varmint stayed under—Bowie-knife came up alone, more dead than alive, and with the pack came ashore.

" 'Thank God,' said I, 'the old villain has got his deserts at last.' Determined to have the body, I cut a grapevine for a rope, and dove down to where I could see the bear in the water, fastened my queer rope to his leg, and fished him, with great difficulty, ashore, Stranger, may I be chawed to death by young alligators, if the thing I looked at wasn't a *she bear, and not the old critter after all*. The way matters got mixed on that island was unaccountably curious, and thinking of it made

---

[9]I.e., failed to fire.

me more than ever convinced that I was hunting the devil himself. I went home that night and took to my bed—the thing was killing me. The entire team of Arkansas in bear hunting, acknowledged himself used up, and the fact sunk into my feelings like a snagged boat will in the Mississippi. I grew as cross as a bear with two cubs and a sore tail.

"The thing got out among my neighbors, and I was asked how come that individ-u-al that never lost a bear when one started? And if that same individ-u-al didn't wear telescopes when he turned a she bear, of ordinary size, into an old he one, a little larger than a horse?

" 'Perhaps,' said I, 'friends'—getting wrathy—'perhaps you want to call somebody a liar.'

" 'Oh, no,' said they, 'we only heard such things as being *rather common* of late, but we don't believe one word of it, oh, no'—and they would ride off and laugh like so many hyenas over a dead nigger.

"It was too much, and I determined to catch that bear, go to Texas, or die—and I made my preparations accordin. I had the pack shut up and rested. I took my rifle to pieces and iled it. I put caps in every pocket about my person, *for fear of the lining.* I then told my neighbors, that on Monday morning—naming the day—I would start THAT BEAR, and bring him home with me, or they might divide my settlement among them, the owner having disappeared.

"Well, stranger, on the morning previous to the great day of my hunting expedition, I went along into the woods, near my house, taking my gun and Bowie-knife along, just *from habit.* And there sitting down also from habit, what should I see, getting over my fence, but *the bear!* Yes, the old varmint was within a hundred yards of me, and the way he *walked over that fence*—stranger, he loomed up like a *black mist,* he seemed so large, and he walked right towards me.

"I raised myself, took deliberate aim, and fired. Instantly the varmint wheeled, gave a yell, and *walked through that fence* like a falling tree would through a cobweb. I started after, but was tripped up by my inexpressibles, which either from habit or the excitement of the moment, were about my heels, and before I had really gathered myself up I heard the old varmint groaning in a thicket near by, like a thousand sinners, and by the time I reached him, he was a corpse.

"Stranger, it took five niggers and myself to put that carcass on a mule's back, and the old long-ears waddled under the load, as if he was foundered in every leg of his body; and with a common whopper of a bear he would have trotted off, and enjoyed himself. 'Twould astonish you to know how big he was: I made a *bedspread of his skin,* and the way it used to cover my bear mattress, and leave several feet on each side to tuck up, would have delighted you. It was in fact a creation bear, and if it had lived in Samson's[10] time, and had met him, in a fair fight, it would have licked him in the twinkling of a dice box. But stranger, I never like the way I hunted, and *missed him.* There is something curious about it I could never understand—and I never was satisfied at his giving in so easy at the last. Perhaps, he had heard of my preparations to hunt him the next day, so he just come in, like Capt. Scott's coon,[11] to save his wind to grunt with in dying. But that ain't likely. My private opinion is, that that bear was an *unhuntable bear, and died when his time come.*"

When the story was ended, our hero sat some minutes with his auditors in a grave silence. I saw that there was a mystery to him connected with the bear whose death he had just related. It was also evident that there was some superstitious awe connected with the affair—a feeling common with all children of the woods,

[10]Samson is the fabled strong man of the Bible (see Judges 13–16).
[11]Tall tales about Captain Scott made him such an excellent marksman that when a raccoon in a tree saw him approaching, he cried, "Don't shoot! I'm a-comin' down."

when they meet with anything out of their everyday experience. He was the first one, however, to break the silence and jumping up, he asked all present to "liquor" before going to bed—a thing which he did, with a number of companions, evidently to his heart's content.

Long before day, I was put ashore at my place of destination, and I can only follow with the reader, in imagination, our Arkansas friend, in his adventures at the Forks of Cypress, on the Mississippi.

1841

JOHNSON JONES HOOPER
(1815–1862)

"It is good to be shifty in a new country." This motto of a confidence man, Simon Suggs, became a popular slogan all over America in the 1840s. Johnson Jones Hooper created him in 1845 in *Some Adventures of Captain Simon Suggs,* a tongue-in-cheek campaign biography. The confidence man was a familiar figure to backwoods and frontier folk. Indeed, those who were not his victim might even admire his craft in bilking the unwary as an art to be envied. And there was no better place to practice the confidence game than the camp meeting, at which itinerant preachers set up temporary temples and set out to save—and sometimes fleece—the local populace.

Hooper was born in North Carolina and settled in Alabama, becoming a lawyer and newspaper editor. In later life, when he became involved in the Civil War on the southern side (he became secretary to the Provisional Congress of the Confederate States), he was embarrassed by his early comic stories. But this did not deter later writers from drawing on him and his materials. Herman Melville adopted a master swindler as his protagonist in his novel *The Confidence-Man* (1857) and set it on a river boat on the Mississippi River, then frontier country. Mark Twain's Duke and Dauphin in *Huckleberry Finn* (1876) were confidence artists like Simon Suggs, and they (like him) made the most of the emotional frenzy of a camp meeting (see Chapter 20). A modern version of the con man as minister is found in Sinclair Lewis's *Elmer Gantry* (1927).

Simon Suggs Attends a Camp Meeting

Captain Suggs found himself as poor at the conclusion of the Creek war[1] as he had been at the beginning. Although no arbitrary, despotic, corrupt and unprincipled judge had fined him a thousand dollars for his proclamation of martial law at Fort Suggs, or the enforcement of its rules in the case of Mrs. Haycock, yet somehow—the thing is alike inexplicable to him and to us—the money which he had contrived by various shifts to obtain, melted away and was gone forever. To a man like the Captain, of intense domestic affections, this state of destitution was

---

[1] In a previous episode, Suggs had taken advantage of a phony rumor of an Indian rebellion, getting himself made a captain, and fleecing by fines one Mrs. Haycock (named below).

most distressing. "He could stand it himself—didn't care a damn for it, no way," he observed, "but the old woman and the children, *that* bothered him."

As he sat one day ruminating upon the unpleasant condition of his financial concerns, Mrs. Suggs informed him that "the sugar and coffee was nigh about out," and that there were not "a dozen j'ints and middlins,[2] *all put together,* in the smoke house."

Suggs bounced up on the instant, exclaiming, "Damn it! *somebody* must suffer!" But whether this remark was intended to convey the idea that he and his family were about to experience the want of the necessaries of life; or that some other, and as yet unknown, individual should "suffer" to prevent that prospective exigency, must be left to the commentators, if perchance any of that ingenious class of persons should hereafter see proper to write notes for this history. It is enough for us that we give all the facts in this connection, so that ignorance of the subsequent conduct of Captain Suggs may not lead to an erroneous judgment in respect to his words.

Having uttered the exclamation we have repeated—and perhaps, hurriedly walked once or twice across the room—Captain Suggs drew on his famous old green-blanket overcoat and ordered his horse, and within five minutes was on his way to a camp meeting, then in full blast on Sandy Creek, twenty miles distant, where he hoped to find amusement, at least. When he arrived there, he found the hollow square of the encampment filled with people, listening to the mid-day sermon, and its dozen accompanying exhortations.

A half-dozen preachers were dispensing the word; the one in the pulpit, a meek-faced old man, of great simplicity and benevolence. His voice was weak and cracked, notwithstanding which, however, he contrived to make himself heard occasionally above the din of the exhorting, the singing, and the shouting which were going on around him. The rest were walking to and fro (engaged in the other exercises we have indicated), among the "mourners"—a host of whom occupied the seat set apart for their especial use—or made personal appeals to the mere spectators.

The excitement was intense. Men and women rolled about on the ground, or lay sobbing or shouting in promiscuous heaps. More than all, the Negroes sang and screamed and prayed. Several, under the influence of what is technically called "the jerks," were plunging and pitching about with convulsive energy. The greatest object of all seemed to be, to see who could make the greatest noise.

> "And each—for madness ruled the hour—
> Would try his own expressive power."[3]

"Bless my poor old soul!" screamed the preacher in the pulpit, "if yonder ain't a squad in that corner that we ain't got one out'n yet! It'll never do"—raising his voice—"you must come out'n that! Brother Fant, fetch up that youngster in the blue coat! I see the Lord's a-workin upon him! fetch him along—glory—yes!—hold to him!"

"Keep the thing warm!" roared a sensual seeming man, of stout mould and florid countenance, who was exhorting among a bevy of young women, upon whom he was lavishing caresses. "Keep the thing warm, breethring!—come to the Lord, honey!" he added, as he vigorously hugged one of the damsels he sought to save.

"Oh, I've got him!" said another in exulting tones, as he led up a gawky youth among the mourners. "I've got him—he tried to git off, but—ha! Lord!" shaking his head as much as to say, it took a smart fellow to escape him—"Ha! Lord"—and he wiped the perspiration from his face with one hand, and with the other,

---

[2] I.e., joints (hams and shoulders) and middle parts of a hog.

[3] From *The Passions: An Ode for Music* (1746), by the British poet William Collins (1721–1759).

patted his neophyte on the shoulder—"he couldn't do it! No! then he tried to ar- gue wi' me—but bless the Lord!—he couldn't do that nuther! Ha! Lord! I tuck him, first in the Old Testament—bless the Lord!—and I argued him all through Kings—then I throwed him into Proverbs—and from that, here we had it up and down, clear down to the New Testament, and then I begun to see it work him! Then we got into Matthew, and from Matthew right straight along to Acts, and *there* I throwed him! Y-e-s—L-o-r-d!" assuming the nasal twang and high pitch which are, in some parts, considered the perfection of rhetorical art—"Y-e-s L-o- r-d! and h-e-r-e he is! Now g-i-t down there," addressing the subject, "and s-e-e if the L-o-r-d won't do something f-o-r you!" Having thus deposited his charge among the mourners, he started out summarily to convert another soul.

"Gl-o-*ree*!" yelled a huge, greasy Negro woman, as in a fit of the jerks, she threw herself convulsively from her feet, and fell like a thousand of brick across a diminutive old man in a little round hat, who was speaking consolation to one of the mourners.

"Good Lord, have Mercy!" ejaculated the little man earnestly and unaffectedly, as he strove to crawl from under the sable mass which was crushing him.

In another part of the square a dozen old women were singing. They were in a state of absolute ecstasy, as their shrill pipes gave forth:

> "I rode on the sky,
> Quite undestified I,
> And the moon it was under my feet!"[4]

Near these last, stood a delicate woman in that hysterical condition in which the nerves are uncontrollable, and which is vulgarly—and almost blasphemously— termed the "holy laugh." A hideous grin distorted her mouth and was accompa- nied with a maniac's chuckle, while every muscle and nerve of the face twitched and jerked in horrible spasms.

Amid all this confusion and excitement Suggs stood unmoved. He viewed the whole affair as a grand deception—a sort of opposition line running against his own—and looked on with a sort of professional jealousy. Sometimes he would mutter running comments upon what passed before him.

"Well, now," said he, as he observed the full-faced brother who was officiating among the women, "that-ere fellow takes *my* eye! There he's been this half-hour, a-figurin among them gals, and 's never said the first word to nobody else. Won- der what's the reason these-here preachers never hugs up the old, ugly women? Never seed one do it in my life—the spirit never moves 'em that way! It's natur, though; and the women, *they* never flocks around one of the old, dried up bree- thring—bet two to one old splinter legs there"—nodding at one of the minis- ters—"won't git a chance to say turkey to a good-lookin gal today! Well! who blames 'em? Natur will be natur, the world over; and I judge, if I was a preacher, I should save the purtiest souls first, myself!"

While the Captain was in the midst of his conversation with himself, he caught the attention of the preacher in the pulpit, who inferring from an indescribable something about his appearance that he was a person of some consequence, im- mediately determined to add him at once to the church if it could be done; and to that end began a vigorous, direct personal attack.

"Breethring," he exclaimed, "I see yonder a man that's a sinner. I *know* he's a sinner! There he stands," pointing at Simon, "a miserable old critter, with his head a-blossomin for the grave! A few more short years, and d-o-w-n he'll go to perdition, lessen the Lord have mer-cy upon him! Come up here you old hoary-

---

[4]Appears to be Hooper's own verse, primarily because of its comic quality. "Undestified" is a play on the Calvinistic "predestination," but here a reversal—"unpredestinated."

headed sinner, a-n-d git down on your knees, a-n-d put up your cry for the Lord to snatch you from the bottomless pit! You're ripe for the devil—you're b-o-u-n-d for hell, and the Lord only knows what'll become on you!"

"Damn it," thought Suggs, "if I only had you down in the crick swamp for a minute or so, *I'd* show you who's *old*! I'd alter your tune *mighty* sudden, you sassy 'ceitful old rascal!" But he judiciously held his tongue and gave no utterance to the thought.

The attention of many having been directed to the Captain by the preacher's remarks, he was soon surrounded by numerous well-meaning, and doubtless very pious persons, each one of whom seemed bent on the application of his own particular recipe for the salvation of souls. For a long time the Captain stood silent, or answered the incessant stream of exhortations only with a sneer; but at length, his countenance began to give token of inward emotion. First his eyelids twitched—then his upper lip quivered—next a transparent drop formed on one of his eye lashes, and a similar one on the tip of his nose—and at last, a sudden bursting of air from nose and mouth told that Captain Suggs was overpowered by his emotions. At the moment of the explosion, he made a feint as if to rush from the crowd, but he was in experienced hands who well knew that the battle was more than half won.

"Hold to him!" said one. "It's a-workin in him as strong as a Dick horse!"[5]

"Pour it into him," said another. "It'll all come right directly!"

"That's the way I love to see 'em do," observed a third. "When you begin to draw the water from their eyes, 'tain't gwine to be long afore you'll have 'em on their knees!"

And so they clung to the Captain manfully, and half dragged, half led him to the mourners' bench; by which he threw himself down, altogether unmanned, and bathed in tears. Great was the rejoicing of the brethren, as they sang, shouted and prayed around him—for by this time it had come to be known that the convicted old man was Captain Simon Suggs, the very chief of sinners[6] in all that region.

The Captain remained grovelling in the dust during the usual time, and gave vent to even more than the requisite number of sobs and groans and heart-piercing cries. At length, when the proper time had arrived, he bounced up, and with a face radiant with joy, commenced a series of vaultings and tumblings, which laid in the shade all previous performances of the sort at that camp meeting. The brethren were in ecstasies at the demonstration of completion of the work; and whenever Suggs shouted "Gloree!" at the top of his lungs, every one of them shouted it back, until the woods rang with echoes.

The effervescence having partially subsided, Suggs was put upon his pins[7] to relate his experience, which he did somewhat in this style—first brushing the tear drops from his eyes, and giving the end of his nose a preparatory wring with his fingers, to free it of the superabundant moisture.

"Friends," he said, "it don't take long to curry a short horse, accordin to the old sayin, and I'll give you the particulars of the way I was brought to a knowledge"—here the Captain wiped his eyes, brushed the tip of his nose and snuffled a little—"in less 'n no time."

"Praise the Lord!" ejaculated a bystander.

"You see I come here full of romancin and devilment, and just to make game of all the proceedins. Well, sure enough, I done so for some time, and was a-thinkin how I should play some trick—"

"Dear soul alive! *Don't* he talk sweet!" cried an old lady in black silk. "Where's

---

[5]A stallion.
[6]See 1 Timothy 1:15. What Paul names himself.
[7]Helped to stand up on his legs.

John Dobbs? You Sukey!" screaming at a Negro woman on the other side of the square—"if you don't hunt up your Mass John in a minute, and have him here to listen to this 'sperience, I'll tuck you up when I git home and give you a hundred and fifty lashes, madam!—see if I don't! Blessed Lord!"—referring again to the Captain's relation—"ain't it a *precious* 'scourse?"[8]

"I was just a-thinkin how I should play some trick to turn it all into ridicule, when they begun to come round me and talk. Long at first, I didn't mind it, but a'ter a little that brother"—pointing to the reverend gentleman who had so successfully carried the unbeliever through the Old and New Testaments and who Simon was convinced was the "big dog of the tanyard"[9]—"that brother spoke a word that struck me clean to the heart and run all over me, like fire in dry grass—"

"*I-I-I* can bring 'em!" cried the preacher alluded to in a tone of exultation—"Lord thou knows if thy servant can't stir 'em up, nobody else needn't try—but the glory ain't mine! I'm a poor worm of the dust," he added, with ill-managed affectation.

"And so from that I felt something a-pullin me inside—"

"Grace! grace! nothin but grace!" exclaimed one; meaning that "grace" had been operating in the Captain's gastric region.

"And then," continued Suggs, "I wanted to git off, but they hilt[10] me, and bimeby[11] I felt so miserable, I had to go yonder"—pointing to the mourners' seat—"and when I lay down there it got worse and worse, and 'peared like somethin was a-mashin down on my back—"

"That was his load of sin," said one of the brethren—"never mind, it'll tumble off presently, see if it don't!" And he shook his professionally and knowingly.

"And it kept a-gittin heavier and heavier, until it looked like it might be a four year old steer, or a pine log, or somethin of that sort—"

"Glory to my soul!" shouted Mrs. Dobbs. "It's the sweetest talk I *ever* hearn! You Sukey! ain't you got John yit? never mind, my lady, I'll settle wi' you!" Sukey quailed before the finger which her mistress shook at her.

"And a'ter a while," Suggs went on, "'peared like I fell into a trance, like, and I seed—"

"Now we'll get the good on it!" cried one of the sanctified.

"And I seed the biggest, longest, riproarinest, blackest, scaliest—" Captain Suggs paused, wiped his brow, and ejaculated, "Ah, L-o-r-d!" so as to give full time for curiosity to become impatience to know what he saw.

"*Serpent*! warn't it?" asked one of the preachers.

"No, not a serpent," replied Suggs, blowing his nose.

"Do tell us *what* it war, soul alive!—where *is* John?" said Mrs. Dobbs.

"Alligator!" said the Captain.

"Alligator!" repeated every woman present, and screamed for very life.

Mrs. Dobbs' nerves were so shaken by the announcement, that after repeating the horrible word, she screamed to Sukey, "You Sukey, I say, you S-u-u-k-e-ey! if you let John come a-nigh this way where the dreadful alliga—pshaw! what am I thinkin 'bout? 'Twarn't nothin but a vision!"

"Well," said the Captain in continuation, "the alligator kept a-comin and a-comin towards me, with his great long jaws a-gapin open like a ten-foot pair of tailor's shears—"

"Oh! oh! oh! Lord! gracious above!" cried the women.

"Satan!" was the laconic ejaculation of the oldest preacher present, who thus informed the congregation that it was the devil which had attacked Suggs in the shape of an alligator.

---

[8]Discourse.
[9]"Big dog" is slang for important personage; the tanyard is an area of the tannery where cattle hides are tanned.

[10]Held.
[11]By and by.

"And then I concluded the jig was up, 'thought I could block his game some way; for I seed his idee was to snap off my head—"

The women screamed again.

"So I fixed myself just like I was perfectly willin for him to take my head, and rather he'd do it as not"—here the women shuddered perceptibly—"and so I hilt my head straight out"—the Captain illustrated by elongating his neck—"and when he come up and was a-gwine to shut down on it, I just pitched in a big rock which choked him to death, and that minute I felt the weight slide off, and I had the best feelins—sorta like you'll have from *good* spirits—anybody every had!"

"Didn't I *tell* you so? Didn't I *tell* you so?" asked the brother who had predicted the off-tumbling of the load of sin. "Ha, Lord! fool *who*! I've been *all* along there!—yes, *all along there*! and I know every inch of the way just as good as I do the road home!" And then he turned round and round, and looked at all, to receive a short tribute to his superior penetration.

Captain Suggs was now the lion of the day. Nobody could pray so well, or exhort so movingly, as "Brother Suggs." Nor did his natural modesty prevent the proper performance of appropriate exercises. With the reverend Bela Bugg (him to whom, under providence, he ascribed his conversion) he was a most especial favorite. They walked, sang, and prayed together for hours.

"Come, come up; there's room for all!" cried Brother Bugg in his evening exhortation. "Come to the seat, and if you won't pray yourselves, let *me* pray for you!"

"Yes!" said Simon, by way of assisting his friend. "It's a game that all can win at! Ante up! ante up, boys—friends I mean—don't back out!"

"There ain't a sinner here," said Bugg, "no matter if his soul's black as a nigger, but what there's room for him!"

"No matter what sort of hand you've got," added Simon in the fulness of his benevolence, "take stock! here am *I*, the wickedest and blindest of sinners—has spent my whole life in the service of the devil—has now come in on *ne'er a pair* and won a *pile*!" And the Captain's face beamed with holy pleasure.

"D-o-n-'t be afeared!" cried the preacher. "Come along! The meanest won't be turned away! Humble yourselves and come!"

"No!" said Simon, still indulging in his favorite style of metaphor. "The bluff game ain't played here! No runnin of a body off! Everybody holds four aces, and when you bet, you win!"

And thus the Captain continued, until the services were concluded, to assist in adding to the number at the mourners' seat. And up to the hour of retiring, he exhibited such enthusiasm in the cause that he was unanimously voted to be the most effective addition the church had made during that meeting.

The next morning, when the preacher of the day first entered the pulpit, he announced that "Brother Simon Suggs," mourning over his past iniquities, and desirous of going to work in the cause as speedily as possible, would take up a collection to found a church in his own neighborhood, at which he hoped to make himself useful as soon as he could prepare himself for the ministry, which the preacher didn't doubt would be in a very few weeks, as Brother Suggs was a man of mighty good *judgment* and of a great discourse. The funds were to be collected by "Brother Suggs," and held in trust by Brother Bela Bugg, who was the financial officer of the circuit, until some arrangement could be made to build a suitable house.

"Yes, breethring," said the Captain, rising to his feet, "I want to start a little 'sociation close to me, and I want you all to help. I'm mighty poor myself, as poor as any of you—don't leave, breethring,"—observing that several of the well-to-do were about to go off—"don't leave. If you ain't able to afford anything, just give us your blessin and it'll be all the same!"

This insinuation did the business, and the sensitive individuals reseated themselves.

"It's mighty little of this world's goods I've got," resumed Suggs, pulling off his hat and holding it before him. "But I'll bury that in the cause anyhow." And he deposited his last five-dollar bill in the hat.

There was a murmur of approbation at the Captain's liberality throughout the assembly.

Suggs now commenced collecting, and very prudently attacked first the gentlemen who had shown a disposition to escape. These, to exculpate themselves from anything like poverty, contributed handsomely.

"Look here, breethring," said the Captain, displaying the bank notes thus received. "Brother Snooks has dropped a five wi' me, and Brother Snodgrass a ten! In course 'tain't expected that you *that ain't as well off as them* will give *as much,* but every one give accordin to their means."

This was another chain shot[12] that raked as it went! Who so low as not to be able to contribute as much as Snooks and Snodgrass?

"Here's all the *small* money I've got about me," said a burly old fellow, ostentatiously handing to Suggs, over the heads of a half dozen, a ten-dollar bill.

"That's what I call magnanimous!" exclaimed the Captain. "That's the way every *rich* man ought to do."

These examples were followed, more or less closely, by almost all present, for Simon had excited the pride of purse in the congregation, and a very handsome sum was collected in a very short time.

The Reverend Mr. Bugg, as soon as he observed that our hero had obtained all that was to be had at that time, went to him and inquired what amount had been collected. The Captain replied that it was still uncounted, but that it couldn't be much under a hundred.

"Well, Brother Suggs, you'd better count it and turn it over to me now. I'm goin to leave presently."

"No!" said Suggs. "Can't do it!"

"Why?—what's the matter?" inquired Bugg.

"It's got to be *prayed over,* first!" said Simon, a heavenly smile illuminating his whole face.

"Well," replied Bugg, "let's go one side and do it!"

"No," said Simon, solemnly.

Mr. Bugg gave a look of inquiry.

"You see that crick swamp?" asked Suggs. "I'm gwine down in *there,* and I'm gwine to lay the money down *so*"—showing how he would place it on the ground—"and I'm gwine to git on these-here knees"—slapping the right one—"and I'm *n-e-v-e-r* gwine to quit the grit until I feel it's got the blessin! And nobody ain't got to be there but me!"

Mr. Bugg greatly admired the Captain's fervent piety, and bidding him God speed, turned off.

Captain Suggs struck for the swamp, sure enough, where his horse was already hitched. "If them fellows ain't done to a cracklin," he muttered to himself as he mounted, "I'll never bet on two pair agin! They're peart[13] at the snap game themselves, but they're badly lewed[14] this hitch! Well! Live and let live is a good old motto, and it's my sentiments adzactly!" And giving the spur to his horse, off he cantered.

1845

---

[12]Cannon shot made up of two balls connected by chains (used by the Navy especially to destroy sails).

[13]Expert.
[14]Cheated.

LITERATURE OF NATIVE AMERICANS

WINNEBAGO   QUECHUAN
TETON SIOUX   DAKOTA
MENOMINI   OJIBWA
OGLALA SIOUX   SENECA
PIMA
PAPAGO   BLACK HAWK
HOPI   SEATTLE
ZUÑI   CHIEF JOSEPH
NAVAJO
OMAHA

"To us the ashes of our ancestors are sacred and their resting place is hallowed ground. You wander far from the graves of your ancestors and seemingly without regret. Your religion was written upon tables of stone by the iron finger of your God so that you could not forget. The Red Man could never comprehend nor remember it. Our religion is the traditions of our ancestors—the dreams of our old men, given them in the solemn hours of night by the Great Spirit; and the visions of our sachems, and is written in the hearts of our people."

Seattle, "The Indians' Night Promises to be Dark"

LITERATURE OF NATIVE AMERICANS

When Columbus "discovered" America in 1492, there were (according to the estimates of historians) between one and two million natives occupying what is now the United States. They shared a common origin in the Orient (probably Mongolia), migrating across a land bridge over the Bering Strait that now separates Russian Siberia and Alaska. They arrived, according to some scientists, about 25,000 years ago; but others have speculated that it might have been 10,000 years earlier or later.

By the time Columbus, while searching for India, found America instead, the peoples in the Americas differed radically one from another. Because he thought he had discovered India, Columbus called all the inhabitants "Indians." They spoke several hundred different dialects, which linguistic scholars have classified into six fundamental language groups. It has been estimated that there were over 600 different cultures. The Indians were primarily hunters of animals and gatherers of seeds, berries, and nuts. Deer was an important food throughout the country, and also the buffalo (or bison), especially on the Great Plains. Tribes along the seashores or streams subsisted on fish. In the Southwest (New Mexico and Arizona), the natives lived in villages (pueblos); elsewhere they were nomadic, especially in the central area of the country where large herds of buffalo roamed. Corn (or maize) was an important crop everywhere, and the turkey was domesticated in some areas. Although a few tribes grew cotton, the main source of clothing and shelter was skins and furs of animals.

The Native Americans had no written language until the early part of the nineteenth century. It was then that Sequoyah (1770?–1843), the son of a Cherokee Indian maiden and a white trader, upon seeing soldiers laughing and crying while reading their mail, suddenly comprehended the importance of writing. He observed to himself: "Words are like wild animals. I must learn to capture them. I will catch them and tame and put them in writing." He created a syllabary of eighty-five characters for the Cherokee language. The syllabary was adapted for other Indian languages in the 1820s.

Although the Native Americans had no literature preserved in writing, they had a rich oral literature, stretching back into the dim, prehistoric period of the past, and handed down from one generation to another. The *Iliad* and the *Odyssey*, the classic Greek epics, were preserved in a similar way. N. Scott Momaday, a contemporary Kiowa, has said, "In the oral tradition one stands in a different relation to language. Words are rare and therefore dear. They are jealously preserved in the ear and in the mind. Words are spoken with great care, and they are heard. They matter, and they must not be taken for granted; they must be taken seriously, and they must be remembered."

The Native Americans believed language could shape and control the world around them. Words were magic, and the utterance of them a serious matter that could affect their lives. They used words ritualistically to repel storms, to induce rain, to ripen crops, to heal a friend or harm an enemy. They used words also as intermediaries between themselves and the supernatural spirit world, the world beyond death. In their profound respect for words, they used language with care and passion, and the result was often a work of great power and beauty.

Anthropologists and linguists have been writing down oral Indian literature, usually in English or Spanish, for over a hundred years. Only a fraction of the vast amount extant has been recorded, but this fraction by now is extraordinarily large. There is much controversy as to translation. Linguistic anthropologists often look upon the Indian stories and songs as cultural artifacts that are useful only when literally translated, word for word. On the other hand, poets and novelists believe that there is a spirit alive in the original that must survive in the translation, requiring thus a recreation in the new language. The simply literal is often ineffective as literature. But distortion can easily corrupt a translation too free, as was especially true in the earlier period when Indian texts took on a Christian veneer from missionary translators. A balance is clearly best, with a translation faithful to the words, spirit, and intention of the original.

For the Indians, the imaginative use of language—in effect, literature—was a part of their daily lives. There were sacred stories, dealing with the myth-laden past, telling of origins, journeys, departures and arrivals; and there were temporal or worldly stories, telling of everyday events, trials, tricks, jokes. The favorite story-telling time was at night, around a fire, the entire community gathering to listen to the storyteller.

Poems were sung or chanted. As William Brandon has observed in the introduction to his collection of Indian poetry *The Magic World* (1971), "Life was a mystical adventure, and making up songs and singing them its most important business." Often a "religious activity," the creation or chanting of poems "transformed the soul to an awareness of the beauty and holiness of the 'permanent real.'" But poems were also made for entertainment, joyous celebration, or sheer indulgence in fantasy. Sometimes, as in the Japanese haiku, a poem seems designed simply to present a single, vivid image.

The art of public speaking figured prominently in Indian life, inasmuch as the leaders were selected in part for their ability to speak and persuade. Most of the speeches that have survived are those addressed to white men in situations of confrontation—at peace parleys or in disputes over lands. Because the Indians shared land communally, they were never able to comprehend the white man's need to claim personal ownership of patches of Mother Earth. As the new settlers moved westward, the Indians retreated and diminished in numbers, their cultures shattered. And their speeches responding to this fate, often bitter and tinged with melancholy, are extraordinarily eloquent. Few readers fail to be moved by them.

In reading Indian literature of whatever genre, it is important to remember that the Indians believed in the sacred power of the word in a way quite foreign to the white man's beliefs about language. Through words the Indians felt their mystical links with Father Sky and Mother Earth, with the lakes, forests, and prairies of the places they temporarily inhabited. As they held no deeds of ownership for plots of land, so they did not claim authorship for a story or poem.

America is by its immigrant nature a pluralistic society with diverse ethnic groups making distinctive contributions to its culture. It can well learn something from the Indian respect for language and its use, as well as Indian respect for the lands and waters, air, sun, and moon to which language relates magically and directly. America can only be enriched and enlightened by paying heed to the imagination, lore, and wisdom embodied in Native American literature, an important part of the national heritage.

ADDITIONAL READING

John G. Neihardt, *Black Elk Speaks: Being the Life Story of a Holy Man of the Oglala Sioux*, 1932 ("as told through" precedes author's name, followed by the Indian name given him, Flaming Rainbow); Margot Astrov, ed., *American Indian Prose and Poetry: An Anthology*, 1946; A. Grove Day, *The Sky Clears: Poetry of the American Indians*, 1951, 1964; William T. Hagan, *American Indians*, 1961; John Bierhorst, ed., *In the Trail of Wind: American Indian Poems and Ritual Orations*, 1971; Jerome Rothenberg, *Shaking the Pumpkin: Traditional Poetry of the Indian North Americas*, 1972; Thomas E. Sanders and Walter W. Peek, ed., *Literature of the American Indian*, 1973; Wayne Moquin and Charles van Doren, eds., *Great Documents in American Indian History*, 1973; Alan R. Velie, ed., *American Indian Literature: An Anthology*, 1979; Kenneth Lincoln, "Native American Literature: 'old like hills, like stars,'" and Lester A. Standiford, "Worlds Made of Dawn," *Three American Literatures*, ed., Houston A. Baker, Jr., 1982; Bernd Peyer, ed., *The Elders Wrote: An Anthology of Early Prose by North American Indians 1768–1931*, 1982; John Bierhorst, ed., *Spells, Prayers & Power Songs of the American Indians*, 1983; Kenneth Lincoln, *Native American Renaissance*, 1983; Paula Gunn Allen, ed., *Studies in American Indian Literature: Critical Essays and Course Designs*, 1983; Russell Thornton, *American Indian Holocaust and Survival: A Population History Since 1492*, 1987; Brian Swann and Arnold Krupat, eds., *I Tell You Now: Autobiographical Essays by Native American Writers*, 1987, and *Recovering the Word: Essays on Native American Literature*, 1987; H. David Brumble III, *American Indian Autobiography*, 1988.

TEXTS

"The Story of My Ancestor Weshgishega," *Crashing Thunder: The Autobiography of an American Indian*, ed. Paul Radin, 1926; "The White Buffalo Calf Pipe," *Teton Sioux Music*, 1918; "The Jealous Ghost," *Folklore of the Menomini Indians*, ed. Alanson Skinner and John V. Satterlee, 1915; "High Horse's Courting," *Black Elk Speaks: Being the Life Story of a Holy Man of the Oglala Sioux*, "as told through" John G. Neihardt (Flaming Rainbow), 1932; poems from *The Magic World: American Indian Songs and Poems*, ed. William Brandon, 1971; speeches from *Indian Oratory: Famous Speeches by Noted Indian Chieftains*, ed. W. C. Vanderwerth, Copyright 1971 by the University of Oklahoma Press..

Tales

The Story of My Ancestor Weshgishega

[WINNEBAGO][1]

When Weshgishega was growing up his father coaxed him to fast. He told him that when Earthmaker had created the various spirits, all the good ones he had created, were placed in charge of something. The gift of bestowing upon man life and victory in war he gave to some; to others, the gift of hunting-powers. Whatever powers the Indians needed in order to live, these he placed in the hands of various spirits. These blessings Weshgishega's father told Weshgishega to attempt to obtain from the spirits.

Thus Weshgishega fasted and tried to obtain something from the spirits. But as he fasted he kept thinking to himself, "Long ago Earthmaker created all the different spirits and he put every one of them in control of something, so people say. He himself must therefore be much more powerful than all the others. As holy as

---

[1]The Winnebago were a tribe of the Sioux Indians, located in eastern Wisconsin.

these spirits are, so assuredly, Earthmaker must be mightier, holier." So he thought. He tried to be blessed by Earthmaker. He thought to himself, "What kind of being is he?" As he fasted Weshgishega thought to himself, "Not even any of the spirits whom Earthmaker created has really known Earthmaker as he actually is; not one of the spirits has he even blessed. I wonder, however, whether Earthmaker would bless me? This is what I am thinking of." So he put himself into a most pitiable condition and uttered his cry to the spirits. He could not stop. "From Earthmaker do I wish to obtain knowledge. If he does not bless me during my fasting I shall assuredly die." So, to the utmost of his power, did he fast. He wished to be blessed only by Earthmaker.

At first he fasted four days; then six; then eight; then ten and finally twelve days. After that he broke his fast. Yet it was quite clear that he had obtained no knowledge, quite clear that he had not been blessed. So he gave up his fasting and when he reached the age of early manhood he married.

He took his wife, and the two of them moved to an out-of-the-way place. There they lived, he and his wife.

Here again he commenced to fast, his wife with him. He wished to be blessed by Earthmaker. This time he felt that most assuredly would he die if Earthmaker did not appear before him in his fasting. "Never has it been told that such a thing could happen, that Earthmaker would bless any one. Yet I shall continue even if I have to die."

After a while a child was born to him. It was a boy. He addressed his wife and asked her advice, saying that they ought to sacrifice their child to Earthmaker. She consented. To Earthmaker therefore they prepared to sacrifice their child. They constructed a platform and placed their child upon it.[2] Then both of them wept bitterly. In the nighttime when the man slept, Earthmaker took pity on him and appeared to him. The man looked at him. He thought, "This, most certainly, is Earthmaker." He wore a soldier's uniform and carried a high cocked hat on his head. He had a very pleasing appearance. Weshgishega looked at him and wondered whether this really was Earthmaker. The figure took one step, then another, and finally disappeared, uttering a cry. It was not Earthmaker; it was a pigeon. The bad spirits were fooling Weshgishega.

Now even more than before did his heart ache, even more than before was his heart wound up in the desire to be blessed by Earthmaker. Now again he fasted and again apparently Earthmaker appeared to him. "Human being, I bless you. Long have you made your cry for a blessing. I am Earthmaker." When Weshgishega looked at him, he saw that he was pleasing in appearance. He looked very handsome and his dress was nice to look upon. He wondered whether this really was Earthmaker. As he looked at the figure it became smaller and smaller and when finally he looked, he noticed that it was a bird.

Then his heart ached even more than before. Bitterly did he cry. Now, for the third time, Earthmaker blessed him saying, "Human being, you have tried to be blessed by Earthmaker and you have caused yourself great suffering. I am Earthmaker and I bless you. You will never be in want of anything; you will be able to understand the languages of your neighbors; you will have a long life; indeed, with everything do I bless you." But, from the very first, this figure did not inspire Weshgishega with confidence and he thought to himself, "Somebody must be fooling me." And so it was; it was a bird.

Then most assuredly did he think that he wished to die for he felt that all the bad birds in the world were trying to make fun of him.

Earthmaker, above where he sits, knew of all this. He heard the man's voice

---

[2]I.e., they killed the child and placed the body on the platform, in accord with the clan burial customs.

and he said, "O Weshgishega, you are crying. I shall come to the earth for you. Your father has told me all." Then when Weshgishega looked, he saw a ray of light extending very distinctly from the sky down to the earth. To the camp it extended. "Weshgishega, you said that you wanted to see me. That, however, cannot be. But I am the ray of light. You have seen me."

Not with any war powers did Earthmaker bless him; only with life.

The White Buffalo Calf Pipe[1]

[TETON SIOUX][2]

In the olden times it was a general custom for the Sioux tribe (especially the Teton band of Sioux) to assemble in a body once at least during the year. This gathering took place usually about that time of midsummer when everything looked beautiful and everybody rejoiced to live to see nature at its best—that was the season when the Sun-dance ceremony took place and vows were made and fulfilled. Sometimes the tribal gathering took place in the fall when wild game was in the best condition, when wild fruits of all kinds were ripe, and when the leaves on the trees and plants were the brightest.

One reason why the people gathered as they did was that the tribe as a whole might celebrate the victories, successes on the warpath, and other good fortunes which had occurred during the year while the bands were scattered and each band was acting somewhat independently. Another reason was that certain rules or laws were made by the head chiefs and other leaders of the tribe, by which each band of the tribe was governed. For instance, if a certain band got into trouble with some other tribe, as the Crows, the Sioux tribe as a whole should be notified. Or if an enemy or enemies came on their hunting grounds the tribe should be notified at once. In this way the Teton band of Sioux was protected as to its territory and its hunting grounds.

After these gatherings there was a scattering of the various bands. On one such occasion the Sans Arc band started toward the west. They were moving from place to place, expecting to find buffalo and other game which they would lay up for their winter supply, but they failed to find anything. A council was called and two young men were selected to go in quest of buffalo and other game. They started on foot. When they were out of sight they each went in a different direction, but met again at a place which they had agreed upon. While they were planning and planning what to do, there appeared from the west a solitary object advancing toward them. It did not look like a buffalo; it looked more like a human being than anything else. They could not make out what it was, but it was coming rapidly. Both considered themselves brave, so they concluded that they would face whatever it might be. They stood still and gazed at it very eagerly. At last they saw that it was a beautiful young maiden. She wore a beautiful fringed buckskin dress, leggings, and moccasins. Her hair was hanging loose except at the left side, where was tied a tuft of shedded buffalo hair. In her right hand she carried a fan made of flat sage. Her face was painted with red vertical stripes. Not knowing what to do or say, they hesitated, saying nothing to her.

She spoke first, thus: "I am sent by the Buffalo tribe to visit the people you

---

[1]This tale fulfills several important functions of myths—it reveals the origin of the special peace pipe, as well as the ways it is to be used and the purposes it serves in ritual and ceremony.

[2]One of the largest Indian confederations of North America, the Sioux were located on the northern plains of the United States; the Tetons were one of the seven tribes of the Sioux.

represent. You have been chosen to perform a difficult task. It is right that you should try to carry out the wishes of your people, and you must try to accomplish your purpose. Go home and tell the chief and headmen to put up a special lodge in the middle of the camp circle, with the door of the lodge and the entrance into the camp toward the direction where the sun rolls off the earth. Let them spread sage at the place of honor, and back of the fireplace let a small square place be prepared. Back of this and the sage let a certain frame, or rack, be made. Right in front of the rack a buffalo skull should be placed. I have something of importance to present to the tribe, which will have a great deal to do with their future welfare. I shall be in the camp about sunrise."

While she was thus speaking to the young men one of them had impure thoughts. A cloud came down and enveloped this young man. When the cloud left the earth the young man was left there—only a skeleton. The Maiden commanded the other young man to turn his back toward her and face in the direction of the camp, then to start for home. He was ordered not to look back.

When the young man came in sight of the camp he ran in a zigzag course, this being a signal required of such parties on returning home from a searching or scouting expedition. The people in the camp were on the alert for the signal, and preparations were begun at once to escort the party home. Just outside the council lodge, in front of the door, an old man qualified to perform the ceremony was waiting anxiously for the party. He knelt in the direction of the coming of the party to receive the report of the expedition. A row of old men were kneeling behind him. The young man arrived at the lodge. Great curiosity was shown by the people on account of the missing member of the party. The report was made, and the people received it with enthusiasm.

The special lodge was made, and the other requirements were carried out. The crier announced in the whole camp what was to take place on the following morning. Great preparations were made for the occasion. Early the next morning, at daybreak, men, women, and children assembled around the special lodge. Young men who were known to bear unblemished characters were chosen to escort the Maiden into the camp. Promptly at sunrise she was in sight. Everybody was anxious. All eyes were fixed on the Maiden. Slowly she walked into the camp. She was dressed as when she first appeared to the two young men except that instead of the sage fan she carried a pipe—the stem was carried with her right hand and the bowl with the left.

The chief, who was qualified and authorized to receive the guest in behalf of the Sioux tribe, sat outside, right in front of the door of the lodge, facing the direction of the coming of the Maiden. When she was at the door the chief stepped aside and made room for her to enter. She entered the lodge, went to the left of the door, and was seated at the place of honor.

The chief made a speech welcoming the Maiden, as follows:

"My dear relatives: This day Wakaŋ'taŋka has again looked down and smiled upon us by sending us this young Maiden, whom we shall recognize and consider as a sister. She has come to our rescue just as we are in great need. Wakaŋ'taŋka wishes us to live. This day we lift up our eyes to the sun, the giver of light, that opens our eyes and gives us this beautiful day to see our visiting sister. Sister, we are glad that you have come to us, and trust that whatever message you have brought we may be able to abide by it. We are poor, but we have a great respect to visitors, especially relatives. It is our custom to serve our guests with some special food. We are at present needy and all we have to offer you is water, that falls from the clouds. Take it, drink it, and remember that we are very poor."

Then braided sweet grass was dipped into a buffalo horn containing rain water and was offered to the Maiden. The chief said, "Sister, we are now ready to hear the good message you have brought." The pipe, which was in the hands of the Maiden, was lowered and placed on the rack. Then the Maiden sipped the water from the sweet grass.

Then, taking up the pipe again, she arose and said:

"My relatives, brothers and sisters: Wakaŋ'taŋka has looked down, and smiles upon us this day because we have met as belonging to one family. The best thing in a family is good feeling toward every member of the family. I am proud to become a member of your family—a sister to you all. The sun is your grandfather, and he is the same to me. Your tribe has the distinction of being always very faithful to promises, and of possessing great respect and reverence toward sacred things. It is known also that nothing but good feeling prevails in the tribe, and that whenever any member has been found guilty of committing any wrong, that member has been cast out and not allowed to mingle with the other members of the tribe. For all these good qualities in the tribe you have been chosen as worthy and deserving of all good gifts. I represent the Buffalo tribe, who have sent you this pipe. You are to receive this pipe in the name of all the common people [Indians]. Take it, and use it according to my directions. The bowl of the pipe is red stone—a stone not very common and found only at a certain place. This pipe shall be used as a peacemaker. The time will come when you shall cease hostilities against other nations. Whenever peace is agreed upon between two tribes or parties this pipe shall be a binding instrument. By this pipe the medicine-men shall be called to administer help to the sick."

Turning to the women, she said:

"My dear sisters, the women: You have a hard life to live in this world, yet without you this life would not be what it is. Wakaŋ'taŋka intends that you shall bear much sorrow—comfort others in time of sorrow. By your hands the family moves. You have been given the knowledge of making clothing and of feeding the family. Wakaŋ'taŋka is with you in your sorrows and joins you in your griefs. He has given you the great gift of kindness toward every living creature on earth. You he has chosen to have a feeling for the dead who are gone. He knows that you remember the dead longer than do the men. He knows that you love your children dearly."

Then turning to the children:

"My little brothers and sisters: Your parents were once little children like you, but in the course of time they became men and women. All living creatures were once small, but if no one took care of them they would never grow up. Your parents love you and have made many sacrifices for your sake in order that Wakaŋ'taŋka may listen to them, and that nothing but good may come to you as you grow up. I have brought this pipe for them, and you shall reap some benefit from it. Learn to respect and reverence this pipe, and above all, lead pure lives. Wakaŋ'taŋka is your great grandfather."

Turning to the men:

"Now my dear brothers: In giving you this pipe you are expected to use it for nothing but good purposes. The tribe as a whole shall depend upon it for their necessary needs. You realize that all your necessities of life come from the earth below, the sky above, and the four winds. Whenever you do anything wrong against these elements they will always take some revenge upon you. You should reverence them. Offer sacrifices through this pipe. When you are in need of buffalo meat, smoke this pipe and ask for what you need and it shall be granted you. On you it depends to be a strong help to the women in the raising of children. Share the women's sorrow. Wakaŋ'taŋka smiles on the man who has a kind feeling for a woman, because the woman is weak. Take this pipe, and offer it to Wakaŋ'taŋka daily. Be good and kind to the little children."

Turning to the chief:

"My older brother: You have been chosen by these people to receive this pipe in the name of the whole Sioux tribe. Wakaŋ'taŋka is pleased and glad this day because you have done what it is required and expected that every good leader should do. By this pipe the tribe shall live. It is your duty to see that this pipe is respected and reverenced. I am proud to be called a sister. May Wakaŋ'taŋka look down on us and take pity on us and provide us with what we need. Now we shall smoke the pipe."

Then she took the buffalo chip which lay on the ground, lighted the pipe, and pointing to the sky with the stem of the pipe, she said, "I offer this to Wakaŋ'taŋka for all the good that comes from above." (Pointing to the earth:) "I offer this to the earth, whence come all good gifts." (Pointing to the cardinal points:) "I offer this to the four winds, whence come all good things." Then she took a puff of the pipe, passed it to the chief, and said, "Now my dear brothers and sisters, I have done the work for which I was sent here and now I will go, but I do not wish any escort. I only ask that the way be cleared before me."

Then, rising, she started, leaving the pipe with the chief, who ordered that the people be quiet until their sister was out of sight. She came out of the tent on the left side, walking very slowly; as soon as she was outside the entrance she turned into a white buffalo calf.[3]

The Jealous Ghost

[MENOMINI][1]

This happened very long ago among the Menomini, and it is the truth.

There was once a man and his wife who had four sons and two daughters. The eldest of the sisters got married and went with her husband and family, but she soon took sick and died. Right in the place where she breathed her last they dressed her in beautiful clothes and buried her, and the rest of the party stayed right there for they did not like to leave her. After a while, the four brothers began to suspect that their brother-in-law was going to leave them because his wife was gone. They liked him so much that they begged him not to go and gave him the other sister in place of his dead wife.

The girl was very young, but he stayed to live with her. One day the old mother took the girl out with her to dig wild potatoes which grew a short distance from their camp. Evening approached, and the old woman said: "Now let's go home," but the daughter continued digging as she was finding more and bigger ones. In the meantime her mother took her pack on her back and started off, saying once more; "Come, let's go home!" But the daughter kept right on digging.

The sun set and it began to get dark. The mother by this time was at home, and the young girl started off to find her. As she was walking along with her load she heard someone behind, saying: "Well, you who are marrying and living with your brother-in-law!" The young wife understood right away that this was her sister who had died so she answered: "Well, it was not my intention to live with him; it is not my fault, my four brothers wanted me to live with him because they had loved our sister so much."

---

[3]The collector of this tale, Frances Densmore, added: "It is said that the chief who received the pipe from the White Buffalo Maiden was Buffalo Stands Upward [in the early eighteenth century]. . . . The pipe has been handed down from one generation to another. . . ."

[1]The Menomini were related to the Algonquians and were located in northern Wisconsin.

The girl was so frightened that she whooped and screamed for help as she hurried through the dark for her house. Her mother and brothers heard her and made a bigger fire to give her light to make for camp. They made birchbark torches and turned out to meet her. The young wife told her mother that a woman had overtaken her and found fault with her because she was living with her own brother-in-law. When the party went out to meet her and bring her to the wigwam they did not see anything or anybody with her, but just as she was about to enter the wigwam door and one of the brothers lifted the door mat for her to go in, she was pushed from behind with such force that she fell head first into the big fire and was burnt to death in a few moments. The mother and brothers saw nobody, but they knew it was the jealous ghost of her dead sister.

Then the mother became so agitated and crazy with rage she went outside their wigwam for a few steps to where her first daughter was buried and dug up her body and pulled her violently out of the grave and flung her around. She threw her down and stripped her, taking off her fancy clothes that they had put on her to show their love. Then the mother spoke to the corpse saying: "Why don't you come to natural life if you have the power of a god?"

Then the distracted mother quit her abuse and left the body lying on the ground naked, taking the pretty clothes to put on the girl who was burned to death and buried her in the elder daughter's grave. The next morning, when the husband went out and saw the body of his first wife lying their naked, it made him very sad, and he did not like it. The old people said to their sons, "Now let us move away from this place." They asked their brother-in-law to go along with them but he replied, "I will remain here until I bury her."

So the old folks and their sons left him, and the husband went out and dragged his first wife's body into the lodge. He took some of her old clothes and dressed her and placed her in his bed, where she lay as though asleep. He himself rested on the other side of the wigwam opposite her, and every time he cooked for himself he offered some of the victuals to her. "Here is your dish, eat!" he would say.

He did this at every meal time, and once as he did this he thought he saw her hand move. It was her shade which had appeared first, like a shadow on the wall, so he thought that after a while she would come to life. He continued to cook, and made some broth or gruel and put some of it in her mouth with a spoon, very slowly, and as the broth went down, she swallowed it. He kept on with this till she really came to life and got up and worked the same as ever.

They both lived right there and stored away meat of all kinds that the husband had killed in hunting, till it happened that some Indians came to camp in the neighborhood. One day the wife's younger brother, who was still a child, saw his brother-in-law when he was out walking and recognized him. He also saw his sister who he knew had died some time ago. He thought it must be another person just like her, it couldn't be she, but when he looked closer he was sure he could not be mistaken. So he went home and told his mother that he had seen his brother-in-law: "Yes, and I saw my eldest sister, too, she has come to life again!"

When the mother learned this she went over to visit her. She knew her but did not say much to her about what had happened to them both. As she went out her daughter gave her some dried meat. The meat was the muscle of deer's legs and when she began to eat it the first bite choked her to death, and then her daughter was even with her.

High Horse's Courting

[Oglala Sioux][1]

You know, in the old days, it was not so very easy to get a girl when you wanted to be married. Sometimes it was hard work for a young man and he had to stand a great deal. Say I am a young man and I have seen a young girl who looks so beautiful to me that I feel all sick when I think about her. I can not just go and tell her about it and then get married if she is willing. I have to be a very sneaky fellow to talk to her at all, and after I have managed to talk to her, that is only the beginning.

Probably for a long time I have been feeling sick about a certain girl because I love her so much, but she will not even look at me, and her parents keep a good watch over her. But I keep feeling worse and worse all the time; so maybe I sneak up to her tepee in the dark and wait until she comes out. Maybe I just wait there all night and don't get any sleep at all and she does not come out. Then I feel sicker than ever about her.

Maybe I hide in the brush by a spring where she sometimes goes to get water, and when she comes by, if nobody is looking, then I jump out and hold her and just make her listen to me. If she likes me too, I can tell that from the way she acts, for she is very bashful and maybe will not say a word or even look at me the first time. So I let her go, and then maybe I sneak around until I can see her father alone, and I tell him how many horses I can give him for his beautiful girl, and by now I am feeling so sick that maybe I would give him all the horses in the world if I had them.

Well, this young man I am telling about was called High Horse, and there was a girl in the village who looked so beautiful to him that he was just sick all over from thinking about her so much and he was getting sicker all the time. The girl was very shy, and her parents thought a great deal of her because they were not young any more and this was the only child they had. So they watched her all day long, and they fixed it so that she would be safe at night too when they were asleep. They thought so much of her that they had made a rawhide bed for her to sleep in, and after they knew that High Horse was sneaking around after her, they took rawhide thongs and tied the girl in bed at night so that nobody could steal her when they were asleep, for they were not sure but that their girl might really want to be stolen.

Well, after High Horse had been sneaking around a good while and hiding and waiting for the girl and getting sicker all the time, he finally caught her alone and made her talk to him. Then he found out that she liked him maybe a little. Of course this did not make him feel well. It made him sicker than ever, but now he felt as brave as a bison bull, and so he went right to her father and said he loved the girl so much that he would give two good horses for her—one of them young and the other one not so very old.

But the old man just waved his hand, meaning for High Horse to go away and quit talking foolishness like that.

High Horse was feeling sicker than ever about it; but there was another young fellow who said he would loan High Horse two ponies and when he got some more horses, why, he could just give them back for the ones he had borrowed.

Then High Horse went back to the old man and said he would give four horses for the girl—two of them young and the other two not hardly old at all. But the old man just waved his hand and would not say anything.

---

[1]The Oglala were a tribe of the Teton Dakota group of Sioux Indians. The speaker of this tale is the Oglala Sioux medicine man, Black Elk, retelling a story told him by Watanye, a friend.

So High Horse sneaked around until he could talk to the girl again, and he asked her to run away with him. He told her he thought he would just fall over and die if she did not. But she said she would not do that; she wanted to be bought like a fine woman. You see she thought a great deal of herself too.

That made High Horse feel so very sick that he could not eat a bite, and he went around with his head hanging down as though he might just fall down and die any time.

Red Deer was another young fellow, and he and High Horse were great comrades, always doing things together. Red Deer saw how High Horse was acting, and he said: "Cousin, what is the matter? Are you sick in the belly? You look as though you were going to die."

Then High Horse told Red Deer how it was, and said he thought he could not stay alive much longer if he could not marry the girl pretty quick.

Red Deer thought awhile about it, and then he said: "Cousin, I have a plan, and if you are man enough to do as I tell you, then everything will be all right. She will not run away with you; her old man will not take four horses; and four horses are all you can get. You must steal her and run away with her. Then afterwhile you can come back and the old man cannot do anything because she will be your woman. Probably she wants you to steal her anyway."

So they planned what High Horse had to do, and he said he loved the girl so much that he was man enough to do anything Red Deer or anybody else could think up.

So this is what they did.

That night late they sneaked up to the girl's tepee and waited until it sounded inside as though the old man and the old woman and the girl were sound asleep. Then High Horse crawled under the tepee with a knife. He had to cut the rawhide thongs first, and then Red Deer, who was pulling up the stakes around that side of the tepee, was going to help drag the girl outside and gag her. After that, High Horse could put her across his pony in front of him and hurry out of there and be happy all the rest of his life.

When High Horse had crawled inside, he felt so nervous that he could hear his heart drumming, and it seemed so loud he felt sure it would 'waken the old folks. But it did not, and afterwhile he began cutting the thongs. Every time he cut one it made a pop and nearly scared him to death. But he was getting along all right and all the thongs were cut down as far as the girl's thighs, when he became so nervous that his knife slipped and stuck the girl. She gave a big, loud yell. Then the old folks jumped up and yelled too. By this time High Horse was outside, and he and Red Deer were running away like antelope. The old man and some other people chased the young men but they got away in the dark and nobody knew who it was.

Well, if you ever wanted a beautiful girl you will know how sick High Horse was now. It was very bad the way he felt, and it looked as though he would starve even if he did not drop over dead sometime.

Red Deer kept thinking about this, and after a few days he went to High Horse and said: "Cousin, take courage! I have another plan, and I am sure, if you are man enough, we can steal her this time." And High Horse said: "I am man enough to do anything anybody can think up, if I can only get that girl."

So this is what they did.

They went away from the village alone, and Red Deer made High Horse strip naked. Then he painted High Horse solid white all over, and after that he painted black stripes all over the white and put black rings around High Horse's eyes. High Horse looked terrible. He looked so terrible that when Red Deer was through painting and took a good look at what he had done, he said it scared even him a little.

"Now," Red Deer said, "if you get caught again, everybody will be so scared they will think you are a bad spirit and will be afraid to chase you."

So when the night was getting old and everybody was sound asleep, they sneaked back to the girl's tepee. High Horse crawled in with his knife, as before, and Red Deer waited outside, ready to drag the girl out and gag her when High Horse had all the thongs cut.

High Horse crept up by the girl's bed and began cutting at the thongs. But he kept thinking, "If they see me they will shoot me because I look so terrible." The girl was restless and kept squirming around in bed, and when a thong was cut, it popped. So High Horse worked very slowly and carefully.

But he must have made some noise, for suddenly the old woman awoke and said to her old man: "Old Man, wake up! There is somebody in this tepee!" But the old man was sleepy and didn't want to be bothered. He said: "Of course there is somebody in this tepee. Go to sleep and don't bother me." Then he snored some more.

But High Horse was so scared by now that he lay very still and as flat to the ground as he could. Now, you see, he had not been sleeping very well for a long time because he was so sick about the girl. And while he was lying there waiting for the old woman to snore, he just forgot everything, even how beautiful the girl was. Red Deer who was lying outside ready to do his part, wondered and wondered what had happened in there, but he did not dare call out to High Horse.

Afterwhile the day began to break and Red Deer had to leave with the two ponies he had staked there for his comrade and girl, or somebody would see him.

So he left.

Now when it was getting light in the tepee, the girl awoke and the first thing she saw was a terrible animal, all white with black stripes on it, lying asleep beside her bed. So she screamed, and then the old woman screamed and the old man yelled. High Horse jumped up, scared almost to death, and he nearly knocked the tepee down getting out of there.

People were coming running from all over the village with guns and bows and axes, and everybody was yelling.

By now High Horse was running so fast that he hardly touched the ground at all, and he looked so terrible that the people fled from him and let him run. Some braves wanted to shoot at him, but the others said he might be some sacred being and it would bring bad trouble to kill him.

High Horse made for the river that was near, and in among the brush he found a hollow tree and dived into it. Afterwhile some braves came there and he could hear them saying that it was some bad spirit that had come out of the water and gone back in again.

That morning the people were ordered to break camp and move away from there. So they did, while High Horse was hiding in his hollow tree.

Now Red Deer had been watching all this from his own tepee and trying to look as though he were as much surprised and scared as all the others. So when the camp moved, he sneaked back to where he had seen his comrade disappear. When he was down there in the brush, he called, and High Horse answered, because he knew his friend's voice. They washed off the paint from High Horse and sat down on the river bank to talk about their troubles.

High Horse said he never would go back to the village as long as he lived and he did not care what happened to him now. He said he was going to go on the war-path all by himself. Red Deer said: "No, cousin, you are not going on the war-path alone, because I am going with you."

So Red Deer got everything ready, and at night they started out on the war-path all alone. After several days they came to a Crow camp just about sundown, and when it was dark they sneaked up to where the Crow horses were grazing, killed the horse guard, who was not thinking about enemies because he thought all the Lakotas[2] were far away, and drove off about a hundred horses.

They got a big start because all the Crow horses stampeded and it was probably morning before the Crow warriors could catch any horses to ride. Red Deer and High Horse fled with their herd three days and nights before they reached the village of their people. Then they drove the whole herd right into the village and up in front of the girl's tepee. The old man was there, and High Horse called out to him and asked if he thought maybe that would be enough horses for his girl. The old man did not wave him away that time. It was not the horses that he wanted. What he wanted was a son who was a real man and good for something.

So High Horse got his girl after all, and I think he deserved her.

Poems and Songs[1]

Pima: *Feast Song*[2]

I stand straight
          singing my shining song
                    to the gods

Harlots come running
          holding blue flowers
                    talking in whispers   5

               (Singers now appear, in two files,
               men and women apart.)

Along the crooked road I'm going
along the crooked road I'm going   10
               going to the rainbows
               westward to the rainbows
               swinging my arms

---

[2]Another name for the Teton Dakota Indians, including the Oglala Sioux. The Crows were a rival tribe.

[1]All translations of the poems and songs are adapted from literal translations (done by anthropologists and linguists) by poet William Brandon and are taken from his book, *The Magic World: American Indian Songs and Poems* (1971). Brandon has provided this explanation: "The people from whom these poems come: *Pima*, village farmers who have lived from ancient prehistoric times along the valleys of the Gila and Salt rivers in the region of present Phoenix, Arizona; their near relatives the *Papago*, of the desert country near present Tucson; the *Hopi*, whose villages in northern Arizona contain some of the oldest continuously occupied sites in North America; *Zuñi*, puebloan residents of western New Mexico; *Navajo*, the largest Indian tribe in the United States, an Apache-related people who occupy an extensive area in and about northeastern Arizona; *Omaha*, a siouan-speaking group on the Missouri River in Nebraska; *Quechan*, the name used today—their own name—for the Colorado River people formerly known as the Yuma; *Dakota*, the real name of the Sioux, chiefly associated with the high plains of the West; *Ojibwa* (sometimes Chippewa, different spellings of the same word) on the shores of Lake Superior and Lake Huron; *Seneca*, one of the Five Nations Iroquois, their homeland between Lake Seneca and the Genesee River in upstate New York."

[2]This footnote and all remaining footnotes are by the translator (or adapter), William Brandon. Adapted from the literal translation in Frank Russell, "The Pima Indians," *Twenty-sixth Annual BAE Report*, Washington, D.C., 1908.

Pima: *A Dancing Song*[3]

Dizzy I run into the bog water
there tadpoles sing among the reeds
tadpoles wearing girdles of bark
      there singing

In the evening land a very blue dragonfly   5
hanging on the water top
touching in his tail

There I run in rattling darkness
cactus flowers in my hair
in rattling darkness   10

        darkness rattling
running to that singing place

Papago: *Elegy Dream Song*[4]

In the great night my heart will go out
darkness will come toward me
    with a sound of rattling
in the great night my heart will go out

I am running toward a range of low mountains   5
from those mountain tops I will see the dawn

I die and lie dead here

I die and lie dead here!

Hopi: *Kachina Song*[5]

Yellow butterflies for corn blossoms
           (with flower-painted maidens' faces)
Blue butterflies over bean blossoms
           (with pollen-painted maidens' faces)
Yellow and blue hovering, hovering,   5

Wild bees singing in and out

Over all black thunder hanging

Over all downpouring rain

---

[3]Adapted from the literal translation in Russell, "The Pima Indians."
[4]Adapted from Frances Densmore, *Papago Music, BAE Bulletin 90*, Washington, D.C., 1929.
[5]Adapted from Natalie Curtis, *The Indians' Book*, New York, 1907, in comparison with a literal translation made with the consultation of Rev. H. R. Voth. The song was composed and sung by a young poet of the time, Koianimptiwa, for a Korosta Kachina Dance, a corn-planting dance in which the kachinas wear rainbow masks.

Zuñi: *Storm Song*[6]

Cover my earth mother
four times with many flowers

Cover the heavens
with high-piled clouds

Cover the earth with fog   5
cover the earth with rains

Cover the earth with great rains
cover the earth with lightnings

Let thunder drum over all the earth
let thunder be heard   10

Let thunder drum over all
over all the six directions of the earth

Navajo: *The War God's Horse Song*[7]

I am the Turquoise Woman's son

On top of Belted Mountain beautiful horses
slim like a weasel

My horse has a hoof like striped agate
his fetlock is like fine eagle plume   5
his legs are like quick lightning

My horse's body is like an eagle-feathered arrow

My horse has a tail like a trailing black cloud

I put flexible goods on my horse's back

The Holy Wind blows through his mane   10
his mane is made of rainbows

My horse's ears are made of round corn

My horse's eyes are made of stars

My horse's head is made of mixed waters
   (from the holy waters)   15
   (he never knows thirst)

My horse's teeth are made of white shell

---

[6]Adapted from Matilda Coxe Stevenson, "The Zuñi Indians," *Twenty-third Annual BAE Report*, Washington, D.C., 1904.
[7]Adapted from Dane and Mary Roberts Coolidge, *The Na-* *vaho Indians*, Boston, 1930. The words to the song were furnished by Tall Kiaah'ni, and interpreted by Louis Watchman.

> The long rainbow is in his mouth for a bridle
> with it I guide him
>
> When my horse neighs   20
> different-colored horses follow
>
> When my horse neighs
> different-colored sheep follow
>
> I am wealthy from my horse
>
> Before me peaceful   25
> Behind me peaceful
> Under me peaceful
> Over me peaceful
> Around me peaceful
> Peaceful voice when he neighs   30
> I am everlasting and peaceful
> I stand for my horse

Navajo: *Lines from the Wind Chant*[8]

The patient was twice bathed, sacredly.

Then his body was painted with the sun on his breast
       and the wind above,
       the moon on his back,
       arrows on his arms,   5
       snakes on his legs
       and on each shoulder a white cross.

A prayer plume they tied to his head
and they painted his face,
       white on the forehead,   10
       red across the eyes,
       yellow across the chin.

They mixed herbs
       and the Blue Jay came
       and the Whirling Winds.   15

The singer stroked the patient's body
and pressed his body to the patient's body.

Have you learned? they asked him
and he answered, Yes.

They sang all night, and the patient learned   20
and was well.

Then he was told to be sure and remember all that he had been taught,
for everything forgotten went back to the gods.

---

[8]Freely adapted from "*Nilth Chiji Bakaji*" (Wind Chant), told by Hasteen Klah, retold in shorter form by Mary C. Wheelwright in *Bulletin No. 4, Museum of Navajo Ceremonial Art*, Santa Fe, 1946, copyright 1946, by the Museum of Navajo Ceremonial Art.

Omaha: *The Rock (Fragment of a Ritual)*[9]

    unmoved
    from time without
    end
    you rest
    there in the midst of the paths   5
    in the midst of the winds
    you rest
    covered with the droppings of birds
    grass growing from your feet
    your head decked with the down of birds   10
    you rest
    in the midst of the winds
    you wait
    Aged one

Three Fragments (Quechuan, Dakota, Ojibwa)[10]

QUECHUAN

The water bug is drawing
    the shadows of the evening
        toward him on the water

DAKOTA

You cannot harm me
    you cannot harm
        one who has dreamed a dream like
        mine

OJIBWA

The bush is sitting under a tree and
singing

Ojibwa: *Firefly Song*[11]

Flickering firefly
        give me light
        light
once more before I sleep

---

[9]Adapted from Alice C. Fletcher and Francis La Flesche, "The Omaha Tribe," in *Twenty-seventh Annual BAE Report,* Washington, D.C., 1911.
[10]From *Frances Densmore and American Indian Music,* Museum of the American Indian, Heye Foundation, New York, 1968.

[11]Adapted from Henry R. Schoolcraft, *Historical and Statistical Information, Respecting the History, Condition, and Prospects of the Indian Tribes of the United States,* Philadelphia, 1851–57.

Dancing firefly   5
    wandering firefly
      light
once more before I sleep

White light sailing
        white light winking   10
just once more before I sleep

Seneca: *A Vision of Handsome Lake*[12]

The day was bright when I went into the planted field
Alone I wandered in the planted field

It was the time of the second hoeing

A maiden appeared and clasped me about the neck
saying   5
    When you leave this earth for the new world above
    we want to follow you

I looked for the maiden
but saw only the long leaves of corn
twined round my shoulders   10

I understood it was the spirit of the corn
speaking
she the sustainer of life

I replied O spirit
    follow me not   15

    but remain here upon the earth
    be strong and faithful to your purpose

Endure

Do not fail the children of women

It is not time for you to follow   20

The word I teach is only in its beginning

---

[12]Slightly altered from Arthur C. Parker, *The Code of Handsome Lake, the Seneca Prophet*, Albany, 1913. Handsome Lake taught a new religion, and brought a literal salvation to the Seneca; he died at Onondaga, New York, in 1815, a few days after relating this, his last vision.

Speeches[1]

BLACK HAWK
(1767–1838)

Chief of the Sauk and Fox Indians, Black Hawk refused to remove his people to the west of the Mississippi in compliance with an 1804 treaty. He roused his people to war with speeches like the one included here, delivered in 1832. In the Black Hawk War of 1832, he and his braves were captured, and Black Hawk sent to Washington to meet with President Andrew Jackson. In 1833, he published his *Autobiography,* defending his actions. He died in 1838, at the age of seventy-two.

"For More Than a Hundred Winters Our Nation Was a Powerful, Happy, and United People"

Head-men, Chiefs, Braves and Warriors of the Sauks: For more than a hundred winters our nation was a powerful, happy and united people. The Great Spirit gave to us a territory, seven hundred miles in length, along the Mississippi, reaching from Prairie du Chien to the mouth of the Illinois river. This vast territory was composed of some of the finest and best land for the home and use of the Indian ever found in this country. The woods and prairies teemed with buffalo, moose, elk, bear and deer, with other game suitable to our enjoyment, while its lakes, rivers, creeks and ponds were alive with the very best kinds of fish, for our food. The islands in the Mississippi were our gardens, where the Great Spirit caused berries, plums and other fruits to grow in great abundance, while the soil, when cultivated, produced corn, beans, pumpkins and squash of the finest quality and largest quantities. Our children were never known to cry of hunger, and no stranger, red or white, was permitted to enter our lodges without finding food and rest. Our nation was respected by all who came in contact with it, for we had the ability as well as the courage to defend and maintain our rights of territory, person and property against the world. Then, indeed, was it an honor to be called a Sauk, for that name was a passport to our people traveling in other territories and among other nations. But an evil day befell us when we became a divided nation, and with that division our glory deserted us, leaving us with the hearts and heels of the rabbit in place of the courage and strength of the bear.

All this was brought about by the long guns, who now claim all our territory east of the Mississippi, including Saukenuk, our ancient village, where all of us were born, raised, lived, hunted, fished and loved, and near which are our corn lands, which have yielded abundant harvests for an hundred winters, and where sleep the bones of our sacred dead, and around which cluster our fondest recollections of heroism and noble deeds of charity done by our fathers, who were Sauks, not only in name, but in courage and action. I thank the Great Spirit for making me a Sauk, and the son of a great Sauk chief, and a lineal descendant of Nanamakee, the founder of our nation.

[1]Speeches reprinted from *Indian Oratory: Famous Speeches by Noted Indian Chieftains,* ed. W. C. Vanderwerth. Copyright © 1971 by the Univ. of Oklahoma Press.

The Great Spirit is the friend and protector of the Sauks, and has accompanied me as your War Chief upon the war-path against our enemies, and has given me skill to direct and you the courage to achieve an hundred victories over our enemies upon the war-path. All this occurred before we became a divided nation. We then had the courage and strength of the bear, but since the division our hearts and heels are like those of the rabbit and fawn. We have neither courage or confidence in our leaders or ourselves, and have fallen a prey to internal jealousies and petty strifes until we are no longer worth of the illustrious name we bear. In a word, we have become subjects of ridicule and badinage,—"there goes a cowardly Sauk." All this has resulted from the white man's accursed fire-water united with our own tribal quarrels and personal jealousies. The Great Spirit created this country for the use and benefit of his red children, and placed them in full possession of it, and we were happy and contented. Why did he send the palefaces across the great ocean to take it from us? When they landed on our territory they were received as long-absent brothers whom the Great Spirit had returned to us. Food and rest were freely given them by our fathers, who treated them all the more kindly on account of their weak and helpless condition. Had our fathers the desire, they could have crushed the intruders out of existence with the same ease we kill the blood-sucking mosquitoes. Little did our fathers then think they were taking to their bosoms, and warming them to life, a lot of torpid, half-frozen and starving vipers, which in a few winters would fix their deadly fangs upon the very bosoms that had nursed and cared for them when they needed help.

From the day when the palefaces landed upon our shores, they have been robbing us of our inheritance, and slowly, but surely, driving us back, back, back towards the setting sun, burning our villages, destroying our growing crops, ravishing our wives and daughters, beating our papooses with cruel sticks, and brutally murdering our people upon the most flimsy pretenses and trivial causes.

Upon our return to Saukenuk from our winter hunting grounds last spring, we found the palefaces in our lodges, and that they had torn down our fences and were plowing our corn lands and getting ready to plant their corn upon the lands which the Sauks have owned and cultivated for so many winters that our memory cannot go back to them. Nor is this all. They claim to own our lands and lodges by right of purchase from the cowardly and treacherous Quashquamme, nearly thirty winters ago, and drive us away from our lodges and fields with kicks of their cruel boots, accompanied with vile cursing and beating with sticks. When returning from an ill-fated day's hunt, wearied and hungry, with my feet stumbling with the weight of sixty-four winters, I was basely charged by two palefaces of killing their hogs, which I indignantly denied because the charges were false, but they told me I lied, and then they took my gun, powder-horn and bullet-pouch from me by violence, and beat me with a hickory stick until blood ran down my back like drops of falling rain, and my body was so lame and sore for a moon that I could not hunt or fish. They brought their accursed fire-water to our village, making wolves of our braves and warriors, and then when we protested against the sale and destroyed their bad spirits, they came with a multitude on horseback, compelling us to flee across the Mississippi for our lives, and then they burned down our ancient village and turned their horses into our growing corn.

They are now running their plows through our graveyards, turning up the bones and ashes of our sacred dead, whose spirits are calling to us from the land of dreams for vengeance on the despoilers. Will the descendants of Nanamakee and our other illustrious dead stand idly by and suffer this sacrilege to be continued? Have they lost their strength and courage, and become squaws and pappooses? The Great Spirit whispers in my ear, no! Then let us be again united as a nation and at once cross the Mississippi, rekindle our watchfires upon our ancient watch-tower, and send forth the war-whoop of the again united Sauks, and our cousins, the Masquawkees, Pottawattamies, Ottawas, Chippewas, Winnebagoes and Kickapoos, will unite with us in avenging our wrongs upon the white pioneers of Illinois.

When we recross the Mississippi with a strong army, the British Father will send us not only guns, tomahawks, spears, knives and ammunition in abundance, but he will also send us British soldiers to fight our battles for us. Then will the deadly arrow and fatal tomahawk hurtle through the air at the hearts and heads of the pale faced invaders, sending their guilty spirits to the white man's place of endless punishment, and should we, while on the warpath, meet the Pauguk, our departing spirits will be led along that path which is strewn with beautiful flowers, laden with the fragrance of patriotism and heroism, which leads to the land of dreams, whence the spirit of our fathers are beckoning us on, to avenge their wrongs.

1832

SEATTLE
(1786–1866)

Chief of the Suquamish and Duwamish tribes, Seattle was friendly to early white settlers in what is now the state of Washington (its capital city is named after him). He was converted by Catholic missionaries in the 1830s. But as white settlement increased, and the area was ceded to the United States by Great Britain in 1846 by her acceptance of the forty-ninth parallel as the boundary between Canada and the United States, the question of land owner-ship became critical. In 1853, the Washington Territory was organized, and a plan for the town of Seattle was filed. The governor visited and addressed the Indians, offering them a reservation in place of the land on which they had settled. In reply, Chief Seattle delivered the following speech through an interpreter. It was taken down on the spot by Dr. Henry Smith, who had learned the Duwamish language in two years. Not without some bitterness, Seattle accepted the offer of a reservation, and two years later signed the Port Elliott Treaty formalizing the agreement.

"The Indians' Night Promises To Be Dark"

Yonder sky that has wept tears of compassion upon my people for centuries un-told, and which to us appears changeless and eternal, may change. Today is fair. Tomorrow it may be overcast with clouds. My words are like the stars that never change. Whatever Seattle says the great chief at Washington can rely upon with as much certainty as he can upon the return of the sun or the seasons. The White Chief says that Big Chief at Washington sends us greetings of friendship and goodwill. This is kind of him for we know he has little need of our friendship in return. His people are many. They are like the grass that covers vast prairies. My people are few. They resemble the scattering trees of a storm-swept plain. The great—and I presume—good White Chief sends us word that he wishes to buy our lands but is willing to allow us enough to live comfortably. This indeed appears just, even generous, for the Red Man no longer has rights that he need respect, and the offer may be wise also, as we are no longer in need of an extensive country.

There was a time when our people covered the land as the waves of a wind-ruffled sea cover its shell paved floor, but that time long since passed away with the greatness of tribes that are now but a mournful memory. I will not dwell on, nor mourn over, our untimely decay, nor reproach my paleface brothers with hastening it as we too may have been somewhat to blame.

Youth is impulsive. When our young men grow angry at some real or imaginary wrong, and disfigure their faces with black paint, it denotes that their hearts are black, and that they are often cruel and relentless, and our old men and old women are unable to restrain them. Thus it has ever been. Thus it was when the white man first began to push our forefathers westward. But let us hope that the hostilities between us may never return. We would have everything to lose and nothing to gain. Revenge by young men is considered gain, even at the cost of their own lives, but old men who stay at home in times of war, and mothers who have sons to lose, know better.

Our good father at Washington—for I presume he is now our father as well as yours, since King George has moved his boundaries further north[1]—our great and good father, I say, sends us word that if we do as he desires he will protect us. His brave warriors will be to us a bristling wall of strength, and his wonderful ships of war will fill our harbors so that our ancient enemies far to the northward—the Hydas and Tsimpsians—will cease to frighten our women, children and old men. Then in reality will he be our father and we his children. But can that ever be? Your God is not our God! Your God loves your people and hates mine. He folds his strong protecting arms lovingly about the pale face and leads him by the hand as a father leads his infant son—but He has forsaken His red children—if they really are His. Our God, the Great Spirit, seems also to have forsaken us. Your God makes your people wax strong every day. Soon they will fill all the land. Our people are ebbing away like a rapidly receding tide that will never return. The white man's God cannot love our people or He would protect them. They seem to be orphans who can look nowhere for help. How then can we be brothers? How can your God become our God and renew our prosperity and awaken in us dreams of returning greatness. If we have a common heavenly father He must be partial—for He came to His paleface children. We never saw Him. He gave you laws but had no word for his red children whose teeming multitudes once filled this vast continent as stars fill the firmament. No; we are two distinct races with separate origins and separate destinies. There is little in common between us.

To us the ashes of our ancestors are sacred and their resting place is hallowed ground. You wander far from the graves of your ancestors and seemingly without regret. Your religion was written upon tables of stone by the iron finger of your God so that you could not forget. The Red Man could never comprehend nor remember it. Our religion is the traditions of our ancestors—the dreams of our old men, given them in the solemn hours of night by the Great Spirit; and the visions of our sachems, and is written in the hearts of our people.

Your dead cease to love you and the land of their nativity as soon as they pass the portals of the tomb and wander way beyond the stars. They are soon forgotten and never return. Our dead never forget the beautiful world that gave them being. They still love its verdant valleys, its murmuring rivers, its magnificent

---

[1] I.e., in 1846, Great Britain accepted the forty-ninth parallel as the dividing line between Canada and the United States, and the present state of Washington, part of the Oregon Territory, came under U.S. control. Queen Victoria was on the throne at the time.

mountains, sequestered vales and verdant lined lakes and bays, and ever yearn in tender, fond affection over the lonely hearted living, and often return from the Happy Hunting Ground to visit, guide, console and comfort them.

Day and night cannot dwell together. The Red Man has ever fled the approach of the White Man, as the morning mist flees before the morning sun.

However, your proposition seems fair and I think that my people will accept it and will retire to the reservation you offer them. Then we will dwell in peace, for the words of the Great White Chief seem to be the words of nature speaking to my people out of dense darkness.

It matters little where we pass the remnant of our days. They will not be many. The Indians' night promises to be dark. Not a single star of hope hovers above his horizon. Sad-voiced winds moan in the distance. Grim fate seems to be on the Red Man's trail, and wherever he goes he will hear the approaching footsteps of his fell destroyer and prepare stolidly to meet his doom, as does the wounded doe that hears the approaching footsteps of the hunter.

A few more moons. A few more winters—and not one of the descendants of the mighty hosts that once moved over this broad land or lived in happy homes, protected by the Great Spirit, will remain to mourn over the graves of a people— once more powerful and hopeful than yours. But why should I mourn at the untimely fate of my people? Tribe follows tribe, and nation follows nation, like the waves of the sea. It is the order of nature, and regret is useless. Your time of decay may be distant, but it will surely come, for even the White Man whose God walked and talked with him as friend with friend, cannot be exempt from the common destiny. We may be brothers after all. We will see.

We will ponder your proposition and when we decide we will let you know. But should we accept it, I here and now make this condition that we will not be denied the privilege without molestation of visiting at any time the tombs of our ancestors, friends and children. Every part of this soil is sacred in the estimation of my people. Every hillside, every valley, every plain and grove, has been hallowed by some sad or happy event in days long vanished. Even the rocks, which seem to be dumb and dead as they swelter in the sun along the silent shore, thrill with memories of stirring events connected with the lives of my people, and the very dust upon which you now stand responds more lovingly to their footsteps than to yours, because it is rich with the blood of our ancestors and our bare feet are conscious of the sympathetic touch. Our departed braves, fond mothers, glad, happy-hearted maidens, and even our little children who lived here and rejoiced here for a brief season, will love these somber solitudes and at eventide they greet shadowy returning spirits. And when the last Red Man shall have perished, and the memory of my tribe shall have become a myth among the White Men, these shores will swarm with the invisible dead of my tribe, and when your children's children think themselves alone in the field, the store, the shop, upon the highway, or in the silence of the pathless woods, they will not be alone. In all the earth there is no place dedicated to solitude. At night when the streets of your cities and villages are silent and you think them deserted, they will throng with the returning hosts that once filled them and still love this beautiful land. The White Man will never be alone.

Let him be just and deal kindly with my people, for the dead are not powerless. Dead, did I say? There is no death, only a change of worlds.

1853

CHIEF JOSEPH
(1840– 1904)

Chief Joseph's tribe was the Nez Percés ("Pierced Nose" in French, from the Indian practice of some tribes), located in the mountainous area of the northwest, in what is now Idaho, Oregon, and Washington. During the gold rush migrations of the 1860s and 1870s, a treaty of cession of lands was fraudulently extracted from some members of the tribe. This led to the uprising by Chief Joseph in 1877. After defeating several United States military expeditions, the Indians were attempting to escape to Canada but were defeated by rugged terrain and the freezing weather. On surrendering to General Oliver O. Howard and General Nelson A. Miles, on October 5, 1877, Chief Joseph delivered a brief and moving speech. General William T. Sherman described the campaign as "one of the most extraordinary wars of which there is any record." Chief Joseph later visited Washington, D.C., and the East in 1903. He died on September 21, 1904.

"I Will Fight No More Forever"

Tell General Howard I know his heart. What he told me before, I have in my heart. I am tired of fighting. Our chiefs are killed. Looking Glass is dead. Toohoolhoolzote is dead. The old men are all dead. It is the young men who say yes and no. He who led on the young men is dead. It is cold and we have no blankets. The little children are freezing to death. My people, some of them, have run away to the hills and have no blankets, no food; no one knows where they are— perhaps freezing to death. I want to have time to look for my children and see how many I can find. Maybe I shall find them among the dead. Hear me, my chiefs. I am tired; my heart is sick and sad. From where the sun now stands I will fight no more forever.

1877

SLAVERY AND THE CIVIL WAR

David Walker
Frederick Douglass
Harriet A. Jacobs
Frances E. W. Harper

Harriet Beecher Stowe
Abraham Lincoln
Walt Whitman

The debate over slavery, beginning around 1830 and rumbling through three decades, may be likened to the gradual gathering of thunderclouds at the slow approach of a mighty storm. There were many thunderclaps and flashes of lightning along the way. One of the first was made by the free black man David Walker in his *Appeal* of 1829 for slaves to unite in their struggle for freedom. The escaped ex-slave Frederick Douglass published a *Narrative* of his life in 1845, describing the brutality of slave life firsthand. After her escape, Harriet A. Jacobs depicted the degradations she suffered under slavery in *Incidents in the Life of a Slave Girl*, published in 1861. A free black poet, Frances E. W. Harper in her 1854 volume of *Poems on Miscellaneous Subjects* wrote with great feeling and compassion of the slave's lot, doomed to family ruptures and separations.

But it was Harriet Beecher Stowe's *Uncle Tom's Cabin*, published in 1852, that gripped the imagination of the country by dramatizing the humanity of blacks treated inhumanely as property. The book has been credited by more than one historian with helping to start the Civil War. Abraham Lincoln (who had read Stowe's book) brought the eloquence of simple, plain speech to mount the political position against slavocracy—as in his "House Divided" address of 1858. The storm broke forth in the full fury of the Civil War shortly after Lincoln's first inauguration as President in 1861. At his second inauguration in 1865, he knew the war was almost over, but within a few weeks he was dead by an assassin's hand. The poet Walt Whitman provided the nation the elegy it needed for mouring him in "When Lilacs Last in the Dooryard Bloom'd." And his *Drum-Taps* poems provided a kind of elegy for all the war dead, the soldiers of both the North and the South.

DAVID WALKER
(1785–1830)

By about 1830, antislavery sentiment had grown so strong in the North as to constitute itself the Abolitionist Movement. William Lloyd Garrison's *The Liberator* began to appear in 1831, demanding immediate and complete emancipation of the slaves. Two years before (1829), a black man, David Walker, had published his *Appeal in Four Articles Together with a Preamble to the Colored Citizens of the World But in Particular and very Expressly to those of the United States of America.*

This remarkable document concluded with an eloquent appeal to the language of the Declaration of Independence: that "all men are created equal; that they are endowed by their creator with certain unalienable rights; that among these are life, liberty and the pursuit of happiness." The contradictions of principle and practice in America were notoriously self-evident.

If Thomas Jefferson's original draft (see Jefferson selections) had been adopted, slavery would have been abolished in 1776. But representatives of slave-holding states at the Continental Congress demanded that condemnation of the "peculiar institution" be stricken from the Declaration or they would vote "nay" and kill it (since it required unanimity). Thus the issue was suppressed in favor of independence in 1776, but soon resurfaced and came to violent resolution in the Civil War (1861–65).

David Walker was born in Wilmington, North Carolina. His father was a slave, but his mother was free. The law held that the mother's status was conferred on the children, meaning that Walker was born free. He eventually settled in Boston, where he ran a store selling second-hand clothes. His *Appeal* envisioned a day when the blacks would "throw off their chains and handcuffs" from their "hands and feet, and their devilish lashes" from off their backs.

Such language frightened slave-owning whites, who passed laws banning the pamphlet. Georgia's governor asked the mayor of Boston to suppress it, but to no avail. When the slave Nat Turner led fellow slaves in rebellion in Virginia in 1831, killing some sixty whites in twenty-four hours, blame was placed on such "inflammatory" documents as Walker's *Appeal.* But by this time, Walker was already dead. Georgia had offered a reward for his death or capture, and there was widespread belief that he had been poisoned.

The distinguished black historian John Hope Franklin, in *From Slavery to Freedom* (1947), has characterized Walker's *Appeal*: "It was one of the most vigorous denunciations of slavery ever to be printed in the United States. In unmistakable language he called upon Negroes to rise up and throw off the yoke of slavery."

ADDITIONAL READING

John Hope Franklin, *From Slavery to Freedom*, 1947, 1967; Stanley Elkins, *Slavery*, 1964; Herbert Aptheker, ed., *One Continual Cry: David Walker's Appeal to the Colored Citizens of the World*, 1965; Eugene D. Genovese, *The Political Economy of Slavery*, 1965; Allen Weinstein, ed., *American Negro Slavery: A Modern Reader*, 1968; Sterling Stuckey, *Slave Culture: Nationalist Theory and the Foundations of Black America*, 1987.

TEXT

David Walker's Appeal, ed. Charles M. Wiltse, 1965.

from Appeal . . .

PREAMBLE
[THIS SYSTEM OF CRUELTY AND OPPRESSION]

My dearly beloved Brethren and Fellow Citizens.

Having travelled over a considerable portion of these United States, and having, in the course of my travels, taken the most accurate observations of things as they exist—the result of my observations has warranted the full and unshaken conviction, that we, (coloured people of these United States,) are the most degraded, wretched, and abject set of beings that ever lived since the world began; and I pray God that none like us ever may live again until time shall be no more. They tell us of the Israelites in Egypt, the Helots in Sparta, and of the Roman Slaves,[1] which last were made up from almost every nation under heaven, whose sufferings under those ancient and heathen nations, were, in comparison with ours, under this enlightened and Christian nation, no more than a cypher—or, in other words, those heathen nations of antiquity, had but little more among them than the name and form of slavery; while wretchedness and endless miseries were reserved, apparently in a phial, to be poured out upon our fathers, ourselves and our children, by *Christian* Americans!

These positions I shall endeavour, by the help of the Lord, to demonstrate in the course of this *Appeal,* to the satisfaction of the most incredulous mind—and may God Almighty, who is the Father of our Lord Jesus Christ, open your hearts to understand and believe the truth.

The *causes,* my brethren, which produce our wretchedness and miseries, are so very numerous and aggravating, that I believe the pen only of a Josephus or a Plutarch,[2] can well enumerate and explain them. Upon subjects, then, of such incomprehensible magnitude, so impenetrable, and so notorious, I shall be obliged to omit a large class of, and content myself with giving you an exposition of a few of those, which do indeed rage to such an alarming pitch, that they cannot but be a perpetual source of terror and dismay to every reflecting mind.

I am fully aware, in making this appeal to my much afflicted and suffering brethren, that I shall not only be assailed by those whose greatest earthly desires are, to keep us in abject ignorance and wretchedness, and who are of the firm conviction that Heaven has designed us and our children to be slaves and *beasts of burden* to them and their children. I say, I do not only expect to be held up to the public as an ignorant, impudent and restless disturber of the public peace, by such avaricious creatures, as well as a mover of insubordination—and perhaps put in prison or to death, for giving a superficial exposition of our miseries, and exposing tyrants. But I am persuaded, that many of my brethren, particularly those who are ignorantly in league with slave-holders or tyrants, who acquire their daily bread by the blood and sweat of their more ignorant brethren—and not a few of those too, who are too ignorant to see an inch beyond their noses, will rise up and call me cursed—Yea, the jealous ones among us will perhaps use more abject subtlety, by affirming that this work is not worth perusing, that we are well situated, and there is no use in trying to better our condition, for we cannot. I will ask one question here.—Can our condition be any worse?—Can it be more mean and abject? If there are any changes, will they not be for the better, though they may appear for the worst at first? Can they get us any lower? Where can they get us?

---

[1] All were made slaves by others declaring themselves masters; Helots came from the town of Helos in Laconia, enslaved by Sparta.

[2] Flavius Josephus (A.D. 37–100?), Jewish military leader and historian; Plutarch (A.D. 46?–120?), Greek moralist and biographer.

They are afraid to treat us worse, for they know well, the day they do it they are gone. But against all accusations which may or can be preferred against me, I appeal to Heaven for my motive in writing—who knows that my object is, if possible, to awaken in the breasts of my afflicted, degraded and slumbering brethren, a spirit of inquiry and investigation respecting our miseries and wretchedness in this *Republican Land of Liberty! ! ! ! !*

The sources from which our miseries are derived, and on which I shall comment, I shall not combine in one, but shall put them under distinct heads and expose them in their turn; in doing which, keeping truth on my side, and not departing from the strictest rules of morality, I shall endeavour to penetrate, search out, and lay them open for your inspection. If you cannot or will not profit by them, I shall have done *my* duty to you, my country and my God.

And as the inhuman system of *slavery*, is the *source* from which most of our miseries proceed, I shall begin with that *curse to nations,* which has spread terror and devastation through so many nations of antiquity, and which is raging to such a pitch at the present day in Spain and in Portugal. It had one tug in England, in France, and in the United States of America; yet the inhabitants thereof, do not learn wisdom, and erase it entirely from their dwellings and from all with whom they have to do. The fact is, the labour of slaves comes so cheap to the avaricious usurpers, and is (as they think) of such great utility to the country where it exists, that those who are actuated by sordid avarice only, overlook the evils, which will as sure as the Lord lives, follow after the good. In fact, they are so happy to keep in ignorance and degradation, and to receive the homage and the labour of the slaves, they forget that God rules in the armies of heaven and among the inhabitants of the earth, having his ears continually open to the cries, tears and groans of his oppressed people; and being a just and holy Being will at one day appear fully in behalf of the oppressed, and arrest the progress of the avaricious oppressors; for although the destruction of the oppressors God may not effect by the oppressed, yet the Lord our God will bring other destructions upon them—for not unfrequently will he cause them to rise up one against another, to be split and divided, and to oppress each other, and sometimes to open hostilities with sword in hand. Some may ask, what is the matter with this united and happy people?— Some say it is the cause of political usurpers, tyrants, oppressors, &c. But has not the Lord an oppressed and suffering people among them? Does the Lord condescend to hear their cries and see their tears in consequence of oppression? Will he let the oppressors rest comfortably and happy always? Will he not cause the very children of the oppressors to rise up against them, and oftimes put them to death? "God works in many ways his wonders to perform."

I will not here speak of the destructions which the Lord brought upon Egypt, in consequence of the oppression and consequent groans of the oppressed—of the hundreds and thousands of Egyptians whom God hurled into the Red Sea for afflicting his people in their land[3]—of the Lord's suffering people in Sparta or Lacedaemon, the land of the truly famous Lycurgus[4]—nor have I time to comment upon the cause which produced the fierceness with which Sylla[5] usurped the title, and absolutely acted as dictator of the Roman people—the conspiracy of Cataline[6]—the conspiracy against, and murder of Cæsar in the Senate house— the spirit with which Marc Antony made himself master of the commonwealth—

---

[3]See Exodus 14:21–27: the fleeing Israelites were able to escape when Moses parted the waters of the Red Sea; when the pharaoh's armies followed in pursuit, the waters drowned them.

[4]The Helots were the slaves in ancient Sparta (also called Lacedaemon); Lycurgus was the renowned law-giver of Sparta (ninth century B.C.), who developed the code that enabled Sparta to produce disciplined soldiers.

[5]Variant of Sulla (138–78 B.C.), ruthless dictator of Rome (82–79 B.C.)

[6]Variant of Catiline (c. 108–62 B.C.), Roman politician who organized a widespread conspiracy for which he was executed.

his associating Octavius and Lipidus with himself in power—their dividing the provinces of Rome among themselves—their attack and defeat, on the plains of Phillippi, of the last defenders of their liberty, (Brutus and Cassius)[7]—the tyranny of Tiberius,[8] and from him to the final overthrow of Constantinople by the Turkish Sultan, Mahomed II.[9] A.D. 1453. I say, I shall not take up time to speak of the *causes* which produced so much wretchedness and massacre among those heathen nations, for I am aware that you know too well, that God is just, as well as merciful!—I shall call your attention a few moments to that *Christian* nation, the Spaniards—while I shall leave almost unnoticed, that avaricious and cruel people, the Portuguese, among whom all true hearted Christians and lovers of Jesus Christ, must evidently see the judgments of God displayed. To show the judgments of God upon the Spaniards, I shall occupy but a little time, leaving a plenty of room for the candid and unprejudiced to reflect.

All persons who are acquainted with history, and particularly the Bible, who are not blinded by the God of this world, and are not actuated solely by avarice—who are able to lay aside prejudice long enough to view candidly and impartially, things as they were, are, and probably will be—who are willing to admit that God made man to serve Him *alone,* and that man should have no other Lord or Lords but Himself—that God Almighty is the *sole proprietor* or *master* of the WHOLE human family, and will not on any consideration admit of a colleague, being unwilling to divide his glory with another—and who can dispense with prejudice long enough to admit that we are *men,* notwithstanding our *improminent noses* and *woolly heads,* and believe that we feel for our fathers, mothers, wives and children, as well as the whites do for theirs.—I say, all who are permitted to see and believe these things, can easily recognize the judgments of God among the Spaniards. Though others may lay the cause of the fierceness with which they cut each other's throats, to some other circumstance, yet they who believe that God is a God of justice, will believe that SLAVERY *is the principal cause.*

While the Spaniards are running about upon the field of battle cutting each other's throats, has not the Lord an afflicted and suffering people in the midst of them, whose cries and groans in consequence of oppression are continually pouring into the ears of the God of justice? Would they not cease to cut each other's throats, if they could? But how can they? The very support which they draw from government to aid them in perpetrating such enormities, does it not arise in a great degree from the wretched victims of oppression among them? And yet they are calling for *Peace!—Peace! !* Will any peace be given unto them? Their destruction may indeed be procrastinated awhile, but can it continue long, while they are oppressing the Lord's people? Has He not the hearts of all men in His hand? Will he suffer one part of his creatures to go on oppressing another like brutes always, with impunity? And yet, those avaricious wretches are calling for *Peace! ! ! !* I declare, it does appear to me, as though some nations think God is asleep, or that he made the Africans for nothing else but to dig their mines and work their farms, or they cannot believe history, sacred or profane. I ask every man who has a heart, and is blessed with the privilege of believing—Is not God a God of justice to *all* his creatures? Do you say he is? Then if he gives peace and tranquillity to tyrants, and permits them to keep our fathers, our mothers, ourselves and our children in eternal ignorance and wretchedness, to support them and their families, would he be to us a God of *justice?* I ask, O ye *Christians! !* who hold us and our children in

---

[7] Brutus and Cassius, assassinators of dictator Julius Caesar (100–44 B.C.), were defeated at Phillippi in 42 B.C. by Marc Antony (c. 83–30 B.C.), who, after the murder of Caesar, recruited armed supporters, and, in 43 B.C., became a member of the governing triumvirate along with Octavian (63 B.C.–14 A.D.) and Lepidus (d. 13 B.C.).

[8] Tiberius (42 B.C.–A.D. 37), second emperor of Rome (A.D. 14–37), became cruel and tyrannical, abolishing freedom in Rome.
[9] Known also as Mohammed the Great, who captured Constantinople in 1453.

the most abject ignorance and degradation, that ever a people were afflicted with since the world began—I say, if God gives you peace and tranquillity, and suffers you thus to go on afflicting us, and our children, who have never given you the least provocation—would he be to us *a God of justice?* If you will allow that we are MEN, who feel for each other, does not the blood of our fathers and of us their children, cry aloud to the Lord of Sabaoth[10] against you, for the cruelties and murders with which you have, and do continue to afflict us. But it is time for me to close my remarks on the suburbs, just to enter more fully into the interior of this system of cruelty and oppression.

1829

FREDERICK DOUGLASS
(1818–1895)

Frederick Douglass was born a slave; his mother was black, his father white. He was never to identify or know his father, and his mother died when he was only eight years old. As a boy, Douglass found himself serving in the Hugh Auld household in Baltimore, Maryland. There he was favored by Mrs. Auld, who began to teach him how to read. But on hearing of the lessons, the master of the household immediately forbade further teaching, commenting, "Learning would spoil the best nigger in the world. . . . It would forever unfit him to be a slave."

Douglass went on to teach himself to read and write, and discovered in a newspaper the efforts of the Abolitionists to free slaves. His master was right. Learning had determined him to escape his bondage. But in the meantime, he lost his position in the Auld household and was sent back to the plantation, where he found himself working as a field hand under an overseer who prided himself on breaking the will of rebellious black youths. After many arbitrary floggings, Douglass decided to resist; he was large and strong, and could have beaten the overseer. His resistance was successful; Douglass later speculated that the overseer did not retaliate because he did not want to tarnish his reputation as a slave breaker.

In any event, Douglass felt his manhood revived. His escape, at the age of twenty-one (described in detail in a passage included here), found him briefly in New York and then in New Bedford, Massachusetts, with the new name of Frederick Douglass (in place of Bailey), a change to prevent his discovery. It was not long before he was involved in antislavery organizations and was lecturing about his life as a slave and his escape.

He was extraordinarily successful on the lecture platform and decided to set his story down on paper. In 1845, he published *Narrative of the Life of Frederick Douglass, an American Slave, Written by Himself.* It was a remarkable success, both popularly and critically. Margaret Fuller, whose *Woman in the Nineteenth Century* had appeared the same year, reviewed the *Narrative* in the *New York Tribune* and praised it highly. She found it "an excellent piece of writing and on that score to be prized as a specimen of the powers of the Black Race, which prejudice persists in disputing."

---

[10]"Lord of Hosts," a term describing all the forces at God's command throughout creation (Psalm 89:6–8.)

Since publication of his *Narrative* put him in jeopardy of arrest and return to slavery, Douglass went to England for two years, lecturing widely and enjoying liberties not afforded by his own country. While there, some of his British acquaintances collected a sum of around $700 to buy his freedom from his former master. Back in the United States, Douglass turned to journalism, founding an abolitionist weekly, *The North Star,* which became *Frederick Douglass's Paper* in 1851. He embraced other causes, too, including women's rights. On the masthead of *The North Star* appeared the motto: "Right is of no sex—Truth is of no Color." He actively supported the right of women to vote.

Later expansions of his *Narrative—My Bondage and My Freedom* in 1855, and *The Life and Times of Frederick Douglass* in 1881 and 1892—turned a cleanly written, clearly focused narrative into a diffuse and sometimes inflated account. The later works were valuable, but could not reproduce the strong impact of the earlier work. Margaret Fuller had been right in saying that, "as a narrative, we have never read one more simple, true, coherent, and warm with genuine feeling."

ADDITIONAL READING

The Life and Writings of Frederick Douglass, 5 vols., ed. Philip S. Foner, 1950–75; *The Frederick Douglass Papers, Series One: Speeches, Debates, and Interviews,* 2 vols, ed. John W. Blassingame, 1979, 1982; *Frederick Douglass: The Narrative and Selected Writings,* ed. Michael Mayer, 1984.

Charles Chesnutt, *Frederick Douglass,* 1899, 1970; Booker T. Washington, *Frederick Douglass,* 1907, 1969; Benjamin Quarles, *Frederick Douglass,* 1948; Philip S. Foner, *Frederick Douglass: A Biography,* 1964; Arna Bontemps, *Free at Last: The Life of Frederick Douglass,* 1971; Philip S. Foner, ed., *Frederick Douglass on Women's Rights,* 1976; Dexter Fisher and Robert B. Stepto, eds., *Afro-American Literature: The Reconstruction of Instruction,* 1979; Dickson J. Preston, *Young Frederick Douglass: The Maryland Years,* 1980; Nathan Irwin Huggins, *Slave and Citizen: The Life of Frederick Douglass,* 1980; Waldo E. Martin, Jr., *The Mind of Frederick Douglass,* 1985; William L. Andrews, *To Tell a Free Story: The First Century of Afro-American Autobiography, 1760–1865,* 1986.

TEXT

Narrative of the Life of Frederick Douglass, an American Slave, Written by Himself, ed. Benjamin Quarles, 1960; *Life and Times of Frederick Douglass,* 1892.

from Narrative of the Life of Frederick Douglass

CHAPTER I
[ORIGINS AND FIRST MEMORIES]

I was born in Tuckahoe, near Hillsborough, and about twelve miles from Easton, in Talbot county, Maryland. I have no accurate knowledge of my age, never having seen any authentic record containing it. By far the larger part of the slaves know as little of their age as horses know of theirs, and it is the wish of most masters within my knowledge to keep their slaves thus ignorant. I do not remember to have ever met a slave who could tell of his birthday. They seldom come nearer to it than planting-time, harvest-time, cherry-time, spring-time, or fall-time. A want of information concerning my own was a source of unhappiness to me even during childhood. The white children could tell their ages. I could not tell why I ought to be deprived of the same privilege. I was not allowed to make any inquiries of my master concerning it. He deemed all such inquiries on the part of a slave improper and impertinent, and evidence of a restless spirit. The nearest estimate I can give makes me now between twenty-seven and twenty-eight years of age. I come to this, from hearing my master say, some time during 1835, I was about seventeen years old.

My mother was named Harriet Bailey. She was the daughter of Isaac and Betsey Bailey, both colored, and quite dark. My mother was of a darker complexion than either my grandmother or grandfather.

My father was a white man. He was admitted to be such by all I ever heard speak of my parentage. The opinion was also whispered that my master was my father; but of the correctness of this opinion, I know nothing; the means of knowing was withheld from me. My mother and I were separated when I was but an infant—before I knew her as my mother. It is a common custom, in the part of Maryland from which I ran away; to part children from their mothers at a very early age. Frequently, before the child has reached its twelfth month, its mother is taken from it, and hired out on some farm a considerable distance off, and the child is placed under the care of an old woman, too old for field labor. For what this separation is done, I do not know, unless it be to hinder the development of the child's affection toward its mother, and to blunt and destroy the natural affection of the mother for the child. This is the inevitable result.

I never saw my mother, to know her as such, more than four or five times in my life; and each of these times was very short in duration, and at night. She was hired by a Mr. Stewart, who lived about twelve miles from my home. She made her journeys to see me in the night, travelling the whole distance on foot, after the performance of her day's work. She was a field hand, and a whipping is the penalty of not being in the field at sunrise, unless a slave has special permission from his or her master to the contrary—a permission which they seldom get, and one that gives to him that gives it the proud name of being a kind master. I do not recollect of ever seeing my mother by the light of day. She was with me in the night. She would lie down with me, and get me to sleep, but long before I waked she was gone. Very little communication ever took place between us. Death soon ended what little we could have while she lived, and with it her hardships and suffering. She died when I was about seven years old, on one of my master's farms, near Lee's Mill. I was not allowed to be present during her illness, at her death, or burial. She was gone long before I knew any thing about it. Never having enjoyed, to any considerable extent, her soothing presence, her tender and watchful care, I received the tidings of her death with much the same emotions I should have probably felt at the death of a stranger.

Called thus suddenly away, she left me without the slightest intimation of who my father was. The whisper that my master was my father, may or may not be true; and, true or false, it is of but little consequence to my purpose whilst the fact remains, in all its glaring odiousness, that slaveholders have ordained, and by law established, that the children of slave women shall in all cases follow the condition of their mothers; and this is done too obviously to administer to their own lusts, and make a gratification of their wicked desires profitable as well as pleasurable; for by this cunning arrangement, the slaveholder, in cases not a few, sustains to his slaves the double relation of master and father.

I know of such cases; and it is worthy of remark that such slaves invariably suffer greater hardships, and have more to contend with, than others. They are, in the first place, a constant offence to their mistress. She is ever disposed to find fault with them; they can seldom do any thing to please her; she is never better pleased than when she sees them under the lash, especially when she suspects her husband of showing to his mulatto children favors which he withholds from his black slaves. The master is frequently compelled to sell this class of his slaves, out of deference to the feelings of his white wife; and, cruel as the deed may strike any one to be, for a man to sell his own children to human flesh-mongers, it is often the dictate of humanity for him to do so; for, unless he does this, he must not only whip them himself, but must stand by and see one white son tie up his brother, of but few shades darker complexion than himself, and ply the gory lash to his naked back; and if he lisp one word of disapproval, it is set down to his parental partiality, and only makes a bad matter worse, both for himself and the slave whom he would protect and defend.

Every year brings with it multitudes of this class of slaves. It was doubtless in consequence of a knowledge of this fact, that one great statesman of the south predicted the downfall of slavery by the inevitable laws of population. Whether this prophecy is ever fulfilled or not, it is nevertheless plain that a very different-looking class of people are springing up at the south, and are now held in slavery, from those originally brought to this country from Africa; and if their increase will do no other good, it will do away the force of the argument, that God cursed Ham,[1] and therefore American slavery is right. If the lineal descendants of Ham are alone to be scripturally enslaved, it is certain that slavery at the south must soon become unscriptural; for thousands are ushered into the world, annually, who, like myself, owe their existence to white fathers, and those fathers most frequently their own masters.

I have had two masters. My first master's name was Anthony. I do not remember his first name. He was generally called Captain Anthony—a title which, I presume, he acquired by sailing a craft on the Chesapeake Bay. He was not considered a rich slaveholder. He owned two or three farms, and about thirty slaves. His farms and slaves were under the care of an overseer. The overseer's name was Plummer. Mr. Plummer was a miserable drunkard, a profane swearer, and a savage monster. He always went armed with a cowskin and a heavy cudgel.[2] I have known him to cut and slash the women's heads so horribly, that even master would be enraged at his cruelty, and would threaten to whip him if he did not mind himself. Master, however, was not a humane slaveholder. It required extraordinary barbarity on the part of an overseer to affect him. He was a cruel man, hardened by a long life of slaveholding. He would at times seem to take great pleasure in whipping a slave. I have often been awakened at the dawn of day by the most heart-rending shrieks of an own aunt of mine, whom he used to tie up to a joist, and whip upon her naked back till she was literally covered with blood. No words, no tears, no prayers, from his gory victim, seemed to move his iron heart from its bloody purpose. The louder she screamed, the harder he whipped; and where the blood ran fastest, there he whipped longest. He would whip her to make her scream, and whip her to make her hush; and not until overcome by fatigue, would he cease to swing the blood-clotted cowskin. I remember the first time I ever witnessed this horrible exhibition. I was quite a child, but I well remember it. I never shall forget it whilst I remember any thing. It was the first of a long series of such outrages, of which I was doomed to be a witness and a participant. It struck me with awful force. It was the blood-stained gate, the entrance to the hell of slavery, through which I was about to pass. It was a most terrible spectacle. I wish I could commit to paper the feelings with which I beheld it.

This occurrence took place very soon after I went to live with my old master, and under the following circumstances. Aunt Hester went out one night,—where

---

[1] Cf. Genesis 9:20–27; one racist view justifying slavery was that God through Noah had placed a curse on his son Ham's offspring, Canaan ("a servant of servants shall he be unto his brethren")—supposedly accounting for the servitude of the black race.
[2] A leather whip and a short club.

or for what I do not know,—and happened to be absent when my master desired her presence. He had ordered her not to go out evenings, and warned her that she must never let him catch her in company with a young man, who was paying attention to her belonging to Colonel Lloyd. The young man's name was Ned Roberts, generally called Lloyd's Ned. Why master was so careful of her, may be safely left to conjecture. She was a woman of noble form, and of graceful proportions, having very few equals, and fewer superiors, in personal appearance, among the colored or white women of our neighborhood.

Aunt Hester had not only disobeyed his orders in going out, but had been found in company with Lloyd's Ned; which circumstance, I found, from what he said while whipping her, was the chief offence. Had he been a man of pure morals himself, he might have been thought interested in protecting the innocence of my aunt; but those who knew him will not suspect him of any such virtue. Before he commenced whipping Aunt Hester, he took her into the kitchen, and stripped her from neck to waist, leaving her neck, shoulders, and back, entirely naked. He then told her to cross her hands, calling her at the same time a d—d b—h. After crossing her hands, he tied them with a strong rope, and led her to a stool under a large hook in the joist, put in for the purpose. He made her get upon the stool, and tied her hands to the hook. She now stood fair for his infernal purpose. Her arms were stretched up at their full length, so that she stood upon the ends of her toes. He then said to her, "Now, you d—d b—h, I'll learn you how to disobey my orders!" and after rolling up his sleeves, he commenced to lay on the heavy cowskin, and soon the warm, red blood (amid heart-rending shrieks from her, and horrid oaths from him) came dripping to the floor. I was so terrified and horror-stricken at the sight, that I hid myself in a closet, and dared not venture out till long after the bloody transaction was over. I expected it would be my turn next. It was all new to me. I had never seen any thing like it before. I had always lived with my grandmother on the outskirts of the plantation, where she was put to raise the children of the younger women. I had therefore been, until now, out of the way of the bloody scenes that often occurred on the plantation.

CHAPTER XI

[Planning and Succeeding in Escape]

I now come to that part of my life during which I planned, and finally succeeded in making, my escape from slavery. But before narrating any of the peculiar circumstances, I deem it proper to make known my intention not to state all the facts connected with the transaction. My reasons for pursuing this course may be understood from the following: First, were I to give a minute statement of all the facts, it is not only possible, but quite probable, that others would thereby be involved in the most embarrassing difficulties. Secondly, such a statement would most undoubtedly induce greater vigilance on the part of slaveholders than has existed heretofore among them; which would, of course be the means of guarding a door whereby some dear brother bondman might escape his galling chains. I deeply regret the necessity that impels me to suppress any thing of importance connected with my experience in slavery. It would afford me great pleasure indeed, as well as materially add to the interest of my narrative, were I at liberty to gratify a curiosity, which I know exists in the minds of many, by an accurate statement of all the facts pertaining to my most fortunate escape. But I must deprive myself of this pleasure, and the curious of the gratification which such a statement would afford. I would allow myself to suffer under the greatest imputations which evil-minded men might suggest, rather than exculpate myself, and thereby run the hazard of closing the slightest avenue by which a brother slave might clear himself of the chains and fetters of slavery.

I have never approved of the very public manner in which some of our western friends have conducted what they call the *underground railroad*, but which, I think, by their open declarations, has been made most emphatically the *upperground railroad*. I honor those good men and women for their noble daring, and applaud them for willingly subjecting themselves to bloody persecution, by openly avowing their participation in the escape of slaves. I, however, can see very little good resulting from such a course, either to themselves or the slaves escaping; while, upon the other hand, I see and feel assured that those open declarations are a positive evil to the slaves remaining, who are seeking to escape. They do nothing towards enlightening the slave, whilst they do much towards enlightening the master. They stimulate him to greater watchfulness, and enhance his power to capture his slave. We owe something to the slaves south of the line as well as to those north of it; and in aiding the latter on their way to freedom, we should be careful to do nothing which would be likely to hinder the former from escaping from slavery. I would keep the merciless slaveholder profoundly ignorant of the means of flight adopted by the slave. I would leave him to imagine himself surrounded by myriads of invisible tormentors, ever ready to snatch from his infernal grasp his trembling prey. Let him be left to feel his way in the dark; let darkness commensurate with his crime hover over him; and let him feel that at every step he takes, in pursuit of the flying bondman, he is running the frightful risk of having his hot brains dashed out by an invisible agency. Let us render the tyrant no aid; let us not hold the light by which he can trace the footprints of our flying brother. But enough of this. I will now proceed to the statement of those facts, connected with my escape, for which I am alone responsible, and for which no one can be made to suffer but myself.

In the early part of the year 1838, I became quite restless. I could see no reason why I should, at the end of each week, pour the reward of my toil into the purse of my master. When I carried to him my weekly wages, he would, after counting the money, look me in the face with a robber-like fierceness, and ask, "Is this all?" He was satisfied with nothing less than the last cent. He would, however, when I made him six dollars, sometimes give me six cents, to encourage me. It had the opposite effect. I regarded it as a sort of admission of my right to the whole. The fact that he gave me any part of my wages was proof, to my mind, that he believed me entitled to the whole of them. I always felt worse for having received any thing; for I feared that the giving me a few cents would ease his conscience, and make him feel himself to be a pretty honorable sort of robber. My discontent grew upon me. I was ever on the look-out for means of escape; and, finding no direct means, I determined to try to hire my time, with a view of getting money with which to make my escape. In the spring of 1838, when Master Thomas came to Baltimore to purchase his spring goods, I got an opportunity, and applied to him to allow me to hire my time. He unhesitatingly refused my request, and told me this was another stratagem by which to escape. He told me I could go nowhere but that he could get me; and that, in the event of my running away, he should spare no pains in his efforts to catch me. He exhorted me to content myself, and be obedient. He told me, if I would be happy, I must lay out no plans for the future. He said, if I behaved myself properly, he would take care of me. Indeed, he advised me to complete thoughtlessness of the future, and taught me to depend solely upon him for happiness. He seemed to see fully the pressing necessity of setting aside my intellectual nature, in order to contentment in slavery. But in spite of him, and even in spite of myself, I continued to think, and to think about the injustice of my enslavement, and the means of escape.

About two months after this, I applied to Master Hugh for the privilege of hiring my time. He was not acquainted with the fact that I had applied to Master Thomas, and had been refused. He too, at first, seemed disposed to refuse; but, after some reflection, he granted me the privilege, and proposed the following term: I was to be allowed all my time, make all contracts with those for whom I worked, and find my own employment; and, in return for this liberty, I was to pay him three dollars at the end of each week; find myself in calking tools, and in board and clothing. My board was two dollars and a half per week. This, with the wear and tear of clothing and calking tools, made my regular expenses about six dollars per week. This amount I was compelled to make up, or relinquish the privilege of hiring my time. Rain or shine, work or no work, at the end of each week the money must be forthcoming, or I must give up my privilege. This arrangement, it will be perceived, was decidedly in my master's favor. It relieved him of all need of looking after me. His money was sure. He received all the benefits of slaveholding without its evils; while I endured all the evils of a slave, and suffered all the care and anxiety of a freeman. I found it a hard bargain. But, hard as it was, I thought it better than the old mode of getting along. It was a step towards freedom to be allowed to bear the responsibilities of a freeman, and I was determined to hold on upon it. I bent myself to the work of making money. I was ready to work at night as well as day, and by the most untiring perseverance and industry, I made enough to meet my expenses, and lay up a little money every week. I went on thus from May till August. Master Hugh then refused to allow me to hire my time longer. The ground for his refusal was a failure on my part, one Saturday night, to pay him for my week's time. This failure was occasioned by my attending a camp meeting about ten miles from Baltimore. During the week, I had entered into an engagement with a number of young friends to start from Baltimore to the camp ground early Saturday evening; and being detained by my employer, I was unable to get down to Master Hugh's without disappointing the company. I knew that Master Hugh was in no special need of the money that night. I therefore decided to go to camp meeting, and upon my return pay him the three dollars. I staid at the camp meeting one day longer than I intended when I left. But as soon as I returned, I called upon him to pay him what he considered his due. I found him very angry; he could scarce restrain his wrath. He said he had a great mind to give me a severe whipping. He wished to know how I dared go out of the city without asking his permission. I told him I hired my time, and while I paid him the price which he asked for it, I did not know that I was bound to ask him when and where I should go. This reply troubled him; and, after reflecting a few moments, he turned to me, and said I should hire my time no longer; that the next thing he should know of, I would be running away. Upon the same plea, he told me to bring my tools and clothing home forthwith. I did so; but instead of seeking work, as I had been accustomed to do previously to hiring my time, I spent the whole week without the performance of a single stroke of work. I did this in retaliation. Saturday night, he called upon me as usual for my week's wages. I told him I had no wages; I had done no work that week. Here we were upon the point of coming to blows. He raved, and swore his determination to get hold of me. I did not allow myself a single word; but was resolved, if he laid the weight of his hand upon me, it should be blow for blow. He did not strike me, but told me that he would find me in constant employment in future. I thought the matter over during the next day, Sunday, and finally resolved upon the third day of September, as the day upon which I would make a second attempt to secure my freedom. I now had three weeks during which to prepare for my journey. Early on Monday morning, before Master Hugh had time to make any engagement for me, I went out and got employment of Mr. Butler, at his ship-yard near the drawbridge, upon what is called the City Block, thus making it unnecessary for him to seek employment for me. At the end of the week, I brought him between eight and nine dollars. He seemed very well pleased, and asked me why I did not do the same the week before. He little knew what my plans were. My object in working steadily was to remove any suspicion he might entertain of my intent to run away; and in this I succeeded admirably. I suppose he thought I was never better satisfied with my condition than at the very time during which I was planning my escape. The second week passed, and again I carried him my full wages; and so well pleased was he, that he gave me twenty-five cents, (quite a large sum for a slaveholder to give a slave,) and bade me to make a good use of it. I told him I would.

Things went on without very smoothly indeed, but within there was trouble. It is impossible for me to describe my feelings as the time of my contemplated start drew near. I had a number of warm-hearted friends in Baltimore,—friends that I loved almost as I did my life,—and the thought of being separated from them forever was painful beyond expression. It is my opinion that thousands would escape from slavery, who now remain, but for the strong cords of affection that bind them to their friends. The thought of leaving my friends was decidedly the most painful thought with which I had to contend. The love of them was my tender point, and shook my decision more than all things else. Besides the pain of separation, the dread and apprehension of a failure exceeded what I had experienced at my first attempt. The appalling defeat I then sustained returned to torment me. I felt assured that, if I failed in this attempt, my case would be a hopeless one—it would seal my fate as a slave forever. I could not hope to get off with any thing less than the severest punishment, and being placed beyond the means of escape. It required no very vivid imagination to depict the most frightful scenes through which I should have to pass, in case I failed. The wretchedness of slavery, and the blessedness of freedom, were perpetually before me. It was life and death with me. But I remained firm, and according to my resolution, on the third day of September, 1838, I left my chains, and succeeded in reaching New York without the slightest interruption of any kind. How I did so,—what means I adopted,—what direction I travelled, and by what mode of conveyance,—I must leave unexplained, for the reasons before mentioned.

I have been frequently asked how I felt when I found myself in a free State. I have never been able to answer the question with any satisfaction to myself. It was a moment of the highest excitement I ever experienced. I suppose I felt as one may imagine the unarmed mariner to feel when he is rescued by a friendly man-of-war from the pursuit of a pirate. In writing to a dear friend, immediately after my arrival at New York, I said I felt like one who had escaped a den of hungry lions. This state of mind, however, very soon subsided; and I was again seized with a feeling of great insecurity and loneliness. I was yet liable to be taken back, and subjected to all the tortures of slavery. This in itself was enough to damp the ardor of my enthusiasm. But the loneliness overcame me. There I was in the midst of thousands, and yet a perfect stranger; without home and without friends, in the midst of thousands of my own brethren—children of a common Father, and yet I dared not to unfold to any one of them my sad condition. I was afraid to speak to any one for fear of speaking to the wrong one, and thereby falling into the hands of money-loving kidnappers, whose business it was to lie in wait for the panting fugitive, as the ferocious beasts of the forest lie in wait for their prey. The motto which I adopted when I started from slavery was this—"Trust no man!" I saw in every white man an enemy, and in almost every colored man cause for distrust. It was a most painful situation; and, to understand it, one must needs experience it, or imagine himself in similar circumstances. Let him be a fugitive slave in a strange land—a land given up to be the hunting-ground for slaveholders—whose inhabitants are legalized kidnappers—where he is every moment subjected to the terrible liability of being seized upon by his fellowmen, as the hideous crocodile seizes upon his prey!—I say, let him place himself in my situation—without home or friends—without money or credit—wanting shelter, and no one to give it—wanting bread, and no money to buy it,—and at the same time let him feel that he is pursued by merciless men-hunters, and in total darkness as to what to do, where to go, or where to stay,—perfectly helpless both as to the means of defence and means of escape,—in the midst of plenty, yet suffering the terrible gnawings of hunger,—in the midst of houses, yet having no home,—among fellow-men, yet feeling as if in the midst of wild beasts, whose greediness to swallow up the trembling and half-famished fugitive is only equalled by that with which the monsters of the deep swallow up the helpless fish upon which they subsist,—I say, let him be placed in this most trying situation,—the situation in which I was placed,—then, and not till then, will he fully appreciate the hardships of, and know how to sympathize with, the toil-worn and whip-scarred fugitive slave.

Thank Heaven, I remained but a short time in this distressed situation. I was relieved from it by the humane hand of Mr. DAVID RUGGLES,[1] whose vigilance, kindness, and perseverance, I shall never forget. I am glad of an opportunity to express, as far as words can, the love and gratitude I bear him. Mr. Ruggles is now afflicted with blindness, and is himself in need of the same kind offices which he was once so forward in the performance of toward others. I had been in New York but a few days, when Mr. Ruggles sought me out, and very kindly took me to his boarding-house at the corner of Church and Lespenard Streets. Mr. Ruggles was then very deeply engaged in the memorable *Darg* case, as well as attending to a number of other fugitive slaves, devising ways and means for their successful escape; and, though watched and hemmed in on almost every side, he seemed to be more than a match for his enemies.

Very soon after I went to Mr. Ruggles, he wished to know of me where I wanted to go; as he deemed it unsafe for me to remain in New York. I told him I was a calker, and should like to go where I could get work. I thought of going to Canada; but he decided against it, and in favor of my going to New Bedford, thinking I should be able to get work there at my trade. At this time, Anna,[2] my intended wife, came on; for I wrote to her immediately after my arrival at New York, (notwithstanding my homeless, houseless, and helpless condition,) informing her of my successful flight, and wishing her to come on forthwith. In a few days after her arrival, Mr. Ruggles called in the Rev. J. W. C. Pennington, who, in the presence of Mr. Ruggles, Mrs. Michaels, and two or three others, performed the marriage ceremony, and gave us a certificate, of which the following is an exact copy:—

"THIS may certify, that I joined together in holy matrimony Frederick Johnson,[3] and Anna Murray, as man and wife, in the presence of Mr. David Ruggles and Mrs. Michaels.

"JAMES W. C. PENNINGTON.

"*New York, Sept.* 15, 1838."

Upon receiving this certificate, and a five-dollar bill from Mr. Ruggles, I shouldered one part of our baggage, and Anna took up the other, and we set out forthwith to take passage on board of the steamboat John W. Richmond for Newport, on our way to New Bedford. Mr. Ruggles gave me a letter to a Mr. Shaw in Newport, and told me, in case my money did not serve me to New Bedford, to stop in Newport and obtain further assistance; but upon our arrival at Newport, we were so anxious to get to a place of safety, that, notwithstanding we lacked the necessary money to pay our fare, we decided to take seats in the stage, and promise to

---

[1]David Ruggles (1810–1849), an Abolitionist, became secretary of the New York Vigilance Committee of the Anti-Slavery Society in 1835. Such Vigilance Committees were organized to raise funds to help slaves escape to freedom.

[2]"She was free" (Douglass's note).

[3]"I had changed my name from Frederick Bailey to that of Johnson" (Douglass's note).

pay when we got to New Bedford. We were encouraged to do this by two excellent gentlemen, residents of New Bedford, whose names I afterward ascertained to be Joseph Ricketson and William C. Taber. They seemed at once to understand our circumstances, and gave us such assurance of their friendliness as put us fully at ease in their presence. It was good indeed to meet with such friends, at such a time. Upon reaching New Bedford, we were directed to the house of Mr. Nathan Johnson, by whom we were kindly received, and hospitably provided for. Both Mr. and Mrs. Johnson took a deep and lively interest in our welfare. They proved themselves quite worthy of the name of abolitionists. When the stage-driver found us unable to pay our fare, he held on upon our baggage as security for the debt. I had but to mention the fact to Mr. Johnson, and he forthwith advanced the money.

We now began to feel a degree of safety, and to prepare ourselves for the duties and responsibilities of a life of freedom. On the morning after our arrival at New Bedford, while at the breakfast-table, the question arose as to what name I should be called by. The name given me by my mother was, "Frederick Augustus Washington Bailey." I, however, had dispensed with the two middle names long before I left Maryland so that I was generally known by the name of "Frederick Bailey." I started from Baltimore bearing the name of "Stanley." When I got to New York, I again changed my name to "Frederick Johnson," and thought that would be the last change. But when I got to New Bedford, I found it necessary again to change my name. The reason of this necessity was, that there were so many Johnsons in New Bedford, it was already quite difficult to distinguish between them. I gave Mr. Johnson the privilege of choosing me a name, but told him he must not take from me the name of "Frederick." I must hold on to that, to preserve a sense of my identity. Mr. Johnson had just been reading the "Lady of the Lake," and at once suggested that my name be "Douglass."[4] From that time until now I have been called "Frederick Douglass;" and as I am more widely known by that name than by either of the others, I shall continue to use it as my own.

I was quite disappointed at the general appearance of things in New Bedford. The impression which I had received respecting the character and condition of the people of the north, I found to be singularly erroneous. I had very strangely supposed, while in slavery, that few of the comforts, and scarcely any of the luxuries, of life were enjoyed at the north, compared with what were enjoyed by the slaveholders of the south. I probably came to this conclusion from the fact that northern people owned no slaves. I supposed that they were about upon a level with the non-slaveholding population of the south. I knew *they* were exceedingly poor, and I had been accustomed to regard their poverty as the necessary consequence of their being nonslaveholders. I had somehow imbibed the opinion that, in the absence of slaves, there could be no wealth, and very little refinement. And upon coming to the north, I expected to meet with a rough, hard-handed, and uncultivated population, living in the most Spartan-like simplicity, knowing nothing of the ease, luxury, pomp, and grandeur of southern slaveholders. Such being my conjectures, any one acquainted with the appearance of New Bedford may very readily infer how palpably I must have seen my mistake.

In the afternoon of the day when I reached New Bedford, I visited the wharves, to take a view of the shipping. Here I found myself surrounded with the strongest proofs of wealth. Lying at the wharves, and riding in the stream, I saw many ships of the finest model, in the best order, and of the largest size. Upon the

---

[4]James Douglas, of Scotland, is a character in *The Lady of the Lake* (1810), a narrative poem by Sir Walter Scott (1771–1832).

right and left, I was walled in by granite warehouses of the widest dimensions, stowed to their utmost capacity with the necessaries and comforts of life. Added to this, almost every body seemed to be at work, but noiselessly so, compared with what I had been accustomed to in Baltimore. There were no loud songs heard from those engaged in loading and unloading ships. I heard no deep oaths or horrid curses on the laborer. I saw no whipping of men; but all seemed to go smoothly on. Every man appeared to understand his work, and went at it with a sober, yet cheerful earnestness, which betokened the deep interest which he felt in what he was doing, as well as a sense of his own dignity as a man. To me this looked exceedingly strange. From the wharves I strolled around and over the town, gazing with wonder and admiration at the splendid churches, beautiful dwellings, and finely-cultivated gardens; evincing an amount of wealth, comfort, taste, and refinement, such as I had never seen in any part of slaveholding Maryland.

Every thing looked clean, new and beautiful. I saw few or no dilapidated houses, with poverty-stricken inmates; no half-naked children and barefooted women, such as I had been accustomed to see in Hillsborough, Easton, St. Michael's, and Baltimore. The people looked more able, stronger, healthier, and happier, than those of Maryland. I was for once made glad by a view of extreme wealth, without being saddened by seeing extreme poverty. But the most astonishing as well as the most interesting thing to me was the condition of the colored people, a great many of whom, like myself, had escaped thither as a refuge from the hunters of men. I found many, who had not been seven years out of their chains, living in finer houses, and evidently enjoying more of the comforts of life, than the average of slaveholders in Maryland. I will venture to assert that my friend Mr. Nathan Johnson (of whom I can say with a grateful heart, "I was hungry, and he gave me meat; I was thirsty, and he gave me drink; I was a stranger, and he took me in")[5] lived in a neater house; dined at a better table; took, paid for, and read, more newspapers; better understood the moral, religious, and political character of the nation,—than nine tenths of the slaveholders in Talbot county, Maryland. Yet Mr. Johnson was a working man. His hands were hardened by toil, and not his alone, but those also of Mrs. Johnson. I found the colored people much more spirited than I had supposed they would be. I found among them a determination to protect each other from the blood-thirsty kidnapper, at all hazards. Soon after my arrival, I was told of a circumstance which illustrated their spirit. A colored man and a fugitive slave were on unfriendly terms. The former was heard to threaten the latter with informing his master of his whereabouts. Straightway a meeting was called among the colored people, under the stereotyped notice, "Business of importance!" The betrayer was invited to attend. The people came at the appointed hour, and organized the meeting by appointing a very religious old gentleman as president, who, I believe, made a prayer, after which he addressed the meeting as follows: *"Friends, we have got him here, and I would recommend that you young men just take him outside the door, and kill him!"* With this, a number of them bolted at him; but they were intercepted by some more timid than themselves, and the betrayer escaped their vengeance, and has not been seen in New Bedford since. I believe there have been no more such threats, and should there be hereafter, I doubt not that death would be the consequence.

I found employment, the third day after my arrival, in stowing a sloop with a load of oil. It was new, dirty, and hard work for me; but I went at it with a glad heart and a willing hand. I was now my own master. It was a happy moment, the rapture of which can be understood only by those who have been slaves. It was the

---

[5]Cf. Matthew 25:35.

first work, the reward of which was to be entirely my own. There was no Master Hugh standing ready, the moment I earned the money, to rob me of it. I worked that day with a pleasure I had never before experienced. I was at work for myself and newly-married wife. It was to me the starting-point of a new existence. When I got through with that job, I went in pursuit of a job of calking; but such was the strength of prejudice against color, among the white calkers, that they refused to work with me, and of course I could get no employment.[6] Finding my trade of no immediate benefit, I threw off my calking habiliments, and prepared myself to do any kind of work I could get to do. Mr. Johnson kindly let me have his wood-horse and saw, and I very soon found myself a plenty of work. There was no work too hard—none too dirty. I was ready to saw wood, shovel coal, carry the hod, sweep the chimney, or roll oil casks,—all of which I did for nearly three years in New Bedford, before I became known to the antislavery world.

In about four months after I went to New Bedford, there came a young man to me, and inquired if I did not wish to take the "Liberator."[7] I told him I did; but, just having made my escape from slavery, I remarked that I was unable to pay for it then. I, however, finally became a subscriber to it. The paper came, and I read it from week to week with such feelings as it would be quite idle for me to attempt to describe. The paper became my meat and my drink. My soul was set all on fire. Its sympathy for my brethren in bonds—its scathing denunciations of slaveholders—its faithful exposures of slavery—and its powerful attacks upon the upholders of the institution—sent a thrill of joy through my soul, such as I had never felt before!

I had not long been a reader of the "Liberator," before I got a pretty correct idea of the principles, measures and spirit of the anti-slavery reform. I took right hold of the cause. I could do but little; but what I could, I did with a joyful heart, and never felt happier than when in an antislavery meeting. I seldom had much to say at the meetings, because what I wanted to say was said so much better by others. But, while attending an anti-slavery convention at Nantucket, on the 11th of August, 1841, I felt strongly moved to speak, and was at the same time much urged to do so by Mr. William C. Coffin, a gentleman who had heard me speak in the colored people's meeting at New Bedford. It was a severe cross, and I took it up reluctantly. The truth was, I felt myself a slave, and the idea of speaking to white people weighed me down. I spoke but a few moments, when I felt a degree of freedom, and said what I desired with considerable ease. From that time until now, I have been engaged in pleading the cause of my brethren—with what success, and with what devotion, I leave those acquainted with my labors to decide.

1845

from Life and Times of Frederick Douglass

SECOND PART

CHAPTER I: ESCAPE FROM SLAVERY

In the first narrative of my experience in slavery, written nearly forty years ago, and in various writings since, I have given the public what I considered very

---

[6]"I am told that colored persons can now get employment at calking in New Bedford—a result of anti-slavery effort" (Douglass's note).
[7]A paper that called for immediate and complete emanci- pation of slaves, published by William Lloyd Garrison (1805–1879) from 1831 to the end of the Civil War in 1865.

good reasons for withholding the manner of my escape. In substance these reasons were, first, that such publication at any time during the existence of slavery might be used by the master against the slave, and prevent the future escape of any who might adopt the same means that I did. The second reason was, if possible, still more binding to silence—for publication of details would certainly have put in peril the persons and property of those who assisted. Murder itself was not more sternly and certainly punished in the State of Maryland than was the aiding and abetting the escape of a slave. Many colored men, for no other crime than that of giving aid to a fugitive slave, have, like Charles T. Torrey,[1] perished in prison. The abolition of slavery in my native State and throughout the country, and the lapse of time, render the caution hitherto observed no longer necessary. But, even since the abolition of slavery, I have sometimes thought it well enough to baffle curiosity by saying that while slavery existed there were good reasons for not telling the manner of my escape, and since slavery had ceased to exist there was no reason for telling it. I shall now, however, cease to avail myself of this formula, and, as far as I can, endeavor to satisfy this very natural curiosity. I should perhaps have yielded to that feeling sooner, had there been anything very heroic or thrilling in the incidents connected with my escape, for I am sorry to say I have nothing of that sort to tell; and yet the courage that could risk betrayal and the bravery which was ready to encounter death if need be, in pursuit of freedom, were essential features in the undertaking. My success was due to address rather than to courage; to good luck rather than to bravery. My means of escape were provided for me by the very men who were making laws to hold and bind me more securely in slavery. It was the custom in the State of Maryland to require of the free colored people to have what were called free papers. This instrument they were required to renew very often, and by charging a fee for this writing, considerable sums from time to time were collected by the State. In these papers the name, age, color, height and form of the free man were described, together with any scars or other marks upon his person which could assist in his identification. This device of slaveholding ingenuity, like other devices of wickedness, in some measure defeated itself—since more than one man could be found to answer the same general description. Hence many slaves could escape by personating the owner of one set of papers; and this was often done as follows: A slave nearly or sufficiently answering the description set forth in the papers, would borrow or hire them till he could by their means escape to a free state, and then, by mail or otherwise, return them to the owner. The operation was a hazardous one for the lender as well as for the borrower. A failure on the part of the fugitive to send back the papers would imperil his benefactor, and the discovery of the papers in possession of the wrong man would imperil both the fugitive and his friend. It was therefore an act of supreme trust on the part of a freeman of color thus to put in jeopardy his own liberty that another might be free. It was, however, not unfrequently bravely done, and was seldom discovered. I was not so fortunate as to sufficiently resemble any of my free acquaintances as to answer the description of their papers. But I had one friend—a sailor—who owned a sailor's protection, which answered somewhat the purpose of free papers—describing his person and certifying to the fact that he was a free American sailor. The instrument had at its head the American eagle, which at once gave it the appearance of an authorized document. This protection did not, when in my hands, describe its bearer very accurately. Indeed, it called for a man much darker than myself, and close examination of it would have caused my arrest at the start. In order to avoid this fatal scrutiny on the part of the railroad official, I had arranged with Isaac

[1]Charles Turner Torrey (1813–1846), abolitionist from Massachusetts who settled in Baltimore and helped escaping slaves; he was arrested and sentenced in 1844 to six years in prison, where he died.

Rolls, a hackman, to bring my baggage to the train just on the moment of starting, and jumped upon the car myself when the train was already in motion. Had I gone into the station and offered to purchase a ticket, I should have been instantly and carefully examined, and undoubtedly arrested. In choosing this plan upon which to act, I considered the jostle of the train, and the natural haste of the conductor in a train crowded with passengers, and relied upon my skill and address in playing the sailor as described in my protection, to do the rest. One element in my favor was the kind feeling which prevailed in Baltimore and other seaports at the time, towards "those who go down to the sea in ships." "Free trade and sailors' rights" expressed the sentiment of the country just then. In my clothing I was rigged out in sailor style. I had on a red shirt and a tarpaulin hat and black cravat, tied in sailor fashion, carelessly and loosely about my neck. My knowledge of ships and sailor's talk came much to my assistance, for I knew a ship from stem to stern, and from keelson to cross-trees,[2] and could talk sailor like an "old salt." On sped the train, and I was well on the way to Havre de Grace before the conductor came into the negro car to collect tickets and examine the papers of his black passengers. This was a critical moment in the drama. My whole future depended upon the decision of this conductor. Agitated I was while this ceremony was proceeding, but still, externally at least, I was apparently calm and self-possessed. He went on with his duty—examining several colored passengers before reaching me. He was somewhat harsh in tone and peremptory in manner until he reached me, when, strangely enough, and to my surprise and relief, his whole manner changed. Seeing that I did not readily produce my free papers, as the other colored persons in the car had done, he said to me in a friendly contrast with that observed towards the others: "I suppose you have your free papers?" To which I answered: "No, sir; I never carry my free papers to sea with me." "But you have something to show that you are a free man, have you not?" "Yes, sir," I answered; "I have a paper with the American eagle on it, that will carry me round the world." With this I drew from my deep sailor's pocket my seaman's protection, as before described. The merest glance at the paper satisfied him, and he took my fare and went on about his business. This moment of time was one of the most anxious I ever experienced. Had the conductor looked closely at the paper, he could not have failed to discover that it called for a very different looking person from myself, and in that case it would have been his duty to arrest me on the instant and send me back to Baltimore from the first station. When he left me with the assurance that I was all right, though much relieved, I realized that I was still in great danger: I was still in Maryland, and subject to arrest at any moment. I saw on the train several persons who would have known me in any other clothes, and I feared they might recognize me, even in my sailor "rig," and report me to the conductor, who would then subject me to a closer examination, which I knew well would be fatal to me.

Though I was not a murderer fleeing from justice, I felt, perhaps, quite as miserable as such a criminal. The train was moving at a very high rate of speed for that time of railroad travel, but to my anxious mind, it was moving far too slowly. Minutes were hours, and hours were days during this part of my flight. After Maryland I was to pass through Delaware—another slave State, where slavecatchers generally awaited their prey, for it was not in the interior of the State, but on its borders, that these human hounds were most vigilant and active. The border lines between slavery and freedom were the dangerous ones, for the fugitives. The heart of no fox or deer, with hungry hounds on his trail, in full chase, could have beaten more anxiously or noisily than did mine from the time I left Balti-

---

[2]Keelson: beams of timber or metal fastened over and along the keel to give support to the ship's frame; cross- trees: two short, horizontal bars on the masthead to spread rigging for holding the mast.

more till I reached Philadelphia. The passage of the Susquehanna river at Havre de Grace was at that time made by ferry-boat, on board of which I met a young colored man by the name of Nichols, who came very near betraying me. He was a "hand" on the boat, but instead of minding his business, he insisted upon knowing me, and asking me dangerous questions as to where I was going, and when I was coming back, etc. I got away from my old and inconvenient acquaintance as soon as I could decently do so, and went to another part of the boat. Once across the river I encountered a new danger. Only a few days before I had been at work on a revenue cutter,[3] in Mr. Price's shipyard, under the care of Captain McGowan. On the meeting at this point of the two trains, the one going south stopped on the track just opposite to the one going north, and it so happened that this Captain McGowan sat at a window where he could see me very distinctly, and would certainly have recognized me had he looked at me but for a second. Fortunately, in the hurry of the moment, he did not see me, and the trains soon passed each other on their respective ways. But this was not the only hair-breadth escape. A German blacksmith, whom I knew well, was on the train with me, and looked at me very intently, as if he thought he had seen me somewhere before in his travels. I really believe he knew me, but had no heart to betray me. At any rate he saw me escaping and held his peace.

The last point of imminent danger, and the one I dreaded most, was Wilmington. Here we left the train and took the steamboat for Philadelphia. In making the change I again apprehended arrest, but no one disturbed me, and I was soon on the broad and beautiful Delaware, speeding away to the Quaker City. On reaching Philadelphia in the afternoon I inquired of a colored man how I could get on to New York? He directed me to the Willow street depot, and thither I went, taking the train that night. I reached New York Tuesday morning, having completed the journey in less than twenty-four hours. Such is briefly the manner of my escape from slavery—and the end of my experience as a slave.

1881

HARRIET A. JACOBS
(1813–1897)

When *Incidents in the Life of a Slave Girl: Written by Herself* appeared in 1861, it was under the pseudonym of Linda Brent and was advertised as "edited" by a famous white author of the time, the abolitionist Lydia Maria Child (1802–1880). In a Preface, the author explained that she had "concealed the names of places, and given persons fictitious names" to protect those who had helped her in her eventual escape. She wrote, she added, "to arouse the women of the North to a realizing sense of the condition of two million of women at the South, still in bondage, suffering what I suffered, and most of them far worse."

Linda Brent's depiction of the "wrongs, and sufferings, and mortifications" peculiar to women in slavery—and especially the degrading sexual harrassment she endured—caused Child to acknowledge in her Introduction that she might be accused of "indecorum" for presenting subjects some might call "delicate" or "indelicate." But Child did so "for the sake of my sisters in bond-

---

[3] Armed sailing vessel used to pursue smugglers.

age." In reference to the 1850 Fugitive Slave Law, she closed with an appeal to "every man" to swear that "no fugitive from Slavery shall ever be sent back to suffer in that loathsome den of corruption and cruelty."

Although Child affirmed the existence of the author and the authenticity of the text ("with trifling exceptions, both the ideas and the language are her own"), many readers were not convinced, and the work was not widely known until well into the twentieth century. It was not until a contemporary scholar, Jean Fagan Yellin, edited and published a new edition in 1987 that the work's claim as an authentic female slave narrative was firmly established. Yellin discovered correspondence and other documents, including important biographical data, that did indeed corroborate Child's assertions that the author existed and that the work was written by the ex-slave herself.

Linda Brent was Harriet Ann Jacobs, born into slavery in Edenton, North Carolina, in 1813. When she was six, her mother died, and then, as she writes, she knew for the first time that she was a slave. When her father, a skilled carpenter, died, she was left with "a great treasure" in her maternal grandmother, Molly Horniblow, who had been freed by a sympathetic owner in 1828 and who continued to live in Edenton.

Jacobs's strong, independent grandmother is a powerful force in her narrative, which concludes with "tender memories" of her. When her first mistress (who had taught her to read and spell) died, the fifteen-year-old Jacobs found herself in a household in which the presiding male, Dr. James Norcom (Dr. Flint in the narrative), repeatedly tried to seduce her. In desperation at her plight, and as a way of holding him at bay, Jacobs began a sexual relationship with a sympathetic white man, a lawyer named Samuel Tredwell Sawyer (Mr. Sands in the narrative), and had a son and daughter by him.

The determined Norcom renewed his demands on Jacobs, and to escape him she went into hiding. He tried to get to her by punishing her children and other relatives, but her lover Sawyer frustrated his efforts by buying the children through a trader and sending them to live in relative freedom with Jacobs's grandmother. In 1835, Jacobs first hid for a time in a swamp, and then later—for seven years—in a cramped, dark garret above her grandmother's attached shed. There she spent an arduous time reading the Bible, sewing, peeping through a one-inch hole at her children (who did not know she was there), and overhearing the slave-hunters conferring about runaways—until her escape to the North in 1842.

Even though she was in the North, Jacobs was not safe. Norcom, and later his daughter, pursued her there, and the danger of her capture and re-enslavement was intensified with the passage in 1850 of the Fugitive Slave Law (part of the Compromise of 1850), which stringently provided for the return of escaped slaves to their owners. Gradually Jacobs came to know a number of the activists in the antislavery movement, and one of them, Amy Post, suggested that she write the story of her life. In 1853, despite her heavy workload, she began to write secretly at night, concealing her enterprise from her unsympathetic employer, the well-known writer-editor, Nathaniel Parker Willis. She completed the work in 1858.

Lydia Maria Child persuaded a Boston firm, Thayer and Eldridge, to publish the book in 1860, but the firm went bankrupt before the book could be issued. Jacobs acquired the already prepared plates, and a Boston printer brought the book out in 1861 "for the author." The following year saw publication of an English edition entitled *The Deeper Wrong: or, Incidents in the Life of a Slave Girl.* Because of the circumstances of the book's publication and the advent of the Civil War, *Incidents* did not receive much attention. Jacobs spent the rest of her life working to raise money for her relief work with slaves and freedmen, but her book was largely forgotten by the time she died in 1897.

In an Introduction to a reprint of Jacobs's book in 1973, Walter Teller pointed out that the work represented "a genre of writing as distinctive to American literature as blues is to American music: the experience that gave rise to slave songs also produced slave narratives. . . . *Incidents in the Life of a Slave Girl* . . . was one of the last and most remarkable of its genre and also one of the very few written by a woman." Whatever minor changes made by the book's first editor, Teller concluded, they did not detract from the "stark realities" of the author's experience and her "straightforward narrative. Her first-hand knowledge of slavery speaks for itself."

ADDITIONAL READING

Incidents in the Life of a Slave Girl by Linda Brent: New Introduction and Notes, ed. Walter Teller, 1973; *Incidents in the Life of a Slave Girl, Written by Herself*, by Harriet A. Jacobs, ed. and with Introduction by Jean Fagan Yellin, 1987.

Bell Hooks, *Ain't I a Woman: Black Women and Feminism*, 1981; Dorothy Sterling, ed., *We Are Your Sisters: Black Women in the Nineteenth Century*, 1984; Jean Fagan Yellin, "Texts and Contexts of Harriet Jacobs's *Incidents in the Life of a Slave Girl*," *The Slave's Narrative*, ed. Charles T. Davis and Henry Louis Gates, Jr., 1985; Minrose C. Gwin, *Black and White Women of the Old South: The Peculiar Sisterhood in American Literature*, 1985; Deborah Gray White, *Ar'n't I a Woman? Female Slaves in the Plantation South*, 1985; Hazel Carby, *Reconstructing Womanhood: The Emergence of the Afro-American Woman Novelist*, 1987; Valerie Smith, *Self-Discovery and Authority in Afro-American Narrative*, 1987; Mary Helen Washington, ed., *Invented Lives: Narratives of Black Women, 1860–1960*, 1987.

TEXT

Incidents in the Life of a Slave Girl: Written by Herself, ed. L. Maria Child, 1861.

from Incidents in the Life of a Slave Girl

V

THE TRIALS OF GIRLHOOD

During the first years of my service in Dr. Flint's family, I was accustomed to share some indulgences with the children of my mistress. Though this seemed to me no more than right, I was grateful for it, and tried to merit the kindness by the faithful discharge of my duties. But I now entered on my fifteenth year—a sad epoch in the life of a slave girl. My master began to whisper foul words in my ear. Young as I was, I could not remain ignorant of their import. I tried to treat them with indifference or contempt. The master's age, my extreme youth, and the fear that his conduct would be reported to my grandmother, made him bear this treatment for many months. He was a crafty man, and resorted to many means to accomplish his purposes. Sometimes he had stormy, terrific ways, that made his victims tremble; sometimes he assumed a gentleness that he thought must surely subdue. Of the two, I preferred his stormy moods, although they left me trembling. He tried his utmost to corrupt the pure principles my grandmother had instilled. He peopled my young mind with unclean images, such as only a vile monster could think of. I turned from him with disgust and hatred. But he was my master. I was compelled to live under the same roof with him—where I saw a man forty years my senior daily violating the most sacred commandments of nature. He told me I was his property; that I must be subject to his will in all things. My soul revolted against the mean tyranny. But where could I turn for protection? No matter whether the slave girl be as black as ebony or as fair as her mistress. In either case, there is no shadow of law to protect her from insult, from violence, or even from death; all these are inflicted by fiends who bear the shape of men. The mistress, who ought to protect the helpless victim, has no other feelings towards her but those of jealousy and rage. The degradation, the wrongs, the vices, that grow out of slavery, are more than I can describe. They are greater than you would willingly believe. Surely, if you credited one half the truths that are told you concerning the helpless millions suffering in this cruel bondage, you at the north would not help to tighten the yoke. You surely would refuse to do for the master, on your own soil, the mean and cruel work which trained bloodhounds and the lowest class of whites do for him at the south.[1]

Every where the years bring to all enough of sin and sorrow; but in slavery the very dawn of life is darkened by these shadows. Even the little child, who is accustomed to wait on her mistress and her children, will learn, before she is twelve years old, why it is that her mistress hates such and such a one among the slaves. Perhaps the child's own mother is among those hated ones. She listens to violent outbreaks of jealous passion, and cannot help understanding what is the cause. She will become prematurely knowing in evil things. Soon she will learn to tremble when she hears her master's footfall. She will be compelled to realize that she is no longer a child. If God has bestowed beauty upon her, it will prove her greatest curse. That which commands admiration in the white woman only hastens the degradation of the female slave. I know that some are too much brutalized by slavery to feel the humiliation of their position; but many slaves feel it most acutely, and shrink from the memory of it. I cannot tell how much I suffered in the presence of these wrongs, nor how I am still pained by the retrospect. My master met me at every turn, reminding me that I belonged to him, and swearing by heaven and earth that he would compel me to submit to him. If I went out for a breath of fresh air, after a day of unwearied toil, his footsteps dogged me. If I knelt by my mother's grave, his dark shadow fell on me even there. The light heart which nature had given me became heavy with sad forebodings. The other slaves in my master's house noticed the change. Many of them pitied me; but none dared to ask the cause. They had no need to inquire. They knew too well the guilty practices under that roof; and they were aware that to speak of them was an offence that never went unpunished.

I longed for some one to confide in. I would have given the world to have laid my head on my grandmother's faithful bosom, and told her all my troubles. But Dr. Flint swore he would kill me, if I was not as silent as the grave. Then, although my grandmother was all in all to me, I feared her as well as loved her. I had been accustomed to look up to her with a respect bordering upon awe. I was very young, and felt shamefaced about telling her such impure things, especially as I knew her to be very strict on such subjects. Moreover, she was a woman of a high spirit. She was usually very quiet in her demeanor; but if her indignation was once roused, it was not very easily quelled. I had been told that she once chased a white gentleman with a loaded pistol, because he insulted one of her daughters. I dreaded the consequences of a violent outbreak; and both pride and fear kept me silent. But though I did not confide in my grandmother, and even evaded her vigilant watchfulness and inquiry, her presence in the neighborhood was some pro-

---

[1]A reference to the stringent Fugitive Slave Law of 1850, part of the Compromise of 1850, which provided for the return of escaped slaves to their owners; the new law encouraged slave hunting and kidnapping in the North.

tection to me. Though she had been a slave, Dr. Flint was afraid of her. He dreaded her scorching rebukes. Moreover, she was known and patronized by many people; and he did not wish to have his villainy made public. It was lucky for me that I did not live on a distant plantation, but in a town not so large that the inhabitants were ignorant of each other's affairs. Bad as are the laws and customs in a slaveholding community, the doctor, as a professional man, deemed it prudent to keep up some outward show of decency.

O, what days and nights of fear and sorrow that man caused me! Reader, it is not to awaken sympathy for myself that I am telling you truthfully what I suffered in slavery. I do it to kindle a flame of compassion in your hearts for my sisters who are still in bondage, suffering as I once suffered.

I once saw two beautiful children playing together. One was a fair white child; the other was her slave, and also her sister. When I saw them embracing each other, and heard their joyous laughter, I turned sadly away from the lovely sight. I foresaw the inevitable blight that would fall on the little slave's heart. I knew how soon her laughter would be changed to sighs. The fair child grew up to be a still fairer woman. From childhood to womanhood her pathway was blooming with flowers, and overarched by a sunny sky. Scarcely one day of her life had been clouded when the sun rose on her happy bridal morning.

How had those years dealt with her slave sister, the little playmate of her childhood? She, also, was very beautiful; but the flowers and sunshine of love were not for her. She drank the cup of sin, and shame, and misery, whereof her persecuted race are compelled to drink.

In view of these things, why are ye silent, ye free men and women of the north? Why do your tongues falter in maintenance of the right? Would that I had more ability! But my heart is so full, and my pen is so weak! There are noble men and women who plead for us, striving to help those who cannot help themselves. God bless them! God give them strength and courage to go on! God bless those, every where, who are laboring to advance the cause of humanity!

from VII

THE LOVER

. . . There was in the neighborhood a young colored carpenter; a free-born man. We had been well acquainted in childhood, and frequently met together afterwards. We became mutually attached, and he proposed to marry me. I loved him with all the ardor of a young girl's first love. But when I reflected that I was a slave, and that the laws gave no sanction to the marriage of such, my heart sank within me. My lover wanted to buy me; but I knew that Dr. Flint was too wilful and arbitrary a man to consent to that arrangement.

•   •   •   •   •   •

There was no hope that the doctor would consent to sell me on any terms. He had an iron will, and was determined to keep me, and to conquer me. My lover was an intelligent and religious man. Even if he could have obtained permission to marry me while I was a slave, the marriage would give him no power to protect me from my master. It would have made him miserable to witness the insults I should have been subjected to. And then, if we had children, I knew they must "follow the condition of the mother." What a terrible blight that would be on the heart of a free, intelligent father! For *his* sake, I felt that I ought not to link his fate with my own unhappy destiny. He was going to Savannah to see about a little property left him by an uncle; and hard as it was to bring my feelings to it, I earnestly entreated him not to come back. I advised him to go to the Free States, where his tongue would not be tied, and where his intelligence would be of more avail to him. He left me, still hoping the day would come when I could be bought. With me the lamp of hope had gone out. The dream of my girlhood was over. I felt lonely and desolate. . . .

X

A PERILOUS PASSAGE IN THE SLAVE GIRL'S LIFE

After my lover went away, Dr. Flint contrived a new plan. He seemed to have an idea that my fear of my mistress was his greatest obstacle. In the blandest tones, he told me that he was going to build a small house for me, in a secluded place, four miles away from the town. I shuddered; but I was constrained to listen, while he talked of his intention to give me a home of my own, and to make a lady of me. Hitherto, I had escaped my dreaded fate, by being in the midst of people. My grandmother had already had high words with my master about me. She had told him pretty plainly what she thought of his character, and there was considerable gossip in the neighborhood about our affairs, to which the open-mouthed jealousy of Mrs. Flint contributed not a little. When my master said he was going to build a house for me, and that he could do it with little trouble and expense, I was in hopes something would happen to frustrate his scheme; but I soon heard that the house was actually begun. I vowed before my Maker that I would never enter it. I had rather toil on the plantation from dawn till dark; I had rather live and die in jail, than drag on, from day to day, through such a living death. I was determined that the master, whom I so hated and loathed, who had blighted the prospects of my youth, and made my life a desert, should not, after my long struggle with him, succeed at last in trampling his victim under his feet. I would do any thing, every thing, for the sake of defeating him. What *could* I do? I thought and thought, till I became desperate, and made a plunge into the abyss.

And now, reader, I come to a period in my unhappy life, which I would gladly forget if I could. The remembrance fills me with sorrow and shame. It pains me to tell you of it; but I have promised to tell you the truth, and I will do it honestly, let it cost me what it may. I will not try to screen myself behind the plea of compulsion from a master; for it was not so. Neither can I plead ignorance or thoughtlessness. For years, my master had done his utmost to pollute my mind with foul images, and to destroy the pure principles inculcated by my grandmother, and the good mistress of my childhood. The influences of slavery had had the same effect on me that they had on other young girls; they had made me prematurely knowing, concerning the evil ways of the world. I knew what I did, and I did it with deliberate calculation.

But, O, ye happy women, whose purity has been sheltered from childhood, who have been free to choose the objects of your affection, whose homes are protected by law, do not judge the poor desolate slave girl too severely! If slavery had been abolished, I, also, could have married the man of my choice; I could have had a home shielded by the laws; and I should have been spared the painful task of confessing what I am now about to relate; but all my prospects had been blighted by slavery. I wanted to keep myself pure; and, under the most adverse circumstances, I tried hard to preserve my self-respect; but I was struggling alone in the powerful grasp of the demon Slavery; and the monster proved too strong for me. I felt as if I was forsaken by God and man; as if all my efforts must be frustrated; and I became reckless in my despair.

I have told you that Dr. Flint's persecutions and his wife's jealousy had given rise to some gossip in the neighborhood. Among others, it chanced that a white unmarried gentleman had obtained some knowledge of the circumstances in which I was placed. He knew my grandmother, and often spoke to me in the street. He became interested for me, and asked questions about my master, which

I answered in part. He expressed a great deal of sympathy, and a wish to aid me. He constantly sought opportunities to see me, and wrote to me frequently. I was a poor slave girl, only fifteen years old.

So much attention from a superior person was, of course, flattering; for human nature is the same in all. I also felt grateful for his sympathy, and encouraged by his kind words. It seemed to me a great thing to have such a friend. By degrees, a more tender feeling crept into my heart. He was an educated and eloquent gentleman; too eloquent, alas, for the poor slave girl who trusted in him. Of course I saw whither all this was tending. I knew the impassable gulf between us; but to be an object of interest to a man who is not married, and who is not her master, is agreeable to the pride and feelings of a slave, if her miserable situation has left her any pride or sentiment. It seems less degrading to give one's self, than to submit to compulsion. There is something akin to freedom in having a lover who has no control over you, except that which he gains by kindness and attachment. A master may treat you as rudely as he pleases, and you dare not speak; moreover, the wrong does not seem so great with an unmarried man, as with one who has a wife to be made unhappy. There may be sophistry in all this; but the condition of a slave confuses all principles of morality, and, in fact, renders the practice of them impossible.

When I found that my master had actually begun to build the lonely cottage, other feelings mixed with those I have described. Revenge, and calculations of interest, were added to flattered vanity and sincere gratitude for kindness. I knew nothing would enrage Dr. Flint so much as to know that I favored another; and it was something to triumph over my tyrant even in that small way. I thought he would revenge himself by selling me, and I was sure my friend, Mr. Sands, would buy me. He was a man of more generosity and feeling than my master, and I thought my freedom could be easily obtained from him. The crisis of my fate now came so near that I was desperate. I shuddered to think of being the mother of children that should be owned by my old tyrant. I knew that as soon as a new fancy took him, his victims were sold far off to get rid of them; especially if they had children. I had seen several women sold, with his babies at the breast. He never allowed his offspring by slaves to remain long in sight of himself and his wife. Of a man who was not my master I could ask to have my children well supported; and in this case, I felt confident I should obtain the boon. I also felt quite sure that they would be made free. With all these thoughts revolving in my mind, and seeing no other way of escaping the doom I so much dreaded, I made a headlong plunge. Pity me, and pardon me, O virtuous reader! You never knew what it is to be a slave; to be entirely unprotected by law or custom; to have the laws reduce you to the condition of a chattel, entirely subject to the will of another. You never exhausted your ingenuity in avoiding the snares, and eluding the power of a hated tyrant; you never shuddered at the sound of his footsteps, and trembled within hearing of his voice. I know I did wrong. No one can feel it more sensibly than I do. The painful and humiliating memory will haunt me to my dying day. Still, in looking back, calmly, on the events of my life, I feel that the slave woman ought not to be judged by the same standard as others.

The months passed on. I had many unhappy hours. I secretly mourned over the sorrow I was bringing on my grandmother, who had so tried to shield me from harm. I knew that I was the greatest comfort of her old age, and that it was a source of pride to her that I had not degraded myself, like most of the slaves. I wanted to confess to her that I was no longer worthy of her love; but could not utter the dreaded words.

As for Dr. Flint, I had a feeling of satisfaction and triumph in the thought of telling *him*. From time to time he told me of his intended arrangements, and I was silent. At last, he came and told me the cottage was completed, and ordered me to go to it. I told him I would never enter it. He said, "I have heard enough of such talk as that. You shall go, if you are carried by force; and you shall remain there."

I replied, "I will never go there. In a few months I shall be a mother."

He stood and looked at me in dumb amazement, and left the house without a word. I thought I should be happy in my triumph over him. But now that the truth was out, and my relatives would hear of it, I felt wretched. Humble as were their circumstances, they had pride in my good character. Now, how could I look them in the face? My self-respect was gone! I had resolved that I would be virtuous, though I was a slave. I had said, "Let the storm beat! I will brave it till I die." And now, how humiliated I felt!

I went to my grandmother. My lips moved to make confession, but the words stuck in my throat. I sat down in the shade of a tree at her door and began to sew. I think she saw something unusual was the matter with me. The mother of slaves is very watchful. She knows there is no security for her children. After they have entered their teens she lives in daily expectation of trouble. This leads to many questions. If the girl is of a sensitive nature, timidity keeps her from answering truthfully, and this well-meant course has a tendency to drive her from maternal counsels. Presently, in came my mistress, like a mad woman, and accused me concerning her husband. My grandmother, whose suspicions had been previously awakened, believed what she said. She exclaimed, "O Linda! has it come to this! I had rather see you dead than to see you as you now are. You are a disgrace to your dead mother." She tore from my fingers my mother's wedding ring and her silver thimble. "Go away!" she exclaimed, "and never come to my house, again." Her reproaches fell so hot and heavy, that they left me no chance to answer. Bitter tears, such as the eyes never shed but once, were my only answer. I rose from my seat, but fell back again, sobbing. She did not speak to me; but the tears were running down her furrowed cheeks, and they scorched me like fire. She had always been so kind to me! *So* kind! How I longed to throw myself at her feet, and tell her all the truth! But she had ordered me to go, and never to come there again. After a few minutes, I mustered strength, and started to obey her. With what feelings did I now close that little gate, which I used to open with such an eager hand in my childhood! It closed upon me with a sound I never heard before.

Where could I go? I was afraid to return to my master's. I walked on recklessly, not caring where I went, or what would become of me. When I had gone four or five miles, fatigue compelled me to stop. I sat down on the stump of an old tree. The stars were shining through the boughs above me. How they mocked me, with their bright, calm light! The hours passed by, and as I sat there alone a chilliness and deadly sickness came over me. I sank on the ground. My mind was full of horrid thoughts. I prayed to die; but the prayer was not answered. At last, with great effort I roused myself, and walked some distance further, to the house of a woman who had been a friend of my mother. When I told her why I was there, she spoke soothingly to me; but I could not be comforted. I thought I could bear my shame if I could only be reconciled to my grandmother. I longed to open my heart to her. I thought if she could know the real state of the case, and all I had been bearing for years, she would perhaps judge me less harshly. My friend advised me to send for her. I did so; but days of agonizing suspense passed before she came. Had she utterly forsaken me? No. She came at last. I knelt before her, and told her things that had poisoned my life; how long I had been persecuted; that I saw no way of escape; and in an hour of extremity I had become desperate. She listened in silence. I told her I would bear any thing and do any thing, if in time I had hopes of obtaining her forgiveness. I begged of her to pity me, for my dead mother's sake. And she did pity me. She did not say, "I forgive you;" but she looked at me lovingly, with her eyes full of tears. She laid her old hand gently on my head, and murmured, "Poor child! Poor child!"

1853–58   *1861*

FRANCES E. W. HARPER
(1825–1911)

Born a free black woman in Baltimore, Maryland, in 1825, Frances Ellen Watkins Harper was orphaned at a very young age. She was adopted by an aunt and uncle who operated a school for free blacks, which Harper attended until she started earning her living as a domestic at the age of fourteen. Finding her way to Ohio, she taught for a period in what was to become Wilburforce University. She soon became active in the antislavery movement, and worked in Pennsylvania in the early 1850s supporting the Underground Railroad in its aid to slaves escaping from their southern masters.

Harper's volume of *Poems on Miscellaneous Subjects* was published in 1854, and she became a popular platform lecturer for the Anti-Slavery Society in the North. She read her poems with great elocutionary skill, holding her audiences enthralled as she assumed the voice she had created in her poem of a slave wife separated from her husband or dramatically described (as in another poem) the desperation of a slave mother deprived of her child. She had mastered the literary forms familiar to her white audiences—the four-line rhymed stanzas with alternating lines of iambic tetrameter and iambic trimeter—through reading such fireside poets as Henry Wadsworth Longfellow.

Married to a widower in 1860, Harper settled with her husband and children on a farm in Ohio. But with his death a few years later, and the end of the Civil War, Harper resumed her career in writing and reform, to which she dedicated the rest of her life. She lectured throughout the South against lynching, an extraordinary feat for a black woman often travelling alone; and she took up the cause of temperance, participating in the crusade against alcohol waged by the Women's Christian Temperance Union. She also campaigned for women's rights and was active in the suffrage movement. Her genius as a reformer was in insisting on the connections of one just cause with another, and the interlinking of them all.

Her *Poems on Miscellaneous Subjects* was extraordinarily popular and was frequently reprinted. She published a new volume of *Poems* in 1871 and still another, *Sketches of Southern Life*, in 1872. In 1869, she published a long narrative poem in blank verse, *Moses: A Story of the Nile*, a recounting of the biblical narrative. Her major fictional achievement was a novel, *Iola Leroy, or Shadows Uplifted*, portraying a family of mixed marriage and spanning the period from before to after the Civil War. It was published in 1892 (when Harper was sixty-seven) and was reprinted in 1969. In his Introduction to the original edition, William Still, author of *The Underground Railroad* (1872), pointed to its embodiment of "the grand and ennobling sentiments which have characterized all [the author's] utterances in laboring for the elevation of the oppressed."

ADDITIONAL READING

William H. Robinson, Jr., ed., *Early Black American Poets*, 1969; Jean Wagner, *Black Poets of the United States: From Paul Laurence Dunbar to Langston Hughes*, 1973; Joan R. Sherman, *Invisible Poets: Afro-Americans of the Nineteenth Century*, 1974; Mary Helen Washington, ed., *Invented Lives: Narratives of Black Women, 1860–1960*, 1987.

TEXT

Poems on Miscellaneous Subjects, 1854.

The Slave Mother

Heard you that shriek? It rose
  So wildly on the air,
It seem'd as if a burden'd heart
  Was breaking in despair.

Saw you those hands so sadly clasped—   5
  The bowed and feeble head—
The shuddering of that fragile form—
  That look of grief and dread?

Saw you the sad, imploring eye?
  Its every glance was pain,   10
As if a storm of agony
  Were sweeping through the brain.

She is a mother pale with fear,
  Her boy clings to her side,
And in her kyrtle[1] vainly tries   15
  His trembling form to hide.

He is not hers, although she bore
  For him a mother's pains;
He is not hers, although her blood
  Is coursing through his veins!   20

He is not hers, for cruel hands
  May rudely tear apart
The only wreath of household love
  That binds her breaking heart.

His love has been a joyous light   25
  That o'er her pathway smiled,
A fountain gushing ever new,
  Amid life's desert wild.

His lightest word has been a tone
  Of music round her heart,   30

---

[1]Variant of "kirtle," a garment or coat reaching to the knees.

Their lives a streamlet blent in one—
　　Oh, Father! must they part?

They tear him from her circling arms,
　　Her last and fond embrace:—
Oh! never more may her sad eyes   35
　　Gaze on his mournful face.

No marvel, then, these bitter shrieks
　　Disturb the listening air;
She is a mother, and her heart
　　Is breaking in despair.   40

　　　　　　　　　　　　　　　　　1854

The Fugitive's Wife

It was my sad and weary lot
　　To toil in slavery;
But one thing cheered my lowly cot—
　　My husband was with me.

One evening, as our children played   5
　　Around our cabin door,
I noticed on his brow a shade
　　I'd never seen before.

And in his eyes a gloomy night
　　Of anguish and despair;—   10
I gazed upon their troubled light,
　　To read the meaning there.

He strained me to his heaving heart—
　　My own beat wild with fear;
I knew not, but I sadly felt   15
　　There must be evil near.

He vainly strove to cast aside
　　The tears that fell like rain:—
Too frail, indeed, is manly pride
　　To strive with grief and pain.   20

Again he clasped me to his breast,
　　And said that we must part:
I tried to speak—but, oh! it seemed
　　An arrow reached my heart.

"Bear not," I cried, "unto your grave,   25
　　The yoke you 've borne from birth,
No longer live a helpless slave,
　　The meanest thing on earth!"

　　　　　　　　　　　　　　　　　1854

HARRIET BEECHER STOWE
(1811–1896)

Uncle Tom's Cabin began appearing serially on June 5, 1851, in the *National Era,* and continued until April 1, 1852. It then appeared as a book, and during its first year sold over 300,000 copies. Its impact was stupendous. Other moralists and intellectuals wrote eloquently against slavery, but had only a fraction of the effect of *Uncle Tom's Cabin.* The reason may be found in the appeal of the victimized characters, Uncle Tom, Eliza, and Topsy; in the scenes that touched chords deep in the national soul; and in the moral passion with which Harriet Beecher Stowe enveloped these characters and scenes.

When *Uncle Tom's Cabin* was turned into a play and produced in 1853, it was an immediate popular success. It played for an astonishing 325 performances on Broadway, becoming the most popular work of its time in one of the most popular art forms. It went on national tour and spectators all over the country could see Uncle Tom beaten by the overseer Simon Legree; or Eliza escaping, child in arms, by stepping from one ice cake to another across the Ohio River; or little Eva dying and ascending to heaven on angel's wings.

In 1862, Harriet Beecher Stowe went to Washington to interview President Abraham Lincoln for a magazine article she was writing. According to her account, when they met, Lincoln greeted her as "the little lady who wrote the book that made this big war!" The remark was of course an exaggeration, but it contained metaphorical truth. The book certainly intensified northern indignation and southern guilt for the searing evils of slavery.

Harriet Beecher was born in Litchfield, Connecticut, into a large family, the seventh of nine children. Her mother died when she was five. Her father, Lyman Beecher, was a well-known and sternly Calvinistic clergyman; two brothers, Henry Ward and Edward, became distinguished preachers. Her sister Catherine established a pioneering school for girls, the Hartford Female Seminary, which Harriet first attended and then assisted under her sister's supervision. In 1832, she moved with her family to Cincinnati, where she witnessed the turmoil surrounding the slavery issue.

Harriet began to write stories for the magazines to earn a few dollars, and in 1836 married Calvin Stowe, a university professor of Greek and theology. In the first four years of marriage there were four children. In 1850, Calvin Stowe accepted a position at Bowdoin College in Maine. There the last of the seven children was born, and Stowe cast about for something to keep her mind preoccupied and to help with family finances. Inspired by a vision in church of a suffering slave, she wrote *Uncle Tom's Cabin, or The Man That Was a Thing* (the original subtitle), and overnight became rich and famous.

Although Stowe continued to write for some thiry-five years, and was recognized as the greatest of American women writers, she never duplicated the phenomenal success of *Uncle Tom's Cabin.* Yet some of the later work, generally classified as "local color" fiction, has been critically acclaimed—including *The Minister's Wooing* (1859) and *Oldtown Folks* (1869).

Literary criticism has always been ambivalent about *Uncle Tom's Cabin,* reluctant to recognize merit in what is often considered a propagandistic novel. In *Patriotic Gore* (1962), Edmund Wilson demolished this point of view: "To expose oneself in maturity to *Uncle Tom* may . . . prove a startling experience.

It is a much more impressive work than one has ever been allowed to suspect. The first thing that strikes one about it is a certain eruptive force. . . . The characters leap into being with . . . vitality. . . . They come before us arguing and struggling, like real people who cannot be quiet."

ADDITIONAL READING

The Life of Harriet Beecher Stowe from Her Letters and Journals, ed. Charles E. Stowe, 1889.

Robert Forrest Wilson, *Crusader in Crinoline: The Life of Harriet Beecher Stowe*, 1941; Charles H. Foster, *The Rungless Ladder: Harriet Beecher Stowe and New England Puritanism*, 1954; Edmund Wilson, *Patriotic Gore*, 1962; John R. Adams, *Harriet Beecher Stowe*, 1963; Johanna Johnston, *Runaway to Heaven: The Story of Harriet Beecher Stowe*, 1963; Edward Wagenknecht, *Harriet Beecher Stowe: The Known and the Unknown*, 1965; Alice C. Crozier, *The Novels of Harriet Beecher Stowe*, 1969; Noel B. Gerson, *Harriet Beecher Stowe: A Biography*, 1976; Edwin Bruce Kirkham, *The Building of Uncle Tom's Cabin*, 1977; Ellen Moer, *Harriet Beecher Stowe and American Literature*, 1978; Elizabeth Ammons, ed., *Critical Essays on Harriet Beecher Stowe*, 1980; Gayle Kimball, *The Religious Ideas of Harriet Beecher Stowe*, 1982; Eric Sundquist, ed., *New Essays on Uncle Tom's Cabin*, 1986.

TEXT

The Writings of Harriet Beecher Stowe, 16 vols., 1896: Vol. I, *Uncle Tom's Cabin: or, Life Among the Lowly.*

from Uncle Tom's Cabin

PREFACE TO THE FIRST EDITION
["To Awaken Sympathy and Feeling"]

THE scenes of this story, as its title indicates, lie among a race hitherto ignored by the associations of polite and refined society; an exotic race, whose ancestors, born beneath a tropic sun, brought with them, and perpetuated to their descendants, a character so essentially unlike the hard and dominant Anglo-Saxon race, as for many years to have won from it only misunderstanding and contempt.

But another and better day is dawning; every influence of literature, of poetry, and of art, in our times, is becoming more and more in unison with the great master chord of Christianity, "good-will to man." The poet, the painter, and the artist now seek out and embellish the common and gentler humanities of life, and, under the allurements of fiction, breathe a humanizing and subduing influence, favorable to the development of the great principles of Christian brotherhood.

The hand of benevolence is everywhere stretched out, searching into abuses, righting wrongs, alleviating distresses, and bringing to the knowledge and sympathies of the world the lowly, the oppressed, and the forgotten. In this general movement, unhappy Africa at last is remembered; Africa, who began the race of civilization and human progress in the dim, gray dawn of early time, but who, for centuries, has lain bound and bleeding at the foot of civilized and Christianized humanity, imploring compassion in vain.

But the heart of the dominant race, who have been her conquerors, her hard masters, has at length been turned towards her in mercy; and it has been seen how far nobler it is in nations to protect the feeble than to oppress them. Thanks be to God, the world has at last outlived the slave-trade!

The object of these sketches is to awaken sympathy and feeling for the African race, as they exist among us; to show their wrongs and sorrows, under a system so necessarily cruel and unjust as to defeat and do away the good effects of all that can be attempted for them, by their best friends, under it. In doing this, the author can sincerely disclaim any invidious feeling towards those individuals who, often without any fault of their own, are involved in the trials and embarrassments of the legal relations of slavery. Experience has shown her that some of the noblest of minds and hearts are often thus involved; and no one knows better than they do, that what may be gathered of the evils of slavery from sketches like these is not the half that could be told of the unspeakable whole.

In the Northern States, these representations may, perhaps, be thought caricatures; in the Southern States are witnesses who know their fidelity. What personal knowledge the author has had, of the truth of incidents such as here are related, will appear in its time. It is a comfort to hope, as so many of the world's sorrows and wrongs have, from age to age, been lived down, so a time shall come when sketches similar to these shall be valuable only as memorials of what has long ceased to be. When an enlightened and Christianized community shall have, on the shores of Africa, laws, language, and literature, drawn from among us, may then, the scenes of the house of bondage be to them like the remembrance of Egypt to the Israelite,—a motive of thankfulness to Him who hath redeemed them! For, while politicians contend, and men are swerved this way and that by conflicting tides of interest and passion, the great cause of human liberty is in the hands of One, of whom it is said:—

> "He shall not fail nor be discouraged
> Till he have set judgment in the earth."[1]

> "He shall deliver the needy when he crieth,
> The poor, and him that hath no helper."[2]

> "He shall redeem their soul from deceit and violence,
> And precious shall their blood be in his sight."[3]

1852

ABRAHAM LINCOLN
(1809–1865)

The most candid word portrait we have of Abraham Lincoln is an autobiography he wrote in 1859. It is exceedingly short and terse. He was born in Hardin County, Kentucky. His parents, he said, were born in Virginia, of "undistinguished families." His mother, "of the name of Hanks," died in his tenth year. His father grew up "literally without education." When he was eight, the family moved from Kentucky to Indiana: "It was a wild region, with many bears and other wild animals, still in the woods." Lincoln wrote of his schooling: "There was absolutely nothing to excite ambition for education. Of course when I came of age I did not know much. Still somehow, I could read, write, and cipher to the Rule of Three; but that was all. I have not been to

---

[1] Isaiah 42:4.
[2] Psalm 72:12.
[3] Psalm 72:14.

school since. The little advance I now have upon this store of education, I have picked up from time to time under the pressure of necessity."

This self-portrait is remarkable not only in its frankness, but also in its simple, lucid, rhythmic style. These are not the sentences of an ignorant man but of one of the finest writers ever to hold the American presidency. Under such handicaps in his youth, how did Lincoln grow up to be one of our greatest presidents—the one who preserved the Union at its time of greatest trial?

He was a self-educated man. From his earliest age, he was an omnivorous reader. He read the Bible, Shakespeare, John Bunyan's *Pilgrim's Progress,* John Milton's *Paradise Lost,* Edward Gibbon's *Decline and Fall of the Roman Empire,* and more. But Lincoln's learning was not the pedantry of mere book knowledge. He assimilated the cadence and rhythm of sentences he read. And he applied to all troublesome questions the shrewd backwoods common sense he grew up with.

Lincoln read for the law and became a lawyer in Springfield, Illinois. He served in the state legislature, and then for a term (1847–49) in the House of Representatives, making himself unpopular by opposing the Mexican War. He joined the new Republican party in 1856 and was its candidate in 1858 for the U.S. Senate from Illinois running against Democrat Stephen A. Douglas.

Lincoln's loss turned out to be a victory, in that the campaign and the Lincoln-Douglas debates on slavery brought him national attention and, two years later, the presidency itself. He was the president challenged to preserve the Union in the nation's trial by fire, the Civil War, and preserve it he did. By the time he was inaugurated for his second term in 1865, assured of victory in the war, he could turn his attention to the healing of the terrible wounds of war. But that task was left to other hands when he was assassinated only six weeks later.

In "Ode Recited at the Harvard Commemoration," James Russell Lowell wrote that Nature, in forming Lincoln, threw aside the "Old-World moulds"—

> And, choosing sweet clay from the breast
> Of the unexhausted West,
> With stuff untainted shaped a hero new,
> Wise, steadfast in the strength of God, and true.

It was a common view that Lincoln represented a kind of new Western man, with a backwoods wisdom and strength that typified America. And the Civil War was popularly deemed the country's somber rite of passage from youth to maturity, from innocence to experience.

ADDITIONAL READING

The Collected Works of Abraham Lincoln, 9 vols., ed. Roy P. Basler et al., 1953–55.

John G. Nicolay and John Hay, *Abraham Lincoln: A History,* 10 vols., 1890; Carl Sandburg, *Abraham Lincoln: The Prairie Years,* 2 vols., 1926; Carl Sandburg, *Abraham Lincoln: The War Years,* 4 vols., 1939; James G. Randall, *Lincoln the President,* 4 vols., 1945–55; Benjamin P. Thomas, *Abraham Lincoln,* 1952; Edmund Wilson, "Abraham Lincoln," *Patriotic Gore,* 1962; Herbert Joseph Edwards and John Erskine Hankins, *Lincoln the Writer: The Development of His Style,* 1962; Steven B. Oates, *With Malice Toward None: The Life of Abraham Lincoln,* 1977; Charles B. Strozier, *Lincoln's Quest for Union: Public and Private Meanings,* 1982; Steven B. Oates, *Abraham Lincoln: The Man Behind the Myths,* 1984; Roger Bruns, *Abraham Lincoln,* 1986.

TEXT

Abraham Lincoln: His Speeches and Writings, ed. Roy P. Basler, 1946.

A House Divided: Speech Delivered at Springfield, Illinois, at the Close of the Republican State Convention. June 16, 1858[1]

If we could first know *where* we are, and *whither* we are tending, we could better judge *what* to do, and *how* to do it.

We are now far into the *fifth* year, since a policy was initiated, with the *avowed* object, and *confident* promise, of putting an end to slavery agitation.

Under the operation of that policy, that agitation has not only, *not ceased*, but has *constantly augmented*.

In my opinion, it *will* not cease, until a *crisis* shall have been reached, and passed—

"A house divided against itself cannot stand."[2]

I believe this government cannot endure, permanently half *slave* and half *free*.

I do not expect the Union to be *dissolved*—I do not expect the house to *fall*—but I *do* expect it will cease to be divided.

It will become *all* one thing, or *all* the other.

Either the *opponents* of slavery, will arrest the further spread of it, and place it where the public mind shall rest in the belief that it is in course of ultimate extinction; or its *advocates* will push it forward, till it shall become alike lawful in *all* the States, *old* as well as *new*—*North* as well as *South*.

Have we no *tendency* to the latter condition?

Let any one who doubts, carefully contemplate that now almost complete legal combination—piece of *machinery* so to speak—compounded of the Nebraska doctrine, and the Dred Scott decision.[3] Let him consider not only *what work* the machinery is adapted to do, and *how well* adapted; but also, let him study the history of its construction, and trace, if he can, or rather *fail*, if he can, to trace the evidences of design, and concert of action, among its chief bosses, from the beginning.

The new year of 1854 found slavery excluded from more than half the States by State Constitutions, and from most of the national territory by congressional prohibition.

Four days later, commenced the struggle, which ended in repealing that congressional prohibition.

This opened all the national territory to slavery; and was the first point gained.

But, so far, *Congress* only, had acted; and an *indorsement* by the people, *real* or *apparent*, was indispensable, to *save* the point already gained, and give chance for more.

This necessity had not been overlooked; but had been provided for, as well as might be, in the notable argument of "squatter sovereignty," otherwise called "*sacred right of self government*," which latter phrase, though expressive of the only rightful basis of any government, was so perverted in this attempted use of it as to amount to just this: That if any *one* man, choose to enslave *another*, no *third* man shall be allowed to object.

That argument was incorporated into the Nebraska bill itself, in the language which follows: "*It being the true intent and meaning of this act not to legislate slavery into*

---

[1] Lincoln's speech accepting the Republican party's nomination for Senator from Illinois, to run against the incumbent Democratic Senator Stephen A. Douglas. Douglas won the election, but Lincoln won the debate—and national attention which would make him president two years later.
[2] Cf. Mark 3:25.
[3] The Kansas-Nebraska Act of 1854 had been introduced by Illinois Senator Douglas and allowed residents of these two territories to decide whether they would be slave states or free; the Dred Scott decision, announced by the Supreme Court in 1857, overturned a lower court decision setting a Negro free on grounds that he had lived in free territory for four years. The Supreme Court ruled that, as a Negro and noncitizen, Scott could not sue for his freedom in the courts, and that temporary residence in free territory did not make him free.

any Territory or State, nor to exclude it therefrom; but to leave the people thereof perfectly free to form and regulate their domestic institutions in their own way, subject only to the Constitution of the United States."

Then opened the roar of loose declamation in favor of "Squatter Sovereignty," and "Sacred right of self government."

"But," said opposition members, "let us be more *specific*—let us *amend* the bill so as to expressly declare that the people of the Territory *may* exclude slavery." "Not we," said the friends of the measure; and down they voted the amendment.

While the Nebraska bill was passing through congress, a *law case,* involving the question of a negro's freedom, by reason of his owner having voluntarily taken him first into a free State and then a territory covered by the congressional prohibition, and held him as a slave for a long time in each, was passing through the U.S. Circuit Court for the District of Missouri; and both Nebraska bill and law suit were brought to a decision in the same month of May, 1854. The negro's name was "Dred Scott," which name now designates the decision finally made in the case.

Before the *then* next Presidential election, the law case came *to,* and was argued *in* the Supreme Court of the United States; but the *decision* of it was deferred until *after* the election. Still, *before* the election, Senator Trumbull, on the floor of the Senate, requests the leading advocate of the Nebraska bill[4] to state *his opinion* whether the people of a territory can constitutionally exclude slavery from their limits; and the latter answers, "That is a question for the Supreme Court."

The election came. Mr. Buchanan[5] was elected, and the *indorsement,* such as it was, secured. That was the *second* point gained. The indorsement, however, fell short of a clear popular majority by nearly four hundred thousand votes, and so, perhaps, was not over-whelmingly reliable and satisfactory.

The *outgoing* President, in his last annual message, as impressively as possible *echoed back* upon the people the *weight* and *authority* of the indorsement.

The Supreme Court met again; *did not* announce their decision, but ordered a re-argument.

The Presidential inauguration came, and still no decision of the court; but the *incoming* President, in his inaugural address, fervently exhorted the people to abide by the forthcoming decision, *whatever it might be.*

Then, in a few days, came the decision.

The reputed author of the Nebraska bill finds an early occasion to make a speech at this capitol indorsing the Dred Scott Decision, and vehemently denouncing all opposition to it.

The new President, too, seizes the early occasion of the Silliman letter[6] to indorse and strongly *construe* that decision, and to express his *astonishment* that any different view had ever been entertained.

At length a squabble springs up between the President and the author of the Nebraska bill, on the *mere* question of *fact,* whether the Lecompton constitution[7] was or was not, in any just sense, made by the people of Kansas; and in that quarrel the latter declares that all he wants is a fair vote for the people, and that he *cares* not whether slavery be voted *down* or voted *up.* I do not understand his declaration that he cares not whether slavery be voted down or voted up, to be intended by him other than as an *apt definition* of the *policy* he would impress upon

---

[4]Stephen A. Douglas (1813–1861); Lyman Trumbull (1813–1896) was Illinois Senator from 1855 to 1873.
[5]James Buchanan (1791–1868), elected U.S. president in 1857 for one term.
[6]Benjamin Silliman (1816–1885) was leader of a Connecticut group that protested to President Buchanan for his support of the proslavery delegates that dominated Kansas's State Constitutional Convention, ignoring the antislavery settlers of the state.
[7]The draft constitution that, if approved, would have admitted Kansas to the Union as a slave state; it was rejected by Kansas voters and the House of Representatives. Lecompton led the proslave Kansans.

the public mind—the *principle* for which he declares he has suffered much, and is ready to suffer to the end.

And well may he cling to that principle. If he has any parental feeling, well may he cling to it. That principle, is the only shred left of his original Nebraska doctrine. Under the Dred Scott decision, "squatter sovereignty" squatted out of existence, tumbled down like temporary scaffolding—like the mold at the foundry served through one blast and fell back into loose sand—helped to carry an election, and then was kicked to the winds. His late *joint* struggle with the Republicans, against the Lecompton Constitution, involves nothing of the original Nebraska doctrine. That struggle was made on a point, the right of a people to make their own constitution, upon which he and the Republicans have never differed.

The several points of the Dred Scott decision, in connection with Senator Douglas' "care not" policy, constitute the piece of machinery, in its *present* state of advancement.

The *working* points of that machinery are:

First, that no negro slave, imported as such from Africa, and no descendant of such slave can ever be a *citizen* of any State, in the sense of that term as used in the Constitution of the United States.

This point is made in order to deprive the negro, in every possible event, of the benefit of that provision of the United States Constitution, which declares that—

"the citizens of each State shall be entitled to all privileges and immunities of citizens in the several States."

Secondly, that "subject to the Constitution of the United States," neither *Congress* nor a *Territorial Legislature* can exclude slavery from any United States Territory.

This point is made in order that individual men may *fill up* the territories with slaves, without danger of losing them as property, and thus enhance the chances of *permanency* to the institution through all the future.

Thirdly, that whether the holding a negro in actual slavery in a free State, makes him free, as against the holder, the United States courts will not decide, but will leave to be decided by the courts of any slave State the negro may be forced into by the master.

This point is made, not to be pressed *immediately;* but, if acquiesced in for a while, and apparently *indorsed* by the people at an election, *then* to sustain the logical conclusion that what Dred Scott's master might lawfully do with Dred Scott, in the free State of Illinois, every other master may lawfully do with any other *one* or one *thousand* slaves, in Illinois, or in any other free State.

Auxiliary to all this, and working hand in hand with it, the Nebraska doctrine, or what is left of it, is to *educate* and *mould* public opinion, at least *Northern* public opinion, to not *care* whether slavery is voted *down* or voted *up.*

This shows exactly where we now *are;* and *partially* also, whither we are tending.

It will throw additional light on the latter, to go back, and run the mind over the string of historical facts already stated. Several things will *now* appear less *dark* and *mysterious* than they did *when* they were transpiring. The people were to be left "perfectly free" "subject only to the Constitution." What the *Constitution* had to do with it, outsiders could not *then* see. Plainly enough *now*, it was an exactly fitted *nitch* for the Dred Scott decision to afterward come in, and declare that *perfect freedom* of the people, to be just no freedom at all.

Why was the amendment, expressly declaring the right of the people to exclude slavery, voted down? Plainly enough *now,* the adoption of it, would have spoiled the nitch for the Dred Scott decision.

Why was the court decision held up? Why, even a Senator's individual opinion withheld, till *after* the Presidential election? Plainly enough *now*, the speaking out *then* would have damaged the *"perfectly free"* argument upon which the election was to be carried.

Why the *outgoing* President's felicitation on the indorsement? Why the delay of a reargument? Why the incoming President's *advance* exhortation in favor of the decision?

These things *look* like the cautious *patting* and *petting* of a spirited horse, preparatory to mounting him, when it is dreaded that he may give the rider a fall.

And why the hasty after indorsements of the decision by the President and others?

We cannot absolutely *know* that all these exact adaptations are the result of preconcert. But when we see a lot of framed timbers, different portions of which we know have been gotten out at different times and places and by different workmen—Stephen, Franklin, Roger, and James, for instance—and we see these timbers joined together, and see they exactly make the frame of a house or a mill, all the tenons and mortises exactly fitting, and all the lengths and proportions of the different pieces exactly adapted to their respective places, and not a piece too many or too few—not omitting even scaffolding—or, if a single piece be lacking, we see the place in the frame exactly fitted and prepared to yet bring such piece in—in *such* a case, we find it impossible not to *believe* that Stephen and Franklin and Roger and James all understood one another from the beginning, and all worked upon a common *plan* or *draft* drawn up before the first lick was struck.

It should not be overlooked that, by the Nebraska bill, the people of a *State* as well as *Territory*, were to be left *"perfectly free" "subject only to the Constitution."*

Why mention a *State*? They were legislating for *territories*, and not *for* or *about* States. Certainly the people of a *State are* and *ought to be* subject to the Constitution of the United States; but why is mention of this *lugged* into this merely *territorial* law? Why are the people of a *territory* and the people of a *state* therein *lumped* together, and their relation to the Constitution therein treated as being *precisely* the same?

While the opinion of the Court, by Chief Justice Taney, in the Dred Scott case, and the separate opinions of all the concurring Judges, expressly declare that the Constitution of the United States neither permits Congress nor a territorial legislature to exclude slavery from any United States territory, they all *omit* to declare whether or not the same Constitution permits a state, or the people of a State, to exclude it.

Possibly, this is a mere *omission;* but who can be *quite* sure, if McLean or Curtis[8] had sought to get into the opinion a declaration of unlimited power in the people of a state to exclude slavery from their limits, just as Chase and Mace[9] sought to get such declaration, in behalf of the people of a territory, into the Nebraska bill—I ask, who can be quite *sure* that it would not have been voted down, in the one case, as it had been in the other?

The nearest approach to the point of declaring the power of a State over slavery, is made by Judge Nelson.[10] He approaches it more than once, using the precise idea, and *almost* the language too, of the Nebraska act. On one occasion his exact language is, "except in cases where the power is restrained by the Constitution of the United States, the law of the State is supreme over the subject of slavery within its jurisdiction."

---

[8]John McLean (1785–1861), lawyer and legislator, and member of the U.S. Supreme Court (1829–61); Benjamin Robbins Curtis (1809–1874), jurist, member of the U.S. Supreme Court (1851–57).
[9]Salmon Portland Chase (1808–1873), active in free-soil movement, U.S. Senator (1849–55); later, Lincoln's Secre-

tary of the Treasury, and Chief Justice of the Supreme Court (1864–73). Daniel Mace (1811–1867), representative from Indiana (1851–57).
[10]Rensselaer Russell Nelson (1826–1904), member of the territorial Supreme Court of Minnesota, appointed by President Buchanan in 1857.

In what *cases* the power of the *states* is so restrained by the U.S. Constitution is left an *open* question, precisely [*sic*] as the same question, as to the restraint on the power of the *territories* was left open in the Nebraska act. Put *that* and *that* together, and we have another nice little nitch, which we may, ere long, see filled with another Supreme Court decision, declaring that the Constitution of the United States does not permit a state to exclude slavery from its limits.

And this may especially be expected if the doctrine of "care not whether slavery be voted *down* or voted *up*," shall gain upon the public mind sufficiently to give promise that such a decision can be maintained when made.

Such a decision is all that slavery now lacks of being alike lawful in all the States.

Welcome or unwelcome, such decision *is* probably coming, and will soon be upon us, unless the power of the present political dynasty shall be met and overthrown. We shall *lie down* pleasantly dreaming that the people of *Missouri* are on the verge of making their State *free;* and we shall *awake* to the *reality*, instead, that the *Supreme* Court has made *Illinois* a *slave* State.

To meet and overthrow the power of that dynasty, is the work now before all those who would prevent that consummation.

That is *what* we have to do.

But *how* can we best do it?

There are those who denounce us *openly* to their *own* friends, and yet whisper *us softly,* that Senator Douglas is the *aptest* instrument there is, with which to effect that object. *They* do *not* tell us, nor has *he* told us, that he *wishes* any such object to be effected. They wish us to *infer* all, from the facts, that he now has a little quarrel with the present head of the dynasty; and that he has regularly voted with us, on a single point, upon which, he and we, have never differed.

They remind us that *he* is a *great* man, and that the largest of *us* are very small ones. Let this be granted. But "a *living dog* is better than a *dead lion.*"[11] Judge Douglas, if not a *dead* lion *for this work,* is at least a *caged* and *toothless* one. How can he oppose the advances of slavery? He don't *care* anything about it. His avowed *mission is impressing* the "public heart" to *care* nothing about it.

A leading Douglas Democratic newspaper thinks Douglas' superior talent will be needed to resist the revival of the African slave trade.

Does Douglas believe an effort to revive that trade is approaching? He has not said so. Does he *really* think so? But if it is, how can he resist it? For years he has labored to prove it a *sacred right* of white men to take negro slaves into the new territories. Can he possibly show that it is *less* a sacred right to *buy* them where they can be bought cheapest? And, unquestionably they can be bought *cheaper* in *Africa* than in *Virginia.*

He has done all in his power to reduce the whole question of slavery to one of a mere *right of property;* and as such, how can *he* oppose the foreign slave trade—how can he refuse that trade in that "property" shall be "perfectly free"—unless he does it as a *protection* to the home production? And as the home *producers* will probably not *ask* the protection, he will be wholly without a ground of opposition.

Senator Douglas holds, we know, that a man may rightfully be *wiser to-day* than he was *yesterday*—that he may rightfully *change* when he finds himself wrong.

But, can we for that reason, run ahead, and *infer* that he *will* make any particular change, of which he, himself, has given no intimation? Can we *safely* base *our* action upon any such *vague* inference?

Now, as ever, I wish to not misrepresent Judge Douglas' *position*, question his *motives*, or do aught that can be personally offensive to him.

---

[11]Cf. Ecclesiastes 9:4.

Whenever, *if ever,* he and we can come together on *principle* so that *our great cause* may have assistance from *his great ability,* I hope to have interposed no adventitious obstacle.

But clearly, he is not *now* with us—he does not *pretend* to be—he does not *promise* to *ever* be.

Our cause, then, must be intrusted to, and conducted by its own undoubted friends—those whose hands are free, whose hearts are in the work—who *do care* for the result.

Two years ago the Republicans of the nation mustered over thirteen hundred thousand strong.

We did this under the single impulse of resistance to a common danger, with every external circumstance against us.

Of *strange, discordant,* and even, *hostile* elements, we gathered from the four winds, and *formed* and fought the battle through, under the constant hot fire of a disciplined, proud, and pampered enemy.

Did we brave all *then* to *falter* now?—now—when that same enemy is *wavering,* dissevered, and belligerent?

The result is not doubtful. We shall not fail—if we stand firm, we shall not fail.

Wise counsels may *accelerate* or *mistakes delay* it, but sooner or later the victory is *sure* to come.

1858

Letter to Horace Greeley[1]

[Paramount Object: To Save the Union]

Executive Mansion,
Washington, August 22, 1862.

Hon. Horace Greeley:
Dear Sir.

I have just read yours of the 19th. addressed to myself through the New-York Tribune. If there be in it any statements, or assumptions of fact, which I may know to be erroneous, I do not, now and here, controvert them. If there be in it any inferences which I may believe to be falsely drawn, I do not now and here, argue against them. If there be perceptable [*sic*] in it an impatient and dictatorial tone, I waive it in deference to an old friend, whose heart I have always supposed to be right.

As to the policy I "seem to be pursuing" as you say, I have not meant to leave any one in doubt.

I would save the Union. I would save it the shortest way under the Constitution. The sooner the national authority can be restored; the nearer the Union will be "the Union as it was." If there be those who would not save the Union, unless they could at the same time *save* slavery, I do not agree with them. If there be those who would not save the Union unless they could at the same time *destroy* slavery, I do not agree with them. My paramount object in this struggle *is* to save the

---

[1] Horace Greeley, in his *New York Tribune,* August 19, 1862, had published "The Prayer of Twenty Million," saying that Lincoln might have threatened, in his Inaugural Address, to emancipate the slaves and he might have adopted sterner measures in dealing with the South. A few weeks earlier, Lincoln had drafted the Emancipation Proclama-tion and was waiting for the right moment to issue it. His letter to Greeley was published in the *National Intelligencer,* August 23, 1862. The next month, on September 22, Lincoln issued the Emancipation Proclamation, setting the date for it to take effect as January 1, 1863.

Union, and is *not* either to save or to destroy slavery. If I could save the Union without freeing *any* slave I would do it, and if I could save it by freeing *all* the slaves, I would do it; and if I could save it by freeing some and leaving others alone I would also do that. What I do about slavery, and the colored race, I do because I believe it helps to save the Union; and what I forbear, I forbear because I do *not* believe it would help to save the Union. I shall do *less* whenever I shall believe what I am doing hurts the cause, and I shall do *more* whenever I shall believe doing more will help the cause. I shall try to correct errors when shown to be errors; and I shall adopt new views so fast as they shall appear to be true views.

I have here stated my purpose according to my view of *official* duty; and I intend no modification of my oft-expressed *personal* wish that all men everywhere could be free.

Yours,
A. Lincoln.

Final Emancipation Proclamation
January 1, 1863

Whereas, on the twentysecond day of September, in the year of our Lord one thousand eight hundred and sixty two a proclamation was issued by the President of the United States, containing, among other things, the following, to wit:

"That on the first day of January, in the year of our Lord one thousand eight hundred and sixty-three, all persons held as slaves within any state, or designated part of a state, the people whereof shall then be in rebellion against the United States, shall be then, thenceforward and forever free; and the Executive Government of the United States, including the military and naval authority thereof, will recognize and maintain the freedom of such persons, and will do no act or acts to repress such persons, or any of them, in any efforts they may make for their actual freedom.

"That the executive will, on the first day of January aforesaid, by proclamation, designate the states and parts of states, if any, in which the people thereof, respectively, shall then be in rebellion against the United States, and the fact that any state, or the people thereof, shall on that day be in good faith represented in the Congress of the United States by members chosen thereto, at elections wherein a majority of the qualified voters of such state shall have participated, shall, in the absence of strong countervailing testimony, be deemed conclusive evidence that such state, and the people thereof, are not then in rebellion against the United States."

Now, therefore I, Abraham Lincoln President of the United States, by virtue of the power in me vested as Commander-in-Chief, of the Army and Navy of the United States in time of actual armed rebellion against authority and government of the United States, and as a fit and necessary war measure for suppressing said rebellion, do on this first day of January, in the year of our Lord one thousand eight hundred and sixty three, and in accordance with my purpose so to do publicly proclaimed for the full period of one hundred days, from the day first above mentioned, order and designate as the States and parts of States wherein the people thereof respectively, are this day in rebellion against the United States, the following, to wit

Arkansas, Texas, Louisiana, (except the Parishes of St. Bernard, Plaquemine, Jefferson, St. Johns, St. Charles, St. James, Ascension, Assumption, Terrebonne, Lafourche, St. Mary, St. Martin, and Orleans, including the City of New-Orleans) Mississippi, Alabama, Florida, Georgia, South-Carolina, North-Carolina, and Virginia, (except the forty-eight counties designated as West Virginia and also the counties of Berkeley, Accomac, Northampton, Elizabeth City, York, Princess-Ann, and Norfolk, including the cities of Norfolk & Portsmouth; and which excepted parts are for the present left precisely as if this proclamation were not issued.

And by virtue of the power and for the purpose aforesaid I do order and declare that all persons held as slaves within said designated States, and parts of States are and henceforward shall be free; and that the Executive government of the United States, including the military and naval authorities thereof, will recognize and maintain the freedom of said persons.

And I hereby enjoin upon the people so declared to be free to abstain from all violence, unless in necessary self-defense; and I recommend to them that in all cases when allowed, they labor faithfully for reasonable wages.

And I further declare and make known, that such persons of suitable condition, will be received into the armed service of the United States to garrison forts, positions, stations and other places, and to man vessels of all sorts in said service.

And upon this act sincerely believed to be an act of justice, warranted by the Constitution upon military necessity, I invoke the considerate judgment of mankind, and the gracious favor of Almighty God.

In witness whereof, I have hereunto set my hand and caused the seal of the United States to be affixed

Done at the city of Washington, this first day of January, in the year of our Lord one thousand eight hundred and sixty three, [L. S.]   and of the Independence of the United States of America the eighty-seventh.

By the President: Abraham Lincoln

William H. Seward,
Secretary of State

Address Delivered at the Dedication
of the Cemetery at Gettysburg
November 19, 1863[1]

Four score and seven years ago our fathers brought forth on this continent, a new nation, conceived in Liberty, and dedicated to the proposition that all men are created equal.

Now we are engaged in a great civil war, testing whether that nation, or any nation so conceived and so dedicated, can long endure. We are met on a great battle-field of that war. We have come to dedicate a portion of that field, as a final

---

[1]Edward Everett, renowned orator, was the featured speaker on the dedication of the Gettysburg National Cemetery where the thousands who died on the battlefield would be buried. President Lincoln was invited as an afterthought and he composed the first draft of his speech on the train to Gettysburg. Everett delivered a polished oration which lasted for two hours. Lincoln delivered his brief remarks next. Later Everett wrote to Lincoln: "I should be glad if I could flatter myself that I came as near to the central idea of the occasion in two hours as you did in two minutes."

resting place for those who here gave their lives that that nation might live. It is altogether fitting and proper that we should do this.

But, in a larger sense, we can not dedicate—we can not consecrate—we can not hallow—this ground. The brave men, living and dead, who struggled here, have consecrated it, far above our poor power to add or detract. The world will little note, nor long remember what we say here, but it can never forget what they did here. It is for us the living, rather, to be dedicated here to the unfinished work which they who fought here have thus far so nobly advanced. It is rather for us to be here dedicated to the great task remaining before us—that from these honored dead we take increased devotion to that cause for which they gave the last full measure of devotion—that we here highly resolve that these dead shall not have died in vain—that this nation, under God, shall have a new birth of freedom—and that government of the people, by the people, for the people, shall not perish from the earth.

Abraham Lincoln.

November 19, 1863.

Second Inaugural Address
March 4, 1865[1]

At this second appearing to take the oath of the presidential office, there is less occasion for an extended address than there was at the first. Then a statement, somewhat in detail, of a course to be pursued, seemed fitting and proper. Now, at the expiration of four years, during which public declarations have been constantly called forth on every point and phase of the great contest which still absorbs the attention, and engrosses the energies of the nation, little that is new could be presented. The progress of our arms, upon which all else chiefly depends, is as well known to the public as to myself; and it is, I trust, reasonably satisfactory and encouraging to all. With high hope for the future, no prediction in regard to it is ventured.

On the occasion corresponding to this four years ago, all thoughts were anxiously directed to an impending civil war. All dreaded it—all sought to avert it. While the inaugeral [*sic*] address was being delivered from this place, devoted altogether to *saving* the Union without war, insurgent agents were in the city seeking to *destroy* it without war—seeking to dissole [*sic*] the Union, and divide effects, by negotiation. Both parties deprecated war; but one of them would *make* war rather than let the nation survive; and the other would *accept* war rather than let it perish. And the war came.

One eighth of the whole population were colored slaves, not distributed generally over the Union, but localized in the Southern part of it. These slaves constituted a peculiar and powerful interest. All knew that this interest was, somehow, the cause of the war. To strengthen, perpetuate, and extend this interest was the object for which the insurgents would rend the Union, even by war; while the government claimed no right to do more than to restrict the territorial enlargement of it. Neither party expected for the war, the magnitude, or the duration, which it has already attained. Neither anticipated that the *cause* of the conflict might cease with, or even before, the conflict itself should cease.[2] Each looked for an easier

---

[1] When Lincoln delivered his "Second Inaugural Address," victory in the Civil War was assured. The Union would be preserved. The speech sounded the note of conciliation—love and forgiveness. Within six weeks, Lincoln was dead at the hands of an assassin.

[2] Slavery had been effectively abolished with the Emancipation Proclamation of January 1, 1863.

triumph, and a result less fundamental and astounding. Both read the same Bible, and pray to the same God; and each invokes His aid against the other. It may seem strange that any men should dare to ask a just God's assistance in wringing their bread from the sweat of other men's faces; but let us judge not that we be not judged.[3] The prayers of both could not be answered; that of neither has been answered fully. The Almighty has his own purposes. "Woe unto the world because of offences! for it must needs be that offences come; but woe to that man by whom the offence cometh!"[4] If we shall suppose that American Slavery is one of those offences which, in the providence of God, must needs come, but which, having continued through His appointed time, He now wills to remove, and that He gives to both North and South, this terrible war, as the woe due to those by whom the offence came, shall we discern therein any departure from those divine attributes which the believers in a Living God always ascribe to Him? Fondly do we hope—fervently do we pray—that this mighty scourge of war may speedily pass away. Yet, if God wills that it continue, until all the wealth piled by the bond-man's two hundred and fifty years of unrequited toil shall be sunk, and until every drop of blood drawn with the lash, shall be paid by another drawn with the sword, as was said three thousand years ago, so still it must be said "the judgments of the Lord, are true and righteous altogether."[5]

With malice toward none; with charity for all; with firmness in the right, as God gives us to see the right, let us strive on to finish the work we are in; to bind up the nation's wounds; to care for him who shall have borne the battle, and for his widow, and his orphan—to do all which may achieve and cherish a just and lasting peace, among ourselves, and with all nations.

1865

WALT WHITMAN
(1819–1892)

When Walt Whitman, an unknown New York poet, published the first edition of *Leaves of Grass* in 1855, he also published, anonymously, three of the rare reviews of the volume, one of which opened: "An American bard at last!" The astonishing thing is not that Whitman promoted himself in these reviews, but that his characterization of himself turned out to be right. When Emerson received a copy of *Leaves of Grass*, he appears to have almost immediately dispatched a letter to Whitman written out of a deep and enthusiastic response to Whitman's poetry. He wrote: "I find it the most extraordinary piece of wit and wisdom that America has yet contributed." In effect, the letter from the most distinguished man of letters in America at the time confirmed Whitman's view of himself.

Leaves of Grass appeared in three editions before the Civil War (1855, 1856, 1860), and it would appear in several editions afterwards, ultimately achieving the magnitude and structure which Whitman endorsed in the so-called Deathbed Edition of 1892. Whitman spent a lifetime in making one book, which as it grew incorporated much of the life the poet lived. It could not have been

---

[3]Cf. Matthew 7:1.
[4]Cf. Matthew 18:7.
[5]Cf. Psalm 19:9.

planned in advance, in substance, because Whitman could not have known in advance what events he was going to experience. It could not have been altered after the fact because it was bound to follow the contour and shape of Whitman's life and no other.

Whitman said that his purpose from the beginning was to express his "own distinctive era and surroundings, America, Democracy." He succeeded, making his book America's great national poem, an epic, with himself as its democratic hero. Its spirit was echoed in its free verse, with its long lines sweeping across the page freed from the encumbrances of traditional and confining patterns and forms. Poetry would never be the same again, once the impact of Whitman's innovations in form were felt. The full impact would not be felt, however, until the twentieth century.

Whitman could not of course have planned to have the Civil War as the ballast and center of his book when he began it in 1855. But when the war began, he went to the battlegrounds in Virginia looking for his wounded brother George. And becoming involved as a nurse or wound-dresser in and around Washington, he could not prevent that cataclysmic national event from becoming the very heart of *Leaves of Grass*. In "A Backward Glance O'er Travel'd Roads," written near the end of his career, Whitman said:

> I went down to the war fields in Virginia (end of 1862), lived thenceforward in camp—saw great battles and the days and nights afterward—partook of all the fluctuations, gloom, despair, hopes again arous'd, courage evoked—death readily risk'd—*the cause,* too—along and filling those agonistic and lurid following years, 1863–'64–'65—the real parturition years (more than 1776–'83) of this henceforth homogeneous Union. Without those three or four years and the experiences they gave, *Leaves of Grass* would not now be existing.

This bit of self-examination, like the reviews of that first edition of *Leaves of Grass,* is remarkable for its accuracy. Whitman saw that the Civil War, not the Revolutionary War, was the real birth of the "homogeneous Union." This perception led to a renegotiation of the literary contract he had made with himself at the beginning of his poetic career. The war re-created America, and it re-created Whitman in making him into the genuine American Bard he had wanted and planned to be.

In 1865, Whitman issued his poems written out of his experiences on the battlefields and in Washington, D.C., as *Drum-Taps*. In April of 1865, just as the war was about to end, Abraham Lincoln was assassinated. Whitman had never met him, but had seen him often passing in the streets of Washington, and had come to like his simple western ways and his humanity, and to identify with his devotion to freedom and democracy. Whitman's reaction to the death was immediate, expressing his and the nation's grief in one of the greatest elegies ever written, "When Lilacs Last in the Dooryard Bloom'd." Lincoln became the setting western star of the poem, and the country's homage to the dead president the common April lilacs growing in the dooryard. This and other Lincoln poems were included in a reissue of the *Drum-Taps* volume in the fall of 1865.

In later editions of *Leaves of Grass,* Whitman placed the "Drum-Taps" and "Memories of President Lincoln" clusters of poems in the book's center. But the war and its results radiate from that position and touch almost every page of the book. Because of the Civil War and Whitman's imaginative engagement with it in *Leaves of Grass,* his achievement is genuinely epic. Like epic poets of antiquity, Whitman was there at the true national beginning and embodied the ideals, aspirations, hopes, and dreams of the young nation entering maturity. Later poets could never have that opportunity. And they would have to come to terms with Whitman. As the mover and shaper of the modernist period, Ezra Pound wrote later in "What I Feel about Walt Whitman" (1909): "He *is* America . . . . He *does* 'chant the crucial stage' and he is the 'voice triumphant.'"

Few persons would have seemed less likely than Whitman to have become what he became. He was born in rural Long Island, the son of a carpenter, in a household nominally Quaker. He had a few years of schooling in Brooklyn. Quitting school, he worked in printing offices and learned the trade. He worked for a time with his father as a carpenter. But gradually he drifted into journalism, and worked as an editor of various Long Island and New York papers—and even a paper in New Orleans for a few months in 1848. He had clearly been a greedy reader of books from the beginning. And his ability to make his way as a journalist showed his gift with language.

He might have had a quite satisfactory career as a journalist for the rest of his life had he not been driven by a deeper sense of his own destiny. One of the greatest of literary mysteries is how Whitman suddenly in 1855, at the age of thirty-six, transformed himself from a skilled journalist and mediocre poet into one of the classic writers of all time—publishing that first edition of *Leaves of Grass.* His reading of Homer and the Bible, Virgil, Shakespeare, and Milton, his passion for the operas then produced frequently in New York, his intense interest in oratory and declamation—these and other elements have been examined as part of that "long foreground" which Emerson guessed he must have had. But finally, critics must throw up their hands and grant Whitman a spark of genius in making himself one of the great originals of all time.

His life became his book, his book his life. He continued to shape it through edition after edition after the Civil War, one of the fanciest, in two volumes, appearing as the Centennial Edition in 1876. He published occasional prose pieces, one of the most important of which was the autobiographical *Specimen Days* in 1882; much of it consisted of vivid episodic reminiscenses of the Civil War. But recognition or popular acclaim as a great poet eluded Whitman, except for bursts of enthusiasm here and there. Emerson never publicly praised Whitman after Whitman used (without asking permission) Emerson's letter to advertise the 1856 edition of *Leaves of Grass.* There were several attacks on him as an obscene poet, and at one point his book was banned in Boston.

But Whitman never gave up his life's work of completing his book. And when he died in 1892, he could rest easy in the knowledge that there were enough passionately committed disciples to take over and preserve the book as he had made it and as he wanted posterity to see it. He could not have known that poets, even though sometimes grudgingly, would grant him the epithet he had set out to claim—the American Bard. Randall Jarrell spoke for them all in 1952 in an admiring (and still valuable) essay, the original title of which put his point succinctly: "Walt Whitman: He Had His Nerve."

ADDITIONAL READING

The Collected Writings of Walt Whitman, ed. Gay Wilson Allen and Sculley Bradley, 1963–.

Newton Arvin, *Whitman*, 1938; Henry Seidel Canby, *Walt Whitman, An American*, 1943; Robert D. Faner, *Walt Whitman and Opera*, 1951; Gay Wilson Allen, *The Solitary Singer: A Crit-*

ical Biography of Walt Whitman, 1955, rev. 1967; Richard Chase, Walt Whitman Reconsidered, 1955; James E. Miller, Jr., A Critical Guide to Leaves of Grass, 1957; Roger Asselineau, The Evolution of Walt Whitman, 2 vols., 1960, 1962; James E. Miller, Jr., Walt Whitman, 1962, rev. 1990; Roy Harvey Pearce, ed., Whitman: A Collection of Critical Essays, 1962; R. W. B. Lewis, ed., The Presence of Walt Whitman, 1962; John C. Broderick, ed., Whitman the Poet, 1962; James E. Miller, Jr., Whitman's "Song of Myself": Origin, Growth, Meaning, 1964; Edwin H. Miller, Walt Whitman's Poetry: A Psychological Journey, 1968; Edwin H. Miller, ed., A Century of Whitman Criticism, 1969; Gay Wilson Allen, A Reader's Guide to Walt Whitman, 1970; Milton Hindus, ed., Whitman: The Critical Heritage, 1971; Joseph Jay Rubin, The Historic Whitman, 1973; Arthur Golden, ed., Walt Whitman: A Collection of Criticism, 1974; Floyd Stovall, The Foreground of Leaves of Grass, 1974; Jerome M. Loving, ed., Civil War Letters of George Washington Whitman, 1975; Gay Wilson Allen, The New Walt Whitman Handbook, 1975, updated 1986; Randall H. Waldron, Mattie: The Letters of Martha Mitchell Whitman, 1978; James E. Miller, Jr., The American Quest for a Supreme Fiction: Whitman's Legacy in the Personal Epic, 1979; Justin Kaplin, Walt Whitman: A Life, 1980; Harold Aspiz, Walt Whitman and the Body Beautiful, 1980; Betsy Erkkila, Walt Whitman among the French, 1980; Jim Perlman, Ed Folson, Dan Campion, eds., Walt Whitman: The Measure of His Song, 1981; Jerome M. Loving, Emerson, Whitman, and the American Muse, 1982; C. Carroll Hollis, Language and Style in Leaves of Grass, 1983; James Woodress, ed., Critical Essays on Walt Whitman, 1983; Paul Zweig, Walt Whitman: The Making of the Poet, 1984; Dennis Berthold and Kenneth Price, eds., Dear Brother Walt: The Letters of Thomas Jefferson Whitman, 1984; David Cavitch, My Soul and I: The Inner Life of Walt Whitman, 1985; Joann P. Krieg, ed., Walt Whitman: Here and Now, 1985; George B. Hutchinson, The Ecstatic Whitman: Literary Shamanism and the Crisis of the Union, 1986; M. Wynn Thomas, The Lunar Light of Whitman's Poetry, 1987; Charley Shively, ed., Calamus Lovers: Walt Whitman's Working-Class Camerados, 1987; Neeli Cherkovski, Whitman's Wild Children, 1988; Kerry C. Larson, Whitman's Drama of Consensus, 1988; Edwin Haviland Miller, Walt Whitman's "Song of Myself": A Mosaic of Interpretations, 1989; M. Jimmie Killingsworth, Whitman's Poetry of the Body, 1989; Thomas Gardner, Discovering Ourselves in Whitman: The Contemporary American Long Poem, 1989; Jeffrey Walker, Bardic Ethos and the American Epic Poem: Whitman, Pound, Crane, Williams, Olson, 1989; Thomas B. Byers, What I Cannot Say: Self, Word, and World in Whitman, Stevens, and Merwin, 1989; Betsy Erkkila, Whitman the Political Poet, 1989; David Kuebrich, Minor Prophecy: Walt Whitman's New American Religion, 1989; Kenneth M. Price, Whitman and Tradition, 1990.

TEXTS

Leaves of Grass, 1891–92; Specimen Days and Collect, 1882.

from Leaves of Grass

from DRUM-TAPS[1]

Cavalry Crossing a Ford

A line in long array where they wind betwixt green islands,
They take a serpentine course, their arms flash in the sun—hark to the
    musical clank,

---

[1] Whitman was over forty when the Civil War began in 1861, and thus too old to be taken as a soldier. But his brother George went to the war and was wounded in 1862 in Virginia. Whitman went to find him and became involved for the duration of the war as an unofficial nurse, visiting hospitals in Washington, D.C., cheering the living and comforting the dying. During his "wound-dresser" period, Whitman wrote "Drum-Taps," a cluster of poems touching on his feelings about and experiences in the war. Drum-Taps appeared as a book in 1865, and was reissued with "Sequel to Drum-Taps" in 1866 (containing poems written on the assassination of President Abraham Lincoln). The poems were added as annexes to a reissue of Leaves of Grass in 1867, and were then integrated with the whole of the new edition of Leaves of Grass that appeared in 1870–71.

Behold the silvery river, in it the splashing horses loitering stop to drink,
Behold the brown-faced men, each group, each person a picture, the
    negligent rest on the saddles,
Some emerge on the opposite bank, others are just entering the
    ford—while,   5
Scarlet and blue and snowy white,
The guidon flags[2] flutter gayly in the wind.

1865, 1871

Bivouac on a Mountain Side

I see before me now a traveling army halting,
Below a fertile valley spread, with barns and the orchards of summer,
Behind, the terraced sides of a mountain, abrupt, in places rising high,
Broken, with rocks, with clinging cedars, with tall shapes dingily seen,
The numerous camp-fires scatter'd near and far, some away up on the
    mountain,   5
The shadowy forms of men and horses, looming, large-sized, flickering,
And over all the sky—the sky! far, far out of reach, studded, breaking out,
    the eternal stars.

1865, 1871

By the Bivouac's Fitful Flame

By the bivouac's fitful flame,
A procession winding around me, solemn and sweet and slow—but
    first I note,
The tents of the sleeping army, the fields' and woods' dim outline,
The darkness lit by spots of kindled fire, the silence,
Like a phantom far or near an occasional figure moving,   5
The shrubs and trees, (as I lift my eyes they seem to be stealthily
    watching me,)
While wind in procession thoughts, O tender and wondrous thoughts,
Of life and death, of home and the past and loved, and of those that
    are far away;
A solemn and slow procession there as I sit on the ground,
By the bivouac's fitful flame.   10

1865, 1867

Come Up from the Fields Father

Come up from the fields father, here's a letter from our Pete,
And come to the front door mother, here's a letter from thy dear son.

---

[2]Flags identifying particular units.

Lo, 'tis autumn,
Lo, where the trees, deeper green, yellower and redder,
Cool and sweeten Ohio's villages with leaves fluttering in the moderate
    wind,   5
Where apples ripe in the orchards hang and grapes on the trellis'd vines,
(Smell you the smell of the grapes on the vines?
Smell you the buckwheat where the bees were lately buzzing?)
Above all, lo, the sky so calm, so transparent after the rain, and with
    wondrous clouds,
Below too, all calm, all vital and beautiful, and the farm prospers well.   10

Down in the fields all prospers well,
But now from the fields come father, come at the daughter's call,
And come to the entry mother, to the front door come right away.

Fast as she can she hurries, something ominous, her steps trembling,
She does not tarry to smooth her hair nor adjust her cap.   15

Open the envelope quickly,
O this is not our son's writing, yet his name is sign'd,

O a strange hand writes for our dear son, O stricken mother's soul!
All swims before her eyes, flashes with black, she catches the main
    words only,
Sentences broken, *gunshot wound in the breast, cavalry skirmish, taken
    to hospital,*   20
At present low, but will soon be better.

Ah now the single figure to me,
Amid all teeming and wealthy Ohio with all its cities and farms,
Sickly white in the face and dull in the head, very faint,
By the jamb of a door leans.   25

Grieve not so, dear mother, (the just-grown daughter speaks through
    her sobs,
The little sisters huddle around speechless and dismay'd,)
See, dearest mother, the letter says Pete will soon be better.

Alas poor boy, he will never be better, (nor may-be needs to be better, that
    brave and simple soul,)
While they stand at home at the door he is dead already,   30
The only son is dead.

But the mother needs to be better,
She with thin form presently drest in black,
By day her meals untouch'd, then at night fitfully sleeping, often waking,
In the midnight waking, weeping, longing with one deep longing,   35
O that she might withdraw unnoticed, silent from life escape and
    withdraw,
To follow, to seek, to be with her dear dead son.

                                      1865, 1867

Vigil Strange I Kept on the Field One Night

Vigil strange I kept on the field one night;
When you my son and my comrade dropt at my side that day,
One look I but gave which your dear eyes return'd with a look I shall
    never forget,
One touch of your hand to mine O boy, reach'd up as you lay on the
    ground,
Then onward I sped in the battle, the even-contested battle,   5
Till late in the night reliev'd to the place at last again I made my way,
Found you in death so cold dear comrade, found your body son of
    responding kisses, (never again on earth responding,)
Bared your face in the starlight, curious the scene, cool blew the
    moderate night-wind,
Long there and then in vigil I stood, dimly around me the battlefield
    spreading,
Vigil wondrous and vigil sweet there in the fragrant silent night,   10
But not a tear fell, not even a long-drawn sigh, long, long I gazed,
Then on the earth partially reclining sat by your side leaning my chin
    in my hands,
Passing sweet hours, immortal and mystic hours with you dearest
    comrade—not a tear, not a word,
Vigil of silence, love and death, vigil for you my son and my soldier,
As onward silently stars aloft, eastward new ones upward stole,   15
Vigil final for you brave boy, (I could not save you, swift was your death,
I faithfully loved you and cared for you living, I think we shall surely
    meet again,)
Till at latest lingering of the night, indeed just as the dawn appear'd,
My comrade I wrapt in his blanket, envelop'd well his form,
Folded the blanket well, tucking it carefully over head and carefully
    under feet,   20
And there and then and bathed by the rising sun, my son in his grave,
    in his rude-dug grave I deposited,
Ending my vigil strange with that, vigil of night and battle-field dim,
Vigil for boy of responding kisses, (never again on earth responding,)
Vigil for comrade swiftly slain, vigil I never forgot, how as day
    brighten'd,
I rose from the chill ground and folded my soldier well in his blanket,   25
And buried him where he fell.

1865, 1867

A March in the Ranks Hard-Prest,
and the Road Unknown

A march in the ranks hard-prest, and the road unknown,
A route through a heavy wood with muffled steps in the darkness,
Our army foil'd with loss severe, and the sullen remnant retreating,
Till after midnight glimmer upon us the lights of a dim-lighted building,
We come to an open space in the woods, and halt by the dim-lighted
    building,   5
'Tis a large old church at the crossing roads, now an impromptu hospital,

Entering but for a minute I see sight beyond all the pictures and poems
   ever made,
Shadows of deepest, deepest black, just lit by moving candles and lamps,
And by one great pitchy torch stationary with wild red flame and clouds
   of smoke,
By these, crowds, groups of forms vaguely I see on the floor, some in
   the pews laid down,   10
At my feet more distinctly a soldier, a mere lad, in danger of bleeding
   to death, (he is shot in the abdomen,)
I stanch the blood temporarily, (the youngster's face is white as a lily,)
Then before I depart I sweep my eyes o'er the scene fain[3] to absorb it all,
Faces, varieties, postures beyond description, most in obscurity, some of
   them dead,
Surgeons operating, attendants holding lights, the smell of ether, the
   odor of blood,   15
The crowd, O the crowd of the bloody forms, the yard outside also
   fill'd,
Some on the bare ground, some on planks or stretchers, some in the
   death-spasm sweating,
An occasional scream or cry, the doctor's shouted orders or calls,
The glisten of the little steel instruments catching the glint of the torches,
These I resume as I chant, I see again the forms, I smell the odor,   20
Then hear outside the orders given, *Fall in, my men, fall in;*
But first I bend to the dying lad, his eyes open, a half-smile gives he me,
Then the eyes close, calmly close, and I speed forth to the darkness,
Resuming, marching, ever in darkness marching, on in the ranks,
The unknown road still marching.   25

                                   1865, 1867

A Sight in Camp
in the Daybreak Gray and Dim

A sight in camp in the daybreak gray and dim,
As from my tent I emerge so early sleepless,
As slow I walk in the cool fresh air the path near by the hospital tent,
Three forms I see on stretchers lying, brought out there untended lying,
Over each the blanket spread, ample brownish woolen blanket,   5
Gray and heavy blanket, folding, covering all.

Curious I halt and silent stand,
Then with light fingers I from the face of the nearest the first just lift the
   blanket;
Who are you elderly man so gaunt and grim, with well gray'd hair, and
   flesh all sunken about the eyes?
Who are you my dear comrade?   10

Then to the second I step—and who are you my child and darling?
Who are you sweet boy with cheeks yet blooming?

---

[3]Reluctantly ready.

Then to the third—a face nor child nor old, very calm, as of beautiful
yellow-white ivory;
Young man I think I know you—I think this face is the face of the
Christ himself,
Dead and divine and brother of all, and here again he lies.   15

1865, 1867

As Toilsome I Wander'd Virginia's Woods

As toilsome I wander'd Virginia's woods,
To the music of rustling leaves kick'd by my feet, (for 'twas autumn,)
I mark'd at the foot of a tree the grave of a soldier;
Mortally wounded he and buried on the retreat, (easily all could I
understand,)
The halt of a mid-day hour, when up! no time to lose—yet this sign left,   5
On a tablet scrawl'd and nail'd on the tree by the grave,
Bold, cautious, true, and my loving comrade.

Long, long I muse, then on my way go wandering,
Many a changeful season to follow, and many a scene of life,
Yet at times through changeful season and scene, abrupt, alone, or in the
crowded street,   10
Comes before me the unknown soldier's grave, comes the inscription rude
in Virginia's woods,
Bold, cautious, true, and my loving comrade.

1865, 1867

The Wound-Dresser

1

An old man bending I come among new faces,
Years looking backward resuming in answer to children,
Come tell us old man, as from young men and maidens that love me,
(Arous'd and angry, I'd thought to beat the alarum, and urge relentless
war,
But soon my fingers fail'd me, my face droop'd and I resign'd myself   5
To sit by the wounded and soothe them, or silently watch the dead;)
Years hence of these scenes, of these furious passions, these chances,
Of unsurpass'd heroes, (was one side so brave? the other was equally
brave;)
Now be witness again, paint the mightiest armies of earth,
Of those armies so rapid so wondrous what saw you to tell us?   10
What stays with you latest and deepest? of curious panics,
Of hard-fought engagements of sieges tremendous what deepest remains?

2

O maidens and young men I love and that love me,
What you ask of my days those the strangest and sudden your talking
recalls,

Soldier alert I arrive after a long march cover'd with sweat and dust,   15
In the nick of time I come, plunge in the fight, loudly shout in the rush
   of successful charge,
Enter the captur'd works—yet lo, like a swift-running river they fade,
Pass and are gone they fade—I dwell not on soldiers' perils or soldiers'
   joys,
(Both I remember well—many of the hardships, few the joys, yet I was
   content.)

But in silence, in dreams' projections,   20
While the world of gain and appearance and mirth goes on,
So soon what is over forgotten, and waves wash the imprints off the sand,
With hinged knees returning I enter the doors, (while for you up there,
Whoever you are, follow without noise and be of strong heart.)

Bearing the bandages, water and sponge,   25
Straight and swift to my wounded I go,
Where they lie on the ground after the battle brought in,
Where their priceless blood reddens the grass the ground,
Or to the rows of the hospital tent, or under the roof'd hospital,
To the long rows of cots up and down each side I return,   30
To each and all one after another I draw near, not one do I miss,
An attendent follows holding a tray, he carries a refuse pail,
Soon to be fill'd with clotted rags and blood, emptied, and fill'd again.

I onward go, I stop,
With hinged knees and steady hand to dress wounds,   35
I am firm with each, the pangs are sharp yet unavoidable,
One turns to me his appealing eyes—poor boy! I never knew you,
Yet I think I could not refuse this moment to die for you, if that would
   save you.

3

On, on I go, (open doors of time! open hospital doors!)
The crush'd head I dress, (poor crazed hand tear not the bandage away,)   40
The neck of the cavalry-man with the bullet through and through I
   examine,
Hard the breathing rattles, quite glazed already the eye, yet life struggles
   hard,
(Come sweet death! be persuaded O beautiful death!
In mercy come quickly.)

From the stump of the arm, the amputated hand,   45
I undo the clotted lint, remove the slough, wash off the matter and
   blood,
Back on his pillow the soldier bends with curv'd neck and side falling
   head,
His eyes are closed, his face is pale, he dares not look on the bloody
   stump,
And has not yet look'd on it.

I dress a wound in the side, deep, deep,   50
But a day or two more, for see the frame all wasted and sinking,
And the yellow-blue countenance see.

I dress the perforated shoulder, the foot with the bullet-wound,
Cleanse the one with a gnawing and putrid gangrene, so sickening, so
    offensive,
While the attendant stands behind aside me holding the tray and pail.   55

I am faithful, I do not give out,
The fractur'd thigh, the knee, the wound in the abdomen,
These and more I dress with impassive hand, (yet deep in my breast a
    fire, a burning flame.)

4

Thus in silence in dreams' projections,
Returning, resuming, I thread my way through the hospitals,   60
The hurt and wounded I pacify with soothing hand,
I sit by the restless all the dark night, some are so young,
Some suffer so much, I recall the experience sweet and sad,
(Many a soldier's loving arms about this neck have cross'd and rested,
Many a soldier's kiss dwells on these bearded lips.)   65

1865, 1881

Dirge for Two Veterans

    The last sunbeam
Lightly falls from the finish'd Sabbath,
On the pavement here, and there beyond it is looking,
    Down a new-made double grave.

    Lo, the moon ascending,   5
Up from the east the silvery round moon,
Beautiful over the house-tops, ghastly, phantom moon,
    Immense and silent moon.

    I see a sad procession,
And I hear the sound of coming full-key'd bugles,   10
All the channels of the city streets they're flooding,
    As with voices and with tears.

    I hear the great drums pounding,
And the small drums steady whirring,
And every blow of the great convulsive drums,   15
    Strikes me through and through.

    For the son is brought with the father,
(In the foremost ranks of the fierce assault they fell,
Two veterans son and father dropt together,
    And the double grave awaits them.)   20

    Now nearer blow the bugles,
And the drums strike more convulsive,
And the daylight o'er the pavement quite has faded,
    And the strong dead-march enwraps me.

In the eastern sky up-buoying,
The sorrowful vast phantom moves illumin'd,
('Tis some mother's large transparent face,
In heaven brighter growing.)   25

O strong dead-march you please me!
O moon immense with your silvery face you soothe me!   30
O my soldiers twain! O my veterans passing to burial!
What I have I also give you.

The moon gives you light,
And the bugles and the drums give you music,
And my heart, O my soldiers, my veterans,   35
My heart gives you love.

1865–66, 1867

The Artilleryman's Vision

While my wife at my side lies slumbering, and the wars are over long,
And my head on the pillow rests at home, and the vacant midnight
    passes,
And through the stillness, through the dark, I hear, just hear, the
    breath of my infant,
There in the room as I wake from sleep this vision presses upon me;
The engagement opens there and then in fantasy unreal,   5
The skirmishers begin, they crawl cautiously ahead, I hear the irregular
    snap! snap!
I hear the sounds of the different missiles, the short *t-h-t! t-h-t!* of the
    rifle-balls,
I see the shells exploding leaving small white clouds, I hear the great
    shells shrieking as they pass,
The grape[4] like the hum and whirr of wind through the trees,
    (tumultuous now the content rages,)
All the scenes at the batteries rise in detail before me again,   10
The crashing and smoking, the pride of the men in their pieces,
The chief-gunner ranges and sights his piece and selects a fuse of the
    right time,
After firing I see him lean aside and look eagerly off to note the effect;
Elsewhere I hear the cry of a regiment charging, (the young colonel leads
    himself this time with brandish'd sword,)
I see the gaps cut by the enemy's volleys, (quickly fill'd up, no delay,) 15
I breathe the suffocating smoke, then the flat clouds hover low concealing
    all;
Now a strange lull for a few seconds, not a shot fired on either side,
Then resumed the chaos louder than ever, with eager calls and orders of
    officers,
While from some distant part of the field the wind wafts to my ears a
    shout of applause, (some special success,)
And ever the sound of the cannon far or near, (rousing even in dreams a
    devilish exultation and all the old mad joy in the depths of my soul,) 20

---

[4]Grape-shot.

And ever the hastening of infantry shifting positions, batteries, cavalry,
    moving hither and thither,
(The falling, dying, I heed not, the wounded dripping and red I heed not,
    some to the rear are hobbling,)
Grime, heat, rush, aides-de-camp galloping by or on a full run,
With the patter of small arms, the warning *s-s-t* of the rifles, (these in my
    vision I hear or see,)
And bombs bursting in air, and at night the vari-color'd rockets.   25

1865, 1881

Look Down Fair Moon

Look down fair moon and bathe this scene,
Pour softly down night's nimbus floods on faces ghastly, swollen, purple,
On the dead on their backs with arms toss'd wide,
Pour down your unstinted nimbus sacred moon.

1865, 1881

Reconciliation

Word over all, beautiful as the sky,
Beautiful that war and all its deeds of carnage must in time be utterly
    lost,
That the hands of the sisters Death and Night incessantly softly wash
    again, and ever again, this soil'd world;
For my enemy is dead, a man divine as myself is dead,
I look where he lies white-faced and still in the coffin—I draw near,   5
Bend down and touch lightly with my lips the white face in the coffin.

1865–66, 1881

How Solemn as One by One

(WASHINGTON CITY, 1865)

How solemn as one by one,
As the ranks returning worn and sweaty, as the men file by where I stand,
As the faces the masks appear, as I glance at the faces studying the masks,
(As I glance upward out of this page studying you, dear friend, whoever
    you are,)
How solemn the thought of my whispering soul to each in the ranks, and
    to you!   5
I see behind each mask that wonder a kindred soul,
O the bullet could never kill what you really are, dear friend,
Nor the bayonet stab what you really are;

The soul! yourself I see, great as any, good as the best,
Waiting secure and content, which the bullet could never kill,   10
Nor the bayonet stab O friend.

1865–66, 1871

As I Lay with My
Head in Your Lap Camerado[5]

As I lay with my head in your lap camerado,
The confession I made I resume, what I said to you and the open air
    I resume,
I know I am restless and make others so,
I know my words are weapons full of danger, full of death,
For I confront peace, security, and all the settled laws, to unsettle
    them,   5
I am more resolute because all have denied me than I could ever have
    been had all accepted me,
I heed not and have never heeded either experience, cautions,
    majorities, nor ridicule,
And the threat of what is call'd hell is little or nothing to me,
And the lure of what is call'd heaven is little or nothing to me;
Dear camerado! I confess I have urged you onward with me, and still
    urge you, without the least idea what is our destination,   10
Or whether we shall be victorious, or utterly quell'd and defeated.

1865–66, 1881

MEMORIES OF PRESIDENT LINCOLN

When Lilacs Last in the Dooryard Bloom'd[1]

1

When lilacs last in the dooryard bloom'd,
And the great star early droop'd in the western sky in the night,
I mourn'd, and yet shall mourn with ever-returning spring.

Ever-returning spring, trinity sure to me you bring,
Lilac blooming perennial and drooping star in the west,   5
And thought of him I love.

---

[5]Intimate companion and sharer; cf. Spanish *camarada*, bed or chamber mate.
[1]President Abraham Lincoln was shot by an assassin on April 14, 1865, and died the next day. The murder shocked the nation; it happened only a few weeks after Lincoln's inauguration for a second term, and only a few days after the Confederacy's General Lee surrendered his armies to the Union's General Grant at Appomattox, effectively ending the Civil War. Whitman wrote in *Specimen Days:* "The day of the murder we heard the news very early in the morning. Mother prepared breakfast—and other meals afterward—as usual; but not a mouthful was eaten all day by either of us. We each drank half a cup of coffee; that was all. We got every newspaper morning and evening, and the frequent extras of that period, and pass'd them silently to each other." April is the month for lilacs in America.

2

O powerful western fallen star!
O shades of night—O moody, tearful night!
O great star disappear'd—O the black murk that hides the star!
O cruel hands that hold me powerless—O helpless soul of me!   10
O harsh surrounding cloud that will not free my soul.

3

In the dooryard fronting an old farm-house near the white-wash'd
    palings,
Stands the lilac-bush tall-growing with heart-shaped leaves of rich
    green,
With many a pointed blossom rising delicate, with the perfume strong
    I love,
With every leaf a miracle—and from this bush in the dooryard,   15
With delicate-color'd blossoms and heart-shaped leaves of rich green,
A sprig with its flower I break.

4

In the swamp in secluded recesses,
A shy and hidden bird is warbling a song.

Solitary the thrush,   20
The hermit withdrawn to himself, avoiding the settlements,
Sings by himself a song.

Song of the bleeding throat,
Death's outlet song of life, (for well dear brother I know,
If thou wast not granted to sing thou would'st surely die.)   25

5

Over the breast of the spring, the land, amid cities,
Amid lanes and through old woods, where lately the violets peep'd
    from the ground, spotting the gray debris,
Amid the grass in the fields each side of the lanes, passing the endless
    grass,
Passing the yellow-spear'd wheat, every grain from its shroud in the
    dark-brown fields uprisen.
Passing the apple-tree blows of white and pink in the orchards,   30
Carrying a corpse to where it shall rest in the grave,
Night and day journeys a coffin.[2]

6

Coffin that passes through lanes and streets,
Through day and night with the great cloud darkening the land,
With the pomp of the inloop'd flags with the cities draped in black,   35
With the show of the States themselves as of crape-veil'd women
    standing,
With processions long and winding and the flambeaus of the night,
With the countless torches lit, with the silent sea of faces and the
    unbared heads,
With the waiting depot, the arriving coffin, and the sombre faces,

---

[2]Lincoln's coffin was placed on a train that first went to
New York and then to Springfield, Illinois, for burial.

With dirges through the night, with the thousand voices rising strong
   and solemn,   40
With all the mournful voices of the dirges pour'd around the coffin,
The dim-lit churches and the shuddering organs—where amid these
   you journey,
With the tolling tolling bells' perpetual clang,
Here, coffin that slowly passes,
I give you my sprig of lilac.   45

                              7

(Nor for you, for one alone,
Blossoms and branches green to coffins all I bring,
For fresh as the morning, thus would I chant a song for you O sane
   and sacred death.

All over bouquets of roses,
O death, I cover you over with roses and early lilies,   50
But mostly and now the lilac that blooms the first,
Copious I break, I break the sprigs from the bushes,
With loaded arms I come, pouring for you,
For you and the coffins all of you O death.)

                              8

O western orb sailing the heaven,   55
Now I know what you must have meant as a month since I walk'd,
As I walk'd in silence the transparent shadowy night,
As I saw you had something to tell as you bent to me night after night,
As you droop'd from the sky low down as if to my side, (while the other
   stars all look'd on,)
As we wander'd together the solemn night, (for something I know not
   what kept me from sleep,)   60
As the night advanced, and I saw on the rim of the west how full you
   were of woe,
As I stood on the rising ground in the breeze in the cool transparent
   night,
As I watch'd where you pass'd and was lost in the netherward black
   of the night,
As my soul in its trouble dissatisfied sank, as where you sad orb,
Concluded, dropt in the night, and was gone.   65

                              9

Sing on there in the swamp,
O singer bashful and tender, I hear your notes, I hear your call,
I hear, I come presently, I understand you,
But a moment I linger, for the lustrous star has detain'd me,
The star my departing comrade holds and detains me.   70

                              10

O how shall I warble myself for the dead one there I loved?
And how shall I deck my song for the large sweet soul that has gone?
And what shall my perfume be for the grave of him I love?

Sea-winds blown from east and west,
Blown from the Eastern sea and blown from the Western sea, till there
   on the prairies meeting,   75
These and with these and the breath of my chant,
I'll perfume the grave of him I love.

11

O what shall I hang on the chamber walls?
And what shall the pictures be that I hang on the walls,
To adorn the burial-house of him I love?   80

Pictures of growing spring and farms and homes,
With the Fourth-month[3] eve at sundown, and the gray smoke lucid and
    bright,
With floods of the yellow gold of the gorgeous, indolent, sinking sun,
    burning, expanding the air,
With the fresh sweet herbage under foot, and the pale green leaves of
    the trees prolific,
In the distance the flowing glaze, the breast of the river, with a
    wind-dapple here and there,   85
With ranging hills on the banks, with many a line against the sky, and
    shadows,
And the city at hand with dwellings so dense, and stacks of chimneys,
And all the scenes of life and the workshops, and the workmen
    homeward returning.

12

Lo, body and soul—this land,
My own Manhattan with spires, and the sparkling and hurrying tides,
    and the ships,   90
The varied and ample land, the South and the North in the light,
    Ohio's shores and flashing Missouri,
And ever the far-spreading prairies cover'd with grass and corn.

Lo, the most excellent sun so calm and haughty,
The violet and purple morn with just-felt breezes,
The gentle soft-born measureless light,   95
The miracle spreading bathing all, the fulfill'd noon,
The coming eve delicious, the welcome night and the stars,
Over my cities shining all, enveloping man and land.

13

Sing on, sing on you gray-brown bird,
Sing from the swamps, the recesses, pour your chant from the
    bushes,   100
Limitless out of the dusk, out of the cedars and pines.

Sing on dearest brother, warble your reedy song,
Loud human song, with voice of uttermost woe.

O liquid and free and tender!
O wild and loose to my soul—O wondrous singer,   105
You only I hear—yet the star holds me, (but will soon depart,)
Yet the lilac with mastering odor holds me.

14

Now while I sat in the day and look'd forth,
In the close of the day with its light and the fields of spring, and the
    farmers preparing their crops,

---

[3]April.

In the large unconscious scenery of my land with its lakes and forests,   110
In the heavenly aerial beauty, (after the perturb'd winds and the
    storms,)
Under the arching heavens of the afternoon swift passing, and the
    voices of children and women,
The many-moving sea-tides, and I saw the ships how they sail'd,
And the summer approaching with richness, and the fields all busy
    with labor,
And the infinite separate houses, how they all went on, each with its
    meals and minutia of daily usages,   115
And the streets how their throbbings throbb'd, and the cities pent—
    lo, then and there,
Falling upon them all and among them all, enveloping me with the
    rest,
Appear'd the cloud, appear'd the long black trail,
And I knew death, its thought, and the sacred knowledge of death.

Then with the knowledge of death as walking one side of me,   120
And the thought of death close-walking the other side of me,
And I in the middle as with companions, and as holding the hands of
    companions,
I fled forth to the hiding receiving night that talks not,
Down to the shores of the water, the path by the swamp in the
    dimness,
To the solemn shadowy cedars and ghostly pines so still.   125

And the singer so shy to the rest receiv'd me,
The gray-brown bird I know receiv'd us comrades three,
And he sang the carol of death, and a verse for him I love.

From deep secluded recesses,
From the fragrant cedars and the ghostly pines so still,   130
Came the carol of the bird.

And the charm of the carol rapt me,
As I held as if by their hands my comrades in the night,
And the voice of my spirit tallied the song of the bird.

Come lovely and soothing death,   135
Undulate round the world, serenely arriving, arriving,
In the day, in the night, to all, to each,
Sooner or later delicate death.

Prais'd be the fathomless universe,
For life and joy, and for objects and knowledge curious,
And for love, sweet love—but praise! praise! praise!   140
For the sure-enwinding arms of cool-enfolding death.

Dark mother always gliding near with soft feet,
Have none chanted for thee a chant of fullest welcome?
Then I chant it for thee, I glorify thee above all,   145
I bring thee a song that when thou must indeed come, come unfalteringly.

Approach strong deliveress,
When it is so, when thou hast taken them I joyously sing the dead,
Lost in the loving floating ocean of thee,
Laved in the flood of thy bliss O death.   150

From me to thee glad serenades,
Dances for thee I propose saluting thee, adornments and feastings for thee,
And the sights of the open landscape and the high-spread sky are fitting,
And life and the fields, and the huge and thoughtful night.

The night in silence under many a star,   155
The ocean shore and the husky whispering wave whose voice I know,
And the soul turning to thee O vast and well-veil'd death,
And the body gratefully nestling close to thee.

Over the tree-tops I float thee a song,
Over the rising and sinking waves, over the myriad fields and the prairies wide,   160
Over the dense-pack'd cities all and the teeming wharves and ways,
I float this carol with joy, with joy to thee O death.

15

To the tally of my soul,
Loud and strong kept up the gray-brown bird,
With pure deliberate notes spreading filling the night.   165

Loud in the pines and cedars dim,
Clear in the freshness moist and the swamp-perfume,
And I with my comrades there in the night.

While my sight that was bound in my eyes unclosed,
As to long panoramas of visions.   170

And I saw askant[4] the armies,
I saw as in noiseless dreams hundreds of battle-flags,
Borne through the smoke of the battles and pierc'd with missiles I
    saw them,
And carried hither and yon through the smoke, and torn and bloody,
And at last but a few shreds left on the staffs, (and all in silence,) 175
And the staffs all splinter'd and broken.

I saw battle-corpses, myriads of them,
And the white skeletons of young men, I saw them,
I saw the debris and debris of all the slain soldiers of the war,
But I saw they were not as was thought,   180
They themselves were fully at rest, they suffer d not,
The living remain'd and suffer'd, the mother suffer'd,
And the wife and the child and the musing comrade suffer'd,
And the armies that remain'd suffer'd.

16

Passing the visions, passing the night,   185
Passing, unloosing the hold of my comrade's hands,
Passing the song of the hermit bird and the tallying song of my soul,
Victorious song, death's outlet song, yet varying ever-altering song,
As low and wailing, yet clear the notes, rising and falling, flooding the
    night,
Sadly sinking and fainting, as warning and warning, and yet again
    bursting with joy,   190
Covering the earth and filling the spread of the heaven,
As that powerful psalm in the night I heard from recesses,

---

[4]With mistrust.

Passing, I leave thee lilac with heart-shaped leaves,
I leave thee there in the door-yard, blooming, returning with spring.

I cease from my song for thee,   195
From my gaze on thee in the west, fronting the west, communing with
    thee,
O comrade lustrous with silver face in the night.

Yet each to keep and all, retrievements out of the night,
The song, the wondrous chant of the gray-brown bird,
And the tallying chant, the echo arous'd in my soul,   200
With the lustrous and drooping star with the countenance full of woe,
With the holders holding my hand nearing the call of the bird,
Comrades mine and I in the midst, and their memory ever to keep,
    for the dead I loved so well,
For the sweetest, wisest soul of all my days and lands—and this for
    his dear sake,
Lilac and star and bird twined with the chant of my soul,   205
There in the fragrant pines and the cedars dusk and dim.

1865   *1865–66, 1881*

O Captain! My Captain![1]

O Captain! my Captain! our fearful trip is done,
The ship has weather'd every rack, the prize we sought is won,
The port is near, the bells I hear, the people all exulting,
While follow eyes the steady keel, the vessel grim and daring;
      But O heart! heart! heart!   5
        O the bleeding drops of red,
          Where on the deck my Captain lies,
          Fallen cold and dead.

O Captain! my Captain! rise up and hear the bells;
Rise up—for you the flag is flung—for you the bugle trills,   10
For you bouquets and ribbon'd wreaths—for you the shores a-crowding,
For you they call, the swaying mass, their eager faces turning;
      Here Captain! dear father!
        This arm beneath your head!
          It is some dream that on the deck,
          You've fallen cold and dead.   15

My Captain does not answer, his lips are pale and still,
My father does not feel my arm, he has no pulse nor will,
The ship is anchor'd safe and sound, its voyage closed and done,
From fearful trip the victor ship comes in with object won: 20
      Exult O shores, and ring O bells!
        But I with mournful tread,
          Walk the deck my Captain lies,
          Fallen cold and dead.

1865, 1871

---

[1]This poem was for long Whitman's most popular. It is a kind of public elegy written for public declamation, while "Lilacs" is more private, more effective in working through genuine grief to some kind of comprehension and reconciliation.

Hush'd Be the Camps To-day

(MAY 4, 1865)

Hush'd be the camps to-day,
And soldiers let us drape our war-worn weapons,
And each with musing soul retire to celebrate,
Our dear commander's death.

No more for him life's stormy conflicts,   5
Nor victory, nor defeat—no more time's dark events,
Charging like ceaseless clouds across the sky.

But sing poet in our name,
Sing of the love we bore him—because you,—dweller in camps, know it
    truly.

As they invault the coffin there,   10
Sing—as they close the doors of earth upon him—one verse,
For the heavy hearts of soldiers.

1865, 1871

This Dust Was Once the Man

This dust was once the man,
Gentle, plain, just and resolute, under whose cautious hand,
Against the foulest crime in history known in any land or age,
Was saved the Union of these States.

1871

from Specimen Days[1]

OPENING OF THE SECESSION WAR

News of the attack on Fort Sumter and *the flag* at Charleston harbor, S. C.,[2] was receiv'd in New York City late at night (13th April, 1861,) and was immediately sent out in extras of the newspapers. I had been to the opera in Fourteenth Street that night, and after the performance was walking down Broadway toward twelve o'clock, on my way to Brooklyn, when I heard in the distance the loud cries of the newsboys, who came presently tearing and yelling up the street, rushing from side to side even more furiously than usual. I bought an extra and cross'd to the Metropolitan hotel (Niblo's) where the great lamps were still brightly blazing, and, with a crowd of others, who gather'd impromptu, read the news, which was evi-

---

[1] Whitman published *Specimen Days,* an unsystematic autobiographical account of his life, in 1882, incorporating *Memoranda During the War* (1875). The vignettes of the Civil War from one who was there as wound-dresser and nurse are both valuable and moving.

[2] The bombardment of Fort Sumter, a Union installation in the harbor of Charleston, South Carolina, by Confederate forces April 12–14, 1861, signalled the beginning of the Civil War.

dently authentic. For the benefit of some who had no papers, one of us read the telegram aloud, while all listened silently and attentively. No remark was made by any of the crowd, which had increas'd to thirty or forty, but all stood a minute or two, I remember, before they dispers'd. I can almost see them there now, under the lamps at midnight again.

DOWN AT THE FRONT

FALMOUTH, VA., *opposite Fredericksburg,*[3] *December 21, 1862.*—Begin my visits among the camp hospitals in the army of the Potomac. Spend a good part of the day in a large brick mansion on the banks of the Rappahannock, used as a hospital since the battle—seems to have receiv'd only the worst cases. Out doors, at the foot of a tree, within ten yards of the front of the house, I notice a heap of amputated feet, legs, arms, hands, &c., a full load for a one-horse cart. Several dead bodies lie near, each cover'd with its brown woolen blanket. In the door-yard, towards the river, are fresh graves, mostly of officers, their names on pieces of barrel-staves or broken boards, stuck in the dirt. (Most of these bodies were subsequently taken up and transported north to their friends.) The large mansion is quite crowded upstairs and down, everything impromptu, no system, all bad enough, but I have no doubt the best that can be done; all the wounds pretty bad, some frightful, the men in their old clothes, unclean and bloody. Some of the wounded are rebel soldiers and officers, prisoners. One, a Mississippian, a captain, hit badly in leg, I talk'd with some time; he ask'd me for papers, which I gave him. (I saw him three months afterward in Washington, with his leg amputated, doing well.) I went through the rooms, downstairs and up. Some of the men were dying. I had nothing to give at that visit, but wrote a few letters to folks home, mothers, &c. Also talk'd to three or four, who seem'd most susceptible to it, and needing it.

AN ARMY HOSPITAL WARD

Let me specialize a visit I made to the collection of barrack-like one-story edifices, Campbell hospital, out on the flats, at the end of the then horse railway route, on Seventh Street. There is a long building appropriated to each ward. Let us go into ward 6. It contains, to-day, I should judge, eighty or a hundred patients, half sick, half wounded. The edifice is nothing but boards, well whitewash'd inside, and the usual slender-framed iron bedsteads, narrow and plain. You walk down the central passage, with a row on either side, their feet towards you, and their heads to the wall. There are fires in large stoves, and the prevailing white of the walls is reliev'd by some ornaments, stars, circles, &c., made of evergreens. The view of the whole edifice and occupants can be taken at once, for there is no partition. You may hear groans or other sounds of unendurable suffering from two or three of the cots, but in the main there is quiet—almost a painful absence of demonstration; but the pallid face, the dull'd eye, and the moisture of the lip, are demonstration enough. Most of these sick or hurt are evidently young fellows from the country, farmers' sons, and such like. Look at the fine large frames, the bright and broad countenances, and the many yet lingering proofs of strong constitution and physique. Look at the patient and mute manner of our American wounded as they lie in such a sad collection; representatives from all New England, and from New York, and New Jersey, and Pennsylvania—indeed from all the States and all the cities—largely from the West. Most of them are entirely without friends or acquaintances here—no familiar face, and hardly a word of ju-

---

[3]The Battle of Fredericksburg in Virginia took place December 13, 1862. The Union's superior forces were wasted in frontal attacks on entrenched Confederate troops. The Union losses, over 12,000, were twice those of the Confederacy.

dicious sympathy or cheer, through their sometimes long and tedious sickness, or the pangs of aggravated wounds.

UNNAMED REMAINS THE BRAVEST SOLDIER

Of scenes like these, I say, who writes—whoe'er can write the story? Of many a score—aye, thousands, North and South, of unwrit heroes, unknown heroisms, incredible, impromptu, first-class desperations—who tells? No history ever—no poem sings, no music sounds, those bravest men of all—those deeds. No formal general's report, nor book in the library, nor column in the paper, embalms the bravest, North or South, East or West. Unnamed, unknown, remain, and still remain, the bravest soldiers.

Our manliest—our boys—our hardy darlings; no picture gives them. Likely, the typic one of them (standing, no doubt, for hundreds, thousands,) crawls aside to some bush-clump, or ferny tuft, on receiving his death-shot—there sheltering a little while, soaking roots, grass and soil, with red blood—the battle advances, retreats, flits from the scene, sweeps by—and there, haply with pain and suffering (yet less, far less, than is supposed,) the last lethargy winds like a serpent round him—the eyes glaze in death—none recks—perhaps the burial-squads, in truce, a week afterwards, search not the secluded spot—and there, at last, the Bravest Soldier crumbles in mother earth, unburied and unknown.

ABRAHAM LINCOLN

August 12th [1863]—I see the President almost every day, as I happen to live where he passes to or from his lodgings out of town. He never sleeps at the White House during the hot season, but has quarters at a healthy location some three miles north of the city, the Soldiers' Home, a United States military establishment. I saw him this morning about 8½ coming in to business, riding on Vermont Avenue, near L Street. He always has a company of twenty-five or thirty cavalry, with sabres drawn and held upright over their shoulders. They say this guard was against his personal wish, but he let his counselors have their way. The party makes no great show in uniform or horses. Mr. Lincoln on the saddle generally rides a good-sized, easy-going gray horse, is dress'd in plain black, somewhat rusty and dusty, wears a black stiff hat, and looks about as ordinary in attire, &c., as the commonest man. A lieutenant, with yellow straps, rides at his left, and following behind, two by two, come the cavalry men, in their yellow-striped jackets. They are generally going at a slow trot, as that is the pace set them by the one they wait upon. The sabres and accoutrements clank, and the entirely unornamental *cortège*[4] as it trots towards Lafayette Square arouses no sensation, only some curious stranger stops and gazes. I see very plainly ABRAHAM LINCOLN's dark brown face, with the deep-cut lines, the eyes, always to me with a deep latent sadness in the expression. We have got so that we exchange bows, and very cordial ones. Sometimes the President goes and comes in an open barouche.[5] The cavalry always accompany him, with drawn sabres. Often I notice as he goes out evenings—and sometimes in the morning, when he returns early—he turns off and halts at the large and handsome residence of the Secretary of War, on K Street, and holds conference there. If in his barouche, I can see from my window he does not alight, but sits in his vehicle, and Mr. Stanton[6] comes out to attend him. Sometimes one of his sons, a boy of ten or twelve, accompanies him, riding at his right on a pony. Earlier in the summer I occasionally saw the President and his wife, toward the latter part of the afternoon, out in a barouche, on a pleasure ride

---

[4]Usually, a ceremonial procession.
[5]Four-wheeled carriage with collapsible hood.
[6]Edwin McMasters Stanton (1814–1869), Secretary of War

in Lincoln's Cabinet and later in Andrew Johnson's (1862–68).

through the city. Mrs. Lincoln was dress'd in complete black, with a long crape veil. The equipage is of the plainest kind, only two horses, and they nothing extra. They pass'd me once very close, and I saw the President in the face fully, as they were moving slowly, and his look, though abstracted, happen'd to be directed steadily in my eye. He bow'd and smiled, but far beneath his smile I noticed well the expression I have alluded to. None of the artists or pictures has caught the deep, though subtle and indirect expression of this man's face. There is something else there. One of the great portrait painters of two or three centuries ago is needed.

SUMMER OF 1864

I am back again in Washington, on my regular daily and nightly rounds. Of course there are many specialties. Dotting a ward here and there are always cases of poor fellows, long-suffering under obstinate wounds, or weak and dishearten'd from typhoid fever, or the like; mark'd cases, needing special and sympathetic nourishment. These I sit down and either talk to, or silently cheer them up. They always like it hugely (and so do I). Each case has its peculiarities, and needs some new adaptation. I have learnt to thus conform—learnt a good deal of hospital wisdom. Some of the poor young chaps, away from home for the first time in their lives, hunger and thirst for affection; this is sometimes the only thing that will reach their condition. The men like to have a pencil, and something to write in. I have given them cheap pocket-diaries, and almanacs for 1864, interleav'd with blank paper. For reading I generally have some old pictorial magazines or story papers—they are always acceptable. Also the morning or evening papers of the day. The best books I do not give, but lend to read through the wards, and then take them to others, and so on; they are very punctual about returning the books. In these wards, or on the field, as I thus continue to go round, I have come to adapt myself to each emergency, after its kind or call, however trivial, however solemn, every one justified and made real under its circumstances—not only visits and cheering talk and little gifts—not only washing and dressing wounds (I have some cases where the patient is unwilling any one should do this but me)—but passages from the Bible, expounding them, prayer at the bedside, explanations of doctrine, &c. (I think I see my friends smiling at this confession, but I was never more in earnest in my life.) In camp and everywhere, I was in the habit of reading or giving recitations to the men. They were very fond of it, and liked declamatory poetical pieces. We would gather in a large group by ourselves, after supper, and spend the time in such readings, or in talking, and occasionally by an amusing game called the game of twenty questions.

THE INAUGURATION

March 4th [1865]—The President very quietly rode down to the Capitol in his own carriage, by himself, on a sharp trot, about noon, either because he wish'd to be on hand to sign bills, or to get rid of marching in line with the absurd procession, the muslin temple of liberty and pasteboard monitor. I saw him on his return, at three o'clock, after the performance was over. He was in his plain two-horse barouche, and look'd very much worn and tired; the lines, indeed, of vast responsibilities, intricate questions, and demands of life and death, cut deeper than ever upon his dark brown face; yet all the old goodness, tenderness, sadness, and canny shrewdness, underneath the furrows. (I never see that man without feeling that he is one to become personally attach'd to, for his combination of purest, heartiest tenderness, and native Western form of manliness.) By his side sat his little boy, of ten years. There were no soldiers, only a lot of civilians on horseback, with huge yellow scarfs over their shoulders, riding around the carriage. (At the inauguration four years ago, he rode down and back again surrounded by a dense mass of arm'd cavalrymen eight deep, with drawn sabres; and there were sharpshooters station'd at every corner on the route.) I ought to make mention of the closing levee[7] of Saturday night last. Never before was such a compact jam in front of the White House—all the grounds fill'd, and away out to the spacious sidewalks. I was there, as I took a notion to go—was in the rush inside with the crowd—surged along the passage-ways, the blue and other rooms, and through the great east room. Crowds of country people, some very funny. Fine music from the Marine Band, off in a side place. I saw Mr. Lincoln, drest all in black, with white kid gloves and a claw-hammer coat,[8] receiving, as in duty bound, shaking hands, looking very disconsolate, and as if he would give anything to be somewhere else.

DEATH OF PRESIDENT LINCOLN

April 16, '65.—I find in my notes of the time, this passage on the death of Abraham Lincoln: He leaves for America's history and biography, so far, not only its most dramatic reminiscence—he leaves, in my opinion, the greatest, best, most characteristic, artistic, moral personality. Not but that he had faults, and show'd them in the Presidency; but honesty, goodness, shrewdness, conscience, and (a new virtue, unknown to other lands, and hardly yet really known here, but the foundation and tie of all, as the future will grandly develop,) UNIONISM, in its truest and amplest sense, form'd the hard-pan of his character. These he seal'd with his life. The tragic splendor of his death, purging, illuminating all, throws round his form, his head, an aureole that will remain and will grow brighter through time, while history lives, and love of country lasts. By many has this Union been help'd; but if one name, one man, must be pick'd out, he, most of all, is the conservator of it, to the future. He was assassinated—but the Union is not assassinated—*ça ira!*[9] One falls and another falls. The soldier drops, sinks like a wave—but the ranks of the ocean eternally press on. Death does its work, obliterates a hundred, a thousand—President, general, captain, private,—but the Nation is immortal.

THREE YEARS SUMM'D UP

During those three years in hospital, camp or field, I made over six hundred visits or tours, and went, as I estimate, counting all, among from eighty thousand to a hundred thousand of the wounded and sick, as sustainer of spirit and body in some degree, in time of need. These visits varied from an hour or two, to all day or night; for with dear or critical cases I generally watch'd all night. Sometimes I took up my quarters in the hospital, and slept or watch'd there several nights in succession. Those three years I consider the greatest privilege and satisfaction, (with all their feverish excitements and physical deprivations and lamentable sights,) and, of course, the most profound lesson of my life. I can say that in my ministerings I comprehended all, whoever came in my way, Northern or Southern, and slighted none. It arous'd and brought out and decided undream'd-of depths of emotion. It has given me my most fervent views of the true *ensemble* and extent of the States. While I was with wounded and sick in thousands of cases from the New England States, and from New York, New Jersey, and Pennsylvania, and from Michigan, Wisconsin, Ohio, Indiana, Illinois, and all the Western States, I was with more or less from all the States, North and South, without exception. I was with many from the border States, especially from Maryland and

---

[7]Reception given by high official.
[8]Tailcoat.
[9]"It _ontinues" (French).

Virginia, and found, during those lurid years 1862–'63, far more Union South-erners, especially Tennesseans, than is supposed. I was with many rebel officers and men among our wounded, and gave them always what I had, and tried to cheer them the same as any. I was among the army teamsters considerably, and, indeed, always found myself drawn to them. Among the black soldiers, wounded or sick, and in the contraband camps, I also took my way whenever in their neigh-borhood, and did what I could for them.

THE MILLION DEAD, TOO, SUMM'D UP

The dead in this war—there they lie, strewing the fields and woods and valleys and battle-fields of the South—Virginia, the Peninsula—Malvern Hill and Fair Oaks—the banks of the Chickahominy—the terraces of Fredericksburg—Antie-tam bridge—the grisly ravines of Manassas—the bloody promenade of the Wil-derness—the varieties of the *strayed* dead, (the estimate of the War Department is 25,000 national soldiers kill'd in battle and never buried at all, 5,000 drown'd—15,000 inhumed by strangers, or on the march in haste, in hitherto unfound local-ities—2,000 graves cover'd by sand and mud by Mississippi freshets, 3,000 carried away by caving-in of banks, &c.,)—Gettysburg, the West, Southwest—Vicks-burg—Chattanooga—the trenches of Petersburg—the numberless battles, camps, hospitals everywhere—the crop reap'd by the mighty reapers, typhoid, dysentery, inflammations—and blackest and loathsomest of all, the dead and liv-ing burial-pits, the prison-pens of Andersonville, Salisbury, Belle Isle, &c., (not Dante's pictured hell and all its woes, its degradations, filthy torments, excell'd those prisons)—the dead, the dead, the dead—*our* dead—or South or North, ours all, (all, all, all, finally dear to me)—or East or West—Atlantic coast or Mis-sissippi valley—somewhere they crawl'd to die, alone, in bushes, low gullies, or on the sides of hills—(there, in secluded spots, their skeletons, bleach'd bones, tufts of hair, buttons, fragments of clothing, are occasionally found yet)—our young men once so handsome and so joyous, taken from us—the son from the mother, the husband from the wife, the dear friend from the dear friend—the clusters of camp graves, in Georgia, the Carolinas, and in Tennessee—the single graves left in the woods or by the roadside, (hundreds, thousands, obliterated)—the corpses floated down the rivers, and caught and lodged, (dozens, scores, floated down the upper Potomac, after the cavalry engagements, the pursuit of Lee, following Get-tysburg)—some lie at the bottom of the sea—the general million, and the special cemeteries in almost all the States—the infinite dead—(the land entire saturated, perfumed with their impalpable ashes' exhalation in Nature's chemistry distill'd, and shall be so forever, in every future grain of wheat and ear of corn, and every flower that grows, and every breath we draw)—not only Northern dead leavening Southern soil—thousands, aye tens of thousands, of Southerners, crumble to-day in Northern earth.

And everywhere among these countless graves—everywhere in the many sol-dier Cemeteries of the Nation, (there are now, I believe, over seventy of them)—as at the time in the vast trenches, the depositories of slain, Northern and South-ern, after the great battles—not only where the scathing trail passed those years, but radiating since in all the peaceful quarters of the land—we see, and ages yet may see, on monuments and gravestones, singly or in masses, to thousands or tens of thousands, the significant word *Unknown*.

(In some of the cemeteries nearly *all* the dead are unknown. At Salisbury, N.C., for instance, the known are only 85, while the unknown are 12,027, and 11,700 of these are buried in trenches. A national monument has been put up here, by or-der of Congress, to mark the spot—but what visible, material monument can ever fittingly commemorate that spot?)

THE REAL WAR WILL NEVER GET IN THE BOOKS

And so good-bye to the war. I know not how it may have been, or may be, to others—to me the main interest I found, (and still, on recollection, find,) in the rank and file of the armies, both sides, and in those specimens amid the hospitals, and even the dead on the field. To me the points illustrating the latent personal character and eligibilities of these States, in the two or three millions of American young and middle-aged men, North and South, embodied in those armies—and especially the one third or one fourth of their number, stricken by wounds or disease at some time in the course of the contest—were of more significance even than the political interests involved. (As so much of a race depends on how it faces death, and how it stands personal anguish and sickness. As, in the glints of emotions under emergencies, and the indirect traits and asides in Plutarch,[10] we get far profounder clues to the antique world than all its more formal history.)

Future years will never know the seething hell and the black infernal background of countless minor scenes and interiors, (not the official surface-courteousness of the Generals, not the few great battles) of the Secession war; and it is best they should not—the real war will never get in the books. In the mushy influences of current times, too, the fervid atmosphere and typical events of those years are in danger of being totally forgotten. I have at night watch'd by the side of a sick man in the hospital, one who could not live many hours. I have seen his eyes flash and burn as he raised himself and recurr'd to the cruelties on his surrender'd brother, and mutilations of the corpse afterward. (See in the preceding pages, the incident at Upperville[11]—the seventeen kill'd as in the description were left there on the ground. After they dropt dead, no one touch'd them—all were made sure of, however. The carcasses were left for the citizens to bury or not, as they chose.)

Such was the war. It was not a quadrille in a ball-room. Its interior history will not only never be written—its practicality, minutiæ of deeds and passions, will never be even suggested. The actual soldier of 1862–'65, North and South, with all his ways, his incredible dauntlessness, habits, practices, tastes, language, his fierce friendship, his appetite, rankness, his superb strength and animality, lawless gait, and a hundred unnamed lights and shades of camp, I say, will never be written—perhaps must not and should not be.

The preceding notes may furnish a few stray glimpses into that life, and into those lurid interiors, never to be fully convey'd to the future. The hospital part of the drama from '61 to '65 deserves indeed to be recorded. Of that many-threaded drama, with its sudden and strange surprises, its confounding of prophecies, its moments of despair, the dread of foreign interference, the interminable campaigns, the bloody battles, the mighty and cumbrous and green armies, the drafts and bounties—the immense money expenditure, like a heavy-pouring constant rain—with, over the whole land, the last three years of the struggle, an unending, universal mourning-wail of women, parents, orphans—the marrow of the tragedy concentrated in those Army Hospitals—(it seem'd sometimes as if the whole interest of the land, North and South, was one vast central hospital, and all the rest of the affair but flanges[12])—those forming the untold and unwritten history of the war—infinitely greater (like life's) than the few scraps and distortions that are ever told or written. Think how much, and of importance, will be—how much, civic and military, has already been—buried in the grave, in eternal darkness.

1882

---

[10]Greek biographer and historian (A.D. 46?–120?).
[11]In "A Glimpse of War's Hell-Scenes," Whitman had described a Confederate attack on a Union hospital train, near Upperville, Virginia; as the Rebels were robbing the train, Union forces arrived and captured seventeen Rebels, all of them summarily executed by grim Union soldiers.
[12]Projecting rim of a wheel, holding it in place and guiding it.

Copyrights and Acknowledgments and Illustration Credits

John Bakeless: Excerpt from "Preface," John Bakeless, *The Eyes of Discovery*. New York: Dover Publications, 1961.

Joel Barlow: "Advice to a Raven in Russia" from "Joel Barlow and Napoleon," reprinted from *The Huntington Library Quarterly* (1938).

William Bartram: Excerpts from *The Travels of William Bartram: Naturalist's Edition*, edited by Francis Harper, Yale Univ. Press. Copyright © 1958 by the Yale Univ. Press.

William Bradford: Excerpts from *Of Plymouth Plantation, 1620–1647* by William Bradford, edited by Samuel Eliot Morison. Copyright 1952 by Samuel Eliot Morison and renewed 1980 by Emily M. Beck. Reprinted by permission of Alfred A. Knopf, Inc.

Anne Bradstreet: Poems and Meditations reprinted by permission of the publishers from *The Works of Anne Bradstreet*, Jeannine Hensley, ed., Cambridge, MA: The Belknap Press of Harvard Univ. Press, Copyright © 1967 by The President and Fellows of Harvard College.

William Byrd: Excerpts reprinted by permission from *The History of the Dividing Line* in *The Prose Works of William Byrd of Westover*, edited by Louis B. Wright. Cambridge, MA: The Belknap Press of Harvard Univ. Press. Copyright 1966 by The President and Fellows of Harvard College. Excerpts from *The Secret Diary of William Byrd of Westover, 1709–1712*, edited by Louis B. Wright and Marion Tinling, The Dietz Press, 1941, and *Another Secret Diary of William Byrd of Westover, 1739–1741, with Letters and Literary Exercises, 1696–1726*, edited by Maude H. Woodfin, trans. and collated by Marion Tinling, The Dietz Press 1942, reprinted by permission of Marion Tinling.

Christopher Columbus: "Letter of Columbus" from *Christopher Columbus, Mariner* by Samuel Eliot Morison. Copyright 1942, 1955 by Samuel Eliot Morison. Copyright © renewed 1983 by Emily Morison Beck. By permission of Little, Brown and Co., in association with The Atlantic Monthly Press.

James Fenimore Cooper: Excerpts from *The Pioneers*, Ch. XXII, and from *The Last of the Mohicans*, Ch. II, reprinted from *The Writing of James Fenimore Cooper*, edited by James F. Beard et al., by permission of the State Univ. of New York Press. Copyright © 1980, 1983. Excerpt from "A Visit from Scott" reprinted by permission from *Gleanings in Europe: France*, edited by Robert E. Spiller, New York: Oxford Univ. Press, 1928. Copyright renewed 1955 by Robert E. Spiller.

Dekanawidah: Excerpts of *The Iroquois Constitution* from *The Magic World* by William Brandon. Reprinted by permission of Harold Ober Associates Inc. Copyright © 1971 by William Brandon.

Emily Dickinson: Reprinted by permission of the publishers and the Trustees of Amherst College from *The Poems of Emily Dickinson*, edited by Thomas H. Johnson. Cambridge, MA: The Belknap Press of Harvard Univ. Press, Copyright 1951, © 1955, 1979, 1983 by The President and Fellows of Harvard College.

Jonathan Edwards: Excepts from *Images or Shadows of Divine Things*, edited by Perry Miller, Yale Univ. Press. Coypright © 1948 Yale Univ. Press. All other excerpts from *The Works of Jonathan Edwards*, edited by Perry Miller and John E. Smith: Vol. I, *Freedom of the Will*, edited by Paul Ramsey; Vol. IV, *The Great Awakening*, edited by G. C. Goen; and Vol. VI, *Scientific and Philosophical Writings*, "Of Insects," edited by Wallace E. Anderson. Yale Univ. Press. Copyright © 1957, 1972, 1980 by Yale Univ. Press.

Ralph Waldo Emerson: Essays reprinted by permission from *The Collected Works of Ralph Waldo Emerson*: Vol. I, *Nature, Addresses, and Lectures;* Vol. II, *Essays, First Series;* Vol. III, *Essays, Second Series*, edited by Alfred R. Ferguson. Cambridge, MA: The Belknap Press of Harvard University Press. Copyright 1971, 1979, 1983 by The President and Fellows of Harvard College. *The Letters of Ralph Waldo Emerson*, 6 vols., edited by Ralph L. Rusk, Columbia Univ. Press, 1939; "To Lydia Jackson, Concord, February 1, 1835" from Vol. I; "To Henry Ware, Jr., Concord, October 8, 1838" from Vol. II; "To Caroline Sturgis, Concord, February 4, 1842" and "To Margaret Fuller, Concord, June 7, 1843" from Vol. III.

Philip Freneau: "On Observing a Large Red-Streak Apple" from *The Last Poems of Philip Freneau*, edited by Lewis Leary. Copyright 1945 by The Trustees of Rutgers College in New Jersey.

Nathaniel Hawthorne: "Wandering to and from over These Deserts" reprinted by permission of the Modern Language Association of America from *The English Notebooks of Nathaniel Hawthorne*, edited by Randall Stewart. Copyright © 1941. All other excerpts reprinted from *The Centenary Edition of the Works of Nathaniel Hawthorne,* edited by William Charvat et al. Columbus: Ohio State Univ. Press, 1962–.

George Washington Harris: From *The Mirth of a Nation: America's Great Dialect Humor,* edited by Walter Blair and Raven I. McDavid, Jr. Univ. of Minnesota Press, 1983.

Johnson Jones Hooper: From *The Mirth of a Nation: America's Great Dialect Humor,* edited by Walter Blair and Raven I. McDavid, Jr. Univ. of Minnesota Press, 1983.

Literature of Native Americans: Poems and Songs: From *The Magic World* by William Brandon. Reprinted by permission of Harold Ober Associates Inc. Copyright © 1971 by William Brandon. Speeches: From *Indian Oratory: Famous Speeches by Noted Indian Chieftains,* ed. W. C. Vanderwerth. Copyright © 1971 by the Univ. of Oklahoma Press. Tales: "High Horse's Courting" reprinted by permission from *Black Elk Speaks* by John G. Neihardt, copyright John G. Neihardt 1932, 1961, 1972. Published by Simon & Schuster Pocket Books and The Univ. of Nebraska Press. "The Jealous Ghost" reprinted with kind permission, Anthropological Papers of the American Museum of Natural History, Vol. XIII, Part III. "The Story of My Ancestor Weshgishega (Winnebago)" by San Blowsnake reprinted from *Crashing Thunder,* by Paul Radin, by permission of Univ. of Nebraska Press. Copyright © 1926, 1954, by Paul Radin. "The White Buffalo Calf Pipe" from *Teton Sioux Music* by Frances Densmore in Smithsonian Institution, U.S. Bureau of American Ethnology Bulletin 61.

Washington Irving: Excerpts from *The Complete Works of Washington Irving,* edited by Henry A. Pochmann et al., Vol. VII, *A History of New York,* edited by Michael L. Black and Nancy B. Black (1984); Vol. VIII, *The Sketch-Book of Geoffrey Crayon, Gent.,* edited by Haskeel Springer (1978); Vol. XXII, *The Crayon Miscellany,* edited by Dahlia Kerby Terrell (1979). Boston: Twayne Publishers. Copyright 1978, 1979, 1984, reprinted with the permission of G. K. Hall & Co., Boston.

Thomas Jefferson: From Thomas Jefferson's *Notes on the State of Virginia,* edited by William Peden. © 1955 The Univ. of North Carolina Press. Published for the Institute of Early American History and Culture. Letters adapted from *The Adams-Jefferson Letters,* edited by Lester J. Cappon. © 1959 The Univ. of North Carolina Press.

Robert Lowell: Excerpt from "Jonathan Edwards in Western Massachusetts" from *Life Studies and For the Union Dead* by Robert Lowell. Copyright © 1956, 1959, 1960, 1961, 1962, 1963, 1964 by Robert Lowell. Reprinted by Farrar, Straus and Giroux, Inc.

Cotton Mather: Excerpts reprinted by permission from the publishers of *Bonifacius: An Essay upon the Good,* edited by David Levin. Cambridge, MA: The Belknap Press of Harvard Univ. Press. Copyright 1966 by The President and Fellows of Harvard College.

Herman Melville: *Billy Budd, Sailor,* edited by Harrison Hayford and Merton M. Sealts, Jr. Chicago: Univ. of Chicago Press. Copyright © 1962 by The Univ. of Chicago. All rights reserved. Letters excerpted from *The Letters of Herman Melville,* edited by Merrell R. Davis and William H. Gilman, Yale Univ. Press. Copyright 1960 Yale Univ. Press. "Letter to Hawthorne, 13 Aug. 1852," by permission of the Houghton Library, Harvard Univ. "Letter to Hawthorne, 25 Oct. 1852" by permission of Henry W. and Albert A. Berg Collection, The New York Public Library, Astor, Lenox and Tilden Foundations. Poems reprinted by permission from *The Collected Poems of Herman Melville* edited by Howard P. Vincent, Hendricks House, Inc.

Edgar Allen Poe: Reprinted by permission from *The Collected Works of Edgar Allen Poe,* Vol. I, *Poems,* Vols. II and III, *Tales and Sketches,* edited by Thomas Ollive Mabbott, Cambridge, MA: Harvard Univ. Press. Copyright 1969, 1978 by The President and Fellows of Harvard College.

Samuel Sewall: Excerpts from *The Diary of Samuel Sewall, 1674–1729,* edited by M. Halsey Thomas. Copyright © 1973 by Farrar, Straus and Giroux, Inc. Reprinted by permission of Farrar, Straus and Giroux, Inc.

Seba Smith: From *The Mirth of a Nation: America's Great Dialect Humor,* edited by Walter Blair and Raven I. McDavid, Jr. Univ. of Minnesota Press, 1983.

Edward Taylor: "Meditation 23 (First Series)" and "Meditation 26 (Second Series)" from Donald E. Stanford, "Nineteen Unpublished Poems by Edward Taylor," in *American Literature* 29:1, pp. 34–35. Copyright © 1957, 1985 Duke Univ. Press. Reprinted by permission of Donald E. Stanford. "Meditation 150 (Second Series)" and "A Fig for Thee Oh! Death" from Donald E. Stanford, *The Poems of Edward Taylor,* Yale Univ. Press, 1960. Reprinted by permission of Donald E. Stanford. All other selections from *The Poetical Works of Edward Taylor,* ed. with an Introduction and Notes by Thomas H. Johnson. Copyright 1939 by Rockland, 1943 by Princeton Univ. Press. Reprinted with permission of Princeton Univ. Press. "Meditation 43 (Second Series)," "Upon a Wasp Chilled with Cold," and

Illustrations

Part I: Sir Walter Raleigh ordering the Standard of Queen Elizabeth to be erected on the Coast of Virginia.

Part II: Amos Doolittle, after Peter Lacour. Federal Hall The Seat of Congress. 1790 engraving (Stokes 1789 B-124). I. N. Phelps Stokes Collection. Miriam & Ira D. Wallach Division of Art, Prints and Photographs. The New York Public Library, Astor, Lenox and Tilden Foundations.

Part III: View of Boston Harbor, from *The Annotated Walden,* Thoreau, ed. Philip Van Doren Stern, Clarkson N. Potter, Inc. New York, 1970.

INDEX

Note: This index includes authors' names (in **boldface**), titles of works (in *italics*), and first lines of poems (in roman type).